D1272979

Presented
TO

Eulan Jones

BY

(self)

ON

_____

I remember the days of old,
I think about
all your deeds,
I meditate on the works
of your hands.

PSALM 143.5

THE
SPIRITUAL
FORMATION
BIBLE

Growing in Intimacy

With God

Through Scripture

New Revised
Standard Version

Zondervan Publishing House
Grand Rapids, Michigan, 49530, U.S.A.

CONTENTS

Alphabetical List of Bible Books iv
Abbreviations iv
How to Use the Spiritual Formation Bible v
About the Upper Room vii
Contributors viii
Getting Started in Spiritual Formation
   WHAT IS SPIRITUAL FORMATION? .x
   PRAYING THE SCRIPTURES xv
   READING THE SCRIPTURES DEVOTIONALLY xx
   MOVING FORWARD IN SPIRITUAL FORMATION xxiii
Preface to the New Revised Standard Version xxvii

OLD TESTAMENT

Genesis 1
Exodus 71
Leviticus 125
MEETING GOD
IN PRAYER 164
Numbers 168
Deuteronomy 225
Joshua 272
MEETING GOD
IN SERVICE 304
Judges 308
Ruth 340
1 Samuel 346
2 Samuel 388
1 Kings 426
2 Kings 468
1 Chronicles 509
MEETING GOD
IN WORSHIP 550
2 Chronicles 554
Ezra 600
Nehemiah 615
Esther 636
Job 647
Psalms 693
MEETING GOD
IN THE CREATED ORDER . 820

Proverbs 824
Ecclesiastes 867
Song of Solomon 879
Isaiah 889
Jeremiah 986
Lamentations 1075
MEETING GOD
IN SCRIPTURE 1086
Ezekiel 1090
Daniel 1158
Hosea 1179
Joel 1195
Amos 1202
Obadiah 1215
Jonah 1218
Micah 1222
Nahum 1232
Habakkuk 1237
Zephaniah 1242
Haggai 1248
Zechariah 1251
Malachi 1264

NEW TESTAMENT

Matthew 1271
Mark 1318
Luke 1347

John 1396
Acts 1432
Romans 1477
MEETING GOD
IN COMMUNITY 1498
1 Corinthians 1502
2 Corinthians 1521
Galatians 1533
Ephesians 1540
Philippians 1547
Colossians 1553
1 Thessalonians 1558
2 Thessalonians 1563
1 Timothy 1567
2 Timothy 1573
MEETING GOD
IN EVERYDAY LIFE 1578
Titus 1582
Philemon 1585
Hebrews 1587
James 1603
1 Peter 1609
2 Peter 1615
1 John 1619
2 John 1625
3 John 1627
Jude 1629
Revelation 1632

Topical Index to Entry Points and Ways of Meeting God   1659
Index of Quotations 1664

Alphabetical List
OF BIBLE BOOKS

The books of the New Testament are in *italic*.

Acts 1432	*James* 1603	Nehemiah 615
Amos 1202	Jeremiah 986	Numbers 168
1 Chronicles 509	Job 647	Obadiah 1215
2 Chronicles 554	Joel 1195	*1 Peter* 1609
Colossians 1553	*John* 1396	*2 Peter* 1615
1 Corinthians 1502	*1 John* 1619	*Philemon* 1585
2 Corinthians 1521	*2 John* 1625	*Philippians* 1547
Daniel 1158	*3 John* 1627	Proverbs 824
Deuteronomy 225	Jonah 1218	Psalms 693
Ecclesiastes 867	Joshua 272	*Revelation* 1632
Ephesians 1540	*Jude* 1629	*Romans* 1477
Esther 636	Judges 308	Ruth 340
Exodus 71	1 Kings 426	1 Samuel 346
Ezekiel 1090	2 Kings 468	2 Samuel 388
Ezra 600	Lamentations 1075	Song of Solomon 879
Galatians 1533	Leviticus 125	*1 Thessalonians* 1558
Genesis 1	*Luke* 1347	*2 Thessalonians* 1563
Habakkuk 1237	Malachi 1264	*1 Timothy* 1567
Haggai 1248	*Mark* 1318	*2 Timothy* 1573
Hebrews 1587	*Matthew* 1271	*Titus* 1582
Hosea 1179	Micah 1222	Zechariah 1251
Isaiah 889	Nahum 1232	Zephaniah 1242

Abbreviations

In the notes to the books of the Old Testament the following abbreviations are used:

Ant.	Josephus, *Antiquities of the Jews*	Josephus	Flavius Josephus (Jewish historian,
Aram	Aramaic		about A.D. 37 to about 95)
Ch, chs	Chapter, chapters	Macc.	The book(s) of the Maccabees
Cn	Correction; made where the text has	Ms(s)	Manuscript(s)
	suffered in transmission and the	MT	The Hebrew of the pointed
	versions provide no satisfactory		Masoretic Text of the Old Testament
	restoration but where the Standard	OL	Old Latin
	Bible Committee agrees with the	Q Ms(s)	Manuscript(s) found at Qumran by
	judgment of competent scholars as		the Dead Sea
	to the most probable reconstruction	Sam	Samaritan Hebrew text of the Old
	of the original text.		Testament
Gk	Septuagint, Greek version of the Old	Syr	Syriac Version of the Old Testament
	Testament	Tg	Targum
Heb	Hebrew of the consonantal	Vg	Vulgate, Latin Version of the Old
	Masoretic Text of the Old Testament		Testament

How to Use
THE SPIRITUAL FORMATION BIBLE

The editors and writers of the *Spiritual Formation Bible* (many associated with *The Upper Room* and *Weavings* magazines) believe that the written Word is a living word, that its readers should come to scripture with the expectancy that God will speak to them. With that in mind The Upper Room and Zondervan Publishing House have teamed up to bring you *The Spiritual Formation Bible*. Spiritual formation, that process whereby we grow in our relationship with God and become conformed to Jesus Christ, takes place as we interact with God's words in scripture. "The Bible is alive, it speaks to me," sixteenth-century reformer Martin Luther once said. "It has feet, it runs after me; it has hands, it lays hold of me." We meet God personally in the Bible.

This Bible provides simple and practical ways to help you listen for a word from God for your own life. Page after page and feature after feature, its attractive, easy-to-use format will help you linger over each precious passage of scripture. Even if your life tends to be harried and hurried, using this Bible will encourage you to dig deeply and read reflectively. It can help you to be "transformed by the renewing of your mind" (Romans 12.2).

The *Spiritual Formation Bible* is designed to help you:
- reflect on the treasured stories and passages of scripture until they come alive for you
- ask while reading the Bible, "What is God saying to me in this passage?"
- read scripture prayerfully, expectantly and in ways that deeply touch you.
- incorporate the riches of classical spiritual wisdom into your prayer times

The *Spiritual Formation Bible* offers you these benefits through the following features:

Getting Started Articles on pages x–xxv will provide a wealth of wisdom on spiritual formation.

Book Introductions at the beginning of each book point to the primary themes of each book of the Bible. They will help you grasp the Bible's great and recurring spiritual truths and provide the context for each book.

Entry Points appear on each page of the Bible text. Each short article is based on a particular passage on or near the page of scripture on which it appears, and each one will lead you to explore themes of special importance for spiritual growth. Each "Entry Point" follows one of the methods of approaching scripture listed in "Meeting God in Scripture" (pages 1086-89). Many of the "Entry Points" contain quotations from spiritual classics to stir your thoughts and emotions. These insightful, reflective notes will help you enter the passage and make it come alive for you in a personal way. They allow you to *listen* to the Bible as never before. They are also linked to articles on "Ways of Meeting God." The entry points were designed to allow you the freedom to interact with scripture at your own pace. You can use these "Entry Points" consecutively by reading through the Bible from Genesis to Revelation, or you can enter the text at any point. You may also want to try an in-depth reading of a particular book or books. Whatever method you choose, the "Entry Points" will assist you in interacting with God's word.

Ways of Meeting God tie many of the "Entry Points," and their corresponding passages to spiritual disciplines or practices that provide a framework and structure for spiritual growth. Each article provides the reader with background that helps make sense of the "big picture." These general articles provide a wonderful resource for individual reflection or small group or church school discussion. Each of the "Ways of Meeting God" articles can be identified by a distinctive woodcut that also identifies that practice in the "Entry Points." Refer to the Table of Contents to locate these articles.

Glimpses from the Classics are brief excerpts from some of the wisest and most profound writings on the spiritual life. You will find these scattered throughout the text in beautiful, full-page calligraphy, providing a feast for the eyes as well as the spirit.

Indexes help you find topics of special relevance to spiritual formation and provide information about the quotations included in this Bible.

New Revised Standard Version Far more important than any of the tools we've provided is the text itself, the Word of God. The Bible you are holding in your hands is a supernaturally powerful book. The life-giving truth it offers is startlingly simple, yet deeply layered. Our prayer for you is that, as you use *The Spiritual Formation Bible,* the Word of God will enter and enrich you with its message of God's love and grace.

About the Upper Room

"THE UPPER ROOM was prayed into existence," a church leader declared. At the worst of the Great Depression in 1935, a group of Texas church people asked for help with family and home worship. In response to that call, an interdenominational daily devotional magazine was created. From that small beginning, the magazine has grown to a publication in sixty-three editions and forty-three languages in more than eighty countries. Domestic circulation alone exceeds two and a quarter million copies per issue. *El Aposento Alto* is the Spanish language edition.

The organization publishes four additional magazines: *Alive Now* and *Weavings: A Journal of the Christian Spiritual Life* for adults; *Pockets* magazine for children and *Devo'Zine* for teens. Upper Room Books publishes a variety of resources in spiritual formation. In addition to publishing, The Upper Room's ministries have grown to include several spiritual formation programs, among them, The Walk to Emmaus, the Academy for Spiritual Formation, the Adventure in Healing and Wholeness, the Pathways Center for Spiritual Leadership and the Living Prayer Center. To find out more, log on to The Upper Room website: www.upperroom.org.

CONTRIBUTORS

THE EDITORS wish to especially thank **Keith Beasley-Topliffe, Jan Johnson, Robert Morris** and **Mary Lou Redding** for the advice and editorial assistance they provided far beyond the call of duty and to the writers who contributed to this project:

ENTRY POINT NOTES

The Reverend Mary Lou Santillan Baert
United Methodist minister and writer, Dallas, TX.
Proverbs

The Reverend Keith Beasley-Topliffe
United Methodist clergyperson and editor of the
Upper Room Spiritual Classics series.
1&2 Chronicles, Acts

The Reverend Eugene Blair
Director of Congregational Development, Northern
Illinois Conference of the United Methodist
church; curriculum writer for United Methodist
Publishing House and the African Methodist Episcopal Church.
1&2 Kings

The Reverend Anne Broyles
A United Methodist minister and writer of novels,
children's books and religious materials, who lives
in Malibu, CA.
Haggai, Zechariah, Lamentations, Nehemiah

Professor Doris Donnelly, Ph.D.
Professor of Theology at John Carroll University,
Cleveland, OH.
and
Ms. Carol Edkins, M.A.
President of Qualified Pension/Profit Sharing
Consultants, Inc. Cleveland, OH.
1&2 Thessalonians, Philemon

Mr. Robert Durback
A former monk of Mepkin Abbey, Order of
Cistercians of the Strict Observance and editor of
Seeds of Hope: A Henri Nouwen Reader
(Doubleday, 1997).
Exodus

Reverend Paul L. Escamilla
Pastor of Munger Place United Methodist Church
in Dallas, TX and author of *Seasons of Communion*
(1984).
James, Habakkuk

The Reverend Bernard John Franklin
A minister of the Presbyterian Church of Aotearoa,
New Zealand, Reverend Franklin ministers in spiri-
tual direction, leadership, teaching and preaching
in Palmerston North, New Zealand.
John, Jeremiah

Eli Fisher, Ph.D.
Associate Editor of *Alive Now* magazine, Nashville,
TN.
Leviticus

The Reverend Kent Ira Groff
Director, Oasis Ministries for Spiritual Development, Inc., Camp Hill, PA, and writer and Presbyterian minister.
Luke

Dr. E. Glenn Hinson
Professor of Spirituality and John Loftis Professor
of Church History, Baptist Theological Seminary,
Richmond, VA.
and
Ms. Stephanie Ford
A graduate of Baptist Theological Seminary in
Richmond, VA as well as graduate studies in spiri-
tuality at The Catholic University of America,
Washington, DC.
Psalms

Dr. Carol Caruth Johnson
Professor of Pastoral Care, Oral Roberts University,
Tulsa, OK and a licensed marriage and family
therapist.
Hosea, Joshua

Ms. Jan Johnson
Journalist, retreat leader, trained spiritual director
and author of *Enjoying the Presence of God* and
Listening to God, Ms. Johnson lives in Simi, CA.
Mark, Judges

Ms. Jan Knight
Editor of *Pockets* magazine, Nashville, TN.
Micah, Amos

The Reverend Robert Corin Morris
Founding Director of Interweave, an interfaith
adult center in Summit, NJ, and an Episcopal
priest.
Isaiah

The Reverend M. Robert Mulholland, Jr.
Vice President and Chief Academic Officer,
Asbury Theological Seminary, Wilmore, KY.
Among his books are *Shaped by the Word* (Upper
Room Books) and *Invitation to a Journey* (IVP).
Revelation

Susan Muto, Ph.D.
Executive Director of the Epiphany Association, Pittsburgh, PA and the author or co-author of over thirty books.
1&2 Corinthians

The Reverend Bruce R. Ough
Senior Pastor, St. Paul's United Methodist Church, Cedar Rapids, IA , and writer.
Joel

Ms. Virginia Stem Owens
Esther

Dr. Elizabeth L. Patterson, M.A., Ph.D.
Associate Dean, School of Theology, Fuller Theological Seminary, Pasadena, CA
Romans

The Reverend Larry Peacock
A United Methodist pastor, retreat leader, author and spiritual director currently serving Malibu United Methodist Church, CA
Ezekiel, Obadiah, Nahum, Zephaniah, Malachi

Ms. Sheila Mary Pritchard, MTh, Dip. R.E.
Teacher, spiritual director, retreat leader; developed the Spiritual Formation department of the Bible College of New Zealand.
1&2 Peter, Jude

Ms. Mary Lou Redding
Managing Editor, *The Upper Room* magazine, Nashville, TN
Numbers, Daniel, Job, Ezra

Dr. Tom Schwanda
An ordained minister in the Reformed Church of America who serves as the associate for spiritual formation and family ministry in the RCA, Grand Rapids, MI
Galatians, Ephesians, Philippians, Colossians, Hebrews, 1,2,3 John

Mr. Gary Thomas
Director of the Center for Evangelical Spirituality, Bellingham, WA and author of *Seeking the Face of God, Sacred Pathways* and *The Glorious Pursuit.*
Matthew, 1&2 Timothy, Titus, Deuteronomy

The Reverend Douglas Vest
Episcopal priest, author, spiritual director and retreat leader, Altadena, CA
Jonah, Ecclesiastes, 1&2 Samuel

Ms. Norvene Vest
Author of *Gathered in the Word* and frequent writer on Benedictine spirituality. Ms. Vest is an Episcopal laywoman who lives with her husband, Douglas, in Altadena, CA
Genesis, Ruth

Wendy Wright
Professor of Theology, Creighton University, Omaha, NE and author of *Sacred Dwelling: A Spirituality of Family Life*
Song of Solomon

WAYS OF MEETING GOD

The Reverend Keith Beasley-Topliffe
United Methodist clergyperson and editor of the *Upper Room Spiritual Classics* series
"Meeting God in Worship" (co-author)

Stephen D. Bryant
Publisher, The Upper Room, Nashville, TN
"Meeting God in Prayer"

Janice T. Grana
Former Editor and Publisher, The Upper Room, now Executive Editor, Upper Room Books, Nashville, TN
"Meeting God in Service"

J.Steven Harper, Ph.D.
Former Dean of the Chapel, The Upper Room, now Vice President and Dean, Asbury Theological Seminary, Orlando Campus
"Meeting God in Scripture"

Reuben P. Job
Former Publisher, The Upper Room, and a retired bishop in the United Methodist Church
"Meeting God in Worship" (co-author)

Timothy Jones
Author, editor and retreat leader, author of *Awake My Soul* and *The Art of Prayer*
"Meeting God in Everyday Life"

Mary Lou Redding
Managing Editor, The Upper Room magazine, Nashville, TN, author of *Breaking and Mending* (1998)
"Meeting God in Community"

Marjorie Thompson
Presbyterian Minister and Director of the Pathways Center for Spiritual Leadership, Nashville, TN; author of *Soul Feast* and *Family: The Forming Center*
"Meeting God in the Created Order"

GETTING STARTED IN SPIRITUAL FORMATION

J. Steven Harper, Ph.D.
Former Dean of the Chapel, The Upper Room, now Vice President and Dean, Asbury Theological Seminary, Orlando Campus.
"Moving Forward in Spiritual Formation"

John Mogabgab
Editor *Weavings* magazine, Nashville, TN and the husband of Marjorie Thompson.
"What is Spiritual Formation?"

The Reverend M. Robert Mulholland, Jr.
Adapted from Chapters Two and Five of *Shaped by the Word: The Power of Scripture in Spiritual Formation* (Upper Room Books,1985) by Jan Johnson
"Reading the Scriptures Devotionally"

Marjorie Thompson
Director, The Pathways Center for Spiritual Leadership, Nashville, TN and the wife of John Mogabgab.
"Praying the Scriptures"

GETTING STARTED
in SPIRITUAL FORMATION

What is Spiritual Formation?

Human beings are creatures of the future. Unlike other inhabitants of creation whose lives are fixed within the boundaries of genetics and instinct, human existence is open-ended, laced with mystery, like moist clay in a potter's hand. We are works in progress, shaped by the constant rhythms of nature and the unexpected turns of history. Sometimes elated and sometimes burdened by our unfinished condition, we live our days conscious that "what we shall be has not yet been revealed (1 John 3.2). A sense of our true identity is always just beyond our grasp, always awaiting us, it seems, just around the next bend in the road.

As nature and history interact with a human existence that is incomplete, pliable and rich with potential, personal formation occurs. Human beings are formed by the sculpting of will, intellect and emotion into a distinct way of being in the world. Such formation of personal character will assume a wide range of expression depending on our location geographically, socially, economically and culturally. Family values, social conventions, cultural assumptions, the great turning points of an epoch, the painful secrets of a heart—these and many other factors combine to form or deform the direction, depth and boundaries of our lives. Formation is therefore a fundamental characteristic of human life. It is happening whether or not we are aware of it, and its effect may as often inhibit as promote the development of healthy, fulfilled humanity.

For people of Biblical faith, nature and history of themselves are not the final sources of personal formation. Rather, they are means through which the God who formed all things molds human beings into the contours of their truest destiny, the unfettered praise of God (see Isaiah 43.21). To be shaped by God's gracious design is a particular expression of personal formation—spiritual formation. Irenaeus, third-century bishop of Lyons, echoed this ancient Biblical theme when he observed that "the glory of God is the human being fully alive." The God known in scripture is a God who continuously forms something out of nothing—earth and heaven, creatures great and small, a people who call upon God's name, the "inward parts" (Psalm 139.13) of every human life. Yet the majestic sweep of God's formational activity never eclipses the intimacy God desires and seeks with us. Having carefully and lovingly formed each of us in the womb, God knows us by name and will not forget us (see Isaiah 43.1; 44.21,24). In Biblical perspective, to be a person means to exist in a relationship of ongoing spiritual formation with the God whose interest in us extends to the very roots of our being.

For Christians, the pattern and fulfillment of God's work of spiritual formation converge in a single figure—Jesus Christ. Jesus is the human being fully alive, fully open to God's work in the world. Simultaneously, Jesus *is* God's work fully alive, fully embodied in the world. For all who are heavily burdened and wearied by the torments of the world, for all who long to dwell in the house of the Lord, Jesus is the level way, the whole truth and the radiant life. Christians are placed daily before the greatest of all choices: to be conformed to the luminous image of Jesus Christ through the gracious assistance of God the Holy Spirit or to be conformed to the ravaged image of the world through the deceitful encouragement of the "cosmic powers of this present darkness" (Romans 12.2; Ephesians 6.10–13).

Spiritual formation in the Christian tradition, then, is a lifelong process through which our new humanity, hidden with Jesus Christ in God, becomes ever more visible and effective through the leading of the Holy Spirit. Spiritual formation at its best has been understood to be at once fully divine and fully human—that is, initiated by God and manifest in both vital communities of faith and in the lives of individual disciples. We see this theme carried through the history of the church, from Paul's introduction of formation in Jesus Christ as the central work of Christian life (Galatians 4.19) to early formational writings such as the *Didache* (second century); to the formative intent of monastic rules; to the shaping purpose of Protestant manuals of piety; to the affirmation of lay formation in the documents of Vatican II; and finally to the current search for practices that open us to God.

In Biblical perspective, to be a person means to exist in a relationship of ongoing spiritual formation with the God whose interest in us extends to the very roots of our being.

Our New Humanity. Our unfinished character leads us to acknowledge that "what we shall be has not yet been revealed." Yet Christians, looking at Jesus Christ, can add with confident hope that "we shall be like him" (1 John 3.2). This hope originates in the hidden dimensions of baptism. Baptism unites us with the full sweep of Christ's life and death, resurrection

and ascension in glory to the eternal communion of love enjoyed by our triune God. In baptism motifs of cleansing from the stain of sin coexist with images of death and rebirth to signal the radically new life we enter through this spiritual birth canal (see John 3.1–6).

At the center of this rebirth from above is the Paschal mystery—the pattern of self-relinquishment and loving availability Jesus freely manifested in his ministry and in his final journey to Jerusalem and Golgotha. This is the mysterious pattern of

God's work in the world, the pattern of loss that brings gain, willing sacrifice that yields abundance, self-forgetfulness that creates a space for the remembering God. It is the pattern that steers our course from bondage to freedom—from the ways of the old Adam, who turned and hid from the one who so lovingly formed him, to the freedom of the new Adam, Jesus Christ, who lives with God in unbroken intimacy.

This unfolding of baptismal grace in daily life, this passing from bondage to freedom, is spiritual formation. Because spiritual formation draws us into the fullness of life in Jesus Christ, it shares the qualities of Jesus Christ. Thus, spiritual formation is eminently personal yet inherently corporate: It erases nothing of our unique humanity but transposes it into a larger reality—the mystical body of Jesus Christ in and through which we are, as the Episcopal *Book of Common Prayer* notes, "very members incorporate" of one another. Spiritual formation is also fully human, reflecting our own decisions, commitments, disciplines and actions. At the same time, spiritual formation is wholly divine, an activity initiated by God and completed by God, in which we have been generously embraced for the sake of the world.

The Holy Spirit's Leading. The sweeping movement of grace by which the world was created and is sustained is orchestrated by God the Holy Spirit. In God's sovereign freedom, the Holy Spirit stirs where he chooses. Remarkably, the Spirit has selected human life as a privileged place of redemptive activity. In the day-to-day rhythms of our life, the Holy Spirit comes to us with gentle persistence, inviting us to join the wondrous dance of life with God. In this holy dance the Spirit always takes the lead, a partner both sensitive and sure. "The spiritual life is the life of God's Spirit in us," notes spiritual writer Marjorie Thompson, "the living interaction between our spirit and the Holy Spirit through which we mature into the full stature of Christ and become more surrendered to the work of the Spirit within and around us."

There are settings and disciplines that prepare us to recognize and respond to the Holy Spirit's invitation. The church, itself at once human and divine—the body of Jesus Christ visible and tangible in the world, as rich with promise as it is with paradox—is the principal context in which to sharpen our spiritual senses. The mere fact of gathering with others on the Lord's Day reminds us that the Holy Spirit continuously draws together what evil strives to scatter. In congregational worship, we hear God's word to us; recall how lavishly God loves us; see this love enacted in baptism; taste its sweetness in the Lord's Supper; and take stock of our response to it in confession, hymn and corporate prayer. Small groups given to prayer, study or outreach also offer places to increase our awareness of the Holy Spirit's leading. In the company of faithful seekers, another person's moment of vulnerability, a truth spoken in love or a story told in trust can awaken insight into ways the Holy Spirit is also present with us. Family life, which Martin Luther placed ahead of the monastery as the true school of charity, provides many opportunities to learn the art of self-forgetfulness. Time spent with the poor and needy instructs us in our own poverty, prepares us to receive more than we bestow from those who often seem so distressingly different and gives the Spirit occasion to teach us the extent of our common humanity.

Personal spiritual practices also prime us to be responsive to the Holy Spirit's approach. The meditative reading of scripture encouraged in this Bible enables us to become at home in God's Word. As this occurs, we develop a growing familiarity with the Holy Spirit who fashioned and continues to dwell in holy writ. According to twelfth-century Cistercian abbot Peter of Celle, such reading is nothing less than "the soul's food, light, lamp, refuge, consolation, and the spice of every spiritual savor." Prayer, that royal road to deepening intimacy with God, will inevitably acquaint us with the guiding grace of the Spirit. It is in the Spirit that we pray and through the Spirit that the inarticulate yearnings of our heart receive coherent expression before God (see Romans 8.27). Various "spiritual fitness" exercises, including abstaining from self-destructive activities and attitudes, allocating personal resources in a godly manner and following simple rules of life, help to remind us that God is the center of each day. Such exercises produce stamina for continued acceptance of the Holy Spirit's invitation to "come and follow."

Following the leading of the Holy Spirit builds in us a growing capacity for extraordinary witness to God's kingdom, such as extending forgiveness where there has been genuine injury. It also reinforces in us the knowledge that our new humanity in Jesus Christ is the work of the Spirit and not our own achievement. In our human weakness, we need the strength and sustenance of the Holy Spirit to maintain the God-ward direction of our life. Such assistance is clearly promised by Jesus: "When the Spirit of truth, comes, he will guide you into all truth" (John 16.13). This truth is what the author of Ephesians calls "the stature of Christ" (Ephesians 4.13). The measure of this truth is nothing other than love. Love is the first gift of the Spirit and the final test of our freedom in Jesus Christ (see 1 Corinthians 13; Galatians 5.22; Colossians 1.8). All other marks of our new humanity—joy, peace, patience, kindness, generosity, faithfulness, self-control—are manifestations of this love, a love that binds us to Jesus Christ in the unity of the Holy Spirit for the sake of the world God loves so much. "If we live by the Spirit, let us also be guided by the Spirit" (Galatians 5.25).

> In a life increasingly given to the guidance of the Holy Spirit, our new humanity in Jesus Christ gradually becomes more visible and effective in the world.

In the World. In a life increasingly given to the guidance of the Holy Spirit, our new humanity in Jesus Christ gradually becomes more visible and effective in the world. Far from removing us from the messiness of the world, spiritual formation plunges us into the middle of the world's rage and suffering. It was to this place of pain and bewilderment that Jesus Christ was sent as the visible image of the invisible God (see John 14.9; Colossians 1.15). It was to this place of bitterness and infirmity that Jesus Christ was sent, not to condemn, but to save (see John 3.17). Those who are being formed in his image take the same path. Love, the full measure of Christian maturity, impels us with kindly urgency in this direction. Love desires to be seen, known, and received, for by these actions it grows wider and deeper. Through us love is extended to the furthest recesses of human sorrow and need. Thus, God's love for the world—in us because we are in Jesus Christ—becomes a sign of hope and a source of transformation in the world.

"No one is richer, no one more powerful, no one more free," observes Thomas à Kempis, "than the person who can give his whole life to God and freely serve others with deep humility and love." To embody in thought, word, and deed the love of God made known in our Lord Jesus Christ is the signal mark of faithful discipleship, the inexhaustible strength of vital congregations and the ultimate goal of spiritual formation.

GETTING STARTED
in SPIRITUAL FORMATION

Praying the Scriptures

A longtime member of a well-established Protestant church recounted a turning point in her spiritual life: She discovered that the Bible could be prayed as well as read. She had read, studied and reflected on the Bible for many years, yet the notion of "praying the scriptures" seemed quite foreign when a friend first suggested it. Nonetheless, as soon as she began to practice praying the scriptures, it made complete sense. For the first time in her adult life, the Bible truly came alive. She experienced the Word of God as "living and active" (Hebrews 4.12), a means through which God searched, invited, challenged and comforted her. It seemed so natural that she felt as if she had spiritually "come home."

To pray the scriptures means to allow the words of the sacred text to form our prayer—either directly or indirectly. Prayer entails heart-to-heart communication with God that moves in both directions. God speaks, we listen and respond; we speak, God listens and responds.

> To pray the scriptures means to allow the words of the sacred text to form our prayer —either directly or indirectly.

To pray the scriptures requires first of all that we approach the Word in a spirit of prayer. We acknowledge that we are seeking the living, active presence of God in and through God's Word. We bring ourselves consciously into the divine presence and affirm the reality of this presence even if we cannot feel it. Whatever we read and reflect on in the Word is part of our ongoing relationship with God.

From this basic stance, we may take any number of approaches to praying the scriptures. One of the most central and ancient practices of Christian prayer is called *lectio divina,* or spiritual reading. In *lectio divina,* we begin by reading and savoring a short passage of scripture. Our inner posture is one of a listening heart filled with an unhurried expectation that God has a message to convey especially suited to our condition and circumstance. We read and ruminate with the ears of our heart open, alert to connections the Spirit may reveal between the passage and our life situation. We ask, "What are you saying to me today, Lord? What am I to hear in this story, parable, prophecy?" Listening in this way requires an attitude of patient receptivity in which we let go of our own agendas and open ourselves to God's shaping purpose.

Lectio Divina. Once we have heard a word that we know is meant for our ears, we are naturally drawn to prayer. From listening we move to speaking—perhaps in anguish, confession or sorrow; perhaps in joy, praise, thanksgiving or adoration; perhaps in anger, confusion or hurt; perhaps in quiet confidence, trust or surrender. Finally, after pouring out our heart to God, we come to rest simply and deeply in that wonderful, loving presence of God. Reading, reflecting, responding and resting—this is the basic rhythm of a venerable and often-used approach to scripture called *lectio divina*.

Perhaps an example will help to bring this rhythm alive in your imagination. Recently I read in 2 Kings about the origins of the people called Samaritans. Samaria once belonged to the ancient kingdom of Israel. When the king of Assyria invaded, taking Israelites captive to his own land, he forcibly repopulated Samaria with people from surrounding regions who decided to worship "the god of the land." The passage reads, "So they worshiped the LORD but also served their own gods, after the manner of the nations from among whom they had been carried away" (2 Kings 17.33). I hadn't read this book in a long time, and I found myself fascinated by the history. It would make for interesting Bible study, I thought, or a good sermon. Then suddenly I heard in my mind's ear a shocking indictment: "You are a Samaritan." Recalling that I was reading for the purpose of prayer, I asked, "Are you really saying that I'm like this, God?" The answer was there in my own heart: Yes, you worship God but also the gods of this land—success, prosperity, "the American Dream." This was clearly a very uncomfortable word that God had addressed personally to me. It prompted me to reflect on all the ways I do, in fact, give my heart and allegiance to the idols of my culture. Recognition of that reality propelled me into prayers of confession and repentance, then prayer for the strength of will to desire God above all else. Finally, I had to confess my guilt to God and rest in the assurance of God's mercy. The whole cycle took perhaps ten or fifteen minutes.

The Ignatian Method. *Lectio divina* is but one way to pray the scriptures. We can also pray the Bible by using our God-given imagination by means of an ancient method referred to as Ignatian. This approach invites us to enter the narrative, picturing the situation and identifying with characters that populate the drama. This may eventually lead us to dialogue beyond what is given in the text, a dialogue that becomes part of our prayer. Some passages of scripture are better suited to this process than others. The Gospels are especially rich in stories that easily engage our imagination as a way to enter into prayer.

Read, for example, a story such as the tax collector and the Pharisee (see Luke 18.9–14). Picture the two men in the temple, the Pharisee standing proudly upfront, grateful not to be like the man behind him. Imagine what it is like to be in the shoes of someone who represents such high standards of righteousness according to Israelite law, who sees his life as a model of religious conduct for others. Have you ever felt like this? If so, in what kinds of situations or with what sorts of people? Then step into the shoes of the tax collector, the hated "tool of Rome." Imagine how many times you have skimmed a hefty sum for yourself from the taxes you have collected from fellow Jews for the Roman occupiers. What emotions are your experiencing—the misery of being an outcast in your own community, the self-loathing that comes from betraying your people and your integrity, the despair at your weakness of character, your desperate hope for mercy from God? With which of these two characters do you most identify? What do you have to say to God about your own experience in relation to these two characters? Do you see how the story and your personal engagement with it lead you into prayer?

This approach to praying the scriptures is rich and fruitful for people who can readily exercise their God-given imagination. Perhaps you can imagine yourself as Peter, looking at the awesome catch of fish, feeling the power of the One standing before you whose eyes you dare not even look into (see Luke 5.1–11). Does this speak to your experience before God? Or perhaps you identify strongly with Martha as your sister sits idly listening to Jesus while you, in an anxious dither, rush to complete meal preparations. Do you hear Jesus' words to you as rebuke or invitation? What are you really longing for in your own heart? (see Luke 10.38–42). Maybe you are in the boat with the disciples facing a sudden and terrifying storm. You sense the limits of your vision and power is limited by your fear. How do Jesus' words affect your spirit as you imagine being part of this story? Are you facing a storm in your life just now? Does identification with the story make your prayer more concrete? Is God speaking a word to you through this passage (see Mark 4.35–41)? Or picture yourself as the woman who suffered from an issue of blood for twelve years, as you shyly thread your way through the crowd to touch the edge of Jesus' clothing. Or as Jairus, desperate for Jesus to come quickly before your daughter dies, watching Jesus turn around to find out who touched him, taking precious time to deal with the needs of someone else before he comes with you to your home (see Mark 5.21–43). Where do you connect with these powerful stories? What insight into yourself, into God, into your relationships comes through praying the Gospels in this way? It can be especially helpful to write down the basic outline of your imaginative encounter with the text, your insights and any dialogue with story characters or with God that naturally occur as part of your prayer.

> The Gospels are especially rich in stories that easily engage our imagination as a way to enter into prayer.

The Prayers and Songs of Scripture. There are other ways to pray scripture as well. The Bible gives us categories for prayer, expands our language for prayer and tutors us in speaking to God as we hear God speak to us through the Word. The Bible contains prayers and canticles (songs) that give us words to pray and praise. Many, such as the Lord's Prayer, the Magnificat and the Canticle of Simeon, have become part of the common prayer of church liturgy. Yet any of these may also give voice to the joys, yearnings and struggles of our personal lives. We truly pray the Lord's Prayer when we take each phrase and make it our own, finding its truth reflected in our beliefs, needs, fears and aspirations. Mary's Magnificat can become our own song of exultation, hope and trust. There are times when we recognize with her that "the Mighty One has done great things for me" (Luke 1.49). We may know from experience what it means to be lifted up from lowliness, or we may see the emptiness of those who seem powerful and self-satisfied. Thus, we know that the truths spoken in Mary's words are universal precisely because they are so personal.

Sometimes we can personalize a passage of scripture by placing our own name in it. Some passages from the books of the Prophets lend themselves to becoming personal prayers as we make ourselves the recipients of God's Word. Take, for example, God's invitation to the abundant life in Isaiah. Insert your name in the blanks to get a feel for how to pray scripture this way:

Ho, _____ who thirsts,
    come to the waters;
and _____ who have no money,
    come, buy and eat!
_____, why do you spend your money for that which is not bread,
    and your labor for that which does not satisfy?
Listen carefully to me, _____, and eat what is good . . .
    listen, so that you may live.
I will make with you an everlasting covenant, _____. (Isaiah 55.1–3)

Here you allow yourself to receive personally the promises (or the judgments) of God and to respond from the heart. Try this out with Isaiah 43.1–7; Jeremiah 1.4–8 or 18.1–6.

Praying the Book of Psalms. The words of scripture can also become words through which we address God directly. Nowhere is this more apparent than in the book of Psalms. The book of Psalms has been called "the prayer book of the Bible" in both the Jewish and Christian traditions. It is a collection of sung prayers that has been used in corporate liturgy from the time of ancient Israel up to the present. Because the psalms range so widely in emotional expression, from the heights of adoration and praise to the depths of vengeful curses against the enemy, they have special pertinence to our prayer life. They teach us to hide nothing from God, but to bring all that is real into the only relationship that can bless the best and heal the worst in us. Surely this is why German theologian Dietrich Bonhoeffer summoned the earthy wit of Martin Luther when he declared, "Whoever has begun to pray the Psalter seriously and regularly will soon give a vacation to other little devotional prayers and say: 'Ah, there is not the juice, the strength, the passion, the fire which

I find in the Psalter' (Luther)" (*Psalms: The Prayer Book of the Bible* [Minneapolis: Augsburg Publishing House, 1970], 25).

Whether in distress, trust, anger or delight, we find that the words of the psalms accompany us into God's presence. The Lord becomes *my* shepherd as well as the shepherd of all those who trust in him (see Psalm 23). It is I who sit down by the rivers of Babylon lamenting my experience of exile with all who know such anguish (see Psalm 137). God is searching my heart in Psalm 139, assuring me that there is no place I can go where God's Spirit is not. Psalm 131 leads me into the peace of resting in the divine embrace like a small child with my mother. I am the poor and needy one who cries out for preservation (see Psalm 86), the one who has transgressed and needs mercy (see Psalm 51). It is I who stand looking in awe at the heavens, marveling that humans like me should count for anything in God's sight (see Psalm 8). In the psalms we find words to express every conceivable human condition and feeling. These prayers give us words to glorify, confess, hope, ask and even curse. In so doing, they give us permission to share our whole being with God.

Sometimes the psalms give us words for intercession as well. The psalm I pray may not fit *my* experience but may very well reflect the experience of another person or group. Recently, praying Psalm 107 led me into intercession for many people.

Trust the Spirit to Guide You. There are, then, many ways to pray the scriptures. To practice any particular way, however, we need to set aside some time each day to listen and respond to God's Word. Even ten to fifteen minutes daily may be sufficient, although if you combine praying scripture with journaling, you will likely need twenty-five to thirty minutes. Seek a regular place for prayer as well, a place that can be free from distracting noise and interruption. Take a few moments to settle yourself peacefully in God's presence and pray for the guidance of the Spirit. Let your body be a partner in prayer; find a comfortable posture that will keep you alert but relaxed. Then simply trust the Spirit to guide you into prayer as your listening, your reflection and your response are shaped by the Word of God. Be patient with your practice. In time, rich blessings will attend you!

Because the psalms range so widely in emotional expression, from the heights of adoration and praise to the depths of vengeful curses against the enemy, they have special pertinence to our prayer life.

GETTING STARTED
in SPIRITUAL FORMATION

Reading Scripture Devotionally

The moment we open a book, a powerful set of habitual practices begins to work. Our culture teaches us learning methods that establish the reader as the controlling power; that person seeks to master the text in order to use it for his or her own purposes. The cognitive, analytical aspects of our beings are hyper-developed in our culture; we tend to think that this is proper—the sharper we are intellectually, the smarter we are; the more quickly we grasp concepts and synthesize them, the more balanced we are.

If we care about responding to God with our whole being, we must love God with all of our mind, using our cognitive abilities. We cannot shirk this. Jesus, however, puts loving God with the heart and soul higher on his list: "You shall love the Lord your God with all your heart, and with all your soul, and with all your mind" (Matthew 22.37). Loving God with all our heart and all our soul precedes loving God with all of our mind. Perhaps the fact that "mind" comes last in the list doesn't mean that it is less important, but it certainly indicates that it is not the only way to respond to God or even the dominant way to respond as our culture asserts. (The order is the same in all three Synoptic Gospels: See Mark 12.30; Luke 10.27.)

Our predominant mode of response, however, is often the rational, cognitive and intellectual. When we make this mindset our only mode of reading scripture, it can be difficult to have "ears to hear." If we want to allow God to use scripture for our spiritual formation, we need to develop another way of reading that allows God's Word to speak transformationally to the deepest levels of our being.

It is wise to filter scripture through the mind, but when that is our primary filter, it can create an imbalance. Can you see the problem that arises here? What if God wishes to meet us in the passage in an intimate way, according to his wisdom, communicating what we need to hear but wish to avoid? It is easy to read scripture in a purely cognitive way and decide that this passage doesn't apply to us. (We frequently even pick out some other troublesome person who should obviously heed this text instead of ourselves!) This purely cognitive way of reading insulates the "door" of our being against God's "knocking." Why? We are not really opening our being at deeper levels to the possibility of meeting God in that passage.

Formational Scripture Reading. *Formational* scripture reading is quite different from what we're used to. Formational scripture reading invites us to open ourselves to allow God to set the agenda for our lives through the text. It facilitates genuine spiritual formation—the process of being conformed to the image of Jesus Christ.

Reading formationally helps us open our "rational filter," which can sift out so much of God's voice. We begin to hear at the heart and soul level. Jesus frequently reminded those who had "ears to hear" (Mark 4.9,23; Luke 8.8; 14.35).

Formational reading often helps us develop those ears to hear. Let me share with you a personal experience of formational reading. I was following a prescribed plan for Bible reading and had come to the exodus event. I'd read about the struggle between God and Pharaoh many times before but only informationally. As I read the daily assigned portion, I sat before it and said, "Lord, what are you seeking to say to me through this?" All sorts of thoughts went through my mind—who said what, Pharaoh's resistance, God's hardening Pharaoh's heart. I got nothing from it after wrestling with it for a week or more. Finally, each day's portion moved one by one through the ten plagues. I was met each time with silence—or my own noisy understanding of the passage.

As I moved toward the end of the passage about the plagues and asked that same question, an answer came: "You are Pharaoh!" "What?" I replied. "Me, Pharaoh? Moses, perhaps, even one of the Hebrews, but Pharaoh? Perhaps a servant or slave, but Pharaoh?" Things began to open up in the text and inside me. I realized that God had given me certain gifts, abilities and personality traits. All these were God's "children," but I had enslaved them to my own purposes, desires, intentions and plans. Truly I was the Pharaoh of my life! I came to the last plague— the death of the firstborn. I saw that for me to cease to be Pharaoh in my life, there had to be a death of my "firstborn" desires to use God's gifts for my own purposes. If those gifts were to be liberated for God's use in my life, I would have to cease to be Pharaoh.

> Formational scripture reading invites us to open ourselves to allow God to set the agenda for our lives through the text.

Characteristics of Formational Scripture Reading.

Depth. Informational reading seeks to cover as much material as possible as quickly as possible, while formational reading involves smaller portions of scripture. The point is not to just get through the text, but to become personally involved in it. Formational reading is concerned with depth, so we may find ourselves "holding on" to just one sentence or paragraph or page for quite a while. We allow the passage to open out to us its deeper dynamics and multiple layers of meaning. We let the text intrude into our life and address us.

Openness. In formational reading, we let the text master us. We come to the text with an openness to hear, to receive and to respond. This may feel risky because it lays us open to unforeseen conclusions.

Humility. Formational reading requires a humble and willing approach, which requires a new inner posture in which we are willing to relinquish our insights and purposes. We stand ourselves before scripture and await its address.

Mystery. Informational reading can be characterized by a problem-solving mentality. When we do respond, we often read our needs and desires into the scripture, asking, Does this passage solve my problems, answer my questions, meet my needs? Formational reading invites us to become open to the whole mystery of God. We allow God to address us however he may wish to do so. Eventually, we may discover that problem-solving dynamics emerge from the encounter, but we relinquish the right to solve our problems with scripture.

Suggestions for Formational Scripture Reading. *Make listening for God's voice a top priority.* Focus your attention on what God is saying to you as you read. Listen for God to speak to you in and through, around and within, over and behind the words. Keep asking yourself, "What is God seeking to say to me in all of this?" Allow the text to become an instrument of God's control in your life. Respond to what you read with your heart and spirit.

Let your response take place down in the deeper levels of your being. Ask yourself questions such as: How do I feel about what is being said? How am I reacting? How am I responding down deep within myself? What is going on inside of me? Then begin to ask yourself "why" questions: Why do I feel this way? Why am I responding in this manner? Why do I have these feelings within?

Let this exercise be an opportunity to get in touch with the deeper layers of your being. What do your reactions tell you about your habits, your attitudes, your perspectives, your responses and your reactions to life? Are you beginning to see something about yourself? Thomas à Kempis said, "A humble knowledge of ourselves is a surer way to God than is the search for depth of learning." That humble knowledge of yourself can come when you read scripture if you balance your cognitive response pattern with this affective response from deep within your being.

Prepare to read by quieting yourself. You can't run in, sit down, pick up the text and read scripture formationally. You have to "center down," to use the old Quaker phrase—become still, relinquish your agenda and acknowledge the presence of God. You may have to relax first in order to do this. When you do this, you may find that no word addresses you out of that text on that day, but the constant discipline of preparing yourself and entering into formational reading will itself be spiritually forming to your soul.

Allow the two kinds of reading—informational and formational—to work together. You may begin reading a scripture passage with informational dynamics, but then you must be sensitive to the need to move to the formational dynamics of reading. Allow yourself to become open and receptive to the intrusion of the living Word of God into your garbled, distorted self. You may get tripped up on an informational point and need to move back to an informational mode. There is a necessary interplay between these two approaches, but you'll ultimately need to arrive at a disciplined development of the formational mode of approaching the text. As we become skilled at shifting to that inner posture of becoming listeners, we develop "ears to hear." We become receptive and accessible to being addressed by the living Word of God.

Getting Started
in Spiritual Formation

Moving Forward in Spiritual Formation

In his article "What is Spiritual Formation," John Mogabgab defines spiritual formation as "a lifelong process through which our new humanity, hidden with Jesus Christ in God, becomes ever more visible and effective through the leading of the Holy Spirit." As noted evangelist E. Stanley Jones said, "We are Christians under construction." Thinking of our spiritual life as a process, as a journey, helps us to continually make progress toward the goal of being conformed to the image of Jesus Christ.

> Thinking of our spiritual life as a process, as a journey, helps us to continually make progress toward the goal of being conformed to the image of Jesus Christ.

First, we journey forward in faith. The Christian life is lived in relationship with Jesus Christ. We express our faith in Jesus through the character and conduct that emerge from that relationship. Our "belief system" is the total expression of who we are and what we do. The ongoing process of spiritual formation begins and continues with faith. Having given ourselves to God through an initial commitment, we subsequently respond to God, so that our faith grows deeper and stronger. The Holy Spirit is the dynamic energy that conforms us to the likeness of Jesus Christ in both personal and social holiness.

We never "graduate" from the spiritual life. Instead, we awaken each day to discovery. Frank Laubach began each day by praying, "God, what are you doing in the world today that I can help you

with?" We move forward in spiritual formation believing that God does indeed invite us into holy partnership.

Second, we move forward with a sense of "fit." When David volunteered to fight Goliath, King Saul clothed him with the royal armor (see 1 Samuel 17.38). Because the armor didn't fit, David gave it back to Saul, preferring his own clothing and his own weaponry—five stones and a slingshot. David's strategy may have been contrary to all standards of military preparedness, but it worked! Likewise, our approach to God in spiritual formation must "fit" each of us individually. The Christian life is a way of the heart, and we must follow our hearts in the way we move forward in spiritual formation. Spiritual formation is not random or subjective, however. On the contrary, the choices we make will conform to the larger patterns of faith development in our lives.

As you use this Bible, you will undoubtedly find that certain approaches will be more valuable and meaningful than others. They may seem more comfortable. Go forward in the directions that have benefited you most. Don't worry about what you are *not* selecting; concentrate on the tradition or path that produces righteousness, peace and joy in your life (see Romans 14.17).

Along the way, you may find yourself circling back to a previous method or expanding into new areas. Just as with clothing so also with the soul, there will come those times when you "outgrow" the methods you are using and feel the need to develop in new and different ways. Remember that outgrowing something does not mean leaving it behind. It merely means increasing the size. You will inevitably arrive at such turning points in your spiritual life. When the time is ripe for change, you will know it. For now, work with the principles and practices that best fuel your desire for deeper life in God.

A sense of "fit" also means tailoring your spiritual practices to the realities of your life. What are you experiencing now? Develop a devotional life that takes your circumstances into consideration. In fact, you will not continue to move forward if you deny your needs and your emotions. When they change, you can alter your particular practices to fit a new circumstance or emotion. God knows what you are going through. Don't be afraid to follow wherever God might be leading you on your spiritual formation journey.

Third, we move forward in the presence of friends. Spiritual formation does not happen in isolation. One sign of our genuine progress is the desire to be in "communion with the saints"—in community with others. Community is the context in which much authentic spiritual formation takes place.

Through community we express our faith in Jesus Christ—a faith that includes the conviction that Jesus has many brothers and sisters whom we are called to love and with whom we are called to live. Our faith community consists of our particular affiliation with a congregation and the related smaller groups that exist within it, as well as our spiritual friends, mentors and teachers. Living in community educates, guides, protects, restores, inspires, forgives, heals and sustains us and sends us out into the world.

Community is also the laboratory in which we learn what it means to be compassionate, not only to fellow Christians, but to people located throughout the world; our community extends to our wider ecumenical and mission associations with Christians around the globe.

The saints are not only those with whom we live in ongoing fellowship—they are those of renown from the past. Being in community with others means developing a devotional life that includes reading and reflecting on the classics of Christian spirituality. Quotations from godly men and women have been scattered throughout this Bible, not only for inspiration, but also as a reminder that the spiritual life is always one of connecting to others. When we read the classics we connect with those who have gone before us. Far from being outdated or irrelevant, the classic writers are part of the great "cloud of witnesses" (see Hebrews 12.1) who both inform us and encourage us in our journey.

We are blessed to have many of the spiritual classics in print today. The Paulist Press series *Classics of Western Spirituality* is one of the most extensive offerings in this regard. The Upper Room has produced *Great Devotional Classics,* a boxed set of booklets with excerpts from the writings of many men and women of Christian history, and has more recently, launched a series entitled *Upper Room Spiritual Classics.*

You can also find individual classics in print. Works like Augustine's *Confessions* or Julian of Norwich's *Revelations of Divine Love* are but two of hundreds of such works available for your enrichment. Anthologies are another wonderful way to connect with the classics. John Baillie's *A Diary of Readings* is one of the best known, containing one-page excerpts for every day of the year. Woodeene Koenig-Bricker's volume *365 Saints* summarizes the thoughts and contributions of well-known and little-known Christians.

> Faith and form are inseparable. Form provides the concrete structure on which spiritual formation is built.

Finally, we move forward by adopting a form. Faith and form are inseparable. Form provides the concrete structure on which spiritual formation is built. We are offered a variety of forms and styles, plans and programs to shape and sustain our discipleship. As we become rooted in the spiritual life, we will likely gravitate toward particular resources and practices that suit us and satisfy our needs. Our choices are determined by factors such as gender, race, personality, faith tradition, age and stage in life. There is nothing wrong with settling into a particular form of spiritual formation. It is as normal as our choices in areas such as literature, art and music. We never have to apologize for finding and developing those patterns to which we are drawn.

God is gracious to provide many avenues for spiritual development. This Bible is designed to provide a means to enter into the scriptures in a very personal way. Or you may find a daily-office format like *The Book of Common Prayer* or *A Guide to Prayer for All God's People* very helpful. You may enjoy feeding for an extensive period of time on the writings of a single author like Oswald Chambers' *My Utmost for His Highest* or Lloyd Ogilvie's *Silent Strength*.

Though it's perfectly acceptable to choose a form that suits us, we also need to be open to broadening our experience by trying new forms, traditions, writers and so on. There is indeed a great variety in the ways God speaks to us. A look back through church history reveals that the saints were not only deeply spiritual people, they were also people with broad interests that expanded and informed their spiritual formation. Catherine of Siena was involved in the political affairs of her day. John Wesley was fascinated with medicine. Peter Marshall was a great game player.

There is a world of blessing and benefit available to us when we embrace all the experiences God offers us. If our spiritual formation is grounded in the Bible, we stand on a sure foundation that enables us to reach upward and outward to every dimension of development that God—who created the earth in all its fullness—has provided.

When you use this Bible you will not only encounter Holy Scripture directly, you will also encounter the elements that will enable you to move forward in spiritual formation: faith, fit, friends and form. These are the roadmaps that will guide your journey—a journey that none of us can plan or control.

The earliest Christian creed contained only three words: "Jesus is Lord!" It was the simplest way believers knew to declare their utter confidence in the risen Christ to lead and guide them into an abundant and everlasting life. Wherever you are right now, there is good news: God loves you more than you can imagine. Move forward with assurance. The best is yet to be!

PREFACE
TO THE NRSV

This preface is addressed to you by the Committee of translators, who wish to explain, as briefly as possible, the origin and character of our work. The publication of our revision is yet another step in the long, continual process of making the Bible available in the form of the English language that is most widely current in our day. To summarize in a single sentence: the New Revised Standard Version of the Bible is an authorized revision of the Revised Standard Version, published in 1952, which was a revision of the American Standard Version, published in 1901, which, in turn, embodied earlier revisions of the King James Version, published in 1611.

In the course of time, the King James Version came to be regarded as "the Authorized Version." With good reason it has been termed "the noblest monument of English prose," and it has entered, as no other book has, into the making of the personal character and the public institutions of the English-speaking peoples. We owe to it an incalculable debt.

Yet the King James Version has serious defects. By the middle of the nineteenth century, the development of biblical studies and the discovery of many biblical manuscripts more ancient than those on which the King James Version was based made it apparent that these defects were so many as to call for revision. The task was begun, by authority of the Church of England, in 1870. The (British) Revised Version of the Bible was published in 1881-1885; and the American Standard Version, its variant embodying the preferences of the American scholars associated with the work, was published, as was mentioned above, in 1901. In 1928 the copyright of the latter was acquired by the International Council of Religious Education and thus passed into the ownership of the Churches of the United States and Canada that were associated in this Council through their boards of education and publication.

The Council appointed a committee of scholars to have charge of the text of the American Standard Version and to undertake inquiry concerning the need for further revision. After studying the questions whether or not revision should be undertaken, and if so, what its nature and extent should be, in 1937 the Council authorized a revision. The scholars who served as members of the Committee worked in two sections, one dealing with the Old Testament and one with the New Testament. In 1946 the Revised Standard Version of the New Testament was published. The publication of the Revised Standard Version of the Bible, containing the Old and New Testaments, took place on September 30, 1952. A translation of the *Apocryphal/Deuterocanonical* Books of the Old Testament followed in 1957. In 1977 this collection was issued in an expanded edition, containing three additional texts received by Eastern Orthodox communions (3 and 4 Maccabees and Psalm 151). Thereafter the Revised Standard Version gained the distinction of being officially authorized for use by all major Christian churches: Protestant, Anglican, Roman Catholic, and Eastern Orthodox.

The Revised Standard Version Bible Committee is a continuing body, comprising about thirty members, both men and women. Ecumenical in representation, it includes scholars affiliated with various Protestant denominations, as well as several Roman Catholic members, an Eastern Orthodox member, and a Jewish member who serves in the Old Testament section. For a period of time the Committee included several members from Canada and from England.

Because no translation of the Bible is perfect or is acceptable to all groups of readers, and because discoveries of older manuscripts and further investigation of linguistic features of the text continue to become available, renderings of the Bible have proliferated. During the years following the publication of the Revised Standard Version, twenty-six other English translations and revisions of the Bible were produced by committees and by individual scholars—not to mention twenty-five other translations and revisions of the New Testament alone. One of the latter was the second edition of the RSV New Testament, issued in 1971, twenty-five years after its initial publication.

Following the publication of the RSV Old Testament in 1952, significant advances were made in the discovery and interpretation of documents in Semitic languages related to Hebrew. In addition to the information that had become available in the late 1940s from the Dead Sea texts of Isaiah and Habakkuk, subsequent acquisitions from the same area brought to light many other early copies of all the books of the Hebrew Scriptures (except Esther), though most of these copies are fragmentary. During the same period early Greek manuscript copies of books of the New Testament also became available.

In order to take these discoveries into account, along with recent studies of documents in Semitic languages related to Hebrew, in 1974 the Policies Committee of the Revised Standard Version, which is a standing committee of the National Council of the Churches of Christ in the U.S.A., authorized the preparation of a revision of the entire RSV Bible.

For the Old Testament the Committee has made use of the *Biblia Hebraica Stuttgartensia* (1977; ed. sec. emendata, 1983). This is an edition of the Hebrew and Aramaic text as current early in the Christian era and fixed by Jewish scholars (the "Masoretes") of the sixth to the ninth centuries. The vowel signs, which were added by the Masoretes, are accepted in the main, but where a more probable and convincing reading can be obtained by assuming different vowels, this has been done. No notes are given in such cases, because the vowel points are less ancient and reliable than the consonants. When an alternative reading given by the Masoretes is translated in a footnote, this is identified by the words "Another reading is."

Departures from the consonantal text of the best manuscripts have been made only where it seems clear that errors in copying had been made before the text was standardized. Most of the corrections adopted are based on the ancient versions (translations into Greek, Aramaic, Syriac, and Latin), which were made prior to the time of the work of the Masoretes and which therefore may reflect earlier forms of the Hebrew text. In such instances a footnote specifies the version or versions from which the correction has been derived and also gives a translation of the Masoretic Text. Where it was deemed appropriate to do so, information is supplied in footnotes from subsidiary Jewish traditions concerning other textual readings (the *Tiqqune Sopherim,* "emendations of the scribes"). These are identified in the footnotes as "Ancient Heb tradition."

Occasionally it is evident that the text has suffered in transmission and that none of the versions provides a satisfactory restoration. Here we can only follow the best judgment of competent scholars as to the most probable reconstruction of the original text. Such reconstructions are indicated in footnotes by the abbreviation Cn ("Correction"), and a translation of the Masoretic Text is added.

For the Apocryphal/Deuterocanonical Books of the Old Testament the Committee has made use of a number of texts. For most of these books the basic Greek text from which the present translation was made is the edition of the Septuagint prepared by Alfred Rahlfs and published by the Württemberg Bible Society (Stuttgart, 1935). For several of the books the more recently published individual volumes of the Göttingen Septuagint project were utilized. For the book of Tobit it was decided to follow the form of the Greek text found in codex Sinaiticus (supported as it is by evidence from Qumran); where this text is defective, it was supplemented and corrected by other Greek manuscripts. For the three Additions to Daniel (namely, Susanna, the Prayer of Azariah and the Song of the Three Jews, and Bel and the Dragon) the Committee continued to use the Greek version attributed to Theodotion (the so-called "Theodotion-Daniel"). In translating Ecclesiasticus (Sirach), while constant reference was made to the Hebrew fragments of a large portion of this book (those discovered at Qumran and Masada as well as those recovered from the Cairo Geniza), the Committee generally followed the Greek text (including verse numbers) published by Joseph Ziegler in the Göttingen Septuagint (1965). But in many places the Committee has translated the Hebrew text when this provides a reading that is clearly superior to the Greek; the Syriac and Latin versions were also consulted throughout and occasionally adopted. The basic text adopted in rendering 2 Esdras is the Latin version given in *Biblia Sacra,* edited by Robert Weber (Stuttgart, 1971). This was supplemented by consulting the Latin text as edited by R. L. Bensly (1895) and by Bruno Violet (1910), as well as by taking into account the several Oriental versions of 2 Esdras, namely, the Syriac, Ethiopic, Arabic (two forms, referred to as Arabic 1 and Arabic 2), Armenian, and Georgian versions. Finally, since the Additions to the Book of Esther are disjointed and quite unintelligible as they stand in most editions of the Apocrypha, we have provided them with their original context by translating the whole of the Greek version of Esther from Robert Hanhart's Göttingen edition (1983).

For the New Testament the Committee has based its work on the most recent edition of *The Greek New Testament,* prepared by an interconfessional and international committee and published by the United Bible Societies (1966; 3rd ed. corrected, 1983; information concerning changes to be introduced into the critical apparatus of the forthcoming 4th edition was available to the Committee). As in that edition, double brackets are used to enclose a few passages that are generally regarded to be later additions to the text, but which we have retained because of their evident antiquity and their importance in the textual tradition. Only in very rare instances have we replaced the text or the punctuation of the Bible Societies' edition by an alternative that seemed to us to be superior. Here and there in the footnotes the phrase, "Other ancient authorities read," identifies alternative readings preserved by Greek manuscripts and early versions. In both Testaments, alternative renderings of the text are indicated by the word "Or."

As for the style of English adopted for the present revision, among the mandates given to the Committee in 1980 by the Division of Education and Ministry of the National Council of Churches of Christ (which now holds the copyright of the RSV Bible) was the directive to continue in the tradition of the King James Bible, but to introduce such changes as are warranted on the basis of accuracy, clarity, euphony, and current English usage. Within the constraints set by the original texts and by the mandates of the Division, the Committee has followed the maxim, "As literal as possible, as free as necessary." As a consequence, the New Revised Standard Version (NRSV) remains essentially a literal translation. Paraphrastic renderings have been adopted only sparingly, and then chiefly to compensate for a deficiency in the English language—the lack of a common gender third person singular pronoun.

During the almost half a century since the publication of the RSV, many in the churches have become sensitive to the danger of linguistic sexism arising from the inherent bias of the English language towards the masculine gender, a bias that in the case of the Bible has often restricted or obscured the meaning of the original text. The mandates from the Division specified that, in references to men and women, masculine-oriented language should be eliminated as far as this can be done without altering passages that reflect the historical situation of ancient patriarchal culture. As can be appreciated, more than once the Committee found that the several mandates stood in tension and even in conflict. The various concerns had to be balanced case by case in order to provide a faithful and acceptable rendering without using contrived English. Only very occasionally has the pronoun "he" or "him" been retained in passages where the reference may have been to a woman as well as to a man; for example, in several legal texts in Leviticus and Deuteronomy. In such instances of formal, legal language, the options of either putting the passage in the plural or of introducing additional nouns to avoid masculine pronouns in English seemed to the Committee to obscure the historic structure and literary character of the original. In the vast majority of cases, however, inclusiveness has been attained by simple rephrasing or by introducing plural forms when this does not distort the meaning of the passage. Of course, in narrative and in parable no attempt was made to generalize the sex of individual persons.

Another aspect of style will be detected by readers who compare the more stately English rendering of the Old Testament with the less formal rendering adopted for the New Testament. For example, the traditional distinction between *shall* and *will* in English has been retained in the Old Testament as appropriate in rendering a document that embodies what may be termed the classic form of Hebrew, while in the New Testament the abandonment of such distinctions in the usage of the future tense in English reflects the more colloquial nature of the koine Greek used by most New Testament authors except when they are quoting the Old Testament.

Careful readers will notice that here and there in the Old Testament the word Lord (or in certain cases God) is printed in capital letters. This represents the traditional manner in English versions of rendering the Divine Name, the "Tetragrammaton" (see the notes on Exodus 3.14, 15), following the precedent of the ancient Greek and Latin translators and the long established practice in the reading of the Hebrew Scriptures in the synagogue. While it is almost if not quite certain that the Name was originally pronounced "Yahweh," this pronunciation was not indicated when the Masoretes added vowel sounds to the consonantal Hebrew text. To the four consonants YHWH of the Name, which had come to be regarded as too sacred to be pronounced, they attached vowel signs indicating that in its place should be read the Hebrew word *Adonai* meaning "Lord" (or *Elohim* meaning "God"). Ancient Greek translators employed the word *Kyrios* ("Lord") for the Name. The Vulgate likewise used the Latin word *Dominus* ("Lord"). The form "Jehovah" is of late medieval origin; it is a combination of the consonants of the Divine Name and the vowels attached to it by the Masoretes but belonging to an entirely different word. Although the American Standard Version (1901) had used "Jehovah" to render the Tetragrammaton (the sound of Y being represented by J and the sound of W by V, as in Latin), for two reasons the Committees that produced the RSV and the NRSV returned to the more familiar usage of the King James Version. (1) The word "Jehovah" does not accurately represent any form of the Name ever used in Hebrew. (2) The use of any proper name for the one and only God, as though there were other gods from whom the true God had to be distinguished, began to be discontinued in Judaism before the Christian era and is inappropriate for the universal faith of the Christian Church.

It will be seen that in the Psalms and in other prayers addressed to God the archaic second person singular pronouns *(thee, thou, thine)* and verb forms *(art, hast, hadst)* are no longer used. Although some readers may regret this change, it should be pointed out that in the original languages neither the Old Testament nor the New makes any linguistic distinction between addressing a human being and addressing the Deity. Furthermore, in the tradition of the King James Version one will not expect to find the use of capital letters for pronouns that refer to the Deity— such capitalization is an unnecessary innovation that has only recently been introduced into a few English translations of the Bible. Finally, we have left to the discretion of the licensed publishers such matters as section headings, cross-references, and clues to the pronunciation of proper names.

This new version seeks to preserve all that is best in the English Bible as it has been known and used through the years. It is intended for use in public reading and congregational worship, as well as in private study, instruction, and meditation. We have resisted the temptation to introduce terms and phrases that merely reflect current moods, and have tried to put the message of the Scriptures in simple, enduring words and expressions that are worthy to stand in the great tradition of the King James Bible and its predecessors.

In traditional Judaism and Christianity, the Bible has been more than a historical document to be preserved or a classic of literature to be cherished and admired; it is recognized as the unique record of God's dealings with people over the ages. The Old Testament sets forth the call of a special people to enter into covenant relation with the God of justice and steadfast love and to bring God's law to the nations. The New Testament records the life and work of Jesus Christ, the one in whom "the Word became flesh," as well as describes the rise and spread of the early Christian Church. The Bible carries its full message, not to those who regard it simply as a noble literary heritage of the past or who wish to use it to enhance political purposes and advance otherwise desirable goals, but to all persons and communities who read it so that they may discern and understand what God is saying to them. That message must not be disguised in phrases that are no longer clear, or hidden under words that have changed or lost their meaning; it must be presented in language that is direct and plain and meaningful to people today. It is the hope and prayer of the translators that this version of the Bible may continue to hold a large place in congregational life and to speak to all readers, young and old alike, helping them to understand and believe and respond to its message.

For the Committee,
BRUCE M. METZGER

OLD TESTAMENT

GENESIS
Created for Relationship

KEY VERSES:

"I am God Almighty; walk before me, and be blameless . . . I will establish my covenant between me and you, and your offspring after you throughout their generations, for an everlasting covenant, to be God to you and to your offspring after you."—Genesis 17.1,7

The book of Genesis contains the "old, old stories" of our faith, the record of God's interaction with his people, an account that has been faithfully handed down to us for our encouragement. Perhaps the elements are so familiar that we overlook the stunning importance of the event itself. God chooses to create to be in covenant with us! We are not separate from, but intimately related to, the unimaginable God. Our relationship with God endures day by day, through challenges, opportunities, losses and joys. Our covenant with God endures though we fall short. Our intimacy with God satisfies our high aspirations for union with every breath and beyond death.

The record of Genesis is fascinating reading, for it is real, even harsh and cruel, yet often piercingly joyful. In its pages we find people not unlike ourselves, whose lives are always under God's watchful eye. Like us, these people are creatures formed by God's hand and inspirited with the very breath of God. Astonishingly, they are transformed even in the midst of their struggles; they deepen in their capacity to respond to God's care.

As you read Genesis slowly and prayerfully, seek to enter into the events described. Step into the "shoes" of the people you meet and ask how their situations might apply to your own life. Each reading is a new opportunity for God to speak to you through the Holy Spirit and for you to marvel at the ways God loved and formed Abraham and Sarah, Isaac and Rebekah, Jacob, Leah and Rachel.

"(I said) Ah, good Lord, how could all things be well, because of the great harm which has come through sin to your creatures? . . . And to this our blessed Lord answered . . . that I should contemplate the glorious atonement, for this atoning is more pleasing to the blessed divinity and more honourable for man's salvation, without comparison, than ever Adam's sin was harmful. So then this is our blessed Lord's intention, and in this teaching we should pay heed to this: For since I have set right the greatest of harms, then it is my will that you should know through this that I shall set right everything which is less."

—JULIAN OF NORWICH,
Showings

God's Word Works

GENESIS 1.9

Over and over we read, "God said . . . And it was so." Verse 9 is one of many such refrains in this first chapter of Genesis. God spoke, and creation leaped into being in joyful response to the overwhelming power of God's Word. Great comfort can be found in knowing that God's Word is *always* fruitful. God doesn't just *try*. God *does*. Is there a place in your prayer today where this fact might bring you assurance? The next time you wonder how anything good can possibly emerge from your current situation, remember that God's response to prayer is immediate, even though the effects may not at first be visible. When God speaks, things happen—both within us and around us!

See *Meeting God in Prayer*

Six Days of Creation and the Sabbath

1 In the beginning when God created*a* the heavens and the earth, ²the earth was a formless void and darkness covered the face of the deep, while a wind from God*b* swept over the face of the waters. ³Then God said, "Let there be light"; and there was light. ⁴And God saw that the light was good; and God separated the light from the darkness. ⁵God called the light Day, and the darkness he called Night. And there was evening and there was morning, the first day.

6 And God said, "Let there be a dome in the midst of the waters, and let it separate the waters from the waters." ⁷So God made the dome and separated the waters that were under the dome from the waters that were above the dome. And it was so. ⁸God called the dome Sky. And there was evening and there was morning, the second day.

9 And God said, "Let the waters under the sky be gathered together into one place, and let the dry land appear." And it was so. ¹⁰God called the dry land Earth, and the waters that were gathered together he called Seas. And God saw that it was good. ¹¹Then God said, "Let the earth put forth vegetation: plants yielding seed, and fruit trees of every kind on earth that bear fruit with the seed in it." And it was so. ¹²The earth brought forth vegetation: plants yielding seed of every kind, and trees of every kind bearing fruit with the seed in it. And God saw that it was good. ¹³And there was evening and there was morning, the third day.

14 And God said, "Let there be lights in the dome of the sky to separate the day from the night; and let them be for signs and for seasons and for days and years, ¹⁵and let them be lights in the dome of the sky to give light upon the earth." And it was so. ¹⁶God made the two great lights—the greater light to rule the day and the lesser light to rule the night—and the stars. ¹⁷God set them in the dome of the sky to give light upon the earth, ¹⁸to rule over the day and over the night, and to separate the light from the darkness. And God saw that it was good. ¹⁹And there was evening and there was morning, the fourth day.

20 And God said, "Let the waters bring forth swarms of living creatures, and let birds fly above the earth across the dome of the sky." ²¹So God created the great sea monsters and every living creature that moves, of every kind, with which the waters swarm, and every winged bird of every kind. And God saw that it was good. ²²God blessed them, saying, "Be fruitful and multiply and fill the waters in the seas, and let birds multiply on the earth." ²³And there was evening and there was morning, the fifth day.

24 And God said, "Let the earth bring forth living creatures of every kind: cattle and creeping things and wild animals of the earth of every kind." And it was so. ²⁵God made the wild animals of the earth of every kind, and the cattle of every kind, and everything that creeps upon the ground of every kind. And God saw that it was good.

a Or *when God began to create* or *In the beginning God created*   *b* Or *while the spirit of God* or *while a mighty wind*

26 Then God said, "Let us make humankind[a] in our image, according to our likeness; and let them have dominion over the fish of the sea, and over the birds of the air, and over the cattle, and over all the wild animals of the earth,[b] and over every creeping thing that creeps upon the earth."
[27] So God created humankind[a] in his image,
in the image of God he created them;[c]
male and female he created them.
[28]God blessed them, and God said to them, "Be fruitful and multiply, and fill the earth and subdue it; and have dominion over the fish of the sea and over the birds of the air and over every living thing that moves upon the earth." [29]God said, "See, I have given you every plant yielding seed that is upon the face of all the earth, and every tree with seed in its fruit; you shall have them for food. [30]And to every beast of the earth, and to every bird of the air, and to everything that creeps on the earth, everything that has the breath of life, I have given every green plant for food." And it was so. [31]God saw everything that he had made, and indeed, it was very good. And there was evening and there was morning, the sixth day.

2 Thus the heavens and the earth were finished, and all their multitude. [2]And on the seventh day God finished the work that he had done, and he rested on the seventh day from all the work that he had done. [3]So God blessed the seventh day and hallowed it, because on it God rested from all the work that he had done in creation.

4 These are the generations of the heavens and the earth when they were created.

Another Account of the Creation

In the day that the LORD God made the earth and the heavens, [5]when no plant of the field was yet in the earth and no herb of the field had yet sprung up—for the LORD God had not caused it to rain upon the earth, and there was no one to till the ground; [6]but a stream would rise from the earth, and water the whole face of the ground— [7]then the LORD God formed man from the dust of the ground,[d] and breathed into his nostrils the breath of life; and the man became a living being. [8]And the LORD God planted a garden in Eden, in the east; and there he put the man whom he had formed. [9]Out of the ground the LORD God made to grow every tree that is pleasant to the sight and good for food, the tree of life also in the midst of the garden, and the tree of the knowledge of good and evil.

10 A river flows out of Eden to water the garden, and from there it divides and becomes four branches. [11]The name of the first is Pishon; it is the one that flows around the whole land of Havilah, where there is gold; [12]and the gold of that land is good; bdellium and onyx stone are there. [13]The name of the second river is Gihon; it is the

God Forms Us

GENESIS 2.7

Here we find a wonderful image of the way God forms us both physically and spiritually. Take a piece of clay or some malleable substance in your hands. Start by just feeling the weight and temperature of the clay you are holding, attentive to its basic nature—its pliability. Begin to knead the clay, gently but firmly working with it until it is soft. Think of a shape and begin to mold the clay to your purpose, noticing both its resistance and its receptivity. Based on this exercise, what do you think spiritual formation means? How is God molding or forming you continually, even today? How do you resist or receive God's attentions?

See *Meeting God in the Created Order*

a Heb adam   b Syr: Heb and over all the earth   c Heb him
d Or formed a man (Heb adam) of dust from the ground (Heb adamah)

It Is Not Good to Be Alone

GENESIS 2.18

Over and over God has found creation "good," but here is something "not good": that the man should be alone. From the very beginning, God has seen that we require not only divine companionship, but also the comfort and assistance that comes from being in community. We long for another who is so like us that we can cry out: "This at last is bone of my bones!" Who has God given you for companionship? Where do you find those who help you to be all that God has made you? Whatever your situation, God intends for you to have a friend of the heart; look for them among the many "givens" of your life.

See Meeting God in Community

one that flows around the whole land of Cush. ¹⁴The name of the third river is Tigris, which flows east of Assyria. And the fourth river is the Euphrates.

15 The LORD God took the man and put him in the garden of Eden to till it and keep it. ¹⁶And the LORD God commanded the man, "You may freely eat of every tree of the garden; ¹⁷but of the tree of the knowledge of good and evil you shall not eat, for in the day that you eat of it you shall die."

18 Then the LORD God said, "It is not good that the man should be alone; I will make him a helper as his partner." ¹⁹So out of the ground the LORD God formed every animal of the field and every bird of the air, and brought them to the man to see what he would call them; and whatever the man called every living creature, that was its name. ²⁰The man gave names to all cattle, and to the birds of the air, and to every animal of the field; but for the man*a* there was not found a helper as his partner. ²¹So the LORD God caused a deep sleep to fall upon the man, and he slept; then he took one of his ribs and closed up its place with flesh. ²²And the rib that the LORD God had taken from the man he made into a woman and brought her to the man. ²³Then the man said,

"This at last is bone of my bones
    and flesh of my flesh;
this one shall be called Woman,*b*
    for out of Man*c* this one was taken."

²⁴Therefore a man leaves his father and his mother and clings to his wife, and they become one flesh. ²⁵And the man and his wife were both naked, and were not ashamed.

The First Sin and Its Punishment

3 Now the serpent was more crafty than any other wild animal that the LORD God had made. He said to the woman, "Did God say, 'You shall not eat from any tree in the garden'?" ²The woman said to the serpent, "We may eat of the fruit of the trees in the garden; ³but God said, 'You shall not eat of the fruit of the tree that is in the middle of the garden, nor shall you touch it, or you shall die.' " ⁴But the serpent said to the woman, "You will not die; ⁵for God knows that when you eat of it your eyes will be opened, and you will be like God,*d* knowing good and evil." ⁶So when the woman saw that the tree was good for food, and that it was a delight to the eyes, and that the tree was to be desired to make one wise, she took of its fruit and ate; and she also gave some to her husband, who was with her, and he ate. ⁷Then the eyes of both were opened, and they knew that they were naked; and they sewed fig leaves together and made loincloths for themselves.

8 They heard the sound of the LORD God walking in the garden at the time of the evening breeze, and the man and his wife hid themselves from the presence of the LORD God among the trees of the garden. ⁹But the LORD God called to the man, and said to him, "Where are you?"

a Or *for Adam*   *b* Heb *ishshah*   *c* Heb *ish*   *d* Or *gods*

¹⁰He said, "I heard the sound of you in the garden, and I was afraid, because I was naked; and I hid myself." ¹¹He said, "Who told you that you were naked? Have you eaten from the tree of which I commanded you not to eat?" ¹²The man said, "The woman whom you gave to be with me, she gave me fruit from the tree, and I ate." ¹³Then the LORD God said to the woman, "What is this that you have done?" The woman said, "The serpent tricked me, and I ate." ¹⁴The LORD God said to the serpent,

"Because you have done this,
> cursed are you among all animals
> and among all wild creatures;
upon your belly you shall go,
> and dust you shall eat
> all the days of your life.
15   I will put enmity between you and the woman,
> and between your offspring and hers;
he will strike your head,
> and you will strike his heel."

¹⁶To the woman he said,

"I will greatly increase your pangs in childbearing;
> in pain you shall bring forth children,
yet your desire shall be for your husband,
> and he shall rule over you."

¹⁷And to the man*ᵃ* he said,

"Because you have listened to the voice of your
>   wife,
> and have eaten of the tree
about which I commanded you,
> 'You shall not eat of it,'
cursed is the ground because of you;
> in toil you shall eat of it all the days of your life;
18   thorns and thistles it shall bring forth for you;
> and you shall eat the plants of the field.
19   By the sweat of your face
> you shall eat bread
until you return to the ground,
> for out of it you were taken;
you are dust,
> and to dust you shall return."

20 The man named his wife Eve,*ᵇ* because she was the mother of all living. ²¹And the LORD God made garments of skins for the man*ᶜ* and for his wife, and clothed them.

22 Then the LORD God said, "See, the man has become like one of us, knowing good and evil; and now, he might reach out his hand and take also from the tree of life, and eat, and live forever"— ²³therefore the LORD God sent him forth from the garden of Eden, to till the ground from which he was taken. ²⁴He drove out the man; and at the east of the garden of Eden he placed the cherubim, and a sword flaming and turning to guard the way to the tree of life.

a Or *to Adam*   *b* In Heb *Eve* resembles the word for *living*
c Or *for Adam*

What Have You Done?

GENESIS 3.13

Amid all the gifts of God, we seem always to want what we don't have. We know better, yet we continue to act in acquisitive or destructive ways. At such moments, God appears before us, asking: "What have you done?" God asks the question, not because he doesn't know the answer, but because he is giving us the opportunity to admit our fault and be forgiven. Admitting sin is also admitting that God's power can strengthen the good in us. Today, ask if there is something God wants you to reassess and repent of. What goodness are you avoiding?

See Meeting God in Prayer

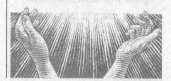

More Than I Can Bear

GENESIS 4.13

Sin brings its own inevitable consequences. Imagine that you are Cain. You have murdered your own brother. You may have felt driven to it, but you also know you deserve punishment. Yet the punishment is crushing, like a too-heavy burden placed upon your shoulders, so that you cannot even stand up. Place yourself in this scene, feeling the weight that burdens you, tasting the bitterness of shame and grief, experiencing the hopeless future.
What is your reaction to God's unexpected grace—the touch of his anointing finger—protecting you from the worst harm? God kneels to share your yoke and lighten your load, sinner that you are. Can you take it in?

See Meeting God in Scripture

Cain Murders Abel

4 Now the man knew his wife Eve, and she conceived and bore Cain, saying, "I have produced*a* a man with the help of the LORD." ²Next she bore his brother Abel. Now Abel was a keeper of sheep, and Cain a tiller of the ground. ³In the course of time Cain brought to the LORD an offering of the fruit of the ground, ⁴and Abel for his part brought of the firstlings of his flock, their fat portions. And the LORD had regard for Abel and his offering, ⁵but for Cain and his offering he had no regard. So Cain was very angry, and his countenance fell. ⁶The LORD said to Cain, "Why are you angry, and why has your countenance fallen? ⁷If you do well, will you not be accepted? And if you do not do well, sin is lurking at the door; its desire is for you, but you must master it."

8 Cain said to his brother Abel, "Let us go out to the field."*b* And when they were in the field, Cain rose up against his brother Abel, and killed him. ⁹Then the LORD said to Cain, "Where is your brother Abel?" He said, "I do not know; am I my brother's keeper?" ¹⁰And the LORD said, "What have you done? Listen; your brother's blood is crying out to me from the ground! ¹¹And now you are cursed from the ground, which has opened its mouth to receive your brother's blood from your hand. ¹²When you till the ground, it will no longer yield to you its strength; you will be a fugitive and a wanderer on the earth." ¹³Cain said to the LORD, "My punishment is greater than I can bear! ¹⁴Today you have driven me away from the soil, and I shall be hidden from your face; I shall be a fugitive and a wanderer on the earth, and anyone who meets me may kill me." ¹⁵Then the LORD said to him, "Not so!*c* Whoever kills Cain will suffer a sevenfold vengeance." And the LORD put a mark on Cain, so that no one who came upon him would kill him. ¹⁶Then Cain went away from the presence of the LORD, and settled in the land of Nod,*d* east of Eden.

Beginnings of Civilization

17 Cain knew his wife, and she conceived and bore Enoch; and he built a city, and named it Enoch after his son Enoch. ¹⁸To Enoch was born Irad; and Irad was the father of Mehujael, and Mehujael the father of Methushael, and Methushael the father of Lamech. ¹⁹Lamech took two wives; the name of the one was Adah, and the name of the other Zillah. ²⁰Adah bore Jabal; he was the ancestor of those who live in tents and have livestock. ²¹His brother's name was Jubal; he was the ancestor of all those who play the lyre and pipe. ²²Zillah bore Tubal-cain, who made all kinds of bronze and iron tools. The sister of Tubal-cain was Naamah.

23 Lamech said to his wives:
"Adah and Zillah, hear my voice;
you wives of Lamech, listen to what I say:
I have killed a man for wounding me,
a young man for striking me.

---

a The verb in Heb resembles the word for *Cain*   *b* Sam Gk Syr Compare Vg: MT lacks *Let us go out to the field*   *c* Gk Syr Vg: Heb *Therefore*
d That is *Wandering*

24   If Cain is avenged sevenfold,
           truly Lamech seventy-sevenfold."

25 Adam knew his wife again, and she bore a son and named him Seth, for she said, "God has appointed[a] for me another child instead of Abel, because Cain killed him." [26]To Seth also a son was born, and he named him Enosh. At that time people began to invoke the name of the LORD.

Adam's Descendants to Noah and His Sons

5 This is the list of the descendants of Adam. When God created humankind,[b] he made them[c] in the likeness of God. [2]Male and female he created them, and he blessed them and named them "Humankind"[b] when they were created.

3 When Adam had lived one hundred thirty years, he became the father of a son in his likeness, according to his image, and named him Seth. [4]The days of Adam after he became the father of Seth were eight hundred years; and he had other sons and daughters. [5]Thus all the days that Adam lived were nine hundred thirty years; and he died.

6 When Seth had lived one hundred five years, he became the father of Enosh. [7]Seth lived after the birth of Enosh eight hundred seven years, and had other sons and daughters. [8]Thus all the days of Seth were nine hundred twelve years; and he died.

9 When Enosh had lived ninety years, he became the father of Kenan. [10]Enosh lived after the birth of Kenan eight hundred fifteen years, and had other sons and daughters. [11]Thus all the days of Enosh were nine hundred five years; and he died.

12 When Kenan had lived seventy years, he became the father of Mahalalel. [13]Kenan lived after the birth of Mahalalel eight hundred and forty years, and had other sons and daughters. [14]Thus all the days of Kenan were nine hundred and ten years; and he died.

15 When Mahalalel had lived sixty-five years, he became the father of Jared. [16]Mahalalel lived after the birth of Jared eight hundred thirty years, and had other sons and daughters. [17]Thus all the days of Mahalalel were eight hundred ninety-five years; and he died.

18 When Jared had lived one hundred sixty-two years he became the father of Enoch. [19]Jared lived after the birth of Enoch eight hundred years, and had other sons and daughters. [20]Thus all the days of Jared were nine hundred sixty-two years; and he died.

21 When Enoch had lived sixty-five years, he became the father of Methuselah. [22]Enoch walked with God after the birth of Methuselah three hundred years, and had other sons and daughters. [23]Thus all the days of Enoch were three hundred sixty-five years. [24]Enoch walked with God; then he was no more, because God took him.

25 When Methuselah had lived one hundred eighty-seven years, he became the father of Lamech. [26]Methuselah lived after the birth of Lamech seven hundred

---

In God's Likeness

GENESIS 5.1

"Dignity is acting as if we believe the facts of our creation are true: that we are indeed created in God's image, that we are created out of love, that we are good because God created us, and that we have the goodness of God within us. Dignity is risking that, as the popular saying goes, 'God don't make junk' . . . Dignity always says we are meant for greater things than those we ever could aspire to. Choosing dignity, then, is not selecting another self-image. It is choosing an openendedness in which we know all our images will be insufficient. It is an act of faith."

—GERALD MAY,
Addiction and Grace

---

a The verb in Heb resembles the word for *Seth*   *b* Heb *adam*   *c* Heb *him*

God's Grief

GENESIS 6.6

Can we imagine God feeling grief? Seeing how far humans have fallen away from his intention for them, God's heart, we are told, is filled with pain. God grieves for the human soul that is dead because of sin. Early Christians thought that the primary remedy for the soul was to weep tears of compunction, sharing God's grief at its misery and folly. Gregory of Nyssa's words at the death of his friend, St. Ephrem, suggest the inevitability of a "flood" of sorrow: "When I start to remember his floods of tears I myself begin to weep, for it is almost impossible to pass dry-eyed through the ocean of his tears." Might this great flood have been caused not only by God's wrath but also by God's sorrow?

eighty-two years, and had other sons and daughters. [27]Thus all the days of Methuselah were nine hundred sixty-nine years; and he died.

28 When Lamech had lived one hundred eighty-two years, he became the father of a son; [29]he named him Noah, saying, "Out of the ground that the LORD has cursed this one shall bring us relief from our work and from the toil of our hands." [30]Lamech lived after the birth of Noah five hundred ninety-five years, and had other sons and daughters. [31]Thus all the days of Lamech were seven hundred seventy-seven years; and he died.

32 After Noah was five hundred years old, Noah became the father of Shem, Ham, and Japheth.

The Wickedness of Humankind

6 When people began to multiply on the face of the ground, and daughters were born to them, [2]the sons of God saw that they were fair; and they took wives for themselves of all that they chose. [3]Then the LORD said, "My spirit shall not abide[a] in mortals forever, for they are flesh; their days shall be one hundred twenty years." [4]The Nephilim were on the earth in those days—and also afterward—when the sons of God went in to the daughters of humans, who bore children to them. These were the heroes that were of old, warriors of renown.

5 The LORD saw that the wickedness of humankind was great in the earth, and that every inclination of the thoughts of their hearts was only evil continually. [6]And the LORD was sorry that he had made humankind on the earth, and it grieved him to his heart. [7]So the LORD said, "I will blot out from the earth the human beings I have created—people together with animals and creeping things and birds of the air, for I am sorry that I have made them." [8]But Noah found favor in the sight of the LORD.

Noah Pleases God

9 These are the descendants of Noah. Noah was a righteous man, blameless in his generation; Noah walked with God. [10]And Noah had three sons, Shem, Ham, and Japheth.

11 Now the earth was corrupt in God's sight, and the earth was filled with violence. [12]And God saw that the earth was corrupt; for all flesh had corrupted its ways upon the earth. [13]And God said to Noah, "I have determined to make an end of all flesh, for the earth is filled with violence because of them; now I am going to destroy them along with the earth. [14]Make yourself an ark of cypress[a] wood; make rooms in the ark, and cover it inside and out with pitch. [15]This is how you are to make it: the length of the ark three hundred cubits, its width fifty cubits, and its height thirty cubits. [16]Make a roof[b] for the ark, and finish it to a cubit above; and put the door of the ark in its side; make it with lower, second, and third decks. [17]For my part, I am going to bring a flood of waters on the earth, to destroy from under heaven all flesh in which is the breath of life; everything that is on the

a Meaning of Heb uncertain   *b* Or *window*

earth shall die. ¹⁸But I will establish my covenant with you; and you shall come into the ark, you, your sons, your wife, and your sons' wives with you. ¹⁹And of every living thing, of all flesh, you shall bring two of every kind into the ark, to keep them alive with you; they shall be male and female. ²⁰Of the birds according to their kinds, and of the animals according to their kinds, of every creeping thing of the ground according to its kind, two of every kind shall come in to you, to keep them alive. ²¹Also take with you every kind of food that is eaten, and store it up; and it shall serve as food for you and for them." ²²Noah did this; he did all that God commanded him.

The Great Flood

7 Then the LORD said to Noah, "Go into the ark, you and all your household, for I have seen that you alone are righteous before me in this generation. ²Take with you seven pairs of all clean animals, the male and its mate; and a pair of the animals that are not clean, the male and its mate; ³and seven pairs of the birds of the air also, male and female, to keep their kind alive on the face of all the earth. ⁴For in seven days I will send rain on the earth for forty days and forty nights; and every living thing that I have made I will blot out from the face of the ground." ⁵And Noah did all that the LORD had commanded him.

6 Noah was six hundred years old when the flood of waters came on the earth. ⁷And Noah with his sons and his wife and his sons' wives went into the ark to escape the waters of the flood. ⁸Of clean animals, and of animals that are not clean, and of birds, and of everything that creeps on the ground, ⁹two and two, male and female, went into the ark with Noah, as God had commanded Noah. ¹⁰And after seven days the waters of the flood came on the earth.

11 In the six hundredth year of Noah's life, in the second month, on the seventeenth day of the month, on that day all the fountains of the great deep burst forth, and the windows of the heavens were opened. ¹²The rain fell on the earth forty days and forty nights. ¹³On the very same day Noah with his sons, Shem and Ham and Japheth, and Noah's wife and the three wives of his sons entered the ark, ¹⁴they and every wild animal of every kind, and all domestic animals of every kind, and every creeping thing that creeps on the earth, and every bird of every kind—every bird, every winged creature. ¹⁵They went into the ark with Noah, two and two of all flesh in which there was the breath of life. ¹⁶And those that entered, male and female of all flesh, went in as God had commanded him; and the LORD shut him in.

17 The flood continued forty days on the earth; and the waters increased, and bore up the ark, and it rose high above the earth. ¹⁸The waters swelled and increased greatly on the earth; and the ark floated on the face of the waters. ¹⁹The waters swelled so mightily on the earth that all the high mountains under the whole heaven were covered; ²⁰the waters swelled above the mountains, covering them fifteen cubits deep. ²¹And all flesh died that moved on the earth, birds, domestic animals, wild animals, all

The Gift of Water

GENESIS 7.11

Water is a critical element in many stories throughout Scripture: in the beginning of creation, in the exodus of the children of Israel from Egypt, and especially in Jesus' baptism. Meditate on the place of water in your life, its power for creation and destruction. Can you recall insights you've experienced during a renewing spring shower or while fishing a rushing stream? Do you remember your own baptism, or one you have attended recently? What truths has God shown you through the gift of water?

See Meeting God in the Created Order

A Sign of Hope

GENESIS 8.11

Place yourself on the crowded deck of Noah's ark, confined for many days in a small space filled with every kind of creature. You have experienced the violent destruction of your whole environment and for days have seen nothing but water. Imagine the eagerness with which you anticipate the return of the dove, the mixture of hope and dread with which you wonder what the future will be. When you see the dove returning, you notice something in its mouth, but what? A freshly plucked olive leaf! Amidst all this loss, new life is emerging! Somewhere a tree grows, and fragile shoots bloom, and a safe place for you is being created. Praise God!

See Meeting God in Scripture

swarming creatures that swarm on the earth, and all human beings; ²²everything on dry land in whose nostrils was the breath of life died. ²³He blotted out every living thing that was on the face of the ground, human beings and animals and creeping things and birds of the air; they were blotted out from the earth. Only Noah was left, and those that were with him in the ark. ²⁴And the waters swelled on the earth for one hundred fifty days.

The Flood Subsides

8 But God remembered Noah and all the wild animals and all the domestic animals that were with him in the ark. And God made a wind blow over the earth, and the waters subsided; ²the fountains of the deep and the windows of the heavens were closed, the rain from the heavens was restrained, ³and the waters gradually receded from the earth. At the end of one hundred fifty days the waters had abated; ⁴and in the seventh month, on the seventeenth day of the month, the ark came to rest on the mountains of Ararat. ⁵The waters continued to abate until the tenth month; in the tenth month, on the first day of the month, the tops of the mountains appeared.

6 At the end of forty days Noah opened the window of the ark that he had made ⁷and sent out the raven; and it went to and fro until the waters were dried up from the earth. ⁸Then he sent out the dove from him, to see if the waters had subsided from the face of the ground; ⁹but the dove found no place to set its foot, and it returned to him to the ark, for the waters were still on the face of the whole earth. So he put out his hand and took it and brought it into the ark with him. ¹⁰He waited another seven days, and again he sent out the dove from the ark; ¹¹and the dove came back to him in the evening, and there in its beak was a freshly plucked olive leaf; so Noah knew that the waters had subsided from the earth. ¹²Then he waited another seven days, and sent out the dove; and it did not return to him any more.

13 In the six hundred first year, in the first month, on the first day of the month, the waters were dried up from the earth; and Noah removed the covering of the ark, and looked, and saw that the face of the ground was drying. ¹⁴In the second month, on the twenty-seventh day of the month, the earth was dry. ¹⁵Then God said to Noah, ¹⁶"Go out of the ark, you and your wife, and your sons and your sons' wives with you. ¹⁷Bring out with you every living thing that is with you of all flesh—birds and animals and every creeping thing that creeps on the earth—so that they may abound on the earth, and be fruitful and multiply on the earth." ¹⁸So Noah went out with his sons and his wife and his sons' wives. ¹⁹And every animal, every creeping thing, and every bird, everything that moves on the earth, went out of the ark by families.

God's Promise to Noah

20 Then Noah built an altar to the LORD, and took of every clean animal and of every clean bird, and offered burnt offerings on the altar. ²¹And when the LORD smelled

the pleasing odor, the LORD said in his heart, "I will never again curse the ground because of humankind, for the inclination of the human heart is evil from youth; nor will I ever again destroy every living creature as I have done. [22] As long as the earth endures,

> seedtime and harvest, cold and heat,
> summer and winter, day and night,
> shall not cease."

The Covenant with Noah

9 God blessed Noah and his sons, and said to them, "Be fruitful and multiply, and fill the earth. [2]The fear and dread of you shall rest on every animal of the earth, and on every bird of the air, on everything that creeps on the ground, and on all the fish of the sea; into your hand they are delivered. [3]Every moving thing that lives shall be food for you; and just as I gave you the green plants, I give you everything. [4]Only, you shall not eat flesh with its life, that is, its blood. [5]For your own lifeblood I will surely require a reckoning: from every animal I will require it and from human beings, each one for the blood of another, I will require a reckoning for human life.

[6] Whoever sheds the blood of a human,
> by a human shall that person's blood be shed;
> for in his own image
> God made humankind.

[7]And you, be fruitful and multiply, abound on the earth and multiply in it."

8 Then God said to Noah and to his sons with him, [9]"As for me, I am establishing my covenant with you and your descendants after you, [10]and with every living creature that is with you, the birds, the domestic animals, and every animal of the earth with you, as many as came out of the ark.[a] [11]I establish my covenant with you, that never again shall all flesh be cut off by the waters of a flood, and never again shall there be a flood to destroy the earth." [12]God said, "This is the sign of the covenant that I make between me and you and every living creature that is with you, for all future generations: [13]I have set my bow in the clouds, and it shall be a sign of the covenant between me and the earth. [14]When I bring clouds over the earth and the bow is seen in the clouds, [15]I will remember my covenant that is between me and you and every living creature of all flesh; and the waters shall never again become a flood to destroy all flesh. [16]When the bow is in the clouds, I will see it and remember the everlasting covenant between God and every living creature of all flesh that is on the earth." [17]God said to Noah, "This is the sign of the covenant that I have established between me and all flesh that is on the earth."

Noah and His Sons

18 The sons of Noah who went out of the ark were Shem, Ham, and Japheth. Ham was the father of Canaan. [19]These three were the sons of Noah; and from these the whole earth was peopled.

My Bow in the Clouds

GENESIS 9.13

A woman who loved rainbows went on a summer retreat. As she walked by water sprinklers that sent drops sparkling into the sunlight, she saw the rainbows they made, and their beauty brought her up short. She had been feeling quite burdened and alone, and the rainbows powerfully spoke to her of God's continuing care. What are you reminded of when you see a rainbow in the clouds? On a white piece of paper, draw a rainbow, noticing the richness of each color of the spectrum: red, orange, yellow, green, blue, indigo and violet. Then give each color a name representing some way in which God has been faithful in your life.

See Meeting God in Everyday Life

---

a Gk: Heb adds *every animal of the earth*

More Value Than a Sparrow

GENESIS 10.1

"In the eyes of God, each particular human spirit had been allotted a particular physical constitution as its appropriate sparring partner. Each person's *flesh and blood* was particular to that person, and had been exquisitely calibrated by God, 'who tests the minds and hearts' [Psalm 7.9], to challenge the potentially mighty spirit of each to stretch beyond itself . . . The gentle precision of God's mercy ensured that each body was adjusted to the peculiar needs of its soul down to the finest details . . . Confronted with their own, irreducibly particular *flesh and blood*, all believers struggled to maintain, in themselves, the huge momentum of their spirit's longing for God."

—PETER BROWN,
The Body and Society

See *Meeting God in the Created Order*

20 Noah, a man of the soil, was the first to plant a vineyard. ²¹He drank some of the wine and became drunk, and he lay uncovered in his tent. ²²And Ham, the father of Canaan, saw the nakedness of his father, and told his two brothers outside. ²³Then Shem and Japheth took a garment, laid it on both their shoulders, and walked backward and covered the nakedness of their father; their faces were turned away, and they did not see their father's nakedness. ²⁴When Noah awoke from his wine and knew what his youngest son had done to him, ²⁵he said,

"Cursed be Canaan;
    lowest of slaves shall he be to his brothers."

²⁶He also said,

"Blessed by the LORD my God be Shem;
    and let Canaan be his slave.
²⁷   May God make space for*ᵃ* Japheth,
    and let him live in the tents of Shem;
    and let Canaan be his slave."

28 After the flood Noah lived three hundred fifty years. ²⁹All the days of Noah were nine hundred fifty years; and he died.

Nations Descended from Noah

10 These are the descendants of Noah's sons, Shem, Ham, and Japheth; children were born to them after the flood.

2 The descendants of Japheth: Gomer, Magog, Madai, Javan, Tubal, Meshech, and Tiras. ³The descendants of Gomer: Ashkenaz, Riphath, and Togarmah. ⁴The descendants of Javan: Elishah, Tarshish, Kittim, and Rodanim.*ᵇ* ⁵From these the coastland peoples spread. These are the descendants of Japheth*ᶜ* in their lands, with their own language, by their families, in their nations.

6 The descendants of Ham: Cush, Egypt, Put, and Canaan. ⁷The descendants of Cush: Seba, Havilah, Sabtah, Raamah, and Sabteca. The descendants of Raamah: Sheba and Dedan. ⁸Cush became the father of Nimrod; he was the first on earth to become a mighty warrior. ⁹He was a mighty hunter before the LORD; therefore it is said, "Like Nimrod a mighty hunter before the LORD." ¹⁰The beginning of his kingdom was Babel, Erech, and Accad, all of them in the land of Shinar. ¹¹From that land he went into Assyria, and built Nineveh, Rehoboth-ir, Calah, and ¹²Resen between Nineveh and Calah; that is the great city. ¹³Egypt became the father of Ludim, Anamim, Lehabim, Naphtuhim, ¹⁴Pathrusim, Casluhim, and Caphtorim, from which the Philistines come.*ᵈ*

15 Canaan became the father of Sidon his firstborn, and Heth, ¹⁶and the Jebusites, the Amorites, the Girgashites, ¹⁷the Hivites, the Arkites, the Sinites, ¹⁸the Arvadites, the Zemarites, and the Hamathites. Afterward the families of the Canaanites spread abroad. ¹⁹And the territory of the Canaanites extended from Sidon, in the direction of Gerar, as far as Gaza, and in the direction of Sodom, Gomorrah, Admah, and Zeboiim, as far as Lasha.

a Heb *yapht,* a play on *Japheth*   *b* Heb Mss Sam Gk See 1 Chr 1.7: MT *Dodanim*   *c* Compare verses 20, 31. Heb lacks *These are the descendants of Japheth*   *d* Cn: Heb *Casluhim, from which the Philistines come, and Caphtorim*

²⁰These are the descendants of Ham, by their families, their languages, their lands, and their nations.

21 To Shem also, the father of all the children of Eber, the elder brother of Japheth, children were born. ²²The descendants of Shem: Elam, Asshur, Arpachshad, Lud, and Aram. ²³The descendants of Aram: Uz, Hul, Gether, and Mash. ²⁴Arpachshad became the father of Shelah; and Shelah became the father of Eber. ²⁵To Eber were born two sons: the name of the one was Peleg,ᵃ for in his days the earth was divided, and his brother's name was Joktan. ²⁶Joktan became the father of Almodad, Sheleph, Hazarmaveth, Jerah, ²⁷Hadoram, Uzal, Diklah, ²⁸Obal, Abimael, Sheba, ²⁹Ophir, Havilah, and Jobab; all these were the descendants of Joktan. ³⁰The territory in which they lived extended from Mesha in the direction of Sephar, the hill country of the east. ³¹These are the descendants of Shem, by their families, their languages, their lands, and their nations.

32 These are the families of Noah's sons, according to their genealogies, in their nations; and from these the nations spread abroad on the earth after the flood.

The Tower of Babel

11 Now the whole earth had one language and the same words. ²And as they migrated from the east,ᵇ they came upon a plain in the land of Shinar and settled there. ³And they said to one another, "Come, let us make bricks, and burn them thoroughly." And they had brick for stone, and bitumen for mortar. ⁴Then they said, "Come, let us build ourselves a city, and a tower with its top in the heavens, and let us make a name for ourselves; otherwise we shall be scattered abroad upon the face of the whole earth." ⁵The Lord came down to see the city and the tower, which mortals had built. ⁶And the Lord said, "Look, they are one people, and they have all one language; and this is only the beginning of what they will do; nothing that they propose to do will now be impossible for them. ⁷Come, let us go down, and confuse their language there, so that they will not understand one another's speech." ⁸So the Lord scattered them abroad from there over the face of all the earth, and they left off building the city. ⁹Therefore it was called Babel, because there the Lord confusedᶜ the language of all the earth; and from there the Lord scattered them abroad over the face of all the earth.

Descendants of Shem

10 These are the descendants of Shem. When Shem was one hundred years old, he became the father of Arpachshad two years after the flood; ¹¹and Shem lived after the birth of Arpachshad five hundred years, and had other sons and daughters.

12 When Arpachshad had lived thirty-five years, he became the father of Shelah; ¹³and Arpachshad lived after

A Name for Ourselves

What is wrong with trying to build a tower to heaven? Don't humans naturally aspire to heavenly things? In this account the problem is with the reason the people are building the tower; it is not to be nearer God, or to glorify God, but to exalt themselves. In our own lives, we often embark on projects designed to help us feel like little gods, in control, independently successful. All such projects, large or small, deny our creatureliness and minimize our dependence upon God. Often it is easier to see others "playing god" than to notice it in ourselves. What is your own most recent "tower" project? What clues show that it is *your* project and not God's?

See Meeting God in Scripture

ᵃ That is *Division*   ᵇ Or *migrated eastward*   ᶜ Heb *balal*, meaning *to confuse*

What Do We Tell?

GENESIS 11.10–26

In this genealogy, each person is defined by name, age at death, and age at birth of the oldest son. If you were to give an account of your life and your family, what would be the important things you would want to tell? Today we rarely name our children when we identify ourselves, much less our own age at their births. When first meeting someone, we are most likely to describe ourselves in terms of our primary occupation. Yet our titles and job descriptions do not paint an adequate picture of who we are. How would you best identify yourself in terms of values important to you? What are the essential things you would want others to know about your life?

See Meeting God in Community

the birth of Shelah four hundred three years, and had other sons and daughters.

14 When Shelah had lived thirty years, he became the father of Eber; [15]and Shelah lived after the birth of Eber four hundred three years, and had other sons and daughters.

16 When Eber had lived thirty-four years, he became the father of Peleg; [17]and Eber lived after the birth of Peleg four hundred thirty years, and had other sons and daughters.

18 When Peleg had lived thirty years, he became the father of Reu; [19]and Peleg lived after the birth of Reu two hundred nine years, and had other sons and daughters.

20 When Reu had lived thirty-two years, he became the father of Serug; [21]and Reu lived after the birth of Serug two hundred seven years, and had other sons and daughters.

22 When Serug had lived thirty years, he became the father of Nahor; [23]and Serug lived after the birth of Nahor two hundred years, and had other sons and daughters.

24 When Nahor had lived twenty-nine years, he became the father of Terah; [25]and Nahor lived after the birth of Terah one hundred nineteen years, and had other sons and daughters.

26 When Terah had lived seventy years, he became the father of Abram, Nahor, and Haran.

Descendants of Terah

27 Now these are the descendants of Terah. Terah was the father of Abram, Nahor, and Haran; and Haran was the father of Lot. [28]Haran died before his father Terah in the land of his birth, in Ur of the Chaldeans. [29]Abram and Nahor took wives; the name of Abram's wife was Sarai, and the name of Nahor's wife was Milcah. She was the daughter of Haran the father of Milcah and Iscah. [30]Now Sarai was barren; she had no child.

31 Terah took his son Abram and his grandson Lot son of Haran, and his daughter-in-law Sarai, his son Abram's wife, and they went out together from Ur of the Chaldeans to go into the land of Canaan; but when they came to Haran, they settled there. [32]The days of Terah were two hundred five years; and Terah died in Haran.

The Call of Abram

12 Now the LORD said to Abram, "Go from your country and your kindred and your father's house to the land that I will show you. [2]I will make of you a great nation, and I will bless you, and make your name great, so that you will be a blessing. [3]I will bless those who bless you, and the one who curses you I will curse; and in you all the families of the earth shall be blessed."[a]

4 So Abram went, as the LORD had told him; and Lot went with him. Abram was seventy-five years old when he departed from Haran. [5]Abram took his wife Sarai and his brother's son Lot, and all the possessions that they had gathered, and the persons whom they had acquired

a Or by you all the families of the earth shall bless themselves

in Haran; and they set forth to go to the land of Canaan. When they had come to the land of Canaan, ⁶Abram passed through the land to the place at Shechem, to the oak*ª* of Moreh. At that time the Canaanites were in the land. ⁷Then the LORD appeared to Abram, and said, "To your offspring*ᵇ* I will give this land." So he built there an altar to the LORD, who had appeared to him. ⁸From there he moved on to the hill country on the east of Bethel, and pitched his tent, with Bethel on the west and Ai on the east; and there he built an altar to the LORD and invoked the name of the LORD. ⁹And Abram journeyed on by stages toward the Negeb.

Abram and Sarai in Egypt

10 Now there was a famine in the land. So Abram went down to Egypt to reside there as an alien, for the famine was severe in the land. ¹¹When he was about to enter Egypt, he said to his wife Sarai, "I know well that you are a woman beautiful in appearance; ¹²and when the Egyptians see you, they will say, 'This is his wife'; then they will kill me, but they will let you live. ¹³Say you are my sister, so that it may go well with me because of you, and that my life may be spared on your account." ¹⁴When Abram entered Egypt the Egyptians saw that the woman was very beautiful. ¹⁵When the officials of Pharaoh saw her, they praised her to Pharaoh. And the woman was taken into Pharaoh's house. ¹⁶And for her sake he dealt well with Abram; and he had sheep, oxen, male donkeys, male and female slaves, female donkeys, and camels.

17 But the LORD afflicted Pharaoh and his house with great plagues because of Sarai, Abram's wife. ¹⁸So Pharaoh called Abram, and said, "What is this you have done to me? Why did you not tell me that she was your wife? ¹⁹Why did you say, 'She is my sister,' so that I took her for my wife? Now then, here is your wife, take her, and be gone." ²⁰And Pharaoh gave his men orders concerning him; and they set him on the way, with his wife and all that he had.

Abram and Lot Separate

13 So Abram went up from Egypt, he and his wife, and all that he had, and Lot with him, into the Negeb.

2 Now Abram was very rich in livestock, in silver, and in gold. ³He journeyed on by stages from the Negeb as far as Bethel, to the place where his tent had been at the beginning, between Bethel and Ai, ⁴to the place where he had made an altar at the first; and there Abram called on the name of the LORD. ⁵Now Lot, who went with Abram, also had flocks and herds and tents, ⁶so that the land could not support both of them living together; for their possessions were so great that they could not live together, ⁷and there was strife between the herders of Abram's livestock and the herders of Lot's livestock. At that time the Canaanites and the Perizzites lived in the land.

The Call

GENESIS 12.1–4

God's covenant with his people begins with this simple yet earthshaking command, stated simply "Leave what you know and go into the unknown." The command is united with a promise of blessing, yet it is no less fearful for that. God calls to each of us: "Leave what you know and go into the unknown. I will be with you and I will bless you, but you must act in faith in response to my word." Usually we are given many opportunities, and we need them, because we often deflect a call, ask for more information, distract ourselves, even run away. When you hear God's call, how do you usually respond? What is your preferred strategy when faced with this breathtaking word?

See Meeting God in Prayer

---

a Or *terebinth*   *b* Heb *seed*

God's Designs

GENESIS 13.2–18

"The Old Testament is the history of a process whereby God prepares the human race for Christ . . . slowly and gradually, but inexorably . . . God speaks and we answer—very inadequately; so he speaks again and again, undeterred by our fumbling replies until he finally speaks the ultimate Word in Jesus. This is the Word we are still striving to answer—not perhaps very successfully, but that does not matter, for God's designs cannot be thwarted in the end, and he can use our very failures as instruments which will achieve his purpose."

—CYPRIAN SMITH, O.S.B.,
The Path of Life

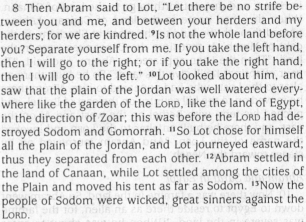

8 Then Abram said to Lot, "Let there be no strife between you and me, and between your herders and my herders; for we are kindred. ⁹Is not the whole land before you? Separate yourself from me. If you take the left hand, then I will go to the right; or if you take the right hand, then I will go to the left." ¹⁰Lot looked about him, and saw that the plain of the Jordan was well watered everywhere like the garden of the LORD, like the land of Egypt, in the direction of Zoar; this was before the LORD had destroyed Sodom and Gomorrah. ¹¹So Lot chose for himself all the plain of the Jordan, and Lot journeyed eastward; thus they separated from each other. ¹²Abram settled in the land of Canaan, while Lot settled among the cities of the Plain and moved his tent as far as Sodom. ¹³Now the people of Sodom were wicked, great sinners against the LORD.

14 The LORD said to Abram, after Lot had separated from him, "Raise your eyes now, and look from the place where you are, northward and southward and eastward and westward; ¹⁵for all the land that you see I will give to you and to your offspring*a* forever. ¹⁶I will make your offspring like the dust of the earth; so that if one can count the dust of the earth, your offspring also can be counted. ¹⁷Rise up, walk through the length and the breadth of the land, for I will give it to you." ¹⁸So Abram moved his tent, and came and settled by the oaks*b* of Mamre, which are at Hebron; and there he built an altar to the LORD.

Lot's Captivity and Rescue

14 In the days of King Amraphel of Shinar, King Arioch of Ellasar, King Chedorlaomer of Elam, and King Tidal of Goiim, ²these kings made war with King Bera of Sodom, King Birsha of Gomorrah, King Shinab of Admah, King Shemeber of Zeboiim, and the king of Bela (that is, Zoar). ³All these joined forces in the Valley of Siddim (that is, the Dead Sea).*c* ⁴Twelve years they had served Chedorlaomer, but in the thirteenth year they rebelled. ⁵In the fourteenth year Chedorlaomer and the kings who were with him came and subdued the Rephaim in Ashteroth-karnaim, the Zuzim in Ham, the Emim in Shaveh-kiriathaim, ⁶and the Horites in the hill country of Seir as far as El-paran on the edge of the wilderness; ⁷then they turned back and came to En-mishpat (that is, Kadesh), and subdued all the country of the Amalekites, and also the Amorites who lived in Hazazon-tamar. ⁸Then the king of Sodom, the king of Gomorrah, the king of Admah, the king of Zeboiim, and the king of Bela (that is, Zoar) went out, and they joined battle in the Valley of Siddim ⁹with King Chedorlaomer of Elam, King Tidal of Goiim, King Amraphel of Shinar, and King Arioch of Ellasar, four kings against five. ¹⁰Now the Valley of Siddim was full of bitumen pits; and as the kings of Sodom and Gomorrah fled, some fell into them, and the rest fled to the hill country. ¹¹So the enemy took all the goods of Sodom and Gomorrah, and all their provisions, and went

a Heb *seed*   *b* Or *terebinths*   *c* Heb *Salt Sea*

their way; [12]they also took Lot, the son of Abram's brother, who lived in Sodom, and his goods, and departed.

13 Then one who had escaped came and told Abram the Hebrew, who was living by the oaks[a] of Mamre the Amorite, brother of Eshcol and of Aner; these were allies of Abram. [14]When Abram heard that his nephew had been taken captive, he led forth his trained men, born in his house, three hundred eighteen of them, and went in pursuit as far as Dan. [15]He divided his forces against them by night, he and his servants, and routed them and pursued them to Hobah, north of Damascus. [16]Then he brought back all the goods, and also brought back his nephew Lot with his goods, and the women and the people.

Abram Blessed by Melchizedek

17 After his return from the defeat of Chedorlaomer and the kings who were with him, the king of Sodom went out to meet him at the Valley of Shaveh (that is, the King's Valley). [18]And King Melchizedek of Salem brought out bread and wine; he was priest of God Most High.[b] [19]He blessed him and said,

"Blessed be Abram by God Most High,[b]
    maker of heaven and earth;
[20]   and blessed be God Most High,[b]
    who has delivered your enemies into your
        hand!"

And Abram gave him one-tenth of everything. [21]Then the king of Sodom said to Abram, "Give me the persons, but take the goods for yourself." [22]But Abram said to the king of Sodom, "I have sworn to the Lord, God Most High,[b] maker of heaven and earth, [23]that I would not take a thread or a sandal-thong or anything that is yours, so that you might not say, 'I have made Abram rich.' [24]I will take nothing but what the young men have eaten, and the share of the men who went with me—Aner, Eshcol, and Mamre. Let them take their share."

God's Covenant with Abram

15 After these things the word of the Lord came to Abram in a vision, "Do not be afraid, Abram, I am your shield; your reward shall be very great." [2]But Abram said, "O Lord God, what will you give me, for I continue childless, and the heir of my house is Eliezer of Damascus?"[c] [3]And Abram said, "You have given me no offspring, and so a slave born in my house is to be my heir." [4]But the word of the Lord came to him, "This man shall not be your heir; no one but your very own issue shall be your heir." [5]He brought him outside and said, "Look toward heaven and count the stars, if you are able to count them." Then he said to him, "So shall your descendants be." [6]And he believed the Lord; and the Lord[d] reckoned it to him as righteousness.

7 Then he said to him, "I am the Lord who brought you from Ur of the Chaldeans, to give you this land to

---

A Sacred Encounter

GENESIS 14.18–20

Who is this priest of God Most High who appears from nowhere with a blessing for Abram? This mystical encounter fascinated the authors of Scripture, with Psalm 110 describing "a priest forever according to the order of Melchizedek" and the book of Hebrews speculating in chapter 7 that the ancient priest prefigured the Son of God. Was there a time in your life when, unexpectedly, you felt that you were in the presence of God Most High? Who else was there, and what happened beforehand? Recall everything about that incident, what you saw and felt, all the sounds and smells you experienced, and above all, what your heart told you. Return to that moment regularly for refreshment and joy!

See *Meeting God in Worship*

---

a Or *terebinths*   *b* Heb *El Elyon*   *c* Meaning of Heb uncertain
d Heb *he*

Covenant

GENESIS 15.17

Perhaps when you were a child you made a pact with a close friend, pricking your fingers to mingle your blood or exchanging rings as a sign of solemn covenant. As we become adults, sometimes we neglect the importance of enacting a ritual to mark the importance of an event. What symbolic actions help you confirm your commitment to something? The next time a rite of passage occurs in your family, think of a special way to make a simple ritual for it: Collect armfuls of flowers and shower them on a graduate. Or at a wedding form a circle around the newly married couple and sing to them. Be imaginative and serious but not solemn.

See Meeting God in Community

possess." ⁸But he said, "O Lord GOD, how am I to know that I shall possess it?" ⁹He said to him, "Bring me a heifer three years old, a female goat three years old, a ram three years old, a turtledove, and a young pigeon." ¹⁰He brought him all these and cut them in two, laying each half over against the other; but he did not cut the birds in two. ¹¹And when birds of prey came down on the carcasses, Abram drove them away.

12 As the sun was going down, a deep sleep fell upon Abram, and a deep and terrifying darkness descended upon him. ¹³Then the LORD*ᵃ* said to Abram, "Know this for certain, that your offspring shall be aliens in a land that is not theirs, and shall be slaves there, and they shall be oppressed for four hundred years; ¹⁴but I will bring judgment on the nation that they serve, and afterward they shall come out with great possessions. ¹⁵As for yourself, you shall go to your ancestors in peace; you shall be buried in a good old age. ¹⁶And they shall come back here in the fourth generation; for the iniquity of the Amorites is not yet complete."

17 When the sun had gone down and it was dark, a smoking fire pot and a flaming torch passed between these pieces. ¹⁸On that day the LORD made a covenant with Abram, saying, "To your descendants I give this land, from the river of Egypt to the great river, the river Euphrates, ¹⁹the land of the Kenites, the Kenizzites, the Kadmonites, ²⁰the Hittites, the Perizzites, the Rephaim, ²¹the Amorites, the Canaanites, the Girgashites, and the Jebusites."

The Birth of Ishmael

16 Now Sarai, Abram's wife, bore him no children. She had an Egyptian slave-girl whose name was Hagar, ²and Sarai said to Abram, "You see that the LORD has prevented me from bearing children; go in to my slave-girl; it may be that I shall obtain children by her." And Abram listened to the voice of Sarai. ³So, after Abram had lived ten years in the land of Canaan, Sarai, Abram's wife, took Hagar the Egyptian, her slave-girl, and gave her to her husband Abram as a wife. ⁴He went in to Hagar, and she conceived; and when she saw that she had conceived, she looked with contempt on her mistress. ⁵Then Sarai said to Abram, "May the wrong done to me be on you! I gave my slave-girl to your embrace, and when she saw that she had conceived, she looked on me with contempt. May the LORD judge between you and me!" ⁶But Abram said to Sarai, "Your slave-girl is in your power; do to her as you please." Then Sarai dealt harshly with her, and she ran away from her.

7 The angel of the LORD found her by a spring of water in the wilderness, the spring on the way to Shur. ⁸And he said, "Hagar, slave-girl of Sarai, where have you come from and where are you going?" She said, "I am running away from my mistress Sarai." ⁹The angel of the LORD said to her, "Return to your mistress, and submit to her." ¹⁰The angel of the LORD also said to her, "I will so greatly

a Heb *he*

multiply your offspring that they cannot be counted for multitude." [11]And the angel of the LORD said to her,

"Now you have conceived and shall bear a son;
   you shall call him Ishmael,[a]
   for the LORD has given heed to your affliction.
[12] He shall be a wild ass of a man,
   with his hand against everyone,
      and everyone's hand against him;
   and he shall live at odds with all his kin."

[13]So she named the LORD who spoke to her, "You are El-roi";[b] for she said, "Have I really seen God and remained alive after seeing him?"[c] [14]Therefore the well was called Beer-lahai-roi;[d] it lies between Kadesh and Bered.

15 Hagar bore Abram a son; and Abram named his son, whom Hagar bore, Ishmael. [16]Abram was eighty-six years old when Hagar bore him[e] Ishmael.

The Sign of the Covenant

17 When Abram was ninety-nine years old, the LORD appeared to Abram, and said to him, "I am God Almighty;[f] walk before me, and be blameless. [2]And I will make my covenant between me and you, and will make you exceedingly numerous." [3]Then Abram fell on his face; and God said to him, [4]"As for me, this is my covenant with you: You shall be the ancestor of a multitude of nations. [5]No longer shall your name be Abram,[g] but your name shall be Abraham;[h] for I have made you the ancestor of a multitude of nations. [6]I will make you exceedingly fruitful; and I will make nations of you, and kings shall come from you. [7]I will establish my covenant between me and you, and your offspring after you throughout their generations, for an everlasting covenant, to be God to you and to your offspring[i] after you. [8]And I will give to you, and to your offspring after you, the land where you are now an alien, all the land of Canaan, for a perpetual holding; and I will be their God."

9 God said to Abraham, "As for you, you shall keep my covenant, you and your offspring after you throughout their generations. [10]This is my covenant, which you shall keep, between me and you and your offspring after you: Every male among you shall be circumcised. [11]You shall circumcise the flesh of your foreskins, and it shall be a sign of the covenant between me and you. [12]Throughout your generations every male among you shall be circumcised when he is eight days old, including the slave born in your house and the one bought with your money from any foreigner who is not of your offspring. [13]Both the slave born in your house and the one bought with your money must be circumcised. So shall my covenant be in your flesh an everlasting covenant. [14]Any uncircumcised male who is not circumcised in the flesh of his foreskin shall be cut off from his people; he has broken my covenant."

15 God said to Abraham, "As for Sarai your wife, you

A New Name

GENESIS 17.5–6

"For the ancients a name, any name, is not simply a conventional designation, but rather *an expression* of a being's place in the universe . . . A proper noun has a mysterious identity with the person named, denoting the nature and function of the person. The name is not simply a label but is so closely linked with the bearer as to contain something of his character . . . To indicate that God is taking possession of their lives, God changes the name of Abraham and Sarah."

—SISTER VANDANA,
Nama Japa: Prayer of the Name

---

a That is *God hears*   b Perhaps *God of seeing* or *God who sees*   c Meaning of Heb uncertain   d That is *the Well of the Living One who sees me*
e Heb *Abram*   f Traditional rendering of Heb *El Shaddai*   g That is *exalted ancestor*   h Here taken to mean *ancestor of a multitude*   i Heb *seed*

Promising the Impossible

GENESIS 17.19

God's first words to creation include the command to be fruitful, and that command is taken seriously by his people. Yet through no fault of their own, Abraham and Sarah are barren. No children arrive, and they believe parenthood is impossible for them. Now God is promising the impossible. In your own life, are you waiting for something you have long desired from God? How might the waiting, the apparent emptiness, be somehow preparing you for the fulfillment God intends to give you? If you were to have the assurance that God would satisfy your desire (though perhaps not as you imagine), could you believe that promise? Why or why not?

See Meeting God in Everyday Life

shall not call her Sarai, but Sarah shall be her name. ¹⁶I will bless her, and moreover I will give you a son by her. I will bless her, and she shall give rise to nations; kings of peoples shall come from her." ¹⁷Then Abraham fell on his face and laughed, and said to himself, "Can a child be born to a man who is a hundred years old? Can Sarah, who is ninety years old, bear a child?" ¹⁸And Abraham said to God, "O that Ishmael might live in your sight!" ¹⁹God said, "No, but your wife Sarah shall bear you a son, and you shall name him Isaac.ᵃ I will establish my covenant with him as an everlasting covenant for his offspring after him. ²⁰As for Ishmael, I have heard you; I will bless him and make him fruitful and exceedingly numerous; he shall be the father of twelve princes, and I will make him a great nation. ²¹But my covenant I will establish with Isaac, whom Sarah shall bear to you at this season next year." ²²And when he had finished talking with him, God went up from Abraham.

23 Then Abraham took his son Ishmael and all the slaves born in his house or bought with his money, every male among the men of Abraham's house, and he circumcised the flesh of their foreskins that very day, as God had said to him. ²⁴Abraham was ninety-nine years old when he was circumcised in the flesh of his foreskin. ²⁵And his son Ishmael was thirteen years old when he was circumcised in the flesh of his foreskin. ²⁶That very day Abraham and his son Ishmael were circumcised; ²⁷and all the men of his house, slaves born in the house and those bought with money from a foreigner, were circumcised with him.

A Son Promised to Abraham and Sarah

18 The Lᴏʀᴅ appeared to Abrahamᵇ by the oaksᶜ of Mamre, as he sat at the entrance of his tent in the heat of the day. ²He looked up and saw three men standing near him. When he saw them, he ran from the tent entrance to meet them, and bowed down to the ground. ³He said, "My lord, if I find favor with you, do not pass by your servant. ⁴Let a little water be brought, and wash your feet, and rest yourselves under the tree. ⁵Let me bring a little bread, that you may refresh yourselves, and after that you may pass on—since you have come to your servant." So they said, "Do as you have said." ⁶And Abraham hastened into the tent to Sarah, and said, "Make ready quickly three measuresᵈ of choice flour, knead it, and make cakes." ⁷Abraham ran to the herd, and took a calf, tender and good, and gave it to the servant, who hastened to prepare it. ⁸Then he took curds and milk and the calf that he had prepared, and set it before them; and he stood by them under the tree while they ate.

9 They said to him, "Where is your wife Sarah?" And he said, "There, in the tent." ¹⁰Then one said, "I will surely return to you in due season, and your wife Sarah shall have a son." And Sarah was listening at the tent entrance behind him. ¹¹Now Abraham and Sarah were old, advanced in age; it had ceased to be with Sarah after the

a That is he laughs   b Heb him   c Or terebinths   d Heb seahs manner of women. [12]So Sarah laughed to herself, saying, "After I have grown old, and my husband is old, shall I have pleasure?" [13]The LORD said to Abraham, "Why did Sarah laugh, and say, 'Shall I indeed bear a child, now that I am old?' [14]Is anything too wonderful for the LORD? At the set time I will return to you, in due season, and Sarah shall have a son." [15]But Sarah denied, saying, "I did not laugh"; for she was afraid. He said, "Oh yes, you did laugh."

Judgment Pronounced on Sodom

16 Then the men set out from there, and they looked toward Sodom; and Abraham went with them to set them on their way. [17]The LORD said, "Shall I hide from Abraham what I am about to do, [18]seeing that Abraham shall become a great and mighty nation, and all the nations of the earth shall be blessed in him?[a] [19]No, for I have chosen[b] him, that he may charge his children and his household after him to keep the way of the LORD by doing righteousness and justice; so that the LORD may bring about for Abraham what he has promised him." [20]Then the LORD said, "How great is the outcry against Sodom and Gomorrah and how very grave their sin! [21]I must go down and see whether they have done altogether according to the outcry that has come to me; and if not, I will know."

22 So the men turned from there, and went toward Sodom, while Abraham remained standing before the LORD.[c] [23]Then Abraham came near and said, "Will you indeed sweep away the righteous with the wicked? [24]Suppose there are fifty righteous within the city; will you then sweep away the place and not forgive it for the fifty righteous who are in it? [25]Far be it from you to do such a thing, to slay the righteous with the wicked, so that the righteous fare as the wicked! Far be that from you! Shall not the Judge of all the earth do what is just?" [26]And the LORD said, "If I find at Sodom fifty righteous in the city, I will forgive the whole place for their sake." [27]Abraham answered, "Let me take it upon myself to speak to the Lord, I who am but dust and ashes. [28]Suppose five of the fifty righteous are lacking? Will you destroy the whole city for lack of five?" And he said, "I will not destroy it if I find forty-five there." [29]Again he spoke to him, "Suppose forty are found there." He answered, "For the sake of forty I will not do it." [30]Then he said, "Oh do not let the Lord be angry if I speak. Suppose thirty are found there." He answered, "I will not do it, if I find thirty there." [31]He said, "Let me take it upon myself to speak to the Lord. Suppose twenty are found there." He answered, "For the sake of twenty I will not destroy it." [32]Then he said, "Oh do not let the Lord be angry if I speak just once more. Suppose ten are found there." He answered, "For the sake of ten I will not destroy it." [33]And the LORD went his way, when he had finished speaking to Abraham; and Abraham returned to his place.

a Or and all the nations of the earth shall bless themselves by him
b Heb known   c Another ancient tradition reads while the LORD remained standing before Abraham

How Many Is Enough?

GENESIS 18.23–24

Abraham ventures to plead with God on behalf of his nephew Lot for the people of Sodom. While we appreciate his loyalty, we are inclined to become impatient as he haggles over numbers. Write the names of ten friends on blank index cards, and lay out all ten cards face up on a flat surface. If it were important, would you walk five miles for these ten people? Now remove five cards at random; for the five remaining friends, would you still walk five miles? Remove one more card; for four friends, would you walk? Remove one; for three friends? Remove one more. At last only two are left: Are they alone worth your trouble?

See Meeting God in Scripture

Wrath and Love

"God's wrath is not incompatible with his love; they are aspects of the same character. His wrath is the clear shining of his light which of its nature burns up injustice and oppression. The opposite of wrath is not love but neutrality: Wrath and love are essentially one. The wrath of God is the Bible's expression for his essential hostility to all evil. The Bible does not see the love and wrath of God as two conflicting impulses, wrath restraining love from time to time; on the contrary, wrath is tempered with mercy . . . To reject, and live apart from, the love of God is to enter the world of wrath, or ruin, or disaster."

—KENNETH LEECH,
True Prayer

See *Meeting God in Community*

The Depravity of Sodom

19 The two angels came to Sodom in the evening, and Lot was sitting in the gateway of Sodom. When Lot saw them, he rose to meet them, and bowed down with his face to the ground. ²He said, "Please, my lords, turn aside to your servant's house and spend the night, and wash your feet; then you can rise early and go on your way." They said, "No; we will spend the night in the square." ³But he urged them strongly; so they turned aside to him and entered his house; and he made them a feast, and baked unleavened bread, and they ate. ⁴But before they lay down, the men of the city, the men of Sodom, both young and old, all the people to the last man, surrounded the house; ⁵and they called to Lot, "Where are the men who came to you tonight? Bring them out to us, so that we may know them." ⁶Lot went out of the door to the men, shut the door after him, ⁷and said, "I beg you, my brothers, do not act so wickedly. ⁸Look, I have two daughters who have not known a man; let me bring them out to you, and do to them as you please; only do nothing to these men, for they have come under the shelter of my roof." ⁹But they replied, "Stand back!" And they said, "This fellow came here as an alien, and he would play the judge! Now we will deal worse with you than with them." Then they pressed hard against the man Lot, and came near the door to break it down. ¹⁰But the men inside reached out their hands and brought Lot into the house with them, and shut the door. ¹¹And they struck with blindness the men who were at the door of the house, both small and great, so that they were unable to find the door.

Sodom and Gomorrah Destroyed

12 Then the men said to Lot, "Have you anyone else here? Sons-in-law, sons, daughters, or anyone you have in the city—bring them out of the place. ¹³For we are about to destroy this place, because the outcry against its people has become great before the LORD, and the LORD has sent us to destroy it." ¹⁴So Lot went out and said to his sons-in-law, who were to marry his daughters, "Up, get out of this place; for the LORD is about to destroy the city." But he seemed to his sons-in-law to be jesting.

15 When morning dawned, the angels urged Lot, saying, "Get up, take your wife and your two daughters who are here, or else you will be consumed in the punishment of the city." ¹⁶But he lingered; so the men seized him and his wife and his two daughters by the hand, the LORD being merciful to him, and they brought him out and left him outside the city. ¹⁷When they had brought them outside, they*ᵃ* said, "Flee for your life; do not look back or stop anywhere in the Plain; flee to the hills, or else you will be consumed." ¹⁸And Lot said to them, "Oh, no, my lords; ¹⁹your servant has found favor with you, and you have shown me great kindness in saving my life; but I cannot flee to the hills, for fear the disaster will overtake me and I die. ²⁰Look, that city is near enough to flee to,

a Gk Syr Vg: Heb *he*

and it is a little one. Let me escape there—is it not a little one?—and my life will be saved!" ²¹He said to him, "Very well, I grant you this favor too, and will not overthrow the city of which you have spoken. ²²Hurry, escape there, for I can do nothing until you arrive there." Therefore the city was called Zoar.ᵃ ²³The sun had risen on the earth when Lot came to Zoar.

24 Then the LORD rained on Sodom and Gomorrah sulfur and fire from the LORD out of heaven; ²⁵and he overthrew those cities, and all the Plain, and all the inhabitants of the cities, and what grew on the ground. ²⁶But Lot's wife, behind him, looked back, and she became a pillar of salt.

27 Abraham went early in the morning to the place where he had stood before the LORD; ²⁸and he looked down toward Sodom and Gomorrah and toward all the land of the Plain and saw the smoke of the land going up like the smoke of a furnace.

29 So it was that, when God destroyed the cities of the Plain, God remembered Abraham, and sent Lot out of the midst of the overthrow, when he overthrew the cities in which Lot had settled.

The Shameful Origin of Moab and Ammon

30 Now Lot went up out of Zoar and settled in the hills with his two daughters, for he was afraid to stay in Zoar; so he lived in a cave with his two daughters. ³¹And the firstborn said to the younger, "Our father is old, and there is not a man on earth to come in to us after the manner of all the world. ³²Come, let us make our father drink wine, and we will lie with him, so that we may preserve offspring through our father." ³³So they made their father drink wine that night; and the firstborn went in, and lay with her father; he did not know when she lay down or when she rose. ³⁴On the next day, the firstborn said to the younger, "Look, I lay last night with my father; let us make him drink wine tonight also; then you go in and lie with him, so that we may preserve offspring through our father." ³⁵So they made their father drink wine that night also; and the younger rose, and lay with him; and he did not know when she lay down or when she rose. ³⁶Thus both the daughters of Lot became pregnant by their father. ³⁷The firstborn bore a son, and named him Moab; he is the ancestor of the Moabites to this day. ³⁸The younger also bore a son and named him Ben-ammi; he is the ancestor of the Ammonites to this day.

Abraham and Sarah at Gerar

20 From there Abraham journeyed toward the region of the Negeb, and settled between Kadesh and Shur. While residing in Gerar as an alien, ²Abraham said of his wife Sarah, "She is my sister." And King Abimelech of Gerar sent and took Sarah. ³But God came to Abimelech in a dream by night, and said to him, "You are about to die because of the woman whom you have taken; for she is a married woman." ⁴Now Abimelech had

Preserve Our Family

GENESIS 19.32

This account troubles us: It seems to suggest that evil begets more evil. Try to imagine the catastrophe that has overtaken these young women who have been betrayed by their father, lost their mother and seen their home leveled. Consider their obligation to be fruitful and to preserve their line. They make the only choice they know in order to choose life in the midst of death. We, too, often find ourselves struggling in deeply troubling situations; how do we choose life? For one month, write in a journal about the little deaths and green shoots of new life you experience each day. Praying for God's help, note how you try to choose life daily.

See Meeting God in Everyday Life

ᵃ That is Little

The Promise Fulfilled

GENESIS 21.2

So much turmoil intervenes in these few verses after God promised an heir to Abraham and Sarah (Genesis 17.19) that we almost forget the promise. Often this happens: Our life with God is filled with ups and downs, with passions and problems, and we cannot see the big picture. By the time God answers a prayer, we have forgotten we asked! What seemed impossible has happened, and we take it for granted rather than receive it as a gift. Is there some answered prayer in your life for which you have neglected to give thanks? Start writing down your prayers today, and in six months look back over your petitions to see how many God has answered.

See Meeting God in Prayer

not approached her; so he said, "Lord, will you destroy an innocent people? 5Did he not himself say to me, 'She is my sister'? And she herself said, 'He is my brother.' I did this in the integrity of my heart and the innocence of my hands." 6Then God said to him in the dream, "Yes, I know that you did this in the integrity of your heart; furthermore it was I who kept you from sinning against me. Therefore I did not let you touch her. 7Now then, return the man's wife; for he is a prophet, and he will pray for you and you shall live. But if you do not restore her, know that you shall surely die, you and all that are yours."

8 So Abimelech rose early in the morning, and called all his servants and told them all these things; and the men were very much afraid. 9Then Abimelech called Abraham, and said to him, "What have you done to us? How have I sinned against you, that you have brought such great guilt on me and my kingdom? You have done things to me that ought not to be done." 10And Abimelech said to Abraham, "What were you thinking of, that you did this thing?" 11Abraham said, "I did it because I thought, There is no fear of God at all in this place, and they will kill me because of my wife. 12Besides, she is indeed my sister, the daughter of my father but not the daughter of my mother; and she became my wife. 13And when God caused me to wander from my father's house, I said to her, 'This is the kindness you must do me: at every place to which we come, say of me, He is my brother.'" 14Then Abimelech took sheep and oxen, and male and female slaves, and gave them to Abraham, and restored his wife Sarah to him. 15Abimelech said, "My land is before you; settle where it pleases you." 16To Sarah he said, "Look, I have given your brother a thousand pieces of silver; it is your exoneration before all who are with you; you are completely vindicated." 17Then Abraham prayed to God; and God healed Abimelech, and also healed his wife and female slaves so that they bore children. 18For the LORD had closed fast all the wombs of the house of Abimelech because of Sarah, Abraham's wife.

The Birth of Isaac

21 The LORD dealt with Sarah as he had said, and the LORD did for Sarah as he had promised. 2Sarah conceived and bore Abraham a son in his old age, at the time of which God had spoken to him. 3Abraham gave the name Isaac to his son whom Sarah bore him. 4And Abraham circumcised his son Isaac when he was eight days old, as God had commanded him. 5Abraham was a hundred years old when his son Isaac was born to him. 6Now Sarah said, "God has brought laughter for me; everyone who hears will laugh with me." 7And she said, "Who would ever have said to Abraham that Sarah would nurse children? Yet I have borne him a son in his old age."

Hagar and Ishmael Sent Away

8 The child grew, and was weaned; and Abraham made a great feast on the day that Isaac was weaned. 9But Sarah saw the son of Hagar the Egyptian, whom she

had borne to Abraham, playing with her son Isaac.ᵃ ¹⁰So she said to Abraham, "Cast out this slave woman with her son; for the son of this slave woman shall not inherit along with my son Isaac." ¹¹The matter was very distressing to Abraham on account of his son. ¹²But God said to Abraham, "Do not be distressed because of the boy and because of your slave woman; whatever Sarah says to you, do as she tells you, for it is through Isaac that offspring shall be named for you. ¹³As for the son of the slave woman, I will make a nation of him also, because he is your offspring." ¹⁴So Abraham rose early in the morning, and took bread and a skin of water, and gave it to Hagar, putting it on her shoulder, along with the child, and sent her away. And she departed, and wandered about in the wilderness of Beer-sheba.

15 When the water in the skin was gone, she cast the child under one of the bushes. ¹⁶Then she went and sat down opposite him a good way off, about the distance of a bowshot; for she said, "Do not let me look on the death of the child." And as she sat opposite him, she lifted up her voice and wept. ¹⁷And God heard the voice of the boy; and the angel of God called to Hagar from heaven, and said to her, "What troubles you, Hagar? Do not be afraid; for God has heard the voice of the boy where he is. ¹⁸Come, lift up the boy and hold him fast with your hand, for I will make a great nation of him." ¹⁹Then God opened her eyes and she saw a well of water. She went, and filled the skin with water, and gave the boy a drink.

20 God was with the boy, and he grew up; he lived in the wilderness, and became an expert with the bow. ²¹He lived in the wilderness of Paran; and his mother got a wife for him from the land of Egypt.

Abraham and Abimelech Make a Covenant

22 At that time Abimelech, with Phicol the commander of his army, said to Abraham, "God is with you in all that you do; ²³now therefore swear to me here by God that you will not deal falsely with me or with my offspring or with my posterity, but as I have dealt loyally with you, you will deal with me and with the land where you have resided as an alien." ²⁴And Abraham said, "I swear it."

25 When Abraham complained to Abimelech about a well of water that Abimelech's servants had seized, ²⁶Abimelech said, "I do not know who has done this; you did not tell me, and I have not heard of it until today." ²⁷So Abraham took sheep and oxen and gave them to Abimelech, and the two men made a covenant. ²⁸Abraham set apart seven ewe lambs of the flock. ²⁹And Abimelech said to Abraham, "What is the meaning of these seven ewe lambs that you have set apart?" ³⁰He said, "These seven ewe lambs you shall accept from my hand, in order that you may be a witness for me that I dug this well." ³¹Therefore that place was called Beer-sheba;ᵇ because there both of them swore an oath. ³²When they had made a covenant at Beer-sheba, Abimelech, with Phicol

And She Wept

GENESIS 21.16

This situation seems unfair to Hagar. In everything, she has done as she was told, and now she is about to lose not only her life, but also her beloved child. Questioning just this kind of justice, Teresa of Avila is reputed to have charged God: "If this is how you treat your friends, no wonder you have so few of them!" What *does* God promise when we dedicate our lives to him? Are we promised that there will be no hardship, no difficulties? Instead, we are promised that we will never be alone. Is that enough for us? In your own difficulties, what is your "well of water"? What restores your hope? What opens your eyes to the utter fullness of God's companionship?

See *Meeting God in Scripture*

---

a Gk Vg: Heb lacks *with her son Isaac*   b That is *Well of seven* or *Well of the oath*

The Test

GENESIS 22.1

What kind of God would present such a test as this? We recoil from this difficult passage, which has caused wise ones to wonder for centuries. Perhaps the real question is "What kind of creatures benefit from such a test?" for no one here is exempt from its rigors. Hagar's hope is tested in the wilderness, as are Sarah's faith in "the impossible" and Lot's capacity for hospitality. Apparently there comes a time in our relationship with God when we need to be tested, even though he already knows our capabilities. Might God's purpose in the tests be to reveal something to us about ourselves? Think of a time when you felt God was absent, yet you sensed that he was testing you. What did you learn?

See Meeting God in Everyday Life

the commander of his army, left and returned to the land of the Philistines. [33]Abraham[a] planted a tamarisk tree in Beer-sheba, and called there on the name of the Lord, the Everlasting God.[b] [34]And Abraham resided as an alien many days in the land of the Philistines.

The Command to Sacrifice Isaac

22 After these things God tested Abraham. He said to him, "Abraham!" And he said, "Here I am." [2]He said, "Take your son, your only son Isaac, whom you love, and go to the land of Moriah, and offer him there as a burnt offering on one of the mountains that I shall show you." [3]So Abraham rose early in the morning, saddled his donkey, and took two of his young men with him, and his son Isaac; he cut the wood for the burnt offering, and set out and went to the place in the distance that God had shown him. [4]On the third day Abraham looked up and saw the place far away. [5]Then Abraham said to his young men, "Stay here with the donkey; the boy and I will go over there; we will worship, and then we will come back to you." [6]Abraham took the wood of the burnt offering and laid it on his son Isaac, and he himself carried the fire and the knife. So the two of them walked on together. [7]Isaac said to his father Abraham, "Father!" And he said, "Here I am, my son." He said, "The fire and the wood are here, but where is the lamb for a burnt offering?" [8]Abraham said, "God himself will provide the lamb for a burnt offering, my son." So the two of them walked on together.

9 When they came to the place that God had shown him, Abraham built an altar there and laid the wood in order. He bound his son Isaac, and laid him on the altar, on top of the wood. [10]Then Abraham reached out his hand and took the knife to kill[c] his son. [11]But the angel of the Lord called to him from heaven, and said, "Abraham, Abraham!" And he said, "Here I am." [12]He said, "Do not lay your hand on the boy or do anything to him; for now I know that you fear God, since you have not withheld your son, your only son, from me." [13]And Abraham looked up and saw a ram, caught in a thicket by its horns. Abraham went and took the ram and offered it up as a burnt offering instead of his son. [14]So Abraham called that place "The Lord will provide";[d] as it is said to this day, "On the mount of the Lord it shall be provided."[e]

15 The angel of the Lord called to Abraham a second time from heaven, [16]and said, "By myself I have sworn, says the Lord: Because you have done this, and have not withheld your son, your only son, [17]I will indeed bless you, and I will make your offspring as numerous as the stars of heaven and as the sand that is on the seashore. And your offspring shall possess the gate of their enemies, [18]and by your offspring shall all the nations of the earth gain blessing for themselves, because you have obeyed my voice." [19]So Abraham returned to his young

a Heb *He*   b Or *the Lord, El Olam*   c Or *to slaughter*   d Or *will see*; Heb traditionally transliterated *Jehovah Jireh*   e Or *he shall be seen*

men, and they arose and went together to Beer-sheba; and Abraham lived at Beer-sheba.

The Children of Nahor

20 Now after these things it was told Abraham, "Milcah also has borne children, to your brother Nahor: ²¹Uz the firstborn, Buz his brother, Kemuel the father of Aram, ²²Chesed, Hazo, Pildash, Jidlaph, and Bethuel." ²³Bethuel became the father of Rebekah. These eight Milcah bore to Nahor, Abraham's brother. ²⁴Moreover, his concubine, whose name was Reumah, bore Tebah, Gaham, Tahash, and Maacah.

Sarah's Death and Burial

23 Sarah lived one hundred twenty-seven years; this was the length of Sarah's life. ²And Sarah died at Kiriath-arba (that is, Hebron) in the land of Canaan; and Abraham went in to mourn for Sarah and to weep for her. ³Abraham rose up from beside his dead, and said to the Hittites, ⁴"I am a stranger and an alien residing among you; give me property among you for a burying place, so that I may bury my dead out of my sight." ⁵The Hittites answered Abraham, ⁶"Hear us, my lord; you are a mighty prince among us. Bury your dead in the choicest of our burial places; none of us will withhold from you any burial ground for burying your dead." ⁷Abraham rose and bowed to the Hittites, the people of the land. ⁸He said to them, "If you are willing that I should bury my dead out of my sight, hear me, and entreat for me Ephron son of Zohar, ⁹so that he may give me the cave of Machpelah, which he owns; it is at the end of his field. For the full price let him give it to me in your presence as a possession for a burying place." ¹⁰Now Ephron was sitting among the Hittites; and Ephron the Hittite answered Abraham in the hearing of the Hittites, of all who went in at the gate of his city, ¹¹"No, my lord, hear me; I give you the field, and I give you the cave that is in it; in the presence of my people I give it to you; bury your dead." ¹²Then Abraham bowed down before the people of the land. ¹³He said to Ephron in the hearing of the people of the land, "If you only will listen to me! I will give the price of the field; accept it from me, so that I may bury my dead there." ¹⁴Ephron answered Abraham, ¹⁵"My lord, listen to me; a piece of land worth four hundred shekels of silver—what is that between you and me? Bury your dead." ¹⁶Abraham agreed with Ephron; and Abraham weighed out for Ephron the silver that he had named in the hearing of the Hittites, four hundred shekels of silver, according to the weights current among the merchants.

17 So the field of Ephron in Machpelah, which was to the east of Mamre, the field with the cave that was in it and all the trees that were in the field, throughout its whole area, passed ¹⁸to Abraham as a possession in the presence of the Hittites, in the presence of all who went in at the gate of his city. ¹⁹After this, Abraham buried Sarah his wife in the cave of the field of Machpelah facing Mamre (that is, Hebron) in the land of Canaan. ²⁰The

Holiness

GENESIS 23.2–4

"As humans, we are holy insofar as we have come into contact with divine holiness . . . The divine initiative cannot be over stressed, but at the same time there is need of our most generous effort and concentration. The hard part is doing our utmost and then having to count it as nothing. Far from seeing ourselves growing in insight and closeness to God, the opposite happens. We are beset by weaknesses of all kinds and fail to make a good show in our own estimation. All we do seems paltry and shabby, even our sufferings are not worthy of the name. We have nothing to fall back on . . . except the one thing which is everything—faith in God's goodness and fidelity."

—RUTH BURROWS,
To Believe in Jesus

The Lord Will Send His Angel Ahead

GENESIS 24.17–21

Enter this scene fully in your imagination. Let your senses create the sight of the well, the smell of the water, the shuffling noises of the tired camels. First imagine yourself as Abraham's servant, entrusted with an important task, praying earnestly for God's help. Now imagine yourself as Rebekah, going about your hard daily work, interrupted by a stranger, asked to do yet more. Finally, imagine that you are the well itself, silent repository of many ancient secrets. Listen carefully for what God speaks to you as you enter each of these roles. When you have explored each in turn, sit quietly for a time, receptive to what God might be saying to you today through this incident in scripture.

See Meeting God in Scripture

field and the cave that is in it passed from the Hittites into Abraham's possession as a burying place.

The Marriage of Isaac and Rebekah

24 Now Abraham was old, well advanced in years; and the LORD had blessed Abraham in all things. ²Abraham said to his servant, the oldest of his house, who had charge of all that he had, "Put your hand under my thigh ³and I will make you swear by the LORD, the God of heaven and earth, that you will not get a wife for my son from the daughters of the Canaanites, among whom I live, ⁴but will go to my country and to my kindred and get a wife for my son Isaac." ⁵The servant said to him, "Perhaps the woman may not be willing to follow me to this land; must I then take your son back to the land from which you came?" ⁶Abraham said to him, "See to it that you do not take my son back there. ⁷The LORD, the God of heaven, who took me from my father's house and from the land of my birth, and who spoke to me and swore to me, 'To your offspring I will give this land,' he will send his angel before you, and you shall take a wife for my son from there. ⁸But if the woman is not willing to follow you, then you will be free from this oath of mine; only you must not take my son back there." ⁹So the servant put his hand under the thigh of Abraham his master and swore to him concerning this matter.

10 Then the servant took ten of his master's camels and departed, taking all kinds of choice gifts from his master; and he set out and went to Aram-naharaim, to the city of Nahor. ¹¹He made the camels kneel down outside the city by the well of water; it was toward evening, the time when women go out to draw water. ¹²And he said, "O LORD, God of my master Abraham, please grant me success today and show steadfast love to my master Abraham. ¹³I am standing here by the spring of water, and the daughters of the townspeople are coming out to draw water. ¹⁴Let the girl to whom I shall say, 'Please offer your jar that I may drink,' and who shall say, 'Drink, and I will water your camels'—let her be the one whom you have appointed for your servant Isaac. By this I shall know that you have shown steadfast love to my master."

15 Before he had finished speaking, there was Rebekah, who was born to Bethuel son of Milcah, the wife of Nahor, Abraham's brother, coming out with her water jar on her shoulder. ¹⁶The girl was very fair to look upon, a virgin, whom no man had known. She went down to the spring, filled her jar, and came up. ¹⁷Then the servant ran to meet her and said, "Please let me sip a little water from your jar." ¹⁸"Drink, my lord," she said, and quickly lowered her jar upon her hand and gave him a drink. ¹⁹When she had finished giving him a drink, she said, "I will draw for your camels also, until they have finished drinking." ²⁰So she quickly emptied her jar into the trough and ran again to the well to draw, and she drew for all his camels. ²¹The man gazed at her in silence to learn whether or not the LORD had made his journey successful.

22 When the camels had finished drinking, the man took a gold nose-ring weighing a half shekel, and two

bracelets for her arms weighing ten gold shekels, ²³and said, "Tell me whose daughter you are. Is there room in your father's house for us to spend the night?" ²⁴She said to him, "I am the daughter of Bethuel son of Milcah, whom she bore to Nahor." ²⁵She added, "We have plenty of straw and fodder and a place to spend the night." ²⁶The man bowed his head and worshiped the LORD ²⁷and said, "Blessed be the LORD, the God of my master Abraham, who has not forsaken his steadfast love and his faithfulness toward my master. As for me, the LORD has led me on the way to the house of my master's kin."

28 Then the girl ran and told her mother's household about these things. ²⁹Rebekah had a brother whose name was Laban; and Laban ran out to the man, to the spring. ³⁰As soon as he had seen the nose-ring, and the bracelets on his sister's arms, and when he heard the words of his sister Rebekah, "Thus the man spoke to me," he went to the man; and there he was, standing by the camels at the spring. ³¹He said, "Come in, O blessed of the LORD. Why do you stand outside when I have prepared the house and a place for the camels?" ³²So the man came into the house; and Laban unloaded the camels, and gave him straw and fodder for the camels, and water to wash his feet and the feet of the men who were with him. ³³Then food was set before him to eat; but he said, "I will not eat until I have told my errand." He said, "Speak on."

34 So he said, "I am Abraham's servant. ³⁵The LORD has greatly blessed my master, and he has become wealthy; he has given him flocks and herds, silver and gold, male and female slaves, camels and donkeys. ³⁶And Sarah my master's wife bore a son to my master when she was old; and he has given him all that he has. ³⁷My master made me swear, saying, 'You shall not take a wife for my son from the daughters of the Canaanites, in whose land I live; ³⁸but you shall go to my father's house, to my kindred, and get a wife for my son.' ³⁹I said to my master, 'Perhaps the woman will not follow me.' ⁴⁰But he said to me, 'The LORD, before whom I walk, will send his angel with you and make your way successful. You shall get a wife for my son from my kindred, from my father's house. ⁴¹Then you will be free from my oath, when you come to my kindred; even if they will not give her to you, you will be free from my oath.'

42 "I came today to the spring, and said, 'O LORD, the God of my master Abraham, if now you will only make successful the way I am going! ⁴³I am standing here by the spring of water; let the young woman who comes out to draw, to whom I shall say, "Please give me a little water from your jar to drink," ⁴⁴and who will say to me, "Drink, and I will draw for your camels also"—let her be the woman whom the LORD has appointed for my master's son.'

45 "Before I had finished speaking in my heart, there was Rebekah coming out with her water jar on her shoulder; and she went down to the spring, and drew. I said to her, 'Please let me drink.' ⁴⁶She quickly let down her jar from her shoulder, and said, 'Drink, and I will also water your camels.' So I drank, and she also watered the camels.

Come, O Blessed

GENESIS 24.31

In the culture of the desert, hospitality is a serious obligation. The stranger depends for life itself on various tribes' willingness to provide shelter, drink and food as he travels through the wilderness. The tribes are also aware that generosity is not merely an obligation. The stranger may bring blessing; angels are often entertained "unawares." What is your response to strangers at your door, especially if they seem "different" from you? Consider making a deliberate decision to give a certain percentage of your time or money for a period of time to the care of someone in need. Do this unconditionally, but be alert to the possibility that Jesus Christ may be revealed in those you encounter (see Matthew 25.34–46).

See Meeting God in Community

From the Lord

GENESIS 24.50–51

How do we know when an opportunity is from the Lord? How do we discern God's desire among several good choices? We know that Abraham's servant has been praying, and we can reasonably assume that Laban, Bethuel and Rebekah root their lives in a regular rhythm of prayer; this is the foundation of all discernment. Today, take the phrase "The thing comes from the Lord" and repeat it over and over until it begins to pulse with the rhythm of your heartbeat. Ponder the phrase; be open not only to ordinary insights, but to images or hymn verses that accompany your reflection. Finally, be receptive to an invitation to be or do something today in response to your meditation in the Spirit.

See Meeting God in Prayer

⁴⁷Then I asked her, 'Whose daughter are you?' She said, 'The daughter of Bethuel, Nahor's son, whom Milcah bore to him.' So I put the ring on her nose, and the bracelets on her arms. ⁴⁸Then I bowed my head and worshiped the Lord, and blessed the Lord, the God of my master Abraham, who had led me by the right way to obtain the daughter of my master's kinsman for his son. ⁴⁹Now then, if you will deal loyally and truly with my master, tell me; and if not, tell me, so that I may turn either to the right hand or to the left."

50 Then Laban and Bethuel answered, "The thing comes from the Lord; we cannot speak to you anything bad or good. ⁵¹Look, Rebekah is before you, take her and go, and let her be the wife of your master's son, as the Lord has spoken."

52 When Abraham's servant heard their words, he bowed himself to the ground before the Lord. ⁵³And the servant brought out jewelry of silver and of gold, and garments, and gave them to Rebekah; he also gave to her brother and to her mother costly ornaments. ⁵⁴Then he and the men who were with him ate and drank, and they spent the night there. When they rose in the morning, he said, "Send me back to my master." ⁵⁵Her brother and her mother said, "Let the girl remain with us a while, at least ten days; after that she may go." ⁵⁶But he said to them, "Do not delay me, since the Lord has made my journey successful; let me go that I may go to my master." ⁵⁷They said, "We will call the girl, and ask her." ⁵⁸And they called Rebekah, and said to her, "Will you go with this man?" She said, "I will." ⁵⁹So they sent away their sister Rebekah and her nurse along with Abraham's servant and his men. ⁶⁰And they blessed Rebekah and said to her,

"May you, our sister, become
    thousands of myriads;
may your offspring gain possession
    of the gates of their foes."

⁶¹Then Rebekah and her maids rose up, mounted the camels, and followed the man; thus the servant took Rebekah, and went his way.

62 Now Isaac had come from*ᵃ* Beer-lahai-roi, and was settled in the Negeb. ⁶³Isaac went out in the evening to walk*ᵇ* in the field; and looking up, he saw camels coming. ⁶⁴And Rebekah looked up, and when she saw Isaac, she slipped quickly from the camel, ⁶⁵and said to the servant, "Who is the man over there, walking in the field to meet us?" The servant said, "It is my master." So she took her veil and covered herself. ⁶⁶And the servant told Isaac all the things that he had done. ⁶⁷Then Isaac brought her into his mother Sarah's tent. He took Rebekah, and she became his wife; and he loved her. So Isaac was comforted after his mother's death.

Abraham Marries Keturah

25 Abraham took another wife, whose name was Keturah. ²She bore him Zimran, Jokshan, Medan, Midian, Ishbak, and Shuah. ³Jokshan was the father of

a Syr Tg: Heb *from coming to*   *b* Meaning of Heb word is uncertain

Sheba and Dedan. The sons of Dedan were Asshurim, Letushim, and Leummim. [4]The sons of Midian were Ephah, Epher, Hanoch, Abida, and Eldaah. All these were the children of Keturah. [5]Abraham gave all he had to Isaac. [6]But to the sons of his concubines Abraham gave gifts, while he was still living, and he sent them away from his son Isaac, eastward to the east country.

The Death of Abraham

7 This is the length of Abraham's life, one hundred seventy-five years. [8]Abraham breathed his last and died in a good old age, an old man and full of years, and was gathered to his people. [9]His sons Isaac and Ishmael buried him in the cave of Machpelah, in the field of Ephron son of Zohar the Hittite, east of Mamre, [10]the field that Abraham purchased from the Hittites. There Abraham was buried, with his wife Sarah. [11]After the death of Abraham God blessed his son Isaac. And Isaac settled at Beer-lahai-roi.

Ishmael's Descendants

12 These are the descendants of Ishmael, Abraham's son, whom Hagar the Egyptian, Sarah's slave-girl, bore to Abraham. [13]These are the names of the sons of Ishmael, named in the order of their birth: Nebaioth, the firstborn of Ishmael; and Kedar, Adbeel, Mibsam, [14]Mishma, Dumah, Massa, [15]Hadad, Tema, Jetur, Naphish, and Kedemah. [16]These are the sons of Ishmael and these are their names, by their villages and by their encampments, twelve princes according to their tribes. [17](This is the length of the life of Ishmael, one hundred thirty-seven years; he breathed his last and died, and was gathered to his people.) [18]They settled from Havilah to Shur, which is opposite Egypt in the direction of Assyria; he settled down[a] alongside of[b] all his people.

The Birth and Youth of Esau and Jacob

19 These are the descendants of Isaac, Abraham's son: Abraham was the father of Isaac, [20]and Isaac was forty years old when he married Rebekah, daughter of Bethuel the Aramean of Paddan-aram, sister of Laban the Aramean. [21]Isaac prayed to the LORD for his wife, because she was barren; and the LORD granted his prayer, and his wife Rebekah conceived. [22]The children struggled together within her; and she said, "If it is to be this way, why do I live?"[c] So she went to inquire of the LORD. [23]And the LORD said to her,

"Two nations are in your womb,
and two peoples born of you shall be divided;
the one shall be stronger than the other,
the elder shall serve the younger."

[24]When her time to give birth was at hand, there were twins in her womb. [25]The first came out red, all his body like a hairy mantle; so they named him Esau. [26]Afterward his brother came out, with his hand gripping Esau's heel;

Living in Conflict

GENESIS 25.22

Again conflict rears its head: The sons of Isaac and Ishmael live in hostility toward one another, and even the babies in Rebekah's womb struggle with each other. In light of the record of Genesis, we might consider that the peace of God that we seek must surely encompass the inevitable conflicts of life. Perhaps our spiritual formation involves not eliminating conflict and suffering, but allowing ourselves to learn how they strengthen us in faith and love. Reflect on some current conflict in your life from which you have prayed for release. Ask God for insight into how you can *live with* the conflict, letting it teach you what he wishes you to learn.

See *Meeting God in Scripture*

---

a Heb *he fell*   b Or *down in opposition to*   c Syr: Meaning of Heb uncertain

The Soul's Birthright

"If self-sacrifice is, as we are told, 'glorious madness,' then certainly undeviating self-assertion is inglorious madness. Either path leads alike to annihilation. We have come upon one of those deep paradoxes of life. To become a person, one must both affirm and deny oneself. Each involves the other. They are not totally different things, but diverse aspects of the same thing. They belong together as indissolubly as the two sides of the board do."

—RUFUS JONES,
Daily Readings from Quaker Spirituality

so he was named Jacob.[a] Isaac was sixty years old when she bore them.

27 When the boys grew up, Esau was a skillful hunter, a man of the field, while Jacob was a quiet man, living in tents. [28]Isaac loved Esau, because he was fond of game; but Rebekah loved Jacob.

Esau Sells His Birthright

29 Once when Jacob was cooking a stew, Esau came in from the field, and he was famished. [30]Esau said to Jacob, "Let me eat some of that red stuff, for I am famished!" (Therefore he was called Edom.[b]) [31]Jacob said, "First sell me your birthright." [32]Esau said, "I am about to die; of what use is a birthright to me?" [33]Jacob said, "Swear to me first."[c] So he swore to him, and sold his birthright to Jacob. [34]Then Jacob gave Esau bread and lentil stew, and he ate and drank, and rose and went his way. Thus Esau despised his birthright.

Isaac and Abimelech

26 Now there was a famine in the land, besides the former famine that had occurred in the days of Abraham. And Isaac went to Gerar, to King Abimelech of the Philistines. [2]The LORD appeared to Isaac[d] and said, "Do not go down to Egypt; settle in the land that I shall show you. [3]Reside in this land as an alien, and I will be with you, and will bless you; for to you and to your descendants I will give all these lands, and I will fulfill the oath that I swore to your father Abraham. [4]I will make your offspring as numerous as the stars of heaven, and will give to your offspring all these lands; and all the nations of the earth shall gain blessing for themselves through your offspring, [5]because Abraham obeyed my voice and kept my charge, my commandments, my statutes, and my laws."

6 So Isaac settled in Gerar. [7]When the men of the place asked him about his wife, he said, "She is my sister"; for he was afraid to say, "My wife," thinking, "or else the men of the place might kill me for the sake of Rebekah, because she is attractive in appearance." [8]When Isaac had been there a long time, King Abimelech of the Philistines looked out of a window and saw him fondling his wife Rebekah. [9]So Abimelech called for Isaac, and said, "So she is your wife! Why then did you say, 'She is my sister'?" Isaac said to him, "Because I thought I might die because of her." [10]Abimelech said, "What is this you have done to us? One of the people might easily have lain with your wife, and you would have brought guilt upon us." [11]So Abimelech warned all the people, saying, "Whoever touches this man or his wife shall be put to death."

12 Isaac sowed seed in that land, and in the same year reaped a hundredfold. The LORD blessed him, [13]and the man became rich; he prospered more and more until he became very wealthy. [14]He had possessions of flocks and herds, and a great household, so that the Philistines en-

a That is *He takes by the heel* or *He supplants*   *b* That is *Red*   *c* Heb *today*
d Heb *him*

vied him. [15](Now the Philistines had stopped up and filled with earth all the wells that his father's servants had dug in the days of his father Abraham.) [16]And Abimelech said to Isaac, "Go away from us; you have become too powerful for us."

17 So Isaac departed from there and camped in the valley of Gerar and settled there. [18]Isaac dug again the wells of water that had been dug in the days of his father Abraham; for the Philistines had stopped them up after the death of Abraham; and he gave them the names that his father had given them. [19]But when Isaac's servants dug in the valley and found there a well of spring water, [20]the herders of Gerar quarreled with Isaac's herders, saying, "The water is ours." So he called the well Esek,[a] because they contended with him. [21]Then they dug another well, and they quarreled over that one also; so he called it Sitnah.[b] [22]He moved from there and dug another well, and they did not quarrel over it; so he called it Rehoboth,[c] saying, "Now the LORD has made room for us, and we shall be fruitful in the land."

23 From there he went up to Beer-sheba. [24]And that very night the LORD appeared to him and said, "I am the God of your father Abraham; do not be afraid, for I am with you and will bless you and make your offspring numerous for my servant Abraham's sake." [25]So he built an altar there, called on the name of the LORD, and pitched his tent there. And there Isaac's servants dug a well.

26 Then Abimelech went to him from Gerar, with Ahuzzath his adviser and Phicol the commander of his army. [27]Isaac said to them, "Why have you come to me, seeing that you hate me and have sent me away from you?" [28]They said, "We see plainly that the LORD has been with you; so we say, let there be an oath between you and us, and let us make a covenant with you [29]so that you will do us no harm, just as we have not touched you and have done to you nothing but good and have sent you away in peace. You are now the blessed of the LORD." [30]So he made them a feast, and they ate and drank. [31]In the morning they rose early and exchanged oaths; and Isaac set them on their way, and they departed from him in peace. [32]That same day Isaac's servants came and told him about the well that they had dug, and said to him, "We have found water!" [33]He called it Shibah;[d] therefore the name of the city is Beer-sheba[e] to this day.

Esau's Hittite Wives

34 When Esau was forty years old, he married Judith daughter of Beeri the Hittite, and Basemath daughter of Elon the Hittite; [35]and they made life bitter for Isaac and Rebekah.

Isaac Blesses Jacob

27 When Isaac was old and his eyes were dim so that he could not see, he called his elder son Esau and said to him, "My son"; and he answered, "Here I am."

---

a That is Contention   b That is Enmity   c That is Broad places or Room
d A word resembling the word for oath   e That is Well of the oath or Well of seven

We Have Found Water!

GENESIS 26.32

Find a lovely bowl and fill it with water. Place the bowl near the main entrance to your home and gather your family around. Thank God for the gift of water and pray together over the bowl. Then, each time any one of you passes through the door, dip your fingers into the bowl and remember that God is with you, blessing your going in and your coming out. Refill the bowl from time to time with fresh water, and keep it there as long as it continues to remind you of God's presence.

See Meeting God in the Created Order

Only Obey My Word

GENESIS 27.13

Many strong wills are clashing in this account, bringing to a head the conflict that has simmered in this family from the beginning. So many people are determined to control the outcome that God's will seems to have been eclipsed. Notice how a stubborn desire to manage things prevails, creating a rigidity that inevitably pits individuals against each other. As you consider these Biblical events, choose one person in this story with whom you most identify. How is that person's situation and motivation like your own? And how unlike yours? How do you resist God's will in your life? In contrast, what can you do to allow God's will to flow through and permeate your life?

See *Meeting God in Scripture*

²He said, "See, I am old; I do not know the day of my death. ³Now then, take your weapons, your quiver and your bow, and go out to the field, and hunt game for me. ⁴Then prepare for me savory food, such as I like, and bring it to me to eat, so that I may bless you before I die."

5 Now Rebekah was listening when Isaac spoke to his son Esau. So when Esau went to the field to hunt for game and bring it, ⁶Rebekah said to her son Jacob, "I heard your father say to your brother Esau, ⁷'Bring me game, and prepare for me savory food to eat, that I may bless you before the LORD before I die.' ⁸Now therefore, my son, obey my word as I command you. ⁹Go to the flock, and get me two choice kids, so that I may prepare from them savory food for your father, such as he likes; ¹⁰and you shall take it to your father to eat, so that he may bless you before he dies." ¹¹But Jacob said to his mother Rebekah, "Look, my brother Esau is a hairy man, and I am a man of smooth skin. ¹²Perhaps my father will feel me, and I shall seem to be mocking him, and bring a curse on myself and not a blessing." ¹³His mother said to him, "Let your curse be on me, my son; only obey my word, and go, get them for me." ¹⁴So he went and got them and brought them to his mother; and his mother prepared savory food, such as his father loved. ¹⁵Then Rebekah took the best garments of her elder son Esau, which were with her in the house, and put them on her younger son Jacob; ¹⁶and she put the skins of the kids on his hands and on the smooth part of his neck. ¹⁷Then she handed the savory food, and the bread that she had prepared, to her son Jacob.

18 So he went in to his father, and said, "My father"; and he said, "Here I am; who are you, my son?" ¹⁹Jacob said to his father, "I am Esau your firstborn. I have done as you told me; now sit up and eat of my game, so that you may bless me." ²⁰But Isaac said to his son, "How is it that you have found it so quickly, my son?" He answered, "Because the LORD your God granted me success." ²¹Then Isaac said to Jacob, "Come near, that I may feel you, my son, to know whether you are really my son Esau or not." ²²So Jacob went up to his father Isaac, who felt him and said, "The voice is Jacob's voice, but the hands are the hands of Esau." ²³He did not recognize him, because his hands were hairy like his brother Esau's hands; so he blessed him. ²⁴He said, "Are you really my son Esau?" He answered, "I am." ²⁵Then he said, "Bring it to me, that I may eat of my son's game and bless you." So he brought it to him, and he ate; and he brought him wine, and he drank. ²⁶Then his father Isaac said to him, "Come near and kiss me, my son." ²⁷So he came near and kissed him; and he smelled the smell of his garments, and blessed him, and said,

"Ah, the smell of my son
    is like the smell of a field that the LORD has
        blessed.
²⁸ May God give you of the dew of heaven,
        and of the fatness of the earth,
        and plenty of grain and wine.
²⁹ Let peoples serve you,

and nations bow down to you.
Be lord over your brothers,
and may your mother's sons bow down to you.
Cursed be everyone who curses you,
and blessed be everyone who blesses you!"

Esau's Lost Blessing

30 As soon as Isaac had finished blessing Jacob, when Jacob had scarcely gone out from the presence of his father Isaac, his brother Esau came in from his hunting. [31]He also prepared savory food, and brought it to his father. And he said to his father, "Let my father sit up and eat of his son's game, so that you may bless me." [32]His father Isaac said to him, "Who are you?" He answered, "I am your firstborn son, Esau." [33]Then Isaac trembled violently, and said, "Who was it then that hunted game and brought it to me, and I ate it all[a] before you came, and I have blessed him?—yes, and blessed he shall be!" [34]When Esau heard his father's words, he cried out with an exceedingly great and bitter cry, and said to his father, "Bless me, me also, father!" [35]But he said, "Your brother came deceitfully, and he has taken away your blessing." [36]Esau said, "Is he not rightly named Jacob?[b] For he has supplanted me these two times. He took away my birthright; and look, now he has taken away my blessing." Then he said, "Have you not reserved a blessing for me?" [37]Isaac answered Esau, "I have already made him your lord, and I have given him all his brothers as servants, and with grain and wine I have sustained him. What then can I do for you, my son?" [38]Esau said to his father, "Have you only one blessing, father? Bless me, me also, father!" And Esau lifted up his voice and wept.

39 Then his father Isaac answered him:
"See, away from[c] the fatness of the earth shall your
home be,
and away from[d] the dew of heaven on high.
[40] By your sword you shall live,
and you shall serve your brother;
but when you break loose,[e]
you shall break his yoke from your neck."

Jacob Escapes Esau's Fury

41 Now Esau hated Jacob because of the blessing with which his father had blessed him, and Esau said to himself, "The days of mourning for my father are approaching; then I will kill my brother Jacob." [42]But the words of her elder son Esau were told to Rebekah; so she sent and called her younger son Jacob and said to him, "Your brother Esau is consoling himself by planning to kill you. [43]Now therefore, my son, obey my voice; flee at once to my brother Laban in Haran, [44]and stay with him a while, until your brother's fury turns away— [45]until your brother's anger against you turns away, and he forgets what you have done to him; then I will send, and bring you

---

He Deceived Me

GENESIS 27.36

Esau's way of handling the conflict seems all too familiar. Each of us has been taken advantage of by someone close to us. At such a time we have a choice: Will we grow bitter and cynical, holding a grudge and waiting for revenge? What other options exist? We can humbly accept the situation, praying for compassion for ourselves and the other, though acting thus requires the grace of God's help. Compare the two choices, recalling first an event about which you grew bitter and vengeful; try to remember how that felt, and notice its effect on your body. Now set that memory aside and bring to mind another event that you accepted fully. Observe the differences and compare the costs.

See Meeting God in Community

---

a Cn: Heb *of all*   b That is *He supplants* or *He takes by the heel*   c Or *See, of*   d Or *and of*   e Meaning of Heb uncertain

Awe and Gladness

GENESIS 28.16–17

"When you had been thinking you were the hunter, it is scary suddenly to discover that all the time you have actually been the hunted one: when you imagined that you had taken the initiative in pursuit of the Holy One and then realize that in truth it was the Holy One who initiated the pursuit. 'How awesome is this place,' declared Jacob when he woke at Bethel; 'this is the house of God.' Yet Jacob had been attracted to that very spot; he had been drawn to it, fascinated by the dream of holy angels. The Holy One is both attractive and terrifying."

—DONALD NICHOLL,
Holiness

See *Meeting God in Worship*

back from there. Why should I lose both of you in one day?"

46 Then Rebekah said to Isaac, "I am weary of my life because of the Hittite women. If Jacob marries one of the Hittite women such as these, one of the women of the land, what good will my life be to me?"

28 Then Isaac called Jacob and blessed him, and charged him, "You shall not marry one of the Canaanite women. ²Go at once to Paddan-aram to the house of Bethuel, your mother's father; and take as wife from there one of the daughters of Laban, your mother's brother. ³May God Almighty[a] bless you and make you fruitful and numerous, that you may become a company of peoples. ⁴May he give to you the blessing of Abraham, to you and to your offspring with you, so that you may take possession of the land where you now live as an alien—land that God gave to Abraham." ⁵Thus Isaac sent Jacob away; and he went to Paddan-aram, to Laban son of Bethuel the Aramean, the brother of Rebekah, Jacob's and Esau's mother.

Esau Marries Ishmael's Daughter

6 Now Esau saw that Isaac had blessed Jacob and sent him away to Paddan-aram to take a wife from there, and that as he blessed him he charged him, "You shall not marry one of the Canaanite women," ⁷and that Jacob had obeyed his father and his mother and gone to Paddan-aram. ⁸So when Esau saw that the Canaanite women did not please his father Isaac, ⁹Esau went to Ishmael and took Mahalath daughter of Abraham's son Ishmael, and sister of Nebaioth, to be his wife in addition to the wives he had.

Jacob's Dream at Bethel

10 Jacob left Beer-sheba and went toward Haran. ¹¹He came to a certain place and stayed there for the night, because the sun had set. Taking one of the stones of the place, he put it under his head and lay down in that place. ¹²And he dreamed that there was a ladder[b] set up on the earth, the top of it reaching to heaven; and the angels of God were ascending and descending on it. ¹³And the LORD stood beside him[c] and said, "I am the LORD, the God of Abraham your father and the God of Isaac; the land on which you lie I will give to you and to your offspring; ¹⁴and your offspring shall be like the dust of the earth, and you shall spread abroad to the west and to the east and to the north and to the south; and all the families of the earth shall be blessed[d] in you and in your offspring. ¹⁵Know that I am with you and will keep you wherever you go, and will bring you back to this land; for I will not leave you until I have done what I have promised you." ¹⁶Then Jacob woke from his sleep and said, "Surely the LORD is in this place—and I did not know it!" ¹⁷And he was afraid, and said, "How awesome is this place! This is

a Traditional rendering of Heb *El Shaddai* b Or *stairway* or *ramp*
c Or *stood above it* d Or *shall bless themselves*

none other than the house of God, and this is the gate of heaven."

18 So Jacob rose early in the morning, and he took the stone that he had put under his head and set it up for a pillar and poured oil on the top of it. [19]He called that place Bethel;[a] but the name of the city was Luz at the first. [20]Then Jacob made a vow, saying, "If God will be with me, and will keep me in this way that I go, and will give me bread to eat and clothing to wear, [21]so that I come again to my father's house in peace, then the LORD shall be my God, [22]and this stone, which I have set up for a pillar, shall be God's house; and of all that you give me I will surely give one-tenth to you."

Jacob Meets Rachel

29 Then Jacob went on his journey, and came to the land of the people of the east. [2]As he looked, he saw a well in the field and three flocks of sheep lying there beside it; for out of that well the flocks were watered. The stone on the well's mouth was large, [3]and when all the flocks were gathered there, the shepherds would roll the stone from the mouth of the well, and water the sheep, and put the stone back in its place on the mouth of the well.

4 Jacob said to them, "My brothers, where do you come from?" They said, "We are from Haran." [5]He said to them, "Do you know Laban son of Nahor?" They said, "We do." [6]He said to them, "Is it well with him?" "Yes," they replied, "and here is his daughter Rachel, coming with the sheep." [7]He said, "Look, it is still broad daylight; it is not time for the animals to be gathered together. Water the sheep, and go, pasture them." [8]But they said, "We cannot until all the flocks are gathered together, and the stone is rolled from the mouth of the well; then we water the sheep."

9 While he was still speaking with them, Rachel came with her father's sheep; for she kept them. [10]Now when Jacob saw Rachel, the daughter of his mother's brother Laban, and the sheep of his mother's brother Laban, Jacob went up and rolled the stone from the well's mouth, and watered the flock of his mother's brother Laban. [11]Then Jacob kissed Rachel, and wept aloud. [12]And Jacob told Rachel that he was her father's kinsman, and that he was Rebekah's son; and she ran and told her father.

13 When Laban heard the news about his sister's son Jacob, he ran to meet him; he embraced him and kissed him, and brought him to his house. Jacob[b] told Laban all these things, [14]and Laban said to him, "Surely you are my bone and my flesh!" And he stayed with him a month.

Jacob Marries Laban's Daughters

15 Then Laban said to Jacob, "Because you are my kinsman, should you therefore serve me for nothing? Tell me, what shall your wages be?" [16]Now Laban had two daughters; the name of the elder was Leah, and the name of the younger was Rachel. [17]Leah's eyes were lovely,[c] and

You Are My Own Flesh and Blood

GENESIS 29.14

What a wonderful feeling to be welcomed as kin! The language Laban uses here is reminiscent of Adam's joyful word to Eve: "This at last is bone of my bones!"(2.23). We feel truly at home when we are with others who have similar features, coloring, speech patterns, gestures or attitudes; no sense of strangeness separates us. Ironically, flesh and blood can separate as well as unite; no person is quite like any other, and often a sense of intimacy can also remind us of a foundational isolation. What helps you feel "at home"—physically, mentally and spiritually? Notice how both similarity and difference play a part in making us feel we have found our place.

See Meeting God in Community

---

a That is *House of God*   *b* Heb *He*   *c* Meaning of Heb uncertain

She Was Not Loved

GENESIS 29.31

Leah's tragedy reminds us how important love is. The whole sad situation created from Jacob's multiple marriages could have been averted if each person—from Laban to Jacob to Leah to Rachel—would have acted more lovingly. Even though God ultimately works through this troubled family to accomplish his will, its members' lack of love causes much suffering and produces jealousy and conflict both in this generation of God's people and in subsequent generations.

In our frail humanity, we are limited in our ability and capacity to love. But God has given us the grace to love (see 1 John 4.7–12), and God has told us what love in action looks like (see 1 Corinthians 13). Practice living today as a conduit through which God's love flows continuously. Start at home. How does this change your usual behavior?

See Meeting God in Everyday Life

Rachel was graceful and beautiful. [18]Jacob loved Rachel; so he said, "I will serve you seven years for your younger daughter Rachel." [19]Laban said, "It is better that I give her to you than that I should give her to any other man; stay with me." [20]So Jacob served seven years for Rachel, and they seemed to him but a few days because of the love he had for her.

21 Then Jacob said to Laban, "Give me my wife that I may go in to her, for my time is completed." [22]So Laban gathered together all the people of the place, and made a feast. [23]But in the evening he took his daughter Leah and brought her to Jacob; and he went in to her. [24](Laban gave his maid Zilpah to his daughter Leah to be her maid.) [25]When morning came, it was Leah! And Jacob said to Laban, "What is this you have done to me? Did I not serve with you for Rachel? Why then have you deceived me?" [26]Laban said, "This is not done in our country—giving the younger before the firstborn. [27]Complete the week of this one, and we will give you the other also in return for serving me another seven years." [28]Jacob did so, and completed her week; then Laban gave him his daughter Rachel as a wife. [29](Laban gave his maid Bilhah to his daughter Rachel to be her maid.) [30]So Jacob went in to Rachel also, and he loved Rachel more than Leah. He served Laban[a] for another seven years.

31 When the LORD saw that Leah was unloved, he opened her womb; but Rachel was barren. [32]Leah conceived and bore a son, and she named him Reuben;[b] for she said, "Because the LORD has looked on my affliction; surely now my husband will love me." [33]She conceived again and bore a son, and said, "Because the LORD has heard[c] that I am hated, he has given me this son also"; and she named him Simeon. [34]Again she conceived and bore a son, and said, "Now this time my husband will be joined[d] to me, because I have borne him three sons"; therefore he was named Levi. [35]She conceived again and bore a son, and said, "This time I will praise[e] the LORD"; therefore she named him Judah; then she ceased bearing.

30 When Rachel saw that she bore Jacob no children, she envied her sister; and she said to Jacob, "Give me children, or I shall die!" [2]Jacob became very angry with Rachel and said, "Am I in the place of God, who has withheld from you the fruit of the womb?" [3]Then she said, "Here is my maid Bilhah; go in to her, that she may bear upon my knees and that I too may have children through her." [4]So she gave him her maid Bilhah as a wife; and Jacob went in to her. [5]And Bilhah conceived and bore Jacob a son. [6]Then Rachel said, "God has judged me, and has also heard my voice and given me a son"; therefore she named him Dan.[f] [7]Rachel's maid Bilhah conceived again and bore Jacob a second son. [8]Then Rachel said, "With mighty wrestlings I have wrestled[g] with my sister, and have prevailed"; so she named him Naphtali.

9 When Leah saw that she had ceased bearing children, she took her maid Zilpah and gave her to Jacob as

---

a Heb *him*   b That is *See, a son*   c Heb *shama*   d Heb *lawah*
e Heb *hodah*   f That is *He judged*   g Heb *niphtal*

a wife. ¹⁰Then Leah's maid Zilpah bore Jacob a son. ¹¹And Leah said, "Good fortune!" so she named him Gad.ᵃ ¹²Leah's maid Zilpah bore Jacob a second son. ¹³And Leah said, "Happy am I! For the women will call me happy"; so she named him Asher.ᵇ

14 In the days of wheat harvest Reuben went and found mandrakes in the field, and brought them to his mother Leah. Then Rachel said to Leah, "Please give me some of your son's mandrakes." ¹⁵But she said to her, "Is it a small matter that you have taken away my husband? Would you take away my son's mandrakes also?" Rachel said, "Then he may lie with you tonight for your son's mandrakes." ¹⁶When Jacob came from the field in the evening, Leah went out to meet him, and said, "You must come in to me; for I have hired you with my son's mandrakes." So he lay with her that night. ¹⁷And God heeded Leah, and she conceived and bore Jacob a fifth son. ¹⁸Leah said, "God has given me my hireᶜ because I gave my maid to my husband"; so she named him Issachar. ¹⁹And Leah conceived again, and she bore Jacob a sixth son. ²⁰Then Leah said, "God has endowed me with a good dowry; now my husband will honorᵈ me, because I have borne him six sons"; so she named him Zebulun. ²¹Afterwards she bore a daughter, and named her Dinah.

22 Then God remembered Rachel, and God heeded her and opened her womb. ²³She conceived and bore a son, and said, "God has taken away my reproach"; ²⁴and she named him Joseph,ᵉ saying, "May the LORD add to me another son!"

Jacob Prospers at Laban's Expense

25 When Rachel had borne Joseph, Jacob said to Laban, "Send me away, that I may go to my own home and country. ²⁶Give me my wives and my children for whom I have served you, and let me go; for you know very well the service I have given you." ²⁷But Laban said to him, "If you will allow me to say so, I have learned by divination that the LORD has blessed me because of you; ²⁸name your wages, and I will give it." ²⁹Jacob said to him, "You yourself know how I have served you, and how your cattle have fared with me. ³⁰For you had little before I came, and it has increased abundantly; and the LORD has blessed you wherever I turned. But now when shall I provide for my own household also?" ³¹He said, "What shall I give you?" Jacob said, "You shall not give me anything; if you will do this for me, I will again feed your flock and keep it: ³²let me pass through all your flock today, removing from it every speckled and spotted sheep and every black lamb, and the spotted and speckled among the goats; and such shall be my wages. ³³So my honesty will answer for me later, when you come to look into my wages with you. Every one that is not speckled and spotted among the goats and black among the lambs, if found with me, shall be counted stolen." ³⁴Laban said, "Good! Let it be as you have said." ³⁵But that day Laban removed

---

My First Responsibility

GENESIS 30.20

Recall that these early generations took quite seriously God's command to be fruitful and multiply. The first responsibility of a couple was to continue their family line, and those who did not have children were pitied and even shamed. Is there anything in your life that you value above everything else? Does its presence or absence make all the difference to you? Look at how you actually live: What do you prize so greatly that you are tempted to hoard it? What do you hold so tightly that you pity those who don't possess it? Is that something you *choose* to value, or has it been a less-than-conscious decision? Does it draw you nearer to God or drive you farther from him?

See Meeting God in Everyday Life

Relocated

GENESIS 30.25,43

"Our life of faith consists in moving with God in terms of (a) being securely *oriented*, (b) being painfully *disoriented*, and (c) being surprisingly *reoriented* . . . [Contrast that with] being well-settled, knowing that life makes sense and God is well placed in heaven, presiding but not bothering . . . [This latter mood] exists in the Bible, but it is a minor theme in the Psalms and is not very provocative. People are driven to poignant prayer and song precisely by *experiences of dislocation and relocation*. It is experiences of being overwhelmed, nearly destroyed, and surprisingly given life which empower us to pray and to sing."

—WALTER BRUEGGEMANN,
Praying the Psalms

See Meeting God in Scripture

the male goats that were striped and spotted, and all the female goats that were speckled and spotted, every one that had white on it, and every lamb that was black, and put them in charge of his sons; [36]and he set a distance of three days' journey between himself and Jacob, while Jacob was pasturing the rest of Laban's flock.

37 Then Jacob took fresh rods of poplar and almond and plane, and peeled white streaks in them, exposing the white of the rods. [38]He set the rods that he had peeled in front of the flocks in the troughs, that is, the watering places, where the flocks came to drink. And since they bred when they came to drink, [39]the flocks bred in front of the rods, and so the flocks produced young that were striped, speckled, and spotted. [40]Jacob separated the lambs, and set the faces of the flocks toward the striped and the completely black animals in the flock of Laban; and he put his own droves apart, and did not put them with Laban's flock. [41]Whenever the stronger of the flock were breeding, Jacob laid the rods in the troughs before the eyes of the flock, that they might breed among the rods, [42]but for the feebler of the flock he did not lay them there; so the feebler were Laban's, and the stronger Jacob's. [43]Thus the man grew exceedingly rich, and had large flocks, and male and female slaves, and camels and donkeys.

Jacob Flees with Family and Flocks

31 Now Jacob heard that the sons of Laban were saying, "Jacob has taken all that was our father's; he has gained all this wealth from what belonged to our father." [2]And Jacob saw that Laban did not regard him as favorably as he did before. [3]Then the LORD said to Jacob, "Return to the land of your ancestors and to your kindred, and I will be with you." [4]So Jacob sent and called Rachel and Leah into the field where his flock was, [5]and said to them, "I see that your father does not regard me as favorably as he did before. But the God of my father has been with me. [6]You know that I have served your father with all my strength; [7]yet your father has cheated me and changed my wages ten times, but God did not permit him to harm me. [8]If he said, 'The speckled shall be your wages,' then all the flock bore speckled; and if he said, 'The striped shall be your wages,' then all the flock bore striped. [9]Thus God has taken away the livestock of your father, and given them to me.

10 During the mating of the flock I once had a dream in which I looked up and saw that the male goats that leaped upon the flock were striped, speckled, and mottled. [11]Then the angel of God said to me in the dream, 'Jacob,' and I said, 'Here I am!' [12]And he said, 'Look up and see that all the goats that leap on the flock are striped, speckled, and mottled; for I have seen all that Laban is doing to you. [13]I am the God of Bethel,[a] where you anointed a pillar and made a vow to me. Now leave this land at once and return to the land of your birth.' " [14]Then Rachel and Leah answered him, "Is there any por-

a Cn: Meaning of Heb uncertain

tion or inheritance left to us in our father's house? ¹⁵Are we not regarded by him as foreigners? For he has sold us, and he has been using up the money given for us. ¹⁶All the property that God has taken away from our father belongs to us and to our children; now then, do whatever God has said to you."

17 So Jacob arose, and set his children and his wives on camels; ¹⁸and he drove away all his livestock, all the property that he had gained, the livestock in his possession that he had acquired in Paddan-aram, to go to his father Isaac in the land of Canaan.

19 Now Laban had gone to shear his sheep, and Rachel stole her father's household gods. ²⁰And Jacob deceived Laban the Aramean, in that he did not tell him that he intended to flee. ²¹So he fled with all that he had; starting out he crossed the Euphrates,ᵃ and set his face toward the hill country of Gilead.

Laban Overtakes Jacob

22 On the third day Laban was told that Jacob had fled. ²³So he took his kinsfolk with him and pursued him for seven days until he caught up with him in the hill country of Gilead. ²⁴But God came to Laban the Aramean in a dream by night, and said to him, "Take heed that you say not a word to Jacob, either good or bad."

25 Laban overtook Jacob. Now Jacob had pitched his tent in the hill country, and Laban with his kinsfolk camped in the hill country of Gilead. ²⁶Laban said to Jacob, "What have you done? You have deceived me, and carried away my daughters like captives of the sword. ²⁷Why did you flee secretly and deceive me and not tell me? I would have sent you away with mirth and songs, with tambourine and lyre. ²⁸And why did you not permit me to kiss my sons and my daughters farewell? What you have done is foolish. ²⁹It is in my power to do you harm; but the God of your father spoke to me last night, saying, 'Take heed that you speak to Jacob neither good nor bad.' ³⁰Even though you had to go because you longed greatly for your father's house, why did you steal my gods?" ³¹Jacob answered Laban, "Because I was afraid, for I thought that you would take your daughters from me by force. ³²But anyone with whom you find your gods shall not live. In the presence of our kinsfolk, point out what I have that is yours, and take it." Now Jacob did not know that Rachel had stolen the gods.ᵇ

33 So Laban went into Jacob's tent, and into Leah's tent, and into the tent of the two maids, but he did not find them. And he went out of Leah's tent, and entered Rachel's. ³⁴Now Rachel had taken the household gods and put them in the camel's saddle, and sat on them. Laban felt all about in the tent, but did not find them. ³⁵And she said to her father, "Let not my lord be angry that I cannot rise before you, for the way of women is upon me." So he searched, but did not find the household gods.

36 Then Jacob became angry, and upbraided Laban. Jacob said to Laban, "What is my offense? What is my

You Made a Vow to Me

GENESIS 31.13

In many ways Jacob is a rascal, weak and morally immature. Yet his heart has been deeply touched by God, and he struggles to stay centered in that relationship.

Again and again God calls us back to our true selves by reminding us that we belong to him. Thankfully, each of us has been given occasional moments of *knowing* that God is with us, and we are meant to return to those moments again and again in memory, continuing to be nourished by them, and allowing them to strengthen our commitment to God. Remember one or two of your own personal "holy encounters." How can you establish a rhythm of deep reflection on their truth?

God Is a Witness

GENESIS 31.50

The stone heap serves as a symbol for Laban and Jacob of their promises to one another. The symbol points to God as a true witness. God is a steady and objective witness to all we are and do, always setting our behavior beside his own loving vision of our intended wholeness. The good news is that we can always turn back to God in fidelity; the "bad" news is that God always notices when we are unfaithful. Can you think of some symbol that will remind you of this loving watchfulness of God in your life? Draw or build that symbol for yourself, and set it up on your desk or in another prominent place.

See *Meeting God in Everyday Life*

sin, that you have hotly pursued me? ³⁷Although you have felt about through all my goods, what have you found of all your household goods? Set it here before my kinsfolk and your kinsfolk, so that they may decide between us two. ³⁸These twenty years I have been with you; your ewes and your female goats have not miscarried, and I have not eaten the rams of your flocks. ³⁹That which was torn by wild beasts I did not bring to you; I bore the loss of it myself; of my hand you required it, whether stolen by day or stolen by night. ⁴⁰It was like this with me: by day the heat consumed me, and the cold by night, and my sleep fled from my eyes. ⁴¹These twenty years I have been in your house; I served you fourteen years for your two daughters, and six years for your flock, and you have changed my wages ten times. ⁴²If the God of my father, the God of Abraham and the Fear^a of Isaac, had not been on my side, surely now you would have sent me away empty-handed. God saw my affliction and the labor of my hands, and rebuked you last night."

Laban and Jacob Make a Covenant

43 Then Laban answered and said to Jacob, "The daughters are my daughters, the children are my children, the flocks are my flocks, and all that you see is mine. But what can I do today about these daughters of mine, or about their children whom they have borne? ⁴⁴Come now, let us make a covenant, you and I; and let it be a witness between you and me." ⁴⁵So Jacob took a stone, and set it up as a pillar. ⁴⁶And Jacob said to his kinsfolk, "Gather stones," and they took stones, and made a heap; and they ate there by the heap. ⁴⁷Laban called it Jegar-sahadutha:^b but Jacob called it Galeed.^c ⁴⁸Laban said, "This heap is a witness between you and me today." Therefore he called it Galeed, ⁴⁹and the pillar^d Mizpah,^e for he said, "The LORD watch between you and me, when we are absent one from the other. ⁵⁰If you ill-treat my daughters, or if you take wives in addition to my daughters, though no one else is with us, remember that God is witness between you and me."

51 Then Laban said to Jacob, "See this heap and see the pillar, which I have set between you and me. ⁵²This heap is a witness, and the pillar is a witness, that I will not pass beyond this heap to you, and you will not pass beyond this heap and this pillar to me, for harm. ⁵³May the God of Abraham and the God of Nahor"—the God of their father—"judge between us." So Jacob swore by the Fear^a of his father Isaac, ⁵⁴and Jacob offered a sacrifice on the height and called his kinsfolk to eat bread; and they ate bread and tarried all night in the hill country.

55^f Early in the morning Laban rose up, and kissed his grandchildren and his daughters and blessed them; then he departed and returned home.

a Meaning of Heb uncertain   b In Aramaic *The heap of witness*
c In Hebrew *The heap of witness*   d Compare Sam: MT lacks *the pillar*
e That is *Watchpost*   f Ch 32.1 in Heb

32

Jacob went on his way and the angels of God met him; ²and when Jacob saw them he said, "This is God's camp!" So he called that place Mahanaim.ᵃ

Jacob Sends Presents to Appease Esau

3 Jacob sent messengers before him to his brother Esau in the land of Seir, the country of Edom, ⁴instructing them, "Thus you shall say to my lord Esau: Thus says your servant Jacob, 'I have lived with Laban as an alien, and stayed until now; ⁵and I have oxen, donkeys, flocks, male and female slaves; and I have sent to tell my lord, in order that I may find favor in your sight.' "

6 The messengers returned to Jacob, saying, "We came to your brother Esau, and he is coming to meet you, and four hundred men are with him." ⁷Then Jacob was greatly afraid and distressed; and he divided the people that were with him, and the flocks and herds and camels, into two companies, ⁸thinking, "If Esau comes to the one company and destroys it, then the company that is left will escape."

9 And Jacob said, "O God of my father Abraham and God of my father Isaac, O LORD who said to me, 'Return to your country and to your kindred, and I will do you good,' ¹⁰I am not worthy of the least of all the steadfast love and all the faithfulness that you have shown to your servant, for with only my staff I crossed this Jordan; and now I have become two companies. ¹¹Deliver me, please, from the hand of my brother, from the hand of Esau, for I am afraid of him; he may come and kill us all, the mothers with the children. ¹²Yet you have said, 'I will surely do you good, and make your offspring as the sand of the sea, which cannot be counted because of their number.' "

13 So he spent that night there, and from what he had with him he took a present for his brother Esau, ¹⁴two hundred female goats and twenty male goats, two hundred ewes and twenty rams, ¹⁵thirty milch camels and their colts, forty cows and ten bulls, twenty female donkeys and ten male donkeys. ¹⁶These he delivered into the hand of his servants, every drove by itself, and said to his servants, "Pass on ahead of me, and put a space between drove and drove." ¹⁷He instructed the foremost, "When Esau my brother meets you, and asks you, 'To whom do you belong? Where are you going? And whose are these ahead of you?' ¹⁸then you shall say, 'They belong to your servant Jacob; they are a present sent to my lord Esau; and moreover he is behind us.' " ¹⁹He likewise instructed the second and the third and all who followed the droves, "You shall say the same thing to Esau when you meet him, ²⁰and you shall say, 'Moreover your servant Jacob is behind us.' " For he thought, "I may appease him with the present that goes ahead of me, and afterwards I shall see his face; perhaps he will accept me." ²¹So the present passed on ahead of him; and he himself spent that night in the camp.

Bless Me

GENESIS 32.24–27

"The divine antagonist seemed anxious to depart as the day was about to dawn; and Jacob held him more convulsively fast, as if aware that the daylight was likely to rob him of his anticipated blessing . . . God is approached more nearly in that which is *indefinite* than in that which is definite and distinct. [God] is felt in *awe* and *wonder* and *worship* rather than in clear *conception*. There is a sense in which *darkness* has more of God than light has. Moments of tender, vague mystery often bring distinctly the feeling of [God's] presence . . . If Jacob had got a word, that word might have satisfied him . . . Instead, [God] impressed on Jacob's soul a religious awe."

—F.W. Robertson,
"Jacob's Wrestling" in *Ten Sermons*

ᵃ Here taken to mean *Two camps*

And They Wept

GENESIS 33.4

Turn back to chapter 27 and read how Jacob and Esau parted. Compare that occasion to this greeting. Jacob's anxiety about the meeting and Esau's need for the company of four hundred men suggest that both vividly remembered their parting. What changed? The tenderness of their reunion can only be called a miracle, a miracle resulting in part from Jacob's intense and touching struggle with God the previous night. Seeing God does change us, even when we struggle through the encounter. Is there something in your life that you need to have transformed? Pray intensely about it, and risk a face to face encounter with the Most High.

See *Meeting God in Prayer*

Jacob Wrestles at Peniel

22 The same night he got up and took his two wives, his two maids, and his eleven children, and crossed the ford of the Jabbok. ²³He took them and sent them across the stream, and likewise everything that he had. ²⁴Jacob was left alone; and a man wrestled with him until daybreak. ²⁵When the man saw that he did not prevail against Jacob, he struck him on the hip socket; and Jacob's hip was put out of joint as he wrestled with him. ²⁶Then he said, "Let me go, for the day is breaking." But Jacob said, "I will not let you go, unless you bless me." ²⁷So he said to him, "What is your name?" And he said, "Jacob." ²⁸Then the man[a] said, "You shall no longer be called Jacob, but Israel,[b] for you have striven with God and with humans,[c] and have prevailed." ²⁹Then Jacob asked him, "Please tell me your name." But he said, "Why is it that you ask my name?" And there he blessed him. ³⁰So Jacob called the place Peniel,[d] saying, "For I have seen God face to face, and yet my life is preserved." ³¹The sun rose upon him as he passed Penuel, limping because of his hip. ³²Therefore to this day the Israelites do not eat the thigh muscle that is on the hip socket, because he struck Jacob on the hip socket at the thigh muscle.

Jacob and Esau Meet

33 Now Jacob looked up and saw Esau coming, and four hundred men with him. So he divided the children among Leah and Rachel and the two maids. ²He put the maids with their children in front, then Leah with her children, and Rachel and Joseph last of all. ³He himself went on ahead of them, bowing himself to the ground seven times, until he came near his brother.

4 But Esau ran to meet him, and embraced him, and fell on his neck and kissed him, and they wept. ⁵When Esau looked up and saw the women and children, he said, "Who are these with you?" Jacob said, "The children whom God has graciously given your servant." ⁶Then the maids drew near, they and their children, and bowed down; ⁷Leah likewise and her children drew near and bowed down; and finally Joseph and Rachel drew near, and they bowed down. ⁸Esau said, "What do you mean by all this company that I met?" Jacob answered, "To find favor with my lord." ⁹But Esau said, "I have enough, my brother; keep what you have for yourself." ¹⁰Jacob said, "No, please; if I find favor with you, then accept my present from my hand; for truly to see your face is like seeing the face of God—since you have received me with such favor. ¹¹Please accept my gift that is brought to you, because God has dealt graciously with me, and because I have everything I want." So he urged him, and he took it.

12 Then Esau said, "Let us journey on our way, and I will go alongside you." ¹³But Jacob said to him, "My lord knows that the children are frail and that the flocks and herds, which are nursing, are a care to me; and if they are overdriven for one day, all the flocks will die. ¹⁴Let my

a Heb *he*   b That is *The one who strives with God* or *God strives*
c Or *with divine and human beings*   d That is *The face of God*

lord pass on ahead of his servant, and I will lead on slowly, according to the pace of the cattle that are before me and according to the pace of the children, until I come to my lord in Seir."

15 So Esau said, "Let me leave with you some of the people who are with me." But he said, "Why should my lord be so kind to me?" ¹⁶So Esau returned that day on his way to Seir. ¹⁷But Jacob journeyed to Succoth,ᵃ and built himself a house, and made booths for his cattle; therefore the place is called Succoth.

Jacob Reaches Shechem

18 Jacob came safely to the city of Shechem, which is in the land of Canaan, on his way from Paddan-aram; and he camped before the city. ¹⁹And from the sons of Hamor, Shechem's father, he bought for one hundred pieces of moneyᵇ the plot of land on which he had pitched his tent. ²⁰There he erected an altar and called it El-Elohe-Israel.ᶜ

The Rape of Dinah

34 Now Dinah the daughter of Leah, whom she had borne to Jacob, went out to visit the women of the region. ²When Shechem son of Hamor the Hivite, prince of the region, saw her, he seized her and lay with her by force. ³And his soul was drawn to Dinah daughter of Jacob; he loved the girl, and spoke tenderly to her. ⁴So Shechem spoke to his father Hamor, saying, "Get me this girl to be my wife."

5 Now Jacob heard that Shechemᵈ had defiled his daughter Dinah; but his sons were with his cattle in the field, so Jacob held his peace until they came. ⁶And Hamor the father of Shechem went out to Jacob to speak with him, ⁷just as the sons of Jacob came in from the field. When they heard of it, the men were indignant and very angry, because he had committed an outrage in Israel by lying with Jacob's daughter, for such a thing ought not to be done.

8 But Hamor spoke with them, saying, "The heart of my son Shechem longs for your daughter; please give her to him in marriage. ⁹Make marriages with us; give your daughters to us, and take our daughters for yourselves. ¹⁰You shall live with us; and the land shall be open to you; live and trade in it, and get property in it." ¹¹Shechem also said to her father and to her brothers, "Let me find favor with you, and whatever you say to me I will give. ¹²Put the marriage present and gift as high as you like, and I will give whatever you ask me; only give me the girl to be my wife."

13 The sons of Jacob answered Shechem and his father Hamor deceitfully, because he had defiled their sister Dinah. ¹⁴They said to them, "We cannot do this thing, to give our sister to one who is uncircumcised, for that would be a disgrace to us. ¹⁵Only on this condition will we consent to you: that you will become as we are and every male among you be circumcised. ¹⁶Then we will give our

The Sins of the Fathers

GENESIS 34.13

Deceit breeds deceit. This family has a history of dishonesty, and even with the reconciliation recently effected between Jacob and Esau, the deeply ingrained tendency to lie and cheat does not disappear. The pride and anger that Jacob's sons display accomplishes nothing except to increase their neighbors' hostility. Today we talk about "family systems"; our modern language struggles with the same troublesome multigenerational patterns that we read about so often in the Biblical account. But the slightest honest effort on our part to break free of "disease" is always supported by God's healing power. Share with someone else one way in which you have been freed from a troublesome family habit through the power of God.

See *Meeting God in Community*

---

a That is *Booths*   *b* Heb *one hundred qesitah*   *c* That is *God, the God of Israel*   *d* Heb *he*

I Will Build an Altar

GENESIS 35.3

"Consecration means dedication to God. It occurs when we claim our deepest desire for God, beneath, above, and beyond all other things. We may not understand the full meaning of consecration: the ups and downs, the joys and agonies of the journey that must follow. And certainly we will be unable to grasp the overarching cosmic meaning of our small assent, the joy it gives to God, the deepening love it will bring to humanity, the universal covenant it has enriched. But our yes comes from some bare recollection of all these things. In a tiny space our hearts can say yes."

—GERALD MAY,
Addiction and Grace

See Meeting God in Worship

daughters to you, and we will take your daughters for ourselves, and we will live among you and become one people. [17]But if you will not listen to us and be circumcised, then we will take our daughter and be gone."

18 Their words pleased Hamor and Hamor's son Shechem. [19]And the young man did not delay to do the thing, because he was delighted with Jacob's daughter. Now he was the most honored of all his family. [20]So Hamor and his son Shechem came to the gate of their city and spoke to the men of their city, saying, [21]"These people are friendly with us; let them live in the land and trade in it, for the land is large enough for them; let us take their daughters in marriage, and let us give them our daughters. [22]Only on this condition will they agree to live among us, to become one people: that every male among us be circumcised as they are circumcised. [23]Will not their livestock, their property, and all their animals be ours? Only let us agree with them, and they will live among us." [24]And all who went out of the city gate heeded Hamor and his son Shechem; and every male was circumcised, all who went out of the gate of his city.

Dinah's Brothers Avenge Their Sister

25 On the third day, when they were still in pain, two of the sons of Jacob, Simeon and Levi, Dinah's brothers, took their swords and came against the city unawares, and killed all the males. [26]They killed Hamor and his son Shechem with the sword, and took Dinah out of Shechem's house, and went away. [27]And the other sons of Jacob came upon the slain, and plundered the city, because their sister had been defiled. [28]They took their flocks and their herds, their donkeys, and whatever was in the city and in the field. [29]All their wealth, all their little ones and their wives, all that was in the houses, they captured and made their prey. [30]Then Jacob said to Simeon and Levi, "You have brought trouble on me by making me odious to the inhabitants of the land, the Canaanites and the Perizzites; my numbers are few, and if they gather themselves against me and attack me, I shall be destroyed, both I and my household." [31]But they said, "Should our sister be treated like a whore?"

Jacob Returns to Bethel

35 God said to Jacob, "Arise, go up to Bethel, and settle there. Make an altar there to the God who appeared to you when you fled from your brother Esau." [2]So Jacob said to his household and to all who were with him, "Put away the foreign gods that are among you, and purify yourselves, and change your clothes; [3]then come, let us go up to Bethel, that I may make an altar there to the God who answered me in the day of my distress and has been with me wherever I have gone." [4]So they gave to Jacob all the foreign gods that they had, and the rings that were in their ears; and Jacob hid them under the oak that was near Shechem.

5 As they journeyed, a terror from God fell upon the cities all around them, so that no one pursued them. [6]Jacob came to Luz (that is, Bethel), which is in the land

of Canaan, he and all the people who were with him, ⁷and there he built an altar and called the place El-bethel,ᵃ because it was there that God had revealed himself to him when he fled from his brother. ⁸And Deborah, Rebekah's nurse, died, and she was buried under an oak below Bethel. So it was called Allon-bacuth.ᵇ

9 God appeared to Jacob again when he came from Paddan-aram, and he blessed him. ¹⁰God said to him, "Your name is Jacob; no longer shall you be called Jacob, but Israel shall be your name." So he was called Israel. ¹¹God said to him, "I am God Almighty:ᶜ be fruitful and multiply; a nation and a company of nations shall come from you, and kings shall spring from you. ¹²The land that I gave to Abraham and Isaac I will give to you, and I will give the land to your offspring after you." ¹³Then God went up from him at the place where he had spoken with him. ¹⁴Jacob set up a pillar in the place where he had spoken with him, a pillar of stone; and he poured out a drink offering on it, and poured oil on it. ¹⁵So Jacob called the place where God had spoken with him Bethel.

The Birth of Benjamin and the Death of Rachel

16 Then they journeyed from Bethel; and when they were still some distance from Ephrath, Rachel was in childbirth, and she had hard labor. ¹⁷When she was in her hard labor, the midwife said to her, "Do not be afraid; for now you will have another son." ¹⁸As her soul was departing (for she died), she named him Ben-oni;ᵈ but his father called him Benjamin.ᵉ ¹⁹So Rachel died, and she was buried on the way to Ephrath (that is, Bethlehem), ²⁰and Jacob set up a pillar at her grave; it is the pillar of Rachel's tomb, which is there to this day. ²¹Israel journeyed on, and pitched his tent beyond the tower of Eder.

22 While Israel lived in that land, Reuben went and lay with Bilhah his father's concubine; and Israel heard of it.

Now the sons of Jacob were twelve. ²³The sons of Leah: Reuben (Jacob's firstborn), Simeon, Levi, Judah, Issachar, and Zebulun. ²⁴The sons of Rachel: Joseph and Benjamin. ²⁵The sons of Bilhah, Rachel's maid: Dan and Naphtali. ²⁶The sons of Zilpah, Leah's maid: Gad and Asher. These were the sons of Jacob who were born to him in Paddan-aram.

The Death of Isaac

27 Jacob came to his father Isaac at Mamre, or Kiriath-arba (that is, Hebron), where Abraham and Isaac had resided as aliens. ²⁸Now the days of Isaac were one hundred eighty years. ²⁹And Isaac breathed his last; he died and was gathered to his people, old and full of days; and his sons Esau and Jacob buried him.

Esau's Descendants

36 These are the descendants of Esau (that is, Edom). ²Esau took his wives from the Canaanites: Adah daughter of Elon the Hittite, Oholibamah daughter of

---

Israel Moved On

GENESIS 35.21

From this point on in the Biblical account, Jacob is sometimes called Jacob and sometimes Israel. Israel is the name the angel gives him, with a blessing, after Jacob spends the night wrestling with God (see 32.28). The name directly refers to the struggle, but it eventually belongs to the nation, the beloved of God. Jacob grows into his new name, and, though his behavior is inconsistent for a time, there is no longer any doubt that he has God's blessing. Think about the name God might have for you, the one that describes your deepest wholeness as his beloved. Do a little research, as if you were going to name a new baby. Let your dreams suggest possibilities; be open to the name that is yours alone.

---

a That is *God of Bethel*   b That is *Oak of weeping*   c Traditional rendering of Heb *El Shaddai*   d That is *Son of my sorrow*   e That is *Son of the right hand* or *Son of the South*

The People of God

GENESIS 36.9

The need that prompted these Biblical listings of generations of God's people also stands behind our contemporary interest in genealogies: Knowing our name is not enough; our identity is connected to and interrelated with a whole people. We ask: Who were my grandparents, and who were theirs? What kind of people were they and what was important to them? The question of *who* I am expands to include the question of *whose* I am. Reading these Biblical accounts, we discover one crucial element of our holy history: We are members of the people of God!

Find several people in your church with whom you share similar interests. Ask them to join you in planning, writing and presenting a short play that dramatizes your understanding of what it means to be the people of God.

See Meeting God in Community

Anah son[a] of Zibeon the Hivite, [3]and Basemath, Ishmael's daughter, sister of Nebaioth. [4]Adah bore Eliphaz to Esau; Basemath bore Reuel; [5]and Oholibamah bore Jeush, Jalam, and Korah. These are the sons of Esau who were born to him in the land of Canaan.

6 Then Esau took his wives, his sons, his daughters, and all the members of his household, his cattle, all his livestock, and all the property he had acquired in the land of Canaan; and he moved to a land some distance from his brother Jacob. [7]For their possessions were too great for them to live together; the land where they were staying could not support them because of their livestock. [8]So Esau settled in the hill country of Seir; Esau is Edom.

9 These are the descendants of Esau, ancestor of the Edomites, in the hill country of Seir. [10]These are the names of Esau's sons: Eliphaz son of Adah the wife of Esau; Reuel, the son of Esau's wife Basemath. [11]The sons of Eliphaz were Teman, Omar, Zepho, Gatam, and Kenaz. [12](Timna was a concubine of Eliphaz, Esau's son; she bore Amalek to Eliphaz.) These were the sons of Adah, Esau's wife. [13]These were the sons of Reuel: Nahath, Zerah, Shammah, and Mizzah. These were the sons of Esau's wife, Basemath. [14]These were the sons of Esau's wife Oholibamah, daughter of Anah son[b] of Zibeon: she bore to Esau Jeush, Jalam, and Korah.

Clans and Kings of Edom

15 These are the clans[c] of the sons of Esau. The sons of Eliphaz the firstborn of Esau: the clans[c] Teman, Omar, Zepho, Kenaz, [16]Korah, Gatam, and Amalek; these are the clans[c] of Eliphaz in the land of Edom; they are the sons of Adah. [17]These are the sons of Esau's son Reuel: the clans[c] Nahath, Zerah, Shammah, and Mizzah; these are the clans[c] of Reuel in the land of Edom; they are the sons of Esau's wife Basemath. [18]These are the sons of Esau's wife Oholibamah: the clans[c] Jeush, Jalam, and Korah; these are the clans[c] born of Esau's wife Oholibamah, the daughter of Anah. [19]These are the sons of Esau (that is, Edom), and these are their clans.[c]

20 These are the sons of Seir the Horite, the inhabitants of the land: Lotan, Shobal, Zibeon, Anah, [21]Dishon, Ezer, and Dishan; these are the clans[c] of the Horites, the sons of Seir in the land of Edom. [22]The sons of Lotan were Hori and Heman; and Lotan's sister was Timna. [23]These are the sons of Shobal: Alvan, Manahath, Ebal, Shepho, and Onam. [24]These are the sons of Zibeon: Aiah and Anah; he is the Anah who found the springs[d] in the wilderness, as he pastured the donkeys of his father Zibeon. [25]These are the children of Anah: Dishon and Oholibamah daughter of Anah. [26]These are the sons of Dishon: Hemdan, Eshban, Ithran, and Cheran. [27]These are the sons of Ezer: Bilhan, Zaavan, and Akan. [28]These are the sons of Dishan: Uz and Aran. [29]These are the clans[c] of the Horites: the clans[c] Lotan, Shobal, Zibeon, Anah, [30]Di-

a Sam Gk Syr: Heb *daughter*   b Gk Syr: Heb *daughter*   c Or *chiefs*
d Meaning of Heb uncertain

shon, Ezer, and Dishan; these are the clans*a* of the Horites, clan by clan*b* in the land of Seir.

31 These are the kings who reigned in the land of Edom, before any king reigned over the Israelites. ³²Bela son of Beor reigned in Edom, the name of his city being Dinhabah. ³³Bela died, and Jobab son of Zerah of Bozrah succeeded him as king. ³⁴Jobab died, and Husham of the land of the Temanites succeeded him as king. ³⁵Husham died, and Hadad son of Bedad, who defeated Midian in the country of Moab, succeeded him as king, the name of his city being Avith. ³⁶Hadad died, and Samlah of Masrekah succeeded him as king. ³⁷Samlah died, and Shaul of Rehoboth on the Euphrates succeeded him as king. ³⁸Shaul died, and Baal-hanan son of Achbor succeeded him as king. ³⁹Baal-hanan son of Achbor died, and Hadar succeeded him as king, the name of his city being Pau; his wife's name was Mehetabel, the daughter of Matred, daughter of Me-zahab.

40 These are the names of the clans*a* of Esau, according to their families and their localities by their names: the clans*a* Timna, Alvah, Jetheth, ⁴¹Oholibamah, Elah, Pinon, ⁴²Kenaz, Teman, Mibzar, ⁴³Magdiel, and Iram; these are the clans*a* of Edom (that is, Esau, the father of Edom), according to their settlements in the land that they held.

Joseph Dreams of Greatness

37 Jacob settled in the land where his father had lived as an alien, the land of Canaan. ²This is the story of the family of Jacob.

Joseph, being seventeen years old, was shepherding the flock with his brothers; he was a helper to the sons of Bilhah and Zilpah, his father's wives; and Joseph brought a bad report of them to their father. ³Now Israel loved Joseph more than any other of his children, because he was the son of his old age; and he had made him a long robe with sleeves.*c* ⁴But when his brothers saw that their father loved him more than all his brothers, they hated him, and could not speak peaceably to him.

5 Once Joseph had a dream, and when he told it to his brothers, they hated him even more. ⁶He said to them, "Listen to this dream that I dreamed. ⁷There we were, binding sheaves in the field. Suddenly my sheaf rose and stood upright; then your sheaves gathered around it, and bowed down to my sheaf." ⁸His brothers said to him, "Are you indeed to reign over us? Are you indeed to have dominion over us?" So they hated him even more because of his dreams and his words.

9 He had another dream, and told it to his brothers, saying, "Look, I have had another dream: the sun, the moon, and eleven stars were bowing down to me." ¹⁰But when he told it to his father and to his brothers, his father rebuked him, and said to him, "What kind of dream is this that you have had? Shall we indeed come, I and your mother and your brothers, and bow to the ground before

---

Life and Death

GENESIS 36.33

"When we compare the present life of man with that time of which we have no knowledge, it seems to me like the swift flight of a lone sparrow through the banqueting-hall in winter . . . . This sparrow flies swiftly in through one door of the hall, and out through another. While he is inside, he is safe from the winter storms; but after a few moments of comfort, he vanishes from sight into the darkness whence he came. Similarly, man appears on earth for a little while, but we know nothing of what went before this life, and what follows. Therefore if [Christianity] can reveal more certain knowledge, it seems only right that we should follow it."

—BEDE,
A History of the English Church and People

See *Meeting God in the Created Order*

---

a Or *chiefs*   *b* Or *chief by chief*   *c* Traditional rendering (compare Gk):
a coat of many colors; Meaning of Heb uncertain

He Kept the Matter in Mind

GENESIS 37.11

Jacob listened intently to his son's dream, and "kept the matter in mind." His words here remind us of Mary, who, on finding Jesus in the temple, treasures the events in her heart (see Luke 2.51). "Treasuring" is noticing that God is mysteriously at work and then reflecting on that work. Is there something in your life that disturbs you even as you sense that God is somehow involved? Be attentive to an event, a thought, idea or dream you may have set aside for safekeeping. Regularly examine and tend it, so that God can eventually illuminate it. Every so often, bring it out from the back of your mind and gently reflect on it, asking God for guidance. Then send it back and remember it again at intervals until illumination comes.

See Meeting God in Prayer

you?" ¹¹So his brothers were jealous of him, but his father kept the matter in mind.

Joseph Is Sold by His Brothers

12 Now his brothers went to pasture their father's flock near Shechem. ¹³And Israel said to Joseph, "Are not your brothers pasturing the flock at Shechem? Come, I will send you to them." He answered, "Here I am." ¹⁴So he said to him, "Go now, see if it is well with your brothers and with the flock; and bring word back to me." So he sent him from the valley of Hebron.

He came to Shechem, ¹⁵and a man found him wandering in the fields; the man asked him, "What are you seeking?" ¹⁶"I am seeking my brothers," he said; "tell me, please, where they are pasturing the flock." ¹⁷The man said, "They have gone away, for I heard them say, 'Let us go to Dothan.' " So Joseph went after his brothers, and found them at Dothan. ¹⁸They saw him from a distance, and before he came near to them, they conspired to kill him. ¹⁹They said to one another, "Here comes this dreamer. ²⁰Come now, let us kill him and throw him into one of the pits; then we shall say that a wild animal has devoured him, and we shall see what will become of his dreams." ²¹But when Reuben heard it, he delivered him out of their hands, saying, "Let us not take his life." ²²Reuben said to them, "Shed no blood; throw him into this pit here in the wilderness, but lay no hand on him"—that he might rescue him out of their hand and restore him to his father. ²³So when Joseph came to his brothers, they stripped him of his robe, the long robe with sleeves*ᵃ* that he wore; ²⁴and they took him and threw him into a pit. The pit was empty; there was no water in it.

25 Then they sat down to eat; and looking up they saw a caravan of Ishmaelites coming from Gilead, with their camels carrying gum, balm, and resin, on their way to carry it down to Egypt. ²⁶Then Judah said to his brothers, "What profit is it if we kill our brother and conceal his blood? ²⁷Come, let us sell him to the Ishmaelites, and not lay our hands on him, for he is our brother, our own flesh." And his brothers agreed. ²⁸When some Midianite traders passed by, they drew Joseph up, lifting him out of the pit, and sold him to the Ishmaelites for twenty pieces of silver. And they took Joseph to Egypt.

29 When Reuben returned to the pit and saw that Joseph was not in the pit, he tore his clothes. ³⁰He returned to his brothers, and said, "The boy is gone; and I, where can I turn?" ³¹Then they took Joseph's robe, slaughtered a goat, and dipped the robe in the blood. ³²They had the long robe with sleeves*ᵃ* taken to their father, and they said, "This we have found; see now whether it is your son's robe or not." ³³He recognized it, and said, "It is my son's robe! A wild animal has devoured him; Joseph is without doubt torn to pieces." ³⁴Then Jacob tore his garments, and put sackcloth on his loins, and mourned for his son many days. ³⁵All his sons and all his daughters sought to comfort him; but he refused to be comforted,

a See note on 37.3

and said, "No, I shall go down to Sheol to my son, mourning." Thus his father bewailed him. ³⁶Meanwhile the Midianites had sold him in Egypt to Potiphar, one of Pharaoh's officials, the captain of the guard.

Judah and Tamar

38 It happened at that time that Judah went down from his brothers and settled near a certain Adullamite whose name was Hirah. ²There Judah saw the daughter of a certain Canaanite whose name was Shua; he married her and went in to her. ³She conceived and bore a son; and he named him Er. ⁴Again she conceived and bore a son whom she named Onan. ⁵Yet again she bore a son, and she named him Shelah. She[a] was in Chezib when she bore him. ⁶Judah took a wife for Er his firstborn; her name was Tamar. ⁷But Er, Judah's firstborn, was wicked in the sight of the Lᴏʀᴅ, and the Lᴏʀᴅ put him to death. ⁸Then Judah said to Onan, "Go in to your brother's wife and perform the duty of a brother-in-law to her; raise up offspring for your brother." ⁹But since Onan knew that the offspring would not be his, he spilled his semen on the ground whenever he went in to his brother's wife, so that he would not give offspring to his brother. ¹⁰What he did was displeasing in the sight of the Lᴏʀᴅ, and he put him to death also. ¹¹Then Judah said to his daughter-in-law Tamar, "Remain a widow in your father's house until my son Shelah grows up"—for he feared that he too would die, like his brothers. So Tamar went to live in her father's house.

12 In course of time the wife of Judah, Shua's daughter, died; when Judah's time of mourning was over,[b] he went up to Timnah to his sheepshearers, he and his friend Hirah the Adullamite. ¹³When Tamar was told, "Your father-in-law is going up to Timnah to shear his sheep," ¹⁴she put off her widow's garments, put on a veil, wrapped herself up, and sat down at the entrance to Enaim, which is on the road to Timnah. She saw that Shelah was grown up, yet she had not been given to him in marriage. ¹⁵When Judah saw her, he thought her to be a prostitute, for she had covered her face. ¹⁶He went over to her at the roadside, and said, "Come, let me come in to you," for he did not know that she was his daughter-in-law. She said, "What will you give me, that you may come in to me?" ¹⁷He answered, "I will send you a kid from the flock." And she said, "Only if you give me a pledge, until you send it." ¹⁸He said, "What pledge shall I give you?" She replied, "Your signet and your cord, and the staff that is in your hand." So he gave them to her, and went in to her, and she conceived by him. ¹⁹Then she got up and went away, and taking off her veil she put on the garments of her widowhood.

20 When Judah sent the kid by his friend the Adullamite, to recover the pledge from the woman, he could not find her. ²¹He asked the townspeople, "Where is the temple prostitute who was at Enaim by the wayside?" But they said, "No prostitute has been here." ²²So he returned

The Ornamented Robe

GENESIS 37.32–35

The robe is a beautiful symbol of love. Think of someone in whom you delight. Then find or buy some bits of beautiful fabric and sew the pieces together in a simple design that suits your fancy. Obtain several lovely buttons or beads and sew them on at random. Don't worry whether your creation looks fashionable or even useful; just pour all your creative, loving energy into making a gift for that person you love. When your creation feels complete to you, give it to that person with a prayer that God will always be with them. Then watch with awe as God cares for your loved one!

See Meeting God in Community

---

a Gk: Heb *He*   b Heb *when Judah was comforted*

More In the Right Than I

GENESIS 38.26

Why this troubling interruption? Genesis shows the lineage of God's people, and Perez, son of Tamar and Judah, is an ancestor of David and ultimately of Jesus. Here Judah admits that Tamar is in the right, for in fearing to lose another of his sons to her, he deprived her of her contribution to the community. This feisty woman fought for her right to bear children. Through them, the Davidic line gains Tamar's shrewdness and courage, as well as Judah's willingness to accept responsibility. Is there something God wants for you that is rightfully yours, but which you have relinquished because of how it might look to others? Write down a few possibilities, and consider whether you are being called to reclaim something for God.

See Meeting God in Everyday Life

to Judah, and said, "I have not found her; moreover the townspeople said, 'No prostitute has been here.' " [23]Judah replied, "Let her keep the things as her own, otherwise we will be laughed at; you see, I sent this kid, and you could not find her."

24 About three months later Judah was told, "Your daughter-in-law Tamar has played the whore; moreover she is pregnant as a result of whoredom." And Judah said, "Bring her out, and let her be burned." [25]As she was being brought out, she sent word to her father-in-law, "It was the owner of these who made me pregnant." And she said, "Take note, please, whose these are, the signet and the cord and the staff." [26]Then Judah acknowledged them and said, "She is more in the right than I, since I did not give her to my son Shelah." And he did not lie with her again.

27 When the time of her delivery came, there were twins in her womb. [28]While she was in labor, one put out a hand; and the midwife took and bound on his hand a crimson thread, saying, "This one came out first." [29]But just then he drew back his hand, and out came his brother; and she said, "What a breach you have made for yourself!" Therefore he was named Perez.[a] [30]Afterward his brother came out with the crimson thread on his hand; and he was named Zerah.[b]

Joseph and Potiphar's Wife

39 Now Joseph was taken down to Egypt, and Potiphar, an officer of Pharaoh, the captain of the guard, an Egyptian, bought him from the Ishmaelites who had brought him down there. [2]The LORD was with Joseph, and he became a successful man; he was in the house of his Egyptian master. [3]His master saw that the LORD was with him, and that the LORD caused all that he did to prosper in his hands. [4]So Joseph found favor in his sight and attended him; he made him overseer of his house and put him in charge of all that he had. [5]From the time that he made him overseer in his house and over all that he had, the LORD blessed the Egyptian's house for Joseph's sake; the blessing of the LORD was on all that he had, in house and field. [6]So he left all that he had in Joseph's charge; and, with him there, he had no concern for anything but the food that he ate.

Now Joseph was handsome and good-looking. [7]And after a time his master's wife cast her eyes on Joseph and said, "Lie with me." [8]But he refused and said to his master's wife, "Look, with me here, my master has no concern about anything in the house, and he has put everything that he has in my hand. [9]He is not greater in this house than I am, nor has he kept back anything from me except yourself, because you are his wife. How then could I do this great wickedness, and sin against God?" [10]And although she spoke to Joseph day after day, he would not consent to lie beside her or to be with her. [11]One day, however, when he went into the house to do

a That is *A breach* *b* That is *Brightness*; perhaps alluding to the crimson thread

his work, and while no one else was in the house, ¹²she caught hold of his garment, saying, "Lie with me!" But he left his garment in her hand, and fled and ran outside. ¹³When she saw that he had left his garment in her hand and had fled outside, ¹⁴she called out to the members of her household and said to them, "See, my husband*ᵃ* has brought among us a Hebrew to insult us! He came in to me to lie with me, and I cried out with a loud voice; ¹⁵and when he heard me raise my voice and cry out, he left his garment beside me, and fled outside." ¹⁶Then she kept his garment by her until his master came home, ¹⁷and she told him the same story, saying, "The Hebrew servant, whom you have brought among us, came in to me to insult me; ¹⁸but as soon as I raised my voice and cried out, he left his garment beside me, and fled outside."

19 When his master heard the words that his wife spoke to him, saying, "This is the way your servant treated me," he became enraged. ²⁰And Joseph's master took him and put him into the prison, the place where the king's prisoners were confined; he remained there in prison. ²¹But the LORD was with Joseph and showed him steadfast love; he gave him favor in the sight of the chief jailer. ²²The chief jailer committed to Joseph's care all the prisoners who were in the prison, and whatever was done there, he was the one who did it. ²³The chief jailer paid no heed to anything that was in Joseph's care, because the LORD was with him; and whatever he did, the LORD made it prosper.

The Dreams of Two Prisoners

40 Some time after this, the cupbearer of the king of Egypt and his baker offended their lord the king of Egypt. ²Pharaoh was angry with his two officers, the chief cupbearer and the chief baker, ³and he put them in custody in the house of the captain of the guard, in the prison where Joseph was confined. ⁴The captain of the guard charged Joseph with them, and he waited on them; and they continued for some time in custody. ⁵One night they both dreamed—the cupbearer and the baker of the king of Egypt, who were confined in the prison—each his own dream, and each dream with its own meaning. ⁶When Joseph came to them in the morning, he saw that they were troubled. ⁷So he asked Pharaoh's officers, who were with him in custody in his master's house, "Why are your faces downcast today?" ⁸They said to him, "We have had dreams, and there is no one to interpret them." And Joseph said to them, "Do not interpretations belong to God? Please tell them to me."

9 So the chief cupbearer told his dream to Joseph, and said to him, "In my dream there was a vine before me, ¹⁰and on the vine there were three branches. As soon as it budded, its blossoms came out and the clusters ripened into grapes. ¹¹Pharaoh's cup was in my hand; and I took the grapes and pressed them into Pharaoh's cup, and placed the cup in Pharaoh's hand." ¹²Then Joseph said to him, "This is its interpretation: the three branches are

The Lord Was With Him

GENESIS 39.2,20–21

"It was just when, because I saw no escape, nothing to wish and no reason to expect any good thing, I abandoned all effort—it was then that the mere necessity I fell back upon proved to be 'the good and perfect and acceptable will of God' on which my soul could rest with a rest and peace that are better to me than any pleasure . . . It is as if my painted roof had been smashed and, instead of the darkness I had dreaded, I had found the stars shining."

—CAROLINE STEPHEN,
Daily Readings from Quaker Spirituality

All Belongs to God

GENESIS 40.1–23

This story of Joseph's life is sometimes called "wisdom" writing, part of the Biblical tradition of seeking how best to live. Observing this series of disasters in that light, we look carefully at Joseph's responses. Above all, Joseph believed that God was with him and that everything is in God's hands. Trusting, he looked for God's presence in all the details of his life, even in his dreams. Are there areas of your life that you have not yet entrusted to God? With what do you think it improbable that God would be concerned: driving the car, making business deals, disciplining children, sitting in noisy airports? Notice one or two areas in which you have kept God at a distance, and deliberately watch for his presence there.

See Meeting God in Everyday Life

three days; ¹³within three days Pharaoh will lift up your head and restore you to your office; and you shall place Pharaoh's cup in his hand, just as you used to do when you were his cupbearer. ¹⁴But remember me when it is well with you; please do me the kindness to make mention of me to Pharaoh, and so get me out of this place. ¹⁵For in fact I was stolen out of the land of the Hebrews; and here also I have done nothing that they should have put me into the dungeon."

16 When the chief baker saw that the interpretation was favorable, he said to Joseph, "I also had a dream: there were three cake baskets on my head, ¹⁷and in the uppermost basket there were all sorts of baked food for Pharaoh, but the birds were eating it out of the basket on my head." ¹⁸And Joseph answered, "This is its interpretation: the three baskets are three days; ¹⁹within three days Pharaoh will lift up your head—from you!—and hang you on a pole; and the birds will eat the flesh from you."

20 On the third day, which was Pharaoh's birthday, he made a feast for all his servants, and lifted up the head of the chief cupbearer and the head of the chief baker among his servants. ²¹He restored the chief cupbearer to his cupbearing, and he placed the cup in Pharaoh's hand; ²²but the chief baker he hanged, just as Joseph had interpreted to them. ²³Yet the chief cupbearer did not remember Joseph, but forgot him.

Joseph Interprets Pharaoh's Dream

41 After two whole years, Pharaoh dreamed that he was standing by the Nile, ²and there came up out of the Nile seven sleek and fat cows, and they grazed in the reed grass. ³Then seven other cows, ugly and thin, came up out of the Nile after them, and stood by the other cows on the bank of the Nile. ⁴The ugly and thin cows ate up the seven sleek and fat cows. And Pharaoh awoke. ⁵Then he fell asleep and dreamed a second time; seven ears of grain, plump and good, were growing on one stalk. ⁶Then seven ears, thin and blighted by the east wind, sprouted after them. ⁷The thin ears swallowed up the seven plump and full ears. Pharaoh awoke, and it was a dream. ⁸In the morning his spirit was troubled; so he sent and called for all the magicians of Egypt and all its wise men. Pharaoh told them his dreams, but there was no one who could interpret them to Pharaoh.

9 Then the chief cupbearer said to Pharaoh, "I remember my faults today. ¹⁰Once Pharaoh was angry with his servants, and put me and the chief baker in custody in the house of the captain of the guard. ¹¹We dreamed on the same night, he and I, each having a dream with its own meaning. ¹²A young Hebrew was there with us, a servant of the captain of the guard. When we told him, he interpreted our dreams to us, giving an interpretation to each according to his dream. ¹³As he interpreted to us, so it turned out; I was restored to my office, and the baker was hanged."

14 Then Pharaoh sent for Joseph, and he was hurriedly brought out of the dungeon. When he had shaved him-

self and changed his clothes, he came in before Pharaoh. ¹⁵And Pharaoh said to Joseph, "I have had a dream, and there is no one who can interpret it. I have heard it said of you that when you hear a dream you can interpret it." ¹⁶Joseph answered Pharaoh, "It is not I; God will give Pharaoh a favorable answer." ¹⁷Then Pharaoh said to Joseph, "In my dream I was standing on the banks of the Nile; ¹⁸and seven cows, fat and sleek, came up out of the Nile and fed in the reed grass. ¹⁹Then seven other cows came up after them, poor, very ugly, and thin. Never had I seen such ugly ones in all the land of Egypt. ²⁰The thin and ugly cows ate up the first seven fat cows, ²¹but when they had eaten them no one would have known that they had done so, for they were still as ugly as before. Then I awoke. ²²I fell asleep a second time*a* and I saw in my dream seven ears of grain, full and good, growing on one stalk, ²³and seven ears, withered, thin, and blighted by the east wind, sprouting after them; ²⁴and the thin ears swallowed up the seven good ears. But when I told it to the magicians, there was no one who could explain it to me."

25 Then Joseph said to Pharaoh, "Pharaoh's dreams are one and the same; God has revealed to Pharaoh what he is about to do. ²⁶The seven good cows are seven years, and the seven good ears are seven years; the dreams are one. ²⁷The seven lean and ugly cows that came up after them are seven years, as are the seven empty ears blighted by the east wind. They are seven years of famine. ²⁸It is as I told Pharaoh; God has shown to Pharaoh what he is about to do. ²⁹There will come seven years of great plenty throughout all the land of Egypt. ³⁰After them there will arise seven years of famine, and all the plenty will be forgotten in the land of Egypt; the famine will consume the land. ³¹The plenty will no longer be known in the land because of the famine that will follow, for it will be very grievous. ³²And the doubling of Pharaoh's dream means that the thing is fixed by God, and God will shortly bring it about. ³³Now therefore let Pharaoh select a man who is discerning and wise, and set him over the land of Egypt. ³⁴Let Pharaoh proceed to appoint overseers over the land, and take one-fifth of the produce of the land of Egypt during the seven plenteous years. ³⁵Let them gather all the food of these good years that are coming, and lay up grain under the authority of Pharaoh for food in the cities, and let them keep it. ³⁶That food shall be a reserve for the land against the seven years of famine that are to befall the land of Egypt, so that the land may not perish through the famine."

Joseph's Rise to Power

37 The proposal pleased Pharaoh and all his servants. ³⁸Pharaoh said to his servants, "Can we find anyone else like this—one in whom is the spirit of God?" ³⁹So Pharaoh said to Joseph, "Since God has shown you all this, there is no one so discerning and wise as you. ⁴⁰You shall be over my house, and all my people shall order them-

Can You Read These Signs?

GENESIS 41.15–16

Imagine that you yourself dreamed these dreams: What might they offer to you from God? Picture the greenish-gray Nile waters flowing past, and imagine seven fat cows grazing among the reeds along the bank. What do such images evoke within you? What feelings arise as you imagine the scene? Now observe seven ugly and thin cows also grazing nearby; in your own musing, how might the two sets of cows interact? What are some symbols of comfort and prosperity for you? Compare them with images of insecurity and want. How is God working with these two themes in your life right now?

See Meeting God in Scripture

---

a Gk Syr Vg: Heb lacks *I fell asleep a second time*

One in Whom Is the Spirit of God

GENESIS 41.38,45

"When you feel by the grace of God that he is calling you to this work, and you intend to respond, lift your heart to God with humble love. And really [attend] God himself who created you, and bought you, and graciously called you to this state of life . . . . It all depends on your desire. A naked intention directed to God, and himself alone, is wholly sufficient. If you want this intention summed up in a word, to retain it more easily, take a short word, preferably of one syllable . . .

And fix this word fast to your heart, so that it is always there come what may. It will be your shield and spear in peace and war alike."

ANONYMOUS,
The Cloud of Unknowing

See *Meeting God in Prayer*

selves as you command; only with regard to the throne will I be greater than you." [41]And Pharaoh said to Joseph, "See, I have set you over all the land of Egypt." [42]Removing his signet ring from his hand, Pharaoh put it on Joseph's hand; he arrayed him in garments of fine linen, and put a gold chain around his neck. [43]He had him ride in the chariot of his second-in-command; and they cried out in front of him, "Bow the knee!"[a] Thus he set him over all the land of Egypt. [44]Moreover Pharaoh said to Joseph, "I am Pharaoh, and without your consent no one shall lift up hand or foot in all the land of Egypt." [45]Pharaoh gave Joseph the name Zaphenath-paneah; and he gave him Asenath daughter of Potiphera, priest of On, as his wife. Thus Joseph gained authority over the land of Egypt.

[46] Joseph was thirty years old when he entered the service of Pharaoh king of Egypt. And Joseph went out from the presence of Pharaoh, and went through all the land of Egypt. [47]During the seven plenteous years the earth produced abundantly. [48]He gathered up all the food of the seven years when there was plenty[b] in the land of Egypt, and stored up food in the cities; he stored up in every city the food from the fields around it. [49]So Joseph stored up grain in such abundance—like the sand of the sea—that he stopped measuring it; it was beyond measure.

[50] Before the years of famine came, Joseph had two sons, whom Asenath daughter of Potiphera, priest of On, bore to him. [51]Joseph named the firstborn Manasseh,[c] "For," he said, "God has made me forget all my hardship and all my father's house." [52]The second he named Ephraim,[d] "For God has made me fruitful in the land of my misfortunes."

[53] The seven years of plenty that prevailed in the land of Egypt came to an end; [54]and the seven years of famine began to come, just as Joseph had said. There was famine in every country, but throughout the land of Egypt there was bread. [55]When all the land of Egypt was famished, the people cried to Pharaoh for bread. Pharaoh said to all the Egyptians, "Go to Joseph; what he says to you, do." [56]And since the famine had spread over all the land, Joseph opened all the storehouses,[e] and sold to the Egyptians, for the famine was severe in the land of Egypt. [57]Moreover, all the world came to Joseph in Egypt to buy grain, because the famine became severe throughout the world.

Joseph's Brothers Go to Egypt

42 When Jacob learned that there was grain in Egypt, he said to his sons, "Why do you keep looking at one another? [2]I have heard," he said, "that there is grain in Egypt; go down and buy grain for us there, that we may live and not die." [3]So ten of Joseph's brothers went down to buy grain in Egypt. [4]But Jacob did not send Jo-

a *Abrek*, apparently an Egyptian word similar in sound to the Hebrew word meaning *to kneel* b Sam Gk: MT *the seven years that were* c That is *Making to forget* d From a Hebrew word meaning *to be fruitful* e Gk Vg Compare Syr: Heb *opened all that was in* (or, *among*) *them*

seph's brother Benjamin with his brothers, for he feared that harm might come to him. ⁵Thus the sons of Israel were among the other people who came to buy grain, for the famine had reached the land of Canaan.

6 Now Joseph was governor over the land; it was he who sold to all the people of the land. And Joseph's brothers came and bowed themselves before him with their faces to the ground. ⁷When Joseph saw his brothers, he recognized them, but he treated them like strangers and spoke harshly to them. "Where do you come from?" he said. They said, "From the land of Canaan, to buy food." ⁸Although Joseph had recognized his brothers, they did not recognize him. ⁹Joseph also remembered the dreams that he had dreamed about them. He said to them, "You are spies; you have come to see the nakedness of the land!" ¹⁰They said to him, "No, my lord; your servants have come to buy food. ¹¹We are all sons of one man; we are honest men; your servants have never been spies." ¹²But he said to them, "No, you have come to see the nakedness of the land!" ¹³They said, "We, your servants, are twelve brothers, the sons of a certain man in the land of Canaan; the youngest, however, is now with our father, and one is no more." ¹⁴But Joseph said to them, "It is just as I have said to you; you are spies! ¹⁵Here is how you shall be tested: as Pharaoh lives, you shall not leave this place unless your youngest brother comes here! ¹⁶Let one of you go and bring your brother, while the rest of you remain in prison, in order that your words may be tested, whether there is truth in you; or else, as Pharaoh lives, surely you are spies." ¹⁷And he put them all together in prison for three days.

18 On the third day Joseph said to them, "Do this and you will live, for I fear God: ¹⁹if you are honest men, let one of your brothers stay here where you are imprisoned. The rest of you shall go and carry grain for the famine of your households, ²⁰and bring your youngest brother to me. Thus your words will be verified, and you shall not die." And they agreed to do so. ²¹They said to one another, "Alas, we are paying the penalty for what we did to our brother; we saw his anguish when he pleaded with us, but we would not listen. That is why this anguish has come upon us." ²²Then Reuben answered them, "Did I not tell you not to wrong the boy? But you would not listen. So now there comes a reckoning for his blood." ²³They did not know that Joseph understood them, since he spoke with them through an interpreter. ²⁴He turned away from them and wept; then he returned and spoke to them. And he picked out Simeon and had him bound before their eyes. ²⁵Joseph then gave orders to fill their bags with grain, to return every man's money to his sack, and to give them provisions for their journey. This was done for them.

Joseph's Brothers Return to Canaan

26 They loaded their donkeys with their grain, and departed. ²⁷When one of them opened his sack to give his donkey fodder at the lodging place, he saw his money at the top of the sack. ²⁸He said to his brothers, "My money

It Came to Pass

GENESIS 42.1–5

This is the record of *God's action* in human history. Sometimes we become so intrigued with the story and the characters' responses that we forget that God is the main actor. Nonetheless, even as God's will is unfolding as it should, we must account for our actions before him. Make a time line for your own life, dividing it into units of ten years. Give each decade a "name" and note your major life tasks and concerns during each period. Then evaluate how you prayed and the quality of your relationship with God during each decade. Finally, look over your time line and notice any patterns in the way God deals with you and the way you typically respond. Pray about what you find.

See Meeting God in Everyday Life

Punished or Invited to Return?

GENESIS 42.21–28

"For your prayer, your journey into God, may you be given a small storm, a little hurricane named after you, persistent enough to get your attention, violent enough to awaken you to new depths, strong enough to shake you to the roots, majestic enough to remind you of your origin: made of earth yet steeped in eternity, frail human dust yet soaked with infinity . . . In the midst of these holy winds, in the midst of this divine wrestling, your storm journey, like all hurricanes, leads you into the eye, into the Eye of God."

—MACRINA WIEDERKEHR,
A Tree Full of Angels

has been put back; here it is in my sack!" At this they lost heart and turned trembling to one another, saying, "What is this that God has done to us?"

29 When they came to their father Jacob in the land of Canaan, they told him all that had happened to them, saying, 30 "The man, the lord of the land, spoke harshly to us, and charged us with spying on the land. 31 But we said to him, 'We are honest men, we are not spies. 32 We are twelve brothers, sons of our father; one is no more, and the youngest is now with our father in the land of Canaan.' 33 Then the man, the lord of the land, said to us, 'By this I shall know that you are honest men: leave one of your brothers with me, take grain for the famine of your households, and go your way. 34 Bring your youngest brother to me, and I shall know that you are not spies but honest men. Then I will release your brother to you, and you may trade in the land.' "

35 As they were emptying their sacks, there in each one's sack was his bag of money. When they and their father saw their bundles of money, they were dismayed. 36 And their father Jacob said to them, "I am the one you have bereaved of children: Joseph is no more, and Simeon is no more, and now you would take Benjamin. All this has happened to me!" 37 Then Reuben said to his father, "You may kill my two sons if I do not bring him back to you. Put him in my hands, and I will bring him back to you." 38 But he said, "My son shall not go down with you, for his brother is dead, and he alone is left. If harm should come to him on the journey that you are to make, you would bring down my gray hairs with sorrow to Sheol."

The Brothers Come Again, Bringing Benjamin

43 Now the famine was severe in the land. 2 And when they had eaten up the grain that they had brought from Egypt, their father said to them, "Go again, buy us a little more food." 3 But Judah said to him, "The man solemnly warned us, saying, 'You shall not see my face unless your brother is with you.' 4 If you will send our brother with us, we will go down and buy you food; 5 but if you will not send him, we will not go down, for the man said to us, 'You shall not see my face, unless your brother is with you.' " 6 Israel said, "Why did you treat me so badly as to tell the man that you had another brother?" 7 They replied, "The man questioned us carefully about ourselves and our kindred, saying, 'Is your father still alive? Have you another brother?' What we told him was in answer to these questions. Could we in any way know that he would say, 'Bring your brother down'?" 8 Then Judah said to his father Israel, "Send the boy with me, and let us be on our way, so that we may live and not die—you and we and also our little ones. 9 I myself will be surety for him; you can hold me accountable for him. If I do not bring him back to you and set him before you, then let me bear the blame forever. 10 If we had not delayed, we would now have returned twice."

11 Then their father Israel said to them, "If it must be so, then do this: take some of the choice fruits of the land in your bags, and carry them down as a present to the

man—a little balm and a little honey, gum, resin, pista-chio nuts, and almonds. ¹²Take double the money with you. Carry back with you the money that was returned in the top of your sacks; perhaps it was an oversight. ¹³Take your brother also, and be on your way again to the man; ¹⁴may God Almighty*a* grant you mercy before the man, so that he may send back your other brother and Benjamin. As for me, if I am bereaved of my children, I am be-reaved." ¹⁵So the men took the present, and they took double the money with them, as well as Benjamin. Then they went on their way down to Egypt, and stood before Joseph.

16 When Joseph saw Benjamin with them, he said to the steward of his house, "Bring the men into the house, and slaughter an animal and make ready, for the men are to dine with me at noon." ¹⁷The man did as Joseph said, and brought the men to Joseph's house. ¹⁸Now the men were afraid because they were brought to Joseph's house, and they said, "It is because of the money, replaced in our sacks the first time, that we have been brought in, so that he may have an opportunity to fall upon us, to make slaves of us and take our donkeys." ¹⁹So they went up to the steward of Joseph's house and spoke with him at the entrance to the house. ²⁰They said, "Oh, my lord, we came down the first time to buy food; ²¹and when we came to the lodging place we opened our sacks, and there was each one's money in the top of his sack, our money in full weight. So we have brought it back with us. ²²More-over we have brought down with us additional money to buy food. We do not know who put our money in our sacks." ²³He replied, "Rest assured, do not be afraid; your God and the God of your father must have put treasure in your sacks for you; I received your money." Then he brought Simeon out to them. ²⁴When the steward*b* had brought the men into Joseph's house, and given them water, and they had washed their feet, and when he had given their donkeys fodder, ²⁵they made the present ready for Joseph's coming at noon, for they had heard that they would dine there.

26 When Joseph came home, they brought him the present that they had carried into the house, and bowed to the ground before him. ²⁷He inquired about their wel-fare, and said, "Is your father well, the old man of whom you spoke? Is he still alive?" ²⁸They said, "Your servant our father is well; he is still alive." And they bowed their heads and did obeisance. ²⁹Then he looked up and saw his brother Benjamin, his mother's son, and said, "Is this your youngest brother, of whom you spoke to me? God be gracious to you, my son!" ³⁰With that, Joseph hurried out, because he was overcome with affection for his brother, and he was about to weep. So he went into a private room and wept there. ³¹Then he washed his face and came out; and controlling himself he said, "Serve the meal." ³²They served him by himself, and them by themselves, and the Egyptians who ate with him by themselves, because the Egyptians could not eat with the Hebrews, for that is an

The Choice Fruits of the Land

GENESIS 43.11

Gum and honey, resin and myrrh, pistachio nuts and al-monds! If money were scarce for you, and you wanted to give a precious gift to someone, a gift that would convey the best of your life, what would you give? Put your five senses to work in your daily environment and notice the pleasant treasure of sight, of smell, of sound, taste and touch. Enjoy fully the gifts God has given you to nour-ish and stimulate your senses, and think of how you might best share them with another. Start today by sharing them with those you live with, by showing them what you see and giving thanks together.

See Meeting God in the Created Order

Can Trouble Be Treasure?

GENESIS 43.23–34

"We who try to evade suffering at any cost may be rejecting the Truth knocking at our door, asking that we sup with him and he with us, including most significantly the drinking of his cup. The Good News is that suffering is not itself alien and terrible, or hostile to the nature of God, but that suffering is that peculiar environment in which the love and power of God can shine most clearly, for it was God who suffered for us, who suffers with us, and shares our travail."

—THOMAS BROWN,
Daily Readings from Quaker Spirituality

abomination to the Egyptians. [33]When they were seated before him, the firstborn according to his birthright and the youngest according to his youth, the men looked at one another in amazement. [34]Portions were taken to them from Joseph's table, but Benjamin's portion was five times as much as any of theirs. So they drank and were merry with him.

Joseph Detains Benjamin

44 Then he commanded the steward of his house, "Fill the men's sacks with food, as much as they can carry, and put each man's money in the top of his sack. [2]Put my cup, the silver cup, in the top of the sack of the youngest, with his money for the grain." And he did as Joseph told him. [3]As soon as the morning was light, the men were sent away with their donkeys. [4]When they had gone only a short distance from the city, Joseph said to his steward, "Go, follow after the men; and when you overtake them, say to them, 'Why have you returned evil for good? Why have you stolen my silver cup?[a] [5]Is it not from this that my lord drinks? Does he not indeed use it for divination? You have done wrong in doing this.' "

6 When he overtook them, he repeated these words to them. [7]They said to him, "Why does my lord speak such words as these? Far be it from your servants that they should do such a thing! [8]Look, the money that we found at the top of our sacks, we brought back to you from the land of Canaan; why then would we steal silver or gold from your lord's house? [9]Should it be found with any one of your servants, let him die; moreover the rest of us will become my lord's slaves." [10]He said, "Even so; in accordance with your words, let it be: he with whom it is found shall become my slave, but the rest of you shall go free." [11]Then each one quickly lowered his sack to the ground, and each opened his sack. [12]He searched, beginning with the eldest and ending with the youngest; and the cup was found in Benjamin's sack. [13]At this they tore their clothes. Then each one loaded his donkey, and they returned to the city.

14 Judah and his brothers came to Joseph's house while he was still there; and they fell to the ground before him. [15]Joseph said to them, "What deed is this that you have done? Do you not know that one such as I can practice divination?" [16]And Judah said, "What can we say to my lord? What can we speak? How can we clear ourselves? God has found out the guilt of your servants; here we are then, my lord's slaves, both we and also the one in whose possession the cup has been found." [17]But he said, "Far be it from me that I should do so! Only the one in whose possession the cup was found shall be my slave; but as for you, go up in peace to your father."

Judah Pleads for Benjamin's Release

18 Then Judah stepped up to him and said, "O my lord, let your servant please speak a word in my lord's ears, and do not be angry with your servant; for you are

a Gk Compare Vg: Heb lacks Why have you stolen my silver cup?

like Pharaoh himself. [19]My lord asked his servants, saying, 'Have you a father or a brother?' [20]And we said to my lord, 'We have a father, an old man, and a young brother, the child of his old age. His brother is dead; he alone is left of his mother's children, and his father loves him.' [21]Then you said to your servants, 'Bring him down to me, so that I may set my eyes on him.' [22]We said to my lord, 'The boy cannot leave his father, for if he should leave his father, his father would die.' [23]Then you said to your servants, 'Unless your youngest brother comes down with you, you shall see my face no more.' [24]When we went back to your servant my father we told him the words of my lord. [25]And when our father said, 'Go again, buy us a little food,' [26]we said, 'We cannot go down. Only if our youngest brother goes with us, will we go down; for we cannot see the man's face unless our youngest brother is with us.' [27]Then your servant my father said to us, 'You know that my wife bore me two sons; [28]one left me, and I said, Surely he has been torn to pieces; and I have never seen him since. [29]If you take this one also from me, and harm comes to him, you will bring down my gray hairs in sorrow to Sheol.' [30]Now therefore, when I come to your servant my father and the boy is not with us, then, as his life is bound up in the boy's life, [31]when he sees that the boy is not with us, he will die; and your servants will bring down the gray hairs of your servant our father with sorrow to Sheol. [32]For your servant became surety for the boy to my father, saying, 'If I do not bring him back to you, then I will bear the blame in the sight of my father all my life.' [33]Now therefore, please let your servant remain as a slave to my lord in place of the boy; and let the boy go back with his brothers. [34]For how can I go back to my father if the boy is not with me? I fear to see the suffering that would come upon my father."

Joseph Reveals Himself to His Brothers

45 Then Joseph could no longer control himself before all those who stood by him, and he cried out, "Send everyone away from me." So no one stayed with him when Joseph made himself known to his brothers. [2]And he wept so loudly that the Egyptians heard it, and the household of Pharaoh heard it. [3]Joseph said to his brothers, "I am Joseph. Is my father still alive?" But his brothers could not answer him, so dismayed were they at his presence.

[4] Then Joseph said to his brothers, "Come closer to me." And they came closer. He said, "I am your brother, Joseph, whom you sold into Egypt. [5]And now do not be distressed, or angry with yourselves, because you sold me here; for God sent me before you to preserve life. [6]For the famine has been in the land these two years; and there are five more years in which there will be neither plowing nor harvest. [7]God sent me before you to preserve for you a remnant on earth, and to keep alive for you many survivors. [8]So it was not you who sent me here, but God; he has made me a father to Pharaoh, and lord of all his house and ruler over all the land of Egypt. [9]Hurry and go up to my father and say to him, 'Thus says your son

Playing Cat and Mouse

GENESIS 44.14–15

Place yourself in this scene, in the role of each character in turn. Imagine that you are Joseph. How do you feel about your brothers' cruelty, your isolation from home, your wish to hurt as you have been hurt? Imagine that you are Reuben, Simeon or Levi, proud and quick to react with physical violence, but out of your element in Pharaoh's courts. Be Judah now, a good but weak man, seldom defending the truth. Or perhaps be Israel, waiting at home, expecting to lose your second beloved son, just as Joseph was taken so long ago. Experience all these emotions in yourself, and offer them one by one to God, asking that your heart be purified, freeing you to cooperate with his divine purpose in your life.

See Meeting God in Scripture

The Eyes of Faith

GENESIS 45.8–15

At last Joseph releases his desire for revenge and sees the events of his life with the eyes of faith. His brothers meant him evil, but God has brought goodness from the harm they intended. With this certainty, Joseph can be forgiving and generous. Seeing how much God has done for him, he weeps in gratitude. Is there a bitterness in your heart that has been eating away at your trust in God? Do not suppress it or act out because of it. Take it to God in prayer, over and over again, weeping in despair and anger if necessary until you can weep in gratitude. If possible, find a friend to travel with you to the depths, bringing his or her own hope alongside to carry you through.

See Meeting God in Prayer

Joseph, God has made me lord of all Egypt; come down to me, do not delay. ¹⁰You shall settle in the land of Goshen, and you shall be near me, you and your children and your children's children, as well as your flocks, your herds, and all that you have. ¹¹I will provide for you there—since there are five more years of famine to come—so that you and your household, and all that you have, will not come to poverty.' ¹²And now your eyes and the eyes of my brother Benjamin see that it is my own mouth that speaks to you. ¹³You must tell my father how greatly I am honored in Egypt, and all that you have seen. Hurry and bring my father down here." ¹⁴Then he fell upon his brother Benjamin's neck and wept, while Benjamin wept upon his neck. ¹⁵And he kissed all his brothers and wept upon them; and after that his brothers talked with him.

16 When the report was heard in Pharaoh's house, "Joseph's brothers have come," Pharaoh and his servants were pleased. ¹⁷Pharaoh said to Joseph, "Say to your brothers, 'Do this: load your animals and go back to the land of Canaan. ¹⁸Take your father and your households and come to me, so that I may give you the best of the land of Egypt, and you may enjoy the fat of the land.' ¹⁹You are further charged to say, 'Do this: take wagons from the land of Egypt for your little ones and for your wives, and bring your father, and come. ²⁰Give no thought to your possessions, for the best of all the land of Egypt is yours.' "

21 The sons of Israel did so. Joseph gave them wagons according to the instruction of Pharaoh, and he gave them provisions for the journey. ²²To each one of them he gave a set of garments; but to Benjamin he gave three hundred pieces of silver and five sets of garments. ²³To his father he sent the following: ten donkeys loaded with the good things of Egypt, and ten female donkeys loaded with grain, bread, and provision for his father on the journey. ²⁴Then he sent his brothers on their way, and as they were leaving he said to them, "Do not quarrel*a* along the way."

25 So they went up out of Egypt and came to their father Jacob in the land of Canaan. ²⁶And they told him, "Joseph is still alive! He is even ruler over all the land of Egypt." He was stunned; he could not believe them. ²⁷But when they told him all the words of Joseph that he had said to them, and when he saw the wagons that Joseph had sent to carry him, the spirit of their father Jacob revived. ²⁸Israel said, "Enough! My son Joseph is still alive. I must go and see him before I die."

Jacob Brings His Whole Family to Egypt

46 When Israel set out on his journey with all that he had and came to Beer-sheba, he offered sacrifices to the God of his father Isaac. ²God spoke to Israel in visions of the night, and said, "Jacob, Jacob." And he said, "Here I am." ³Then he said, "I am God,*b* the God of your father; do not be afraid to go down to Egypt, for I will

a Or *be agitated*   *b* Heb *the God*

make of you a great nation there. [4]I myself will go down with you to Egypt, and I will also bring you up again; and Joseph's own hand shall close your eyes."

5 Then Jacob set out from Beer-sheba; and the sons of Israel carried their father Jacob, their little ones, and their wives, in the wagons that Pharaoh had sent to carry him. [6]They also took their livestock and the goods that they had acquired in the land of Canaan, and they came into Egypt, Jacob and all his offspring with him, [7]his sons, and his sons' sons with him, his daughters, and his sons' daughters; all his offspring he brought with him into Egypt.

8 Now these are the names of the Israelites, Jacob and his offspring, who came to Egypt. Reuben, Jacob's firstborn, [9]and the children of Reuben: Hanoch, Pallu, Hezron, and Carmi. [10]The children of Simeon: Jemuel, Jamin, Ohad, Jachin, Zohar, and Shaul,[a] the son of a Canaanite woman. [11]The children of Levi: Gershon, Kohath, and Merari. [12]The children of Judah: Er, Onan, Shelah, Perez, and Zerah (but Er and Onan died in the land of Canaan); and the children of Perez were Hezron and Hamul. [13]The children of Issachar: Tola, Puvah, Jashub,[b] and Shimron. [14]The children of Zebulun: Sered, Elon, and Jahleel [15](these are the sons of Leah, whom she bore to Jacob in Paddan-aram, together with his daughter Dinah; in all his sons and his daughters numbered thirty-three). [16]The children of Gad: Ziphion, Haggi, Shuni, Ezbon, Eri, Arodi, and Areli. [17]The children of Asher: Imnah, Ishvah, Ishvi, Beriah, and their sister Serah. The children of Beriah: Heber and Malchiel [18](these are the children of Zilpah, whom Laban gave to his daughter Leah; and these she bore to Jacob—sixteen persons). [19]The children of Jacob's wife Rachel: Joseph and Benjamin. [20]To Joseph in the land of Egypt were born Manasseh and Ephraim, whom Asenath daughter of Potiphera, priest of On, bore to him. [21]The children of Benjamin: Bela, Becher, Ashbel, Gera, Naaman, Ehi, Rosh, Muppim, Huppim, and Ard [22](these are the children of Rachel, who were born to Jacob—fourteen persons in all). [23]The children of Dan: Hashum.[c] [24]The children of Naphtali: Jahzeel, Guni, Jezer, and Shillem [25](these are the children of Bilhah, whom Laban gave to his daughter Rachel, and these she bore to Jacob—seven persons in all). [26]All the persons belonging to Jacob who came into Egypt, who were his own offspring, not including the wives of his sons, were sixty-six persons in all. [27]The children of Joseph, who were born to him in Egypt, were two; all the persons of the house of Jacob who came into Egypt were seventy.

Jacob Settles in Goshen

28 Israel[d] sent Judah ahead to Joseph to lead the way before him into Goshen. When they came to the land of Goshen, [29]Joseph made ready his chariot and went up to meet his father Israel in Goshen. He presented himself to him, fell on his neck, and wept on his neck a good while.

a Or *Saul*   b Compare Sam Gk Num 26.24; 1 Chr 7.1: MT *Iob*
c Gk: Heb *Hushim*   d Heb *He*

Enough!

GENESIS 45.26–28

At first Israel is disbelieving, but when he sees the full wagons he believes. Perhaps there are some small parts within yourself that even today are "holdouts"; you're not yet willing to trust in God's care—you're waiting for a "sign" like the wagons or Jesus' wounded hands and side. But seldom can anything important be proven with certainty: How can you prove that you love someone? There is always a place for faith beside reason. Think back on times when your God has strengthened your faith. Recall what was going on in your life beforehand, what actually happened, and what occurred afterward. Based on those experiences, how can you create a more receptive climate within yourself for deepening faith today?

See Meeting God in Everyday Life

Reconciled and Restored

GENESIS 46.29–30

In a grand sweep of God's divine love, Joseph is restored to his beloved father Jacob. God's generosity is astounding. Through a remarkable chain of events, God's people are saved from famine, and a family, split apart by jealousy, is reconciled and restored.

God is concerned for your family as well. Has your family experienced a rift or an estrangement that seems irreconcilable? Keeping the story of Joseph and his family in mind, write a prayer that lays all the complicated emotions and issues before God. Make that prayer your ministry to your family by repeating it often.

See Meeting God in Prayer

³⁰Israel said to Joseph, "I can die now, having seen for myself that you are still alive." ³¹Joseph said to his brothers and to his father's household, "I will go up and tell Pharaoh, and will say to him, 'My brothers and my father's household, who were in the land of Canaan, have come to me. ³²The men are shepherds, for they have been keepers of livestock; and they have brought their flocks, and their herds, and all that they have.' ³³When Pharaoh calls you, and says, 'What is your occupation?' ³⁴you shall say, 'Your servants have been keepers of livestock from our youth even until now, both we and our ancestors'— in order that you may settle in the land of Goshen, because all shepherds are abhorrent to the Egyptians."

47 So Joseph went and told Pharaoh, "My father and my brothers, with their flocks and herds and all that they possess, have come from the land of Canaan; they are now in the land of Goshen." ²From among his brothers he took five men and presented them to Pharaoh. ³Pharaoh said to his brothers, "What is your occupation?" And they said to Pharaoh, "Your servants are shepherds, as our ancestors were." ⁴They said to Pharaoh, "We have come to reside as aliens in the land; for there is no pasture for your servants' flocks because the famine is severe in the land of Canaan. Now, we ask you, let your servants settle in the land of Goshen." ⁵Then Pharaoh said to Joseph, "Your father and your brothers have come to you. ⁶The land of Egypt is before you; settle your father and your brothers in the best part of the land; let them live in the land of Goshen; and if you know that there are capable men among them, put them in charge of my livestock."

7 Then Joseph brought in his father Jacob, and presented him before Pharaoh, and Jacob blessed Pharaoh. ⁸Pharaoh said to Jacob, "How many are the years of your life?" ⁹Jacob said to Pharaoh, "The years of my earthly sojourn are one hundred thirty; few and hard have been the years of my life. They do not compare with the years of the life of my ancestors during their long sojourn." ¹⁰Then Jacob blessed Pharaoh, and went out from the presence of Pharaoh. ¹¹Joseph settled his father and his brothers, and granted them a holding in the land of Egypt, in the best part of the land, in the land of Rameses, as Pharaoh had instructed. ¹²And Joseph provided his father, his brothers, and all his father's household with food, according to the number of their dependents.

The Famine in Egypt

13 Now there was no food in all the land, for the famine was very severe. The land of Egypt and the land of Canaan languished because of the famine. ¹⁴Joseph collected all the money to be found in the land of Egypt and in the land of Canaan, in exchange for the grain that they bought; and Joseph brought the money into Pharaoh's house. ¹⁵When the money from the land of Egypt and from the land of Canaan was spent, all the Egyptians came to Joseph, and said, "Give us food! Why should we die before your eyes? For our money is gone." ¹⁶And Joseph answered, "Give me your livestock, and I

will give you food in exchange for your livestock, if your money is gone." [17]So they brought their livestock to Joseph; and Joseph gave them food in exchange for the horses, the flocks, the herds, and the donkeys. That year he supplied them with food in exchange for all their livestock. [18]When that year was ended, they came to him the following year, and said to him, "We can not hide from my lord that our money is all spent; and the herds of cattle are my lord's. There is nothing left in the sight of my lord but our bodies and our lands. [19]Shall we die before your eyes, both we and our land? Buy us and our land in exchange for food. We with our land will become slaves to Pharaoh; just give us seed, so that we may live and not die, and that the land may not become desolate."

20 So Joseph bought all the land of Egypt for Pharaoh. All the Egyptians sold their fields, because the famine was severe upon them; and the land became Pharaoh's. [21]As for the people, he made slaves of them[a] from one end of Egypt to the other. [22]Only the land of the priests he did not buy; for the priests had a fixed allowance from Pharaoh, and lived on the allowance that Pharaoh gave them; therefore they did not sell their land. [23]Then Joseph said to the people, "Now that I have this day bought you and your land for Pharaoh, here is seed for you; sow the land. [24]And at the harvests you shall give one-fifth to Pharaoh, and four-fifths shall be your own, as seed for the field and as food for yourselves and your households, and as food for your little ones." [25]They said, "You have saved our lives; may it please my lord, we will be slaves to Pharaoh." [26]So Joseph made it a statute concerning the land of Egypt, and it stands to this day, that Pharaoh should have the fifth. The land of the priests alone did not become Pharaoh's.

The Last Days of Jacob

27 Thus Israel settled in the land of Egypt, in the region of Goshen; and they gained possessions in it, and were fruitful and multiplied exceedingly. [28]Jacob lived in the land of Egypt seventeen years; so the days of Jacob, the years of his life, were one hundred forty-seven years.

29 When the time of Israel's death drew near, he called his son Joseph and said to him, "If I have found favor with you, put your hand under my thigh and promise to deal loyally and truly with me. Do not bury me in Egypt. [30]When I lie down with my ancestors, carry me out of Egypt and bury me in their burial place." He answered, "I will do as you have said." [31]And he said, "Swear to me"; and he swore to him. Then Israel bowed himself on the head of his bed.

Jacob Blesses Joseph's Sons

48 After this Joseph was told, "Your father is ill." So he took with him his two sons, Manasseh and Ephraim. [2]When Jacob was told, "Your son Joseph has come to you," he[b] summoned his strength and sat up in

Jacob Blessed Pharaoh

GENESIS 47.7–10

How moving to see the dignified old patriarch blessing the pharaoh of all Egypt! Contrast this picture with that of the younger Jacob, conniving for his brother's birthright. Jacob has walked with God all the days of his life, and he bears the mark of God's shaping. His spiritual transformation is almost imperceptible as it is happening; yet at the end of his life God's glory shines through him. Every one of us is invited to the same deepening, loving relationship with God. It may involve difficulties; certainly it will involve counting ourselves as part of the whole people of God. Today, in the midst of all the practical matters of your life, how can you best cooperate with God in your transformation?

See Meeting God in Everyday Life

---

a Sam Gk Compare Vg: MT *He removed them to the cities*   *b* Heb *Israel*

God Blessed Me

GENESIS 48.3–4

We bless others because we have been blessed. At life's end, we can gratefully recall moments when we felt God's presence and blessing. Such moments may be intangible and incommunicable, yet they are the most real events of our lives. God gives us these "moments of meeting" for our joy, for our formation into his likeness. God's blessings are formative for us when we recall them often, ponder them and allow grace to enlarge our hearts. Think back over your experience of God and remember several sacred times of encounter with him. Begin a regular discipline of dwelling within those cherished moments. If you do not remember such times, watch attentively for the way God is trying to reach you even now.

See Meeting God in Prayer

bed. ³And Jacob said to Joseph, "God Almighty[a] appeared to me at Luz in the land of Canaan, and he blessed me, ⁴and said to me, 'I am going to make you fruitful and increase your numbers; I will make of you a company of peoples, and will give this land to your offspring after you for a perpetual holding.' ⁵Therefore your two sons, who were born to you in the land of Egypt before I came to you in Egypt, are now mine; Ephraim and Manasseh shall be mine, just as Reuben and Simeon are. ⁶As for the offspring born to you after them, they shall be yours. They shall be recorded under the names of their brothers with regard to their inheritance. ⁷For when I came from Paddan, Rachel, alas, died in the land of Canaan on the way, while there was still some distance to go to Ephrath; and I buried her there on the way to Ephrath" (that is, Bethlehem).

8 When Israel saw Joseph's sons, he said, "Who are these?" ⁹Joseph said to his father, "They are my sons, whom God has given me here." And he said, "Bring them to me, please, that I may bless them." ¹⁰Now the eyes of Israel were dim with age, and he could not see well. So Joseph brought them near him; and he kissed them and embraced them. ¹¹Israel said to Joseph, "I did not expect to see your face; and here God has let me see your children also." ¹²Then Joseph removed them from his father's knees,[b] and he bowed himself with his face to the earth. ¹³Joseph took them both, Ephraim in his right hand toward Israel's left, and Manasseh in his left hand toward Israel's right, and brought them near him. ¹⁴But Israel stretched out his right hand and laid it on the head of Ephraim, who was the younger, and his left hand on the head of Manasseh, crossing his hands, for Manasseh was the firstborn. ¹⁵He blessed Joseph, and said,

"The God before whom my ancestors Abraham
and Isaac walked,
the God who has been my shepherd all my life to
this day,
¹⁶ the angel who has redeemed me from all harm,
bless the boys;
and in them let my name be perpetuated, and the
name of my ancestors Abraham and Isaac;
and let them grow into a multitude on the earth."

17 When Joseph saw that his father laid his right hand on the head of Ephraim, it displeased him; so he took his father's hand, to remove it from Ephraim's head to Manasseh's head. ¹⁸Joseph said to his father, "Not so, my father! Since this one is the firstborn, put your right hand on his head." ¹⁹But his father refused, and said, "I know, my son, I know; he also shall become a people, and he also shall be great. Nevertheless his younger brother shall be greater than he, and his offspring shall become a multitude of nations." ²⁰So he blessed them that day, saying,

"By you[c] Israel will invoke blessings, saying,
'God make you[c] like Ephraim and like Manasseh.'"

So he put Ephraim ahead of Manasseh. ²¹Then Israel said

a Traditional rendering of Heb *El Shaddai*   *b* Heb *from his knees*   *c* you here is singular in Heb

to Joseph, "I am about to die, but God will be with you and will bring you again to the land of your ancestors. [22]I now give to you one portion[a] more than to your brothers, the portion[a] that I took from the hand of the Amorites with my sword and with my bow."

Jacob's Last Words to His Sons

49 Then Jacob called his sons, and said: "Gather around, that I may tell you what will happen to you in days to come.
2   Assemble and hear, O sons of Jacob;
          listen to Israel your father.

3   Reuben, you are my firstborn,
          my might and the first fruits of my vigor,
          excelling in rank and excelling in power.
4   Unstable as water, you shall no longer excel
          because you went up onto your father's bed;
          then you defiled it—you[b] went up onto my
             couch!

5   Simeon and Levi are brothers;
          weapons of violence are their swords.
6   May I never come into their council;
          may I not be joined to their company—
       for in their anger they killed men,
          and at their whim they hamstrung oxen.
7   Cursed be their anger, for it is fierce,
          and their wrath, for it is cruel!
       I will divide them in Jacob,
          and scatter them in Israel.

8   Judah, your brothers shall praise you;
          your hand shall be on the neck of your enemies;
          your father's sons shall bow down before you.
9   Judah is a lion's whelp;
          from the prey, my son, you have gone up.
       He crouches down, he stretches out like a lion,
          like a lioness—who dares rouse him up?
10   The scepter shall not depart from Judah,
          nor the ruler's staff from between his feet,
       until tribute comes to him;[c]
          and the obedience of the peoples is his.
11   Binding his foal to the vine
          and his donkey's colt to the choice vine,
       he washes his garments in wine
          and his robe in the blood of grapes;
12   his eyes are darker than wine,
          and his teeth whiter than milk.

13   Zebulun shall settle at the shore of the sea;
          he shall be a haven for ships,
          and his border shall be at Sidon.

14   Issachar is a strong donkey,

---

a Or *mountain slope* (Heb *shekem*, a play on the name of the town and district of Shechem)   b Gk Syr Tg: Heb *he*   c Or *until Shiloh comes* or *until he comes to Shiloh* or (with Syr) *until he comes to whom it belongs*

God Who Has Been My Shepherd

GENESIS 48.15–16

"Loving, tender Lord! My mind has from the earliest days of my childhood sought something with an earnest thirst of longing, Lord, and what that is I have not yet perfectly apprehended. Lord, I have now for many a year been in hot pursuit of it, and never yet have I been able to succeed, for I know not aright what it is. And yet it is something that draws my heart and my soul after it, and without which I can never attain full repose."

—HENRY SUSO,
Works

God of the Future As Well As the Past

GENESIS 49.3–27

Judah is probably the most promising of Leah's sons, and Jacob is generous in blessing him. He remembers the past as he did in blessing his other sons, but here Jacob, in his blessing, looks also to Judah's future, as God does. Our God has been with us in all that is completed, but God also draws us toward the "not yet," the promised fulfillment both of his reign and of our place in it. Can you envision God standing in the future, calling you forth to your very best, unfolding the potential he has given you? Does that possibility change the way you think about the present? Write a poem expressing what you feel and imagine about God's calling and blessing of what is yet to be.

lying down between the sheepfolds;
15 he saw that a resting place was good,
   and that the land was pleasant;
so he bowed his shoulder to the burden,
   and became a slave at forced labor.

16 Dan shall judge his people
   as one of the tribes of Israel.
17 Dan shall be a snake by the roadside,
   a viper along the path,
that bites the horse's heels
   so that its rider falls backward.

18 I wait for your salvation, O LORD.

19 Gad shall be raided by raiders,
   but he shall raid at their heels.

20 Asher's*a* food shall be rich,
   and he shall provide royal delicacies.

21 Naphtali is a doe let loose
   that bears lovely fawns.*b*

22 Joseph is a fruitful bough,
   a fruitful bough by a spring;
   his branches run over the wall.*c*
23 The archers fiercely attacked him;
   they shot at him and pressed him hard.
24 Yet his bow remained taut,
   and his arms*d* were made agile
by the hands of the Mighty One of Jacob,
   by the name of the Shepherd, the Rock of Israel,
25 by the God of your father, who will help you,
   by the Almighty*e* who will bless you
   with blessings of heaven above,
blessings of the deep that lies beneath,
   blessings of the breasts and of the womb.
26 The blessings of your father
   are stronger than the blessings of the eternal
      mountains,
   the bounties*f* of the everlasting hills;
may they be on the head of Joseph,
   on the brow of him who was set apart from his
      brothers.

27 Benjamin is a ravenous wolf,
   in the morning devouring the prey,
   and at evening dividing the spoil."

28 All these are the twelve tribes of Israel, and this is what their father said to them when he blessed them, blessing each one of them with a suitable blessing.

a Gk Vg Syr: Heb *From Asher*   *b* Or *that gives beautiful words*
c Meaning of Heb uncertain   *d* Heb *the arms of his hands*   *e* Traditional
rendering of Heb *Shaddai*   *f* Cn Compare Gk: Heb *of my progenitors to the boundaries*

Jacob's Death and Burial

29 Then he charged them, saying to them, "I am about to be gathered to my people. Bury me with my ancestors—in the cave in the field of Ephron the Hittite, ³⁰in the cave in the field at Machpelah, near Mamre, in the land of Canaan, in the field that Abraham bought from Ephron the Hittite as a burial site. ³¹There Abraham and his wife Sarah were buried; there Isaac and his wife Rebekah were buried; and there I buried Leah— ³²the field and the cave that is in it were purchased from the Hittites." ³³When Jacob ended his charge to his sons, he drew up his feet into the bed, breathed his last, and was gathered to his people.

50 Then Joseph threw himself on his father's face and wept over him and kissed him. ²Joseph commanded the physicians in his service to embalm his father. So the physicians embalmed Israel; ³they spent forty days in doing this, for that is the time required for embalming. And the Egyptians wept for him seventy days.

4 When the days of weeping for him were past, Joseph addressed the household of Pharaoh, "If now I have found favor with you, please speak to Pharaoh as follows: ⁵My father made me swear an oath; he said, 'I am about to die. In the tomb that I hewed out for myself in the land of Canaan, there you shall bury me.' Now therefore let me go up, so that I may bury my father; then I will return." ⁶Pharaoh answered, "Go up, and bury your father, as he made you swear to do."

7 So Joseph went up to bury his father. With him went up all the servants of Pharaoh, the elders of his household, and all the elders of the land of Egypt, ⁸as well as all the household of Joseph, his brothers, and his father's household. Only their children, their flocks, and their herds were left in the land of Goshen. ⁹Both chariots and charioteers went up with him. It was a very great company. ¹⁰When they came to the threshing floor of Atad, which is beyond the Jordan, they held there a very great and sorrowful lamentation; and he observed a time of mourning for his father seven days. ¹¹When the Canaanite inhabitants of the land saw the mourning on the threshing floor of Atad, they said, "This is a grievous mourning on the part of the Egyptians." Therefore the place was named Abel-mizraim;ᵃ it is beyond the Jordan. ¹²Thus his sons did for him as he had instructed them. ¹³They carried him to the land of Canaan and buried him in the cave of the field at Machpelah, the field near Mamre, which Abraham bought as a burial site from Ephron the Hittite. ¹⁴After he had buried his father, Joseph returned to Egypt with his brothers and all who had gone up with him to bury his father.

Joseph Forgives His Brothers

15 Realizing that their father was dead, Joseph's brothers said, "What if Joseph still bears a grudge against us and pays us back in full for all the wrong that we did to him?" ¹⁶So they approachedᵇ Joseph, saying, "Your father

---

The Almighty Who Blesses

GENESIS 49.24-25

We bless God and God blesses us and that is everything. But what *is* blessing? The essence of blessing is to be in relationship with Almighty God, to be dedicated to him and encouraged by him. Apart from that relationship, blessing makes no sense. If you were to describe blessing to someone who did not speak English, could you communicate its meaning with gestures or signs? Decide on a nonverbal "explanation" and see whether your best friend can understand it. How about developing a game of "holy charades" in which each team tries to identify words of faith as they are wordlessly acted out by the other team?

See Meeting God in Everyday Life

ᵃ That is *mourning* (or *meadow*) *of Egypt*   ᵇ Gk Syr: Heb *they commanded*

He Reassured Them

GENESIS 50.21

"To conclude your meditation . . . you must gather a little devotional bouquet. I explain my meaning. People who have been walking about in a beautiful garden do not like to leave without gathering in their hands four or five flowers to smell and keep for the rest of the day. In the same way, when our soul has carefully considered by meditation a certain mystery, we should select one, two, or three points that we liked best and that are most adapted to our improvement, think frequently about them, and smell them spiritually during the rest of the day."

—FRANCIS DE SALES,
Introduction to the Devout Life

See Meeting God in Prayer

gave this instruction before he died, [17]'Say to Joseph: I beg you, forgive the crime of your brothers and the wrong they did in harming you.' Now therefore please forgive the crime of the servants of the God of your father." Joseph wept when they spoke to him. [18]Then his brothers also wept,[a] fell down before him, and said, "We are here as your slaves." [19]But Joseph said to them, "Do not be afraid! Am I in the place of God? [20]Even though you intended to do harm to me, God intended it for good, in order to preserve a numerous people, as he is doing today. [21]So have no fear; I myself will provide for you and your little ones." In this way he reassured them, speaking kindly to them.

Joseph's Last Days and Death

22 So Joseph remained in Egypt, he and his father's household; and Joseph lived one hundred ten years. [23]Joseph saw Ephraim's children of the third generation; the children of Machir son of Manasseh were also born on Joseph's knees.

24 Then Joseph said to his brothers, "I am about to die; but God will surely come to you, and bring you up out of this land to the land that he swore to Abraham, to Isaac, and to Jacob." [25]So Joseph made the Israelites swear, saying, "When God comes to you, you shall carry up my bones from here." [26]And Joseph died, being one hundred ten years old; he was embalmed and placed in a coffin in Egypt.

a Cn: Heb *also came*

EXODUS
Journey From Bondage to Liberation

KEY VERSE:

Then the Lord said, "I have observed the misery of my people who are in Egypt; I have heard their cry on account of their taskmasters. Indeed, I know their sufferings."—Exodus 3.7

Among all the books of the canon, Biblical writers quote or refer to Exodus more often than any other book. Though numerically second in the vast collection of the Hebrew scriptures, it has played a foundational role in the development of both Hebrew and Christian traditions. The earliest Christian writers carefully probed this book as they gave expression to the message and meaning of the life of Jesus.

Exodus abounds with themes of profound relevance to the Christian life. As you prayerfully read this book, give special attention to the symbols and images (such as the sacrificial lamb) that resurface in the Gospels. Try to identify with the new nation of Israel as they experience God's hand in their corporate life. Be alert especially to these events and images: the giving of the manna or bread of life, the guiding presence of fire and cloud, the centrality of the tabernacle and tent, and the mountain as a meeting place with God.

Don't read Exodus as a spectator! Watch for opportunities to put yourself in the story, to interact with the narrative. In what ways can you identify with Moses? His self-doubt? His hesitancy to answer God's call to take responsibility for others? His frustration? Or, as you follow Moses up the mountain to converse with God as "one speaks to a friend" (Exodus 33.11), do you find yourself hungering for intimacy with God? The Exodus story is ultimately the story of all God's people from age to age, and it can become your story too.

"Lord God, in the new covenant you shed light on the miracles you worked in ancient times: the Red Sea is a symbol of our baptism, and the nation you freed from slavery is a sign of your Christian people."

—Roman Missal,
"Prayer at Easter Vigil"

Transitions

EXODUS 1.1–12

"Now a new king arose over Egypt, who did not know Joseph." In one chilling sentence the fate of a people is sealed. The comforts and certainties they have known will be shattered. Who of us cannot look back on our own lives and recall a loss that seemed to mark the end of our world: a divorce, a downsizing, the death of a child? What spiritual truths do you cling to when you believe you have lost everything? Or what wise and holy person do you trust to say the helpful thing? Do you have a group of people, a spiritual family, that sustains you during dark periods? If you have these aids in your life, thank God for them; if not, ask for God's presence to sustain you and to help you find other divine solutions.

See Meeting God in Everyday Life

1 These are the names of the sons of Israel who came to Egypt with Jacob, each with his household: ²Reuben, Simeon, Levi, and Judah, ³Issachar, Zebulun, and Benjamin, ⁴Dan and Naphtali, Gad and Asher. ⁵The total number of people born to Jacob was seventy. Joseph was already in Egypt. ⁶Then Joseph died, and all his brothers, and that whole generation. ⁷But the Israelites were fruitful and prolific; they multiplied and grew exceedingly strong, so that the land was filled with them.

The Israelites Are Oppressed

8 Now a new king arose over Egypt, who did not know Joseph. ⁹He said to his people, "Look, the Israelite people are more numerous and more powerful than we. ¹⁰Come, let us deal shrewdly with them, or they will increase and, in the event of war, join our enemies and fight against us and escape from the land." ¹¹Therefore they set taskmasters over them to oppress them with forced labor. They built supply cities, Pithom and Rameses, for Pharaoh. ¹²But the more they were oppressed, the more they multiplied and spread, so that the Egyptians came to dread the Israelites. ¹³The Egyptians became ruthless in imposing tasks on the Israelites, ¹⁴and made their lives bitter with hard service in mortar and brick and in every kind of field labor. They were ruthless in all the tasks that they imposed on them.

15 The king of Egypt said to the Hebrew midwives, one of whom was named Shiphrah and the other Puah, ¹⁶"When you act as midwives to the Hebrew women, and see them on the birthstool, if it is a boy, kill him; but if it is a girl, she shall live." ¹⁷But the midwives feared God; they did not do as the king of Egypt commanded them, but they let the boys live. ¹⁸So the king of Egypt summoned the midwives and said to them, "Why have you done this, and allowed the boys to live?" ¹⁹The midwives said to Pharaoh, "Because the Hebrew women are not like the Egyptian women; for they are vigorous and give birth before the midwife comes to them." ²⁰So God dealt well with the midwives; and the people multiplied and became very strong. ²¹And because the midwives feared God, he gave them families. ²²Then Pharaoh commanded all his people, "Every boy that is born to the Hebrews*ᵃ* you shall throw into the Nile, but you shall let every girl live."

Birth and Youth of Moses

2 Now a man from the house of Levi went and married a Levite woman. ²The woman conceived and bore a son; and when she saw that he was a fine baby, she hid him three months. ³When she could hide him no longer she got a papyrus basket for him, and plastered it with bitumen and pitch; she put the child in it and placed it among the reeds on the bank of the river. ⁴His sister stood at a distance, to see what would happen to him.

5 The daughter of Pharaoh came down to bathe at the river, while her attendants walked beside the river. She saw the basket among the reeds and sent her maid to bring it. ⁶When she opened it, she saw the child. He was crying, and she took pity on him. "This must be one of the Hebrews' children," she said. ⁷Then his sister said to Phar-

a Sam Gk Tg: Heb lacks *to the Hebrews*

aoh's daughter, "Shall I go and get you a nurse from the Hebrew women to nurse the child for you?" [8]Pharaoh's daughter said to her, "Yes." So the girl went and called the child's mother. [9]Pharaoh's daughter said to her, "Take this child and nurse it for me, and I will give you your wages." So the woman took the child and nursed it. [10]When the child grew up, she brought him to Pharaoh's daughter, and she took him as her son. She named him Moses,[a] "because," she said, "I drew him out[b] of the water."

Moses Flees to Midian

11 One day, after Moses had grown up, he went out to his people and saw their forced labor. He saw an Egyptian beating a Hebrew, one of his kinsfolk. [12]He looked this way and that, and seeing no one he killed the Egyptian and hid him in the sand. [13]When he went out the next day, he saw two Hebrews fighting; and he said to the one who was in the wrong, "Why do you strike your fellow Hebrew?" [14]He answered, "Who made you a ruler and judge over us? Do you mean to kill me as you killed the Egyptian?" Then Moses was afraid and thought, "Surely the thing is known." [15]When Pharaoh heard of it, he sought to kill Moses.

But Moses fled from Pharaoh. He settled in the land of Midian, and sat down by a well. [16]The priest of Midian had seven daughters. They came to draw water, and filled the troughs to water their father's flock. [17]But some shepherds came and drove them away. Moses got up and came to their defense and watered their flock. [18]When they returned to their father Reuel, he said, "How is it that you have come back so soon today?" [19]They said, "An Egyptian helped us against the shepherds; he even drew water for us and watered the flock." [20]He said to his daughters, "Where is he? Why did you leave the man? Invite him to break bread." [21]Moses agreed to stay with the man, and he gave Moses his daughter Zipporah in marriage. [22]She bore a son, and he named him Gershom; for he said, "I have been an alien[c] residing in a foreign land."

23 After a long time the king of Egypt died. The Israelites groaned under their slavery, and cried out. Out of the slavery their cry for help rose up to God. [24]God heard their groaning, and God remembered his covenant with Abraham, Isaac, and Jacob. [25]God looked upon the Israelites, and God took notice of them.

Moses at the Burning Bush

3 Moses was keeping the flock of his father-in-law Jethro, the priest of Midian; he led his flock beyond the wilderness, and came to Horeb, the mountain of God. [2]There the angel of the LORD appeared to him in a flame of fire out of a bush; he looked, and the bush was blazing, yet it was not consumed. [3]Then Moses said, "I must turn aside and look at this great sight, and see why the bush is not burned up." [4]When the LORD saw that he had turned aside to see, God called to him out of the bush, "Moses, Moses!" And he said, "Here I am." [5]Then he said, "Come no closer! Remove the sandals from your feet, for the place on which you are standing is holy ground." [6]He said further, "I am the God of your father, the God of Abraham, the God of Isaac, and the

Baby in a Basket

EXODUS 2.6–14

The story of the baby Moses in the basket reveals a strange paradox: Pharaoh's power is threatened by the weakness of an infant. How can this be? In a way, the baby's salvation lies in his helplessness, in the fact that what happens next hinges on God's intervention. The little baby floats quietly in a basket right into the halls of power.

When we are humble, we learn to depend on a power beyond ourselves. Reflect on how you handle the threatening and troubling situations in your life. The next time you find yourself a basket case, think of Moses floating in his little ark. Let go. Let God.

---

a Heb *Mosheh*   *b* Heb *mashah*   *c* Heb *ger*

Burning Bushes

EXODUS 3.1–12

The burning bush can be seen as a metaphor for all of creation—it is afire with God. This story illustrates that any place can become a meeting place with God and that God can break into our lives when we least expect it. Who would have thought simply going to work in the morning (as Moses did) could lead to an experience that would turn one's whole life around? When we encounter God we come to a deeper level of awareness of the Presence that is around us, within us and yet beyond us.

Have you ever had a "burning bush" experience? Think back on a person or event that gave you a special sense of encounter with the Holy One. How has that experience changed your life? Form the habit of imagining the people you see on the street, the trees on the neighborhood lawns, the place where you spend most of your day, ablaze with fire. What you see with your soul may be truer than what you see with your physical eyes.

See Meeting God in Everyday Life

God of Jacob." And Moses hid his face, for he was afraid to look at God.

7 Then the LORD said, "I have observed the misery of my people who are in Egypt; I have heard their cry on account of their taskmasters. Indeed, I know their sufferings, [8]and I have come down to deliver them from the Egyptians, and to bring them up out of that land to a good and broad land, a land flowing with milk and honey, to the country of the Canaanites, the Hittites, the Amorites, the Perizzites, the Hivites, and the Jebusites. [9]The cry of the Israelites has now come to me; I have also seen how the Egyptians oppress them. [10]So come, I will send you to Pharaoh to bring my people, the Israelites, out of Egypt." [11]But Moses said to God, "Who am I that I should go to Pharaoh, and bring the Israelites out of Egypt?" [12]He said, "I will be with you; and this shall be the sign for you that it is I who sent you: when you have brought the people out of Egypt, you shall worship God on this mountain."

The Divine Name Revealed

13 But Moses said to God, "If I come to the Israelites and say to them, 'The God of your ancestors has sent me to you,' and they ask me, 'What is his name?' what shall I say to them?" [14]God said to Moses, "I AM WHO I AM."[a] He said further, "Thus you shall say to the Israelites, 'I AM has sent me to you.' " [15]God also said to Moses, "Thus you shall say to the Israelites, 'The LORD,[b] the God of your ancestors, the God of Abraham, the God of Isaac, and the God of Jacob, has sent me to you':

This is my name forever,
and this my title for all generations.

[16]Go and assemble the elders of Israel, and say to them, 'The LORD, the God of your ancestors, the God of Abraham, of Isaac, and of Jacob, has appeared to me, saying: I have given heed to you and to what has been done to you in Egypt. [17]I declare that I will bring you up out of the misery of Egypt, to the land of the Canaanites, the Hittites, the Amorites, the Perizzites, the Hivites, and the Jebusites, a land flowing with milk and honey.' [18]They will listen to your voice; and you and the elders of Israel shall go to the king of Egypt and say to him, 'The LORD, the God of the Hebrews, has met with us; let us now go a three days' journey into the wilderness, so that we may sacrifice to the LORD our God.' [19]I know, however, that the king of Egypt will not let you go unless compelled by a mighty hand.[c] [20]So I will stretch out my hand and strike Egypt with all my wonders that I will perform in it; after that he will let you go. [21]I will bring this people into such favor with the Egyptians that, when you go, you will not go empty-handed; [22]each woman shall ask her neighbor and any woman living in the neighbor's house for jewelry of silver and of gold, and clothing, and you shall put them on your sons and on your daughters; and so you shall plunder the Egyptians."

a Or *I AM WHAT I AM* or *I WILL BE WHAT I WILL BE*   *b* The word "LORD" when spelled with capital letters stands for the divine name, *YHWH,* which is here connected with the verb *hayah,* "to be"   *c* Gk Vg: Heb *no, not by a mighty hand*

Moses' Miraculous Power

4 Then Moses answered, "But suppose they do not believe me or listen to me, but say, 'The LORD did not appear to you.' " ²The LORD said to him, "What is that in your hand?" He said, "A staff." ³And he said, "Throw it on the ground." So he threw the staff on the ground, and it became a snake; and Moses drew back from it. ⁴Then the LORD said to Moses, "Reach out your hand, and seize it by the tail"— so he reached out his hand and grasped it, and it became a staff in his hand— ⁵"so that they may believe that the LORD, the God of their ancestors, the God of Abraham, the God of Isaac, and the God of Jacob, has appeared to you."

6 Again, the LORD said to him, "Put your hand inside your cloak." He put his hand into his cloak; and when he took it out, his hand was leprous,ᵃ as white as snow. ⁷Then God said, "Put your hand back into your cloak"—so he put his hand back into his cloak, and when he took it out, it was restored like the rest of his body— ⁸"If they will not believe you or heed the first sign, they may believe the second sign. ⁹If they will not believe even these two signs or heed you, you shall take some water from the Nile and pour it on the dry ground; and the water that you shall take from the Nile will become blood on the dry ground."

10 But Moses said to the LORD, "O my Lord, I have never been eloquent, neither in the past nor even now that you have spoken to your servant; but I am slow of speech and slow of tongue." ¹¹Then the LORD said to him, "Who gives speech to mortals? Who makes them mute or deaf, seeing or blind? Is it not I, the LORD? ¹²Now go, and I will be with your mouth and teach you what you are to speak." ¹³But he said, "O my Lord, please send someone else." ¹⁴Then the anger of the LORD was kindled against Moses and he said, "What of your brother Aaron the Levite? I know that he can speak fluently; even now he is coming out to meet you, and when he sees you his heart will be glad. ¹⁵You shall speak to him and put the words in his mouth; and I will be with your mouth and with his mouth, and will teach you what you shall do. ¹⁶He indeed shall speak for you to the people; he shall serve as a mouth for you, and you shall serve as God for him. ¹⁷Take in your hand this staff, with which you shall perform the signs."

Moses Returns to Egypt

18 Moses went back to his father-in-law Jethro and said to him, "Please let me go back to my kindred in Egypt and see whether they are still living." And Jethro said to Moses, "Go in peace." ¹⁹The LORD said to Moses in Midian, "Go back to Egypt; for all those who were seeking your life are dead." ²⁰So Moses took his wife and his sons, put them on a donkey, and went back to the land of Egypt; and Moses carried the staff of God in his hand.

21 And the LORD said to Moses, "When you go back to Egypt, see that you perform before Pharaoh all the wonders that I have put in your power; but I will harden his heart, so that he will not let the people go. ²²Then you shall say to Pharaoh, 'Thus says the LORD: Israel is my firstborn son. ²³I said to you, "Let my son go that he may worship me." But you refused to let him go; now I will kill your firstborn son.' "

ᵃ A term for several skin diseases; precise meaning uncertain

Closing the Credibility Gap

EXODUS 4.1–17

"But suppose they do not believe me or listen to me?" This is the question that haunts the soul of every preacher and minister and teacher. The same question should haunt the mind of every Christian. What sign shall we give to the people we speak to? What proof shall we offer today to convince others that we speak in the name of God? We want to offer a sign of credibility to those with whom we work, to our families, to friends, and even to our enemies. God speaks to us as he spoke to Moses: "I will be with your mouth and teach you what you are to speak." Today, before you speak, ask yourself: "Is what I am about to say necessary? And if it is necessary, is God in it?"

See Meeting God in Community

The Sign That Convinces

EXODUS 4.21–31

"Even if it is perhaps possible for doctors to cure patients even when the doctors hardly believe in the value of life, Christian ministers will never be able to minister if their own most personal faith and insight into life do not form the core of their pastoral work. So ministry and spirituality never can be separated. Ministry is not an eight-to-five job but primarily a way of life, which is for others to see and understand so that liberation can become a possibility."

—HENRI J. M. NOUWEN,
Creative Ministry

24 On the way, at a place where they spent the night, the LORD met him and tried to kill him. [25]But Zipporah took a flint and cut off her son's foreskin, and touched Moses'[a] feet with it, and said, "Truly you are a bridegroom of blood to me!" [26]So he let him alone. It was then she said, "A bridegroom of blood by circumcision."

27 The LORD said to Aaron, "Go into the wilderness to meet Moses." So he went; and he met him at the mountain of God and kissed him. [28]Moses told Aaron all the words of the LORD with which he had sent him, and all the signs with which he had charged him. [29]Then Moses and Aaron went and assembled all the elders of the Israelites. [30]Aaron spoke all the words that the LORD had spoken to Moses, and performed the signs in the sight of the people. [31]The people believed; and when they heard that the LORD had given heed to the Israelites and that he had seen their misery, they bowed down and worshiped.

Bricks without Straw

5 Afterward Moses and Aaron went to Pharaoh and said, "Thus says the LORD, the God of Israel, 'Let my people go, so that they may celebrate a festival to me in the wilderness.' " [2]But Pharaoh said, "Who is the LORD, that I should heed him and let Israel go? I do not know the LORD, and I will not let Israel go." [3]Then they said, "The God of the Hebrews has revealed himself to us; let us go a three days' journey into the wilderness to sacrifice to the LORD our God, or he will fall upon us with pestilence or sword." [4]But the king of Egypt said to them, "Moses and Aaron, why are you taking the people away from their work? Get to your labors!" [5]Pharaoh continued, "Now they are more numerous than the people of the land[b] and yet you want them to stop working!" [6]That same day Pharaoh commanded the taskmasters of the people, as well as their supervisors, [7]"You shall no longer give the people straw to make bricks, as before; let them go and gather straw for themselves. [8]But you shall require of them the same quantity of bricks as they have made previously; do not diminish it, for they are lazy; that is why they cry, 'Let us go and offer sacrifice to our God.' [9]Let heavier work be laid on them; then they will labor at it and pay no attention to deceptive words."

10 So the taskmasters and the supervisors of the people went out and said to the people, "Thus says Pharaoh, 'I will not give you straw. [11]Go and get straw yourselves, wherever you can find it; but your work will not be lessened in the least.' " [12]So the people scattered throughout the land of Egypt, to gather stubble for straw. [13]The taskmasters were urgent, saying, "Complete your work, the same daily assignment as when you were given straw." [14]And the supervisors of the Israelites, whom Pharaoh's taskmasters had set over them, were beaten, and were asked, "Why did you not finish the required quantity of bricks yesterday and today, as you did before?"

15 Then the Israelite supervisors came to Pharaoh and cried, "Why do you treat your servants like this? [16]No straw is given to your servants, yet they say to us, 'Make bricks!' Look how your servants are beaten! You are unjust to your own people."[c] [17]He said, "You are lazy, lazy; that is why you

a Heb *his*   b Sam: Heb *The people of the land are now many*
c Gk Compare Syr Vg: Heb *beaten, and the sin of your people*

say, 'Let us go and sacrifice to the LORD.' ¹⁸Go now, and work; for no straw shall be given you, but you shall still deliver the same number of bricks." ¹⁹The Israelite supervisors saw that they were in trouble when they were told, "You shall not lessen your daily number of bricks." ²⁰As they left Pharaoh, they came upon Moses and Aaron who were waiting to meet them. ²¹They said to them, "The LORD look upon you and judge! You have brought us into bad odor with Pharaoh and his officials, and have put a sword in their hand to kill us."

22 Then Moses turned again to the LORD and said, "O LORD, why have you mistreated this people? Why did you ever send me? ²³Since I first came to Pharaoh to speak in your name, he has mistreated this people, and you have done nothing at all to deliver your people."

Israel's Deliverance Assured

6 Then the LORD said to Moses, "Now you shall see what I will do to Pharaoh: Indeed, by a mighty hand he will let them go; by a mighty hand he will drive them out of his land."

2 God also spoke to Moses and said to him: "I am the LORD. ³I appeared to Abraham, Isaac, and Jacob as God Almighty,ᵃ but by my name 'The LORD'ᵇ I did not make myself known to them. ⁴I also established my covenant with them, to give them the land of Canaan, the land in which they resided as aliens. ⁵I have also heard the groaning of the Israelites whom the Egyptians are holding as slaves, and I have remembered my covenant. ⁶Say therefore to the Israelites, 'I am the LORD, and I will free you from the burdens of the Egyptians and deliver you from slavery to them. I will redeem you with an outstretched arm and with mighty acts of judgment. ⁷I will take you as my people, and I will be your God. You shall know that I am the LORD your God, who has freed you from the burdens of the Egyptians. ⁸I will bring you into the land that I swore to give to Abraham, Isaac, and Jacob; I will give it to you for a possession. I am the LORD.' " ⁹Moses told this to the Israelites; but they would not listen to Moses, because of their broken spirit and their cruel slavery.

10 Then the LORD spoke to Moses, ¹¹"Go and tell Pharaoh king of Egypt to let the Israelites go out of his land." ¹²But Moses spoke to the LORD, "The Israelites have not listened to me; how then shall Pharaoh listen to me, poor speaker that I am?"ᶜ ¹³Thus the LORD spoke to Moses and Aaron, and gave them orders regarding the Israelites and Pharaoh king of Egypt, charging them to free the Israelites from the land of Egypt.

The Genealogy of Moses and Aaron

14 The following are the heads of their ancestral houses: the sons of Reuben, the firstborn of Israel: Hanoch, Pallu, Hezron, and Carmi; these are the families of Reuben. ¹⁵The sons of Simeon: Jemuel, Jamin, Ohad, Jachin, Zohar, and Shaul,ᵈ the son of a Canaanite woman; these are the families of Simeon. ¹⁶The following are the names of the sons of Levi according to their genealogies: Gershon,ᵉ Kohath, and Merari, and the length of Levi's life was one hundred thirty-seven years. ¹⁷The sons of Gershon:ᵉ Libni and Shimei, by their families. ¹⁸The sons of Kohath: Amram, Izhar, Hebron, and

Remember the Covenant

EXODUS 6.2–8

God tells Moses that the groans of the enslaved Hebrew people were heard and that "I have remembered my covenant." With words that echo throughout the Bible as the very definition of this covenant, God says, "I will take you as my people, and I will be your God."

There comes a time when every faithful person wonders if God has heard them in their distress. Take time today to find or create some symbol of God's covenant with you so that you will remember that God hears you. Make it as durable as possible to remind you of the permanency of God's plans. Perhaps you can write it on official-looking paper as if it were a law passed by Congress: "Be it resolved, I am your God and you are my people." Or have a stone mason engrave these words on a large piece of masonry, or have them written on a bracelet of some fine metal. Ask God in prayer to help you keep this covenant ever before your eyes.

See Meeting God in Scripture

a Traditional rendering of Heb *El Shaddai*   b Heb *YHWH*; see note at 3.15
c Heb *me? I am uncircumcised of lips*   d Or *Saul*   e Also spelled *Gershom*; see 2.22

Fulfilling the Dream

EXODUS 6.12–13,26–27

As believers, we are the privileged recipients of divine revelation. But we also discover that, like Moses, we are commissioned to carry that revelation to others, even when it means controversy, even when we address issues that may upset others, even when it means breaking through the barriers of discouragement. Where do we find the courage to do so? Make a list of the controversial issues that divide people in your family or community today. What issues need to be addressed? How can you prepare to say the things that need to be said? (See 2 Timothy 4.2 for guidelines.) Like Moses, ask God to prepare the way for you.

See *Meeting God in Community*

Uzziel, and the length of Kohath's life was one hundred thirty-three years. ¹⁹The sons of Merari: Mahli and Mushi. These are the families of the Levites according to their genealogies. ²⁰Amram married Jochebed his father's sister and she bore him Aaron and Moses, and the length of Amram's life was one hundred thirty-seven years. ²¹The sons of Izhar: Korah, Nepheg, and Zichri. ²²The sons of Uzziel: Mishael, Elzaphan, and Sithri. ²³Aaron married Elisheba, daughter of Amminadab and sister of Nahshon, and she bore him Nadab, Abihu, Eleazar, and Ithamar. ²⁴The sons of Korah: Assir, Elkanah, and Abiasaph; these are the families of the Korahites. ²⁵Aaron's son Eleazar married one of the daughters of Putiel, and she bore him Phinehas. These are the heads of the ancestral houses of the Levites by their families.

26 It was this same Aaron and Moses to whom the LORD said, "Bring the Israelites out of the land of Egypt, company by company." ²⁷It was they who spoke to Pharaoh king of Egypt to bring the Israelites out of Egypt, the same Moses and Aaron.

Moses and Aaron Obey God's Commands

28 On the day when the LORD spoke to Moses in the land of Egypt, ²⁹he said to him, "I am the LORD; tell Pharaoh king of Egypt all that I am speaking to you." ³⁰But Moses said in the LORD's presence, "Since I am a poor speaker,ᵃ why would Pharaoh listen to me?"

7 The LORD said to Moses, "See, I have made you like God to Pharaoh, and your brother Aaron shall be your prophet. ²You shall speak all that I command you, and your brother Aaron shall tell Pharaoh to let the Israelites go out of his land. ³But I will harden Pharaoh's heart, and I will multiply my signs and wonders in the land of Egypt. ⁴When Pharaoh does not listen to you, I will lay my hand upon Egypt and bring my people the Israelites, company by company, out of the land of Egypt by great acts of judgment. ⁵The Egyptians shall know that I am the LORD, when I stretch out my hand against Egypt and bring the Israelites out from among them." ⁶Moses and Aaron did so; they did just as the LORD commanded them. ⁷Moses was eighty years old and Aaron eighty-three when they spoke to Pharaoh.

Aaron's Miraculous Rod

8 The LORD said to Moses and Aaron, ⁹"When Pharaoh says to you, 'Perform a wonder,' then you shall say to Aaron, 'Take your staff and throw it down before Pharaoh, and it will become a snake.' " ¹⁰So Moses and Aaron went to Pharaoh and did as the LORD had commanded; Aaron threw down his staff before Pharaoh and his officials, and it became a snake. ¹¹Then Pharaoh summoned the wise men and the sorcerers; and they also, the magicians of Egypt, did the same by their secret arts. ¹²Each one threw down his staff, and they became snakes; but Aaron's staff swallowed up theirs. ¹³Still Pharaoh's heart was hardened, and he would not listen to them, as the LORD had said.

The First Plague: Water Turned to Blood

14 Then the LORD said to Moses, "Pharaoh's heart is hardened; he refuses to let the people go. ¹⁵Go to Pharaoh

a Heb *am uncircumcised of lips*; see 6.12

in the morning, as he is going out to the water; stand by at the river bank to meet him, and take in your hand the staff that was turned into a snake. ¹⁶Say to him, 'The LORD, the God of the Hebrews, sent me to you to say, "Let my people go, so that they may worship me in the wilderness." But until now you have not listened. ¹⁷Thus says the LORD, "By this you shall know that I am the LORD." See, with the staff that is in my hand I will strike the water that is in the Nile, and it shall be turned to blood. ¹⁸The fish in the river shall die, the river itself shall stink, and the Egyptians shall be unable to drink water from the Nile.' " ¹⁹The LORD said to Moses, "Say to Aaron, 'Take your staff and stretch out your hand over the waters of Egypt—over its rivers, its canals, and its ponds, and all its pools of water—so that they may become blood; and there shall be blood throughout the whole land of Egypt, even in vessels of wood and in vessels of stone.' "

20 Moses and Aaron did just as the LORD commanded. In the sight of Pharaoh and of his officials he lifted up the staff and struck the water in the river, and all the water in the river was turned into blood, ²¹and the fish in the river died. The river stank so that the Egyptians could not drink its water, and there was blood throughout the whole land of Egypt. ²²But the magicians of Egypt did the same by their secret arts; so Pharaoh's heart remained hardened, and he would not listen to them, as the LORD had said. ²³Pharaoh turned and went into his house, and he did not take even this to heart. ²⁴And all the Egyptians had to dig along the Nile for water to drink, for they could not drink the water of the river.

25 Seven days passed after the LORD had struck the Nile.

The Second Plague: Frogs

8ᵃ Then the LORD said to Moses, "Go to Pharaoh and say to him, 'Thus says the LORD: Let my people go, so that they may worship me. ²If you refuse to let them go, I will plague your whole country with frogs. ³The river shall swarm with frogs; they shall come up into your palace, into your bedchamber and your bed, and into the houses of your officials and of your people,ᵇ and into your ovens and your kneading bowls. ⁴The frogs shall come up on you and on your people and on all your officials.' " ⁵ᶜAnd the LORD said to Moses, "Say to Aaron, 'Stretch out your hand with your staff over the rivers, the canals, and the pools, and make frogs come up on the land of Egypt.' " ⁶So Aaron stretched out his hand over the waters of Egypt; and the frogs came up and covered the land of Egypt. ⁷But the magicians did the same by their secret arts, and brought frogs up on the land of Egypt.

8 Then Pharaoh called Moses and Aaron, and said, "Pray to the LORD to take away the frogs from me and my people, and I will let the people go to sacrifice to the LORD." ⁹Moses said to Pharaoh, "Kindly tell me when I am to pray for you and for your officials and for your people, that the frogs may be removed from you and your houses and be left only in the Nile." ¹⁰And he said, "Tomorrow." Moses said, "As you say! So that you may know that there is no one like the LORD our God, ¹¹the frogs shall leave you and your houses and your officials and your people; they shall be left

Turning Rivers to Blood

EXODUS 7.14–25

Whole rivers turned into blood? At first sight this miracle seems beyond belief. Yet it issues a powerful statement that commands our attention: God speaks to us through the signs and forces of nature. Sometimes it is not hard to hear. We willingly listen to God speaking to us through the beauty of a sunrise or a rushing, foaming waterfall. But do we listen as carefully when God speaks to us through a calamity such as a hurricane or tornado?

By using Moses to change rivers into blood, God gave Pharaoh a strong message: God, the creator of all, was not to be trifled with. Spend time now contemplating the awesome power of God, who sees the nations as "a drop from a bucket," who "takes up the isles like fine dust" (Isaiah 40.15). Draw a picture of a tornado, volcano, sunrise or waterfall, or find a picture in a magazine. Place it on your refrigerator or at your work station to remind you of God's awesome power.

See Meeting God in the Created Order

---

a Ch 7.26 in Heb   *b* Gk: Heb *upon your people*   *c* Ch 8.1 in Heb

Frogs, Gnats and Flies

EXODUS 8.1–24

Frogs, gnats and flies do not ordinarily claim much of our attention. They are nuisances we merely tolerate—at least until they get in our soup or crawl up our pants, or climb our walls, or burrow their way under our bed sheets. Pharaoh, too, took these creatures for granted until they became God's means to get his attention. Then Pharaoh listened—for a while. When relief came in answer to Moses' prayer, Pharaoh went back to his old ways.

Reflect now on ways petty annoyances such as heavy traffic, cold symptoms and lost keys can become occasions for turning to God. Ask God to help you be spiritually sensitive to what you can learn from the daily nuisances and irritations of life.

See Meeting God in Everyday Life

only in the Nile." ¹²Then Moses and Aaron went out from Pharaoh; and Moses cried out to the LORD concerning the frogs that he had brought upon Pharaoh.*ᵃ* ¹³And the LORD did as Moses requested: the frogs died in the houses, the courtyards, and the fields. ¹⁴And they gathered them together in heaps, and the land stank. ¹⁵But when Pharaoh saw that there was a respite, he hardened his heart, and would not listen to them, just as the LORD had said.

The Third Plague: Gnats

16 Then the LORD said to Moses, "Say to Aaron, 'Stretch out your staff and strike the dust of the earth, so that it may become gnats throughout the whole land of Egypt.' " ¹⁷And they did so; Aaron stretched out his hand with his staff and struck the dust of the earth, and gnats came on humans and animals alike; all the dust of the earth turned into gnats throughout the whole land of Egypt. ¹⁸The magicians tried to produce gnats by their secret arts, but they could not. There were gnats on both humans and animals. ¹⁹And the magicians said to Pharaoh, "This is the finger of God!" But Pharaoh's heart was hardened, and he would not listen to them, just as the LORD had said.

The Fourth Plague: Flies

20 Then the LORD said to Moses, "Rise early in the morning and present yourself before Pharaoh, as he goes out to the water, and say to him, 'Thus says the LORD: Let my people go, so that they may worship me. ²¹For if you will not let my people go, I will send swarms of flies on you, your officials, and your people, and into your houses; and the houses of the Egyptians shall be filled with swarms of flies; so also the land where they live. ²²But on that day I will set apart the land of Goshen, where my people live, so that no swarms of flies shall be there, that you may know that I the LORD am in this land. ²³Thus I will make a distinction*ᵇ* between my people and your people. This sign shall appear tomorrow.' " ²⁴The LORD did so, and great swarms of flies came into the house of Pharaoh and into his officials' houses; in all of Egypt the land was ruined because of the flies.

25 Then Pharaoh summoned Moses and Aaron, and said, "Go, sacrifice to your God within the land." ²⁶But Moses said, "It would not be right to do so; for the sacrifices that we offer to the LORD our God are offensive to the Egyptians. If we offer in the sight of the Egyptians sacrifices that are offensive to them, will they not stone us? ²⁷We must go a three days' journey into the wilderness and sacrifice to the LORD our God as he commands us." ²⁸So Pharaoh said, "I will let you go to sacrifice to the LORD your God in the wilderness, provided you do not go very far away. Pray for me." ²⁹Then Moses said, "As soon as I leave you, I will pray to the LORD that the swarms of flies may depart tomorrow from Pharaoh, from his officials, and from his people; only do not let Pharaoh again deal falsely by not letting the people go to sacrifice to the LORD."

30 So Moses went out from Pharaoh and prayed to the LORD. ³¹And the LORD did as Moses asked: he removed the swarms of flies from Pharaoh, from his officials, and from

a Or frogs, as he had agreed with Pharaoh   b Gk Vg: Heb will set redemption

his people; not one remained. ³²But Pharaoh hardened his heart this time also, and would not let the people go.

The Fifth Plague: Livestock Diseased

9 Then the Lord said to Moses, "Go to Pharaoh, and say to him, 'Thus says the Lord, the God of the Hebrews: Let my people go, so that they may worship me. ²For if you refuse to let them go and still hold them, ³the hand of the Lord will strike with a deadly pestilence your livestock in the field: the horses, the donkeys, the camels, the herds, and the flocks. ⁴But the Lord will make a distinction between the livestock of Israel and the livestock of Egypt, so that nothing shall die of all that belongs to the Israelites.' " ⁵The Lord set a time, saying, "Tomorrow the Lord will do this thing in the land." ⁶And on the next day the Lord did so; all the livestock of the Egyptians died, but of the livestock of the Israelites not one died. ⁷Pharaoh inquired and found that not one of the livestock of the Israelites was dead. But the heart of Pharaoh was hardened, and he would not let the people go.

The Sixth Plague: Boils

8 Then the Lord said to Moses and Aaron, "Take handfuls of soot from the kiln, and let Moses throw it in the air in the sight of Pharaoh. ⁹It shall become fine dust all over the land of Egypt, and shall cause festering boils on humans and animals throughout the whole land of Egypt." ¹⁰So they took soot from the kiln, and stood before Pharaoh, and Moses threw it in the air, and it caused festering boils on humans and animals. ¹¹The magicians could not stand before Moses because of the boils, for the boils afflicted the magicians as well as all the Egyptians. ¹²But the Lord hardened the heart of Pharaoh, and he would not listen to them, just as the Lord had spoken to Moses.

The Seventh Plague: Thunder and Hail

13 Then the Lord said to Moses, "Rise up early in the morning and present yourself before Pharaoh, and say to him, 'Thus says the Lord, the God of the Hebrews: Let my people go, so that they may worship me. ¹⁴For this time I will send all my plagues upon you yourself, and upon your officials, and upon your people, so that you may know that there is no one like me in all the earth. ¹⁵For by now I could have stretched out my hand and struck you and your people with pestilence, and you would have been cut off from the earth. ¹⁶But this is why I have let you live: to show you my power, and to make my name resound through all the earth. ¹⁷You are still exalting yourself against my people, and will not let them go. ¹⁸Tomorrow at this time I will cause the heaviest hail to fall that has ever fallen in Egypt from the day it was founded until now. ¹⁹Send, therefore, and have your livestock and everything that you have in the open field brought to a secure place; every human or animal that is in the open field and is not brought under shelter will die when the hail comes down upon them.' " ²⁰Those officials of Pharaoh who feared the word of the Lord hurried their slaves and livestock off to a secure place. ²¹Those who did not regard the word of the Lord left their slaves and livestock in the open field.

22 The Lord said to Moses, "Stretch out your hand to-

A Temporary Peace

EXODUS 8.25–31

Because of Israel's faithfulness, God stops the plague of flies. Moses' prayer restores calm to the land once again. Peace, said Augustine, is "the order of tranquillity." In this case peace is restored when Israel—and even Pharaoh—are in harmony with the will of God. In Pharaoh's case, however, the submission to God's "order of tranquillity" never becomes more than a short-lived intention.

How do you come to know the will of God? What are the means God uses to get across a message to you? How can you make hearing God's will more than a temporary project? In what ways might God come alongside you to help you remain faithful?

Hailstones and Stonewalling

EXODUS 9.13–26

The story seems to go around and around in circles. Moses uses his big stick. Pharaoh backs off. Moses relents. Pharaoh reneges. Moses calls down hailstones. Pharaoh stonewalls. Moses looks weak. Pharaoh looks strong. But Pharaoh's strength is not strength of character, but the brick-wall stubbornness of entrenched attitudes that keep him in bondage. Being in control is the only mode of operation Pharaoh has known. Giving it up seems more threatening to him than having stars fall down around him. In contrast, Moses can afford to take short-term losses because he knows who is ultimately in control.

Ask yourself whose behavior your behavior most resembles. In which areas in your life do you insist on having control? What would happen if you turned control over to God?

See Meeting God in Scripture

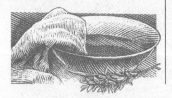

ward heaven so that hail may fall on the whole land of Egypt, on humans and animals and all the plants of the field in the land of Egypt." ²³Then Moses stretched out his staff toward heaven, and the LORD sent thunder and hail, and fire came down on the earth. And the LORD rained hail on the land of Egypt; ²⁴there was hail with fire flashing continually in the midst of it, such heavy hail as had never fallen in all the land of Egypt since it became a nation. ²⁵The hail struck down everything that was in the open field throughout all the land of Egypt, both human and animal; the hail also struck down all the plants of the field, and shattered every tree in the field. ²⁶Only in the land of Goshen, where the Israelites were, there was no hail.

27 Then Pharaoh summoned Moses and Aaron, and said to them, "This time I have sinned; the LORD is in the right, and I and my people are in the wrong. ²⁸Pray to the LORD! Enough of God's thunder and hail! I will let you go; you need stay no longer." ²⁹Moses said to him, "As soon as I have gone out of the city, I will stretch out my hands to the LORD; the thunder will cease, and there will be no more hail, so that you may know that the earth is the LORD's. ³⁰But as for you and your officials, I know that you do not yet fear the LORD God." ³¹(Now the flax and the barley were ruined, for the barley was in the ear and the flax was in bud. ³²But the wheat and the spelt were not ruined, for they are late in coming up.) ³³So Moses left Pharaoh, went out of the city, and stretched out his hands to the LORD; then the thunder and the hail ceased, and the rain no longer poured down on the earth. ³⁴But when Pharaoh saw that the rain and the hail and the thunder had ceased, he sinned once more and hardened his heart, he and his officials. ³⁵So the heart of Pharaoh was hardened, and he would not let the Israelites go, just as the LORD had spoken through Moses.

The Eighth Plague: Locusts

10 Then the LORD said to Moses, "Go to Pharaoh; for I have hardened his heart and the heart of his officials, in order that I may show these signs of mine among them, ²and that you may tell your children and grandchildren how I have made fools of the Egyptians and what signs I have done among them—so that you may know that I am the LORD."

3 So Moses and Aaron went to Pharaoh, and said to him, "Thus says the LORD, the God of the Hebrews, 'How long will you refuse to humble yourself before me? Let my people go, so that they may worship me. ⁴For if you refuse to let my people go, tomorrow I will bring locusts into your country. ⁵They shall cover the surface of the land, so that no one will be able to see the land. They shall devour the last remnant left you after the hail, and they shall devour every tree of yours that grows in the field. ⁶They shall fill your houses, and the houses of all your officials and of all the Egyptians—something that neither your parents nor your grandparents have seen, from the day they came on earth to this day.' " Then he turned and went out from Pharaoh.

7 Pharaoh's officials said to him, "How long shall this fellow be a snare to us? Let the people go, so that they may worship the LORD their God; do you not yet understand that Egypt is ruined?" ⁸So Moses and Aaron were brought back

to Pharaoh, and he said to them, "Go, worship the LORD your God! But which ones are to go?" ⁹Moses said, "We will go with our young and our old; we will go with our sons and daughters and with our flocks and herds, because we have the LORD's festival to celebrate." ¹⁰He said to them, "The LORD indeed will be with you, if ever I let your little ones go with you! Plainly, you have some evil purpose in mind. ¹¹No, never! Your men may go and worship the LORD, for that is what you are asking." And they were driven out from Pharaoh's presence.

12 Then the LORD said to Moses, "Stretch out your hand over the land of Egypt, so that the locusts may come upon it and eat every plant in the land, all that the hail has left." ¹³So Moses stretched out his staff over the land of Egypt, and the LORD brought an east wind upon the land all that day and all that night; when morning came, the east wind had brought the locusts. ¹⁴The locusts came upon all the land of Egypt and settled on the whole country of Egypt, such a dense swarm of locusts as had never been before, nor ever shall be again. ¹⁵They covered the surface of the whole land, so that the land was black; and they ate all the plants in the land and all the fruit of the trees that the hail had left; nothing green was left, no tree, no plant in the field, in all the land of Egypt. ¹⁶Pharaoh hurriedly summoned Moses and Aaron and said, "I have sinned against the LORD your God, and against you. ¹⁷Do forgive my sin just this once, and pray to the LORD your God that at the least he remove this deadly thing from me." ¹⁸So he went out from Pharaoh and prayed to the LORD. ¹⁹The LORD changed the wind into a very strong west wind, which lifted the locusts and drove them into the Red Sea;ᵃ not a single locust was left in all the country of Egypt. ²⁰But the LORD hardened Pharaoh's heart, and he would not let the Israelites go.

The Ninth Plague: Darkness

21 Then the LORD said to Moses, "Stretch out your hand toward heaven so that there may be darkness over the land of Egypt, a darkness that can be felt." ²²So Moses stretched out his hand toward heaven, and there was dense darkness in all the land of Egypt for three days. ²³People could not see one another, and for three days they could not move from where they were; but all the Israelites had light where they lived. ²⁴Then Pharaoh summoned Moses, and said, "Go, worship the LORD. Only your flocks and your herds shall remain behind. Even your children may go with you." ²⁵But Moses said, "You must also let us have sacrifices and burnt offerings to sacrifice to the LORD our God. ²⁶Our livestock also must go with us; not a hoof shall be left behind, for we must choose some of them for the worship of the LORD our God, and we will not know what to use to worship the LORD until we arrive there." ²⁷But the LORD hardened Pharaoh's heart, and he was unwilling to let them go. ²⁸Then Pharaoh said to him, "Get away from me! Take care that you do not see my face again, for on the day you see my face you shall die." ²⁹Moses said, "Just as you say! I will never see your face again."

Pharaoh's Dilemma

EXODUS 10.7–19

Pharaoh faced a troubling dilemma. If he let the Israelites go it would devastate the economy. He needed the Hebrew slaves to maintain and continue capital expansion. In the same way, much resistance to ending slavery in the United States came from economic fears in a region dependent on slave labor.

There may be areas in our lives that need to be yielded to God but that, if done, would cause some troubling dislocation. Perhaps your job does not glorify God, but to consider leaving it creates economic fears. Maybe you have long been feuding with someone, and to make amends would be a painful process. Ask God in prayer to reveal these areas to you—perhaps some you have been unwilling to think about. Next ask God for the strength to face them and then follow the Lord's will in everything.

See Meeting God in Prayer

Zero Hour: Midnight

EXODUS 11.4

The standoff between Moses and Pharaoh is coming to a climax. The hour is set: Midnight is the turning point. It is an hour of deep darkness—the hour when all is still. It is the hour of expectation and decision—marking both an end and a new beginning. This story invites us to see the midnight hour both as a symbol of death and of liberation. Set your alarm tonight for midnight. Once awake, sit in complete silence for fifteen minutes in an attitude of expectation toward God before going back to sleep.

See Meeting God in Scripture

Warning of the Final Plague

11 The LORD said to Moses, "I will bring one more plague upon Pharaoh and upon Egypt; afterwards he will let you go from here; indeed, when he lets you go, he will drive you away. [2]Tell the people that every man is to ask his neighbor and every woman is to ask her neighbor for objects of silver and gold." [3]The LORD gave the people favor in the sight of the Egyptians. Moreover, Moses himself was a man of great importance in the land of Egypt, in the sight of Pharaoh's officials and in the sight of the people.

4 Moses said, "Thus says the LORD: About midnight I will go out through Egypt. [5]Every firstborn in the land of Egypt shall die, from the firstborn of Pharaoh who sits on his throne to the firstborn of the female slave who is behind the handmill, and all the firstborn of the livestock. [6]Then there will be a loud cry throughout the whole land of Egypt, such as has never been or will ever be again. [7]But not a dog shall growl at any of the Israelites—not at people, not at animals—so that you may know that the LORD makes a distinction between Egypt and Israel. [8]Then all these officials of yours shall come down to me, and bow low to me, saying, 'Leave us, you and all the people who follow you.' After that I will leave." And in hot anger he left Pharaoh.

9 The LORD said to Moses, "Pharaoh will not listen to you, in order that my wonders may be multiplied in the land of Egypt." [10]Moses and Aaron performed all these wonders before Pharaoh; but the LORD hardened Pharaoh's heart, and he did not let the people of Israel go out of his land.

The First Passover Instituted

12 The LORD said to Moses and Aaron in the land of Egypt: [2]This month shall mark for you the beginning of months; it shall be the first month of the year for you. [3]Tell the whole congregation of Israel that on the tenth of this month they are to take a lamb for each family, a lamb for each household. [4]If a household is too small for a whole lamb, it shall join its closest neighbor in obtaining one; the lamb shall be divided in proportion to the number of people who eat of it. [5]Your lamb shall be without blemish, a year-old male; you may take it from the sheep or from the goats. [6]You shall keep it until the fourteenth day of this month; then the whole assembled congregation of Israel shall slaughter it at twilight. [7]They shall take some of the blood and put it on the two doorposts and the lintel of the houses in which they eat it. [8]They shall eat the lamb that same night; they shall eat it roasted over the fire with unleavened bread and bitter herbs. [9]Do not eat any of it raw or boiled in water, but roasted over the fire, with its head, legs, and inner organs. [10]You shall let none of it remain until the morning; anything that remains until the morning you shall burn. [11]This is how you shall eat it: your loins girded, your sandals on your feet, and your staff in your hand; and you shall eat it hurriedly. It is the passover of the LORD. [12]For I will pass through the land of Egypt that night, and I will strike down every firstborn in the land of Egypt, both human beings and animals; on all the gods of Egypt I will execute judgments: I am the LORD. [13]The blood shall be a sign for you on the houses where you live: when

I see the blood, I will pass over you, and no plague shall destroy you when I strike the land of Egypt.

14 This day shall be a day of remembrance for you. You shall celebrate it as a festival to the LORD; throughout your generations you shall observe it as a perpetual ordinance. [15]Seven days you shall eat unleavened bread; on the first day you shall remove leaven from your houses, for whoever eats leavened bread from the first day until the seventh day shall be cut off from Israel. [16]On the first day you shall hold a solemn assembly, and on the seventh day a solemn assembly; no work shall be done on those days; only what everyone must eat, that alone may be prepared by you. [17]You shall observe the festival of unleavened bread, for on this very day I brought your companies out of the land of Egypt: you shall observe this day throughout your generations as a perpetual ordinance. [18]In the first month, from the evening of the fourteenth day until the evening of the twenty-first day, you shall eat unleavened bread. [19]For seven days no leaven shall be found in your houses; for whoever eats what is leavened shall be cut off from the congregation of Israel, whether an alien or a native of the land. [20]You shall eat nothing leavened; in all your settlements you shall eat unleavened bread.

21 Then Moses called all the elders of Israel and said to them, "Go, select lambs for your families, and slaughter the passover lamb. [22]Take a bunch of hyssop, dip it in the blood that is in the basin, and touch the lintel and the two doorposts with the blood in the basin. None of you shall go outside the door of your house until morning. [23]For the LORD will pass through to strike down the Egyptians; when he sees the blood on the lintel and on the two doorposts, the LORD will pass over that door and will not allow the destroyer to enter your houses to strike you down. [24]You shall observe this rite as a perpetual ordinance for you and your children. [25]When you come to the land that the LORD will give you, as he has promised, you shall keep this observance. [26]And when your children ask you, 'What do you mean by this observance?' [27]you shall say, 'It is the passover sacrifice to the LORD, for he passed over the houses of the Israelites in Egypt, when he struck down the Egyptians but spared our houses.' " And the people bowed down and worshiped.

28 The Israelites went and did just as the LORD had commanded Moses and Aaron.

The Tenth Plague: Death of the Firstborn

29 At midnight the LORD struck down all the firstborn in the land of Egypt, from the firstborn of Pharaoh who sat on his throne to the firstborn of the prisoner who was in the dungeon, and all the firstborn of the livestock. [30]Pharaoh arose in the night, he and all his officials and all the Egyptians; and there was a loud cry in Egypt, for there was not a house without someone dead. [31]Then he summoned Moses and Aaron in the night, and said, "Rise up, go away from my people, both you and the Israelites! Go, worship the LORD, as you said. [32]Take your flocks and your herds, as you said, and be gone. And bring a blessing on me too!"

The Exodus: From Rameses to Succoth

33 The Egyptians urged the people to hasten their de-

Passover

EXODUS 12.3–13

Here we read of a departure made in haste, but this is not a story to be read in haste. It holds the key to the meaning of many symbols that will resurface in New Testament writings. It should be read with one finger holding your place in Exodus and another holding your place in the Gospels and related New Testament writings. Note the parallel: John the Baptist refers to Jesus as the "Lamb of God" (John 1.36); and the Evangelist John fixes the hour of Jesus' sentencing at noon, the hour at which priests began to slaughter Passover lambs in the temple (John 19.14). Let the symbol of the paschal lamb in Exodus shed light on your reading whenever you turn to the four Gospels and other New Testament passages.

See *Meeting God in Scripture*

Death of the Firstborn

EXODUS 12.29–13.1

Midnight has come. Pharaoh, who has turned a deaf ear to the voice of Moses, listens to the booming voice of Death. Henceforth the symbol of the firstborn as a sign of liberation becomes deeply etched in the communal memory of the Hebrew people. So much so that the coming of the Messiah is heralded with the words: "And she gave birth to her firstborn son" (Luke 2.7).

Identify those people, events or objects in your life—the ones that seem to give you a new freedom, fresh strength or renewed joy—that you might label "firstborn." Can you see them as gifts from God? How do you offer these back to God in thanksgiving and gratitude?

See *Meeting God in Community*

parture from the land, for they said, "We shall all be dead." [34]So the people took their dough before it was leavened, with their kneading bowls wrapped up in their cloaks on their shoulders. [35]The Israelites had done as Moses told them; they had asked the Egyptians for jewelry of silver and gold, and for clothing, [36]and the LORD had given the people favor in the sight of the Egyptians, so that they let them have what they asked. And so they plundered the Egyptians.

37 The Israelites journeyed from Rameses to Succoth, about six hundred thousand men on foot, besides children. [38]A mixed crowd also went up with them, and livestock in great numbers, both flocks and herds. [39]They baked unleavened cakes of the dough that they had brought out of Egypt; it was not leavened, because they were driven out of Egypt and could not wait, nor had they prepared any provisions for themselves.

40 The time that the Israelites had lived in Egypt was four hundred thirty years. [41]At the end of four hundred thirty years, on that very day, all the companies of the LORD went out from the land of Egypt. [42]That was for the LORD a night of vigil, to bring them out of the land of Egypt. That same night is a vigil to be kept for the LORD by all the Israelites throughout their generations.

Directions for the Passover

43 The LORD said to Moses and Aaron: This is the ordinance for the passover: no foreigner shall eat of it, [44]but any slave who has been purchased may eat of it after he has been circumcised; [45]no bound or hired servant may eat of it. [46]It shall be eaten in one house; you shall not take any of the animal outside the house, and you shall not break any of its bones. [47]The whole congregation of Israel shall celebrate it. [48]If an alien who resides with you wants to celebrate the passover to the LORD, all his males shall be circumcised; then he may draw near to celebrate it; he shall be regarded as a native of the land. But no uncircumcised person shall eat of it; [49]there shall be one law for the native and for the alien who resides among you.

50 All the Israelites did just as the LORD had commanded Moses and Aaron. [51]That very day the LORD brought the Israelites out of the land of Egypt, company by company.

13 The LORD said to Moses: [2]Consecrate to me all the firstborn; whatever is the first to open the womb among the Israelites, of human beings and animals, is mine.

The Festival of Unleavened Bread

3 Moses said to the people, "Remember this day on which you came out of Egypt, out of the house of slavery, because the LORD brought you out from there by strength of hand; no leavened bread shall be eaten. [4]Today, in the month of Abib, you are going out. [5]When the LORD brings you into the land of the Canaanites, the Hittites, the Amorites, the Hivites, and the Jebusites, which he swore to your ancestors to give you, a land flowing with milk and honey, you shall keep this observance in this month. [6]Seven days you shall eat unleavened bread, and on the seventh day there shall be a festival to the LORD. [7]Unleavened bread shall be eaten for seven days; no leavened bread shall be

seen in your possession, and no leaven shall be seen among you in all your territory. [8]You shall tell your child on that day, 'It is because of what the LORD did for me when I came out of Egypt.' [9]It shall serve for you as a sign on your hand and as a reminder on your forehead, so that the teaching of the LORD may be on your lips; for with a strong hand the LORD brought you out of Egypt. [10]You shall keep this ordinance at its proper time from year to year.

The Consecration of the Firstborn

11 "When the LORD has brought you into the land of the Canaanites, as he swore to you and your ancestors, and has given it to you, [12]you shall set apart to the LORD all that first opens the womb. All the firstborn of your livestock that are males shall be the LORD's. [13]But every firstborn donkey you shall redeem with a sheep; if you do not redeem it, you must break its neck. Every firstborn male among your children you shall redeem. [14]When in the future your child asks you, 'What does this mean?' you shall answer, 'By strength of hand the LORD brought us out of Egypt, from the house of slavery. [15]When Pharaoh stubbornly refused to let us go, the LORD killed all the firstborn in the land of Egypt, from human firstborn to the firstborn of animals. Therefore I sacrifice to the LORD every male that first opens the womb, but every firstborn of my sons I redeem.' [16]It shall serve as a sign on your hand and as an emblem[a] on your forehead that by strength of hand the LORD brought us out of Egypt."

The Pillars of Cloud and Fire

17 When Pharaoh let the people go, God did not lead them by way of the land of the Philistines, although that was nearer; for God thought, "If the people face war, they may change their minds and return to Egypt." [18]So God led the people by the roundabout way of the wilderness toward the Red Sea.[b] The Israelites went up out of the land of Egypt prepared for battle. [19]And Moses took with him the bones of Joseph who had required a solemn oath of the Israelites, saying, "God will surely take notice of you, and then you must carry my bones with you from here." [20]They set out from Succoth, and camped at Etham, on the edge of the wilderness. [21]The LORD went in front of them in a pillar of cloud by day, to lead them along the way, and in a pillar of fire by night, to give them light, so that they might travel by day and by night. [22]Neither the pillar of cloud by day nor the pillar of fire by night left its place in front of the people.

Crossing the Red Sea

14 Then the LORD said to Moses: [2]Tell the Israelites to turn back and camp in front of Pi-hahiroth, between Migdol and the sea, in front of Baal-zephon; you shall camp opposite it, by the sea. [3]Pharaoh will say of the Israelites, "They are wandering aimlessly in the land; the wilderness has closed in on them." [4]I will harden Pharaoh's heart, and he will pursue them, so that I will gain glory for myself over Pharaoh and all his army; and the Egyptians shall know that I am the LORD. And they did so.

5 When the king of Egypt was told that the people had fled, the minds of Pharaoh and his officials were changed

The First Commandment

EXODUS 13.3–10

Before ever reaching Mount Sinai Moses gives his people a commandment: *Remember*. If we do remember then everything else falls into place. These exhortations to remember should not be left to fossilize in their original context, but should be lifted out and converted into the context of our own lives. We are all busy. That is why we must set aside specific times that belong to God alone, times we call to mind or "re-collect" what God has said or done.

What events have been important in your personal journey, bringing you to where you are today? What signposts or "memory points" have you built into your day to remind you of the presence of God?

See Meeting God in Everyday Life

Exodus

This chapter contains one of the most repeated, most passed-along stories of God's people. God's leading of Israel out of captivity provides a central metaphor for both the Old and New Testaments. Its almost universal appeal has to do not only with the drama and power of the story itself, but also its meaning for our own journeys of faith.

Let Moses' uplifted staff provide you with an image of God's caring power in your life. The army of the Egyptians chasing you might represent the dangers you face. As God parts the waters, see his intervention in your life—things he has done to save you. Look back and see the miracles, the parted waters you have passed through, the shore of safety to which a loving God has brought you.

toward the people, and they said, "What have we done, letting Israel leave our service?" 6So he had his chariot made ready, and took his army with him; 7he took six hundred picked chariots and all the other chariots of Egypt with officers over all of them. 8The LORD hardened the heart of Pharaoh king of Egypt and he pursued the Israelites, who were going out boldly. 9The Egyptians pursued them, all Pharaoh's horses and chariots, his chariot drivers and his army; they overtook them camped by the sea, by Pi-hahiroth, in front of Baal-zephon.

10 As Pharaoh drew near, the Israelites looked back, and there were the Egyptians advancing on them. In great fear the Israelites cried out to the LORD. 11They said to Moses, "Was it because there were no graves in Egypt that you have taken us away to die in the wilderness? What have you done to us, bringing us out of Egypt? 12Is this not the very thing we told you in Egypt, 'Let us alone and let us serve the Egyptians'? For it would have been better for us to serve the Egyptians than to die in the wilderness." 13But Moses said to the people, "Do not be afraid, stand firm, and see the deliverance that the LORD will accomplish for you today; for the Egyptians whom you see today you shall never see again. 14The LORD will fight for you, and you have only to keep still."

15 Then the LORD said to Moses, "Why do you cry out to me? Tell the Israelites to go forward. 16But you lift up your staff, and stretch out your hand over the sea and divide it, that the Israelites may go into the sea on dry ground. 17Then I will harden the hearts of the Egyptians so that they will go in after them; and so I will gain glory for myself over Pharaoh and all his army, his chariots, and his chariot drivers. 18And the Egyptians shall know that I am the LORD, when I have gained glory for myself over Pharaoh, his chariots, and his chariot drivers."

19 The angel of God who was going before the Israelite army moved and went behind them; and the pillar of cloud moved from in front of them and took its place behind them. 20It came between the army of Egypt and the army of Israel. And so the cloud was there with the darkness, and it lit up the night; one did not come near the other all night.

21 Then Moses stretched out his hand over the sea. The LORD drove the sea back by a strong east wind all night, and turned the sea into dry land; and the waters were divided. 22The Israelites went into the sea on dry ground, the waters forming a wall for them on their right and on their left. 23The Egyptians pursued, and went into the sea after them, all of Pharaoh's horses, chariots, and chariot drivers. 24At the morning watch the LORD in the pillar of fire and cloud looked down upon the Egyptian army, and threw the Egyptian army into panic. 25He clogged*a* their chariot wheels so that they turned with difficulty. The Egyptians said, "Let us flee from the Israelites, for the LORD is fighting for them against Egypt."

The Pursuers Drowned

26 Then the LORD said to Moses, "Stretch out your hand over the sea, so that the water may come back upon the Egyptians, upon their chariots and chariot drivers." 27So Moses stretched out his hand over the sea, and at dawn the

a Sam Gk Syr: MT removed

sea returned to its normal depth. As the Egyptians fled before it, the LORD tossed the Egyptians into the sea. [28]The waters returned and covered the chariots and the chariot drivers, the entire army of Pharaoh that had followed them into the sea; not one of them remained. [29]But the Israelites walked on dry ground through the sea, the waters forming a wall for them on their right and on their left.

30 Thus the LORD saved Israel that day from the Egyptians; and Israel saw the Egyptians dead on the seashore. [31]Israel saw the great work that the LORD did against the Egyptians. So the people feared the LORD and believed in the LORD and in his servant Moses.

The Song of Moses

15 Then Moses and the Israelites sang this song to the LORD:

    "I will sing to the LORD, for he has triumphed
        gloriously;
    horse and rider he has thrown into the sea.
[2] The LORD is my strength and my might,[a]
    and he has become my salvation;
    this is my God, and I will praise him,
      my father's God, and I will exalt him.
[3] The LORD is a warrior;
    the LORD is his name.

[4] "Pharaoh's chariots and his army he cast into the sea;
    his picked officers were sunk in the Red Sea.[b]
[5] The floods covered them;
    they went down into the depths like a stone.
[6] Your right hand, O LORD, glorious in power—
    your right hand, O LORD, shattered the enemy.
[7] In the greatness of your majesty you overthrew
      your adversaries;
    you sent out your fury, it consumed them like
      stubble.
[8] At the blast of your nostrils the waters piled up,
    the floods stood up in a heap;
    the deeps congealed in the heart of the sea.
[9] The enemy said, 'I will pursue, I will overtake,
    I will divide the spoil, my desire shall have its fill
      of them.
    I will draw my sword, my hand shall destroy them.'
[10] You blew with your wind, the sea covered them;
    they sank like lead in the mighty waters.

[11] "Who is like you, O LORD, among the gods?
    Who is like you, majestic in holiness,
    awesome in splendor, doing wonders?
[12] You stretched out your right hand,
    the earth swallowed them.

[13] "In your steadfast love you led the people whom
      you redeemed;
    you guided them by your strength to your holy
      abode.
[14] The peoples heard, they trembled;
    pangs seized the inhabitants of Philistia.
[15] Then the chiefs of Edom were dismayed;

Following God's Ways

EXODUS 14.21–31

"God wants to lead us. Not all the ways of humans are God's leading. For a long time we can walk our own paths. On those we are pawns of coincidence, whether they bring good luck or misfortune. Our own ways always lead in a circle back to ourselves. But when God leads our ways, they guide us to him. God's ways guide us to God. God leads us through happiness and unhappiness always and only towards God. In this we recognize God's ways."

—DIETRICH BONHOEFFER,
The Mystery of Easter

Something to Sing About

EXODUS 15.1–18

This is one of many great songs found throughout the Bible. Many of the psalms are written as songs. There are also songs in Isaiah at 12.1–6, 55.6–11 and elsewhere. In the New Testament we think of the Song of Mary (Luke 1.46–55), the Song of Simeon (Luke 2.29–32), the Song of Christ Jesus (Philippians 2.6–11) and many others. Then, like now, certain occasions seem to call for music and singing, songs like "Happy Birthday" and The National Anthem.

Try to think now of songs that are especially appropriate at important times. Perhaps you have favorite hymns or songs that are particularly meaningful. Find recordings to play or write down the words of the songs. Then offer these tunes or words to God when you pray. Or you may play or hum the music alone as prayers without words. Thank God for the meaning and beauty of music.

See Meeting God in Worship

trembling seized the leaders of Moab;
all the inhabitants of Canaan melted away.
16 Terror and dread fell upon them;
by the might of your arm, they became still as a stone
until your people, O LORD, passed by,
until the people whom you acquired passed by.
17 You brought them in and planted them on the mountain of your own possession,
the place, O LORD, that you made your abode,
the sanctuary, O LORD, that your hands have established.
18 The LORD will reign forever and ever."

19 When the horses of Pharaoh with his chariots and his chariot drivers went into the sea, the LORD brought back the waters of the sea upon them; but the Israelites walked through the sea on dry ground.

The Song of Miriam

20 Then the prophet Miriam, Aaron's sister, took a tambourine in her hand; and all the women went out after her with tambourines and with dancing. 21 And Miriam sang to them:

"Sing to the LORD, for he has triumphed gloriously;
horse and rider he has thrown into the sea."

Bitter Water Made Sweet

22 Then Moses ordered Israel to set out from the Red Sea,[a] and they went into the wilderness of Shur. They went three days in the wilderness and found no water. 23 When they came to Marah, they could not drink the water of Marah because it was bitter. That is why it was called Marah.[b] 24 And the people complained against Moses, saying, "What shall we drink?" 25 He cried out to the LORD; and the LORD showed him a piece of wood;[c] he threw it into the water, and the water became sweet.

There the LORD[d] made for them a statute and an ordinance and there he put them to the test. 26 He said, "If you will listen carefully to the voice of the LORD your God, and do what is right in his sight, and give heed to his commandments and keep all his statutes, I will not bring upon you any of the diseases that I brought upon the Egyptians; for I am the LORD who heals you."

27 Then they came to Elim, where there were twelve springs of water and seventy palm trees; and they camped there by the water.

Bread from Heaven

16 The whole congregation of the Israelites set out from Elim; and Israel came to the wilderness of Sin, which is between Elim and Sinai, on the fifteenth day of the second month after they had departed from the land of Egypt. 2 The whole congregation of the Israelites complained against Moses and Aaron in the wilderness. 3 The Israelites said to them, "If only we had died by the hand of the LORD in the land of Egypt, when we sat by the fleshpots and ate our fill of bread; for you have brought us out into this wilderness to kill this whole assembly with hunger."

4 Then the LORD said to Moses, "I am going to rain bread

a Or Sea of Reeds   b That is Bitterness   c Or a tree   d Heb he from heaven for you, and each day the people shall go out and gather enough for that day. In that way I will test them, whether they will follow my instruction or not. ⁵On the sixth day, when they prepare what they bring in, it will be twice as much as they gather on other days." ⁶So Moses and Aaron said to all the Israelites, "In the evening you shall know that it was the LORD who brought you out of the land of Egypt, ⁷and in the morning you shall see the glory of the LORD, because he has heard your complaining against the LORD. For what are we, that you complain against us?" ⁸And Moses said, "When the LORD gives you meat to eat in the evening and your fill of bread in the morning, because the LORD has heard the complaining that you utter against him—what are we? Your complaining is not against us but against the LORD."

9 Then Moses said to Aaron, "Say to the whole congregation of the Israelites, 'Draw near to the LORD, for he has heard your complaining.' " ¹⁰And as Aaron spoke to the whole congregation of the Israelites, they looked toward the wilderness, and the glory of the LORD appeared in the cloud. ¹¹The LORD spoke to Moses and said, ¹²"I have heard the complaining of the Israelites; say to them, 'At twilight you shall eat meat, and in the morning you shall have your fill of bread; then you shall know that I am the LORD your God.' "

13 In the evening quails came up and covered the camp; and in the morning there was a layer of dew around the camp. ¹⁴When the layer of dew lifted, there on the surface of the wilderness was a fine flaky substance, as fine as frost on the ground. ¹⁵When the Israelites saw it, they said to one another, "What is it?"ᵃ For they did not know what it was. Moses said to them, "It is the bread that the LORD has given you to eat. ¹⁶This is what the LORD has commanded: 'Gather as much of it as each of you needs, an omer to a person according to the number of persons, all providing for those in their own tents.' " ¹⁷The Israelites did so, some gathering more, some less. ¹⁸But when they measured it with an omer, those who gathered much had nothing over, and those who gathered little had no shortage; they gathered as much as each of them needed. ¹⁹And Moses said to them, "Let no one leave any of it over until morning." ²⁰But they did not listen to Moses; some left part of it until morning, and it bred worms and became foul. And Moses was angry with them. ²¹Morning by morning they gathered it, as much as each needed; but when the sun grew hot, it melted.

22 On the sixth day they gathered twice as much food, two omers apiece. When all the leaders of the congregation came and told Moses, ²³he said to them, "This is what the LORD has commanded: 'Tomorrow is a day of solemn rest, a holy sabbath to the LORD; bake what you want to bake and boil what you want to boil, and all that is left over put aside to be kept until morning.' " ²⁴So they put it aside until morning, as Moses commanded them; and it did not become foul, and there were no worms in it. ²⁵Moses said, "Eat it today, for today is a sabbath to the LORD; today you will not find it in the field. ²⁶Six days you shall gather it; but on the seventh day, which is a sabbath, there will be none."

27 On the seventh day some of the people went out to

Bread From Heaven

EXODUS 16.4–12

Perhaps we can best appreciate the story of bread from heaven by getting in touch with bread from the kitchen table. Pick up a fresh loaf of homemade bread or one you have just brought home from the store. Hold it in your hands. Feel the weight of it. Inhale the aroma of baked grain. Compare your experience of bread from the kitchen with the Israelites' search for manna in the wilderness. How is it that while the desert wanderers complained in the midst of dire necessity, we complain today in the midst of abundance? What do you find yourself complaining about most? Turn it around and say a prayer of thanksgiving for the person, experience or challenge you are taking for granted. Make a list of the sustaining, life-giving things in your life that might be symbolized by bread and thank God for each of them. Be thankful for all the things God provides for your sustenance.

See Meeting God in Everyday Life

ᵃ Or *"It is manna"* (Heb *man hu*, see verse 31)

Freedom From Want

EXODUS 16.13–36

"It is not God's will that we should remain in need. He would fulfill all our needs by delivering us from all possessions and giving us Himself in exchange. If we would belong to His love, we must remain always empty of everything else, not in order to be in need, but precisely because possessions make us needy."

—THOMAS MERTON,
No Man Is an Island

gather, and they found none. [28]The LORD said to Moses, "How long will you refuse to keep my commandments and instructions? [29]See! The LORD has given you the sabbath, therefore on the sixth day he gives you food for two days; each of you stay where you are; do not leave your place on the seventh day." [30]So the people rested on the seventh day.

31 The house of Israel called it manna; it was like coriander seed, white, and the taste of it was like wafers made with honey. [32]Moses said, "This is what the LORD has commanded: 'Let an omer of it be kept throughout your generations, in order that they may see the food with which I fed you in the wilderness, when I brought you out of the land of Egypt.' " [33]And Moses said to Aaron, "Take a jar, and put an omer of manna in it, and place it before the LORD, to be kept throughout your generations." [34]As the LORD commanded Moses, so Aaron placed it before the covenant,[a] for safekeeping. [35]The Israelites ate manna forty years, until they came to a habitable land; they ate manna, until they came to the border of the land of Canaan. [36]An omer is a tenth of an ephah.

Water from the Rock

17 From the wilderness of Sin the whole congregation of the Israelites journeyed by stages, as the LORD commanded. They camped at Rephidim, but there was no water for the people to drink. [2]The people quarreled with Moses, and said, "Give us water to drink." Moses said to them, "Why do you quarrel with me? Why do you test the LORD?" [3]But the people thirsted there for water; and the people complained against Moses and said, "Why did you bring us out of Egypt, to kill us and our children and livestock with thirst?" [4]So Moses cried out to the LORD, "What shall I do with this people? They are almost ready to stone me." [5]The LORD said to Moses, "Go on ahead of the people, and take some of the elders of Israel with you; take in your hand the staff with which you struck the Nile, and go. [6]I will be standing there in front of you on the rock at Horeb. Strike the rock, and water will come out of it, so that the people may drink." Moses did so, in the sight of the elders of Israel. [7]He called the place Massah[b] and Meribah,[c] because the Israelites quarreled and tested the LORD, saying, "Is the LORD among us or not?"

Amalek Attacks Israel and Is Defeated

8 Then Amalek came and fought with Israel at Rephidim. [9]Moses said to Joshua, "Choose some men for us and go out, fight with Amalek. Tomorrow I will stand on the top of the hill with the staff of God in my hand." [10]So Joshua did as Moses told him, and fought with Amalek, while Moses, Aaron, and Hur went up to the top of the hill. [11]Whenever Moses held up his hand, Israel prevailed; and whenever he lowered his hand, Amalek prevailed. [12]But Moses' hands grew weary; so they took a stone and put it under him, and he sat on it. Aaron and Hur held up his hands, one on one side, and the other on the other side; so his hands were steady until the sun set. [13]And Joshua defeated Amalek and his people with the sword.

14 Then the LORD said to Moses, "Write this as a re-

a Or *treaty* or *testimony*; Heb *eduth*   *b* That is *Test*   *c* That is *Quarrel* minder in a book and recite it in the hearing of Joshua: I will utterly blot out the remembrance of Amalek from under heaven." [15]And Moses built an altar and called it, The LORD is my banner. [16]He said, "A hand upon the banner of the LORD![a] The LORD will have war with Amalek from generation to generation."

Jethro's Advice

18 Jethro, the priest of Midian, Moses' father-in-law, heard of all that God had done for Moses and for his people Israel, how the LORD had brought Israel out of Egypt. [2]After Moses had sent away his wife Zipporah, his father-in-law Jethro took her back, [3]along with her two sons. The name of the one was Gershom (for he said, "I have been an alien[b] in a foreign land"), [4]and the name of the other, Eliezer[c] (for he said, "The God of my father was my help, and delivered me from the sword of Pharaoh"). [5]Jethro, Moses' father-in-law, came into the wilderness where Moses was encamped at the mountain of God, bringing Moses' sons and wife to him. [6]He sent word to Moses, "I, your father-in-law Jethro, am coming to you, with your wife and her two sons." [7]Moses went out to meet his father-in-law; he bowed down and kissed him; each asked after the other's welfare, and they went into the tent. [8]Then Moses told his father-in-law all that the LORD had done to Pharaoh and to the Egyptians for Israel's sake, all the hardship that had beset them on the way, and how the LORD had delivered them. [9]Jethro rejoiced for all the good that the LORD had done to Israel, in delivering them from the Egyptians.

10 Jethro said, "Blessed be the LORD, who has delivered you from the Egyptians and from Pharaoh. [11]Now I know that the LORD is greater than all gods, because he delivered the people from the Egyptians,[d] when they dealt arrogantly with them." [12]And Jethro, Moses' father-in-law, brought a burnt offering and sacrifices to God; and Aaron came with all the elders of Israel to eat bread with Moses' father-in-law in the presence of God.

13 The next day Moses sat as judge for the people, while the people stood around him from morning until evening. [14]When Moses' father-in-law saw all that he was doing for the people, he said, "What is this that you are doing for the people? Why do you sit alone, while all the people stand around you from morning until evening?" [15]Moses said to his father-in-law, "Because the people come to me to inquire of God. [16]When they have a dispute, they come to me and I decide between one person and another, and I make known to them the statutes and instructions of God." [17]Moses' father-in-law said to him, "What you are doing is not good. [18]You will surely wear yourself out, both you and these people with you. For the task is too heavy for you; you cannot do it alone. [19]Now listen to me. I will give you counsel, and God be with you! You should represent the people before God, and you should bring their cases before God; [20]teach them the statutes and instructions and make known to them the way they are to go and the things they are to do. [21]You should also look for able men among all the people, men who fear God, are trustworthy, and hate dishonest gain; set such men over them as officers over thou-

Water From the Rock

EXODUS 17.6

Moses got water the hard way. First, he risked being stoned by the impatient people he led. Second, he found himself driven to seek divine intervention. Third, he had to search for a rock. Finally, he had to strike the rock with a very special stick. Finding water was an act of faith.

All most of us have to do to find water is turn on the faucet. Most of us have never lived in an area where water—the basis of life—is scarce, a subject for daily concern.

Think of a day, perhaps a hot one, when you grew very thirsty. Remember the very moment the first sip of cool water hit your mouth. Recall the sense of relief, of refreshment. Can you recall a spiritual experience that felt like a cool drink of water? Perhaps it was an answered prayer, an insight into scripture, a real sense of God's presence. Give thanks for all the ways God slakes our spiritual thirst.

See Meeting God in the Created Order

---

a Cn: Meaning of Heb uncertain   *b* Heb *ger*   *c* Heb *Eli,* my God; *ezer,* help
d The clause *because . . . Egyptians* has been transposed from verse 10

The Leader's Burden

EXODUS 18.13–27

Jethro offers good advice to Moses. Like so many of us, Moses' idea is to do everything himself. Jethro knows this allows for no weakness or failure and that it is unrealistic. In a sentence that must have rung in Moses ear, Jethro said to him, "You should represent the people before God."

Can you remember a time when someone represented you before God? Perhaps you felt dry spiritually and found it difficult to pray. Give God great thanks if you have friends like that. If not, ask God to help you find the sort of person who can pray for you when you need it and for whom you can pray as well.

See *Meeting God in Prayer*

sands, hundreds, fifties and tens. ²²Let them sit as judges for the people at all times; let them bring every important case to you, but decide every minor case themselves. So it will be easier for you, and they will bear the burden with you. ²³If you do this, and God so commands you, then you will be able to endure, and all these people will go to their home in peace."

24 So Moses listened to his father-in-law and did all that he had said. ²⁵Moses chose able men from all Israel and appointed them as heads over the people, as officers over thousands, hundreds, fifties, and tens. ²⁶And they judged the people at all times; hard cases they brought to Moses, but any minor case they decided themselves. ²⁷Then Moses let his father-in-law depart, and he went off to his own country.

The Israelites Reach Mount Sinai

19 On the third new moon after the Israelites had gone out of the land of Egypt, on that very day, they came into the wilderness of Sinai. ²They had journeyed from Rephidim, entered the wilderness of Sinai, and camped in the wilderness; Israel camped there in front of the mountain. ³Then Moses went up to God; the Lord called to him from the mountain, saying, "Thus you shall say to the house of Jacob, and tell the Israelites: ⁴You have seen what I did to the Egyptians, and how I bore you on eagles' wings and brought you to myself. ⁵Now therefore, if you obey my voice and keep my covenant, you shall be my treasured possession out of all the peoples. Indeed, the whole earth is mine, ⁶but you shall be for me a priestly kingdom and a holy nation. These are the words that you shall speak to the Israelites."

7 So Moses came, summoned the elders of the people, and set before them all these words that the Lord had commanded him. ⁸The people all answered as one: "Everything that the Lord has spoken we will do." Moses reported the words of the people to the Lord. ⁹Then the Lord said to Moses, "I am going to come to you in a dense cloud, in order that the people may hear when I speak with you and so trust you ever after."

The People Consecrated

When Moses had told the words of the people to the Lord, ¹⁰the Lord said to Moses: "Go to the people and consecrate them today and tomorrow. Have them wash their clothes ¹¹and prepare for the third day, because on the third day the Lord will come down upon Mount Sinai in the sight of all the people. ¹²You shall set limits for the people all around, saying, 'Be careful not to go up the mountain or to touch the edge of it. Any who touch the mountain shall be put to death. ¹³No hand shall touch them, but they shall be stoned or shot with arrows;ᵃ whether animal or human being, they shall not live.' When the trumpet sounds a long blast, they may go up on the mountain." ¹⁴So Moses went down from the mountain to the people. He consecrated the people, and they washed their clothes. ¹⁵And he said to the people, "Prepare for the third day; do not go near a woman."

16 On the morning of the third day there was thunder

a Heb lacks *with arrows*

and lightning, as well as a thick cloud on the mountain, and a blast of a trumpet so loud that all the people who were in the camp trembled. ¹⁷Moses brought the people out of the camp to meet God. They took their stand at the foot of the mountain. ¹⁸Now Mount Sinai was wrapped in smoke, because the LORD had descended upon it in fire; the smoke went up like the smoke of a kiln, while the whole mountain shook violently. ¹⁹As the blast of the trumpet grew louder and louder, Moses would speak and God would answer him in thunder. ²⁰When the LORD descended upon Mount Sinai, to the top of the mountain, the LORD summoned Moses to the top of the mountain, and Moses went up. ²¹Then the LORD said to Moses, "Go down and warn the people not to break through to the LORD to look; otherwise many of them will perish. ²²Even the priests who approach the LORD must consecrate themselves or the LORD will break out against them." ²³Moses said to the LORD, "The people are not permitted to come up to Mount Sinai; for you yourself warned us, saying, 'Set limits around the mountain and keep it holy.' " ²⁴The LORD said to him, "Go down, and come up bringing Aaron with you; but do not let either the priests or the people break through to come up to the LORD; otherwise he will break out against them." ²⁵So Moses went down to the people and told them.

The Ten Commandments

20 Then God spoke all these words:

2 I am the LORD your God, who brought you out of the land of Egypt, out of the house of slavery; ³you shall have no other gods before*ᵃ* me.

4 You shall not make for yourself an idol, whether in the form of anything that is in heaven above, or that is on the earth beneath, or that is in the water under the earth. ⁵You shall not bow down to them or worship them; for I the LORD your God am a jealous God, punishing children for the iniquity of parents, to the third and the fourth generation of those who reject me, ⁶but showing steadfast love to the thousandth generation*ᵇ* of those who love me and keep my commandments.

7 You shall not make wrongful use of the name of the LORD your God, for the LORD will not acquit anyone who misuses his name.

8 Remember the sabbath day, and keep it holy. ⁹Six days you shall labor and do all your work. ¹⁰But the seventh day is a sabbath to the LORD your God; you shall not do any work—you, your son or your daughter, your male or female slave, your livestock, or the alien resident in your towns. ¹¹For in six days the LORD made heaven and earth, the sea, and all that is in them, but rested the seventh day; therefore the LORD blessed the sabbath day and consecrated it.

12 Honor your father and your mother, so that your days may be long in the land that the LORD your God is giving you.

13 You shall not murder.*ᶜ*

14 You shall not commit adultery.

15 You shall not steal.

16 You shall not bear false witness against your neighbor.

17 You shall not covet your neighbor's house; you shall

Peak Experience

EXODUS 19.1–25

Chapters 19 and 20 are the very heart of the book of Exodus, the dramatic climax. These pages are more to be "dwelt in" than analyzed or studied. In this chapter, we are ushered into the Presence of the Holy One. Here we remove our shoes. Place yourself in the scene. Look. Listen. Allow yourself to stand with the community in the Presence. Stay here. Forget the clock. After you have left the scene, take the memory of it with you. Dwell on it. Return to the mountain, again and again.

See Meeting God in Worship

---

a Or *besides*   *b* Or *to thousands*   *c* Or *kill*

The Ten Commandments

EXODUS 20.1–21

Kathleen Norris, author of the award-winning *Cloister Walk*, decided one day to search through the four Gospels to sift out a set of "imperatives" that might be juxtaposed to the commandments of the Old Testament. The result was a poem she published under the title "Imperatives":

> "Look at the birds
> Consider the lilies
> Drink ye all of it
> Ask
> Seek
> Knock
> Enter by the narrow gate

> "Do not be anxious
> Judge not; do not give dogs
>   what is holy
> Go: be it done for you
> Do not be afraid
> Maiden, arise
> Young man, I say arise

> "Stretch out your hand
> Stand up, be still

> "Rise, let us be going . . .
> Love
> Forgive
> Remember me."

—KATHLEEN NORRIS,
"Little Girls In Church"

not covet your neighbor's wife, or male or female slave, or ox, or donkey, or anything that belongs to your neighbor.

18 When all the people witnessed the thunder and lightning, the sound of the trumpet, and the mountain smoking, they were afraid[a] and trembled and stood at a distance, ¹⁹and said to Moses, "You speak to us, and we will listen; but do not let God speak to us, or we will die." ²⁰Moses said to the people, "Do not be afraid; for God has come only to test you and to put the fear of him upon you so that you do not sin." ²¹Then the people stood at a distance, while Moses drew near to the thick darkness where God was.

The Law concerning the Altar

22 The LORD said to Moses: Thus you shall say to the Israelites: "You have seen for yourselves that I spoke with you from heaven. ²³You shall not make gods of silver alongside me, nor shall you make for yourselves gods of gold. ²⁴You need make for me only an altar of earth and sacrifice on it your burnt offerings and your offerings of well-being, your sheep and your oxen; in every place where I cause my name to be remembered I will come to you and bless you. ²⁵But if you make for me an altar of stone, do not build it of hewn stones; for if you use a chisel upon it you profane it. ²⁶You shall not go up by steps to my altar, so that your nakedness may not be exposed on it."

The Law concerning Slaves

21 These are the ordinances that you shall set before them:

2 When you buy a male Hebrew slave, he shall serve six years, but in the seventh he shall go out a free person, without debt. ³If he comes in single, he shall go out single; if he comes in married, then his wife shall go out with him. ⁴If his master gives him a wife and she bears him sons or daughters, the wife and her children shall be her master's and he shall go out alone. ⁵But if the slave declares, "I love my master, my wife, and my children; I will not go out a free person," ⁶then his master shall bring him before God.[b] He shall be brought to the door or the doorpost; and his master shall pierce his ear with an awl; and he shall serve him for life.

7 When a man sells his daughter as a slave, she shall not go out as the male slaves do. ⁸If she does not please her master, who designated her for himself, then he shall let her be redeemed; he shall have no right to sell her to a foreign people, since he has dealt unfairly with her. ⁹If he designates her for his son, he shall deal with her as with a daughter. ¹⁰If he takes another wife to himself, he shall not diminish the food, clothing, or marital rights of the first wife.[c] ¹¹And if he does not do these three things for her, she shall go out without debt, without payment of money.

The Law concerning Violence

12 Whoever strikes a person mortally shall be put to death. ¹³If it was not premeditated, but came about by an act of God, then I will appoint for you a place to which the killer may flee. ¹⁴But if someone willfully attacks and kills another by treachery, you shall take the killer from my altar for execution.

a Sam Gk Syr Vg: MT *they saw*   *b* Or *to the judges*   *c* Heb *of her*

15 Whoever strikes father or mother shall be put to death.

16 Whoever kidnaps a person, whether that person has been sold or is still held in possession, shall be put to death.

17 Whoever curses father or mother shall be put to death.

18 When individuals quarrel and one strikes the other with a stone or fist so that the injured party, though not dead, is confined to bed, ¹⁹but recovers and walks around outside with the help of a staff, then the assailant shall be free of liability, except to pay for the loss of time, and to arrange for full recovery.

20 When a slaveowner strikes a male or female slave with a rod and the slave dies immediately, the owner shall be punished. ²¹But if the slave survives a day or two, there is no punishment; for the slave is the owner's property.

22 When people who are fighting injure a pregnant woman so that there is a miscarriage, and yet no further harm follows, the one responsible shall be fined what the woman's husband demands, paying as much as the judges determine. ²³If any harm follows, then you shall give life for life, ²⁴eye for eye, tooth for tooth, hand for hand, foot for foot, ²⁵burn for burn, wound for wound, stripe for stripe.

26 When a slaveowner strikes the eye of a male or female slave, destroying it, the owner shall let the slave go, a free person, to compensate for the eye. ²⁷If the owner knocks out a tooth of a male or female slave, the slave shall be let go, a free person, to compensate for the tooth.

Laws concerning Property

28 When an ox gores a man or a woman to death, the ox shall be stoned, and its flesh shall not be eaten; but the owner of the ox shall not be liable. ²⁹If the ox has been accustomed to gore in the past, and its owner has been warned but has not restrained it, and it kills a man or a woman, the ox shall be stoned, and its owner also shall be put to death. ³⁰If a ransom is imposed on the owner, then the owner shall pay whatever is imposed for the redemption of the victim's life. ³¹If it gores a boy or a girl, the owner shall be dealt with according to this same rule. ³²If the ox gores a male or female slave, the owner shall pay to the slaveowner thirty shekels of silver, and the ox shall be stoned.

33 If someone leaves a pit open, or digs a pit and does not cover it, and an ox or a donkey falls into it, ³⁴the owner of the pit shall make restitution, giving money to its owner, but keeping the dead animal.

35 If someone's ox hurts the ox of another, so that it dies, then they shall sell the live ox and divide the price of it; and the dead animal they shall also divide. ³⁶But if it was known that the ox was accustomed to gore in the past, and its owner has not restrained it, the owner shall restore ox for ox, but keep the dead animal.

Laws of Restitution

22 *a* When someone steals an ox or a sheep, and slaughters it or sells it, the thief shall pay five oxen for an ox, and four sheep for a sheep.*b* The thief shall make restitution, but if unable to do so, shall be sold for the theft.

An Eye for an Eye?

EXODUS 21.23–25

What are we to make of this well-known law of retaliation? It helps to remember that its balanced approach represented a great advance among ancient legal systems, a softening influence among a people sometimes known for casual cruelty and escalating retribution. Later, Jesus was to go even further with the law of love, insisting that believers turn the other cheek and go the extra mile (see Matthew 5.38–42).

When have you been tempted to take revenge? Think about people against whom you may harbor hard or harsh feelings. Write down their names. One by one, pray about the hurt each one has caused you. Seek God's help for the difficult process of forgiveness and reconciliation. Ask God if there is anything you need to do to make something right, or if you need to take the risk of confronting someone.

See Meeting God in Community

---

a Ch 21.37 in Heb   *b* Verses 2, 3, and 4 rearranged thus: 3b, 4, 2, 3a

Whatsoever You Do . . .

EXODUS 22.5–9

"Keep in mind that each of you has your own vineyard. But every one is joined to your neighbors' vineyards without any dividing lines. They are so joined together, in fact, that you cannot do good or evil for yourself without doing the same for your neighbors."

—CATHERINE OF SIENA,
The Dialogue

See Meeting God in Community

⁴When the animal, whether ox or donkey or sheep, is found alive in the thief's possession, the thief shall pay double.

2*ᵃ* If a thief is found breaking in, and is beaten to death, no bloodguilt is incurred; ³but if it happens after sunrise, bloodguilt is incurred.

5 When someone causes a field or vineyard to be grazed over, or lets livestock loose to graze in someone else's field, restitution shall be made from the best in the owner's field or vineyard.

6 When fire breaks out and catches in thorns so that the stacked grain or the standing grain or the field is consumed, the one who started the fire shall make full restitution.

7 When someone delivers to a neighbor money or goods for safekeeping, and they are stolen from the neighbor's house, then the thief, if caught, shall pay double. ⁸If the thief is not caught, the owner of the house shall be brought before God,*ᵇ* to determine whether or not the owner had laid hands on the neighbor's goods.

9 In any case of disputed ownership involving ox, donkey, sheep, clothing, or any other loss, of which one party says, "This is mine," the case of both parties shall come before God;*ᵇ* the one whom God condemns*ᶜ* shall pay double to the other.

10 When someone delivers to another a donkey, ox, sheep, or any other animal for safekeeping, and it dies or is injured or is carried off, without anyone seeing it, ¹¹an oath before the LORD shall decide between the two of them that the one has not laid hands on the property of the other; the owner shall accept the oath, and no restitution shall be made. ¹²But if it was stolen, restitution shall be made to its owner. ¹³If it was mangled by beasts, let it be brought as evidence; restitution shall not be made for the mangled remains.

14 When someone borrows an animal from another and it is injured or dies, the owner not being present, full restitution shall be made. ¹⁵If the owner was present, there shall be no restitution; if it was hired, only the hiring fee is due.

Social and Religious Laws

16 When a man seduces a virgin who is not engaged to be married, and lies with her, he shall give the bride-price for her and make her his wife. ¹⁷But if her father refuses to give her to him, he shall pay an amount equal to the bride-price for virgins.

18 You shall not permit a female sorcerer to live.

19 Whoever lies with an animal shall be put to death.

20 Whoever sacrifices to any god, other than the LORD alone, shall be devoted to destruction.

21 You shall not wrong or oppress a resident alien, for you were aliens in the land of Egypt. ²²You shall not abuse any widow or orphan. ²³If you do abuse them, when they cry out to me, I will surely heed their cry; ²⁴my wrath will burn, and I will kill you with the sword, and your wives shall become widows and your children orphans.

25 If you lend money to my people, to the poor among you, you shall not deal with them as a creditor; you shall not exact interest from them. ²⁶If you take your neighbor's

a Ch 22.1 in Heb   *b* Or *before the judges*   *c* Or *the judges condemn* cloak in pawn, you shall restore it before the sun goes down; [27]for it may be your neighbor's only clothing to use as cover; in what else shall that person sleep? And if your neighbor cries out to me, I will listen, for I am compassionate.

28 You shall not revile God, or curse a leader of your people.

29 You shall not delay to make offerings from the fullness of your harvest and from the outflow of your presses.[a]

The firstborn of your sons you shall give to me. [30]You shall do the same with your oxen and with your sheep: seven days it shall remain with its mother; on the eighth day you shall give it to me.

31 You shall be people consecrated to me; therefore you shall not eat any meat that is mangled by beasts in the field; you shall throw it to the dogs.

Justice for All

23 You shall not spread a false report. You shall not join hands with the wicked to act as a malicious witness. [2]You shall not follow a majority in wrongdoing; when you bear witness in a lawsuit, you shall not side with the majority so as to pervert justice; [3]nor shall you be partial to the poor in a lawsuit.

4 When you come upon your enemy's ox or donkey going astray, you shall bring it back.

5 When you see the donkey of one who hates you lying under its burden and you would hold back from setting it free, you must help to set it free.[a]

6 You shall not pervert the justice due to your poor in their lawsuits. [7]Keep far from a false charge, and do not kill the innocent and those in the right, for I will not acquit the guilty. [8]You shall take no bribe, for a bribe blinds the officials, and subverts the cause of those who are in the right.

9 You shall not oppress a resident alien; you know the heart of an alien, for you were aliens in the land of Egypt.

Sabbatical Year and Sabbath

10 For six years you shall sow your land and gather in its yield; [11]but the seventh year you shall let it rest and lie fallow, so that the poor of your people may eat; and what they leave the wild animals may eat. You shall do the same with your vineyard, and with your olive orchard.

12 Six days you shall do your work, but on the seventh day you shall rest, so that your ox and your donkey may have relief, and your homeborn slave and the resident alien may be refreshed. [13]Be attentive to all that I have said to you. Do not invoke the names of other gods; do not let them be heard on your lips.

The Annual Festivals

14 Three times in the year you shall hold a festival for me. [15]You shall observe the festival of unleavened bread; as I commanded you, you shall eat unleavened bread for seven days at the appointed time in the month of Abib, for in it you came out of Egypt.

No one shall appear before me empty-handed.

16 You shall observe the festival of harvest, of the first fruits of your labor, of what you sow in the field. You shall

Sinai and Our Life Together

EXODUS 22.16–23.9

God sets a lengthy series of laws before Moses and the people. As we read through them, we can see an amazing thing—a nation is brought into being. For in the end, this is a purpose of the laws: They define how the people will live together in health and righteousness to the glory of God.

On a sheet of paper, make a list of the rules that govern the life of your family, your smaller community of faith or your church. What are the unspoken rules? Is it taken for granted, for instance, that if someone asks for prayers, you will all pray for that person? Do you honor confidences and refuse to gossip? If someone is in need, do you take what actions you can to help? Perhaps there are other things you can do as a family or as a church that will glorify God and promote loving relationships.

See Meeting God in Community

Remember Your Angel

EXODUS 23.20

God sends an angel in front of the people to guard them and to bring them "to the place that I have prepared." Even though they trekked through the wilderness, they knew they were not alone.

These words invite your personal response. Hear them as though they are spoken to you. Think back to earlier stages in your own journey when it seemed difficult, if not impossible, to go on. Remember how, in spite of overwhelming problems, emotional or financial struggles, perhaps even moral lapses, God walked with you and assisted you. You made it after all. Make this promise of presence and protection the basis of grateful prayer.

See Meeting God in Everyday Life

observe the festival of ingathering at the end of the year, when you gather in from the field the fruit of your labor. [17]Three times in the year all your males shall appear before the Lord GOD.

18 You shall not offer the blood of my sacrifice with anything leavened, or let the fat of my festival remain until the morning.

19 The choicest of the first fruits of your ground you shall bring into the house of the LORD your God.

You shall not boil a kid in its mother's milk.

The Conquest of Canaan Promised

20 I am going to send an angel in front of you, to guard you on the way and to bring you to the place that I have prepared. [21]Be attentive to him and listen to his voice; do not rebel against him, for he will not pardon your transgression; for my name is in him.

22 But if you listen attentively to his voice and do all that I say, then I will be an enemy to your enemies and a foe to your foes.

23 When my angel goes in front of you, and brings you to the Amorites, the Hittites, the Perizzites, the Canaanites, the Hivites, and the Jebusites, and I blot them out, [24]you shall not bow down to their gods, or worship them, or follow their practices, but you shall utterly demolish them and break their pillars in pieces. [25]You shall worship the LORD your God, and I[a] will bless your bread and your water; and I will take sickness away from among you. [26]No one shall miscarry or be barren in your land; I will fulfill the number of your days. [27]I will send my terror in front of you, and will throw into confusion all the people against whom you shall come, and I will make all your enemies turn their backs to you. [28]And I will send the pestilence[b] in front of you, which shall drive out the Hivites, the Canaanites, and the Hittites from before you. [29]I will not drive them out from before you in one year, or the land would become desolate and the wild animals would multiply against you. [30]Little by little I will drive them out from before you, until you have increased and possess the land. [31]I will set your borders from the Red Sea[c] to the sea of the Philistines, and from the wilderness to the Euphrates; for I will hand over to you the inhabitants of the land, and you shall drive them out before you. [32]You shall make no covenant with them and their gods. [33]They shall not live in your land, or they will make you sin against me; for if you worship their gods, it will surely be a snare to you.

The Blood of the Covenant

24 Then he said to Moses, "Come up to the LORD, you and Aaron, Nadab, and Abihu, and seventy of the elders of Israel, and worship at a distance. [2]Moses alone shall come near the LORD; but the others shall not come near, and the people shall not come up with him."

3 Moses came and told the people all the words of the LORD and all the ordinances; and all the people answered with one voice, and said, "All the words that the LORD has spoken we will do." [4]And Moses wrote down all the words of the LORD. He rose early in the morning, and built an altar

a Gk Vg: Heb *he*   *b* Or *hornets*: Meaning of Heb uncertain   *c* Or *Sea of Reeds*

at the foot of the mountain, and set up twelve pillars, corresponding to the twelve tribes of Israel. [5]He sent young men of the people of Israel, who offered burnt offerings and sacrificed oxen as offerings of well-being to the LORD. [6]Moses took half of the blood and put it in basins, and half of the blood he dashed against the altar. [7]Then he took the book of the covenant, and read it in the hearing of the people; and they said, "All that the LORD has spoken we will do, and we will be obedient." [8]Moses took the blood and dashed it on the people, and said, "See the blood of the covenant that the LORD has made with you in accordance with all these words."

On the Mountain with God

9 Then Moses and Aaron, Nadab, and Abihu, and seventy of the elders of Israel went up, [10]and they saw the God of Israel. Under his feet there was something like a pavement of sapphire stone, like the very heaven for clearness. [11]God[a] did not lay his hand on the chief men of the people of Israel; also they beheld God, and they ate and drank.

12 The LORD said to Moses, "Come up to me on the mountain, and wait there; and I will give you the tablets of stone, with the law and the commandment, which I have written for their instruction." [13]So Moses set out with his assistant Joshua, and Moses went up into the mountain of God. [14]To the elders he had said, "Wait here for us, until we come to you again; for Aaron and Hur are with you; whoever has a dispute may go to them."

15 Then Moses went up on the mountain, and the cloud covered the mountain. [16]The glory of the LORD settled on Mount Sinai, and the cloud covered it for six days; on the seventh day he called to Moses out of the cloud. [17]Now the appearance of the glory of the LORD was like a devouring fire on the top of the mountain in the sight of the people of Israel. [18]Moses entered the cloud, and went up on the mountain. Moses was on the mountain for forty days and forty nights.

Offerings for the Tabernacle

25 The LORD said to Moses: [2]Tell the Israelites to take for me an offering; from all whose hearts prompt them to give you shall receive the offering for me. [3]This is the offering that you shall receive from them: gold, silver, and bronze, [4]blue, purple, and crimson yarns and fine linen, goats' hair, [5]tanned rams' skins, fine leather,[b] acacia wood, [6]oil for the lamps, spices for the anointing oil and for the fragrant incense, [7]onyx stones and gems to be set in the ephod and for the breastpiece. [8]And have them make me a sanctuary, so that I may dwell among them. [9]In accordance with all that I show you concerning the pattern of the tabernacle and of all its furniture, so you shall make it.

The Ark of the Covenant

10 They shall make an ark of acacia wood; it shall be two and a half cubits long, a cubit and a half wide, and a cubit and a half high. [11]You shall overlay it with pure gold, inside and outside you shall overlay it, and you shall make a molding of gold upon it all around. [12]You shall cast four rings of gold for it and put them on its four feet, two rings

Entering the Cloud

EXODUS 24.12–18

There is a Moses inside every one of us, hungering to break away from the ordinary and everyday, to explore frontiers, to ascend the heights, to get close to the heart of God.

When was the last time you set apart a time and a place to be alone with God, to allow God to speak to you? Explore the possibilities of finding a monastic or lay retreat center that offers weekend or extended retreats. And don't overlook the resources nearest you: a solitary walk in the park, a place at the water's edge to watch a sunrise or sunset. The glory of the Lord awaits you.

See Meeting God in Prayer

A Matter of the Heart

EXODUS 25.10–30

Moses was not commanded to build the tabernacle by himself. It was to be a community effort. Building resources were to come "from all whose hearts prompt them to give" (v.2). Likewise, religious leaders are facilitators at the service of the community, not independent entities. Community worship is meant to provide a way for everyone in the body of Christ to participate.

Take time now to reflect on the role you fill in your worshiping community. What personal contribution can you make to public worship? Prayerfully think about volunteering to work as an usher, scripture reader, minister of the bread or cup, hospitality helper, or whatever gift your heart prompts you to give.

See Meeting God in Service

on the one side of it, and two rings on the other side. ¹³You shall make poles of acacia wood, and overlay them with gold. ¹⁴And you shall put the poles into the rings on the sides of the ark, by which to carry the ark. ¹⁵The poles shall remain in the rings of the ark; they shall not be taken from it. ¹⁶You shall put into the ark the covenant*ᵃ* that I shall give you.

17 Then you shall make a mercy seat*ᵇ* of pure gold; two cubits and a half shall be its length, and a cubit and a half its width. ¹⁸You shall make two cherubim of gold; you shall make them of hammered work, at the two ends of the mercy seat.*ᶜ* ¹⁹Make one cherub at the one end, and one cherub at the other; of one piece with the mercy seat*ᶜ* you shall make the cherubim at its two ends. ²⁰The cherubim shall spread out their wings above, overshadowing the mercy seat*ᶜ* with their wings. They shall face one to another; the faces of the cherubim shall be turned toward the mercy seat.*ᶜ* ²¹You shall put the mercy seat*ᶜ* on the top of the ark; and in the ark you shall put the covenant*ᵃ* that I shall give you. ²²There I will meet with you, and from above the mercy seat,*ᶜ* from between the two cherubim that are on the ark of the covenant,*ᵃ* I will deliver to you all my commands for the Israelites.

The Table for the Bread of the Presence

23 You shall make a table of acacia wood, two cubits long, one cubit wide, and a cubit and a half high. ²⁴You shall overlay it with pure gold, and make a molding of gold around it. ²⁵You shall make around it a rim a handbreadth wide, and a molding of gold around the rim. ²⁶You shall make for it four rings of gold, and fasten the rings to the four corners at its four legs. ²⁷The rings that hold the poles used for carrying the table shall be close to the rim. ²⁸You shall make the poles of acacia wood, and overlay them with gold, and the table shall be carried with these. ²⁹You shall make its plates and dishes for incense, and its flagons and bowls with which to pour drink offerings; you shall make them of pure gold. ³⁰And you shall set the bread of the Presence on the table before me always.

The Lampstand

31 You shall make a lampstand of pure gold. The base and the shaft of the lampstand shall be made of hammered work; its cups, its calyxes, and its petals shall be of one piece with it; ³²and there shall be six branches going out of its sides, three branches of the lampstand out of one side of it and three branches of the lampstand out of the other side of it; ³³three cups shaped like almond blossoms, each with calyx and petals, on one branch, and three cups shaped like almond blossoms, each with calyx and petals, on the other branch—so for the six branches going out of the lampstand. ³⁴On the lampstand itself there shall be four cups shaped like almond blossoms, each with its calyxes and petals. ³⁵There shall be a calyx of one piece with it under the first pair of branches, a calyx of one piece with it under the next pair of branches, and a calyx of one piece with it under the last pair of branches—so for the six branches that go out of the lampstand. ³⁶Their calyxes and their branches shall be of one piece with it, the whole of it

a Or *treaty*, or *testimony*; Heb *eduth*   *b* Or *a cover*   *c* Or *the cover*

one hammered piece of pure gold. [37]You shall make the seven lamps for it; and the lamps shall be set up so as to give light on the space in front of it. [38]Its snuffers and trays shall be of pure gold. [39]It, and all these utensils, shall be made from a talent of pure gold. [40]And see that you make them according to the pattern for them, which is being shown you on the mountain.

The Tabernacle

26 Moreover you shall make the tabernacle with ten curtains of fine twisted linen, and blue, purple, and crimson yarns; you shall make them with cherubim skillfully worked into them. [2]The length of each curtain shall be twenty-eight cubits, and the width of each curtain four cubits; all the curtains shall be of the same size. [3]Five curtains shall be joined to one another; and the other five curtains shall be joined to one another. [4]You shall make loops of blue on the edge of the outermost curtain in the first set; and likewise you shall make loops on the edge of the outermost curtain in the second set. [5]You shall make fifty loops on the one curtain, and you shall make fifty loops on the edge of the curtain that is in the second set; the loops shall be opposite one another. [6]You shall make fifty clasps of gold, and join the curtains to one another with the clasps, so that the tabernacle may be one whole.

7 You shall also make curtains of goats' hair for a tent over the tabernacle; you shall make eleven curtains. [8]The length of each curtain shall be thirty cubits, and the width of each curtain four cubits; the eleven curtains shall be of the same size. [9]You shall join five curtains by themselves, and six curtains by themselves, and the sixth curtain you shall double over at the front of the tent. [10]You shall make fifty loops on the edge of the curtain that is outermost in one set, and fifty loops on the edge of the curtain that is outermost in the second set.

11 You shall make fifty clasps of bronze, and put the clasps into the loops, and join the tent together, so that it may be one whole. [12]The part that remains of the curtains of the tent, the half curtain that remains, shall hang over the back of the tabernacle. [13]The cubit on the one side, and the cubit on the other side, of what remains in the length of the curtains of the tent, shall hang over the sides of the tabernacle, on this side and that side, to cover it. [14]You shall make for the tent a covering of tanned rams' skins and an outer covering of fine leather.[a]

The Framework

15 You shall make upright frames of acacia wood for the tabernacle. [16]Ten cubits shall be the length of a frame, and a cubit and a half the width of each frame. [17]There shall be two pegs in each frame to fit the frames together; you shall make these for all the frames of the tabernacle. [18]You shall make the frames for the tabernacle: twenty frames for the south side; [19]and you shall make forty bases of silver under the twenty frames, two bases under the first frame for its two pegs, and two bases under the next frame for its two pegs; [20]and for the second side of the tabernacle, on the north side twenty frames, [21]and their forty bases of silver, two bases under the first frame, and two bases under the

---

Curtains and Light

EXODUS 26. 1–14

As you read the details of God's instructions to Moses for the furnishings of the tabernacle, you may be struck by the importance given to curtains. Stop and reflect on the role curtains play in ordinary home life. Closed, they provide privacy, a space where we can be alone. Open, they invite rays of golden sunlight. Curtains in the tabernacle can speak to us powerfully as symbols of God's nearness, but also of God's hiddenness. Recall the experiences in your life when God seemed most present. Next recall when God seemed most hidden.

Set your alarm and get up a few minutes before dawn. Go to a window and open the curtains. In the quiet of early morning, experience the transition from darkness to light. Greet the dawn with the prayer of your heart as the God present also in darkness embraces you with the light of a new day.

See Meeting God in Everyday Life

Making a Sanctuary

EXODUS 26.26–37

"God wishes . . . that we make a sanctuary for him. For he promises that if we make a sanctuary for him, he can be seen by us . . . This, therefore, is the sanctuary which the Lord wishes to be constructed . . . knowing without doubt that he who makes a sanctuary for the Lord by the purity of his own heart and body will himself see God. Let us, therefore, also make a sanctuary for the Lord both collectively and individually."

—ORIGEN OF ALEXANDRIA,
Homilies On Exodus

See Meeting God in Prayer

next frame; ²²and for the rear of the tabernacle westward you shall make six frames. ²³You shall make two frames for corners of the tabernacle in the rear; ²⁴they shall be separate beneath, but joined at the top, at the first ring; it shall be the same with both of them; they shall form the two corners. ²⁵And so there shall be eight frames, with their bases of silver, sixteen bases; two bases under the first frame, and two bases under the next frame.

26 You shall make bars of acacia wood, five for the frames of the one side of the tabernacle, ²⁷and five bars for the frames of the other side of the tabernacle, and five bars for the frames of the side of the tabernacle at the rear westward. ²⁸The middle bar, halfway up the frames, shall pass through from end to end. ²⁹You shall overlay the frames with gold, and shall make their rings of gold to hold the bars; and you shall overlay the bars with gold. ³⁰Then you shall erect the tabernacle according to the plan for it that you were shown on the mountain.

The Curtain

31 You shall make a curtain of blue, purple, and crimson yarns, and of fine twisted linen; it shall be made with cherubim skillfully worked into it. ³²You shall hang it on four pillars of acacia overlaid with gold, which have hooks of gold and rest on four bases of silver. ³³You shall hang the curtain under the clasps, and bring the ark of the covenant[a] in there, within the curtain; and the curtain shall separate for you the holy place from the most holy. ³⁴You shall put the mercy seat[b] on the ark of the covenant[a] in the most holy place. ³⁵You shall set the table outside the curtain, and the lampstand on the south side of the tabernacle opposite the table; and you shall put the table on the north side.

36 You shall make a screen for the entrance of the tent, of blue, purple, and crimson yarns, and of fine twisted linen, embroidered with needlework. ³⁷You shall make for the screen five pillars of acacia, and overlay them with gold; their hooks shall be of gold, and you shall cast five bases of bronze for them.

The Altar of Burnt Offering

27 You shall make the altar of acacia wood, five cubits long and five cubits wide; the altar shall be square, and it shall be three cubits high. ²You shall make horns for it on its four corners; its horns shall be of one piece with it, and you shall overlay it with bronze. ³You shall make pots for it to receive its ashes, and shovels and basins and forks and firepans; you shall make all its utensils of bronze. ⁴You shall also make for it a grating, a network of bronze; and on the net you shall make four bronze rings at its four corners. ⁵You shall set it under the ledge of the altar so that the net shall extend halfway down the altar. ⁶You shall make poles for the altar, poles of acacia wood, and overlay them with bronze; ⁷the poles shall be put through the rings, so that the poles shall be on the two sides of the altar when it is carried. ⁸You shall make it hollow, with boards. They shall be made just as you were shown on the mountain.

The Court and Its Hangings

9 You shall make the court of the tabernacle. On the

a Or *treaty*, or *testimony*; Heb *eduth*   *b* Or *the cover*

south side the court shall have hangings of fine twisted linen one hundred cubits long for that side; [10]its twenty pillars and their twenty bases shall be of bronze, but the hooks of the pillars and their bands shall be of silver. [11]Likewise for its length on the north side there shall be hangings one hundred cubits long, their pillars twenty and their bases twenty, of bronze, but the hooks of the pillars and their bands shall be of silver. [12]For the width of the court on the west side there shall be fifty cubits of hangings, with ten pillars and ten bases. [13]The width of the court on the front to the east shall be fifty cubits. [14]There shall be fifteen cubits of hangings on the one side, with three pillars and three bases. [15]There shall be fifteen cubits of hangings on the other side, with three pillars and three bases. [16]For the gate of the court there shall be a screen twenty cubits long, of blue, purple, and crimson yarns, and of fine twisted linen, embroidered with needlework; it shall have four pillars and with them four bases. [17]All the pillars around the court shall be banded with silver; their hooks shall be of silver, and their bases of bronze. [18]The length of the court shall be one hundred cubits, the width fifty, and the height five cubits, with hangings of fine twisted linen and bases of bronze. [19]All the utensils of the tabernacle for every use, and all its pegs and all the pegs of the court, shall be of bronze.

The Oil for the Lamp

20 You shall further command the Israelites to bring you pure oil of beaten olives for the light, so that a lamp may be set up to burn regularly. [21]In the tent of meeting, outside the curtain that is before the covenant,[a] Aaron and his sons shall tend it from evening to morning before the LORD. It shall be a perpetual ordinance to be observed throughout their generations by the Israelites.

Vestments for the Priesthood

28 Then bring near to you your brother Aaron, and his sons with him, from among the Israelites, to serve me as priests—Aaron and Aaron's sons, Nadab and Abihu, Eleazar and Ithamar. [2]You shall make sacred vestments for the glorious adornment of your brother Aaron. [3]And you shall speak to all who have ability, whom I have endowed with skill, that they make Aaron's vestments to consecrate him for my priesthood. [4]These are the vestments that they shall make: a breastpiece, an ephod, a robe, a checkered tunic, a turban, and a sash. When they make these sacred vestments for your brother Aaron and his sons to serve me as priests, [5]they shall use gold, blue, purple, and crimson yarns, and fine linen.

The Ephod

6 They shall make the ephod of gold, of blue, purple, and crimson yarns, and of fine twisted linen, skillfully worked. [7]It shall have two shoulder-pieces attached to its two edges, so that it may be joined together. [8]The decorated band on it shall be of the same workmanship and materials, of gold, of blue, purple, and crimson yarns, and of fine twisted linen. [9]You shall take two onyx stones, and engrave on them the names of the sons of Israel, [10]six of their names

A Lamp to Burn Regularly

EXODUS 27.20–21

Note the importance placed on keeping a lamp burning at all times. Candlelight has always had a special place in both religious and civil festive celebrations. Lighting a candle before a meal or before saying a prayer can be an effective way to instill in those gathered a sense of the sacred. Let candles light the family table or the places where you pray. Consider lighting a candle now, letting the light remind you of Jesus the light of the world.

a Or *treaty*, or *testimony*; Heb *eduth*

Our Great High Priest

"Surely he has borne our
infirmities
and carried our diseases;
yet we accounted him stricken,
struck down by God, and
afflicted.

"But he was wounded for our
transgressions,
crushed for our iniquities;
upon him was the punishment
that made us whole,
and by his bruises we are
healed.

Out of his anguish he shall see
light;
he shall find satisfaction
through his knowledge.
The righteous one, f my
servant, shall make
many righteous,
and he shall bear their
iniquities.

—Isaiah 53.4–5,11

on the one stone, and the names of the remaining six on the other stone, in the order of their birth. ¹¹As a gem-cutter engraves signets, so you shall engrave the two stones with the names of the sons of Israel; you shall mount them in settings of gold filigree. ¹²You shall set the two stones on the shoulder-pieces of the ephod, as stones of remembrance for the sons of Israel; and Aaron shall bear their names before the LORD on his two shoulders for remembrance. ¹³You shall make settings of gold filigree, ¹⁴and two chains of pure gold, twisted like cords; and you shall attach the corded chains to the settings.

The Breastplate

15 You shall make a breastpiece of judgment, in skilled work; you shall make it in the style of the ephod; of gold, of blue and purple and crimson yarns, and of fine twisted linen you shall make it. ¹⁶It shall be square and doubled, a span in length and a span in width. ¹⁷You shall set in it four rows of stones. A row of carnelian,ᵃ chrysolite, and emerald shall be the first row; ¹⁸and the second row a turquoise, a sapphireᵇ and a moonstone; ¹⁹and the third row a jacinth, an agate, and an amethyst; ²⁰and the fourth row a beryl, an onyx, and a jasper; they shall be set in gold filigree. ²¹There shall be twelve stones with names corresponding to the names of the sons of Israel; they shall be like signets, each engraved with its name, for the twelve tribes. ²²You shall make for the breastpiece chains of pure gold, twisted like cords; ²³and you shall make for the breastpiece two rings of gold, and put the two rings on the two edges of the breastpiece. ²⁴You shall put the two cords of gold in the two rings at the edges of the breastpiece; ²⁵the two ends of the two cords you shall attach to the two settings, and so attach it in front to the shoulder-pieces of the ephod. ²⁶You shall make two rings of gold, and put them at the two ends of the breastpiece, on its inside edge next to the ephod. ²⁷You shall make two rings of gold, and attach them in front to the lower part of the two shoulder-pieces of the ephod, at its joining above the decorated band of the ephod. ²⁸The breastpiece shall be bound by its rings to the rings of the ephod with a blue cord, so that it may lie on the decorated band of the ephod, and so that the breastpiece shall not come loose from the ephod. ²⁹So Aaron shall bear the names of the sons of Israel in the breastpiece of judgment on his heart when he goes into the holy place, for a continual remembrance before the LORD. ³⁰In the breastpiece of judgment you shall put the Urim and the Thummim, and they shall be on Aaron's heart when he goes in before the LORD; thus Aaron shall bear the judgment of the Israelites on his heart before the LORD continually.

Other Priestly Vestments

31 You shall make the robe of the ephod all of blue. ³²It shall have an opening for the head in the middle of it, with a woven binding around the opening, like the opening in a coat of mail,ᶜ so that it may not be torn. ³³On its lower hem you shall make pomegranates of blue, purple, and crimson yarns, all around the lower hem, with bells of gold between them all around— ³⁴a golden bell and a pomegranate alter-

a The identity of several of these stones is uncertain   *b* Or *lapis lazuli*
c Meaning of Heb uncertain

nating all around the lower hem of the robe. ³⁵Aaron shall wear it when he ministers, and its sound shall be heard when he goes into the holy place before the LORD, and when he comes out, so that he may not die.

36 You shall make a rosette of pure gold, and engrave on it, like the engraving of a signet, "Holy to the LORD." ³⁷You shall fasten it on the turban with a blue cord; it shall be on the front of the turban. ³⁸It shall be on Aaron's forehead, and Aaron shall take on himself any guilt incurred in the holy offering that the Israelites consecrate as their sacred donations; it shall always be on his forehead, in order that they may find favor before the LORD.

39 You shall make the checkered tunic of fine linen, and you shall make a turban of fine linen, and you shall make a sash embroidered with needlework.

40 For Aaron's sons you shall make tunics and sashes and headdresses; you shall make them for their glorious adornment. ⁴¹You shall put them on your brother Aaron, and on his sons with him, and shall anoint them and ordain them and consecrate them, so that they may serve me as priests. ⁴²You shall make for them linen undergarments to cover their naked flesh; they shall reach from the hips to the thighs; ⁴³Aaron and his sons shall wear them when they go into the tent of meeting, or when they come near the altar to minister in the holy place; or they will bring guilt on themselves and die. This shall be a perpetual ordinance for him and for his descendants after him.

The Ordination of the Priests

29 Now this is what you shall do to them to consecrate them, so that they may serve me as priests. Take one young bull and two rams without blemish, ²and unleavened bread, unleavened cakes mixed with oil, and unleavened wafers spread with oil. You shall make them of choice wheat flour. ³You shall put them in one basket and bring them in the basket, and bring the bull and the two rams. ⁴You shall bring Aaron and his sons to the entrance of the tent of meeting, and wash them with water. ⁵Then you shall take the vestments, and put on Aaron the tunic and the robe of the ephod, and the ephod, and the breastpiece, and gird him with the decorated band of the ephod; ⁶and you shall set the turban on his head, and put the holy diadem on the turban. ⁷You shall take the anointing oil, and pour it on his head and anoint him. ⁸Then you shall bring his sons, and put tunics on them, ⁹and you shall gird them with sashes[a] and tie headdresses on them; and the priesthood shall be theirs by a perpetual ordinance. You shall then ordain Aaron and his sons.

10 You shall bring the bull in front of the tent of meeting. Aaron and his sons shall lay their hands on the head of the bull, ¹¹and you shall slaughter the bull before the LORD, at the entrance of the tent of meeting, ¹²and shall take some of the blood of the bull and put it on the horns of the altar with your finger, and all the rest of the blood you shall pour out at the base of the altar. ¹³You shall take all the fat that covers the entrails, and the appendage of the liver, and the two kidneys with the fat that is on them, and turn them into smoke on the altar. ¹⁴But the flesh of the bull, and its

a Gk: Heb sashes, Aaron and his sons

Living to Make Intercession

EXODUS 28.29–40

Notice that Aaron, when approaching the holy place, is directed to "bear the names of the sons of Israel in the breastplate of judgement on his heart." With this passage in mind, notice how the New Testament letter to the Hebrews refers to the risen Christ entering the heavenly sanctuary: "He is able for all time to save those who approach God through him, since he always lives to make intercession for them" (Hebrews 7.25). Reflect on the implications of knowing that the risen Jesus enters the heavenly sanctuary bearing your name in his heart. In what ways do you find encouragement in your praying from knowing that Jesus intercedes for you?

See Meeting God in Prayer

Ritual Sacrifices: A Contemporary Reading

EXODUS 29.1–34

Trying to understand the religious rituals of ancient times can be a challenge to modern believers. While we no longer slaughter cattle and burn livestock in our houses of worship, the vividness of Old Testament animal sacrifice still reminds us of the seriousness with which God views wrongdoing; restoration of what is broken by sin is never a casual affair.

Now that Jesus has come, abolishing forever the need for animal sacrifices, reflect prayerfully on God's costly, forgiving grace. What areas do you need to bring to God for an assurance of forgiveness? If it helps, write them down. Lift them up to God, reminding yourself that his love overcomes what separates you from him.

See Meeting God in Scripture

skin, and its dung, you shall burn with fire outside the camp; it is a sin offering.

15 Then you shall take one of the rams, and Aaron and his sons shall lay their hands on the head of the ram, [16]and you shall slaughter the ram, and shall take its blood and dash it against all sides of the altar. [17]Then you shall cut the ram into its parts, and wash its entrails and its legs, and put them with its parts and its head, [18]and turn the whole ram into smoke on the altar; it is a burnt offering to the LORD; it is a pleasing odor, an offering by fire to the LORD.

19 You shall take the other ram; and Aaron and his sons shall lay their hands on the head of the ram, [20]and you shall slaughter the ram, and take some of its blood and put it on the lobe of Aaron's right ear and on the lobes of the right ears of his sons, and on the thumbs of their right hands, and on the big toes of their right feet, and dash the rest of the blood against all sides of the altar. [21]Then you shall take some of the blood that is on the altar, and some of the anointing oil, and sprinkle it on Aaron and his vestments and on his sons and his sons' vestments with him; then he and his vestments shall be holy, as well as his sons and his sons' vestments.

22 You shall also take the fat of the ram, the fat tail, the fat that covers the entrails, the appendage of the liver, the two kidneys with the fat that is on them, and the right thigh (for it is a ram of ordination), [23]and one loaf of bread, one cake of bread made with oil, and one wafer, out of the basket of unleavened bread that is before the LORD; [24]and you shall place all these on the palms of Aaron and on the palms of his sons, and raise them as an elevation offering before the LORD. [25]Then you shall take them from their hands, and turn them into smoke on the altar on top of the burnt offering of pleasing odor before the LORD; it is an offering by fire to the LORD.

26 You shall take the breast of the ram of Aaron's ordination and raise it as an elevation offering before the LORD; and it shall be your portion. [27]You shall consecrate the breast that was raised as an elevation offering and the thigh that was raised as an elevation offering from the ram of ordination, from that which belonged to Aaron and his sons. [28]These things shall be a perpetual ordinance for Aaron and his sons from the Israelites, for this is an offering; and it shall be an offering by the Israelites from their sacrifice of offerings of well-being, their offering to the LORD.

29 The sacred vestments of Aaron shall be passed on to his sons after him; they shall be anointed in them and ordained in them. [30]The son who is priest in his place shall wear them seven days, when he comes into the tent of meeting to minister in the holy place.

31 You shall take the ram of ordination, and boil its flesh in a holy place; [32]and Aaron and his sons shall eat the flesh of the ram and the bread that is in the basket, at the entrance of the tent of meeting. [33]They themselves shall eat the food by which atonement is made, to ordain and consecrate them, but no one else shall eat of them, because they are holy. [34]If any of the flesh for the ordination, or of the bread, remains until the morning, then you shall burn the remainder with fire; it shall not be eaten, because it is holy.

35 Thus you shall do to Aaron and to his sons, just as I have commanded you; through seven days you shall ordain them. ³⁶Also every day you shall offer a bull as a sin offering for atonement. Also you shall offer a sin offering for the altar, when you make atonement for it, and shall anoint it, to consecrate it. ³⁷Seven days you shall make atonement for the altar, and consecrate it, and the altar shall be most holy; whatever touches the altar shall become holy.

The Daily Offerings

38 Now this is what you shall offer on the altar: two lambs a year old regularly each day. ³⁹One lamb you shall offer in the morning, and the other lamb you shall offer in the evening; ⁴⁰and with the first lamb one-tenth of a measure of choice flour mixed with one-fourth of a hin of beaten oil, and one-fourth of a hin of wine for a drink offering. ⁴¹And the other lamb you shall offer in the evening, and shall offer with it a grain offering and its drink offering, as in the morning, for a pleasing odor, an offering by fire to the LORD. ⁴²It shall be a regular burnt offering throughout your generations at the entrance of the tent of meeting before the LORD, where I will meet with you, to speak to you there. ⁴³I will meet with the Israelites there, and it shall be sanctified by my glory; ⁴⁴I will consecrate the tent of meeting and the altar; Aaron also and his sons I will consecrate, to serve me as priests. ⁴⁵I will dwell among the Israelites, and I will be their God. ⁴⁶And they shall know that I am the LORD their God, who brought them out of the land of Egypt that I might dwell among them; I am the LORD their God.

The Altar of Incense

30 You shall make an altar on which to offer incense; you shall make it of acacia wood. ²It shall be one cubit long, and one cubit wide; it shall be square, and shall be two cubits high; its horns shall be of one piece with it. ³You shall overlay it with pure gold, its top, and its sides all around and its horns; and you shall make for it a molding of gold all around. ⁴And you shall make two golden rings for it; under its molding on two opposite sides of it you shall make them, and they shall hold the poles with which to carry it. ⁵You shall make the poles of acacia wood, and overlay them with gold. ⁶You shall place it in front of the curtain that is above the ark of the covenant,ᵃ in front of the mercy seatᵇ that is over the covenant,ᵃ where I will meet with you. ⁷Aaron shall offer fragrant incense on it; every morning when he dresses the lamps he shall offer it, ⁸and when Aaron sets up the lamps in the evening, he shall offer it, a regular incense offering before the LORD throughout your generations. ⁹You shall not offer unholy incense on it, or a burnt offering, or a grain offering; and you shall not pour a drink offering on it. ¹⁰Once a year Aaron shall perform the rite of atonement on its horns. Throughout your generations he shall perform the atonement for it once a year with the blood of the atoning sin offering. It is most holy to the LORD.

The Half Shekel for the Sanctuary

11 The LORD spoke to Moses: ¹²When you take a census of the Israelites to register them, at registration all of them

Ritual and Daily Life

EXODUS 29.29–46

What we do regularly has a way of seeping into our minds and influencing our daily behavior. Rituals such as those described in these verses, far from being irrelevant, can form a kind of backbone of religious life. Referring to the Tent of Meeting where offerings were made, God tells Moses, "I will meet with you, to speak to you there."

What role do rituals or spiritual habits play in your experience of faith and worship? Do they ever get in the way of your experience of God? Can you think of ways in which habitual practices enhance your worship? Pray about your participation in worship. How can it continue to keep your faith vital and growing?

See Meeting God in Worship

Precious Oils

EXODUS 30.22–38

Moses is commanded here to prepare oil for anointing with the rarest and most precious spices and perfumes. The oil is to be used only for sacred purposes in the sanctuary. What is marked with oil is thus declared holy and consecrated to God. Moses is to anoint not only Aaron and his sons, but practically everything!

Make a precious ointment yourself with mineral or baby oil and add your favorite fragrances to it. Today, or on some significant occasion, anoint your spouse, your children and your home. Use some appropriate words like, "You are set aside for God's work," or "You are sealed with this oil in the royal priesthood of Jesus Christ." Like another Moses you will be proclaiming their true worth in the Lord's eyes, and giving new sight to your own.

See Meeting God in Everyday Life

shall give a ransom for their lives to the LORD, so that no plague may come upon them for being registered. [13]This is what each one who is registered shall give: half a shekel according to the shekel of the sanctuary (the shekel is twenty gerahs), half a shekel as an offering to the LORD. [14]Each one who is registered, from twenty years old and upward, shall give the LORD's offering. [15]The rich shall not give more, and the poor shall not give less, than the half shekel, when you bring this offering to the LORD to make atonement for your lives. [16]You shall take the atonement money from the Israelites and shall designate it for the service of the tent of meeting; before the LORD it will be a reminder to the Israelites of the ransom given for your lives.

The Bronze Basin

17 The LORD spoke to Moses: [18]You shall make a bronze basin with a bronze stand for washing. You shall put it between the tent of meeting and the altar, and you shall put water in it; [19]with the water[a] Aaron and his sons shall wash their hands and their feet. [20]When they go into the tent of meeting, or when they come near the altar to minister, to make an offering by fire to the LORD, they shall wash with water, so that they may not die. [21]They shall wash their hands and their feet, so that they may not die: it shall be a perpetual ordinance for them, for him and for his descendants throughout their generations.

The Anointing Oil and Incense

22 The LORD spoke to Moses: [23]Take the finest spices: of liquid myrrh five hundred shekels, and of sweet-smelling cinnamon half as much, that is, two hundred fifty, and two hundred fifty of aromatic cane, [24]and five hundred of cassia—measured by the sanctuary shekel—and a hin of olive oil; [25]and you shall make of these a sacred anointing oil blended as by the perfumer; it shall be a holy anointing oil. [26]With it you shall anoint the tent of meeting and the ark of the covenant,[b] [27]and the table and all its utensils, and the lampstand and its utensils, and the altar of incense, [28]and the altar of burnt offering with all its utensils, and the basin with its stand; [29]you shall consecrate them, so that they may be most holy; whatever touches them will become holy. [30]You shall anoint Aaron and his sons, and consecrate them, in order that they may serve me as priests. [31]You shall say to the Israelites, "This shall be my holy anointing oil throughout your generations. [32]It shall not be used in any ordinary anointing of the body, and you shall make no other like it in composition; it is holy, and it shall be holy to you. [33]Whoever compounds any like it or whoever puts any of it on an unqualified person shall be cut off from the people."

34 The LORD said to Moses: Take sweet spices, stacte, and onycha, and galbanum, sweet spices with pure frankincense (an equal part of each), [35]and make an incense blended as by the perfumer, seasoned with salt, pure and holy; [36]and you shall beat some of it into powder, and put part of it before the covenant[b] in the tent of meeting where I shall meet with you; it shall be for you most holy. [37]When you make incense according to this composition, you shall not make it for yourselves; it shall be regarded by you as

a Heb *it*   *b* Or *treaty,* or *testimony;* Heb *eduth* holy to the LORD. ³⁸Whoever makes any like it to use as perfume shall be cut off from the people.

Bezalel and Oholiab

31 The LORD spoke to Moses: ²See, I have called by name Bezalel son of Uri son of Hur, of the tribe of Judah: ³and I have filled him with divine spirit,ᵃ with ability, intelligence, and knowledge in every kind of craft, ⁴to devise artistic designs, to work in gold, silver, and bronze, ⁵in cutting stones for setting, and in carving wood, in every kind of craft. ⁶Moreover, I have appointed with him Oholiab son of Ahisamach, of the tribe of Dan; and I have given skill to all the skillful, so that they may make all that I have commanded you: ⁷the tent of meeting, and the ark of the covenant,ᵇ and the mercy seatᶜ that is on it, and all the furnishings of the tent, ⁸the table and its utensils, and the pure lampstand with all its utensils, and the altar of incense, ⁹and the altar of burnt offering with all its utensils, and the basin with its stand, ¹⁰and the finely worked vestments, the holy vestments for the priest Aaron and the vestments of his sons, for their service as priests, ¹¹and the anointing oil and the fragrant incense for the holy place. They shall do just as I have commanded you.

The Sabbath Law

12 The LORD said to Moses: ¹³You yourself are to speak to the Israelites: "You shall keep my sabbaths, for this is a sign between me and you throughout your generations, given in order that you may know that I, the LORD, sanctify you. ¹⁴You shall keep the sabbath, because it is holy for you; everyone who profanes it shall be put to death; whoever does any work on it shall be cut off from among the people. ¹⁵Six days shall work be done, but the seventh day is a sabbath of solemn rest, holy to the LORD; whoever does any work on the sabbath day shall be put to death. ¹⁶Therefore the Israelites shall keep the sabbath, observing the sabbath throughout their generations, as a perpetual covenant. ¹⁷It is a sign forever between me and the people of Israel that in six days the LORD made heaven and earth, and on the seventh day he rested, and was refreshed."

The Two Tablets of the Covenant

18 When Godᵈ finished speaking with Moses on Mount Sinai, he gave him the two tablets of the covenant,ᵇ tablets of stone, written with the finger of God.

The Golden Calf

32 When the people saw that Moses delayed to come down from the mountain, the people gathered around Aaron, and said to him, "Come, make gods for us, who shall go before us; as for this Moses, the man who brought us up out of the land of Egypt, we do not know what has become of him." ²Aaron said to them, "Take off the gold rings that are on the ears of your wives, your sons, and your daughters, and bring them to me." ³So all the people took off the gold rings from their ears, and brought them to Aaron. ⁴He took the gold from them, formed it in

a Or *with the spirit of God*   b Or *treaty*, or *testimony*; Heb *eduth*   c Or *the cover*   d Heb *he*

A Time to Rest

EXODUS 31.12–17

After giving Moses a detailed list of things to be done, God follows with a very different command, a command to set aside a day for "doing nothing"—or so it seems. Resting on the sabbath, however, is not so much about what we do or don't do, but rather about taking time to remember who we are and to whom we belong. The key words in this passage are in verse 13: "In order that you may know that I, the LORD, sanctify you." Keeping a day of rest helps us recall our individual and community identities. It helps us stay moving in the right direction in daily life.

What plans can you make now to ensure that your next day of rest will be truly a day to remember and worship? If necessary, take out a calendar and write in the words: *Rest and worship!*

See Meeting God in Worship

The Golden Calf

EXODUS 32.1–10

It is easy for us to sit in judgment on the Israelites for their blatant infidelity to God, the One who had done so much for them. Worship so foolish a thing as a golden calf? We would never do a thing like that, but we do have a great respect for a thriving "bull" stock market! In a world increasingly divided between the "haves" and "have-nots," we need to supplement Bible reading with reflection on another book. The next time you want to pray, reach for your checkbook. Where does your money go? Ask God to lead and guide you as you order your financial commitments.

See Meeting God in Everyday Life

a mold,*a* and cast an image of a calf; and they said, "These are your gods, O Israel, who brought you up out of the land of Egypt!" ⁵When Aaron saw this, he built an altar before it; and Aaron made proclamation and said, "Tomorrow shall be a festival to the LORD." ⁶They rose early the next day, and offered burnt offerings and brought sacrifices of well-being; and the people sat down to eat and drink, and rose up to revel.

7 The LORD said to Moses, "Go down at once! Your people, whom you brought up out of the land of Egypt, have acted perversely; ⁸they have been quick to turn aside from the way that I commanded them; they have cast for themselves an image of a calf, and have worshiped it and sacrificed to it, and said, 'These are your gods, O Israel, who brought you up out of the land of Egypt!' " ⁹The LORD said to Moses, "I have seen this people, how stiff-necked they are. ¹⁰Now let me alone, so that my wrath may burn hot against them and I may consume them; and of you I will make a great nation."

11 But Moses implored the LORD his God, and said, "O LORD, why does your wrath burn hot against your people, whom you brought out of the land of Egypt with great power and with a mighty hand? ¹²Why should the Egyptians say, 'It was with evil intent that he brought them out to kill them in the mountains, and to consume them from the face of the earth'? Turn from your fierce wrath; change your mind and do not bring disaster on your people. ¹³Remember Abraham, Isaac, and Israel, your servants, how you swore to them by your own self, saying to them, 'I will multiply your descendants like the stars of heaven, and all this land that I have promised I will give to your descendants, and they shall inherit it forever.' " ¹⁴And the LORD changed his mind about the disaster that he planned to bring on his people.

15 Then Moses turned and went down from the mountain, carrying the two tablets of the covenant*b* in his hands, tablets that were written on both sides, written on the front and on the back. ¹⁶The tablets were the work of God, and the writing was the writing of God, engraved upon the tablets. ¹⁷When Joshua heard the noise of the people as they shouted, he said to Moses, "There is a noise of war in the camp." ¹⁸But he said,

"It is not the sound made by victors,
or the sound made by losers;
it is the sound of revelers that I hear."

¹⁹As soon as he came near the camp and saw the calf and the dancing, Moses' anger burned hot, and he threw the tablets from his hands and broke them at the foot of the mountain. ²⁰He took the calf that they had made, burned it with fire, ground it to powder, scattered it on the water, and made the Israelites drink it.

21 Moses said to Aaron, "What did this people do to you that you have brought so great a sin upon them?" ²²And Aaron said, "Do not let the anger of my lord burn hot; you know the people, that they are bent on evil. ²³They said to me, 'Make us gods, who shall go before us; as for this Moses, the man who brought us up out of the land of Egypt, we do not know what has become of him.' ²⁴So I

a Or *fashioned it with a graving tool*; Meaning of Heb uncertain
b Or *treaty*, or *testimony*; Heb *eduth*

said to them, 'Whoever has gold, take it off'; so they gave it to me, and I threw it into the fire, and out came this calf!"

25 When Moses saw that the people were running wild (for Aaron had let them run wild, to the derision of their enemies), [26]then Moses stood in the gate of the camp, and said, "Who is on the Lord's side? Come to me!" And all the sons of Levi gathered around him. [27]He said to them, "Thus says the Lord, the God of Israel, 'Put your sword on your side, each of you! Go back and forth from gate to gate throughout the camp, and each of you kill your brother, your friend, and your neighbor.' " [28]The sons of Levi did as Moses commanded, and about three thousand of the people fell on that day. [29]Moses said, "Today you have ordained yourselves[a] for the service of the Lord, each one at the cost of a son or a brother, and so have brought a blessing on yourselves this day."

30 On the next day Moses said to the people, "You have sinned a great sin. But now I will go up to the Lord; perhaps I can make atonement for your sin." [31]So Moses returned to the Lord and said, "Alas, this people has sinned a great sin; they have made for themselves gods of gold. [32]But now, if you will only forgive their sin—but if not, blot me out of the book that you have written." [33]But the Lord said to Moses, "Whoever has sinned against me I will blot out of my book. [34]But now go, lead the people to the place about which I have spoken to you; see, my angel shall go in front of you. Nevertheless, when the day comes for punishment, I will punish them for their sin."

35 Then the Lord sent a plague on the people, because they made the calf—the one that Aaron made.

The Command to Leave Sinai

33 The Lord said to Moses, "Go, leave this place, you and the people whom you have brought up out of the land of Egypt, and go to the land of which I swore to Abraham, Isaac, and Jacob, saying, 'To your descendants I will give it.' [2]I will send an angel before you, and I will drive out the Canaanites, the Amorites, the Hittites, the Perizzites, the Hivites, and the Jebusites. [3]Go up to a land flowing with milk and honey; but I will not go up among you, or I would consume you on the way, for you are a stiff-necked people."

4 When the people heard these harsh words, they mourned, and no one put on ornaments. [5]For the Lord had said to Moses, "Say to the Israelites, 'You are a stiff-necked people; if for a single moment I should go up among you, I would consume you. So now take off your ornaments, and I will decide what to do to you.' " [6]Therefore the Israelites stripped themselves of their ornaments, from Mount Horeb onward.

The Tent outside the Camp

7 Now Moses used to take the tent and pitch it outside the camp, far off from the camp; he called it the tent of meeting. And everyone who sought the Lord would go out to the tent of meeting, which was outside the camp. [8]Whenever Moses went out to the tent, all the people would rise and stand, each of them, at the entrance of their tents and watch Moses until he had gone into the tent. [9]When

From Administration to Contemplation

EXODUS 33.1–11

While we have been given glimpses in preceding chapters of Moses' privileged access to conversations with God, for the greater part we've seen Moses in his role as leader or administrator. Here we tiptoe, as it were, into the most private chamber of his dwelling, the place where we discover that the Lord speaks to Moses "face to face, as one speaks to a friend." This story contains one of the most sublime passages in all the inspired scriptures—a passage that invites attentive reading and deep reflection. It bids us to enter quietly into the scene, bringing with us our own hunger for intimate communion with God.

See Meeting God in Prayer

---

a Gk Vg Compare Tg: Heb *Today ordain yourselves*

"While My Glory Passes By . . ."

EXODUS 33.18–23

"Moses, who eagerly seeks to behold God, is now taught how he can behold him: to follow God wherever he might lead is to behold God. His passing by signifies his guiding the one who follows, for someone who does not know the way cannot complete his journey safely in any other way than by following behind his guide. He who leads, then, by guidance shows the way to the one following. He who follows will not turn aside from the right way if he always keeps the back of his leader in view."

—GREGORY OF NYSSA,
The Life of Moses

Moses entered the tent, the pillar of cloud would descend and stand at the entrance of the tent, and the LORD would speak with Moses. ¹⁰When all the people saw the pillar of cloud standing at the entrance of the tent, all the people would rise and bow down, all of them, at the entrance of their tent. ¹¹Thus the LORD used to speak to Moses face to face, as one speaks to a friend. Then he would return to the camp; but his young assistant, Joshua son of Nun, would not leave the tent.

Moses' Intercession

12 Moses said to the LORD, "See, you have said to me, 'Bring up this people'; but you have not let me know whom you will send with me. Yet you have said, 'I know you by name, and you have also found favor in my sight.' ¹³Now if I have found favor in your sight, show me your ways, so that I may know you and find favor in your sight. Consider too that this nation is your people." ¹⁴He said, "My presence will go with you, and I will give you rest." ¹⁵And he said to him, "If your presence will not go, do not carry us up from here. ¹⁶For how shall it be known that I have found favor in your sight, I and your people, unless you go with us? In this way, we shall be distinct, I and your people, from every people on the face of the earth."

17 The LORD said to Moses, "I will do the very thing that you have asked; for you have found favor in my sight, and I know you by name." ¹⁸Moses said, "Show me your glory, I pray." ¹⁹And he said, "I will make all my goodness pass before you, and will proclaim before you the name, 'The LORD';ᵃ and I will be gracious to whom I will be gracious, and will show mercy on whom I will show mercy. ²⁰But," he said, "you cannot see my face; for no one shall see me and live." ²¹And the LORD continued, "See, there is a place by me where you shall stand on the rock; ²²and while my glory passes by I will put you in a cleft of the rock, and I will cover you with my hand until I have passed by; ²³then I will take away my hand, and you shall see my back; but my face shall not be seen."

Moses Makes New Tablets

34 The LORD said to Moses, "Cut two tablets of stone like the former ones, and I will write on the tablets the words that were on the former tablets, which you broke. ²Be ready in the morning, and come up in the morning to Mount Sinai and present yourself there to me, on the top of the mountain. ³No one shall come up with you, and do not let anyone be seen throughout all the mountain; and do not let flocks or herds graze in front of that mountain." ⁴So Moses cut two tablets of stone like the former ones; and he rose early in the morning and went up on Mount Sinai, as the LORD had commanded him, and took in his hand the two tablets of stone. ⁵The LORD descended in the cloud and stood with him there, and proclaimed the name, "The LORD."ᵃ ⁶The LORD passed before him, and proclaimed,

"The LORD, the LORD,
a God merciful and gracious,
slow to anger,
and abounding in steadfast love and faithfulness,

a Heb *YHWH;* see note at 3.15

7   keeping steadfast love for the thousandth
      generation,[a]
  forgiving iniquity and transgression and sin,
  yet by no means clearing the guilty,
  but visiting the iniquity of the parents
  upon the children
  and the children's children,
  to the third and the fourth generation."

8 And Moses quickly bowed his head toward the earth, and worshiped. **9** He said, "If now I have found favor in your sight, O Lord, I pray, let the Lord go with us. Although this is a stiff-necked people, pardon our iniquity and our sin, and take us for your inheritance."

The Covenant Renewed

10 He said: I hereby make a covenant. Before all your people I will perform marvels, such as have not been performed in all the earth or in any nation; and all the people among whom you live shall see the work of the LORD; for it is an awesome thing that I will do with you.

11 Observe what I command you today. See, I will drive out before you the Amorites, the Canaanites, the Hittites, the Perizzites, the Hivites, and the Jebusites. **12** Take care not to make a covenant with the inhabitants of the land to which you are going, or it will become a snare among you. **13** You shall tear down their altars, break their pillars, and cut down their sacred poles[b] **14** (for you shall worship no other god, because the LORD, whose name is Jealous, is a jealous God). **15** You shall not make a covenant with the inhabitants of the land, for when they prostitute themselves to their gods and sacrifice to their gods, someone among them will invite you, and you will eat of the sacrifice. **16** And you will take wives from among their daughters for your sons, and their daughters who prostitute themselves to their gods will make your sons also prostitute themselves to their gods.

17 You shall not make cast idols.

18 You shall keep the festival of unleavened bread. Seven days you shall eat unleavened bread, as I commanded you, at the time appointed in the month of Abib; for in the month of Abib you came out from Egypt.

19 All that first opens the womb is mine, all your male[c] livestock, the firstborn of cow and sheep. **20** The firstborn of a donkey you shall redeem with a lamb, or if you will not redeem it you shall break its neck. All the firstborn of your sons you shall redeem.

No one shall appear before me empty-handed.

21 Six days you shall work, but on the seventh day you shall rest; even in plowing time and in harvest time you shall rest. **22** You shall observe the festival of weeks, the first fruits of wheat harvest, and the festival of ingathering at the turn of the year. **23** Three times in the year all your males shall appear before the LORD God, the God of Israel. **24** For I will cast out nations before you, and enlarge your borders; no one shall covet your land when you go up to appear before the LORD your God three times in the year.

25 You shall not offer the blood of my sacrifice with

The Compassionate and Gracious God

EXODUS 34.4–14

Through this passage we have the privilege of going with Moses to Mount Sinai. Begin by thinking about the laborious work of chiseling two stone tablets, a task that could take days. Imagine that you are carrying them up the mist-shrouded mountain—the exertion robbing you of breath. Now you are at the pinnacle, gripped by a sense of expectancy and uncertainty. Suddenly—dramatically—God appears in front of you and declares himself, "The LORD, the LORD, a God merciful and gracious, slow to anger, and abounding in steadfast love and faithfulness, keeping steadfast love for the thousandth generation, forgiving iniquity and transgression and sin."

Be still before God for a while. Let God's words sink into your soul. What is your response? How is it like or unlike Moses' response? What is God saying to you personally in this passage?

See Meeting God in Scripture

---

a Or *for thousands*   b Heb *Asherim*   c Gk Theodotion Vg Tg: Meaning of Heb uncertain

The Face of Moses

EXODUS 34.27–35

Inevitably our faces mirror our inner disposition to others. Moses was so intensely present with God, and God with Moses, that God's presence radiated from his face.

Sometimes a face turned resolutely and lovingly to God will finally be the most powerful word we can utter. Think about your own facial expressions and demeanor. Do they reflect the indwelling presence of God? In your preparation for ministry and service, what role does spending time in God's presence play? How does it show? Reflect on these words of an old theology professor who enjoyed saying to his students: "By the time you reach the age of forty, you are responsible for your face."

See *Meeting God in Worship*

leaven, and the sacrifice of the festival of the passover shall not be left until the morning.

26 The best of the first fruits of your ground you shall bring to the house of the LORD your God.

You shall not boil a kid in its mother's milk.

27 The LORD said to Moses: Write these words; in accordance with these words I have made a covenant with you and with Israel. [28] He was there with the LORD forty days and forty nights; he neither ate bread nor drank water. And he wrote on the tablets the words of the covenant, the ten commandments. [a]

The Shining Face of Moses

29 Moses came down from Mount Sinai. As he came down from the mountain with the two tablets of the covenant[b] in his hand, Moses did not know that the skin of his face shone because he had been talking with God. [30] When Aaron and all the Israelites saw Moses, the skin of his face was shining, and they were afraid to come near him. [31] But Moses called to them; and Aaron and all the leaders of the congregation returned to him, and Moses spoke with them. [32] Afterward all the Israelites came near, and he gave them in commandment all that the LORD had spoken with him on Mount Sinai. [33] When Moses had finished speaking with them, he put a veil on his face; [34] but whenever Moses went in before the LORD to speak with him, he would take the veil off, until he came out; and when he came out, and told the Israelites what he had been commanded, [35] the Israelites would see the face of Moses, that the skin of his face was shining; and Moses would put the veil on his face again, until he went in to speak with him.

Sabbath Regulations

35 Moses assembled all the congregation of the Israelites and said to them: These are the things that the LORD has commanded you to do:

2 Six days shall work be done, but on the seventh day you shall have a holy sabbath of solemn rest to the LORD; whoever does any work on it shall be put to death. [3] You shall kindle no fire in all your dwellings on the sabbath day.

Preparations for Making the Tabernacle

4 Moses said to all the congregation of the Israelites: This is the thing that the LORD has commanded: [5] Take from among you an offering to the LORD; let whoever is of a generous heart bring the LORD's offering: gold, silver, and bronze; [6] blue, purple, and crimson yarns, and fine linen; goats' hair, [7] tanned rams' skins, and fine leather;[c] acacia wood, [8] oil for the light, spices for the anointing oil and for the fragrant incense, [9] and onyx stones and gems to be set in the ephod and the breastpiece.

10 All who are skillful among you shall come and make all that the LORD has commanded: the tabernacle, [11] its tent and its covering, its clasps and its frames, its bars, its pillars, and its bases; [12] the ark with its poles, the mercy seat,[d] and the curtain for the screen; [13] the table with its poles and all its utensils, and the bread of the Presence; [14] the lampstand also for the light, with its utensils and its lamps, and

a Heb *words*   *b* Or *treaty*, or *testimony*; Heb *eduth*   *c* Meaning of Heb uncertain   *d* Or *the cover*

the oil for the light; [15]and the altar of incense, with its poles, and the anointing oil and the fragrant incense, and the screen for the entrance, the entrance of the tabernacle; [16]the altar of burnt offering, with its grating of bronze, its poles, and all its utensils, the basin with its stand; [17]the hangings of the court, its pillars and its bases, and the screen for the gate of the court; [18]the pegs of the tabernacle and the pegs of the court, and their cords; [19]the finely worked vestments for ministering in the holy place, the holy vestments for the priest Aaron, and the vestments of his sons, for their service as priests.

Offerings for the Tabernacle

20 Then all the congregation of the Israelites withdrew from the presence of Moses. [21]And they came, everyone whose heart was stirred, and everyone whose spirit was willing, and brought the LORD's offering to be used for the tent of meeting, and for all its service, and for the sacred vestments. [22]So they came, both men and women; all who were of a willing heart brought brooches and earrings and signet rings and pendants, all sorts of gold objects, everyone bringing an offering of gold to the LORD. [23]And everyone who possessed blue or purple or crimson yarn or fine linen or goats' hair or tanned rams' skins or fine leather,[a] brought them. [24]Everyone who could make an offering of silver or bronze brought it as the LORD's offering; and everyone who possessed acacia wood of any use in the work, brought it. [25]All the skillful women spun with their hands, and brought what they had spun in blue and purple and crimson yarns and fine linen; [26]all the women whose hearts moved them to use their skill spun the goats' hair. [27]And the leaders brought onyx stones and gems to be set in the ephod and the breastpiece, [28]and spices and oil for the light, and for the anointing oil, and for the fragrant incense. [29]All the Israelite men and women whose hearts made them willing to bring anything for the work that the LORD had commanded by Moses to be done, brought it as a freewill offering to the LORD.

Bezalel and Oholiab

30 Then Moses said to the Israelites: See, the LORD has called by name Bezalel son of Uri son of Hur, of the tribe of Judah; [31]he has filled him with divine spirit,[b] with skill, intelligence, and knowledge in every kind of craft, [32]to devise artistic designs, to work in gold, silver, and bronze, [33]in cutting stones for setting, and in carving wood, in every kind of craft. [34]And he has inspired him to teach, both him and Oholiab son of Ahisamach, of the tribe of Dan. [35]He has filled them with skill to do every kind of work done by an artisan or by a designer or by an embroiderer in blue, purple, and crimson yarns, and in fine linen, or by a weaver—by any sort of artisan or skilled designer.

36 Bezalel and Oholiab and every skillful one to whom the LORD has given skill and understanding to know how to do any work in the construction of the sanctuary shall work in accordance with all that the LORD has commanded.

2 Moses then called Bezalel and Oholiab and every skillful one to whom the LORD had given skill, everyone whose

The Spirituality of Art

EXODUS 35.30

Bezalel could be a kind of patron saint to artists and other creative types. His name figures prominently, and his craftsmanship is celebrated, in the following verses. While due credit is given to his coworker Oholiab, Moses obviously gives his highest praise to Bezalel. Bezalel challenges our cultural tendency to separate the secular from the sacred in the artistic realm. He is obviously gifted in arts and crafts; his example teaches us that we can pray not only with folded hands, but with busy hands. Hands that carve wood or sweep a paintbrush or cut stone give glory to God also. What worthwhile things do you do with your hands? Ask God to use your creative talents to bring good to others and honor to him.

See *Meeting God in Everyday Life*

Curtains, Rings, Pegs and Frames

EXODUS 36.10–19

It is hard to read passages like this that give meticulous attention to detail and not wonder why. Why so much attention to the minute details of the furnishings of the tabernacle? Attention to detail, however, can be an indication of excitement and enthusiasm. Listen to new homeowners talk about the house they have just had built! No detail is spared!

The next time you attend worship or join in a small-group Bible study, pay careful attention to details: the chair you sit in, the walls and windows that surround you, any objects with liturgical or spiritual significance. Especially pay attention to those things that remind you of the presence of God in your midst. Ask God to open your eyes and allow the experience to become an expedition of visual discovery.

See Meeting God in Everyday Life

heart was stirred to come to do the work; ³and they received from Moses all the freewill offerings that the Israelites had brought for doing the work on the sanctuary. They still kept bringing him freewill offerings every morning, ⁴so that all the artisans who were doing every sort of task on the sanctuary came, each from the task being performed, ⁵and said to Moses, "The people are bringing much more than enough for doing the work that the Lᴏʀᴅ has commanded us to do." ⁶So Moses gave command, and word was proclaimed throughout the camp: "No man or woman is to make anything else as an offering for the sanctuary." So the people were restrained from bringing; ⁷for what they had already brought was more than enough to do all the work.

Construction of the Tabernacle

8 All those with skill among the workers made the tabernacle with ten curtains; they were made of fine twisted linen, and blue, purple, and crimson yarns, with cherubim skillfully worked into them. ⁹The length of each curtain was twenty-eight cubits, and the width of each curtain four cubits; all the curtains were of the same size.

10 He joined five curtains to one another, and the other five curtains he joined to one another. ¹¹He made loops of blue on the edge of the outermost curtain of the first set; likewise he made them on the edge of the outermost curtain of the second set; ¹²he made fifty loops on the one curtain, and he made fifty loops on the edge of the curtain that was in the second set; the loops were opposite one another. ¹³And he made fifty clasps of gold, and joined the curtains one to the other with clasps; so the tabernacle was one whole.

14 He also made curtains of goats' hair for a tent over the tabernacle; he made eleven curtains. ¹⁵The length of each curtain was thirty cubits, and the width of each curtain four cubits; the eleven curtains were of the same size. ¹⁶He joined five curtains by themselves, and six curtains by themselves. ¹⁷He made fifty loops on the edge of the outermost curtain of the one set, and fifty loops on the edge of the other connecting curtain. ¹⁸He made fifty clasps of bronze to join the tent together so that it might be one whole. ¹⁹And he made for the tent a covering of tanned rams' skins and an outer covering of fine leather.ᵃ

20 Then he made the upright frames for the tabernacle of acacia wood. ²¹Ten cubits was the length of a frame, and a cubit and a half the width of each frame. ²²Each frame had two pegs for fitting together; he did this for all the frames of the tabernacle. ²³The frames for the tabernacle he made in this way: twenty frames for the south side; ²⁴and he made forty bases of silver under the twenty frames, two bases under the first frame for its two pegs, and two bases under the next frame for its two pegs. ²⁵For the second side of the tabernacle, on the north side, he made twenty frames ²⁶and their forty bases of silver, two bases under the first frame and two bases under the next frame. ²⁷For the rear of the tabernacle westward he made six frames. ²⁸He made two frames for corners of the tabernacle in the rear. ²⁹They were separate beneath, but joined at the top, at the first ring; he made two of them in this

a Meaning of Heb uncertain

way, for the two corners. **30**There were eight frames with their bases of silver: sixteen bases, under every frame two bases.

31 He made bars of acacia wood, five for the frames of the one side of the tabernacle, **32**and five bars for the frames of the other side of the tabernacle, and five bars for the frames of the tabernacle at the rear westward. **33**He made the middle bar to pass through from end to end halfway up the frames. **34**And he overlaid the frames with gold, and made rings of gold for them to hold the bars, and overlaid the bars with gold.

35 He made the curtain of blue, purple, and crimson yarns, and fine twisted linen, with cherubim skillfully worked into it. **36**For it he made four pillars of acacia, and overlaid them with gold; their hooks were of gold, and he cast for them four bases of silver. **37**He also made a screen for the entrance to the tent, of blue, purple, and crimson yarns, and fine twisted linen, embroidered with needle-work; **38**and its five pillars with their hooks. He overlaid their capitals and their bases with gold, but their five bases were of bronze.

Making the Ark of the Covenant

37 Bezalel made the ark of acacia wood; it was two and a half cubits long, a cubit and a half wide, and a cubit and a half high. **2**He overlaid it with pure gold inside and outside, and made a molding of gold around it. **3**He cast for it four rings of gold for its four feet, two rings on its one side and two rings on its other side. **4**He made poles of acacia wood, and overlaid them with gold, **5**and put the poles into the rings on the sides of the ark, to carry the ark. **6**He made a mercy seat*a* of pure gold; two cubits and a half was its length, and a cubit and a half its width. **7**He made two cherubim of hammered gold; at the two ends of the mercy seat*b* he made them, **8**one cherub at the one end, and one cherub at the other end; of one piece with the mercy seat*b* he made the cherubim at its two ends. **9**The cherubim spread out their wings above, overshadowing the mercy seat*b* with their wings. They faced one another; the faces of the cherubim were turned toward the mercy seat.*b*

Making the Table for the Bread of the Presence

10 He also made the table of acacia wood, two cubits long, one cubit wide, and a cubit and a half high. **11**He over-laid it with pure gold, and made a molding of gold around it. **12**He made around it a rim a handbreadth wide, and made a molding of gold around the rim. **13**He cast for it four rings of gold, and fastened the rings to the four corners at its four legs. **14**The rings that held the poles used for car-rying the table were close to the rim. **15**He made the poles of acacia wood to carry the table, and overlaid them with gold. **16**And he made the vessels of pure gold that were to be on the table, its plates and dishes for incense, and its bowls and flagons with which to pour drink offerings.

Making the Lampstand

17 He also made the lampstand of pure gold. The base and the shaft of the lampstand were made of hammered work; its cups, its calyxes, and its petals were of one piece

The Angels on the Ark

EXODUS 37.6–9

The cherubim mentioned in these verses are heavenly be-ings often depicted in scripture in mysterious fashion. Descrip-tions of cherubim are always tantalizingly brief, just as is the spare, simple picture painted here. We could wish for more details, for a peek into vast heavenly realities, but here we content ourselves with knowing that the gold representations of cherubim are to remind the people of the holiness and sanctity of the ark and its con-tents.

What do you think it means that the cherubim are shown with wings spread upward? In what ways might angels have served as a reminder to the people of a God of glory and grace? Find a picture of an angel—or sketch your own. How can pondering God's heavenly realm invest your thoughts and actions with greater reverence?

See Meeting God in Scripture

Preparing for Worship

EXODUS 37.25—38.17

"Why, then, do I not long more ardently for your adorable presence? Why do I not prepare myself with greater care to receive your sacred gifts, since those holy patriarchs and prophets of old, as well as kings and princes with all their people, have shown such affectionate devotion for the worship of God?"

—THOMAS À KEMPIS,
The Imitation of Christ

See *Meeting God in Worship*

with it. [18]There were six branches going out of its sides, three branches of the lampstand out of one side of it and three branches of the lampstand out of the other side of it; [19]three cups shaped like almond blossoms, each with calyx and petals, on one branch, and three cups shaped like almond blossoms, each with calyx and petals, on the other branch—so for the six branches going out of the lampstand. [20]On the lampstand itself there were four cups shaped like almond blossoms, each with its calyxes and petals. [21]There was a calyx of one piece with it under the first pair of branches, a calyx of one piece with it under the next pair of branches, and a calyx of one piece with it under the last pair of branches. [22]Their calyxes and their branches were of one piece with it, the whole of it one hammered piece of pure gold. [23]He made its seven lamps and its snuffers and its trays of pure gold. [24]He made it and all its utensils of a talent of pure gold.

Making the Altar of Incense

25 He made the altar of incense of acacia wood, one cubit long, and one cubit wide; it was square, and was two cubits high; its horns were of one piece with it. [26]He overlaid it with pure gold, its top, and its sides all around, and its horns; and he made for it a molding of gold all around, [27]and made two golden rings for it under its molding, on two opposite sides of it, to hold the poles with which to carry it. [28]And he made the poles of acacia wood, and overlaid them with gold.

Making the Anointing Oil and the Incense

29 He made the holy anointing oil also, and the pure fragrant incense, blended as by the perfumer.

Making the Altar of Burnt Offering

38 He made the altar of burnt offering also of acacia wood; it was five cubits long, and five cubits wide; it was square, and three cubits high. [2]He made horns for it on its four corners; its horns were of one piece with it, and he overlaid it with bronze. [3]He made all the utensils of the altar, the pots, the shovels, the basins, the forks, and the firepans: all its utensils he made of bronze. [4]He made for the altar a grating, a network of bronze, under its ledge, extending halfway down. [5]He cast four rings on the four corners of the bronze grating to hold the poles; [6]he made the poles of acacia wood, and overlaid them with bronze. [7]And he put the poles through the rings on the sides of the altar, to carry it with them; he made it hollow, with boards.

8 He made the basin of bronze with its stand of bronze, from the mirrors of the women who served at the entrance to the tent of meeting.

Making the Court of the Tabernacle

9 He made the court; for the south side the hangings of the court were of fine twisted linen, one hundred cubits long; [10]its twenty pillars and their twenty bases were of bronze, but the hooks of the pillars and their bands were of silver. [11]For the north side there were hangings one hundred cubits long; its twenty pillars and their twenty bases were of bronze, but the hooks of the pillars and their bands were of silver. [12]For the west side there were hangings fifty

cubits long, with ten pillars and ten bases; the hooks of the pillars and their bands were of silver. [13]And for the front to the east, fifty cubits. [14]The hangings for one side of the gate were fifteen cubits, with three pillars and three bases. [15]And so for the other side; on each side of the gate of the court were hangings of fifteen cubits, with three pillars and three bases. [16]All the hangings around the court were of fine twisted linen. [17]The bases for the pillars were of bronze, but the hooks of the pillars and their bands were of silver; the overlaying of their capitals was also of silver, and all the pillars of the court were banded with silver. [18]The screen for the entrance to the court was embroidered with needlework in blue, purple, and crimson yarns and fine twisted linen. It was twenty cubits long and, along the width of it, five cubits high, corresponding to the hangings of the court. [19]There were four pillars; their four bases were of bronze, their hooks of silver, and the overlaying of their capitals and their bands of silver. [20]All the pegs for the tabernacle and for the court all around were of bronze.

Materials of the Tabernacle

21 These are the records of the tabernacle, the tabernacle of the covenant,[a] which were drawn up at the commandment of Moses, the work of the Levites being under the direction of Ithamar son of the priest Aaron. [22]Bezalel son of Uri son of Hur, of the tribe of Judah, made all that the LORD commanded Moses; [23]and with him was Oholiab son of Ahisamach, of the tribe of Dan, engraver, designer, and embroiderer in blue, purple, and crimson yarns, and in fine linen.

24 All the gold that was used for the work, in all the construction of the sanctuary, the gold from the offering, was twenty-nine talents and seven hundred thirty shekels, measured by the sanctuary shekel. [25]The silver from those of the congregation who were counted was one hundred talents and one thousand seven hundred seventy-five shekels, measured by the sanctuary shekel; [26]a beka a head (that is, half a shekel, measured by the sanctuary shekel), for everyone who was counted in the census, from twenty years old and upward, for six hundred three thousand, five hundred fifty men. [27]The hundred talents of silver were for casting the bases of the sanctuary, and the bases of the curtain; one hundred bases for the hundred talents, a talent for a base. [28]Of the thousand seven hundred seventy-five shekels he made hooks for the pillars, and overlaid their capitals and made bands for them. [29]The bronze that was contributed was seventy talents, and two thousand four hundred shekels; [30]with it he made the bases for the entrance of the tent of meeting, the bronze altar and the bronze grating for it and all the utensils of the altar, [31]the bases all around the court, and the bases of the gate of the court, all the pegs of the tabernacle, and all the pegs around the court.

Making the Vestments for the Priesthood

39 Of the blue, purple, and crimson yarns they made finely worked vestments, for ministering in the holy place; they made the sacred vestments for Aaron; as the LORD had commanded Moses.

a Or *treaty*, or *testimony*; Heb *eduth*

Unstinting Preparation

EXODUS 38.18–39.4

These verses reveal the great care and expense the people of Israel invested in the worship of God. There was to be no scrimping! Even the curtain for the entrance to the temple courtyard used the best: blue, purple and crimson yarn and finely twisted linen.

In what ways can you make your worship this coming Sabbath a matter of careful preparation and unstinting self-offering? Begin, even now, to prepare to meet and worship God. Make yourself a small card or note with the word *worship* on it to carry around with you. Pull it out occasionally or post it in a prominent place so it can remind you to get ready for heartfelt participation in your Lord's Day celebration.

See Meeting God in Worship

The Work of a Skilled Craftsman

EXODUS 39.2–7

The priestly garments were carefully and elaborately constructed to signify to the people that worshiping God was an awesome privilege and not to be undertaken carelessly or casually—God is honored by the work of a skilled craftsman.

Think about your talents and gifts. What can you offer God in worship today? Might it be a song played or sung with all your heart? A few moments of your undivided attention spent in prayer? A poem that expresses your gratitude to God or a sketch that shows your appreciation for God's creation? Whatever you offer to God in worship, offer your best.

See Meeting God in Worship

2 He made the ephod of gold, of blue, purple, and crimson yarns, and of fine twisted linen. ³Gold leaf was hammered out and cut into threads to work into the blue, purple, and crimson yarns and into the fine twisted linen, in skilled design. ⁴They made for the ephod shoulder-pieces, joined to it at its two edges. ⁵The decorated band on it was of the same materials and workmanship, of gold, of blue, purple, and crimson yarns, and of fine twisted linen; as the LORD had commanded Moses.

6 The onyx stones were prepared, enclosed in settings of gold filigree and engraved like the engravings of a signet, according to the names of the sons of Israel. ⁷He set them on the shoulder-pieces of the ephod, to be stones of remembrance for the sons of Israel; as the LORD had commanded Moses.

8 He made the breastpiece, in skilled work, like the work of the ephod, of gold, of blue, purple, and crimson yarns, and of fine twisted linen. ⁹It was square; the breastpiece was made double, a span in length and a span in width when doubled. ¹⁰They set in it four rows of stones. A row of carnelian,ᵃ chrysolite, and emerald was the first row; ¹¹and the second row, a turquoise, a sapphire,ᵇ and a moonstone; ¹²and the third row, a jacinth, an agate, and an amethyst; ¹³and the fourth row, a beryl, an onyx, and a jasper; they were enclosed in settings of gold filigree. ¹⁴There were twelve stones with names corresponding to the names of the sons of Israel; they were like signets, each engraved with its name, for the twelve tribes. ¹⁵They made on the breastpiece chains of pure gold, twisted like cords; ¹⁶and they made two settings of gold filigree and two gold rings, and put the two rings on the two edges of the breastpiece; ¹⁷and they put the two cords of gold in the two rings at the edges of the breastpiece. ¹⁸Two ends of the two cords they had attached to the two settings of filigree; in this way they attached it in front to the shoulder-pieces of the ephod. ¹⁹Then they made two rings of gold, and put them at the two ends of the breastpiece, on its inside edge next to the ephod. ²⁰They made two rings of gold, and attached them in front to the lower part of the two shoulder-pieces of the ephod, at its joining above the decorated band of the ephod. ²¹They bound the breastpiece by its rings to the rings of the ephod with a blue cord, so that it should lie on the decorated band of the ephod, and that the breastpiece should not come loose from the ephod; as the LORD had commanded Moses.

22 He also made the robe of the ephod woven all of blue yarn; ²³and the opening of the robe in the middle of it was like the opening in a coat of mail,ᶜ with a binding around the opening, so that it might not be torn. ²⁴On the lower hem of the robe they made pomegranates of blue, purple, and crimson yarns, and of fine twisted linen. ²⁵They also made bells of pure gold, and put the bells between the pomegranates on the lower hem of the robe all around, between the pomegranates; ²⁶a bell and a pomegranate, a bell and a pomegranate all around on the lower hem of the robe for ministering; as the LORD had commanded Moses.

27 They also made the tunics, woven of fine linen, for Aaron and his sons, ²⁸and the turban of fine linen, and the

ᵃ The identification of several of these stones is uncertain   ᵇ Or *lapis lazuli*   ᶜ Meaning of Heb uncertain

headdresses of fine linen, and the linen undergarments of fine twisted linen, ²⁹and the sash of fine twisted linen, and of blue, purple, and crimson yarns, embroidered with needlework; as the LORD had commanded Moses.

30 They made the rosette of the holy diadem of pure gold, and wrote on it an inscription, like the engraving of a signet, "Holy to the LORD." ³¹They tied to it a blue cord, to fasten it on the turban above; as the LORD had commanded Moses.

The Work Completed

32 In this way all the work of the tabernacle of the tent of meeting was finished; the Israelites had done everything just as the LORD had commanded Moses. ³³Then they brought the tabernacle to Moses, the tent and all its utensils, its hooks, its frames, its bars, its pillars, and its bases; ³⁴the covering of tanned rams' skins and the covering of fine leather,ᵃ and the curtain for the screen; ³⁵the ark of the covenantᵇ with its poles and the mercy seat;ᶜ ³⁶the table with all its utensils, and the bread of the Presence; ³⁷the pure lampstand with its lamps set on it and all its utensils, and the oil for the light; ³⁸the golden altar, the anointing oil and the fragrant incense, and the screen for the entrance of the tent; ³⁹the bronze altar, and its grating of bronze, its poles, and all its utensils; the basin with its stand; ⁴⁰the hangings of the court, its pillars, and its bases, and the screen for the gate of the court, its cords, and its pegs; and all the utensils for the service of the tabernacle, for the tent of meeting; ⁴¹the finely worked vestments for ministering in the holy place, the sacred vestments for the priest Aaron, and the vestments of his sons to serve as priests. ⁴²The Israelites had done all of the work just as the LORD had commanded Moses. ⁴³When Moses saw that they had done all the work just as the LORD had commanded, he blessed them.

The Tabernacle Erected and Its Equipment Installed

40 The LORD spoke to Moses: ²On the first day of the first month you shall set up the tabernacle of the tent of meeting. ³You shall put in it the ark of the covenant,ᵇ and you shall screen the ark with the curtain. ⁴You shall bring in the table, and arrange its setting; and you shall bring in the lampstand, and set up its lamps. ⁵You shall put the golden altar for incense before the ark of the covenant,ᵇ and set up the screen for the entrance of the tabernacle. ⁶You shall set the altar of burnt offering before the entrance of the tabernacle of the tent of meeting, ⁷and place the basin between the tent of meeting and the altar, and put water in it. ⁸You shall set up the court all around, and hang up the screen for the gate of the court. ⁹Then you shall take the anointing oil, and anoint the tabernacle and all that is in it, and consecrate it and all its furniture, so that it shall become holy. ¹⁰You shall also anoint the altar of burnt offering and all its utensils, and consecrate the altar, so that the altar shall be most holy. ¹¹You shall also anoint the basin with its stand, and consecrate it. ¹²Then you shall bring Aaron and his sons to the entrance of the tent of meeting, and shall wash them with water, ¹³and put on

---

Just as the Lord Had Commanded

EXODUS 39.32–40.16

In the space of these two chapters alone the phrase "as the LORD had commanded Moses" is repeated eighteen times with only minor variations. In each case, Moses and the people completed some work that God had commanded them to do. Most significant of all is the completion of the tabernacle (the tent of meeting), which is henceforth a sacred sign to the people of the God who dwells in their midst.

What symbolizes God's presence to you? For some, it is the people they love most of all. For others it may be a beautiful picture, a family Bible, some family heirloom. Find or make some object that reminds you of the place where you most frequently worship God. Put it in some important place in your home. Or if it is portable, keep it in your wallet or purse all the time. Each time you see or touch this object, remind yourself that God is in this place, indeed in every place.

See Meeting God in Everyday Life

ᵃ Meaning of Heb uncertain   ᵇ Or *treaty*, or *testimony*; Heb *eduth*
ᶜ Or *the cover*

God's Sweet and Awesome Presence

"As the soul goes ever after God with love so true, imbued with the spirit of suffering for His sake, God's majesty often and regularly grants it joy, and visits it sweetly and delectably in the spirit; for the boundless love of Christ, the Word, cannot see the afflictions of his lover without comforting him or her."

—JOHN OF THE CROSS,
The Dark Night of the Soul

Aaron the sacred vestments, and you shall anoint him and consecrate him, so that he may serve me as priest. [14]You shall bring his sons also and put tunics on them, [15]and anoint them, as you anointed their father, that they may serve me as priests: and their anointing shall admit them to a perpetual priesthood throughout all generations to come.

16 Moses did everything just as the LORD had commanded him. [17]In the first month in the second year, on the first day of the month, the tabernacle was set up. [18]Moses set up the tabernacle; he laid its bases, and set up its frames, and put in its poles, and raised up its pillars; [19]and he spread the tent over the tabernacle, and put the covering of the tent over it; as the LORD had commanded Moses. [20]He took the covenant[a] and put it into the ark, and put the poles on the ark, and set the mercy seat[b] above the ark; [21]and he brought the ark into the tabernacle, and set up the curtain for screening, and screened the ark of the covenant;[a] as the LORD had commanded Moses. [22]He put the table in the tent of meeting, on the north side of the tabernacle, outside the curtain, [23]and set the bread in order on it before the LORD; as the LORD had commanded Moses. [24]He put the lampstand in the tent of meeting, opposite the table on the south side of the tabernacle, [25]and set up the lamps before the LORD; as the LORD had commanded Moses. [26]He put the golden altar in the tent of meeting before the curtain, [27]and offered fragrant incense on it; as the LORD had commanded Moses. [28]He also put in place the screen for the entrance of the tabernacle. [29]He set the altar of burnt offering at the entrance of the tabernacle of the tent of meeting, and offered on it the burnt offering and the grain offering as the LORD had commanded Moses. [30]He set the basin between the tent of meeting and the altar, and put water in it for washing, [31]with which Moses and Aaron and his sons washed their hands and their feet. [32]When they went into the tent of meeting, and when they approached the altar, they washed; as the LORD had commanded Moses. [33]He set up the court around the tabernacle and the altar, and put up the screen at the gate of the court. So Moses finished the work.

The Cloud and the Glory

34 Then the cloud covered the tent of meeting, and the glory of the LORD filled the tabernacle. [35]Moses was not able to enter the tent of meeting because the cloud settled upon it, and the glory of the LORD filled the tabernacle. [36]Whenever the cloud was taken up from the tabernacle, the Israelites would set out on each stage of their journey; [37]but if the cloud was not taken up, then they did not set out until the day that it was taken up. [38]For the cloud of the LORD was on the tabernacle by day, and fire was in the cloud[c] by night, before the eyes of all the house of Israel at each stage of their journey.

a Or *treaty*, or *testimony*; Heb *eduth*   *b* Or *the cover*   *c* Heb *it*

LEVITICUS

For the Common Good

KEY VERSE:

"You shall be holy, for I the LORD your God am holy."—Leviticus 19.2

or many Christians, Leviticus is perhaps the most difficult book of the Bible from which to draw spiritual guidance. We wonder, "What do all these ancient laws about sacrifice have to do with me, anyhow? And haven't they all been nullified in the death and resurrection of Jesus?"

Yet if you have ever struggled with working out the complex connections among grace, obedience, repentance and forgiveness then Leviticus has a great deal to say. The book of Leviticus demonstrates how the people of Israel, as a nation and as individuals, could maintain a righteous relationship with God and receive the blessings that accompany that relationship.

Leviticus teaches us that the proper response to God's saving grace is to live holy lives, lives that are an imitation of God's holiness. In addition, Leviticus demonstrates that God understood that the ancient Israelites, like all humans, were not perfect and so provided a way for them to atone for their sins. Finally, Leviticus shows that empty ritual and blind compliance are not true worship. As Jesus and the prophets so clearly recognized and preached, and as the laws of Leviticus make clear, the most ornate worship services are no substitute for the ultimate requirements of God's instruction, or Torah: "Love the LORD your God with all your heart, and with all your soul, and with all your might," and "love your neighbor as yourself" (Deuteronomy 6.5; Leviticus 19.18).

As you read Leviticus, be open to experiencing God's forgiveness even as you seek to live out these great commandments.

"Christ came provided with the Holy Spirit after a peculiar manner . . . that he might separate us from the world, and unite us in the hope of an eternal inheritance."

—JOHN CALVIN,
Institutes of the Christian Religion

Offering God Our Best

LEVITICUS 1.2,14; 2.1–3

Livestock, poultry and grain were important sources of wealth and security in the era before hard currency. Leviticus begins by describing proper sacrifices, outlining those things the Israelites could give to God from their abundance in recognition that everything was a gift.

Compose a mental checklist of your physical possessions. Suppose that you could no longer offer monetary gifts to God but were required to offer something from your non-monetary possessions. What do you own that would be a worthy gift for the Lord? Would you be willing to part with it? What are some non-material ways that you can offer gifts to the Giver of Life?

See Meeting God in Service

The Burnt Offering

1 The Lord summoned Moses and spoke to him from the tent of meeting, saying: ²Speak to the people of Israel and say to them: When any of you bring an offering of livestock to the Lord, you shall bring your offering from the herd or from the flock.

3 If the offering is a burnt offering from the herd, you shall offer a male without blemish; you shall bring it to the entrance of the tent of meeting, for acceptance in your behalf before the Lord. ⁴You shall lay your hand on the head of the burnt offering, and it shall be acceptable in your behalf as atonement for you. ⁵The bull shall be slaughtered before the Lord; and Aaron's sons the priests shall offer the blood, dashing the blood against all sides of the altar that is at the entrance of the tent of meeting. ⁶The burnt offering shall be flayed and cut up into its parts. ⁷The sons of the priest Aaron shall put fire on the altar and arrange wood on the fire. ⁸Aaron's sons the priests shall arrange the parts, with the head and the suet, on the wood that is on the fire on the altar; ⁹but its entrails and its legs shall be washed with water. Then the priest shall turn the whole into smoke on the altar as a burnt offering, an offering by fire of pleasing odor to the Lord.

10 If your gift for a burnt offering is from the flock, from the sheep or goats, your offering shall be a male without blemish. ¹¹It shall be slaughtered on the north side of the altar before the Lord, and Aaron's sons the priests shall dash its blood against all sides of the altar. ¹²It shall be cut up into its parts, with its head and its suet, and the priest shall arrange them on the wood that is on the fire on the altar; ¹³but the entrails and the legs shall be washed with water. Then the priest shall offer the whole and turn it into smoke on the altar; it is a burnt offering, an offering by fire of pleasing odor to the Lord.

14 If your offering to the Lord is a burnt offering of birds, you shall choose your offering from turtledoves or pigeons. ¹⁵The priest shall bring it to the altar and wring off its head, and turn it into smoke on the altar; and its blood shall be drained out against the side of the altar. ¹⁶He shall remove its crop with its contents[a] and throw it at the east side of the altar, in the place for ashes. ¹⁷He shall tear it open by its wings without severing it. Then the priest shall turn it into smoke on the altar, on the wood that is on the fire; it is a burnt offering, an offering by fire of pleasing odor to the Lord.

Grain Offerings

2 When anyone presents a grain offering to the Lord, the offering shall be of choice flour; the worshiper shall pour oil on it, and put frankincense on it, ²and bring it to Aaron's sons the priests. After taking from it a handful of the choice flour and oil, with all its frankincense, the priest shall turn this token portion into smoke on the altar, an offering by fire of pleasing odor to the Lord. ³And what is left of the grain offering shall be for Aaron and his sons, a most holy part of the offerings by fire to the Lord.

4 When you present a grain offering baked in the oven, it shall be of choice flour: unleavened cakes mixed with oil,

a Meaning of Heb uncertain

or unleavened wafers spread with oil. ⁵If your offering is grain prepared on a griddle, it shall be of choice flour mixed with oil, unleavened; ⁶break it in pieces, and pour oil on it; it is a grain offering. ⁷If your offering is grain prepared in a pan, it shall be made of choice flour in oil. ⁸You shall bring to the LORD the grain offering that is prepared in any of these ways; and when it is presented to the priest, he shall take it to the altar. ⁹The priest shall remove from the grain offering its token portion and turn this into smoke on the altar, an offering by fire of pleasing odor to the LORD. ¹⁰And what is left of the grain offering shall be for Aaron and his sons; it is a most holy part of the offerings by fire to the LORD.

11 No grain offering that you bring to the LORD shall be made with leaven, for you must not turn any leaven or honey into smoke as an offering by fire to the LORD. ¹²You may bring them to the LORD as an offering of choice products, but they shall not be offered on the altar for a pleasing odor. ¹³You shall not omit from your grain offerings the salt of the covenant with your God; with all your offerings you shall offer salt.

14 If you bring a grain offering of first fruits to the LORD, you shall bring as the grain offering of your first fruits coarse new grain from fresh ears, parched with fire. ¹⁵You shall add oil to it and lay frankincense on it; it is a grain offering. ¹⁶And the priest shall turn a token portion of it into smoke—some of the coarse grain and oil with all its frankincense; it is an offering by fire to the LORD.

Offerings of Well-Being

3 If the offering is a sacrifice of well-being, if you offer an animal of the herd, whether male or female, you shall offer one without blemish before the LORD. ²You shall lay your hand on the head of the offering and slaughter it at the entrance of the tent of meeting; and Aaron's sons the priests shall dash the blood against all sides of the altar. ³You shall offer from the sacrifice of well-being, as an offering by fire to the LORD, the fat that covers the entrails and all the fat that is around the entrails; ⁴the two kidneys with the fat that is on them at the loins, and the appendage of the liver, which he shall remove with the kidneys. ⁵Then Aaron's sons shall turn these into smoke on the altar, with the burnt offering that is on the wood on the fire, as an offering by fire of pleasing odor to the LORD.

6 If your offering for a sacrifice of well-being to the LORD is from the flock, male or female, you shall offer one without blemish. ⁷If you present a sheep as your offering, you shall bring it before the LORD ⁸and lay your hand on the head of the offering. It shall be slaughtered before the tent of meeting, and Aaron's sons shall dash its blood against all sides of the altar. ⁹You shall present its fat from the sacrifice of well-being, as an offering by fire to the LORD: the whole broad tail, which shall be removed close to the backbone, the fat that covers the entrails, and all the fat that is around the entrails; ¹⁰the two kidneys with the fat that is on them at the loins, and the appendage of the liver, which you shall remove with the kidneys. ¹¹Then the priest shall turn these into smoke on the altar as a food offering by fire to the LORD.

Celebrating God's Kingdom

LEVITICUS 3.1–17

"A sacrifice of well-being" was only offered in part on the altar. The meat from these animals was shared with God and the priests, but the bulk of the meat was used to provide a feast for the donor's family in celebration of the goodness of creation and God's generosity. Similarly, fellowship meals, which included even prostitutes and other social outcasts, were also a primary feature of Jesus' earthly mission.

What role do communal meals serve in your church and family? What are other ways that you or your faith community celebrate the presence of God and God's blessings? How does your celebration include those who are less fortunate?

See Meeting God in Community

This Is My Body, Broken for You

LEVITICUS 4.1–21

Sin offerings allowed an individual or the community the opportunity to repent and reestablish their relationship with God. Failing to do so placed the community in grave danger.

Imagine yourself as an ancient Israelite: You are choosing a sacrificial animal, standing at the entrance to the tabernacle or temple and watching the priests attend to your sacrifice. There are meat and fat burning on the altar and blood is being sprinkled around. What do you see, smell, hear and feel?

Recall Jesus' words at the Last Supper: "This is my body . . . this is my blood." Remember his death on the cross. Ancient Israelites offered sacrifices when they sinned. In what ways does Jesus' death on the cross parallel (and so replace) a sin offering? In what ways does it transcend it? In what ways (rites or prayers) do you and your community confess your sin and appropriate Jesus' once-and-for-all sacrifice?

See Meeting God in Worship

12 If your offering is a goat, you shall bring it before the LORD [13]and lay your hand on its head; it shall be slaughtered before the tent of meeting; and the sons of Aaron shall dash its blood against all sides of the altar. [14]You shall present as your offering from it, as an offering by fire to the LORD, the fat that covers the entrails, and all the fat that is around the entrails; [15]the two kidneys with the fat that is on them at the loins, and the appendage of the liver, which you shall remove with the kidneys. [16]Then the priest shall turn these into smoke on the altar as a food offering by fire for a pleasing odor.

All fat is the LORD's. [17]It shall be a perpetual statute throughout your generations, in all your settlements: you must not eat any fat or any blood.

Sin Offerings

4 The LORD spoke to Moses, saying, [2]Speak to the people of Israel, saying: When anyone sins unintentionally in any of the LORD's commandments about things not to be done, and does any one of them:

3 If it is the anointed priest who sins, thus bringing guilt on the people, he shall offer for the sin that he has committed a bull of the herd without blemish as a sin offering to the LORD. [4]He shall bring the bull to the entrance of the tent of meeting before the LORD and lay his hand on the head of the bull; the bull shall be slaughtered before the LORD. [5]The anointed priest shall take some of the blood of the bull and bring it into the tent of meeting. [6]The priest shall dip his finger in the blood and sprinkle some of the blood seven times before the LORD in front of the curtain of the sanctuary. [7]The priest shall put some of the blood on the horns of the altar of fragrant incense that is in the tent of meeting before the LORD; and the rest of the blood of the bull he shall pour out at the base of the altar of burnt offering, which is at the entrance of the tent of meeting. [8]He shall remove all the fat from the bull of sin offering: the fat that covers the entrails and all the fat that is around the entrails; [9]the two kidneys with the fat that is on them at the loins, and the appendage of the liver, which he shall remove with the kidneys, [10]just as these are removed from the ox of the sacrifice of well-being. The priest shall turn them into smoke upon the altar of burnt offering. [11]But the skin of the bull and all its flesh, as well as its head, its legs, its entrails, and its dung— [12]all the rest of the bull—he shall carry out to a clean place outside the camp, to the ash heap, and shall burn it on a wood fire; at the ash heap it shall be burned.

13 If the whole congregation of Israel errs unintentionally and the matter escapes the notice of the assembly, and they do any one of the things that by the LORD's commandments ought not to be done and incur guilt; [14]when the sin that they have committed becomes known, the assembly shall offer a bull of the herd for a sin offering and bring it before the tent of meeting. [15]The elders of the congregation shall lay their hands on the head of the bull before the LORD, and the bull shall be slaughtered before the LORD. [16]The anointed priest shall bring some of the blood of the bull into the tent of meeting, [17]and the priest shall dip his finger in the blood and sprinkle it seven times before the LORD, in front of the curtain. [18]He shall put some of the

blood on the horns of the altar that is before the LORD in the tent of meeting; and the rest of the blood he shall pour out at the base of the altar of burnt offering that is at the entrance of the tent of meeting. ¹⁹He shall remove all its fat and turn it into smoke on the altar. ²⁰He shall do with the bull just as is done with the bull of sin offering; he shall do the same with this. The priest shall make atonement for them, and they shall be forgiven. ²¹He shall carry the bull outside the camp, and burn it as he burned the first bull; it is the sin offering for the assembly.

22 When a ruler sins, doing unintentionally any one of all the things that by commandments of the LORD his God ought not to be done and incurs guilt, ²³once the sin that he has committed is made known to him, he shall bring as his offering a male goat without blemish. ²⁴He shall lay his hand on the head of the goat; it shall be slaughtered at the spot where the burnt offering is slaughtered before the LORD; it is a sin offering. ²⁵The priest shall take some of the blood of the sin offering with his finger and put it on the horns of the altar of burnt offering, and pour out the rest of its blood at the base of the altar of burnt offering. ²⁶All its fat he shall turn into smoke on the altar, like the fat of the sacrifice of well-being. Thus the priest shall make atonement on his behalf for his sin, and he shall be forgiven.

27 If anyone of the ordinary people among you sins unintentionally in doing any one of the things that by the LORD's commandments ought not to be done and incurs guilt, ²⁸when the sin that you have committed is made known to you, you shall bring a female goat without blemish as your offering, for the sin that you have committed. ²⁹You shall lay your hand on the head of the sin offering; and the sin offering shall be slaughtered at the place of the burnt offering. ³⁰The priest shall take some of its blood with his finger and put it on the horns of the altar of burnt offering, and he shall pour out the rest of its blood at the base of the altar. ³¹He shall remove all its fat, as the fat is removed from the offering of well-being, and the priest shall turn it into smoke on the altar for a pleasing odor to the LORD. Thus the priest shall make atonement on your behalf, and you shall be forgiven.

32 If the offering you bring as a sin offering is a sheep, you shall bring a female without blemish. ³³You shall lay your hand on the head of the sin offering; and it shall be slaughtered as a sin offering at the spot where the burnt offering is slaughtered. ³⁴The priest shall take some of the blood of the sin offering with his finger and put it on the horns of the altar of burnt offering, and pour out the rest of its blood at the base of the altar. ³⁵You shall remove all its fat, as the fat of the sheep is removed from the sacrifice of well-being, and the priest shall turn it into smoke on the altar, with the offerings by fire to the LORD. Thus the priest shall make atonement on your behalf for the sin that you have committed, and you shall be forgiven.

5 When any of you sin in that you have heard a public adjuration to testify and—though able to testify as one who has seen or learned of the matter—do not speak up, you are subject to punishment. ²Or when any of you touch any unclean thing—whether the carcass of an unclean beast or the carcass of unclean livestock or the carcass of an unclean swarming thing—and are unaware of it, you

Confession Is Good for the Soul

LEVITICUS 5.1–6

In Levitical law, atoning for one's sin requires a two-part ritual involving a public confession and the actual sacrifice. Because even private sins might have serious consequences for the community, public confession is vital.

Look at your daily paper and find stories that illustrate how an individual's sin can be detrimental, even destructive, for the community at large. What are some sins that you might commit that would be detrimental for your community? What is your own "ritual" when you realize that you have sinned? Does it involve just yourself, or does it include your community as well? What makes public confession important?

See Meeting God in Community

Forgive Us Our Debts

LEVITICUS 5.6—6.6

Scripture often refers to sin as debt. "Guilt offerings" or "restitution offerings" allow for repayment for breaches of faith against property, especially when things of sacred value were misused. The person must restore the item, pay a twenty percent penalty and offer a "guilt offering to God."

Identify times when just saying "I'm sorry" (either your own apology or someone else's apology to you), even when meant sincerely, left you feeling unfulfilled. Why might just saying "I'm sorry" not be enough? Have you ever made a donation as an act of contrition? Make a list of other nonverbal ways in which one can express repentance.

See Meeting God in Community

have become unclean, and are guilty. [3]Or when you touch human uncleanness—any uncleanness by which one can become unclean—and are unaware of it, when you come to know it, you shall be guilty. [4]Or when any of you utter aloud a rash oath for a bad or a good purpose, whatever people utter in an oath, and are unaware of it, when you come to know it, you shall in any of these be guilty. [5]When you realize your guilt in any of these, you shall confess the sin that you have committed. [6]And you shall bring to the LORD, as your penalty for the sin that you have committed, a female from the flock, a sheep or a goat, as a sin offering; and the priest shall make atonement on your behalf for your sin.

7 But if you cannot afford a sheep, you shall bring to the LORD, as your penalty for the sin that you have committed, two turtledoves or two pigeons, one for a sin offering and the other for a burnt offering. [8]You shall bring them to the priest, who shall offer first the one for the sin offering, wringing its head at the nape without severing it. [9]He shall sprinkle some of the blood of the sin offering on the side of the altar, while the rest of the blood shall be drained out at the base of the altar; it is a sin offering. [10]And the second he shall offer for a burnt offering according to the regulation. Thus the priest shall make atonement on your behalf for the sin that you have committed, and you shall be forgiven.

11 But if you cannot afford two turtledoves or two pigeons, you shall bring as your offering for the sin that you have committed one-tenth of an ephah of choice flour for a sin offering; you shall not put oil on it or lay frankincense on it, for it is a sin offering. [12]You shall bring it to the priest, and the priest shall scoop up a handful of it as its memorial portion, and turn this into smoke on the altar, with the offerings by fire to the LORD; it is a sin offering. [13]Thus the priest shall make atonement on your behalf for whichever of these sins you have committed, and you shall be forgiven. Like the grain offering, the rest shall be for the priest.

Offerings with Restitution

14 The LORD spoke to Moses, saying: [15]When any of you commit a trespass and sin unintentionally in any of the holy things of the LORD, you shall bring, as your guilt offering to the LORD, a ram without blemish from the flock, convertible into silver by the sanctuary shekel; it is a guilt offering. [16]And you shall make restitution for the holy thing in which you were remiss, and shall add one-fifth to it and give it to the priest. The priest shall make atonement on your behalf with the ram of the guilt offering, and you shall be forgiven.

17 If any of you sin without knowing it, doing any of the things that by the LORD's commandments ought not to be done, you have incurred guilt, and are subject to punishment. [18]You shall bring to the priest a ram without blemish from the flock, or the equivalent, as a guilt offering; and the priest shall make atonement on your behalf for the error that you committed unintentionally, and you shall be forgiven. [19]It is a guilt offering; you have incurred guilt before the LORD.

6 *a* The LORD spoke to Moses, saying: ²When any of you sin and commit a trespass against the LORD by deceiving a neighbor in a matter of a deposit or a pledge, or by robbery, or if you have defrauded a neighbor, ³or have found something lost and lied about it—if you swear falsely regarding any of the various things that one may do and sin thereby— ⁴when you have sinned and realize your guilt, and would restore what you took by robbery or by fraud or the deposit that was committed to you, or the lost thing that you found, ⁵or anything else about which you have sworn falsely, you shall repay the principal amount and shall add one-fifth to it. You shall pay it to its owner when you realize your guilt. ⁶And you shall bring to the priest, as your guilt offering to the LORD, a ram without blemish from the flock, or its equivalent, for a guilt offering. ⁷The priest shall make atonement on your behalf before the LORD, and you shall be forgiven for any of the things that one may do and incur guilt thereby.

Instructions concerning Sacrifices

8 *b* The LORD spoke to Moses, saying: ⁹Command Aaron and his sons, saying: This is the ritual of the burnt offering. The burnt offering itself shall remain on the hearth upon the altar all night until the morning, while the fire on the altar shall be kept burning. ¹⁰The priest shall put on his linen vestments after putting on his linen undergarments next to his body; and he shall take up the ashes to which the fire has reduced the burnt offering on the altar, and place them beside the altar. ¹¹Then he shall take off his vestments and put on other garments, and carry the ashes out to a clean place outside the camp. ¹²The fire on the altar shall be kept burning; it shall not go out. Every morning the priest shall add wood to it, lay out the burnt offering on it, and turn into smoke the fat pieces of the offerings of well-being. ¹³A perpetual fire shall be kept burning on the altar; it shall not go out.

14 This is the ritual of the grain offering: The sons of Aaron shall offer it before the LORD, in front of the altar. ¹⁵They shall take from it a handful of the choice flour and oil of the grain offering, with all the frankincense that is on the offering, and they shall turn its memorial portion into smoke on the altar as a pleasing odor to the LORD. ¹⁶Aaron and his sons shall eat what is left of it; it shall be eaten as unleavened cakes in a holy place; in the court of the tent of meeting they shall eat it. ¹⁷It shall not be baked with leaven. I have given it as their portion of my offerings by fire; it is most holy, like the sin offering and the guilt offering. ¹⁸Every male among the descendants of Aaron shall eat of it, as their perpetual due throughout your generations, from the LORD's offerings by fire; anything that touches them shall become holy.

19 The LORD spoke to Moses, saying: ²⁰This is the offering that Aaron and his sons shall offer to the LORD on the day when he is anointed: one-tenth of an ephah of choice flour as a regular offering, half of it in the morning and half in the evening. ²¹It shall be made with oil on a griddle; you shall bring it well soaked, as a grain offering of baked *c* pieces, and you shall present it as a pleasing odor to the

---

Keep a Fire Burning

LEVITICUS 6.13

Light a candle and watch it burn for several minutes. Time (or estimate) how long it takes to burn down. Calculate the number of candles that would be required to keep the same flame burning uninterrupted for a week, a year.

Imagine that you live in the time of Jeremiah and you are going to worship at the temple in Jerusalem. You watch the priest lay your sacrifice on the altar. What might your feelings be when you realize that the fire that is burning on the altar is the same fire that has burned uninterrupted for over seven hundred years—the same fire that burned before Aaron and Moses (see 9.24)? As you watch the portion of your sacrifice being burned on the altar, ponder what it means to say that God is a consuming fire.

See Meeting God in Worship

Keeping the Community Pure

LEVITICUS 7.20–21

Because the covenant with God defines the nation, being cut off or separated from it is a terrible event. It is just the opposite of what God intends for his people—to be partakers of the covenant. In ancient Israel the priests would decide whether a person should be cut off from the community.

Picture an occasion (real or hypothetical) when this passage would be applicable to your spiritual community. What might be your response toward someone who has been "cut off"? Jesus specifically charges us, "Do not judge, so that you may not be judged" (Matthew 7.1). Does this command negate the requirement to exclude known sinners from the church (see also 1 Corinthians 5.1–5; Ephesians 5.3)? Who would make that decision in your community? When have you been tempted to usurp God's role as judge? Was someone "cut off" from your faith community as a result? What effects might this have on the community as a whole?

See Meeting God in Community

LORD. ²²And so the priest, anointed from among Aaron's descendants as a successor, shall prepare it; it is the LORD'S—a perpetual due—to be turned entirely into smoke. ²³Every grain offering of a priest shall be wholly burned; it shall not be eaten.

24 The LORD spoke to Moses, saying: ²⁵Speak to Aaron and his sons, saying: This is the ritual of the sin offering. The sin offering shall be slaughtered before the LORD at the spot where the burnt offering is slaughtered; it is most holy. ²⁶The priest who offers it as a sin offering shall eat of it; it shall be eaten in a holy place, in the court of the tent of meeting. ²⁷Whatever touches its flesh shall become holy; and when any of its blood is spattered on a garment, you shall wash the bespattered part in a holy place. ²⁸An earthen vessel in which it was boiled shall be broken; but if it is boiled in a bronze vessel, that shall be scoured and rinsed in water. ²⁹Every male among the priests shall eat of it; it is most holy. ³⁰But no sin offering shall be eaten from which any blood is brought into the tent of meeting for atonement in the holy place; it shall be burned with fire.

7 This is the ritual of the guilt offering. It is most holy; ²at the spot where the burnt offering is slaughtered, they shall slaughter the guilt offering, and its blood shall be dashed against all sides of the altar. ³All its fat shall be offered: the broad tail, the fat that covers the entrails, ⁴the two kidneys with the fat that is on them at the loins, and the appendage of the liver, which shall be removed with the kidneys. ⁵The priest shall turn them into smoke on the altar as an offering by fire to the LORD; it is a guilt offering. ⁶Every male among the priests shall eat of it; it shall be eaten in a holy place; it is most holy.

7 The guilt offering is like the sin offering, there is the same ritual for them; the priest who makes atonement with it shall have it. ⁸So, too, the priest who offers anyone's burnt offering shall keep the skin of the burnt offering that he has offered. ⁹And every grain offering baked in the oven, and all that is prepared in a pan or on a griddle, shall belong to the priest who offers it. ¹⁰But every other grain offering, mixed with oil or dry, shall belong to all the sons of Aaron equally.

Further Instructions

11 This is the ritual of the sacrifice of the offering of well-being that one may offer to the LORD. ¹²If you offer it for thanksgiving, you shall offer with the thank offering unleavened cakes mixed with oil, unleavened wafers spread with oil, and cakes of choice flour well soaked in oil. ¹³With your thanksgiving sacrifice of well-being you shall bring your offering with cakes of leavened bread. ¹⁴From this you shall offer one cake from each offering, as a gift to the LORD; it shall belong to the priest who dashes the blood of the offering of well-being. ¹⁵And the flesh of your thanksgiving sacrifice of well-being shall be eaten on the day it is offered; you shall not leave any of it until morning. ¹⁶But if the sacrifice you offer is a votive offering or a freewill offering, it shall be eaten on the day that you offer your sacrifice, and what is left of it shall be eaten the next day; ¹⁷but what is left of the flesh of the sacrifice shall be burned up on the third day. ¹⁸If any of the flesh of your sacrifice of well-being is eaten on the third day, it shall not be accept-

able, nor shall it be credited to the one who offers it; it shall be an abomination, and the one who eats of it shall incur guilt.

19 Flesh that touches any unclean thing shall not be eaten; it shall be burned up. As for other flesh, all who are clean may eat such flesh. 20But those who eat flesh from the LORD's sacrifice of well-being while in a state of uncleanness shall be cut off from their kin. 21When any one of you touches any unclean thing—human uncleanness or an unclean animal or any unclean creature—and then eats flesh from the LORD's sacrifice of well-being, you shall be cut off from your kin.

22 The LORD spoke to Moses, saying: 23Speak to the people of Israel, saying: You shall eat no fat of ox or sheep or goat. 24The fat of an animal that died or was torn by wild animals may be put to any other use, but you must not eat it. 25If any one of you eats the fat from an animal of which an offering by fire may be made to the LORD, you who eat it shall be cut off from your kin. 26You must not eat any blood whatever, either of bird or of animal, in any of your settlements. 27Any one of you who eats any blood shall be cut off from your kin.

28 The LORD spoke to Moses, saying: 29Speak to the people of Israel, saying: Any one of you who would offer to the LORD your sacrifice of well-being must yourself bring to the LORD your offering from your sacrifice of well-being. 30Your own hands shall bring the LORD's offering by fire; you shall bring the fat with the breast, so that the breast may be raised as an elevation offering before the LORD. 31The priest shall turn the fat into smoke on the altar, but the breast shall belong to Aaron and his sons. 32And the right thigh from your sacrifices of well-being you shall give to the priest as an offering; 33the one among the sons of Aaron who offers the blood and fat of the offering of well-being shall have the right thigh for a portion. 34For I have taken the breast of the elevation offering, and the thigh that is offered, from the people of Israel, from their sacrifices of well-being, and have given them to Aaron the priest and to his sons, as a perpetual due from the people of Israel. 35This is the portion allotted to Aaron and to his sons from the offerings made by fire to the LORD, once they have been brought forward to serve the LORD as priests; 36these the LORD commanded to be given them, when he anointed them, as a perpetual due from the people of Israel throughout their generations.

37 This is the ritual of the burnt offering, the grain offering, the sin offering, the guilt offering, the offering of ordination, and the sacrifice of well-being, 38which the LORD commanded Moses on Mount Sinai, when he commanded the people of Israel to bring their offerings to the LORD, in the wilderness of Sinai.

The Rites of Ordination

8 The LORD spoke to Moses, saying: 2Take Aaron and his sons with him, the vestments, the anointing oil, the bull of sin offering, the two rams, and the basket of unleavened bread; 3and assemble the whole congregation at the entrance of the tent of meeting. 4And Moses did as the LORD commanded him. When the congregation was assembled at the entrance of the tent of meeting, 5Moses said to the

God's Portion

LEVITICUS 7.22–27

Blood is forbidden because it contains life (see 17.11) and effects atonement (by substituting one life for another). Fat is forbidden because it is God's portion (see 3.16). Thus, all blood and fat are holy and, in some sense, a part of every meal becomes an offering to God.

Ancient Israelites offered their sacrificial portions from food and animals that they had raised in their own gardens and herds. Because they had to work hard, often under adverse conditions, just to survive, giving away food was a hardship, truly a sacrifice. Grill a piece of prepackaged meat on a barbecue. Experience the aroma and smoke. Imagine what it must have been like to be in the temple compound where sacrifices were continually burning.

What is the spiritual cost to a society such as ours that eats prepackaged food as opposed to raising it?

See Meeting God in the Created Order

Rites of Ordination

LEVITICUS 8.10–13

In the sight of all the community, Moses anoints and consecrates the tabernacle and Aaron and his sons, fulfilling the command of God (see Exodus 30.22–33). From this point on, the tabernacle, all its furnishings, and Aaron and his sons are set apart for service to God.

Christians are called to be "separated" from the world in which they live. Make a list of five ways that your Christian faith distinguishes you and your faith community from the culture around you. Make a second list of ways that you and your faith community are more like the culture than you might wish to be. Take your lists before God, asking God to strengthen you in your attempts to be faithfully set apart.

See Meeting God in Community

congregation, "This is what the LORD has commanded to be done."

6 Then Moses brought Aaron and his sons forward, and washed them with water. [7]He put the tunic on him, fastened the sash around him, clothed him with the robe, and put the ephod on him. He then put the decorated band of the ephod around him, tying the ephod to him with it. [8]He placed the breastpiece on him, and in the breastpiece he put the Urim and the Thummim. [9]And he set the turban on his head, and on the turban, in front, he set the golden ornament, the holy crown, as the LORD commanded Moses.

10 Then Moses took the anointing oil and anointed the tabernacle and all that was in it, and consecrated them. [11]He sprinkled some of it on the altar seven times, and anointed the altar and all its utensils, and the basin and its base, to consecrate them. [12]He poured some of the anointing oil on Aaron's head and anointed him, to consecrate him. [13]And Moses brought forward Aaron's sons, and clothed them with tunics, and fastened sashes around them, and tied headdresses on them, as the LORD commanded Moses.

14 He led forward the bull of sin offering; and Aaron and his sons laid their hands upon the head of the bull of sin offering, [15]and it was slaughtered. Moses took the blood and with his finger put some on each of the horns of the altar, purifying the altar; then he poured out the blood at the base of the altar. Thus he consecrated it, to make atonement for it. [16]Moses took all the fat that was around the entrails, and the appendage of the liver, and the two kidneys with their fat, and turned them into smoke on the altar. [17]But the bull itself, its skin and flesh and its dung, he burned with fire outside the camp, as the LORD commanded Moses.

18 Then he brought forward the ram of burnt offering. Aaron and his sons laid their hands on the head of the ram, [19]and it was slaughtered. Moses dashed the blood against all sides of the altar. [20]The ram was cut into its parts, and Moses turned into smoke the head and the parts and the suet. [21]And after the entrails and the legs were washed with water, Moses turned into smoke the whole ram on the altar; it was a burnt offering for a pleasing odor, an offering by fire to the LORD, as the LORD commanded Moses.

22 Then he brought forward the second ram, the ram of ordination. Aaron and his sons laid their hands on the head of the ram, [23]and it was slaughtered. Moses took some of its blood and put it on the lobe of Aaron's right ear and on the thumb of his right hand and on the big toe of his right foot. [24]After Aaron's sons were brought forward, Moses put some of the blood on the lobes of their right ears and on the thumbs of their right hands and on the big toes of their right feet; and Moses dashed the rest of the blood against all sides of the altar. [25]He took the fat—the broad tail, all the fat that was around the entrails, the appendage of the liver, and the two kidneys with their fat—and the right thigh. [26]From the basket of unleavened bread that was before the LORD, he took one cake of unleavened bread, one cake of bread with oil, and one wafer, and placed them on the fat and on the right thigh. [27]He placed all these on the palms of Aaron and on the palms of his sons, and raised them as an elevation offering before the LORD. [28]Then Moses took them from their hands and turned them into smoke on the altar

with the burnt offering. This was an ordination offering for a pleasing odor, an offering by fire to the LORD. ²⁹Moses took the breast and raised it as an elevation offering before the LORD; it was Moses' portion of the ram of ordination, as the LORD commanded Moses.

30 Then Moses took some of the anointing oil and some of the blood that was on the altar and sprinkled them on Aaron and his vestments, and also on his sons and their vestments. Thus he consecrated Aaron and his vestments, and also his sons and their vestments.

31 And Moses said to Aaron and his sons, "Boil the flesh at the entrance of the tent of meeting, and eat it there with the bread that is in the basket of ordination offerings, as I was commanded, 'Aaron and his sons shall eat it'; ³²and what remains of the flesh and the bread you shall burn with fire. ³³You shall not go outside the entrance of the tent of meeting for seven days, until the day when your period of ordination is completed. For it will take seven days to ordain you; ³⁴as has been done today, the LORD has commanded to be done to make atonement for you. ³⁵You shall remain at the entrance of the tent of meeting day and night for seven days, keeping the LORD's charge so that you do not die; for so I am commanded." ³⁶Aaron and his sons did all the things that the LORD commanded through Moses.

Aaron's Priesthood Inaugurated

9 On the eighth day Moses summoned Aaron and his sons and the elders of Israel. ²He said to Aaron, "Take a bull calf for a sin offering and a ram for a burnt offering, without blemish, and offer them before the LORD. ³And say to the people of Israel, 'Take a male goat for a sin offering; a calf and a lamb, yearlings without blemish, for a burnt offering; ⁴and an ox and a ram for an offering of well-being to sacrifice before the LORD; and a grain offering mixed with oil. For today the LORD will appear to you.'" ⁵They brought what Moses commanded to the front of the tent of meeting; and the whole congregation drew near and stood before the LORD. ⁶And Moses said, "This is the thing that the LORD commanded you to do, so that the glory of the LORD may appear to you." ⁷Then Moses said to Aaron, "Draw near to the altar and sacrifice your sin offering and your burnt offering, and make atonement for yourself and for the people; and sacrifice the offering of the people, and make atonement for them; as the LORD has commanded."

8 Aaron drew near to the altar, and slaughtered the calf of the sin offering, which was for himself. ⁹The sons of Aaron presented the blood to him, and he dipped his finger in the blood and put it on the horns of the altar; and the rest of the blood he poured out at the base of the altar. ¹⁰But the fat, the kidneys, and the appendage of the liver from the sin offering he turned into smoke on the altar, as the LORD commanded Moses; ¹¹and the flesh and the skin he burned with fire outside the camp.

12 Then he slaughtered the burnt offering. Aaron's sons brought him the blood, and he dashed it against all sides of the altar. ¹³And they brought him the burnt offering piece by piece, and the head, which he turned into smoke on the altar. ¹⁴He washed the entrails and the legs and, with the burnt offering, turned them into smoke on the altar.

Completely Burned

LEVITICUS 8.31–9.17

By Levitical law, a whole burnt offering was to be completely burned up and the ashes properly disposed of, removing the guilt from the person offering the sacrifice.

On a piece of paper, record some past sins that have separated you from others and from God. Now contemplate any current sins that may be standing between you and God and record them as well. Offer the paper as your sacrifice to God and burn it. Take the ashes outside and blow them into the wind.

See *Meeting God in Scripture*

Fire From the Lord

LEVITICUS 9.23–24

Imagine yourself watching as Aaron lays the sacrificial portions on the altar; the fire suddenly shoots out from the presence of the LORD and consumes them. What are you feeling—awe, fear, joy, excitement?

Recall a time in your life when you suddenly and unexpectedly experienced the presence of God. Where were you? In worship? In private meditation? What emotions did you experience then? What are some of the ways you experience God's presence today?

See Meeting God in Scripture

15 Next he presented the people's offering. He took the goat of the sin offering that was for the people, and slaughtered it, and presented it as a sin offering like the first one. [16]He presented the burnt offering, and sacrificed it according to regulation. [17]He presented the grain offering, and, taking a handful of it, he turned it into smoke on the altar, in addition to the burnt offering of the morning.

18 He slaughtered the ox and the ram as a sacrifice of well-being for the people. Aaron's sons brought him the blood, which he dashed against all sides of the altar, [19]and the fat of the ox and of the ram—the broad tail, the fat that covers the entrails, the two kidneys and the fat on them,*a* and the appendage of the liver. [20]They first laid the fat on the breasts, and the fat was turned into smoke on the altar; [21]and the breasts and the right thigh Aaron raised as an elevation offering before the LORD, as Moses had commanded.

22 Aaron lifted his hands toward the people and blessed them; and he came down after sacrificing the sin offering, the burnt offering, and the offering of well-being. [23]Moses and Aaron entered the tent of meeting, and then came out and blessed the people; and the glory of the LORD appeared to all the people. [24]Fire came out from the LORD and consumed the burnt offering and the fat on the altar; and when all the people saw it, they shouted and fell on their faces.

Nadab and Abihu

10 Now Aaron's sons, Nadab and Abihu, each took his censer, put fire in it, and laid incense on it; and they offered unholy fire before the LORD, such as he had not commanded them. [2]And fire came out from the presence of the LORD and consumed them, and they died before the LORD. [3]Then Moses said to Aaron, "This is what the LORD meant when he said,

'Through those who are near me
    I will show myself holy,
and before all the people
    I will be glorified.' "
And Aaron was silent.

4 Moses summoned Mishael and Elzaphan, sons of Uzziel the uncle of Aaron, and said to them, "Come forward, and carry your kinsmen away from the front of the sanctuary to a place outside the camp." [5]They came forward and carried them by their tunics out of the camp, as Moses had ordered. [6]And Moses said to Aaron and to his sons Eleazar and Ithamar, "Do not dishevel your hair, and do not tear your vestments, or you will die and wrath will strike all the congregation; but your kindred, the whole house of Israel, may mourn the burning that the LORD has sent. [7]You shall not go outside the entrance of the tent of meeting, or you will die; for the anointing oil of the LORD is on you." And they did as Moses had ordered.

8 And the LORD spoke to Aaron: [9]Drink no wine or strong drink, neither you nor your sons, when you enter the tent of meeting, that you may not die; it is a statute forever throughout your generations. [10]You are to distinguish between the holy and the common, and between the unclean and the clean; [11]and you are to teach the people of Israel all

a Gk: Heb *the broad tail, and that which covers, and the kidneys* the statutes that the LORD has spoken to them through Moses.

12 Moses spoke to Aaron and to his remaining sons, Eleazar and Ithamar: Take the grain offering that is left from the LORD's offerings by fire, and eat it unleavened beside the altar, for it is most holy; [13]you shall eat it in a holy place, because it is your due and your sons' due, from the offerings by fire to the LORD; for so I am commanded. [14]But the breast that is elevated and the thigh that is raised, you and your sons and daughters as well may eat in any clean place; for they have been assigned to you and your children from the sacrifices of the offerings of well-being of the people of Israel. [15]The thigh that is raised and the breast that is elevated they shall bring, together with the offerings by fire of the fat, to raise for an elevation offering before the LORD; they are to be your due and that of your children forever, as the LORD has commanded.

16 Then Moses made inquiry about the goat of the sin offering, and—it had already been burned! He was angry with Eleazar and Ithamar, Aaron's remaining sons, and said, [17]"Why did you not eat the sin offering in the sacred area? For it is most holy, and God[a] has given it to you that you may remove the guilt of the congregation, to make atonement on their behalf before the LORD. [18]Its blood was not brought into the inner part of the sanctuary. You should certainly have eaten it in the sanctuary, as I commanded." [19]And Aaron spoke to Moses, "See, today they offered their sin offering and their burnt offering before the LORD; and yet such things as these have befallen me! If I had eaten the sin offering today, would it have been agreeable to the LORD?" [20]And when Moses heard that, he agreed.

Clean and Unclean Foods

11 The LORD spoke to Moses and Aaron, saying to them: [2]Speak to the people of Israel, saying:

From among all the land animals, these are the creatures that you may eat. [3]Any animal that has divided hoofs and is cleft-footed and chews the cud—such you may eat. [4]But among those that chew the cud or have divided hoofs, you shall not eat the following: the camel, for even though it chews the cud, it does not have divided hoofs; it is unclean for you. [5]The rock badger, for even though it chews the cud, it does not have divided hoofs; it is unclean for you. [6]The hare, for even though it chews the cud, it does not have divided hoofs; it is unclean for you. [7]The pig, for even though it has divided hoofs and is cleft-footed, it does not chew the cud; it is unclean for you. [8]Of their flesh you shall not eat, and their carcasses you shall not touch; they are unclean for you.

9 These you may eat, of all that are in the waters. Everything in the waters that has fins and scales, whether in the seas or in the streams—such you may eat. [10]But anything in the seas or the streams that does not have fins and scales, of the swarming creatures in the waters and among all the other living creatures that are in the waters—they are detestable to you [11]and detestable they shall remain. Of their flesh you shall not eat, and their carcasses you shall regard as detestable. [12]Everything in the waters that does not have fins and scales is detestable to you.

Removing the Guilt

LEVITICUS 10.17

The New Testament builds on this verse to describe Jesus' role in removing our sin (1 Peter 2.24; John 1.29). God has placed all of our sin on the cross with Jesus and has removed it.

God has removed our sin. Explore the implications of what that means. Does this include only our past misdeeds or also any sins we may commit in the future? If future sins are included, does that mean Christians have no restrictions placed on their actions? What is the meaning of salvation if there is no punishment for sin? If future sins are not automatically included, what rituals are available for Christians to confess their sin and once again be at peace with God?

See Meeting God in Scripture

Clean and Unclean

LEVITICUS 11.22–12.1

"Moses . . . describes the clean and unclean beasts, and says that all beasts which are not cloven-footed and chew their cud, shall be unclean. This refers to people who are not cloven-hoofed, that is, those who rush aimlessly into life, and snatch up whatever crosses their path and follow it. But the clean beasts are they who act with the discrimination of the spirit in external matters and in things relating to doctrine. They retain what they observe to be in harmony with the Scriptures, but whatever has no basis in the Scriptures and is a valueless human trifle, they reject."

—MARTIN LUTHER,
Sermons

See Meeting God in Scripture

13 These you shall regard as detestable among the birds. They shall not be eaten; they are an abomination: the eagle, the vulture, the osprey, ¹⁴the buzzard, the kite of any kind; ¹⁵every raven of any kind; ¹⁶the ostrich, the nighthawk, the sea gull, the hawk of any kind; ¹⁷the little owl, the cormorant, the great owl, ¹⁸the water hen, the desert owl,*ᵃ* the carrion vulture, ¹⁹the stork, the heron of any kind, the hoopoe, and the bat.*ᵇ*
20 All winged insects that walk upon all fours are detestable to you. ²¹But among the winged insects that walk on all fours you may eat those that have jointed legs above their feet, with which to leap on the ground. ²²Of them you may eat: the locust according to its kind, the bald locust according to its kind, the cricket according to its kind, and the grasshopper according to its kind. ²³But all other winged insects that have four feet are detestable to you.

Unclean Animals

24 By these you shall become unclean; whoever touches the carcass of any of them shall be unclean until the evening, ²⁵and whoever carries any part of the carcass of any of them shall wash his clothes and be unclean until the evening. ²⁶Every animal that has divided hoofs but is not cleft-footed or does not chew the cud is unclean for you; everyone who touches one of them shall be unclean. ²⁷All that walk on their paws, among the animals that walk on all fours, are unclean for you; whoever touches the carcass of any of them shall be unclean until the evening, ²⁸and the one who carries the carcass shall wash his clothes and be unclean until the evening; they are unclean for you.
29 These are unclean for you among the creatures that swarm upon the earth: the weasel, the mouse, the great lizard according to its kind, ³⁰the gecko, the land crocodile, the lizard, the sand lizard, and the chameleon. ³¹These are unclean for you among all that swarm; whoever touches one of them when they are dead shall be unclean until the evening. ³²And anything upon which any of them falls when they are dead shall be unclean, whether an article of wood or cloth or skin or sacking, any article that is used for any purpose; it shall be dipped into water, and it shall be unclean until the evening, and then it shall be clean. ³³And if any of them falls into any earthen vessel, all that is in it shall be unclean, and you shall break the vessel. ³⁴Any food that could be eaten shall be unclean if water from any such vessel comes upon it; and any liquid that could be drunk shall be unclean if it was in any such vessel. ³⁵Everything on which any part of the carcass falls shall be unclean; whether an oven or stove, it shall be broken in pieces; they are unclean, and shall remain unclean for you. ³⁶But a spring or a cistern holding water shall be clean, while whatever touches the carcass in it shall be unclean. ³⁷If any part of their carcass falls upon any seed set aside for sowing, it is clean; ³⁸but if water is put on the seed and any part of their carcass falls on it, it is unclean for you.
39 If an animal of which you may eat dies, anyone who touches its carcass shall be unclean until the evening. ⁴⁰Those who eat of its carcass shall wash their clothes and be unclean until the evening; and those who carry the car-

---

a Or *pelican*   *b* Identification of several of the birds in verses 13-19 is uncertain cass shall wash their clothes and be unclean until the evening.

41 All creatures that swarm upon the earth are detestable; they shall not be eaten. ⁴²Whatever moves on its belly, and whatever moves on all fours, or whatever has many feet, all the creatures that swarm upon the earth, you shall not eat; for they are detestable. ⁴³You shall not make yourselves detestable with any creature that swarms; you shall not defile yourselves with them, and so become unclean. ⁴⁴For I am the Lord your God; sanctify yourselves therefore, and be holy, for I am holy. You shall not defile yourselves with any swarming creature that moves on the earth. ⁴⁵For I am the Lord who brought you up from the land of Egypt, to be your God; you shall be holy, for I am holy.

46 This is the law pertaining to land animal and bird and every living creature that moves through the waters and every creature that swarms upon the earth, ⁴⁷to make a distinction between the unclean and the clean, and between the living creature that may be eaten and the living creature that may not be eaten.

Purification of Women after Childbirth

12 The Lord spoke to Moses, saying: ²Speak to the people of Israel, saying:

If a woman conceives and bears a male child, she shall be ceremonially unclean seven days; as at the time of her menstruation, she shall be unclean. ³On the eighth day the flesh of his foreskin shall be circumcised. ⁴Her time of blood purification shall be thirty-three days; she shall not touch any holy thing, or come into the sanctuary, until the days of her purification are completed. ⁵If she bears a female child, she shall be unclean two weeks, as in her menstruation; her time of blood purification shall be sixty-six days.

6 When the days of her purification are completed, whether for a son or for a daughter, she shall bring to the priest at the entrance of the tent of meeting a lamb in its first year for a burnt offering, and a pigeon or a turtledove for a sin offering. ⁷He shall offer it before the Lord, and make atonement on her behalf; then she shall be clean from her flow of blood. This is the law for her who bears a child, male or female. ⁸If she cannot afford a sheep, she shall take two turtledoves or two pigeons, one for a burnt offering and the other for a sin offering; and the priest shall make atonement on her behalf, and she shall be clean.

Leprosy, Varieties and Symptoms

13 The Lord spoke to Moses and Aaron, saying:
2 When a person has on the skin of his body a swelling or an eruption or a spot, and it turns into a leprous*ᵃ* disease on the skin of his body, he shall be brought to Aaron the priest or to one of his sons the priests. ³The priest shall examine the disease on the skin of his body, and if the hair in the diseased area has turned white and the disease appears to be deeper than the skin of his body, it is a leprous*ᵃ* disease; after the priest has examined him he shall pronounce him ceremonially unclean. ⁴But if the spot is white in the skin of his body, and appears no deep-

Purification

LEVITICUS 12.1–8

According to Levitical law, childbirth is a milestone in a woman's life that is marked by a special religious observance. It is meant to be a holy occasion, a time to bring a family closer to God, and is not meant to be a burden to those who are not well-off. The offering Joseph and Mary offered when they brought Jesus to the temple was the offering mandated for the poor (see Luke 2.24). What does the fact that our Savior was born to a poor family rather than to a wealthy, powerful one signify to us? What does this tell us about God's nature? Why do you think we are surprised that God appeared to humans in so humble a form? What does that tell us about human nature?

Examine your own actions and feelings: Do you show deference or respect for wealth and power? How might you react when you encounter a homeless person asking for help?

See Meeting God in Community

---

a A term for several skin diseases; precise meaning uncertain

Prayer of Thanks

LEVITICUS 13.12

"Thanks, thanks to thee, O Eternal Father, for thou hast not despised me, the work of thy hands, nor turned thy face from me, nor despised my desires; thou, the Light, hast not regarded my darkness; thou, true Life, has not regarded my living death; thou, the Physician, hast not been repelled by my grave infirmities; thou, the Eternal Purity, hast not considered the many miseries of which I am full; thou, who art the Infinite, hast overlooked that I am finite; thou, who are Wisdom, but overlooked my folly; thy wisdom, thy goodness, thy clemency, thy infinite good, have overlooked these infinite evils and sins, and the many others which are in me."

—CATHERINE OF SIENA,
The Dialogue

See Meeting God in Prayer

er than the skin, and the hair in it has not turned white, the priest shall confine the diseased person for seven days. [5]The priest shall examine him on the seventh day, and if he sees that the disease is checked and the disease has not spread in the skin, then the priest shall confine him seven days more. [6]The priest shall examine him again on the seventh day, and if the disease has abated and the disease has not spread in the skin, the priest shall pronounce him clean; it is only an eruption; and he shall wash his clothes, and be clean. [7]But if the eruption spreads in the skin after he has shown himself to the priest for his cleansing, he shall appear again before the priest. [8]The priest shall make an examination, and if the eruption has spread in the skin, the priest shall pronounce him unclean; it is a leprous[a] disease.

9 When a person contracts a leprous[a] disease, he shall be brought to the priest. [10]The priest shall make an examination, and if there is a white swelling in the skin that has turned the hair white, and there is quick raw flesh in the swelling, [11]it is a chronic leprous[a] disease in the skin of his body. The priest shall pronounce him unclean; he shall not confine him, for he is unclean. [12]But if the disease breaks out in the skin, so that it covers all the skin of the diseased person from head to foot, so far as the priest can see, [13]then the priest shall make an examination, and if the disease has covered all his body, he shall pronounce him clean of the disease; since it has all turned white, he is clean. [14]But if raw flesh ever appears on him, he shall be unclean; [15]the priest shall examine the raw flesh and pronounce him unclean. Raw flesh is unclean, for it is a leprous[a] disease. [16]But if the raw flesh again turns white, he shall come to the priest; [17]the priest shall examine him, and if the disease has turned white, the priest shall pronounce the diseased person clean. He is clean.

18 When there is on the skin of one's body a boil that has healed, [19]and in the place of the boil there appears a white swelling or a reddish-white spot, it shall be shown to the priest. [20]The priest shall make an examination, and if it appears deeper than the skin and its hair has turned white, the priest shall pronounce him unclean; this is a leprous[a] disease, broken out in the boil. [21]But if the priest examines it and the hair on it is not white, nor is it deeper than the skin but has abated, the priest shall confine him seven days. [22]If it spreads in the skin, the priest shall pronounce him unclean; it is diseased. [23]But if the spot remains in one place and does not spread, it is the scar of the boil; the priest shall pronounce him clean.

24 Or, when the body has a burn on the skin and the raw flesh of the burn becomes a spot, reddish-white or white, [25]the priest shall examine it. If the hair in the spot has turned white and it appears deeper than the skin, it is a leprous[a] disease; it has broken out in the burn, and the priest shall pronounce him unclean. This is a leprous[a] disease. [26]But if the priest examines it and the hair in the spot is not white, and it is no deeper than the skin but has abated, the priest shall confine him seven days. [27]The priest shall examine him the seventh day; if it is spreading in the skin, the priest shall pronounce him unclean. This is a leprous[a] disease. [28]But if the spot remains in one place and

a A term for several skin diseases; precise meaning uncertain

does not spread in the skin but has abated, it is a swelling from the burn, and the priest shall pronounce him clean; for it is the scar of the burn.

29 When a man or woman has a disease on the head or in the beard, ³⁰the priest shall examine the disease. If it appears deeper than the skin and the hair in it is yellow and thin, the priest shall pronounce him unclean; it is an itch, a leprous[a] disease of the head or the beard. ³¹If the priest examines the itching disease, and it appears no deeper than the skin and there is no black hair in it, the priest shall confine the person with the itching disease for seven days. ³²On the seventh day the priest shall examine the itch; if the itch has not spread, and there is no yellow hair in it, and the itch appears to be no deeper than the skin, ³³he shall shave, but the itch he shall not shave. The priest shall confine the person with the itch for seven days more. ³⁴On the seventh day the priest shall examine the itch; if the itch has not spread in the skin and it appears to be no deeper than the skin, the priest shall pronounce him clean. He shall wash his clothes and be clean. ³⁵But if the itch spreads in the skin after he was pronounced clean, ³⁶the priest shall examine him. If the itch has spread in the skin, the priest need not seek for the yellow hair; he is unclean. ³⁷But if in his eyes the itch is checked, and black hair has grown in it, the itch is healed, he is clean; and the priest shall pronounce him clean.

38 When a man or a woman has spots on the skin of the body, white spots, ³⁹the priest shall make an examination, and if the spots on the skin of the body are of a dull white, it is a rash that has broken out on the skin; he is clean.

40 If anyone loses the hair from his head, he is bald but he is clean. ⁴¹If he loses the hair from his forehead and temples, he has baldness of the forehead but he is clean. ⁴²But if there is on the bald head or the bald forehead a reddish-white diseased spot, it is a leprous[a] disease breaking out on his bald head or his bald forehead. ⁴³The priest shall examine him; if the diseased swelling is reddish-white on his bald head or on his bald forehead, which resembles a leprous[a] disease in the skin of the body, ⁴⁴he is leprous,[a] he is unclean. The priest shall pronounce him unclean; the disease is on his head.

45 The person who has the leprous[a] disease shall wear torn clothes and let the hair of his head be disheveled; and he shall cover his upper lip and cry out, "Unclean, unclean." ⁴⁶He shall remain unclean as long as he has the disease; he is unclean. He shall live alone; his dwelling shall be outside the camp.

47 Concerning clothing: when a leprous[a] disease appears in it, in woolen or linen cloth, ⁴⁸in warp or woof of linen or wool, or in a skin or in anything made of skin, ⁴⁹if the disease shows greenish or reddish in the garment, whether in warp or woof or in skin or in anything made of skin, it is a leprous[a] disease and shall be shown to the priest. ⁵⁰The priest shall examine the disease, and put the diseased article aside for seven days. ⁵¹He shall examine the disease on the seventh day. If the disease has spread in the cloth, in warp or woof, or in the skin, whatever be the use of the skin, this is a spreading leprous[a] disease; it is unclean. ⁵²He shall burn the clothing, whether diseased in

Unclean, Unclean!

LEVITICUS 13.45–46

To protect the other members of the community, those with "leprous diseases" are forced to live separately, wear special clothes and warn others to stay away.

In our society, certain groups are treated as if they were lepers and forced into virtual isolation. Can you think of people whom you or your immediate circle of friends treat as if they were lepers? What is it about them that makes you uncomfortable? What types of things have you or others done to make them feel unwanted? How do you suppose they feel? Share your thoughts with God and pray for those people.

See Meeting God in Service

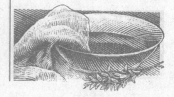

Coming Home

LEVITICUS 13.59—14.19

The term translated "guilt offering" in this passage is sometimes called a "purification offering." It signifies that the individual is ready to return to active participation in the community.

Recall a time when you or someone you know has been ill or injured and absent from your faith community for an extended period. In what ways was your community diminished by the absence? Write or perform an act of praise or a prayer (perhaps based on a familiar scriptural passage) to welcome someone back into normal communion with the community after a prolonged absence.

See Meeting God in Community

warp or woof, woolen or linen, or anything of skin, for it is a spreading leprous[a] disease; it shall be burned in fire.

53 If the priest makes an examination, and the disease has not spread in the clothing, in warp or woof or in anything of skin, [54]the priest shall command them to wash the article in which the disease appears, and he shall put it aside seven days more. [55]The priest shall examine the diseased article after it has been washed. If the diseased spot has not changed color, though the disease has not spread, it is unclean; you shall burn it in fire, whether the leprous[a] spot is on the inside or on the outside.

56 If the priest makes an examination, and the disease has abated after it is washed, he shall tear the spot out of the cloth, in warp or woof, or out of skin. [57]If it appears again in the garment, in warp or woof, or in anything of skin, it is spreading; you shall burn with fire that in which the disease appears. [58]But the cloth, warp or woof, or anything of skin from which the disease disappears when you have washed it, shall then be washed a second time, and it shall be clean.

59 This is the ritual for a leprous[a] disease in a cloth of wool or linen, either in warp or woof, or in anything of skin, to decide whether it is clean or unclean.

Purification of Lepers and Leprous Houses

14 The LORD spoke to Moses, saying: [2]This shall be the ritual for the leprous[a] person at the time of his cleansing:

He shall be brought to the priest; [3]the priest shall go out of the camp, and the priest shall make an examination. If the disease is healed in the leprous[a] person, [4]the priest shall command that two living clean birds and cedarwood and crimson yarn and hyssop be brought for the one who is to be cleansed. [5]The priest shall command that one of the birds be slaughtered over fresh water in an earthen vessel. [6]He shall take the living bird with the cedarwood and the crimson yarn and the hyssop, and dip them and the living bird in the blood of the bird that was slaughtered over the fresh water. [7]He shall sprinkle it seven times upon the one who is to be cleansed of the leprous[a] disease; then he shall pronounce him clean, and he shall let the living bird go into the open field. [8]The one who is to be cleansed shall wash his clothes, and shave off all his hair, and bathe himself in water, and he shall be clean. After that he shall come into the camp, but shall live outside his tent seven days. [9]On the seventh day he shall shave all his hair: of head, beard, eyebrows; he shall shave all his hair. Then he shall wash his clothes, and bathe his body in water, and he shall be clean.

10 On the eighth day he shall take two male lambs without blemish, and one ewe lamb in its first year without blemish, and a grain offering of three-tenths of an ephah of choice flour mixed with oil, and one log[b] of oil. [11]The priest who cleanses shall set the person to be cleansed, along with these things, before the LORD, at the entrance of the tent of meeting. [12]The priest shall take one of the lambs, and offer it as a guilt offering, along with the log[b] of oil, and raise them as an elevation offering before the LORD. [13]He

a A term for several skin diseases; precise meaning uncertain   b A liquid measure shall slaughter the lamb in the place where the sin offering and the burnt offering are slaughtered in the holy place; for the guilt offering, like the sin offering, belongs to the priest: it is most holy. ¹⁴The priest shall take some of the blood of the guilt offering and put it on the lobe of the right ear of the one to be cleansed, and on the thumb of the right hand, and on the big toe of the right foot. ¹⁵The priest shall take some of the log*ᵃ* of oil and pour it into the palm of his own left hand, ¹⁶and dip his right finger in the oil that is in his left hand and sprinkle some oil with his finger seven times before the Lᴏʀᴅ. ¹⁷Some of the oil that remains in his hand the priest shall put on the lobe of the right ear of the one to be cleansed, and on the thumb of the right hand, and on the big toe of the right foot, on top of the blood of the guilt offering. ¹⁸The rest of the oil that is in the priest's hand he shall put on the head of the one to be cleansed. Then the priest shall make atonement on his behalf before the Lᴏʀᴅ: ¹⁹the priest shall offer the sin offering, to make atonement for the one to be cleansed from his uncleanness. Afterward he shall slaughter the burnt offering; ²⁰and the priest shall offer the burnt offering and the grain offering on the altar. Thus the priest shall make atonement on his behalf and he shall be clean.

21 But if he is poor and cannot afford so much, he shall take one male lamb for a guilt offering to be elevated, to make atonement on his behalf, and one-tenth of an ephah of choice flour mixed with oil for a grain offering and a log*ᵃ* of oil; ²²also two turtledoves or two pigeons, such as he can afford, one for a sin offering and the other for a burnt offering. ²³On the eighth day he shall bring them for his cleansing to the priest, to the entrance of the tent of meeting, before the Lᴏʀᴅ; ²⁴and the priest shall take the lamb of the guilt offering and the log*ᵃ* of oil, and the priest shall raise them as an elevation offering before the Lᴏʀᴅ. ²⁵The priest shall slaughter the lamb of the guilt offering and shall take some of the blood of the guilt offering, and put it on the lobe of the right ear of the one to be cleansed, and on the thumb of the right hand, and on the big toe of the right foot. ²⁶The priest shall pour some of the oil into the palm of his own left hand, ²⁷and shall sprinkle with his right finger some of the oil that is in his left hand seven times before the Lᴏʀᴅ. ²⁸The priest shall put some of the oil that is in his hand on the lobe of the right ear of the one to be cleansed, and on the thumb of the right hand, and on the big toe of the right foot, where the blood of the guilt offering was placed. ²⁹The rest of the oil that is in the priest's hand he shall put on the head of the one to be cleansed, to make atonement on his behalf before the Lᴏʀᴅ. ³⁰And he shall offer, of the turtledoves or pigeons such as he can afford, ³¹one*ᵇ* for a sin offering and the other for a burnt offering, along with a grain offering; and the priest shall make atonement before the Lᴏʀᴅ on behalf of the one being cleansed. ³²This is the ritual for the one who has a leprous*ᶜ* disease, who cannot afford the offerings for his cleansing.

33 The Lᴏʀᴅ spoke to Moses and Aaron, saying:

34 When you come into the land of Canaan, which I give you for a possession, and I put a leprous*ᶜ* disease in a house in the land of your possession, ³⁵the owner of the

Diseased Houses

LEVITICUS 14.34–42

Buildings as well as people can be "diseased" and contaminate the community. As you read this passage, identify "houses" or neighborhoods that might be considered "unclean" in your own community, perhaps due to illegal or immoral activity. What are ways that they "infect" your community and the individuals comprising it? As a Christian, what are things that, based on the ministry of Jesus, you feel called to do to help "purify" your community?

See Meeting God in Service

---

a A liquid measure   *b* Gk Syr: Heb *afford,* ³¹*such as he can afford, one*
c A term for several skin diseases; precise meaning uncertain

Cleaning House

LEVITICUS 14.43-53

These rituals for removing mildew from a dwelling may seem rather strange to us today. Yet left untreated, mildew could spread and destroy the dwelling. The Israelites' homes were to conform to God's standards of holiness and cleanliness.

When Jesus Christ comes into our lives, he sweeps our sins out the door. Choose some area of your house or apartment to clean or organize today. As you do so, meditate with gratitude on how Jesus has destroyed the power of sin—and continues to cleanse and transform you.

See Meeting God in Prayer

house shall come and tell the priest, saying, "There seems to me to be some sort of disease in my house." ³⁶The priest shall command that they empty the house before the priest goes to examine the disease, or all that is in the house will become unclean; and afterward the priest shall go in to inspect the house. ³⁷He shall examine the disease; if the disease is in the walls of the house with greenish or reddish spots, and if it appears to be deeper than the surface, ³⁸the priest shall go outside to the door of the house and shut up the house seven days. ³⁹The priest shall come again on the seventh day and make an inspection; if the disease has spread in the walls of the house, ⁴⁰the priest shall command that the stones in which the disease appears be taken out and thrown into an unclean place outside the city. ⁴¹He shall have the inside of the house scraped thoroughly, and the plaster that is scraped off shall be dumped in an unclean place outside the city. ⁴²They shall take other stones and put them in the place of those stones, and take other plaster and plaster the house.

43 If the disease breaks out again in the house, after he has taken out the stones and scraped the house and plastered it, ⁴⁴the priest shall go and make inspection; if the disease has spread in the house, it is a spreading leprous*ᵃ* disease in the house; it is unclean. ⁴⁵He shall have the house torn down, its stones and timber and all the plaster of the house, and taken outside the city to an unclean place. ⁴⁶All who enter the house while it is shut up shall be unclean until the evening; ⁴⁷and all who sleep in the house shall wash their clothes; and all who eat in the house shall wash their clothes.

48 If the priest comes and makes an inspection, and the disease has not spread in the house after the house was plastered, the priest shall pronounce the house clean; the disease is healed. ⁴⁹For the cleansing of the house he shall take two birds, with cedarwood and crimson yarn and hyssop, ⁵⁰and shall slaughter one of the birds over fresh water in an earthen vessel, ⁵¹and shall take the cedarwood and the hyssop and the crimson yarn, along with the living bird, and dip them in the blood of the slaughtered bird and the fresh water, and sprinkle the house seven times. ⁵²Thus he shall cleanse the house with the blood of the bird, and with the fresh water, and with the living bird, and with the cedarwood and hyssop and crimson yarn; ⁵³and he shall let the living bird go out of the city into the open field; so he shall make atonement for the house, and it shall be clean.

54 This is the ritual for any leprous*ᵃ* disease: for an itch, ⁵⁵for leprous*ᵃ* diseases in clothing and houses, ⁵⁶and for a swelling or an eruption or a spot, ⁵⁷to determine when it is unclean and when it is clean. This is the ritual for leprous*ᵃ* diseases.

Concerning Bodily Discharges

15 The LORD spoke to Moses and Aaron, saying: ²Speak to the people of Israel and say to them:

When any man has a discharge from his member,*ᵇ* his discharge makes him ceremonially unclean. ³The uncleanness of his discharge is this: whether his member*ᵇ* flows with his discharge, or his member*ᵇ* is stopped from discharging, it is uncleanness for him. ⁴Every bed on which

a A term for several skin diseases; precise meaning uncertain   *b* Heb *flesh*

the one with the discharge lies shall be unclean; and everything on which he sits shall be unclean. ⁵Anyone who touches his bed shall wash his clothes, and bathe in water, and be unclean until the evening. ⁶All who sit on anything on which the one with the discharge has sat shall wash their clothes, and bathe in water, and be unclean until the evening. ⁷All who touch the body of the one with the discharge shall wash their clothes, and bathe in water, and be unclean until the evening. ⁸If the one with the discharge spits on persons who are clean, then they shall wash their clothes, and bathe in water, and be unclean until the evening. ⁹Any saddle on which the one with the discharge rides shall be unclean. ¹⁰All who touch anything that was under him shall be unclean until the evening, and all who carry such a thing shall wash their clothes, and bathe in water, and be unclean until the evening. ¹¹All those whom the one with the discharge touches without his having rinsed his hands in water shall wash their clothes, and bathe in water, and be unclean until the evening. ¹²Any earthen vessel that the one with the discharge touches shall be broken; and every vessel of wood shall be rinsed in water.

13 When the one with a discharge is cleansed of his discharge, he shall count seven days for his cleansing; he shall wash his clothes and bathe his body in fresh water, and he shall be clean. ¹⁴On the eighth day he shall take two turtledoves or two pigeons and come before the LORD to the entrance of the tent of meeting and give them to the priest. ¹⁵The priest shall offer them, one for a sin offering and the other for a burnt offering; and the priest shall make atonement on his behalf before the LORD for his discharge.

16 If a man has an emission of semen, he shall bathe his whole body in water, and be unclean until the evening. ¹⁷Everything made of cloth or of skin on which the semen falls shall be washed with water, and be unclean until the evening. ¹⁸If a man lies with a woman and has an emission of semen, both of them shall bathe in water, and be unclean until the evening.

19 When a woman has a discharge of blood that is her regular discharge from her body, she shall be in her impurity for seven days, and whoever touches her shall be unclean until the evening. ²⁰Everything upon which she lies during her impurity shall be unclean; everything also upon which she sits shall be unclean. ²¹Whoever touches her bed shall wash his clothes, and bathe in water, and be unclean until the evening; ²²Whoever touches anything upon which she sits shall wash his clothes, and bathe in water, and be unclean until the evening; ²³whether it is the bed or anything upon which she sits, when he touches it he shall be unclean until the evening. ²⁴If any man lies with her, and her impurity falls on him, he shall be unclean seven days; and every bed on which he lies shall be unclean.

25 If a woman has a discharge of blood for many days, not at the time of her impurity, or if she has a discharge beyond the time of her impurity, all the days of the discharge she shall continue in uncleanness; as in the days of her impurity, she shall be unclean. ²⁶Every bed on which she lies during all the days of her discharge shall be treated as the bed of her impurity; and everything on which she sits shall be unclean, as in the uncleanness of her impurity. ²⁷Who-

Separate From Uncleanness

LEVITICUS 15.1–31

Make a list of the people with whom you come into contact on a normal workday. Now, assuming everyone on your list comes into contact with approximately the same number of people daily, calculate how many people's lives you might affect, directly or indirectly, in a single day.

Suppose that you "infected" each person you encountered by your attitude, either positive or negative. Would you infect them with joy, apathy, indifference, concern, anger? Write a statement: "Today I will infect people with my _____." List five ways you can accomplish this goal.

See Meeting God in Everyday Life

The Day of Atonement

LEVITICUS 16.2–20

Read this passage aloud slowly, imagining yourself as a member of the crowd watching Aaron performing these rites on the very first Day of Atonement. Listen for words that appeal to your senses, and let them help you to become part of the story itself. Then ponder this question: How important is it to have a set, yearly ritual to purify both the people and their place of worship? Other passages, such as Joshua 24.1–27, indicate that yearly renewal included a recitation of God's saving acts and a reaffirmation of the people's commitment to God. Why are these elements important? Which elements speak most strongly to you at this moment? Share your feelings with God.

See *Meeting God in Worship*

ever touches these things shall be unclean, and shall wash his clothes, and bathe in water, and be unclean until the evening. ²⁸If she is cleansed of her discharge, she shall count seven days, and after that she shall be clean. ²⁹On the eighth day she shall take two turtledoves or two pigeons and bring them to the priest at the entrance of the tent of meeting. ³⁰The priest shall offer one for a sin offering and the other for a burnt offering; and the priest shall make atonement on her behalf before the LORD for her unclean discharge.

31 Thus you shall keep the people of Israel separate from their uncleanness, so that they do not die in their uncleanness by defiling my tabernacle that is in their midst.

32 This is the ritual for those who have a discharge: for him who has an emission of semen, becoming unclean thereby, ³³for her who is in the infirmity of her period, for anyone, male or female, who has a discharge, and for the man who lies with a woman who is unclean.

The Day of Atonement

16 The LORD spoke to Moses after the death of the two sons of Aaron, when they drew near before the LORD and died. ²The LORD said to Moses:

Tell your brother Aaron not to come just at any time into the sanctuary inside the curtain before the mercy seat*ᵃ* that is upon the ark, or he will die; for I appear in the cloud upon the mercy seat.*ᵃ* ³Thus shall Aaron come into the holy place: with a young bull for a sin offering and a ram for a burnt offering. ⁴He shall put on the holy linen tunic, and shall have the linen undergarments next to his body, fasten the linen sash, and wear the linen turban; these are the holy vestments. He shall bathe his body in water, and then put them on. ⁵He shall take from the congregation of the people of Israel two male goats for a sin offering, and one ram for a burnt offering.

6 Aaron shall offer the bull as a sin offering for himself, and shall make atonement for himself and for his house. ⁷He shall take the two goats and set them before the LORD at the entrance of the tent of meeting; ⁸and Aaron shall cast lots on the two goats, one lot for the LORD and the other lot for Azazel.*ᵇ* ⁹Aaron shall present the goat on which the lot fell for the LORD, and offer it as a sin offering; ¹⁰but the goat on which the lot fell for Azazel*ᵇ* shall be presented alive before the LORD to make atonement over it, that it may be sent away into the wilderness to Azazel.*ᵇ*

11 Aaron shall present the bull as a sin offering for himself, and shall make atonement for himself and for his house; he shall slaughter the bull as a sin offering for himself. ¹²He shall take a censer full of coals of fire from the altar before the LORD, and two handfuls of crushed sweet incense, and he shall bring it inside the curtain ¹³and put the incense on the fire before the LORD, that the cloud of the incense may cover the mercy seat*ᵃ* that is upon the covenant,*ᶜ* or he will die. ¹⁴He shall take some of the blood of the bull, and sprinkle it with his finger on the front of the mercy seat,*ᵃ* and before the mercy seat*ᵃ* he shall sprinkle the blood with his finger seven times.

15 He shall slaughter the goat of the sin offering that is

a Or *the cover*   *b* Traditionally rendered *a scapegoat*   *c* Or *treaty*, or *testament*; Heb *eduth*

for the people and bring its blood inside the curtain, and do with its blood as he did with the blood of the bull, sprinkling it upon the mercy seat[a] and before the mercy seat.[a] [16]Thus he shall make atonement for the sanctuary, because of the uncleannesses of the people of Israel, and because of their transgressions, all their sins; and so he shall do for the tent of meeting, which remains with them in the midst of their uncleannesses. [17]No one shall be in the tent of meeting from the time he enters to make atonement in the sanctuary until he comes out and has made atonement for himself and for his house and for all the assembly of Israel. [18]Then he shall go out to the altar that is before the LORD and make atonement on its behalf, and shall take some of the blood of the bull and of the blood of the goat, and put it on each of the horns of the altar. [19]He shall sprinkle some of the blood on it with his finger seven times, and cleanse it and hallow it from the uncleannesses of the people of Israel.

20 When he has finished atoning for the holy place and the tent of meeting and the altar, he shall present the live goat. [21]Then Aaron shall lay both his hands on the head of the live goat, and confess over it all the iniquities of the people of Israel, and all their transgressions, all their sins, putting them on the head of the goat, and sending it away into the wilderness by means of someone designated for the task.[b] [22]The goat shall bear on itself all their iniquities to a barren region; and the goat shall be set free in the wilderness.

23 Then Aaron shall enter the tent of meeting, and shall take off the linen vestments that he put on when he went into the holy place, and shall leave them there. [24]He shall bathe his body in water in a holy place, and put on his vestments; then he shall come out and offer his burnt offering and the burnt offering of the people, making atonement for himself and for the people. [25]The fat of the sin offering he shall turn into smoke on the altar. [26]The one who sets the goat free for Azazel[c] shall wash his clothes and bathe his body in water, and afterward may come into the camp. [27]The bull of the sin offering and the goat of the sin offering, whose blood was brought in to make atonement in the holy place, shall be taken outside the camp; their skin and their flesh and their dung shall be consumed in fire. [28]The one who burns them shall wash his clothes and bathe his body in water, and afterward may come into the camp.

29 This shall be a statute to you forever: In the seventh month, on the tenth day of the month, you shall deny yourselves,[d] and shall do no work, neither the citizen nor the alien who resides among you. [30]For on this day atonement shall be made for you, to cleanse you; from all your sins you shall be clean before the LORD. [31]It is a sabbath of complete rest to you, and you shall deny yourselves;[d] it is a statute forever. [32]The priest who is anointed and consecrated as priest in his father's place shall make atonement, wearing the linen vestments, the holy vestments. [33]He shall make atonement for the sanctuary, and he shall make atonement for the tent of meeting and for the altar, and he shall make atonement for the priests and for all the people of the assembly. [34]This shall be an everlasting statute for

The Scapegoat

LEVITICUS 16.21–22

As you read these two verses, meditate on the actions taking place and their underlying meaning. Given that all other animal sacrifices are slaughtered, why do you suppose this sacrifice is not? What is the symbolic meaning of laying hands on the goat and then sending it into the wilderness?

Find a stuffed animal. As you read this passage again, place your hands on the animal and imagine that your sins are being transferred to it. What feelings does this action arouse in you? How has Jesus replaced the scapegoat? Offer a prayer to God describing your feelings.

See Meeting God in Scripture

---

a Or *the cover*   *b* Meaning of Heb uncertain   *c* Traditionally rendered *a scapegoat*   *d* Or *shall fast*

The Law and Grace

LEVITICUS 17.8–18.17

"The Lord Himself not only shows us the evil we are to avoid and the good we are to do (which is all that the letter of the law can do), but also helps us to avoid evil and to do good—things that are impossible without the spirit of grace. If grace is lacking, the law is there simply to make culprits and to slay; for this reason, the Apostle said: "The letter kills, but the Spirit gives life" (2 Corinthians 3.6). He, therefore, who uses the law according to the law learns from it good and evil, and, trusting not in his own strength, has recourse to grace, which enable[s] him to avoid evil and to do good. But when has a [person] recourse to grace, except when the steps of [that person] are directed by the Lord and he delighteth in His way? Therefore, even the desire for the help of grace is itself the beginning of grace."

—AUGUSTINE,
"Admonition and Grace"

you, to make atonement for the people of Israel once in the year for all their sins. And Moses did as the LORD had commanded him.

The Slaughtering of Animals

17 The LORD spoke to Moses: 2 Speak to Aaron and his sons and to all the people of Israel and say to them: This is what the LORD has commanded. ³If anyone of the house of Israel slaughters an ox or a lamb or a goat in the camp, or slaughters it outside the camp, ⁴and does not bring it to the entrance of the tent of meeting, to present it as an offering to the LORD before the tabernacle of the LORD, he shall be held guilty of bloodshed; he has shed blood, and he shall be cut off from the people. ⁵This is in order that the people of Israel may bring their sacrifices that they offer in the open field, that they may bring them to the LORD, to the priest at the entrance of the tent of meeting, and offer them as sacrifices of well-being to the LORD. ⁶The priest shall dash the blood against the altar of the LORD at the entrance of the tent of meeting, and turn the fat into smoke as a pleasing odor to the LORD, ⁷so that they may no longer offer their sacrifices for goat-demons, to whom they prostitute themselves. This shall be a statute forever to them throughout their generations.

8 And say to them further: Anyone of the house of Israel or of the aliens who reside among them who offers a burnt offering or sacrifice, ⁹and does not bring it to the entrance of the tent of meeting, to sacrifice it to the LORD, shall be cut off from the people.

Eating Blood Prohibited

10 If anyone of the house of Israel or of the aliens who reside among them eats any blood, I will set my face against that person who eats blood, and will cut that person off from the people. ¹¹For the life of the flesh is in the blood; and I have given it to you for making atonement for your lives on the altar; for, as life, it is the blood that makes atonement. ¹²Therefore I have said to the people of Israel: No person among you shall eat blood, nor shall any alien who resides among you eat blood. ¹³And anyone of the people of Israel, or of the aliens who reside among them, who hunts down an animal or bird that may be eaten shall pour out its blood and cover it with earth.

14 For the life of every creature—its blood is its life; therefore I have said to the people of Israel: You shall not eat the blood of any creature, for the life of every creature is its blood; whoever eats it shall be cut off. ¹⁵All persons, citizens or aliens, who eat what dies of itself or what has been torn by wild animals, shall wash their clothes, and bathe themselves in water, and be unclean until the evening; then they shall be clean. ¹⁶But if they do not wash themselves or bathe their body, they shall bear their guilt.

Sexual Relations

18 The LORD spoke to Moses, saying: 2 Speak to the people of Israel and say to them: I am the LORD your God. ³You shall not do as they do in the land of Egypt, where you lived, and you shall not do as they do in the land of Canaan, to which I am bringing you. You shall not follow their statutes. ⁴My ordinances you shall observe and my statutes you shall keep, following them: I am the LORD your God. ⁵You shall keep my statutes and my ordinances; by doing so one shall live: I am the LORD.

6 None of you shall approach anyone near of kin to uncover nakedness: I am the LORD. ⁷You shall not uncover the nakedness of your father, which is the nakedness of your mother; she is your mother, you shall not uncover her nakedness. ⁸You shall not uncover the nakedness of your father's wife; it is the nakedness of your father. ⁹You shall not uncover the nakedness of your sister, your father's daughter or your mother's daughter, whether born at home or born abroad. ¹⁰You shall not uncover the nakedness of your son's daughter or of your daughter's daughter, for their nakedness is your own nakedness. ¹¹You shall not uncover the nakedness of your father's wife's daughter, begotten by your father, since she is your sister. ¹²You shall not uncover the nakedness of your father's sister; she is your father's flesh. ¹³You shall not uncover the nakedness of your mother's sister, for she is your mother's flesh. ¹⁴You shall not uncover the nakedness of your father's brother, that is, you shall not approach his wife; she is your aunt. ¹⁵You shall not uncover the nakedness of your daughter-in-law: she is your son's wife; you shall not uncover her nakedness. ¹⁶You shall not uncover the nakedness of your brother's wife; it is your brother's nakedness. ¹⁷You shall not uncover the nakedness of a woman and her daughter, and you shall not take*a* her son's daughter or her daughter's daughter to uncover her nakedness; they are your*b* flesh; it is depravity. ¹⁸And you shall not take*a* a woman as a rival to her sister, uncovering her nakedness while her sister is still alive.

19 You shall not approach a woman to uncover her nakedness while she is in her menstrual uncleanness. ²⁰You shall not have sexual relations with your kinsman's wife, and defile yourself with her. ²¹You shall not give any of your offspring to sacrifice them*c* to Molech, and so profane the name of your God: I am the LORD. ²²You shall not lie with a male as with a woman; it is an abomination. ²³You shall not have sexual relations with any animal and defile yourself with it, nor shall any woman give herself to an animal to have sexual relations with it: it is perversion.

24 Do not defile yourselves in any of these ways, for by all these practices the nations I am casting out before you have defiled themselves. ²⁵Thus the land became defiled; and I punished it for its iniquity, and the land vomited out its inhabitants. ²⁶But you shall keep my statutes and my ordinances and commit none of these abominations, either the citizen or the alien who resides among you ²⁷(for the inhabitants of the land, who were before you, committed all of these abominations, and the land became defiled); ²⁸otherwise the land will vomit you out for defiling it, as it vomited out the nation that was before you. ²⁹For whoever commits any of these abominations shall be cut off from their people. ³⁰So keep my charge not to commit any of these abominations that were done before you, and not to defile yourselves by them: I am the LORD your God.

Be Holy, for I Am Holy

LEVITICUS 18.30—19.2

Read verses 1–2, then read 18.1–5. At the heart of these verses lies the major presupposition that forms the basis of all of God's charges against human sin, namely, that God's values are not human values (see Isaiah 55.6–9).

Write the headings "God's Values" and "Human Values" on a piece of paper. Read chapters 18 and 19 all the way through more slowly, making lists under the columns based on what you read. Compare and contrast them. What do these passages tell you about God's nature, as compared to human nature? What changes are you called to make in your life after looking at these passages?

See Meeting God in Scripture

Love Your Neighbor as Yourself

LEVITICUS 19.18

Does it surprise you that the rule of life that Christians equate so strongly with the New Testament—where it is quoted by Jesus (see Matthew 22.37–39), Paul (see Galatians 5.14) and James (see James 2.8)—is actually the core of the Old Testament's call to obedience?

Jesus quoted the Torah (the body of Jewish law) to condemn the self-righteous Pharisees, who were considered "experts" at interpreting and living it. Pharisees had turned this command into a way of excluding others by narrowing the definition of neighbor so much that it was practically meaningless. They twisted God's intent—to build up the community—into its exact opposite. What does the command to "Love your neighbor as yourself" mean to you? Within your understanding of grace, what does it require of you?

See Meeting God in Community

Ritual and Moral Holiness

19 The LORD spoke to Moses, saying: 2 Speak to all the congregation of the people of Israel and say to them: You shall be holy, for I the LORD your God am holy. ³You shall each revere your mother and father, and you shall keep my sabbaths: I am the LORD your God. ⁴Do not turn to idols or make cast images for yourselves: I am the LORD your God.

5 When you offer a sacrifice of well-being to the LORD, offer it in such a way that it is acceptable in your behalf. ⁶It shall be eaten on the same day you offer it, or on the next day; and anything left over until the third day shall be consumed in fire. ⁷If it is eaten at all on the third day, it is an abomination; it will not be acceptable. ⁸All who eat it shall be subject to punishment, because they have profaned what is holy to the LORD; and any such person shall be cut off from the people.

9 When you reap the harvest of your land, you shall not reap to the very edges of your field, or gather the gleanings of your harvest. ¹⁰You shall not strip your vineyard bare, or gather the fallen grapes of your vineyard; you shall leave them for the poor and the alien: I am the LORD your God.

11 You shall not steal; you shall not deal falsely; and you shall not lie to one another. ¹²And you shall not swear falsely by my name, profaning the name of your God: I am the LORD.

13 You shall not defraud your neighbor; you shall not steal; and you shall not keep for yourself the wages of a laborer until morning. ¹⁴You shall not revile the deaf or put a stumbling block before the blind; you shall fear your God: I am the LORD.

15 You shall not render an unjust judgment; you shall not be partial to the poor or defer to the great: with justice you shall judge your neighbor. ¹⁶You shall not go around as a slanderer[a] among your people, and you shall not profit by the blood[b] of your neighbor: I am the LORD.

17 You shall not hate in your heart anyone of your kin; you shall reprove your neighbor, or you will incur guilt yourself. ¹⁸You shall not take vengeance or bear a grudge against any of your people, but you shall love your neighbor as yourself: I am the LORD.

19 You shall keep my statutes. You shall not let your animals breed with a different kind; you shall not sow your field with two kinds of seed; nor shall you put on a garment made of two different materials.

20 If a man has sexual relations with a woman who is a slave, designated for another man but not ransomed or given her freedom, an inquiry shall be held. They shall not be put to death, since she has not been freed; ²¹but he shall bring a guilt offering for himself to the LORD, at the entrance of the tent of meeting, a ram as guilt offering. ²²And the priest shall make atonement for him with the ram of guilt offering before the LORD for his sin that he committed; and the sin he committed shall be forgiven him.

23 When you come into the land and plant all kinds of trees for food, then you shall regard their fruit as forbidden;[c] three years it shall be forbidden[d] to you, it must not

---

a Meaning of Heb uncertain   *b* Heb *stand against the blood*   *c* Heb *as their uncircumcision*   *d* Heb *uncircumcision*

be eaten. ²⁴In the fourth year all their fruit shall be set apart for rejoicing in the LORD. ²⁵But in the fifth year you may eat of their fruit, that their yield may be increased for you: I am the LORD your God.

26 You shall not eat anything with its blood. You shall not practice augury or witchcraft. ²⁷You shall not round off the hair on your temples or mar the edges of your beard. ²⁸You shall not make any gashes in your flesh for the dead or tattoo any marks upon you: I am the LORD.

29 Do not profane your daughter by making her a prostitute, that the land not become prostituted and full of depravity. ³⁰You shall keep my sabbaths and reverence my sanctuary: I am the LORD.

31 Do not turn to mediums or wizards; do not seek them out, to be defiled by them: I am the LORD your God.

32 You shall rise before the aged, and defer to the old; and you shall fear your God: I am the LORD.

33 When an alien resides with you in your land, you shall not oppress the alien. ³⁴The alien who resides with you shall be to you as the citizen among you; you shall love the alien as yourself, for you were aliens in the land of Egypt: I am the LORD your God.

35 You shall not cheat in measuring length, weight, or quantity. ³⁶You shall have honest balances, honest weights, an honest ephah, and an honest hin: I am the LORD your God, who brought you out of the land of Egypt. ³⁷You shall keep all my statutes and all my ordinances, and observe them: I am the LORD.

Penalties for Violations of Holiness

20 The LORD spoke to Moses, saying: ²Say further to the people of Israel:

Any of the people of Israel, or of the aliens who reside in Israel, who give any of their offspring to Molech shall be put to death; the people of the land shall stone them to death. ³I myself will set my face against them, and will cut them off from the people, because they have given of their offspring to Molech, defiling my sanctuary and profaning my holy name. ⁴And if the people of the land should ever close their eyes to them, when they give of their offspring to Molech, and do not put them to death, ⁵I myself will set my face against them and against their family, and will cut them off from among their people, them and all who follow them in prostituting themselves to Molech.

6 If any turn to mediums and wizards, prostituting themselves to them, I will set my face against them, and will cut them off from the people. ⁷Consecrate yourselves therefore, and be holy; for I am the LORD your God. ⁸Keep my statutes, and observe them; I am the LORD; I sanctify you. ⁹All who curse father or mother shall be put to death; having cursed father or mother, their blood is upon them.

10 If a man commits adultery with the wife of*ᵃ* his neighbor, both the adulterer and the adulteress shall be put to death. ¹¹The man who lies with his father's wife has uncovered his father's nakedness; both of them shall be put to death; their blood is upon them. ¹²If a man lies with his daughter-in-law, both of them shall be put to death; they have committed perversion, their blood is upon them. ¹³If a man lies with a male as with a woman, both of them have

---

I Am the Lord Your God

LEVITICUS 20.1–5

Chapter 20 is similar to chapter 18 in many ways. The harsh punishments called for in this chapter may be difficult for us to comprehend and accept. Even more difficult is to draw spiritual guidance from them. Most of the actions described in chapters 18 and 20, however, are not only violations against God, but are also actions that threaten the fabric of society itself. Passages such as these teach us just how society's values differ from God's.

Verse 4 warns that "If the people of the land should ever close their eyes [to the worship of Molech]," God will personally step in and punish the evildoers. In addition, the nation itself will be punished for disobedience (see verses 22–26). Make a list of ways that our society has "closed its eyes" to things that are an "abomination" to God. Are there ways that you, personally, are guilty of "closing your eyes" by being part of a society based on oppression?

See Meeting God in Community

---

a Heb repeats *if a man commits adultery with the wife of*

The Conduct of Leaders

LEVITICUS 21.1–14

Priests are held to a stricter standard than the average Israelite; the standard for the high priest is even more so. Similarly, the standard for overseers and deacons is high in the New Testament church (see 1 Timothy 3).

How important is it for a community that its leaders, whether religious or secular, be held to a stricter code of behavior than its lay people? Some Christian denominations choose their leaders by lot from a pool of qualified candidates, believing that God's Spirit will determine the final choice. What are some arguments for and against this procedure?

See Meeting God in Community

committed an abomination; they shall be put to death; their blood is upon them. ¹⁴If a man takes a wife and her mother also, it is depravity; they shall be burned to death, both he and they, that there may be no depravity among you. ¹⁵If a man has sexual relations with an animal, he shall be put to death; and you shall kill the animal. ¹⁶If a woman approaches any animal and has sexual relations with it, you shall kill the woman and the animal; they shall be put to death, their blood is upon them.

17 If a man takes his sister, a daughter of his father or a daughter of his mother, and sees her nakedness, and she sees his nakedness, it is a disgrace, and they shall be cut off in the sight of their people; he has uncovered his sister's nakedness, he shall be subject to punishment. ¹⁸If a man lies with a woman having her sickness and uncovers her nakedness, he has laid bare her flow and she has laid bare her flow of blood; both of them shall be cut off from their people. ¹⁹You shall not uncover the nakedness of your mother's sister or of your father's sister, for that is to lay bare one's own flesh; they shall be subject to punishment. ²⁰If a man lies with his uncle's wife, he has uncovered his uncle's nakedness; they shall be subject to punishment; they shall die childless. ²¹If a man takes his brother's wife, it is impurity; he has uncovered his brother's nakedness; they shall be childless.

22 You shall keep all my statutes and all my ordinances, and observe them, so that the land to which I bring you to settle in may not vomit you out. ²³You shall not follow the practices of the nation that I am driving out before you. Because they did all these things, I abhorred them. ²⁴But I have said to you: You shall inherit their land, and I will give it to you to possess, a land flowing with milk and honey. I am the LORD your God; I have separated you from the peoples. ²⁵You shall therefore make a distinction between the clean animal and the unclean, and between the unclean bird and the clean; you shall not bring abomination on yourselves by animal or by bird or by anything with which the ground teems, which I have set apart for you to hold unclean. ²⁶You shall be holy to me; for I the LORD am holy, and I have separated you from the other peoples to be mine.

27 A man or a woman who is a medium or a wizard shall be put to death; they shall be stoned to death, their blood is upon them.

The Holiness of Priests

21 The LORD said to Moses: Speak to the priests, the sons of Aaron, and say to them:

No one shall defile himself for a dead person among his relatives, ²except for his nearest kin: his mother, his father, his son, his daughter, his brother; ³likewise, for a virgin sister, close to him because she has had no husband, he may defile himself for her. ⁴But he shall not defile himself as a husband among his people and so profane himself. ⁵They shall not make bald spots upon their heads, or shave off the edges of their beards, or make any gashes in their flesh. ⁶They shall be holy to their God, and not profane the name of their God; for they offer the LORD's offerings by fire, the food of their God; therefore they shall be holy. ⁷They shall not marry a prostitute or a woman who has been defiled; neither shall they marry a woman divorced from her husband. For they are holy to their God, **8**and you shall treat them as holy, since they offer the food of your God; they shall be holy to you, for I the LORD, I who sanctify you, am holy. **9**When the daughter of a priest profanes herself through prostitution, she profanes her father; she shall be burned to death.

10 The priest who is exalted above his fellows, on whose head the anointing oil has been poured and who has been consecrated to wear the vestments, shall not dishevel his hair, nor tear his vestments. **11**He shall not go where there is a dead body; he shall not defile himself even for his father or mother. **12**He shall not go outside the sanctuary and thus profane the sanctuary of his God; for the consecration of the anointing oil of his God is upon him: I am the LORD. **13**He shall marry only a woman who is a virgin. **14**A widow, or a divorced woman, or a woman who has been defiled, a prostitute, these he shall not marry. He shall marry a virgin of his own kin, **15**that he may not profane his offspring among his kin; for I am the LORD; I sanctify him.

16 The LORD spoke to Moses, saying: **17**Speak to Aaron and say: No one of your offspring throughout their generations who has a blemish may approach to offer the food of his God. **18**For no one who has a blemish shall draw near, one who is blind or lame, or one who has a mutilated face or a limb too long, **19**or one who has a broken foot or a broken hand, **20**or a hunchback, or a dwarf, or a man with a blemish in his eyes or an itching disease or scabs or crushed testicles. **21**No descendant of Aaron the priest who has a blemish shall come near to offer the LORD's offerings by fire; since he has a blemish, he shall not come near to offer the food of his God. **22**He may eat the food of his God, of the most holy as well as of the holy. **23**But he shall not come near the curtain or approach the altar, because he has a blemish, that he may not profane my sanctuaries; for I am the LORD; I sanctify them. **24**Thus Moses spoke to Aaron and to his sons and to all the people of Israel.

The Use of Holy Offerings

22 The LORD spoke to Moses, saying: **2**Direct Aaron and his sons to deal carefully with the sacred donations of the people of Israel, which they dedicate to me, so that they may not profane my holy name; I am the LORD. **3**Say to them: If anyone among all your offspring throughout your generations comes near the sacred donations, which the people of Israel dedicate to the LORD, while he is in a state of uncleanness, that person shall be cut off from my presence: I am the LORD. **4**No one of Aaron's offspring who has a leprous*ᵃ* disease or suffers a discharge may eat of the sacred donations until he is clean. Whoever touches anything made unclean by a corpse or a man who has had an emission of semen, **5**and whoever touches any swarming thing by which he may be made unclean or any human being by whom he may be made unclean—whatever his uncleanness may be— **6**the person who touches any such shall be unclean until evening and shall not eat of the sacred donations unless he has washed his body in water. **7**When the sun sets he shall be clean; and afterward he may eat of the sacred donations, for they are his food. **8**That which died or was torn by wild animals he shall not

---

Sacred Donations

LEVITICUS 22.1–13

The "sacred donations" mentioned in this chapter are the portions of sacrificial animals received by the priests, and to some extent these portions represent their wages. Even so, the priests were not allowed to use them as they pleased.

Try to rewrite Leviticus 22.1–13 in your own words. Contemplate why the demands for obedience and penalties for disobedience were so much stricter for priests. What might be the effect on a society if it fails to hold its leadership accountable? What might be the effect if leadership is held to too strict a standard?

See Meeting God in Community

---

a A term for several skin diseases; precise meaning uncertain

Acceptable Offerings

LEVITICUS 22.19,29

Read these verses aloud. What does it mean to offer a sacrifice "so that it may be acceptable in your behalf"? What are ways that one might offer a sacrifice that would make it unacceptable?

While Christians believe that Jesus was *the* offering for our sin, we are also told by the apostle Paul to offer our bodies as "a living sacrifice." In what ways might we try to offer our lives with wrong or mixed motives?

Think about your own worship practices and those of the congregation you are part of. Are there aspects about your worship that might make it unacceptable? Offer these things in prayer to God.

See Meeting God in Worship

eat, becoming unclean by it: I am the LORD. ⁹They shall keep my charge, so that they may not incur guilt and die in the sanctuary*a* for having profaned it: I am the LORD; I sanctify them.

10 No lay person shall eat of the sacred donations. No bound or hired servant of the priest shall eat of the sacred donations; ¹¹but if a priest acquires anyone by purchase, the person may eat of them; and those that are born in his house may eat of his food. ¹²If a priest's daughter marries a layman, she shall not eat of the offering of the sacred donations; ¹³but if a priest's daughter is widowed or divorced, without offspring, and returns to her father's house, as in her youth, she may eat of her father's food. No lay person shall eat of it. ¹⁴If a man eats of the sacred donation unintentionally, he shall add one-fifth of its value to it, and give the sacred donation to the priest. ¹⁵No one shall profane the sacred donations of the people of Israel, which they offer to the LORD, ¹⁶causing them to bear guilt requiring a guilt offering, by eating their sacred donations: for I am the LORD; I sanctify them.

Acceptable Offerings

17 The LORD spoke to Moses, saying: ¹⁸Speak to Aaron and his sons and all the people of Israel and say to them: When anyone of the house of Israel or of the aliens residing in Israel presents an offering, whether in payment of a vow or as a freewill offering that is offered to the LORD as a burnt offering, ¹⁹to be acceptable in your behalf it shall be a male without blemish, of the cattle or the sheep or the goats. ²⁰You shall not offer anything that has a blemish, for it will not be acceptable in your behalf.

21 When anyone offers a sacrifice of well-being to the LORD, in fulfillment of a vow or as a freewill offering, from the herd or from the flock, to be acceptable it must be perfect; there shall be no blemish in it. ²²Anything blind, or injured, or maimed, or having a discharge or an itch or scabs—these you shall not offer to the LORD or put any of them on the altar as offerings by fire to the LORD. ²³An ox or a lamb that has a limb too long or too short you may present for a freewill offering; but it will not be accepted for a vow. ²⁴Any animal that has its testicles bruised or crushed or torn or cut, you shall not offer to the LORD; such you shall not do within your land, ²⁵nor shall you accept any such animals from a foreigner to offer as food to your God; since they are mutilated, with a blemish in them, they shall not be accepted in your behalf.

26 The LORD spoke to Moses, saying: ²⁷When an ox or a sheep or a goat is born, it shall remain seven days with its mother, and from the eighth day on it shall be acceptable as the LORD's offering by fire. ²⁸But you shall not slaughter, from the herd or the flock, an animal with its young on the same day. ²⁹When you sacrifice a thanksgiving offering to the LORD, you shall sacrifice it so that it may be acceptable in your behalf. ³⁰It shall be eaten on the same day; you shall not leave any of it until morning: I am the LORD.

31 Thus you shall keep my commandments and observe them: I am the LORD. ³²You shall not profane my holy name, that I may be sanctified among the people of Israel:

a Vg: Heb *incur guilt for it and die in it*

I am the LORD; I sanctify you, 33I who brought you out of the land of Egypt to be your God: I am the LORD.

Appointed Festivals

23 The LORD spoke to Moses, saying: 2Speak to the people of Israel and say to them: These are the appointed festivals of the LORD that you shall proclaim as holy convocations, my appointed festivals.

The Sabbath, Passover, and Unleavened Bread

3 Six days shall work be done; but the seventh day is a sabbath of complete rest, a holy convocation; you shall do no work: it is a sabbath to the LORD throughout your settlements.

4 These are the appointed festivals of the LORD, the holy convocations, which you shall celebrate at the time appointed for them. 5In the first month, on the fourteenth day of the month, at twilight,a there shall be a passover offering to the LORD, 6and on the fifteenth day of the same month is the festival of unleavened bread to the LORD; seven days you shall eat unleavened bread. 7On the first day you shall have a holy convocation; you shall not work at your occupations. 8For seven days you shall present the LORD's offerings by fire; on the seventh day there shall be a holy convocation: you shall not work at your occupations.

The Offering of First Fruits

9 The LORD spoke to Moses: 10Speak to the people of Israel and say to them: When you enter the land that I am giving you and you reap its harvest, you shall bring the sheaf of the first fruits of your harvest to the priest. 11He shall raise the sheaf before the LORD, that you may find acceptance; on the day after the sabbath the priest shall raise it. 12On the day when you raise the sheaf, you shall offer a lamb a year old, without blemish, as a burnt offering to the LORD. 13And the grain offering with it shall be two-tenths of an ephah of choice flour mixed with oil, an offering by fire of pleasing odor to the LORD; and the drink offering with it shall be of wine, one-fourth of a hin. 14You shall eat no bread or parched grain or fresh ears until that very day, until you have brought the offering of your God: it is a statute forever throughout your generations in all your settlements.

The Festival of Weeks

15 And from the day after the sabbath, from the day on which you bring the sheaf of the elevation offering, you shall count off seven weeks; they shall be complete. 16You shall count until the day after the seventh sabbath, fifty days; then you shall present an offering of new grain to the LORD. 17You shall bring from your settlements two loaves of bread as an elevation offering, each made of two-tenths of an ephah; they shall be of choice flour, baked with leaven, as first fruits to the LORD. 18You shall present with the bread seven lambs a year old without blemish, one young bull, and two rams; they shall be a burnt offering to the LORD, along with their grain offering and their drink offerings, an offering by fire of pleasing odor to the LORD. 19You shall also

Remember the Sabbath

LEVITICUS 23.3

The Hebrew word *sabbath* comes from the root word "to stop." God delivered the Israelites from harsh slavery and required that for one day out of every seven everyone should rest from the daily routine. Jesus taught that the sabbath was created for humans, and not vice versa. Given this background, what are the implications of the sabbath regulations?

What is your view of the sabbath? Does your weekly routine include a "sabbath"? Consider celebrating the sabbath as an act of faith, a way of letting go of your normal routine and your worldly concerns, and trusting God to provide what you need.

See Meeting God in Worship

---

a Heb *between the two evenings*

The Earth Is the Lord's

LEVITICUS 23.37–38

The largest part of the offerings the Hebrew people brought were the fruits of the field. If you have a vegetable or flower garden, arrange an offering from it in a basket. If you don't have a garden, prepare an offering basket using produce you buy (or use canned goods). Place the basket in a prominent place in your home. Write a special prayer of thanksgiving to use as a blessing at meals (or read Psalm 67). After a week, use the food to prepare a special meal of thanks, or give the food (or a monetary donation) to a food bank or other organization that helps to feed the poor.

See Meeting God in Service

offer one male goat for a sin offering, and two male lambs a year old as a sacrifice of well-being. ²⁰The priest shall raise them with the bread of the first fruits as an elevation offering before the LORD, together with the two lambs; they shall be holy to the LORD for the priest. ²¹On that same day you shall make proclamation; you shall hold a holy convocation; you shall not work at your occupations. This is a statute forever in all your settlements throughout your generations.

22 When you reap the harvest of your land, you shall not reap to the very edges of your field, or gather the gleanings of your harvest; you shall leave them for the poor and for the alien: I am the LORD your God.

The Festival of Trumpets

23 The LORD spoke to Moses, saying: ²⁴Speak to the people of Israel, saying: In the seventh month, on the first day of the month, you shall observe a day of complete rest, a holy convocation commemorated with trumpet blasts. ²⁵You shall not work at your occupations; and you shall present the LORD's offering by fire.

The Day of Atonement

26 The LORD spoke to Moses, saying: ²⁷Now, the tenth day of this seventh month is the day of atonement; it shall be a holy convocation for you: you shall deny yourselves[a] and present the LORD's offering by fire; ²⁸and you shall do no work during that entire day; for it is a day of atonement, to make atonement on your behalf before the LORD your God. ²⁹For anyone who does not practice self-denial[b] during that entire day shall be cut off from the people. ³⁰And anyone who does any work during that entire day, such a one I will destroy from the midst of the people. ³¹You shall do no work: it is a statute forever throughout your generations in all your settlements. ³²It shall be to you a sabbath of complete rest, and you shall deny yourselves;[a] on the ninth day of the month at evening, from evening to evening you shall keep your sabbath.

The Festival of Booths

33 The LORD spoke to Moses, saying: ³⁴Speak to the people of Israel, saying: On the fifteenth day of this seventh month, and lasting seven days, there shall be the festival of booths[c] to the LORD. ³⁵The first day shall be a holy convocation; you shall not work at your occupations. ³⁶Seven days you shall present the LORD's offerings by fire; on the eighth day you shall observe a holy convocation and present the LORD's offerings by fire; it is a solemn assembly; you shall not work at your occupations.

37 These are the appointed festivals of the LORD, which you shall celebrate as times of holy convocation, for presenting to the LORD offerings by fire—burnt offerings and grain offerings, sacrifices and drink offerings, each on its proper day— ³⁸apart from the sabbaths of the LORD, and apart from your gifts, and apart from all your votive offerings, and apart from all your freewill offerings, which you give to the LORD.

39 Now, the fifteenth day of the seventh month, when you have gathered in the produce of the land, you shall

a Or *shall fast*   *b* Or *does not fast*   *c* Or *tabernacles*: Heb *succoth*

keep the festival of the LORD, lasting seven days; a complete rest on the first day, and a complete rest on the eighth day. ⁴⁰On the first day you shall take the fruit of majestic*ᵃ* trees, branches of palm trees, boughs of leafy trees, and willows of the brook; and you shall rejoice before the LORD your God for seven days. ⁴¹You shall keep it as a festival to the LORD seven days in the year; you shall keep it in the seventh month as a statute forever throughout your generations. ⁴²You shall live in booths for seven days; all that are citizens in Israel shall live in booths, ⁴³so that your generations may know that I made the people of Israel live in booths when I brought them out of the land of Egypt: I am the LORD your God.

44 Thus Moses declared to the people of Israel the appointed festivals of the LORD.

The Lamp

24 The LORD spoke to Moses, saying: ²Command the people of Israel to bring you pure oil of beaten olives for the lamp, that a light may be kept burning regularly. ³Aaron shall set it up in the tent of meeting, outside the curtain of the covenant,*ᵇ* to burn from evening to morning before the LORD regularly; it shall be a statute forever throughout your generations. ⁴He shall set up the lamps on the lampstand of pure gold*ᶜ* before the LORD regularly.

The Bread for the Tabernacle

5 You shall take choice flour, and bake twelve loaves of it; two-tenths of an ephah shall be in each loaf. ⁶You shall place them in two rows, six in a row, on the table of pure gold.*ᵈ* ⁷You shall put pure frankincense with each row, to be a token offering for the bread, as an offering by fire to the LORD. ⁸Every sabbath day Aaron shall set them in order before the LORD regularly as a commitment of the people of Israel, as a covenant forever. ⁹They shall be for Aaron and his descendants, who shall eat them in a holy place, for they are most holy portions for him from the offerings by fire to the LORD, a perpetual due.

Blasphemy and Its Punishment

10 A man whose mother was an Israelite and whose father was an Egyptian came out among the people of Israel; and the Israelite woman's son and a certain Israelite began fighting in the camp. ¹¹The Israelite woman's son blasphemed the Name in a curse. And they brought him to Moses—now his mother's name was Shelomith, daughter of Dibri, of the tribe of Dan— ¹²and they put him in custody, until the decision of the LORD should be made clear to them.

13 The LORD said to Moses, saying: ¹⁴Take the blasphemer outside the camp; and let all who were within hearing lay their hands on his head, and let the whole congregation stone him. ¹⁵And speak to the people of Israel, saying: Anyone who curses God shall bear the sin. ¹⁶One who blasphemes the name of the LORD shall be put to death; the whole congregation shall stone the blasphemer. Aliens as well as citizens, when they blaspheme the Name, shall be

Eye for Eye, Tooth for Tooth

LEVITICUS 24.13–21

This so-called "law of retaliation," which for many people symbolizes the harshness of the Old Testament law, is actually an attempt to prevent a punishment from exceeding the crime. Rather than retribution, the major purpose of the law codes is to restore the community to its original state. What is more, this law was rarely interpreted literally. With the exception of murder, crimes of bodily injury were normally settled by paying the injured person a fine.

When does our society still demand "eye for eye, tooth for tooth"? Read Matthew 5.38–42. How does Jesus' interpretation counter traditional thinking? Are his demands practical? What might the effect be on an individual or on a society that strictly follows this command without exception?

See Meeting God in Community

---

a Meaning of Heb uncertain   *b* Or *treaty*, or *testament*; Heb *eduth*
c Heb *pure lampstand*   *d* Heb *pure table*

The Year of Jubilee

LEVITICUS 25.1–55

The year of jubilee was a year when the slate was wiped clean and Israel returned to its original state: All debts were forgiven, all Israelite slaves were freed, all land was returned to its original owners (and owners to their land!) and the land was to lie fallow.

Imagine yourself as a wealthy Israelite, and read this passage again. Imagine yourself as a poor Israelite. How do your emotions change?

For Isaiah, the year of jubilee symbolized God's coming reign on earth (Isaiah 62.1–4); for Jesus, it symbolized his ministry and the kingdom of God (Luke 4.18–21). Write your own description of God's reign with Leviticus 25 as a model. What would be the result of a jubilee year (or even a sabbatical year) on our economy?

See *Meeting God in Community*

put to death. [17]Anyone who kills a human being shall be put to death. [18]Anyone who kills an animal shall make restitution for it, life for life. [19]Anyone who maims another shall suffer the same injury in return: [20]fracture for fracture, eye for eye, tooth for tooth; the injury inflicted is the injury to be suffered. [21]One who kills an animal shall make restitution for it; but one who kills a human being shall be put to death. [22]You shall have one law for the alien and for the citizen: for I am the LORD your God. [23]Moses spoke thus to the people of Israel; and they took the blasphemer outside the camp, and stoned him to death. The people of Israel did as the LORD had commanded Moses.

The Sabbatical Year

25 The LORD spoke to Moses on Mount Sinai, saying: [2]Speak to the people of Israel and say to them: When you enter the land that I am giving you, the land shall observe a sabbath for the LORD. [3]Six years you shall sow your field, and six years you shall prune your vineyard, and gather in their yield; [4]but in the seventh year there shall be a sabbath of complete rest for the land, a sabbath for the LORD: you shall not sow your field or prune your vineyard. [5]You shall not reap the aftergrowth of your harvest or gather the grapes of your unpruned vine: it shall be a year of complete rest for the land. [6]You may eat what the land yields during its sabbath—you, your male and female slaves, your hired and your bound laborers who live with you; [7]for your livestock also, and for the wild animals in your land all its yield shall be for food.

The Year of Jubilee

8 You shall count off seven weeks[a] of years, seven times seven years, so that the period of seven weeks of years gives forty-nine years. [9]Then you shall have the trumpet sounded loud; on the tenth day of the seventh month—on the day of atonement—you shall have the trumpet sounded throughout all your land. [10]And you shall hallow the fiftieth year and you shall proclaim liberty throughout the land to all its inhabitants. It shall be a jubilee for you: you shall return, every one of you, to your property and every one of you to your family. [11]That fiftieth year shall be a jubilee for you: you shall not sow, or reap the aftergrowth, or harvest the unpruned vines. [12]For it is a jubilee; it shall be holy to you: you shall eat only what the field itself produces.

13 In this year of jubilee you shall return, every one of you, to your property. [14]When you make a sale to your neighbor or buy from your neighbor, you shall not cheat one another. [15]When you buy from your neighbor, you shall pay only for the number of years since the jubilee; the seller shall charge you only for the remaining crop years. [16]If the years are more, you shall increase the price, and if the years are fewer, you shall diminish the price; for it is a certain number of harvests that are being sold to you. [17]You shall not cheat one another, but you shall fear your God; for I am the LORD your God.

18 You shall observe my statutes and faithfully keep my ordinances, so that you may live on the land securely. [19]The land will yield its fruit, and you will eat your fill and live on it securely. [20]Should you ask, "What shall we eat in the sev-

a Or *sabbaths*

enth year, if we may not sow or gather in our crop?" ²¹I will order my blessing for you in the sixth year, so that it will yield a crop for three years. ²²When you sow in the eighth year, you will be eating from the old crop; until the ninth year, when its produce comes in, you shall eat the old. ²³The land shall not be sold in perpetuity, for the land is mine; with me you are but aliens and tenants. ²⁴Throughout the land that you hold, you shall provide for the redemption of the land.

25 If anyone of your kin falls into difficulty and sells a piece of property, then the next of kin shall come and redeem what the relative has sold. ²⁶If the person has no one to redeem it, but then prospers and finds sufficient means to do so, ²⁷the years since its sale shall be computed and the difference shall be refunded to the person to whom it was sold, and the property shall be returned. ²⁸But if there are not sufficient means to recover it, what was sold shall remain with the purchaser until the year of jubilee; in the jubilee it shall be released, and the property shall be returned.

29 If anyone sells a dwelling house in a walled city, it may be redeemed until a year has elapsed since its sale; the right of redemption shall be one year. ³⁰If it is not redeemed before a full year has elapsed, a house that is in a walled city shall pass in perpetuity to the purchaser, throughout the generations; it shall not be released in the jubilee. ³¹But houses in villages that have no walls around them shall be classed as open country; they may be redeemed, and they shall be released in the jubilee. ³²As for the cities of the Levites, the Levites shall forever have the right of redemption of the houses in the cities belonging to them. ³³Such property as may be redeemed from the Levites—houses sold in a city belonging to them—shall be released in the jubilee; because the houses in the cities of the Levites are their possession among the people of Israel. ³⁴But the open land around their cities may not be sold; for that is their possession for all time.

35 If any of your kin fall into difficulty and become dependent on you,ᵃ you shall support them; they shall live with you as though resident aliens. ³⁶Do not take interest in advance or otherwise make a profit from them, but fear your God; let them live with you. ³⁷You shall not lend them your money at interest taken in advance, or provide them food at a profit. ³⁸I am the LORD your God, who brought you out of the land of Egypt, to give you the land of Canaan, to be your God.

39 If any who are dependent on you become so impoverished that they sell themselves to you, you shall not make them serve as slaves. ⁴⁰They shall remain with you as hired or bound laborers. They shall serve with you until the year of the jubilee. ⁴¹Then they and their children with them shall be free from your authority; they shall go back to their own family and return to their ancestral property. ⁴²For they are my servants, whom I brought out of the land of Egypt; they shall not be sold as slaves are sold. ⁴³You shall not rule over them with harshness, but shall fear your God. ⁴⁴As for the male and female slaves whom you may have, it is from the nations around you that you may acquire male and female slaves. ⁴⁵You may also acquire them from

But Fear Your God

LEVITICUS 25.36–37

Throughout chapters 24 and 25, these guidelines about property ownership and monetary ethics are accented with the phrase, "I am the LORD your God" (24.22; 25.17,37). Verse 36 of chapter 25 underlines the principle that determines all financial and business dealings—indeed, all of life, with the phrase: "but fear your God." Write out each of these phrases. In a few words or a paragraph, write down what each one means to you. Why would God be interested in your financial transactions? Make it personal. Think of some of the financial and business dealings you may have carried out in the last month or some of the interactions you may have had at work or school. How does each one appear when scrutinized in the light of these two phrases?

See Meeting God in Everyday Life

The Fruit of Obedience

LEVITICUS 26.3–13

We are saved by God's grace. Our obedience is to be a joyous response to God's saving acts (in the case of Israel, this was deliverance from slavery in Egypt; for Christians, it is deliverance from the bondage of sin through Jesus' death and resurrection). But God has also promised further blessings for obedient individuals and communities.

Read these verses slowly, as if God were speaking directly to you and your faith community. What emotions do these verses prompt within you? Share them with God in prayer. Contemplate the difference between honest obedience as a joyous response to both God's past saving acts and your anticipation of future blessings, and obedience based primarily on the hope of reward. Could you, like Job, lose everything and still praise God (see Job 13.15)? Contemplate whether your obedience is motivated by joy, hope of reward or fear of punishment. Offer your response to God.

See Meeting God in Scripture

among the aliens residing with you, and from their families that are with you, who have been born in your land; and they may be your property. ⁴⁶You may keep them as a possession for your children after you, for them to inherit as property. These you may treat as slaves, but as for your fellow Israelites, no one shall rule over the other with harshness.

47 If resident aliens among you prosper, and if any of your kin fall into difficulty with one of them and sell themselves to an alien, or to a branch of the alien's family, ⁴⁸after they have sold themselves they shall have the right of redemption; one of their brothers may redeem them, ⁴⁹or their uncle or their uncle's son may redeem them, or anyone of their family who is of their own flesh may redeem them; or if they prosper they may redeem themselves. ⁵⁰They shall compute with the purchaser the total from the year when they sold themselves to the alien until the jubilee year; the price of the sale shall be applied to the number of years: the time they were with the owner shall be rated as the time of a hired laborer. ⁵¹If many years remain, they shall pay for their redemption in proportion to the purchase price; ⁵²and if few years remain until the jubilee year, they shall compute thus: according to the years involved they shall make payment for their redemption. ⁵³As a laborer hired by the year they shall be under the alien's authority, who shall not, however, rule with harshness over them in your sight. ⁵⁴And if they have not been redeemed in any of these ways, they and their children with them shall go free in the jubilee year. ⁵⁵For to me the people of Israel are servants; they are my servants whom I brought out from the land of Egypt: I am the LORD your God.

Rewards for Obedience

26 You shall make for yourselves no idols and erect no carved images or pillars, and you shall not place figured stones in your land, to worship at them; for I am the LORD your God. ²You shall keep my sabbaths and reverence my sanctuary: I am the LORD.

3 If you follow my statutes and keep my commandments and observe them faithfully, ⁴I will give you your rains in their season, and the land shall yield its produce, and the trees of the field shall yield their fruit. ⁵Your threshing shall overtake the vintage, and the vintage shall overtake the sowing; you shall eat your bread to the full, and live securely in your land. ⁶And I will grant peace in the land, and you shall lie down, and no one shall make you afraid; I will remove dangerous animals from the land, and no sword shall go through your land. ⁷You shall give chase to your enemies, and they shall fall before you by the sword. ⁸Five of you shall give chase to a hundred, and a hundred of you shall give chase to ten thousand; your enemies shall fall before you by the sword. ⁹I will look with favor upon you and make you fruitful and multiply you; and I will maintain my covenant with you. ¹⁰You shall eat old grain long stored, and you shall have to clear out the old to make way for the new. ¹¹I will place my dwelling in your midst, and I shall not abhor you. ¹²And I will walk among you, and will be your God, and you shall be my people. ¹³I am the LORD your God who brought you out of the land of

Egypt, to be their slaves no more; I have broken the bars of your yoke and made you walk erect.

Penalties for Disobedience

14 But if you will not obey me, and do not observe all these commandments, ¹⁵if you spurn my statutes, and abhor my ordinances, so that you will not observe all my commandments, and you break my covenant, ¹⁶I in turn will do this to you: I will bring terror on you; consumption and fever that waste the eyes and cause life to pine away. You shall sow your seed in vain, for your enemies shall eat it. ¹⁷I will set my face against you, and you shall be struck down by your enemies; your foes shall rule over you, and you shall flee though no one pursues you. ¹⁸And if in spite of this you will not obey me, I will continue to punish you sevenfold for your sins. ¹⁹I will break your proud glory, and I will make your sky like iron and your earth like copper. ²⁰Your strength shall be spent to no purpose: your land shall not yield its produce, and the trees of the land shall not yield their fruit.

21 If you continue hostile to me, and will not obey me, I will continue to plague you sevenfold for your sins. ²²I will let loose wild animals against you, and they shall bereave you of your children and destroy your livestock; they shall make you few in number, and your roads shall be deserted.

23 If in spite of these punishments you have not turned back to me, but continue hostile to me, ²⁴then I too will continue hostile to you: I myself will strike you sevenfold for your sins. ²⁵I will bring the sword against you, executing vengeance for the covenant; and if you withdraw within your cities, I will send pestilence among you, and you shall be delivered into enemy hands. ²⁶When I break your staff of bread, ten women shall bake your bread in a single oven, and they shall dole out your bread by weight; and though you eat, you shall not be satisfied.

27 But if, despite this, you disobey me, and continue hostile to me, ²⁸I will continue hostile to you in fury; I in turn will punish you myself sevenfold for your sins. ²⁹You shall eat the flesh of your sons, and you shall eat the flesh of your daughters. ³⁰I will destroy your high places and cut down your incense altars; I will heap your carcasses on the carcasses of your idols. I will abhor you. ³¹I will lay your cities waste, will make your sanctuaries desolate, and I will not smell your pleasing odors. ³²I will devastate the land, so that your enemies who come to settle in it shall be appalled at it. ³³And you I will scatter among the nations, and I will unsheathe the sword against you; your land shall be a desolation, and your cities a waste.

34 Then the land shall enjoy*a* its sabbath years as long as it lies desolate, while you are in the land of your enemies; then the land shall rest, and enjoy*a* its sabbath years. ³⁵As long as it lies desolate, it shall have the rest it did not have on your sabbaths when you were living on it. ³⁶And as for those of you who survive, I will send faintness into their hearts in the lands of their enemies; the sound of a driven leaf shall put them to flight, and they shall flee as one flees from the sword, and they shall fall though no one pursues. ³⁷They shall stumble over one another, as if to escape a sword, though no one pursues; and you shall have no

The Land Must Rest

LEVITICUS 26.23–26

As God declared the day of sabbath rest for men and women to be renewed and to rest from labor, so he declared a year of sabbath rest for the land. Why do you think God wanted the land to rest? How might the people have survived without cultivating the land? How might they have prepared for the sabbath year? What is God saying to you about creation through this passage? What might you do in response?

See Meeting God in Scripture

And to God, the Things That Are God's

LEVITICUS 27.2–23

Chapter 27 deals with the payment of vows, which were offerings usually given as expressions of thanks in special circumstances. Items themselves, or their value (plus twenty percent), could be donated.

When you have unexpected windfalls or times of joy, is your first reaction to thank God and make a special offering? Think of times when it might be appropriate for you or your faith community to make a special donation to God. Some churches include a budget line in capital improvements as a special donation to serve as a reminder that all things come from God. What are other ways that we can go beyond our normal requirement to honor God?

Put a jar or bank in a conspicuous place in your home. Then, whenever you buy a gift for a friend or something for yourself, make a donation to God as well. Decide ahead of time which charity will receive the money.

See Meeting God in Service

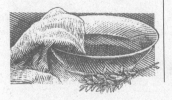

power to stand against your enemies. ³⁸You shall perish among the nations, and the land of your enemies shall devour you. ³⁹And those of you who survive shall languish in the land of your enemies because of their iniquities; also they shall languish because of the iniquities of their ancestors.

40 But if they confess their iniquity and the iniquity of their ancestors, in that they committed treachery against me and, moreover, that they continued hostile to me— ⁴¹so that I, in turn, continued hostile to them and brought them into the land of their enemies; if then their uncircumcised heart is humbled and they make amends for their iniquity, ⁴²then will I remember my covenant with Jacob; I will remember also my covenant with Isaac and also my covenant with Abraham, and I will remember the land. ⁴³For the land shall be deserted by them, and enjoy*ᵃ* its sabbath years by lying desolate without them, while they shall make amends for their iniquity, because they dared to spurn my ordinances, and they abhorred my statutes. ⁴⁴Yet for all that, when they are in the land of their enemies, I will not spurn them, or abhor them so as to destroy them utterly and break my covenant with them; for I am the LORD their God; ⁴⁵but I will remember in their favor the covenant with their ancestors whom I brought out of the land of Egypt in the sight of the nations, to be their God: I am the LORD.

46 These are the statutes and ordinances and laws that the LORD established between himself and the people of Israel on Mount Sinai through Moses.

Votive Offerings

27 The LORD spoke to Moses, saying: ²Speak to the people of Israel and say to them: When a person makes an explicit vow to the LORD concerning the equivalent for a human being, ³the equivalent for a male shall be: from twenty to sixty years of age the equivalent shall be fifty shekels of silver by the sanctuary shekel. ⁴If the person is a female, the equivalent is thirty shekels. ⁵If the age is from five to twenty years of age, the equivalent is twenty shekels for a male and ten shekels for a female. ⁶If the age is from one month to five years, the equivalent for a male is five shekels of silver, and for a female the equivalent is three shekels of silver. ⁷And if the person is sixty years old or over, then the equivalent for a male is fifteen shekels, and for a female ten shekels. ⁸If any cannot afford the equivalent, they shall be brought before the priest and the priest shall assess them; the priest shall assess them according to what each one making a vow can afford.

9 If it concerns an animal that may be brought as an offering to the LORD, any such that may be given to the LORD shall be holy. ¹⁰Another shall not be exchanged or substituted for it, either good for bad or bad for good; and if one animal is substituted for another, both that one and its substitute shall be holy. ¹¹If it concerns any unclean animal that may not be brought as an offering to the LORD, the animal shall be presented before the priest. ¹²The priest shall assess it: whether good or bad, according to the assessment of the priest, so it shall be. ¹³But if it is to be redeemed, one-fifth must be added to the assessment.

a Or make up for

14 If a person consecrates a house to the LORD, the priest shall assess it: whether good or bad, as the priest assesses it, so it shall stand. 15And if the one who consecrates the house wishes to redeem it, one-fifth shall be added to its assessed value, and it shall revert to the original owner.

16 If a person consecrates to the LORD any inherited landholding, its assessment shall be in accordance with its seed requirements: fifty shekels of silver to a homer of barley seed. 17If the person consecrates the field as of the year of jubilee, that assessment shall stand; 18but if the field is consecrated after the jubilee, the priest shall compute the price for it according to the years that remain until the year of jubilee, and the assessment shall be reduced. 19And if the one who consecrates the field wishes to redeem it, then one-fifth shall be added to its assessed value, and it shall revert to the original owner; 20but if the field is not redeemed, or if it has been sold to someone else, it shall no longer be redeemable. 21But when the field is released in the jubilee, it shall be holy to the LORD as a devoted field; it becomes the priest's holding. 22If someone consecrates to the LORD a field that has been purchased, which is not a part of the inherited landholding, 23the priest shall compute for it the proportionate assessment up to the year of jubilee, and the assessment shall be paid as of that day, a sacred donation to the LORD. 24In the year of jubilee the field shall return to the one from whom it was bought, whose holding the land is. 25All assessments shall be by the sanctuary shekel: twenty gerahs shall make a shekel.

26 A firstling of animals, however, which as a firstling belongs to the LORD, cannot be consecrated by anyone; whether ox or sheep, it is the LORD's. 27If it is an unclean animal, it shall be ransomed at its assessment, with one-fifth added; if it is not redeemed, it shall be sold at its assessment.

28 Nothing that a person owns that has been devoted to destruction for the LORD, be it human or animal, or inherited landholding, may be sold or redeemed; every devoted thing is most holy to the LORD. 29No human beings who have been devoted to destruction can be ransomed; they shall be put to death.

30 All tithes from the land, whether the seed from the ground or the fruit from the tree, are the LORD's; they are holy to the LORD. 31If persons wish to redeem any of their tithes, they must add one-fifth to them. 32All tithes of herd and flock, every tenth one that passes under the shepherd's staff, shall be holy to the LORD. 33Let no one inquire whether it is good or bad, or make substitution for it; if one makes substitution for it, then both it and the substitute shall be holy and cannot be redeemed.

34 These are the commandments that the LORD gave to Moses for the people of Israel on Mount Sinai.

What Belongs to the Lord

LEVITICUS 27.26

Suppose you were to take an article of clothing from your spouse's closet, wrap it up and give it to him or her for Christmas. What kind of response might you expect?

Giving to God what already belongs to him is not a gift. What can you give to God that goes beyond your normal tithe or usual offering? Such a gift is voluntary, but not to be entered into lightly or casually. Consider giving a special gift of devotion to God today. Will it be monetary? A gift of service?

See Meeting God in Worship

WAYS of MEETING GOD

Meeting God in Prayer

Many Christians suffer under the assumption that they should automatically know how to pray. If someone has a real relationship with God, the reasoning goes, prayer should flow spontaneously from the heart. And it often does.

Sometimes, however, we need guidance—we need to learn to pray. Prayer grows out of a relationship with God that is permeated by grace and love and is therefore preeminently communion—wordless, spirit-to-spirit oneness with God.

> **The Lord's Prayer is not just a prayer to *say* but, more significantly, a *way* to pray.**

But prayer is also conversation with God. And just as toddlers learn to talk by listening and mimicking the words of their parents, so we learn to pray by using the words God has given us. In the pages of the Bible we discover not only teaching about prayer but ancient prayers that help us dialogue with God today. "Repeating God's words after [God]," wrote Dietrich Bonhoeffer, "we begin to pray to [God]."

The Lord's Prayer. One very meaningful way to "repeat God's words" in our prayers is through the prayer Jesus gave his disciples—the Lord's Prayer. In Luke 11.1–13 an anonymous disciple comes to Jesus saying, "Lord, teach us to pray, as John taught his disciples." The man is making an understandable request; a Jewish rabbi in that time often gave his followers an outline for prayer that expressed the unique characteristics of his teaching, an exercise that brought the group together around a common identity. But behind the disciple's request lies a deeper need. He wants to know how to both *commune* and *communicate* with God. Many of us still make the same request as this disciple. Jesus' response can enrich and transform our praying. In fact, many consider the "discovery" of this prayer as a turning point in their prayer life. The Lord's Prayer is not just a prayer to *say* but, more significantly, a *way* to pray. More than a formula to recite, the Lord's Prayer guides us through three successive movements of opening ourselves to God.

Adoration. "Father, hallowed be your name. Your kingdom come." Adoration celebrates our communion with God. It brings us into conscious awareness of the reality of God with us. Adoration focuses our attention on God, liberating us from focusing on ourselves and setting the context for all true prayer. In adoration we align our lives with God's purposes; we gladly let go of lesser attachments and give God's love full control of our hearts and minds. We respond with gratitude to the God who first called us into a loving relationship.

An act of adoration may consist of slowly repeating the words, "Father, holy and honored be your name" for a period of time, letting Jesus' name for God give expression to our love and praise as God's children. We may build on these trusted words with psalms of praise or familiar hymns that come to mind. Our prayer may give way to improvisation: words of our own, images, songs and other spontaneous expressions of praise and thanksgiving that we verbalize or write. Adoration may consist of quiet reading and reflection on scripture verses and spiritual classics that bring us into God's presence.

Petition. "Give us each day our daily bread . . . and do not bring us to the time of trial." Petition is asking God for what we need, especially for those things we need in order to continue in our communion with him. When adoration has set the proper context for prayer—a focus on God and his kingdom—no need or concern is too small to bring to him. Jesus said, "Ask, and it will be given you; search, and you will find; knock, and the door will be opened for you" (Matthew 7.7). In doing so, we daily acknowledge this all-embracing truth about our lives: We are creatures who are utterly dependent on our loving Creator. Petition is the expression of our total dependence on God for everything: our existence, bread and water, relationships and community, grace and destiny.

Petition invites us to bring to God no less than the totality of our daily lives: our joys and struggles, hopes and hurts, desires and disappointments, loves and hates, pleas and resentments, and our need for healing and for change. By opening ourselves fully to God, we allow God to meet our true needs; God may also kindle in us a desire to question some of our perceived needs. By presenting to God every desire and request, we allow God to bless worthy dreams, to expose not-so-worthy dreams and to give us a passion for God's own dreams. Far from being self-centered, petition is the avenue through which God sustains us in grace and transforms our daily lives. It expresses our faith that God is committed to giving us all we truly need in order to grow in grace and truth.

Contrition. "Forgive us our sins, for we ourselves forgive everyone indebted to us." Contrition seeks grace to restore our communion with God. It is acknowledging the relationships that exist between God and ourselves and ourselves and our neighbor. It is admitting that there are areas in which we have failed. Contrition is the inner chamber of decision and transformation where sin and grace meet, where, with Jesus, we die to sin and rise with him to new life. In contrition we allow God's love to melt our hate, his forgiveness to wash away our guilt and his Spirit to move us to change. "If we say that we have no sin, we deceive ourselves, and the truth is not in us," John writes. "If we confess our sins, he who is faithful and just will forgive us our sins and cleanse us from all unrighteousness" (1 John 1.8–9).

Contrition is also opening to God those parts of our lives that have been closed to him. We humbly confess our unfaithfulness and surrender the sin at work within us to the mercy of God. We receive God's forgiveness and take steps to turn around and live in grateful cooperation with the redeeming love of God. We pray for the sort of world God wants and for the ability to be the sort of people God desires us to be. The prayer Jesus taught us is a pattern for opening ourselves up to God—for transforming our lives.

The Lord's Prayer, then, is both a prayer and a formula for prayer. Dietrich Bonhoeffer says of it, "Every prayer is contained in it . . . All the prayers of Holy Scripture are summarized in the Lord's Prayer, and are contained in its immeasurable breadth."

> The prayer Jesus taught us is a pattern for opening ourselves up to God —for transforming our lives.

Praying the Bible. Notwithstanding the centrality of the Lord's Prayer, there is much to be learned about praying other prayers of the Bible. Perhaps no other book of the Bible has been prayed more frequently than the book of Psalms. Of the Psalter, the collection of psalms, Martin Luther once wrote, "It penetrates the Lord's Prayer and the Lord's Prayer penetrates it, so that it is possible to understand one on the basis of the other and to bring them into joyful harmony." No wonder some call Psalms the "prayer book of the Bible." The psalms can help us find prayerful expression for all of our life before God: from lamentations to praises, from doubt to joy. For example, "The LORD is my shepherd, I shall not want" (Psalm 23.1) may serve to lead us into actual conversation with God. "You are my shepherd, Lord," we might say. "Thank you for promising to provide what I need."

Any Biblical passage that speaks to us can be woven into our praying. This is a powerful way to enter into the heart of scripture. Praying through the Ten Commandments can become a prayer of self-examination. Praying through the parables helps us understand God's values. Praying through 1 Corinthians 13 aligns us with God's heart of love for others.

In a liturgy in which the prayers of adoration, confession and petition are from scripture—whether in the form of readings, hymns or canticles—the body of

Christ, past and present, prays with one voice. Even in our private prayers we are, in one sense, never alone when we pray using the words and phrases of the Bible; we are praying the book common to God's people everywhere and in every time—the whole family of God. We pray with the same words that God's people have prayed throughout the ages.

In praying from scripture, the passage often suggests what form the prayer should take. For example, scriptural prayers are often preparatory to silent prayer. Prayers of intercession—based, perhaps, on one of Paul's letters—in which we vocalize our love and longings for others, are especially fitted to spoken, public prayer. Passages that express adoration, when prayed aloud, impress our minds and hearts with God's majesty and goodness.

Being Quiet Before God. Learning to be quiet and to rest with God is essential in prayer. Silence is the discipline of pushing aside words, busyness and noise in order to create space within for God. Someone once asked a spiritual adviser, "What should I do when I pray?" "Don't do anything," was the response. "Just love." The experience of stillness provides a space within which we can, unhurried, recognize God's presence. Some find "centering prayer," the repetition of a single word or phrase, to be an aid to this kind of quiet communion. In what some have called "contemplative prayer," the words and forms recede altogether. Prayer becomes a simple, restful experience of basking in the Lord's presence. Rich silences—not of our own making—allow us to commune with God. Our prayers may even alternate between articulated words and these quieter, less verbal times.

Whether we pray with the depth and breadth of the Lord's Prayer or recite a verse of a psalm, whether our words are many or few, whether we actively intercede or simply rest in God's presence, prayer is an intimate meeting with God.

See Page 304 for the next Ways of Meeting God *article.*

NUMBERS
Wandering in the Wilderness

KEY VERSE:

The people spoke against God and against Moses, "Why have you brought us up out of Egypt, to die in the wilderness? For there is no food and no water, and we detest this miserable food."—Numbers 21.5

"The people in the wilderness deserved reproof, not because they desired meat, but because in their desire they murmured against the Lord."

—AUGUSTINE,
Confessions

The book of Numbers portrays God's people at what may be their worst—ungrateful and inattentive. Traveling toward the promised land, they do not seem to make much real progress. Though they have left Egypt physically, they have not left it behind emotionally and spiritually. Every time something goes wrong or they become unhappy, they criticize Moses and, by association, God. They complain about the manna and water God miraculously gives them. The Israelites harbor jealousy, fight among themselves, offer "unholy fire" before the Lord, intermarry with women God tells them to avoid, and publicly criticize one another. They appear to learn their lessons—but then turn and make the same mistakes again. God becomes angry with the people, but still loves them and repeatedly forgives them.

In short, the book of Numbers shows us a portrait of the relationship between imperfect people and the Holy One who loves and guides them in spite of their stubbornness. The Israelites are shown God's glory in unmistakable ways; when they listen and obey, they move toward the good life that God offers.

Our journey today, like that of the Israelites—from bondage to what God has promised us—is often anything but a straight line or smooth sailing. But we journey with a patient and faithful God. Perhaps the greatest lesson from the book of Numbers is that when we are willing to listen and follow, God is always ready to speak to us and guide us.

The First Census of Israel

1 The LORD spoke to Moses in the wilderness of Sinai, in the tent of meeting, on the first day of the second month, in the second year after they had come out of the land of Egypt, saying: ²Take a census of the whole congregation of Israelites, in their clans, by ancestral houses, according to the number of names, every male individually; ³from twenty years old and upward, everyone in Israel able to go to war. You and Aaron shall enroll them, company by company. ⁴A man from each tribe shall be with you, each man the head of his ancestral house. ⁵These are the names of the men who shall assist you:

From Reuben, Elizur son of Shedeur.
⁶ From Simeon, Shelumiel son of Zurishaddai.
⁷ From Judah, Nahshon son of Amminadab.
⁸ From Issachar, Nethanel son of Zuar.
⁹ From Zebulun, Eliab son of Helon.
¹⁰ From the sons of Joseph:
from Ephraim, Elishama son of Ammihud;
from Manasseh, Gamaliel son of Pedahzur.
¹¹ From Benjamin, Abidan son of Gideoni.
¹² From Dan, Ahiezer son of Ammishaddai.
¹³ From Asher, Pagiel son of Ochran.
¹⁴ From Gad, Eliasaph son of Deuel.
¹⁵ From Naphtali, Ahira son of Enan.

¹⁶These were the ones chosen from the congregation, the leaders of their ancestral tribes, the heads of the divisions of Israel.

17 Moses and Aaron took these men who had been designated by name, ¹⁸and on the first day of the second month they assembled the whole congregation together. They registered themselves in their clans, by their ancestral houses, according to the number of names from twenty years old and upward, individually, ¹⁹as the LORD commanded Moses. So he enrolled them in the wilderness of Sinai.

20 The descendants of Reuben, Israel's firstborn, their lineage, in their clans, by their ancestral houses, according to the number of names, individually, every male from twenty years old and upward, everyone able to go to war: ²¹those enrolled of the tribe of Reuben were forty-six thousand five hundred.

22 The descendants of Simeon, their lineage, in their clans, by their ancestral houses, those of them that were numbered, according to the number of names, individually, every male from twenty years old and upward, everyone able to go to war: ²³those enrolled of the tribe of Simeon were fifty-nine thousand three hundred.

24 The descendants of Gad, their lineage, in their clans, by their ancestral houses, according to the number of the names, from twenty years old and upward, everyone able to go to war: ²⁵those enrolled of the tribe of Gad were forty-five thousand six hundred fifty.

26 The descendants of Judah, their lineage, in their clans, by their ancestral houses, according to the number of names, from twenty years old and upward, everyone able to go to war: ²⁷those enrolled of the tribe of Judah were seventy-four thousand six hundred.

28 The descendants of Issachar, their lineage, in their clans, by their ancestral houses, according to the number

A Big Job

NUMBERS 1.2–5

Moses is given charge of the whole congregation of Israelites. Imagine over six hundred thousand able-bodied men; the women, children and men not able to fight were not even counted! The crowd must have stretched as far as the eye could see! But Moses does a very sensible thing—he subdivides the group by tribe, by clan, by houses, by age and by gender, and then he chooses people to help him govern.

Consider a task, group or project God has given into your charge. The task may look overwhelming or the goal seem unreachable. Following Moses' example, divide the task into smaller components. Ask God for insight into what you can do today and whom you should ask to help you. What do you need strength for immediately, and what can you place in God's keeping until another time?

See Meeting God in Everyday Life

Unapproachably Holy

NUMBERS 1.48–53

The tabernacle of the covenant was a holy place, so holy that ordinary people could not come close to it. The Levites encamped around the tabernacle as a sort of buffer between the incredible power of God's holiness and the people.

Think about a time when you had a strong sense of the holiness of God. Where were you? What did you feel? Envision God's holy presence surrounding you now, perhaps as light or warmth. If there is a lamp near you, hold your hand in the light. As you move your hand closer to the light, what do you see? How does what you see change as you get nearer to the light? What do you see about yourself as you contemplate God's holiness?

See Meeting God in Worship

of names, from twenty years old and upward, everyone able to go to war: ²⁹those enrolled of the tribe of Issachar were fifty-four thousand four hundred.

30 The descendants of Zebulun, their lineage, in their clans, by their ancestral houses, according to the number of names, from twenty years old and upward, everyone able to go to war: ³¹those enrolled of the tribe of Zebulun were fifty-seven thousand four hundred.

32 The descendants of Joseph, namely, the descendants of Ephraim, their lineage, in their clans, by their ancestral houses, according to the number of names, from twenty years old and upward, everyone able to go to war: ³³those enrolled of the tribe of Ephraim were forty thousand five hundred.

34 The descendants of Manasseh, their lineage, in their clans, by their ancestral houses, according to the number of names, from twenty years old and upward, everyone able to go to war: ³⁵those enrolled of the tribe of Manasseh were thirty-two thousand two hundred.

36 The descendants of Benjamin, their lineage, in their clans, by their ancestral houses, according to the number of names, from twenty years old and upward, everyone able to go to war: ³⁷those enrolled of the tribe of Benjamin were thirty-five thousand four hundred.

38 The descendants of Dan, their lineage, in their clans, by their ancestral houses, according to the number of names, from twenty years old and upward, everyone able to go to war: ³⁹those enrolled of the tribe of Dan were sixty-two thousand seven hundred.

40 The descendants of Asher, their lineage, in their clans, by their ancestral houses, according to the number of names, from twenty years old and upward, everyone able to go to war: ⁴¹those enrolled of the tribe of Asher were forty-one thousand five hundred.

42 The descendants of Naphtali, their lineage, in their clans, by their ancestral houses, according to the number of names, from twenty years old and upward, everyone able to go to war: ⁴³those enrolled of the tribe of Naphtali were fifty-three thousand four hundred.

44 These are those who were enrolled, whom Moses and Aaron enrolled with the help of the leaders of Israel, twelve men, each representing his ancestral house. ⁴⁵So the whole number of the Israelites, by their ancestral houses, from twenty years old and upward, everyone able to go to war in Israel— ⁴⁶their whole number was six hundred three thousand five hundred fifty. ⁴⁷The Levites, however, were not numbered by their ancestral tribe along with them.

48 The LORD had said to Moses: ⁴⁹Only the tribe of Levi you shall not enroll, and you shall not take a census of them with the other Israelites. ⁵⁰Rather you shall appoint the Levites over the tabernacle of the covenant,ᵃ and over all its equipment, and over all that belongs to it; they are to carry the tabernacle and all its equipment, and they shall tend it, and shall camp around the tabernacle. ⁵¹When the tabernacle is to set out, the Levites shall take it down; and when the tabernacle is to be pitched, the Levites shall set it up. And any outsider who comes near shall be put to death. ⁵²The other Israelites shall camp in

a Or treaty, or testimony; Heb eduth

their respective regimental camps, by companies; ⁵³but the Levites shall camp around the tabernacle of the covenant,ᵃ that there may be no wrath on the congregation of the Israelites; and the Levites shall perform the guard duty of the tabernacle of the covenant.ᵃ ⁵⁴The Israelites did so; they did just as the LORD commanded Moses.

The Order of Encampment and Marching

2 The LORD spoke to Moses and Aaron, saying: ²The Israelites shall camp each in their respective regiments, under ensigns by their ancestral houses; they shall camp facing the tent of meeting on every side. ³Those to camp on the east side toward the sunrise shall be of the regimental encampment of Judah by companies. The leader of the people of Judah shall be Nahshon son of Amminadab, ⁴with a company as enrolled of seventy-four thousand six hundred. ⁵Those to camp next to him shall be the tribe of Issachar. The leader of the Issacharites shall be Nethanel son of Zuar, ⁶with a company as enrolled of fifty-four thousand four hundred. ⁷Then the tribe of Zebulun: The leader of the Zebulunites shall be Eliab son of Helon, ⁸with a company as enrolled of fifty-seven thousand four hundred. ⁹The total enrollment of the camp of Judah, by companies, is one hundred eighty-six thousand four hundred. They shall set out first on the march.

10 On the south side shall be the regimental encampment of Reuben by companies. The leader of the Reubenites shall be Elizur son of Shedeur, ¹¹with a company as enrolled of forty-six thousand five hundred. ¹²And those to camp next to him shall be the tribe of Simeon. The leader of the Simeonites shall be Shelumiel son of Zurishaddai, ¹³with a company as enrolled of fifty-nine thousand three hundred. ¹⁴Then the tribe of Gad: The leader of the Gadites shall be Eliasaph son of Reuel, ¹⁵with a company as enrolled of forty-five thousand six hundred fifty. ¹⁶The total enrollment of the camp of Reuben, by companies, is one hundred fifty-one thousand four hundred fifty. They shall set out second.

17 The tent of meeting, with the camp of the Levites, shall set out in the center of the camps; they shall set out just as they camp, each in position, by their regiments.

18 On the west side shall be the regimental encampment of Ephraim by companies. The leader of the people of Ephraim shall be Elishama son of Ammihud, ¹⁹with a company as enrolled of forty thousand five hundred. ²⁰Next to him shall be the tribe of Manasseh. The leader of the people of Manasseh shall be Gamaliel son of Pedahzur, ²¹with a company as enrolled of thirty-two thousand two hundred. ²²Then the tribe of Benjamin: The leader of the Benjaminites shall be Abidan son of Gideoni, ²³with a company as enrolled of thirty-five thousand four hundred. ²⁴The total enrollment of the camp of Ephraim, by companies, is one hundred eight thousand one hundred. They shall set out third on the march.

25 On the north side shall be the regimental encampment of Dan by companies. The leader of the Danites shall be Ahiezer son of Ammishaddai, ²⁶with a company as enrolled of sixty-two thousand seven hundred. ²⁷Those to camp next to him shall be the tribe of Asher. The leader

The Center of the Circle

NUMBERS 2.2,17–34

The tent of meeting, where the people meet God, is placed in the center of their camp; God's dwelling is at the center of their lives.

What is at the center of your life? Draw a circle to represent your waking hours on a typical day and subdivide it to represent how you spend your time. Does the picture created by the circle reflect what you want to be most important in your life? Do you see changes that you want to make?

See Meeting God in Everyday Life

Children Gone Wrong

NUMBERS 3.2–4

Two of Aaron's sons serve faithfully with him as priests, but two of them make unacceptable offerings to God. This "unholy fire" is an affront to God, and the two men die.

Picture Aaron grieving for his disobedient sons, perhaps for some time even before they died. The difficulties that led to their death probably began long before this moment.

Many faithful parents have some children who follow God's way and others who do not. Do you know parents who are in pain because of difficulties with troubled children, children whose actions may even be life-threatening? In your prayers, hold them and their children before God. What kind of help and support can you offer them?

See *Meeting God in Service*

of the Asherites shall be Pagiel son of Ochran, [28]with a company as enrolled of forty-one thousand five hundred. [29]Then the tribe of Naphtali: The leader of the Naphtalites shall be Ahira son of Enan, [30]with a company as enrolled of fifty-three thousand four hundred. [31]The total enrollment of the camp of Dan is one hundred fifty-seven thousand six hundred. They shall set out last, by companies.[a]

32 This was the enrollment of the Israelites by their ancestral houses; the total enrollment in the camps by their companies was six hundred three thousand five hundred fifty. [33]Just as the LORD had commanded Moses, the Levites were not enrolled among the other Israelites.

34 The Israelites did just as the LORD had commanded Moses: They camped by regiments, and they set out the same way, everyone by clans, according to ancestral houses.

The Sons of Aaron

3 This is the lineage of Aaron and Moses at the time when the LORD spoke with Moses on Mount Sinai. [2]These are the names of the sons of Aaron: Nadab the firstborn, and Abihu, Eleazar, and Ithamar; [3]these are the names of the sons of Aaron, the anointed priests, whom he ordained to minister as priests. [4]Nadab and Abihu died before the LORD when they offered unholy fire before the LORD in the wilderness of Sinai, and they had no children. Eleazar and Ithamar served as priests in the lifetime of their father Aaron.

The Duties of the Levites

5 Then the LORD spoke to Moses, saying: [6]Bring the tribe of Levi near, and set them before Aaron the priest, so that they may assist him. [7]They shall perform duties for him and for the whole congregation in front of the tent of meeting, doing service at the tabernacle; [8]they shall be in charge of all the furnishings of the tent of meeting, and attend to the duties for the Israelites as they do service at the tabernacle. [9]You shall give the Levites to Aaron and his descendants; they are unreservedly given to him from among the Israelites. [10]But you shall make a register of Aaron and his descendants; it is they who shall attend to the priesthood, and any outsider who comes near shall be put to death.

11 Then the LORD spoke to Moses, saying: [12]I hereby accept the Levites from among the Israelites as substitutes for all the firstborn that open the womb among the Israelites. The Levites shall be mine, [13]for all the firstborn are mine; when I killed all the firstborn in the land of Egypt, I consecrated for my own all the firstborn in Israel, both human and animal; they shall be mine. I am the LORD.

A Census of the Levites

14 Then the LORD spoke to Moses in the wilderness of Sinai, saying: [15]Enroll the Levites by ancestral houses and by clans. You shall enroll every male from a month old and upward. [16]So Moses enrolled them according to the word of the LORD, as he was commanded. [17]The following were the sons of Levi, by their names: Gershon, Kohath, and Merari. [18]These are the names of the sons of Gershon

a Compare verses 9, 16, 24: Heb *by their regiments*

by their clans: Libni and Shimei. ¹⁹The sons of Kohath by their clans: Amram, Izhar, Hebron, and Uzziel. ²⁰The sons of Merari by their clans: Mahli and Mushi. These are the clans of the Levites, by their ancestral houses.

21 To Gershon belonged the clan of the Libnites and the clan of the Shimeites; these were the clans of the Gershonites. ²²Their enrollment, counting all the males from a month old and upward, was seven thousand five hundred. ²³The clans of the Gershonites were to camp behind the tabernacle on the west, ²⁴with Eliasaph son of Lael as head of the ancestral house of the Gershonites. ²⁵The responsibility of the sons of Gershon in the tent of meeting was to be the tabernacle, the tent with its covering, the screen for the entrance of the tent of meeting, ²⁶the hangings of the court, the screen for the entrance of the court that is around the tabernacle and the altar, and its cords—all the service pertaining to these.

27 To Kohath belonged the clan of the Amramites, the clan of the Izharites, the clan of the Hebronites, and the clan of the Uzzielites; these are the clans of the Kohathites. ²⁸Counting all the males, from a month old and upward, there were eight thousand six hundred, attending to the duties of the sanctuary. ²⁹The clans of the Kohathites were to camp on the south side of the tabernacle, ³⁰with Elizaphan son of Uzziel as head of the ancestral house of the clans of the Kohathites. ³¹Their responsibility was to be the ark, the table, the lampstand, the altars, the vessels of the sanctuary with which the priests minister, and the screen—all the service pertaining to these. ³²Eleazar son of Aaron the priest was to be chief over the leaders of the Levites, and to have oversight of those who had charge of the sanctuary.

33 To Merari belonged the clan of the Mahlites and the clan of the Mushites: these are the clans of Merari. ³⁴Their enrollment, counting all the males from a month old and upward, was six thousand two hundred. ³⁵The head of the ancestral house of the clans of Merari was Zuriel son of Abihail; they were to camp on the north side of the tabernacle. ³⁶The responsibility assigned to the sons of Merari was to be the frames of the tabernacle, the bars, the pillars, the bases, and all their accessories—all the service pertaining to these; ³⁷also the pillars of the court all around, with their bases and pegs and cords.

38 Those who were to camp in front of the tabernacle on the east—in front of the tent of meeting toward the east—were Moses and Aaron and Aaron's sons, having charge of the rites within the sanctuary, whatever had to be done for the Israelites; and any outsider who came near was to be put to death. ³⁹The total enrollment of the Levites whom Moses and Aaron enrolled at the commandment of the LORD, by their clans, all the males from a month old and upward, was twenty-two thousand.

The Redemption of the Firstborn

40 Then the LORD said to Moses: Enroll all the firstborn males of the Israelites, from a month old and upward, and count their names. ⁴¹But you shall accept the Levites for me—I am the LORD—as substitutes for all the firstborn among the Israelites, and the livestock of the Levites as substitutes for all the firstborn among the

A Clear Claim

NUMBERS 3.44–45

"I am the LORD," God said. The Levites are to be set apart for God. God is sovereign, and God's claim is absolute.

Today's culture promotes individualism that encourages us to think we are autonomous, self-contained, free to determine our own way. What absolute claims does God make on your life? Is your list different today than it was at some point in the past? Do you feel resistance to the idea that God is sovereign and has claim on you? In what areas do you try to bargain with God to ask less of you?

livestock of the Israelites. ⁴²So Moses enrolled all the firstborn among the Israelites, as the LORD commanded him. ⁴³The total enrollment, all the firstborn males from a month old and upward, counting the number of names, was twenty-two thousand two hundred seventy-three.

44 Then the LORD spoke to Moses, saying: ⁴⁵Accept the Levites as substitutes for all the firstborn among the Israelites, and the livestock of the Levites as substitutes for their livestock; and the Levites shall be mine. I am the LORD. ⁴⁶As the price of redemption of the two hundred seventy-three of the firstborn of the Israelites, over and above the number of the Levites, ⁴⁷you shall accept five shekels apiece, reckoning by the shekel of the sanctuary, a shekel of twenty gerahs. ⁴⁸Give to Aaron and his sons the money by which the excess number of them is redeemed. ⁴⁹So Moses took the redemption money from those who were over and above those redeemed by the Levites; ⁵⁰from the firstborn of the Israelites he took the money, one thousand three hundred sixty-five shekels, reckoned by the shekel of the sanctuary; ⁵¹and Moses gave the redemption money to Aaron and his sons, according to the word of the LORD, as the LORD had commanded Moses.

The Kohathites

4 The LORD spoke to Moses and Aaron, saying: ²Take a census of the Kohathites separate from the other Levites, by their clans and their ancestral houses, ³from thirty years old up to fifty years old, all who qualify to do work relating to the tent of meeting. ⁴The service of the Kohathites relating to the tent of meeting concerns the most holy things.

5 When the camp is to set out, Aaron and his sons shall go in and take down the screening curtain, and cover the ark of the covenant*a* with it; ⁶then they shall put on it a covering of fine leather,*b* and spread over that a cloth all of blue, and shall put its poles in place. ⁷Over the table of the bread of the Presence they shall spread a blue cloth, and put on it the plates, the dishes for incense, the bowls, and the flagons for the drink offering; the regular bread also shall be on it; ⁸then they shall spread over them a crimson cloth, and cover it with a covering of fine leather,*b* and shall put its poles in place. ⁹They shall take a blue cloth, and cover the lampstand for the light, with its lamps, its snuffers, its trays, and all the vessels for oil with which it is supplied; ¹⁰and they shall put it with all its utensils in a covering of fine leather,*b* and put it on the carrying frame. ¹¹Over the golden altar they shall spread a blue cloth, and cover it with a covering of fine leather,*b* and shall put its poles in place; ¹²and they shall take all the utensils of the service that are used in the sanctuary, and put them in a blue cloth, and cover them with a covering of fine leather,*b* and put them on the carrying frame. ¹³They shall take away the ashes from the altar, and spread a purple cloth over it; ¹⁴and they shall put on it all the utensils of the altar, which are used for the service there, the firepans, the forks, the shovels, and the basins, all the utensils of

a Or *treaty*, or *testimony*; Heb *eduth*   *b* Meaning of Heb uncertain

the altar; and they shall spread on it a covering of fine leather,*a* and shall put its poles in place. ¹⁵When Aaron and his sons have finished covering the sanctuary and all the furnishings of the sanctuary, as the camp sets out, after that the Kohathites shall come to carry these, but they must not touch the holy things, or they will die. These are the things of the tent of meeting that the Kohathites are to carry.

16 Eleazar son of Aaron the priest shall have charge of the oil for the light, the fragrant incense, the regular grain offering, and the anointing oil, the oversight of all the tabernacle and all that is in it, in the sanctuary and in its utensils.

17 Then the LORD spoke to Moses and Aaron, saying: ¹⁸You must not let the tribe of the clans of the Kohathites be destroyed from among the Levites. ¹⁹This is how you must deal with them in order that they may live and not die when they come near to the most holy things: Aaron and his sons shall go in and assign each to a particular task or burden. ²⁰But the Kohathites*b* must not go in to look on the holy things even for a moment; otherwise they will die.

The Gershonites and Merarites

21 Then the LORD spoke to Moses, saying: ²²Take a census of the Gershonites also, by their ancestral houses and by their clans; ²³from thirty years old up to fifty years old you shall enroll them, all who qualify to do work in the tent of meeting. ²⁴This is the service of the clans of the Gershonites, in serving and bearing burdens: ²⁵They shall carry the curtains of the tabernacle, and the tent of meeting with its covering, and the outer covering of fine leather*a* that is on top of it, and the screen for the entrance of the tent of meeting, ²⁶and the hangings of the court, and the screen for the entrance of the gate of the court that is around the tabernacle and the altar, and their cords, and all the equipment for their service; and they shall do all that needs to be done with regard to them. ²⁷All the service of the Gershonites shall be at the command of Aaron and his sons, in all that they are to carry, and in all that they have to do; and you shall assign to their charge all that they are to carry. ²⁸This is the service of the clans of the Gershonites relating to the tent of meeting, and their responsibilities are to be under the oversight of Ithamar son of Aaron the priest.

29 As for the Merarites, you shall enroll them by their clans and their ancestral houses; ³⁰from thirty years old up to fifty years old you shall enroll them, everyone who qualifies to do the work of the tent of meeting. ³¹This is what they are charged to carry, as the whole of their service in the tent of meeting: the frames of the tabernacle, with its bars, pillars, and bases, ³²and the pillars of the court all around with their bases, pegs, and cords, with all their equipment and all their related service; and you shall assign by name the objects that they are required to carry. ³³This is the service of the clans of the Merarites, the whole of their service relating to the tent of meeting, under the hand of Ithamar son of Aaron the priest.

---

a Meaning of Heb uncertain   *b* Heb *they*

Special Moments

NUMBERS 4.5–15

The vessels and supplies for the sanctuary are revered and handled in specific ways because they represent contact with God. The people's manner with them is evidence that they have a profound sense of God's holiness.

Sacraments and rituals of worship such as Holy Communion, the wedding ceremony, or praying the Lord's Prayer aloud with other believers, call us to step aside from our routines. The extraordinary language and symbolic movements make these moments different from others, to remind us that God is present in a special way for a special purpose. We may feel comforted, welcomed, challenged by other believers and bound to them. Think about a ritual that holds power for you. What does it show you about God? How can you prepare to approach that ritual with deeper attentiveness?

See Meeting God in Worship

Strong Backs, Servant Hearts

NUMBERS 4.46–49

The Levites served according to their individual abilities. For instance, only those who were physically strong were expected to carry heavy loads.

Likewise, God calls us according to our unique aptitudes. But we often overlook our more "everyday" human attributes like having a strong back or being able to repair machines or grow flowers. Some of us can organize; some can do accounting; some can greet people warmly and make them feel welcome; some can make plants grow. Think about such abilities and how God might use them. Which of your natural aptitudes and interests do you use to serve God? What skills and aptitudes are you working to develop for God's use in the future?

See Meeting God in Everyday Life

Census of the Levites

34 So Moses and Aaron and the leaders of the congregation enrolled the Kohathites, by their clans and their ancestral houses, ³⁵from thirty years old up to fifty years old, everyone who qualified for work relating to the tent of meeting; ³⁶and their enrollment by clans was two thousand seven hundred fifty. ³⁷This was the enrollment of the clans of the Kohathites, all who served at the tent of meeting, whom Moses and Aaron enrolled according to the commandment of the LORD by Moses.

38 The enrollment of the Gershonites, by their clans and their ancestral houses, ³⁹from thirty years old up to fifty years old, everyone who qualified for work relating to the tent of meeting— ⁴⁰their enrollment by their clans and their ancestral houses was two thousand six hundred thirty. ⁴¹This was the enrollment of the clans of the Gershonites, all who served at the tent of meeting, whom Moses and Aaron enrolled according to the commandment of the LORD.

42 The enrollment of the clans of the Merarites, by their clans and their ancestral houses, ⁴³from thirty years old up to fifty years old, everyone who qualified for work relating to the tent of meeting— ⁴⁴their enrollment by their clans was three thousand two hundred. ⁴⁵This is the enrollment of the clans of the Merarites, whom Moses and Aaron enrolled according to the commandment of the LORD by Moses.

46 All those who were enrolled of the Levites, whom Moses and Aaron and the leaders of Israel enrolled, by their clans and their ancestral houses, ⁴⁷from thirty years old up to fifty years old, everyone who qualified to do the work of service and the work of bearing burdens relating to the tent of meeting, ⁴⁸their enrollment was eight thousand five hundred eighty. ⁴⁹According to the commandment of the LORD through Moses they were appointed to their several tasks of serving or carrying; thus they were enrolled by him, as the LORD commanded Moses.

Unclean Persons

5 The LORD spoke to Moses, saying: ²Command the Israelites to put out of the camp everyone who is leprous,ᵃ or has a discharge, and everyone who is unclean through contact with a corpse; ³you shall put out both male and female, putting them outside the camp; they must not defile their camp, where I dwell among them. ⁴The Israelites did so, putting them outside the camp; as the LORD had spoken to Moses, so the Israelites did.

Confession and Restitution

5 The LORD spoke to Moses, saying: ⁶Speak to the Israelites: When a man or a woman wrongs another, breaking faith with the LORD, that person incurs guilt ⁷and shall confess the sin that has been committed. The person shall make full restitution for the wrong, adding one-fifth to it, and giving it to the one who was wronged. ⁸If the injured party has no next of kin to whom restitution may be made for the wrong, the restitution for wrong shall go to

ᵃ A term for several skin diseases; precise meaning uncertain the LORD for the priest, in addition to the ram of atonement with which atonement is made for the guilty party. ⁹Among all the sacred donations of the Israelites, every gift that they bring to the priest shall be his. ¹⁰The sacred donations of all are their own; whatever anyone gives to the priest shall be his.

Concerning an Unfaithful Wife

11 The LORD spoke to Moses, saying: ¹²Speak to the Israelites and say to them: If any man's wife goes astray and is unfaithful to him, ¹³if a man has had intercourse with her but it is hidden from her husband, so that she is undetected though she has defiled herself, and there is no witness against her since she was not caught in the act; ¹⁴if a spirit of jealousy comes on him, and he is jealous of his wife who has defiled herself; or if a spirit of jealousy comes on him, and he is jealous of his wife, though she has not defiled herself; ¹⁵then the man shall bring his wife to the priest. And he shall bring the offering required for her, one-tenth of an ephah of barley flour. He shall pour no oil on it and put no frankincense on it, for it is a grain offering of jealousy, a grain offering of remembrance, bringing iniquity to remembrance.

16 Then the priest shall bring her near, and set her before the LORD; ¹⁷the priest shall take holy water in an earthen vessel, and take some of the dust that is on the floor of the tabernacle and put it into the water. ¹⁸The priest shall set the woman before the LORD, dishevel the woman's hair, and place in her hands the grain offering of remembrance, which is the grain offering of jealousy. In his own hand the priest shall have the water of bitterness that brings the curse. ¹⁹Then the priest shall make her take an oath, saying, "If no man has lain with you, if you have not turned aside to uncleanness while under your husband's authority, be immune to this water of bitterness that brings the curse. ²⁰But if you have gone astray while under your husband's authority, if you have defiled yourself and some man other than your husband has had intercourse with you," ²¹—let the priest make the woman take the oath of the curse and say to the woman—"the LORD make you an execration and an oath among your people, when the LORD makes your uterus drop, your womb discharge; ²²now may this water that brings the curse enter your bowels and make your womb discharge, your uterus drop!" And the woman shall say, "Amen. Amen."

23 Then the priest shall put these curses in writing, and wash them off into the water of bitterness. ²⁴He shall make the woman drink the water of bitterness that brings the curse, and the water that brings the curse shall enter her and cause bitter pain. ²⁵The priest shall take the grain offering of jealousy out of the woman's hand, and shall elevate the grain offering before the LORD and bring it to the altar; ²⁶and the priest shall take a handful of the grain offering, as its memorial portion, and turn it into smoke on the altar, and afterward shall make the woman drink the water. ²⁷When he has made her drink the water, then, if she has defiled herself and has been unfaithful to her husband, the water that brings the curse shall enter into her and cause bitter

Broken Threads

NUMBERS 5.5–15

God's rules about their life together protected the Israelites and reinforced the importance of community.

God's Word indicates to us that what we do affects others (see Romans 12.5–21; Ephesians 2.19–22). Our relationships with God and with other people are part of a single piece of fabric. Pick up a piece of fabric and examine it. What would happen if you broke some threads? What happens if several threads are cut or torn? Now turn your mind to the fabric of relationships in your life. Are there torn places? Are the edges fraying? Picture yourself going to someone with whom you have some difficulty. What do you need to say? What do you need to do?

See Meeting God in Community

Vows and Gestures

NUMBERS 6.1–8

Some people make special commitments to God to live by particular disciplines. They may engage in special activities such as daily, structured times of prayer or Bible reading. Or they may abstain from food or from some activity. Nazirites neither cut their hair nor ate or drank any product of the vine. What marks you as someone who serves God? What is the evidence in your life that proves you a believer? What value do you see in special vows?

pain, and her womb shall discharge, her uterus drop, and the woman shall become an execration among her people. ²⁸But if the woman has not defiled herself and is clean, then she shall be immune and be able to conceive children.

29 This is the law in cases of jealousy, when a wife, while under her husband's authority, goes astray and defiles herself, ³⁰or when a spirit of jealousy comes on a man and he is jealous of his wife; then he shall set the woman before the LORD, and the priest shall apply this entire law to her. ³¹The man shall be free from iniquity, but the woman shall bear her iniquity.

The Nazirites

6 The LORD spoke to Moses, saying: ²Speak to the Israelites and say to them: When either men or women make a special vow, the vow of a nazirite,ᵃ to separate themselves to the LORD, ³they shall separate themselves from wine and strong drink; they shall drink no wine vinegar or other vinegar, and shall not drink any grape juice or eat grapes, fresh or dried. ⁴All their days as naziritesᵇ they shall eat nothing that is produced by the grapevine, not even the seeds or the skins.

5 All the days of their nazirite vow no razor shall come upon the head; until the time is completed for which they separate themselves to the LORD, they shall be holy; they shall let the locks of the head grow long.

6 All the days that they separate themselves to the LORD they shall not go near a corpse. ⁷Even if their father or mother, brother or sister, should die, they may not defile themselves; because their consecration to God is upon the head. ⁸All their days as naziritesᵇ they are holy to the LORD.

9 If someone dies very suddenly nearby, defiling the consecrated head, then they shall shave the head on the day of their cleansing; on the seventh day they shall shave it. ¹⁰On the eighth day they shall bring two turtledoves or two young pigeons to the priest at the entrance of the tent of meeting, ¹¹and the priest shall offer one as a sin offering and the other as a burnt offering, and make atonement for them, because they incurred guilt by reason of the corpse. They shall sanctify the head that same day, ¹²and separate themselves to the LORD for their days as nazirites,ᵇ and bring a male lamb a year old as a guilt offering. The former time shall be void, because the consecrated head was defiled.

13 This is the law for the naziritesᵇ when the time of their consecration has been completed: they shall be brought to the entrance of the tent of meeting, ¹⁴and they shall offer their gift to the LORD, one male lamb a year old without blemish as a burnt offering, one ewe lamb a year old without blemish as a sin offering, one ram without blemish as an offering of well-being, ¹⁵and a basket of unleavened bread, cakes of choice flour mixed with oil and unleavened wafers spread with oil, with their grain offering and their drink offerings. ¹⁶The priest shall present them before the LORD and offer their sin offering and burnt offering, ¹⁷and shall offer the ram as a sacrifice of

a That is one separated or one consecrated   b That is those separated or those consecrated

well-being to the LORD, with the basket of unleavened bread; the priest also shall make the accompanying grain offering and drink offering. [18]Then the nazirites[a] shall shave the consecrated head at the entrance of the tent of meeting, and shall take the hair from the consecrated head and put it on the fire under the sacrifice of well-being. [19]The priest shall take the shoulder of the ram, when it is boiled, and one unleavened cake out of the basket, and one unleavened wafer, and shall put them in the palms of the nazirites,[a] after they have shaved the consecrated head. [20]Then the priest shall elevate them as an elevation offering before the LORD; they are a holy portion for the priest, together with the breast that is elevated and the thigh that is offered. After that the nazirites[a] may drink wine.

21 This is the law for the nazirites[a] who take a vow. Their offering to the LORD must be in accordance with the nazirite[b] vow, apart from what else they can afford. In accordance with whatever vow they take, so they shall do, following the law for their consecration.

The Priestly Benediction

22 The LORD spoke to Moses, saying: [23]Speak to Aaron and his sons, saying, Thus you shall bless the Israelites: You shall say to them,

[24] The LORD bless you and keep you;
[25] the LORD make his face to shine upon you, and be
           gracious to you;
[26] the LORD lift up his countenance upon you, and
           give you peace.

27 So they shall put my name on the Israelites, and I will bless them.

Offerings of the Leaders

7 On the day when Moses had finished setting up the tabernacle, and had anointed and consecrated it with all its furnishings, and had anointed and consecrated the altar with all its utensils, [2]the leaders of Israel, heads of their ancestral houses, the leaders of the tribes, who were over those who were enrolled, made offerings. [3]They brought their offerings before the LORD, six covered wagons and twelve oxen, a wagon for every two of the leaders, and for each one an ox; they presented them before the tabernacle. [4]Then the LORD said to Moses: [5]Accept these from them, that they may be used in doing the service of the tent of meeting, and give them to the Levites, to each according to his service. [6]So Moses took the wagons and the oxen, and gave them to the Levites. [7]Two wagons and four oxen he gave to the Gershonites, according to their service; [8]and four wagons and eight oxen he gave to the Merarites, according to their service, under the direction of Ithamar son of Aaron the priest. [9]But to the Kohathites he gave none, because they were charged with the care of the holy things that had to be carried on the shoulders.

10 The leaders also presented offerings for the dedication of the altar at the time when it was anointed; the leaders presented their offering before the altar. [11]The

---

The Power to Bless

NUMBERS 6.22–27

Blessing another in the name of God is a powerful act. Bidding God's face to "shine upon" someone is asking God to turn toward them and work for their good. When we "put [God's] name on" someone, we do something important. Think of those you know who need God's help. In your mind, envision God's power surrounding them. Hold them in the light that shines from God's face. Bless them in the name of God.

See Meeting God in Prayer

---

a That is *those separated* or *those consecrated*   b That is *one separated* or *one consecrated*

Ordinary Gifts

NUMBERS 7.23,29,35,41,47

The sacrifice of well-being signifies thanksgiving for the day-by-day sustenance God provides. We too can mark our gratitude daily for God's ordinary gifts. Practices such as giving thanks at mealtime, praying for those we love, and keeping a journal record of where we see God at work can become our "sacrifice of well-being." What are you grateful for? What "ordinary" gifts from God make your life better, day by day? How does your gratitude show in your words and actions?

See Meeting God in Everyday Life

LORD said to Moses: They shall present their offerings, one leader each day, for the dedication of the altar.

12 The one who presented his offering the first day was Nahshon son of Amminadab, of the tribe of Judah; 13his offering was one silver plate weighing one hundred thirty shekels, one silver basin weighing seventy shekels, according to the shekel of the sanctuary, both of them full of choice flour mixed with oil for a grain offering; 14one golden dish weighing ten shekels, full of incense; 15one young bull, one ram, one male lamb a year old, for a burnt offering; 16one male goat for a sin offering; 17and for the sacrifice of well-being, two oxen, five rams, five male goats, and five male lambs a year old. This was the offering of Nahshon son of Amminadab.

18 On the second day Nethanel son of Zuar, the leader of Issachar, presented an offering; 19he presented for his offering one silver plate weighing one hundred thirty shekels, one silver basin weighing seventy shekels, according to the shekel of the sanctuary, both of them full of choice flour mixed with oil for a grain offering; 20one golden dish weighing ten shekels, full of incense; 21one young bull, one ram, one male lamb a year old, as a burnt offering; 22one male goat as a sin offering; 23and for the sacrifice of well-being, two oxen, five rams, five male goats, and five male lambs a year old. This was the offering of Nethanel son of Zuar.

24 On the third day Eliab son of Helon, the leader of the Zebulunites: 25his offering was one silver plate weighing one hundred thirty shekels, one silver basin weighing seventy shekels, according to the shekel of the sanctuary, both of them full of choice flour mixed with oil for a grain offering; 26one golden dish weighing ten shekels, full of incense; 27one young bull, one ram, one male lamb a year old, for a burnt offering; 28one male goat for a sin offering; 29and for the sacrifice of well-being, two oxen, five rams, five male goats, and five male lambs a year old. This was the offering of Eliab son of Helon.

30 On the fourth day Elizur son of Shedeur, the leader of the Reubenites: 31his offering was one silver plate weighing one hundred thirty shekels, one silver basin weighing seventy shekels, according to the shekel of the sanctuary, both of them full of choice flour mixed with oil for a grain offering; 32one golden dish weighing ten shekels, full of incense; 33one young bull, one ram, one male lamb a year old, for a burnt offering; 34one male goat for a sin offering; 35and for the sacrifice of well-being, two oxen, five rams, five male goats, and five male lambs a year old. This was the offering of Elizur son of Shedeur.

36 On the fifth day Shelumiel son of Zurishaddai, the leader of the Simeonites: 37his offering was one silver plate weighing one hundred thirty shekels, one silver basin weighing seventy shekels, according to the shekel of the sanctuary, both of them full of choice flour mixed with oil for a grain offering; 38one golden dish weighing ten shekels, full of incense; 39one young bull, one ram, one male lamb a year old, for a burnt offering; 40one male goat for a sin offering; 41and for the sacrifice of well-being, two oxen, five rams, five male goats, and five male

lambs a year old. This was the offering of Shelumiel son of Zurishaddai.

42 On the sixth day Eliasaph son of Deuel, the leader of the Gadites: ⁴³his offering was one silver plate weighing one hundred thirty shekels, one silver basin weighing seventy shekels, according to the shekel of the sanctuary, both of them full of choice flour mixed with oil for a grain offering; ⁴⁴one golden dish weighing ten shekels, full of incense; ⁴⁵one young bull, one ram, one male lamb a year old, for a burnt offering; ⁴⁶one male goat for a sin offering; ⁴⁷and for the sacrifice of well-being, two oxen, five rams, five male goats, and five male lambs a year old. This was the offering of Eliasaph son of Deuel.

48 On the seventh day Elishama son of Ammihud, the leader of the Ephraimites: ⁴⁹his offering was one silver plate weighing one hundred thirty shekels, one silver basin weighing seventy shekels, according to the shekel of the sanctuary, both of them full of choice flour mixed with oil for a grain offering; ⁵⁰one golden dish weighing ten shekels, full of incense; ⁵¹one young bull, one ram, one male lamb a year old, for a burnt offering; ⁵²one male goat for a sin offering; ⁵³and for the sacrifice of well-being, two oxen, five rams, five male goats, and five male lambs a year old. This was the offering of Elishama son of Ammihud.

54 On the eighth day Gamaliel son of Pedahzur, the leader of the Manassites: ⁵⁵his offering was one silver plate weighing one hundred thirty shekels, one silver basin weighing seventy shekels, according to the shekel of the sanctuary, both of them full of choice flour mixed with oil for a grain offering; ⁵⁶one golden dish weighing ten shekels, full of incense; ⁵⁷one young bull, one ram, one male lamb a year old, for a burnt offering; ⁵⁸one male goat for a sin offering; ⁵⁹and for the sacrifice of well-being, two oxen, five rams, five male goats, and five male lambs a year old. This was the offering of Gamaliel son of Pedahzur.

60 On the ninth day Abidan son of Gideoni, the leader of the Benjaminites: ⁶¹his offering was one silver plate weighing one hundred thirty shekels, one silver basin weighing seventy shekels, according to the shekel of the sanctuary, both of them full of choice flour mixed with oil for a grain offering; ⁶²one golden dish weighing ten shekels, full of incense; ⁶³one young bull, one ram, one male lamb a year old, for a burnt offering; ⁶⁴one male goat for a sin offering; ⁶⁵and for the sacrifice of well-being, two oxen, five rams, five male goats, and five male lambs a year old. This was the offering of Abidan son of Gideoni.

66 On the tenth day Ahiezer son of Ammishaddai, the leader of the Danites: ⁶⁷his offering was one silver plate weighing one hundred thirty shekels, one silver basin weighing seventy shekels, according to the shekel of the sanctuary, both of them full of choice flour mixed with oil for a grain offering; ⁶⁸one golden dish weighing ten shekels, full of incense; ⁶⁹one young bull, one ram, one male lamb a year old, for a burnt offering; ⁷⁰one male goat for a sin offering; ⁷¹and for the sacrifice of well-being, two oxen, five rams, five male goats, and five male

Majestic Procession

NUMBERS 7.12–83

The measured cadence of this account suggests the magnificence of the ceremony of the dedication of the altar. Envision yourself among the watchers as each leader brings the tribe's finest goods in offering. See the sheen of the gold and silver and fine clothing you have helped carry from Egypt. Sense the air of celebration and excitement building more and more each day. With Moses' blessing from God echoing in your heart (vv. 24–26), feel the anticipation as the altar is readied for the presence of the Lord. What is happening within you?

See Meeting God in Scripture

A Place to Meet God

NUMBERS 7.89

After many days of setting up, anointing and preparing the altar and the tent of meeting with the finest the tribes had to offer, the climactic moment arrives. Moses enters the tent of meeting and hears the voice of God. "Thus it spoke to him."

Where do you speak with the Lord? Do you have a special place reserved for prayer and reflection? Consider clearing a corner of your house or apartment for just this holy use. Furnish it with objects that represent the finest things you own—a beautiful candle, flowers, a picture, a lovely tablecloth. Find time every day to go to your special place to listen to God.

See Meeting God in Worship

lambs a year old. This was the offering of Ahiezer son of Ammishaddai.

72 On the eleventh day Pagiel son of Ochran, the leader of the Asherites: [73]his offering was one silver plate weighing one hundred thirty shekels, one silver basin weighing seventy shekels, according to the shekel of the sanctuary, both of them full of choice flour mixed with oil for a grain offering; [74]one golden dish weighing ten shekels, full of incense; [75]one young bull, one ram, one male lamb a year old, for a burnt offering; [76]one male goat for a sin offering; [77]and for the sacrifice of well-being, two oxen, five rams, five male goats, and five male lambs a year old. This was the offering of Pagiel son of Ochran.

78 On the twelfth day Ahira son of Enan, the leader of the Naphtalites: [79]his offering was one silver plate weighing one hundred thirty shekels, one silver basin weighing seventy shekels, according to the shekel of the sanctuary, both of them full of choice flour mixed with oil for a grain offering; [80]one golden dish weighing ten shekels, full of incense; [81]one young bull, one ram, one male lamb a year old, for a burnt offering; [82]one male goat for a sin offering; [83]and for the sacrifice of well-being, two oxen, five rams, five male goats, and five male lambs a year old. This was the offering of Ahira son of Enan.

84 This was the dedication offering for the altar, at the time when it was anointed, from the leaders of Israel: twelve silver plates, twelve silver basins, twelve golden dishes, [85]each silver plate weighing one hundred thirty shekels and each basin seventy, all the silver of the vessels two thousand four hundred shekels according to the shekel of the sanctuary, [86]the twelve golden dishes, full of incense, weighing ten shekels apiece according to the shekel of the sanctuary, all the gold of the dishes being one hundred twenty shekels; [87]all the livestock for the burnt offering twelve bulls, twelve rams, twelve male lambs a year old, with their grain offering; and twelve male goats for a sin offering; [88]and all the livestock for the sacrifice of well-being twenty-four bulls, the rams sixty, the male goats sixty, the male lambs a year old sixty. This was the dedication offering for the altar, after it was anointed.

89 When Moses went into the tent of meeting to speak with the LORD,[a] he would hear the voice speaking to him from above the mercy seat[b] that was on the ark of the covenant[c] from between the two cherubim; thus it spoke to him.

The Seven Lamps

8 The LORD spoke to Moses, saying: [2]Speak to Aaron and say to him: When you set up the lamps, the seven lamps shall give light in front of the lampstand. [3]Aaron did so; he set up its lamps to give light in front of the lampstand, as the LORD had commanded Moses. [4]Now this was how the lampstand was made, out of hammered work of gold. From its base to its flowers, it was hammered work; according to the pattern that the LORD had shown Moses, so he made the lampstand.

a Heb *him*   *b* Or *the cover*   *c* Or *treaty*, or *testimony*; Heb *eduth*

Consecration and Service of the Levites

5 The LORD spoke to Moses, saying: ⁶Take the Levites from among the Israelites and cleanse them. ⁷Thus you shall do to them, to cleanse them: sprinkle the water of purification on them, have them shave their whole body with a razor and wash their clothes, and so cleanse themselves. ⁸Then let them take a young bull and its grain offering of choice flour mixed with oil, and you shall take another young bull for a sin offering. ⁹You shall bring the Levites before the tent of meeting, and assemble the whole congregation of the Israelites. ¹⁰When you bring the Levites before the LORD, the Israelites shall lay their hands on the Levites, ¹¹and Aaron shall present the Levites before the LORD as an elevation offering from the Israelites, that they may do the service of the LORD. ¹²The Levites shall lay their hands on the heads of the bulls, and he shall offer the one for a sin offering and the other for a burnt offering to the LORD, to make atonement for the Levites. ¹³Then you shall have the Levites stand before Aaron and his sons, and you shall present them as an elevation offering to the LORD.

14 Thus you shall separate the Levites from among the other Israelites, and the Levites shall be mine. ¹⁵Thereafter the Levites may go in to do service at the tent of meeting, once you have cleansed them and presented them as an elevation offering. ¹⁶For they are unreservedly given to me from among the Israelites; I have taken them for myself, in place of all that open the womb, the firstborn of all the Israelites. ¹⁷For all the firstborn among the Israelites are mine, both human and animal. On the day that I struck down all the firstborn in the land of Egypt I consecrated them for myself, ¹⁸but I have taken the Levites in place of all the firstborn among the Israelites. ¹⁹Moreover, I have given the Levites as a gift to Aaron and his sons from among the Israelites, to do the service for the Israelites at the tent of meeting, and to make atonement for the Israelites, in order that there may be no plague among the Israelites for coming too close to the sanctuary.

20 Moses and Aaron and the whole congregation of the Israelites did with the Levites accordingly; the Israelites did with the Levites just as the LORD had commanded Moses concerning them. ²¹The Levites purified themselves from sin and washed their clothes; then Aaron presented them as an elevation offering before the LORD, and Aaron made atonement for them to cleanse them. ²²Thereafter the Levites went in to do their service in the tent of meeting in attendance on Aaron and his sons. As the LORD had commanded Moses concerning the Levites, so they did with them.

23 The LORD spoke to Moses, saying: ²⁴This applies to the Levites: from twenty-five years old and upward they shall begin to do duty in the service of the tent of meeting; ²⁵and from the age of fifty years they shall retire from the duty of the service and serve no more. ²⁶They may assist their brothers in the tent of meeting in carrying out their duties, but they shall perform no service. Thus you shall do with the Levites in assigning their duties.

Jesus, Our Atonement

NUMBERS 8.5–13

"In the days of his flesh, Jesus offered up prayers and supplications, with loud cries and tears, to the one who was able to save him from death, and he was heard because of his reverent submission. Although he was a Son, he learned obedience through what he suffered; and having been made perfect, he became the source of eternal salvation for all who obey him, having been designated by God a high priest according to the order of Melchizedek."

—Hebrews 5.7–10

Time to Remember

NUMBERS 9.1–2

Even though the people are in the wilderness, they are to keep the Passover as a reminder of what God has done for them.

When you are in a "wilderness"—a spiritually bleak place—what practices keep you in touch with God? Can you think of a practice such as attending worship, reading the Bible, writing in your journal, receiving Holy Communion, or some other discipline that may have begun as a duty but has become a window to God's grace? Make work of learning about one new regular discipline you may not have tried before.

See *Meeting God in Worship*

The Passover at Sinai

9 The LORD spoke to Moses in the wilderness of Sinai, in the first month of the second year after they had come out of the land of Egypt, saying: ²Let the Israelites keep the passover at its appointed time. ³On the fourteenth day of this month, at twilight,ᵃ you shall keep it at its appointed time; according to all its statutes and all its regulations you shall keep it. ⁴So Moses told the Israelites that they should keep the passover. ⁵They kept the passover in the first month, on the fourteenth day of the month, at twilight,ᵃ in the wilderness of Sinai. Just as the LORD had commanded Moses, so the Israelites did. ⁶Now there were certain people who were unclean through touching a corpse, so that they could not keep the passover on that day. They came before Moses and Aaron on that day, ⁷and said to him, "Although we are unclean through touching a corpse, why must we be kept from presenting the LORD's offering at its appointed time among the Israelites?" ⁸Moses spoke to them, "Wait, so that I may hear what the LORD will command concerning you."

9 The LORD spoke to Moses, saying: ¹⁰Speak to the Israelites, saying: Anyone of you or your descendants who is unclean through touching a corpse, or is away on a journey, shall still keep the passover to the LORD. ¹¹In the second month on the fourteenth day, at twilight,ᵃ they shall keep it; they shall eat it with unleavened bread and bitter herbs. ¹²They shall leave none of it until morning, nor break a bone of it; according to all the statute for the passover they shall keep it. ¹³But anyone who is clean and is not on a journey, and yet refrains from keeping the passover, shall be cut off from the people for not presenting the LORD's offering at its appointed time; such a one shall bear the consequences for the sin. ¹⁴Any alien residing among you who wishes to keep the passover to the LORD shall do so according to the statute of the passover and according to its regulation; you shall have one statute for both the resident alien and the native.

The Cloud and the Fire

15 On the day the tabernacle was set up, the cloud covered the tabernacle, the tent of the covenant;ᵇ and from evening until morning it was over the tabernacle, having the appearance of fire. ¹⁶It was always so: the cloud covered it by dayᶜ and the appearance of fire by night. ¹⁷Whenever the cloud lifted from over the tent, then the Israelites would set out; and in the place where the cloud settled down, there the Israelites would camp. ¹⁸At the command of the LORD the Israelites would set out, and at the command of the LORD they would camp. As long as the cloud rested over the tabernacle, they would remain in camp. ¹⁹Even when the cloud continued over the tabernacle many days, the Israelites would keep the charge of the LORD, and would not set out. ²⁰Sometimes the cloud would remain a few days over the tabernacle, and according to the command of the LORD they would

---

a Heb *between the two evenings*   *b* Or *treaty*, or *testimony*; Heb *eduth*
c Gk Syr Vg: Heb lacks *by day*

remain in camp; then according to the command of the LORD they would set out. ²¹Sometimes the cloud would remain from evening until morning; and when the cloud lifted in the morning, they would set out, or if it continued for a day and a night, when the cloud lifted they would set out. ²²Whether it was two days, or a month, or a longer time, that the cloud continued over the tabernacle, resting upon it, the Israelites would remain in camp and would not set out; but when it lifted they would set out. ²³At the command of the LORD they would camp, and at the command of the LORD they would set out. They kept the charge of the LORD, at the command of the LORD by Moses.

The Silver Trumpets

10 The LORD spoke to Moses, saying: ²Make two silver trumpets; you shall make them of hammered work; and you shall use them for summoning the congregation, and for breaking camp. ³When both are blown, the whole congregation shall assemble before you at the entrance of the tent of meeting. ⁴But if only one is blown, then the leaders, the heads of the tribes of Israel, shall assemble before you. ⁵When you blow an alarm, the camps on the east side shall set out; ⁶when you blow a second alarm, the camps on the south side shall set out. An alarm is to be blown whenever they are to set out. ⁷But when the assembly is to be gathered, you shall blow, but you shall not sound an alarm. ⁸The sons of Aaron, the priests, shall blow the trumpets; this shall be a perpetual institution for you throughout your generations. ⁹When you go to war in your land against the adversary who oppresses you, you shall sound an alarm with the trumpets, so that you may be remembered before the LORD your God and be saved from your enemies. ¹⁰Also on your days of rejoicing, at your appointed festivals, and at the beginnings of your months, you shall blow the trumpets over your burnt offerings and over your sacrifices of well-being; they shall serve as a reminder on your behalf before the LORD your God: I am the LORD your God.

Departure from Sinai

11 In the second year, in the second month, on the twentieth day of the month, the cloud lifted from over the tabernacle of the covenant.ᵃ ¹²Then the Israelites set out by stages from the wilderness of Sinai, and the cloud settled down in the wilderness of Paran. ¹³They set out for the first time at the command of the LORD by Moses. ¹⁴The standard of the camp of Judah set out first, company by company, and over the whole company was Nahshon son of Amminadab. ¹⁵Over the company of the tribe of Issachar was Nethanel son of Zuar; ¹⁶and over the company of the tribe of Zebulun was Eliab son of Helon.

17 Then the tabernacle was taken down, and the Gershonites and the Merarites, who carried the tabernacle, set out. ¹⁸Next the standard of the camp of Reuben set out, company by company; and over the whole company was Elizur son of Shedeur. ¹⁹Over the company of the tribe of Simeon was Shelumiel son of Zurishaddai, ²⁰and

Desert, Mountains, Plain?

NUMBERS 10.12

Look back over your life. Consider your spiritual journey and the terrain through which you have passed. Close your eyes and consider the terrain of your life right now. What picture comes to mind? Are you in a desert? Are you camping at an oasis, a place of refreshment? Are you living in a fruitful plain and enjoying its abundance? Are you struggling to scale mountains? Are you living in the middle of a bustling city? Through what people and experiences is God present for you in your situation? Give thanks for the ways God has been with you in those places and is with you now.

ᵃ Or *treaty*, or *testimony*; Heb *eduth*

An Experienced Guide

NUMBERS 10.29–32

We know people like Hobab—those who know "the lay of the land" and can guide us. Who functions in your life as a spiritual guide? Who has helped you in the past to see important things and to find your way through difficulties?

We can also be like Hobab for others. What help can you offer someone you know who is going through spiritual, emotional or vocational terrain with which you are familiar?

See Meeting God in Community

over the company of the tribe of Gad was Eliasaph son of Deuel.

21 Then the Kohathites, who carried the holy things, set out; and the tabernacle was set up before their arrival. 22 Next the standard of the Ephraimite camp set out, company by company, and over the whole company was Elishama son of Ammihud. 23 Over the company of the tribe of Manasseh was Gamaliel son of Pedahzur, 24 and over the company of the tribe of Benjamin was Abidan son of Gideoni.

25 Then the standard of the camp of Dan, acting as the rear guard of all the camps, set out, company by company, and over the whole company was Ahiezer son of Ammishaddai. 26 Over the company of the tribe of Asher was Pagiel son of Ochran, 27 and over the company of the tribe of Naphtali was Ahira son of Enan. 28 This was the order of march of the Israelites, company by company, when they set out.

29 Moses said to Hobab son of Reuel the Midianite, Moses' father-in-law, "We are setting out for the place of which the LORD said, 'I will give it to you'; come with us, and we will treat you well; for the LORD has promised good to Israel." 30 But he said to him, "I will not go, but I will go back to my own land and to my kindred." 31 He said, "Do not leave us, for you know where we should camp in the wilderness, and you will serve as eyes for us. 32 Moreover, if you go with us, whatever good the LORD does for us, the same we will do for you."

33 So they set out from the mount of the LORD three days' journey with the ark of the covenant of the LORD going before them three days' journey, to seek out a resting place for them, 34 the cloud of the LORD being over them by day when they set out from the camp.

35 Whenever the ark set out, Moses would say,

"Arise, O LORD, let your enemies be scattered,
    and your foes flee before you."

36 And whenever it came to rest, he would say,

"Return, O LORD of the ten thousand thousands of
    Israel." [a]

Complaining in the Desert

11 Now when the people complained in the hearing of the LORD about their misfortunes, the LORD heard it and his anger was kindled. Then the fire of the LORD burned against them, and consumed some outlying parts of the camp. 2 But the people cried out to Moses; and Moses prayed to the LORD, and the fire abated. 3 So that place was called Taberah, [b] because the fire of the LORD burned against them.

4 The rabble among them had a strong craving; and the Israelites also wept again, and said, "If only we had meat to eat! 5 We remember the fish we used to eat in Egypt for nothing, the cucumbers, the melons, the leeks, the onions, and the garlic; 6 but now our strength is dried up, and there is nothing at all but this manna to look at."

7 Now the manna was like coriander seed, and its color was like the color of gum resin. 8 The people went around and gathered it, ground it in mills or beat it in mortars, then boiled it in pots and made cakes of it; and

a Meaning of Heb uncertain   *b* That is *Burning*

the taste of it was like the taste of cakes baked with oil. [9]When the dew fell on the camp in the night, the manna would fall with it.

10 Moses heard the people weeping throughout their families, all at the entrances of their tents. Then the LORD became very angry, and Moses was displeased. [11]So Moses said to the LORD, "Why have you treated your servant so badly? Why have I not found favor in your sight, that you lay the burden of all this people on me? [12]Did I conceive all this people? Did I give birth to them, that you should say to me, 'Carry them in your bosom, as a nurse carries a sucking child,' to the land that you promised on oath to their ancestors? [13]Where am I to get meat to give to all this people? For they come weeping to me and say, 'Give us meat to eat!' [14]I am not able to carry all this people alone, for they are too heavy for me. [15]If this is the way you are going to treat me, put me to death at once—if I have found favor in your sight—and do not let me see my misery."

The Seventy Elders

16 So the LORD said to Moses, "Gather for me seventy of the elders of Israel, whom you know to be the elders of the people and officers over them; bring them to the tent of meeting, and have them take their place there with you. [17]I will come down and talk with you there; and I will take some of the spirit that is on you and put it on them; and they shall bear the burden of the people along with you so that you will not bear it all by yourself. [18]And say to the people: Consecrate yourselves for tomorrow, and you shall eat meat; for you have wailed in the hearing of the LORD, saying, 'If only we had meat to eat! Surely it was better for us in Egypt.' Therefore the LORD will give you meat, and you shall eat. [19]You shall eat not only one day, or two days, or five days, or ten days, or twenty days, [20]but for a whole month—until it comes out of your nostrils and becomes loathsome to you—because you have rejected the LORD who is among you, and have wailed before him, saying, 'Why did we ever leave Egypt?' " [21]But Moses said, "The people I am with number six hundred thousand on foot; and you say, 'I will give them meat, that they may eat for a whole month'! [22]Are there enough flocks and herds to slaughter for them? Are there enough fish in the sea to catch for them?" [23]The LORD said to Moses, "Is the LORD's power limited?[a] Now you shall see whether my word will come true for you or not."

24 So Moses went out and told the people the words of the LORD; and he gathered seventy elders of the people, and placed them all around the tent. [25]Then the LORD came down in the cloud and spoke to him, and took some of the spirit that was on him and put it on the seventy elders; and when the spirit rested upon them, they prophesied. But they did not do so again.

26 Two men remained in the camp, one named Eldad, and the other named Medad, and the spirit rested on them; they were among those registered, but they had not gone out to the tent, and so they prophesied in the camp. [27]And a young man ran and told Moses, "Eldad and

A Weary Leader

NUMBERS 11.10–17

Moses was so overwhelmed by the task of leading the people that he asked God to put him to death. God's solution was less spectacular but considerably healthier. God told Moses to gather helpers.

Our leaders are often overworked, and they often feel unappreciated. Pray for the leaders in your community, both the public leaders and those who work behind the scenes. In addition to praying for them, consider what else you can do to lighten their load.

See Meeting God in Community

---

a Heb LORD's *hand too short?*

Open Rebellion

NUMBERS 12.1–13

Aaron and Miriam rebel against Moses' leadership. They are jealous of his close relationship with God and criticize him. Yet when Miriam is stricken with leprosy Moses prays fervently for her healing.

Imagine yourself in Moses' shoes, facing two people who oppose you. What emotions do you experience? What do you want to do? Do you respond with compassion? What resources help you do so? How can you draw on these resources when coping with some difficult relationship you are facing now?

See *Meeting God in Community*

Medad are prophesying in the camp." [28]And Joshua son of Nun, the assistant of Moses, one of his chosen men,[a] said, "My lord Moses, stop them!" [29]But Moses said to him, "Are you jealous for my sake? Would that all the LORD's people were prophets, and that the LORD would put his spirit on them!" [30]And Moses and the elders of Israel returned to the camp.

The Quails

31 Then a wind went out from the LORD, and it brought quails from the sea and let them fall beside the camp, about a day's journey on this side and a day's journey on the other side, all around the camp, about two cubits deep on the ground. [32]So the people worked all that day and night and all the next day, gathering the quails; the least anyone gathered was ten homers; and they spread them out for themselves all around the camp. [33]But while the meat was still between their teeth, before it was consumed, the anger of the LORD was kindled against the people, and the LORD struck the people with a very great plague. [34]So that place was called Kibroth-hattaavah,[b] because there they buried the people who had the craving. [35]From Kibroth-hattaavah the people journeyed to Hazeroth.

Aaron and Miriam Jealous of Moses

12 While they were at Hazeroth, Miriam and Aaron spoke against Moses because of the Cushite woman whom he had married (for he had indeed married a Cushite woman); [2]and they said, "Has the LORD spoken only through Moses? Has he not spoken through us also?" And the LORD heard it. [3]Now the man Moses was very humble,[c] more so than anyone else on the face of the earth. [4]Suddenly the LORD said to Moses, Aaron, and Miriam, "Come out, you three, to the tent of meeting." So the three of them came out. [5]Then the LORD came down in a pillar of cloud, and stood at the entrance of the tent, and called Aaron and Miriam; and they both came forward. [6]And he said, "Hear my words:

When there are prophets among you,
    I the LORD make myself known to them in
       visions;
    I speak to them in dreams.
[7] Not so with my servant Moses;
    he is entrusted with all my house.
[8] With him I speak face to face— clearly, not in
    riddles;
    and he beholds the form of the LORD.
Why then were you not afraid to speak against my servant Moses?" [9]And the anger of the LORD was kindled against them, and he departed.

10 When the cloud went away from over the tent, Miriam had become leprous,[d] as white as snow. And Aaron turned towards Miriam and saw that she was leprous. [11]Then Aaron said to Moses, "Oh, my lord, do not punish us[e] for a sin that we have so foolishly committed. [12]Do not let her be like one stillborn, whose flesh is half con-

---

a Or *of Moses from his youth*   *b* That is *Graves of craving*   *c* Or *devout*
d A term for several skin diseases; precise meaning uncertain   *e* Heb *do not lay sin upon us*

sumed when it comes out of its mother's womb." ¹³And Moses cried to the LORD, "O God, please heal her." ¹⁴But the LORD said to Moses, "If her father had but spit in her face, would she not bear her shame for seven days? Let her be shut out of the camp for seven days, and after that she may be brought in again." ¹⁵So Miriam was shut out of the camp for seven days; and the people did not set out on the march until Miriam had been brought in again. ¹⁶After that the people set out from Hazeroth, and camped in the wilderness of Paran.

Spies Sent into Canaan

13 The LORD said to Moses, ²"Send men to spy out the land of Canaan, which I am giving to the Israelites; from each of their ancestral tribes you shall send a man, every one a leader among them." ³So Moses sent them from the wilderness of Paran, according to the command of the LORD, all of them leading men among the Israelites. ⁴These were their names: From the tribe of Reuben, Shammua son of Zaccur; ⁵from the tribe of Simeon, Shaphat son of Hori; ⁶from the tribe of Judah, Caleb son of Jephunneh; ⁷from the tribe of Issachar, Igal son of Joseph; ⁸from the tribe of Ephraim, Hoshea son of Nun; ⁹from the tribe of Benjamin, Palti son of Raphu; ¹⁰from the tribe of Zebulun, Gaddiel son of Sodi; ¹¹from the tribe of Joseph (that is, from the tribe of Manasseh), Gaddi son of Susi; ¹²from the tribe of Dan, Ammiel son of Gemalli; ¹³from the tribe of Asher, Sethur son of Michael; ¹⁴from the tribe of Naphtali, Nahbi son of Vophsi; ¹⁵from the tribe of Gad, Geuel son of Machi. ¹⁶These were the names of the men whom Moses sent to spy out the land. And Moses changed the name of Hoshea son of Nun to Joshua.

17 Moses sent them to spy out the land of Canaan, and said to them, "Go up there into the Negeb, and go up into the hill country, ¹⁸and see what the land is like, and whether the people who live in it are strong or weak, whether they are few or many, ¹⁹and whether the land they live in is good or bad, and whether the towns that they live in are unwalled or fortified, ²⁰and whether the land is rich or poor, and whether there are trees in it or not. Be bold, and bring some of the fruit of the land." Now it was the season of the first ripe grapes.

21 So they went up and spied out the land from the wilderness of Zin to Rehob, near Lebo-hamath. ²²They went up into the Negeb, and came to Hebron; and Ahiman, Sheshai, and Talmai, the Anakites, were there. (Hebron was built seven years before Zoan in Egypt.) ²³And they came to the Wadi Eshcol, and cut down from there a branch with a single cluster of grapes, and they carried it on a pole between two of them. They also brought some pomegranates and figs. ²⁴That place was called the Wadi Eshcol,ᵃ because of the cluster that the Israelites cut down from there.

The Report of the Spies

25 At the end of forty days they returned from spying out the land. ²⁶And they came to Moses and Aaron and to all the congregation of the Israelites in the wilderness of Paran, at Kadesh; they brought back word to them and to

No More Than Grasshoppers!

NUMBERS 13.25–33

The scouts come back to report that the inhabitants of the land are like giants. Alongside them the Israelite scouts feel no bigger than grasshoppers.

The way we perceive reality depends on the frame of reference we use when we look at problems. Relying on our human perceptions can make us feel overwhelmed. Take a magnifying glass and hold it above this page. Move the glass and notice how the print seems to grow and shrink. Does the size of the print actually change? Of course it doesn't, but the lens changes our perception. Think about a time when you faced a task that seemed impossible. How did you see yourself? Do you see yourself and the task differently now? What demanding tasks are you facing today, and how can you find a godly perspective on them?

See Meeting God in Everyday Life

ᵃ That is *Cluster*

Facing the Consequences

NUMBERS 14.18–23

The kind of fruit we grow depends on the kind of seeds we sow. Our behavior has consequences. If we overeat, we gain weight. If we don't exercise, our muscles become weak. If we mistreat others, relationships deteriorate. And the consequences may affect others, even across generations. What patterns of behavior in your life have had negative consequences for you or for those you love? In what areas do you need God's help in changing those patterns? What patterns have had good consequences? What practices such as daily prayer or Bible study have been especially helpful to you in your faith?

See Meeting God in Community

all the congregation, and showed them the fruit of the land. ²⁷And they told him, "We came to the land to which you sent us; it flows with milk and honey, and this is its fruit. ²⁸Yet the people who live in the land are strong, and the towns are fortified and very large; and besides, we saw the descendants of Anak there. ²⁹The Amalekites live in the land of the Negeb; the Hittites, the Jebusites, and the Amorites live in the hill country; and the Canaanites live by the sea, and along the Jordan."

30 But Caleb quieted the people before Moses, and said, "Let us go up at once and occupy it, for we are well able to overcome it." ³¹Then the men who had gone up with him said, "We are not able to go up against this people, for they are stronger than we." ³²So they brought to the Israelites an unfavorable report of the land that they had spied out, saying, "The land that we have gone through as spies is a land that devours its inhabitants; and all the people that we saw in it are of great size. ³³There we saw the Nephilim (the Anakites come from the Nephilim); and to ourselves we seemed like grasshoppers, and so we seemed to them."

The People Rebel

14 Then all the congregation raised a loud cry, and the people wept that night. ²And all the Israelites complained against Moses and Aaron; the whole congregation said to them, "Would that we had died in the land of Egypt! Or would that we had died in this wilderness! ³Why is the LORD bringing us into this land to fall by the sword? Our wives and our little ones will become booty; would it not be better for us to go back to Egypt?" ⁴So they said to one another, "Let us choose a captain, and go back to Egypt."

5 Then Moses and Aaron fell on their faces before all the assembly of the congregation of the Israelites. ⁶And Joshua son of Nun and Caleb son of Jephunneh, who were among those who had spied out the land, tore their clothes ⁷and said to all the congregation of the Israelites, "The land that we went through as spies is an exceedingly good land. ⁸If the LORD is pleased with us, he will bring us into this land and give it to us, a land that flows with milk and honey. ⁹Only, do not rebel against the LORD; and do not fear the people of the land, for they are no more than bread for us; their protection is removed from them, and the LORD is with us; do not fear them." ¹⁰But the whole congregation threatened to stone them.

Then the glory of the LORD appeared at the tent of meeting to all the Israelites. ¹¹And the LORD said to Moses, "How long will this people despise me? And how long will they refuse to believe in me, in spite of all the signs that I have done among them? ¹²I will strike them with pestilence and disinherit them, and I will make of you a nation greater and mightier than they."

Moses Intercedes for the People

13 But Moses said to the LORD, "Then the Egyptians will hear of it, for in your might you brought up this people from among them, ¹⁴and they will tell the inhabitants of this land. They have heard that you, O LORD, are in the midst of this people; for you, O LORD, are seen face to

face, and your cloud stands over them and you go in front of them, in a pillar of cloud by day and in a pillar of fire by night. ¹⁵Now if you kill this people all at one time, then the nations who have heard about you will say, ¹⁶'It is because the LORD was not able to bring this people into the land he swore to give them that he has slaughtered them in the wilderness.' ¹⁷And now, therefore, let the power of the LORD be great in the way that you promised when you spoke, saying,

¹⁸ 'The LORD is slow to anger,
  and abounding in steadfast love,
  forgiving iniquity and transgression,
  but by no means clearing the guilty,
  visiting the iniquity of the parents
  upon the children
  to the third and the fourth generation.'

¹⁹Forgive the iniquity of this people according to the greatness of your steadfast love, just as you have pardoned this people, from Egypt even until now."

20 Then the LORD said, "I do forgive, just as you have asked; ²¹nevertheless—as I live, and as all the earth shall be filled with the glory of the LORD— ²²none of the people who have seen my glory and the signs that I did in Egypt and in the wilderness, and yet have tested me these ten times and have not obeyed my voice, ²³shall see the land that I swore to give to their ancestors; none of those who despised me shall see it. ²⁴But my servant Caleb, because he has a different spirit and has followed me wholeheartedly, I will bring into the land into which he went, and his descendants shall possess it. ²⁵Now, since the Amalekites and the Canaanites live in the valleys, turn tomorrow and set out for the wilderness by the way to the Red Sea."ᵃ

An Attempted Invasion is Repulsed

26 And the LORD spoke to Moses and to Aaron, saying: ²⁷How long shall this wicked congregation complain against me? I have heard the complaints of the Israelites, which they complain against me. ²⁸Say to them, "As I live," says the LORD, "I will do to you the very things I heard you say: ²⁹your dead bodies shall fall in this very wilderness; and of all your number, included in the census, from twenty years old and upward, who have complained against me, ³⁰not one of you shall come into the land in which I swore to settle you, except Caleb son of Jephunneh and Joshua son of Nun. ³¹But your little ones, who you said would become booty, I will bring in, and they shall know the land that you have despised. ³²But as for you, your dead bodies shall fall in this wilderness. ³³And your children shall be shepherds in the wilderness for forty years, and shall suffer for your faithlessness, until the last of your dead bodies lies in the wilderness. ³⁴According to the number of the days in which you spied out the land, forty days, for every day a year, you shall bear your iniquity, forty years, and you shall know my displeasure." ³⁵I the LORD have spoken; surely I will do thus to all this wicked congregation gathered together against me: in this wilderness they shall come to a full end, and there they shall die.

Without Reservation

NUMBERS 14.24

Think about what it would mean to give yourself to God wholly, without reservation. What images come to mind? What would your life look like if you completely depended on God and allowed God into every part of it? What do you feel as you consider the idea? Consider whether there are areas that you want to open more fully to God and areas that you are withholding from God. What can you do to entrust yourself more completely to the love that sustains you and carries you along?

New in Town?

NUMBERS 15.14–16

God's people are commanded to include outsiders in their worship. Visualize your community of faith at a typical gathering. Are the people all of the same ethnic background or social class? If your community is diverse, what does the diversity add to your life together? If it isn't diverse, what can you do to make your worship setting more welcoming? Consider also how you can better incorporate new people into the life of your church, communicating your values and history to the new members even as you learn from them in turn.

See Meeting God in Community

36 And the men whom Moses sent to spy out the land, who returned and made all the congregation complain against him by bringing a bad report about the land—³⁷the men who brought an unfavorable report about the land died by a plague before the Lord. ³⁸But Joshua son of Nun and Caleb son of Jephunneh alone remained alive, of those men who went to spy out the land.

39 When Moses told these words to all the Israelites, the people mourned greatly. ⁴⁰They rose early in the morning and went up to the heights of the hill country, saying, "Here we are. We will go up to the place that the Lord has promised, for we have sinned." ⁴¹But Moses said, "Why do you continue to transgress the command of the Lord? That will not succeed. ⁴²Do not go up, for the Lord is not with you; do not let yourselves be struck down before your enemies. ⁴³For the Amalekites and the Canaanites will confront you there, and you shall fall by the sword; because you have turned back from following the Lord, the Lord will not be with you." ⁴⁴But they presumed to go up to the heights of the hill country, even though the ark of the covenant of the Lord, and Moses, had not left the camp. ⁴⁵Then the Amalekites and the Canaanites who lived in that hill country came down and defeated them, pursuing them as far as Hormah.

Various Offerings

15 The Lord spoke to Moses, saying: ²Speak to the Israelites and say to them: When you come into the land you are to inhabit, which I am giving you, ³and you make an offering by fire to the Lord from the herd or from the flock—whether a burnt offering or a sacrifice, to fulfill a vow or as a freewill offering or at your appointed festivals—to make a pleasing odor for the Lord, ⁴then whoever presents such an offering to the Lord shall present also a grain offering, one-tenth of an ephah of choice flour, mixed with one-fourth of a hin of oil. ⁵Moreover, you shall offer one-fourth of a hin of wine as a drink offering with the burnt offering or the sacrifice, for each lamb. ⁶For a ram, you shall offer a grain offering, two-tenths of an ephah of choice flour mixed with one-third of a hin of oil; ⁷and as a drink offering you shall offer one-third of a hin of wine, a pleasing odor to the Lord. ⁸When you offer a bull as a burnt offering or a sacrifice, to fulfill a vow or as an offering of well-being to the Lord, ⁹then you shall present with the bull a grain offering, three-tenths of an ephah of choice flour, mixed with half a hin of oil, ¹⁰and you shall present as a drink offering half a hin of wine, as an offering by fire, a pleasing odor to the Lord.

11 Thus it shall be done for each ox or ram, or for each of the male lambs or the kids. ¹²According to the number that you offer, so you shall do with each and every one. ¹³Every native Israelite shall do these things in this way, in presenting an offering by fire, a pleasing odor to the Lord. ¹⁴An alien who lives with you, or who takes up permanent residence among you, and wishes to offer an offering by fire, a pleasing odor to the Lord, shall do as you do. ¹⁵As for the assembly, there shall be for both you and the resident alien a single statute, a perpetual statute

throughout your generations; you and the alien shall be alike before the LORD. [16]You and the alien who resides with you shall have the same law and the same ordinance.

17 The LORD spoke to Moses, saying: [18]Speak to the Israelites and say to them: After you come into the land to which I am bringing you, [19]whenever you eat of the bread of the land, you shall present a donation to the LORD. [20]From your first batch of dough you shall present a loaf as a donation; you shall present it just as you present a donation from the threshing floor. [21]Throughout your generations you shall give to the LORD a donation from the first of your batch of dough.

22 But if you unintentionally fail to observe all these commandments that the LORD has spoken to Moses— [23]everything that the LORD has commanded you by Moses, from the day the LORD gave commandment and thereafter, throughout your generations— [24]then if it was done unintentionally without the knowledge of the congregation, the whole congregation shall offer one young bull for a burnt offering, a pleasing odor to the LORD, together with its grain offering and its drink offering, according to the ordinance, and one male goat for a sin offering. [25]The priest shall make atonement for all the congregation of the Israelites, and they shall be forgiven; it was unintentional, and they have brought their offering, an offering by fire to the LORD, and their sin offering before the LORD, for their error. [26]All the congregation of the Israelites shall be forgiven, as well as the aliens residing among them, because the whole people was involved in the error.

27 An individual who sins unintentionally shall present a female goat a year old for a sin offering. [28]And the priest shall make atonement before the LORD for the one who commits an error, when it is unintentional, to make atonement for the person, who then shall be forgiven. [29]For both the native among the Israelites and the alien residing among them—you shall have the same law for anyone who acts in error. [30]But whoever acts high-handedly, whether a native or an alien, affronts the LORD, and shall be cut off from among the people. [31]Because of having despised the word of the LORD and broken his commandment, such a person shall be utterly cut off and bear the guilt.

Penalty for Violating the Sabbath

32 When the Israelites were in the wilderness, they found a man gathering sticks on the sabbath day. [33]Those who found him gathering sticks brought him to Moses, Aaron, and to the whole congregation. [34]They put him in custody, because it was not clear what should be done to him. [35]Then the LORD said to Moses, "The man shall be put to death; all the congregation shall stone him outside the camp." [36]The whole congregation brought him outside the camp and stoned him to death, just as the LORD had commanded Moses.

Fringes on Garments

37 The LORD said to Moses: [38]Speak to the Israelites, and tell them to make fringes on the corners of their gar-

Your Calls to Prayer

NUMBERS 15.37–41

The blue cords are to remind the Israelites of what God has done for them. For many Christian believers throughout the centuries, the chiming of a clock on the hour has signified a reminder—a call to prayer that bids them pause momentarily, recognize God's presence and give thanks. Sounds, objects or experiences can be a personal call to prayer still today. Seeing objects that remind us of a favorite friend or relative can become a call to pray for them; waiting for a phone to be answered can remind us to pray for willingness to listen to God. For the next twenty-four hours pay attention to small reminders of people and situations, and consider how each of them may become your call to prayer.

See Meeting God in Everyday Life

Fierce Holiness

NUMBERS 16.19–34

Moses warned the people to stay away from Korah and his followers. Then the ground opened and swallowed up those who were unholy! Put yourself in the place of one of those watching. What do you see and hear? What do you feel? What does this scene convey to you about God's call to be holy? Does this scene suggest to you how to pray?

See *Meeting God in Scripture*

ments throughout their generations and to put a blue cord on the fringe at each corner. ³⁹You have the fringe so that, when you see it, you will remember all the commandments of the LORD and do them, and not follow the lust of your own heart and your own eyes. ⁴⁰So you shall remember and do all my commandments, and you shall be holy to your God. ⁴¹I am the LORD your God, who brought you out of the land of Egypt, to be your God: I am the LORD your God.

Revolt of Korah, Dathan, and Abiram

16 Now Korah son of Izhar son of Kohath son of Levi, along with Dathan and Abiram sons of Eliab, and On son of Peleth—descendants of Reuben—took ²two hundred fifty Israelite men, leaders of the congregation, chosen from the assembly, well-known men,ᵃ and they confronted Moses. ³They assembled against Moses and against Aaron, and said to them, "You have gone too far! All the congregation are holy, every one of them, and the LORD is among them. So why then do you exalt yourselves above the assembly of the LORD?" ⁴When Moses heard it, he fell on his face. ⁵Then he said to Korah and all his company, "In the morning the LORD will make known who is his, and who is holy, and who will be allowed to approach him; the one whom he will choose he will allow to approach him. ⁶Do this: take censers, Korah and all yourᵇ company, ⁷and tomorrow put fire in them, and lay incense on them before the LORD; and the man whom the LORD chooses shall be the holy one. You Levites have gone too far!" ⁸Then Moses said to Korah, "Hear now, you Levites! ⁹Is it too little for you that the God of Israel has separated you from the congregation of Israel, to allow you to approach him in order to perform the duties of the LORD's tabernacle, and to stand before the congregation and serve them? ¹⁰He has allowed you to approach him, and all your brother Levites with you; yet you seek the priesthood as well! ¹¹Therefore you and all your company have gathered together against the LORD. What is Aaron that you rail against him?"

12 Moses sent for Dathan and Abiram sons of Eliab; but they said, "We will not come! ¹³Is it too little that you have brought us up out of a land flowing with milk and honey to kill us in the wilderness, that you must also lord it over us? ¹⁴It is clear you have not brought us into a land flowing with milk and honey, or given us an inheritance of fields and vineyards. Would you put out the eyes of these men? We will not come!"

15 Moses was very angry and said to the LORD, "Pay no attention to their offering. I have not taken one donkey from them, and I have not harmed any one of them." ¹⁶And Moses said to Korah, "As for you and all your company, be present tomorrow before the LORD, you and they and Aaron; ¹⁷and let each one of you take his censer, and put incense on it, and each one of you present his censer before the LORD, two hundred fifty censers; you also, and Aaron, each his censer." ¹⁸So each man took his censer, and they put fire in the censers and laid incense on them,

---

a Cn: Heb *and they confronted Moses, and two hundred fifty men . . . well-known men*   *b* Heb *his*

and they stood at the entrance of the tent of meeting with Moses and Aaron. ¹⁹Then Korah assembled the whole congregation against them at the entrance of the tent of meeting. And the glory of the LORD appeared to the whole congregation.

20 Then the LORD spoke to Moses and to Aaron, saying: ²¹Separate yourselves from this congregation, so that I may consume them in a moment. ²²They fell on their faces, and said, "O God, the God of the spirits of all flesh, shall one person sin and you become angry with the whole congregation?"

23 And the LORD spoke to Moses, saying: ²⁴Say to the congregation: Get away from the dwellings of Korah, Dathan, and Abiram. ²⁵So Moses got up and went to Dathan and Abiram; the elders of Israel followed him. ²⁶He said to the congregation, "Turn away from the tents of these wicked men, and touch nothing of theirs, or you will be swept away for all their sins." ²⁷So they got away from the dwellings of Korah, Dathan, and Abiram; and Dathan and Abiram came out and stood at the entrance of their tents, together with their wives, their children, and their little ones. ²⁸And Moses said, "This is how you shall know that the LORD has sent me to do all these works; it has not been of my own accord: ²⁹If these people die a natural death, or if a natural fate comes on them, then the LORD has not sent me. ³⁰But if the LORD creates something new, and the ground opens its mouth and swallows them up, with all that belongs to them, and they go down alive into Sheol, then you shall know that these men have despised the LORD."

31 As soon as he finished speaking all these words, the ground under them was split apart. ³²The earth opened its mouth and swallowed them up, along with their households—everyone who belonged to Korah and all their goods. ³³So they with all that belonged to them went down alive into Sheol; the earth closed over them, and they perished from the midst of the assembly. ³⁴All Israel around them fled at their outcry, for they said, "The earth will swallow us too!" ³⁵And fire came out from the LORD and consumed the two hundred fifty men offering the incense.

36ᵃ Then the LORD spoke to Moses, saying: ³⁷Tell Eleazar son of Aaron the priest to take the censers out of the blaze; then scatter the fire far and wide. ³⁸For the censers of these sinners have become holy at the cost of their lives. Make them into hammered plates as a covering for the altar, for they presented them before the LORD and they became holy. Thus they shall be a sign to the Israelites. ³⁹So Eleazar the priest took the bronze censers that had been presented by those who were burned; and they were hammered out as a covering for the altar— ⁴⁰a reminder to the Israelites that no outsider, who is not of the descendants of Aaron, shall approach to offer incense before the LORD, so as not to become like Korah and his company—just as the LORD had said to him through Moses.

41 On the next day, however, the whole congregation of the Israelites rebelled against Moses and against Aaron, saying, "You have killed the people of the LORD." ⁴²And

The Fragrance of Mercy

NUMBERS 16.41–48

Imagine yourself in this scene. Breathe deeply. Inhale the burning incense that Aaron is carrying in the censer. What does mercy "smell" like? Aaron could condemn these rebellious people to suffer for their sin. Instead, he walks among them, effecting reconciliation, bringing healing.

Do you know people who need someone to "burn incense for them," someone to represent God's mercy and love in a way that they can recognize? What can you carry with you as a reminder to burn the incense of grace and mercy for others?

See Meeting God in Community

---

a Ch 17.1 in Heb

A Dangerous Gift

NUMBERS 17.8; 18.6–8

Overnight, Aaron's staff buds, blossoms and bears fruit. His priesthood is a God-given gift, a special calling. What evidence might you see that God has called someone for a special role? What gifts do leaders need in order to care for God's people effectively? What are your leadership gifts, and in what ways are you exercising them for God's kingdom?

See Meeting God in Community

when the congregation had assembled against them, Moses and Aaron turned toward the tent of meeting; the cloud had covered it and the glory of the LORD appeared. ⁴³Then Moses and Aaron came to the front of the tent of meeting, ⁴⁴and the LORD spoke to Moses, saying, ⁴⁵"Get away from this congregation, so that I may consume them in a moment." And they fell on their faces. ⁴⁶Moses said to Aaron, "Take your censer, put fire on it from the altar and lay incense on it, and carry it quickly to the congregation and make atonement for them. For wrath has gone out from the LORD; the plague has begun." ⁴⁷So Aaron took it as Moses had ordered, and ran into the middle of the assembly, where the plague had already begun among the people. He put on the incense, and made atonement for the people. ⁴⁸He stood between the dead and the living; and the plague was stopped. ⁴⁹Those who died by the plague were fourteen thousand seven hundred, besides those who died in the affair of Korah. ⁵⁰When the plague was stopped, Aaron returned to Moses at the entrance of the tent of meeting.

The Budding of Aaron's Rod

17ᵃ The LORD spoke to Moses, saying: ²Speak to the Israelites, and get twelve staffs from them, one for each ancestral house, from all the leaders of their ancestral houses. Write each man's name on his staff, ³and write Aaron's name on the staff of Levi. For there shall be one staff for the head of each ancestral house. ⁴Place them in the tent of meeting before the covenant,ᵇ where I meet with you. ⁵And the staff of the man whom I choose shall sprout; thus I will put a stop to the complaints of the Israelites that they continually make against you. ⁶Moses spoke to the Israelites; and all their leaders gave him staffs, one for each leader, according to their ancestral houses, twelve staffs; and the staff of Aaron was among theirs. ⁷So Moses placed the staffs before the LORD in the tent of the covenant.ᵇ

8 When Moses went into the tent of the covenantᵇ on the next day, the staff of Aaron for the house of Levi had sprouted. It put forth buds, produced blossoms, and bore ripe almonds. ⁹Then Moses brought out all the staffs from before the LORD to all the Israelites; and they looked, and each man took his staff. ¹⁰And the LORD said to Moses, "Put back the staff of Aaron before the covenant,ᵇ to be kept as a warning to rebels, so that you may make an end of their complaints against me, or else they will die." ¹¹Moses did so; just as the LORD commanded him, so he did.

12 The Israelites said to Moses, "We are perishing; we are lost, all of us are lost! ¹³Everyone who approaches the tabernacle of the LORD will die. Are we all to perish?"

Responsibility of Priests and Levites

18 The LORD said to Aaron: You and your sons and your ancestral house with you shall bear responsibility for offenses connected with the sanctuary, while you and your sons alone shall bear responsibility for offenses connected with the priesthood. ²So bring with you also your brothers of the tribe of Levi, your ancestral tribe,

a Ch 17.16 in Heb   *b* Or *treaty*, or *testimony*; Heb *eduth*

in order that they may be joined to you, and serve you while you and your sons with you are in front of the tent of the covenant.*ᵃ* **³**They shall perform duties for you and for the whole tent. But they must not approach either the utensils of the sanctuary or the altar, otherwise both they and you will die. **⁴**They are attached to you in order to perform the duties of the tent of meeting, for all the service of the tent; no outsider shall approach you. **⁵**You yourselves shall perform the duties of the sanctuary and the duties of the altar, so that wrath may never again come upon the Israelites. **⁶**It is I who now take your brother Levites from among the Israelites; they are now yours as a gift, dedicated to the LORD, to perform the service of the tent of meeting. **⁷**But you and your sons with you shall diligently perform your priestly duties in all that concerns the altar and the area behind the curtain. I give your priesthood as a gift;*ᵇ* any outsider who approaches shall be put to death.

The Priests' Portion

8 The LORD spoke to Aaron: I have given you charge of the offerings made to me, all the holy gifts of the Israelites; I have given them to you and your sons as a priestly portion due you in perpetuity. **⁹**This shall be yours from the most holy things, reserved from the fire: every offering of theirs that they render to me as a most holy thing, whether grain offering, sin offering, or guilt offering, shall belong to you and your sons. **¹⁰**As a most holy thing you shall eat it; every male may eat it; it shall be holy to you. **¹¹**This also is yours: I have given to you, together with your sons and daughters, as a perpetual due, whatever is set aside from the gifts of all the elevation offerings of the Israelites; everyone who is clean in your house may eat them. **¹²**All the best of the oil and all the best of the wine and of the grain, the choice produce that they give to the LORD, I have given to you. **¹³**The first fruits of all that is in their land, which they bring to the LORD, shall be yours; everyone who is clean in your house may eat of it. **¹⁴**Every devoted thing in Israel shall be yours. **¹⁵**The first issue of the womb of all creatures, human and animal, which is offered to the LORD, shall be yours; but the firstborn of human beings you shall redeem, and the firstborn of unclean animals you shall redeem. **¹⁶**Their redemption price, reckoned from one month of age, you shall fix at five shekels of silver, according to the shekel of the sanctuary (that is, twenty gerahs). **¹⁷**But the firstborn of a cow, or the firstborn of a sheep, or the firstborn of a goat, you shall not redeem; they are holy. You shall dash their blood on the altar, and shall turn their fat into smoke as an offering by fire for a pleasing odor to the LORD; **¹⁸**but their flesh shall be yours, just as the breast that is elevated and as the right thigh are yours. **¹⁹**All the holy offerings that the Israelites present to the LORD I have given to you, together with your sons and daughters, as a perpetual due; it is a covenant of salt forever before the LORD for you and your descendants as well. **²⁰**Then the LORD said to Aaron: You shall have no allotment in their land, nor shall you have any share among them; I am your share and your possession among the Israelites.

A Secure Possession

NUMBERS 18.20

Listen as God communicates to you, "I am your share and your possession." Mull over that thought. What does it mean to you? Think about your dearest possession. How do you care for it? How do you care for your most important relationships? Consider what you can do to show your gratitude for the gift of God's presence in your life.

God's Portion

NUMBERS 18:29

Because God gives to us, we are to give to others. We often think of giving only in terms of money, but this passage tells the Levites to share the best and holiest of all that God has given them. Think back over the last few weeks and list in your mind how you have given to those you love, to the church, to your job, to your community. Do you find it easier to give money than time? How do you give of your personal strengths and talents? Are there gifts that you choose not to share?

See Meeting God in Service

21 To the Levites I have given every tithe in Israel for a possession in return for the service that they perform, the service in the tent of meeting. ²²From now on the Israelites shall no longer approach the tent of meeting, or else they will incur guilt and die. ²³But the Levites shall perform the service of the tent of meeting, and they shall bear responsibility for their own offenses; it shall be a perpetual statute throughout your generations. But among the Israelites they shall have no allotment, ²⁴because I have given to the Levites as their portion the tithe of the Israelites, which they set apart as an offering to the LORD. Therefore I have said of them that they shall have no allotment among the Israelites.

25 Then the LORD spoke to Moses, saying: ²⁶You shall speak to the Levites, saying: When you receive from the Israelites the tithe that I have given you from them for your portion, you shall set apart an offering from it to the LORD, a tithe of the tithe. ²⁷It shall be reckoned to you as your gift, the same as the grain of the threshing floor and the fullness of the wine press. ²⁸Thus you also shall set apart an offering to the LORD from all the tithes that you receive from the Israelites; and from them you shall give the LORD's offering to the priest Aaron. ²⁹Out of all the gifts to you, you shall set apart every offering due to the LORD; the best of all of them is the part to be consecrated. ³⁰Say also to them: When you have set apart the best of it, then the rest shall be reckoned to the Levites as produce of the threshing floor, and as produce of the wine press. ³¹You may eat it in any place, you and your households; for it is your payment for your service in the tent of meeting. ³²You shall incur no guilt by reason of it, when you have offered the best of it. But you shall not profane the holy gifts of the Israelites, on pain of death.

Ceremony of the Red Heifer

19 The LORD spoke to Moses and Aaron, saying: ²This is a statute of the law that the LORD has commanded: Tell the Israelites to bring you a red heifer without defect, in which there is no blemish and on which no yoke has been laid. ³You shall give it to the priest Eleazar, and it shall be taken outside the camp and slaughtered in his presence. ⁴The priest Eleazar shall take some of its blood with his finger and sprinkle it seven times towards the front of the tent of meeting. ⁵Then the heifer shall be burned in his sight; its skin, its flesh, and its blood, with its dung, shall be burned. ⁶The priest shall take cedarwood, hyssop, and crimson material, and throw them into the fire in which the heifer is burning. ⁷Then the priest shall wash his clothes and bathe his body in water, and afterwards he may come into the camp; but the priest shall remain unclean until evening. ⁸The one who burns the heifer*ᵃ* shall wash his clothes in water and bathe his body in water; he shall remain unclean until evening. ⁹Then someone who is clean shall gather up the ashes of the heifer, and deposit them outside the camp in a clean place; and they shall be kept for the congregation of the Israelites for the water for cleansing. It is a purification offering. ¹⁰The one who gathers the ashes of the heifer shall wash his clothes and be unclean until evening.

a Heb *it*

This shall be a perpetual statute for the Israelites and for the alien residing among them. ¹¹Those who touch the dead body of any human being shall be unclean seven days. ¹²They shall purify themselves with the water on the third day and on the seventh day, and so be clean; but if they do not purify themselves on the third day and on the seventh day, they will not become clean. ¹³All who touch a corpse, the body of a human being who has died, and do not purify themselves, defile the tabernacle of the Lord; such persons shall be cut off from Israel. Since water for cleansing was not dashed on them, they remain unclean; their uncleanness is still on them.

14 This is the law when someone dies in a tent: everyone who comes into the tent, and everyone who is in the tent, shall be unclean seven days. ¹⁵And every open vessel with no cover fastened on it is unclean. ¹⁶Whoever in the open field touches one who has been killed by a sword, or who has died naturally,ᵃ or a human bone, or a grave, shall be unclean seven days. ¹⁷For the unclean they shall take some ashes of the burnt purification offering, and running water shall be added in a vessel; ¹⁸then a clean person shall take hyssop, dip it in the water, and sprinkle it on the tent, on all the furnishings, on the persons who were there, and on whoever touched the bone, the slain, the corpse, or the grave. ¹⁹The clean person shall sprinkle the unclean ones on the third day and on the seventh day, thus purifying them on the seventh day. Then they shall wash their clothes and bathe themselves in water, and at evening they shall be clean. ²⁰Any who are unclean but do not purify themselves, those persons shall be cut off from the assembly, for they have defiled the sanctuary of the Lord. Since the water for cleansing has not been dashed on them, they are unclean.

21 It shall be a perpetual statute for them. The one who sprinkles the water for cleansing shall wash his clothes, and whoever touches the water for cleansing shall be unclean until evening. ²²Whatever the unclean person touches shall be unclean, and anyone who touches it shall be unclean until evening.

The Waters of Meribah

20 The Israelites, the whole congregation, came into the wilderness of Zin in the first month, and the people stayed in Kadesh. Miriam died there, and was buried there.

2 Now there was no water for the congregation; so they gathered together against Moses and against Aaron. ³The people quarreled with Moses and said, "Would that we had died when our kindred died before the Lord! ⁴Why have you brought the assembly of the Lord into this wilderness for us and our livestock to die here? ⁵Why have you brought us up out of Egypt, to bring us to this wretched place? It is no place for grain, or figs, or vines, or pomegranates; and there is no water to drink." ⁶Then Moses and Aaron went away from the assembly to the entrance of the tent of meeting; they fell on their faces, and the glory of the Lord appeared to them. ⁷The Lord spoke to Moses, saying: ⁸Take the staff, and assemble the con-

---

Made Pure

NUMBERS 19.7–8

Water is a recurring, powerful symbol of cleansing in the Bible. The next time you bathe or shower, pour water over yourself or stand still under the running water. As the water flows over you, imagine that it is God's grace washing you, cleansing you inwardly as you bathe outwardly. In what area of your mind and emotions do you need cleansing? In what ways do you want God to wipe the slate clean and give you a fresh start? What do you need to let go of and allow to drain away? Whatever it is, picture it being washed away by God's cleansing love.

See Meeting God in the Created Order

Again? Again?

NUMBERS 20.1–12

The Israelites witness many miracles and are sustained daily by heaven-sent manna, yet they still fail to trust God and to rely on his goodness. We may wonder how they remain so stubborn, but think for a moment. Most of us have an arena of continuing struggle in our spiritual life, some fear or area of worry that we wrestle with year after year, some attitude in which we resist God's grace. What is your arena of continuing challenge? Where do you struggle to be faithful? How have you experienced God's grace in the times you have failed? What progress have you made and where do you still need to grow in faithfulness?

gregation, you and your brother Aaron, and command the rock before their eyes to yield its water. Thus you shall bring water out of the rock for them; thus you shall provide drink for the congregation and their livestock.

9 So Moses took the staff from before the LORD, as he had commanded him. ¹⁰Moses and Aaron gathered the assembly together before the rock, and he said to them, "Listen, you rebels, shall we bring water for you out of this rock?" ¹¹Then Moses lifted up his hand and struck the rock twice with his staff; water came out abundantly, and the congregation and their livestock drank. ¹²But the LORD said to Moses and Aaron, "Because you did not trust in me, to show my holiness before the eyes of the Israelites, therefore you shall not bring this assembly into the land that I have given them." ¹³These are the waters of Meribah,ᵃ where the people of Israel quarreled with the LORD, and by which he showed his holiness.

Passage through Edom Refused

14 Moses sent messengers from Kadesh to the king of Edom, "Thus says your brother Israel: You know all the adversity that has befallen us: ¹⁵how our ancestors went down to Egypt, and we lived in Egypt a long time; and the Egyptians oppressed us and our ancestors; ¹⁶and when we cried to the LORD, he heard our voice, and sent an angel and brought us out of Egypt; and here we are in Kadesh, a town on the edge of your territory. ¹⁷Now let us pass through your land. We will not pass through field or vineyard, or drink water from any well; we will go along the King's Highway, not turning aside to the right hand or to the left until we have passed through your territory."

18 But Edom said to him, "You shall not pass through, or we will come out with the sword against you." ¹⁹The Israelites said to him, "We will stay on the highway; and if we drink of your water, we and our livestock, then we will pay for it. It is only a small matter; just let us pass through on foot." ²⁰But he said, "You shall not pass through." And Edom came out against them with a large force, heavily armed. ²¹Thus Edom refused to give Israel passage through their territory; so Israel turned away from them.

The Death of Aaron

22 They set out from Kadesh, and the Israelites, the whole congregation, came to Mount Hor. ²³Then the LORD said to Moses and Aaron at Mount Hor, on the border of the land of Edom, ²⁴"Let Aaron be gathered to his people. For he shall not enter the land that I have given to the Israelites, because you rebelled against my command at the waters of Meribah. ²⁵Take Aaron and his son Eleazar, and bring them up Mount Hor; ²⁶strip Aaron of his vestments, and put them on his son Eleazar. But Aaron shall be gathered to his people,ᵇ and shall die there." ²⁷Moses did as the LORD had commanded; they went up Mount Hor in the sight of the whole congregation. ²⁸Moses stripped Aaron of his vestments, and put them on his son Eleazar; and Aaron died there on the top of the mountain. Moses and Eleazar came down from the mountain. ²⁹When all the congregation saw that Aaron had died, all the house of Israel mourned for Aaron thirty days.

a That is *Quarrel*   b Heb lacks *to his people*

The Bronze Serpent

21 When the Canaanite, the king of Arad, who lived in the Negeb, heard that Israel was coming by the way of Atharim, he fought against Israel and took some of them captive. ²Then Israel made a vow to the LORD and said, "If you will indeed give this people into our hands, then we will utterly destroy their towns." ³The LORD listened to the voice of Israel, and handed over the Canaanites; and they utterly destroyed them and their towns; so the place was called Hormah.ᵃ

4 From Mount Hor they set out by the way to the Red Sea,ᵇ to go around the land of Edom; but the people became impatient on the way. ⁵The people spoke against God and against Moses, "Why have you brought us up out of Egypt to die in the wilderness? For there is no food and no water, and we detest this miserable food." ⁶Then the LORD sent poisonousᶜ serpents among the people, and they bit the people, so that many Israelites died. ⁷The people came to Moses and said, "We have sinned by speaking against the LORD and against you; pray to the LORD to take away the serpents from us." So Moses prayed for the people. ⁸And the LORD said to Moses, "Make a poisonousᵈ serpent, and set it on a pole; and everyone who is bitten shall look at it and live." ⁹So Moses made a serpent of bronze, and put it upon a pole; and whenever a serpent bit someone, that person would look at the serpent of bronze and live.

The Journey to Moab

10 The Israelites set out, and camped in Oboth. ¹¹They set out from Oboth, and camped at Iye-abarim, in the wilderness bordering Moab toward the sunrise. ¹²From there they set out, and camped in the Wadi Zered. ¹³From there they set out, and camped on the other side of the Arnon, inᵉ the wilderness that extends from the boundary of the Amorites; for the Arnon is the boundary of Moab, between Moab and the Amorites. ¹⁴Wherefore it is said in the Book of the Wars of the LORD,

"Waheb in Suphah and the wadis.
The Arnon ¹⁵and the slopes of the wadis
that extend to the seat of Ar,
and lie along the border of Moab."ᶠ

16 From there they continued to Beer;ᵍ that is the well of which the LORD said to Moses, "Gather the people together, and I will give them water." ¹⁷Then Israel sang this song:

"Spring up, O well!—Sing to it!—
¹⁸ the well that the leaders sank,
that the nobles of the people dug,
with the scepter, with the staff."

From the wilderness to Mattanah, ¹⁹from Mattanah to Nahaliel, from Nahaliel to Bamoth, ²⁰and from Bamoth to the valley lying in the region of Moab by the top of Pisgah that overlooks the wasteland.ʰ

ᵃ Heb *Destruction*   ᵇ Or *Sea of Reeds*   ᶜ Or *fiery*; Heb *seraphim*
ᵈ Or *fiery*; Heb *seraph*   ᵉ Gk: Heb *which is in*   ᶠ Meaning of Heb
uncertain   ᵍ That is *Well*   ʰ Or *Jeshimon*

Your Song of Praise

NUMBERS 21.17–18

God provides water in the wilderness, and in response the people sing a song of praise. Make a list of good things God has done for you—things that you can celebrate today. Think of a familiar hymn of praise and thanksgiving, or compose your own. Sing it aloud, adding items from your list as part of the song. It doesn't matter if you don't sing well or can't carry a tune. Just make a "joyful noise" before God.

See Meeting God in Worship

Making War

NUMBERS 21.32–35

"Briefly, in this tempest, there is no help for it but to wait upon the mercy of God, Who suddenly, at the most unlooked-for hour, with a single word, or on some chance occasion, lifts the whole of this burden from the soul, so that it seems as if it has never been clouded over, but is full of sunshine and far happier than it was before. Then, like one who has escaped from a perilous battle and gained the victory, the soul keeps praising Our Lord, for it is He Who has fought and enabled it to conquer. It knows very well that it did not itself do the fighting. For it saw that all the weapons with which it could defend itself were in the hands of the enemy, and it was thus clearly aware of its misery and realized how little we can do of ourselves if the Lord should forsake us."

—TERESA OF AVILA,
The Interior Castle

King Sihon Defeated

21 Then Israel sent messengers to King Sihon of the Amorites, saying, [22] "Let me pass through your land; we will not turn aside into field or vineyard; we will not drink the water of any well; we will go by the King's Highway until we have passed through your territory." [23] But Sihon would not allow Israel to pass through his territory. Sihon gathered all his people together, and went out against Israel to the wilderness; he came to Jahaz, and fought against Israel. [24] Israel put him to the sword, and took possession of his land from the Arnon to the Jabbok, as far as to the Ammonites; for the boundary of the Ammonites was strong. [25] Israel took all these towns, and Israel settled in all the towns of the Amorites, in Heshbon, and in all its villages. [26] For Heshbon was the city of King Sihon of the Amorites, who had fought against the former king of Moab and captured all his land as far as the Arnon. [27] Therefore the ballad singers say,

"Come to Heshbon, let it be built;
let the city of Sihon be established.
[28]   For fire came out from Heshbon,
flame from the city of Sihon.
It devoured Ar of Moab,
and swallowed up[a] the heights of the Arnon.
[29]   Woe to you, O Moab!
You are undone, O people of Chemosh!
He has made his sons fugitives,
and his daughters captives,
to an Amorite king, Sihon.
[30]   So their posterity perished
from Heshbon[b] to Dibon,
and we laid waste until fire spread to Medeba."[c]

31 Thus Israel settled in the land of the Amorites. [32] Moses sent to spy out Jazer; and they captured its villages, and dispossessed the Amorites who were there.

King Og Defeated

33 Then they turned and went up the road to Bashan; and King Og of Bashan came out against them, he and all his people, to battle at Edrei. [34] But the LORD said to Moses, "Do not be afraid of him; for I have given him into your hand, with all his people, and all his land. You shall do to him as you did to King Sihon of the Amorites, who ruled in Heshbon." [35] So they killed him, his sons, and all his people, until there was no survivor left; and they took possession of his land.

Balak Summons Balaam to Curse Israel

22 The Israelites set out, and camped in the plains of Moab across the Jordan from Jericho. [2] Now Balak son of Zippor saw all that Israel had done to the Amorites. [3] Moab was in great dread of the people, because they were so numerous; Moab was overcome with fear of the people of Israel. [4] And Moab said to the elders of Midian, "This horde will now lick up all that is around us, as an ox licks up the grass of the field." Now Balak son of Zippor was king of Moab at that time. [5] He sent messen-

a Gk: Heb *and the lords of*   *b* Gk: Heb *we have shot at them; Heshbon has perished*   *c* Compare Sam Gk: Meaning of MT uncertain

gers to Balaam son of Beor at Pethor, which is on the Euphrates, in the land of Amaw,ᵃ to summon him, saying, "A people has come out of Egypt; they have spread over the face of the earth, and they have settled next to me. ⁶Come now, curse this people for me, since they are stronger than I; perhaps I shall be able to defeat them and drive them from the land; for I know that whomever you bless is blessed, and whomever you curse is cursed."

7 So the elders of Moab and the elders of Midian departed with the fees for divination in their hand; and they came to Balaam, and gave him Balak's message. ⁸He said to them, "Stay here tonight, and I will bring back word to you, just as the LORD speaks to me"; so the officials of Moab stayed with Balaam. ⁹God came to Balaam and said, "Who are these men with you?" ¹⁰Balaam said to God, "King Balak son of Zippor of Moab, has sent me this message: ¹¹'A people has come out of Egypt and has spread over the face of the earth; now come, curse them for me; perhaps I shall be able to fight against them and drive them out.' " ¹²God said to Balaam, "You shall not go with them; you shall not curse the people, for they are blessed." ¹³So Balaam rose in the morning, and said to the officials of Balak, "Go to your own land, for the LORD has refused to let me go with you." ¹⁴So the officials of Moab rose and went to Balak, and said, "Balaam refuses to come with us."

15 Once again Balak sent officials, more numerous and more distinguished than these. ¹⁶They came to Balaam and said to him, "Thus says Balak son of Zippor: 'Do not let anything hinder you from coming to me; ¹⁷for I will surely do you great honor, and whatever you say to me I will do; come, curse this people for me.' " ¹⁸But Balaam replied to the servants of Balak, "Although Balak were to give me his house full of silver and gold, I could not go beyond the command of the LORD my God, to do less or more. ¹⁹You remain here, as the others did, so that I may learn what more the LORD may say to me." ²⁰That night God came to Balaam and said to him, "If the men have come to summon you, get up and go with them; but do only what I tell you to do." ²¹So Balaam got up in the morning, saddled his donkey, and went with the officials of Moab.

Balaam, the Donkey, and the Angel

22 God's anger was kindled because he was going, and the angel of the LORD took his stand in the road as his adversary. Now he was riding on the donkey, and his two servants were with him. ²³The donkey saw the angel of the LORD standing in the road, with a drawn sword in his hand; so the donkey turned off the road, and went into the field; and Balaam struck the donkey, to turn it back onto the road. ²⁴Then the angel of the LORD stood in a narrow path between the vineyards, with a wall on either side. ²⁵When the donkey saw the angel of the LORD, it scraped against the wall, and scraped Balaam's foot against the wall; so he struck it again. ²⁶Then the angel of the LORD went ahead, and stood in a narrow place, where there was no way to turn either to the right or to the left.

A Word From God

NUMBERS 22.18

Think about a dilemma or a decision you are facing. Ask God to show you what you should do in the situation. Wait quietly. If you do not receive immediate guidance, can you wait and do nothing until God gives you direction? Balaam waited for God's leading; he told Balak that he would not go beyond what God said.

As you read and think about this scripture passage, listen for God's guidance. Ask for strength to do what God tells you to do, even if it is to do nothing.

See Meeting God in Everyday Life

Pressured to Speak

NUMBERS 22.38

Balaam and Balak are engaged in a tug of war over words—but not just any words. Balak wants Balaam to curse God's people. Each time Balaam consults his oracle he is told not to curse them, but Balak keeps asking him to do it anyway, trying to get him to compromise.

Think of a time when you have felt pressured to do or say something that you felt was wrong. Perhaps something like this is going on in your life right now. At such times, in what ways can you ask for help and guidance from God and others?

See *Meeting God in Everyday Life*

27When the donkey saw the angel of the LORD, it lay down under Balaam; and Balaam's anger was kindled, and he struck the donkey with his staff. 28Then the LORD opened the mouth of the donkey, and it said to Balaam, "What have I done to you, that you have struck me these three times?" 29Balaam said to the donkey, "Because you have made a fool of me! I wish I had a sword in my hand! I would kill you right now!" 30But the donkey said to Balaam, "Am I not your donkey, which you have ridden all your life to this day? Have I been in the habit of treating you this way?" And he said, "No."

31 Then the LORD opened the eyes of Balaam, and he saw the angel of the LORD standing in the road, with his drawn sword in his hand; and he bowed down, falling on his face. 32The angel of the LORD said to him, "Why have you struck your donkey these three times? I have come out as an adversary, because your way is perverse*a* before me. 33The donkey saw me, and turned away from me these three times. If it had not turned away from me, surely just now I would have killed you and let it live." 34Then Balaam said to the angel of the LORD, "I have sinned, for I did not know that you were standing in the road to oppose me. Now therefore, if it is displeasing to you, I will return home." 35The angel of the LORD said to Balaam, "Go with the men; but speak only what I tell you to speak." So Balaam went on with the officials of Balak.

36 When Balak heard that Balaam had come, he went out to meet him at Ir-moab, on the boundary formed by the Arnon, at the farthest point of the boundary. 37Balak said to Balaam, "Did I not send to summon you? Why did you not come to me? Am I not able to honor you?" 38Balaam said to Balak, "I have come to you now, but do I have power to say just anything? The word God puts in my mouth, that is what I must say." 39Then Balaam went with Balak, and they came to Kiriath-huzoth. 40Balak sacrificed oxen and sheep, and sent them to Balaam and to the officials who were with him.

Balaam's First Oracle

41 On the next day Balak took Balaam and brought him up to Bamoth-baal; and from there he could see part **23** of the people of Israel.*b* 1Then Balaam said to Balak, "Build me seven altars here, and prepare seven bulls and seven rams for me." 2Balak did as Balaam had said; and Balak and Balaam offered a bull and a ram on each altar. 3Then Balaam said to Balak, "Stay here beside your burnt offerings while I go aside. Perhaps the LORD will come to meet me. Whatever he shows me I will tell you." And he went to a bare height.

4 Then God met Balaam; and Balaam said to him, "I have arranged the seven altars, and have offered a bull and a ram on each altar." 5The LORD put a word in Balaam's mouth, and said, "Return to Balak, and this is what you must say." 6So he returned to Balak,*c* who was standing beside his burnt offerings with all the officials of Moab. 7Then Balaam*d* uttered his oracle, saying:

a Meaning of Heb uncertain   *b* Heb lacks *of Israel*   *c* Heb *him*
d Heb *he*

"Balak has brought me from Aram,
    the king of Moab from the eastern mountains:
'Come, curse Jacob for me;
    Come, denounce Israel!'
8 How can I curse whom God has not cursed?
    How can I denounce those whom the LORD has
      not denounced?
9 For from the top of the crags I see him,
    from the hills I behold him;
  Here is a people living alone,
    and not reckoning itself among the nations!
10 Who can count the dust of Jacob,
    or number the dust-cloud*a* of Israel?
  Let me die the death of the upright,
    and let my end be like his!"

11 Then Balak said to Balaam, "What have you done to me? I brought you to curse my enemies, but now you have done nothing but bless them." 12He answered, "Must I not take care to say what the LORD puts into my mouth?"

Balaam's Second Oracle

13 So Balak said to him, "Come with me to another place from which you may see them; you shall see only part of them, and shall not see them all; then curse them for me from there." 14So he took him to the field of Zophim, to the top of Pisgah. He built seven altars, and offered a bull and a ram on each altar. 15Balaam said to Balak, "Stand here beside your burnt offerings, while I meet the LORD over there." 16The LORD met Balaam, put a word into his mouth, and said, "Return to Balak, and this is what you shall say." 17When he came to him, he was standing beside his burnt offerings with the officials of Moab. Balak said to him, "What has the LORD said?" 18Then Balaam uttered his oracle, saying:

"Rise, Balak, and hear;
    listen to me, O son of Zippor:
19 God is not a human being, that he should lie,
    or a mortal, that he should change his mind.
  Has he promised, and will he not do it?
  Has he spoken, and will he not fulfill it?
20 See, I received a command to bless;
    he has blessed, and I cannot revoke it.
21 He has not beheld misfortune in Jacob;
    nor has he seen trouble in Israel.
  The LORD their God is with them,
    acclaimed as a king among them.
22 God, who brings them out of Egypt,
    is like the horns of a wild ox for them.
23 Surely there is no enchantment against Jacob,
    no divination against Israel;
  now it shall be said of Jacob and Israel,
    'See what God has done!'
24 Look, a people rising up like a lioness,
    and rousing itself like a lion!
  It does not lie down until it has eaten the prey
    and drunk the blood of the slain."

25 Then Balak said to Balaam, "Do not curse them at all, and do not bless them at all." 26But Balaam answered

Speak Up!

NUMBERS 23.12

Balaam seems an unlikely candidate for a prophet of God, yet God uses him to utter the truth to Balak, a mission Balaam cannot resist: "Must I not take care to say what the LORD puts into my mouth?"

We sometimes find ourselves with a word from God in our mouth—a word of truth, encouragement or comfort—yet we hold back because we're afraid we might sound overly pious, or because we just don't want to deal with the emotions such words might invoke. Can you think of occasions when you held back from speaking a word from the Lord? When you did speak up? What was the result? How does this passage give you courage to speak up next time?

See Meeting God in Community

A Beautiful Vision

NUMBERS 24.3–7

As the Spirit of God comes upon him, Balaam describes the abundance and verdancy of the new land in which the Israelites will dwell. What does the kingdom of heaven look like from where you stand? What does it smell and feel like? What do you hear? Using paint, pencil, words, music or whatever creative medium you wish, create a representation of your vision of the kingdom of heaven.

Balak, "Did I not tell you, 'Whatever the LORD says, that is what I must do'?"

27 So Balak said to Balaam, "Come now, I will take you to another place; perhaps it will please God that you may curse them for me from there." [28]So Balak took Balaam to the top of Peor, which overlooks the wasteland.[a] [29]Balaam said to Balak, "Build me seven altars here, and prepare seven bulls and seven rams for me." [30]So Balak did as Balaam had said, and offered a bull and a ram on each altar.

Balaam's Third Oracle

24 Now Balaam saw that it pleased the LORD to bless Israel, so he did not go, as at other times, to look for omens, but set his face toward the wilderness. [2]Balaam looked up and saw Israel camping tribe by tribe. Then the spirit of God came upon him, [3]and he uttered his oracle, saying:

> "The oracle of Balaam son of Beor,
>> the oracle of the man whose eye is clear,[b]
> [4] the oracle of one who hears the words of God,
>> who sees the vision of the Almighty,[c]
>> who falls down, but with eyes uncovered:
> [5] how fair are your tents, O Jacob,
>> your encampments, O Israel!
> [6] Like palm groves that stretch far away,
>> like gardens beside a river,
> like aloes that the LORD has planted,
>> like cedar trees beside the waters.
> [7] Water shall flow from his buckets,
>> and his seed shall have abundant water,
> his king shall be higher than Agag,
>> and his kingdom shall be exalted.
> [8] God who brings him out of Egypt,
>> is like the horns of a wild ox for him;
> he shall devour the nations that are his foes
>> and break their bones.
> He shall strike with his arrows.[d]
> [9] He crouched, he lay down like a lion,
>> and like a lioness; who will rouse him up?
> Blessed is everyone who blesses you,
>> and cursed is everyone who curses you."

10 Then Balak's anger was kindled against Balaam, and he struck his hands together. Balak said to Balaam, "I summoned you to curse my enemies, but instead you have blessed them these three times. [11]Now be off with you! Go home! I said, 'I will reward you richly,' but the LORD has denied you any reward." [12]And Balaam said to Balak, "Did I not tell your messengers whom you sent to me, [13]'If Balak should give me his house full of silver and gold, I would not be able to go beyond the word of the LORD, to do either good or bad of my own will; what the LORD says, that is what I will say'? [14]So now, I am going to my people; let me advise you what this people will do to your people in days to come."

Balaam's Fourth Oracle

15 So he uttered his oracle, saying:
> "The oracle of Balaam son of Beor,

---

a Or overlooks Jeshimon   b Or closed or open   c Traditional rendering of Heb Shaddai   d Meaning of Heb uncertain

the oracle of the man whose eye is clear,[a]
16 the oracle of one who hears the words of God,
    and knows the knowledge of the Most High,[b]
who sees the vision of the Almighty,[c]
    who falls down, but with his eyes uncovered:
17 I see him, but not now;
    I behold him, but not near—
a star shall come out of Jacob,
    and a scepter shall rise out of Israel;
it shall crush the borderlands[d] of Moab,
    and the territory[e] of all the Shethites.
18 Edom will become a possession,
    Seir a possession of its enemies,[f]
    while Israel does valiantly.
19 One out of Jacob shall rule,
    and destroy the survivors of Ir."

20 Then he looked on Amalek, and uttered his oracle, saying:
"First among the nations was Amalek,
    but its end is to perish forever."

21 Then he looked on the Kenite, and uttered his oracle, saying:
"Enduring is your dwelling place,
    and your nest is set in the rock;
22 yet Kain is destined for burning.
    How long shall Asshur take you away captive?"
23 Again he uttered his oracle, saying:
"Alas, who shall live when God does this?
24   But ships shall come from Kittim
and shall afflict Asshur and Eber;
    and he also shall perish forever."

25 Then Balaam got up and went back to his place, and Balak also went his way.

Worship of Baal of Peor

25 While Israel was staying at Shittim, the people began to have sexual relations with the women of Moab. 2These invited the people to the sacrifices of their gods, and the people ate and bowed down to their gods. 3Thus Israel yoked itself to the Baal of Peor, and the LORD's anger was kindled against Israel. 4The LORD said to Moses, "Take all the chiefs of the people, and impale them in the sun before the LORD, in order that the fierce anger of the LORD may turn away from Israel." 5And Moses said to the judges of Israel, "Each of you shall kill any of your people who have yoked themselves to the Baal of Peor."

6 Just then one of the Israelites came and brought a Midianite woman into his family, in the sight of Moses and in the sight of the whole congregation of the Israelites, while they were weeping at the entrance of the tent of meeting. 7When Phinehas son of Eleazar, son of Aaron the priest, saw it, he got up and left the congregation. Taking a spear in his hand, 8he went after the Israelite man into the tent, and pierced the two of them, the Israelite and the woman, through the belly. So the plague was stopped among the people of Israel. 9Nevertheless those that died by the plague were twenty-four thousand.

Purging the Camp

NUMBERS 25.1–5

Alliances with the Moabites were pulling the Israelites away from God. They were allowing themselves to be "mismatched with unbelievers" (2 Corinthians 6.14). Paul is referring to the way matched oxen are yoked together. Physical yokes like those used on oxen are not familiar in our urban culture, but we have various other kinds of yokes—marriage, legal contracts, relationships with employers or employees—that directly influence us. Think about the "yokes" you share with others right now. Are they helping you to walk in the direction God wants for you? In what ways might you be yoked to people or activities from which you need to be free?

Think about someone who supports you in growing toward being the person God wants you to be. List the traits that make your alliance with that person healthy and beneficial.

See Meeting God in Community

---

a Or *closed* or *open*   b Or *of Elyon*   c Traditional rendering of Heb *Shaddai*   d Or *forehead*   e Some Mss read *skull*   f Heb *Seir, its enemies, a possession*

The People of God

NUMBERS 26.3–18

Some of the names here are slightly familiar—perhaps the names of the twelve tribes. But most of these names are unfamiliar. Yet these people are important to us because they passed their faith from generation to generation. Picture in your mind the generations of believers that stretch back through the centuries, crossing continents and oceans. Whom do you see? What sacrifices did they make for the faith? What do you feel? Which of the gifts they gave us do you especially value today?

See Meeting God in Community

10 The LORD spoke to Moses, saying: [11]"Phinehas son of Eleazar, son of Aaron the priest, has turned back my wrath from the Israelites by manifesting such zeal among them on my behalf that in my jealousy I did not consume the Israelites. [12]Therefore say, 'I hereby grant him my covenant of peace. [13]It shall be for him and for his descendants after him a covenant of perpetual priesthood, because he was zealous for his God, and made atonement for the Israelites.' "

14 The name of the slain Israelite man, who was killed with the Midianite woman, was Zimri son of Salu, head of an ancestral house belonging to the Simeonites. [15]The name of the Midianite woman who was killed was Cozbi daughter of Zur, who was the head of a clan, an ancestral house in Midian.

16 The LORD said to Moses, [17]"Harass the Midianites, and defeat them; [18]for they have harassed you by the trickery with which they deceived you in the affair of Peor, and in the affair of Cozbi, the daughter of a leader of Midian, their sister; she was killed on the day of the plague that resulted from Peor."

A Census of the New Generation

26 After the plague the LORD said to Moses and to Eleazar son of Aaron the priest, [2]"Take a census of the whole congregation of the Israelites, from twenty years old and upward, by their ancestral houses, everyone in Israel able to go to war." [3]Moses and Eleazar the priest spoke with them in the plains of Moab by the Jordan opposite Jericho, saying, [4]"Take a census of the people,[a] from twenty years old and upward," as the LORD commanded Moses.

The Israelites, who came out of the land of Egypt, were:
5 Reuben, the firstborn of Israel. The descendants of Reuben: of Hanoch, the clan of the Hanochites; of Pallu, the clan of the Palluites; [6]of Hezron, the clan of the Hezronites; of Carmi, the clan of the Carmites. [7]These are the clans of the Reubenites; the number of those enrolled was forty-three thousand seven hundred thirty. [8]And the descendants of Pallu: Eliab. [9]The descendants of Eliab: Nemuel, Dathan, and Abiram. These are the same Dathan and Abiram, chosen from the congregation, who rebelled against Moses and Aaron in the company of Korah, when they rebelled against the LORD, [10]and the earth opened its mouth and swallowed them up along with Korah, when that company died, when the fire devoured two hundred fifty men; and they became a warning. [11]Notwithstanding, the sons of Korah did not die.

12 The descendants of Simeon by their clans: of Nemuel, the clan of the Nemuelites; of Jamin, the clan of the Jaminites; of Jachin, the clan of the Jachinites; [13]of Zerah, the clan of the Zerahites; of Shaul, the clan of the Shaulites.[b] [14]These are the clans of the Simeonites, twenty-two thousand two hundred.

15 The children of Gad by their clans: of Zephon, the clan of the Zephonites; of Haggi, the clan of the Haggites; of Shuni, the clan of the Shunites; [16]of Ozni, the clan of the Oznites; of Eri, the clan of the Erites; [17]of Arod, the

a Heb lacks *take a census of the people*: Compare verse 2   *b* Or *Saul . . .*
Saulites

clan of the Arodites; of Areli, the clan of the Arelites. [18]These are the clans of the Gadites: the number of those enrolled was forty thousand five hundred.

19 The sons of Judah: Er and Onan; Er and Onan died in the land of Canaan. [20]The descendants of Judah by their clans were: of Shelah, the clan of the Shelanites; of Perez, the clan of the Perezites; of Zerah, the clan of the Zerahites. [21]The descendants of Perez were: of Hezron, the clan of the Hezronites; of Hamul, the clan of the Hamulites. [22]These are the clans of Judah: the number of those enrolled was seventy-six thousand five hundred.

23 The descendants of Issachar by their clans: of Tola, the clan of the Tolaites; of Puvah, the clan of the Punites; [24]of Jashub, the clan of the Jashubites; of Shimron, the clan of the Shimronites. [25]These are the clans of Issachar: sixty-four thousand three hundred enrolled.

26 The descendants of Zebulun by their clans: of Sered, the clan of the Seredites; of Elon, the clan of the Elonites; of Jahleel, the clan of the Jahleelites. [27]These are the clans of the Zebulunites; the number of those enrolled was sixty thousand five hundred.

28 The sons of Joseph by their clans: Manasseh and Ephraim. [29]The descendants of Manasseh: of Machir, the clan of the Machirites; and Machir was the father of Gilead; of Gilead, the clan of the Gileadites. [30]These are the descendants of Gilead: of Iezer, the clan of the Iezerites; of Helek, the clan of the Helekites; [31]and of Asriel, the clan of the Asrielites; and of Shechem, the clan of the Shechemites; [32]and of Shemida, the clan of the Shemidaites; and of Hepher, the clan of the Hepherites. [33]Now Zelophehad son of Hepher had no sons, but daughters: and the names of the daughters of Zelophehad were Mahlah, Noah, Hoglah, Milcah, and Tirzah. [34]These are the clans of Manasseh; the number of those enrolled was fifty-two thousand seven hundred.

35 These are the descendants of Ephraim according to their clans: of Shuthelah, the clan of the Shuthelahites; of Becher, the clan of the Becherites; of Tahan, the clan of the Tahanites. [36]And these are the descendants of Shuthelah: of Eran, the clan of the Eranites. [37]These are the clans of the Ephraimites: the number of those enrolled was thirty-two thousand five hundred. These are the descendants of Joseph by their clans.

38 The descendants of Benjamin by their clans: of Bela, the clan of the Belaites; of Ashbel, the clan of the Ashbelites; of Ahiram, the clan of the Ahiramites; [39]of Shephupham, the clan of the Shuphamites; of Hupham, the clan of the Huphamites. [40]And the sons of Bela were Ard and Naaman: of Ard, the clan of the Ardites; of Naaman, the clan of the Naamites. [41]These are the descendants of Benjamin by their clans; the number of those enrolled was forty-five thousand six hundred.

42 These are the descendants of Dan by their clans: of Shuham, the clan of the Shuhamites. These are the clans of Dan by their clans. [43]All the clans of the Shuhamites: sixty-four thousand four hundred enrolled.

44 The descendants of Asher by their families: of Imnah, the clan of the Imnites; of Ishvi, the clan of the Ishvites; of Beriah, the clan of the Beriites. [45]Of the descendants of Beriah: of Heber, the clan of the Heberites;

A Faith Family Tree

NUMBERS 26.28–34

Look at your ancestors in your personal faith heritage and lineage. What faith traditions shaped the lives of your parents, grandparents, greatgrandparents? Can you trace more than one faith among your biological kin? Beyond family, who are your faith ancestors? What relationships, writers, artists or places have shaped your ways of believing and worshiping?

Draw a "faith family tree," placing yourself at its base. On the branches and trunk nearest you, write in the strongest influences in your spiritual life. On other branches, place names or descriptions of other such influences. As you remember and realize more, add branches to your "tree of faith" picture.

See Meeting God in Community

According to Need

NUMBERS 26.52–56

The land is apportioned to the tribes according to their size and how much each tribe needs to survive. Larger tribes with more people are given more land, and smaller tribes are given less land. Many of us are accustomed to abundance in many areas of our lives, and we tend to think in terms of what we want rather than what we need. Examine your closets. How many coats do you have? How many pairs of shoes? How many changes of clothes? Do you have more than you need? In what other areas of your life do you have abundance—in education, money, specialized skills, energy and physical stamina? Think of at least one way you can share what you have in abundance with those who need it, then do it.

See Meeting God in Service

of Malchiel, the clan of the Malchielites. ⁴⁶And the name of the daughter of Asher was Serah. ⁴⁷These are the clans of the Asherites: the number of those enrolled was fifty-three thousand four hundred.

48 The descendants of Naphtali by their clans: of Jahzeel, the clan of the Jahzeelites; of Guni, the clan of the Gunites; ⁴⁹of Jezer, the clan of the Jezerites; of Shillem, the clan of the Shillemites. ⁵⁰These are the Naphtalites*a* by their clans: the number of those enrolled was forty-five thousand four hundred.

51 This was the number of the Israelites enrolled: six hundred and one thousand seven hundred thirty.

52 The LORD spoke to Moses, saying: ⁵³To these the land shall be apportioned for inheritance according to the number of names. ⁵⁴To a large tribe you shall give a large inheritance, and to a small tribe you shall give a small inheritance; every tribe shall be given its inheritance according to its enrollment. ⁵⁵But the land shall be apportioned by lot; according to the names of their ancestral tribes they shall inherit. ⁵⁶Their inheritance shall be apportioned according to lot between the larger and the smaller.

57 This is the enrollment of the Levites by their clans: of Gershon, the clan of the Gershonites; of Kohath, the clan of the Kohathites; of Merari, the clan of the Merarites. ⁵⁸These are the clans of Levi: the clan of the Libnites, the clan of the Hebronites, the clan of the Mahlites, the clan of the Mushites, the clan of the Korahites. Now Kohath was the father of Amram. ⁵⁹The name of Amram's wife was Jochebed daughter of Levi, who was born to Levi in Egypt; and she bore to Amram: Aaron, Moses, and their sister Miriam. ⁶⁰To Aaron were born Nadab, Abihu, Eleazar, and Ithamar. ⁶¹But Nadab and Abihu died when they offered unholy fire before the LORD. ⁶²The number of those enrolled was twenty-three thousand, every male one month old and upward; for they were not enrolled among the Israelites because there was no allotment given to them among the Israelites.

63 These were those enrolled by Moses and Eleazar the priest, who enrolled the Israelites in the plains of Moab by the Jordan opposite Jericho. ⁶⁴Among these there was not one of those enrolled by Moses and Aaron the priest, who had enrolled the Israelites in the wilderness of Sinai. ⁶⁵For the LORD had said of them, "They shall die in the wilderness." Not one of them was left, except Caleb son of Jephunneh and Joshua son of Nun.

The Daughters of Zelophehad

27 Then the daughters of Zelophehad came forward. Zelophehad was son of Hepher son of Gilead son of Machir son of Manasseh son of Joseph, a member of the Manassite clans. The names of his daughters were: Mahlah, Noah, Hoglah, Milcah, and Tirzah. ²They stood before Moses, Eleazar the priest, the leaders, and all the congregation, at the entrance of the tent of meeting, and they said, ³"Our father died in the wilderness; he was not among the company of those who gathered themselves together against the LORD in the company of Korah, but died for his own sin; and he had no sons. ⁴Why should

a Heb *clans of Naphtali*

the name of our father be taken away from his clan because he had no son? Give to us a possession among our father's brothers."

5 Moses brought their case before the LORD. ⁶And the LORD spoke to Moses, saying: ⁷The daughters of Zelophehad are right in what they are saying; you shall indeed let them possess an inheritance among their father's brothers and pass the inheritance of their father on to them. ⁸You shall also say to the Israelites, "If a man dies, and has no son, then you shall pass his inheritance on to his daughter. ⁹If he has no daughter, then you shall give his inheritance to his brothers. ¹⁰If he has no brothers, then you shall give his inheritance to his father's brothers. ¹¹And if his father has no brothers, then you shall give his inheritance to the nearest kinsman of his clan, and he shall possess it. It shall be for the Israelites a statute and ordinance, as the LORD commanded Moses."

Joshua Appointed Moses' Successor

12 The LORD said to Moses, "Go up this mountain of the Abarim range, and see the land that I have given to the Israelites. ¹³When you have seen it, you also shall be gathered to your people, as your brother Aaron was, ¹⁴because you rebelled against my word in the wilderness of Zin when the congregation quarreled with me.ᵃ You did not show my holiness before their eyes at the waters." (These are the waters of Meribath-kadesh in the wilderness of Zin.) ¹⁵Moses spoke to the LORD, saying, ¹⁶"Let the LORD, the God of the spirits of all flesh, appoint someone over the congregation ¹⁷who shall go out before them and come in before them, who shall lead them out and bring them in, so that the congregation of the LORD may not be like sheep without a shepherd." ¹⁸So the LORD said to Moses, "Take Joshua son of Nun, a man in whom is the spirit, and lay your hand upon him; ¹⁹have him stand before Eleazar the priest and all the congregation, and commission him in their sight. ²⁰You shall give him some of your authority, so that all the congregation of the Israelites may obey. ²¹But he shall stand before Eleazar the priest, who shall inquire for him by the decision of the Urim before the LORD; at his word they shall go out, and at his word they shall come in, both he and all the Israelites with him, the whole congregation." ²²So Moses did as the LORD commanded him. He took Joshua and had him stand before Eleazar the priest and the whole congregation; ²³he laid his hands on him and commissioned him—as the LORD had directed through Moses.

Daily Offerings

28 The LORD spoke to Moses, saying: ²Command the Israelites, and say to them: My offering, the food for my offerings by fire, my pleasing odor, you shall take care to offer to me at its appointed time. ³And you shall say to them, This is the offering by fire that you shall offer to the LORD: two male lambs a year old without blemish, daily, as a regular offering. ⁴One lamb you shall offer in the morning, and the other lamb you shall offer at twi-

Stand Up and Speak

NUMBERS 27.1–5

Mahlah and her sisters join together and speak out for their rights. Imagine standing up in the assembly before all the people, asking Moses to change the rules. Would you be quaking inwardly, outwardly or both? What kinds of issues might be serious enough to call for such action? These women feel they are being treated unfairly, and they say so. Moses listens. This is a new situation, and it calls for new ways of dealing with people.

Have you ever spoken out when you saw someone being treated unfairly? When you are being treated unfairly, do you tend to speak up, or do you avoid confrontation? What situations in our time call for new rules, new ways of dealing with people? What does this model offer us for these situations?

See Meeting God in Community

---

a Heb lacks *with me*

Pleasing to God

NUMBERS 28.6,8

The sacrifices carefully prepared and offered are a "pleasing odor" to God. Similarly, God is pleased with the fragrant offering of Christ's sacrifice (Ephesians 5.2). The image helps us understand that God is pleased with offerings made with an honest and righteous heart.

Try the practice of using fragrance in your worship time. Bring a scented candle, a bundle of fresh herbs, spices or potpourri to your prayer place. Let the fragrance represent your wholehearted and obedient offering of worship, prayer and repentance before God.

See Meeting God in Worship

light;[a] [5]also one-tenth of an ephah of choice flour for a grain offering, mixed with one-fourth of a hin of beaten oil. [6]It is a regular burnt offering, ordained at Mount Sinai for a pleasing odor, an offering by fire to the LORD. [7]Its drink offering shall be one-fourth of a hin for each lamb; in the sanctuary you shall pour out a drink offering of strong drink to the LORD. [8]The other lamb you shall offer at twilight[a] with a grain offering and a drink offering like the one in the morning; you shall offer it as an offering by fire, a pleasing odor to the LORD.

Sabbath Offerings

9 On the sabbath day: two male lambs a year old without blemish, and two-tenths of an ephah of choice flour for a grain offering, mixed with oil, and its drink offering— [10]this is the burnt offering for every sabbath, in addition to the regular burnt offering and its drink offering.

Monthly Offerings

11 At the beginnings of your months you shall offer a burnt offering to the LORD: two young bulls, one ram, seven male lambs a year old without blemish; [12]also three-tenths of an ephah of choice flour for a grain offering, mixed with oil, for each bull; and two-tenths of choice flour for a grain offering, mixed with oil, for the one ram; [13]and one-tenth of choice flour mixed with oil as a grain offering for every lamb—a burnt offering of pleasing odor, an offering by fire to the LORD. [14]Their drink offerings shall be half a hin of wine for a bull, one-third of a hin for a ram, and one-fourth of a hin for a lamb. This is the burnt offering of every month throughout the months of the year. [15]And there shall be one male goat for a sin offering to the LORD; it shall be offered in addition to the regular burnt offering and its drink offering.

Offerings at Passover

16 On the fourteenth day of the first month there shall be a passover offering to the LORD. [17]And on the fifteenth day of this month is a festival; seven days shall unleavened bread be eaten. [18]On the first day there shall be a holy convocation. You shall not work at your occupations. [19]You shall offer an offering by fire, a burnt offering to the LORD: two young bulls, one ram, and seven male lambs a year old; see that they are without blemish. [20]Their grain offering shall be of choice flour mixed with oil: three-tenths of an ephah shall you offer for a bull, and two-tenths for a ram; [21]one-tenth shall you offer for each of the seven lambs; [22]also one male goat for a sin offering, to make atonement for you. [23]You shall offer these in addition to the burnt offering of the morning, which belongs to the regular burnt offering. [24]In the same way you shall offer daily, for seven days, the food of an offering by fire, a pleasing odor to the LORD; it shall be offered in addition to the regular burnt offering and its drink offering. [25]And on the seventh day you shall have a holy convocation; you shall not work at your occupations.

a Heb *between the two evenings*

Offerings at the Festival of Weeks

26 On the day of the first fruits, when you offer a grain offering of new grain to the LORD at your festival of weeks, you shall have a holy convocation; you shall not work at your occupations. 27You shall offer a burnt offering, a pleasing odor to the LORD: two young bulls, one ram, seven male lambs a year old. 28Their grain offering shall be of choice flour mixed with oil, three-tenths of an ephah for each bull, two-tenths for one ram, 29one-tenth for each of the seven lambs; 30with one male goat, to make atonement for you. 31In addition to the regular burnt offering with its grain offering, you shall offer them and their drink offering. They shall be without blemish.

Offerings at the Festival of Trumpets

29 On the first day of the seventh month you shall have a holy convocation; you shall not work at your occupations. It is a day for you to blow the trumpets, 2and you shall offer a burnt offering, a pleasing odor to the LORD: one young bull, one ram, seven male lambs a year old without blemish. 3Their grain offering shall be of choice flour mixed with oil, three-tenths of one ephah for the bull, two-tenths for the ram, 4and one-tenth for each of the seven lambs; 5with one male goat for a sin offering, to make atonement for you. 6These are in addition to the burnt offering of the new moon and its grain offering, and the regular burnt offering and its grain offering, and their drink offerings, according to the ordinance for them, a pleasing odor, an offering by fire to the LORD.

Offerings on the Day of Atonement

7 On the tenth day of this seventh month you shall have a holy convocation, and deny yourselves;*a* you shall do no work. 8You shall offer a burnt offering to the LORD, a pleasing odor: one young bull, one ram, seven male lambs a year old. They shall be without blemish. 9Their grain offering shall be of choice flour mixed with oil, three-tenths of an ephah for the bull, two-tenths for the one ram, 10one-tenth for each of the seven lambs; 11with one male goat for a sin offering, in addition to the sin offering of atonement, and the regular burnt offering and its grain offering, and their drink offerings.

Offerings at the Festival of Booths

12 On the fifteenth day of the seventh month you shall have a holy convocation; you shall not work at your occupations. You shall celebrate a festival to the LORD seven days. 13You shall offer a burnt offering, an offering by fire, a pleasing odor to the LORD: thirteen young bulls, two rams, fourteen male lambs a year old. They shall be without blemish. 14Their grain offering shall be of choice flour mixed with oil, three-tenths of an ephah for each of the thirteen bulls, two-tenths for each of the two rams, 15and one-tenth for each of the fourteen lambs; 16also one male goat for a sin offering, in addition to the regular burnt offering, its grain offering and its drink offering.

a Or *and fast*

Set the Date

NUMBERS 28.25–26; 29.1

The Israelites set aside a special time to hold a "holy convocation" or sacred assembly, during which they would rest from their regular work. Think about your calendar. When can you set aside some time to spend with God, a special time for prayer, Bible study, spiritual reading and simply resting in God's presence, in addition to your usual worship or service? Perhaps you can participate in a retreat alone or with others. If you cannot take an entire day or weekend, consider setting aside a few hours on Saturday mornings or a few afternoons this month. God longs for time with you as loved ones long for time with their beloved. God will meet you whenever and wherever you make a meeting place. Make an appointment to meet with God.

See Meeting God in Prayer

Do What Is Right

NUMBERS 29.12–38

"It is the duty of every one to be firm in that which they certainly know is right for them."

—JOHN WOOLMAN,
The Journal of John Woolman

17 On the second day: twelve young bulls, two rams, fourteen male lambs a year old without blemish, [18]with the grain offering and the drink offerings for the bulls, for the rams, and for the lambs, as prescribed in accordance with their number; [19]also one male goat for a sin offering, in addition to the regular burnt offering and its grain offering, and their drink offerings.

20 On the third day: eleven bulls, two rams, fourteen male lambs a year old without blemish, [21]with the grain offering and the drink offerings for the bulls, for the rams, and for the lambs, as prescribed in accordance with their number; [22]also one male goat for a sin offering, in addition to the regular burnt offering and its grain offering and its drink offering.

23 On the fourth day: ten bulls, two rams, fourteen male lambs a year old without blemish, [24]with the grain offering and the drink offerings for the bulls, for the rams, and for the lambs, as prescribed in accordance with their number; [25]also one male goat for a sin offering, in addition to the regular burnt offering, its grain offering and its drink offering.

26 On the fifth day: nine bulls, two rams, fourteen male lambs a year old without blemish, [27]with the grain offering and the drink offerings for the bulls, for the rams, and for the lambs, as prescribed in accordance with their number; [28]also one male goat for a sin offering, in addition to the regular burnt offering and its grain offering and its drink offering.

29 On the sixth day: eight bulls, two rams, fourteen male lambs a year old without blemish, [30]with the grain offering and the drink offerings for the bulls, for the rams, and for the lambs, as prescribed in accordance with their number; [31]also one male goat for a sin offering, in addition to the regular burnt offering, its grain offering, and its drink offerings.

32 On the seventh day: seven bulls, two rams, fourteen male lambs a year old without blemish, [33]with the grain offering and the drink offerings for the bulls, for the rams, and for the lambs, as prescribed in accordance with their number; [34]also one male goat for a sin offering, besides the regular burnt offering, its grain offering, and its drink offering.

35 On the eighth day you shall have a solemn assembly; you shall not work at your occupations. [36]You shall offer a burnt offering, an offering by fire, a pleasing odor to the LORD: one bull, one ram, seven male lambs a year old without blemish, [37]and the grain offering and the drink offerings for the bull, for the ram, and for the lambs, as prescribed in accordance with their number; [38]also one male goat for a sin offering, in addition to the regular burnt offering and its grain offering and its drink offering.

39 These you shall offer to the LORD at your appointed festivals, in addition to your votive offerings and your freewill offerings, as your burnt offerings, your grain offerings, your drink offerings, and your offerings of well-being.

40[a] So Moses told the Israelites everything just as the LORD had commanded Moses.

a Ch 30.1 in Heb

Vows Made by Women

30 Then Moses said to the heads of the tribes of the Israelites: This is what the LORD has commanded. ²When a man makes a vow to the LORD, or swears an oath to bind himself by a pledge, he shall not break his word; he shall do according to all that proceeds out of his mouth.

3 When a woman makes a vow to the LORD, or binds herself by a pledge, while within her father's house, in her youth, ⁴and her father hears of her vow or her pledge by which she has bound herself, and says nothing to her; then all her vows shall stand, and any pledge by which she has bound herself shall stand. ⁵But if her father expresses disapproval to her at the time that he hears of it, no vow of hers, and no pledge by which she has bound herself, shall stand; and the LORD will forgive her, because her father had expressed to her his disapproval.

6 If she marries, while obligated by her vows or any thoughtless utterance of her lips by which she has bound herself, ⁷and her husband hears of it and says nothing to her at the time that he hears, then her vows shall stand, and her pledges by which she has bound herself shall stand. ⁸But if, at the time that her husband hears of it, he expresses disapproval to her, then he shall nullify the vow by which she was obligated, or the thoughtless utterance of her lips, by which she bound herself; and the LORD will forgive her. ⁹(But every vow of a widow or of a divorced woman, by which she has bound herself, shall be binding upon her.) ¹⁰And if she made a vow in her husband's house, or bound herself by a pledge with an oath, ¹¹and her husband heard it and said nothing to her, and did not express disapproval to her, then all her vows shall stand, and any pledge by which she bound herself shall stand. ¹²But if her husband nullifies them at the time that he hears them, then whatever proceeds out of her lips concerning her vows, or concerning her pledge of herself, shall not stand. Her husband has nullified them, and the LORD will forgive her. ¹³Any vow or any binding oath to deny herself,ᵃ her husband may allow to stand, or her husband may nullify. ¹⁴But if her husband says nothing to her from day to day,ᵇ then he validates all her vows, or all her pledges, by which she is obligated; he has validated them, because he said nothing to her at the time that he heard of them. ¹⁵But if he nullifies them some time after he has heard of them, then he shall bear her guilt.

16 These are the statutes that the LORD commanded Moses concerning a husband and his wife, and a father and his daughter while she is still young and in her father's house.

War against Midian

31 The LORD spoke to Moses, saying, ²"Avenge the Israelites on the Midianites; afterward you shall be gathered to your people." ³So Moses said to the people, "Arm some of your number for the war, so that they may go against Midian, to execute the LORD's vengeance on Midian. ⁴You shall send a thousand from each of the tribes of Israel to the war." ⁵So out of the thousands of

---

Supporting the Vows

NUMBERS 30.1–15

This passage describes the role the Israelites assumed, by their verbal or tacit assent, in vows made by others. A similar principle is invoked in the traditional marriage ceremony when the officiant asks the gathered witnesses to assent to the lawfulness of the marriage, "If anyone knows any reason why this man and this woman may not be lawfully joined, let them speak now or forever hold their peace."

We can learn from this passage that we are not to hinder others in keeping their vows. We have a responsibility to uphold those close to us in keeping their commitments to God. Who supports you in your faith? What can you do to support those you care about in living their faith?

See *Meeting God in Community*

Purity of Heart

NUMBERS 31.20–24

"Be exceedingly quick to turn aside from the slightest thing leading to impurity, for it is an evil that approaches stealthily and in which the very smallest beginnings are apt to grow rapidly."

—FRANCIS DE SALES,
Introduction to the Devout Life

Israel, a thousand from each tribe were conscripted, twelve thousand armed for battle. 6Moses sent them to the war, a thousand from each tribe, along with Phinehas son of Eleazar the priest,*a* with the vessels of the sanctuary and the trumpets for sounding the alarm in his hand. 7They did battle against Midian, as the LORD had commanded Moses, and killed every male. 8They killed the kings of Midian: Evi, Rekem, Zur, Hur, and Reba, the five kings of Midian, in addition to others who were slain by them; and they also killed Balaam son of Beor with the sword. 9The Israelites took the women of Midian and their little ones captive; and they took all their cattle, their flocks, and all their goods as booty. 10All their towns where they had settled, and all their encampments, they burned, 11but they took all the spoil and all the booty, both people and animals. 12Then they brought the captives and the booty and the spoil to Moses, to Eleazar the priest, and to the congregation of the Israelites, at the camp on the plains of Moab by the Jordan at Jericho.

Return from the War

13 Moses, Eleazar the priest, and all the leaders of the congregation went to meet them outside the camp. 14Moses became angry with the officers of the army, the commanders of thousands and the commanders of hundreds, who had come from service in the war. 15Moses said to them, "Have you allowed all the women to live? 16These women here, on Balaam's advice, made the Israelites act treacherously against the LORD in the affair of Peor, so that the plague came among the congregation of the LORD. 17Now therefore, kill every male among the little ones, and kill every woman who has known a man by sleeping with him. 18But all the young girls who have not known a man by sleeping with him, keep alive for yourselves. 19Camp outside the camp seven days; whoever of you has killed any person or touched a corpse, purify yourselves and your captives on the third and on the seventh day. 20You shall purify every garment, every article of skin, everything made of goats' hair, and every article of wood."

21 Eleazar the priest said to the troops who had gone to battle: "This is the statute of the law that the LORD has commanded Moses: 22gold, silver, bronze, iron, tin, and lead— 23everything that can withstand fire, shall be passed through fire, and it shall be clean. Nevertheless it shall also be purified with the water for purification; and whatever cannot withstand fire, shall be passed through the water. 24You must wash your clothes on the seventh day, and you shall be clean; afterward you may come into the camp."

Disposition of Captives and Booty

25 The LORD spoke to Moses, saying, 26"You and Eleazar the priest and the heads of the ancestral houses of the congregation make an inventory of the booty captured, both human and animal. 27Divide the booty into two parts, between the warriors who went out to battle and all the congregation. 28From the share of the warriors who

a Gk: Heb adds *to the war*

went out to battle, set aside as tribute for the Lord, one item out of every five hundred, whether persons, oxen, donkeys, sheep, or goats. ²⁹Take it from their half and give it to Eleazar the priest as an offering to the Lord. ³⁰But from the Israelites' half you shall take one out of every fifty, whether persons, oxen, donkeys, sheep, or goats— all the animals—and give them to the Levites who have charge of the tabernacle of the Lord."

31 Then Moses and Eleazar the priest did as the Lord had commanded Moses:

32 The booty remaining from the spoil that the troops had taken totaled six hundred seventy-five thousand sheep, ³³seventy-two thousand oxen, ³⁴sixty-one thousand donkeys, ³⁵and thirty-two thousand persons in all, women who had not known a man by sleeping with him.

36 The half-share, the portion of those who had gone out to war, was in number three hundred thirty-seven thousand five hundred sheep and goats, ³⁷and the Lord's tribute of sheep and goats was six hundred seventy-five. ³⁸The oxen were thirty-six thousand, of which the Lord's tribute was seventy-two. ³⁹The donkeys were thirty thousand five hundred, of which the Lord's tribute was sixty-one. ⁴⁰The persons were sixteen thousand, of which the Lord's tribute was thirty-two persons. ⁴¹Moses gave the tribute, the offering for the Lord, to Eleazar the priest, as the Lord had commanded Moses.

42 As for the Israelites' half, which Moses separated from that of the troops, ⁴³the congregation's half was three hundred thirty-seven thousand five hundred sheep and goats, ⁴⁴thirty-six thousand oxen, ⁴⁵thirty thousand five hundred donkeys, ⁴⁶and sixteen thousand persons. ⁴⁷From the Israelites' half Moses took one of every fifty, both of persons and of animals, and gave them to the Levites who had charge of the tabernacle of the Lord; as the Lord had commanded Moses.

48 Then the officers who were over the thousands of the army, the commanders of thousands and the commanders of hundreds, approached Moses, ⁴⁹and said to Moses, "Your servants have counted the warriors who are under our command, and not one of us is missing. ⁵⁰And we have brought the Lord's offering, what each of us found, articles of gold, armlets and bracelets, signet rings, earrings, and pendants, to make atonement for ourselves before the Lord." ⁵¹Moses and Eleazar the priest received the gold from them, all in the form of crafted articles. ⁵²And all the gold of the offering that they offered to the Lord, from the commanders of thousands and the commanders of hundreds, was sixteen thousand seven hundred fifty shekels. ⁵³(The troops had all taken plunder for themselves.) ⁵⁴So Moses and Eleazar the priest received the gold from the commanders of thousands and of hundreds, and brought it into the tent of meeting as a memorial for the Israelites before the Lord.

Conquest and Division of Transjordan

32 Now the Reubenites and the Gadites owned a very great number of cattle. When they saw that the land of Jazer and the land of Gilead was a good place for

---

For the Good of All

NUMBERS 32.1–5,16–19

The Reubenites and the Gadites settle themselves comfortably on the fine grazing land of the near side of the Jordan and ask to be excused from entering Caanan. Moses, however, is angry because they have put their own needs ahead of God's plan and the welfare and the unity of the entire nation.

While we may find prosperity and comfort individually, some of God's greatest blessings are given to us in community. Make a list of those attitudes and possessions that you value for your own comfort and prosperity. Now make a list of the blessings you find in community. Analyze your lists. Do the two lists conflict? Do your attitudes or possessions conflict with the priorities and needs of your faith community? Do any of the things you hold dear interfere with the unity of the body of Christ?

See Meeting God in Community

Cause and Effect

NUMBERS 32.15,20,29

Moses repeats the "if, then" pattern several times in this passage, making sure that the Reubenites and Gadites understand that their choices will have clear consequences and that turning away from God will have an undesirable result.

Though God forgives us when we make selfish and stubborn choices, he does sometimes let us suffer the consequences for our decisions. Many of our difficulties are consequences of our own acts. What consequences have taught you valuable lessons? What consequences are you struggling with now and what are you learning in the process?

See *Meeting God in Everyday Life*

cattle, ²the Gadites and the Reubenites came and spoke to Moses, to Eleazar the priest, and to the leaders of the congregation, saying, ³"Ataroth, Dibon, Jazer, Nimrah, Heshbon, Elealeh, Sebam, Nebo, and Beon— ⁴the land that the LORD subdued before the congregation of Israel—is a land for cattle; and your servants have cattle." ⁵They continued, "If we have found favor in your sight, let this land be given to your servants for a possession; do not make us cross the Jordan."

6 But Moses said to the Gadites and to the Reubenites, "Shall your brothers go to war while you sit here? ⁷Why will you discourage the hearts of the Israelites from going over into the land that the LORD has given them? ⁸Your fathers did this, when I sent them from Kadesh-barnea to see the land. ⁹When they went up to the Wadi Eshcol and saw the land, they discouraged the hearts of the Israelites from going into the land that the LORD had given them. ¹⁰The LORD's anger was kindled on that day and he swore, saying, ¹¹'Surely none of the people who came up out of Egypt, from twenty years old and upward, shall see the land that I swore to give to Abraham, to Isaac, and to Jacob, because they have not unreservedly followed me— ¹²none except Caleb son of Jephunneh the Kenizzite and Joshua son of Nun, for they have unreservedly followed the LORD.' ¹³And the LORD's anger was kindled against Israel, and he made them wander in the wilderness for forty years, until all the generation that had done evil in the sight of the LORD had disappeared. ¹⁴And now you, a brood of sinners, have risen in place of your fathers, to increase the LORD's fierce anger against Israel! ¹⁵If you turn away from following him, he will again abandon them in the wilderness; and you will destroy all this people."

16 Then they came up to him and said, "We will build sheepfolds here for our flocks, and towns for our little ones, ¹⁷but we will take up arms as a vanguard*a* before the Israelites, until we have brought them to their place. Meanwhile our little ones will stay in the fortified towns because of the inhabitants of the land. ¹⁸We will not return to our homes until all the Israelites have obtained their inheritance. ¹⁹We will not inherit with them on the other side of the Jordan and beyond, because our inheritance has come to us on this side of the Jordan to the east."

20 So Moses said to them, "If you do this—if you take up arms to go before the LORD for the war, ²¹and all those of you who bear arms cross the Jordan before the LORD, until he has driven out his enemies from before him ²²and the land is subdued before the LORD—then after that you may return and be free of obligation to the LORD and to Israel, and this land shall be your possession before the LORD. ²³But if you do not do this, you have sinned against the LORD; and be sure your sin will find you out. ²⁴Build towns for your little ones, and folds for your flocks; but do what you have promised."

25 Then the Gadites and the Reubenites said to Moses, "Your servants will do as my lord commands. ²⁶Our little ones, our wives, our flocks, and all our livestock shall remain there in the towns of Gilead; ²⁷but your servants will

a Cn: Heb *hurrying*

cross over, everyone armed for war, to do battle for the LORD, just as my lord orders."

28 So Moses gave command concerning them to Eleazar the priest, to Joshua son of Nun, and to the heads of the ancestral houses of the Israelite tribes. ²⁹And Moses said to them, "If the Gadites and the Reubenites, everyone armed for battle before the LORD, will cross over the Jordan with you and the land shall be subdued before you, then you shall give them the land of Gilead for a possession; ³⁰but if they will not cross over with you armed, they shall have possessions among you in the land of Canaan." ³¹The Gadites and the Reubenites answered, "As the LORD has spoken to your servants, so we will do. ³²We will cross over armed before the LORD into the land of Canaan, but the possession of our inheritance shall remain with us on this side of*ᵃ* the Jordan."

33 Moses gave to them—to the Gadites and to the Reubenites and to the half-tribe of Manasseh son of Joseph—the kingdom of King Sihon of the Amorites and the kingdom of King Og of Bashan, the land and its towns, with the territories of the surrounding towns. ³⁴And the Gadites rebuilt Dibon, Ataroth, Aroer, ³⁵Atroth-shophan, Jazer, Jogbehah, ³⁶Beth-nimrah, and Beth-haran, fortified cities, and folds for sheep. ³⁷And the Reubenites rebuilt Heshbon, Elealeh, Kiriathaim, ³⁸Nebo, and Baal-meon (some names being changed), and Sibmah; and they gave names to the towns that they rebuilt. ³⁹The descendants of Machir son of Manasseh went to Gilead, captured it, and dispossessed the Amorites who were there; ⁴⁰so Moses gave Gilead to Machir son of Manasseh, and he settled there. ⁴¹Jair son of Manasseh went and captured their villages, and renamed them Havvoth-jair.*ᵇ* ⁴²And Nobah went and captured Kenath and its villages, and renamed it Nobah after himself.

The Stages of Israel's Journey from Egypt

33 These are the stages by which the Israelites went out of the land of Egypt in military formation under the leadership of Moses and Aaron. ²Moses wrote down their starting points, stage by stage, by command of the LORD; and these are their stages according to their starting places. ³They set out from Rameses in the first month, on the fifteenth day of the first month; on the day after the passover the Israelites went out boldly in the sight of all the Egyptians, ⁴while the Egyptians were burying all their firstborn, whom the LORD had struck down among them. The LORD executed judgments even against their gods.

5 So the Israelites set out from Rameses, and camped at Succoth. ⁶They set out from Succoth, and camped at Etham, which is on the edge of the wilderness. ⁷They set out from Etham, and turned back to Pi-hahiroth, which faces Baal-zephon; and they camped before Migdol. ⁸They set out from Pi-hahiroth, passed through the sea into the wilderness, went a three days' journey in the wilderness of Etham, and camped at Marah. ⁹They set out from Marah and came to Elim; at Elim there were twelve springs of water and seventy palm trees, and they camped there. ¹⁰They set out from Elim and camped by

Your Lifeline

NUMBERS 33.1–2

Record the stages of your journey, as Moses recorded the journey of the Israelites. (If you keep a spiritual journal, you may want to record this.) Draw a horizontal line to represent your life. Beginning with your birth year, mark off five- or ten-year sections on the line. Above the line, list significant events within each time span. Below the line, list spiritual milestones or some wisdom you have gained from each period. Did you spend time wandering in the wilderness? If you were writing a book about your life, what would the chapter titles be? What would the title of the last chapter be? Do you see any patterns in your journey so far? Take some time to reflect on where you started and where you are today.

See Meeting God in Everyday Life

Vestiges of the Old Life

NUMBERS 33.51–55

Moderation is not necessarily a Biblical ideal, it seems. Again in this passage, the Israelites hear that it must be all or nothing. Moses demands that the people demolish all the "high places," every vestige of idols and idol worship. If they allow any trace to remain, these will become "barbs" in their eyes and "thorns" in their sides.

Though we say we want to follow God, we may try to keep some of our old ways, perhaps some old relationships. In what ways are your past actions like a barb to you? What bad habit is like a thorn in your side? Are there areas in which you still need to let go of habits or activities that keep you from serving God with all your heart? What do you need to do in order to be free of them?

See Meeting God in Everyday Life

the Red Sea.*ᵃ* ¹¹They set out from the Red Seaᵃ and camped in the wilderness of Sin. ¹²They set out from the wilderness of Sin and camped at Dophkah. ¹³They set out from Dophkah and camped at Alush. ¹⁴They set out from Alush and camped at Rephidim, where there was no water for the people to drink. ¹⁵They set out from Rephidim and camped in the wilderness of Sinai. ¹⁶They set out from the wilderness of Sinai and camped at Kibroth-hattaavah. ¹⁷They set out from Kibroth-hattaavah and camped at Hazeroth. ¹⁸They set out from Hazeroth and camped at Rithmah. ¹⁹They set out from Rithmah and camped at Rimmon-perez. ²⁰They set out from Rimmon-perez and camped at Libnah. ²¹They set out from Libnah and camped at Rissah. ²²They set out from Rissah and camped at Kehelathah. ²³They set out from Kehelathah and camped at Mount Shepher. ²⁴They set out from Mount Shepher and camped at Haradah. ²⁵They set out from Haradah and camped at Makheloth. ²⁶They set out from Makheloth and camped at Tahath. ²⁷They set out from Tahath and camped at Terah. ²⁸They set out from Terah and camped at Mithkah. ²⁹They set out from Mithkah and camped at Hashmonah. ³⁰They set out from Hashmonah and camped at Moseroth. ³¹They set out from Moseroth and camped at Bene-jaakan. ³²They set out from Bene-jaakan and camped at Hor-haggidgad. ³³They set out from Hor-haggidgad and camped at Jotbathah. ³⁴They set out from Jotbathah and camped at Abronah. ³⁵They set out from Abronah and camped at Ezion-geber. ³⁶They set out from Ezion-geber and camped in the wilderness of Zin (that is, Kadesh). ³⁷They set out from Kadesh and camped at Mount Hor, on the edge of the land of Edom.

38 Aaron the priest went up Mount Hor at the command of the LORD and died there in the fortieth year after the Israelites had come out of the land of Egypt, on the first day of the fifth month. ³⁹Aaron was one hundred twenty-three years old when he died on Mount Hor.

40 The Canaanite, the king of Arad, who lived in the Negeb in the land of Canaan, heard of the coming of the Israelites.

41 They set out from Mount Hor and camped at Zalmonah. ⁴²They set out from Zalmonah and camped at Punon. ⁴³They set out from Punon and camped at Oboth. ⁴⁴They set out from Oboth and camped at Iye-abarim, in the territory of Moab. ⁴⁵They set out from Iyim and camped at Dibon-gad. ⁴⁶They set out from Dibon-gad and camped at Almon-diblathaim. ⁴⁷They set out from Almon-diblathaim and camped in the mountains of Abarim, before Nebo. ⁴⁸They set out from the mountains of Abarim and camped in the plains of Moab by the Jordan at Jericho; ⁴⁹they camped by the Jordan from Beth-jeshimoth as far as Abel-shittim in the plains of Moab.

Directions for the Conquest of Canaan

50 In the plains of Moab by the Jordan at Jericho, the LORD spoke to Moses, saying: ⁵¹Speak to the Israelites, and say to them: When you cross over the Jordan into the land of Canaan, ⁵²you shall drive out all the inhabitants of the land from before you, destroy all their figured stones, de-

a Or Sea of Reeds

stroy all their cast images, and demolish all their high places. ⁵³You shall take possession of the land and settle in it, for I have given you the land to possess. ⁵⁴You shall apportion the land by lot according to your clans; to a large one you shall give a large inheritance, and to a small one you shall give a small inheritance; the inheritance shall belong to the person on whom the lot falls; according to your ancestral tribes you shall inherit. ⁵⁵But if you do not drive out the inhabitants of the land from before you, then those whom you let remain shall be as barbs in your eyes and thorns in your sides; they shall trouble you in the land where you are settling. ⁵⁶And I will do to you as I thought to do to them.

The Boundaries of the Land

34 The LORD spoke to Moses, saying: ²Command the Israelites, and say to them: When you enter the land of Canaan (this is the land that shall fall to you for an inheritance, the land of Canaan, defined by its boundaries), ³your south sector shall extend from the wilderness of Zin along the side of Edom. Your southern boundary shall begin from the end of the Dead Sea*a* on the east; ⁴your boundary shall turn south of the ascent of Akrabbim, and cross to Zin, and its outer limit shall be south of Kadesh-barnea; then it shall go on to Hazar-addar, and cross to Azmon; ⁵the boundary shall turn from Azmon to the Wadi of Egypt, and its termination shall be at the Sea.

6 For the western boundary, you shall have the Great Sea and its*b* coast; this shall be your western boundary.

7 This shall be your northern boundary: from the Great Sea you shall mark out your line to Mount Hor; ⁸from Mount Hor you shall mark it out to Lebo-hamath, and the outer limit of the boundary shall be at Zedad; ⁹then the boundary shall extend to Ziphron, and its end shall be at Hazar-enan; this shall be your northern boundary.

10 You shall mark out your eastern boundary from Hazar-enan to Shepham; ¹¹and the boundary shall continue down from Shepham to Riblah on the east side of Ain; and the boundary shall go down, and reach the eastern slope of the sea of Chinnereth; ¹²and the boundary shall go down to the Jordan, and its end shall be at the Dead Sea.*a* This shall be your land with its boundaries all around.

13 Moses commanded the Israelites, saying: This is the land that you shall inherit by lot, which the LORD has commanded to give to the nine tribes and to the half-tribe; ¹⁴for the tribe of the Reubenites by their ancestral houses and the tribe of the Gadites by their ancestral houses have taken their inheritance, and also the half-tribe of Manasseh; ¹⁵the two tribes and the half-tribe have taken their inheritance beyond the Jordan at Jericho eastward, toward the sunrise.

Tribal Leaders

16 The LORD spoke to Moses, saying: ¹⁷These are the names of the men who shall apportion the land to you for inheritance: the priest Eleazar and Joshua son of Nun. ¹⁸You shall take one leader of every tribe to apportion the

Your Boundaries

NUMBERS 34.1–15

God gave the Israelites a specific area as their domain; God gives us opportunities and responsibilities. The outline of the modern country of Israel looks roughly like a wide, shortened necktie. Draw this shape to represent your life and what God has given you. Subdivide the shape into portions, labeling the parts to show the things on which you spend time, energy and care. Put your major concerns in the center of your "country," as Jerusalem is in the center of Israel. Draw the same shape again and label it to show what you want to be spending time, energy and care on five years from now.

a Heb *Salt Sea*   b Syr: Heb lacks *its*

Cities of Refuge

NUMBERS 35.9–15

This passage invites us to consider our attitudes toward mercy. Recall a death that has touched your community. Perhaps someone driving under the influence of alcohol has caused the deaths of an entire family, or someone playing a prank has caused a young person to be killed. Would your church be willing to be a "city of refuge" for the person or persons who caused the death(s)? What would people's reactions be if the person who caused a death were to stand up in your worship service and ask for help? What if the family of the victim were also a part of your congregation? How can we respond to both perpetrator and victim with mercy? God calls for mercy. How can you extend mercy in these and other less serious everyday situations?

See Meeting God in Community

land for inheritance. ¹⁹These are the names of the men: Of the tribe of Judah, Caleb son of Jephunneh. ²⁰Of the tribe of the Simeonites, Shemuel son of Ammihud. ²¹Of the tribe of Benjamin, Elidad son of Chislon. ²²Of the tribe of the Danites a leader, Bukki son of Jogli. ²³Of the Josephites: of the tribe of the Manassites a leader, Hanniel son of Ephod, ²⁴and of the tribe of the Ephraimites a leader, Kemuel son of Shiphtan. ²⁵Of the tribe of the Zebulunites a leader, Eli-zaphan son of Parnach. ²⁶Of the tribe of the Issacharites a leader, Paltiel son of Azzan. ²⁷And of the tribe of the Asherites a leader, Ahihud son of Shelomi. ²⁸Of the tribe of the Naphtalites a leader, Pedahel son of Ammihud. ²⁹These were the ones whom the LORD commanded to apportion the inheritance for the Israelites in the land of Canaan.

Cities for the Levites

35 In the plains of Moab by the Jordan at Jericho, the LORD spoke to Moses, saying: ²Command the Israelites to give, from the inheritance that they possess, towns for the Levites to live in; you shall also give to the Levites pasture lands surrounding the towns. ³The towns shall be theirs to live in, and their pasture lands shall be for their cattle, for their livestock, and for all their animals. ⁴The pasture lands of the towns, which you shall give to the Levites, shall reach from the wall of the town outward a thousand cubits all around. ⁵You shall measure, outside the town, for the east side two thousand cubits, for the south side two thousand cubits, for the west side two thousand cubits, and for the north side two thousand cubits, with the town in the middle; this shall belong to them as pasture land for their towns.

6 The towns that you give to the Levites shall include the six cities of refuge, where you shall permit a slayer to flee, and in addition to them you shall give forty-two towns. ⁷The towns that you give to the Levites shall total forty-eight, with their pasture lands. ⁸And as for the towns that you shall give from the possession of the Israelites, from the larger tribes you shall take many, and from the smaller tribes you shall take few; each, in proportion to the inheritance that it obtains, shall give of its towns to the Levites.

Cities of Refuge

9 The LORD spoke to Moses, saying: ¹⁰Speak to the Israelites, and say to them: When you cross the Jordan into the land of Canaan, ¹¹then you shall select cities to be cities of refuge for you, so that a slayer who kills a person without intent may flee there. ¹²The cities shall be for you a refuge from the avenger, so that the slayer may not die until there is a trial before the congregation.

13 The cities that you designate shall be six cities of refuge for you: ¹⁴you shall designate three cities beyond the Jordan, and three cities in the land of Canaan, to be cities of refuge. ¹⁵These six cities shall serve as refuge for the Israelites, for the resident or transient alien among them, so that anyone who kills a person without intent may flee there.

Concerning Murder and Blood Revenge

16 But anyone who strikes another with an iron object, and death ensues, is a murderer; the murderer shall be put to death. [17]Or anyone who strikes another with a stone in hand that could cause death, and death ensues, is a murderer; the murderer shall be put to death. [18]Or anyone who strikes another with a weapon of wood in hand that could cause death, and death ensues, is a murderer; the murderer shall be put to death. [19]The avenger of blood is the one who shall put the murderer to death; when they meet, the avenger of blood shall execute the sentence. [20]Likewise, if someone pushes another from hatred, or hurls something at another, lying in wait, and death ensues, [21]or in enmity strikes another with the hand, and death ensues, then the one who struck the blow shall be put to death; that person is a murderer; the avenger of blood shall put the murderer to death, when they meet.

22 But if someone pushes another suddenly without enmity, or hurls any object without lying in wait, [23]or, while handling any stone that could cause death, unintentionally[a] drops it on another and death ensues, though they were not enemies, and no harm was intended, [24]then the congregation shall judge between the slayer and the avenger of blood, in accordance with these ordinances; [25]and the congregation shall rescue the slayer from the avenger of blood. Then the congregation shall send the slayer back to the original city of refuge. The slayer shall live in it until the death of the high priest who was anointed with the holy oil. [26]But if the slayer shall at any time go outside the bounds of the original city of refuge, [27]and is found by the avenger of blood outside the bounds of the city of refuge, and is killed by the avenger, no bloodguilt shall be incurred. [28]For the slayer must remain in the city of refuge until the death of the high priest; but after the death of the high priest the slayer may return home.

29 These things shall be a statute and ordinance for you throughout your generations wherever you live.

30 If anyone kills another, the murderer shall be put to death on the evidence of witnesses; but no one shall be put to death on the testimony of a single witness. [31]Moreover you shall accept no ransom for the life of a murderer who is subject to the death penalty; a murderer must be put to death. [32]Nor shall you accept ransom for one who has fled to a city of refuge, enabling the fugitive to return to live in the land before the death of the high priest. [33]You shall not pollute the land in which you live; for blood pollutes the land, and no expiation can be made for the land, for the blood that is shed in it, except by the blood of the one who shed it. [34]You shall not defile the land in which you live, in which I also dwell; for I the LORD dwell among the Israelites.

Marriage of Female Heirs

36 The heads of the ancestral houses of the clans of the descendants of Gilead son of Machir son of Manasseh, of the Josephite clans, came forward and

---

God's Dwelling

NUMBERS 35.22–34

Violence "pollutes" the land, and pollution is unacceptable because God dwells with the Israelites. The passage suggests that we seek justice as a way of honoring God, who dwells among us. How might we deal with violence to make our communities places that reflect the presence of God? If violence pollutes the places where it occurs, how can we pray and act to cleanse our surroundings of violence? What can you do to help victims of violence?

See Meeting God in Service

---

a Heb *without seeing*

Women's Rights?

NUMBERS 36.1–7

The women of Israel had not been allowed to inherit property, but Moses changed the rules in order to give these women an inheritance—because it was the just, fair thing to do.

In modern times, changes in written and unwritten "rules" have allowed women to be employed, vote for candidates for political office, be educated, hold political office and be ordained as clergy. Think about your life. What changes in society's "rules" about ethnic groups, social class, gender roles and occupations have affected you? Where do you see need for change so that people may be treated more fairly? Making such changes because they are just and right is part of doing God's work in the world. How are you seeking God's justice in the community?

See *Meeting God in Community*

spoke in the presence of Moses and the leaders, the heads of the ancestral houses of the Israelites; [2]they said, "The LORD commanded my lord to give the land for inheritance by lot to the Israelites; and my lord was commanded by the LORD to give the inheritance of our brother Zelophehad to his daughters. [3]But if they are married into another Israelite tribe, then their inheritance will be taken from the inheritance of our ancestors and added to the inheritance of the tribe into which they marry; so it will be taken away from the allotted portion of our inheritance. [4]And when the jubilee of the Israelites comes, then their inheritance will be added to the inheritance of the tribe into which they have married; and their inheritance will be taken from the inheritance of our ancestral tribe."

5 Then Moses commanded the Israelites according to the word of the LORD, saying, "The descendants of the tribe of Joseph are right in what they are saying. [6]This is what the LORD commands concerning the daughters of Zelophehad, 'Let them marry whom they think best; only it must be into a clan of their father's tribe that they are married, [7]so that no inheritance of the Israelites shall be transferred from one tribe to another; for all Israelites shall retain the inheritance of their ancestral tribes. [8]Every daughter who possesses an inheritance in any tribe of the Israelites shall marry one from the clan of her father's tribe, so that all Israelites may continue to possess their ancestral inheritance. [9]No inheritance shall be transferred from one tribe to another; for each of the tribes of the Israelites shall retain its own inheritance.' "

10 The daughters of Zelophehad did as the LORD had commanded Moses. [11]Mahlah, Tirzah, Hoglah, Milcah, and Noah, the daughters of Zelophehad, married sons of their father's brothers. [12]They were married into the clans of the descendants of Manasseh son of Joseph, and their inheritance remained in the tribe of their father's clan.

13 These are the commandments and the ordinances that the LORD commanded through Moses to the Israelites in the plains of Moab by the Jordan at Jericho.

DEUTERONOMY

Remember to Remember

KEY VERSES:

"So acknowledge today and take to heart that the LORD is God in heaven above and on the earth beneath; there is no other. Keep his statutes and his commandments, which I am commanding you today for your own well-being and that of your descendants after you, so that you may long remain in the land that the LORD your God is giving you for all time."—Deuteronomy 4.39–40

Have you ever given a farewell address? Imagine Moses' situation. In the process of transferring the leadership of Israel to Joshua, he delivers this address to prepare God's people to enter the promised land. God had performed many miracles during the previous years, but almost everyone who had witnessed his mighty works had died in the wilderness. And yet, somehow, Moses must make known all that God has done, direct the people with various laws and decrees, and show them a vision of the future that they might experience—depending on whether the people remember their relationship with God or go their own way.

The key theme in Deuteronomy is "remembering to remember." And as the book of Deuteronomy opens, Moses is obviously intent on embedding the memory of God's faithfulness to Israel into the hearts of his listeners. Israel is urged to remember the past, remember the present obligations and remember the future that the people might build.

In his classic work *Letters and Papers from Prison*, the German-Christian martyr Dietrich Bonhoeffer called forgetfulness "the great problem of Christian ministry." In what ways do you think this might be so? As you read this foundational book of the Old Testament, ask God to open your heart to the past, to make you sensitive to God's claim on your life today and to help you anticipate your vivid future with the Lord of your life. See if you don't agree that your memories and your faith are inextricably entwined as you walk with God.

> "Turning myself towards my most gracious and merciful God, I desire, purpose, and am irrevocably resolved to serve and love him now and forever; and to this end, I give and consecrate to him my soul with all its powers, my heart with all its affections, and my body with all its senses . . . to be forever his loyal, obedient, and faithful creature."
>
> —FRANCIS DE SALES,
> *Introduction to the Devout Life*

A Corporate Challenge

DEUTERONOMY 1.3–8

Imagine that you are present when Moses calls the Israelites together after forty years of wandering and says, "Okay, now it's time to go in and take possession of the promised land." Listen in on some of the conversations that are taking place among your neighbors. What are some of their worries? Fears? Hopes?

If Moses showed up at your church with a similar call to action—not to war, certainly, but to a risky, corporate challenge—how do you think you would respond? How would other church members respond?

See Meeting God in Scripture

Events at Horeb Recalled

1 These are the words that Moses spoke to all Israel beyond the Jordan—in the wilderness, on the plain opposite Suph, between Paran and Tophel, Laban, Hazeroth, and Dizahab. ²(By the way of Mount Seir it takes eleven days to reach Kadesh-barnea from Horeb.) ³In the fortieth year, on the first day of the eleventh month, Moses spoke to the Israelites just as the LORD had commanded him to speak to them. ⁴This was after he had defeated King Sihon of the Amorites, who reigned in Heshbon, and King Og of Bashan, who reigned in Ashtaroth and*ᵃ* in Edrei. ⁵Beyond the Jordan in the land of Moab, Moses undertook to expound this law as follows:

6 The LORD our God spoke to us at Horeb, saying, "You have stayed long enough at this mountain. ⁷Resume your journey, and go into the hill country of the Amorites as well as into the neighboring regions—the Arabah, the hill country, the Shephelah, the Negeb, and the seacoast—the land of the Canaanites and the Lebanon, as far as the great river, the river Euphrates. ⁸See, I have set the land before you; go in and take possession of the land that I*ᵇ* swore to your ancestors, to Abraham, to Isaac, and to Jacob, to give to them and to their descendants after them."

Appointment of Tribal Leaders

9 At that time I said to you, "I am unable by myself to bear you. ¹⁰The LORD your God has multiplied you, so that today you are as numerous as the stars of heaven. ¹¹May the LORD, the God of your ancestors, increase you a thousand times more and bless you, as he has promised you! ¹²But how can I bear the heavy burden of your disputes all by myself? ¹³Choose for each of your tribes individuals who are wise, discerning, and reputable to be your leaders." ¹⁴You answered me, "The plan you have proposed is a good one." ¹⁵So I took the leaders of your tribes, wise and reputable individuals, and installed them as leaders over you, commanders of thousands, commanders of hundreds, commanders of fifties, commanders of tens, and officials, throughout your tribes. ¹⁶I charged your judges at that time: "Give the members of your community a fair hearing, and judge rightly between one person and another, whether citizen or resident alien. ¹⁷You must not be partial in judging: hear out the small and the great alike; you shall not be intimidated by anyone, for the judgment is God's. Any case that is too hard for you, bring to me, and I will hear it." ¹⁸So I charged you at that time with all the things that you should do.

Israel's Refusal to Enter the Land

19 Then, just as the LORD our God had ordered us, we set out from Horeb and went through all that great and terrible wilderness that you saw, on the way to the hill country of the Amorites, until we reached Kadesh-barnea. ²⁰I said to you, "You have reached the hill country of the Amorites, which the LORD our God is giving us. ²¹See, the LORD your God has given the land to you; go up, take possession, as the LORD, the God of your ancestors, has promised you; do not fear or be dismayed."

22 All of you came to me and said, "Let us send men ahead of us to explore the land for us and bring back a report

a Gk Syr Vg Compare Josh 12.4: Heb lacks *and*   *b* Sam Gk: MT *the* LORD

to us regarding the route by which we should go up and the cities we will come to." ²³The plan seemed good to me, and I selected twelve of you, one from each tribe. ²⁴They set out and went up into the hill country, and when they reached the Valley of Eshcol they spied it out ²⁵and gathered some of the land's produce, which they brought down to us. They brought back a report to us, and said, "It is a good land that the LORD our God is giving us."

26 But you were unwilling to go up. You rebelled against the command of the LORD your God; ²⁷you grumbled in your tents and said, "It is because the LORD hates us that he has brought us out of the land of Egypt, to hand us over to the Amorites to destroy us. ²⁸Where are we headed? Our kindred have made our hearts melt by reporting, 'The people are stronger and taller than we; the cities are large and fortified up to heaven! We actually saw there the offspring of the Anakim!' " ²⁹I said to you, "Have no dread or fear of them. ³⁰The LORD your God, who goes before you, is the one who will fight for you, just as he did for you in Egypt before your very eyes, ³¹and in the wilderness, where you saw how the LORD your God carried you, just as one carries a child, all the way that you traveled until you reached this place. ³²But in spite of this, you have no trust in the LORD your God, ³³who goes before you on the way to seek out a place for you to camp, in fire by night, and in the cloud by day, to show you the route you should take."

The Penalty for Israel's Rebellion

34 When the LORD heard your words, he was wrathful and swore: ³⁵"Not one of these—not one of this evil generation— shall see the good land that I swore to give to your ancestors, ³⁶except Caleb son of Jephunneh. He shall see it, and to him and to his descendants I will give the land on which he set foot, because of his complete fidelity to the LORD." ³⁷Even with me the LORD was angry on your account, saying, "You also shall not enter there. ³⁸Joshua son of Nun, your assistant, shall enter there; encourage him, for he is the one who will secure Israel's possession of it. ³⁹And as for your little ones, who you thought would become booty, your children, who today do not yet know right from wrong, they shall enter there; to them I will give it, and they shall take possession of it. ⁴⁰But as for you, journey back into the wilderness, in the direction of the Red Sea."ᵃ

41 You answered me, "We have sinned against the LORD! We are ready to go up and fight, just as the LORD our God commanded us." So all of you strapped on your battle gear, and thought it easy to go up into the hill country. ⁴²The LORD said to me, "Say to them, 'Do not go up and do not fight, for I am not in the midst of you; otherwise you will be defeated by your enemies.' " ⁴³Although I told you, you would not listen. You rebelled against the command of the LORD and presumptuously went up into the hill country. ⁴⁴The Amorites who lived in that hill country then came out against you and chased you as bees do. They beat you down in Seir as far as Hormah. ⁴⁵When you returned and wept before the LORD, the LORD would neither heed your voice nor pay you any attention.

A Father's Burden

DEUTERONOMY 1.31

If you have a young child, take her for a walk around the block, praying as you carry her. Use this experience to imagine how the Lord might carry a nation as a father carries his son or daughter. If you don't have a young child, go to a mall and study the expressions of children and the expressions of their parents. Try to enter into the experience from both perspectives—the emotions and challenges of the parent, and the security and needs of the child. Now imagine God carrying your church as a parent would carry a child. How might this affect your church's leadership, relationships and mission if the church were to picture itself this way?

Walking Through Others' Blessings

DEUTERONOMY 2.4–5,9,19

Place yourself in the sandals of an Israelite. You have been wandering for forty years and most of your life is behind you. Now you pass through land belonging to Esau's descendants—the Moabites and the Ammonites. You're hungry for your own land, but God makes you walk through somebody else's land as you wait. Describe the envy you might feel. How hard is it to wait? Does someone else's good fortune make it even more difficult to wait for your own land?

In your present life, do you see anything owned or experienced by your neighbor or fellow church member that makes it hard for you to be content with what you have? What can you learn from the experience of the Israelites?

See Meeting God in Community

The Desert Years

46 After you had stayed at Kadesh as many days as you did, [1]we journeyed back into the wilderness, in the direction of the Red Sea,*a* as the LORD had told me and skirted Mount Seir for many days. [2]Then the LORD said to me: [3]"You have been skirting this hill country long enough. Head north, [4]and charge the people as follows: You are about to pass through the territory of your kindred, the descendants of Esau, who live in Seir. They will be afraid of you, so, be very careful [5]not to engage in battle with them, for I will not give you even so much as a foot's length of their land, since I have given Mount Seir to Esau as a possession. [6]You shall purchase food from them for money, so that you may eat; and you shall also buy water from them for money, so that you may drink. [7]Surely the LORD your God has blessed you in all your undertakings; he knows your going through this great wilderness. These forty years the LORD your God has been with you; you have lacked nothing." [8]So we passed by our kin, the descendants of Esau who live in Seir, leaving behind the route of the Arabah, and leaving behind Elath and Ezion-geber.

When we had headed out along the route of the wilderness of Moab, [9]the LORD said to me: "Do not harass Moab or engage them in battle, for I will not give you any of its land as a possession, since I have given Ar as a possession to the descendants of Lot." [10](The Emim—a large and numerous people, as tall as the Anakim—had formerly inhabited it. [11]Like the Anakim, they are usually reckoned as Rephaim, though the Moabites call them Emim. [12]Moreover, the Horim had formerly inhabited Seir, but the descendants of Esau dispossessed them, destroying them and settling in their place, as Israel has done in the land that the LORD gave them as a possession.) [13]"Now then, proceed to cross over the Wadi Zered."

So we crossed over the Wadi Zered. [14]And the length of time we had traveled from Kadesh-barnea until we crossed the Wadi Zered was thirty-eight years, until the entire generation of warriors had perished from the camp, as the LORD had sworn concerning them. [15]Indeed, the LORD's own hand was against them, to root them out from the camp, until all had perished.

16 Just as soon as all the warriors had died off from among the people, [17]the LORD spoke to me, saying, [18]"Today you are going to cross the boundary of Moab at Ar. [19]When you approach the frontier of the Ammonites, do not harass them or engage them in battle, for I will not give the land of the Ammonites to you as a possession, because I have given it to the descendants of Lot." [20](It also is usually reckoned as a land of Rephaim. Rephaim formerly inhabited it, though the Ammonites call them Zamzummim, [21]a strong and numerous people, as tall as the Anakim. But the LORD destroyed them from before the Ammonites so that they could dispossess them and settle in their place. [22]He did the same for the descendants of Esau, who live in Seir, by destroying the Horim before them so that they could dispossess them and settle in their place even to this day. [23]As for the Avvim, who had lived in settlements in the vicinity of Gaza, the Caphtorim, who came from Caphtor, destroyed them and settled in their place.) [24]"Proceed on your journey and cross the Wadi Arnon. See, I have handed over to you King Sihon the Amorite of Heshbon, and his land. Begin to take possession by en-

a Or *Sea of Reeds*

gaging him in battle. ²⁵This day I will begin to put the dread and fear of you upon the peoples everywhere under heaven; when they hear report of you, they will tremble and be in anguish because of you."

Defeat of King Sihon

26 So I sent messengers from the wilderness of Kedemoth to King Sihon of Heshbon with the following terms of peace: ²⁷"If you let me pass through your land, I will travel only along the road; I will turn aside neither to the right nor to the left. ²⁸You shall sell me food for money, so that I may eat, and supply me water for money, so that I may drink. Only allow me to pass through on foot— ²⁹just as the descendants of Esau who live in Seir have done for me and likewise the Moabites who live in Ar—until I cross the Jordan into the land that the LORD our God is giving us." ³⁰But King Sihon of Heshbon was not willing to let us pass through, for the LORD your God had hardened his spirit and made his heart defiant in order to hand him over to you, as he has now done.

31 The LORD said to me, "See, I have begun to give Sihon and his land over to you. Begin now to take possession of his land." ³²So when Sihon came out against us, he and all his people for battle at Jahaz, ³³the LORD our God gave him over to us; and we struck him down, along with his offspring and all his people. ³⁴At that time we captured all his towns, and in each town we utterly destroyed men, women, and children. We left not a single survivor. ³⁵Only the livestock we kept as spoil for ourselves, as well as the plunder of the towns that we had captured. ³⁶From Aroer on the edge of the Wadi Arnon (including the town that is in the wadi itself) as far as Gilead, there was no citadel too high for us. The LORD our God gave everything to us. ³⁷You did not encroach, however, on the land of the Ammonites, avoiding the whole upper region of the Wadi Jabbok as well as the towns of the hill country, just as*ᵃ* the LORD our God had charged.

Defeat of King Og

3 When we headed up the road to Bashan, King Og of Bashan came out against us, he and all his people, for battle at Edrei. ²The LORD said to me, "Do not fear him, for I have handed him over to you, along with his people and his land. Do to him as you did to King Sihon of the Amorites, who reigned in Heshbon." ³So the LORD our God also handed over to us King Og of Bashan and all his people. We struck him down until not a single survivor was left. ⁴At that time we captured all his towns; there was no citadel that we did not take from them—sixty towns, the whole region of Argob, the kingdom of Og in Bashan. ⁵All these were fortress towns with high walls, double gates, and bars, besides a great many villages. ⁶And we utterly destroyed them, as we had done to King Sihon of Heshbon, in each city utterly destroying men, women, and children. ⁷But all the livestock and the plunder of the towns we kept as spoil for ourselves.

8 So at that time we took from the two kings of the Amorites the land beyond the Jordan, from the Wadi Arnon to Mount Hermon ⁹(the Sidonians call Hermon Sirion, while the Amorites call it Senir), ¹⁰all the towns of the tableland, the whole of Gilead, and all of Bashan, as far as Salecah and Edrei, towns of Og's kingdom in Bashan. ¹¹(Now only King Og

A Masked Entrance

DEUTERONOMY 2.30–32

The Israelites are out in the desert; they need food to eat, water to drink and a road to travel on. The local king brings his army out to "greet" them. Things couldn't look worse, but then God says, "See, I have begun to give Sihon and his land over to you. Begin now to take possession of his land." In the midst of what looks like certain disaster, God tells Moses to go on the offensive, because God has already begun to deliver the Israelites.

Is there a bleak situation in your life that God might look at differently from the way you do? Can you recall a moment that looked ominous but proved instead to be a prelude to God's redeeming entrance?

See Meeting God in Everyday Life

a Gk Tg: Heb and all

Sacrificial Service

DEUTERONOMY 3.19–20

Have you ever missed time with your family because you were helping someone else? What did that teach you about unselfishness? Service? Godly love? To more fully experience this passage, go out on an unusually cold or hot day, leave the shelter of your heated or air-conditioned house and perform a service out-of-doors for someone else. As you do this, prayerfully consider the self-denial the Reubenites and Gadites must have endured to fight their brothers' battles when their own land was already won. What temptations must they have faced? How might their hearts have changed after they returned home?

See Meeting God in Community

of Bashan was left of the remnant of the Rephaim. In fact his bed, an iron bed, can still be seen in Rabbah of the Ammonites. By the common cubit it is nine cubits long and four cubits wide.) [12]As for the land that we took possession of at that time, I gave to the Reubenites and Gadites the territory north of Aroer,[a] that is on the edge of the Wadi Arnon, as well as half the hill country of Gilead with its towns, [13]and I gave to the half-tribe of Manasseh the rest of Gilead and all of Bashan, Og's kingdom. (The whole region of Argob: all that portion of Bashan used to be called a land of Rephaim; [14]Jair the Manassite acquired the whole region of Argob as far as the border of the Geshurites and the Maacathites, and he named them—that is, Bashan—after himself, Havvoth-jair,[b] as it is to this day.) [15]To Machir I gave Gilead. [16]And to the Reubenites and the Gadites I gave the territory from Gilead as far as the Wadi Arnon, with the middle of the wadi as a boundary, and up to the Jabbok, the wadi being boundary of the Ammonites; [17]the Arabah also, with the Jordan and its banks, from Chinnereth down to the sea of the Arabah, the Dead Sea,[c] with the lower slopes of Pisgah on the east.

18 At that time, I charged you as follows: "Although the LORD your God has given you this land to occupy, all your troops shall cross over armed as the vanguard of your Israelite kin. [19]Only your wives, your children, and your livestock—I know that you have much livestock—shall stay behind in the towns that I have given to you. [20]When the LORD gives rest to your kindred, as to you, and they too have occupied the land that the LORD your God is giving them beyond the Jordan, then each of you may return to the property that I have given to you." [21]And I charged Joshua as well at that time, saying: "Your own eyes have seen everything that the LORD your God has done to these two kings; so the LORD will do to all the kingdoms into which you are about to cross. [22]Do not fear them, for it is the LORD your God who fights for you."

Moses Views Canaan from Pisgah

23 At that time, too, I entreated the LORD, saying: [24]"O Lord GOD, you have only begun to show your servant your greatness and your might; what god in heaven or on earth can perform deeds and mighty acts like yours! [25]Let me cross over to see the good land beyond the Jordan, that good hill country and the Lebanon." [26]But the LORD was angry with me on your account and would not heed me. The LORD said to me, "Enough from you! Never speak to me of this matter again! [27]Go up to the top of Pisgah and look around you to the west, to the north, to the south, and to the east. Look well, for you shall not cross over this Jordan. [28]But charge Joshua, and encourage and strengthen him, because it is he who shall cross over at the head of this people and who shall secure their possession of the land that you will see." [29]So we remained in the valley opposite Beth-peor.

Moses Commands Obedience

4 So now, Israel, give heed to the statutes and ordinances that I am teaching you to observe, so that you may live to enter and occupy the land that the LORD, the God of your ancestors, is giving you. [2]You must neither add anything to what I command you nor take away anything from it, but keep the commandments of the LORD your God with which I am charg-

a Heb territory from Aroer   b That is Settlement of Jair   c Heb Salt Sea ing you. ³You have seen for yourselves what the Lord did with regard to the Baal of Peor—how the Lord your God destroyed from among you everyone who followed the Baal of Peor, ⁴while those of you who held fast to the Lord your God are all alive today.

5 See, just as the Lord my God has charged me, I now teach you statutes and ordinances for you to observe in the land that you are about to enter and occupy. ⁶You must observe them diligently, for this will show your wisdom and discernment to the peoples, who, when they hear all these statutes, will say, "Surely this great nation is a wise and discerning people!" ⁷For what other great nation has a god so near to it as the Lord our God is whenever we call to him? ⁸And what other great nation has statutes and ordinances as just as this entire law that I am setting before you today?

9 But take care and watch yourselves closely, so as neither to forget the things that your eyes have seen nor to let them slip from your mind all the days of your life; make them known to your children and your children's children— ¹⁰how you once stood before the Lord your God at Horeb, when the Lord said to me, "Assemble the people for me, and I will let them hear my words, so that they may learn to fear me as long as they live on the earth, and may teach their children so"; ¹¹you approached and stood at the foot of the mountain while the mountain was blazing up to the very heavens, shrouded in dark clouds. ¹²Then the Lord spoke to you out of the fire. You heard the sound of words but saw no form; there was only a voice. ¹³He declared to you his covenant, which he charged you to observe, that is, the ten commandments;ᵃ and he wrote them on two stone tablets. ¹⁴And the Lord charged me at that time to teach you statutes and ordinances for you to observe in the land that you are about to cross into and occupy.

15 Since you saw no form when the Lord spoke to you at Horeb out of the fire, take care and watch yourselves closely, ¹⁶so that you do not act corruptly by making an idol for yourselves, in the form of any figure—the likeness of male or female, ¹⁷the likeness of any animal that is on the earth, the likeness of any winged bird that flies in the air, ¹⁸the likeness of anything that creeps on the ground, the likeness of any fish that is in the water under the earth. ¹⁹And when you look up to the heavens and see the sun, the moon, and the stars, all the host of heaven, do not be led astray and bow down to them and serve them, things that the Lord your God has allotted to all the peoples everywhere under heaven. ²⁰But the Lord has taken you and brought you out of the iron-smelter, out of Egypt, to become a people of his very own possession, as you are now.

21 The Lord was angry with me because of you, and he vowed that I should not cross the Jordan and that I should not enter the good land that the Lord your God is giving for your possession. ²²For I am going to die in this land without crossing over the Jordan, but you are going to cross over to take possession of that good land. ²³So be careful not to forget the covenant that the Lord your God made with you, and not to make for yourselves an idol in the form of anything that the Lord your God has forbidden you. ²⁴For the Lord your God is a devouring fire, a jealous God.

25 When you have had children and children's children,

ᵃ Heb *the ten words*

Close Watch

DEUTERONOMY 4.9

"If thou canst not continually recollect thyself, yet do it sometimes, at least once a day, namely, in the morning or at night. In the morning fix thy good purpose; and at night examine thyself what thou hast done, how thou hast behaved thyself in word, deed, and thought; for in these perhaps thou hast oftentimes offended both God and thy neighbor. Gird up thy loins like a man against the evil assaults of the devil; bridle thy riotous appetite, and thou shalt be the better able to keep under all the unruly desires of the flesh."

—THOMAS À KEMPIS, *The Imitation of Christ*

Remember to Remember

DEUTERONOMY 4.23

Can you remember your 16th birthday? How about your 21st? What about a less momentous one, say, your 19th? Read Deuteronomy 6.6–9; 8.10–14; 9.7. How does God encourage Israel to remember important events? Can you think of any ways you can create contemporary equivalents that will help you "remember to remember"? To what holidays might you pay particular attention? What has happened in your life that you want to remember? What memories do you want to pass on to your children? How might you make that happen? Reflect on the many ways that remembering is important to our faith.

See Meeting God in Everyday Life

and become complacent in the land, if you act corruptly by making an idol in the form of anything, thus doing what is evil in the sight of the LORD your God, and provoking him to anger, ²⁶I call heaven and earth to witness against you today that you will soon utterly perish from the land that you are crossing the Jordan to occupy; you will not live long on it, but will be utterly destroyed. ²⁷The LORD will scatter you among the peoples; only a few of you will be left among the nations where the LORD will lead you. ²⁸There you will serve other gods made by human hands, objects of wood and stone that neither see, nor hear, nor eat, nor smell. ²⁹From there you will seek the LORD your God, and you will find him if you search after him with all your heart and soul. ³⁰In your distress, when all these things have happened to you in time to come, you will return to the LORD your God and heed him. ³¹Because the LORD your God is a merciful God, he will neither abandon you nor destroy you; he will not forget the covenant with your ancestors that he swore to them.

32 For ask now about former ages, long before your own, ever since the day that God created human beings on the earth; ask from one end of heaven to the other: has anything so great as this ever happened or has its like ever been heard of? ³³Has any people ever heard the voice of a god speaking out of a fire, as you have heard, and lived? ³⁴Or has any god ever attempted to go and take a nation for himself from the midst of another nation, by trials, by signs and wonders, by war, by a mighty hand and an outstretched arm, and by terrifying displays of power, as the LORD your God did for you in Egypt before your very eyes? ³⁵To you it was shown so that you would acknowledge that the LORD is God; there is no other besides him. ³⁶From heaven he made you hear his voice to discipline you. On earth he showed you his great fire, while you heard his words coming out of the fire. ³⁷And because he loved your ancestors, he chose their descendants after them. He brought you out of Egypt with his own presence, by his great power, ³⁸driving out before you nations greater and mightier than yourselves, to bring you in, giving you their land for a possession, as it is still today. ³⁹So acknowledge today and take to heart that the LORD is God in heaven above and on the earth beneath; there is no other. ⁴⁰Keep his statutes and his commandments, which I am commanding you today for your own well-being and that of your descendants after you, so that you may long remain in the land that the LORD your God is giving you for all time.

Cities of Refuge East of the Jordan

41 Then Moses set apart on the east side of the Jordan three cities ⁴²to which a homicide could flee, someone who unintentionally kills another person, the two not having been at enmity before; the homicide could flee to one of these cities and live: ⁴³Bezer in the wilderness on the tableland belonging to the Reubenites, Ramoth in Gilead belonging to the Gadites, and Golan in Bashan belonging to the Manassites.

Transition to the Second Address

44 This is the law that Moses set before the Israelites. ⁴⁵These are the decrees and the statutes and ordinances that Moses spoke to the Israelites when they had come out of Egypt, ⁴⁶beyond the Jordan in the valley opposite Beth-peor, in the land of King Sihon of the Amorites, who reigned at Heshbon, whom Moses and the Israelites defeated when

they came out of Egypt. ⁴⁷They occupied his land and the land of King Og of Bashan, the two kings of the Amorites on the eastern side of the Jordan: ⁴⁸from Aroer, which is on the edge of the Wadi Arnon, as far as Mount Sirion*ᵃ* (that is, Hermon), ⁴⁹together with all the Arabah on the east side of the Jordan as far as the Sea of the Arabah, under the slopes of Pisgah.

The Ten Commandments

5 Moses convened all Israel, and said to them:
Hear, O Israel, the statutes and ordinances that I am addressing to you today; you shall learn them and observe them diligently. ²The LORD our God made a covenant with us at Horeb. ³Not with our ancestors did the LORD make this covenant, but with us, who are all of us here alive today. ⁴The LORD spoke with you face to face at the mountain, out of the fire. ⁵(At that time I was standing between the LORD and you to declare to you the words*ᵇ* of the LORD; for you were afraid because of the fire and did not go up the mountain.) And he said:

6 I am the LORD your God, who brought you out of the land of Egypt, out of the house of slavery; ⁷you shall have no other gods before*ᶜ* me.

8 You shall not make for yourself an idol, whether in the form of anything that is in heaven above, or that is on the earth beneath, or that is in the water under the earth. ⁹You shall not bow down to them or worship them; for I the LORD your God am a jealous God, punishing children for the iniquity of parents, to the third and fourth generation of those who reject me, ¹⁰but showing steadfast love to the thousandth generation*ᵈ* of those who love me and keep my commandments.

11 You shall not make wrongful use of the name of the LORD your God, for the LORD will not acquit anyone who misuses his name.

12 Observe the sabbath day and keep it holy, as the LORD your God commanded you. ¹³Six days you shall labor and do all your work. ¹⁴But the seventh day is a sabbath to the LORD your God; you shall not do any work—you, or your son or your daughter, or your male or female slave, or your ox or your donkey, or any of your livestock, or the resident alien in your towns, so that your male and female slave may rest as well as you. ¹⁵Remember that you were a slave in the land of Egypt, and the LORD your God brought you out from there with a mighty hand and an outstretched arm; therefore the LORD your God commanded you to keep the sabbath day.

16 Honor your father and your mother, as the LORD your God commanded you, so that your days may be long and that it may go well with you in the land that the LORD your God is giving you.

17 You shall not murder.*ᵉ*

18 Neither shall you commit adultery.

19 Neither shall you steal.

20 Neither shall you bear false witness against your neighbor.

21 Neither shall you covet your neighbor's wife.

Neither shall you desire your neighbor's house, or field, or male or female slave, or ox, or donkey, or anything that belongs to your neighbor.

The Ten Evaluations

DEUTERONOMY 5.6–21

Martin Luther encouraged Christians to pray through the Ten Commandments each day as a form of spiritual evaluation. Christians are to look at each commandment both positively and negatively: that is, the negative commandment not to steal leads to reflection on the positive virtue of giving; the positive commandment to honor our parents invites reflection on how we might have dishonored them. Using this framework, pray through each commandment. Allow God time to speak to your heart about the positive and negative elements of each one. This will be an evaluative prayer, so have pen and paper handy in case the Lord brings to mind someone with whom you need to set things right.

See Meeting God in Prayer

---

a Syr: Heb *Sion*   *b* Q Mss Sam Gk Syr Vg Tg: MT *word*   *c* Or *besides*
d Or *to thousands*   *e* Or *kill*

A Dramatic Entrance

DEUTERONOMY 5.22–23

Get out some drawing materials and, based on these two verses, try to re-create (in symbolic form) the encounter between God and Israel. How will you depict the loud voice, the fire, the cloud, the thick darkness? Next, draw a symbolic representation of how God has met you recently. Think about the images you chose. What might they tell you about your prayer life? How does God most often approach you? How would you react if God were to approach you as he did the Israelites?

See Meeting God in Scripture

Moses the Mediator of God's Will

22 These words the LORD spoke with a loud voice to your whole assembly at the mountain, out of the fire, the cloud, and the thick darkness, and he added no more. He wrote them on two stone tablets, and gave them to me. ²³When you heard the voice out of the darkness, while the mountain was burning with fire, you approached me, all the heads of your tribes and your elders; ²⁴and you said, "Look, the LORD our God has shown us his glory and greatness, and we have heard his voice out of the fire. Today we have seen that God may speak to someone and the person may still live. ²⁵So now why should we die? For this great fire will consume us; if we hear the voice of the LORD our God any longer, we shall die. ²⁶For who is there of all flesh that has heard the voice of the living God speaking out of fire, as we have, and remained alive? ²⁷Go near, you yourself, and hear all that the LORD our God will say. Then tell us everything that the LORD our God tells you, and we will listen and do it."

28 The LORD heard your words when you spoke to me, and the LORD said to me: "I have heard the words of this people, which they have spoken to you; they are right in all that they have spoken. ²⁹If only they had such a mind as this, to fear me and to keep all my commandments always, so that it might go well with them and with their children forever! ³⁰Go say to them, 'Return to your tents.' ³¹But you, stand here by me, and I will tell you all the commandments, the statutes and the ordinances, that you shall teach them, so that they may do them in the land that I am giving them to possess." ³²You must therefore be careful to do as the LORD your God has commanded you; you shall not turn to the right or to the left. ³³You must follow exactly the path that the LORD your God has commanded you, so that you may live, and that it may go well with you, and that you may live long in the land that you are to possess.

The Great Commandment

6 Now this is the commandment—the statutes and the ordinances—that the LORD your God charged me to teach you to observe in the land that you are about to cross into and occupy, ²so that you and your children and your children's children may fear the LORD your God all the days of your life, and keep all his decrees and his commandments that I am commanding you, so that your days may be long. ³Hear therefore, O Israel, and observe them diligently, so that it may go well with you, and so that you may multiply greatly in a land flowing with milk and honey, as the LORD, the God of your ancestors, has promised you.

4 Hear, O Israel: The LORD is our God, the LORD alone.ᵃ ⁵You shall love the LORD your God with all your heart, and with all your soul, and with all your might. ⁶Keep these words that I am commanding you today in your heart. ⁷Recite them to your children and talk about them when you are at home and when you are away, when you lie down and when you rise. ⁸Bind them as a sign on your hand, fix them as an emblemᵇ on your forehead, ⁹and write them on the doorposts of your house and on your gates.

---

a Or *The LORD our God is one LORD,* or *The LORD our God, the LORD is one,* or *The LORD is our God, the LORD is one*   b Or *as a frontlet*

Caution against Disobedience

10 When the LORD your God has brought you into the land that he swore to your ancestors, to Abraham, to Isaac, and to Jacob, to give you—a land with fine, large cities that you did not build, ¹¹houses filled with all sorts of goods that you did not fill, hewn cisterns that you did not hew, vineyards and olive groves that you did not plant—and when you have eaten your fill, ¹²take care that you do not forget the LORD, who brought you out of the land of Egypt, out of the house of slavery. ¹³The LORD your God you shall fear; him you shall serve, and by his name alone you shall swear. ¹⁴Do not follow other gods, any of the gods of the peoples who are all around you, ¹⁵because the LORD your God, who is present with you, is a jealous God. The anger of the LORD your God would be kindled against you and he would destroy you from the face of the earth.

16 Do not put the LORD your God to the test, as you tested him at Massah. ¹⁷You must diligently keep the commandments of the LORD your God, and his decrees, and his statutes that he has commanded you. ¹⁸Do what is right and good in the sight of the LORD, so that it may go well with you, and so that you may go in and occupy the good land that the LORD swore to your ancestors to give you, ¹⁹thrusting out all your enemies from before you, as the LORD has promised.

20 When your children ask you in time to come, "What is the meaning of the decrees and the statutes and the ordinances that the LORD our God has commanded you?" ²¹then you shall say to your children, "We were Pharaoh's slaves in Egypt, but the LORD brought us out of Egypt with a mighty hand. ²²The LORD displayed before our eyes great and awesome signs and wonders against Egypt, against Pharaoh and all his household. ²³He brought us out from there in order to bring us in, to give us the land that he promised on oath to our ancestors. ²⁴Then the LORD commanded us to observe all these statutes, to fear the LORD our God, for our lasting good, so as to keep us alive, as is now the case. ²⁵If we diligently observe this entire commandment before the LORD our God, as he has commanded us, we will be in the right."

A Chosen People

7 When the LORD your God brings you into the land that you are about to enter and occupy, and he clears away many nations before you—the Hittites, the Girgashites, the Amorites, the Canaanites, the Perizzites, the Hivites, and the Jebusites, seven nations mightier and more numerous than you— ²and when the LORD your God gives them over to you and you defeat them, then you must utterly destroy them. Make no covenant with them and show them no mercy. ³Do not intermarry with them, giving your daughters to their sons or taking their daughters for your sons, ⁴for that would turn away your children from following me, to serve other gods. Then the anger of the LORD would be kindled against you, and he would destroy you quickly. ⁵But this is how you must deal with them: break down their altars, smash their pillars, hew down their sacred poles,^a and burn their idols with fire. ⁶For you are a people holy to the LORD your God; the LORD your God has chosen you out of all the peoples on earth to be his people, his treasured possession.

7 It was not because you were more numerous than any

Milk and Honey

DEUTERONOMY 6.3

Invite some friends over, take them into your kitchen, and sample some milk and honey. Think about (and discuss) the qualities of milk, particularly its life-giving nutrients. Also consider the nature of honey, particularly its sweet flavor. Reflect on the larger implications of God's promise to bring Israel into a land "flowing" with these two elements. Look at your current situation: How has God provided you with nourishing "milk"? Do you see any evidence of sweet "honey"? Why do you think God chose these two food items to describe the promised land?

See *Meeting God in Everyday Life*

Sweet, Happy Devotion

DEUTERONOMY 7.17

"They who discouraged the Israelites from going into the
land of promise told them it
was a country which devoured
its inhabitants . . . It is in this
manner . . . that the world de-
fames holy devotion, representing devout persons as a
peevish, gloomy, and sullen
race of men, pretending that
devotion begets melancholy and
insupportable humors. But as
Joshua and Caleb protested that
the promised land was not only
good and fair, but also that the
possession of it would be sweet
and agreeable, so the Holy
Ghost . . . and our Savior . . .
assure us that a devout life is a
life of all others the most
sweet, happy, and amiable."
—FRANCIS DE SALES,
Introduction to the Devout Life

other people that the LORD set his heart on you and chose you—for you were the fewest of all peoples. [8]It was because the LORD loved you and kept the oath that he swore to your ancestors, that the LORD has brought you out with a mighty hand, and redeemed you from the house of slavery, from the hand of Pharaoh king of Egypt. [9]Know therefore that the LORD your God is God, the faithful God who maintains covenant loyalty with those who love him and keep his command-ments, to a thousand generations, [10]and who repays in their own person those who reject him. He does not delay but re-pays in their own person those who reject him. [11]Therefore, observe diligently the commandment—the statutes and the ordinances—that I am commanding you today.

Blessings for Obedience

12 If you heed these ordinances, by diligently observing them, the LORD your God will maintain with you the covenant loyalty that he swore to your ancestors; [13]he will love you, bless you, and multiply you; he will bless the fruit of your womb and the fruit of your ground, your grain and your wine and your oil, the increase of your cattle and the issue of your flock, in the land that he swore to your ancestors to give you. [14]You shall be the most blessed of peoples, with neither steril-ity nor barrenness among you or your livestock. [15]The LORD will turn away from you every illness; all the dread diseases of Egypt that you experienced, he will not inflict on you, but he will lay them on all who hate you. [16]You shall devour all the peoples that the LORD your God is giving over to you, showing them no pity; you shall not serve their gods, for that would be a snare to you.

17 If you say to yourself, "These nations are more numer-ous than I; how can I dispossess them?" [18]do not be afraid of them. Just remember what the LORD your God did to Pharaoh and to all Egypt, [19]the great trials that your eyes saw, the signs and wonders, the mighty hand and the outstretched arm by which the LORD your God brought you out. The LORD your God will do the same to all the peoples of whom you are afraid. [20]Moreover, the LORD your God will send the pestilence[a] against them, until even the survivors and the fugitives are destroyed. [21]Have no dread of them, for the LORD your God, who is present with you, is a great and awesome God. [22]The LORD your God will clear away these nations before you little by little; you will not be able to make a quick end of them, otherwise the wild animals would become too numerous for you. [23]But the LORD your God will give them over to you, and throw them into great panic, until they are destroyed. [24]He will hand their kings over to you and you shall blot out their name from under heaven; no one will be able to stand against you, until you have destroyed them. [25]The images of their gods you shall burn with fire. Do not covet the silver or the gold that is on them and take it for yourself, because you could be ensnared by it; for it is abhorrent to the LORD your God. [26]Do not bring an abhorrent thing into your house, or you will be set apart for destruction like it. You must utterly detest and abhor it, for it is set apart for destruction.

A Warning Not to Forget God in Prosperity

8 This entire commandment that I command you today you must diligently observe, so that you may live and in-

a Or *hornets*: Meaning of Heb uncertain

crease, and go in and occupy the land that the LORD promised on oath to your ancestors. ²Remember the long way that the LORD your God has led you these forty years in the wilderness, in order to humble you, testing you to know what was in your heart, whether or not you would keep his commandments. ³He humbled you by letting you hunger, then by feeding you with manna, with which neither you nor your ancestors were acquainted, in order to make you understand that one does not live by bread alone, but by every word that comes from the mouth of the LORD.ᵃ ⁴The clothes on your back did not wear out and your feet did not swell these forty years. ⁵Know then in your heart that as a parent disciplines a child so the LORD your God disciplines you. ⁶Therefore keep the commandments of the LORD your God, by walking in his ways and by fearing him. ⁷For the LORD your God is bringing you into a good land, a land with flowing streams, with springs and underground waters welling up in valleys and hills, ⁸a land of wheat and barley, of vines and fig trees and pomegranates, a land of olive trees and honey, ⁹a land where you may eat bread without scarcity, where you will lack nothing, a land whose stones are iron and from whose hills you may mine copper. ¹⁰You shall eat your fill and bless the LORD your God for the good land that he has given you.

11 Take care that you do not forget the LORD your God, by failing to keep his commandments, his ordinances, and his statutes, which I am commanding you today. ¹²When you have eaten your fill and have built fine houses and live in them, ¹³and when your herds and flocks have multiplied, and your silver and gold is multiplied, and all that you have is multiplied, ¹⁴then do not exalt yourself, forgetting the LORD your God, who brought you out of the land of Egypt, out of the house of slavery, ¹⁵who led you through the great and terrible wilderness, an arid wasteland with poisonousᵇ snakes and scorpions. He made water flow for you from flint rock, ¹⁶and fed you in the wilderness with manna that your ancestors did not know, to humble you and to test you, and in the end to do you good. ¹⁷Do not say to yourself, "My power and the might of my own hand have gotten me this wealth." ¹⁸But remember the LORD your God, for it is he who gives you power to get wealth, so that he may confirm his covenant that he swore to your ancestors, as he is doing today. ¹⁹If you do forget the LORD your God and follow other gods to serve and worship them, I solemnly warn you today that you shall surely perish. ²⁰Like the nations that the LORD is destroying before you, so shall you perish, because you would not obey the voice of the LORD your God.

The Consequences of Rebelling against God

9 Hear, O Israel! You are about to cross the Jordan today, to go in and dispossess nations larger and mightier than you, great cities, fortified to the heavens, ²a strong and tall people, the offspring of the Anakim, whom you know. You have heard it said of them, "Who can stand up to the Anakim?" ³Know then today that the LORD your God is the one who crosses over before you as a devouring fire; he will defeat them and subdue them before you, so that you may dispossess and destroy them quickly, as the LORD has promised you.

4 When the LORD your God thrusts them out before you,

Don't Forget

DEUTERONOMY 8.1–20

Moses declares to the Israelites that God is eager to bless them. Go through chapter 8 and write down the types of blessings Moses promises in the future (particularly vv.7–10, 12–13). Next, go back through this chapter and compare the future blessings with the past sojourn in the wilderness (particularly vv.4,14–16).

Consider your own life before and after you began actively following God. Have any blessings tempted you to forget your need for God? Have you forgotten what life was like without God? How can your memory of God's deliverance in the past enhance your thankfulness today? How can you fully enjoy God's blessings without losing sight of the One who provided them?

---

a Or *by anything that the* LORD *decrees*   *b* Or *fiery*; Heb *seraph*

A Devouring Fire

DEUTERONOMY 9.3,15

Twice in this chapter, Moses uses the image of fire to describe God's dealings with people. Build a fire in a fireplace, and burn several different items—newspaper, a piece of wood, and one or two other items of your choosing. As you see the items consumed, reflect on how God will go before you as "a devouring fire." Notice how quickly the paper burns compared to the wood. What comfort can you take from the thought that God precedes his people as a devouring fire? What challenges are you facing that you wish God would destroy?

See Meeting God in Everyday Life

do not say to yourself, "It is because of my righteousness that the LORD has brought me in to occupy this land"; it is rather because of the wickedness of these nations that the LORD is dispossessing them before you. ⁵It is not because of your righteousness or the uprightness of your heart that you are going in to occupy their land; but because of the wickedness of these nations the LORD your God is dispossessing them before you, in order to fulfill the promise that the LORD made on oath to your ancestors, to Abraham, to Isaac, and to Jacob.

6 Know, then, that the LORD your God is not giving you this good land to occupy because of your righteousness; for you are a stubborn people. ⁷Remember and do not forget how you provoked the LORD your God to wrath in the wilderness; you have been rebellious against the LORD from the day you came out of the land of Egypt until you came to this place.

8 Even at Horeb you provoked the LORD to wrath, and the LORD was so angry with you that he was ready to destroy you. ⁹When I went up the mountain to receive the stone tablets, the tablets of the covenant that the LORD made with you, I remained on the mountain forty days and forty nights; I neither ate bread nor drank water. ¹⁰And the LORD gave me the two stone tablets written with the finger of God; on them were all the words that the LORD had spoken to you at the mountain out of the fire on the day of the assembly. ¹¹At the end of forty days and forty nights the LORD gave me the two stone tablets, the tablets of the covenant. ¹²Then the LORD said to me, "Get up, go down quickly from here, for your people whom you have brought from Egypt have acted corruptly. They have been quick to turn from the way that I commanded them; they have cast an image for themselves." ¹³Furthermore the LORD said to me, "I have seen that this people is indeed a stubborn people. ¹⁴Let me alone that I may destroy them and blot out their name from under heaven; and I will make of you a nation mightier and more numerous than they."

15 So I turned and went down from the mountain, while the mountain was ablaze; the two tablets of the covenant were in my two hands. ¹⁶Then I saw that you had indeed sinned against the LORD your God, by casting for yourselves an image of a calf; you had been quick to turn from the way that the LORD had commanded you. ¹⁷So I took hold of the two tablets and flung them from my two hands, smashing them before your eyes. ¹⁸Then I lay prostrate before the LORD as before, forty days and forty nights; I neither ate bread nor drank water, because of all the sin you had committed, provoking the LORD by doing what was evil in his sight. ¹⁹For I was afraid that the anger that the LORD bore against you was so fierce that he would destroy you. But the LORD listened to me that time also. ²⁰The LORD was so angry with Aaron that he was ready to destroy him, but I interceded also on behalf of Aaron at that same time. ²¹Then I took the sinful thing you had made, the calf, and burned it with fire and crushed it, grinding it thoroughly, until it was reduced to dust; and I threw the dust of it into the stream that runs down the mountain.

22 At Taberah also, and at Massah, and at Kibroth-hattaavah, you provoked the LORD to wrath. ²³And when the LORD sent you from Kadesh-barnea, saying, "Go up and occupy the land that I have given you," you rebelled against the command of the LORD your God, neither trusting him nor

obeying him. [24]You have been rebellious against the Lord as long as he has[a] known you.

25 Throughout the forty days and forty nights that I lay prostrate before the Lord when the Lord intended to destroy you, [26]I prayed to the Lord and said, "Lord God, do not destroy the people who are your very own possession, whom you redeemed in your greatness, whom you brought out of Egypt with a mighty hand. [27]Remember your servants, Abraham, Isaac, and Jacob; pay no attention to the stubbornness of this people, their wickedness and their sin, [28]otherwise the land from which you have brought us might say, 'Because the Lord was not able to bring them into the land that he promised them, and because he hated them, he has brought them out to let them die in the wilderness.' [29]For they are the people of your very own possession, whom you brought out by your great power and by your outstretched arm."

The Second Pair of Tablets

10 At that time the Lord said to me, "Carve out two tablets of stone like the former ones, and come up to me on the mountain, and make an ark of wood. [2]I will write on the tablets the words that were on the former tablets, which you smashed, and you shall put them in the ark." [3]So I made an ark of acacia wood, cut two tablets of stone like the former ones, and went up the mountain with the two tablets in my hand. [4]Then he wrote on the tablets the same words as before, the ten commandments[b] that the Lord had spoken to you on the mountain out of the fire on the day of the assembly; and the Lord gave them to me. [5]So I turned and came down from the mountain, and put the tablets in the ark that I had made; and there they are, as the Lord commanded me.

6 (The Israelites journeyed from Beeroth-bene-jaakan[c] to Moserah. There Aaron died, and there he was buried; his son Eleazar succeeded him as priest. [7]From there they journeyed to Gudgodah, and from Gudgodah to Jotbathah, a land with flowing streams. [8]At that time the Lord set apart the tribe of Levi to carry the ark of the covenant of the Lord, to stand before the Lord to minister to him, and to bless in his name, to this day. [9]Therefore Levi has no allotment or inheritance with his kindred; the Lord is his inheritance, as the Lord your God promised him.)

10 I stayed on the mountain forty days and forty nights, as I had done the first time. And once again the Lord listened to me. The Lord was unwilling to destroy you. [11]The Lord said to me, "Get up, go on your journey at the head of the people, that they may go in and occupy the land that I swore to their ancestors to give them."

The Essence of the Law

12 So now, O Israel, what does the Lord your God require of you? Only to fear the Lord your God, to walk in all his ways, to love him, to serve the Lord your God with all your heart and with all your soul, [13]and to keep the commandments of the Lord your God[d] and his decrees that I am commanding you today, for your own well-being. [14]Although heaven and the heaven of heavens belong to the Lord your God, the earth with all that is in it, [15]yet the Lord set his heart in love on your ancestors alone and chose you, their descendants after them,

Hunger and Thirst

DEUTERONOMY 9.18

Have you ever responded to a spiritual challenge by fasting? Why do you think so many people in the Bible regularly engaged in fasting? What can we learn spiritually from our hunger and thirst? How might fasting help us to focus on God? How does fasting promote true contrition and repentance? If you've never fasted, consider skipping one or two meals, and devote to prayer the time that you'd normally spend preparing the food, eating it and cleaning up afterwards.

See Meeting God in Prayer

---

a Sam Gk: MT *I have*   b Heb *the ten words*   c Or *the wells of the Bene-jaakan*   d Q Ms Gk Syr: MT lacks *your God*

Pure Love for God

"Whosoever seeketh of God anything besides God, doth not love God purely. If a wife loved her husband because he is rich, she is not pure, for she loveth not her husband, but the gold of her husband . . . Who so seeks from God any other reward but God, and for it would serve God, esteems what he wishes to receive, more than Him from whom he would receive it. What then? Hath God no reward? None, save Himself. The reward of God is God Himself."

—AUGUSTINE,
Sermons and Expositions

out of all the peoples, as it is today. ¹⁶Circumcise, then, the foreskin of your heart, and do not be stubborn any longer. ¹⁷For the LORD your God is God of gods and Lord of lords, the great God, mighty and awesome, who is not partial and takes no bribe, ¹⁸who executes justice for the orphan and the widow, and who loves the strangers, providing them food and clothing. ¹⁹You shall also love the stranger, for you were strangers in the land of Egypt. ²⁰You shall fear the LORD your God; him alone you shall worship; to him you shall hold fast, and by his name you shall swear. ²¹He is your praise; he is your God, who has done for you these great and awesome things that your own eyes have seen. ²²Your ancestors went down to Egypt seventy persons; and now the LORD your God has made you as numerous as the stars in heaven.

Rewards for Obedience

11 You shall love the LORD your God, therefore, and keep his charge, his decrees, his ordinances, and his commandments always. ²Remember today that it was not your children (who have not known or seen the discipline of the LORD your God), but it is you who must acknowledge his greatness, his mighty hand and his outstretched arm, ³his signs and his deeds that he did in Egypt to Pharaoh, the king of Egypt, and to all his land; ⁴what he did to the Egyptian army, to their horses and chariots, how he made the water of the Red Sea*ᵃ* flow over them as they pursued you, so that the LORD has destroyed them to this day; ⁵what he did to you in the wilderness, until you came to this place; ⁶and what he did to Dathan and Abiram, sons of Eliab son of Reuben, how in the midst of all Israel the earth opened its mouth and swallowed them up, along with their households, their tents, and every living being in their company; ⁷for it is your own eyes that have seen every great deed that the LORD did.

8 Keep, then, this entire commandment that I am commanding you today, so that you may have strength to go in and occupy the land that you are crossing over to occupy, ⁹and so that you may live long in the land that the LORD swore to your ancestors to give them and to their descendants, a land flowing with milk and honey. ¹⁰For the land that you are about to enter to occupy is not like the land of Egypt, from which you have come, where you sow your seed and irrigate by foot like a vegetable garden. ¹¹But the land that you are crossing over to occupy is a land of hills and valleys, watered by rain from the sky, ¹²a land that the LORD your God looks after. The eyes of the LORD your God are always on it, from the beginning of the year to the end of the year.

13 If you will only heed his every commandment*ᵇ* that I am commanding you today—loving the LORD your God, and serving him with all your heart and with all your soul— ¹⁴then he*ᶜ* will give the rain for your land in its season, the early rain and the later rain, and you will gather in your grain, your wine, and your oil; ¹⁵and he*ᶜ* will give grass in your fields for your livestock, and you will eat your fill. ¹⁶Take care, or you will be seduced into turning away, serving other gods and worshiping them, ¹⁷for then the anger of the LORD will be kindled against you and he will shut up the heavens, so that there will be no rain and the land will yield no fruit; then you

---

a Or *Sea of Reeds*   *b* Compare Gk: Heb *my commandments*   *c* Sam Gk Vg: MT *I*

will perish quickly off the good land that the LORD is giving you.

18 You shall put these words of mine in your heart and soul, and you shall bind them as a sign on your hand, and fix them as an emblem[a] on your forehead. [19]Teach them to your children, talking about them when you are at home and when you are away, when you lie down and when you rise. [20]Write them on the doorposts of your house and on your gates, [21]so that your days and the days of your children may be multiplied in the land that the LORD swore to your ancestors to give them, as long as the heavens are above the earth.

22 If you will diligently observe this entire commandment that I am commanding you, loving the LORD your God, walking in all his ways, and holding fast to him, [23]then the LORD will drive out all these nations before you, and you will dispossess nations larger and mightier than yourselves. [24]Every place on which you set foot shall be yours; your territory shall extend from the wilderness to the Lebanon and from the River, the river Euphrates, to the Western Sea. [25]No one will be able to stand against you; the LORD your God will put the fear and dread of you on all the land on which you set foot, as he promised you.

26 See, I am setting before you today a blessing and a curse: [27]the blessing, if you obey the commandments of the LORD your God that I am commanding you today; [28]and the curse, if you do not obey the commandments of the LORD your God, but turn from the way that I am commanding you today, to follow other gods that you have not known.

29 When the LORD your God has brought you into the land that you are entering to occupy, you shall set the blessing on Mount Gerizim and the curse on Mount Ebal. [30]As you know, they are beyond the Jordan, some distance to the west, in the land of the Canaanites who live in the Arabah, opposite Gilgal, beside the oak[b] of Moreh.

31 When you cross the Jordan to go in to occupy the land that the LORD your God is giving you, and when you occupy it and live in it, [32]you must diligently observe all the statutes and ordinances that I am setting before you today.

Pagan Shrines to Be Destroyed

12 These are the statutes and ordinances that you must diligently observe in the land that the LORD, the God of your ancestors, has given you to occupy all the days that you live on the earth. [2] You must demolish completely all the places where the nations whom you are about to dispossess served their gods, on the mountain heights, on the hills, and under every leafy tree. [3]Break down their altars, smash their pillars, burn their sacred poles[c] with fire, and hew down the idols of their gods, and thus blot out their name from their places. [4]You shall not worship the LORD your God in such ways. [5]But you shall seek the place that the LORD your God will choose out of all your tribes as his habitation to put his name there. You shall go there, [6]bringing there your burnt offerings and your sacrifices, your tithes and your donations, your votive gifts, your freewill offerings, and the firstlings of your herds and flocks. [7]And you shall eat there in the presence of the LORD your God, you and

---

Remembering With Symbols

DEUTERONOMY 11.18

The Christian church has often made elaborate use of symbols to help its adherents "remember to remember." Byzantine churches, for example, were frequently designed in the shape of a cross. In art, the Holy Spirit was often symbolized as fire or a dove; the Trinity has been symbolized by a triangle or three interlocking circles. Some branches of the church have used colors to mark the seasons of the church year: white for Easter and Christmas, red for Pentecost, purple for Lent and Advent. Think about some ways you might incorporate symbols into your life to help you remember eternal truths. Think of a symbol you can carry with you—perhaps while you drive in your car—or one you can put on the main entrance of your home. (See Numbers 15.37–40.)

See Meeting God in Everyday Life

Remembering With Gifts

DEUTERONOMY 12.6,11

God has ordained the tithe—giving a portion of our goods and resources to his work—as one of the ways to help us remember that the Lord is the source of all blessings. Instead of mindlessly dropping a check in the offering plate or the mail, try to make your giving a spiritually enriching experience, an expression of a worshipful and grateful heart. The next time you write out a check to a favorite charity or ministry, consciously connect it with a blessing God has given you: "Lord, this is in honor of the health you've given us"; "Lord, thank you for providing us with our children"; "Lord, thank you for keeping us warm and well fed."

See *Meeting God in Community*

your households together, rejoicing in all the undertakings in which the LORD your God has blessed you.

8 You shall not act as we are acting here today, all of us according to our own desires, [9]for you have not yet come into the rest and the possession that the LORD your God is giving you. [10]When you cross over the Jordan and live in the land that the LORD your God is allotting to you, and when he gives you rest from your enemies all around so that you live in safety, [11]then you shall bring everything that I command you to the place that the LORD your God will choose as a dwelling for his name: your burnt offerings and your sacrifices, your tithes and your donations, and all your choice votive gifts that you vow to the LORD. [12]And you shall rejoice before the LORD your God, you together with your sons and your daughters, your male and female slaves, and the Levites who reside in your towns (since they have no allotment or inheritance with you).

A Prescribed Place of Worship

13 Take care that you do not offer your burnt offerings at any place you happen to see. [14]But only at the place that the LORD will choose in one of your tribes—there you shall offer your burnt offerings and there you shall do everything I command you.

15 Yet whenever you desire you may slaughter and eat meat within any of your towns, according to the blessing that the LORD your God has given you; the unclean and the clean may eat of it, as they would of gazelle or deer. [16]The blood, however, you must not eat; you shall pour it out on the ground like water. [17]Nor may you eat within your towns the tithe of your grain, your wine, and your oil, the firstlings of your herds and your flocks, any of your votive gifts that you vow, your freewill offerings, or your donations; [18]these you shall eat in the presence of the LORD your God at the place that the LORD your God will choose, you together with your son and your daughter, your male and female slaves, and the Levites resident in your towns, rejoicing in the presence of the LORD your God in all your undertakings. [19]Take care that you do not neglect the Levite as long as you live in your land.

20 When the LORD your God enlarges your territory, as he has promised you, and you say, "I am going to eat some meat," because you wish to eat meat, you may eat meat whenever you have the desire. [21]If the place where the LORD your God will choose to put his name is too far from you, and you slaughter as I have commanded you any of your herd or flock that the LORD has given you, then you may eat within your towns whenever you desire. [22]Indeed, just as gazelle or deer is eaten, so you may eat it; the unclean and the clean alike may eat it. [23]Only be sure that you do not eat the blood; for the blood is the life, and you shall not eat the life with the meat. [24]Do not eat it; you shall pour it out on the ground like water. [25]Do not eat it, so that all may go well with you and your children after you, because you do what is right in the sight of the LORD. [26]But the sacred donations that are due from you, and your votive gifts, you shall bring to the place that the LORD will choose. [27]You shall present your burnt offerings, both the meat and the blood, on the altar of the LORD your God; the blood of your other sacrifices shall be poured out beside[a] the altar of the LORD your God, but the meat you may eat.

a Or on

28 Be careful to obey all these words that I command you today,[a] so that it may go well with you and with your children after you forever, because you will be doing what is good and right in the sight of the LORD your God.

Warning against Idolatry

29 When the LORD your God has cut off before you the nations whom you are about to enter to dispossess them, when you have dispossessed them and live in their land, [30]take care that you are not snared into imitating them, after they have been destroyed before you: do not inquire concerning their gods, saying, "How did these nations worship their gods? I also want to do the same." [31]You must not do the same for the LORD your God, because every abhorrent thing that the LORD hates they have done for their gods. They would even burn their sons and their daughters in the fire to their gods. [32][b]You must diligently observe everything that I command you; do not add to it or take anything from it.

13 [c] If prophets or those who divine by dreams appear among you and promise you omens or portents, [2]and the omens or the portents declared by them take place, and they say, "Let us follow other gods" (whom you have not known) "and let us serve them," [3]you must not heed the words of those prophets or those who divine by dreams; for the LORD your God is testing you, to know whether you indeed love the LORD your God with all your heart and soul. [4]The LORD your God you shall follow, him alone you shall fear, his commandments you shall keep, his voice you shall obey, him you shall serve, and to him you shall hold fast. [5]But those prophets or those who divine by dreams shall be put to death for having spoken treason against the LORD your God—who brought you out of the land of Egypt and redeemed you from the house of slavery—to turn you from the way in which the LORD your God commanded you to walk. So you shall purge the evil from your midst.

6 If anyone secretly entices you—even if it is your brother, your father's son or[d] your mother's son, or your own son or daughter, or the wife you embrace, or your most intimate friend—saying, "Let us go worship other gods," whom neither you nor your ancestors have known, [7]any of the gods of the peoples that are around you, whether near you or far away from you, from one end of the earth to the other, [8]you must not yield to or heed any such persons. Show them no pity or compassion and do not shield them. [9]But you shall surely kill them; your own hand shall be first against them to execute them, and afterwards the hand of all the people. [10]Stone them to death for trying to turn you away from the LORD your God, who brought you out of the land of Egypt, out of the house of slavery. [11]Then all Israel shall hear and be afraid, and never again do any such wickedness.

12 If you hear it said about one of the towns that the LORD your God is giving you to live in, [13]that scoundrels from among you have gone out and led the inhabitants of the town astray, saying, "Let us go and worship other gods," whom you have not known, [14]then you shall inquire and make a thorough investigation. If the charge is established that such an abhorrent thing has been done among you, [15]you shall put the inhabitants of that town to the sword, utterly destroying

Hold Fast

DEUTERONOMY 13.4

Have you ever climbed rocks and mountains, or gone water-skiing? If you have, you know the importance of "holding fast" to something. Imagine that a rope is the only thing keeping you from falling hundreds of feet. How tightly would you clasp it?

What are some of the ways we can "hold fast" to God? Moses mentions two ways in this verse—keeping God's commands and serving him—but can you think of any others? Picture yourself holding tightly to a rope. What insights come to mind as you meditate on this passage?

See Meeting God in Scripture

---

a Gk Sam Syr: MT lacks *today*   *b* Ch 13.1 in Heb   *c* Ch 13.2 in Heb
d Sam Gk Compare Tg: MT lacks *your father's son or*

Health and Remembering

DEUTERONOMY 14.1–3

"For the love of God, therefore, regulate yourself prudently both in body and in soul and secure your health as much as you can. And if beyond your power sickness does come to you, be patient and await God's mercy with meekness. At such times, everything is good enough. In fact, it is often true that patience in sickness and in other kinds of trouble is much more pleasing to God than any other devotion you might make when you have your health."

—ANONYMOUS,
The Cloud of Unknowing

it and everything in it—even putting its livestock to the sword. [16]All of its spoil you shall gather into its public square; then burn the town and all its spoil with fire, as a whole burnt offering to the LORD your God. It shall remain a perpetual ruin, never to be rebuilt. [17]Do not let anything devoted to destruction stick to your hand, so that the LORD may turn from his fierce anger and show you compassion, and in his compassion multiply you, as he swore to your ancestors, [18]if you obey the voice of the LORD your God by keeping all his commandments that I am commanding you today, doing what is right in the sight of the LORD your God.

Pagan Practices Forbidden

14 You are children of the LORD your God. You must not lacerate yourselves or shave your forelocks for the dead. [2]For you are a people holy to the LORD your God; it is you the LORD has chosen out of all the peoples on earth to be his people, his treasured possession.

Clean and Unclean Foods

3 You shall not eat any abhorrent thing. [4]These are the animals you may eat: the ox, the sheep, the goat, [5]the deer, the gazelle, the roebuck, the wild goat, the ibex, the antelope, and the mountain-sheep. [6]Any animal that divides the hoof and has the hoof cleft in two, and chews the cud, among the animals, you may eat. [7]Yet of those that chew the cud or have the hoof cleft you shall not eat these: the camel, the hare, and the rock badger, because they chew the cud but do not divide the hoof; they are unclean for you. [8]And the pig, because it divides the hoof but does not chew the cud, is unclean for you. You shall not eat their meat, and you shall not touch their carcasses.

9 Of all that live in water you may eat these: whatever has fins and scales you may eat. [10]And whatever does not have fins and scales you shall not eat; it is unclean for you.

11 You may eat any clean birds. [12]But these are the ones that you shall not eat: the eagle, the vulture, the osprey, [13]the buzzard, the kite of any kind; [14]every raven of any kind; [15]the ostrich, the nighthawk, the sea gull, the hawk of any kind; [16]the little owl and the great owl, the water hen [17]and the desert owl,[a] the carrion vulture and the cormorant, [18]the stork, the heron of any kind; the hoopoe and the bat.[b] [19]And all winged insects are unclean for you; they shall not be eaten. [20]You may eat any clean winged creature.

21 You shall not eat anything that dies of itself; you may give it to aliens residing in your towns for them to eat, or you may sell it to a foreigner. For you are a people holy to the LORD your God.

You shall not boil a kid in its mother's milk.

Regulations concerning Tithes

22 Set apart a tithe of all the yield of your seed that is brought in yearly from the field. [23]In the presence of the LORD your God, in the place that he will choose as a dwelling for his name, you shall eat the tithe of your grain, your wine, and your oil, as well as the firstlings of your herd and flock, so that you may learn to fear the LORD your God always. [24]But if, when the LORD your God has blessed you, the distance is so

---

a Or *pelican*   *b* Identification of several of the birds in verses 12-18 is uncertain

great that you are unable to transport it, because the place where the LORD your God will choose to set his name is too far away from you, [25]then you may turn it into money. With the money secure in hand, go to the place that the LORD your God will choose; [26]spend the money for whatever you wish— oxen, sheep, wine, strong drink, or whatever you desire. And you shall eat there in the presence of the LORD your God, you and your household rejoicing together. [27]As for the Levites resident in your towns, do not neglect them, because they have no allotment or inheritance with you.

28 Every third year you shall bring out the full tithe of your produce for that year, and store it within your towns; [29]the Levites, because they have no allotment or inheritance with you, as well as the resident aliens, the orphans, and the widows in your towns, may come and eat their fill so that the LORD your God may bless you in all the work that you undertake.

Laws concerning the Sabbatical Year

15 Every seventh year you shall grant a remission of debts. [2]And this is the manner of the remission: every creditor shall remit the claim that is held against a neighbor, not exacting it of a neighbor who is a member of the community, because the LORD's remission has been proclaimed. [3]Of a foreigner you may exact it, but you must remit your claim on whatever any member of your community owes you. [4]There will, however, be no one in need among you, because the LORD is sure to bless you in the land that the LORD your God is giving you as a possession to occupy, [5]if only you will obey the LORD your God by diligently observing this entire commandment that I command you today. [6]When the LORD your God has blessed you, as he promised you, you will lend to many nations, but you will not borrow; you will rule over many nations, but they will not rule over you.

7 If there is among you anyone in need, a member of your community in any of your towns within the land that the LORD your God is giving you, do not be hard-hearted or tight-fisted toward your needy neighbor. [8]You should rather open your hand, willingly lending enough to meet the need, whatever it may be. [9]Be careful that you do not entertain a mean thought, thinking, "The seventh year, the year of remission, is near," and therefore view your needy neighbor with hostility and give nothing; your neighbor might cry to the LORD against you, and you would incur guilt. [10]Give liberally and be ungrudging when you do so, for on this account the LORD your God will bless you in all your work and in all that you undertake. [11]Since there will never cease to be some in need on the earth, I therefore command you, "Open your hand to the poor and needy neighbor in your land."

12 If a member of your community, whether a Hebrew man or a Hebrew woman, is sold[a] to you and works for you six years, in the seventh year you shall set that person free. [13]And when you send a male slave[b] out from you a free person, you shall not send him out empty-handed. [14]Provide liberally out of your flock, your threshing floor, and your wine press, thus giving to him some of the bounty with which the LORD your God has blessed you. [15]Remember that you were a slave in the land of Egypt, and the LORD your God redeemed you; for this reason I lay this command upon you today. [16]But

---

Remember With a Party

DEUTERONOMY 14.26

Have you ever thought of organizing a party specifically to celebrate God's goodness? Here the Israelites are commanded to take some of the money they have set aside and buy their favorite food and drink so that they can celebrate the Lord's presence. Consider planning such an affair. Whom would you invite (see 15.11)? What would you serve? What activities would you want to organize? On what would the celebration focus? As an act of worship, take the next step and actually hold such a party. Celebrate God!

See Meeting God in Worship

---

a Or sells himself or herself   b Heb him

Remember With Food

DEUTERONOMY 16.1–3

To enter into the spirit of the verse, make a list of foods that will help you remember God's work in history. We often bake Christmas cookies, for example, but what can you do during the rest of the year? What foods might you prepare around Easter or Pentecost to help you commemorate those days? A number of books are available to tell you how to you cook a Passover meal and organize a seder table. Your family might remember God's work through Esther and Mordecai by making *Hamantashen*, triangular-shaped cookies resembling the hat that Haman wore. Get creative and "pray with your oven." How can you help your family remember God with food?

See Meeting God in Everyday Life

if he says to you, "I will not go out from you," because he loves you and your household, since he is well off with you, [17]then you shall take an awl and thrust it through his earlobe into the door, and he shall be your slave[a] forever.

You shall do the same with regard to your female slave.[b]

18 Do not consider it a hardship when you send them out from you free persons, because for six years they have given you services worth the wages of hired laborers; and the LORD your God will bless you in all that you do.

The Firstborn of Livestock

19 Every firstling male born of your herd and flock you shall consecrate to the LORD your God; you shall not do work with your firstling ox nor shear the firstling of your flock. [20]You shall eat it, you together with your household, in the presence of the LORD your God year by year at the place that the LORD will choose. [21]But if it has any defect—any serious defect, such as lameness or blindness—you shall not sacrifice it to the LORD your God; [22]within your towns you may eat it, the unclean and the clean alike, as you would a gazelle or deer. [23]Its blood, however, you must not eat; you shall pour it out on the ground like water.

The Passover Reviewed

16 Observe the month[c] of Abib by keeping the passover to the LORD your God, for in the month of Abib the LORD your God brought you out of Egypt by night. [2]You shall offer the passover sacrifice to the LORD your God, from the flock and the herd, at the place that the LORD will choose as a dwelling for his name. [3]You must not eat with it anything leavened. For seven days you shall eat unleavened bread with it—the bread of affliction—because you came out of the land of Egypt in great haste, so that all the days of your life you may remember the day of your departure from the land of Egypt. [4]No leaven shall be seen with you in all your territory for seven days; and none of the meat of what you slaughter on the evening of the first day shall remain until morning. [5]You are not permitted to offer the passover sacrifice within any of your towns that the LORD your God is giving you. [6]But at the place that the LORD your God will choose as a dwelling for his name, only there shall you offer the passover sacrifice, in the evening at sunset, the time of day when you departed from Egypt. [7]You shall cook it and eat it at the place that the LORD your God will choose; the next morning you may go back to your tents. [8]For six days you shall continue to eat unleavened bread, and on the seventh day there shall be a solemn assembly for the LORD your God, when you shall do no work.

The Festival of Weeks Reviewed

9 You shall count seven weeks; begin to count the seven weeks from the time the sickle is first put to the standing grain. [10]Then you shall keep the festival of weeks to the LORD your God, contributing a freewill offering in proportion to the blessing that you have received from the LORD your God. [11]Rejoice before the LORD your God—you and your sons and your daughters, your male and female slaves, the Levites resident in your towns, as well as the strangers, the orphans, and the widows who are among you—at the place that the LORD your

a Or *bondman*   *b* Or *bondwoman*   *c* Or *new moon*

God will choose as a dwelling for his name. ¹²Remember that you were a slave in Egypt, and diligently observe these statutes.

The Festival of Booths Reviewed

13 You shall keep the festival of booths[a] for seven days, when you have gathered in the produce from your threshing floor and your wine press. ¹⁴Rejoice during your festival, you and your sons and your daughters, your male and female slaves, as well as the Levites, the strangers, the orphans, and the widows resident in your towns. ¹⁵Seven days you shall keep the festival to the LORD your God at the place that the LORD will choose; for the LORD your God will bless you in all your produce and in all your undertakings, and you shall surely celebrate.

16 Three times a year all your males shall appear before the LORD your God at the place that he will choose: at the festival of unleavened bread, at the festival of weeks, and at the festival of booths.[a] They shall not appear before the LORD empty-handed; ¹⁷all shall give as they are able, according to the blessing of the LORD your God that he has given you.

Municipal Judges and Officers

18 You shall appoint judges and officials throughout your tribes, in all your towns that the LORD your God is giving you, and they shall render just decisions for the people. ¹⁹You must not distort justice; you must not show partiality; and you must not accept bribes, for a bribe blinds the eyes of the wise and subverts the cause of those who are in the right. ²⁰Justice, and only justice, you shall pursue, so that you may live and occupy the land that the LORD your God is giving you.

Forbidden Forms of Worship

21 You shall not plant any tree as a sacred pole[b] beside the altar that you make for the LORD your God; ²²nor shall you set up a stone pillar—things that the LORD your God hates.

17 You must not sacrifice to the LORD your God an ox or a sheep that has a defect, anything seriously wrong; for that is abhorrent to the LORD your God.

2 If there is found among you, in one of your towns that the LORD your God is giving you, a man or woman who does what is evil in the sight of the LORD your God, and transgresses his covenant ³by going to serve other gods and worshiping them—whether the sun or the moon or any of the host of heaven, which I have forbidden— ⁴and if it is reported to you or you hear of it, and you make a thorough inquiry, and the charge is proved true that such an abhorrent thing has occurred in Israel, ⁵then you shall bring out to your gates that man or that woman who has committed this crime and you shall stone the man or woman to death. ⁶On the evidence of two or three witnesses the death sentence shall be executed; a person must not be put to death on the evidence of only one witness. ⁷The hands of the witnesses shall be the first raised against the person to execute the death penalty, and afterward the hands of all the people. So you shall purge the evil from your midst.

Legal Decisions by Priests and Judges

8 If a judicial decision is too difficult for you to make be-

A House of Mirrors

DEUTERONOMY 16.18–20

Have you ever walked through a carnival "house of mirrors"? Try to imagine what it would be like to walk through a dark place where you've never been before, to look into mirrors that distort your image into funny or grotesque shapes and to walk on planks that move so that you're unsure of your footing. Imagine what it would be like *living* in that world. Now compare that with living in the world as we know it—defined shapes, solid ground, well-lit corridors. According to Moses, doing business and making laws according to greed, bribery and unfairness distort our world. How would you describe the way *you* do business or approach the law? Do others feel as if they are in a house of mirrors when they do business with you? Write down a code of ethics for the way you do business. What "laws" are the basis for your actions?

See Meeting God in Everyday Life

Leading Under Authority

DEUTERONOMY 17.18–20

Why do you think it is important for the king to consciously place himself under God's authority? What might happen if he considers himself autonomous, the final word for how the kingdom is to be run? What types of authority has God placed in your hands? How do God's laws, commands and scriptures direct you to behave in these situations? How might your leadership be shaped by remembering not to consider yourself better than those you lead? Is there a symbol you can develop (a facsimile of the scrolled copy of the law the king was to make, for example) to help you remember God's authority over you?

See Meeting God in Community

tween one kind of bloodshed and another, one kind of legal right and another, or one kind of assault and another—any such matters of dispute in your towns—then you shall immediately go up to the place that the LORD your God will choose, [9]where you shall consult with the levitical priests and the judge who is in office in those days; they shall announce to you the decision in the case. [10]Carry out exactly the decision that they announce to you from the place that the LORD will choose, diligently observing everything they instruct you. [11]You must carry out fully the law that they interpret for you or the ruling that they announce to you; do not turn aside from the decision that they announce to you, either to the right or to the left. [12]As for anyone who presumes to disobey the priest appointed to minister there to the LORD your God, or the judge, that person shall die. So you shall purge the evil from Israel. [13]All the people will hear and be afraid, and will not act presumptuously again.

Limitations of Royal Authority

14 When you have come into the land that the LORD your God is giving you, and have taken possession of it and settled in it, and you say, "I will set a king over me, like all the nations that are around me," [15]you may indeed set over you a king whom the LORD your God will choose. One of your own community you may set as king over you; you are not permitted to put a foreigner over you, who is not of your own community. [16]Even so, he must not acquire many horses for himself, or return the people to Egypt in order to acquire more horses, since the LORD has said to you, "You must never return that way again." [17]And he must not acquire many wives for himself, or else his heart will turn away; also silver and gold he must not acquire in great quantity for himself. [18]When he has taken the throne of his kingdom, he shall have a copy of this law written for him in the presence of the levitical priests. [19]It shall remain with him and he shall read in it all the days of his life, so that he may learn to fear the LORD his God, diligently observing all the words of this law and these statutes, [20]neither exalting himself above other members of the community nor turning aside from the commandment, either to the right or to the left, so that he and his descendants may reign long over his kingdom in Israel.

Privileges of Priests and Levites

18 The levitical priests, the whole tribe of Levi, shall have no allotment or inheritance within Israel. They may eat the sacrifices that are the LORD's portion[a] [2]but they shall have no inheritance among the other members of the community; the LORD is their inheritance, as he promised them.

3 This shall be the priests' due from the people, from those offering a sacrifice, whether an ox or a sheep: they shall give to the priest the shoulder, the two jowls, and the stomach. [4]The first fruits of your grain, your wine, and your oil, as well as the first of the fleece of your sheep, you shall give him. [5]For the LORD your God has chosen Levi[b] out of all your tribes, to stand and minister in the name of the LORD, him and his sons for all time.

6 If a Levite leaves any of your towns, from wherever he has been residing in Israel, and comes to the place that the LORD will choose (and he may come whenever he wishes),

a Meaning of Heb uncertain   *b* Heb *him*

[7]then he may minister in the name of the LORD his God, like all his fellow-Levites who stand to minister there before the LORD. [8]They shall have equal portions to eat, even though they have income from the sale of family possessions.[a]

Child-Sacrifice, Divination, and Magic Prohibited

9 When you come into the land that the LORD your God is giving you, you must not learn to imitate the abhorrent practices of those nations. [10]No one shall be found among you who makes a son or daughter pass through fire, or who practices divination, or is a soothsayer, or an augur, or a sorcerer, [11]or one who casts spells, or who consults ghosts or spirits, or who seeks oracles from the dead. [12]For whoever does these things is abhorrent to the LORD; it is because of such abhorrent practices that the LORD your God is driving them out before you. [13]You must remain completely loyal to the LORD your God. [14]Although these nations that you are about to dispossess do give heed to soothsayers and diviners, as for you, the LORD your God does not permit you to do so.

A New Prophet Like Moses

15 The LORD your God will raise up for you a prophet[b] like me from among your own people; you shall heed such a prophet.[c] [16]This is what you requested of the LORD your God at Horeb on the day of the assembly when you said: "If I hear the voice of the LORD my God any more, or ever again see this great fire, I will die." [17]Then the LORD replied to me: "They are right in what they have said. [18]I will raise up for them a prophet[b] like you from among their own people; I will put my words in the mouth of the prophet,[d] who shall speak to them everything that I command. [19]Anyone who does not heed the words that the prophet[e] shall speak in my name, I myself will hold accountable. [20]But any prophet who speaks in the name of other gods, or who presumes to speak in my name a word that I have not commanded the prophet to speak—that prophet shall die." [21]You may say to yourself, "How can we recognize a word that the LORD has not spoken?" [22]If a prophet speaks in the name of the LORD but the thing does not take place or prove true, it is a word that the LORD has not spoken. The prophet has spoken it presumptuously; do not be frightened by it.

Laws concerning the Cities of Refuge

19 When the LORD your God has cut off the nations whose land the LORD your God is giving you, and you have dispossessed them and settled in their towns and in their houses, [2]you shall set apart three cities in the land that the LORD your God is giving you to possess. [3]You shall calculate the distances[f] and divide into three regions the land that the LORD your God gives you as a possession, so that any homicide can flee to one of them.

4 Now this is the case of a homicide who might flee there and live, that is, someone who has killed another person unintentionally when the two had not been at enmity before: [5]Suppose someone goes into the forest with another to cut wood, and when one of them swings the ax to cut down a tree, the head slips from the handle and strikes the other person who then dies; the killer may flee to one of these cities

Refuge and Mercy

DEUTERONOMY 19.1–7

Have you ever unintentionally harmed someone? Imagine yourself in a situation such as the one described in verse 5. You are cutting wood with a good friend when an accident occurs and your friend is killed. What goes through your mind? Now remember that the friend's family is obligated to kill you in order to honor its relative. What are you feeling now? Map out in your mind (or on paper) how God specifically instructed the cities of refuge to be made accessible. What does this attention to detail say about God's mercy? In what ways do you or someone you know need "refuge" today?

See Meeting God in Community

---

a Meaning of Heb uncertain   *b* Or *prophets*   *c* Or *such prophets*
d Or *mouths of the prophets*   *e* Heb *he*   *f* Or *prepare roads to them*

Strength From the Past

DEUTERONOMY 20.1

Moses tells the Israelites to overcome their fear by remembering God's provision in the past—the same God who brought them out of Egypt would continue to fight their battles in the future. Spend some time writing a history of God's provision in your life. You might want to write it in the form of a poem, a song, a list or a short narrative that consists of the key moments in your life—moments when God delivered you from trials or provided strength to handle them. What will you title this work of remembering? Is there a general theme that flows throughout? Are you going through a current trial in which you need to remember how God has helped you in the past?

See Meeting God in Everyday Life

and live. 6But if the distance is too great, the avenger of blood in hot anger might pursue and overtake and put the killer to death, although a death sentence was not deserved, since the two had not been at enmity before. 7Therefore I command you: You shall set apart three cities.

8 If the Lord your God enlarges your territory, as he swore to your ancestors—and he will give you all the land that he promised your ancestors to give you, 9provided you diligently observe this entire commandment that I command you today, by loving the Lord your God and walking always in his ways—then you shall add three more cities to these three, 10so that the blood of an innocent person may not be shed in the land that the Lord your God is giving you as an inheritance, thereby bringing bloodguilt upon you.

11 But if someone at enmity with another lies in wait and attacks and takes the life of that person, and flees into one of these cities, 12then the elders of the killer's city shall send to have the culprit taken from there and handed over to the avenger of blood to be put to death. 13Show no pity; you shall purge the guilt of innocent blood from Israel, so that it may go well with you.

Property Boundaries

14 You must not move your neighbor's boundary marker, set up by former generations, on the property that will be allotted to you in the land that the Lord your God is giving you to possess.

Law concerning Witnesses

15 A single witness shall not suffice to convict a person of any crime or wrongdoing in connection with any offense that may be committed. Only on the evidence of two or three witnesses shall a charge be sustained. 16If a malicious witness comes forward to accuse someone of wrongdoing, 17then both parties to the dispute shall appear before the Lord, before the priests and the judges who are in office in those days, 18and the judges shall make a thorough inquiry. If the witness is a false witness, having testified falsely against another, 19then you shall do to the false witness just as the false witness had meant to do to the other. So you shall purge the evil from your midst. 20The rest shall hear and be afraid, and a crime such as this shall never again be committed among you. 21Show no pity: life for life, eye for eye, tooth for tooth, hand for hand, foot for foot.

Rules of Warfare

20 When you go out to war against your enemies, and see horses and chariots, an army larger than your own, you shall not be afraid of them; for the Lord your God is with you, who brought you up from the land of Egypt. 2Before you engage in battle, the priest shall come forward and speak to the troops, 3and shall say to them: "Hear, O Israel! Today you are drawing near to do battle against your enemies. Do not lose heart, or be afraid, or panic, or be in dread of them; 4for it is the Lord your God who goes with you, to fight for you against your enemies, to give you victory." 5Then the officials shall address the troops, saying, "Has anyone built a new house but not dedicated it? He should go back to his house, or he might die in the battle and another dedicate it. 6Has anyone planted a vineyard but not yet enjoyed its fruit? He should go back to his house, or he might die in the

battle and another be first to enjoy its fruit. ⁷Has anyone become engaged to a woman but not yet married her? He should go back to his house, or he might die in the battle and another marry her." ⁸The officials shall continue to address the troops, saying, "Is anyone afraid or disheartened? He should go back to his house, or he might cause the heart of his comrades to melt like his own." ⁹When the officials have finished addressing the troops, then the commanders shall take charge of them.

10 When you draw near to a town to fight against it, offer it terms of peace. ¹¹If it accepts your terms of peace and surrenders to you, then all the people in it shall serve you at forced labor. ¹²If it does not submit to you peacefully, but makes war against you, then you shall besiege it; ¹³and when the LORD your God gives it into your hand, you shall put all its males to the sword. ¹⁴You may, however, take as your booty the women, the children, livestock, and everything else in the town, all its spoil. You may enjoy the spoil of your enemies, which the LORD your God has given you. ¹⁵Thus you shall treat all the towns that are very far from you, which are not towns of the nations here. ¹⁶But as for the towns of these peoples that the LORD your God is giving you as an inheritance, you must not let anything that breathes remain alive. ¹⁷You shall annihilate them—the Hittites and the Amorites, the Canaanites and the Perizzites, the Hivites and the Jebusites—just as the LORD your God has commanded, ¹⁸so that they may not teach you to do all the abhorrent things that they do for their gods, and you thus sin against the LORD your God.

19 If you besiege a town for a long time, making war against it in order to take it, you must not destroy its trees by wielding an ax against them. Although you may take food from them, you must not cut them down. Are trees in the field human beings that they should come under siege from you? ²⁰You may destroy only the trees that you know do not produce food; you may cut them down for use in building siegeworks against the town that makes war with you, until it falls.

Law concerning Murder by Persons Unknown

21 If, in the land that the LORD your God is giving you to possess, a body is found lying in open country, and it is not known who struck the person down, ²then your elders and your judges shall come out to measure the distances to the towns that are near the body. ³The elders of the town nearest the body shall take a heifer that has never been worked, one that has not pulled in the yoke; ⁴the elders of that town shall bring the heifer down to a wadi with running water, which is neither plowed nor sown, and shall break the heifer's neck there in the wadi. ⁵Then the priests, the sons of Levi, shall come forward, for the LORD your God has chosen them to minister to him and to pronounce blessings in the name of the LORD, and by their decision all cases of dispute and assault shall be settled. ⁶All the elders of that town nearest the body shall wash their hands over the heifer whose neck was broken in the wadi, ⁷and they shall declare: "Our hands did not shed this blood, nor were we witnesses to it. ⁸Absolve, O LORD, your people Israel, whom you redeemed; do not let the guilt of innocent blood remain in the midst of your people Israel." Then they will be absolved of bloodguilt. ⁹So you shall purge the guilt of innocent blood from your

Loving God's Creation

DEUTERONOMY 20.19–20

Whether this command has to do with the humane treatment of wildlife or with preservation of the food supply, it calls for a gentle concern for the natural world. Christians have a long tradition of appreciating the beauty of creation and caring for nature. How might your care and stewardship of creation be considered a form of prayer, worship and service toward God? Reflect on ways that you might show your allegiance to the Creator by caring for the earth.

See Meeting God in the Created Order

A New Start

DEUTERONOMY 21.10–14

When a captive woman shaved her head, cut her nails and discarded her clothes, her actions could be rituals of mourning or symbolic of her subjugation. One commentator suggests that such actions may have been symbolic of initiation into a new way of life: "It is with new hair, nails and clothes that she enters on her new life as a married woman in Israel." Have you ever considered changing your outward appearance to reflect an inner, spiritual change —shaving your beard, cutting your hair, choosing a new style of clothing? What change in appearance would be most appropriate in your life? How might it symbolize or direct your prayers throughout the day?

See Meeting God in Everyday Life

midst, because you must do what is right in the sight of the LORD.

Female Captives

10 When you go out to war against your enemies, and the LORD your God hands them over to you and you take them captive, [11]suppose you see among the captives a beautiful woman whom you desire and want to marry, [12]and so you bring her home to your house: she shall shave her head, pare her nails, [13]discard her captive's garb, and shall remain in your house a full month, mourning for her father and mother; after that you may go in to her and be her husband, and she shall be your wife. [14]But if you are not satisfied with her, you shall let her go free and not sell her for money. You must not treat her as a slave, since you have dishonored her.

The Right of the Firstborn

15 If a man has two wives, one of them loved and the other disliked, and if both the loved and the disliked have borne him sons, the firstborn being the son of the one who is disliked, [16]then on the day when he wills his possessions to his sons, he is not permitted to treat the son of the loved as the firstborn in preference to the son of the disliked, who is the firstborn. [17]He must acknowledge as firstborn the son of the one who is disliked, giving him a double portion[a] of all that he has; since he is the first issue of his virility, the right of the firstborn is his.

Rebellious Children

18 If someone has a stubborn and rebellious son who will not obey his father and mother, who does not heed them when they discipline him, [19]then his father and his mother shall take hold of him and bring him out to the elders of his town at the gate of that place. [20]They shall say to the elders of his town, "This son of ours is stubborn and rebellious. He will not obey us. He is a glutton and a drunkard." [21]Then all the men of the town shall stone him to death. So you shall purge the evil from your midst; and all Israel will hear, and be afraid.

Miscellaneous Laws

22 When someone is convicted of a crime punishable by death and is executed, and you hang him on a tree, [23]his corpse must not remain all night upon the tree; you shall bury him that same day, for anyone hung on a tree is under God's curse. You must not defile the land that the LORD your God is giving you for possession.

22 You shall not watch your neighbor's ox or sheep straying away and ignore them; you shall take them back to their owner. [2]If the owner does not reside near you or you do not know who the owner is, you shall bring it to your own house, and it shall remain with you until the owner claims it; then you shall return it. [3]You shall do the same with a neighbor's donkey; you shall do the same with a neighbor's garment; and you shall do the same with anything else that your neighbor loses and you find. You may not withhold your help.

4 You shall not see your neighbor's donkey or ox fallen on the road and ignore it; you shall help to lift it up.

5 A woman shall not wear a man's apparel, nor shall a

a Heb *two-thirds*

man put on a woman's garment; for whoever does such things is abhorrent to the LORD your God.

6 If you come on a bird's nest, in any tree or on the ground, with fledglings or eggs, with the mother sitting on the fledglings or on the eggs, you shall not take the mother with the young. [7]Let the mother go, taking only the young for yourself, in order that it may go well with you and you may live long.

8 When you build a new house, you shall make a parapet for your roof; otherwise you might have bloodguilt on your house, if anyone should fall from it.

9 You shall not sow your vineyard with a second kind of seed, or the whole yield will have to be forfeited, both the crop that you have sown and the yield of the vineyard itself.

10 You shall not plow with an ox and a donkey yoked together.

11 You shall not wear clothes made of wool and linen woven together.

12 You shall make tassels on the four corners of the cloak with which you cover yourself.

Laws concerning Sexual Relations

13 Suppose a man marries a woman, but after going in to her, he dislikes her [14]and makes up charges against her, slandering her by saying, "I married this woman; but when I lay with her, I did not find evidence of her virginity." [15]The father of the young woman and her mother shall then submit the evidence of the young woman's virginity to the elders of the city at the gate. [16]The father of the young woman shall say to the elders: "I gave my daughter in marriage to this man but he dislikes her; [17]now he has made up charges against her, saying, 'I did not find evidence of your daughter's virginity.' But here is the evidence of my daughter's virginity." Then they shall spread out the cloth before the elders of the town. [18]The elders of that town shall take the man and punish him; [19]they shall fine him one hundred shekels of silver (which they shall give to the young woman's father) because he has slandered a virgin of Israel. She shall remain his wife; he shall not be permitted to divorce her as long as he lives.

20 If, however, this charge is true, that evidence of the young woman's virginity was not found, [21]then they shall bring the young woman out to the entrance of her father's house and the men of her town shall stone her to death, because she committed a disgraceful act in Israel by prostituting herself in her father's house. So you shall purge the evil from your midst.

22 If a man is caught lying with the wife of another man, both of them shall die, the man who lay with the woman as well as the woman. So you shall purge the evil from Israel.

23 If there is a young woman, a virgin already engaged to be married, and a man meets her in the town and lies with her, [24]you shall bring both of them to the gate of that town and stone them to death, the young woman because she did not cry for help in the town and the man because he violated his neighbor's wife. So you shall purge the evil from your midst.

25 But if the man meets the engaged woman in the open country, and the man seizes her and lies with her, then only the man who lay with her shall die. [26]You shall do nothing to the young woman; the young woman has not committed an offense punishable by death, because this case is like that of

Right Desires

DEUTERONOMY 22.13–30

"Desire not that which is at a great distance, nor that which cannot happen for a long time, as many do, who, by this means, weary and distract their hearts unprofitably. If a married woman desires to be a nun, to what purpose? If I desire to buy my neighbor's goods before he is willing to sell them, is it not a loss of time to entertain this desire? . . . I can by no means approve that persons should desire to amuse themselves in any other kind of life than that in which they are already engaged; nor in any exercises that are incompatible with their present condition; for this dissipates the heart, and makes it unfit for its necessary occupations."

—FRANCIS DE SALES,
Introduction to the Devout Life

Holy Business

DEUTERONOMY 23.19–20

Many people compartmentalize their lives, relegating religion and faith to a weekly worship service; Deuteronomy, however, contains many passages that stress the practical, everyday nature of true faith and worship. Imagine that you are the CEO of a major corporation, or perhaps a land developer, banker, landlord or small-business owner. How would remembering God daily affect the way you do business? Now reflect on your vocational calling. If Moses were writing about what you do, what changes in your daily routine might he suggest?

See Meeting God in Everyday Life

someone who attacks and murders a neighbor. [27]Since he found her in the open country, the engaged woman may have cried for help, but there was no one to rescue her.

28 If a man meets a virgin who is not engaged, and seizes her and lies with her, and they are caught in the act, [29]the man who lay with her shall give fifty shekels of silver to the young woman's father, and she shall become his wife. Because he violated her he shall not be permitted to divorce her as long as he lives.

30[a] A man shall not marry his father's wife, thereby violating his father's rights.[b]

Those Excluded from the Assembly

23 No one whose testicles are crushed or whose penis is cut off shall be admitted to the assembly of the LORD.

2 Those born of an illicit union shall not be admitted to the assembly of the LORD. Even to the tenth generation, none of their descendants shall be admitted to the assembly of the LORD.

3 No Ammonite or Moabite shall be admitted to the assembly of the LORD. Even to the tenth generation, none of their descendants shall be admitted to the assembly of the LORD, [4]because they did not meet you with food and water on your journey out of Egypt, and because they hired against you Balaam son of Beor, from Pethor of Mesopotamia, to curse you. [5](Yet the LORD your God refused to heed Balaam; the LORD your God turned the curse into a blessing for you, because the LORD your God loved you.) [6]You shall never promote their welfare or their prosperity as long as you live.

7 You shall not abhor any of the Edomites, for they are your kin. You shall not abhor any of the Egyptians, because you were an alien residing in their land. [8]The children of the third generation that are born to them may be admitted to the assembly of the LORD.

Sanitary, Ritual, and Humanitarian Precepts

9 When you are encamped against your enemies you shall guard against any impropriety.

10 If one of you becomes unclean because of a nocturnal emission, then he shall go outside the camp; he must not come within the camp. [11]When evening comes, he shall wash himself with water, and when the sun has set, he may come back into the camp.

12 You shall have a designated area outside the camp to which you shall go. [13]With your utensils you shall have a trowel; when you relieve yourself outside, you shall dig a hole with it and then cover up your excrement. [14]Because the LORD your God travels along with your camp, to save you and to hand over your enemies to you, therefore your camp must be holy, so that he may not see anything indecent among you and turn away from you.

15 Slaves who have escaped to you from their owners shall not be given back to them. [16]They shall reside with you, in your midst, in any place they choose in any one of your towns, wherever they please; you shall not oppress them.

17 None of the daughters of Israel shall be a temple prostitute; none of the sons of Israel shall be a temple prostitute. [18]You shall not bring the fee of a prostitute or the wages of a male prostitute[c] into the house of the LORD your God in pay-

254

a Ch 23.1 in Heb   *b* Heb *uncovering his father's skirt*   *c* Heb *a dog* ment for any vow, for both of these are abhorrent to the LORD your God.

19 You shall not charge interest on loans to another Israelite, interest on money, interest on provisions, interest on anything that is lent. ²⁰On loans to a foreigner you may charge interest, but on loans to another Israelite you may not charge interest, so that the LORD your God may bless you in all your undertakings in the land that you are about to enter and possess.

21 If you make a vow to the LORD your God, do not postpone fulfilling it; for the LORD your God will surely require it of you, and you would incur guilt. ²²But if you refrain from vowing, you will not incur guilt. ²³Whatever your lips utter you must diligently perform, just as you have freely vowed to the LORD your God with your own mouth.

24 If you go into your neighbor's vineyard, you may eat your fill of grapes, as many as you wish, but you shall not put any in a container.

25 If you go into your neighbor's standing grain, you may pluck the ears with your hand, but you shall not put a sickle to your neighbor's standing grain.

Laws concerning Marriage and Divorce

24 Suppose a man enters into marriage with a woman, but she does not please him because he finds something objectionable about her, and so he writes her a certificate of divorce, puts it in her hand, and sends her out of his house; she then leaves his house ²and goes off to become another man's wife. ³Then suppose the second man dislikes her, writes her a bill of divorce, puts it in her hand, and sends her out of his house (or the second man who married her dies); ⁴her first husband, who sent her away, is not permitted to take her again to be his wife after she has been defiled; for that would be abhorrent to the LORD, and you shall not bring guilt on the land that the LORD your God is giving you as a possession.

Miscellaneous Laws

5 When a man is newly married, he shall not go out with the army or be charged with any related duty. He shall be free at home one year, to be happy with the wife whom he has married.

6 No one shall take a mill or an upper millstone in pledge, for that would be taking a life in pledge.

7 If someone is caught kidnaping another Israelite, enslaving or selling the Israelite, then that kidnaper shall die. So you shall purge the evil from your midst.

8 Guard against an outbreak of a leprous*a* skin disease by being very careful; you shall carefully observe whatever the levitical priests instruct you, just as I have commanded them. ⁹Remember what the LORD your God did to Miriam on your journey out of Egypt.

10 When you make your neighbor a loan of any kind, you shall not go into the house to take the pledge. ¹¹You shall wait outside, while the person to whom you are making the loan brings the pledge out to you. ¹²If the person is poor, you shall not sleep in the garment given you as*b* the pledge. ¹³You shall give the pledge back by sunset, so that your neighbor may

a A term for several skin diseases; precise meaning uncertain
b Heb lacks *the garment given you as*

Holy Happiness

DEUTERONOMY 24.5

Does it surprise you that serving God might require you to take time off to focus on making someone else happy? Why do you think this pleases God? What sort of limits might be placed on this form of remembering God? Reflect on how it would touch you emotionally if someone were to go out of his or her way to please one of your close family members. What might this reveal about God? Given your life circumstances, how can you remember God today by making someone else happy?

See *Meeting God in Service*

Holy Living

DEUTERONOMY 23.15—25.19

This passage offers the Israelites guidelines for many aspects of life—covering everything from eating too much from a neighbor's garden to paying wages on time to honest weights and measures. As varied as these laws are, the principles underlying them are familiar and simple: justice, honesty, compassion and so forth.

As you read through this list of laws, see whether you can discern the Biblical principle that each law upholds. Beside each law, jot down this principle in the margin of your Bible. Think of some of the laws and mores that govern our day-to-day life. What Biblical principles do they uphold, if any? How do common sense, self-control, courtesy and thoughtfulness grow from these principles?

Use this exercise as a springboard for examining your own behavior. What principles govern your actions as you drive your car, shop for groceries, write out your monthly bills or gather with others in the lunchroom?

See *Meeting God in Everyday Life*

sleep in the cloak and bless you; and it will be to your credit before the LORD your God.

14 You shall not withhold the wages of poor and needy laborers, whether other Israelites or aliens who reside in your land in one of your towns. ¹⁵You shall pay them their wages daily before sunset, because they are poor and their livelihood depends on them; otherwise they might cry to the LORD against you, and you would incur guilt.

16 Parents shall not be put to death for their children, nor shall children be put to death for their parents; only for their own crimes may persons be put to death.

17 You shall not deprive a resident alien or an orphan of justice; you shall not take a widow's garment in pledge. ¹⁸Remember that you were a slave in Egypt and the LORD your God redeemed you from there; therefore I command you to do this.

19 When you reap your harvest in your field and forget a sheaf in the field, you shall not go back to get it; it shall be left for the alien, the orphan, and the widow, so that the LORD your God may bless you in all your undertakings. ²⁰When you beat your olive trees, do not strip what is left; it shall be for the alien, the orphan, and the widow.

21 When you gather the grapes of your vineyard, do not glean what is left; it shall be for the alien, the orphan, and the widow. ²²Remember that you were a slave in the land of Egypt; therefore I am commanding you to do this.

25 Suppose two persons have a dispute and enter into litigation, and the judges decide between them, declaring one to be in the right and the other to be in the wrong. ²If the one in the wrong deserves to be flogged, the judge shall make that person lie down and be beaten in his presence with the number of lashes proportionate to the offense. ³Forty lashes may be given but not more; if more lashes than these are given, your neighbor will be degraded in your sight.

4 You shall not muzzle an ox while it is treading out the grain.

Levirate Marriage

5 When brothers reside together, and one of them dies and has no son, the wife of the deceased shall not be married outside the family to a stranger. Her husband's brother shall go in to her, taking her in marriage, and performing the duty of a husband's brother to her, ⁶and the firstborn whom she bears shall succeed to the name of the deceased brother, so that his name may not be blotted out of Israel. ⁷But if the man has no desire to marry his brother's widow, then his brother's widow shall go up to the elders at the gate and say, "My husband's brother refuses to perpetuate his brother's name in Israel; he will not perform the duty of a husband's brother to me." ⁸Then the elders of his town shall summon him and speak to him. If he persists, saying, "I have no desire to marry her," ⁹then his brother's wife shall go up to him in the presence of the elders, pull his sandal off his foot, spit in his face, and declare, "This is what is done to the man who does not build up his brother's house." ¹⁰Throughout Israel his family shall be known as "the house of him whose sandal was pulled off."

Various Commands

11 If men get into a fight with one another, and the wife of one intervenes to rescue her husband from the grip of his op-

ponent by reaching out and seizing his genitals, [12]you shall cut off her hand; show no pity.

13 You shall not have in your bag two kinds of weights, large and small. [14]You shall not have in your house two kinds of measures, large and small. [15]You shall have only a full and honest weight; you shall have only a full and honest measure, so that your days may be long in the land that the LORD your God is giving you. [16]For all who do such things, all who act dishonestly, are abhorrent to the LORD your God.

17 Remember what Amalek did to you on your journey out of Egypt, [18]how he attacked you on the way, when you were faint and weary, and struck down all who lagged behind you; he did not fear God. [19]Therefore when the LORD your God has given you rest from all your enemies on every hand, in the land that the LORD your God is giving you as an inheritance to possess, you shall blot out the remembrance of Amalek from under heaven; do not forget.

First Fruits and Tithes

26 When you have come into the land that the LORD your God is giving you as an inheritance to possess, and you possess it, and settle in it, [2]you shall take some of the first of all the fruit of the ground, which you harvest from the land that the LORD your God is giving you, and you shall put it in a basket and go to the place that the LORD your God will choose as a dwelling for his name. [3]You shall go to the priest who is in office at that time, and say to him, "Today I declare to the LORD your God that I have come into the land that the LORD swore to our ancestors to give us." [4]When the priest takes the basket from your hand and sets it down before the altar of the LORD your God, [5]you shall make this response before the LORD your God: "A wandering Aramean was my ancestor; he went down into Egypt and lived there as an alien, few in number, and there he became a great nation, mighty and populous. [6]When the Egyptians treated us harshly and afflicted us, by imposing hard labor on us, [7]we cried to the LORD, the God of our ancestors; the LORD heard our voice and saw our affliction, our toil, and our oppression. [8]The LORD brought us out of Egypt with a mighty hand and an outstretched arm, with a terrifying display of power, and with signs and wonders; [9]and he brought us into this place and gave us this land, a land flowing with milk and honey. [10]So now I bring the first of the fruit of the ground that you, O LORD, have given me." You shall set it down before the LORD your God and bow down before the LORD your God. [11]Then you, together with the Levites and the aliens who reside among you, shall celebrate with all the bounty that the LORD your God has given to you and to your house.

12 When you have finished paying all the tithe of your produce in the third year (which is the year of the tithe), giving it to the Levites, the aliens, the orphans, and the widows, so that they may eat their fill within your towns, [13]then you shall say before the LORD your God: "I have removed the sacred portion from the house, and I have given it to the Levites, the resident aliens, the orphans, and the widows, in accordance with your entire commandment that you commanded me; I have neither transgressed nor forgotten any of your commandments: [14]I have not eaten of it while in mourning; I have not removed any of it while I was unclean; and I have not offered any of it to the dead. I have obeyed the LORD my God, doing just as you commanded me. [15]Look down from your

Holy History

DEUTERONOMY 26.1–11

The Israelites are commanded to give the first fruits of their labor and their tithes as a way of remembering God's provision throughout the generations. In this way, remembering becomes a spiritual discipline. Reflect on (or even better, write out) your "spiritual autobiography." How many generations does your family's faith go back? Or perhaps you are the first person in your family to come to faith. Either way, in this autobiography recount the moment when your faith became a personal matter. Tell how God has nurtured you spiritually through the years. How does your history ultimately connect with that of the nation of Israel? With the early church? With the advent of your denomination or congregation? What kind of response does such remembering elicit from you?

See Meeting God in Community

A Visible Reminder

DEUTERONOMY 27.1–8

Moses and the people of Israel built an altar of stone to remind them of the presence of the Lord with them. How might such an altar help them remember God's commandments and laws? Gather your family or roommates together and discuss how you might create such a visible reminder in your home of God's claim on your life. Is there a work of calligraphy, a piece of art or a symbol you can think of? Where will you place it?

See Meeting God in Everyday Life

holy habitation, from heaven, and bless your people Israel and the ground that you have given us, as you swore to our ancestors—a land flowing with milk and honey."

Concluding Exhortation

16 This very day the Lord your God is commanding you to observe these statutes and ordinances; so observe them diligently with all your heart and with all your soul. [17]Today you have obtained the Lord's agreement: to be your God; and for you to walk in his ways, to keep his statutes, his commandments, and his ordinances, and to obey him. [18]Today the Lord has obtained your agreement: to be his treasured people, as he promised you, and to keep his commandments; [19]for him to set you high above all nations that he has made, in praise and in fame and in honor; and for you to be a people holy to the Lord your God, as he promised.

The Inscribed Stones and Altar on Mount Ebal

27 Then Moses and the elders of Israel charged all the people as follows: Keep the entire commandment that I am commanding you today. [2]On the day that you cross over the Jordan into the land that the Lord your God is giving you, you shall set up large stones and cover them with plaster. [3]You shall write on them all the words of this law when you have crossed over, to enter the land that the Lord your God is giving you, a land flowing with milk and honey, as the Lord, the God of your ancestors, promised you. [4]So when you have crossed over the Jordan, you shall set up these stones, about which I am commanding you today, on Mount Ebal, and you shall cover them with plaster. [5]And you shall build an altar there to the Lord your God, an altar of stones on which you have not used an iron tool. [6]You must build the altar of the Lord your God of unhewn[a] stones. Then offer up burnt offerings on it to the Lord your God, [7]make sacrifices of well-being, and eat them there, rejoicing before the Lord your God. [8]You shall write on the stones all the words of this law very clearly.

9 Then Moses and the levitical priests spoke to all Israel, saying: Keep silence and hear, O Israel! This very day you have become the people of the Lord your God. [10]Therefore obey the Lord your God, observing his commandments and his statutes that I am commanding you today.

Twelve Curses

11 The same day Moses charged the people as follows: [12]When you have crossed over the Jordan, these shall stand on Mount Gerizim for the blessing of the people: Simeon, Levi, Judah, Issachar, Joseph, and Benjamin. [13]And these shall stand on Mount Ebal for the curse: Reuben, Gad, Asher, Zebulun, Dan, and Naphtali. [14]Then the Levites shall declare in a loud voice to all the Israelites:

15 "Cursed be anyone who makes an idol or casts an image, anything abhorrent to the Lord, the work of an artisan, and sets it up in secret." All the people shall respond, saying, "Amen!"

16 "Cursed be anyone who dishonors father or mother." All the people shall say, "Amen!"

17 "Cursed be anyone who moves a neighbor's boundary marker." All the people shall say, "Amen!"

a Heb whole

18 "Cursed be anyone who misleads a blind person on the road." All the people shall say, "Amen!"

19 "Cursed be anyone who deprives the alien, the orphan, and the widow of justice." All the people shall say, "Amen!"

20 "Cursed be anyone who lies with his father's wife, because he has violated his father's rights."[a] All the people shall say, "Amen!"

21 "Cursed be anyone who lies with any animal." All the people shall say, "Amen!"

22 "Cursed be anyone who lies with his sister, whether the daughter of his father or the daughter of his mother." All the people shall say, "Amen!"

23 "Cursed be anyone who lies with his mother-in-law." All the people shall say, "Amen!"

24 "Cursed be anyone who strikes down a neighbor in secret." All the people shall say, "Amen!"

25 "Cursed be anyone who takes a bribe to shed innocent blood." All the people shall say, "Amen!"

26 "Cursed be anyone who does not uphold the words of this law by observing them." All the people shall say, "Amen!"

Blessings for Obedience

28 If you will only obey the LORD your God, by diligently observing all his commandments that I am commanding you today, the LORD your God will set you high above all the nations of the earth; ²all these blessings shall come upon you and overtake you, if you obey the LORD your God:

3 Blessed shall you be in the city, and blessed shall you be in the field.

4 Blessed shall be the fruit of your womb, the fruit of your ground, and the fruit of your livestock, both the increase of your cattle and the issue of your flock.

5 Blessed shall be your basket and your kneading bowl.

6 Blessed shall you be when you come in, and blessed shall you be when you go out.

7 The LORD will cause your enemies who rise against you to be defeated before you; they shall come out against you one way, and flee before you seven ways. ⁸The LORD will command the blessing upon you in your barns, and in all that you undertake; he will bless you in the land that the LORD your God is giving you. ⁹The LORD will establish you as his holy people, as he has sworn to you, if you keep the commandments of the LORD your God and walk in his ways. ¹⁰All the peoples of the earth shall see that you are called by the name of the LORD, and they shall be afraid of you. ¹¹The LORD will make you abound in prosperity, in the fruit of your womb, in the fruit of your livestock, and in the fruit of your ground in the land that the LORD swore to your ancestors to give you. ¹²The LORD will open for you his rich storehouse, the heavens, to give the rain of your land in its season and to bless all your undertakings. You will lend to many nations, but you will not borrow. ¹³The LORD will make you the head, and not the tail; you shall be only at the top, and not at the bottom—if you obey the commandments of the LORD your God, which I am commanding you today, by diligently observing them, ¹⁴and if you do not turn aside from any of the words that I am commanding you today, either to the right or to the left, following other gods to serve them.

Abundant Blessings

DEUTERONOMY 28.2–15

Write a poem about God's blessings using this passage as a starting point. Moses dwells on blessings within an agrarian society, but what might be some of the modern, especially urban, equivalents? Now go through the curses beginning in 28.16, also thinking of modern-day examples. What are some of the worst misfortunes you can imagine? Have you experienced any of these blessings or curses? How do they draw you into God's presence? How do they create questions and doubts, or perhaps anger, in your mind? How does your understanding of the death and resurrection of Jesus affect the way you read this passage in Deuteronomy?

See Meeting God in Scripture

---

a Heb *uncovered his father's skirt*

Remembering Through Adversity

DEUTERONOMY 28.32–35

Have you ever been in a situation where, regardless of how hard you worked, you just couldn't seem to meet all your financial obligations? What did you do with the frustration? Have you ever faced persistent medical problems, or even a severe case of the flu that lingered too long? How have these difficult moments pointed you toward eternity? What is your greatest difficulty today? How can you use it to remember God rather than grow bitter toward him?

See Meeting God in Everyday Life

Warnings against Disobedience

15 But if you will not obey the LORD your God by diligently observing all his commandments and decrees, which I am commanding you today, then all these curses shall come upon you and overtake you:

16 Cursed shall you be in the city, and cursed shall you be in the field.

17 Cursed shall be your basket and your kneading bowl.

18 Cursed shall be the fruit of your womb, the fruit of your ground, the increase of your cattle and the issue of your flock.

19 Cursed shall you be when you come in, and cursed shall you be when you go out.

20 The LORD will send upon you disaster, panic, and frustration in everything you attempt to do, until you are destroyed and perish quickly, on account of the evil of your deeds, because you have forsaken me. ²¹The LORD will make the pestilence cling to you until it has consumed you off the land that you are entering to possess. ²²The LORD will afflict you with consumption, fever, inflammation, with fiery heat and drought, and with blight and mildew; they shall pursue you until you perish. ²³The sky over your head shall be bronze, and the earth under you iron. ²⁴The LORD will change the rain of your land into powder, and only dust shall come down upon you from the sky until you are destroyed.

25 The LORD will cause you to be defeated before your enemies; you shall go out against them one way and flee before them seven ways. You shall become an object of horror to all the kingdoms of the earth. ²⁶Your corpses shall be food for every bird of the air and animal of the earth, and there shall be no one to frighten them away. ²⁷The LORD will afflict you with the boils of Egypt, with ulcers, scurvy, and itch, of which you cannot be healed. ²⁸The LORD will afflict you with madness, blindness, and confusion of mind; ²⁹you shall grope about at noon as blind people grope in darkness, but you shall be unable to find your way; and you shall be continually abused and robbed, without anyone to help. ³⁰You shall become engaged to a woman, but another man shall lie with her. You shall build a house, but not live in it. You shall plant a vineyard, but not enjoy its fruit. ³¹Your ox shall be butchered before your eyes, but you shall not eat of it. Your donkey shall be stolen in front of you, and shall not be restored to you. Your sheep shall be given to your enemies, without anyone to help you. ³²Your sons and daughters shall be given to another people, while you look on; you will strain your eyes looking for them all day but be powerless to do anything. ³³A people whom you do not know shall eat up the fruit of your ground and of all your labors; you shall be continually abused and crushed, ³⁴and driven mad by the sight that your eyes shall see. ³⁵The LORD will strike you on the knees and on the legs with grievous boils of which you cannot be healed, from the sole of your foot to the crown of your head. ³⁶The LORD will bring you, and the king whom you set over you, to a nation that neither you nor your ancestors have known, where you shall serve other gods, of wood and stone. ³⁷You shall become an object of horror, a proverb, and a byword among all the peoples where the LORD will lead you.

38 You shall carry much seed into the field but shall gather little in, for the locust shall consume it. ³⁹You shall plant vineyards and dress them, but you shall neither drink the wine nor gather the grapes, for the worm shall eat them. ⁴⁰You shall have olive trees throughout all your territory, but

you shall not anoint yourself with the oil, for your olives shall drop off. **41**You shall have sons and daughters, but they shall not remain yours, for they shall go into captivity. **42**All your trees and the fruit of your ground the cicada shall take over. **43**Aliens residing among you shall ascend above you higher and higher, while you shall descend lower and lower. **44**They shall lend to you but you shall not lend to them; they shall be the head and you shall be the tail.

45 All these curses shall come upon you, pursuing and overtaking you until you are destroyed, because you did not obey the LORD your God, by observing the commandments and the decrees that he commanded you. **46**They shall be among you and your descendants as a sign and a portent forever.

47 Because you did not serve the LORD your God joyfully and with gladness of heart for the abundance of everything, **48**therefore you shall serve your enemies whom the LORD will send against you, in hunger and thirst, in nakedness and lack of everything. He will put an iron yoke on your neck until he has destroyed you. **49**The LORD will bring a nation from far away, from the end of the earth, to swoop down on you like an eagle, a nation whose language you do not understand, **50**a grim-faced nation showing no respect to the old or favor to the young. **51**It shall consume the fruit of your livestock and the fruit of your ground until you are destroyed, leaving you neither grain, wine, and oil, nor the increase of your cattle and the issue of your flock, until it has made you perish. **52**It shall besiege you in all your towns until your high and fortified walls, in which you trusted, come down throughout your land; it shall besiege you in all your towns throughout the land that the LORD your God has given you. **53**In the desperate straits to which the enemy siege reduces you, you will eat the fruit of your womb, the flesh of your own sons and daughters whom the LORD your God has given you. **54**Even the most refined and gentle of men among you will begrudge food to his own brother, to the wife whom he embraces, and to the last of his remaining children, **55**giving to none of them any of the flesh of his children whom he is eating, because nothing else remains to him, in the desperate straits to which the enemy siege will reduce you in all your towns. **56**She who is the most refined and gentle among you, so gentle and refined that she does not venture to set the sole of her foot on the ground, will begrudge food to the husband whom she embraces, to her own son, and to her own daughter, **57**begrudging even the afterbirth that comes out from between her thighs, and the children that she bears, because she is eating them in secret for lack of anything else, in the desperate straits to which the enemy siege will reduce you in your towns.

58 If you do not diligently observe all the words of this law that are written in this book, fearing this glorious and awesome name, the LORD your God, **59**then the LORD will overwhelm both you and your offspring with severe and lasting afflictions and grievous and lasting maladies. **60**He will bring back upon you all the diseases of Egypt, of which you were in dread, and they shall cling to you. **61**Every other malady and affliction, even though not recorded in the book of this law, the LORD will inflict on you until you are destroyed. **62**Although once you were as numerous as the stars in heaven, you shall be left few in number, because you did not obey the LORD your God. **63**And just as the LORD took delight in making you prosperous and numerous, so the LORD will take delight in

Living in the Present

DEUTERONOMY 28.58–67

"Let each of us examine his thoughts; he will find them wholly concerned with the past or the future. We almost never think of the present, and if we do think of it, it is only to see what light it throws on our plans for the future. The present is never our end. The past and the present are our means, the future alone our end. Thus we never actually live, but hope to live, and since we are always planning how to be happy, it is inevitable that we should never be so."

—BLAISE PASCAL,
Pensees

Covenant Keeper

DEUTERONOMY 29.9–15

Have you ever signed a contract when buying a house or car? What kind of thought did you give it beforehand? How did you feel as you signed your name on the dotted line? Have you ever signed a contract that you didn't read first? Keeping in mind the death and resurrection of Jesus Christ, and using scripture (see 2 Corinthians 3.6; Hebrews 8–9) as a guide, write out an agreement between yourself and God. What does God expect of you, and what does he promise in return? How willing are you to sign this covenant? How might reflecting on its terms help you to mature spiritually?

See Meeting God in Scripture

bringing you to ruin and destruction; you shall be plucked off the land that you are entering to possess. 64The LORD will scatter you among all peoples, from one end of the earth to the other; and there you shall serve other gods, of wood and stone, which neither you nor your ancestors have known. 65Among those nations you shall find no ease, no resting place for the sole of your foot. There the LORD will give you a trembling heart, failing eyes, and a languishing spirit. 66Your life shall hang in doubt before you; night and day you shall be in dread, with no assurance of your life. 67In the morning you shall say, "If only it were evening!" and at evening you shall say, "If only it were morning!"—because of the dread that your heart shall feel and the sights that your eyes shall see. 68The LORD will bring you back in ships to Egypt, by a route that I promised you would never see again; and there you shall offer yourselves for sale to your enemies as male and female slaves, but there will be no buyer.

29 *a* These are the words of the covenant that the LORD commanded Moses to make with the Israelites in the land of Moab, in addition to the covenant that he had made with them at Horeb.

The Covenant Renewed in Moab

2*b* Moses summoned all Israel and said to them: You have seen all that the LORD did before your eyes in the land of Egypt, to Pharaoh and to all his servants and to all his land, 3the great trials that your eyes saw, the signs, and those great wonders. 4But to this day the LORD has not given you a mind to understand, or eyes to see, or ears to hear. 5I have led you forty years in the wilderness. The clothes on your back have not worn out, and the sandals on your feet have not worn out; 6you have not eaten bread, and you have not drunk wine or strong drink—so that you may know that I am the LORD your God. 7When you came to this place, King Sihon of Heshbon and King Og of Bashan came out against us for battle, but we defeated them. 8We took their land and gave it as an inheritance to the Reubenites, the Gadites, and the half-tribe of Manasseh. 9Therefore diligently observe the words of this covenant, in order that you may succeed*c* in everything that you do.

10 You stand assembled today, all of you, before the LORD your God—the leaders of your tribes,*d* your elders, and your officials, all the men of Israel, 11your children, your women, and the aliens who are in your camp, both those who cut your wood and those who draw your water— 12to enter into the covenant of the LORD your God, sworn by an oath, which the LORD your God is making with you today; 13in order that he may establish you today as his people, and that he may be your God, as he promised you and as he swore to your ancestors, to Abraham, to Isaac, and to Jacob. 14I am making this covenant, sworn by an oath, not only with you who stand here with us today before the LORD our God, 15but also with those who are not here with us today. 16You know how we lived in the land of Egypt, and how we came through the midst of the nations through which you passed. 17You have seen their detestable things, the filthy idols of wood and stone, of silver and gold, that were among them. 18It may be that there is among you a man or woman, or a family or

a Ch 28.69 in Heb   *b* Ch 29.1 in Heb   *c* Or *deal wisely*   *d* Gk Syr: Heb *your leaders, your tribes*

tribe, whose heart is already turning away from the LORD our God to serve the gods of those nations. It may be that there is among you a root sprouting poisonous and bitter growth. [19]All who hear the words of this oath and bless themselves, thinking in their hearts, "We are safe even though we go our own stubborn ways" (thus bringing disaster on moist and dry alike)[a]— [20]the LORD will be unwilling to pardon them, for the LORD's anger and passion will smoke against them. All the curses written in this book will descend on them, and the LORD will blot out their names from under heaven. [21]The LORD will single them out from all the tribes of Israel for calamity, in accordance with all the curses of the covenant written in this book of the law. [22]The next generation, your children who rise up after you, as well as the foreigner who comes from a distant country, will see the devastation of that land and the afflictions with which the LORD has afflicted it— [23]all its soil burned out by sulfur and salt, nothing planted, nothing sprouting, unable to support any vegetation, like the destruction of Sodom and Gomorrah, Admah and Zeboiim, which the LORD destroyed in his fierce anger— [24]they and indeed all the nations will wonder, "Why has the LORD done thus to this land? What caused this great display of anger?" [25]They will conclude, "It is because they abandoned the covenant of the LORD, the God of their ancestors, which he made with them when he brought them out of the land of Egypt. [26]They turned and served other gods, worshiping them, gods whom they had not known and whom he had not allotted to them; [27]so the anger of the LORD was kindled against that land, bringing on it every curse written in this book. [28]The LORD uprooted them from their land in anger, fury, and great wrath, and cast them into another land, as is now the case." [29]The secret things belong to the LORD our God, but the revealed things belong to us and to our children forever, to observe all the words of this law.

God's Fidelity Assured

30 When all these things have happened to you, the blessings and the curses that I have set before you, if you call them to mind among all the nations where the LORD your God has driven you, [2]and return to the LORD your God, and you and your children obey him with all your heart and with all your soul, just as I am commanding you today, [3]then the LORD your God will restore your fortunes and have compassion on you, gathering you again from all the peoples among whom the LORD your God has scattered you. [4]Even if you are exiled to the ends of the world,[b] from there the LORD your God will gather you, and from there he will bring you back. [5]The LORD your God will bring you into the land that your ancestors possessed, and you will possess it; he will make you more prosperous and numerous than your ancestors.

6 Moreover, the LORD your God will circumcise your heart and the heart of your descendants, so that you will love the LORD your God with all your heart and with all your soul, in order that you may live. [7]The LORD your God will put all these curses on your enemies and on the adversaries who took advantage of you. [8]Then you shall again obey the LORD, observing all his commandments that I am commanding you today, [9]and the LORD your God will make you abundantly prosper-

An Angry Enemy

DEUTERONOMY 29.18–38

Although at times scripture urges us to take comfort in God, other passages remind us of how terrible a foe God could be. The next time you're in a small group—at a dinner or a Bible study—ask the provocative question, "What would it be like to have God for an enemy?" Consider all the ways that an angry, all-seeing, all-powerful, ever-present God could make someone's life absolutely miserable. Discuss how God could make war on his enemy physically as well as emotionally and spiritually. How might this discussion affect how you choose to respond to God? How might this reality affect your relationship with Jesus Christ?

Within Reach

DEUTERONOMY 30.11–14

What if following God's way required you to climb to the top of Mount Everest or cross an ocean in a rowboat? How would you assess the risks and the rewards? Moses here says that doing God's will is not impossible or even as difficult as one of these challenges. What does it mean to you that God's Word is not far away, but "in your mouth and in your heart"?

See Meeting God in Scripture

ous in all your undertakings, in the fruit of your body, in the fruit of your livestock, and in the fruit of your soil. For the LORD will again take delight in prospering you, just as he delighted in prospering your ancestors, [10]when you obey the LORD your God by observing his commandments and decrees that are written in this book of the law, because you turn to the LORD your God with all your heart and with all your soul.

Exhortation to Choose Life

11 Surely, this commandment that I am commanding you today is not too hard for you, nor is it too far away. [12]It is not in heaven, that you should say, "Who will go up to heaven for us, and get it for us so that we may hear it and observe it?" [13]Neither is it beyond the sea, that you should say, "Who will cross to the other side of the sea for us, and get it for us so that we may hear it and observe it?" [14]No, the word is very near to you; it is in your mouth and in your heart for you to observe.

15 See, I have set before you today life and prosperity, death and adversity. [16]If you obey the commandments of the LORD your God[a] that I am commanding you today, by loving the LORD your God, walking in his ways, and observing his commandments, decrees, and ordinances, then you shall live and become numerous, and the LORD your God will bless you in the land that you are entering to possess. [17]But if your heart turns away and you do not hear, but are led astray to bow down to other gods and serve them, [18]I declare to you today that you shall perish; you shall not live long in the land that you are crossing the Jordan to enter and possess. [19]I call heaven and earth to witness against you today that I have set before you life and death, blessings and curses. Choose life so that you and your descendants may live, [20]loving the LORD your God, obeying him, and holding fast to him; for that means life to you and length of days, so that you may live in the land that the LORD swore to give to your ancestors, to Abraham, to Isaac, and to Jacob.

Joshua Becomes Moses' Successor

31 When Moses had finished speaking all[b] these words to all Israel, [2]he said to them: "I am now one hundred twenty years old. I am no longer able to get about, and the LORD has told me, 'You shall not cross over this Jordan.' [3]The LORD your God himself will cross over before you. He will destroy these nations before you, and you shall dispossess them. Joshua also will cross over before you, as the LORD promised. [4]The LORD will do to them as he did to Sihon and Og, the kings of the Amorites, and to their land, when he destroyed them. [5]The LORD will give them over to you and you shall deal with them in full accord with the command that I have given to you. [6]Be strong and bold; have no fear or dread of them, because it is the LORD your God who goes with you; he will not fail you or forsake you."

7 Then Moses summoned Joshua and said to him in the sight of all Israel: "Be strong and bold, for you are the one who will go with this people into the land that the LORD has sworn to their ancestors to give them; and you will put them in possession of it. [8]It is the LORD who goes before you. He

a Gk: Heb lacks *If you obey the commandments of the LORD your God*
b Q Ms Gk: MT *Moses went and spoke*

will be with you; he will not fail you or forsake you. Do not fear or be dismayed."

The Law to Be Read Every Seventh Year

9 Then Moses wrote down this law, and gave it to the priests, the sons of Levi, who carried the ark of the covenant of the LORD, and to all the elders of Israel. [10]Moses commanded them: "Every seventh year, in the scheduled year of remission, during the festival of booths,[a] [11]when all Israel comes to appear before the LORD your God at the place that he will choose, you shall read this law before all Israel in their hearing. [12]Assemble the people—men, women, and children, as well as the aliens residing in your towns—so that they may hear and learn to fear the LORD your God and to observe diligently all the words of this law, [13]and so that their children, who have not known it, may hear and learn to fear the LORD your God, as long as you live in the land that you are crossing over the Jordan to possess."

Moses and Joshua Receive God's Charge

14 The LORD said to Moses, "Your time to die is near; call Joshua and present yourselves in the tent of meeting, so that I may commission him." So Moses and Joshua went and presented themselves in the tent of meeting, [15]and the LORD appeared at the tent in a pillar of cloud; the pillar of cloud stood at the entrance to the tent.

16 The LORD said to Moses, "Soon you will lie down with your ancestors. Then this people will begin to prostitute themselves to the foreign gods in their midst, the gods of the land into which they are going; they will forsake me, breaking my covenant that I have made with them. [17]My anger will be kindled against them in that day. I will forsake them and hide my face from them; they will become easy prey, and many terrible troubles will come upon them. In that day they will say, 'Have not these troubles come upon us because our God is not in our midst?' [18]On that day I will surely hide my face on account of all the evil they have done by turning to other gods. [19]Now therefore write this song, and teach it to the Israelites; put it in their mouths, in order that this song may be a witness for me against the Israelites. [20]For when I have brought them into the land flowing with milk and honey, which I promised on oath to their ancestors, and they have eaten their fill and grown fat, they will turn to other gods and serve them, despising me and breaking my covenant. [21]And when many terrible troubles come upon them, this song will confront them as a witness, because it will not be lost from the mouths of their descendants. For I know what they are inclined to do even now, before I have brought them into the land that I promised them on oath." [22]That very day Moses wrote this song and taught it to the Israelites.

23 Then the LORD commissioned Joshua son of Nun and said, "Be strong and bold, for you shall bring the Israelites into the land that I promised them; I will be with you."

24 When Moses had finished writing down in a book the words of this law to the very end, [25]Moses commanded the Levites who carried the ark of the covenant of the LORD, saying, [26]"Take this book of the law and put it beside the ark of the covenant of the LORD your God; let it remain there as a witness against you. [27]For I know well how rebellious and

a Or *tabernacles*; Heb *succoth*

Last Words

DEUTERONOMY 31.14

Moses is given an opportunity that many of us will never have—he knows that his death is at hand. If God were to tell you that you had just one year left to live, how would you spend it? What relationships would you need to address? On what form of ministry would you focus? How would you re-prioritize your life? Whom would you want to train or to whom would you want to give special instructions before you died?

Natural Insights

DEUTERONOMY 32.2,4

Moses uses natural images to capture the beauty of God's truth. Meditate on these images: God's teaching dropping like rain, condensing like dew or like gentle rain on grass. Next spend some time on the image of God as the Rock. What security does this thought provide for you? Can you find any other natural images in scripture that especially appeal to you? What natural image (or images) would *you* use to describe God's teaching and protection?

See Meeting God in the Created Order

stubborn you are. If you already have been so rebellious toward the LORD while I am still alive among you, how much more after my death! ²⁸Assemble to me all the elders of your tribes and your officials, so that I may recite these words in their hearing and call heaven and earth to witness against them. ²⁹For I know that after my death you will surely act corruptly, turning aside from the way that I have commanded you. In time to come trouble will befall you, because you will do what is evil in the sight of the LORD, provoking him to anger through the work of your hands."

The Song of Moses

30 Then Moses recited the words of this song, to the very end, in the hearing of the whole assembly of Israel:

32 Give ear, O heavens, and I will speak;
   let the earth hear the words of my mouth.
² May my teaching drop like the rain,
   my speech condense like the dew;
 like gentle rain on grass,
   like showers on new growth.
³ For I will proclaim the name of the LORD;
   ascribe greatness to our God!

⁴ The Rock, his work is perfect,
   and all his ways are just.
 A faithful God, without deceit,
   just and upright is he;
⁵ yet his degenerate children have dealt falsely with
      him,ᵃ
   a perverse and crooked generation.
⁶ Do you thus repay the LORD,
   O foolish and senseless people?
 Is not he your father, who created you,
   who made you and established you?
⁷ Remember the days of old,
   consider the years long past;
 ask your father, and he will inform you;
   your elders, and they will tell you.
⁸ When the Most Highᵇ apportioned the nations,
   when he divided humankind,
 he fixed the boundaries of the peoples
   according to the number of the gods;ᶜ
⁹ the LORD's own portion was his people,
   Jacob his allotted share.

¹⁰ He sustainedᵈ him in a desert land,
   in a howling wilderness waste;
 he shielded him, cared for him,
   guarded him as the apple of his eye.
¹¹ As an eagle stirs up its nest,
   and hovers over its young;
 as it spreads its wings, takes them up,
   and bears them aloft on its pinions,
¹² the LORD alone guided him;
   no foreign god was with him.
¹³ He set him atop the heights of the land,
   and fed him withᵉ produce of the field;
 he nursed him with honey from the crags,

---

a Meaning of Heb uncertain   *b* Traditional rendering of Heb *Elyon*
c Q Ms Compare Gk Tg: MT *the Israelites*   *d* Sam Gk Compare Tg: MT *found*   *e* Sam Gk Syr Tg: MT *he ate*

with oil from flinty rock;
14 curds from the herd, and milk from the flock,
    with fat of lambs and rams;
Bashan bulls and goats,
    together with the choicest wheat—
you drank fine wine from the blood of grapes.
15 Jacob ate his fill;[a]
    Jeshurun grew fat, and kicked.
    You grew fat, bloated, and gorged!
He abandoned God who made him,
    and scoffed at the Rock of his salvation.
16 They made him jealous with strange gods,
    with abhorrent things they provoked him.
17 They sacrificed to demons, not God,
    to deities they had never known,
to new ones recently arrived,
    whom your ancestors had not feared.
18 You were unmindful of the Rock that bore you;[b]
    you forgot the God who gave you birth.

19 The LORD saw it, and was jealous;[c]
    he spurned[d] his sons and daughters.
20 He said: I will hide my face from them,
    I will see what their end will be;
for they are a perverse generation,
    children in whom there is no faithfulness.
21 They made me jealous with what is no god,
    provoked me with their idols.
So I will make them jealous with what is no people,
    provoke them with a foolish nation.
22 For a fire is kindled by my anger,
    and burns to the depths of Sheol;
it devours the earth and its increase,
    and sets on fire the foundations of the mountains.
23 I will heap disasters upon them,
    spend my arrows against them:
24 wasting hunger,
    burning consumption,
    bitter pestilence.
The teeth of beasts I will send against them,
    with venom of things crawling in the dust.
25 In the street the sword shall bereave,
    and in the chambers terror,
for young man and woman alike,
    nursing child and old gray head.
26 I thought to scatter them[e]
    and blot out the memory of them from
        humankind;
27 but I feared provocation by the enemy,
    for their adversaries might misunderstand
and say, "Our hand is triumphant;
    it was not the LORD who did all this."

28 They are a nation void of sense;
    there is no understanding in them.
29 If they were wise, they would understand this;
    they would discern what the end would be.
30 How could one have routed a thousand,

Relational Insights

DEUTERONOMY 32.6,8,15

How might thinking about God as Father create a different understanding from meditating on God as Creator? What insights might you gain by reflecting on other names for God used in these verses, including Most High and Rock of Salvation? List some of the other names for God (see Exodus 17.15; Daniel 7.9) mentioned in the Bible. Which image is most meaningful to you? Which image is most difficult for you to relate to? Why do you think scripture describes God with many metaphors rather than just one?

---

a Q Mss Sam Gk: MT lacks *Jacob ate his fill*   b Or *that begot you*
c Q Mss Gk: MT lacks *was jealous*   d Cn: Heb *he spurned because of provocation*   e Gk: Meaning of Heb uncertain

A Final Denial

DEUTERONOMY 32.48–52

What might Moses' emotions have been as he looked out over the promised land and knew that he would not enter it? If you were in Moses' situation, would seeing the land make it harder or easier to accept God's denial? Is there anything in your life that God seems to be denying you? Do you think God is denying you because you have disobeyed, or is there another reason? Imagine having a conversation with Moses on Mount Nebo. What might he say to encourage you as you struggle to accept God's denial of what you desire?

See Meeting God in Scripture

and two put a myriad to flight,
unless their Rock had sold them,
the LORD had given them up?

31 Indeed their rock is not like our Rock;
our enemies are fools. *a*

32 Their vine comes from the vinestock of Sodom,
from the vineyards of Gomorrah;
their grapes are grapes of poison,
their clusters are bitter;

33 their wine is the poison of serpents,
the cruel venom of asps.

34 Is not this laid up in store with me,
sealed up in my treasuries?

35 Vengeance is mine, and recompense,
for the time when their foot shall slip;
because the day of their calamity is at hand,
their doom comes swiftly.

36 Indeed the LORD will vindicate his people,
have compassion on his servants,
when he sees that their power is gone,
neither bond nor free remaining.

37 Then he will say: Where are their gods,
the rock in which they took refuge,

38 who ate the fat of their sacrifices,
and drank the wine of their libations?
Let them rise up and help you,
let them be your protection!

39 See now that I, even I, am he;
there is no god besides me.
I kill and I make alive;
I wound and I heal;
and no one can deliver from my hand.

40 For I lift up my hand to heaven,
and swear: As I live forever,

41 when I whet my flashing sword,
and my hand takes hold on judgment;
I will take vengeance on my adversaries,
and will repay those who hate me.

42 I will make my arrows drunk with blood,
and my sword shall devour flesh—
with the blood of the slain and the captives,
from the long-haired enemy.

43 Praise, O heavens,*b* his people,
worship him, all you gods!*c*
For he will avenge the blood of his children,*d*
and take vengeance on his adversaries;
he will repay those who hate him,*e*
and cleanse the land for his people.*e*

44 Moses came and recited all the words of this song in the hearing of the people, he and Joshua*f* son of Nun. 45When Moses had finished reciting all these words to all Israel, 46he said to them: "Take to heart all the words that I am giving in witness against you today; give them as a command to your children, so that they may diligently observe all the words of

a Gk: Meaning of Heb uncertain   *b* Q Ms Gk: MT *nations*   *c* Q Ms Gk: MT lacks this line   *d* Q Ms Gk: MT *his servants*   *e* Q Ms Sam Gk Vg: MT *his land his people*   *f* Sam Gk Syr Vg: MT *Hoshea*

this law. ⁴⁷This is no trifling matter for you, but rather your very life; through it you may live long in the land that you are crossing over the Jordan to possess."

Moses' Death Foretold

48 On that very day the LORD addressed Moses as follows: ⁴⁹"Ascend this mountain of the Abarim, Mount Nebo, which is in the land of Moab, across from Jericho, and view the land of Canaan, which I am giving to the Israelites for a possession; ⁵⁰you shall die there on the mountain that you ascend and shall be gathered to your kin, as your brother Aaron died on Mount Hor and was gathered to his kin; ⁵¹because both of you broke faith with me among the Israelites at the waters of Meribath-kadesh in the wilderness of Zin, by failing to maintain my holiness among the Israelites. ⁵²Although you may view the land from a distance, you shall not enter it—the land that I am giving to the Israelites."

Moses' Final Blessing on Israel

33 This is the blessing with which Moses, the man of God, blessed the Israelites before his death. ²He said:
> The LORD came from Sinai,
>   and dawned from Seir upon us;^a
>   he shone forth from Mount Paran.
> With him were myriads of holy ones;^b
>   at his right, a host of his own.^c
> ³ Indeed, O favorite among^d peoples,
>   all his holy ones were in your charge;
> they marched at your heels,
>   accepted direction from you.
> ⁴ Moses charged us with the law,
>   as a possession for the assembly of Jacob.
> ⁵ There arose a king in Jeshurun,
>   when the leaders of the people assembled—
>   the united tribes of Israel.

> ⁶ May Reuben live, and not die out,
>   even though his numbers are few.

⁷And this he said of Judah:
> O LORD, give heed to Judah,
>   and bring him to his people;
> strengthen his hands for him,^e
>   and be a help against his adversaries.

⁸And of Levi he said:
> Give to Levi^f your Thummim,
>   and your Urim to your loyal one,
> whom you tested at Massah,
>   with whom you contended at the waters of
>   Meribah;
> ⁹ who said of his father and mother,
>   "I regard them not";
> he ignored his kin,
>   and did not acknowledge his children.
> For they observed your word,
>   and kept your covenant.

a Gk Syr Vg Compare Tg: Heb *upon them*   *b* Cn Compare Gk Sam Syr Vg: MT *He came from Ribeboth-kodesh.*   *c* Cn Compare Gk: meaning of Heb uncertain   *d* Or *O lover of the*   *e* Cn: Heb *with his hands he contended*   *f* Q Ms Gk: MT lacks *Give to Levi*

The Lord's Beloved

DEUTERONOMY 33.1–12

"Blessed is he that understandeth what it is to love Jesus, and to despise himself for Jesus' sake. Thou oughtest to leave thy beloved, for thy Beloved; for Jesus will be loved alone above all things. The love of things created is deceitful and inconstant; the love of Jesus is faithful and lasting. He that cleaveth unto creatures, shall fall with that which is frail; he that embraceth Jesus, shall stand firmly for ever. Love Him and keep Him for thy friend, who, when all go away, will not forsake thee, nor suffer thee to perish in the end."

—THOMAS À KEMPIS,
The Imitation of Christ

A Secure Shelter

DEUTERONOMY 33.26–29

This is Moses' final address to Israel. He has led this people through an astounding, perilous and miracle-laden journey, and now he is about to leave them with a final portrait of the God they know, love and serve. Moses wants Israel to remember a God who "rides through the heavens" and the skies, an eternal God of refuge who drives out enemies, who provides basic needs even to the point of abundance and who acts as a shield, help and sword. Spend a few minutes meditating on each image. How can you personally draw security from such a God? What aspect of God's shelter and care is most precious and meaningful to you? Drawing from your own experience and vocabulary, how would you describe God to someone else?

See *Meeting God in Scripture*

10 They teach Jacob your ordinances,
      and Israel your law;
   they place incense before you,
      and whole burnt offerings on your altar.
11 Bless, O LORD, his substance,
      and accept the work of his hands;
   crush the loins of his adversaries,
      of those that hate him, so that they do not rise
         again.

12 Of Benjamin he said:
   The beloved of the LORD rests in safety—
      the High God*a* surrounds him all day long—
      the beloved*b* rests between his shoulders.

13 And of Joseph he said:
   Blessed by the LORD be his land,
      with the choice gifts of heaven above,
      and of the deep that lies beneath;
14   with the choice fruits of the sun,
      and the rich yield of the months;
15   with the finest produce of the ancient mountains,
      and the abundance of the everlasting hills;
16   with the choice gifts of the earth and its fullness,
      and the favor of the one who dwells on Sinai.*c*
   Let these come on the head of Joseph,
      on the brow of the prince among his brothers.
17   A firstborn*d* bull—majesty is his!
      His horns are the horns of a wild ox;
   with them he gores the peoples,
      driving them to*e* the ends of the earth;
   such are the myriads of Ephraim,
      such the thousands of Manasseh.

18 And of Zebulun he said:
   Rejoice, Zebulun, in your going out;
      and Issachar, in your tents.
19   They call peoples to the mountain;
      there they offer the right sacrifices;
   for they suck the affluence of the seas
      and the hidden treasures of the sand.

20 And of Gad he said:
   Blessed be the enlargement of Gad!
      Gad lives like a lion;
      he tears at arm and scalp.
21   He chose the best for himself,
      for there a commander's allotment was reserved;
   he came at the head of the people,
      he executed the justice of the LORD,
      and his ordinances for Israel.

22 And of Dan he said:
   Dan is a lion's whelp
      that leaps forth from Bashan.

23 And of Naphtali he said:
   O Naphtali, sated with favor,

a Heb *above him*   *b* Heb *he*   *c* Cn: Heb *in the bush*   *d* Q Ms Gk Syr Vg: MT *His firstborn*   *e* Cn: Heb *the peoples, together*

full of the blessing of the LORD,
possess the west and the south.

24 And of Asher he said:
Most blessed of sons be Asher;
may he be the favorite of his brothers,
and may he dip his foot in oil.
25 Your bars are iron and bronze;
and as your days, so is your strength.

26 There is none like God, O Jeshurun,
who rides through the heavens to your help,
majestic through the skies.
27 He subdues the ancient gods,*a*
shatters*b* the forces of old;*c*
he drove out the enemy before you,
and said, "Destroy!"
28 So Israel lives in safety,
untroubled is Jacob's abode*d*
in a land of grain and wine,
where the heavens drop down dew.
29 Happy are you, O Israel! Who is like you,
a people saved by the LORD,
the shield of your help,
and the sword of your triumph!
Your enemies shall come fawning to you,
and you shall tread on their backs.

Moses Dies and Is Buried in the Land of Moab

34 Then Moses went up from the plains of Moab to Mount Nebo, to the top of Pisgah, which is opposite Jericho, and the LORD showed him the whole land: Gilead as far as Dan, 2 all Naphtali, the land of Ephraim and Manasseh, all the land of Judah as far as the Western Sea, 3 the Negeb, and the Plain—that is, the valley of Jericho, the city of palm trees—as far as Zoar. 4 The LORD said to him, "This is the land of which I swore to Abraham, to Isaac, and to Jacob, saying, 'I will give it to your descendants'; I have let you see it with your eyes, but you shall not cross over there." 5 Then Moses, the servant of the LORD, died there in the land of Moab, at the LORD's command. 6 He was buried in a valley in the land of Moab, opposite Beth-peor, but no one knows his burial place to this day. 7 Moses was one hundred twenty years old when he died; his sight was unimpaired and his vigor had not abated. 8 The Israelites wept for Moses in the plains of Moab thirty days; then the period of mourning for Moses was ended.

9 Joshua son of Nun was full of the spirit of wisdom, because Moses had laid his hands on him; and the Israelites obeyed him, doing as the LORD had commanded Moses.

10 Never since has there arisen a prophet in Israel like Moses, whom the LORD knew face to face. 11 He was unequaled for all the signs and wonders that the LORD sent him to perform in the land of Egypt, against Pharaoh and all his servants and his entire land, 12 and for all the mighty deeds and all the terrifying displays of power that Moses performed in the sight of all Israel.

Passing of the Spiritual Guard

DEUTERONOMY 34.8–10

Has someone who was very influential in your spiritual life passed away? How did this loss affect your faith? What do you think it was like for the Israelites to grieve over Moses? What comfort did God provide them? Moses was a singular character (see 34.11–12), but now that the Holy Spirit has come, how might we approach the death of an influential person differently from the way the Israelites did?

---

a Or *The eternal God is a dwelling place*   *b* Cn: Heb *from underneath*
c Or *the everlasting arms*   *d* Or *fountain*

JOSHUA
Good News of Second Chances

KEY VERSE:

"No one shall be able to stand against you all the days of your life. As I was with Moses, so I will be with you; I will not fail you or forsake you."—Joshua 1.5

"If you and I are to be made by God into people for God's purposes, it will depend largely on the courage with which we respond to God. It won't be worked by God's action alone . . . It works through our brave and willing cooperation, our active acceptance and use of all the material we are offered, even everything that damages our vanity and opposes our self-will."

—EVELYN UNDERHILL,
The Ways of the Spirit

When the book of Joshua opens, Israel is still journeying to the promised land. Though God knows Israel's rebellious history, he gives the people another chance to possess the land promised them. Under Joshua's leadership (and with God's intervention) they finally cross the Jordan River and take control of Canaan. Though God's goals for them have not changed, entering and possessing the land requires of them renewed courage, perseverance and faith. The Israelites face a difficult task—to conquer and settle the land. The good news is that God is with them every step of the way.

As spiritual pilgrims in quest of our own land of promise, we can be encouraged by this story of renewed faith as the Israelites finally take possession of God's gift. The book of Joshua suggests abundant parallels between conquering a geographic Canaan and a spiritual Canaan. How are we called to exercise courage when facing the enemies of our souls? What does perseverance in daily spiritual practice look like in our lives? What do we allow to hinder us from possessing our inheritance? How is God giving us a second chance to renew our relationship with him? How is God giving us opportunity to cover new spiritual ground?

God's Commission to Joshua

1 After the death of Moses the servant of the LORD, the LORD spoke to Joshua son of Nun, Moses' assistant, saying, ²"My servant Moses is dead. Now proceed to cross the Jordan, you and all this people, into the land that I am giving to them, to the Israelites. ³Every place that the sole of your foot will tread upon I have given to you, as I promised to Moses. ⁴From the wilderness and the Lebanon as far as the great river, the river Euphrates, all the land of the Hittites, to the Great Sea in the west shall be your territory. ⁵No one shall be able to stand against you all the days of your life. As I was with Moses, so I will be with you; I will not fail you or forsake you. ⁶Be strong and courageous; for you shall put this people in possession of the land that I swore to their ancestors to give them. ⁷Only be strong and very courageous, being careful to act in accordance with all the law that my servant Moses commanded you; do not turn from it to the right hand or to the left, so that you may be successful wherever you go. ⁸This book of the law shall not depart out of your mouth; you shall meditate on it day and night, so that you may be careful to act in accordance with all that is written in it. For then you shall make your way prosperous, and then you shall be successful. ⁹I hereby command you: Be strong and courageous; do not be frightened or dismayed, for the LORD your God is with you wherever you go."

Preparations for the Invasion

10 Then Joshua commanded the officers of the people, ¹¹"Pass through the camp, and command the people: 'Prepare your provisions; for in three days you are to cross over the Jordan, to go in to take possession of the land that the LORD your God gives you to possess.' "

12 To the Reubenites, the Gadites, and the half-tribe of Manasseh Joshua said, ¹³"Remember the word that Moses the servant of the LORD commanded you, saying, 'The LORD your God is providing you a place of rest, and will give you this land.' ¹⁴Your wives, your little ones, and your livestock shall remain in the land that Moses gave you beyond the Jordan. But all the warriors among you shall cross over armed before your kindred and shall help them, ¹⁵until the LORD gives rest to your kindred as well as to you, and they too take possession of the land that the LORD your God is giving them. Then you shall return to your own land and take possession of it, the land that Moses the servant of the LORD gave you beyond the Jordan to the east."

16 They answered Joshua: "All that you have commanded us we will do, and wherever you send us we will go. ¹⁷Just as we obeyed Moses in all things, so we will obey you. Only may the LORD your God be with you, as he was with Moses! ¹⁸Whoever rebels against your orders and disobeys your words, whatever you command, shall be put to death. Only be strong and courageous."

Spies Sent to Jericho

2 Then Joshua son of Nun sent two men secretly from Shittim as spies, saying, "Go, view the land, especially Jericho." So they went, and entered the house of a prostitute whose name was Rahab, and spent the night there. ²The king of Jericho was told, "Some Israelites have come

Fighting and Faith

JOSHUA 1.1–9

God suggests to the people through Joshua that taking Canaan will require faith, courage and great effort. Is there a parallel to our spiritual lives today? Do we have to fight to possess what God has already promised? How do we wage such a fight? In what ways are we strengthened in our inner being by exercising faith in possessing the promises of God? In what areas of your life is God calling you to fight? This is God's word to you: "Be strong and courageous . . . for the LORD your God is with you wherever you go" (v.9).

Spies for the Lord

JOSHUA 2.1–7

"The soul, then, touched with the love of Christ the Spouse, and longing to attain to his grace and gain his goodwill, goes forth here disguised with that disguise which most vividly represents the affections of its spirit and which will protect it most securely on its journey from its adversaries and enemies, which are the devil, the world and the flesh."

—JOHN OF THE CROSS,
The Dark Night of the Soul

here tonight to search out the land." ³Then the king of Jericho sent orders to Rahab, "Bring out the men who have come to you, who entered your house, for they have come only to search out the whole land." ⁴But the woman took the two men and hid them. Then she said, "True, the men came to me, but I did not know where they came from. ⁵And when it was time to close the gate at dark, the men went out. Where the men went I do not know. Pursue them quickly, for you can overtake them." ⁶She had, however, brought them up to the roof and hidden them with the stalks of flax that she had laid out on the roof. ⁷So the men pursued them on the way to the Jordan as far as the fords. As soon as the pursuers had gone out, the gate was shut.

8 Before they went to sleep, she came up to them on the roof ⁹and said to the men: "I know that the LORD has given you the land, and that dread of you has fallen on us, and that all the inhabitants of the land melt in fear before you. ¹⁰For we have heard how the LORD dried up the water of the Red Sea*a* before you when you came out of Egypt, and what you did to the two kings of the Amorites that were beyond the Jordan, to Sihon and Og, whom you utterly destroyed. ¹¹As soon as we heard it, our hearts melted, and there was no courage left in any of us because of you. The LORD your God is indeed God in heaven above and on earth below. ¹²Now then, since I have dealt kindly with you, swear to me by the LORD that you in turn will deal kindly with my family. Give me a sign of good faith ¹³that you will spare my father and mother, my brothers and sisters, and all who belong to them, and deliver our lives from death." ¹⁴The men said to her, "Our life for yours! If you do not tell this business of ours, then we will deal kindly and faithfully with you when the LORD gives us the land."

15 Then she let them down by a rope through the window, for her house was on the outer side of the city wall and she resided within the wall itself. ¹⁶She said to them, "Go toward the hill country, so that the pursuers may not come upon you. Hide yourselves there three days, until the pursuers have returned; then afterward you may go your way." ¹⁷The men said to her, "We will be released from this oath that you have made us swear to you ¹⁸if we invade the land and you do not tie this crimson cord in the window through which you let us down, and you do not gather into your house your father and mother, your brothers, and all your family. ¹⁹If any of you go out of the doors of your house into the street, they shall be responsible for their own death, and we shall be innocent; but if a hand is laid upon any who are with you in the house, we shall bear the responsibility for their death. ²⁰But if you tell this business of ours, then we shall be released from this oath that you made us swear to you." ²¹She said, "According to your words, so be it." She sent them away and they departed. Then she tied the crimson cord in the window.

22 They departed and went into the hill country and stayed there three days, until the pursuers returned. The pursuers had searched all along the way and found nothing. ²³Then the two men came down again from the hill country. They crossed over, came to Joshua son of Nun, and told him all that had happened to them. ²⁴They said to Joshua, "Truly the LORD has given all the land into our hands;

a Or *Sea of Reeds*

moreover all the inhabitants of the land melt in fear before us."

Israel Crosses the Jordan

3 Early in the morning Joshua rose and set out from Shittim with all the Israelites, and they came to the Jordan. They camped there before crossing over. ²At the end of three days the officers went through the camp ³and commanded the people, "When you see the ark of the covenant of the LORD your God being carried by the levitical priests, then you shall set out from your place. Follow it, ⁴so that you may know the way you should go, for you have not passed this way before. Yet there shall be a space between you and it, a distance of about two thousand cubits; do not come any nearer to it." ⁵Then Joshua said to the people, "Sanctify yourselves; for tomorrow the LORD will do wonders among you." ⁶To the priests Joshua said, "Take up the ark of the covenant, and pass on in front of the people." So they took up the ark of the covenant and went in front of the people.

7 The LORD said to Joshua, "This day I will begin to exalt you in the sight of all Israel, so that they may know that I will be with you as I was with Moses. ⁸You are the one who shall command the priests who bear the ark of the covenant, 'When you come to the edge of the waters of the Jordan, you shall stand still in the Jordan.'" ⁹Joshua then said to the Israelites, "Draw near and hear the words of the LORD your God." ¹⁰Joshua said, "By this you shall know that among you is the living God who without fail will drive out from before you the Canaanites, Hittites, Hivites, Perizzites, Girgashites, Amorites, and Jebusites: ¹¹the ark of the covenant of the Lord of all the earth is going to pass before you into the Jordan. ¹²So now select twelve men from the tribes of Israel, one from each tribe. ¹³When the soles of the feet of the priests who bear the ark of the LORD, the Lord of all the earth, rest in the waters of the Jordan, the waters of the Jordan flowing from above shall be cut off; they shall stand in a single heap."

14 When the people set out from their tents to cross over the Jordan, the priests bearing the ark of the covenant were in front of the people. ¹⁵Now the Jordan overflows all its banks throughout the time of harvest. So when those who bore the ark had come to the Jordan, and the feet of the priests bearing the ark were dipped in the edge of the water, ¹⁶the waters flowing from above stood still, rising up in a single heap far off at Adam, the city that is beside Zarethan, while those flowing toward the sea of the Arabah, the Dead Sea,ᵃ were wholly cut off. Then the people crossed over opposite Jericho. ¹⁷While all Israel were crossing over on dry ground, the priests who bore the ark of the covenant of the LORD stood on dry ground in the middle of the Jordan, until the entire nation finished crossing over the Jordan.

Twelve Stones Set Up at Gilgal

4 When the entire nation had finished crossing over the Jordan, the LORD said to Joshua: ²"Select twelve men from the people, one from each tribe, ³and command them, 'Take twelve stones from here out of the middle of

---

Wet Feet

JOSHUA 3.1–17

The waters of the Jordan River part, but not until the feet of the priests touch the water. How is God calling you to get your feet "wet" through actions of faith? What waters are waiting to roll back in response to your steps? Meditate on God's challenge to step in and walk forward. What might be the outcome of your boldness?

See Meeting God in Everyday Life

Stones of Memory

JOSHUA 4.5–7

The people of Israel set up a memorial of stones from the bed of the river to commemorate the miraculous crossing. Find a stone you can hold in your hands. As you hold it, think about times when God has brought you through the raging waters of trouble and confusion. Remember times when God's presence and touch seemed especially real. As you thank God for those times, put the stone in a place where you will be able to see it. Let it serve as a "memorial" of God's love and grace.

See Meeting God in Everyday Life

the Jordan, from the place where the priests' feet stood, carry them over with you, and lay them down in the place where you camp tonight.' " ⁴Then Joshua summoned the twelve men from the Israelites, whom he had appointed, one from each tribe. ⁵Joshua said to them, "Pass on before the ark of the LORD your God into the middle of the Jordan, and each of you take up a stone on his shoulder, one for each of the tribes of the Israelites, ⁶so that this may be a sign among you. When your children ask in time to come, 'What do those stones mean to you?' ⁷then you shall tell them that the waters of the Jordan were cut off in front of the ark of the covenant of the LORD. When it crossed over the Jordan, the waters of the Jordan were cut off. So these stones shall be to the Israelites a memorial forever."

8 The Israelites did as Joshua commanded. They took up twelve stones out of the middle of the Jordan, according to the number of the tribes of the Israelites, as the LORD told Joshua, carried them over with them to the place where they camped, and laid them down there. ⁹(Joshua set up twelve stones in the middle of the Jordan, in the place where the feet of the priests bearing the ark of the covenant had stood; and they are there to this day.)

10 The priests who bore the ark remained standing in the middle of the Jordan, until everything was finished that the LORD commanded Joshua to tell the people, according to all that Moses had commanded Joshua. The people crossed over in haste. ¹¹As soon as all the people had finished crossing over, the ark of the LORD, and the priests, crossed over in front of the people. ¹²The Reubenites, the Gadites, and the half-tribe of Manasseh crossed over armed before the Israelites, as Moses had ordered them. ¹³About forty thousand armed for war crossed over before the LORD to the plains of Jericho for battle.

14 On that day the LORD exalted Joshua in the sight of all Israel; and they stood in awe of him, as they had stood in awe of Moses, all the days of his life.

15 The LORD said to Joshua, ¹⁶"Command the priests who bear the ark of the covenant,ᵃ to come up out of the Jordan." ¹⁷Joshua therefore commanded the priests, "Come up out of the Jordan." ¹⁸When the priests bearing the ark of the covenant of the LORD came up from the middle of the Jordan, and the soles of the priests' feet touched dry ground, the waters of the Jordan returned to their place and overflowed all its banks, as before.

19 The people came up out of the Jordan on the tenth day of the first month, and they camped in Gilgal on the east border of Jericho. ²⁰Those twelve stones, which they had taken out of the Jordan, Joshua set up in Gilgal, ²¹saying to the Israelites, "When your children ask their parents in time to come, 'What do these stones mean?' ²²then you shall let your children know, 'Israel crossed over the Jordan here on dry ground.' ²³For the LORD your God dried up the waters of the Jordan for you until you crossed over, as the LORD your God did to the Red Sea,ᵇ which he dried up for us until we crossed over, ²⁴so that all the peoples of the earth may know that the hand of the LORD is mighty, and so that you may fear the LORD your God forever."

a Or treaty, or testimony; Heb eduth   b Or Sea of Reeds

The New Generation Circumcised

5 When all the kings of the Amorites beyond the Jordan to the west, and all the kings of the Canaanites by the sea, heard that the LORD had dried up the waters of the Jordan for the Israelites until they had crossed over, their hearts melted, and there was no longer any spirit in them, because of the Israelites.

2 At that time the LORD said to Joshua, "Make flint knives and circumcise the Israelites a second time." ³So Joshua made flint knives, and circumcised the Israelites at Gibeath-haaraloth.ᵃ ⁴This is the reason why Joshua circumcised them: all the males of the people who came out of Egypt, all the warriors, had died during the journey through the wilderness after they had come out of Egypt. ⁵Although all the people who came out had been circumcised, yet all the people born on the journey through the wilderness after they had come out of Egypt had not been circumcised. ⁶For the Israelites traveled forty years in the wilderness, until all the nation, the warriors who came out of Egypt, perished, not having listened to the voice of the LORD. To them the LORD swore that he would not let them see the land that he had sworn to their ancestors to give us, a land flowing with milk and honey. ⁷So it was their children, whom he raised up in their place, that Joshua circumcised; for they were uncircumcised, because they had not been circumcised on the way.

8 When the circumcising of all the nation was done, they remained in their places in the camp until they were healed. ⁹The LORD said to Joshua, "Today I have rolled away from you the disgrace of Egypt." And so that place is called Gilgalᵇ to this day.

The Passover at Gilgal

10 While the Israelites were camped in Gilgal they kept the passover in the evening on the fourteenth day of the month in the plains of Jericho. ¹¹On the day after the passover, on that very day, they ate the produce of the land, unleavened cakes and parched grain. ¹²The manna ceased on the day they ate the produce of the land, and the Israelites no longer had manna; they ate the crops of the land of Canaan that year.

Joshua's Vision

13 Once when Joshua was by Jericho, he looked up and saw a man standing before him with a drawn sword in his hand. Joshua went to him and said to him, "Are you one of us, or one of our adversaries?" ¹⁴He replied, "Neither; but as commander of the army of the LORD I have now come." And Joshua fell on his face to the earth and worshiped, and he said to him, "What do you command your servant, my lord?" ¹⁵The commander of the army of the LORD said to Joshua, "Remove the sandals from your feet, for the place where you stand is holy." And Joshua did so.

Jericho Taken and Destroyed

6 Now Jericho was shut up inside and out because of the Israelites; no one came out and no one went in. ²The LORD said to Joshua, "See, I have handed Jericho over to

---

Manna No More

JOSHUA 5.10–12

"O most blessed grace, which makes the poor in spirit rich in virtues, which renders one who is rich in many good things humble of heart, come, descend upon me, fill me quickly with your consolation lest my soul faint with weariness and dryness of mind. Let me find grace in your sight, I beg, Lord, for your grace is enough for me, even though I obtain none of the things which nature desires."

—THOMAS À KEMPIS,
The Imitation of Christ

---

a That is *the Hill of the Foreskins*   *b* Related to Heb *galal* to roll

Do Not Raise Your Voices

JOSHUA 6.8–11

God gives explicit instructions to Joshua on how to take Jericho. There is a time for the army to march in silence and a time to shout—and take the city.

Can silence and shouting have their places in the spiritual life? How might silence be an act of obedience (see Psalm 46.10)? How might shouting initiate an act of power (see Mark 10.47)? In what way is God calling you to be silent or to speak out?

See Meeting God in Service

you, along with its king and soldiers. ³You shall march around the city, all the warriors circling the city once. Thus you shall do for six days, ⁴with seven priests bearing seven trumpets of rams' horns before the ark. On the seventh day you shall march around the city seven times, the priests blowing the trumpets. ⁵When they make a long blast with the ram's horn, as soon as you hear the sound of the trumpet, then all the people shall shout with a great shout; and the wall of the city will fall down flat, and all the people shall charge straight ahead." ⁶So Joshua son of Nun summoned the priests and said to them, "Take up the ark of the covenant, and have seven priests carry seven trumpets of rams' horns in front of the ark of the Lord." ⁷To the people he said, "Go forward and march around the city; have the armed men pass on before the ark of the Lord."

8 As Joshua had commanded the people, the seven priests carrying the seven trumpets of rams' horns before the Lord went forward, blowing the trumpets, with the ark of the covenant of the Lord following them. ⁹And the armed men went before the priests who blew the trumpets; the rear guard came after the ark, while the trumpets blew continually. ¹⁰To the people Joshua gave this command: "You shall not shout or let your voice be heard, nor shall you utter a word, until the day I tell you to shout. Then you shall shout." ¹¹So the ark of the Lord went around the city, circling it once; and they came into the camp, and spent the night in the camp.

12 Then Joshua rose early in the morning, and the priests took up the ark of the Lord. ¹³The seven priests carrying the seven trumpets of rams' horns before the ark of the Lord passed on, blowing the trumpets continually. The armed men went before them, and the rear guard came after the ark of the Lord, while the trumpets blew continually. ¹⁴On the second day they marched around the city once and then returned to the camp. They did this for six days.

15 On the seventh day they rose early, at dawn, and marched around the city in the same manner seven times. It was only on that day that they marched around the city seven times. ¹⁶And at the seventh time, when the priests had blown the trumpets, Joshua said to the people, "Shout! For the Lord has given you the city. ¹⁷The city and all that is in it shall be devoted to the Lord for destruction. Only Rahab the prostitute and all who are with her in her house shall live because she hid the messengers we sent. ¹⁸As for you, keep away from the things devoted to destruction, so as not to covet*a* and take any of the devoted things and make the camp of Israel an object for destruction, bringing trouble upon it. ¹⁹But all silver and gold, and vessels of bronze and iron, are sacred to the Lord; they shall go into the treasury of the Lord." ²⁰So the people shouted, and the trumpets were blown. As soon as the people heard the sound of the trumpets, they raised a great shout, and the wall fell down flat; so the people charged straight ahead into the city and captured it. ²¹Then they devoted to destruction by the edge of the sword all in the city, both men and women, young and old, oxen, sheep, and donkeys.

22 Joshua said to the two men who had spied out the land, "Go into the prostitute's house, and bring the woman

a Gk: Heb *devote to destruction* Compare 7.21

out of it and all who belong to her, as you swore to her." ²³So the young men who had been spies went in and brought Rahab out, along with her father, her mother, her brothers, and all who belonged to her—they brought all her kindred out—and set them outside the camp of Israel. ²⁴They burned down the city, and everything in it; only the silver and gold, and the vessels of bronze and iron, they put into the treasury of the house of the LORD. ²⁵But Rahab the prostitute, with her family and all who belonged to her, Joshua spared. Her family*a* has lived in Israel ever since. For she hid the messengers whom Joshua sent to spy out Jericho.

26 Joshua then pronounced this oath, saying,

"Cursed before the LORD be anyone who tries
to build this city—this Jericho!

At the cost of his firstborn he shall lay its
foundation,

and at the cost of his youngest he shall set up its
gates!"

27 So the LORD was with Joshua; and his fame was in all the land.

The Sin of Achan and Its Punishment

7 But the Israelites broke faith in regard to the devoted things: Achan son of Carmi son of Zabdi son of Zerah, of the tribe of Judah, took some of the devoted things; and the anger of the LORD burned against the Israelites.

2 Joshua sent men from Jericho to Ai, which is near Beth-aven, east of Bethel, and said to them, "Go up and spy out the land." And the men went up and spied out Ai. ³Then they returned to Joshua and said to him, "Not all the people need go up; about two or three thousand men should go up and attack Ai. Since they are so few, do not make the whole people toil up there." ⁴So about three thousand of the people went up there; and they fled before the men of Ai. ⁵The men of Ai killed about thirty-six of them, chasing them from outside the gate as far as Shebarim and killing them on the slope. The hearts of the people melted and turned to water.

6 Then Joshua tore his clothes, and fell to the ground on his face before the ark of the LORD until the evening, he and the elders of Israel; and they put dust on their heads. ⁷Joshua said, "Ah, Lord GOD! Why have you brought this people across the Jordan at all, to hand us over to the Amorites so as to destroy us? Would that we had been content to settle beyond the Jordan! ⁸O Lord, what can I say, now that Israel has turned their backs to their enemies! ⁹The Canaanites and all the inhabitants of the land will hear of it, and surround us, and cut off our name from the earth. Then what will you do for your great name?"

10 The LORD said to Joshua, "Stand up! Why have you fallen upon your face? ¹¹Israel has sinned; they have transgressed my covenant that I imposed on them. They have taken some of the devoted things; they have stolen, they have acted deceitfully, and they have put them among their own belongings. ¹²Therefore the Israelites are unable to stand before their enemies; they turn their backs to their enemies, because they have become a thing devoted for destruction themselves. I will be with you no more, unless

---

Small Sins, Big Consequences

JOSHUA 7.1–5

Achan takes some of the gold and silver set apart for God from the spoils of Jericho. It seems to be only a little thing. Yet in God's eyes his action counts as the whole people breaking faith. It brings disaster as God withdraws his help from the army of Israel.

Can you recall an occasion when your "private" actions had consequences for a larger group—your family, your friends, your church, your company? Did it seem like a "little thing" at first? When did you realize that your actions had consequences for others? What did you learn from the experience? Ask God to help you see the big picture as you look at your own life.

See Meeting God in Community

---

a Heb She

Hidden Things

JOSHUA 7.13–15

Achan tries to hide his dishonest actions, yet God still knows all about them. In what ways do you try to hide from God? At what point does hiding your sin become exhausting enough to bring you to confession and repentance before the Lord? Why does the all-seeing God want us to open the door to our own hidden things? If you are able, invite God into the "hidden" places of your heart. Offer them to God; ask God to bring healing and cleansing. If you cannot yet make the invitation, ask for the grace to be more open and honest.

See Meeting God in Prayer

you destroy the devoted things from among you. ¹³Proceed to sanctify the people, and say, 'Sanctify yourselves for tomorrow; for thus says the LORD, the God of Israel, "There are devoted things among you, O Israel; you will be unable to stand before your enemies until you take away the devoted things from among you." ¹⁴In the morning therefore you shall come forward tribe by tribe. The tribe that the LORD takes shall come near by clans, the clan that the LORD takes shall come near by households, and the household that the LORD takes shall come near one by one. ¹⁵And the one who is taken as having the devoted things shall be burned with fire, together with all that he has, for having transgressed the covenant of the LORD, and for having done an outrageous thing in Israel.' "

16 So Joshua rose early in the morning, and brought Israel near tribe by tribe, and the tribe of Judah was taken. ¹⁷He brought near the clans of Judah, and the clan of the Zerahites was taken; and he brought near the clan of the Zerahites, family by family,ᵃ and Zabdi was taken. ¹⁸And he brought near his household one by one, and Achan son of Carmi son of Zabdi son of Zerah, of the tribe of Judah, was taken. ¹⁹Then Joshua said to Achan, "My son, give glory to the LORD God of Israel and make confession to him. Tell me now what you have done; do not hide it from me." ²⁰And Achan answered Joshua, "It is true; I am the one who sinned against the LORD God of Israel. This is what I did: ²¹when I saw among the spoil a beautiful mantle from Shinar, and two hundred shekels of silver, and a bar of gold weighing fifty shekels, then I coveted them and took them. They now lie hidden in the ground inside my tent, with the silver underneath."

22 So Joshua sent messengers, and they ran to the tent; and there it was, hidden in his tent with the silver underneath. ²³They took them out of the tent and brought them to Joshua and all the Israelites; and they spread them out before the LORD. ²⁴Then Joshua and all Israel with him took Achan son of Zerah, with the silver, the mantle, and the bar of gold, with his sons and daughters, with his oxen, donkeys, and sheep, and his tent and all that he had; and they brought them up to the Valley of Achor. ²⁵Joshua said, "Why did you bring trouble on us? The LORD is bringing trouble on you today." And all Israel stoned him to death; they burned them with fire, cast stones on them, ²⁶and raised over him a great heap of stones that remains to this day. Then the LORD turned from his burning anger. Therefore that place to this day is called the Valley of Achor.ᵇ

Ai Captured by a Stratagem and Destroyed

8 Then the LORD said to Joshua, "Do not fear or be dismayed; take all the fighting men with you, and go up now to Ai. See, I have handed over to you the king of Ai with his people, his city, and his land. ²You shall do to Ai and its king as you did to Jericho and its king; only its spoil and its livestock you may take as booty for yourselves. Set an ambush against the city, behind it."

3 So Joshua and all the fighting men set out to go up against Ai. Joshua chose thirty thousand warriors and sent them out by night ⁴with the command, "You shall lie in ambush against the city, behind it; do not go very far from the

a Mss Syr: MT *man by man*   *b* That is *Trouble*

city, but all of you stay alert. [5]I and all the people who are with me will approach the city. When they come out against us, as before, we shall flee from them. [6]They will come out after us until we have drawn them away from the city; for they will say, 'They are fleeing from us, as before.' While we flee from them, [7]you shall rise up from the ambush and seize the city; for the LORD your God will give it into your hand. [8]And when you have taken the city, you shall set the city on fire, doing as the LORD has ordered; see, I have commanded you." [9]So Joshua sent them out; and they went to the place of ambush, and lay between Bethel and Ai, to the west of Ai; but Joshua spent that night in the camp.[a]

10 In the morning Joshua rose early and mustered the people, and went up, with the elders of Israel, before the people to Ai. [11]All the fighting men who were with him went up, and drew near before the city, and camped on the north side of Ai, with a ravine between them and Ai. [12]Taking about five thousand men, he set them in ambush between Bethel and Ai, to the west of the city. [13]So they stationed the forces, the main encampment that was north of the city and its rear guard west of the city. But Joshua spent that night in the valley. [14]When the king of Ai saw this, he and all his people, the inhabitants of the city, hurried out early in the morning to the meeting place facing the Arabah to meet Israel in battle; but he did not know that there was an ambush against him behind the city. [15]And Joshua and all Israel made a pretense of being beaten before them, and fled in the direction of the wilderness. [16]So all the people who were in the city were called together to pursue them, and as they pursued Joshua they were drawn away from the city. [17]There was not a man left in Ai or Bethel who did not go out after Israel; they left the city open, and pursued Israel.

18 Then the LORD said to Joshua, "Stretch out the sword that is in your hand toward Ai; for I will give it into your hand." And Joshua stretched out the sword that was in his hand toward the city. [19]As soon as he stretched out his hand, the troops in ambush rose quickly out of their place and rushed forward. They entered the city, took it, and at once set the city on fire. [20]So when the men of Ai looked back, the smoke of the city was rising to the sky. They had no power to flee this way or that, for the people who fled to the wilderness turned back against the pursuers. [21]When Joshua and all Israel saw that the ambush had taken the city and that the smoke of the city was rising, then they turned back and struck down the men of Ai. [22]And the others came out from the city against them; so they were surrounded by Israelites, some on one side, and some on the other; and Israel struck them down until no one was left who survived or escaped. [23]But the king of Ai was taken alive and brought to Joshua.

24 When Israel had finished slaughtering all the inhabitants of Ai in the open wilderness where they pursued them, and when all of them to the very last had fallen by the edge of the sword, all Israel returned to Ai, and attacked it with the edge of the sword. [25]The total of those who fell that day, both men and women, was twelve thousand—all the people of Ai. [26]For Joshua did not draw back his hand,

Conquest a Different Way

JOSHUA 8.3–23

Though Ai, like Jericho, is Joshua's to conquer, God's strategy for defeating Ai is very different than the strategy used in defeating Jericho. Joshua and his army draw all the inhabitants of Ai completely outside the city walls, with the gates standing open.

What diverse ways and means has God used to defeat the enemies of your soul? How do Israel's experiences encourage you? What enemy do you face now? Ask God for guidance in developing a plan to defeat this enemy. Be open to new ways of defeating spiritual enemies.

Including the Strangers

JOSHUA 8.30–35

In triumph Joshua reads the book of the law to all the people, including the strangers who lived among the citizens of the land. God's Word was for all the people. God's Word addresses all areas of our lives, including those we haven't yet yielded to God. Write a journal page identifying areas you have surrendered to God and areas you haven't submitted to the authority of God's Word. Write a conversation between these varied aspects of your life. What is God saying to you through this exercise?

See Meeting God in Scripture

with which he stretched out the sword, until he had utterly destroyed all the inhabitants of Ai. ²⁷Only the livestock and the spoil of that city Israel took as their booty, according to the word of the LORD that he had issued to Joshua. ²⁸So Joshua burned Ai, and made it forever a heap of ruins, as it is to this day. ²⁹And he hanged the king of Ai on a tree until evening; and at sunset Joshua commanded, and they took his body down from the tree, threw it down at the entrance of the gate of the city, and raised over it a great heap of stones, which stands there to this day.

Joshua Renews the Covenant

30 Then Joshua built on Mount Ebal an altar to the LORD, the God of Israel, ³¹just as Moses the servant of the LORD had commanded the Israelites, as it is written in the book of the law of Moses, "an altar of unhewn*ᵃ* stones, on which no iron tool has been used"; and they offered on it burnt offerings to the LORD, and sacrificed offerings of well-being. ³²And there, in the presence of the Israelites, Joshua*ᵇ* wrote on the stones a copy of the law of Moses, which he had written. ³³All Israel, alien as well as citizen, with their elders and officers and their judges, stood on opposite sides of the ark in front of the levitical priests who carried the ark of the covenant of the LORD, half of them in front of Mount Gerizim and half of them in front of Mount Ebal, as Moses the servant of the LORD had commanded at the first, that they should bless the people of Israel. ³⁴And afterward he read all the words of the law, blessings and curses, according to all that is written in the book of the law. ³⁵There was not a word of all that Moses commanded that Joshua did not read before all the assembly of Israel, and the women, and the little ones, and the aliens who resided among them.

The Gibeonites Save Themselves by Trickery

9 Now when all the kings who were beyond the Jordan in the hill country and in the lowland all along the coast of the Great Sea toward Lebanon—the Hittites, the Amorites, the Canaanites, the Perizzites, the Hivites, and the Jebusites—heard of this, ²they gathered together with one accord to fight Joshua and Israel.

3 But when the inhabitants of Gibeon heard what Joshua had done to Jericho and to Ai, ⁴they on their part acted with cunning: they went and prepared provisions,*ᶜ* and took worn-out sacks for their donkeys, and wineskins, worn-out and torn and mended, ⁵with worn-out, patched sandals on their feet, and worn-out clothes; and all their provisions were dry and moldy. ⁶They went to Joshua in the camp at Gilgal, and said to him and to the Israelites, "We have come from a far country; so now make a treaty with us." ⁷But the Israelites said to the Hivites, "Perhaps you live among us; then how can we make a treaty with you?" ⁸They said to Joshua, "We are your servants." And Joshua said to them, "Who are you? And where do you come from?" ⁹They said to him, "Your servants have come from a very far country, because of the name of the LORD your God; for we have heard a report of him, of all that he did in Egypt, ¹⁰and of all that he did to the two kings of the Amorites who were beyond the Jordan, King Sihon of Heshbon, and King Og of Bashan who lived in Ashtaroth. ¹¹So

a Heb *whole* *b* Heb *he* *c* Cn: Meaning of Heb uncertain our elders and all the inhabitants of our country said to us, 'Take provisions in your hand for the journey; go to meet them, and say to them, "We are your servants; come now, make a treaty with us." ' ¹²Here is our bread; it was still warm when we took it from our houses as our food for the journey, on the day we set out to come to you, but now, see, it is dry and moldy; ¹³these wineskins were new when we filled them, and see, they are burst; and these garments and sandals of ours are worn out from the very long journey." ¹⁴So the leaders*a* partook of their provisions, and did not ask direction from the LORD. ¹⁵And Joshua made peace with them, guaranteeing their lives by a treaty; and the leaders of the congregation swore an oath to them.

16 But when three days had passed after they had made a treaty with them, they heard that they were their neighbors and were living among them. ¹⁷So the Israelites set out and reached their cities on the third day. Now their cities were Gibeon, Chephirah, Beeroth, and Kiriath-jearim. ¹⁸But the Israelites did not attack them, because the leaders of the congregation had sworn to them by the LORD, the God of Israel. Then all the congregation murmured against the leaders. ¹⁹But all the leaders said to all the congregation, "We have sworn to them by the LORD, the God of Israel, and now we must not touch them. ²⁰This is what we will do to them: We will let them live, so that wrath may not come upon us, because of the oath that we swore to them." ²¹The leaders said to them, "Let them live." So they became hewers of wood and drawers of water for all the congregation, as the leaders had decided concerning them.

22 Joshua summoned them, and said to them, "Why did you deceive us, saying, 'We are very far from you,' while in fact you are living among us? ²³Now therefore you are cursed, and some of you shall always be slaves, hewers of wood and drawers of water for the house of my God." ²⁴They answered Joshua, "Because it was told to your servants for a certainty that the LORD your God had commanded his servant Moses to give you all the land, and to destroy all the inhabitants of the land before you; so we were in great fear for our lives because of you, and did this thing. ²⁵And now we are in your hand: do as it seems good and right in your sight to do to us." ²⁶This is what he did for them: he saved them from the Israelites; and they did not kill them. ²⁷But on that day Joshua made them hewers of wood and drawers of water for the congregation and for the altar of the LORD, to continue to this day, in the place that he should choose.

The Sun Stands Still

10 When King Adoni-zedek of Jerusalem heard how Joshua had taken Ai, and had utterly destroyed it, doing to Ai and its king as he had done to Jericho and its king, and how the inhabitants of Gibeon had made peace with Israel and were among them, ²he*b* became greatly frightened, because Gibeon was a large city, like one of the royal cities, and was larger than Ai, and all its men were warriors. ³So King Adoni-zedek of Jerusalem sent a message to King Hoham of Hebron, to King Piram of Jarmuth, to King Japhia of Lachish, and to King Debir of Eglon, saying, ⁴"Come up and help me, and let us attack Gibeon; for

a Gk: Heb *men*   *b* Heb *they*

Inquire First

JOSHUA 9.3–15

When the people of Gibeon come to Joshua, he judges them by their appearance and makes a hasty alliance without bothering to consult God. Joshua finds himself trapped by his shortsightedness.

Meeting deadlines, responding to the demands of family life, coping with fatigue or feeling "stressed" often tempt us to go ahead with plans without inquiring about God's will in the situation. In what ways does failing to inquire of the Lord make you vulnerable to attack, difficulty, failure, damage? What kinds of pressures cause you to step out with your own power of reasoning and make assumptions without consulting God directly? What issue needs prayerful consultation right now, before you rush into action?

See Meeting God in Everyday Life

When God Listens to Humans

JOSHUA 10.6–14

Envision yourself in Joshua's army of the Lord. You have fought all day. You are tired but exhilarated. Feel the heat of the sun, smell the parched earth and trampled grass, hear the buzzing of insects attracted to the sweat running down your neck. Hear Joshua's voice as he addresses the troops. How do you feel as you hear him command the sun and moon to stand still? What do you see in the sky?

In what extraordinary ways has God answered Joshua's prayer and given victory to Israel? What will you tell your children about this day? What is God saying to you through this drama?

See Meeting God in Scripture

it has made peace with Joshua and with the Israelites." ⁵Then the five kings of the Amorites—the king of Jerusalem, the king of Hebron, the king of Jarmuth, the king of Lachish, and the king of Eglon—gathered their forces, and went up with all their armies and camped against Gibeon, and made war against it.

6 And the Gibeonites sent to Joshua at the camp in Gilgal, saying, "Do not abandon your servants; come up to us quickly, and save us, and help us; for all the kings of the Amorites who live in the hill country are gathered against us." ⁷So Joshua went up from Gilgal, he and all the fighting force with him, all the mighty warriors. ⁸The LORD said to Joshua, "Do not fear them, for I have handed them over to you; not one of them shall stand before you." ⁹So Joshua came upon them suddenly, having marched up all night from Gilgal. ¹⁰And the LORD threw them into a panic before Israel, who inflicted a great slaughter on them at Gibeon, chased them by the way of the ascent of Beth-horon, and struck them down as far as Azekah and Makkedah. ¹¹As they fled before Israel, while they were going down the slope of Beth-horon, the LORD threw down huge stones from heaven on them as far as Azekah, and they died; there were more who died because of the hailstones than the Israelites killed with the sword.

12 On the day when the LORD gave the Amorites over to the Israelites, Joshua spoke to the LORD; and he said in the sight of Israel,

"Sun, stand still at Gibeon,
    and Moon, in the valley of Aijalon."
¹³   And the sun stood still, and the moon stopped,
    until the nation took vengeance on their enemies.

Is this not written in the Book of Jashar? The sun stopped in midheaven, and did not hurry to set for about a whole day. ¹⁴There has been no day like it before or since, when the LORD heeded a human voice; for the LORD fought for Israel.

15 Then Joshua returned, and all Israel with him, to the camp at Gilgal.

Five Kings Defeated

16 Meanwhile, these five kings fled and hid themselves in the cave at Makkedah. ¹⁷And it was told Joshua, "The five kings have been found, hidden in the cave at Makkedah." ¹⁸Joshua said, "Roll large stones against the mouth of the cave, and set men by it to guard them; ¹⁹but do not stay there yourselves; pursue your enemies, and attack them from the rear. Do not let them enter their towns, for the LORD your God has given them into your hand." ²⁰When Joshua and the Israelites had finished inflicting a very great slaughter on them, until they were wiped out, and when the survivors had entered into the fortified towns, ²¹all the people returned safe to Joshua in the camp at Makkedah; no one dared to speak*ᵃ* against any of the Israelites.

22 Then Joshua said, "Open the mouth of the cave, and bring those five kings out to me from the cave." ²³They did so, and brought the five kings out to him from the cave, the king of Jerusalem, the king of Hebron, the king of Jarmuth, the king of Lachish, and the king of Eglon. ²⁴When they brought the kings out to Joshua, Joshua summoned all the Israelites, and said to the chiefs of the warriors who had

a Heb moved his tongue

gone with him, "Come near, put your feet on the necks of these kings." Then they came near and put their feet on their necks. 25And Joshua said to them, "Do not be afraid or dismayed; be strong and courageous; for thus the LORD will do to all the enemies against whom you fight." 26Afterward Joshua struck them down and put them to death, and he hung them on five trees. And they hung on the trees until evening. 27At sunset Joshua commanded, and they took them down from the trees and threw them into the cave where they had hidden themselves; they set large stones against the mouth of the cave, which remain to this very day.

28 Joshua took Makkedah on that day, and struck it and its king with the edge of the sword; he utterly destroyed every person in it; he left no one remaining. And he did to the king of Makkedah as he had done to the king of Jericho.

29 Then Joshua passed on from Makkedah, and all Israel with him, to Libnah, and fought against Libnah. 30The LORD gave it also and its king into the hand of Israel; and he struck it with the edge of the sword, and every person in it; he left no one remaining in it; and he did to its king as he had done to the king of Jericho.

31 Next Joshua passed on from Libnah, and all Israel with him, to Lachish, and laid siege to it, and assaulted it. 32The LORD gave Lachish into the hand of Israel, and he took it on the second day, and struck it with the edge of the sword, and every person in it, as he had done to Libnah.

33 Then King Horam of Gezer came up to help Lachish; and Joshua struck him and his people, leaving him no survivors.

34 From Lachish Joshua passed on with all Israel to Eglon; and they laid siege to it, and assaulted it; 35and they took it that day, and struck it with the edge of the sword; and every person in it he utterly destroyed that day, as he had done to Lachish.

36 Then Joshua went up with all Israel from Eglon to Hebron; they assaulted it, 37and took it, and struck it with the edge of the sword, and its king and its towns, and every person in it; he left no one remaining, just as he had done to Eglon, and utterly destroyed it with every person in it.

38 Then Joshua, with all Israel, turned back to Debir and assaulted it, 39and he took it with its king and all its towns; they struck them with the edge of the sword, and utterly destroyed every person in it; he left no one remaining; just as he had done to Hebron, and, as he had done to Libnah and its king, so he did to Debir and its king.

40 So Joshua defeated the whole land, the hill country and the Negeb and the lowland and the slopes, and all their kings; he left no one remaining, but utterly destroyed all that breathed, as the LORD God of Israel commanded. 41And Joshua defeated them from Kadesh-barnea to Gaza, and all the country of Goshen, as far as Gibeon. 42Joshua took all these kings and their land at one time, because the LORD God of Israel fought for Israel. 43Then Joshua returned, and all Israel with him, to the camp at Gilgal.

The United Kings of Northern Canaan Defeated

11 When King Jabin of Hazor heard of this, he sent to King Jobab of Madon, to the king of Shimron, to the king of Achshaph, 2and to the kings who were in the north-

Conquering With Burning Passion

JOSHUA 11.10–11

"When God calls . . . God bids us to come and burn—burn with a new love, a new desire, that will take all the mixed and muddled desires and ambitions and burn till it has refined all that was God-given in them and purged out all that was going in other directions."

—N. T. WRIGHT,
The Crown and the Fire

ern hill country, and in the Arabah south of Chinneroth, and in the lowland, and in Naphoth-dor on the west, ³to the Canaanites in the east and the west, the Amorites, the Hittites, the Perizzites, and the Jebusites in the hill country, and the Hivites under Hermon in the land of Mizpah. ⁴They came out, with all their troops, a great army, in number like the sand on the seashore, with very many horses and chariots. ⁵All these kings joined their forces, and came and camped together at the waters of Merom, to fight with Israel.

6 And the Lord said to Joshua, "Do not be afraid of them, for tomorrow at this time I will hand over all of them, slain, to Israel; you shall hamstring their horses, and burn their chariots with fire." ⁷So Joshua came suddenly upon them with all his fighting force, by the waters of Merom, and fell upon them. ⁸And the Lord handed them over to Israel, who attacked them and chased them as far as Great Sidon and Misrephoth-maim, and eastward as far as the valley of Mizpeh. They struck them down, until they had left no one remaining. ⁹And Joshua did to them as the Lord commanded him; he hamstrung their horses, and burned their chariots with fire.

10 Joshua turned back at that time, and took Hazor, and struck its king down with the sword. Before that time Hazor was the head of all those kingdoms. ¹¹And they put to the sword all who were in it, utterly destroying them; there was no one left who breathed, and he burned Hazor with fire. ¹²And all the towns of those kings, and all their kings, Joshua took, and struck them with the edge of the sword, utterly destroying them, as Moses the servant of the Lord had commanded. ¹³But Israel burned none of the towns that stood on mounds except Hazor, which Joshua did burn. ¹⁴All the spoil of these towns, and the livestock, the Israelites took for their booty; but all the people they struck down with the edge of the sword, until they had destroyed them, and they did not leave any who breathed. ¹⁵As the Lord had commanded his servant Moses, so Moses commanded Joshua, and so Joshua did; he left nothing undone of all that the Lord had commanded Moses.

Summary of Joshua's Conquests

16 So Joshua took all that land: the hill country and all the Negeb and all the land of Goshen and the lowland and the Arabah and the hill country of Israel and its lowland, ¹⁷from Mount Halak, which rises toward Seir, as far as Baalgad in the valley of Lebanon below Mount Hermon. He took all their kings, struck them down, and put them to death. ¹⁸Joshua made war a long time with all those kings. ¹⁹There was not a town that made peace with the Israelites, except the Hivites, the inhabitants of Gibeon; all were taken in battle. ²⁰For it was the Lord's doing to harden their hearts so that they would come against Israel in battle, in order that they might be utterly destroyed, and might receive no mercy, but be exterminated, just as the Lord had commanded Moses.

21 At that time Joshua came and wiped out the Anakim from the hill country, from Hebron, from Debir, from Anab, and from all the hill country of Judah, and from all the hill country of Israel; Joshua utterly destroyed them with their towns. ²²None of the Anakim was left in the land of the Is-

Let no day
pass by without reading
some portion of the

sacred Scriptures
and giving some space to

meditation;
for nothing feeds the soul
so well as those sacred studies do.

THEONAS OF ALEXANDRIA (C. 300)

The Epistle of Theonas

Scripture
is like a river,
broad and deep,

shallow enough here
for the lamb to go wading,
but deep enough there
for the elephant to swim.

GREGORY THE GREAT (540-604)

Moralia in Iob, Book I

Even when carrying out
needful tasks,
keep meditating inwardly
and praying.
Thus you can grasp the
depths of divine Scripture
and the power hidden in it,
and "pray without ceasing."

ABBA PHILIMON (LATE SIXTH CENTURY?)
The Philokalia (Volume Two)

Reading

seeks for the sweetness
of a blessed life,
meditation perceives it,
prayer asks for it,
contemplation tastes it.

GUIGO II (D. 1188)
The Ladder of Monks

raelites; some remained only in Gaza, in Gath, and in Ashdod. 23So Joshua took the whole land, according to all that the LORD had spoken to Moses; and Joshua gave it for an inheritance to Israel according to their tribal allotments. And the land had rest from war.

The Kings Conquered by Moses

12 Now these are the kings of the land, whom the Israelites defeated, whose land they occupied beyond the Jordan toward the east, from the Wadi Arnon to Mount Hermon, with all the Arabah eastward: 2King Sihon of the Amorites who lived at Heshbon, and ruled from Aroer, which is on the edge of the Wadi Arnon, and from the middle of the valley as far as the river Jabbok, the boundary of the Ammonites, that is, half of Gilead, 3and the Arabah to the Sea of Chinneroth eastward, and in the direction of Beth-jeshimoth, to the sea of the Arabah, the Dead Sea,*a* southward to the foot of the slopes of Pisgah; 4and King Og*b* of Bashan, one of the last of the Rephaim, who lived at Ashtaroth and at Edrei 5and ruled over Mount Hermon and Salecah and all Bashan to the boundary of the Geshurites and the Maacathites, and over half of Gilead to the boundary of King Sihon of Heshbon. 6Moses, the servant of the LORD, and the Israelites defeated them; and Moses the servant of the LORD gave their land for a possession to the Reubenites and the Gadites and the half-tribe of Manasseh.

The Kings Conquered by Joshua

7 The following are the kings of the land whom Joshua and the Israelites defeated on the west side of the Jordan, from Baal-gad in the valley of Lebanon to Mount Halak, that rises toward Seir (and Joshua gave their land to the tribes of Israel as a possession according to their allotments, 8in the hill country, in the lowland, in the Arabah, in the slopes, in the wilderness, and in the Negeb, the land of the Hittites, Amorites, Canaanites, Perizzites, Hivites, and Jebusites):

9	the king of Jericho	one
	the king of Ai, which is next to Bethel	one
10	the king of Jerusalem	one
	the king of Hebron	one
11	the king of Jarmuth	one
	the king of Lachish	one
12	the king of Eglon	one
	the king of Gezer	one
13	the king of Debir	one
	the king of Geder	one
14	the king of Hormah	one
	the king of Arad	one
15	the king of Libnah	one
	the king of Adullam	one
16	the king of Makkedah	one
	the king of Bethel	one
17	the king of Tappuah	one
	the king of Hepher	one
18	the king of Aphek	one
	the king of Lasharon	one
19	the king of Madon	one
	the king of Hazor	one
20	the king of Shimron-meron	one

a Heb *Salt Sea*   *b* Gk: Heb *the boundary of King Og*

Resting From War

JOSHUA 11.21–23

Even when God required much warfare from the Israelites so that they could possess the land, there did come a time of rest and distribution of the fruits of victory.

In what ways are you enjoying the fruits of your obedience to God? When do you know you are experiencing God-ordained rest? How can you tell when it is time to do spiritual battle? How do you know when it is time to rest? What time is it now?

See Meeting God in the Created Order

God at All Ages and Stages

JOSHUA 13.1–7

Although Joshua is now very old, there is more land yet to be taken. In spite of Joshua's age, God wants to use him.

We are never too old to be used by God and to exercise our faith in obedience. To what new challenge is God calling you? Do you feel too old, too tired? What will be the source of your strength to continue to actively obey God?

See Meeting God in Service

	the king of Achshaph	one
21	the king of Taanach	one
	the king of Megiddo	one
22	the king of Kedesh	one
	the king of Jokneam in Carmel	one
23	the king of Dor in Naphath-dor	one
	the king of Goiim in Galilee,[a]	one
24	the king of Tirzah	one

thirty-one kings in all.

The Parts of Canaan Still Unconquered

13 Now Joshua was old and advanced in years; and the LORD said to him, "You are old and advanced in years, and very much of the land still remains to be possessed. ²This is the land that still remains: all the regions of the Philistines, and all those of the Geshurites ³(from the Shihor, which is east of Egypt, northward to the boundary of Ekron, it is reckoned as Canaanite; there are five rulers of the Philistines, those of Gaza, Ashdod, Ashkelon, Gath, and Ekron), and those of the Avvim ⁴in the south; all the land of the Canaanites, and Mearah that belongs to the Sidonians, to Aphek, to the boundary of the Amorites, ⁵and the land of the Gebalites, and all Lebanon, toward the east, from Baal-gad below Mount Hermon to Lebo-hamath, ⁶all the inhabitants of the hill country from Lebanon to Misrephoth-maim, even all the Sidonians. I will myself drive them out from before the Israelites; only allot the land to Israel for an inheritance, as I have commanded you. ⁷Now therefore divide this land for an inheritance for the nine tribes and the half-tribe of Manasseh."

The Territory East of the Jordan

8 With the other half-tribe of Manasseh[b] the Reubenites and the Gadites received their inheritance, which Moses gave them, beyond the Jordan eastward, as Moses the servant of the LORD gave them: ⁹from Aroer, which is on the edge of the Wadi Arnon, and the town that is in the middle of the valley, and all the tableland from[c] Medeba as far as Dibon; ¹⁰and all the cities of King Sihon of the Amorites, who reigned in Heshbon, as far as the boundary of the Ammonites; ¹¹and Gilead, and the region of the Geshurites and Maacathites, and all Mount Hermon, and all Bashan to Salecah; ¹²all the kingdom of Og in Bashan, who reigned in Ashtaroth and in Edrei (he alone was left of the survivors of the Rephaim); these Moses had defeated and driven out. ¹³Yet the Israelites did not drive out the Geshurites or the Maacathites; but Geshur and Maacath live within Israel to this day.

14 To the tribe of Levi alone Moses gave no inheritance; the offerings by fire to the LORD God of Israel are their inheritance, as he said to them.

The Territory of Reuben

15 Moses gave an inheritance to the tribe of the Reubenites according to their clans. ¹⁶Their territory was from Aroer, which is on the edge of the Wadi Arnon, and the town that is in the middle of the valley, and all the tableland by Medeba; ¹⁷with Heshbon, and all its towns that are in the tableland; Dibon, and Bamoth-baal, and Beth-baal-

a Gk: Heb *Gilgal*   *b* Cn: Heb *With it*   *c* Compare Gk: Heb lacks *from*

meon, [18]and Jahaz, and Kedemoth, and Mephaath, [19]and Kiriathaim, and Sibmah, and Zereth-shahar on the hill of the valley, [20]and Beth-peor, and the slopes of Pisgah, and Beth-jeshimoth, [21]that is, all the towns of the tableland, and all the kingdom of King Sihon of the Amorites, who reigned in Heshbon, whom Moses defeated with the leaders of Midian, Evi and Rekem and Zur and Hur and Reba, as princes of Sihon, who lived in the land. [22]Along with the rest of those they put to death, the Israelites also put to the sword Balaam son of Beor, who practiced divination. [23]And the border of the Reubenites was the Jordan and its banks. This was the inheritance of the Reubenites according to their families with their towns and villages.

The Territory of Gad

24 Moses gave an inheritance also to the tribe of the Gadites, according to their families. [25]Their territory was Jazer, and all the towns of Gilead, and half the land of the Ammonites, to Aroer, which is east of Rabbah, [26]and from Heshbon to Ramath-mizpeh and Betonim, and from Mahanaim to the territory of Debir,[a] [27]and in the valley Beth-haram, Beth-nimrah, Succoth, and Zaphon, the rest of the kingdom of King Sihon of Heshbon, the Jordan and its banks, as far as the lower end of the Sea of Chinnereth, eastward beyond the Jordan. [28]This is the inheritance of the Gadites according to their clans, with their towns and villages.

The Territory of the Half-Tribe of Manasseh (East)

29 Moses gave an inheritance to the half-tribe of Manasseh; it was allotted to the half-tribe of the Manassites according to their families. [30]Their territory extended from Mahanaim, through all Bashan, the whole kingdom of King Og of Bashan, and all the settlements of Jair, which are in Bashan, sixty towns, [31]and half of Gilead, and Ashtaroth, and Edrei, the towns of the kingdom of Og in Bashan; these were allotted to the people of Machir son of Manasseh according to their clans—for half the Machirites.

32 These are the inheritances that Moses distributed in the plains of Moab, beyond the Jordan east of Jericho. [33]But to the tribe of Levi Moses gave no inheritance; the LORD God of Israel is their inheritance, as he said to them.

The Distribution of Territory West of the Jordan

14 These are the inheritances that the Israelites received in the land of Canaan, which the priest Eleazar, and Joshua son of Nun, and the heads of the families of the tribes of the Israelites distributed to them. [2]Their inheritance was by lot, as the LORD had commanded Moses for the nine and one-half tribes. [3]For Moses had given an inheritance to the two and one-half tribes beyond the Jordan; but to the Levites he gave no inheritance among them. [4]For the people of Joseph were two tribes, Manasseh and Ephraim; and no portion was given to the Levites in the land, but only towns to live in, with their pasture lands for their flocks and herds. [5]The Israelites did as the LORD commanded Moses; they allotted the land.

a Gk Syr Vg: Heb *Lidebir*

Our Divine Inheritance

JOSHUA 13.32–33

"This divine king, full of mercy and goodness, far from chastising me, embraces me with love, makes me eat at his table, serves me with his own hands, gives me the key of his treasures; God converses and delights himself with me incessantly, in a thousand and a thousand ways . . . It is thus I consider myself from time to time in God's holy presence."

—BROTHER LAWRENCE,
The Practice of the Presence of God

Testimony of an Explorer

JOSHUA 14.6–12

Caleb recounts his life of service to God and God's people. Now, at eighty-five, he asks not for retirement, but for a new challenge—a territory to conquer and make his own for God's sake.

Give some thought to your own aging. Do you fear it or welcome it? "You have made my days a few handbreaths," confesses the psalmist (Psalm 39.5). What plans can you make now to ensure that you live vigorously in the Lord in your later years? What spiritual habits can you form now to prepare you for faithful service even when you are old?

See Meeting God in Service

Hebron Allotted to Caleb

6 Then the people of Judah came to Joshua at Gilgal; and Caleb son of Jephunneh the Kenizzite said to him, "You know what the LORD said to Moses the man of God in Kadesh-barnea concerning you and me. ⁷I was forty years old when Moses the servant of the LORD sent me from Kadesh-barnea to spy out the land; and I brought him an honest report. ⁸But my companions who went up with me made the heart of the people melt; yet I wholeheartedly followed the LORD my God. ⁹And Moses swore on that day, saying, 'Surely the land on which your foot has trodden shall be an inheritance for you and your children forever, because you have wholeheartedly followed the LORD my God.' ¹⁰And now, as you see, the LORD has kept me alive, as he said, these forty-five years since the time that the LORD spoke this word to Moses, while Israel was journeying through the wilderness; and here I am today, eighty-five years old. ¹¹I am still as strong today as I was on the day that Moses sent me; my strength now is as my strength was then, for war, and for going and coming. ¹²So now give me this hill country of which the LORD spoke on that day; for you heard on that day how the Anakim were there, with great fortified cities; it may be that the LORD will be with me, and I shall drive them out, as the LORD said."

13 Then Joshua blessed him, and gave Hebron to Caleb son of Jephunneh for an inheritance. ¹⁴So Hebron became the inheritance of Caleb son of Jephunneh the Kenizzite to this day, because he wholeheartedly followed the LORD, the God of Israel. ¹⁵Now the name of Hebron formerly was Kiriath-arba;ᵃ this Arba wasᵇ the greatest man among the Anakim. And the land had rest from war.

The Territory of Judah

15 The lot for the tribe of the people of Judah according to their families reached southward to the boundary of Edom, to the wilderness of Zin at the farthest south. ²And their south boundary ran from the end of the Dead Sea,ᶜ from the bay that faces southward; ³it goes out southward of the ascent of Akrabbim, passes along to Zin, and goes up south of Kadesh-barnea, along by Hezron, up to Addar, makes a turn to Karka, ⁴passes along to Azmon, goes out by the Wadi of Egypt, and comes to its end at the sea. This shall be your south boundary. ⁵And the east boundary is the Dead Sea,ᶜ to the mouth of the Jordan. And the boundary on the north side runs from the bay of the sea at the mouth of the Jordan; ⁶and the boundary goes up to Beth-hoglah, and passes along north of Beth-arabah; and the boundary goes up to the Stone of Bohan, Reuben's son; ⁷and the boundary goes up to Debir from the Valley of Achor, and so northward, turning toward Gilgal, which is opposite the ascent of Adummim, which is on the south side of the valley; and the boundary passes along to the waters of En-shemesh, and ends at En-rogel; ⁸then the boundary goes up by the valley of the son of Hinnom at the southern slope of the Jebusites (that is, Jerusalem); and the boundary goes up to the top of the mountain that lies over against the valley of Hinnom, on the west, at the northern end of the valley of Rephaim; ⁹then the boundary

a That is *the city of Arba*   *b* Heb lacks *this Arba was*   *c* Heb *Salt Sea*

extends from the top of the mountain to the spring of the Waters of Nephtoah, and from there to the towns of Mount Ephron; then the boundary bends around to Baalah (that is, Kiriath-jearim); [10]and the boundary circles west of Baalah to Mount Seir, passes along to the northern slope of Mount Jearim (that is, Chesalon), and goes down to Beth-shemesh, and passes along by Timnah; [11]the boundary goes out to the slope of the hill north of Ekron, then the boundary bends around to Shikkeron, and passes along to Mount Baalah, and goes out to Jabneel; then the boundary comes to an end at the sea. [12]And the west boundary was the Mediterranean with its coast. This is the boundary surrounding the people of Judah according to their families.

Caleb Occupies His Portion

13 According to the commandment of the LORD to Joshua, he gave to Caleb son of Jephunneh a portion among the people of Judah, Kiriath-arba,[a] that is, Hebron (Arba was the father of Anak). [14]And Caleb drove out from there the three sons of Anak: Sheshai, Ahiman, and Talmai, the descendants of Anak. [15]From there he went up against the inhabitants of Debir; now the name of Debir formerly was Kiriath-sepher. [16]And Caleb said, "Whoever attacks Kiriath-sepher and takes it, to him I will give my daughter Achsah as wife." [17]Othniel son of Kenaz, the brother of Caleb, took it; and he gave him his daughter Achsah as wife. [18]When she came to him, she urged her to ask her father for a field. As she dismounted from her donkey, Caleb said to her, "What do you wish?" [19]She said to him, "Give me a present; since you have set me in the land of the Negeb, give me springs of water as well." So Caleb gave her the upper springs and the lower springs.

The Towns of Judah

20 This is the inheritance of the tribe of the people of Judah according to their families. [21]The towns belonging to the tribe of the people of Judah in the extreme south, toward the boundary of Edom, were Kabzeel, Eder, Jagur, [22]Kinah, Dimonah, Adadah, [23]Kedesh, Hazor, Ithnan, [24]Ziph, Telem, Bealoth, [25]Hazor-hadattah, Kerioth-hezron (that is, Hazor), [26]Amam, Shema, Moladah, [27]Hazar-gaddah, Heshmon, Beth-pelet, [28]Hazar-shual, Beer-sheba, Biziothiah, [29]Baalah, Iim, Ezem, [30]Eltolad, Chesil, Hormah, [31]Ziklag, Madmannah, Sansannah, [32]Lebaoth, Shilhim, Ain, and Rimmon: in all, twenty-nine towns, with their villages.

33 And in the lowland, Eshtaol, Zorah, Ashnah, [34]Zanoah, En-gannim, Tappuah, Enam, [35]Jarmuth, Adullam, Socoh, Azekah, [36]Shaaraim, Adithaim, Gederah, Gederothaim: fourteen towns with their villages.

37 Zenan, Hadashah, Migdal-gad, [38]Dilan, Mizpeh, Jokthe-el, [39]Lachish, Bozkath, Eglon, [40]Cabbon, Lahmam, Chitlish, [41]Gederoth, Beth-dagon, Naamah, and Makkedah: sixteen towns with their villages.

42 Libnah, Ether, Ashan, [43]Iphtah, Ashnah, Nezib, [44]Keilah, Achzib, and Mareshah: nine towns with their villages.

45 Ekron, with its dependencies and its villages; [46]from Ekron to the sea, all that were near Ashdod, with their villages.

47 Ashdod, its towns and its villages; Gaza, its towns

Give Me Springs of Water

JOSHUA 15.15–19

Caleb's daughter, Achsah, is a reward for a conqueror. Not only does her husband receive land along with his bride, but, at Achsah's request, also receives springs of water. This bride knows that the land must have a source of water to keep it fruitful, to make things grow and to nourish it.

What images come to mind when you think of springs of water? What do these images convey to you about your source of spiritual nourishment and sustenance? Spend some time sitting quietly, picturing God's love—God's Spirit—welling up in your heart, nurturing your spirit and overflowing to those around you.

See Meeting God in the Created Order

---

a That is *the city of Arba*

The Wilderness and Hills of Life

JOSHUA 16.1–3

This passage outlines the allotment of land to Ephraim and Manasseh. This allotment encompasses both hill country and wilderness. While that geography has a very physical significance for the people, it also carries spiritual meaning.

Throughout scripture, hills and deserts, or wilderness areas, have symbolic as well as literal significance. Walk in memory through the spiritual "deserts" of your life. Feel again the dryness of those times when spiritual refreshment seemed meager and experience again the heat of pressure to "look" Christian even though you didn't "feel" Christian; recollect the disappointment in the mirage of ritual without meaning. Recall also the climb up hills of spiritual challenge. How did God beckon you onward up the hill or across the wilderness? How have you learned to dwell both in the hills and in the wilderness as you respond to God's direction?

See Meeting God in Everyday Life

and its villages; to the Wadi of Egypt, and the Great Sea with its coast.

48 And in the hill country, Shamir, Jattir, Socoh, ⁴⁹Dannah, Kiriath-sannah (that is, Debir), ⁵⁰Anab, Eshtemoh, Anim, ⁵¹Goshen, Holon, and Giloh: eleven towns with their villages.

52 Arab, Dumah, Eshan, ⁵³Janim, Beth-tappuah, Aphekah, ⁵⁴Humtah, Kiriath-arba (that is, Hebron), and Zior: nine towns with their villages.

55 Maon, Carmel, Ziph, Juttah, ⁵⁶Jezreel, Jokdeam, Zanoah, ⁵⁷Kain, Gibeah, and Timnah: ten towns with their villages.

58 Halhul, Beth-zur, Gedor, ⁵⁹Maarath, Beth-anoth, and Eltekon: six towns with their villages.

60 Kiriath-baal (that is, Kiriath-jearim) and Rabbah: two towns with their villages.

61 In the wilderness, Beth-arabah, Middin, Secacah, ⁶²Nibshan, the City of Salt, and En-gedi: six towns with their villages.

63 But the people of Judah could not drive out the Jebusites, the inhabitants of Jerusalem; so the Jebusites live with the people of Judah in Jerusalem to this day.

The Territory of Ephraim

16 The allotment of the Josephites went from the Jordan by Jericho, east of the waters of Jericho, into the wilderness, going up from Jericho into the hill country to Bethel; ²then going from Bethel to Luz, it passes along to Ataroth, the territory of the Archites; ³then it goes down westward to the territory of the Japhletites, as far as the territory of Lower Beth-horon, then to Gezer, and it ends at the sea.

4 The Josephites—Manasseh and Ephraim—received their inheritance.

5 The territory of the Ephraimites by their families was as follows: the boundary of their inheritance on the east was Ataroth-addar as far as Upper Beth-horon, ⁶and the boundary goes from there to the sea; on the north is Michmethath; then on the east the boundary makes a turn toward Taanath-shiloh, and passes along beyond it on the east to Janoah, ⁷then it goes down from Janoah to Ataroth and to Naarah, and touches Jericho, ending at the Jordan. ⁸From Tappuah the boundary goes westward to the Wadi Kanah, and ends at the sea. Such is the inheritance of the tribe of the Ephraimites by their families, ⁹together with the towns that were set apart for the Ephraimites within the inheritance of the Manassites, all those towns with their villages. ¹⁰They did not, however, drive out the Canaanites who lived in Gezer: so the Canaanites have lived within Ephraim to this day but have been made to do forced labor.

The Other Half-Tribe of Manasseh (West)

17 Then allotment was made to the tribe of Manasseh, for he was the firstborn of Joseph. To Machir the firstborn of Manasseh, the father of Gilead, were allotted Gilead and Bashan, because he was a warrior. ²And allotments were made to the rest of the tribe of Manasseh, by their families, Abiezer, Helek, Asriel, Shechem, Hepher, and Shemida; these were the male descendants of Manasseh son of Joseph, by their families.

3 Now Zelophehad son of Hepher son of Gilead son of Machir son of Manasseh had no sons, but only daughters; and these are the names of his daughters: Mahlah, Noah, Hoglah, Milcah, and Tirzah. 4They came before the priest Eleazar and Joshua son of Nun and the leaders, and said, "The LORD commanded Moses to give us an inheritance along with our male kin." So according to the commandment of the LORD he gave them an inheritance among the kinsmen of their father. 5Thus there fell to Manasseh ten portions, besides the land of Gilead and Bashan, which is on the other side of the Jordan, 6because the daughters of Manasseh received an inheritance along with his sons. The land of Gilead was allotted to the rest of the Manassites.

7 The territory of Manasseh reached from Asher to Michmethath, which is east of Shechem; then the boundary goes along southward to the inhabitants of En-tappuah. 8The land of Tappuah belonged to Manasseh, but the town of Tappuah on the boundary of Manasseh belonged to the Ephraimites. 9Then the boundary went down to the Wadi Kanah. The towns here, to the south of the wadi, among the towns of Manasseh, belong to Ephraim. Then the boundary of Manasseh goes along the north side of the wadi and ends at the sea. 10The land to the south is Ephraim's and that to the north is Manasseh's, with the sea forming its boundary; on the north Asher is reached, and on the east Issachar. 11Within Issachar and Asher, Manasseh had Beth-shean and its villages, Ibleam and its villages, the inhabitants of Dor and its villages, the inhabitants of En-dor and its villages, the inhabitants of Taanach and its villages, and the inhabitants of Megiddo and its villages (the third is Naphath).*a* 12Yet the Manassites could not take possession of those towns; but the Canaanites continued to live in that land. 13But when the Israelites grew strong, they put the Canaanites to forced labor, but did not utterly drive them out.

The Tribe of Joseph Protests

14 The tribe of Joseph spoke to Joshua, saying, "Why have you given me but one lot and one portion as an inheritance, since we are a numerous people, whom all along the LORD has blessed?" 15And Joshua said to them, "If you are a numerous people, go up to the forest, and clear ground there for yourselves in the land of the Perizzites and the Rephaim, since the hill country of Ephraim is too narrow for you." 16The tribe of Joseph said, "The hill country is not enough for us; yet all the Canaanites who live in the plain have chariots of iron, both those in Beth-shean and its villages and those in the Valley of Jezreel." 17Then Joshua said to the house of Joseph, to Ephraim and Manasseh, "You are indeed a numerous people, and have great power; you shall not have one lot only, 18but the hill country shall be yours, for though it is a forest, you shall clear it and possess it to its farthest borders; for you shall drive out the Canaanites, though they have chariots of iron, and though they are strong."

Stand Up and Be Counted

JOSHUA 17.3–6

What amazing women these daughters of Zelophehad must have been to stand up and demand their right to be counted along with the male heirs of Manasseh! They got what they asked for—their own portion of the promised land.

Can you think of an occasion when you were overlooked because of your gender or age or race or some other aspect of your identity? Did you have the courage to stand up and insist on being counted? How has God encouraged you to do so? In what ways do you need to remind others that you, too, are one of God's people?

See Meeting God in Community

When Will You Possess the Land?

JOSHUA 18.3

"When I say 'Yes' to God, I am taking the first step along that road which is as direct as the air path of the migratory bird . . . My every moment, my every fiber and sinew must be coordinated to the purposes of God. Words aren't enough; they often darken knowledge. Deeds aren't enough; they often hide God. My whole nature must be God's to use as God will. Results are not my concern."

—MURIEL LESTER,
Dare We Face Facts

The Territories of the Remaining Tribes

18 Then the whole congregation of the Israelites assembled at Shiloh, and set up the tent of meeting there. The land lay subdued before them.

2 There remained among the Israelites seven tribes whose inheritance had not yet been apportioned. ³So Joshua said to the Israelites, "How long will you be slack about going in and taking possession of the land that the LORD, the God of your ancestors, has given you? ⁴Provide three men from each tribe, and I will send them out that they may begin to go throughout the land, writing a description of it with a view to their inheritances. Then come back to me. ⁵They shall divide it into seven portions, Judah continuing in its territory on the south, and the house of Joseph in their territory on the north. ⁶You shall describe the land in seven divisions and bring the description here to me; and I will cast lots for you here before the LORD our God. ⁷The Levites have no portion among you, for the priesthood of the LORD is their heritage; and Gad and Reuben and the half-tribe of Manasseh have received their inheritance beyond the Jordan eastward, which Moses the servant of the LORD gave them."

8 So the men started on their way; and Joshua charged those who went to write the description of the land, saying, "Go throughout the land and write a description of it, and come back to me; and I will cast lots for you here before the LORD in Shiloh." ⁹So the men went and traversed the land and set down in a book a description of it by towns in seven divisions; then they came back to Joshua in the camp at Shiloh, ¹⁰and Joshua cast lots for them in Shiloh before the LORD; and there Joshua apportioned the land to the Israelites, to each a portion.

The Territory of Benjamin

11 The lot of the tribe of Benjamin according to its families came up, and the territory allotted to it fell between the tribe of Judah and the tribe of Joseph. ¹²On the north side their boundary began at the Jordan; then the boundary goes up to the slope of Jericho on the north, then up through the hill country westward; and it ends at the wilderness of Beth-aven. ¹³From there the boundary passes along southward in the direction of Luz, to the slope of Luz (that is, Bethel), then the boundary goes down to Ataroth-addar, on the mountain that lies south of Lower Beth-horon. ¹⁴Then the boundary goes in another direction, turning on the western side southward from the mountain that lies to the south, opposite Beth-horon, and it ends at Kiriath-baal (that is, Kiriath-jearim), a town belonging to the tribe of Judah. This forms the western side. ¹⁵The southern side begins at the outskirts of Kiriath-jearim; and the boundary goes from there to Ephron,ᵃ to the spring of the Waters of Nephtoah; ¹⁶then the boundary goes down to the border of the mountain that overlooks the valley of the son of Hinnom, which is at the north end of the valley of Rephaim; and it then goes down the valley of Hinnom, south of the slope of the Jebusites, and downward to En-rogel; ¹⁷then it bends in a northerly direction going on to En-shemesh, and from there goes to Geliloth, which is opposite

a Cn See 15.9. Heb *westward*

the ascent of Adummim; then it goes down to the Stone of Bohan, Reuben's son; [18]and passing on to the north of the slope of Beth-arabah[a] it goes down to the Arabah; [19]then the boundary passes on to the north of the slope of Beth-hoglah; and the boundary ends at the northern bay of the Dead Sea,[b] at the south end of the Jordan: this is the southern border. [20]The Jordan forms its boundary on the eastern side. This is the inheritance of the tribe of Benjamin, according to its families, boundary by boundary all around.

21 Now the towns of the tribe of Benjamin according to their families were Jericho, Beth-hoglah, Emek-keziz, [22]Beth-arabah, Zemaraim, Bethel, [23]Avvim, Parah, Ophrah, [24]Chephar-ammoni, Ophni, and Geba—twelve towns with their villages: [25]Gibeon, Ramah, Beeroth, [26]Mizpeh, Chephirah, Mozah, [27]Rekem, Irpeel, Taralah, [28]Zela, Haeleph, Jebus[c] (that is, Jerusalem), Gibeah[d] and Kiriath-jearim[e]—fourteen towns with their villages. This is the inheritance of the tribe of Benjamin according to its families.

The Territory of Simeon

19 The second lot came out for Simeon, for the tribe of Simeon, according to its families; its inheritance lay within the inheritance of the tribe of Judah. [2]It had for its inheritance Beer-sheba, Sheba, Moladah, [3]Hazar-shual, Balah, Ezem, [4]Eltolad, Bethul, Hormah, [5]Ziklag, Beth-marcaboth, Hazar-susah, [6]Beth-lebaoth, and Sharuhen—thirteen towns with their villages; [7]Ain, Rimmon, Ether, and Ashan—four towns with their villages; [8]together with all the villages all around these towns as far as Baalath-beer, Ramah of the Negeb. This was the inheritance of the tribe of Simeon according to its families. [9]The inheritance of the tribe of Simeon formed part of the territory of Judah; because the portion of the tribe of Judah was too large for them, the tribe of Simeon obtained an inheritance within their inheritance.

The Territory of Zebulun

10 The third lot came up for the tribe of Zebulun, according to its families. The boundary of its inheritance reached as far as Sarid; [11]then its boundary goes up westward, and on to Maralah, and touches Dabbesheth, then the wadi that is east of Jokneam; [12]from Sarid it goes in the other direction eastward toward the sunrise to the boundary of Chisloth-tabor; from there it goes to Daberath, then up to Japhia; [13]from there it passes along on the east toward the sunrise to Gath-hepher, to Eth-kazin, and going on to Rimmon it bends toward Neah; [14]then on the north the boundary makes a turn to Hannathon, and it ends at the valley of Iphtah-el; [15]and Kattath, Nahalal, Shimron, Idalah, and Bethlehem—twelve towns with their villages. [16]This is the inheritance of the tribe of Zebulun, according to its families—these towns with their villages.

The Territory of Issachar

17 The fourth lot came out for Issachar, for the tribe of Issachar, according to its families. [18]Its territory included Jezreel, Chesulloth, Shunem, [19]Hapharaim, Shion, Anaharath, [20]Rabbith, Kishion, Ebez, [21]Remeth, En-gannim,

---

Your Lot in Life

JOSHUA 19.1–9

The leaders of Israel draw lots to decide the homeland for each tribe. The tribe of Simeon doesn't get a homeland of its own—just some towns in the territory of Judah.

What is your lot in life? What are the givens into which you were born? Some may have nothing to do with accomplishments and choices—family, nation, religion, social status. Others may be chosen or earned. What do you do with your givens? Do you wish they were different, wondering, "If only . . ."? Or do you accept them as a starting point and move on? Do you proudly embrace them as your heritage? How have they had a part in forming you? Spend some time thanking God for your lot in life.

See Meeting God in Everyday Life

---

a Gk: Heb *to the slope over against the Arabah*   *b* Heb *Salt Sea*   *c* Gk Syr Vg: Heb *the Jebusite*   *d* Heb *Gibeath*   *e* Gk: Heb *Kiriath*

Boundaries of Inheritance

JOSHUA 19.24–31

The lists of boundaries occupy substantial space in this chapter. Why is it important to know one's boundaries geographically? Why might it be important to know them emotionally and spiritually?

Our spiritual boundaries define our very character, the sort of person we are, just like the boundaries of a baseball field define the game. Boundaries also define what we may and may not do. What are the boundaries that God asks you to observe? Do you feel fenced in by such boundaries or liberated to enjoy the extent of them? Do you focus more on the "don'ts" of your spiritual life or on the freedoms of living in obedience to God?

See *Meeting God in the Created Order*

En-haddah, Beth-pazzez; [22]the boundary also touches Tabor, Shahazumah, and Beth-shemesh, and its boundary ends at the Jordan—sixteen towns with their villages. [23]This is the inheritance of the tribe of Issachar, according to its families—the towns with their villages.

The Territory of Asher

24 The fifth lot came out for the tribe of Asher according to its families. [25]Its boundary included Helkath, Hali, Beten, Achshaph, [26]Allammelech, Amad, and Mishal; on the west it touches Carmel and Shihor-libnath, [27]then it turns eastward, goes to Beth-dagon, and touches Zebulun and the valley of Iphtah-el northward to Beth-emek and Neiel; then it continues in the north to Cabul, [28]Ebron, Rehob, Hammon, Kanah, as far as Great Sidon; [29]then the boundary turns to Ramah, reaching to the fortified city of Tyre; then the boundary turns to Hosah, and it ends at the sea; Mahalab,[a] Achzib, [30]Ummah, Aphek, and Rehob—twenty-two towns with their villages. [31]This is the inheritance of the tribe of Asher according to its families—these towns with their villages.

The Territory of Naphtali

32 The sixth lot came out for the tribe of Naphtali, for the tribe of Naphtali, according to its families. [33]And its boundary ran from Heleph, from the oak in Zaanannim, and Adami-nekeb, and Jabneel, as far as Lakkum; and it ended at the Jordan; [34]then the boundary turns westward to Aznoth-tabor, and goes from there to Hukkok, touching Zebulun at the south, and Asher on the west, and Judah on the east at the Jordan. [35]The fortified towns are Ziddim, Zer, Hammath, Rakkath, Chinnereth, [36]Adamah, Ramah, Hazor, [37]Kedesh, Edrei, En-hazor, [38]Iron, Migdal-el, Horem, Bethanath, and Beth-shemesh—nineteen towns with their villages. [39]This is the inheritance of the tribe of Naphtali according to its families—the towns with their villages.

The Territory of Dan

40 The seventh lot came out for the tribe of Dan, according to its families. [41]The territory of its inheritance included Zorah, Eshtaol, Ir-shemesh, [42]Shaalabbin, Aijalon, Ithlah, [43]Elon, Timnah, Ekron, [44]Eltekeh, Gibbethon, Baalath, [45]Jehud, Bene-berak, Gath-rimmon, [46]Me-jarkon, and Rakkon at the border opposite Joppa. [47]When the territory of the Danites was lost to them, the Danites went up and fought against Leshem, and after capturing it and putting it to the sword, they took possession of it and settled in it, calling Leshem, Dan, after their ancestor Dan. [48]This is the inheritance of the tribe of Dan, according to their families—these towns with their villages.

Joshua's Inheritance

49 When they had finished distributing the several territories of the land as inheritances, the Israelites gave an inheritance among them to Joshua son of Nun. [50]By command of the LORD they gave him the town that he asked for, Timnath-serah in the hill country of Ephraim; he rebuilt the town, and settled in it.

51 These are the inheritances that the priest Eleazar and

a Cn Compare Gk: Heb *Mehebel*

Joshua son of Nun and the heads of the families of the tribes of the Israelites distributed by lot at Shiloh before the LORD, at the entrance of the tent of meeting. So they finished dividing the land.

The Cities of Refuge

20 Then the LORD spoke to Joshua, saying, ²"Say to the Israelites, 'Appoint the cities of refuge, of which I spoke to you through Moses, ³so that anyone who kills a person without intent or by mistake may flee there; they shall be for you a refuge from the avenger of blood. ⁴The slayer shall flee to one of these cities and shall stand at the entrance of the gate of the city, and explain the case to the elders of that city; then the fugitive shall be taken into the city, and given a place, and shall remain with them. ⁵And if the avenger of blood is in pursuit, they shall not give up the slayer, because the neighbor was killed by mistake, there having been no enmity between them before. ⁶The slayer shall remain in that city until there is a trial before the congregation, until the death of the one who is high priest at the time: then the slayer may return home, to the town in which the deed was done.' "

7 So they set apart Kedesh in Galilee in the hill country of Naphtali, and Shechem in the hill country of Ephraim, and Kiriath-arba (that is, Hebron) in the hill country of Judah. ⁸And beyond the Jordan east of Jericho, they appointed Bezer in the wilderness on the tableland, from the tribe of Reuben, and Ramoth in Gilead, from the tribe of Gad, and Golan in Bashan, from the tribe of Manasseh. ⁹These were the cities designated for all the Israelites, and for the aliens residing among them, that anyone who killed a person without intent could flee there, so as not to die by the hand of the avenger of blood, until there was a trial before the congregation.

Cities Allotted to the Levites

21 Then the heads of the families of the Levites came to the priest Eleazar and to Joshua son of Nun and to the heads of the families of the tribes of the Israelites; ²they said to them at Shiloh in the land of Canaan, "The LORD commanded through Moses that we be given towns to live in, along with their pasture lands for our livestock." ³So by command of the LORD the Israelites gave to the Levites the following towns and pasture lands out of their inheritance.

4 The lot came out for the families of the Kohathites. So those Levites who were descendants of Aaron the priest received by lot thirteen towns from the tribes of Judah, Simeon, and Benjamin.

5 The rest of the Kohathites received by lot ten towns from the families of the tribe of Ephraim, from the tribe of Dan, and the half-tribe of Manasseh.

6 The Gershonites received by lot thirteen towns from the families of the tribe of Issachar, from the tribe of Asher, from the tribe of Naphtali, and from the half-tribe of Manasseh in Bashan.

7 The Merarites according to their families received twelve towns from the tribe of Reuben, the tribe of Gad, and the tribe of Zebulun.

8 These towns and their pasture lands the Israelites gave

Cities of Refuge

JOSHUA 20.1–9

God provides places of refuge for those in need of protection and shelter, especially for the unjustly accused. Can you think of people and places that God has placed in your life that function as places of refuge for you? How and when do you make use of them? In what ways can friends, family or fellow church members give you refuge? How has the Word of God been your refuge? You might close by singing and meditating on a hymn of refuge, such as "A Mighty Fortress Is Our God" or "Rock of Ages" or "O God, Our Help in Ages Past."

See *Meeting God in Community*

Open Hands to Receive Inheritance

JOSHUA 21.4–8

The Levites have no territory of their own but rather receive towns scattered throughout the promised land. Like many who devote themselves to God's service today, they were open to going wherever God sent them. Open and close your hands. Notice how these gestures hinder or assist your power to receive. How does the power to receive depend on the willingness to be open? What is the power of the open hand? Of the closed hand? What does God want you to receive? What is hindering you?

by lot to the Levites, as the LORD had commanded through Moses.

9 Out of the tribe of Judah and the tribe of Simeon they gave the following towns mentioned by name, 10which went to the descendants of Aaron, one of the families of the Kohathites who belonged to the Levites, since the lot fell to them first. 11They gave them Kiriath-arba (Arba being the father of Anak), that is Hebron, in the hill country of Judah, along with the pasture lands around it. 12But the fields of the town and its villages had been given to Caleb son of Jephunneh as his holding.

13 To the descendants of Aaron the priest they gave Hebron, the city of refuge for the slayer, with its pasture lands, Libnah with its pasture lands, 14Jattir with its pasture lands, Eshtemoa with its pasture lands, 15Holon with its pasture lands, Debir with its pasture lands, 16Ain with its pasture lands, Juttah with its pasture lands, and Beth-shemesh with its pasture lands—nine towns out of these two tribes. 17Out of the tribe of Benjamin: Gibeon with its pasture lands, Geba with its pasture lands, 18Anathoth with its pasture lands, and Almon with its pasture lands—four towns. 19The towns of the descendants of Aaron—the priests—were thirteen in all, with their pasture lands.

20 As to the rest of the Kohathites belonging to the Kohathite families of the Levites, the towns allotted to them were out of the tribe of Ephraim. 21To them were given Shechem, the city of refuge for the slayer, with its pasture lands in the hill country of Ephraim, Gezer with its pasture lands, 22Kibzaim with its pasture lands, and Beth-horon with its pasture lands—four towns. 23Out of the tribe of Dan: Elteke with its pasture lands, Gibbethon with its pasture lands, 24Aijalon with its pasture lands, Gath-rimmon with its pasture lands—four towns. 25Out of the half-tribe of Manasseh: Taanach with its pasture lands, and Gath-rimmon with its pasture lands—two towns. 26The towns of the families of the rest of the Kohathites were ten in all, with their pasture lands.

27 To the Gershonites, one of the families of the Levites, were given out of the half-tribe of Manasseh, Golan in Bashan with its pasture lands, the city of refuge for the slayer, and Beeshterah with its pasture lands—two towns. 28Out of the tribe of Issachar: Kishion with its pasture lands, Daberath with its pasture lands, 29Jarmuth with its pasture lands, En-gannim with its pasture lands—four towns. 30Out of the tribe of Asher: Mishal with its pasture lands, Abdon with its pasture lands, 31Helkath with its pasture lands, and Rehob with its pasture lands—four towns. 32Out of the tribe of Naphtali: Kedesh in Galilee with its pasture lands, the city of refuge for the slayer, Hammoth-dor with its pasture lands, and Kartan with its pasture lands—three towns. 33The towns of the several families of the Gershonites were in all thirteen, with their pasture lands.

34 To the rest of the Levites—the Merarite families—were given out of the tribe of Zebulun: Jokneam with its pasture lands, Kartah with its pasture lands, 35Dimnah with its pasture lands, Nahalal with its pasture lands—four towns. 36Out of the tribe of Reuben: Bezer with its pasture lands, Jahzah with its pasture lands, 37Kedemoth with its pasture lands, and Mephaath with its pasture lands—four towns. 38Out of the tribe of Gad: Ramoth in Gilead with its

pasture lands, the city of refuge for the slayer, Mahanaim with its pasture lands, [39]Heshbon with its pasture lands, Jazer with its pasture lands—four towns in all. [40]As for the towns of the several Merarite families, that is, the remainder of the families of the Levites, those allotted to them were twelve in all.

41 The towns of the Levites within the holdings of the Israelites were in all forty-eight towns with their pasture lands. [42]Each of these towns had its pasture lands around it; so it was with all these towns.

43 Thus the LORD gave to Israel all the land that he swore to their ancestors that he would give them; and having taken possession of it, they settled there. [44]And the LORD gave them rest on every side just as he had sworn to their ancestors; not one of all their enemies had withstood them, for the LORD had given all their enemies into their hands. [45]Not one of all the good promises that the LORD had made to the house of Israel had failed; all came to pass.

The Eastern Tribes Return to Their Territory

22 Then Joshua summoned the Reubenites, the Gadites, and the half-tribe of Manasseh, [2]and said to them, "You have observed all that Moses the servant of the LORD commanded you, and have obeyed me in all that I have commanded you; [3]you have not forsaken your kindred these many days, down to this day, but have been careful to keep the charge of the LORD your God. [4]And now the LORD your God has given rest to your kindred, as he promised them; therefore turn and go to your tents in the land where your possession lies, which Moses the servant of the LORD gave you on the other side of the Jordan. [5]Take good care to observe the commandment and instruction that Moses the servant of the LORD commanded you, to love the LORD your God, to walk in all his ways, to keep his commandments, and to hold fast to him, and to serve him with all your heart and with all your soul." [6]So Joshua blessed them and sent them away, and they went to their tents.

7 Now to the one half of the tribe of Manasseh Moses had given a possession in Bashan; but to the other half Joshua had given a possession beside their fellow Israelites in the land west of the Jordan. And when Joshua sent them away to their tents and blessed them, [8]he said to them, "Go back to your tents with much wealth, and with very much livestock, with silver, gold, bronze, and iron, and with a great quantity of clothing; divide the spoil of your enemies with your kindred." [9]So the Reubenites and the Gadites and the half-tribe of Manasseh returned home, parting from the Israelites at Shiloh, which is in the land of Canaan, to go to the land of Gilead, their own land of which they had taken possession by command of the LORD through Moses.

A Memorial Altar East of the Jordan

10 When they came to the region[a] near the Jordan that lies in the land of Canaan, the Reubenites and the Gadites and the half-tribe of Manasseh built there an altar by the Jordan, an altar of great size. [11]The Israelites heard that the Reubenites and the Gadites and the half-tribe of Manasseh had built an altar at the frontier of the land of Canaan, in

---

a Or to Geliloth

Cross Over Into the Lord's Land

JOSHUA 22.16–19

The tribes who had land east of the Jordan are settled and comfortable. Yet they fear being left out of the blessings God seems to promise to the tribes to the west. Rather than remain part of the whole people of God and join those in the west, where the war of conquest continued, some in the eastern tribes set up their own temple.

Are you settled and comfortable in your spiritual life? What choices must you make in order to move from your "comfort zone" to God's land of blessing? What must you leave behind? What concrete things can you do this day, this week, to make this move? How might your personal obedience to God affect your spiritual community as a whole? How do the spiritual choices of others affect you? How does your life extend the invitation, "Cross over into the LORD's land"?

See Meeting God in Community

the region*a* near the Jordan, on the side that belongs to the Israelites. ¹²And when the people of Israel heard of it, the whole assembly of the Israelites gathered at Shiloh, to make war against them.

13 Then the Israelites sent the priest Phinehas son of Eleazar to the Reubenites and the Gadites and the half-tribe of Manasseh, in the land of Gilead, ¹⁴and with him ten chiefs, one from each of the tribal families of Israel, every one of them the head of a family among the clans of Israel. ¹⁵They came to the Reubenites, the Gadites, and the half-tribe of Manasseh, in the land of Gilead, and they said to them, ¹⁶"Thus says the whole congregation of the LORD, 'What is this treachery that you have committed against the God of Israel in turning away today from following the LORD, by building yourselves an altar today in rebellion against the LORD? ¹⁷Have we not had enough of the sin at Peor from which even yet we have not cleansed ourselves, and for which a plague came upon the congregation of the LORD, ¹⁸that you must turn away today from following the LORD! If you rebel against the LORD today, he will be angry with the whole congregation of Israel tomorrow. ¹⁹But now, if your land is unclean, cross over into the LORD's land where the LORD's tabernacle now stands, and take for yourselves a possession among us; only do not rebel against the LORD, or rebel against us*b* by building yourselves an altar other than the altar of the LORD our God. ²⁰Did not Achan son of Zerah break faith in the matter of the devoted things, and wrath fell upon all the congregation of Israel? And he did not perish alone for his iniquity!' "

21 Then the Reubenites, the Gadites, and the half-tribe of Manasseh said in answer to the heads of the families of Israel, ²²"The LORD, God of gods! The LORD, God of gods! He knows; and let Israel itself know! If it was in rebellion or in breach of faith toward the LORD, do not spare us today ²³for building an altar to turn away from following the LORD; or if we did so to offer burnt offerings or grain offerings or offerings of well-being on it, may the LORD himself take vengeance. ²⁴No! We did it from fear that in time to come your children might say to our children, 'What have you to do with the LORD, the God of Israel? ²⁵For the LORD has made the Jordan a boundary between us and you, you Reubenites and Gadites; you have no portion in the LORD.' So your children might make our children cease to worship the LORD. ²⁶Therefore we said, 'Let us now build an altar, not for burnt offering, nor for sacrifice, ²⁷but to be a witness between us and you, and between the generations after us, that we do perform the service of the LORD in his presence with our burnt offerings and sacrifices and offerings of well-being; so that your children may never say to our children in time to come, "You have no portion in the LORD." ' ²⁸And we thought, If this should be said to us or to our descendants in time to come, we could say, 'Look at this copy of the altar of the LORD, which our ancestors made, not for burnt offerings, nor for sacrifice, but to be a witness between us and you.' ²⁹Far be it from us that we should rebel against the LORD, and turn away this day from following the LORD by building an altar for burnt offering, grain offering, or sacrifice, other than the altar of the LORD our God that stands before his tabernacle!"

a Or *at Geliloth*   *b* Or *make rebels of us*

30 When the priest Phinehas and the chiefs of the congregation, the heads of the families of Israel who were with him, heard the words that the Reubenites and the Gadites and the Manassites spoke, they were satisfied. ³¹The priest Phinehas son of Eleazar said to the Reubenites and the Gadites and the Manassites, "Today we know that the LORD is among us, because you have not committed this treachery against the LORD; now you have saved the Israelites from the hand of the LORD."

32 Then the priest Phinehas son of Eleazar and the chiefs returned from the Reubenites and the Gadites in the land of Gilead to the land of Canaan, to the Israelites, and brought back word to them. ³³The report pleased the Israelites; and the Israelites blessed God and spoke no more of making war against them, to destroy the land where the Reubenites and the Gadites were settled. ³⁴The Reubenites and the Gadites called the altar Witness;ᵃ "For," said they, "it is a witness between us that the LORD is God."

Joshua Exhorts the People

23 A long time afterward, when the LORD had given rest to Israel from all their enemies all around, and Joshua was old and well advanced in years, ²Joshua summoned all Israel, their elders and heads, their judges and officers, and said to them, "I am now old and well advanced in years; ³and you have seen all that the LORD your God has done to all these nations for your sake, for it is the LORD your God who has fought for you. ⁴I have allotted to you as an inheritance for your tribes those nations that remain, along with all the nations that I have already cut off, from the Jordan to the Great Sea in the west. ⁵The LORD your God will push them back before you, and drive them out of your sight; and you shall possess their land, as the LORD your God promised you. ⁶Therefore be very steadfast to observe and do all that is written in the book of the law of Moses, turning aside from it neither to the right nor to the left, ⁷so that you may not be mixed with these nations left here among you, or make mention of the names of their gods, or swear by them, or serve them, or bow yourselves down to them, ⁸but hold fast to the LORD your God, as you have done to this day. ⁹For the LORD has driven out before you great and strong nations; and as for you, no one has been able to withstand you to this day. ¹⁰One of you puts to flight a thousand, since it is the LORD your God who fights for you, as he promised you. ¹¹Be very careful, therefore, to love the LORD your God. ¹²For if you turn back, and join the survivors of these nations left here among you, and intermarry with them, so that you marry their women and they yours, ¹³know assuredly that the LORD your God will not continue to drive out these nations before you; but they shall be a snare and a trap for you, a scourge on your sides, and thorns in your eyes, until you perish from this good land that the LORD your God has given you.

14 "And now I am about to go the way of all the earth, and you know in your hearts and souls, all of you, that not one thing has failed of all the good things that the LORD your God promised concerning you; all have come to pass for you, not one of them has failed. ¹⁵But just as all the good things that the LORD your God promised concerning

Remembering to Remember

JOSHUA 23.2–11

"When would there be enough time to recount all thy great blessings that you bestow on us . . . especially as I am hastening on to still greater mercies? For my memory recalls them to me and it is pleasant to confess them to you, O Lord: the inward goads by which you subdued me and how you brought me low, leveling the mountains and hills of my thoughts, straightening my crookedness, and smoothing my rough ways."

—AUGUSTINE,
Confessions

ᵃ Cn Compare Syr: Heb lacks *Witness*

Enjoying the Plantings of Others

JOSHUA 24.13

What vineyards or gardens—spiritual benefits—have you enjoyed, which you neither planted nor cultivated? Bring God into the scene with you as you walk in these lush places. What is God saying to you about your inheritance?

Give praise to God for what has come your way in the spiritual journey without effort on your part. Examine your heart to see if you have ever taken this effortless abundance for granted. Offer your repentance to God if there are ways in which you have not lived in gratitude for the plantings of others.

Contemplate the images of fruition, plenty, provision—all unearned bounty. How do these images speak of the nature of God? Are you content to admire the beauty rather than taste the fruit? Wait and listen in God's presence.

See *Meeting God in Prayer*

you have been fulfilled for you, so the LORD will bring upon you all the bad things, until he has destroyed you from this good land that the LORD your God has given you. ¹⁶If you transgress the covenant of the LORD your God, which he enjoined on you, and go and serve other gods and bow down to them, then the anger of the LORD will be kindled against you, and you shall perish quickly from the good land that he has given to you."

The Tribes Renew the Covenant

24 Then Joshua gathered all the tribes of Israel to Shechem, and summoned the elders, the heads, the judges, and the officers of Israel; and they presented themselves before God. ²And Joshua said to all the people, "Thus says the LORD, the God of Israel: Long ago your ancestors—Terah and his sons Abraham and Nahor—lived beyond the Euphrates and served other gods. ³Then I took your father Abraham from beyond the River and led him through all the land of Canaan and made his offspring many. I gave him Isaac; ⁴and to Isaac I gave Jacob and Esau. I gave Esau the hill country of Seir to possess, but Jacob and his children went down to Egypt. ⁵Then I sent Moses and Aaron, and I plagued Egypt with what I did in its midst; and afterwards I brought you out. ⁶When I brought your ancestors out of Egypt, you came to the sea; and the Egyptians pursued your ancestors with chariots and horsemen to the Red Sea.ᵃ ⁷When they cried out to the LORD, he put darkness between you and the Egyptians, and made the sea come upon them and cover them; and your eyes saw what I did to Egypt. Afterwards you lived in the wilderness a long time. ⁸Then I brought you to the land of the Amorites, who lived on the other side of the Jordan; they fought with you, and I handed them over to you, and you took possession of their land, and I destroyed them before you. ⁹Then King Balak son of Zippor of Moab, set out to fight against Israel. He sent and invited Balaam son of Beor to curse you, ¹⁰but I would not listen to Balaam; therefore he blessed you; so I rescued you out of his hand. ¹¹When you went over the Jordan and came to Jericho, the citizens of Jericho fought against you, and also the Amorites, the Perizzites, the Canaanites, the Hittites, the Girgashites, the Hivites, and the Jebusites; and I handed them over to you. ¹²I sent the hornetᵇ ahead of you, which drove out before you the two kings of the Amorites; it was not by your sword or by your bow. ¹³I gave you a land on which you had not labored, and towns that you had not built, and you live in them; you eat the fruit of vineyards and oliveyards that you did not plant.

14 "Now therefore revere the LORD, and serve him in sincerity and in faithfulness; put away the gods that your ancestors served beyond the River and in Egypt, and serve the LORD. ¹⁵Now if you are unwilling to serve the LORD, choose this day whom you will serve, whether the gods your ancestors served in the region beyond the River or the gods of the Amorites in whose land you are living; but as for me and my household, we will serve the LORD."

16 Then the people answered, "Far be it from us that we should forsake the LORD to serve other gods; ¹⁷for it is the LORD our God who brought us and our ancestors up from the land of Egypt, out of the house of slavery, and who did

a Or *Sea of Reeds*   *b* Meaning of Heb uncertain

those great signs in our sight. He protected us along all the way that we went, and among all the peoples through whom we passed; [18]and the LORD drove out before us all the peoples, the Amorites who lived in the land. Therefore we also will serve the LORD, for he is our God."

19 But Joshua said to the people, "You cannot serve the LORD, for he is a holy God. He is a jealous God; he will not forgive your transgressions or your sins. [20]If you forsake the LORD and serve foreign gods, then he will turn and do you harm, and consume you, after having done you good." [21]And the people said to Joshua, "No, we will serve the LORD!" [22]Then Joshua said to the people, "You are witnesses against yourselves that you have chosen the LORD, to serve him." And they said, "We are witnesses." [23]He said, "Then put away the foreign gods that are among you, and incline your hearts to the LORD, the God of Israel." [24]The people said to Joshua, "The LORD our God we will serve, and him we will obey." [25]So Joshua made a covenant with the people that day, and made statutes and ordinances for them at Shechem. [26]Joshua wrote these words in the book of the law of God; and he took a large stone, and set it up there under the oak in the sanctuary of the LORD. [27]Joshua said to all the people, "See, this stone shall be a witness against us; for it has heard all the words of the LORD that he spoke to us; therefore it shall be a witness against you, if you deal falsely with your God." [28]So Joshua sent the people away to their inheritances.

Death of Joshua and Eleazar

29 After these things Joshua son of Nun, the servant of the LORD, died, being one hundred ten years old. [30]They buried him in his own inheritance at Timnath-serah, which is in the hill country of Ephraim, north of Mount Gaash.

31 Israel served the LORD all the days of Joshua, and all the days of the elders who outlived Joshua and had known all the work that the LORD did for Israel.

32 The bones of Joseph, which the Israelites had brought up from Egypt, were buried at Shechem, in the portion of ground that Jacob had bought from the children of Hamor, the father of Shechem, for one hundred pieces of money;[a] it became an inheritance of the descendants of Joseph.

33 Eleazar son of Aaron died; and they buried him at Gibeah, the town of his son Phinehas, which had been given him in the hill country of Ephraim.

Choosing Faithfulness to the End

JOSHUA 24.29–31

"My Lord God, I have no idea where I am going. I do not see the road ahead of me, I cannot know for certain where it will end. Nor do I really know myself, and the fact that I think I am following your will does not mean that I am actually doing so. But I believe that the desire to please you does in fact please you. And I hope I have that desire in all that I am doing. I hope that I will never do anything apart from that desire. And I know that if I do this you will lead me by the right road, though I may know nothing about it. Therefore I will trust you always though I may seem to be lost and in the shadow of death. I will not fear, for you are ever with me, and you will never leave me to face my perils alone."

—THOMAS MERTON,
Thoughts in Solitude

WAYS of MEETING GOD

Meeting God in Service

Ten chairs were pulled closely together in a circle, but we were all leaning forward to catch Mary Jean's words. She seldom spoke during our small-group meetings, yet this week she seemed eager to talk. She described the time she had spent working in a community center and the relentless problems of poverty, addiction and abuse she had encountered there. Tears came to her eyes as she concluded, "I feel helpless as I look at these families and see their suffering. What does God expect of me? How can I make a difference?"

We learn to see God by opening our eyes and actively looking for opportunities to serve others.

Like Mary Jean, we may struggle to see just how God acts in a world of great suffering. And when it comes to our own role, we often don't know where to begin or what God might be asking of us. We sometimes feel overwhelmed or we want to turn away from the realities that surround us. Yet as we begin to serve others, we often find our hesitations fading. We discover that when we help others we encounter God. We meet God in the midst of our efforts. This can happen in several ways.

Learning to Look. We learn to see God by opening our eyes and actively looking for opportunities to serve others. From the beginning of his ministry, Jesus constantly stayed alert to people and their needs. It was one reason why he came. Jesus read from the book of Isaiah in the synagogue at Nazareth, applying these words to himself:

> "The Spirit of the Lord is upon me,
>> because he has anointed me
>> to bring good news to the poor.
> He has sent me to proclaim release to the captives
>> and recovery of sight to the blind,
> to let the oppressed go free,
>> to proclaim the year of the Lord's favor."—Luke 4.18–19

Every day as he traveled with his disciples Jesus healed and fed and loved people. A number of stories in the Gospels tell us that Jesus acted because he was moved with compassion. As painful as it must have been sometimes, he did not turn aside from seeing people suffer.

Jesus not only saw the sufferings of human beings but also became involved in people's suffering to heal and bring new life. The story of the widow of Nain in Luke 7.11–17 illustrates this. As Jesus travels with his disciples and a crowd of followers, he encounters a funeral procession. The widow, he discovers, has lost her only son. Jesus sees her grief with eyes of compassion, knowing that as a widow she has been completely dependent on her son. Now she has no one—and nothing. Jesus says to her, "Do not weep," and raises the young man back to life. Then we find the words, "Jesus gave him to his mother" (v.15). What compassion and mercy are captured in those words!

Again and again Jesus actively seeks the sick and needy. He goes directly to them; he notices their pain and suffering and responds with divine grace and love. The common activities of his life—travels, conversations, seemingly chance meetings with people—become the settings for expressions of his caring alertness. He appropriately perceives himself as a servant of God, and in serving God he ministers to those God loves.

Learning to Listen. In the Gospel of John, Jesus demonstrates that this open-eyed attitude of caring was not to be confined only to his own ministry but was to characterize the lives of his followers as well. Jesus washed the disciples' feet as they gathered to celebrate the festival of the Passover, in part to remind us of our proper posture before others: "You call me Teacher and Lord—and you are right, for that is what I am. So if I, your Lord and Teacher, have washed your feet, you also ought to wash one another's feet" (John 13.13–14). Not only do we open our eyes to need; we also listen to those we serve. We cannot know how to help others if we simply barge in to "fix" a list of problems we think we see in them. We must serve others with gentle openness to them and with a willingness to relinquish our own agenda. We listen to their ideas and hopes and longings.

To listen requires a quieting of our own interests and experiences so that we can become open not only in that particular relationship but also to the ways in which God is present in the relationship. Henri J. M. Nouwen writes, "Real training for service asks for a hard and often painful process of self-emptying. The main problem of service is to be the way without being 'in the way.' "

Learning to become more open to others teaches us many things. Openness cultivates in us an attitude of honesty. We see ourselves, as well as others, more clearly. Then we are able to open ourselves to God—to let him have those parts of us that are wounded and in need of healing and forgiveness. Just as we speak of God's love for and forgiveness of others, so we can claim that healing in our own lives.

Our lives may be deeply changed as we serve others. As those we serve share their own pilgrimages, we see how God has been a part of their experiences. Their vision of God may enlarge ours. Their words, feelings and desires may challenge us in surprising ways. When twentieth-century spiritual writer Evelyn Underhill went to Baron von Hÿgel for guidance about her relationship with God, he recommended that she spend a designated amount of time each week directly serving the poor so as to break open her heart to the needs of people and open her up more fully to experience God's grace. As a result she met a woman named Laura Rose, the beginning of a relationship that was to become deeply significant for Underhill's spiritual growth.

Learning to Love. To looking and listening we add loving—of the most radical, sacrificial kind. It is easy to be captured by our own special interests and by self-absorption. When we follow Jesus, however, normal priorities get turned upside down. We confront what German pastor and theologian Dietrich Bonhoeffer called "the cost of discipleship."

God thereby transforms our self-interest into a new awareness of our interdependence. We identify the ways in which we need one another in order to grow in faithfulness. We find a new identity by centering our lives in the One who is the light of the world and who calls us to let our lights "shine before others, so that they may see [our] good works and give glory to [our] Father in heaven" (Matthew 5.16). We realize that nothing matters more than bringing people to Jesus for healing and salvation.

Little by little our hearts, which can so easily become hardened to the needs of others, are changed into caring and compassionate hearts. Thomas Kelly, in his book, *A Testament of Devotion*, captures this phenomenon in these words: "God plucks the world out of our hearts, loosening the chains of attachment. And He hurls the world into our hearts, where we and He together carry it in infinitely tender love."

Resources to Get Us Through. The radical call to service does not pose for us an impossible duty, however. God promises to give us the power and resources we need through the indwelling Spirit of Jesus. Paul wrote to the new converts in the first-century church in Corinth to remind them of their calling. Paul pointed out that he had come to them in weakness, fear and trembling, but that God had used him to demonstrate the power of

> The radical call to service does not pose for us an impossible duty . . . God promises to give us the power and resources we need through the indwelling Spirit of Jesus.

306

the Spirit (see 1 Corinthians 1.18–31; 2.6–13). What freedom there is in knowing that God can use us in spite of our weaknesses!

Indeed, power is released through our vulnerability. It is through our vulnerabilities that we learn the nature of God's sufficiency. The only way in which we can confront head-on the pain of a suffering world is through utter reliance on God's grace. We can take to heart God's word to Paul, "My grace is sufficient for you, for power is made perfect in weakness" (2 Corinthians 12.9).

Jesus is inviting us to love the world as he loves. Paul encouraged a congregation of Christians who were undergoing much struggle by reminding them that they were a letter of Christ, written not with ink but with the Spirit of the living God (2 Corinthians 3.2–3). What a word of promise for today! We go in the power of the Spirit. The Spirit speaks in and through what we do.

"Christian ministry," writes James Fenhagen, "is more than doing good. Ministry is an act of service performed either consciously or unconsciously in the name of Christ. Ministry is Jesus Christ expressing his life through us." When we are tempted to run and hide because the needs of the world are overwhelming and we feel helpless to make a difference, we can remember that we do not go alone. We venture out boldly, not because we underestimate or devalue the needs and woundedness of others, but because we trust in the steadfast and abiding love of God.

In serving the needs of others in society, we meet God. We find joy, as Brother Lawrence found centuries ago, "doing little things for the love of God." And as we grow, we learn more about the love of Jesus and what it means to share it with others. This prayer in Ephesians describes what it means to mature in our relationship with Jesus: "I pray that, according to the riches of his glory, he may grant that you may be strengthened in your inner being with power through his Spirit, and that Christ may dwell in your hearts through faith, as you are being rooted and grounded in love" (Ephesians 3.16–17).

See Page 550 for the next Ways of Meeting God *article.*

JUDGES

God's Imperfect People

Whenever the LORD raised up judges for them, the LORD was with the judge, and he delivered them from the hand of their enemies all the days of the judge; for the LORD would be moved to pity by their groaning because of those who persecuted and oppressed them.—Judges 2.18

"The worst things that happen do not happen because a few people are monstrously wicked, but because most people are like us. When we grasp that, we begin to realize that our need is not merely for moving quietly on in the way we are going; our need is for radical change, to find a power that is going to turn us into somebody else."

—WILLIAM TEMPLE,
Christian Faith and Life

Within this Bible designed to help you listen to God, you are reading a book that shows what happens when people listen mostly to themselves. The book of Judges presents an account of twelve military heroes who deliver Israel from its oppressors. Not all of these judges are heroes in every sense—one is an assassin (Ehud) and another is sexually promiscuous (Samson). Yet God has raised them up to carry out his will in Israel and, for the most part, the judges are willing to follow the will of the Lord.

The judges' interest in doing God's will is significant because the Israelites are mostly interested in doing their own will; "all the people did what was right in their own eyes" (17.6; 21.25) because "there was no king in Israel" (17.6; 18.1). The Israelites lived to please themselves and experienced this cycle six times in three centuries: apostasy (wandering from God); oppression (domination by other things and other nations); renewal and repentance (returning to God); deliverance by a dynamic leader (freedom based on God-provided human help).

The book of Judges drives home the truth that people who lose their spiritual commitment wander into idolatry and anarchy. This book may be disturbing to read, for it recounts massive civil war, violence, abuse of women, and power-grabbing leaders. But allow God to use this book to help you grow in wisdom. Imagine how differently this book would read if the Israelites had sought God more consistently. Perhaps reading Judges will help you ponder possible cycles in your own spiritual life and prompt you to examine your willingness to listen to God.

Israel's Failure to Complete the Conquest of Canaan

1 After the death of Joshua, the Israelites inquired of the LORD, "Who shall go up first for us against the Canaanites, to fight against them?" ²The LORD said, "Judah shall go up. I hereby give the land into his hand." ³Judah said to his brother Simeon, "Come up with me into the territory allotted to me, that we may fight against the Canaanites; then I too will go with you into the territory allotted to you." So Simeon went with him. ⁴Then Judah went up and the LORD gave the Canaanites and the Perizzites into their hand; and they defeated ten thousand of them at Bezek. ⁵They came upon Adoni-bezek at Bezek, and fought against him, and defeated the Canaanites and the Perizzites. ⁶Adoni-bezek fled; but they pursued him, and caught him, and cut off his thumbs and big toes. ⁷Adoni-bezek said, "Seventy kings with their thumbs and big toes cut off used to pick up scraps under my table; as I have done, so God has paid me back." They brought him to Jerusalem, and he died there.

8 Then the people of Judah fought against Jerusalem and took it. They put it to the sword and set the city on fire. ⁹Afterward the people of Judah went down to fight against the Canaanites who lived in the hill country, in the Negeb, and in the lowland. ¹⁰Judah went against the Canaanites who lived in Hebron (the name of Hebron was formerly Kiriath-arba); and they defeated Sheshai and Ahiman and Talmai.

11 From there they went against the inhabitants of Debir (the name of Debir was formerly Kiriath-sepher). ¹²Then Caleb said, "Whoever attacks Kiriath-sepher and takes it, I will give him my daughter Achsah as wife." ¹³And Othniel son of Kenaz, Caleb's younger brother, took it; and he gave him his daughter Achsah as wife. ¹⁴When she came to him, she urged him to ask her father for a field. As she dismounted from her donkey, Caleb said to her, "What do you wish?" ¹⁵She said to him, "Give me a present; since you have set me in the land of the Negeb, give me also Gulloth-mayim."ᵃ So Caleb gave her Upper Gulloth and Lower Gulloth.

16 The descendants of Hobabᵇ the Kenite, Moses' father-in-law, went up with the people of Judah from the city of palms into the wilderness of Judah, which lies in the Negeb near Arad. Then they went and settled with the Amalekites.ᶜ ¹⁷Judah went with his brother Simeon, and they defeated the Canaanites who inhabited Zephath, and devoted it to destruction. So the city was called Hormah. ¹⁸Judah took Gaza with its territory, Ashkelon with its territory, and Ekron with its territory. ¹⁹The LORD was with Judah, and he took possession of the hill country, but could not drive out the inhabitants of the plain, because they had chariots of iron. ²⁰Hebron was given to Caleb, as Moses had said; and he drove out from it the three sons of Anak. ²¹But the Benjaminites did not drive out the Jebusites who lived in Jerusalem; so the Jebusites have lived in Jerusalem among the Benjaminites to this day.

22 The house of Joseph also went up against Bethel; and the LORD was with them. ²³The house of Joseph sent out spies to Bethel (the name of the city was formerly Luz). ²⁴When the spies saw a man coming out of the city, they said to him, "Show us the way into the city, and we will deal

a That is Basins of Water   b Gk: Heb lacks Hobab   c See 1 Sam 15.6; Heb people

---

Willing to Give

JUDGES 1.14–15

Although Achsah has to abide by the customary way of being married off as a daughter, she enjoys an unusually generous relationship with her father Caleb. He asks her a question that stands out: "What do you wish?" We often hear similar words, such as "What may I do for you?" used in a customer service context, but why not let them help us develop a giving heart?

Picture the people to whom you could easily say, "What may I do for you?" How does it feel to be so open and vulnerable with them? Imagine yourself answering their request as Caleb did (giving Achsah both the upper and lower basins of water). How do you feel about being so generous?

See Meeting God in Community

Divine Confrontation

JUDGES 2.1–5

The confrontational words of the angel make the Israelites weep. Ponder how the angel of the Lord goes out of the way to make a personal appearance, driving home to the Israelites the real consequences of their behavior.

Reread Judges 2.1–5, absorbing the words and phrases of the angel of the Lord. Pick a word or phrase on which to reflect. Why is this important for you? Rest in silence, staying open for any impressions from God. How does this passage touch your life today?

See Meeting God in Scripture

kindly with you." [25]So he showed them the way into the city; and they put the city to the sword, but they let the man and all his family go. [26]So the man went to the land of the Hittites and built a city, and named it Luz; that is its name to this day.

27 Manasseh did not drive out the inhabitants of Beth-shean and its villages, or Taanach and its villages, or the inhabitants of Dor and its villages, or the inhabitants of Ibleam and its villages, or the inhabitants of Megiddo and its villages; but the Canaanites continued to live in that land. [28]When Israel grew strong, they put the Canaanites to forced labor, but did not in fact drive them out.

29 And Ephraim did not drive out the Canaanites who lived in Gezer; but the Canaanites lived among them in Gezer.

30 Zebulun did not drive out the inhabitants of Kitron, or the inhabitants of Nahalol; but the Canaanites lived among them, and became subject to forced labor.

31 Asher did not drive out the inhabitants of Acco, or the inhabitants of Sidon, or of Ahlab, or of Achzib, or of Helbah, or of Aphik, or of Rehob; [32]but the Asherites lived among the Canaanites, the inhabitants of the land; for they did not drive them out.

33 Naphtali did not drive out the inhabitants of Beth-shemesh, or the inhabitants of Beth-anath, but lived among the Canaanites, the inhabitants of the land; nevertheless the inhabitants of Beth-shemesh and of Beth-anath became subject to forced labor for them.

34 The Amorites pressed the Danites back into the hill country; they did not allow them to come down to the plain. [35]The Amorites continued to live in Har-heres, in Aijalon, and in Shaalbim, but the hand of the house of Joseph rested heavily on them, and they became subject to forced labor. [36]The border of the Amorites ran from the ascent of Akrabbim, from Sela and upward.

Israel's Disobedience

2 Now the angel of the LORD went up from Gilgal to Bochim, and said, "I brought you up from Egypt, and brought you into the land that I had promised to your ancestors. I said, 'I will never break my covenant with you. [2]For your part, do not make a covenant with the inhabitants of this land; tear down their altars.' But you have not obeyed my command. See what you have done! [3]So now I say, I will not drive them out before you; but they shall become adversaries[a] to you, and their gods shall be a snare to you." [4]When the angel of the LORD spoke these words to all the Israelites, the people lifted up their voices and wept. [5]So they named that place Bochim,[b] and there they sacrificed to the LORD.

Death of Joshua

6 When Joshua dismissed the people, the Israelites all went to their own inheritances to take possession of the land. [7]The people worshiped the LORD all the days of Joshua, and all the days of the elders who outlived Joshua, who had seen all the great work that the LORD had done for Israel. [8]Joshua son of Nun, the servant of the LORD, died at the age of one hundred ten years. [9]So they buried him within the bounds of his inheritance in Timnath-heres, in the hill country of Ephraim, north of Mount Gaash. [10]Moreover, that

a OL Vg Compare Gk: Heb *sides*   *b* That is *Weepers*

whole generation was gathered to their ancestors, and another generation grew up after them, who did not know the LORD or the work that he had done for Israel.

Israel's Unfaithfulness

11 Then the Israelites did what was evil in the sight of the LORD and worshiped the Baals; [12]and they abandoned the LORD, the God of their ancestors, who had brought them out of the land of Egypt; they followed other gods, from among the gods of the peoples who were all around them, and bowed down to them; and they provoked the LORD to anger. [13]They abandoned the LORD, and worshiped Baal and the Astartes. [14]So the anger of the LORD was kindled against Israel, and he gave them over to plunderers who plundered them, and he sold them into the power of their enemies all around, so that they could no longer withstand their enemies. [15]Whenever they marched out, the hand of the LORD was against them to bring misfortune, as the LORD had warned them and sworn to them; and they were in great distress.

16 Then the LORD raised up judges, who delivered them out of the power of those who plundered them. [17]Yet they did not listen even to their judges; for they lusted after other gods and bowed down to them. They soon turned aside from the way in which their ancestors had walked, who had obeyed the commandments of the LORD; they did not follow their example. [18]Whenever the LORD raised up judges for them, the LORD was with the judge, and he delivered them from the hand of their enemies all the days of the judge; for the LORD would be moved to pity by their groaning because of those who persecuted and oppressed them. [19]But whenever the judge died, they would relapse and behave worse than their ancestors, following other gods, worshiping them and bowing down to them. They would not drop any of their practices or their stubborn ways. [20]So the anger of the LORD was kindled against Israel; and he said, "Because this people have transgressed my covenant that I commanded their ancestors, and have not obeyed my voice, [21]I will no longer drive out before them any of the nations that Joshua left when he died." [22]In order to test Israel, whether or not they would take care to walk in the way of the LORD as their ancestors did, [23]the LORD had left those nations, not driving them out at once, and had not handed them over to Joshua.

Nations Remaining in the Land

3 Now these are the nations that the LORD left to test all those in Israel who had no experience of any war in Canaan [2](it was only that successive generations of Israelites might know war, to teach those who had no experience of it before): [3]the five lords of the Philistines, and all the Canaanites, and the Sidonians, and the Hivites who lived on Mount Lebanon, from Mount Baal-hermon as far as Lebo-hamath. [4]They were for the testing of Israel, to know whether Israel would obey the commandments of the LORD, which he commanded their ancestors by Moses. [5]So the Israelites lived among the Canaanites, the Hittites, the Amorites, the Perizzites, the Hivites, and the Jebusites; [6]and they took their daughters as wives for themselves, and their own daughters they gave to their sons; and they worshiped their gods.

Leaning Too Hard

JUDGES 2.16–19

Just as the Israelites rely too much on the judges to inspire them to obey, we in our celebrity-driven society often rely excessively on others to inspire, instruct and comfort us. What does this passage say about the way God works in people's lives? What does it say about the way humans behave in relation to leaders? What does this passage suggest to you as a leader? As a follower? What do you most need to say to God regarding this passage?

See Meeting God in Community

Your Deliverer

JUDGES 3.12–15

The Israelites' behavior forms a pattern through the book of Judges: The Israelites wander from God; they are captured; God provides a deliverer. Ponder the word "deliverer." Consider times in your life when you have wandered and God provided a deliverer—perhaps the deliverer was a person or an event or a group of people. If you could have a deliverer now, from what would you want to be delivered? What possible forms could that deliverer take?

Othniel

7 The Israelites did what was evil in the sight of the LORD, forgetting the LORD their God, and worshiping the Baals and the Asherahs. ⁸Therefore the anger of the LORD was kindled against Israel, and he sold them into the hand of King Cushan-rishathaim of Aram-naharaim; and the Israelites served Cushan-rishathaim eight years. ⁹But when the Israelites cried out to the LORD, the LORD raised up a deliverer for the Israelites, who delivered them, Othniel son of Kenaz, Caleb's younger brother. ¹⁰The spirit of the LORD came upon him, and he judged Israel; he went out to war, and the LORD gave King Cushan-rishathaim of Aram into his hand; and his hand prevailed over Cushan-rishathaim. ¹¹So the land had rest forty years. Then Othniel son of Kenaz died.

Ehud

12 The Israelites again did what was evil in the sight of the LORD; and the LORD strengthened King Eglon of Moab against Israel, because they had done what was evil in the sight of the LORD. ¹³In alliance with the Ammonites and the Amalekites, he went and defeated Israel; and they took possession of the city of palms. ¹⁴So the Israelites served King Eglon of Moab eighteen years.

15 But when the Israelites cried out to the LORD, the LORD raised up for them a deliverer, Ehud son of Gera, the Benjaminite, a left-handed man. The Israelites sent tribute by him to King Eglon of Moab. ¹⁶Ehud made for himself a sword with two edges, a cubit in length; and he fastened it on his right thigh under his clothes. ¹⁷Then he presented the tribute to King Eglon of Moab. Now Eglon was a very fat man. ¹⁸When Ehud had finished presenting the tribute, he sent the people who carried the tribute on their way. ¹⁹But he himself turned back at the sculptured stones near Gilgal, and said, "I have a secret message for you, O king." So the king said,ᵃ "Silence!" and all his attendants went out from his presence. ²⁰Ehud came to him, while he was sitting alone in his cool roof chamber, and said, "I have a message from God for you." So he rose from his seat. ²¹Then Ehud reached with his left hand, took the sword from his right thigh, and thrust it into Eglon'sᵇ belly; ²²the hilt also went in after the blade, and the fat closed over the blade, for he did not draw the sword out of his belly; and the dirt came out.ᶜ ²³Then Ehud went out into the vestibule,ᵈ and closed the doors of the roof chamber on him, and locked them.

24 After he had gone, the servants came. When they saw that the doors of the roof chamber were locked, they thought, "He must be relieving himselfᵉ in the cool chamber." ²⁵So they waited until they were embarrassed. When he still did not open the doors of the roof chamber, they took the key and opened them. There was their lord lying dead on the floor.

26 Ehud escaped while they delayed, and passed beyond the sculptured stones, and escaped to Seirah. ²⁷When he arrived, he sounded the trumpet in the hill country of Ephraim; and the Israelites went down with him from the hill country, having him at their head. ²⁸He said to them, "Follow after me; for the LORD has given your enemies the Mo-

a Heb *he said* b Heb *his* c With Tg Vg: Meaning of Heb uncertain
d Meaning of Heb uncertain e Heb *covering his feet*

abites into your hand." So they went down after him, and seized the fords of the Jordan against the Moabites, and allowed no one to cross over. ²⁹At that time they killed about ten thousand of the Moabites, all strong, able-bodied men; no one escaped. ³⁰So Moab was subdued that day under the hand of Israel. And the land had rest eighty years.

Shamgar

31 After him came Shamgar son of Anath, who killed six hundred of the Philistines with an oxgoad. He too delivered Israel.

Deborah and Barak

4 The Israelites again did what was evil in the sight of the LORD, after Ehud died. ²So the LORD sold them into the hand of King Jabin of Canaan, who reigned in Hazor; the commander of his army was Sisera, who lived in Harosheth-ha-goiim. ³Then the Israelites cried out to the LORD for help; for he had nine hundred chariots of iron, and had oppressed the Israelites cruelly twenty years.

4 At that time Deborah, a prophetess, wife of Lappidoth, was judging Israel. ⁵She used to sit under the palm of Deborah between Ramah and Bethel in the hill country of Ephraim; and the Israelites came up to her for judgment. ⁶She sent and summoned Barak son of Abinoam from Kedesh in Naphtali, and said to him, "The LORD, the God of Israel, commands you, 'Go, take position at Mount Tabor, bringing ten thousand from the tribe of Naphtali and the tribe of Zebulun. ⁷I will draw out Sisera, the general of Jabin's army, to meet you by the Wadi Kishon with his chariots and his troops; and I will give him into your hand.'" ⁸Barak said to her, "If you will go with me, I will go; but if you will not go with me, I will not go." ⁹And she said, "I will surely go with you; nevertheless, the road on which you are going will not lead to your glory, for the LORD will sell Sisera into the hand of a woman." Then Deborah got up and went with Barak to Kedesh. ¹⁰Barak summoned Zebulun and Naphtali to Kedesh; and ten thousand warriors went up behind him; and Deborah went up with him.

11 Now Heber the Kenite had separated from the other Kenites,^a that is, the descendants of Hobab the father-in-law of Moses, and had encamped as far away as Elon-bezaanannim, which is near Kedesh.

12 When Sisera was told that Barak son of Abinoam had gone up to Mount Tabor, ¹³Sisera called out all his chariots, nine hundred chariots of iron, and all the troops who were with him, from Harosheth-ha-goiim to the Wadi Kishon. ¹⁴Then Deborah said to Barak, "Up! For this is the day on which the LORD has given Sisera into your hand. The LORD is indeed going out before you." So Barak went down from Mount Tabor with ten thousand warriors following him. ¹⁵And the LORD threw Sisera and all his chariots and all his army into a panic^b before Barak; Sisera got down from his chariot and fled away on foot, ¹⁶while Barak pursued the chariots and the army to Harosheth-ha-goiim. All the army of Sisera fell by the sword; no one was left.

17 Now Sisera had fled away on foot to the tent of Jael wife of Heber the Kenite; for there was peace between King Jabin of Hazor and the clan of Heber the Kenite. ¹⁸Jael came

God Goes Before You

JUDGES 4.14

Deborah's wisdom leads her to expect God to go before the Israelites and to do the hard work ahead of time.

Get out your calendar of things to do this week or month. Pick an item and pray that God will go before you. How does it change the way you approach an activity when you understand that God goes before you? How does it change the way you think or feel about it and about the people involved in it?

See Meeting God in Everyday Life

Making Melody

JUDGES 5.1–3

Occasionally things go well in the nation. Deborah and Barak burst into song when the Israelites offer themselves in service. They thank God because they realize that the people's willingness to serve the Lord is a sign of spiritual wholeness.

Consider your favorite way to "make melody"—whistling, humming, or singing in the shower. For whom are you willing to offer yourself? Whom would you love to see praising God and making music because you willingly served them?

See *Meeting God in Worship*

out to meet Sisera, and said to him, "Turn aside, my lord, turn aside to me; have no fear." So he turned aside to her into the tent, and she covered him with a rug. [19]Then he said to her, "Please give me a little water to drink; for I am thirsty." So she opened a skin of milk and gave him a drink and covered him. [20]He said to her, "Stand at the entrance of the tent, and if anybody comes and asks you, 'Is anyone here?' say, 'No.'" [21]But Jael wife of Heber took a tent peg, and took a hammer in her hand, and went softly to him and drove the peg into his temple, until it went down into the ground—he was lying fast asleep from weariness—and he died. [22]Then, as Barak came in pursuit of Sisera, Jael went out to meet him, and said to him, "Come, and I will show you the man whom you are seeking." So he went into her tent; and there was Sisera lying dead, with the tent peg in his temple.

23 So on that day God subdued King Jabin of Canaan before the Israelites. [24]Then the hand of the Israelites bore harder and harder on King Jabin of Canaan, until they destroyed King Jabin of Canaan.

The Song of Deborah

5 Then Deborah and Barak son of Abinoam sang on that day, saying:

2 "When locks are long in Israel,
 when the people offer themselves willingly—
  bless[a] the LORD!

3 "Hear, O kings; give ear, O princes;
  to the LORD I will sing,
 I will make melody to the LORD, the God of Israel.

4 "LORD, when you went out from Seir,
  when you marched from the region of Edom,
 the earth trembled,
  and the heavens poured,
  the clouds indeed poured water.
5 The mountains quaked before the LORD, the One of
   Sinai,
  before the LORD, the God of Israel.

6 "In the days of Shamgar son of Anath,
  in the days of Jael, caravans ceased
  and travelers kept to the byways.
7 The peasantry prospered in Israel,
  they grew fat on plunder,
 because you arose, Deborah,
  arose as a mother in Israel.
8 When new gods were chosen,
  then war was in the gates.
 Was shield or spear to be seen
  among forty thousand in Israel?
9 My heart goes out to the commanders of Israel
  who offered themselves willingly among the
    people.
 Bless the LORD.

10 "Tell of it, you who ride on white donkeys,
  you who sit on rich carpets[b]

a Or *You who offer yourselves willingly among the people, bless*   b Meaning of Heb uncertain

and you who walk by the way.
11 To the sound of musicians[a] at the watering places,
there they repeat the triumphs of the LORD,
the triumphs of his peasantry in Israel.

"Then down to the gates marched the people of the
LORD.

12 "Awake, awake, Deborah!
Awake, awake, utter a song!
Arise, Barak, lead away your captives,
O son of Abinoam.
13 Then down marched the remnant of the noble;
the people of the LORD marched down for him[b]
against the mighty.
14 From Ephraim they set out[c] into the valley,[d]
following you, Benjamin, with your kin;
from Machir marched down the commanders,
and from Zebulun those who bear the marshal's
staff;
15 the chiefs of Issachar came with Deborah,
and Issachar faithful to Barak;
into the valley they rushed out at his heels.
Among the clans of Reuben
there were great searchings of heart.
16 Why did you tarry among the sheepfolds,
to hear the piping for the flocks?
Among the clans of Reuben
there were great searchings of heart.
17 Gilead stayed beyond the Jordan;
and Dan, why did he abide with the ships?
Asher sat still at the coast of the sea,
settling down by his landings.
18 Zebulun is a people that scorned death;
Naphtali too, on the heights of the field.

19 "The kings came, they fought;
then fought the kings of Canaan,
at Taanach, by the waters of Megiddo;
they got no spoils of silver.
20 The stars fought from heaven,
from their courses they fought against Sisera.
21 The torrent Kishon swept them away,
the onrushing torrent, the torrent Kishon.
March on, my soul, with might!

22 "Then loud beat the horses' hoofs
with the galloping, galloping of his steeds.

23 "Curse Meroz, says the angel of the LORD,
curse bitterly its inhabitants,
because they did not come to the help of the LORD,
to the help of the LORD against the mighty.

24 "Most blessed of women be Jael,
the wife of Heber the Kenite,
of tent-dwelling women most blessed.
25 He asked water and she gave him milk,

Searching the Heart

JUDGES 5.15–18

The tribes of Reuben, Dan, Gilead and Asher stay behind, probably because they live some distance from the threat of violence, yet "there are great searchings of heart" while others risk their lives rushing into the valley with Deborah and Barak.

Consider a skirmish taking place in your life—a family disagreement, a work conflict or a church squabble. What are you called to do—to "stay at the campfire" or "tarry among the sheepfolds" away from the clash of words, or to "rush into the valley" and contribute what you can? In either case, what does it mean to "search your heart"? How can you behave with integrity and mercy toward the people involved? How is God calling you to make the best of an imperfect situation?

See Meeting God in Community

---

a Meaning of Heb uncertain   b Gk: Heb *me*   c Cn: Heb *From Ephraim
their root*   d Gk: Heb *in Amalek*

Protesting to the Angel

JUDGES 6.11–14

How would you behave if an angel appeared to you? Would you have some protest to offer as Gideon does: "If the LORD is with us . . ."?

Let God address you in this passage as you read it aloud. Then shut your eyes and listen for the words or phrases that echo in your heart. Slowly turn the words over in your heart without trying too hard to turn them into a "message." Sitting quietly, offering protests if you need to, listen for a word from God.

See Meeting God in Scripture

she brought him curds in a lordly bowl.

26 She put her hand to the tent peg
   and her right hand to the workmen's mallet;
she struck Sisera a blow,
   she crushed his head,
   she shattered and pierced his temple.

27 He sank, he fell,
   he lay still at her feet;
at her feet he sank, he fell;
   where he sank, there he fell dead.

28 "Out of the window she peered,
   the mother of Sisera gazed*a* through the lattice:
'Why is his chariot so long in coming?
   Why tarry the hoofbeats of his chariots?'

29 Her wisest ladies make answer,
   indeed, she answers the question herself:

30 'Are they not finding and dividing the spoil?—
   A girl or two for every man;
spoil of dyed stuffs for Sisera,
   spoil of dyed stuffs embroidered,
   two pieces of dyed work embroidered for my
      neck as spoil?'

31 "So perish all your enemies, O LORD!
   But may your friends be like the sun as it rises in
      its might."

And the land had rest forty years.

The Midianite Oppression

6 The Israelites did what was evil in the sight of the LORD, and the LORD gave them into the hand of Midian seven years. ²The hand of Midian prevailed over Israel; and because of Midian the Israelites provided for themselves hiding places in the mountains, caves and strongholds. ³For whenever the Israelites put in seed, the Midianites and the Amalekites and the people of the east would come up against them. ⁴They would encamp against them and destroy the produce of the land, as far as the neighborhood of Gaza, and leave no sustenance in Israel, and no sheep or ox or donkey. ⁵For they and their livestock would come up, and they would even bring their tents, as thick as locusts; neither they nor their camels could be counted; so they wasted the land as they came in. ⁶Thus Israel was greatly impoverished because of Midian; and the Israelites cried out to the LORD for help.

7 When the Israelites cried to the LORD on account of the Midianites, ⁸the LORD sent a prophet to the Israelites; and he said to them, "Thus says the LORD, the God of Israel: I led you up from Egypt, and brought you out of the house of slavery; ⁹and I delivered you from the hand of the Egyptians, and from the hand of all who oppressed you, and drove them out before you, and gave you their land; ¹⁰and I said to you, 'I am the LORD your God; you shall not pay reverence to the gods of the Amorites, in whose land you live.' But you have not given heed to my voice."

a Gk Compare Tg: Heb *exclaimed*

The Call of Gideon

11 Now the angel of the LORD came and sat under the oak at Ophrah, which belonged to Joash the Abiezrite, as his son Gideon was beating out wheat in the wine press, to hide it from the Midianites. [12]The angel of the LORD appeared to him and said to him, "The LORD is with you, you mighty warrior." [13]Gideon answered him, "But sir, if the LORD is with us, why then has all this happened to us? And where are all his wonderful deeds that our ancestors recounted to us, saying, 'Did not the LORD bring us up from Egypt?' But now the LORD has cast us off, and given us into the hand of Midian." [14]Then the LORD turned to him and said, "Go in this might of yours and deliver Israel from the hand of Midian; I hereby commission you." [15]He responded, "But sir, how can I deliver Israel? My clan is the weakest in Manasseh, and I am the least in my family." [16]The LORD said to him, "But I will be with you, and you shall strike down the Midianites, every one of them." [17]Then he said to him, "If now I have found favor with you, then show me a sign that it is you who speak with me. [18]Do not depart from here until I come to you, and bring out my present, and set it before you." And he said, "I will stay until you return."

19 So Gideon went into his house and prepared a kid, and unleavened cakes from an ephah of flour; the meat he put in a basket, and the broth he put in a pot, and brought them to him under the oak and presented them. [20]The angel of God said to him, "Take the meat and the unleavened cakes, and put them on this rock, and pour out the broth." And he did so. [21]Then the angel of the LORD reached out the tip of the staff that was in his hand, and touched the meat and the unleavened cakes; and fire sprang up from the rock and consumed the meat and the unleavened cakes; and the angel of the LORD vanished from his sight. [22]Then Gideon perceived that it was the angel of the LORD; and Gideon said, "Help me, Lord GOD! For I have seen the angel of the LORD face to face." [23]But the LORD said to him, "Peace be to you; do not fear, you shall not die." [24]Then Gideon built an altar there to the LORD, and called it, The LORD is peace. To this day it still stands at Ophrah, which belongs to the Abiezrites.

25 That night the LORD said to him, "Take your father's bull, the second bull seven years old, and pull down the altar of Baal that belongs to your father, and cut down the sacred pole[a] that is beside it; [26]and build an altar to the LORD your God on the top of the stronghold here, in proper order; then take the second bull, and offer it as a burnt offering with the wood of the sacred pole[a] that you shall cut down." [27]So Gideon took ten of his servants, and did as the LORD had told him; but because he was too afraid of his family and the townspeople to do it by day, he did it by night.

Gideon Destroys the Altar of Baal

28 When the townspeople rose early in the morning, the altar of Baal was broken down, and the sacred pole[a] beside it was cut down, and the second bull was offered on the altar that had been built. [29]So they said to one another, "Who has done this?" After searching and inquiring, they were told, "Gideon son of Joash did it." [30]Then the townspeople said to Joash, "Bring out your son, so that he may die, for he has

---

Holy Moments

JUDGES 6.22–24

Gideon converses with an angel and lives to tell about it (although we don't know if he actually told anyone). What does this passage tell us about God? That God is quick to declare peace and calm Gideon's fears?

Consider a situation in which you may frighten, intimidate or confuse someone. Picture the person's face for a moment. How could you communicate to the person the peace God speaks to Gideon? With what gesture or facial expression could you communicate: "Peace be to you; do not fear"?

---

a Heb Asherah

In God's Strength

JUDGES 7.2

Gideon's role as judge is about more than driving out Israel's enemies. If the people pay attention, both Israel and Gideon may discover greater trust in God.

Ponder the words God speaks to Gideon. Let God fill in the blanks for you: "The _____ are too many for me to _____." Look at your personal belongings—your books, your personal telephone book, your clothes closet, maybe even your kitchen cabinet. What strengths have you relied on? Have you gathered too much and worked too hard?

If nothing comes to mind, turn that statement over to your subconscious in an effort to hear God. Check back in a few days to see if you've heard anything.

See Meeting God in Everyday Life

pulled down the altar of Baal and cut down the sacred pole[a] beside it." [31]But Joash said to all who were arrayed against him, "Will you contend for Baal? Or will you defend his cause? Whoever contends for him shall be put to death by morning. If he is a god, let him contend for himself, because his altar has been pulled down." [32]Therefore on that day Gideon[b] was called Jerubbaal, that is to say, "Let Baal contend against him," because he pulled down his altar.

33 Then all the Midianites and the Amalekites and the people of the east came together, and crossing the Jordan they encamped in the Valley of Jezreel. [34]But the spirit of the LORD took possession of Gideon; and he sounded the trumpet, and the Abiezrites were called out to follow him. [35]He sent messengers throughout all Manasseh, and they too were called out to follow him. He also sent messengers to Asher, Zebulun, and Naphtali, and they went up to meet them.

The Sign of the Fleece

36 Then Gideon said to God, "In order to see whether you will deliver Israel by my hand, as you have said, [37]I am going to lay a fleece of wool on the threshing floor; if there is dew on the fleece alone, and it is dry on all the ground, then I shall know that you will deliver Israel by my hand, as you have said." [38]And it was so. When he rose early next morning and squeezed the fleece, he wrung enough dew from the fleece to fill a bowl with water. [39]Then Gideon said to God, "Do not let your anger burn against me, let me speak one more time; let me, please, make trial with the fleece just once more; let it be dry only on the fleece, and on all the ground let there be dew." [40]And God did so that night. It was dry on the fleece only, and on all the ground there was dew.

Gideon Surprises and Routs the Midianites

7 Then Jerubbaal (that is, Gideon) and all the troops that were with him rose early and encamped beside the spring of Harod; and the camp of Midian was north of them, below[c] the hill of Moreh, in the valley.

2 The LORD said to Gideon, "The troops with you are too many for me to give the Midianites into their hand. Israel would only take the credit away from me, saying, 'My own hand has delivered me.' [3]Now therefore proclaim this in the hearing of the troops, 'Whoever is fearful and trembling, let him return home.' " Thus Gideon sifted them out;[d] twenty-two thousand returned, and ten thousand remained.

4 Then the LORD said to Gideon, "The troops are still too many; take them down to the water and I will sift them out for you there. When I say, 'This one shall go with you,' he shall go with you; and when I say, 'This one shall not go with you,' he shall not go." [5]So he brought the troops down to the water; and the LORD said to Gideon, "All those who lap the water with their tongues, as a dog laps, you shall put to one side; all those who kneel down to drink, putting their hands to their mouths,[e] you shall put to the other side." [6]The number of those that lapped was three hundred; but all the rest of the troops knelt down to drink water. [7]Then the LORD said to Gideon, "With the three hundred that lapped I will deliver you, and give the Midianites into your hand. Let all the oth-

---

a Heb *Asherah*   *b* Heb *he*   *c* Heb *from*   *d* Cn: Heb *home, and depart from Mount Gilead' "*   *e* Heb places the words *putting their hands to their mouths* after the word *lapped* in verse 6

ers go to their homes." [8]So he took the jars of the troops from their hands,[a] and their trumpets; and he sent all the rest of Israel back to their own tents, but retained the three hundred. The camp of Midian was below him in the valley.

9 That same night the LORD said to him, "Get up, attack the camp; for I have given it into your hand. [10]But if you fear to attack, go down to the camp with your servant Purah; [11]and you shall hear what they say, and afterward your hands shall be strengthened to attack the camp." Then he went down with his servant Purah to the outposts of the armed men that were in the camp. [12]The Midianites and the Amalekites and all the people of the east lay along the valley as thick as locusts; and their camels were without number, countless as the sand on the seashore. [13]When Gideon arrived, there was a man telling a dream to his comrade; and he said, "I had a dream, and in it a cake of barley bread tumbled into the camp of Midian, and came to the tent, and struck it so that it fell; it turned upside down, and the tent collapsed." [14]And his comrade answered, "This is no other than the sword of Gideon son of Joash, a man of Israel; into his hand God has given Midian and all the army."

15 When Gideon heard the telling of the dream and its interpretation, he worshiped; and he returned to the camp of Israel, and said, "Get up; for the LORD has given the army of Midian into your hand." [16]After he divided the three hundred men into three companies, and put trumpets into the hands of all of them, and empty jars, with torches inside the jars, [17]he said to them, "Look at me, and do the same; when I come to the outskirts of the camp, do as I do. [18]When I blow the trumpet, I and all who are with me, then you also blow the trumpets around the whole camp, and shout, 'For the LORD and for Gideon!' "

19 So Gideon and the hundred who were with him came to the outskirts of the camp at the beginning of the middle watch, when they had just set the watch; and they blew the trumpets and smashed the jars that were in their hands. [20]So the three companies blew the trumpets and broke the jars, holding in their left hands the torches, and in their right hands the trumpets to blow; and they cried, "A sword for the LORD and for Gideon!" [21]Every man stood in his place all around the camp, and all the men in camp ran; they cried out and fled. [22]When they blew the three hundred trumpets, the LORD set every man's sword against his fellow and against all the army; and the army fled as far as Beth-shittah toward Zererah,[b] as far as the border of Abel-meholah, by Tabbath. [23]And the men of Israel were called out from Naphtali and from Asher and from all Manasseh, and they pursued after the Midianites.

24 Then Gideon sent messengers throughout all the hill country of Ephraim, saying, "Come down against the Midianites and seize the waters against them, as far as Beth-barah, and also the Jordan." So all the men of Ephraim were called out, and they seized the waters as far as Beth-barah, and also the Jordan. [25]They captured the two captains of Midian, Oreb and Zeeb; they killed Oreb at the rock of Oreb, and Zeeb they killed at the wine press of Zeeb, as they pursued the Midianites. They brought the heads of Oreb and Zeeb to Gideon beyond the Jordan.

Dreaming of God's Will

JUDGES 7.13–15

Gideon takes dreams seriously. Even though both the dreamer and the interpreter are non-Israelites, Gideon recognizes the voice of God and acts upon what God says.

Do you listen to your dreams? Your friends' dreams? How open are you to hear God speaking in ways that seem unconventional?

Reread these three verses. See if you can sense the excitement of the two friends who hear God. Pick a word or phrase from the passage on which to reflect. Why is this important for you? Rest in silence, being open for any impressions from God. What might God be saying to you?

See *Meeting God in Prayer*

---

a Cn: Heb *So the people took provisions in their hands*   b Another reading is *Zeredah*

Power Plays

JUDGES 8.22–23

After Gideon frees Israel from its oppressors, he is asked to rule over Israel—to be a king, if not in name then at least in practice. It would be a natural position for Gideon to accept if he wanted to grab the power, but instead he insists that Israel must be governed by God alone.

Would such an offer—to be ruler over a country—entice you? If not that, what sort of power does attract you? Ask God what you need to know today about acquiring power and giving him sovereignty. In what ways do you grab for power?

See Meeting God in Community

Gideon's Triumph and Vengeance

8 Then the Ephraimites said to him, "What have you done to us, not to call us when you went to fight against the Midianites?" And they upbraided him violently. [2]So he said to them, "What have I done now in comparison with you? Is not the gleaning of the grapes of Ephraim better than the vintage of Abiezer? [3]God has given into your hands the captains of Midian, Oreb and Zeeb; what have I been able to do in comparison with you?" When he said this, their anger against him subsided.

4 Then Gideon came to the Jordan and crossed over, he and the three hundred who were with him, exhausted and famished.[a] [5]So he said to the people of Succoth, "Please give some loaves of bread to my followers, for they are exhausted, and I am pursuing Zebah and Zalmunna, the kings of Midian." [6]But the officials of Succoth said, "Do you already have in your possession the hands of Zebah and Zalmunna, that we should give bread to your army?" [7]Gideon replied, "Well then, when the LORD has given Zebah and Zalmunna into my hand, I will trample your flesh on the thorns of the wilderness and on briers." [8]From there he went up to Penuel, and made the same request of them; and the people of Penuel answered him as the people of Succoth had answered. [9]So he said to the people of Penuel, "When I come back victorious, I will break down this tower."

10 Now Zebah and Zalmunna were in Karkor with their army, about fifteen thousand men, all who were left of all the army of the people of the east; for one hundred twenty thousand men bearing arms had fallen. [11]So Gideon went up by the caravan route east of Nobah and Jogbehah, and attacked the army; for the army was off its guard. [12]Zebah and Zalmunna fled; and he pursued them and took the two kings of Midian, Zebah and Zalmunna, and threw all the army into a panic.

13 When Gideon son of Joash returned from the battle by the ascent of Heres, [14]he caught a young man, one of the people of Succoth, and questioned him; and he listed for him the officials and elders of Succoth, seventy-seven people. [15]Then he came to the people of Succoth, and said, "Here are Zebah and Zalmunna, about whom you taunted me, saying, 'Do you already have in your possession the hands of Zebah and Zalmunna, that we should give bread to your troops who are exhausted?' " [16]So he took the elders of the city and he took thorns of the wilderness and briers and with them trampled[b] the people of Succoth. [17]He also broke down the tower of Penuel, and killed the men of the city.

18 Then he said to Zebah and Zalmunna, "What about the men whom you killed at Tabor?" They answered, "As you are, so were they, every one of them; they resembled the sons of a king." [19]And he replied, "They were my brothers, the sons of my mother; as the LORD lives, if you had saved them alive, I would not kill you." [20]So he said to Jether his firstborn, "Go kill them!" But the boy did not draw his sword, for he was afraid, because he was still a boy. [21]Then Zebah and Zalmunna said, "You come and kill us; for as the man is, so is his strength." So Gideon proceeded to kill Zebah and Zalmunna; and he took the crescents that were on the necks of their camels.

a Gk: Heb *pursuing*   *b* With verse 7, Compare Gk: Heb *he taught*

Gideon's Idolatry

22 Then the Israelites said to Gideon, "Rule over us, you and your son and your grandson also; for you have delivered us out of the hand of Midian." ²³Gideon said to them, "I will not rule over you, and my son will not rule over you; the LORD will rule over you." ²⁴Then Gideon said to them, "Let me make a request of you; each of you give me an earring he has taken as booty." (For the enemy*a* had golden earrings, because they were Ishmaelites.) ²⁵"We will willingly give them," they answered. So they spread a garment, and each threw into it an earring he had taken as booty. ²⁶The weight of the golden earrings that he requested was one thousand seven hundred shekels of gold (apart from the crescents and the pendants and the purple garments worn by the kings of Midian, and the collars that were on the necks of their camels). ²⁷Gideon made an ephod of it and put it in his town, in Ophrah; and all Israel prostituted themselves to it there, and it became a snare to Gideon and to his family. ²⁸So Midian was subdued before the Israelites, and they lifted up their heads no more. So the land had rest forty years in the days of Gideon.

Death of Gideon

29 Jerubbaal son of Joash went to live in his own house. ³⁰Now Gideon had seventy sons, his own offspring, for he had many wives. ³¹His concubine who was in Shechem also bore him a son, and he named him Abimelech. ³²Then Gideon son of Joash died at a good old age, and was buried in the tomb of his father Joash at Ophrah of the Abiezrites.

33 As soon as Gideon died, the Israelites relapsed and prostituted themselves with the Baals, making Baal-berith their god. ³⁴The Israelites did not remember the LORD their God, who had rescued them from the hand of all their enemies on every side; ³⁵and they did not exhibit loyalty to the house of Jerubbaal (that is, Gideon) in return for all the good that he had done to Israel.

Abimelech Attempts to Establish a Monarchy

9 Now Abimelech son of Jerubbaal went to Shechem to his mother's kinsfolk and said to them and to the whole clan of his mother's family, ²"Say in the hearing of all the lords of Shechem, 'Which is better for you, that all seventy of the sons of Jerubbaal rule over you, or that one rule over you?' Remember also that I am your bone and your flesh." ³So his mother's kinsfolk spoke all these words on his behalf in the hearing of all the lords of Shechem; and their hearts inclined to follow Abimelech, for they said, "He is our brother." ⁴They gave him seventy pieces of silver out of the temple of Baal-berith with which Abimelech hired worthless and reckless fellows, who followed him. ⁵He went to his father's house at Ophrah, and killed his brothers the sons of Jerubbaal, seventy men, on one stone; but Jotham, the youngest son of Jerubbaal, survived, for he hid himself. ⁶Then all the lords of Shechem and all Beth-millo came together, and they went and made Abimelech king, by the oak of the pillar*b* at Shechem.

a Heb *they*   *b* Cn: Meaning of Heb uncertain

Speaking Up Against Injustice

JUDGES 9.1–22

After Abimelech slaughters the seventy (minus one) sons of Jerubbaal, Jotham risks his life by speaking out against this injustice. It's interesting how Jotham does so by using an allegory about an olive tree, a fig tree, a vine and a bramble—everyday objects to his listeners.

Consider an injustice you've witnessed recently—an unfair law, a group unjustly punished, a helpless person oppressed. Write a few sentences to describe what needs to be said about this situation. Is there possibly a story to be told? How could you use everyday objects to make the dilemma more understandable to people who could do something to alleviate the situation? Write out your story or draw an illustrated version of it.

See Meeting God in Community

A Relationship Rooted in Treachery

JUDGES 9.23–24

The author of Judges declares that God sent the evil spirit between Abimelech and the citizens of Shechem. Ponder: Was the spirit a supernatural being, or was it the attitude of bitterness and distrust that had permeated the relationship from its inception, rooted as it was in the murder of Jerubbaal's (Gideon's) sons?

Is there a troubling relationship in your experience—a relationship that has "gone sour"? Can you trace the present problems to earlier ones? Ask God to show you how you might have done wrong. Ask God for the grace to heal the mistakes of the past and mend the relationship. Take whatever action God suggests to you.

See Meeting God in Community

The Parable of the Trees

7 When it was told to Jotham, he went and stood on the top of Mount Gerizim, and cried aloud and said to them, "Listen to me, you lords of Shechem, so that God may listen to you.

8   The trees once went out
     to anoint a king over themselves.
   So they said to the olive tree,
     'Reign over us.'
9   The olive tree answered them,
     'Shall I stop producing my rich oil
      by which gods and mortals are honored,
     and go to sway over the trees?'
10   Then the trees said to the fig tree,
     'You come and reign over us.'
11   But the fig tree answered them,
     'Shall I stop producing my sweetness
     and my delicious fruit,
     and go to sway over the trees?'
12   Then the trees said to the vine,
     'You come and reign over us.'
13   But the vine said to them,
     'Shall I stop producing my wine
     that cheers gods and mortals,
     and go to sway over the trees?'
14   So all the trees said to the bramble,
     'You come and reign over us.'
15   And the bramble said to the trees,
     'If in good faith you are anointing me king over
      you,
     then come and take refuge in my shade;
     but if not, let fire come out of the bramble
     and devour the cedars of Lebanon.'

16 "Now therefore, if you acted in good faith and honor when you made Abimelech king, and if you have dealt well with Jerubbaal and his house, and have done to him as his actions deserved— 17for my father fought for you, and risked his life, and rescued you from the hand of Midian; 18but you have risen up against my father's house this day, and have killed his sons, seventy men on one stone, and have made Abimelech, the son of his slave woman, king over the lords of Shechem, because he is your kinsman— 19if, I say, you have acted in good faith and honor with Jerubbaal and with his house this day, then rejoice in Abimelech, and let him also rejoice in you; 20but if not, let fire come out from Abimelech, and devour the lords of Shechem, and Beth-millo; and let fire come out from the lords of Shechem, and from Beth-millo, and devour Abimelech." 21Then Jotham ran away and fled, going to Beer, where he remained for fear of his brother Abimelech.

The Downfall of Abimelech

22 Abimelech ruled over Israel three years. 23But God sent an evil spirit between Abimelech and the lords of Shechem; and the lords of Shechem dealt treacherously with Abimelech. 24This happened so that the violence done to the seventy sons of Jerubbaal might be avenged[a] and their blood be laid on their brother Abimelech, who killed them,

a Heb might come

and on the lords of Shechem, who strengthened his hands to kill his brothers. 25So, out of hostility to him, the lords of Shechem set ambushes on the mountain tops. They robbed all who passed by them along that way; and it was reported to Abimelech.

26 When Gaal son of Ebed moved into Shechem with his kinsfolk, the lords of Shechem put confidence in him. 27They went out into the field and gathered the grapes from their vineyards, trod them, and celebrated. Then they went into the temple of their god, ate and drank, and ridiculed Abimelech. 28Gaal son of Ebed said, "Who is Abimelech, and who are we of Shechem, that we should serve him? Did not the son of Jerubbaal and Zebul his officer serve the men of Hamor father of Shechem? Why then should we serve him? 29If only this people were under my command! Then I would remove Abimelech; I would say*a* to him, 'Increase your army, and come out.' "

30 When Zebul the ruler of the city heard the words of Gaal son of Ebed, his anger was kindled. 31He sent messengers to Abimelech at Arumah,*b* saying, "Look, Gaal son of Ebed and his kinsfolk have come to Shechem, and they are stirring up*c* the city against you. 32Now therefore, go by night, you and the troops that are with you, and lie in wait in the fields. 33Then early in the morning, as soon as the sun rises, get up and rush on the city; and when he and the troops that are with him come out against you, you may deal with them as best you can."

34 So Abimelech and all the troops with him got up by night and lay in wait against Shechem in four companies. 35When Gaal son of Ebed went out and stood in the entrance of the gate of the city, Abimelech and the troops with him rose from the ambush. 36And when Gaal saw them, he said to Zebul, "Look, people are coming down from the mountain tops!" And Zebul said to him, "The shadows on the mountains look like people to you." 37Gaal spoke again and said, "Look, people are coming down from Tabbur-erez, and one company is coming from the direction of Elon-meonenim."*d* 38Then Zebul said to him, "Where is your boast*e* now, you who said, 'Who is Abimelech, that we should serve him?' Are not these the troops you made light of? Go out now and fight with them." 39So Gaal went out at the head of the lords of Shechem, and fought with Abimelech. 40Abimelech chased him, and he fled before him. Many fell wounded, up to the entrance of the gate. 41So Abimelech resided at Arumah; and Zebul drove out Gaal and his kinsfolk, so that they could not live on at Shechem.

42 On the following day the people went out into the fields. When Abimelech was told, 43he took his troops and divided them into three companies, and lay in wait in the fields. When he looked and saw the people coming out of the city, he rose against them and killed them. 44Abimelech and the company that was*f* with him rushed forward and stood at the entrance of the gate of the city, while the two companies rushed on all who were in the fields and killed them. 45Abimelech fought against the city all that day; he took the city, and killed the people that were in it; and he razed the city and sowed it with salt.

a Gk: Heb *and he said*   *b* Cn See 9.41. Heb *Tormah*   *c* Cn: Heb *are besieging*   *d* That is *Diviners' Oak*   *e* Heb *mouth*   *f* Vg and some Gk Mss: Heb *companies that were*

God in the News

JUDGES 9.42–57

When we read the newspaper, many events seem to randomly occur, but the eyes of God do not stray from human affairs. Abimelech, a bloodthirsty man, is not allowed to rage on indefinitely but is instead brought to a quick and shameful end. The newspapers of that day would have claimed that the woman dropped the stone on him and that Abimelech then asked his armor-bearer to kill him. But the truth is that God intervened.

Pick up a newspaper and peruse the stories. What situations are full of injustice? In which situation is God likely to intervene? How is God calling you to intercede so that justice and mercy prevail?

See Meeting God in Community

Cry for Rescue

JUDGES 10.10–15

Many people today would question your sanity if you said you regularly hold dialogues with God, but that's what is happening between Israel and God. Israel cries out; God answers, identifying its wrong behavior; then Israel confesses its sin.

Notice the rhythm of the conversation between God and Israel. Pick a word or phrase that resonates with you. Why is it important for you? Rest in silence, being open to whatever conversation you may need to have with God. What do you believe God is trying to communicate to you today?

See Meeting God in Scripture

46 When all the lords of the Tower of Shechem heard of it, they entered the stronghold of the temple of El-berith. [47]Abimelech was told that all the lords of the Tower of Shechem were gathered together. [48]So Abimelech went up to Mount Zalmon, he and all the troops that were with him. Abimelech took an ax in his hand, cut down a bundle of brushwood, and took it up and laid it on his shoulder. Then he said to the troops with him, "What you have seen me do, do quickly, as I have done." [49]So every one of the troops cut down a bundle and following Abimelech put it against the stronghold, and they set the stronghold on fire over them, so that all the people of the Tower of Shechem also died, about a thousand men and women.

50 Then Abimelech went to Thebez, and encamped against Thebez, and took it. [51]But there was a strong tower within the city, and all the men and women and all the lords of the city fled to it and shut themselves in; and they went to the roof of the tower. [52]Abimelech came to the tower, and fought against it, and came near to the entrance of the tower to burn it with fire. [53]But a certain woman threw an upper millstone on Abimelech's head, and crushed his skull. [54]Immediately he called to the young man who carried his armor and said to him, "Draw your sword and kill me, so people will not say about me, 'A woman killed him.' " So the young man thrust him through, and he died. [55]When the Israelites saw that Abimelech was dead, they all went home. [56]Thus God repaid Abimelech for the crime he committed against his father in killing his seventy brothers; [57]and God also made all the wickedness of the people of Shechem fall back on their heads, and on them came the curse of Jotham son of Jerubbaal.

Tola and Jair

10 After Abimelech, Tola son of Puah son of Dodo, a man of Issachar, who lived at Shamir in the hill country of Ephraim, rose to deliver Israel. [2]He judged Israel twenty-three years. Then he died, and was buried at Shamir.

3 After him came Jair the Gileadite, who judged Israel twenty-two years. [4]He had thirty sons who rode on thirty donkeys; and they had thirty towns, which are in the land of Gilead, and are called Havvoth-jair to this day. [5]Jair died, and was buried in Kamon.

Oppression by the Ammonites

6 The Israelites again did what was evil in the sight of the LORD, worshiping the Baals and the Astartes, the gods of Aram, the gods of Sidon, the gods of Moab, the gods of the Ammonites, and the gods of the Philistines. Thus they abandoned the LORD, and did not worship him. [7]So the anger of the LORD was kindled against Israel, and he sold them into the hand of the Philistines and into the hand of the Ammonites, [8]and they crushed and oppressed the Israelites that year. For eighteen years they oppressed all the Israelites that were beyond the Jordan in the land of the Amorites, which is in Gilead. [9]The Ammonites also crossed the Jordan to fight against Judah and against Benjamin and against the house of Ephraim; so that Israel was greatly distressed.

10 So the Israelites cried to the LORD, saying, "We have sinned against you, because we have abandoned our God and have worshiped the Baals." [11]And the LORD said to the

Israelites, "Did I not deliver you[a] from the Egyptians and from the Amorites, from the Ammonites and from the Philistines? [12]The Sidonians also, and the Amalekites, and the Maonites, oppressed you; and you cried to me, and I delivered you out of their hand. [13]Yet you have abandoned me and worshiped other gods; therefore I will deliver you no more. [14]Go and cry to the gods whom you have chosen; let them deliver you in the time of your distress." [15]And the Israelites said to the LORD, "We have sinned; do to us whatever seems good to you; but deliver us this day!" [16]So they put away the foreign gods from among them and worshiped the LORD; and he could no longer bear to see Israel suffer.

17 Then the Ammonites were called to arms, and they encamped in Gilead; and the Israelites came together, and they encamped at Mizpah. [18]The commanders of the people of Gilead said to one another, "Who will begin the fight against the Ammonites? He shall be head over all the inhabitants of Gilead."

Jephthah

11 Now Jephthah the Gileadite, the son of a prostitute, was a mighty warrior. Gilead was the father of Jephthah. [2]Gilead's wife also bore him sons; and when his wife's sons grew up, they drove Jephthah away, saying to him, "You shall not inherit anything in our father's house; for you are the son of another woman." [3]Then Jephthah fled from his brothers and lived in the land of Tob. Outlaws collected around Jephthah and went raiding with him.

4 After a time the Ammonites made war against Israel. [5]And when the Ammonites made war against Israel, the elders of Gilead went to bring Jephthah from the land of Tob. [6]They said to Jephthah, "Come and be our commander, so that we may fight with the Ammonites." [7]But Jephthah said to the elders of Gilead, "Are you not the very ones who rejected me and drove me out of my father's house? So why do you come to me now when you are in trouble?" [8]The elders of Gilead said to Jephthah, "Nevertheless, we have now turned back to you, so that you may go with us and fight with the Ammonites, and become head over us, over all the inhabitants of Gilead." [9]Jephthah said to the elders of Gilead, "If you bring me home again to fight with the Ammonites, and the LORD gives them over to me, I will be your head." [10]And the elders of Gilead said to Jephthah, "The LORD will be witness between us; we will surely do as you say." [11]So Jephthah went with the elders of Gilead, and the people made him head and commander over them; and Jephthah spoke all his words before the LORD at Mizpah.

12 Then Jephthah sent messengers to the king of the Ammonites and said, "What is there between you and me, that you have come to me to fight against my land?" [13]The king of the Ammonites answered the messengers of Jephthah, "Because Israel, on coming from Egypt, took away my land from the Arnon to the Jabbok and to the Jordan; now therefore restore it peaceably." [14]Once again Jephthah sent messengers to the king of the Ammonites [15]and said to him: "Thus says Jephthah: Israel did not take away the land of Moab or the land of the Ammonites, [16]but when they came up from Egypt, Israel went through the wilderness to the Red Sea[b] and came to Kadesh. [17]Israel then sent messengers to

Grace to Pass Through

JUDGES 11.17–19

Israel asks permission to pass through Edom, Moab and the land of the Amorites on the way to the promised land, but these nations do not give it. They may feel threatened by the possibility of aggression, sabotage or intermarriage.

Who is passing through your life? A new coworker, a new in-law, a new neighbor? You might consider this person bothersome or even threatening, but take a moment to pray for this person, asking God to show you what you need to know about him or her.

See Meeting God in Community

An Acceptable Sacrifice

JUDGES 11.34–40

"And when a deep consideration had from the secret bottom
of my soul drawn together and
heaped up all my misery in the
sight of my heart, there arose a
mighty storm, bringing a shower of tears . . . I cast myself
down I know not how, under a
certain fig tree, giving full vent
to my tears; and the floods of
mine eyes gushed out an acceptable sacrifice to Thee."

—AUGUSTINE,
Confessions

the king of Edom, saying, 'Let us pass through your land'; but the king of Edom would not listen. They also sent to the king of Moab, but he would not consent. So Israel remained at Kadesh. [18]Then they journeyed through the wilderness, went around the land of Edom and the land of Moab, arrived on the east side of the land of Moab, and camped on the other side of the Arnon. They did not enter the territory of Moab, for the Arnon was the boundary of Moab. [19]Israel then sent messengers to King Sihon of the Amorites, king of Heshbon; and Israel said to him, 'Let us pass through your land to our country.' [20]But Sihon did not trust Israel to pass through his territory; so Sihon gathered all his people together, and encamped at Jahaz, and fought with Israel. [21]Then the LORD, the God of Israel, gave Sihon and all his people into the hand of Israel, and they defeated them; so Israel occupied all the land of the Amorites, who inhabited that country. [22]They occupied all the territory of the Amorites from the Arnon to the Jabbok and from the wilderness to the Jordan. [23]So now the LORD, the God of Israel, has conquered the Amorites for the benefit of his people Israel. Do you intend to take their place? [24]Should you not possess what your god Chemosh gives you to possess? And should we not be the ones to possess everything that the LORD our God has conquered for our benefit? [25]Now are you any better than King Balak son of Zippor of Moab? Did he ever enter into conflict with Israel, or did he ever go to war with them? [26]While Israel lived in Heshbon and its villages, and in Aroer and its villages, and in all the towns that are along the Arnon, three hundred years, why did you not recover them within that time? [27]It is not I who have sinned against you, but you are the one who does me wrong by making war on me. Let the LORD, who is judge, decide today for the Israelites or for the Ammonites." [28]But the king of the Ammonites did not heed the message that Jephthah sent him.

Jephthah's Vow

29 Then the spirit of the LORD came upon Jephthah, and he passed through Gilead and Manasseh. He passed on to Mizpah of Gilead, and from Mizpah of Gilead he passed on to the Ammonites. [30]And Jephthah made a vow to the LORD, and said, "If you will give the Ammonites into my hand, [31]then whoever comes out of the doors of my house to meet me, when I return victorious from the Ammonites, shall be the LORD's, to be offered up by me as a burnt offering." [32]So Jephthah crossed over to the Ammonites to fight against them; and the LORD gave them into his hand. [33]He inflicted a massive defeat on them from Aroer to the neighborhood of Minnith, twenty towns, and as far as Abel-keramim. So the Ammonites were subdued before the people of Israel.

Jephthah's Daughter

34 Then Jephthah came to his home at Mizpah; and there was his daughter coming out to meet him with timbrels and with dancing. She was his only child; he had no son or daughter except her. [35]When he saw her, he tore his clothes, and said, "Alas, my daughter! You have brought me very low; you have become the cause of great trouble to me. For I have opened my mouth to the LORD, and I cannot take back my vow." [36]She said to him, "My father, if you have opened your mouth to the LORD, do to me according to what has gone out

of your mouth, now that the LORD has given you vengeance against your enemies, the Ammonites." [37]And she said to her father, "Let this thing be done for me: Grant me two months, so that I may go and wander[a] on the mountains, and bewail my virginity, my companions and I." [38]"Go," he said and sent her away for two months. So she departed, she and her companions, and bewailed her virginity on the mountains. [39]At the end of two months, she returned to her father, who did with her according to the vow he had made. She had never slept with a man. So there arose an Israelite custom that [40]for four days every year the daughters of Israel would go out to lament the daughter of Jephthah the Gileadite.

Intertribal Dissension

12 The men of Ephraim were called to arms, and they crossed to Zaphon and said to Jephthah, "Why did you cross over to fight against the Ammonites, and did not call us to go with you? We will burn your house down over you!" [2]Jephthah said to them, "My people and I were engaged in conflict with the Ammonites who oppressed us[b] severely. But when I called you, you did not deliver me from their hand. [3]When I saw that you would not deliver me, I took my life in my hand, and crossed over against the Ammonites, and the LORD gave them into my hand. Why then have you come up to me this day, to fight against me?" [4]Then Jephthah gathered all the men of Gilead and fought with Ephraim; and the men of Gilead defeated Ephraim, because they said, "You are fugitives from Ephraim, you Gileadites—in the heart of Ephraim and Manasseh."[c] [5]Then the Gileadites took the fords of the Jordan against the Ephraimites. Whenever one of the fugitives of Ephraim said, "Let me go over," the men of Gilead would say to him, "Are you an Ephraimite?" When he said, "No," [6]they said to him, "Then say Shibboleth," and he said, "Sibboleth," for he could not pronounce it right. Then they seized him and killed him at the fords of the Jordan. Forty-two thousand of the Ephraimites fell at that time.

7 Jephthah judged Israel six years. Then Jephthah the Gileadite died, and was buried in his town in Gilead.[d]

Ibzan, Elon, and Abdon

8 After him Ibzan of Bethlehem judged Israel. [9]He had thirty sons. He gave his thirty daughters in marriage outside his clan and brought in thirty young women from outside for his sons. He judged Israel seven years. [10]Then Ibzan died, and was buried at Bethlehem.

11 After him Elon the Zebulunite judged Israel; and he judged Israel ten years. [12]Then Elon the Zebulunite died, and was buried at Aijalon in the land of Zebulun.

13 After him Abdon son of Hillel the Pirathonite judged Israel. [14]He had forty sons and thirty grandsons, who rode on seventy donkeys; he judged Israel eight years. [15]Then Abdon son of Hillel the Pirathonite died, and was buried at Pirathon in the land of Ephraim, in the hill country of the Amalekites.

a Cn: Heb *go down*   b Gk OL, Syr H: Heb lacks *who oppressed us*
c Meaning of Heb uncertain: Gk omits *because . . . Manasseh*   d Gk: Heb *in the towns of Gilead*

Asking for Further Instructions

JUDGES 13.2–16

Put yourself in the place of Manoah and his wife. You are being granted a request you've probably despaired of ever receiving. A stranger—actually an angel—promises you a child. This angel instructs you to bring up the boy as a nazirite, so you ask the angel to teach you how to do that.

What great gifts has God given to you, in the sense of having "the desires of your heart" granted? (Psalm 37.4). What do you need God to teach you further about those gifts?

See Meeting God in Prayer

Faces to the Ground

JUDGES 13.17–21

Imagine yourself and someone close to you experiencing the things Manoah and his wife experience: They are told they are speaking to a person with a name that is "too wonderful," and they watch an angel ascend in a flame. In awe they lie down with their faces to the ground.

What would cause you to be that awestruck? Consider praying in that face-to-the-ground position or some other position you rarely use, such as kneeling or bowing. What sort of prayers come out of your mouth in that position? Are they words of human humility or a testament to God's majesty? What do you need to say to God?

See *Meeting God in Worship*

The Birth of Samson

13 The Israelites again did what was evil in the sight of the LORD, and the LORD gave them into the hand of the Philistines forty years.

2 There was a certain man of Zorah, of the tribe of the Danites, whose name was Manoah. His wife was barren, having borne no children. ³And the angel of the LORD appeared to the woman and said to her, "Although you are barren, having borne no children, you shall conceive and bear a son. ⁴Now be careful not to drink wine or strong drink, or to eat anything unclean, ⁵for you shall conceive and bear a son. No razor is to come on his head, for the boy shall be a nazirite[a] to God from birth. It is he who shall begin to deliver Israel from the hand of the Philistines." ⁶Then the woman came and told her husband, "A man of God came to me, and his appearance was like that of an angel[b] of God, most awe-inspiring; I did not ask him where he came from, and he did not tell me his name; ⁷but he said to me, 'You shall conceive and bear a son. So then drink no wine or strong drink, and eat nothing unclean, for the boy shall be a nazirite[a] to God from birth to the day of his death.' "

8 Then Manoah entreated the LORD, and said, "O LORD, I pray, let the man of God whom you sent come to us again and teach us what we are to do concerning the boy who will be born." ⁹God listened to Manoah, and the angel of God came again to the woman as she sat in the field; but her husband Manoah was not with her. ¹⁰So the woman ran quickly and told her husband, "The man who came to me the other day has appeared to me." ¹¹Manoah got up and followed his wife, and came to the man and said to him, "Are you the man who spoke to this woman?" And he said, "I am." ¹²Then Manoah said, "Now when your words come true, what is to be the boy's rule of life; what is he to do?" ¹³The angel of the LORD said to Manoah, "Let the woman give heed to all that I said to her. ¹⁴She may not eat of anything that comes from the vine. She is not to drink wine or strong drink, or eat any unclean thing. She is to observe everything that I commanded her."

15 Manoah said to the angel of the LORD, "Allow us to detain you, and prepare a kid for you." ¹⁶The angel of the LORD said to Manoah, "If you detain me, I will not eat your food; but if you want to prepare a burnt offering, then offer it to the LORD." (For Manoah did not know that he was the angel of the LORD.) ¹⁷Then Manoah said to the angel of the LORD, "What is your name, so that we may honor you when your words come true?" ¹⁸But the angel of the LORD said to him, "Why do you ask my name? It is too wonderful."

19 So Manoah took the kid with the grain offering, and offered it on the rock to the LORD, to him who works[c] wonders.[d] ²⁰When the flame went up toward heaven from the altar, the angel of the LORD ascended in the flame of the altar while Manoah and his wife looked on; and they fell on their faces to the ground. ²¹The angel of the LORD did not appear again to Manoah and his wife. Then Manoah realized that it was the angel of the LORD. ²²And Manoah said to his wife, "We shall surely die, for we have seen God." ²³But his wife said to him, "If the LORD had meant to kill us, he would not

---

a That is one separated or one consecrated   b Or the angel   c Gk Vg: Heb and working   d Heb wonders, while Manoah and his wife looked on

have accepted a burnt offering and a grain offering at our hands, or shown us all these things, or now announced to us such things as these."

24 The woman bore a son, and named him Samson. The boy grew, and the LORD blessed him. [25]The spirit of the LORD began to stir him in Mahaneh-dan, between Zorah and Eshtaol.

Samson's Marriage

14 Once Samson went down to Timnah, and at Timnah he saw a Philistine woman. [2]Then he came up, and told his father and mother, "I saw a Philistine woman at Timnah; now get her for me as my wife." [3]But his father and mother said to him, "Is there not a woman among your kin, or among all our[a] people, that you must go to take a wife from the uncircumcised Philistines?" But Samson said to his father, "Get her for me, because she pleases me." [4]His father and mother did not know that this was from the LORD; for he was seeking a pretext to act against the Philistines. At that time the Philistines had dominion over Israel.

5 Then Samson went down with his father and mother to Timnah. When he came to the vineyards of Timnah, suddenly a young lion roared at him. [6]The spirit of the LORD rushed on him, and he tore the lion apart barehanded as one might tear apart a kid. But he did not tell his father or his mother what he had done. [7]Then he went down and talked with the woman, and she pleased Samson. [8]After a while he returned to marry her, and he turned aside to see the carcass of the lion, and there was a swarm of bees in the body of the lion, and honey. [9]He scraped it out into his hands, and went on, eating as he went. When he came to his father and mother, he gave some to them, and they ate it. But he did not tell them that he had taken the honey from the carcass of the lion.

10 His father went down to the woman, and Samson made a feast there as the young men were accustomed to do. [11]When the people saw him, they brought thirty companions to be with him. [12]Samson said to them, "Let me now put a riddle to you. If you can explain it to me within the seven days of the feast, and find it out, then I will give you thirty linen garments and thirty festal garments. [13]But if you cannot explain it to me, then you shall give me thirty linen garments and thirty festal garments." So they said to him, "Ask your riddle; let us hear it." [14]He said to them,

"Out of the eater came something to eat.
Out of the strong came something sweet."

But for three days they could not explain the riddle.

15 On the fourth[b] day they said to Samson's wife, "Coax your husband to explain the riddle to us, or we will burn you and your father's house with fire. Have you invited us here to impoverish us?" [16]So Samson's wife wept before him, saying, "You hate me; you do not really love me. You have asked a riddle of my people, but you have not explained it to me." He said to her, "Look, I have not told my father or my mother. Why should I tell you?" [17]She wept before him the seven days that their feast lasted; and because she nagged him, on the seventh day he told her. Then she explained the riddle to her people. [18]The men of the town said to him on the seventh day before the sun went down,

"What is sweeter than honey?

Tales of Manipulation

JUDGES 14.13–20

Samson's wife manipulates him with tears and accusations. Enter this story for a moment from the perspective of God's unseen heart. How does it feel to watch a man whom you've set aside for special service being manipulated? How does it feel to watch him respond?

Take a few minutes to grieve with God over the people in this world who are being manipulated. Include yourself as one who has been manipulated. Include others whom you have manipulated.

See *Meeting God in Community*

Power of the Spirit

JUDGES 15.14

When the Spirit comes over Samson, Samson has great physical power to free himself from the Philistines. What important work is God calling you to do—work that is important in God's eyes, but perhaps not in society's? What sort of power of the Spirit do you need in order to do this work? What are the ropes binding your hands at this time—ropes that God's Spirit can rip away?

See Meeting God in Service

What is stronger than a lion?"
And he said to them,

"If you had not plowed with my heifer,
you would not have found out my riddle."

[19]Then the spirit of the LORD rushed on him, and he went down to Ashkelon. He killed thirty men of the town, took their spoil, and gave the festal garments to those who had explained the riddle. In hot anger he went back to his father's house. [20]And Samson's wife was given to his companion, who had been his best man.

Samson Defeats the Philistines

15 After a while, at the time of the wheat harvest, Samson went to visit his wife, bringing along a kid. He said, "I want to go into my wife's room." But her father would not allow him to go in. [2]Her father said, "I was sure that you had rejected her; so I gave her to your companion. Is not her younger sister prettier than she? Why not take her instead?" [3]Samson said to them, "This time, when I do mischief to the Philistines, I will be without blame." [4]So Samson went and caught three hundred foxes, and took some torches; and he turned the foxes[a] tail to tail, and put a torch between each pair of tails. [5]When he had set fire to the torches, he let the foxes go into the standing grain of the Philistines, and burned up the shocks and the standing grain, as well as the vineyards and[b] olive groves. [6]Then the Philistines asked, "Who has done this?" And they said, "Samson, the son-in-law of the Timnite, because he has taken Samson's wife and given her to his companion." So the Philistines came up, and burned her and her father. [7]Samson said to them, "If this is what you do, I swear I will not stop until I have taken revenge on you." [8]He struck them down hip and thigh with great slaughter; and he went down and stayed in the cleft of the rock of Etam.

9 Then the Philistines came up and encamped in Judah, and made a raid on Lehi. [10]The men of Judah said, "Why have you come up against us?" They said, "We have come up to bind Samson, to do to him as he did to us." [11]Then three thousand men of Judah went down to the cleft of the rock of Etam, and they said to Samson, "Do you not know that the Philistines are rulers over us? What then have you done to us?" He replied, "As they did to me, so I have done to them." [12]They said to him, "We have come down to bind you, so that we may give you into the hands of the Philistines." Samson answered them, "Swear to me that you yourselves will not attack me." [13]They said to him, "No, we will only bind you and give you into their hands; we will not kill you." So they bound him with two new ropes, and brought him up from the rock.

14 When he came to Lehi, the Philistines came shouting to meet him; and the spirit of the LORD rushed on him, and the ropes that were on his arms became like flax that has caught fire, and his bonds melted off his hands. [15]Then he found a fresh jawbone of a donkey, reached down and took it, and with it he killed a thousand men. [16]And Samson said,

"With the jawbone of a donkey,
heaps upon heaps,
with the jawbone of a donkey
I have slain a thousand men."

[17]When he had finished speaking, he threw away the jawbone; and that place was called Ramath-lehi.[c]

a Heb *them*   *b* Gk Tg Vg: Heb lacks *and*   *c* That is *The Hill of the Jawbone*

18 By then he was very thirsty, and he called on the LORD, saying, "You have granted this great victory by the hand of your servant. Am I now to die of thirst, and fall into the hands of the uncircumcised?" ¹⁹So God split open the hollow place that is at Lehi, and water came from it. When he drank, his spirit returned, and he revived. Therefore it was named En-hakkore,ᵃ which is at Lehi to this day. ²⁰And he judged Israel in the days of the Philistines twenty years.

Samson and Delilah

16 Once Samson went to Gaza, where he saw a prostitute and went in to her. ²The Gazites were told,ᵇ "Samson has come here." So they circled around and lay in wait for him all night at the city gate. They kept quiet all night, thinking, "Let us wait until the light of the morning; then we will kill him." ³But Samson lay only until midnight. Then at midnight he rose up, took hold of the doors of the city gate and the two posts, pulled them up, bar and all, put them on his shoulders, and carried them to the top of the hill that is in front of Hebron.

4 After this he fell in love with a woman in the valley of Sorek, whose name was Delilah. ⁵The lords of the Philistines came to her and said to her, "Coax him, and find out what makes his strength so great, and how we may overpower him, so that we may bind him in order to subdue him; and we will each give you eleven hundred pieces of silver." ⁶So Delilah said to Samson, "Please tell me what makes your strength so great, and how you could be bound, so that one could subdue you." ⁷Samson said to her, "If they bind me with seven fresh bowstrings that are not dried out, then I shall become weak, and be like anyone else." ⁸Then the lords of the Philistines brought her seven fresh bowstrings that had not dried out, and she bound him with them. ⁹While men were lying in wait in an inner chamber, she said to him, "The Philistines are upon you, Samson!" But he snapped the bowstrings, as a strand of fiber snaps when it touches the fire. So the secret of his strength was not known.

10 Then Delilah said to Samson, "You have mocked me and told me lies; please tell me how you could be bound." ¹¹He said to her, "If they bind me with new ropes that have not been used, then I shall become weak, and be like anyone else." ¹²So Delilah took new ropes and bound him with them, and said to him, "The Philistines are upon you, Samson!" (The men lying in wait were in an inner chamber.) But he snapped the ropes off his arms like a thread.

13 Then Delilah said to Samson, "Until now you have mocked me and told me lies; tell me how you could be bound." He said to her, "If you weave the seven locks of my head with the web and make it tight with the pin, then I shall become weak, and be like anyone else." ¹⁴So while he slept, Delilah took the seven locks of his head and wove them into the web,ᶜ and made them tight with the pin. Then she said to him, "The Philistines are upon you, Samson!" But he awoke from his sleep, and pulled away the pin, the loom, and the web.

15 Then she said to him, "How can you say, 'I love you,' when your heart is not with me? You have mocked me three times now and have not told me what makes your strength

Failing–in Spite of Advantages

JUDGES 16.15–20

Samson, divinely appointed by God to save Israel, is allowed to fail. What does this passage say about the nature of God in relation to human failure? What does it say about human nature that Samson, so blessed with loving parents and nazirite righteousness, can fail so miserably? How does this passage lead you to pray? In what areas have you failed? How do you feel about those failures? How do you think God sees your failures? After you ponder these questions, read Ephesians 1.1–8.

See Meeting God in Everyday Life

---

a That is *The Spring of the One who Called*   b Gk: Heb lacks *were told*
c Compare Gk: in verses 13-14, Heb lacks *and make it tight . . . into the web*

The Destruction of a Soul

JUDGES 16.26–31

"A man will have a great and long struggle with himself, before he fully learns to master self and to turn his whole affection towards God. When a man relies on himself, he easily turns aside to human consolations. But a true lover of Christ, and a diligent pursuer of virtue, does not fall back upon consolations, nor seek such sensible sweetnesses; he prefers hard trials and would wish to undergo severe labours for Christ. The devil sleeps not, neither is the flesh yet dead; therefore you must not cease to prepare yourself for the battle; for on the right hand and on the left are enemies that never rest."

—THOMAS À KEMPIS,
The Imitation of Christ

so great." ¹⁶Finally, after she had nagged him with her words day after day, and pestered him, he was tired to death. ¹⁷So he told her his whole secret, and said to her, "A razor has never come upon my head; for I have been a nazirite*a* to God from my mother's womb. If my head were shaved, then my strength would leave me; I would become weak, and be like anyone else."

18 When Delilah realized that he had told her his whole secret, she sent and called the lords of the Philistines, saying, "This time come up, for he has told his whole secret to me." Then the lords of the Philistines came up to her, and brought the money in their hands. ¹⁹She let him fall asleep on her lap; and she called a man, and had him shave off the seven locks of his head. He began to weaken,*b* and his strength left him. ²⁰Then she said, "The Philistines are upon you, Samson!" When he awoke from his sleep, he thought, "I will go out as at other times, and shake myself free." But he did not know that the LORD had left him. ²¹So the Philistines seized him and gouged out his eyes. They brought him down to Gaza and bound him with bronze shackles; and he ground at the mill in the prison. ²²But the hair of his head began to grow again after it had been shaved.

Samson's Death

23 Now the lords of the Philistines gathered to offer a great sacrifice to their god Dagon, and to rejoice; for they said, "Our god has given Samson our enemy into our hand." ²⁴When the people saw him, they praised their god; for they said, "Our god has given our enemy into our hand, the ravager of our country, who has killed many of us." ²⁵And when their hearts were merry, they said, "Call Samson, and let him entertain us." So they called Samson out of the prison, and he performed for them. They made him stand between the pillars; ²⁶and Samson said to the attendant who held him by the hand, "Let me feel the pillars on which the house rests, so that I may lean against them." ²⁷Now the house was full of men and women; all the lords of the Philistines were there, and on the roof there were about three thousand men and women, who looked on while Samson performed.

28 Then Samson called to the LORD and said, "Lord GOD, remember me and strengthen me only this once, O God, so that with this one act of revenge I may pay back the Philistines for my two eyes."*c* ²⁹And Samson grasped the two middle pillars on which the house rested, and he leaned his weight against them, his right hand on the one and his left hand on the other. ³⁰Then Samson said, "Let me die with the Philistines." He strained with all his might; and the house fell on the lords and all the people who were in it. So those he killed at his death were more than those he had killed during his life. ³¹Then his brothers and all his family came down and took him and brought him up and buried him between Zorah and Eshtaol in the tomb of his father Manoah. He had judged Israel twenty years.

Micah and the Levite

17 There was a man in the hill country of Ephraim whose name was Micah. ²He said to his mother, "The eleven hundred pieces of silver that were taken from

a That is one separated or one consecrated   *b* Gk: Heb She began to torment him   *c* Or so that I may be avenged upon the Philistines for one of my two eyes

you, about which you uttered a curse, and even spoke it in my hearing,—that silver is in my possession; I took it; but now I will return it to you."*a* And his mother said, "May my son be blessed by the LORD!" ³Then he returned the eleven hundred pieces of silver to his mother; and his mother said, "I consecrate the silver to the LORD from my hand for my son, to make an idol of cast metal." ⁴So when he returned the money to his mother, his mother took two hundred pieces of silver, and gave it to the silversmith, who made it into an idol of cast metal; and it was in the house of Micah. ⁵This man Micah had a shrine, and he made an ephod and teraphim, and installed one of his sons, who became his priest. ⁶In those days there was no king in Israel; all the people did what was right in their own eyes.

7 Now there was a young man of Bethlehem in Judah, of the clan of Judah. He was a Levite residing there. ⁸This man left the town of Bethlehem in Judah, to live wherever he could find a place. He came to the house of Micah in the hill country of Ephraim to carry on his work.*b* ⁹Micah said to him, "From where do you come?" He replied, "I am a Levite of Bethlehem in Judah, and I am going to live wherever I can find a place." ¹⁰Then Micah said to him, "Stay with me, and be to me a father and a priest, and I will give you ten pieces of silver a year, a set of clothes, and your living."*c* ¹¹The Levite agreed to stay with the man; and the young man became to him like one of his sons. ¹²So Micah installed the Levite, and the young man became his priest, and was in the house of Micah. ¹³Then Micah said, "Now I know that the LORD will prosper me, because the Levite has become my priest."

The Migration of Dan

18 In those days there was no king in Israel. And in those days the tribe of the Danites was seeking for itself a territory to live in; for until then no territory among the tribes of Israel had been allotted to them. ²So the Danites sent five valiant men from the whole number of their clan, from Zorah and from Eshtaol, to spy out the land and to explore it; and they said to them, "Go, explore the land." When they came to the hill country of Ephraim, to the house of Micah, they stayed there. ³While they were at Micah's house, they recognized the voice of the young Levite; so they went over and asked him, "Who brought you here? What are you doing in this place? What is your business here?" ⁴He said to them, "Micah did such and such for me, and he hired me, and I have become his priest." ⁵Then they said to him, "Inquire of God that we may know whether the mission we are undertaking will succeed." ⁶The priest replied, "Go in peace. The mission you are on is under the eye of the LORD."

7 The five men went on, and when they came to Laish, they observed the people who were there living securely, after the manner of the Sidonians, quiet and unsuspecting, lacking*d* nothing on earth, and possessing wealth.*e* Furthermore, they were far from the Sidonians and had no dealings with Aram.*f* ⁸When they came to their kinsfolk at Zorah and Eshtaol, they said to them, "What do you report?" ⁹They said, "Come, let us go up against them; for we have seen the

Minding My Own Business

JUDGES 18.7

The people of Laish live an ideal life of safety, security and prosperity. God's imperfect people, the Danites, decide to conquer the people of Laish, who are without help because they have "no dealings with Aram." What does the unwitting isolation of this content, prosperous people say about human nature? What does this passage say about how isolation can make you vulnerable to ruthless people? What does it suggest about how you might pray? What does it suggest about what you need to do?

See Meeting God in Community

---

a The words *but now I will return it to you* are transposed from the end of verse 3 in Heb   *b* Or *Ephraim, continuing his journey*   *c* Heb *living, and the Levite went*   *d* Cn Compare 18.10: Meaning of Heb uncertain   *e* Meaning of Heb uncertain   *f* Symmachus: Heb *with anyone*

Because "I Can"

JUDGES 18.18–26

The Danites steal from Micah and later subdue Laish with no thought of whether doing these things is consistent with God's will or morally right. They do them because they want to do them; they have the power to do them. They give in to the human inclination to treat the powerless in any way they choose.

Imagine for a moment that the Danite men seek God in the matter. What possible solutions might God suggest to escape their dilemma (which is that "until then no territory among the tribes of Israel had been allotted to them" [18.1])?

See Meeting God in Scripture

land, and it is very good. Will you do nothing? Do not be slow to go, but enter in and possess the land. ¹⁰When you go, you will come to an unsuspecting people. The land is broad—God has indeed given it into your hands—a place where there is no lack of anything on earth."

11 Six hundred men of the Danite clan, armed with weapons of war, set out from Zorah and Eshtaol, ¹²and went up and encamped at Kiriath-jearim in Judah. On this account that place is called Mahaneh-dan*ᵃ* to this day; it is west of Kiriath-jearim. ¹³From there they passed on to the hill country of Ephraim, and came to the house of Micah.

14 Then the five men who had gone to spy out the land (that is, Laish) said to their comrades, "Do you know that in these buildings there are an ephod, teraphim, and an idol of cast metal? Now therefore consider what you will do." ¹⁵So they turned in that direction and came to the house of the young Levite, at the home of Micah, and greeted him. ¹⁶While the six hundred men of the Danites, armed with their weapons of war, stood by the entrance of the gate, ¹⁷the five men who had gone to spy out the land proceeded to enter and take the idol of cast metal, the ephod, and the teraphim.*ᵇ* The priest was standing by the entrance of the gate with the six hundred men armed with weapons of war. ¹⁸When the men went into Micah's house and took the idol of cast metal, the ephod, and the teraphim, the priest said to them, "What are you doing?" ¹⁹They said to him, "Keep quiet! Put your hand over your mouth, and come with us, and be to us a father and a priest. Is it better for you to be priest to the house of one person, or to be priest to a tribe and clan in Israel?" ²⁰Then the priest accepted the offer. He took the ephod, the teraphim, and the idol, and went along with the people.

21 So they resumed their journey, putting the little ones, the livestock, and the goods in front of them. ²²When they were some distance from the home of Micah, the men who were in the houses near Micah's house were called out, and they overtook the Danites. ²³They shouted to the Danites, who turned around and said to Micah, "What is the matter that you come with such a company?" ²⁴He replied, "You take my gods that I made, and the priest, and go away, and what have I left? How then can you ask me, 'What is the matter?' " ²⁵And the Danites said to him, "You had better not let your voice be heard among us or else hot-tempered fellows will attack you, and you will lose your life and the lives of your household." ²⁶Then the Danites went their way. When Micah saw that they were too strong for him, he turned and went back to his home.

The Danites Settle in Laish

27 The Danites, having taken what Micah had made, and the priest who belonged to him, came to Laish, to a people quiet and unsuspecting, put them to the sword, and burned down the city. ²⁸There was no deliverer, because it was far from Sidon and they had no dealings with Aram.*ᶜ* It was in the valley that belongs to Beth-rehob. They rebuilt the city, and lived in it. ²⁹They named the city Dan, after their ancestor Dan, who was born to Israel; but the name of the city was formerly Laish. ³⁰Then the Danites set up the idol for themselves.

a That is *Camp of Dan*   *b* Compare 17.4, 5; 18.14: Heb *teraphim and the cast metal*   *c* Cn Compare verse 7: Heb *with anyone*

Jonathan son of Gershom, son of Moses,[a] and his sons were priests to the tribe of the Danites until the time the land went into captivity. [31]So they maintained as their own Micah's idol that he had made, as long as the house of God was at Shiloh.

The Levite's Concubine

19 In those days, when there was no king in Israel, a certain Levite, residing in the remote parts of the hill country of Ephraim, took to himself a concubine from Bethlehem in Judah. [2]But his concubine became angry with[b] him, and she went away from him to her father's house at Bethlehem in Judah, and was there some four months. [3]Then her husband set out after her, to speak tenderly to her and bring her back. He had with him his servant and a couple of donkeys. When he reached[c] her father's house, the girl's father saw him and came with joy to meet him. [4]His father-in-law, the girl's father, made him stay, and he remained with him three days; so they ate and drank, and he[d] stayed there. [5]On the fourth day they got up early in the morning, and he prepared to go; but the girl's father said to his son-in-law, "Fortify yourself with a bit of food, and after that you may go." [6]So the two men sat and ate and drank together; and the girl's father said to the man, "Why not spend the night and enjoy yourself?" [7]When the man got up to go, his father-in-law kept urging him until he spent the night there again. [8]On the fifth day he got up early in the morning to leave; and the girl's father said, "Fortify yourself." So they lingered[e] until the day declined, and the two of them ate and drank.[f] [9]When the man with his concubine and his servant got up to leave, his father-in-law, the girl's father, said to him, "Look, the day has worn on until it is almost evening. Spend the night. See, the day has drawn to a close. Spend the night here and enjoy yourself. Tomorrow you can get up early in the morning for your journey, and go home."

10 But the man would not spend the night; he got up and departed, and arrived opposite Jebus (that is, Jerusalem). He had with him a couple of saddled donkeys, and his concubine was with him. [11]When they were near Jebus, the day was far spent, and the servant said to his master, "Come now, let us turn aside to this city of the Jebusites, and spend the night in it." [12]But his master said to him, "We will not turn aside into a city of foreigners, who do not belong to the people of Israel; but we will continue on to Gibeah." [13]Then he said to his servant, "Come, let us try to reach one of these places, and spend the night at Gibeah or at Ramah." [14]So they passed on and went their way; and the sun went down on them near Gibeah, which belongs to Benjamin. [15]They turned aside there, to go in and spend the night at Gibeah. He went in and sat down in the open square of the city, but no one took them in to spend the night.

16 Then at evening there was an old man coming from his work in the field. The man was from the hill country of Ephraim, and he was residing in Gibeah. (The people of the place were Benjaminites.) [17]When the old man looked up and saw the wayfarer in the open square of the city, he said, "Where are you going and where do you come from?" [18]He answered him, "We are passing from Bethlehem in Judah to

---

Sin on Sin, Sorrow on Sorrow

JUDGES 19–20

One sin leads to another in these disquieting passages, and each sinful choice—each decision made without calling on God—is compounded until the tragic conflict mushrooms into widespread death and destruction.

Are you involved in a conflict today? A small difference of opinion? A seemingly minor personality conflict? How can you stop it from mushrooming? By saying a quick prayer before you reply to criticism or a sharp word? By choosing words of reconciliation rather than retort? By choosing humility and offering an apology rather than striking out in defensiveness? By asking God how the conflict might be resolved with fairness and justice?

See Meeting God in Community

---

a Another reading is *son of Manasseh*   b Gk OL: Heb *prostituted herself against*   c Gk: Heb *she brought him*   d Compare verse 7 and Gk: Heb *they*   e Cn: Heb *Linger*   f Gk: Heb lacks *and drank*

Paying Attention to Tragedy

JUDGES 19.29–30

Why does the Levite do such a shocking thing? Apparently he wants to get the twelve tribes' attention and knows that sending body parts will serve just that purpose. Sometimes God will allow us to be alarmed and appalled.

In the face of our dulled sensitivity, others may feel the need to be overly dramatic in order to get our attention. Consider the requests your coworkers and children have made of you today. What would it take for you to consider them seriously? Or even better, as you open your mail today, open and read the pleas for donations you receive. Ask God, "What would it take to cultivate an inner person that is readily sensitive to others?"

See Meeting God in Community

the remote parts of the hill country of Ephraim, from which I come. I went to Bethlehem in Judah; and I am going to my home.[a] Nobody has offered to take me in. [19]We your servants have straw and fodder for our donkeys, with bread and wine for me and the woman and the young man along with us. We need nothing more." [20]The old man said, "Peace be to you. I will care for all your wants; only do not spend the night in the square." [21]So he brought him into his house, and fed the donkeys; they washed their feet, and ate and drank.

Gibeah's Crime

22 While they were enjoying themselves, the men of the city, a perverse lot, surrounded the house, and started pounding on the door. They said to the old man, the master of the house, "Bring out the man who came into your house, so that we may have intercourse with him." [23]And the man, the master of the house, went out to them and said to them, "No, my brothers, do not act so wickedly. Since this man is my guest, do not do this vile thing. [24]Here are my virgin daughter and his concubine; let me bring them out now. Ravish them and do whatever you want to them; but against this man do not do such a vile thing." [25]But the men would not listen to him. So the man seized his concubine, and put her out to them. They wantonly raped her, and abused her all through the night until the morning. And as the dawn began to break, they let her go. [26]As morning appeared, the woman came and fell down at the door of the man's house where her master was, until it was light.

27 In the morning her master got up, opened the doors of the house, and when he went out to go on his way, there was his concubine lying at the door of the house, with her hands on the threshold. [28]"Get up," he said to her, "we are going." But there was no answer. Then he put her on the donkey; and the man set out for his home. [29]When he had entered his house, he took a knife, and grasping his concubine he cut her into twelve pieces, limb by limb, and sent her throughout all the territory of Israel. [30]Then he commanded the men whom he sent, saying, "Thus shall you say to all the Israelites, 'Has such a thing ever happened[b] since the day that the Israelites came up from the land of Egypt until this day? Consider it, take counsel, and speak out.'"

The Other Tribes Attack Benjamin

20 Then all the Israelites came out, from Dan to Beersheba, including the land of Gilead, and the congregation assembled in one body before the LORD at Mizpah. [2]The chiefs of all the people, of all the tribes of Israel, presented themselves in the assembly of the people of God, four hundred thousand foot-soldiers bearing arms. [3](Now the Benjaminites heard that the people of Israel had gone up to Mizpah.) And the Israelites said, "Tell us, how did this criminal act come about?" [4]The Levite, the husband of the woman who was murdered, answered, "I came to Gibeah that belongs to Benjamin, I and my concubine, to spend the night. [5]The lords of Gibeah rose up against me, and surrounded the house at night. They intended to kill me, and they raped my concubine until she died. [6]Then I took my concubine and cut her into pieces, and sent her throughout

a Gk Compare 19.29. Heb *to the house of the LORD*   b Compare Gk: Heb
[30]*And all who saw it said, "Such a thing has not happened or been seen*

the whole extent of Israel's territory; for they have committed a vile outrage in Israel. ⁷So now, you Israelites, all of you, give your advice and counsel here."

8 All the people got up as one, saying, "We will not any of us go to our tents, nor will any of us return to our houses. ⁹But now this is what we will do to Gibeah: we will go up^a against it by lot. ¹⁰We will take ten men of a hundred throughout all the tribes of Israel, and a hundred of a thousand, and a thousand of ten thousand, to bring provisions for the troops, who are going to repay^b Gibeah of Benjamin for all the disgrace that they have done in Israel." ¹¹So all the men of Israel gathered against the city, united as one.

12 The tribes of Israel sent men through all the tribe of Benjamin, saying, "What crime is this that has been committed among you? ¹³Now then, hand over those scoundrels in Gibeah, so that we may put them to death, and purge the evil from Israel." But the Benjaminites would not listen to their kinsfolk, the Israelites. ¹⁴The Benjaminites came together out of the towns to Gibeah, to go out to battle against the Israelites. ¹⁵On that day the Benjaminites mustered twenty-six thousand armed men from their towns, besides the inhabitants of Gibeah. ¹⁶Of all this force, there were seven hundred picked men who were left-handed; every one could sling a stone at a hair, and not miss. ¹⁷And the Israelites, apart from Benjamin, mustered four hundred thousand armed men, all of them warriors.

18 The Israelites proceeded to go up to Bethel, where they inquired of God, "Which of us shall go up first to battle against the Benjaminites?" And the LORD answered, "Judah shall go up first."

19 Then the Israelites got up in the morning, and encamped against Gibeah. ²⁰The Israelites went out to battle against Benjamin; and the Israelites drew up the battle line against them at Gibeah. ²¹The Benjaminites came out of Gibeah, and struck down on that day twenty-two thousand of the Israelites. ²³ᶜThe Israelites went up and wept before the LORD until the evening; and they inquired of the LORD, "Shall we again draw near to battle against our kinsfolk the Benjaminites?" And the LORD said, "Go up against them." ²²The Israelites took courage, and again formed the battle line in the same place where they had formed it on the first day.

24 So the Israelites advanced against the Benjaminites the second day. ²⁵Benjamin moved out against them from Gibeah the second day, and struck down eighteen thousand of the Israelites, all of them armed men. ²⁶Then all the Israelites, the whole army, went back to Bethel and wept, sitting there before the LORD; they fasted that day until evening. Then they offered burnt offerings and sacrifices of well-being before the LORD. ²⁷And the Israelites inquired of the LORD (for the ark of the covenant of God was there in those days, ²⁸and Phinehas son of Eleazar, son of Aaron, ministered before it in those days), saying, "Shall we go out once more to battle against our kinsfolk the Benjaminites, or shall we desist?" The LORD answered, "Go up, for tomorrow I will give them into your hand."

29 So Israel stationed men in ambush around Gibeah. ³⁰Then the Israelites went up against the Benjaminites on the third day, and set themselves in array against Gibeah, as be-

---

a Gk: Heb lacks *we will go up*   b Compare Gk: Meaning of Heb uncertain
c Verses 22 and 23 are transposed

Righteous Anger Is Never Enough

JUDGES 20.26–28

Shocked by the evil committed by the city of Gibeah, Israel comes against the city and its tribe. Being on the right side isn't enough, and appropriately they seek God—weeping, fasting, inquiring and offering themselves to God.

Notice the many outward ways Israel worships God. Pick a word, phrase or movement described in this passage that impresses you. Why is it important for you? To what service is God calling you? In what ways do you need to worship before you begin to serve?

See Meeting God in Worship

Mercy for the Wicked

JUDGES 21.1–5

The first hint of mercy for the tribe of Benjamin occurs in the writer's description of their fighters: "courageous" (20.44,46). Suddenly Israel—a country made up of distant but related tribes—realizes that it has been fighting its own people and that it must take steps to preserve the nation.

If you have pictures of your family or friends in your wallet or hanging on the wall of your home, look at these pictures. Whom, if anyone, have you declared war on? Whom would you like to declare war on? Whom would you judge to be unredeemable? What can you do to restore them to the family? Pray that they be restored.

See *Meeting God in Community*

fore. ³¹When the Benjaminites went out against the army, they were drawn away from the city. As before they began to inflict casualties on the troops, along the main roads, one of which goes up to Bethel and the other to Gibeah, as well as in the open country, killing about thirty men of Israel. ³²The Benjaminites thought, "They are being routed before us, as previously." But the Israelites said, "Let us retreat and draw them away from the city toward the roads." ³³The main body of the Israelites drew back its battle line to Baal-tamar, while those Israelites who were in ambush rushed out of their place west*a* of Geba. ³⁴There came against Gibeah ten thousand picked men out of all Israel, and the battle was fierce. But the Benjaminites did not realize that disaster was close upon them.

35 The LORD defeated Benjamin before Israel; and the Israelites destroyed twenty-five thousand one hundred men of Benjamin that day, all of them armed.

36 Then the Benjaminites saw that they were defeated.*b*
The Israelites gave ground to Benjamin, because they trusted to the troops in ambush that they had stationed against Gibeah. ³⁷The troops in ambush rushed quickly upon Gibeah. Then they put the whole city to the sword. ³⁸Now the agreement between the main body of Israel and the men in ambush was that when they sent up a cloud of smoke out of the city ³⁹the main body of Israel should turn in battle. But Benjamin had begun to inflict casualties on the Israelites, killing about thirty of them; so they thought, "Surely they are defeated before us, as in the first battle." ⁴⁰But when the cloud, a column of smoke, began to rise out of the city, the Benjaminites looked behind them—and there was the whole city going up in smoke toward the sky! ⁴¹Then the main body of Israel turned, and the Benjaminites were dismayed, for they saw that disaster was close upon them. ⁴²Therefore they turned away from the Israelites in the direction of the wilderness; but the battle overtook them, and those who came out of the city*c* were slaughtering them in between.*d* ⁴³Cutting down*e* the Benjaminites, they pursued them from Nohah*f* and trod them down as far as a place east of Gibeah. ⁴⁴Eighteen thousand Benjaminites fell, all of them courageous fighters. ⁴⁵When they turned and fled toward the wilderness to the rock of Rimmon, five thousand of them were cut down on the main roads, and they were pursued as far as Gidom, and two thousand of them were slain. ⁴⁶So all who fell that day of Benjamin were twenty-five thousand arms-bearing men, all of them courageous fighters. ⁴⁷But six hundred turned and fled toward the wilderness to the rock of Rimmon, and remained at the rock of Rimmon for four months. ⁴⁸Meanwhile, the Israelites turned back against the Benjaminites, and put them to the sword—the city, the people, the animals, and all that remained. Also the remaining towns they set on fire.

The Benjaminites Saved from Extinction

21 Now the Israelites had sworn at Mizpah, "No one of us shall give his daughter in marriage to Benjamin." ²And the people came to Bethel, and sat there until evening before God, and they lifted up their voices and wept bitterly. ³They said, "O LORD, the God of Israel, why has it come to pass that

a Gk Vg: Heb *in the plain*   *b* This sentence is continued by verse 45.
c Compare Vg and some Gk Mss: Heb *cities*   *d* Compare Syr: Meaning of Heb uncertain   *e* Gk: Heb *Surrounding*   *f* Gk: Heb *pursued them at their resting place*

today there should be one tribe lacking in Israel?" ⁴On the next day, the people got up early, and built an altar there, and offered burnt offerings and sacrifices of well-being. ⁵Then the Israelites said, "Which of all the tribes of Israel did not come up in the assembly to the LORD?" For a solemn oath had been taken concerning whoever did not come up to the LORD to Mizpah, saying, "That one shall be put to death." ⁶But the Israelites had compassion for Benjamin their kin, and said, "One tribe is cut off from Israel this day. ⁷What shall we do for wives for those who are left, since we have sworn by the LORD that we will not give them any of our daughters as wives?"

8 Then they said, "Is there anyone from the tribes of Israel who did not come up to the LORD to Mizpah?" It turned out that no one from Jabesh-gilead had come to the camp, to the assembly. ⁹For when the roll was called among the people, not one of the inhabitants of Jabesh-gilead was there. ¹⁰So the congregation sent twelve thousand soldiers there and commanded them, "Go, put the inhabitants of Jabesh-gilead to the sword, including the women and the little ones. ¹¹This is what you shall do; every male and every woman that has lain with a male you shall devote to destruction." ¹²And they found among the inhabitants of Jabesh-gilead four hundred young virgins who had never slept with a man and brought them to the camp at Shiloh, which is in the land of Canaan.

13 Then the whole congregation sent word to the Benjaminites who were at the rock of Rimmon, and proclaimed peace to them. ¹⁴Benjamin returned at that time; and they gave them the women whom they had saved alive of the women of Jabesh-gilead; but they did not suffice for them.

15 The people had compassion on Benjamin because the LORD had made a breach in the tribes of Israel. ¹⁶So the elders of the congregation said, "What shall we do for wives for those who are left, since there are no women left in Benjamin?" ¹⁷And they said, "There must be heirs for the survivors of Benjamin, in order that a tribe may not be blotted out from Israel. ¹⁸Yet we cannot give any of our daughters to them as wives." For the Israelites had sworn, "Cursed be anyone who gives a wife to Benjamin." ¹⁹So they said, "Look, the yearly festival of the LORD is taking place at Shiloh, which is north of Bethel, on the east of the highway that goes up from Bethel to Shechem, and south of Lebonah." ²⁰And they instructed the Benjaminites, saying, "Go and lie in wait in the vineyards, ²¹and watch; when the young women of Shiloh come out to dance in the dances, then come out of the vineyards and each of you carry off a wife for himself from the young women of Shiloh, and go to the land of Benjamin. ²²Then if their fathers or their brothers come to complain to us, we will say to them, 'Be generous and allow us to have them; because we did not capture in battle a wife for each man. But neither did you incur guilt by giving your daughters to them.' " ²³The Benjaminites did so; they took wives for each of them from the dancers whom they abducted. Then they went and returned to their territory, and rebuilt the towns, and lived in them. ²⁴So the Israelites departed from there at that time by tribes and families, and they went out from there to their own territories.

25 In those days there was no king in Israel; all the people did what was right in their own eyes.

Conscience

JUDGES 21.25

"Some people even say that so long as a man follows his conscience he cannot be committing sin. Certainly a man should follow his conscience; but that is not the whole of his duty. Still more important is it to enlighten the conscience itself, lest 'the light that is in us be darkness' (Matthew 6.23) . . . But we shall not set ourselves that standard, to say nothing of attaining it, if we are left to our own resource. And we do not know what the perfection of God is until we have seen it in Christ."

—WILLIAM TEMPLE,
Christus Veritas

RUTH
The Power of Relationships

KEY VERSE:

"Where you go, I will go; where you lodge, I will lodge; your people shall be my people, and your God my God."—Ruth 1.16

Set squarely within the daily life of common people, the book of Ruth tells a story about people who need God and how God responds. The story demonstrates that, though mysterious and unpredictable, God's provision can be sought confidently in the midst of ordinary human problems. The enduring power of the story of Ruth and Naomi rests in the fact that two outcast women—one a foreigner and one an elderly widow—become significant links in the family line of the Christ child. God's grace often comes in surprising ways.

This story also reminds us that God uses people from unexpected places in unexpected ways. Ruth is not a Hebrew; she cannot inherit a claim to the promises of God to Israel, yet God blesses her with compassion, resourcefulness and courage. Her faith and love transform a tragic situation into a joyous one.

Redemption—rescuing and reclaiming one apart or adrift—is the central theme of the book of Ruth. The focus is on the management of the land and family obligations, but the story teaches us a more profound meaning of redemption: God gives new life in abundance where only death and emptiness are expected. And while God is easing Naomi's and Ruth's need, he is also bringing about his purposes for the whole nation.

Ask yourself where you least expect to find God at work, and give new attention to that place or those people. If you feel like an "outcast," ask God what he might be seeking from you and ask him to bring about transformation. Expect to be surprised!

Elimelech's Family Goes to Moab

1 In the days when the judges ruled, there was a famine in the land, and a certain man of Bethlehem in Judah went to live in the country of Moab, he and his wife and two sons. ²The name of the man was Elimelech and the name of his wife Naomi, and the names of his two sons were Mahlon and Chilion; they were Ephrathites from Bethlehem in Judah. They went into the country of Moab and remained there. ³But Elimelech, the husband of Naomi, died, and she was left with her two sons. ⁴These took Moabite wives; the name of the one was Orpah and the name of the other Ruth. When they had lived there about ten years, ⁵both Mahlon and Chilion also died, so that the woman was left without her two sons and her husband.

Naomi and Her Moabite Daughters-in-Law

6 Then she started to return with her daughters-in-law from the country of Moab, for she had heard in the country of Moab that the LORD had considered his people and given them food. ⁷So she set out from the place where she had been living, she and her two daughters-in-law, and they went on their way to go back to the land of Judah. ⁸But Naomi said to her two daughters-in-law, "Go back each of you to your mother's house. May the LORD deal kindly with you, as you have dealt with the dead and with me. ⁹The LORD grant that you may find security, each of you in the house of your husband." Then she kissed them, and they wept aloud. ¹⁰They said to her, "No, we will return with you to your people." ¹¹But Naomi said, "Turn back, my daughters, why will you go with me? Do I still have sons in my womb that they may become your husbands? ¹²Turn back, my daughters, go your way, for I am too old to have a husband. Even if I thought there was hope for me, even if I should have a husband tonight and bear sons, ¹³would you then wait until they were grown? Would you then refrain from marrying? No, my daughters, it has been far more bitter for me than for you, because the hand of the LORD has turned against me." ¹⁴Then they wept aloud again. Orpah kissed her mother-in-law, but Ruth clung to her.

15 So she said, "See, your sister-in-law has gone back to her people and to her gods; return after your sister-in-law." ¹⁶But Ruth said,

"Do not press me to leave you
    or to turn back from following you!
Where you go, I will go;
    where you lodge, I will lodge;
your people shall be my people,
    and your God my God.
¹⁷ Where you die, I will die—
    there will I be buried.
May the LORD do thus and so to me,
    and more as well,
    if even death parts me from you!"

¹⁸When Naomi saw that she was determined to go with her, she said no more to her.

19 So the two of them went on until they came to Bethlehem. When they came to Bethlehem, the whole town

How Bitter to Be Alone!

RUTH 1.20–21

Naomi's life had been full of family love, even in the midst of famine. But she now feels empty and bitter, and she blames God. Enter Ruth, her daughter-in-law, a Moabite "outsider" whose kindness moves her to share Naomi's isolation rather than return to "her own" people. Do the situations of either of these women remind you of an important time in your own life—when loss and grief, and even bitterness, threatened to overwhelm you? Or when love called you to do something others considered foolish or risky? Recall such a time, remembering how despair and hope mingled with one another. What happened to change your sense of emptiness?

See Meeting God in Community

A Place of Safety

RUTH 2.12

God's care is like the wings of a mother bird, gently covering her baby chicks, keeping them warm and safe from harm. The image of shelter under wings is repeated later in the story when Ruth asks Boaz to spread the corner of his cloak over her (see 3.9). What image comes to your mind when you think of safety, security and generous care? Perhaps you think of a hearth fire, or a cozy old chair, or a childhood treehouse. Imagine yourself now sheltered in this way within God's loving embrace. Explore what you feel in that secure and welcoming place.

was stirred because of them; and the women said, "Is this Naomi?" [20]She said to them,

> "Call me no longer Naomi,[a]
>   call me Mara,[b]
>   for the Almighty[c] has dealt bitterly with me.
> [21] I went away full,
>   but the LORD has brought me back empty;
>   why call me Naomi
>   when the LORD has dealt harshly with[d] me,
>   and the Almighty[c] has brought calamity upon me?"

22 So Naomi returned together with Ruth the Moabite, her daughter-in-law, who came back with her from the country of Moab. They came to Bethlehem at the beginning of the barley harvest.

Ruth Meets Boaz

2 Now Naomi had a kinsman on her husband's side, a prominent rich man, of the family of Elimelech, whose name was Boaz. [2]And Ruth the Moabite said to Naomi, "Let me go to the field and glean among the ears of grain, behind someone in whose sight I may find favor." She said to her, "Go, my daughter." [3]So she went. She came and gleaned in the field behind the reapers. As it happened, she came to the part of the field belonging to Boaz, who was of the family of Elimelech. [4]Just then Boaz came from Bethlehem. He said to the reapers, "The LORD be with you." They answered, "The LORD bless you." [5]Then Boaz said to his servant who was in charge of the reapers, "To whom does this young woman belong?" [6]The servant who was in charge of the reapers answered, "She is the Moabite who came back with Naomi from the country of Moab. [7]She said, 'Please, let me glean and gather among the sheaves behind the reapers.' So she came, and she has been on her feet from early this morning until now, without resting even for a moment."[e]

8 Then Boaz said to Ruth, "Now listen, my daughter, do not go to glean in another field or leave this one, but keep close to my young women. [9]Keep your eyes on the field that is being reaped, and follow behind them. I have ordered the young men not to bother you. If you get thirsty, go to the vessels and drink from what the young men have drawn." [10]Then she fell prostrate, with her face to the ground, and said to him, "Why have I found favor in your sight, that you should take notice of me, when I am a foreigner?" [11]But Boaz answered her, "All that you have done for your mother-in-law since the death of your husband has been fully told me, and how you left your father and mother and your native land and came to a people that you did not know before. [12]May the LORD reward you for your deeds, and may you have a full reward from the LORD, the God of Israel, under whose wings you have come for refuge!" [13]Then she said, "May I continue to find favor in your sight, my lord, for you have comforted me and spoken kindly to your servant, even though I am not one of your servants."

14 At mealtime Boaz said to her, "Come here, and eat

a That is *Pleasant*   b That is *Bitter*   c Traditional rendering of Heb *Shaddai*   d Or *has testified against*   e Compare Gk Vg: Meaning of Heb uncertain

some of this bread, and dip your morsel in the sour wine." So she sat beside the reapers, and he heaped up for her some parched grain. She ate until she was satisfied, and she had some left over. ¹⁵When she got up to glean, Boaz instructed his young men, "Let her glean even among the standing sheaves, and do not reproach her. ¹⁶You must also pull out some handfuls for her from the bundles, and leave them for her to glean, and do not rebuke her."

17 So she gleaned in the field until evening. Then she beat out what she had gleaned, and it was about an ephah of barley. ¹⁸She picked it up and came into the town, and her mother-in-law saw how much she had gleaned. Then she took out and gave her what was left over after she herself had been satisfied. ¹⁹Her mother-in-law said to her, "Where did you glean today? And where have you worked? Blessed be the man who took notice of you." So she told her mother-in-law with whom she had worked, and said, "The name of the man with whom I worked today is Boaz." ²⁰Then Naomi said to her daughter-in-law, "Blessed be he by the Lord, whose kindness has not forsaken the living or the dead!" Naomi also said to her, "The man is a relative of ours, one of our nearest kin."ᵃ ²¹Then Ruth the Moabite said, "He even said to me, 'Stay close by my servants, until they have finished all my harvest.' " ²²Naomi said to Ruth, her daughter-in-law, "It is better, my daughter, that you go out with his young women, otherwise you might be bothered in another field." ²³So she stayed close to the young women of Boaz, gleaning until the end of the barley and wheat harvests; and she lived with her mother-in-law.

Ruth and Boaz at the Threshing Floor

3 Naomi her mother-in-law said to her, "My daughter, I need to seek some security for you, so that it may be well with you. ²Now here is our kinsman Boaz, with whose young women you have been working. See, he is winnowing barley tonight at the threshing floor. ³Now wash and anoint yourself, and put on your best clothes and go down to the threshing floor; but do not make yourself known to the man until he has finished eating and drinking. ⁴When he lies down, observe the place where he lies; then, go and uncover his feet and lie down; and he will tell you what to do." ⁵She said to her, "All that you tell me I will do."

6 So she went down to the threshing floor and did just as her mother-in-law had instructed her. ⁷When Boaz had eaten and drunk, and he was in a contented mood, he went to lie down at the end of the heap of grain. Then she came stealthily and uncovered his feet, and lay down. ⁸At midnight the man was startled, and turned over, and there, lying at his feet, was a woman! ⁹He said, "Who are you?" And she answered, "I am Ruth, your servant; spread your cloak over your servant, for you are next-of-kin."ᵃ ¹⁰He said, "May you be blessed by the Lord, my daughter; this last instance of your loyalty is better than the first; you have not gone after young men, whether poor or rich. ¹¹And now, my daughter, do not be afraid, I will do for you all that you ask, for all the assembly of my people know that you are a

Who Is My Mother and Brother and Sister?

RUTH 3.10–12

Naomi calls Ruth "daughter", as does Boaz (v.11). Neither Naomi nor Boaz can mean the word literally, yet the term highlights the meaning of kinship in this story about "strangers." Despite the differences of their backgrounds, a deep bond develops among Naomi, Ruth and Boaz, the essence of which is kindness. When you think of kindness, what feelings arise? Can you imagine a smell or a taste that evokes feelings of kindness in you, such as hot milk and cookies before jumping into a warm bed? Do you find it easier to be kind to a stranger or to a family member? What is the difference between your response when you expect kindness from another and your response when kindness comes "out of the blue"?

See Meeting God in Service

A Tender Interlude

RUTH 3.1–18

Having met Boaz and experienced his kindness and generosity, Ruth goes to the threshing floor at night to make a discreet request for marriage. As you read this tender interlude between Boaz and Ruth, enter the scene for yourself. Sense Ruth's excitement and nervousness as she dresses and perfumes herself to visit Boaz. Feel the damp coolness of the night air as she walks toward the threshing floor. Smell the dusty fragrance of the grain piles in the threshing shed. Imagine Boaz's sleepy surprise as he wakes to find Ruth at his feet and feel the emotion of their quiet talk in the predawn. How is God's tender care for us reflected in this story?

See Meeting God in Scripture

worthy woman. ¹²But now, though it is true that I am a near kinsman, there is another kinsman more closely related than I. ¹³Remain this night, and in the morning, if he will act as next-of-kin*ᵃ* for you, good; let him do it. If he is not willing to act as next-of-kin*ᵃ* for you, then, as the LORD lives, I will act as next-of-kin*ᵃ* for you. Lie down until the morning."

14 So she lay at his feet until morning, but got up before one person could recognize another; for he said, "It must not be known that the woman came to the threshing floor." ¹⁵Then he said, "Bring the cloak you are wearing and hold it out." So she held it, and he measured out six measures of barley, and put it on her back; then he went into the city. ¹⁶She came to her mother-in-law, who said, "How did things go with you,*ᵇ* my daughter?" Then she told her all that the man had done for her, ¹⁷saying, "He gave me these six measures of barley, for he said, 'Do not go back to your mother-in-law empty-handed.' " ¹⁸She replied, "Wait, my daughter, until you learn how the matter turns out, for the man will not rest, but will settle the matter today."

The Marriage of Boaz and Ruth

4 No sooner had Boaz gone up to the gate and sat down there than the next-of-kin,*ᵃ* of whom Boaz had spoken, came passing by. So Boaz said, "Come over, friend; sit down here." And he went over and sat down. ²Then Boaz took ten men of the elders of the city, and said, "Sit down here"; so they sat down. ³He then said to the next-of-kin,*ᵃ* "Naomi, who has come back from the country of Moab, is selling the parcel of land that belonged to our kinsman Elimelech. ⁴So I thought I would tell you of it, and say: Buy it in the presence of those sitting here, and in the presence of the elders of my people. If you will redeem it, redeem it; but if you will not, tell me, so that I may know; for there is no one prior to you to redeem it, and I come after you." So he said, "I will redeem it." ⁵Then Boaz said, "The day you acquire the field from the hand of Naomi, you are also acquiring Ruth*ᶜ* the Moabite, the widow of the dead man, to maintain the dead man's name on his inheritance." ⁶At this, the next-of-kin*ᵃ* said, "I cannot redeem it for myself without damaging my own inheritance. Take my right of redemption yourself, for I cannot redeem it."

7 Now this was the custom in former times in Israel concerning redeeming and exchanging: to confirm a transaction, the one took off a sandal and gave it to the other; this was the manner of attesting in Israel. ⁸So when the next-of-kin*ᵃ* said to Boaz, "Acquire it for yourself," he took off his sandal. ⁹Then Boaz said to the elders and all the people, "Today you are witnesses that I have acquired from the hand of Naomi all that belonged to Elimelech and all that belonged to Chilion and Mahlon. ¹⁰I have also acquired Ruth the Moabite, the wife of Mahlon, to be my wife, to maintain the dead man's name on his inheritance, in order that the name of the dead may not be cut off from his kindred and from the gate of his native place; today you are witnesses." ¹¹Then all the people who were

a Or *one with the right to redeem*   *b* Or *"Who are you,*   *c* OL Vg: Heb *from the hand of Naomi and from Ruth*

at the gate, along with the elders, said, "We are witnesses. May the LORD make the woman who is coming into your house like Rachel and Leah, who together built up the house of Israel. May you produce children in Ephrathah and bestow a name in Bethlehem; [12]and, through the children that the LORD will give you by this young woman, may your house be like the house of Perez, whom Tamar bore to Judah."

The Genealogy of David

13 So Boaz took Ruth and she became his wife. When they came together, the LORD made her conceive, and she bore a son. [14]Then the women said to Naomi, "Blessed be the LORD, who has not left you this day without next-of-kin;[a] and may his name be renowned in Israel! [15]He shall be to you a restorer of life and a nourisher of your old age; for your daughter-in-law who loves you, who is more to you than seven sons, has borne him." [16]Then Naomi took the child and laid him in her bosom, and became his nurse. [17]The women of the neighborhood gave him a name, saying, "A son has been born to Naomi." They named him Obed; he became the father of Jesse, the father of David.

18 Now these are the descendants of Perez: Perez became the father of Hezron, [19]Hezron of Ram, Ram of Amminadab, [20]Amminadab of Nahshon, Nahshon of Salmon, [21]Salmon of Boaz, Boaz of Obed, [22]Obed of Jesse, and Jesse of David.

God's Mysterious Ways

RUTH 4.17

The son of Ruth and Boaz will be Jesse's father and David's grandfather. What an unexpected surprise that this family's troubles should culminate in the kingship of David, and later the birth of the Lord Jesus Christ! If you were to tell this story with puppets, how would you show the special qualities of this family? They had no status or wealth; why would God choose them? What sort of a puppet would you make for God? Or would God be offstage all the time? What action scene could convey how God is working in this story to bring about such a wonderful outcome?

See Meeting God in Scripture

---

1 SAMUEL
Learning to Listen

KEY VERSE:
"Speak, LORD, for your servant is listening." —1 Samuel 3.9

"Listen carefully, my son, to the master's instructions, and attend to them with the ear of your heart. This is the advice from a father who loves you; welcome it, and faithfully put it into practice. The labor of obedience will bring you back to him from whom you had drifted through the sloth of disobedience. This message of mine is for you, then, if you are ready to give up your own will, once for all, and armed with the strong and noble weapons of obedience to do battle for the true King, Christ the Lord."

—Prologue,
The Rule of Saint Benedict

The book of 1 Samuel unfolds like a historical novel, interweaving the lives of the prophet Samuel, King Saul and his family, and David, the God-appointed heir to the throne of Israel. The nation of Israel is struggling to remain loyal to God as its only supreme Ruler and still survive among surrounding nations that boast superior technology, military organization and government. Israel, by contrast, relies on a loose tribal confederacy rooted in ancient, sacred law and a faith in God's intervention to save.

We can profitably approach the book of 1 Samuel by praying the words of one of its early characters: "Speak, LORD, for your servant is listening." Just as the boy Samuel learned early in life to listen deeply (3.1–10), so can we. We can hear God's voice in this story telling us of his own character and his actions among humans. We can hear about our own struggles; we too are sometimes pulled between obedient loyalty to God and the temptation to put our trust in self-chosen causes, ideas and preferences. We can listen for what it means to be a person after God's own heart and see how God blesses those who listen. We can claim the promise that God directs and changes human lives today as he did long ago.

Prepare yourself to realize that promise for yourself as you absorb yourself in the reflections and activities suggested in each entry point. As you read ancient words about God's anointed leaders—the kings and prophets—let them guide you into a deeper relationship with God's Anointed, Jesus the Christ.

Samuel's Birth and Dedication

1 There was a certain man of Ramathaim, a Zuphite[a] from the hill country of Ephraim, whose name was Elkanah son of Jeroham son of Elihu son of Tohu son of Zuph, an Ephraimite. ²He had two wives; the name of the one was Hannah, and the name of the other Peninnah. Peninnah had children, but Hannah had no children.

3 Now this man used to go up year by year from his town to worship and to sacrifice to the LORD of hosts at Shiloh, where the two sons of Eli, Hophni and Phinehas, were priests of the LORD. ⁴On the day when Elkanah sacrificed, he would give portions to his wife Peninnah and to all her sons and daughters; ⁵but to Hannah he gave a double portion,[b] because he loved her, though the LORD had closed her womb. ⁶Her rival used to provoke her severely, to irritate her, because the LORD had closed her womb. ⁷So it went on year by year; as often as she went up to the house of the LORD, she used to provoke her. Therefore Hannah wept and would not eat. ⁸Her husband Elkanah said to her, "Hannah, why do you weep? Why do you not eat? Why is your heart sad? Am I not more to you than ten sons?"

9 After they had eaten and drunk at Shiloh, Hannah rose and presented herself before the LORD.[c] Now Eli the priest was sitting on the seat beside the doorpost of the temple of the LORD. ¹⁰She was deeply distressed and prayed to the LORD, and wept bitterly. ¹¹She made this vow: "O LORD of hosts, if only you will look on the misery of your servant, and remember me, and not forget your servant, but will give to your servant a male child, then I will set him before you as a nazirite[d] until the day of his death. He shall drink neither wine nor intoxicants,[e] and no razor shall touch his head."

12 As she continued praying before the LORD, Eli observed her mouth. ¹³Hannah was praying silently; only her lips moved, but her voice was not heard; therefore Eli thought she was drunk. ¹⁴So Eli said to her, "How long will you make a drunken spectacle of yourself? Put away your wine." ¹⁵But Hannah answered, "No, my lord, I am a woman deeply troubled; I have drunk neither wine nor strong drink, but I have been pouring out my soul before the LORD. ¹⁶Do not regard your servant as a worthless woman, for I have been speaking out of my great anxiety and vexation all this time." ¹⁷Then Eli answered, "Go in peace; the God of Israel grant the petition you have made to him." ¹⁸And she said, "Let your servant find favor in your sight." Then the woman went to her quarters,[f] ate and drank with her husband,[g] and her countenance was sad no longer.[h]

19 They rose early in the morning and worshiped before the LORD; then they went back to their house at Ramah. Elkanah knew his wife Hannah, and the LORD remembered her. ²⁰In due time Hannah conceived and bore a son. She named him Samuel, for she said, "I have asked him of the LORD."

"If You . . . Then I Will"

1 SAMUEL 1.3–11

Hannah's inability to have a child has affected her deeply. She weeps, loses her appetite, endures taunts from a rival and receives tender treatment from her understanding husband. But Hannah's prayers are not for her own benefit. Hannah promises God that she will offer back the very gift she asks for: the child for whom she yearns.

Take stock of at least one of the gifts God has given you. Now act out the offering of that gift: if it is singing, sing now; if writing, jot down the nucleus of an idea to expand; if caring for others, plan a specific caring action for another, then embrace yourself as a rehearsal for that action. Use your talent imaginatively, expressively and thankfully.

See Meeting God in Service

---

a Compare Gk and 1 Chr 6.35-36: Heb *Ramathaim-zophim*
b Syr: Meaning of Heb uncertain   c Gk: Heb lacks *and presented herself before the LORD*   d That is *one separated* or *one consecrated*
e Cn Compare Gk Q Ms 1.22: MT *then I will give him to the LORD all the days of his life*   f Gk: Heb *went her way*   g Gk: Heb lacks *and drank with her husband*   h Gk: Meaning of Heb uncertain

Given Over to the Lord

1 SAMUEL 1.27–28

"I am sometimes almost terrified at the scope of the demands made upon me, at the perfection of the self-abandonment required of me; yet outside of such absoluteness can be no salvation. In God we live every commonplace as well as most exalted moment of our being. To trust *in Him* when no need is pressing, when things seem going right of themselves, may be harder than when things seem going wrong."

—GEORGE MACDONALD,
George MacDonald: 365 Readings

21 The man Elkanah and all his household went up to offer to the LORD the yearly sacrifice, and to pay his vow. 22But Hannah did not go up, for she said to her husband, "As soon as the child is weaned, I will bring him, that he may appear in the presence of the LORD, and remain there forever; I will offer him as a nazirite*a* for all time."*b* 23Her husband Elkanah said to her, "Do what seems best to you, wait until you have weaned him; only—may the LORD establish his word."*c* So the woman remained and nursed her son, until she weaned him. 24When she had weaned him, she took him up with her, along with a three-year-old bull,*d* an ephah of flour, and a skin of wine. She brought him to the house of the LORD at Shiloh; and the child was young. 25Then they slaughtered the bull, and they brought the child to Eli. 26And she said, "Oh, my lord! As you live, my lord, I am the woman who was standing here in your presence, praying to the LORD. 27For this child I prayed; and the LORD has granted me the petition that I made to him. 28Therefore I have lent him to the LORD; as long as he lives, he is given to the LORD."

She left him there for*e* the LORD.

Hannah's Prayer

2 Hannah prayed and said,
"My heart exults in the LORD;
   my strength is exalted in my God.*f*
My mouth derides my enemies,
   because I rejoice in my*g* victory.

2 "There is no Holy One like the LORD,
   no one besides you;
   there is no Rock like our God.
3 Talk no more so very proudly,
   let not arrogance come from your mouth;
for the LORD is a God of knowledge,
   and by him actions are weighed.
4 The bows of the mighty are broken,
   but the feeble gird on strength.
5 Those who were full have hired themselves out for
      bread,
   but those who were hungry are fat with spoil.
The barren has borne seven,
   but she who has many children is forlorn.
6 The LORD kills and brings to life;
   he brings down to Sheol and raises up.
7 The LORD makes poor and makes rich;
   he brings low, he also exalts.
8 He raises up the poor from the dust;
   he lifts the needy from the ash heap,
to make them sit with princes
   and inherit a seat of honor.*h*
For the pillars of the earth are the LORD's,
   and on them he has set the world.

---

a That is *one separated* or *one consecrated*   *b* Cn Compare Q Ms: MT lacks *I will offer him as a nazirite for all time*   *c* MT: Q Ms Gk Compare Syr *that which goes out of your mouth*   *d* Q Ms Gk Syr: MT *three bulls* *e* Gk (Compare Q Ms) and Gk at 2.11: MT *And he* (that is, Elkanah) *worshiped there before*   *f* Gk: Heb the LORD   *g* Q Ms: MT *your*   *h* Gk (Compare Q Ms) adds *He grants the vow of the one who vows, and blesses the years of the just*

9 "He will guard the feet of his faithful ones,
  but the wicked shall be cut off in darkness;
  for not by might does one prevail.
10 The Lord! His adversaries shall be shattered;
  the Most High[a] will thunder in heaven.
  The Lord will judge the ends of the earth;
  he will give strength to his king,
  and exalt the power of his anointed."

Eli's Wicked Sons

11 Then Elkanah went home to Ramah, while the boy remained to minister to the Lord, in the presence of the priest Eli.

12 Now the sons of Eli were scoundrels; they had no regard for the Lord 13or for the duties of the priests to the people. When anyone offered sacrifice, the priest's servant would come, while the meat was boiling, with a three-pronged fork in his hand, 14and he would thrust it into the pan, or kettle, or caldron, or pot; all that the fork brought up the priest would take for himself.[b] This is what they did at Shiloh to all the Israelites who came there. 15Moreover, before the fat was burned, the priest's servant would come and say to the one who was sacrificing, "Give meat for the priest to roast; for he will not accept boiled meat from you, but only raw." 16And if the man said to him, "Let them burn the fat first, and then take whatever you wish," he would say, "No, you must give it now; if not, I will take it by force." 17Thus the sin of the young men was very great in the sight of the Lord; for they treated the offerings of the Lord with contempt.

The Child Samuel at Shiloh

18 Samuel was ministering before the Lord, a boy wearing a linen ephod. 19His mother used to make for him a little robe and take it to him each year, when she went up with her husband to offer the yearly sacrifice. 20Then Eli would bless Elkanah and his wife, and say, "May the Lord repay[c] you with children by this woman for the gift that she made to[d] the Lord"; and then they would return to their home.

21 And[e] the Lord took note of Hannah; she conceived and bore three sons and two daughters. And the boy Samuel grew up in the presence of the Lord.

Prophecy against Eli's Household

22 Now Eli was very old. He heard all that his sons were doing to all Israel, and how they lay with the women who served at the entrance to the tent of meeting. 23He said to them, "Why do you do such things? For I hear of your evil dealings from all these people. 24No, my sons; it is not a good report that I hear the people of the Lord spreading abroad. 25If one person sins against another, someone can intercede for the sinner with the Lord;[f] but if someone sins against the Lord, who can make intercession?" But they would not listen to the voice of their father; for it was the will of the Lord to kill them.

---

a Cn Heb *against him he*   b Gk Syr Vg: Heb *with it*   c Q Ms Gk: MT *give*
d Q Ms Gk: MT *for the petition that she asked of*   e Q Ms Gk: MT *When*
f Gk Compare Q Ms: MT *another, God will mediate for him*

Growing in the Presence of the Lord

1 SAMUEL 2.21

Samuel grew up in the presence of God, the writer tells us. In what ways might that be said about your life?

Prayerfully recall how God has been quietly present in your life in times of distress or loneliness as well as in times of progress and achievement. Do you picture a judgmental or a loving Presence, an intimate or a somewhat distant God? Recall your responses to God during and after the crises, and in the midst of the successes. Make a simple drawing expressing how you have grown through these periods. Then stand up to your full stature as you offer the drawing to God in thankfulness for that abiding presence.

See Meeting God in Prayer

Called a Third Time

1 SAMUEL 3.1–20

With old Eli's advice, young Samuel realizes that it is God who calls in the night. Then Eli tells Samuel how to listen and respond.

Participants in the monastic tradition take a vow "to hear," which moves them beyond mere obedience. Those who listen deeply for God's voice—and hear it—act in spiritual agreement with one another rather than simply obey a rule.

Practice your listening skills. Walk to a window, look outside for thirty seconds or so, then close your eyes for several minutes. Attend to whatever comes to your ears—traffic noise, birds, playing children, the sounds of your own movements. Return to your chair and think about what or whom you listen to most regularly: family members, television, your work supervisor or someone else. How might you hear God speaking through these things? How might you listen more carefully to what God has to tell you?

See Meeting God in Prayer

26 Now the boy Samuel continued to grow both in stature and in favor with the LORD and with the people.

27 A man of God came to Eli and said to him, "Thus the LORD has said, 'I revealed[a] myself to the family of your ancestor in Egypt when they were slaves[b] to the house of Pharaoh. [28]I chose him out of all the tribes of Israel to be my priest, to go up to my altar, to offer incense, to wear an ephod before me; and I gave to the family of your ancestor all my offerings by fire from the people of Israel. [29]Why then look with greedy eye[c] at my sacrifices and my offerings that I commanded, and honor your sons more than me by fattening yourselves on the choicest parts of every offering of my people Israel?' [30]Therefore the LORD the God of Israel declares: 'I promised that your family and the family of your ancestor should go in and out before me forever'; but now the LORD declares: 'Far be it from me; for those who honor me I will honor, and those who despise me shall be treated with contempt. [31]See, a time is coming when I will cut off your strength and the strength of your ancestor's family, so that no one in your family will live to old age. [32]Then in distress you will look with greedy eye[d] on all the prosperity that shall be bestowed upon Israel; and no one in your family shall ever live to old age. [33]The only one of you whom I shall not cut off from my altar shall be spared to weep out his[e] eyes and grieve his[f] heart; all the members of your household shall die by the sword.[g] [34]The fate of your two sons, Hophni and Phinehas, shall be the sign to you—both of them shall die on the same day. [35]I will raise up for myself a faithful priest, who shall do according to what is in my heart and in my mind. I will build him a sure house, and he shall go in and out before my anointed one forever. [36]Everyone who is left in your family shall come to implore him for a piece of silver or a loaf of bread, and shall say, Please put me in one of the priest's places, that I may eat a morsel of bread.' "

Samuel's Calling and Prophetic Activity

3 Now the boy Samuel was ministering to the LORD under Eli. The word of the LORD was rare in those days; visions were not widespread.

2 At that time Eli, whose eyesight had begun to grow dim so that he could not see, was lying down in his room; [3]the lamp of God had not yet gone out, and Samuel was lying down in the temple of the LORD, where the ark of God was. [4]Then the LORD called, "Samuel! Samuel!"[h] and he said, "Here I am!" [5]and ran to Eli, and said, "Here I am, for you called me." But he said, "I did not call; lie down again." So he went and lay down. [6]The LORD called again, "Samuel!" Samuel got up and went to Eli, and said, "Here I am, for you called me." But he said, "I did not call, my son; lie down again." [7]Now Samuel did not yet know the LORD, and the word of the LORD had not yet been revealed to him. [8]The LORD called Samuel again, a third time. And he got up and went to Eli, and said, "Here I am, for you called me." Then Eli perceived that the LORD was calling the boy. [9]Therefore Eli said to Samuel, "Go, lie down; and if he calls

---

a Gk Tg Syr: Heb *Did I reveal*   *b* Q Ms Gk: MT lacks *slaves*   *c* Q Ms Gk: MT *then kick*   *d* Q Ms Gk: MT *will kick*   *e* Q Ms Gk: MT *your*   *f* Q Ms Gk: Heb *your*   *g* Q Ms See Gk: MT *die like mortals*   *h* Q Ms Gk See 3.10: MT *the LORD called Samuel*

you, you shall say, 'Speak, LORD, for your servant is listening.' " So Samuel went and lay down in his place.

10 Now the LORD came and stood there, calling as before, "Samuel! Samuel!" And Samuel said, "Speak, for your servant is listening." ¹¹Then the LORD said to Samuel, "See, I am about to do something in Israel that will make both ears of anyone who hears of it tingle. ¹²On that day I will fulfill against Eli all that I have spoken concerning his house, from beginning to end. ¹³For I have told him that I am about to punish his house forever, for the iniquity that he knew, because his sons were blaspheming God,ᵃ and he did not restrain them. ¹⁴Therefore I swear to the house of Eli that the iniquity of Eli's house shall not be expiated by sacrifice or offering forever."

15 Samuel lay there until morning; then he opened the doors of the house of the LORD. Samuel was afraid to tell the vision to Eli. ¹⁶But Eli called Samuel and said, "Samuel, my son." He said, "Here I am." ¹⁷Eli said, "What was it that he told you? Do not hide it from me. May God do so to you and more also, if you hide anything from me of all that he told you." ¹⁸So Samuel told him everything and hid nothing from him. Then he said, "It is the LORD; let him do what seems good to him."

19 As Samuel grew up, the LORD was with him and let none of his words fall to the ground. ²⁰And all Israel from Dan to Beer-sheba knew that Samuel was a trustworthy prophet of the LORD. ²¹The LORD continued to appear at Shiloh, for the LORD revealed himself to Samuel at Shiloh by the word of the LORD. ¹And the word of Samuel came to 4 all Israel.

The Ark of God Captured

In those days the Philistines mustered for war against Israel,ᵇ and Israel went out to battle against them;ᶜ they encamped at Ebenezer, and the Philistines encamped at Aphek. ²The Philistines drew up in line against Israel, and when the battle was joined,ᵈ Israel was defeated by the Philistines, who killed about four thousand men on the field of battle. ³When the troops came to the camp, the elders of Israel said, "Why has the LORD put us to rout today before the Philistines? Let us bring the ark of the covenant of the LORD here from Shiloh, so that he may come among us and save us from the power of our enemies." ⁴So the people sent to Shiloh, and brought from there the ark of the covenant of the LORD of hosts, who is enthroned on the cherubim. The two sons of Eli, Hophni and Phinehas, were there with the ark of the covenant of God.

5 When the ark of the covenant of the LORD came into the camp, all Israel gave a mighty shout, so that the earth resounded. ⁶When the Philistines heard the noise of the shouting, they said, "What does this great shouting in the camp of the Hebrews mean?" When they learned that the ark of the LORD had come to the camp, ⁷the Philistines were afraid; for they said, "Gods haveᵉ come into the camp." They also said, "Woe to us! For nothing like this has happened before. ⁸Woe to us! Who can deliver us from the power of these mighty gods? These are the gods who struck

A God Too Small?

1 SAMUEL 4.3

In crisis, Israel turns to the ways they have known God in the past, fetching the neglected ark of the covenant to lead them into a battle. But the symbol of God's presence in the past cannot help them unless they have a living relationship with God in the present.

Sometimes our ideas about God grow more meaningful through the years while others restrict our faith. On paper, draw sketches of at least two ways you thought about God during your childhood and your teen years; or describe in writing how you perceived God during those years. Now sketch or describe some of the ways you have held God at a distance. Finally, draw or write about a way in which you can now let God's Spirit move recognizably in your life. Leave your Bible open until your next reading to signify that you do not want to limit God's presence in your life.

a Another reading is *for themselves*   b Gk: Heb lacks *In those days the Philistines mustered for war against Israel*   c Gk: Heb *against the Philistines*   d Meaning of Heb uncertain   e Or *A god has*

News of Loss

1 SAMUEL 4.21

How awful it is to be the one at home wondering about the safety of loved ones in wartime! Loss can strike unexpectedly at any moment. Old Eli, receiving the news that both his sons have perished and that the ark is captured, dies. His daughter-in-law, in grief, names his grandson Ichabod as she mourns the loss of the divine presence and the nation's glory.

In times of loss—of a loved one, a job, health, confidence, hope, even of a precious object—we might feel deep pain, perhaps perceiving our loss as abandonment by God. Bring to mind two or more such losses of the past; then acknowledge what pain may remain, and ask God now to help you deal with the hurt. Resolve to reach out within the next three days to someone who is struggling with a loss and try to listen to that person rather than advise him or her. Write down the name of that person now.

See Meeting God in Community

the Egyptians with every sort of plague in the wilderness. ⁹Take courage, and be men, O Philistines, in order not to become slaves to the Hebrews as they have been to you; be men and fight."

10 So the Philistines fought; Israel was defeated, and they fled, everyone to his home. There was a very great slaughter, for there fell of Israel thirty thousand foot soldiers. ¹¹The ark of God was captured; and the two sons of Eli, Hophni and Phinehas, died.

Death of Eli

12 A man of Benjamin ran from the battle line, and came to Shiloh the same day, with his clothes torn and with earth upon his head. ¹³When he arrived, Eli was sitting upon his seat by the road watching, for his heart trembled for the ark of God. When the man came into the city and told the news, all the city cried out. ¹⁴When Eli heard the sound of the outcry, he said, "What is this uproar?" Then the man came quickly and told Eli. ¹⁵Now Eli was ninety-eight years old and his eyes were set, so that he could not see. ¹⁶The man said to Eli, "I have just come from the battle; I fled from the battle today." He said, "How did it go, my son?" ¹⁷The messenger replied, "Israel has fled before the Philistines, and there has also been a great slaughter among the troops; your two sons also, Hophni and Phinehas, are dead, and the ark of God has been captured." ¹⁸When he mentioned the ark of God, Eli*ᵃ* fell over backward from his seat by the side of the gate; and his neck was broken and he died, for he was an old man, and heavy. He had judged Israel forty years.

19 Now his daughter-in-law, the wife of Phinehas, was pregnant, about to give birth. When she heard the news that the ark of God was captured, and that her father-in-law and her husband were dead, she bowed and gave birth; for her labor pains overwhelmed her. ²⁰As she was about to die, the women attending her said to her, "Do not be afraid, for you have borne a son." But she did not answer or give heed. ²¹She named the child Ichabod, meaning, "The glory has departed from Israel," because the ark of God had been captured and because of her father-in-law and her husband. ²²She said, "The glory has departed from Israel, for the ark of God has been captured."

The Philistines and the Ark

5 When the Philistines captured the ark of God, they brought it from Ebenezer to Ashdod; ²then the Philistines took the ark of God and brought it into the house of Dagon and placed it beside Dagon. ³When the people of Ashdod rose early the next day, there was Dagon, fallen on his face to the ground before the ark of the LORD. So they took Dagon and put him back in his place. ⁴But when they rose early on the next morning, Dagon had fallen on his face to the ground before the ark of the LORD, and the head of Dagon and both his hands were lying cut off upon the threshold; only the trunk ofᵇ Dagon was left to him. ⁵This is why the priests of Dagon and all who enter the house of Dagon do not step on the threshold of Dagon in Ashdod to this day.

6 The hand of the LORD was heavy upon the people of

a Heb *he*   *b* Heb lacks *the trunk of*

Ashdod, and he terrified and struck them with tumors, both in Ashdod and in its territory. ⁷And when the inhabitants of Ashdod saw how things were, they said, "The ark of the God of Israel must not remain with us; for his hand is heavy on us and on our god Dagon." ⁸So they sent and gathered together all the lords of the Philistines, and said, "What shall we do with the ark of the God of Israel?" The inhabitants of Gath replied, "Let the ark of God be moved on to us."ᵃ So they moved the ark of the God of Israel to Gath.ᵇ ⁹But after they had brought it to Gath,ᶜ the hand of the LORD was against the city, causing a very great panic; he struck the inhabitants of the city, both young and old, so that tumors broke out on them. ¹⁰So they sent the ark of the God of Israelᵈ to Ekron. But when the ark of God came to Ekron, the people of Ekron cried out, "Whyᵉ have they brought around to usᶠ the ark of the God of Israel to kill usᶠ and ourᵍ people?" ¹¹They sent therefore and gathered together all the lords of the Philistines, and said, "Send away the ark of the God of Israel, and let it return to its own place, that it may not kill us and our people." For there was a deathly panicʰ throughout the whole city. The hand of God was very heavy there; ¹²those who did not die were stricken with tumors, and the cry of the city went up to heaven.

The Ark Returned to Israel

6 The ark of the LORD was in the country of the Philistines seven months. ²Then the Philistines called for the priests and the diviners and said, "What shall we do with the ark of the LORD? Tell us what we should send with it to its place." ³They said, "If you send away the ark of the God of Israel, do not send it empty, but by all means return him a guilt offering. Then you will be healed and will be ransomed;ⁱ will not his hand then turn from you?" ⁴And they said, "What is the guilt offering that we shall return to him?" They answered, "Five gold tumors and five gold mice, according to the number of the lords of the Philistines; for the same plague was upon all of you and upon your lords. ⁵So you must make images of your tumors and images of your mice that ravage the land, and give glory to the God of Israel; perhaps he will lighten his hand on you and your gods and your land. ⁶Why should you harden your hearts as the Egyptians and Pharaoh hardened their hearts? After he had made fools of them, did they not let the people go, and they departed? ⁷Now then, get ready a new cart and two milch cows that have never borne a yoke, and yoke the cows to the cart, but take their calves home, away from them. ⁸Take the ark of the LORD and place it on the cart, and put in a box at its side the figures of gold, which you are returning to him as a guilt offering. Then send it off, and let it go its way. ⁹And watch; if it goes up on the way to its own land, to Beth-shemesh, then it is he who has done us this great harm; but if not, then we shall know that it is not his hand that struck us; it happened to us by chance."

ᵃ Gk Compare Q Ms: MT *They answered, "Let the ark of the God of Israel be brought around to us to Gath."*   ᵇ Gk: Heb lacks *to Gath*   ᶜ Q Ms: MT lacks *to Gath*   ᵈ Q Ms Gk: MT lacks *of Israel*   ᵉ Q Ms Gk: MT lacks *Why*   ᶠ Heb *me*   ᵍ Heb *my*   ʰ Q Ms reads *a panic from the LORD*   ⁱ Q Ms Gk: MT *and it will be known to you*

The Most Important Occasions

1 SAMUEL 5.8–9

Rather than return the ark empty, the Philistines place highly symbolic objects in a chest beside it. Mainly they intended to mollify the Israelites' God. But perhaps they also knew that such important events must be accompanied by something purely ceremonial. Even today, the life of the nation and the community is marked by times of ceremony: the Fourth of July, Thanksgiving Day, a presidential inauguration.

What celebrations do you observe? Which ones mean the most to you? What important events do you like to remember by planning something special? What moments in your journey of faith do you celebrate? Look back over your life and the life of your family and choose four or five of the most important events. Do you observe these events with some sort of ceremony? If not, perhaps with your closest family and friends, you can plan ways to remember the turning points in your life and the life of your family.

See *Meeting God in Everyday Life*

Water, Water

1 SAMUEL 7.6

As part of its ritual of repentance, Israel pours out water, the most common, essential, life-sustaining resource on earth. We can survive without food for weeks but without water for only a short while. How we regard and use water is representative of how we treat the gift of life itself.

Our water usually comes from faucets and bottle dispensers, but what would be the nearest natural source supplying your home if these modern systems failed? Enjoy the gift of water now, giving thanks in several ways. Hold up a glass filled with water and look through it at the sky. Taste the water, sipping it very slowly, as you continue your thanksgiving. Pour the water back and forth between two glasses, enjoying the sound. Pour out the water, perhaps over your hands and down your arms, recalling your baptism (or what you have been told about it). Ponder and repent of the ways you may squander water or use it without gratitude, then dedicate your hands to handle water gratefully.

See Meeting God in the Created Order

10 The men did so; they took two milch cows and yoked them to the cart, and shut up their calves at home. ¹¹They put the ark of the LORD on the cart, and the box with the gold mice and the images of their tumors. ¹²The cows went straight in the direction of Beth-shemesh along one highway, lowing as they went; they turned neither to the right nor to the left, and the lords of the Philistines went after them as far as the border of Beth-shemesh.

13 Now the people of Beth-shemesh were reaping their wheat harvest in the valley. When they looked up and saw the ark, they went with rejoicing to meet it.ᵃ ¹⁴The cart came into the field of Joshua of Beth-shemesh, and stopped there. A large stone was there; so they split up the wood of the cart and offered the cows as a burnt offering to the LORD. ¹⁵The Levites took down the ark of the LORD and the box that was beside it, in which were the gold objects, and set them upon the large stone. Then the people of Beth-shemesh offered burnt offerings and presented sacrifices on that day to the LORD. ¹⁶When the five lords of the Philistines saw it, they returned that day to Ekron.

17 These are the gold tumors, which the Philistines returned as a guilt offering to the LORD: one for Ashdod, one for Gaza, one for Ashkelon, one for Gath, one for Ekron; ¹⁸also the gold mice, according to the number of all the cities of the Philistines belonging to the five lords, both fortified cities and unwalled villages. The great stone, beside which they set down the ark of the LORD, is a witness to this day in the field of Joshua of Beth-shemesh.

The Ark at Kiriath-jearim

19 The descendants of Jeconiah did not rejoice with the people of Beth-shemesh when they greetedᵇ the ark of the LORD; and he killed seventy men of them.ᶜ The people mourned because the LORD had made a great slaughter among the people. ²⁰Then the people of Beth-shemesh said, "Who is able to stand before the LORD, this holy God? To whom shall he go so that we may be rid of him?" ²¹So they sent messengers to the inhabitants of Kiriath-jearim, saying, "The Philistines have returned the ark of the LORD. Come down and take it up to you." ¹And the people of Kiriath-jearim came and took up the ark of the LORD, and brought it to the house of Abinadab on the hill. They consecrated his son, Eleazar, to have charge of the ark of the LORD.

2 From the day that the ark was lodged at Kiriath-jearim, a long time passed, some twenty years, and all the house of Israel lamentedᵈ after the LORD.

Samuel as Judge

3 Then Samuel said to all the house of Israel, "If you are returning to the LORD with all your heart, then put away the foreign gods and the Astartes from among you. Direct your heart to the LORD, and serve him only, and he will deliver you out of the hand of the Philistines." ⁴So Israel put away the Baals and the Astartes, and they served the LORD only.

5 Then Samuel said, "Gather all Israel at Mizpah, and I will pray to the LORD for you." ⁶So they gathered at Mizpah,

a Gk: Heb *rejoiced to see it*   b Gk: Heb *And he killed some of the people of Beth-shemesh, because they looked into*   c Heb *killed seventy men, fifty thousand men*   d Meaning of Heb uncertain

354

and drew water and poured it out before the LORD. They fasted that day, and said, "We have sinned against the LORD." And Samuel judged the people of Israel at Mizpah.

7 When the Philistines heard that the people of Israel had gathered at Mizpah, the lords of the Philistines went up against Israel. And when the people of Israel heard of it they were afraid of the Philistines. ⁸The people of Israel said to Samuel, "Do not cease to cry out to the LORD our God for us, and pray that he may save us from the hand of the Philistines." ⁹So Samuel took a sucking lamb and offered it as a whole burnt offering to the LORD; Samuel cried out to the LORD for Israel, and the LORD answered him. ¹⁰As Samuel was offering up the burnt offering, the Philistines drew near to attack Israel; but the LORD thundered with a mighty voice that day against the Philistines and threw them into confusion; and they were routed before Israel. ¹¹And the men of Israel went out of Mizpah and pursued the Philistines, and struck them down as far as beyond Beth-car.

12 Then Samuel took a stone and set it up between Mizpah and Jeshanah,ᵃ and named it Ebenezer;ᵇ for he said, "Thus far the LORD has helped us." ¹³So the Philistines were subdued and did not again enter the territory of Israel; the hand of the LORD was against the Philistines all the days of Samuel. ¹⁴The towns that the Philistines had taken from Israel were restored to Israel, from Ekron to Gath; and Israel recovered their territory from the hand of the Philistines. There was peace also between Israel and the Amorites.

15 Samuel judged Israel all the days of his life. ¹⁶He went on a circuit year by year to Bethel, Gilgal, and Mizpah; and he judged Israel in all these places. ¹⁷Then he would come back to Ramah, for his home was there; he administered justice there to Israel, and built there an altar to the LORD.

Israel Demands a King

8 When Samuel became old, he made his sons judges over Israel. ²The name of his firstborn son was Joel, and the name of his second, Abijah; they were judges in Beer-sheba. ³Yet his sons did not follow in his ways, but turned aside after gain; they took bribes and perverted justice.

4 Then all the elders of Israel gathered together and came to Samuel at Ramah, ⁵and said to him, "You are old and your sons do not follow in your ways; appoint for us, then, a king to govern us, like other nations." ⁶But the thing displeased Samuel when they said, "Give us a king to govern us." Samuel prayed to the LORD, ⁷and the LORD said to Samuel, "Listen to the voice of the people in all that they say to you; for they have not rejected you, but they have rejected me from being king over them. ⁸Just as they have done to me,ᶜ from the day I brought them up out of Egypt to this day, forsaking me and serving other gods, so also they are doing to you. ⁹Now then, listen to their voice; only—you shall solemnly warn them, and show them the ways of the king who shall reign over them."

10 So Samuel reported all the words of the LORD to the people who were asking him for a king. ¹¹He said, "These will be the ways of the king who will reign over you: he will take your sons and appoint them to his chariots and to be his horsemen, and to run before his chariots; ¹²and he will

O God, Help!

1 SAMUEL 7.2–17

"[Each service of daily prayer begins with] 'O God, make speed to save me: O Lord, make haste to help me'[see Psalm 40.13]. This verse has rightly been selected from the whole Bible for this purpose. It fits every mood and temper of human nature, every temptation, every circumstance. It contains an invocation of God, a humble confession of faith, a reverent watchfulness, a meditation upon our frailty, a confidence in God's answer, an assurance of ever-present support."

—JOHN CASSIAN,
Conference X on Prayer

See *Meeting God in Prayer*

ᵃ Gk Syr: Heb *Shen*   ᵇ That is *Stone of Help*   ᶜ Gk: Heb lacks *to me*

Keeping Up With the Neighbors

1 SAMUEL 8.19–20

The Israelites shout, "We are determined to have a king," bypassing God as their promised leader, the only dependable source of certainty amidst hostile forces. The people's motives are clear: They covet the political securities their neighbors seem to enjoy. Their insistence takes precedence over God's ways. How like a basic human inclination: "I want to be true to myself and God's ways, but I don't want to miss out on the advantages others enjoy." What is it about the lives of those who may not follow God that makes you less willing to trust God's pattern for your life? In what ways are you willing to compromise your values to be like that other person, or to fit into another group? Can you trust God to guide you? Pray for assistance in following the path God has set before you.

See Meeting God in Everyday Life

appoint for himself commanders of thousands and commanders of fifties, and some to plow his ground and to reap his harvest, and to make his implements of war and the equipment of his chariots. ¹³He will take your daughters to be perfumers and cooks and bakers. ¹⁴He will take the best of your fields and vineyards and olive orchards and give them to his courtiers. ¹⁵He will take one-tenth of your grain and of your vineyards and give it to his officers and his courtiers. ¹⁶He will take your male and female slaves, and the best of your cattleᵃ and donkeys, and put them to his work. ¹⁷He will take one-tenth of your flocks, and you shall be his slaves. ¹⁸And in that day you will cry out because of your king, whom you have chosen for yourselves; but the LORD will not answer you in that day."

Israel's Request for a King Granted

19 But the people refused to listen to the voice of Samuel; they said, "No! but we are determined to have a king over us, ²⁰so that we also may be like other nations, and that our king may govern us and go out before us and fight our battles." ²¹When Samuel had heard all the words of the people, he repeated them in the ears of the LORD. ²²The LORD said to Samuel, "Listen to their voice and set a king over them." Samuel then said to the people of Israel, "Each of you return home."

Saul Chosen to Be King

9 There was a man of Benjamin whose name was Kish son of Abiel son of Zeror son of Becorath son of Aphiah, a Benjaminite, a man of wealth. ²He had a son whose name was Saul, a handsome young man. There was not a man among the people of Israel more handsome than he; he stood head and shoulders above everyone else.

3 Now the donkeys of Kish, Saul's father, had strayed. So Kish said to his son Saul, "Take one of the boys with you; go and look for the donkeys." ⁴He passed through the hill country of Ephraim and passed through the land of Shalishah, but they did not find them. And they passed through the land of Shaalim, but they were not there. Then he passed through the land of Benjamin, but they did not find them.

5 When they came to the land of Zuph, Saul said to the boy who was with him, "Let us turn back, or my father will stop worrying about the donkeys and worry about us." ⁶But he said to him, "There is a man of God in this town; he is a man held in honor. Whatever he says always comes true. Let us go there now; perhaps he will tell us about the journey on which we have set out." ⁷Then Saul replied to the boy, "But if we go, what can we bring the man? For the bread in our sacks is gone, and there is no present to bring to the man of God. What have we?" ⁸The boy answered Saul again, "Here, I have with me a quarter shekel of silver; I will give it to the man of God, to tell us our way." ⁹(Formerly in Israel, anyone who went to inquire of God would say, "Come, let us go to the seer"; for the one who is now called a prophet was formerly called a seer.) ¹⁰Saul said to the boy, "Good; come, let us go." So they went to the town where the man of God was.

11 As they went up the hill to the town, they met some

a Gk: Heb *young men*

girls coming out to draw water, and said to them, "Is the seer here?" [12]They answered, "Yes, there he is just ahead of you. Hurry; he has come just now to the town, because the people have a sacrifice today at the shrine. [13]As soon as you enter the town, you will find him, before he goes up to the shrine to eat. For the people will not eat until he comes, since he must bless the sacrifice; afterward those eat who are invited. Now go up, for you will meet him immediately." [14]So they went up to the town. As they were entering the town, they saw Samuel coming out toward them on his way up to the shrine.

15 Now the day before Saul came, the LORD had revealed to Samuel: [16]"Tomorrow about this time I will send to you a man from the land of Benjamin, and you shall anoint him to be ruler over my people Israel. He shall save my people from the hand of the Philistines; for I have seen the suffering of[a] my people, because their outcry has come to me." [17]When Samuel saw Saul, the LORD told him, "Here is the man of whom I spoke to you. He it is who shall rule over my people." [18]Then Saul approached Samuel inside the gate, and said, "Tell me, please, where is the house of the seer?" [19]Samuel answered Saul, "I am the seer; go up before me to the shrine, for today you shall eat with me, and in the morning I will let you go and will tell you all that is on your mind. [20]As for your donkeys that were lost three days ago, give no further thought to them, for they have been found. And on whom is all Israel's desire fixed, if not on you and on all your ancestral house?" [21]Saul answered, "I am only a Benjaminite, from the least of the tribes of Israel, and my family is the humblest of all the families of the tribe of Benjamin. Why then have you spoken to me in this way?"

22 Then Samuel took Saul and his servant-boy and brought them into the hall, and gave them a place at the head of those who had been invited, of whom there were about thirty. [23]And Samuel said to the cook, "Bring the portion I gave you, the one I asked you to put aside." [24]The cook took up the thigh and what went with it[b] and set them before Saul. Samuel said, "See, what was kept is set before you. Eat; for it is set[c] before you at the appointed time, so that you might eat with the guests."[d]

So Saul ate with Samuel that day. [25]When they came down from the shrine into the town, a bed was spread for Saul[e] on the roof, and he lay down to sleep.[f] [26]Then at the break of dawn[g] Samuel called to Saul upon the roof, "Get up, so that I may send you on your way." Saul got up, and both he and Samuel went out into the street.

Samuel Anoints Saul

27 As they were going down to the outskirts of the town, Samuel said to Saul, "Tell the boy to go on before us, and when he has passed on, stop here yourself for a while, that 10 I may make known to you the word of God." [1]Samuel took a vial of oil and poured it on his head, and kissed him; he said, "The LORD has anointed you ruler over his people Israel. You shall reign over the people of the

Sacred Meals

1 SAMUEL 9.11–14

Sacred meals such as the Sabbath dinner, Passover and the Eucharist play a large part in religious observance to this day. But making mealtime an opportunity for holiness is also something you can do in daily life.

Look at the room where you usually eat meals. In what way is it conducive to creating a sacred space for a sacred meal? What might you change or add? You may wish to add candles or a lamp to remind you of the inner light God imparts. A small picture, flowers, or a souvenir from a place which once brought you contentment also helps create a reflective and meaningful environment.

Prayer, heartfelt conversation, laughter, singing, and mindfulness at meals can all contribute to a sense of the sacred. Sharing a meal with others is a powerful reminder of community, but even dining alone can be an entryway to grace.

See Meeting God in Everyday Life

---

a Gk: Heb lacks *the suffering of*   b Meaning of Heb uncertain   c Q Ms Gk: MT *it was kept*   d Cn: Heb *it was kept for you, saying, I have invited the people*   e Gk: Heb *and he spoke with Saul*   f Gk: Heb lacks *and he lay down to sleep*   g Gk: Heb *and they arose early and at break of dawn*

A Spiritual Overhaul

1 SAMUEL 10.6

Clever Samuel! He has already anointed Saul as the new king, yet he has made no public announcement. There is much political intrigue here, but the real life-changing act is God's, as Samuel prophesies: "The spirit of the LORD will possess you, and you will be turned into a different person."

How unsettling, that the person you know best will be changed! Can you trust God—really trust—if your life is significantly changed? Try taking a threefold inventory of the state of your soul: Very specifically, what do you think God would really like to change in you? What will you relinquish to make room for the change? What decision or action will you make at this moment to invite God to initiate the change?

See Meeting God in Everyday Life

LORD and you will save them from the hand of their enemies all around. Now this shall be the sign to you that the LORD has anointed you ruler[a] over his heritage: [2]When you depart from me today you will meet two men by Rachel's tomb in the territory of Benjamin at Zelzah; they will say to you, 'The donkeys that you went to seek are found, and now your father has stopped worrying about them and is worrying about you, saying: What shall I do about my son?' [3]Then you shall go on from there further and come to the oak of Tabor; three men going up to God at Bethel will meet you there, one carrying three kids, another carrying three loaves of bread, and another carrying a skin of wine. [4]They will greet you and give you two loaves of bread, which you shall accept from them. [5]After that you shall come to Gibe-ath-elohim,[b] at the place where the Philistine garrison is; there, as you come to the town, you will meet a band of prophets coming down from the shrine with harp, tambourine, flute, and lyre playing in front of them; they will be in a prophetic frenzy. [6]Then the spirit of the LORD will possess you, and you will be in a prophetic frenzy along with them and be turned into a different person. [7]Now when these signs meet you, do whatever you see fit to do, for God is with you. [8]And you shall go down to Gilgal ahead of me; then I will come down to you to present burnt offerings and offer sacrifices of well-being. Seven days you shall wait, until I come to you and show you what you shall do."

Saul Prophesies

9 As he turned away to leave Samuel, God gave him another heart; and all these signs were fulfilled that day. [10]When they were going from there[c] to Gibeah,[d] a band of prophets met him; and the spirit of God possessed him, and he fell into a prophetic frenzy along with them. [11]When all who knew him before saw how he prophesied with the prophets, the people said to one another, "What has come over the son of Kish? Is Saul also among the prophets?" [12]A man of the place answered, "And who is their father?" Therefore it became a proverb, "Is Saul also among the prophets?" [13]When his prophetic frenzy had ended, he went home.[e]

14 Saul's uncle said to him and to the boy, "Where did you go?" And he replied, "To seek the donkeys; and when we saw they were not to be found, we went to Samuel." [15]Saul's uncle said, "Tell me what Samuel said to you." [16]Saul said to his uncle, "He told us that the donkeys had been found." But about the matter of the kingship, of which Samuel had spoken, he did not tell him anything.

Saul Proclaimed King

17 Samuel summoned the people to the LORD at Mizpah [18]and said to them,[f] "Thus says the LORD, the God of Israel, 'I brought up Israel out of Egypt, and I rescued you from the hand of the Egyptians and from the hand of all the kingdoms that were oppressing you.' [19]But today you have rejected your God, who saves you from all your calamities and your distresses; and you have said, 'No! but set a king

---

a Gk: Heb lacks *over his people Israel. You shall . . . anointed you ruler*
b Or *the Hill of God*   c Gk: Heb *they came there*   d Or *the hill*
e Cn: Heb *he came to the shrine*   f Heb *to the people of Israel*

over us.' Now therefore present yourselves before the Lord by your tribes and by your clans."

20 Then Samuel brought all the tribes of Israel near, and the tribe of Benjamin was taken by lot. ²¹He brought the tribe of Benjamin near by its families, and the family of the Matrites was taken by lot. Finally he brought the family of the Matrites near man by man,ᵃ and Saul the son of Kish was taken by lot. But when they sought him, he could not be found. ²²So they inquired again of the Lord, "Did the man come here?"ᵇ and the Lord said, "See, he has hidden himself among the baggage." ²³Then they ran and brought him from there. When he took his stand among the people, he was head and shoulders taller than any of them. ²⁴Samuel said to all the people, "Do you see the one whom the Lord has chosen? There is no one like him among all the people." And all the people shouted, "Long live the king!"

25 Samuel told the people the rights and duties of the kingship; and he wrote them in a book and laid it up before the Lord. Then Samuel sent all the people back to their homes. ²⁶Saul also went to his home at Gibeah, and with him went warriors whose hearts God had touched. ²⁷But some worthless fellows said, "How can this man save us?" They despised him and brought him no present. But he held his peace.

Now Nahash, king of the Ammonites, had been grievously oppressing the Gadites and the Reubenites. He would gouge out the right eye of each of them and would not grant Israel a deliverer. No one was left of the Israelites across the Jordan whose right eye Nahash, king of the Ammonites, had not gouged out. But there were seven thousand men who had escaped from the Ammonites and had entered Jabesh-gilead.ᶜ

Saul Defeats the Ammonites

11 About a month later,ᵈ Nahash the Ammonite went up and besieged Jabesh-gilead; and all the men of Jabesh said to Nahash, "Make a treaty with us, and we will serve you." ²But Nahash the Ammonite said to them, "On this condition I will make a treaty with you, namely that I gouge out everyone's right eye, and thus put disgrace upon all Israel." ³The elders of Jabesh said to him, "Give us seven days' respite that we may send messengers through all the territory of Israel. Then, if there is no one to save us, we will give ourselves up to you." ⁴When the messengers came to Gibeah of Saul, they reported the matter in the hearing of the people; and all the people wept aloud.

5 Now Saul was coming from the field behind the oxen; and Saul said, "What is the matter with the people, that they are weeping?" So they told him the message from the inhabitants of Jabesh. ⁶And the spirit of God came upon Saul in power when he heard these words, and his anger was greatly kindled. ⁷He took a yoke of oxen, and cut them in pieces and sent them throughout all the territory of Israel by messengers, saying, "Whoever does not come out after Saul and Samuel, so shall it be done to his oxen!" Then the dread of the Lord fell upon the people, and they

Offerings of Well-Being

1 SAMUEL 11.1–15

Saul is on the throne as king. Even those who initially objected are convinced after a military victory won against high odds. (Affirmation seems to come easily after victories!) This time they are united in ratifying his kingship "before the Lord." They act out this renewal with an offering of well-being.

Another name for a ritual of acceptance is "fellowship offering." You can make a "fellowship offering" today in a note to or in conversation with a friend, in which you express how important they are to you and how you value their friendship. If you plan to write a note, at least outline it now; if you plan to make a telephone call, at least write down the number and the time when you plan to call.

See *Meeting God in Community*

a Gk: Heb lacks *Finally . . . man by man*   b Gk: Heb *Is there yet a man to come here?*   c Q Ms Compare Josephus, *Antiquities* VI.v.1 (68-71): MT lacks *Now Nahash . . . entered Jabesh-gilead.*   d Q Ms Gk: MT lacks *About a month later*

Stop Doing; Take Stock

1 SAMUEL 12.15–16

How often we hear, "Don't just stand there; do something!" In his farewell speech to his people, Samuel reverses the clauses: "Don't just keep doing; stand still, and pay attention." After sketching the history of the people, and warning of the risks of giving up God's primary guidance in exchange for a king who is an able warrior, Samuel calls rain down upon the very day of the wheat harvest. The people are stopped in their tracks, both literally and emotionally, and called to reflect on their relationship with God.

In silence, take stock of your relationship with God. Recall the times, if you can, when God caught your attention or changed the direction of your life. How did it happen? What means or circumstances did God use to catch your attention? How did you respond? Slowly? Right away? In what ways might God be calling you today to trust his guidance more completely?

See *Meeting God in Everyday Life*

came out as one. [8]When he mustered them at Bezek, those from Israel were three hundred thousand, and those from Judah seventy[a] thousand. [9]They said to the messengers who had come, "Thus shall you say to the inhabitants of Jabesh-gilead: 'Tomorrow, by the time the sun is hot, you shall have deliverance.' " When the messengers came and told the inhabitants of Jabesh, they rejoiced. [10]So the inhabitants of Jabesh said, "Tomorrow we will give ourselves up to you, and you may do to us whatever seems good to you." [11]The next day Saul put the people in three companies. At the morning watch they came into the camp and cut down the Ammonites until the heat of the day; and those who survived were scattered, so that no two of them were left together.

12 The people said to Samuel, "Who is it that said, 'Shall Saul reign over us?' Give them to us so that we may put them to death." [13]But Saul said, "No one shall be put to death this day, for today the LORD has brought deliverance to Israel."

14 Samuel said to the people, "Come, let us go to Gilgal and there renew the kingship." [15]So all the people went to Gilgal, and there they made Saul king before the LORD in Gilgal. There they sacrificed offerings of well-being before the LORD, and there Saul and all the Israelites rejoiced greatly.

Samuel's Farewell Address

12 Samuel said to all Israel, "I have listened to you in all that you have said to me, and have set a king over you. [2]See, it is the king who leads you now; I am old and gray, but my sons are with you. I have led you from my youth until this day. [3]Here I am; testify against me before the LORD and before his anointed. Whose ox have I taken? Or whose donkey have I taken? Or whom have I defrauded? Whom have I oppressed? Or from whose hand have I taken a bribe to blind my eyes with it? Testify against me[b] and I will restore it to you." [4]They said, "You have not defrauded us or oppressed us or taken anything from the hand of anyone." [5]He said to them, "The LORD is witness against you, and his anointed is witness this day, that you have not found anything in my hand." And they said, "He is witness."

6 Samuel said to the people, "The LORD is witness, who[c] appointed Moses and Aaron and brought your ancestors up out of the land of Egypt. [7]Now therefore take your stand, so that I may enter into judgment with you before the LORD, and I will declare to you[d] all the saving deeds of the LORD that he performed for you and for your ancestors. [8]When Jacob went into Egypt and the Egyptians oppressed them,[e] then your ancestors cried to the LORD and the LORD sent Moses and Aaron, who brought forth your ancestors out of Egypt, and settled them in this place. [9]But they forgot the LORD their God; and he sold them into the hand of Sisera, commander of the army of King Jabin of[f] Hazor, and into the hand of the Philistines, and into the hand of the king of Moab; and they fought against them. [10]Then they cried to the LORD, and said, 'We have sinned, because we have for-

a Q Ms Gk: MT *thirty*   *b* Gk: Heb lacks *Testify against me*   *c* Gk: Heb lacks *is witness, who*   *d* Gk: Heb lacks *and I will declare to you*   *e* Gk: Heb lacks *and the Egyptians oppressed them*   *f* Gk: Heb lacks *King Jabin of*

saken the LORD, and have served the Baals and the Astartes; but now rescue us out of the hand of our enemies, and we will serve you.' [11]And the LORD sent Jerubbaal and Barak,[a] and Jephthah, and Samson,[b] and rescued you out of the hand of your enemies on every side; and you lived in safety. [12]But when you saw that King Nahash of the Ammonites came against you, you said to me, 'No, but a king shall reign over us,' though the LORD your God was your king. [13]See, here is the king whom you have chosen, for whom you have asked; see, the LORD has set a king over you. [14]If you will fear the LORD and serve him and heed his voice and not rebel against the commandment of the LORD, and if both you and the king who reigns over you will follow the LORD your God, it will be well; [15]but if you will not heed the voice of the LORD, but rebel against the commandment of the LORD, then the hand of the LORD will be against you and your king.[c] [16]Now therefore take your stand and see this great thing that the LORD will do before your eyes. [17]Is it not the wheat harvest today? I will call upon the LORD, that he may send thunder and rain; and you shall know and see that the wickedness that you have done in the sight of the LORD is great in demanding a king for yourselves." [18]So Samuel called upon the LORD, and the LORD sent thunder and rain that day; and all the people greatly feared the LORD and Samuel.

19 All the people said to Samuel, "Pray to the LORD your God for your servants, so that we may not die; for we have added to all our sins the evil of demanding a king for ourselves." [20]And Samuel said to the people, "Do not be afraid; you have done all this evil, yet do not turn aside from following the LORD, but serve the LORD with all your heart; [21]and do not turn aside after useless things that cannot profit or save, for they are useless. [22]For the LORD will not cast away his people, for his great name's sake, because it has pleased the LORD to make you a people for himself. [23]Moreover as for me, far be it from me that I should sin against the LORD by ceasing to pray for you; and I will instruct you in the good and the right way. [24]Only fear the LORD, and serve him faithfully with all your heart; for consider what great things he has done for you. [25]But if you still do wickedly, you shall be swept away, both you and your king."

Saul's Unlawful Sacrifice

13 Saul was . . .[d] years old when he began to reign; and he reigned . . . and two[e] years over Israel.

2 Saul chose three thousand out of Israel; two thousand were with Saul in Michmash and the hill country of Bethel, and a thousand were with Jonathan in Gibeah of Benjamin; the rest of the people he sent home to their tents. [3]Jonathan defeated the garrison of the Philistines that was at Geba; and the Philistines heard of it. And Saul blew the trumpet throughout all the land, saying, "Let the Hebrews hear!" [4]When all Israel heard that Saul had defeated the garrison of the Philistines, and also that Israel had become odious to the Philistines, the people were called out to join Saul at Gilgal.

Halfway Is Not Wholehearted

1 SAMUEL 12.20

"Meister Eckhart wrote: 'There are plenty to follow our Lord half-way, but not the other half. They will give up possessions, friends and honors, but it touches them too closely to disown themselves.' It is just this astonishing life which is willing to follow Him the other half, sincerely to disown itself, this life which intends complete obedience, without any reservations, that I would propose to you in all humility, in all boldness, in all seriousness."

—THOMAS KELLY,
A Testament of Devotion

See Meeting God in Service

---

a Gk Syr: Heb *Bedan*   b Gk: Heb *Samuel*   c Gk: Heb *and your ancestors*
d The number is lacking in the Heb text (the verse is lacking in the Septuagint).   e *Two* is not the entire number; something has dropped out.

Unarmed—but Prepared

1 SAMUEL 13.22

What a challenge for military leadership: The new warrior-king Saul has troops but no weapons with which to arm them! Yet God will give them victory.

Recall a time when you felt totally unprepared for an important meeting or duty, yet things turned out because something intervened: a sudden inspiration, a coincidence, a lead from an understanding person who helped you. Consider how this unexpected help equipped you for your task. In what ways did it represent God-given strength or ability? Take time now to thank God for a specific instance when divine help made the difference.

5 The Philistines mustered to fight with Israel, thirty thousand chariots, and six thousand horsemen, and troops like the sand on the seashore in multitude; they came up and encamped at Michmash, to the east of Beth-aven. ⁶When the Israelites saw that they were in distress (for the troops were hard pressed), the people hid themselves in caves and in holes and in rocks and in tombs and in cisterns. ⁷Some Hebrews crossed the Jordan to the land of Gad and Gilead. Saul was still at Gilgal, and all the people followed him trembling.

8 He waited seven days, the time appointed by Samuel; but Samuel did not come to Gilgal, and the people began to slip away from Saul.ᵃ ⁹So Saul said, "Bring the burnt offering here to me, and the offerings of well-being." And he offered the burnt offering. ¹⁰As soon as he had finished offering the burnt offering, Samuel arrived; and Saul went out to meet him and salute him. ¹¹Samuel said, "What have you done?" Saul replied, "When I saw that the people were slipping away from me, and that you did not come within the days appointed, and that the Philistines were mustering at Michmash, ¹²I said, 'Now the Philistines will come down upon me at Gilgal, and I have not entreated the favor of the LORD'; so I forced myself, and offered the burnt offering." ¹³Samuel said to Saul, "You have done foolishly; you have not kept the commandment of the LORD your God, which he commanded you. The LORD would have established your kingdom over Israel forever, ¹⁴but now your kingdom will not continue; the LORD has sought out a man after his own heart; and the LORD has appointed him to be ruler over his people, because you have not kept what the LORD commanded you." ¹⁵And Samuel left and went on his way from Gilgal.ᵇ The rest of the people followed Saul to join the army; they went up from Gilgal toward Gibeah of Benjamin.ᶜ

Preparations for Battle

Saul counted the people who were present with him, about six hundred men. ¹⁶Saul, his son Jonathan, and the people who were present with them stayed in Geba of Benjamin; but the Philistines encamped at Michmash. ¹⁷And raiders came out of the camp of the Philistines in three companies; one company turned toward Ophrah, to the land of Shual, ¹⁸another company turned toward Bethhoron, and another company turned toward the mountainᵈ that looks down upon the valley of Zeboim toward the wilderness.

19 Now there was no smith to be found throughout all the land of Israel; for the Philistines said, "The Hebrews must not make swords or spears for themselves"; ²⁰so all the Israelites went down to the Philistines to sharpen their plowshares, mattocks, axes, or sickles;ᵉ ²¹The charge was two-thirds of a shekelᶠ for the plowshares and for the mattocks, and one-third of a shekel for sharpening the axes and for setting the goads.ᵍ ²²So on the day of the battle neither sword nor spear was to be found in the possession of any of the people with Saul and Jonathan; but Saul and his son Jonathan had them.

ᵃ Heb *him*   ᵇ Gk: Heb *went up from Gilgal to Gibeah of Benjamin*
ᶜ Gk: Heb lacks *The rest . . . of Benjamin*   ᵈ Cn Compare Gk: Heb *toward the border*   ᵉ Gk: Heb *plowshare*   ᶠ Heb *was a pim*   ᵍ Cn: Meaning of Heb uncertain

Jonathan Surprises and Routs the Philistines

23 Now a garrison of the Philistines had gone out to the pass of Michmash. **14** [1]One day Jonathan son of Saul said to the young man who carried his armor, "Come, let us go over to the Philistine garrison on the other side." But he did not tell his father. [2]Saul was staying in the outskirts of Gibeah under the pomegranate tree that is at Migron; the troops that were with him were about six hundred men, [3]along with Ahijah son of Ahitub, Ichabod's brother, son of Phinehas son of Eli, the priest of the Lord in Shiloh, carrying an ephod. Now the people did not know that Jonathan had gone. [4]In the pass,[a] by which Jonathan tried to go over to the Philistine garrison, there was a rocky crag on one side and a rocky crag on the other; the name of the one was Bozez, and the name of the other Seneh. [5]One crag rose on the north in front of Michmash, and the other on the south in front of Geba.

6 Jonathan said to the young man who carried his armor, "Come, let us go over to the garrison of these uncircumcised; it may be that the Lord will act for us; for nothing can hinder the Lord from saving by many or by few." [7]His armor-bearer said to him, "Do all that your mind inclines to.[b] I am with you; as your mind is, so is mine."[c] [8]Then Jonathan said, "Now we will cross over to those men and will show ourselves to them. [9]If they say to us, 'Wait until we come to you,' then we will stand still in our place, and we will not go up to them. [10]But if they say, 'Come up to us,' then we will go up; for the Lord has given them into our hand. That will be the sign for us." [11]So both of them showed themselves to the garrison of the Philistines; and the Philistines said, "Look, Hebrews are coming out of the holes where they have hidden themselves." [12]The men of the garrison hailed Jonathan and his armor-bearer, saying, "Come up to us, and we will show you something." Jonathan said to his armor-bearer, "Come up after me; for the Lord has given them into the hand of Israel." [13]Then Jonathan climbed up on his hands and feet, with his armor-bearer following after him. The Philistines[d] fell before Jonathan, and his armor-bearer, coming after him, killed them. [14]In that first slaughter Jonathan and his armor-bearer killed about twenty men within an area about half a furrow long in an acre[e] of land. [15]There was a panic in the camp, in the field, and among all the people; the garrison and even the raiders trembled; the earth quaked; and it became a very great panic.

16 Saul's lookouts in Gibeah of Benjamin were watching as the multitude was surging back and forth.[f] [17]Then Saul said to the troops that were with him, "Call the roll and see who has gone from us." When they had called the roll, Jonathan and his armor-bearer were not there. [18]Saul said to Ahijah, "Bring the ark[g] of God here." For at that time the ark[g] of God went with the Israelites. [19]While Saul was talking to the priest, the tumult in the camp of the Philistines increased more and more; and Saul said to the priest, "Withdraw your hand." [20]Then Saul and all the people who were with him rallied and went into the battle; and every sword was against the other, so that there was very great confu-

---

Heroism or Imprudence?

1 SAMUEL 14.8–14

Visualize Jonathan and his armor-bearer as they struggle up a very steep ascent, exposing themselves to great risk yet dispatching many enemies in the process. For a similar accomplishment today they might well be awarded Medals of Honor!

Take five minutes to reflect on these verses. Listen for a word or short phrase that attracts you and repeat it silently ten or more times. Imagine yourself in the scene and dwell there for a minute or more. How does what you experience or feel relate to your life? For the next two or three days, listen for an invitation from God as revealed through that word or phrase.

See Meeting God in Scripture

---

a Heb *Between the passes*   b Gk: Heb *Do all that is in your mind. Turn*
c Gk: Heb lacks *so is mine*   d Heb *They*   e Heb *yoke*   f Gk: Heb *they went and there*   g Gk *the ephod*

Rescued by the Crowd

1 SAMUEL 14.36–45

A crowd challenges the king about what they consider the unfair treatment of Jonathan, who is threatened with death because he did something he didn't know was banned. Their argument is not simply that Jonathan has delivered them from defeat, but that he did so with God's help.

Recall a time when you defended someone unjustly accused. Or remember a time when you joined, or wanted to join, a group protest against what you considered to be an injustice upheld by law or custom. What led you to take this stand? How did it feel to behave counter to prevailing opinion or law? How much of your action was prompted by a sense of God's call? Ask God for courage to stand firm when justice requires it.

See Meeting God in Community

sion. ²¹Now the Hebrews who previously had been with the Philistines and had gone up with them into the camp turned and joined the Israelites who were with Saul and Jonathan. ²²Likewise, when all the Israelites who had gone into hiding in the hill country of Ephraim heard that the Philistines were fleeing, they too followed closely after them in the battle. ²³So the LORD gave Israel the victory that day.

The battle passed beyond Beth-aven, and the troops with Saul numbered altogether about ten thousand men. The battle spread out over the hill country of Ephraim.

Saul's Rash Oath

24 Now Saul committed a very rash act on that day.[a] He had laid an oath on the troops, saying, "Cursed be anyone who eats food before it is evening and I have been avenged on my enemies." So none of the troops tasted food. ²⁵All the troops[b] came upon a honeycomb; and there was honey on the ground. ²⁶When the troops came upon the honeycomb, the honey was dripping out; but they did not put their hands to their mouths, for they feared the oath. ²⁷But Jonathan had not heard his father charge the troops with the oath; so he extended the staff that was in his hand, and dipped the tip of it in the honeycomb, and put his hand to his mouth; and his eyes brightened. ²⁸Then one of the soldiers said, "Your father strictly charged the troops with an oath, saying, 'Cursed be anyone who eats food this day.' And so the troops are faint." ²⁹Then Jonathan said, "My father has troubled the land; see how my eyes have brightened because I tasted a little of this honey. ³⁰How much better if today the troops had eaten freely of the spoil taken from their enemies; for now the slaughter among the Philistines has not been great."

31 After they had struck down the Philistines that day from Michmash to Aijalon, the troops were very faint; ³²so the troops flew upon the spoil, and took sheep and oxen and calves, and slaughtered them on the ground; and the troops ate them with the blood. ³³Then it was reported to Saul, "Look, the troops are sinning against the LORD by eating with the blood." And he said, "You have dealt treacherously; roll a large stone before me here."[c] ³⁴Saul said, "Disperse yourselves among the troops, and say to them, 'Let all bring their oxen or their sheep, and slaughter them here, and eat; and do not sin against the LORD by eating with the blood.' " So all of the troops brought their oxen with them that night, and slaughtered them there. ³⁵And Saul built an altar to the LORD; it was the first altar that he built to the LORD.

Jonathan in Danger of Death

36 Then Saul said, "Let us go down after the Philistines by night and despoil them until the morning light; let us not leave one of them." They said, "Do whatever seems good to you." But the priest said, "Let us draw near to God here." ³⁷So Saul inquired of God, "Shall I go down after the Philistines? Will you give them into the hand of Israel?" But he did not answer him that day. ³⁸Saul said, "Come here, all you leaders of the people; and let us find out how this sin has arisen today. ³⁹For as the LORD lives who saves Israel,

a Gk: Heb The Israelites were distressed that day   b Heb land   c Gk: Heb me this day

even if it is in my son Jonathan, he shall surely die!" But there was no one among all the people who answered him. **40**He said to all Israel, "You shall be on one side, and I and my son Jonathan will be on the other side." The people said to Saul, "Do what seems good to you." **41**Then Saul said, "O LORD God of Israel, why have you not answered your servant today? If this guilt is in me or in my son Jonathan, O LORD God of Israel, give Urim; but if this guilt is in your people Israel,*a* give Thummim." And Jonathan and Saul were indicated by the lot, but the people were cleared. **42**Then Saul said, "Cast the lot between me and my son Jonathan." And Jonathan was taken.

43 Then Saul said to Jonathan, "Tell me what you have done." Jonathan told him, "I tasted a little honey with the tip of the staff that was in my hand; here I am, I will die." **44**Saul said, "God do so to me and more also; you shall surely die, Jonathan!" **45**Then the people said to Saul, "Shall Jonathan die, who has accomplished this great victory in Israel? Far from it! As the LORD lives, not one hair of his head shall fall to the ground; for he has worked with God today." So the people ransomed Jonathan, and he did not die. **46**Then Saul withdrew from pursuing the Philistines; and the Philistines went to their own place.

Saul's Continuing Wars

47 When Saul had taken the kingship over Israel, he fought against all his enemies on every side—against Moab, against the Ammonites, against Edom, against the kings of Zobah, and against the Philistines; wherever he turned he routed them. **48**He did valiantly, and struck down the Amalekites, and rescued Israel out of the hands of those who plundered them.

49 Now the sons of Saul were Jonathan, Ishvi, and Malchishua; and the names of his two daughters were these: the name of the firstborn was Merab, and the name of the younger, Michal. **50**The name of Saul's wife was Ahinoam daughter of Ahimaaz. And the name of the commander of his army was Abner son of Ner, Saul's uncle; **51**Kish was the father of Saul, and Ner the father of Abner was the son of Abiel.

52 There was hard fighting against the Philistines all the days of Saul; and when Saul saw any strong or valiant warrior, he took him into his service.

Saul Defeats the Amalekites but Spares Their King

15 Samuel said to Saul, "The LORD sent me to anoint you king over his people Israel; now therefore listen to the words of the LORD. **2**Thus says the LORD of hosts, 'I will punish the Amalekites for what they did in opposing the Israelites when they came up out of Egypt. **3**Now go and attack Amalek, and utterly destroy all that they have; do not spare them, but kill both man and woman, child and infant, ox and sheep, camel and donkey.' "

4 So Saul summoned the people, and numbered them in Telaim, two hundred thousand foot soldiers, and ten thousand soldiers of Judah. **5**Saul came to the city of the Amalekites and lay in wait in the valley. **6**Saul said to the Kenites, "Go! Leave! Withdraw from among the Amalekites, or I will destroy you with them; for you showed kindness to all

---

Recruiting for the Lord's Service

1 SAMUEL 14.52

"If a person would gain spiritual freedom and not be continually troubled, let him begin by not being afraid of the Cross and he will find that the Lord will help him to bear it; he will then advance happily and find profit in everything. It is now clear that, if no water is coming from the well, we ourselves can put none into it. But of course we must not be careless: water must always be drawn when there is any there, for at such a time God's will is that we should use it so that He may multiply our virtues."

—TERESA OF AVILA,
The Life of Teresa of Jesus

See *Meeting God in Service*

---

a Vg Compare Gk: Heb *41Saul said to the LORD, the God of Israel*

Holding and Releasing

1 SAMUEL 15.24–27

Like Saul, hunger for acceptance by others can weaken our resolve to "[speak] the truth in love (Ephesians 4.15)." It can even lead us to compromise our standards.

Consider ways in which you may be hesitating to speak honestly to someone involved in destructive behavior because you fear their response—or lack of response. As you pray about the matter, grip tightly some part of your clothing as a symbol of any insistence on your part to control or change the other person. Signify letting go of your need for control by releasing your garment. Commend that person to God's life-changing power. Prayerfully consider how to wait for receptivity in that person, and how to speak to him or her.

See *Meeting God in Community*

the people of Israel when they came up out of Egypt." So the Kenites withdrew from the Amalekites. ⁷Saul defeated the Amalekites, from Havilah as far as Shur, which is east of Egypt. ⁸He took King Agag of the Amalekites alive, but utterly destroyed all the people with the edge of the sword. ⁹Saul and the people spared Agag, and the best of the sheep and of the cattle and of the fatlings, and the lambs, and all that was valuable, and would not utterly destroy them; all that was despised and worthless they utterly destroyed.

Saul Rejected as King

10 The word of the LORD came to Samuel: ¹¹"I regret that I made Saul king, for he has turned back from following me, and has not carried out my commands." Samuel was angry; and he cried out to the LORD all night. ¹²Samuel rose early in the morning to meet Saul, and Samuel was told, "Saul went to Carmel, where he set up a monument for himself, and on returning he passed on down to Gilgal." ¹³When Samuel came to Saul, Saul said to him, "May you be blessed by the LORD; I have carried out the command of the LORD." ¹⁴But Samuel said, "What then is this bleating of sheep in my ears, and the lowing of cattle that I hear?" ¹⁵Saul said, "They have brought them from the Amalekites; for the people spared the best of the sheep and the cattle, to sacrifice to the LORD your God; but the rest we have utterly destroyed." ¹⁶Then Samuel said to Saul, "Stop! I will tell you what the LORD said to me last night." He replied, "Speak."

17 Samuel said, "Though you are little in your own eyes, are you not the head of the tribes of Israel? The LORD anointed you king over Israel. ¹⁸And the LORD sent you on a mission, and said, 'Go, utterly destroy the sinners, the Amalekites, and fight against them until they are consumed.' ¹⁹Why then did you not obey the voice of the LORD? Why did you swoop down on the spoil, and do what was evil in the sight of the LORD?" ²⁰Saul said to Samuel, "I have obeyed the voice of the LORD, I have gone on the mission on which the LORD sent me, I have brought Agag the king of Amalek, and I have utterly destroyed the Amalekites. ²¹But from the spoil the people took sheep and cattle, the best of the things devoted to destruction, to sacrifice to the LORD your God in Gilgal." ²²And Samuel said,

"Has the LORD as great delight in burnt offerings
and sacrifices,
as in obedience to the voice of the LORD?
Surely, to obey is better than sacrifice,
and to heed than the fat of rams.
²³ For rebellion is no less a sin than divination,
and stubbornness is like iniquity and idolatry.
Because you have rejected the word of the LORD,
he has also rejected you from being king."

24 Saul said to Samuel, "I have sinned; for I have transgressed the commandment of the LORD and your words, because I feared the people and obeyed their voice. ²⁵Now therefore, I pray, pardon my sin, and return with me, so that I may worship the LORD." ²⁶Samuel said to Saul, "I will not return with you; for you have rejected the word of the LORD, and the LORD has rejected you from being king over Israel." ²⁷As Samuel turned to go away, Saul caught hold of the hem of his robe, and it tore. ²⁸And Samuel said to him, "The LORD has torn the kingdom of Israel from you this

very day, and has given it to a neighbor of yours, who is better than you. ²⁹Moreover the Glory of Israel will not recant*ᵃ* or change his mind; for he is not a mortal, that he should change his mind." ³⁰Then Saul*ᵇ* said, "I have sinned; yet honor me now before the elders of my people and before Israel, and return with me, so that I may worship the LORD your God." ³¹So Samuel turned back after Saul; and Saul worshiped the LORD.

32 Then Samuel said, "Bring Agag king of the Amalekites here to me." And Agag came to him haltingly.*ᶜ* Agag said, "Surely this is the bitterness of death."*ᵈ* ³³But Samuel said,

"As your sword has made women childless,
so your mother shall be childless among
women."

And Samuel hewed Agag in pieces before the LORD in Gilgal.

34 Then Samuel went to Ramah; and Saul went up to his house in Gibeah of Saul. ³⁵Samuel did not see Saul again until the day of his death, but Samuel grieved over Saul. And the LORD was sorry that he had made Saul king over Israel.

David Anointed as King

16 The LORD said to Samuel, "How long will you grieve over Saul? I have rejected him from being king over Israel. Fill your horn with oil and set out; I will send you to Jesse the Bethlehemite, for I have provided for myself a king among his sons." ²Samuel said, "How can I go? If Saul hears of it, he will kill me." And the LORD said, "Take a heifer with you, and say, 'I have come to sacrifice to the LORD.' ³Invite Jesse to the sacrifice, and I will show you what you shall do; and you shall anoint for me the one whom I name to you." ⁴Samuel did what the LORD commanded, and came to Bethlehem. The elders of the city came to meet him trembling, and said, "Do you come peaceably?" ⁵He said, "Peaceably; I have come to sacrifice to the LORD; sanctify yourselves and come with me to the sacrifice." And he sanctified Jesse and his sons and invited them to the sacrifice.

6 When they came, he looked on Eliab and thought, "Surely the LORD's anointed is now before the LORD."*ᵉ* ⁷But the LORD said to Samuel, "Do not look on his appearance or on the height of his stature, because I have rejected him; for the LORD does not see as mortals see; they look on the outward appearance, but the LORD looks on the heart." ⁸Then Jesse called Abinadab, and made him pass before Samuel. He said, "Neither has the LORD chosen this one." ⁹Then Jesse made Shammah pass by. And he said, "Neither has the LORD chosen this one." ¹⁰Jesse made seven of his sons pass before Samuel, and Samuel said to Jesse, "The LORD has not chosen any of these." ¹¹Samuel said to Jesse, "Are all your sons here?" And he said, "There remains yet the youngest, but he is keeping the sheep." And Samuel said to Jesse, "Send and bring him; for we will not sit down until he comes here." ¹²He sent and brought him in. Now he was ruddy, and had beautiful eyes, and was handsome. The LORD said, "Rise and anoint him; for this is the one." ¹³Then

Looking on the Heart

1 SAMUEL 16.7

Samuel has warned Saul (see 13.13–14) that the Lord will remove him as king in favor of one "after [the LORD's] own heart." Samuel is guided by the Lord in his search for the new king, learning that man looks "on the outward appearance, but the LORD looks on the heart," the core of one's being.

Recall a time when your evaluation of a person's character or suitability for service relied mainly on outward appearance. Did this prove to be misleading or cause problems later? Consider now how God can help you look at people rightly, as the Lord sees them. Pray about a relationship with someone in which having new eyes might make all the difference.

See Meeting God in Service

---

a Q Ms Gk: MT *deceive*   *b* Heb *he*   *c* Cn Compare Gk: Meaning of Heb uncertain   *d* Q Ms Gk: MT *Surely the bitterness of death is past*   *e* Heb *him*

Sweet Music

1 SAMUEL 16.23

Shakespeare often gets the credit, but William Congreve actually wrote the words: "Music has charms to soothe a savage breast, to soften rocks, or bend a knotted oak." When Saul is beset by an evil spirit, David's music brings him tenderness and peace.

What music soothes your "savage breast"? What hymns or sacred songs draw you toward a calm and peaceful trust in God? Sing such a hymn to yourself, or turn on background music as you read or reread this passage. What phrases or Bible verses deepen your trust in God's peace-giving power? Recite prayerfully a phrase or Bible verse, either on a single note or in a simple melody, as music of praise from your heart.

See Meeting God in Worship

Samuel took the horn of oil, and anointed him in the presence of his brothers; and the spirit of the LORD came mightily upon David from that day forward. Samuel then set out and went to Ramah.

David Plays the Lyre for Saul

14 Now the spirit of the LORD departed from Saul, and an evil spirit from the LORD tormented him. [15]And Saul's servants said to him, "See now, an evil spirit from God is tormenting you. [16]Let our lord now command the servants who attend you to look for someone who is skillful in playing the lyre; and when the evil spirit from God is upon you, he will play it, and you will feel better." [17]So Saul said to his servants, "Provide for me someone who can play well, and bring him to me." [18]One of the young men answered, "I have seen a son of Jesse the Bethlehemite who is skillful in playing, a man of valor, a warrior, prudent in speech, and a man of good presence; and the LORD is with him." [19]So Saul sent messengers to Jesse, and said, "Send me your son David who is with the sheep." [20]Jesse took a donkey loaded with bread, a skin of wine, and a kid, and sent them by his son David to Saul. [21]And David came to Saul, and entered his service. Saul loved him greatly, and he became his armor-bearer. [22]Saul sent to Jesse, saying, "Let David remain in my service, for he has found favor in my sight." [23]And whenever the evil spirit from God came upon Saul, David took the lyre and played it with his hand, and Saul would be relieved and feel better, and the evil spirit would depart from him.

David and Goliath

17 Now the Philistines gathered their armies for battle; they were gathered at Socoh, which belongs to Judah, and encamped between Socoh and Azekah, in Ephes-dammim. [2]Saul and the Israelites gathered and encamped in the valley of Elah, and formed ranks against the Philistines. [3]The Philistines stood on the mountain on the one side, and Israel stood on the mountain on the other side, with a valley between them. [4]And there came out from the camp of the Philistines a champion named Goliath, of Gath, whose height was six[a] cubits and a span. [5]He had a helmet of bronze on his head, and he was armed with a coat of mail; the weight of the coat was five thousand shekels of bronze. [6]He had greaves of bronze on his legs and a javelin of bronze slung between his shoulders. [7]The shaft of his spear was like a weaver's beam, and his spear's head weighed six hundred shekels of iron; and his shield-bearer went before him. [8]He stood and shouted to the ranks of Israel, "Why have you come out to draw up for battle? Am I not a Philistine, and are you not servants of Saul? Choose a man for yourselves, and let him come down to me. [9]If he is able to fight with me and kill me, then we will be your servants; but if I prevail against him and kill him, then you shall be our servants and serve us." [10]And the Philistine said, "Today I defy the ranks of Israel! Give me a man, that we may fight together." [11]When Saul and all Israel heard these words of the Philistine, they were dismayed and greatly afraid.

12 Now David was the son of an Ephrathite of Bethlehem in Judah, named Jesse, who had eight sons. In the

a MT: Q Ms Gk four

days of Saul the man was already old and advanced in years.[a] 13The three eldest sons of Jesse had followed Saul to the battle; the names of his three sons who went to the battle were Eliab the firstborn, and next to him Abinadab, and the third Shammah. 14David was the youngest; the three eldest followed Saul, 15but David went back and forth from Saul to feed his father's sheep at Bethlehem. 16For forty days the Philistine came forward and took his stand, morning and evening.

17 Jesse said to his son David, "Take for your brothers an ephah of this parched grain and these ten loaves, and carry them quickly to the camp to your brothers; 18also take these ten cheeses to the commander of their thousand. See how your brothers fare, and bring some token from them."

19 Now Saul, and they, and all the men of Israel, were in the valley of Elah, fighting with the Philistines. 20David rose early in the morning, left the sheep with a keeper, took the provisions, and went as Jesse had commanded him. He came to the encampment as the army was going forth to the battle line, shouting the war cry. 21Israel and the Philistines drew up for battle, army against army. 22David left the things in charge of the keeper of the baggage, ran to the ranks, and went and greeted his brothers. 23As he talked with them, the champion, the Philistine of Gath, Goliath by name, came up out of the ranks of the Philistines, and spoke the same words as before. And David heard him.

24 All the Israelites, when they saw the man, fled from him and were very much afraid. 25The Israelites said, "Have you seen this man who has come up? Surely he has come up to defy Israel. The king will greatly enrich the man who kills him, and will give him his daughter and make his family free in Israel." 26David said to the men who stood by him, "What shall be done for the man who kills this Philistine, and takes away the reproach from Israel? For who is this uncircumcised Philistine that he should defy the armies of the living God?" 27The people answered him in the same way, "So shall it be done for the man who kills him."

28 His eldest brother Eliab heard him talking to the men; and Eliab's anger was kindled against David. He said, "Why have you come down? With whom have you left those few sheep in the wilderness? I know your presumption and the evil of your heart; for you have come down just to see the battle." 29David said, "What have I done now? It was only a question." 30He turned away from him toward another and spoke in the same way; and the people answered him again as before.

31 When the words that David spoke were heard, they repeated them before Saul; and he sent for him. 32David said to Saul, "Let no one's heart fail because of him; your servant will go and fight with this Philistine." 33Saul said to David, "You are not able to go against this Philistine to fight with him; for you are just a boy, and he has been a warrior from his youth." 34But David said to Saul, "Your servant used to keep sheep for his father; and whenever a lion or a bear came, and took a lamb from the flock, 35I went after it and struck it down, rescuing the lamb from its mouth; and if it turned against me, I would catch it by the jaw, strike it down, and kill it. 36Your servant has killed both lions and bears; and this uncircumcised Philistine shall be like one of

God's Plans

1 SAMUEL 17.17–37

This well-known passage describes the most significant turning point in young David's life. Imagine that you are David, given a perfectly ordinary task by your father. Think of the long—and perhaps monotonous—walk to the battlefront. When you arrive, you sense the tension in the air. You smell campfires all around you, hear the sounds of an army, see soldiers everywhere. When you ask a few questions, your brothers tell you about Goliath and his challenge; you hear fear in everyone's voice. You feel the weight of adult armor and know you can hardly move under it. You feel small and weak.

Suddenly you know that God intends for you to take the lead and confront the Philistine giant. Despite all evidence to the contrary, you still are certain that God has work for you to do in this situation.

In your own life today, pray that God will allow you this same certainty of divine guidance when you need it, even in the most unlikely of situations.

See Meeting God in Service

One Smooth Stone Is Enough

1 SAMUEL 17.49

One small stone doesn't seem potent enough to slay a giant, but David's aim is good, and the sling sends the missile at high velocity. Just as a knife with the sharpest possible edge cuts best, the smallest stone, with all of David's prayer-driven energy behind it—sinks into the body of the Philistines' strongest champion.

Take a moment now to think about your weaknesses—not your sins, but those areas in your life where you may not be especially gifted. Perhaps you don't speak well in public (like Moses) or you suffer some physical affliction (like Paul). Think of areas in your life where you feel inadequate. Read 2 Corinthians 12.7–9 where God says to Paul: "My grace is sufficient for you, for power is made perfect in weakness." If it helps, write down the list of weaknesses. Read each one and try to imagine how the power of God can shine through, not merely *despite* that weakness but *because* of it. Offer those weaknesses to God. Ask God to use your weaknesses as well as your strengths.

See *Meeting God in Service*

them, since he has defied the armies of the living God." ³⁷ David said, "The LORD, who saved me from the paw of the lion and from the paw of the bear, will save me from the hand of this Philistine." So Saul said to David, "Go, and may the LORD be with you!"

38 Saul clothed David with his armor; he put a bronze helmet on his head and clothed him with a coat of mail. ³⁹ David strapped Saul's sword over the armor, and he tried in vain to walk, for he was not used to them. Then David said to Saul, "I cannot walk with these; for I am not used to them." So David removed them. ⁴⁰ Then he took his staff in his hand, and chose five smooth stones from the wadi, and put them in his shepherd's bag, in the pouch; his sling was in his hand, and he drew near to the Philistine.

41 The Philistine came on and drew near to David, with his shield-bearer in front of him. ⁴² When the Philistine looked and saw David, he disdained him, for he was only a youth, ruddy and handsome in appearance. ⁴³ The Philistine said to David, "Am I a dog, that you come to me with sticks?" And the Philistine cursed David by his gods. ⁴⁴ The Philistine said to David, "Come to me, and I will give your flesh to the birds of the air and to the wild animals of the field." ⁴⁵ But David said to the Philistine, "You come to me with sword and spear and javelin; but I come to you in the name of the LORD of hosts, the God of the armies of Israel, whom you have defied. ⁴⁶ This very day the LORD will deliver you into my hand, and I will strike you down and cut off your head; and I will give the dead bodies of the Philistine army this very day to the birds of the air and to the wild animals of the earth, so that all the earth may know that there is a God in Israel, ⁴⁷ and that all this assembly may know that the LORD does not save by sword and spear; for the battle is the LORD's and he will give you into our hand."

48 When the Philistine drew nearer to meet David, David ran quickly toward the battle line to meet the Philistine. ⁴⁹ David put his hand in his bag, took out a stone, slung it, and struck the Philistine on his forehead; the stone sank into his forehead, and he fell face down on the ground.

50 So David prevailed over the Philistine with a sling and a stone, striking down the Philistine and killing him; there was no sword in David's hand. ⁵¹ Then David ran and stood over the Philistine; he grasped his sword, drew it out of its sheath, and killed him; then he cut off his head with it.

When the Philistines saw that their champion was dead, they fled. ⁵² The troops of Israel and Judah rose up with a shout and pursued the Philistines as far as Gath^a and the gates of Ekron, so that the wounded Philistines fell on the way from Shaaraim as far as Gath and Ekron. ⁵³ The Israelites came back from chasing the Philistines, and they plundered their camp. ⁵⁴ David took the head of the Philistine and brought it to Jerusalem; but he put his armor in his tent.

55 When Saul saw David go out against the Philistine, he said to Abner, the commander of the army, "Abner, whose son is this young man?" Abner said, "As your soul lives, O king, I do not know." ⁵⁶ The king said, "Inquire whose son the stripling is." ⁵⁷ On David's return from killing the Philistine, Abner took him and brought him before Saul, with the head of the Philistine in his hand. ⁵⁸ Saul said to him,

a Gk Syr: Heb *Gai*

"Whose son are you, young man?" And David answered, "I am the son of your servant Jesse the Bethlehemite."

Jonathan's Covenant with David

18 When David[a] had finished speaking to Saul, the soul of Jonathan was bound to the soul of David, and Jonathan loved him as his own soul. ²Saul took him that day and would not let him return to his father's house. ³Then Jonathan made a covenant with David, because he loved him as his own soul. ⁴Jonathan stripped himself of the robe that he was wearing, and gave it to David, and his armor, and even his sword and his bow and his belt. ⁵David went out and was successful wherever Saul sent him; as a result, Saul set him over the army. And all the people, even the servants of Saul, approved.

6 As they were coming home, when David returned from killing the Philistine, the women came out of all the towns of Israel, singing and dancing, to meet King Saul, with tambourines, with songs of joy, and with musical instruments.[b] ⁷And the women sang to one another as they made merry,

"Saul has killed his thousands,
    and David his ten thousands."

⁸Saul was very angry, for this saying displeased him. He said, "They have ascribed to David ten thousands, and to me they have ascribed thousands; what more can he have but the kingdom?" ⁹So Saul eyed David from that day on.

Saul Tries to Kill David

10 The next day an evil spirit from God rushed upon Saul, and he raved within his house, while David was playing the lyre, as he did day by day. Saul had his spear in his hand; ¹¹and Saul threw the spear, for he thought, "I will pin David to the wall." But David eluded him twice.

12 Saul was afraid of David, because the LORD was with him but had departed from Saul. ¹³So Saul removed him from his presence, and made him a commander of a thousand; and David marched out and came in, leading the army. ¹⁴David had success in all his undertakings; for the LORD was with him. ¹⁵When Saul saw that he had great success, he stood in awe of him. ¹⁶But all Israel and Judah loved David; for it was he who marched out and came in leading them.

David Marries Michal

17 Then Saul said to David, "Here is my elder daughter Merab; I will give her to you as a wife; only be valiant for me and fight the LORD's battles." For Saul thought, "I will not raise a hand against him; let the Philistines deal with him." ¹⁸David said to Saul, "Who am I and who are my kinsfolk, my father's family in Israel, that I should be son-in-law to the king?" ¹⁹But at the time when Saul's daughter Merab should have been given to David, she was given to Adriel the Meholathite as a wife.

20 Now Saul's daughter Michal loved David. Saul was told, and the thing pleased him. ²¹Saul thought, "Let me give her to him that she may be a snare for him and that the hand of the Philistines may be against him." Therefore Saul said to David a second time,[c] "You shall now be

---

Friendship

1 SAMUEL 18.1

"What happiness, what security, what joy to have someone to whom you dare to speak on terms of equality as to another self; one to whom you need have no fear to confess your failings; one to whom you can unblushingly make known what progress you have made in the spiritual life; one to whom you can entrust all the secrets of your heart and before whom you can place all your plans!"

—AELRED OF RIEVAULX,
Spiritual Friendship

See Meeting God in Community

The Corrosiveness of Envy

1 SAMUEL 19.9–10

For Saul, what may have begun as competition now spins out of control on a slippery slope, downhill from envy to attempted murder.

Competition, like many words in English that refer to human relationships, begins with the Latin prefix *com*, meaning "together with." In competition, the "together with" can be wholesome or unhealthy. Make a list, using a dictionary if need be, of a number of relational words beginning with *com*—comrade, compassion and companionable, for example. Consider how each of these words apply to your relationships with several people. Then prayerfully consider how Jesus Christ would view each of these people. How can God help you to keep these relationships free of envy and competitiveness?

See *Meeting God in Community*

my son-in-law." ²²Saul commanded his servants, "Speak to David in private and say, 'See, the king is delighted with you, and all his servants love you; now then, become the king's son-in-law.' " ²³So Saul's servants reported these words to David in private. And David said, "Does it seem to you a little thing to become the king's son-in-law, seeing that I am a poor man and of no repute?" ²⁴The servants of Saul told him, "This is what David said." ²⁵Then Saul said, "Thus shall you say to David, 'The king desires no marriage present except a hundred foreskins of the Philistines, that he may be avenged on the king's enemies.' " Now Saul planned to make David fall by the hand of the Philistines. ²⁶When his servants told David these words, David was well pleased to be the king's son-in-law. Before the time had expired, ²⁷David rose and went, along with his men, and killed one hundred*a* of the Philistines; and David brought their foreskins, which were given in full number to the king, that he might become the king's son-in-law. Saul gave him his daughter Michal as a wife. ²⁸But when Saul realized that the LORD was with David, and that Saul's daughter Michal loved him, ²⁹Saul was still more afraid of David. So Saul was David's enemy from that time forward.

30 Then the commanders of the Philistines came out to battle; and as often as they came out, David had more success than all the servants of Saul, so that his fame became very great.

Jonathan Intercedes for David

19 Saul spoke with his son Jonathan and with all his servants about killing David. But Saul's son Jonathan took great delight in David. ²Jonathan told David, "My father Saul is trying to kill you; therefore be on guard tomorrow morning; stay in a secret place and hide yourself. ³I will go out and stand beside my father in the field where you are, and I will speak to my father about you; if I learn anything I will tell you." ⁴Jonathan spoke well of David to his father Saul, saying to him, "The king should not sin against his servant David, because he has not sinned against you, and because his deeds have been of good service to you; ⁵for he took his life in his hand when he attacked the Philistine, and the LORD brought about a great victory for all Israel. You saw it, and rejoiced; why then will you sin against an innocent person by killing David without cause?" ⁶Saul heeded the voice of Jonathan; Saul swore, "As the LORD lives, he shall not be put to death." ⁷So Jonathan called David and related all these things to him. Jonathan then brought David to Saul, and he was in his presence as before.

Michal Helps David Escape from Saul

8 Again there was war, and David went out to fight the Philistines. He launched a heavy attack on them, so that they fled before him. ⁹Then an evil spirit from the LORD came upon Saul, as he sat in his house with his spear in his hand, while David was playing music. ¹⁰Saul sought to pin David to the wall with the spear; but he eluded Saul, so that he struck the spear into the wall. David fled and escaped that night.

a Gk Compare 2 Sam 3.14: Heb *two hundred*

11 Saul sent messengers to David's house to keep watch over him, planning to kill him in the morning. David's wife Michal told him, "If you do not save your life tonight, tomorrow you will be killed." ¹²So Michal let David down through the window; he fled away and escaped. ¹³Michal took an idol*ᵃ* and laid it on the bed; she put a net*ᵇ* of goats' hair on its head, and covered it with the clothes. ¹⁴When Saul sent messengers to take David, she said, "He is sick." ¹⁵Then Saul sent the messengers to see David for themselves. He said, "Bring him up to me in the bed, that I may kill him." ¹⁶When the messengers came in, the idol*ᶜ* was in the bed, with the covering*ᵇ* of goats' hair on its head. ¹⁷Saul said to Michal, "Why have you deceived me like this, and let my enemy go, so that he has escaped?" Michal answered Saul, "He said to me, 'Let me go; why should I kill you?' "

David Joins Samuel in Ramah

18 Now David fled and escaped; he came to Samuel at Ramah, and told him all that Saul had done to him. He and Samuel went and settled at Naioth. ¹⁹Saul was told, "David is at Naioth in Ramah." ²⁰Then Saul sent messengers to take David. When they saw the company of the prophets in a frenzy, with Samuel standing in charge of*ᵇ* them, the spirit of God came upon the messengers of Saul, and they also fell into a prophetic frenzy. ²¹When Saul was told, he sent other messengers, and they also fell into a frenzy. Saul sent messengers again the third time, and they also fell into a frenzy. ²²Then he himself went to Ramah. He came to the great well that is in Secu;*ᵈ* he asked, "Where are Samuel and David?" And someone said, "They are at Naioth in Ramah." ²³He went there, toward Naioth in Ramah; and the spirit of God came upon him. As he was going, he fell into a prophetic frenzy, until he came to Naioth in Ramah. ²⁴He too stripped off his clothes, and he too fell into a frenzy before Samuel. He lay naked all that day and all that night. Therefore it is said, "Is Saul also among the prophets?"

The Friendship of David and Jonathan

20 David fled from Naioth in Ramah. He came before Jonathan and said, "What have I done? What is my guilt? And what is my sin against your father that he is trying to take my life?" ²He said to him, "Far from it! You shall not die. My father does nothing either great or small without disclosing it to me; and why should my father hide this from me? Never!" ³But David also swore, "Your father knows well that you like me; and he thinks, 'Do not let Jonathan know this, or he will be grieved.' But truly, as the LORD lives and as you yourself live, there is but a step between me and death." ⁴Then Jonathan said to David, "Whatever you say, I will do for you." ⁵David said to Jonathan, "Tomorrow is the new moon, and I should not fail to sit with the king at the meal; but let me go, so that I may hide in the field until the third evening. ⁶If your father misses me at all, then say, 'David earnestly asked leave of me to run to Bethlehem his city; for there is a yearly sacrifice there for all the family.' ⁷If he says, 'Good!' it will be well with your servant; but if he is angry, then know that evil has

The Spirit's Power

1 SAMUEL 19.23

Soldiers sent to capture David fail in their assignment, but the Spirit of God invades their hearts. So it is with two other groups, and finally Saul himself ventures to handle the matter—and he too is caught up in the Spirit power.

Recall the feelings that accompanied a profound spiritual experience you may have had—an awakening to God, a sense of God's call, your conversion to Jesus Christ as your Savior and Lord. What commitments did you make in such a moment? Did you share your excitement with others? How long did you keep reminding yourself that something special had occurred? How have those feelings and commitments changed since then? In what ways do you now seek the Spirit's refreshment?

See Meeting God in Everyday Life

---

a Heb *took the teraphim*   *b* Meaning of Heb uncertain   *c* Heb *the teraphim*   *d* Gk reads *to the well of the threshing floor on the bare height*

Spiritual Murder

1 SAMUEL 20.30–32

"It may be infinitely less evil to murder a man than to refuse to forgive him. The former may be an act of a moment of passion: the latter is the heart's choice. It is spiritual murder, the worst, to hate, to brood over the feeling that excludes, that, in our microcosm, kills the image, the idea of the hated."

—GEORGE MACDONALD

George MacDonald, 365 Readings

been determined by him. ⁸Therefore deal kindly with your servant, for you have brought your servant into a sacred covenant*a* with you. But if there is guilt in me, kill me yourself; why should you bring me to your father?" ⁹Jonathan said, "Far be it from you! If I knew that it was decided by my father that evil should come upon you, would I not tell you?" ¹⁰Then David said to Jonathan, "Who will tell me if your father answers you harshly?" ¹¹Jonathan replied to David, "Come, let us go out into the field." So they both went out into the field.

12 Jonathan said to David, "By the LORD, the God of Israel! When I have sounded out my father, about this time tomorrow, or on the third day, if he is well disposed toward David, shall I not then send and disclose it to you? ¹³But if my father intends to do you harm, the LORD do so to Jonathan, and more also, if I do not disclose it to you, and send you away, so that you may go in safety. May the LORD be with you, as he has been with my father. ¹⁴If I am still alive, show me the faithful love of the LORD; but if I die,*b* ¹⁵never cut off your faithful love from my house, even if the LORD were to cut off every one of the enemies of David from the face of the earth." ¹⁶Thus Jonathan made a covenant with the house of David, saying, "May the LORD seek out the enemies of David." ¹⁷Jonathan made David swear again by his love for him; for he loved him as he loved his own life.

18 Jonathan said to him, "Tomorrow is the new moon; you will be missed, because your place will be empty. ¹⁹On the day after tomorrow, you shall go a long way down; go to the place where you hid yourself earlier, and remain beside the stone there.*b* ²⁰I will shoot three arrows to the side of it, as though I shot at a mark. ²¹Then I will send the boy, saying, 'Go, find the arrows.' If I say to the boy, 'Look, the arrows are on this side of you, collect them,' then you are to come, for, as the LORD lives, it is safe for you and there is no danger. ²²But if I say to the young man, 'Look, the arrows are beyond you,' then go; for the LORD has sent you away. ²³As for the matter about which you and I have spoken, the LORD is witness*c* between you and me forever."

24 So David hid himself in the field. When the new moon came, the king sat at the feast to eat. ²⁵The king sat upon his seat, as at other times, upon the seat by the wall. Jonathan stood, while Abner sat by Saul's side; but David's place was empty.

26 Saul did not say anything that day; for he thought, "Something has befallen him; he is not clean, surely he is not clean." ²⁷But on the second day, the day after the new moon, David's place was empty. And Saul said to his son Jonathan, "Why has the son of Jesse not come to the feast, either yesterday or today?" ²⁸Jonathan answered Saul, "David earnestly asked leave of me to go to Bethlehem; ²⁹he said, 'Let me go; for our family is holding a sacrifice in the city, and my brother has commanded me to be there. So now, if I have found favor in your sight, let me get away, and see my brothers.' For this reason he has not come to the king's table."

30 Then Saul's anger was kindled against Jonathan. He said to him, "You son of a perverse, rebellious woman! Do I not know that you have chosen the son of Jesse to your

a Heb *a covenant of the LORD*   *b* Meaning of Heb uncertain   *c* Gk: Heb lacks *witness* own shame, and to the shame of your mother's nakedness? ³¹For as long as the son of Jesse lives upon the earth, neither you nor your kingdom shall be established. Now send and bring him to me, for he shall surely die." ³²Then Jonathan answered his father Saul, "Why should he be put to death? What has he done?" ³³But Saul threw his spear at him to strike him; so Jonathan knew that it was the decision of his father to put David to death. ³⁴Jonathan rose from the table in fierce anger and ate no food on the second day of the month, for he was grieved for David, and because his father had disgraced him.

35 In the morning Jonathan went out into the field to the appointment with David, and with him was a little boy. ³⁶He said to the boy, "Run and find the arrows that I shoot." As the boy ran, he shot an arrow beyond him. ³⁷When the boy came to the place where Jonathan's arrow had fallen, Jonathan called after the boy and said, "Is the arrow not beyond you?" ³⁸Jonathan called after the boy, "Hurry, be quick, do not linger." So Jonathan's boy gathered up the arrows and came to his master. ³⁹But the boy knew nothing; only Jonathan and David knew the arrangement. ⁴⁰Jonathan gave his weapons to the boy and said to him, "Go and carry them to the city." ⁴¹As soon as the boy had gone, David rose from beside the stone heap*a* and prostrated himself with his face to the ground. He bowed three times, and they kissed each other, and wept with each other; David wept the more.*b* ⁴²Then Jonathan said to David, "Go in peace, since both of us have sworn in the name of the LORD, saying, 'The LORD shall be between me and you, and between my descendants and your descendants, forever.' " He got up and left; and Jonathan went into the city.*c*

David and the Holy Bread

21 *d* David came to Nob to the priest Ahimelech. Ahimelech came trembling to meet David, and said to him, "Why are you alone, and no one with you?" ²David said to the priest Ahimelech, "The king has charged me with a matter, and said to me, 'No one must know anything of the matter about which I send you, and with which I have charged you.' I have made an appointment*e* with the young men for such and such a place. ³Now then, what have you at hand? Give me five loaves of bread, or whatever is here." ⁴The priest answered David, "I have no ordinary bread at hand, only holy bread—provided that the young men have kept themselves from women." ⁵David answered the priest, "Indeed women have been kept from us as always when I go on an expedition; the vessels of the young men are holy even when it is a common journey; how much more today will their vessels be holy?" ⁶So the priest gave him the holy bread; for there was no bread there except the bread of the Presence, which is removed from before the LORD, to be replaced by hot bread on the day it is taken away.

7 Now a certain man of the servants of Saul was there that day, detained before the LORD; his name was Doeg the Edomite, the chief of Saul's shepherds.

8 David said to Ahimelech, "Is there no spear or sword

The Gift of Hospitality

> 1 SAMUEL 21.4–6

The priest gave David the "bread of the Presence" to feed his hungry men. This bread was a sign of hospitality, presented as a meal to a God who did not eat! Hospitality to hungry humans took precedence over symbolic hospitality to God when the priest had validated David's motives and honesty. Just so, *The Rule of Saint Benedict*, for centuries the basis of monastic life, reads, "All guests . . . are to be welcomed as Christ" (chapter 53). What physical signs around your home convey to others that they are truly welcomed? Do you have a clear address number, a door ornament, color around your entryway, a doormat announcing "Welcome" or your family name, a doorbell that works? How do you express welcome and hospitality? Is there a cordial answering of the telephone, a courteous greeting of even unexpected arrivals, a welcoming refreshment? Consider what more you might do to welcome all guests as Christ.

See Meeting God in Community

---

a Gk: Heb *from beside the south*   *b* Vg: Meaning of Heb uncertain   *c* This sentence is 21.1 in Heb   *d* Ch 21.2 in Heb   *e* Q Ms Vg Compare Gk: Meaning of MT uncertain

Really Together

1 SAMUEL 22.2

David gathered about him "everyone who was in distress, and everyone who was in debt, and everyone who was discontented . . . and he became captain over them. Those who were with him numbered about four hundred." Another great leader, Martin Luther King, Jr., in a speech on August 28, 1963, saw a similar gathering: "I have a dream that one day on the red hills of Georgia the sons of former slaves and the sons of former slave owners will be able to sit down together at the table of brotherhood." Thank God for the ways in which common needs or common causes draw you and others together.

See Meeting God in Community

here with you? I did not bring my sword or my weapons with me, because the king's business required haste." ⁹The priest said, "The sword of Goliath the Philistine, whom you killed in the valley of Elah, is here wrapped in a cloth behind the ephod; if you will take that, take it, for there is none here except that one." David said, "There is none like it; give it to me."

David Flees to Gath

10 David rose and fled that day from Saul; he went to King Achish of Gath. ¹¹The servants of Achish said to him, "Is this not David the king of the land? Did they not sing to one another of him in dances,

'Saul has killed his thousands,
and David his ten thousands'?"

¹²David took these words to heart and was very much afraid of King Achish of Gath. ¹³So he changed his behavior before them; he pretended to be mad when in their presence.ᵃ He scratched marks on the doors of the gate, and let his spittle run down his beard. ¹⁴Achish said to his servants, "Look, you see the man is mad; why then have you brought him to me? ¹⁵Do I lack madmen, that you have brought this fellow to play the madman in my presence? Shall this fellow come into my house?"

David and His Followers at Adullam

22 David left there and escaped to the cave of Adullam; when his brothers and all his father's house heard of it, they went down there to him. ²Everyone who was in distress, and everyone who was in debt, and everyone who was discontented gathered to him; and he became captain over them. Those who were with him numbered about four hundred.

3 David went from there to Mizpeh of Moab. He said to the king of Moab, "Please let my father and mother comeᵇ to you, until I know what God will do for me." ⁴He left them with the king of Moab, and they stayed with him all the time that David was in the stronghold. ⁵Then the prophet Gad said to David, "Do not remain in the stronghold; leave, and go into the land of Judah." So David left, and went into the forest of Hereth.

Saul Slaughters the Priests at Nob

6 Saul heard that David and those who were with him had been located. Saul was sitting at Gibeah, under the tamarisk tree on the height, with his spear in his hand, and all his servants were standing around him. ⁷Saul said to his servants who stood around him, "Hear now, you Benjaminites; will the son of Jesse give every one of you fields and vineyards, will he make you all commanders of thousands and commanders of hundreds? ⁸Is that why all of you have conspired against me? No one discloses to me when my son makes a league with the son of Jesse, none of you is sorry for me or discloses to me that my son has stirred up my servant against me, to lie in wait, as he is doing today." ⁹Doeg the Edomite, who was in charge of Saul's servants, answered, "I saw the son of Jesse coming to Nob, to Ahimelech son of Ahitub; ¹⁰he inquired of the

a Heb *in their hands*   *b* Syr Vg: Heb *come out*

LORD for him, gave him provisions, and gave him the sword of Goliath the Philistine."

11 The king sent for the priest Ahimelech son of Ahitub and for all his father's house, the priests who were at Nob; and all of them came to the king. ¹²Saul said, "Listen now, son of Ahitub." He answered, "Here I am, my lord." ¹³Saul said to him, "Why have you conspired against me, you and the son of Jesse, by giving him bread and a sword, and by inquiring of God for him, so that he has risen against me, to lie in wait, as he is doing today?"

14 Then Ahimelech answered the king, "Who among all your servants is so faithful as David? He is the king's son-in-law, and is quick*ᵃ* to do your bidding, and is honored in your house. ¹⁵Is today the first time that I have inquired of God for him? By no means! Do not let the king impute anything to his servant or to any member of my father's house; for your servant has known nothing of all this, much or little." ¹⁶The king said, "You shall surely die, Ahimelech, you and all your father's house." ¹⁷The king said to the guard who stood around him, "Turn and kill the priests of the LORD, because their hand also is with David; they knew that he fled, and did not disclose it to me." But the servants of the king would not raise their hand to attack the priests of the LORD. ¹⁸Then the king said to Doeg, "You, Doeg, turn and attack the priests." Doeg the Edomite turned and attacked the priests; on that day he killed eighty-five who wore the linen ephod. ¹⁹Nob, the city of the priests, he put to the sword; men and women, children and infants, oxen, donkeys, and sheep, he put to the sword.

20 But one of the sons of Ahimelech son of Ahitub, named Abiathar, escaped and fled after David. ²¹Abiathar told David that Saul had killed the priests of the LORD. ²²David said to Abiathar, "I knew on that day, when Doeg the Edomite was there, that he would surely tell Saul. I am responsible*ᵇ* for the lives of all your father's house. ²³Stay with me, and do not be afraid; for the one who seeks my life seeks your life; you will be safe with me."

David Saves the City of Keilah

23 Now they told David, "The Philistines are fighting against Keilah, and are robbing the threshing floors." ²David inquired of the LORD, "Shall I go and attack these Philistines?" The LORD said to David, "Go and attack the Philistines and save Keilah." ³But David's men said to him, "Look, we are afraid here in Judah; how much more then if we go to Keilah against the armies of the Philistines?" ⁴Then David inquired of the LORD again. The LORD answered him, "Yes, go down to Keilah; for I will give the Philistines into your hand." ⁵So David and his men went to Keilah, fought with the Philistines, brought away their livestock, and dealt them a heavy defeat. Thus David rescued the inhabitants of Keilah.

6 When Abiathar son of Ahimelech fled to David at Keilah, he came down with an ephod in his hand. ⁷Now it was told Saul that David had come to Keilah. And Saul said, "God has given*ᶜ* him into my hand; for he has shut himself in by entering a town that has gates and bars." ⁸Saul summoned all the people to war, to go down to Keilah, to be-

Timely Guidance

1 SAMUEL 23.6–9

When David seeks guidance from God by means of the mysterious ephod about what Saul will do next, he is rewarded with clear answers. Have you ever had an experience where you seemed clearly guided by the Spirit about a situation in your life? How did the guidance come—through an idea, dream, feeling, friend or passage of scripture? When you are in difficulty or in a quandary, what or whom do you consult to find trustworthy guidance? Make a list of the ways you feel God provides guidance to human beings, and notice which ones you have experienced yourself.

a Heb *and turns aside*   *b* Gk Vg: Meaning of Heb uncertain   *c* Gk Tg: Heb *made a stranger of*

Guides for the Soul

1 SAMUEL 23.16–18

"In the Book of Proverbs it says, 'Those who have no guidance fall like leaves but there is safety in much counsel' [see Proverbs 11.14]. Take a good look at this saying. Brothers, look at what Scripture is teaching us. It assures us that we should not set ourselves up as guide posts, that we should not consider ourselves sagacious, that we should not believe we can direct ourselves. We need assistance, we need guidance in addition to God's grace. No one is more wretched, no one is more easily caught unawares, than a man who has no one to guide him along the road to God."

—DOROTHEOS OF GAZA,
Discourses and Sayings

See Meeting God in Community

siege David and his men. [9]When David learned that Saul was plotting evil against him, he said to the priest Abiathar, "Bring the ephod here." [10]David said, "O LORD, the God of Israel, your servant has heard that Saul seeks to come to Keilah, to destroy the city on my account. [11]And now, will[a] Saul come down as your servant has heard? O LORD, the God of Israel, I beseech you, tell your servant." The LORD said, "He will come down." [12]Then David said, "Will the men of Keilah surrender me and my men into the hand of Saul?" The LORD said, "They will surrender you." [13]Then David and his men, who were about six hundred, set out and left Keilah; they wandered wherever they could go. When Saul was told that David had escaped from Keilah, he gave up the expedition. [14]David remained in the strongholds in the wilderness, in the hill country of the Wilderness of Ziph. Saul sought him every day, but the LORD[b] did not give him into his hand.

David Eludes Saul in the Wilderness

15 David was in the Wilderness of Ziph at Horesh when he learned that[c] Saul had come out to seek his life. [16]Saul's son Jonathan set out and came to David at Horesh; there he strengthened his hand through the LORD.[d] [17]He said to him, "Do not be afraid; for the hand of my father Saul shall not find you; you shall be king over Israel, and I shall be second to you; my father Saul also knows that this is so." [18]Then the two of them made a covenant before the LORD; David remained at Horesh, and Jonathan went home.

19 Then some Ziphites went up to Saul at Gibeah and said, "David is hiding among us in the strongholds of Horesh, on the hill of Hachilah, which is south of Jeshimon. [20]Now, O king, whenever you wish to come down, do so; and our part will be to surrender him into the king's hand." [21]Saul said, "May you be blessed by the LORD for showing me compassion! [22]Go and make sure once more; find out exactly where he is, and who has seen him there; for I am told that he is very cunning. [23]Look around and learn all the hiding places where he lurks, and come back to me with sure information. Then I will go with you; and if he is in the land, I will search him out among all the thousands of Judah." [24]So they set out and went to Ziph ahead of Saul.

David and his men were in the wilderness of Maon, in the Arabah to the south of Jeshimon. [25]Saul and his men went to search for him. When David was told, he went down to the rock and stayed in the wilderness of Maon. When Saul heard that, he pursued David into the wilderness of Maon. [26]Saul went on one side of the mountain, and David and his men on the other side of the mountain. David was hurrying to get away from Saul, while Saul and his men were closing in on David and his men to capture them. [27]Then a messenger came to Saul, saying, "Hurry and come; for the Philistines have made a raid on the land." [28]So Saul stopped pursuing David, and went against the Philistines; therefore that place was called the Rock of Escape.[e] [29]David then went up from there, and lived in the strongholds of En-gedi.

a Q Ms Compare Gk: MT *Will the men of Keilah surrender me into his hand? Will* *b* Q Ms Gk: MT *God* *c* Or *saw that* *d* Compare Q Ms Gk: MT *God* *e* Or *Rock of Division*; Meaning of Heb uncertain *f* Ch 24.1 in Heb

David Spares Saul's Life

24 When Saul returned from following the Philistines, he was told, "David is in the wilderness of En-gedi." ²Then Saul took three thousand chosen men out of all Israel, and went to look for David and his men in the direction of the Rocks of the Wild Goats. ³He came to the sheepfolds beside the road, where there was a cave; and Saul went in to relieve himself.ᵃ Now David and his men were sitting in the innermost parts of the cave. ⁴The men of David said to him, "Here is the day of which the LORD said to you, 'I will give your enemy into your hand, and you shall do to him as it seems good to you.' " Then David went and stealthily cut off a corner of Saul's cloak. ⁵Afterward David was stricken to the heart because he had cut off a corner of Saul's cloak. ⁶He said to his men, "The LORD forbid that I should do this thing to my lord, the LORD's anointed, to raise my hand against him; for he is the LORD's anointed." ⁷So David scolded his men severely and did not permit them to attack Saul. Then Saul got up and left the cave, and went on his way.

8 Afterwards David also rose up and went out of the cave and called after Saul, "My lord the king!" When Saul looked behind him, David bowed with his face to the ground, and did obeisance. ⁹David said to Saul, "Why do you listen to the words of those who say, 'David seeks to do you harm'? ¹⁰This very day your eyes have seen how the LORD gave you into my hand in the cave; and some urged me to kill you, but I sparedᵇ you. I said, 'I will not raise my hand against my lord; for he is the LORD's anointed.' ¹¹See, my father, see the corner of your cloak in my hand; for by the fact that I cut off the corner of your cloak, and did not kill you, you may know for certain that there is no wrong or treason in my hands. I have not sinned against you, though you are hunting me to take my life. ¹²May the LORD judge between me and you! May the LORD avenge me on you; but my hand shall not be against you. ¹³As the ancient proverb says, 'Out of the wicked comes forth wickedness'; but my hand shall not be against you. ¹⁴Against whom has the king of Israel come out? Whom do you pursue? A dead dog? A single flea? ¹⁵May the LORD therefore be judge, and give sentence between me and you. May he see to it, and plead my cause, and vindicate me against you."

16 When David had finished speaking these words to Saul, Saul said, "Is this your voice, my son David?" Saul lifted up his voice and wept. ¹⁷He said to David, "You are more righteous than I; for you have repaid me good, whereas I have repaid you evil. ¹⁸Today you have explained how you have dealt well with me, in that you did not kill me when the LORD put me into your hands. ¹⁹For who has ever found an enemy, and sent the enemy safely away? So may the LORD reward you with good for what you have done to me this day. ²⁰Now I know that you shall surely be king, and that the kingdom of Israel shall be established in your hand. ²¹Swear to me therefore by the LORD that you will not cut off my descendants after me, and that you will not wipe out my name from my father's house." ²²So David swore this to Saul. Then Saul went home; but David and his men went up to the stronghold.

ᵃ Heb *to cover his feet* ᵇ Gk Syr Tg Vg: Heb *it* (my eye) *spared*

God's Judgment in Relationships

1 SAMUEL 24.15

David, not swayed by his troops who want him to dispatch the erratic King Saul (see 24.4), leaves the judgment up to God, saying "May the LORD therefore be judge, and give sentence between me and you." He expects God to act decisively to vindicate him in the face of Saul's attack.

How do you think God's judgment works in day-to-day life? How, and for what reasons, does God judge and decide between people? How is that judgment made manifest? Through arguments and disagreements? In court decisions? By the Spirit's work in the innermost conscience? In what ways does God's judgment feel hard and painful to you? In what ways is God's judgment constructive? Make a list of the ways judgment from God can be constructive and life-giving.

See Meeting God in Community

Intercession That Makes for Peace

1 SAMUEL 25.2–37

"O God, you made us in your own image and redeemed us through Jesus your Son: Look with compassion on the whole human family; take away the arrogance and hatred which infect our hearts; break down the walls that separate us; unite us in bonds of love; and work through our struggle and confusion to accomplish your purposes on earth; that, in your good time, all nations and races may serve you in harmony around your heavenly throne; through Jesus Christ our Lord."

—"Prayer for the Human Family,"
The Episcopal *Book of Common Prayer*

Death of Samuel

25 Now Samuel died; and all Israel assembled and mourned for him. They buried him at his home in Ramah.

Then David got up and went down to the wilderness of Paran.

David and the Wife of Nabal

2 There was a man in Maon, whose property was in Carmel. The man was very rich; he had three thousand sheep and a thousand goats. He was shearing his sheep in Carmel. ³Now the name of the man was Nabal, and the name of his wife Abigail. The woman was clever and beautiful, but the man was surly and mean; he was a Calebite. ⁴David heard in the wilderness that Nabal was shearing his sheep. ⁵So David sent ten young men; and David said to the young men, "Go up to Carmel, and go to Nabal, and greet him in my name. ⁶Thus you shall salute him: 'Peace be to you, and peace be to your house, and peace be to all that you have. ⁷I hear that you have shearers; now your shepherds have been with us, and we did them no harm, and they missed nothing, all the time they were in Carmel. ⁸Ask your young men, and they will tell you. Therefore let my young men find favor in your sight; for we have come on a feast day. Please give whatever you have at hand to your servants and to your son David.'"

9 When David's young men came, they said all this to Nabal in the name of David; and then they waited. ¹⁰But Nabal answered David's servants, "Who is David? Who is the son of Jesse? There are many servants today who are breaking away from their masters. ¹¹Shall I take my bread and my water and the meat that I have butchered for my shearers, and give it to men who come from I do not know where?" ¹²So David's young men turned away, and came back and told him all this. ¹³David said to his men, "Every man strap on his sword!" And every one of them strapped on his sword; David also strapped on his sword; and about four hundred men went up after David, while two hundred remained with the baggage.

14 But one of the young men told Abigail, Nabal's wife, "David sent messengers out of the wilderness to salute our master; and he shouted insults at them. ¹⁵Yet the men were very good to us, and we suffered no harm, and we never missed anything when we were in the fields, as long as we were with them; ¹⁶they were a wall to us both by night and by day, all the while we were with them keeping the sheep. ¹⁷Now therefore know this and consider what you should do; for evil has been decided against our master and against all his house; he is so ill-natured that no one can speak to him."

18 Then Abigail hurried and took two hundred loaves, two skins of wine, five sheep ready dressed, five measures of parched grain, one hundred clusters of raisins, and two hundred cakes of figs. She loaded them on donkeys ¹⁹and said to her young men, "Go on ahead of me; I am coming after you." But she did not tell her husband Nabal. ²⁰As she rode on the donkey and came down under cover of the mountain, David and his men came down toward her; and she met them. ²¹Now David had said, "Surely it was in vain that I protected all that this fellow has in the wilderness, so that nothing was missed of all that belonged to him; but he

has returned me evil for good. ²²God do so to David[a] and more also, if by morning I leave so much as one male of all who belong to him."

23 When Abigail saw David, she hurried and alighted from the donkey, and fell before David on her face, bowing to the ground. ²⁴She fell at his feet and said, "Upon me alone, my lord, be the guilt; please let your servant speak in your ears, and hear the words of your servant. ²⁵My lord, do not take seriously this ill-natured fellow, Nabal; for as his name is, so is he; Nabal[b] is his name, and folly is with him; but I, your servant, did not see the young men of my lord, whom you sent.

26 "Now then, my lord, as the Lord lives, and as you yourself live, since the Lord has restrained you from blood-guilt and from taking vengeance with your own hand, now let your enemies and those who seek to do evil to my lord be like Nabal. ²⁷And now let this present that your servant has brought to my lord be given to the young men who follow my lord. ²⁸Please forgive the trespass of your servant; for the Lord will certainly make my lord a sure house, because my lord is fighting the battles of the Lord; and evil shall not be found in you so long as you live. ²⁹If anyone should rise up to pursue you and to seek your life, the life of my lord shall be bound in the bundle of the living under the care of the Lord your God; but the lives of your enemies he shall sling out as from the hollow of a sling. ³⁰When the Lord has done to my lord according to all the good that he has spoken concerning you, and has appointed you prince over Israel, ³¹my lord shall have no cause of grief, or pangs of conscience, for having shed blood without cause or for having saved himself. And when the Lord has dealt well with my lord, then remember your servant."

32 David said to Abigail, "Blessed be the Lord, the God of Israel, who sent you to meet me today! ³³Blessed be your good sense, and blessed be you, who have kept me today from bloodguilt and from avenging myself by my own hand! ³⁴For as surely as the Lord the God of Israel lives, who has restrained me from hurting you, unless you had hurried and come to meet me, truly by morning there would not have been left to Nabal so much as one male." ³⁵Then David received from her hand what she had brought him; he said to her, "Go up to your house in peace; see, I have heeded your voice, and I have granted your petition."

36 Abigail came to Nabal; he was holding a feast in his house, like the feast of a king. Nabal's heart was merry within him, for he was very drunk; so she told him nothing at all until the morning light. ³⁷In the morning, when the wine had gone out of Nabal, his wife told him these things, and his heart died within him; he became like a stone. ³⁸About ten days later the Lord struck Nabal, and he died.

39 When David heard that Nabal was dead, he said, "Blessed be the Lord who has judged the case of Nabal's insult to me, and has kept back his servant from evil; the Lord has returned the evildoing of Nabal upon his own head." Then David sent and wooed Abigail, to make her his wife. ⁴⁰When David's servants came to Abigail at Carmel, they said to her, "David has sent us to you to take you to him as his wife." ⁴¹She rose and bowed down, with her face to the ground, and said, "Your servant is a slave to wash the feet of

The Power of Goodness

1 SAMUEL 25.32–33

Reinhold Niebuhr wrote in *Beyond Tragedy*: "Goodness, armed with power, is corrupted; and pure love without power is destroyed." Abigail's sensible intercession saves David from misusing his power by launching a bloodbath. As his temper subsides, David realizes that Abigail's transparent goodness has brought about this change of heart.

Recall one or more persons who have brought such goodness into your life, perhaps saving you from an unwise or destructive course of action. Calling upon this lived experience, make a list of the attributes of a "good person." Prudence might be one, and gentleness another; try to think of at least ten other qualities. Prayerfully consider how you might cultivate such virtues.

See Meeting God in Community

Holy Reading

1 SAMUEL 26.5–25

Slowly read the story of David's encounter with Saul and Abner, looking for a word or phrase that attracts you. Then close your eyes and repeat it silently. Be open to what comes into your mind—other words, feelings, images, even sensations of touch and smell—in association with the word or phrase. What might the Spirit be trying to bring to your mind by guiding you to this word or phrase? For the next few days, be receptive to an invitation from God about how you might live or what you might do.

See Meeting God in Scripture

the servants of my lord." [42]Abigail got up hurriedly and rode away on a donkey; her five maids attended her. She went after the messengers of David and became his wife.

43 David also married Ahinoam of Jezreel; both of them became his wives. [44]Saul had given his daughter Michal, David's wife, to Palti son of Laish, who was from Gallim.

David Spares Saul's Life a Second Time

26 Then the Ziphites came to Saul at Gibeah, saying, "David is in hiding on the hill of Hachilah, which is opposite Jeshimon."[a] [2]So Saul rose and went down to the Wilderness of Ziph, with three thousand chosen men of Israel, to seek David in the Wilderness of Ziph. [3]Saul encamped on the hill of Hachilah, which is opposite Jeshimon[a] beside the road. But David remained in the wilderness. When he learned that Saul had come after him into the wilderness, [4]David sent out spies, and learned that Saul had indeed arrived. [5]Then David set out and came to the place where Saul had encamped; and David saw the place where Saul lay, with Abner son of Ner, the commander of his army. Saul was lying within the encampment, while the army was encamped around him.

6 Then David said to Ahimelech the Hittite, and to Joab's brother Abishai son of Zeruiah, "Who will go down with me into the camp to Saul?" Abishai said, "I will go down with you." [7]So David and Abishai went to the army by night; there Saul lay sleeping within the encampment, with his spear stuck in the ground at his head; and Abner and the army lay around him. [8]Abishai said to David, "God has given your enemy into your hand today; now therefore let me pin him to the ground with one stroke of the spear; I will not strike him twice." [9]But David said to Abishai, "Do not destroy him; for who can raise his hand against the LORD's anointed, and be guiltless?" [10]David said, "As the LORD lives, the LORD will strike him down; or his day will come to die; or he will go down into battle and perish. [11]The LORD forbid that I should raise my hand against the LORD's anointed; but now take the spear that is at his head, and the water jar, and let us go." [12]So David took the spear that was at Saul's head and the water jar, and they went away. No one saw it, or knew it, nor did anyone awake; for they were all asleep, because a deep sleep from the LORD had fallen upon them.

13 Then David went over to the other side, and stood on top of a hill far away, with a great distance between them. [14]David called to the army and to Abner son of Ner, saying, "Abner! Will you not answer?" Then Abner replied, "Who are you that calls to the king?" [15]David said to Abner, "Are you not a man? Who is like you in Israel? Why then have you not kept watch over your lord the king? For one of the people came in to destroy your lord the king. [16]This thing that you have done is not good. As the LORD lives, you deserve to die, because you have not kept watch over your lord, the LORD's anointed. See now, where is the king's spear, or the water jar that was at his head?"

17 Saul recognized David's voice, and said, "Is this your voice, my son David?" David said, "It is my voice, my lord, O king." [18]And he added, "Why does my lord pursue his servant? For what have I done? What guilt is on my hands?

a Or opposite the wasteland

[19] Now therefore let my lord the king hear the words of his servant. If it is the LORD who has stirred you up against me, may he accept an offering; but if it is mortals, may they be cursed before the LORD, for they have driven me out today from my share in the heritage of the LORD, saying, 'Go, serve other gods.' [20] Now therefore, do not let my blood fall to the ground, away from the presence of the LORD; for the king of Israel has come out to seek a single flea, like one who hunts a partridge in the mountains."

21 Then Saul said, "I have done wrong; come back, my son David, for I will never harm you again, because my life was precious in your sight today; I have been a fool, and have made a great mistake." [22] David replied, "Here is the spear, O king! Let one of the young men come over and get it. [23] The LORD rewards everyone for his righteousness and his faithfulness; for the LORD gave you into my hand today, but I would not raise my hand against the LORD's anointed. [24] As your life was precious today in my sight, so may my life be precious in the sight of the LORD, and may he rescue me from all tribulation." [25] Then Saul said to David, "Blessed be you, my son David! You will do many things and will succeed in them." So David went his way, and Saul returned to his place.

David Serves King Achish of Gath

27 David said in his heart, "I shall now perish one day by the hand of Saul; there is nothing better for me than to escape to the land of the Philistines; then Saul will despair of seeking me any longer within the borders of Israel, and I shall escape out of his hand." [2] So David set out and went over, he and the six hundred men who were with him, to King Achish son of Maoch of Gath. [3] David stayed with Achish at Gath, he and his troops, every man with his household, and David with his two wives, Ahinoam of Jezreel, and Abigail of Carmel, Nabal's widow. [4] When Saul was told that David had fled to Gath, he no longer sought for him.

5 Then David said to Achish, "If I have found favor in your sight, let a place be given me in one of the country towns, so that I may live there; for why should your servant live in the royal city with you?" [6] So that day Achish gave him Ziklag; therefore Ziklag has belonged to the kings of Judah to this day. [7] The length of time that David lived in the country of the Philistines was one year and four months.

8 Now David and his men went up and made raids on the Geshurites, the Girzites, and the Amalekites; for these were the landed settlements from Telam[a] on the way to Shur and on to the land of Egypt. [9] David struck the land, leaving neither man nor woman alive, but took away the sheep, the oxen, the donkeys, the camels, and the clothing, and came back to Achish. [10] When Achish asked, "Against whom[b] have you made a raid today?" David would say, "Against the Negeb of Judah," or "Against the Negeb of the Jerahmeelites," or, "Against the Negeb of the Kenites." [11] David left neither man nor woman alive to be brought back to Gath, thinking, "They might tell about us, and say, 'David has done so and so.'" Such was his practice all the time he lived in the country of the Philistines. [12] Achish trusted David, thinking, "He has made himself utterly ab-

---

To Whom Vengeance Belongs

1 SAMUEL 26.21–25

Saul responds, although only temporarily, with insight when David consistently refrains from vengeance, even when opportunity puts Saul at his mercy. David's respect, even kindness, touches Saul's heart. Have you ever received mercy when vengeance might have been an understandable response? How did it feel? Did it change your behavior? Have you ever felt such grace from God—a generous goodness in the face of your hostile or heedless behavior? Bring a person who has hurt you, or sought to harm you, into your heart and mind now. Consider that person in the light of God's mercy to you, and shed that light on him or her.

See Meeting God in Prayer

---

a Compare Gk 15.4: Heb *from of old*   *b* Q Ms Gk Vg: MT lacks *whom*

Abandoned by God?

1 SAMUEL 28.5–15

Saul, knowing that God has abandoned him, is desperate enough to disturb the departed Samuel by consulting a medium. Lonely and afraid, he tells Samuel, "God has turned away from me and answers me no more, either by prophets or by dreams."

How do you feel when God seems absent? What's missing when God seems far away? What is your understanding of such a situation? Do you feel God has actually left you, or do you assume that arid periods are a natural part of the ups and downs of any spiritual journey? What do you do to continue your relationship with God when you feel out of touch?

See *Meeting God in Prayer*

horrent to his people Israel; therefore he shall always be my servant."

28 In those days the Philistines gathered their forces for war, to fight against Israel. Achish said to David, "You know, of course, that you and your men are to go out with me in the army." ²David said to Achish, "Very well, then you shall know what your servant can do." Achish said to David, "Very well, I will make you my bodyguard for life."

Saul Consults a Medium

3 Now Samuel had died, and all Israel had mourned for him and buried him in Ramah, his own city. Saul had expelled the mediums and the wizards from the land. ⁴The Philistines assembled, and came and encamped at Shunem. Saul gathered all Israel, and they encamped at Gilboa. ⁵When Saul saw the army of the Philistines, he was afraid, and his heart trembled greatly. ⁶When Saul inquired of the Lord, the Lord did not answer him, not by dreams, or by Urim, or by prophets. ⁷Then Saul said to his servants, "Seek out for me a woman who is a medium, so that I may go to her and inquire of her." His servants said to him, "There is a medium at Endor."

8 So Saul disguised himself and put on other clothes and went there, he and two men with him. They came to the woman by night. And he said, "Consult a spirit for me, and bring up for me the one whom I name to you." ⁹The woman said to him, "Surely you know what Saul has done, how he has cut off the mediums and the wizards from the land. Why then are you laying a snare for my life to bring about my death?" ¹⁰But Saul swore to her by the Lord, "As the Lord lives, no punishment shall come upon you for this thing." ¹¹Then the woman said, "Whom shall I bring up for you?" He answered, "Bring up Samuel for me." ¹²When the woman saw Samuel, she cried out with a loud voice; and the woman said to Saul, "Why have you deceived me? You are Saul!" ¹³The king said to her, "Have no fear; what do you see?" The woman said to Saul, "I see a divine being*a* coming up out of the ground." ¹⁴He said to her, "What is his appearance?" She said, "An old man is coming up; he is wrapped in a robe." So Saul knew that it was Samuel, and he bowed with his face to the ground, and did obeisance.

15 Then Samuel said to Saul, "Why have you disturbed me by bringing me up?" Saul answered, "I am in great distress, for the Philistines are warring against me, and God has turned away from me and answers me no more, either by prophets or by dreams; so I have summoned you to tell me what I should do." ¹⁶Samuel said, "Why then do you ask me, since the Lord has turned from you and become your enemy? ¹⁷The Lord has done to you just as he spoke by me; for the Lord has torn the kingdom out of your hand, and given it to your neighbor, David. ¹⁸Because you did not obey the voice of the Lord, and did not carry out his fierce wrath against Amalek, therefore the Lord has done this thing to you today. ¹⁹Moreover the Lord will give Israel along with you into the hands of the Philistines; and tomorrow you and your sons shall be with me; the Lord will also give the army of Israel into the hands of the Philistines."

a Or *a god*; or *gods*

20 Immediately Saul fell full length on the ground, filled with fear because of the words of Samuel; and there was no strength in him, for he had eaten nothing all day and all night. ²¹The woman came to Saul, and when she saw that he was terrified, she said to him, "Your servant has listened to you; I have taken my life in my hand, and have listened to what you have said to me. ²²Now therefore, you also listen to your servant; let me set a morsel of bread before you. Eat, that you may have strength when you go on your way." ²³He refused, and said, "I will not eat." But his servants, together with the woman, urged him; and he listened to their words. So he got up from the ground and sat on the bed. ²⁴Now the woman had a fatted calf in the house. She quickly slaughtered it, and she took flour, kneaded it, and baked unleavened cakes. ²⁵She put them before Saul and his servants, and they ate. Then they rose and went away that night.

The Philistines Reject David

29 Now the Philistines gathered all their forces at Aphek, while the Israelites were encamped by the fountain that is in Jezreel. ²As the lords of the Philistines were passing on by hundreds and by thousands, and David and his men were passing on in the rear with Achish, ³the commanders of the Philistines said, "What are these Hebrews doing here?" Achish said to the commanders of the Philistines, "Is this not David, the servant of King Saul of Israel, who has been with me now for days and years? Since he deserted to me I have found no fault in him to this day." ⁴But the commanders of the Philistines were angry with him; and the commanders of the Philistines said to him, "Send the man back, so that he may return to the place that you have assigned to him; he shall not go down with us to battle, or else he may become an adversary to us in the battle. For how could this fellow reconcile himself to his lord? Would it not be with the heads of the men here? ⁵Is this not David, of whom they sing to one another in dances,

'Saul has killed his thousands,
and David his ten thousands'?"

6 Then Achish called David and said to him, "As the LORD lives, you have been honest, and to me it seems right that you should march out and in with me in the campaign; for I have found nothing wrong in you from the day of your coming to me until today. Nevertheless the lords do not approve of you. ⁷So go back now; and go peaceably; do nothing to displease the lords of the Philistines." ⁸David said to Achish, "But what have I done? What have you found in your servant from the day I entered your service until now, that I should not go and fight against the enemies of my lord the king?" ⁹Achish replied to David, "I know that you are as blameless in my sight as an angel of God; nevertheless, the commanders of the Philistines have said, 'He shall not go up with us to the battle.' ¹⁰Now then rise early in the morning, you and the servants of your lord who came with you, and go to the place that I appointed for you. As for the evil report, do not take it to heart, for you have done well before me.^a Start early in the morning, and leave as soon as you have light." ¹¹So David set out with his men early in the

---

Where Is Home?

1 SAMUEL 29.6—30.5

David, sent home from battle, finds the place sacked and deserted, the wives, children and elderly captured. How like the present time it is, when more human beings are displaced from their homelands than at any other time in history!

Pray for those refugees and prisoners. What attitudes and spiritual resources do they need? Are there ways in which you feel emotionally or spiritually displaced? Reflect on what Jesus said about himself: "Foxes have holes, and birds of the air have nests; but the Son of Man has nowhere to lay his head" (Matthew 8.20). How might inviting Jesus into your life more deeply help you find a spiritual "home" in the universe and resources to deal with your displacement?

See Meeting God in Community

---

a Gk: Heb lacks *and go to the place . . . done well before me*

Locating Your Roots

1 SAMUEL 30.11–13

How would you answer David's question: "To whom do you belong. Where are you from?" The Egyptian slave defines himself by his country of origin and his owner. Dietrich Bonhoeffer wrote when imprisoned by the Nazis: "Who am I? Am I then all that which other men tell of?" (*Letters and Papers from Prison*).

Am I more concerned about "who I am" in the eyes of others than "whose I am"? Draw a tree (like a family tree) of your commitments, and rank them by importance. To whom or what do you primarily belong? Who or what is at the bottom of the list? Are you satisfied with the priorities this tree illustrates? Read Psalm 139.1–14 as you ponder.

See Meeting God in Prayer

morning, to return to the land of the Philistines. But the Philistines went up to Jezreel.

David Avenges the Destruction of Ziklag

30 Now when David and his men came to Ziklag on the third day, the Amalekites had made a raid on the Negeb and on Ziklag. They had attacked Ziklag, burned it down, ²and taken captive the women and all*ᵃ* who were in it, both small and great; they killed none of them, but carried them off, and went their way. ³When David and his men came to the city, they found it burned down, and their wives and sons and daughters taken captive. ⁴Then David and the people who were with him raised their voices and wept, until they had no more strength to weep. ⁵David's two wives also had been taken captive, Ahinoam of Jezreel, and Abigail the widow of Nabal of Carmel. ⁶David was in great danger; for the people spoke of stoning him, because all the people were bitter in spirit for their sons and daughters. But David strengthened himself in the LORD his God.

7 David said to the priest Abiathar son of Ahimelech, "Bring me the ephod." So Abiathar brought the ephod to David. ⁸David inquired of the LORD, "Shall I pursue this band? Shall I overtake them?" He answered him, "Pursue; for you shall surely overtake and shall surely rescue." ⁹So David set out, he and the six hundred men who were with him. They came to the Wadi Besor, where those stayed who were left behind. ¹⁰But David went on with the pursuit, he and four hundred men; two hundred stayed behind, too exhausted to cross the Wadi Besor.

11 In the open country they found an Egyptian, and brought him to David. They gave him bread and he ate; they gave him water to drink; ¹²they also gave him a piece of fig cake and two clusters of raisins. When he had eaten, his spirit revived; for he had not eaten bread or drunk water for three days and three nights. ¹³Then David said to him, "To whom do you belong? Where are you from?" He said, "I am a young man of Egypt, servant to an Amalekite. My master left me behind because I fell sick three days ago. ¹⁴We had made a raid on the Negeb of the Cherethites and on that which belongs to Judah and on the Negeb of Caleb; and we burned Ziklag down." ¹⁵David said to him, "Will you take me down to this raiding party?" He said, "Swear to me by God that you will not kill me, or hand me over to my master, and I will take you down to them."

16 When he had taken him down, they were spread out all over the ground, eating and drinking and dancing, because of the great amount of spoil they had taken from the land of the Philistines and from the land of Judah. ¹⁷David attacked them from twilight until the evening of the next day. Not one of them escaped, except four hundred young men, who mounted camels and fled. ¹⁸David recovered all that the Amalekites had taken; and David rescued his two wives. ¹⁹Nothing was missing, whether small or great, sons or daughters, spoil or anything that had been taken; David brought back everything. ²⁰David also captured all the flocks and herds, which were driven ahead of the other cattle; people said, "This is David's spoil."

21 Then David came to the two hundred men who had been too exhausted to follow David, and who had been left

a Gk: Heb lacks *and all*

at the Wadi Besor. They went out to meet David and to meet the people who were with him. When David drew near to the people he saluted them. ²²Then all the corrupt and worthless fellows among the men who had gone with David said, "Because they did not go with us, we will not give them any of the spoil that we have recovered, except that each man may take his wife and children, and leave." ²³But David said, "You shall not do so, my brothers, with what the LORD has given us; he has preserved us and handed over to us the raiding party that attacked us. ²⁴Who would listen to you in this matter? For the share of the one who goes down into the battle shall be the same as the share of the one who stays by the baggage; they shall share alike." ²⁵From that day forward he made it a statute and an ordinance for Israel; it continues to the present day.

26 When David came to Ziklag, he sent part of the spoil to his friends, the elders of Judah, saying, "Here is a present for you from the spoil of the enemies of the LORD"; ²⁷it was for those in Bethel, in Ramoth of the Negeb, in Jattir, ²⁸in Aroer, in Siphmoth, in Eshtemoa, ²⁹in Racal, in the towns of the Jerahmeelites, in the towns of the Kenites, ³⁰in Hormah, in Bor-ashan, in Athach, ³¹in Hebron, all the places where David and his men had roamed.

The Death of Saul and His Sons

31 Now the Philistines fought against Israel; and the men of Israel fled before the Philistines, and many fell[a] on Mount Gilboa. ²The Philistines overtook Saul and his sons; and the Philistines killed Jonathan and Abinadab and Malchishua, the sons of Saul. ³The battle pressed hard upon Saul; the archers found him, and he was badly wounded by them. ⁴Then Saul said to his armor-bearer, "Draw your sword and thrust me through with it, so that these uncircumcised may not come and thrust me through, and make sport of me." But his armor-bearer was unwilling; for he was terrified. So Saul took his own sword and fell upon it. ⁵When his armor-bearer saw that Saul was dead, he also fell upon his sword and died with him. ⁶So Saul and his three sons and his armor-bearer and all his men died together on the same day. ⁷When the men of Israel who were on the other side of the valley and those beyond the Jordan saw that the men of Israel had fled and that Saul and his sons were dead, they forsook their towns and fled; and the Philistines came and occupied them.

8 The next day, when the Philistines came to strip the dead, they found Saul and his three sons fallen on Mount Gilboa. ⁹They cut off his head, stripped off his armor, and sent messengers throughout the land of the Philistines to carry the good news to the houses of their idols and to the people. ¹⁰They put his armor in the temple of Astarte;[b] and they fastened his body to the wall of Beth-shan. ¹¹But when the inhabitants of Jabesh-gilead heard what the Philistines had done to Saul, ¹²all the valiant men set out, traveled all night long, and took the body of Saul and the bodies of his sons from the wall of Beth-shan. They came to Jabesh and burned them there. ¹³Then they took their bones and buried them under the tamarisk tree in Jabesh, and fasted seven days.

Losing the Vision

1 SAMUEL 31.1–4

Saul has fallen from being a visionary, charismatic leader to a lost and despairing wreck of a man. Imaginatively review the tale of his fall, perhaps drawing a diagram of his downward spiral. How did he lose the call that raised him up to service? What did he allow to isolate him from those who could have been most helpful, especially the God who had called him? In what ways did he try to manage alone instead of listening and obeying?

Do you have a "community of faith"—companions in the faith with whom you can be open and honest and who can do the same with you? Make a list of the most important "spiritual friends" in your life. Pray for them individually and ask God that all of you together may help keep one another faithful. Talk to your spiritual friends and share this resolution openly with them; ask them for their prayers for you.

See Meeting God in Community

2 SAMUEL
Seduced by Power

KEY VERSE:

David then perceived that the Lord had established him king over Israel, and that he had exalted his kingdom for the sake of his people Israel.—2 Samuel 5.12

"The battle you are to fight is within you . . . Your enemy comes out of your own heart. We shall not fight, as the men of former times . . . against men on earth, but against principalities and authorities, against the cosmic powers of this dark world . . . We also arm ourselves and bestir ourselves to do battle, but against those enemies which come forth from our own hearts, evil thoughts, thefts, lies about other people, blasphemies, and all other enemies of our soul that are like them . . . For if we prevail against these enemies, we shall lay hold on the spiritual forces well enough and throw them out of that kingdom which they have set up within us."

—ORIGEN OF ALEXANDRIA,
Homily on Joshua

In 2 Samuel, the young King David comes into his own. His story is full of power struggles, duplicity, tragedy and the violence of war. Presented as "the Lord's anointed," David evokes both admiration and dislike. A musician and a soldier, brave and passionate, he dances with joy, sings praises to God and mourns his sons—all with his whole heart. But personal ambition causes David to trample on other people's lives, and his actions illustrate Lord Acton's maxim: "Power corrupts and absolute power corrupts absolutely." David, however, is remarkable in that, having surrounded himself with advisers unafraid to confront his hypocrisy, he *listens*—to them, to his own conscience and to the God he loves. His imperfect life is lived in constant relationship with the Divine One who is the true sovereign and Israel's only security.

The book of 2 Samuel can be read quickly as a compelling story or contemplated slowly. You may identify with the Lord's call to missions—a call that is both daunting and inspiring. You may mourn with David at the tragedies involving his children, reflecting on the difficulties and ambiguities of parenting. You may find yourself pondering the similarities between these ancient characters and events and some of today's public figures and media headlines. But be sure to look through the windows of this story into your own soul—in the ways you deal with the temptations inherent in power and influence. Like David, stay aware of the real, enduring power that reposes in God and is lived out in the Lord's Anointed, "great David's greater Son."

David Mourns for Saul and Jonathan

1 After the death of Saul, when David had returned from defeating the Amalekites, David remained two days in Ziklag. ²On the third day, a man came from Saul's camp, with his clothes torn and dirt on his head. When he came to David, he fell to the ground and did obeisance. ³David said to him, "Where have you come from?" He said to him, "I have escaped from the camp of Israel." ⁴David said to him, "How did things go? Tell me!" He answered, "The army fled from the battle, but also many of the army fell and died; and Saul and his son Jonathan also died." ⁵Then David asked the young man who was reporting to him, "How do you know that Saul and his son Jonathan died?" ⁶The young man reporting to him said, "I happened to be on Mount Gilboa; and there was Saul leaning on his spear, while the chariots and the horsemen drew close to him. ⁷When he looked behind him, he saw me, and called to me. I answered, 'Here sir.' ⁸And he said to me, 'Who are you?' I answered him, 'I am an Amalekite.' ⁹He said to me, 'Come, stand over me and kill me; for convulsions have seized me, and yet my life still lingers.' ¹⁰So I stood over him, and killed him, for I knew that he could not live after he had fallen. I took the crown that was on his head and the armlet that was on his arm, and I have brought them here to my lord."

11 Then David took hold of his clothes and tore them; and all the men who were with him did the same. ¹²They mourned and wept, and fasted until evening for Saul and for his son Jonathan, and for the army of the LORD and for the house of Israel, because they had fallen by the sword. ¹³David said to the young man who had reported to him, "Where do you come from?" He answered, "I am the son of a resident alien, an Amalekite." ¹⁴David said to him, "Were you not afraid to lift your hand to destroy the LORD's anointed?" ¹⁵Then David called one of the young men and said, "Come here and strike him down." So he struck him down and he died. ¹⁶David said to him, "Your blood be on your head; for your own mouth has testified against you, saying, 'I have killed the LORD's anointed.' "

17 David intoned this lamentation over Saul and his son Jonathan. ¹⁸(He ordered that The Song of the Bow*a* be taught to the people of Judah; it is written in the Book of Jashar.) He said:

¹⁹ Your glory, O Israel, lies slain upon your high places!
       How the mighty have fallen!
²⁰ Tell it not in Gath,
       proclaim it not in the streets of Ashkelon;
   or the daughters of the Philistines will rejoice,
       the daughters of the uncircumcised will exult.

²¹ You mountains of Gilboa,
       let there be no dew or rain upon you,
       nor bounteous fields!*b*
   For there the shield of the mighty was defiled,
       the shield of Saul, anointed with oil no more.

²² From the blood of the slain,
       from the fat of the mighty,

---

a Heb *that The Bow*   *b* Meaning of Heb uncertain

Ancient Enemies

2 SAMUEL 1.13–16

The Amalekites, Israel's enemy from the time of Moses, have been part of Saul's downfall (see 1 Samuel 15.18–19). Now David gives orders to execute the young Amalekite who claimed to slay King Saul, for he has "lift[ed his] hand to destroy the LORD's anointed." What do you suppose God thinks of David's act of revenge? Do you believe that God takes sides in the conflicts of history, especially when one of the parties to the conflict, like the Amalekites, engages in especially vicious, unjust or destructive behavior? What emotions arise in you when you encounter, or read about, people who belong to such an unjust group or nation? What temptations toward revenge have you felt in your conflicts with other people? How would you pray for those other people; what might you need to ask God for in order to help you relate justly to them?

See Meeting God in Prayer

The Mighty Are Fallen

2 SAMUEL 1.25–26

Quietly reflect on any relationships you may have had in your life that have affected you deeply—perhaps a relationship that has bound you to the soul of the other person, as David and Jonathan were bound together (see 1 Samuel 18.1). What was it about that other person that you loved, respected, and admired? What gifts does that friendship still give you? Remember what it was like to lose that person—or imagine what it might be like to lose him or her. Enter into the emotions of David's lament over the deaths of Saul and Jonathan by reading the text two or three times, aloud; in each repetition, vary the emotion expressed: anger, quiet mourning, bitterness or gentle affection, for instance. Then thank God for that friendship and its enduring effect in your life.

See Meeting God in Community

the bow of Jonathan did not turn back,
nor the sword of Saul return empty.

23 Saul and Jonathan, beloved and lovely!
In life and in death they were not divided;
they were swifter than eagles,
they were stronger than lions.

24 O daughters of Israel, weep over Saul,
who clothed you with crimson, in luxury,
who put ornaments of gold on your apparel.

25 How the mighty have fallen
in the midst of the battle!

Jonathan lies slain upon your high places.
26 I am distressed for you, my brother Jonathan;
greatly beloved were you to me;
your love to me was wonderful,
passing the love of women.

27 How the mighty have fallen,
and the weapons of war perished!

David Anointed King of Judah

2 After this David inquired of the LORD, "Shall I go up into any of the cities of Judah?" The LORD said to him, "Go up." David said, "To which shall I go up?" He said, "To Hebron." ²So David went up there, along with his two wives, Ahinoam of Jezreel, and Abigail the widow of Nabal of Carmel. ³David brought up the men who were with him, every one with his household; and they settled in the towns of Hebron. ⁴Then the people of Judah came, and there they anointed David king over the house of Judah.

When they told David, "It was the people of Jabesh-gilead who buried Saul," ⁵David sent messengers to the people of Jabesh-gilead, and said to them, "May you be blessed by the LORD, because you showed this loyalty to Saul your lord, and buried him! ⁶Now may the LORD show steadfast love and faithfulness to you! And I too will reward you because you have done this thing. ⁷Therefore let your hands be strong, and be valiant; for Saul your lord is dead, and the house of Judah has anointed me king over them."

Ishbaal King of Israel

8 But Abner son of Ner, commander of Saul's army, had taken Ishbaal[a] son of Saul, and brought him over to Mahanaim. ⁹He made him king over Gilead, the Ashurites, Jezreel, Ephraim, Benjamin, and over all Israel. ¹⁰Ishbaal,[a] Saul's son, was forty years old when he began to reign over Israel, and he reigned two years. But the house of Judah followed David. ¹¹The time that David was king in Hebron over the house of Judah was seven years and six months.

a Gk Compare 1 Chr 8.33; 9.39: Heb *Ish-bosheth*, "man of shame"

The Battle of Gibeon

12 Abner son of Ner, and the servants of Ishbaal[a] son of Saul, went out from Mahanaim to Gibeon. [13]Joab son of Zeruiah, and the servants of David, went out and met them at the pool of Gibeon. One group sat on one side of the pool, while the other sat on the other side of the pool. [14]Abner said to Joab, "Let the young men come forward and have a contest before us." Joab said, "Let them come forward." [15]So they came forward and were counted as they passed by, twelve for Benjamin and Ishbaal[a] son of Saul, and twelve of the servants of David. [16]Each grasped his opponent by the head, and thrust his sword in his opponent's side; so they fell down together. Therefore that place was called Helkath-hazzurim,[b] which is at Gibeon. [17]The battle was very fierce that day; and Abner and the men of Israel were beaten by the servants of David.

18 The three sons of Zeruiah were there, Joab, Abishai, and Asahel. Now Asahel was as swift of foot as a wild gazelle. [19]Asahel pursued Abner, turning neither to the right nor to the left as he followed him. [20]Then Abner looked back and said, "Is it you, Asahel?" He answered, "Yes, it is." [21]Abner said to him, "Turn to your right or to your left, and seize one of the young men, and take his spoil." But Asahel would not turn away from following him. [22]Abner said again to Asahel, "Turn away from following me; why should I strike you to the ground? How then could I show my face to your brother Joab?" [23]But he refused to turn away. So Abner struck him in the stomach with the butt of his spear, so that the spear came out at his back. He fell there, and died where he lay. And all those who came to the place where Asahel had fallen and died, stood still.

24 But Joab and Abishai pursued Abner. As the sun was going down they came to the hill of Ammah, which lies before Giah on the way to the wilderness of Gibeon. [25]The Benjaminites rallied around Abner and formed a single band; they took their stand on the top of a hill. [26]Then Abner called to Joab, "Is the sword to keep devouring forever? Do you not know that the end will be bitter? How long will it be before you order your people to turn from the pursuit of their kinsmen?" [27]Joab said, "As God lives, if you had not spoken, the people would have continued to pursue their kinsmen, not stopping until morning." [28]Joab sounded the trumpet and all the people stopped; they no longer pursued Israel or engaged in battle any further.

29 Abner and his men traveled all that night through the Arabah; they crossed the Jordan, and, marching the whole forenoon,[c] they came to Mahanaim. [30]Joab returned from the pursuit of Abner; and when he had gathered all the people together, there were missing of David's servants nineteen men besides Asahel. [31]But the servants of David had killed of Benjamin three hundred sixty of Abner's men. [32]They took up Asahel and buried him in the tomb of his father, which was at Bethlehem. Joab and his men marched all night, and the day broke upon them at Hebron.

---

a Gk Compare 1 Chr 8.33; 9.39: Heb Ish-bosheth, "man of shame"   b That is Field of Sword-edges   c Meaning of Heb uncertain

Civil War Begins

2 SAMUEL 2.14–17

"Let's have the young men fight," the leaders and generals of the world say. The Civil War's General Sherman said, "War is hell! It is only those who have neither fired a shot nor heard the shrieks and groans of the wounded who cry aloud for blood, more vengeance, more desolation." Sherman's frank assessment of America's Civil War applies equally well to the dozen or more such conflicts being fought by young men and women in the world today. Bring to mind a contemporary civil conflict by reading the daily paper or a news magazine or by asking others to help you. Pray for sanity and peace in each country racked by such strife.

See Meeting God in Prayer

Victimized by the Powers That Be

2 SAMUEL 3.15–16

Paltiel follows behind his wife, weeping; Michal must remain silent because she is now "owned" as David's property. Their lives are once again fodder for the power struggle between Saul and David. In what ways are innocent lives today disrupted and destroyed by such powerful forces—institutions or individuals? What incidents have you personally witnessed when weakness or difference in age, race, gender, wealth or ability has been exploited or punished? In what ways have you participated in such exploitation—or been the object of it? How would you pray for the perpetrators of such injustices? Spend some time with a trusted friend sharing your insights, perhaps praying together about them.

See Meeting God in Community

Abner Defects to David

3 There was a long war between the house of Saul and the house of David; David grew stronger and stronger, while the house of Saul became weaker and weaker.

2 Sons were born to David at Hebron: his firstborn was Amnon, of Ahinoam of Jezreel; ³his second, Chileab, of Abigail the widow of Nabal of Carmel; the third, Absalom son of Maacah, daughter of King Talmai of Geshur; ⁴the fourth, Adonijah son of Haggith; the fifth, Shephatiah son of Abital; ⁵and the sixth, Ithream, of David's wife Eglah. These were born to David in Hebron.

6 While there was war between the house of Saul and the house of David, Abner was making himself strong in the house of Saul. ⁷Now Saul had a concubine whose name was Rizpah daughter of Aiah. And Ishbaal*a* said to Abner, "Why have you gone in to my father's concubine?" ⁸The words of Ishbaal*b* made Abner very angry; he said, "Am I a dog's head for Judah? Today I keep showing loyalty to the house of your father Saul, to his brothers, and to his friends, and have not given you into the hand of David; and yet you charge me now with a crime concerning this woman. ⁹So may God do to Abner and so may he add to it! For just what the LORD has sworn to David, that will I accomplish for him, ¹⁰to transfer the kingdom from the house of Saul, and set up the throne of David over Israel and over Judah, from Dan to Beersheba." ¹¹And Ishbaal*a* could not answer Abner another word, because he feared him.

12 Abner sent messengers to David at Hebron,*c* saying, "To whom does the land belong? Make your covenant with me, and I will give you my support to bring all Israel over to you." ¹³He said, "Good; I will make a covenant with you. But one thing I require of you: you shall never appear in my presence unless you bring Saul's daughter Michal when you come to see me." ¹⁴Then David sent messengers to Saul's son Ishbaal,*d* saying, "Give me my wife Michal, to whom I became engaged at the price of one hundred foreskins of the Philistines." ¹⁵Ishbaal*d* sent and took her from her husband Paltiel the son of Laish. ¹⁶But her husband went with her, weeping as he walked behind her all the way to Bahurim. Then Abner said to him, "Go back home!" So he went back.

17 Abner sent word to the elders of Israel, saying, "For some time past you have been seeking David as king over you. ¹⁸Now then bring it about; for the LORD has promised David: Through my servant David I will save my people Israel from the hand of the Philistines, and from all their enemies." ¹⁹Abner also spoke directly to the Benjaminites; then Abner went to tell David at Hebron all that Israel and the whole house of Benjamin were ready to do.

20 When Abner came with twenty men to David at Hebron, David made a feast for Abner and the men who were with him. ²¹Abner said to David, "Let me go and rally all Israel to my lord the king, in order that they may make a covenant with you, and that you may reign over all that your heart desires." So David dismissed Abner, and he went away in peace.

---

a Heb *And he*   *b* Gk Compare 1 Chr 8.33; 9.39: Heb *Ish-bosheth*, "man of shame"   *c* Gk: Heb *where he was*   *d* Heb *Ish-bosheth*

Abner Is Killed by Joab

22 Just then the servants of David arrived with Joab from a raid, bringing much spoil with them. But Abner was not with David at Hebron, for David*a* had dismissed him, and he had gone away in peace. ²³When Joab and all the army that was with him came, it was told Joab, "Abner son of Ner came to the king, and he has dismissed him, and he has gone away in peace." ²⁴Then Joab went to the king and said, "What have you done? Abner came to you; why did you dismiss him, so that he got away? ²⁵You know that Abner son of Ner came to deceive you, and to learn your comings and goings and to learn all that you are doing."

26 When Joab came out from David's presence, he sent messengers after Abner, and they brought him back from the cistern of Sirah; but David did not know about it. ²⁷When Abner returned to Hebron, Joab took him aside in the gateway to speak with him privately, and there he stabbed him in the stomach. So he died for shedding*b* the blood of Asahel, Joab's*c* brother. ²⁸Afterward, when David heard of it, he said, "I and my kingdom are forever guiltless before the Lord for the blood of Abner son of Ner. ²⁹May the guilt*d* fall on the head of Joab, and on all his father's house; and may the house of Joab never be without one who has a discharge, or who is leprous,*e* or who holds a spindle, or who falls by the sword, or who lacks food!" ³⁰So Joab and his brother Abishai murdered Abner because he had killed their brother Asahel in the battle at Gibeon.

31 Then David said to Joab and to all the people who were with him, "Tear your clothes, and put on sackcloth, and mourn over Abner." And King David followed the bier. ³²They buried Abner at Hebron. The king lifted up his voice and wept at the grave of Abner, and all the people wept. ³³The king lamented for Abner, saying,

"Should Abner die as a fool dies?
³⁴ Your hands were not bound,
    your feet were not fettered;
  as one falls before the wicked
      you have fallen."

And all the people wept over him again. ³⁵Then all the people came to persuade David to eat something while it was still day; but David swore, saying, "So may God do to me, and more, if I taste bread or anything else before the sun goes down!" ³⁶All the people took notice of it, and it pleased them; just as everything the king did pleased all the people. ³⁷So all the people and all Israel understood that day that the king had no part in the killing of Abner son of Ner. ³⁸And the king said to his servants, "Do you not know that a prince and a great man has fallen this day in Israel? ³⁹Today I am powerless, even though anointed king; these men, the sons of Zeruiah, are too violent for me. The Lord pay back the one who does wickedly in accordance with his wickedness!"

Chief Mourner

2 SAMUEL 3.31

David's public mourning for Abner (walking behind the bier, weeping aloud at his tomb, singing a lament, fasting) was a comfort to his people: They "took notice of it, and it pleased them" (3.36). All grief is deeply personal, but at moments of corporate loss, we look to our leaders to express our feelings by their words and actions. When Princess Diana was killed in a car accident in August, 1997, the British royal family was criticized for their reserved response, resulting in an uncharacteristically emotional address by Queen Elizabeth. What have been the times of grief and loss in your own life, especially those shared by others? Whose vocal lament or behavior comforted you? In what situations have you been called upon to be chief mourner, or one of the lead mourners? What words or deeds best express authentic sympathy and comfort? How does God's presence help?

See Meeting God in Community

---

a Heb *he*   *b* Heb lacks *shedding*   *c* Heb *his*   *d* Heb *May it*   *e* A term for several skin diseases; precise meaning uncertain

Images of Leadership

2 SAMUEL 5.1–3

David is now king over the land, and the clans of Israel acknowledge that God has made him shepherd of the people. The pledge of loyalty springs easily to their lips because their new leader fits the image of the king they want and need. Brave and strong, David is the human representative of the God who leads them as a nation. In a few minutes of silence, consider the characteristics of righteous leadership. What makes for good leadership in a nation? A work force? A spiritual community? A family? What are the leadership qualities manifested in the God of the Bible, and in God's human manifestation in Jesus Christ, the Good Shepherd? How are these qualities reflected in your own life?

See *Meeting God in Community*

Ishbaal Assassinated

4 When Saul's son Ishbaal[a] heard that Abner had died at Hebron, his courage failed, and all Israel was dismayed. [2]Saul's son had two captains of raiding bands; the name of the one was Baanah, and the name of the other Rechab. They were sons of Rimmon a Benjaminite from Beeroth—for Beeroth is considered to belong to Benjamin. [3](Now the people of Beeroth had fled to Gittaim and are there as resident aliens to this day).

4 Saul's son Jonathan had a son who was crippled in his feet. He was five years old when the news about Saul and Jonathan came from Jezreel. His nurse picked him up and fled; and, in her haste to flee, it happened that he fell and became lame. His name was Mephibosheth.[b]

5 Now the sons of Rimmon the Beerothite, Rechab and Baanah, set out, and about the heat of the day they came to the house of Ishbaal,[c] while he was taking his noonday rest. [6]They came inside the house as though to take wheat, and they struck him in the stomach; then Rechab and his brother Baanah escaped.[d] [7]Now they had come into the house while he was lying on his couch in his bedchamber; they attacked him, killed him, and beheaded him. Then they took his head and traveled by way of the Arabah all night long. [8]They brought the head of Ishbaal[c] to David at Hebron and said to the king, "Here is the head of Ishbaal,[c] son of Saul, your enemy, who sought your life; the LORD has avenged my lord the king this day on Saul and on his offspring."

9 David answered Rechab and his brother Baanah, the sons of Rimmon the Beerothite, "As the LORD lives, who has redeemed my life out of every adversity, [10]when the one who told me, 'See, Saul is dead,' thought he was bringing good news, I seized him and killed him at Ziklag—this was the reward I gave him for his news. [11]How much more then, when wicked men have killed a righteous man on his bed in his own house! And now shall I not require his blood at your hand, and destroy you from the earth?" [12]So David commanded the young men, and they killed them; they cut off their hands and feet, and hung their bodies beside the pool at Hebron. But the head of Ishbaal[c] they took and buried in the tomb of Abner at Hebron.

David Anointed King of All Israel

5 Then all the tribes of Israel came to David at Hebron, and said, "Look, we are your bone and flesh. [2]For some time, while Saul was king over us, it was you who led out Israel and brought it in. The LORD said to you: It is you who shall be shepherd of my people Israel, you who shall be ruler over Israel." [3]So all the elders of Israel came to the king at Hebron; and King David made a covenant with them at Hebron before the LORD, and they anointed David king over Israel. [4]David was thirty years old when he began to reign, and he reigned forty years. [5]At Hebron he reigned over Judah seven years and six months; and at Jerusalem he reigned over all Israel and Judah thirty-three years.

---

a Heb lacks *Ishbaal*   b In 1 Chr 8.34 and 9.40, *Merib-baal*   c Heb *Ish-bosheth*   d Meaning of Heb of verse 6 uncertain

Jerusalem Made Capital of the United Kingdom

6 The king and his men marched to Jerusalem against the Jebusites, the inhabitants of the land, who said to David, "You will not come in here, even the blind and the lame will turn you back"—thinking, "David cannot come in here." [7]Nevertheless David took the stronghold of Zion, which is now the city of David. [8]David had said on that day, "Whoever would strike down the Jebusites, let him get up the water shaft to attack the lame and the blind, those whom David hates."[a] Therefore it is said, "The blind and the lame shall not come into the house." [9]David occupied the stronghold, and named it the city of David. David built the city all around from the Millo inward. [10]And David became greater and greater, for the LORD, the God of hosts, was with him.

11 King Hiram of Tyre sent messengers to David, along with cedar trees, and carpenters and masons who built David a house. [12]David then perceived that the LORD had established him king over Israel, and that he had exalted his kingdom for the sake of his people Israel.

13 In Jerusalem, after he came from Hebron, David took more concubines and wives; and more sons and daughters were born to David. [14]These are the names of those who were born to him in Jerusalem: Shammua, Shobab, Nathan, Solomon, [15]Ibhar, Elishua, Nepheg, Japhia, [16]Elishama, Eliada, and Eliphelet.

Philistine Attack Repulsed

17 When the Philistines heard that David had been anointed king over Israel, all the Philistines went up in search of David; but David heard about it and went down to the stronghold. [18]Now the Philistines had come and spread out in the valley of Rephaim. [19]David inquired of the LORD, "Shall I go up against the Philistines? Will you give them into my hand?" The LORD said to David, "Go up; for I will certainly give the Philistines into your hand." [20]So David came to Baal-perazim, and David defeated them there. He said, "The LORD has burst forth against[b] my enemies before me, like a bursting flood." Therefore that place is called Baal-perazim.[c] [21]The Philistines abandoned their idols there, and David and his men carried them away.

22 Once again the Philistines came up, and were spread out in the valley of Rephaim. [23]When David inquired of the LORD, he said, "You shall not go up; go around to their rear, and come upon them opposite the balsam trees. [24]When you hear the sound of marching in the tops of the balsam trees, then be on the alert; for then the LORD has gone out before you to strike down the army of the Philistines." [25]David did just as the LORD had commanded him; and he struck down the Philistines from Geba all the way to Gezer.

David Brings the Ark to Jerusalem

6 David again gathered all the chosen men of Israel, thirty thousand. [2]David and all the people with him set out and went from Baale-judah, to bring up from there

---

The Constant Presence of God

2 SAMUEL 5.17–25

"Alas . . . we do not see God, who is present with us; and, though faith assures us of His presence, yet, not beholding Him with our eyes, we too often forget Him and behave ourselves as though He were at a distance from us; for, although we well know that He is present in all things, yet, not reflecting on it, we act as if we knew it not. Therefore, before prayer, we must always excite in our souls a lively apprehension of the presence of God, such as David conceived when he exclaimed: 'If I ascend up into heaven, O my God, thou art there; if I descend into hell, thou art there!' . . . When, therefore, you come to prayer, you must say with your whole heart and in your heart, 'O my heart! Be attentive, for God is truly here.' "

—FRANCIS DE SALES,
Introduction to the Devout Life

See Meeting God in Prayer

Dancing Before the Lord

2 SAMUEL 6.16

I cannot dance, O Lord
unless you lead me.
If you will
that I leap joyfully
then you must be the first
to dance
and sing.

Then, and only then,
will I leap for love.

Then I will soar
from love to knowledge,
from knowledge to fruition
from fruition to beyond
all human sense.

And there
I will remain
and circle for evermore.
—MECHTILD OF MAGDEBURG

See *Meeting God in Worship*

the ark of God, which is called by the name of the Lord of hosts who is enthroned on the cherubim. ³They carried the ark of God on a new cart, and brought it out of the house of Abinadab, which was on the hill. Uzzah and Ahio,ᵃ the sons of Abinadab, were driving the new cart ⁴with the ark of God;ᵇ and Ahioᵃ went in front of the ark. ⁵David and all the house of Israel were dancing before the Lord with all their might, with songsᶜ and lyres and harps and tambourines and castanets and cymbals.

6 When they came to the threshing floor of Nacon, Uzzah reached out his hand to the ark of God and took hold of it, for the oxen shook it. ⁷The anger of the Lord was kindled against Uzzah; and God struck him there because he reached out his hand to the ark;ᵈ and he died there beside the ark of God. ⁸David was angry because the Lord had burst forth with an outburst upon Uzzah; so that place is called Perez-uzzah,ᵉ to this day. ⁹David was afraid of the Lord that day; he said, "How can the ark of the Lord come into my care?" ¹⁰So David was unwilling to take the ark of the Lord into his care in the city of David; instead David took it to the house of Obed-edom the Gittite. ¹¹The ark of the Lord remained in the house of Obed-edom the Gittite three months; and the Lord blessed Obed-edom and all his household.

12 It was told King David, "The Lord has blessed the household of Obed-edom and all that belongs to him, because of the ark of God." So David went and brought up the ark of God from the house of Obed-edom to the city of David with rejoicing; ¹³and when those who bore the ark of the Lord had gone six paces, he sacrificed an ox and a fatling. ¹⁴David danced before the Lord with all his might; David was girded with a linen ephod. ¹⁵So David and all the house of Israel brought up the ark of the Lord with shouting, and with the sound of the trumpet.

16 As the ark of the Lord came into the city of David, Michal daughter of Saul looked out of the window, and saw King David leaping and dancing before the Lord; and she despised him in her heart.

17 They brought in the ark of the Lord, and set it in its place, inside the tent that David had pitched for it; and David offered burnt offerings and offerings of well-being before the Lord. ¹⁸When David had finished offering the burnt offerings and the offerings of well-being, he blessed the people in the name of the Lord of hosts, ¹⁹and distributed food among all the people, the whole multitude of Israel, both men and women, to each a cake of bread, a portion of meat,ᶠ and a cake of raisins. Then all the people went back to their homes.

20 David returned to bless his household. But Michal the daughter of Saul came out to meet David, and said, "How the king of Israel honored himself today, uncovering himself today before the eyes of his servants' maids, as any vulgar fellow might shamelessly uncover himself!" ²¹David said to Michal, "It was before the Lord, who chose me in place of your father and all his household, to appoint me as prince over Israel, the people of the Lord,

a Or *and his brother*　　*b* Compare Gk: Heb *and brought it out of the house of Abinadab, which was on the hill with the ark of God*　　*c* Q Ms Gk 1 Chr 13.8: Heb *fir trees*　　*d* 1 Chr 13.10 Compare Q Ms: Meaning of Heb uncertain　　*e* That is *Bursting Out Against Uzzah*　　*f* Vg: Meaning of Heb uncertain

that I have danced before the LORD. [22]I will make myself yet more contemptible than this, and I will be abased in my own eyes; but by the maids of whom you have spoken, by them I shall be held in honor." [23]And Michal the daughter of Saul had no child to the day of her death.

God's Covenant with David

7 Now when the king was settled in his house, and the LORD had given him rest from all his enemies around him, [2]the king said to the prophet Nathan, "See now, I am living in a house of cedar, but the ark of God stays in a tent." [3]Nathan said to the king, "Go, do all that you have in mind; for the LORD is with you."

4 But that same night the word of the LORD came to Nathan: [5]Go and tell my servant David: Thus says the LORD: Are you the one to build me a house to live in? [6]I have not lived in a house since the day I brought up the people of Israel from Egypt to this day, but I have been moving about in a tent and a tabernacle. [7]Wherever I have moved about among all the people of Israel, did I ever speak a word with any of the tribal leaders[a] of Israel, whom I commanded to shepherd my people Israel, saying, "Why have you not built me a house of cedar?" [8]Now therefore thus you shall say to my servant David: Thus says the LORD of hosts: I took you from the pasture, from following the sheep to be prince over my people Israel; [9]and I have been with you wherever you went, and have cut off all your enemies from before you; and I will make for you a great name, like the name of the great ones of the earth. [10]And I will appoint a place for my people Israel and will plant them, so that they may live in their own place, and be disturbed no more; and evildoers shall afflict them no more, as formerly, [11]from the time that I appointed judges over my people Israel; and I will give you rest from all your enemies. Moreover the LORD declares to you that the LORD will make you a house. [12]When your days are fulfilled and you lie down with your ancestors, I will raise up your offspring after you, who shall come forth from your body, and I will establish his kingdom. [13]He shall build a house for my name, and I will establish the throne of his kingdom forever. [14]I will be a father to him, and he shall be a son to me. When he commits iniquity, I will punish him with a rod such as mortals use, with blows inflicted by human beings. [15]But I will not take[b] my steadfast love from him, as I took it from Saul, whom I put away from before you. [16]Your house and your kingdom shall be made sure forever before me;[c] your throne shall be established forever. [17]In accordance with all these words and with all this vision, Nathan spoke to David.

David's Prayer

18 Then King David went in and sat before the LORD, and said, "Who am I, O Lord GOD, and what is my house, that you have brought me thus far? [19]And yet this was a small thing in your eyes, O Lord GOD; you have spoken also of your servant's house for a great while to come.

I Will Give You Rest

2 SAMUEL 7.1

An ancient prayer for a service at the end of the day says, "Guide us waking, O Lord, and guard us sleeping; that awake we may watch with Christ, and asleep we may rest in peace." The purpose of resting in the Lord is not merely to relax and refresh ourselves; resting is also eliminating distractions so that we may be fully aware of the presence of God.

Before going to sleep tonight, after you turn the lights out, repeat to yourself several times, "I rest in the Lord." If you wake up before morning, lie very still and say the name of Jesus, or say again, "I rest in the Lord." Use this exercise anytime you take a break from work or stop for a period of relaxation.

See *Meeting God in Everyday Life*

---

a Or *any of the tribes*   b Gk Syr Vg 1 Chr 17.13: Heb *shall not depart*
c Gk Heb Mss: MT *before you*; Compare 2 Sam 7.26, 29

"You Have Brought Me Thus Far"

2 SAMUEL 7.18–29

The expression "brought thus far" suggests a journey taken with a special guide. Struck by Nathan's words, David declares, "May this be instruction for the people, O Lord GOD!" Consider how God has brought you to this point by drawing a trail map for your own life. Imagine a hiking trail that begins with your birth and label that event on a large sheet of paper. Proceed down the imaginary trail, marking on your map the high moments, narrow ways, verdant valleys, patches, inspiration points, caves, islands and other features that describe events in your life. In what direction do you think God wishes to take you next?

See Meeting God in Everyday Life

May this be instruction for the people,[a] O Lord GOD! [20]And what more can David say to you? For you know your servant, O Lord GOD! [21]Because of your promise, and according to your own heart, you have wrought all this greatness, so that your servant may know it. [22]Therefore you are great, O LORD God; for there is no one like you, and there is no God besides you, according to all that we have heard with our ears. [23]Who is like your people, like Israel? Is there another[b] nation on earth whose God went to redeem it as a people, and to make a name for himself, doing great and awesome things for them,[c] by driving out[d] before his people nations and their gods?[e] [24]And you established your people Israel for yourself to be your people forever; and you, O LORD, became their God. [25]And now, O LORD God, as for the word that you have spoken concerning your servant and concerning his house, confirm it forever; do as you have promised. [26]Thus your name will be magnified forever in the saying, 'The LORD of hosts is God over Israel'; and the house of your servant David will be established before you. [27]For you, O LORD of hosts, the God of Israel, have made this revelation to your servant, saying, 'I will build you a house'; therefore your servant has found courage to pray this prayer to you. [28]And now, O Lord GOD, you are God, and your words are true, and you have promised this good thing to your servant; [29]now therefore may it please you to bless the house of your servant, so that it may continue forever before you; for you, O Lord GOD, have spoken, and with your blessing shall the house of your servant be blessed forever."

David's Wars

8 Some time afterward, David attacked the Philistines and subdued them; David took Metheg-ammah out of the hand of the Philistines.

2 He also defeated the Moabites and, making them lie down on the ground, measured them off with a cord; he measured two lengths of cord for those who were to be put to death, and one length[f] for those who were to be spared. And the Moabites became servants to David and brought tribute.

3 David also struck down King Hadadezer son of Rehob of Zobah, as he went to restore his monument[g] at the river Euphrates. [4]David took from him one thousand seven hundred horsemen, and twenty thousand foot soldiers. David hamstrung all the chariot horses, but left enough for a hundred chariots. [5]When the Arameans of Damascus came to help King Hadadezer of Zobah, David killed twenty-two thousand men of the Arameans. [6]Then David put garrisons among the Arameans of Damascus; and the Arameans became servants to David and brought tribute. The LORD gave victory to David wherever he went. [7]David took the gold shields that were carried by the servants of Hadadezer, and brought them to Jerusalem. [8]From Betah and from Berothai, towns of Hadadezer, King David took a great amount of bronze.

a Meaning of Heb uncertain   b Gk: Heb one   c Heb you   d Gk 1 Chr 17.21: Heb for your land   e Cn: Heb before your people, whom you redeemed for yourself from Egypt, nations and its gods   f Heb one full length
g Compare 1 Sam 15.12 and 2 Sam 18.18

9 When King Toi of Hamath heard that David had defeated the whole army of Hadadezer, [10]Toi sent his son Joram to King David, to greet him and to congratulate him because he had fought against Hadadezer and defeated him. Now Hadadezer had often been at war with Toi. Joram brought with him articles of silver, gold, and bronze; [11]these also King David dedicated to the LORD, together with the silver and gold that he dedicated from all the nations he subdued, [12]from Edom, Moab, the Ammonites, the Philistines, Amalek, and from the spoil of King Hadadezer son of Rehob of Zobah.

13 David won a name for himself. When he returned, he killed eighteen thousand Edomites[a] in the Valley of Salt. [14]He put garrisons in Edom; throughout all Edom he put garrisons, and all the Edomites became David's servants. And the LORD gave victory to David wherever he went.

David's Officers

15 So David reigned over all Israel; and David administered justice and equity to all his people. [16]Joab son of Zeruiah was over the army; Jehoshaphat son of Ahilud was recorder; [17]Zadok son of Ahitub and Ahimelech son of Abiathar were priests; Seraiah was secretary; [18]Benaiah son of Jehoiada was over[b] the Cherethites and the Pelethites; and David's sons were priests.

David's Kindness to Mephibosheth

9 David asked, "Is there still anyone left of the house of Saul to whom I may show kindness for Jonathan's sake?" [2]Now there was a servant of the house of Saul whose name was Ziba, and he was summoned to David. The king said to him, "Are you Ziba?" And he said, "At your service!" [3]The king said, "Is there anyone remaining of the house of Saul to whom I may show the kindness of God?" Ziba said to the king, "There remains a son of Jonathan; he is crippled in his feet." [4]The king said to him, "Where is he?" Ziba said to the king, "He is in the house of Machir son of Ammiel, at Lo-debar." [5]Then King David sent and brought him from the house of Machir son of Ammiel, at Lo-debar. [6]Mephibosheth[c] son of Jonathan son of Saul came to David, and fell on his face and did obeisance. David said, "Mephibosheth!"[c] He answered, "I am your servant." [7]David said to him, "Do not be afraid, for I will show you kindness for the sake of your father Jonathan; I will restore to you all the land of your grandfather Saul, and you yourself shall eat at my table always." [8]He did obeisance and said, "What is your servant, that you should look upon a dead dog such as I?"

9 Then the king summoned Saul's servant Ziba, and said to him, "All that belonged to Saul and to all his house I have given to your master's grandson. [10]You and your sons and your servants shall till the land for him, and shall bring in the produce, so that your master's grandson may have food to eat; but your master's grandson Mephibosheth[c] shall always eat at my table." Now Ziba had

---

a Gk: Heb *returned from striking down eighteen thousand Arameans*   b Syr Tg Vg 20.23; 1 Chr 18.17: Heb lacks *was over*   c Or *Merib-baal:* See 4.4 note

---

A Vow Fulfilled

2 SAMUEL 9.1–6

David asks, "Is there still anyone . . . to whom I may show kindness?" By vowing protection for Jonathan's descendants, he turns away from a custom that permitted the slaying of all surviving members of a former dynasty; his love for Jonathan lives on in his kindly treatment of Jonathan's crippled son. We also often benefit from the affections for, and promises made to, our parents, ancestors or friends. On a small piece of paper, write the names of people who have treated you kindly "for the sake" of another person. Use the paper as a bookmark, reminding you for the next three days to look intentionally for ways to extend kindness to someone else.

See Meeting God in Service

Humiliation and Humility

2 SAMUEL 10.4–5

Curiously, both "humiliate" and "humble" come from the Latin word *humus*, meaning soil. When we are humiliated, we may feel like "dirt," like the disgraced warriors in the story. Humility, on the other hand, connotes having one's feet on the ground of reality, being clear in one's self-assessment. As Dag Hammarskjöld wrote in *Markings*: "Humility is just as much the opposite of self-abasement as it is of self-exaltation. To be humble is [not to make comparisons]." Recall moments when you have felt humiliated. Then, by contrast, consider what it means to see yourself humbly, simply as you are, without comparison to someone else. Go to a mirror now and describe yourself in your own words. Then imagine that God sees what you see, hears what you have said, and loves you just as you are.

See Meeting God in Prayer

fifteen sons and twenty servants. ¹¹Then Ziba said to the king, "According to all that my lord the king commands his servant, so your servant will do." Mephibosheth*ª* ate at David's*ᵇ* table, like one of the king's sons. ¹²Mephibosheth*ª* had a young son whose name was Mica. And all who lived in Ziba's house became Mephibosheth's*ᶜ* servants. ¹³Mephibosheth*ª* lived in Jerusalem, for he always ate at the king's table. Now he was lame in both his feet.

The Ammonites and Arameans Are Defeated

10 Some time afterward, the king of the Ammonites died, and his son Hanun succeeded him. ²David said, "I will deal loyally with Hanun son of Nahash, just as his father dealt loyally with me." So David sent envoys to console him concerning his father. When David's envoys came into the land of the Ammonites, ³the princes of the Ammonites said to their lord Hanun, "Do you really think that David is honoring your father just because he has sent messengers with condolences to you? Has not David sent his envoys to you to search the city, to spy it out, and to overthrow it?" ⁴So Hanun seized David's envoys, shaved off half the beard of each, cut off their garments in the middle at their hips, and sent them away. ⁵When David was told, he sent to meet them, for the men were greatly ashamed. The king said, "Remain at Jericho until your beards have grown, and then return."

6 When the Ammonites saw that they had become odious to David, the Ammonites sent and hired the Arameans of Beth-rehob and the Arameans of Zobah, twenty thousand foot soldiers, as well as the king of Maacah, one thousand men, and the men of Tob, twelve thousand men. ⁷When David heard of it, he sent Joab and all the army with the warriors. ⁸The Ammonites came out and drew up in battle array at the entrance of the gate; but the Arameans of Zobah and of Rehob, and the men of Tob and Maacah, were by themselves in the open country.

9 When Joab saw that the battle was set against him both in front and in the rear, he chose some of the picked men of Israel, and arrayed them against the Arameans; ¹⁰the rest of his men he put in the charge of his brother Abishai, and he arrayed them against the Ammonites. ¹¹He said, "If the Arameans are too strong for me, then you shall help me; but if the Ammonites are too strong for you, then I will come and help you. ¹²Be strong, and let us be courageous for the sake of our people, and for the cities of our God; and may the Lord do what seems good to him." ¹³So Joab and the people who were with him moved forward into battle against the Arameans; and they fled before him. ¹⁴When the Ammonites saw that the Arameans fled, they likewise fled before Abishai, and entered the city. Then Joab returned from fighting against the Ammonites, and came to Jerusalem.

15 But when the Arameans saw that they had been defeated by Israel, they gathered themselves together. ¹⁶Hadadezer sent and brought out the Arameans who were beyond the Euphrates; and they came to Helam, with Shobach the commander of the army of Hadadezer

a Or *Merib-baal*: See 4.4 note   *b* Gk: Heb *my*   *c* Or *Merib-baal's*: See 4.4 note

at their head. [17]When it was told David, he gathered all Israel together, and crossed the Jordan, and came to Helam. The Arameans arrayed themselves against David and fought with him. [18]The Arameans fled before Israel; and David killed of the Arameans seven hundred chariot teams, and forty thousand horsemen,[a] and wounded Shobach the commander of their army, so that he died there. [19]When all the kings who were servants of Hadadezer saw that they had been defeated by Israel, they made peace with Israel, and became subject to them. So the Arameans were afraid to help the Ammonites any more.

David Commits Adultery with Bathsheba

11 In the spring of the year, the time when kings go out to battle, David sent Joab with his officers and all Israel with him; they ravaged the Ammonites, and besieged Rabbah. But David remained at Jerusalem.

[2] It happened, late one afternoon, when David rose from his couch and was walking about on the roof of the king's house, that he saw from the roof a woman bathing; the woman was very beautiful. [3]David sent someone to inquire about the woman. It was reported, "This is Bathsheba daughter of Eliam, the wife of Uriah the Hittite." [4]So David sent messengers to get her, and she came to him, and he lay with her. (Now she was purifying herself after her period.) Then she returned to her house. [5]The woman conceived; and she sent and told David, "I am pregnant."

[6] So David sent word to Joab, "Send me Uriah the Hittite." And Joab sent Uriah to David. [7]When Uriah came to him, David asked how Joab and the people fared, and how the war was going. [8]Then David said to Uriah, "Go down to your house, and wash your feet." Uriah went out of the king's house, and there followed him a present from the king. [9]But Uriah slept at the entrance of the king's house with all the servants of his lord, and did not go down to his house. [10]When they told David, "Uriah did not go down to his house," David said to Uriah, "You have just come from a journey. Why did you not go down to your house?" [11]Uriah said to David, "The ark and Israel and Judah remain in booths;[b] and my lord Joab and the servants of my lord are camping in the open field; shall I then go to my house, to eat and to drink, and to lie with my wife? As you live, and as your soul lives, I will not do such a thing." [12]Then David said to Uriah, "Remain here today also, and tomorrow I will send you back." So Uriah remained in Jerusalem that day. On the next day, [13]David invited him to eat and drink in his presence and made him drunk; and in the evening he went out to lie on his couch with the servants of his lord, but he did not go down to his house.

David Has Uriah Killed

[14] In the morning David wrote a letter to Joab, and sent it by the hand of Uriah. [15]In the letter he wrote, "Set Uriah in the forefront of the hardest fighting, and then draw back from him, so that he may be struck down and die." [16]As Joab was besieging the city, he assigned Uriah

---

Friends in Need

2 SAMUEL 10.11–12

How reassuring it is to have someone to depend on in times of need. And how validating to know that others are willing to call on us in their difficult periods. Think of your own times of need, recollecting two people still living who have come to your aid. Write or call to let these people know that you still treasure their past support. If you are going through a difficult time right now, ask for support from someone else. Reach out to offer help to someone who has been on your mind; tell them you have been thinking warmly of them and hope that all is well. Ask what you might do to help them.

See Meeting God in Community

---

a 1 Chr 19.18 and some Gk Mss read *foot soldiers*   *b* Or at Succoth

Good Greed?

2 SAMUEL 11.27–12.7

In his 1986 commencement address at the University of California at Berkeley, trader Ivan Boesky asserted: "Greed is all right . . . . Greed is healthy. You can be greedy and still feel good about yourself." David might have been comforted by such an adviser, but instead he had Nathan, whose rebuke helped him recognize and repent of his greediness in arranging Uriah's death and marrying Bathsheba. In what areas of your life are you greedy, taking more than you need and failing to be grateful for what you have received? Are there "Ivans" inside you or around you who encourage you to rationalize this behavior as good? Do you have a "Nathan," someone who challenges you to confront your weaknesses and helps you to be your best self?

See Meeting God in Service

to the place where he knew there were valiant warriors. [17]The men of the city came out and fought with Joab; and some of the servants of David among the people fell. Uriah the Hittite was killed as well. [18]Then Joab sent and told David all the news about the fighting; [19]and he instructed the messenger, "When you have finished telling the king all the news about the fighting, [20]then, if the king's anger rises, and if he says to you, 'Why did you go so near the city to fight? Did you not know that they would shoot from the wall? [21]Who killed Abimelech son of Jerubbaal?[a] Did not a woman throw an upper millstone on him from the wall, so that he died at Thebez? Why did you go so near the wall?' then you shall say, 'Your servant Uriah the Hittite is dead too.' "

22 So the messenger went, and came and told David all that Joab had sent him to tell. [23]The messenger said to David, "The men gained an advantage over us, and came out against us in the field; but we drove them back to the entrance of the gate. [24]Then the archers shot at your servants from the wall; some of the king's servants are dead; and your servant Uriah the Hittite is dead also." [25]David said to the messenger, "Thus you shall say to Joab, 'Do not let this matter trouble you, for the sword devours now one and now another; press your attack on the city, and overthrow it.' And encourage him."

26 When the wife of Uriah heard that her husband was dead, she made lamentation for him. [27]When the mourning was over, David sent and brought her to his house, and she became his wife, and bore him a son.

Nathan Condemns David

But the thing that David had done displeased the Lord, **12** [1]and the Lord sent Nathan to David. He came to him, and said to him, "There were two men in a certain city, the one rich and the other poor. [2]The rich man had very many flocks and herds; [3]but the poor man had nothing but one little ewe lamb, which he had bought. He brought it up, and it grew up with him and with his children; it used to eat of his meager fare, and drink from his cup, and lie in his bosom, and it was like a daughter to him. [4]Now there came a traveler to the rich man, and he was loath to take one of his own flock or herd to prepare for the wayfarer who had come to him, but he took the poor man's lamb, and prepared that for the guest who had come to him." [5]Then David's anger was greatly kindled against the man. He said to Nathan, "As the Lord lives, the man who has done this deserves to die; [6]he shall restore the lamb fourfold, because he did this thing, and because he had no pity."

7 Nathan said to David, "You are the man! Thus says the Lord, the God of Israel: I anointed you king over Israel, and I rescued you from the hand of Saul; [8]I gave you your master's house, and your master's wives into your bosom, and gave you the house of Israel and of Judah; and if that had been too little, I would have added as much more. [9]Why have you despised the word of the Lord, to do what is evil in his sight? You have struck down Uriah the Hittite with the sword, and have taken his wife

a Gk Syr Judg 7.1: Heb *Jerubbesheth*

to be your wife, and have killed him with the sword of the Ammonites. [10]Now therefore the sword shall never depart from your house, for you have despised me, and have taken the wife of Uriah the Hittite to be your wife. [11]Thus says the LORD: I will raise up trouble against you from within your own house; and I will take your wives before your eyes, and give them to your neighbor, and he shall lie with your wives in the sight of this very sun. [12]For you did it secretly; but I will do this thing before all Israel, and before the sun." [13]David said to Nathan, "I have sinned against the LORD." Nathan said to David, "Now the LORD has put away your sin; you shall not die. [14]Nevertheless, because by this deed you have utterly scorned the LORD,[a] the child that is born to you shall die." [15]Then Nathan went to his house.

Bathsheba's Child Dies

The LORD struck the child that Uriah's wife bore to David, and it became very ill. [16]David therefore pleaded with God for the child; David fasted, and went in and lay all night on the ground. [17]The elders of his house stood beside him, urging him to rise from the ground; but he would not, nor did he eat food with them. [18]On the seventh day the child died. And the servants of David were afraid to tell him that the child was dead; for they said, "While the child was still alive, we spoke to him, and he did not listen to us; how then can we tell him the child is dead? He may do himself some harm." [19]But when David saw that his servants were whispering together, he perceived that the child was dead; and David said to his servants, "Is the child dead?" They said, "He is dead."

20 Then David rose from the ground, washed, anointed himself, and changed his clothes. He went into the house of the LORD, and worshiped; he then went to his own house; and when he asked, they set food before him and he ate. [21]Then his servants said to him, "What is this thing that you have done? You fasted and wept for the child while it was alive; but when the child died, you rose and ate food." [22]He said, "While the child was still alive, I fasted and wept; for I said, 'Who knows? The LORD may be gracious to me, and the child may live.' [23]But now he is dead; why should I fast? Can I bring him back again? I shall go to him, but he will not return to me."

Solomon Is Born

24 Then David consoled his wife Bathsheba, and went to her, and lay with her; and she bore a son, and he named him Solomon. The LORD loved him, [25]and sent a message by the prophet Nathan; so he named him Jedidiah,[b] because of the LORD.

The Ammonites Crushed

26 Now Joab fought against Rabbah of the Ammonites, and took the royal city. [27]Joab sent messengers to David, and said, "I have fought against Rabbah; moreover, I have taken the water city. [28]Now, then, gather the rest of the people together, and encamp against the city,

Pleading for Another

2 SAMUEL 12.16

David's pleading and fasting constitute a prayer of intercession, which in his day was a priestly act of loving identification with a suffering person.

For whom are you called to intercede today? Bring one or more persons into your heart and mind. In love, try to identify with their need or distress. Then, holding them in your heart, open yourself to God's love for them as you understand that love. Let that love flow through you toward those in need.

See Meeting God in Prayer

---

a Ancient scribal tradition: Compare 1 Sam 25.22 note: Heb *scorned the enemies of the LORD*   b That is *Beloved of the LORD*

Good and Evil

2 SAMUEL 13.5

"Evil is changed into good when it is received in patience through the love of God; while good is changed into evil when we become attached to it through the love of self. True good lies only in detachment, and abandonment to God. You are now in the trial; put yourself confidently and without reserve into his hand. What would I not sacrifice to see you once more restored in body, but heartily sick of the love of the world! Attachment to ourselves is a thousand times more infectious than a contagious poison, for it contains the venom of self. I pray for you with all my heart."

—FRANÇOIS FÈNELON,
Spiritual Letters (Letter 7)

and take it; or I myself will take the city, and it will be called by my name." [29]So David gathered all the people together and went to Rabbah, and fought against it and took it. [30]He took the crown of Milcom[a] from his head; the weight of it was a talent of gold, and in it was a precious stone; and it was placed on David's head. He also brought forth the spoil of the city, a very great amount. [31]He brought out the people who were in it, and set them to work with saws and iron picks and iron axes, or sent them to the brickworks. Thus he did to all the cities of the Ammonites. Then David and all the people returned to Jerusalem.

Amnon and Tamar

13 Some time passed. David's son Absalom had a beautiful sister whose name was Tamar; and David's son Amnon fell in love with her. [2]Amnon was so tormented that he made himself ill because of his sister Tamar, for she was a virgin and it seemed impossible to Amnon to do anything to her. [3]But Amnon had a friend whose name was Jonadab, the son of David's brother Shimeah; and Jonadab was a very crafty man. [4]He said to him, "O son of the king, why are you so haggard morning after morning? Will you not tell me?" Amnon said to him, "I love Tamar, my brother Absalom's sister." [5]Jonadab said to him, "Lie down on your bed, and pretend to be ill; and when your father comes to see you, say to him, 'Let my sister Tamar come and give me something to eat, and prepare the food in my sight, so that I may see it and eat it from her hand.'" [6]So Amnon lay down, and pretended to be ill; and when the king came to see him, Amnon said to the king, "Please let my sister Tamar come and make a couple of cakes in my sight, so that I may eat from her hand."

7 Then David sent home to Tamar, saying, "Go to your brother Amnon's house, and prepare food for him." [8]So Tamar went to her brother Amnon's house, where he was lying down. She took dough, kneaded it, made cakes in his sight, and baked the cakes. [9]Then she took the pan and set them[b] out before him, but he refused to eat. Amnon said, "Send out everyone from me." So everyone went out from him. [10]Then Amnon said to Tamar, "Bring the food into the chamber, so that I may eat from your hand." So Tamar took the cakes she had made, and brought them into the chamber to Amnon her brother. [11]But when she brought them near him to eat, he took hold of her, and said to her, "Come, lie with me, my sister." [12]She answered him, "No, my brother, do not force me; for such a thing is not done in Israel; do not do anything so vile! [13]As for me, where could I carry my shame? And as for you, you would be as one of the scoundrels in Israel. Now therefore, I beg you, speak to the king; for he will not withhold me from you." [14]But he would not listen to her; and being stronger than she, he forced her and lay with her.

15 Then Amnon was seized with a very great loathing for her; indeed, his loathing was even greater than the lust he had felt for her. Amnon said to her, "Get out!"

a Gk See 1 Kings 11.5, 33: Heb *their kings*   *b* Heb *and poured*

¹⁶But she said to him, "No, my brother;ᵃ for this wrong in sending me away is greater than the other that you did to me." But he would not listen to her. ¹⁷He called the young man who served him and said, "Put this woman out of my presence, and bolt the door after her." ¹⁸(Now she was wearing a long robe with sleeves; for this is how the virgin daughters of the king were clothed in earlier times.ᵇ) So his servant put her out, and bolted the door after her. ¹⁹But Tamar put ashes on her head, and tore the long robe that she was wearing; she put her hand on her head, and went away, crying aloud as she went.

20 Her brother Absalom said to her, "Has Amnon your brother been with you? Be quiet for now, my sister; he is your brother; do not take this to heart." So Tamar remained, a desolate woman, in her brother Absalom's house. ²¹When King David heard of all these things, he became very angry, but he would not punish his son Amnon, because he loved him, for he was his firstborn.ᶜ ²²But Absalom spoke to Amnon neither good nor bad; for Absalom hated Amnon, because he had raped his sister Tamar.

Absalom Avenges the Violation of His Sister

23 After two full years Absalom had sheepshearers at Baal-hazor, which is near Ephraim, and Absalom invited all the king's sons. ²⁴Absalom came to the king, and said, "Your servant has sheepshearers; will the king and his servants please go with your servant?" ²⁵But the king said to Absalom, "No, my son, let us not all go, or else we will be burdensome to you." He pressed him, but he would not go but gave him his blessing. ²⁶Then Absalom said, "If not, please let my brother Amnon go with us." The king said to him, "Why should he go with you?" ²⁷But Absalom pressed him until he let Amnon and all the king's sons go with him. Absalom made a feast like a king's feast.ᵈ ²⁸Then Absalom commanded his servants, "Watch when Amnon's heart is merry with wine, and when I say to you, 'Strike Amnon,' then kill him. Do not be afraid; have I not myself commanded you? Be courageous and valiant." ²⁹So the servants of Absalom did to Amnon as Absalom had commanded. Then all the king's sons rose, and each mounted his mule and fled.

30 While they were on the way, the report came to David that Absalom had killed all the king's sons, and not one of them was left. ³¹The king rose, tore his garments, and lay on the ground; and all his servants who were standing by tore their garments. ³²But Jonadab, the son of David's brother Shimeah, said, "Let not my lord suppose that they have killed all the young men the king's sons; Amnon alone is dead. This has been determined by Absalom from the day Amnonᵉ raped his sister Tamar. ³³Now therefore, do not let my lord the king take it to heart, as if all the king's sons were dead; for Amnon alone is dead."

34 But Absalom fled. When the young man who kept

Violent Cruelty

2 SAMUEL 13.15

The story of Tamar, Amnon and Jonadab is hard to read for it is a story of cruelty, abuse and neglect. But we may also realize through this story that God does not hide his face from the hardest things in life. Through this story we see that evil is real and that God does not gloss over this reality.

Pray today for anyone you know who is or has been abused. Set aside a special time each day this week and offer to God's care all people who suffer from violence within their families. Pray for people who are afraid. Pray for those people who try to protect the weaker and more vulnerable members of our communities.

See Meeting God in Community

---

a Cn Compare Gk Vg: Meaning of Heb uncertain   *b* Cn: Heb *were clothed in robes*   *c* Q Ms Gk: MT lacks *but he would not punish . . . firstborn*
d Gk Compare Q Ms: MT lacks *Absalom made a feast like a king's feast*
e Heb *he*

Justice

2 SAMUEL 14.4–13

Like Nathan's earlier tale of the little ewe lamb (chapter 12), Joab's hired "wise woman" spins a tale about her family's threatened clan feud and bloodbath. She, too, makes the point that the king's principles do not necessarily carry over into his concrete decisions—in this case, to call his own son Absalom out of exile. We, too, may not always practice what we preach, calling for justice for oppressed groups while avoiding contact with their members or neglecting to bring justice into our own relationships, work situation or families. Can you think of areas where your abstract principles are not practiced concretely? The Choristers' Prayer of the Royal School of Church Music asks God that "what we sing [or say] with our lips we may believe in our hearts and what we believe in our hearts, we may show forth in our lives." Let this be your prayer today.

See Meeting God in Service

watch looked up, he saw many people coming from the Horonaim road[a] by the side of the mountain. [35]Jonadab said to the king, "See, the king's sons have come; as your servant said, so it has come about." [36]As soon as he had finished speaking, the king's sons arrived, and raised their voices and wept; and the king and all his servants also wept very bitterly.

37 But Absalom fled, and went to Talmai son of Ammihud, king of Geshur. David mourned for his son day after day. [38]Absalom, having fled to Geshur, stayed there three years. [39]And the heart of[b] the king went out, yearning for Absalom; for he was now consoled over the death of Amnon.

Absalom Returns to Jerusalem

14 Now Joab son of Zeruiah perceived that the king's mind was on Absalom. [2]Joab sent to Tekoa and brought from there a wise woman. He said to her, "Pretend to be a mourner; put on mourning garments, do not anoint yourself with oil, but behave like a woman who has been mourning many days for the dead. [3]Go to the king and speak to him as follows." And Joab put the words into her mouth.

4 When the woman of Tekoa came to the king, she fell on her face to the ground and did obeisance, and said, "Help, O king!" [5]The king asked her, "What is your trouble?" She answered, "Alas, I am a widow; my husband is dead. [6]Your servant had two sons, and they fought with one another in the field; there was no one to part them, and one struck the other and killed him. [7]Now the whole family has risen against your servant. They say, 'Give up the man who struck his brother, so that we may kill him for the life of his brother whom he murdered, even if we destroy the heir as well.' Thus they would quench my one remaining ember, and leave to my husband neither name nor remnant on the face of the earth."

8 Then the king said to the woman, "Go to your house, and I will give orders concerning you." [9]The woman of Tekoa said to the king, "On me be the guilt, my lord the king, and on my father's house; let the king and his throne be guiltless." [10]The king said, "If anyone says anything to you, bring him to me, and he shall never touch you again." [11]Then she said, "Please, may the king keep the Lord your God in mind, so that the avenger of blood may kill no more, and my son not be destroyed." He said, "As the Lord lives, not one hair of your son shall fall to the ground."

12 Then the woman said, "Please let your servant speak a word to my lord the king." He said, "Speak." [13]The woman said, "Why then have you planned such a thing against the people of God? For in giving this decision the king convicts himself, inasmuch as the king does not bring his banished one home again. [14]We must all die; we are like water spilled on the ground, which cannot be gathered up. But God will not take away a life; he will devise plans so as not to keep an outcast banished forever from his presence.[c] [15]Now I have come to say this to my

a Cn Compare Gk: Heb *the road behind him*   b Q Ms Gk: MT *And David*
c Meaning of Heb uncertain

lord the king because the people have made me afraid; your servant thought, 'I will speak to the king; it may be that the king will perform the request of his servant. [16]For the king will hear, and deliver his servant from the hand of the man who would cut both me and my son off from the heritage of God.' [17]Your servant thought, 'The word of my lord the king will set me at rest'; for my lord the king is like the angel of God, discerning good and evil. The LORD your God be with you!"

18 Then the king answered the woman, "Do not withhold from me anything I ask you." The woman said, "Let my lord the king speak." [19]The king said, "Is the hand of Joab with you in all this?" The woman answered and said, "As surely as you live, my lord the king, one cannot turn right or left from anything that my lord the king has said. For it was your servant Joab who commanded me; it was he who put all these words into the mouth of your servant. [20]In order to change the course of affairs your servant Joab did this. But my lord has wisdom like the wisdom of the angel of God to know all things that are on the earth."

21 Then the king said to Joab, "Very well, I grant this; go, bring back the young man Absalom." [22]Joab prostrated himself with his face to the ground and did obeisance, and blessed the king; and Joab said, "Today your servant knows that I have found favor in your sight, my lord the king, in that the king has granted the request of his servant." [23]So Joab set off, went to Geshur, and brought Absalom to Jerusalem. [24]The king said, "Let him go to his own house; he is not to come into my presence." So Absalom went to his own house, and did not come into the king's presence.

David Forgives Absalom

25 Now in all Israel there was no one to be praised so much for his beauty as Absalom; from the sole of his foot to the crown of his head there was no blemish in him. [26]When he cut the hair of his head (for at the end of every year he used to cut it; when it was heavy on him, he cut it), he weighed the hair of his head, two hundred shekels by the king's weight. [27]There were born to Absalom three sons, and one daughter whose name was Tamar; she was a beautiful woman.

28 So Absalom lived two full years in Jerusalem, without coming into the king's presence. [29]Then Absalom sent for Joab to send him to the king; but Joab would not come to him. He sent a second time, but Joab would not come. [30]Then he said to his servants, "Look, Joab's field is next to mine, and he has barley there; go and set it on fire." So Absalom's servants set the field on fire. [31]Then Joab rose and went to Absalom at his house, and said to him, "Why have your servants set my field on fire?" [32]Absalom answered Joab, "Look, I sent word to you: Come here, that I may send you to the king with the question, 'Why have I come from Geshur? It would be better for me to be there still.' Now let me go into the king's presence; if there is guilt in me, let him kill me!" [33]Then Joab went to the king and told him; and he summoned Absalom. So he came to the king and prostrated himself with his face to the ground before the king; and the king kissed Absalom.

Conspiracies of Silence

2 SAMUEL 15.10–12

"In Germany they came first for the Communists, and I didn't speak up because I wasn't a Communist. Then they came for the Jews, and I didn't speak up because I wasn't a Jew. Then they came for the trade unionists, and I didn't speak up because I wasn't a trade unionist. Then they came for the Catholics, and I didn't speak up because I was a Protestant. Then they came for me, and by that time, there was no one left to speak up."

—Attributed to Pastor Martin Niemoeller

Absalom Usurps the Throne

15 After this Absalom got himself a chariot and horses, and fifty men to run ahead of him. ²Absalom used to rise early and stand beside the road into the gate; and when anyone brought a suit before the king for judgment, Absalom would call out and say, "From what city are you?" When the person said, "Your servant is of such and such a tribe in Israel," ³Absalom would say, "See, your claims are good and right; but there is no one deputed by the king to hear you." ⁴Absalom said moreover, "If only I were judge in the land! Then all who had a suit or cause might come to me, and I would give them justice." ⁵Whenever people came near to do obeisance to him, he would put out his hand and take hold of them, and kiss them. ⁶Thus Absalom did to every Israelite who came to the king for judgment; so Absalom stole the hearts of the people of Israel.

7 At the end of four[a] years Absalom said to the king, "Please let me go to Hebron and pay the vow that I have made to the LORD. ⁸For your servant made a vow while I lived at Geshur in Aram: If the LORD will indeed bring me back to Jerusalem, then I will worship the LORD in Hebron."[b] ⁹The king said to him, "Go in peace." So he got up, and went to Hebron. ¹⁰But Absalom sent secret messengers throughout all the tribes of Israel, saying, "As soon as you hear the sound of the trumpet, then shout: Absalom has become king at Hebron!" ¹¹Two hundred men from Jerusalem went with Absalom; they were invited guests, and they went in their innocence, knowing nothing of the matter. ¹²While Absalom was offering the sacrifices, he sent for[c] Ahithophel the Gilonite, David's counselor, from his city Giloh. The conspiracy grew in strength, and the people with Absalom kept increasing.

David Flees from Jerusalem

13 A messenger came to David, saying, "The hearts of the Israelites have gone after Absalom." ¹⁴Then David said to all his officials who were with him at Jerusalem, "Get up! Let us flee, or there will be no escape for us from Absalom. Hurry, or he will soon overtake us, and bring disaster down upon us, and attack the city with the edge of the sword." ¹⁵The king's officials said to the king, "Your servants are ready to do whatever our lord the king decides." ¹⁶So the king left, followed by all his household, except ten concubines whom he left behind to look after the house. ¹⁷The king left, followed by all the people; and they stopped at the last house. ¹⁸All his officials passed by him; and all the Cherethites, and all the Pelethites, and all the six hundred Gittites who had followed him from Gath, passed on before the king.

19 Then the king said to Ittai the Gittite, "Why are you also coming with us? Go back, and stay with the king; for you are a foreigner, and also an exile from your home. ²⁰You came only yesterday, and shall I today make you wander about with us, while I go wherever I can? Go back, and take your kinsfolk with you; and may the LORD show[d]

a Gk Syr: Heb *forty*   b Gk Mss: Heb lacks *in Hebron*   c Or *he sent*
d Gk Compare 2.6: Heb lacks *may the LORD show*

steadfast love and faithfulness to you." ²¹But Ittai answered the king, "As the LORD lives, and as my lord the king lives, wherever my lord the king may be, whether for death or for life, there also your servant will be." ²²David said to Ittai, "Go then, march on." So Ittai the Gittite marched on, with all his men and all the little ones who were with him. ²³The whole country wept aloud as all the people passed by; the king crossed the Wadi Kidron, and all the people moved on toward the wilderness.

24 Abiathar came up, and Zadok also, with all the Levites, carrying the ark of the covenant of God. They set down the ark of God, until the people had all passed out of the city. ²⁵Then the king said to Zadok, "Carry the ark of God back into the city. If I find favor in the eyes of the LORD, he will bring me back and let me see both it and the place where it stays. ²⁶But if he says, 'I take no pleasure in you,' here I am, let him do to me what seems good to him." ²⁷The king also said to the priest Zadok, "Look,ᵃ go back to the city in peace, you and Abiathar,ᵇ with your two sons, Ahimaaz your son, and Jonathan son of Abiathar. ²⁸See, I will wait at the fords of the wilderness until word comes from you to inform me." ²⁹So Zadok and Abiathar carried the ark of God back to Jerusalem, and they remained there.

30 But David went up the ascent of the Mount of Olives, weeping as he went, with his head covered and walking barefoot; and all the people who were with him covered their heads and went up, weeping as they went. ³¹David was told that Ahithophel was among the conspirators with Absalom. And David said, "O LORD, I pray you, turn the counsel of Ahithophel into foolishness."

Hushai Becomes David's Spy

32 When David came to the summit, where God was worshiped, Hushai the Archite came to meet him with his coat torn and earth on his head. ³³David said to him, "If you go on with me, you will be a burden to me. ³⁴But if you return to the city and say to Absalom, 'I will be your servant, O king; as I have been your father's servant in time past, so now I will be your servant,' then you will defeat for me the counsel of Ahithophel. ³⁵The priests Zadok and Abiathar will be with you there. So whatever you hear from the king's house, tell it to the priests Zadok and Abiathar. ³⁶Their two sons are with them there, Zadok's son Ahimaaz and Abiathar's son Jonathan; and by them you shall report to me everything you hear." ³⁷So Hushai, David's friend, came into the city, just as Absalom was entering Jerusalem.

David's Adversaries

16 When David had passed a little beyond the summit, Ziba the servant of Mephiboshethᶜ met him, with a couple of donkeys saddled, carrying two hundred loaves of bread, one hundred bunches of raisins, one hundred of summer fruits, and one skin of wine. ²The king said to Ziba, "Why have you brought these?" Ziba answered, "The donkeys are for the king's household to

Fidelity

2 SAMUEL 15.21

Ittai the Gittite pledges that in life or death, "Wherever my lord the king may be . . . there also your servant will be." Such fidelity is particularly striking today, when people are shifting residences, work places, relationships and church affiliations with such frequency. To what values, and to which people, do you commit yourself? What commitments have you made—to yourself, to others, to your community and to God—that involve real pledges of fidelity? How do you nurture these commitments to help them become stronger? How do you stay faithful to old commitments as you move on to new interests? Take your current commitments to prayer, being open to any ideas that come regarding how to strengthen them; be open to new commitments you may be called to make.

See *Meeting God in Community*

---

a Gk: Heb *Are you a seer* or *Do you see?*   b Cn: Heb lacks *and Abiathar*
c Or *Merib-baal*: See 4.4 note

Cursing and Blessing

2 SAMUEL 16.5–7

When Shimei curses David, saying, "Disaster has overtaken you; for you are a man of blood," the refugee king does not retaliate. In what situations do you feel called to "curse" by blasting someone personally, or by sounding off about some social issue? Christians are called to bless and not curse (see Luke 6.28), a principle founded on the belief that goodness can overcome evil, and blessings can counteract curses. Consider how you might reframe your "curse" into a more positive declaration of objection or challenge—and follow up on the issue by communicating with a government official or business leader.

See Meeting God in Everyday Life

ride, the bread and summer fruit for the young men to eat, and the wine is for those to drink who faint in the wilderness." ³The king said, "And where is your master's son?" Ziba said to the king, "He remains in Jerusalem; for he said, 'Today the house of Israel will give me back my grandfather's kingdom.' " ⁴Then the king said to Ziba, "All that belonged to Mephibosheth*a* is now yours." Ziba said, "I do obeisance; let me find favor in your sight, my lord the king."

Shimei Curses David

5 When King David came to Bahurim, a man of the family of the house of Saul came out whose name was Shimei son of Gera; he came out cursing. ⁶He threw stones at David and at all the servants of King David; now all the people and all the warriors were on his right and on his left. ⁷Shimei shouted while he cursed, "Out! Out! Murderer! Scoundrel! ⁸The LORD has avenged on all of you the blood of the house of Saul, in whose place you have reigned; and the LORD has given the kingdom into the hand of your son Absalom. See, disaster has overtaken you; for you are a man of blood."

9 Then Abishai son of Zeruiah said to the king, "Why should this dead dog curse my lord the king? Let me go over and take off his head." ¹⁰But the king said, "What have I to do with you, you sons of Zeruiah? If he is cursing because the LORD has said to him, 'Curse David,' who then shall say, 'Why have you done so?' " ¹¹David said to Abishai and to all his servants, "My own son seeks my life; how much more now may this Benjaminite! Let him alone, and let him curse; for the LORD has bidden him. ¹²It may be that the LORD will look on my distress,*b* and the LORD will repay me with good for this cursing of me today." ¹³So David and his men went on the road, while Shimei went along on the hillside opposite him and cursed as he went, throwing stones and flinging dust at him. ¹⁴The king and all the people who were with him arrived weary at the Jordan;*c* and there he refreshed himself.

The Counsel of Ahithophel

15 Now Absalom and all the Israelites*d* came to Jerusalem; Ahithophel was with him. ¹⁶When Hushai the Archite, David's friend, came to Absalom, Hushai said to Absalom, "Long live the king! Long live the king!" ¹⁷Absalom said to Hushai, "Is this your loyalty to your friend? Why did you not go with your friend?" ¹⁸Hushai said to Absalom, "No; but the one whom the LORD and this people and all the Israelites have chosen, his I will be, and with him I will remain. ¹⁹Moreover, whom should I serve? Should it not be his son? Just as I have served your father, so I will serve you."

20 Then Absalom said to Ahithophel, "Give us your counsel; what shall we do?" ²¹Ahithophel said to Absalom, "Go in to your father's concubines, the ones he has left to look after the house; and all Israel will hear that you have made yourself odious to your father, and the hands of all

---

a Or *Merib-baal:* See 4.4 note   *b* Gk Vg: Heb *iniquity*   *c* Gk: Heb lacks *at the Jordan*   *d* Gk: Heb *all the people, the men of Israel*

who are with you will be strengthened." ²²So they pitched a tent for Absalom upon the roof; and Absalom went in to his father's concubines in the sight of all Israel. ²³Now in those days the counsel that Ahithophel gave was as if one consulted the oracle^a of God; so all the counsel of Ahithophel was esteemed, both by David and by Absalom.

17 Moreover Ahithophel said to Absalom, "Let me choose twelve thousand men, and I will set out and pursue David tonight. ²I will come upon him while he is weary and discouraged, and throw him into a panic; and all the people who are with him will flee. I will strike down only the king, ³and I will bring all the people back to you as a bride comes home to her husband. You seek the life of only one man,^b and all the people will be at peace." ⁴The advice pleased Absalom and all the elders of Israel.

The Counsel of Hushai

5 Then Absalom said, "Call Hushai the Archite also, and let us hear too what he has to say." ⁶When Hushai came to Absalom, Absalom said to him, "This is what Ahithophel has said; shall we do as he advises? If not, you tell us." ⁷Then Hushai said to Absalom, "This time the counsel that Ahithophel has given is not good." ⁸Hushai continued, "You know that your father and his men are warriors, and that they are enraged, like a bear robbed of her cubs in the field. Besides, your father is expert in war; he will not spend the night with the troops. ⁹Even now he has hidden himself in one of the pits, or in some other place. And when some of our troops^c fall at the first attack, whoever hears it will say, 'There has been a slaughter among the troops who follow Absalom.' ¹⁰Then even the valiant warrior, whose heart is like the heart of a lion, will utterly melt with fear; for all Israel knows that your father is a warrior, and that those who are with him are valiant warriors. ¹¹But my counsel is that all Israel be gathered to you, from Dan to Beer-sheba, like the sand by the sea for multitude, and that you go to battle in person. ¹²So we shall come upon him in whatever place he may be found, and we shall light on him as the dew falls on the ground; and he will not survive, nor will any of those with him. ¹³If he withdraws into a city, then all Israel will bring ropes to that city, and we shall drag it into the valley, until not even a pebble is to be found there." ¹⁴Absalom and all the men of Israel said, "The counsel of Hushai the Archite is better than the counsel of Ahithophel." For the LORD had ordained to defeat the good counsel of Ahithophel, so that the LORD might bring ruin on Absalom.

Hushai Warns David to Escape

15 Then Hushai said to the priests Zadok and Abiathar, "Thus and so did Ahithophel counsel Absalom and the elders of Israel; and thus and so I have counseled. ¹⁶Therefore send quickly and tell David, 'Do not lodge tonight at the fords of the wilderness, but by all means

Advice Is Easily Given

2 SAMUEL 17.7

Absalom rejects Ahithophel's sage advice for a bold strike against David in favor of the more cautious counsel of Hushai, thus dooming his cause. On what occasions in your life have you rejected the advice of wise and experienced souls in favor of more comforting counsel? When have you chosen, unwisely, the cautious and careful course when the bold, decisive one would have been more fruitful? What qualities make for a good adviser? Who have been your most trusted advisers—the people whose counsel has proven most accurate and helpful? Are there occasions when you have felt that the counsel you received through another was, in truth, the guidance of God?

See Meeting God in Community

Leadership and Authority

2 SAMUEL 18.3

"You are worth ten thousand of us," the men tell David, recognizing the innate authority of inspiring leadership on the battlefield and firm discipline applied well. The Gospels describe Jesus, the Son of David, as one who speaks with authority.

Such authority arises from how one conducts oneself, not merely from appointment or election. Who are the people you look up to as having authentic authority? What characteristics do they have?

What is the main source of your authority: age, size, assertiveness, hierarchy at work, parental status? How much of your authority comes from your status, and how much comes from your character and actions? In what ways do you use your authority for the good of others? How is your exercise of authority Christlike?

See Meeting God in Service

cross over; otherwise the king and all the people who are with him will be swallowed up.'" [17]Jonathan and Ahimaaz were waiting at En-rogel; a servant-girl used to go and tell them, and they would go and tell King David; for they could not risk being seen entering the city. [18]But a boy saw them, and told Absalom; so both of them went away quickly, and came to the house of a man at Bahurim, who had a well in his courtyard; and they went down into it. [19]The man's wife took a covering, stretched it over the well's mouth, and spread out grain on it; and nothing was known of it. [20]When Absalom's servants came to the woman at the house, they said, "Where are Ahimaaz and Jonathan?" The woman said to them, "They have crossed over the brook[a] of water." And when they had searched and could not find them, they returned to Jerusalem.

21 After they had gone, the men came up out of the well, and went and told King David. They said to David, "Go and cross the water quickly; for thus and so has Ahithophel counseled against you." [22]So David and all the people who were with him set out and crossed the Jordan; by daybreak not one was left who had not crossed the Jordan.

23 When Ahithophel saw that his counsel was not followed, he saddled his donkey and went off home to his own city. He set his house in order, and hanged himself; he died and was buried in the tomb of his father.

24 Then David came to Mahanaim, while Absalom crossed the Jordan with all the men of Israel. [25]Now Absalom had set Amasa over the army in the place of Joab. Amasa was the son of a man named Ithra the Ishmaelite,[b] who had married Abigal daughter of Nahash, sister of Zeruiah, Joab's mother. [26]The Israelites and Absalom encamped in the land of Gilead.

27 When David came to Mahanaim, Shobi son of Nahash from Rabbah of the Ammonites, and Machir son of Ammiel from Lo-debar, and Barzillai the Gileadite from Rogelim, [28]brought beds, basins, and earthen vessels, wheat, barley, meal, parched grain, beans and lentils,[c] [29]honey and curds, sheep, and cheese from the herd, for David and the people with him to eat; for they said, "The troops are hungry and weary and thirsty in the wilderness."

The Defeat and Death of Absalom

18 Then David mustered the men who were with him, and set over them commanders of thousands and commanders of hundreds. [2]And David divided the army into three groups:[d] one third under the command of Joab, one third under the command of Abishai son of Zeruiah, Joab's brother, and one third under the command of Ittai the Gittite. The king said to the men, "I myself will also go out with you." [3]But the men said, "You shall not go out. For if we flee, they will not care about us. If half of us die, they will not care about us. But you are worth ten thousand of us;[e] therefore it is better that you send us

---

a Meaning of Heb uncertain   *b* 1 Chr 2.17: Heb *Israelite*   *c* Heb *and lentils and parched grain*   *d* Gk: Heb *sent forth the army*   *e* Gk Vg Symmachus: Heb *for now there are ten thousand such as we*

help from the city." ⁴The king said to them, "Whatever seems best to you I will do." So the king stood at the side of the gate, while all the army marched out by hundreds and by thousands. ⁵The king ordered Joab and Abishai and Ittai, saying, "Deal gently for my sake with the young man Absalom." And all the people heard when the king gave orders to all the commanders concerning Absalom.

6 So the army went out into the field against Israel; and the battle was fought in the forest of Ephraim. ⁷The men of Israel were defeated there by the servants of David, and the slaughter there was great on that day, twenty thousand men. ⁸The battle spread over the face of all the country; and the forest claimed more victims that day than the sword.

9 Absalom happened to meet the servants of David. Absalom was riding on his mule, and the mule went under the thick branches of a great oak. His head caught fast in the oak, and he was left hanging*a* between heaven and earth, while the mule that was under him went on. ¹⁰A man saw it, and told Joab, "I saw Absalom hanging in an oak." ¹¹Joab said to the man who told him, "What, you saw him! Why then did you not strike him there to the ground? I would have been glad to give you ten pieces of silver and a belt." ¹²But the man said to Joab, "Even if I felt in my hand the weight of a thousand pieces of silver, I would not raise my hand against the king's son; for in our hearing the king commanded you and Abishai and Ittai, saying: For my sake protect the young man Absalom! ¹³On the other hand, if I had dealt treacherously against his life*b* (and there is nothing hidden from the king), then you yourself would have stood aloof." ¹⁴Joab said, "I will not waste time like this with you." He took three spears in his hand, and thrust them into the heart of Absalom, while he was still alive in the oak. ¹⁵And ten young men, Joab's armor-bearers, surrounded Absalom and struck him, and killed him.

16 Then Joab sounded the trumpet, and the troops came back from pursuing Israel, for Joab restrained the troops. ¹⁷They took Absalom, threw him into a great pit in the forest, and raised over him a very great heap of stones. Meanwhile all the Israelites fled to their homes. ¹⁸Now Absalom in his lifetime had taken and set up for himself a pillar that is in the King's Valley, for he said, "I have no son to keep my name in remembrance"; he called the pillar by his own name. It is called Absalom's Monument to this day.

David Hears of Absalom's Death

19 Then Ahimaaz son of Zadok said, "Let me run, and carry tidings to the king that the LORD has delivered him from the power of his enemies." ²⁰Joab said to him, "You are not to carry tidings today; you may carry tidings another day, but today you shall not do so, because the king's son is dead." ²¹Then Joab said to a Cushite, "Go, tell the king what you have seen." The Cushite bowed before Joab, and ran. ²²Then Ahimaaz son of Zadok said again to Joab, "Come what may, let me also run after the

Remembrance

2 SAMUEL 18.18

Very likely there was little or no writing on Absalom's monument. Even today, our gravestones often list only a name and the dates of birth and death. Draw the outline of a tombstone, or a pillar like Absalom's, and write on it what you would like to be remembered for: your accomplishments, relationships with God and others, aspirations, commitments, enduring loves. Then consider, in prayer, what sort of monument you are erecting with your life, and what God might wish to say about it.

See Meeting God in Everyday Life

---

a Gk Syr Tg: Heb *was put*   *b* Another reading is *at the risk of my life*

Deep Love

2 SAMUEL 18.33

"O my son Absalom! . . . Would I had died instead of you!" David's indulgent fondness for Absalom, though rooted in genuine, parental love, has led to this tragedy. Now his loud grieving demoralizes the very troops who have saved his kingship. Yet his capacity to give his whole heart to others and to God lies at the center of David's greatness.

Ponder the mystery of such love in your own life. Have your mistakes sometimes been overlooked or forgiven because of another's fondness for you? Have you treated other people close to your heart over-generously, even indulgently? What are some of the warning signs that fondness is leading to indulgence that ought to be challenged? How do you think God seeks to challenge our behavior while still loving us deeply?

Cushite." And Joab said, "Why will you run, my son, seeing that you have no reward[a] for the tidings?" 23"Come what may," he said, "I will run." So he said to him, "Run." Then Ahimaaz ran by the way of the Plain, and outran the Cushite.

24 Now David was sitting between the two gates. The sentinel went up to the roof of the gate by the wall, and when he looked up, he saw a man running alone. 25The sentinel shouted and told the king. The king said, "If he is alone, there are tidings in his mouth." He kept coming, and drew near. 26Then the sentinel saw another man running; and the sentinel called to the gatekeeper and said, "See, another man running alone!" The king said, "He also is bringing tidings." 27The sentinel said, "I think the running of the first one is like the running of Ahimaaz son of Zadok." The king said, "He is a good man, and comes with good tidings."

28 Then Ahimaaz cried out to the king, "All is well!" He prostrated himself before the king with his face to the ground, and said, "Blessed be the LORD your God, who has delivered up the men who raised their hand against my lord the king." 29The king said, "Is it well with the young man Absalom?" Ahimaaz answered, "When Joab sent your servant,[b] I saw a great tumult, but I do not know what it was." 30The king said, "Turn aside, and stand here." So he turned aside, and stood still.

31 Then the Cushite came; and the Cushite said, "Good tidings for my lord the king! For the LORD has vindicated you this day, delivering you from the power of all who rose up against you." 32The king said to the Cushite, "Is it well with the young man Absalom?" The Cushite answered, "May the enemies of my lord the king, and all who rise up to do you harm, be like that young man."

David Mourns for Absalom

33[c] The king was deeply moved, and went up to the chamber over the gate, and wept; and as he went, he said, "O my son Absalom, my son, my son Absalom! Would I had died instead of you, O Absalom, my son, my son!"

19 It was told Joab, "The king is weeping and mourning for Absalom." 2So the victory that day was turned into mourning for all the troops; for the troops heard that day, "The king is grieving for his son." 3The troops stole into the city that day as soldiers steal in who are ashamed when they flee in battle. 4The king covered his face, and the king cried with a loud voice, "O my son Absalom, O Absalom, my son, my son!" 5Then Joab came into the house to the king, and said, "Today you have covered with shame the faces of all your officers who have saved your life today, and the lives of your sons and your daughters, and the lives of your wives and your concubines, 6for love of those who hate you and for hatred of those who love you. You have made it clear today that commanders and officers are nothing to you; for I perceive that if Absalom were alive and all of us were dead today, then you would be

---

a Meaning of Heb uncertain   *b* Heb *the king's servant, your servant*
c Ch 19.1 in Heb

pleased. ⁷So go out at once and speak kindly to your servants; for I swear by the LORD, if you do not go, not a man will stay with you this night; and this will be worse for you than any disaster that has come upon you from your youth until now." ⁸Then the king got up and took his seat in the gate. The troops were all told, "See, the king is sitting in the gate"; and all the troops came before the king.

David Recalled to Jerusalem

Meanwhile, all the Israelites had fled to their homes. ⁹All the people were disputing throughout all the tribes of Israel, saying, "The king delivered us from the hand of our enemies, and saved us from the hand of the Philistines; and now he has fled out of the land because of Absalom. ¹⁰But Absalom, whom we anointed over us, is dead in battle. Now therefore why do you say nothing about bringing the king back?"

11 King David sent this message to the priests Zadok and Abiathar, "Say to the elders of Judah, 'Why should you be the last to bring the king back to his house? The talk of all Israel has come to the king.ᵃ ¹²You are my kin, you are my bone and my flesh; why then should you be the last to bring back the king?' ¹³And say to Amasa, 'Are you not my bone and my flesh? So may God do to me, and more, if you are not the commander of my army from now on, in place of Joab.' " ¹⁴Amasaᵇ swayed the hearts of all the people of Judah as one, and they sent word to the king, "Return, both you and all your servants." ¹⁵So the king came back to the Jordan; and Judah came to Gilgal to meet the king and to bring him over the Jordan.

16 Shimei son of Gera, the Benjaminite, from Bahurim, hurried to come down with the people of Judah to meet King David; ¹⁷with him were a thousand people from Benjamin. And Ziba, the servant of the house of Saul, with his fifteen sons and his twenty servants, rushed down to the Jordan ahead of the king, ¹⁸while the crossing was taking place,ᶜ to bring over the king's household, and to do his pleasure.

David's Mercy to Shimei

Shimei son of Gera fell down before the king, as he was about to cross the Jordan, ¹⁹and said to the king, "May my lord not hold me guilty or remember how your servant did wrong on the day my lord the king left Jerusalem; may the king not bear it in mind. ²⁰For your servant knows that I have sinned; therefore, see, I have come this day, the first of all the house of Joseph to come down to meet my lord the king." ²¹Abishai son of Zeruiah answered, "Shall not Shimei be put to death for this, because he cursed the LORD's anointed?" ²²But David said, "What have I to do with you, you sons of Zeruiah, that you should today become an adversary to me? Shall anyone be put to death in Israel this day? For do I not know that I am this day king over Israel?" ²³The king said to Shimei, "You shall not die." And the king gave him his oath.

Returning Home

2 SAMUEL 19.14–18

David returns to Judah and Jerusalem in a humble, grateful and forgiving spirit. Consider the many "returns" you have made in your life: to important places, to relationships with people, to a lapsed discipline, to a belief or moral behavior. In each act of return, what have you had to be grateful for? What might you have had to forgive in others, or in yourself? As a token of several possible returns in your life, make a point of pausing as you approach your residence or place of work the next few times. Be aware of your first glimpse of the building and its surroundings, of what you treasure there, of the spirit that characterizes your life there, of things that need forgiving, and of how God's abiding presence is manifested to you there.

See Meeting God in Everyday Life

Age and Beauty

2 SAMUEL 19.35

Our youth-glorifying society is often ready to agree with Barzillai's characterization of the aged as an "added burden" because of perceived diminished capabilities. But David accords him the respect he deserves. First, enter into Barzillai's self-estimation: Imagine how it must feel to no longer be able to "discern what is pleasant and what is not," to lose the sensations of taste and hearing? Second, say aloud Augustine's lament, "Too late I loved you, O Beauty ever ancient and ever new! . . . Behold, you were within me" (*Confessions* X.27). Take David's place in the story, and ponder how this "Beauty" is made manifest in those of advanced age. Then begin today, before it is "too late," to use all your senses (inner and outer) to find specific examples of God's beauty in yourself, in others and in the world.

See Meeting God in the Created Order

David and Mephibosheth Meet

24 Mephibosheth[a] grandson of Saul came down to meet the king; he had not taken care of his feet, or trimmed his beard, or washed his clothes, from the day the king left until the day he came back in safety. 25When he came from Jerusalem to meet the king, the king said to him, "Why did you not go with me, Mephibosheth?"[a] 26He answered, "My lord, O king, my servant deceived me; for your servant said to him, 'Saddle a donkey for me,[b] so that I may ride on it and go with the king.' For your servant is lame. 27He has slandered your servant to my lord the king. But my lord the king is like the angel of God; do therefore what seems good to you. 28For all my father's house were doomed to death before my lord the king; but you set your servant among those who eat at your table. What further right have I, then, to appeal to the king?" 29The king said to him, "Why speak any more of your affairs? I have decided: you and Ziba shall divide the land." 30Mephibosheth[a] said to the king, "Let him take it all, since my lord the king has arrived home safely."

David's Kindness to Barzillai

31 Now Barzillai the Gileadite had come down from Rogelim; he went on with the king to the Jordan, to escort him over the Jordan. 32Barzillai was a very aged man, eighty years old. He had provided the king with food while he stayed at Mahanaim, for he was a very wealthy man. 33The king said to Barzillai, "Come over with me, and I will provide for you in Jerusalem at my side." 34But Barzillai said to the king, "How many years have I still to live, that I should go up with the king to Jerusalem? 35Today I am eighty years old; can I discern what is pleasant and what is not? Can your servant taste what he eats or what he drinks? Can I still listen to the voice of singing men and singing women? Why then should your servant be an added burden to my lord the king? 36Your servant will go a little way over the Jordan with the king. Why should the king recompense me with such a reward? 37Please let your servant return, so that I may die in my own town, near the graves of my father and my mother. But here is your servant Chimham; let him go over with my lord the king; and do for him whatever seems good to you." 38The king answered, "Chimham shall go over with me, and I will do for him whatever seems good to you; and all that you desire of me I will do for you." 39Then all the people crossed over the Jordan, and the king crossed over; the king kissed Barzillai and blessed him, and he returned to his own home. 40The king went on to Gilgal, and Chimham went on with him; all the people of Judah, and also half the people of Israel, brought the king on his way.

41 Then all the people of Israel came to the king, and said to him, "Why have our kindred the people of Judah stolen you away, and brought the king and his household over the Jordan, and all David's men with him?" 42All the people of Judah answered the people of Israel, "Because the king is near of kin to us. Why then are you angry over

a Or *Merib-baal:* See 4.4 note   *b* Gk Syr Vg: Heb *said, 'I will saddle a donkey for myself*

this matter? Have we eaten at all at the king's expense? Or has he given us any gift?" ⁴³But the people of Israel answered the people of Judah, "We have ten shares in the king, and in David also we have more than you. Why then did you despise us? Were we not the first to speak of bringing back our king?" But the words of the people of Judah were fiercer than the words of the people of Israel.

The Rebellion of Sheba

20 Now a scoundrel named Sheba son of Bichri, a Benjaminite, happened to be there. He sounded the trumpet and cried out,

"We have no portion in David,
no share in the son of Jesse!
Everyone to your tents, O Israel!"

²So all the people of Israel withdrew from David and followed Sheba son of Bichri; but the people of Judah followed their king steadfastly from the Jordan to Jerusalem.

3 David came to his house at Jerusalem; and the king took the ten concubines whom he had left to look after the house, and put them in a house under guard, and provided for them, but did not go in to them. So they were shut up until the day of their death, living as if in widowhood.

4 Then the king said to Amasa, "Call the men of Judah together to me within three days, and be here yourself." ⁵So Amasa went to summon Judah; but he delayed beyond the set time that had been appointed him. ⁶David said to Abishai, "Now Sheba son of Bichri will do us more harm than Absalom; take your lord's servants and pursue him, or he will find fortified cities for himself, and escape from us." ⁷Joab's men went out after him, along with the Cherethites, the Pelethites, and all the warriors; they went out from Jerusalem to pursue Sheba son of Bichri. ⁸When they were at the large stone that is in Gibeon, Amasa came to meet them. Now Joab was wearing a soldier's garment and over it was a belt with a sword in its sheath fastened at his waist; as he went forward it fell out. ⁹Joab said to Amasa, "Is it well with you, my brother?" And Joab took Amasa by the beard with his right hand to kiss him. ¹⁰But Amasa did not notice the sword in Joab's hand; Joab struck him in the belly so that his entrails poured out on the ground, and he died. He did not strike a second blow.

Then Joab and his brother Abishai pursued Sheba son of Bichri. ¹¹And one of Joab's men took his stand by Amasa, and said, "Whoever favors Joab, and whoever is for David, let him follow Joab." ¹²Amasa lay wallowing in his blood on the highway, and the man saw that all the people were stopping. Since he saw that all who came by him were stopping, he carried Amasa from the highway into a field, and threw a garment over him. ¹³Once he was removed from the highway, all the people went on after Joab to pursue Sheba son of Bichri.

14 Sheba[a] passed through all the tribes of Israel to Abel of Beth-maacah;[b] and all the Bichrites[c] assembled, and

Going Along With the Crowd

2 SAMUEL 20.2

The fickleness of David's troops is no surprise to us, tugged about by instant fads and rising and falling tides of popular opinion. The desire to be "in" is a nonviolent expression of mob mentality. Take a paper and make three columns on it. In the first column, list the messages you are receiving daily from the media and other people about what's "in" and "essential" right now. Then make a list of the core values on the basis of which you decide what is really worthwhile among these many choices. Finally, list ways in which you can resist this cultural pressure and find the strength to be steadfast, like the men of Judah who "followed their king."

See Meeting God in Everyday Life

Famine

2 SAMUEL 21.1

Hunger is as near to us as the newspaper headlines—and not just in far-off deserts but in our own communities. Pray at one meal each day this week, "O Lord, help me truly to know how my rich diet affects scarce resources that feed my sisters and brothers around your abundant earth." Keep a list of your discoveries and use it to consider ways to simplify your diet, contributing any monetary savings to hunger-fighting organizations. Explore ways to share your time, talent or treasure with food banks and soup kitchens in your community; you will then become part of the solution rather than part of the problem.

See Meeting God in the Created Order

followed him inside. ¹⁵Joab's forces*a* came and besieged him in Abel of Beth-maacah; they threw up a siege ramp against the city, and it stood against the rampart. Joab's forces were battering the wall to break it down. ¹⁶Then a wise woman called from the city, "Listen! Listen! Tell Joab, 'Come here, I want to speak to you.' " ¹⁷He came near her; and the woman said, "Are you Joab?" He answered, "I am." Then she said to him, "Listen to the words of your servant." He answered, "I am listening." ¹⁸Then she said, "They used to say in the old days, 'Let them inquire at Abel'; and so they would settle a matter. ¹⁹I am one of those who are peaceable and faithful in Israel; you seek to destroy a city that is a mother in Israel; why will you swallow up the heritage of the LORD?" ²⁰Joab answered, "Far be it from me, far be it, that I should swallow up or destroy! ²¹That is not the case! But a man of the hill country of Ephraim, called Sheba son of Bichri, has lifted up his hand against King David; give him up alone, and I will withdraw from the city." The woman said to Joab, "His head shall be thrown over the wall to you." ²²Then the woman went to all the people with her wise plan. And they cut off the head of Sheba son of Bichri, and threw it out to Joab. So he blew the trumpet, and they dispersed from the city, and all went to their homes, while Joab returned to Jerusalem to the king.

23 Now Joab was in command of all the army of Israel;*b* Benaiah son of Jehoiada was in command of the Cherethites and the Pelethites; ²⁴Adoram was in charge of the forced labor; Jehoshaphat son of Ahilud was the recorder; ²⁵Sheva was secretary; Zadok and Abiathar were priests; ²⁶and Ira the Jairite was also David's priest.

David Avenges the Gibeonites

21 Now there was a famine in the days of David for three years, year after year; and David inquired of the LORD. The LORD said, "There is bloodguilt on Saul and on his house, because he put the Gibeonites to death." ²So the king called the Gibeonites and spoke to them. (Now the Gibeonites were not of the people of Israel, but of the remnant of the Amorites; although the people of Israel had sworn to spare them, Saul had tried to wipe them out in his zeal for the people of Israel and Judah.) ³David said to the Gibeonites, "What shall I do for you? How shall I make expiation, that you may bless the heritage of the LORD?" ⁴The Gibeonites said to him, "It is not a matter of silver or gold between us and Saul or his house; neither is it for us to put anyone to death in Israel." He said, "What do you say that I should do for you?" ⁵They said to the king, "The man who consumed us and planned to destroy us, so that we should have no place in all the territory of Israel— ⁶let seven of his sons be handed over to us, and we will impale them before the LORD at Gibeon on the mountain of the LORD."*c* The king said, "I will hand them over."

7 But the king spared Mephibosheth,*d* the son of Saul's son Jonathan, because of the oath of the LORD that was

a Heb *They*   *b* Cn: Heb *Joab to all the army, Israel*   *c* Cn Compare Gk and 21.9: Heb *at Gibeah of Saul, the chosen of the LORD*   *d* Or *Merib-baal*: See 4.4 note

between them, between David and Jonathan son of Saul. ⁸The king took the two sons of Rizpah daughter of Aiah, whom she bore to Saul, Armoni and Mephibosheth;ᵃ and the five sons of Merabᵇ daughter of Saul, whom she bore to Adriel son of Barzillai the Meholathite; ⁹he gave them into the hands of the Gibeonites, and they impaled them on the mountain before the LORD. The seven of them perished together. They were put to death in the first days of harvest, at the beginning of barley harvest.

10 Then Rizpah the daughter of Aiah took sackcloth, and spread it on a rock for herself, from the beginning of harvest until rain fell on them from the heavens; she did not allow the birds of the air to come on the bodiesᶜ by day, or the wild animals by night. ¹¹When David was told what Rizpah daughter of Aiah, the concubine of Saul, had done, ¹²David went and took the bones of Saul and the bones of his son Jonathan from the people of Jabesh-gilead, who had stolen them from the public square of Bethshan, where the Philistines had hung them up, on the day the Philistines killed Saul on Gilboa. ¹³He brought up from there the bones of Saul and the bones of his son Jonathan; and they gathered the bones of those who had been impaled. ¹⁴They buried the bones of Saul and of his son Jonathan in the land of Benjamin in Zela, in the tomb of his father Kish; they did all that the king commanded. After that, God heeded supplications for the land.

Exploits of David's Men

15 The Philistines went to war again with Israel, and David went down together with his servants. They fought against the Philistines, and David grew weary. ¹⁶Ishbi-benob, one of the descendants of the giants, whose spear weighed three hundred shekels of bronze, and who was fitted out with new weapons,ᵈ said he would kill David. ¹⁷But Abishai son of Zeruiah came to his aid, and attacked the Philistine and killed him. Then David's men swore to him, "You shall not go out with us to battle any longer, so that you do not quench the lamp of Israel."

18 After this a battle took place with the Philistines, at Gob; then Sibbecai the Hushathite killed Saph, who was one of the descendants of the giants. ¹⁹Then there was another battle with the Philistines at Gob; and Elhanan son of Jaare-oregim, the Bethlehemite, killed Goliath the Gittite, the shaft of whose spear was like a weaver's beam. ²⁰There was again war at Gath, where there was a man of great size, who had six fingers on each hand, and six toes on each foot, twenty-four in number; he too was descended from the giants. ²¹When he taunted Israel, Jonathan son of David's brother Shimei, killed him. ²²These four were descended from the giants in Gath; they fell by the hands of David and his servants.

David's Song of Thanksgiving

22 David spoke to the LORD the words of this song on the day when the LORD delivered him from the hand of all his enemies, and from the hand of Saul. ²He said:

ᵃ Or *Merib-baal*: See 4.4 note   ᵇ Two Heb Mss Syr Compare Gk: MT *Michal*   ᶜ Heb *them*   ᵈ Heb *was belted anew*

God's Delight

2 SAMUEL 22.20

Why didn't the Lord leave David and his fighters to fend for themselves? God's love is often difficult to accept, perhaps because it seems too good to be true, especially for "just plain me!" The "broad place" of God's love for us is unfamiliar at first, accustomed as we are to the narrowness of self-deprecation. To the mirror you look into most frequently, attach a piece of paper or card bearing these words: "God delights in me; I am loved eternally." Read those words aloud now and daily for as many days or months as the paper remains intact.

See Meeting God in Everyday Life

The LORD is my rock, my fortress, and my deliverer,
3   my God, my rock, in whom I take refuge,
my shield and the horn of my salvation,
    my stronghold and my refuge,
    my savior; you save me from violence.
4   I call upon the LORD, who is worthy to be praised,
    and I am saved from my enemies.
5   For the waves of death encompassed me,
    the torrents of perdition assailed me;
6   the cords of Sheol entangled me,
    the snares of death confronted me.
7   In my distress I called upon the LORD;
    to my God I called.
From his temple he heard my voice,
    and my cry came to his ears.
8   Then the earth reeled and rocked;
    the foundations of the heavens trembled
    and quaked, because he was angry.
9   Smoke went up from his nostrils,
    and devouring fire from his mouth;
    glowing coals flamed forth from him.
10   He bowed the heavens, and came down;
    thick darkness was under his feet.
11   He rode on a cherub, and flew;
    he was seen upon the wings of the wind.
12   He made darkness around him a canopy,
    thick clouds, a gathering of water.
13   Out of the brightness before him
    coals of fire flamed forth.
14   The LORD thundered from heaven;
    the Most High uttered his voice.
15   He sent out arrows, and scattered them
    —lightning, and routed them.
16   Then the channels of the sea were seen,
    the foundations of the world were laid bare
at the rebuke of the LORD,
    at the blast of the breath of his nostrils.

17   He reached from on high, he took me,
    he drew me out of mighty waters.
18   He delivered me from my strong enemy,
    from those who hated me;
    for they were too mighty for me.
19   They came upon me in the day of my calamity,
    but the LORD was my stay.
20   He brought me out into a broad place;
    he delivered me, because he delighted in me.

21   The LORD rewarded me according to my
        righteousness;
        according to the cleanness of my hands he
        recompensed me.
22   For I have kept the ways of the LORD,
    and have not wickedly departed from my God.
23   For all his ordinances were before me,
    and from his statutes I did not turn aside.

24 I was blameless before him,
  and I kept myself from guilt.
25 Therefore the LORD has recompensed me according
    to my righteousness,
  according to my cleanness in his sight.

26 With the loyal you show yourself loyal;
  with the blameless you show yourself blameless;
27 with the pure you show yourself pure,
  and with the crooked you show yourself
    perverse.
28 You deliver a humble people,
  but your eyes are upon the haughty to bring
    them down.
29 Indeed, you are my lamp, O LORD,
  the LORD lightens my darkness.
30 By you I can crush a troop,
  and by my God I can leap over a wall.
31 This God—his way is perfect;
  the promise of the LORD proves true;
  he is a shield for all who take refuge in him.

32 For who is God, but the LORD?
  And who is a rock, except our God?
33 The God who has girded me with strength*a*
  has opened wide my path.*b*
34 He made my*c* feet like the feet of deer,
  and set me secure on the heights.
35 He trains my hands for war,
  so that my arms can bend a bow of bronze.
36 You have given me the shield of your salvation,
  and your help*d* has made me great.
37 You have made me stride freely,
  and my feet do not slip;
38 I pursued my enemies and destroyed them,
  and did not turn back until they were consumed.
39 I consumed them; I struck them down, so that they
    did not rise;
  they fell under my feet.
40 For you girded me with strength for the battle;
  you made my assailants sink under me.
41 You made my enemies turn their backs to me,
  those who hated me, and I destroyed them.
42 They looked, but there was no one to save them;
  they cried to the LORD, but he did not answer
    them.
43 I beat them fine like the dust of the earth,
  I crushed them and stamped them down like the
    mire of the streets.

44 You delivered me from strife with the peoples;*e*
  you kept me as the head of the nations;
  people whom I had not known served me.
45 Foreigners came cringing to me;
  as soon as they heard of me, they obeyed me.

Darkness Into Light

2 SAMUEL 22.29

The beautiful light of God's presence in art and nature is one of the best antidotes to the darkness of "worldly cares." As Johann von Goethe said, "A person should hear a little music, read a little poetry and see a fine picture every day in order that worldly cares may not obliterate the sense of the beautiful which God has implanted in the human soul." Revise your schedule today to include at least fifteen minutes to listen to peaceful music, read poetry about nature, meditate before a painting or reflect on a photograph that reminds you of your relationship with God. Or, weather permitting, go outdoors to admire the sunrise or sunset. Let your immersion in beauty end with a prayer of thanksgiving to the One who is the source of beauty.

See Meeting God in the Created Order

---

a Q Ms Gk Syr Vg Compare Ps 18.32: MT *God is my strong refuge*
b Meaning of Heb uncertain   *c* Another reading is *his*   *d* Q Ms: MT *your answering*   *e* Gk: Heb *from strife with my people*

I Will Sing Praises

2 SAMUEL 22.48–50

William Wordsworth viewed poetry as the "spontaneous overflow of powerful feelings; it takes its origins from emotion recollected in tranquillity." Sit quietly and focus on your breathing for a few moments, preparing to write a psalm about an experience of powerful emotion in your life. Recall a difficult situation in which you feel God came to your aid. Revisit the emotions you experienced before and after God's assistance became evident. Write your own psalm in three or four verses, expressing how difficulty gave way to deliverance and how your feelings in the midst of difficulty yielded to feelings of gratitude and praise.

See Meeting God in Worship

46 Foreigners lost heart,
and came trembling out of their strongholds.

47 The LORD lives! Blessed be my rock,
and exalted be my God, the rock of my salvation,

48 the God who gave me vengeance
and brought down peoples under me,

49 who brought me out from my enemies;
you exalted me above my adversaries,
you delivered me from the violent.

50 For this I will extol you, O LORD, among the nations,
and sing praises to your name.

51 He is a tower of salvation for his king,
and shows steadfast love to his anointed,
to David and his descendants forever.

The Last Words of David

23 Now these are the last words of David:
The oracle of David, son of Jesse,
the oracle of the man whom God exalted,*a*
the anointed of the God of Jacob,
the favorite of the Strong One of Israel:

2 The spirit of the LORD speaks through me,
his word is upon my tongue.

3 The God of Israel has spoken,
the Rock of Israel has said to me:
One who rules over people justly,
ruling in the fear of God,

4 is like the light of morning,
like the sun rising on a cloudless morning,
gleaming from the rain on the grassy land.

5 Is not my house like this with God?
For he has made with me an everlasting covenant,
ordered in all things and secure.
Will he not cause to prosper
all my help and my desire?

6 But the godless are*b* all like thorns that are thrown away;
for they cannot be picked up with the hand;

7 to touch them one uses an iron bar
or the shaft of a spear.
And they are entirely consumed in fire on the spot.*c*

David's Mighty Men

8 These are the names of the warriors whom David had: Josheb-basshebeth a Tahchemonite; he was chief of the Three;*d* he wielded his spear*e* against eight hundred whom he killed at one time.

9 Next to him among the three warriors was Eleazar son of Dodo son of Ahohi. He was with David when they

a Q Ms: MT *who was raised on high*   *b* Heb *But worthlessness*   *c* Heb *in sitting*   *d* Gk Vg Compare 1 Chr 11.11: Meaning of Heb uncertain
e 1 Chr 11.11: Meaning of Heb uncertain

defied the Philistines who were gathered there for battle. The Israelites withdrew, [10]but he stood his ground. He struck down the Philistines until his arm grew weary, though his hand clung to the sword. The LORD brought about a great victory that day. Then the people came back to him—but only to strip the dead.

11 Next to him was Shammah son of Agee, the Hararite. The Philistines gathered together at Lehi, where there was a plot of ground full of lentils; and the army fled from the Philistines. [12]But he took his stand in the middle of the plot, defended it, and killed the Philistines; and the LORD brought about a great victory.

13 Towards the beginning of harvest three of the thirty[a] chiefs went down to join David at the cave of Adullam, while a band of Philistines was encamped in the valley of Rephaim. [14]David was then in the stronghold; and the garrison of the Philistines was then at Bethlehem. [15]David said longingly, "O that someone would give me water to drink from the well of Bethlehem that is by the gate!" [16]Then the three warriors broke through the camp of the Philistines, drew water from the well of Bethlehem that was by the gate, and brought it to David. But he would not drink of it; he poured it out to the LORD, [17]for he said, "The LORD forbid that I should do this. Can I drink the blood of the men who went at the risk of their lives?" Therefore he would not drink it. The three warriors did these things.

18 Now Abishai son of Zeruiah, the brother of Joab, was chief of the Thirty.[b] With his spear he fought against three hundred men and killed them, and won a name beside the Three. [19]He was the most renowned of the Thirty,[c] and became their commander; but he did not attain to the Three.

20 Benaiah son of Jehoiada was a valiant warrior[d] from Kabzeel, a doer of great deeds; he struck down two sons of Ariel[e] of Moab. He also went down and killed a lion in a pit on a day when snow had fallen. [21]And he killed an Egyptian, a handsome man. The Egyptian had a spear in his hand; but Benaiah went against him with a staff, snatched the spear out of the Egyptian's hand, and killed him with his own spear. [22]Such were the things Benaiah son of Jehoiada did, and won a name beside the three warriors. [23]He was renowned among the Thirty, but he did not attain to the Three. And David put him in charge of his bodyguard.

24 Among the Thirty were Asahel brother of Joab; Elhanan son of Dodo of Bethlehem; [25]Shammah of Harod; Elika of Harod; [26]Helez the Paltite; Ira son of Ikkesh of Tekoa; [27]Abiezer of Anathoth; Mebunnai the Hushathite; [28]Zalmon the Ahohite; Maharai of Netophah; [29]Heleb son of Baanah of Netophah; Ittai son of Ribai of Gibeah of the Benjaminites; [30]Benaiah of Pirathon; Hiddai of the torrents of Gaash; [31]Abi-albon the Arbathite; Azmaveth of Bahurim; [32]Eliahba of Shaalbon; the sons of Jashen: Jonathan [33]son of[f] Shammah the Hararite; Ahiam son of Sharar the Hararite; [34]Eliphelet son of Ahasbai of Maa-

In the Pits

2 SAMUEL 23.20–22

Imaginatively place yourself in this one-paragraph story, seeing yourself as Benaiah. Imagine the sensations of your feet on the snow, the rush of adrenaline as you struggle with the lion. Then begin to invite memories of your own struggles with "lions" or in "pits" in your life. Perhaps you recall an incident when you found yourself in an awkward and hostile situation. Or maybe you recall being "in the pits" emotionally. Especially recall how you vanquished the lion or got out of the pit, whether by your own mental discipline, through strength or guidance gained in prayer, or by another person's assistance. Say a prayer of thanksgiving to God, or write a grateful note to your "rescuer," expressing gratitude for this deliverance.

See Meeting God in Scripture

a Heb adds head   b Two Heb Mss Syr: MT *Three*   c Syr Compare 1 Chr 11.25: Heb *Was he the most renowned of the Three?*   d Another reading is *the son of Ish-hai*   e Gk: Heb lacks *sons of*   f Gk: Heb lacks *son of*

Your Hall of Fame

2 SAMUEL 23.8–39

Who are some of the top thirty "mighty men" and women in your life? Make a list of five persons whom you have admired during the course of your life, and recount their exploits. Then write a second list of five characters in the Bible whom you have admired or perhaps tried to emulate. Pair up people from your admiration list with people from your Biblical list by noting similar characteristics. Imagine yourself speaking to each one in turn about what they mean to you, then thank God for what their presence or inspiration has meant in your life.

See Meeting God in Scripture

cah; Eliam son of Ahithophel the Gilonite; ³⁵Hezro*ᵃ* of Carmel; Paarai the Arbite; ³⁶Igal son of Nathan of Zobah; Bani the Gadite; ³⁷Zelek the Ammonite; Naharai of Beeroth, the armor-bearer of Joab son of Zeruiah; ³⁸Ira the Ithrite; Gareb the Ithrite; ³⁹Uriah the Hittite—thirty-seven in all.

David's Census of Israel and Judah

24 Again the anger of the LORD was kindled against Israel, and he incited David against them, saying, "Go, count the people of Israel and Judah." ²So the king said to Joab and the commanders of the army,*ᵇ* who were with him, "Go through all the tribes of Israel, from Dan to Beer-sheba, and take a census of the people, so that I may know how many there are." ³But Joab said to the king, "May the LORD your God increase the number of the people a hundredfold, while the eyes of my lord the king can still see it! But why does my lord the king want to do this?" ⁴But the king's word prevailed against Joab and the commanders of the army. So Joab and the commanders of the army went out from the presence of the king to take a census of the people of Israel. ⁵They crossed the Jordan, and began from*ᶜ* Aroer and from the city that is in the middle of the valley, toward Gad and on to Jazer. ⁶Then they came to Gilead, and to Kadesh in the land of the Hittites;*ᵈ* and they came to Dan, and from Dan*ᵉ* they went around to Sidon, ⁷and came to the fortress of Tyre and to all the cities of the Hivites and Canaanites; and they went out to the Negeb of Judah at Beer-sheba. ⁸So when they had gone through all the land, they came back to Jerusalem at the end of nine months and twenty days. ⁹Joab reported to the king the number of those who had been recorded: in Israel there were eight hundred thousand soldiers able to draw the sword, and those of Judah were five hundred thousand.

Judgment on David's Sin

10 But afterward, David was stricken to the heart because he had numbered the people. David said to the LORD, "I have sinned greatly in what I have done. But now, O LORD, I pray you, take away the guilt of your servant; for I have done very foolishly." ¹¹When David rose in the morning, the word of the LORD came to the prophet Gad, David's seer, saying, ¹²"Go and say to David: Thus says the LORD: Three things I offer*ᶠ* you; choose one of them, and I will do it to you." ¹³So Gad came to David and told him; he asked him, "Shall three*ᵍ* years of famine come to you on your land? Or will you flee three months before your foes while they pursue you? Or shall there be three days' pestilence in your land? Now consider, and decide what answer I shall return to the one who sent me." ¹⁴Then David said to Gad, "I am in great distress; let us fall into the hand of the LORD, for his mercy is great; but let me not fall into human hands."

15 So the LORD sent a pestilence on Israel from that morning until the appointed time; and seventy thousand

a Another reading is *Hezrai*   *b* 1 Chr 21.2 Gk: Heb *to Joab the commander of the army*   *c* Gk Mss: Heb *encamped in Aroer south of*   *d* Gk: Heb *to the land of Tahtim-hodshi*   *e* Cn Compare Gk: Heb *they came to Dan-jaan and*   *f* Or *hold over*   *g* 1 Chr 21.12 Gk: Heb *seven*

of the people died, from Dan to Beer-sheba. [16]But when the angel stretched out his hand toward Jerusalem to destroy it, the LORD relented concerning the evil, and said to the angel who was bringing destruction among the people, "It is enough; now stay your hand." The angel of the LORD was then by the threshing floor of Araunah the Jebusite. [17]When David saw the angel who was destroying the people, he said to the LORD, "I alone have sinned, and I alone have done wickedly; but these sheep, what have they done? Let your hand, I pray, be against me and against my father's house."

David's Altar on the Threshing Floor

18 That day Gad came to David and said to him, "Go up and erect an altar to the LORD on the threshing floor of Araunah the Jebusite." [19]Following Gad's instructions, David went up, as the LORD had commanded. [20]When Araunah looked down, he saw the king and his servants coming toward him; and Araunah went out and prostrated himself before the king with his face to the ground. [21]Araunah said, "Why has my lord the king come to his servant?" David said, "To buy the threshing floor from you in order to build an altar to the LORD, so that the plague may be averted from the people." [22]Then Araunah said to David, "Let my lord the king take and offer up what seems good to him; here are the oxen for the burnt offering, and the threshing sledges and the yokes of the oxen for the wood. [23]All this, O king, Araunah gives to the king." And Araunah said to the king, "May the LORD your God respond favorably to you."

24 But the king said to Araunah, "No, but I will buy them from you for a price; I will not offer burnt offerings to the LORD my God that cost me nothing." So David bought the threshing floor and the oxen for fifty shekels of silver. [25]David built there an altar to the LORD, and offered burnt offerings and offerings of well-being. So the LORD answered his supplication for the land, and the plague was averted from Israel.

Conscience: Nag or Friend?

2 SAMUEL 24.10–17

After the census, David came to his senses, "stricken to the heart," recognizing that he had behaved "very foolishly." Conscience can remind us of the persons we really are when we are not "on camera." Such reminders from the heart can sometimes be upsetting and persistent, often because we have not completed the work that conscience reveals is still undone. Acknowledge a continuing discomfort traceable to something you have done or left undone. Ask yourself why you have not dealt with the issue that continues to overshadow you. Resolve to take corrective action when that becomes possible. At this moment, write words that clearly describe what is troubling you, say these words in confession to God, and pray for help in releasing the burden and making all possible amends.

See Meeting God in Prayer

1 KINGS
Making Room for God

"God hates evil because it deprives man of the highest joy of which he is capable and the fullness of life for which he was designed. But His attitude to the sinner is unvarying love and compassion, a longing that he may 'turn from his wickedness and live.' "

—LESLIE D. WEATHERHEAD,
Time for God

The book of 1 Kings can be read as the history of a nation on a collision course with itself.

The harsh judgment of history turns a glaring spotlight on the deeds of its kings. The ancient Israelites are learning life's lessons the hard way. The people of Israel have sought the counsel of God and the wisdom of the prophets, but they do not heed, hear or respond to the call to wholeness.

The account in 1 Kings tells a harsh tale of national tragedy and spiritual bankruptcy. Ignorance and pride battle with wisdom; greed and lust diminish prosperity. The people call on prophets—such as the great Elijah—for counsel, then ignore, persecute or even kill them. The ancient Israelite kingdom is divided into two rival nations, north and south, because the nation has lost sight of its spiritual source, the Lord God.

As you read 1 Kings, meditate on how the cycle of sin, repentance and restoration repeats itself. Consider how that same cycle occurs in your own life. As you read and study 1 Kings, look at your life and see where the call to act *now* for change strikes home.

Disobedience, evil, hatred, racism and indifference have been around since the earliest days of humankind. Countless others have already endured many of the personal and national struggles we experience today, yet the presence and love of our forgiving God is not new either! At the heart of the story in 1 Kings is the gracious One who promises to be faithful to us in love regardless of the chaos we create.

The Struggle for the Succession

1 King David was old and advanced in years; and although they covered him with clothes, he could not get warm. ²So his servants said to him, "Let a young virgin be sought for my lord the king, and let her wait on the king, and be his attendant; let her lie in your bosom, so that my lord the king may be warm." ³So they searched for a beautiful girl throughout all the territory of Israel, and found Abishag the Shunammite, and brought her to the king. ⁴The girl was very beautiful. She became the king's attendant and served him, but the king did not know her sexually.

5 Now Adonijah son of Haggith exalted himself, saying, "I will be king"; he prepared for himself chariots and horsemen, and fifty men to run before him. ⁶His father had never at any time displeased him by asking, "Why have you done thus and so?" He was also a very handsome man, and he was born next after Absalom. ⁷He conferred with Joab son of Zeruiah and with the priest Abiathar, and they supported Adonijah. ⁸But the priest Zadok, and Benaiah son of Jehoiada, and the prophet Nathan, and Shimei, and Rei, and David's own warriors did not side with Adonijah.

9 Adonijah sacrificed sheep, oxen, and fatted cattle by the stone Zoheleth, which is beside En-rogel, and he invited all his brothers, the king's sons, and all the royal officials of Judah, ¹⁰but he did not invite the prophet Nathan or Benaiah or the warriors or his brother Solomon.

11 Then Nathan said to Bathsheba, Solomon's mother, "Have you not heard that Adonijah son of Haggith has become king and our lord David does not know it? ¹²Now therefore come, let me give you advice, so that you may save your own life and the life of your son Solomon. ¹³Go in at once to King David, and say to him, 'Did you not, my lord the king, swear to your servant, saying: Your son Solomon shall succeed me as king, and he shall sit on my throne? Why then is Adonijah king?' ¹⁴Then while you are still there speaking with the king, I will come in after you and confirm your words."

15 So Bathsheba went to the king in his room. The king was very old; Abishag the Shunammite was attending the king. ¹⁶Bathsheba bowed and did obeisance to the king, and the king said, "What do you wish?" ¹⁷She said to him, "My lord, you swore to your servant by the Lord your God, saying: Your son Solomon shall succeed me as king, and he shall sit on my throne. ¹⁸But now suddenly Adonijah has become king, though you, my lord the king, do not know it. ¹⁹He has sacrificed oxen, fatted cattle, and sheep in abundance, and has invited all the children of the king, the priest Abiathar, and Joab the commander of the army; but your servant Solomon he has not invited. ²⁰But you, my lord the king—the eyes of all Israel are on you to tell them who shall sit on the throne of my lord the king after him. ²¹Otherwise it will come to pass, when my lord the king sleeps with his ancestors, that my son Solomon and I will be counted offenders."

22 While she was still speaking with the king, the prophet Nathan came in. ²³The king was told, "Here is the prophet Nathan." When he came in before the king, he did obeisance to the king, with his face to the ground.

Legacy

1 KINGS 1.5–11

Even as King David nears death, the legacy of his dysfunctional family and rocky marriages catches up with him. His son Adonijah connives to become king as Absalom had done before him.

Prayerfully consider the legacy, both for good and ill, that previous generations have given to you. What recurrent patterns of behavior of previous generations do you see in your family life today? What major influences for good shaped you in childhood (consider the habits of parents, grandparents, and other close family and friends)? What influences were less helpful, or even harmful? In prayer, hold the image of each family member in your mind as you pray God's blessing on him or her.

See Meeting God in Everyday Life

Getting Ahead

1 KINGS 1.23–27

It is hard to blame Adonijah for wanting to get ahead. After all, don't we encourage our sons and daughters to do the same? To be ambitious is not necessarily sinful. But ambition is too often blind and driven, and it leads to a costly downfall. As you reflect on your life, pray that you will be able to discern the fine line between healthy ambition and sin. As you go through the day, be prayerfully aware of how ambition is at work in your encounters. Ponder what desires fuel these ambitions—and note when the ambition leads you to behave in destructive ways. Take note of how you are climbing the ladder of success and ask God to help you view your actions through his eyes.

²⁴Nathan said, "My lord the king, have you said, 'Adonijah shall succeed me as king, and he shall sit on my throne'? ²⁵For today he has gone down and has sacrificed oxen, fatted cattle, and sheep in abundance, and has invited all the king's children, Joab the commander^a of the army, and the priest Abiathar, who are now eating and drinking before him, and saying, 'Long live King Adonijah!' ²⁶But he did not invite me, your servant, and the priest Zadok, and Benaiah son of Jehoiada, and your servant Solomon. ²⁷Has this thing been brought about by my lord the king and you have not let your servants know who should sit on the throne of my lord the king after him?"

The Accession of Solomon

28 King David answered, "Summon Bathsheba to me." So she came into the king's presence, and stood before the king. ²⁹The king swore, saying, "As the LORD lives, who has saved my life from every adversity, ³⁰as I swore to you by the LORD, the God of Israel, 'Your son Solomon shall succeed me as king, and he shall sit on my throne in my place,' so will I do this day." ³¹Then Bathsheba bowed with her face to the ground, and did obeisance to the king, and said, "May my lord King David live forever!"

32 King David said, "Summon to me the priest Zadok, the prophet Nathan, and Benaiah son of Jehoiada." When they came before the king, ³³the king said to them, "Take with you the servants of your lord, and have my son Solomon ride on my own mule, and bring him down to Gihon. ³⁴There let the priest Zadok and the prophet Nathan anoint him king over Israel; then blow the trumpet, and say, 'Long live King Solomon!' ³⁵You shall go up following him. Let him enter and sit on my throne; he shall be king in my place; for I have appointed him to be ruler over Israel and over Judah." ³⁶Benaiah son of Jehoiada answered the king, "Amen! May the LORD, the God of my lord the king, so ordain. ³⁷As the LORD has been with my lord the king, so may he be with Solomon, and make his throne greater than the throne of my lord King David."

38 So the priest Zadok, the prophet Nathan, and Benaiah son of Jehoiada, and the Cherethites and the Pelethites, went down and had Solomon ride on King David's mule, and led him to Gihon. ³⁹There the priest Zadok took the horn of oil from the tent and anointed Solomon. Then they blew the trumpet, and all the people said, "Long live King Solomon!" ⁴⁰And all the people went up following him, playing on pipes and rejoicing with great joy, so that the earth quaked at their noise.

41 Adonijah and all the guests who were with him heard it as they finished feasting. When Joab heard the sound of the trumpet, he said, "Why is the city in an uproar?" ⁴²While he was still speaking, Jonathan son of the priest Abiathar arrived. Adonijah said, "Come in, for you are a worthy man and surely you bring good news." ⁴³Jonathan answered Adonijah, "No, for our lord King David has made Solomon king; ⁴⁴the king has sent with him the priest Zadok, the prophet Nathan, and Benaiah son of Jehoiada, and the Cherethites and the Pelethites; and they had him ride on the king's mule; ⁴⁵the priest Zadok and the prophet Nathan have anointed him king at Gihon; and

a Gk: Heb *the commanders*

they have gone up from there rejoicing, so that the city is in an uproar. This is the noise that you heard. [46]Solomon now sits on the royal throne. [47]Moreover the king's servants came to congratulate our lord King David, saying, 'May God make the name of Solomon more famous than yours, and make his throne greater than your throne.' The king bowed in worship on the bed [48]and went on to pray thus, 'Blessed be the LORD, the God of Israel, who today has granted one of my offspring[a] to sit on my throne and permitted me to witness it.' "

49 Then all the guests of Adonijah got up trembling and went their own ways. [50]Adonijah, fearing Solomon, got up and went to grasp the horns of the altar. [51]Solomon was informed, "Adonijah is afraid of King Solomon; see, he has laid hold of the horns of the altar, saying, 'Let King Solomon swear to me first that he will not kill his servant with the sword.' " [52]So Solomon responded, "If he proves to be a worthy man, not one of his hairs shall fall to the ground; but if wickedness is found in him, he shall die." [53]Then King Solomon sent to have him brought down from the altar. He came to do obeisance to King Solomon; and Solomon said to him, "Go home."

David's Instruction to Solomon

2 When David's time to die drew near, he charged his son Solomon, saying: [2]"I am about to go the way of all the earth. Be strong, be courageous, [3]and keep the charge of the LORD your God, walking in his ways and keeping his statutes, his commandments, his ordinances, and his testimonies, as it is written in the law of Moses, so that you may prosper in all that you do and wherever you turn. [4]Then the LORD will establish his word that he spoke concerning me: 'If your heirs take heed to their way, to walk before me in faithfulness with all their heart and with all their soul, there shall not fail you a successor on the throne of Israel.'

5 "Moreover you know also what Joab son of Zeruiah did to me, how he dealt with the two commanders of the armies of Israel, Abner son of Ner, and Amasa son of Jether, whom he murdered, retaliating in time of peace for blood that had been shed in war, and putting the blood of war on the belt around his waist, and on the sandals on his feet. [6]Act therefore according to your wisdom, but do not let his gray head go down to Sheol in peace. [7]Deal loyally, however, with the sons of Barzillai the Gileadite, and let them be among those who eat at your table; for with such loyalty they met me when I fled from your brother Absalom. [8]There is also with you Shimei son of Gera, the Benjaminite from Bahurim, who cursed me with a terrible curse on the day when I went to Mahanaim; but when he came down to meet me at the Jordan, I swore to him by the LORD, 'I will not put you to death with the sword.' [9]Therefore do not hold him guiltless, for you are a wise man; you will know what you ought to do to him, and you must bring his gray head down with blood to Sheol."

Death of David

10 Then David slept with his ancestors, and was buried in the city of David. [11]The time that David reigned over Is-

A Father and His Son

1 KINGS 2.1–4

David charges his son Solomon to be a wise ruler. Each generation wants "the best" for the next. Think about the children you know—within your sphere of influence—whether you are a parent, a relative, a teacher or a member of a community with children. What hopes do you have for these children? What hopes do you think God may have for them? What blessings or struggles have children brought into your life? How have these children affected your relationship with God? How would you pray today for them?

See Meeting God in Community

Solomon Consolidates His Reign

1 KINGS 2.12–29

"David's kingdom was established into the hands of Solomon. How Solomon ruled and lived personally remained to be seen. We may feel established in our lives, our marriage, spiritual journey, or career. There is a danger that we can get too comfortable. We must reflect daily on how we are living before the Lord. God is present. The purpose of spiritual discipline is to help us recognize what is already a fact and to open us up to the reality of God in human life. The best life we can live is a life oriented toward God. To live any other way is to rebel against our Creator and to destroy what we were made to be."

—WILLIAM O. PAULSELL,
Taste and See

rael was forty years; he reigned seven years in Hebron, and thirty-three years in Jerusalem. [12]So Solomon sat on the throne of his father David; and his kingdom was firmly established.

Solomon Consolidates His Reign

13 Then Adonijah son of Haggith came to Bathsheba, Solomon's mother. She asked, "Do you come peaceably?" He said, "Peaceably." [14]Then he said, "May I have a word with you?" She said, "Go on." [15]He said, "You know that the kingdom was mine, and that all Israel expected me to reign; however, the kingdom has turned about and become my brother's, for it was his from the LORD. [16]And now I have one request to make of you; do not refuse me." She said to him, "Go on." [17]He said, "Please ask King Solomon—he will not refuse you—to give me Abishag the Shunammite as my wife." [18]Bathsheba said, "Very well; I will speak to the king on your behalf."

19 So Bathsheba went to King Solomon, to speak to him on behalf of Adonijah. The king rose to meet her, and bowed down to her; then he sat on his throne, and had a throne brought for the king's mother, and she sat on his right. [20]Then she said, "I have one small request to make of you; do not refuse me." And the king said to her, "Make your request, my mother; for I will not refuse you." [21]She said, "Let Abishag the Shunammite be given to your brother Adonijah as his wife." [22]King Solomon answered his mother, "And why do you ask Abishag the Shunammite for Adonijah? Ask for him the kingdom as well! For he is my elder brother; ask not only for him but also for the priest Abiathar and for Joab son of Zeruiah!" [23]Then King Solomon swore by the LORD, "So may God do to me, and more also, for Adonijah has devised this scheme at the risk of his life! [24]Now therefore as the LORD lives, who has established me and placed me on the throne of my father David, and who has made me a house as he promised, today Adonijah shall be put to death." [25]So King Solomon sent Benaiah son of Jehoiada; he struck him down, and he died.

26 The king said to the priest Abiathar, "Go to Anathoth, to your estate; for you deserve death. But I will not at this time put you to death, because you carried the ark of the Lord GOD before my father David, and because you shared in all the hardships my father endured." [27]So Solomon banished Abiathar from being priest to the LORD, thus fulfilling the word of the LORD that he had spoken concerning the house of Eli in Shiloh.

28 When the news came to Joab—for Joab had supported Adonijah though he had not supported Absalom—Joab fled to the tent of the LORD and grasped the horns of the altar. [29]When it was told King Solomon, "Joab has fled to the tent of the LORD and now is beside the altar," Solomon sent Benaiah son of Jehoiada, saying, "Go, strike him down." [30]So Benaiah came to the tent of the LORD and said to him, "The king commands, 'Come out.' " But he said, "No, I will die here." Then Benaiah brought the king word again, saying, "Thus said Joab, and thus he answered me." [31]The king replied to him, "Do as he has said, strike him down and bury him; and thus take away from me and from my father's house the guilt for the

blood that Joab shed without cause. ³²The Lord will bring back his bloody deeds on his own head, because, without the knowledge of my father David, he attacked and killed with the sword two men more righteous and better than himself, Abner son of Ner, commander of the army of Israel, and Amasa son of Jether, commander of the army of Judah. ³³So shall their blood come back on the head of Joab and on the head of his descendants forever; but to David, and to his descendants, and to his house, and to his throne, there shall be peace from the Lord forevermore." ³⁴Then Benaiah son of Jehoiada went up and struck him down and killed him; and he was buried at his own house near the wilderness. ³⁵The king put Benaiah son of Jehoiada over the army in his place, and the king put the priest Zadok in the place of Abiathar.

36 Then the king sent and summoned Shimei, and said to him, "Build yourself a house in Jerusalem, and live there, and do not go out from there to any place whatever. ³⁷For on the day you go out, and cross the Wadi Kidron, know for certain that you shall die; your blood shall be on your own head." ³⁸And Shimei said to the king, "The sentence is fair; as my lord the king has said, so will your servant do." So Shimei lived in Jerusalem many days.

39 But it happened at the end of three years that two of Shimei's slaves ran away to King Achish son of Maacah of Gath. When it was told Shimei, "Your slaves are in Gath," ⁴⁰Shimei arose and saddled a donkey, and went to Achish in Gath, to search for his slaves; Shimei went and brought his slaves from Gath. ⁴¹When Solomon was told that Shimei had gone from Jerusalem to Gath and returned, ⁴²the king sent and summoned Shimei, and said to him, "Did I not make you swear by the Lord, and solemnly adjure you, saying, 'Know for certain that on the day you go out and go to any place whatever, you shall die'? And you said to me, 'The sentence is fair; I accept.' ⁴³Why then have you not kept your oath to the Lord and the commandment with which I charged you?" ⁴⁴The king also said to Shimei, "You know in your own heart all the evil that you did to my father David; so the Lord will bring back your evil on your own head. ⁴⁵But King Solomon shall be blessed, and the throne of David shall be established before the Lord forever." ⁴⁶Then the king commanded Benaiah son of Jehoiada; and he went out and struck him down, and he died.

So the kingdom was established in the hand of Solomon.

Solomon's Prayer for Wisdom

3 Solomon made a marriage alliance with Pharaoh king of Egypt; he took Pharaoh's daughter and brought her into the city of David, until he had finished building his own house and the house of the Lord and the wall around Jerusalem. ²The people were sacrificing at the high places, however, because no house had yet been built for the name of the Lord.

3 Solomon loved the Lord, walking in the statutes of his father David; only, he sacrificed and offered incense at the high places. ⁴The king went to Gibeon to sacrifice there, for that was the principal high place; Solomon used

Joab's Fate

1 KINGS 2.31–34

Personal characteristics and traits can be strengths in one phase of our lives and become our undoing in another phase. Joab, King David's general, is struck down for plotting with Adonijah for the throne of King David.

A strong and confident commander, warrior, strategist and leader, Joab has been overconfident in deciding what is best for David. That self-confident, commanding style now leads him to disaster.

What are your primary strengths, talents and gifts? How have they changed over time? Have the same talents been used for both good and ill? In what areas is God calling you to grow? In which situations are you relying on your own confidence rather than seeking God's will?

See Meeting God in Service

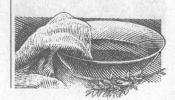

Solomon's Wisdom

1 KINGS 3.9–14

Solomon is given a "wise and discerning mind." In the Bible, wisdom is the exercise of sound and reverent judgment. The test of true wisdom is how well it is applied in day-to-day practice. The wise are those who, through faithfulness to the commandments of God, live well. Through spiritual knowledge, combined with practical experience, they are able to give astute counsel about navigating life's pitfalls.

Reflect with gratitude on your own life: Who are some of the wise mentors you have known? When have you called upon them for their wisdom? In what areas of your own life are you blessed with wisdom? When do others call upon you for that wisdom?

See Meeting God in Community

to offer a thousand burnt offerings on that altar. [5]At Gibeon the LORD appeared to Solomon in a dream by night; and God said, "Ask what I should give you." [6]And Solomon said, "You have shown great and steadfast love to your servant my father David, because he walked before you in faithfulness, in righteousness, and in uprightness of heart toward you; and you have kept for him this great and steadfast love, and have given him a son to sit on his throne today. [7]And now, O LORD my God, you have made your servant king in place of my father David, although I am only a little child; I do not know how to go out or come in. [8]And your servant is in the midst of the people whom you have chosen, a great people, so numerous they cannot be numbered or counted. [9]Give your servant therefore an understanding mind to govern your people, able to discern between good and evil; for who can govern this your great people?"

10 It pleased the Lord that Solomon had asked this. [11]God said to him, "Because you have asked this, and have not asked for yourself long life or riches, or for the life of your enemies, but have asked for yourself understanding to discern what is right, [12]I now do according to your word. Indeed I give you a wise and discerning mind; no one like you has been before you and no one like you shall arise after you. [13]I give you also what you have not asked, both riches and honor all your life; no other king shall compare with you. [14]If you will walk in my ways, keeping my statutes and my commandments, as your father David walked, then I will lengthen your life."

15 Then Solomon awoke; it had been a dream. He came to Jerusalem where he stood before the ark of the covenant of the LORD. He offered up burnt offerings and offerings of well-being, and provided a feast for all his servants.

Solomon's Wisdom in Judgment

16 Later, two women who were prostitutes came to the king and stood before him. [17]The one woman said, "Please, my lord, this woman and I live in the same house; and I gave birth while she was in the house. [18]Then on the third day after I gave birth, this woman also gave birth. We were together; there was no one else with us in the house, only the two of us were in the house. [19]Then this woman's son died in the night, because she lay on him. [20]She got up in the middle of the night and took my son from beside me while your servant slept. She laid him at her breast, and laid her dead son at my breast. [21]When I rose in the morning to nurse my son, I saw that he was dead; but when I looked at him closely in the morning, clearly it was not the son I had borne." [22]But the other woman said, "No, the living son is mine, and the dead son is yours." The first said, "No, the dead son is yours, and the living son is mine." So they argued before the king.

23 Then the king said, "The one says, 'This is my son that is alive, and your son is dead'; while the other says, 'Not so! Your son is dead, and my son is the living one.' " [24]So the king said, "Bring me a sword," and they brought a sword before the king. [25]The king said, "Divide the living boy in two; then give half to the one, and half to the

other." ²⁶But the woman whose son was alive said to the king—because compassion for her son burned within her—"Please, my lord, give her the living boy; certainly do not kill him!" The other said, "It shall be neither mine nor yours; divide it." ²⁷Then the king responded: "Give the first woman the living boy; do not kill him. She is his mother." ²⁸All Israel heard of the judgment that the king had rendered; and they stood in awe of the king, because they perceived that the wisdom of God was in him, to execute justice.

Solomon's Administrative Officers

4 King Solomon was king over all Israel, ²and these were his high officials: Azariah son of Zadok was the priest; ³Elihoreph and Ahijah sons of Shisha were secretaries; Jehoshaphat son of Ahilud was recorder; ⁴Benaiah son of Jehoiada was in command of the army; Zadok and Abiathar were priests; ⁵Azariah son of Nathan was over the officials; Zabud son of Nathan was priest and king's friend; ⁶Ahishar was in charge of the palace; and Adoniram son of Abda was in charge of the forced labor.

7 Solomon had twelve officials over all Israel, who provided food for the king and his household; each one had to make provision for one month in the year. ⁸These were their names: Ben-hur, in the hill country of Ephraim; ⁹Ben-deker, in Makaz, Shaalbim, Beth-shemesh, and Elon-beth-hanan; ¹⁰Ben-hesed, in Arubboth (to him belonged Socoh and all the land of Hepher); ¹¹Ben-abinadab, in all Naphath-dor (he had Taphath, Solomon's daughter, as his wife); ¹²Baana son of Ahilud, in Taanach, Megiddo, and all Beth-shean, which is beside Zarethan below Jezreel, and from Beth-shean to Abel-meholah, as far as the other side of Jokmeam; ¹³Ben-geber, in Ramoth-gilead (he had the villages of Jair son of Manasseh, which are in Gilead, and he had the region of Argob, which is in Bashan, sixty great cities with walls and bronze bars); ¹⁴Ahinadab son of Iddo, in Mahanaim; ¹⁵Ahimaaz, in Naphtali (he had taken Basemath, Solomon's daughter, as his wife); ¹⁶Baana son of Hushai, in Asher and Bealoth; ¹⁷Jehoshaphat son of Paruah, in Issachar; ¹⁸Shimei son of Ela, in Benjamin; ¹⁹Geber son of Uri, in the land of Gilead, the country of King Sihon of the Amorites and of King Og of Bashan. And there was one official in the land of Judah.

Magnificence of Solomon's Rule

20 Judah and Israel were as numerous as the sand by the sea; they ate and drank and were happy. ²¹ᵃSolomon was sovereign over all the kingdoms from the Euphrates to the land of the Philistines, even to the border of Egypt; they brought tribute and served Solomon all the days of his life.

22 Solomon's provision for one day was thirty cors of choice flour, and sixty cors of meal, ²³ten fat oxen, and twenty pasture-fed cattle, one hundred sheep, besides deer, gazelles, roebucks, and fatted fowl. ²⁴For he had dominion over all the region west of the Euphrates from Tiphsah to Gaza, over all the kings west of the Euphrates; and he had peace on all sides. ²⁵During Solomon's lifetime Judah and Israel lived in safety, from Dan even to

---

The Path to Wisdom

1 KINGS 3.28

"If one is to have true wisdom, it is not enough merely to have a handbook in one's hands, it is also necessary that a great zeal be kindled in one's heart."

—AUGUSTINE, *Enchiridion*

David's Dream Deferred

1 KINGS 5.1–4

David's fondest dream was to build a temple for the Lord, but his dream was put on hold—permanently. Regardless, dreaming is not a luxury for the child of God. Dreams are what form our spirits and lives. What happens to us when dreams are deferred? Do our dreams just go away and become forgotten pieces of our lives? Do we hang on to them in hopes of future fulfillment? What dreams do you have? Which ones are alive and active? Which dreams have been deferred? Pray for discernment about which dreams to hold on to, and about which dreams to let go.

See Meeting God in Prayer

Beer-sheba, all of them under their vines and fig trees. ²⁶Solomon also had forty thousand stalls of horses for his chariots, and twelve thousand horsemen. ²⁷Those officials supplied provisions for King Solomon and for all who came to King Solomon's table, each one in his month; they let nothing be lacking. ²⁸They also brought to the required place barley and straw for the horses and swift steeds, each according to his charge.

Fame of Solomon's Wisdom

29 God gave Solomon very great wisdom, discernment, and breadth of understanding as vast as the sand on the seashore, ³⁰so that Solomon's wisdom surpassed the wisdom of all the people of the east, and all the wisdom of Egypt. ³¹He was wiser than anyone else, wiser than Ethan the Ezrahite, and Heman, Calcol, and Darda, children of Mahol; his fame spread throughout all the surrounding nations. ³²He composed three thousand proverbs, and his songs numbered a thousand and five. ³³He would speak of trees, from the cedar that is in the Lebanon to the hyssop that grows in the wall; he would speak of animals, and birds, and reptiles, and fish. ³⁴People came from all the nations to hear the wisdom of Solomon; they came from all the kings of the earth who had heard of his wisdom.

Preparations and Materials for the Temple

5 *ᵃ* Now King Hiram of Tyre sent his servants to Solomon, when he heard that they had anointed him king in place of his father; for Hiram had always been a friend to David. ²Solomon sent word to Hiram, saying, ³"You know that my father David could not build a house for the name of the LORD his God because of the warfare with which his enemies surrounded him, until the LORD put them under the soles of his feet.*ᵇ* ⁴But now the LORD my God has given me rest on every side; there is neither adversary nor misfortune. ⁵So I intend to build a house for the name of the LORD my God, as the LORD said to my father David, 'Your son, whom I will set on your throne in your place, shall build the house for my name.' ⁶Therefore command that cedars from the Lebanon be cut for me. My servants will join your servants, and I will give you whatever wages you set for your servants; for you know that there is no one among us who knows how to cut timber like the Sidonians."

7 When Hiram heard the words of Solomon, he rejoiced greatly, and said, "Blessed be the LORD today, who has given to David a wise son to be over this great people." ⁸Hiram sent word to Solomon, "I have heard the message that you have sent to me; I will fulfill all your needs in the matter of cedar and cypress timber. ⁹My servants shall bring it down to the sea from the Lebanon; I will make it into rafts to go by sea to the place you indicate. I will have them broken up there for you to take away. And you shall meet my needs by providing food for my household." ¹⁰So Hiram supplied Solomon's every need for timber of cedar and cypress. ¹¹Solomon in turn gave Hiram twenty thousand cors of wheat as food for his household, and twenty cors of fine oil.

a Ch 5.15 in Heb   *b* Gk Tg Vg: Heb *my feet* or *his feet*

Solomon gave this to Hiram year by year. ¹²So the LORD gave Solomon wisdom, as he promised him. There was peace between Hiram and Solomon; and the two of them made a treaty.

13 King Solomon conscripted forced labor out of all Israel; the levy numbered thirty thousand men. ¹⁴He sent them to the Lebanon, ten thousand a month in shifts; they would be a month in the Lebanon and two months at home; Adoniram was in charge of the forced labor. ¹⁵Solomon also had seventy thousand laborers and eighty thousand stonecutters in the hill country, ¹⁶besides Solomon's three thousand three hundred supervisors who were over the work, having charge of the people who did the work. ¹⁷At the king's command, they quarried out great, costly stones in order to lay the foundation of the house with dressed stones. ¹⁸So Solomon's builders and Hiram's builders and the Gebalites did the stonecutting and prepared the timber and the stone to build the house.

Solomon Builds the Temple

6 In the four hundred eightieth year after the Israelites came out of the land of Egypt, in the fourth year of Solomon's reign over Israel, in the month of Ziv, which is the second month, he began to build the house of the LORD. ²The house that King Solomon built for the LORD was sixty cubits long, twenty cubits wide, and thirty cubits high. ³The vestibule in front of the nave of the house was twenty cubits wide, across the width of the house. Its depth was ten cubits in front of the house. ⁴For the house he made windows with recessed frames.ᵃ ⁵He also built a structure against the wall of the house, running around the walls of the house, both the nave and the inner sanctuary; and he made side chambers all around. ⁶The lowest storyᵇ was five cubits wide, the middle one was six cubits wide, and the third was seven cubits wide; for around the outside of the house he made offsets on the wall in order that the supporting beams should not be inserted into the walls of the house.

7 The house was built with stone finished at the quarry, so that neither hammer nor ax nor any tool of iron was heard in the temple while it was being built.

8 The entrance for the middle story was on the south side of the house: one went up by winding stairs to the middle story, and from the middle story to the third. ⁹So he built the house, and finished it; he roofed the house with beams and planks of cedar. ¹⁰He built the structure against the whole house, each storyᶜ five cubits high, and it was joined to the house with timbers of cedar.

11 Now the word of the LORD came to Solomon, ¹²"Concerning this house that you are building, if you will walk in my statutes, obey my ordinances, and keep all my commandments by walking in them, then I will establish my promise with you, which I made to your father David. ¹³I will dwell among the children of Israel, and will not forsake my people Israel."

14 So Solomon built the house, and finished it. ¹⁵He lined the walls of the house on the inside with boards of

---

ᵃ Gk: Meaning of Heb uncertain   ᵇ Gk: Heb *structure*   ᶜ Heb lacks *each story*

When God Answers Yes or No

1 KINGS 5.5

God does not always say "yes" to all our hopes and dreams. God said "no" to David's aspiration to build the temple. Because God wanted a peacemaker and not a warrior to build the temple, he said "yes" to Solomon instead. Our hopes, dreams and possibilities are often unfulfilled because God says, "No, not now." Do Solomon's and David's experiences resemble your own experiences? What is your prayer for the dreams of your life? When have you yearned to accomplish something personal only to hear that clear "no"? How did that "no" affect your relationship with God?

An Eternal Presence

1 KINGS 6.14

The temple is a sign of God's presence in the lives of his people. Through such signs and symbols God reaches out to embrace us in relationship. Prayerfully recall from your experience some of the signs of the presence of God. It may be a building, a community of faith, a relationship or a specific occasion. Bring it into focus in your memory, recalling sights, colors, smells, sounds, emotions and conversations that mark the sign in your memory. Remember the particular spiritual quality of your "sign"—a spirit of love, peace, hope, comfort, encouragement or challenge. Now, in that living recollection of your "temple," give thanks to God and store that memory in your heart for future thanksgiving.

See *Meeting God in Worship*

cedar; from the floor of the house to the rafters of the ceiling, he covered them on the inside with wood; and he covered the floor of the house with boards of cypress. ¹⁶He built twenty cubits of the rear of the house with boards of cedar from the floor to the rafters, and he built this within as an inner sanctuary, as the most holy place. ¹⁷The house, that is, the nave in front of the inner sanctuary, was forty cubits long. ¹⁸The cedar within the house had carvings of gourds and open flowers; all was cedar, no stone was seen. ¹⁹The inner sanctuary he prepared in the innermost part of the house, to set there the ark of the covenant of the LORD. ²⁰The interior of the inner sanctuary was twenty cubits long, twenty cubits wide, and twenty cubits high; he overlaid it with pure gold. He also overlaid the altar with cedar.^a ²¹Solomon overlaid the inside of the house with pure gold, then he drew chains of gold across, in front of the inner sanctuary, and overlaid it with gold. ²²Next he overlaid the whole house with gold, in order that the whole house might be perfect; even the whole altar that belonged to the inner sanctuary he overlaid with gold.

The Furnishings of the Temple

23 In the inner sanctuary he made two cherubim of olivewood, each ten cubits high. ²⁴Five cubits was the length of one wing of the cherub, and five cubits the length of the other wing of the cherub; it was ten cubits from the tip of one wing to the tip of the other. ²⁵The other cherub also measured ten cubits; both cherubim had the same measure and the same form. ²⁶The height of one cherub was ten cubits, and so was that of the other cherub. ²⁷He put the cherubim in the innermost part of the house; the wings of the cherubim were spread out so that a wing of one was touching the one wall, and a wing of the other cherub was touching the other wall; their other wings toward the center of the house were touching wing to wing. ²⁸He also overlaid the cherubim with gold.

29 He carved the walls of the house all around about with carved engravings of cherubim, palm trees, and open flowers, in the inner and outer rooms. ³⁰The floor of the house he overlaid with gold, in the inner and outer rooms.

31 For the entrance to the inner sanctuary he made doors of olivewood; the lintel and the doorposts were five-sided.^a ³²He covered the two doors of olivewood with carvings of cherubim, palm trees, and open flowers; he overlaid them with gold, and spread gold on the cherubim and on the palm trees.

33 So also he made for the entrance to the nave doorposts of olivewood, four-sided each, ³⁴and two doors of cypress wood; the two leaves of the one door were folding, and the two leaves of the other door were folding. ³⁵He carved cherubim, palm trees, and open flowers, overlaying them with gold evenly applied upon the carved work. ³⁶He built the inner court with three courses of dressed stone to one course of cedar beams.

37 In the fourth year the foundation of the house of the LORD was laid, in the month of Ziv. ³⁸In the eleventh year,

a Meaning of Heb uncertain

in the month of Bul, which is the eighth month, the house was finished in all its parts, and according to all its specifications. He was seven years in building it.

Solomon's Palace and Other Buildings

7 Solomon was building his own house thirteen years, and he finished his entire house.

2 He built the House of the Forest of the Lebanon one hundred cubits long, fifty cubits wide, and thirty cubits high, built on four rows of cedar pillars, with cedar beams on the pillars. ³It was roofed with cedar on the forty-five rafters, fifteen in each row, which were on the pillars. ⁴There were window frames in the three rows, facing each other in the three rows. ⁵All the doorways and doorposts had four-sided frames, opposite, facing each other in the three rows.

6 He made the Hall of Pillars fifty cubits long and thirty cubits wide. There was a porch in front with pillars, and a canopy in front of them.

7 He made the Hall of the Throne where he was to pronounce judgment, the Hall of Justice, covered with cedar from floor to floor.

8 His own house where he would reside, in the other court back of the hall, was of the same construction. Solomon also made a house like this hall for Pharaoh's daughter, whom he had taken in marriage.

9 All these were made of costly stones, cut according to measure, sawed with saws, back and front, from the foundation to the coping, and from outside to the great court. ¹⁰The foundation was of costly stones, huge stones, stones of eight and ten cubits. ¹¹There were costly stones above, cut to measure, and cedarwood. ¹²The great court had three courses of dressed stone to one layer of cedar beams all around; so had the inner court of the house of the LORD, and the vestibule of the house.

Products of Hiram the Bronzeworker

13 Now King Solomon invited and received Hiram from Tyre. ¹⁴He was the son of a widow of the tribe of Naphtali, whose father, a man of Tyre, had been an artisan in bronze; he was full of skill, intelligence, and knowledge in working bronze. He came to King Solomon, and did all his work.

15 He cast two pillars of bronze. Eighteen cubits was the height of the one, and a cord of twelve cubits would encircle it; the second pillar was the same.ᵃ ¹⁶He also made two capitals of molten bronze, to set on the tops of the pillars; the height of the one capital was five cubits, and the height of the other capital was five cubits. ¹⁷There were nets of checker work with wreaths of chain work for the capitals on the tops of the pillars; sevenᵇ for the one capital, and sevenᵇ for the other capital. ¹⁸He made the columns with two rows around each latticework to cover the capitals that were above the pomegranates; he did the same with the other capital. ¹⁹Now the capitals that were on the tops of the pillars in the vestibule were of lily-work, four cubits high. ²⁰The capitals were on the two pillars and also above the rounded projection that was beside the lat-

---

Building Our Life for God

1 KINGS 6.38—7.1

Solomon spent seven years building the house of God and thirteen years building his own palace. What does this say about Solomon's priorities? What can we learn from them? Examine your priorities. How have you been building your life and career? Name a foundational principle (for example, integrity, love, creativity) for each area of your life (for example, career, family, avocation). What are some of the things you have accomplished in each area? What are your goals and priorities for each? How have these priorities come into conflict with each other? With your life of the spirit?

See Meeting God in Everyday Life

Articles of Worship

1 KINGS 7.13–30

Our modern articles of worship are different than those used in Solomon's temple, but the purpose of sacred things remains the same. The Israelites used iron and bronze, fire and priests, sacrificial offerings and basins. Our hymnals, altars, stained glass windows and pulpits look different, but their purpose is still to lead hearts and minds to give honor and glory to God.

How do you prepare yourself to enter into worship? What elements of the building or the order of service most help you to worship God? What inward and outward obstacles impede your worship? How is your daily and weekly journey affected by missed opportunities for worship?

See *Meeting God in Worship*

ticework; there were two hundred pomegranates in rows all around; and so with the other capital. ²¹He set up the pillars at the vestibule of the temple; he set up the pillar on the south and called it Jachin; and he set up the pillar on the north and called it Boaz. ²²On the tops of the pillars was lily-work. Thus the work of the pillars was finished.

23 Then he made the molten sea; it was round, ten cubits from brim to brim, and five cubits high. A line of thirty cubits would encircle it completely. ²⁴Under its brim were panels all around it, each of ten cubits, surrounding the sea; there were two rows of panels, cast when it was cast. ²⁵It stood on twelve oxen, three facing north, three facing west, three facing south, and three facing east; the sea was set on them. The hindquarters of each were toward the inside. ²⁶Its thickness was a handbreadth; its brim was made like the brim of a cup, like the flower of a lily; it held two thousand baths.ᵃ

27 He also made the ten stands of bronze; each stand was four cubits long, four cubits wide, and three cubits high. ²⁸This was the construction of the stands: they had borders; the borders were within the frames; ²⁹on the borders that were set in the frames were lions, oxen, and cherubim. On the frames, both above and below the lions and oxen, there were wreaths of beveled work. ³⁰Each stand had four bronze wheels and axles of bronze; at the four corners were supports for a basin. The supports were cast with wreaths at the side of each. ³¹Its opening was within the crown whose height was one cubit; its opening was round, as a pedestal is made; it was a cubit and a half wide. At its opening there were carvings; its borders were four-sided, not round. ³²The four wheels were underneath the borders; the axles of the wheels were in the stands; and the height of a wheel was a cubit and a half. ³³The wheels were made like a chariot wheel; their axles, their rims, their spokes, and their hubs were all cast. ³⁴There were four supports at the four corners of each stand; the supports were of one piece with the stands. ³⁵On the top of the stand there was a round band half a cubit high; on the top of the stand, its stays and its borders were of one piece with it. ³⁶On the surfaces of its stays and on its borders he carved cherubim, lions, and palm trees, where each had space, with wreaths all around. ³⁷In this way he made the ten stands; all of them were cast alike, with the same size and the same form.

38 He made ten basins of bronze; each basin held forty baths,ᵃ each basin measured four cubits; there was a basin for each of the ten stands. ³⁹He set five of the stands on the south side of the house, and five on the north side of the house; he set the sea on the southeast corner of the house.

40 Hiram also made the pots, the shovels, and the basins. So Hiram finished all the work that he did for King Solomon on the house of the LORD: ⁴¹the two pillars, the two bowls of the capitals that were on the tops of the pillars, the two latticeworks to cover the two bowls of the capitals that were on the tops of the pillars; ⁴²the four hundred pomegranates for the two latticeworks, two rows

a A Heb measure of volume

of pomegranates for each latticework, to cover the two bowls of the capitals that were on the pillars; ⁴³the ten stands, the ten basins on the stands; ⁴⁴the one sea, and the twelve oxen underneath the sea.

45 The pots, the shovels, and the basins, all these vessels that Hiram made for King Solomon for the house of the LORD were of burnished bronze. ⁴⁶In the plain of the Jordan the king cast them, in the clay ground between Succoth and Zarethan. ⁴⁷Solomon left all the vessels unweighed, because there were so many of them; the weight of the bronze was not determined.

48 So Solomon made all the vessels that were in the house of the LORD: the golden altar, the golden table for the bread of the Presence, ⁴⁹the lampstands of pure gold, five on the south side and five on the north, in front of the inner sanctuary; the flowers, the lamps, and the tongs, of gold; ⁵⁰the cups, snuffers, basins, dishes for incense, and firepans, of pure gold; the sockets for the doors of the innermost part of the house, the most holy place, and for the doors of the nave of the temple, of gold.

51 Thus all the work that King Solomon did on the house of the LORD was finished. Solomon brought in the things that his father David had dedicated, the silver, the gold, and the vessels, and stored them in the treasuries of the house of the LORD.

Dedication of the Temple

8 Then Solomon assembled the elders of Israel and all the heads of the tribes, the leaders of the ancestral houses of the Israelites, before King Solomon in Jerusalem, to bring up the ark of the covenant of the LORD out of the city of David, which is Zion. ²All the people of Israel assembled to King Solomon at the festival in the month Ethanim, which is the seventh month. ³And all the elders of Israel came, and the priests carried the ark. ⁴So they brought up the ark of the LORD, the tent of meeting, and all the holy vessels that were in the tent; the priests and the Levites brought them up. ⁵King Solomon and all the congregation of Israel, who had assembled before him, were with him before the ark, sacrificing so many sheep and oxen that they could not be counted or numbered. ⁶Then the priests brought the ark of the covenant of the LORD to its place, in the inner sanctuary of the house, in the most holy place, underneath the wings of the cherubim. ⁷For the cherubim spread out their wings over the place of the ark, so that the cherubim made a covering above the ark and its poles. ⁸The poles were so long that the ends of the poles were seen from the holy place in front of the inner sanctuary; but they could not be seen from outside; they are there to this day. ⁹There was nothing in the ark except the two tablets of stone that Moses had placed there at Horeb, where the LORD made a covenant with the Israelites, when they came out of the land of Egypt. ¹⁰And when the priests came out of the holy place, a cloud filled the house of the LORD, ¹¹so that the priests could not stand to minister because of the cloud; for the glory of the LORD filled the house of the LORD.

Dedicated Contributions

1 KINGS 7.50

Solomon goes to great lengths to build the temple; he makes fine vessels for the temple. There are far simpler contributions that we can make to the places in which we worship. Such an act can be a response to God's love for us.

Have you ever thought about what you contribute to your place of worship? Do you sew, bake bread, arrange flowers, read or sing? Can you make banners or altar cloths? Your worshiping community can use your gifts and skills to draw people closer to God. Pray about what contributions you could make to help your worship community draw closer to God.

See Meeting God in Worship

God's Dwelling Place

1 KINGS 8.12–21

"God, who is wholly present everywhere, [dwells] in those whom he has made into His most blessed temple or temples, delivering them from the power of darkness and translating them into the Kingdom of the Son of his Love [see Colossians 1.13]. God dwells within each one singly as in His temples, and in all of them gathered together as His temple . . . But in his indwelling, he is received more fully by some, less by others."

—AUGUSTINE,
"On the Presence of God," Letter 187

12 Then Solomon said,
    "The LORD has said that he would dwell in thick
        darkness.
13   I have built you an exalted house,
        a place for you to dwell in forever."

Solomon's Speech

14 Then the king turned around and blessed all the assembly of Israel, while all the assembly of Israel stood. [15]He said, "Blessed be the LORD, the God of Israel, who with his hand has fulfilled what he promised with his mouth to my father David, saying, [16]'Since the day that I brought my people Israel out of Egypt, I have not chosen a city from any of the tribes of Israel in which to build a house, that my name might be there; but I chose David to be over my people Israel.' [17]My father David had it in mind to build a house for the name of the LORD, the God of Israel. [18]But the LORD said to my father David, 'You did well to consider building a house for my name; [19]nevertheless you shall not build the house, but your son who shall be born to you shall build the house for my name.' [20]Now the LORD has upheld the promise that he made; for I have risen in the place of my father David; I sit on the throne of Israel, as the LORD promised, and have built the house for the name of the LORD, the God of Israel. [21]There I have provided a place for the ark, in which is the covenant of the LORD that he made with our ancestors when he brought them out of the land of Egypt."

Solomon's Prayer of Dedication

22 Then Solomon stood before the altar of the LORD in the presence of all the assembly of Israel, and spread out his hands to heaven. [23]He said, "O LORD, God of Israel, there is no God like you in heaven above or on earth beneath, keeping covenant and steadfast love for your servants who walk before you with all their heart, [24]the covenant that you kept for your servant my father David as you declared to him; you promised with your mouth and have this day fulfilled with your hand. [25]Therefore, O LORD, God of Israel, keep for your servant my father David that which you promised him, saying, 'There shall never fail you a successor before me to sit on the throne of Israel, if only your children look to their way, to walk before me as you have walked before me.' [26]Therefore, O God of Israel, let your word be confirmed, which you promised to your servant my father David.

27 "But will God indeed dwell on the earth? Even heaven and the highest heaven cannot contain you, much less this house that I have built! [28]Regard your servant's prayer and his plea, O LORD my God, heeding the cry and the prayer that your servant prays to you today; [29]that your eyes may be open night and day toward this house, the place of which you said, 'My name shall be there,' that you may heed the prayer that your servant prays toward this place. [30]Hear the plea of your servant and of your people Israel when they pray toward this place; O hear in heaven your dwelling place; heed and forgive.

31 "If someone sins against a neighbor and is given an oath to swear, and comes and swears before your altar in this house, ³²then hear in heaven, and act, and judge your servants, condemning the guilty by bringing their conduct on their own head, and vindicating the righteous by rewarding them according to their righteousness.

33 "When your people Israel, having sinned against you, are defeated before an enemy but turn again to you, confess your name, pray and plead with you in this house, ³⁴then hear in heaven, forgive the sin of your people Israel, and bring them again to the land that you gave to their ancestors.

35 "When heaven is shut up and there is no rain because they have sinned against you, and then they pray toward this place, confess your name, and turn from their sin, because you punish*a* them, ³⁶then hear in heaven, and forgive the sin of your servants, your people Israel, when you teach them the good way in which they should walk; and grant rain on your land, which you have given to your people as an inheritance.

37 "If there is famine in the land, if there is plague, blight, mildew, locust, or caterpillar; if their enemy besieges them in any*b* of their cities; whatever plague, whatever sickness there is; ³⁸whatever prayer, whatever plea there is from any individual or from all your people Israel, all knowing the afflictions of their own hearts so that they stretch out their hands toward this house; ³⁹then hear in heaven your dwelling place, forgive, act, and render to all whose hearts you know—according to all their ways, for only you know what is in every human heart— ⁴⁰so that they may fear you all the days that they live in the land that you gave to our ancestors.

41 "Likewise when a foreigner, who is not of your people Israel, comes from a distant land because of your name ⁴²—for they shall hear of your great name, your mighty hand, and your outstretched arm—when a foreigner comes and prays toward this house, ⁴³then hear in heaven your dwelling place, and do according to all that the foreigner calls to you, so that all the peoples of the earth may know your name and fear you, as do your people Israel, and so that they may know that your name has been invoked on this house that I have built.

44 "If your people go out to battle against their enemy, by whatever way you shall send them, and they pray to the LORD toward the city that you have chosen and the house that I have built for your name, ⁴⁵then hear in heaven their prayer and their plea, and maintain their cause.

46 "If they sin against you—for there is no one who does not sin—and you are angry with them and give them to an enemy, so that they are carried away captive to the land of the enemy, far off or near; ⁴⁷yet if they come to their senses in the land to which they have been taken captive, and repent, and plead with you in the land of their captors, saying, 'We have sinned, and have done wrong; we have acted wickedly'; ⁴⁸if they repent with all their heart and soul in the land of their enemies, who took them captive, and pray to you toward their land,

Prayer of Dedication

1 KINGS 8.20–30

Solomon dedicates the temple for "the name of the LORD"; God's name represents every aspect of his being. Look through your house, home and family. Walk about your own house, considering how it, and the activities that take place within it, can be more deeply consecrated to God. In each place, frame a prayer of dedication. Where in your house are reminders of God's glory and presence? In what rooms have forgiveness and reconciliation been sought and received? Where are the places of hospitality and prayer? How is the frailty of the humans residing there in evidence? You might pray this prayer: "Day by day, week by week, help us to make our home a sacred place dedicated to you, a place where we may dwell in harmony, peace and joy. Amen."

See Meeting God in Everyday Life

---

a Or *when you answer* *b* Gk Syr: Heb *in the land*

When God's People Repent

1 KINGS 8.46–53

Sometimes defeat or frustration is a sign that we are on the wrong track. We realize we have missed opportunities and blundered and blown more chances than we care to admit. Sometimes the darkness of despair covers the light of hope. Somehow, though, life goes on; miraculously, so does God's forgiveness. Like ancient Israel, we can start over with each new day. Turning toward God from wherever we are, confessing all before our loving God, we can let go of the past and embrace the future. What are your unforgiven blunders and mistakes? How is the past holding you down? What is God calling you to do and to become? Trusting God, tell all to God and accept the new, clean slate he offers.

See Meeting God in Prayer

which you gave to their ancestors, the city that you have chosen, and the house that I have built for your name; [49]then hear in heaven your dwelling place their prayer and their plea, maintain their cause [50]and forgive your people who have sinned against you, and all their transgressions that they have committed against you; and grant them compassion in the sight of their captors, so that they may have compassion on them [51](for they are your people and heritage, which you brought out of Egypt, from the midst of the iron-smelter). [52]Let your eyes be open to the plea of your servant, and to the plea of your people Israel, listening to them whenever they call to you. [53]For you have separated them from among all the peoples of the earth, to be your heritage, just as you promised through Moses, your servant, when you brought our ancestors out of Egypt, O Lord GOD."

Solomon Blesses the Assembly

54 Now when Solomon finished offering all this prayer and this plea to the LORD, he arose from facing the altar of the LORD, where he had knelt with hands outstretched toward heaven; [55]he stood and blessed the assembly of Israel with a loud voice:

56 "Blessed be the LORD, who has given rest to his people Israel according to all that he promised; not one word has failed of all his good promise, which he spoke through his servant Moses. [57]The LORD our God be with us, as he was with our ancestors; may he not leave us or abandon us, [58]but incline our hearts to him, to walk in all his ways, and to keep his commandments, his statutes, and his ordinances, which he commanded our ancestors. [59]Let these words of mine, with which I pleaded before the LORD, be near to the LORD our God day and night, and may he maintain the cause of his servant and the cause of his people Israel, as each day requires; [60]so that all the peoples of the earth may know that the LORD is God; there is no other. [61]Therefore devote yourselves completely to the LORD our God, walking in his statutes and keeping his commandments, as at this day."

Solomon Offers Sacrifices

62 Then the king, and all Israel with him, offered sacrifice before the LORD. [63]Solomon offered as sacrifices of well-being to the LORD twenty-two thousand oxen and one hundred twenty thousand sheep. So the king and all the people of Israel dedicated the house of the LORD. [64]The same day the king consecrated the middle of the court that was in front of the house of the LORD; for there he offered the burnt offerings and the grain offerings and the fat pieces of the sacrifices of well-being, because the bronze altar that was before the LORD was too small to receive the burnt offerings and the grain offerings and the fat pieces of the sacrifices of well-being.

65 So Solomon held the festival at that time, and all Israel with him—a great assembly, people from Lebo-hamath to the Wadi of Egypt—before the LORD our God, seven days.[a] [66]On the eighth day he sent the people away; and they blessed the king, and went to their tents, joyful and in good spirits because of all the goodness that the

a Compare Gk: Heb *seven days and seven days, fourteen days*

LORD had shown to his servant David and to his people Israel.

God Appears Again to Solomon

9 When Solomon had finished building the house of the LORD and the king's house and all that Solomon desired to build, ²the LORD appeared to Solomon a second time, as he had appeared to him at Gibeon. ³The LORD said to him, "I have heard your prayer and your plea, which you made before me; I have consecrated this house that you have built, and put my name there forever; my eyes and my heart will be there for all time. ⁴As for you, if you will walk before me, as David your father walked, with integrity of heart and uprightness, doing according to all that I have commanded you, and keeping my statutes and my ordinances, ⁵then I will establish your royal throne over Israel forever, as I promised your father David, saying, 'There shall not fail you a successor on the throne of Israel.'

6 "If you turn aside from following me, you or your children, and do not keep my commandments and my statutes that I have set before you, but go and serve other gods and worship them, ⁷then I will cut Israel off from the land that I have given them; and the house that I have consecrated for my name I will cast out of my sight; and Israel will become a proverb and a taunt among all peoples. ⁸This house will become a heap of ruins;ᵃ everyone passing by it will be astonished, and will hiss; and they will say, 'Why has the LORD done such a thing to this land and to this house?' ⁹Then they will say, 'Because they have forsaken the LORD their God, who brought their ancestors out of the land of Egypt, and embraced other gods, worshiping them and serving them; therefore the LORD has brought this disaster upon them.' "

10 At the end of twenty years, in which Solomon had built the two houses, the house of the LORD and the king's house, ¹¹King Hiram of Tyre having supplied Solomon with cedar and cypress timber and gold, as much as he desired, King Solomon gave to Hiram twenty cities in the land of Galilee. ¹²But when Hiram came from Tyre to see the cities that Solomon had given him, they did not please him. ¹³Therefore he said, "What kind of cities are these that you have given me, my brother?" So they are called the land of Cabulᵇ to this day. ¹⁴But Hiram had sent to the king one hundred twenty talents of gold.

Other Acts of Solomon

15 This is the account of the forced labor that King Solomon conscripted to build the house of the LORD and his own house, the Millo and the wall of Jerusalem, Hazor, Megiddo, Gezer ¹⁶(Pharaoh king of Egypt had gone up and captured Gezer and burned it down, had killed the Canaanites who lived in the city, and had given it as dowry to his daughter, Solomon's wife; ¹⁷so Solomon rebuilt Gezer), Lower Beth-horon, ¹⁸Baalath, Tamar in the wilderness, within the land, ¹⁹as well as all of Solomon's storage cities, the cities for his chariots, the

---

Praying for the Basics

1 KINGS 8.56–61

Solomon's blessing concludes with the simple plea that God "may maintain the cause of his servant and the cause of his people Israel, as each day requires" and that the people will be devoted to God in their daily lives. Suppose you were to ask for such a blessing on your life. Envision the day ahead and imagine God's blessing pouring forth on all the events you anticipate. Craft a prayer, in your mind or on paper, for this day. Include the simple basics you really require *today* to "maintain [your] cause" in service to God's purposes, to your family's essential needs, and to the most urgent needs of your community and nation. Pray your prayer two or three times during the day.

See Meeting God in Everyday Life

ᵃ Syr Old Latin: Heb *will become high*   ᵇ Perhaps meaning *a land good for nothing*

Wandering Away From Real Relationship

1 KINGS 9.15–26

Amid all the building projects Solomon launched (the temple, his own palace, the supporting terraces and the wall) he still "completed the house," fulfilling his temple obligations.

When life's duties press in on you, how well do you maintain your spiritual disciplines? When is busyness most likely to crowd out your times of practicing the presence of God? Ask God to help you cultivate your spiritual life despite the demands on your time. How can you practice God's presence even amid the busyness of life?

See Meeting God in Everyday Life

cities for his cavalry, and whatever Solomon desired to build, in Jerusalem, in Lebanon, and in all the land of his dominion. ²⁰All the people who were left of the Amorites, the Hittites, the Perizzites, the Hivites, and the Jebusites, who were not of the people of Israel— ²¹their descendants who were still left in the land, whom the Israelites were unable to destroy completely—these Solomon conscripted for slave labor, and so they are to this day. ²²But of the Israelites Solomon made no slaves; they were the soldiers, they were his officials, his commanders, his captains, and the commanders of his chariotry and cavalry.

23 These were the chief officers who were over Solomon's work: five hundred fifty, who had charge of the people who carried on the work.

24 But Pharaoh's daughter went up from the city of David to her own house that Solomon had built for her; then he built the Millo.

25 Three times a year Solomon used to offer up burnt offerings and sacrifices of well-being on the altar that he built for the LORD, offering incense*a* before the LORD. So he completed the house.

Solomon's Commercial Activity

26 King Solomon built a fleet of ships at Ezion-geber, which is near Eloth on the shore of the Red Sea,*b* in the land of Edom. ²⁷Hiram sent his servants with the fleet, sailors who were familiar with the sea, together with the servants of Solomon. ²⁸They went to Ophir, and imported from there four hundred twenty talents of gold, which they delivered to King Solomon.

Visit of the Queen of Sheba

10 When the queen of Sheba heard of the fame of Solomon (fame due to*c* the name of the LORD), she came to test him with hard questions. ²She came to Jerusalem with a very great retinue, with camels bearing spices, and very much gold, and precious stones; and when she came to Solomon, she told him all that was on her mind. ³Solomon answered all her questions; there was nothing hidden from the king that he could not explain to her. ⁴When the queen of Sheba had observed all the wisdom of Solomon, the house that he had built, ⁵the food of his table, the seating of his officials, and the attendance of his servants, their clothing, his valets, and his burnt offerings that he offered at the house of the LORD, there was no more spirit in her.

6 So she said to the king, "The report was true that I heard in my own land of your accomplishments and of your wisdom, ⁷but I did not believe the reports until I came and my own eyes had seen it. Not even half had been told me; your wisdom and prosperity far surpass the report that I had heard. ⁸Happy are your wives!*d* Happy are these your servants, who continually attend you and hear your wisdom! ⁹Blessed be the LORD your God, who has delighted in you and set you on the throne of Israel! Because the LORD loved Israel forever, he has made you king to execute justice and righteousness." ¹⁰Then she

---

a Gk: Heb *offering incense with it that was*   *b* Or *Sea of Reeds*
c Meaning of Heb uncertain   *d* Gk Syr: Heb *men*

gave the king one hundred twenty talents of gold, a great quantity of spices, and precious stones; never again did spices come in such quantity as that which the queen of Sheba gave to King Solomon.

11 Moreover, the fleet of Hiram, which carried gold from Ophir, brought from Ophir a great quantity of almug wood and precious stones. ¹²From the almug wood the king made supports for the house of the LORD, and for the king's house, lyres also and harps for the singers; no such almug wood has come or been seen to this day.

13 Meanwhile King Solomon gave to the queen of Sheba every desire that she expressed, as well as what he gave her out of Solomon's royal bounty. Then she returned to her own land, with her servants.

14 The weight of gold that came to Solomon in one year was six hundred sixty-six talents of gold, ¹⁵besides that which came from the traders and from the business of the merchants, and from all the kings of Arabia and the governors of the land. ¹⁶King Solomon made two hundred large shields of beaten gold; six hundred shekels of gold went into each large shield. ¹⁷He made three hundred shields of beaten gold; three minas of gold went into each shield; and the king put them in the House of the Forest of Lebanon. ¹⁸The king also made a great ivory throne, and overlaid it with the finest gold. ¹⁹The throne had six steps. The top of the throne was rounded in the back, and on each side of the seat were arm rests and two lions standing beside the arm rests, ²⁰while twelve lions were standing, one on each end of a step on the six steps. Nothing like it was ever made in any kingdom. ²¹All King Solomon's drinking vessels were of gold, and all the vessels of the House of the Forest of Lebanon were of pure gold; none were of silver—it was not considered as anything in the days of Solomon. ²²For the king had a fleet of ships of Tarshish at sea with the fleet of Hiram. Once every three years the fleet of ships of Tarshish used to come bringing gold, silver, ivory, apes, and peacocks.ᵃ

23 Thus King Solomon excelled all the kings of the earth in riches and in wisdom. ²⁴The whole earth sought the presence of Solomon to hear his wisdom, which God had put into his mind. ²⁵Every one of them brought a present, objects of silver and gold, garments, weaponry, spices, horses, and mules, so much year by year.

26 Solomon gathered together chariots and horses; he had fourteen hundred chariots and twelve thousand horses, which he stationed in the chariot cities and with the king in Jerusalem. ²⁷The king made silver as common in Jerusalem as stones, and he made cedars as numerous as the sycamores of the Shephelah. ²⁸Solomon's import of horses was from Egypt and Kue, and the king's traders received them from Kue at a price. ²⁹A chariot could be imported from Egypt for six hundred shekels of silver, and a horse for one hundred fifty; so through the king's traders they were exported to all the kings of the Hittites and the kings of Aram.

Hard Questions for a Famous King

1 KINGS 10.1–9

After a contest and a series of riddles, proverbs and quizzes, the queen of Sheba decides that Solomon is indeed as wise as she had been told. The queen leaves in awe of him. Imagine that you are talking with Solomon, the wisest man who ever lived. What questions would you ask him about the source of his wisdom? What would you want to learn from him? What would you want to glean from an encounter with him? How might his answers help you lead a more faithful life?

A Marriage of Convenience

1 KINGS 11.1–10

Solomon's wisdom in public affairs was not reflected in his personal life. If Solomon knew the right way to live, what pressures might have caused him to make "marriages of convenience" with lesser gods?

What choices of convenience have you made that conflict with your real values? What pressures and inner weaknesses led you to such choices? When have you chosen to resist convenient choices for the sake of God's way? What gave you the strength to resist? What consequences in your spiritual life have these choices led to?

See Meeting God in Community

Solomon's Errors

11 King Solomon loved many foreign women along with the daughter of Pharaoh: Moabite, Ammonite, Edomite, Sidonian, and Hittite women, ²from the nations concerning which the LORD had said to the Israelites, "You shall not enter into marriage with them, neither shall they with you; for they will surely incline your heart to follow their gods"; Solomon clung to these in love. ³Among his wives were seven hundred princesses and three hundred concubines; and his wives turned away his heart. ⁴For when Solomon was old, his wives turned away his heart after other gods; and his heart was not true to the LORD his God, as was the heart of his father David. ⁵For Solomon followed Astarte the goddess of the Sidonians, and Milcom the abomination of the Ammonites. ⁶So Solomon did what was evil in the sight of the LORD, and did not completely follow the LORD, as his father David had done. ⁷Then Solomon built a high place for Chemosh the abomination of Moab, and for Molech the abomination of the Ammonites, on the mountain east of Jerusalem. ⁸He did the same for all his foreign wives, who offered incense and sacrificed to their gods.

9 Then the LORD was angry with Solomon, because his heart had turned away from the LORD, the God of Israel, who had appeared to him twice, ¹⁰and had commanded him concerning this matter, that he should not follow other gods; but he did not observe what the LORD commanded. ¹¹Therefore the LORD said to Solomon, "Since this has been your mind and you have not kept my covenant and my statutes that I have commanded you, I will surely tear the kingdom from you and give it to your servant. ¹²Yet for the sake of your father David I will not do it in your lifetime; I will tear it out of the hand of your son. ¹³I will not, however, tear away the entire kingdom; I will give one tribe to your son, for the sake of my servant David and for the sake of Jerusalem, which I have chosen."

Adversaries of Solomon

14 Then the LORD raised up an adversary against Solomon, Hadad the Edomite; he was of the royal house in Edom. ¹⁵For when David was in Edom, and Joab the commander of the army went up to bury the dead, he killed every male in Edom ¹⁶(for Joab and all Israel remained there six months, until he had eliminated every male in Edom); ¹⁷but Hadad fled to Egypt with some Edomites who were servants of his father. He was a young boy at that time. ¹⁸They set out from Midian and came to Paran; they took people with them from Paran and came to Egypt, to Pharaoh king of Egypt, who gave him a house, assigned him an allowance of food, and gave him land. ¹⁹Hadad found great favor in the sight of Pharaoh, so that he gave him his sister-in-law for a wife, the sister of Queen Tahpenes. ²⁰The sister of Tahpenes gave birth by him to his son Genubath, whom Tahpenes weaned in Pharaoh's house; Genubath was in Pharaoh's house among the children of Pharaoh. ²¹When Hadad heard in Egypt that David slept with his ancestors and that Joab the commander of the army was dead, Hadad said to

Pharaoh, "Let me depart, that I may go to my own country." [22]But Pharaoh said to him, "What do you lack with me that you now seek to go to your own country?" And he said, "No, do let me go."

23 God raised up another adversary against Solomon,[a] Rezon son of Eliada, who had fled from his master, King Hadadezer of Zobah. [24]He gathered followers around him and became leader of a marauding band, after the slaughter by David; they went to Damascus, settled there, and made him king in Damascus. [25]He was an adversary of Israel all the days of Solomon, making trouble as Hadad did; he despised Israel and reigned over Aram.

Jeroboam's Rebellion

26 Jeroboam son of Nebat, an Ephraimite of Zeredah, a servant of Solomon, whose mother's name was Zeruah, a widow, rebelled against the king. [27]The following was the reason he rebelled against the king. Solomon built the Millo, and closed up the gap in the wall[b] of the city of his father David. [28]The man Jeroboam was very able, and when Solomon saw that the young man was industrious he gave him charge over all the forced labor of the house of Joseph. [29]About that time, when Jeroboam was leaving Jerusalem, the prophet Ahijah the Shilonite found him on the road. Ahijah had clothed himself with a new garment. The two of them were alone in the open country [30]when Ahijah laid hold of the new garment he was wearing and tore it into twelve pieces. [31]He then said to Jeroboam: Take for yourself ten pieces; for thus says the LORD, the God of Israel, "See, I am about to tear the kingdom from the hand of Solomon, and will give you ten tribes. [32]One tribe will remain his, for the sake of my servant David and for the sake of Jerusalem, the city that I have chosen out of all the tribes of Israel. [33]This is because he has[c] forsaken me, worshiped Astarte the goddess of the Sidonians, Chemosh the god of Moab, and Milcom the god of the Ammonites, and has[c] not walked in my ways, doing what is right in my sight and keeping my statutes and my ordinances, as his father David did. [34]Nevertheless I will not take the whole kingdom away from him but will make him ruler all the days of his life, for the sake of my servant David whom I chose and who did keep my commandments and my statutes; [35]but I will take the kingdom away from his son and give it to you—that is, the ten tribes. [36]Yet to his son I will give one tribe, so that my servant David may always have a lamp before me in Jerusalem, the city where I have chosen to put my name. [37]I will take you, and you shall reign over all that your soul desires; you shall be king over Israel. [38]If you will listen to all that I command you, walk in my ways, and do what is right in my sight by keeping my statutes and my commandments, as David my servant did, I will be with you, and will build you an enduring house, as I built for David, and I will give Israel to you. [39]For this reason I will punish the descendants of David, but not forever." [40]Solomon sought therefore to kill Jeroboam; but Jeroboam promptly fled to Egypt, to King Shi-

Solomon Humbled

1 KINGS 11.9–15

"They teach, 'Be strong as a leopard, swift as an eagle, to do the will of thy Father who is in heaven,' in order to instruct you that there should be no pride before God. Elijah taught, 'If a man exalts the glory of God, and diminishes his own glory, God's glory will be exalted and his own too, but if he diminishes God's glory, and exalts his own, then God's glory remains what it was, but the man's glory is diminished' "

—*The Talmud,*
Numbers Rabba, Bemidhar, IV, 20

---

a Heb *him*   *b* Heb lacks *in the wall*   *c* Gk Syr Vg: Heb *they have*

Death of the King

1 KINGS 11.41–43

Solomon "slept with his ancestors"; his passing was no doubt noted with elaborate funeral rituals. Funerals can be routine and impersonal or genuine celebrations of the life of one of God's children. Planning your own funeral rites can be both a great help to your family and a testimony of faith. Spend some time envisioning your own funeral, not just the service but the events surrounding it. Should it be small and quiet or more of a celebration? What hymns would you like sung? What readings—from scripture, poetry or books—are especially meaningful to you? How do you want your faith in God to be exemplified in this celebration?

See Meeting God in Everyday Life

shak of Egypt, and remained in Egypt until the death of Solomon.

Death of Solomon

41 Now the rest of the acts of Solomon, all that he did as well as his wisdom, are they not written in the Book of the Acts of Solomon? 42The time that Solomon reigned in Jerusalem over all Israel was forty years. 43Solomon slept with his ancestors and was buried in the city of his father David; and his son Rehoboam succeeded him.

The Northern Tribes Secede

12 Rehoboam went to Shechem, for all Israel had come to Shechem to make him king. 2When Jeroboam son of Nebat heard of it (for he was still in Egypt, where he had fled from King Solomon), then Jeroboam returned from*a* Egypt. 3And they sent and called him; and Jeroboam and all the assembly of Israel came and said to Rehoboam, 4"Your father made our yoke heavy. Now therefore lighten the hard service of your father and his heavy yoke that he placed on us, and we will serve you." 5He said to them, "Go away for three days, then come again to me." So the people went away.

6 Then King Rehoboam took counsel with the older men who had attended his father Solomon while he was still alive, saying, "How do you advise me to answer this people?" 7They answered him, "If you will be a servant to this people today and serve them, and speak good words to them when you answer them, then they will be your servants forever." 8But he disregarded the advice that the older men gave him, and consulted with the young men who had grown up with him and now attended him. 9He said to them, "What do you advise that we answer this people who have said to me, 'Lighten the yoke that your father put on us'?" 10The young men who had grown up with him said to him, "Thus you should say to this people who spoke to you, 'Your father made our yoke heavy, but you must lighten it for us'; thus you should say to them, 'My little finger is thicker than my father's loins. 11Now, whereas my father laid on you a heavy yoke, I will add to your yoke. My father disciplined you with whips, but I will discipline you with scorpions.' "

12 So Jeroboam and all the people came to Rehoboam the third day, as the king had said, "Come to me again the third day." 13The king answered the people harshly. He disregarded the advice that the older men had given him 14and spoke to them according to the advice of the young men, "My father made your yoke heavy, but I will add to your yoke; my father disciplined you with whips, but I will discipline you with scorpions." 15So the king did not listen to the people, because it was a turn of affairs brought about by the LORD that he might fulfill his word, which the LORD had spoken by Ahijah the Shilonite to Jeroboam son of Nebat.

16 When all Israel saw that the king would not listen to them, the people answered the king,

"What share do we have in David?

a Gk Vg Compare 2 Chr 10.2: Heb *lived in*

We have no inheritance in the son of Jesse.
To your tents, O Israel!
Look now to your own house, O David."

So Israel went away to their tents. [17]But Rehoboam reigned over the Israelites who were living in the towns of Judah. [18]When King Rehoboam sent Adoram, who was taskmaster over the forced labor, all Israel stoned him to death. King Rehoboam then hurriedly mounted his chariot to flee to Jerusalem. [19]So Israel has been in rebellion against the house of David to this day.

First Dynasty: Jeroboam Reigns over Israel

20 When all Israel heard that Jeroboam had returned, they sent and called him to the assembly and made him king over all Israel. There was no one who followed the house of David, except the tribe of Judah alone.

21 When Rehoboam came to Jerusalem, he assembled all the house of Judah and the tribe of Benjamin, one hundred eighty thousand chosen troops to fight against the house of Israel, to restore the kingdom to Rehoboam son of Solomon. [22]But the word of God came to Shemaiah the man of God: [23]Say to King Rehoboam of Judah, son of Solomon, and to all the house of Judah and Benjamin, and to the rest of the people, [24]"Thus says the LORD, You shall not go up or fight against your kindred the people of Israel. Let everyone go home, for this thing is from me." So they heeded the word of the LORD and went home again, according to the word of the LORD.

Jeroboam's Golden Calves

25 Then Jeroboam built Shechem in the hill country of Ephraim, and resided there; he went out from there and built Penuel. [26]Then Jeroboam said to himself, "Now the kingdom may well revert to the house of David. [27]If this people continues to go up to offer sacrifices in the house of the LORD at Jerusalem, the heart of this people will turn again to their master, King Rehoboam of Judah; they will kill me and return to King Rehoboam of Judah." [28]So the king took counsel, and made two calves of gold. He said to the people,[a] "You have gone up to Jerusalem long enough. Here are your gods, O Israel, who brought you up out of the land of Egypt." [29]He set one in Bethel, and the other he put in Dan. [30]And this thing became a sin, for the people went to worship before the one at Bethel and before the other as far as Dan.[b] [31]He also made houses[c] on high places, and appointed priests from among all the people, who were not Levites. [32]Jeroboam appointed a festival on the fifteenth day of the eighth month like the festival that was in Judah, and he offered sacrifices on the altar; so he did in Bethel, sacrificing to the calves that he had made. And he placed in Bethel the priests of the high places that he had made. [33]He went up to the altar that he had made in Bethel on the fifteenth day in the eighth month, in the month that he alone had devised; he appointed a festival for the people of Israel, and he went up to the altar to offer incense.

a Gk: Heb to them   b Compare Gk: Heb went to the one as far as Dan
c Gk Vg Compare 13.32: Heb a house

Hard Consequences of Wrong Choices

1 KINGS 12.1–15

Picture yourself as the new leader of all Israel. The people are assembled before you with one request: that the harsh conditions of forced labor imposed by the previous leader be lightened. You have two choices. You can listen to your elders and follow their advice to lighten the load of the people; or you can listen to the voices of your peers, who have their own ideas about how you should rule. Bring to mind the times when your own unwise decisions may have caused harm—times when you have heeded the wrong advice. How have you handled the consequences that came with making such mistakes? What did you learn? How did you relate to God in such situations?

See Meeting God in Prayer

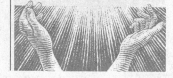

Disrupting Worship

1 KINGS 13.1–10

After reading the narrative of this passage, imagine this incident step by step. Notice how beautiful the sanctuary is. Listen to the reactions of the priests and King Jeroboam. Hear the tone of the prophet's voice and see his facial expression. Is his voice soft or loud, harsh or compassionate? Now imagine a similar scene happening in a contemporary house of worship, perhaps your own. What judgments would the prophet make about the worship of your congregation. What would he say about the people's lives? Let the prophet now turn to you and tell you what you may need to hear about the way you worship God.

See Meeting God in Worship

A Man of God from Judah

13 While Jeroboam was standing by the altar to offer incense, a man of God came out of Judah by the word of the LORD to Bethel ²and proclaimed against the altar by the word of the LORD, and said, "O altar, altar, thus says the LORD: 'A son shall be born to the house of David, Josiah by name; and he shall sacrifice on you the priests of the high places who offer incense on you, and human bones shall be burned on you.' " ³He gave a sign the same day, saying, "This is the sign that the LORD has spoken: 'The altar shall be torn down, and the ashes that are on it shall be poured out.' " ⁴When the king heard what the man of God cried out against the altar at Bethel, Jeroboam stretched out his hand from the altar, saying, "Seize him!" But the hand that he stretched out against him withered so that he could not draw it back to himself. ⁵The altar also was torn down, and the ashes poured out from the altar, according to the sign that the man of God had given by the word of the LORD. ⁶The king said to the man of God, "Entreat now the favor of the LORD your God, and pray for me, so that my hand may be restored to me." So the man of God entreated the LORD; and the king's hand was restored to him, and became as it was before. ⁷Then the king said to the man of God, "Come home with me and dine, and I will give you a gift." ⁸But the man of God said to the king, "If you give me half your kingdom, I will not go in with you; nor will I eat food or drink water in this place. ⁹For thus I was commanded by the word of the LORD: You shall not eat food, or drink water, or return by the way that you came." ¹⁰So he went another way, and did not return by the way that he had come to Bethel.

11 Now there lived an old prophet in Bethel. One of his sons came and told him all that the man of God had done that day in Bethel; the words also that he had spoken to the king, they told to their father. ¹²Their father said to them, "Which way did he go?" And his sons showed him the way that the man of God who came from Judah had gone. ¹³Then he said to his sons, "Saddle a donkey for me." So they saddled a donkey for him, and he mounted it. ¹⁴He went after the man of God, and found him sitting under an oak tree. He said to him, "Are you the man of God who came from Judah?" He answered, "I am." ¹⁵Then he said to him, "Come home with me and eat some food." ¹⁶But he said, "I cannot return with you, or go in with you; nor will I eat food or drink water with you in this place; ¹⁷for it was said to me by the word of the LORD: You shall not eat food or drink water there, or return by the way that you came." ¹⁸Then the other*a* said to him, "I also am a prophet as you are, and an angel spoke to me by the word of the LORD: Bring him back with you into your house so that he may eat food and drink water." But he was deceiving him. ¹⁹Then the man of God*a* went back with him, and ate food and drank water in his house.

20 As they were sitting at the table, the word of the LORD came to the prophet who had brought him back; ²¹and he proclaimed to the man of God who came from

a Heb *he*

Judah, "Thus says the LORD: Because you have disobeyed the word of the LORD, and have not kept the commandment that the LORD your God commanded you, ²²but have come back and have eaten food and drunk water in the place of which he said to you, 'Eat no food, and drink no water,' your body shall not come to your ancestral tomb." ²³After the man of God[a] had eaten food and had drunk, they saddled for him a donkey belonging to the prophet who had brought him back. ²⁴Then as he went away, a lion met him on the road and killed him. His body was thrown in the road, and the donkey stood beside it; the lion also stood beside the body. ²⁵People passed by and saw the body thrown in the road, with the lion standing by the body. And they came and told it in the town where the old prophet lived.

26 When the prophet who had brought him back from the way heard of it, he said, "It is the man of God who disobeyed the word of the LORD; therefore the LORD has given him to the lion, which has torn him and killed him according to the word that the LORD spoke to him." ²⁷Then he said to his sons, "Saddle a donkey for me." So they saddled one, ²⁸and he went and found the body thrown in the road, with the donkey and the lion standing beside the body. The lion had not eaten the body or attacked the donkey. ²⁹The prophet took up the body of the man of God, laid it on the donkey, and brought it back to the city,[b] to mourn and to bury him. ³⁰He laid the body in his own grave; and they mourned over him, saying, "Alas, my brother!" ³¹After he had buried him, he said to his sons, "When I die, bury me in the grave in which the man of God is buried; lay my bones beside his bones. ³²For the saying that he proclaimed by the word of the LORD against the altar in Bethel, and against all the houses of the high places that are in the cities of Samaria, shall surely come to pass."

33 Even after this event Jeroboam did not turn from his evil way, but made priests for the high places again from among all the people; any who wanted to be priests he consecrated for the high places. ³⁴This matter became sin to the house of Jeroboam, so as to cut it off and to destroy it from the face of the earth.

Judgment on the House of Jeroboam

14 At that time Abijah son of Jeroboam fell sick. ²Jeroboam said to his wife, "Go, disguise yourself, so that it will not be known that you are the wife of Jeroboam, and go to Shiloh; for the prophet Ahijah is there, who said of me that I should be king over this people. ³Take with you ten loaves, some cakes, and a jar of honey, and go to him; he will tell you what shall happen to the child."

4 Jeroboam's wife did so; she set out and went to Shiloh, and came to the house of Ahijah. Now Ahijah could not see, for his eyes were dim because of his age. ⁵But the LORD said to Ahijah, "The wife of Jeroboam is coming to inquire of you concerning her son; for he is sick. Thus and thus you shall say to her."

When she came, she pretended to be another woman. ⁶But when Ahijah heard the sound of her feet, as she

Facing Lions

1 KINGS 13.20–25

In the Old Testament, stories about David, Samson and Daniel all include lions. In ancient times lions were a common threat to flocks and occasionally to people, attacking and destroying without warning.

Attacks in this life come from many places and take many forms—physical illness, financial loss or spiritual struggles. Think back on the various attacks you have experienced. When were you attacked without warning? What form did the lion take? In what ways was God present with you through the experience? How did this experience change your relationship with God?

See Meeting God in Everyday Life

---

a Heb *he*   *b* Gk: Heb *he came to the town of the old prophet*

Justice and the Unjust King

1 KINGS 14.1–18

"Do not sneer at justice, for it is one of the three feet of the world, for the sages taught that the world stands on three things: justice, truth and peace. Therefore reflect that if you pervert justice, you shake the world . . . It is written, 'To do justice and righteousness is better than sacrifice' [Proverbs 21.3]. For . . . sacrifices can occur only in this world, but righteousness and justice are for this world and the world to come." (Rabbi Simeon, b. Gamaliel, 2nd century B.C.)

—*The Talmud,*
Deuteronomy Rabba, Shofetim, V, 1 and 3

came in at the door, he said, "Come in, wife of Jeroboam; why do you pretend to be another? For I am charged with heavy tidings for you. [7]Go, tell Jeroboam, 'Thus says the LORD, the God of Israel: Because I exalted you from among the people, made you leader over my people Israel, [8]and tore the kingdom away from the house of David to give it to you; yet you have not been like my servant David, who kept my commandments and followed me with all his heart, doing only that which was right in my sight, [9]but you have done evil above all those who were before you and have gone and made for yourself other gods, and cast images, provoking me to anger, and have thrust me behind your back; [10]therefore, I will bring evil upon the house of Jeroboam. I will cut off from Jeroboam every male, both bond and free in Israel, and will consume the house of Jeroboam, just as one burns up dung until it is all gone. [11]Anyone belonging to Jeroboam who dies in the city, the dogs shall eat; and anyone who dies in the open country, the birds of the air shall eat; for the LORD has spoken.' [12]Therefore set out, go to your house. When your feet enter the city, the child shall die. [13]All Israel shall mourn for him and bury him; for he alone of Jeroboam's family shall come to the grave, because in him there is found something pleasing to the LORD, the God of Israel, in the house of Jeroboam. [14]Moreover the LORD will raise up for himself a king over Israel, who shall cut off the house of Jeroboam today, even right now![a]

15 "The LORD will strike Israel, as a reed is shaken in the water; he will root up Israel out of this good land that he gave to their ancestors, and scatter them beyond the Euphrates, because they have made their sacred poles,[b] provoking the LORD to anger. [16]He will give Israel up because of the sins of Jeroboam, which he sinned and which he caused Israel to commit."

17 Then Jeroboam's wife got up and went away, and she came to Tirzah. As she came to the threshold of the house, the child died. [18]All Israel buried him and mourned for him, according to the word of the LORD, which he spoke by his servant the prophet Ahijah.

Death of Jeroboam

19 Now the rest of the acts of Jeroboam, how he warred and how he reigned, are written in the Book of the Annals of the Kings of Israel. [20]The time that Jeroboam reigned was twenty-two years; then he slept with his ancestors, and his son Nadab succeeded him.

Rehoboam Reigns over Judah

21 Now Rehoboam son of Solomon reigned in Judah. Rehoboam was forty-one years old when he began to reign, and he reigned seventeen years in Jerusalem, the city that the LORD had chosen out of all the tribes of Israel, to put his name there. His mother's name was Naamah the Ammonite. [22]Judah did what was evil in the sight of the LORD; they provoked him to jealousy with their sins that they committed, more than all that their ancestors had done. [23]For they also built for themselves high places, pillars, and sacred poles[b] on every high hill and under

a Meaning of Heb uncertain   *b* Heb *Asherim*

every green tree; [24]there were also male temple prostitutes in the land. They committed all the abominations of the nations that the LORD drove out before the people of Israel.

25 In the fifth year of King Rehoboam, King Shishak of Egypt came up against Jerusalem; [26]he took away the treasures of the house of the LORD and the treasures of the king's house; he took everything. He also took away all the shields of gold that Solomon had made; [27]so King Rehoboam made shields of bronze instead, and committed them to the hands of the officers of the guard, who kept the door of the king's house. [28]As often as the king went into the house of the LORD, the guard carried them and brought them back to the guardroom.

29 Now the rest of the acts of Rehoboam, and all that he did, are they not written in the Book of the Annals of the Kings of Judah? [30]There was war between Rehoboam and Jeroboam continually. [31]Rehoboam slept with his ancestors and was buried with his ancestors in the city of David. His mother's name was Naamah the Ammonite. His son Abijam succeeded him.

Abijam Reigns over Judah: Idolatry and War

15 Now in the eighteenth year of King Jeroboam son of Nebat, Abijam began to reign over Judah. [2]He reigned for three years in Jerusalem. His mother's name was Maacah daughter of Abishalom. [3]He committed all the sins that his father did before him; his heart was not true to the LORD his God, like the heart of his father David. [4]Nevertheless for David's sake the LORD his God gave him a lamp in Jerusalem, setting up his son after him, and establishing Jerusalem; [5]because David did what was right in the sight of the LORD, and did not turn aside from anything that he commanded him all the days of his life, except in the matter of Uriah the Hittite. [6]The war begun between Rehoboam and Jeroboam continued all the days of his life. [7]The rest of the acts of Abijam, and all that he did, are they not written in the Book of the Annals of the Kings of Judah? There was war between Abijam and Jeroboam. [8]Abijam slept with his ancestors, and they buried him in the city of David. Then his son Asa succeeded him.

Asa Reigns over Judah

9 In the twentieth year of King Jeroboam of Israel, Asa began to reign over Judah; [10]he reigned forty-one years in Jerusalem. His mother's name was Maacah daughter of Abishalom. [11]Asa did what was right in the sight of the LORD, as his father David had done. [12]He put away the male temple prostitutes out of the land, and removed all the idols that his ancestors had made. [13]He also removed his mother Maacah from being queen mother, because she had made an abominable image for Asherah; Asa cut down her image and burned it at the Wadi Kidron. [14]But the high places were not taken away. Nevertheless the heart of Asa was true to the LORD all his days. [15]He brought into the house of the LORD the votive gifts of his father and his own votive gifts—silver, gold, and utensils.

The Temple and Palace Plundered

1 KINGS 14.25–26

God's judgment on the people's idolatry, evil and sin is executed by foreign armies. Riches that took years to accumulate are plundered overnight, initiating a time of great social, political and religious change.

How are the "riches" of your own community or nation being "plundered" because of individual or communal sin? How have decisions made by our leaders, local and national, diminished the moral and spiritual quality of life? What changes in the nation upset or encourage you? What leaders attract your attention by their stands for or against what you consider God's values? Consider these concerns as your call to specific prayer; spend time praying for the nation and its leaders.

See Meeting God in Community

Return to the Sovereign God

1 KINGS 15.9–24

"If God is indeed sovereign, it is utter foolishness to ignore the One who is in complete control. Our lives cannot possibly be what they were intended to be apart from the Source of life. The folly of resisting the Power that transcends all powers of men is so obvious it is difficult to understand why we do it. Quite clearly, life can be what it should be only when it is lived in a conscious relationship with God."

—WILLIAM O. PAULSELL,
Taste and See

Alliance with Aram against Israel

16 There was war between Asa and King Baasha of Israel all their days. [17]King Baasha of Israel went up against Judah, and built Ramah, to prevent anyone from going out or coming in to King Asa of Judah. [18]Then Asa took all the silver and the gold that were left in the treasures of the house of the LORD and the treasures of the king's house, and gave them into the hands of his servants. King Asa sent them to King Ben-hadad son of Tabrimmon son of Hezion of Aram, who resided in Damascus, saying, [19]"Let there be an alliance between me and you, like that between my father and your father: I am sending you a present of silver and gold; go, break your alliance with King Baasha of Israel, so that he may withdraw from me." [20]Ben-hadad listened to King Asa, and sent the commanders of his armies against the cities of Israel. He conquered Ijon, Dan, Abel-beth-maacah, and all Chinneroth, with all the land of Naphtali. [21]When Baasha heard of it, he stopped building Ramah and lived in Tirzah. [22]Then King Asa made a proclamation to all Judah, none was exempt: they carried away the stones of Ramah and its timber, with which Baasha had been building; with them King Asa built Geba of Benjamin and Mizpah. [23]Now the rest of all the acts of Asa, all his power, all that he did, and the cities that he built, are they not written in the Book of the Annals of the Kings of Judah? But in his old age he was diseased in his feet. [24]Then Asa slept with his ancestors, and was buried with his ancestors in the city of his father David; his son Jehoshaphat succeeded him.

Nadab Reigns over Israel

25 Nadab son of Jeroboam began to reign over Israel in the second year of King Asa of Judah; he reigned over Israel two years. [26]He did what was evil in the sight of the LORD, walking in the way of his ancestor and in the sin that he caused Israel to commit.

27 Baasha son of Ahijah, of the house of Issachar, conspired against him; and Baasha struck him down at Gibbethon, which belonged to the Philistines; for Nadab and all Israel were laying siege to Gibbethon. [28]So Baasha killed Nadab[a] in the third year of King Asa of Judah, and succeeded him. [29]As soon as he was king, he killed all the house of Jeroboam; he left to the house of Jeroboam not one that breathed, until he had destroyed it, according to the word of the LORD that he spoke by his servant Ahijah the Shilonite— [30]because of the sins of Jeroboam that he committed and that he caused Israel to commit, and because of the anger to which he provoked the LORD, the God of Israel.

31 Now the rest of the acts of Nadab, and all that he did, are they not written in the Book of the Annals of the Kings of Israel? [32]There was war between Asa and King Baasha of Israel all their days.

Second Dynasty: Baasha Reigns over Israel

33 In the third year of King Asa of Judah, Baasha son of Ahijah began to reign over all Israel at Tirzah; he

a Heb *him*

reigned twenty-four years. [34]He did what was evil in the sight of the LORD, walking in the way of Jeroboam and in the sin that he caused Israel to commit.

16 The word of the LORD came to Jehu son of Hanani against Baasha, saying, [2]"Since I exalted you out of the dust and made you leader over my people Israel, and you have walked in the way of Jeroboam, and have caused my people Israel to sin, provoking me to anger with their sins, [3]therefore, I will consume Baasha and his house, and I will make your house like the house of Jeroboam son of Nebat. [4]Anyone belonging to Baasha who dies in the city the dogs shall eat; and anyone of his who dies in the field the birds of the air shall eat."

5 Now the rest of the acts of Baasha, what he did, and his power, are they not written in the Book of the Annals of the Kings of Israel? [6]Baasha slept with his ancestors, and was buried at Tirzah; and his son Elah succeeded him. [7]Moreover the word of the LORD came by the prophet Jehu son of Hanani against Baasha and his house, both because of all the evil that he did in the sight of the LORD, provoking him to anger with the work of his hands, in being like the house of Jeroboam, and also because he destroyed it.

Elah Reigns over Israel

8 In the twenty-sixth year of King Asa of Judah, Elah son of Baasha began to reign over Israel in Tirzah; he reigned two years. [9]But his servant Zimri, commander of half his chariots, conspired against him. When he was at Tirzah, drinking himself drunk in the house of Arza, who was in charge of the palace at Tirzah, [10]Zimri came in and struck him down and killed him, in the twenty-seventh year of King Asa of Judah, and succeeded him.

11 When he began to reign, as soon as he had seated himself on his throne, he killed all the house of Baasha; he did not leave him a single male of his kindred or his friends. [12]Thus Zimri destroyed all the house of Baasha, according to the word of the LORD, which he spoke against Baasha by the prophet Jehu— [13]because of all the sins of Baasha and the sins of his son Elah that they committed, and that they caused Israel to commit, provoking the LORD God of Israel to anger with their idols. [14]Now the rest of the acts of Elah, and all that he did, are they not written in the Book of the Annals of the Kings of Israel?

Third Dynasty: Zimri Reigns over Israel

15 In the twenty-seventh year of King Asa of Judah, Zimri reigned seven days in Tirzah. Now the troops were encamped against Gibbethon, which belonged to the Philistines, [16]and the troops who were encamped heard it said, "Zimri has conspired, and he has killed the king"; therefore all Israel made Omri, the commander of the army, king over Israel that day in the camp. [17]So Omri went up from Gibbethon, and all Israel with him, and they besieged Tirzah. [18]When Zimri saw that the city was taken, he went into the citadel of the king's house; he burned down the king's house over himself with fire, and died— [19]because of the sins that he committed, doing evil in the sight of the LORD, walking in the way of Jeroboam,

God Alone

1 KINGS 16.1–4

Over the door of the guest house of a famous American Trappist monastery are the words "God alone." Baasha is judged severely, as are most of the kings, for not making "God alone" his aim. When we firmly and decisively decide to live for God alone, our activities, problems, anxieties and hopes begin to fit into place. Life can have new orderliness and peace.

Is this a basic value for your life? Look at your schedule for today and the rest of the week. What times are set aside for God and God alone? What occasions are available for prayer and reflection? When are there times for relationships and family? What changes do you have to make in order to make time for these things?

See *Meeting God in Everyday Life*

The Problem of Human Evil

1 KINGS 16.29–30

"Evil is in opposition to life. Evil, then, for the moment, is that force, residing either inside or outside human beings, that seeks to kill life or liveliness. And goodness is its opposite. Goodness promotes life and liveliness."

—M. SCOTT PECK,
People of the Lie

and for the sin that he committed, causing Israel to sin. ²⁰ Now the rest of the acts of Zimri, and the conspiracy that he made, are they not written in the Book of the Annals of the Kings of Israel?

Fourth Dynasty: Omri Reigns over Israel

21 Then the people of Israel were divided into two parts; half of the people followed Tibni son of Ginath, to make him king, and half followed Omri. ²² But the people who followed Omri overcame the people who followed Tibni son of Ginath; so Tibni died, and Omri became king. ²³ In the thirty-first year of King Asa of Judah, Omri began to reign over Israel; he reigned for twelve years, six of them in Tirzah.

Samaria the New Capital

24 He bought the hill of Samaria from Shemer for two talents of silver; he fortified the hill, and called the city that he built, Samaria, after the name of Shemer, the owner of the hill.

25 Omri did what was evil in the sight of the LORD; he did more evil than all who were before him. ²⁶ For he walked in all the way of Jeroboam son of Nebat, and in the sins that he caused Israel to commit, provoking the LORD, the God of Israel, to anger by their idols. ²⁷ Now the rest of the acts of Omri that he did, and the power that he showed, are they not written in the Book of the Annals of the Kings of Israel? ²⁸ Omri slept with his ancestors, and was buried in Samaria; his son Ahab succeeded him.

Ahab Reigns over Israel

29 In the thirty-eighth year of King Asa of Judah, Ahab son of Omri began to reign over Israel; Ahab son of Omri reigned over Israel in Samaria twenty-two years. ³⁰ Ahab son of Omri did evil in the sight of the LORD more than all who were before him.

Ahab Marries Jezebel and Worships Baal

31 And as if it had been a light thing for him to walk in the sins of Jeroboam son of Nebat, he took as his wife Jezebel daughter of King Ethbaal of the Sidonians, and went and served Baal, and worshiped him. ³² He erected an altar for Baal in the house of Baal, which he built in Samaria. ³³ Ahab also made a sacred pole.^a Ahab did more to provoke the anger of the LORD, the God of Israel, than had all the kings of Israel who were before him. ³⁴ In his days Hiel of Bethel built Jericho; he laid its foundation at the cost of Abiram his firstborn, and set up its gates at the cost of his youngest son Segub, according to the word of the LORD, which he spoke by Joshua son of Nun.

Elijah Predicts a Drought

17 Now Elijah the Tishbite, of Tishbe^b in Gilead, said to Ahab, "As the LORD the God of Israel lives, before whom I stand, there shall be neither dew nor rain these years, except by my word." ² The word of the LORD came to him, saying, ³ "Go from here and turn eastward, and hide yourself by the Wadi Cherith, which is east of the

a Heb *Asherah*   *b* Gk: Heb *of the settlers*

Jordan. ⁴You shall drink from the wadi, and I have commanded the ravens to feed you there." ⁵So he went and did according to the word of the LORD; he went and lived by the Wadi Cherith, which is east of the Jordan. ⁶The ravens brought him bread and meat in the morning, and bread and meat in the evening; and he drank from the wadi. ⁷But after a while the wadi dried up, because there was no rain in the land.

The Widow of Zarephath

8 Then the word of the LORD came to him, saying, ⁹"Go now to Zarephath, which belongs to Sidon, and live there; for I have commanded a widow there to feed you." ¹⁰So he set out and went to Zarephath. When he came to the gate of the town, a widow was there gathering sticks; he called to her and said, "Bring me a little water in a vessel, so that I may drink." ¹¹As she was going to bring it, he called to her and said, "Bring me a morsel of bread in your hand." ¹²But she said, "As the LORD your God lives, I have nothing baked, only a handful of meal in a jar, and a little oil in a jug; I am now gathering a couple of sticks, so that I may go home and prepare it for myself and my son, that we may eat it, and die." ¹³Elijah said to her, "Do not be afraid; go and do as you have said; but first make me a little cake of it and bring it to me, and afterwards make something for yourself and your son. ¹⁴For thus says the LORD the God of Israel: The jar of meal will not be emptied and the jug of oil will not fail until the day that the LORD sends rain on the earth." ¹⁵She went and did as Elijah said, so that she as well as he and her household ate for many days. ¹⁶The jar of meal was not emptied, neither did the jug of oil fail, according to the word of the LORD that he spoke by Elijah.

Elijah Revives the Widow's Son

17 After this the son of the woman, the mistress of the house, became ill; his illness was so severe that there was no breath left in him. ¹⁸She then said to Elijah, "What have you against me, O man of God? You have come to me to bring my sin to remembrance, and to cause the death of my son!" ¹⁹But he said to her, "Give me your son." He took him from her bosom, carried him up into the upper chamber where he was lodging, and laid him on his own bed. ²⁰He cried out to the LORD, "O LORD my God, have you brought calamity even upon the widow with whom I am staying, by killing her son?" ²¹Then he stretched himself upon the child three times, and cried out to the LORD, "O LORD my God, let this child's life come into him again." ²²The LORD listened to the voice of Elijah; the life of the child came into him again, and he revived. ²³Elijah took the child, brought him down from the upper chamber into the house, and gave him to his mother; then Elijah said, "See, your son is alive." ²⁴So the woman said to Elijah, "Now I know that you are a man of God, and that the word of the LORD in your mouth is truth."

Help From Unlikely Sources

1 KINGS 17.1–16

God turned to ravens (unclean birds) and to a widow—a foreigner from Jezebel's home territory—to care for the prophet Elijah. This zealous prophet is called to go stand for the Lord against the corrupt mainstream, yet God takes care of him by means Elijah might have prejudged negatively.

God uses unexpected sources to teach us lessons. In what ways has God provided you with help from surprising sources? In what ways has God's help in the past broadened your expectations of how God may bring help in the future? When has God helped you unexpectedly? What have been some of the unexpected places where you have found God's help?

Spiritual Burnout

1 KINGS 18.20–22

Ahab and Jezebel chase Elijah. The people of Israel say nothing in response to Elijah's call to worship God. It hardly seems surprising, therefore, that Elijah would say, "I, even I only, am left a prophet of the LORD." Recall a time when you felt discouraged and alone and perhaps unable to see God acting. What brought your perspective back into focus? What spiritual resources can save you from spiritual depletion?

See Meeting God in Prayer

Elijah's Message to Ahab

18 After many days the word of the LORD came to Elijah, in the third year of the drought,[a] saying, "Go, present yourself to Ahab; I will send rain on the earth." ²So Elijah went to present himself to Ahab. The famine was severe in Samaria. ³Ahab summoned Obadiah, who was in charge of the palace. (Now Obadiah revered the LORD greatly; ⁴when Jezebel was killing off the prophets of the LORD, Obadiah took a hundred prophets, hid them fifty to a cave, and provided them with bread and water.) ⁵Then Ahab said to Obadiah, "Go through the land to all the springs of water and to all the wadis; perhaps we may find grass to keep the horses and mules alive, and not lose some of the animals." ⁶So they divided the land between them to pass through it; Ahab went in one direction by himself, and Obadiah went in another direction by himself.

7 As Obadiah was on the way, Elijah met him; Obadiah recognized him, fell on his face, and said, "Is it you, my lord Elijah?" ⁸He answered him, "It is I. Go, tell your lord that Elijah is here." ⁹And he said, "How have I sinned, that you would hand your servant over to Ahab, to kill me? ¹⁰As the LORD your God lives, there is no nation or kingdom to which my lord has not sent to seek you; and when they would say, 'He is not here,' he would require an oath of the kingdom or nation, that they had not found you. ¹¹But now you say, 'Go, tell your lord that Elijah is here.' ¹²As soon as I have gone from you, the spirit of the LORD will carry you I know not where; so, when I come and tell Ahab and he cannot find you, he will kill me, although I your servant have revered the LORD from my youth. ¹³Has it not been told my lord what I did when Jezebel killed the prophets of the LORD, how I hid a hundred of the LORD's prophets fifty to a cave, and provided them with bread and water? ¹⁴Yet now you say, 'Go, tell your lord that Elijah is here'; he will surely kill me." ¹⁵Elijah said, "As the LORD of hosts lives, before whom I stand, I will surely show myself to him today." ¹⁶So Obadiah went to meet Ahab, and told him; and Ahab went to meet Elijah.

17 When Ahab saw Elijah, Ahab said to him, "Is it you, you troubler of Israel?" ¹⁸He answered, "I have not troubled Israel; but you have, and your father's house, because you have forsaken the commandments of the LORD and followed the Baals. ¹⁹Now therefore have all Israel assemble for me at Mount Carmel, with the four hundred fifty prophets of Baal and the four hundred prophets of Asherah, who eat at Jezebel's table."

Elijah's Triumph over the Priests of Baal

20 So Ahab sent to all the Israelites, and assembled the prophets at Mount Carmel. ²¹Elijah then came near to all the people, and said, "How long will you go limping with two different opinions? If the LORD is God, follow him; but if Baal, then follow him." The people did not answer him a word. ²²Then Elijah said to the people, "I, even I only, am left a prophet of the LORD; but Baal's prophets number four hundred fifty. ²³Let two bulls be given to us; let

a Heb lacks *of the drought*

them choose one bull for themselves, cut it in pieces, and lay it on the wood, but put no fire to it; I will prepare the other bull and lay it on the wood, but put no fire to it. ²⁴Then you call on the name of your god and I will call on the name of the LORD; the god who answers by fire is indeed God." All the people answered, "Well spoken!" ²⁵Then Elijah said to the prophets of Baal, "Choose for yourselves one bull and prepare it first, for you are many; then call on the name of your god, but put no fire to it." ²⁶So they took the bull that was given them, prepared it, and called on the name of Baal from morning until noon, crying, "O Baal, answer us!" But there was no voice, and no answer. They limped about the altar that they had made. ²⁷At noon Elijah mocked them, saying, "Cry aloud! Surely he is a god; either he is meditating, or he has wandered away, or he is on a journey, or perhaps he is asleep and must be awakened." ²⁸Then they cried aloud and, as was their custom, they cut themselves with swords and lances until the blood gushed out over them. ²⁹As midday passed, they raved on until the time of the offering of the oblation, but there was no voice, no answer, and no response.

30 Then Elijah said to all the people, "Come closer to me"; and all the people came closer to him. First he repaired the altar of the LORD that had been thrown down; ³¹Elijah took twelve stones, according to the number of the tribes of the sons of Jacob, to whom the word of the LORD came, saying, "Israel shall be your name"; ³²with the stones he built an altar in the name of the LORD. Then he made a trench around the altar, large enough to contain two measures of seed. ³³Next he put the wood in order, cut the bull in pieces, and laid it on the wood. He said, "Fill four jars with water and pour it on the burnt offering and on the wood." ³⁴Then he said, "Do it a second time"; and they did it a second time. Again he said, "Do it a third time"; and they did it a third time, ³⁵so that the water ran all around the altar, and filled the trench also with water.

36 At the time of the offering of the oblation, the prophet Elijah came near and said, "O LORD, God of Abraham, Isaac, and Israel, let it be known this day that you are God in Israel, that I am your servant, and that I have done all these things at your bidding. ³⁷Answer me, O LORD, answer me, so that this people may know that you, O LORD, are God, and that you have turned their hearts back." ³⁸Then the fire of the LORD fell and consumed the burnt offering, the wood, the stones, and the dust, and even licked up the water that was in the trench. ³⁹When all the people saw it, they fell on their faces and said, "The LORD indeed is God; the LORD indeed is God." ⁴⁰Elijah said to them, "Seize the prophets of Baal; do not let one of them escape." Then they seized them; and Elijah brought them down to the Wadi Kishon, and killed them there.

The Drought Ends

41 Elijah said to Ahab, "Go up, eat and drink; for there is a sound of rushing rain." ⁴²So Ahab went up to eat and to drink. Elijah went up to the top of Carmel; there he bowed himself down upon the earth and put his face be-

Elijah and the Priests of Baal

1 KINGS 18.20–40

Read the dramatic narrative of Elijah's confrontation with the priests of Baal, and their defeat. Then pray that you may be open to God's living word for you in this text. Now read the passage again more slowly. Look for any word, phrase or scene that seems to leap off the page at you, or that calls to you for further thought. Write down each notable phrase as you read through the passage, then choose one phrase or scene to spend time with. Let it fill your mind and heart. Be open to the living voice of the Spirit to show you how this might apply to your life today.

See Meeting God in Scripture

Victory, Exhaustion and Restoration

1 KINGS 19.1–18

Imagine that you are the prophet Elijah. After your stunning victory, you suddenly have to flee for your life. You are alone in the battle for righteousness. God leads you into the wilderness, providing you with shelter and sending an angel to deliver food. Experience the wind, the earthquake and the fire, then, "a sound of sheer silence." Listen as God reminds you that you are not alone, that he is still with you and that you have more work to do. As you step back out onto the road and continue the journey, how are you different? Note your emotions and give thanks to God.

See Meeting God in Scripture

tween his knees. ⁴³He said to his servant, "Go up now, look toward the sea." He went up and looked, and said, "There is nothing." Then he said, "Go again seven times." ⁴⁴At the seventh time he said, "Look, a little cloud no bigger than a person's hand is rising out of the sea." Then he said, "Go say to Ahab, 'Harness your chariot and go down before the rain stops you.' " ⁴⁵In a little while the heavens grew black with clouds and wind; there was a heavy rain. Ahab rode off and went to Jezreel. ⁴⁶But the hand of the LORD was on Elijah; he girded up his loins and ran in front of Ahab to the entrance of Jezreel.

Elijah Flees from Jezebel

19 Ahab told Jezebel all that Elijah had done, and how he had killed all the prophets with the sword. ²Then Jezebel sent a messenger to Elijah, saying, "So may the gods do to me, and more also, if I do not make your life like the life of one of them by this time tomorrow." ³Then he was afraid; he got up and fled for his life, and came to Beer-sheba, which belongs to Judah; he left his servant there.

4 But he himself went a day's journey into the wilderness, and came and sat down under a solitary broom tree. He asked that he might die: "It is enough; now, O LORD, take away my life, for I am no better than my ancestors." ⁵Then he lay down under the broom tree and fell asleep. Suddenly an angel touched him and said to him, "Get up and eat." ⁶He looked, and there at his head was a cake baked on hot stones, and a jar of water. He ate and drank, and lay down again. ⁷The angel of the LORD came a second time, touched him, and said, "Get up and eat, otherwise the journey will be too much for you." ⁸He got up, and ate and drank; then he went in the strength of that food forty days and forty nights to Horeb the mount of God. ⁹At that place he came to a cave, and spent the night there.

Then the word of the LORD came to him, saying, "What are you doing here, Elijah?" ¹⁰He answered, "I have been very zealous for the LORD, the God of hosts; for the Israelites have forsaken your covenant, thrown down your altars, and killed your prophets with the sword. I alone am left, and they are seeking my life, to take it away."

Elijah Meets God at Horeb

11 He said, "Go out and stand on the mountain before the LORD, for the LORD is about to pass by." Now there was a great wind, so strong that it was splitting mountains and breaking rocks in pieces before the LORD, but the LORD was not in the wind; and after the wind an earthquake, but the LORD was not in the earthquake; ¹²and after the earthquake a fire, but the LORD was not in the fire; and after the fire a sound of sheer silence. ¹³When Elijah heard it, he wrapped his face in his mantle and went out and stood at the entrance of the cave. Then there came a voice to him that said, "What are you doing here, Elijah?" ¹⁴He answered, "I have been very zealous for the LORD, the God of hosts; for the Israelites have forsaken your covenant, thrown down your altars,

and killed your prophets with the sword. I alone am left, and they are seeking my life, to take it away." ¹⁵Then the LORD said to him, "Go, return on your way to the wilderness of Damascus; when you arrive, you shall anoint Hazael as king over Aram. ¹⁶Also you shall anoint Jehu son of Nimshi as king over Israel; and you shall anoint Elisha son of Shaphat of Abel-meholah as prophet in your place. ¹⁷Whoever escapes from the sword of Hazael, Jehu shall kill; and whoever escapes from the sword of Jehu, Elisha shall kill. ¹⁸Yet I will leave seven thousand in Israel, all the knees that have not bowed to Baal, and every mouth that has not kissed him."

Elisha Becomes Elijah's Disciple

19 So he set out from there, and found Elisha son of Shaphat, who was plowing. There were twelve yoke of oxen ahead of him, and he was with the twelfth. Elijah passed by him and threw his mantle over him. ²⁰He left the oxen, ran after Elijah, and said, "Let me kiss my father and my mother, and then I will follow you." Then Elijah*ᵃ* said to him, "Go back again; for what have I done to you?" ²¹He returned from following him, took the yoke of oxen, and slaughtered them; using the equipment from the oxen, he boiled their flesh, and gave it to the people, and they ate. Then he set out and followed Elijah, and became his servant.

Ahab's Wars with the Arameans

20 King Ben-hadad of Aram gathered all his army together; thirty-two kings were with him, along with horses and chariots. He marched against Samaria, laid siege to it, and attacked it. ²Then he sent messengers into the city to King Ahab of Israel, and said to him: "Thus says Ben-hadad: ³Your silver and gold are mine; your fairest wives and children also are mine." ⁴The king of Israel answered, "As you say, my lord, O king, I am yours, and all that I have." ⁵The messengers came again and said: "Thus says Ben-hadad: I sent to you, saying, 'Deliver to me your silver and gold, your wives and children'; ⁶nevertheless I will send my servants to you tomorrow about this time, and they shall search your house and the houses of your servants, and lay hands on whatever pleases them,*ᵇ* and take it away."

7 Then the king of Israel called all the elders of the land, and said, "Look now! See how this man is seeking trouble; for he sent to me for my wives, my children, my silver, and my gold; and I did not refuse him." ⁸Then all the elders and all the people said to him, "Do not listen or consent." ⁹So he said to the messengers of Ben-hadad, "Tell my lord the king: All that you first demanded of your servant I will do; but this thing I cannot do." The messengers left and brought him word again. ¹⁰Ben-hadad sent to him and said, "The gods do so to me, and more also, if the dust of Samaria will provide a handful for each of the people who follow me." ¹¹The king of Israel answered, "Tell him: One who puts on armor should not brag like one who takes it off." ¹²When Ben-hadad heard this message—now he had been drinking with the kings

Passing the Mantle

1 KINGS 19.19–21

The mantle was the prophet's most important article of clothing. An animal skin covered with hair, it served as a coat, a blanket, a satchel to carry goods and a bundle to sit on, as well as security for a debt. A prophet's mantle identified him as a man of God.

Search your photo album, house, garage and attic. What are the most important things you own? What possessions, perhaps those that have been passed down through generations, are rich with meaning? What items indicate your family's heritage and spiritual identity? Gather these things together and decide how to preserve them. How do they tell the story of your life or the story of your family and heritage?

See *Meeting God in Everyday Life*

Untapped Skill in the Young

1 KINGS 20.13–22

Israel faces a formidable challenge: Ben-hadad and his thirty-two kings besiege Samaria. But a prophet is able to discern real hope in the situation. Victory will come from the "young men who serve the district governors" rather than from the old, the trusted and the experienced. What trends among those younger than yourself do you see as positive and hopeful? If you are discouraged by what you see in younger people, prayerfully ask God to show you what you may have overlooked. What young people do you know who are gifted and willing to serve God and humankind? How can you support them? Pray now for guidance in how to encourage those younger than yourself.

See Meeting God in Service

in the booths—he said to his men, "Take your positions!" And they took their positions against the city.

Prophetic Opposition to Ahab

13 Then a certain prophet came up to King Ahab of Israel and said, "Thus says the LORD, Have you seen all this great multitude? Look, I will give it into your hand today; and you shall know that I am the LORD." ¹⁴Ahab said, "By whom?" He said, "Thus says the LORD, By the young men who serve the district governors." Then he said, "Who shall begin the battle?" He answered, "You." ¹⁵Then he mustered the young men who served the district governors, two hundred thirty-two; after them he mustered all the people of Israel, seven thousand.

16 They went out at noon, while Ben-hadad was drinking himself drunk in the booths, he and the thirty-two kings allied with him. ¹⁷The young men who served the district governors went out first. Ben-hadad had sent out scouts,ᵃ and they reported to him, "Men have come out from Samaria." ¹⁸He said, "If they have come out for peace, take them alive; if they have come out for war, take them alive."

19 But these had already come out of the city: the young men who served the district governors, and the army that followed them. ²⁰Each killed his man; the Arameans fled and Israel pursued them, but King Ben-hadad of Aram escaped on a horse with the cavalry. ²¹The king of Israel went out, attacked the horses and chariots, and defeated the Arameans with a great slaughter.

22 Then the prophet approached the king of Israel and said to him, "Come, strengthen yourself, and consider well what you have to do; for in the spring the king of Aram will come up against you."

The Arameans Are Defeated

23 The servants of the king of Aram said to him, "Their gods are gods of the hills, and so they were stronger than we; but let us fight against them in the plain, and surely we shall be stronger than they. ²⁴Also do this: remove the kings, each from his post, and put commanders in place of them; ²⁵and muster an army like the army that you have lost, horse for horse, and chariot for chariot; then we will fight against them in the plain, and surely we shall be stronger than they." He heeded their voice, and did so.

26 In the spring Ben-hadad mustered the Arameans and went up to Aphek to fight against Israel. ²⁷After the Israelites had been mustered and provisioned, they went out to engage them; the people of Israel encamped opposite them like two little flocks of goats, while the Arameans filled the country. ²⁸A man of God approached and said to the king of Israel, "Thus says the LORD: Because the Arameans have said, 'The LORD is a god of the hills but he is not a god of the valleys,' therefore I will give all this great multitude into your hand, and you shall know that I am the LORD." ²⁹They encamped opposite one another seven days. Then on the seventh day the battle began; the Israelites killed one hundred thousand Aramean foot soldiers in one day. ³⁰The rest fled into the city of Aphek;

a Heb lacks *scouts*

and the wall fell on twenty-seven thousand men that were left.

Ben-hadad also fled, and entered the city to hide. [31]His servants said to him, "Look, we have heard that the kings of the house of Israel are merciful kings; let us put sackcloth around our waists and ropes on our heads, and go out to the king of Israel; perhaps he will spare your life." [32]So they tied sackcloth around their waists, put ropes on their heads, went to the king of Israel, and said, "Your servant Ben-hadad says, 'Please let me live.' " And he said, "Is he still alive? He is my brother." [33]Now the men were watching for an omen; they quickly took it up from him and said, "Yes, Ben-hadad is your brother." Then he said, "Go and bring him." So Ben-hadad came out to him; and he had him come up into the chariot. [34]Ben-hadad[a] said to him, "I will restore the towns that my father took from your father; and you may establish bazaars for yourself in Damascus, as my father did in Samaria." The king of Israel responded,[b] "I will let you go on those terms." So he made a treaty with him and let him go.

A Prophet Condemns Ahab

35 At the command of the LORD a certain member of a company of prophets[c] said to another, "Strike me!" But the man refused to strike him. [36]Then he said to him, "Because you have not obeyed the voice of the LORD, as soon as you have left me, a lion will kill you." And when he had left him, a lion met him and killed him. [37]Then he found another man and said, "Strike me!" So the man hit him, striking and wounding him. [38]Then the prophet departed, and waited for the king along the road, disguising himself with a bandage over his eyes. [39]As the king passed by, he cried to the king and said, "Your servant went out into the thick of the battle; then a soldier turned and brought a man to me, and said, 'Guard this man; if he is missing, your life shall be given for his life, or else you shall pay a talent of silver.' [40]While your servant was busy here and there, he was gone." The king of Israel said to him, "So shall your judgment be; you yourself have decided it." [41]Then he quickly took the bandage away from his eyes. The king of Israel recognized him as one of the prophets. [42]Then he said to him, "Thus says the LORD, 'Because you have let the man go whom I had devoted to destruction, therefore your life shall be for his life, and your people for his people.' " [43]The king of Israel set out toward home, resentful and sullen, and came to Samaria.

Naboth's Vineyard

21 Later the following events took place: Naboth the Jezreelite had a vineyard in Jezreel, beside the palace of King Ahab of Samaria. [2]And Ahab said to Naboth, "Give me your vineyard, so that I may have it for a vegetable garden, because it is near my house; I will give you a better vineyard for it; or, if it seems good to you, I will give you its value in money." [3]But Naboth said to Ahab, "The LORD forbid that I should give you my ancestral inheritance." [4]Ahab went home resentful and sullen

a Heb He   b Heb lacks The king of Israel responded   c Heb of the sons of the prophets

Wavering Between Obedience and Disobedience

1 KINGS 20.30–31

This book's litany continues, tale after tale, of people who waver between doing right and doing evil—between following God and following their own way. While God presents them with countless opportunities to return to him and pursue order and justice, they refuse to repent and to accept God's forgiveness. The results are devastating. Ponder this: Repentance is an act of change, restoration and grace. Remember times when you have repented or accepted the repentance of others.

How has repentance and forgiveness been a part of your journey with God? What role has forgiveness played in your relationships? How do you express your repentance to God and others? How do you express forgiveness?

At this time, is there any situation that requires you to repent? Is there anyone who needs your forgiveness? Ask God to give you courage to remedy this situation. Ask how you might do so.

See Meeting God in Prayer

King Ahab's Greed

1 KINGS 21.4–7

"Then [Jesus] told them a parable: 'The land of a rich man produced abundantly. And he thought to himself, "What should I do, for I have no place to store my crops?" Then he said, "I will do this: I will pull down my barns and build larger ones, and there I will store all my grain and my goods. And I will say to my soul, Soul, you have ample goods laid up for many years; relax, eat, drink, be merry." But God said to him, "You fool! This very night your life is being demanded of you. And the things you have prepared, whose will they be?" So it is with those who store up treasures for themselves but are not rich toward God.' "

—Luke 12.15–21

because of what Naboth the Jezreelite had said to him; for he had said, "I will not give you my ancestral inheritance." He lay down on his bed, turned away his face, and would not eat.

5 His wife Jezebel came to him and said, "Why are you so depressed that you will not eat?" 6He said to her, "Because I spoke to Naboth the Jezreelite and said to him, 'Give me your vineyard for money; or else, if you prefer, I will give you another vineyard for it'; but he answered, 'I will not give you my vineyard.' " 7His wife Jezebel said to him, "Do you now govern Israel? Get up, eat some food, and be cheerful; I will give you the vineyard of Naboth the Jezreelite."

8 So she wrote letters in Ahab's name and sealed them with his seal; she sent the letters to the elders and the nobles who lived with Naboth in his city. 9She wrote in the letters, "Proclaim a fast, and seat Naboth at the head of the assembly; 10seat two scoundrels opposite him, and have them bring a charge against him, saying, 'You have cursed God and the king.' Then take him out, and stone him to death." 11The men of his city, the elders and the nobles who lived in his city, did as Jezebel had sent word to them. Just as it was written in the letters that she had sent to them, 12they proclaimed a fast and seated Naboth at the head of the assembly. 13The two scoundrels came in and sat opposite him; and the scoundrels brought a charge against him, in the presence of the people, saying, "Naboth cursed God and the king." So they took him outside the city, and stoned him to death. 14Then they sent to Jezebel, saying, "Naboth has been stoned; he is dead."

15 As soon as Jezebel heard that Naboth had been stoned and was dead, Jezebel said to Ahab, "Go, take possession of the vineyard of Naboth the Jezreelite, which he refused to give you for money; for Naboth is not alive, but dead." 16As soon as Ahab heard that Naboth was dead, Ahab set out to go down to the vineyard of Naboth the Jezreelite, to take possession of it.

Elijah Pronounces God's Sentence

17 Then the word of the LORD came to Elijah the Tishbite, saying: 18Go down to meet King Ahab of Israel, who rules[a] in Samaria; he is now in the vineyard of Naboth, where he has gone to take possession. 19You shall say to him, "Thus says the LORD: Have you killed, and also taken possession?" You shall say to him, "Thus says the LORD: In the place where dogs licked up the blood of Naboth, dogs will also lick up your blood."

20 Ahab said to Elijah, "Have you found me, O my enemy?" He answered, "I have found you. Because you have sold yourself to do what is evil in the sight of the LORD, 21I will bring disaster on you; I will consume you, and will cut off from Ahab every male, bond or free, in Israel; 22and I will make your house like the house of Jeroboam son of Nebat, and like the house of Baasha son of Ahijah, because you have provoked me to anger and have caused Israel to sin. 23Also concerning Jezebel the LORD said, 'The dogs shall eat Jezebel within the bounds of Jezreel.' 24Anyone belonging to Ahab who dies in the city the

a Heb *who is*

dogs shall eat; and anyone of his who dies in the open country the birds of the air shall eat."

25 (Indeed, there was no one like Ahab, who sold himself to do what was evil in the sight of the Lord, urged on by his wife Jezebel. ²⁶He acted most abominably in going after idols, as the Amorites had done, whom the Lord drove out before the Israelites.)

27 When Ahab heard those words, he tore his clothes and put sackcloth over his bare flesh; he fasted, lay in the sackcloth, and went about dejectedly. ²⁸Then the word of the Lord came to Elijah the Tishbite: ²⁹"Have you seen how Ahab has humbled himself before me? Because he has humbled himself before me, I will not bring the disaster in his days; but in his son's days I will bring the disaster on his house."

Joint Campaign with Judah against Aram

22 For three years Aram and Israel continued without war. ²But in the third year King Jehoshaphat of Judah came down to the king of Israel. ³The king of Israel said to his servants, "Do you know that Ramoth-gilead belongs to us, yet we are doing nothing to take it out of the hand of the king of Aram?" ⁴He said to Jehoshaphat, "Will you go with me to battle at Ramoth-gilead?" Jehoshaphat replied to the king of Israel, "I am as you are; my people are your people, my horses are your horses."

5 But Jehoshaphat also said to the king of Israel, "Inquire first for the word of the Lord." ⁶Then the king of Israel gathered the prophets together, about four hundred of them, and said to them, "Shall I go to battle against Ramoth-gilead, or shall I refrain?" They said, "Go up; for the Lord will give it into the hand of the king." ⁷But Jehoshaphat said, "Is there no other prophet of the Lord here of whom we may inquire?" ⁸The king of Israel said to Jehoshaphat, "There is still one other by whom we may inquire of the Lord, Micaiah son of Imlah; but I hate him, for he never prophesies anything favorable about me, but only disaster." Jehoshaphat said, "Let the king not say such a thing." ⁹Then the king of Israel summoned an officer and said, "Bring quickly Micaiah son of Imlah." ¹⁰Now the king of Israel and King Jehoshaphat of Judah were sitting on their thrones, arrayed in their robes, at the threshing floor at the entrance of the gate of Samaria; and all the prophets were prophesying before them. ¹¹Zedekiah son of Chenaanah made for himself horns of iron, and he said, "Thus says the Lord: With these you shall gore the Arameans until they are destroyed." ¹²All the prophets were prophesying the same and saying, "Go up to Ramoth-gilead and triumph; the Lord will give it into the hand of the king."

Micaiah Predicts Failure

13 The messenger who had gone to summon Micaiah said to him, "Look, the words of the prophets with one accord are favorable to the king; let your word be like the word of one of them, and speak favorably." ¹⁴But Micaiah said, "As the Lord lives, whatever the Lord says to me, that I will speak."

15 When he had come to the king, the king said to him, "Micaiah, shall we go to Ramoth-gilead to battle, or

King Ahab's Repentance

1 KINGS 21.25–29

According to this report, Ahab "acted most abominably in going after idols." But because he repented in deep humility, God spared him from full and immediate punishment for his deeds. Often we think that the guilt for the worst things we have done will be with us forever. The same God who forgave Ahab forgives us today. Make a list of the idols in your life or sketch a picture of each one. You might want to construct a model of an idol from materials you have at hand. Which of your senses led you to these idols—touch, smell, taste, sight or hearing? Ask God to give you the grace you need to be freed from the power of these idols so that you can worship the one true God. As a symbol of your repentance, destroy the idols or burn the list as you offer a prayer of rededication.

See Meeting God in Prayer

Micaiah's Prophecy

1 KINGS 22.17–18

Micaiah is a man of conviction and forthright speech and the courage to go against the easy words of the false prophets. We may sometimes wonder whether anyone is speaking for God in the midst of all of the easy speeches, comforting lies and destructive forces in our culture. Can you name anyone who speaks the uncomfortable truth to kings, presidents and other leaders about their false sense of security in power, weapons or each other? Imagine that you are the prophet Micaiah. Write a prayer for your nation and its leaders from Micaiah's perspective. Use it in your daily devotions this week. What do you need and what do our leaders need? What should be the church's role in speaking out against injustice? How is God calling you to be a voice such as Micaiah's?

See Meeting God in Service

shall we refrain?" He answered him, "Go up and triumph; the Lord will give it into the hand of the king." ¹⁶But the king said to him, "How many times must I make you swear to tell me nothing but the truth in the name of the Lord?" ¹⁷Then Micaiah*a* said, "I saw all Israel scattered on the mountains, like sheep that have no shepherd; and the Lord said, 'These have no master; let each one go home in peace.' " ¹⁸The king of Israel said to Jehoshaphat, "Did I not tell you that he would not prophesy anything favorable about me, but only disaster?"

19 Then Micaiah*a* said, "Therefore hear the word of the Lord: I saw the Lord sitting on his throne, with all the host of heaven standing beside him to the right and to the left of him. ²⁰And the Lord said, 'Who will entice Ahab, so that he may go up and fall at Ramoth-gilead?' Then one said one thing, and another said another, ²¹until a spirit came forward and stood before the Lord, saying, 'I will entice him.' ²²'How?' the Lord asked him. He replied, 'I will go out and be a lying spirit in the mouth of all his prophets.' Then the Lord*a* said, 'You are to entice him, and you shall succeed; go out and do it.' ²³So you see, the Lord has put a lying spirit in the mouth of all these your prophets; the Lord has decreed disaster for you."

24 Then Zedekiah son of Chenaanah came up to Micaiah, slapped him on the cheek, and said, "Which way did the spirit of the Lord pass from me to speak to you?" ²⁵Micaiah replied, "You will find out on that day when you go in to hide in an inner chamber." ²⁶The king of Israel then ordered, "Take Micaiah, and return him to Amon the governor of the city and to Joash the king's son, ²⁷and say, 'Thus says the king: Put this fellow in prison, and feed him on reduced rations of bread and water until I come in peace.' " ²⁸Micaiah said, "If you return in peace, the Lord has not spoken by me." And he said, "Hear, you peoples, all of you!"

Defeat and Death of Ahab

29 So the king of Israel and King Jehoshaphat of Judah went up to Ramoth-gilead. ³⁰The king of Israel said to Jehoshaphat, "I will disguise myself and go into battle, but you wear your robes." So the king of Israel disguised himself and went into battle. ³¹Now the king of Aram had commanded the thirty-two captains of his chariots, "Fight with no one small or great, but only with the king of Israel." ³²When the captains of the chariots saw Jehoshaphat, they said, "It is surely the king of Israel." So they turned to fight against him; and Jehoshaphat cried out. ³³When the captains of the chariots saw that it was not the king of Israel, they turned back from pursuing him. ³⁴But a certain man drew his bow and unknowingly struck the king of Israel between the scale armor and the breastplate; so he said to the driver of his chariot, "Turn around, and carry me out of the battle, for I am wounded." ³⁵The battle grew hot that day, and the king was propped up in his chariot facing the Arameans, until at evening he died; the blood from the wound had flowed into the bottom of the chariot. ³⁶Then about sunset a shout went through the

a Heb *he*

army, "Every man to his city, and every man to his country!"

37 So the king died, and was brought to Samaria; they buried the king in Samaria. **38**They washed the chariot by the pool of Samaria; the dogs licked up his blood, and the prostitutes washed themselves in it,*a* according to the word of the Lord that he had spoken. **39**Now the rest of the acts of Ahab, and all that he did, and the ivory house that he built, and all the cities that he built, are they not written in the Book of the Annals of the Kings of Israel? **40**So Ahab slept with his ancestors; and his son Ahaziah succeeded him.

Jehoshaphat Reigns over Judah

41 Jehoshaphat son of Asa began to reign over Judah in the fourth year of King Ahab of Israel. **42**Jehoshaphat was thirty-five years old when he began to reign, and he reigned twenty-five years in Jerusalem. His mother's name was Azubah daughter of Shilhi. **43**He walked in all the way of his father Asa; he did not turn aside from it, doing what was right in the sight of the Lord; yet the high places were not taken away, and the people still sacrificed and offered incense on the high places. **44**Jehoshaphat also made peace with the king of Israel.

45 Now the rest of the acts of Jehoshaphat, and his power that he showed, and how he waged war, are they not written in the Book of the Annals of the Kings of Judah? **46**The remnant of the male temple prostitutes who were still in the land in the days of his father Asa, he exterminated.

47 There was no king in Edom; a deputy was king. **48**Jehoshaphat made ships of the Tarshish type to go to Ophir for gold; but they did not go, for the ships were wrecked at Ezion-geber. **49**Then Ahaziah son of Ahab said to Jehoshaphat, "Let my servants go with your servants in the ships," but Jehoshaphat was not willing. **50**Jehoshaphat slept with his ancestors and was buried with his ancestors in the city of his father David; his son Jehoram succeeded him.

Ahaziah Reigns over Israel

51 Ahaziah son of Ahab began to reign over Israel in Samaria in the seventeenth year of King Jehoshaphat of Judah; he reigned two years over Israel. **52**He did what was evil in the sight of the Lord, and walked in the way of his father and mother, and in the way of Jeroboam son of Nebat, who caused Israel to sin. **53**He served Baal and worshiped him; he provoked the Lord, the God of Israel, to anger, just as his father had done.

Final Judgment

1 KINGS 22.37–40

Review this national tragedy by drawing a simple time line of the events in 1 Kings. Make a list of the major national mistakes in this tale of disobedience, and note the instances of righteousness and obedience. Note on the time line the leaders who ignore God and whose wrongdoing leads to lifestyles of blatant wickedness. Note God's prophets and others who call the people to return to God. Conclude by praying for the present day: "Gracious God, may we never forget that you are the source of life and hope. May we acknowledge you as the guide and inspiration for our living. May we, your people, always be light, hope and peace to all people. Amen."

---

a Heb lacks *in it*

2 KINGS

Our Weakness, God's Power

KEY VERSES:

Yet the LORD warned Israel and Judah by every prophet and every seer, saying, "Turn from your evil ways and keep my commandments and my statutes, in accordance with all the law that I commanded your ancestors and that I sent to you by my servants the prophets." They would not listen but were stubborn, as their ancestors had been, who did not believe in the LORD their God.—2 Kings 17.13–14

"Most of our conflicts and difficulties come from trying to deal with the spiritual and practical aspects of life separately instead of realizing them as parts of a whole. If our practical life is centered on our own interests, cluttered up by our possessions, distracted by ambitions, passions, wants and worries, beset by a sense of our own rights and importance, or anxieties for our own future, or longings for our own success, we need not expect that our spiritual life will be a contrast to all of this."

—EVELYN UNDERHILL,
The Spiritual Life

The book of 2 Kings continues the saga of the dearth of God-centered leadership among Israel's kings. It describes Israel's downward slide away from God and into idolatry and immorality—an era of kings who do "evil in the sight of the LORD" by imitating the sins of other nations. Once a great nation built by David, Israel is now divided and surrounded by powerful enemies and teeters on the verge of complete destruction.

Thirty prophets, most notably Elijah and Elisha, call the alarm using signs, miracles, warnings and proclamations—to no avail. Both kingdoms continue to turn from God and are ultimately exiled. Is there any word from the Lord in this desperate and lost situation? The book of 2 Kings demonstrates all too clearly the fate of those who stubbornly refuse to follow God's commandments. There is hope however. The God of the covenant always offers hope and restoration. A remnant is taken to Babylon to be called into new faithfulness and to receive God's blessings.

Consider how some of these destructive patterns may be at work in our own day. What are some of the unwise choices and destructive actions that undermine the health and spirit of the nation? How might we be "exiled" from the blessings we enjoy today if we do not face our own behavior squarely?

God still needs faithful and courageous people who are willing to proclaim the truth. As you read, search your own heart for how you can be part of God's remnant of faithful people today.

Elijah Denounces Ahaziah

1 After the death of Ahab, Moab rebelled against Israel. 2 Ahaziah had fallen through the lattice in his upper chamber in Samaria, and lay injured; so he sent messengers, telling them, "Go, inquire of Baal-zebub, the god of Ekron, whether I shall recover from this injury." ³But the angel of the LORD said to Elijah the Tishbite, "Get up, go to meet the messengers of the king of Samaria, and say to them, 'Is it because there is no God in Israel that you are going to inquire of Baal-zebub, the god of Ekron?' ⁴Now therefore thus says the LORD, 'You shall not leave the bed to which you have gone, but you shall surely die.' " So Elijah went.

5 The messengers returned to the king, who said to them, "Why have you returned?" ⁶They answered him, "There came a man to meet us, who said to us, 'Go back to the king who sent you, and say to him: Thus says the LORD: Is it because there is no God in Israel that you are sending to inquire of Baal-zebub, the god of Ekron? Therefore you shall not leave the bed to which you have gone, but shall surely die.' " ⁷He said to them, "What sort of man was he who came to meet you and told you these things?" ⁸They answered him, "A hairy man, with a leather belt around his waist." He said, "It is Elijah the Tishbite."

9 Then the king sent to him a captain of fifty with his fifty men. He went up to Elijah, who was sitting on the top of a hill, and said to him, "O man of God, the king says, 'Come down.' " ¹⁰But Elijah answered the captain of fifty, "If I am a man of God, let fire come down from heaven and consume you and your fifty." Then fire came down from heaven, and consumed him and his fifty.

11 Again the king sent to him another captain of fifty with his fifty. He went up*a* and said to him, "O man of God, this is the king's order: Come down quickly!" ¹²But Elijah answered them, "If I am a man of God, let fire come down from heaven and consume you and your fifty." Then the fire of God came down from heaven and consumed him and his fifty.

13 Again the king sent the captain of a third fifty with his fifty. So the third captain of fifty went up, and came and fell on his knees before Elijah, and entreated him, "O man of God, please let my life, and the life of these fifty servants of yours, be precious in your sight. ¹⁴Look, fire came down from heaven and consumed the two former captains of fifty men with their fifties; but now let my life be precious in your sight." ¹⁵Then the angel of the LORD said to Elijah, "Go down with him; do not be afraid of him." So he set out and went down with him to the king, ¹⁶and said to him, "Thus says the LORD: Because you have sent messengers to inquire of Baal-zebub, the god of Ekron,—is it because there is no God in Israel to inquire of his word?—therefore you shall not leave the bed to which you have gone, but you shall surely die."

Death of Ahaziah

17 So he died according to the word of the LORD that

a Gk Compare verses 9, 13: Heb *He answered*

Pictures of a Troubled World

2 KINGS 1.1–8

Leaf through some favorite magazines and periodicals. List the characteristics of the culture these publications represent. In what ways does our world look much like the world in the opening chapters of 2 Kings? What false gods does contemporary culture worship? What aspects of that culture allure you to wander from what is good and true? What is your hope for God's people in these times? What role might you play in proclaiming truth and hope? Make a collage, if you wish, of both the good and evil of our society, using pages from the publications; then spend time praying for God's Spirit to work among us.

See Meeting God in Prayer

Elijah's Ascension

2 KINGS 2.1–16

Like Enoch before him (Genesis 5.24) and Jesus after him (Luke 24.51), Elijah "ascended" into God's heavenly presence. Read the passage, then imagine that you can craft your own cinematic version of this dramatic event. Find your own role as a participant. Are you Elisha? One of the company of the prophets? As you imagine the poignant parting from your master, let your God-given imagination give life to the fiery horses and chariot. What happens within you as Elijah bestows the Spirit on you? You may choose to imagine the story more than once, taking different roles each time, in order to write this story deeply in your heart.

See Meeting God in Scripture

Elijah had spoken. His brother,[a] Jehoram succeeded him as king in the second year of King Jehoram son of Jehoshaphat of Judah, because Ahaziah had no son. [18]Now the rest of the acts of Ahaziah that he did, are they not written in the Book of the Annals of the Kings of Israel?

Elijah Ascends to Heaven

2 Now when the LORD was about to take Elijah up to heaven by a whirlwind, Elijah and Elisha were on their way from Gilgal. [2]Elijah said to Elisha, "Stay here; for the LORD has sent me as far as Bethel." But Elisha said, "As the LORD lives, and as you yourself live, I will not leave you." So they went down to Bethel. [3]The company of prophets[b] who were in Bethel came out to Elisha, and said to him, "Do you know that today the LORD will take your master away from you?" And he said, "Yes, I know; keep silent."

4 Elijah said to him, "Elisha, stay here; for the LORD has sent me to Jericho." But he said, "As the LORD lives, and as you yourself live, I will not leave you." So they came to Jericho. [5]The company of prophets[b] who were at Jericho drew near to Elisha, and said to him, "Do you know that today the LORD will take your master away from you?" And he answered, "Yes, I know; be silent."

6 Then Elijah said to him, "Stay here; for the LORD has sent me to the Jordan." But he said, "As the LORD lives, and as you yourself live, I will not leave you." So the two of them went on. [7]Fifty men of the company of prophets[b] also went, and stood at some distance from them, as they both were standing by the Jordan. [8]Then Elijah took his mantle and rolled it up, and struck the water; the water was parted to the one side and to the other, until the two of them crossed on dry ground.

9 When they had crossed, Elijah said to Elisha, "Tell me what I may do for you, before I am taken from you." Elisha said, "Please let me inherit a double share of your spirit." [10]He responded, "You have asked a hard thing; yet, if you see me as I am being taken from you, it will be granted you; if not, it will not." [11]As they continued walking and talking, a chariot of fire and horses of fire separated the two of them, and Elijah ascended in a whirlwind into heaven. [12]Elisha kept watching and crying out, "Father, father! The chariots of Israel and its horsemen!" But when he could no longer see him, he grasped his own clothes and tore them in two pieces.

Elisha Succeeds Elijah

13 He picked up the mantle of Elijah that had fallen from him, and went back and stood on the bank of the Jordan. [14]He took the mantle of Elijah that had fallen from him, and struck the water, saying, "Where is the LORD, the God of Elijah?" When he had struck the water, the water was parted to the one side and to the other, and Elisha went over.

15 When the company of prophets[b] who were at Jericho saw him at a distance, they declared, "The spirit of Elijah rests on Elisha." They came to meet him and bowed to the ground before him. [16]They said to him, "See now, we have fifty strong men among your servants;

a Gk Syr: Heb lacks *His brother*   *b* Heb *sons of the prophets* please let them go and seek your master; it may be that the spirit of the LORD has caught him up and thrown him down on some mountain or into some valley." He responded, "No, do not send them." [17]But when they urged him until he was ashamed, he said, "Send them." So they sent fifty men who searched for three days but did not find him. [18]When they came back to him (he had remained at Jericho), he said to them, "Did I not say to you, Do not go?"

Elisha Performs Miracles

19 Now the people of the city said to Elisha, "The location of this city is good, as my lord sees; but the water is bad, and the land is unfruitful." [20]He said, "Bring me a new bowl, and put salt in it." So they brought it to him. [21]Then he went to the spring of water and threw the salt into it, and said, "Thus says the LORD, I have made this water wholesome; from now on neither death nor miscarriage shall come from it." [22]So the water has been wholesome to this day, according to the word that Elisha spoke.

23 He went up from there to Bethel; and while he was going up on the way, some small boys came out of the city and jeered at him, saying, "Go away, baldhead! Go away, baldhead!" [24]When he turned around and saw them, he cursed them in the name of the LORD. Then two she-bears came out of the woods and mauled forty-two of the boys. [25]From there he went on to Mount Carmel, and then returned to Samaria.

Jehoram Reigns over Israel

3 In the eighteenth year of King Jehoshaphat of Judah, Jehoram son of Ahab became king over Israel in Samaria; he reigned twelve years. [2]He did what was evil in the sight of the LORD, though not like his father and mother, for he removed the pillar of Baal that his father had made. [3]Nevertheless he clung to the sin of Jeroboam son of Nebat, which he caused Israel to commit; he did not depart from it.

War with Moab

4 Now King Mesha of Moab was a sheep breeder, who used to deliver to the king of Israel one hundred thousand lambs, and the wool of one hundred thousand rams. [5]But when Ahab died, the king of Moab rebelled against the king of Israel. [6]So King Jehoram marched out of Samaria at that time and mustered all Israel. [7]As he went he sent word to King Jehoshaphat of Judah, "The king of Moab has rebelled against me; will you go with me to battle against Moab?" He answered, "I will; I am with you, my people are your people, my horses are your horses." [8]Then he asked, "By which way shall we march?" Jehoram answered, "By the way of the wilderness of Edom."

9 So the king of Israel, the king of Judah, and the king of Edom set out; and when they had made a roundabout march of seven days, there was no water for the army or for the animals that were with them. [10]Then the king of Israel said, "Alas! The LORD has summoned us, three kings, only to be handed over to Moab." [11]But Jehoshaphat said,

The Simplicity of Service

2 KINGS 3.11

Elisha learned the art of service, in part, through simple acts such as pouring water on the hands of his master and teacher. Sometimes it is the simplest acts that have the greatest meaning. Look at your hands for a moment. Reflect on the many tasks that you have accomplished today with them. What would your life be without them? For which menial, but important, tasks have you used your hands today? How have you touched or served people? How can you find ways to do so tomorrow? What is your prayer for the use of your hands?

See *Meeting God in Service*

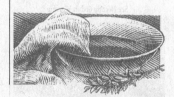

Music's Spiritual Power

2 KINGS 3.12—4.3

Elisha calls for a musician, knowing that music will help him be more open to the "power of the LORD." How does music make you more receptive to God, more aware of God's presence? Make a list of your own "top ten" spiritual songs, including hymns, classical pieces and popular tunes. Take time now to find a hymnal, other printed music or a recording. Then play or sing one of these musical selections as you open your heart and mind to the presence of God here and now. Keep the list near your prayer or study space to use on other days as a prelude or postlude to your devotions.

See Meeting God in Worship

"Is there no prophet of the LORD here, through whom we may inquire of the LORD?" Then one of the servants of the king of Israel answered, "Elisha son of Shaphat, who used to pour water on the hands of Elijah, is here." [12]Jehoshaphat said, "The word of the LORD is with him." So the king of Israel and Jehoshaphat and the king of Edom went down to him.

13 Elisha said to the king of Israel, "What have I to do with you? Go to your father's prophets or to your mother's." But the king of Israel said to him, "No; it is the LORD who has summoned us, three kings, only to be handed over to Moab." [14]Elisha said, "As the LORD of hosts lives, whom I serve, were it not that I have regard for King Jehoshaphat of Judah, I would give you neither a look nor a glance. [15]But get me a musician." And then, while the musician was playing, the power of the LORD came on him. [16]And he said, "Thus says the LORD, 'I will make this wadi full of pools.' [17]For thus says the LORD, 'You shall see neither wind nor rain, but the wadi shall be filled with water, so that you shall drink, you, your cattle, and your animals.' [18]This is only a trifle in the sight of the LORD, for he will also hand Moab over to you. [19]You shall conquer every fortified city and every choice city; every good tree you shall fell, all springs of water you shall stop up, and every good piece of land you shall ruin with stones." [20]The next day, about the time of the morning offering, suddenly water began to flow from the direction of Edom, until the country was filled with water.

21 When all the Moabites heard that the kings had come up to fight against them, all who were able to put on armor, from the youngest to the oldest, were called out and were drawn up at the frontier. [22]When they rose early in the morning, and the sun shone upon the water, the Moabites saw the water opposite them as red as blood. [23]They said, "This is blood; the kings must have fought together, and killed one another. Now then, Moab, to the spoil!" [24]But when they came to the camp of Israel, the Israelites rose up and attacked the Moabites, who fled before them; as they entered Moab they continued the attack.[a] [25]The cities they overturned, and on every good piece of land everyone threw a stone, until it was covered; every spring of water they stopped up, and every good tree they felled. Only at Kir-hareseth did the stone walls remain, until the slingers surrounded and attacked it. [26]When the king of Moab saw that the battle was going against him, he took with him seven hundred swordsmen to break through, opposite the king of Edom; but they could not. [27]Then he took his firstborn son who was to succeed him, and offered him as a burnt offering on the wall. And great wrath came upon Israel, so they withdrew from him and returned to their own land.

Elisha and the Widow's Oil

4 Now the wife of a member of the company of prophets[b] cried to Elisha, "Your servant my husband is

---

a Compare Gk Syr: Meaning of Heb uncertain   *b* Heb *the sons of the prophets*

dead; and you know that your servant feared the LORD, but a creditor has come to take my two children as slaves." ²Elisha said to her, "What shall I do for you? Tell me, what do you have in the house?" She answered, "Your servant has nothing in the house, except a jar of oil." ³He said, "Go outside, borrow vessels from all your neighbors, empty vessels and not just a few. ⁴Then go in, and shut the door behind you and your children, and start pouring into all these vessels; when each is full, set it aside." ⁵So she left him and shut the door behind her and her children; they kept bringing vessels to her, and she kept pouring. ⁶When the vessels were full, she said to her son, "Bring me another vessel." But he said to her, "There are no more." Then the oil stopped flowing. ⁷She came and told the man of God, and he said, "Go sell the oil and pay your debts, and you and your children can live on the rest."

Elisha Raises the Shunammite's Son

8 One day Elisha was passing through Shunem, where a wealthy woman lived, who urged him to have a meal. So whenever he passed that way, he would stop there for a meal. ⁹She said to her husband, "Look, I am sure that this man who regularly passes our way is a holy man of God. ¹⁰Let us make a small roof chamber with walls, and put there for him a bed, a table, a chair, and a lamp, so that he can stay there whenever he comes to us."

11 One day when he came there, he went up to the chamber and lay down there. ¹²He said to his servant Gehazi, "Call the Shunammite woman." When he had called her, she stood before him. ¹³He said to him, "Say to her, Since you have taken all this trouble for us, what may be done for you? Would you have a word spoken on your behalf to the king or to the commander of the army?" She answered, "I live among my own people." ¹⁴He said, "What then may be done for her?" Gehazi answered, "Well, she has no son, and her husband is old." ¹⁵He said, "Call her." When he had called her, she stood at the door. ¹⁶He said, "At this season, in due time, you shall embrace a son." She replied, "No, my lord, O man of God; do not deceive your servant."

17 The woman conceived and bore a son at that season, in due time, as Elisha had declared to her.

18 When the child was older, he went out one day to his father among the reapers. ¹⁹He complained to his father, "Oh, my head, my head!" The father said to his servant, "Carry him to his mother." ²⁰He carried him and brought him to his mother; the child sat on her lap until noon, and he died. ²¹She went up and laid him on the bed of the man of God, closed the door on him, and left. ²²Then she called to her husband, and said, "Send me one of the servants and one of the donkeys, so that I may quickly go to the man of God and come back again." ²³He said, "Why go to him today? It is neither new moon nor sabbath." She said, "It will be all right." ²⁴Then she saddled the donkey and said to her servant, "Urge the animal on; do not hold back for me unless I tell you." ²⁵So she set out, and came to the man of God at Mount Carmel.

Pouring Out Blessings

2 KINGS 4.1–7

Even though God had ordered creditors and rich people not to take advantage of debtors in extreme need (Leviticus 25.39), this woman and her children are in danger of being sold into slavery. The compassionate prophet responds with instructions for her, which she follows in faith, and God blesses her abundantly. Review your financial history: How has your faith been tested in financial matters? Has it ever seemed as if you were at the end of your resources? Have you ever experienced receiving or offering compassion in money matters? In what other ways has God poured out blessings on you in hard times? How does the way you spend your money reflect an active compassion in your life?

See Meeting God in Everyday Life

A Mother's Faith

2 KINGS 4.27–44

Elisha, whose name means "God's healing and salvation," brings God's healing love to the son of a widow, in much the same way that Jesus healed the daughter of Jairus (Mark 5.35–43). Read the entire passage through once, then see the story imaginatively through the eyes of the mother. Reach out your arms and hold your afflicted son on your lap. What emotions churn within you as you search for the prophet? Imagine approaching the prophet and kneeling at his feet. You wonder what is transpiring behind the closed doors of the prophet's room; you joyfully receive your restored son. Pray that God will help grow such faith in your own heart.

See Meeting God in Scripture

When the man of God saw her coming, he said to Gehazi his servant, "Look, there is the Shunammite woman; [26]run at once to meet her, and say to her, Are you all right? Is your husband all right? Is the child all right?" She answered, "It is all right." [27]When she came to the man of God at the mountain, she caught hold of his feet. Gehazi approached to push her away. But the man of God said, "Let her alone, for she is in bitter distress; the LORD has hidden it from me and has not told me." [28]Then she said, "Did I ask my lord for a son? Did I not say, Do not mislead me?" [29]He said to Gehazi, "Gird up your loins, and take my staff in your hand, and go. If you meet anyone, give no greeting, and if anyone greets you, do not answer; and lay my staff on the face of the child." [30]Then the mother of the child said, "As the LORD lives, and as you yourself live, I will not leave without you." So he rose up and followed her. [31]Gehazi went on ahead and laid the staff on the face of the child, but there was no sound or sign of life. He came back to meet him and told him, "The child has not awakened."

[32] When Elisha came into the house, he saw the child lying dead on his bed. [33]So he went in and closed the door on the two of them, and prayed to the LORD. [34]Then he got up on the bed[a] and lay upon the child, putting his mouth upon his mouth, his eyes upon his eyes, and his hands upon his hands; and while he lay bent over him, the flesh of the child became warm. [35]He got down, walked once to and fro in the room, then got up again and bent over him; the child sneezed seven times, and the child opened his eyes. [36]Elisha[b] summoned Gehazi and said, "Call the Shunammite woman." So he called her. When she came to him, he said, "Take your son." [37]She came and fell at his feet, bowing to the ground; then she took her son and left.

Elisha Purifies the Pot of Stew

[38] When Elisha returned to Gilgal, there was a famine in the land. As the company of prophets was[c] sitting before him, he said to his servant, "Put the large pot on, and make some stew for the company of prophets."[d] [39]One of them went out into the field to gather herbs; he found a wild vine and gathered from it a lapful of wild gourds, and came and cut them up into the pot of stew, not knowing what they were. [40]They served some for the men to eat. But while they were eating the stew, they cried out, "O man of God, there is death in the pot!" They could not eat it. [41]He said, "Then bring some flour." He threw it into the pot, and said, "Serve the people and let them eat." And there was nothing harmful in the pot.

Elisha Feeds One Hundred Men

[42] A man came from Baal-shalishah, bringing food from the first fruits to the man of God: twenty loaves of barley and fresh ears of grain in his sack. Elisha said, "Give it to the people and let them eat." [43]But his servant said, "How can I set this before a hundred people?" So he repeated, "Give it to the people and let them eat, for thus says the LORD, 'They shall eat and have some left.'" [44]He

---

*a Heb lacks on the bed   .b Heb he   c Heb sons of the prophets were
d Heb sons of the prophets*

set it before them, they ate, and had some left, according to the word of the LORD.

The Healing of Naaman

5 Naaman, commander of the army of the king of Aram, was a great man and in high favor with his master, because by him the LORD had given victory to Aram. The man, though a mighty warrior, suffered from leprosy.[a] [2]Now the Arameans on one of their raids had taken a young girl captive from the land of Israel, and she served Naaman's wife. [3]She said to her mistress, "If only my lord were with the prophet who is in Samaria! He would cure him of his leprosy."[a] [4]So Naaman[b] went in and told his lord just what the girl from the land of Israel had said. [5]And the king of Aram said, "Go then, and I will send along a letter to the king of Israel."

He went, taking with him ten talents of silver, six thousand shekels of gold, and ten sets of garments. [6]He brought the letter to the king of Israel, which read, "When this letter reaches you, know that I have sent to you my servant Naaman, that you may cure him of his leprosy."[a] [7]When the king of Israel read the letter, he tore his clothes and said, "Am I God, to give death or life, that this man sends word to me to cure a man of his leprosy?[a] Just look and see how he is trying to pick a quarrel with me."

8 But when Elisha the man of God heard that the king of Israel had torn his clothes, he sent a message to the king, "Why have you torn your clothes? Let him come to me, that he may learn that there is a prophet in Israel." [9]So Naaman came with his horses and chariots, and halted at the entrance of Elisha's house. [10]Elisha sent a messenger to him, saying, "Go, wash in the Jordan seven times, and your flesh shall be restored and you shall be clean." [11]But Naaman became angry and went away, saying, "I thought that for me he would surely come out, and stand and call on the name of the LORD his God, and would wave his hand over the spot, and cure the leprosy![a] [12]Are not Abana[c] and Pharpar, the rivers of Damascus, better than all the waters of Israel? Could I not wash in them, and be clean?" He turned and went away in a rage. [13]But his servants approached and said to him, "Father, if the prophet had commanded you to do something difficult, would you not have done it? How much more, when all he said to you was, 'Wash, and be clean'?" [14]So he went down and immersed himself seven times in the Jordan, according to the word of the man of God; his flesh was restored like the flesh of a young boy, and he was clean.

15 Then he returned to the man of God, he and all his company; he came and stood before him and said, "Now I know that there is no God in all the earth except in Israel; please accept a present from your servant." [16]But he said, "As the LORD lives, whom I serve, I will accept nothing!" He urged him to accept, but he refused. [17]Then Naaman said, "If not, please let two mule-loads of earth be given to your servant; for your servant will no longer offer burnt offering or sacrifice to any god except the LORD. [18]But may the LORD pardon your servant on one count:

Stubbornness, Foolishness and Faith

2 KINGS 5.1–14

As desperate as Naaman is to have his leprosy cured, he is furious that Elisha does not show up in person. He is more concerned about the perceived insult than about humbly following the instructions of Elisha's messenger. Pride jeopardizes Naaman's chance to be healed.

Pride has long been acknowledged as the source of many other sins. This is a good time to take stock of where sinful pride occurs in your own life. Ask someone whom you love and trust (and who loves and trusts you) for help. List two or three areas in your life where pride undermines your closeness to God. What are the sources of pride in these areas? What is the difference between pride and wholesome confidence? Ask God to show you ways to be free from sinful pride.

See *Meeting God in Community*

---

a A term for several skin diseases; precise meaning uncertain   b Heb *he*
c Another reading is *Amana*

A Servant's Deceit and Greed

2 KINGS 5.19–27

"Avarice is selfishness, expressed in hoarding what we don't need, refusing to share. Covetousness is selfishness expressed in desiring what other people have that we don't, or specifically desiring something that belongs to someone else. Greed is selfishness expressed in always wanting more. Someone defined enough as 'a little more than what you have.'"

—MAXIE DUNNAM,
KIMBERLY DUNNAM REISMAN,
Workbook on the Seven Deadly Sins

when my master goes into the house of Rimmon to worship there, leaning on my arm, and I bow down in the house of Rimmon, when I do bow down in the house of Rimmon, may the LORD pardon your servant on this one count." [19]He said to him, "Go in peace."

Gehazi's Greed

But when Naaman had gone from him a short distance, [20]Gehazi, the servant of Elisha the man of God, thought, "My master has let that Aramean Naaman off too lightly by not accepting from him what he offered. As the LORD lives, I will run after him and get something out of him." [21]So Gehazi went after Naaman. When Naaman saw someone running after him, he jumped down from the chariot to meet him and said, "Is everything all right?" [22]He replied, "Yes, but my master has sent me to say, 'Two members of a company of prophets[a] have just come to me from the hill country of Ephraim; please give them a talent of silver and two changes of clothing.' " [23]Naaman said, "Please accept two talents." He urged him, and tied up two talents of silver in two bags, with two changes of clothing, and gave them to two of his servants, who carried them in front of Gehazi.[b] [24]When he came to the citadel, he took the bags[c] from them, and stored them inside; he dismissed the men, and they left.

25 He went in and stood before his master; and Elisha said to him, "Where have you been, Gehazi?" He answered, "Your servant has not gone anywhere at all." [26]But he said to him, "Did I not go with you in spirit when someone left his chariot to meet you? Is this a time to accept money and to accept clothing, olive orchards and vineyards, sheep and oxen, and male and female slaves? [27]Therefore the leprosy[d] of Naaman shall cling to you, and to your descendants forever." So he left his presence leprous,[d] as white as snow.

The Miracle of the Ax Head

6 Now the company of prophets[a] said to Elisha, "As you see, the place where we live under your charge is too small for us. [2]Let us go to the Jordan, and let us collect logs there, one for each of us, and build a place there for us to live." He answered, "Do so." [3]Then one of them said, "Please come with your servants." And he answered, "I will." [4]So he went with them. When they came to the Jordan, they cut down trees. [5]But as one was felling a log, his ax head fell into the water; he cried out, "Alas, master! It was borrowed." [6]Then the man of God said, "Where did it fall?" When he showed him the place, he cut off a stick, and threw it in there, and made the iron float. [7]He said, "Pick it up." So he reached out his hand and took it.

The Aramean Attack Is Thwarted

8 Once when the king of Aram was at war with Israel, he took counsel with his officers. He said, "At such and such a place shall be my camp." [9]But the man of God sent

a Heb *sons of the prophets*   *b* Heb *him*   *c* Heb lacks *the bags*   *d* A term for several skin diseases; precise meaning uncertain

word to the king of Israel, "Take care not to pass this place, because the Arameans are going down there." ¹⁰The king of Israel sent word to the place of which the man of God spoke. More than once or twice he warned such a place[a] so that it was on the alert.

11 The mind of the king of Aram was greatly perturbed because of this; he called his officers and said to them, "Now tell me who among us sides with the king of Israel?" ¹²Then one of his officers said, "No one, my lord king. It is Elisha, the prophet in Israel, who tells the king of Israel the words that you speak in your bedchamber." ¹³He said, "Go and find where he is; I will send and seize him." He was told, "He is in Dothan." ¹⁴So he sent horses and chariots there and a great army; they came by night, and surrounded the city.

15 When an attendant of the man of God rose early in the morning and went out, an army with horses and chariots was all around the city. His servant said, "Alas, master! What shall we do?" ¹⁶He replied, "Do not be afraid, for there are more with us than there are with them." ¹⁷Then Elisha prayed: "O LORD, please open his eyes that he may see." So the LORD opened the eyes of the servant, and he saw; the mountain was full of horses and chariots of fire all around Elisha. ¹⁸When the Arameans[b] came down against him, Elisha prayed to the LORD, and said, "Strike this people, please, with blindness." So he struck them with blindness as Elisha had asked. ¹⁹Elisha said to them, "This is not the way, and this is not the city; follow me, and I will bring you to the man whom you seek." And he led them to Samaria.

20 As soon as they entered Samaria, Elisha said, "O LORD, open the eyes of these men so that they may see." The LORD opened their eyes, and they saw that they were inside Samaria. ²¹When the king of Israel saw them he said to Elisha, "Father, shall I kill them? Shall I kill them?" ²²He answered, "No! Did you capture with your sword and your bow those whom you want to kill? Set food and water before them so that they may eat and drink; and let them go to their master." ²³So he prepared for them a great feast; after they ate and drank, he sent them on their way, and they went to their master. And the Arameans no longer came raiding into the land of Israel.

Ben-hadad's Siege of Samaria

24 Some time later King Ben-hadad of Aram mustered his entire army; he marched against Samaria and laid siege to it. ²⁵As the siege continued, famine in Samaria became so great that a donkey's head was sold for eighty shekels of silver, and one-fourth of a kab of dove's dung for five shekels of silver. ²⁶Now as the king of Israel was walking on the city wall, a woman cried out to him, "Help, my lord king!" ²⁷He said, "No! Let the LORD help you. How can I help you? From the threshing floor or from the wine press?" ²⁸But then the king asked her, "What is your complaint?" She answered, "This woman said to me, 'Give up your son; we will eat him today, and we will eat my son tomorrow.' ²⁹So we cooked my son and ate him. The next

Invisible Support

2 KINGS 6.11–17

Elisha is surrounded by enemy warriors, but he knows that "there are more with us than there are with them." Imagine that you are Elisha's attendant, spiritually blind to the presence of God's invisible aid. Imagine that your eyes are opened to see that "the mountain [is] full of horses and chariots of fire." Transpose this vision into your own life. Bring to mind a situation where you may feel "surrounded" by opposing or unhelpful forces. Ask God to oppose the negative powers at work in your situation. Through images, feelings or words, confirm to your mind and heart the reality of God's presence. Repeat: "There are more with me than I realize."

See Meeting God in Scripture

Don't Just Sit There!

2 KINGS 7.3–7

These four lepers are sure they are all alone and headed for certain death. No one wants these outcasts. They are faced with famine in the city and the Aramean army outside the city. They decide they might as well get up and do something—and they find that God has already acted, and their lives are spared.

Perhaps there was a time in your life when you felt you were all alone and destined to die—emotionally, spiritually or physically. In what form did rescue come? How do you see the hand of God in your predicament? Is there a situation in your life where are you just "sitting around," waiting for the worst to happen? What do you need to get up and do while trusting in God's help?

day I said to her, 'Give up your son and we will eat him.' But she has hidden her son." ³⁰When the king heard the words of the woman he tore his clothes—now since he was walking on the city wall, the people could see that he had sackcloth on his body underneath— ³¹and he said, "So may God do to me, and more, if the head of Elisha son of Shaphat stays on his shoulders today." ³²So he dispatched a man from his presence.

Now Elisha was sitting in his house, and the elders were sitting with him. Before the messenger arrived, Elisha said to the elders, "Are you aware that this murderer has sent someone to take off my head? When the messenger comes, see that you shut the door and hold it closed against him. Is not the sound of his master's feet behind him?" ³³While he was still speaking with them, the king*ᵃ* came down to him and said, "This trouble is from the LORD! Why should I hope in the LORD any longer?" 7 ¹But Elisha said, "Hear the word of the LORD: thus says the LORD, Tomorrow about this time a measure of choice meal shall be sold for a shekel, and two measures of barley for a shekel, at the gate of Samaria." ²Then the captain on whose hand the king leaned said to the man of God, "Even if the LORD were to make windows in the sky, could such a thing happen?" But he said, "You shall see it with your own eyes, but you shall not eat from it."

The Arameans Flee

3 Now there were four leprous*ᵇ* men outside the city gate, who said to one another, "Why should we sit here until we die? ⁴If we say, 'Let us enter the city,' the famine is in the city, and we shall die there; but if we sit here, we shall also die. Therefore, let us desert to the Aramean camp; if they spare our lives, we shall live; and if they kill us, we shall but die." ⁵So they arose at twilight to go to the Aramean camp; but when they came to the edge of the Aramean camp, there was no one there at all. ⁶For the Lord had caused the Aramean army to hear the sound of chariots, and of horses, the sound of a great army, so that they said to one another, "The king of Israel has hired the kings of the Hittites and the kings of Egypt to fight against us." ⁷So they fled away in the twilight and abandoned their tents, their horses, and their donkeys leaving the camp just as it was, and fled for their lives. ⁸When these leprous*ᵇ* men had come to the edge of the camp, they went into a tent, ate and drank, carried off silver, gold, and clothing, and went and hid them. Then they came back, entered another tent, carried off things from it, and went and hid them.

9 Then they said to one another, "What we are doing is wrong. This is a day of good news; if we are silent and wait until the morning light, we will be found guilty; therefore let us go and tell the king's household." ¹⁰So they came and called to the gatekeepers of the city, and told them, "We went to the Aramean camp, but there was no one to be seen or heard there, nothing but the horses tied, the donkeys tied, and the tents as they

a See 7.2: Heb *messenger*   *b* A term for several skin diseases; precise meaning uncertain

were." [11]Then the gatekeepers called out and proclaimed it to the king's household. [12]The king got up in the night, and said to his servants, "I will tell you what the Arameans have prepared against us. They know that we are starving; so they have left the camp to hide themselves in the open country, thinking, 'When they come out of the city, we shall take them alive and get into the city.'" [13]One of his servants said, "Let some men take five of the remaining horses, since those left here will suffer the fate of the whole multitude of Israel that have perished already;[a] let us send and find out." [14]So they took two mounted men, and the king sent them after the Aramean army, saying, "Go and find out." [15]So they went after them as far as the Jordan; the whole way was littered with garments and equipment that the Arameans had thrown away in their haste. So the messengers returned, and told the king.

16 Then the people went out, and plundered the camp of the Arameans. So a measure of choice meal was sold for a shekel, and two measures of barley for a shekel, according to the word of the LORD. [17]Now the king had appointed the captain on whose hand he leaned to have charge of the gate; the people trampled him to death in the gate, just as the man of God had said when the king came down to him. [18]For when the man of God had said to the king, "Two measures of barley shall be sold for a shekel, and a measure of choice meal for a shekel, about this time tomorrow in the gate of Samaria," [19]the captain had answered the man of God, "Even if the LORD were to make windows in the sky, could such a thing happen?" And he had answered, "You shall see it with your own eyes, but you shall not eat from it." [20]It did indeed happen to him; the people trampled him to death in the gate.

The Shunammite Woman's Land Restored

8 Now Elisha had said to the woman whose son he had restored to life, "Get up and go with your household, and settle wherever you can; for the LORD has called for a famine, and it will come on the land for seven years." [2]So the woman got up and did according to the word of the man of God; she went with her household and settled in the land of the Philistines seven years. [3]At the end of the seven years, when the woman returned from the land of the Philistines, she set out to appeal to the king for her house and her land. [4]Now the king was talking with Gehazi the servant of the man of God, saying, "Tell me all the great things that Elisha has done." [5]While he was telling the king how Elisha had restored a dead person to life, the woman whose son he had restored to life appealed to the king for her house and her land. Gehazi said, "My lord king, here is the woman, and here is her son whom Elisha restored to life." [6]When the king questioned the woman, she told him. So the king appointed an official for her, saying, "Restore all that was hers, together with all the revenue of the fields from the day that she left the land until now."

A Simple Act of Kindness

2 KINGS 8.1–6

This story reflects Elisha's kindness and concern for the well-being of the widow. His ministry to her is both public and private. Read through the story, imagining the feelings and thoughts of the characters. How might it feel to be so dependent on someone else? What does Elisha's ministry teach you about God? How does the widow's need and your need reflect the needs of every human being? How do Elisha's actions reflect God's concern for others? Does this time of reflection suggest any specific actions you might take to express God's concern to the people around you?

See Meeting God in Service

---

a Compare Gk Syr Vg: Meaning of Heb uncertain

Weeping for Israel

The prophet weeps in sorrow over the destruction Hazael will visit upon Israel. Tears can be a burden or a release, an act of joy or an act of sorrow. When someone cries in our presence, they are sharing an expression of deepest emotion. Tears lovingly received can be a blessing from God. Remember the last time you shared tears with someone. What brings tears of joy and what brings tears of sorrow? How have tears expressed your deepest emotions? How do you respond to the tears of others? When have you been in Elisha's position—knowing the necessity of harsh actions, yet sorrowful about the pain they may cause?

Death of Ben-hadad

7 Elisha went to Damascus while King Ben-hadad of Aram was ill. When it was told him, "The man of God has come here," [8]the king said to Hazael, "Take a present with you and go to meet the man of God. Inquire of the LORD through him, whether I shall recover from this illness." [9]So Hazael went to meet him, taking a present with him, all kinds of goods of Damascus, forty camel loads. When he entered and stood before him, he said, "Your son King Ben-hadad of Aram has sent me to you, saying, 'Shall I recover from this illness?' " [10]Elisha said to him, "Go, say to him, 'You shall certainly recover'; but the LORD has shown me that he shall certainly die." [11]He fixed his gaze and stared at him, until he was ashamed. Then the man of God wept. [12]Hazael asked, "Why does my lord weep?" He answered, "Because I know the evil that you will do to the people of Israel; you will set their fortresses on fire, you will kill their young men with the sword, dash in pieces their little ones, and rip up their pregnant women." [13]Hazael said, "What is your servant, who is a mere dog, that he should do this great thing?" Elisha answered, "The LORD has shown me that you are to be king over Aram." [14]Then he left Elisha, and went to his master Ben-hadad,[a] who said to him, "What did Elisha say to you?" And he answered, "He told me that you would certainly recover." [15]But the next day he took the bed-cover and dipped it in water and spread it over the king's face, until he died. And Hazael succeeded him.

Jehoram Reigns over Judah

16 In the fifth year of King Joram son of Ahab of Israel,[b] Jehoram son of King Jehoshaphat of Judah began to reign. [17]He was thirty-two years old when he became king, and he reigned eight years in Jerusalem. [18]He walked in the way of the kings of Israel, as the house of Ahab had done, for the daughter of Ahab was his wife. He did what was evil in the sight of the LORD. [19]Yet the LORD would not destroy Judah, for the sake of his servant David, since he had promised to give a lamp to him and to his descendants forever.

20 In his days Edom revolted against the rule of Judah, and set up a king of their own. [21]Then Joram crossed over to Zair with all his chariots. He set out by night and attacked the Edomites and their chariot commanders who had surrounded him;[c] but his army fled home. [22]So Edom has been in revolt against the rule of Judah to this day. Libnah also revolted at the same time. [23]Now the rest of the acts of Joram, and all that he did, are they not written in the Book of the Annals of the Kings of Judah? [24]So Joram slept with his ancestors, and was buried with them in the city of David; his son Ahaziah succeeded him.

Ahaziah Reigns over Judah

25 In the twelfth year of King Joram son of Ahab of Israel, Ahaziah son of King Jehoram of Judah began to reign. [26]Ahaziah was twenty-two years old when he began to reign; he reigned one year in Jerusalem. His mother's

a Heb lacks *Ben-hadad*   *b* Gk Syr: Heb adds *Jehoshaphat being king of Judah.*   *c* Meaning of Heb uncertain

name was Athaliah, a granddaughter of King Omri of Israel. ²⁷He also walked in the way of the house of Ahab, doing what was evil in the sight of the LORD, as the house of Ahab had done, for he was son-in-law to the house of Ahab.

28 He went with Joram son of Ahab to wage war against King Hazael of Aram at Ramoth-gilead, where the Arameans wounded Joram. ²⁹King Joram returned to be healed in Jezreel of the wounds that the Arameans had inflicted on him at Ramah, when he fought against King Hazael of Aram. King Ahaziah son of Jehoram of Judah went down to see Joram son of Ahab in Jezreel, because he was wounded.

Anointing of Jehu

9 Then the prophet Elisha called a member of the company of prophets*a* and said to him, "Gird up your loins; take this flask of oil in your hand, and go to Ramoth-gilead. ²When you arrive, look there for Jehu son of Jehoshaphat, son of Nimshi; go in and get him to leave his companions, and take him into an inner chamber. ³Then take the flask of oil, pour it on his head, and say, 'Thus says the LORD: I anoint you king over Israel.' Then open the door and flee; do not linger."

4 So the young man, the young prophet, went to Ramoth-gilead. ⁵He arrived while the commanders of the army were in council, and he announced, "I have a message for you, commander." "For which one of us?" asked Jehu. "For you, commander." ⁶So Jehu*b* got up and went inside; the young man poured the oil on his head, saying to him, "Thus says the LORD the God of Israel: I anoint you king over the people of the LORD, over Israel. ⁷You shall strike down the house of your master Ahab, so that I may avenge on Jezebel the blood of my servants the prophets, and the blood of all the servants of the LORD. ⁸For the whole house of Ahab shall perish; I will cut off from Ahab every male, bond or free, in Israel. ⁹I will make the house of Ahab like the house of Jeroboam son of Nebat, and like the house of Baasha son of Ahijah. ¹⁰The dogs shall eat Jezebel in the territory of Jezreel, and no one shall bury her." Then he opened the door and fled.

11 When Jehu came back to his master's officers, they said to him, "Is everything all right? Why did that madman come to you?" He answered them, "You know the sort and how they babble." ¹²They said, "Liar! Come on, tell us!" So he said, "This is just what he said to me: 'Thus says the LORD, I anoint you king over Israel.' " ¹³Then hurriedly they all took their cloaks and spread them for him on the bare*c* steps; and they blew the trumpet, and proclaimed, "Jehu is king."

Joram of Israel Killed

14 Thus Jehu son of Jehoshaphat son of Nimshi conspired against Joram. Joram with all Israel had been on guard at Ramoth-gilead against King Hazael of Aram; ¹⁵but King Joram had returned to be healed in Jezreel of the wounds that the Arameans had inflicted on him, when he fought against King Hazael of Aram. So Jehu said, "If this

---

Anointed for Service

2 KINGS 9.1–3

Anointing symbolizes divine empowerment to render specific service. God raised up and anointed servants. Sometimes they were obscure and unknown before their call, sometimes they were not even from the "chosen people."

Picture in your mind the great leaders of the past century—people through whom God has judged, restored or healed others. Who will be raised up in our own day of crisis? Spend time praying for them, whomever they might be, and thanking God for their anointed service. What other situations are in need of God-inspired leadership? Spend time praying for such leaders in situations (global or local) that are close to your heart.

See Meeting God in Prayer

---

a Heb *sons of the prophets*   *b* Heb *he*   *c* Meaning of Heb uncertain

Jehu's Zeal

2 KINGS 9.20

Jehu "drives like a maniac" as he is used as an instrument of justice for God. He is a passionate reformer, set apart to clean up the spiritual mess with the cry, "See my zeal for the LORD" (10.16).

What are the passions of your heart? What people or issues do you care about passionately? Make a list of the roles you assume every day—husband, wife, friend, parent and so forth. What passions do you express in each role? How can your passions be consecrated to the Lord? Is there a special ministry or work that may be calling you to new or deeper consecration? Ask God to redeem and sanctify your passions.

See Meeting God in Everyday Life

is your wish, then let no one slip out of the city to go and tell the news in Jezreel." ¹⁶Then Jehu mounted his chariot and went to Jezreel, where Joram was lying ill. King Ahaziah of Judah had come down to visit Joram.

17 In Jezreel, the sentinel standing on the tower spied the company of Jehu arriving, and said, "I see a company." Joram said, "Take a horseman; send him to meet them, and let him say, 'Is it peace?' " ¹⁸So the horseman went to meet him; he said, "Thus says the king, 'Is it peace?' " Jehu responded, "What have you to do with peace? Fall in behind me." The sentinel reported, saying, "The messenger reached them, but he is not coming back." ¹⁹Then he sent out a second horseman, who came to them and said, "Thus says the king, 'Is it peace?' " Jehu answered, "What have you to do with peace? Fall in behind me." ²⁰Again the sentinel reported, "He reached them, but he is not coming back. It looks like the driving of Jehu son of Nimshi; for he drives like a maniac."

21 Joram said, "Get ready." And they got his chariot ready. Then King Joram of Israel and King Ahaziah of Judah set out, each in his chariot, and went to meet Jehu; they met him at the property of Naboth the Jezreelite. ²²When Joram saw Jehu, he said, "Is it peace, Jehu?" He answered, "What peace can there be, so long as the many whoredoms and sorceries of your mother Jezebel continue?" ²³Then Joram reined about and fled, saying to Ahaziah, "Treason, Ahaziah!" ²⁴Jehu drew his bow with all his strength, and shot Joram between the shoulders, so that the arrow pierced his heart; and he sank in his chariot. ²⁵Jehu said to his aide Bidkar, "Lift him out, and throw him on the plot of ground belonging to Naboth the Jezreelite; for remember, when you and I rode side by side behind his father Ahab how the LORD uttered this oracle against him: ²⁶'For the blood of Naboth and for the blood of his children that I saw yesterday, says the LORD, I swear I will repay you on this very plot of ground.' Now therefore lift him out and throw him on the plot of ground, in accordance with the word of the LORD."

Ahaziah of Judah Killed

27 When King Ahaziah of Judah saw this, he fled in the direction of Beth-haggan. Jehu pursued him, saying, "Shoot him also!" And they shot him*a* in the chariot at the ascent to Gur, which is by Ibleam. Then he fled to Megiddo, and died there. ²⁸His officers carried him in a chariot to Jerusalem, and buried him in his tomb with his ancestors in the city of David.

29 In the eleventh year of Joram son of Ahab, Ahaziah began to reign over Judah.

Jezebel's Violent Death

30 When Jehu came to Jezreel, Jezebel heard of it; she painted her eyes, and adorned her head, and looked out of the window. ³¹As Jehu entered the gate, she said, "Is it peace, Zimri, murderer of your master?" ³²He looked up to the window and said, "Who is on my side? Who?" Two or three eunuchs looked out at him. ³³He said, "Throw her down." So they threw her down; some of her blood spat-

a Syr Vg Compare Gk: Heb lacks *and they shot him*

tered on the wall and on the horses, which trampled on her. ³⁴Then he went in and ate and drank; he said, "See to that cursed woman and bury her; for she is a king's daughter." ³⁵But when they went to bury her, they found no more of her than the skull and the feet and the palms of her hands. ³⁶When they came back and told him, he said, "This is the word of the LORD, which he spoke by his servant Elijah the Tishbite, 'In the territory of Jezreel the dogs shall eat the flesh of Jezebel; ³⁷the corpse of Jezebel shall be like dung on the field in the territory of Jezreel, so that no one can say, This is Jezebel.' "

Massacre of Ahab's Descendants

10 Now Ahab had seventy sons in Samaria. So Jehu wrote letters and sent them to Samaria, to the rulers of Jezreel,ᵃ to the elders, and to the guardians of the sons ofᵇ Ahab, saying, ²"Since your master's sons are with you and you have at your disposal chariots and horses, a fortified city, and weapons, ³select the son of your master who is the best qualified, set him on his father's throne, and fight for your master's house." ⁴But they were utterly terrified and said, "Look, two kings could not withstand him; how then can we stand?" ⁵So the steward of the palace, and the governor of the city, along with the elders and the guardians, sent word to Jehu: "We are your servants; we will do anything you say. We will not make anyone king; do whatever you think right." ⁶Then he wrote them a second letter, saying, "If you are on my side, and if you are ready to obey me, take the heads of your master's sons and come to me at Jezreel tomorrow at this time." Now the king's sons, seventy persons, were with the leaders of the city, who were charged with their upbringing. ⁷When the letter reached them, they took the king's sons and killed them, seventy persons; they put their heads in baskets and sent them to him at Jezreel. ⁸When the messenger came and told him, "They have brought the heads of the king's sons," he said, "Lay them in two heaps at the entrance of the gate until the morning." ⁹Then in the morning when he went out, he stood and said to all the people, "You are innocent. It was I who conspired against my master and killed him; but who struck down all these? ¹⁰Know then that there shall fall to the earth nothing of the word of the LORD, which the LORD spoke concerning the house of Ahab; for the LORD has done what he said through his servant Elijah." ¹¹So Jehu killed all who were left of the house of Ahab in Jezreel, all his leaders, close friends, and priests, until he left him no survivor.

12 Then he set out and went to Samaria. On the way, when he was at Beth-eked of the Shepherds, ¹³Jehu met relatives of King Ahaziah of Judah and said, "Who are you?" They answered, "We are kin of Ahaziah; we have come down to visit the royal princes and the sons of the queen mother." ¹⁴He said, "Take them alive." They took them alive, and slaughtered them at the pit of Beth-eked, forty-two in all; he spared none of them.

15 When he left there, he met Jehonadab son of Rechab coming to meet him; he greeted him, and said to

Human Brutality

2 KINGS 9.27—10.9

At times the violence and brutality detailed in Biblical accounts can seem overwhelming and puzzling; we wonder how a loving God can allow such suffering. Yet violence and death are the consequences of human evil. How do you think God feels about such violence? How are people today like the people in this passage? What is your prayer for those who suffer violence? Cultivate the habit of praying—as you listen to the news broadcast or read the newspaper—for all who suffer brutality at the hands of others.

See Meeting God in Service

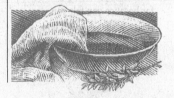

---

a Or *of the city*; Vg Compare Gk   *b* Gk: Heb lacks *of the sons of*

Going Too Far

2 KINGS 10.9–17

Jehu leaves no survivors, destroying Ahab's family and supporters in a bloodbath. Elijah's prophecy is fulfilled, but Jehu goes too far. He would later be punished for his excessive brutality. Sometimes personal ambition, zeal, power and cruelty become mixed with holy causes. A genuine calling to do good can become a destructive weapon if not wielded in genuine love. Where do you think people of faith go too far in a misguided zeal, even though the cause is just? When have you, or those you know, been injured by overzealous people? When have you ever gone too far because you felt you were right? What harm did your zeal cause? Is there a way, now, to make amends?

him, "Is your heart as true to mine as mine is to yours?"[a] Jehonadab answered, "It is." Jehu said,[b] "If it is, give me your hand." So he gave him his hand. Jehu took him up with him into the chariot. **16**He said, "Come with me, and see my zeal for the Lord." So he[c] had him ride in his chariot. **17**When he came to Samaria, he killed all who were left to Ahab in Samaria, until he had wiped them out, according to the word of the Lord that he spoke to Elijah.

Slaughter of Worshipers of Baal

18 Then Jehu assembled all the people and said to them, "Ahab offered Baal small service; but Jehu will offer much more. **19**Now therefore summon to me all the prophets of Baal, all his worshipers, and all his priests; let none be missing, for I have a great sacrifice to offer to Baal; whoever is missing shall not live." But Jehu was acting with cunning in order to destroy the worshipers of Baal. **20**Jehu decreed, "Sanctify a solemn assembly for Baal." So they proclaimed it. **21**Jehu sent word throughout all Israel; all the worshipers of Baal came, so that there was no one left who did not come. They entered the temple of Baal, until the temple of Baal was filled from wall to wall. **22**He said to the keeper of the wardrobe, "Bring out the vestments for all the worshipers of Baal." So he brought out the vestments for them. **23**Then Jehu entered the temple of Baal with Jehonadab son of Rechab; he said to the worshipers of Baal, "Search and see that there is no worshiper of the Lord here among you, but only worshipers of Baal." **24**Then they proceeded to offer sacrifices and burnt offerings.

Now Jehu had stationed eighty men outside, saying, "Whoever allows any of those to escape whom I deliver into your hands shall forfeit his life." **25**As soon as he had finished presenting the burnt offering, Jehu said to the guards and to the officers, "Come in and kill them; let no one escape." So they put them to the sword. The guards and the officers threw them out, and then went into the citadel of the temple of Baal. **26**They brought out the pillar[d] that was in the temple of Baal, and burned it. **27**Then they demolished the pillar of Baal, and destroyed the temple of Baal, and made it a latrine to this day.

28 Thus Jehu wiped out Baal from Israel. **29**But Jehu did not turn aside from the sins of Jeroboam son of Nebat, which he caused Israel to commit—the golden calves that were in Bethel and in Dan. **30**The Lord said to Jehu, "Because you have done well in carrying out what I consider right, and in accordance with all that was in my heart have dealt with the house of Ahab, your sons of the fourth generation shall sit on the throne of Israel." **31**But Jehu was not careful to follow the law of the Lord the God of Israel with all his heart; he did not turn from the sins of Jeroboam, which he caused Israel to commit.

Death of Jehu

32 In those days the Lord began to trim off parts of Is-

---

a Gk: Heb *Is it right with your heart, as my heart is with your heart?*
b Gk: Heb lacks *Jehu said*   *c* Gk Syr Tg: Heb *they*   *d* Gk Vg Syr Tg: Heb *pillars*

rael. Hazael defeated them throughout the territory of Israel: [33]from the Jordan eastward, all the land of Gilead, the Gadites, the Reubenites, and the Manassites, from Aroer, which is by the Wadi Arnon, that is, Gilead and Bashan. [34]Now the rest of the acts of Jehu, all that he did, and all his power, are they not written in the Book of the Annals of the Kings of Israel? [35]So Jehu slept with his ancestors, and they buried him in Samaria. His son Jehoahaz succeeded him. [36]The time that Jehu reigned over Israel in Samaria was twenty-eight years.

Athaliah Reigns over Judah

11 Now when Athaliah, Ahaziah's mother, saw that her son was dead, she set about to destroy all the royal family. [2]But Jehosheba, King Joram's daughter, Ahaziah's sister, took Joash son of Ahaziah, and stole him away from among the king's children who were about to be killed; she put[a] him and his nurse in a bedroom. Thus she[b] hid him from Athaliah, so that he was not killed; [3]he remained with her six years, hidden in the house of the LORD, while Athaliah reigned over the land.

Jehoiada Anoints the Child Joash

4 But in the seventh year Jehoiada summoned the captains of the Carites and of the guards and had them come to him in the house of the LORD. He made a covenant with them and put them under oath in the house of the LORD; then he showed them the king's son. [5]He commanded them, "This is what you are to do: one-third of you, those who go off duty on the sabbath and guard the king's house [6](another third being at the gate Sur and a third at the gate behind the guards), shall guard the palace; [7]and your two divisions that come on duty in force on the sabbath and guard the house of the LORD[c] [8]shall surround the king, each with weapons in hand; and whoever approaches the ranks is to be killed. Be with the king in his comings and goings."

9 The captains did according to all that the priest Jehoiada commanded; each brought his men who were to go off duty on the sabbath, with those who were to come on duty on the sabbath, and came to the priest Jehoiada. [10]The priest delivered to the captains the spears and shields that had been King David's, which were in the house of the LORD; [11]the guards stood, every man with his weapons in his hand, from the south side of the house to the north side of the house, around the altar and the house, to guard the king on every side. [12]Then he brought out the king's son, put the crown on him, and gave him the covenant;[d] they proclaimed him king, and anointed him; they clapped their hands and shouted, "Long live the king!"

Death of Athaliah

13 When Athaliah heard the noise of the guard and of the people, she went into the house of the LORD to the people; [14]when she looked, there was the king standing by the pillar, according to custom, with the captains and the

Joash, a Special Baby

2 KINGS 11.1–11

The young king, hidden for six years, is finally crowned. He is another special child rescued from death, as were Moses, Isaac and Jesus. Reread the story, putting yourself in Jehosheba's shoes. Hear the call of God to save the infant prince. Experience the tension of stealing Joash and his nurse away to the hidden bedroom and the despair of knowing you cannot save all your nephews. Or put on Joash's shoes; imagine six years of hiding and fear. With relief, hear the faithful few calling you to serve God's ways; feel the excitement of your crowning. Reflect on ways in which you might hear God's call to be a Jehosheba preserving what is vulnerable, or a Joash coming out of hiding to do good.

See Meeting God in Scripture

a With 2 Chr 22.11: Heb lacks *she put*   *b* Gk Syr Vg Compare 2 Chr 22.11: Heb *they*   *c* Heb *the LORD to the king*   *d* Or *treaty* or *testimony*; Heb *eduth*

Jehoiada, a Good Teacher

2 KINGS 11.17–12.3

Good teachers have a lasting influence on our lives. We read in this passage how the priest Jehoiada instructs both the people and the king in the ways of the Lord. Review the passage. How does Jehoiada's correct instruction lead the people toward spiritual renewal? What impact did this one man have on the religious life of the people?

Make a list of the people who have been inspirational teachers in your life. In what ways did their teaching reflect spirituality, wholeness and maturity? In what ways do you want to be like them? How can you mentor others as you have been mentored? Take time to call or write your teachers and mentors, thanking them for their inspiration.

See Meeting God in Community

trumpeters beside the king, and all the people of the land rejoicing and blowing trumpets. Athaliah tore her clothes and cried, "Treason! Treason!" ¹⁵Then the priest Jehoiada commanded the captains who were set over the army, "Bring her out between the ranks, and kill with the sword anyone who follows her." For the priest said, "Let her not be killed in the house of the LORD." ¹⁶So they laid hands on her; she went through the horses' entrance to the king's house, and there she was put to death.

17 Jehoiada made a covenant between the LORD and the king and people, that they should be the LORD's people; also between the king and the people. ¹⁸Then all the people of the land went to the house of Baal, and tore it down; his altars and his images they broke in pieces, and they killed Mattan, the priest of Baal, before the altars. The priest posted guards over the house of the LORD. ¹⁹He took the captains, the Carites, the guards, and all the people of the land; then they brought the king down from the house of the LORD, marching through the gate of the guards to the king's house. He took his seat on the throne of the kings. ²⁰So all the people of the land rejoiced; and the city was quiet after Athaliah had been killed with the sword at the king's house.

21ᵃ Jehoashᵇ was seven years old when he began to reign.

The Temple Repaired

12 In the seventh year of Jehu, Jehoash began to reign; he reigned forty years in Jerusalem. His mother's name was Zibiah of Beer-sheba. ²Jehoash did what was right in the sight of the LORD all his days, because the priest Jehoiada instructed him. ³Nevertheless the high places were not taken away; the people continued to sacrifice and make offerings on the high places.

4 Jehoash said to the priests, "All the money offered as sacred donations that is brought into the house of the LORD, the money for which each person is assessed—the money from the assessment of persons—and the money from the voluntary offerings brought into the house of the LORD, ⁵let the priests receive from each of the donors; and let them repair the house wherever any need of repairs is discovered." ⁶But by the twenty-third year of King Jehoash the priests had made no repairs on the house. ⁷Therefore King Jehoash summoned the priest Jehoiada with the other priests and said to them, "Why are you not repairing the house? Now therefore do not accept any more money from your donors but hand it over for the repair of the house." ⁸So the priests agreed that they would neither accept more money from the people nor repair the house.

9 Then the priest Jehoiada took a chest, made a hole in its lid, and set it beside the altar on the right side as one entered the house of the LORD; the priests who guarded the threshold put in it all the money that was brought into the house of the LORD. ¹⁰Whenever they saw that there was a great deal of money in the chest, the king's secretary and the high priest went up, counted the money that was found in the house of the LORD, and tied it up in bags. ¹¹They would give the money that was weighed out into

ᵃ Ch 12.1 in Heb   ᵇ Another spelling is *Joash*; see verse 19

the hands of the workers who had the oversight of the house of the LORD; then they paid it out to the carpenters and the builders who worked on the house of the LORD, [12]to the masons and the stonecutters, as well as to buy timber and quarried stone for making repairs on the house of the LORD, as well as for any outlay for repairs of the house. [13]But for the house of the LORD no basins of silver, snuffers, bowls, trumpets, or any vessels of gold, or of silver, were made from the money that was brought into the house of the LORD, [14]for that was given to the workers who were repairing the house of the LORD with it. [15]They did not ask an accounting from those into whose hand they delivered the money to pay out to the workers, for they dealt honestly. [16]The money from the guilt offerings and the money from the sin offerings was not brought into the house of the LORD; it belonged to the priests.

Hazael Threatens Jerusalem

17 At that time King Hazael of Aram went up, fought against Gath, and took it. But when Hazael set his face to go up against Jerusalem, [18]King Jehoash of Judah took all the votive gifts that Jehoshaphat, Jehoram, and Ahaziah, his ancestors, the kings of Judah, had dedicated, as well as his own votive gifts, all the gold that was found in the treasuries of the house of the LORD and of the king's house, and sent these to King Hazael of Aram. Then Hazael withdrew from Jerusalem.

Death of Joash

19 Now the rest of the acts of Joash, and all that he did, are they not written in the Book of the Annals of the Kings of Judah? [20]His servants arose, devised a conspiracy, and killed Joash in the house of Millo, on the way that goes down to Silla. [21]It was Jozacar son of Shimeath and Jehozabad son of Shomer, his servants, who struck him down, so that he died. He was buried with his ancestors in the city of David; then his son Amaziah succeeded him.

Jehoahaz Reigns over Israel

13 In the twenty-third year of King Joash son of Ahaziah of Judah, Jehoahaz son of Jehu began to reign over Israel in Samaria; he reigned seventeen years. [2]He did what was evil in the sight of the LORD, and followed the sins of Jeroboam son of Nebat, which he caused Israel to sin; he did not depart from them. [3]The anger of the LORD was kindled against Israel, so that he gave them repeatedly into the hand of King Hazael of Aram, then into the hand of Ben-hadad son of Hazael. [4]But Jehoahaz entreated the LORD, and the LORD heeded him; for he saw the oppression of Israel, how the king of Aram oppressed them. [5]Therefore the LORD gave Israel a savior, so that they escaped from the hand of the Arameans; and the people of Israel lived in their homes as formerly. [6]Nevertheless they did not depart from the sins of the house of Jeroboam, which he caused Israel to sin, but walked[a] in them; the sacred pole[b] also remained in Samaria. [7]So Jehoahaz was left with an army of not more than fifty horsemen, ten chariots and ten thousand footmen; for the king of Aram had

Praying in a Crisis

2 KINGS 13.1–5

Jehoahaz is introduced by the refrain used for most of the kings of Israel and Judah: "He did what was evil in the sight of the LORD." But during his reign, when King Hazael of Aram threatens, Jehoahaz calls on the Lord for help and is answered with "a savior," probably an Assyrian king who draws Hazael's attention away from Israel for the moment. How often have you gone along, doing your own thing, and then in a troubled moment called on the Lord to save you? Remember the times when you have been helped in such a way or have been given another chance to live more fully for God. Relive one such experience in your mind right now. How did you grow from that experience? How did you resolve to change your life? What lasting effects has it had?

See *Meeting God in Everyday Life*

Settling for Halfhearted Faith

2 KINGS 13.15–19

"No one is ever really at ease in facing what we call 'life' and 'death' without religious faith. The trouble with many people today is that they have not found a God big enough for modern needs. While their experience of life has grown in a score of directions, and their emotional horizons have been expanded to the point of bewilderment by world events and by scientific discoveries, their ideas of God have remained largely static."

—J. B. PHILLIPS,
Your God Is Too Small

destroyed them and made them like the dust at threshing. 8Now the rest of the acts of Jehoahaz and all that he did, including his might, are they not written in the Book of the Annals of the Kings of Israel? 9So Jehoahaz slept with his ancestors, and they buried him in Samaria; then his son Joash succeeded him.

Jehoash Reigns over Israel

10 In the thirty-seventh year of King Joash of Judah, Jehoash son of Jehoahaz began to reign over Israel in Samaria; he reigned sixteen years. 11He also did what was evil in the sight of the LORD; he did not depart from all the sins of Jeroboam son of Nebat, which he caused Israel to sin, but he walked in them. 12Now the rest of the acts of Joash, and all that he did, as well as the might with which he fought against King Amaziah of Judah, are they not written in the Book of the Annals of the Kings of Israel? 13So Joash slept with his ancestors, and Jeroboam sat upon his throne; Joash was buried in Samaria with the kings of Israel.

Death of Elisha

14 Now when Elisha had fallen sick with the illness of which he was to die, King Joash of Israel went down to him, and wept before him, crying, "My father, my father! The chariots of Israel and its horsemen!" 15Elisha said to him, "Take a bow and arrows"; so he took a bow and arrows. 16Then he said to the king of Israel, "Draw the bow"; and he drew it. Elisha laid his hands on the king's hands. 17Then he said, "Open the window eastward"; and he opened it. Elisha said, "Shoot"; and he shot. Then he said, "The LORD's arrow of victory, the arrow of victory over Aram! For you shall fight the Arameans in Aphek until you have made an end of them." 18He continued, "Take the arrows"; and he took them. He said to the king of Israel, "Strike the ground with them"; he struck three times, and stopped. 19Then the man of God was angry with him, and said, "You should have struck five or six times; then you would have struck down Aram until you had made an end of it, but now you will strike down Aram only three times."

20 So Elisha died, and they buried him. Now bands of Moabites used to invade the land in the spring of the year. 21As a man was being buried, a marauding band was seen and the man was thrown into the grave of Elisha; as soon as the man touched the bones of Elisha, he came to life and stood on his feet.

Israel Recaptures Cities from Aram

22 Now King Hazael of Aram oppressed Israel all the days of Jehoahaz. 23But the LORD was gracious to them and had compassion on them; he turned toward them, because of his covenant with Abraham, Isaac, and Jacob, and would not destroy them; nor has he banished them from his presence until now.

24 When King Hazael of Aram died, his son Ben-hadad succeeded him. 25Then Jehoash son of Jehoahaz took again from Ben-hadad son of Hazael the towns that he had taken from his father Jehoahaz in war. Three times Joash defeated him and recovered the towns of Israel.

Amaziah Reigns over Judah

14 In the second year of King Joash son of Joahaz of Israel, King Amaziah son of Joash of Judah, began to reign. ²He was twenty-five years old when he began to reign, and he reigned twenty-nine years in Jerusalem. His mother's name was Jehoaddin of Jerusalem. ³He did what was right in the sight of the Lord, yet not like his ancestor David; in all things he did as his father Joash had done. ⁴But the high places were not removed; the people still sacrificed and made offerings on the high places. ⁵As soon as the royal power was firmly in his hand he killed his servants who had murdered his father the king. ⁶But he did not put to death the children of the murderers; according to what is written in the book of the law of Moses, where the Lord commanded, "The parents shall not be put to death for the children, or the children be put to death for the parents; but all shall be put to death for their own sins."

7 He killed ten thousand Edomites in the Valley of Salt and took Sela by storm; he called it Jokthe-el, which is its name to this day.

8 Then Amaziah sent messengers to King Jehoash son of Jehoahaz, son of Jehu, of Israel, saying, "Come, let us look one another in the face." ⁹King Jehoash of Israel sent word to King Amaziah of Judah, "A thornbush on Lebanon sent to a cedar on Lebanon, saying, 'Give your daughter to my son for a wife'; but a wild animal of Lebanon passed by and trampled down the thornbush. ¹⁰You have indeed defeated Edom, and your heart has lifted you up. Be content with your glory, and stay at home; for why should you provoke trouble so that you fall, you and Judah with you?"

11 But Amaziah would not listen. So King Jehoash of Israel went up; he and King Amaziah of Judah faced one another in battle at Beth-shemesh, which belongs to Judah. ¹²Judah was defeated by Israel; everyone fled home. ¹³King Jehoash of Israel captured King Amaziah of Judah son of Jehoash, son of Ahaziah, at Beth-shemesh; he came to Jerusalem, and broke down the wall of Jerusalem from the Ephraim Gate to the Corner Gate, a distance of four hundred cubits. ¹⁴He seized all the gold and silver, and all the vessels that were found in the house of the Lord and in the treasuries of the king's house, as well as hostages; then he returned to Samaria.

15 Now the rest of the acts that Jehoash did, his might, and how he fought with King Amaziah of Judah, are they not written in the Book of the Annals of the Kings of Israel? ¹⁶Jehoash slept with his ancestors, and was buried in Samaria with the kings of Israel; then his son Jeroboam succeeded him.

17 King Amaziah son of Joash of Judah lived fifteen years after the death of King Jehoash son of Jehoahaz of Israel. ¹⁸Now the rest of the deeds of Amaziah, are they not written in the Book of the Annals of the Kings of Judah? ¹⁹They made a conspiracy against him in Jerusalem, and he fled to Lachish. But they sent after him to Lachish, and killed him there. ²⁰They brought him on horses; he was buried in Jerusalem with his ancestors in the city of David. ²¹All the people of Judah took Azariah, who was sixteen years old, and made him king to succeed

A Parable of Warning

2 KINGS 14.9–11

We have all experienced times when a task seemed greater than our abilities. King Amaziah, flushed with pride in his victory over the Edomites, rejects King Jehoash's warning parable, overrates his own strength and is soundly defeated. Stepping out into life with hope, ambition and dreams is one thing; to overestimate our ability to produce is another. How often is it that you have not listened to your own inner warnings or those of others and you were soundly defeated? It has been said that defeat is not fatal, nor is it final. What does defeat do to your relationship with God? How do you respond to defeat or disappointment? What do you do to get back on your feet?

See Meeting God in Service

Following the Ways of Others

2 KINGS 14.23–24

The sins of a dynasty live on in succeeding rulers. Likewise, those around us are affected by the way we treat them, live our lives and make decisions. We want the good we do today to be remembered tomorrow. Consider your own "dynasty" by gathering pictures of your own family, friends, relatives and children. How have you made a difference in their lives? Can you recall specific situations in which your influence became apparent? Holding each picture in turn, pray for those who are within your sphere of influence: "Loving God, in this world of evil, selfishness and suffering, let me live before you in such a way as to make a difference to this person. Amen."

See Meeting God in Community

his father Amaziah. ²²He rebuilt Elath and restored it to Judah, after King Amaziah*a* slept with his ancestors.

Jeroboam II Reigns over Israel

23 In the fifteenth year of King Amaziah son of Joash of Judah, King Jeroboam son of Joash of Israel began to reign in Samaria; he reigned forty-one years. ²⁴He did what was evil in the sight of the LORD; he did not depart from all the sins of Jeroboam son of Nebat, which he caused Israel to sin. ²⁵He restored the border of Israel from Lebo-hamath as far as the Sea of the Arabah, according to the word of the LORD, the God of Israel, which he spoke by his servant Jonah son of Amittai, the prophet, who was from Gath-hepher. ²⁶For the LORD saw that the distress of Israel was very bitter; there was no one left, bond or free, and no one to help Israel. ²⁷But the LORD had not said that he would blot out the name of Israel from under heaven, so he saved them by the hand of Jeroboam son of Joash.

28 Now the rest of the acts of Jeroboam, and all that he did, and his might, how he fought, and how he recovered for Israel Damascus and Hamath, which had belonged to Judah, are they not written in the Book of the Annals of the Kings of Israel? ²⁹Jeroboam slept with his ancestors, the kings of Israel; his son Zechariah succeeded him.

Azariah Reigns over Judah

15 In the twenty-seventh year of King Jeroboam of Israel King Azariah son of Amaziah of Judah began to reign. ²He was sixteen years old when he began to reign, and he reigned fifty-two years in Jerusalem. His mother's name was Jecoliah of Jerusalem. ³He did what was right in the sight of the LORD, just as his father Amaziah had done. ⁴Nevertheless the high places were not taken away; the people still sacrificed and made offerings on the high places. ⁵The LORD struck the king, so that he was leprous*b* to the day of his death, and lived in a separate house. Jotham the king's son was in charge of the palace, governing the people of the land. ⁶Now the rest of the acts of Azariah, and all that he did, are they not written in the Book of the Annals of the Kings of Judah? ⁷Azariah slept with his ancestors; they buried him with his ancestors in the city of David; his son Jotham succeeded him.

Zechariah Reigns over Israel

8 In the thirty-eighth year of King Azariah of Judah, Zechariah son of Jeroboam reigned over Israel in Samaria six months. ⁹He did what was evil in the sight of the LORD, as his ancestors had done. He did not depart from the sins of Jeroboam son of Nebat, which he caused Israel to sin. ¹⁰Shallum son of Jabesh conspired against him, and struck him down in public and killed him, and reigned in place of him. ¹¹Now the rest of the deeds of Zechariah are written in the Book of the Annals of the Kings of Israel. ¹²This was the promise of the LORD that he gave to Jehu, "Your sons shall sit on the throne of Israel to the fourth generation." And so it happened.

a Heb *the king*   *b* A term for several skin diseases; precise meaning uncertain

Shallum Reigns over Israel

13 Shallum son of Jabesh began to reign in the thirty-ninth year of King Uzziah of Judah; he reigned one month in Samaria. ¹⁴Then Menahem son of Gadi came up from Tirzah and came to Samaria; he struck down Shallum son of Jabesh in Samaria and killed him; he reigned in place of him. ¹⁵Now the rest of the deeds of Shallum, including the conspiracy that he made, are written in the Book of the Annals of the Kings of Israel. ¹⁶At that time Menahem sacked Tiphsah, all who were in it and its territory from Tirzah on; because they did not open it to him, he sacked it. He ripped open all the pregnant women in it.

Menahem Reigns over Israel

17 In the thirty-ninth year of King Azariah of Judah, Menahem son of Gadi began to reign over Israel; he reigned ten years in Samaria. ¹⁸He did what was evil in the sight of the LORD; he did not depart all his days from any of the sins of Jeroboam son of Nebat, which he caused Israel to sin. ¹⁹King Pul of Assyria came against the land; Menahem gave Pul a thousand talents of silver, so that he might help him confirm his hold on the royal power. ²⁰Menahem exacted the money from Israel, that is, from all the wealthy, fifty shekels of silver from each one, to give to the king of Assyria. So the king of Assyria turned back, and did not stay there in the land. ²¹Now the rest of the deeds of Menahem, and all that he did, are they not written in the Book of the Annals of the Kings of Israel? ²²Menahem slept with his ancestors, and his son Pekahiah succeeded him.

Pekahiah Reigns over Israel

23 In the fiftieth year of King Azariah of Judah, Pekahiah son of Menahem began to reign over Israel in Samaria; he reigned two years. ²⁴He did what was evil in the sight of the LORD; he did not turn away from the sins of Jeroboam son of Nebat, which he caused Israel to sin. ²⁵Pekah son of Remaliah, his captain, conspired against him with fifty of the Gileadites, and attacked him in Samaria, in the citadel of the palace along with Argob and Arieh; he killed him, and reigned in place of him. ²⁶Now the rest of the deeds of Pekahiah, and all that he did, are written in the Book of the Annals of the Kings of Israel.

Pekah Reigns over Israel

27 In the fifty-second year of King Azariah of Judah, Pekah son of Remaliah began to reign over Israel in Samaria; he reigned twenty years. ²⁸He did what was evil in the sight of the LORD; he did not depart from the sins of Jeroboam son of Nebat, which he caused Israel to sin.

29 In the days of King Pekah of Israel, King Tiglath-pileser of Assyria came and captured Ijon, Abel-beth-maacah, Janoah, Kedesh, Hazor, Gilead, and Galilee, all the land of Naphtali; and he carried the people captive to Assyria. ³⁰Then Hoshea son of Elah made a conspiracy against Pekah son of Remaliah, attacked him, and killed him; he reigned in place of him, in the twentieth year of Jotham son of Uzziah. ³¹Now the rest of the acts of Pekah,

The Annals of the Kings

2 KINGS 15.8–26

Several times in these pages the writer refers to the Annals of the Kings of Israel. This was probably an official government record, which has, unfortunately, been lost. As you read these passages, try to imagine that someday you will write the annals of your own life. What characteristics would someone reading your annals see in your history? What would be the highlights of your spiritual journey? Try writing your annals for the past year, looking particularly for the times and events in which the hand of God was clearly evident.

See Meeting God in Everyday Life

Crisis, Judgment and Condemnation

2 KINGS 16.1–7

Read Isaiah 7.1–17, a passage referring to this time in Ahaz's life, in which Isaiah counsels Ahaz to stand firm and trust in God. In this 2 Kings account we see Ahaz capitulating to Assyrian domination rather than taking any such advice.

When faced with crisis, where do you turn for help first? How do you seek God's aid? In what ways have you found God's help in past crises? If the crisis is because of your own misdeeds or mistakes, how does your own spirit speak to you when you realize judgment is at hand? Is there a difference between God's judgment and God's condemnation? What does "there is therefore now no condemnation for those who are in Christ Jesus" (Romans 8.1) mean to you?

and all that he did, are written in the Book of the Annals of the Kings of Israel.

Jotham Reigns over Judah

32 In the second year of King Pekah son of Remaliah of Israel, King Jotham son of Uzziah of Judah began to reign. [33]He was twenty-five years old when he began to reign and reigned sixteen years in Jerusalem. His mother's name was Jerusha daughter of Zadok. [34]He did what was right in the sight of the LORD, just as his father Uzziah had done. [35]Nevertheless the high places were not removed; the people still sacrificed and made offerings on the high places. He built the upper gate of the house of the LORD. [36]Now the rest of the acts of Jotham, and all that he did, are they not written in the Book of the Annals of the Kings of Judah? [37]In those days the LORD began to send King Rezin of Aram and Pekah son of Remaliah against Judah. [38]Jotham slept with his ancestors, and was buried with his ancestors in the city of David, his ancestor; his son Ahaz succeeded him.

Ahaz Reigns over Judah

16 In the seventeenth year of Pekah son of Remaliah, King Ahaz son of Jotham of Judah began to reign. [2]Ahaz was twenty years old when he began to reign; he reigned sixteen years in Jerusalem. He did not do what was right in the sight of the LORD his God, as his ancestor David had done, [3]but he walked in the way of the kings of Israel. He even made his son pass through fire, according to the abominable practices of the nations whom the LORD drove out before the people of Israel. [4]He sacrificed and made offerings on the high places, on the hills, and under every green tree.

5 Then King Rezin of Aram and King Pekah son of Remaliah of Israel came up to wage war on Jerusalem; they besieged Ahaz but could not conquer him. [6]At that time the king of Edom[a] recovered Elath for Edom,[b] and drove the Judeans from Elath; and the Edomites came to Elath, where they live to this day. [7]Ahaz sent messengers to King Tiglath-pileser of Assyria, saying, "I am your servant and your son. Come up, and rescue me from the hand of the king of Aram and from the hand of the king of Israel, who are attacking me." [8]Ahaz also took the silver and gold found in the house of the LORD and in the treasures of the king's house, and sent a present to the king of Assyria. [9]The king of Assyria listened to him; the king of Assyria marched up against Damascus, and took it, carrying its people captive to Kir; then he killed Rezin.

10 When King Ahaz went to Damascus to meet King Tiglath-pileser of Assyria, he saw the altar that was at Damascus. King Ahaz sent to the priest Uriah a model of the altar, and its pattern, exact in all its details. [11]The priest Uriah built the altar; in accordance with all that King Ahaz had sent from Damascus, just so did the priest Uriah build it, before King Ahaz arrived from Damascus. [12]When the king came from Damascus, the king viewed the altar. Then the king drew near to the altar, went up on it, [13]and offered his burnt offering and his grain offering, poured his

a Cn: Heb *King Rezin of Aram*   *b* Cn: Heb *Aram*

drink offering, and dashed the blood of his offerings of well-being against the altar. [14]The bronze altar that was before the LORD he removed from the front of the house, from the place between his altar and the house of the LORD, and put it on the north side of his altar. [15]King Ahaz commanded the priest Uriah, saying, "Upon the great altar offer the morning burnt offering, and the evening grain offering, and the king's burnt offering, and his grain offering, with the burnt offering of all the people of the land, their grain offering, and their drink offering; then dash against it all the blood of the burnt offering, and all the blood of the sacrifice; but the bronze altar shall be for me to inquire by." [16]The priest Uriah did everything that King Ahaz commanded.

17 Then King Ahaz cut off the frames of the stands, and removed the laver from them; he removed the sea from the bronze oxen that were under it, and put it on a pediment of stone. [18]The covered portal for use on the sabbath that had been built inside the palace, and the outer entrance for the king he removed from[a] the house of the LORD. He did this because of the king of Assyria. [19]Now the rest of the acts of Ahaz that he did, are they not written in the Book of the Annals of the Kings of Judah? [20]Ahaz slept with his ancestors, and was buried with his ancestors in the city of David; his son Hezekiah succeeded him.

Hoshea Reigns over Israel

17 In the twelfth year of King Ahaz of Judah, Hoshea son of Elah began to reign in Samaria over Israel; he reigned nine years. [2]He did what was evil in the sight of the LORD, yet not like the kings of Israel who were before him. [3]King Shalmaneser of Assyria came up against him; Hoshea became his vassal, and paid him tribute. [4]But the king of Assyria found treachery in Hoshea; for he had sent messengers to King So of Egypt, and offered no tribute to the king of Assyria, as he had done year by year; therefore the king of Assyria confined him and imprisoned him.

Israel Carried Captive to Assyria

5 Then the king of Assyria invaded all the land and came to Samaria; for three years he besieged it. [6]In the ninth year of Hoshea the king of Assyria captured Samaria; he carried the Israelites away to Assyria. He placed them in Halah, on the Habor, the river of Gozan, and in the cities of the Medes.

7 This occurred because the people of Israel had sinned against the LORD their God, who had brought them up out of the land of Egypt from under the hand of Pharaoh king of Egypt. They had worshiped other gods [8]and walked in the customs of the nations whom the LORD drove out before the people of Israel, and in the customs that the kings of Israel had introduced.[b] [9]The people of Israel secretly did things that were not right against the LORD their God. They built for themselves high places at all their towns, from watchtower to fortified city; [10]they set up for themselves pillars and sacred poles[c] on every high hill and under every green tree; [11]there they made offerings on all the

First Wave of Destruction

2 KINGS 17.5–7

Assyria invades, but the worst is still to come. Israel will be exiled, eventually becoming the "ten lost tribes." While this passage tells us that Israel's exile came as divine judgment, it also reminds us of the ever-present reality of international turmoil. The cost of conflict in terms of deaths, suffering, upheaval and sorrow cannot be counted. Today's world is full of slaves and refugees created by political invasions and war. Children are especially vulnerable at these times.

God can work through our prayers and deeds to bring about peace and justice. Look at a map of the world. Where are wars occurring now? From what countries are refugees fleeing? Where are they taking sanctuary? How can you become involved in giving aid to these victims? How might a nation's spiritual renewal make a difference? Use your map as a guide to prayer for governments at war and for the people who suffer.

Conformed to God's Will

2 KINGS 17.17

The people of Israel have conformed to the destructive ways of the nations around them, bringing displeasure to God's heart. Following social norms founded on unsound principles and evil practices leads Israel to ruin.

Reflect on your actions in light of the Word of God by reading Romans 12.1–2. In what ways have you conformed to this world? What needs to be changed so that you conform to the Word and will of God? What do you need to cultivate in order to become aligned with God's love and justice? Pray daily for the grace and power to live for God.

high places, as the nations did whom the LORD carried away before them. They did wicked things, provoking the LORD to anger; [12]they served idols, of which the LORD had said to them, "You shall not do this." [13]Yet the LORD warned Israel and Judah by every prophet and every seer, saying, "Turn from your evil ways and keep my commandments and my statutes, in accordance with all the law that I commanded your ancestors and that I sent to you by my servants the prophets." [14]They would not listen but were stubborn, as their ancestors had been, who did not believe in the LORD their God. [15]They despised his statutes, and his covenant that he made with their ancestors, and the warnings that he gave them. They went after false idols and became false; they followed the nations that were around them, concerning whom the LORD had commanded them that they should not do as they did. [16]They rejected all the commandments of the LORD their God and made for themselves cast images of two calves; they made a sacred pole,[a] worshiped all the host of heaven, and served Baal. [17]They made their sons and their daughters pass through fire; they used divination and augury; and they sold themselves to do evil in the sight of the LORD, provoking him to anger. [18]Therefore the LORD was very angry with Israel and removed them out of his sight; none was left but the tribe of Judah alone.

19 Judah also did not keep the commandments of the LORD their God but walked in the customs that Israel had introduced. [20]The LORD rejected all the descendants of Israel; he punished them and gave them into the hand of plunderers, until he had banished them from his presence.

21 When he had torn Israel from the house of David, they made Jeroboam son of Nebat king. Jeroboam drove Israel from following the LORD and made them commit great sin. [22]The people of Israel continued in all the sins that Jeroboam committed; they did not depart from them [23]until the LORD removed Israel out of his sight, as he had foretold through all his servants the prophets. So Israel was exiled from their own land to Assyria until this day.

Assyria Resettles Samaria

24 The king of Assyria brought people from Babylon, Cuthah, Avva, Hamath, and Sepharvaim, and placed them in the cities of Samaria in place of the people of Israel; they took possession of Samaria, and settled in its cities. [25]When they first settled there, they did not worship the LORD; therefore the LORD sent lions among them, which killed some of them. [26]So the king of Assyria was told, "The nations that you have carried away and placed in the cities of Samaria do not know the law of the god of the land; therefore he has sent lions among them; they are killing them, because they do not know the law of the god of the land." [27]Then the king of Assyria commanded, "Send there one of the priests whom you carried away from there; let him[b] go and live there, and teach them the law of the god of the land." [28]So one of the priests whom they had carried away from Samaria came and lived in Bethel; he taught them how they should worship the LORD.

29 But every nation still made gods of its own and put

a Heb *Asherah*   *b* Syr Vg: Heb *them*

them in the shrines of the high places that the people of Samaria had made, every nation in the cities in which they lived; [30]the people of Babylon made Succoth-benoth, the people of Cuth made Nergal, the people of Hamath made Ashima; [31]the Avvites made Nibhaz and Tartak; the Sepharvites burned their children in the fire to Adrammelech and Anammelech, the gods of Sepharvaim. [32]They also worshiped the LORD and appointed from among themselves all sorts of people as priests of the high places, who sacrificed for them in the shrines of the high places. [33]So they worshiped the LORD but also served their own gods, after the manner of the nations from among whom they had been carried away. [34]To this day they continue to practice their former customs.

They do not worship the LORD and they do not follow the statutes or the ordinances or the law or the commandment that the LORD commanded the children of Jacob, whom he named Israel. [35]The LORD had made a covenant with them and commanded them, "You shall not worship other gods or bow yourselves to them or serve them or sacrifice to them, [36]but you shall worship the LORD, who brought you out of the land of Egypt with great power and with an outstretched arm; you shall bow yourselves to him, and to him you shall sacrifice. [37]The statutes and the ordinances and the law and the commandment that he wrote for you, you shall always be careful to observe. You shall not worship other gods; [38]you shall not forget the covenant that I have made with you. You shall not worship other gods, [39]but you shall worship the LORD your God; he will deliver you out of the hand of all your enemies." [40]They would not listen, however, but they continued to practice their former custom.

41 So these nations worshiped the LORD, but also served their carved images; to this day their children and their children's children continue to do as their ancestors did.

Hezekiah's Reign over Judah

18 In the third year of King Hoshea son of Elah of Israel, Hezekiah son of King Ahaz of Judah began to reign. [2]He was twenty-five years old when he began to reign; he reigned twenty-nine years in Jerusalem. His mother's name was Abi daughter of Zechariah. [3]He did what was right in the sight of the LORD just as his ancestor David had done. [4]He removed the high places, broke down the pillars, and cut down the sacred pole.[a] He broke in pieces the bronze serpent that Moses had made, for until those days the people of Israel had made offerings to it; it was called Nehushtan. [5]He trusted in the LORD the God of Israel; so that there was no one like him among all the kings of Judah after him, or among those who were before him. [6]For he held fast to the LORD; he did not depart from following him but kept the commandments that the LORD commanded Moses. [7]The LORD was with him; wherever he went, he prospered. He rebelled against the king of Assyria and would not serve him. [8]He attacked the Philistines as far as Gaza and its territory, from watchtower to fortified city.

Spiritual Housecleaning

2 KINGS 18.1–4

Hezekiah does not hesitate to discard time-honored customs and objects that impede the people's pure worship of God. The high places and sacred poles, long beloved, are destroyed. Even Moses' bronze serpent, used idolatrously, is broken into pieces. Take stock of your own practices. What habits or customs are impeding your response to God's purposes—such as aimless television watching or purposeless reading? What is one habit you can begin discarding today? What will you put in its place? Prayerfully make a decision. If actually throwing something out helps enact this decision, do so as soon as you finish your prayer.

See Meeting God in Everyday Life

---

a Heb *Asherah*

A Good King in Hard Times

2 KINGS 18.5–8

Hezekiah's strong, moral, focused leadership leads to reform and revival. He is the only good king in one hundred years, and "there was no one like him among all the kings of Judah" because he followed God closely and kept God's commands. The nation's downfall was postponed.

Who are the good leaders of our day? Have you ever thought about calling them or writing a letter in support of their good efforts? Think about what you want to say to them; then call, write, fax or send an e-mail message to them. Let them know that you pray for them. Encourage them to do what is "right in the sight of the LORD."

See Meeting God in Community

9 In the fourth year of King Hezekiah, which was the seventh year of King Hoshea son of Elah of Israel, King Shalmaneser of Assyria came up against Samaria, besieged it, [10]and at the end of three years, took it. In the sixth year of Hezekiah, which was the ninth year of King Hoshea of Israel, Samaria was taken. [11]The king of Assyria carried the Israelites away to Assyria, settled them in Halah, on the Habor, the river of Gozan, and in the cities of the Medes, [12]because they did not obey the voice of the LORD their God but transgressed his covenant—all that Moses the servant of the LORD had commanded; they neither listened nor obeyed.

Sennacherib Invades Judah

13 In the fourteenth year of King Hezekiah, King Sennacherib of Assyria came up against all the fortified cities of Judah and captured them. [14]King Hezekiah of Judah sent to the king of Assyria at Lachish, saying, "I have done wrong; withdraw from me; whatever you impose on me I will bear." The king of Assyria demanded of King Hezekiah of Judah three hundred talents of silver and thirty talents of gold. [15]Hezekiah gave him all the silver that was found in the house of the LORD and in the treasuries of the king's house. [16]At that time Hezekiah stripped the gold from the doors of the temple of the LORD, and from the doorposts that King Hezekiah of Judah had overlaid and gave it to the king of Assyria. [17]The king of Assyria sent the Tartan, the Rabsaris, and the Rabshakeh with a great army from Lachish to King Hezekiah at Jerusalem. They went up and came to Jerusalem. When they arrived, they came and stood by the conduit of the upper pool, which is on the highway to the Fuller's Field. [18]When they called for the king, there came out to them Eliakim son of Hilkiah, who was in charge of the palace, and Shebnah the secretary, and Joah son of Asaph, the recorder.

19 The Rabshakeh said to them, "Say to Hezekiah: Thus says the great king, the king of Assyria: On what do you base this confidence of yours? [20]Do you think that mere words are strategy and power for war? On whom do you now rely, that you have rebelled against me? [21]See, you are relying now on Egypt, that broken reed of a staff, which will pierce the hand of anyone who leans on it. Such is Pharaoh king of Egypt to all who rely on him. [22]But if you say to me, 'We rely on the LORD our God,' is it not he whose high places and altars Hezekiah has removed, saying to Judah and to Jerusalem, 'You shall worship before this altar in Jerusalem'? [23]Come now, make a wager with my master the king of Assyria: I will give you two thousand horses, if you are able on your part to set riders on them. [24]How then can you repulse a single captain among the least of my master's servants, when you rely on Egypt for chariots and for horsemen? [25]Moreover, is it without the LORD that I have come up against this place to destroy it? The LORD said to me, Go up against this land, and destroy it."

26 Then Eliakim son of Hilkiah, and Shebnah, and Joah said to the Rabshakeh, "Please speak to your servants in the Aramaic language, for we understand it; do not speak to us in the language of Judah within the hearing of the people who are on the wall." [27]But the Rabshakeh said to

them, "Has my master sent me to speak these words to your master and to you, and not to the people sitting on the wall, who are doomed with you to eat their own dung and to drink their own urine?"

28 Then the Rabshakeh stood and called out in a loud voice in the language of Judah, "Hear the word of the great king, the king of Assyria! ²⁹Thus says the king: 'Do not let Hezekiah deceive you, for he will not be able to deliver you out of my hand. ³⁰Do not let Hezekiah make you rely on the LORD by saying, The LORD will surely deliver us, and this city will not be given into the hand of the king of Assyria.' ³¹Do not listen to Hezekiah; for thus says the king of Assyria: 'Make your peace with me and come out to me; then every one of you will eat from your own vine and your own fig tree, and drink water from your own cistern, ³²until I come and take you away to a land like your own land, a land of grain and wine, a land of bread and vineyards, a land of olive oil and honey, that you may live and not die. Do not listen to Hezekiah when he misleads you by saying, The LORD will deliver us. ³³Has any of the gods of the nations ever delivered its land out of the hand of the king of Assyria? ³⁴Where are the gods of Hamath and Arpad? Where are the gods of Sepharvaim, Hena, and Ivvah? Have they delivered Samaria out of my hand? ³⁵Who among all the gods of the countries have delivered their countries out of my hand, that the LORD should deliver Jerusalem out of my hand?' "

36 But the people were silent and answered him not a word, for the king's command was, "Do not answer him." ³⁷Then Eliakim son of Hilkiah, who was in charge of the palace, and Shebna the secretary, and Joah son of Asaph, the recorder, came to Hezekiah with their clothes torn and told him the words of the Rabshakeh.

Hezekiah Consults Isaiah

19 When King Hezekiah heard it, he tore his clothes, covered himself with sackcloth, and went into the house of the LORD. ²And he sent Eliakim, who was in charge of the palace, and Shebna the secretary, and the senior priests, covered with sackcloth, to the prophet Isaiah son of Amoz. ³They said to him, "Thus says Hezekiah, This day is a day of distress, of rebuke, and of disgrace; children have come to the birth, and there is no strength to bring them forth. ⁴It may be that the LORD your God heard all the words of the Rabshakeh, whom his master the king of Assyria has sent to mock the living God, and will rebuke the words that the LORD your God has heard; therefore lift up your prayer for the remnant that is left." ⁵When the servants of King Hezekiah came to Isaiah, ⁶Isaiah said to them, "Say to your master, 'Thus says the LORD: Do not be afraid because of the words that you have heard, with which the servants of the king of Assyria have reviled me. ⁷I myself will put a spirit in him, so that he shall hear a rumor and return to his own land; I will cause him to fall by the sword in his own land.' "

Sennacherib's Threat

8 The Rabshakeh returned, and found the king of Assyria fighting against Libnah; for he had heard that the

Enemies at the Gate

2 KINGS 18.17–25

Unexpected trouble arises in the midst of good times: An enemy is trying to convince Hezekiah and Judah that God is not with them. What unexpected enemies—a health problem, financial concerns, family troubles, employment issues or other matters—have you had to face that threatened to shake your faith in God's providential care? When your faith is tested, who or what helps you? Pray, "Help me, O mighty God, to see how you have helped when enemies have marched up to the gate of my life. I thank you that when I am threatened or discouraged, attacked or misunderstood, you are my help and shield. Amen."

See Meeting God in Prayer

Birthing the New

2 KINGS 19.3–7

Just as the nation is being re-born, a threat arises. Hezekiah laments, likening the situation to a woman without the "strength to bring . . . forth" her child; he turns to the Lord and his prophet Isaiah. God says, "Do not be afraid." When has opposition threatened to stop something you were trying to accomplish? When have you felt so discouraged that you did not have "the strength to bring . . . forth"? What gave you strength to carry on? Prayerfully imagine yourself in one of those past situations, or in a current dilemma; ask God to show you where "the strength to bring . . . forth" can be found. Repeat quietly, as you envision the situation, "Thus says the LORD: 'Do not be afraid.' "

See Meeting God in Prayer

king had left Lachish. [9]When the king[a] heard concerning King Tirhakah of Ethiopia,[b] "See, he has set out to fight against you," he sent messengers again to Hezekiah, saying, [10]"Thus shall you speak to King Hezekiah of Judah: Do not let your God on whom you rely deceive you by promising that Jerusalem will not be given into the hand of the king of Assyria. [11]See, you have heard what the kings of Assyria have done to all lands, destroying them utterly. Shall you be delivered? [12]Have the gods of the nations delivered them, the nations that my predecessors destroyed, Gozan, Haran, Rezeph, and the people of Eden who were in Telassar? [13]Where is the king of Hamath, the king of Arpad, the king of the city of Sepharvaim, the king of Hena, or the king of Ivvah?"

Hezekiah's Prayer

14 Hezekiah received the letter from the hand of the messengers and read it; then Hezekiah went up to the house of the LORD and spread it before the LORD. [15]And Hezekiah prayed before the LORD, and said: "O LORD the God of Israel, who are enthroned above the cherubim, you are God, you alone, of all the kingdoms of the earth; you have made heaven and earth. [16]Incline your ear, O LORD, and hear; open your eyes, O LORD, and see; hear the words of Sennacherib, which he has sent to mock the living God. [17]Truly, O LORD, the kings of Assyria have laid waste the nations and their lands, [18]and have hurled their gods into the fire, though they were no gods but the work of human hands—wood and stone—and so they were destroyed. [19]So now, O LORD our God, save us, I pray you, from his hand, so that all the kingdoms of the earth may know that you, O LORD, are God alone."

20 Then Isaiah son of Amoz sent to Hezekiah, saying, "Thus says the LORD, the God of Israel: I have heard your prayer to me about King Sennacherib of Assyria. [21]This is the word that the LORD has spoken concerning him:

> She despises you, she scorns you—
>   virgin daughter Zion;
> she tosses her head—behind your back,
>   daughter Jerusalem.

[22]   "Whom have you mocked and reviled?
>   Against whom have you raised your voice
> and haughtily lifted your eyes?
>   Against the Holy One of Israel!

[23]   By your messengers you have mocked the Lord,
>   and you have said, 'With my many chariots
> I have gone up the heights of the mountains,
>   to the far recesses of Lebanon;
> I felled its tallest cedars,
>   its choicest cypresses;
> I entered its farthest retreat,
>   its densest forest.

[24]   I dug wells
>   and drank foreign waters,
> I dried up with the sole of my foot
>   all the streams of Egypt.'

a Heb *he*   *b* Or *Nubia*; Heb *Cush*

25 "Have you not heard
      that I determined it long ago?
I planned from days of old
      what now I bring to pass,
that you should make fortified cities
      crash into heaps of ruins,
26 while their inhabitants, shorn of strength,
      are dismayed and confounded;
they have become like plants of the field
      and like tender grass,
like grass on the housetops,
      blighted before it is grown.

27 "But I know your rising*a* and your sitting,
      your going out and coming in,
      and your raging against me.
28 Because you have raged against me
      and your arrogance has come to my ears,
I will put my hook in your nose
      and my bit in your mouth;
I will turn you back on the way
      by which you came.

29 "And this shall be the sign for you: This year you shall eat what grows of itself, and in the second year what springs from that; then in the third year sow, reap, plant vineyards, and eat their fruit. ³⁰The surviving remnant of the house of Judah shall again take root downward, and bear fruit upward; ³¹for from Jerusalem a remnant shall go out, and from Mount Zion a band of survivors. The zeal of the LORD of hosts will do this.

32 "Therefore thus says the LORD concerning the king of Assyria: He shall not come into this city, shoot an arrow there, come before it with a shield, or cast up a siege ramp against it. ³³By the way that he came, by the same he shall return; he shall not come into this city, says the LORD. ³⁴For I will defend this city to save it, for my own sake and for the sake of my servant David."

Sennacherib's Defeat and Death

35 That very night the angel of the LORD set out and struck down one hundred eighty-five thousand in the camp of the Assyrians; when morning dawned, they were all dead bodies. ³⁶Then King Sennacherib of Assyria left, went home, and lived at Nineveh. ³⁷As he was worshiping in the house of his god Nisroch, his sons Adrammelech and Sharezer killed him with the sword, and they escaped into the land of Ararat. His son Esar-haddon succeeded him.

Hezekiah's Illness

20 In those days Hezekiah became sick and was at the point of death. The prophet Isaiah son of Amoz came to him, and said to him, "Thus says the LORD: Set your house in order, for you shall die; you shall not recover." ²Then Hezekiah turned his face to the wall and prayed to the LORD: ³"Remember now, O LORD, I implore you, how I have walked before you in faithfulness with a

---

A Fruitful Remnant

2 KINGS 19.30–31

God promises that a small remnant will "take root" after the fall of David's kingdom, and that from the exiles he will bring new growth for the nation's future. Even a small thing, held in faith, can be the sprout of new life. God can use the bare remnants of a relationship, small hopes, simple deeds and small groups for renewal.

When you look back over your life, how have you received hope and inspiration from such small things? In what ways has God used a small remnant of faithful people to bring new life to you—to your family, church and community? Give thanks: "Loving God, help me to know how to offer small things to you so that you can use them to bring new life. I thank you that you use humble things to do great things for you."

See Meeting God in Service

A King's Desperation and Vanity

2 KINGS 20.1–14

Hezekiah turns to God in his illness and is granted an additional fifteen years of life. Safely delivered, he now shows off his wealth to impress envoys from Babylon. How quickly he turns God's blessings into a show of vanity! He prays for healing, he gets well and then, in all-too-human fashion, Hezekiah ignores the source of all goodness!

Think back to a significant illness in your life or in the life of a loved one. Remember your journey and how you sought after, and received, spiritual or physical recovery. Perhaps you are still longing for recovery. What have you learned through your experience about your relationship to God, to your family and to your friends? What changes in outlook and behavior did you make?

See *Meeting God in Service*

whole heart, and have done what is good in your sight." Hezekiah wept bitterly. ⁴Before Isaiah had gone out of the middle court, the word of the LORD came to him: ⁵"Turn back, and say to Hezekiah prince of my people, Thus says the LORD, the God of your ancestor David: I have heard your prayer, I have seen your tears; indeed, I will heal you; on the third day you shall go up to the house of the LORD. ⁶I will add fifteen years to your life. I will deliver you and this city out of the hand of the king of Assyria; I will defend this city for my own sake and for my servant David's sake." ⁷Then Isaiah said, "Bring a lump of figs. Let them take it and apply it to the boil, so that he may recover."

8 Hezekiah said to Isaiah, "What shall be the sign that the LORD will heal me, and that I shall go up to the house of the LORD on the third day?" ⁹Isaiah said, "This is the sign to you from the LORD, that the LORD will do the thing that he has promised: the shadow has now advanced ten intervals; shall it retreat ten intervals?" ¹⁰Hezekiah answered, "It is normal for the shadow to lengthen ten intervals; rather let the shadow retreat ten intervals." ¹¹The prophet Isaiah cried to the LORD; and he brought the shadow back the ten intervals, by which the sun[a] had declined on the dial of Ahaz.

Envoys from Babylon

12 At that time King Merodach-baladan son of Baladan of Babylon sent envoys with letters and a present to Hezekiah, for he had heard that Hezekiah had been sick. ¹³Hezekiah welcomed them;[b] he showed them all his treasure house, the silver, the gold, the spices, the precious oil, his armory, all that was found in his storehouses; there was nothing in his house or in all his realm that Hezekiah did not show them. ¹⁴Then the prophet Isaiah came to King Hezekiah, and said to him, "What did these men say? From where did they come to you?" Hezekiah answered, "They have come from a far country, from Babylon." ¹⁵He said, "What have they seen in your house?" Hezekiah answered, "They have seen all that is in my house; there is nothing in my storehouses that I did not show them."

16 Then Isaiah said to Hezekiah, "Hear the word of the LORD: ¹⁷Days are coming when all that is in your house, and that which your ancestors have stored up until this day, shall be carried to Babylon; nothing shall be left, says the LORD. ¹⁸Some of your own sons who are born to you shall be taken away; they shall be eunuchs in the palace of the king of Babylon." ¹⁹Then Hezekiah said to Isaiah, "The word of the LORD that you have spoken is good." For he thought, "Why not, if there will be peace and security in my days?"

Death of Hezekiah

20 The rest of the deeds of Hezekiah, all his power, how he made the pool and the conduit and brought water into the city, are they not written in the Book of the Annals of the Kings of Judah? ²¹Hezekiah slept with his ancestors; and his son Manasseh succeeded him.

---

a Syr See Isa 38.8 and Tg: Heb *it*   b Gk Vg Syr: Heb *When Hezekiah heard about them*

Manasseh Reigns over Judah

21 Manasseh was twelve years old when he began to reign; he reigned fifty-five years in Jerusalem. His mother's name was Hephzibah. ²He did what was evil in the sight of the LORD, following the abominable practices of the nations that the LORD drove out before the people of Israel. ³For he rebuilt the high places that his father Hezekiah had destroyed; he erected altars for Baal, made a sacred pole,ᵃ as King Ahab of Israel had done, worshiped all the host of heaven, and served them. ⁴He built altars in the house of the LORD, of which the LORD had said, "In Jerusalem I will put my name." ⁵He built altars for all the host of heaven in the two courts of the house of the LORD. ⁶He made his son pass through fire; he practiced soothsaying and augury, and dealt with mediums and with wizards. He did much evil in the sight of the LORD, provoking him to anger. ⁷The carved image of Asherah that he had made he set in the house of which the LORD said to David and to his son Solomon, "In this house, and in Jerusalem, which I have chosen out of all the tribes of Israel, I will put my name forever; ⁸I will not cause the feet of Israel to wander any more out of the land that I gave to their ancestors, if only they will be careful to do according to all that I have commanded them, and according to all the law that my servant Moses commanded them." ⁹But they did not listen; Manasseh misled them to do more evil than the nations had done that the LORD destroyed before the people of Israel.

10 The LORD said by his servants the prophets, ¹¹"Because King Manasseh of Judah has committed these abominations, has done things more wicked than all that the Amorites did, who were before him, and has caused Judah also to sin with his idols; ¹²therefore thus says the LORD, the God of Israel, I am bringing upon Jerusalem and Judah such evil that the ears of everyone who hears of it will tingle. ¹³I will stretch over Jerusalem the measuring line for Samaria, and the plummet for the house of Ahab; I will wipe Jerusalem as one wipes a dish, wiping it and turning it upside down. ¹⁴I will cast off the remnant of my heritage, and give them into the hand of their enemies; they shall become a prey and a spoil to all their enemies, ¹⁵because they have done what is evil in my sight and have provoked me to anger, since the day their ancestors came out of Egypt, even to this day."

16 Moreover Manasseh shed very much innocent blood, until he had filled Jerusalem from one end to another, besides the sin that he caused Judah to sin so that they did what was evil in the sight of the LORD.

17 Now the rest of the acts of Manasseh, all that he did, and the sin that he committed, are they not written in the Book of the Annals of the Kings of Judah? ¹⁸Manasseh slept with his ancestors, and was buried in the garden of his house, in the garden of Uzza. His son Amon succeeded him.

Amon Reigns over Judah

19 Amon was twenty-two years old when he began to reign; he reigned two years in Jerusalem. His mother's

---

True Treasures

2 KINGS 20.12–15

Recovered from his illness, Hezekiah takes pleasure and pride in flaunting his great treasures to the Babylonian envoys.

Prayerfully wander through your own house or around your property, noting all your treasures, giving thanks where appropriate as you remember how these objects came into your life. Then sit quietly and make a list of the less tangible treasures you possess—relationships, values, ideas, skills—that cannot be taken away by fire, flood or violence. Spend time giving thanks for all these treasures, inner and outer, and ask for guidance in how to pass them on to specific people in the next generation.

See Meeting God in Everyday Life

The Measuring Line

2 KINGS 21.13–26

As Manasseh and Amon reverse the good of King Hezekiah's reforms, God declares that he will measure Judah with a "measuring line." What do you think the divine measuring line is comprised of? What are the minimum standards for survival? What are the divine Judge's standards for a truly godly nation? What might be uppermost in the mind of the Shepherd of nations regarding the needs of the world today? How does God communicate his standards to the leaders and peoples of nations in our day? In what ways are God's judgments shown to a nation? As you pray for God's will to be done "on earth as it is in heaven," what is most important to pray for today? Pray that prayer now.

See Meeting God in Prayer

name was Meshullemeth daughter of Haruz of Jotbah. [20]He did what was evil in the sight of the LORD, as his father Manasseh had done. [21]He walked in all the way in which his father walked, served the idols that his father served, and worshiped them; [22]he abandoned the LORD, the God of his ancestors, and did not walk in the way of the LORD. [23]The servants of Amon conspired against him, and killed the king in his house. [24]But the people of the land killed all those who had conspired against King Amon, and the people of the land made his son Josiah king in place of him. [25]Now the rest of the acts of Amon that he did, are they not written in the Book of the Annals of the Kings of Judah? [26]He was buried in his tomb in the garden of Uzza; then his son Josiah succeeded him.

Josiah Reigns over Judah

22 Josiah was eight years old when he began to reign; he reigned thirty-one years in Jerusalem. His mother's name was Jedidah daughter of Adaiah of Bozkath. [2]He did what was right in the sight of the LORD, and walked in all the way of his father David; he did not turn aside to the right or to the left.

Hilkiah Finds the Book of the Law

3 In the eighteenth year of King Josiah, the king sent Shaphan son of Azaliah, son of Meshullam, the secretary, to the house of the LORD, saying, [4]"Go up to the high priest Hilkiah, and have him count the entire sum of the money that has been brought into the house of the LORD, which the keepers of the threshold have collected from the people; [5]let it be given into the hand of the workers who have the oversight of the house of the LORD; let them give it to the workers who are at the house of the LORD, repairing the house, [6]that is, to the carpenters, to the builders, to the masons; and let them use it to buy timber and quarried stone to repair the house. [7]But no accounting shall be asked from them for the money that is delivered into their hand, for they deal honestly."

8 The high priest Hilkiah said to Shaphan the secretary, "I have found the book of the law in the house of the LORD." When Hilkiah gave the book to Shaphan, he read it. [9]Then Shaphan the secretary came to the king, and reported to the king, "Your servants have emptied out the money that was found in the house, and have delivered it into the hand of the workers who have oversight of the house of the LORD." [10]Shaphan the secretary informed the king, "The priest Hilkiah has given me a book." Shaphan then read it aloud to the king.

11 When the king heard the words of the book of the law, he tore his clothes. [12]Then the king commanded the priest Hilkiah, Ahikam son of Shaphan, Achbor son of Micaiah, Shaphan the secretary, and the king's servant Asaiah, saying, [13]"Go, inquire of the LORD for me, for the people, and for all Judah, concerning the words of this book that has been found; for great is the wrath of the LORD that is kindled against us, because our ancestors did not obey the words of this book, to do according to all that is written concerning us."

14 So the priest Hilkiah, Ahikam, Achbor, Shaphan, and Asaiah went to the prophetess Huldah the wife of Shallum

son of Tikvah, son of Harhas, keeper of the wardrobe; she resided in Jerusalem in the Second Quarter, where they consulted her. ¹⁵She declared to them, "Thus says the LORD, the God of Israel: Tell the man who sent you to me, ¹⁶Thus says the LORD, I will indeed bring disaster on this place and on its inhabitants—all the words of the book that the king of Judah has read. ¹⁷Because they have abandoned me and have made offerings to other gods, so that they have provoked me to anger with all the work of their hands, therefore my wrath will be kindled against this place, and it will not be quenched. ¹⁸But as to the king of Judah, who sent you to inquire of the LORD, thus shall you say to him, Thus says the LORD, the God of Israel: Regarding the words that you have heard, ¹⁹because your heart was penitent, and you humbled yourself before the LORD, when you heard how I spoke against this place, and against its inhabitants, that they should become a desolation and a curse, and because you have torn your clothes and wept before me, I also have heard you, says the LORD. ²⁰Therefore, I will gather you to your ancestors, and you shall be gathered to your grave in peace; your eyes shall not see all the disaster that I will bring on this place." They took the message back to the king.

Josiah's Reformation

23 Then the king directed that all the elders of Judah and Jerusalem should be gathered to him. ²The king went up to the house of the LORD, and with him went all the people of Judah, all the inhabitants of Jerusalem, the priests, the prophets, and all the people, both small and great; he read in their hearing all the words of the book of the covenant that had been found in the house of the LORD. ³The king stood by the pillar and made a covenant before the LORD, to follow the LORD, keeping his commandments, his decrees, and his statutes, with all his heart and all his soul, to perform the words of this covenant that were written in this book. All the people joined in the covenant.

4 The king commanded the high priest Hilkiah, the priests of the second order, and the guardians of the threshold, to bring out of the temple of the LORD all the vessels made for Baal, for Asherah, and for all the host of heaven; he burned them outside Jerusalem in the fields of the Kidron, and carried their ashes to Bethel. ⁵He deposed the idolatrous priests whom the kings of Judah had ordained to make offerings in the high places at the cities of Judah and around Jerusalem; those also who made offerings to Baal, to the sun, the moon, the constellations, and all the host of the heavens. ⁶He brought out the image of*ᵃ* Asherah from the house of the LORD, outside Jerusalem, to the Wadi Kidron, burned it at the Wadi Kidron, beat it to dust and threw the dust of it upon the graves of the common people. ⁷He broke down the houses of the male temple prostitutes that were in the house of the LORD, where the women did weaving for Asherah. ⁸He brought all the priests out of the towns of Judah, and defiled the high places where the priests had made offerings, from Geba to Beer-sheba; he broke down the high places of the gates

a Heb lacks *image of*

Hearing and Response

2 KINGS 22.8–20

Josiah begins following God's way from the beginning of his reign, when he was eight years old. At age twenty-six, he reads the newly found scroll, probably the book of Deuteronomy, and responds with lament and with readiness to institute reforms. His quick repentance speaks well of his childhood spiritual formation. Think about your childhood. How did you hear about God? Were you schooled in the church? If so, what kinds of memories do you have about that experience and those who taught you? How was your spiritual life nurtured in other ways? What books or ideas have helped you grow and develop more mature ideas about God?

See Meeting God in Worship

Celebrating the Passover

2 KINGS 23.21

Turn to Deuteronomy 16 and read the instructions for keeping the passover. It had been generations since Israel celebrated this yearly feast in the manner the "lost book" demanded. God rejoices in celebration, and the Passover feast commemorates God's saving power to the people of Israel.

God wants us to live life and have life to the fullest. Which celebrations do you enjoy most? How does that day of celebration demonstrate God's goodness? What brings you joy that might deserve its own special celebration? Make a list of events you have celebrated recently. Make another list of events you want to celebrate and make specific plans to do so!

See Meeting God in Worship

that were at the entrance of the gate of Joshua the governor of the city, which were on the left at the gate of the city. [9]The priests of the high places, however, did not come up to the altar of the LORD in Jerusalem, but ate unleavened bread among their kindred. [10]He defiled Topheth, which is in the valley of Ben-hinnom, so that no one would make a son or a daughter pass through fire as an offering to Molech. [11]He removed the horses that the kings of Judah had dedicated to the sun, at the entrance to the house of the LORD, by the chamber of the eunuch Nathan-melech, which was in the precincts;[a] then he burned the chariots of the sun with fire. [12]The altars on the roof of the upper chamber of Ahaz, which the kings of Judah had made, and the altars that Manasseh had made in the two courts of the house of the LORD, he pulled down from there and broke in pieces, and threw the rubble into the Wadi Kidron. [13]The king defiled the high places that were east of Jerusalem, to the south of the Mount of Destruction, which King Solomon of Israel had built for Astarte the abomination of the Sidonians, for Chemosh the abomination of Moab, and for Milcom the abomination of the Ammonites. [14]He broke the pillars in pieces, cut down the sacred poles,[b] and covered the sites with human bones.

15 Moreover, the altar at Bethel, the high place erected by Jeroboam son of Nebat, who caused Israel to sin—he pulled down that altar along with the high place. He burned the high place, crushing it to dust; he also burned the sacred pole.[c] [16]As Josiah turned, he saw the tombs there on the mount; and he sent and took the bones out of the tombs, and burned them on the altar, and defiled it, according to the word of the LORD that the man of God proclaimed,[d] when Jeroboam stood by the altar at the festival; he turned and looked up at the tomb of the man of God who had predicted these things. [17]Then he said, "What is that monument that I see?" The people of the city told him, "It is the tomb of the man of God who came from Judah and predicted these things that you have done against the altar at Bethel." [18]He said, "Let him rest; let no one move his bones." So they let his bones alone, with the bones of the prophet who came out of Samaria. [19]Moreover, Josiah removed all the shrines of the high places that were in the towns of Samaria, which kings of Israel had made, provoking the LORD to anger; he did to them just as he had done at Bethel. [20]He slaughtered on the altars all the priests of the high places who were there, and burned human bones on them. Then he returned to Jerusalem.

The Passover Celebrated

21 The king commanded all the people, "Keep the passover to the LORD your God as prescribed in this book of the covenant." [22]No such passover had been kept since the days of the judges who judged Israel, even during all the days of the kings of Israel and of the kings of Judah; [23]but in the eighteenth year of King Josiah this passover was kept to the LORD in Jerusalem.

24 Moreover Josiah put away the mediums, wizards, teraphim,[e] idols, and all the abominations that were seen

---

a Meaning of Heb uncertain   *b* Heb *Asherim*   *c* Heb *Asherah*
d Gk: Heb *proclaimed, who had predicted these things*   *e* Or *household gods*

in the land of Judah and in Jerusalem, so that he established the words of the law that were written in the book that the priest Hilkiah had found in the house of the LORD. ²⁵Before him there was no king like him, who turned to the LORD with all his heart, with all his soul, and with all his might, according to all the law of Moses; nor did any like him arise after him.

26 Still the LORD did not turn from the fierceness of his great wrath, by which his anger was kindled against Judah, because of all the provocations with which Manasseh had provoked him. ²⁷The LORD said, "I will remove Judah also out of my sight, as I have removed Israel; and I will reject this city that I have chosen, Jerusalem, and the house of which I said, My name shall be there."

Josiah Dies in Battle

28 Now the rest of the acts of Josiah, and all that he did, are they not written in the Book of the Annals of the Kings of Judah? ²⁹In his days Pharaoh Neco king of Egypt went up to the king of Assyria to the river Euphrates. King Josiah went to meet him; but when Pharaoh Neco met him at Megiddo, he killed him. ³⁰His servants carried him dead in a chariot from Megiddo, brought him to Jerusalem, and buried him in his own tomb. The people of the land took Jehoahaz son of Josiah, anointed him, and made him king in place of his father.

Reign and Captivity of Jehoahaz

31 Jehoahaz was twenty-three years old when he began to reign; he reigned three months in Jerusalem. His mother's name was Hamutal daughter of Jeremiah of Libnah. ³²He did what was evil in the sight of the LORD, just as his ancestors had done. ³³Pharaoh Neco confined him at Riblah in the land of Hamath, so that he might not reign in Jerusalem, and imposed tribute on the land of one hundred talents of silver and a talent of gold. ³⁴Pharaoh Neco made Eliakim son of Josiah king in place of his father Josiah, and changed his name to Jehoiakim. But he took Jehoahaz away; he came to Egypt, and died there. ³⁵Jehoiakim gave the silver and the gold to Pharaoh, but he taxed the land in order to meet Pharaoh's demand for money. He exacted the silver and the gold from the people of the land, from all according to their assessment, to give it to Pharaoh Neco.

Jehoiakim Reigns over Judah

36 Jehoiakim was twenty-five years old when he began to reign; he reigned eleven years in Jerusalem. His mother's name was Zebidah daughter of Pedaiah of Rumah. ³⁷He did what was evil in the sight of the LORD, just as all his ancestors had done.

Judah Overrun by Enemies

24 In his days King Nebuchadnezzar of Babylon came up; Jehoiakim became his servant for three years; then he turned and rebelled against him. ²The LORD sent against him bands of the Chaldeans, bands of the Arameans, bands of the Moabites, and bands of the Ammonites; he sent them against Judah to destroy it, according to the word of the LORD that he spoke by his

Service to God

2 KINGS 23.21–25

"Men and women, rich and poor must . . . walk before God in the same wise and holy spirit, in the same denial of all vain tempers, and in the same discipline and care of their souls; not only because they have all the same rational nature and are servants of the same God, but because they all need the same holiness to make them fit for the same happiness to which they are called. It is therefore absolutely necessary for all Christians, whether men or women, to consider themselves as persons that are devoted to holiness and so order their common ways of life by such rules of reason and piety as may turn it into continual service unto Almighty God."

—WILLIAM LAW,
A Serious Call to a Devout and Holy Life

A New World Power

2 KINGS 24.1–7

Now Babylon, after defeating Assyria and Egypt, reduces Judah—once triumphant—to vassal status. As this story draws to a close, its lessons are clear: Power is fleeting. Without God, no nation can endure for long. Yet nations and individuals still strive after the fleeting "number one" status, seeking temporal power rather than investing in things that last.

When have you wanted to be first? How did this desire or accomplishment affect your relationship to God—to other people? What values do you feel are more enduring than the rewards of being number one?

servants the prophets. ³Surely this came upon Judah at the command of the LORD, to remove them out of his sight, for the sins of Manasseh, for all that he had committed, ⁴and also for the innocent blood that he had shed; for he filled Jerusalem with innocent blood, and the LORD was not willing to pardon. ⁵Now the rest of the deeds of Jehoiakim, and all that he did, are they not written in the Book of the Annals of the Kings of Judah? ⁶So Jehoiakim slept with his ancestors; then his son Jehoiachin succeeded him. ⁷The king of Egypt did not come again out of his land, for the king of Babylon had taken over all that belonged to the king of Egypt from the Wadi of Egypt to the River Euphrates.

Reign and Captivity of Jehoiachin

8 Jehoiachin was eighteen years old when he began to reign; he reigned three months in Jerusalem. His mother's name was Nehushta daughter of Elnathan of Jerusalem. ⁹He did what was evil in the sight of the LORD, just as his father had done.

10 At that time the servants of King Nebuchadnezzar of Babylon came up to Jerusalem, and the city was besieged. ¹¹King Nebuchadnezzar of Babylon came to the city, while his servants were besieging it; ¹²King Jehoiachin of Judah gave himself up to the king of Babylon, himself, his mother, his servants, his officers, and his palace officials. The king of Babylon took him prisoner in the eighth year of his reign.

Capture of Jerusalem

13 He carried off all the treasures of the house of the LORD, and the treasures of the king's house; he cut in pieces all the vessels of gold in the temple of the LORD, which King Solomon of Israel had made, all this as the LORD had foretold. ¹⁴He carried away all Jerusalem, all the officials, all the warriors, ten thousand captives, all the artisans and the smiths; no one remained, except the poorest people of the land. ¹⁵He carried away Jehoiachin to Babylon; the king's mother, the king's wives, his officials, and the elite of the land, he took into captivity from Jerusalem to Babylon. ¹⁶The king of Babylon brought captive to Babylon all the men of valor, seven thousand, the artisans and the smiths, one thousand, all of them strong and fit for war. ¹⁷The king of Babylon made Mattaniah, Jehoiachin's uncle, king in his place, and changed his name to Zedekiah.

Zedekiah Reigns over Judah

18 Zedekiah was twenty-one years old when he began to reign; he reigned eleven years in Jerusalem. His mother's name was Hamutal daughter of Jeremiah of Libnah. ¹⁹He did what was evil in the sight of the LORD, just as Jehoiakim had done. ²⁰Indeed, Jerusalem and Judah so angered the LORD that he expelled them from his presence.

The Fall and Captivity of Judah

25 Zedekiah rebelled against the king of Babylon. ¹And in the ninth year of his reign, in the tenth month, on the tenth day of the month, King Nebuchadnezzar of

Babylon came with all his army against Jerusalem, and laid siege to it; they built siegeworks against it all around. ²So the city was besieged until the eleventh year of King Zedekiah. ³On the ninth day of the fourth month the famine became so severe in the city that there was no food for the people of the land. ⁴Then a breach was made in the city wall;ᵃ the king with all the soldiers fledᵇ by night by the way of the gate between the two walls, by the king's garden, though the Chaldeans were all around the city. They went in the direction of the Arabah. ⁵But the army of the Chaldeans pursued the king, and overtook him in the plains of Jericho; all his army was scattered, deserting him. ⁶Then they captured the king and brought him up to the king of Babylon at Riblah, who passed sentence on him. ⁷They slaughtered the sons of Zedekiah before his eyes, then put out the eyes of Zedekiah; they bound him in fetters and took him to Babylon.

8 In the fifth month, on the seventh day of the month—which was the nineteenth year of King Nebuchadnezzar, king of Babylon—Nebuzaradan, the captain of the bodyguard, a servant of the king of Babylon, came to Jerusalem. ⁹He burned the house of the LORD, the king's house, and all the houses of Jerusalem; every great house he burned down. ¹⁰All the army of the Chaldeans who were with the captain of the guard broke down the walls around Jerusalem. ¹¹Nebuzaradan the captain of the guard carried into exile the rest of the people who were left in the city and the deserters who had defected to the king of Babylon—all the rest of the population. ¹²But the captain of the guard left some of the poorest people of the land to be vinedressers and tillers of the soil.

13 The bronze pillars that were in the house of the LORD, as well as the stands and the bronze sea that were in the house of the LORD, the Chaldeans broke in pieces, and carried the bronze to Babylon. ¹⁴They took away the pots, the shovels, the snuffers, the dishes for incense, and all the bronze vessels used in the temple service, ¹⁵as well as the firepans and the basins. What was made of gold the captain of the guard took away for the gold, and what was made of silver, for the silver. ¹⁶As for the two pillars, the one sea, and the stands, which Solomon had made for the house of the LORD, the bronze of all these vessels was beyond weighing. ¹⁷The height of the one pillar was eighteen cubits, and on it was a bronze capital; the height of the capital was three cubits; latticework and pomegranates, all of bronze, were on the capital all around. The second pillar had the same, with the latticework.

18 The captain of the guard took the chief priest Seraiah, the second priest Zephaniah, and the three guardians of the threshold; ¹⁹from the city he took an officer who had been in command of the soldiers, and five men of the king's council who were found in the city; the secretary who was the commander of the army who mustered the people of the land; and sixty men of the people of the land who were found in the city. ²⁰Nebuzaradan the captain of the guard took them, and brought them to the king of Babylon at Riblah. ²¹The king of Babylon struck them down

Broken Walls

2 KINGS 25.10

The enemy tears down Jerusalem's walls as a final act of humiliation. In Biblical times, a city without walls was doomed, unprotected from wild animals, marauders and enemies.

We often think of walls as being symbolic of that which protects us from harm, shelters the vulnerable aspects of our soul, and marks the emotional boundaries between people. But walls have the potential to divide us destructively.

Reflect on your key relationships with others. How does your behavior respect healthy boundaries between yourself and others? In what ways may you be trespassing those boundaries? Are there unhelpful walls that need to be torn down? After making a list of these walls, prayerfully consider how to strengthen the life-giving walls and dismantle the divisive ones.

See Meeting God in Community

---

a Heb lacks *wall*   b Gk Compare Jer 39.4; 52.7: Heb lacks *the king* and lacks *fled*

Expelled From God's Presence

2 KINGS 25.27–30

After ignoring the warnings of the prophets for so long, the people of Jerusalem and Judah are carried to Babylon in exile, cast out of God's presence (see 24.20).

Exile has become a powerful symbol in Jewish liturgy and in Christian prayer of the experience of God's hiddenness. Sing or say prayerfully the hymn, "O come, O come, Emmanuel, and ransom captive Israel, that mourns in lowly exile here, until the Son of God appear." As you sing or speak the words again and again, remember situations in which God seemed hidden from you. Bring to mind similar situations in the lives of those you know. Conclude with the refrain: "Rejoice! Rejoice! Emmanuel shall come to thee, O Israel!"

See Meeting God in Worship

and put them to death at Riblah in the land of Hamath. So Judah went into exile out of its land.

Gedaliah Made Governor of Judah

22 He appointed Gedaliah son of Ahikam son of Shaphan as governor over the people who remained in the land of Judah, whom King Nebuchadnezzar of Babylon had left. ²³Now when all the captains of the forces and their men heard that the king of Babylon had appointed Gedaliah as governor, they came with their men to Gedaliah at Mizpah, namely, Ishmael son of Nethaniah, Johanan son of Kareah, Seraiah son of Tanhumeth the Netophathite, and Jaazaniah son of the Maacathite. ²⁴Gedaliah swore to them and their men, saying, "Do not be afraid because of the Chaldean officials; live in the land, serve the king of Babylon, and it shall be well with you." ²⁵But in the seventh month, Ishmael son of Nethaniah son of Elishama, of the royal family, came with ten men; they struck down Gedaliah so that he died, along with the Judeans and Chaldeans who were with him at Mizpah. ²⁶Then all the people, high and low,ᵃ and the captains of the forces set out and went to Egypt; for they were afraid of the Chaldeans.

Jehoiachin Released from Prison

27 In the thirty-seventh year of the exile of King Jehoiachin of Judah, in the twelfth month, on the twenty-seventh day of the month, King Evil-merodach of Babylon, in the year that he began to reign, released King Jehoiachin of Judah from prison; ²⁸he spoke kindly to him, and gave him a seat above the other seats of the kings who were with him in Babylon. ²⁹So Jehoiachin put aside his prison clothes. Every day of his life he dined regularly in the king's presence. ³⁰For his allowance, a regular allowance was given him by the king, a portion every day, as long as he lived.

a Or young and old

1 CHRONICLES

The People of God

KEY VERSE:

So all the elders of Israel came to the king at Hebron, and David made a covenant with them at Hebron before the LORD. And they anointed David king over Israel, according to the word of the LORD by Samuel.—1 Chronicles 11.3

If you glance through this book, you will notice the large number of names. Everywhere are long lists of names: the generations from Adam to Abraham, the many families descended from the twelve sons of Jacob, the officials of David's court, the priests and Levites who served before the Lord. So many people!

Some of the names have Biblical stories connected to them. Some we know from other references. But most are no more than names and titles, yet each name represents one of God's people. Each had a unique role to play in the history of Israel. No doubt many would be surprised that anyone remembers them at all today, three thousand years later.

They are remembered because God still has faithful followers who know they are part of a long tradition. God's people still tell the old, old stories. As people of God—the church—we continue to worship God with prayer, song, musical instruments and dance. We continue to organize and take on special responsibilities to deal with practical matters. We continue to struggle to know how to be faithful in a confusing and often hostile world.

As you read this book, consider your place among God's people. How are you tied into the tradition through your family and your church? What is your special role within your church or within the church as a whole? To what deeper involvement is God calling you?

"At all times and in every race, anyone who fears God and does what is right has been acceptable to him [see Acts 10.35]. God has, however, willed to make people holy and save them, not as individuals without any bond or link between them, but rather to make them into a people who might acknowledge him and serve him in holiness. He therefore chose the Israelite race to be his own people and established a covenant with it. He gradually instructed this people—in its history manifesting both himself and the decree of his will—and made it holy unto himself."

—SECOND VATICAN COUNCIL, *Lumen Gentium*, Chapter 2

Children of Abraham

1 CHRONICLES 1.28

Here is a reminder that the people of God, the children of Abraham, include both the descendants of Isaac (the Jews and, by adoption, Christians) and the descendants of Ishmael (the Arabs). The same point is brought out in the Koran. The struggles in the Middle East today, then, are family quarrels. With a globe or atlas in front of you, spend some time in prayer for all the children of Abraham, that their fighting may cease and that they may rediscover their unity as Abraham's children.

See Meeting God in Community

From Adam to Abraham

1 Adam, Seth, Enosh; ²Kenan, Mahalalel, Jared; ³Enoch, Methuselah, Lamech; ⁴Noah, Shem, Ham, and Japheth.

5 The descendants of Japheth: Gomer, Magog, Madai, Javan, Tubal, Meshech, and Tiras. ⁶The descendants of Gomer: Ashkenaz, Diphath,ᵃ and Togarmah. ⁷The descendants of Javan: Elishah, Tarshish, Kittim, and Rodanim.ᵇ

8 The descendants of Ham: Cush, Egypt, Put, and Canaan. ⁹The descendants of Cush: Seba, Havilah, Sabta, Raama, and Sabteca. The descendants of Raamah: Sheba and Dedan. ¹⁰Cush became the father of Nimrod; he was the first to be a mighty one on the earth.

11 Egypt became the father of Ludim, Anamim, Lehabim, Naphtuhim, ¹²Pathrusim, Casluhim, and Caphtorim, from whom the Philistines come.ᶜ

13 Canaan became the father of Sidon his firstborn, and Heth, ¹⁴and the Jebusites, the Amorites, the Girgashites, ¹⁵the Hivites, the Arkites, the Sinites, ¹⁶the Arvadites, the Zemarites, and the Hamathites.

17 The descendants of Shem: Elam, Asshur, Arpachshad, Lud, Aram, Uz, Hul, Gether, and Meshech.ᵈ ¹⁸Arpachshad became the father of Shelah; and Shelah became the father of Eber. ¹⁹To Eber were born two sons: the name of the one was Peleg (for in his days the earth was divided), and the name of his brother Joktan. ²⁰Joktan became the father of Almodad, Sheleph, Hazarmaveth, Jerah, ²¹Hadoram, Uzal, Diklah, ²²Ebal, Abimael, Sheba, ²³Ophir, Havilah, and Jobab; all these were the descendants of Joktan.

24 Shem, Arpachshad, Shelah; ²⁵Eber, Peleg, Reu; ²⁶Serug, Nahor, Terah; ²⁷Abram, that is, Abraham.

From Abraham to Jacob

28 The sons of Abraham: Isaac and Ishmael. ²⁹These are their genealogies: the firstborn of Ishmael, Nebaioth; and Kedar, Adbeel, Mibsam, ³⁰Mishma, Dumah, Massa, Hadad, Tema, ³¹Jetur, Naphish, and Kedemah. These are the sons of Ishmael. ³²The sons of Keturah, Abraham's concubine: she bore Zimran, Jokshan, Medan, Midian, Ishbak, and Shuah. The sons of Jokshan: Sheba and Dedan. ³³The sons of Midian: Ephah, Epher, Hanoch, Abida, and Eldaah. All these were the descendants of Keturah.

34 Abraham became the father of Isaac. The sons of Isaac: Esau and Israel. ³⁵The sons of Esau: Eliphaz, Reuel, Jeush, Jalam, and Korah. ³⁶The sons of Eliphaz: Teman, Omar, Zephi, Gatam, Kenaz, Timna, and Amalek. ³⁷The sons of Reuel: Nahath, Zerah, Shammah, and Mizzah.

38 The sons of Seir: Lotan, Shobal, Zibeon, Anah, Dishon, Ezer, and Dishan. ³⁹The sons of Lotan: Hori and Homam; and Lotan's sister was Timna. ⁴⁰The sons of Sho-

a Gen 10.3 *Ripath*; See Gk Vg   *b* Gen 10.4 *Dodanim*; See Syr Vg
c Heb *Casluhim, from which the Philistines come, Caphtorim*; See Am 9.7, Jer 47.4   *d* *Mash* in Gen 10.23

510

bal: Alian, Manahath, Ebal, Shephi, and Onam. The sons of Zibeon: Aiah and Anah. ⁴¹The sons of Anah: Dishon. The sons of Dishon: Hamran, Eshban, Ithran, and Cheran. ⁴²The sons of Ezer: Bilhan, Zaavan, and Jaakan.ᵃ The sons of Dishan:ᵇ Uz and Aran.

43 These are the kings who reigned in the land of Edom before any king reigned over the Israelites: Bela son of Beor, whose city was called Dinhabah. ⁴⁴When Bela died, Jobab son of Zerah of Bozrah succeeded him. ⁴⁵When Jobab died, Husham of the land of the Temanites succeeded him. ⁴⁶When Husham died, Hadad son of Bedad, who defeated Midian in the country of Moab, succeeded him; and the name of his city was Avith. ⁴⁷When Hadad died, Samlah of Masrekah succeeded him. ⁴⁸When Samlah died, Shaulᶜ of Rehoboth on the Euphrates succeeded him. ⁴⁹When Shaulᶜ died, Baal-hanan son of Achbor succeeded him. ⁵⁰When Baal-hanan died, Hadad succeeded him; the name of his city was Pai, and his wife's name Mehetabel daughter of Matred, daughter of Me-zahab. ⁵¹And Hadad died.

The clansᵈ of Edom were: clansᵈ Timna, Aliah,ᵉ Jetheth, ⁵²Oholibamah, Elah, Pinon, ⁵³Kenaz, Teman, Mibzar, ⁵⁴Magdiel, and Iram; these are the clansᵈ of Edom.

The Sons of Israel and the Descendants of Judah

2 These are the sons of Israel: Reuben, Simeon, Levi, Judah, Issachar, Zebulun, ²Dan, Joseph, Benjamin, Naphtali, Gad, and Asher. ³The sons of Judah: Er, Onan, and Shelah; these three the Canaanite woman Bath-shua bore to him. Now Er, Judah's firstborn, was wicked in the sight of the LORD, and he put him to death. ⁴His daughter-in-law Tamar also bore him Perez and Zerah. Judah had five sons in all.

5 The sons of Perez: Hezron and Hamul. ⁶The sons of Zerah: Zimri, Ethan, Heman, Calcol, and Dara,ᶠ five in all. ⁷The sons of Carmi: Achar, the troubler of Israel, who transgressed in the matter of the devoted thing; ⁸and Ethan's son was Azariah.

9 The sons of Hezron, who were born to him: Jerahmeel, Ram, and Chelubai. ¹⁰Ram became the father of Amminadab, and Amminadab became the father of Nahshon, prince of the sons of Judah. ¹¹Nahshon became the father of Salma, Salma of Boaz, ¹²Boaz of Obed, Obed of Jesse. ¹³Jesse became the father of Eliab his firstborn, Abinadab the second, Shimea the third, ¹⁴Nethanel the fourth, Raddai the fifth, ¹⁵Ozem the sixth, David the seventh; ¹⁶and their sisters were Zeruiah and Abigail. The sons of Zeruiah: Abishai, Joab, and Asahel, three. ¹⁷Abigail bore Amasa, and the father of Amasa was Jether the Ishmaelite.

18 Caleb son of Hezron had children by his wife Azu-

People of God

1 CHRONICLES 2.1–55

"The people of God are the Church made visible in the world. It is they who must convince the world of the reality of the gospel or leave it unconvinced. There can be no evasion or delegation of this responsibility; the Church is either faithful as a witnessing and serving community, or it loses its vitality and its impact on an unbelieving world."

—*The Book of Discipline of the United Methodist Church* (1992)

---

a Or *and Akan*; See Gen 36.27   b See 1.38: Heb *Dishon*   c Or *Saul*
d Or *chiefs*   e Or *Alvah*; See Gen 36.40   f Or *Darda*; Compare Syr Tg some Gk Mss; See 1 Kings 4.31

Desire for Children

1 CHRONICLES 2.34–35

People have always taken extraordinary steps in order to have a child to carry on the family name. Today many couples struggle to become parents, whether through complex medical procedures or through adoption. Pray for those who seek to share their love with a child. Pray for the clinics, adoption agencies and foster care programs that help them. Pray also for all women who consider their pregnancies a problem; pray for them as they face critical choices. You might also want to thank God for the parents who gave you life or raised you or for your own children.

See Meeting God in Community

bah, and by Jerioth; these were her sons: Jesher, Shobab, and Ardon. ¹⁹When Azubah died, Caleb married Ephrath, who bore him Hur. ²⁰Hur became the father of Uri, and Uri became the father of Bezalel.

21 Afterward Hezron went in to the daughter of Machir father of Gilead, whom he married when he was sixty years old; and she bore him Segub; ²²and Segub became the father of Jair, who had twenty-three towns in the land of Gilead. ²³But Geshur and Aram took from them Havvoth-jair, Kenath and its villages, sixty towns. All these were descendants of Machir, father of Gilead. ²⁴After the death of Hezron, in Caleb-ephrathah, Abijah wife of Hezron bore him Ashhur, father of Tekoa.

25 The sons of Jerahmeel, the firstborn of Hezron: Ram his firstborn, Bunah, Oren, Ozem, and Ahijah. ²⁶Jerahmeel also had another wife, whose name was Atarah; she was the mother of Onam. ²⁷The sons of Ram, the firstborn of Jerahmeel: Maaz, Jamin, and Eker. ²⁸The sons of Onam: Shammai and Jada. The sons of Shammai: Nadab and Abishur. ²⁹The name of Abishur's wife was Abihail, and she bore him Ahban and Molid. ³⁰The sons of Nadab: Seled and Appaim; and Seled died childless. ³¹The son*ᵃ* of Appaim: Ishi. The son*ᵃ* of Ishi: Sheshan. The son*ᵃ* of Sheshan: Ahlai. ³²The sons of Jada, Shammai's brother: Jether and Jonathan; and Jether died childless. ³³The sons of Jonathan: Peleth and Zaza. These were the descendants of Jerahmeel. ³⁴Now Sheshan had no sons, only daughters; but Sheshan had an Egyptian slave, whose name was Jarha. ³⁵So Sheshan gave his daughter in marriage to his slave Jarha; and she bore him Attai. ³⁶Attai became the father of Nathan, and Nathan of Zabad. ³⁷Zabad became the father of Ephlal, and Ephlal of Obed. ³⁸Obed became the father of Jehu, and Jehu of Azariah. ³⁹Azariah became the father of Helez, and Helez of Eleasah. ⁴⁰Eleasah became the father of Sismai, and Sismai of Shallum. ⁴¹Shallum became the father of Jekamiah, and Jekamiah of Elishama.

42 The sons of Caleb brother of Jerahmeel: Mesha*ᵇ* his firstborn, who was father of Ziph. The sons of Mareshah father of Hebron. ⁴³The sons of Hebron: Korah, Tappuah, Rekem, and Shema. ⁴⁴Shema became father of Raham, father of Jorkeam; and Rekem became the father of Shammai. ⁴⁵The son of Shammai: Maon; and Maon was the father of Beth-zur. ⁴⁶Ephah also, Caleb's concubine, bore Haran, Moza, and Gazez; and Haran became the father of Gazez. ⁴⁷The sons of Jahdai: Regem, Jotham, Geshan, Pelet, Ephah, and Shaaph. ⁴⁸Maacah, Caleb's concubine, bore Sheber and Tirhanah. ⁴⁹She also bore Shaaph father of Madmannah, Sheva father of Machbenah and father of Gibea; and the daughter of Caleb was Achsah. ⁵⁰These were the descendants of Caleb.

The sons*ᶜ* of Hur the firstborn of Ephrathah: Shobal father of Kiriath-jearim, ⁵¹Salma father of Bethlehem, and

a Heb sons   *b* Gk reads *Mareshah*   *c* Gk Vg: Heb *son*

Hareph father of Beth-gader. ⁵²Shobal father of Kiriath-je-arim had other sons: Haroeh, half of the Menuhoth. ⁵³And the families of Kiriath-jearim: the Ithrites, the Puthites, the Shumathites, and the Mishraites; from these came the Zorathites and the Eshtaolites. ⁵⁴The sons of Salma: Bethlehem, the Netophathites, Atroth-beth-joab, and half of the Manahathites, the Zorites. ⁵⁵The families also of the scribes that lived at Jabez: the Tirathites, the Shimeathites, and the Sucathites. These are the Kenites who came from Hammath, father of the house of Rechab.

Descendants of David and Solomon

3 These are the sons of David who were born to him in Hebron: the firstborn Amnon, by Ahinoam the Jezreelite; the second Daniel, by Abigail the Carmelite; ²the third Absalom, son of Maacah, daughter of King Talmai of Geshur; the fourth Adonijah, son of Haggith; ³the fifth Shephatiah, by Abital; the sixth Ithream, by his wife Eglah; ⁴six were born to him in Hebron, where he reigned for seven years and six months. And he reigned thirty-three years in Jerusalem. ⁵These were born to him in Jerusalem: Shimea, Shobab, Nathan, and Solomon, four by Bath-shua, daughter of Ammiel; ⁶then Ibhar, Elishama, Eliphelet, ⁷Nogah, Nepheg, Japhia, ⁸Elishama, Eliada, and Eliphelet, nine. ⁹All these were David's sons, besides the sons of the concubines; and Tamar was their sister.

10 The descendants of Solomon: Rehoboam, Abijah his son, Asa his son, Jehoshaphat his son, ¹¹Joram his son, Ahaziah his son, Joash his son, ¹²Amaziah his son, Azariah his son, Jotham his son, ¹³Ahaz his son, Hezekiah his son, Manasseh his son, ¹⁴Amon his son, Josiah his son. ¹⁵The sons of Josiah: Johanan the firstborn, the second Jehoiakim, the third Zedekiah, the fourth Shallum. ¹⁶The descendants of Jehoiakim: Jeconiah his son, Zedekiah his son; ¹⁷and the sons of Jeconiah, the captive: Shealtiel his son, ¹⁸Malchiram, Pedaiah, Shenazzar, Jekamiah, Hoshama, and Nedabiah; ¹⁹The sons of Pedaiah: Zerubbabel and Shimei; and the sons of Zerubbabel: Meshullam and Hananiah, and Shelomith was their sister; ²⁰and Hashubah, Ohel, Berechiah, Hasadiah, and Jushab-hesed, five. ²¹The sons of Hananiah: Pelatiah and Jeshaiah, his son*ᵃ* Rephaiah, his son*ᵃ* Arnan, his son*ᵃ* Obadiah, his son*ᵃ* Shecaniah. ²²The son*ᵇ* of Shecaniah: Shemaiah. And the sons of Shemaiah: Hattush, Igal, Bariah, Neariah, and Shaphat, six. ²³The sons of Neariah: Elioenai, Hizkiah, and Azrikam, three. ²⁴The sons of Elioenai: Hodaviah, Eliashib, Pelaiah, Akkub, Johanan, Delaiah, and Anani, seven.

Descendants of Judah

4 The sons of Judah: Perez, Hezron, Carmi, Hur, and Shobal. ²Reaiah son of Shobal became the father of Jahath, and Jahath became the father of Ahumai and Lahad.

a Gk Compare Syr Vg: Heb *sons of*   *b* Heb *sons*

Jabez

This is the whole story of Jabez, who is mentioned only once in the Bible. He was born; he prayed; his prayer was heard. Look at his prayer. It is quite simple: God, help me, be with me, protect me. How many of your prayers, especially short spontaneous prayers, ask simply for God's help, presence or protection? You might pray with Jabez—take time to dwell on each of his petitions. What kind of help do you most want from God? How would you like to experience God's presence with you? From what do you seek God's protection?

See Meeting God in Prayer

These were the families of the Zorathites. ³These were the sons[a] of Etam: Jezreel, Ishma, and Idbash; and the name of their sister was Hazzelelponi, ⁴and Penuel was the father of Gedor, and Ezer the father of Hushah. These were the sons of Hur, the firstborn of Ephrathah, the father of Bethlehem. ⁵Ashhur father of Tekoa had two wives, Helah and Naarah; ⁶Naarah bore him Ahuzzam, Hepher, Temeni, and Haahashtari.[b] These were the sons of Naarah. ⁷The sons of Helah: Zereth, Izhar,[c] and Ethnan. ⁸Koz became the father of Anub, Zobebah, and the families of Aharhel son of Harum. ⁹Jabez was honored more than his brothers; and his mother named him Jabez, saying, "Because I bore him in pain." ¹⁰Jabez called on the God of Israel, saying, "Oh that you would bless me and enlarge my border, and that your hand might be with me, and that you would keep me from hurt and harm!" And God granted what he asked. ¹¹Chelub the brother of Shuhah became the father of Mehir, who was the father of Eshton. ¹²Eshton became the father of Beth-rapha, Paseah, and Tehinnah the father of Ir-nahash. These are the men of Recah. ¹³The sons of Kenaz: Othniel and Seraiah; and the sons of Othniel: Hathath and Meonothai.[d] ¹⁴Meonothai became the father of Ophrah; and Seraiah became the father of Joab father of Ge-harashim,[e] so-called because they were artisans. ¹⁵The sons of Caleb son of Jephunneh: Iru, Elah, and Naam; and the son[f] of Elah: Kenaz. ¹⁶The sons of Jehallelel: Ziph, Ziphah, Tiria, and Asarel. ¹⁷The sons of Ezrah: Jether, Mered, Epher, and Jalon. These are the sons of Bithiah, daughter of Pharaoh, whom Mered married;[g] and she conceived and bore[h] Miriam, Shammai, and Ishbah father of Eshtemoa. ¹⁸And his Judean wife bore Jered father of Gedor, Heber father of Soco, and Jekuthiel father of Zanoah. ¹⁹The sons of the wife of Hodiah, the sister of Naham, were the fathers of Keilah the Garmite and Eshtemoa the Maacathite. ²⁰The sons of Shimon: Amnon, Rinnah, Ben-hanan, and Tilon. The sons of Ishi: Zoheth and Ben-zoheth. ²¹The sons of Shelah son of Judah: Er father of Lecah, Laadah father of Mareshah, and the families of the guild of linen workers at Beth-ashbea; ²²and Jokim, and the men of Cozeba, and Joash, and Saraph, who married into Moab but returned to Lehem[i] (now the records[j] are ancient). ²³These were the potters and inhabitants of Netaim and Gederah; they lived there with the king in his service.

Descendants of Simeon

24 The sons of Simeon: Nemuel, Jamin, Jarib, Zerah, Shaul;[k] ²⁵Shallum was his son, Mibsam his son, Mishma his son. ²⁶The sons of Mishma: Hammuel his son, Zaccur

a Gk Compare Vg: Heb *the father*   b Or *Ahashtari*   c Another reading is *Zohar*   d Gk Vg: Heb lacks *and Meonothai*   e That is *Valley of artisans*
f Heb *sons*   g The clause: *These are . . . married* is transposed from verse 18   h Heb lacks *and bore*   i Vg Compare Gk: Heb *and Jashubi-lahem*
j Or *matters*   k Or *Saul*

his son, Shimei his son. ²⁷Shimei had sixteen sons and six daughters; but his brothers did not have many children, nor did all their family multiply like the Judeans. ²⁸They lived in Beer-sheba, Moladah, Hazar-shual, ²⁹Bilhah, Ezem, Tolad, ³⁰Bethuel, Hormah, Ziklag, ³¹Beth-marcaboth, Hazar-susim, Beth-biri, and Shaaraim. These were their towns until David became king. ³²And their villages were Etam, Ain, Rimmon, Tochen, and Ashan, five towns, ³³along with all their villages that were around these towns as far as Baal. These were their settlements. And they kept a genealogical record.

34 Meshobab, Jamlech, Joshah son of Amaziah, ³⁵Joel, Jehu son of Joshibiah son of Seraiah son of Asiel, ³⁶Elioenai, Jaakobah, Jeshohaiah, Asaiah, Adiel, Jesimiel, Benaiah, ³⁷Ziza son of Shiphi son of Allon son of Jedaiah son of Shimri son of Shemaiah— ³⁸these mentioned by name were leaders in their families, and their clans increased greatly. ³⁹They journeyed to the entrance of Gedor, to the east side of the valley, to seek pasture for their flocks, ⁴⁰where they found rich, good pasture, and the land was very broad, quiet, and peaceful; for the former inhabitants there belonged to Ham. ⁴¹These, registered by name, came in the days of King Hezekiah of Judah, and attacked their tents and the Meunim who were found there, and exterminated them to this day, and settled in their place, because there was pasture there for their flocks. ⁴²And some of them, five hundred men of the Simeonites, went to Mount Seir, having as their leaders Pelatiah, Neariah, Rephaiah, and Uzziel, sons of Ishi; ⁴³they destroyed the remnant of the Amalekites that had escaped, and they have lived there to this day.

Descendants of Reuben

5 The sons of Reuben the firstborn of Israel. (He was the firstborn, but because he defiled his father's bed his birthright was given to the sons of Joseph son of Israel, so that he is not enrolled in the genealogy according to the birthright; ²though Judah became prominent among his brothers and a ruler came from him, yet the birthright belonged to Joseph.) ³The sons of Reuben, the firstborn of Israel: Hanoch, Pallu, Hezron, and Carmi. ⁴The sons of Joel: Shemaiah his son, Gog his son, Shimei his son, ⁵Micah his son, Reaiah his son, Baal his son, ⁶Beerah his son, whom King Tilgath-pilneser of Assyria carried away into exile; he was a chieftain of the Reubenites. ⁷And his kindred by their families, when the genealogy of their generations was reckoned: the chief, Jeiel, and Zechariah, ⁸and Bela son of Azaz, son of Shema, son of Joel, who lived in Aroer, as far as Nebo and Baal-meon. ⁹He also lived to the east as far as the beginning of the desert this side of the Euphrates, because their cattle had multiplied in the land of Gilead. ¹⁰And in the days of Saul they made war on the Hagrites, who fell by their hand; and they lived in their tents throughout all the region east of Gilead.

Fitting In

1 CHRONICLES 5.23–26

The half-tribe of Manasseh adapted to the culture they found in the land they conquered, and they eventually worshiped other gods. The result was their destruction.

We are often faced with conflicts between what God calls us to be and to do and what others do in the society around us. Where do you experience such conflicts in your own life? What are the outcomes of these conflicts? What "other gods" vie for your allegiance and your devotion? What does it cost you to resist them? What does it cost you to give in to them? Ask for God's help to remain faithful despite the temptation to fit in.

See Meeting God in Everyday Life

Descendants of Gad

11 The sons of Gad lived beside them in the land of Bashan as far as Salecah: ¹²Joel the chief, Shapham the second, Janai, and Shaphat in Bashan. ¹³And their kindred according to their clans: Michael, Meshullam, Sheba, Jorai, Jacan, Zia, and Eber, seven. ¹⁴These were the sons of Abihail son of Huri, son of Jaroah, son of Gilead, son of Michael, son of Jeshishai, son of Jahdo, son of Buz; ¹⁵Ahi son of Abdiel, son of Guni, was chief in their clan; ¹⁶and they lived in Gilead, in Bashan and in its towns, and in all the pasture lands of Sharon to their limits. ¹⁷All of these were enrolled by genealogies in the days of King Jotham of Judah, and in the days of King Jeroboam of Israel.

18 The Reubenites, the Gadites, and the half-tribe of Manasseh had valiant warriors, who carried shield and sword, and drew the bow, expert in war, forty-four thousand seven hundred sixty, ready for service. ¹⁹They made war on the Hagrites, Jetur, Naphish, and Nodab; ²⁰and when they received help against them, the Hagrites and all who were with them were given into their hands, for they cried to God in the battle, and he granted their entreaty because they trusted in him. ²¹They captured their livestock: fifty thousand of their camels, two hundred fifty thousand sheep, two thousand donkeys, and one hundred thousand captives. ²²Many fell slain, because the war was of God. And they lived in their territory until the exile.

The Half-Tribe of Manasseh

23 The members of the half-tribe of Manasseh lived in the land; they were very numerous from Bashan to Baal-hermon, Senir, and Mount Hermon. ²⁴These were the heads of their clans: Epher,ᵃ Ishi, Eliel, Azriel, Jeremiah, Hodaviah, and Jahdiel, mighty warriors, famous men, heads of their clans. ²⁵But they transgressed against the God of their ancestors, and prostituted themselves to the gods of the peoples of the land, whom God had destroyed before them. ²⁶So the God of Israel stirred up the spirit of King Pul of Assyria, the spirit of King Tilgath-pilneser of Assyria, and he carried them away, namely, the Reubenites, the Gadites, and the half-tribe of Manasseh, and brought them to Halah, Habor, Hara, and the river Gozan, to this day.

Descendants of Levi

6ᵇ The sons of Levi: Gershom,ᶜ Kohath, and Merari. ²The sons of Kohath: Amram, Izhar, Hebron, and Uzziel. ³The children of Amram: Aaron, Moses, and Miriam. The sons of Aaron: Nadab, Abihu, Eleazar, and Ithamar. ⁴Eleazar became the father of Phinehas, Phinehas of Abishua, ⁵Abishua of Bukki, Bukki of Uzzi, ⁶Uzzi of Zerahiah, Zerahiah of Meraioth, ⁷Meraioth of Amariah, Amari-

a Gk Vg: Heb *and Epher*   b Ch 5.27 in Heb   c Heb *Gershon,* variant of *Gershom;* See 6.16

ah of Ahitub, [8]Ahitub of Zadok, Zadok of Ahimaaz, [9]Ahimaaz of Azariah, Azariah of Johanan, [10]and Johanan of Azariah (it was he who served as priest in the house that Solomon built in Jerusalem). [11]Azariah became the father of Amariah, Amariah of Ahitub, [12]Ahitub of Zadok, Zadok of Shallum, [13]Shallum of Hilkiah, Hilkiah of Azariah, [14]Azariah of Seraiah, Seraiah of Jehozadak; [15]and Jehozadak went into exile when the Lord sent Judah and Jerusalem into exile by the hand of Nebuchadnezzar.

[16][a] The sons of Levi: Gershom, Kohath, and Merari. [17]These are the names of the sons of Gershom: Libni and Shimei. [18]The sons of Kohath: Amram, Izhar, Hebron, and Uzziel. [19]The sons of Merari: Mahli and Mushi. These are the clans of the Levites according to their ancestry. [20]Of Gershom: Libni his son, Jahath his son, Zimmah his son, [21]Joah his son, Iddo his son, Zerah his son, Jeatherai his son. [22]The sons of Kohath: Amminadab his son, Korah his son, Assir his son, [23]Elkanah his son, Ebiasaph his son, Assir his son, [24]Tahath his son, Uriel his son, Uzziah his son, and Shaul his son. [25]The sons of Elkanah: Amasai and Ahimoth, [26]Elkanah his son, Zophai his son, Nahath his son, [27]Eliab his son, Jeroham his son, Elkanah his son. [28]The sons of Samuel: Joel[b] his firstborn, the second Abijah.[c] [29]The sons of Merari: Mahli, Libni his son, Shimei his son, Uzzah his son, [30]Shimea his son, Haggiah his son, and Asaiah his son.

Musicians Appointed by David

31 These are the men whom David put in charge of the service of song in the house of the Lord, after the ark came to rest there. [32]They ministered with song before the tabernacle of the tent of meeting, until Solomon had built the house of the Lord in Jerusalem; and they performed their service in due order. [33]These are the men who served; and their sons were: Of the Kohathites: Heman, the singer, son of Joel, son of Samuel, [34]son of Elkanah, son of Jeroham, son of Eliel, son of Toah, [35]son of Zuph, son of Elkanah, son of Mahath, son of Amasai, [36]son of Elkanah, son of Joel, son of Azariah, son of Zephaniah, [37]son of Tahath, son of Assir, son of Ebiasaph, son of Korah, [38]son of Izhar, son of Kohath, son of Levi, son of Israel; [39]and his brother Asaph, who stood on his right, namely, Asaph son of Berechiah, son of Shimea, [40]son of Michael, son of Baaseiah, son of Malchijah, [41]son of Ethni, son of Zerah, son of Adaiah, [42]son of Ethan, son of Zimmah, son of Shimei, [43]son of Jahath, son of Gershom, son of Levi. [44]On the left were their kindred the sons of Merari: Ethan son of Kishi, son of Abdi, son of Malluch, [45]son of Hashabiah, son of Amaziah, son of Hilkiah, [46]son of Amzi, son of Bani, son of Shemer, [47]son of Mahli, son of Mushi, son of Merari, son of Levi; [48]and their kindred the Levites were

Ministering With Song

1 CHRONICLES 6.31–48

Here is your chance to be a Kohathite, ministering with song before the Lord. Which hymns or gospel songs particularly speak to you? Which ones lift your heart in praise? Sing one or two now, aloud if possible. You might go a step further and write your own song of praise. If coming up with words and music seems too difficult, you might try creating a tune for a favorite verse of scripture or writing new words to a familiar tune. If all else fails, just make a joyful noise to the Lord!

See Meeting God in Worship

---

a Ch 6.1 in Heb   *b* Gk Syr Compare verse 33 and 1 Sam 8.2: Heb lacks *Joel*   *c* Heb reads *Vashni, and Abijah* for *the second Abijah*, taking *the second* as a proper name

Through the Ages

1 CHRONICLES 6.61–80

"Forward through the ages,
    in unbroken line,
move the faithful spirits at
    the call divine;
gifts in differing measure,
    hearts of one accord,
manifold the service, one
    the sure reward.
Wider grows the kingdom,
    reign of love and light;
for it we must labor, till our
    faith is sight.
Prophets have proclaimed it,
    martyrs testified,
poets sung its glory, heroes
    for it died.
Forward through the ages,
    in unbroken line,
move the faithful spirits at
    the call divine."

—FREDERICK LUCIAN HOSMER

appointed for all the service of the tabernacle of the house of God.

49 But Aaron and his sons made offerings on the altar of burnt offering and on the altar of incense, doing all the work of the most holy place, to make atonement for Israel, according to all that Moses the servant of God had commanded. ⁵⁰These are the sons of Aaron: Eleazar his son, Phinehas his son, Abishua his son, ⁵¹Bukki his son, Uzzi his son, Zerahiah his son, ⁵²Meraioth his son, Amariah his son, Ahitub his son, ⁵³Zadok his son, Ahimaaz his son.

Settlements of the Levites

54 These are their dwelling places according to their settlements within their borders: to the sons of Aaron of the families of Kohathites—for the lot fell to them first— ⁵⁵to them they gave Hebron in the land of Judah and its surrounding pasture lands, ⁵⁶but the fields of the city and its villages they gave to Caleb son of Jephunneh. ⁵⁷To the sons of Aaron they gave the cities of refuge: Hebron, Libnah with its pasture lands, Jattir, Eshtemoa with its pasture lands, ⁵⁸Hilen*a* with its pasture lands, Debir with its pasture lands, ⁵⁹Ashan with its pasture lands, and Bethshemesh with its pasture lands. ⁶⁰From the tribe of Benjamin, Geba with its pasture lands, Alemeth with its pasture lands, and Anathoth with its pasture lands. All their towns throughout their families were thirteen.

61 To the rest of the Kohathites were given by lot out of the family of the tribe, out of the half-tribe, the half of Manasseh, ten towns. ⁶²To the Gershomites according to their families were allotted thirteen towns out of the tribes of Issachar, Asher, Naphtali, and Manasseh in Bashan. ⁶³To the Merarites according to their families were allotted twelve towns out of the tribes of Reuben, Gad, and Zebulun. ⁶⁴So the people of Israel gave the Levites the towns with their pasture lands. ⁶⁵They also gave them by lot out of the tribes of Judah, Simeon, and Benjamin these towns that are mentioned by name.

66 And some of the families of the sons of Kohath had towns of their territory out of the tribe of Ephraim. ⁶⁷They were given the cities of refuge: Shechem with its pasture lands in the hill country of Ephraim, Gezer with its pasture lands, ⁶⁸Jokmeam with its pasture lands, Beth-horon with its pasture lands, ⁶⁹Aijalon with its pasture lands, Gath-rimmon with its pasture lands; ⁷⁰and out of the half-tribe of Manasseh, Aner with its pasture lands, and Bileam with its pasture lands, for the rest of the families of the Kohathites.

71 To the Gershomites: out of the half-tribe of Manasseh: Golan in Bashan with its pasture lands and Ashtaroth with its pasture lands; ⁷²and out of the tribe of Issachar: Kedesh with its pasture lands, Daberath*b* with its pasture lands, ⁷³Ramoth with its pasture lands, and Anem with its

a Other readings *Hilez, Holon;* See Josh 21.15   *b* Or *Dobrath*

pasture lands; ⁷⁴out of the tribe of Asher: Mashal with its pasture lands, Abdon with its pasture lands, ⁷⁵Hukok with its pasture lands, and Rehob with its pasture lands; ⁷⁶and out of the tribe of Naphtali: Kedesh in Galilee with its pasture lands, Hammon with its pasture lands, and Kiriathaim with its pasture lands. ⁷⁷To the rest of the Merarites out of the tribe of Zebulun: Rimmono with its pasture lands, Tabor with its pasture lands, ⁷⁸and across the Jordan from Jericho, on the east side of the Jordan, out of the tribe of Reuben: Bezer in the steppe with its pasture lands, Jahzah with its pasture lands, ⁷⁹Kedemoth with its pasture lands, and Mephaath with its pasture lands; ⁸⁰and out of the tribe of Gad: Ramoth in Gilead with its pasture lands, Mahanaim with its pasture lands, ⁸¹Heshbon with its pasture lands, and Jazer with its pasture lands.

Descendants of Issachar

7 The sons*^a* of Issachar: Tola, Puah, Jashub, and Shimron, four. ²The sons of Tola: Uzzi, Rephaiah, Jeriel, Jahmai, Ibsam, and Shemuel, heads of their ancestral houses, namely of Tola, mighty warriors of their generations, their number in the days of David being twenty-two thousand six hundred. ³The son*^b* of Uzzi: Izrahiah. And the sons of Izrahiah: Michael, Obadiah, Joel, and Isshiah, five, all of them chiefs; ⁴and along with them, by their generations, according to their ancestral houses, were units of the fighting force, thirty-six thousand, for they had many wives and sons. ⁵Their kindred belonging to all the families of Issachar were in all eighty-seven thousand mighty warriors, enrolled by genealogy.

Descendants of Benjamin

6 The sons of Benjamin: Bela, Becher, and Jediael, three. ⁷The sons of Bela: Ezbon, Uzzi, Uzziel, Jerimoth, and Iri, five, heads of ancestral houses, mighty warriors; and their enrollment by genealogies was twenty-two thousand thirty-four. ⁸The sons of Becher: Zemirah, Joash, Eliezer, Elioenai, Omri, Jeremoth, Abijah, Anathoth, and Alemeth. All these were the sons of Becher; ⁹and their enrollment by genealogies, according to their generations, as heads of their ancestral houses, mighty warriors, was twenty thousand two hundred. ¹⁰The sons of Jediael: Bilhan. And the sons of Bilhan: Jeush, Benjamin, Ehud, Chenaanah, Zethan, Tarshish, and Ahishahar. ¹¹All these were the sons of Jediael according to the heads of their ancestral houses, mighty warriors, seventeen thousand two hundred, ready for service in war. ¹²And Shuppim and Huppim were the sons of Ir, Hushim the son*^b* of Aher.

Descendants of Naphtali

13 The descendants of Naphtali: Jahziel, Guni, Jezer, and Shallum, the descendants of Bilhah.

Christ's Whole Body

1 CHRONICLES 6.72–7.12

Tribe after tribe and name after name—these verses may not be the most inspiring passages of scripture, but they can serve to remind us of the vast number of people who have worshiped God throughout the centuries, as well as the number of people around the globe who worship him today. Each name is more than a statistic—it represents a person who lived and worked, laughed and cried, and who faced challenges of life and faith.

Sometimes we can become dull to statistics about churches that are being persecuted and people who are suffering. We may tend to ignore the individuals behind those statistics. Take time to pray through your denominational list of mission locations, or pray with an atlas open before you, asking God to give you a heart for the real people—his people—who live behind the statistics.

See Meeting God in Community

Life From the Ashes

1 CHRONICLES 7.20–24

These verses form a curious side note to this list of allotments. They tell a sad tale of two sons who went down to their land to claim their livestock and were killed. Ephraim mourned for many days; even the birth of another son couldn't erase the pain of his family's misfortune. His daughter is mentioned though as a construction supervisor, an unusual position for a woman in this patriarchal society.

Tragedy and loss often change families forever. The pain of loss remains even though the family must "keep on keeping on." Still, through God's grace, new life can grow out of loss. Wisdom grows out of pain. Family members may find strengths they never knew they had and fill new roles. They find that their loss helps them help others. Have you and your family suffered tragedy and loss? How is God's grace helping you go on, to grow, to find new wisdom in your tragedy? Reflect on how new life can grow out of ashes.

Descendants of Manasseh

14 The sons of Manasseh: Asriel, whom his Aramean concubine bore; she bore Machir the father of Gilead. [15]And Machir took a wife for Huppim and for Shuppim. The name of his sister was Maacah. And the name of the second was Zelophehad; and Zelophehad had daughters. [16]Maacah the wife of Machir bore a son, and she named him Peresh; the name of his brother was Sheresh; and his sons were Ulam and Rekem. [17]The son[a] of Ulam: Bedan. These were the sons of Gilead son of Machir, son of Manasseh. [18]And his sister Hammolecheth bore Ishhod, Abiezer, and Mahlah. [19]The sons of Shemida were Ahian, Shechem, Likhi, and Aniam.

Descendants of Ephraim

20 The sons of Ephraim: Shuthelah, and Bered his son, Tahath his son, Eleadah his son, Tahath his son, [21]Zabad his son, Shuthelah his son, and Ezer and Elead. Now the people of Gath, who were born in the land, killed them, because they came down to raid their cattle. [22]And their father Ephraim mourned many days, and his brothers came to comfort him. [23]Ephraim[b] went in to his wife, and she conceived and bore a son; and he named him Beriah, because disaster[c] had befallen his house. [24]His daughter was Sheerah, who built both Lower and Upper Beth-horon, and Uzzen-sheerah. [25]Rephah was his son, Resheph his son, Telah his son, Tahan his son, [26]Ladan his son, Ammihud his son, Elishama his son, [27]Nun[d] his son, Joshua his son. [28]Their possessions and settlements were Bethel and its towns, and eastward Naaran, and westward Gezer and its towns, Shechem and its towns, as far as Ayyah and its towns; [29]also along the borders of the Manassites, Beth-shean and its towns, Taanach and its towns, Megiddo and its towns, Dor and its towns. In these lived the sons of Joseph son of Israel.

Descendants of Asher

30 The sons of Asher: Imnah, Ishvah, Ishvi, Beriah, and their sister Serah. [31]The sons of Beriah: Heber and Malchiel, who was the father of Birzaith. [32]Heber became the father of Japhlet, Shomer, Hotham, and their sister Shua. [33]The sons of Japhlet: Pasach, Bimhal, and Ashvath. These are the sons of Japhlet. [34]The sons of Shemer: Ahi, Rohgah, Hubbah, and Aram. [35]The sons of Helem[e] his brother: Zophah, Imna, Shelesh, and Amal. [36]The sons of Zophah: Suah, Harnepher, Shual, Beri, Imrah, [37]Bezer, Hod, Shamma, Shilshah, Ithran, and Beera. [38]The sons of Jether: Jephunneh, Pispa, and Ara. [39]The sons of Ulla: Arah, Hanniel, and Rizia. [40]All of these were men of Asher, heads of ancestral houses, select mighty warriors, chief of

a Heb *sons*   b Heb *He*   c Heb *beraah*   d Here spelled *Non*; see Ex 33.11   e Or *Hotham*; see 7.32

the princes. Their number enrolled by genealogies, for service in war, was twenty-six thousand men.

Descendants of Benjamin

8 Benjamin became the father of Bela his firstborn, Ashbel the second, Aharah the third, [2]Nohah the fourth, and Rapha the fifth. [3]And Bela had sons: Addar, Gera, Abihud,[a] [4]Abishua, Naaman, Ahoah, [5]Gera, Shephuphan, and Huram. [6]These are the sons of Ehud (they were heads of ancestral houses of the inhabitants of Geba, and they were carried into exile to Manahath): [7]Naaman,[b] Ahijah, and Gera, that is, Heglam,[c] who became the father of Uzza and Ahihud. [8]And Shaharaim had sons in the country of Moab after he had sent away his wives Hushim and Baara. [9]He had sons by his wife Hodesh: Jobab, Zibia, Mesha, Malcam, [10]Jeuz, Sachia, and Mirmah. These were his sons, heads of ancestral houses. [11]He also had sons by Hushim: Abitub and Elpaal. [12]The sons of Elpaal: Eber, Misham, and Shemed, who built Ono and Lod with its towns, [13]and Beriah and Shema (they were heads of ancestral houses of the inhabitants of Aijalon, who put to flight the inhabitants of Gath); [14]and Ahio, Shashak, and Jeremoth. [15]Zebadiah, Arad, Eder, [16]Michael, Ishpah, and Joha were sons of Beriah. [17]Zebadiah, Meshullam, Hizki, Heber, [18]Ishmerai, Izliah, and Jobab were the sons of Elpaal. [19]Jakim, Zichri, Zabdi, [20]Elienai, Zillethai, Eliel, [21]Adaiah, Beraiah, and Shimrath were the sons of Shimei. [22]Ishpan, Eber, Eliel, [23]Abdon, Zichri, Hanan, [24]Hananiah, Elam, Anthothijah, [25]Iphdeiah, and Penuel were the sons of Shashak. [26]Shamsherai, Shehariah, Athaliah, [27]Jaareshiah, Elijah, and Zichri were the sons of Jeroham. [28]These were the heads of ancestral houses, according to their generations, chiefs. These lived in Jerusalem.

29 Jeiel[d] the father of Gibeon lived in Gibeon, and the name of his wife was Maacah. [30]His firstborn son: Abdon, then Zur, Kish, Baal,[e] Nadab, [31]Gedor, Ahio, Zecher, [32]and Mikloth, who became the father of Shimeah. Now these also lived opposite their kindred in Jerusalem, with their kindred. [33]Ner became the father of Kish, Kish of Saul,[f] Saul[f] of Jonathan, Malchishua, Abinadab, and Esh-baal; [34]and the son of Jonathan was Merib-baal; and Merib-baal became the father of Micah. [35]The sons of Micah: Pithon, Melech, Tarea, and Ahaz. [36]Ahaz became the father of Jehoaddah; and Jehoaddah became the father of Alemeth, Azmaveth, and Zimri; Zimri became the father of Moza. [37]Moza became the father of Binea; Raphah was his son, Eleasah his son, Azel his son. [38]Azel had six sons, and these are their names: Azrikam, Bocheru, Ishmael, Sheariah, Obadiah, and Hanan; all these were the sons of Azel. [39]The sons of his brother Eshek: Ulam his firstborn, Jeush the second, and Eliphelet the third. [40]The sons of Ulam

---

A Living Structure

1 CHRONICLES 8.1

"The Church is a living structure, made up of live building stones. They are far from perfect; they need to be dressed and hewn if they are to fit into the building. And yet it is a perfect building. The mystery is this: the life of this building does not reside in its parts, but rather in the living, gathering Holy Spirit. Its unity does not result from assembling the parts that make it up or from an agreement of opinions. By nature the stones are spiritually dead. But the Holy Spirit awakens them to life by joining them together in a new unity."

—EBERHARD ARNOLD,
God's Revolution

---

a Or *father of Ehud;* see 8.6   b Heb *and Naaman*   c Or *he carried them into exile*   d Compare 9.35: Heb lacks *Jeiel*   e Gk Ms adds *Ner;* Compare 8.33 and 9.36   f Or *Shaul*

Into Exile

1 CHRONICLES 9.1

For the Chronicler, the story is simple: "And Judah was taken into exile . . . because of their unfaithfulness." It may not be so clear for us when we feel isolated, exiled, cut off from the people and places we have loved. Still, God can help bring us home. Ask for God's help in looking at your feelings of exile. What have you done to cause broken relationships? What can you do to mend them? How can God help you to return from exile? What breaks can be repaired only by God's grace? Offer God your brokenness and receive God's healing.

See Meeting God in Community

were mighty warriors, archers, having many children and grandchildren, one hundred fifty. All these were Benjaminites.

9 So all Israel was enrolled by genealogies; and these are written in the Book of the Kings of Israel. And Judah was taken into exile in Babylon because of their unfaithfulness. ²Now the first to live again in their possessions in their towns were Israelites, priests, Levites, and temple servants.

Inhabitants of Jerusalem after the Exile

3 And some of the people of Judah, Benjamin, Ephraim, and Manasseh lived in Jerusalem: ⁴Uthai son of Ammihud, son of Omri, son of Imri, son of Bani, from the sons of Perez son of Judah. ⁵And of the Shilonites: Asaiah the firstborn, and his sons. ⁶Of the sons of Zerah: Jeuel and their kin, six hundred ninety. ⁷Of the Benjaminites: Sallu son of Meshullam, son of Hodaviah, son of Hassenuah, ⁸Ibneiah son of Jeroham, Elah son of Uzzi, son of Michri, and Meshullam son of Shephatiah, son of Reuel, son of Ibnijah; ⁹and their kindred according to their generations, nine hundred fifty-six. All these were heads of families according to their ancestral houses.

Priestly Families

10 Of the priests: Jedaiah, Jehoiarib, Jachin, ¹¹and Azariah son of Hilkiah, son of Meshullam, son of Zadok, son of Meraioth, son of Ahitub, the chief officer of the house of God; ¹²and Adaiah son of Jeroham, son of Pashhur, son of Malchijah, and Maasai son of Adiel, son of Jahzerah, son of Meshullam, son of Meshillemith, son of Immer; ¹³besides their kindred, heads of their ancestral houses, one thousand seven hundred sixty, qualified for the work of the service of the house of God.

Levitical Families

14 Of the Levites: Shemaiah son of Hasshub, son of Azrikam, son of Hashabiah, of the sons of Merari; ¹⁵and Bakbakkar, Heresh, Galal, and Mattaniah son of Mica, son of Zichri, son of Asaph; ¹⁶and Obadiah son of Shemaiah, son of Galal, son of Jeduthun, and Berechiah son of Asa, son of Elkanah, who lived in the villages of the Netophathites.

17 The gatekeepers were: Shallum, Akkub, Talmon, Ahiman; and their kindred Shallum was the chief, ¹⁸stationed previously in the king's gate on the east side. These were the gatekeepers of the camp of the Levites. ¹⁹Shallum son of Kore, son of Ebiasaph, son of Korah, and his kindred of his ancestral house, the Korahites, were in charge of the work of the service, guardians of the thresholds of the tent, as their ancestors had been in charge of the camp of the LORD, guardians of the entrance. ²⁰And Phinehas son of Eleazar was chief over them in former times; the LORD was with him. ²¹Zechariah son of Meshelemiah was gatekeeper at the entrance of the tent of meeting. ²²All these, who were chosen as gatekeepers at the thresholds, were

two hundred twelve. They were enrolled by genealogies in their villages. David and the seer Samuel established them in their office of trust. ²³So they and their descendants were in charge of the gates of the house of the LORD, that is, the house of the tent, as guards. ²⁴The gatekeepers were on the four sides, east, west, north, and south; ²⁵and their kindred who were in their villages were obliged to come in every seven days, in turn, to be with them; ²⁶for the four chief gatekeepers, who were Levites, were in charge of the chambers and the treasures of the house of God. ²⁷And they would spend the night near the house of God; for on them lay the duty of watching, and they had charge of opening it every morning.

28 Some of them had charge of the utensils of service, for they were required to count them when they were brought in and taken out. ²⁹Others of them were appointed over the furniture, and over all the holy utensils, also over the choice flour, the wine, the oil, the incense, and the spices. ³⁰Others, of the sons of the priests, prepared the mixing of the spices, ³¹and Mattithiah, one of the Levites, the firstborn of Shallum the Korahite, was in charge of making the flat cakes. ³²Also some of their kindred of the Kohathites had charge of the rows of bread, to prepare them for each sabbath.

33 Now these are the singers, the heads of ancestral houses of the Levites, living in the chambers of the temple free from other service, for they were on duty day and night. ³⁴These were heads of ancestral houses of the Levites, according to their generations; these leaders lived in Jerusalem.

The Family of King Saul

35 In Gibeon lived the father of Gibeon, Jeiel, and the name of his wife was Maacah. ³⁶His firstborn son was Abdon, then Zur, Kish, Baal, Ner, Nadab, ³⁷Gedor, Ahio, Zechariah, and Mikloth; ³⁸and Mikloth became the father of Shimeam; and these also lived opposite their kindred in Jerusalem, with their kindred. ³⁹Ner became the father of Kish, Kish of Saul, Saul of Jonathan, Malchishua, Abinadab, and Esh-baal; ⁴⁰and the son of Jonathan was Merib-baal; and Merib-baal became the father of Micah. ⁴¹The sons of Micah: Pithon, Melech, Tahrea, and Ahaz;ᵃ ⁴²and Ahaz became the father of Jarah, and Jarah of Alemeth, Azmaveth, and Zimri; and Zimri became the father of Moza. ⁴³Moza became the father of Binea; and Rephaiah was his son, Eleasah his son, Azel his son. ⁴⁴Azel had six sons, and these are their names: Azrikam, Bocheru, Ishmael, Sheariah, Obadiah, and Hanan; these were the sons of Azel.

Death of Saul and His Sons

10 Now the Philistines fought against Israel; and the men of Israel fled before the Philistines, and fell

ᵃ Compare 8.35: Heb lacks *and Ahaz*

God in the Details

1 CHRONICLES 9.28

Even counting the knives and spoons can be a holy task if offered to the Lord. Spiritual writers call this "the sacrament of the present moment." As you go about your chores today—cleaning the house, pulling the weeds, doing the laundry, taking out the trash—invite God to be with you. Thank God for giving you work to do and ability to do it. At first it will take a lot of effort to remember God, to let God's presence light up even the most tedious tasks. But as you continue to "practice the presence of God" it will become easier.

See Meeting God in Everyday Life

Good Intentions

1 CHRONICLES 10.13–14

The sins for which Saul is condemned, failing to follow God's instructions (see 1 Samuel 13.1–15) and consulting a medium (see 1 Samuel 28.3–25), represent good intentions gone bad. When have you done the wrong thing for what seemed the right reasons? How did your good reasons block you from admitting that what you did was wrong? Are there still such situations in your life that are unresolved? Ask God to help you let go of self-righteousness so that you can confess your wrongdoing both to God and to those who might have been hurt by it. Ask for forgiveness and mercy so that God's love can cleanse your heart.

See Meeting God in Prayer

slain on Mount Gilboa. ²The Philistines overtook Saul and his sons; and the Philistines killed Jonathan and Abinadab and Malchishua, sons of Saul. ³The battle pressed hard on Saul; and the archers found him, and he was wounded by the archers. ⁴Then Saul said to his armor-bearer, "Draw your sword, and thrust me through with it, so that these uncircumcised may not come and make sport of me." But his armor-bearer was unwilling, for he was terrified. So Saul took his own sword and fell on it. ⁵When his armor-bearer saw that Saul was dead, he also fell on his sword and died. ⁶Thus Saul died; he and his three sons and all his house died together. ⁷When all the men of Israel who were in the valley saw that the army[a] had fled and that Saul and his sons were dead, they abandoned their towns and fled; and the Philistines came and occupied them.

8 The next day when the Philistines came to strip the dead, they found Saul and his sons fallen on Mount Gilboa. ⁹They stripped him and took his head and his armor, and sent messengers throughout the land of the Philistines to carry the good news to their idols and to the people. ¹⁰They put his armor in the temple of their gods, and fastened his head in the temple of Dagon. ¹¹But when all Jabesh-gilead heard everything that the Philistines had done to Saul, ¹²all the valiant warriors got up and took away the body of Saul and the bodies of his sons, and brought them to Jabesh. Then they buried their bones under the oak in Jabesh, and fasted seven days.

13 So Saul died for his unfaithfulness; he was unfaithful to the LORD in that he did not keep the command of the LORD; moreover, he had consulted a medium, seeking guidance, ¹⁴and did not seek guidance from the LORD. Therefore the LORD[b] put him to death and turned the kingdom over to David son of Jesse.

David Anointed King of All Israel

11 Then all Israel gathered together to David at Hebron and said, "See, we are your bone and flesh. ²For some time now, even while Saul was king, it was you who commanded the army of Israel. The LORD your God said to you: It is you who shall be shepherd of my people Israel, you who shall be ruler over my people Israel." ³So all the elders of Israel came to the king at Hebron, and David made a covenant with them at Hebron before the LORD. And they anointed David king over Israel, according to the word of the LORD by Samuel.

Jerusalem Captured

4 David and all Israel marched to Jerusalem, that is Jebus, where the Jebusites were, the inhabitants of the land. ⁵The inhabitants of Jebus said to David, "You will not come in here." Nevertheless David took the stronghold of Zion, now the city of David. ⁶David had said, "Whoever

a Heb *they*   *b* Heb *he*

attacks the Jebusites first shall be chief and commander." And Joab son of Zeruiah went up first, so he became chief. [7]David resided in the stronghold; therefore it was called the city of David. [8]He built the city all around, from the Millo in complete circuit; and Joab repaired the rest of the city. [9]And David became greater and greater, for the LORD of hosts was with him.

David's Mighty Men and Their Exploits

10 Now these are the chiefs of David's warriors, who gave him strong support in his kingdom, together with all Israel, to make him king, according to the word of the LORD concerning Israel. [11]This is an account of David's mighty warriors: Jashobeam, son of Hachmoni,[a] was chief of the Three;[b] he wielded his spear against three hundred whom he killed at one time.

12 And next to him among the three warriors was Eleazar son of Dodo, the Ahohite. [13]He was with David at Pasdammim when the Philistines were gathered there for battle. There was a plot of ground full of barley. Now the people had fled from the Philistines, [14]but he and David took their stand in the middle of the plot, defended it, and killed the Philistines; and the LORD saved them by a great victory.

15 Three of the thirty chiefs went down to the rock to David at the cave of Adullam, while the army of Philistines was encamped in the valley of Rephaim. [16]David was then in the stronghold; and the garrison of the Philistines was then at Bethlehem. [17]David said longingly, "O that someone would give me water to drink from the well of Bethlehem that is by the gate!" [18]Then the Three broke through the camp of the Philistines, and drew water from the well of Bethlehem that was by the gate, and they brought it to David. But David would not drink of it; he poured it out to the LORD, [19]and said, "My God forbid that I should do this. Can I drink the blood of these men? For at the risk of their lives they brought it." Therefore he would not drink it. The three warriors did these things.

20 Now Abishai,[c] the brother of Joab, was chief of the Thirty.[d] With his spear he fought against three hundred and killed them, and won a name beside the Three. [21]He was the most renowned[e] of the Thirty,[d] and became their commander; but he did not attain to the Three.

22 Benaiah son of Jehoiada was a valiant man[f] of Kabzeel, a doer of great deeds; he struck down two sons of[g] Ariel of Moab. He also went down and killed a lion in a pit on a day when snow had fallen. [23]And he killed an Egyptian, a man of great stature, five cubits tall. The Egyptian had in his hand a spear like a weaver's beam; but Benaiah went against him with a staff, snatched the spear out of

A Gift Too Precious

1 CHRONICLES 11.10–19

Try to imagine the scene. David is hiding in a cave while the Philistines occupy his hometown of Bethlehem. See the cave, the guards on watch. Hear the commotion as three of his companions come running and gasping to David, holding aloft a water skin. It is water from the well of Bethlehem. Notice the fresh bloodstains, the bandaged wounds. David pours out the water, saying it has become their blood and can be offered only to God. How do you respond to David's action? When have you received a gift that was too precious to be kept for yourself? What was it? How did you offer it to God? What precious gift do you keep for your own use? How might you use it to glorify God?

See Meeting God in Scripture

---

a Or *a Hachmonite*   b Compare 2 Sam 23.8: Heb *Thirty* or *captains*
c Gk Vg Tg Compare 2 Sam 23.18: Heb *Abshai*   d Syr: Heb *Three*
e Compare 2 Sam 23.19: Heb *more renowned among the two*   f Syr: Heb *the son of a valiant man*   g See 2 Sam 23.20: Heb lacks *sons of*

Celestial Warfare

"Do you, however, whom the celestial warfare has enlisted in the spiritual camp, only observe a discipline uncorrupted and chastened in the virtues of religion. Be constant as well in prayer as in reading. Now speak with God, now let God speak with you. Let God instruct you in his precepts. Let God direct you. Whom God has made rich, none shall make poor. In fact, there can be no poverty to one whose breast has once been supplied with heavenly food."

—CYPRIAN OF CARTHAGE,
Letter 1

the Egyptian's hand, and killed him with his own spear. [24]Such were the things Benaiah son of Jehoiada did, and he won a name beside the three warriors. [25]He was renowned among the Thirty, but he did not attain to the Three. And David put him in charge of his bodyguard.

26 The warriors of the armies were Asahel brother of Joab, Elhanan son of Dodo of Bethlehem, [27]Shammoth of Harod,[a] Helez the Pelonite, [28]Ira son of Ikkesh of Tekoa, Abiezer of Anathoth, [29]Sibbecai the Hushathite, Ilai the Ahohite, [30]Maharai of Netophah, Heled son of Baanah of Netophah, [31]Ithai son of Ribai of Gibeah of the Benjaminites, Benaiah of Pirathon, [32]Hurai of the wadis of Gaash, Abiel the Arbathite, [33]Azmaveth of Baharum, Eliahba of Shaalbon, [34]Hashem[b] the Gizonite, Jonathan son of Shagee the Hararite, [35]Ahiam son of Sachar the Hararite, Eliphal son of Ur, [36]Hepher the Mecherathite, Ahijah the Pelonite, [37]Hezro of Carmel, Naarai son of Ezbai, [38]Joel the brother of Nathan, Mibhar son of Hagri, [39]Zelek the Ammonite, Naharai of Beeroth, the armor-bearer of Joab son of Zeruiah, [40]Ira the Ithrite, Gareb the Ithrite, [41]Uriah the Hittite, Zabad son of Ahlai, [42]Adina son of Shiza the Reubenite, a leader of the Reubenites, and thirty with him, [43]Hanan son of Maacah, and Joshaphat the Mithnite, [44]Uzzia the Ashterathite, Shama and Jeiel sons of Hotham the Aroerite, [45]Jediael son of Shimri, and his brother Joha the Tizite, [46]Eliel the Mahavite, and Jeribai and Joshaviah sons of Elnaam, and Ithmah the Moabite, [47]Eliel, and Obed, and Jaasiel the Mezobaite.

David's Followers in the Wilderness

12 The following are those who came to David at Ziklag, while he could not move about freely because of Saul son of Kish; they were among the mighty warriors who helped him in war. [2]They were archers, and could shoot arrows and sling stones with either the right hand or the left; they were Benjaminites, Saul's kindred. [3]The chief was Ahiezer, then Joash, both sons of Shemaah of Gibeah; also Jeziel and Pelet sons of Azmaveth; Beracah, Jehu of Anathoth, [4]Ishmaiah of Gibeon, a warrior among the Thirty and a leader over the Thirty; Jeremiah,[c] Jahaziel, Johanan, Jozabad of Gederah, [5]Eluzai,[d] Jerimoth, Bealiah, Shemariah, Shephatiah the Haruphite; [6]Elkanah, Isshiah, Azarel, Joezer, and Jashobeam, the Korahites; [7]and Joelah and Zebadiah, sons of Jeroham of Gedor.

8 From the Gadites there went over to David at the stronghold in the wilderness mighty and experienced warriors, expert with shield and spear, whose faces were like the faces of lions, and who were swift as gazelles on the mountains: [9]Ezer the chief, Obadiah second, Eliab third, [10]Mishmannah fourth, Jeremiah fifth, [11]Attai sixth, Eliel seventh, [12]Johanan eighth, Elzabad ninth, [13]Jeremiah tenth, Machbannai eleventh. [14]These Gadites were officers

---

a Compare 2 Sam 23.25: Heb *the Harorite*   b Compare Gk and 2 Sam 23.32: Heb *the sons of Hashem*   c Heb verse 5   d Heb verse 6

of the army, the least equal to a hundred and the greatest to a thousand. ¹⁵These are the men who crossed the Jordan in the first month, when it was overflowing all its banks, and put to flight all those in the valleys, to the east and to the west.

16 Some Benjaminites and Judahites came to the stronghold to David. ¹⁷David went out to meet them and said to them, "If you have come to me in friendship, to help me, then my heart will be knit to you; but if you have come to betray me to my adversaries, though my hands have done no wrong, then may the God of our ancestors see and give judgment." ¹⁸Then the spirit came upon Amasai, chief of the Thirty, and he said,

"We are yours, O David;
    and with you, O son of Jesse!
Peace, peace to you,
    and peace to the one who helps you!
For your God is the one who helps you."

Then David received them, and made them officers of his troops.

19 Some of the Manassites deserted to David when he came with the Philistines for the battle against Saul. (Yet he did not help them, for the rulers of the Philistines took counsel and sent him away, saying, "He will desert to his master Saul at the cost of our heads.") ²⁰As he went to Ziklag these Manassites deserted to him: Adnah, Jozabad, Jediael, Michael, Jozabad, Elihu, and Zillethai, chiefs of the thousands in Manasseh. ²¹They helped David against the band of raiders,ᵃ for they were all warriors and commanders in the army. ²²Indeed from day to day people kept coming to David to help him, until there was a great army, like an army of God.

David's Army at Hebron

23 These are the numbers of the divisions of the armed troops who came to David in Hebron to turn the kingdom of Saul over to him, according to the word of the LORD. ²⁴The people of Judah bearing shield and spear numbered six thousand eight hundred armed troops. ²⁵Of the Simeonites, mighty warriors, seven thousand one hundred. ²⁶Of the Levites four thousand six hundred. ²⁷Jehoiada, leader of the house of Aaron, and with him three thousand seven hundred. ²⁸Zadok, a young warrior, and twenty-two commanders from his own ancestral house. ²⁹Of the Benjaminites, the kindred of Saul, three thousand, of whom the majority had continued to keep their allegiance to the house of Saul. ³⁰Of the Ephraimites, twenty thousand eight hundred, mighty warriors, notables in their ancestral houses. ³¹Of the half-tribe of Manasseh, eighteen thousand, who were expressly named to come and make

God Will Help

1 CHRONICLES 12.1–18

"If God is for us," asks Paul, "who is against us?" (Romans 8.31). Here David's companions promise him loyalty because they know that God will help him. Their statement of affirmation might be a good one to use as a breath prayer. Sit quietly, eyes closed, and repeat to yourself: "God is the one who helps me." Time it to your breathing by saying "God is the one" as you breathe in and "who helps me" as you breathe out. If you find your thoughts wandering, come back to the breath prayer. You might close your prayer time with the Lord's Prayer. During the day, stop from time to time to repeat the prayer.

See Meeting God in Prayer

Discernment

1 CHRONICLES 13.2

David knows what he wants to do, but he still puts the decision before the people and before the Lord. What major decision is hanging over you? Which of your friends can you ask, "Does this seem good to you?" How can you discern what is the will of the Lord? Perhaps you could gather a few trusted friends and pray together for guidance before discussing the pros and cons of each possibility. Ask God to guide and inspire your time together.

See Meeting God in Community

David king. ³²Of Issachar, those who had understanding of the times, to know what Israel ought to do, two hundred chiefs, and all their kindred under their command. ³³Of Zebulun, fifty thousand seasoned troops, equipped for battle with all the weapons of war, to help David*ᵃ* with singleness of purpose. ³⁴Of Naphtali, a thousand commanders, with whom there were thirty-seven thousand armed with shield and spear. ³⁵Of the Danites, twenty-eight thousand six hundred equipped for battle. ³⁶Of Asher, forty thousand seasoned troops ready for battle. ³⁷Of the Reubenites and Gadites and the half-tribe of Manasseh from beyond the Jordan, one hundred twenty thousand armed with all the weapons of war.

38 All these, warriors arrayed in battle order, came to Hebron with full intent to make David king over all Israel; likewise all the rest of Israel were of a single mind to make David king. ³⁹They were there with David for three days, eating and drinking, for their kindred had provided for them. ⁴⁰And also their neighbors, from as far away as Issachar and Zebulun and Naphtali, came bringing food on donkeys, camels, mules, and oxen—abundant provisions of meal, cakes of figs, clusters of raisins, wine, oil, oxen, and sheep, for there was joy in Israel.

The Ark Brought from Kiriath-jearim

13 David consulted with the commanders of the thousands and of the hundreds, with every leader. ²David said to the whole assembly of Israel, "If it seems good to you, and if it is the will of the Lᴏʀᴅ our God, let us send abroad to our kindred who remain in all the land of Israel, including the priests and Levites in the cities that have pasture lands, that they may come together to us. ³Then let us bring again the ark of our God to us; for we did not turn to it in the days of Saul." ⁴The whole assembly agreed to do so, for the thing pleased all the people.

5 So David assembled all Israel from the Shihor of Egypt to Lebo-hamath, to bring the ark of God from Kiriath-jearim. ⁶And David and all Israel went up to Baalah, that is, to Kiriath-jearim, which belongs to Judah, to bring up from there the ark of God, the Lᴏʀᴅ, who is enthroned on the cherubim, which is called by his*ᵇ* name. ⁷They carried the ark of God on a new cart, from the house of Abinadab, and Uzzah and Ahio*ᶜ* were driving the cart. ⁸David and all Israel were dancing before God with all their might, with song and lyres and harps and tambourines and cymbals and trumpets.

9 When they came to the threshing floor of Chidon, Uzzah put out his hand to hold the ark, for the oxen shook it. ¹⁰The anger of the Lᴏʀᴅ was kindled against Uzzah; he struck him down because he put out his hand to the ark; and he died there before God. ¹¹David was angry because the Lᴏʀᴅ had burst out against Uzzah; so that place is

a Gk: Heb lacks *David*   *b* Heb lacks *his*   *c* Or *and his brother*

called Perez-uzzah[a] to this day. [12]David was afraid of God that day; he said, "How can I bring the ark of God into my care?" [13]So David did not take the ark into his care into the city of David; he took it instead to the house of Obed-edom the Gittite. [14]The ark of God remained with the household of Obed-edom in his house three months, and the LORD blessed the household of Obed-edom and all that he had.

David Established at Jerusalem

14 King Hiram of Tyre sent messengers to David, along with cedar logs, and masons and carpenters to build a house for him. [2]David then perceived that the LORD had established him as king over Israel, and that his kingdom was highly exalted for the sake of his people Israel.

3 David took more wives in Jerusalem, and David became the father of more sons and daughters. [4]These are the names of the children whom he had in Jerusalem: Shammua, Shobab, and Nathan; Solomon, [5]Ibhar, Elishua, and Elpelet; [6]Nogah, Nepheg, and Japhia; [7]Elishama, Beeliada, and Eliphelet.

Defeat of the Philistines

8 When the Philistines heard that David had been anointed king over all Israel, all the Philistines went up in search of David; and David heard of it and went out against them. [9]Now the Philistines had come and made a raid in the valley of Rephaim. [10]David inquired of God, "Shall I go up against the Philistines? Will you give them into my hand?" The LORD said to him, "Go up, and I will give them into your hand." [11]So he went up to Baal-perazim, and David defeated them there. David said, "God has burst out[b] against my enemies by my hand, like a bursting flood." Therefore that place is called Baal-perazim.[c] [12]They abandoned their gods there, and at David's command they were burned.

13 Once again the Philistines made a raid in the valley. [14]When David again inquired of God, God said to him, "You shall not go up after them; go around and come on them opposite the balsam trees. [15]When you hear the sound of marching in the tops of the balsam trees, then go out to battle; for God has gone out before you to strike down the army of the Philistines." [16]David did as God had commanded him, and they struck down the Philistine army from Gibeon to Gezer. [17]The fame of David went out into all lands, and the LORD brought the fear of him on all nations.

The Ark Brought to Jerusalem

15 David[d] built houses for himself in the city of David, and he prepared a place for the ark of God and

Keeping Your Distance

1 CHRONICLES 13.11–12

When David saw that God's wrath had "burst out" against Uzzah, he was afraid. The fear of getting too close to such an awesome God or the fear of drawing God's attention to our own sinfulness can be a major block to a deeper relationship. What are the fears that keep you at a distance from God? Try drawing a picture to express your fear. Then draw a second picture to express God's love for you. As you look at the two pictures, let the one depicting God's love cover over the other, overwhelming your fear. Let God's love come into your heart and banish every fear. As the apostle John writes, "Perfect love casts out fear" (1 John 4.18).

See Meeting God in Prayer

---

a That is *Bursting Out Against Uzzah*   *b* Heb *paraz*   *c* That is *Lord of Bursting Out*   *d* Heb *He*

Lover of Harmony

1 CHRONICLES 15.16–24

"Now David was a man skilled in songs, who dearly loved musical harmony, not with a vulgar delight, but with a believing disposition, and by it served his God, who is the true God, by the mystical representation of a great thing. For the rational and well-ordered concord of diverse sounds in harmonious variety suggests the compact unity of the well-ordered city."

—AUGUSTINE,
The City of God

pitched a tent for it. ²Then David commanded that no one but the Levites were to carry the ark of God, for the LORD had chosen them to carry the ark of the LORD and to minister to him forever. ³David assembled all Israel in Jerusalem to bring up the ark of the LORD to its place, which he had prepared for it. ⁴Then David gathered together the descendants of Aaron and the Levites: ⁵of the sons of Kohath, Uriel the chief, with one hundred twenty of his kindred; ⁶of the sons of Merari, Asaiah the chief, with two hundred twenty of his kindred; ⁷of the sons of Gershom, Joel the chief, with one hundred thirty of his kindred; ⁸of the sons of Elizaphan, Shemaiah the chief, with two hundred of his kindred; ⁹of the sons of Hebron, Eliel the chief, with eighty of his kindred; ¹⁰of the sons of Uzziel, Amminadab the chief, with one hundred twelve of his kindred.

11 David summoned the priests Zadok and Abiathar, and the Levites Uriel, Asaiah, Joel, Shemaiah, Eliel, and Amminadab. ¹²He said to them, "You are the heads of families of the Levites; sanctify yourselves, you and your kindred, so that you may bring up the ark of the LORD, the God of Israel, to the place that I have prepared for it. ¹³Because you did not carry it the first time,ᵃ the LORD our God burst out against us, because we did not give it proper care." ¹⁴So the priests and the Levites sanctified themselves to bring up the ark of the LORD, the God of Israel. ¹⁵And the Levites carried the ark of God on their shoulders with the poles, as Moses had commanded according to the word of the LORD.

16 David also commanded the chiefs of the Levites to appoint their kindred as the singers to play on musical instruments, on harps and lyres and cymbals, to raise loud sounds of joy. ¹⁷So the Levites appointed Heman son of Joel; and of his kindred Asaph son of Berechiah; and of the sons of Merari, their kindred, Ethan son of Kushaiah; ¹⁸and with them their kindred of the second order, Zechariah, Jaaziel, Shemiramoth, Jehiel, Unni, Eliab, Benaiah, Maaseiah, Mattithiah, Eliphelehu, and Mikneiah, and the gatekeepers Obed-edom and Jeiel. ¹⁹The singers Heman, Asaph, and Ethan were to sound bronze cymbals; ²⁰Zechariah, Aziel, Shemiramoth, Jehiel, Unni, Eliab, Maaseiah, and Benaiah were to play harps according to Alamoth; ²¹but Mattithiah, Eliphelehu, Mikneiah, Obed-edom, Jeiel, and Azaziah were to lead with lyres according to the Sheminith. ²²Chenaniah, leader of the Levites in music, was to direct the music, for he understood it. ²³Berechiah and Elkanah were to be gatekeepers for the ark. ²⁴Shebaniah, Joshaphat, Nethanel, Amasai, Zechariah, Benaiah, and Eliezer, the priests, were to blow the trumpets before the ark of God. Obed-edom and Jehiah also were to be gatekeepers for the ark.

25 So David and the elders of Israel, and the command-

a Meaning of Heb uncertain

ers of the thousands, went to bring up the ark of the covenant of the Lord from the house of Obed-edom with rejoicing. ²⁶And because God helped the Levites who were carrying the ark of the covenant of the Lord, they sacrificed seven bulls and seven rams. ²⁷David was clothed with a robe of fine linen, as also were all the Levites who were carrying the ark, and the singers, and Chenaniah the leader of the music of the singers; and David wore a linen ephod. ²⁸So all Israel brought up the ark of the covenant of the Lord with shouting, to the sound of the horn, trumpets, and cymbals, and made loud music on harps and lyres.

29 As the ark of the covenant of the Lord came to the city of David, Michal daughter of Saul looked out of the window, and saw King David leaping and dancing; and she despised him in her heart.

The Ark Placed in the Tent

16 They brought in the ark of God, and set it inside the tent that David had pitched for it; and they offered burnt offerings and offerings of well-being before God. ²When David had finished offering the burnt offerings and the offerings of well-being, he blessed the people in the name of the Lord; ³and he distributed to every person in Israel—man and woman alike—to each a loaf of bread, a portion of meat,ᵃ and a cake of raisins.

4 He appointed certain of the Levites as ministers before the ark of the Lord, to invoke, to thank, and to praise the Lord, the God of Israel. ⁵Asaph was the chief, and second to him Zechariah, Jeiel, Shemiramoth, Jehiel, Mattithiah, Eliab, Benaiah, Obed-edom, and Jeiel, with harps and lyres; Asaph was to sound the cymbals, ⁶and the priests Benaiah and Jahaziel were to blow trumpets regularly, before the ark of the covenant of God.

David's Psalm of Thanksgiving

7 Then on that day David first appointed the singing of praises to the Lord by Asaph and his kindred.

8   O give thanks to the Lord, call on his name,
     make known his deeds among the peoples.
9   Sing to him, sing praises to him,
     tell of all his wonderful works.
10   Glory in his holy name;
     let the hearts of those who seek the Lord rejoice.
11   Seek the Lord and his strength,
     seek his presence continually.
12   Remember the wonderful works he has done,
     his miracles, and the judgments he uttered,
13   O offspring of his servant Israel,ᵇ
     children of Jacob, his chosen ones.

14   He is the Lord our God;

Dancing Before the Lord

1 CHRONICLES 15.29

David was "leaping and dancing" to show his love for God. What body language do you use to communicate with God? Do you come before God hunched over like a cowering slave? Do you lift your hands in praise? Do you dance? Try praising God through movement. Select some music that can lift your heart and that might help you move. Find a space where you can move freely, even if only to sway or clap your hands or spin around. Let the music flow through you to express your love for God in sound and rhythm. Let the Holy Spirit guide you. You will probably want to assure yourself of privacy when you try this. Remember Michal. Observers might not understand.

See Meeting God in Worship

---

a Compare Gk Syr Vg: Meaning of Heb uncertain   *b* Another reading is *Abraham* (compare Ps 105.6)

Glory Due God's Name

1 CHRONICLES 16.28–30

How do you ascribe glory and strength to God? What words or images come to mind when you hear the words "the glory of God" or "the power of God"? Linger over each word or image. What offering can you bring to such a God? How can you glorify God by your actions as well as by your words? Be as specific as you can, trying to name at least five things you can do today or tomorrow to give God glory.

See Meeting God in Worship

his judgments are in all the earth.

15 Remember his covenant forever,
    the word that he commanded, for a thousand generations,
16 the covenant that he made with Abraham,
    his sworn promise to Isaac,
17 which he confirmed to Jacob as a statute,
    to Israel as an everlasting covenant,
18 saying, "To you I will give the land of Canaan
    as your portion for an inheritance."

19 When they were few in number,
    of little account, and strangers in the land,[a]
20 wandering from nation to nation,
    from one kingdom to another people,
21 he allowed no one to oppress them;
    he rebuked kings on their account,
22 saying, "Do not touch my anointed ones;
    do my prophets no harm."

23 Sing to the LORD, all the earth.
    Tell of his salvation from day to day.
24 Declare his glory among the nations,
    his marvelous works among all the peoples.
25 For great is the LORD, and greatly to be praised;
    he is to be revered above all gods.
26 For all the gods of the peoples are idols,
    but the LORD made the heavens.
27 Honor and majesty are before him;
    strength and joy are in his place.

28 Ascribe to the LORD, O families of the peoples,
    ascribe to the LORD glory and strength.
29 Ascribe to the LORD the glory due his name;
    bring an offering, and come before him.
    Worship the LORD in holy splendor;
30   tremble before him, all the earth.
    The world is firmly established; it shall never be moved.
31 Let the heavens be glad, and let the earth rejoice,
    and let them say among the nations, "The LORD is king!"
32 Let the sea roar, and all that fills it;
    let the field exult, and everything in it.
33 Then shall the trees of the forest sing for joy
    before the LORD, for he comes to judge the earth.
34 O give thanks to the LORD, for he is good;
    for his steadfast love endures forever.

35 Say also:
    "Save us, O God of our salvation,

a Heb *in it*

and gather and rescue us from among the
nations,
that we may give thanks to your holy name,
and glory in your praise.
³⁶ Blessed be the LORD, the God of Israel,
from everlasting to everlasting."
Then all the people said "Amen!" and praised the LORD.

Regular Worship Maintained

37 David left Asaph and his kinsfolk there before the
ark of the covenant of the LORD to minister regularly before the ark as each day required, ³⁸and also Obed-edom
and his^a sixty-eight kinsfolk; while Obed-edom son of Jeduthun and Hosah were to be gatekeepers. ³⁹And he left
the priest Zadok and his kindred the priests before the
tabernacle of the LORD in the high place that was at Gibeon, ⁴⁰to offer burnt offerings to the LORD on the altar of
burnt offering regularly, morning and evening, according
to all that is written in the law of the LORD that he commanded Israel. ⁴¹With them were Heman and Jeduthun,
and the rest of those chosen and expressly named to render thanks to the LORD, for his steadfast love endures forever. ⁴²Heman and Jeduthun had with them trumpets and
cymbals for the music, and instruments for sacred song.
The sons of Jeduthun were appointed to the gate.

43 Then all the people departed to their homes, and
David went home to bless his household.

God's Covenant with David

17 Now when David settled in his house, David said to
the prophet Nathan, "I am living in a house of
cedar, but the ark of the covenant of the LORD is under a
tent." ²Nathan said to David, "Do all that you have in
mind, for God is with you."

3 But that same night the word of the LORD came to Nathan, saying: ⁴Go and tell my servant David: Thus says the
LORD: You shall not build me a house to live in. ⁵For I have
not lived in a house since the day I brought out Israel to
this very day, but I have lived in a tent and a tabernacle.^b
⁶Wherever I have moved about among all Israel, did I ever
speak a word with any of the judges of Israel, whom I
commanded to shepherd my people, saying, Why have
you not built me a house of cedar? ⁷Now therefore thus
you shall say to my servant David: Thus says the LORD of
hosts: I took you from the pasture, from following the
sheep, to be ruler over my people Israel; ⁸and I have been
with you wherever you went, and have cut off all your enemies before you; and I will make for you a name, like the
name of the great ones of the earth. ⁹I will appoint a place
for my people Israel, and will plant them, so that they may
live in their own place, and be disturbed no more; and
evildoers shall wear them down no more, as they did for-

Bowing to Authority

1 CHRONICLES 17.1–5

How could Nathan object to
David's plans? David was God's
chosen king! Besides, David's
plans glorified God (even if they
added to David's glory too).
But God had other plans. When
have you gone along with
something you weren't sure
about just because someone in
authority asked you to? When
have you followed your own
conscience, even if it meant
contradicting "the boss"? Ask
for God's help to be attentive to
God's call in the midst of daily
pressures from family, friends,
employers and others under
whose authority you have
placed yourself.

See Meeting God in Everyday Life

Grace Reaches Everyone

1 CHRONICLES 17.16

"Thy sovereign grace to all
    extends,
Immense and unconfined;
From age to age it never
    ends;
It reaches all mankind.
Throughout the world its
    breadth is known,
Wide as infinity;
So wide, it never passed by
    one,
Or it had passed by me."

—CHARLES WESLEY

merly, [10]from the time that I appointed judges over my people Israel; and I will subdue all your enemies.

Moreover I declare to you that the LORD will build you a house. [11]When your days are fulfilled to go to be with your ancestors, I will raise up your offspring after you, one of your own sons, and I will establish his kingdom. [12]He shall build a house for me, and I will establish his throne forever. [13]I will be a father to him, and he shall be a son to me. I will not take my steadfast love from him, as I took it from him who was before you, [14]but I will confirm him in my house and in my kingdom forever, and his throne shall be established forever. [15]In accordance with all these words and all this vision, Nathan spoke to David.

David's Prayer

16 Then King David went in and sat before the LORD, and said, "Who am I, O LORD God, and what is my house, that you have brought me thus far? [17]And even this was a small thing in your sight, O God; you have also spoken of your servant's house for a great while to come. You regard me as someone of high rank,[a] O LORD God! [18]And what more can David say to you for honoring your servant? You know your servant. [19]For your servant's sake, O LORD, and according to your own heart, you have done all these great deeds, making known all these great things. [20]There is no one like you, O LORD, and there is no God besides you, according to all that we have heard with our ears. [21]Who is like your people Israel, one nation on the earth whom God went to redeem to be his people, making for yourself a name for great and terrible things, in driving out nations before your people whom you redeemed from Egypt? [22]And you made your people Israel to be your people forever; and you, O LORD, became their God.

23 "And now, O LORD, as for the word that you have spoken concerning your servant and concerning his house, let it be established forever, and do as you have promised. [24]Thus your name will be established and magnified forever in the saying, 'The LORD of hosts, the God of Israel, is Israel's God'; and the house of your servant David will be established in your presence. [25]For you, my God, have revealed to your servant that you will build a house for him; therefore your servant has found it possible to pray before you. [26]And now, O LORD, you are God, and you have promised this good thing to your servant; [27]therefore may it please you to bless the house of your servant, that it may continue forever before you. For you, O LORD, have blessed and are blessed[b] forever."

David's Kingdom Established and Extended

18 Some time afterward, David attacked the Philistines and subdued them; he took Gath and its villages from the Philistines.

a Meaning of Heb uncertain   *b* Or *and it is blessed*

2 He defeated Moab, and the Moabites became subject to David and brought tribute.

3 David also struck down King Hadadezer of Zobah, toward Hamath,*a* as he went to set up a monument at the river Euphrates. ⁴David took from him one thousand chariots, seven thousand cavalry, and twenty thousand foot soldiers. David hamstrung all the chariot horses, but left one hundred of them. ⁵When the Arameans of Damascus came to help King Hadadezer of Zobah, David killed twenty-two thousand Arameans. ⁶Then David put garrisons*b* in Aram of Damascus; and the Arameans became subject to David, and brought tribute. The LORD gave victory to David wherever he went. ⁷David took the gold shields that were carried by the servants of Hadadezer, and brought them to Jerusalem. ⁸From Tibhath and from Cun, cities of Hadadezer, David took a vast quantity of bronze; with it Solomon made the bronze sea and the pillars and the vessels of bronze.

9 When King Tou of Hamath heard that David had defeated the whole army of King Hadadezer of Zobah, ¹⁰he sent his son Hadoram to King David, to greet him and to congratulate him, because he had fought against Hadadezer and defeated him. Now Hadadezer had often been at war with Tou. He sent all sorts of articles of gold, of silver, and of bronze; ¹¹these also King David dedicated to the LORD, together with the silver and gold that he had carried off from all the nations, from Edom, Moab, the Ammonites, the Philistines, and Amalek.

12 Abishai son of Zeruiah killed eighteen thousand Edomites in the Valley of Salt. ¹³He put garrisons in Edom; and all the Edomites became subject to David. And the LORD gave victory to David wherever he went.

David's Administration

14 So David reigned over all Israel; and he administered justice and equity to all his people. ¹⁵Joab son of Zeruiah was over the army; Jehoshaphat son of Ahilud was recorder; ¹⁶Zadok son of Ahitub and Ahimelech son of Abiathar were priests; Shavsha was secretary; ¹⁷Benaiah son of Jehoiada was over the Cherethites and the Pelethites; and David's sons were the chief officials in the service of the king.

Defeat of the Ammonites and Arameans

19 Some time afterward, King Nahash of the Ammonites died, and his son succeeded him. ²David said, "I will deal loyally with Hanun son of Nahash, for his father dealt loyally with me." So David sent messengers to console him concerning his father. When David's servants came to Hanun in the land of the Ammonites, to console him, ³the officials of the Ammonites said to Hanun, "Do you think, because David has sent consolers to you, that

---

David's Prayer

1 CHRONICLES 17.16–27

Read this passage using the method of *lectio divina*. Read the passage through twice carefully. What words or phrases strike you as meaningful? Write them down. Choose one or two and spend some time with them. Write down some of the images that come to mind. Rest in receptive silence. What is God saying to you through this word or phrase? What is your response? Pray accordingly.

---

a Meaning of Heb uncertain   *b* Gk Vg 2 Sam 8.6 Compare Syr: Heb lacks *garrisons*

Simple Prayer

1 CHRONICLES 19.10–15

Abba Macarius was asked, "How should one pray?" The old man said, "There is no need at all to make long discourses; it is enough to stretch out one's hands and say, 'Lord, as you will, and as you know, have mercy.' And if the conflict grows any fiercer say, 'Lord, help!' He knows very well what we need and he shows us his mercy."

—MACARIUS THE GREAT,
Sayings of the Desert Fathers

See Meeting God in Prayer

he is honoring your father? Have not his servants come to you to search and to overthrow and to spy out the land?" ⁴So Hanun seized David's servants, shaved them, cut off their garments in the middle at their hips, and sent them away; ⁵and they departed. When David was told about the men, he sent messengers to them, for they felt greatly humiliated. The king said, "Remain at Jericho until your beards have grown, and then return."

6 When the Ammonites saw that they had made themselves odious to David, Hanun and the Ammonites sent a thousand talents of silver to hire chariots and cavalry from Mesopotamia, from Aram-maacah and from Zobah. ⁷They hired thirty-two thousand chariots and the king of Maacah with his army, who came and camped before Medeba. And the Ammonites were mustered from their cities and came to battle. ⁸When David heard of it, he sent Joab and all the army of the warriors. ⁹The Ammonites came out and drew up in battle array at the entrance of the city, and the kings who had come were by themselves in the open country.

10 When Joab saw that the line of battle was set against him both in front and in the rear, he chose some of the picked men of Israel and arrayed them against the Arameans; ¹¹the rest of his troops he put in the charge of his brother Abishai, and they were arrayed against the Ammonites. ¹²He said, "If the Arameans are too strong for me, then you shall help me; but if the Ammonites are too strong for you, then I will help you. ¹³Be strong, and let us be courageous for our people and for the cities of our God; and may the LORD do what seems good to him." ¹⁴So Joab and the troops who were with him advanced toward the Arameans for battle; and they fled before him. ¹⁵When the Ammonites saw that the Arameans fled, they likewise fled before Abishai, Joab's brother, and entered the city. Then Joab came to Jerusalem.

16 But when the Arameans saw that they had been defeated by Israel, they sent messengers and brought out the Arameans who were beyond the Euphrates, with Shophach the commander of the army of Hadadezer at their head. ¹⁷When David was informed, he gathered all Israel together, crossed the Jordan, came to them, and drew up his forces against them. When David set the battle in array against the Arameans, they fought with him. ¹⁸The Arameans fled before Israel; and David killed seven thousand Aramean charioteers and forty thousand foot soldiers, and also killed Shophach the commander of their army. ¹⁹When the servants of Hadadezer saw that they had been defeated by Israel, they made peace with David, and became subject to him. So the Arameans were not willing to help the Ammonites any more.

Siege and Capture of Rabbah

20 In the spring of the year, the time when kings go out to battle, Joab led out the army, ravaged the country of the Ammonites, and came and besieged Rab-

bah. But David remained at Jerusalem. Joab attacked Rabbah, and overthrew it. ²David took the crown of Milcom*ᵃ* from his head; he found that it weighed a talent of gold, and in it was a precious stone; and it was placed on David's head. He also brought out the booty of the city, a very great amount. ³He brought out the people who were in it, and set them to work*ᵇ* with saws and iron picks and axes.*ᶜ* Thus David did to all the cities of the Ammonites. Then David and all the people returned to Jerusalem.

Exploits against the Philistines

4 After this, war broke out with the Philistines at Gezer; then Sibbecai the Hushathite killed Sippai, who was one of the descendants of the giants; and the Philistines were subdued. ⁵Again there was war with the Philistines; and Elhanan son of Jair killed Lahmi the brother of Goliath the Gittite, the shaft of whose spear was like a weaver's beam. ⁶Again there was war at Gath, where there was a man of great size, who had six fingers on each hand, and six toes on each foot, twenty-four in number; he also was descended from the giants. ⁷When he taunted Israel, Jonathan son of Shimea, David's brother, killed him. ⁸These were descended from the giants in Gath; they fell by the hand of David and his servants.

The Census and Plague

21 Satan stood up against Israel, and incited David to count the people of Israel. ²So David said to Joab and the commanders of the army, "Go, number Israel, from Beer-sheba to Dan, and bring me a report, so that I may know their number." ³But Joab said, "May the Lᴏʀᴅ increase the number of his people a hundredfold! Are they not, my lord the king, all of them my lord's servants? Why then should my lord require this? Why should he bring guilt on Israel?" ⁴But the king's word prevailed against Joab. So Joab departed and went throughout all Israel, and came back to Jerusalem. ⁵Joab gave the total count of the people to David. In all Israel there were one million one hundred thousand men who drew the sword, and in Judah four hundred seventy thousand who drew the sword. ⁶But he did not include Levi and Benjamin in the numbering, for the king's command was abhorrent to Joab.

7 But God was displeased with this thing, and he struck Israel. ⁸David said to God, "I have sinned greatly in that I have done this thing. But now, I pray you, take away the guilt of your servant; for I have done very foolishly." ⁹The Lᴏʀᴅ spoke to Gad, David's seer, saying, ¹⁰"Go and say to David, 'Thus says the Lᴏʀᴅ: Three things I offer you; choose one of them, so that I may do it to you.'" ¹¹So Gad came to David and said to him, "Thus says the Lᴏʀᴅ, 'Take your choice: ¹²either three years of famine; or three months of devastation by your foes, while the sword of

They Might Be Giants

1 CHRONICLES 20.4–8

The people of God still have to face giants. But today's giants are more likely to be the faceless giants of corporations, nations and social problems. What are the giants attacking you, your family, your church or your community? Do they need to be fought, or can they be engaged and redeemed? You might spend some time imagining one of these giants. What does it look like? Try talking with it. Writing out your conversation could help to keep you focused. You might want to invite God into the conversation to mediate your dispute or to advise you on how to proceed.

See Meeting God in Everyday Life

a Gk Vg See 1 Kings 11.5, 33; MT *of their king*   *b* Compare 2 Sam 12.31; Heb *and he sawed*   *c* Compare 2 Sam 12.31; Heb *saws*

Justice or Mercy?

1 CHRONICLES 21.11–13

Human ideas of justice center on retribution. But God offers mercy even while we are in the midst of suffering the consequences of our actions. Our call is to be merciful as God is merciful (see Luke 6.36). Where in your life are you aching for someone to "fall into human hands"? Try praying for that person or persons. Ask God to break into their lives, to offer them mercy and forgiveness even if you cannot do so. You might also ask God to fill you with love so that you, too, can offer mercy. What can you do to be an agent of mercy rather than retribution?

See *Meeting God in Community*

your enemies overtakes you; or three days of the sword of the LORD, pestilence on the land, and the angel of the LORD destroying throughout all the territory of Israel.' Now decide what answer I shall return to the one who sent me." [13]Then David said to Gad, "I am in great distress; let me fall into the hand of the LORD, for his mercy is very great; but let me not fall into human hands."

14 So the LORD sent a pestilence on Israel; and seventy thousand persons fell in Israel. [15]And God sent an angel to Jerusalem to destroy it; but when he was about to destroy it, the LORD took note and relented concerning the calamity; he said to the destroying angel, "Enough! Stay your hand." The angel of the LORD was then standing by the threshing floor of Ornan the Jebusite. [16]David looked up and saw the angel of the LORD standing between earth and heaven, and in his hand a drawn sword stretched out over Jerusalem. Then David and the elders, clothed in sackcloth, fell on their faces. [17]And David said to God, "Was it not I who gave the command to count the people? It is I who have sinned and done very wickedly. But these sheep, what have they done? Let your hand, I pray, O LORD my God, be against me and against my father's house; but do not let your people be plagued!"

David's Altar and Sacrifice

18 Then the angel of the LORD commanded Gad to tell David that he should go up and erect an altar to the LORD on the threshing floor of Ornan the Jebusite. [19]So David went up following Gad's instructions, which he had spoken in the name of the LORD. [20]Ornan turned and saw the angel; and while his four sons who were with him hid themselves, Ornan continued to thresh wheat. [21]As David came to Ornan, Ornan looked and saw David; he went out from the threshing floor, and did obeisance to David with his face to the ground. [22]David said to Ornan, "Give me the site of the threshing floor that I may build on it an altar to the LORD—give it to me at its full price—so that the plague may be averted from the people." [23]Then Ornan said to David, "Take it; and let my lord the king do what seems good to him; see, I present the oxen for burnt offerings, and the threshing sledges for the wood, and the wheat for a grain offering. I give it all." [24]But King David said to Ornan, "No; I will buy them for the full price. I will not take for the LORD what is yours, nor offer burnt offerings that cost me nothing." [25]So David paid Ornan six hundred shekels of gold by weight for the site. [26]David built there an altar to the LORD and presented burnt offerings and offerings of well-being. He called upon the LORD, and he answered him with fire from heaven on the altar of burnt offering. [27]Then the LORD commanded the angel, and he put his sword back into its sheath.

The Place Chosen for the Temple

28 At that time, when David saw that the LORD had answered him at the threshing floor of Ornan the Jebusite, he

made his sacrifices there. ²⁹For the tabernacle of the LORD, which Moses had made in the wilderness, and the altar of burnt offering were at that time in the high place at Gibeon; ³⁰but David could not go before it to inquire of God, for he was afraid of the sword of the angel of the LORD. 22 ¹Then David said, "Here shall be the house of the LORD God and here the altar of burnt offering for Israel."

David Prepares to Build the Temple

2 David gave orders to gather together the aliens who were residing in the land of Israel, and he set stonecutters to prepare dressed stones for building the house of God. ³David also provided great stores of iron for nails for the doors of the gates and for clamps, as well as bronze in quantities beyond weighing, ⁴and cedar logs without number—for the Sidonians and Tyrians brought great quantities of cedar to David. ⁵For David said, "My son Solomon is young and inexperienced, and the house that is to be built for the LORD must be exceedingly magnificent, famous and glorified throughout all lands; I will therefore make preparation for it." So David provided materials in great quantity before his death.

David's Charge to Solomon and the Leaders

6 Then he called for his son Solomon and charged him to build a house for the LORD, the God of Israel. ⁷David said to Solomon, "My son, I had planned to build a house to the name of the LORD my God. ⁸But the word of the LORD came to me, saying, 'You have shed much blood and have waged great wars; you shall not build a house to my name, because you have shed so much blood in my sight on the earth. ⁹See, a son shall be born to you; he shall be a man of peace. I will give him peace from all his enemies on every side; for his name shall be Solomon,ᵃ and I will give peaceᵇ and quiet to Israel in his days. ¹⁰He shall build a house for my name. He shall be a son to me, and I will be a father to him, and I will establish his royal throne in Israel forever.' ¹¹Now, my son, the LORD be with you, so that you may succeed in building the house of the LORD your God, as he has spoken concerning you. ¹²Only, may the LORD grant you discretion and understanding, so that when he gives you charge over Israel you may keep the law of the LORD your God. ¹³Then you will prosper if you are careful to observe the statutes and the ordinances that the LORD commanded Moses for Israel. Be strong and of good courage. Do not be afraid or dismayed. ¹⁴With great pains I have provided for the house of the LORD one hundred thousand talents of gold, one million talents of silver, and bronze and iron beyond weighing, for there is so much of it; timber and stone too I have provided. To these you must add more. ¹⁵You have an abundance of workers:

Words for the Leader

1 CHRONICLES 22.6–13

David's prayer and charge to Solomon might make a good blessing for any national leader. You might use this passage as a basis for prayer for the leader of your nation. Ask God to grant him or her discretion and understanding, strength and courage, confidence and, above all, care in seeking God's will as an individual and as a leader. You might also send a note of encouragement, letting the leader know about your prayer.

See Meeting God in Service

Gifts Are to Be Used

1 CHRONICLES 22.14–19

"I was made to see that the Holy Ghost never intended that [those] who have gifts and abilities should bury them in the earth, but rather did command and stir up such to the exercise of their gift, and also did commend those that were apt and ready so to do . . . Wherefore, though of myself of all the saints the most unworthy, yet I, but with great fear and trembling at the sight of my own weakness, did set upon the work, and did according to my gift, and the proportion of my faith, preach that blessed Gospel that God has showed me in the holy word of truth."

—JOHN BUNYAN,
Grace Abounding

stonecutters, masons, carpenters, and all kinds of artisans without number, skilled in working [16]gold, silver, bronze, and iron. Now begin the work, and the LORD be with you."

17 David also commanded all the leaders of Israel to help his son Solomon, saying, [18]"Is not the LORD your God with you? Has he not given you peace on every side? For he has delivered the inhabitants of the land into my hand; and the land is subdued before the LORD and his people. [19]Now set your mind and heart to seek the LORD your God. Go and build the sanctuary of the LORD God so that the ark of the covenant of the LORD and the holy vessels of God may be brought into a house built for the name of the LORD."

Families of the Levites and Their Functions

23 When David was old and full of days, he made his son Solomon king over Israel.
2 David assembled all the leaders of Israel and the priests and the Levites. [3]The Levites, thirty years old and upward, were counted, and the total was thirty-eight thousand. [4]"Twenty-four thousand of these," David said, "shall have charge of the work in the house of the LORD, six thousand shall be officers and judges, [5]four thousand gatekeepers, and four thousand shall offer praises to the LORD with the instruments that I have made for praise." [6]And David organized them in divisions corresponding to the sons of Levi: Gershon,[a] Kohath, and Merari.

7 The sons of Gershon[b] were Ladan and Shimei. [8]The sons of Ladan: Jehiel the chief, Zetham, and Joel, three. [9]The sons of Shimei: Shelomoth, Haziel, and Haran, three. These were the heads of families of Ladan. [10]And the sons of Shimei: Jahath, Zina, Jeush, and Beriah. These four were the sons of Shimei. [11]Jahath was the chief, and Zizah the second; but Jeush and Beriah did not have many sons, so they were enrolled as a single family.

12 The sons of Kohath: Amram, Izhar, Hebron, and Uzziel, four. [13]The sons of Amram: Aaron and Moses. Aaron was set apart to consecrate the most holy things, so that he and his sons forever should make offerings before the LORD, and minister to him and pronounce blessings in his name forever; [14]but as for Moses the man of God, his sons were to be reckoned among the tribe of Levi. [15]The sons of Moses: Gershom and Eliezer. [16]The sons of Gershom: Shebuel the chief. [17]The sons of Eliezer: Rehabiah the chief; Eliezer had no other sons, but the sons of Rehabiah were very numerous. [18]The sons of Izhar: Shelomith the chief. [19]The sons of Hebron: Jeriah the chief, Amariah the second, Jahaziel the third, and Jekameam the fourth. [20]The sons of Uzziel: Micah the chief and Isshiah the second.

21 The sons of Merari: Mahli and Mushi. The sons of Mahli: Eleazar and Kish. [22]Eleazar died having no sons, but only daughters; their kindred, the sons of Kish, married

---

a Or *Gershom*; See 1 Chr 6.1, note, and 23.15   *b* Vg Compare Gk Syr: Heb *to the Gershonite*

them. ²³The sons of Mushi: Mahli, Eder, and Jeremoth, three.

24 These were the sons of Levi by their ancestral houses, the heads of families as they were enrolled according to the number of the names of the individuals from twenty years old and upward who were to do the work for the service of the house of the LORD. ²⁵For David said, "The LORD, the God of Israel, has given rest to his people; and he resides in Jerusalem forever. ²⁶And so the Levites no longer need to carry the tabernacle or any of the things for its service"— ²⁷for according to the last words of David these were the number of the Levites from twenty years old and upward— ²⁸"but their duty shall be to assist the descendants of Aaron for the service of the house of the LORD, having the care of the courts and the chambers, the cleansing of all that is holy, and any work for the service of the house of God; ²⁹to assist also with the rows of bread, the choice flour for the grain offering, the wafers of unleavened bread, the baked offering, the offering mixed with oil, and all measures of quantity or size. ³⁰And they shall stand every morning, thanking and praising the LORD, and likewise at evening, ³¹and whenever burnt offerings are offered to the LORD on sabbaths, new moons, and appointed festivals, according to the number required of them, regularly before the LORD. ³²Thus they shall keep charge of the tent of meeting and the sanctuary, and shall attend the descendants of Aaron, their kindred, for the service of the house of the LORD."

Divisions of the Priests

24 The divisions of the descendants of Aaron were these. The sons of Aaron: Nadab, Abihu, Eleazar, and Ithamar. ²But Nadab and Abihu died before their father, and had no sons; so Eleazar and Ithamar became the priests. ³Along with Zadok of the sons of Eleazar, and Ahimelech of the sons of Ithamar, David organized them according to the appointed duties in their service. ⁴Since more chief men were found among the sons of Eleazar than among the sons of Ithamar, they organized them under sixteen heads of ancestral houses of the sons of Eleazar, and eight of the sons of Ithamar. ⁵They organized them by lot, all alike, for there were officers of the sanctuary and officers of God among both the sons of Eleazar and the sons of Ithamar. ⁶The scribe Shemaiah son of Nethanel, a Levite, recorded them in the presence of the king, and the officers, and Zadok the priest, and Ahimelech son of Abiathar, and the heads of ancestral houses of the priests and of the Levites; one ancestral house being chosen for Eleazar and one chosen for Ithamar.

7 The first lot fell to Jehoiarib, the second to Jedaiah, ⁸the third to Harim, the fourth to Seorim, ⁹the fifth to Malchijah, the sixth to Mijamin, ¹⁰the seventh to Hakkoz, the eighth to Abijah, ¹¹the ninth to Jeshua, the tenth to Shecaniah, ¹²the eleventh to Eliashib, the twelfth to Jakim, ¹³the thirteenth to Huppah, the fourteenth to Jeshebeab,

New Times, New Duties

1 CHRONICLES 23.25–28

With the ark of the covenant settled in Jerusalem, the traditional duty of the Levites, who tended the tabernacle, is ended. But there is still plenty for them to do. What traditional church activities have been meaningful to you but are now passing away? How do you respond to their passing? What new activities could you take part in? How can your gifts (both spiritual and natural) and your experience be used to serve the present needs of your church or your community? You might want to thank God for what has been and ask for God's help to be open to new challenges and new opportunities.

See *Meeting God in Service*

God's Word Through Music

1 CHRONICLES 25.1

To prophesy is to speak God's message. Here are people set apart to prophesy through music. Great music has the power to lift us up and to inspire us. Try letting music carry you in prayer. Find a place where you can relax and listen undisturbed. Select music that can allow your spirit to soar freely, whether it be a Bach fugue, a Beethoven symphony, a Stravinsky tone poem or some other composition that inspires you. Do not try to analyze the music. Simply offer the time to God and let the music speak. You might want to avoid music with lyrics, for words would suggest a particular direction. Allow yourself to rest in God's presence.

See Meeting God in Worship

[14]the fifteenth to Bilgah, the sixteenth to Immer, [15]the seventeenth to Hezir, the eighteenth to Happizzez, [16]the nineteenth to Pethahiah, the twentieth to Jehezkel, [17]the twenty-first to Jachin, the twenty-second to Gamul, [18]the twenty-third to Delaiah, the twenty-fourth to Maaziah. [19]These had as their appointed duty in their service to enter the house of the LORD according to the procedure established for them by their ancestor Aaron, as the LORD God of Israel had commanded him.

Other Levites

20 And of the rest of the sons of Levi: of the sons of Amram, Shubael; of the sons of Shubael, Jehdeiah. [21]Of Rehabiah: of the sons of Rehabiah, Isshiah the chief. [22]Of the Izharites, Shelomoth; of the sons of Shelomoth, Jahath. [23]The sons of Hebron:[a] Jeriah the chief,[b] Amariah the second, Jahaziel the third, Jekameam the fourth. [24]The sons of Uzziel, Micah; of the sons of Micah, Shamir. [25]The brother of Micah, Isshiah; of the sons of Isshiah, Zechariah. [26]The sons of Merari: Mahli and Mushi. The sons of Jaaziah: Beno.[c] [27]The sons of Merari: of Jaaziah, Beno,[c] Shoham, Zaccur, and Ibri. [28]Of Mahli: Eleazar, who had no sons. [29]Of Kish, the sons of Kish: Jerahmeel. [30]The sons of Mushi: Mahli, Eder, and Jerimoth. These were the sons of the Levites according to their ancestral houses. [31]These also cast lots corresponding to their kindred, the descendants of Aaron, in the presence of King David, Zadok, Ahimelech, and the heads of ancestral houses of the priests and of the Levites, the chief as well as the youngest brother.

The Temple Musicians

25 David and the officers of the army also set apart for the service the sons of Asaph, and of Heman, and of Jeduthun, who should prophesy with lyres, harps, and cymbals. The list of those who did the work and of their duties was: [2]Of the sons of Asaph: Zaccur, Joseph, Nethaniah, and Asarelah, sons of Asaph, under the direction of Asaph, who prophesied under the direction of the king. [3]Of Jeduthun, the sons of Jeduthun: Gedaliah, Zeri, Jeshaiah, Shimei,[d] Hashabiah, and Mattithiah, six, under the direction of their father Jeduthun, who prophesied with the lyre in thanksgiving and praise to the LORD. [4]Of Heman, the sons of Heman: Bukkiah, Mattaniah, Uzziel, Shebuel, and Jerimoth, Hananiah, Hanani, Eliathah, Giddalti, and Romamti-ezer, Joshbekashah, Mallothi, Hothir, Mahazioth. [5]All these were the sons of Heman the king's seer, according to the promise of God to exalt him; for God had given Heman fourteen sons and three daughters. [6]They were all under the direction of their father for the music in the house of the LORD with cymbals, harps, and lyres for the service of the house of God. Asaph, Jeduthun, and Heman were under the order of the king. [7]They and

a See 23.19: Heb lacks *Hebron* *b* See 23.19: Heb lacks *the chief*
c Or *his son*: Meaning of Heb uncertain *d* One Ms: Gk: MT lacks *Shimei*

their kindred, who were trained in singing to the Lord, all of whom were skillful, numbered two hundred eighty-eight. ⁸And they cast lots for their duties, small and great, teacher and pupil alike.

9 The first lot fell for Asaph to Joseph; the second to Gedaliah, to him and his brothers and his sons, twelve; ¹⁰the third to Zaccur, his sons and his brothers, twelve; ¹¹the fourth to Izri, his sons and his brothers, twelve; ¹²the fifth to Nethaniah, his sons and his brothers, twelve; ¹³the sixth to Bukkiah, his sons and his brothers, twelve; ¹⁴the seventh to Jesarelah,ᵃ his sons and his brothers, twelve; ¹⁵the eighth to Jeshaiah, his sons and his brothers, twelve; ¹⁶the ninth to Mattaniah, his sons and his brothers, twelve; ¹⁷the tenth to Shimei, his sons and his brothers, twelve; ¹⁸the eleventh to Azarel, his sons and his brothers, twelve; ¹⁹the twelfth to Hashabiah, his sons and his brothers, twelve; ²⁰to the thirteenth, Shubael, his sons and his brothers, twelve; ²¹to the fourteenth, Mattithiah, his sons and his brothers, twelve; ²²to the fifteenth, to Jeremoth, his sons and his brothers, twelve; ²³to the sixteenth, to Hananiah, his sons and his brothers, twelve; ²⁴to the seventeenth, to Joshbekashah, his sons and his brothers, twelve; ²⁵to the eighteenth, to Hanani, his sons and his brothers, twelve; ²⁶to the nineteenth, to Mallothi, his sons and his brothers, twelve; ²⁷to the twentieth, to Eliathah, his sons and his brothers, twelve; ²⁸to the twenty-first, to Hothir, his sons and his brothers, twelve; ²⁹to the twenty-second, to Giddalti, his sons and his brothers, twelve; ³⁰to the twenty-third, to Mahazioth, his sons and his brothers, twelve; ³¹to the twenty-fourth, to Romamti-ezer, his sons and his brothers, twelve.

The Gatekeepers

26 As for the divisions of the gatekeepers: of the Korahites, Meshelemiah son of Kore, of the sons of Asaph. ²Meshelemiah had sons: Zechariah the firstborn, Jediael the second, Zebadiah the third, Jathniel the fourth, ³Elam the fifth, Jehohanan the sixth, Eliehoenai the seventh. ⁴Obed-edom had sons: Shemaiah the firstborn, Jehozabad the second, Joah the third, Sachar the fourth, Nethanel the fifth, ⁵Ammiel the sixth, Issachar the seventh, Peullethai the eighth; for God blessed him. ⁶Also to his son Shemaiah sons were born who exercised authority in their ancestral houses, for they were men of great ability. ⁷The sons of Shemaiah: Othni, Rephael, Obed, and Elzabad, whose brothers were able men, Elihu and Semachiah. ⁸All these, sons of Obed-edom with their sons and brothers, were able men qualified for the service; sixty-two of Obed-edom. ⁹Meshelemiah had sons and brothers, able men, eighteen. ¹⁰Hosah, of the sons of Merari, had sons: Shimri the chief (for though he was not the firstborn, his father made him chief), ¹¹Hilkiah the second,

Called to a Special Place

1 CHRONICLES 25.6–31

"Each one of us has some kind of vocation. We are all called by God to share in his life and in His Kingdom. Each one of us is called to a special place in the Kingdom. If we find that place we will be happy. If we do not find it, we can never be completely happy. For each one of us, there is only one thing necessary: to fulfill our own destiny, according to God's will, to be what God wants us to be."

—THOMAS MERTON,
No Man Is an Island

ᵃ Or *Asarelah*; see 25.2

Gatekeepers

1 CHRONICLES 25.31–26.26

The gatekeepers guarded the temple entrances against theft and defilement. They also probably gathered offerings and physically cared for the temple. They were required to be "capable" and "able" and have "the strength to do the work."

Who are the "gatekeepers" of the church today? Pastors, deacons, elders, church-school teachers and parents? Anyone who is a disciple of Jesus? In what way are you a "gatekeeper" of God's truth? What makes you able to do your job well? How can you strengthen yourself to do the work of defending the faith and keeping it secure? For what do you need to ask God in order to qualify as a gatekeeper of the faith?

See *Meeting God in Community*

Tebaliah the third, Zechariah the fourth: all the sons and brothers of Hosah totaled thirteen.

12 These divisions of the gatekeepers, corresponding to their leaders, had duties, just as their kindred did, ministering in the house of the LORD; [13]and they cast lots by ancestral houses, small and great alike, for their gates. [14]The lot for the east fell to Shelemiah. They cast lots also for his son Zechariah, a prudent counselor, and his lot came out for the north. [15]Obed-edom's came out for the south, and to his sons was allotted the storehouse. [16]For Shuppim and Hosah it came out for the west, at the gate of Shallecheth on the ascending road. Guard corresponded to guard. [17]On the east there were six Levites each day,[a] on the north four each day, on the south four each day, as well as two and two at the storehouse; [18]and for the colonnade[b] on the west there were four at the road and two at the colonnade.[b] [19]These were the divisions of the gatekeepers among the Korahites and the sons of Merari.

The Treasurers, Officers, and Judges

20 And of the Levites, Ahijah had charge of the treasuries of the house of God and the treasuries of the dedicated gifts. [21]The sons of Ladan, the sons of the Gershonites belonging to Ladan, the heads of families belonging to Ladan the Gershonite: Jehieli.[c]

22 The sons of Jehieli, Zetham and his brother Joel, were in charge of the treasuries of the house of the LORD. [23]Of the Amramites, the Izharites, the Hebronites, and the Uzzielites: [24]Shebuel son of Gershom, son of Moses, was chief officer in charge of the treasuries. [25]His brothers: from Eliezer were his son Rehabiah, his son Jeshaiah, his son Joram, his son Zichri, and his son Shelomoth. [26]This Shelomoth and his brothers were in charge of all the treasuries of the dedicated gifts that King David, and the heads of families, and the officers of the thousands and the hundreds, and the commanders of the army, had dedicated. [27]From booty won in battles they dedicated gifts for the maintenance of the house of the LORD. [28]Also all that Samuel the seer, and Saul son of Kish, and Abner son of Ner, and Joab son of Zeruiah had dedicated—all dedicated gifts were in the care of Shelomoth[d] and his brothers.

29 Of the Izharites, Chenaniah and his sons were appointed to outside duties for Israel, as officers and judges. [30]Of the Hebronites, Hashabiah and his brothers, one thousand seven hundred men of ability, had the oversight of Israel west of the Jordan for all the work of the LORD and for the service of the king. [31]Of the Hebronites, Jerijah was chief of the Hebronites. (In the fortieth year of David's reign search was made, of whatever genealogy or family, and men of great ability among them were found at Jazer

---

a Gk: Heb lacks *each day*   b Heb *parbar*: meaning uncertain
c The Hebrew text of verse 21 is confused   d Gk Compare 26.28: Heb *Shelomith*

in Gilead.) ³²King David appointed him and his brothers, two thousand seven hundred men of ability, heads of families, to have the oversight of the Reubenites, the Gadites, and the half-tribe of the Manassites for everything pertaining to God and for the affairs of the king.

The Military Divisions

27 This is the list of the people of Israel, the heads of families, the commanders of the thousands and the hundreds, and their officers who served the king in all matters concerning the divisions that came and went, month after month throughout the year, each division numbering twenty-four thousand:

2 Jashobeam son of Zabdiel was in charge of the first division in the first month; in his division were twenty-four thousand. ³He was a descendant of Perez, and was chief of all the commanders of the army for the first month. ⁴Dodai the Ahohite was in charge of the division of the second month; Mikloth was the chief officer of his division. In his division were twenty-four thousand. ⁵The third commander, for the third month, was Benaiah son of the priest Jehoiada, as chief; in his division were twenty-four thousand. ⁶This is the Benaiah who was a mighty man of the Thirty and in command of the Thirty; his son Ammizabad was in charge of his division.ᵃ ⁷Asahel brother of Joab was fourth, for the fourth month, and his son Zebadiah after him; in his division were twenty-four thousand. ⁸The fifth commander, for the fifth month, was Shamhuth, the Izrahite; in his division were twenty-four thousand. ⁹Sixth, for the sixth month, was Ira son of Ikkesh the Tekoite; in his division were twenty-four thousand. ¹⁰Seventh, for the seventh month, was Helez the Pelonite, of the Ephraimites; in his division were twenty-four thousand. ¹¹Eighth, for the eighth month, was Sibbecai the Hushathite, of the Zerahites; in his division were twenty-four thousand. ¹²Ninth, for the ninth month, was Abiezer of Anathoth, a Benjaminite; in his division were twenty-four thousand. ¹³Tenth, for the tenth month, was Maharai of Netophah, of the Zerahites; in his division were twenty-four thousand. ¹⁴Eleventh, for the eleventh month, was Benaiah of Pirathon, of the Ephraimites; in his division were twenty-four thousand. ¹⁵Twelfth, for the twelfth month, was Heldai the Netophathite, of Othniel; in his division were twenty-four thousand.

Leaders of Tribes

16 Over the tribes of Israel, for the Reubenites, Eliezer son of Zichri was chief officer; for the Simeonites, Shephatiah son of Maacah; ¹⁷for Levi, Hashabiah son of Kemuel; for Aaron, Zadok; ¹⁸for Judah, Elihu, one of David's brothers; for Issachar, Omri son of Michael; ¹⁹for Zebulun, Ishmaiah son of Obadiah; for Naphtali, Jerimoth son of

Seeking Ability

Much of this book has listed people in terms of their families and their family duties. Now we are told that some were sought out, not on the basis of the genealogical records of their families but because they were people "of great ability." What parts of your life have been determined by family roles, traditions or expectations? Where have you been able to use your unique abilities and interests? How has God called you from the "expected" and set you free to be fully yourself? To what further growth is God calling you?

See Meeting God in the Created Order

ᵃ Gk Vg: Heb *Ammizabad was his division*

Stewardship

1 CHRONICLES 27.25

One of the most thankless jobs can be caring for the finances of God's people. Spend some time in prayer for the treasurer and other financial officers of your church, or for those in similar roles in other charitable organizations. You might thank God for them and pray that they be filled with God's love. Pray similarly for those who collect the offering and those who count it. If you don't know who they are, find out! When you next see them, tell them you appreciate the work they do.

See Meeting God in Service

Azriel; [20]for the Ephraimites, Hoshea son of Azaziah; for the half-tribe of Manasseh, Joel son of Pedaiah; [21]for the half-tribe of Manasseh in Gilead, Iddo son of Zechariah; for Benjamin, Jaasiel son of Abner; [22]for Dan, Azarel son of Jeroham. These were the leaders of the tribes of Israel. [23]David did not count those below twenty years of age, for the LORD had promised to make Israel as numerous as the stars of heaven. [24]Joab son of Zeruiah began to count them, but did not finish; yet wrath came upon Israel for this, and the number was not entered into the account of the Annals of King David.

Other Civic Officials

25 Over the king's treasuries was Azmaveth son of Adiel. Over the treasuries in the country, in the cities, in the villages and in the towers, was Jonathan son of Uzziah. [26]Over those who did the work of the field, tilling the soil, was Ezri son of Chelub. [27]Over the vineyards was Shimei the Ramathite. Over the produce of the vineyards for the wine cellars was Zabdi the Shiphmite. [28]Over the olive and sycamore trees in the Shephelah was Baal-hanan the Gederite. Over the stores of oil was Joash. [29]Over the herds that pastured in Sharon was Shitrai the Sharonite. Over the herds in the valleys was Shaphat son of Adlai. [30]Over the camels was Obil the Ishmaelite. Over the donkeys was Jehdeiah the Meronothite. Over the flocks was Jaziz the Hagrite. [31]All these were stewards of King David's property.

32 Jonathan, David's uncle, was a counselor, being a man of understanding and a scribe; Jehiel son of Hachmoni attended the king's sons. [33]Ahithophel was the king's counselor, and Hushai the Archite was the king's friend. [34]After Ahithophel came Jehoiada son of Benaiah, and Abiathar. Joab was commander of the king's army.

Solomon Instructed to Build the Temple

28 David assembled at Jerusalem all the officials of Israel, the officials of the tribes, the officers of the divisions that served the king, the commanders of the thousands, the commanders of the hundreds, the stewards of all the property and cattle of the king and his sons, together with the palace officials, the mighty warriors, and all the warriors. [2]Then King David rose to his feet and said: "Hear me, my brothers and my people. I had planned to build a house of rest for the ark of the covenant of the LORD, for the footstool of our God; and I made preparations for building. [3]But God said to me, 'You shall not build a house for my name, for you are a warrior and have shed blood.' [4]Yet the LORD God of Israel chose me from all my ancestral house to be king over Israel forever; for he chose Judah as leader, and in the house of Judah my father's house, and among my father's sons he took delight in making me king over all Israel. [5]And of all my sons, for the LORD has given me many, he has chosen my son Solomon to sit upon the throne of the kingdom of the LORD

over Israel. ⁶He said to me, 'It is your son Solomon who shall build my house and my courts, for I have chosen him to be a son to me, and I will be a father to him. ⁷I will establish his kingdom forever if he continues resolute in keeping my commandments and my ordinances, as he is today.' ⁸Now therefore in the sight of all Israel, the assembly of the Lord, and in the hearing of our God, observe and search out all the commandments of the Lord your God; that you may possess this good land, and leave it for an inheritance to your children after you forever.

9 "And you, my son Solomon, know the God of your father, and serve him with single mind and willing heart; for the Lord searches every mind, and understands every plan and thought. If you seek him, he will be found by you; but if you forsake him, he will abandon you forever. ¹⁰Take heed now, for the Lord has chosen you to build a house as the sanctuary; be strong, and act."

11 Then David gave his son Solomon the plan of the vestibule of the temple, and of its houses, its treasuries, its upper rooms, and its inner chambers, and of the room for the mercy seat;ᵃ ¹²and the plan of all that he had in mind: for the courts of the house of the Lord, all the surrounding chambers, the treasuries of the house of God, and the treasuries for dedicated gifts; ¹³for the divisions of the priests and of the Levites, and all the work of the service in the house of the Lord; for all the vessels for the service in the house of the Lord, ¹⁴the weight of gold for all golden vessels for each service, the weight of silver vessels for each service, ¹⁵the weight of the golden lampstands and their lamps, the weight of gold for each lampstand and its lamps, the weight of silver for a lampstand and its lamps, according to the use of each in the service, ¹⁶the weight of gold for each table for the rows of bread, the silver for the silver tables, ¹⁷and pure gold for the forks, the basins, and the cups; for the golden bowls and the weight of each; for the silver bowls and the weight of each; ¹⁸for the altar of incense made of refined gold, and its weight; also his plan for the golden chariot of the cherubim that spread their wings and covered the ark of the covenant of the Lord.

19 "All this, in writing at the Lord's direction, he made clear to me—the plan of all the works."

20 David said further to his son Solomon, "Be strong and of good courage, and act. Do not be afraid or dismayed; for the Lord God, my God, is with you. He will not fail you or forsake you, until all the work for the service of the house of the Lord is finished. ²¹Here are the divisions of the priests and the Levites for all the service of the house of God; and with you in all the work will be every volunteer who has skill for any kind of service; also the officers and all the people will be wholly at your command."

With a Willing Heart

1 CHRONICLES 28.2–10

Sometimes it is hard for us to pray "with single mind and willing heart." Instead, our thoughts run in many directions: praying, thinking over the things we have to do, monitoring our devotional "temperature," listening to cars going by or to the TV playing in the next room. One way of focusing our thoughts is through a breath prayer. Try using the phrase "with single mind and willing heart" as a breath prayer, repeating it to yourself slowly with each breath. Don't become discouraged if you find your thoughts wandering. Simply repeat the phrase. Let it affirm your intention to serve God completely and willingly. You might end your prayer time by slowly praying the Lord's Prayer.

See Meeting God in Prayer

---

a Or the cover

Blessing God

1 CHRONICLES 29.10–13

Read this passage slowly. Let David's prayer of praise become your own. Think of the blessings you have received and how you have experienced God's glory. If a phrase or a word claims your attention, stay with it for a while. When you reach the end of the passage, return to the beginning until the praise is echoing in your mind and you can carry thanks and praise from your prayer time into the rest of your day.

See Meeting God in Worship

Offerings for Building the Temple

29 King David said to the whole assembly, "My son Solomon, whom alone God has chosen, is young and inexperienced, and the work is great; for the temple*a* will not be for mortals but for the LORD God. ²So I have provided for the house of my God, so far as I was able, the gold for the things of gold, the silver for the things of silver, and the bronze for the things of bronze, the iron for the things of iron, and wood for the things of wood, besides great quantities of onyx and stones for setting, antimony, colored stones, all sorts of precious stones, and marble in abundance. ³Moreover, in addition to all that I have provided for the holy house, I have a treasure of my own of gold and silver, and because of my devotion to the house of my God I give it to the house of my God: ⁴three thousand talents of gold, of the gold of Ophir, and seven thousand talents of refined silver, for overlaying the walls of the house, ⁵and for all the work to be done by artisans, gold for the things of gold and silver for the things of silver. Who then will offer willingly, consecrating themselves today to the LORD?"

6 Then the leaders of ancestral houses made their freewill offerings, as did also the leaders of the tribes, the commanders of the thousands and of the hundreds, and the officers over the king's work. ⁷They gave for the service of the house of God five thousand talents and ten thousand darics of gold, ten thousand talents of silver, eighteen thousand talents of bronze, and one hundred thousand talents of iron. ⁸Whoever had precious stones gave them to the treasury of the house of the LORD, into the care of Jehiel the Gershonite. ⁹Then the people rejoiced because these had given willingly, for with single mind they had offered freely to the LORD; King David also rejoiced greatly.

David's Praise to God

10 Then David blessed the LORD in the presence of all the assembly; David said: "Blessed are you, O LORD, the God of our ancestor Israel, forever and ever. ¹¹Yours, O LORD, are the greatness, the power, the glory, the victory, and the majesty; for all that is in the heavens and on the earth is yours; yours is the kingdom, O LORD, and you are exalted as head above all. ¹²Riches and honor come from you, and you rule over all. In your hand are power and might; and it is in your hand to make great and to give strength to all. ¹³And now, our God, we give thanks to you and praise your glorious name.

14 "But who am I, and what is my people, that we should be able to make this freewill offering? For all things come from you, and of your own have we given you. ¹⁵For we are aliens and transients before you, as were all our ancestors; our days on the earth are like a shadow, and

a Heb *fortress*

there is no hope. ¹⁶O LORD our God, all this abundance that we have provided for building you a house for your holy name comes from your hand and is all your own. ¹⁷I know, my God, that you search the heart, and take pleasure in uprightness; in the uprightness of my heart I have freely offered all these things, and now I have seen your people, who are present here, offering freely and joyously to you. ¹⁸O LORD, the God of Abraham, Isaac, and Israel, our ancestors, keep forever such purposes and thoughts in the hearts of your people, and direct their hearts toward you. ¹⁹Grant to my son Solomon that with single mind he may keep your commandments, your decrees, and your statutes, performing all of them, and that he may build the temple*a* for which I have made provision."

20 Then David said to the whole assembly, "Bless the LORD your God." And all the assembly blessed the LORD, the God of their ancestors, and bowed their heads and prostrated themselves before the LORD and the king. ²¹On the next day they offered sacrifices and burnt offerings to the LORD, a thousand bulls, a thousand rams, and a thousand lambs, with their libations, and sacrifices in abundance for all Israel; ²²and they ate and drank before the LORD on that day with great joy.

Solomon Anointed King

They made David's son Solomon king a second time; they anointed him as the LORD's prince, and Zadok as priest. ²³Then Solomon sat on the throne of the LORD, succeeding his father David as king; he prospered, and all Israel obeyed him. ²⁴All the leaders and the mighty warriors, and also all the sons of King David, pledged their allegiance to King Solomon. ²⁵The LORD highly exalted Solomon in the sight of all Israel, and bestowed upon him such royal majesty as had not been on any king before him in Israel.

Summary of David's Reign

26 Thus David son of Jesse reigned over all Israel. ²⁷The period that he reigned over Israel was forty years; he reigned seven years in Hebron, and thirty-three years in Jerusalem. ²⁸He died in a good old age, full of days, riches, and honor; and his son Solomon succeeded him. ²⁹Now the acts of King David, from first to last, are written in the records of the seer Samuel, and in the records of the prophet Nathan, and in the records of the seer Gad, ³⁰with accounts of all his rule and his might and of the events that befell him and Israel and all the kingdoms of the earth.

Epitaph

1 CHRONICLES 29.26–30

These few verses serve as David's obituary. Try writing your own obituary. Whom do you leave behind? What legacy will you leave them? What noteworthy accomplishments or events are included? How is your imaginary obituary different from what would be written if you died right now? What needs to change in your life? How is your imaginary obituary different from your hopes and dreams? How is it different from what you sense God is calling you to be? How can God help you come closer to these ideals?

---

a Heb *fortress*

WAYS of MEETING GOD

Meeting God in Worship

The Bible places worship at the heart of life with God—and it is no wonder that it should do so. Over and over scripture invites us to praise God—to "ascribe to the LORD the glory due his name; bring an offering, and come before him. Worship the LORD in holy splendor" (1 Chronicles 16.29).

From the sacrificial offerings of Cain and Abel (see Genesis 4) to the expressions of the saints worshiping around the throne of God in the new Jerusalem (see Revelation 21–22), the act of worship is woven throughout scripture like a glittering thread. Noah leaves the ark and immediately builds an altar to make an offering of thanksgiving. The Israelites escape from Pharaoh at the Red Sea and begin to dance and sing God's praise. God offers detailed instruction about the settings, times and forms of worship (Exodus 25–31; Leviticus 1–8,16,23; Numbers 28–29). The book of Psalms is the Bible's own hymnal, offering choruses of praise, cries for help, prayers of confession and songs of thanksgiving. We read of the earliest Christians devoting themselves "to the apostles' teaching and fellowship, to the breaking of bread and the prayers" (Acts 2.42). Paul offers advice about the conduct of worship (see 1 Corinthians 11,14) and expects that his letters will be read to the gathered community (see Colossians 4.16).

For many of us the impulse to worship seems instinctive. The human heart cries: "O God, you are my God, I seek you, my soul thirsts for you; my flesh faints for you" (Psalm 63.1). In one sense, at least, seeking God comes naturally; we long for God because we have been created for companionship

> **W**orship begins with God reaching out to the ones he made. God floods our lives with blessing, and we give thanks: "O give thanks to the LORD, for he is good, for his steadfast love endures forever" (Psalm 136.1).

with God. As Augustine prayed, "You move us to delight in praising you; for you have formed us for yourself, and our hearts are restless till they find rest in you."

Worship, however, is more than the human soul reaching out to God. Worship begins with God reaching out to the ones he made. God floods our lives with blessing, and we give thanks: "O give thanks to the LORD, for he is good, for his steadfast love endures forever" (Psalm 136.1). God utters a prophetic word of warning that cuts us to the heart, and we cry out for mercy and forgiveness, individually (see Psalm 51) or even nationally (see Jonah 3). God comes to us in Jesus Christ, saying, in effect, "See who I am, what I am like, how I love you. This is what I expect. I offer you myself and the full inheritance that is yours as my faithful children." And we fall on our knees and say, "My Lord and my God!" (John 20.28).

Worship Is Personal. Worship involves an immediate, personal response to God. In worship we remember personally how God has acted in our past. In worship we hear God's voice, silence, music, preaching and the testimony of other believers in Jesus. In worship we experience the presence of Jesus Christ and hear his life-giving word to each of us in our particular time and situation.

Worship Is Corporate. However, we cannot do without the benefits of worship in the midst of the faithful congregation (see Matthew 18.20; Acts 2.1–4,42–47). Whenever we pray the opening words of the Lord's Prayer, "Our Father," we recognize that we never really pray or worship alone. There will always be times when we must stand in God's presence together. "I was glad," says the psalmist, "when they said to me, 'Let us go to the house of the LORD!' " (Psalm 122.1). In corporate worship we discern ourselves more clearly as walking with other Christians, together seeking God and following Jesus. Here, bowed before God or gathered at Christ's table, we are reminded again of the equality of all God's children. For here none is excluded because of race, status, gender, health, economics, language or age. We are united in "one body and one Spirit . . . one Lord, one faith, one baptism, one God and Father of all" (Ephesians 4.4–6).

In corporate worship sisters and brothers help us to hear and interpret God's Word. Each one has truth to share, and together we can hear and see so much more of God and of the gospel than we could ever hear or see alone. The gathered community of believers not only holds us accountable to God but also holds us close to God. In those moments during which our memories or our wills fail and we would otherwise drift away from God and from the abundant life in Jesus, the rest of the body of Christ upholds us and even carries us until we are able to walk again. Acts of worship—sharing a meal, passing the peace, baptizing new Christians—allow us to practice the sharing and forgiveness of Christian love that we carry from our worship into our world.

Corporate worship pushes back the horizons of our self-centered world and reminds us of our identity as people of God. As we participate in the baptism of a child or adult, the conversion of an individual or the reception of new members into the church, we are reminded of and given opportunity to renew our own covenant with God. As we share in the Lord's Supper, we unite to "proclaim the Lord's death until he comes" (1 Corinthians 11.26). In corporate worship, it is easier to remember who we are, from where we have come and where we are going. We encounter God in ways in which we would not have met him on our own. This awareness helps us to live more faithful lives as followers of Jesus Christ.

Public worship acknowledges that our relationship with God requires a corporate expression that is rooted in tradition. The Jewish cycle of festivals and gatherings at sabbath synagogues offered the people regular opportunities to worship, to "tell the old, old story," and to hear again God's instruction on how to live as his anointed, set-apart people. In a similar way the holy days of the church year and the weekly worship services offer Christians such opportunities. Worship becomes an occasion for meeting God. Such regular worship transforms our spirits until we become more and more like our Master, Jesus Christ.

> Christian worship that is anchored in the Bible may take on a variety of forms while remaining faithful and faith-centered. But through it all God's Word is proclaimed and our lives are touched—our hearts transformed.

Worship Is Biblical. Both the words and the manner of Christian worship are grounded in the Bible. This holds true for private worship, which may consist of reflecting on a passage of scripture or praying psalms; the same holds true for public worship in which the Bible provides the lessons for the day and the basis for a sermon or homily. The Bible may also provide the basis for a call to worship, words of assurance, responsive readings and hymns. Prayers at baptism recall Biblical references to water, including the passage concerning Jesus' own baptism. Prayers at Communion refer to the actions of Jesus at the Last Supper as recorded in the Gospels and 1 Corinthians 11, particularly in verses 23-29.

Worship Is Transforming. Christian worship that is anchored in the Bible may take on a variety of forms while remaining faithful and faith-centered. But through it all God's Word is proclaimed and our lives are touched—our hearts transformed. Unfortunately, the act of worship can become routine. The truth is, we frequently attend worship services from a sense of duty or custom rather than with any hope of encountering God. If we wish to be transformed by worship—if we truly want to meet God—we must adopt three essential practices.

We are to worship *regularly*. We need regular times and places for personal and corporate worship. Without such regularity we are likely to forget or to allow other things to crowd out life's most important relationship. But the life given to God and lived intentionally in God's presence is always secure and sustained. Luke tells us that Jesus on the Sabbath day "went into the synagogue . . . as was his custom" (Luke 4.16).

We are to worship *reverently*. When we enter our church or the special place set aside for worship in our home, we need to consciously focus our minds and hearts. In worship we remember, reflect, plead, offer and receive as we come intentionally into the presence of the One who created us in love. We come not only seeking God's gifts and presence but also offering all that we are and all that we hope to become as our gift of response.

We are to worship *expectantly*. If we are not listening for God to speak to us, we are not likely to hear. In Christian community we help each other to be strong enough to hear the prophetic word calling us to righteousness and humble enough to hear the hopeful word calling us to receive the gift of God's salvation. God enables us to use the gifts of the Spirit in ways that are humble—and sometimes dramatic—in order to make hearing him possible (see Romans 12.6–8; 1 Corinthians 12.1–13; Ephesians 4.11–13). God can reach out to us not only in scripture and sermon but also in the songs we sing, the prayers we pray and the love of those around us.

See Page 820 for the next Ways of Meeting God article.

2 CHRONICLES

Covenants Broken, Covenants Renewed

KEY VERSE:

The king stood in his place and made a covenant before the LORD, to follow the LORD, keeping his commandments, his decrees, and his statutes, with all his heart and all his soul, to perform the words of the covenant that were written in this book.—2 Chronicles 34.31

"Fri. 25. [December 1747]— We met at four, and solemnly rejoiced in God our Savior. I found much revival in my own soul this day; and so did many others also. Both this and the following days, I strongly urged the wholly giving up ourselves to God, and renewing in every point our covenant, that the Lord should be our God."

—JOHN WESLEY,
Journal

Covenant is one of the key concepts in the Old Testament. A covenant is a binding agreement, a promise to behave in a particular way toward another person or group. God makes covenants with Noah (Genesis 9), Abraham (Genesis 15), the Israelites (Exodus 19—24) and David (2 Samuel 7). The prophets call the people to return to covenant faithfulness while reminding them that God is always faithful—"gracious and merciful, slow to anger, and abounding in steadfast love" (Joel 2.13). Jeremiah looks to a new day when God's covenant will be written directly on our hearts (Jeremiah 31.31–34).

In this second part of the Chronicler's account, references to covenant are myriad. Bad kings break the covenant or fail to keep it. Good kings keep the covenant with God. Great kings are reformers who restore the covenant, especially Hezekiah (chapters 29—31) and Josiah (chapters 34—35). No other measure—not peace at home or victory in battle—can measure a king's true worth.

In our baptism, God seals his amazing promise that he will forever be our gracious and forgiving God. He calls us to put our trust in Jesus and to respond in obedience. We renew this covenant in many ways throughout our lives: when we take part in the baptism of another, in confirmation and other special services of baptismal renewal, and when we gather at the Lord's Table. As you read 2 Chronicles seek to renew your own covenant with your sovereign and loving God.

Solomon Requests Wisdom

1 Solomon son of David established himself in his kingdom; the LORD his God was with him and made him exceedingly great.

2 Solomon summoned all Israel, the commanders of the thousands and of the hundreds, the judges, and all the leaders of all Israel, the heads of families. ³Then Solomon, and the whole assembly with him, went to the high place that was at Gibeon; for God's tent of meeting, which Moses the servant of the LORD had made in the wilderness, was there. ⁴(But David had brought the ark of God up from Kiriath-jearim to the place that David had prepared for it; for he had pitched a tent for it in Jerusalem.) ⁵Moreover the bronze altar that Bezalel son of Uri, son of Hur, had made, was there in front of the tabernacle of the LORD. And Solomon and the assembly inquired at it. ⁶Solomon went up there to the bronze altar before the LORD, which was at the tent of meeting, and offered a thousand burnt offerings on it.

7 That night God appeared to Solomon, and said to him, "Ask what I should give you." ⁸Solomon said to God, "You have shown great and steadfast love to my father David, and have made me succeed him as king. ⁹O LORD God, let your promise to my father David now be fulfilled, for you have made me king over a people as numerous as the dust of the earth. ¹⁰Give me now wisdom and knowledge to go out and come in before this people, for who can rule this great people of yours?" ¹¹God answered Solomon, "Because this was in your heart, and you have not asked for possessions, wealth, honor, or the life of those who hate you, and have not even asked for long life, but have asked for wisdom and knowledge for yourself that you may rule my people over whom I have made you king, ¹²wisdom and knowledge are granted to you. I will also give you riches, possessions, and honor, such as none of the kings had who were before you, and none after you shall have the like." ¹³So Solomon came from*a* the high place at Gibeon, from the tent of meeting, to Jerusalem. And he reigned over Israel.

Solomon's Military and Commercial Activity

14 Solomon gathered together chariots and horses; he had fourteen hundred chariots and twelve thousand horses, which he stationed in the chariot cities and with the king in Jerusalem. ¹⁵The king made silver and gold as common in Jerusalem as stone, and he made cedar as plentiful as the sycamore of the Shephelah. ¹⁶Solomon's horses were imported from Egypt and Kue; the king's traders received them from Kue at the prevailing price. ¹⁷They imported from Egypt, and then exported, a chariot for six hundred shekels of silver, and a horse for one hundred fifty; so through them these were exported to all the kings of the Hittites and the kings of Aram.

Preparations for Building the Temple

2 *b* Solomon decided to build a temple for the name of the LORD, and a royal palace for himself. ²*c* Solomon conscripted seventy thousand laborers and eighty thou-

---

A Question to Ponder

2 CHRONICLES 1.7

How would you respond if God said to you what he said to Solomon: "Ask what I should give you"? What would you ask for? How would God respond? This might be a good question to explore in writing. Spell out the dialogue between God and yourself. When you have finished, read aloud what you have written. What have you learned from this second reading?

---

a Gk Vg: Heb *to*   *b* Ch 1.18 in Heb   *c* Ch 2.1 in Heb

Who Am I?

2 CHRONICLES 2.6

Solomon explains that the task of building a temple for God is overwhelming, so he asks for help. What task is God calling you to perform? What is your part in building up God's people into a living temple? What can you do on your own? What kind of help do you need? Who might provide that help? Who might know where you can find help? Ask God to give you both help and helpers for the task ahead.

See Meeting God in Service

sand stonecutters in the hill country, with three thousand six hundred to oversee them.

Alliance with Huram of Tyre

3 Solomon sent word to King Huram of Tyre: "Once you dealt with my father David and sent him cedar to build himself a house to live in. ⁴I am now about to build a house for the name of the LORD my God and dedicate it to him for offering fragrant incense before him, and for the regular offering of the rows of bread, and for burnt offerings morning and evening, on the sabbaths and the new moons and the appointed festivals of the LORD our God, as ordained forever for Israel. ⁵The house that I am about to build will be great, for our God is greater than other gods. ⁶But who is able to build him a house, since heaven, even highest heaven, cannot contain him? Who am I to build a house for him, except as a place to make offerings before him? ⁷So now send me an artisan skilled to work in gold, silver, bronze, and iron, and in purple, crimson, and blue fabrics, trained also in engraving, to join the skilled workers who are with me in Judah and Jerusalem, whom my father David provided. ⁸Send me also cedar, cypress, and algum timber from Lebanon, for I know that your servants are skilled in cutting Lebanon timber. My servants will work with your servants ⁹to prepare timber for me in abundance, for the house I am about to build will be great and wonderful. ¹⁰I will provide for your servants, those who cut the timber, twenty thousand cors of crushed wheat, twenty thousand cors of barley, twenty thousand baths*a* of wine, and twenty thousand baths of oil."

11 Then King Huram of Tyre answered in a letter that he sent to Solomon, "Because the LORD loves his people he has made you king over them." ¹²Huram also said, "Blessed be the LORD God of Israel, who made heaven and earth, who has given King David a wise son, endowed with discretion and understanding, who will build a temple for the LORD, and a royal palace for himself.

13 "I have dispatched Huram-abi, a skilled artisan, endowed with understanding, ¹⁴the son of one of the Danite women, his father a Tyrian. He is trained to work in gold, silver, bronze, iron, stone, and wood, and in purple, blue, and crimson fabrics and fine linen, and to do all sorts of engraving and execute any design that may be assigned him, with your artisans, the artisans of my lord, your father David. ¹⁵Now, as for the wheat, barley, oil, and wine, of which my lord has spoken, let him send them to his servants. ¹⁶We will cut whatever timber you need from Lebanon, and bring it to you as rafts by sea to Joppa; you will take it up to Jerusalem."

17 Then Solomon took a census of all the aliens who were residing in the land of Israel, after the census that his father David had taken; and there were found to be one hundred fifty-three thousand six hundred. ¹⁸Seventy thousand of them he assigned as laborers, eighty thousand as stonecutters in the hill country, and three thousand six hundred as overseers to make the people work.

a A Hebrew measure of volume

Solomon Builds the Temple

3 Solomon began to build the house of the LORD in Jerusalem on Mount Moriah, where the LORD had appeared to his father David, at the place that David had designated, on the threshing floor of Ornan the Jebusite. [2] He began to build on the second day of the second month of the fourth year of his reign. [3] These are Solomon's measurements[a] for building the house of God: the length, in cubits of the old standard, was sixty cubits, and the width twenty cubits. [4] The vestibule in front of the nave of the house was twenty cubits long, across the width of the house;[b] and its height was one hundred twenty cubits. He overlaid it on the inside with pure gold. [5] The nave he lined with cypress, covered it with fine gold, and made palms and chains on it. [6] He adorned the house with settings of precious stones. The gold was gold from Parvaim. [7] So he lined the house with gold—its beams, its thresholds, its walls, and its doors; and he carved cherubim on the walls.

8 He made the most holy place; its length, corresponding to the width of the house, was twenty cubits, and its width was twenty cubits; he overlaid it with six hundred talents of fine gold. [9] The weight of the nails was fifty shekels of gold. He overlaid the upper chambers with gold.

10 In the most holy place he made two carved cherubim and overlaid[c] them with gold. [11] The wings of the cherubim together extended twenty cubits: one wing of the one, five cubits long, touched the wall of the house, and its other wing, five cubits long, touched the wing of the other cherub; [12] and of this cherub, one wing, five cubits long, touched the wall of the house, and the other wing, also five cubits long, was joined to the wing of the first cherub. [13] The wings of these cherubim extended twenty cubits; the cherubim[d] stood on their feet, facing the nave. [14] And Solomon[e] made the curtain of blue and purple and crimson fabrics and fine linen, and worked cherubim into it.

15 In front of the house he made two pillars thirty-five cubits high, with a capital of five cubits on the top of each. [16] He made encircling[f] chains and put them on the tops of the pillars; and he made one hundred pomegranates, and put them on the chains. [17] He set up the pillars in front of the temple, one on the right, the other on the left; the one on the right he called Jachin, and the one on the left, Boaz.

Furnishings of the Temple

4 He made an altar of bronze, twenty cubits long, twenty cubits wide, and ten cubits high. [2] Then he made the molten sea; it was round, ten cubits from rim to rim, and five cubits high. A line of thirty cubits would encircle it completely. [3] Under it were panels all around, each of ten cubits, surrounding the sea; there were two rows of panels, cast when it was cast. [4] It stood on twelve oxen, three facing north, three facing west, three facing south, and three facing east; the sea was set on them. The hindquarters of

---

A House of Stories

2 CHRONICLES 3.1

A church is a holy place, not only because of its use, but also because of the people who have helped to build it. In your imagination—or perhaps in reality—take a walk through your church. What are the stories it tells? Notice windows and pictures that may tell Biblical stories. What places or objects evoke memories of particular people or events? Thank God for your church as a house of stories.

See Meeting God in Worship

---

a Syr: Heb *foundations*   *b* Compare 1 Kings 6.3: Meaning of Heb uncertain   *c* Heb *they overlaid*   *d* Heb *they*   *e* Heb *he*   *f* Cn: Heb *in the inner sanctuary*

A House of Praise

2 CHRONICLES 4.7

Take another walk through your church. This time notice things in terms of their use in the church. There may be lampstands, special doors and basins, as in the temple of Solomon. There may be books and pews and musical instruments. How is each item a part of the worship of God? How do these items contribute to the work of God's people? How about you? What is your part in the worship and work of your church? How do you think God wants to use you?

See Meeting God in Worship

each were toward the inside. ⁵Its thickness was a handbreadth; its rim was made like the rim of a cup, like the flower of a lily; it held three thousand baths.ᵃ ⁶He also made ten basins in which to wash, and set five on the right side, and five on the left. In these they were to rinse what was used for the burnt offering. The sea was for the priests to wash in.

7 He made ten golden lampstands as prescribed, and set them in the temple, five on the south side and five on the north. ⁸He also made ten tables and placed them in the temple, five on the right side and five on the left. And he made one hundred basins of gold. ⁹He made the court of the priests, and the great court, and doors for the court; he overlaid their doors with bronze. ¹⁰He set the sea at the southeast corner of the house.

11 And Huram made the pots, the shovels, and the basins. Thus Huram finished the work that he did for King Solomon on the house of God: ¹²the two pillars, the bowls, and the two capitals on the top of the pillars; and the two latticeworks to cover the two bowls of the capitals that were on the top of the pillars; ¹³the four hundred pomegranates for the two latticeworks, two rows of pomegranates for each latticework, to cover the two bowls of the capitals that were on the pillars. ¹⁴He made the stands, the basins on the stands, ¹⁵the one sea, and the twelve oxen underneath it. ¹⁶The pots, the shovels, the forks, and all the equipment for these Huram-abi made of burnished bronze for King Solomon for the house of the LORD. ¹⁷In the plain of the Jordan the king cast them, in the clay ground between Succoth and Zeredah. ¹⁸Solomon made all these things in great quantities, so that the weight of the bronze was not determined.

19 So Solomon made all the things that were in the house of God: the golden altar, the tables for the bread of the Presence, ²⁰the lampstands and their lamps of pure gold to burn before the inner sanctuary, as prescribed; ²¹the flowers, the lamps, and the tongs, of purest gold; ²²the snuffers, basins, ladles, and firepans, of pure gold. As for the entrance to the temple: the inner doors to the most holy place and the doors of the nave of the temple were of gold.

5 Thus all the work that Solomon did for the house of the LORD was finished. Solomon brought in the things that his father David had dedicated, and stored the silver, the gold, and all the vessels in the treasuries of the house of God.

The Ark Brought into the Temple

2 Then Solomon assembled the elders of Israel and all the heads of the tribes, the leaders of the ancestral houses of the people of Israel, in Jerusalem, to bring up the ark of the covenant of the LORD out of the city of David, which is Zion. ³And all the Israelites assembled before the king at the festival that is in the seventh month. ⁴And all the elders of Israel came, and the Levites carried the ark. ⁵So they brought up the ark, the tent of meeting, and all the holy vessels that were in the tent; the priests and the Levites brought them up. ⁶King Solomon and all the congregation of Israel, who had assembled before him, were

a A Hebrew measure of volume

before the ark, sacrificing so many sheep and oxen that they could not be numbered or counted. ⁷Then the priests brought the ark of the covenant of the LORD to its place, in the inner sanctuary of the house, in the most holy place, underneath the wings of the cherubim. ⁸For the cherubim spread out their wings over the place of the ark, so that the cherubim made a covering above the ark and its poles. ⁹The poles were so long that the ends of the poles were seen from the holy place in front of the inner sanctuary; but they could not be seen from outside; they are there to this day. ¹⁰There was nothing in the ark except the two tablets that Moses put there at Horeb, where the LORD made a covenant*a* with the people of Israel after they came out of Egypt.

11 Now when the priests came out of the holy place (for all the priests who were present had sanctified themselves, without regard to their divisions), ¹²all the levitical singers, Asaph, Heman, and Jeduthun, their sons and kindred, arrayed in fine linen, with cymbals, harps, and lyres, stood east of the altar with one hundred twenty priests who were trumpeters. ¹³It was the duty of the trumpeters and singers to make themselves heard in unison in praise and thanksgiving to the LORD, and when the song was raised, with trumpets and cymbals and other musical instruments, in praise to the LORD,

"For he is good,
    for his steadfast love endures forever,"
the house, the house of the LORD, was filled with a cloud, ¹⁴so that the priests could not stand to minister because of the cloud; for the glory of the LORD filled the house of God.

Dedication of the Temple

6 Then Solomon said, "The LORD has said that he would reside in thick darkness. ²I have built you an exalted house, a place for you to reside in forever."

3 Then the king turned around and blessed all the assembly of Israel, while all the assembly of Israel stood. ⁴And he said, "Blessed be the LORD, the God of Israel, who with his hand has fulfilled what he promised with his mouth to my father David, saying, ⁵'Since the day that I brought my people out of the land of Egypt, I have not chosen a city from any of the tribes of Israel in which to build a house, so that my name might be there, and I chose no one as ruler over my people Israel; ⁶but I have chosen Jerusalem in order that my name may be there, and I have chosen David to be over my people Israel.' ⁷My father David had it in mind to build a house for the name of the LORD, the God of Israel. ⁸But the LORD said to my father David, 'You did well to consider building a house for my name; ⁹nevertheless you shall not build the house, but your son who shall be born to you shall build the house for my name.' ¹⁰Now the LORD has fulfilled his promise that he made; for I have succeeded my father David, and sit on the throne of Israel, as the LORD promised, and have built the house for the name of the LORD, the God of Israel. ¹¹There I have set the ark, in which is the covenant of the LORD that he made with the people of Israel."

a Heb lacks *a covenant*

In the Thick Darkness

2 CHRONICLES 5.11–6.1

"Try as you might, this darkness and this cloud will remain between you and your God. You will feel frustrated, for your mind will be unable to grasp him, and your heart will not relish the delight of his love. But learn to be at home in this darkness. Return to it as often as you can, letting your spirit cry out to him whom you love. For if, in this life, you hope to feel and see God as he is in himself it must be within this darkness and this cloud."

—ANONYMOUS,
The Cloud of Unknowing

Promises Fulfilled

2 CHRONICLES 6.14–15

Think back through your life. What promises did God make to you? What promises have been proclaimed in God's name? How have you experienced promises fulfilled? You might want to write down some experiences that come to mind. You might make a litany by reading one of those experiences aloud and then repeating verse 14. What promises are still awaiting fulfillment?

Solomon's Prayer of Dedication

12 Then Solomon*a* stood before the altar of the LORD in the presence of the whole assembly of Israel, and spread out his hands. [13] Solomon had made a bronze platform five cubits long, five cubits wide, and three cubits high, and had set it in the court; and he stood on it. Then he knelt on his knees in the presence of the whole assembly of Israel, and spread out his hands toward heaven. [14] He said, "O LORD, God of Israel, there is no God like you, in heaven or on earth, keeping covenant in steadfast love with your servants who walk before you with all their heart— [15] you who have kept for your servant, my father David, what you promised to him. Indeed, you promised with your mouth and this day have fulfilled with your hand. [16] Therefore, O LORD, God of Israel, keep for your servant, my father David, that which you promised him, saying, 'There shall never fail you a successor before me to sit on the throne of Israel, if only your children keep to their way, to walk in my law as you have walked before me.' [17] Therefore, O LORD, God of Israel, let your word be confirmed, which you promised to your servant David.

18 "But will God indeed reside with mortals on earth? Even heaven and the highest heaven cannot contain you, how much less this house that I have built! [19] Regard your servant's prayer and his plea, O LORD my God, heeding the cry and the prayer that your servant prays to you. [20] May your eyes be open day and night toward this house, the place where you promised to set your name, and may you heed the prayer that your servant prays toward this place. [21] And hear the plea of your servant and of your people Israel, when they pray toward this place; may you hear from heaven your dwelling place; hear and forgive.

22 "If someone sins against another and is required to take an oath and comes and swears before your altar in this house, [23] may you hear from heaven, and act, and judge your servants, repaying the guilty by bringing their conduct on their own head, and vindicating those who are in the right by rewarding them in accordance with their righteousness.

24 "When your people Israel, having sinned against you, are defeated before an enemy but turn again to you, confess your name, pray and plead with you in this house, [25] may you hear from heaven, and forgive the sin of your people Israel, and bring them again to the land that you gave to them and to their ancestors.

26 "When heaven is shut up and there is no rain because they have sinned against you, and then they pray toward this place, confess your name, and turn from their sin, because you punish them, [27] may you hear in heaven, forgive the sin of your servants, your people Israel, when you teach them the good way in which they should walk; and send down rain upon your land, which you have given to your people as an inheritance.

28 "If there is famine in the land, if there is plague, blight, mildew, locust, or caterpillar; if their enemies besiege them in any of the settlements of the lands; whatever suffering, whatever sickness there is; [29] whatever prayer,

a Heb he

whatever plea from any individual or from all your people Israel, all knowing their own suffering and their own sorrows so that they stretch out their hands toward this house; ³⁰may you hear from heaven, your dwelling place, forgive, and render to all whose heart you know, according to all their ways, for only you know the human heart. ³¹Thus may they fear you and walk in your ways all the days that they live in the land that you gave to our ancestors.

32 "Likewise when foreigners, who are not of your people Israel, come from a distant land because of your great name, and your mighty hand, and your outstretched arm, when they come and pray toward this house, ³³may you hear from heaven your dwelling place, and do whatever the foreigners ask of you, in order that all the peoples of the earth may know your name and fear you, as do your people Israel, and that they may know that your name has been invoked on this house that I have built.

34 "If your people go out to battle against their enemies, by whatever way you shall send them, and they pray to you toward this city that you have chosen and the house that I have built for your name, ³⁵then hear from heaven their prayer and their plea, and maintain their cause.

36 "If they sin against you—for there is no one who does not sin—and you are angry with them and give them to an enemy, so that they are carried away captive to a land far or near; ³⁷then if they come to their senses in the land to which they have been taken captive, and repent, and plead with you in the land of their captivity, saying, 'We have sinned, and have done wrong; we have acted wickedly'; ³⁸if they repent with all their heart and soul in the land of their captivity, to which they were taken captive, and pray toward their land, which you gave to their ancestors, the city that you have chosen, and the house that I have built for your name, ³⁹then hear from heaven your dwelling place their prayer and their pleas, maintain their cause and forgive your people who have sinned against you. ⁴⁰Now, O my God, let your eyes be open and your ears attentive to prayer from this place.

⁴¹ "Now rise up, O Lᴏʀᴅ God, and go to your resting place,
   you and the ark of your might.
Let your priests, O Lᴏʀᴅ God, be clothed with salvation,
   and let your faithful rejoice in your goodness.
⁴² O Lᴏʀᴅ God, do not reject your anointed one.
   Remember your steadfast love for your servant David."

Solomon Dedicates the Temple

7 When Solomon had ended his prayer, fire came down from heaven and consumed the burnt offering and the sacrifices; and the glory of the Lᴏʀᴅ filled the temple. ²The priests could not enter the house of the Lᴏʀᴅ, because the glory of the Lᴏʀᴅ filled the Lᴏʀᴅ's house. ³When all the people of Israel saw the fire come down and the glory of the Lᴏʀᴅ on the temple, they bowed down on the pave-

Outsiders Welcome!

2 CHRONICLES 6.32–33

What an amazing request! Solomon asks that even foreigners may find the temple to be a place where they can encounter God and receive God's blessings. How are strangers made to feel welcome at your church? How are they reminded that they are outsiders? What might be done to help them feel at home? To bring them into God's presence? How might God use you to accomplish this?

See Meeting God in Community

Awesome Glory

2 CHRONICLES 7.1–3

When you encounter God's glory, words just aren't enough to express what you feel. You can't even think straight. So don't try. Simply relax and give yourself over to adoration. You might try repeating the single word "glory" to provide a focus, to keep your mind from running about wildly. Or you might prefer to repeat the affirmation "God's love endures forever" as a breath prayer, that is, saying it once slowly with each breath. If you become distracted, simply return to the prayer word or breath prayer. You might end by singing the Doxology or by praying the Lord's Prayer.

See Meeting God in Worship

ment with their faces to the ground, and worshiped and gave thanks to the LORD, saying,

"For he is good,
for his steadfast love endures forever."

4 Then the king and all the people offered sacrifice before the LORD. ⁵King Solomon offered as a sacrifice twenty-two thousand oxen and one hundred twenty thousand sheep. So the king and all the people dedicated the house of God. ⁶The priests stood at their posts; the Levites also, with the instruments for music to the LORD that King David had made for giving thanks to the LORD—for his steadfast love endures forever—whenever David offered praises by their ministry. Opposite them the priests sounded trumpets; and all Israel stood.

7 Solomon consecrated the middle of the court that was in front of the house of the LORD; for there he offered the burnt offerings and the fat of the offerings of well-being because the bronze altar Solomon had made could not hold the burnt offering and the grain offering and the fat parts.

8 At that time Solomon held the festival for seven days, and all Israel with him, a very great congregation, from Lebo-hamath to the Wadi of Egypt. ⁹On the eighth day they held a solemn assembly; for they had observed the dedication of the altar seven days and the festival seven days. ¹⁰On the twenty-third day of the seventh month he sent the people away to their homes, joyful and in good spirits because of the goodness that the LORD had shown to David and to Solomon and to his people Israel.

11 Thus Solomon finished the house of the LORD and the king's house; all that Solomon had planned to do in the house of the LORD and in his own house he successfully accomplished.

God's Second Appearance to Solomon

12 Then the LORD appeared to Solomon in the night and said to him: "I have heard your prayer, and have chosen this place for myself as a house of sacrifice. ¹³When I shut up the heavens so that there is no rain, or command the locust to devour the land, or send pestilence among my people, ¹⁴if my people who are called by my name humble themselves, pray, seek my face, and turn from their wicked ways, then I will hear from heaven, and will forgive their sin and heal their land. ¹⁵Now my eyes will be open and my ears attentive to the prayer that is made in this place. ¹⁶For now I have chosen and consecrated this house so that my name may be there forever; my eyes and my heart will be there for all time. ¹⁷As for you, if you walk before me, as your father David walked, doing according to all that I have commanded you and keeping my statutes and my ordinances, ¹⁸then I will establish your royal throne, as I made covenant with your father David saying, 'You shall never lack a successor to rule over Israel.'

19 "But if you*ᵃ* turn aside and forsake my statutes and my commandments that I have set before you, and go and serve other gods and worship them, ²⁰then I will pluck you*ᵇ* up from the land that I have given you;*ᵇ* and this house, which I have consecrated for my name, I will cast

a The word *you* in this verse is plural   *b* Heb *them*

out of my sight, and will make it a proverb and a byword among all peoples. ²¹And regarding this house, now exalted, everyone passing by will be astonished, and say, 'Why has the LORD done such a thing to this land and to this house?' ²²Then they will say, 'Because they abandoned the LORD the God of their ancestors who brought them out of the land of Egypt, and they adopted other gods, and worshiped them and served them; therefore he has brought all this calamity upon them.' "

Various Activities of Solomon

8 At the end of twenty years, during which Solomon had built the house of the LORD and his own house, ²Solomon rebuilt the cities that Huram had given to him, and settled the people of Israel in them.

3 Solomon went to Hamath-zobah, and captured it. ⁴He built Tadmor in the wilderness and all the storage towns that he built in Hamath. ⁵He also built Upper Beth-horon and Lower Beth-horon, fortified cities, with walls, gates, and bars, ⁶and Baalath, as well as all Solomon's storage towns, and all the towns for his chariots, the towns for his cavalry, and whatever Solomon desired to build, in Jerusalem, in Lebanon, and in all the land of his dominion. ⁷All the people who were left of the Hittites, the Amorites, the Perizzites, the Hivites, and the Jebusites, who were not of Israel, ⁸from their descendants who were still left in the land, whom the people of Israel had not destroyed—these Solomon conscripted for forced labor, as is still the case today. ⁹But of the people of Israel Solomon made no slaves for his work; they were soldiers, and his officers, the commanders of his chariotry and cavalry. ¹⁰These were the chief officers of King Solomon, two hundred fifty of them, who exercised authority over the people.

11 Solomon brought Pharaoh's daughter from the city of David to the house that he had built for her, for he said, "My wife shall not live in the house of King David of Israel, for the places to which the ark of the LORD has come are holy."

12 Then Solomon offered up burnt offerings to the LORD on the altar of the LORD that he had built in front of the vestibule, ¹³as the duty of each day required, offering according to the commandment of Moses for the sabbaths, the new moons, and the three annual festivals—the festival of unleavened bread, the festival of weeks, and the festival of booths. ¹⁴According to the ordinance of his father David, he appointed the divisions of the priests for their service, and the Levites for their offices of praise and ministry alongside the priests as the duty of each day required, and the gatekeepers in their divisions for the several gates; for so David the man of God had commanded. ¹⁵They did not turn away from what the king had commanded the priests and Levites regarding anything at all, or regarding the treasuries.

16 Thus all the work of Solomon was accomplished from*a* the day the foundation of the house of the LORD was laid until the house of the LORD was finished completely.

17 Then Solomon went to Ezion-geber and Eloth on the shore of the sea, in the land of Edom. ¹⁸Huram sent him, in the care of his servants, ships and servants fa-

National Repentance

2 CHRONICLES 7.14

Imagine that you have been asked to lead a time of national repentance based on this verse. What national sins would you recount as part of the humbling process? What actions, symbolic or practical, would you call for? What prayer would you offer to lead the nation in seeking God's face? How would you proclaim the good news that God will forgive the nation's sin and heal the land? Now that you have all these great ideas, how will you use them?

See Meeting God in Community

Prayer for the King

2 CHRONICLES 9.8

The queen of Sheba, seeing all that Solomon has built and hearing his wisdom, is inspired to bless God. What qualities or actions of the leaders of your country, your state or your community inspire you? You might want to spend some time in prayer for these leaders, thanking God for the good you see in them and asking God to strengthen or inspire them where you see faults. You might also write to them to let them know you are holding them up in prayer.

See Meeting God in Community

miliar with the sea. They went to Ophir, together with the servants of Solomon, and imported from there four hundred fifty talents of gold and brought it to King Solomon.

Visit of the Queen of Sheba

9 When the queen of Sheba heard of the fame of Solomon, she came to Jerusalem to test him with hard questions, having a very great retinue and camels bearing spices and very much gold and precious stones. When she came to Solomon, she discussed with him all that was on her mind. ²Solomon answered all her questions; there was nothing hidden from Solomon that he could not explain to her. ³When the queen of Sheba had observed the wisdom of Solomon, the house that he had built, ⁴the food of his table, the seating of his officials, and the attendance of his servants, and their clothing, his valets, and their clothing, and his burnt offerings*a* that he offered at the house of the LORD, there was no more spirit left in her.

5 So she said to the king, "The report was true that I heard in my own land of your accomplishments and of your wisdom, ⁶but I did not believe the*b* reports until I came and my own eyes saw it. Not even half of the greatness of your wisdom had been told to me; you far surpass the report that I had heard. ⁷Happy are your people! Happy are these your servants, who continually attend you and hear your wisdom! ⁸Blessed be the LORD your God, who has delighted in you and set you on his throne as king for the LORD your God. Because your God loved Israel and would establish them forever, he has made you king over them, that you may execute justice and righteousness." ⁹Then she gave the king one hundred twenty talents of gold, a very great quantity of spices, and precious stones: there were no spices such as those that the queen of Sheba gave to King Solomon.

10 Moreover the servants of Huram and the servants of Solomon who brought gold from Ophir brought algum wood and precious stones. ¹¹From the algum wood, the king made steps*c* for the house of the LORD and for the king's house, lyres also and harps for the singers; there never was seen the like of them before in the land of Judah.

12 Meanwhile King Solomon granted the queen of Sheba every desire that she expressed, well beyond what she had brought to the king. Then she returned to her own land, with her servants.

Solomon's Great Wealth

13 The weight of gold that came to Solomon in one year was six hundred sixty-six talents of gold, ¹⁴besides that which the traders and merchants brought; and all the kings of Arabia and the governors of the land brought gold and silver to Solomon. ¹⁵King Solomon made two hundred large shields of beaten gold; six hundred shekels of beaten gold went into each large shield. ¹⁶He made three hundred shields of beaten gold; three hundred shekels of gold went into each shield; and the king put them in the House of the

---

a Gk Syr Vg 1 Kings 10.5: Heb *ascent*   *b* Heb *their*   *c* Gk Vg: Meaning of Heb uncertain

Forest of Lebanon. ¹⁷The king also made a great ivory throne, and overlaid it with pure gold. ¹⁸The throne had six steps and a footstool of gold, which were attached to the throne, and on each side of the seat were arm rests and two lions standing beside the arm rests, ¹⁹while twelve lions were standing, one on each end of a step on the six steps. The like of it was never made in any kingdom. ²⁰All King Solomon's drinking vessels were of gold, and all the vessels of the House of the Forest of Lebanon were of pure gold; silver was not considered as anything in the days of Solomon. ²¹For the king's ships went to Tarshish with the servants of Huram; once every three years the ships of Tarshish used to come bringing gold, silver, ivory, apes, and peacocks.ᵃ

22 Thus King Solomon excelled all the kings of the earth in riches and in wisdom. ²³All the kings of the earth sought the presence of Solomon to hear his wisdom, which God had put into his mind. ²⁴Every one of them brought a present, objects of silver and gold, garments, weaponry, spices, horses, and mules, so much year by year. ²⁵Solomon had four thousand stalls for horses and chariots, and twelve thousand horses, which he stationed in the chariot cities and with the king in Jerusalem. ²⁶He ruled over all the kings from the Euphrates to the land of the Philistines, and to the border of Egypt. ²⁷The king made silver as common in Jerusalem as stone, and cedar as plentiful as the sycamore of the Shephelah. ²⁸Horses were imported for Solomon from Egypt and from all lands.

Death of Solomon

29 Now the rest of the acts of Solomon, from first to last, are they not written in the history of the prophet Nathan, and in the prophecy of Ahijah the Shilonite, and in the visions of the seer Iddo concerning Jeroboam son of Nebat? ³⁰Solomon reigned in Jerusalem over all Israel forty years. ³¹Solomon slept with his ancestors and was buried in the city of his father David; and his son Rehoboam succeeded him.

The Revolt against Rehoboam

10 Rehoboam went to Shechem, for all Israel had come to Shechem to make him king. ²When Jeroboam son of Nebat heard of it (for he was in Egypt, where he had fled from King Solomon), then Jeroboam returned from Egypt. ³They sent and called him; and Jeroboam and all Israel came and said to Rehoboam, ⁴"Your father made our yoke heavy. Now therefore lighten the hard service of your father and his heavy yoke that he placed on us, and we will serve you." ⁵He said to them, "Come to me again in three days." So the people went away.

6 Then King Rehoboam took counsel with the older men who had attended his father Solomon while he was still alive, saying, "How do you advise me to answer this people?" ⁷They answered him, "If you will be kind to this people and please them, and speak good words to them, then they will be your servants forever." ⁸But he rejected the advice that the older men gave him, and consulted the

---

Signs of Greatness

2 CHRONICLES 9.13–28

Solomon surrounds himself with the trappings of wealth and power as signs of his greatness. What would some equivalent signs be today? Think about the lifestyles of the rich and famous or about monumental government buildings. What do you look for as indications of greatness in a person? What makes a person great in your eyes? What impression would you like to make on others? What impression do you think you do make? (You might want to discuss this with someone you can trust to be honest.) How do you need to change in order to match your standards of greatness? How do your ambitions differ from what God is calling you to be?

ᵃ Or *baboons*

Temptations to Evil

2 CHRONICLES 10.6–11

"Inconstancy of mind, and a weak confidence in God, are the beginning of all temptations to evil. For as a ship without a rudder is driven to and fro by the waves so those who are remiss and give up their resolution are in many ways tempted. As fire tries iron, so temptation tries the just. We often know not what we can do; but temptation reveals what we are."

—THOMAS À KEMPIS,
The Imitation of Christ

young men who had grown up with him and now attended him. ⁹He said to them, "What do you advise that we answer this people who have said to me, 'Lighten the yoke that your father put on us'?" ¹⁰The young men who had grown up with him said to him, "Thus should you speak to the people who said to you, 'Your father made our yoke heavy, but you must lighten it for us'; tell them, 'My little finger is thicker than my father's loins. ¹¹Now, whereas my father laid on you a heavy yoke, I will add to your yoke. My father disciplined you with whips, but I will discipline you with scorpions.' "

12 So Jeroboam and all the people came to Rehoboam the third day, as the king had said, "Come to me again the third day." ¹³The king answered them harshly. King Rehoboam rejected the advice of the older men; ¹⁴he spoke to them in accordance with the advice of the young men, "My father made your yoke heavy, but I will add to it; my father disciplined you with whips, but I will discipline you with scorpions." ¹⁵So the king did not listen to the people, because it was a turn of affairs brought about by God so that the LORD might fulfill his word, which he had spoken by Ahijah the Shilonite to Jeroboam son of Nebat.

16 When all Israel saw that the king would not listen to them, the people answered the king,

"What share do we have in David?
We have no inheritance in the son of Jesse.
Each of you to your tents, O Israel!
Look now to your own house, O David."

So all Israel departed to their tents. ¹⁷But Rehoboam reigned over the people of Israel who were living in the cities of Judah. ¹⁸When King Rehoboam sent Hadoram, who was taskmaster over the forced labor, the people of Israel stoned him to death. King Rehoboam hurriedly mounted his chariot to flee to Jerusalem. ¹⁹So Israel has been in rebellion against the house of David to this day.

Judah and Benjamin Fortified

11 When Rehoboam came to Jerusalem, he assembled one hundred eighty thousand chosen troops of the house of Judah and Benjamin to fight against Israel, to restore the kingdom to Rehoboam. ²But the word of the LORD came to Shemaiah the man of God: ³Say to King Rehoboam of Judah, son of Solomon, and to all Israel in Judah and Benjamin, ⁴"Thus says the LORD: You shall not go up or fight against your kindred. Let everyone return home, for this thing is from me." So they heeded the word of the LORD and turned back from the expedition against Jeroboam.

5 Rehoboam resided in Jerusalem, and he built cities for defense in Judah. ⁶He built up Bethlehem, Etam, Tekoa, ⁷Beth-zur, Soco, Adullam, ⁸Gath, Mareshah, Ziph, ⁹Adoraim, Lachish, Azekah, ¹⁰Zorah, Aijalon, and Hebron, fortified cities that are in Judah and in Benjamin. ¹¹He made the fortresses strong, and put commanders in them, and stores of food, oil, and wine. ¹²He also put large shields and spears in all the cities, and made them very strong. So he held Judah and Benjamin.

Priests and Levites Support Rehoboam

13 The priests and the Levites who were in all Israel presented themselves to him from all their territories. ¹⁴The Levites had left their common lands and their holdings and had come to Judah and Jerusalem, because Jeroboam and his sons had prevented them from serving as priests of the Lord, ¹⁵and had appointed his own priests for the high places, and for the goat-demons, and for the calves that he had made. ¹⁶Those who had set their hearts to seek the Lord God of Israel came after them from all the tribes of Israel to Jerusalem to sacrifice to the Lord, the God of their ancestors. ¹⁷They strengthened the kingdom of Judah, and for three years they made Rehoboam son of Solomon secure, for they walked for three years in the way of David and Solomon.

Rehoboam's Marriages

18 Rehoboam took as his wife Mahalath daughter of Jerimoth son of David, and of Abihail daughter of Eliab son of Jesse. ¹⁹She bore him sons: Jeush, Shemariah, and Zaham. ²⁰After her he took Maacah daughter of Absalom, who bore him Abijah, Attai, Ziza, and Shelomith. ²¹Rehoboam loved Maacah daughter of Absalom more than all his other wives and concubines (he took eighteen wives and sixty concubines, and became the father of twenty-eight sons and sixty daughters). ²²Rehoboam appointed Abijah son of Maacah as chief prince among his brothers, for he intended to make him king. ²³He dealt wisely, and distributed some of his sons through all the districts of Judah and Benjamin, in all the fortified cities; he gave them abundant provisions, and found many wives for them.

Egypt Attacks Judah

12 When the rule of Rehoboam was established and he grew strong, he abandoned the law of the Lord, he and all Israel with him. ²In the fifth year of King Rehoboam, because they had been unfaithful to the Lord, King Shishak of Egypt came up against Jerusalem ³with twelve hundred chariots and sixty thousand cavalry. A countless army came with him from Egypt—Libyans, Sukkiim, and Ethiopians.ᵃ ⁴He took the fortified cities of Judah and came as far as Jerusalem. ⁵Then the prophet Shemaiah came to Rehoboam and to the officers of Judah, who had gathered at Jerusalem because of Shishak, and said to them, "Thus says the Lord: You abandoned me, so I have abandoned you to the hand of Shishak." ⁶Then the officers of Israel and the king humbled themselves and said, "The Lord is in the right." ⁷When the Lord saw that they humbled themselves, the word of the Lord came to Shemaiah, saying: "They have humbled themselves; I will not destroy them, but I will grant them some deliverance, and my wrath shall not be poured out on Jerusalem by the hand of Shishak. ⁸Nevertheless they shall be his servants, so that they may know the difference between serving me and serving the kingdoms of other lands."

9 So King Shishak of Egypt came up against Jerusalem;

Outgrowing God

2 CHRONICLES 12.1–12

Rehoboam seems to be like many people who feel they have outgrown their need for God. Some leave the church when they leave their parents' home. Some get so caught up in working and raising a family that it seems easy to skip attending worship services or to omit quiet times with God. Where can you see this happening in your own life? Where is your love growing cold? What former activities no longer seem important? You might ask God to fan the flame of the Spirit in your heart. You might also seek new, more mature ways of relating to God and living out your devotion to God.

See Meeting God in Prayer

he took away the treasures of the house of the LORD and the treasures of the king's house; he took everything. He also took away the shields of gold that Solomon had made; ¹⁰but King Rehoboam made in place of them shields of bronze, and committed them to the hands of the officers of the guard, who kept the door of the king's house. ¹¹Whenever the king went into the house of the LORD, the guard would come along bearing them, and would then bring them back to the guardroom. ¹²Because he humbled himself the wrath of the LORD turned from him, so as not to destroy them completely; moreover, conditions were good in Judah.

Death of Rehoboam

13 So King Rehoboam established himself in Jerusalem and reigned. Rehoboam was forty-one years old when he began to reign; he reigned seventeen years in Jerusalem, the city that the LORD had chosen out of all the tribes of Israel to put his name there. His mother's name was Naamah the Ammonite. ¹⁴He did evil, for he did not set his heart to seek the LORD.

15 Now the acts of Rehoboam, from first to last, are they not written in the records of the prophet Shemaiah and of the seer Iddo, recorded by genealogy? There were continual wars between Rehoboam and Jeroboam. ¹⁶Rehoboam slept with his ancestors and was buried in the city of David; and his son Abijah succeeded him.

Abijah Reigns over Judah

13 In the eighteenth year of King Jeroboam, Abijah began to reign over Judah. ²He reigned for three years in Jerusalem. His mother's name was Micaiah daughter of Uriel of Gibeah.

Now there was war between Abijah and Jeroboam. ³Abijah engaged in battle, having an army of valiant warriors, four hundred thousand picked men; and Jeroboam drew up his line of battle against him with eight hundred thousand picked mighty warriors. ⁴Then Abijah stood on the slope of Mount Zemaraim that is in the hill country of Ephraim, and said, "Listen to me, Jeroboam and all Israel! ⁵Do you not know that the LORD God of Israel gave the kingship over Israel forever to David and his sons by a covenant of salt? ⁶Yet Jeroboam son of Nebat, a servant of Solomon son of David, rose up and rebelled against his lord; ⁷and certain worthless scoundrels gathered around him and defied Rehoboam son of Solomon, when Rehoboam was young and irresolute and could not withstand them.

8 "And now you think that you can withstand the kingdom of the LORD in the hand of the sons of David, because you are a great multitude and have with you the golden calves that Jeroboam made as gods for you. ⁹Have you not driven out the priests of the LORD, the descendants of Aaron, and the Levites, and made priests for yourselves like the peoples of other lands? Whoever comes to be consecrated with a young bull or seven rams becomes a priest of what are no gods. ¹⁰But as for us, the LORD is our God, and we have not abandoned him. We have priests ministering to the LORD who are descendants of Aaron, and Levites for their service.

[11]They offer to the LORD every morning and every evening burnt offerings and fragrant incense, set out the rows of bread on the table of pure gold, and care for the golden lampstand so that its lamps may burn every evening; for we keep the charge of the LORD our God, but you have abandoned him. [12]See, God is with us at our head, and his priests have their battle trumpets to sound the call to battle against you. O Israelites, do not fight against the LORD, the God of your ancestors; for you cannot succeed."

13 Jeroboam had sent an ambush around to come on them from behind; thus his troops[a] were in front of Judah, and the ambush was behind them. [14]When Judah turned, the battle was in front of them and behind them. They cried out to the LORD, and the priests blew the trumpets. [15]Then the people of Judah raised the battle shout. And when the people of Judah shouted, God defeated Jeroboam and all Israel before Abijah and Judah. [16]The Israelites fled before Judah, and God gave them into their hands. [17]Abijah and his army defeated them with great slaughter; five hundred thousand picked men of Israel fell slain. [18]Thus the Israelites were subdued at that time, and the people of Judah prevailed, because they relied on the LORD, the God of their ancestors. [19]Abijah pursued Jeroboam, and took cities from him: Bethel with its villages and Jeshanah with its villages and Ephron[b] with its villages. [20]Jeroboam did not recover his power in the days of Abijah; the LORD struck him down, and he died. [21]But Abijah grew strong. He took fourteen wives, and became the father of twenty-two sons and sixteen daughters. [22]The rest of the acts of Abijah, his behavior and his deeds, are written in the story of the prophet Iddo.

Asa Reigns

14[c] So Abijah slept with his ancestors, and they buried him in the city of David. His son Asa succeeded him. In his days the land had rest for ten years. [2][d]Asa did what was good and right in the sight of the LORD his God. [3]He took away the foreign altars and the high places, broke down the pillars, hewed down the sacred poles,[e] [4]and commanded Judah to seek the LORD, the God of their ancestors, and to keep the law and the commandment. [5]He also removed from all the cities of Judah the high places and the incense altars. And the kingdom had rest under him. [6]He built fortified cities in Judah while the land had rest. He had no war in those years, for the LORD gave him peace. [7]He said to Judah, "Let us build these cities, and surround them with walls and towers, gates and bars; the land is still ours because we have sought the LORD our God; we have sought him, and he has given us peace on every side." So they built and prospered. [8]Asa had an army of three hundred thousand from Judah, armed with large shields and spears, and two hundred eighty thousand troops from Benjamin who carried shields and drew bows; all these were mighty warriors.

a Heb *they*   *b* Another reading is *Ephrain*   *c* Ch 13.23 in Heb
d Ch 14.1 in Heb   *e* Heb *Asherim*
569

Clever Plans

2 CHRONICLES 13.13–15

Jeroboam makes careful and clever plans for trapping the army of Judah and gaining victory. But God has other plans. When have your plans been overthrown? Do you see that as a tragedy? Or can you see it as God leading you in another direction? What have you learned from plans gone wrong? Where is God leading you today? How can you best cooperate with God's leading?

See Meeting God in Prayer

I Need Thee Every Hour

2 CHRONICLES 14.11

"I need thee every hour,
   most gracious Lord;
no tender voice like thine
   can peace afford.
I need thee, O I need thee,
   every hour I need thee;
O bless me now, my Savior,
   I come to thee.
I need thee every hour, in
   joy or pain;
come quickly and abide, or
   life is vain.
I need thee, O I need thee,
   every hour I need thee;
O bless me now, my Savior,
   I come to thee."

—ANNIE S. HAWKS

Ethiopian Invasion Repulsed

9 Zerah the Ethiopian[a] came out against them with an army of a million men and three hundred chariots, and came as far as Mareshah. [10]Asa went out to meet him, and they drew up their lines of battle in the valley of Zephathah at Mareshah. [11]Asa cried to the LORD his God, "O LORD, there is no difference for you between helping the mighty and the weak. Help us, O LORD our God, for we rely on you, and in your name we have come against this multitude. O LORD, you are our God; let no mortal prevail against you." [12]So the LORD defeated the Ethiopians[b] before Asa and before Judah, and the Ethiopians[b] fled. [13]Asa and the army with him pursued them as far as Gerar, and the Ethiopians[b] fell until no one remained alive; for they were broken before the LORD and his army. The people of Judah[c] carried away a great quantity of booty. [14]They defeated all the cities around Gerar, for the fear of the LORD was on them. They plundered all the cities; for there was much plunder in them. [15]They also attacked the tents of those who had livestock,[d] and carried away sheep and goats in abundance, and camels. Then they returned to Jerusalem.

15 The spirit of God came upon Azariah son of Oded. [2]He went out to meet Asa and said to him, "Hear me, Asa, and all Judah and Benjamin: The LORD is with you, while you are with him. If you seek him, he will be found by you, but if you abandon him, he will abandon you. [3]For a long time Israel was without the true God, and without a teaching priest, and without law; [4]but when in their distress they turned to the LORD, the God of Israel, and sought him, he was found by them. [5]In those times it was not safe for anyone to go or come, for great disturbances afflicted all the inhabitants of the lands. [6]They were broken in pieces, nation against nation and city against city, for God troubled them with every sort of distress. [7]But you, take courage! Do not let your hands be weak, for your work shall be rewarded."

8 When Asa heard these words, the prophecy of Azariah son of Oded,[e] he took courage, and put away the abominable idols from all the land of Judah and Benjamin and from the towns that he had taken in the hill country of Ephraim. He repaired the altar of the LORD that was in front of the vestibule of the house of the LORD.[f] [9]He gathered all Judah and Benjamin, and those from Ephraim, Manasseh, and Simeon who were residing as aliens with them, for great numbers had deserted to him from Israel when they saw that the LORD his God was with him. [10]They were gathered at Jerusalem in the third month of the fifteenth year of the reign of Asa. [11]They sacrificed to the LORD on that day, from the booty that they had brought, seven hundred oxen and seven thousand sheep. [12]They entered into a covenant to seek the LORD, the God of their ancestors, with all their heart and with all their soul. [13]Whoever would not seek the LORD, the God of Israel, should be put to death, whether young or old, man or woman. [14]They took an oath to the LORD with a loud voice, and with shouting, and with trumpets, and with

---

a Or Nubian; Heb Cushite   b Or Nubians; Heb Cushites   c Heb They
d Meaning of Heb uncertain   e Compare Syr Vg: Heb the prophecy, the
prophet Obed   f Heb the vestibule of the LORD

horns. ¹⁵All Judah rejoiced over the oath; for they had sworn with all their heart, and had sought him with their whole desire, and he was found by them, and the LORD gave them rest all around.

16 King Asa even removed his mother Maacah from being queen mother because she had made an abominable image for Asherah. Asa cut down her image, crushed it, and burned it at the Wadi Kidron. ¹⁷But the high places were not taken out of Israel. Nevertheless the heart of Asa was true all his days. ¹⁸He brought into the house of God the votive gifts of his father and his own votive gifts—silver, gold, and utensils. ¹⁹And there was no more war until the thirty-fifth year of the reign of Asa.

Alliance with Aram Condemned

16 In the thirty-sixth year of the reign of Asa, King Baasha of Israel went up against Judah, and built Ramah, to prevent anyone from going out or coming into the territory of*a* King Asa of Judah. ²Then Asa took silver and gold from the treasures of the house of the LORD and the king's house, and sent them to King Ben-hadad of Aram, who resided in Damascus, saying, ³"Let there be an alliance between me and you, like that between my father and your father; I am sending to you silver and gold; go, break your alliance with King Baasha of Israel, so that he may withdraw from me." ⁴Ben-hadad listened to King Asa, and sent the commanders of his armies against the cities of Israel. They conquered Ijon, Dan, Abel-maim, and all the store-cities of Naphtali. ⁵When Baasha heard of it, he stopped building Ramah, and let his work cease. ⁶Then King Asa brought all Judah, and they carried away the stones of Ramah and its timber, with which Baasha had been building, and with them he built up Geba and Mizpah.

7 At that time the seer Hanani came to King Asa of Judah, and said to him, "Because you relied on the king of Aram, and did not rely on the LORD your God, the army of the king of Aram has escaped you. ⁸Were not the Ethiopians*b* and the Libyans a huge army with exceedingly many chariots and cavalry? Yet because you relied on the LORD, he gave them into your hand. ⁹For the eyes of the LORD range throughout the entire earth, to strengthen those whose heart is true to him. You have done foolishly in this; for from now on you will have wars." ¹⁰Then Asa was angry with the seer, and put him in the stocks, in prison, for he was in a rage with him because of this. And Asa inflicted cruelties on some of the people at the same time.

Asa's Disease and Death

11 The acts of Asa, from first to last, are written in the Book of the Kings of Judah and Israel. ¹²In the thirty-ninth year of his reign Asa was diseased in his feet, and his disease became severe; yet even in his disease he did not seek the LORD, but sought help from physicians. ¹³Then Asa slept with his ancestors, dying in the forty-first year of his reign. ¹⁴They buried him in the tomb that he had hewn out for himself in the city of David. They laid him on a bier

a Heb lacks *the territory of*   *b* Or Nubians; Heb Cushites

A Joyful Oath

2 CHRONICLES 15.12–15

The people of Judah find joy and rest in a renewed covenant. Spend some time remembering the promises you have already made as a Christian. What vows did you take when you joined your church? What faith have you proclaimed by reciting creeds? What private promises have you made to God? How well do your actions reflect what you have said? What steps can you take to renew the covenant you have already made? Write down a proclamation of your desire to renew your covenant with God and ask God to bless it.

See Meeting God in Prayer

Holy Medicine

2 CHRONICLES 16.12–14

Asa is faulted, not for calling in the doctors, but for failing to call on God. How can you become involved in asking God for healing for yourself or for others? If your church announces, in the bulletin or during worship, the names of those who are sick, you might continue to pray for those people during the week. You might add to that list the names of friends and family members who also need prayer for healing. If your church has regularly scheduled healing services, you might attend one or more. If a healing service is not available, you might ask about starting such a healing ministry.

See *Meeting God in Service*

that had been filled with various kinds of spices prepared by the perfumer's art; and they made a very great fire in his honor.

Jehoshaphat's Reign

17 His son Jehoshaphat succeeded him, and strengthened himself against Israel. [2]He placed forces in all the fortified cities of Judah, and set garrisons in the land of Judah, and in the cities of Ephraim that his father Asa had taken. [3]The LORD was with Jehoshaphat, because he walked in the earlier ways of his father;[a] he did not seek the Baals, [4]but sought the God of his father and walked in his commandments, and not according to the ways of Israel. [5]Therefore the LORD established the kingdom in his hand. All Judah brought tribute to Jehoshaphat, and he had great riches and honor. [6]His heart was courageous in the ways of the LORD; and furthermore he removed the high places and the sacred poles[b] from Judah.

7 In the third year of his reign he sent his officials, Benhail, Obadiah, Zechariah, Nethanel, and Micaiah, to teach in the cities of Judah. [8]With them were the Levites, Shemaiah, Nethaniah, Zebadiah, Asahel, Shemiramoth, Jehonathan, Adonijah, Tobijah, and Tob-adonijah; and with these Levites, the priests Elishama and Jehoram. [9]They taught in Judah, having the book of the law of the LORD with them; they went around through all the cities of Judah and taught among the people.

10 The fear of the LORD fell on all the kingdoms of the lands around Judah, and they did not make war against Jehoshaphat. [11]Some of the Philistines brought Jehoshaphat presents, and silver for tribute; and the Arabs also brought him seven thousand seven hundred rams and seven thousand seven hundred male goats. [12]Jehoshaphat grew steadily greater. He built fortresses and storage cities in Judah. [13]He carried out great works in the cities of Judah. He had soldiers, mighty warriors, in Jerusalem. [14]This was the muster of them by ancestral houses: Of Judah, the commanders of the thousands: Adnah the commander, with three hundred thousand mighty warriors, [15]and next to him Jehohanan the commander, with two hundred eighty thousand, [16]and next to him Amasiah son of Zichri, a volunteer for the service of the LORD, with two hundred thousand mighty warriors. [17]Of Benjamin: Eliada, a mighty warrior, with two hundred thousand armed with bow and shield, [18]and next to him Jehozabad with one hundred eighty thousand armed for war. [19]These were in the service of the king, besides those whom the king had placed in the fortified cities throughout all Judah.

Micaiah Predicts Failure

18 Now Jehoshaphat had great riches and honor; and he made a marriage alliance with Ahab. [2]After some years he went down to Ahab in Samaria. Ahab slaughtered an abundance of sheep and oxen for him and for the people who were with him, and induced him to go up against Ramoth-gilead. [3]King Ahab of Israel said to King Jehoshaphat of Judah, "Will you go with

a Another reading is *his father David*   *b* Heb *Asherim* me to Ramoth-gilead?" He answered him, "I am with you, my people are your people. We will be with you in the war."

4 But Jehoshaphat also said to the king of Israel, "Inquire first for the word of the Lord." 5Then the king of Israel gathered the prophets together, four hundred of them, and said to them, "Shall we go to battle against Ramoth-gilead, or shall I refrain?" They said, "Go up; for God will give it into the hand of the king." 6But Jehoshaphat said, "Is there no other prophet of the Lord here of whom we may inquire?" 7The king of Israel said to Jehoshaphat, "There is still one other by whom we may inquire of the Lord, Micaiah son of Imlah; but I hate him, for he never prophesies anything favorable about me, but only disaster." Jehoshaphat said, "Let the king not say such a thing." 8Then the king of Israel summoned an officer and said, "Bring quickly Micaiah son of Imlah." 9Now the king of Israel and King Jehoshaphat of Judah were sitting on their thrones, arrayed in their robes; and they were sitting at the threshing floor at the entrance of the gate of Samaria; and all the prophets were prophesying before them. 10Zedekiah son of Chenaanah made for himself horns of iron, and he said, "Thus says the Lord: With these you shall gore the Arameans until they are destroyed." 11All the prophets were prophesying the same and saying, "Go up to Ramoth-gilead and triumph; the Lord will give it into the hand of the king."

12 The messenger who had gone to summon Micaiah said to him, "Look, the words of the prophets with one accord are favorable to the king; let your word be like the word of one of them, and speak favorably." 13But Micaiah said, "As the Lord lives, whatever my God says, that I will speak."

14 When he had come to the king, the king said to him, "Micaiah, shall we go to Ramoth-gilead to battle, or shall I refrain?" He answered, "Go up and triumph; they will be given into your hand." 15But the king said to him, "How many times must I make you swear to tell me nothing but the truth in the name of the Lord?" 16Then Micaiah[a] said, "I saw all Israel scattered on the mountains, like sheep without a shepherd; and the Lord said, 'These have no master; let each one go home in peace.' " 17The king of Israel said to Jehoshaphat, "Did I not tell you that he would not prophesy anything favorable about me, but only disaster?"

18 Then Micaiah[a] said, "Therefore hear the word of the Lord: I saw the Lord sitting on his throne, with all the host of heaven standing to the right and to the left of him. 19And the Lord said, 'Who will entice King Ahab of Israel, so that he may go up and fall at Ramoth-gilead?' Then one said one thing, and another said another, 20until a spirit came forward and stood before the Lord, saying, 'I will entice him.' The Lord asked him, 'How?' 21He replied, 'I will go out and be a lying spirit in the mouth of all his prophets.' Then the Lord[a] said, 'You are to entice him, and you shall succeed; go out and do it.' 22So you see, the Lord has put a lying spirit in the mouth of these your prophets; the Lord has decreed disaster for you."

No Bad News

2 CHRONICLES 18.7

King Ahab rejects the prophet Micaiah, not because what Micaiah says is untrue, but because what he says is unpleasant. Do you find yourself doing the same thing? What unpleasant truths do you try to ignore? What people do you avoid because they have told you things you did not want to hear? In prayer God often confronts us with deep truths about ourselves. Does unwillingness to face such truths block you from deeper prayer and from growing closer to God? It might help to talk with an intimate friend or spiritual mentor. Such conversation may encourage you to allow yourself to hear what God has to say.

How Can You Know?

2 CHRONICLES 18.25–27

Discernment is difficult. Sometimes it is not easy to know whether a word or a perceived call to action is really from God. As Ahab waffles between conflicting prophecies, Micaiah offers a suggestion: Ahab should do what he wants and see what happens. If things turn out as Micaiah predicted, he was right. What decision has stumped you, so that you cannot tell what is really God's will? Can you explore one choice, trusting God to give you greater clarity somewhere down the road? You might reaffirm your trust in God as you step out in faith.

See Meeting God in Everyday Life

23 Then Zedekiah son of Chenaanah came up to Micaiah, slapped him on the cheek, and said, "Which way did the spirit of the LORD pass from me to speak to you?" 24Micaiah replied, "You will find out on that day when you go in to hide in an inner chamber." 25The king of Israel then ordered, "Take Micaiah, and return him to Amon the governor of the city and to Joash the king's son; 26and say, 'Thus says the king: Put this fellow in prison, and feed him on reduced rations of bread and water until I return in peace.' " 27Micaiah said, "If you return in peace, the LORD has not spoken by me." And he said, "Hear, you peoples, all of you!"

Defeat and Death of Ahab

28 So the king of Israel and King Jehoshaphat of Judah went up to Ramoth-gilead. 29The king of Israel said to Jehoshaphat, "I will disguise myself and go into battle, but you wear your robes." So the king of Israel disguised himself, and they went into battle. 30Now the king of Aram had commanded the captains of his chariots, "Fight with no one small or great, but only with the king of Israel." 31When the captains of the chariots saw Jehoshaphat, they said, "It is the king of Israel." So they turned to fight against him; and Jehoshaphat cried out, and the LORD helped him. God drew them away from him, 32for when the captains of the chariots saw that it was not the king of Israel, they turned back from pursuing him. 33But a certain man drew his bow and unknowingly struck the king of Israel between the scale armor and the breastplate; so he said to the driver of his chariot, "Turn around, and carry me out of the battle, for I am wounded." 34The battle grew hot that day, and the king of Israel propped himself up in his chariot facing the Arameans until evening; then at sunset he died.

19 King Jehoshaphat of Judah returned in safety to his house in Jerusalem. 2Jehu son of Hanani the seer went out to meet him and said to King Jehoshaphat, "Should you help the wicked and love those who hate the LORD? Because of this, wrath has gone out against you from the LORD. 3Nevertheless, some good is found in you, for you destroyed the sacred poles[a] out of the land, and have set your heart to seek God."

The Reforms of Jehoshaphat

4 Jehoshaphat resided at Jerusalem; then he went out again among the people, from Beer-sheba to the hill country of Ephraim, and brought them back to the LORD, the God of their ancestors. 5He appointed judges in the land in all the fortified cities of Judah, city by city, 6and said to the judges, "Consider what you are doing, for you judge not on behalf of human beings but on the LORD's behalf; he is with you in giving judgment. 7Now, let the fear of the LORD be upon you; take care what you do, for there is no perversion of justice with the LORD our God, or partiality, or taking of bribes."

8 Moreover in Jerusalem Jehoshaphat appointed certain Levites and priests and heads of families of Israel, to give judgment for the LORD and to decide disputed cases. They had their seat at Jerusalem. 9He charged them: "This is

a Heb *Asheroth*

how you shall act: in the fear of the Lord, in faithfulness, and with your whole heart; ¹⁰whenever a case comes to you from your kindred who live in their cities, concerning bloodshed, law or commandment, statutes or ordinances, then you shall instruct them, so that they may not incur guilt before the Lord and wrath may not come on you and your kindred. Do so, and you will not incur guilt. ¹¹See, Amariah the chief priest is over you in all matters of the Lord; and Zebadiah son of Ishmael, the governor of the house of Judah, in all the king's matters; and the Levites will serve you as officers. Deal courageously, and may the Lord be with the good!"

Invasion from the East

20 After this the Moabites and Ammonites, and with them some of the Meunites,ᵃ came against Jehoshaphat for battle. ²Messengersᵇ came and told Jehoshaphat, "A great multitude is coming against you from Edom,ᶜ from beyond the sea; already they are at Hazazon-tamar" (that is, En-gedi). ³Jehoshaphat was afraid; he set himself to seek the Lord, and proclaimed a fast throughout all Judah. ⁴Judah assembled to seek help from the Lord; from all the towns of Judah they came to seek the Lord.

Jehoshaphat's Prayer and Victory

5 Jehoshaphat stood in the assembly of Judah and Jerusalem, in the house of the Lord, before the new court, ⁶and said, "O Lord, God of our ancestors, are you not God in heaven? Do you not rule over all the kingdoms of the nations? In your hand are power and might, so that no one is able to withstand you. ⁷Did you not, O our God, drive out the inhabitants of this land before your people Israel, and give it forever to the descendants of your friend Abraham? ⁸They have lived in it, and in it have built you a sanctuary for your name, saying, ⁹'If disaster comes upon us, the sword, judgment,ᵈ or pestilence, or famine, we will stand before this house, and before you, for your name is in this house, and cry to you in our distress, and you will hear and save.' ¹⁰See now, the people of Ammon, Moab, and Mount Seir, whom you would not let Israel invade when they came from the land of Egypt, and whom they avoided and did not destroy— ¹¹they reward us by coming to drive us out of your possession that you have given us to inherit. ¹²O our God, will you not execute judgment upon them? For we are powerless against this great multitude that is coming against us. We do not know what to do, but our eyes are on you."

13 Meanwhile all Judah stood before the Lord, with their little ones, their wives, and their children. ¹⁴Then the spirit of the Lord came upon Jahaziel son of Zechariah, son of Benaiah, son of Jeiel, son of Mattaniah, a Levite of the sons of Asaph, in the middle of the assembly. ¹⁵He said, "Listen, all Judah and inhabitants of Jerusalem, and King Jehoshaphat: Thus says the Lord to you: 'Do not fear or be dismayed at this great multitude; for the battle is not yours but God's. ¹⁶Tomorrow go down against them;

Shades of Gray

2 CHRONICLES 19.2–3

The Chronicler, like most of us, tends to see characters as either good or evil. Here, though, Jehu lifts up both the good and the evil in Jehoshaphat's actions. As a result, Jehoshaphat's good resolve is strengthened. Think of one person whom you dislike. What good points can you list about that person? How can you encourage that good? Where can you see Jesus in that person? Thank God for Jesus' presence in that person's life. These are ways of loving your enemies. You might want to repeat this exercise several times, thinking of other people whom you dislike.

See Meeting God in Community

ᵃ Compare 26.7: Heb *Ammonites*   ᵇ Heb *They*   ᶜ One Ms: MT *Aram*
ᵈ Or *the sword of judgment*

The Battle Is God's

2 CHRONICLES 20.5–30

It is not only invading armies that leave people feeling powerless. Temptations, habits and oppressive situations can all overwhelm us. What makes you feel helpless? Let God fight for you. You might pray in words similar to those used by Jehoshaphat: "Lord, I am powerless against _____. I do not know what to do. My eyes are on you." Then hear for yourself the prophet's word of hope: "Do not fear or be dismayed . . . for the battle is not yours but God's."

See Meeting God in Scripture

they will come up by the ascent of Ziz; you will find them at the end of the valley, before the wilderness of Jeruel. ¹⁷This battle is not for you to fight; take your position, stand still, and see the victory of the LORD on your behalf, O Judah and Jerusalem.' Do not fear or be dismayed; tomorrow go out against them, and the LORD will be with you."

18 Then Jehoshaphat bowed down with his face to the ground, and all Judah and the inhabitants of Jerusalem fell down before the LORD, worshiping the LORD. ¹⁹And the Levites, of the Kohathites and the Korahites, stood up to praise the LORD, the God of Israel, with a very loud voice.

20 They rose early in the morning and went out into the wilderness of Tekoa; and as they went out, Jehoshaphat stood and said, "Listen to me, O Judah and inhabitants of Jerusalem! Believe in the LORD your God and you will be established; believe his prophets." ²¹When he had taken counsel with the people, he appointed those who were to sing to the LORD and praise him in holy splendor, as they went before the army, saying,

"Give thanks to the LORD,
     for his steadfast love endures forever."

²²As they began to sing and praise, the LORD set an ambush against the Ammonites, Moab, and Mount Seir, who had come against Judah, so that they were routed. ²³For the Ammonites and Moab attacked the inhabitants of Mount Seir, destroying them utterly; and when they had made an end of the inhabitants of Seir, they all helped to destroy one another.

24 When Judah came to the watchtower of the wilderness, they looked toward the multitude; they were corpses lying on the ground; no one had escaped. ²⁵When Jehoshaphat and his people came to take the booty from them, they found livestock*a* in great numbers, goods, clothing, and precious things, which they took for themselves until they could carry no more. They spent three days taking the booty, because of its abundance. ²⁶On the fourth day they assembled in the Valley of Beracah, for there they blessed the LORD; therefore that place has been called the Valley of Beracah*b* to this day. ²⁷Then all the people of Judah and Jerusalem, with Jehoshaphat at their head, returned to Jerusalem with joy, for the LORD had enabled them to rejoice over their enemies. ²⁸They came to Jerusalem, with harps and lyres and trumpets, to the house of the LORD. ²⁹The fear of God came on all the kingdoms of the countries when they heard that the LORD had fought against the enemies of Israel. ³⁰And the realm of Jehoshaphat was quiet, for his God gave him rest all around.

The End of Jehoshaphat's Reign

31 So Jehoshaphat reigned over Judah. He was thirty-five years old when he began to reign; he reigned twenty-five years in Jerusalem. His mother's name was Azubah daughter of Shilhi. ³²He walked in the way of his father Asa and did not turn aside from it, doing what was right in the sight of the LORD. ³³Yet the high places were not removed;

a Gk: Heb *among them*   *b* That is *Blessing*

the people had not yet set their hearts upon the God of their ancestors.

34 Now the rest of the acts of Jehoshaphat, from first to last, are written in the Annals of Jehu son of Hanani, which are recorded in the Book of the Kings of Israel.

35 After this King Jehoshaphat of Judah joined with King Ahaziah of Israel, who did wickedly. ³⁶He joined him in building ships to go to Tarshish; they built the ships in Ezion-geber. ³⁷Then Eliezer son of Dodavahu of Mareshah prophesied against Jehoshaphat, saying, "Because you have joined with Ahaziah, the LORD will destroy what you have made." And the ships were wrecked and were not able to go to Tarshish.

Jehoram's Reign

21 Jehoshaphat slept with his ancestors and was buried with his ancestors in the city of David; his son Jehoram succeeded him. ²He had brothers, the sons of Jehoshaphat: Azariah, Jehiel, Zechariah, Azariah, Michael, and Shephatiah; all these were the sons of King Jehoshaphat of Judah.ᵃ ³Their father gave them many gifts, of silver, gold, and valuable possessions, together with fortified cities in Judah; but he gave the kingdom to Jehoram, because he was the firstborn. ⁴When Jehoram had ascended the throne of his father and was established, he put all his brothers to the sword, and also some of the officials of Israel. ⁵Jehoram was thirty-two years old when he began to reign; he reigned eight years in Jerusalem. ⁶He walked in the way of the kings of Israel, as the house of Ahab had done; for the daughter of Ahab was his wife. He did what was evil in the sight of the LORD. ⁷Yet the LORD would not destroy the house of David because of the covenant that he had made with David, and since he had promised to give a lamp to him and to his descendants forever.

Revolt of Edom

8 In his days Edom revolted against the rule of Judah and set up a king of their own. ⁹Then Jehoram crossed over with his commanders and all his chariots. He set out by night and attacked the Edomites, who had surrounded him and his chariot commanders. ¹⁰So Edom has been in revolt against the rule of Judah to this day. At that time Libnah also revolted against his rule, because he had forsaken the LORD, the God of his ancestors.

Elijah's Letter

11 Moreover he made high places in the hill country of Judah, and led the inhabitants of Jerusalem into unfaithfulness, and made Judah go astray. ¹²A letter came to him from the prophet Elijah, saying: "Thus says the LORD, the God of your father David: Because you have not walked in the ways of your father Jehoshaphat or in the ways of King Asa of Judah, ¹³but have walked in the way of the kings of Israel, and have led Judah and the inhabitants of Jerusalem into unfaithfulness, as the house of Ahab led Israel into unfaithfulness, and because you also have killed your brothers, members of your father's house, who were better than yourself, ¹⁴see, the LORD

Great Is the Lord!

2 CHRONICLES 20.26–30

"Great are you, O Lord, and greatly to be praised; great is your power, and your understanding is beyond measure. And people, being a part of your creation, desire to praise you—people who bear about with them their mortality, the witness of their sin, even the witness that you oppose the proud. Nevertheless, people, this part of your creation, desire to praise you. You move us to delight in praising you; for you have formed us for yourself, and our hearts are restless until they find rest in you."

—AUGUSTINE,
Confessions

ᵃ Gk Syr: Heb *Israel*

A Letter From a Prophet

2 CHRONICLES 21.12–15

Jehoram receives a rather con-
victing letter from Elijah containing a point-by-point
indictment of his behavior.
Imagine that God asked Elijah
to write to you about the way
you are walking. What would
the letter say? Actually writing
a letter out may be helpful; perhaps you could begin it, "Thus
says the LORD." What is your response to this letter? For what
do you need to ask God's forgiveness? For what do you need
to make amends to others?
What is God pleased with in
your life?

See Meeting God in Everyday Life

will bring a great plague on your people, your children,
your wives, and all your possessions, [15]and you yourself
will have a severe sickness with a disease of your bowels, until your bowels come out, day after day, because
of the disease."

16 The LORD aroused against Jehoram the anger of the
Philistines and of the Arabs who are near the Ethiopians.[a] [17]They came up against Judah, invaded it, and carried away all the possessions they found that belonged to
the king's house, along with his sons and his wives, so
that no son was left to him except Jehoahaz, his youngest
son.

Disease and Death of Jehoram

18 After all this the LORD struck him in his bowels with
an incurable disease. [19]In course of time, at the end of two
years, his bowels came out because of the disease, and he
died in great agony. His people made no fire in his honor,
like the fires made for his ancestors. [20]He was thirty-two
years old when he began to reign; he reigned eight years
in Jerusalem. He departed with no one's regret. They
buried him in the city of David, but not in the tombs of the
kings.

Ahaziah's Reign

22 The inhabitants of Jerusalem made his youngest
son Ahaziah king as his successor; for the troops
who came with the Arabs to the camp had killed all the
older sons. So Ahaziah son of Jehoram reigned as king of
Judah. [2]Ahaziah was forty-two years old when he began to
reign; he reigned one year in Jerusalem. His mother's
name was Athaliah, a granddaughter of Omri. [3]He also
walked in the ways of the house of Ahab, for his mother
was his counselor in doing wickedly. [4]He did what was evil
in the sight of the LORD, as the house of Ahab had done;
for after the death of his father they were his counselors,
to his ruin. [5]He even followed their advice, and went with
Jehoram son of King Ahab of Israel to make war against
King Hazael of Aram at Ramoth-gilead. The Arameans
wounded Joram, [6]and he returned to be healed in Jezreel
of the wounds that he had received at Ramah, when he
fought King Hazael of Aram. And Ahaziah son of King Jehoram of Judah went down to see Joram son of Ahab in
Jezreel, because he was sick.

7 But it was ordained by God that the downfall of Ahaziah should come about through his going to visit Joram.
For when he came there he went out with Jehoram to
meet Jehu son of Nimshi, whom the LORD had anointed to
destroy the house of Ahab. [8]When Jehu was executing
judgment on the house of Ahab, he met the officials of
Judah and the sons of Ahaziah's brothers, who attended
Ahaziah, and he killed them. [9]He searched for Ahaziah,
who was captured while hiding in Samaria and was
brought to Jehu, and put to death. They buried him, for
they said, "He is the grandson of Jehoshaphat, who sought
the LORD with all his heart." And the house of Ahaziah had
no one able to rule the kingdom.

a Or Nubians; Heb Cushites

Athaliah Seizes the Throne

10 Now when Athaliah, Ahaziah's mother, saw that her son was dead, she set about to destroy all the royal family of the house of Judah. ¹¹But Jehoshabeath, the king's daughter, took Joash son of Ahaziah, and stole him away from among the king's children who were about to be killed; she put him and his nurse in a bedroom. Thus Jehoshabeath, daughter of King Jehoram and wife of the priest Jehoiada—because she was a sister of Ahaziah—hid him from Athaliah, so that she did not kill him; ¹²he remained with them six years, hidden in the house of God, while Athaliah reigned over the land.

23 But in the seventh year Jehoiada took courage, and entered into a compact with the commanders of the hundreds, Azariah son of Jeroham, Ishmael son of Jehohanan, Azariah son of Obed, Maaseiah son of Adaiah, and Elishaphat son of Zichri. ²They went around through Judah and gathered the Levites from all the towns of Judah, and the heads of families of Israel, and they came to Jerusalem. ³Then the whole assembly made a covenant with the king in the house of God. Jehoiada[a] said to them, "Here is the king's son! Let him reign, as the LORD promised concerning the sons of David. ⁴This is what you are to do: one-third of you, priests and Levites, who come on duty on the sabbath, shall be gatekeepers, ⁵one-third shall be at the king's house, and one-third at the Gate of the Foundation; and all the people shall be in the courts of the house of the LORD. ⁶Do not let anyone enter the house of the LORD except the priests and ministering Levites; they may enter, for they are holy, but all the other[b] people shall observe the instructions of the LORD. ⁷The Levites shall surround the king, each with his weapons in his hand; and whoever enters the house shall be killed. Stay with the king in his comings and goings."

Joash Crowned King

8 The Levites and all Judah did according to all that the priest Jehoiada commanded; each brought his men, who were to come on duty on the sabbath, with those who were to go off duty on the sabbath; for the priest Jehoiada did not dismiss the divisions. ⁹The priest Jehoiada delivered to the captains the spears and the large and small shields that had been King David's, which were in the house of God; ¹⁰and he set all the people as a guard for the king, everyone with weapon in hand, from the south side of the house to the north side of the house, around the altar and the house. ¹¹Then he brought out the king's son, put the crown on him, and gave him the covenant;[c] they proclaimed him king, and Jehoiada and his sons anointed him; and they shouted, "Long live the king!"

Athaliah Murdered

12 When Athaliah heard the noise of the people running and praising the king, she went into the house of the LORD to the people; ¹³and when she looked, there was the king

Rescuing the Persecuted

2 CHRONICLES 22.11–12

Protecting the helpless has always been a significant calling for God's people. Just as Jehoshabeath and the priests helped to protect Joash, so Christians have been involved in protecting escaped slaves along the Underground Railroad and in helping Jews hiding from Nazi persecution. How might you be involved in helping the helpless today? You might explore the refugee relief opportunities of your denomination or wider efforts such as those provided by Amnesty International. You might ask God if you should be more directly involved, perhaps by opening your home to a refugee family or volunteering to go to a refugee camp. As you watch or read news reports about refugees, take time to ask God, "Is there anything you want me to do?"

See Meeting God in Community

a Heb *He*   b Heb lacks *other*   c Or *treaty*, or *testimony*; Heb *eduth*

Renewed Hope

2 CHRONICLES 23.1–21

Try to imagine this scene of violent revolution and restored hope. Imagine yourself in Jerusalem, listening to the series of surprising commands and announcements from Jehoiada (vv.3–7,11,14,16). What emotions run through you? Where do you find yourself participating? Some scholars have suggested that Isaiah 9.2–7, so often associated with the birth of Jesus, may originally have been used for Joash's coronation. You might read that passage as you think about this one and the new hope that comes with the end of any oppressive regime. What oppressive powers need to be overthrown in your own life? You might ask God to come and rule in your heart, in order to restore hope, peace and joy.

See Meeting God in Scripture

standing by his pillar at the entrance, and the captains and the trumpeters beside the king, and all the people of the land rejoicing and blowing trumpets, and the singers with their musical instruments leading in the celebration. Athaliah tore her clothes, and cried, "Treason! Treason!" [14]Then the priest Jehoiada brought out the captains who were set over the army, saying to them, "Bring her out between the ranks; anyone who follows her is to be put to the sword." For the priest said, "Do not put her to death in the house of the LORD." [15]So they laid hands on her; she went into the entrance of the Horse Gate of the king's house, and there they put her to death.

16 Jehoiada made a covenant between himself and all the people and the king that they should be the LORD's people. [17]Then all the people went to the house of Baal, and tore it down; his altars and his images they broke in pieces, and they killed Mattan, the priest of Baal, in front of the altars. [18]Jehoiada assigned the care of the house of the LORD to the levitical priests whom David had organized to be in charge of the house of the LORD, to offer burnt offerings to the LORD, as it is written in the law of Moses, with rejoicing and with singing, according to the order of David. [19]He stationed the gatekeepers at the gates of the house of the LORD so that no one should enter who was in any way unclean. [20]And he took the captains, the nobles, the governors of the people, and all the people of the land, and they brought the king down from the house of the LORD, marching through the upper gate to the king's house. They set the king on the royal throne. [21]So all the people of the land rejoiced, and the city was quiet after Athaliah had been killed with the sword.

Joash Repairs the Temple

24 Joash was seven years old when he began to reign; he reigned forty years in Jerusalem; his mother's name was Zibiah of Beer-sheba. [2]Joash did what was right in the sight of the LORD all the days of the priest Jehoiada. [3]Jehoiada got two wives for him, and he became the father of sons and daughters.

4 Some time afterward Joash decided to restore the house of the LORD. [5]He assembled the priests and the Levites and said to them, "Go out to the cities of Judah and gather money from all Israel to repair the house of your God, year by year; and see that you act quickly." But the Levites did not act quickly. [6]So the king summoned Jehoiada the chief, and said to him, "Why have you not required the Levites to bring in from Judah and Jerusalem the tax levied by Moses, the servant of the LORD, on[a] the congregation of Israel for the tent of the covenant?"[b] [7]For the children of Athaliah, that wicked woman, had broken into the house of God, and had even used all the dedicated things of the house of the LORD for the Baals.

8 So the king gave command, and they made a chest, and set it outside the gate of the house of the LORD. [9]A proclamation was made throughout Judah and Jerusalem to bring in for the LORD the tax that Moses the servant of God laid on Israel in the wilderness. [10]All the leaders and all the people rejoiced and brought their tax and dropped

a Compare Vg: Heb *and*   *b* Or *treaty,* or *testimony;* Heb *eduth*

it into the chest until it was full. ¹¹Whenever the chest was brought to the king's officers by the Levites, when they saw that there was a large amount of money in it, the king's secretary and the officer of the chief priest would come and empty the chest and take it and return it to its place. So they did day after day, and collected money in abundance. ¹²The king and Jehoiada gave it to those who had charge of the work of the house of the LORD, and they hired masons and carpenters to restore the house of the LORD, and also workers in iron and bronze to repair the house of the LORD. ¹³So those who were engaged in the work labored, and the repairing went forward at their hands, and they restored the house of God to its proper condition and strengthened it. ¹⁴When they had finished, they brought the rest of the money to the king and Jehoiada, and with it were made utensils for the house of the LORD, utensils for the service and for the burnt offerings, and ladles, and vessels of gold and silver. They offered burnt offerings in the house of the LORD regularly all the days of Jehoiada.

Apostasy of Joash

15 But Jehoiada grew old and full of days, and died; he was one hundred thirty years old at his death. ¹⁶And they buried him in the city of David among the kings, because he had done good in Israel, and for God and his house.

17 Now after the death of Jehoiada the officials of Judah came and did obeisance to the king; then the king listened to them. ¹⁸They abandoned the house of the LORD, the God of their ancestors, and served the sacred poles^a and the idols. And wrath came upon Judah and Jerusalem for this guilt of theirs. ¹⁹Yet he sent prophets among them to bring them back to the LORD; they testified against them, but they would not listen.

20 Then the spirit of God took possession of^b Zechariah son of the priest Jehoiada; he stood above the people and said to them, "Thus says God: Why do you transgress the commandments of the LORD, so that you cannot prosper? Because you have forsaken the LORD, he has also forsaken you." ²¹But they conspired against him, and by command of the king they stoned him to death in the court of the house of the LORD. ²²King Joash did not remember the kindness that Jehoiada, Zechariah's father, had shown him, but killed his son. As he was dying, he said, "May the LORD see and avenge!"

Death of Joash

23 At the end of the year the army of Aram came up against Joash. They came to Judah and Jerusalem, and destroyed all the officials of the people from among them, and sent all the booty they took to the king of Damascus. ²⁴Although the army of Aram had come with few men, the LORD delivered into their hand a very great army, because they had abandoned the LORD, the God of their ancestors. Thus they executed judgment on Joash.

25 When they had withdrawn, leaving him severely wounded, his servants conspired against him because of the blood of the son^c of the priest Jehoiada, and they killed him on his bed. So he died; and they buried him in the

---

Take, Lord, Receive

2 CHRONICLES 24.8–9

"Take, Lord, and receive all my liberty, my memory, my understanding, and my entire will, all that I have and possess. Thou hast given all to me. To Thee, O Lord, I return it. All is Thine, dispose of it wholly according to Thy will. Give me Thy love and Thy grace, for this is sufficient for me."

—IGNATIUS OF LOYOLA,
The Spiritual Exercises, 234

---

a Heb *Asherim*   *b* Heb *clothed itself with*   *c* Gk Vg: Heb *sons*

Halfhearted Love

2 CHRONICLES 25.2

What a sad statement to have to make about anyone: "He did what was right . . . yet not with a true heart." Yet all of us experience times when we are doing something we know is good, but we are just going through the motions. Our hearts aren't in it. What are those things for you? Why have they become dull, halfhearted routine? Are you burned out? Are you doing too many different things? Ask for God's guidance as you look at changes you might make in your life. What are the things you *can* do wholeheartedly? How can you build on that core?

See *Meeting God in Service*

city of David, but they did not bury him in the tombs of the kings. ²⁶Those who conspired against him were Zabad son of Shimeath the Ammonite, and Jehozabad son of Shimrith the Moabite. ²⁷Accounts of his sons, and of the many oracles against him, and of the rebuilding*a* of the house of God are written in the Commentary on the Book of the Kings. And his son Amaziah succeeded him.

Reign of Amaziah

25 Amaziah was twenty-five years old when he began to reign, and he reigned twenty-nine years in Jerusalem. His mother's name was Jehoaddan of Jerusalem. ²He did what was right in the sight of the LORD, yet not with a true heart. ³As soon as the royal power was firmly in his hand he killed his servants who had murdered his father the king. ⁴But he did not put their children to death, according to what is written in the law, in the book of Moses, where the LORD commanded, "The parents shall not be put to death for the children, or the children be put to death for the parents; but all shall be put to death for their own sins."

Slaughter of the Edomites

5 Amaziah assembled the people of Judah, and set them by ancestral houses under commanders of the thousands and of the hundreds for all Judah and Benjamin. He mustered those twenty years old and upward, and found that they were three hundred thousand picked troops fit for war, able to handle spear and shield. ⁶He also hired one hundred thousand mighty warriors from Israel for one hundred talents of silver. ⁷But a man of God came to him and said, "O king, do not let the army of Israel go with you, for the LORD is not with Israel—all these Ephraimites. ⁸Rather, go by yourself and act; be strong in battle, or God will fling you down before the enemy; for God has power to help or to overthrow." ⁹Amaziah said to the man of God, "But what shall we do about the hundred talents that I have given to the army of Israel?" The man of God answered, "The LORD is able to give you much more than this." ¹⁰Then Amaziah discharged the army that had come to him from Ephraim, letting them go home again. But they became very angry with Judah, and returned home in fierce anger.

11 Amaziah took courage, and led out his people; he went to the Valley of Salt, and struck down ten thousand men of Seir. ¹²The people of Judah captured another ten thousand alive, took them to the top of Sela, and threw them down from the top of Sela, so that all of them were dashed to pieces. ¹³But the men of the army whom Amaziah sent back, not letting them go with him to battle, fell on the cities of Judah from Samaria to Beth-horon; they killed three thousand people in them, and took much booty.

14 Now after Amaziah came from the slaughter of the Edomites, he brought the gods of the people of Seir, set them up as his gods, and worshiped them, making offerings to them. ¹⁵The LORD was angry with Amaziah and sent to him a prophet, who said to him, "Why have you resorted to a people's gods who could not deliver their own

a Heb *founding*

people from your hand?" ¹⁶But as he was speaking the king*a* said to him, "Have we made you a royal counselor? Stop! Why should you be put to death?" So the prophet stopped, but said, "I know that God has determined to destroy you, because you have done this and have not listened to my advice."

Israel Defeats Judah

17 Then King Amaziah of Judah took counsel and sent to King Joash son of Jehoahaz son of Jehu of Israel, saying, "Come, let us look one another in the face." ¹⁸King Joash of Israel sent word to King Amaziah of Judah, "A thornbush on Lebanon sent to a cedar on Lebanon, saying, 'Give your daughter to my son for a wife'; but a wild animal of Lebanon passed by and trampled down the thornbush. ¹⁹You say, 'See, I have defeated Edom,' and your heart has lifted you up in boastfulness. Now stay at home; why should you provoke trouble so that you fall, you and Judah with you?"

20 But Amaziah would not listen—it was God's doing, in order to hand them over, because they had sought the gods of Edom. ²¹So King Joash of Israel went up; and he and King Amaziah of Judah faced one another in battle at Bethshemesh, which belongs to Judah. ²²Judah was defeated by Israel; everyone fled home. ²³King Joash of Israel captured King Amaziah of Judah, son of Joash, son of Ahaziah, at Beth-shemesh; he brought him to Jerusalem, and broke down the wall of Jerusalem from the Ephraim Gate to the Corner Gate, a distance of four hundred cubits. ²⁴He seized all the gold and silver, and all the vessels that were found in the house of God, and Obed-edom with them; he seized also the treasuries of the king's house, also hostages; then he returned to Samaria.

Death of Amaziah

25 King Amaziah son of Joash of Judah, lived fifteen years after the death of King Joash son of Jehoahaz of Israel. ²⁶Now the rest of the deeds of Amaziah, from first to last, are they not written in the Book of the Kings of Judah and Israel? ²⁷From the time that Amaziah turned away from the LORD they made a conspiracy against him in Jerusalem, and he fled to Lachish. But they sent after him to Lachish, and killed him there. ²⁸They brought him back on horses; he was buried with his ancestors in the city of David.

Reign of Uzziah

26 Then all the people of Judah took Uzziah, who was sixteen years old, and made him king to succeed his father Amaziah. ²He rebuilt Eloth and restored it to Judah, after the king slept with his ancestors. ³Uzziah was sixteen years old when he began to reign, and he reigned fifty-two years in Jerusalem. His mother's name was Jecoliah of Jerusalem. ⁴He did what was right in the sight of the LORD, just as his father Amaziah had done. ⁵He set himself to seek God in the days of Zechariah, who instructed him in the fear of God; and as long as he sought the LORD, God made him prosper.

6 He went out and made war against the Philistines,

Worshiping Defeated Powers

2 CHRONICLES 25.14–15

What could Amaziah have been thinking? Why, if he had defeated the Edomites, might he have wanted to make offerings to their gods? In what ways do you give honor to powers such as consumerism, nationalism, racism or sexism, powers which have already been defeated by Jesus Christ? What other powers have you set up in the temple of your heart alongside him? Why do you keep them there? You might want to invite God to cleanse your heart of such false allegiances and make a renewed covenant to have no other gods before God. The prayers "Take, Lord, Receive" and "A Covenant Prayer" (see Entry Points at 24.8–9 and 29.4) might be good models.

See Meeting God in Prayer

Pride and Presumption

2 CHRONICLES 26.16–18

It is all too easy when things are going well for us to begin to think that we have God in our back pockets. Like Uzziah, we can begin to believe we have a special status that sets us above the usual rules for God's people. When in your life has success led to presumption? Do you find yourself distracted in worship by your critical thoughts? Do you evaluate others not by how well they are using their gifts, but by how their accomplishments compare to yours? Have you tried to take over tasks assigned to others because you think you could do better? You might ask God to grant you the humility to accept your limited role in your church and community and to help you to appreciate others as they go about their tasks.

See *Meeting God in Community*

and broke down the wall of Gath and the wall of Jabneh and the wall of Ashdod; he built cities in the territory of Ashdod and elsewhere among the Philistines. ⁷God helped him against the Philistines, against the Arabs who lived in Gur-baal, and against the Meunites. ⁸The Ammonites paid tribute to Uzziah, and his fame spread even to the border of Egypt, for he became very strong. ⁹Moreover Uzziah built towers in Jerusalem at the Corner Gate, at the Valley Gate, and at the Angle, and fortified them. ¹⁰He built towers in the wilderness and hewed out many cisterns, for he had large herds, both in the Shephelah and in the plain, and he had farmers and vinedressers in the hills and in the fertile lands, for he loved the soil. ¹¹Moreover Uzziah had an army of soldiers, fit for war, in divisions according to the numbers in the muster made by the secretary Jeiel and the officer Maaseiah, under the direction of Hananiah, one of the king's commanders. ¹²The whole number of the heads of ancestral houses of mighty warriors was two thousand six hundred. ¹³Under their command was an army of three hundred seven thousand five hundred, who could make war with mighty power, to help the king against the enemy. ¹⁴Uzziah provided for all the army the shields, spears, helmets, coats of mail, bows, and stones for slinging. ¹⁵In Jerusalem he set up machines, invented by skilled workers, on the towers and the corners for shooting arrows and large stones. And his fame spread far, for he was marvelously helped until he became strong.

Pride and Apostasy

16 But when he had become strong he grew proud, to his destruction. For he was false to the LORD his God, and entered the temple of the LORD to make offering on the altar of incense. ¹⁷But the priest Azariah went in after him, with eighty priests of the LORD who were men of valor; ¹⁸they withstood King Uzziah, and said to him, "It is not for you, Uzziah, to make offering to the LORD, but for the priests the descendants of Aaron, who are consecrated to make offering. Go out of the sanctuary; for you have done wrong, and it will bring you no honor from the LORD God." ¹⁹Then Uzziah was angry. Now he had a censer in his hand to make offering, and when he became angry with the priests a leprous*ᵃ* disease broke out on his forehead, in the presence of the priests in the house of the LORD, by the altar of incense. ²⁰When the chief priest Azariah, and all the priests, looked at him, he was leprous*ᵃ* in his forehead. They hurried him out, and he himself hurried to get out, because the LORD had struck him. ²¹King Uzziah was leprous*ᵃ* to the day of his death, and being leprous*ᵃ* lived in a separate house, for he was excluded from the house of the LORD. His son Jotham was in charge of the palace of the king, governing the people of the land.

22 Now the rest of the acts of Uzziah, from first to last, the prophet Isaiah son of Amoz wrote. ²³Uzziah slept with his ancestors; they buried him near his ancestors in the burial field that belonged to the kings, for they said, "He is leprous."*ᵃ* His son Jotham succeeded him.

a A term for several skin diseases; precise meaning uncertain

Reign of Jotham

27 Jotham was twenty-five years old when he began to reign; he reigned sixteen years in Jerusalem. His mother's name was Jerushah daughter of Zadok. ²He did what was right in the sight of the LORD just as his father Uzziah had done—only he did not invade the temple of the LORD. But the people still followed corrupt practices. ³He built the upper gate of the house of the LORD, and did extensive building on the wall of Ophel. ⁴Moreover he built cities in the hill country of Judah, and forts and towers on the wooded hills. ⁵He fought with the king of the Ammonites and prevailed against them. The Ammonites gave him that year one hundred talents of silver, ten thousand cors of wheat and ten thousand of barley. The Ammonites paid him the same amount in the second and the third years. ⁶So Jotham became strong because he ordered his ways before the LORD his God. ⁷Now the rest of the acts of Jotham, and all his wars and his ways, are written in the Book of the Kings of Israel and Judah. ⁸He was twenty-five years old when he began to reign; he reigned sixteen years in Jerusalem. ⁹Jotham slept with his ancestors, and they buried him in the city of David; and his son Ahaz succeeded him.

Reign of Ahaz

28 Ahaz was twenty years old when he began to reign; he reigned sixteen years in Jerusalem. He did not do what was right in the sight of the LORD, as his ancestor David had done, ²but he walked in the ways of the kings of Israel. He even made cast images for the Baals; ³and he made offerings in the valley of the son of Hinnom, and made his sons pass through fire, according to the abominable practices of the nations whom the LORD drove out before the people of Israel. ⁴He sacrificed and made offerings on the high places, on the hills, and under every green tree.

Aram and Israel Defeat Judah

5 Therefore the LORD his God gave him into the hand of the king of Aram, who defeated him and took captive a great number of his people and brought them to Damascus. He was also given into the hand of the king of Israel, who defeated him with great slaughter. ⁶Pekah son of Remaliah killed one hundred twenty thousand in Judah in one day, all of them valiant warriors, because they had abandoned the LORD, the God of their ancestors. ⁷And Zichri, a mighty warrior of Ephraim, killed the king's son Maaseiah, Azrikam the commander of the palace, and Elkanah the next in authority to the king.

Intervention of Oded

8 The people of Israel took captive two hundred thousand of their kin, women, sons, and daughters; they also took much booty from them and brought the booty to Samaria. ⁹But a prophet of the LORD was there, whose name was Oded; he went out to meet the army that came to Samaria, and said to them, "Because the LORD, the God of your ancestors, was angry with Judah, he gave them into your hand, but you have killed them in a rage that has reached up to heaven. ¹⁰Now you intend to subjugate the

A Covenant Prayer

2 CHRONICLES 28.8

"I am no longer my own,
but thine.
Put me to what thou wilt,
rank me with whom
thou wilt.
Put me to doing, put me to
suffering.
Let me be employed by thee
or laid aside for thee,
exalted for thee or brought
low for thee.
Let me be full, let me be
empty.
Let me have all things, let
me have nothing.
I freely and heartily yield all
things
to thy pleasure and
disposal.
And now, O glorious and
blessed God,
Father, Son, and Holy
Spirit,
thou art mine, and I am
thine. So be it.
And the covenant which I
have made on earth,
let it be ratified in heaven.
Amen."

—GEORGE B. ROBSON

people of Judah and Jerusalem, male and female, as your slaves. But what have you except sins against the LORD your God? [11]Now hear me, and send back the captives whom you have taken from your kindred, for the fierce wrath of the LORD is upon you." [12]Moreover, certain chiefs of the Ephraimites, Azariah son of Johanan, Berechiah son of Meshillemoth, Jehizkiah son of Shallum, and Amasa son of Hadlai, stood up against those who were coming from the war, [13]and said to them, "You shall not bring the captives in here, for you propose to bring on us guilt against the LORD in addition to our present sins and guilt. For our guilt is already great, and there is fierce wrath against Israel." [14]So the warriors left the captives and the booty before the officials and all the assembly. [15]Then those who were mentioned by name got up and took the captives, and with the booty they clothed all that were naked among them; they clothed them, gave them sandals, provided them with food and drink, and anointed them; and carrying all the feeble among them on donkeys, they brought them to their kindred at Jericho, the city of palm trees. Then they returned to Samaria.

Assyria Refuses to Help Judah

16 At that time King Ahaz sent to the king[a] of Assyria for help. [17]For the Edomites had again invaded and defeated Judah, and carried away captives. [18]And the Philistines had made raids on the cities in the Shephelah and the Negeb of Judah, and had taken Beth-shemesh, Aijalon, Gederoth, Soco with its villages, Timnah with its villages, and Gimzo with its villages; and they settled there. [19]For the LORD brought Judah low because of King Ahaz of Israel, for he had behaved without restraint in Judah and had been faithless to the LORD. [20]So King Tilgath-pilneser of Assyria came against him, and oppressed him instead of strengthening him. [21]For Ahaz plundered the house of the LORD and the houses of the king and of the officials, and gave tribute to the king of Assyria; but it did not help him.

Apostasy and Death of Ahaz

22 In the time of his distress he became yet more faithless to the LORD—this same King Ahaz. [23]For he sacrificed to the gods of Damascus, which had defeated him, and said, "Because the gods of the kings of Aram helped them, I will sacrifice to them so that they may help me." But they were the ruin of him, and of all Israel. [24]Ahaz gathered together the utensils of the house of God, and cut in pieces the utensils of the house of God. He shut up the doors of the house of the LORD and made himself altars in every corner of Jerusalem. [25]In every city of Judah he made high places to make offerings to other gods, provoking to anger the LORD, the God of his ancestors. [26]Now the rest of his acts and all his ways, from first to last, are written in the Book of the Kings of Judah and Israel. [27]Ahaz slept with his ancestors, and they buried him in the city, in Jerusalem; but they did not bring him into the tombs of the kings of Israel. His son Hezekiah succeeded him.

a Gk Syr Vg Compare 2 Kings 16.7: Heb *kings*

Reign of Hezekiah

29 Hezekiah began to reign when he was twenty-five years old; he reigned twenty-nine years in Jerusalem. His mother's name was Abijah daughter of Zechariah. ²He did what was right in the sight of the LORD, just as his ancestor David had done.

The Temple Cleansed

3 In the first year of his reign, in the first month, he opened the doors of the house of the LORD and repaired them. ⁴He brought in the priests and the Levites and assembled them in the square on the east. ⁵He said to them, "Listen to me, Levites! Sanctify yourselves, and sanctify the house of the LORD, the God of your ancestors, and carry out the filth from the holy place. ⁶For our ancestors have been unfaithful and have done what was evil in the sight of the LORD our God; they have forsaken him, and have turned away their faces from the dwelling of the LORD, and turned their backs. ⁷They also shut the doors of the vestibule and put out the lamps, and have not offered incense or made burnt offerings in the holy place to the God of Israel. ⁸Therefore the wrath of the LORD came upon Judah and Jerusalem, and he has made them an object of horror, of astonishment, and of hissing, as you see with your own eyes. ⁹Our fathers have fallen by the sword and our sons and our daughters and our wives are in captivity for this. ¹⁰Now it is in my heart to make a covenant with the LORD, the God of Israel, so that his fierce anger may turn away from us. ¹¹My sons, do not now be negligent, for the LORD has chosen you to stand in his presence to minister to him, and to be his ministers and make offerings to him."

12 Then the Levites arose, Mahath son of Amasai, and Joel son of Azariah, of the sons of the Kohathites; and of the sons of Merari, Kish son of Abdi, and Azariah son of Jehallelel; and of the Gershonites, Joah son of Zimmah, and Eden son of Joah; ¹³and of the sons of Elizaphan, Shimri and Jeuel; and of the sons of Asaph, Zechariah and Mattaniah; ¹⁴and of the sons of Heman, Jehuel and Shimei; and of the sons of Jeduthun, Shemaiah and Uzziel. ¹⁵They gathered their brothers, sanctified themselves, and went in as the king had commanded, by the words of the LORD, to cleanse the house of the LORD. ¹⁶The priests went into the inner part of the house of the LORD to cleanse it, and they brought out all the unclean things that they found in the temple of the LORD into the court of the house of the LORD; and the Levites took them and carried them out to the Wadi Kidron. ¹⁷They began to sanctify on the first day of the first month, and on the eighth day of the month they came to the vestibule of the LORD; then for eight days they sanctified the house of the LORD, and on the sixteenth day of the first month they finished. ¹⁸Then they went inside to King Hezekiah and said, "We have cleansed all the house of the LORD, the altar of burnt offering and all its utensils, and the table for the rows of bread and all its utensils. ¹⁹All the utensils that King Ahaz repudiated during his reign when he was faithless, we have made ready and sanctified; see, they are in front of the altar of the LORD."

Time of Cleansing

2 CHRONICLES 29.5–11

Try to imagine yourself present during this time of religious renewal and cleansing. See the animals being slaughtered as atoning sacrifices. Smell the blood and the smoke. Hear trumpets blaring, cymbals clashing, crowds singing. Join in the shouts of praise. Listen to the prayers and proclamations. What parts of this scene do you find particularly moving? What disturbs you? If you were to design a service of cleansing and renewal for your church, what actions, symbolic or direct, would you include?

See *Meeting God in Worship*

The Sacrifice We Can Offer

2 CHRONICLES 29.20–30

"The Lord doesn't look so much at the greatness of our works as at the love with which they are done. And if we do what we can, his Majesty will enable us each day to do more and more, provided that we do not quickly tire. But during the little while this life lasts—and perhaps it will last a shorter time than each one thinks—let us offer the Lord interiorly and exteriorly the sacrifice we can."

—TERESA OF AVILA,
The Interior Castle

Temple Worship Restored

20 Then King Hezekiah rose early, assembled the officials of the city, and went up to the house of the LORD. ²¹They brought seven bulls, seven rams, seven lambs, and seven male goats for a sin offering for the kingdom and for the sanctuary and for Judah. He commanded the priests the descendants of Aaron to offer them on the altar of the LORD. ²²So they slaughtered the bulls, and the priests received the blood and dashed it against the altar; they slaughtered the rams and their blood was dashed against the altar; they also slaughtered the lambs and their blood was dashed against the altar. ²³Then the male goats for the sin offering were brought to the king and the assembly; they laid their hands on them, ²⁴and the priests slaughtered them and made a sin offering with their blood at the altar, to make atonement for all Israel. For the king commanded that the burnt offering and the sin offering should be made for all Israel.

25 He stationed the Levites in the house of the LORD with cymbals, harps, and lyres, according to the commandment of David and of Gad the king's seer and of the prophet Nathan, for the commandment was from the LORD through his prophets. ²⁶The Levites stood with the instruments of David, and the priests with the trumpets. ²⁷Then Hezekiah commanded that the burnt offering be offered on the altar. When the burnt offering began, the song to the LORD began also, and the trumpets, accompanied by the instruments of King David of Israel. ²⁸The whole assembly worshiped, the singers sang, and the trumpeters sounded; all this continued until the burnt offering was finished. ²⁹When the offering was finished, the king and all who were present with him bowed down and worshiped. ³⁰King Hezekiah and the officials commanded the Levites to sing praises to the LORD with the words of David and of the seer Asaph. They sang praises with gladness, and they bowed down and worshiped.

31 Then Hezekiah said, "You have now consecrated yourselves to the LORD; come near, bring sacrifices and thank offerings to the house of the LORD." The assembly brought sacrifices and thank offerings; and all who were of a willing heart brought burnt offerings. ³²The number of the burnt offerings that the assembly brought was seventy bulls, one hundred rams, and two hundred lambs; all these were for a burnt offering to the LORD. ³³The consecrated offerings were six hundred bulls and three thousand sheep. ³⁴But the priests were too few and could not skin all the burnt offerings, so, until other priests had sanctified themselves, their kindred, the Levites, helped them until the work was finished—for the Levites were more conscientious*a* than the priests in sanctifying themselves. ³⁵Besides the great number of burnt offerings there was the fat of the offerings of well-being, and there were the drink offerings for the burnt offerings. Thus the service of the house of the LORD was restored. ³⁶And Hezekiah and all the people rejoiced because of what God had done for the people; for the thing had come about suddenly.

a Heb *upright in heart*

The Great Passover

30 Hezekiah sent word to all Israel and Judah, and wrote letters also to Ephraim and Manasseh, that they should come to the house of the LORD at Jerusalem, to keep the passover to the LORD the God of Israel. ²For the king and his officials and all the assembly in Jerusalem had taken counsel to keep the passover in the second month ³(for they could not keep it at its proper time because the priests had not sanctified themselves in sufficient number, nor had the people assembled in Jerusalem). ⁴The plan seemed right to the king and all the assembly. ⁵So they decreed to make a proclamation throughout all Israel, from Beer-sheba to Dan, that the people should come and keep the passover to the LORD the God of Israel, at Jerusalem; for they had not kept it in great numbers as prescribed. ⁶So couriers went throughout all Israel and Judah with letters from the king and his officials, as the king had commanded, saying, "O people of Israel, return to the LORD, the God of Abraham, Isaac, and Israel, so that he may turn again to the remnant of you who have escaped from the hand of the kings of Assyria. ⁷Do not be like your ancestors and your kindred, who were faithless to the LORD God of their ancestors, so that he made them a desolation, as you see. ⁸Do not now be stiff-necked as your ancestors were, but yield yourselves to the LORD and come to his sanctuary, which he has sanctified forever, and serve the LORD your God, so that his fierce anger may turn away from you. ⁹For as you return to the LORD, your kindred and your children will find compassion with their captors, and return to this land. For the LORD your God is gracious and merciful, and will not turn away his face from you, if you return to him."

10 So the couriers went from city to city through the country of Ephraim and Manasseh, and as far as Zebulun; but they laughed them to scorn, and mocked them. ¹¹Only a few from Asher, Manasseh, and Zebulun humbled themselves and came to Jerusalem. ¹²The hand of God was also on Judah to give them one heart to do what the king and the officials commanded by the word of the LORD.

13 Many people came together in Jerusalem to keep the festival of unleavened bread in the second month, a very large assembly. ¹⁴They set to work and removed the altars that were in Jerusalem, and all the altars for offering incense they took away and threw into the Wadi Kidron. ¹⁵They slaughtered the passover lamb on the fourteenth day of the second month. The priests and the Levites were ashamed, and they sanctified themselves and brought burnt offerings into the house of the LORD. ¹⁶They took their accustomed posts according to the law of Moses the man of God; the priests dashed the blood that they received[a] from the hands of the Levites. ¹⁷For there were many in the assembly who had not sanctified themselves; therefore the Levites had to slaughter the passover lamb for everyone who was not clean, to make it holy to the LORD. ¹⁸For a multitude of the people, many of them from Ephraim, Manasseh, Issachar, and Zebulun, had not cleansed themselves, yet they ate the passover otherwise than as prescribed. But Hezekiah prayed for them, saying,

---

Prayer for Return

2 CHRONICLES 30.6–9

Carefully read this call to the people of Israel to return to God. As you read, think of people who have left their churches or become inactive. Remember them in prayer. First simply commend them to God's care. Ask God to reach out to them and gently call them to return. Then ask God to show you ways in which you might invite them to return. You might want to call them or visit them. If so, you will probably need to ask for patience to listen to grievances without becoming defensive.

See Meeting God in Community

---

a Heb lacks *that they received*

Rules Aren't Everything

2 CHRONICLES 30.18–20,25–26

For one moment "business as usual" is suspended and people are invited to come to God without worrying about all the traditional rules of cleanliness. What are the special rules—mostly unwritten—that serve as barriers to people who might want to come to your church? You might try to list "rules" involving standards of dress or cleanliness, proper behavior, literacy (do people have to be able to read to participate?), social or economic status, or anything else you can think of. As you review the list, which rules are important to you personally? Why? What can you do to make your church more welcoming to all who seek to encounter God?

See Meeting God in Community

"The good LORD pardon all ¹⁹who set their hearts to seek God, the LORD the God of their ancestors, even though not in accordance with the sanctuary's rules of cleanness." ²⁰The LORD heard Hezekiah, and healed the people. ²¹The people of Israel who were present at Jerusalem kept the festival of unleavened bread seven days with great gladness; and the Levites and the priests praised the LORD day by day, accompanied by loud instruments for the LORD. ²²Hezekiah spoke encouragingly to all the Levites who showed good skill in the service of the LORD. So the people ate the food of the festival for seven days, sacrificing offerings of well-being and giving thanks to the LORD the God of their ancestors.

23 Then the whole assembly agreed together to keep the festival for another seven days; so they kept it for another seven days with gladness. ²⁴For King Hezekiah of Judah gave the assembly a thousand bulls and seven thousand sheep for offerings, and the officials gave the assembly a thousand bulls and ten thousand sheep. The priests sanctified themselves in great numbers. ²⁵The whole assembly of Judah, the priests and the Levites, and the whole assembly that came out of Israel, and the resident aliens who came out of the land of Israel, and the resident aliens who lived in Judah, rejoiced. ²⁶There was great joy in Jerusalem, for since the time of Solomon son of King David of Israel there had been nothing like this in Jerusalem. ²⁷Then the priests and the Levites stood up and blessed the people, and their voice was heard; their prayer came to his holy dwelling in heaven.

Pagan Shrines Destroyed

31 Now when all this was finished, all Israel who were present went out to the cities of Judah and broke down the pillars, hewed down the sacred poles,*ᵃ* and pulled down the high places and the altars throughout all Judah and Benjamin, and in Ephraim and Manasseh, until they had destroyed them all. Then all the people of Israel returned to their cities, all to their individual properties.

2 Hezekiah appointed the divisions of the priests and of the Levites, division by division, everyone according to his service, the priests and the Levites, for burnt offerings and offerings of well-being, to minister in the gates of the camp of the LORD and to give thanks and praise. ³The contribution of the king from his own possessions was for the burnt offerings: the burnt offerings of morning and evening, and the burnt offerings for the sabbaths, the new moons, and the appointed festivals, as it is written in the law of the LORD. ⁴He commanded the people who lived in Jerusalem to give the portion due to the priests and the Levites, so that they might devote themselves to the law of the LORD. ⁵As soon as the word spread, the people of Israel gave in abundance the first fruits of grain, wine, oil, honey, and of all the produce of the field; and they brought in abundantly the tithe of everything. ⁶The people of Israel and Judah who lived in the cities of Judah also brought in the tithe of cattle and sheep, and the tithe of the dedicated things that had been consecrated to the LORD their God, and laid them in heaps. ⁷In the third month they began to pile up the heaps, and finished them in the sev-

a Heb Asherim

enth month. [8]When Hezekiah and the officials came and saw the heaps, they blessed the LORD and his people Israel. [9]Hezekiah questioned the priests and the Levites about the heaps. [10]The chief priest Azariah, who was of the house of Zadok, answered him, "Since they began to bring the contributions into the house of the LORD, we have had enough to eat and have plenty to spare; for the LORD has blessed his people, so that we have this great supply left over."

Reorganization of Priests and Levites

11 Then Hezekiah commanded them to prepare storechambers in the house of the LORD; and they prepared them. [12]Faithfully they brought in the contributions, the tithes and the dedicated things. The chief officer in charge of them was Conaniah the Levite, with his brother Shimei as second; [13]while Jehiel, Azaziah, Nahath, Asahel, Jerimoth, Jozabad, Eliel, Ismachiah, Mahath, and Benaiah were overseers assisting Conaniah and his brother Shimei, by the appointment of King Hezekiah and of Azariah the chief officer of the house of God. [14]Kore son of Imnah the Levite, keeper of the east gate, was in charge of the freewill offerings to God, to apportion the contribution reserved for the LORD and the most holy offerings. [15]Eden, Miniamin, Jeshua, Shemaiah, Amariah, and Shecaniah were faithfully assisting him in the cities of the priests, to distribute the portions to their kindred, old and young alike, by divisions, [16]except those enrolled by genealogy, males from three years old and upwards, all who entered the house of the LORD as the duty of each day required, for their service according to their offices, by their divisions. [17]The enrollment of the priests was according to their ancestral houses; that of the Levites from twenty years old and upwards was according to their offices, by their divisions. [18]The priests were enrolled with all their little children, their wives, their sons, and their daughters, the whole multitude; for they were faithful in keeping themselves holy. [19]And for the descendants of Aaron, the priests, who were in the fields of common land belonging to their towns, town by town, the people designated by name were to distribute portions to every male among the priests and to everyone among the Levites who was enrolled.

20 Hezekiah did this throughout all Judah; he did what was good and right and faithful before the LORD his God. [21]And every work that he undertook in the service of the house of God, and in accordance with the law and the commandments, to seek his God, he did with all his heart; and he prospered.

Sennacherib's Invasion

32 After these things and these acts of faithfulness, King Sennacherib of Assyria came and invaded Judah and encamped against the fortified cities, thinking to win them for himself. [2]When Hezekiah saw that Sennacherib had come and intended to fight against Jerusalem, [3]he planned with his officers and his warriors to stop the flow of the springs that were outside the city; and they helped him. [4]A great many people were gathered, and they stopped all the springs and the wadi that

Thanksgiving

2 CHRONICLES 31.11

"With praise and adoration to God comes thanksgiving to him for his good gifts. In the devotional life these moods are intertwined, and we discuss them separately only for the sake of further analysis of the place of gratitude in prayer. We ought to praise God anyway for being what he is, quite regardless of our particular blessings. Otherwise, our worship is not centered in God but in ourselves. Yet praise leads normally to the mood of thanksgiving for God's bounties."

—GEORGIA HARKNESS,
Prayer and the Common Life

Trust God and Be Ready

2 CHRONICLES 32.7–8

Prayer is not an alternative to preparing for battle but an essential part of it. Hezekiah makes all the standard military preparations, but he insists that the deciding factor is that God will fight with them. What battles are you fighting or preparing to fight? Which ones are God's battles too? What preparations do you need to make? What must you surrender to God's care? You might want to turn the entire battle over to God by offering your efforts and your preparations to God's service. Repeat to yourself, "With us is the LORD our God, to help us and to fight our battles."

See Meeting God in Prayer

flowed through the land, saying, "Why should the Assyrian kings come and find water in abundance?" [5]Hezekiah[a] set to work resolutely and built up the entire wall that was broken down, and raised towers on it,[b] and outside it he built another wall; he also strengthened the Millo in the city of David, and made weapons and shields in abundance. [6]He appointed combat commanders over the people, and gathered them together to him in the square at the gate of the city and spoke encouragingly to them, saying, [7]"Be strong and of good courage. Do not be afraid or dismayed before the king of Assyria and all the horde that is with him; for there is one greater with us than with him. [8]With him is an arm of flesh; but with us is the LORD our God, to help us and to fight our battles." The people were encouraged by the words of King Hezekiah of Judah.

9 After this, while King Sennacherib of Assyria was at Lachish with all his forces, he sent his servants to Jerusalem to King Hezekiah of Judah and to all the people of Judah that were in Jerusalem, saying, [10]"Thus says King Sennacherib of Assyria: On what are you relying, that you undergo the siege of Jerusalem? [11]Is not Hezekiah misleading you, handing you over to die by famine and by thirst, when he tells you, 'The LORD our God will save us from the hand of the king of Assyria'? [12]Was it not this same Hezekiah who took away his high places and his altars and commanded Judah and Jerusalem, saying, 'Before one altar you shall worship, and upon it you shall make your offerings'? [13]Do you not know what I and my ancestors have done to all the peoples of other lands? Were the gods of the nations of those lands at all able to save their lands out of my hand? [14]Who among all the gods of those nations that my ancestors utterly destroyed was able to save his people from my hand, that your God should be able to save you from my hand? [15]Now therefore do not let Hezekiah deceive you or mislead you in this fashion, and do not believe him, for no god of any nation or kingdom has been able to save his people from my hand or from the hand of my ancestors. How much less will your God save you out of my hand!"

16 His servants said still more against the Lord GOD and against his servant Hezekiah. [17]He also wrote letters to throw contempt on the LORD the God of Israel and to speak against him, saying, "Just as the gods of the nations in other lands did not rescue their people from my hands, so the God of Hezekiah will not rescue his people from my hand." [18]They shouted it with a loud voice in the language of Judah to the people of Jerusalem who were on the wall, to frighten and terrify them, in order that they might take the city. [19]They spoke of the God of Jerusalem as if he were like the gods of the peoples of the earth, which are the work of human hands.

Sennacherib's Defeat and Death

20 Then King Hezekiah and the prophet Isaiah son of Amoz prayed because of this and cried to heaven. [21]And the LORD sent an angel who cut off all the mighty warriors and commanders and officers in the camp of the king of Assyria. So he returned in disgrace to his own land. When he came into the house of his god, some of his own sons

a Heb *He*   *b* Vg: Heb *and raised on the towers*

struck him down there with the sword. ²²So the LORD saved Hezekiah and the inhabitants of Jerusalem from the hand of King Sennacherib of Assyria and from the hand of all his enemies; he gave them rest*a* on every side. ²³Many brought gifts to the LORD in Jerusalem and precious things to King Hezekiah of Judah, so that he was exalted in the sight of all nations from that time onward.

Hezekiah's Sickness

24 In those days Hezekiah became sick and was at the point of death. He prayed to the LORD, and he answered him and gave him a sign. ²⁵But Hezekiah did not respond according to the benefit done to him, for his heart was proud. Therefore wrath came upon him and upon Judah and Jerusalem. ²⁶Then Hezekiah humbled himself for the pride of his heart, both he and the inhabitants of Jerusalem, so that the wrath of the LORD did not come upon them in the days of Hezekiah.

Hezekiah's Prosperity and Achievements

27 Hezekiah had very great riches and honor; and he made for himself treasuries for silver, for gold, for precious stones, for spices, for shields, and for all kinds of costly objects; ²⁸storehouses also for the yield of grain, wine, and oil; and stalls for all kinds of cattle, and sheepfolds.*b* ²⁹He likewise provided cities for himself, and flocks and herds in abundance; for God had given him very great possessions. ³⁰This same Hezekiah closed the upper outlet of the waters of Gihon and directed them down to the west side of the city of David. Hezekiah prospered in all his works. ³¹So also in the matter of the envoys of the officials of Babylon, who had been sent to him to inquire about the sign that had been done in the land, God left him to himself, in order to test him and to know all that was in his heart.

32 Now the rest of the acts of Hezekiah, and his good deeds, are written in the vision of the prophet Isaiah son of Amoz in the Book of the Kings of Judah and Israel. ³³Hezekiah slept with his ancestors, and they buried him on the ascent to the tombs of the descendants of David; and all Judah and the inhabitants of Jerusalem did him honor at his death. His son Manasseh succeeded him.

Reign of Manasseh

33 Manasseh was twelve years old when he began to reign; he reigned fifty-five years in Jerusalem. ²He did what was evil in the sight of the LORD, according to the abominable practices of the nations whom the LORD drove out before the people of Israel. ³For he rebuilt the high places that his father Hezekiah had pulled down, and erected altars to the Baals, made sacred poles,*c* worshiped all the host of heaven, and served them. ⁴He built altars in the house of the LORD, of which the LORD had said, "In Jerusalem shall my name be forever." ⁵He built altars for all the host of heaven in the two courts of the house of the LORD. ⁶He made his son pass through fire in the valley of the son of Hinnom, practiced soothsaying and augury and sorcery, and dealt with mediums and with wizards. He did much evil in the sight of the LORD, provoking him to anger. ⁷The carved image of the idol that he had made he set in

---

God Welcomes Repentance

2 CHRONICLES 32.24–26

A soldier asked Abba Mius if God accepted repentance. After the old man had taught him many things he said, "Tell me, my dear, if your cloak is torn, do you throw it away?" He replied, "No, I mend it and use it again." The old man said to him, "If you are so careful about your cloak, will not God be equally careful about his creature?"

—MIUS OF BELOS,
Sayings of the Desert Fathers

---

a Gk Vg: Heb *guided them*   *b* Gk Vg: Heb *flocks for folds*   *c* Heb *Asheroth*

Never Too Late

2 CHRONICLES 33.10–13

It is never too late to repent
and receive God's forgiveness
and grace. Even after Manasseh
has brought disaster to himself
and God's people, he still can
turn to God and be restored.
Are there sins for which you
have been afraid to ask God's
forgiveness? Ask now. You
might turn to God and ask for
the grace of a new start. You
might also take special notice
(on television and in newspapers and novels) of others who
have received God's gift of love
after making disasters of their
lives.

See Meeting God in Prayer

the house of God, of which God said to David and to his
son Solomon, "In this house, and in Jerusalem, which I
have chosen out of all the tribes of Israel, I will put my
name forever; [8]I will never again remove the feet of Israel
from the land that I appointed for your ancestors, if only
they will be careful to do all that I have commanded them,
all the law, the statutes, and the ordinances given through
Moses." [9]Manasseh misled Judah and the inhabitants of
Jerusalem, so that they did more evil than the nations
whom the LORD had destroyed before the people of Israel.

Manasseh Restored after Repentance

10 The LORD spoke to Manasseh and to his people, but
they gave no heed. [11]Therefore the LORD brought against
them the commanders of the army of the king of Assyria,
who took Manasseh captive in manacles, bound him with
fetters, and brought him to Babylon. [12]While he was in distress he entreated the favor of the LORD his God and humbled himself greatly before the God of his ancestors. [13]He
prayed to him, and God received his entreaty, heard his
plea, and restored him again to Jerusalem and to his kingdom. Then Manasseh knew that the LORD indeed was God.

14 Afterward he built an outer wall for the city of David
west of Gihon, in the valley, reaching the entrance at the
Fish Gate; he carried it around Ophel, and raised it to a
very great height. He also put commanders of the army in
all the fortified cities in Judah. [15]He took away the foreign
gods and the idol from the house of the LORD, and all the
altars that he had built on the mountain of the house of
the LORD and in Jerusalem, and he threw them out of the
city. [16]He also restored the altar of the LORD and offered on
it sacrifices of well-being and of thanksgiving; and he commanded Judah to serve the LORD the God of Israel. [17]The
people, however, still sacrificed at the high places, but only
to the LORD their God.

Death of Manasseh

18 Now the rest of the acts of Manasseh, his prayer to
his God, and the words of the seers who spoke to him in
the name of the LORD God of Israel, these are in the Annals
of the Kings of Israel. [19]His prayer, and how God received
his entreaty, all his sin and his faithlessness, the sites on
which he built high places and set up the sacred poles[a]
and the images, before he humbled himself, these are
written in the records of the seers.[b] [20]So Manasseh slept
with his ancestors, and they buried him in his house. His
son Amon succeeded him.

Amon's Reign and Death

21 Amon was twenty-two years old when he began to
reign; he reigned two years in Jerusalem. [22]He did what
was evil in the sight of the LORD, as his father Manasseh
had done. Amon sacrificed to all the images that his father
Manasseh had made, and served them. [23]He did not humble himself before the LORD, as his father Manasseh had
humbled himself, but this Amon incurred more and more
guilt. [24]His servants conspired against him and killed him
in his house. [25]But the people of the land killed all those

a Heb *Asherim*   *b* One Ms Gk: MT *of Hozai*

who had conspired against King Amon; and the people of the land made his son Josiah king to succeed him.

Reign of Josiah

34 Josiah was eight years old when he began to reign; he reigned thirty-one years in Jerusalem. ²He did what was right in the sight of the LORD, and walked in the ways of his ancestor David; he did not turn aside to the right or to the left. ³For in the eighth year of his reign, while he was still a boy, he began to seek the God of his ancestor David, and in the twelfth year he began to purge Judah and Jerusalem of the high places, the sacred poles,ᵃ and the carved and the cast images. ⁴In his presence they pulled down the altars of the Baals; he demolished the incense altars that stood above them. He broke down the sacred polesᵃ and the carved and the cast images; he made dust of them and scattered it over the graves of those who had sacrificed to them. ⁵He also burned the bones of the priests on their altars, and purged Judah and Jerusalem. ⁶In the towns of Manasseh, Ephraim, and Simeon, and as far as Naphtali, in their ruinsᵇ all around, ⁷he broke down the altars, beat the sacred polesᵃ and the images into powder, and demolished all the incense altars throughout all the land of Israel. Then he returned to Jerusalem.

Discovery of the Book of the Law

8 In the eighteenth year of his reign, when he had purged the land and the house, he sent Shaphan son of Azaliah, Maaseiah the governor of the city, and Joah son of Joahaz, the recorder, to repair the house of the LORD his God. ⁹They came to the high priest Hilkiah and delivered the money that had been brought into the house of God, which the Levites, the keepers of the threshold, had collected from Manasseh and Ephraim and from all the remnant of Israel and from all Judah and Benjamin and from the inhabitants of Jerusalem. ¹⁰They delivered it to the workers who had the oversight of the house of the LORD, and the workers who were working in the house of the LORD gave it for repairing and restoring the house. ¹¹They gave it to the carpenters and the builders to buy quarried stone, and timber for binders, and beams for the buildings that the kings of Judah had let go to ruin. ¹²The people did the work faithfully. Over them were appointed the Levites Jahath and Obadiah, of the sons of Merari, along with Zechariah and Meshullam, of the sons of the Kohathites, to have oversight. Other Levites, all skillful with instruments of music, ¹³were over the burden bearers and directed all who did work in every kind of service; and some of the Levites were scribes, and officials, and gatekeepers.

14 While they were bringing out the money that had been brought into the house of the LORD, the priest Hilkiah found the book of the law of the LORD given through Moses. ¹⁵Hilkiah said to the secretary Shaphan, "I have found the book of the law in the house of the LORD"; and Hilkiah gave the book to Shaphan. ¹⁶Shaphan brought the book to the king, and further reported to the king, "All that was committed to your servants they are doing. ¹⁷They have emptied out the money that was found in the house of the LORD and have delivered it into the hand of the over-

Destroying Idols

2 CHRONICLES 34.3–7

As you read this vivid account of Josiah pulling down idols and destroying their altars, consider the idols that may be in your life. What are the possessions, organizations, places that seem to have power over you—that seem to be able to command you? You might imagine yourself pulling them from their places of honor and making dust of them. How can you bring your imagining into reality? What things need to be eliminated from your life? What can be redeemed? How can things that use you and that require your time and attention become things that you can use to serve God? You might start by offering or consecrating these things to God's service.

See *Meeting God in Everyday Life*

a Heb *Asherim*   b Meaning of Heb uncertain

Discovering the Bible

2 CHRONICLES 34.29–32

Try to imagine yourself in the crowd as the newly discovered scroll is read. Because some scholars believe that this scroll was the book of Deuteronomy, you might get a sense of the occasion by reading Deuteronomy 29–30 aloud. What is your mood as you hear yourself read these words? How do these words apply to your life and to the life of your community? What response would you make? What would it mean for you to act "according to the covenant of God"? What specific changes do you need to make in the way you have been living?

See Meeting God in Everyday Life

seers and the workers." [18]The secretary Shaphan informed the king, "The priest Hilkiah has given me a book." Shaphan then read it aloud to the king.

19 When the king heard the words of the law he tore his clothes. [20]Then the king commanded Hilkiah, Ahikam son of Shaphan, Abdon son of Micah, the secretary Shaphan, and the king's servant Asaiah: [21]"Go, inquire of the LORD for me and for those who are left in Israel and in Judah, concerning the words of the book that has been found; for the wrath of the LORD that is poured out on us is great, because our ancestors did not keep the word of the LORD, to act in accordance with all that is written in this book."

The Prophet Huldah Consulted

22 So Hilkiah and those whom the king had sent went to the prophet Huldah, the wife of Shallum son of Tokhath son of Hasrah, keeper of the wardrobe (who lived in Jerusalem in the Second Quarter) and spoke to her to that effect. [23]She declared to them, "Thus says the LORD, the God of Israel: Tell the man who sent you to me, [24]Thus says the LORD: I will indeed bring disaster upon this place and upon its inhabitants, all the curses that are written in the book that was read before the king of Judah. [25]Because they have forsaken me and have made offerings to other gods, so that they have provoked me to anger with all the works of their hands, my wrath will be poured out on this place and will not be quenched. [26]But as to the king of Judah, who sent you to inquire of the LORD, thus shall you say to him: Thus says the LORD, the God of Israel: Regarding the words that you have heard, [27]because your heart was penitent and you humbled yourself before God when you heard his words against this place and its inhabitants, and you have humbled yourself before me, and have torn your clothes and wept before me, I also have heard you, says the LORD. [28]I will gather you to your ancestors and you shall be gathered to your grave in peace; your eyes shall not see all the disaster that I will bring on this place and its inhabitants." They took the message back to the king.

The Covenant Renewed

29 Then the king sent word and gathered together all the elders of Judah and Jerusalem. [30]The king went up to the house of the LORD, with all the people of Judah, the inhabitants of Jerusalem, the priests and the Levites, all the people both great and small; he read in their hearing all the words of the book of the covenant that had been found in the house of the LORD. [31]The king stood in his place and made a covenant before the LORD, to follow the LORD, keeping his commandments, his decrees, and his statutes, with all his heart and all his soul, to perform the words of the covenant that were written in this book. [32]Then he made all who were present in Jerusalem and in Benjamin pledge themselves to it. And the inhabitants of Jerusalem acted according to the covenant of God, the God of their ancestors. [33]Josiah took away all the abominations from all the territory that belonged to the people of Israel, and made all who were in Israel worship the LORD their God. All his days they did not turn away from following the LORD the God of their ancestors.

Celebration of the Passover

35 Josiah kept a passover to the LORD in Jerusalem; they slaughtered the passover lamb on the fourteenth day of the first month. ²He appointed the priests to their offices and encouraged them in the service of the house of the LORD. ³He said to the Levites who taught all Israel and who were holy to the LORD, "Put the holy ark in the house that Solomon son of David, king of Israel, built; you need no longer carry it on your shoulders. Now serve the LORD your God and his people Israel. ⁴Make preparations by your ancestral houses by your divisions, following the written directions of King David of Israel and the written directions of his son Solomon. ⁵Take position in the holy place according to the groupings of the ancestral houses of your kindred the people, and let there be Levites for each division of an ancestral house.ᵃ ⁶Slaughter the passover lamb, sanctify yourselves, and on behalf of your kindred make preparations, acting according to the word of the LORD by Moses."

7 Then Josiah contributed to the people, as passover offerings for all that were present, lambs and kids from the flock to the number of thirty thousand, and three thousand bulls; these were from the king's possessions. ⁸His officials contributed willingly to the people, to the priests, and to the Levites. Hilkiah, Zechariah, and Jehiel, the chief officers of the house of God, gave to the priests for the passover offerings two thousand six hundred lambs and kids and three hundred bulls. ⁹Conaniah also, and his brothers Shemaiah and Nethanel, and Hashabiah and Jeiel and Jozabad, the chiefs of the Levites, gave to the Levites for the passover offerings five thousand lambs and kids and five hundred bulls.

10 When the service had been prepared for, the priests stood in their place, and the Levites in their divisions according to the king's command. ¹¹They slaughtered the passover lamb, and the priests dashed the blood that they receivedᵇ from them, while the Levites did the skinning. ¹²They set aside the burnt offerings so that they might distribute them according to the groupings of the ancestral houses of the people, to offer to the LORD, as it is written in the book of Moses. And they did the same with the bulls. ¹³They roasted the passover lamb with fire according to the ordinance; and they boiled the holy offerings in pots, in caldrons, and in pans, and carried them quickly to all the people. ¹⁴Afterward they made preparations for themselves and for the priests, because the priests the descendants of Aaron were occupied in offering the burnt offerings and the fat parts until night; so the Levites made preparations for themselves and for the priests, the descendants of Aaron. ¹⁵The singers, the descendants of Asaph, were in their place according to the command of David, and Asaph, and Heman, and the king's seer Jeduthun. The gatekeepers were at each gate; they did not need to interrupt their service, for their kindred the Levites made preparations for them.

16 So all the service of the LORD was prepared that day, to keep the passover and to offer burnt offerings on the altar of the LORD, according to the command of King Josiah. ¹⁷The people of Israel who were present kept the passover

In Every Generation

2 CHRONICLES 35.10–11

"In every generation, let all people look on themselves as if they came forth out of Egypt . . . It was not only our ancestors that the Holy One (blessed be he) redeemed, but he redeemed us as well along with them . . . . Therefore we are bound to thank, praise, laud, glorify, exalt, honor, bless, extol, and adore God who performed all these miracles for our ancestors and for us. God has brought us forth from slavery to freedom, from sorrow to joy, from mourning to holiday, from darkness to great light, and from bondage to redemption. Therefore let us recite before God a new song: Praise the Lord!"

—*THE PASSOVER HAGGADAH*,
Traditional

---

a Meaning of Heb uncertain   *b* Heb lacks *that they received*

Lamentation

Josiah's death is lamentable, not only because a righteous king is dead, but also because he represented Israel's last great hope for freedom. What are the losses in your life that are suffocating your hopes? You might offer your own lament, crying to God over destroyed plans, dashed hopes, lost friends and painful mistakes. Offer God your sorrow. If you have trouble putting your feelings into words, you might "prime the pump" by reading the book of Lamentations. As you mourn the past, be open to hearing God's gracious call to new beginnings.

See Meeting God in Everyday Life

at that time, and the festival of unleavened bread seven days. ¹⁸No passover like it had been kept in Israel since the days of the prophet Samuel; none of the kings of Israel had kept such a passover as was kept by Josiah, by the priests and the Levites, by all Judah and Israel who were present, and by the inhabitants of Jerusalem. ¹⁹In the eighteenth year of the reign of Josiah this passover was kept.

Defeat by Pharaoh Neco and Death of Josiah

20 After all this, when Josiah had set the temple in order, King Neco of Egypt went up to fight at Carchemish on the Euphrates, and Josiah went out against him. ²¹But Neco^a sent envoys to him, saying, "What have I to do with you, king of Judah? I am not coming against you today, but against the house with which I am at war; and God has commanded me to hurry. Cease opposing God, who is with me, so that he will not destroy you." ²²But Josiah would not turn away from him, but disguised himself in order to fight with him. He did not listen to the words of Neco from the mouth of God, but joined battle in the plain of Megiddo. ²³The archers shot King Josiah; and the king said to his servants, "Take me away, for I am badly wounded." ²⁴So his servants took him out of the chariot and carried him in his second chariot^b and brought him to Jerusalem. There he died, and was buried in the tombs of his ancestors. All Judah and Jerusalem mourned for Josiah. ²⁵Jeremiah also uttered a lament for Josiah, and all the singing men and singing women have spoken of Josiah in their laments to this day. They made these a custom in Israel; they are recorded in the Laments. ²⁶Now the rest of the acts of Josiah and his faithful deeds in accordance with what is written in the law of the LORD, ²⁷and his acts, first and last, are written in the Book of the Kings of Israel and Judah.

Reign of Jehoahaz

36 The people of the land took Jehoahaz son of Josiah and made him king to succeed his father in Jerusalem. ²Jehoahaz was twenty-three years old when he began to reign; he reigned three months in Jerusalem. ³Then the king of Egypt deposed him in Jerusalem and laid on the land a tribute of one hundred talents of silver and one talent of gold. ⁴The king of Egypt made his brother Eliakim king over Judah and Jerusalem, and changed his name to Jehoiakim; but Neco took his brother Jehoahaz and carried him to Egypt.

Reign and Captivity of Jehoiakim

5 Jehoiakim was twenty-five years old when he began to reign; he reigned eleven years in Jerusalem. He did what was evil in the sight of the LORD his God. ⁶Against him King Nebuchadnezzar of Babylon came up, and bound him with fetters to take him to Babylon. ⁷Nebuchadnezzar also carried some of the vessels of the house of the LORD to Babylon and put them in his palace in Babylon. ⁸Now the rest of the acts of Jehoiakim, and the abominations that he did, and what was found against him, are written in the Book of the Kings of Israel and Judah; and his son Jehoiachin succeeded him.

a Heb *he*   *b* Or *the chariot of his deputy*

Reign and Captivity of Jehoiachin

9 Jehoiachin was eight years old when he began to reign; he reigned three months and ten days in Jerusalem. He did what was evil in the sight of the LORD. ¹⁰In the spring of the year King Nebuchadnezzar sent and brought him to Babylon, along with the precious vessels of the house of the LORD, and made his brother Zedekiah king over Judah and Jerusalem.

Reign of Zedekiah

11 Zedekiah was twenty-one years old when he began to reign; he reigned eleven years in Jerusalem. ¹²He did what was evil in the sight of the LORD his God. He did not humble himself before the prophet Jeremiah who spoke from the mouth of the LORD. ¹³He also rebelled against King Nebuchadnezzar, who had made him swear by God; he stiffened his neck and hardened his heart against turning to the LORD, the God of Israel. ¹⁴All the leading priests and the people also were exceedingly unfaithful, following all the abominations of the nations; and they polluted the house of the LORD that he had consecrated in Jerusalem.

The Fall of Jerusalem

15 The LORD, the God of their ancestors, sent persistently to them by his messengers, because he had compassion on his people and on his dwelling place; ¹⁶but they kept mocking the messengers of God, despising his words, and scoffing at his prophets, until the wrath of the LORD against his people became so great that there was no remedy.
17 Therefore he brought up against them the king of the Chaldeans, who killed their youths with the sword in the house of their sanctuary, and had no compassion on young man or young woman, the aged or the feeble; he gave them all into his hand. ¹⁸All the vessels of the house of God, large and small, and the treasures of the house of the LORD, and the treasures of the king and of his officials, all these he brought to Babylon. ¹⁹They burned the house of God, broke down the wall of Jerusalem, burned all its palaces with fire, and destroyed all its precious vessels. ²⁰He took into exile in Babylon those who had escaped from the sword, and they became servants to him and to his sons until the establishment of the kingdom of Persia, ²¹to fulfill the word of the LORD by the mouth of Jeremiah, until the land had made up for its sabbaths. All the days that it lay desolate it kept sabbath, to fulfill seventy years.

Cyrus Proclaims Liberty for the Exiles

22 In the first year of King Cyrus of Persia, in fulfillment of the word of the LORD spoken by Jeremiah, the LORD stirred up the spirit of King Cyrus of Persia so that he sent a herald throughout all his kingdom and also declared in a written edict: ²³"Thus says King Cyrus of Persia: The LORD, the God of heaven, has given me all the kingdoms of the earth, and he has charged me to build him a house at Jerusalem, which is in Judah. Whoever is among you of all his people, may the LORD his God be with him! Let him go up."

The Last Word

2 CHRONICLES 36.15–16

The book of 1 Chronicles ended with an epitaph for a king; the book of 2 Chronicles ends with an epitaph for a nation. And what a sad one it is! God's people ignored warning after warning until it was too late and disaster came. Where have you seen this pattern in your life? In your community? What warnings are you hearing now? What warnings do you need to pass on to others? How can you respond to these warnings? What actions can you take? What words of hope can you proclaim along with the words of warning?

See Meeting God in Community

EZRA
Rebuilding and Reclaiming

KEY VERSE:

With joy they celebrated the festival of unleavened bread seven days; for the LORD had made them joyful, and had turned the heart of the king of Assyria to them, so that he aided them in the work on the house of God, the God of Israel.—Ezra 6.22

"Now my heart began to ache and fear again I might meet with disappointment at the last . . . at which point I began to consider whether one who had sinned as I have might with confidence trust the faithfulness of God . . . And as I was in a muse about this thing, that Scripture came home to me, 'Mercy triumphs over judgment!' [James 2.13]. This was a wonderment to me; yet truly I am apt to think it was of God; for the word of the law and wrath must give place to the word of life and grace."

—JOHN BUNYAN,
Grace Abounding

There are plenty of instances in history where a nation was exiled and never received its homeland back. Think, for example, of the Armenians, who have suffered massacres and who are without their ancient land; and think of the Kurdish people, now spread out in Turkey, Iraq and elsewhere. Yet, against all odds, God restored the people of Israel to Jerusalem and made provision for rebuilding the temple. Of course, Israel was not just any nation exiled and the temple was not just any temple destroyed. This nation was the chosen of the one, true God. They had worshiped God in the temple that lay in ruins: "By the rivers of Babylon—there we sat down and there we wept when we remembered Zion" (Psalm 137.1).

Beneath the rather dry lists and the copies of official documents and decrees in the book of Ezra, this is a dramatic story—a resurrection story. What seems like the death of a nation is, in reality, new life. Have you ever been forced to live away from home for an extended period of time? Do you know people who are refugees from their homes? Try to place yourself in this story. Imagine the emotions God's people experience as they return to their ancient land: "The wonder of it! We never expected this! Is it too good to be true? How could we have imagined that God would forget the covenant, that God would no longer be gracious and loving toward us?" While Israel may be faithless, God is forever faithful!

End of the Babylonian Captivity

1 In the first year of King Cyrus of Persia, in order that the word of the LORD by the mouth of Jeremiah might be accomplished, the LORD stirred up the spirit of King Cyrus of Persia so that he sent a herald throughout all his kingdom, and also in a written edict declared:
2 "Thus says King Cyrus of Persia: The LORD, the God of heaven, has given me all the kingdoms of the earth, and he has charged me to build him a house at Jerusalem in Judah. ³Any of those among you who are of his people—may their God be with them!—are now permitted to go up to Jerusalem in Judah, and rebuild the house of the LORD, the God of Israel—he is the God who is in Jerusalem; ⁴and let all survivors, in whatever place they reside, be assisted by the people of their place with silver and gold, with goods and with animals, besides freewill offerings for the house of God in Jerusalem."

5 The heads of the families of Judah and Benjamin, and the priests and the Levites—everyone whose spirit God had stirred—got ready to go up and rebuild the house of the LORD in Jerusalem. ⁶All their neighbors aided them with silver vessels, with gold, with goods, with animals, and with valuable gifts, besides all that was freely offered. ⁷King Cyrus himself brought out the vessels of the house of the LORD that Nebuchadnezzar had carried away from Jerusalem and placed in the house of his gods. ⁸King Cyrus of Persia had them released into the charge of Mithredath the treasurer, who counted them out to Sheshbazzar the prince of Judah. ⁹And this was the inventory: gold basins, thirty; silver basins, one thousand; knives,ᵃ twenty-nine; ¹⁰gold bowls, thirty; other silver bowls, four hundred ten; other vessels, one thousand; ¹¹the total of the gold and silver vessels was five thousand four hundred. All these Sheshbazzar brought up, when the exiles were brought up from Babylonia to Jerusalem.

List of the Returned Exiles

2 Now these were the people of the province who came from those captive exiles whom King Nebuchadnezzar of Babylon had carried captive to Babylonia; they returned to Jerusalem and Judah, all to their own towns. ²They came with Zerubbabel, Jeshua, Nehemiah, Seraiah, Reelaiah, Mordecai, Bilshan, Mispar, Bigvai, Rehum, and Baanah.

The number of the Israelite people: ³the descendants of Parosh, two thousand one hundred seventy-two. ⁴Of Shephatiah, three hundred seventy-two. ⁵Of Arah, seven hundred seventy-five. ⁶Of Pahath-moab, namely the descendants of Jeshua and Joab, two thousand eight hundred twelve. ⁷Of Elam, one thousand two hundred fifty-four. ⁸Of Zattu, nine hundred forty-five. ⁹Of Zaccai, seven hundred sixty. ¹⁰Of Bani, six hundred forty-two. ¹¹Of Bebai, six hundred twenty-three. ¹²Of Azgad, one thousand two hundred twenty-two. ¹³Of Adonikam, six

---

The Kingdoms of This World

EZRA 1.1,5

While we are accustomed to looking for God's hand in the details of our daily lives, we sometimes fail to see God working out his purposes among the nations of the world. Here, at the very beginning of the book, we are alerted to the fact that God moved the leaders to take action.

Today, watch the news broadcast or read the newspaper and list the world leaders whose names are prominent. Keep their names before you as you pray this week and offer each of them to God's care. Pray that they will be open to God's leading. Listen for God's leading in your prayer. What does God wish for these leaders? What does God want you to pray for when you hold the nations of the world before God?

See Meeting God in Prayer

Generation to Generation

EZRA 2.36–61

Through the long years of exile, the Hebrew people did not lose their identity or forget their fathers and mothers in the faith. Their commitment to remember those who served God was especially strong. Priests, Levites, temple servants, Solomon's servants—the people recorded their names and remembered how they had served.

If you come from a family that has been faithful to God for generations, how did your family maintain that tradition? What special beliefs and understandings were prevalent in your family? Do you remember things your parents and grandparents did or said to help preserve your family's worship of God? If you are the first in your family to worship God, what can you do to establish an allegiance to God that will last for generations?

See *Meeting God in Community*

hundred sixty-six. [14]Of Bigvai, two thousand fifty-six. [15]Of Adin, four hundred fifty-four. [16]Of Ater, namely of Hezekiah, ninety-eight. [17]Of Bezai, three hundred twenty-three. [18]Of Jorah, one hundred twelve. [19]Of Hashum, two hundred twenty-three. [20]Of Gibbar, ninety-five. [21]Of Bethlehem, one hundred twenty-three. [22]The people of Netophah, fifty-six. [23]Of Anathoth, one hundred twenty-eight. [24]The descendants of Azmaveth, forty-two. [25]Of Kiriatharim, Chephirah, and Beeroth, seven hundred forty-three. [26]Of Ramah and Geba, six hundred twenty-one. [27]The people of Michmas, one hundred twenty-two. [28]Of Bethel and Ai, two hundred twenty-three. [29]The descendants of Nebo, fifty-two. [30]Of Magbish, one hundred fifty-six. [31]Of the other Elam, one thousand two hundred fifty-four. [32]Of Harim, three hundred twenty. [33]Of Lod, Hadid, and Ono, seven hundred twenty-five. [34]Of Jericho, three hundred forty-five. [35]Of Senaah, three thousand six hundred thirty.

36 The priests: the descendants of Jedaiah, of the house of Jeshua, nine hundred seventy-three. [37]Of Immer, one thousand fifty-two. [38]Of Pashhur, one thousand two hundred forty-seven. [39]Of Harim, one thousand seventeen.

40 The Levites: the descendants of Jeshua and Kadmiel, of the descendants of Hodaviah, seventy-four. [41]The singers: the descendants of Asaph, one hundred twenty-eight. [42]The descendants of the gatekeepers: of Shallum, of Ater, of Talmon, of Akkub, of Hatita, and of Shobai, in all one hundred thirty-nine.

43 The temple servants: the descendants of Ziha, Hasupha, Tabbaoth, [44]Keros, Siaha, Padon, [45]Lebanah, Hagabah, Akkub, [46]Hagab, Shamlai, Hanan, [47]Giddel, Gahar, Reaiah, [48]Rezin, Nekoda, Gazzam, [49]Uzza, Paseah, Besai, [50]Asnah, Meunim, Nephisim, [51]Bakbuk, Hakupha, Harhur, [52]Bazluth, Mehida, Harsha, [53]Barkos, Sisera, Temah, [54]Neziah, and Hatipha.

55 The descendants of Solomon's servants: Sotai, Hassophereth, Peruda, [56]Jaalah, Darkon, Giddel, [57]Shephatiah, Hattil, Pochereth-hazzebaim, and Ami.

58 All the temple servants and the descendants of Solomon's servants were three hundred ninety-two.

59 The following were those who came up from Telmelah, Tel-harsha, Cherub, Addan, and Immer, though they could not prove their families or their descent, whether they belonged to Israel: [60]the descendants of Delaiah, Tobiah, and Nekoda, six hundred fifty-two. [61]Also, of the descendants of the priests: the descendants of Habaiah, Hakkoz, and Barzillai (who had married one of the daughters of Barzillai the Gileadite, and was called by their name). [62]These looked for their entries in the genealogical records, but they were not found there, and so they were excluded from the priesthood as unclean; [63]the governor told them that they were not to partake of the most holy food, until there should be a priest to consult Urim and Thummim.

64 The whole assembly together was forty-two thousand three hundred sixty, [65]besides their male and female servants, of whom there were seven thousand three hun-

dred thirty-seven; and they had two hundred male and female singers. ⁶⁶They had seven hundred thirty-six horses, two hundred forty-five mules, ⁶⁷four hundred thirty-five camels, and six thousand seven hundred twenty donkeys.

68 As soon as they came to the house of the Lord in Jerusalem, some of the heads of families made freewill offerings for the house of God, to erect it on its site. ⁶⁹According to their resources they gave to the building fund sixty-one thousand darics of gold, five thousand minas of silver, and one hundred priestly robes.

70 The priests, the Levites, and some of the people lived in Jerusalem and its vicinity;ᵃ and the singers, the gatekeepers, and the temple servants lived in their towns, and all Israel in their towns.

Worship Restored at Jerusalem

3 When the seventh month came, and the Israelites were in the towns, the people gathered together in Jerusalem. ²Then Jeshua son of Jozadak, with his fellow priests, and Zerubbabel son of Shealtiel with his kin set out to build the altar of the God of Israel, to offer burnt offerings on it, as prescribed in the law of Moses the man of God. ³They set up the altar on its foundation, because they were in dread of the neighboring peoples, and they offered burnt offerings upon it to the Lord, morning and evening. ⁴And they kept the festival of booths,ᵇ as prescribed, and offered the daily burnt offerings by number according to the ordinance, as required for each day, ⁵and after that the regular burnt offerings, the offerings at the new moon and at all the sacred festivals of the Lord, and the offerings of everyone who made a freewill offering to the Lord. ⁶From the first day of the seventh month they began to offer burnt offerings to the Lord. But the foundation of the temple of the Lord was not yet laid. ⁷So they gave money to the masons and the carpenters, and food, drink, and oil to the Sidonians and the Tyrians to bring cedar trees from Lebanon to the sea, to Joppa, according to the grant that they had from King Cyrus of Persia.

Foundation Laid for the Temple

8 In the second year after their arrival at the house of God at Jerusalem, in the second month, Zerubbabel son of Shealtiel and Jeshua son of Jozadak made a beginning, together with the rest of their people, the priests and the Levites and all who had come to Jerusalem from the captivity. They appointed the Levites, from twenty years old and upward, to have the oversight of the work on the house of the Lord. ⁹And Jeshua with his sons and his kin, and Kadmiel and his sons, Binnui and Hodaviahᶜ along with the sons of Henadad, the Levites, their sons and kin, together took charge of the workers in the house of God.

10 When the builders laid the foundation of the temple of the Lord, the priests in their vestments were stationed

A Great Assembly of Faithful People

EZRA 2.64–69

Try to picture yourself among the vast horde of people—tired and dusty—nearing the end of a very long walk from your country of exile. You stand on tiptoe to see over the heads of the people in front of you, longing for the first glimpse of Jerusalem. Word spreads through the crowd that the heads of families are to meet at the site where the temple will be built in order to contribute to its construction. Perhaps this is the very first thing you will do, even before you go to look for your ancestral home. The crowd grows quiet as, finally in Jerusalem, everyone begins to picture a new temple and how they will again worship God in Jerusalem.

Now, try to picture the people of God gathering in your church each week. Imagine that this coming sabbath day is the first day back for all of you after a lengthy absence. What special items might you bring? How would the leaders mark this event in a special way? What songs would you sing? What sort of prayers would you pray?

See Meeting God in Worship

---

a 1 Esdras 5.46: Heb lacks *lived in Jerusalem and its vicinity*
b Or *tabernacles*; Heb *succoth*   c Compare 2.40; Neh 7.43; 1 Esdras 5.58: Heb *sons of Judah*

A New Beginning

EZRA 3.10–13

The people gather for a grand celebration. They never thought this would happen—a new foundation for a new temple. The shouts of joy are loud enough to be heard far away. But astonishingly, those who remember the old temple weep just as loudly as those who shout for joy.

Every new beginning is also an occasion of loss. Something old is abandoned; something new takes its place. We cannot be sure what the future will bring. Sometimes the old things should be abandoned; the new beginning is a necessary thing.

Think back on the times in which you have made a new beginning. Make a list of these on paper. In each case, what was left behind? How did you see God's hand in your new beginning? Even in retrospect, offer each new beginning to God in prayer.

See *Meeting God in Everyday Life*

to praise the LORD with trumpets, and the Levites, the sons of Asaph, with cymbals, according to the directions of King David of Israel; [11]and they sang responsively, praising and giving thanks to the LORD,

"For he is good,
    for his steadfast love endures forever toward
        Israel."

And all the people responded with a great shout when they praised the LORD, because the foundation of the house of the LORD was laid. [12]But many of the priests and Levites and heads of families, old people who had seen the first house on its foundations, wept with a loud voice when they saw this house, though many shouted aloud for joy, [13]so that the people could not distinguish the sound of the joyful shout from the sound of the people's weeping, for the people shouted so loudly that the sound was heard far away.

Resistance to Rebuilding the Temple

4 When the adversaries of Judah and Benjamin heard that the returned exiles were building a temple to the LORD, the God of Israel, [2]they approached Zerubbabel and the heads of families and said to them, "Let us build with you, for we worship your God as you do, and we have been sacrificing to him ever since the days of King Esarhaddon of Assyria who brought us here." [3]But Zerubbabel, Jeshua, and the rest of the heads of families in Israel said to them, "You shall have no part with us in building a house to our God; but we alone will build to the LORD, the God of Israel, as King Cyrus of Persia has commanded us."

4 Then the people of the land discouraged the people of Judah, and made them afraid to build, [5]and they bribed officials to frustrate their plan throughout the reign of King Cyrus of Persia and until the reign of King Darius of Persia.

Rebuilding of Jerusalem Opposed

6 In the reign of Ahasuerus, in his accession year, they wrote an accusation against the inhabitants of Judah and Jerusalem.

7 And in the days of Artaxerxes, Bishlam and Mithredath and Tabeel and the rest of their associates wrote to King Artaxerxes of Persia; the letter was written in Aramaic and translated.[a] [8]Rehum the royal deputy and Shimshai the scribe wrote a letter against Jerusalem to King Artaxerxes as follows [9](then Rehum the royal deputy, Shimshai the scribe, and the rest of their associates, the judges, the envoys, the officials, the Persians, the people of Erech, the Babylonians, the people of Susa, that is, the Elamites, [10]and the rest of the nations whom the great and noble Osnappar deported and settled in the cities of Samaria and in the rest of the province Beyond the River

a Heb adds *in Aramaic,* indicating that 4.8–6.18 is in Aramaic. Another interpretation is *The letter was written in the Aramaic script and set forth in the Aramaic language*

wrote—and now [11]this is a copy of the letter that they sent):

"To King Artaxerxes: Your servants, the people of the province Beyond the River, send greeting. And now [12]may it be known to the king that the Jews who came up from you to us have gone to Jerusalem. They are rebuilding that rebellious and wicked city; they are finishing the walls and repairing the foundations. [13]Now may it be known to the king that, if this city is rebuilt and the walls finished, they will not pay tribute, custom, or toll, and the royal revenue will be reduced. [14]Now because we share the salt of the palace and it is not fitting for us to witness the king's dishonor, therefore we send and inform the king, [15]so that a search may be made in the annals of your ancestors. You will discover in the annals that this is a rebellious city, hurtful to kings and provinces, and that sedition was stirred up in it from long ago. On that account this city was laid waste. [16]We make known to the king that, if this city is rebuilt and its walls finished, you will then have no possession in the province Beyond the River."

17 The king sent an answer: "To Rehum the royal deputy and Shimshai the scribe and the rest of their associates who live in Samaria and in the rest of the province Beyond the River, greeting. And now [18]the letter that you sent to us has been read in translation before me. [19]So I made a decree, and someone searched and discovered that this city has risen against kings from long ago, and that rebellion and sedition have been made in it. [20]Jerusalem has had mighty kings who ruled over the whole province Beyond the River, to whom tribute, custom, and toll were paid. [21]Therefore issue an order that these people be made to cease, and that this city not be rebuilt, until I make a decree. [22]Moreover, take care not to be slack in this matter; why should damage grow to the hurt of the king?"

23 Then when the copy of King Artaxerxes' letter was read before Rehum and the scribe Shimshai and their associates, they hurried to the Jews in Jerusalem and by force and power made them cease. [24]At that time the work on the house of God in Jerusalem stopped and was discontinued until the second year of the reign of King Darius of Persia.

Restoration of the Temple Resumed

5 Now the prophets, Haggai[a] and Zechariah son of Iddo, prophesied to the Jews who were in Judah and Jerusalem, in the name of the God of Israel who was over them. [2]Then Zerubbabel son of Shealtiel and Jeshua son of Jozadak set out to rebuild the house of God in Jerusalem; and with them were the prophets of God, helping them.

3 At the same time Tattenai the governor of the province Beyond the River and Shethar-bozenai and their associates came to them and spoke to them thus, "Who

Discouragement and Fear

EZRA 4.6–16

No wonder the people of Judah are discouraged and afraid (v.4). The rebuilding of the temple means everything to them. This is their defining moment, the very thing they dared to hope for during the long years in exile. They might ask themselves, "Why do these people want to stop us? Will our fondest dreams never be fulfilled?"

Sometime when you are alone and quiet, stand up and close your eyes. Imagine yourself standing beside the foundation of the yet-to-be-completed temple. Imagine the fear and discouragement of the people of God. Ask yourself the despairing questions they must have asked. Reach out and touch the massive stones of the foundation. Now remember your resource in trying times—the massive strength of God upholding you. There is a small group standing near you: What can you say to them to help restore their hope?

See Meeting God in Scripture

---

a Aram adds *the prophet*

Servants of God

EZRA 5.11

"Invocation is made as follows: your soul, having realized God's presence, will prostrate itself with the utmost reverence, acknowledging its unworthiness to abide before God's Sovereign Majesty; and yet knowing that God of his goodness would have you come, you must ask God for grace to serve and worship him."

—FRANCIS DE SALES,
Introduction to the Devout Life

See *Meeting God in Worship*

gave you a decree to build this house and to finish this structure?" [4]They[a] also asked them this, "What are the names of the men who are building this building?" [5]But the eye of their God was upon the elders of the Jews, and they did not stop them until a report reached Darius and then answer was returned by letter in reply to it.

6 The copy of the letter that Tattenai the governor of the province Beyond the River and Shethar-bozenai and his associates the envoys who were in the province Beyond the River sent to King Darius; [7]they sent him a report, in which was written as follows: "To Darius the king, all peace! [8]May it be known to the king that we went to the province of Judah, to the house of the great God. It is being built of hewn stone, and timber is laid in the walls; this work is being done diligently and prospers in their hands. [9]Then we spoke to those elders and asked them, 'Who gave you a decree to build this house and to finish this structure?' [10]We also asked them their names, for your information, so that we might write down the names of the men at their head. [11]This was their reply to us: 'We are the servants of the God of heaven and earth, and we are rebuilding the house that was built many years ago, which a great king of Israel built and finished. [12]But because our ancestors had angered the God of heaven, he gave them into the hand of King Nebuchadnezzar of Babylon, the Chaldean, who destroyed this house and carried away the people to Babylonia. [13]However, King Cyrus of Babylon, in the first year of his reign, made a decree that this house of God should be rebuilt. [14]Moreover, the gold and silver vessels of the house of God, which Nebuchadnezzar had taken out of the temple in Jerusalem and had brought into the temple of Babylon, these King Cyrus took out of the temple of Babylon, and they were delivered to a man named Sheshbazzar, whom he had made governor. [15]He said to him, "Take these vessels; go and put them in the temple in Jerusalem, and let the house of God be rebuilt on its site." [16]Then this Sheshbazzar came and laid the foundations of the house of God in Jerusalem; and from that time until now it has been under construction, and it is not yet finished.' [17]And now, if it seems good to the king, have a search made in the royal archives there in Babylon, to see whether a decree was issued by King Cyrus for the rebuilding of this house of God in Jerusalem. Let the king send us his pleasure in this matter."

The Decree of Darius

6 Then King Darius made a decree, and they searched the archives where the documents were stored in Babylon. [2]But it was in Ecbatana, the capital in the province of Media, that a scroll was found on which this was written: "A record. [3]In the first year of his reign, King Cyrus issued a decree: Concerning the house of God at Jerusalem, let the house be rebuilt, the place where sacrifices are offered and burnt offerings are brought;[b] its

a Gk Syr: Aram *We*   *b* Meaning of Aram uncertain

height shall be sixty cubits and its width sixty cubits, [4]with three courses of hewn stones and one course of timber; let the cost be paid from the royal treasury. [5]Moreover, let the gold and silver vessels of the house of God, which Nebuchadnezzar took out of the temple in Jerusalem and brought to Babylon, be restored and brought back to the temple in Jerusalem, each to its place; you shall put them in the house of God."

6 "Now you, Tattenai, governor of the province Beyond the River, Shethar-bozenai, and you, their associates, the envoys in the province Beyond the River, keep away; [7]let the work on this house of God alone; let the governor of the Jews and the elders of the Jews rebuild this house of God on its site. [8]Moreover I make a decree regarding what you shall do for these elders of the Jews for the rebuilding of this house of God: the cost is to be paid to these people, in full and without delay, from the royal revenue, the tribute of the province Beyond the River. [9]Whatever is needed—young bulls, rams, or sheep for burnt offerings to the God of heaven, wheat, salt, wine, or oil, as the priests in Jerusalem require—let that be given to them day by day without fail, [10]so that they may offer pleasing sacrifices to the God of heaven, and pray for the life of the king and his children. [11]Furthermore I decree that if anyone alters this edict, a beam shall be pulled out of the house of the perpetrator, who then shall be impaled on it. The house shall be made a dunghill. [12]May the God who has established his name there overthrow any king or people that shall put forth a hand to alter this, or to destroy this house of God in Jerusalem. I, Darius, make a decree; let it be done with all diligence."

Completion and Dedication of the Temple

13 Then, according to the word sent by King Darius, Tattenai, the governor of the province Beyond the River, Shethar-bozenai, and their associates did with all diligence what King Darius had ordered. [14]So the elders of the Jews built and prospered, through the prophesying of the prophet Haggai and Zechariah son of Iddo. They finished their building by command of the God of Israel and by decree of Cyrus, Darius, and King Artaxerxes of Persia; [15]and this house was finished on the third day of the month of Adar, in the sixth year of the reign of King Darius.

16 The people of Israel, the priests and the Levites, and the rest of the returned exiles, celebrated the dedication of this house of God with joy. [17]They offered at the dedication of this house of God one hundred bulls, two hundred rams, four hundred lambs, and as a sin offering for all Israel, twelve male goats, according to the number of the tribes of Israel. [18]Then they set the priests in their divisions and the Levites in their courses for the service of God at Jerusalem, as it is written in the book of Moses.

The Passover Celebrated

19 On the fourteenth day of the first month the returned exiles kept the passover. [20]For both the priests

Celebration

EZRA 6.13–22

The temple is finished! The house of God has been rebuilt! What joy is in the hearts of God's people. Draw a party hat and write on it what you want to celebrate today. Celebrate with joy what God is building within you. In what areas is God rebuilding and renovating you? How can you celebrate that? What areas are still unfinished? What are the "stones and mortar" God will use to build you up?

See Meeting God in Everyday Life

and the Levites had purified themselves; all of them were clean. So they killed the passover lamb for all the returned exiles, for their fellow priests, and for themselves. ²¹It was eaten by the people of Israel who had returned from exile, and also by all who had joined them and separated themselves from the pollutions of the nations of the land to worship the LORD, the God of Israel. ²²With joy they celebrated the festival of unleavened bread seven days; for the LORD had made them joyful, and had turned the heart of the king of Assyria to them, so that he aided them in the work on the house of God, the God of Israel.

The Coming and Work of Ezra

7 After this, in the reign of King Artaxerxes of Persia, Ezra son of Seraiah, son of Azariah, son of Hilkiah, ²son of Shallum, son of Zadok, son of Ahitub, ³son of Amariah, son of Azariah, son of Meraioth, ⁴son of Zerahiah, son of Uzzi, son of Bukki, ⁵son of Abishua, son of Phinehas, son of Eleazar, son of the chief priest Aaron— ⁶this Ezra went up from Babylonia. He was a scribe skilled in the law of Moses that the LORD the God of Israel had given; and the king granted him all that he asked, for the hand of the LORD his God was upon him.

7 Some of the people of Israel, and some of the priests and Levites, the singers and gatekeepers, and the temple servants also went up to Jerusalem, in the seventh year of King Artaxerxes. ⁸They came to Jerusalem in the fifth month, which was in the seventh year of the king. ⁹On the first day of the first month the journey up from Babylon was begun, and on the first day of the fifth month he came to Jerusalem, for the gracious hand of his God was upon him. ¹⁰For Ezra had set his heart to study the law of the LORD, and to do it, and to teach the statutes and ordinances in Israel.

The Letter of Artaxerxes to Ezra

11 This is a copy of the letter that King Artaxerxes gave to the priest Ezra, the scribe, a scholar of the text of the commandments of the LORD and his statutes for Israel: ¹²"Artaxerxes, king of kings, to the priest Ezra, the scribe of the law of the God of heaven: Peace.ᵃ And now ¹³I decree that any of the people of Israel or their priests or Levites in my kingdom who freely offers to go to Jerusalem may go with you. ¹⁴For you are sent by the king and his seven counselors to make inquiries about Judah and Jerusalem according to the law of your God, which is in your hand, ¹⁵and also to convey the silver and gold that the king and his counselors have freely offered to the God of Israel, whose dwelling is in Jerusalem, ¹⁶with all the silver and gold that you shall find in the whole province of Babylonia, and with the freewill offerings of the people and the priests, given willingly for the house of their God in Jerusalem. ¹⁷With this money, then, you shall with all diligence buy bulls, rams, and lambs, and their grain of-

a Syr Vg 1 Esdras 8.9: Aram *Perfect*

ferings and their drink offerings, and you shall offer them on the altar of the house of your God in Jerusalem. ¹⁸Whatever seems good to you and your colleagues to do with the rest of the silver and gold, you may do, according to the will of your God. ¹⁹The vessels that have been given you for the service of the house of your God, you shall deliver before the God of Jerusalem. ²⁰And whatever else is required for the house of your God, which you are responsible for providing, you may provide out of the king's treasury.

21 "I, King Artaxerxes, decree to all the treasurers in the province Beyond the River: Whatever the priest Ezra, the scribe of the law of the God of heaven, requires of you, let it be done with all diligence, ²²up to one hundred talents of silver, one hundred cors of wheat, one hundred baths*a* of wine, one hundred baths*a* of oil, and unlimited salt. ²³Whatever is commanded by the God of heaven, let it be done with zeal for the house of the God of heaven, or wrath will come upon the realm of the king and his heirs. ²⁴We also notify you that it shall not be lawful to impose tribute, custom, or toll on any of the priests, the Levites, the singers, the doorkeepers, the temple servants, or other servants of this house of God.

25 "And you, Ezra, according to the God-given wisdom you possess, appoint magistrates and judges who may judge all the people in the province Beyond the River who know the laws of your God; and you shall teach those who do not know them. ²⁶All who will not obey the law of your God and the law of the king, let judgment be strictly executed on them, whether for death or for banishment or for confiscation of their goods or for imprisonment."

27 Blessed be the LORD, the God of our ancestors, who put such a thing as this into the heart of the king to glorify the house of the LORD in Jerusalem, ²⁸and who extended to me steadfast love before the king and his counselors, and before all the king's mighty officers. I took courage, for the hand of the LORD my God was upon me, and I gathered leaders from Israel to go up with me.

Heads of Families Who Returned with Ezra

8 These are their family heads, and this is the genealogy of those who went up with me from Babylonia, in the reign of King Artaxerxes: ²Of the descendants of Phinehas, Gershom. Of Ithamar, Daniel. Of David, Hattush, ³of the descendants of Shecaniah. Of Parosh, Zechariah, with whom were registered one hundred fifty males. ⁴Of the descendants of Pahath-moab, Eliehoenai son of Zerahiah, and with him two hundred males. ⁵Of the descendants of Zattu,*b* Shecaniah son of Jahaziel, and with him three hundred males. ⁶Of the descendants of Adin, Ebed son of Jonathan, and with him fifty males. ⁷Of the descendants of Elam, Jeshaiah son of Athaliah, and with him seventy males. ⁸Of the descendants of Shephatiah, Zebadiah son of Michael, and with him eighty males. ⁹Of the descendants of Joab, Obadiah son

---

A Commission From God

EZRA 7.11–20

Ezra is a fortunate man. He has in his hand a decree in which the king commissions Ezra with a specific task. Moreover, the king has given Ezra silver and gold to accomplish his task.

What has God commissioned you to do? Find a special sheet of handmade paper or one that looks like parchment. With any pen that will make bold letters, write out a decree from God to yourself. What has God decreed for your life? What specific jobs does God intend for you to perform? What means has God provided you with to accomplish his will?

See Meeting God in Service

Leaders of Faith

EZRA 8.16

In this recital of names we may lose sight of the real people to whom the names belong. Some are known as leaders and others are known as men of learning. In such a close-knit community, the talents of each leader and scholar are well known.

Who are the leaders in your community of faith? Who are the people others go to for advice? Are there people whose native gifts or life experiences have made them especially wise? Uphold these people in prayer. Write down their names (perhaps in a prayer journal, if you keep one) and pray for each person specifically. Make a point of encouraging and thanking each person for their gifts. Inform the leaders in your faith community of those who have been a blessing to you in your journey.

See Meeting God in Community

of Jehiel, and with him two hundred eighteen males. [10]Of the descendants of Bani,[a] Shelomith son of Josiphiah, and with him one hundred sixty males. [11]Of the descendants of Bebai, Zechariah son of Bebai, and with him twenty-eight males. [12]Of the descendants of Azgad, Johanan son of Hakkatan, and with him one hundred ten males. [13]Of the descendants of Adonikam, those who came later, their names being Eliphelet, Jeuel, and Shemaiah, and with them sixty males. [14]Of the descendants of Bigvai, Uthai and Zaccur, and with them seventy males.

Servants for the Temple

15 I gathered them by the river that runs to Ahava, and there we camped three days. As I reviewed the people and the priests, I found there none of the descendants of Levi. [16]Then I sent for Eliezer, Ariel, Shemaiah, Elnathan, Jarib, Elnathan, Nathan, Zechariah, and Meshullam, who were leaders, and for Joiarib and Elnathan, who were wise, [17]and sent them to Iddo, the leader at the place called Casiphia, telling them what to say to Iddo and his colleagues the temple servants at Casiphia, namely, to send us ministers for the house of our God. [18]Since the gracious hand of our God was upon us, they brought us a man of discretion, of the descendants of Mahli son of Levi son of Israel, namely Sherebiah, with his sons and kin, eighteen; [19]also Hashabiah and with him Jeshaiah of the descendants of Merari, with his kin and their sons, twenty; [20]besides two hundred twenty of the temple servants, whom David and his officials had set apart to attend the Levites. These were all mentioned by name.

Fasting and Prayer for Protection

21 Then I proclaimed a fast there, at the river Ahava, that we might deny ourselves[b] before our God, to seek from him a safe journey for ourselves, our children, and all our possessions. [22]For I was ashamed to ask the king for a band of soldiers and cavalry to protect us against the enemy on our way, since we had told the king that the hand of our God is gracious to all who seek him, but his power and his wrath are against all who forsake him. [23]So we fasted and petitioned our God for this, and he listened to our entreaty.

Gifts for the Temple

24 Then I set apart twelve of the leading priests: Sherebiah, Hashabiah, and ten of their kin with them. [25]And I weighed out to them the silver and the gold and the vessels, the offering for the house of our God that the king, his counselors, his lords, and all Israel there present had offered; [26]I weighed out into their hand six hundred fifty talents of silver, and one hundred silver vessels worth . . . talents,[c] and one hundred talents of gold, [27]twenty gold bowls worth a thousand darics, and two vessels of fine polished bronze as precious as gold. [28]And I said to them,

a Gk 1 Esdras 8.36: Heb lacks *Bani*   *b* Or *might fast*   *c* The number of talents is lacking

"You are holy to the LORD, and the vessels are holy; and the silver and the gold are a freewill offering to the LORD, the God of your ancestors. [29]Guard them and keep them until you weigh them before the chief priests and the Levites and the heads of families in Israel at Jerusalem, within the chambers of the house of the LORD." [30]So the priests and the Levites took over the silver, the gold, and the vessels as they were weighed out, to bring them to Jerusalem, to the house of our God.

The Return to Jerusalem

31 Then we left the river Ahava on the twelfth day of the first month, to go to Jerusalem; the hand of our God was upon us, and he delivered us from the hand of the enemy and from ambushes along the way. [32]We came to Jerusalem and remained there three days. [33]On the fourth day, within the house of our God, the silver, the gold, and the vessels were weighed into the hands of the priest Meremoth son of Uriah, and with him was Eleazar son of Phinehas, and with them were the Levites, Jozabad son of Jeshua and Noadiah son of Binnui. [34]The total was counted and weighed, and the weight of everything was recorded.

35 At that time those who had come from captivity, the returned exiles, offered burnt offerings to the God of Israel, twelve bulls for all Israel, ninety-six rams, seventy-seven lambs, and as a sin offering twelve male goats; all this was a burnt offering to the LORD. [36]They also delivered the king's commissions to the king's satraps and to the governors of the province Beyond the River; and they supported the people and the house of God.

Denunciation of Mixed Marriages

9 After these things had been done, the officials approached me and said, "The people of Israel, the priests, and the Levites have not separated themselves from the peoples of the lands with their abominations, from the Canaanites, the Hittites, the Perizzites, the Jebusites, the Ammonites, the Moabites, the Egyptians, and the Amorites. [2]For they have taken some of their daughters as wives for themselves and for their sons. Thus the holy seed has mixed itself with the peoples of the lands, and in this faithlessness the officials and leaders have led the way." [3]When I heard this, I tore my garment and my mantle, and pulled hair from my head and beard, and sat appalled. [4]Then all who trembled at the words of the God of Israel, because of the faithlessness of the returned exiles, gathered around me while I sat appalled until the evening sacrifice.

Ezra's Prayer

5 At the evening sacrifice I got up from my fasting, with my garments and my mantle torn, and fell on my knees, spread out my hands to the LORD my God, [6]and said,

"O my God, I am too ashamed and embarrassed to lift my face to you, my God, for our iniquities have risen higher than our heads, and our guilt has mounted up to

A Fast Before the Lord

EZRA 8.21–23

When Ezra stops the whole procession and declares a fast, he is not initiating an unfamiliar practice. Fasting has a long tradition; for thousands of years many have found fasting to be a useful, even powerful, spiritual exercise. Fasting is an act that declares that we rely on God—not on ourselves.

Fasting need not only be abstinence from food. We may decide for a period of time to abstain from other consumer goods as an offering to God. Try to think of several things you might do without for a period of time, perhaps rich or sweet foods, television or maybe all media, some luxury items, forms of entertainment or a new item of clothing. Then plan for a period of time—perhaps a week or a month—when you will do without these things. Each day during that period, turn your attention away from yourself and toward the One who loves you.

See *Meeting God in Everyday Life*

Ashamed in God's Presence

EZRA 9.5–15

Ezra uses an inclusive "we" when he confesses the people's iniquities before God. Ezra so identifies with his people that he feels complicity in their guilt. Whether our guilt is communal or individual, the common experience of humanity is the need for forgiveness.

Painful as it may be, recall a time when you felt keenly ashamed. A good time to do this is during some strenuous activity such as gardening or exercising. Let the dirt and sweat symbolize your guilt. Then take a shower or a bath and think of the soap and warm water as representative of the forgiveness of God. Experience God's cleansing love as you picture your faults and shortcomings disappearing down the drain.

See Meeting God in Everyday Life

the heavens. ⁷From the days of our ancestors to this day we have been deep in guilt, and for our iniquities we, our kings, and our priests have been handed over to the kings of the lands, to the sword, to captivity, to plundering, and to utter shame, as is now the case. ⁸But now for a brief moment favor has been shown by the LORD our God, who has left us a remnant, and given us a stake in his holy place, in order that he*a* may brighten our eyes and grant us a little sustenance in our slavery. ⁹For we are slaves; yet our God has not forsaken us in our slavery, but has extended to us his steadfast love before the kings of Persia, to give us new life to set up the house of our God, to repair its ruins, and to give us a wall in Judea and Jerusalem.

10 "And now, our God, what shall we say after this? For we have forsaken your commandments, ¹¹which you commanded by your servants the prophets, saying, 'The land that you are entering to possess is a land unclean with the pollutions of the peoples of the lands, with their abominations. They have filled it from end to end with their uncleanness. ¹²Therefore do not give your daughters to their sons, neither take their daughters for your sons, and never seek their peace or prosperity, so that you may be strong and eat the good of the land and leave it for an inheritance to your children forever.' ¹³After all that has come upon us for our evil deeds and for our great guilt, seeing that you, our God, have punished us less than our iniquities deserved and have given us such a remnant as this, ¹⁴shall we break your commandments again and intermarry with the peoples who practice these abominations? Would you not be angry with us until you destroy us without remnant or survivor? ¹⁵O LORD, God of Israel, you are just, but we have escaped as a remnant, as is now the case. Here we are before you in our guilt, though no one can face you because of this."

The People's Response

10 While Ezra prayed and made confession, weeping and throwing himself down before the house of God, a very great assembly of men, women, and children gathered to him out of Israel; the people also wept bitterly. ²Shecaniah son of Jehiel, of the descendants of Elam, addressed Ezra, saying, "We have broken faith with our God and have married foreign women from the peoples of the land, but even now there is hope for Israel in spite of this. ³So now let us make a covenant with our God to send away all these wives and their children, according to the counsel of my lord and of those who tremble at the commandment of our God; and let it be done according to the law. ⁴Take action, for it is your duty, and we are with you; be strong, and do it." ⁵Then Ezra stood up and made the leading priests, the Levites, and all Israel swear that they would do as had been said. So they swore.

a Heb *our God*

Foreign Wives and Their Children Rejected

6 Then Ezra withdrew from before the house of God, and went to the chamber of Jehohanan son of Eliashib, where he spent the night.[a] He did not eat bread or drink water, for he was mourning over the faithlessness of the exiles. [7]They made a proclamation throughout Judah and Jerusalem to all the returned exiles that they should assemble at Jerusalem, [8]and that if any did not come within three days, by order of the officials and the elders all their property should be forfeited, and they themselves banned from the congregation of the exiles.

9 Then all the people of Judah and Benjamin assembled at Jerusalem within the three days; it was the ninth month, on the twentieth day of the month. All the people sat in the open square before the house of God, trembling because of this matter and because of the heavy rain. [10]Then Ezra the priest stood up and said to them, "You have trespassed and married foreign women, and so increased the guilt of Israel. [11]Now make confession to the Lord the God of your ancestors, and do his will; separate yourselves from the peoples of the land and from the foreign wives." [12]Then all the assembly answered with a loud voice, "It is so; we must do as you have said. [13]But the people are many, and it is a time of heavy rain; we cannot stand in the open. Nor is this a task for one day or for two, for many of us have transgressed in this matter. [14]Let our officials represent the whole assembly, and let all in our towns who have taken foreign wives come at appointed times, and with them the elders and judges of every town, until the fierce wrath of our God on this account is averted from us." [15]Only Jonathan son of Asahel and Jahzeiah son of Tikvah opposed this, and Meshullam and Shabbethai the Levites supported them.

16 Then the returned exiles did so. Ezra the priest selected men,[b] heads of families, according to their families, each of them designated by name. On the first day of the tenth month they sat down to examine the matter. [17]By the first day of the first month they had come to the end of all the men who had married foreign women.

18 There were found of the descendants of the priests who had married foreign women, of the descendants of Jeshua son of Jozadak and his brothers: Maaseiah, Eliezer, Jarib, and Gedaliah. [19]They pledged themselves to send away their wives, and their guilt offering was a ram of the flock for their guilt. [20]Of the descendants of Immer: Hanani and Zebadiah. [21]Of the descendants of Harim: Maaseiah, Elijah, Shemaiah, Jehiel, and Uzziah. [22]Of the descendants of Pashhur: Elioenai, Maaseiah, Ishmael, Nethanel, Jozabad, and Elasah.

23 Of the Levites: Jozabad, Shimei, Kelaiah (that is, Kelita), Pethahiah, Judah, and Eliezer. [24]Of the singers: Eliashib. Of the gatekeepers: Shallum, Telem, and Uri.

Grieving God's Heart

EZRA 10.6

Ezra's grief represents God's grief as the prophet mourns the self-destructive failures of the people. We all too easily slip into thinking that God is distant, unsympathetic, unemotional. Perhaps we rarely stop to think that we individually and collectively might be breaking God's heart. As you take an inner inventory, what thoughts and behaviors might break God's heart? Why do you think God grieves over them? Now consider your family, your faith community and your nation. What collective acts and assumptions of these groups might cause God grief? In both arenas, personal and public, what steps can we take to warm God's heart?

---

a 1 Esdras 9.2: Heb *where he went*   *b* 1 Esdras 9.16: Syr: Heb *And there were selected Ezra,*

Hard Choices

EZRA 10.44

Despite the moral ambiguity of the actions described in this verse (and the preceding chapters), the fact remains that no such bitter and difficult choices would have been necessary if the Hebrew men had obeyed the law of God in the first place. The difficulty of restoring faithfulness is complicated by the snowball effect: Bad decisions lead to other bad decisions; sooner or later hard choices have to be made.

Think of three or four major decisions in your life, both good and bad. On an unlined piece of paper, draw a "family tree" for each one. Show on this diagram how your decisions resulted from earlier choices. There may be more than one line of choices leading to each decision. Try to trace this process to the present time. Now offer all this to God. For those decisions that have led to difficult times, ask God for ways to redeem the situation. For decisions that in retrospect were wise ones, thank God for wisdom and understanding.

See Meeting God in Everyday Life

25 And of Israel: of the descendants of Parosh: Ramiah, Izziah, Malchijah, Mijamin, Eleazar, Hashabiah,*a* and Benaiah. **26**Of the descendants of Elam: Mattaniah, Zechariah, Jehiel, Abdi, Jeremoth, and Elijah. **27**Of the descendants of Zattu: Elioenai, Eliashib, Mattaniah, Jeremoth, Zabad, and Aziza. **28**Of the descendants of Bebai: Jehohanan, Hananiah, Zabbai, and Athlai. **29**Of the descendants of Bani: Meshullam, Malluch, Adaiah, Jashub, Sheal, and Jeremoth. **30**Of the descendants of Pahathmoab: Adna, Chelal, Benaiah, Maaseiah, Mattaniah, Bezalel, Binnui, and Manasseh. **31**Of the descendants of Harim: Eliezer, Isshijah, Malchijah, Shemaiah, Shimeon, **32**Benjamin, Malluch, and Shemariah. **33**Of the descendants of Hashum: Mattenai, Mattattah, Zabad, Eliphelet, Jeremai, Manasseh, and Shimei. **34**Of the descendants of Bani: Maadai, Amram, Uel, **35**Benaiah, Bedeiah, Cheluhi, **36**Vaniah, Meremoth, Eliashib, **37**Mattaniah, Mattenai, and Jaasu. **38**Of the descendants of Binnui:*b* Shimei, **39**Shelemiah, Nathan, Adaiah, **40**Machnadebai, Shashai, Sharai, **41**Azarel, Shelemiah, Shemariah, **42**Shallum, Amariah, and Joseph. **43**Of the descendants of Nebo: Jeiel, Mattithiah, Zabad, Zebina, Jaddai, Joel, and Benaiah. **44**All these had married foreign women, and they sent them away with their children.*c*

a 1 Esdras 9.26 Gk: Heb *Malchijah*   *b* Gk: Heb *Bani, Binnui*   *c* 1 Esdras 9.36; Meaning of Heb uncertain

NEHEMIAH

Remember Who You Are

KEY VERSES:

Then I said to them, "You see the trouble we are in, how Jerusalem lies in ruins with its gates burned. Come, let us rebuild the wall of Jerusalem, so that we may no longer suffer disgrace." I told them that the hand of my God had been gracious upon me, and also the words that the king had spoken to me. Then they said, "Let us start building!" So they committed themselves to the common good.—Nehemiah 2.17–18

The task that Nehemiah and his people faced was formidable. With limited resources, and in the midst of political pressure and sabotage, they began to rebuild the walls of their beloved city Jerusalem. Under the guidance of Ezra, they had reconstructed the temple, but the challenges of rebuilding had demoralized them. In this book, we see how Nehemiah's reliance on and faith in God helped him lead his people to successfully accomplish a task and restore his people's courage and renew their respect and appreciation for God's Word. Nehemiah was a man of action, but he was also a man of deep faith. Because he lived in relationship with the all-knowing God, he knew when to pray and when to act.

In the book of Nehemiah, we find more than an historical account of God's people at a certain point in time; we discover a reminder that we are partners with God. We are not exiles recently returned to our homeland. Our destroyed city walls do not need to be rebuilt. Yet we are called just as surely to be builders of faithful lives, relationships and communities. If you ever face these tasks with feelings of being overwhelmed or inadequate, you'll be able to identify with Nehemiah. Just as surely as he struggled with issues of motivation, fatigue and criticism, so too do we today. But this book also offers inspiration to lean on the living God as we go about our building tasks.

> "God is our creator. God made us in his image and likeness. Therefore we are creators. [God] gave us a garden to till and cultivate. We became co-creators by our responsible acts, whether in bringing forth children, or producing food, furniture or clothing. The joy of creativeness should be ours."
> —DOROTHY DAY,
> *The Long Loneliness*

On Our Knees Before God

NEHEMIAH 1.3–11

Upon hearing the "state of the union" of his beloved Jerusalem and her people, Nehemiah went into mourning. What would the future hold for those who had survived exile? Nehemiah's faith in God's loving covenant prompted him to offer a prayer of confession for himself and all the Israelites because he was sure of his future with God. Think about your own congregation or denomination. Have there been times when you fell on your knees before God, seeking corporate forgiveness or renewal? Did you feel God was attentive to your prayer? Give thanks to God, who shows us our wrongdoing but always stands ready to hear our prayers of repentance and pronounce his forgiveness.

See *Meeting God in Prayer*

Nehemiah Prays for His People

1 The words of Nehemiah son of Hacaliah. In the month of Chislev, in the twentieth year, while I was in Susa the capital, ²one of my brothers, Hanani, came with certain men from Judah; and I asked them about the Jews that survived, those who had escaped the captivity, and about Jerusalem. ³They replied, "The survivors there in the province who escaped captivity are in great trouble and shame; the wall of Jerusalem is broken down, and its gates have been destroyed by fire."

4 When I heard these words I sat down and wept, and mourned for days, fasting and praying before the God of heaven. ⁵I said, "O LORD God of heaven, the great and awesome God who keeps covenant and steadfast love with those who love him and keep his commandments; ⁶let your ear be attentive and your eyes open to hear the prayer of your servant that I now pray before you day and night for your servants, the people of Israel, confessing the sins of the people of Israel, which we have sinned against you. Both I and my family have sinned. ⁷We have offended you deeply, failing to keep the commandments, the statutes, and the ordinances that you commanded your servant Moses. ⁸Remember the word that you commanded your servant Moses, 'If you are unfaithful, I will scatter you among the peoples; ⁹but if you return to me and keep my commandments and do them, though your outcasts are under the farthest skies, I will gather them from there and bring them to the place at which I have chosen to establish my name.' ¹⁰They are your servants and your people, whom you redeemed by your great power and your strong hand. ¹¹O Lord, let your ear be attentive to the prayer of your servant, and to the prayer of your servants who delight in revering your name. Give success to your servant today, and grant him mercy in the sight of this man!"

At the time, I was cupbearer to the king.

Nehemiah Sent to Judah

2 In the month of Nisan, in the twentieth year of King Artaxerxes, when wine was served him, I carried the wine and gave it to the king. Now, I had never been sad in his presence before. ²So the king said to me, "Why is your face sad, since you are not sick? This can only be sadness of the heart." Then I was very much afraid. ³I said to the king, "May the king live forever! Why should my face not be sad, when the city, the place of my ancestors' graves, lies waste, and its gates have been destroyed by fire?" ⁴Then the king said to me, "What do you request?" So I prayed to the God of heaven. ⁵Then I said to the king, "If it pleases the king, and if your servant has found favor with you, I ask that you send me to Judah, to the city of my ancestors' graves, so that I may rebuild it." ⁶The king said to me (the queen also was sitting beside him), "How long will you be gone, and when will you return?" So it pleased the king to send me, and I set him a date. ⁷Then I said to the king, "If it pleases the king, let letters be given me to the governors of the province Beyond the River, that they may grant me passage until I ar-

rive in Judah; [8]and a letter to Asaph, the keeper of the king's forest, directing him to give me timber to make beams for the gates of the temple fortress, and for the wall of the city, and for the house that I shall occupy." And the king granted me what I asked, for the gracious hand of my God was upon me.

9 Then I came to the governors of the province Beyond the River, and gave them the king's letters. Now the king had sent officers of the army and cavalry with me. [10]When Sanballat the Horonite and Tobiah the Ammonite official heard this, it displeased them greatly that someone had come to seek the welfare of the people of Israel.

Nehemiah's Inspection of the Walls

11 So I came to Jerusalem and was there for three days. [12]Then I got up during the night, I and a few men with me; I told no one what my God had put into my heart to do for Jerusalem. The only animal I took was the animal I rode. [13]I went out by night by the Valley Gate past the Dragon's Spring and to the Dung Gate, and I inspected the walls of Jerusalem that had been broken down and its gates that had been destroyed by fire. [14]Then I went on to the Fountain Gate and to the King's Pool; but there was no place for the animal I was riding to continue. [15]So I went up by way of the valley by night and inspected the wall. Then I turned back and entered by the Valley Gate, and so returned. [16]The officials did not know where I had gone or what I was doing; I had not yet told the Jews, the priests, the nobles, the officials, and the rest that were to do the work.

Decision to Restore the Walls

17 Then I said to them, "You see the trouble we are in, how Jerusalem lies in ruins with its gates burned. Come, let us rebuild the wall of Jerusalem, so that we may no longer suffer disgrace." [18]I told them that the hand of my God had been gracious upon me, and also the words that the king had spoken to me. Then they said, "Let us start building!" So they committed themselves to the common good. [19]But when Sanballat the Horonite and Tobiah the Ammonite official, and Geshem the Arab heard of it, they mocked and ridiculed us, saying, "What is this that you are doing? Are you rebelling against the king?" [20]Then I replied to them, "The God of heaven is the one who will give us success, and we his servants are going to start building; but you have no share or claim or historic right in Jerusalem."

Organization of the Work

3 Then the high priest Eliashib set to work with his fellow priests and rebuilt the Sheep Gate. They consecrated it and set up its doors; they consecrated it as far as the Tower of the Hundred and as far as the Tower of Hananel. [2]And the men of Jericho built next to him. And next to them[a] Zaccur son of Imri built.

a Heb him

God's Gracious Hand

NEHEMIAH 2.17–18

Nehemiah's message is straightforward: We're in trouble; Jerusalem is in ruins; we need to rebuild.

We've all had times when our own lives have crumbled and fallen into ruins: A marriage has failed or a friendship has ended; we have lost a job, have had to claim bankruptcy, have moved to a new city or have lost a loved one. Using paper and markers or paints, draw a time line of your life, designating the times when you have needed to rebuild your life. Were you able to feel, as Nehemiah did, that "the hand of [your] God had been gracious upon [you]?" On your time line, draw a small hand to note those times when you especially felt God's presence. As you look at your sketch, how often did God's healing presence coincide with rebuilding? If your life is in ruins right now, offer it to God with your palms open and your hands outstretched. Ask God to place his gracious hand upon you today.

See Meeting God in Everyday Life

God's Beautiful Work

NEHEMIAH 3.3–19

"There is something very beautiful in work which is well and precisely done. It is a participation in the activity of God, who makes all things well and wisely, beautiful to the last detail."

—JEAN VANIER,
Community and Growth

See *Meeting God in Everyday Life*

3 The sons of Hassenaah built the Fish Gate; they laid its beams and set up its doors, its bolts, and its bars. ⁴Next to them Meremoth son of Uriah son of Hakkoz made repairs. Next to them Meshullam son of Berechiah son of Meshezabel made repairs. Next to them Zadok son of Baana made repairs. ⁵Next to them the Tekoites made repairs; but their nobles would not put their shoulders to the work of their Lord.ᵃ

6 Joiada son of Paseah and Meshullam son of Besodeiah repaired the Old Gate; they laid its beams and set up its doors, its bolts, and its bars. ⁷Next to them repairs were made by Melatiah the Gibeonite and Jadon the Meronothite—the men of Gibeon and of Mizpah—who were under the jurisdiction ofᵇ the governor of the province Beyond the River. ⁸Next to them Uzziel son of Harhaiah, one of the goldsmiths, made repairs. Next to him Hananiah, one of the perfumers, made repairs; and they restored Jerusalem as far as the Broad Wall. ⁹Next to them Rephaiah son of Hur, ruler of half the district ofᶜ Jerusalem, made repairs. ¹⁰Next to them Jedaiah son of Harumaph made repairs opposite his house; and next to him Hattush son of Hashabneiah made repairs. ¹¹Malchijah son of Harim and Hasshub son of Pahath-moab repaired another section and the Tower of the Ovens. ¹²Next to him Shallum son of Hallohesh, ruler of half the district ofᶜ Jerusalem, made repairs, he and his daughters.

13 Hanun and the inhabitants of Zanoah repaired the Valley Gate; they rebuilt it and set up its doors, its bolts, and its bars, and repaired a thousand cubits of the wall, as far as the Dung Gate.

14 Malchijah son of Rechab, ruler of the district ofᵈ Beth-haccherem, repaired the Dung Gate; he rebuilt it and set up its doors, its bolts, and its bars.

15 And Shallum son of Col-hozeh, ruler of the district ofᵈ Mizpah, repaired the Fountain Gate; he rebuilt it and covered it and set up its doors, its bolts, and its bars; and he built the wall of the Pool of Shelah of the king's garden, as far as the stairs that go down from the City of David. ¹⁶After him Nehemiah son of Azbuk, ruler of half the district ofᶜ Beth-zur, repaired from a point opposite the graves of David, as far as the artificial pool and the house of the warriors. ¹⁷After him the Levites made repairs: Rehum son of Bani; next to him Hashabiah, ruler of half the district ofᶜ Keilah, made repairs for his district. ¹⁸After him their kin made repairs: Binnui,ᵉ son of Henadad, ruler of half the district ofᶜ Keilah; ¹⁹next to him Ezer son of Jeshua, rulerᶠ of Mizpah, repaired another section opposite the ascent to the armory at the Angle. ²⁰After him Baruch son of Zabbai repaired another section from the Angle to the door of the house of the high priest Eliashib. ²¹After him Meremoth son of Uriah son of Hakkoz repaired another section from the door of the house of Eliashib to the end of the house of Eliashib. ²²After him the priests, the men of the surrounding area,

a Or *lords*   *b* Meaning of Heb uncertain   *c* Or *supervisor of half the portion assigned to*   *d* Or *supervisor of the portion assigned to*   *e* Gk Syr Compare verse 24, 10.9: Heb *Bavvai*   *f* Or *supervisor*

made repairs. ²³After them Benjamin and Hasshub made repairs opposite their house. After them Azariah son of Maaseiah son of Ananiah made repairs beside his own house. ²⁴After him Binnui son of Henadad repaired another section, from the house of Azariah to the Angle and to the corner. ²⁵Palal son of Uzai repaired opposite the Angle and the tower projecting from the upper house of the king at the court of the guard. After him Pedaiah son of Parosh ²⁶and the temple servants living[a] on Ophel made repairs up to a point opposite the Water Gate on the east and the projecting tower. ²⁷After him the Tekoites repaired another section opposite the great projecting tower as far as the wall of Ophel.

28 Above the Horse Gate the priests made repairs, each one opposite his own house. ²⁹After them Zadok son of Immer made repairs opposite his own house. After him Shemaiah son of Shecaniah, the keeper of the East Gate, made repairs. ³⁰After him Hananiah son of Shelemiah and Hanun sixth son of Zalaph repaired another section. After him Meshullam son of Berechiah made repairs opposite his living quarters. ³¹After him Malchijah, one of the goldsmiths, made repairs as far as the house of the temple servants and of the merchants, opposite the Muster Gate,[b] and to the upper room of the corner. ³²And between the upper room of the corner and the Sheep Gate the goldsmiths and the merchants made repairs.

Hostile Plots Thwarted

4[c] Now when Sanballat heard that we were building the wall, he was angry and greatly enraged, and he mocked the Jews. ²He said in the presence of his associates and of the army of Samaria, "What are these feeble Jews doing? Will they restore things? Will they sacrifice? Will they finish it in a day? Will they revive the stones out of the heaps of rubbish—and burned ones at that?" ³Tobiah the Ammonite was beside him, and he said, "That stone wall they are building—any fox going up on it would break it down!" ⁴Hear, O our God, for we are despised; turn their taunt back on their own heads, and give them over as plunder in a land of captivity. ⁵Do not cover their guilt, and do not let their sin be blotted out from your sight; for they have hurled insults in the face of the builders.

6 So we rebuilt the wall, and all the wall was joined together to half its height; for the people had a mind to work.

7[d] But when Sanballat and Tobiah and the Arabs and the Ammonites and the Ashdodites heard that the repairing of the walls of Jerusalem was going forward and the gaps were beginning to be closed, they were very angry, ⁸and all plotted together to come and fight against Jerusalem and to cause confusion in it. ⁹So we prayed to our God, and set a guard as a protection against them day and night.

Remembering God Brings Courage

NEHEMIAH 4.1–18

Read this story slowly and meditatively. As you read, imagine that you are a laborer or worker-guard rebuilding the wall. What do you see? What do you hear? How do the stones feel beneath your hands? How well do you work with a sword in your belt? How do you respond to the insults and threats of those who oppose the work? Do Nehemiah's words, "Remember the LORD, who is great and awesome," give you courage?

See Meeting God in Scripture

---

a Cn: Heb *were living*   b Or *Hammiphkad Gate*   c Ch 3.33 in Heb
d Ch 4.1 in Heb

Symbols of Our Work in God

NEHEMIAH 4.19–20

When the trumpet sounds, every worker is reminded of the God who has brought them together, even though they work on separate parts of the wall. Whom do you consider your work team for God? What symbolizes the way you were brought together? Think of a sound, logo, smell or symbol of your common life in God. It might be the communion chalice, a denominational logo, the view of your church doors, a hammer and saw, or the smell of incense. When you have something in mind, take a few minutes to meditate on the image, giving thanks for the opportunity to work with others for God.

See Meeting God in Service

10 But Judah said, "The strength of the burden bearers is failing, and there is too much rubbish so that we are unable to work on the wall." [11]And our enemies said, "They will not know or see anything before we come upon them and kill them and stop the work." [12]When the Jews who lived near them came, they said to us ten times, "From all the places where they live[a] they will come up against us."[b] [13]So in the lowest parts of the space behind the wall, in open places, I stationed the people according to their families,[c] with their swords, their spears, and their bows. [14]After I looked these things over, I stood up and said to the nobles and the officials and the rest of the people, "Do not be afraid of them. Remember the LORD, who is great and awesome, and fight for your kin, your sons, your daughters, your wives, and your homes."

15 When our enemies heard that their plot was known to us, and that God had frustrated it, we all returned to the wall, each to his work. [16]From that day on, half of my servants worked on construction, and half held the spears, shields, bows, and body-armor; and the leaders posted themselves behind the whole house of Judah, [17]who were building the wall. The burden bearers carried their loads in such a way that each labored on the work with one hand and with the other held a weapon. [18]And each of the builders had his sword strapped at his side while he built. The man who sounded the trumpet was beside me. [19]And I said to the nobles, the officials, and the rest of the people, "The work is great and widely spread out, and we are separated far from one another on the wall. [20]Rally to us wherever you hear the sound of the trumpet. Our God will fight for us."

21 So we labored at the work, and half of them held the spears from break of dawn until the stars came out. [22]I also said to the people at that time, "Let every man and his servant pass the night inside Jerusalem, so that they may be a guard for us by night and may labor by day." [23]So neither I nor my brothers nor my servants nor the men of the guard who followed me ever took off our clothes; each kept his weapon in his right hand.[d]

Nehemiah Deals with Oppression

5 Now there was a great outcry of the people and of their wives against their Jewish kin. [2]For there were those who said, "With our sons and our daughters, we are many; we must get grain, so that we may eat and stay alive." [3]There were also those who said, "We are having to pledge our fields, our vineyards, and our houses in order to get grain during the famine." [4]And there were those who said, "We are having to borrow money on our fields and vineyards to pay the king's tax. [5]Now our flesh is the same as that of our kindred; our children are the same as their children; and yet we are forcing our sons and daughters to be slaves, and some of our daughters have been ravished; we are powerless, and our fields and vineyards now belong to others."

a Cn: Heb *you return* *b* Compare Gk Syr: Meaning of Heb uncertain
c Meaning of Heb uncertain *d* Cn: Heb *each his weapon the water*

6 I was very angry when I heard their outcry and these complaints. ⁷After thinking it over, I brought charges against the nobles and the officials; I said to them, "You are all taking interest from your own people." And I called a great assembly to deal with them, ⁸and said to them, "As far as we were able, we have bought back our Jewish kindred who had been sold to other nations; but now you are selling your own kin, who must then be bought back by us!" They were silent, and could not find a word to say. ⁹So I said, "The thing that you are doing is not good. Should you not walk in the fear of our God, to prevent the taunts of the nations our enemies? ¹⁰Moreover I and my brothers and my servants are lending them money and grain. Let us stop this taking of interest. ¹¹Restore to them, this very day, their fields, their vineyards, their olive orchards, and their houses, and the interest on money, grain, wine, and oil that you have been exacting from them." ¹²Then they said, "We will restore everything and demand nothing more from them. We will do as you say." And I called the priests, and made them take an oath to do as they had promised. ¹³I also shook out the fold of my garment and said, "So may God shake out everyone from house and from property who does not perform this promise. Thus may they be shaken out and emptied." And all the assembly said, "Amen," and praised the LORD. And the people did as they had promised.

The Generosity of Nehemiah

14 Moreover from the time that I was appointed to be their governor in the land of Judah, from the twentieth year to the thirty-second year of King Artaxerxes, twelve years, neither I nor my brothers ate the food allowance of the governor. ¹⁵The former governors who were before me laid heavy burdens on the people, and took food and wine from them, besides forty shekels of silver. Even their servants lorded it over the people. But I did not do so, because of the fear of God. ¹⁶Indeed, I devoted myself to the work on this wall, and acquired no land; and all my servants were gathered there for the work. ¹⁷Moreover there were at my table one hundred fifty people, Jews and officials, besides those who came to us from the nations around us. ¹⁸Now that which was prepared for one day was one ox and six choice sheep; also fowls were prepared for me, and every ten days skins of wine in abundance; yet with all this I did not demand the food allowance of the governor, because of the heavy burden of labor on the people. ¹⁹Remember for my good, O my God, all that I have done for this people.

Intrigues of Enemies Foiled

6 Now when it was reported to Sanballat and Tobiah and to Geshem the Arab and to the rest of our enemies that I had built the wall and that there was no gap left in it (though up to that time I had not set up the doors in the gates), ²Sanballat and Geshem sent to me, saying, "Come and let us meet together in one of the villages in the plain of Ono." But they intended to do me harm. ³So

Doing What Is Right

NEHEMIAH 5.5–13

"O Lord and master of my life, take from me the spirit of sloth, faintheartedness, lust of power, and idle talk. But give to thy servant rather the spirit of chastity, humility, patience, and love. Yea, O Lord and King, grant me to see my own errors and not to judge my [neighbor], for Thou art blessed from ages to ages."

—EPHRAIM OF SYRIA

Strengthen My Hands

NEHEMIAH 6.5–9

Stretch your hands out in front of you. Examine them closely. Notice the uniqueness of your fingernails, your veins, the shape of your fingers, the wrinkles of your knuckles, the colors of your skin. Name some of the jobs your hands have done in the past. What tasks do your hands accomplish on a daily basis? How have your hands shown mercy and compassion? If your own hands were included in a photo of many hands, how would you know which ones were yours? After you have taken time to examine your fingers and the palms and backs of your hands, meditate on the gift that your hands are. Repeat Nehemiah's prayer, "Now, O God, strengthen my hands," several times, trusting that your prayer will be answered.

See Meeting God in Service

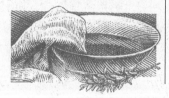

I sent messengers to them, saying, "I am doing a great work and I cannot come down. Why should the work stop while I leave it to come down to you?" ⁴They sent to me four times in this way, and I answered them in the same manner. ⁵In the same way Sanballat for the fifth time sent his servant to me with an open letter in his hand. ⁶In it was written, "It is reported among the nations—and Geshem*ᵃ* also says it—that you and the Jews intend to rebel; that is why you are building the wall; and according to this report you wish to become their king. ⁷You have also set up prophets to proclaim in Jerusalem concerning you, 'There is a king in Judah!' And now it will be reported to the king according to these words. So come, therefore, and let us confer together." ⁸Then I sent to him, saying, "No such things as you say have been done; you are inventing them out of your own mind" ⁹—for they all wanted to frighten us, thinking, "Their hands will drop from the work, and it will not be done." But now, O God, strengthen my hands.

10 One day when I went into the house of Shemaiah son of Delaiah son of Mehetabel, who was confined to his house, he said, "Let us meet together in the house of God, within the temple, and let us close the doors of the temple, for they are coming to kill you; indeed, tonight they are coming to kill you." ¹¹But I said, "Should a man like me run away? Would a man like me go into the temple to save his life? I will not go in!" ¹²Then I perceived and saw that God had not sent him at all, but he had pronounced the prophecy against me because Tobiah and Sanballat had hired him. ¹³He was hired for this purpose, to intimidate me and make me sin by acting in this way, and so they could give me a bad name, in order to taunt me. ¹⁴Remember Tobiah and Sanballat, O my God, according to these things that they did, and also the prophetess Noadiah and the rest of the prophets who wanted to make me afraid.

The Wall Completed

15 So the wall was finished on the twenty-fifth day of the month Elul, in fifty-two days. ¹⁶And when all our enemies heard of it, all the nations around us were afraid*ᵇ* and fell greatly in their own esteem; for they perceived that this work had been accomplished with the help of our God. ¹⁷Moreover in those days the nobles of Judah sent many letters to Tobiah, and Tobiah's letters came to them. ¹⁸For many in Judah were bound by oath to him, because he was the son-in-law of Shecaniah son of Arah: and his son Jehohanan had married the daughter of Meshullam son of Berechiah. ¹⁹Also they spoke of his good deeds in my presence, and reported my words to him. And Tobiah sent letters to intimidate me.

7 Now when the wall had been built and I had set up the doors, and the gatekeepers, the singers, and the Levites had been appointed, ²I gave my brother Hanani charge over Jerusalem, along with Hananiah the com-

a Heb *Gashmu*   *b* Another reading is *saw*

mander of the citadel—for he was a faithful man and feared God more than many. ³And I said to them, "The gates of Jerusalem are not to be opened until the sun is hot; while the gatekeepers*a* are still standing guard, let them shut and bar the doors. Appoint guards from among the inhabitants of Jerusalem, some at their watch posts, and others before their own houses." ⁴The city was wide and large, but the people within it were few and no houses had been built.

Lists of the Returned Exiles

5 Then my God put it into my mind to assemble the nobles and the officials and the people to be enrolled by genealogy. And I found the book of the genealogy of those who were the first to come back, and I found the following written in it:

6 These are the people of the province who came up out of the captivity of those exiles whom King Nebuchadnezzar of Babylon had carried into exile; they returned to Jerusalem and Judah, each to his town. ⁷They came with Zerubbabel, Jeshua, Nehemiah, Azariah, Raamiah, Nahamani, Mordecai, Bilshan, Mispereth, Bigvai, Nehum, Baanah.

The number of the Israelite people: ⁸the descendants of Parosh, two thousand one hundred seventy-two. ⁹Of Shephatiah, three hundred seventy-two. ¹⁰Of Arah, six hundred fifty-two. ¹¹Of Pahath-moab, namely the descendants of Jeshua and Joab, two thousand eight hundred eighteen. ¹²Of Elam, one thousand two hundred fifty-four. ¹³Of Zattu, eight hundred forty-five. ¹⁴Of Zaccai, seven hundred sixty. ¹⁵Of Binnui, six hundred forty-eight. ¹⁶Of Bebai, six hundred twenty-eight. ¹⁷Of Azgad, two thousand three hundred twenty-two. ¹⁸Of Adonikam, six hundred sixty-seven. ¹⁹Of Bigvai, two thousand sixty-seven. ²⁰Of Adin, six hundred fifty-five. ²¹Of Ater, namely of Hezekiah, ninety-eight. ²²Of Hashum, three hundred twenty-eight. ²³Of Bezai, three hundred twenty-four. ²⁴Of Hariph, one hundred twelve. ²⁵Of Gibeon, ninety-five. ²⁶The people of Bethlehem and Netophah, one hundred eighty-eight. ²⁷Of Anathoth, one hundred twenty-eight. ²⁸Of Beth-azmaveth, forty-two. ²⁹Of Kiriath-jearim, Chephirah, and Beeroth, seven hundred forty-three. ³⁰Of Ramah and Geba, six hundred twenty-one. ³¹Of Michmas, one hundred twenty-two. ³²Of Bethel and Ai, one hundred twenty-three. ³³Of the other Nebo, fifty-two. ³⁴The descendants of the other Elam, one thousand two hundred fifty-four. ³⁵Of Harim, three hundred twenty. ³⁶Of Jericho, three hundred forty-five. ³⁷Of Lod, Hadid, and Ono, seven hundred twenty-one. ³⁸Of Senaah, three thousand nine hundred thirty.

39 The priests: the descendants of Jedaiah, namely the house of Jeshua, nine hundred seventy-three. ⁴⁰Of Immer, one thousand fifty-two. ⁴¹Of Pashhur, one thousand two hundred forty-seven. ⁴²Of Harim, one thousand seventeen.

Building Relationships

NEHEMIAH 7.4

Building can take many forms. Structures are constructed from brick, stucco, wood, steel—one brick, one nail, one trowel of plaster at a time. Relationships, however, are built with conversations, time spent together, common interests and goals, and a common faith—one word, one action, one gesture at a time. Each of us builds relationships on a daily basis. With whom are you presently building a new or continued relationship? What "tools" do you bring to the task? What "tools" do you need to sharpen or acquire? How do you see God as a partner in the construction effort?

See *Meeting God in Community*

My Spiritual Genealogy

NEHEMIAH 7.44–69

Genealogies are important in the Bible. Long passages list generation after generation and number the members of various clans and groups. The practice seems strange, in a way, to our modern minds. Most of us can name parents, grandparents, and perhaps great- and great-great-grandparents. Few of us, though, can name our ancestors back to the beginning of time or list the number of people in our extended family group.

While we do not tend to pay as much attention to family trees as the Israelites did, there is great value in thinking about people whose lives have influenced us and who have nurtured us spiritually. Who in your life has been a spiritual guide? A relative, friend, mentor or historical figure? Name some people who have helped you to know God and to live as God's beloved child.

See Meeting God in Community

43 The Levites: the descendants of Jeshua, namely of Kadmiel of the descendants of Hodevah, seventy-four. [44] The singers: the descendants of Asaph, one hundred forty-eight. [45] The gatekeepers: the descendants of Shallum, of Ater, of Talmon, of Akkub, of Hatita, of Shobai, one hundred thirty-eight.

46 The temple servants: the descendants of Ziha, of Hasupha, of Tabbaoth, [47] of Keros, of Sia, of Padon, [48] of Lebana, of Hagaba, of Shalmai, [49] of Hanan, of Giddel, of Gahar, [50] of Reaiah, of Rezin, of Nekoda, [51] of Gazzam, of Uzza, of Paseah, [52] of Besai, of Meunim, of Nephushesim, [53] of Bakbuk, of Hakupha, of Harhur, [54] of Bazlith, of Mehida, of Harsha, [55] of Barkos, of Sisera, of Temah, [56] of Neziah, of Hatipha.

57 The descendants of Solomon's servants: of Sotai, of Sophereth, of Perida, [58] of Jaala, of Darkon, of Giddel, [59] of Shephatiah, of Hattil, of Pochereth-hazzebaim, of Amon.

60 All the temple servants and the descendants of Solomon's servants were three hundred ninety-two.

61 The following were those who came up from Tel-melah, Tel-harsha, Cherub, Addon, and Immer, but they could not prove their ancestral houses or their descent, whether they belonged to Israel: [62] the descendants of Delaiah, of Tobiah, of Nekoda, six hundred forty-two. [63] Also, of the priests: the descendants of Hobaiah, of Hakkoz, of Barzillai (who had married one of the daughters of Barzillai the Gileadite and was called by their name). [64] These sought their registration among those enrolled in the genealogies, but it was not found there, so they were excluded from the priesthood as unclean; [65] the governor told them that they were not to partake of the most holy food, until a priest with Urim and Thummim should come.

66 The whole assembly together was forty-two thousand three hundred sixty, [67] besides their male and female slaves, of whom there were seven thousand three hundred thirty-seven; and they had two hundred forty-five singers, male and female. [68] They had seven hundred thirty-six horses, two hundred forty-five mules,[a] [69] four hundred thirty-five camels, and six thousand seven hundred twenty donkeys.

70 Now some of the heads of ancestral houses contributed to the work. The governor gave to the treasury one thousand darics of gold, fifty basins, and five hundred thirty priestly robes. [71] And some of the heads of ancestral houses gave into the building fund twenty thousand darics of gold and two thousand two hundred minas of silver. [72] And what the rest of the people gave was twenty thousand darics of gold, two thousand minas of silver, and sixty-seven priestly robes.

73 So the priests, the Levites, the gatekeepers, the singers, some of the people, the temple servants, and all Israel settled in their towns.

a Ezra 2.66 and the margins of some Hebrew Mss: MT lacks *They had . . . forty-five mules*

Ezra Summons the People to Obey the Law

8 When the seventh month came—the people of Israel being settled in their towns— [1] all the people gathered together into the square before the Water Gate. They told the scribe Ezra to bring the book of the law of Moses, which the LORD had given to Israel. [2] Accordingly, the priest Ezra brought the law before the assembly, both men and women and all who could hear with understanding. This was on the first day of the seventh month. [3] He read from it facing the square before the Water Gate from early morning until midday, in the presence of the men and the women and those who could understand; and the ears of all the people were attentive to the book of the law. [4] The scribe Ezra stood on a wooden platform that had been made for the purpose; and beside him stood Mattithiah, Shema, Anaiah, Uriah, Hilkiah, and Maaseiah on his right hand; and Pedaiah, Mishael, Malchijah, Hashum, Hash-baddanah, Zechariah, and Meshullam on his left hand. [5] And Ezra opened the book in the sight of all the people, for he was standing above all the people; and when he opened it, all the people stood up. [6] Then Ezra blessed the LORD, the great God, and all the people answered, "Amen, Amen," lifting up their hands. Then they bowed their heads and worshiped the LORD with their faces to the ground. [7] Also Jeshua, Bani, Sherebiah, Jamin, Akkub, Shabbethai, Hodiah, Maaseiah, Kelita, Azariah, Jozabad, Hanan, Pelaiah, the Levites,[a] helped the people to understand the law, while the people remained in their places. [8] So they read from the book, from the law of God, with interpretation. They gave the sense, so that the people understood the reading.

9 And Nehemiah, who was the governor, and Ezra the priest and scribe, and the Levites who taught the people said to all the people, "This day is holy to the LORD your God; do not mourn or weep." For all the people wept when they heard the words of the law. [10] Then he said to them, "Go your way, eat the fat and drink sweet wine and send portions of them to those for whom nothing is prepared, for this day is holy to our LORD; and do not be grieved, for the joy of the LORD is your strength." [11] So the Levites stilled all the people, saying, "Be quiet, for this day is holy; do not be grieved." [12] And all the people went their way to eat and drink and to send portions and to make great rejoicing, because they had understood the words that were declared to them.

The Festival of Booths Celebrated

13 On the second day the heads of ancestral houses of all the people, with the priests and the Levites, came together to the scribe Ezra in order to study the words of the law. [14] And they found it written in the law, which the LORD had commanded by Moses, that the people of Israel should live in booths[b] during the festival of the seventh month, [15] and that they should publish and proclaim in

Joyfully Listening to God's Voice

NEHEMIAH 8.2–12

Can you imagine standing for five or six hours while scripture is read? The people who gather in assembly before Ezra listen attentively to the book of the law, bow down and worship, and "[weep] when they [hear] the words of the law," grieving as they understand how they have not lived according to God's ways. But Nehemiah proclaims God's grace: "Do not be grieved, for the joy of the LORD is your strength." Read verse 12 again. What is your response to this story? How can you relate to the emotions of the people?

What does this story say about how God relates to us? How does the experience of listening to God's Word being read differ from the experience of reading it yourself? What can you learn from these ancient believers about listening to the reading of scripture?

See Meeting God in Scripture

Time to Party!

NEHEMIAH 8.17

The Israelites have much to celebrate. The wall is complete, they are settling into their homeland and the community has heard scripture read aloud. It is time to feast! Enjoying a long-standing tradition, they gather branches of lovely greenery and make shelters (booths) in which to celebrate once again the festival of booths. How does your faith community celebrate? Do you have regular times when you joyfully commemorate all the good that happens in your communal or individual lives? Consider celebrating with a springtime or summer camping trip to commemorate Paul's words from the New Testament: "Rejoice in the Lord always; again I will say, Rejoice." (Philippians 4.4).

See Meeting God in Community

all their towns and in Jerusalem as follows, "Go out to the hills and bring branches of olive, wild olive, myrtle, palm, and other leafy trees to make booths,*a* as it is written." ¹⁶So the people went out and brought them, and made booths*a* for themselves, each on the roofs of their houses, and in their courts and in the courts of the house of God, and in the square at the Water Gate and in the square at the Gate of Ephraim. ¹⁷And all the assembly of those who had returned from the captivity made booths*a* and lived in them; for from the days of Jeshua son of Nun to that day the people of Israel had not done so. And there was very great rejoicing. ¹⁸And day by day, from the first day to the last day, he read from the book of the law of God. They kept the festival seven days; and on the eighth day there was a solemn assembly, according to the ordinance.

National Confession

9 Now on the twenty-fourth day of this month the people of Israel were assembled with fasting and in sackcloth, and with earth on their heads.*b* ²Then those of Israelite descent separated themselves from all foreigners, and stood and confessed their sins and the iniquities of their ancestors. ³They stood up in their place and read from the book of the law of the LORD their God for a fourth part of the day, and for another fourth they made confession and worshiped the LORD their God. ⁴Then Jeshua, Bani, Kadmiel, Shebaniah, Bunni, Sherebiah, Bani, and Chenani stood on the stairs of the Levites and cried out with a loud voice to the LORD their God. ⁵Then the Levites, Jeshua, Kadmiel, Bani, Hashabneiah, Sherebiah, Hodiah, Shebaniah, and Pethahiah, said, "Stand up and bless the LORD your God from everlasting to everlasting. Blessed be your glorious name, which is exalted above all blessing and praise."

6 And Ezra said:*c* "You are the LORD, you alone; you have made heaven, the heaven of heavens, with all their host, the earth and all that is on it, the seas and all that is in them. To all of them you give life, and the host of heaven worships you. ⁷You are the LORD, the God who chose Abram and brought him out of Ur of the Chaldeans and gave him the name Abraham; ⁸and you found his heart faithful before you, and made with him a covenant to give to his descendants the land of the Canaanite, the Hittite, the Amorite, the Perizzite, the Jebusite, and the Girgashite; and you have fulfilled your promise, for you are righteous.

9 "And you saw the distress of our ancestors in Egypt and heard their cry at the Red Sea.*d* ¹⁰You performed signs and wonders against Pharaoh and all his servants and all the people of his land, for you knew that they acted insolently against our ancestors. You made a name for yourself, which remains to this day. ¹¹And you divided the sea before them, so that they passed through the sea on dry land, but you threw their pursuers into the

a Or *tabernacles*; Heb *succoth*   *b* Heb *on them*   *c* Gk: Heb lacks *And Ezra said*   *d* Or *Sea of Reeds* depths, like a stone into mighty waters. [12]Moreover, you led them by day with a pillar of cloud, and by night with a pillar of fire, to give them light on the way in which they should go. [13]You came down also upon Mount Sinai, and spoke with them from heaven, and gave them right ordinances and true laws, good statutes and commandments, [14]and you made known your holy sabbath to them and gave them commandments and statutes and a law through your servant Moses. [15]For their hunger you gave them bread from heaven, and for their thirst you brought water for them out of the rock, and you told them to go in to possess the land that you swore to give them.

16 "But they and our ancestors acted presumptuously and stiffened their necks and did not obey your commandments; [17]they refused to obey, and were not mindful of the wonders that you performed among them; but they stiffened their necks and determined to return to their slavery in Egypt. But you are a God ready to forgive, gracious and merciful, slow to anger and abounding in steadfast love, and you did not forsake them. [18]Even when they had cast an image of a calf for themselves and said, 'This is your God who brought you up out of Egypt,' and had committed great blasphemies, [19]you in your great mercies did not forsake them in the wilderness; the pillar of cloud that led them in the way did not leave them by day, nor the pillar of fire by night that gave them light on the way by which they should go. [20]You gave your good spirit to instruct them, and did not withhold your manna from their mouths, and gave them water for their thirst. [21]Forty years you sustained them in the wilderness so that they lacked nothing; their clothes did not wear out and their feet did not swell. [22]And you gave them kingdoms and peoples, and allotted to them every corner,[a] so they took possession of the land of King Sihon of Heshbon and the land of King Og of Bashan. [23]You multiplied their descendants like the stars of heaven, and brought them into the land that you had told their ancestors to enter and possess. [24]So the descendants went in and possessed the land, and you subdued before them the inhabitants of the land, the Canaanites, and gave them into their hands, with their kings and the peoples of the land, to do with them as they pleased. [25]And they captured fortress cities and a rich land, and took possession of houses filled with all sorts of goods, hewn cisterns, vineyards, olive orchards, and fruit trees in abundance; so they ate, and were filled and became fat, and delighted themselves in your great goodness.

26 "Nevertheless they were disobedient and rebelled against you and cast your law behind their backs and killed your prophets, who had warned them in order to turn them back to you, and they committed great blasphemies. [27]Therefore you gave them into the hands of their enemies, who made them suffer. Then in the time

God in the Details

NEHEMIAH 9.19–21

The Levites recite their history, recalling how, in the wilderness of Sinai, God had provided pillars of cloud and fire as a constant guide, food and water, and all manner of sustenance for their survival. Focus on verse 21. "Their clothes did not wear out and their feet did not swell." God cared about the big picture (providing cloud and fire to show them the way) and the small details (no one can walk far with swollen or blistered feet). Most of us remember the large gifts from God—our lives, food, our families. Take time to consider the small gifts God may be giving you—the intense colors of a patch of pansies, the patience to handle a conflict with graciousness, a good night's sleep.

See Meeting God in Everyday Life

A Binding Agreement

NEHEMIAH 9.38

Most of us operate on an "oral agreement" with God. We listen to scripture and think about God. We attend worship and express our devotion and love in prayer and song. Take the time to write out your end of a "firm agreement" as the Israelites did. List those things you commit to (such as, I will honor you as my God, I will always tell the truth, I promise to share your love), then carefully rewrite or type your agreement on an elegant piece of stationery or paper. Date and sign it, and place it in your Bible.

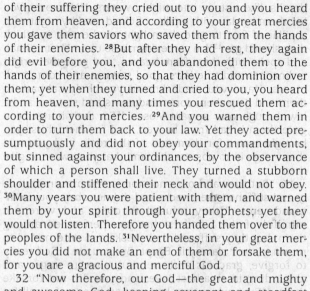

of their suffering they cried out to you and you heard them from heaven, and according to your great mercies you gave them saviors who saved them from the hands of their enemies. 28But after they had rest, they again did evil before you, and you abandoned them to the hands of their enemies, so that they had dominion over them; yet when they turned and cried to you, you heard from heaven, and many times you rescued them according to your mercies. 29And you warned them in order to turn them back to your law. Yet they acted presumptuously and did not obey your commandments, but sinned against your ordinances, by the observance of which a person shall live. They turned a stubborn shoulder and stiffened their neck and would not obey. 30Many years you were patient with them, and warned them by your spirit through your prophets; yet they would not listen. Therefore you handed them over to the peoples of the lands. 31Nevertheless, in your great mercies you did not make an end of them or forsake them, for you are a gracious and merciful God.

32 "Now therefore, our God—the great and mighty and awesome God, keeping covenant and steadfast love—do not treat lightly all the hardship that has come upon us, upon our kings, our officials, our priests, our prophets, our ancestors, and all your people, since the time of the kings of Assyria until today. 33You have been just in all that has come upon us, for you have dealt faithfully and we have acted wickedly; 34our kings, our officials, our priests, and our ancestors have not kept your law or heeded the commandments and the warnings that you gave them. 35Even in their own kingdom, and in the great goodness you bestowed on them, and in the large and rich land that you set before them, they did not serve you and did not turn from their wicked works. 36Here we are, slaves to this day—slaves in the land that you gave to our ancestors to enjoy its fruit and its good gifts. 37Its rich yield goes to the kings whom you have set over us because of our sins; they have power also over our bodies and over our livestock at their pleasure, and we are in great distress."

Those Who Signed the Covenant

38*a* Because of all this we make a firm agreement in writing, and on that sealed document are inscribed the names of our officials, our Levites, and our priests.

10 *b* Upon the sealed document are the names of Nehemiah the governor, son of Hacaliah, and Zedekiah; 2Seraiah, Azariah, Jeremiah, 3Pashhur, Amariah, Malchijah, 4Hattush, Shebaniah, Malluch, 5Harim, Meremoth, Obadiah, 6Daniel, Ginnethon, Baruch, 7Meshullam, Abijah, Mijamin, 8Maaziah, Bilgai, Shemaiah; these are the priests. 9And the Levites: Jeshua son of Azaniah, Binnui of the sons of Henadad, Kadmiel; 10and their associates, Shebaniah, Hodiah, Kelita, Pelaiah, Hanan, 11Mica, Rehob, Hashabiah, 12Zaccur, Sherebiah,

a Ch 10.1 in Heb   *b* Ch 10.2 in Heb

Shebaniah, [13]Hodiah, Bani, Beninu. [14]The leaders of the people: Parosh, Pahath-moab, Elam, Zattu, Bani, [15]Bunni, Azgad, Bebai, [16]Adonijah, Bigvai, Adin, [17]Ater, Hezekiah, Azzur, [18]Hodiah, Hashum, Bezai, [19]Hariph, Anathoth, Nebai, [20]Magpiash, Meshullam, Hezir, [21]Meshezabel, Zadok, Jaddua, [22]Pelatiah, Hanan, Anaiah, [23]Hoshea, Hananiah, Hasshub, [24]Hallohesh, Pilha, Shobek, [25]Rehum, Hashabnah, Maaseiah, [26]Ahiah, Hanan, Anan, [27]Malluch, Harim, and Baanah.

Summary of the Covenant

28 The rest of the people, the priests, the Levites, the gatekeepers, the singers, the temple servants, and all who have separated themselves from the peoples of the lands to adhere to the law of God, their wives, their sons, their daughters, all who have knowledge and understanding, [29]join with their kin, their nobles, and enter into a curse and an oath to walk in God's law, which was given by Moses the servant of God, and to observe and do all the commandments of the LORD our Lord and his ordinances and his statutes. [30]We will not give our daughters to the peoples of the land or take their daughters for our sons; [31]and if the peoples of the land bring in merchandise or any grain on the sabbath day to sell, we will not buy it from them on the sabbath or on a holy day; and we will forego the crops of the seventh year and the exaction of every debt.

32 We also lay on ourselves the obligation to charge ourselves yearly one-third of a shekel for the service of the house of our God: [33]for the rows of bread, the regular grain offering, the regular burnt offering, the sabbaths, the new moons, the appointed festivals, the sacred donations, and the sin offerings to make atonement for Israel, and for all the work of the house of our God. [34]We have also cast lots among the priests, the Levites, and the people, for the wood offering, to bring it into the house of our God, by ancestral houses, at appointed times, year by year, to burn on the altar of the LORD our God, as it is written in the law. [35]We obligate ourselves to bring the first fruits of our soil and the first fruits of all fruit of every tree, year by year, to the house of the LORD; [36]also to bring to the house of our God, to the priests who minister in the house of our God, the firstborn of our sons and of our livestock, as it is written in the law, and the firstlings of our herds and of our flocks; [37]and to bring the first of our dough, and our contributions, the fruit of every tree, the wine and the oil, to the priests, to the chambers of the house of our God; and to bring to the Levites the tithes from our soil, for it is the Levites who collect the tithes in all our rural towns. [38]And the priest, the descendant of Aaron, shall be with the Levites when the Levites receive the tithes; and the Levites shall bring up a tithe of the tithes to the house of our God, to the chambers of the storehouse. [39]For the people of Israel and the sons of Levi shall bring the contribution of grain, wine, and oil to the storerooms where the vessels of the sanctuary are, and where the priests that minister, and the

God in All Our Work

NEHEMIAH 10.28–29

"My God, since You are with me, and since it is Your will that I should apply my mind to these outward things, I pray that You will give me the grace to remain with You and to keep company with You. But so that my work may be better, Lord, work with me; receive my work and possess all my affections. Amen."

—BROTHER LAWRENCE,
The Practice of the Presence of God

Gifts for the Storeroom of God

NEHEMIAH 10.35–39

Imagine that you are sitting outside the house of God, watching the stream of people who are walking toward the temple. The people are lined up as far as you can see, their arms laden with offerings. A lamb squirms in a shepherd's arms. Two brothers bring sacks of grain carefully balanced on a cart. People holding bags of fruits and vegetables mingle with those pulling calves by leather reins. What animal sounds do you hear? Do you smell the ripeness of fresh fruit? What colors and textures illumine the gifts piled outside the door of God's house? What expressions are on the faces of those who gladly bring gifts of their firstborn and the first fruits of their crops? And what have you brought?

See *Meeting God in Worship*

gatekeepers and the singers are. We will not neglect the house of our God.

Population of the City Increased

11 Now the leaders of the people lived in Jerusalem; and the rest of the people cast lots to bring one out of ten to live in the holy city Jerusalem, while nine-tenths remained in the other towns. ²And the people blessed all those who willingly offered to live in Jerusalem.

3 These are the leaders of the province who lived in Jerusalem; but in the towns of Judah all lived on their property in their towns: Israel, the priests, the Levites, the temple servants, and the descendants of Solomon's servants. ⁴And in Jerusalem lived some of the Judahites and of the Benjaminites. Of the Judahites: Athaiah son of Uzziah son of Zechariah son of Amariah son of Shephatiah son of Mahalalel, of the descendants of Perez; ⁵and Maaseiah son of Baruch son of Col-hozeh son of Hazaiah son of Adaiah son of Joiarib son of Zechariah son of the Shilonite. ⁶All the descendants of Perez who lived in Jerusalem were four hundred sixty-eight valiant warriors.

7 And these are the Benjaminites: Sallu son of Meshullam son of Joed son of Pedaiah son of Kolaiah son of Maaseiah son of Ithiel son of Jeshaiah. ⁸And his brothers*ᵃ* Gabbai, Sallai: nine hundred twenty-eight. ⁹Joel son of Zichri was their overseer; and Judah son of Hassenuah was second in charge of the city.

10 Of the priests: Jedaiah son of Joiarib, Jachin, ¹¹Seraiah son of Hilkiah son of Meshullam son of Zadok son of Meraioth son of Ahitub, officer of the house of God, ¹²and their associates who did the work of the house, eight hundred twenty-two; and Adaiah son of Jeroham son of Pelaliah son of Amzi son of Zechariah son of Pashhur son of Malchijah, ¹³and his associates, heads of ancestral houses, two hundred forty-two; and Amashsai son of Azarel son of Ahzai son of Meshillemoth son of Immer, ¹⁴and their associates, valiant warriors, one hundred twenty-eight; their overseer was Zabdiel son of Haggedolim.

15 And of the Levites: Shemaiah son of Hasshub son of Azrikam son of Hashabiah son of Bunni; ¹⁶and Shabbethai and Jozabad, of the leaders of the Levites, who were over the outside work of the house of God; ¹⁷and Mattaniah son of Mica son of Zabdi son of Asaph, who was the leader to begin the thanksgiving in prayer, and Bakbukiah, the second among his associates; and Abda son of Shammua son of Galal son of Jeduthun. ¹⁸All the Levites in the holy city were two hundred eighty-four.

19 The gatekeepers, Akkub, Talmon and their associates, who kept watch at the gates, were one hundred seventy-two. ²⁰And the rest of Israel, and of the priests and the Levites, were in all the towns of Judah, all of them in their inheritance. ²¹But the temple servants lived on

a Gk Mss: Heb *And after him*

Ophel; and Ziha and Gishpa were over the temple servants.

22 The overseer of the Levites in Jerusalem was Uzzi son of Bani son of Hashabiah son of Mattaniah son of Mica, of the descendants of Asaph, the singers, in charge of the work of the house of God. ²³For there was a command from the king concerning them, and a settled provision for the singers, as was required every day. ²⁴And Pethahiah son of Meshezabel, of the descendants of Zerah son of Judah, was at the king's hand in all matters concerning the people.

Villages outside Jerusalem

25 And as for the villages, with their fields, some of the people of Judah lived in Kiriath-arba and its villages, and in Dibon and its villages, and in Jekabzeel and its villages, ²⁶and in Jeshua and in Moladah and Beth-pelet, ²⁷in Hazar-shual, in Beer-sheba and its villages, ²⁸in Ziklag, in Meconah and its villages, ²⁹in En-rimmon, in Zorah, in Jarmuth, ³⁰Zanoah, Adullam, and their villages, Lachish and its fields, and Azekah and its villages. So they camped from Beer-sheba to the valley of Hinnom. ³¹The people of Benjamin also lived from Geba onward, at Michmash, Aija, Bethel and its villages, ³²Anathoth, Nob, Ananiah, ³³Hazor, Ramah, Gittaim, ³⁴Hadid, Zeboim, Neballat, ³⁵Lod, and Ono, the valley of artisans. ³⁶And certain divisions of the Levites in Judah were joined to Benjamin.

A List of Priests and Levites

12 These are the priests and the Levites who came up with Zerubbabel son of Shealtiel, and Jeshua: Seraiah, Jeremiah, Ezra, ²Amariah, Malluch, Hattush, ³Shecaniah, Rehum, Meremoth, ⁴Iddo, Ginnethoi, Abijah, ⁵Mijamin, Maadiah, Bilgah, ⁶Shemaiah, Joiarib, Jedaiah, ⁷Sallu, Amok, Hilkiah, Jedaiah. These were the leaders of the priests and of their associates in the days of Jeshua.

8 And the Levites: Jeshua, Binnui, Kadmiel, Sherebiah, Judah, and Mattaniah, who with his associates was in charge of the songs of thanksgiving. ⁹And Bakbukiah and Unno their associates stood opposite them in the service. ¹⁰Jeshua was the father of Joiakim, Joiakim the father of Eliashib, Eliashib the father of Joiada, ¹¹Joiada the father of Jonathan, and Jonathan the father of Jaddua.

12 In the days of Joiakim the priests, heads of ancestral houses, were: of Seraiah, Meraiah; of Jeremiah, Hananiah; ¹³of Ezra, Meshullam; of Amariah, Jehohanan; ¹⁴of Malluchi, Jonathan; of Shebaniah, Joseph; ¹⁵of Harim, Adna; of Meraioth, Helkai; ¹⁶of Iddo, Zechariah; of Ginnethon, Meshullam; ¹⁷of Abijah, Zichri; of Miniamin, of Moadiah, Piltai; ¹⁸of Bilgah, Shammua; of Shemaiah, Jehonathan; ¹⁹of Joiarib, Mattenai; of Jedaiah, Uzzi; ²⁰of Sallai, Kallai; of Amok, Eber; ²¹of Hilkiah, Hashabiah; of Jedaiah, Nethanel.

22 As for the Levites, in the days of Eliashib, Joiada, Johanan, and Jaddua, there were recorded the heads of an-

God's Work of Transformation

NEHEMIAH 11.13–36

"Our whole life is to be poised on a certain glad expectancy of God; taking each moment, incident, choice and opportunity as material placed in our hand by the Creator whose whole intricate and mysterious process moved toward the triumph of Charity, and who has given each living spirit a tiny part in this vast work of transformation."

—EVELYN UNDERHILL,
The School of Charity

Meeting Through Music

NEHEMIAH 12.27

Harps, voices, flutes, lyres, trumpets, tambourines and cymbals join in joyful euphony to praise and worship God. Who can fathom the fullness of the way music communicates with God and other believers? How does music play a part in your faith? Do you love to sing hymns and praise songs? Do you play an instrument to connect with God? Is listening to religious music important in your spiritual life? Spend some time singing, playing an instrument or listening to music that brings you closer to God.

See Meeting God in Worship

cestral houses; also the priests until the reign of Darius the Persian. ²³The Levites, heads of ancestral houses, were recorded in the Book of the Annals until the days of Johanan son of Eliashib. ²⁴And the leaders of the Levites: Hashabiah, Sherebiah, and Jeshua son of Kadmiel, with their associates over against them, to praise and to give thanks, according to the commandment of David the man of God, section opposite to section. ²⁵Mattaniah, Bakbukiah, Obadiah, Meshullam, Talmon, and Akkub were gatekeepers standing guard at the storehouses of the gates. ²⁶These were in the days of Joiakim son of Jeshua son of Jozadak, and in the days of the governor Nehemiah and of the priest Ezra, the scribe.

Dedication of the City Wall

27 Now at the dedication of the wall of Jerusalem they sought out the Levites in all their places, to bring them to Jerusalem to celebrate the dedication with rejoicing, with thanksgivings and with singing, with cymbals, harps, and lyres. ²⁸The companies of the singers gathered together from the circuit around Jerusalem and from the villages of the Netophathites; ²⁹also from Beth-gilgal and from the region of Geba and Azmaveth; for the singers had built for themselves villages around Jerusalem. ³⁰And the priests and the Levites purified themselves; and they purified the people and the gates and the wall.

31 Then I brought the leaders of Judah up onto the wall, and appointed two great companies that gave thanks and went in procession. One went to the right on the wall to the Dung Gate; ³²and after them went Hoshaiah and half the officials of Judah, ³³and Azariah, Ezra, Meshullam, ³⁴Judah, Benjamin, Shemaiah, and Jeremiah, ³⁵and some of the young priests with trumpets: Zechariah son of Jonathan son of Shemaiah son of Mattaniah son of Micaiah son of Zaccur son of Asaph; ³⁶and his kindred, Shemaiah, Azarel, Milalai, Gilalai, Maai, Nethanel, Judah, and Hanani, with the musical instruments of David the man of God; and the scribe Ezra went in front of them. ³⁷At the Fountain Gate, in front of them, they went straight up by the stairs of the city of David, at the ascent of the wall, above the house of David, to the Water Gate on the east.

38 The other company of those who gave thanks went to the left,ᵃ and I followed them with half of the people on the wall, above the Tower of the Ovens, to the Broad Wall, ³⁹and above the Gate of Ephraim, and by the Old Gate, and by the Fish Gate and the Tower of Hananel and the Tower of the Hundred, to the Sheep Gate; and they came to a halt at the Gate of the Guard. ⁴⁰So both companies of those who gave thanks stood in the house of God, and I and half of the officials with me; ⁴¹and the priests Eliakim, Maaseiah, Miniamin, Micaiah, Elioenai, Zechariah, and Hananiah, with trumpets; ⁴²and Maaseiah, Shemaiah, Eleazar, Uzzi, Jehohanan, Malchijah, Elam, and Ezer. And the singers sang with Jezrahiah as their leader. ⁴³They of-

a Cn: Heb *opposite*

fered great sacrifices that day and rejoiced, for God had made them rejoice with great joy; the women and children also rejoiced. The joy of Jerusalem was heard far away.

Temple Responsibilities

44 On that day men were appointed over the chambers for the stores, the contributions, the first fruits, and the tithes, to gather into them the portions required by the law for the priests and for the Levites from the fields belonging to the towns; for Judah rejoiced over the priests and the Levites who ministered. ⁴⁵They performed the service of their God and the service of purification, as did the singers and the gatekeepers, according to the command of David and his son Solomon. ⁴⁶For in the days of David and Asaph long ago there was a leader of the singers, and there were songs of praise and thanksgiving to God. ⁴⁷In the days of Zerubbabel and in the days of Nehemiah all Israel gave the daily portions for the singers and the gatekeepers. They set apart that which was for the Levites; and the Levites set apart that which was for the descendants of Aaron.

Foreigners Separated from Israel

13 On that day they read from the book of Moses in the hearing of the people; and in it was found written that no Ammonite or Moabite should ever enter the assembly of God, ²because they did not meet the Israelites with bread and water, but hired Balaam against them to curse them—yet our God turned the curse into a blessing. ³When the people heard the law, they separated from Israel all those of foreign descent.

The Reforms of Nehemiah

4 Now before this, the priest Eliashib, who was appointed over the chambers of the house of our God, and who was related to Tobiah, ⁵prepared for Tobiah a large room where they had previously put the grain offering, the frankincense, the vessels, and the tithes of grain, wine, and oil, which were given by commandment to the Levites, singers, and gatekeepers, and the contributions for the priests. ⁶While this was taking place I was not in Jerusalem, for in the thirty-second year of King Artaxerxes of Babylon I went to the king. After some time I asked leave of the king ⁷and returned to Jerusalem. I then discovered the wrong that Eliashib had done on behalf of Tobiah, preparing a room for him in the courts of the house of God. ⁸And I was very angry, and I threw all the household furniture of Tobiah out of the room. ⁹Then I gave orders and they cleansed the chambers, and I brought back the vessels of the house of God, with the grain offering and the frankincense.

10 I also found out that the portions of the Levites had not been given to them; so that the Levites and the singers, who had conducted the service, had gone back to their fields. ¹¹So I remonstrated with the officials and said, "Why is the house of God forsaken?" And I gathered them together and set them in their stations. ¹²Then all Judah

Thus Rejoicing

NEHEMIAH 12.43

How has God given you joy? Set a timer for two minutes. Put pen to paper and see how many joys you can list in that short time. Jot down whatever comes to you—big and little things, those that seem important and those that appear insignificant. If after writing furiously for a time you draw a blank, think about a different aspect of your life (past, present, family, friends, work, faith community, creation) to inspire new ideas. When the timer sounds, reread your list of joys and thank God for giving them to you.

See Meeting God in Prayer

Turning a Curse Into a Blessing

NEHEMIAH 13.1–14

Have you ever tried to repair a shattered vase? Worked hard to restore a relationship that had gone sour? Found yourself genuinely loving a person who had previously been difficult to even like? Has disaster or tragedy befallen you—and only later did you see blessings come from what had seemed the worst possible scenario? In the miracle of God's loving power, what seems negative can often lead to something positive, as verse 2 illustrates. Is there something in your life right now that feels as though it is unredeemable? Offer that situation to God, who can make all things new.

See Meeting God in Everyday Life

brought the tithe of the grain, wine, and oil into the storehouses. ¹³And I appointed as treasurers over the storehouses the priest Shelemiah, the scribe Zadok, and Pedaiah of the Levites, and as their assistant Hanan son of Zaccur son of Mattaniah, for they were considered faithful; and their duty was to distribute to their associates. ¹⁴Remember me, O my God, concerning this, and do not wipe out my good deeds that I have done for the house of my God and for his service.

Sabbath Reforms Begun

15 In those days I saw in Judah people treading wine presses on the sabbath, and bringing in heaps of grain and loading them on donkeys; and also wine, grapes, figs, and all kinds of burdens, which they brought into Jerusalem on the sabbath day; and I warned them at that time against selling food. ¹⁶Tyrians also, who lived in the city, brought in fish and all kinds of merchandise and sold them on the sabbath to the people of Judah, and in Jerusalem. ¹⁷Then I remonstrated with the nobles of Judah and said to them, "What is this evil thing that you are doing, profaning the sabbath day? ¹⁸Did not your ancestors act in this way, and did not our God bring all this disaster on us and on this city? Yet you bring more wrath on Israel by profaning the sabbath."

19 When it began to be dark at the gates of Jerusalem before the sabbath, I commanded that the doors should be shut and gave orders that they should not be opened until after the sabbath. And I set some of my servants over the gates, to prevent any burden from being brought in on the sabbath day. ²⁰Then the merchants and sellers of all kinds of merchandise spent the night outside Jerusalem once or twice. ²¹But I warned them and said to them, "Why do you spend the night in front of the wall? If you do so again, I will lay hands on you." From that time on they did not come on the sabbath. ²²And I commanded the Levites that they should purify themselves and come and guard the gates, to keep the sabbath day holy. Remember this also in my favor, O my God, and spare me according to the greatness of your steadfast love.

Mixed Marriages Condemned

23 In those days also I saw Jews who had married women of Ashdod, Ammon, and Moab; ²⁴and half of their children spoke the language of Ashdod, and they could not speak the language of Judah, but spoke the language of various peoples. ²⁵And I contended with them and cursed them and beat some of them and pulled out their hair; and I made them take an oath in the name of God, saying, "You shall not give your daughters to their sons, or take their daughters for your sons or for yourselves. ²⁶Did not King Solomon of Israel sin on account of such women? Among the many nations there was no king like him, and he was beloved by his God, and God made him king over all Israel; nevertheless, foreign women made even him to sin. ²⁷Shall we then listen to you and do all

this great evil and act treacherously against our God by marrying foreign women?"

28 And one of the sons of Jehoiada, son of the high priest Eliashib, was the son-in-law of Sanballat the Horonite; I chased him away from me. ²⁹Remember them, O my God, because they have defiled the priesthood, the covenant of the priests and the Levites.

30 Thus I cleansed them from everything foreign, and I established the duties of the priests and Levites, each in his work; ³¹and I provided for the wood offering, at appointed times, and for the first fruits. Remember me, O my God, for good.

Serving God Faithfully

NEHEMIAH 13.31

Nehemiah served God throughout his life. Sometimes he had success (the wall was rebuilt) and sometimes, when his people did not follow God's laws, he felt frustrated. This last chapter of Nehemiah ends with the plaintive statement, "Remember me, O my God, for good." When have you felt that your endeavors for God were not successful despite your best efforts? When did you simply have to trust that God knew you well enough to understand both the highs and the lows of your circumstances? Offer your own "Remember me for good" prayer in the belief that God will acknowledge all you do and deem you faithful.

See Meeting God in Prayer

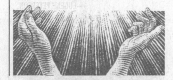

ESTHER
Courage to Be Faithful

KEY VERSE:
"Who knows? Perhaps you have come to royal dignity for just such a time as this."—Esther 4.14

> "Most of the time we are not living in a crisis in which we are conscious of our need of God, yet everything we do is critical to our faith, and God is critically involved in it. All day long we are doing eternally important things without knowing it. All through the day we inadvertently speak words that enter people's lives and change them in minor or major ways, and we never know it."
>
> —EUGENE PETERSON,
> *Reversed Thunder*

Every year in late winter Jews celebrate the Feast of Purim to commemorate their deliverance from those in a position to destroy them. This book is the story of how that feast came into being. The Jews living in exile in Persia are first threatened with extermination and then granted the sort of vindication the psalmists continually pleaded with God to pursue on their behalf.

This is also a story of irony, a dark comedy that reveals the posturing of the proud as foolishness. First, the ruler of the entire Middle East is thwarted by his wife when he tries to display her as a trophy at a feast. Then the scheming Haman, jealous of another's reward, ends up being hanged on his own gallows. The mighty fall and the lowly are raised up.

How is this reversal accomplished? By militia groups and palace coups? No. By an orphan girl isolated in the Persian harem. Counseled by her uncle, Mordecai, she first hides her identity as a Jew, revealing it only when her privileged position allows her to intercede on behalf of her people. She risks her life, yet fulfills her true destiny—one greater than she had ever dreamed.

Stuck in our everyday routine, we may find it difficult to remember our deepest identity as members of the body of Christ. To revive your awareness of that identity, consider carefully how much of your energy you expend on personal advancement. Compare that to your concern for the community of faith that sustains you. What risks do you take on behalf of that body?

Consider your destiny. Ask yourself, "Who knows for what purpose I have been brought to this time and place?"

King Ahasuerus Deposes Queen Vashti

1 This happened in the days of Ahasuerus, the same Ahasuerus who ruled over one hundred twenty-seven provinces from India to Ethiopia.*a* ²In those days when King Ahasuerus sat on his royal throne in the citadel of Susa, ³in the third year of his reign, he gave a banquet for all his officials and ministers. The army of Persia and Media and the nobles and governors of the provinces were present, ⁴while he displayed the great wealth of his kingdom and the splendor and pomp of his majesty for many days, one hundred eighty days in all.

5 When these days were completed, the king gave for all the people present in the citadel of Susa, both great and small, a banquet lasting for seven days, in the court of the garden of the king's palace. ⁶There were white cotton curtains and blue hangings tied with cords of fine linen and purple to silver rings*b* and marble pillars. There were couches of gold and silver on a mosaic pavement of porphyry, marble, mother-of-pearl, and colored stones. ⁷Drinks were served in golden goblets, goblets of different kinds, and the royal wine was lavished according to the bounty of the king. ⁸Drinking was by flagons, without restraint; for the king had given orders to all the officials of his palace to do as each one desired. ⁹Furthermore, Queen Vashti gave a banquet for the women in the palace of King Ahasuerus.

10 On the seventh day, when the king was merry with wine, he commanded Mehuman, Biztha, Harbona, Bigtha and Abagtha, Zethar and Carkas, the seven eunuchs who attended him, ¹¹to bring Queen Vashti before the king, wearing the royal crown, in order to show the peoples and the officials her beauty; for she was fair to behold. ¹²But Queen Vashti refused to come at the king's command conveyed by the eunuchs. At this the king was enraged, and his anger burned within him.

13 Then the king consulted the sages who knew the laws*c* (for this was the king's procedure toward all who were versed in law and custom, ¹⁴and those next to him were Carshena, Shethar, Admatha, Tarshish, Meres, Marsena, and Memucan, the seven officials of Persia and Media, who had access to the king, and sat first in the kingdom): ¹⁵"According to the law, what is to be done to Queen Vashti because she has not performed the command of King Ahasuerus conveyed by the eunuchs?" ¹⁶Then Memucan said in the presence of the king and the officials, "Not only has Queen Vashti done wrong to the king, but also to all the officials and all the peoples who are in all the provinces of King Ahasuerus. ¹⁷For this deed of the queen will be made known to all women, causing them to look with contempt on their husbands, since they will say, 'King Ahasuerus commanded Queen Vashti to be brought before him, and she did not come.' ¹⁸This very day the noble ladies of Persia and Media who have heard of the queen's behavior will rebel against*d* the king's officials, and there will be no end of contempt and wrath! ¹⁹If it pleases the king, let a royal order go out from him, and let it be written among the laws of the Persians and the Medes so that it may not be altered,

People and Prizes

ESTHER 1.4–12

Conspicuous consumption often goes beyond acquiring a beautifully furnished home and entertaining royally. The process can become addictive. Intoxicated with ownership, we seek to enlarge our identities by adding to our possessions. Sometimes we even seek to possess and control other people.

Look around your house—in the closets, the living room, the garage. Which objects were acquired for their beauty or usefulness? Were any bought to impress others with your importance?

Look at the people you love. Do you ever use them to feel good about yourself? If your child brings home a report card with poor grades, do you respond in anger because you believe it reflects badly on you?

See *Meeting God in Everyday Life*

a Or *Nubia*; Heb *Cush*   *b* Or *rods*   *c* Cn: Heb *times*   *d* Cn: Heb *will tell*

The Need for Mentors

ESTHER 2.10–11

A true mentor not only encourages another to reach his or her potential and instructs his or her student but also actively seeks the student's advancement. Every athlete needs a coach who can continue to guide and counsel, even after the athlete's abilities and fame surpass the teacher's. We need experienced spiritual tutors to track our progress.

Imagine yourself in Esther's predicament full of unfamiliar people and bizarre circumstances. God brings to you a person, full of wisdom and deep concern, who paces back and forth waiting to see you and help you. How would this make you feel?

Consider any strange circumstances you are now encountering. Whom might you ask to become your mentor?

See Meeting God in Community

that Vashti is never again to come before King Ahasuerus; and let the king give her royal position to another who is better than she. ²⁰So when the decree made by the king is proclaimed throughout all his kingdom, vast as it is, all women will give honor to their husbands, high and low alike."

21 This advice pleased the king and the officials, and the king did as Memucan proposed; ²²he sent letters to all the royal provinces, to every province in its own script and to every people in its own language, declaring that every man should be master in his own house.ᵃ

Esther Becomes Queen

2 After these things, when the anger of King Ahasuerus had abated, he remembered Vashti and what she had done and what had been decreed against her. ²Then the king's servants who attended him said, "Let beautiful young virgins be sought out for the king. ³And let the king appoint commissioners in all the provinces of his kingdom to gather all the beautiful young virgins to the harem in the citadel of Susa under custody of Hegai, the king's eunuch, who is in charge of the women; let their cosmetic treatments be given them. ⁴And let the girl who pleases the king be queen instead of Vashti." This pleased the king, and he did so.

5 Now there was a Jew in the citadel of Susa whose name was Mordecai son of Jair son of Shimei son of Kish, a Benjaminite. ⁶Kishᵇ had been carried away from Jerusalem among the captives carried away with King Jeconiah of Judah, whom King Nebuchadnezzar of Babylon had carried away. ⁷Mordecaiᶜ had brought up Hadassah, that is Esther, his cousin, for she had neither father nor mother; the girl was fair and beautiful, and when her father and her mother died, Mordecai adopted her as his own daughter. ⁸So when the king's order and his edict were proclaimed, and when many young women were gathered in the citadel of Susa in custody of Hegai, Esther also was taken into the king's palace and put in custody of Hegai, who had charge of the women. ⁹The girl pleased him and won his favor, and he quickly provided her with her cosmetic treatments and her portion of food, and with seven chosen maids from the king's palace, and advanced her and her maids to the best place in the harem. ¹⁰Esther did not reveal her people or kindred, for Mordecai had charged her not to tell. ¹¹Every day Mordecai would walk around in front of the court of the harem, to learn how Esther was and how she fared.

12 The turn came for each girl to go in to King Ahasuerus, after being twelve months under the regulations for the women, since this was the regular period of their cosmetic treatment, six months with oil of myrrh and six months with perfumes and cosmetics for women. ¹³When the girl went in to the king she was given whatever she asked for to take with her from the harem to the king's palace. ¹⁴In the evening she went in; then in the morning she came back to the second harem in custody of Shaashgaz, the king's eunuch, who was in charge of the

---

a Heb adds *and speak according to the language of his people*   b Heb *a Benjamite* ⁶*who*   c Heb *He*

concubines; she did not go in to the king again, unless the king delighted in her and she was summoned by name.

15 When the turn came for Esther daughter of Abihail the uncle of Mordecai, who had adopted her as his own daughter, to go in to the king, she asked for nothing except what Hegai the king's eunuch, who had charge of the women, advised. Now Esther was admired by all who saw her. ¹⁶When Esther was taken to King Ahasuerus in his royal palace in the tenth month, which is the month of Tebeth, in the seventh year of his reign, ¹⁷the king loved Esther more than all the other women; of all the virgins she won his favor and devotion, so that he set the royal crown on her head and made her queen instead of Vashti. ¹⁸Then the king gave a great banquet to all his officials and ministers—"Esther's banquet." He also granted a holiday[a] to the provinces, and gave gifts with royal liberality.

Mordecai Discovers a Plot

19 When the virgins were being gathered together,[b] Mordecai was sitting at the king's gate. ²⁰Now Esther had not revealed her kindred or her people, as Mordecai had charged her; for Esther obeyed Mordecai just as when she was brought up by him. ²¹In those days, while Mordecai was sitting at the king's gate, Bigthan and Teresh, two of the king's eunuchs, who guarded the threshold, became angry and conspired to assassinate[c] King Ahasuerus. ²²But the matter came to the knowledge of Mordecai, and he told it to Queen Esther, and Esther told the king in the name of Mordecai. ²³When the affair was investigated and found to be so, both the men were hanged on the gallows. It was recorded in the book of the annals in the presence of the king.

Haman Undertakes to Destroy the Jews

3 After these things King Ahasuerus promoted Haman son of Hammedatha the Agagite, and advanced him and set his seat above all the officials who were with him. ²And all the king's servants who were at the king's gate bowed down and did obeisance to Haman; for the king had so commanded concerning him. But Mordecai did not bow down or do obeisance. ³Then the king's servants who were at the king's gate said to Mordecai, "Why do you disobey the king's command?" ⁴When they spoke to him day after day and he would not listen to them, they told Haman, in order to see whether Mordecai's words would avail; for he had told them that he was a Jew. ⁵When Haman saw that Mordecai did not bow down or do obeisance to him, Haman was infuriated. ⁶But he thought it beneath him to lay hands on Mordecai alone. So, having been told who Mordecai's people were, Haman plotted to destroy all the Jews, the people of Mordecai, throughout the whole kingdom of Ahasuerus.

7 In the first month, which is the month of Nisan, in the twelfth year of King Ahasuerus, they cast Pur—which means "the lot"—before Haman for the day and for the month, and the lot fell on the thirteenth day[d] of the twelfth month, which is the month of Adar. ⁸Then Haman said to

a Or an amnesty   b Heb adds a second time   c Heb to lay hands on
d Cn Compare Gk and verse 13 below: Heb the twelfth month

639

Refusing to Kneel

ESTHER 3.2-4

Being a Jew meant acknowledging that only God is worthy of worship. Much as Mordecai did in Persia, Christians today live both as citizens and as strangers in this world. We are surrounded by people whose values we may not share and with whom we may disagree on numerous issues.

Reread Esther 3.2-4. Notice what word or phrase or action attracts your attention. Reflect on this word or phrase or action. Why is it meaningful to you?

Remain silent and open for insight from God—perhaps about divided loyalties or frustrating disagreements. In what way does this passage touch your life today?

See Meeting God in Scripture

Sharing Suffering

ESTHER 4.1,5

Compassion means, literally, to "suffer with." The ancient world had active means of portraying this shared anguish and showing solidarity with sufferers. Esther makes an effort to discover the cause of Mordecai's grief.

Do you seek to discover the cause of suffering even if it does not affect you directly? Do you try to guard against hearing such unpleasant information? What means do we have at our disposal for suffering with other parts of the body of Christ? How is grief expressed publicly in your church?

See Meeting God in Community

King Ahasuerus, "There is a certain people scattered and separated among the peoples in all the provinces of your kingdom; their laws are different from those of every other people, and they do not keep the king's laws, so that it is not appropriate for the king to tolerate them. ⁹If it pleases the king, let a decree be issued for their destruction, and I will pay ten thousand talents of silver into the hands of those who have charge of the king's business, so that they may put it into the king's treasuries." ¹⁰So the king took his signet ring from his hand and gave it to Haman son of Hammedatha the Agagite, the enemy of the Jews. ¹¹The king said to Haman, "The money is given to you, and the people as well, to do with them as it seems good to you."

12 Then the king's secretaries were summoned on the thirteenth day of the first month, and an edict, according to all that Haman commanded, was written to the king's satraps and to the governors over all the provinces and to the officials of all the peoples, to every province in its own script and every people in its own language; it was written in the name of King Ahasuerus and sealed with the king's ring. ¹³Letters were sent by couriers to all the king's provinces, giving orders to destroy, to kill, and to annihilate all Jews, young and old, women and children, in one day, the thirteenth day of the twelfth month, which is the month of Adar, and to plunder their goods. ¹⁴A copy of the document was to be issued as a decree in every province by proclamation, calling on all the peoples to be ready for that day. ¹⁵The couriers went quickly by order of the king, and the decree was issued in the citadel of Susa. The king and Haman sat down to drink; but the city of Susa was thrown into confusion.

Esther Agrees to Help the Jews

4 When Mordecai learned all that had been done, Mordecai tore his clothes and put on sackcloth and ashes, and went through the city, wailing with a loud and bitter cry; ²he went up to the entrance of the king's gate, for no one might enter the king's gate clothed with sackcloth. ³In every province, wherever the king's command and his decree came, there was great mourning among the Jews, with fasting and weeping and lamenting, and most of them lay in sackcloth and ashes.

4 When Esther's maids and her eunuchs came and told her, the queen was deeply distressed; she sent garments to clothe Mordecai, so that he might take off his sackcloth; but he would not accept them. ⁵Then Esther called for Hathach, one of the king's eunuchs, who had been appointed to attend her, and ordered him to go to Mordecai to learn what was happening and why. ⁶Hathach went out to Mordecai in the open square of the city in front of the king's gate, ⁷and Mordecai told him all that had happened to him, and the exact sum of money that Haman had promised to pay into the king's treasuries for the destruction of the Jews. ⁸Mordecai also gave him a copy of the written decree issued in Susa for their destruction, that he might show it to Esther, explain it to her, and charge her to go to the king to make supplication to him and entreat him for her people.

9 Hathach went and told Esther what Mordecai had said. ¹⁰Then Esther spoke to Hathach and gave him a message for Mordecai, saying, ¹¹"All the king's servants and the people of the king's provinces know that if any man or woman goes to the king inside the inner court without being called, there is but one law—all alike are to be put to death. Only if the king holds out the golden scepter to someone, may that person live. I myself have not been called to come in to the king for thirty days." ¹²When they told Mordecai what Esther had said, ¹³Mordecai told them to reply to Esther, "Do not think that in the king's palace you will escape any more than all the other Jews. ¹⁴For if you keep silence at such a time as this, relief and deliverance will rise for the Jews from another quarter, but you and your father's family will perish. Who knows? Perhaps you have come to royal dignity for just such a time as this." ¹⁵Then Esther said in reply to Mordecai, ¹⁶"Go, gather all the Jews to be found in Susa, and hold a fast on my behalf, and neither eat nor drink for three days, night or day. I and my maids will also fast as you do. After that I will go to the king, though it is against the law; and if I perish, I perish." ¹⁷Mordecai then went away and did everything as Esther had ordered him.

Esther's Banquet

5 On the third day Esther put on her royal robes and stood in the inner court of the king's palace, opposite the king's hall. The king was sitting on his royal throne inside the palace opposite the entrance to the palace. ²As soon as the king saw Queen Esther standing in the court, she won his favor and he held out to her the golden scepter that was in his hand. Then Esther approached and touched the top of the scepter. ³The king said to her, "What is it, Queen Esther? What is your request? It shall be given you, even to the half of my kingdom." ⁴Then Esther said, "If it pleases the king, let the king and Haman come today to a banquet that I have prepared for the king." ⁵Then the king said, "Bring Haman quickly, so that we may do as Esther desires." So the king and Haman came to the banquet that Esther had prepared. ⁶While they were drinking wine, the king said to Esther, "What is your petition? It shall be granted you. And what is your request? Even to the half of my kingdom, it shall be fulfilled." ⁷Then Esther said, "This is my petition and request: ⁸If I have won the king's favor, and if it pleases the king to grant my petition and fulfill my request, let the king and Haman come tomorrow to the banquet that I will prepare for them, and then I will do as the king has said."

Haman Plans to Have Mordecai Hanged

9 Haman went out that day happy and in good spirits. But when Haman saw Mordecai in the king's gate, and observed that he neither rose nor trembled before him, he was infuriated with Mordecai; ¹⁰nevertheless Haman restrained himself and went home. Then he sent and called for his friends and his wife Zeresh, ¹¹and Haman recounted to them the splendor of his riches, the number of his sons, all the promotions with which the king had hon-

On the Way to Freedom

ESTHER 4.14

"Do and dare what is right, not swayed by the whim of the moment. Bravely take hold of the real, not dallying now with what might be. Not in the flight of ideas but only in action is freedom. Make up your mind and come out into the tempest of living. God's command is enough and your faith in him to sustain you. Then at last freedom will welcome your spirit among great rejoicing."
—DIETRICH BONHOEFFER,
Ethics

641

The Rival's Reward

ESTHER 6.6

In a twist of irony, the proud Haman puts the noose around his own neck as he mistakes "the man whom the king wishes to honor" for himself. The wonderful reward he dreams up for himself turns into his worst nightmare when the reward goes to his enemy instead.

Write down ways you secretly dream of being recognized for your worth—perhaps by winning a marathon, getting a raise or graduating *magna cum laude*. Then think of someone with whom you feel competitive—a sibling, a coworker or even a spouse. Now imagine that person receiving the rewards on your list instead of you. How does that feel? What would need to happen in order for you to congratulate him or her with a pure heart?

See Meeting God in Everyday Life

ored him, and how he had advanced him above the officials and the ministers of the king. [12]Haman added, "Even Queen Esther let no one but myself come with the king to the banquet that she prepared. Tomorrow also I am invited by her, together with the king. [13]Yet all this does me no good so long as I see the Jew Mordecai sitting at the king's gate." [14]Then his wife Zeresh and all his friends said to him, "Let a gallows fifty cubits high be made, and in the morning tell the king to have Mordecai hanged on it; then go with the king to the banquet in good spirits." This advice pleased Haman, and he had the gallows made.

The King Honors Mordecai

6 On that night the king could not sleep, and he gave orders to bring the book of records, the annals, and they were read to the king. [2]It was found written how Mordecai had told about Bigthana and Teresh, two of the king's eunuchs, who guarded the threshold, and who had conspired to assassinate[a] King Ahasuerus. [3]Then the king said, "What honor or distinction has been bestowed on Mordecai for this?" The king's servants who attended him said, "Nothing has been done for him." [4]The king said, "Who is in the court?" Now Haman had just entered the outer court of the king's palace to speak to the king about having Mordecai hanged on the gallows that he had prepared for him. [5]So the king's servants told him, "Haman is there, standing in the court." The king said, "Let him come in." [6]So Haman came in, and the king said to him, "What shall be done for the man whom the king wishes to honor?" Haman said to himself, "Whom would the king wish to honor more than me?" [7]So Haman said to the king, "For the man whom the king wishes to honor, [8]let royal robes be brought, which the king has worn, and a horse that the king has ridden, with a royal crown on its head. [9]Let the robes and the horse be handed over to one of the king's most noble officials; let him[b] robe the man whom the king wishes to honor, and let him[b] conduct the man on horseback through the open square of the city, proclaiming before him: 'Thus shall it be done for the man whom the king wishes to honor.' " [10]Then the king said to Haman, "Quickly, take the robes and the horse, as you have said, and do so to the Jew Mordecai who sits at the king's gate. Leave out nothing that you have mentioned." [11]So Haman took the robes and the horse and robed Mordecai and led him riding through the open square of the city, proclaiming, "Thus shall it be done for the man whom the king wishes to honor."

12 Then Mordecai returned to the king's gate, but Haman hurried to his house, mourning and with his head covered. [13]When Haman told his wife Zeresh and all his friends everything that had happened to him, his advisers and his wife Zeresh said to him, "If Mordecai, before whom your downfall has begun, is of the Jewish people, you will not prevail against him, but will surely fall before him."

a Heb *to lay hands on*   *b* Heb *them*

Haman's Downfall and Mordecai's Advancement

14 While they were still talking with him, the king's eunuchs arrived and hurried Haman off to the banquet that 7 Esther had prepared. ¹So the king and Haman went in to feast with Queen Esther. ²On the second day, as they were drinking wine, the king again said to Esther, "What is your petition, Queen Esther? It shall be granted you. And what is your request? Even to the half of my kingdom, it shall be fulfilled." ³Then Queen Esther answered, "If I have won your favor, O king, and if it pleases the king, let my life be given me—that is my petition— and the lives of my people—that is my request. ⁴For we have been sold, I and my people, to be destroyed, to be killed, and to be annihilated. If we had been sold merely as slaves, men and women, I would have held my peace; but no enemy can compensate for this damage to the king."ᵃ ⁵Then King Ahasuerus said to Queen Esther, "Who is he, and where is he, who has presumed to do this?" ⁶Esther said, "A foe and enemy, this wicked Haman!" Then Haman was terrified before the king and the queen. ⁷The king rose from the feast in wrath and went into the palace garden, but Haman stayed to beg his life from Queen Esther, for he saw that the king had determined to destroy him. ⁸When the king returned from the palace garden to the banquet hall, Haman had thrown himself on the couch where Esther was reclining; and the king said, "Will he even assault the queen in my presence, in my own house?" As the words left the mouth of the king, they covered Haman's face. ⁹Then Harbona, one of the eunuchs in attendance on the king, said, "Look, the very gallows that Haman has prepared for Mordecai, whose word saved the king, stands at Haman's house, fifty cubits high." And the king said, "Hang him on that." ¹⁰So they hanged Haman on the gallows that he had prepared for Mordecai. Then the anger of the king abated.

Esther Saves the Jews

8 On that day King Ahasuerus gave to Queen Esther the house of Haman, the enemy of the Jews; and Mordecai came before the king, for Esther had told what he was to her. ²Then the king took off his signet ring, which he had taken from Haman, and gave it to Mordecai. So Esther set Mordecai over the house of Haman.

3 Then Esther spoke again to the king; she fell at his feet, weeping and pleading with him to avert the evil design of Haman the Agagite and the plot that he had devised against the Jews. ⁴The king held out the golden scepter to Esther, ⁵and Esther rose and stood before the king. She said, "If it pleases the king, and if I have won his favor, and if the thing seems right before the king, and I have his approval, let an order be written to revoke the letters devised by Haman son of Hammedatha the Agagite, which he wrote giving orders to destroy the Jews who are in all the provinces of the king. ⁶For how can I bear to see the calamity that is coming on my people? Or how can I bear to see the destruction of my kindred?" ⁷Then King Ahasuerus said to Queen Esther and to the Jew Mordecai, "See, I have given Esther the house of

---

---

a Meaning of Heb uncertain

Rescue and Rejoicing

ESTHER 8.16–17

The Jews' prayers are answered when the king grants them rights of assembly and self-protection. Mourning turns to joy as the Jews feast in celebration of their rescue.

Celebrating times of deliverance is important. Consider the problems or situations from which God has delivered you in the last year. Take a few minutes to celebrate one or two of them by writing about them, by allowing yourself a treat or by thinking about your deliverance as you perform an appropriate action, such as rocking your now-healthy baby, driving in your repaired car or holding the letter that welcomes you to your new job.

See Meeting God in Everyday Life

Haman, and they have hanged him on the gallows, because he plotted to lay hands on the Jews. ⁸You may write as you please with regard to the Jews, in the name of the king, and seal it with the king's ring; for an edict written in the name of the king and sealed with the king's ring cannot be revoked."

9 The king's secretaries were summoned at that time, in the third month, which is the month of Sivan, on the twenty-third day; and an edict was written, according to all that Mordecai commanded, to the Jews and to the satraps and the governors and the officials of the provinces from India to Ethiopia,ᵃ one hundred twenty-seven provinces, to every province in its own script and to every people in its own language, and also to the Jews in their script and their language. ¹⁰He wrote letters in the name of King Ahasuerus, sealed them with the king's ring, and sent them by mounted couriers riding on fast steeds bred from the royal herd.ᵇ ¹¹By these letters the king allowed the Jews who were in every city to assemble and defend their lives, to destroy, to kill, and to annihilate any armed force of any people or province that might attack them, with their children and women, and to plunder their goods ¹²on a single day throughout all the provinces of King Ahasuerus, on the thirteenth day of the twelfth month, which is the month of Adar. ¹³A copy of the writ was to be issued as a decree in every province and published to all peoples, and the Jews were to be ready on that day to take revenge on their enemies. ¹⁴So the couriers, mounted on their swift royal steeds, hurried out, urged by the king's command. The decree was issued in the citadel of Susa.

15 Then Mordecai went out from the presence of the king, wearing royal robes of blue and white, with a great golden crown and a mantle of fine linen and purple, while the city of Susa shouted and rejoiced. ¹⁶For the Jews there was light and gladness, joy and honor. ¹⁷In every province and in every city, wherever the king's command and his edict came, there was gladness and joy among the Jews, a festival and a holiday. Furthermore, many of the peoples of the country professed to be Jews, because the fear of the Jews had fallen upon them.

Destruction of the Enemies of the Jews

9 Now in the twelfth month, which is the month of Adar, on the thirteenth day, when the king's command and edict were about to be executed, on the very day when the enemies of the Jews hoped to gain power over them, but which had been changed to a day when the Jews would gain power over their foes, ²the Jews gathered in their cities throughout all the provinces of King Ahasuerus to lay hands on those who had sought their ruin; and no one could withstand them, because the fear of them had fallen upon all peoples. ³All the officials of the provinces, the satraps and the governors, and the royal officials were supporting the Jews, because the fear of Mordecai had fallen upon them. ⁴For Mordecai was powerful in the king's house, and his fame spread throughout all the provinces as the man Mordecai grew more and more powerful. ⁵So the Jews struck down all their enemies with the sword, slaugh-

ᵃ Or *Nubia*; Heb *Cush*   ᵇ Meaning of Heb uncertain

tering, and destroying them, and did as they pleased to those who hated them. ⁶In the citadel of Susa the Jews killed and destroyed five hundred people. ⁷They killed Parshandatha, Dalphon, Aspatha, ⁸Poratha, Adalia, Aridatha, ⁹Parmashta, Arisai, Aridai, Vaizatha, ¹⁰the ten sons of Haman son of Hammedatha, the enemy of the Jews; but they did not touch the plunder.

11 That very day the number of those killed in the citadel of Susa was reported to the king. ¹²The king said to Queen Esther, "In the citadel of Susa the Jews have killed five hundred people and also the ten sons of Haman. What have they done in the rest of the king's provinces? Now what is your petition? It shall be granted you. And what further is your request? It shall be fulfilled." ¹³Esther said, "If it pleases the king, let the Jews who are in Susa be allowed tomorrow also to do according to this day's edict, and let the ten sons of Haman be hanged on the gallows." ¹⁴So the king commanded this to be done; a decree was issued in Susa, and the ten sons of Haman were hanged. ¹⁵The Jews who were in Susa gathered also on the fourteenth day of the month of Adar and they killed three hundred persons in Susa; but they did not touch the plunder.

16 Now the other Jews who were in the king's provinces also gathered to defend their lives, and gained relief from their enemies, and killed seventy-five thousand of those who hated them; but they laid no hands on the plunder. ¹⁷This was on the thirteenth day of the month of Adar, and on the fourteenth day they rested and made that a day of feasting and gladness.

The Feast of Purim Inaugurated

18 But the Jews who were in Susa gathered on the thirteenth day and on the fourteenth, and rested on the fifteenth day, making that a day of feasting and gladness. ¹⁹Therefore the Jews of the villages, who live in the open towns, hold the fourteenth day of the month of Adar as a day for gladness and feasting, a holiday on which they send gifts of food to one another.

20 Mordecai recorded these things, and sent letters to all the Jews who were in all the provinces of King Ahasuerus, both near and far, ²¹enjoining them that they should keep the fourteenth day of the month Adar and also the fifteenth day of the same month, year by year, ²²as the days on which the Jews gained relief from their enemies, and as the month that had been turned for them from sorrow into gladness and from mourning into a holiday; that they should make them days of feasting and gladness, days for sending gifts of food to one another and presents to the poor. ²³So the Jews adopted as a custom what they had begun to do, as Mordecai had written to them.

24 Haman son of Hammedatha the Agagite, the enemy of all the Jews, had plotted against the Jews to destroy them, and had cast Pur—that is "the lot"—to crush and destroy them; ²⁵but when Esther came before the king, he gave orders in writing that the wicked plot that he had devised against the Jews should come upon his own head, and that he and his sons should be hanged on the gallows. ²⁶Therefore these days are called Purim, from the word Pur. Thus because of all that was written

The Widening Circle

ESTHER 9.20–22

Mordecai sends instructions to the Jews in all the provinces to celebrate their deliverance by sharing food with others and showering the poor with gifts. This celebration ensures that no one is left out and it further deepens the exiled people's sense of community.

Read the passage again slowly. Listen for a word or phrase that draws your attention. Wait for something to happen apart from yourself. Reflect on this word or phrase. What comes to you as you turn it over in your mind? Pray that phrase back to God. How does it sound as a prayer? Rest in silence, letting the text work its way throughout the layers of who you are.

See Meeting God in Scripture

Commemoration

ESTHER 9.28

"Lest we forget" marks many a soldier's tombstone. "Remember!" begins every passover celebration. We remember the Lord's death in every celebration of the Lord's Supper. Memory is essential to being human. Commemoration acknowledges and honors God's saving acts among us. The past is not obsolete or irrelevant. We do not invent the life of faith; we come to a dynamic and personal faith within the context of the traditions our spiritual ancestors have shaped and preserved for us. What have you inherited from your spiritual forebears? Thank God for their faithfulness. Make a list of what you would like your children or some future generation to remember about your spiritual life.

See Meeting God in Community

in this letter, and of what they had faced in this matter, and of what had happened to them, [27]the Jews established and accepted as a custom for themselves and their descendants and all who joined them, that without fail they would continue to observe these two days every year, as it was written and at the time appointed. [28]These days should be remembered and kept throughout every generation, in every family, province, and city; and these days of Purim should never fall into disuse among the Jews, nor should the commemoration of these days cease among their descendants.

29 Queen Esther daughter of Abihail, along with the Jew Mordecai, gave full written authority, confirming this second letter about Purim. [30]Letters were sent wishing peace and security to all the Jews, to the one hundred twenty-seven provinces of the kingdom of Ahasuerus, [31]and giving orders that these days of Purim should be observed at their appointed seasons, as the Jew Mordecai and Queen Esther enjoined on the Jews, just as they had laid down for themselves and for their descendants regulations concerning their fasts and their lamentations. [32]The command of Queen Esther fixed these practices of Purim, and it was recorded in writing.

10 King Ahasuerus laid tribute on the land and on the islands of the sea. [2]All the acts of his power and might, and the full account of the high honor of Mordecai, to which the king advanced him, are they not written in the annals of the kings of Media and Persia? [3]For Mordecai the Jew was next in rank to King Ahasuerus, and he was powerful among the Jews and popular with his many kindred, for he sought the good of his people and interceded for the welfare of all his descendants.

JOB

When Bad Things Happen

KEY VERSE:
"I had heard of you by the hearing of the ear, but now my eye sees you."—Job 42.5

Read the book of Job as a drama being played out on a stage. Act I begins with Job living in happiness and prosperity. Then, through one calamity after another, Job loses everything—his livestock, his servants, his children, his health. In Act II Job converses with his friends, who try to help him make sense of his suffering. In Act III Job speaks directly with God, and Job grasps—apparently for the first time—the depth of God's power and love. Job knows he has personally encountered the Eternal God: "I had heard of you by the hearing of the ear, but now my eye sees you" (42.5).

The book of Job endures as a drama because it addresses the reality of suffering. Not surprisingly, Job struggles more with the crisis of faith going on within himself than he does with what has happened to him externally. But Job persists in loving God—refusing to curse God—in spite of all his deeply felt losses. He never abandons his own honest, relentless and tormented pursuit of God.

All of us eventually travel the way of suffering. As we journey into its darkness, we may find ourselves tempted to doubt God's goodness, mercy and love. But Job gives us the courage to face honestly our hard questions and to wrestle with God. Like Job, we may meet God face-to-face at a depth we have not known before. Like Job, we can come to know that when all we have is taken away, God is enough.

> "It is well for those who find themselves in the dark night of the soul to persevere in patience . . . Let them trust in God, who does not abandon those who seek God with a simple and right heart, and will not fail to give them what is needful for the road, until he brings them into the clear and pure light of love."
>
> —JOHN OF THE CROSS,
> *The Dark Night of the Soul*

When Hardship Overtakes the Upright

JOB 1.1

From the first few words of the book we learn that Job is blameless and upright. This is the point on which the whole of the book of Job turns: He does not deserve the various calamities that befall him. He has done nothing wrong, though his friends later argue the contrary. The book of Job shows us that bad things happen to good people, and that we may have to struggle to be faithful when things seem unfair.

Perhaps you, like Job, are experiencing pain or distress. What questions do you bring to God? If you or someone you love is enduring great pain or loss, hold yourself or that other person in silence before God. Simply be still. Wait patiently.

Job and His Family

1 There was once a man in the land of Uz whose name was Job. That man was blameless and upright, one who feared God and turned away from evil. ²There were born to him seven sons and three daughters. ³He had seven thousand sheep, three thousand camels, five hundred yoke of oxen, five hundred donkeys, and very many servants; so that this man was the greatest of all the people of the east. ⁴His sons used to go and hold feasts in one another's houses in turn; and they would send and invite their three sisters to eat and drink with them. ⁵And when the feast days had run their course, Job would send and sanctify them, and he would rise early in the morning and offer burnt offerings according to the number of them all; for Job said, "It may be that my children have sinned, and cursed God in their hearts." This is what Job always did.

Attack on Job's Character

6 One day the heavenly beings[a] came to present themselves before the LORD, and Satan[b] also came among them. ⁷The LORD said to Satan,[b] "Where have you come from?" Satan[b] answered the LORD, "From going to and fro on the earth, and from walking up and down on it." ⁸The LORD said to Satan,[b] "Have you considered my servant Job? There is no one like him on the earth, a blameless and upright man who fears God and turns away from evil." ⁹Then Satan[b] answered the LORD, "Does Job fear God for nothing? ¹⁰Have you not put a fence around him and his house and all that he has, on every side? You have blessed the work of his hands, and his possessions have increased in the land. ¹¹But stretch out your hand now, and touch all that he has, and he will curse you to your face." ¹²The LORD said to Satan,[b] "Very well, all that he has is in your power; only do not stretch out your hand against him!" So Satan[b] went out from the presence of the LORD.

Job Loses Property and Children

13 One day when his sons and daughters were eating and drinking wine in the eldest brother's house, ¹⁴a messenger came to Job and said, "The oxen were plowing and the donkeys were feeding beside them, ¹⁵and the Sabeans fell on them and carried them off, and killed the servants with the edge of the sword; I alone have escaped to tell you." ¹⁶While he was still speaking, another came and said, "The fire of God fell from heaven and burned up the sheep and the servants, and consumed them; I alone have escaped to tell you." ¹⁷While he was still speaking, another came and said, "The Chaldeans formed three columns, made a raid on the camels and carried them off, and killed the servants with the edge of the sword; I alone have escaped to tell you." ¹⁸While he was still speaking, another came and said, "Your sons and daughters were eating and drinking wine in their eldest brother's house, ¹⁹and suddenly a great wind came across the desert, struck the four corners of the house, and it fell on the young people, and they are dead; I alone have escaped to tell you."

20 Then Job arose, tore his robe, shaved his head, and fell on the ground and worshiped. ²¹He said, "Naked I came

a Heb *sons of God*   *b* Or *the Accuser*; Heb *ha-satan* from my mother's womb, and naked shall I return there; the LORD gave, and the LORD has taken away; blessed be the name of the LORD."

22 In all this Job did not sin or charge God with wrong-doing.

Attack on Job's Health

2 One day the heavenly beings[a] came to present themselves before the LORD, and Satan[b] also came among them to present himself before the LORD. ²The LORD said to Satan,[b] "Where have you come from?" Satan[b] answered the LORD, "From going to and fro on the earth, and from walking up and down on it." ³The LORD said to Satan,[b] "Have you considered my servant Job? There is no one like him on the earth, a blameless and upright man who fears God and turns away from evil. He still persists in his integrity, although you incited me against him, to destroy him for no reason." ⁴Then Satan[b] answered the LORD, "Skin for skin! All that people have they will give to save their lives.[c] ⁵But stretch out your hand now and touch his bone and his flesh, and he will curse you to your face." ⁶The LORD said to Satan,[b] "Very well, he is in your power; only spare his life."

7 So Satan[b] went out from the presence of the LORD, and inflicted loathsome sores on Job from the sole of his foot to the crown of his head. ⁸Job[d] took a potsherd with which to scrape himself, and sat among the ashes.

9 Then his wife said to him, "Do you still persist in your integrity? Curse[e] God, and die." ¹⁰But he said to her, "You speak as any foolish woman would speak. Shall we receive the good at the hand of God, and not receive the bad?" In all this Job did not sin with his lips.

Job's Three Friends

11 Now when Job's three friends heard of all these troubles that had come upon him, each of them set out from his home—Eliphaz the Temanite, Bildad the Shuhite, and Zophar the Naamathite. They met together to go and console and comfort him. ¹²When they saw him from a distance, they did not recognize him, and they raised their voices and wept aloud; they tore their robes and threw dust in the air upon their heads. ¹³They sat with him on the ground seven days and seven nights, and no one spoke a word to him, for they saw that his suffering was very great.

Job Curses the Day He Was Born

3 After this Job opened his mouth and cursed the day of his birth. ²Job said:
³ "Let the day perish in which I was born,
      and the night that said,
      'A man-child is conceived.'
⁴ Let that day be darkness!
      May God above not seek it,
      or light shine on it.
⁵ Let gloom and deep darkness claim it.
      Let clouds settle upon it;
      let the blackness of the day terrify it.

Wordless Comfort

JOB 2.11–13

Job's friends come to Job to "console and comfort him." For seven days they throw dust on their heads (a sign of grieving) and sit with him; no one says a word. At this point, Job's friends model compassionate friendship—patient presence with someone in a difficult situation.

When have you experienced such wordless comfort? Do you have friends with whom no words are necessary? Give thanks for those who understand you and stand with you emotionally, especially when you grieve. Consider whether there is someone who needs your presence and support. How can you indicate your concern and support if you are not able to be physically present with someone you care about during his or her hard times?

See Meeting God in Service

---

a Heb *sons of God*   *b* Or *the Accuser*; Heb *ha-satan*   *c* Or *All that the man has he will give for his life*   *d* Heb *He*   *e* Heb *Bless*

Honest With God

JOB 3.1–15

In strong language, Job wishes that he had died at birth and compares death to release and freedom. This is not a picture of someone tiptoeing into God's presence, whispering mild displeasure. Job rails at God, expressing his anguish in complete openness and honesty.

Following Job's example, offer to God your honest feelings, whatever they are. What do you want to say to God? Express the deepest pain or the deepest joy in your heart. God listens to us and welcomes the open expression of all of our emotions.

See Meeting God in Prayer

6   That night—let thick darkness seize it!
     let it not rejoice among the days of the year;
     let it not come into the number of the months.
7   Yes, let that night be barren;
     let no joyful cry be heard[a] in it.
8   Let those curse it who curse the Sea,[b]
     those who are skilled to rouse up Leviathan.
9   Let the stars of its dawn be dark;
     let it hope for light, but have none;
     may it not see the eyelids of the morning—
10   because it did not shut the doors of my mother's
          womb,
     and hide trouble from my eyes.
11   "Why did I not die at birth,
     come forth from the womb and expire?
12   Why were there knees to receive me,
     or breasts for me to suck?
13   Now I would be lying down and quiet;
     I would be asleep; then I would be at rest
14   with kings and counselors of the earth
     who rebuild ruins for themselves,
15   or with princes who have gold,
     who fill their houses with silver.
16   Or why was I not buried like a stillborn child,
     like an infant that never sees the light?
17   There the wicked cease from troubling,
     and there the weary are at rest.
18   There the prisoners are at ease together;
     they do not hear the voice of the taskmaster.
19   The small and the great are there,
     and the slaves are free from their masters.

20   "Why is light given to one in misery,
     and life to the bitter in soul,
21   who long for death, but it does not come,
     and dig for it more than for hidden treasures;
22   who rejoice exceedingly,
     and are glad when they find the grave?
23   Why is light given to one who cannot see the way,
     whom God has fenced in?
24   For my sighing comes like[c] my bread,
     and my groanings are poured out like water.
25   Truly the thing that I fear comes upon me,
     and what I dread befalls me.
26   I am not at ease, nor am I quiet;
     I have no rest; but trouble comes."

Eliphaz Speaks: Job Has Sinned

4 Then Eliphaz the Temanite answered:
2 "If one ventures a word with you, will you be offended?
     But who can keep from speaking?
3   See, you have instructed many;
     you have strengthened the weak hands.
4   Your words have supported those who were
          stumbling,
     and you have made firm the feeble knees.
5   But now it has come to you, and you are impatient;
     it touches you, and you are dismayed.

a Heb *come*   *b* Cn: Heb *day*   *c* Heb *before*

⁶ Is not your fear of God your confidence,
and the integrity of your ways your hope?

⁷ "Think now, who that was innocent ever perished?
Or where were the upright cut off?
⁸ As I have seen, those who plow iniquity
and sow trouble reap the same.
⁹ By the breath of God they perish,
and by the blast of his anger they are consumed.
¹⁰ The roar of the lion, the voice of the fierce lion,
and the teeth of the young lions are broken.
¹¹ The strong lion perishes for lack of prey,
and the whelps of the lioness are scattered.

¹² "Now a word came stealing to me,
my ear received the whisper of it.
¹³ Amid thoughts from visions of the night,
when deep sleep falls on mortals,
¹⁴ dread came upon me, and trembling,
which made all my bones shake.
¹⁵ A spirit glided past my face;
the hair of my flesh bristled.
¹⁶ It stood still,
but I could not discern its appearance.
A form was before my eyes;
there was silence, then I heard a voice:
¹⁷ 'Can mortals be righteous before*a* God?
Can human beings be pure before*a* their Maker?
¹⁸ Even in his servants he puts no trust,
and his angels he charges with error;
¹⁹ how much more those who live in houses of clay,
whose foundation is in the dust,
who are crushed like a moth.
²⁰ Between morning and evening they are destroyed;
they perish forever without any regarding it.
²¹ Their tent-cord is plucked up within them,
and they die devoid of wisdom.'

Job Is Corrected by God

5 "Call now; is there anyone who will answer you?
To which of the holy ones will you turn?
² Surely vexation kills the fool,
and jealousy slays the simple.
³ I have seen fools taking root,
but suddenly I cursed their dwelling.
⁴ Their children are far from safety,
they are crushed in the gate,
and there is no one to deliver them.
⁵ The hungry eat their harvest,
and they take it even out of the thorns;*b*
and the thirsty*c* pant after their wealth.
⁶ For misery does not come from the earth,
nor does trouble sprout from the ground;
⁷ but human beings are born to trouble
just as sparks*d* fly upward.

⁸ "As for me, I would seek God,
and to God I would commit my cause.

---

a Or *more than*   *b* Meaning of Heb uncertain   *c* Aquila Symmachus Syr
Vg: Heb *snare*   *d* Or *birds*; Heb *sons of Resheph*

Breaking the Silence

JOB 4.1–6

Eliphaz, Bildad and Zophar care about Job and have come a long way to be with him. But one of the trials Job has to bear is hearing advice from his friends. Eliphaz breaks the seven-day silence by offering Job the first of many pieces of advice: Be a good example. Job has taught others, Eliphaz says, and now has the opportunity to practice what he preaches. Though well-meaning, these words do not help Job.

When we experience difficulty, people often struggle to find something helpful to say to us. Imagine yourself in a desperate situation; someone says to you, "Be a good Christian. Show others how strong you are. People are watching." How would this make you feel? What would you want someone to say to you? What lessons does Job's friend offer you for helping those you care about?

See Meeting God in Community

More Advice

JOB 5.8,17–21

"God is disciplining you," is the next admonition. We know from Job 1.9–12 that these calamities have not come from God, though Job's friend says otherwise. Have you ever said or heard words like these: "God is trying to teach you something through this. Just pay attention and you'll see it"?

Make a point of being prepared to comfort others before you are called to do so. Perhaps you could ask a few people who have experienced loss what kinds of words and advice helped them most when they were suffering. Read a book about comforting the grieving. Collect a file of encouraging and empathetic poetry or prayers to share with someone who is grieving.

See Meeting God in Everyday Life

9   He does great things and unsearchable,
    marvelous things without number.
10 He gives rain on the earth
    and sends waters on the fields;
11 he sets on high those who are lowly,
    and those who mourn are lifted to safety.
12 He frustrates the devices of the crafty,
    so that their hands achieve no success.
13 He takes the wise in their own craftiness;
    and the schemes of the wily are brought to a
    quick end.
14 They meet with darkness in the daytime,
    and grope at noonday as in the night.
15 But he saves the needy from the sword of their
    mouth,
    from the hand of the mighty.
16 So the poor have hope,
    and injustice shuts its mouth.

17 "How happy is the one whom God reproves;
    therefore do not despise the discipline of the
    Almighty.[a]
18 For he wounds, but he binds up;
    he strikes, but his hands heal.
19 He will deliver you from six troubles;
    in seven no harm shall touch you.
20 In famine he will redeem you from death,
    and in war from the power of the sword.
21 You shall be hidden from the scourge of the tongue,
    and shall not fear destruction when it comes.
22 At destruction and famine you shall laugh,
    and shall not fear the wild animals of the earth.
23 For you shall be in league with the stones of the
    field,
    and the wild animals shall be at peace with you.
24 You shall know that your tent is safe,
    you shall inspect your fold and miss nothing.
25 You shall know that your descendants will be
    many,
    and your offspring like the grass of the earth.
26 You shall come to your grave in ripe old age,
    as a shock of grain comes up to the threshing
    floor in its season.
27 See, we have searched this out; it is true.
    Hear, and know it for yourself."

Job Replies: My Complaint Is Just

6 Then Job answered:
2 "O that my vexation were weighed,
    and all my calamity laid in the balances!
3 For then it would be heavier than the sand of the
    sea;
    therefore my words have been rash.
4 For the arrows of the Almighty[a] are in me;
    my spirit drinks their poison;
    the terrors of God are arrayed against me.
5 Does the wild ass bray over its grass,
    or the ox low over its fodder?
6 Can that which is tasteless be eaten without salt,

a Traditional rendering of Heb Shaddai

or is there any flavor in the juice of mallows?*a*

7   My appetite refuses to touch them;
    they are like food that is loathsome to me.*a*

8   "O that I might have my request,
    and that God would grant my desire;
9   that it would please God to crush me,
    that he would let loose his hand and cut me off!
10 This would be my consolation;
    I would even exult*a* in unrelenting pain;
    for I have not denied the words of the Holy One.
11 What is my strength, that I should wait?
    And what is my end, that I should be patient?
12 Is my strength the strength of stones,
    or is my flesh bronze?
13 In truth I have no help in me,
    and any resource is driven from me.

14 "Those who withhold*b* kindness from a friend
    forsake the fear of the Almighty.*c*
15 My companions are treacherous like a torrent-bed,
    like freshets that pass away,
16 that run dark with ice,
    turbid with melting snow.
17 In time of heat they disappear;
    when it is hot, they vanish from their place.
18 The caravans turn aside from their course;
    they go up into the waste, and perish.
19 The caravans of Tema look,
    the travelers of Sheba hope.
20 They are disappointed because they were
        confident;
    they come there and are confounded.
21 Such you have now become to me;*d*
    you see my calamity, and are afraid.
22 Have I said, 'Make me a gift'?
    Or, 'From your wealth offer a bribe for me'?
23 Or, 'Save me from an opponent's hand'?
    Or, 'Ransom me from the hand of oppressors'?

24 "Teach me, and I will be silent;
    make me understand how I have gone wrong.
25 How forceful are honest words!
    But your reproof, what does it reprove?
26 Do you think that you can reprove words,
    as if the speech of the desperate were wind?
27 You would even cast lots over the orphan,
    and bargain over your friend.

28 "But now, be pleased to look at me;
    for I will not lie to your face.
29 Turn, I pray, let no wrong be done.
    Turn now, my vindication is at stake.
30 Is there any wrong on my tongue?
    Cannot my taste discern calamity?

People of Flesh

JOB 6.8–17

Job compares his friends to streams that evaporate when the weather gets hot. Job's friends offer him no refreshment; they do not follow him into the darkness of his pain, grief and loss. Job says, "Is my flesh bronze?" (v.12). In other words, he cannot shut off his feelings as if he were inanimate. While he has great faith, he acknowledges that his emotions are real, and he refuses to deny them.

Are you a good listener? When someone pours out his or her feelings to you, do you minimize their emotions or deny that person's right to experience those emotions? Or do you acknowledge their feelings as real and legitimate, even if they are hard to listen to? Practice being a good listener. The next time someone expresses an emotion to you, show them you are open to hear. Reflect that emotion back to them without judging or minimizing it.

See Meeting God in Service

---

a Meaning of Heb uncertain   *b* Syr Vg Compare Tg: Meaning of Heb uncertain   *c* Traditional rendering of Heb *Shaddai*   *d* Cn Compare Gk Syr: Meaning of Heb uncertain

No Sugarcoating

JOB 7.11–15

Great suffering often begets great honesty. Job doesn't sugarcoat his experience with polite distance. He complains bitterly. Job's honesty allows us to identify with him in his pain.

In spoken prayer or in your personal journal, pour out your complaints to God. God can take it. Be utterly honest about your experience. Trust that God is able to accept the full range of your emotions as he did Job's.

See Meeting God in Prayer

Job: My Suffering Is without End

7 "Do not human beings have a hard service on earth,
and are not their days like the days of a laborer?
2 Like a slave who longs for the shadow,
and like laborers who look for their wages,
3 so I am allotted months of emptiness,
and nights of misery are apportioned to me.
4 When I lie down I say, 'When shall I rise?'
But the night is long,
and I am full of tossing until dawn.
5 My flesh is clothed with worms and dirt;
my skin hardens, then breaks out again.
6 My days are swifter than a weaver's shuttle,
and come to their end without hope.*a*

7 "Remember that my life is a breath;
my eye will never again see good.
8 The eye that beholds me will see me no more;
while your eyes are upon me, I shall be gone.
9 As the cloud fades and vanishes,
so those who go down to Sheol do not come up;
10 they return no more to their houses,
nor do their places know them any more.

11 "Therefore I will not restrain my mouth;
I will speak in the anguish of my spirit;
I will complain in the bitterness of my soul.
12 Am I the Sea, or the Dragon,
that you set a guard over me?
13 When I say, 'My bed will comfort me,
my couch will ease my complaint,'
14 then you scare me with dreams
and terrify me with visions,
15 so that I would choose strangling
and death rather than this body.
16 I loathe my life; I would not live forever.
Let me alone, for my days are a breath.
17 What are human beings, that you make so much of them,
that you set your mind on them,
18 visit them every morning,
test them every moment?
19 Will you not look away from me for a while,
let me alone until I swallow my spittle?
20 If I sin, what do I do to you, you watcher of humanity?
Why have you made me your target?
Why have I become a burden to you?
21 Why do you not pardon my transgression
and take away my iniquity?
For now I shall lie in the earth;
you will seek me, but I shall not be."

Bildad Speaks: Job Should Repent

8 Then Bildad the Shuhite answered:
2 "How long will you say these things,
and the words of your mouth be a great wind?
3 Does God pervert justice?

a Or as the thread runs out

Or does the Almighty[a] pervert the right?
4 If your children sinned against him,
    he delivered them into the power of their
        transgression.
5 If you will seek God
    and make supplication to the Almighty,[a]
6 if you are pure and upright,
    surely then he will rouse himself for you
    and restore to you your rightful place.
7 Though your beginning was small,
    your latter days will be very great.

8 "For inquire now of bygone generations,
    and consider what their ancestors have found;
9 for we are but of yesterday, and we know nothing,
    for our days on earth are but a shadow.
10 Will they not teach you and tell you
    and utter words out of their understanding?

11 "Can papyrus grow where there is no marsh?
    Can reeds flourish where there is no water?
12 While yet in flower and not cut down,
    they wither before any other plant.
13 Such are the paths of all who forget God;
    the hope of the godless shall perish.
14 Their confidence is gossamer,
    a spider's house their trust.
15 If one leans against its house, it will not stand;
    if one lays hold of it, it will not endure.
16 The wicked thrive[b] before the sun,
    and their shoots spread over the garden.
17 Their roots twine around the stoneheap;
    they live among the rocks.[c]
18 If they are destroyed from their place,
    then it will deny them, saying, 'I have never seen
        you.'
19 See, these are their happy ways,[d]
    and out of the earth still others will spring.

20 "See, God will not reject a blameless person,
    nor take the hand of evildoers.
21 He will yet fill your mouth with laughter,
    and your lips with shouts of joy.
22 Those who hate you will be clothed with shame,
    and the tent of the wicked will be no more."

Job Replies: There Is No Mediator

9 Then Job answered:
2 "Indeed I know that this is so;
    but how can a mortal be just before God?
3 If one wished to contend with him,
    one could not answer him once in a thousand.
4 He is wise in heart, and mighty in strength
    —who has resisted him, and succeeded?—
5 he who removes mountains, and they do not know
        it,
    when he overturns them in his anger;
6 who shakes the earth out of its place,

Another Strategy

JOB 8.1–7

Bildad offers another bit of advice: Take action. Repent. Do something. Job has the power to end his suffering if he'll just admit his sin, and then God will restore all that he has lost. Bildad's words are an attempt to protect his belief that he has power over what happens to himself. If Bildad were to admit that Job is innocent and righteous, then he would have to admit that his own good behavior is not a shield for himself either. But the truth is that loss, suffering and pain often strike for reasons that are not apparent. There is no defense against disaster.

Looking for reasons for suffering tempts us to think that we can control what happens to us. For example, we think that if we eat right, we won't ever get cancer. If we save money, we will always have financial security. Such rationalization tempts us to ignore our fears and hide from them. What are some of the thought processes you use to insulate yourself from fear? After you identify them, acknowledge them and offer your need to rationalize suffering, and your fear of suffering, to God.

a Traditional rendering of Heb Shaddai   b Heb He thrives   c Gk Vg:
Meaning of Heb uncertain   d Meaning of Heb uncertain

Innocent!

JOB 9.14–22

Job knows his suffering is not caused by anything he has done or left undone. Yet he also acknowledges God's power—and is mystified that there seems to be no justice; calamity comes to "both the blameless and the wicked." This shakes Job's concept of God, but the examination is part of Job's wrestling with what has happened to him.

Life often forces us to rethink what we believe. How have your beliefs changed over time as you have journeyed with God? What do you affirm in your heart as true about God? Write a creed that you can say with honesty and conviction: "I believe that God . . . ." or "I believe in a God who . . ." Include several statements. Repeat your creed as a way to begin your times of prayer.

See Meeting God in Prayer

and its pillars tremble;

7 who commands the sun, and it does not rise;
   who seals up the stars;

8 who alone stretched out the heavens
   and trampled the waves of the Sea;*a*

9 who made the Bear and Orion,
   the Pleiades and the chambers of the south;

10 who does great things beyond understanding,
   and marvelous things without number.

11 Look, he passes by me, and I do not see him;
   he moves on, but I do not perceive him.

12 He snatches away; who can stop him?
   Who will say to him, 'What are you doing?'

13 "God will not turn back his anger;
   the helpers of Rahab bowed beneath him.

14 How then can I answer him,
   choosing my words with him?

15 Though I am innocent, I cannot answer him;
   I must appeal for mercy to my accuser.*b*

16 If I summoned him and he answered me,
   I do not believe that he would listen to my voice.

17 For he crushes me with a tempest,
   and multiplies my wounds without cause;

18 he will not let me get my breath,
   but fills me with bitterness.

19 If it is a contest of strength, he is the strong one!
   If it is a matter of justice, who can summon him?*c*

20 Though I am innocent, my own mouth would condemn me;
   though I am blameless, he would prove me perverse.

21 I am blameless; I do not know myself;
   I loathe my life.

22 It is all one; therefore I say,
   he destroys both the blameless and the wicked.

23 When disaster brings sudden death,
   he mocks at the calamity*d* of the innocent.

24 The earth is given into the hand of the wicked;
   he covers the eyes of its judges—
   if it is not he, who then is it?

25 "My days are swifter than a runner;
   they flee away, they see no good.

26 They go by like skiffs of reed,
   like an eagle swooping on the prey.

27 If I say, 'I will forget my complaint;
   I will put off my sad countenance and be of good cheer,'

28 I become afraid of all my suffering,
   for I know you will not hold me innocent.

29 I shall be condemned;
   why then do I labor in vain?

30 If I wash myself with soap
   and cleanse my hands with lye,

31 yet you will plunge me into filth,
   and my own clothes will abhor me.

---

a Or *trampled the back of the sea dragon*   *b* Or *for my right*   *c* Compare Gk: Heb *me*   *d* Meaning of Heb uncertain

³² For he is not a mortal, as I am, that I might answer
    him,
      that we should come to trial together.
³³ There is no umpire^a between us,
      who might lay his hand on us both.
³⁴ If he would take his rod away from me,
      and not let dread of him terrify me,
³⁵ then I would speak without fear of him,
      for I know I am not what I am thought to be.^b

Job: I Loathe My Life

10 "I loathe my life;
      I will give free utterance to my complaint;
      I will speak in the bitterness of my soul.
² I will say to God, Do not condemn me;
      let me know why you contend against me.
³ Does it seem good to you to oppress,
      to despise the work of your hands
      and favor the schemes of the wicked?
⁴ Do you have eyes of flesh?
      Do you see as humans see?
⁵ Are your days like the days of mortals,
      or your years like human years,
⁶ that you seek out my iniquity
      and search for my sin,
⁷ although you know that I am not guilty,
      and there is no one to deliver out of your hand?
⁸ Your hands fashioned and made me;
      and now you turn and destroy me.^c
⁹ Remember that you fashioned me like clay;
      and will you turn me to dust again?
¹⁰ Did you not pour me out like milk
      and curdle me like cheese?
¹¹ You clothed me with skin and flesh,
      and knit me together with bones and sinews.
¹² You have granted me life and steadfast love,
      and your care has preserved my spirit.
¹³ Yet these things you hid in your heart;
      I know that this was your purpose.
¹⁴ If I sin, you watch me,
      and do not acquit me of my iniquity.
¹⁵ If I am wicked, woe to me!
      If I am righteous, I cannot lift up my head,
    for I am filled with disgrace
      and look upon my affliction.
¹⁶ Bold as a lion you hunt me;
      you repeat your exploits against me.
¹⁷ You renew your witnesses against me,
      and increase your vexation toward me;
      you bring fresh troops against me.^d
¹⁸ "Why did you bring me forth from the womb?
      Would that I had died before any eye had seen
        me,
¹⁹ and were as though I had not been,
      carried from the womb to the grave.

---

a Another reading is *Would that there were an umpire*   *b* Cn: Heb *for I am
not so in myself*   *c* Cn Compare Gk Syr: Heb *made me together all around,
and you destroy me*   *d* Cn Compare Gk: Heb *toward me; changes and a troop
are with me*

Put on a Happy Face

JOB 9.27

Job tells his friends that he could put his questions and struggles out of his mind and "forget [his] complaint . . . and be of good cheer." But that would not be honest, and Job is an honest man. He refuses to run from his questions and struggles. He relentlessly pursues God.

Sometimes it *is* necessary to do what Job suggests—to temporarily set aside our pain and struggles. We have to go to work or to school or take care of daily responsibilities. But we also need a safe place and non-threatening, open relationships in which to deal with our concerns. What people or places offer you the opportunity to be completely honest without hiding your feelings? Thank God for these people, times and places. How can you offer such an opportunity and place of hospitality to others?

See Meeting God in Service

Pushing Away

JOB 10.18–22

"Let me die," Job says in despair. He says that being alone would be better than being with his friends. Job pushes away his comforters; it seems as if he is even pushing God away. Do you sometimes prefer solitude to being with others? Do you experience God's presence more in solitude or more when you are with other believers? How does God call to you when life seems pointless and dark? Through scripture? Through relationships with others? Through music? Consider how you can reach out to someone who feels as Job does here. How can you accept their desire for privacy and still support them?

See Meeting God in Service

20 Are not the days of my life few?*a*
Let me alone, that I may find a little comfort*b*
21 before I go, never to return,
to the land of gloom and deep darkness,
22 the land of gloom*c* and chaos,
where light is like darkness."

Zophar Speaks: Job's Guilt Deserves Punishment

11 Then Zophar the Naamathite answered:
2 "Should a multitude of words go unanswered,
and should one full of talk be vindicated?
3 Should your babble put others to silence,
and when you mock, shall no one shame you?
4 For you say, 'My conduct*d* is pure,
and I am clean in God's*e* sight.'
5 But O that God would speak,
and open his lips to you,
6 and that he would tell you the secrets of wisdom!
For wisdom is many-sided.*f*
Know then that God exacts of you less than your
guilt deserves.

7 "Can you find out the deep things of God?
Can you find out the limit of the Almighty?*g*
8 It is higher than heaven*h*—what can you do?
Deeper than Sheol—what can you know?
9 Its measure is longer than the earth,
and broader than the sea.
10 If he passes through, and imprisons,
and assembles for judgment, who can hinder
him?
11 For he knows those who are worthless;
when he sees iniquity, will he not consider it?
12 But a stupid person will get understanding,
when a wild ass is born human.*f*

13 "If you direct your heart rightly,
you will stretch out your hands toward him.
14 If iniquity is in your hand, put it far away,
and do not let wickedness reside in your tents.
15 Surely then you will lift up your face without
blemish;
you will be secure, and will not fear.
16 You will forget your misery;
you will remember it as waters that have passed
away.
17 And your life will be brighter than the noonday;
its darkness will be like the morning.
18 And you will have confidence, because there is
hope;
you will be protected*i* and take your rest in
safety.
19 You will lie down, and no one will make you afraid;
many will entreat your favor.
20 But the eyes of the wicked will fail;

a Cn Compare Gk Syr: Heb *Are not my days few? Let him cease!* b Heb *that
I may brighten up a little* c Heb *gloom as darkness, deep darkness*
d Gk: Heb *teaching* e Heb *your* f Meaning of Heb uncertain
g Traditional rendering of Heb *Shaddai* h Heb *The heights of heaven*
i Or *you will look around*

all way of escape will be lost to them,
and their hope is to breathe their last."

Job Replies: I Am a Laughingstock

12 Then Job answered:
² "No doubt you are the people,
and wisdom will die with you.

³ But I have understanding as well as you;
I am not inferior to you.
Who does not know such things as these?

⁴ I am a laughingstock to my friends;
I, who called upon God and he answered me,
a just and blameless man, I am a laughingstock.

⁵ Those at ease have contempt for misfortune,ᵃ
but it is ready for those whose feet are unstable.

⁶ The tents of robbers are at peace,
and those who provoke God are secure,
who bring their god in their hands.ᵇ

⁷ "But ask the animals, and they will teach you;
the birds of the air, and they will tell you;

⁸ ask the plants of the earth,ᶜ and they will teach you;
and the fish of the sea will declare to you.

⁹ Who among all these does not know
that the hand of the Lᴏʀᴅ has done this?

¹⁰ In his hand is the life of every living thing
and the breath of every human being.

¹¹ Does not the ear test words
as the palate tastes food?

¹² Is wisdom with the aged,
and understanding in length of days?

¹³ "With Godᵈ are wisdom and strength;
he has counsel and understanding.

¹⁴ If he tears down, no one can rebuild;
if he shuts someone in, no one can open up.

¹⁵ If he withholds the waters, they dry up;
if he sends them out, they overwhelm the land.

¹⁶ With him are strength and wisdom;
the deceived and the deceiver are his.

¹⁷ He leads counselors away stripped,
and makes fools of judges.

¹⁸ He looses the sash of kings,
and binds a waistcloth on their loins.

¹⁹ He leads priests away stripped,
and overthrows the mighty.

²⁰ He deprives of speech those who are trusted,
and takes away the discernment of the elders.

²¹ He pours contempt on princes,
and looses the belt of the strong.

²² He uncovers the deeps out of darkness,
and brings deep darkness to light.

²³ He makes nations great, then destroys them;
he enlarges nations, then leads them away.

²⁴ He strips understanding from the leadersᵉ of the
earth,
and makes them wander in a pathless waste.

Right Thinking

JOB 11.13–18

If you devote your heart to him, argues Zophar, God will reward you. What a seductive argument this is! If we believe a particular way and do particular things, God will make us successful. Have you heard people say things like this?

We may broaden this way of thinking even more to say that we can influence the way God treats us by becoming better people. Are you tempted to believe that you earn God's love when you do certain things or when you refrain from doing other things? Pray for the faith to believe that God loves you and embraces you just as you are. Ask God for the grace to demonstrate the same kind of acceptance to the people you love.

See Meeting God in Prayer

ᵃ Meaning of Heb uncertain   ᵇ Or *whom God brought forth by his hand;*
Meaning of Heb uncertain   ᶜ Or *speak to the earth*   ᵈ Heb *him*
ᵉ Heb adds *of the people*

Without a Word

JOB 13.4–5

Sometimes speaking is the wrong way to try to help someone in pain, as Job so vividly demonstrates here. Recall a time when someone helped you without saying a word, and give thanks. What did that person do that helped you? For the next twenty-four hours, challenge yourself to find ways to support, encourage, and comfort others without offering advice or even without speaking.

See Meeting God in Service

25 They grope in the dark without light;
     he makes them stagger like a drunkard.

13 "Look, my eye has seen all this,
     my ear has heard and understood it.
2 What you know, I also know;
     I am not inferior to you.
3 But I would speak to the Almighty,*a*
     and I desire to argue my case with God.
4 As for you, you whitewash with lies;
     all of you are worthless physicians.
5 If you would only keep silent,
     that would be your wisdom!
6 Hear now my reasoning,
     and listen to the pleadings of my lips.
7 Will you speak falsely for God,
     and speak deceitfully for him?
8 Will you show partiality toward him,
     will you plead the case for God?
9 Will it be well with you when he searches you out?
     Or can you deceive him, as one person deceives another?
10 He will surely rebuke you
     if in secret you show partiality.
11 Will not his majesty terrify you,
     and the dread of him fall upon you?
12 Your maxims are proverbs of ashes,
     your defenses are defenses of clay.

13 "Let me have silence, and I will speak,
     and let come on me what may.
14 I will take my flesh in my teeth,
     and put my life in my hand.*b*
15 See, he will kill me; I have no hope;*c*
     but I will defend my ways to his face.
16 This will be my salvation,
     that the godless shall not come before him.
17 Listen carefully to my words,
     and let my declaration be in your ears.
18 I have indeed prepared my case;
     I know that I shall be vindicated.
19 Who is there that will contend with me?
     For then I would be silent and die.

Job's Despondent Prayer

20 Only grant two things to me,
     then I will not hide myself from your face:
21 withdraw your hand far from me,
     and do not let dread of you terrify me.
22 Then call, and I will answer;
     or let me speak, and you reply to me.
23 How many are my iniquities and my sins?
     Make me know my transgression and my sin.
24 Why do you hide your face,
     and count me as your enemy?
25 Will you frighten a windblown leaf
     and pursue dry chaff?

a Traditional rendering of Heb *Shaddai*   *b* Gk: Heb *Why should I take . . . in my hand?*   *c* Or *Though he kill me, yet I will trust in him*

26 For you write bitter things against me,
    and make me reap[a] the iniquities of my youth.
27 You put my feet in the stocks,
    and watch all my paths;
    you set a bound to the soles of my feet.
28 One wastes away like a rotten thing,
    like a garment that is moth-eaten.

14 "A mortal, born of woman, few of days and full
    of trouble,
2 comes up like a flower and withers,
    flees like a shadow and does not last.
3 Do you fix your eyes on such a one?
    Do you bring me into judgment with you?
4 Who can bring a clean thing out of an unclean?
    No one can.
5 Since their days are determined,
    and the number of their months is known to you,
    and you have appointed the bounds that they
      cannot pass,
6 look away from them, and desist,[b]
    that they may enjoy, like laborers, their days.

7 "For there is hope for a tree,
    if it is cut down, that it will sprout again,
    and that its shoots will not cease.
8 Though its root grows old in the earth,
    and its stump dies in the ground,
9 yet at the scent of water it will bud
    and put forth branches like a young plant.
10 But mortals die, and are laid low;
    humans expire, and where are they?
11 As waters fail from a lake,
    and a river wastes away and dries up,
12 so mortals lie down and do not rise again;
    until the heavens are no more, they will not
      awake
    or be roused out of their sleep.
13 O that you would hide me in Sheol,
    that you would conceal me until your wrath is
      past,
    that you would appoint me a set time, and
      remember me!
14 If mortals die, will they live again?
    All the days of my service I would wait
    until my release should come.
15 You would call, and I would answer you;
    you would long for the work of your hands.
16 For then you would not[c] number my steps,
    you would not keep watch over my sin;
17 my transgression would be sealed up in a bag,
    and you would cover over my iniquity.

18 "But the mountain falls and crumbles away,
    and the rock is removed from its place;
19 the waters wear away the stones;
    the torrents wash away the soil of the earth;
    so you destroy the hope of mortals.

Any One of Us

JOB 13.22–24

Reading the book of Job can make us feel very vulnerable. If such disasters can happen to a good man like Job, we must consider that tragedy can strike any one of us.

Here Job cries out in prayer, remaining vulnerable and reaching out to God even in his terrible situation. Job clings to God and will not let go. What ways of worshiping or praying help you to cling to God during difficult times? What are some of the hymns you might sing when you are down? Think of some music CDs you might use as "music therapy" the next time you are tense, anxious or depressed—music that will help calm you and help you focus on God in prayer. Set them aside for just such an occasion.

See Meeting God in Worship

---

a Heb *inherit*   *b* Cn: Heb *that they may desist*   *c* Syr: Heb lacks *not*

Protecting God's Reputation

JOB 15.4-5

Eliphaz offers another painful comment: Job is calling the faith into question, undermining religion and interfering with others' devotion to God by his response to his tragedy. Job's friend seems more interested in protecting his perception of "the faith" than in helping Job. Job is alone.

Have you ever felt completely alone before God—when it seemed as if "religion" had nothing to offer you? Have you ever been abruptly counseled to put aside your needs and your pain and to think of others first? Or have you felt pressured to keep your struggles quiet in order to be a "good witness"? In prayer, sit alone in a dark room. Ask God to hold on to you when others leave you.

See Meeting God in Prayer

20 You prevail forever against them, and they pass away;
    you change their countenance, and send them away.
21 Their children come to honor, and they do not know it;
    they are brought low, and it goes unnoticed.
22 They feel only the pain of their own bodies,
    and mourn only for themselves."

Eliphaz Speaks: Job Undermines Religion

15 Then Eliphaz the Temanite answered:
2 "Should the wise answer with windy knowledge,
    and fill themselves with the east wind?
3 Should they argue in unprofitable talk,
    or in words with which they can do no good?
4 But you are doing away with the fear of God,
    and hindering meditation before God.
5 For your iniquity teaches your mouth,
    and you choose the tongue of the crafty.
6 Your own mouth condemns you, and not I;
    your own lips testify against you.

7 "Are you the firstborn of the human race?
    Were you brought forth before the hills?
8 Have you listened in the council of God?
    And do you limit wisdom to yourself?
9 What do you know that we do not know?
    What do you understand that is not clear to us?
10 The gray-haired and the aged are on our side,
    those older than your father.
11 Are the consolations of God too small for you,
    or the word that deals gently with you?
12 Why does your heart carry you away,
    and why do your eyes flash,[a]
13 so that you turn your spirit against God,
    and let such words go out of your mouth?
14 What are mortals, that they can be clean?
    Or those born of woman, that they can be righteous?
15 God puts no trust even in his holy ones,
    and the heavens are not clean in his sight;
16 how much less one who is abominable and corrupt,
    one who drinks iniquity like water!

17 "I will show you; listen to me;
    what I have seen I will declare—
18 what sages have told,
    and their ancestors have not hidden,
19 to whom alone the land was given,
    and no stranger passed among them.
20 The wicked writhe in pain all their days,
    through all the years that are laid up for the ruthless.
21 Terrifying sounds are in their ears;
    in prosperity the destroyer will come upon them.
22 They despair of returning from darkness,
    and they are destined for the sword.

a Meaning of Heb uncertain

23 They wander abroad for bread, saying, 'Where is
   it?'
   They know that a day of darkness is ready at
   hand;
24 distress and anguish terrify them;
   they prevail against them, like a king prepared for
   battle.
25 Because they stretched out their hands against God,
   and bid defiance to the Almighty,*a*
26 running stubbornly against him
   with a thick-bossed shield;
27 because they have covered their faces with their fat,
   and gathered fat upon their loins,
28 they will live in desolate cities,
   in houses that no one should inhabit,
   houses destined to become heaps of ruins;
29 they will not be rich, and their wealth will not
   endure,
   nor will they strike root in the earth;*b*
30 they will not escape from darkness;
   the flame will dry up their shoots,
   and their blossom*c* will be swept away*d* by the
   wind.
31 Let them not trust in emptiness, deceiving
   themselves;
   for emptiness will be their recompense.
32 It will be paid in full before their time,
   and their branch will not be green.
33 They will shake off their unripe grape, like the vine,
   and cast off their blossoms, like the olive tree.
34 For the company of the godless is barren,
   and fire consumes the tents of bribery.
35 They conceive mischief and bring forth evil
   and their heart prepares deceit."

Job Reaffirms His Innocence

16 Then Job answered:
2 "I have heard many such things;
   miserable comforters are you all.
3 Have windy words no limit?
   Or what provokes you that you keep on talking?
4 I also could talk as you do,
   if you were in my place;
   I could join words together against you,
   and shake my head at you.
5 I could encourage you with my mouth,
   and the solace of my lips would assuage your
   pain.

6 "If I speak, my pain is not assuaged,
   and if I forbear, how much of it leaves me?
7 Surely now God has worn me out;
   he has*e* made desolate all my company.
8 And he has*e* shriveled me up,
   which is a witness against me;
   my leanness has risen up against me,
   and it testifies to my face.

Naked and Alone

JOB 16.1–4

Job sits naked in the dirt; his family, possessions and health are all gone. He has nothing and is nothing; his friends don't understand the depth of his emotions.

Friends cannot always understand; sometimes, because of their own fears and doubts, they fail to be able or available to help us when we most need them. Think of a friend who has failed you, someone you counted on for help but who did not deliver. Pray for that friend and for your relationship. Think of another time when this same friend helped you and showed faithful care; express your thanks in whatever way would be meaningful to you. How does that friend's faithfulness provide an image of God's reliable and loving presence?

See Meeting God in Community

---

a Traditional rendering of Heb *Shaddai*   *b* Vg: Meaning of Heb uncertain
c Gk: Heb *mouth*   *d* Cn: Heb *will depart*   *e* Heb *you have*

Injury or Heartache?

JOB 16.11–17

Job feels assaulted. He expresses his inner pain in graphic metaphors, using images of injury to his body. His physical pain is difficult, but his heartache is even more bruising.

Think about times of anguish and upheaval when you feel assaulted by life. Much is made these days of the ways our emotions affect our bodies. Do you have headaches, an upset stomach, backaches, chest pains, a stiff neck or muscle aches? In difficult times, what would help you pay attention to the signals of distress that your body sends? Sit in God's presence and open your hands with palms upward as a way of opening yourself to God. What emotional, spiritual or physical pain do you offer to God?

See Meeting God in Prayer

9   He has torn me in his wrath, and hated me;
  he has gnashed his teeth at me;
  my adversary sharpens his eyes against me.
10 They have gaped at me with their mouths;
  they have struck me insolently on the cheek;
  they mass themselves together against me.
11 God gives me up to the ungodly,
  and casts me into the hands of the wicked.
12 I was at ease, and he broke me in two;
  he seized me by the neck and dashed me to pieces;
  he set me up as his target;
13 his archers surround me.
  He slashes open my kidneys, and shows no mercy;
  he pours out my gall on the ground.
14 He bursts upon me again and again;
  he rushes at me like a warrior.
15 I have sewed sackcloth upon my skin,
  and have laid my strength in the dust.
16 My face is red with weeping,
  and deep darkness is on my eyelids,
17 though there is no violence in my hands,
  and my prayer is pure.

18 "O earth, do not cover my blood;
  let my outcry find no resting place.
19 Even now, in fact, my witness is in heaven,
  and he that vouches for me is on high.
20 My friends scorn me;
  my eye pours out tears to God,
21 that he would maintain the right of a mortal with God,
  as*a* one does for a neighbor.
22 For when a few years have come,
  I shall go the way from which I shall not return.

Job Prays for Relief

17 My spirit is broken, my days are extinct,
  the grave is ready for me.
2   Surely there are mockers around me,
  and my eye dwells on their provocation.

3   "Lay down a pledge for me with yourself;
  who is there that will give surety for me?
4   Since you have closed their minds to understanding,
  therefore you will not let them triumph.
5   Those who denounce friends for reward—
  the eyes of their children will fail.

6   "He has made me a byword of the peoples,
  and I am one before whom people spit.
7   My eye has grown dim from grief,
  and all my members are like a shadow.
8   The upright are appalled at this,
  and the innocent stir themselves up against the godless.
9   Yet the righteous hold to their way,

a Syr Vg Tg: Heb *and*

and they that have clean hands grow stronger
  and stronger.
10 But you, come back now, all of you,
  and I shall not find a sensible person among you.
11 My days are past, my plans are broken off,
  the desires of my heart.
12 They make night into day;
  'The light,' they say, 'is near to the darkness.'*a*
13 If I look for Sheol as my house,
  if I spread my couch in darkness,
14 if I say to the Pit, 'You are my father,'
  and to the worm, 'My mother,' or 'My sister,'
15 where then is my hope?
  Who will see my hope?
16 Will it go down to the bars of Sheol?
  Shall we descend together into the dust?"

Bildad Speaks: God Punishes the Wicked

18 Then Bildad the Shuhite answered:
2 "How long will you hunt for words?
  Consider, and then we shall speak.
3 Why are we counted as cattle?
  Why are we stupid in your sight?
4 You who tear yourself in your anger—
  shall the earth be forsaken because of you,
  or the rock be removed out of its place?

5 "Surely the light of the wicked is put out,
  and the flame of their fire does not shine.
6 The light is dark in their tent,
  and the lamp above them is put out.
7 Their strong steps are shortened,
  and their own schemes throw them down.
8 For they are thrust into a net by their own feet,
  and they walk into a pitfall.
9 A trap seizes them by the heel;
  a snare lays hold of them.
10 A rope is hid for them in the ground,
  a trap for them in the path.
11 Terrors frighten them on every side,
  and chase them at their heels.
12 Their strength is consumed by hunger,*b*
  and calamity is ready for their stumbling.
13 By disease their skin is consumed,*c*
  the firstborn of Death consumes their limbs.
14 They are torn from the tent in which they trusted,
  and are brought to the king of terrors.
15 In their tents nothing remains;
  sulfur is scattered upon their habitations.
16 Their roots dry up beneath,
  and their branches wither above.
17 Their memory perishes from the earth,
  and they have no name in the street.
18 They are thrust from light into darkness,
  and driven out of the world.
19 They have no offspring or descendant among their
  people,
  and no survivor where they used to live.

Where Hope Is Found

JOB 17.15

"This is the first and principal benefit caused by [the] arid and dark night of [the soul]: the knowledge of oneself and of one's misery . . . These aridities and this emptiness of the faculties, compared with the abundance which the soul experienced before and the difficulty it now finds in good works, make it recognize its own lowliness . . . which in the time of its prosperity it was unable to see."

—JOHN OF THE CROSS,
The Dark Night of the Soul

---

a Meaning of Heb uncertain   *b* Or *Disaster is hungry for them*
c Cn: Heb *It consumes the limbs of his skin*

To Hurt or To Heal?

JOB 19.1–5

Job cries out for mercy. His friends torment him and "break [him] in pieces with words."

Words have power both to hurt and to heal. Words spoken to us by others shape our perceptions of ourselves; with our words we influence the perceptions others have of themselves. Looking back over your life, think of incidents where negative or hurtful words have been spoken to you. Think of negative or hurtful words you have spoken to others. Now ask God to mend the negative effects those words have had. Then think of life-giving words spoken to you, perhaps when you were a child, which may have helped you to feel loved or capable or deeply valued by God. Give thanks for those who have spoken such words to you. Reflect on how you can speak healing and life to those you encounter day by day.

See *Meeting God in Everyday Life*

20 They of the west are appalled at their fate,
　　and horror seizes those of the east.
21 Surely such are the dwellings of the ungodly,
　　such is the place of those who do not know God."

Job Replies: I Know That My Redeemer Lives

19 Then Job answered:
2 "How long will you torment me,
　　and break me in pieces with words?
3 These ten times you have cast reproach upon me;
　　are you not ashamed to wrong me?
4 And even if it is true that I have erred,
　　my error remains with me.
5 If indeed you magnify yourselves against me,
　　and make my humiliation an argument against me,
6 know then that God has put me in the wrong,
　　and closed his net around me.
7 Even when I cry out, 'Violence!' I am not answered;
　　I call aloud, but there is no justice.
8 He has walled up my way so that I cannot pass,
　　and he has set darkness upon my paths.
9 He has stripped my glory from me,
　　and taken the crown from my head.
10 He breaks me down on every side, and I am gone,
　　he has uprooted my hope like a tree.
11 He has kindled his wrath against me,
　　and counts me as his adversary.
12 His troops come on together;
　　they have thrown up siegeworks[a] against me,
　　and encamp around my tent.

13 "He has put my family far from me,
　　and my acquaintances are wholly estranged from me.
14 My relatives and my close friends have failed me;
15 the guests in my house have forgotten me;
my serving girls count me as a stranger;
　　I have become an alien in their eyes.
16 I call to my servant, but he gives me no answer;
　　I must myself plead with him.
17 My breath is repulsive to my wife;
　　I am loathsome to my own family.
18 Even young children despise me;
　　when I rise, they talk against me.
19 All my intimate friends abhor me,
　　and those whom I loved have turned against me.
20 My bones cling to my skin and to my flesh,
　　and I have escaped by the skin of my teeth.
21 Have pity on me, have pity on me, O you my friends,
　　for the hand of God has touched me!
22 Why do you, like God, pursue me,
　　never satisfied with my flesh?

23 "O that my words were written down!
　　O that they were inscribed in a book!
24 O that with an iron pen and with lead
　　they were engraved on a rock forever!

a Cn: Heb *their way*

25 For I know that my Redeemer*ᵃ* lives,
   and that at the last he*ᵇ* will stand upon the earth;*ᶜ*
26 and after my skin has been thus destroyed,
   then in*ᵈ* my flesh I shall see God,*ᵉ*
27 whom I shall see on my side,*ᶠ*
   and my eyes shall behold, and not another.
   My heart faints within me!
28 If you say, 'How we will persecute him!'
   and, 'The root of the matter is found in him';
29 be afraid of the sword,
   for wrath brings the punishment of the sword,
   so that you may know there is a judgment."

Zophar Speaks: Wickedness Receives Just Retribution

20 Then Zophar the Naamathite answered:
   2 "Pay attention! My thoughts urge me to answer,
      because of the agitation within me.
3 I hear censure that insults me,
   and a spirit beyond my understanding answers
      me.
4 Do you not know this from of old,
   ever since mortals were placed on earth,
5 that the exulting of the wicked is short,
   and the joy of the godless is but for a moment?
6 Even though they mount up high as the heavens,
   and their head reaches to the clouds,
7 they will perish forever like their own dung;
   those who have seen them will say, 'Where are
      they?'
8 They will fly away like a dream, and not be found;
   they will be chased away like a vision of the
      night.
9 The eye that saw them will see them no more,
   nor will their place behold them any longer.
10 Their children will seek the favor of the poor,
   and their hands will give back their wealth.
11 Their bodies, once full of youth,
   will lie down in the dust with them.
12 "Though wickedness is sweet in their mouth,
   though they hide it under their tongues,
13 though they are loath to let it go,
   and hold it in their mouths,
14 yet their food is turned in their stomachs;
   it is the venom of asps within them.
15 They swallow down riches and vomit them up
      again;
   God casts them out of their bellies.
16 They will suck the poison of asps;
   the tongue of a viper will kill them.
17 They will not look on the rivers,
   the streams flowing with honey and curds.
18 They will give back the fruit of their toil,
   and will not swallow it down;
from the profit of their trading
   they will get no enjoyment.
19 For they have crushed and abandoned the poor,
   they have seized a house that they did not build.

My Redeemer Lives

JOB 19.25–27

These famous verses contain the central truth of the book of Job: In the darkness of suffering, Job affirms that he will see God—if not in this life, then in eternity. He refuses to give up on God, remaining in relationship even when no comfort comes and his questions are unanswered.

Why do you continue to pray despite trouble and suffering? If you have ceased to pray, what is it about God that keeps you from abandoning God altogether? Close your eyes. Imagine yourself in a dark place, looking for God. What do you see? Can you see the road on which you travel or what surrounds you? Can you see God? If darkness is all you can see right now, as an expression of your faith and desire to see God, repeat Job's words in your heart: "I know that my Redeemer lives."

See Meeting God in Prayer

a Or *Vindicator*   *b* Or *that he the Last*   *c* Heb *dust*   *d* Or *without*
e Meaning of Heb of this verse uncertain   *f* Or *for myself*

667

What They Deserve

JOB 21.7–12

Zophar has said that the wicked are punished and that Job's problems are proof of his wickedness. Job challenges this, pointing out that the wicked often prosper.

That often seems to be the case. Drug dealers get rich. Tax evaders send their children to exclusive and expensive schools. People who hurt others for pleasure sleep at night and continue their tortures in the light of day. On a smaller scale, those who cheat and lie are promoted while honest and diligent workers go unnoticed and without reward. Alongside Job, we ask God for explanations.

If you have been harmed by wickedness, or if your life has been limited by wounds and scars, place the offender in God's hands as you pray. Ask for the willingness and grace to forgive that person and to trust God to uphold justice. Or reflect on recent news stories of cruelty and suffering, and hold the people involved before God in prayer.

See Meeting God in Prayer

20 "They knew no quiet in their bellies;
　　in their greed they let nothing escape.
21 There was nothing left after they had eaten;
　　therefore their prosperity will not endure.
22 In full sufficiency they will be in distress;
　　all the force of misery will come upon them.
23 To fill their belly to the full
　　God*a* will send his fierce anger into them,
　　and rain it upon them as their food.*b*
24 They will flee from an iron weapon;
　　a bronze arrow will strike them through.
25 It is drawn forth and comes out of their body,
　　and the glittering point comes out of their gall;
　　terrors come upon them.
26 Utter darkness is laid up for their treasures;
　　a fire fanned by no one will devour them;
　　what is left in their tent will be consumed.
27 The heavens will reveal their iniquity,
　　and the earth will rise up against them.
28 The possessions of their house will be carried
　　away,
　　dragged off in the day of God's*c* wrath.
29 This is the portion of the wicked from God,
　　the heritage decreed for them by God."

Job Replies: The Wicked Often Go Unpunished

21 Then Job answered:
2 "Listen carefully to my words,
　　and let this be your consolation.
3 Bear with me, and I will speak;
　　then after I have spoken, mock on.
4 As for me, is my complaint addressed to mortals?
　　Why should I not be impatient?
5 Look at me, and be appalled,
　　and lay your hand upon your mouth.
6 When I think of it I am dismayed,
　　and shuddering seizes my flesh.
7 Why do the wicked live on,
　　reach old age, and grow mighty in power?
8 Their children are established in their presence,
　　and their offspring before their eyes.
9 Their houses are safe from fear,
　　and no rod of God is upon them.
10 Their bull breeds without fail;
　　their cow calves and never miscarries.
11 They send out their little ones like a flock,
　　and their children dance around.
12 They sing to the tambourine and the lyre,
　　and rejoice to the sound of the pipe.
13 They spend their days in prosperity,
　　and in peace they go down to Sheol.
14 They say to God, 'Leave us alone!
　　We do not desire to know your ways.
15 What is the Almighty,*d* that we should serve him?
　　And what profit do we get if we pray to him?'
16 Is not their prosperity indeed their own
　　achievement?*e*
　　The plans of the wicked are repugnant to me.

a Heb *he*　*b* Cn: Meaning of Heb uncertain　*c* Heb *his*　*d* Traditional rendering of Heb *Shaddai*　*e* Heb *in their hand*

17 "How often is the lamp of the wicked put out?
How often does calamity come upon them?
How often does God*a* distribute pains in his
anger?

18 How often are they like straw before the wind,
and like chaff that the storm carries away?

19 You say, 'God stores up their iniquity for their
children.'
Let it be paid back to them, so that they may
know it.

20 Let their own eyes see their destruction,
and let them drink of the wrath of the Almighty.*b*

21 For what do they care for their household after
them,
when the number of their months is cut off?

22 Will any teach God knowledge,
seeing that he judges those that are on high?

23 One dies in full prosperity,
being wholly at ease and secure,

24 his loins full of milk
and the marrow of his bones moist.

25 Another dies in bitterness of soul,
never having tasted of good.

26 They lie down alike in the dust,
and the worms cover them.

27 "Oh, I know your thoughts,
and your schemes to wrong me.

28 For you say, 'Where is the house of the prince?
Where is the tent in which the wicked lived?'

29 Have you not asked those who travel the roads,
and do you not accept their testimony,

30 that the wicked are spared in the day of calamity,
and are rescued in the day of wrath?

31 Who declares their way to their face,
and who repays them for what they have done?

32 When they are carried to the grave,
a watch is kept over their tomb.

33 The clods of the valley are sweet to them;
everyone will follow after,
and those who went before are innumerable.

34 How then will you comfort me with empty
nothings?
There is nothing left of your answers but
falsehood."

Eliphaz Speaks: Job's Wickedness Is Great

22 Then Eliphaz the Temanite answered:
2 "Can a mortal be of use to God?
Can even the wisest be of service to him?

3 Is it any pleasure to the Almighty*b* if you are
righteous,
or is it gain to him if you make your ways
blameless?

4 Is it for your piety that he reproves you,
and enters into judgment with you?

5 Is not your wickedness great?
There is no end to your iniquities.

The Road of Pain

JOB 21.34

Once again, Job tells his friends
that he takes no comfort in
their useless, empty talk.

Often in traveling the road
of suffering, we find ourselves
without comfort—with no map
to guide us. There are no easy
answers, and even those who
want to help seem unable to do
so. Their actions may even in-
tensify our anguish.

Walk in God's presence on
behalf of someone who is traveling the dark road of pain. Picture God walking in silence and
love alongside you and that
person, present though unseen.
Walk with God in the silence.

See Meeting God in Community

A New Reason

JOB 22.21–22

Job's friends have apparently given up on getting Job to admit that he has done wrong. Now Eliphaz takes another tack, saying that Job is suffering because he hasn't done enough that is right. If he had done more good things, he would not be in this mess. Believing that doing good can insulate us from pain and loss is a trap, but Job's friends are still struggling to find a way to assure themselves that what has happened to Job will not happen to them.

What do you cling to for security—as your assurance that nothing bad is going to happen to you? What do you fear losing? Talk honestly with God in prayer about this. What does God say to you?

See Meeting God in Prayer

6 For you have exacted pledges from your family for
      no reason,
   and stripped the naked of their clothing.
7 You have given no water to the weary to drink,
   and you have withheld bread from the hungry.
8 The powerful possess the land,
   and the favored live in it.
9 You have sent widows away empty-handed,
   and the arms of the orphans you have crushed.*a*
10 Therefore snares are around you,
   and sudden terror overwhelms you,
11 or darkness so that you cannot see;
   a flood of water covers you.

12 "Is not God high in the heavens?
   See the highest stars, how lofty they are!
13 Therefore you say, 'What does God know?
   Can he judge through the deep darkness?
14 Thick clouds enwrap him, so that he does not see,
   and he walks on the dome of heaven.'
15 Will you keep to the old way
   that the wicked have trod?
16 They were snatched away before their time;
   their foundation was washed away by a flood.
17 They said to God, 'Leave us alone,'
   and 'What can the Almighty*b* do to us?'*c*
18 Yet he filled their houses with good things—
   but the plans of the wicked are repugnant to me.
19 The righteous see it and are glad;
   the innocent laugh them to scorn,
20 saying, 'Surely our adversaries are cut off,
   and what they left, the fire has consumed.'

21 "Agree with God,*d* and be at peace;
   in this way good will come to you.
22 Receive instruction from his mouth,
   and lay up his words in your heart.
23 If you return to the Almighty,*b* you will be restored,
   if you remove unrighteousness from your tents,
24 if you treat gold like dust,
   and gold of Ophir like the stones of the
      torrent-bed,
25 and if the Almighty*b* is your gold
   and your precious silver,
26 then you will delight yourself in the Almighty,*b*
   and lift up your face to God.
27 You will pray to him, and he will hear you,
   and you will pay your vows.
28 You will decide on a matter, and it will be
      established for you,
   and light will shine on your ways.
29 When others are humiliated, you say it is pride;
   for he saves the humble.
30 He will deliver even those who are guilty;
   they will escape because of the cleanness of your
      hands."*e*

a Gk Syr Tg Vg: Heb *were crushed*   *b* Traditional rendering of Heb *Shaddai*
c Gk Syr: Heb *them*   *d* Heb *him*   *e* Meaning of Heb uncertain

It is easy to see that the sacred Scriptures, which so far surpass all gifts and graces of human endeavor, breathe something divine.

JOHN CALVIN (1509-1564)

Institutes of Christian Religion, Book One

We pray

to see life as it is,
to *understand* it and to
make it *better* than it was.
We pray so that reality
can break into our *souls*
and give us back our

awareness of the

Divine Presence in *life.*

JOAN CHITTISTER, O.S.B.

Wisdom Distilled from the Daily

If God's word is so full of consolations, what overflowing springs shall we find in God himself? If the promise is so sweet, what will the performance be?

RICHARD BAXTER (1615-1691)

The Saints' Everlasting Rest

When *in reading Scripture you meet with a passage that seems to give your heart a new motion toward God, turn it into the form of a petition, and give it a place in your prayers.*

WILLIAM LAW (1686-1761)

A Serious Call to a Devout and Holy Life

Job Replies: My Complaint Is Bitter

23 Then Job answered:
2 "Today also my complaint is bitter;[a]
his[b] hand is heavy despite my groaning.
3 Oh, that I knew where I might find him,
that I might come even to his dwelling!
4 I would lay my case before him,
and fill my mouth with arguments.
5 I would learn what he would answer me,
and understand what he would say to me.
6 Would he contend with me in the greatness of his
power?
No; but he would give heed to me.
7 There an upright person could reason with him,
and I should be acquitted forever by my judge.

8 "If I go forward, he is not there;
or backward, I cannot perceive him;
9 on the left he hides, and I cannot behold him;
I turn[c] to the right, but I cannot see him.
10 But he knows the way that I take;
when he has tested me, I shall come out like
gold.
11 My foot has held fast to his steps;
I have kept his way and have not turned aside.
12 I have not departed from the commandment of his
lips;
I have treasured in[d] my bosom the words of his
mouth.
13 But he stands alone and who can dissuade him?
What he desires, that he does.
14 For he will complete what he appoints for me;
and many such things are in his mind.
15 Therefore I am terrified at his presence;
when I consider, I am in dread of him.
16 God has made my heart faint;
the Almighty[e] has terrified me;
17 If only I could vanish in darkness,
and thick darkness would cover my face![f]

Job Complains of Violence on the Earth

24 "Why are times not kept by the Almighty,[e]
and why do those who know him never see his days?
2 The wicked[g] remove landmarks;
they seize flocks and pasture them.
3 They drive away the donkey of the orphan;
they take the widow's ox for a pledge.
4 They thrust the needy off the road;
the poor of the earth all hide themselves.
5 Like wild asses in the desert
they go out to their toil,
scavenging in the wasteland
food for their young.
6 They reap in a field not their own
and they glean in the vineyard of the wicked.

Traveling Blind

JOB 23.8–11

"You may find a kind of darkness around your mind, as it were a cloud of unknowing. You seem to feel nothing in your will except a naked intent toward God. However hard you try to do something about it, this darkness and this cloud remain between you and God. It seems as though you neither see God by the light of understanding nor feel God in the sweetness of love and affection. But learn to live with this darkness, crying out always to him whom you love."

—ANONYMOUS,
The Cloud of Unknowing

---

a Syr Vg Tg: Heb *rebellious*   *b* Gk Syr: Heb *my*   *c* Syr Vg: Heb *he turns*
d Gk Vg: Heb *from*   *e* Traditional rendering of Heb *Shaddai*   *f* Or *But I
am not destroyed by the darkness; he has concealed the thick darkness from me*
g Gk: Heb *they*

Souls That Cry Out

JOB 24.9–12

This passage sounds like a recap of the evening news: baby selling, homelessness, hunger, adultery, violence in the city—and yet God seems to do nothing. Job laments God's lack of response.

Think about the community in which you live. Through whom is God working to help the hungry, the homeless and the victims of violence? In what way is God using you now to respond to these situations? In what ways is God calling you to respond on his behalf to those in need?

See Meeting God in Service

7   They lie all night naked, without clothing,
       and have no covering in the cold.
8   They are wet with the rain of the mountains,
       and cling to the rock for want of shelter.

9   "There are those who snatch the orphan child from
           the breast,
       and take as a pledge the infant of the poor.
10 They go about naked, without clothing;
       though hungry, they carry the sheaves;
11 between their terraces*a* they press out oil;
       they tread the wine presses, but suffer thirst.
12 From the city the dying groan,
       and the throat of the wounded cries for help;
       yet God pays no attention to their prayer.

13 "There are those who rebel against the light,
       who are not acquainted with its ways,
       and do not stay in its paths.
14 The murderer rises at dusk
       to kill the poor and needy,
       and in the night is like a thief.
15 The eye of the adulterer also waits for the twilight,
       saying, 'No eye will see me';
       and he disguises his face.
16 In the dark they dig through houses;
       by day they shut themselves up;
       they do not know the light.
17 For deep darkness is morning to all of them;
       for they are friends with the terrors of deep
           darkness.

18 "Swift are they on the face of the waters;
       their portion in the land is cursed;
       no treader turns toward their vineyards.
19 Drought and heat snatch away the snow waters;
       so does Sheol those who have sinned.
20 The womb forgets them;
       the worm finds them sweet;
     they are no longer remembered;
       so wickedness is broken like a tree.

21 "They harm*b* the childless woman,
       and do no good to the widow.
22 Yet God*c* prolongs the life of the mighty by his
           power;
       they rise up when they despair of life.
23 He gives them security, and they are supported;
       his eyes are upon their ways.
24 They are exalted a little while, and then are gone;
       they wither and fade like the mallow;*d*
       they are cut off like the heads of grain.
25 If it is not so, who will prove me a liar,
       and show that there is nothing in what I say?"

---

a Meaning of Heb uncertain   *b* Gk Tg: Heb *feed on* or *associate with*
c Heb *he*   *d* Gk: Heb *like all others*

Bildad Speaks: How Can a Mortal Be Righteous Before God?

25 Then Bildad the Shuhite answered:
² "Dominion and fear are with God;ᵃ
he makes peace in his high heaven.
³ Is there any number to his armies?
Upon whom does his light not arise?
⁴ How then can a mortal be righteous before God?
How can one born of woman be pure?
⁵ If even the moon is not bright
and the stars are not pure in his sight,
⁶ how much less a mortal, who is a maggot,
and a human being, who is a worm!"

Job Replies: God's Majesty Is Unsearchable

26 Then Job answered:
² "How you have helped one who has no power!
How you have assisted the arm that has no
strength!
³ How you have counseled one who has no wisdom,
and given much good advice!
⁴ With whose help have you uttered words,
and whose spirit has come forth from you?
⁵ The shades below tremble,
the waters and their inhabitants.
⁶ Sheol is naked before God,
and Abaddon has no covering.
⁷ He stretches out Zaphonᵇ over the void,
and hangs the earth upon nothing.
⁸ He binds up the waters in his thick clouds,
and the cloud is not torn open by them.
⁹ He covers the face of the full moon,
and spreads over it his cloud.
¹⁰ He has described a circle on the face of the waters,
at the boundary between light and darkness.
¹¹ The pillars of heaven tremble,
and are astounded at his rebuke.
¹² By his power he stilled the Sea;
by his understanding he struck down Rahab.
¹³ By his wind the heavens were made fair;
his hand pierced the fleeing serpent.
¹⁴ These are indeed but the outskirts of his ways;
and how small a whisper do we hear of him!
But the thunder of his power who can
understand?"

Job Maintains His Integrity

27 Job again took up his discourse and said:
² "As God lives, who has taken away my right,
and the Almighty,ᶜ who has made my soul bitter,
³ as long as my breath is in me
and the spirit of God is in my nostrils,
⁴ my lips will not speak falsehood,
and my tongue will not utter deceit.
⁵ Far be it from me to say that you are right;
until I die I will not put away my integrity from
me.

Awesome—and Out There?

JOB 25.2–6

Bildad speaks reverently, almost fearfully, of God's holiness and power—an awesome, unreachable God. In contrast, we flawed humans are "maggots" and "worms." Bildad cannot understand the give-and-take, confrontational intimacy that characterizes Job's relationship with God. Job's closeness to God seems arrogant to him.

Some of us have a reverence for God's holiness but cannot, or do not, embrace the image of God as our loving Father who desires intimacy with us. Such perceptions keep God at a distance. Are you able to speak to God openly about your anger and disappointments, as you would to a trusted family member, or do you see God as a cool, immovable judge? Do you picture yourself standing with head down before God's throne or sitting on God's lap? Consider where your images of God come from and whether your relationship with God is more like Bildad's or Job's.

See Meeting God in Scripture

ᵃ Heb *him*   ᵇ Or *the North*   ᶜ Traditional rendering of Heb *Shaddai*

Where Is Hope?

JOB 27.7–12

Job here declares that he must proclaim the power and the ways of the Almighty to those who do not know him so that they may have hope of delight and deliverance.

The world today suffers from a chronic shortage of hope. Even though many cannot identify or articulate their hopelessness, it's easy to see on faces in crowds, easy to hear on talk shows, apparent in the tough speech of children who have lost their innocence too early in life. What can we do but be ready to respond, as Job does, with words of faith? Be prepared to offer words of encouragement and hope—that God will hear, save, love and rescue them. Write out a paragraph or two articulating what God has done in your life recently so that you can share your hope with others. Update it from time to time to keep it fresh and current.

See Meeting God in Service

6   I hold fast my righteousness, and will not let it go;
      my heart does not reproach me for any of my
         days.

7   "May my enemy be like the wicked,
      and may my opponent be like the unrighteous.
8   For what is the hope of the godless when God cuts
         them off,
      when God takes away their lives?
9   Will God hear their cry
      when trouble comes upon them?
10 Will they take delight in the Almighty?[a]
      Will they call upon God at all times?
11 I will teach you concerning the hand of God;
      that which is with the Almighty[a] I will not
         conceal.
12 All of you have seen it yourselves;
      why then have you become altogether vain?

13 "This is the portion of the wicked with God,
      and the heritage that oppressors receive from the
         Almighty:[a]
14 If their children are multiplied, it is for the sword;
      and their offspring have not enough to eat.
15 Those who survive them the pestilence buries,
      and their widows make no lamentation.
16 Though they heap up silver like dust,
      and pile up clothing like clay—
17 they may pile it up, but the just will wear it,
      and the innocent will divide the silver.
18 They build their houses like nests,
      like booths made by sentinels of the vineyard.
19 They go to bed with wealth, but will do so no more;
      they open their eyes, and it is gone.
20 Terrors overtake them like a flood;
      in the night a whirlwind carries them off.
21 The east wind lifts them up and they are gone;
      it sweeps them out of their place.
22 It[b] hurls at them without pity;
      they flee from its[c] power in headlong flight.
23 It[b] claps its[c] hands at them,
      and hisses at them from its[c] place.

Interlude: Where Wisdom Is Found

28 "Surely there is a mine for silver,
      and a place for gold to be refined.
2   Iron is taken out of the earth,
      and copper is smelted from ore.
3   Miners put[d] an end to darkness,
      and search out to the farthest bound
         the ore in gloom and deep darkness.
4   They open shafts in a valley away from human
         habitation;
      they are forgotten by travelers,
      they sway suspended, remote from people.
5   As for the earth, out of it comes bread;
      but underneath it is turned up as by fire.

a Traditional rendering of Heb *Shaddai*   *b* Or *He* (that is God)   *c* Or *his*
d Heb *He puts*

⁶ Its stones are the place of sapphires,^{*a*}
and its dust contains gold.

⁷ "That path no bird of prey knows,
and the falcon's eye has not seen it.
⁸ The proud wild animals have not trodden it;
the lion has not passed over it.

⁹ "They put their hand to the flinty rock,
and overturn mountains by the roots.
¹⁰ They cut out channels in the rocks,
and their eyes see every precious thing.
¹¹ The sources of the rivers they probe;^{*b*}
hidden things they bring to light.

¹² "But where shall wisdom be found?
And where is the place of understanding?
¹³ Mortals do not know the way to it,^{*c*}
and it is not found in the land of the living.
¹⁴ The deep says, 'It is not in me,'
and the sea says, 'It is not with me.'
¹⁵ It cannot be gotten for gold,
and silver cannot be weighed out as its price.
¹⁶ It cannot be valued in the gold of Ophir,
in precious onyx or sapphire.^{*a*}
¹⁷ Gold and glass cannot equal it,
nor can it be exchanged for jewels of fine gold.
¹⁸ No mention shall be made of coral or of crystal;
the price of wisdom is above pearls.
¹⁹ The chrysolite of Ethiopia^{*d*} cannot compare with it,
nor can it be valued in pure gold.

²⁰ "Where then does wisdom come from?
And where is the place of understanding?
²¹ It is hidden from the eyes of all living,
and concealed from the birds of the air.
²² Abaddon and Death say,
'We have heard a rumor of it with our ears.'

²³ "God understands the way to it,
and he knows its place.
²⁴ For he looks to the ends of the earth,
and sees everything under the heavens.
²⁵ When he gave to the wind its weight,
and apportioned out the waters by measure;
²⁶ when he made a decree for the rain,
and a way for the thunderbolt;
²⁷ then he saw it and declared it;
he established it, and searched it out.
²⁸ And he said to humankind,
'Truly, the fear of the Lord, that is wisdom;
and to depart from evil is understanding.' "

Job Finishes His Defense

29 Job again took up his discourse and said:
² "O that I were as in the months of old,
as in the days when God watched over me;

Sapphire Mines

JOB 28.1–13

Truly precious, priceless things are often mined from deep, dark places. This hymn to wisdom tells us that wisdom is more priceless than sapphires or gold.

What nuggets of wisdom have you discovered in unexpected places? As you have struggled with life's challenges, what "precious stones" have you uncovered? Find an object to symbolize something you have discovered about God or yourself. Put this object in a place where you can see it when you pray to remind you to prospect for wisdom in dark days.

The "Good Old Days"

JOB 29.2–6

The memory of better days of honor and prosperity stands in poignant relief against the dark backdrop of Job's suffering. For a time, Job revels in what used to be.

Do you wistfully remember an easy, pleasant time in your life, the "good old days," when life was easier for you than it is now? Pull out some old photos and spend time thinking about what was going on in your life at the time the photos were taken, or pull out and reread your journal from that time—perhaps even an old checkbook register. What people and situations come to mind as you do so? What made those "good old days" good? How do those memories enrich your life? How can you express gratitude to God for those times now?

See Meeting God in Everyday Life

3 when his lamp shone over my head,
 and by his light I walked through darkness;
4 when I was in my prime,
 when the friendship of God was upon my tent;
5 when the Almighty*a* was still with me,
 when my children were around me;
6 when my steps were washed with milk,
 and the rock poured out for me streams of oil!
7 When I went out to the gate of the city,
 when I took my seat in the square,
8 the young men saw me and withdrew,
 and the aged rose up and stood;
9 the nobles refrained from talking,
 and laid their hands on their mouths;
10 the voices of princes were hushed,
 and their tongues stuck to the roof of their mouths.
11 When the ear heard, it commended me,
 and when the eye saw, it approved;
12 because I delivered the poor who cried,
 and the orphan who had no helper.
13 The blessing of the wretched came upon me,
 and I caused the widow's heart to sing for joy.
14 I put on righteousness, and it clothed me;
 my justice was like a robe and a turban.
15 I was eyes to the blind,
 and feet to the lame.
16 I was a father to the needy,
 and I championed the cause of the stranger.
17 I broke the fangs of the unrighteous,
 and made them drop their prey from their teeth.
18 Then I thought, 'I shall die in my nest,
 and I shall multiply my days like the phoenix;*b*
19 my roots spread out to the waters,
 with the dew all night on my branches;
20 my glory was fresh with me,
 and my bow ever new in my hand.'

21 "They listened to me, and waited,
 and kept silence for my counsel.
22 After I spoke they did not speak again,
 and my word dropped upon them like dew.*c*
23 They waited for me as for the rain;
 they opened their mouths as for the spring rain.
24 I smiled on them when they had no confidence;
 and the light of my countenance they did not extinguish.*d*
25 I chose their way, and sat as chief,
 and I lived like a king among his troops,
 like one who comforts mourners.

30 "But now they make sport of me,
 those who are younger than I,
 whose fathers I would have disdained
 to set with the dogs of my flock.
2 What could I gain from the strength of their hands?
 All their vigor is gone.

---

a Traditional rendering of Heb *Shaddai*   *b* Or *like sand*   *c* Heb lacks *like dew*   *d* Meaning of Heb uncertain

3 Through want and hard hunger
    they gnaw the dry and desolate ground,
4 they pick mallow and the leaves of bushes,
    and to warm themselves the roots of broom.
5 They are driven out from society;
    people shout after them as after a thief.
6 In the gullies of wadis they must live,
    in holes in the ground, and in the rocks.
7 Among the bushes they bray;
    under the nettles they huddle together.
8 A senseless, disreputable brood,
    they have been whipped out of the land.

9 "And now they mock me in song;
    I am a byword to them.
10 They abhor me, they keep aloof from me;
    they do not hesitate to spit at the sight of me.
11 Because God has loosed my bowstring and
      humbled me,
    they have cast off restraint in my presence.
12 On my right hand the rabble rise up;
    they send me sprawling,
    and build roads for my ruin.
13 They break up my path,
    they promote my calamity;
    no one restrains*a* them.
14 As through a wide breach they come;
    amid the crash they roll on.
15 Terrors are turned upon me;
    my honor is pursued as by the wind,
    and my prosperity has passed away like a cloud.

16 "And now my soul is poured out within me;
    days of affliction have taken hold of me.
17 The night racks my bones,
    and the pain that gnaws me takes no rest.
18 With violence he seizes my garment;*b*
    he grasps me by*c* the collar of my tunic.
19 He has cast me into the mire,
    and I have become like dust and ashes.
20 I cry to you and you do not answer me;
    I stand, and you merely look at me.
21 You have turned cruel to me;
    with the might of your hand you persecute me.
22 You lift me up on the wind, you make me ride on it,
    and you toss me about in the roar of the storm.
23 I know that you will bring me to death,
    and to the house appointed for all living.

24 "Surely one does not turn against the needy,*d*
    when in disaster they cry for help.*e*
25 Did I not weep for those whose day was hard?
    Was not my soul grieved for the poor?
26 But when I looked for good, evil came;
    and when I waited for light, darkness came.
27 My inward parts are in turmoil, and are never still;
    days of affliction come to meet me.

Tossing and Turning

JOB 30.16–17

Job's days are full of affliction, and his nights provide him with little rest. He cannot sleep. What are the signs of distress when your soul is not at ease? Do you, like Job, toss and turn through the night? Are your patterns of eating and working disturbed? Do you find yourself irritable with those near you?

When you go to bed tonight, take inventory of your cares and worries—even the small irritations in your life. Acknowledge and admit them, and then commit them to God's care. Write a bedtime prayer committing your worries to God and keep it on your nightstand.

See Meeting God in Prayer

a Cn: Heb *helps*   *b* Gk: Heb *my garment is disfigured*   *c* Heb *like*
d Heb *ruin*   *e* Cn: Meaning of Heb uncertain

Areas of Discipleship

JOB 31.1–23

Job offers us a pattern for examining our conscience regarding relationships as he looks at himself in relation to God, his family, his slaves and the helpless. If we put that in modern terms, we might examine our relationship to God, our family relationships, our work relationships and our ministry to the needy in the community.

Examine yourself in these areas. In which area is your discipleship strongest? Which area needs more attention and diligence? This examination could be done regularly or during a spiritual retreat. In each category, list the persons and situations that come to mind, asking God to show you what action to take in each area and how to pray regarding that area.

See Meeting God in Everyday Life

28 I go about in sunless gloom;
   I stand up in the assembly and cry for help.
29 I am a brother of jackals,
   and a companion of ostriches.
30 My skin turns black and falls from me,
   and my bones burn with heat.
31 My lyre is turned to mourning,
   and my pipe to the voice of those who weep.

31 "I have made a covenant with my eyes;
   how then could I look upon a virgin?
2 What would be my portion from God above,
   and my heritage from the Almighty[a] on high?
3 Does not calamity befall the unrighteous,
   and disaster the workers of iniquity?
4 Does he not see my ways,
   and number all my steps?

5 "If I have walked with falsehood,
   and my foot has hurried to deceit—
6 let me be weighed in a just balance,
   and let God know my integrity!—
7 if my step has turned aside from the way,
   and my heart has followed my eyes,
   and if any spot has clung to my hands;
8 then let me sow, and another eat;
   and let what grows for me be rooted out.

9 "If my heart has been enticed by a woman,
   and I have lain in wait at my neighbor's door;
10 then let my wife grind for another,
   and let other men kneel over her.
11 For that would be a heinous crime;
   that would be a criminal offense;
12 for that would be a fire consuming down to Abaddon,
   and it would burn to the root all my harvest.

13 "If I have rejected the cause of my male or female
      slaves,
   when they brought a complaint against me;
14 what then shall I do when God rises up?
   When he makes inquiry, what shall I answer him?
15 Did not he who made me in the womb make them?
   And did not one fashion us in the womb?

16 "If I have withheld anything that the poor desired,
   or have caused the eyes of the widow to fail,
17 or have eaten my morsel alone,
   and the orphan has not eaten from it—
18 for from my youth I reared the orphan[b] like a father,
   and from my mother's womb I guided the
      widow[c]—
19 if I have seen anyone perish for lack of clothing,
   or a poor person without covering,
20 whose loins have not blessed me,
   and who was not warmed with the fleece of my
      sheep;
21 if I have raised my hand against the orphan,
   because I saw I had supporters at the gate;

a Traditional rendering of Heb *Shaddai*   *b* Heb *him*   *c* Heb *her*

22 then let my shoulder blade fall from my shoulder,
    and let my arm be broken from its socket.
23 For I was in terror of calamity from God,
    and I could not have faced his majesty.

24 "If I have made gold my trust,
    or called fine gold my confidence;
25 if I have rejoiced because my wealth was great,
    or because my hand had gotten much;
26 if I have looked at the sun*a* when it shone,
    or the moon moving in splendor,
27 and my heart has been secretly enticed,
    and my mouth has kissed my hand;
28 this also would be an iniquity to be punished by the judges,
    for I should have been false to God above.

29 "If I have rejoiced at the ruin of those who hated me,
    or exulted when evil overtook them—
30 I have not let my mouth sin
    by asking for their lives with a curse—
31 if those of my tent ever said,
    'O that we might be sated with his flesh!'*b*—
32 the stranger has not lodged in the street;
    I have opened my doors to the traveler—
33 if I have concealed my transgressions as others do,*c*
    by hiding my iniquity in my bosom,
34 because I stood in great fear of the multitude,
    and the contempt of families terrified me,
    so that I kept silence, and did not go out of doors—
35 O that I had one to hear me!
    (Here is my signature! Let the Almighty*d* answer me!)
    O that I had the indictment written by my adversary!
36 Surely I would carry it on my shoulder;
    I would bind it on me like a crown;
37 I would give him an account of all my steps;
    like a prince I would approach him.

38 "If my land has cried out against me,
    and its furrows have wept together;
39 if I have eaten its yield without payment,
    and caused the death of its owners;
40 let thorns grow instead of wheat,
    and foul weeds instead of barley."

The words of Job are ended.

Elihu Rebukes Job's Friends

32 So these three men ceased to answer Job, because he was righteous in his own eyes. 2 Then Elihu son of Barachel the Buzite, of the family of Ram, became angry. He was angry at Job because he justified himself rather than God; 3 he was angry also at Job's three friends because they had found no answer, though they had declared Job to be in the wrong.*e* 4 Now Elihu had waited to speak to Job,

---

Looking at Values

JOB 31.24–40

Job's self-examination continues. After looking at his behavior toward God and other people, Job looks at his attitudes, ethics and values. He has not trusted in his wealth; he has wished good even for his enemies; he has shown hospitality to strangers; he has been responsible in the use of the land God has given him.

Job offers us a pattern for examination of our values and attitudes. In what do you place your trust—your abilities and achievements, or God's faithfulness? Do the attitudes of your heart mirror God's love, justice and mercy? How are you contributing to your community by upholding values God has set? How are you seeking to be a faithful steward of the resources God has given you, including your body and the earth itself? Give thanks for God's help where you are doing well, and ask for help in areas where you are not doing as well.

See Meeting God in Community

---

a Heb *the light*   *b* Meaning of Heb uncertain   *c* Or *as Adam did*
d Traditional rendering of Heb *Shaddai*   *e* Another ancient tradition reads
answer, and had put God in the wrong

God Speaks Through Pain

JOB 32.18–20

"God whispers to us in our pleasures, speaks to us in our conscience, but shouts in our pains."

—C. S. LEWIS,
The Problem of Pain

because they were older than he. [5]But when Elihu saw that there was no answer in the mouths of these three men, he became angry.

6 Elihu son of Barachel the Buzite answered:

"I am young in years,
and you are aged;
therefore I was timid and afraid
to declare my opinion to you.
[7] I said, 'Let days speak,
and many years teach wisdom.'
[8] But truly it is the spirit in a mortal,
the breath of the Almighty,[a] that makes for
understanding.
[9] It is not the old[b] that are wise,
nor the aged that understand what is right.
[10] Therefore I say, 'Listen to me;
let me also declare my opinion.'

[11] "See, I waited for your words,
I listened for your wise sayings,
while you searched out what to say.
[12] I gave you my attention,
but there was in fact no one that confuted Job,
no one among you that answered his words.
[13] Yet do not say, 'We have found wisdom;
God may vanquish him, not a human.'
[14] He has not directed his words against me,
and I will not answer him with your speeches.

[15] "They are dismayed, they answer no more;
they have not a word to say.
[16] And am I to wait, because they do not speak,
because they stand there, and answer no more?
[17] I also will give my answer;
I also will declare my opinion.
[18] For I am full of words;
the spirit within me constrains me.
[19] My heart is indeed like wine that has no vent;
like new wineskins, it is ready to burst.
[20] I must speak, so that I may find relief;
I must open my lips and answer.
[21] I will not show partiality to any person
or use flattery toward anyone.
[22] For I do not know how to flatter—
or my Maker would soon put an end to me!

Elihu Rebukes Job

33 "But now, hear my speech, O Job,
and listen to all my words.
[2] See, I open my mouth;
the tongue in my mouth speaks.
[3] My words declare the uprightness of my heart,
and what my lips know they speak sincerely.
[4] The spirit of God has made me,
and the breath of the Almighty[a] gives me life.
[5] Answer me, if you can;
set your words in order before me; take your stand.
[6] See, before God I am as you are;
I too was formed from a piece of clay.

a Traditional rendering of Heb *Shaddai*   b Gk Syr Vg: Heb *many*

7 No fear of me need terrify you;
  my pressure will not be heavy on you.

8 "Surely, you have spoken in my hearing,
  and I have heard the sound of your words.
9 You say, 'I am clean, without transgression;
  I am pure, and there is no iniquity in me.
10 Look, he finds occasions against me,
  he counts me as his enemy;
11 he puts my feet in the stocks,
  and watches all my paths.'

12 "But in this you are not right. I will answer you:
  God is greater than any mortal.
13 Why do you contend against him,
  saying, 'He will answer none of my[a] words'?
14 For God speaks in one way,
  and in two, though people do not perceive it.
15 In a dream, in a vision of the night,
  when deep sleep falls on mortals,
  while they slumber on their beds,
16 then he opens their ears,
  and terrifies them with warnings,
17 that he may turn them aside from their deeds,
  and keep them from pride,
18 to spare their souls from the Pit,
  their lives from traversing the River.
19 They are also chastened with pain upon their beds,
  and with continual strife in their bones,
20 so that their lives loathe bread,
  and their appetites dainty food.
21 Their flesh is so wasted away that it cannot be
    seen;
  and their bones, once invisible, now stick out.
22 Their souls draw near the Pit,
  and their lives to those who bring death.
23 Then, if there should be for one of them an angel,
  a mediator, one of a thousand,
  one who declares a person upright,
24 and he is gracious to that person, and says,
  'Deliver him from going down into the Pit;
  I have found a ransom;
25 let his flesh become fresh with youth;
  let him return to the days of his youthful vigor';
26 then he prays to God, and is accepted by him,
  he comes into his presence with joy,
  and God[b] repays him for his righteousness.
27 That person sings to others and says,
  'I sinned, and perverted what was right,
  and it was not paid back to me.
28 He has redeemed my soul from going down to the
    Pit,
  and my life shall see the light.'

29 "God indeed does all these things,
  twice, three times, with mortals,
30 to bring back their souls from the Pit,
  so that they may see the light of life.[c]

Lessons in Suffering

JOB 33.12–20

Elihu is right—God does sometimes teach us through suffering to live more fully in his presence. Yet those lessons may not become apparent to us until the pain has subsided and the wounds have healed. We may not be able to perceive suffering's teaching until we gain the perspective of time.

Look back over times of suffering and darkness in your life. What life lessons did God teach you? How have those times changed and matured you? How has your faith blossomed as a result of those times?

See Meeting God in Everyday Life

a Compare Gk: Heb *his*   b Heb *he*   c Syr: Heb *to be lighted with the light of life*

God's Persistence

JOB 33.29–33

Elihu proclaims that God is not a silent God who is far removed. On the contrary, God keeps coming to us, calling to us, rescuing us and turning us away from our sin. God takes the initiative in seeking us.

How has God sought you repeatedly? Through whom has God reached out to you? Consider how God wants to reach out through you to those who are in pain or are searching for meaning and joy in their lives. Give thanks for God's persistence in your life and in the lives of those who have not yet realized that God is seeking them.

See Meeting God in Service

31 Pay heed, Job, listen to me;
  be silent, and I will speak.
32 If you have anything to say, answer me;
  speak, for I desire to justify you.
33 If not, listen to me;
  be silent, and I will teach you wisdom."

Elihu Proclaims God's Justice

34 Then Elihu continued and said:
2 "Hear my words, you wise men,
  and give ear to me, you who know;
3 for the ear tests words
  as the palate tastes food.
4 Let us choose what is right;
  let us determine among ourselves what is good.
5 For Job has said, 'I am innocent,
  and God has taken away my right;
6 in spite of being right I am counted a liar;
  my wound is incurable, though I am without
    transgression.'
7 Who is there like Job,
  who drinks up scoffing like water,
8 who goes in company with evildoers
  and walks with the wicked?
9 For he has said, 'It profits one nothing
  to take delight in God.'

10 "Therefore, hear me, you who have sense,
  far be it from God that he should do wickedness,
  and from the Almighty*a* that he should do wrong.
11 For according to their deeds he will repay them,
  and according to their ways he will make it befall
    them.
12 Of a truth, God will not do wickedly,
  and the Almighty*a* will not pervert justice.
13 Who gave him charge over the earth
  and who laid on him*b* the whole world?
14 If he should take back his spirit*c* to himself,
  and gather to himself his breath,
15 all flesh would perish together,
  and all mortals return to dust.

16 "If you have understanding, hear this;
  listen to what I say.
17 Shall one who hates justice govern?
  Will you condemn one who is righteous and
    mighty,
18 who says to a king, 'You scoundrel!'
  and to princes, 'You wicked men!';
19 who shows no partiality to nobles,
  nor regards the rich more than the poor,
  for they are all the work of his hands?
20 In a moment they die;
  at midnight the people are shaken and pass
    away,
  and the mighty are taken away by no human
    hand.

a Traditional rendering of Heb *Shaddai* *b* Heb lacks *on him* *c* Heb *his heart his spirit*

21 "For his eyes are upon the ways of mortals,
   and he sees all their steps.
22 There is no gloom or deep darkness
   where evildoers may hide themselves.
23 For he has not appointed a time[a] for anyone
   to go before God in judgment.
24 He shatters the mighty without investigation,
   and sets others in their place.
25 Thus, knowing their works,
   he overturns them in the night, and they are
     crushed.
26 He strikes them for their wickedness
   while others look on,
27 because they turned aside from following him,
   and had no regard for any of his ways,
28 so that they caused the cry of the poor to come to
     him,
   and he heard the cry of the afflicted—
29 When he is quiet, who can condemn?
   When he hides his face, who can behold him,
   whether it be a nation or an individual?—
30 so that the godless should not reign,
   or those who ensnare the people.

31 "For has anyone said to God,
   'I have endured punishment; I will not offend any
     more;
32 teach me what I do not see;
   if I have done iniquity, I will do it no more'?
33 Will he then pay back to suit you,
   because you reject it?
   For you must choose, and not I;
   therefore declare what you know.[b]
34 Those who have sense will say to me,
   and the wise who hear me will say,
35 'Job speaks without knowledge,
   his words are without insight.'
36 Would that Job were tried to the limit,
   because his answers are those of the wicked.
37 For he adds rebellion to his sin;
   he claps his hands among us,
   and multiplies his words against God."

Elihu Condemns Self-Righteousness

35 Elihu continued and said:
2 "Do you think this to be just?
   You say, 'I am in the right before God.'
3 If you ask, 'What advantage have I?
   How am I better off than if I had sinned?'
4 I will answer you
   and your friends with you.
5 Look at the heavens and see;
   observe the clouds, which are higher than you.
6 If you have sinned, what do you accomplish against
     him?
   And if your transgressions are multiplied, what
     do you do to him?
7 If you are righteous, what do you give to him;
   or what does he receive from your hand?

Teach Me What I Do Not See

JOB 34.31–32

Although Elihu is mistakenly telling Job to repent, he rightly indicates that the first step of repentance is to acknowledge sin. That can be difficult because we are often blind to our faults and weaknesses. The psalmist, in Psalm 139, asks God to illumine the sinfulness of his heart: "Search me, O God, and know my heart . . . See if there is any wicked way in me, and lead me in the way everlasting" (Psalm 139.23–24).

Using these verses in Job and in Psalm 139 as a starting point, write a prayer of repentance, asking God to illuminate your heart and show you what you need to confess. Keep this prayer in your Bible and use it whenever God calls you to repentance.

See Meeting God in Scripture

---

a Cn: Heb *yet*   b Meaning of Heb of verses 29-33 uncertain

The God Above

JOB 35.6–12

"In this universe, even what is called evil, when it is rightly ordered and kept in its place, commends the good more eminently, since good things yield greater pleasure and praise when compared to the bad things. For the Omnipotent God, whom even the heathen acknowledge as the Supreme Power over all, would not allow any evil in his works, unless in his omnipotence and goodness, as the Supreme Good, he is able to bring forth good out of evil."

—AUGUSTINE,
Enchiridion

8 Your wickedness affects others like you,
and your righteousness, other human beings.

9 "Because of the multitude of oppressions people cry out;
they call for help because of the arm of the mighty.

10 But no one says, 'Where is God my Maker,
who gives strength in the night,

11 who teaches us more than the animals of the earth,
and makes us wiser than the birds of the air?'

12 There they cry out, but he does not answer,
because of the pride of evildoers.

13 Surely God does not hear an empty cry,
nor does the Almighty*ª* regard it.

14 How much less when you say that you do not see him,
that the case is before him, and you are waiting for him!

15 And now, because his anger does not punish,
and he does not greatly heed transgression,*ᵇ*

16 Job opens his mouth in empty talk,
he multiplies words without knowledge."

Elihu Exalts God's Goodness

36 Elihu continued and said:

2 "Bear with me a little, and I will show you,
for I have yet something to say on God's behalf.

3 I will bring my knowledge from far away,
and ascribe righteousness to my Maker.

4 For truly my words are not false;
one who is perfect in knowledge is with you.

5 "Surely God is mighty and does not despise any;
he is mighty in strength of understanding.

6 He does not keep the wicked alive,
but gives the afflicted their right.

7 He does not withdraw his eyes from the righteous,
but with kings on the throne
he sets them forever, and they are exalted.

8 And if they are bound in fetters
and caught in the cords of affliction,

9 then he declares to them their work
and their transgressions, that they are behaving arrogantly.

10 He opens their ears to instruction,
and commands that they return from iniquity.

11 If they listen, and serve him,
they complete their days in prosperity,
and their years in pleasantness.

12 But if they do not listen, they shall perish by the sword,
and die without knowledge.

13 "The godless in heart cherish anger;
they do not cry for help when he binds them.

14 They die in their youth,
and their life ends in shame.*ᶜ*

a Traditional rendering of Heb *Shaddai*   *b* Theodotion Symmachus
Compare Vg: Meaning of Heb uncertain   *c* Heb *ends among the temple prostitutes*

15 He delivers the afflicted by their affliction,
and opens their ear by adversity.

16 He also allured you out of distress
into a broad place where there was no constraint,
and what was set on your table was full of
fatness.

17 "But you are obsessed with the case of the wicked;
judgment and justice seize you.

18 Beware that wrath does not entice you into
scoffing,
and do not let the greatness of the ransom turn
you aside.

19 Will your cry avail to keep you from distress,
or will all the force of your strength?

20 Do not long for the night,
when peoples are cut off in their place.

21 Beware! Do not turn to iniquity;
because of that you have been tried by affliction.

22 See, God is exalted in his power;
who is a teacher like him?

23 Who has prescribed for him his way,
or who can say, 'You have done wrong'?

Elihu Proclaims God's Majesty

24 "Remember to extol his work,
of which mortals have sung.

25 All people have looked on it;
everyone watches it from far away.

26 Surely God is great, and we do not know him;
the number of his years is unsearchable.

27 For he draws up the drops of water;
he distills[a] his mist in rain,

28 which the skies pour down
and drop upon mortals abundantly.

29 Can anyone understand the spreading of the clouds,
the thunderings of his pavilion?

30 See, he scatters his lightning around him
and covers the roots of the sea.

31 For by these he governs peoples;
he gives food in abundance.

32 He covers his hands with the lightning,
and commands it to strike the mark.

33 Its crashing[b] tells about him;
he is jealous[b] with anger against iniquity.

37 "At this also my heart trembles,
and leaps out of its place.

2 Listen, listen to the thunder of his voice
and the rumbling that comes from his mouth.

3 Under the whole heaven he lets it loose,
and his lightning to the corners of the earth.

4 After it his voice roars;
he thunders with his majestic voice
and he does not restrain the lightnings[c] when his
voice is heard.

5 God thunders wondrously with his voice;
he does great things that we cannot comprehend.

My Favorite Obsession

JOB 36.17

Elihu points out that Job is obsessed with the question of whether life is fair—that Job spends too much time worrying about whether the wicked will be punished and the righteous rewarded. Elihu says that this preoccupation keeps Job from hearing God and seeing God at work in his life.

It's true we can spend so much time intellectualizing about God that we have little time to spend with God. Or we can become so busy working for God that we forget to look to him. Or we can become so caught up in our own compelling interests, even positive ones such as staying healthy or doing a good job, that we cannot sense God's nearness. What do you spend most of your time thinking about? Make a list of what has occupied your thoughts and taken up your time over the last twenty-four hours. Do these thoughts and activities reflect attention to God?

See Meeting God in Everyday Life

---

a Cn: Heb *they distill*   *b* Meaning of Heb uncertain   *c* Heb *them*

Amazing!

JOB 37.1–18

Elihu trembles as he considers the wondrous works of God's hand. He lists some of the wonders that awe him: thunder and lightning, snow and rain, the heavens.

What is the most awe-inspiring sight you have ever seen? Do natural wonders turn your mind toward God? Become a psalmist; choose some natural wonder and write a psalm about how it reveals God to you, or sing a hymn (one already published or one you make up) about the power of God.

See Meeting God in the Created Order

6 For to the snow he says, 'Fall on the earth';
   and the shower of rain, his heavy shower of rain,
7 serves as a sign on everyone's hand,
   so that all whom he has made may know it.[a]
8 Then the animals go into their lairs
   and remain in their dens.
9 From its chamber comes the whirlwind,
   and cold from the scattering winds.
10 By the breath of God ice is given,
   and the broad waters are frozen fast.
11 He loads the thick cloud with moisture;
   the clouds scatter his lightning.
12 They turn round and round by his guidance,
   to accomplish all that he commands them
   on the face of the habitable world.
13 Whether for correction, or for his land,
   or for love, he causes it to happen.

14 "Hear this, O Job;
   stop and consider the wondrous works of God.
15 Do you know how God lays his command upon them,
   and causes the lightning of his cloud to shine?
16 Do you know the balancings of the clouds,
   the wondrous works of the one whose knowledge is perfect,
17 you whose garments are hot
   when the earth is still because of the south wind?
18 Can you, like him, spread out the skies,
   hard as a molten mirror?
19 Teach us what we shall say to him;
   we cannot draw up our case because of darkness.
20 Should he be told that I want to speak?
   Did anyone ever wish to be swallowed up?
21 Now, no one can look on the light
   when it is bright in the skies,
   when the wind has passed and cleared them.
22 Out of the north comes golden splendor;
   around God is awesome majesty.
23 The Almighty[b]—we cannot find him;
   he is great in power and justice,
   and abundant righteousness he will not violate.
24 Therefore mortals fear him;
   he does not regard any who are wise in their own conceit."

The LORD Answers Job

38 Then the LORD answered Job out of the whirlwind:
2 "Who is this that darkens counsel by words without knowledge?
3 Gird up your loins like a man,
   I will question you, and you shall declare to me.

4 "Where were you when I laid the foundation of the earth?
   Tell me, if you have understanding.
5 Who determined its measurements—surely you know!

---

a Meaning of Heb of verse 7 uncertain   *b* Traditional rendering of Heb *Shaddai*

Or who stretched the line upon it?
6 On what were its bases sunk,
  or who laid its cornerstone
7 when the morning stars sang together
  and all the heavenly beings[a] shouted for joy?

8 "Or who shut in the sea with doors
  when it burst out from the womb?—
9 when I made the clouds its garment,
  and thick darkness its swaddling band,
10 and prescribed bounds for it,
  and set bars and doors,
11 and said, 'Thus far shall you come, and no farther,
  and here shall your proud waves be stopped'?

12 "Have you commanded the morning since your
    days began,
  and caused the dawn to know its place,
13 so that it might take hold of the skirts of the earth,
  and the wicked be shaken out of it?
14 It is changed like clay under the seal,
  and it is dyed[b] like a garment.
15 Light is withheld from the wicked,
  and their uplifted arm is broken.

16 "Have you entered into the springs of the sea,
  or walked in the recesses of the deep?
17 Have the gates of death been revealed to you,
  or have you seen the gates of deep darkness?
18 Have you comprehended the expanse of the earth?
  Declare, if you know all this.

19 "Where is the way to the dwelling of light,
  and where is the place of darkness,
20 that you may take it to its territory
  and that you may discern the paths to its home?
21 Surely you know, for you were born then,
  and the number of your days is great!

22 "Have you entered the storehouses of the snow,
  or have you seen the storehouses of the hail,
23 which I have reserved for the time of trouble,
  for the day of battle and war?
24 What is the way to the place where the light is
    distributed,
  or where the east wind is scattered upon the earth?

25 "Who has cut a channel for the torrents of rain,
  and a way for the thunderbolt,
26 to bring rain on a land where no one lives,
  on the desert, which is empty of human life,
27 to satisfy the waste and desolate land,
  and to make the ground put forth grass?

28 "Has the rain a father,
  or who has begotten the drops of dew?
29 From whose womb did the ice come forth,
  and who has given birth to the hoarfrost of
    heaven?

Good Morning, Lord

JOB 38.12–21

God challenges Job to consider how little Job knows of what God has made. God sounds a bit sarcastic: "Surely you know, for you were born then [when light and darkness were created]."

Some morning soon, set your alarm to go off before dawn and rise early. Go outside or sit where you can see the sky as it becomes light and consider how the landscape changes as morning comes. What feelings rise up within you? Give thanks for God's love that is renewed with each new day. Some night soon when the sky is clear, go outside and look at the stars. Lie on your back and try to count the stars. Identify the constellations that are visible. If you don't know their names, find out.

See Meeting God in the Created Order

Where Wisdom Resides

JOB 38.36

Who bestows wisdom and understanding? God alone. Where does wisdom reside? In God alone.

On a piece of paper, write down some of the things that you "just don't understand." After you have made your list, present it as an offering to God: set the paper in a dish or bowl and burn it by lighting a match to it. As the smoke rises, allow it to represent your struggles and lack of understanding. Release them to God and trust that God knows what you do not know and is at work to carry out his plans.

See Meeting God in Prayer

30 The waters become hard like stone,
and the face of the deep is frozen.

31 "Can you bind the chains of the Pleiades,
or loose the cords of Orion?

32 Can you lead forth the Mazzaroth in their season,
or can you guide the Bear with its children?

33 Do you know the ordinances of the heavens?
Can you establish their rule on the earth?

34 "Can you lift up your voice to the clouds,
so that a flood of waters may cover you?

35 Can you send forth lightnings, so that they may go
and say to you, 'Here we are'?

36 Who has put wisdom in the inward parts,[a]
or given understanding to the mind?[a]

37 Who has the wisdom to number the clouds?
Or who can tilt the waterskins of the heavens,

38 when the dust runs into a mass
and the clods cling together?

39 "Can you hunt the prey for the lion,
or satisfy the appetite of the young lions,

40 when they crouch in their dens,
or lie in wait in their covert?

41 Who provides for the raven its prey,
when its young ones cry to God,
and wander about for lack of food?

39 "Do you know when the mountain goats give birth?
Do you observe the calving of the deer?

2 Can you number the months that they fulfill,
and do you know the time when they give birth,

3 when they crouch to give birth to their offspring,
and are delivered of their young?

4 Their young ones become strong, they grow up in the open;
they go forth, and do not return to them.

5 "Who has let the wild ass go free?
Who has loosed the bonds of the swift ass,

6 to which I have given the steppe for its home,
the salt land for its dwelling place?

7 It scorns the tumult of the city;
it does not hear the shouts of the driver.

8 It ranges the mountains as its pasture,
and it searches after every green thing.

9 "Is the wild ox willing to serve you?
Will it spend the night at your crib?

10 Can you tie it in the furrow with ropes,
or will it harrow the valleys after you?

11 Will you depend on it because its strength is great,
and will you hand over your labor to it?

12 Do you have faith in it that it will return,
and bring your grain to your threshing floor?[b]

a Meaning of Heb uncertain   *b* Heb *your grain and your threshing floor*

13 "The ostrich's wings flap wildly,
   though its pinions lack plumage.[a]
14 For it leaves its eggs to the earth,
   and lets them be warmed on the ground,
15 forgetting that a foot may crush them,
   and that a wild animal may trample them.
16 It deals cruelly with its young, as if they were not its
       own;
   though its labor should be in vain, yet it has no
       fear;
17 because God has made it forget wisdom,
   and given it no share in understanding.
18 When it spreads its plumes aloft,[a]
   it laughs at the horse and its rider.

19 "Do you give the horse its might?
   Do you clothe its neck with mane?
20 Do you make it leap like the locust?
   Its majestic snorting is terrible.
21 It paws[b] violently, exults mightily;
   it goes out to meet the weapons.
22 It laughs at fear, and is not dismayed;
   it does not turn back from the sword.
23 Upon it rattle the quiver,
   the flashing spear, and the javelin.
24 With fierceness and rage it swallows the ground;
   it cannot stand still at the sound of the trumpet.
25 When the trumpet sounds, it says 'Aha!'
   From a distance it smells the battle,
   the thunder of the captains, and the shouting.

26 "Is it by your wisdom that the hawk soars,
   and spreads its wings toward the south?
27 Is it at your command that the eagle mounts up
   and makes its nest on high?
28 It lives on the rock and makes its home
   in the fastness of the rocky crag.
29 From there it spies the prey;
   its eyes see it from far away.
30 Its young ones suck up blood;
   and where the slain are, there it is."

40

And the LORD said to Job:
2 "Shall a faultfinder contend with the Almighty?[c]
Anyone who argues with God must respond."

Job's Response to God

3 Then Job answered the LORD:
4 "See, I am of small account; what shall I answer
       you?
   I lay my hand on my mouth.
5 I have spoken once, and I will not answer;
   twice, but will proceed no further."

God's Challenge to Job

6 Then the LORD answered Job out of the whirlwind:
7 "Gird up your loins like a man;
   I will question you, and you declare to me.

In Silence

JOB 40.1–5

God demands a response from Job. Job answers by not answering. Job is silent before the whirlwind out of which God speaks.

In the end, words cannot adequately express our suffering and trials and pain and darkness. Nor can words adequately express to God our awe and praise. We come in silence before a powerful, all-knowing God. Make it a priority to set aside an hour to spend in silence. Avoid conversation. Turn off the television, stereo or computer. Put aside books and magazines. Be silent before the Creator of Behemoth and Leviathan.

See Meeting God in Worship

---

a Meaning of Heb uncertain   *b* Gk Syr Vg: Heb *they dig*   *c* Traditional
rendering of Heb *Shaddai*

Evidence of God

JOB 40.10–11

"God's essence, indeed, is incomprehensible, utterly transcending all human thought; but on each of God's works his glory is engraven in characters so bright, so distinct, and so illustrious, that none, however dull and illiterate, can plead ignorance as their excuse. Hence, with perfect truth, the Psalmist exclaims, 'He wraps himself with light as with a garment,' (Psalm 104.2); as if he had said that God for the first time was arrayed in visible attire when, in the creation of the world, he displayed those glorious banners, on which, to whatever side we turn, we behold his perfections visibly portrayed."

—JOHN CALVIN,
Institutes of the Christian Religion

8 Will you even put me in the wrong?
　　Will you condemn me that you may be justified?
9 Have you an arm like God,
　　and can you thunder with a voice like his?

10 "Deck yourself with majesty and dignity;
　　clothe yourself with glory and splendor.
11 Pour out the overflowings of your anger,
　　and look on all who are proud, and abase them.
12 Look on all who are proud, and bring them low;
　　tread down the wicked where they stand.
13 Hide them all in the dust together;
　　bind their faces in the world below.*a*
14 Then I will also acknowledge to you
　　that your own right hand can give you victory.

15 "Look at Behemoth,
　　which I made just as I made you;
　　it eats grass like an ox.
16 Its strength is in its loins,
　　and its power in the muscles of its belly.
17 It makes its tail stiff like a cedar;
　　the sinews of its thighs are knit together.
18 Its bones are tubes of bronze,
　　its limbs like bars of iron.

19 "It is the first of the great acts of God—
　　only its Maker can approach it with the sword.
20 For the mountains yield food for it
　　where all the wild animals play.
21 Under the lotus plants it lies,
　　in the covert of the reeds and in the marsh.
22 The lotus trees cover it for shade;
　　the willows of the wadi surround it.
23 Even if the river is turbulent, it is not frightened;
　　it is confident though Jordan rushes against its mouth.
24 Can one take it with hooks*b*
　　or pierce its nose with a snare?

41 *c* "Can you draw out Leviathan*d* with a fishhook,
　　or press down its tongue with a cord?
2 Can you put a rope in its nose,
　　or pierce its jaw with a hook?
3 Will it make many supplications to you?
　　Will it speak soft words to you?
4 Will it make a covenant with you
　　to be taken as your servant forever?
5 Will you play with it as with a bird,
　　or will you put it on leash for your girls?
6 Will traders bargain over it?
　　Will they divide it up among the merchants?
7 Can you fill its skin with harpoons,
　　or its head with fishing spears?
8 Lay hands on it;
　　think of the battle; you will not do it again!

a Heb *the hidden place*　*b* Cn: Heb *in his eyes*　*c* Ch 40.25 in Heb
d Or *the crocodile*

9[a] Any hope of capturing it[b] will be disappointed;
  were not even the gods[c] overwhelmed at the sight of it?

10 No one is so fierce as to dare to stir it up.
  Who can stand before it?[d]

11 Who can confront it[d] and be safe?[e]
  —under the whole heaven, who?[f]

12 "I will not keep silence concerning its limbs,
  or its mighty strength, or its splendid frame.

13 Who can strip off its outer garment?
  Who can penetrate its double coat of mail?[g]

14 Who can open the doors of its face?
  There is terror all around its teeth.

15 Its back[h] is made of shields in rows,
  shut up closely as with a seal.

16 One is so near to another
  that no air can come between them.

17 They are joined one to another;
  they clasp each other and cannot be separated.

18 Its sneezes flash forth light,
  and its eyes are like the eyelids of the dawn.

19 From its mouth go flaming torches;
  sparks of fire leap out.

20 Out of its nostrils comes smoke,
  as from a boiling pot and burning rushes.

21 Its breath kindles coals,
  and a flame comes out of its mouth.

22 In its neck abides strength,
  and terror dances before it.

23 The folds of its flesh cling together;
  it is firmly cast and immovable.

24 Its heart is as hard as stone,
  as hard as the lower millstone.

25 When it raises itself up the gods are afraid;
  at the crashing they are beside themselves.

26 Though the sword reaches it, it does not avail,
  nor does the spear, the dart, or the javelin.

27 It counts iron as straw,
  and bronze as rotten wood.

28 The arrow cannot make it flee;
  slingstones, for it, are turned to chaff.

29 Clubs are counted as chaff;
  it laughs at the rattle of javelins.

30 Its underparts are like sharp potsherds;
  it spreads itself like a threshing sledge on the mire.

31 It makes the deep boil like a pot;
  it makes the sea like a pot of ointment.

32 It leaves a shining wake behind it;
  one would think the deep to be white-haired.

33 On earth it has no equal,
  a creature without fear.

34 It surveys everything that is lofty;
  it is king over all that are proud."

a Ch 41.1 in Heb   b Heb of it   c Cn Compare Symmachus Syr: Heb one is   d Heb me   e Gk: Heb that I shall repay   f Heb to me   g Gk: Heb bridle   h Cn Compare Gk Vg: Heb pride

The Mighty Beast

JOB 41.12–34

This picture of Leviathan, the great monster of the deep, is like the loud, triumphant ending of a great symphony—intended to leave us in awe, to stop us in our tracks. What music comes to mind as you think of this picture? Listen to Haydn's oratorio *Creation*, to Grofé's *Grand Canyon Suite*, to Dvořák's symphony *From the New World* or to some exultant song of praise. What emotions does the music evoke? Then read again the poetry of 41.12–34. Compare your reactions to the music with your reactions to the words of this passage. How can you express your awe and wonder at all God has done? What moves you to praise God?

See *Meeting God in Worship*

Beyond the Questions

JOB 42.5

The affirmation that Job makes shows how he has moved from thinking and talking about God to encountering God personally—one of the greatest leaps in the spiritual life. Job has grown beyond discussing theology with his friends. He has grown beyond wanting God to answer him. Now, hearing God's voice, he sees that the goal is not an exchange of ideas but a relationship. Being with God is more important than understanding God.

Can you point to a moment when God became real to you in a way that caused you to put aside all your questions and simply rest in him? Sit in God's presence now and put aside your thoughts. Open yourself to receive God. Welcome God, even when you do not understand and even when your questions go unanswered.

See Meeting God in Prayer

Job Is Humbled and Satisfied

42 Then Job answered the LORD:
2 "I know that you can do all things,
    and that no purpose of yours can be thwarted.
3 'Who is this that hides counsel without knowledge?'
    Therefore I have uttered what I did not understand,
    things too wonderful for me, which I did not
        know.
4 'Hear, and I will speak;
    I will question you, and you declare to me.'
5 I had heard of you by the hearing of the ear,
    but now my eye sees you;
6 therefore I despise myself,
    and repent in dust and ashes."

Job's Friends Are Humiliated

7 After the LORD had spoken these words to Job, the LORD said to Eliphaz the Temanite: "My wrath is kindled against you and against your two friends; for you have not spoken of me what is right, as my servant Job has. 8Now therefore take seven bulls and seven rams, and go to my servant Job, and offer up for yourselves a burnt offering; and my servant Job shall pray for you, for I will accept his prayer not to deal with you according to your folly; for you have not spoken of me what is right, as my servant Job has done." 9So Eliphaz the Temanite and Bildad the Shuhite and Zophar the Naamathite went and did what the LORD had told them; and the LORD accepted Job's prayer.

Job's Fortunes Are Restored Twofold

10 And the LORD restored the fortunes of Job when he had prayed for his friends; and the LORD gave Job twice as much as he had before. 11Then there came to him all his brothers and sisters and all who had known him before, and they ate bread with him in his house; they showed him sympathy and comforted him for all the evil that the LORD had brought upon him; and each of them gave him a piece of money*a* and a gold ring. 12The LORD blessed the latter days of Job more than his beginning; and he had fourteen thousand sheep, six thousand camels, a thousand yoke of oxen, and a thousand donkeys. 13He also had seven sons and three daughters. 14He named the first Jemimah, the second Keziah, and the third Keren-happuch. 15In all the land there were no women so beautiful as Job's daughters; and their father gave them an inheritance along with their brothers. 16After this Job lived one hundred and forty years, and saw his children, and his children's children, four generations. 17And Job died, old and full of days.

a Heb a qesitah

THE PSALMS

Honest to God

KEY VERSE:

Your word is a lamp to my feet and a light to my path.—Psalm 119.105

The life of prayer, like life itself, is not always happy and peaceful. Into prayer we take our anxieties, loneliness and discouragement along with our joy, awe and celebration. In order to deepen any intimate relationship, we must be honest about our feelings. Relating to the God of the universe is no different. In fact, God knows us better than we know ourselves and always desires "truth in the inward being" (Psalm 51.6).

The book of Psalms demonstrates such honest prayer. It contains songs of praise and prayers of lament, hymns celebrating God's steadfast love and prayers for vindication against enemies. The psalmists recall God's faithful love to his people and extol the marvels of his created order. As we read we share the psalmists' loneliness, sickness, grief and dread. We experience with them the ups and downs of their genuine spiritual journeys.

Perhaps no other book in the Bible has been read and meditated on as much as the book of Psalms. In most monasteries, the psalms are recited from morning until night. Through prayerful repetition, the psalms reach deeper and deeper into our hearts. When we "pray the psalms," we find new dimensions in our relationship with God. The psalms are a sanctuary of prayer to which we may daily retreat and find crucial nourishment for our hearts.

> "The psalms are more than language. They contain within themselves the silence of high mountains and the silence of heaven . . . [and] become the Tabernacle of God in which we are protected forever from the rage of the city of business, from the racket of human opinions."
>
> —THOMAS MERTON,
> *Bread in the Wilderness*

Deeply Rooted

PSALM 1.1–3

One legacy we receive from the Old Testament writers is their dedication to the "law of the LORD" and to its significance in daily life. By meditating on scripture over and over, this psalmist grows roots "like [trees] planted by streams of water." The practice of *lectio divina*, or divine reading, is a way to become "rooted" in scripture. Choose a verse and repeat it silently to yourself a few times. Listen to what God may be saying to you. You may hear the Spirit ask, "How strong are your roots? Are you planting yourself by streams of water? What are those streams?"

See Meeting God in Prayer

BOOK I

(Psalms 1-41)

Psalm 1

1 Happy are those
　　who do not follow the advice of the wicked,
　or take the path that sinners tread,
　　or sit in the seat of scoffers;
2 but their delight is in the law of the LORD,
　　and on his law they meditate day and night.
3 They are like trees
　　planted by streams of water,
　which yield their fruit in its season,
　　and their leaves do not wither.
　In all that they do, they prosper.

4 The wicked are not so,
　　but are like chaff that the wind drives away.
5 Therefore the wicked will not stand in the
　　　judgment,
　　nor sinners in the congregation of the righteous;
6 for the LORD watches over the way of the righteous,
　　but the way of the wicked will perish.

Psalm 2

1 Why do the nations conspire,
　　and the peoples plot in vain?
2 The kings of the earth set themselves,
　　and the rulers take counsel together,
　　against the LORD and his anointed, saying,
3 "Let us burst their bonds asunder,
　　and cast their cords from us."

4 He who sits in the heavens laughs;
　　the LORD has them in derision.
5 Then he will speak to them in his wrath,
　　and terrify them in his fury, saying,
6 "I have set my king on Zion, my holy hill."

7 I will tell of the decree of the LORD:
　He said to me, "You are my son;
　　today I have begotten you.
8 Ask of me, and I will make the nations your
　　　heritage,
　　and the ends of the earth your possession.
9 You shall break them with a rod of iron,
　　and dash them in pieces like a potter's vessel."

10 Now therefore, O kings, be wise;
　　be warned, O rulers of the earth.
11 Serve the LORD with fear,
　　with trembling 12kiss his feet,*a*
　or he will be angry, and you will perish in the way;
　　for his wrath is quickly kindled.

Happy are all who take refuge in him.

a Cn: Meaning of Heb of verses 11b and 12a is uncertain

Psalm 3

A Psalm of David, when he fled from his son Absalom.

1 O Lord, how many are my foes!
   Many are rising against me;
2 many are saying to me,
   "There is no help for you[a] in God."   *Selah*

3 But you, O Lord, are a shield around me,
   my glory, and the one who lifts up my head.
4 I cry aloud to the Lord,
   and he answers me from his holy hill.   *Selah*

5 I lie down and sleep;
   I wake again, for the Lord sustains me.
6 I am not afraid of ten thousands of people
   who have set themselves against me all around.

7 Rise up, O Lord!
   Deliver me, O my God!
For you strike all my enemies on the cheek;
   you break the teeth of the wicked.

8 Deliverance belongs to the Lord;
   may your blessing be on your people!   *Selah*

Psalm 4

To the leader: with stringed instruments. A Psalm of David.

1 Answer me when I call, O God of my right!
   You gave me room when I was in distress.
   Be gracious to me, and hear my prayer.

2 How long, you people, shall my honor suffer
      shame?
   How long will you love vain words, and seek after
      lies?   *Selah*
3 But know that the Lord has set apart the faithful for
      himself;
   the Lord hears when I call to him.

4 When you are disturbed,[b] do not sin;
   ponder it on your beds, and be silent.   *Selah*
5 Offer right sacrifices,
   and put your trust in the Lord.

6 There are many who say, "O that we might see
      some good!
   Let the light of your face shine on us, O Lord!"
7 You have put gladness in my heart
   more than when their grain and wine abound.

8 I will both lie down and sleep in peace;
   for you alone, O Lord, make me lie down in
      safety.

A Constant Source of Help

PSALM 3.3–5

The psalmist faces danger and adversity but reminds himself that the Lord is a shield surrounding him; he sleeps and awakes in the assurance that God is sustaining him. What images of God's presence comfort you and remind you of your Lord's steadfast care? In the Psalms, metaphors for God's nearness include shepherd, light, rock and shield. English mystic Julian of Norwich envisioned all creation as a hazelnut carried in the palm of the divine hand. As you go to sleep this night and wake up in the morning, meditate for a few minutes on a favorite image of God's protection.

See Meeting God in Worship

Morning With God

PSALM 5.1–3

How easy it is to begin the day in a mad rush of getting ready—finding missing socks and eating burnt toast—and forget to begin the day in God's presence. By beginning the day in prayer, if only for several minutes, we join the psalmist in "watching" for God. We offer our sighs, hopes, worries and dreams on the altar of our hearts before our daily concerns distract us. God desires that we watch in humble expectancy.

In your journal or with a close friend, consider practical ways that you might begin your day with God. Perhaps, for a week, you might set your alarm twenty minutes earlier than you usually do; use that extra time to meditate on a psalm, read a devotional book or offer your prayer before God in silence.

See Meeting God in Prayer

Psalm 5

To the leader: for the flutes. A Psalm of David.

1 Give ear to my words, O Lᴏʀᴅ;
  give heed to my sighing.
2 Listen to the sound of my cry,
  my King and my God,
  for to you I pray.
3 O Lᴏʀᴅ, in the morning you hear my voice;
  in the morning I plead my case to you, and
    watch.

4 For you are not a God who delights in wickedness;
  evil will not sojourn with you.
5 The boastful will not stand before your eyes;
  you hate all evildoers.
6 You destroy those who speak lies;
  the Lᴏʀᴅ abhors the bloodthirsty and deceitful.

7 But I, through the abundance of your steadfast love,
    will enter your house,
  I will bow down toward your holy temple
    in awe of you.
8 Lead me, O Lᴏʀᴅ, in your righteousness
    because of my enemies;
  make your way straight before me.

9 For there is no truth in their mouths;
    their hearts are destruction;
  their throats are open graves;
    they flatter with their tongues.
10 Make them bear their guilt, O God;
    let them fall by their own counsels;
  because of their many transgressions cast them out,
    for they have rebelled against you.

11 But let all who take refuge in you rejoice;
    let them ever sing for joy.
  Spread your protection over them,
    so that those who love your name may exult in
      you.
12 For you bless the righteous, O Lᴏʀᴅ;
    you cover them with favor as with a shield.

Psalm 6

To the leader: with stringed instruments; according to The
  Sheminith. A Psalm of David.

1 O Lᴏʀᴅ, do not rebuke me in your anger,
    or discipline me in your wrath.
2 Be gracious to me, O Lᴏʀᴅ, for I am languishing;
    O Lᴏʀᴅ, heal me, for my bones are shaking with
      terror.
3 My soul also is struck with terror,
    while you, O Lᴏʀᴅ—how long?

4 Turn, O Lᴏʀᴅ, save my life;
    deliver me for the sake of your steadfast love.
5 For in death there is no remembrance of you;
    in Sheol who can give you praise?

6 I am weary with my moaning;
   every night I flood my bed with tears;
   I drench my couch with my weeping.
7 My eyes waste away because of grief;
   they grow weak because of all my foes.

8 Depart from me, all you workers of evil,
   for the LORD has heard the sound of my
     weeping.
9 The LORD has heard my supplication;
   the LORD accepts my prayer.
10 All my enemies shall be ashamed and struck with
    terror;
   they shall turn back, and in a moment be put to
    shame.

Psalm 7

A Shiggaion of David, which he sang to the LORD concerning
Cush, a Benjaminite.

1 O LORD my God, in you I take refuge;
   save me from all my pursuers, and deliver me,
2 or like a lion they will tear me apart;
   they will drag me away, with no one to rescue.

3 O LORD my God, if I have done this,
   if there is wrong in my hands,
4 if I have repaid my ally with harm
   or plundered my foe without cause,
5 then let the enemy pursue and overtake me,
   trample my life to the ground,
   and lay my soul in the dust.   *Selah*

6 Rise up, O LORD, in your anger;
   lift yourself up against the fury of my enemies;
   awake, O my God;[a] you have appointed a
    judgment.
7 Let the assembly of the peoples be gathered around
    you,
   and over it take your seat[b] on high.
8 The LORD judges the peoples;
   judge me, O LORD, according to my
    righteousness
   and according to the integrity that is in me.

9 O let the evil of the wicked come to an end,
   but establish the righteous,
you who test the minds and hearts,
   O righteous God.
10 God is my shield,
   who saves the upright in heart.
11 God is a righteous judge,
   and a God who has indignation every day.

12 If one does not repent, God[c] will whet his sword;
   he has bent and strung his bow;
13 he has prepared his deadly weapons,
   making his arrows fiery shafts.

How Long?

PSALM 6.6–8

The constant pain of chronic illness and the utter loneliness of deep grief—these are realities the psalmist deals with openly before God. "Where are you, God? Why is it taking so long?" he cries out, groaning in his weariness before God. Jesus himself felt a sense of abandonment at the cross, saying "Why have you forsaken me?" (Matthew 27.46). These feelings are natural; there is no need to withhold them in prayer, for God already knows what is yet unspoken. What feelings are you trying to hide from God—anguish, despair, fear? Are you angry with God about something? On a small piece of paper, list one or more of your hidden feelings, and hold the list in your hand as you pray a prayer of waiting.

See Meeting God in Prayer

a Or *awake for me*   b Cn: Heb *return*   c Heb *he*

God's Ordering

PSALM 8.3–6

One way to understand the meaning of "dominion" is to liken it to the loving care of a parent for a child. It is remarkable that God entrusts human beings with a major role in the care of the earth. Following the Franciscan model of faithfulness in action, write down in your journal five things you can do this week to lovingly care for your home and garden, your town or city and the earth and sky. As modern mystic Pierre Teilhard de Chardin invites: "Try, with God's help, to perceive the connection—even physical and natural—which binds your labor with the building of the kingdom of heaven."

See Meeting God in the Created Order

14 See how they conceive evil,
    and are pregnant with mischief,
    and bring forth lies.
15 They make a pit, digging it out,
    and fall into the hole that they have made.
16 Their mischief returns upon their own heads,
    and on their own heads their violence descends.

17 I will give to the LORD the thanks due to his
    righteousness,
    and sing praise to the name of the LORD, the Most
    High.

Psalm 8

To the leader: according to The Gittith. A Psalm of David.

1 O LORD, our Sovereign,
    how majestic is your name in all the earth!

You have set your glory above the heavens.
2   Out of the mouths of babes and infants
you have founded a bulwark because of your foes,
    to silence the enemy and the avenger.

3 When I look at your heavens, the work of your
    fingers,
    the moon and the stars that you have established;
4 what are human beings that you are mindful of
    them,
    mortals*a* that you care for them?

5 Yet you have made them a little lower than God,*b*
    and crowned them with glory and honor.
6 You have given them dominion over the works of
    your hands;
    you have put all things under their feet,
7 all sheep and oxen,
    and also the beasts of the field,
8 the birds of the air, and the fish of the sea,
    whatever passes along the paths of the seas.

9 O LORD, our Sovereign,
    how majestic is your name in all the earth!

Psalm 9

To the leader: according to Muth-labben. A Psalm of David.

1 I will give thanks to the LORD with my whole heart;
    I will tell of all your wonderful deeds.
2 I will be glad and exult in you;
    I will sing praise to your name, O Most High.

3 When my enemies turned back,
    they stumbled and perished before you.
4 For you have maintained my just cause;
    you have sat on the throne giving righteous
    judgment.

a Heb *ben adam*, lit. *son of man*   *b* Or *than the divine beings* or *angels*: Heb *elohim*

5 You have rebuked the nations, you have destroyed
        the wicked;
    you have blotted out their name forever and ever.
6 The enemies have vanished in everlasting ruins;
        their cities you have rooted out;
        the very memory of them has perished.

7 But the LORD sits enthroned forever,
        he has established his throne for judgment.
8 He judges the world with righteousness;
        he judges the peoples with equity.

9 The LORD is a stronghold for the oppressed,
        a stronghold in times of trouble.
10 And those who know your name put their trust in
        you,
    for you, O LORD, have not forsaken those who
        seek you.

11 Sing praises to the LORD, who dwells in Zion.
        Declare his deeds among the peoples.
12 For he who avenges blood is mindful of them;
        he does not forget the cry of the afflicted.

13 Be gracious to me, O LORD.
        See what I suffer from those who hate me;
        you are the one who lifts me up from the gates of
        death,
14 so that I may recount all your praises,
        and, in the gates of daughter Zion,
        rejoice in your deliverance.

15 The nations have sunk in the pit that they made;
        in the net that they hid has their own foot been
        caught.
16 The LORD has made himself known, he has
        executed judgment;
    the wicked are snared in the work of their own
        hands.   *Higgaion. Selah*

17 The wicked shall depart to Sheol,
        all the nations that forget God.

18 For the needy shall not always be forgotten,
        nor the hope of the poor perish forever.

19 Rise up, O LORD! Do not let mortals prevail;
        let the nations be judged before you.
20 Put them in fear, O LORD;
        let the nations know that they are only human.
                                                    Selah

Psalm 10

1 Why, O LORD, do you stand far off?
        Why do you hide yourself in times of trouble?
2 In arrogance the wicked persecute the poor—
        let them be caught in the schemes they have
        devised.

Knowing God's Name

PSALM 9.10

Think of the name of someone you love. Whom do you picture when you hear that name? Perhaps you see a favorite aunt who cared for you when you were small or a dear friend who always makes you laugh. When you "know" a name, you know the person behind the name; when we know the name of Jesus Christ, we know God's infinite love and saving grace. Take five minutes to meditate on the name for God that reminds you of God's steadfast love. Close your eyes, say the name quietly to yourself and reflect on the images that emerge.

See Meeting God in Worship

699

Hope for the Hopeless

PSALM 10.17–18

In Matthew 5.5, Jesus makes the startling proclamation: "Blessed are the meek, for they will inherit the earth." The meek are "the orphan and the oppressed" of this psalm, and the psalmist expresses his feelings of hopelessness on their behalf. God seems far away, while the "wicked" crush the poor. Yet as Jesus called the meek "blessed," so also there is a note of hope in the last verses of this psalm.

We may feel that "God has forgotten" when we read headlines about a baby being drowned in a bathtub by an abusive parent or about children dying of hunger by the tens of thousands every day. Today choose one newspaper headline about a troubling incident and pray in hopeful intercession for that situation.

See Meeting God in Service

3 For the wicked boast of the desires of their heart,
those greedy for gain curse and renounce the LORD.
4 In the pride of their countenance the wicked say,
"God will not seek it out";
all their thoughts are, "There is no God."

5 Their ways prosper at all times;
your judgments are on high, out of their sight;
as for their foes, they scoff at them.
6 They think in their heart, "We shall not be moved;
throughout all generations we shall not meet
adversity."

7 Their mouths are filled with cursing and deceit and
oppression;
under their tongues are mischief and iniquity.
8 They sit in ambush in the villages;
in hiding places they murder the innocent.

Their eyes stealthily watch for the helpless;
9 they lurk in secret like a lion in its covert;
they lurk that they may seize the poor;
they seize the poor and drag them off in their net.

10 They stoop, they crouch,
and the helpless fall by their might.
11 They think in their heart, "God has forgotten,
he has hidden his face, he will never see it."

12 Rise up, O LORD; O God, lift up your hand;
do not forget the oppressed.
13 Why do the wicked renounce God,
and say in their hearts, "You will not call us to
account"?

14 But you do see! Indeed you note trouble and grief,
that you may take it into your hands;
the helpless commit themselves to you;
you have been the helper of the orphan.

15 Break the arm of the wicked and evildoers;
seek out their wickedness until you find none.
16 The LORD is king forever and ever;
the nations shall perish from his land.

17 O LORD, you will hear the desire of the meek;
you will strengthen their heart, you will incline
your ear
18 to do justice for the orphan and the oppressed,
so that those from earth may strike terror no
more.*a*

Psalm 11

To the leader. Of David.

1 In the LORD I take refuge; how can you say to me,
"Flee like a bird to the mountains;*b*

---

a Meaning of Heb uncertain   *b* Gk Syr Jerome Tg: Heb *flee to your mountain, O bird*

2 for look, the wicked bend the bow,
   they have fitted their arrow to the string,
   to shoot in the dark at the upright in heart.
3 If the foundations are destroyed,
   what can the righteous do?"

4 The Lord is in his holy temple;
   the Lord's throne is in heaven.
   His eyes behold, his gaze examines humankind.
5 The Lord tests the righteous and the wicked,
   and his soul hates the lover of violence.
6 On the wicked he will rain coals of fire and sulfur;
   a scorching wind shall be the portion of their cup.
7 For the Lord is righteous;
   he loves righteous deeds;
   the upright shall behold his face.

Psalm 12

To the leader: according to The Sheminith. A Psalm of David.

1 Help, O Lord, for there is no longer anyone who is
       godly;
   the faithful have disappeared from humankind.
2 They utter lies to each other;
   with flattering lips and a double heart they speak.

3 May the Lord cut off all flattering lips,
   the tongue that makes great boasts,
4 those who say, "With our tongues we will prevail;
   our lips are our own—who is our master?"

5 "Because the poor are despoiled, because the
       needy groan,
   I will now rise up," says the Lord;
   "I will place them in the safety for which they
       long."
6 The promises of the Lord are promises that are
       pure,
   silver refined in a furnace on the ground,
   purified seven times.

7 You, O Lord, will protect us;
   you will guard us from this generation forever.
8 On every side the wicked prowl,
   as vileness is exalted among humankind.

Psalm 13

To the leader. A Psalm of David.

1 How long, O Lord? Will you forget me forever?
   How long will you hide your face from me?
2 How long must I bear pain[a] in my soul,
   and have sorrow in my heart all day long?
   How long shall my enemy be exalted over me?

3 Consider and answer me, O Lord my God!
   Give light to my eyes, or I will sleep the sleep of
       death,

God's Faithfulness in Despair

PSALM 13.1–6

Mystic Simone Weil wrote, "At the bottom of the heart of every human being, from earliest infancy until the tomb, there is something that goes on indomitably expecting, in the teeth of all experience of crimes committed, suffered, and witnessed, that good and not evil will be done to him. It is this above all that is sacred in every human being." The psalmist also "expects" God's loving faithfulness. He even believes one day he will "sing to the Lord, because [God] has dealt bountifully with me." In your journal, reflect on one of your deepest hopes about a difficult situation. Find or make an object to symbolize it. Offer that hope to God in a prayer of expectancy.

---

a Syr: Heb *hold counsels*

Worship: The Heart's Examination

PSALM 15.1–5

Theologian Karl Barth tells a story of a professor who would often ask his students, "How are things with your heart?" When we worship God, we face the same question. In coming to God's sanctuary, the psalmist asks himself the hard questions about whether he has been faithful to God's law: "Have I been honest? Have I honored God even though it might have hurt me? Have I benefited from the distress of the disadvantaged or weak?" As you prepare for worship this week, consider these questions in personal prayer, in your journal or with a close friend.

See Meeting God in Worship

4 and my enemy will say, "I have prevailed";
   my foes will rejoice because I am shaken.

5 But I trusted in your steadfast love;
   my heart shall rejoice in your salvation.
6 I will sing to the LORD,
   because he has dealt bountifully with me.

Psalm 14

To the leader. Of David.

1 Fools say in their hearts, "There is no God."
   They are corrupt, they do abominable deeds;
   there is no one who does good.

2 The LORD looks down from heaven on humankind
   to see if there are any who are wise,
   who seek after God.

3 They have all gone astray, they are all alike perverse;
   there is no one who does good,
   no, not one.

4 Have they no knowledge, all the evildoers
   who eat up my people as they eat bread,
   and do not call upon the LORD?

5 There they shall be in great terror,
   for God is with the company of the righteous.
6 You would confound the plans of the poor,
   but the LORD is their refuge.

7 O that deliverance for Israel would come from Zion!
   When the LORD restores the fortunes of his people,
   Jacob will rejoice; Israel will be glad.

Psalm 15

A Psalm of David.

1 O LORD, who may abide in your tent?
   Who may dwell on your holy hill?

2 Those who walk blamelessly, and do what is right,
   and speak the truth from their heart;
3 who do not slander with their tongue,
   and do no evil to their friends,
   nor take up a reproach against their neighbors;
4 in whose eyes the wicked are despised,
   but who honor those who fear the LORD;
   who stand by their oath even to their hurt;
5 who do not lend money at interest,
   and do not take a bribe against the innocent.

Those who do these things shall never be moved.

Psalm 16

A Miktam of David.

1 Protect me, O God, for in you I take refuge.
2 I say to the LORD, "You are my Lord;
I have no good apart from you."*a*

3 As for the holy ones in the land, they are the noble,
in whom is all my delight.

4 Those who choose another god multiply their
sorrows;*b*
their drink offerings of blood I will not pour out
or take their names upon my lips.

5 The LORD is my chosen portion and my cup;
you hold my lot.
6 The boundary lines have fallen for me in pleasant
places;
I have a goodly heritage.

7 I bless the LORD who gives me counsel;
in the night also my heart instructs me.
8 I keep the LORD always before me;
because he is at my right hand, I shall not be
moved.

9 Therefore my heart is glad, and my soul rejoices;
my body also rests secure.
10 For you do not give me up to Sheol,
or let your faithful one see the Pit.

11 You show me the path of life.
In your presence there is fullness of joy;
in your right hand are pleasures forevermore.

Psalm 17

A Prayer of David.

1 Hear a just cause, O LORD; attend to my cry;
give ear to my prayer from lips free of deceit.
2 From you let my vindication come;
let your eyes see the right.

3 If you try my heart, if you visit me by night,
if you test me, you will find no wickedness in me;
my mouth does not transgress.
4 As for what others do, by the word of your lips
I have avoided the ways of the violent.
5 My steps have held fast to your paths;
my feet have not slipped.

6 I call upon you, for you will answer me, O God;
incline your ear to me, hear my words.
7 Wondrously show your steadfast love,
O savior of those who seek refuge
from their adversaries at your right hand.

The Path of Life: Fullness of Joy

PSALM 16.11

One of the recurring themes in the Psalms is that God's path is a way of life. In the old favorite, Psalm 23, the psalmist claims God's mercy and goodness all along this path of life. The delights along the path with God are not material, but spiritual. What are the spiritual gifts you have found along your path? What moments in the last twenty-four hours do you feel grateful for? How have you experienced grace in this past week? Reflect on ways you have known God's presence in your life.

See Meeting God in Everyday Life

---

a Jerome Tg: Meaning of Heb uncertain   *b* Cn: Meaning of Heb uncertain

The Apple of God's Eye

The psalmist is by no means timid when he prays, "Guard me as the apple of [your] eye." Indeed, if we look into God's eyes deeply enough, we will find more and more love, but it is a love that is not always easy for us to accept. "The great spiritual call of the Beloved Children of God," Henri Nouwen writes, "is to pull their brokenness away from the shadow of the curse and put it under the light of the blessing."

On your bathroom mirror or the dashboard of your car, affix a Scripture passage that expresses God's blessing, such as "You are precious in my sight, and honored, and I love you" (Isaiah 43.4), or "I have loved you with an everlasting love; therefore I have continued my faithfulness to you" (Jeremiah 31.3).

See Meeting God in Scripture

8 Guard me as the apple of the eye;
  hide me in the shadow of your wings,
9 from the wicked who despoil me,
  my deadly enemies who surround me.
10 They close their hearts to pity;
  with their mouths they speak arrogantly.
11 They track me down;[a] now they surround me;
  they set their eyes to cast me to the ground.
12 They are like a lion eager to tear,
  like a young lion lurking in ambush.

13 Rise up, O LORD, confront them, overthrow them!
  By your sword deliver my life from the wicked,
14 from mortals—by your hand, O LORD—
  from mortals whose portion in life is in this world.
May their bellies be filled with what you have stored up for them;
  may their children have more than enough;
  may they leave something over to their little ones.

15 As for me, I shall behold your face in righteousness;
  when I awake I shall be satisfied, beholding your likeness.

Psalm 18

To the leader. A Psalm of David the servant of the LORD, who addressed the words of this song to the LORD on the day when the LORD delivered him from the hand of all his enemies, and from the hand of Saul. He said:

1 I love you, O LORD, my strength.
2 The LORD is my rock, my fortress, and my deliverer,
  my God, my rock in whom I take refuge,
  my shield, and the horn of my salvation, my stronghold.
3 I call upon the LORD, who is worthy to be praised,
  so I shall be saved from my enemies.

4 The cords of death encompassed me;
  the torrents of perdition assailed me;
5 the cords of Sheol entangled me;
  the snares of death confronted me.

6 In my distress I called upon the LORD;
  to my God I cried for help.
From his temple he heard my voice,
  and my cry to him reached his ears.

7 Then the earth reeled and rocked;
  the foundations also of the mountains trembled
  and quaked, because he was angry.
8 Smoke went up from his nostrils,
  and devouring fire from his mouth;
  glowing coals flamed forth from him.
9 He bowed the heavens, and came down;
  thick darkness was under his feet.

a One Ms Compare Syr: MT *Our steps*

¹⁰ He rode on a cherub, and flew;
    he came swiftly upon the wings of the wind.
¹¹ He made darkness his covering around him,
    his canopy thick clouds dark with water.
¹² Out of the brightness before him
    there broke through his clouds
    hailstones and coals of fire.
¹³ The LORD also thundered in the heavens,
    and the Most High uttered his voice.^a
¹⁴ And he sent out his arrows, and scattered them;
    he flashed forth lightnings, and routed them.
¹⁵ Then the channels of the sea were seen,
    and the foundations of the world were laid bare
    at your rebuke, O LORD,
    at the blast of the breath of your nostrils.

¹⁶ He reached down from on high, he took me;
    he drew me out of mighty waters.
¹⁷ He delivered me from my strong enemy,
    and from those who hated me;
    for they were too mighty for me.
¹⁸ They confronted me in the day of my calamity;
    but the LORD was my support.
¹⁹ He brought me out into a broad place;
    he delivered me, because he delighted in me.

²⁰ The LORD rewarded me according to my
    righteousness;
    according to the cleanness of my hands he
    recompensed me.
²¹ For I have kept the ways of the LORD,
    and have not wickedly departed from my God.
²² For all his ordinances were before me,
    and his statutes I did not put away from me.
²³ I was blameless before him,
    and I kept myself from guilt.
²⁴ Therefore the LORD has recompensed me according
    to my righteousness,
    according to the cleanness of my hands in his
    sight.

²⁵ With the loyal you show yourself loyal;
    with the blameless you show yourself blameless;
²⁶ with the pure you show yourself pure;
    and with the crooked you show yourself perverse.
²⁷ For you deliver a humble people,
    but the haughty eyes you bring down.
²⁸ It is you who light my lamp;
    the LORD, my God, lights up my darkness.
²⁹ By you I can crush a troop,
    and by my God I can leap over a wall.
³⁰ This God—his way is perfect;
    the promise of the LORD proves true;
    he is a shield for all who take refuge in him.

³¹ For who is God except the LORD?
    And who is a rock besides our God?—
³² the God who girded me with strength,
    and made my way safe.

---

a Gk See 2 Sam 22.14: Heb adds *hailstones and coals of fire*

The Lamp of God

PSALM 18.28

Light is often used as a metaphor for Jesus Christ. The Gospel of John points out that through Jesus Christ we are able to see and to understand what is true. As we read this psalm, we see vivid images of the Christ-light guiding us out of darkness. What is the light of Christ inviting you to see in your heart and life? Do you need God to illuminate an area in your life currently obstructed by "clouds"? As you go through your day, picture this divine light surrounding you and ask God for insights about this cloudy situation.

See Meeting God in Everyday Life

God's Saving Presence

PSALM 18.35–36

The psalmist is not distant and polite in his devotional life. With fiery honesty the psalmist prays for victory over his enemies. We may feel uncomfortable with the violence of the psalmist's emotion and with God's intervention in the battle scenario; it seems primitive and strange to our twentieth-century minds.

There are no doubt moments in your life when God seems to have broadened the place for your steps in unseen and inexplicable ways. In your journal or on a piece of paper, mark off periods of your life in ten-year increments (i.e., 1–10, 10–20, 20–30, and so forth). For each time period, recall a special moment of God's inspiration or intervention.

See Meeting God in Everyday Life

33 He made my feet like the feet of a deer,
   and set me secure on the heights.
34 He trains my hands for war,
   so that my arms can bend a bow of bronze.
35 You have given me the shield of your salvation,
   and your right hand has supported me;
   your help[a] has made me great.
36 You gave me a wide place for my steps under me,
   and my feet did not slip.
37 I pursued my enemies and overtook them;
   and did not turn back until they were consumed.
38 I struck them down, so that they were not able to rise;
   they fell under my feet.
39 For you girded me with strength for the battle;
   you made my assailants sink under me.
40 You made my enemies turn their backs to me,
   and those who hated me I destroyed.
41 They cried for help, but there was no one to save them;
   they cried to the LORD, but he did not answer them.
42 I beat them fine, like dust before the wind;
   I cast them out like the mire of the streets.

43 You delivered me from strife with the peoples;[b]
   you made me head of the nations;
   people whom I had not known served me.
44 As soon as they heard of me they obeyed me;
   foreigners came cringing to me.
45 Foreigners lost heart,
   and came trembling out of their strongholds.

46 The LORD lives! Blessed be my rock,
   and exalted be the God of my salvation,
47 the God who gave me vengeance
   and subdued peoples under me;
48 who delivered me from my enemies;
   indeed, you exalted me above my adversaries;
   you delivered me from the violent.

49 For this I will extol you, O LORD, among the nations,
   and sing praises to your name.
50 Great triumphs he gives to his king,
   and shows steadfast love to his anointed,
   to David and his descendants forever.

Psalm 19

To the leader. A Psalm of David.

1 The heavens are telling the glory of God;
   and the firmament[c] proclaims his handiwork.
2 Day to day pours forth speech,
   and night to night declares knowledge.
3 There is no speech, nor are there words;
   their voice is not heard;
4 yet their voice[d] goes out through all the earth,
   and their words to the end of the world.

a Or *gentleness*   *b* Gk Tg: Heb *people*   *c* Or *dome*   *d* Gk Jerome
Compare Syr: Heb *line*

In the heavens[a] he has set a tent for the sun,
5 which comes out like a bridegroom from his
        wedding canopy,
    and like a strong man runs its course with joy.
6 Its rising is from the end of the heavens,
    and its circuit to the end of them;
    and nothing is hid from its heat.

7 The law of the LORD is perfect,
    reviving the soul;
    the decrees of the LORD are sure,
    making wise the simple;
8 the precepts of the LORD are right,
    rejoicing the heart;
    the commandment of the LORD is clear,
    enlightening the eyes;
9 the fear of the LORD is pure,
    enduring forever;
    the ordinances of the LORD are true
    and righteous altogether.
10 More to be desired are they than gold,
    even much fine gold;
    sweeter also than honey,
    and drippings of the honeycomb.

11 Moreover by them is your servant warned;
    in keeping them there is great reward.
12 But who can detect their errors?
    Clear me from hidden faults.
13 Keep back your servant also from the insolent;[b]
    do not let them have dominion over me.
    Then I shall be blameless,
    and innocent of great transgression.

14 Let the words of my mouth and the meditation of
        my heart
    be acceptable to you,
    O LORD, my rock and my redeemer.

Psalm 20

To the leader. A Psalm of David.

1 The LORD answer you in the day of trouble!
    The name of the God of Jacob protect you!
2 May he send you help from the sanctuary,
    and give you support from Zion.
3 May he remember all your offerings,
    and regard with favor your burnt sacrifices. *Selah*

4 May he grant you your heart's desire,
    and fulfill all your plans.
5 May we shout for joy over your victory,
    and in the name of our God set up our banners.
    May the LORD fulfill all your petitions.

6 Now I know that the LORD will help his anointed;
    he will answer him from his holy heaven
    with mighty victories by his right hand.

Sweeter Than Honey

PSALM 19.7–10

The Torah, or the Law of Moses, is central to the spirituality of the Hebrew people. The "law of the LORD," the psalmist reflects here, offers wisdom more valuable than riches and more satisfying than any sweetness. Why do we neglect Scripture, the centerpiece of our Christian lives? And when the words become all too familiar and we know the stories by heart, how are we to listen afresh to God's words?

Try reading this psalm as you would a love letter. What gifts do you receive from Scripture? What do you desire from God's truth?

See Meeting God in Scripture

---

a Heb *In them*   *b* Or *from proud thoughts*

Feeling Forsaken

PSALM 22.1

These familiar words, echoed by Jesus on the cross (Matthew 27.46; Mark 15.34), convey the utter loneliness of desperate suffering. Jesus suffered physically from torturous nails and from the pain of suffocation, but he also suffered psychologically. Abandoned by the One he loved most, Jesus cried out in terror.

You may also be waiting for God in loneliness or despairing grief, feeling you cannot find a way to hope. Cry out—as Jesus did—to the heavenly Father. God invites your honest emotions.

See Meeting God in Prayer

7 Some take pride in chariots, and some in horses,
 but our pride is in the name of the LORD our God.
8 They will collapse and fall,
 but we shall rise and stand upright.

9 Give victory to the king, O LORD;
 answer us when we call.[a]

Psalm 21

To the leader. A Psalm of David.

1 In your strength the king rejoices, O LORD,
 and in your help how greatly he exults!
2 You have given him his heart's desire,
 and have not withheld the request of his lips.
Selah
3 For you meet him with rich blessings;
 you set a crown of fine gold on his head.
4 He asked you for life; you gave it to him—
 length of days forever and ever.
5 His glory is great through your help;
 splendor and majesty you bestow on him.
6 You bestow on him blessings forever;
 you make him glad with the joy of your presence.
7 For the king trusts in the LORD,
 and through the steadfast love of the Most High
 he shall not be moved.

8 Your hand will find out all your enemies;
 your right hand will find out those who hate you.
9 You will make them like a fiery furnace
 when you appear.
The LORD will swallow them up in his wrath,
 and fire will consume them.
10 You will destroy their offspring from the earth,
 and their children from among humankind.
11 If they plan evil against you,
 if they devise mischief, they will not succeed.
12 For you will put them to flight;
 you will aim at their faces with your bows.

13 Be exalted, O LORD, in your strength!
 We will sing and praise your power.

Psalm 22

To the leader: according to The Deer of the Dawn.
A Psalm of David.

1 My God, my God, why have you forsaken me?
 Why are you so far from helping me, from the
 words of my groaning?
2 O my God, I cry by day, but you do not answer;
 and by night, but find no rest.

3 Yet you are holy,
 enthroned on the praises of Israel.
4 In you our ancestors trusted;
 they trusted, and you delivered them.

a Gk: Heb *give victory, O LORD; let the King answer us when we call*

5   To you they cried, and were saved;
       in you they trusted, and were not put to shame.

6   But I am a worm, and not human;
       scorned by others, and despised by the people.
7   All who see me mock at me;
       they make mouths at me, they shake their heads;
8   "Commit your cause to the LORD; let him deliver—
       let him rescue the one in whom he delights!"

9   Yet it was you who took me from the womb;
       you kept me safe on my mother's breast.
10 On you I was cast from my birth,
       and since my mother bore me you have been my
          God.
11 Do not be far from me,
       for trouble is near
       and there is no one to help.

12 Many bulls encircle me,
       strong bulls of Bashan surround me;
13 they open wide their mouths at me,
       like a ravening and roaring lion.

14 I am poured out like water,
       and all my bones are out of joint;
     my heart is like wax;
       it is melted within my breast;
15 my mouth*a* is dried up like a potsherd,
       and my tongue sticks to my jaws;
       you lay me in the dust of death.

16 For dogs are all around me;
       a company of evildoers encircles me.
     My hands and feet have shriveled;*b*
17 I can count all my bones.
     They stare and gloat over me;
18 they divide my clothes among themselves,
       and for my clothing they cast lots.

19 But you, O LORD, do not be far away!
       O my help, come quickly to my aid!
20 Deliver my soul from the sword,
       my life*c* from the power of the dog!
21 Save me from the mouth of the lion!

     From the horns of the wild oxen you have rescued*d*
          me.
22 I will tell of your name to my brothers and sisters;*e*
       in the midst of the congregation I will praise you:
23 You who fear the LORD, praise him!
       All you offspring of Jacob, glorify him;
       stand in awe of him, all you offspring of Israel!
24 For he did not despise or abhor
       the affliction of the afflicted;
     he did not hide his face from me,*f*
       but heard when I*g* cried to him.

Loved From Birth

PSALM 22.9–10

In the middle of this psalm about terrible suffering and forsakenness, the psalmist remembers that even in the womb he was protected by an unseen hand. We don't have to ask God to be present, for he is always with us; rather, we need to ask for an *awareness* of God's eternal presence. The mystic Meister Eckhart says, "You do not need to seek him here or there, he is no further off than the door of your heart."

What helps you to stay conscious of God's presence during the day? Find an object, such as a seashell or a picture from nature, that you can put on your desk or a table to remind you of God's nearness.

See Meeting God in the Created Order

---

a Cn: Heb *strength*   *b* Meaning of Heb uncertain   *c* Heb *my only one*
d Heb *answered*   *e* Or *kindred*   *f* Heb *him*   *g* Heb *he*

The Lord, My Shepherd

PSALM 23.1–6

Because this beautiful, comforting psalm is very familiar, you may be inclined to rush past it. Instead, try to savor the words through the practice of divine reading—reading Scripture slowly and listening for what speaks to you. Read the psalm; then close your Bible and try to recite it from memory. Pause after each verse. Listen for a word or phrase that seems to speak to you. Perhaps "my shepherd" or "still waters" or "my cup overflows" catches your attention. Let the images or feelings that emerge rest gently on your heart. What is God inviting you to think or pray about today?

See Meeting God in Scripture

25   From you comes my praise in the great
          congregation;
       my vows I will pay before those who fear
          him.
26   The poor[a] shall eat and be satisfied;
       those who seek him shall praise the LORD.
       May your hearts live forever!

27   All the ends of the earth shall remember
       and turn to the LORD;
     and all the families of the nations
       shall worship before him.[b]
28   For dominion belongs to the LORD,
       and he rules over the nations.

29   To him,[c] indeed, shall all who sleep in[d] the earth
          bow down;
       before him shall bow all who go down to the
          dust,
       and I shall live for him.[e]
30   Posterity will serve him;
       future generations will be told about the Lord,
31   and[f] proclaim his deliverance to a people yet
          unborn,
       saying that he has done it.

Psalm 23

A Psalm of David.

1   The LORD is my shepherd, I shall not want.
2   He makes me lie down in green pastures;
     he leads me beside still waters;[g]
3   he restores my soul.[h]
     He leads me in right paths[i]
       for his name's sake.

4   Even though I walk through the darkest valley,[j]
       I fear no evil;
     for you are with me;
       your rod and your staff—
       they comfort me.

5   You prepare a table before me
       in the presence of my enemies;
     you anoint my head with oil;
       my cup overflows.
6   Surely[k] goodness and mercy[l] shall follow me
       all the days of my life,
     and I shall dwell in the house of the LORD
       my whole life long.[m]

a Or *afflicted*   b Gk Syr Jerome: Heb *you*   c Cn: Heb *They have eaten and*
d Cn: Heb *all the fat ones*   e Compare Gk Syr Vg: Heb *and he who cannot
keep himself alive*   f Compare Gk: Heb *it will be told about the Lord to the
generation,* [31]*they will come and*   g Heb *waters of rest*   h Or *life*
i Or *paths of righteousness*   j Or *the valley of the shadow of death*
k Or *Only*   l Or *kindness*   m Heb *for length of days*

Psalm 24

Of David. A Psalm.

1 The earth is the LORD's and all that is in it,
    the world, and those who live in it;
2 for he has founded it on the seas,
    and established it on the rivers.

3 Who shall ascend the hill of the LORD?
    And who shall stand in his holy place?
4 Those who have clean hands and pure hearts,
    who do not lift up their souls to what is false,
    and do not swear deceitfully.
5 They will receive blessing from the LORD,
    and vindication from the God of their salvation.
6 Such is the company of those who seek him,
    who seek the face of the God of Jacob.[a]   Selah

7 Lift up your heads, O gates!
    and be lifted up, O ancient doors!
    that the King of glory may come in.
8 Who is the King of glory?
    The LORD, strong and mighty,
    the LORD, mighty in battle.
9 Lift up your heads, O gates!
    and be lifted up, O ancient doors!
    that the King of glory may come in.
10 Who is this King of glory?
    The LORD of hosts,
    he is the King of glory.   Selah

Psalm 25

Of David.

1 To you, O LORD, I lift up my soul.
2 O my God, in you I trust;
    do not let me be put to shame;
    do not let my enemies exult over me.
3 Do not let those who wait for you be put to shame;
    let them be ashamed who are wantonly
        treacherous.

4 Make me to know your ways, O LORD;
    teach me your paths.
5 Lead me in your truth, and teach me,
    for you are the God of my salvation;
    for you I wait all day long.

6 Be mindful of your mercy, O LORD, and of your
        steadfast love,
    for they have been from of old.
7 Do not remember the sins of my youth or my
        transgressions;
    according to your steadfast love remember me,
    for your goodness' sake, O LORD!

8 Good and upright is the LORD;
    therefore he instructs sinners in the way.

Our Precious Earth

PSALM 24.1–2

The earth is precious because it belongs to God, who designed an orderly and beautiful home for all creatures. Francis of Assisi lived daily in this knowledge—his image graces many gardens today because he loved the Creator and the creation. Consider which aspects of God's creation speak to you as you read a few verses from Francis's *The Canticle of Brother Sun:*

> Praised be You, my Lord,
>   through Brother Wind,
> and through the air, cloudy
>   and serene, and every
>   kind of weather
> through which You give
>   sustenance to Your
>   creatures.
> Praised be You, my Lord,
>   through Sister Water,
> which is very useful and
>   humble and precious
>   and chaste.

Try writing a verse or two of your own.

See Meeting God in the Created Order

---

a Gk Syr: Heb *your face, O Jacob*

Humility Before God

PSALM 25.9–10

The psalmist says that God "leads the humble in what is right." When we become humble, we discover that God's ways are "loving and faithful." In what ways may God be calling you to humility in your daily life? In what ways does your schedule demand anxious efficiency rather than humble availability to God in every moment? How are you treating others you meet in your busy day?

See *Meeting God in Everyday Life*

9 He leads the humble in what is right,
   and teaches the humble his way.
10 All the paths of the Lord are steadfast love and faithfulness,
   for those who keep his covenant and his decrees.

11 For your name's sake, O Lord,
   pardon my guilt, for it is great.
12 Who are they that fear the Lord?
   He will teach them the way that they should choose.
13 They will abide in prosperity,
   and their children shall possess the land.
14 The friendship of the Lord is for those who fear him,
   and he makes his covenant known to them.
15 My eyes are ever toward the Lord,
   for he will pluck my feet out of the net.

16 Turn to me and be gracious to me,
   for I am lonely and afflicted.
17 Relieve the troubles of my heart,
   and bring me*a* out of my distress.
18 Consider my affliction and my trouble,
   and forgive all my sins.

19 Consider how many are my foes,
   and with what violent hatred they hate me.
20 O guard my life, and deliver me;
   do not let me be put to shame, for I take refuge in you.
21 May integrity and uprightness preserve me,
   for I wait for you.

22 Redeem Israel, O God,
   out of all its troubles.

Psalm 26
Of David.

1 Vindicate me, O Lord,
   for I have walked in my integrity,
   and I have trusted in the Lord without wavering.
2 Prove me, O Lord, and try me;
   test my heart and mind.
3 For your steadfast love is before my eyes,
   and I walk in faithfulness to you.*b*

4 I do not sit with the worthless,
   nor do I consort with hypocrites;
5 I hate the company of evildoers,
   and will not sit with the wicked.

6 I wash my hands in innocence,
   and go around your altar, O Lord,
7 singing aloud a song of thanksgiving,
   and telling all your wondrous deeds.

a Or *The troubles of my heart are enlarged; bring me*   *b* Or *in your faithfulness*

8 O LORD, I love the house in which you dwell,
    and the place where your glory abides.
9 Do not sweep me away with sinners,
    nor my life with the bloodthirsty,
10 those in whose hands are evil devices,
    and whose right hands are full of bribes.

11 But as for me, I walk in my integrity;
    redeem me, and be gracious to me.
12 My foot stands on level ground;
    in the great congregation I will bless the LORD.

Psalm 27

Of David.

1 The LORD is my light and my salvation;
    whom shall I fear?
The LORD is the stronghold[a] of my life;
    of whom shall I be afraid?

2 When evildoers assail me
    to devour my flesh—
my adversaries and foes—
    they shall stumble and fall.

3 Though an army encamp against me,
    my heart shall not fear;
though war rise up against me,
    yet I will be confident.

4 One thing I asked of the LORD,
    that will I seek after:
to live in the house of the LORD
    all the days of my life,
to behold the beauty of the LORD,
    and to inquire in his temple.

5 For he will hide me in his shelter
    in the day of trouble;
he will conceal me under the cover of his tent;
    he will set me high on a rock.

6 Now my head is lifted up
    above my enemies all around me,
and I will offer in his tent
    sacrifices with shouts of joy;
I will sing and make melody to the LORD.

7 Hear, O LORD, when I cry aloud,
    be gracious to me and answer me!
8 "Come," my heart says, "seek his face!"
    Your face, LORD, do I seek.
9 Do not hide your face from me.

Do not turn your servant away in anger,
    you who have been my help.
Do not cast me off, do not forsake me,
    O God of my salvation!

Waiting for God

PSALM 27.14

Waiting is difficult, especially in our age of high-speed technology. We tend to think that change should be instantaneous in ourselves, in others and in our situations. Yet again and again the psalmist admonishes us to wait for the Lord (Psalms 37.7; 62.5; 130.5). God's vision of time is much keener than ours. What problem is causing you to feel anxious or impatient? Can you surrender it to the Lord? You may choose to write all of your concerns about the situation in your journal or on a piece of paper. In silence, lay these concerns before God.

See Meeting God in Prayer

Beyond Words

PSALM 28.1–2

In *Praying the Psalms*, Walter
Brueggemann describes the Pit
as a "powerless, gray existence
where one is removed from joy
and discourse with God."
Sometimes we feel, as the
psalmist does, that we are in
the Pit, that God won't—or
can't—hear our cries. In a gesture beyond words, the
psalmist lifts up his hands in
petition toward God's sanctuary.

Recall a time when you have
felt you were in the Pit. How do
you express your pain and loneliness to God? What gesture or
words might express your anguish to God? If you seem to be
in a pit right now, remember
the One who hears even your
sighs that words cannot express.

See Meeting God in Prayer

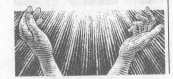

10 If my father and mother forsake me,
  the LORD will take me up.

11 Teach me your way, O LORD,
  and lead me on a level path
  because of my enemies.
12 Do not give me up to the will of my adversaries,
  for false witnesses have risen against me,
  and they are breathing out violence.

13 I believe that I shall see the goodness of the LORD
  in the land of the living.
14 Wait for the LORD;
  be strong, and let your heart take courage;
  wait for the LORD!

Psalm 28

Of David.

1 To you, O LORD, I call;
  my rock, do not refuse to hear me,
for if you are silent to me,
  I shall be like those who go down to the Pit.
2 Hear the voice of my supplication,
  as I cry to you for help,
as I lift up my hands
  toward your most holy sanctuary.[a]

3 Do not drag me away with the wicked,
  with those who are workers of evil,
who speak peace with their neighbors,
  while mischief is in their hearts.
4 Repay them according to their work,
  and according to the evil of their deeds;
repay them according to the work of their hands;
  render them their due reward.
5 Because they do not regard the works of the LORD,
  or the work of his hands,
he will break them down and build them up no
    more.

6 Blessed be the LORD,
  for he has heard the sound of my pleadings.
7 The LORD is my strength and my shield;
  in him my heart trusts;
so I am helped, and my heart exults,
  and with my song I give thanks to him.

8 The LORD is the strength of his people;
  he is the saving refuge of his anointed.
9 O save your people, and bless your heritage;
  be their shepherd, and carry them forever.

Psalm 29

A Psalm of David.

1 Ascribe to the LORD, O heavenly beings,[b]
  ascribe to the LORD glory and strength.

a Heb *your innermost sanctuary*   *b* Heb *sons of gods*

2 Ascribe to the LORD the glory of his name;
   worship the LORD in holy splendor.

3 The voice of the LORD is over the waters;
   the God of glory thunders,
   the LORD, over mighty waters.
4 The voice of the LORD is powerful;
   the voice of the LORD is full of majesty.

5 The voice of the LORD breaks the cedars;
   the LORD breaks the cedars of Lebanon.
6 He makes Lebanon skip like a calf,
   and Sirion like a young wild ox.

7 The voice of the LORD flashes forth flames of fire.
8 The voice of the LORD shakes the wilderness;
   the LORD shakes the wilderness of Kadesh.

9 The voice of the LORD causes the oaks to whirl,[a]
   and strips the forest bare;
   and in his temple all say, "Glory!"

10 The LORD sits enthroned over the flood;
   the LORD sits enthroned as king forever.
11 May the LORD give strength to his people!
   May the LORD bless his people with peace!

Psalm 30

A Psalm. A Song at the dedication of the temple. Of David.

1 I will extol you, O LORD, for you have drawn me up,
   and did not let my foes rejoice over me.
2 O LORD my God, I cried to you for help,
   and you have healed me.
3 O LORD, you brought up my soul from Sheol,
   restored me to life from among those gone down
      to the Pit.[b]

4 Sing praises to the LORD, O you his faithful ones,
   and give thanks to his holy name.
5 For his anger is but for a moment;
   his favor is for a lifetime.
Weeping may linger for the night,
   but joy comes with the morning.

6 As for me, I said in my prosperity,
   "I shall never be moved."
7 By your favor, O LORD,
   you had established me as a strong mountain;
you hid your face;
   I was dismayed.

8 To you, O LORD, I cried,
   and to the LORD I made supplication:
9 "What profit is there in my death,
   if I go down to the Pit?
Will the dust praise you?
   Will it tell of your faithfulness?

Joy in God's Morning

PSALM 30.4–5

We human beings are sometimes reluctant to accept forgiveness. We continue to recall our sins and failures, unable to forgive ourselves even when God has forgiven us. We know that nothing will separate us from the love of God in Christ Jesus (see Romans 8.39), but we often act as if we are unforgivable—disbelieving that God's anger "is but for a moment; his favor is for a lifetime." Are you holding a particular sin against yourself? Have you done something that you believe God can't forgive? What burden are you carrying needlessly into God's joy-filled morning?

See Meeting God in Prayer

a Or *causes the deer to calve*   b Or *that I should not go down to the Pit*

In God's Hand

PSALM 31.5

"As the life of prayer deepens it brings a gradual realization . . . . Through all the vicissitudes of trial, sin and conflict, the ground of the soul is rooted in [God's] life; that country from which we are exiled, yet which is our home . . . The ultimate humble trust of the little creature which first dared to say Abba! Father! is placed in the Absolute love; and finds in the simple return to God the Unchanging, that personal and permanent relation which is the ground of prayer."

—EVELYN UNDERHILL,
Abba

10 Hear, O LORD, and be gracious to me!
    O LORD, be my helper!"

11 You have turned my mourning into dancing;
    you have taken off my sackcloth
    and clothed me with joy,
12 so that my soul[a] may praise you and not be silent.
    O LORD my God, I will give thanks to you forever.

Psalm 31

To the leader. A Psalm of David.

1 In you, O LORD, I seek refuge;
    do not let me ever be put to shame;
    in your righteousness deliver me.
2 Incline your ear to me;
    rescue me speedily.
    Be a rock of refuge for me,
    a strong fortress to save me.

3 You are indeed my rock and my fortress;
    for your name's sake lead me and guide me,
4 take me out of the net that is hidden for me,
    for you are my refuge.
5 Into your hand I commit my spirit;
    you have redeemed me, O LORD, faithful God.

6 You hate[b] those who pay regard to worthless idols,
    but I trust in the LORD.
7 I will exult and rejoice in your steadfast love,
    because you have seen my affliction;
    you have taken heed of my adversities,
8 and have not delivered me into the hand of the
        enemy;
    you have set my feet in a broad place.

9 Be gracious to me, O LORD, for I am in distress;
    my eye wastes away from grief,
    my soul and body also.
10 For my life is spent with sorrow,
    and my years with sighing;
    my strength fails because of my misery,[c]
    and my bones waste away.

11 I am the scorn of all my adversaries,
    a horror[d] to my neighbors,
    an object of dread to my acquaintances;
    those who see me in the street flee from me.
12 I have passed out of mind like one who is dead;
    I have become like a broken vessel.
13 For I hear the whispering of many—
    terror all around!—
    as they scheme together against me,
    as they plot to take my life.

14 But I trust in you, O LORD;
    I say, "You are my God."

a Heb *that glory*   b One Heb Ms Gk Syr Jerome: MT *I hate*   c Gk Syr:
Heb *my iniquity*   d Cn: Heb *exceedingly*

15 My times are in your hand;
  deliver me from the hand of my enemies and
    persecutors.
16 Let your face shine upon your servant;
  save me in your steadfast love.
17 Do not let me be put to shame, O LORD,
  for I call on you;
let the wicked be put to shame;
  let them go dumbfounded to Sheol.
18 Let the lying lips be stilled
  that speak insolently against the righteous
  with pride and contempt.

19 O how abundant is your goodness
  that you have laid up for those who fear you,
and accomplished for those who take refuge in you,
  in the sight of everyone!
20 In the shelter of your presence you hide them
    from human plots;
you hold them safe under your shelter
  from contentious tongues.

21 Blessed be the LORD,
  for he has wondrously shown his steadfast love to
    me
  when I was beset as a city under siege.
22 I had said in my alarm,
  "I am driven far[a] from your sight."
But you heard my supplications
  when I cried out to you for help.

23 Love the LORD, all you his saints.
  The LORD preserves the faithful,
  but abundantly repays the one who acts
    haughtily.
24 Be strong, and let your heart take courage,
  all you who wait for the LORD.

Psalm 32

Of David. A Maskil.

1 Happy are those whose transgression is forgiven,
  whose sin is covered.
2 Happy are those to whom the LORD imputes no
    iniquity,
  and in whose spirit there is no deceit.

3 While I kept silence, my body wasted away
  through my groaning all day long.
4 For day and night your hand was heavy upon me;
  my strength was dried up[b] as by the heat of
    summer.   *Selah*

5 Then I acknowledged my sin to you,
  and I did not hide my iniquity;
I said, "I will confess my transgressions to the
  LORD,"
  and you forgave the guilt of my sin.   *Selah*

The Call to Confession

PSALM 32.3–5

God's hand is "heavy" upon the psalmist; the writer feels the weight of guilt until he openly acknowledges his sin before God. Often it is hard to admit our sins and our failures to do what is right. Yet we know that when we confess, "he who is faithful and just will forgive us our sins and cleanse us from all unrighteousness" (1 John 1.9). Julian of Norwich declared that wrath is an earthly problem, but heaven is founded on mercy: "For the ground of mercy is in love; and the working of mercy is our being kept in love." Confession, oral or written, can help to free you from guilt. Is there a trusted soul friend you might share with? Or perhaps you could write a letter to God.

See Meeting God in Community

a Another reading is *cut off*   b Meaning of Heb uncertain

Celebrating God's Goodness

PSALM 33.1–5

Because the psalms are so often read without music, we may forget that many of them were *songs* of praise. The psalmist calls his hearers to "sing to [God] a new song; play skillfully . . . with loud shouts" Praise declares God's goodness, reminds us of God's love and compassion, and opens our souls to hope. Reflect on your last twenty-four hours. When did you feel thankful? Did you gratefully witness an act of kindness? Did you stand breathless before a sunset? Did you feel God's grace in a stranger's smile? Offer these moments to God in praise.

See Meeting God in Worship

6   Therefore let all who are faithful
    offer prayer to you;
at a time of distress,*a* the rush of mighty waters
    shall not reach them.
7   You are a hiding place for me;
    you preserve me from trouble;
    you surround me with glad cries of deliverance.
                                   Selah

8   I will instruct you and teach you the way you should
       go;
    I will counsel you with my eye upon you.
9   Do not be like a horse or a mule, without
       understanding,
    whose temper must be curbed with bit and
       bridle,
    else it will not stay near you.

10   Many are the torments of the wicked,
    but steadfast love surrounds those who trust in
       the LORD.
11   Be glad in the LORD and rejoice, O righteous,
    and shout for joy, all you upright in heart.

Psalm 33

1   Rejoice in the LORD, O you righteous.
    Praise befits the upright.
2   Praise the LORD with the lyre;
    make melody to him with the harp of ten strings.
3   Sing to him a new song;
    play skillfully on the strings, with loud shouts.

4   For the word of the LORD is upright,
    and all his work is done in faithfulness.
5   He loves righteousness and justice;
    the earth is full of the steadfast love of the LORD.

6   By the word of the LORD the heavens were made,
    and all their host by the breath of his mouth.
7   He gathered the waters of the sea as in a bottle;
    he put the deeps in storehouses.

8   Let all the earth fear the LORD;
    let all the inhabitants of the world stand in awe of
       him.
9   For he spoke, and it came to be;
    he commanded, and it stood firm.

10   The LORD brings the counsel of the nations to
       nothing;
    he frustrates the plans of the peoples.
11   The counsel of the LORD stands forever,
    the thoughts of his heart to all generations.
12   Happy is the nation whose God is the LORD,
    the people whom he has chosen as his heritage.

13   The LORD looks down from heaven;
    he sees all humankind.

a Cn: Heb *at a time of finding only*

14 From where he sits enthroned he watches
   all the inhabitants of the earth—
15 he who fashions the hearts of them all,
   and observes all their deeds.
16 A king is not saved by his great army;
   a warrior is not delivered by his great strength.
17 The war horse is a vain hope for victory,
   and by its great might it cannot save.

18 Truly the eye of the LORD is on those who fear him,
   on those who hope in his steadfast love,
19 to deliver their soul from death,
   and to keep them alive in famine.

20 Our soul waits for the LORD;
   he is our help and shield.
21 Our heart is glad in him,
   because we trust in his holy name.
22 Let your steadfast love, O LORD, be upon us,
   even as we hope in you.

Psalm 34

*Of David, when he feigned madness before Abimelech,
so that he drove him out, and he went away.*

1 I will bless the LORD at all times;
   his praise shall continually be in my mouth.
2 My soul makes its boast in the LORD;
   let the humble hear and be glad.
3 O magnify the LORD with me,
   and let us exalt his name together.

4 I sought the LORD, and he answered me,
   and delivered me from all my fears.
5 Look to him, and be radiant;
   so your*ᵃ* faces shall never be ashamed.
6 This poor soul cried, and was heard by the LORD,
   and was saved from every trouble.
7 The angel of the LORD encamps
   around those who fear him, and delivers them.
8 O taste and see that the LORD is good;
   happy are those who take refuge in him.
9 O fear the LORD, you his holy ones,
   for those who fear him have no want.
10 The young lions suffer want and hunger,
   but those who seek the LORD lack no good thing.

11 Come, O children, listen to me;
   I will teach you the fear of the LORD.
12 Which of you desires life,
   and covets many days to enjoy good?
13 Keep your tongue from evil,
   and your lips from speaking deceit.
14 Depart from evil, and do good;
   seek peace, and pursue it.

15 The eyes of the LORD are on the righteous,
   and his ears are open to their cry.

A Recipe for Life

PSALM 34.11–14

The psalmist explains that to live in "the fear of the LORD" is to live fully within God's design. This recipe is uncomplicated: Speak the truth, do good and pursue peace. As you consider the week ahead, what activities in your life reflect God's intentions? Think of a person to whom you need to speak the truth in love. Perhaps you could call or visit someone who is homebound. Perhaps you could support a conflict resolution program at a local school. How do you pray and live according to God's "recipe"?

See Meeting God in Service

---

a Gk Syr Jerome: Heb *their*

Cleansing Honesty

PSALM 35.4–8

The desire for vengeance is readily apparent in the book of Psalms. Walter Brueggemann points out that the yearning for vengeance "is not only *there* in the Psalms, but it is *here* in the human heart" as well. Though we may not be as blunt as the psalmist, we too carry grudges. By hiding them and staying silent, we hold on to them, but in naming our resentments and offering them to God, we receive freedom and grace. When we "pray" our feelings to God, those feelings lose their power over us. Take some time to write about any bitterness you may be secretly nursing. Fold up the paper you wrote on and hold it in your open palms in a prayer of relinquishment.

See Meeting God in Prayer

16 The face of the LORD is against evildoers,
    to cut off the remembrance of them from the
    earth.
17 When the righteous cry for help, the LORD hears,
    and rescues them from all their troubles.
18 The LORD is near to the brokenhearted,
    and saves the crushed in spirit.

19 Many are the afflictions of the righteous,
    but the LORD rescues them from them all.
20 He keeps all their bones;
    not one of them will be broken.
21 Evil brings death to the wicked,
    and those who hate the righteous will be
    condemned.
22 The LORD redeems the life of his servants;
    none of those who take refuge in him will be
    condemned.

Psalm 35

Of David.

1 Contend, O LORD, with those who contend with me;
    fight against those who fight against me!
2 Take hold of shield and buckler,
    and rise up to help me!
3 Draw the spear and javelin
    against my pursuers;
say to my soul,
    "I am your salvation."

4 Let them be put to shame and dishonor
    who seek after my life.
Let them be turned back and confounded
    who devise evil against me.
5 Let them be like chaff before the wind,
    with the angel of the LORD driving them on.
6 Let their way be dark and slippery,
    with the angel of the LORD pursuing them.

7 For without cause they hid their net[a] for me;
    without cause they dug a pit[b] for my life.
8 Let ruin come on them unawares.
And let the net that they hid ensnare them;
    let them fall in it—to their ruin.

9 Then my soul shall rejoice in the LORD,
    exulting in his deliverance.
10 All my bones shall say,
    "O LORD, who is like you?
You deliver the weak
    from those too strong for them,
    the weak and needy from those who despoil
    them."

11 Malicious witnesses rise up;
    they ask me about things I do not know.

a Heb *a pit, their net*   *b* The word *pit* is transposed from the preceding line

12　They repay me evil for good;
　　　my soul is forlorn.
13　But as for me, when they were sick,
　　　I wore sackcloth;
　　　I afflicted myself with fasting.
　　I prayed with head bowed*a* on my bosom,
14　　as though I grieved for a friend or a brother;
　　I went about as one who laments for a mother,
　　　bowed down and in mourning.

15　But at my stumbling they gathered in glee,
　　　they gathered together against me;
　　ruffians whom I did not know
　　　tore at me without ceasing;
16　they impiously mocked more and more,*b*
　　　gnashing at me with their teeth.

17　How long, O Lord, will you look on?
　　　Rescue me from their ravages,
　　　my life from the lions!
18　Then I will thank you in the great congregation;
　　　in the mighty throng I will praise you.

19　Do not let my treacherous enemies rejoice over me,
　　　or those who hate me without cause wink the
　　　　eye.
20　For they do not speak peace,
　　　but they conceive deceitful words
　　　against those who are quiet in the land.
21　They open wide their mouths against me;
　　　they say, "Aha, Aha,
　　　our eyes have seen it."

22　You have seen, O Lord; do not be silent!
　　　O Lord, do not be far from me!
23　Wake up! Bestir yourself for my defense,
　　　for my cause, my God and my Lord!
24　Vindicate me, O Lord, my God,
　　　according to your righteousness,
　　　and do not let them rejoice over me.
25　Do not let them say to themselves,
　　　"Aha, we have our heart's desire."
　　Do not let them say, "We have swallowed you*c* up."

26　Let all those who rejoice at my calamity
　　　be put to shame and confusion;
　　let those who exalt themselves against me
　　　be clothed with shame and dishonor.

27　Let those who desire my vindication
　　　shout for joy and be glad,
　　　and say evermore,
　　"Great is the Lord,
　　　who delights in the welfare of his servant."
28　Then my tongue shall tell of your righteousness
　　　and of your praise all day long.

Spiritual Fulfillment

PSALM 35.9,27–28

"Then God shall be all our love, all we desire and seek and follow, all we think, all our life and speech and breath. The unity which now is between Father and Son shall be poured into our feelings and our minds: and as he loves us with a pure, sincere, unbreakable charity we on our side shall be linked to him by a lasting affection that nothing can spoil."

—JOHN CASSIAN,
The Conferences of Cassian

a Or *My prayer turned back*　　*b* Cn Compare Gk: Heb *like the profanest of mockers of a cake*　　*c* Heb *him*

Delight and Desire

PSALM 37.4

Delight is a word that is often used for children. Children delight in doing somersaults or watching a cat chase a bug. They possess the innocent joy of discovery and the willingness to give their whole being to that joy. When we delight in God, our deepest desires for love, significance and justice are met in God. What are the desires of your heart? How do you pray about them? Where is God in your deepest longing? Do you sense God's delight in the dreams of your heart? Reflect in a time of quiet prayer or in your journal.

See Meeting God in Prayer

Psalm 36

To the leader. Of David, the servant of the LORD.

1 Transgression speaks to the wicked
  deep in their hearts;
there is no fear of God
  before their eyes.
2 For they flatter themselves in their own eyes
  that their iniquity cannot be found out and hated.
3 The words of their mouths are mischief and deceit;
  they have ceased to act wisely and do good.
4 They plot mischief while on their beds;
  they are set on a way that is not good;
  they do not reject evil.

5 Your steadfast love, O LORD, extends to the heavens,
  your faithfulness to the clouds.
6 Your righteousness is like the mighty mountains,
  your judgments are like the great deep;
  you save humans and animals alike, O LORD.

7 How precious is your steadfast love, O God!
  All people may take refuge in the shadow of your
    wings.
8 They feast on the abundance of your house,
  and you give them drink from the river of your
    delights.
9 For with you is the fountain of life;
  in your light we see light.

10 O continue your steadfast love to those who know
    you,
  and your salvation to the upright of heart!
11 Do not let the foot of the arrogant tread on me,
  or the hand of the wicked drive me away.
12 There the evildoers lie prostrate;
  they are thrust down, unable to rise.

Psalm 37

Of David.

1 Do not fret because of the wicked;
  do not be envious of wrongdoers,
2 for they will soon fade like the grass,
  and wither like the green herb.

3 Trust in the LORD, and do good;
  so you will live in the land, and enjoy security.
4 Take delight in the LORD,
  and he will give you the desires of your heart.

5 Commit your way to the LORD;
  trust in him, and he will act.
6 He will make your vindication shine like the light,
  and the justice of your cause like the noonday.

7 Be still before the LORD, and wait patiently for him;
  do not fret over those who prosper in their way,
  over those who carry out evil devices.

8 Refrain from anger, and forsake wrath.
 Do not fret—it leads only to evil.
9 For the wicked shall be cut off,
 but those who wait for the LORD shall inherit the
 land.

10 Yet a little while, and the wicked will be no more;
 though you look diligently for their place, they
 will not be there.
11 But the meek shall inherit the land,
 and delight themselves in abundant prosperity.

12 The wicked plot against the righteous,
 and gnash their teeth at them;
13 but the LORD laughs at the wicked,
 for he sees that their day is coming.

14 The wicked draw the sword and bend their bows
 to bring down the poor and needy,
 to kill those who walk uprightly;
15 their sword shall enter their own heart,
 and their bows shall be broken.

16 Better is a little that the righteous person has
 than the abundance of many wicked.
17 For the arms of the wicked shall be broken,
 but the LORD upholds the righteous.

18 The LORD knows the days of the blameless,
 and their heritage will abide forever;
19 they are not put to shame in evil times,
 in the days of famine they have abundance.

20 But the wicked perish,
 and the enemies of the LORD are like the glory of
 the pastures;
 they vanish—like smoke they vanish away.

21 The wicked borrow, and do not pay back,
 but the righteous are generous and keep giving;
22 for those blessed by the LORD shall inherit the land,
 but those cursed by him shall be cut off.

23 Our steps*a* are made firm by the LORD,
 when he delights in our*b* way;
24 though we stumble,*c* we*d* shall not fall headlong,
 for the LORD holds us*e* by the hand.

25 I have been young, and now am old,
 yet I have not seen the righteous forsaken
 or their children begging bread.
26 They are ever giving liberally and lending,
 and their children become a blessing.

27 Depart from evil, and do good;
 so you shall abide forever.
28 For the LORD loves justice;
 he will not forsake his faithful ones.

God Enjoys Us

PSALM 37.23–24

God delights in those who walk in kindness and justice. In our faithful actions, large and small, we add to God's joy. According to Julian of Norwich, God enjoys us as a parent does a small child. Even our stumbling—our sin—does not lessen God's tender, enduring love for us. "And when we fall, quickly he raises us by the clasping of his love and touching of his grace." Consider God's delight in you, and in the personality and gifts that are unique to you. Imagine God doting on you as a loving parent, treating you as one would treat a toddler who falls and scrapes a knee.

---

a Heb *A man's steps*   *b* Heb *his*   *c* Heb *he stumbles*   *d* Heb *he*
e Heb *him*

God's Presence in Loneliness

PSALM 38.9–11

The psalmist is honest about the pain of his loneliness. Friends seem to have forgotten him, or they don't know how to respond to his terrible sickness. He fights feelings of deep depression—"for the light of my eyes—it also has gone from me." Yet he is also aware of the presence of the Lord who sees his hurt and hears his sighs. God is near to the lonely, healing the brokenhearted (Psalm 34.18). How do you experience God in times of loneliness or depression? What might God be saying to you in your pain? How do you talk to God in such desperate moments? Explore these questions with a close friend.

See Meeting God in Community

The righteous shall be kept safe forever,
but the children of the wicked shall be cut off.
29 The righteous shall inherit the land,
and live in it forever.

30 The mouths of the righteous utter wisdom,
and their tongues speak justice.
31 The law of their God is in their hearts;
their steps do not slip.

32 The wicked watch for the righteous,
and seek to kill them.
33 The LORD will not abandon them to their power,
or let them be condemned when they are
brought to trial.

34 Wait for the LORD, and keep to his way,
and he will exalt you to inherit the land;
you will look on the destruction of the wicked.

35 I have seen the wicked oppressing,
and towering like a cedar of Lebanon.*a*
36 Again I*b* passed by, and they were no more;
though I sought them, they could not be found.

37 Mark the blameless, and behold the upright,
for there is posterity for the peaceable.
38 But transgressors shall be altogether destroyed;
the posterity of the wicked shall be cut off.

39 The salvation of the righteous is from the LORD;
he is their refuge in the time of trouble.
40 The LORD helps them and rescues them;
he rescues them from the wicked, and saves them,
because they take refuge in him.

Psalm 38

A Psalm of David, for the memorial offering.

1 O LORD, do not rebuke me in your anger,
or discipline me in your wrath.
2 For your arrows have sunk into me,
and your hand has come down on me.
3 There is no soundness in my flesh
because of your indignation;
there is no health in my bones
because of my sin.
4 For my iniquities have gone over my head;
they weigh like a burden too heavy for me.

5 My wounds grow foul and fester
because of my foolishness;
6 I am utterly bowed down and prostrate;
all day long I go around mourning.
7 For my loins are filled with burning,
and there is no soundness in my flesh.

a Gk: Meaning of Heb uncertain   *b* Gk Syr Jerome: Heb *he*

8 I am utterly spent and crushed;
    I groan because of the tumult of my heart.

9 O Lord, all my longing is known to you;
    my sighing is not hidden from you.

10 My heart throbs, my strength fails me;
    as for the light of my eyes—it also has gone from
        me.

11 My friends and companions stand aloof from my
        affliction,
    and my neighbors stand far off.

12 Those who seek my life lay their snares;
    those who seek to hurt me speak of ruin,
    and meditate treachery all day long.

13 But I am like the deaf, I do not hear;
    like the mute, who cannot speak.

14 Truly, I am like one who does not hear,
    and in whose mouth is no retort.

15 But it is for you, O Lord, that I wait;
    it is you, O Lord my God, who will answer.

16 For I pray, "Only do not let them rejoice over me,
    those who boast against me when my foot slips."

17 For I am ready to fall,
    and my pain is ever with me.

18 I confess my iniquity;
    I am sorry for my sin.

19 Those who are my foes without cause[a] are mighty,
    and many are those who hate me wrongfully.

20 Those who render me evil for good
    are my adversaries because I follow after good.

21 Do not forsake me, O Lord;
    O my God, do not be far from me;

22 make haste to help me,
    O Lord, my salvation.

Psalm 39

To the leader: to Jeduthun. A Psalm of David.

1 I said, "I will guard my ways
    that I may not sin with my tongue;
    I will keep a muzzle on my mouth
    as long as the wicked are in my presence."

2 I was silent and still;
    I held my peace to no avail;
    my distress grew worse,

3   my heart became hot within me.
    While I mused, the fire burned;
    then I spoke with my tongue:

4 "Lord, let me know my end,
    and what is the measure of my days;
    let me know how fleeting my life is.

5 You have made my days a few handbreadths,

Why, God?

PSALM 39.4–10

"I am worn out," the psalmist cries. "Forgive me and stop punishing me." Sometimes, like the psalmist, we feel that our suffering is the result of God's chastisement. In our humanity we associate pain with punishment. Although God is not a punishing parent, we may be burdened by that mistaken image. We may secretly believe we deserve illnesses, natural catastrophes or emotional distress.

What passages can you discover that will remind you of the truth of God's tenderness in times of pain—the parable of the forgiving father and the prodigal son (see Luke 15.11–32), the simple verse that declares that "God is love" (1 John 4.8), examples of Jesus' healing compassion, or some other Biblical image? Meditate on the passage or image that speaks most vividly to you of God's tenderness.

See Meeting God in Scripture

Sharing the Good News

PSALM 40.9–10

The tradition of giving one's testimony strengthens the community of believers. Sometimes quiet people leave this responsibility to extroverts, but each of us has a unique story to tell. Reflect on your experience of community. How might you tell your story? Do you participate in a small group where sharing is encouraged? Do you meet with a soul friend? How are you witnessing to the presence of God in your life?

See Meeting God in Community

and my lifetime is as nothing in your sight.
Surely everyone stands as a mere breath. *Selah*
6   Surely everyone goes about like a shadow.
Surely for nothing they are in turmoil;
     they heap up, and do not know who will gather.

7   "And now, O Lord, what do I wait for?
     My hope is in you.
8   Deliver me from all my transgressions.
     Do not make me the scorn of the fool.
9   I am silent; I do not open my mouth,
     for it is you who have done it.
10   Remove your stroke from me;
     I am worn down by the blows[a] of your hand.

11   "You chastise mortals
     in punishment for sin,
consuming like a moth what is dear to them;
     surely everyone is a mere breath. *Selah*

12   "Hear my prayer, O LORD,
     and give ear to my cry;
     do not hold your peace at my tears.
For I am your passing guest,
     an alien, like all my forebears.
13   Turn your gaze away from me, that I may smile
          again,
     before I depart and am no more."

Psalm 40

To the leader. Of David. A Psalm.

1   I waited patiently for the LORD;
     he inclined to me and heard my cry.
2   He drew me up from the desolate pit,[b]
     out of the miry bog,
and set my feet upon a rock,
     making my steps secure.
3   He put a new song in my mouth,
     a song of praise to our God.
Many will see and fear,
     and put their trust in the LORD.

4   Happy are those who make
     the LORD their trust,
who do not turn to the proud,
     to those who go astray after false gods.
5   You have multiplied, O LORD my God,
     your wondrous deeds and your thoughts toward
          us;
     none can compare with you.
Were I to proclaim and tell of them,
     they would be more than can be counted.

6   Sacrifice and offering you do not desire,
     but you have given me an open ear.[c]
Burnt offering and sin offering
     you have not required.

a Heb *hostility*   *b* Cn: Heb *pit of tumult*   *c* Heb *ears you have dug for me*

7 Then I said, "Here I am;
   in the scroll of the book it is written of me.[a]
8 I delight to do your will, O my God;
   your law is within my heart."

9 I have told the glad news of deliverance
   in the great congregation;
   see, I have not restrained my lips,
   as you know, O LORD.
10 I have not hidden your saving help within my heart,
   I have spoken of your faithfulness and your
      salvation;
   I have not concealed your steadfast love and your
      faithfulness
   from the great congregation.

11 Do not, O LORD, withhold
   your mercy from me;
   let your steadfast love and your faithfulness
   keep me safe forever.
12 For evils have encompassed me
   without number;
   my iniquities have overtaken me,
   until I cannot see;
   they are more than the hairs of my head,
   and my heart fails me.

13 Be pleased, O LORD, to deliver me;
   O LORD, make haste to help me.
14 Let all those be put to shame and confusion
   who seek to snatch away my life;
   let those be turned back and brought to dishonor
   who desire my hurt.
15 Let those be appalled because of their shame
   who say to me, "Aha, Aha!"

16 But may all who seek you
   rejoice and be glad in you;
   may those who love your salvation
   say continually, "Great is the LORD!"
17 As for me, I am poor and needy,
   but the Lord takes thought for me.
   You are my help and my deliverer;
   do not delay, O my God.

Psalm 41

To the leader. A Psalm of David.

1 Happy are those who consider the poor;[b]
   the LORD delivers them in the day of trouble.
2 The LORD protects them and keeps them alive;
   they are called happy in the land.
   You do not give them up to the will of their
      enemies.
3 The LORD sustains them on their sickbed;
   in their illness you heal all their infirmities.[c]

Seeking God Always

PSALM 40.16

"Love knows no measure, but is fervent without measure . . . . He who is thus a spiritual lover knows well what that voice means which says: 'You, Lord God, are my whole love and my desire. You are all mine, and I all Yours. Dissolve my heart into Your love so that I may know how sweet it is to serve You and how joyful it is to praise You.' "

—THOMAS À KEMPIS,
The Imitation of Christ

---

a Meaning of Heb uncertain   b Or weak   c Heb you change all his bed

Thirsting for God

PSALM 42.1–2

Thirst is such a powerful longing that it displaces all others. Though the psalmist longs for God's help in the midst of physical thirst and danger, this metaphor also offers a profound spiritual image: Our relationship with God is as essential to our spiritual well-being as water is to our physical well-being.

What are you thirsty for? Is your schedule so crowded that it leaves you thirsty for time alone with God? Are you feeling dryness in your devotional habits? Are you needing a time away in retreat? Consider these questions for a few minutes and then list in your journal whatever comes to you—even half-finished sentences, images, ideas. Let your heart speak.

See Meeting God in Everyday Life

4 As for me, I said, "O LORD, be gracious to me;
 heal me, for I have sinned against you."
5 My enemies wonder in malice
 when I will die, and my name perish.
6 And when they come to see me, they utter empty words,
 while their hearts gather mischief;
 when they go out, they tell it abroad.
7 All who hate me whisper together about me;
 they imagine the worst for me.

8 They think that a deadly thing has fastened on me,
 that I will not rise again from where I lie.
9 Even my bosom friend in whom I trusted,
 who ate of my bread, has lifted the heel against me.
10 But you, O LORD, be gracious to me,
 and raise me up, that I may repay them.

11 By this I know that you are pleased with me;
 because my enemy has not triumphed over me.
12 But you have upheld me because of my integrity,
 and set me in your presence forever.

13 Blessed be the LORD, the God of Israel,
 from everlasting to everlasting.
 Amen and Amen.

BOOK II

(Psalms 42–72)

Psalm 42

To the leader. A Maskil of the Korahites.

1 As a deer longs for flowing streams,
 so my soul longs for you, O God.
2 My soul thirsts for God,
 for the living God.
When shall I come and behold
 the face of God?
3 My tears have been my food
 day and night,
while people say to me continually,
 "Where is your God?"

4 These things I remember,
 as I pour out my soul:
how I went with the throng,*a*
 and led them in procession to the house of God,
with glad shouts and songs of thanksgiving,
 a multitude keeping festival.
5 Why are you cast down, O my soul,
 and why are you disquieted within me?
Hope in God; for I shall again praise him,
 my help 6and my God.

My soul is cast down within me;
 therefore I remember you

a Meaning of Heb uncertain

from the land of Jordan and of Hermon,
   from Mount Mizar.
7 Deep calls to deep
   at the thunder of your cataracts;
all your waves and your billows
   have gone over me.
8 By day the Lord commands his steadfast love,
   and at night his song is with me,
   a prayer to the God of my life.

9 I say to God, my rock,
   "Why have you forgotten me?
Why must I walk about mournfully
   because the enemy oppresses me?"
10 As with a deadly wound in my body,
   my adversaries taunt me,
while they say to me continually,
   "Where is your God?"

11 Why are you cast down, O my soul,
   and why are you disquieted within me?
Hope in God; for I shall again praise him,
   my help and my God.

Psalm 43

1 Vindicate me, O God, and defend my cause
   against an ungodly people;
from those who are deceitful and unjust
   deliver me!
2 For you are the God in whom I take refuge;
   why have you cast me off?
Why must I walk about mournfully
   because of the oppression of the enemy?

3 O send out your light and your truth;
   let them lead me;
let them bring me to your holy hill
   and to your dwelling.
4 Then I will go to the altar of God,
   to God my exceeding joy;
and I will praise you with the harp,
   O God, my God.

5 Why are you cast down, O my soul,
   and why are you disquieted within me?
Hope in God; for I shall again praise him,
   my help and my God.

Psalm 44

To the leader. Of the Korahites. A Maskil.

1 We have heard with our ears, O God,
   our ancestors have told us,
what deeds you performed in their days,
   in the days of old:
2 you with your own hand drove out the nations,
   but them you planted;
you afflicted the peoples,
   but them you set free;

God's Steadfast Love

PSALM 42.7–8

The image of a quiet stream suggests tranquillity, while a crashing wave speaks of power. Images of water can convey strength, beauty, terror or peace. The psalmist recognizes water's spiritual symbolism: God's voice is heard as "deep calls to deep at the thunder of your [waterfalls]." Imagine with the psalmist the strong waves of God's power, the blue depths of the ocean, the sheer beauty of a waterfall. Can you feel the spray against your face? Hear the rush of the water against the rocks? Smell the moist, cool air? What are some other ways water symbolizes God's desire to refresh your spirit daily?

See Meeting God in the Created Order

Remembering Our Story

PSALM 44.1–3

The psalmist begins by recounting the story of Israel's birth: how the people came to the promised land. Thomas Merton observes that when we read the Psalms, "we too are leaving Egypt." For each of us also has a story to tell of spiritual roots and times of transformation and growth, as well as times of drifting. By retracing our spiritual journeys, we see God's hand in our lives. Record some highlights of your spiritual story or make descriptive notes on a time line of your life. Share your story or time line with a mentor, spiritual friend or trusted small group.

See *Meeting God in Community*

3 for not by their own sword did they win the land,
   nor did their own arm give them victory;
but your right hand, and your arm,
   and the light of your countenance,
   for you delighted in them.

4 You are my King and my God;
   you command*a* victories for Jacob.
5 Through you we push down our foes;
   through your name we tread down our assailants.
6 For not in my bow do I trust,
   nor can my sword save me.
7 But you have saved us from our foes,
   and have put to confusion those who hate us.
8 In God we have boasted continually,
   and we will give thanks to your name forever.
                                                    Selah

9 Yet you have rejected us and abased us,
   and have not gone out with our armies.
10 You made us turn back from the foe,
   and our enemies have gotten spoil.
11 You have made us like sheep for slaughter,
   and have scattered us among the nations.
12 You have sold your people for a trifle,
   demanding no high price for them.

13 You have made us the taunt of our neighbors,
   the derision and scorn of those around us.
14 You have made us a byword among the nations,
   a laughingstock*b* among the peoples.
15 All day long my disgrace is before me,
   and shame has covered my face
16 at the words of the taunters and revilers,
   at the sight of the enemy and the avenger.

17 All this has come upon us,
   yet we have not forgotten you,
   or been false to your covenant.
18 Our heart has not turned back,
   nor have our steps departed from your way,
19 yet you have broken us in the haunt of jackals,
   and covered us with deep darkness.

20 If we had forgotten the name of our God,
   or spread out our hands to a strange god,
21 would not God discover this?
   For he knows the secrets of the heart.
22 Because of you we are being killed all day long,
   and accounted as sheep for the slaughter.

23 Rouse yourself! Why do you sleep, O Lord?
   Awake, do not cast us off forever!
24 Why do you hide your face?
   Why do you forget our affliction and oppression?
25 For we sink down to the dust;
   our bodies cling to the ground.
26 Rise up, come to our help.
   Redeem us for the sake of your steadfast love.

a Gk Syr: Heb *You are my King, O God; command*   *b* Heb *a shaking of the head*

Psalm 45

To the leader: according to Lilies. Of the Korahites. A Maskil.
A love song.

1 My heart overflows with a goodly theme;
    I address my verses to the king;
    my tongue is like the pen of a ready scribe.

2 You are the most handsome of men;
    grace is poured upon your lips;
    therefore God has blessed you forever.
3 Gird your sword on your thigh, O mighty one,
    in your glory and majesty.

4 In your majesty ride on victoriously
    for the cause of truth and to defend[a] the right;
    let your right hand teach you dread deeds.
5 Your arrows are sharp
    in the heart of the king's enemies;
    the peoples fall under you.

6 Your throne, O God,[b] endures forever and ever.
    Your royal scepter is a scepter of equity;
7   you love righteousness and hate wickedness.
Therefore God, your God, has anointed you
    with the oil of gladness beyond your companions;
8   your robes are all fragrant with myrrh and aloes
        and cassia.
From ivory palaces stringed instruments make you
        glad;
9   daughters of kings are among your ladies of honor;
    at your right hand stands the queen in gold of
        Ophir.

10 Hear, O daughter, consider and incline your ear;
    forget your people and your father's house,
11   and the king will desire your beauty.
Since he is your lord, bow to him;
12   the people[c] of Tyre will seek your favor with gifts,
    the richest of the people [13]with all kinds of wealth.

The princess is decked in her chamber with
        gold-woven robes;[d]
14   in many-colored robes she is led to the king;
    behind her the virgins, her companions, follow.
15 With joy and gladness they are led along
    as they enter the palace of the king.

16 In the place of ancestors you, O king,[e] shall have
        sons;
    you will make them princes in all the earth.
17 I will cause your name to be celebrated in all
        generations;
    therefore the peoples will praise you forever and
        ever.

a Cn: Heb *and the meekness of*   b Or *Your throne is a throne of God, it*
c Heb *daughter*   d Or *people.* [13]*All glorious is the princess within, gold
embroidery is her clothing*   e Heb lacks *O king*

Your Own Psalm

PSALM 45.1

Spiritual writers throughout the centuries have expressed their overflowing love for God in verse and song. Augustine writes, "Thou didst send forth Thy beams and shine upon me and chase away my blindness . . . Thou didst touch me, and I have burned for Thy peace." What do you do with your heart's "overflow"? What form might your own psalm take? Do you sing, play an instrument, paint, mold clay, write poetry? Take ten or fifteen minutes to experiment. Perhaps you might compose a song, draw a picture or create a collage.

See *Meeting God in Worship*

Our Refuge

PSALM 46.1–3

More than a dozen times, the Psalms refer to God as a refuge—a refuge "for the oppressed" (Psalm 9.9), for "the poor" (Psalm 14.6) and "in the day of my distress" (Psalm 59.16). Here in Psalm 46, God is a refuge from the ravages of earthquakes and floods. The spiritual life is also beset by "climate changes." In what specific areas of your life have you found God to be your refuge and strength? What devotional practices help you to find a spiritual center in times of stress? Draw a symbolic expression of God as your refuge.

See Meeting God in Scripture

Psalm 46

To the leader. Of the Korahites. According to Alamoth. A Song.

1　God is our refuge and strength,
　　a very present*a* help in trouble.
2　Therefore we will not fear, though the earth should change,
　　though the mountains shake in the heart of the sea;
3　though its waters roar and foam,
　　though the mountains tremble with its tumult. *Selah*

4　There is a river whose streams make glad the city of God,
　　the holy habitation of the Most High.
5　God is in the midst of the city;*b* it shall not be moved;
　　God will help it when the morning dawns.
6　The nations are in an uproar, the kingdoms totter;
　　he utters his voice, the earth melts.
7　The LORD of hosts is with us;
　　the God of Jacob is our refuge.*c* *Selah*

8　Come, behold the works of the LORD;
　　see what desolations he has brought on the earth.
9　He makes wars cease to the end of the earth;
　　he breaks the bow, and shatters the spear;
　　he burns the shields with fire.
10　"Be still, and know that I am God!
　　I am exalted among the nations,
　　I am exalted in the earth."
11　The LORD of hosts is with us;
　　the God of Jacob is our refuge.*c* *Selah*

Psalm 47

To the leader. Of the Korahites. A Psalm.

1　Clap your hands, all you peoples;
　　shout to God with loud songs of joy.
2　For the LORD, the Most High, is awesome,
　　a great king over all the earth.
3　He subdued peoples under us,
　　and nations under our feet.
4　He chose our heritage for us,
　　the pride of Jacob whom he loves. *Selah*

5　God has gone up with a shout,
　　the LORD with the sound of a trumpet.
6　Sing praises to God, sing praises;
　　sing praises to our King, sing praises.
7　For God is the king of all the earth;
　　sing praises with a psalm.*d*

8　God is king over the nations;
　　God sits on his holy throne.
9　The princes of the peoples gather
　　as the people of the God of Abraham.
　　For the shields of the earth belong to God;
　　he is highly exalted.

a Or *well proved*　*b* Heb *of it*　*c* Or *fortress*　*d* Heb *Maskil*

Psalm 48

A Song. A Psalm of the Korahites.

1 Great is the LORD and greatly to be praised
    in the city of our God.
His holy mountain, 2beautiful in elevation,
    is the joy of all the earth,
Mount Zion, in the far north,
    the city of the great King.
3 Within its citadels God
    has shown himself a sure defense.

4 Then the kings assembled,
    they came on together.
5 As soon as they saw it, they were astounded;
    they were in panic, they took to flight;
6 trembling took hold of them there,
    pains as of a woman in labor,
7 as when an east wind shatters
    the ships of Tarshish.
8 As we have heard, so have we seen
    in the city of the LORD of hosts,
in the city of our God,
    which God establishes forever.   *Selah*

9 We ponder your steadfast love, O God,
    in the midst of your temple.
10 Your name, O God, like your praise,
    reaches to the ends of the earth.
Your right hand is filled with victory.
11   Let Mount Zion be glad,
let the towns*a* of Judah rejoice
    because of your judgments.

12 Walk about Zion, go all around it,
    count its towers,
13 consider well its ramparts;
    go through its citadels,
that you may tell the next generation
14   that this is God,
our God forever and ever.
    He will be our guide forever.

Psalm 49

To the leader. Of the Korahites. A Psalm.

1 Hear this, all you peoples;
    give ear, all inhabitants of the world,
2 both low and high,
    rich and poor together.
3 My mouth shall speak wisdom;
    the meditation of my heart shall be understanding.
4 I will incline my ear to a proverb;
    I will solve my riddle to the music of the harp.

5 Why should I fear in times of trouble,
    when the iniquity of my persecutors surrounds
        me,

Let Zion Be Glad

PSALM 48.1–4

The city of Zion, Jerusalem, is an actual city, but it is also a spiritual one. A longing for Zion is also a yearning for the fulfillment of the prophetic vision of a holy city of peace, justice and compassion. The kingdom of heaven that Jesus proclaims is very much like this vision. How are you living Jesus' prayer that God's kingdom come on earth as in heaven? Where might God be inviting you to give your time, energy and love in order to "let your light shine"? In what small way can you extend God's reign today?

See Meeting God in Service

---

a Heb *daughters*

A Different Perspective

PSALM 49.16–17

The psalmist speaks to an age-old issue: the power of money. As he explains, the influence of wealth is transitory, for in death we leave all possessions and all material security behind. Consider the place of money and possessions in your life. Where do you find your security? How does our culture's preoccupation with "things" affect your sense of self-worth? How might possessions be distracting you? Richard Foster, in *Freedom of Simplicity*, urges us to enjoy rather than possess. One doesn't have to own parks, beaches, country roads or blue skies in order to enjoy them. What are you enjoying in your life?

See Meeting God in Everyday Life

6 those who trust in their wealth
    and boast of the abundance of their riches?
7 Truly, no ransom avails for one's life,*a*
    there is no price one can give to God for it.
8 For the ransom of life is costly,
    and can never suffice,
9 that one should live on forever
    and never see the grave.*b*

10 When we look at the wise, they die;
    fool and dolt perish together
    and leave their wealth to others.
11 Their graves*c* are their homes forever,
    their dwelling places to all generations,
    though they named lands their own.
12 Mortals cannot abide in their pomp;
    they are like the animals that perish.

13 Such is the fate of the foolhardy,
    the end of those*d* who are pleased with their lot.
        Selah
14 Like sheep they are appointed for Sheol;
    Death shall be their shepherd;
straight to the grave they descend,*e*
    and their form shall waste away;
    Sheol shall be their home.*f*
15 But God will ransom my soul from the power of Sheol,
    for he will receive me.   *Selah*

16 Do not be afraid when some become rich,
    when the wealth of their houses increases.
17 For when they die they will carry nothing away;
    their wealth will not go down after them.
18 Though in their lifetime they count themselves happy
    —for you are praised when you do well for yourself—
19 they*g* will go to the company of their ancestors,
    who will never again see the light.
20 Mortals cannot abide in their pomp;
    they are like the animals that perish.

Psalm 50

A Psalm of Asaph.

1 The mighty one, God the LORD,
    speaks and summons the earth
    from the rising of the sun to its setting.
2 Out of Zion, the perfection of beauty,
    God shines forth.

3 Our God comes and does not keep silence,
    before him is a devouring fire,
    and a mighty tempest all around him.
4 He calls to the heavens above
    and to the earth, that he may judge his people:

a Another reading is *no one can ransom a brother*   *b* Heb *the pit*
c Gk Syr Compare Tg: Heb *their inward* (thought)   *d* Tg: Heb *after them*
e Cn: Heb *the upright shall have dominion over them in the morning*
f Meaning of Heb uncertain   *g* Cn: Heb *you*

5 "Gather to me my faithful ones,
  who made a covenant with me by sacrifice!"
6 The heavens declare his righteousness,
  for God himself is judge.   *Selah*

7 "Hear, O my people, and I will speak,
  O Israel, I will testify against you.
  I am God, your God.
8 Not for your sacrifices do I rebuke you;
  your burnt offerings are continually before me.
9 I will not accept a bull from your house,
  or goats from your folds.
10 For every wild animal of the forest is mine,
  the cattle on a thousand hills.
11 I know all the birds of the air,[a]
  and all that moves in the field is mine.

12 "If I were hungry, I would not tell you,
  for the world and all that is in it is mine.
13 Do I eat the flesh of bulls,
  or drink the blood of goats?
14 Offer to God a sacrifice of thanksgiving,[b]
  and pay your vows to the Most High;
15 Call on me in the day of trouble;
  I will deliver you, and you shall glorify me."

16 But to the wicked God says:
  "What right have you to recite my statutes,
  or take my covenant on your lips?
17 For you hate discipline,
  and you cast my words behind you.
18 You make friends with a thief when you see one,
  and you keep company with adulterers.

19 "You give your mouth free rein for evil,
  and your tongue frames deceit.
20 You sit and speak against your kin;
  you slander your own mother's child.
21 These things you have done and I have been silent;
  you thought that I was one just like yourself.
  But now I rebuke you, and lay the charge before
    you.

22 "Mark this, then, you who forget God,
  or I will tear you apart, and there will be no one
    to deliver.
23 Those who bring thanksgiving as their sacrifice
    honor me;
  to those who go the right way[c]
  I will show the salvation of God."

Psalm 51

To the leader. A Psalm of David, when the prophet Nathan
came to him, after he had gone in to Bathsheba.

1 Have mercy on me, O God,
  according to your steadfast love;

A Thanksgiving Offering

PSALM 50.14

God desires our praise. It is a simple request, but often we find it hard to comply because we come before God with our anxieties and forget to offer our gratitude. Yet praise is a natural response to God when we stop to notice the Lord's great gifts. When we see the canopy of stars on a winter night, we feel awe. When the sun peeks out after days of rain, a sense of thankfulness wells up in our hearts.

Offer God thanks for three things in the natural world that you have noticed in the last few days. As you remember each one, pause and let a mental picture take shape. Allow your joy to well up—and whisper a "thank you" to God.

See Meeting God in the Created Order

---

a Gk Syr Tg: Heb *mountains*   b Or *make thanksgiving your sacrifice to God*
c Heb *who set a way*

A Pure Heart

PSALM 51.10

The psalmist's desire is also ours: to be clean, whole, free from pretense. Yet opening our hearts before God can be scary. We are careful to protect our self-images—even before God, who knows each of us intimately.

Some spiritual writers suggest the discipline of a "daily examen" so as to experience God's cleansing grace. At the end of the day, take several minutes to review the day, recalling times you protected your ego and times you were open. If you remember becoming defensive, you might pray, "Lord, have mercy." If you notice very little self-concern, offer a word of thanksgiving. To aid your recollection, you might record these insights in your journal.

See Meeting God in Everyday Life

according to your abundant mercy
    blot out my transgressions.
2 Wash me thoroughly from my iniquity,
    and cleanse me from my sin.

3 For I know my transgressions,
    and my sin is ever before me.
4 Against you, you alone, have I sinned,
    and done what is evil in your sight,
so that you are justified in your sentence
    and blameless when you pass judgment.
5 Indeed, I was born guilty,
    a sinner when my mother conceived me.

6 You desire truth in the inward being;*a*
    therefore teach me wisdom in my secret heart.
7 Purge me with hyssop, and I shall be clean;
    wash me, and I shall be whiter than snow.
8 Let me hear joy and gladness;
    let the bones that you have crushed rejoice.
9 Hide your face from my sins,
    and blot out all my iniquities.

10 Create in me a clean heart, O God,
    and put a new and right*b* spirit within me.
11 Do not cast me away from your presence,
    and do not take your holy spirit from me.
12 Restore to me the joy of your salvation,
    and sustain in me a willing*c* spirit.

13 Then I will teach transgressors your ways,
    and sinners will return to you.
14 Deliver me from bloodshed, O God,
    O God of my salvation,
    and my tongue will sing aloud of your deliverance.

15 O Lord, open my lips,
    and my mouth will declare your praise.
16 For you have no delight in sacrifice;
    if I were to give a burnt offering, you would not
    be pleased.
17 The sacrifice acceptable to God*d* is a broken spirit;
    a broken and contrite heart, O God, you will not
    despise.

18 Do good to Zion in your good pleasure;
    rebuild the walls of Jerusalem,
19 then you will delight in right sacrifices,
    in burnt offerings and whole burnt offerings;
    then bulls will be offered on your altar.

Psalm 52

To the leader. A Maskil of David, when Doeg the Edomite came to Saul and said to him, "David has come to the house of Ahimelech."

1 Why do you boast, O mighty one,
    of mischief done against the godly?*e*

a Meaning of Heb uncertain   *b* Or *steadfast*   *c* Or *generous*   *d* Or *My sacrifice, O God,*   *e* Cn Compare Syr: Heb *the kindness of God*

All day long ²you are plotting destruction.
Your tongue is like a sharp razor,
  you worker of treachery.

3 You love evil more than good,
  and lying more than speaking the truth.   *Selah*
4 You love all words that devour,
  O deceitful tongue.

5 But God will break you down forever;
  he will snatch and tear you from your tent;
  he will uproot you from the land of the living.
                                                Selah

6 The righteous will see, and fear,
  and will laugh at the evildoer,*a* saying,
7 "See the one who would not take
  refuge in God,
but trusted in abundant riches,
  and sought refuge in wealth!"*b*

8 But I am like a green olive tree
  in the house of God.
I trust in the steadfast love of God
  forever and ever.
9 I will thank you forever,
  because of what you have done.
In the presence of the faithful
  I will proclaim*c* your name, for it is good.

Psalm 53

To the leader: according to Mahalath. A Maskil of David.

1 Fools say in their hearts, "There is no God."
  They are corrupt, they commit abominable acts;
  there is no one who does good.

2 God looks down from heaven on humankind
  to see if there are any who are wise,
  who seek after God.

3 They have all fallen away, they are all alike perverse;
  there is no one who does good,
  no, not one.

4 Have they no knowledge, those evildoers,
  who eat up my people as they eat bread,
  and do not call upon God?

5 There they shall be in great terror,
  in terror such as has not been.
For God will scatter the bones of the ungodly;*d*
  they will be put to shame,*e* for God has rejected
  them.

6 O that deliverance for Israel would come from Zion!
  When God restores the fortunes of his people,
  Jacob will rejoice; Israel will be glad.

A Flourishing Olive Tree

PSALM 52.8

Trees are visible symbols of the spiritual life. From Psalm 1 we learned that those who delight in God's way like "trees planted by streams of water, which yields their fruit in its season" (Psalm 1.3). Rooted in the house of God, this "flourishing" olive tree also symbolizes the soul who trusts God's steadfast love. How is your spiritual life like a tree? Where are your roots finding nourishment? What source of light gives growth to your leaves? Are you withering in places? How are you tending the tree of your spirit?

See Meeting God in Scripture

---

a Heb *him*   *b* Syr Tg: Heb *in his destruction*   *c* Cn: Heb *wait for*
d Cn Compare Gk Syr: Heb *him who encamps against you*   *e* Gk: Heb *you have put (them) to shame*

A God Who Hears

PSALM 54.2

The psalmist holds nothing back from the Maker of the universe—he rejoices, complains, petitions, cries and agonizes. Even in the face of heaven's apparent silence, the psalmist waits and hopes. Over and over, stories of the Hebrew faithful demonstrate that prayer is a "two-way street." God hears, and God responds. God delivers, comforts, shields and loves steadfastly. Do you pray believing that God hears you—even your sighs, your complaints and your everyday concerns? Do you think of God as a "listener"? Reflect on this in your journal.

Psalm 54

To the leader: with stringed instruments. A Maskil of David, when the Ziphites went and told Saul, "David is in hiding among us."

1 Save me, O God, by your name,
  and vindicate me by your might.
2 Hear my prayer, O God;
  give ear to the words of my mouth.

3 For the insolent have risen against me,
  the ruthless seek my life;
  they do not set God before them.   *Selah*

4 But surely, God is my helper;
  the Lord is the upholder of[a] my life.
5 He will repay my enemies for their evil.
  In your faithfulness, put an end to them.

6 With a freewill offering I will sacrifice to you;
  I will give thanks to your name, O LORD, for it is good.
7 For he has delivered me from every trouble,
  and my eye has looked in triumph on my enemies.

Psalm 55

To the leader: with stringed instruments. A Maskil of David.

1 Give ear to my prayer, O God;
  do not hide yourself from my supplication.
2 Attend to me, and answer me;
  I am troubled in my complaint.
I am distraught 3by the noise of the enemy,
  because of the clamor of the wicked.
For they bring[b] trouble upon me,
  and in anger they cherish enmity against me.

4 My heart is in anguish within me,
  the terrors of death have fallen upon me.
5 Fear and trembling come upon me,
  and horror overwhelms me.
6 And I say, "O that I had wings like a dove!
  I would fly away and be at rest;
7 truly, I would flee far away;
  I would lodge in the wilderness;   *Selah*
8 I would hurry to find a shelter for myself
  from the raging wind and tempest."

9 Confuse, O Lord, confound their speech;
  for I see violence and strife in the city.
10 Day and night they go around it
  on its walls,
and iniquity and trouble are within it;
11 ruin is in its midst;
oppression and fraud
  do not depart from its marketplace.

a Gk Syr Jerome: Heb *is of those who uphold* or *is with those who uphold*
b Cn Compare Gk: Heb *they cause to totter*

12 It is not enemies who taunt me—
    I could bear that;
  it is not adversaries who deal insolently with me—
    I could hide from them.
13 But it is you, my equal,
    my companion, my familiar friend,
14 with whom I kept pleasant company;
    we walked in the house of God with the throng.
15 Let death come upon them;
    let them go down alive to Sheol;
  for evil is in their homes and in their hearts.

16 But I call upon God,
    and the LORD will save me.
17 Evening and morning and at noon
    I utter my complaint and moan,
    and he will hear my voice.
18 He will redeem me unharmed
    from the battle that I wage,
    for many are arrayed against me.
19 God, who is enthroned from of old,   *Selah*
    will hear, and will humble them—
  because they do not change,
    and do not fear God.

20 My companion laid hands on a friend
    and violated a covenant with me[a]
21 with speech smoother than butter,
    but with a heart set on war;
  with words that were softer than oil,
    but in fact were drawn swords.

22 Cast your burden[b] on the LORD,
    and he will sustain you;
  he will never permit
    the righteous to be moved.

23 But you, O God, will cast them down
    into the lowest pit;
  the bloodthirsty and treacherous
    shall not live out half their days.
  But I will trust in you.

Psalm 56

To the leader: according to The Dove on Far-off Terebinths. Of David. A Miktam, when the Philistines seized him in Gath.

1 Be gracious to me, O God, for people trample on me;
    all day long foes oppress me;
2 my enemies trample on me all day long,
    for many fight against me.
  O Most High, 3when I am afraid,
    I put my trust in you.
4 In God, whose word I praise,
    in God I trust; I am not afraid;
    what can flesh do to me?

Letting Go of Cares

PSALM 55.22

"Cast your burden on the LORD," the psalmist urges. His charge is also a call to faith, because to let go we must trust that God will sustain us. Thus the prayer of petition is also a prayer of hope. Henri Nouwen, in *With Open Hands*, writes, "Our numerous requests simply become the concrete way of saying that we trust in the fullness of God's goodness, which he wants to share with us . . . . Fear and anxiety fade away." What burden do you long to cast on the Lord? What is weighing you down? Imagine letting go of it. In what ways does your prayer of petition bring you hope?

See Meeting God in Prayer

Learning to Trust

PSALM 56.3

"When I am afraid, I put my trust in you" is easy to say but hard to live out. For when fear enters the heart, it often seems to take over—the mind races, the heart beats faster and a "fight or flight" reaction kicks in.

Former prisoners of war often say that verses learned from childhood helped them deal with fear. How can you prepare to combat fear before you experience it? Do you have favorite passages that you can "call up"? Try to memorize all or part of Psalm 121 or another short passage that expresses trust in God. Repeat it often as a reminder of God's care for you. Keep it as a source of spiritual comfort for difficult times.

See Meeting God in Scripture

5 All day long they seek to injure my cause;
  all their thoughts are against me for evil.
6 They stir up strife, they lurk,
  they watch my steps.
  As they hoped to have my life,
7   so repay^a them for their crime;
  in wrath cast down the peoples, O God!

8 You have kept count of my tossings;
  put my tears in your bottle.
  Are they not in your record?
9 Then my enemies will retreat
  in the day when I call.
  This I know, that^b God is for me.
10 In God, whose word I praise,
  in the LORD, whose word I praise,
11 in God I trust; I am not afraid.
  What can a mere mortal do to me?

12 My vows to you I must perform, O God;
  I will render thank offerings to you.
13 For you have delivered my soul from death,
  and my feet from falling,
  so that I may walk before God
  in the light of life.

Psalm 57

To the leader: Do Not Destroy. Of David. A Miktam,
when he fled from Saul, in the cave.

1 Be merciful to me, O God, be merciful to me,
  for in you my soul takes refuge;
  in the shadow of your wings I will take refuge,
  until the destroying storms pass by.
2 I cry to God Most High,
  to God who fulfills his purpose for me.
3 He will send from heaven and save me,
  he will put to shame those who trample on me.
                                        Selah
God will send forth his steadfast love and his
  faithfulness.

4 I lie down among lions
  that greedily devour^c human prey;
  their teeth are spears and arrows,
  their tongues sharp swords.

5 Be exalted, O God, above the heavens.
  Let your glory be over all the earth.

6 They set a net for my steps;
  my soul was bowed down.
  They dug a pit in my path,
  but they have fallen into it themselves. *Selah*
7 My heart is steadfast, O God,
  my heart is steadfast.
  I will sing and make melody.
8   Awake, my soul!

a Cn: Heb *rescue*   *b* Or *because*   *c* Cn: Heb *are aflame for*

Awake, O harp and lyre!
   I will awake the dawn.
9 I will give thanks to you, O Lord, among the peoples;
   I will sing praises to you among the nations.
10 For your steadfast love is as high as the heavens;
   your faithfulness extends to the clouds.

11 Be exalted, O God, above the heavens.
   Let your glory be over all the earth.

Psalm 58

To the leader: Do Not Destroy. Of David. A Miktam.

1 Do you indeed decree what is right, you gods?[a]
   Do you judge people fairly?
2 No, in your hearts you devise wrongs;
   your hands deal out violence on earth.

3 The wicked go astray from the womb;
   they err from their birth, speaking lies.
4 They have venom like the venom of a serpent,
   like the deaf adder that stops its ear,
5 so that it does not hear the voice of charmers
   or of the cunning enchanter.

6 O God, break the teeth in their mouths;
   tear out the fangs of the young lions, O LORD!
7 Let them vanish like water that runs away;
   like grass let them be trodden down[b] and wither.
8 Let them be like the snail that dissolves into slime;
   like the untimely birth that never sees the sun.
9 Sooner than your pots can feel the heat of thorns,
   whether green or ablaze, may he sweep them
   away!

10 The righteous will rejoice when they see vengeance
   done;
   they will bathe their feet in the blood of the
   wicked.
11 People will say, "Surely there is a reward for the
   righteous;
   surely there is a God who judges on earth."

Psalm 59

To the leader: Do Not Destroy. Of David. A Miktam, when Saul
ordered his house to be watched in order to kill him.

1 Deliver me from my enemies, O my God;
   protect me from those who rise up against me.
2 Deliver me from those who work evil;
   from the bloodthirsty save me.

3 Even now they lie in wait for my life;
   the mighty stir up strife against me.
   For no transgression or sin of mine, O LORD,
4   for no fault of mine, they run and make ready.

Rouse yourself, come to my help and see!

A Steadfast Heart

PSALM 57.7–10

The psalmist interrupts his litany of anxiety-ridden petitions with the exclamation, "Awake, my soul!" He reminds himself of God's steadfast love and unending faithfulness—and tells God that he, too, is trying to be faithful. Spiritual disciplines or practices are ways through which we meet God, who "awakens" our souls to faithfulness. Although methods don't make us holy, commitment to a daily devotional time, a prayer partner, small groups and worship can help us energize our spiritual lives.

In your journal, review your daily spiritual habits. What disciplines might you add or revise?

See Meeting God in Everyday Life

---

a Or *mighty lords*   *b* Cn: Meaning of Heb uncertain

Consecration to God

PSALM 59.9

"O dear child! The best possible life is this: to do our utmost to content God with love, and above all to trust in him. For we come closest to him by confidence; for true prayer is nothing else than pure abandonment to him, with perfect fidelity to trust him in all that he is . . . Take care that God be honored by you and by all those whom you can help, with effort, with self-sacrifice, with counsel, and with all that you can do."

—HADEWIJCH OF ANTWERP,
The Complete Works

See Meeting God in Service

5   You, LORD God of hosts, are God of Israel.
      Awake to punish all the nations;
          spare none of those who treacherously plot evil.
                                                    Selah

6   Each evening they come back,
          howling like dogs
          and prowling about the city.
7   There they are, bellowing with their mouths,
          with sharp words[a] on their lips—
          for "Who," they think,[b] "will hear us?"

8   But you laugh at them, O LORD;
          you hold all the nations in derision.
9   O my strength, I will watch for you;
          for you, O God, are my fortress.
10   My God in his steadfast love will meet me;
          my God will let me look in triumph on my
              enemies.

11   Do not kill them, or my people may forget;
          make them totter by your power, and bring them
              down,
          O Lord, our shield.
12   For the sin of their mouths, the words of their lips,
          let them be trapped in their pride.
      For the cursing and lies that they utter,
13   consume them in wrath;
          consume them until they are no more.
      Then it will be known to the ends of the earth
          that God rules over Jacob.   *Selah*

14   Each evening they come back,
          howling like dogs
          and prowling about the city.
15   They roam about for food,
          and growl if they do not get their fill.

16   But I will sing of your might;
          I will sing aloud of your steadfast love in the
              morning.
      For you have been a fortress for me
          and a refuge in the day of my distress.
17   O my strength, I will sing praises to you,
          for you, O God, are my fortress,
          the God who shows me steadfast love.

Psalm 60

To the leader: according to the Lily of the Covenant. A Miktam
of David; for instruction; when he struggled with Aram-
naharaim and with Aram-zobah, and when Joab on his return
killed twelve thousand Edomites in the Valley of Salt.

1   O God, you have rejected us, broken our defenses;
          you have been angry; now restore us!
2   You have caused the land to quake; you have torn it
              open;
          repair the cracks in it, for it is tottering.

a Heb *with swords*   *b* Heb lacks *they think*

3 You have made your people suffer hard things;
  you have given us wine to drink that made us reel.

4 You have set up a banner for those who fear you,
  to rally to it out of bowshot.[a]   *Selah*
5 Give victory with your right hand, and answer us,[b]
  so that those whom you love may be rescued.

6 God has promised in his sanctuary:[c]
  "With exultation I will divide up Shechem,
  and portion out the Vale of Succoth.
7 Gilead is mine, and Manasseh is mine;
  Ephraim is my helmet;
  Judah is my scepter.
8 Moab is my washbasin;
  on Edom I hurl my shoe;
  over Philistia I shout in triumph."

9 Who will bring me to the fortified city?
  Who will lead me to Edom?
10 Have you not rejected us, O God?
  You do not go out, O God, with our armies.
11 O grant us help against the foe,
  for human help is worthless.
12 With God we shall do valiantly;
  it is he who will tread down our foes.

Psalm 61

To the leader: with stringed instruments. Of David.

1 Hear my cry, O God;
  listen to my prayer.
2 From the end of the earth I call to you,
  when my heart is faint.

  Lead me to the rock
  that is higher than I;
3 for you are my refuge,
  a strong tower against the enemy.

4 Let me abide in your tent forever,
  find refuge under the shelter of your wings.
                                              Selah
5 For you, O God, have heard my vows;
  you have given me the heritage of those who fear
    your name.

6 Prolong the life of the king;
  may his years endure to all generations!
7 May he be enthroned forever before God;
  appoint steadfast love and faithfulness to watch
    over him!

8 So I will always sing praises to your name,
  as I pay my vows day after day.

---

a Gk Syr Jerome: Heb *because of the truth*   b Another reading is *me*
c Or *by his holiness*

A Higher Rock

PSALM 61.1–3

There are times when, like the psalmist, we cry out to God from what seems like the "end of the earth." We feel vulnerable and weary; we cannot see what is ahead; we don't know what to do. Reaching out to God with all of our being, we take an unseen hand and climb to a new perspective—"to the rock that is higher." Recall an experience in which you felt God's presence and help. How was God your "rock"? How did God's grace renew your soul? Record this experience in your journal, or rewrite these verses, adding your story of deliverance to the one expressed by the psalmist.

See Meeting God in Scripture

A Silence Beyond Petitions

PSALM 62.5

Waiting in silence before God is hard for many of us. Although God's heart cherishes spoken prayers of petition, praise and longing, God also desires our simple, *attentive* silence. "It is in this solitude," says Henri Nouwen, "that we discover that being is more important than having, and that we are worth more than the result of our efforts." When we quiet ourselves, we become open to God's voice and leading. Try starting with a few minutes of silence. Close your eyes or focus them on an object, such as a candle or a familiar picture. Some people find that holding a coffee cup or a smooth stone is "centering." Consecrate this time of silence to God.

See Meeting God in Prayer

Psalm 62

To the leader: according to Jeduthun. A Psalm of David.

1 For God alone my soul waits in silence;
   from him comes my salvation.
2 He alone is my rock and my salvation,
   my fortress; I shall never be shaken.

3 How long will you assail a person,
   will you batter your victim, all of you,
   as you would a leaning wall, a tottering fence?
4 Their only plan is to bring down a person of
     prominence.
   They take pleasure in falsehood;
they bless with their mouths,
   but inwardly they curse.   *Selah*

5 For God alone my soul waits in silence,
   for my hope is from him.
6 He alone is my rock and my salvation,
   my fortress; I shall not be shaken.
7 On God rests my deliverance and my honor;
   my mighty rock, my refuge is in God.

8 Trust in him at all times, O people;
   pour out your heart before him;
   God is a refuge for us.   *Selah*

9 Those of low estate are but a breath,
   those of high estate are a delusion;
in the balances they go up;
   they are together lighter than a breath.
10 Put no confidence in extortion,
   and set no vain hopes on robbery;
     if riches increase, do not set your heart on
       them.

11 Once God has spoken;
   twice have I heard this:
that power belongs to God,
12   and steadfast love belongs to you, O Lord.
For you repay to all
   according to their work.

Psalm 63

A Psalm of David, when he was in the Wilderness of Judah.

1 O God, you are my God, I seek you,
   my soul thirsts for you;
my flesh faints for you,
   as in a dry and weary land where there is no
     water.
2 So I have looked upon you in the sanctuary,
   beholding your power and glory.
3 Because your steadfast love is better than life,
   my lips will praise you.
4 So I will bless you as long as I live;
   I will lift up my hands and call on your name.

5 My soul is satisfied as with a rich feast,[a]
     and my mouth praises you with joyful lips
6 when I think of you on my bed,
     and meditate on you in the watches of the night;
7 for you have been my help,
     and in the shadow of your wings I sing for joy.
8 My soul clings to you;
     your right hand upholds me.

9 But those who seek to destroy my life
     shall go down into the depths of the earth;
10 they shall be given over to the power of the sword,
     they shall be prey for jackals.
11 But the king shall rejoice in God;
     all who swear by him shall exult,
     for the mouths of liars will be stopped.

Psalm 64

To the leader. A Psalm of David.

1 Hear my voice, O God, in my complaint;
     preserve my life from the dread enemy.
2 Hide me from the secret plots of the wicked,
     from the scheming of evildoers,
3 who whet their tongues like swords,
     who aim bitter words like arrows,
4 shooting from ambush at the blameless;
     they shoot suddenly and without fear.
5 They hold fast to their evil purpose;
     they talk of laying snares secretly,
   thinking, "Who can see us?[b]
6   Who can search out our crimes?[c]
   We have thought out a cunningly conceived plot."
     For the human heart and mind are deep.

7 But God will shoot his arrow at them;
     they will be wounded suddenly.
8 Because of their tongue he will bring them to ruin;[d]
     all who see them will shake with horror.
9 Then everyone will fear;
     they will tell what God has brought about,
     and ponder what he has done.

10 Let the righteous rejoice in the LORD
     and take refuge in him.
   Let all the upright in heart glory.

Psalm 65

To the leader. A Psalm of David. A Song.

1 Praise is due to you,
     O God, in Zion;
   and to you shall vows be performed,
2   O you who answer prayer!
   To you all flesh shall come.
3 When deeds of iniquity overwhelm us,
     you forgive our transgressions.

The Longing for God

PSALM 63.1–8

The psalmist paints a vivid picture of his desire for God: "My flesh pants for you, as in a dry and weary land where there is no water." Having seen God in the sanctuary, his life is saturated with love for God. Even during the night watches, he is compelled to meditate on God's comforting presence. Bernard of Clairvaux wrote that love for God is "an affection, not a contract . . . It has its reward in what it loves." How fervent is your desire for God? How do you see God in the sanctuary of your heart? God is the Beloved. In what ways do you experience this truth?

See *Meeting God in Worship.*

---

a Heb *with fat and fatness*   b Syr: Heb *them*   c Cn: Heb *They search out crimes*   d Cn: Heb *They will bring him to ruin, their tongue being against them*

Hope

PSALM 65.5

Hope is a very important word in the Psalms. In the midst of this psalm about creation's beauty, we encounter the psalmist's conviction that God is "the hope of all the ends of the earth." Some days when the newspaper tells us another sad story of conflict across the ocean and the television shows us the desolate faces of hungry people, it is hard to feel that hope. An overload of bad news can numb our hearts. As a way of remaining faithful to God's undying love for the world, take a story or issue from the world news and make it a focus of intercessory prayer for the day (or perhaps for the week). Be a partner with God in hope as you pray.

See Meeting God in Prayer

4 Happy are those whom you choose and bring near
    to live in your courts.
We shall be satisfied with the goodness of your
    house,
    your holy temple.

5 By awesome deeds you answer us with
        deliverance,
    O God of our salvation;
you are the hope of all the ends of the earth
    and of the farthest seas.
6 By your*a* strength you established the mountains;
    you are girded with might.
7 You silence the roaring of the seas,
    the roaring of their waves,
    the tumult of the peoples.
8 Those who live at earth's farthest bounds are awed
        by your signs;
you make the gateways of the morning and the
        evening shout for joy.

9 You visit the earth and water it,
    you greatly enrich it;
the river of God is full of water;
    you provide the people with grain,
    for so you have prepared it.
10 You water its furrows abundantly,
    settling its ridges,
softening it with showers,
    and blessing its growth.
11 You crown the year with your bounty;
    your wagon tracks overflow with richness.
12 The pastures of the wilderness overflow,
    the hills gird themselves with joy,
13 the meadows clothe themselves with flocks,
    the valleys deck themselves with grain,
    they shout and sing together for joy.

Psalm 66

To the leader. A Song. A Psalm.

1 Make a joyful noise to God, all the earth;
2   sing the glory of his name;
    give to him glorious praise.
3 Say to God, "How awesome are your deeds!
    Because of your great power, your enemies
        cringe before you.
4 All the earth worships you;
    they sing praises to you,
    sing praises to your name."   *Selah*

5 Come and see what God has done:
    he is awesome in his deeds among mortals.
6 He turned the sea into dry land;
    they passed through the river on foot.
There we rejoiced in him,
7   who rules by his might forever,

a Gk Jerome: Heb *his*

whose eyes keep watch on the nations—
 let the rebellious not exalt themselves.   *Selah*
8 Bless our God, O peoples,
 let the sound of his praise be heard,
9 who has kept us among the living,
 and has not let our feet slip.
10 For you, O God, have tested us;
 you have tried us as silver is tried.
11 You brought us into the net;
 you laid burdens on our backs;
12 you let people ride over our heads;
 we went through fire and through water;
yet you have brought us out to a spacious place.*a*

13 I will come into your house with burnt offerings;
 I will pay you my vows,
14 those that my lips uttered
 and my mouth promised when I was in trouble.
15 I will offer to you burnt offerings of fatlings,
 with the smoke of the sacrifice of rams;
I will make an offering of bulls and goats.   *Selah*

16 Come and hear, all you who fear God,
 and I will tell what he has done for me.
17 I cried aloud to him,
 and he was extolled with my tongue.
18 If I had cherished iniquity in my heart,
 the Lord would not have listened.
19 But truly God has listened;
 he has given heed to the words of my prayer.

20 Blessed be God,
 because he has not rejected my prayer
 or removed his steadfast love from me.

Psalm 67

To the leader: with stringed instruments. A Psalm. A Song.

1 May God be gracious to us and bless us
 and make his face to shine upon us,   *Selah*
2 that your way may be known upon earth,
 your saving power among all nations.
3 Let the peoples praise you, O God;
 let all the peoples praise you.

4 Let the nations be glad and sing for joy,
 for you judge the peoples with equity
 and guide the nations upon earth.   *Selah*
5 Let the peoples praise you, O God;
 let all the peoples praise you.

6 The earth has yielded its increase;
 God, our God, has blessed us.
7 May God continue to bless us;
 let all the ends of the earth revere him.

Worship

PSALM 67.1–4

The word *worship* means "to declare what is worthy." Here the psalmist praises God's justice and guidance. He sings about God's goodness and saving power. Through worship, we proclaim God's value to others. What do you declare is "worthy" by your worship? What are you saying about God—both to God and to others? In your conversations in the next twenty-four hours, consider how you might praise God in specific ways—through noticing something in nature, in a job situation, in a newborn baby.

See *Meeting God in Worship*

---

a Cn Compare Gk Syr Jerome Tg: Heb *to a saturation*

A Father's Care

PSALM 68.5–6

Although Jesus would later use "Father" as an affectionate name for God, this name for God is used only twice in the Psalms. It is significant, then, to see how it is used here. The psalmist says that God is a protective father of the orphan and a defender of the widow—the very people who were the most vulnerable in ancient times. Who are the most defenseless in your world, in your locality? In what practical ways is God leading you to help "protect" them? In Jesus' parable of the "great dinner," he extends the table to people who are poor, disabled and homeless (Luke 14.16–24). How are you extending God's table?

See Meeting God in Service

Psalm 68

To the leader. Of David. A Psalm. A Song.

1 Let God rise up, let his enemies be scattered;
  let those who hate him flee before him.
2 As smoke is driven away, so drive them away;
  as wax melts before the fire,
  let the wicked perish before God.
3 But let the righteous be joyful;
  let them exult before God;
  let them be jubilant with joy.

4 Sing to God, sing praises to his name;
  lift up a song to him who rides upon the clouds[a]—
  his name is the LORD—
  be exultant before him.

5 Father of orphans and protector of widows
  is God in his holy habitation.
6 God gives the desolate a home to live in;
  he leads out the prisoners to prosperity,
  but the rebellious live in a parched land.

7 O God, when you went out before your people,
  when you marched through the wilderness,   Selah
8 the earth quaked, the heavens poured down rain
  at the presence of God, the God of Sinai,
  at the presence of God, the God of Israel.
9 Rain in abundance, O God, you showered abroad;
  you restored your heritage when it languished;
10 your flock found a dwelling in it;
  in your goodness, O God, you provided for the
    needy.

11 The Lord gives the command;
  great is the company of those[b] who bore the
    tidings:
12 "The kings of the armies, they flee, they flee!"
  The women at home divide the spoil,
13   though they stay among the sheepfolds—
  the wings of a dove covered with silver,
    its pinions with green gold.
14 When the Almighty[c] scattered kings there,
  snow fell on Zalmon.

15 O mighty mountain, mountain of Bashan;
  O many-peaked mountain, mountain of Bashan!
16 Why do you look with envy, O many-peaked
    mountain,
  at the mount that God desired for his abode,
  where the LORD will reside forever?

17 With mighty chariotry, twice ten thousand,
  thousands upon thousands,
  the Lord came from Sinai into the holy place.[d]
18 You ascended the high mount,
  leading captives in your train

a Or *cast up a highway for him who rides through the deserts*   b Or *company of the women*   c Traditional rendering of Heb *Shaddai*   d Cn: Heb *The Lord among them Sinai in the holy* (place)

and receiving gifts from people,
even from those who rebel against the LORD God's
abiding there.
19 Blessed be the Lord,
who daily bears us up;
God is our salvation. *Selah*
20 Our God is a God of salvation,
and to GOD, the Lord, belongs escape from death.

21 But God will shatter the heads of his enemies,
the hairy crown of those who walk in their guilty
ways.
22 The Lord said,
"I will bring them back from Bashan,
I will bring them back from the depths of the sea,
23 so that you may bathe*ᵃ* your feet in blood,
so that the tongues of your dogs may have their
share from the foe."

24 Your solemn processions are seen,*ᵇ* O God,
the processions of my God, my King, into the
sanctuary—
25 the singers in front, the musicians last,
between them girls playing tambourines:
26 "Bless God in the great congregation,
the LORD, O you who are of Israel's fountain!"
27 There is Benjamin, the least of them, in the lead,
the princes of Judah in a body,
the princes of Zebulun, the princes of Naphtali.

28 Summon your might, O God;
show your strength, O God, as you have done for
us before.
29 Because of your temple at Jerusalem
kings bear gifts to you.
30 Rebuke the wild animals that live among the reeds,
the herd of bulls with the calves of the peoples.
Trample*ᶜ* under foot those who lust after tribute;
scatter the peoples who delight in war.*ᵈ*
31 Let bronze be brought from Egypt;
let Ethiopia*ᵉ* hasten to stretch out its hands to
God.

32 Sing to God, O kingdoms of the earth;
sing praises to the Lord, *Selah*
33 O rider in the heavens, the ancient heavens;
listen, he sends out his voice, his mighty voice.
34 Ascribe power to God,
whose majesty is over Israel;
and whose power is in the skies.
35 Awesome is God in his*ᶠ* sanctuary,
the God of Israel;
he gives power and strength to his people.

Blessed be God!

a Gk Syr Tg: Heb *shatter*   *b* Or *have been seen*   *c* Cn: Heb *Trampling*
d Meaning of Heb of verse 30 is uncertain   *e* Or *Nubia*; Heb *Cush*
f Gk: Heb *from your*

Worshiping in Body

PSALM 68.24–27

We express praise in many
ways. Some of us praise God in
song, others in dance, drawing,
throwing pottery, playing a
sport, writing, carpentry or pho-
tography. In what creative expressions, gifts or pleasures do
you find yourself reaching out
to God? How might you consecrate your hobbies as praise
and worship? God delights in
your joy, in your own particular
"tambourine." Remember that
God seeks the offering of your
heart, not the offering of perfection.

See *Meeting God in Worship*

In God's Time

PSALM 69.13–16

"The spiritual life is, first of all, a patient waiting, that is, a waiting in suffering, during which the many experiences of unfulfillment remind us of God's absence. But it also is a waiting in expectation which allows us to recognize the first signs of the coming of God in the center of our pains . . . It is in the center of our longing for the absent God that we discover his footprints."

—HENRI J.M. NOUWEN,
Reaching Out: The Three Movements
of the Spiritual Life

Psalm 69

To the leader: according to Lilies. Of David.

1 Save me, O God,
    for the waters have come up to my neck.
2 I sink in deep mire,
    where there is no foothold;
I have come into deep waters,
    and the flood sweeps over me.
3 I am weary with my crying;
    my throat is parched.
My eyes grow dim
    with waiting for my God.

4 More in number than the hairs of my head
    are those who hate me without cause;
many are those who would destroy me,
    my enemies who accuse me falsely.
What I did not steal
    must I now restore?
5 O God, you know my folly;
    the wrongs I have done are not hidden from you.

6 Do not let those who hope in you be put to shame
      because of me,
    O Lord GOD of hosts;
do not let those who seek you be dishonored
      because of me,
    O God of Israel.
7 It is for your sake that I have borne reproach,
    that shame has covered my face.
8 I have become a stranger to my kindred,
    an alien to my mother's children.

9 It is zeal for your house that has consumed me;
    the insults of those who insult you have fallen on
      me.
10 When I humbled my soul with fasting,[a]
    they insulted me for doing so.
11 When I made sackcloth my clothing,
    I became a byword to them.
12 I am the subject of gossip for those who sit in the
      gate,
    and the drunkards make songs about me.

13 But as for me, my prayer is to you, O LORD.
    At an acceptable time, O God,
    in the abundance of your steadfast love, answer
      me.
With your faithful help 14rescue me
    from sinking in the mire;
let me be delivered from my enemies
    and from the deep waters.
15 Do not let the flood sweep over me,
    or the deep swallow me up,
    or the Pit close its mouth over me.

16 Answer me, O LORD, for your steadfast love is good;
    according to your abundant mercy, turn to me.

a Gk Syr: Heb *I wept, with fasting my soul*, or *I made my soul mourn with fasting*

17 Do not hide your face from your servant,
for I am in distress—make haste to answer me.
18 Draw near to me, redeem me,
set me free because of my enemies.

19 You know the insults I receive,
and my shame and dishonor;
my foes are all known to you.
20 Insults have broken my heart,
so that I am in despair.
I looked for pity, but there was none;
and for comforters, but I found none.
21 They gave me poison for food,
and for my thirst they gave me vinegar to drink.

22 Let their table be a trap for them,
a snare for their allies.
23 Let their eyes be darkened so that they cannot see,
and make their loins tremble continually.
24 Pour out your indignation upon them,
and let your burning anger overtake them.
25 May their camp be a desolation;
let no one live in their tents.
26 For they persecute those whom you have struck
down,
and those whom you have wounded, they attack
still more.*a*
27 Add guilt to their guilt;
may they have no acquittal from you.
28 Let them be blotted out of the book of the living;
let them not be enrolled among the righteous.
29 But I am lowly and in pain;
let your salvation, O God, protect me.

30 I will praise the name of God with a song;
I will magnify him with thanksgiving.
31 This will please the Lord more than an ox
or a bull with horns and hoofs.
32 Let the oppressed see it and be glad;
you who seek God, let your hearts revive.
33 For the Lord hears the needy,
and does not despise his own that are in bonds.

34 Let heaven and earth praise him,
the seas and everything that moves in them.
35 For God will save Zion
and rebuild the cities of Judah;
and his servants shall live*b* there and possess it;
36 the children of his servants shall inherit it,
and those who love his name shall live in it.

Psalm 70

To the leader. Of David, for the memorial offering.

1 Be pleased, O God, to deliver me.
O Lord, make haste to help me!
2 Let those be put to shame and confusion
who seek my life.

Giving What You Have to Give

PSALM 69.30–33

In Hebrew religious tradition, the sacrifice of one's finest livestock was highly valued, but this kind of offering was impossible for those in exile or for the poor. Yet as this psalm proclaims, God is more concerned with the heart than with any external sacrifice. We may tend to look at the talents of others and think that what we have to offer is not as good as their contribution. God desires your love, the gift of your self. What are your unique gifts? Try listing ten of your gifts on a sheet of paper (or in your journal). Which ones give you joy? Which ones are you drawn to? How could they be your offering to God?

See Meeting God in Service

---

a Gk Syr: Heb *recount the pain of*   *b* Syr: Heb *and they shall live*

Seeking God

PSALM 70.4

Jesus says that what we seek, we will find (Matthew 7.7), that where our hearts are, therein is our treasure (Matthew 6.21). To treasure the kingdom of heaven is to find God. Indeed, God is faithful to "be found" when we seek God with all of our hearts (Jeremiah 29.13). We may too easily become distracted from our heart's greatest desire. What is calling you? What distracts you from your desire for God? How do you attend to your deepest longing? Sit in silence for five minutes, then write whatever comes to you in response to these questions. God honors even your *desire* to desire him.

See *Meeting God in Prayer*

Let those be turned back and brought to dishonor
who desire to hurt me.
3 Let those who say, "Aha, Aha!"
turn back because of their shame.

4 Let all who seek you
rejoice and be glad in you.
Let those who love your salvation
say evermore, "God is great!"
5 But I am poor and needy;
hasten to me, O God!
You are my help and my deliverer;
O LORD, do not delay!

Psalm 71

1 In you, O LORD, I take refuge;
let me never be put to shame.
2 In your righteousness deliver me and rescue me;
incline your ear to me and save me.
3 Be to me a rock of refuge,
a strong fortress,[a] to save me,
for you are my rock and my fortress.

4 Rescue me, O my God, from the hand of the wicked,
from the grasp of the unjust and cruel.
5 For you, O Lord, are my hope,
my trust, O LORD, from my youth.
6 Upon you I have leaned from my birth;
it was you who took me from my mother's womb.
My praise is continually of you.

7 I have been like a portent to many,
but you are my strong refuge.
8 My mouth is filled with your praise,
and with your glory all day long.
9 Do not cast me off in the time of old age;
do not forsake me when my strength is spent.
10 For my enemies speak concerning me,
and those who watch for my life consult together.
11 They say, "Pursue and seize that person
whom God has forsaken,
for there is no one to deliver."

12 O God, do not be far from me;
O my God, make haste to help me!
13 Let my accusers be put to shame and consumed;
let those who seek to hurt me
be covered with scorn and disgrace.
14 But I will hope continually,
and will praise you yet more and more.
15 My mouth will tell of your righteous acts,
of your deeds of salvation all day long,
though their number is past my knowledge.
16 I will come praising the mighty deeds of the Lord GOD,
I will praise your righteousness, yours alone.

17 O God, from my youth you have taught me,
and I still proclaim your wondrous deeds.

a Gk Compare 31.3: Heb *to come continually you have commanded*

18 So even to old age and gray hairs,
    O God, do not forsake me,
until I proclaim your might
    to all the generations to come.*a*
Your power ¹⁹and your righteousness, O God,
    reach the high heavens.

You who have done great things,
    O God, who is like you?
20 You who have made me see many troubles and
        calamities
    will revive me again;
from the depths of the earth
    you will bring me up again.
21 You will increase my honor,
    and comfort me once again.

22 I will also praise you with the harp
    for your faithfulness, O my God;
I will sing praises to you with the lyre,
    O Holy One of Israel.
23 My lips will shout for joy
    when I sing praises to you;
    my soul also, which you have rescued.
24 All day long my tongue will talk of your righteous
        help,
    for those who tried to do me harm
        have been put to shame, and disgraced.

Psalm 72

Of Solomon.

1 Give the king your justice, O God,
    and your righteousness to a king's son.
2 May he judge your people with righteousness,
    and your poor with justice.
3 May the mountains yield prosperity for the people,
    and the hills, in righteousness.
4 May he defend the cause of the poor of the people,
    give deliverance to the needy,
    and crush the oppressor.

5 May he live*b* while the sun endures,
    and as long as the moon, throughout all generations.
6 May he be like rain that falls on the mown grass,
    like showers that water the earth.
7 In his days may righteousness flourish
    and peace abound, until the moon is no more.

8 May he have dominion from sea to sea,
    and from the River to the ends of the earth.
9 May his foes*c* bow down before him,
    and his enemies lick the dust.
10 May the kings of Tarshish and of the isles
        render him tribute,
    may the kings of Sheba and Seba
        bring gifts.

Naming Mentors

PSALM 71.18

The psalmist prays for a long life, long enough to tell "the story" to the next generation. For how do we discover our faith? We learn its truths from our parents, from teachers and ministers, and from those who have walked before us. We fathom faith's depths in the stories of Abraham, Sarah, Moses, Deborah, Peter and Paul. Our mentors may be the respected and well-known saints of the Christian tradition, teachers and writers of the present day, or the "ordinary" saints in our own families and faith communities. Think about who your mentors are. Make a list of four or five of them, and leave space to write down what each mentor has "bequeathed" to you spiritually. Then pause and offer thanksgiving for each one.

See Meeting God in Community

a Gk Compare Syr: Heb *to a generation, to all that come*   *b* Gk: Heb *may they fear you*   *c* Cn: Heb *those who live in the wilderness*

Precious in God's Sight

PSALM 72.12–14

This psalm is sometimes entitled "The Reign of the Messiah." From our Christian perspective, we can see how Jesus fulfilled this vision. He responded to the poor and needy, healed the sick and preached a new kingdom where the first would be last and the last first. God's kingdom is based on care for the poor and the promotion of justice. Look carefully at the word *precious*. Other words such as *dear, beloved, valuable* and *cherished* come to mind. As you write a check to a charity or take food to a local shelter, offer the prayer of this psalm in thanksgiving: "God, I am grateful for these persons you so cherish."

See Meeting God in Service

11 May all kings fall down before him,
      all nations give him service.

12 For he delivers the needy when they call,
      the poor and those who have no helper.
13 He has pity on the weak and the needy,
      and saves the lives of the needy.
14 From oppression and violence he redeems their life;
      and precious is their blood in his sight.

15 Long may he live!
      May gold of Sheba be given to him.
    May prayer be made for him continually,
      and blessings invoked for him all day long.
16 May there be abundance of grain in the land;
      may it wave on the tops of the mountains;
      may its fruit be like Lebanon;
    and may people blossom in the cities
      like the grass of the field.
17 May his name endure forever,
      his fame continue as long as the sun.
    May all nations be blessed in him;[a]
      may they pronounce him happy.

18 Blessed be the LORD, the God of Israel,
      who alone does wondrous things.
19 Blessed be his glorious name forever;
      may his glory fill the whole earth.
          Amen and Amen.

20 The prayers of David son of Jesse are ended.

BOOK III

(Psalms 73–89)

Psalm 73

A Psalm of Asaph.

1 Truly God is good to the upright,[b]
      to those who are pure in heart.
2 But as for me, my feet had almost stumbled;
      my steps had nearly slipped.
3 For I was envious of the arrogant;
      I saw the prosperity of the wicked.

4 For they have no pain;
      their bodies are sound and sleek.
5 They are not in trouble as others are;
      they are not plagued like other people.
6 Therefore pride is their necklace;
      violence covers them like a garment.
7 Their eyes swell out with fatness;
      their hearts overflow with follies.
8 They scoff and speak with malice;
      loftily they threaten oppression.
9 They set their mouths against heaven,
      and their tongues range over the earth.

a Or *bless themselves by him*   *b* Or *good to Israel*

¹⁰ Therefore the people turn and praise them,ᵃ
and find no fault in them.ᵇ
¹¹ And they say, "How can God know?
Is there knowledge in the Most High?"
¹² Such are the wicked;
always at ease, they increase in riches.
¹³ All in vain I have kept my heart clean
and washed my hands in innocence.
¹⁴ For all day long I have been plagued,
and am punished every morning.

¹⁵ If I had said, "I will talk on in this way,"
I would have been untrue to the circle of your
children.
¹⁶ But when I thought how to understand this,
it seemed to me a wearisome task,
¹⁷ until I went into the sanctuary of God;
then I perceived their end.
¹⁸ Truly you set them in slippery places;
you make them fall to ruin.
¹⁹ How they are destroyed in a moment,
swept away utterly by terrors!
²⁰ They areᶜ like a dream when one awakes;
on awaking you despise their phantoms.

²¹ When my soul was embittered,
when I was pricked in heart,
²² I was stupid and ignorant;
I was like a brute beast toward you.
²³ Nevertheless I am continually with you;
you hold my right hand.
²⁴ You guide me with your counsel,
and afterward you will receive me with honor.ᵈ
²⁵ Whom have I in heaven but you?
And there is nothing on earth that I desire other
than you.
²⁶ My flesh and my heart may fail,
but God is the strengthᵉ of my heart and my
portion forever.

²⁷ Indeed, those who are far from you will perish;
you put an end to those who are false to you.
²⁸ But for me it is good to be near God;
I have made the Lord GOD my refuge,
to tell of all your works.

Psalm 74

A Maskil of Asaph.

¹ O God, why do you cast us off forever?
Why does your anger smoke against the sheep of
your pasture?
² Remember your congregation, which you acquired
long ago,
which you redeemed to be the tribe of your
heritage.
Remember Mount Zion, where you came to dwell.

Losing Our Way

PSALM 73.21–26

How often we wander away from God as we journey. We become distracted by anger or envy, by our individual successes or failures, and by the overcrowding of our lives. We may act, as the psalmist laments, like "a brute beast toward [God]." Yet God is ever faithful—holding us, loving us, guiding us. Augustine writes, "Late have I loved Thee, O Beauty so ancient and so new; late have I loved Thee! For behold Thou wert within me, and I outside." How have you been "looking outside" for the source of your spiritual life? What areas of your life do you need to recommit to God? Make an appointment with yourself in your journal or with a spiritual adviser to consider these questions.

See Meeting God in Community

---

a Cn: Heb *his people return here*   *b* Cn: Heb *abundant waters are drained by them*   *c* Cn: Heb *Lord*   *d* Or *to glory*   *e* Heb *rock*

755

When It Is Hard to See

PSALM 74.10–12

Even deeply committed believers sometimes feel that God is distant. A family member suffers from a life-threatening illness; the headline in the local paper announces a gruesome murder across town; a good friend seems far away. The psalmist is honest about his feelings of doubt: Where is God? Why doesn't God do something? Yet he reminds himself: God is always working "salvation in the earth."

What might God be leading you to do about a discouraging situation—offer prayers of intercession, give time and energy to a local youth program, share your honest feelings of grief with a friend?

See Meeting God in Service

3 Direct your steps to the perpetual ruins;
   the enemy has destroyed everything in the sanctuary.

4 Your foes have roared within your holy place;
   they set up their emblems there.

5 At the upper entrance they hacked
   the wooden trellis with axes.*a*

6 And then, with hatchets and hammers,
   they smashed all its carved work.

7 They set your sanctuary on fire;
   they desecrated the dwelling place of your name,
   bringing it to the ground.

8 They said to themselves, "We will utterly subdue them";
   they burned all the meeting places of God in the land.

9 We do not see our emblems;
   there is no longer any prophet,
   and there is no one among us who knows how long.

10 How long, O God, is the foe to scoff?
   Is the enemy to revile your name forever?

11 Why do you hold back your hand;
   why do you keep your hand in*b* your bosom?

12 Yet God my King is from of old,
   working salvation in the earth.

13 You divided the sea by your might;
   you broke the heads of the dragons in the waters.

14 You crushed the heads of Leviathan;
   you gave him as food*c* for the creatures of the wilderness.

15 You cut openings for springs and torrents;
   you dried up ever-flowing streams.

16 Yours is the day, yours also the night;
   you established the luminaries*d* and the sun.

17 You have fixed all the bounds of the earth;
   you made summer and winter.

18 Remember this, O LORD, how the enemy scoffs,
   and an impious people reviles your name.

19 Do not deliver the soul of your dove to the wild animals;
   do not forget the life of your poor forever.

20 Have regard for your*e* covenant,
   for the dark places of the land are full of the haunts of violence.

21 Do not let the downtrodden be put to shame;
   let the poor and needy praise your name.

22 Rise up, O God, plead your cause;
   remember how the impious scoff at you all day long.

23 Do not forget the clamor of your foes,
   the uproar of your adversaries that goes up continually.

---

a Cn Compare Gk Syr: Meaning of Heb uncertain   *b* Cn: Heb *do you consume your right hand from*   *c* Heb *food for the people*   *d* Or *moon*; Heb *light*   *e* Gk Syr: Heb *the*

Psalm 75

To the leader: Do Not Destroy. A Psalm of Asaph. A Song.

1 We give thanks to you, O God;
    we give thanks; your name is near.
    People tell of your wondrous deeds.

2 At the set time that I appoint
    I will judge with equity.
3 When the earth totters, with all its inhabitants,
    it is I who keep its pillars steady.   *Selah*
4 I say to the boastful, "Do not boast,"
    and to the wicked, "Do not lift up your horn;
5 do not lift up your horn on high,
    or speak with insolent neck."

6 For not from the east or from the west
    and not from the wilderness comes lifting up;
7 but it is God who executes judgment,
    putting down one and lifting up another.
8 For in the hand of the Lord there is a cup
    with foaming wine, well mixed;
    he will pour a draught from it,
    and all the wicked of the earth
    shall drain it down to the dregs.
9 But I will rejoice*ᵃ* forever;
    I will sing praises to the God of Jacob.

10 All the horns of the wicked I will cut off,
    but the horns of the righteous shall be exalted.

Psalm 76

To the leader: with stringed instruments. A Psalm of Asaph.
A Song.

1 In Judah God is known,
    his name is great in Israel.
2 His abode has been established in Salem,
    his dwelling place in Zion.
3 There he broke the flashing arrows,
    the shield, the sword, and the weapons of war.
        Selah

4 Glorious are you, more majestic
    than the everlasting mountains.*ᵇ*
5 The stouthearted were stripped of their spoil;
    they sank into sleep;
none of the troops
    was able to lift a hand.
6 At your rebuke, O God of Jacob,
    both rider and horse lay stunned.

7 But you indeed are awesome!
    Who can stand before you
    when once your anger is roused?
8 From the heavens you uttered judgment;
    the earth feared and was still
9 when God rose up to establish judgment,
    to save all the oppressed of the earth.   *Selah*

a Gk: Heb *declare*   *b* Gk: Heb *the mountains of prey*

The Judgment of God

PSALM 75.6–9

As you read this psalm of judgment, you might think of Jesus' image of the Son of Man separating the "sheep" from the "goats" (Matthew 25.32). We encounter God's sifting, purifying love in our experience of inward spiritual transformation. Spiritual writers refer to this as the "death of the ego" or the "dark night of the soul." In order for God's life to grow in us, our old attitudes, prejudices and self-preoccupation must perish. In what ways have you experienced the "dark night"? How would you describe the process of "dying" to your old self and of finding new life in Jesus Christ? In what areas do you see new life? How is God still leading you to let go of your old self?

Before Dawn

PSALM 77.6

Monastics typically rise while it is still dark, for in the stillness before dawn, the soul is quiet, unhurried. The day has not rushed in yet with all of its duties. In both the silence and the chanting of psalms, the monastic meditates. Meditation is a time to consecrate one's heart to God, a time of wordless communion with God. As an experiment this week, set your alarm clock ten minutes earlier than usual. Using a candle, recite the Lord's Prayer slowly or repeat a favorite psalm; rest in God's presence for several minutes of silent contemplation.

See Meeting God in Scripture

10 Human wrath serves only to praise you,
   when you bind the last bit of your[a] wrath around you.
11 Make vows to the LORD your God, and perform them;
   let all who are around him bring gifts
   to the one who is awesome,
12 who cuts off the spirit of princes,
   who inspires fear in the kings of the earth.

Psalm 77

To the leader: according to Jeduthun. Of Asaph. A Psalm.

1 I cry aloud to God,
   aloud to God, that he may hear me.
2 In the day of my trouble I seek the Lord;
   in the night my hand is stretched out without wearying;
   my soul refuses to be comforted.
3 I think of God, and I moan;
   I meditate, and my spirit faints.   *Selah*

4 You keep my eyelids from closing;
   I am so troubled that I cannot speak.
5 I consider the days of old,
   and remember the years of long ago.
6 I commune[b] with my heart in the night;
   I meditate and search my spirit:[c]
7 "Will the Lord spurn forever,
   and never again be favorable?
8 Has his steadfast love ceased forever?
   Are his promises at an end for all time?
9 Has God forgotten to be gracious?
   Has he in anger shut up his compassion?"   *Selah*
10 And I say, "It is my grief
   that the right hand of the Most High has changed."

11 I will call to mind the deeds of the LORD;
   I will remember your wonders of old.
12 I will meditate on all your work,
   and muse on your mighty deeds.
13 Your way, O God, is holy.
   What god is so great as our God?
14 You are the God who works wonders;
   you have displayed your might among the peoples.
15 With your strong arm you redeemed your people,
   the descendants of Jacob and Joseph.   *Selah*

16 When the waters saw you, O God,
   when the waters saw you, they were afraid;
   the very deep trembled.
17 The clouds poured out water;
   the skies thundered;
   your arrows flashed on every side.
18 The crash of your thunder was in the whirlwind;
   your lightnings lit up the world;
   the earth trembled and shook.

a Heb lacks *your*   *b* Gk Syr: Heb *My music*   *c* Syr Jerome: Heb *my spirit searches*

19 Your way was through the sea,
    your path, through the mighty waters;
    yet your footprints were unseen.
20 You led your people like a flock
    by the hand of Moses and Aaron.

Psalm 78

A Maskil of Asaph.

1 Give ear, O my people, to my teaching;
    incline your ears to the words of my mouth.
2 I will open my mouth in a parable;
    I will utter dark sayings from of old,
3 things that we have heard and known,
    that our ancestors have told us.
4 We will not hide them from their children;
    we will tell to the coming generation
the glorious deeds of the LORD, and his might,
    and the wonders that he has done.

5 He established a decree in Jacob,
    and appointed a law in Israel,
which he commanded our ancestors
    to teach to their children;
6 that the next generation might know them,
    the children yet unborn,
and rise up and tell them to their children,
7 so that they should set their hope in God,
and not forget the works of God,
    but keep his commandments;
8 and that they should not be like their ancestors,
    a stubborn and rebellious generation,
a generation whose heart was not steadfast,
    whose spirit was not faithful to God.

9 The Ephraimites, armed with[a] the bow,
    turned back on the day of battle.
10 They did not keep God's covenant,
    but refused to walk according to his law.
11 They forgot what he had done,
    and the miracles that he had shown them.
12 In the sight of their ancestors he worked marvels
    in the land of Egypt, in the fields of Zoan.
13 He divided the sea and let them pass through it,
    and made the waters stand like a heap.
14 In the daytime he led them with a cloud,
    and all night long with a fiery light.
15 He split rocks open in the wilderness,
    and gave them drink abundantly as from the deep.
16 He made streams come out of the rock,
    and caused waters to flow down like rivers.

17 Yet they sinned still more against him,
    rebelling against the Most High in the desert.
18 They tested God in their heart
    by demanding the food they craved.
19 They spoke against God, saying,
    "Can God spread a table in the wilderness?

Becoming a Mentor

PSALM 78.2–4

Each one of us in the body of Christ is called to encourage others (1 Corinthians 12.7). One important spiritual ministry is parenting—fostering faith in our children. Or we may minister to others through being in regular prayer for them, teaching or leading a small group, visiting someone who is sick or in prison, tutoring at a local school or spending time with a new Christian. Reflect on your current relationships. How might you be an encouraging presence in another person's life?

See Meeting God in Service

---

a Heb *armed with shooting*

Being Human

PSALM 78.38–39

God is compassionate toward us—even in our frailty. As we draw closer to God, our weakness—our humanness—becomes all the more obvious. For as John of the Cross observed, "Freedom cannot abide in a heart dominated by desires, in a slave's heart. It abides in a liberated heart, in a child's heart." Although we are set free by grace, being human, we allow our hearts to become enslaved to sin over and over again. We may even think we have arrived on a higher spiritual plane, but then we realize we have taken on spiritual pride. What are some of the stumbling blocks that keep you from fully accepting God's grace? Invite God's penetrating gaze of love. How is God inviting you to embrace new freedom?

See Meeting God in Prayer

20 Even though he struck the rock so that water
    gushed out
  and torrents overflowed,
can he also give bread,
  or provide meat for his people?"

21 Therefore, when the LORD heard, he was full of rage;
  a fire was kindled against Jacob,
  his anger mounted against Israel,
22 because they had no faith in God,
  and did not trust his saving power.
23 Yet he commanded the skies above,
  and opened the doors of heaven;
24 he rained down on them manna to eat,
  and gave them the grain of heaven.
25 Mortals ate of the bread of angels;
  he sent them food in abundance.
26 He caused the east wind to blow in the heavens,
  and by his power he led out the south wind;
27 he rained flesh upon them like dust,
  winged birds like the sand of the seas;
28 he let them fall within their camp,
  all around their dwellings.
29 And they ate and were well filled,
  for he gave them what they craved.
30 But before they had satisfied their craving,
  while the food was still in their mouths,
31 the anger of God rose against them
  and he killed the strongest of them,
  and laid low the flower of Israel.

32 In spite of all this they still sinned;
  they did not believe in his wonders.
33 So he made their days vanish like a breath,
  and their years in terror.
34 When he killed them, they sought for him;
  they repented and sought God earnestly.
35 They remembered that God was their rock,
  the Most High God their redeemer.
36 But they flattered him with their mouths;
  they lied to him with their tongues.
37 Their heart was not steadfast toward him;
  they were not true to his covenant.
38 Yet he, being compassionate,
    forgave their iniquity,
    and did not destroy them;
  often he restrained his anger,
    and did not stir up all his wrath.
39 He remembered that they were but flesh,
  a wind that passes and does not come again.
40 How often they rebelled against him in the wilderness
  and grieved him in the desert!
41 They tested God again and again,
  and provoked the Holy One of Israel.
42 They did not keep in mind his power,
  or the day when he redeemed them from the foe;
43 when he displayed his signs in Egypt,
  and his miracles in the fields of Zoan.
44 He turned their rivers to blood,
  so that they could not drink of their streams.

45 He sent among them swarms of flies, which
        devoured them,
      and frogs, which destroyed them.
46 He gave their crops to the caterpillar,
      and the fruit of their labor to the locust.
47 He destroyed their vines with hail,
      and their sycamores with frost.
48 He gave over their cattle to the hail,
      and their flocks to thunderbolts.
49 He let loose on them his fierce anger,
      wrath, indignation, and distress,
      a company of destroying angels.
50 He made a path for his anger;
      he did not spare them from death,
      but gave their lives over to the plague.
51 He struck all the firstborn in Egypt,
      the first issue of their strength in the tents of Ham.
52 Then he led out his people like sheep,
      and guided them in the wilderness like a flock.
53 He led them in safety, so that they were not afraid;
      but the sea overwhelmed their enemies.
54 And he brought them to his holy hill,
      to the mountain that his right hand had won.
55 He drove out nations before them;
      he apportioned them for a possession
      and settled the tribes of Israel in their tents.

56 Yet they tested the Most High God,
      and rebelled against him.
      They did not observe his decrees,
57 but turned away and were faithless like their
        ancestors;
      they twisted like a treacherous bow.
58 For they provoked him to anger with their high
        places;
      they moved him to jealousy with their idols.
59 When God heard, he was full of wrath,
      and he utterly rejected Israel.
60 He abandoned his dwelling at Shiloh,
      the tent where he dwelt among mortals,
61 and delivered his power to captivity,
      his glory to the hand of the foe.
62 He gave his people to the sword,
      and vented his wrath on his heritage.
63 Fire devoured their young men,
      and their girls had no marriage song.
64 Their priests fell by the sword,
      and their widows made no lamentation.
65 Then the Lord awoke as from sleep,
      like a warrior shouting because of wine.
66 He put his adversaries to rout;
      he put them to everlasting disgrace.

67 He rejected the tent of Joseph,
      he did not choose the tribe of Ephraim;
68 but he chose the tribe of Judah,
      Mount Zion, which he loves.
69 He built his sanctuary like the high heavens,
      like the earth, which he has founded forever.

Hearing God's Voice in the Wilderness

PSALM 78.52–53

The psalmist remembers how, like an attentive shepherd, God faithfully led the people of Israel through the wilderness by means of a cloud by day and fire in the cloud by night (see Exodus 40.38). Quakers often use the metaphor of traveling in the light: By following even small signs of divine light, one finds that more and more light becomes apparent. "Travels begin at the breakings of day," Friend Isaac Pennington wrote in 1665, "wherein are but glimmerings, or little light . . . yet *there* must the traveller begin . . . and in his faithful travel the light will break in on him more and more." How do you discern God's guiding voice in your life? At what point in your day do you take time to listen, to wait for God's guidance? Perhaps you can begin right now.

See Meeting God in Everyday Life

The Healing of the Generations

PSALM 79.8–9

The psalmist is speaking here about the destruction of Jerusalem and thus the continuing grief in Israel's spirit. In the spiritual life, we may also have concerns about how the sins of our forebears affect our souls. How have you been affected by the fears, prejudices and hurts of your parents, grandparents and great-grandparents? God's compassion can reach into our past. Take a few minutes in quiet reflection to call up in your memory one hurt you have carried as a result of someone's failure; perhaps you feel negative emotions toward God as a parent to you. Imagine God's loving concern for your pain and offer that pain to him. Feel God's unending mercy and love healing your heart.

See Meeting God in Prayer

70 He chose his servant David,
    and took him from the sheepfolds;
71 from tending the nursing ewes he brought him
    to be the shepherd of his people Jacob,
    of Israel, his inheritance.
72 With upright heart he tended them,
    and guided them with skillful hand.

Psalm 79

A Psalm of Asaph.

1 O God, the nations have come into your inheritance;
    they have defiled your holy temple;
    they have laid Jerusalem in ruins.
2 They have given the bodies of your servants
    to the birds of the air for food,
    the flesh of your faithful to the wild animals of
        the earth.
3 They have poured out their blood like water
    all around Jerusalem,
    and there was no one to bury them.
4 We have become a taunt to our neighbors,
    mocked and derided by those around us.

5 How long, O LORD? Will you be angry forever?
    Will your jealous wrath burn like fire?
6 Pour out your anger on the nations
    that do not know you,
and on the kingdoms
    that do not call on your name.
7 For they have devoured Jacob
    and laid waste his habitation.

8 Do not remember against us the iniquities of our
        ancestors;
    let your compassion come speedily to meet us,
    for we are brought very low.
9 Help us, O God of our salvation,
    for the glory of your name;
deliver us, and forgive our sins,
    for your name's sake.
10 Why should the nations say,
    "Where is their God?"
Let the avenging of the outpoured blood of your
        servants
    be known among the nations before our eyes.

11 Let the groans of the prisoners come before you;
    according to your great power preserve those
        doomed to die.
12 Return sevenfold into the bosom of our neighbors
    the taunts with which they taunted you, O Lord!
13 Then we your people, the flock of your pasture,
    will give thanks to you forever;
    from generation to generation we will recount
        your praise.

Psalm 80

To the leader: on Lilies, a Covenant. Of Asaph. A Psalm.

1 Give ear, O Shepherd of Israel,
   you who lead Joseph like a flock!
   You who are enthroned upon the cherubim, shine
      forth
2   before Ephraim and Benjamin and Manasseh.
   Stir up your might,
      and come to save us!

3 Restore us, O God;
   let your face shine, that we may be saved.

4 O Lord God of hosts,
   how long will you be angry with your people's
      prayers?
5 You have fed them with the bread of tears,
   and given them tears to drink in full measure.
6 You make us the scorn[a] of our neighbors;
   our enemies laugh among themselves.

7 Restore us, O God of hosts;
   let your face shine, that we may be saved.

8 You brought a vine out of Egypt;
   you drove out the nations and planted it.
9 You cleared the ground for it;
   it took deep root and filled the land.
10 The mountains were covered with its shade,
   the mighty cedars with its branches;
11 it sent out its branches to the sea,
   and its shoots to the River.
12 Why then have you broken down its walls,
   so that all who pass along the way pluck its fruit?
13 The boar from the forest ravages it,
   and all that move in the field feed on it.

14 Turn again, O God of hosts;
   look down from heaven, and see;
   have regard for this vine,
15   the stock that your right hand planted.[b]
16 They have burned it with fire, they have cut it down;[c]
   may they perish at the rebuke of your countenance.
17 But let your hand be upon the one at your right hand,
   the one whom you made strong for yourself.
18 Then we will never turn back from you;
   give us life, and we will call on your name.

19 Restore us, O Lord God of hosts;
   let your face shine, that we may be saved.

Psalm 81

To the leader: according to The Gittith. Of Asaph.

1 Sing aloud to God our strength;
   shout for joy to the God of Jacob.

God's Shining Face

PSALM 80.3,19

Noted psychologist Erik Erikson believes that one of our earliest experiences of the sacred occurs when we are infants. We experience what God is like through the loving face of our mother (or our primary caregiver). It is a face of love and tenderness, and we experience being loved without condition. Julian of Norwich speaks of Jesus' motherly love for us: "Thus he is our Mother in kind by the working of grace . . . . And he wills that we know it. For he desires to have all of our love attached to him."

Imagine God's face turned toward you with such shining tenderness. God's eyes are full of love for you; God smiles at you and sings to you gently.

See Meeting God in Scripture

---

a Syr: Heb *strife*   *b* Heb adds *from verse 17 and upon the one whom you made strong for yourself*   *c* Cn: Heb *it is cut down*

The Idolatry of Attachment

PSALM 81.9–10

Most of us are not tempted to worship other deities and images. We believe, as Israel learned, that God is unseen spirit. Idolatry for us is usually more insidious; sometimes our idols are our addictions. As psychiatrist and spiritual writer Gerald May explains, addiction is the attachment of our desire for God to objects, and such attachment "can indeed deaden our responsiveness to grace." Typically, we can name addictions to pornography or nicotine while overlooking more "acceptable" ones, such as addictions to approval, neatness, television, revenge or the Internet! What are your attachments? Study one of your "addictions" over the course of a week. How does it distract you from trusting the Spirit of God in your life? Offer your addictions by name to God and ask him to free you and fill you with himself.

2 Raise a song, sound the tambourine,
      the sweet lyre with the harp.
3 Blow the trumpet at the new moon,
      at the full moon, on our festal day.
4 For it is a statute for Israel,
      an ordinance of the God of Jacob.
5 He made it a decree in Joseph,
      when he went out over*a* the land of Egypt.

I hear a voice I had not known:
6 "I relieved your*b* shoulder of the burden;
      your*b* hands were freed from the basket.
7 In distress you called, and I rescued you;
      I answered you in the secret place of thunder;
      I tested you at the waters of Meribah.   *Selah*
8 Hear, O my people, while I admonish you;
      O Israel, if you would but listen to me!
9 There shall be no strange god among you;
      you shall not bow down to a foreign god.
10 I am the LORD your God,
      who brought you up out of the land of Egypt.
      Open your mouth wide and I will fill it.

11 "But my people did not listen to my voice;
      Israel would not submit to me.
12 So I gave them over to their stubborn hearts,
      to follow their own counsels.
13 O that my people would listen to me,
      that Israel would walk in my ways!
14 Then I would quickly subdue their enemies,
      and turn my hand against their foes.
15 Those who hate the LORD would cringe before him,
      and their doom would last forever.
16 I would feed you*c* with the finest of the wheat,
      and with honey from the rock I would satisfy
         you."

Psalm 82

A Psalm of Asaph.

1 God has taken his place in the divine council;
      in the midst of the gods he holds judgment:
2 "How long will you judge unjustly
      and show partiality to the wicked?   *Selah*
3 Give justice to the weak and the orphan;
      maintain the right of the lowly and the destitute.
4 Rescue the weak and the needy;
      deliver them from the hand of the wicked."

5 They have neither knowledge nor understanding,
      they walk around in darkness;
      all the foundations of the earth are shaken.

6 I say, "You are gods,
      children of the Most High, all of you;
7 nevertheless, you shall die like mortals,
      and fall like any prince."*d*

a Or *against*   *b* Heb *his*   *c* Cn Compare verse 16b: Heb *he would feed him*   *d* Or *fall as one man, O princes*

8 Rise up, O God, judge the earth;
  for all the nations belong to you!

Psalm 83

A Song. A Psalm of Asaph.

1 O God, do not keep silence;
  do not hold your peace or be still, O God!
2 Even now your enemies are in tumult;
  those who hate you have raised their heads.
3 They lay crafty plans against your people;
  they consult together against those you protect.
4 They say, "Come, let us wipe them out as a nation;
  let the name of Israel be remembered no more."
5 They conspire with one accord;
  against you they make a covenant—
6 the tents of Edom and the Ishmaelites,
  Moab and the Hagrites,
7 Gebal and Ammon and Amalek,
  Philistia with the inhabitants of Tyre;
8 Assyria also has joined them;
  they are the strong arm of the children of Lot.
  Selah

9 Do to them as you did to Midian,
  as to Sisera and Jabin at the Wadi Kishon,
10 who were destroyed at En-dor,
  who became dung for the ground.
11 Make their nobles like Oreb and Zeeb,
  all their princes like Zebah and Zalmunna,
12 who said, "Let us take the pastures of God
  for our own possession."

13 O my God, make them like whirling dust,[a]
  like chaff before the wind.
14 As fire consumes the forest,
  as the flame sets the mountains ablaze,
15 so pursue them with your tempest
  and terrify them with your hurricane.
16 Fill their faces with shame,
  so that they may seek your name, O Lord.
17 Let them be put to shame and dismayed forever;
  let them perish in disgrace.
18 Let them know that you alone,
  whose name is the Lord,
  are the Most High over all the earth.

Psalm 84

*To the leader: according to The Gittith. Of the Korahites.
A Psalm.*

1 How lovely is your dwelling place,
  O Lord of hosts!
2 My soul longs, indeed it faints
  for the courts of the Lord;
  my heart and my flesh sing for joy
  to the living God.

A Just Judge

PSALM 82.5,8

In this psalm, God's justice and compassion are integral to the "foundations of the earth"; all of God's creation is founded on righteousness. Meditate on the nature of God. What signs do you see of God's order in creation, in our system of laws, in the caring community of the church? What does it mean to "give justice to the weak" and "maintain the right of the lowly and the destitute" (v.3) in our world today? In what ways might God be leading you to build justice in your community? Share your reflections with a friend.

See Meeting God in Service

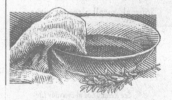

---

a Or *a tumbleweed*

Water in the Desert

PSALM 84.5–7

The Valley of Baca is an arid, desert-like place on the way to Jerusalem. In our hearts, we may also find a desert—a desert of grief and loneliness or of dryness in prayer. In her dry times, Teresa of Avila found nourishment in God's gracious "springs": "[God] produces this delight with the greatest peace and quiet and sweetness in the very interior part of our selves . . . This water overflows through all the dwelling places [of the soul]." Recall a time when you felt God's love "watering you" in a desert experience. What does it mean to rest in God's provision rather than in your own efforts? In your journal, recall a recent situation in which you experienced a "spring" of spiritual refreshment.

See Meeting God in Everyday Life

3 Even the sparrow finds a home,
    and the swallow a nest for herself,
    where she may lay her young,
at your altars, O LORD of hosts,
    my King and my God.
4 Happy are those who live in your house,
    ever singing your praise.   *Selah*

5 Happy are those whose strength is in you,
    in whose heart are the highways to Zion.[a]
6 As they go through the valley of Baca
    they make it a place of springs;
    the early rain also covers it with pools.
7 They go from strength to strength;
    the God of gods will be seen in Zion.

8 O LORD God of hosts, hear my prayer;
    give ear, O God of Jacob!   *Selah*
9 Behold our shield, O God;
    look on the face of your anointed.

10 For a day in your courts is better
    than a thousand elsewhere.
I would rather be a doorkeeper in the house of my
    God
    than live in the tents of wickedness.
11 For the LORD God is a sun and shield;
    he bestows favor and honor.
No good thing does the LORD withhold
    from those who walk uprightly.
12 O LORD of hosts,
    happy is everyone who trusts in you.

Psalm 85

To the leader. Of the Korahites. A Psalm.

1 LORD, you were favorable to your land;
    you restored the fortunes of Jacob.
2 You forgave the iniquity of your people;
    you pardoned all their sin.   *Selah*
3 You withdrew all your wrath;
    you turned from your hot anger.

4 Restore us again, O God of our salvation,
    and put away your indignation toward us.
5 Will you be angry with us forever?
    Will you prolong your anger to all generations?
6 Will you not revive us again,
    so that your people may rejoice in you?
7 Show us your steadfast love, O LORD,
    and grant us your salvation.

8 Let me hear what God the LORD will speak,
    for he will speak peace to his people,
    to his faithful, to those who turn to him in their
        hearts.[b]
9 Surely his salvation is at hand for those who fear him,
    that his glory may dwell in our land.

a Heb lacks *to Zion*   *b* Gk: Heb *but let them not turn back to folly*

10 Steadfast love and faithfulness will meet;
　　righteousness and peace will kiss each other.
11 Faithfulness will spring up from the ground,
　　and righteousness will look down from the sky.
12 The LORD will give what is good,
　　and our land will yield its increase.
13 Righteousness will go before him,
　　and will make a path for his steps.

Psalm 86

A Prayer of David.

1 Incline your ear, O LORD, and answer me,
　　for I am poor and needy.
2 Preserve my life, for I am devoted to you;
　　save your servant who trusts in you.
　You are my God; ³be gracious to me, O Lord,
　　for to you do I cry all day long.
4 Gladden the soul of your servant,
　　for to you, O Lord, I lift up my soul.
5 For you, O Lord, are good and forgiving,
　　abounding in steadfast love to all who call on you.
6 Give ear, O LORD, to my prayer;
　　listen to my cry of supplication.
7 In the day of my trouble I call on you,
　　for you will answer me.

8 There is none like you among the gods, O Lord,
　　nor are there any works like yours.
9 All the nations you have made shall come
　　and bow down before you, O Lord,
　　and shall glorify your name.
10 For you are great and do wondrous things;
　　you alone are God.
11 Teach me your way, O LORD,
　　that I may walk in your truth;
　　give me an undivided heart to revere your name.
12 I give thanks to you, O Lord my God, with my
　　　whole heart,
　　and I will glorify your name forever.
13 For great is your steadfast love toward me;
　　you have delivered my soul from the depths of
　　　Sheol.

14 O God, the insolent rise up against me;
　　a band of ruffians seeks my life,
　　and they do not set you before them.
15 But you, O Lord, are a God merciful and gracious,
　　slow to anger and abounding in steadfast love
　　　and faithfulness.
16 Turn to me and be gracious to me;
　　give your strength to your servant;
　　save the child of your serving girl.
17 Show me a sign of your favor,
　　so that those who hate me may see it and be put
　　　to shame,
　　because you, LORD, have helped me and
　　　comforted me.

The Steadfast Mercy of God

PSALM 86.15

Thomas Merton wrote that in God there is "mercy within mercy within mercy." God's mercy and compassion are greater than we could ever imagine. Jesus told many parables to help us grasp how wide and long and high and deep God's love is (see Ephesians 3.18): The shepherd leaves his flock in search of one lost sheep, a father welcomes home a son who has disgraced the family name, the outsider rescues a dying traveler. Reflect on the word *mercy* and what it means to you. When have you felt God's mercy? What image, symbol or piece of music expresses mercy to you? In your devotions throughout the coming week, use this symbol or musical piece as a way to focus on God's merciful love.

See Meeting God in Scripture

Complaining to God

PSALM 88.8-9

Laments and complaints express feelings of depression, frustration and weariness. We want so much to show the Lord only our gratitude and faith that we may feel uncomfortable speaking to God with such honesty. Yet the psalmist does not soften his negative feelings. For God knows our thoughts and remembers our human vulnerability. How do you express your honest feelings to God? Do you write in a journal, share with a spiritual mentor or friend, pray with upstretched hands toward a starlit sky or with a quiet sigh when you are alone? God hears the cry of your heart. What feelings might you be hiding from God?

See Meeting God in Prayer

Psalm 87

Of the Korahites. A Psalm. A Song.

1 On the holy mount stands the city he founded;
2 the LORD loves the gates of Zion
more than all the dwellings of Jacob.
3 Glorious things are spoken of you,
O city of God.   *Selah*

4 Among those who know me I mention Rahab and
Babylon;
Philistia too, and Tyre, with Ethiopia*ᵃ*—
"This one was born there," they say.

5 And of Zion it shall be said,
"This one and that one were born in it";
for the Most High himself will establish it.
6 The LORD records, as he registers the peoples,
"This one was born there."   *Selah*

7 Singers and dancers alike say,
"All my springs are in you."

Psalm 88

A Song. A Psalm of the Korahites. To the leader: according
to Mahalath Leannoth. A Maskil of Heman the Ezrahite.

1 O LORD, God of my salvation,
when, at night, I cry out in your presence,
2 let my prayer come before you;
incline your ear to my cry.

3 For my soul is full of troubles,
and my life draws near to Sheol.
4 I am counted among those who go down to the Pit;
I am like those who have no help,
5 like those forsaken among the dead,
like the slain that lie in the grave,
like those whom you remember no more,
for they are cut off from your hand.
6 You have put me in the depths of the Pit,
in the regions dark and deep.
7 Your wrath lies heavy upon me,
and you overwhelm me with all your waves.   *Selah*

8 You have caused my companions to shun me;
you have made me a thing of horror to them.
I am shut in so that I cannot escape;
9 my eye grows dim through sorrow.
Every day I call on you, O LORD;
I spread out my hands to you.
10 Do you work wonders for the dead?
Do the shades rise up to praise you?   *Selah*
11 Is your steadfast love declared in the grave,
or your faithfulness in Abaddon?
12 Are your wonders known in the darkness,
or your saving help in the land of forgetfulness?

a Or *Nubia;* Heb *Cush*

13 But I, O LORD, cry out to you;
　　in the morning my prayer comes before you.
14 O LORD, why do you cast me off?
　　Why do you hide your face from me?
15 Wretched and close to death from my youth up,
　　I suffer your terrors; I am desperate.*a*
16 Your wrath has swept over me;
　　your dread assaults destroy me.
17 They surround me like a flood all day long;
　　from all sides they close in on me.
18 You have caused friend and neighbor to shun me;
　　my companions are in darkness.

Psalm 89

A Maskil of Ethan the Ezrahite.

1 I will sing of your steadfast love, O LORD,*b* forever;
　　with my mouth I will proclaim your faithfulness
　　　　to all generations.
2 I declare that your steadfast love is established
　　　　forever;
　　your faithfulness is as firm as the heavens.

3 You said, "I have made a covenant with my chosen
　　　　one,
　　I have sworn to my servant David:
4 'I will establish your descendants forever,
　　and build your throne for all generations.' " *Selah*

5 Let the heavens praise your wonders, O LORD,
　　your faithfulness in the assembly of the holy
　　　　ones.
6 For who in the skies can be compared to the LORD?
　　Who among the heavenly beings is like the LORD,
7 a God feared in the council of the holy ones,
　　great and awesome*c* above all that are around
　　　　him?
8 O LORD God of hosts,
　　who is as mighty as you, O LORD?
　　Your faithfulness surrounds you.
9 You rule the raging of the sea;
　　when its waves rise, you still them.
10 You crushed Rahab like a carcass;
　　you scattered your enemies with your mighty
　　　　arm.
11 The heavens are yours, the earth also is yours;
　　the world and all that is in it—you have founded
　　　　them.
12 The north and the south*d*—you created them;
　　Tabor and Hermon joyously praise your name.
13 You have a mighty arm;
　　strong is your hand, high your right hand.
14 Righteousness and justice are the foundation of
　　　　your throne;
　　steadfast love and faithfulness go before you.
15 Happy are the people who know the festal shout,

Incomparable

PSALM 89.6–8

Isaiah had a heavenly vision in which he saw angels calling to one another, "Holy, holy, holy is the LORD of hosts" (Isaiah 6.3). Awe is our natural response to the majesty and holiness of God; worship is the natural expression we use to extol God's immanence, his indwelling presence in the world. Although God oversees galaxy upon galaxy in a vast, intricate universe, he faithfully offers mercy and love to us small, and often wayward, human beings. Reflect on your expression of awe toward God. What is a favorite hymn that expresses it? Recite the words or sing it on the way to work this week.

See *Meeting God in Worship*

---

a Meaning of Heb uncertain　　*b* Gk: Heb *the steadfast love of the LORD*
c Gk Syr: Heb *greatly awesome*　　*d* Or *Zaphon and Yamin*

God's Steadfast Love

PSALM 89.33

"Maybe we still do not fully believe that God's Spirit is, indeed, the Spirit of love, always leading us deeper into love. Maybe we still distrust the Spirit, afraid to be led to places where our freedom is taken away. Maybe we still think of God's Spirit as an enemy who wants something of us that is not good for us. But God is love, only love, and God's Spirit is the Spirit of love longing to guide us to the place where the deepest desires of our heart can be fulfilled."

—HENRI J.M. NOUWEN,
Here and Now

who walk, O LORD, in the light of your
 countenance;
16 they exult in your name all day long,
 and extol^a your righteousness.

17 For you are the glory of their strength;
 by your favor our horn is exalted.
18 For our shield belongs to the LORD,
 our king to the Holy One of Israel.

19 Then you spoke in a vision to your faithful one, and
 said:
 "I have set the crown^b on one who is mighty,
 I have exalted one chosen from the people.
20 I have found my servant David;
 with my holy oil I have anointed him;
21 my hand shall always remain with him;
 my arm also shall strengthen him.
22 The enemy shall not outwit him,
 the wicked shall not humble him.
23 I will crush his foes before him
 and strike down those who hate him.
24 My faithfulness and steadfast love shall be with him;
 and in my name his horn shall be exalted.
25 I will set his hand on the sea
 and his right hand on the rivers.
26 He shall cry to me, 'You are my Father,
 my God, and the Rock of my salvation!'
27 I will make him the firstborn,
 the highest of the kings of the earth.
28 Forever I will keep my steadfast love for him,
 and my covenant with him will stand firm.
29 I will establish his line forever,
 and his throne as long as the heavens endure.
30 If his children forsake my law
 and do not walk according to my ordinances,
31 if they violate my statutes
 and do not keep my commandments,
32 then I will punish their transgression with the rod
 and their iniquity with scourges;
33 but I will not remove from him my steadfast love,
 or be false to my faithfulness.
34 I will not violate my covenant,
 or alter the word that went forth from my lips.
35 Once and for all I have sworn by my holiness;
 I will not lie to David.
36 His line shall continue forever,
 and his throne endure before me like the sun.
37 It shall be established forever like the moon,
 an enduring witness in the skies."   *Selah*

38 But now you have spurned and rejected him;
 you are full of wrath against your anointed.
39 You have renounced the covenant with your
 servant;
 you have defiled his crown in the dust.
40 You have broken through all his walls;
 you have laid his strongholds in ruins.
41 All who pass by plunder him;
 he has become the scorn of his neighbors.

a Cn: Heb *are exalted in*   *b* Cn: Heb *help*

42 You have exalted the right hand of his foes;
   you have made all his enemies rejoice.
43 Moreover, you have turned back the edge of his
   sword,
   and you have not supported him in battle.
44 You have removed the scepter from his hand,[a]
   and hurled his throne to the ground.
45 You have cut short the days of his youth;
   you have covered him with shame.   *Selah*

46 How long, O LORD? Will you hide yourself forever?
   How long will your wrath burn like fire?
47 Remember how short my time is—[b]
   for what vanity you have created all mortals!
48 Who can live and never see death?
   Who can escape the power of Sheol?   *Selah*

49 Lord, where is your steadfast love of old,
   which by your faithfulness you swore to David?
50 Remember, O Lord, how your servant is taunted;
   how I bear in my bosom the insults of the peoples,[c]
51 with which your enemies taunt, O LORD,
   with which they taunted the footsteps of your
   anointed.

52 Blessed be the LORD forever.
   Amen and Amen.

BOOK IV

(Psalms 90–106)

Psalm 90

A Prayer of Moses, the man of God.

1 Lord, you have been our dwelling place[d]
   in all generations.
2 Before the mountains were brought forth,
   or ever you had formed the earth and the world,
   from everlasting to everlasting you are God.

3 You turn us[e] back to dust,
   and say, "Turn back, you mortals."
4 For a thousand years in your sight
   are like yesterday when it is past,
   or like a watch in the night.

5 You sweep them away; they are like a dream,
   like grass that is renewed in the morning;
6 in the morning it flourishes and is renewed;
   in the evening it fades and withers.

7 For we are consumed by your anger;
   by your wrath we are overwhelmed.
8 You have set our iniquities before you,
   our secret sins in the light of your countenance.

In God's Time

PSALM 90.1–4

The eternal nature of God is hard for us to grasp because we measure our lives in terms of past and present. Yet God, who has an infinite understanding of the future, suggests to our hearts a vision we cannot begin to fathom. We try to control our lives, but God invites us to open our hearts to what spiritual writer Thomas Kelly calls the "Eternal Now," God's eternal plan in each and every second. What aspects of your life are you trying to control? In what areas do you need to "let go and let God"? Offer these areas in a brief prayer of surrender throughout the day.

See Meeting God in Everyday Life

a Cn: Heb *removed his cleanness*   b Meaning of Heb uncertain
c Cn: Heb *bosom all of many peoples*   d Another reading is *our refuge*
e Heb *humankind*

God's Shelter

PSALM 91.1–4

Fear abounds in us. Rightly, we are concerned about the rise of violence, about the dim prospect for peace in many areas of the world and about the world our grandchildren will inherit. The psalmist feels danger too, but he controls his fear by calling to mind these powerful and comforting images of God. With the psalmist, imagine this experience of protection. As your enemies pursue you, you are swept up in the warm, strong, soft wings and borne up, up, away from your enemies and into a high shelter of safety. You relax and lie down, knowing that you are resting near the heart of the Almighty God. Pray with a sense of God's love surrounding you.

9 For all our days pass away under your wrath;
   our years come to an end[a] like a sigh.
10 The days of our life are seventy years,
   or perhaps eighty, if we are strong;
even then their span[b] is only toil and trouble;
   they are soon gone, and we fly away.

11 Who considers the power of your anger?
   Your wrath is as great as the fear that is due you.
12 So teach us to count our days
   that we may gain a wise heart.

13 Turn, O Lord! How long?
   Have compassion on your servants!
14 Satisfy us in the morning with your steadfast love,
   so that we may rejoice and be glad all our days.
15 Make us glad as many days as you have afflicted us,
   and as many years as we have seen evil.
16 Let your work be manifest to your servants,
   and your glorious power to their children.
17 Let the favor of the Lord our God be upon us,
   and prosper for us the work of our hands—
   O prosper the work of our hands!

Psalm 91

1 You who live in the shelter of the Most High,
   who abide in the shadow of the Almighty,[c]
2 will say to the Lord, "My refuge and my fortress;
   my God, in whom I trust."
3 For he will deliver you from the snare of the fowler
   and from the deadly pestilence;
4 he will cover you with his pinions,
   and under his wings you will find refuge;
   his faithfulness is a shield and buckler.
5 You will not fear the terror of the night,
   or the arrow that flies by day,
6 or the pestilence that stalks in darkness,
   or the destruction that wastes at noonday.

7 A thousand may fall at your side,
   ten thousand at your right hand,
   but it will not come near you.
8 You will only look with your eyes
   and see the punishment of the wicked.

9 Because you have made the Lord your refuge,[d]
   the Most High your dwelling place,
10 no evil shall befall you,
   no scourge come near your tent.

11 For he will command his angels concerning you
   to guard you in all your ways.
12 On their hands they will bear you up,
   so that you will not dash your foot against a
   stone.
13 You will tread on the lion and the adder,

---

a Syr: Heb *we bring our years to an end* b Cn Compare Gk Syr Jerome Tg: Heb *pride* c Traditional rendering of Heb *Shaddai* d Cn: Heb *Because you, Lord, are my refuge; you have made*

the young lion and the serpent you will trample
under foot.

14 Those who love me, I will deliver;
I will protect those who know my name.
15 When they call to me, I will answer them;
I will be with them in trouble,
I will rescue them and honor them.
16 With long life I will satisfy them,
and show them my salvation.

Psalm 92

A Psalm. A Song for the Sabbath Day.

1 It is good to give thanks to the LORD,
to sing praises to your name, O Most High;
2 to declare your steadfast love in the morning,
and your faithfulness by night,
3 to the music of the lute and the harp,
to the melody of the lyre.
4 For you, O LORD, have made me glad by your work;
at the works of your hands I sing for joy.

5 How great are your works, O LORD!
Your thoughts are very deep!
6 The dullard cannot know,
the stupid cannot understand this:
7 though the wicked sprout like grass
and all evildoers flourish,
they are doomed to destruction forever,
8 but you, O LORD, are on high forever.
9 For your enemies, O LORD,
for your enemies shall perish;
all evildoers shall be scattered.

10 But you have exalted my horn like that of the wild ox;
you have poured over me*a* fresh oil.
11 My eyes have seen the downfall of my enemies;
my ears have heard the doom of my evil assailants.

12 The righteous flourish like the palm tree,
and grow like a cedar in Lebanon.
13 They are planted in the house of the LORD;
they flourish in the courts of our God.
14 In old age they still produce fruit;
they are always green and full of sap,
15 showing that the LORD is upright;
he is my rock, and there is no unrighteousness in
him.

Psalm 93

1 The LORD is king, he is robed in majesty;
the LORD is robed, he is girded with strength.
He has established the world; it shall never be
moved;
2 your throne is established from of old;
you are from everlasting.

Longevity in the Spirit

PSALM 92.12–15

The palm tree and the cedars of Lebanon are symbols of longevity. As the psalmist proclaims, those who are rooted in God's ways flourish into old age; "they are always green." We live in a culture obsessed with looking young, but this "green" about which the psalmist writes is not external. It is a vibrancy cultivated through a life of prayer, devotion and worship. Think of people you know who continue to "bloom" in old age. What signs do you see of their spiritual lives? How have they handled the loss of physical youth? What habits of the heart do they encourage in you?

See Meeting God in Community

a Syr: Meaning of Heb uncertain

Remembering

PSALM 94.17–19

We may easily remember the negative experiences of our lives; and rightly, we should be honest with God about those past hurts. But how good are we at remembering our experiences of grace and life-giving joy? Praise is a spiritual discipline, a choice of the heart. Like the psalmist, we can *choose* to remember God's grace. Take ten minutes to pause and consider God's gifts in your life. When have you experienced God in unexpected places? How have people in your life shown you love? What natural beauty have you enjoyed? What opportunities or lessons have come out of your struggles? You might write your responses in your journal or compose a collage of pictures and symbols of God's gifts.

See Meeting God in Everyday Life

3 The floods have lifted up, O LORD,
the floods have lifted up their voice;
the floods lift up their roaring.
4 More majestic than the thunders of mighty waters,
more majestic than the waves[a] of the sea,
majestic on high is the LORD!

5 Your decrees are very sure;
holiness befits your house,
O LORD, forevermore.

Psalm 94

1 O LORD, you God of vengeance,
you God of vengeance, shine forth!
2 Rise up, O judge of the earth;
give to the proud what they deserve!
3 O LORD, how long shall the wicked,
how long shall the wicked exult?

4 They pour out their arrogant words;
all the evildoers boast.
5 They crush your people, O LORD,
and afflict your heritage.
6 They kill the widow and the stranger,
they murder the orphan,
7 and they say, "The LORD does not see;
the God of Jacob does not perceive."

8 Understand, O dullest of the people;
fools, when will you be wise?
9 He who planted the ear, does he not hear?
He who formed the eye, does he not see?
10 He who disciplines the nations,
he who teaches knowledge to humankind,
does he not chastise?
11 The LORD knows our thoughts,[b]
that they are but an empty breath.

12 Happy are those whom you discipline, O LORD,
and whom you teach out of your law,
13 giving them respite from days of trouble,
until a pit is dug for the wicked.
14 For the LORD will not forsake his people;
he will not abandon his heritage;
15 for justice will return to the righteous,
and all the upright in heart will follow it.

16 Who rises up for me against the wicked?
Who stands up for me against evildoers?
17 If the LORD had not been my help,
my soul would soon have lived in the land of
silence.
18 When I thought, "My foot is slipping,"
your steadfast love, O LORD, held me up.
19 When the cares of my heart are many,
your consolations cheer my soul.
20 Can wicked rulers be allied with you,
those who contrive mischief by statute?

a Cn: Heb *majestic are the waves*   *b* Heb *the thoughts of humankind*

21 They band together against the life of the righteous,
and condemn the innocent to death.
22 But the LORD has become my stronghold,
and my God the rock of my refuge.
23 He will repay them for their iniquity
and wipe them out for their wickedness;
the LORD our God will wipe them out.

Psalm 95

1 O come, let us sing to the LORD;
let us make a joyful noise to the rock of our
salvation!
2 Let us come into his presence with thanksgiving;
let us make a joyful noise to him with songs of
praise!
3 For the LORD is a great God,
and a great King above all gods.
4 In his hand are the depths of the earth;
the heights of the mountains are his also.
5 The sea is his, for he made it,
and the dry land, which his hands have formed.

6 O come, let us worship and bow down,
let us kneel before the LORD, our Maker!
7 For he is our God,
and we are the people of his pasture,
and the sheep of his hand.

O that today you would listen to his voice!
8 Do not harden your hearts, as at Meribah,
as on the day at Massah in the wilderness,
9 when your ancestors tested me,
and put me to the proof, though they had seen
my work.
10 For forty years I loathed that generation
and said, "They are a people whose hearts go
astray,
and they do not regard my ways."
11 Therefore in my anger I swore,
"They shall not enter my rest."

Psalm 96

1 O sing to the LORD a new song;
sing to the LORD, all the earth.
2 Sing to the LORD, bless his name;
tell of his salvation from day to day.
3 Declare his glory among the nations,
his marvelous works among all the peoples.
4 For great is the LORD, and greatly to be praised;
he is to be revered above all gods.
5 For all the gods of the peoples are idols,
but the LORD made the heavens.
6 Honor and majesty are before him;
strength and beauty are in his sanctuary.

7 Ascribe to the LORD, O families of the peoples,
ascribe to the LORD glory and strength.

Hearing or Hardening?

PSALM 95.7–8

The Biblical metaphor of "hardening one's heart" aptly describes the gradual process that takes place in a relationship when we stop listening, turn away or become self-absorbed. This may happen in our relationship with God, as it did for the Hebrew people. Quakers use the word *tender* to describe the opposite spiritual process of becoming more sensitive to God's voice. How do you keep your heart tender before God? Find an object from nature, perhaps a stone or a feather, that you can put on your desk or nightstand as a reminder to remain open to God.

The Call to Unending Worship

PSALM 96.8–13

"This flowing forth of God constantly demands a flowing back again, for God is a flowing and ebbing sea which ceaselessly flows out into all his beloved . . . To this end, all spirits ceaselessly come together and produce a burning flame of love, so that they might bring to fulfillment the work of loving God according to his nobility. The power of reason shows clearly that this is impossible for creatures, but love constantly wishes to bring its love to fulfillment."

—JOHN RUUSBROEC,
The Spiritual Espousals

8 Ascribe to the LORD the glory due his name;
   bring an offering, and come into his courts.
9 Worship the LORD in holy splendor;
   tremble before him, all the earth.

10 Say among the nations, "The LORD is king!
    The world is firmly established; it shall never be
        moved.
    He will judge the peoples with equity."
11 Let the heavens be glad, and let the earth rejoice;
    let the sea roar, and all that fills it;
12 let the field exult, and everything in it.
    Then shall all the trees of the forest sing for joy
13   before the LORD; for he is coming,
    for he is coming to judge the earth.
    He will judge the world with righteousness,
        and the peoples with his truth.

Psalm 97

1 The LORD is king! Let the earth rejoice;
   let the many coastlands be glad!
2 Clouds and thick darkness are all around him;
   righteousness and justice are the foundation of
       his throne.
3 Fire goes before him,
   and consumes his adversaries on every side.
4 His lightnings light up the world;
   the earth sees and trembles.
5 The mountains melt like wax before the LORD,
   before the Lord of all the earth.

6 The heavens proclaim his righteousness,
   and all the peoples behold his glory.
7 All worshipers of images are put to shame,
   those who make their boast in worthless idols;
   all gods bow down before him.
8 Zion hears and is glad,
   and the towns[a] of Judah rejoice,
   because of your judgments, O God.
9 For you, O LORD, are most high over all the earth;
   you are exalted far above all gods.

10 The LORD loves those who hate[b] evil;
    he guards the lives of his faithful;
    he rescues them from the hand of the wicked.
11 Light dawns[c] for the righteous,
    and joy for the upright in heart.
12 Rejoice in the LORD, O you righteous,
    and give thanks to his holy name!

Psalm 98

A Psalm.

1 O sing to the LORD a new song,
   for he has done marvelous things.
   His right hand and his holy arm

a Heb *daughters*   b Cn: Heb *You who love the LORD hate*   c Gk Syr
Jerome: Heb *is sown*

776

have gotten him victory.
2 The LORD has made known his victory;
  he has revealed his vindication in the sight of the
    nations.
3 He has remembered his steadfast love and
  faithfulness
    to the house of Israel.
All the ends of the earth have seen
  the victory of our God.

4 Make a joyful noise to the LORD, all the earth;
  break forth into joyous song and sing praises.
5 Sing praises to the LORD with the lyre,
  with the lyre and the sound of melody.
6 With trumpets and the sound of the horn
  make a joyful noise before the King, the LORD.

7 Let the sea roar, and all that fills it;
  the world and those who live in it.
8 Let the floods clap their hands;
  let the hills sing together for joy
9 at the presence of the LORD, for he is coming
  to judge the earth.
He will judge the world with righteousness,
  and the peoples with equity.

Psalm 99

1 The LORD is king; let the peoples tremble!
  He sits enthroned upon the cherubim; let the
    earth quake!
2 The LORD is great in Zion;
  he is exalted over all the peoples.
3 Let them praise your great and awesome name.
  Holy is he!
4 Mighty King,[a] lover of justice,
  you have established equity;
you have executed justice
  and righteousness in Jacob.
5 Extol the LORD our God;
  worship at his footstool.
  Holy is he!

6 Moses and Aaron were among his priests,
  Samuel also was among those who called on his
    name.
  They cried to the LORD, and he answered them.
7 He spoke to them in the pillar of cloud;
  they kept his decrees,
  and the statutes that he gave them.

8 O LORD our God, you answered them;
  you were a forgiving God to them,
  but an avenger of their wrongdoings.
9 Extol the LORD our God,
  and worship at his holy mountain;
  for the LORD our God is holy.

Joy Throughout the Earth

PSALM 98.4–9

Praise is not limited to human creatures. While the psalmist utters praise with his mouth, the earth makes a "joyful noise" in countless ways. God enjoys the brilliant color of a wildflower in the middle of a deserted field, a young lion running in tall grass and an ocean with its panoply of life. Our praise is not isolated from the rest of creation's. Make an appointment with nature to sit in awe or take a walk, joining your thanks to the praise of God throughout the earth.

See Meeting God in the Created Order

---

a Cn: Heb *And a king's strength*

Belonging to God

PSALM 100.3

We belong to God. It is a profound truth, yet one that we easily forget. The image of God as an attentive shepherd abounds in Scripture. Belonging to this loving Shepherd, we are watched and cared for with infinite tenderness. What reminds you that you belong to God? What images, songs or Bible verses remind you of God's constancy and care? How might you live today in that reality? Consider how beloved you are in God's eyes.

See Meeting God in Scripture

Psalm 100

A Psalm of thanksgiving.

1 Make a joyful noise to the LORD, all the earth.
2   Worship the LORD with gladness;
    come into his presence with singing.

3 Know that the LORD is God.
    It is he that made us, and we are his;*
    we are his people, and the sheep of his pasture.

4 Enter his gates with thanksgiving,
    and his courts with praise.
    Give thanks to him, bless his name.

5 For the LORD is good;
    his steadfast love endures forever,
    and his faithfulness to all generations.

Psalm 101

Of David. A Psalm.

1 I will sing of loyalty and of justice;
    to you, O LORD, I will sing.
2 I will study the way that is blameless.
    When shall I attain it?

  I will walk with integrity of heart
    within my house;
3 I will not set before my eyes
    anything that is base.

  I hate the work of those who fall away;
    it shall not cling to me.
4 Perverseness of heart shall be far from me;
    I will know nothing of evil.

5 One who secretly slanders a neighbor
    I will destroy.
  A haughty look and an arrogant heart
    I will not tolerate.

6 I will look with favor on the faithful in the land,
    so that they may live with me;
  whoever walks in the way that is blameless
    shall minister to me.

7 No one who practices deceit
    shall remain in my house;
  no one who utters lies
    shall continue in my presence.

8 Morning by morning I will destroy
    all the wicked in the land,
  cutting off all evildoers
    from the city of the LORD.

778   *a* Another reading is *and not we ourselves*

Psalm 102

A prayer of one afflicted, when faint and pleading before the LORD.

1 Hear my prayer, O LORD;
   let my cry come to you.
2 Do not hide your face from me
   in the day of my distress.
   Incline your ear to me;
   answer me speedily in the day when I call.

3 For my days pass away like smoke,
   and my bones burn like a furnace.
4 My heart is stricken and withered like grass;
   I am too wasted to eat my bread.
5 Because of my loud groaning
   my bones cling to my skin.
6 I am like an owl of the wilderness,
   like a little owl of the waste places.
7 I lie awake;
   I am like a lonely bird on the housetop.
8 All day long my enemies taunt me;
   those who deride me use my name for a curse.
9 For I eat ashes like bread,
   and mingle tears with my drink,
10 because of your indignation and anger;
    for you have lifted me up and thrown me aside.
11 My days are like an evening shadow;
    I wither away like grass.

12 But you, O LORD, are enthroned forever;
    your name endures to all generations.
13 You will rise up and have compassion on Zion,
    for it is time to favor it;
    the appointed time has come.
14 For your servants hold its stones dear,
    and have pity on its dust.
15 The nations will fear the name of the LORD,
    and all the kings of the earth your glory.
16 For the LORD will build up Zion;
    he will appear in his glory.
17 He will regard the prayer of the destitute,
    and will not despise their prayer.

18 Let this be recorded for a generation to come,
    so that a people yet unborn may praise the LORD:
19 that he looked down from his holy height,
    from heaven the LORD looked at the earth,
20 to hear the groans of the prisoners,
    to set free those who were doomed to die;
21 so that the name of the LORD may be declared in
       Zion,
    and his praise in Jerusalem,
22 when peoples gather together,
    and kingdoms, to worship the LORD.

23 He has broken my strength in midcourse;
    he has shortened my days.
24 "O my God," I say, "do not take me away
    at the midpoint of my life,

Facing Despair

PSALM 102.1–7

The psalmist's words poignantly illustrate the ache of the human heart in its pain and grief. Persons facing a life-threatening illness know what it is like to be too depleted to eat. Those who know the loss of a loved one have felt like the "owl of the waste places"—lying awake at night, tossing and turning.

God is intimately aware of our deepest heartaches. When have you felt such hopelessness? How was God with you in that despair? Is someone in your life facing this kind of pain? How might you enable that person to feel God's nearness—sitting with him or her, offering an intercessory prayer, writing a note?

See Meeting God in Service

Bless the Lord, O My Soul

PSALM 103.1–5

What does it mean to bless the Lord with "all that is within me"? It means that with our whole hearts, we celebrate God's goodness and rejoice in his steadfast love and mercy. Read the passage slowly, and as you come across a word or phrase that strikes you, pause there. Close your eyes and say the word or phrase to yourself. What associations do you make with these words? What touches you? What do you sense God inviting you to consider in response?

See Meeting God in Scripture

you whose years endure
throughout all generations."

25 Long ago you laid the foundation of the earth,
and the heavens are the work of your hands.
26 They will perish, but you endure;
they will all wear out like a garment.
You change them like clothing, and they pass away;
27 but you are the same, and your years have no end.
28 The children of your servants shall live secure;
their offspring shall be established in your presence.

Psalm 103

Of David.

1 Bless the LORD, O my soul,
and all that is within me,
bless his holy name.
2 Bless the LORD, O my soul,
and do not forget all his benefits—
3 who forgives all your iniquity,
who heals all your diseases,
4 who redeems your life from the Pit,
who crowns you with steadfast love and mercy,
5 who satisfies you with good as long as you live*a*
so that your youth is renewed like the eagle's.

6 The LORD works vindication
and justice for all who are oppressed.
7 He made known his ways to Moses,
his acts to the people of Israel.
8 The LORD is merciful and gracious,
slow to anger and abounding in steadfast love.
9 He will not always accuse,
nor will he keep his anger forever.
10 He does not deal with us according to our sins,
nor repay us according to our iniquities.
11 For as the heavens are high above the earth,
so great is his steadfast love toward those who
fear him;
12 as far as the east is from the west,
so far he removes our transgressions from us.
13 As a father has compassion for his children,
so the LORD has compassion for those who fear
him.
14 For he knows how we were made;
he remembers that we are dust.

15 As for mortals, their days are like grass;
they flourish like a flower of the field;
16 for the wind passes over it, and it is gone,
and its place knows it no more.
17 But the steadfast love of the LORD is from
everlasting to everlasting
on those who fear him,
and his righteousness to children's children,
18 to those who keep his covenant
and remember to do his commandments.

a Meaning of Heb uncertain

19 The LORD has established his throne in the heavens,
    and his kingdom rules over all.
20 Bless the LORD, O you his angels,
    you mighty ones who do his bidding,
    obedient to his spoken word.
21 Bless the LORD, all his hosts,
    his ministers that do his will.
22 Bless the LORD, all his works,
    in all places of his dominion.
Bless the LORD, O my soul.

Psalm 104

1 Bless the LORD, O my soul.
    O LORD my God, you are very great.
You are clothed with honor and majesty,
2   wrapped in light as with a garment.
You stretch out the heavens like a tent,
3   you set the beams of your*a* chambers on the
        waters,
you make the clouds your*a* chariot,
    you ride on the wings of the wind,
4 you make the winds your*a* messengers,
    fire and flame your*a* ministers.
5 You set the earth on its foundations,
    so that it shall never be shaken.
6 You cover it with the deep as with a garment;
    the waters stood above the mountains.
7 At your rebuke they flee;
    at the sound of your thunder they take to flight.
8 They rose up to the mountains, ran down to the
        valleys
    to the place that you appointed for them.
9 You set a boundary that they may not pass,
    so that they might not again cover the earth.

10 You make springs gush forth in the valleys;
    they flow between the hills,
11 giving drink to every wild animal;
    the wild asses quench their thirst.
12 By the streams*b* the birds of the air have their
        habitation;
    they sing among the branches.
13 From your lofty abode you water the mountains;
    the earth is satisfied with the fruit of your work.

14 You cause the grass to grow for the cattle,
    and plants for people to use,*c*
to bring forth food from the earth,
15   and wine to gladden the human heart,
oil to make the face shine,
    and bread to strengthen the human heart.
16 The trees of the LORD are watered abundantly,
    the cedars of Lebanon that he planted.
17 In them the birds build their nests;
    the stork has its home in the fir trees.
18 The high mountains are for the wild goats;
    the rocks are a refuge for the coneys.

Wisdom in the Created Order

PSALM 104.24

Psalm 104 is a celebration of God as the Creator. The psalmist praises God's marvelous, ingenious ordering. Everything—from the sun that gives us light to the grass the cattle feed on—is intricately connected. Scientific knowledge only enhances the wonder of God's wisdom in this design. In your neighborhood, contemplate God's wisdom in creation. What birds frequent your backyard? What trees line your street? If you see a lot of concrete and not much green, where might you go to enjoy God's creation? Praise God *in specifics* this day for the divine wisdom displayed in creation.

See Meeting God in the Created Order

Feasting on God's Abundance

PSALM 104.33–34

Here the psalmist celebrates the abundance of God's gifts. Once we have tasted of God's presence in prayer, we desire more and more. John Ruusbroec writes, "At each new touch our spirit falls into a state of hunger and thirst and wishes in this storm of love thoroughly to savor [it]." The prayer of silence—like centering prayer—is one way to savor God's abundance. For the next five minutes, sit in silent openness before God with your eyes closed or focused on a simple object.

See Meeting God in Prayer

19 You have made the moon to mark the seasons;
    the sun knows its time for setting.
20 You make darkness, and it is night,
    when all the animals of the forest come creeping out.
21 The young lions roar for their prey,
    seeking their food from God.
22 When the sun rises, they withdraw
    and lie down in their dens.
23 People go out to their work
    and to their labor until the evening.

24 O Lord, how manifold are your works!
    In wisdom you have made them all;
    the earth is full of your creatures.
25 Yonder is the sea, great and wide,
    creeping things innumerable are there,
    living things both small and great.
26 There go the ships,
    and Leviathan that you formed to sport in it.

27 These all look to you
    to give them their food in due season;
28 when you give to them, they gather it up;
    when you open your hand, they are filled with good things.
29 When you hide your face, they are dismayed;
    when you take away their breath, they die
    and return to their dust.
30 When you send forth your spirit,[a] they are created;
    and you renew the face of the ground.

31 May the glory of the Lord endure forever;
    may the Lord rejoice in his works—
32 who looks on the earth and it trembles,
    who touches the mountains and they smoke.
33 I will sing to the Lord as long as I live;
    I will sing praise to my God while I have being.
34 May my meditation be pleasing to him,
    for I rejoice in the Lord.
35 Let sinners be consumed from the earth,
    and let the wicked be no more.
    Bless the Lord, O my soul.
    Praise the Lord!

Psalm 105

1 O give thanks to the Lord, call on his name,
   make known his deeds among the peoples.
2 Sing to him, sing praises to him;
   tell of all his wonderful works.
3 Glory in his holy name;
   let the hearts of those who seek the Lord rejoice.
4 Seek the Lord and his strength;
   seek his presence continually.
5 Remember the wonderful works he has done,
   his miracles, and the judgments he has uttered,
6 O offspring of his servant Abraham,[b]
   children of Jacob, his chosen ones.

a Or *your breath*   *b* Another reading is *Israel* (compare 1 Chr 16.13)

7 He is the LORD our God;
  his judgments are in all the earth.
8 He is mindful of his covenant forever,
  of the word that he commanded, for a thousand
    generations,
9 the covenant that he made with Abraham,
  his sworn promise to Isaac,
10 which he confirmed to Jacob as a statute,
  to Israel as an everlasting covenant,
11 saying, "To you I will give the land of Canaan
  as your portion for an inheritance."

12 When they were few in number,
  of little account, and strangers in it,
13 wandering from nation to nation,
  from one kingdom to another people,
14 he allowed no one to oppress them;
  he rebuked kings on their account,
15 saying, "Do not touch my anointed ones;
  do my prophets no harm."

16 When he summoned famine against the land,
  and broke every staff of bread,
17 he had sent a man ahead of them,
  Joseph, who was sold as a slave.
18 His feet were hurt with fetters,
  his neck was put in a collar of iron;
19 until what he had said came to pass,
  the word of the LORD kept testing him.
20 The king sent and released him;
  the ruler of the peoples set him free.
21 He made him lord of his house,
  and ruler of all his possessions,
22 to instruct[a] his officials at his pleasure,
  and to teach his elders wisdom.

23 Then Israel came to Egypt;
  Jacob lived as an alien in the land of Ham.
24 And the LORD made his people very fruitful,
  and made them stronger than their foes,
25 whose hearts he then turned to hate his people,
  to deal craftily with his servants.

26 He sent his servant Moses,
  and Aaron whom he had chosen.
27 They performed his signs among them,
  and miracles in the land of Ham.
28 He sent darkness, and made the land dark;
  they rebelled[b] against his words.
29 He turned their waters into blood,
  and caused their fish to die.
30 Their land swarmed with frogs,
  even in the chambers of their kings.
31 He spoke, and there came swarms of flies,
  and gnats throughout their country.
32 He gave them hail for rain,
  and lightning that flashed through their land.
33 He struck their vines and fig trees,
  and shattered the trees of their country.

Exodus Faith

PSALM 105

The psalmist recalls the miraculous exodus and how God led the Hebrew people out of Egypt. Their ordeal, a long walk through the rugged desert, required trust in God's grace. Often our lives require God's grace too. We cannot know ahead of time how God will lead us. We cannot imagine the grace-bearing manna that God will provide. What is your exodus story? How has God delivered you? Where is God making a way for you in "the desert"? With a spiritual mentor or close friend, or in your journal, reflect on your journey of exodus.

See Meeting God in Everyday Life

a Gk Syr Jerome: Heb *to bind*   b Cn Compare Gk Syr: Heb *they did not rebel*

Facing Our Sin

PSALM 106.6–7

In Psalm 105, we remembered the Hebrews' joy in the exodus, but here we face the darkness of human sin in the same story. How often aren't we like the Hebrew people! Amidst the joy of our new salvation, or on the heels of intimate communion with God, we turn away from God's voice. We coldly ignore a coworker, we yell at our children or we don't bring our whole hearts to the devotional life. What does obedience to God mean to you? Do you detect coldness within yourself toward God or others? With a trusted mentor or friend, examine your heart thoughtfully.

See Meeting God in Prayer

34 He spoke, and the locusts came,
    and young locusts without number;
35 they devoured all the vegetation in their land,
    and ate up the fruit of their ground.
36 He struck down all the firstborn in their land,
    the first issue of all their strength.

37 Then he brought Israel[a] out with silver and gold,
    and there was no one among their tribes who stumbled.
38 Egypt was glad when they departed,
    for dread of them had fallen upon it.
39 He spread a cloud for a covering,
    and fire to give light by night.
40 They asked, and he brought quails,
    and gave them food from heaven in abundance.
41 He opened the rock, and water gushed out;
    it flowed through the desert like a river.
42 For he remembered his holy promise,
    and Abraham, his servant.

43 So he brought his people out with joy,
    his chosen ones with singing.
44 He gave them the lands of the nations,
    and they took possession of the wealth of the peoples,
45 that they might keep his statutes
    and observe his laws.
    Praise the LORD!

Psalm 106

1 Praise the LORD!
    O give thanks to the LORD, for he is good;
    for his steadfast love endures forever.
2 Who can utter the mighty doings of the LORD,
    or declare all his praise?
3 Happy are those who observe justice,
    who do righteousness at all times.

4 Remember me, O LORD, when you show favor to your people;
    help me when you deliver them;
5 that I may see the prosperity of your chosen ones,
    that I may rejoice in the gladness of your nation,
    that I may glory in your heritage.

6 Both we and our ancestors have sinned;
    we have committed iniquity, have done wickedly.
7 Our ancestors, when they were in Egypt,
    did not consider your wonderful works;
    they did not remember the abundance of your steadfast love,
    but rebelled against the Most High[b] at the Red Sea.[c]
8 Yet he saved them for his name's sake,
    so that he might make known his mighty power.
9 He rebuked the Red Sea,[c] and it became dry;
    he led them through the deep as through a desert.

a Heb *them*   b Cn Compare 78.17, 56: Heb *rebelled at the sea*   c Or *Sea of Reeds*

¹⁰ So he saved them from the hand of the foe,
　　and delivered them from the hand of the enemy.
¹¹ The waters covered their adversaries;
　　not one of them was left.
¹² Then they believed his words;
　　they sang his praise.

¹³ But they soon forgot his works;
　　they did not wait for his counsel.
¹⁴ But they had a wanton craving in the wilderness,
　　and put God to the test in the desert;
¹⁵ he gave them what they asked,
　　but sent a wasting disease among them.

¹⁶ They were jealous of Moses in the camp,
　　and of Aaron, the holy one of the LORD.
¹⁷ The earth opened and swallowed up Dathan,
　　and covered the faction of Abiram.
¹⁸ Fire also broke out in their company;
　　the flame burned up the wicked.

¹⁹ They made a calf at Horeb
　　and worshiped a cast image.
²⁰ They exchanged the glory of God^a
　　for the image of an ox that eats grass.
²¹ They forgot God, their Savior,
　　who had done great things in Egypt,
²² wondrous works in the land of Ham,
　　and awesome deeds by the Red Sea.^b
²³ Therefore he said he would destroy them—
　　had not Moses, his chosen one,
stood in the breach before him,
　　to turn away his wrath from destroying them.

²⁴ Then they despised the pleasant land,
　　having no faith in his promise.
²⁵ They grumbled in their tents,
　　and did not obey the voice of the LORD.
²⁶ Therefore he raised his hand and swore to them
　　that he would make them fall in the wilderness,
²⁷ and would disperse^c their descendants among the
　　nations,
　　scattering them over the lands.

²⁸ Then they attached themselves to the Baal of Peor,
　　and ate sacrifices offered to the dead;
²⁹ they provoked the LORD to anger with their deeds,
　　and a plague broke out among them.
³⁰ Then Phinehas stood up and interceded,
　　and the plague was stopped.
³¹ And that has been reckoned to him as righteousness
　　from generation to generation forever.

³² They angered the LORD^d at the waters of Meribah,
　　and it went ill with Moses on their account;
³³ for they made his spirit bitter,
　　and he spoke words that were rash.

A New Way to Love

PSALM 106.32–43

God does not vacillate when it comes to righteousness, nor is God devoid of anger. Yet in responding to human sin, God is ever compassionate, which, explains scholar Walter Brueggemann, is "possible only because God bears the pain of vengeance." Jesus proclaims this radical way of loving when he revises the "eye for an eye" version of justice: "If anyone strikes you on the right cheek, turn the other also" (Matthew 5.39). How do you deal with the natural feelings of vengeance that rise up within you? Is there an old bitterness or vendetta that you feed? How might you offer these old hurts to God?

See Meeting God in Prayer

---

^a Compare Gk Mss: Heb *exchanged their glory*　　^b Or *Sea of Reeds*
^c Syr Compare Ezek 20.23: Heb *cause to fall*　　^d Heb *him*

God's Compassion

We cannot imagine the immensity of God's love for us. It is as high as the endless sky and as tender as a father's compassion for his children. Evelyn Underhill writes, "When we look out towards this Love that moves the stars and stirs in the child's heart . . . we see our human situation from a fresh angle; and [we] perceive that it is both more humble and dependent, and more splendid, than we had dreamed." What fresh perspective does God's extraordinary love stir in you? On a small piece of paper, write your response to this question. Tape it in the front of your Bible, and read it frequently throughout the next month.

34 They did not destroy the peoples,
    as the LORD commanded them,
35 but they mingled with the nations
    and learned to do as they did.
36 They served their idols,
    which became a snare to them.
37 They sacrificed their sons
    and their daughters to the demons;
38 they poured out innocent blood,
    the blood of their sons and daughters,
    whom they sacrificed to the idols of Canaan;
    and the land was polluted with blood.
39 Thus they became unclean by their acts,
    and prostituted themselves in their doings.

40 Then the anger of the LORD was kindled against his
        people,
    and he abhorred his heritage;
41 he gave them into the hand of the nations,
    so that those who hated them ruled over them.
42 Their enemies oppressed them,
    and they were brought into subjection under their
        power.
43 Many times he delivered them,
    but they were rebellious in their purposes,
    and were brought low through their iniquity.
44 Nevertheless he regarded their distress
    when he heard their cry.
45 For their sake he remembered his covenant,
    and showed compassion according to the
        abundance of his steadfast love.
46 He caused them to be pitied
    by all who held them captive.

47 Save us, O LORD our God,
    and gather us from among the nations,
    that we may give thanks to your holy name
    and glory in your praise.

48 Blessed be the LORD, the God of Israel,
    from everlasting to everlasting.
    And let all the people say, "Amen."
    Praise the LORD!

BOOK V

(Psalms 107–150)

Psalm 107

1 O give thanks to the LORD, for he is good;
    for his steadfast love endures forever.
2 Let the redeemed of the LORD say so,
    those he redeemed from trouble
3 and gathered in from the lands,
    from the east and from the west,
    from the north and from the south.[a]

a Cn: Heb *sea*

4 Some wandered in desert wastes,
   finding no way to an inhabited town;
5 hungry and thirsty,
   their soul fainted within them.
6 Then they cried to the LORD in their trouble,
   and he delivered them from their distress;
7 he led them by a straight way,
   until they reached an inhabited town.
8 Let them thank the LORD for his steadfast love,
   for his wonderful works to humankind.
9 For he satisfies the thirsty,
   and the hungry he fills with good things.

10 Some sat in darkness and in gloom,
    prisoners in misery and in irons,
11 for they had rebelled against the words of God,
    and spurned the counsel of the Most High.
12 Their hearts were bowed down with hard labor;
    they fell down, with no one to help.
13 Then they cried to the LORD in their trouble,
    and he saved them from their distress;
14 he brought them out of darkness and gloom,
    and broke their bonds asunder.
15 Let them thank the LORD for his steadfast love,
    for his wonderful works to humankind.
16 For he shatters the doors of bronze,
    and cuts in two the bars of iron.

17 Some were sick[a] through their sinful ways,
    and because of their iniquities endured affliction;
18 they loathed any kind of food,
    and they drew near to the gates of death.
19 Then they cried to the LORD in their trouble,
    and he saved them from their distress;
20 he sent out his word and healed them,
    and delivered them from destruction.
21 Let them thank the LORD for his steadfast love,
    for his wonderful works to humankind.
22 And let them offer thanksgiving sacrifices,
    and tell of his deeds with songs of joy.

23 Some went down to the sea in ships,
    doing business on the mighty waters;
24 they saw the deeds of the LORD,
    his wondrous works in the deep.
25 For he commanded and raised the stormy wind,
    which lifted up the waves of the sea.
26 They mounted up to heaven, they went down to the
       depths;
    their courage melted away in their calamity;
27 they reeled and staggered like drunkards,
    and were at their wits' end.
28 Then they cried to the LORD in their trouble,
    and he brought them out from their distress;
29 he made the storm be still,
    and the waves of the sea were hushed.
30 Then they were glad because they had quiet,
    and he brought them to their desired haven.

Let the Redeemed Say So

PSALM 107.1–16

The psalmist praises God's deliverance of the Hebrew people from exile, from the perils of the desert and from the chains of their oppressors. Likewise, Jesus Christ's death and resurrection are the means of God's deliverance for believers: We pass through a "Red Sea" of transformation, arriving to find new life on the other side. Following the model provided by verses 4–9 and 10–15, write a short psalm of praise or, using colored pencils or crayons, draw a symbolic picture illustrating God's merciful love in your life.

a Cn: Heb *fools*

787

A Prayer for God's Kingdom

PSALM 108.5

In the Lord's Prayer, Jesus prays in simple but powerful words: "Your kingdom come. Your will be done, on earth as it is in heaven" (Matthew 6.10). Jesus, as well as the psalmist, reveals that prayer is not a private matter but a vocation that touches the whole world! Our prayers of intercession for world hunger, for peace and for the spread of Christian faith have an impact. In prayer we join in partnership with God in healing the world. In what ways might God be inviting you to a deeper life of intercessory prayer for the world? In a church school class or small group, you might offer this question for discussion.

See Meeting God in Prayer

31 Let them thank the LORD for his steadfast love,
   for his wonderful works to humankind.
32 Let them extol him in the congregation of the people,
   and praise him in the assembly of the elders.
33 He turns rivers into a desert,
   springs of water into thirsty ground,
34 a fruitful land into a salty waste,
   because of the wickedness of its inhabitants.
35 He turns a desert into pools of water,
   a parched land into springs of water.
36 And there he lets the hungry live,
   and they establish a town to live in;
37 they sow fields, and plant vineyards,
   and get a fruitful yield.
38 By his blessing they multiply greatly,
   and he does not let their cattle decrease.

39 When they are diminished and brought low
   through oppression, trouble, and sorrow,
40 he pours contempt on princes
   and makes them wander in trackless wastes;
41 but he raises up the needy out of distress,
   and makes their families like flocks.
42 The upright see it and are glad;
   and all wickedness stops its mouth.
43 Let those who are wise give heed to these things,
   and consider the steadfast love of the LORD.

Psalm 108

A Song. A Psalm of David.

1 My heart is steadfast, O God, my heart is steadfast;*a*
   I will sing and make melody.
   Awake, my soul!*b*
2 Awake, O harp and lyre!
   I will awake the dawn.
3 I will give thanks to you, O LORD, among the peoples,
   and I will sing praises to you among the nations.
4 For your steadfast love is higher than the heavens,
   and your faithfulness reaches to the clouds.

5 Be exalted, O God, above the heavens,
   and let your glory be over all the earth.
6 Give victory with your right hand, and answer me,
   so that those whom you love may be rescued.

7 God has promised in his sanctuary:*c*
   "With exultation I will divide up Shechem,
   and portion out the Vale of Succoth.
8 Gilead is mine; Manasseh is mine;
   Ephraim is my helmet;
   Judah is my scepter.
9 Moab is my washbasin;
   on Edom I hurl my shoe;
   over Philistia I shout in triumph."

---

a Heb Mss Gk Syr: MT lacks *my heart is steadfast*   *b* Compare 57.8: Heb also *my soul*   *c* Or *by his holiness*

10 Who will bring me to the fortified city?
   Who will lead me to Edom?
11 Have you not rejected us, O God?
   You do not go out, O God, with our armies.
12 O grant us help against the foe,
   for human help is worthless.
13 With God we shall do valiantly;
   it is he who will tread down our foes.

Psalm 109

To the leader. Of David. A Psalm.

1 Do not be silent, O God of my praise.
2 For wicked and deceitful mouths are opened
         against me,
     speaking against me with lying tongues.
3 They beset me with words of hate,
     and attack me without cause.
4 In return for my love they accuse me,
     even while I make prayer for them.ᵃ
5 So they reward me evil for good,
     and hatred for my love.

6 They say,ᵇ "Appoint a wicked man against him;
     let an accuser stand on his right.
7 When he is tried, let him be found guilty;
     let his prayer be counted as sin.
8 May his days be few;
     may another seize his position.
9 May his children be orphans,
     and his wife a widow.
10 May his children wander about and beg;
     may they be driven out ofᶜ the ruins they inhabit.
11 May the creditor seize all that he has;
     may strangers plunder the fruits of his toil.
12 May there be no one to do him a kindness,
     nor anyone to pity his orphaned children.
13 May his posterity be cut off;
     may his name be blotted out in the second
         generation.
14 May the iniquity of his fatherᵈ be remembered
         before the LORD,
     and do not let the sin of his mother be blotted
         out.
15 Let them be before the LORD continually,
     and may hisᵉ memory be cut off from the earth.
16 For he did not remember to show kindness,
     but pursued the poor and needy
     and the brokenhearted to their death.
17 He loved to curse; let curses come on him.
     He did not like blessing; may it be far from him.
18 He clothed himself with cursing as his coat,
     may it soak into his body like water,
     like oil into his bones.
19 May it be like a garment that he wraps around
         himself,
     like a belt that he wears every day."

The Cry of the Poor

PSALM 109.16–24

The psalmist trusts that God hears the cries of people who are poor, sick and needy. Indeed, throughout the Bible it is clear that God has a special love for the poor. Jesus spoke out frequently and unmistakably on their behalf and often blessed them. Who are the needy in your community? How do you treat the poor? Perhaps you can discover a literacy program needing volunteers or an older person who cannot pay his or her utility bills. Look at the year ahead. What is one spiritual habit you could acquire that would extend God's love to "the least of these" (see Matthew 25.40)?

See Meeting God in Service

a Syr: Heb *I prayer*   b Heb lacks *They say*   c Gk: Heb *and seek*
d Cn: Heb *fathers*   e Gk: Heb *their*

Trustworthy Precepts

PSALM 111.7–10

Just as God is a wise Creator (Psalm 104), so he is a discerning Teacher. God's instruction is eternally trustworthy. We truly "fear" the Lord when we value God's wisdom above that of our culture and even that of our own best intentions. How do you discern God's wisdom? In what areas do you need to begin to practice what you know to be wise and true? In your journal, or on a piece of paper, consider the ways you acquire wisdom from God: your prayer life, your experience of Scripture, spiritual mentors, community worship. What are you learning in each of these areas?

See Meeting God in Community

20 May that be the reward of my accusers from the LORD,
   of those who speak evil against my life.
21 But you, O LORD my Lord,
   act on my behalf for your name's sake;
   because your steadfast love is good, deliver me.
22 For I am poor and needy,
   and my heart is pierced within me.
23 I am gone like a shadow at evening;
   I am shaken off like a locust.
24 My knees are weak through fasting;
   my body has become gaunt.
25 I am an object of scorn to my accusers;
   when they see me, they shake their heads.

26 Help me, O LORD my God!
   Save me according to your steadfast love.
27 Let them know that this is your hand;
   you, O LORD, have done it.
28 Let them curse, but you will bless.
   Let my assailants be put to shame;[a] may your
   servant be glad.
29 May my accusers be clothed with dishonor;
   may they be wrapped in their own shame as in a
   mantle.
30 With my mouth I will give great thanks to the LORD;
   I will praise him in the midst of the throng.
31 For he stands at the right hand of the needy,
   to save them from those who would condemn
   them to death.

Psalm 110

Of David. A Psalm.

1 The LORD says to my lord,
   "Sit at my right hand
until I make your enemies your footstool."

2 The LORD sends out from Zion
   your mighty scepter.
   Rule in the midst of your foes.
3 Your people will offer themselves willingly
   on the day you lead your forces
   on the holy mountains.[b]
From the womb of the morning,
   like dew, your youth[c] will come to you.
4 The LORD has sworn and will not change his mind,
   "You are a priest forever according to the order of
   Melchizedek."[d]

5 The Lord is at your right hand;
   he will shatter kings on the day of his wrath.
6 He will execute judgment among the nations,
   filling them with corpses;
   he will shatter heads
   over the wide earth.
7 He will drink from the stream by the path;
   therefore he will lift up his head.

a Gk: Heb *They have risen up and have been put to shame*   b Another
reading is *in holy splendor*   c Cn: Heb *the dew of your youth*   d Or *forever,
a rightful king by my edict*

Psalm 111

1 Praise the LORD!
  I will give thanks to the LORD with my whole heart,
    in the company of the upright, in the congregation.
2 Great are the works of the LORD,
    studied by all who delight in them.
3 Full of honor and majesty is his work,
    and his righteousness endures forever.
4 He has gained renown by his wonderful deeds;
    the LORD is gracious and merciful.
5 He provides food for those who fear him;
    he is ever mindful of his covenant.
6 He has shown his people the power of his works,
    in giving them the heritage of the nations.
7 The works of his hands are faithful and just;
    all his precepts are trustworthy.
8 They are established forever and ever,
    to be performed with faithfulness and uprightness.
9 He sent redemption to his people;
    he has commanded his covenant forever.
    Holy and awesome is his name.
10 The fear of the LORD is the beginning of wisdom;
    all those who practice it*a* have a good
        understanding.
    His praise endures forever.

Psalm 112

1 Praise the LORD!
  Happy are those who fear the LORD,
    who greatly delight in his commandments.
2 Their descendants will be mighty in the land;
    the generation of the upright will be blessed.
3 Wealth and riches are in their houses,
    and their righteousness endures forever.
4 They rise in the darkness as a light for the upright;
    they are gracious, merciful, and righteous.
5 It is well with those who deal generously and lend,
    who conduct their affairs with justice.
6 For the righteous will never be moved;
    they will be remembered forever.
7 They are not afraid of evil tidings;
    their hearts are firm, secure in the LORD.
8 Their hearts are steady, they will not be afraid;
    in the end they will look in triumph on their foes.
9 They have distributed freely, they have given to the
        poor;
    their righteousness endures forever;
    their horn is exalted in honor.
10 The wicked see it and are angry;
    they gnash their teeth and melt away;
    the desire of the wicked comes to nothing.

Psalm 113

1 Praise the LORD!
  Praise, O servants of the LORD;
    praise the name of the LORD.

a Gk Syr: Heb *them*

The Fear of the Lord

PSALM 112.1–9

In the Psalms, the "fear of the LORD" (111.10) refers to awe and worship and then to the practice of obedience. If our words mean something to us, then our lives will reflect them. What are the characteristics of those who fear God? The psalmist says that daily they "delight" in God's ways, are kind to others, are not anxious and are generous to the poor. How do you worship God with your life? How might you consciously consecrate your daily activities to God? Perhaps, as you walk to a business meeting, you might pray for the persons involved. When you pause at traffic lights, pray for persons you will meet during the day.

See Meeting God in Worship

The Answer to Modern Idolatry

PSALM 115.3–7

"The living God, the God Who is God and not a philosopher's abstraction, lies infinitely beyond the reach of anything our eyes can see or our minds can understand . . . If nothing that can be seen can either be God or represent him to us as he is, then to find God we must pass beyond everything that can be seen and enter into darkness. Since nothing that can be heard is God, to find him we must enter into silence."

—THOMAS MERTON,
New Seeds of Contemplation

2 Blessed be the name of the LORD
    from this time on and forevermore.
3 From the rising of the sun to its setting
    the name of the LORD is to be praised.
4 The LORD is high above all nations,
    and his glory above the heavens.

5 Who is like the LORD our God,
    who is seated on high,
6 who looks far down
    on the heavens and the earth?
7 He raises the poor from the dust,
    and lifts the needy from the ash heap,
8 to make them sit with princes,
    with the princes of his people.
9 He gives the barren woman a home,
    making her the joyous mother of children.
    Praise the LORD!

Psalm 114

1 When Israel went out from Egypt,
    the house of Jacob from a people of strange
        language,
2 Judah became God's*a* sanctuary,
    Israel his dominion.

3 The sea looked and fled;
    Jordan turned back.
4 The mountains skipped like rams,
    the hills like lambs.

5 Why is it, O sea, that you flee?
    O Jordan, that you turn back?
6 O mountains, that you skip like rams?
    O hills, like lambs?

7 Tremble, O earth, at the presence of the LORD,
    at the presence of the God of Jacob,
8 who turns the rock into a pool of water,
    the flint into a spring of water.

Psalm 115

1 Not to us, O LORD, not to us, but to your name give
        glory,
    for the sake of your steadfast love and your
        faithfulness.
2 Why should the nations say,
    "Where is their God?"

3 Our God is in the heavens;
    he does whatever he pleases.
4 Their idols are silver and gold,
    the work of human hands.
5 They have mouths, but do not speak;
    eyes, but do not see.
6 They have ears, but do not hear;
    noses, but do not smell.

a Heb *his*

7 They have hands, but do not feel;
   feet, but do not walk;
   they make no sound in their throats.
8 Those who make them are like them;
   so are all who trust in them.

9 O Israel, trust in the LORD!
   He is their help and their shield.
10 O house of Aaron, trust in the LORD!
   He is their help and their shield.
11 You who fear the LORD, trust in the LORD!
   He is their help and their shield.

12 The LORD has been mindful of us; he will bless us;
   he will bless the house of Israel;
   he will bless the house of Aaron;
13 he will bless those who fear the LORD,
   both small and great.

14 May the LORD give you increase,
   both you and your children.
15 May you be blessed by the LORD,
   who made heaven and earth.

16 The heavens are the LORD's heavens,
   but the earth he has given to human beings.
17 The dead do not praise the LORD,
   nor do any that go down into silence.
18 But we will bless the LORD
   from this time on and forevermore.
   Praise the LORD!

Psalm 116

1 I love the LORD, because he has heard
   my voice and my supplications.
2 Because he inclined his ear to me,
   therefore I will call on him as long as I live.
3 The snares of death encompassed me;
   the pangs of Sheol laid hold on me;
   I suffered distress and anguish.
4 Then I called on the name of the LORD:
   "O LORD, I pray, save my life!"

5 Gracious is the LORD, and righteous;
   our God is merciful.
6 The LORD protects the simple;
   when I was brought low, he saved me.
7 Return, O my soul, to your rest,
   for the LORD has dealt bountifully with you.

8 For you have delivered my soul from death,
   my eyes from tears,
   my feet from stumbling.
9 I walk before the LORD
   in the land of the living.
10 I kept my faith, even when I said,
   "I am greatly afflicted";
11 I said in my consternation,
   "Everyone is a liar."

Resting in God

PSALM 116.5–7

Worry and stress have become constant companions for many of us in our busy culture. We might not be facing "the snares of death" (v.3), but we often live anxiously—bombarded by activities, information, appointments and debts. We find it hard to "rest" in God's mercy and bounty. What are some ways you might practice resting in God? Try sitting in silence for fifteen minutes before others in the household get up, taking a prayerful walk during a lunch break, or putting on the headphones and listening to meditative music for twenty minutes when you get home in the afternoon. Try one new "habit" of rest for three weeks.

See Meeting God in Everyday Life

Echoes of Praise

PSALM 118.1–4

In this litany of thanksgiving, we can almost hear the cantor calling to the people, priests and those who fear God to praise God's unending love. Consider the echoes of the liturgy that you hear in sabbath worship: the call to worship, the hymn choruses, the scripture readings. Repeating litanies of praise and thanksgiving are like saying "I love you" over and over—it reinforces that truth in our hearts and minds. How do you carry the reverberations from sabbath worship into your daily life? Instead of throwing away the bulletin, use it. Choose a Biblical passage, a hymn or a call to worship, and make it your daily devotion over the course of a week.

See Meeting God in Worship

12 What shall I return to the LORD
   for all his bounty to me?
13 I will lift up the cup of salvation
   and call on the name of the LORD,
14 I will pay my vows to the LORD
   in the presence of all his people.
15 Precious in the sight of the LORD
   is the death of his faithful ones.
16 O LORD, I am your servant;
   I am your servant, the child of your serving girl.
   You have loosed my bonds.
17 I will offer to you a thanksgiving sacrifice
   and call on the name of the LORD.
18 I will pay my vows to the LORD
   in the presence of all his people,
19 in the courts of the house of the LORD,
   in your midst, O Jerusalem.
Praise the LORD!

Psalm 117

1 Praise the LORD, all you nations!
   Extol him, all you peoples!
2 For great is his steadfast love toward us,
   and the faithfulness of the LORD endures forever.
Praise the LORD!

Psalm 118

1 O give thanks to the LORD, for he is good;
   his steadfast love endures forever!

2 Let Israel say,
   "His steadfast love endures forever."
3 Let the house of Aaron say,
   "His steadfast love endures forever."
4 Let those who fear the LORD say,
   "His steadfast love endures forever."

5 Out of my distress I called on the LORD;
   the LORD answered me and set me in a broad
      place.
6 With the LORD on my side I do not fear.
   What can mortals do to me?
7 The LORD is on my side to help me;
   I shall look in triumph on those who hate me.
8 It is better to take refuge in the LORD
   than to put confidence in mortals.
9 It is better to take refuge in the LORD
   than to put confidence in princes.

10 All nations surrounded me;
   in the name of the LORD I cut them off!
11 They surrounded me, surrounded me on every side;
   in the name of the LORD I cut them off!
12 They surrounded me like bees;
   they blazed*a* like a fire of thorns;
   in the name of the LORD I cut them off!

a Gk: Heb *were extinguished*

13 I was pushed hard,[a] so that I was falling,
   but the LORD helped me.
14 The LORD is my strength and my might;
   he has become my salvation.

15 There are glad songs of victory in the tents of the
   righteous:
   "The right hand of the LORD does valiantly;
16 the right hand of the LORD is exalted;
   the right hand of the LORD does valiantly."
17 I shall not die, but I shall live,
   and recount the deeds of the LORD.
18 The LORD has punished me severely,
   but he did not give me over to death.

19 Open to me the gates of righteousness,
   that I may enter through them
   and give thanks to the LORD.

20 This is the gate of the LORD;
   the righteous shall enter through it.

21 I thank you that you have answered me
   and have become my salvation.
22 The stone that the builders rejected
   has become the chief cornerstone.
23 This is the LORD's doing;
   it is marvelous in our eyes.
24 This is the day that the LORD has made;
   let us rejoice and be glad in it.[b]
25 Save us, we beseech you, O LORD!
   O LORD, we beseech you, give us success!

26 Blessed is the one who comes in the name of the
   LORD.[c]
   We bless you from the house of the LORD.
27 The LORD is God,
   and he has given us light.
   Bind the festal procession with branches,
   up to the horns of the altar.[d]

28 You are my God, and I will give thanks to you;
   you are my God, I will extol you.

29 O give thanks to the LORD, for he is good,
   for his steadfast love endures forever.

Psalm 119

1 Happy are those whose way is blameless,
   who walk in the law of the LORD.
2 Happy are those who keep his decrees,
   who seek him with their whole heart,
3 who also do no wrong,
   but walk in his ways.
4 You have commanded your precepts
   to be kept diligently.

The Rejected Stone

PSALM 118.22–24

These verses, particularly 22 and 23, are often quoted in the New Testament (Matthew 21.42; 1 Peter 2.7) as a reference to the coming of Jesus Christ, for the rejected One has become what is most precious. This is often true for our inner spiritual selves as well. We may reject a part of ourselves because it seems weak but later realize that it is a strength. Perhaps it causes us to rely on God more. Or perhaps we discover that our "weakness" is a diamond in the rough that needs to be honed and shaped. In your journal or with a soul friend, reflect on what you reject in yourself: a tendency to talk too much or too little, a certain compulsivity. What might God be showing you through it?

---

a Gk Syr Jerome: Heb *You pushed me hard*   b Or *in him*   c Or *Blessed in the name of the LORD is the one who comes*   d Meaning of Heb uncertain

Running in God's Way

PSALM 119.30–35

The law is celebrated throughout Psalm 119. The psalmist delights in the law, for he has found that it is his source of strength and understanding. He feeds there. In monastic life, all 150 psalms are chanted each week. There is wisdom in nourishing the heart continuously with God's instruction in scripture. How do you nourish your soul with scripture? Have you cultivated a daily habit? One way to begin is to select one of the Gospels and read it meditatively (not more than ten to fifteen verses each day) or read a psalm every morning as part of a devotion or choose a favorite passage and spend a week memorizing it.

See Meeting God in Scripture

5 O that my ways may be steadfast
    in keeping your statutes!
6 Then I shall not be put to shame,
    having my eyes fixed on all your
       commandments.
7 I will praise you with an upright heart,
    when I learn your righteous ordinances.
8 I will observe your statutes;
    do not utterly forsake me.

9 How can young people keep their way pure?
    By guarding it according to your word.
10 With my whole heart I seek you;
    do not let me stray from your commandments.
11 I treasure your word in my heart,
    so that I may not sin against you.
12 Blessed are you, O LORD;
    teach me your statutes.
13 With my lips I declare
    all the ordinances of your mouth.
14 I delight in the way of your decrees
    as much as in all riches.
15 I will meditate on your precepts,
    and fix my eyes on your ways.
16 I will delight in your statutes;
    I will not forget your word.

17 Deal bountifully with your servant,
    so that I may live and observe your word.
18 Open my eyes, so that I may behold
    wondrous things out of your law.
19 I live as an alien in the land;
    do not hide your commandments from me.
20 My soul is consumed with longing
    for your ordinances at all times.
21 You rebuke the insolent, accursed ones,
    who wander from your commandments;
22 take away from me their scorn and contempt,
    for I have kept your decrees.
23 Even though princes sit plotting against me,
    your servant will meditate on your statutes.
24 Your decrees are my delight,
    they are my counselors.

25 My soul clings to the dust;
    revive me according to your word.
26 When I told of my ways, you answered me;
    teach me your statutes.
27 Make me understand the way of your precepts,
    and I will meditate on your wondrous works.
28 My soul melts away for sorrow;
    strengthen me according to your word.
29 Put false ways far from me;
    and graciously teach me your law.
30 I have chosen the way of faithfulness;
    I set your ordinances before me.
31 I cling to your decrees, O LORD;
    let me not be put to shame.
32 I run the way of your commandments,
    for you enlarge my understanding.

33 Teach me, O LORD, the way of your statutes,
and I will observe it to the end.
34 Give me understanding, that I may keep your law
and observe it with my whole heart.
35 Lead me in the path of your commandments,
for I delight in it.
36 Turn my heart to your decrees,
and not to selfish gain.
37 Turn my eyes from looking at vanities;
give me life in your ways.
38 Confirm to your servant your promise,
which is for those who fear you.
39 Turn away the disgrace that I dread,
for your ordinances are good.
40 See, I have longed for your precepts;
in your righteousness give me life.

41 Let your steadfast love come to me, O LORD,
your salvation according to your promise.
42 Then I shall have an answer for those who taunt me,
for I trust in your word.
43 Do not take the word of truth utterly out of my
mouth,
for my hope is in your ordinances.
44 I will keep your law continually,
forever and ever.
45 I shall walk at liberty,
for I have sought your precepts.
46 I will also speak of your decrees before kings,
and shall not be put to shame;
47 I find my delight in your commandments,
because I love them.
48 I revere your commandments, which I love,
and I will meditate on your statutes.

49 Remember your word to your servant,
in which you have made me hope.
50 This is my comfort in my distress,
that your promise gives me life.
51 The arrogant utterly deride me,
but I do not turn away from your law.
52 When I think of your ordinances from of old,
I take comfort, O LORD.
53 Hot indignation seizes me because of the wicked,
those who forsake your law.
54 Your statutes have been my songs
wherever I make my home.
55 I remember your name in the night, O LORD,
and keep your law.
56 This blessing has fallen to me,
for I have kept your precepts.

57 The LORD is my portion;
I promise to keep your words.
58 I implore your favor with all my heart;
be gracious to me according to your promise.
59 When I think of your ways,
I turn my feet to your decrees;
60 I hurry and do not delay
to keep your commandments.

True Freedom

PSALM 119.45

Here the psalmist declares the spiritual freedom found in seeking God's ways. Freedom is something to be treasured. Prisoners, slaves and day laborers understand its preciousness; one who is shackled by an addiction longs for liberty. Often in the world today, a self-centered materialism parades as freedom. Yet Jesus calls us to a much different freedom when he says, "Strive first for the kingdom of God and his righteousness, and all these things will be given to you as well" (Matthew 6.33). Where is God calling you to detachment? In what practical ways do you give priority to God's ways in your life?

See Meeting God in Everyday Life

Humility

PSALM 119.67

The word in this verse translated "humbled" can also mean "afflicted." The psalmist reminds us that good can come out of difficult, humbling circumstances. Reflect on a time in your life in which you went "astray" and found some painful event the catalyst for a renewed, more faithful walk with God. Ask God to allow the lesson or renewal to be an ongoing part of your life.

See Meeting God in Everyday Life

61 Though the cords of the wicked ensnare me,
   I do not forget your law.
62 At midnight I rise to praise you,
   because of your righteous ordinances.
63 I am a companion of all who fear you,
   of those who keep your precepts.
64 The earth, O LORD, is full of your steadfast love;
   teach me your statutes.

65 You have dealt well with your servant,
   O LORD, according to your word.
66 Teach me good judgment and knowledge,
   for I believe in your commandments.
67 Before I was humbled I went astray,
   but now I keep your word.
68 You are good and do good;
   teach me your statutes.
69 The arrogant smear me with lies,
   but with my whole heart I keep your precepts.
70 Their hearts are fat and gross,
   but I delight in your law.
71 It is good for me that I was humbled,
   so that I might learn your statutes.
72 The law of your mouth is better to me
   than thousands of gold and silver pieces.

73 Your hands have made and fashioned me;
   give me understanding that I may learn your
     commandments.
74 Those who fear you shall see me and rejoice,
   because I have hoped in your word.
75 I know, O LORD, that your judgments are right,
   and that in faithfulness you have humbled me.
76 Let your steadfast love become my comfort
   according to your promise to your servant.
77 Let your mercy come to me, that I may live;
   for your law is my delight.
78 Let the arrogant be put to shame,
   because they have subverted me with guile;
   as for me, I will meditate on your precepts.
79 Let those who fear you turn to me,
   so that they may know your decrees.
80 May my heart be blameless in your statutes,
   so that I may not be put to shame.

81 My soul languishes for your salvation;
   I hope in your word.
82 My eyes fail with watching for your promise;
   I ask, "When will you comfort me?"
83 For I have become like a wineskin in the smoke,
   yet I have not forgotten your statutes.
84 How long must your servant endure?
   When will you judge those who persecute me?
85 The arrogant have dug pitfalls for me;
   they flout your law.
86 All your commandments are enduring;
   I am persecuted without cause; help me!
87 They have almost made an end of me on earth;
   but I have not forsaken your precepts.

88 In your steadfast love spare my life,
    so that I may keep the decrees of your mouth.

89 The LORD exists forever;
    your word is firmly fixed in heaven.
90 Your faithfulness endures to all generations;
    you have established the earth, and it stands fast.
91 By your appointment they stand today,
    for all things are your servants.
92 If your law had not been my delight,
    I would have perished in my misery.
93 I will never forget your precepts,
    for by them you have given me life.
94 I am yours; save me,
    for I have sought your precepts.
95 The wicked lie in wait to destroy me,
    but I consider your decrees.
96 I have seen a limit to all perfection,
    but your commandment is exceedingly broad.

97 Oh, how I love your law!
    It is my meditation all day long.
98 Your commandment makes me wiser than my
        enemies,
    for it is always with me.
99 I have more understanding than all my teachers,
    for your decrees are my meditation.
100 I understand more than the aged,
    for I keep your precepts.
101 I hold back my feet from every evil way,
    in order to keep your word.
102 I do not turn away from your ordinances,
    for you have taught me.
103 How sweet are your words to my taste,
    sweeter than honey to my mouth!
104 Through your precepts I get understanding;
    therefore I hate every false way.

105 Your word is a lamp to my feet
    and a light to my path.
106 I have sworn an oath and confirmed it,
    to observe your righteous ordinances.
107 I am severely afflicted;
    give me life, O LORD, according to your word.
108 Accept my offerings of praise, O LORD,
    and teach me your ordinances.
109 I hold my life in my hand continually,
    but I do not forget your law.
110 The wicked have laid a snare for me,
    but I do not stray from your precepts.
111 Your decrees are my heritage forever;
    they are the joy of my heart.
112 I incline my heart to perform your statutes
    forever, to the end.

113 I hate the double-minded,
    but I love your law.
114 You are my hiding place and my shield;
    I hope in your word.

Heart Wisdom

PSALM 119.97–100

Meditation is a word that is used in many ways today. A person may meditate in silence, meditate on a new idea or even meditate on what to eat at a favorite restaurant. But here the psalmist describes meditation as bringing scripture into the heart. He says, "It is always with me." How do you keep scripture "always" with you? Try reading slowly through the Bible, memorizing verses that touch you, and taking part in a small group where scripture is shared (not necessarily studied). This week, commit (or recommit) to an approach of "dwelling in" scripture.

See *Meeting God in Scripture*

Discernment

PSALM 119.130

The psalmist beautifully reminds us that the "unfolding" of scripture offers guidance for our lives. There are times when we do not know what to do next or when we are making a difficult choice between two "goods." Through the reflective reading of a psalm, a Gospel passage or a chapter of an epistle, "light" and "understanding" may come through a word or phrase at that very moment or perhaps even later during the day. When you face a difficult decision, take a few moments to surrender it to God in prayer, and then prayerfully read a chosen passage. See what wisdom emerges.

See Meeting God in Scripture

115 Go away from me, you evildoers,
   that I may keep the commandments of my God.
116 Uphold me according to your promise, that I may live,
   and let me not be put to shame in my hope.
117 Hold me up, that I may be safe
   and have regard for your statutes continually.
118 You spurn all who go astray from your statutes;
   for their cunning is in vain.
119 All the wicked of the earth you count as dross;
   therefore I love your decrees.
120 My flesh trembles for fear of you,
   and I am afraid of your judgments.

121 I have done what is just and right;
   do not leave me to my oppressors.
122 Guarantee your servant's well-being;
   do not let the godless oppress me.
123 My eyes fail from watching for your salvation,
   and for the fulfillment of your righteous promise.
124 Deal with your servant according to your steadfast love,
   and teach me your statutes.
125 I am your servant; give me understanding,
   so that I may know your decrees.
126 It is time for the Lord to act,
   for your law has been broken.
127 Truly I love your commandments
   more than gold, more than fine gold.
128 Truly I direct my steps by all your precepts;*a*
   I hate every false way.

129 Your decrees are wonderful;
   therefore my soul keeps them.
130 The unfolding of your words gives light;
   it imparts understanding to the simple.
131 With open mouth I pant,
   because I long for your commandments.
132 Turn to me and be gracious to me,
   as is your custom toward those who love your name.
133 Keep my steps steady according to your promise,
   and never let iniquity have dominion over me.
134 Redeem me from human oppression,
   that I may keep your precepts.
135 Make your face shine upon your servant,
   and teach me your statutes.
136 My eyes shed streams of tears
   because your law is not kept.

137 You are righteous, O Lord,
   and your judgments are right.
138 You have appointed your decrees in righteousness
   and in all faithfulness.
139 My zeal consumes me
   because my foes forget your words.
140 Your promise is well tried,
   and your servant loves it.

a Gk Jerome: Meaning of Heb uncertain

141 I am small and despised,
    yet I do not forget your precepts.
142 Your righteousness is an everlasting righteousness,
    and your law is the truth.
143 Trouble and anguish have come upon me,
    but your commandments are my delight.
144 Your decrees are righteous forever;
    give me understanding that I may live.

145 With my whole heart I cry; answer me, O LORD.
    I will keep your statutes.
146 I cry to you; save me,
    that I may observe your decrees.
147 I rise before dawn and cry for help;
    I put my hope in your words.
148 My eyes are awake before each watch of the night,
    that I may meditate on your promise.
149 In your steadfast love hear my voice;
    O LORD, in your justice preserve my life.
150 Those who persecute me with evil purpose draw
      near;
    they are far from your law.
151 Yet you are near, O LORD,
    and all your commandments are true.
152 Long ago I learned from your decrees
    that you have established them forever.

153 Look on my misery and rescue me,
    for I do not forget your law.
154 Plead my cause and redeem me;
    give me life according to your promise.
155 Salvation is far from the wicked,
    for they do not seek your statutes.
156 Great is your mercy, O LORD;
    give me life according to your justice.
157 Many are my persecutors and my adversaries,
    yet I do not swerve from your decrees.
158 I look at the faithless with disgust,
    because they do not keep your commands.
159 Consider how I love your precepts;
    preserve my life according to your steadfast love.
160 The sum of your word is truth;
    and every one of your righteous ordinances
      endures forever.

161 Princes persecute me without cause,
    but my heart stands in awe of your words.
162 I rejoice at your word
    like one who finds great spoil.
163 I hate and abhor falsehood,
    but I love your law.
164 Seven times a day I praise you
    for your righteous ordinances.
165 Great peace have those who love your law;
    nothing can make them stumble.
166 I hope for your salvation, O LORD,
    and I fulfill your commandments.
167 My soul keeps your decrees;
    I love them exceedingly.

Praying the Psalter

PSALM 119.147–148

"The more deeply we grow into the psalms and the more often we pray them as our own, the more simple and rich will our prayer become."

—DIETRICH BONHOEFFER,
Life Together

See Meeting God in Prayer

Always There

PSALM 121.1–4

This psalm speaks peace to our deepest fears. Every night, each of us must abandon consciousness for several hours. Our surrender to sleep—while God neither slumbers nor sleeps—symbolizes the truth that we are always held in God's presence regardless of our awareness. God is near and watching over us. What worries or fears make you anxious about your safety, your health, your work or your children? Make a list of three of your concerns. In the same way that you "let go" for sleep, offer these worries to God. If you think it may be helpful, put your list where you can see it and offer these concerns to God throughout the day.

See *Meeting God in Everyday Life*

168 I keep your precepts and decrees,
    for all my ways are before you.

169 Let my cry come before you, O LORD;
    give me understanding according to your word.

170 Let my supplication come before you;
    deliver me according to your promise.

171 My lips will pour forth praise,
    because you teach me your statutes.

172 My tongue will sing of your promise,
    for all your commandments are right.

173 Let your hand be ready to help me,
    for I have chosen your precepts.

174 I long for your salvation, O LORD,
    and your law is my delight.

175 Let me live that I may praise you,
    and let your ordinances help me.

176 I have gone astray like a lost sheep; seek out your
        servant,
    for I do not forget your commandments.

Psalm 120

A Song of Ascents.

1 In my distress I cry to the LORD,
    that he may answer me:

2 "Deliver me, O LORD,
    from lying lips,
    from a deceitful tongue."

3 What shall be given to you?
    And what more shall be done to you,
        you deceitful tongue?

4 A warrior's sharp arrows,
    with glowing coals of the broom tree!

5 Woe is me, that I am an alien in Meshech,
    that I must live among the tents of Kedar.

6 Too long have I had my dwelling
    among those who hate peace.

7 I am for peace;
    but when I speak,
    they are for war.

Psalm 121

A Song of Ascents.

1 I lift up my eyes to the hills—
    from where will my help come?

2 My help comes from the LORD,
    who made heaven and earth.

3 He will not let your foot be moved;
    he who keeps you will not slumber.

4 He who keeps Israel
    will neither slumber nor sleep.

5 The LORD is your keeper;
    the LORD is your shade at your right hand.

6 The sun shall not strike you by day,
    nor the moon by night.

7 The LORD will keep you from all evil;
    he will keep your life.
8 The LORD will keep
    your going out and your coming in
    from this time on and forevermore.

Psalm 122

A Song of Ascents. Of David.

1 I was glad when they said to me,
    "Let us go to the house of the LORD!"
2 Our feet are standing
    within your gates, O Jerusalem.

3 Jerusalem—built as a city
    that is bound firmly together.
4 To it the tribes go up,
    the tribes of the LORD,
as was decreed for Israel,
    to give thanks to the name of the LORD.
5 For there the thrones for judgment were set up,
    the thrones of the house of David.

6 Pray for the peace of Jerusalem:
    "May they prosper who love you.
7 Peace be within your walls,
    and security within your towers."
8 For the sake of my relatives and friends
    I will say, "Peace be within you."
9 For the sake of the house of the LORD our God,
    I will seek your good.

Psalm 123

A Song of Ascents.

1 To you I lift up my eyes,
    O you who are enthroned in the heavens!
2 As the eyes of servants
    look to the hand of their master,
as the eyes of a maid
    to the hand of her mistress,
so our eyes look to the LORD our God,
    until he has mercy upon us.

3 Have mercy upon us, O LORD, have mercy upon us,
    for we have had more than enough of contempt.
4 Our soul has had more than its fill
    of the scorn of those who are at ease,
    of the contempt of the proud.

Psalm 124

A Song of Ascents. Of David.

1 If it had not been the LORD who was on our side
    —let Israel now say—

Pilgrimage

PSALM 122.1–2

We are hearing about pilgrimages more and more frequently. People are making pilgrimages to Israel, to Assisi, to Ireland and to Scotland. Walking the streets where Jesus walked, worshiping "with" Francis and recovering the roots of Celtic Christian faith enrich the soul. Visiting an old family home or the church of your childhood may also be a "pilgrimage." Even if you cannot travel physically, you may do so in spirit. Using colored pencils, markers or paints, draw a picture of a "sacred place" from your childhood. Below your picture, write a word that comes to mind as you recall this place.

See Meeting God in Everyday Life

Returning Home

PSALM 126.1–3

Can you remember coming home after being gone for a long period of time or after enduring a terrible experience? How glad you were to see the familiar sights of home and the faces of those you love! Here the psalmist is recalling such a return from exile: "Our mouth was filled with laughter." So, too, God is always welcoming us "home." In each moment of every day, we are invited to remember that God is ever near. God's steadfast love always surrounds us, even when we don't recognize it. As you pray during the day, take a moment in silence to rest in the "home" of God's presence.

See Meeting God in Everyday Life

2 if it had not been the LORD who was on our side,
   when our enemies attacked us,
3 then they would have swallowed us up alive,
   when their anger was kindled against us;
4 then the flood would have swept us away,
   the torrent would have gone over us;
5 then over us would have gone
   the raging waters.

6 Blessed be the LORD,
   who has not given us
   as prey to their teeth.
7 We have escaped like a bird
   from the snare of the fowlers;
   the snare is broken,
   and we have escaped.

8 Our help is in the name of the LORD,
   who made heaven and earth.

Psalm 125

A Song of Ascents.

1 Those who trust in the LORD are like Mount Zion,
   which cannot be moved, but abides forever.
2 As the mountains surround Jerusalem,
   so the LORD surrounds his people,
   from this time on and forevermore.
3 For the scepter of wickedness shall not rest
   on the land allotted to the righteous,
   so that the righteous might not stretch out
   their hands to do wrong.
4 Do good, O LORD, to those who are good,
   and to those who are upright in their hearts.
5 But those who turn aside to their own crooked ways
   the LORD will lead away with evildoers.
   Peace be upon Israel!

Psalm 126

A Song of Ascents.

1 When the LORD restored the fortunes of Zion,[a]
   we were like those who dream.
2 Then our mouth was filled with laughter,
   and our tongue with shouts of joy;
   then it was said among the nations,
   "The LORD has done great things for them."
3 The LORD has done great things for us,
   and we rejoiced.

4 Restore our fortunes, O LORD,
   like the watercourses in the Negeb.
5 May those who sow in tears
   reap with shouts of joy.
6 Those who go out weeping,
   bearing the seed for sowing,
   shall come home with shouts of joy,
   carrying their sheaves.

a Or brought back those who returned to Zion

Psalm 127

A Song of Ascents. Of Solomon.

1 Unless the LORD builds the house,
  those who build it labor in vain.
 Unless the LORD guards the city,
  the guard keeps watch in vain.
2 It is in vain that you rise up early
  and go late to rest,
 eating the bread of anxious toil;
  for he gives sleep to his beloved.*a*

3 Sons are indeed a heritage from the LORD,
  the fruit of the womb a reward.
4 Like arrows in the hand of a warrior
  are the sons of one's youth.
5 Happy is the man who has
  his quiver full of them.
 He shall not be put to shame
  when he speaks with his enemies in the gate.

Psalm 128

A Song of Ascents.

1 Happy is everyone who fears the LORD,
  who walks in his ways.
2 You shall eat the fruit of the labor of your hands;
  you shall be happy, and it shall go well with you.

3 Your wife will be like a fruitful vine
  within your house;
 your children will be like olive shoots
  around your table.
4 Thus shall the man be blessed
  who fears the LORD.

5 The LORD bless you from Zion.
  May you see the prosperity of Jerusalem
  all the days of your life.
6 May you see your children's children.
  Peace be upon Israel!

Psalm 129

A Song of Ascents.

1 "Often have they attacked me from my youth"
  —let Israel now say—
2 "often have they attacked me from my youth,
  yet they have not prevailed against me.
3 The plowers plowed on my back;
  they made their furrows long."
4 The LORD is righteous;
  he has cut the cords of the wicked.
5 May all who hate Zion
  be put to shame and turned backward.
6 Let them be like the grass on the housetops
  that withers before it grows up,

a Or for he provides for his beloved during sleep

The Problem With Vanity

PSALM 127.1–2

Vanity is an old-fashioned word, but full of meaning. It can refer to "egotism" and "self-concern," but it can also mean "futility" and "hollowness." In *vain* we do things on our own and for our own benefit—we "build our houses" without the Lord. Our culture values independence and such self-sufficiency, but the spiritual life calls us to nourish ourselves by putting down deeper roots. Daily immersion in scripture, prayer and community (spiritual friends and mentors) helps us check our tendency toward vanity. In what areas of your life are you trying to do things under your own steam? Where is God inviting you to let go of control and learn humility?

See *Meeting God in Community*

More Than Those Who Watch for the Morning

PSALM 130.5–6

Security officers and night shift workers know how hard it is to stay awake in the hours just before dawn. Drowsiness may overcome even the strongest will. Yet the psalmist desires God with all of himself, even more than the one struggling to stay awake until morning. Ignatius shares the psalmist's commitment: "Take, O Lord, and receive all my liberty, my memory, my understanding, and my entire will, all that I have and possess." How often do you consecrate your attention and intentions to God? What simple prayer of consecration might you offer to God as you go through this day?

See Meeting God in Prayer

7 with which reapers do not fill their hands
or binders of sheaves their arms,
8 while those who pass by do not say,
"The blessing of the LORD be upon you!
We bless you in the name of the LORD!"

Psalm 130

A Song of Ascents.

1 Out of the depths I cry to you, O LORD.
2 Lord, hear my voice!
Let your ears be attentive
to the voice of my supplications!

3 If you, O LORD, should mark iniquities,
Lord, who could stand?
4 But there is forgiveness with you,
so that you may be revered.

5 I wait for the LORD, my soul waits,
and in his word I hope;
6 my soul waits for the Lord
more than those who watch for the morning,
more than those who watch for the morning.

7 O Israel, hope in the LORD!
For with the LORD there is steadfast love,
and with him is great power to redeem.
8 It is he who will redeem Israel
from all its iniquities.

Psalm 131

A Song of Ascents. Of David.

1 O LORD, my heart is not lifted up,
my eyes are not raised too high;
I do not occupy myself with things
too great and too marvelous for me.
2 But I have calmed and quieted my soul,
like a weaned child with its mother;
my soul is like the weaned child that is with me.[a]

3 O Israel, hope in the LORD
from this time on and forevermore.

Psalm 132

A Song of Ascents.

1 O LORD, remember in David's favor
all the hardships he endured;
2 how he swore to the LORD
and vowed to the Mighty One of Jacob,
3 "I will not enter my house
or get into my bed;
4 I will not give sleep to my eyes
or slumber to my eyelids,

a Or my soul within me is like a weaned child

5 until I find a place for the Lord,
   a dwelling place for the Mighty One of Jacob."

6 We heard of it in Ephrathah;
   we found it in the fields of Jaar.
7 "Let us go to his dwelling place;
   let us worship at his footstool."

8 Rise up, O Lord, and go to your resting place,
   you and the ark of your might.
9 Let your priests be clothed with righteousness,
   and let your faithful shout for joy.
10 For your servant David's sake
   do not turn away the face of your anointed one.

11 The Lord swore to David a sure oath
   from which he will not turn back:
   "One of the sons of your body
   I will set on your throne.
12 If your sons keep my covenant
   and my decrees that I shall teach them,
   their sons also, forevermore,
   shall sit on your throne."

13 For the Lord has chosen Zion;
   he has desired it for his habitation:
14 "This is my resting place forever;
   here I will reside, for I have desired it.
15 I will abundantly bless its provisions;
   I will satisfy its poor with bread.
16 Its priests I will clothe with salvation,
   and its faithful will shout for joy.
17 There I will cause a horn to sprout up for David;
   I have prepared a lamp for my anointed one.
18 His enemies I will clothe with disgrace,
   but on him, his crown will gleam.'"

Psalm 133

A Song of Ascents.

1 How very good and pleasant it is
   when kindred live together in unity!
2 It is like the precious oil on the head,
   running down upon the beard,
   on the beard of Aaron,
   running down over the collar of his robes.
3 It is like the dew of Hermon,
   which falls on the mountains of Zion.
   For there the Lord ordained his blessing,
   life forevermore.

Psalm 134

A Song of Ascents.

1 Come, bless the Lord, all you servants of the Lord,
   who stand by night in the house of the Lord!
2 Lift up your hands to the holy place,
   and bless the Lord.

Unity: The Precious Gift

PSALM 133.1–3

The psalmist writes about how precious unity is, especially in families and communities. Yet how hard it is for us to achieve. Disagreements, hurts, indifference and self-concern divide us. Unity requires that we work continually at forgiving one another. Brother Roger of the ecumenical Taizé community writes, "A conversion takes place in the very depths of our being when, even though we are rejected or humiliated, we entrust to God, at once, those who have wounded us." What hurts or wounds are separating you from another person or community? What act of reconciliation might God be leading you to do?

See Meeting God in Community

God's Goodness

PSALM 135.3

The psalmist's song begins by extolling God's goodness. Many of us remember the familiar table grace: "God is great; God is good. Let us thank him for our food." How is God good? Eternally loving? Merciful? Just and compassionate? Make a list of God's good qualities. Write your own litany of praise, for example, "Praise the Lord, for the Lord is kind; sing to God for God's endless love."

See Meeting God in Worship

3 May the Lord, maker of heaven and earth,
   bless you from Zion.

Psalm 135

1 Praise the Lord!
   Praise the name of the Lord;
   give praise, O servants of the Lord,
2 you that stand in the house of the Lord,
   in the courts of the house of our God.
3 Praise the Lord, for the Lord is good;
   sing to his name, for he is gracious.
4 For the Lord has chosen Jacob for himself,
   Israel as his own possession.

5 For I know that the Lord is great;
   our Lord is above all gods.
6 Whatever the Lord pleases he does,
   in heaven and on earth,
   in the seas and all deeps.
7 He it is who makes the clouds rise at the end of the
   earth;
   he makes lightnings for the rain
   and brings out the wind from his storehouses.

8 He it was who struck down the firstborn of Egypt,
   both human beings and animals;
9 he sent signs and wonders
   into your midst, O Egypt,
   against Pharaoh and all his servants.
10 He struck down many nations
   and killed mighty kings—
11 Sihon, king of the Amorites,
   and Og, king of Bashan,
   and all the kingdoms of Canaan—
12 and gave their land as a heritage,
   a heritage to his people Israel.

13 Your name, O Lord, endures forever,
   your renown, O Lord, throughout all ages.
14 For the Lord will vindicate his people,
   and have compassion on his servants.

15 The idols of the nations are silver and gold,
   the work of human hands.
16 They have mouths, but they do not speak;
   they have eyes, but they do not see;
17 they have ears, but they do not hear,
   and there is no breath in their mouths.
18 Those who make them
   and all who trust them
   shall become like them.

19 O house of Israel, bless the Lord!
   O house of Aaron, bless the Lord!
20 O house of Levi, bless the Lord!
   You that fear the Lord, bless the Lord!
21 Blessed be the Lord from Zion,
   he who resides in Jerusalem.
   Praise the Lord!

Psalm 136

1 O give thanks to the Lord, for he is good,
   for his steadfast love endures forever.
2 O give thanks to the God of gods,
   for his steadfast love endures forever.
3 O give thanks to the Lord of lords,
   for his steadfast love endures forever;

4 who alone does great wonders,
   for his steadfast love endures forever;
5 who by understanding made the heavens,
   for his steadfast love endures forever;
6 who spread out the earth on the waters,
   for his steadfast love endures forever;
7 who made the great lights,
   for his steadfast love endures forever;
8 the sun to rule over the day,
   for his steadfast love endures forever;
9 the moon and stars to rule over the night,
   for his steadfast love endures forever;

10 who struck Egypt through their firstborn,
   for his steadfast love endures forever;
11 and brought Israel out from among them,
   for his steadfast love endures forever;
12 with a strong hand and an outstretched arm,
   for his steadfast love endures forever;
13 who divided the Red Sea*a* in two,
   for his steadfast love endures forever;
14 and made Israel pass through the midst of it,
   for his steadfast love endures forever;
15 but overthrew Pharaoh and his army in the Red
   Sea,*a*
   for his steadfast love endures forever;
16 who led his people through the wilderness,
   for his steadfast love endures forever;
17 who struck down great kings,
   for his steadfast love endures forever;
18 and killed famous kings,
   for his steadfast love endures forever;
19 Sihon, king of the Amorites,
   for his steadfast love endures forever;
20 and Og, king of Bashan,
   for his steadfast love endures forever;
21 and gave their land as a heritage,
   for his steadfast love endures forever;
22 a heritage to his servant Israel,
   for his steadfast love endures forever.

23 It is he who remembered us in our low estate,
   for his steadfast love endures forever;
24 and rescued us from our foes,
   for his steadfast love endures forever;
25 who gives food to all flesh,
   for his steadfast love endures forever.

26 O give thanks to the God of heaven,
   for his steadfast love endures forever.

a Or *Sea of Reeds*

The Echo of Love

PSALM 136.2–9

Throughout this hymn of praise, the psalmist sings of God's faithful, enduring love. Divine love is the echo throughout the narratives of creation, the account of the exodus from Egypt and the stories of Hebrew nationhood. Love is the echo in your story as well: You are born, and God loves you. You take your first steps, and God delights in you. You enjoy a sunset, and God smiles with you. Think back through the events of the last twenty-four hours. As you remember each event, speak this echoing refrain to yourself: "And God loves me." Reflect on the sense of God's love and presence that this meditation fosters.

See Meeting God in Scripture

With a Whole Heart

PSALM 138.1–2

The psalmist reiterates what Jesus called the greatest commandment of all: Love God with all of your heart, soul and mind (See Matthew 22.37; Deuteronomy 6.5). Yet we often worship God with divided hearts and disinterested minds. We tune out the scripture passages that are read, we mouth the words to the hymns and we leave the worship service without a rekindled heart. How do we keep our first love vital and growing? Worship requires attention. At the next worship service you attend, consecrate your heart to God as you enter the sanctuary. Close your eyes for a few minutes as you listen to the music. Pay attention to your heart.

See *Meeting God in Worship*

Psalm 137

1 By the rivers of Babylon—
   there we sat down and there we wept
   when we remembered Zion.
2 On the willows[a] there
   we hung up our harps.
3 For there our captors
   asked us for songs,
and our tormentors asked for mirth, saying,
   "Sing us one of the songs of Zion!"

4 How could we sing the LORD's song
   in a foreign land?
5 If I forget you, O Jerusalem,
   let my right hand wither!
6 Let my tongue cling to the roof of my mouth,
   if I do not remember you,
if I do not set Jerusalem
   above my highest joy.

7 Remember, O LORD, against the Edomites
   the day of Jerusalem's fall,
how they said, "Tear it down! Tear it down!
   Down to its foundations!"
8 O daughter Babylon, you devastator![b]
   Happy shall they be who pay you back
   what you have done to us!
9 Happy shall they be who take your little ones
   and dash them against the rock!

Psalm 138

Of David.

1 I give you thanks, O LORD, with my whole heart;
   before the gods I sing your praise;
2 I bow down toward your holy temple
   and give thanks to your name for your steadfast
      love and your faithfulness;
   for you have exalted your name and your word
   above everything.[c]
3 On the day I called, you answered me,
   you increased my strength of soul.[d]

4 All the kings of the earth shall praise you, O LORD,
   for they have heard the words of your mouth.
5 They shall sing of the ways of the LORD,
   for great is the glory of the LORD.
6 For though the LORD is high, he regards the lowly;
   but the haughty he perceives from far away.

7 Though I walk in the midst of trouble,
   you preserve me against the wrath of my
      enemies;
   you stretch out your hand,
      and your right hand delivers me.

---

a Or poplars   *b* Or *you who are devastated*   *c* Cn: Heb *you have exalted your word above all your name*   *d* Syr Compare Gk Tg: Heb *you made me arrogant in my soul with strength*

8 The LORD will fulfill his purpose for me;
   your steadfast love, O LORD, endures forever.
   Do not forsake the work of your hands.

Psalm 139

To the leader. Of David. A Psalm.

1 O LORD, you have searched me and known me.
2 You know when I sit down and when I rise up;
   you discern my thoughts from far away.
3 You search out my path and my lying down,
   and are acquainted with all my ways.
4 Even before a word is on my tongue,
   O LORD, you know it completely.
5 You hem me in, behind and before,
   and lay your hand upon me.
6 Such knowledge is too wonderful for me;
   it is so high that I cannot attain it.

7 Where can I go from your spirit?
   Or where can I flee from your presence?
8 If I ascend to heaven, you are there;
   if I make my bed in Sheol, you are there.
9 If I take the wings of the morning
   and settle at the farthest limits of the sea,
10 even there your hand shall lead me,
   and your right hand shall hold me fast.
11 If I say, "Surely the darkness shall cover me,
   and the light around me become night,"
12 even the darkness is not dark to you;
   the night is as bright as the day,
   for darkness is as light to you.

13 For it was you who formed my inward parts;
   you knit me together in my mother's womb.
14 I praise you, for I am fearfully and wonderfully
       made.
   Wonderful are your works;
   that I know very well.
15 My frame was not hidden from you,
   when I was being made in secret,
   intricately woven in the depths of the earth.
16 Your eyes beheld my unformed substance.
   In your book were written
   all the days that were formed for me,
   when none of them as yet existed.
17 How weighty to me are your thoughts, O God!
   How vast is the sum of them!
18 I try to count them—they are more than the sand;
   I come to the end[a]—I am still with you.

19 O that you would kill the wicked, O God,
   and that the bloodthirsty would depart from
       me—
20 those who speak of you maliciously,
   and lift themselves up against you for evil![b]

Search Me, O God

PSALM 139

The psalmist David exhibits an extraordinary sensitivity to God's presence even to the point of knowing that God has been intimately involved in every day of the singer's life. David's whole life span has been orchestrated by the Master Composer.

Are you aware of God's design for your life? Ask God to help you write a life mission statement, whether you're in the early stages of your life or you have many years behind you. What did God have in mind for you when your body was still being formed? How is God forming you spiritually now? Who does God want you to become? What are your dreams, your goals, your special abilities, your spiritual gifts? How does God want to use them? Dare to pray boldly. Dare to dream boldly.

See Meeting God in Prayer

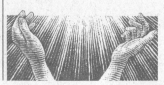

The Unruly Tongue

PSALM 141.3

The image of the psalmist is quite vivid. He prays to God to "keep watch over the door" of his lips. In the letter of James, the tongue is compared to a small fire that can set a vast forest ablaze (James 3.5–6)! Most of us have had the experience of thoughtlessly saying the wrong thing and hurting someone. Gossip and idle speculation are even more insidious. As you go through the day, listen to yourself speak. Are you speaking unfairly, rashly and thoughtlessly? If you hear yourself speaking in one of these ways, say to yourself, "Lord, have mercy." Begin anew in the next moment.

See Meeting God in Everyday Life

21 Do I not hate those who hate you, O LORD?
    And do I not loathe those who rise up against
        you?
22 I hate them with perfect hatred;
    I count them my enemies.
23 Search me, O God, and know my heart;
    test me and know my thoughts.
24 See if there is any wicked*ᵃ* way in me,
    and lead me in the way everlasting.*ᵇ*

Psalm 140

To the leader. A Psalm of David.

1 Deliver me, O LORD, from evildoers;
    protect me from those who are violent,
2 who plan evil things in their minds
    and stir up wars continually.
3 They make their tongue sharp as a snake's,
    and under their lips is the venom of vipers.   *Selah*

4 Guard me, O LORD, from the hands of the wicked;
    protect me from the violent
    who have planned my downfall.
5 The arrogant have hidden a trap for me,
    and with cords they have spread a net,*ᶜ*
    along the road they have set snares for me.   *Selah*

6 I say to the LORD, "You are my God;
    give ear, O LORD, to the voice of my
        supplications."
7 O LORD, my Lord, my strong deliverer,
    you have covered my head in the day of battle.
8 Do not grant, O LORD, the desires of the wicked;
    do not further their evil plot.*ᵈ*   *Selah*

9 Those who surround me lift up their heads;*ᵉ*
    let the mischief of their lips overwhelm them!
10 Let burning coals fall on them!
    Let them be flung into pits, no more to rise!
11 Do not let the slanderer be established in the land;
    let evil speedily hunt down the violent!

12 I know that the LORD maintains the cause of the
        needy,
    and executes justice for the poor.
13 Surely the righteous shall give thanks to your name;
    the upright shall live in your presence.

Psalm 141

A Psalm of David.

1 I call upon you, O LORD; come quickly to me;
    give ear to my voice when I call to you.

---

a Heb *hurtful*   *b* Or *the ancient way.* Compare Jer 6.16   *c* Or *they have
spread cords as a net*   *d* Heb adds *they are exalted*   *e* Cn Compare Gk:
Heb *those who surround me are uplifted in head*; Heb divides verses 8 and 9
differently

2   Let my prayer be counted as incense before you,
     and the lifting up of my hands as an evening
       sacrifice.

3   Set a guard over my mouth, O LORD;
     keep watch over the door of my lips.

4   Do not turn my heart to any evil,
     to busy myself with wicked deeds
  in company with those who work iniquity;
     do not let me eat of their delicacies.

5   Let the righteous strike me;
     let the faithful correct me.
  Never let the oil of the wicked anoint my head,*a*
     for my prayer is continually*b* against their wicked
      deeds.

6   When they are given over to those who shall
     condemn them,
    then they shall learn that my words were
      pleasant.

7   Like a rock that one breaks apart and shatters on
     the land,
    so shall their bones be strewn at the mouth of
      Sheol.*c*

8   But my eyes are turned toward you, O GOD, my
     Lord;
    in you I seek refuge; do not leave me defenseless.

9   Keep me from the trap that they have laid for me,
     and from the snares of evildoers.

10   Let the wicked fall into their own nets,
     while I alone escape.

Psalm 142

A Maskil of David. When he was in the cave. A Prayer.

1   With my voice I cry to the LORD;
     with my voice I make supplication to the LORD.

2   I pour out my complaint before him;
     I tell my trouble before him.

3   When my spirit is faint,
     you know my way.

  In the path where I walk
     they have hidden a trap for me.

4   Look on my right hand and see—
     there is no one who takes notice of me;
  no refuge remains to me;
     no one cares for me.

5   I cry to you, O LORD;
     I say, "You are my refuge,
     my portion in the land of the living."

6   Give heed to my cry,
     for I am brought very low.

God Knows the Way

PSALM 142.1–3

The psalmist remembers God's faithfulness to the weak: "When my spirit is faint, you who know my way." We see our own weakness every day—a stubborn habit we cannot seem to change, a relationship that is not working despite our best efforts. We experience situations that we cannot fix; we cannot even see solutions, let alone work them out. Nevertheless we are reluctant to acknowledge that we are lost and need to wait for God. Yet in the moment we surrender to God, we find new strength, new insight, new hope. In your journal, or on a piece of paper, reflect on the situations and weaknesses that discourage you. What are you trying to control? What might God be gracefully inviting you to risk?

See Meeting God in Everyday Life

---

a Gk: Meaning of Heb uncertain   *b* Cn: Heb *for continually and my prayer*
c Meaning of Heb of verses 5-7 is uncertain

Beginning With God

PSALM 143.8

With each new day, we have a fresh beginning in God's love and faithfulness. Here, the psalmist seeks God's presence from the first light of day. Although each of us has a unique body clock, there is something significant about beginning and ending the day with God. You do not need to be a "morning person" to consecrate the start of your day to God. Perhaps as you drink your coffee, tea or juice, you could close your eyes and offer your day to God. Or when you take your shower, you could thank God for the gift of water and a new day. As you drive to work, you could offer intercessory prayer for persons on your list.

See Meeting God in Everyday Life

Save me from my persecutors,
    for they are too strong for me.
7 Bring me out of prison,
    so that I may give thanks to your name.
The righteous will surround me,
    for you will deal bountifully with me.

Psalm 143

A Psalm of David.

1 Hear my prayer, O LORD;
    give ear to my supplications in your faithfulness;
    answer me in your righteousness.
2 Do not enter into judgment with your servant,
    for no one living is righteous before you.

3 For the enemy has pursued me,
    crushing my life to the ground,
    making me sit in darkness like those long dead.
4 Therefore my spirit faints within me;
    my heart within me is appalled.

5 I remember the days of old,
    I think about all your deeds,
    I meditate on the works of your hands.
6 I stretch out my hands to you;
    my soul thirsts for you like a parched land.   *Selah*

7 Answer me quickly, O LORD;
    my spirit fails.
Do not hide your face from me,
    or I shall be like those who go down to the Pit.
8 Let me hear of your steadfast love in the morning,
    for in you I put my trust.
Teach me the way I should go,
    for to you I lift up my soul.

9 Save me, O LORD, from my enemies;
    I have fled to you for refuge.*a*
10 Teach me to do your will,
    for you are my God.
Let your good spirit lead me
    on a level path.

11 For your name's sake, O LORD, preserve my life.
    In your righteousness bring me out of trouble.
12 In your steadfast love cut off my enemies,
    and destroy all my adversaries,
    for I am your servant.

Psalm 144

Of David.

1 Blessed be the LORD, my rock,
    who trains my hands for war, and my fingers for
      battle;
2 my rock*b* and my fortress,

a One Heb Ms Gk: MT *to you I have hidden*   *b* With 18.2 and 2 Sam 22.2:
Heb *my steadfast love*

my stronghold and my deliverer,
my shield, in whom I take refuge,
   who subdues the peoples[a] under me.

3 O LORD, what are human beings that you regard
      them,
   or mortals that you think of them?
4 They are like a breath;
   their days are like a passing shadow.

5 Bow your heavens, O LORD, and come down;
   touch the mountains so that they smoke.
6 Make the lightning flash and scatter them;
   send out your arrows and rout them.
7 Stretch out your hand from on high;
      set me free and rescue me from the mighty
         waters,
   from the hand of aliens,
8 whose mouths speak lies,
   and whose right hands are false.

9 I will sing a new song to you, O God;
   upon a ten-stringed harp I will play to you,
10 the one who gives victory to kings,
   who rescues his servant David.
11 Rescue me from the cruel sword,
      and deliver me from the hand of aliens,
   whose mouths speak lies,
      and whose right hands are false.

12 May our sons in their youth
      be like plants full grown,
   our daughters like corner pillars,
      cut for the building of a palace.
13 May our barns be filled,
      with produce of every kind;
   may our sheep increase by thousands,
      by tens of thousands in our fields,
14   and may our cattle be heavy with young.
   May there be no breach in the walls,[b] no exile,
      and no cry of distress in our streets.

15 Happy are the people to whom such blessings fall;
   happy are the people whose God is the LORD.

Psalm 145

Praise. Of David.

1 I will extol you, my God and King,
   and bless your name forever and ever.
2 Every day I will bless you,
   and praise your name forever and ever.
3 Great is the LORD, and greatly to be praised;
   his greatness is unsearchable.

4 One generation shall laud your works to another,
   and shall declare your mighty acts.

Across the Generations

PSALM 145.3–6

A gift from our Jewish spiritual heritage is its rich oral tradition. Grandparents tell their grandchildren the stories of creation, of the exodus, of God's provision in the desert and of God's continuing faithfulness. Likewise, the church has grown spiritually through telling and retelling the stories of Jesus. However, too often in our very own families we neglect to tell the meaningful stories of our own spiritual journeys. What stories of God's grace do you need to tell to someone in your family? What moments of awe at God's majesty and love in the past week do you need to share? How do you talk about your faith with loved ones?

See Meeting God in Everyday Life

---

a Heb Mss Syr Aquila Jerome: MT *my people*   *b* Heb lacks *in the walls*

The Spiritual Life

PSALM 146.3–6

"[A] spiritual life is a life which is controlled by a gradually developing sense of the Eternal, of God and his transcendent reality: an increasing capacity for him, so that our relation to God becomes the chief thing about us, exceeding and also conditioning our relationship with each other . . . For, what it means for us is surely this: that we are meant, beyond the physical, to contribute to, indeed collaborate in, God's spiritual creation."

—EVELYN UNDERHILL,
The Spiritual Life

5 On the glorious splendor of your majesty,
  and on your wondrous works, I will meditate.
6 The might of your awesome deeds shall be
    proclaimed,
  and I will declare your greatness.
7 They shall celebrate the fame of your abundant
    goodness,
  and shall sing aloud of your righteousness.

8 The LORD is gracious and merciful,
  slow to anger and abounding in steadfast love.
9 The LORD is good to all,
  and his compassion is over all that he has made.

10 All your works shall give thanks to you, O LORD,
   and all your faithful shall bless you.
11 They shall speak of the glory of your kingdom,
   and tell of your power,
12 to make known to all people your[a] mighty deeds,
   and the glorious splendor of your[b] kingdom.
13 Your kingdom is an everlasting kingdom,
   and your dominion endures throughout all
     generations.

The LORD is faithful in all his words,
  and gracious in all his deeds.[c]
14 The LORD upholds all who are falling,
   and raises up all who are bowed down.
15 The eyes of all look to you,
   and you give them their food in due season.
16 You open your hand,
   satisfying the desire of every living thing.
17 The LORD is just in all his ways,
   and kind in all his doings.
18 The LORD is near to all who call on him,
   to all who call on him in truth.
19 He fulfills the desire of all who fear him;
   he also hears their cry, and saves them.
20 The LORD watches over all who love him,
   but all the wicked he will destroy.

21 My mouth will speak the praise of the LORD,
   and all flesh will bless his holy name forever and
     ever.

Psalm 146

1 Praise the LORD!
  Praise the LORD, O my soul!
2 I will praise the LORD as long as I live;
  I will sing praises to my God all my life long.

3 Do not put your trust in princes,
  in mortals, in whom there is no help.
4 When their breath departs, they return to the earth;
  on that very day their plans perish.

---

a Gk Jerome Syr: Heb *his*   *b* Heb *his*   *c* These two lines supplied by
Q Ms Gk Syr

⁵ Happy are those whose help is the God of Jacob,
   whose hope is in the LORD their God,
⁶ who made heaven and earth,
   the sea, and all that is in them;
   who keeps faith forever;
⁷ who executes justice for the oppressed;
   who gives food to the hungry.

The LORD sets the prisoners free;
⁸ the LORD opens the eyes of the blind.
The LORD lifts up those who are bowed down;
   the LORD loves the righteous.
⁹ The LORD watches over the strangers;
   he upholds the orphan and the widow,
   but the way of the wicked he brings to ruin.

¹⁰ The LORD will reign forever,
   your God, O Zion, for all generations.
Praise the LORD!

Psalm 147

¹ Praise the LORD!
How good it is to sing praises to our God;
   for he is gracious, and a song of praise is fitting.
² The LORD builds up Jerusalem;
   he gathers the outcasts of Israel.
³ He heals the brokenhearted,
   and binds up their wounds.
⁴ He determines the number of the stars;
   he gives to all of them their names.
⁵ Great is our Lord, and abundant in power;
   his understanding is beyond measure.
⁶ The LORD lifts up the downtrodden;
   he casts the wicked to the ground.

⁷ Sing to the LORD with thanksgiving;
   make melody to our God on the lyre.
⁸ He covers the heavens with clouds,
   prepares rain for the earth,
   makes grass grow on the hills.
⁹ He gives to the animals their food,
   and to the young ravens when they cry.
¹⁰ His delight is not in the strength of the horse,
   nor his pleasure in the speed of a runner;[a]
¹¹ but the LORD takes pleasure in those who fear him,
   in those who hope in his steadfast love.

¹² Praise the LORD, O Jerusalem!
   Praise your God, O Zion!
¹³ For he strengthens the bars of your gates;
   he blesses your children within you.
¹⁴ He grants peace[b] within your borders;
   he fills you with the finest of wheat.
¹⁵ He sends out his command to the earth;
   his word runs swiftly.
¹⁶ He gives snow like wool;
   he scatters frost like ashes.

A Godly Balance

PSALM 147.3–6

The psalmist reflects on the amazing paradox: The God of the universe, who names the stars and has an understanding that "is beyond measure," is also concerned with each unique person, poor and grief-stricken as each may be. Even though there are billions of stars in the divine purview, God calls each one of us tenderly. God "heals the brokenhearted." What does this say about God's nature? What is the image of God that you see in your mind's eye? Take five minutes to reflect on this image, then share your thoughts and feelings in your journal or on a sheet of paper.

See Meeting God in the Created Order

a Heb *legs of a person*   *b* Or *prosperity*

It All Comes Down to Praise

PSALM 148.1–12

Praise is a refrain in the Psalms from beginning to end. Here, the psalmist calls all creation—animate and inanimate—to join a universal chorus of thanksgiving. Even sea creatures, stormy winds and small creatures are invited to sing along. The Psalms reveal that praise is a natural response to God's Word. Think of concrete ways by which you might praise God. Could you set aside a small table in a quiet room of your house where you place symbols of God's presence? Could you plant your garden as an act of worship? What creative offering of praise can you make?

See Meeting God in the Created Order

17 He hurls down hail like crumbs—
     who can stand before his cold?
18 He sends out his word, and melts them;
     he makes his wind blow, and the waters flow.
19 He declares his word to Jacob,
     his statutes and ordinances to Israel.
20 He has not dealt thus with any other nation;
     they do not know his ordinances.
     Praise the LORD!

Psalm 148

1 Praise the LORD!
   Praise the LORD from the heavens;
     praise him in the heights!
2 Praise him, all his angels;
     praise him, all his host!

3 Praise him, sun and moon;
     praise him, all you shining stars!
4 Praise him, you highest heavens,
     and you waters above the heavens!

5 Let them praise the name of the LORD,
     for he commanded and they were created.
6 He established them forever and ever;
     he fixed their bounds, which cannot be passed.*a*

7 Praise the LORD from the earth,
     you sea monsters and all deeps,
8 fire and hail, snow and frost,
     stormy wind fulfilling his command!

9 Mountains and all hills,
     fruit trees and all cedars!
10 Wild animals and all cattle,
     creeping things and flying birds!

11 Kings of the earth and all peoples,
     princes and all rulers of the earth!
12 Young men and women alike,
     old and young together!

13 Let them praise the name of the LORD,
     for his name alone is exalted;
     his glory is above earth and heaven.
14 He has raised up a horn for his people,
     praise for all his faithful,
     for the people of Israel who are close to him.
     Praise the LORD!

Psalm 149

1 Praise the LORD!
   Sing to the LORD a new song,
     his praise in the assembly of the faithful.
2 Let Israel be glad in its Maker;
     let the children of Zion rejoice in their King.

a Or he set a law that cannot pass away

³ Let them praise his name with dancing,
    making melody to him with tambourine and lyre.
⁴ For the LORD takes pleasure in his people;
    he adorns the humble with victory.
⁵ Let the faithful exult in glory;
    let them sing for joy on their couches.
⁶ Let the high praises of God be in their throats
    and two-edged swords in their hands,
⁷ to execute vengeance on the nations
    and punishment on the peoples,
⁸ to bind their kings with fetters
    and their nobles with chains of iron,
⁹ to execute on them the judgment decreed.
    This is glory for all his faithful ones.
    Praise the LORD!

Psalm 150

¹ Praise the LORD!
    Praise God in his sanctuary;
        praise him in his mighty firmament!ᵃ
² Praise him for his mighty deeds;
    praise him according to his surpassing greatness!

³ Praise him with trumpet sound;
    praise him with lute and harp!
⁴ Praise him with tambourine and dance;
    praise him with strings and pipe!
⁵ Praise him with clanging cymbals;
    praise him with loud clashing cymbals!
⁶ Let everything that breathes praise the LORD!
    Praise the LORD!

Clanging Cymbals

PSALM 150.1–6

Noise pollution is a growing problem today. Airplanes fly over residential neighborhoods, music blares from open car windows and even our Saturday morning quiet is broken by buzzing power tools. But loud sounds can also be offered to God in worship. To rejoice with your whole heart may take your loudest voice and your brassiest instruments—trumpets, tambourines and loud clashing cymbals. How do you make music to the God of the universe? How do you declare your praise? During a period of time when you can be alone, or perhaps together with a few close friends, experiment with loud worship.

---

a Or *dome*

WAYS of MEETING GOD

Meeting God in the Created Order

A man, weary with responsibilities, slips out of his front door and makes his way to a neighborhood park. Walking through dappled sunlight and shade and breathing deeply of the fresh air, he begins to relax. He thinks about all of his obligations and commitments and begins to gain perspective on his schedule. He senses God's Spirit refreshing him.

A child who lives in a difficult family situation finds refuge and solace in a backyard garden. Jesus is her companion. The quiet beauty of the flowers and the pungency of the herbs assure her of his presence. She tells him about her confusion and pain and knows that he understands.

A woman wakes up at dawn. Hearing birds calling, she opens the tent flap to gaze at a vista she hiked eight miles to see. Rose-gold streaks of light glance off mountain peaks and are mirrored in the still lake before her. The sheer extravagance of the beauty she beholds so grips her that words melt away. She finds herself drawn into wordless, awestruck communion with God.

Have you experienced something similar? From the dawn of civilization, human beings have encountered God's divine presence in the natural world. Poets and mystics of every age have seen God in the orderliness, splendor and mystery of creation. The wonders of earth and sky reminded them—as they remind us—of God's transcendence and holiness. "Earth's crammed with heaven," wrote the poet Elizabeth Barrett Browning, "and every common bush afire with God."

Scripture offers an abundance of insight into the practice of meeting God in the created order. Our

> **P**oets and mystics of every age have seen God in the orderliness, splendor and mystery of creation. The wonders of earth and sky reminded them—as they remind us—of God's transcendence and holiness.

understanding grows from the Biblical teachings concerning God's creation of the universe, humankind's fall from grace, Jesus' saving work and the restoration of all things at the end of time.

The Order of Creation. This world is the theater for the display of God's majesty and holiness. The psalmist wrote,

> The heavens are telling the glory of God;
> and the firmament proclaims his handiwork.
> Day to day pours forth speech,
> and night to night declares knowledge.
> There is no speech, nor are there words;
> their voice is not heard;
> yet their voice goes out through all the earth,
> and their words to the end of the world.—Psalm 19.1–4

The psalmist David knew well that the creation communicates volumes about the Creator, for everything God has made bears the stamp of divine wisdom, power and love. The God who is "unsearchable" (see Romans 11.33) becomes known in part through "his handiwork." Writes the apostle Paul, "Ever since the creation of the world his eternal power and divine nature, invisible thought they are, have been understood and seen through the things he has made" (Romans 1.20).

Time and again the Christian church has affirmed this intimate relationship between the Creator and creation. Eastern Orthodox churches teach that God made all matter to be "Spirit-bearing"; it can therefore communicate God's grace and presence. The Celtic Christianity of the British Isles developed a spiritual path known for earthiness—praying while kindling a hearth fire, milking a cow or tilling the ground. The early monk Benedict viewed life from a similar perspective. Benedictines (as his followers are called) encouraged people to see God in and through the ordinariness of daily work. Francis of Assisi in the thirteenth century is renowned for his love of every creature, each of whom he counted as a brother or sister. Francis preached to birds and animals, believing that the whole of creation was subject to redemption. Centuries later the Swiss Protestant reformer John Calvin wrote, "Wherever you cast your eyes, there is no spot in the universe wherein you cannot discern at least some sparks of [God's] glory." All of these diverse Christian traditions suggest an earth that is truly "crammed with heaven." The nineteenth-century Jesuit poet Gerard Manley Hopkins expressed this idea: "The earth is filled with the grandeur of God. It will flame out, like shining from shook foil."

One of the simplest ways to meet God is to contemplate his creation. Looking out of a window, taking a walk under the stars or going for a leisurely drive reminds us that the hand of the Artist is revealed in the art. Sea lions and hyacinths, volcanoes and hummingbirds speak volumes about the creative imagination of the God who made them. Contemplating the wonder of creation can move us to pray more deeply: "Through every grass blade in the thousand, thousand grasses . . . through the song-notes and the marked feathers of the birds . . . through the soft warm air, the flecks of clouds dissolving—I used them all for prayer" wrote Richard Jefferies.

The more we see God's character and purpose revealed in each living creature, the greater our wonder and gratitude. Indeed, it seems as though everything exists to praise God. Angels and all heavenly beings; sun, moon and stars; mountains and waters; birds, beasts and sea creatures; every kind of weather; women and men, young and old—all are fashioned to praise the Creator we see in creation (see Psalm 148).

The Crown of Creation. The creation stories in Genesis show how God gives preeminence to human beings in the created order. Indeed, we were fashioned as the final act of the drama of creation—the crown of creation that bears the stamp of God's own image and likeness. We do not comprehend fully what it means to be made in the divine image, but we do know that God confers extraordinary dignity on us. In Psalm 8, David muses on the wonderful fact that human beings, seemingly so insignificant in comparison to the vast marvels of this universe, should have been made but "a little lower than God" (Psalm 8.5). Truly we are "fearfully and wonderfully made" (Psalm 139.14).

Yet while we were created to reflect the very goodness of God, we know that human beings have lost the ability to reflect anything but a distorted image of him. The Bible states clearly that human sin has tragic consequences for the whole of creation:

> The earth dries up and withers,
>   the world languishes . . .
> The earth lies polluted
>   under its inhabitants;
> for they have transgressed laws . . .
> [and] broken the everlasting covenant.
> Therefore a curse devours the earth,
>   and its inhabitants suffer for their guilt.
>
> —Isaiah 24.4–6

No century has demonstrated this reality more clearly than the twentieth. Greed and injustice have brought the earth's ecosystems to the edge of peril.

Just as we can reflect on what creation may reveal to us of *God's* character, so we can ask what God may reveal to us through creation about *our* character. Are we wisely using the resources we have been given? Do we really believe that creation reflects God's glory—enough to preserve its beauty so that all people can see God? Should we interpret the earth's distress signals as a call to repentance?

Looking out a window, taking a walk under the stars or going for a leisurely drive reminds us that the hand of the Artist is revealed in the art.

822

Because the order of creation has been fractured by sin, we look to the order of salvation for its healing. Jesus Christ is God's answer to the groans of a creation subjected to the "bondage [of] decay" (Romans 8.21). Jesus "is the image of the invisible God, the firstborn of all creation" (Colossians 1.15). In him the clarity and purity of the image of God are restored to us. But Jesus embodies more than merely our true humanity in God. He is also the One in whom "all things have been created, both in heaven and on earth" (v.16) and in whom "all things hold together" (v.17). As Paul declares, "through him God was pleased to reconcile to himself all things, whether on earth or in heaven" (v.20). And Jesus' coming points to the future restoration of the entire created order. Our salvation in Jesus Christ includes a promise whose full flower we cannot yet see. By hope we believe the seed of redemption will bear fruit in the transfiguration of all that we know and experience. God's creation will one day become what it was intended to be.

The Bodies God Has Made. We must take seriously another implication of the miracle of incarnation—that Jesus took on the form and body of a human being. God's Word "became flesh and lived among us" (John 1.14). This event makes the human body—bones, tendons, blood cells, heart, brain—a chosen instrument of salvation. God sees it as a worthy vehicle for the completion of divine purposes. We may not, then, dismiss or denigrate our bodies. Indeed, Jesus speaks of his own body as the temple of God (see John 2.21). Paul tells the Corinthians that they, too, are God's temple because God's Spirit dwells in them (see 1 Corinthians 3.16–17). Therefore, we must think of our bodies and spirits as an integrated being, and we must care for our whole self. How we treat our physical selves—eating a balanced diet, exercising regularly, getting enough sleep—has spiritual implications. We honor God in our bodies when we keep the sabbath holy, taking a day each week to cease from labor and to worship and enjoy God's gifts. In our hard driving, stress-filled culture in which we tend to value ourselves and others on the basis of what we produce, rest becomes all the more essential; the wisdom of the Sabbath commandment becomes more readily apparent.

The fact that we sometimes find it hard to draw back from our frantic schedules only makes it more necessary to ensure that we set aside a time for rest. Place your cares in God's capable hands, then take time to pray and to play. Enjoy your most precious relationships.

Even more, rest in God and contemplate the beauty and mystery of life. Allow yourself to be absorbed by the innocent delight of a toddler's face, the quiet of an evening sky, the brilliant hues of an autumn leaf. God's creation is to be enjoyed as we let it point us back in reverence to the glorious mystery of the One who brought it into being.

See Page 1086 for the next Ways of Meeting God *article.*

PROVERBS

Wisdom Day by Day

KEY VERSE:

*The beginning of wisdom is this: Get wisdom, and whatever else you get,
get insight.—Proverbs 4.7*

"My soul's house is cramped.
Expand it, so that you may
enter in. It is in ruins. Restore
it. It must offend your eyes. I
confess and know it, but who
will cleanse it? To whom shall
I cry but to you? Clear me from
hidden faults, O Lord, and keep
back your servant also from
those of others."

—AUGUSTINE,
Confessions

Proverbs is perhaps the most practical book in
the Bible. These words of wisdom grew out of
the common experiences of human life. The
teachers of ancient times were eager to share what
they had learned about life. Their insights helped
them in their daily living and in their relationships.
The reward of wisdom is a better and happier life.
Thus, this "treasure" is more precious than silver or
gold and worthy of passing on. The sayings here
cover a variety of themes: love, friendship, marriage, poverty, wealth, and others.

Individual proverbs summarize wisdom that has
been proven true in varied situations. But they are
not absolute or applicable in every circumstance. If
not taken in proper context, some may even contradict each other: "Too many cooks spoil the broth,"
but "Many hands make light work." True wisdom is
not simply knowing the sayings of the wise but also
knowing when and how to apply them.

Some proverbs may trouble us. The question of
why evil besets innocent people, for example, may
continue to baffle and disturb us as we meditate on
some adages in this book. Nevertheless, the wisdom
we find here can help us walk in the Spirit in the
midst of our doubts and all that life offers—good or
bad. Remember that getting insight does not mean
finding quick answers. As you read and ponder,
allow your soul, heart and mind to wrestle with the
sages and, like Jacob wrestling with an angel, to
hold on until you receive a blessing.

1

The proverbs of Solomon son of David, king of Israel:

Prologue

2 For learning about wisdom and instruction,
      for understanding words of insight,
3 for gaining instruction in wise dealing,
      righteousness, justice, and equity;
4 to teach shrewdness to the simple,
      knowledge and prudence to the young—
5 let the wise also hear and gain in learning,
      and the discerning acquire skill,
6 to understand a proverb and a figure,
      the words of the wise and their riddles.

7 The fear of the LORD is the beginning of
         knowledge;
      fools despise wisdom and instruction.

Warnings against Evil Companions

8 Hear, my child, your father's instruction,
      and do not reject your mother's teaching;
9 for they are a fair garland for your head,
      and pendants for your neck.
10 My child, if sinners entice you,
      do not consent.
11 If they say, "Come with us, let us lie in wait for
         blood;
      let us wantonly ambush the innocent;
12 like Sheol let us swallow them alive
      and whole, like those who go down to the Pit.
13 We shall find all kinds of costly things;
      we shall fill our houses with booty.
14 Throw in your lot among us;
      we will all have one purse"—
15 my child, do not walk in their way,
      keep your foot from their paths;
16 for their feet run to evil,
      and they hurry to shed blood.
17 For in vain is the net baited
      while the bird is looking on;
18 yet they lie in wait—to kill themselves!
      and set an ambush—for their own lives!
19 Such is the end^a of all who are greedy for gain;
      it takes away the life of its possessors.

The Call of Wisdom

20 Wisdom cries out in the street;
      in the squares she raises her voice.
21 At the busiest corner she cries out;
      at the entrance of the city gates she speaks:
22 "How long, O simple ones, will you love being
         simple?
      How long will scoffers delight in their scoffing

a Gk: Heb are the ways

Parental Teaching

PROVERBS 1.8–9

For good or for ill, much of who we are—how we think and behave—comes from our parents or others who raised us. In the midst of a conversation we may think, "I sound just like my mother." We may try to clinch an argument with, "Well, that's what my father always said."

Think of recent times when you have "heard" your parents' voices guiding you. What are some of the bits of wisdom you have received from them? Some "parental proverbs" may be sources of great strength or steadiness. Take time to give God thanks for these gifts. Other parental "teachings" may have trained you for prejudice or fearfulness. Ask God for help in discerning the difference. Ask God to let the wisdom of Proverbs become a source of insight and delight.

See Meeting God in Everyday Life

Wisdom's Invitation

PROVERBS 1.20–33

Wisdom (a feminine noun in Hebrew) is depicted as a woman so eager to attract listeners that she raises her voice out on the streets. Imagine yourself there, listening to her call as she offers you the gift of God's wisdom. In what areas of your life are you particularly in need of wisdom? What is holding you back from seeking God's help? The simple would rather not waste the energy required to think deeply. Scoffers turn their backs on God. Fools prefer to live by their own wits. Why do you hesitate to accept wisdom's offer? Ask God for help in employing wisdom in the choices you will face today.

See Meeting God in Scripture

and fools hate knowledge?
23 Give heed to my reproof;
  I will pour out my thoughts to you;
  I will make my words known to you.
24 Because I have called and you refused,
    have stretched out my hand and no one heeded,
25 and because you have ignored all my counsel
    and would have none of my reproof,
26 I also will laugh at your calamity;
    I will mock when panic strikes you,
27 when panic strikes you like a storm,
    and your calamity comes like a whirlwind,
    when distress and anguish come upon you.
28 Then they will call upon me, but I will not answer;
    they will seek me diligently, but will not find me.
29 Because they hated knowledge
    and did not choose the fear of the LORD,
30 would have none of my counsel,
    and despised all my reproof,
31 therefore they shall eat the fruit of their way
    and be sated with their own devices.
32 For waywardness kills the simple,
    and the complacency of fools destroys them;
33 but those who listen to me will be secure
    and will live at ease, without dread of disaster."

The Value of Wisdom

2 My child, if you accept my words
  and treasure up my commandments within you,
2 making your ear attentive to wisdom
    and inclining your heart to understanding;
3 if you indeed cry out for insight,
    and raise your voice for understanding;
4 if you seek it like silver,
    and search for it as for hidden treasures—
5 then you will understand the fear of the LORD
    and find the knowledge of God.
6 For the LORD gives wisdom;
    from his mouth come knowledge and understanding;
7 he stores up sound wisdom for the upright;
    he is a shield to those who walk blamelessly,
8 guarding the paths of justice
    and preserving the way of his faithful ones.
9 Then you will understand righteousness and justice
    and equity, every good path;
10 for wisdom will come into your heart,
    and knowledge will be pleasant to your soul;
11 prudence will watch over you;
    and understanding will guard you.
12 It will save you from the way of evil,
    from those who speak perversely,

13 who forsake the paths of uprightness
 to walk in the ways of darkness,
14 who rejoice in doing evil
 and delight in the perverseness of evil;
15 those whose paths are crooked,
 and who are devious in their ways.

16 You will be saved from the loose*a* woman,
 from the adulteress with her smooth words,
17 who forsakes the partner of her youth
 and forgets her sacred covenant;
18 for her way*b* leads down to death,
 and her paths to the shades;
19 those who go to her never come back,
 nor do they regain the paths of life.

20 Therefore walk in the way of the good,
 and keep to the paths of the just.
21 For the upright will abide in the land,
 and the innocent will remain in it;
22 but the wicked will be cut off from the land,
 and the treacherous will be rooted out of it.

Admonition to Trust and Honor God

3 My child, do not forget my teaching,
 but let your heart keep my commandments;
2 for length of days and years of life
 and abundant welfare they will give you.

3 Do not let loyalty and faithfulness forsake you;
 bind them around your neck,
 write them on the tablet of your heart.
4 So you will find favor and good repute
 in the sight of God and of people.

5 Trust in the LORD with all your heart,
 and do not rely on your own insight.
6 In all your ways acknowledge him,
 and he will make straight your paths.
7 Do not be wise in your own eyes;
 fear the LORD, and turn away from evil.
8 It will be a healing for your flesh
 and a refreshment for your body.

9 Honor the LORD with your substance
 and with the first fruits of all your produce;
10 then your barns will be filled with plenty,
 and your vats will be bursting with wine.

11 My child, do not despise the LORD's discipline
 or be weary of his reproof,
12 for the LORD reproves the one he loves,
 as a father the son in whom he delights.

a Heb strange b Cn: Heb house

Trust and Obey

PROVERBS 3.5–7

"If a faithful soul accepts God's will and purpose in all simplicity, he will reach perfection without ever realizing it, just as a sick person who swallows his medicine obediently will be cured, although he neither knows nor cares about medicine."

—JEAN-PIERRE DE CAUSSADE,
Abandonment to Divine Providence

Being a Good Neighbor

PROVERBS 3.27–30

Proverbs can be extremely practical and down-to-earth. Take these proverbs about how to deal with neighbors. They tell us to help when we can, not when we want, and according to our neighbors' needs, not according to our feeling of generosity. In short, we should love our neighbors. Yet in our mobile, busy society, we often do not even know who our neighbors are.

Who are your neighbors? Do you know them well enough to name them before God? To lift up their concerns and needs? You might draw a small map of your immediate neighborhood, labeling other houses (or neighboring apartments) as well as you can. What steps do you need to take to be able to fill it in more completely? Post the map where it will remind you to pray for your neighbors regularly. Ask God to let this discipline guide you in being a better neighbor to them.

See Meeting God in Service

The True Wealth

13 Happy are those who find wisdom,
   and those who get understanding,

14 for her income is better than silver,
   and her revenue better than gold.

15 She is more precious than jewels,
   and nothing you desire can compare with her.

16 Long life is in her right hand;
   in her left hand are riches and honor.

17 Her ways are ways of pleasantness,
   and all her paths are peace.

18 She is a tree of life to those who lay hold of her;
   those who hold her fast are called happy.

God's Wisdom in Creation

19 The Lord by wisdom founded the earth;
   by understanding he established the heavens;

20 by his knowledge the deeps broke open,
   and the clouds drop down the dew.

The True Security

21 My child, do not let these escape from your sight:
   keep sound wisdom and prudence,

22 and they will be life for your soul
   and adornment for your neck.

23 Then you will walk on your way securely
   and your foot will not stumble.

24 If you sit down,*a* you will not be afraid;
   when you lie down, your sleep will be sweet.

25 Do not be afraid of sudden panic,
   or of the storm that strikes the wicked;

26 for the Lord will be your confidence
   and will keep your foot from being caught.

27 Do not withhold good from those to whom it is due,*b*
   when it is in your power to do it.

28 Do not say to your neighbor, "Go, and come again,
   tomorrow I will give it"—when you have it with you.

29 Do not plan harm against your neighbor
   who lives trustingly beside you.

30 Do not quarrel with anyone without cause,
   when no harm has been done to you.

31 Do not envy the violent
   and do not choose any of their ways;

32 for the perverse are an abomination to the Lord,
   but the upright are in his confidence.

33 The Lord's curse is on the house of the wicked,
   but he blesses the abode of the righteous.

34 Toward the scorners he is scornful,
   but to the humble he shows favor.

a Gk: Heb *lie down*   *b* Heb *from its owners*

35 The wise will inherit honor,
  but stubborn fools, disgrace.

Parental Advice

4 Listen, children, to a father's instruction,
  and be attentive, that you may gain[a] insight;
2 for I give you good precepts:
  do not forsake my teaching.
3 When I was a son with my father,
  tender, and my mother's favorite,
4 he taught me, and said to me,
  "Let your heart hold fast my words;
  keep my commandments, and live.
5 Get wisdom; get insight: do not forget, nor turn
  away
  from the words of my mouth.
6 Do not forsake her, and she will keep you;
  love her, and she will guard you.
7 The beginning of wisdom is this: Get wisdom,
  and whatever else you get, get insight.
8 Prize her highly, and she will exalt you;
  she will honor you if you embrace her.
9 She will place on your head a fair garland;
  she will bestow on you a beautiful crown."

Admonition to Keep to the Right Path

10 Hear, my child, and accept my words,
  that the years of your life may be many.
11 I have taught you the way of wisdom;
  I have led you in the paths of uprightness.
12 When you walk, your step will not be hampered;
  and if you run, you will not stumble.
13 Keep hold of instruction; do not let go;
  guard her, for she is your life.
14 Do not enter the path of the wicked,
  and do not walk in the way of evildoers.
15 Avoid it; do not go on it;
  turn away from it and pass on.
16 For they cannot sleep unless they have done
  wrong;
  they are robbed of sleep unless they have made
  someone stumble.
17 For they eat the bread of wickedness
  and drink the wine of violence.
18 But the path of the righteous is like the light of
  dawn,
  which shines brighter and brighter until full
  day.
19 The way of the wicked is like deep darkness;
  they do not know what they stumble over.
20 My child, be attentive to my words;
  incline your ear to my sayings.
21 Do not let them escape from your sight;
  keep them within your heart.

a Heb *know*

Succeeding in God's Way

PROVERBS 4.10–27

Throughout life we have been given much advice about what to do and what not to do. Much of it is aimed at helping us succeed in life. But life is more than being successful. The wise teacher knows there is a better way. Read this passage again, slowly and reflectively. What words or phrases are most meaningful to you? Write down three key words or phrases on a small piece of paper. Fold it and put it in your pocket or keep it handy so that throughout the day you may take it out and read it. Make the words or phrases your own. Begin now to succeed in God's way.

See Meeting God in Scripture

Attractive Foolishness

PROVERBS 5.7–14

These proverbs pull no punches. Foolishness, they freely admit, can be very attractive, even seductive. Furthermore, it seems so much easier, so much less demanding. Clearly, foolishness has much more advertising potential than wisdom.

Ask God to let wisdom walk with you today, pointing out the ways foolishness calls to you. Pay attention to the seductive claims of advertisements. Which ones do you find particularly tempting? Let wisdom lead you away. Listen to her reproof when you give in to temptation. Try to take no action today without first seeking God's wisdom.

See Meeting God in Everyday Life

22 For they are life to those who find them,
   and healing to all their flesh.
23 Keep your heart with all vigilance,
   for from it flow the springs of life.
24 Put away from you crooked speech,
   and put devious talk far from you.
25 Let your eyes look directly forward,
   and your gaze be straight before you.
26 Keep straight the path of your feet,
   and all your ways will be sure.
27 Do not swerve to the right or to the left;
   turn your foot away from evil.

Warning against Impurity and Infidelity

5 My child, be attentive to my wisdom;
   incline your ear to my understanding,
2 so that you may hold on to prudence,
   and your lips may guard knowledge.
3 For the lips of a loose*a* woman drip honey,
   and her speech is smoother than oil;
4 but in the end she is bitter as wormwood,
   sharp as a two-edged sword.
5 Her feet go down to death;
   her steps follow the path to Sheol.
6 She does not keep straight to the path of life;
   her ways wander, and she does not know it.

7 And now, my child,*b* listen to me,
   and do not depart from the words of my mouth.
8 Keep your way far from her,
   and do not go near the door of her house;
9 or you will give your honor to others,
   and your years to the merciless,
10 and strangers will take their fill of your wealth,
   and your labors will go to the house of an alien;
11 and at the end of your life you will groan,
   when your flesh and body are consumed,
12 and you say, "Oh, how I hated discipline,
   and my heart despised reproof!
13 I did not listen to the voice of my teachers
   or incline my ear to my instructors.
14 Now I am at the point of utter ruin
   in the public assembly."

15 Drink water from your own cistern,
   flowing water from your own well.
16 Should your springs be scattered abroad,
   streams of water in the streets?
17 Let them be for yourself alone,
   and not for sharing with strangers.
18 Let your fountain be blessed,
   and rejoice in the wife of your youth,
19 a lovely deer, a graceful doe.
   May her breasts satisfy you at all times;

a Heb *strange*   *b* Gk Vg: Heb *children*

may you be intoxicated always by her love.

20 Why should you be intoxicated, my son, by another woman
   and embrace the bosom of an adulteress?

21 For human ways are under the eyes of the LORD,
   and he examines all their paths.

22 The iniquities of the wicked ensnare them,
   and they are caught in the toils of their sin.

23 They die for lack of discipline,
   and because of their great folly they are lost.

Practical Admonitions

6 My child, if you have given your pledge to your neighbor,
   if you have bound yourself to another,[a]

2 you are snared by the utterance of your lips,[b]
   caught by the words of your mouth.

3 So do this, my child, and save yourself,
   for you have come into your neighbor's power:
   go, hurry,[c] and plead with your neighbor.

4 Give your eyes no sleep
   and your eyelids no slumber;

5 save yourself like a gazelle from the hunter,[d]
   like a bird from the hand of the fowler.

6 Go to the ant, you lazybones;
   consider its ways, and be wise.

7 Without having any chief
   or officer or ruler,

8 it prepares its food in summer,
   and gathers its sustenance in harvest.

9 How long will you lie there, O lazybones?
   When will you rise from your sleep?

10 A little sleep, a little slumber,
   a little folding of the hands to rest,

11 and poverty will come upon you like a robber,
   and want, like an armed warrior.

12 A scoundrel and a villain
   goes around with crooked speech,

13 winking the eyes, shuffling the feet,
   pointing the fingers,

14 with perverted mind devising evil,
   continually sowing discord;

15 on such a one calamity will descend suddenly;
   in a moment, damage beyond repair.

16 There are six things that the LORD hates,
   seven that are an abomination to him:

17 haughty eyes, a lying tongue,
   and hands that shed innocent blood,

18 a heart that devises wicked plans,
   feet that hurry to run to evil,

A Look Inward

PROVERBS 6.16–19

To take an honest look at one's life can be uncomfortable. Scripture has a way of touching a sensitive nerve and making one feel vulnerable. These verses list actions that are offensive to God. They point out exactly what the Lord hates. The teachers of wisdom want to help their listeners take an honest look inward and to discover for themselves if there is anything in them that is causing Almighty God pain.

After reading these verses, sit quietly. Let God hold you as you take stock of each of the seven behaviors. In what ways do you see them in your own actions? In what ways do you need to seek God's forgiveness? In what ways do you need to ask forgiveness from others? Allow yourself to experience God's love, forgiveness and transforming grace.

---

a Or *a stranger*   *b* Cn Compare Gk Syr: Heb *the words of your mouth*
c Or *humble yourself*   *d* Cn: Heb *from the hand*

Seeking Wisdom

PROVERBS 7.1–4

The beginning of wisdom is the most sincere desire for instruction, and concern for instruction is love of her, and love of her is the keeping of her laws, and giving heed to her laws is assurance of immortality, and immortality brings one near to God; so the desire for wisdom leads to a kingdom.

—*Wisdom of Solomon, Old Testament Apocrypha, NRSV*

19 a lying witness who testifies falsely,
　　and one who sows discord in a family.

20 My child, keep your father's commandment,
　　and do not forsake your mother's teaching.
21 Bind them upon your heart always;
　　tie them around your neck.
22 When you walk, they*a* will lead you;
　　when you lie down, they*a* will watch over you;
　　and when you awake, they*a* will talk with you.
23 For the commandment is a lamp and the
　　　teaching a light,
　　and the reproofs of discipline are the way of
　　　life,
24 to preserve you from the wife of another,*b*
　　from the smooth tongue of the adulteress.
25 Do not desire her beauty in your heart,
　　and do not let her capture you with her
　　　eyelashes;
26 for a prostitute's fee is only a loaf of bread,*c*
　　but the wife of another stalks a man's very life.
27 Can fire be carried in the bosom
　　without burning one's clothes?
28 Or can one walk on hot coals
　　without scorching the feet?
29 So is he who sleeps with his neighbor's wife;
　　no one who touches her will go unpunished.
30 Thieves are not despised who steal only
　　to satisfy their appetite when they are hungry.
31 Yet if they are caught, they will pay sevenfold;
　　they will forfeit all the goods of their house.
32 But he who commits adultery has no sense;
　　he who does it destroys himself.
33 He will get wounds and dishonor,
　　and his disgrace will not be wiped away.
34 For jealousy arouses a husband's fury,
　　and he shows no restraint when he takes
　　　revenge.
35 He will accept no compensation,
　　and refuses a bribe no matter how great.

The False Attractions of Adultery

7 My child, keep my words
　　and store up my commandments with you;
2 keep my commandments and live,
　　keep my teachings as the apple of your eye;
3 bind them on your fingers,
　　write them on the tablet of your heart.
4 Say to wisdom, "You are my sister,"
　　and call insight your intimate friend,
5 that they may keep you from the loose*d* woman,
　　from the adulteress with her smooth words.

a Heb *it*　*b* Gk: MT *the evil woman*　*c* Cn Compare Gk Syr Vg Tg: Heb *for because of a harlot to a piece of bread*　*d* Heb *strange*

6   For at the window of my house
       I looked out through my lattice,
7   and I saw among the simple ones,
       I observed among the youths,
       a young man without sense,
8   passing along the street near her corner,
       taking the road to her house
9   in the twilight, in the evening,
       at the time of night and darkness.

10 Then a woman comes toward him,
       decked out like a prostitute, wily of heart.[a]
11 She is loud and wayward;
       her feet do not stay at home;
12 now in the street, now in the squares,
       and at every corner she lies in wait.
13 She seizes him and kisses him,
       and with impudent face she says to him:
14 "I had to offer sacrifices,
       and today I have paid my vows;
15 so now I have come out to meet you,
       to seek you eagerly, and I have found you!
16 I have decked my couch with coverings,
       colored spreads of Egyptian linen;
17 I have perfumed my bed with myrrh,
       aloes, and cinnamon.
18 Come, let us take our fill of love until morning;
       let us delight ourselves with love.
19 For my husband is not at home;
       he has gone on a long journey.
20 He took a bag of money with him;
       he will not come home until full moon."

21 With much seductive speech she persuades him;
       with her smooth talk she compels him.
22 Right away he follows her,
       and goes like an ox to the slaughter,
   or bounds like a stag toward the trap[b]
23   until an arrow pierces its entrails.
   He is like a bird rushing into a snare,
       not knowing that it will cost him his life.

24 And now, my children, listen to me,
       and be attentive to the words of my mouth.
25 Do not let your hearts turn aside to her ways;
       do not stray into her paths.
26 for many are those she has laid low,
       and numerous are her victims.
27 Her house is the way to Sheol,
       going down to the chambers of death.

An Evening Review

PROVERBS 8.5–8

This passage might be a good starting place for a review of the day. Think back over the last twenty-four hours. What have you learned? What wisdom have you gained? Now think about the things you have said, the conversations you have had. Have you spoken "noble things" and uttered truth? Or has wickedness come from your lips? Listen to yourself and let God's wisdom comment on what you hear yourself saying. Where do you need forgiveness or guidance? You might conclude with the psalmist's plea, "May the words of my mouth and the meditation of my heart be pleasing in your sight, O Lord, my rock and my redeemer" (Psalm 19.14).

See Meeting God in Scripture

---

a Meaning of Heb uncertain   *b* Cn Compare Gk: Meaning of Heb uncertain

Wisdom at Creation

PROVERBS 8.22–31

Use your imagination to enter into this passage. Picture the earth, fresh and new. Imagine God looking out upon this world and pronouncing each and every aspect "Good!" Now see wisdom dancing with delight at the wonder of the world. Join in that dance of delight, at least in your imagination, echoing wisdom's praise of God's goodness in making the world and the people in it. You might want to get up and dance or spin with a small child's enthusiasm. God delights in your rejoicing.

See *Meeting God in Scripture*

The Gifts of Wisdom

8 Does not wisdom call,
  and does not understanding raise her voice?
2 On the heights, beside the way,
  at the crossroads she takes her stand;
3 beside the gates in front of the town,
  at the entrance of the portals she cries out:
4 "To you, O people, I call,
  and my cry is to all that live.
5 O simple ones, learn prudence;
  acquire intelligence, you who lack it.
6 Hear, for I will speak noble things,
  and from my lips will come what is right;
7 for my mouth will utter truth;
  wickedness is an abomination to my lips.
8 All the words of my mouth are righteous;
  there is nothing twisted or crooked in them.
9 They are all straight to one who understands
  and right to those who find knowledge.
10 Take my instruction instead of silver,
  and knowledge rather than choice gold;
11 for wisdom is better than jewels,
  and all that you may desire cannot compare
    with her.
12 I, wisdom, live with prudence,*a*
  and I attain knowledge and discretion.
13 The fear of the Lord is hatred of evil.
  Pride and arrogance and the way of evil
    and perverted speech I hate.
14 I have good advice and sound wisdom;
  I have insight, I have strength.
15 By me kings reign,
  and rulers decree what is just;
16 by me rulers rule,
  and nobles, all who govern rightly.
17 I love those who love me,
  and those who seek me diligently find me.
18 Riches and honor are with me,
  enduring wealth and prosperity.
19 My fruit is better than gold, even fine gold,
  and my yield than choice silver.
20 I walk in the way of righteousness,
  along the paths of justice,
21 endowing with wealth those who love me,
  and filling their treasuries.

Wisdom's Part in Creation

22 The Lord created me at the beginning*b* of his
    work,*c*
  the first of his acts of long ago.
23 Ages ago I was set up,
  at the first, before the beginning of the earth.

a Meaning of Heb uncertain   *b* Or *me as the beginning*   *c* Heb *way*

24 When there were no depths I was brought forth,
   when there were no springs abounding with
      water.
25 Before the mountains had been shaped,
   before the hills, I was brought forth—
26 when he had not yet made earth and fields,*a*
   or the world's first bits of soil.
27 When he established the heavens, I was there,
   when he drew a circle on the face of the deep,
28 when he made firm the skies above,
   when he established the fountains of the deep,
29 when he assigned to the sea its limit,
   so that the waters might not transgress his
      command,
   when he marked out the foundations of the earth,
30 then I was beside him, like a master worker;*b*
   and I was daily his*c* delight,
   rejoicing before him always,
31 rejoicing in his inhabited world
   and delighting in the human race.

32 "And now, my children, listen to me:
   happy are those who keep my ways.
33 Hear instruction and be wise,
   and do not neglect it.
34 Happy is the one who listens to me,
   watching daily at my gates,
   waiting beside my doors.
35 For whoever finds me finds life
   and obtains favor from the LORD;
36 but those who miss me injure themselves;
   all who hate me love death."

Wisdom's Feast

9 Wisdom has built her house,
   she has hewn her seven pillars.
2 She has slaughtered her animals, she has mixed
      her wine,
   she has also set her table.
3 She has sent out her servant-girls, she calls
   from the highest places in the town,
4 "You that are simple, turn in here!"
   To those without sense she says,
5 "Come, eat of my bread
   and drink of the wine I have mixed.
6 Lay aside immaturity,*d* and live,
   and walk in the way of insight."

General Maxims

7 Whoever corrects a scoffer wins abuse;
   whoever rebukes the wicked gets hurt.
8 A scoffer who is rebuked will only hate you;
   the wise, when rebuked, will love you.

Walking by Insight

PROVERBS 9.6

Many magazines from time to time print self-assessment questionnaires to help readers gauge their level of maturity. We may choose to ponder the results and gain some insights about ourselves from them or we may decide to ignore them. The problem is not so much knowing what we need to do but rather choosing to do it. The sages of old counseled their hearers to lay aside immaturity lest it negatively affect their way of living.

What immature ways of thinking and living do you cling to? What is one thing you can begin to do today to think and behave in a more mature fashion? Ask for God's help. You might use the following brief prayer: "I need God's sense of order. I need God's sense. I need God." Copy this prayer and keep it to use when habits of immaturity creep back into your life.

See Meeting God in Everyday Life

a Meaning of Heb uncertain   b Another reading is *little child*
c Gk: Heb lacks *his*   d Or *simpleness*

Hatred and Love

PROVERBS 10.12

Picture a kettle boiling over a fire. Let the kettle represent your soul, the fire your anger. As the contents boil, what old hurts or resentments bubble up to the surface? How long have they been there? Imagine putting a cover on the pot and holding it firmly in place. The contents boil even more furiously. Simply covering the pot is not enough; you have to put out the fire. Now ask God to pour his love over the kettle and the fire. At first you may see only steam, but gradually God's love quenches the fire, and the contents of the kettle stops boiling furiously. Let God's love pour into your heart, quenching your anger and healing old wounds. Thank God for loving you, forgiving you and healing you.

See Meeting God in Scripture

9 Give instruction[a] to the wise, and they will
        become wiser still;
    teach the righteous and they will gain in
        learning.
10 The fear of the LORD is the beginning of wisdom,
        and the knowledge of the Holy One is insight.
11 For by me your days will be multiplied,
        and years will be added to your life.
12 If you are wise, you are wise for yourself;
        if you scoff, you alone will bear it.

Folly's Invitation and Promise

13 The foolish woman is loud;
        she is ignorant and knows nothing.
14 She sits at the door of her house,
        on a seat at the high places of the town,
15 calling to those who pass by,
        who are going straight on their way,
16 "You who are simple, turn in here!"
        And to those without sense she says,
17 "Stolen water is sweet,
        and bread eaten in secret is pleasant."
18 But they do not know that the dead[b] are there,
        that her guests are in the depths of Sheol.

Wise Sayings of Solomon

10
The proverbs of Solomon.

    A wise child makes a glad father,
        but a foolish child is a mother's grief.
2   Treasures gained by wickedness do not profit,
        but righteousness delivers from death.
3   The LORD does not let the righteous go hungry,
        but he thwarts the craving of the wicked.
4   A slack hand causes poverty,
        but the hand of the diligent makes rich.
5   A child who gathers in summer is prudent,
        but a child who sleeps in harvest brings shame.
6   Blessings are on the head of the righteous,
        but the mouth of the wicked conceals violence.
7   The memory of the righteous is a blessing,
        but the name of the wicked will rot.
8   The wise of heart will heed commandments,
        but a babbling fool will come to ruin.
9   Whoever walks in integrity walks securely,
        but whoever follows perverse ways will be
            found out.
10 Whoever winks the eye causes trouble,
        but the one who rebukes boldly makes peace.[c]
11 The mouth of the righteous is a fountain of life,
        but the mouth of the wicked conceals violence.
12 Hatred stirs up strife,
        but love covers all offenses.

a Heb lacks *instruction*   *b* Heb *shades*   *c* Gk: Heb *but a babbling fool
will come to ruin*

13 On the lips of one who has understanding
    wisdom is found,
    but a rod is for the back of one who lacks
      sense.
14 The wise lay up knowledge,
    but the babbling of a fool brings ruin near.
15 The wealth of the rich is their fortress;
    the poverty of the poor is their ruin.
16 The wage of the righteous leads to life,
    the gain of the wicked to sin.
17 Whoever heeds instruction is on the path to life,
    but one who rejects a rebuke goes astray.
18 Lying lips conceal hatred,
    and whoever utters slander is a fool.
19 When words are many, transgression is not
    lacking,
    but the prudent are restrained in speech.
20 The tongue of the righteous is choice silver;
    the mind of the wicked is of little worth.
21 The lips of the righteous feed many,
    but fools die for lack of sense.
22 The blessing of the Lord makes rich,
    and he adds no sorrow with it.[a]
23 Doing wrong is like sport to a fool,
    but wise conduct is pleasure to a person of
      understanding.
24 What the wicked dread will come upon them,
    but the desire of the righteous will be granted.
25 When the tempest passes, the wicked are no
    more,
    but the righteous are established forever.
26 Like vinegar to the teeth, and smoke to the eyes,
    so are the lazy to their employers.
27 The fear of the Lord prolongs life,
    but the years of the wicked will be short.
28 The hope of the righteous ends in gladness,
    but the expectation of the wicked comes to
      nothing.
29 The way of the Lord is a stronghold for the
    upright,
    but destruction for evildoers.
30 The righteous will never be removed,
    but the wicked will not remain in the land.
31 The mouth of the righteous brings forth wisdom,
    but the perverse tongue will be cut off.
32 The lips of the righteous know what is acceptable,
    but the mouth of the wicked what is perverse.

11 A false balance is an abomination to the Lord,
    but an accurate weight is his delight.
2 When pride comes, then comes disgrace;
    but wisdom is with the humble.
3 The integrity of the upright guides them,
    but the crookedness of the treacherous destroys
      them.

Wise Business Practices

PROVERBS 11.1–4

The sages remind us that wisdom is not only applicable to how we live our personal, private lives. Wisdom also informs our public conduct. Here the sages speak about business practices. How does your business look when held up to the bright light of wisdom? What are the ways you, or those at the company you work for, cut corners? Are there problems that you can correct? You might invite God to be present with you as you work today and to review your conduct with you. What does God see? Is it "an abomination" or "a delight"?

See Meeting God in Everyday Life

---

a Or *and toil adds nothing to it*

Generosity

PROVERBS 11.24–26

The generous, says Solomon, are blessed. The miserly end up miserable. And in these proverbs, generosity is defined not only as giving freely but also as making goods available at a fair price to those who need them. Spend some time making out two lists. In the first list include examples of your generosity; on the second list write down some ways in which you hold back from giving. Go beyond money and other things to the ways you share or hold back your time, your affection, your presence, your skills. Dig as deeply as you can in making these lists. Then invite God to review them with you. What does God applaud? What does God criticize? What do you want to change? Ask God to help you learn the wisdom of generosity.

See Meeting God in Service

4 Riches do not profit in the day of wrath,
　　but righteousness delivers from death.
5 The righteousness of the blameless keeps their ways straight,
　　but the wicked fall by their own wickedness.
6 The righteousness of the upright saves them,
　　but the treacherous are taken captive by their schemes.
7 When the wicked die, their hope perishes,
　　and the expectation of the godless comes to nothing.
8 The righteous are delivered from trouble,
　　and the wicked get into it instead.
9 With their mouths the godless would destroy their neighbors,
　　but by knowledge the righteous are delivered.
10 When it goes well with the righteous, the city rejoices;
　　and when the wicked perish, there is jubilation.
11 By the blessing of the upright a city is exalted,
　　but it is overthrown by the mouth of the wicked.
12 Whoever belittles another lacks sense,
　　but an intelligent person remains silent.
13 A gossip goes about telling secrets,
　　but one who is trustworthy in spirit keeps a confidence.
14 Where there is no guidance, a nation*a* falls,
　　but in an abundance of counselors there is safety.
15 To guarantee loans for a stranger brings trouble,
　　but there is safety in refusing to do so.
16 A gracious woman gets honor,
　　but she who hates virtue is covered with shame.*b*
　　The timid become destitute,*c*
　　but the aggressive gain riches.
17 Those who are kind reward themselves,
　　but the cruel do themselves harm.
18 The wicked earn no real gain,
　　but those who sow righteousness get a true reward.
19 Whoever is steadfast in righteousness will live,
　　but whoever pursues evil will die.
20 Crooked minds are an abomination to the LORD,
　　but those of blameless ways are his delight.
21 Be assured, the wicked will not go unpunished,
　　but those who are righteous will escape.
22 Like a gold ring in a pig's snout
　　is a beautiful woman without good sense.
23 The desire of the righteous ends only in good;
　　the expectation of the wicked in wrath.
24 Some give freely, yet grow all the richer;
　　others withhold what is due, and only suffer want.

a Or *an army*　*b* Compare Gk Syr: Heb lacks *but she . . . shame*
c Gk: Heb lacks *The timid . . . destitute*

25 A generous person will be enriched,
and one who gives water will get water.
26 The people curse those who hold back grain,
but a blessing is on the head of those who sell
it.
27 Whoever diligently seeks good seeks favor,
but evil comes to the one who searches for it.
28 Those who trust in their riches will wither,[a]
but the righteous will flourish like green leaves.
29 Those who trouble their households will inherit
wind,
and the fool will be servant to the wise.
30 The fruit of the righteous is a tree of life,
but violence[b] takes lives away.
31 If the righteous are repaid on earth,
how much more the wicked and the sinner!

12 Whoever loves discipline loves knowledge,
but those who hate to be rebuked are stupid.
2 The good obtain favor from the LORD,
but those who devise evil he condemns.
3 No one finds security by wickedness,
but the root of the righteous will never be
moved.
4 A good wife is the crown of her husband,
but she who brings shame is like rottenness in
his bones.
5 The thoughts of the righteous are just;
the advice of the wicked is treacherous.
6 The words of the wicked are a deadly ambush,
but the speech of the upright delivers them.
7 The wicked are overthrown and are no more,
but the house of the righteous will stand.
8 One is commended for good sense,
but a perverse mind is despised.
9 Better to be despised and have a servant,
than to be self-important and lack food.
10 The righteous know the needs of their animals,
but the mercy of the wicked is cruel.
11 Those who till their land will have plenty of food,
but those who follow worthless pursuits have
no sense.
12 The wicked covet the proceeds of wickedness,[c]
but the root of the righteous bears fruit.
13 The evil are ensnared by the transgression of
their lips,
but the righteous escape from trouble.
14 From the fruit of the mouth one is filled with
good things,
and manual labor has its reward.
15 Fools think their own way is right,
but the wise listen to advice.
16 Fools show their anger at once,
but the prudent ignore an insult.

Prayer for God's Wisdom in All We Do

PROVERBS 12.15–20

God be in my head, and in
my understanding;
God be in my eyes, and in
my looking;
God be in my mouth, and in
my speaking;
God be in my heart, and in
my thinking;
God be at my end, and at
my departing.

—*The Sarum Primer*

a Cn: Heb *fall*   b Cn Compare Gk Syr: Heb *a wise man*   c Or *covet the catch of the wicked*

Hope Deferred

PROVERBS 13.12

Look at your life in the light of this proverb. What fulfilled longings have helped you feel alive and strong? What are the deferred hopes that make your heart sick? You might want to write two lists—one of fulfilled longings and one of deferred hopes—so you can consider them more fully. Do you need to let go of any of these deferred hopes so that healing can begin? What actions can you take to bring others closer to fulfillment? What help do you need from God in order to carry out these actions? What cooperation do you need from other people? What hopes can you turn over to God, to let him fulfill them or not fulfill them in his own time and according to his will? Finish your prayer time by returning to the fulfilled desires that have been a tree of life for you. Thank God for them.

See Meeting God in Service

17 Whoever speaks the truth gives honest evidence,
    but a false witness speaks deceitfully.
18 Rash words are like sword thrusts,
    but the tongue of the wise brings healing.
19 Truthful lips endure forever,
    but a lying tongue lasts only a moment.
20 Deceit is in the mind of those who plan evil,
    but those who counsel peace have joy.
21 No harm happens to the righteous,
    but the wicked are filled with trouble.
22 Lying lips are an abomination to the LORD,
    but those who act faithfully are his delight.
23 One who is clever conceals knowledge,
    but the mind of a fool[a] broadcasts folly.
24 The hand of the diligent will rule,
    while the lazy will be put to forced labor.
25 Anxiety weighs down the human heart,
    but a good word cheers it up.
26 The righteous gives good advice to friends,[b]
    but the way of the wicked leads astray.
27 The lazy do not roast[c] their game,
    but the diligent obtain precious wealth.[c]
28 In the path of righteousness there is life,
    in walking its path there is no death.

13 A wise child loves discipline,[d]
    but a scoffer does not listen to rebuke.
2 From the fruit of their words good persons eat
        good things,
    but the desire of the treacherous is for
        wrongdoing.
3 Those who guard their mouths preserve their lives;
    those who open wide their lips come to ruin.
4 The appetite of the lazy craves, and gets nothing,
    while the appetite of the diligent is richly
        supplied.
5 The righteous hate falsehood,
    but the wicked act shamefully and disgracefully.
6 Righteousness guards one whose way is upright,
    but sin overthrows the wicked.
7 Some pretend to be rich, yet have nothing;
    others pretend to be poor, yet have great
        wealth.
8 Wealth is a ransom for a person's life,
    but the poor get no threats.
9 The light of the righteous rejoices,
    but the lamp of the wicked goes out.
10 By insolence the heedless make strife,
    but wisdom is with those who take advice.
11 Wealth hastily gotten[e] will dwindle,
    but those who gather little by little will increase
        it.
12 Hope deferred makes the heart sick,
    but a desire fulfilled is a tree of life.

a Heb *the heart of fools*   *b* Syr: Meaning of Heb uncertain   *c* Meaning of Heb uncertain   *d* Cn: Heb *A wise child the discipline of his father*   *e* Gk Vg: Heb *from vanity*

13 Those who despise the word bring destruction on
   themselves,
   but those who respect the commandment will
   be rewarded.

14 The teaching of the wise is a fountain of life,
   so that one may avoid the snares of death.

15 Good sense wins favor,
   but the way of the faithless is their ruin.[a]

16 The clever do all things intelligently,
   but the fool displays folly.

17 A bad messenger brings trouble,
   but a faithful envoy, healing.

18 Poverty and disgrace are for the one who ignores
   instruction,
   but one who heeds reproof is honored.

19 A desire realized is sweet to the soul,
   but to turn away from evil is an abomination to
   fools.

20 Whoever walks with the wise becomes wise,
   but the companion of fools suffers harm.

21 Misfortune pursues sinners,
   but prosperity rewards the righteous.

22 The good leave an inheritance to their children's
   children,
   but the sinner's wealth is laid up for the
   righteous.

23 The field of the poor may yield much food,
   but it is swept away through injustice.

24 Those who spare the rod hate their children,
   but those who love them are diligent to
   discipline them.

25 The righteous have enough to satisfy their
   appetite,
   but the belly of the wicked is empty.

14 The wise woman[b] builds her house,
   but the foolish tears it down with her own hands.

2 Those who walk uprightly fear the LORD,
   but one who is devious in conduct despises
   him.

3 The talk of fools is a rod for their backs,[c]
   but the lips of the wise preserve them.

4 Where there are no oxen, there is no grain;
   abundant crops come by the strength of the ox.

5 A faithful witness does not lie,
   but a false witness breathes out lies.

6 A scoffer seeks wisdom in vain,
   but knowledge is easy for one who
   understands.

7 Leave the presence of a fool,
   for there you do not find words of knowledge.

8 It is the wisdom of the clever to understand
   where they go,
   but the folly of fools misleads.

Systemic Injustice

PROVERBS 13.23

Although the sages encouraged hard work, diligence and thrift, they knew that the poor could still lose everything through the injustice of the rich or powerful. Spend some time in intercessory prayer for those who are the victims of injustice or oppression. You might let the newspaper or television news reports guide you to specific cases. Or you might think of individuals or groups you have known personally who have been crushed by circumstances beyond their control. You might also ask God to show you any ways in which you have been part of oppressive systems or in which your prosperity is the result of the poor being "swept away." What can you change in your life to help break the power of systemic injustice?

See Meeting God in Prayer

---

a Cn Compare Gk Syr Vg Tg: Heb *is enduring*   b Heb *Wisdom of women*
c Cn: Heb *a rod of pride*

Serenity

PROVERBS 14.29–30

"God, give us grace to accept with serenity the things that cannot be changed, courage to change the things that should be changed, and the wisdom to distinguish the one from the other."

—REINHOLD NIEBUHR,
Justice and Mercy

9 Fools mock at the guilt offering,[a]
   but the upright enjoy God's favor.
10 The heart knows its own bitterness,
   and no stranger shares its joy.
11 The house of the wicked is destroyed,
   but the tent of the upright flourishes.
12 There is a way that seems right to a person,
   but its end is the way to death.[b]
13 Even in laughter the heart is sad,
   and the end of joy is grief.
14 The perverse get what their ways deserve,
   and the good, what their deeds deserve.[c]
15 The simple believe everything,
   but the clever consider their steps.
16 The wise are cautious and turn away from evil,
   but the fool throws off restraint and is careless.
17 One who is quick-tempered acts foolishly,
   and the schemer is hated.
18 The simple are adorned with[d] folly,
   but the clever are crowned with knowledge.
19 The evil bow down before the good,
   the wicked at the gates of the righteous.
20 The poor are disliked even by their neighbors,
   but the rich have many friends.
21 Those who despise their neighbors are sinners,
   but happy are those who are kind to the poor.
22 Do they not err that plan evil?
   Those who plan good find loyalty and
      faithfulness.
23 In all toil there is profit,
   but mere talk leads only to poverty.
24 The crown of the wise is their wisdom,[e]
   but folly is the garland[f] of fools.
25 A truthful witness saves lives,
   but one who utters lies is a betrayer.
26 In the fear of the LORD one has strong confidence,
   and one's children will have a refuge.
27 The fear of the LORD is a fountain of life,
   so that one may avoid the snares of death.
28 The glory of a king is a multitude of people;
   without people a prince is ruined.
29 Whoever is slow to anger has great
      understanding,
   but one who has a hasty temper exalts folly.
30 A tranquil mind gives life to the flesh,
   but passion makes the bones rot.
31 Those who oppress the poor insult their Maker,
   but those who are kind to the needy honor
      him.
32 The wicked are overthrown by their evildoing,
   but the righteous find a refuge in their
      integrity.[g]

a Meaning of Heb uncertain   b Heb *ways of death*   c Cn: Heb *from upon him*   d Or *inherit*   e Cn Compare Gk: Heb *riches*   f Cn: Heb *is the folly*   g Gk Syr: Heb *in their death*

³³ Wisdom is at home in the mind of one who has
    understanding,
  but it is not[a] known in the heart of fools.
³⁴ Righteousness exalts a nation,
  but sin is a reproach to any people.
³⁵ A servant who deals wisely has the king's favor,
  but his wrath falls on one who acts shamefully.

15
¹ A soft answer turns away wrath,
  but a harsh word stirs up anger.
² The tongue of the wise dispenses knowledge,[b]
  but the mouths of fools pour out folly.
³ The eyes of the LORD are in every place,
  keeping watch on the evil and the good.
⁴ A gentle tongue is a tree of life,
  but perverseness in it breaks the spirit.
⁵ A fool despises a parent's instruction,
  but the one who heeds admonition is prudent.
⁶ In the house of the righteous there is much
    treasure,
  but trouble befalls the income of the wicked.
⁷ The lips of the wise spread knowledge;
  not so the minds of fools.
⁸ The sacrifice of the wicked is an abomination to
    the LORD,
  but the prayer of the upright is his delight.
⁹ The way of the wicked is an abomination to the
    LORD,
  but he loves the one who pursues
    righteousness.
¹⁰ There is severe discipline for one who forsakes
    the way,
  but one who hates a rebuke will die.
¹¹ Sheol and Abaddon lie open before the LORD,
  how much more human hearts!
¹² Scoffers do not like to be rebuked;
  they will not go to the wise.
¹³ A glad heart makes a cheerful countenance,
  but by sorrow of heart the spirit is broken.
¹⁴ The mind of one who has understanding seeks
    knowledge,
  but the mouths of fools feed on folly.
¹⁵ All the days of the poor are hard,
  but a cheerful heart has a continual feast.
¹⁶ Better is a little with the fear of the LORD
  than great treasure and trouble with it.
¹⁷ Better is a dinner of vegetables where love is
  than a fatted ox and hatred with it.
¹⁸ Those who are hot-tempered stir up strife,
  but those who are slow to anger calm
    contention.
¹⁹ The way of the lazy is overgrown with thorns,
  but the path of the upright is a level highway.
²⁰ A wise child makes a glad father,
  but the foolish despise their mothers.

Simplicity

PROVERBS 15.16–17

Setting priorities can be extremely difficult with so many people, things and events clamoring for our attention. These proverbs suggest that two things are primary: loving God and having loving relationships with family and friends. Take a look at your life in light of these proverbs. Look at your appointment calendar (if you have one) or make a list of your scheduled activities. How do God, family and friends fit into your schedule? What activities might you give up to allow more time for your most important relationships? Simplifying your life can require painful choices. You might ask God for help in making decisions that can lead to a simpler and richer life and for strength to follow through on the decisions you have made.

See Meeting God in Everyday Life

Gaining Understanding

PROVERBS 15.32–33

Opportunities to listen to wise thinkers or to ignore life-giving advice abound. In our search for transformation, we can ask God to help us evaluate what is precious and what is offensive in the Lord's eyes. But to want instruction and to seek instruction do not necessarily imply that we will heed instruction. In our fast-moving society, few of us take time to listen to instruction unless we find it absolutely necessary.

Think back over the last few days. What good advice or thoughtful criticism has been offered to you? What have you chosen to ignore? Try to write down a few specific examples. Consider each one as you ask yourself, "Why did I ignore this? How would I have to change if I paid attention to this? Is God calling to me through this offer of wisdom? What do I need to do?" Ask God to guide you in being more open to instruction in the coming days.

See Meeting God in Community

21 Folly is a joy to one who has no sense,
  but a person of understanding walks straight
   ahead.
22 Without counsel, plans go wrong,
  but with many advisers they succeed.
23 To make an apt answer is a joy to anyone,
  and a word in season, how good it is!
24 For the wise the path of life leads upward,
  in order to avoid Sheol below.
25 The Lord tears down the house of the proud,
  but maintains the widow's boundaries.
26 Evil plans are an abomination to the Lord,
  but gracious words are pure.
27 Those who are greedy for unjust gain make
   trouble for their households,
  but those who hate bribes will live.
28 The mind of the righteous ponders how to
   answer,
  but the mouth of the wicked pours out evil.
29 The Lord is far from the wicked,
  but he hears the prayer of the righteous.
30 The light of the eyes rejoices the heart,
  and good news refreshes the body.
31 The ear that heeds wholesome admonition
  will lodge among the wise.
32 Those who ignore instruction despise themselves,
  but those who heed admonition gain
   understanding.
33 The fear of the Lord is instruction in wisdom,
  and humility goes before honor.

16 The plans of the mind belong to mortals,
  but the answer of the tongue is from the Lord.
2 All one's ways may be pure in one's own eyes,
  but the Lord weighs the spirit.
3 Commit your work to the Lord,
  and your plans will be established.
4 The Lord has made everything for its purpose,
  even the wicked for the day of trouble.
5 All those who are arrogant are an abomination to
   the Lord;
  be assured, they will not go unpunished.
6 By loyalty and faithfulness iniquity is atoned for,
  and by the fear of the Lord one avoids evil.
7 When the ways of people please the Lord,
  he causes even their enemies to be at peace
   with them.
8 Better is a little with righteousness
  than large income with injustice.
9 The human mind plans the way,
  but the Lord directs the steps.
10 Inspired decisions are on the lips of a king;
  his mouth does not sin in judgment.
11 Honest balances and scales are the Lord's;
  all the weights in the bag are his work.

12 It is an abomination to kings to do evil,
  for the throne is established by righteousness.
13 Righteous lips are the delight of a king,
  and he loves those who speak what is right.
14 A king's wrath is a messenger of death,
  and whoever is wise will appease it.
15 In the light of a king's face there is life,
  and his favor is like the clouds that bring the
    spring rain.
16 How much better to get wisdom than gold!
  To get understanding is to be chosen rather
    than silver.
17 The highway of the upright avoids evil;
  those who guard their way preserve their lives.
18 Pride goes before destruction,
  and a haughty spirit before a fall.
19 It is better to be of a lowly spirit among the poor
  than to divide the spoil with the proud.
20 Those who are attentive to a matter will prosper,
  and happy are those who trust in the LORD.
21 The wise of heart is called perceptive,
  and pleasant speech increases persuasiveness.
22 Wisdom is a fountain of life to one who has it,
  but folly is the punishment of fools.
23 The mind of the wise makes their speech
    judicious,
  and adds persuasiveness to their lips.
24 Pleasant words are like a honeycomb,
  sweetness to the soul and health to the body.
25 Sometimes there is a way that seems to be right,
  but in the end it is the way to death.
26 The appetite of workers works for them;
  their hunger urges them on.
27 Scoundrels concoct evil,
  and their speech is like a scorching fire.
28 A perverse person spreads strife,
  and a whisperer separates close friends.
29 The violent entice their neighbors,
  and lead them in a way that is not good.
30 One who winks the eyes plans[a] perverse things;
  one who compresses the lips brings evil to
    pass.
31 Gray hair is a crown of glory;
  it is gained in a righteous life.
32 One who is slow to anger is better than the
    mighty,
  and one whose temper is controlled than one
    who captures a city.
33 The lot is cast into the lap,
  but the decision is the LORD's alone.

17 Better is a dry morsel with quiet
  than a house full of feasting with strife.
2 A slave who deals wisely will rule over a child
  who acts shamefully,

Better Than Silver or Gold

PROVERBS 16.16–17

"As all wisdom, love, and goodness proceed from God, so nothing but love, wisdom, and goodness can lead to God. When you love that which God loves, you act with God, you join yourself to God. When you love what God dislikes, then you oppose God and separate yourself from God. This is the true and right way: think what God loves and love it yourself with all your heart."

—WILLIAM LAW,
A Serious Call to a Devout and Holy Life

Projects

PROVERBS 17.12

Today's English Version of the Bible renders the last half of this verse, ". . . than to meet some fool busy with a stupid project." Even the most inspired idea can become a "stupid project" when it becomes our project and not God's inspiration. What are the current projects in your life? (Working your way through this Bible might be one project, for example.) When have you become so intent on a project that you have snapped at anyone who interrupted you? You might spend some time offering your projects back to God, reconsecrating them to God's service. Such a prayer time might include thanksgiving for what you have accomplished or learned as well as confession for times in which you have wandered away from the original inspiration.

See Meeting God in Service

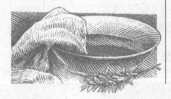

and will share the inheritance as one of the family.

3 The crucible is for silver, and the furnace is for gold,
   but the LORD tests the heart.
4 An evildoer listens to wicked lips;
   and a liar gives heed to a mischievous tongue.
5 Those who mock the poor insult their Maker;
   those who are glad at calamity will not go unpunished.
6 Grandchildren are the crown of the aged,
   and the glory of children is their parents.
7 Fine speech is not becoming to a fool;
   still less is false speech to a ruler.[a]
8 A bribe is like a magic stone in the eyes of those who give it;
   wherever they turn they prosper.
9 One who forgives an affront fosters friendship,
   but one who dwells on disputes will alienate a friend.
10 A rebuke strikes deeper into a discerning person
   than a hundred blows into a fool.
11 Evil people seek only rebellion,
   but a cruel messenger will be sent against them.
12 Better to meet a she-bear robbed of its cubs
   than to confront a fool immersed in folly.
13 Evil will not depart from the house
   of one who returns evil for good.
14 The beginning of strife is like letting out water;
   so stop before the quarrel breaks out.
15 One who justifies the wicked and one who condemns the righteous
   are both alike an abomination to the LORD.
16 Why should fools have a price in hand
   to buy wisdom, when they have no mind to learn?
17 A friend loves at all times,
   and kinsfolk are born to share adversity.
18 It is senseless to give a pledge,
   to become surety for a neighbor.
19 One who loves transgression loves strife;
   one who builds a high threshold invites broken bones.
20 The crooked of mind do not prosper,
   and the perverse of tongue fall into calamity.
21 The one who begets a fool gets trouble;
   the parent of a fool has no joy.
22 A cheerful heart is a good medicine,
   but a downcast spirit dries up the bones.
23 The wicked accept a concealed bribe
   to pervert the ways of justice.
24 The discerning person looks to wisdom,
   but the eyes of a fool to the ends of the earth.

a Or *a noble person*

25 Foolish children are a grief to their father
  and bitterness to her who bore them.
26 To impose a fine on the innocent is not right,
  or to flog the noble for their integrity.
27 One who spares words is knowledgeable;
  one who is cool in spirit has understanding.
28 Even fools who keep silent are considered wise;
  when they close their lips, they are deemed
    intelligent.

18 The one who lives alone is self-indulgent,
  showing contempt for all who have sound
    judgment.*a*
2 A fool takes no pleasure in understanding,
  but only in expressing personal opinion.
3 When wickedness comes, contempt comes also;
  and with dishonor comes disgrace.
4 The words of the mouth are deep waters;
  the fountain of wisdom is a gushing stream.
5 It is not right to be partial to the guilty,
  or to subvert the innocent in judgment.
6 A fool's lips bring strife,
  and a fool's mouth invites a flogging.
7 The mouths of fools are their ruin,
  and their lips a snare to themselves.
8 The words of a whisperer are like delicious
    morsels;
  they go down into the inner parts of the body.
9 One who is slack in work
  is close kin to a vandal.
10 The name of the Lord is a strong tower;
  the righteous run into it and are safe.
11 The wealth of the rich is their strong city;
  in their imagination it is like a high wall.
12 Before destruction one's heart is haughty,
  but humility goes before honor.
13 If one gives answer before hearing,
  it is folly and shame.
14 The human spirit will endure sickness;
  but a broken spirit—who can bear?
15 An intelligent mind acquires knowledge,
  and the ear of the wise seeks knowledge.
16 A gift opens doors;
  it gives access to the great.
17 The one who first states a case seems right,
  until the other comes and cross-examines.
18 Casting the lot puts an end to disputes
  and decides between powerful contenders.
19 An ally offended is stronger than a city;*b*
  such quarreling is like the bars of a castle.
20 From the fruit of the mouth one's stomach is
    satisfied;
  the yield of the lips brings satisfaction.
21 Death and life are in the power of the tongue,
  and those who love it will eat its fruits.

The Name of the Lord

PROVERBS 18.10

Let your imagination play with the image in this verse. Picture a strong tower, a place of safety for you. Imagine that you are outside the tower, under attack. What is attacking you? As you are driven back toward the tower, you call on the name of the Lord. At once the tower gate opens and you can run inside to safety. Your enemy can no longer reach you. You are safe in the tower of the Lord's strength and goodness.

You might want to draw or paint a picture of yourself safe within the tower while enemies lurk outside. You might conclude your prayer time by singing a hymn such as "A Mighty Fortress Is Our God" or "Rock of Ages" or "The Rock That is Higher Than I."

See Meeting God in Scripture

---

a Meaning of Heb uncertain   *b* Gk Syr Vg Tg: Meaning of Heb uncertain

Living or Dying

PROVERBS 19.16

The word *commandment* frightens many people because they think of something very rigid and binding. Using the word instruction instead may ease some of the tension. The author of this proverb feels strongly enough about what his beliefs are that he promises life to those who obey instructions (commandments). This saying is not a warranty for a long life but a guarantee for a more meaningful life regardless of the number of years. Choosing not to listen to instruction or to the commandments leads to death—a joyless life of angst, a despotic posture toward others, a defiant spirit toward God.

God's Word becomes flesh only when we know it, love it and live it. Spend some time reviewing the Ten Commandments (Exodus 20.1–17) and Jesus' Great Commandment (Matthew 22.34–40). How well does your life reflect God's instructions?

See Meeting God in Prayer

22 He who finds a wife finds a good thing,
and obtains favor from the LORD.
23 The poor use entreaties,
but the rich answer roughly.
24 Some*a* friends play at friendship*b*
but a true friend sticks closer than one's
nearest kin.

19 Better the poor walking in integrity
than one perverse of speech who is a fool.
2 Desire without knowledge is not good,
and one who moves too hurriedly misses the
way.
3 One's own folly leads to ruin,
yet the heart rages against the LORD.
4 Wealth brings many friends,
but the poor are left friendless.
5 A false witness will not go unpunished,
and a liar will not escape.
6 Many seek the favor of the generous,
and everyone is a friend to a giver of gifts.
7 If the poor are hated even by their kin,
how much more are they shunned by their
friends!
When they call after them, they are not there.*c*
8 To get wisdom is to love oneself;
to keep understanding is to prosper.
9 A false witness will not go unpunished,
and the liar will perish.
10 It is not fitting for a fool to live in luxury,
much less for a slave to rule over princes.
11 Those with good sense are slow to anger,
and it is their glory to overlook an offense.
12 A king's anger is like the growling of a lion,
but his favor is like dew on the grass.
13 A stupid child is ruin to a father,
and a wife's quarreling is a continual dripping
of rain.
14 House and wealth are inherited from parents,
but a prudent wife is from the LORD.
15 Laziness brings on deep sleep;
an idle person will suffer hunger.
16 Those who keep the commandment will live;
those who are heedless of their ways will die.
17 Whoever is kind to the poor lends to the LORD,
and will be repaid in full.
18 Discipline your children while there is hope;
do not set your heart on their destruction.
19 A violent tempered person will pay the penalty;
if you effect a rescue, you will only have to do
it again.*c*
20 Listen to advice and accept instruction,
that you may gain wisdom for the future.

a Syr Tg: Heb *A man of*   *b* Cn Compare Syr Vg Tg: Meaning of Heb
uncertain   *c* Meaning of Heb uncertain

21 The human mind may devise many plans,
  but it is the purpose of the LORD that will be
    established.
22 What is desirable in a person is loyalty,
  and it is better to be poor than a liar.
23 The fear of the LORD is life indeed;
  filled with it one rests secure
  and suffers no harm.
24 The lazy person buries a hand in the dish,
  and will not even bring it back to the mouth.
25 Strike a scoffer, and the simple will learn
    prudence;
  reprove the intelligent, and they will gain
    knowledge.
26 Those who do violence to their father and chase
    away their mother
  are children who cause shame and bring
    reproach.
27 Cease straying, my child, from the words of
    knowledge,
  in order that you may hear instruction.
28 A worthless witness mocks at justice,
  and the mouth of the wicked devours iniquity.
29 Condemnation is ready for scoffers,
  and flogging for the backs of fools.

20 Wine is a mocker, strong drink a brawler,
  and whoever is led astray by it is not wise.
2 The dread anger of a king is like the growling of a
    lion;
  anyone who provokes him to anger forfeits life
    itself.
3 It is honorable to refrain from strife,
  but every fool is quick to quarrel.
4 The lazy person does not plow in season;
  harvest comes, and there is nothing to be
    found.
5 The purposes in the human mind are like deep
    water,
  but the intelligent will draw them out.
6 Many proclaim themselves loyal,
  but who can find one worthy of trust?
7 The righteous walk in integrity—
  happy are the children who follow them!
8 A king who sits on the throne of judgment
  winnows all evil with his eyes.
9 Who can say, "I have made my heart clean;
  I am pure from my sin"?
10 Diverse weights and diverse measures
  are both alike an abomination to the LORD.
11 Even children make themselves known by their
    acts,
  by whether what they do is pure and right.
12 The hearing ear and the seeing eye—
  the LORD has made them both.
13 Do not love sleep, or else you will come to
    poverty;

Anger and Hatred

PROVERBS 20.3

"When anger tries to burn up my tabernacle, I will look to the goodness of God, whom anger never touched; and thus I will be sweeter than the air, which in its gentleness moistens the earth, and have spiritual joy because virtues are beginning to show themselves in me. And thus I will feel God's goodness.

"And when hatred tries to darken me, I will look to the mercy and the martyrdom of the Son of God, and so restrain my flesh, and in faithful memory receive the sweet fragrance of the roses that spring from thorns. And so I will acknowledge my Redeemer."

—HILDEGARD OF BINGEN,
Scivias

849

Waiting for the Lord

PROVERBS 20.22

Waiting for the Lord often makes us nervous because we do not know when or how God will respond. When evil touches our lives, we want immediate action. The silence and the waiting cause us to wonder if God really values us or cares at all. Often our impatience pushes us to take control away from God. The Lord is well aware of all that happens to us. Our instructions are not to repay evil ourselves but to wait for the Lord's help.

When do you find yourself eager to repay evil? What longing for revenge festers in your soul? Sit quietly in God's presence. Imagine plucking that longing from your heart and offering it to God. You might say, "Here, God, I will let you manage this for me. Take it from my heart. Teach me to wait in patience for your help."

See Meeting God in Prayer

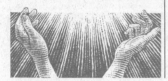

open your eyes, and you will have plenty of
bread.
14 "Bad, bad," says the buyer,
then goes away and boasts.
15 There is gold, and abundance of costly stones;
but the lips informed by knowledge are a
precious jewel.
16 Take the garment of one who has given surety for
a stranger;
seize the pledge given as surety for foreigners.
17 Bread gained by deceit is sweet,
but afterward the mouth will be full of gravel.
18 Plans are established by taking advice;
wage war by following wise guidance.
19 A gossip reveals secrets;
therefore do not associate with a babbler.
20 If you curse father or mother,
your lamp will go out in utter darkness.
21 An estate quickly acquired in the beginning
will not be blessed in the end.
22 Do not say, "I will repay evil";
wait for the LORD, and he will help you.
23 Differing weights are an abomination to the LORD,
and false scales are not good.
24 All our steps are ordered by the LORD;
how then can we understand our own ways?
25 It is a snare for one to say rashly, "It is holy,"
and begin to reflect only after making a vow.
26 A wise king winnows the wicked,
and drives the wheel over them.
27 The human spirit is the lamp of the LORD,
searching every inmost part.
28 Loyalty and faithfulness preserve the king,
and his throne is upheld by righteousness. *a*
29 The glory of youths is their strength,
but the beauty of the aged is their gray hair.
30 Blows that wound cleanse away evil;
beatings make clean the innermost parts.

21 The king's heart is a stream of water in the
hand of the LORD;
he turns it wherever he will.
2 All deeds are right in the sight of the doer,
but the LORD weighs the heart.
3 To do righteousness and justice
is more acceptable to the LORD than sacrifice.
4 Haughty eyes and a proud heart—
the lamp of the wicked—are sin.
5 The plans of the diligent lead surely to
abundance,
but everyone who is hasty comes only to want.
6 The getting of treasures by a lying tongue
is a fleeting vapor and a snare*b* of death.
7 The violence of the wicked will sweep them away,
because they refuse to do what is just.

a Gk: Heb *loyalty*   *b* Gk: Heb *seekers*

8 The way of the guilty is crooked,
  but the conduct of the pure is right.
9 It is better to live in a corner of the housetop
  than in a house shared with a contentious wife.
10 The souls of the wicked desire evil;
  their neighbors find no mercy in their eyes.
11 When a scoffer is punished, the simple become
  wiser;
  when the wise are instructed, they increase in
  knowledge.
12 The Righteous One observes the house of the
  wicked;
  he casts the wicked down to ruin.
13 If you close your ear to the cry of the poor,
  you will cry out and not be heard.
14 A gift in secret averts anger;
  and a concealed bribe in the bosom, strong
  wrath.
15 When justice is done, it is a joy to the righteous,
  but dismay to evildoers.
16 Whoever wanders from the way of understanding
  will rest in the assembly of the dead.
17 Whoever loves pleasure will suffer want;
  whoever loves wine and oil will not be rich.
18 The wicked is a ransom for the righteous,
  and the faithless for the upright.
19 It is better to live in a desert land
  than with a contentious and fretful wife.
20 Precious treasure remains*a* in the house of the
  wise,
  but the fool devours it.
21 Whoever pursues righteousness and kindness
  will find life*b* and honor.
22 One wise person went up against a city of
  warriors
  and brought down the stronghold in which they
  trusted.
23 To watch over mouth and tongue
  is to keep out of trouble.
24 The proud, haughty person, named "Scoffer,"
  acts with arrogant pride.
25 The craving of the lazy person is fatal,
  for lazy hands refuse to labor.
26 All day long the wicked covet,*c*
  but the righteous give and do not hold back.
27 The sacrifice of the wicked is an abomination;
  how much more when brought with evil intent.
28 A false witness will perish,
  but a good listener will testify successfully.
29 The wicked put on a bold face,
  but the upright give thought to*d* their ways.
30 No wisdom, no understanding, no counsel,
  can avail against the LORD.

The Lord Weighs the Heart

PROVERBS 21.2

Those of us who have gone to
church most of our lives know
what the better way is if we
have listened well. We may
consider ourselves wise in our
own eyes, but outward actions
form the true test of wisdom.
We may fool ourselves or be
blind to our inmost motives,
but God looks at the heart and
knows what our real purpose is.

You might ask God for the
gift of insight so that you can
see yourself as God sees you.
What would you do if you knew
what God sees and how God
weighs your heart? One way to
begin might be to write a dialogue between yourself and
God. Begin with the question,
"God, what do you see when
you look at me?" Write out
what you think God might answer. How do you respond?

See Meeting God in Everyday Life

---

a Gk: Heb *and oil*   *b* Gk: Heb *life and righteousness*   *c* Gk: Heb *all day
long one covets covetously*   *d* Another reading is *establish*

Precious in God's Sight

PROVERBS 22.2

It is so easy to notice what makes us different from those around us and to zero in on those differences. Here the sage reminds us of what we have in common with all others: God made us all. As you go through your day, take time to notice the people around you. Say to yourself, "This person is God's creation and precious in God's sight." If you know the person's name, use it. When you find yourself in conflict with someone, say again, "This person is God's creation and precious in God's sight." As you look back over the day, thank God for the many different and precious gifts God has given you in the people you have encountered.

See Meeting God in Everyday Life

31 The horse is made ready for the day of battle,
but the victory belongs to the LORD.

22 A good name is to be chosen rather than great riches,
and favor is better than silver or gold.

2 The rich and the poor have this in common:
the LORD is the maker of them all.

3 The clever see danger and hide;
but the simple go on, and suffer for it.

4 The reward for humility and fear of the LORD
is riches and honor and life.

5 Thorns and snares are in the way of the perverse;
the cautious will keep far from them.

6 Train children in the right way,
and when old, they will not stray.

7 The rich rule over the poor,
and the borrower is the slave of the lender.

8 Whoever sows injustice will reap calamity,
and the rod of anger will fail.

9 Those who are generous are blessed,
for they share their bread with the poor.

10 Drive out a scoffer, and strife goes out;
quarreling and abuse will cease.

11 Those who love a pure heart and are gracious in speech
will have the king as a friend.

12 The eyes of the LORD keep watch over knowledge,
but he overthrows the words of the faithless.

13 The lazy person says, "There is a lion outside!
I shall be killed in the streets!"

14 The mouth of a loose*a* woman is a deep pit;
he with whom the LORD is angry falls into it.

15 Folly is bound up in the heart of a boy,
but the rod of discipline drives it far away.

16 Oppressing the poor in order to enrich oneself,
and giving to the rich, will lead only to loss.

Sayings of the Wise

17 The words of the wise:

Incline your ear and hear my words,*b*
and apply your mind to my teaching;

18 for it will be pleasant if you keep them within you,
if all of them are ready on your lips.

19 So that your trust may be in the LORD,
I have made them known to you today—yes, to you.

20 Have I not written for you thirty sayings
of admonition and knowledge,

21 to show you what is right and true,
so that you may give a true answer to those who sent you?

a Heb *strange*   *b* Cn Compare Gk: Heb *Incline your ear, and hear the words of the wise*

22 Do not rob the poor because they are poor,
    or crush the afflicted at the gate;
23 for the LORD pleads their cause
    and despoils of life those who despoil them.
24 Make no friends with those given to anger,
    and do not associate with hotheads,
25 or you may learn their ways
    and entangle yourself in a snare.
26 Do not be one of those who give pledges,
    who become surety for debts.
27 If you have nothing with which to pay,
    why should your bed be taken from under you?
28 Do not remove the ancient landmark
    that your ancestors set up.
29 Do you see those who are skillful in their work?
    They will serve kings;
    they will not serve common people.

23 When you sit down to eat with a ruler,
    observe carefully what[a] is before you,
2 and put a knife to your throat
    if you have a big appetite.
3 Do not desire the ruler's[b] delicacies,
    for they are deceptive food.
4 Do not wear yourself out to get rich;
    be wise enough to desist.
5 When your eyes light upon it, it is gone;
    for suddenly it takes wings to itself,
    flying like an eagle toward heaven.
6 Do not eat the bread of the stingy;
    do not desire their delicacies;
7 for like a hair in the throat, so are they.[c]
    "Eat and drink!" they say to you;
    but they do not mean it.
8 You will vomit up the little you have eaten,
    and you will waste your pleasant words.
9 Do not speak in the hearing of a fool,
    who will only despise the wisdom of your
        words.
10 Do not remove an ancient landmark
    or encroach on the fields of orphans,
11 for their redeemer is strong;
    he will plead their cause against you.
12 Apply your mind to instruction
    and your ear to words of knowledge.
13 Do not withhold discipline from your children;
    if you beat them with a rod, they will not die.
14 If you beat them with the rod,
    you will save their lives from Sheol.
15 My child, if your heart is wise,
    my heart too will be glad.
16 My soul will rejoice
    when your lips speak what is right.

Ancient Wisdom

PROVERBS 22.17–23.11

These "words of the wise" closely parallel the teachings of Amenemope, an Egyptian sage from several centuries before the time of Solomon. But they have been reworked in light of Israel's understanding of God. Read through these sayings slowly. When one in particular seems to speak to you, stay with it for a while. Why did it intrigue you? What does it have to say to you? What changes does it suggest for the way you live? You might write out your reflections.

Another approach is to try rewording these ancient sayings to fit your own time and situation. What sayings would you adapt? What sayings do you find hard to apply to your life? Where do you find yourself in full agreement with these ancient bits of wisdom?

See *Meeting God in Scripture*

The Mark Of Holiness

PROVERBS 23.23

"Holiness is a state of soul in which all the powers of the body and mind are consciously given up to God; and the witness of holiness is that testimony which the Holy Spirit bears with our spirit that the offering is accepted through Christ. The work is accomplished the moment we lay our all upon the altar."

—PHOEBE PALMER,
Entire Devotion to God

17 Do not let your heart envy sinners,
   but always continue in the fear of the LORD.
18 Surely there is a future,
   and your hope will not be cut off.

19 Hear, my child, and be wise,
   and direct your mind in the way.
20 Do not be among winebibbers,
   or among gluttonous eaters of meat;
21 for the drunkard and the glutton will come to
      poverty,
   and drowsiness will clothe them with rags.

22 Listen to your father who begot you,
   and do not despise your mother when she is
      old.
23 Buy truth, and do not sell it;
   buy wisdom, instruction, and understanding.
24 The father of the righteous will greatly rejoice;
   he who begets a wise son will be glad in him.
25 Let your father and mother be glad;
   let her who bore you rejoice.

26 My child, give me your heart,
   and let your eyes observe[a] my ways.
27 For a prostitute is a deep pit;
   an adulteress[b] is a narrow well.
28 She lies in wait like a robber
   and increases the number of the faithless.

29 Who has woe? Who has sorrow?
   Who has strife? Who has complaining?
   Who has wounds without cause?
   Who has redness of eyes?
30 Those who linger late over wine,
   those who keep trying mixed wines.
31 Do not look at wine when it is red,
   when it sparkles in the cup
   and goes down smoothly.
32 At the last it bites like a serpent,
   and stings like an adder.
33 Your eyes will see strange things,
   and your mind utter perverse things.
34 You will be like one who lies down in the midst of
      the sea,
   like one who lies on the top of a mast.[c]
35 "They struck me," you will say,[d] "but I was not
      hurt;
   they beat me, but I did not feel it.
   When shall I awake?
   I will seek another drink."

24 Do not envy the wicked,
   nor desire to be with them;

854

a Another reading is *delight in*   *b* Heb *an alien woman*   *c* Meaning of
Heb uncertain   *d* Gk Syr Vg Tg: Heb lacks *you will say*

2   for their minds devise violence,
        and their lips talk of mischief.

3   By wisdom a house is built,
        and by understanding it is established;
4   by knowledge the rooms are filled
        with all precious and pleasant riches.
5   Wise warriors are mightier than strong ones,ª
        and those who have knowledge than those who
            have strength;
6   for by wise guidance you can wage your war,
        and in abundance of counselors there is victory.
7   Wisdom is too high for fools;
        in the gate they do not open their mouths.

8   Whoever plans to do evil
        will be called a mischief-maker.
9   The devising of folly is sin,
        and the scoffer is an abomination to all.

10   If you faint in the day of adversity,
        your strength being small;
11   if you hold back from rescuing those taken away
            to death,
        those who go staggering to the slaughter;
12   if you say, "Look, we did not know this"—
        does not he who weighs the heart perceive it?
     Does not he who keeps watch over your soul
            know it?
        And will he not repay all according to their
            deeds?

13   My child, eat honey, for it is good,
        and the drippings of the honeycomb are sweet
            to your taste.
14   Know that wisdom is such to your soul;
        if you find it, you will find a future,
        and your hope will not be cut off.

15   Do not lie in wait like an outlaw against the home
            of the righteous;
        do no violence to the place where the righteous
            live;
16   for though they fall seven times, they will rise
            again;
        but the wicked are overthrown by calamity.

17   Do not rejoice when your enemies fall,
        and do not let your heart be glad when they
            stumble,
18   or else the LORD will see it and be displeased,
        and turn away his anger from them.

Building Houses

PROVERBS 24.3–4

What does your dream house look like? Picture it mentally. You have the land, the plans, all the necessary financial resources, and you will have the last word on every single detail. It is your house, built to your own liking—but not in one day.

You also have a spiritual house, which you are constructing from day to day. Let the foundation be wisdom, instruction, discipline and understanding. The rooms of your spiritual home need to be filled. What will go into each room? Here, too, you have the final word. But transformation does not happen overnight. It is not that God needs more time to accomplish the task. Rather, you need space from day to day to adjust to the construction process. It takes a lifetime to grow in godliness. How can God, the Master Builder, help you?

See Meeting God in Worship

Schadenfreude

PROVERBS 24.17–20

Schadenfreude is a rather imposing German word that means "injury joy." It refers to the glee that comes over us when someone we don't like suffers harm: We laugh when a pompous person slips on a banana peel; we cheer when the villain is blown to pieces in a movie. But Proverbs tells us not to rejoice when enemies fall, even if that fall is the result of God's wrath!

Who are your enemies? If that word seems too strong, who are the people you find yourself opposed to at work or in your church? Try praying for them, asking God for their conversion rather than their destruction. After all, if they are destroyed, you may feel a moment's *schadenfreude*. But if they repent, there will be true joy in heaven.

See Meeting God in Prayer

---

19 Do not fret because of evildoers.
    Do not envy the wicked;
20 for the evil have no future;
    the lamp of the wicked will go out.

21 My child, fear the LORD and the king,
    and do not disobey either of them;[a]
22 for disaster comes from them suddenly,
    and who knows the ruin that both can bring?

Further Sayings of the Wise

23   These also are sayings of the wise:

    Partiality in judging is not good.
24 Whoever says to the wicked, "You are innocent,"
    will be cursed by peoples, abhorred by nations;
25 but those who rebuke the wicked will have
      delight,
    and a good blessing will come upon them.
26 One who gives an honest answer
    gives a kiss on the lips.

27 Prepare your work outside,
    get everything ready for you in the field;
    and after that build your house.

28 Do not be a witness against your neighbor
      without cause,
    and do not deceive with your lips.
29 Do not say, "I will do to others as they have done
      to me;
    I will pay them back for what they have done."

30 I passed by the field of one who was lazy,
    by the vineyard of a stupid person;
31 and see, it was all overgrown with thorns;
    the ground was covered with nettles,
    and its stone wall was broken down.
32 Then I saw and considered it;
    I looked and received instruction.
33 A little sleep, a little slumber,
    a little folding of the hands to rest,
34 and poverty will come upon you like a robber,
    and want, like an armed warrior.

Further Wise Sayings of Solomon

25 These are other proverbs of Solomon that the officials of King Hezekiah of Judah copied.

2 It is the glory of God to conceal things,
    but the glory of kings is to search things out.
3 Like the heavens for height, like the earth for
      depth,
    so the mind of kings is unsearchable.

a Gk: Heb *do not associate with those who change*

4 Take away the dross from the silver,
 and the smith has material for a vessel;

5 take away the wicked from the presence of the
  king,
 and his throne will be established in
  righteousness.

6 Do not put yourself forward in the king's
  presence
 or stand in the place of the great;

7 for it is better to be told, "Come up here,"
 than to be put lower in the presence of a noble.

What your eyes have seen
8 do not hastily bring into court;
for[a] what will you do in the end,
 when your neighbor puts you to shame?

9 Argue your case with your neighbor directly,
 and do not disclose another's secret;

10 or else someone who hears you will bring shame
  upon you,
 and your ill repute will have no end.

11 A word fitly spoken
 is like apples of gold in a setting of silver.

12 Like a gold ring or an ornament of gold
 is a wise rebuke to a listening ear.

13 Like the cold of snow in the time of harvest
 are faithful messengers to those who send them;
 they refresh the spirit of their masters.

14 Like clouds and wind without rain
 is one who boasts of a gift never given.

15 With patience a ruler may be persuaded,
 and a soft tongue can break bones.

16 If you have found honey, eat only enough for you,
 or else, having too much, you will vomit it.

17 Let your foot be seldom in your neighbor's house,
 otherwise the neighbor will become weary of
  you and hate you.

18 Like a war club, a sword, or a sharp arrow
 is one who bears false witness against a
  neighbor.

19 Like a bad tooth or a lame foot
 is trust in a faithless person in time of trouble.

20 Like vinegar on a wound[b]
 is one who sings songs to a heavy heart.
Like a moth in clothing or a worm in wood,
 sorrow gnaws at the human heart.[c]

21 If your enemies are hungry, give them bread to
  eat;
 and if they are thirsty, give them water to
  drink;

22 for you will heap coals of fire on their heads,
 and the LORD will reward you.

Words Fitly Spoken or Written

PROVERBS 25.11–12

The tongue and the pen are powerful weapons. We can use them to bless or to curse, to praise or to insult, to encourage or to destroy. Here, words aptly spoken are compared to apples of gold in silver settings.

Try to pay attention throughout the day to the words you speak. Do your words offer wisdom or sarcasm? Do they build up or cut down? What proverbs do you quote to others? What are your favorite sayings? What do they say about you and your values?

At the end of the day, review with God what you have said. What words have been fitly spoken? What words do you regret? Ask for God's help to speak more wisely in the future.

See Meeting God in Everyday Life

---

a Cn: Heb *or else*   *b* Gk: Heb *Like one who takes off a garment on a cold day, like vinegar on lye*   *c* Gk Syr Tg: Heb lacks *Like a moth . . . human heart*

Love of Enemies

PROVERBS 25.21–26

When the wise teacher tells us to do good to our enemies and thereby heap burning coals on them, the point is that acts of kindness, not revenge, will prick their consciences. Revenge or "getting even" only perpetuates the cycle of violence and harm.

Try to remember someone who has actively wished you harm. Perhaps this is a present situation. Offer this situation to God in prayer. How do you suppose God reacts to this conflict? What might God say to your adversary? What might God say to you? Ask God to help you as you probe the attitudes and inclinations of your heart.

See Meeting God in Prayer

23 The north wind produces rain,
 and a backbiting tongue, angry looks.
24 It is better to live in a corner of the housetop
 than in a house shared with a contentious wife.
25 Like cold water to a thirsty soul,
 so is good news from a far country.
26 Like a muddied spring or a polluted fountain
 are the righteous who give way before the
 wicked.
27 It is not good to eat much honey,
 or to seek honor on top of honor.
28 Like a city breached, without walls,
 is one who lacks self-control.

26 Like snow in summer or rain in harvest,
 so honor is not fitting for a fool.
2 Like a sparrow in its flitting, like a swallow in its
 flying,
 an undeserved curse goes nowhere.
3 A whip for the horse, a bridle for the donkey,
 and a rod for the back of fools.
4 Do not answer fools according to their folly,
 or you will be a fool yourself.
5 Answer fools according to their folly,
 or they will be wise in their own eyes.
6 It is like cutting off one's foot and drinking down
 violence,
 to send a message by a fool.
7 The legs of a disabled person hang limp;
 so does a proverb in the mouth of a fool.
8 It is like binding a stone in a sling
 to give honor to a fool.
9 Like a thornbush brandished by the hand of a
 drunkard
 is a proverb in the mouth of a fool.
10 Like an archer who wounds everybody
 is one who hires a passing fool or drunkard.[a]
11 Like a dog that returns to its vomit
 is a fool who reverts to his folly.
12 Do you see persons wise in their own eyes?
 There is more hope for fools than for them.
13 The lazy person says, "There is a lion in the road!
 There is a lion in the streets!"
14 As a door turns on its hinges,
 so does a lazy person in bed.
15 The lazy person buries a hand in the dish,
 and is too tired to bring it back to the mouth.
16 The lazy person is wiser in self-esteem
 than seven who can answer discreetly.
17 Like somebody who takes a passing dog by the
 ears
 is one who meddles in the quarrel of another.
18 Like a maniac who shoots deadly firebrands and
 arrows,

a Meaning of Heb uncertain

19 so is one who deceives a neighbor
   and says, "I am only joking!"
20 For lack of wood the fire goes out,
   and where there is no whisperer, quarreling
   ceases.
21 As charcoal is to hot embers and wood to fire,
   so is a quarrelsome person for kindling strife.
22 The words of a whisperer are like delicious
   morsels;
   they go down into the inner parts of the body.
23 Like the glaze*a* covering an earthen vessel
   are smooth*b* lips with an evil heart.
24 An enemy dissembles in speaking
   while harboring deceit within;
25 when an enemy speaks graciously, do not believe
   it,
   for there are seven abominations concealed
   within;
26 though hatred is covered with guile,
   the enemy's wickedness will be exposed in the
   assembly.
27 Whoever digs a pit will fall into it,
   and a stone will come back on the one who
   starts it rolling.
28 A lying tongue hates its victims,
   and a flattering mouth works ruin.

27 Do not boast about tomorrow,
   for you do not know what a day may bring.
2 Let another praise you, and not your own mouth—
   a stranger, and not your own lips.
3 A stone is heavy, and sand is weighty,
   but a fool's provocation is heavier than both.
4 Wrath is cruel, anger is overwhelming,
   but who is able to stand before jealousy?
5 Better is open rebuke
   than hidden love.
6 Well meant are the wounds a friend inflicts,
   but profuse are the kisses of an enemy.
7 The sated appetite spurns honey,
   but to a ravenous appetite even the bitter is
   sweet.
8 Like a bird that strays from its nest
   is one who strays from home.
9 Perfume and incense make the heart glad,
   but the soul is torn by trouble.*c*
10 Do not forsake your friend or the friend of your
   parent;
   do not go to the house of your kindred in the
   day of your calamity.
   Better is a neighbor who is nearby
   than kindred who are far away.
11 Be wise, my child, and make my heart glad,
   so that I may answer whoever reproaches me.

Today, Tomorrow or Never

PROVERBS 27.1

Sometimes even the best-laid plans can tumble to pieces around us. We do not really know what tomorrow may bring. If we listen, though, we can hear God's voice in the midst of disaster or failure, calling us to a new direction or a new start.

Ask for God's help to be open to his plan for your future. One way to do this is to dwell on each of the petitions in the Lord's Prayer as a request for God's help and guidance for the here-and-now. For instance, you might pray, "Not my will but yours be done in me, now, here on earth, as your will is eternally fulfilled in heaven." Take as much time as you need with each line before moving on. If you don't have time to finish the whole Lord's Prayer, come back to it another day.

See Meeting God in Prayer

---

a Cn: Heb *silver of dross*   *b* Gk: Heb *burning*   *c* Gk: Heb *the sweetness of a friend is better than one's own counsel*

Unhelpful Help

PROVERBS 27.14

Which kind of help do you give to others? Ask God to help you look honestly at the help you offer. In particular, look at whether you offer your help more to meet your own needs or to meet the needs of the one you are helping. Is the assistance you offer what that person really needs or what you think he or she needs? Have you asked? What more can you do? How can you ensure that your help is a blessing rather than an annoyance or a hindrance? Where does God call you to reach out to others? You might conclude by offering whatever efforts you make to the glory of God alone.

See Meeting God in Service

12 The clever see danger and hide;
  but the simple go on, and suffer for it.
13 Take the garment of one who has given surety for
    a stranger;
  seize the pledge given as surety for foreigners.*a*
14 Whoever blesses a neighbor with a loud voice,
  rising early in the morning,
  will be counted as cursing.
15 A continual dripping on a rainy day
  and a contentious wife are alike;
16 to restrain her is to restrain the wind
  or to grasp oil in the right hand.*b*
17 Iron sharpens iron,
  and one person sharpens the wits*c* of another.
18 Anyone who tends a fig tree will eat its fruit,
  and anyone who takes care of a master will be
    honored.
19 Just as water reflects the face,
  so one human heart reflects another.
20 Sheol and Abaddon are never satisfied,
  and human eyes are never satisfied.
21 The crucible is for silver, and the furnace is for
    gold,
  so a person is tested*d* by being praised.
22 Crush a fool in a mortar with a pestle
  along with crushed grain,
  but the folly will not be driven out.
23 Know well the condition of your flocks,
  and give attention to your herds;
24 for riches do not last forever,
  nor a crown for all generations.
25 When the grass is gone, and new growth appears,
  and the herbage of the mountains is gathered,
26 the lambs will provide your clothing,
  and the goats the price of a field;
27 there will be enough goats' milk for your food,
  for the food of your household
  and nourishment for your servant-girls.

28 The wicked flee when no one pursues,
  but the righteous are as bold as a lion.
2 When a land rebels
  it has many rulers;
  but with an intelligent ruler
  there is lasting order.*b*
3 A ruler*e* who oppresses the poor
  is a beating rain that leaves no food.
4 Those who forsake the law praise the wicked,
  but those who keep the law struggle against
    them.
5 The evil do not understand justice,
  but those who seek the LORD understand it
    completely.

a Vg and 20.16: Heb *for a foreign woman*   *b* Meaning of Heb uncertain
c Heb *face*   *d* Heb lacks *is tested*   *e* Cn: Heb *A poor person*

⁶ Better to be poor and walk in integrity
  than to be crooked in one's ways even though
    rich.
⁷ Those who keep the law are wise children,
  but companions of gluttons shame their
    parents.
⁸ One who augments wealth by exorbitant interest
  gathers it for another who is kind to the poor.
⁹ When one will not listen to the law,
  even one's prayers are an abomination.
¹⁰ Those who mislead the upright into evil ways
  will fall into pits of their own making,
  but the blameless will have a goodly
    inheritance.
¹¹ The rich is wise in self-esteem,
  but an intelligent poor person sees through the
    pose.
¹² When the righteous triumph, there is great glory,
  but when the wicked prevail, people go into
    hiding.
¹³ No one who conceals transgressions will prosper,
  but one who confesses and forsakes them will
    obtain mercy.
¹⁴ Happy is the one who is never without fear,
  but one who is hard-hearted will fall into
    calamity.
¹⁵ Like a roaring lion or a charging bear
  is a wicked ruler over a poor people.
¹⁶ A ruler who lacks understanding is a cruel
    oppressor;
  but one who hates unjust gain will enjoy a long
    life.
¹⁷ If someone is burdened with the blood of
    another,
  let that killer be a fugitive until death;
  let no one offer assistance.
¹⁸ One who walks in integrity will be safe,
  but whoever follows crooked ways will fall into
    the Pit.ᵃ
¹⁹ Anyone who tills the land will have plenty of
    bread,
  but one who follows worthless pursuits will
    have plenty of poverty.
²⁰ The faithful will abound with blessings,
  but one who is in a hurry to be rich will not go
    unpunished.
²¹ To show partiality is not good—
  yet for a piece of bread a person may do
    wrong.
²² The miser is in a hurry to get rich
  and does not know that loss is sure to come.
²³ Whoever rebukes a person will afterward find
    more favor
  than one who flatters with the tongue.

On the Way

PROVERBS 28.13

It is not easy for anyone to confess wrongdoing. Eve and Adam couldn't. Neither could the snake. The proverbs claim that if we conceal our transgressions, we will not prosper. More agonizing than that, perhaps, is living in fear that someone will find out. So our first impulse usually is to hide and to pretend that all is well. Confession can be a freeing spiritual experience. When we recognize our condition before God, we are reminded of our helplessness and God's grace.

Place yourself in God's presence and unburden your heart in confession. You might use a formal prayer of confession from a hymnal or prayer book, or you might use Psalm 51 as a starting point. Say to yourself and believe, "I have a covenant relationship with God. I will trust God's mercy as I confess."

See Meeting God in Prayer

---

a Syr: Heb fall all at once

The Rights of the Poor

PROVERBS 29.7

The belief that the poor will always be around prevents some people from looking seriously at the issue of poverty and justice. The wicked have no understanding of the rights of the poor; they can always list reasons why the poor deserve their poverty.

Being faithful leads us beyond mere belief in the one true God. How would you respond if someone told you that you share responsibility before God for the plight of all of God's children? Overwhelming, isn't it? What concrete action can you take to help at least some of the poor? Listen for God's call. What is the first step you can take in response?

See Meeting God in Service

24 Anyone who robs father or mother
and says, "That is no crime,"
is partner to a thug.
25 The greedy person stirs up strife,
but whoever trusts in the LORD will be enriched.
26 Those who trust in their own wits are fools;
but those who walk in wisdom come through safely.
27 Whoever gives to the poor will lack nothing,
but one who turns a blind eye will get many a curse.
28 When the wicked prevail, people go into hiding;
but when they perish, the righteous increase.

29 One who is often reproved, yet remains stubborn,
will suddenly be broken beyond healing.
2 When the righteous are in authority, the people rejoice;
but when the wicked rule, the people groan.
3 A child who loves wisdom makes a parent glad,
but to keep company with prostitutes is to squander one's substance.
4 By justice a king gives stability to the land,
but one who makes heavy exactions ruins it.
5 Whoever flatters a neighbor
is spreading a net for the neighbor's feet.
6 In the transgression of the evil there is a snare,
but the righteous sing and rejoice.
7 The righteous know the rights of the poor;
the wicked have no such understanding.
8 Scoffers set a city aflame,
but the wise turn away wrath.
9 If the wise go to law with fools,
there is ranting and ridicule without relief.
10 The bloodthirsty hate the blameless,
and they seek the life of the upright.
11 A fool gives full vent to anger,
but the wise quietly holds it back.
12 If a ruler listens to falsehood,
all his officials will be wicked.
13 The poor and the oppressor have this in common:
the LORD gives light to the eyes of both.
14 If a king judges the poor with equity,
his throne will be established forever.
15 The rod and reproof give wisdom,
but a mother is disgraced by a neglected child.
16 When the wicked are in authority, transgression increases,
but the righteous will look upon their downfall.
17 Discipline your children, and they will give you rest;
they will give delight to your heart.
18 Where there is no prophecy, the people cast off restraint,
but happy are those who keep the law.

¹⁹ By mere words servants are not disciplined,
  for though they understand, they will not give
   heed.
²⁰ Do you see someone who is hasty in speech?
  There is more hope for a fool than for anyone
   like that.
²¹ A slave pampered from childhood
  will come to a bad end.ᵃ
²² One given to anger stirs up strife,
  and the hothead causes much transgression.
²³ A person's pride will bring humiliation,
  but one who is lowly in spirit will obtain honor.
²⁴ To be a partner of a thief is to hate one's own life;
  one hears the victim's curse, but discloses
   nothing.ᵇ
²⁵ The fear of othersᶜ lays a snare,
  but one who trusts in the LORD is secure.
²⁶ Many seek the favor of a ruler,
  but it is from the LORD that one gets justice.
²⁷ The unjust are an abomination to the righteous,
  but the upright are an abomination to the
   wicked.

Sayings of Agur

30 The words of Agur son of Jakeh. An oracle.

Thus says the man: I am weary, O God,
  I am weary, O God. How can I prevail?ᵈ
² Surely I am too stupid to be human;
  I do not have human understanding.
³ I have not learned wisdom,
  nor have I knowledge of the holy ones.ᵉ
⁴ Who has ascended to heaven and come down?
  Who has gathered the wind in the hollow of the
   hand?
Who has wrapped up the waters in a garment?
  Who has established all the ends of the earth?
What is the person's name?
  And what is the name of the person's child?
   Surely you know!

⁵ Every word of God proves true;
  he is a shield to those who take refuge in him.
⁶ Do not add to his words,
  or else he will rebuke you, and you will be
   found a liar.

⁷ Two things I ask of you;
  do not deny them to me before I die:
⁸ Remove far from me falsehood and lying;
  give me neither poverty nor riches;
   feed me with the food that I need,

Taking Time

PROVERBS 29.20

Often we pride ourselves on being quick to speak, on always having a ready answer. We know, though, that speaking too quickly often gets us into trouble. Cutting remarks, careless comments and poor advice tumble out of our mouths.

Try for one day to be slow to speak. Take a deep breath before replying to a question or commenting on something you see. During that breath, you might offer a silent prayer such as, "God grant me wisdom when I speak," breathing in over the first four syllables and out over the last four.

One way to prepare for a day of slow and careful speech would be to sit quietly for several minutes. As you sit, breathe slowly and repeat that prayer with each breath. This might also be a good way to prepare for a meeting.

See Meeting God in Prayer

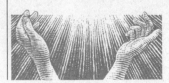

ᵃ Vg: Meaning of Heb uncertain ᵇ Meaning of Heb uncertain
ᶜ Or *human fear* ᵈ Or *I am spent*. Meaning of Heb uncertain
ᵉ Or *Holy One*

Playing the Fool With God's Word

PROVERBS 30.5–9

"No one is more foolish than one who forces the meaning of the Scriptures or finds fault with them so as to demonstrate his own knowledge—or, rather, his own ignorance. What kind of knowledge can result from adapting the meaning of the Scriptures to suit one's own likes and from daring to alter their words? The true sage is one who regards the text as authoritative and discovers, through the wisdom of the Spirit, the hidden mysteries to which the divine Scriptures bear witness."

—PETER OF DAMASKOS,
The Philokalia, Volume III

9 or I shall be full, and deny you,
and say, "Who is the LORD?"
or I shall be poor, and steal,
and profane the name of my God.

10 Do not slander a servant to a master,
or the servant will curse you, and you will be
held guilty.

11 There are those who curse their fathers
and do not bless their mothers.
12 There are those who are pure in their own eyes
yet are not cleansed of their filthiness.
13 There are those—how lofty are their eyes,
how high their eyelids lift!—
14 there are those whose teeth are swords,
whose teeth are knives,
to devour the poor from off the earth,
the needy from among mortals.

15 The leech*a* has two daughters;
"Give, give," they cry.
Three things are never satisfied;
four never say, "Enough":
16 Sheol, the barren womb,
the earth ever thirsty for water,
and the fire that never says, "Enough."*a*

17 The eye that mocks a father
and scorns to obey a mother
will be pecked out by the ravens of the valley
and eaten by the vultures.

18 Three things are too wonderful for me;
four I do not understand:
19 the way of an eagle in the sky,
the way of a snake on a rock,
the way of a ship on the high seas,
and the way of a man with a girl.

20 This is the way of an adulteress:
she eats, and wipes her mouth,
and says, "I have done no wrong."

21 Under three things the earth trembles;
under four it cannot bear up:
22 a slave when he becomes king,
and a fool when glutted with food;
23 an unloved woman when she gets a husband,
and a maid when she succeeds her mistress.

24 Four things on earth are small,
yet they are exceedingly wise:

a Meaning of Heb uncertain

25 the ants are a people without strength,
    yet they provide their food in the summer;
26 the badgers are a people without power,
    yet they make their homes in the rocks;
27 the locusts have no king,
    yet all of them march in rank;
28 the lizard*a* can be grasped in the hand,
    yet it is found in kings' palaces.

29 Three things are stately in their stride;
    four are stately in their gait:
30 the lion, which is mightiest among wild animals
    and does not turn back before any;
31 the strutting rooster,*b* the he-goat,
    and a king striding before*c* his people.

32 If you have been foolish, exalting yourself,
    or if you have been devising evil,
    put your hand on your mouth.
33 For as pressing milk produces curds,
    and pressing the nose produces blood,
    so pressing anger produces strife.

The Teaching of King Lemuel's Mother

31 The words of King Lemuel. An oracle that his mother taught him:

2 No, my son! No, son of my womb!
    No, son of my vows!
3 Do not give your strength to women,
    your ways to those who destroy kings.
4 It is not for kings, O Lemuel,
    it is not for kings to drink wine,
    or for rulers to desire*d* strong drink;
5 or else they will drink and forget what has been
      decreed,
    and will pervert the rights of all the afflicted.
6 Give strong drink to one who is perishing,
    and wine to those in bitter distress;
7 let them drink and forget their poverty,
    and remember their misery no more.
8 Speak out for those who cannot speak,
    for the rights of all the destitute.*e*
9 Speak out, judge righteously,
    defend the rights of the poor and needy.

Ode to a Capable Wife

10 A capable wife who can find?
    She is far more precious than jewels.
11 The heart of her husband trusts in her,
    and he will have no lack of gain.
12 She does him good, and not harm,
    all the days of her life.

A Voice for the Voiceless

PROVERBS 31.8–9

The sage challenges us to speak out and defend the powerless, whose voice is not heard; the poor, who struggle to survive; and the destitute, who have nothing. Some of life's defining moments come as we are invited and challenged to speak out for the voiceless. Henri J. M. Nouwen said, "Compassion without confrontation fades quickly into fruitless sentimental commiseration." What is he trying to tell us? If we are called to speak for the oppressed, how can we live this out? Ask God to keep you alert for surprising encounters that offer you opportunities to be a voice for the voiceless. Ask for the courage to accept such opportunities. You might conclude your prayer time by singing Frances R. Havergal's hymn "Lord, Speak to Me, That I May Speak" or S. Ralph Harlow's "O Young and Fearless Prophet."

See Meeting God in Service

---

a Or *spider*   *b* Gk Syr Tg Compare Vg: Meaning of Heb uncertain
c Meaning of Heb uncertain   *d* Cn: Heb *where*   *e* Heb *all children of passing away*

A Working Mother

PROVERBS 31.10–31

This poem in praise of a working mother is an acrostic; each verse begins with a different letter of the Hebrew alphabet, in order from *Aleph* to *Taw*. This woman is the embodiment of wisdom in action, doing everything she does with forethought and excellence and enabling others in her family to do their best as well.

Who has been an embodiment of wisdom in your life? You might try to create an acrostic in praise of that person, listing qualities that make him or her praiseworthy or that exemplify wisdom in action. You might use the person's name, title or their relationship to you as a basis for the acrostic. (For example, think of the song "MOTHER," which begins, "M is for the million things she gave me.") If the person is still living, make a good copy of the poem and give it to him or her. In any case, thank God for the gift of this person in your life.

See Meeting God in Everyday Life

13 She seeks wool and flax,
   and works with willing hands.

14 She is like the ships of the merchant,
   she brings her food from far away.

15 She rises while it is still night
   and provides food for her household
   and tasks for her servant-girls.

16 She considers a field and buys it;
   with the fruit of her hands she plants a
      vineyard.

17 She girds herself with strength,
   and makes her arms strong.

18 She perceives that her merchandise is profitable.
   Her lamp does not go out at night.

19 She puts her hands to the distaff,
   and her hands hold the spindle.

20 She opens her hand to the poor,
   and reaches out her hands to the needy.

21 She is not afraid for her household when it
      snows,
   for all her household are clothed in crimson.

22 She makes herself coverings;
   her clothing is fine linen and purple.

23 Her husband is known in the city gates,
   taking his seat among the elders of the land.

24 She makes linen garments and sells them;
   she supplies the merchant with sashes.

25 Strength and dignity are her clothing,
   and she laughs at the time to come.

26 She opens her mouth with wisdom,
   and the teaching of kindness is on her tongue.

27 She looks well to the ways of her household,
   and does not eat the bread of idleness.

28 Her children rise up and call her happy;
   her husband too, and he praises her:

29 "Many women have done excellently,
   but you surpass them all."

30 Charm is deceitful, and beauty is vain,
   but a woman who fears the LORD is to be
      praised.

31 Give her a share in the fruit of her hands,
   and let her works praise her in the city gates.

ECCLESIASTES

A Search for Meaning

KEY VERSE:

He has made everything suitable for its time; moreover he has put a sense of past and future into their minds, yet they cannot find out what God has done from the beginning to the end.

—Ecclesiastes 3.11

Ecclesiastes explores the meaning of life, and its words often seem to reflect Thoreau's famous quotation, "The mass of men lead lives of quiet desperation." The author, called "the Teacher," is not as conclusive in his exploration as we would like him to be; at times he seems uncertain about God's ways. We might wonder why he sends all of these mixed messages. He confesses that his past choices have included the pursuit of pleasure, achievement and riches (2.1–11; 4.13–16; 5.1—6.12). Even though the Teacher has found all three, he struggles with disillusionment. In contrast, his parting words seem sure of the purpose of life: "Fear God, and keep his commandments; for that is the whole duty of everyone." We identify with his struggle to find meaning in the weariness of everyday life, a universal struggle to this day; yet beyond the recitation of troubles, his words soar with hope, "I know that whatever God does endures forever" (3.14).

As you read this book of wisdom, take time to ponder the "big picture"—the meaning and purpose of life—but don't forget to make a daily effort to look with wonder at God's creation. Learn from the Teacher about the meaninglessness of acquisition, knowledge and work in and of themselves—but also learn that your ultimate purpose in everything you do is to know, love and serve God. Even as you acknowledge the ambiguities of life, remain open to the rich and mysterious ways in which God will reveal its meaning to you.

> "The present moment holds infinite riches beyond your wildest dreams but you will only enjoy them to the extent of your faith and love. The more a soul loves, the more it longs, the more it hopes, the more it finds."
>
> —JEAN-PIERRE DE CAUSSADE,
> *The Sacrament of the Present*

Summarized

ECCLESIASTES 1.1–18

Your first response might be to think that the Teacher should have developed a rosier outlook on life. Take time to reflect on your life with some one-word summaries. What one word would you use in place of "meaningless" or "vanity" to summarize your life at present? What words best describe your search for meaning and purpose? What sort of picture do these words suggest?

See Meeting God in Scripture

Reflections of a Royal Philosopher

1 The words of the Teacher,[a] the son of David, king in Jerusalem.
2 Vanity of vanities, says the Teacher,[a]
vanity of vanities! All is vanity.
3 What do people gain from all the toil
at which they toil under the sun?
4 A generation goes, and a generation comes,
but the earth remains forever.
5 The sun rises and the sun goes down,
and hurries to the place where it rises.
6 The wind blows to the south,
and goes around to the north;
round and round goes the wind,
and on its circuits the wind returns.
7 All streams run to the sea,
but the sea is not full;
to the place where the streams flow,
there they continue to flow.
8 All things[b] are wearisome;
more than one can express;
the eye is not satisfied with seeing,
or the ear filled with hearing.
9 What has been is what will be,
and what has been done is what will be done;
there is nothing new under the sun.
10 Is there a thing of which it is said,
"See, this is new"?
It has already been,
in the ages before us.
11 The people of long ago are not remembered,
nor will there be any remembrance
of people yet to come
by those who come after them.

The Futility of Seeking Wisdom

12 I, the Teacher,[a] when king over Israel in Jerusalem, 13 applied my mind to seek and to search out by wisdom all that is done under heaven; it is an unhappy business that God has given to human beings to be busy with. 14 I saw all the deeds that are done under the sun; and see, all is vanity and a chasing after wind.[c]
15 What is crooked cannot be made straight,
and what is lacking cannot be counted.
16 I said to myself, "I have acquired great wisdom, surpassing all who were over Jerusalem before me; and my mind has had great experience of wisdom and knowledge." 17 And I applied my mind to know wisdom and to know madness and folly. I perceived that this also is but a chasing after wind.[c]
18 For in much wisdom is much vexation,
and those who increase knowledge increase
sorrow.

The Futility of Self-Indulgence

2 I said to myself, "Come now, I will make a test of pleasure; enjoy yourself." But again, this also was

---

a Heb *Qoheleth*, traditionally rendered *Preacher*   b Or *words*   c Or *a feeding on wind.* See Hos 12.1

vanity. [2]I said of laughter, "It is mad," and of pleasure, "What use is it?" [3]I searched with my mind how to cheer my body with wine—my mind still guiding me with wisdom—and how to lay hold on folly, until I might see what was good for mortals to do under heaven during the few days of their life. [4]I made great works; I built houses and planted vineyards for myself; [5]I made myself gardens and parks, and planted in them all kinds of fruit trees. [6]I made myself pools from which to water the forest of growing trees. [7]I bought male and female slaves, and had slaves who were born in my house; I also had great possessions of herds and flocks, more than any who had been before me in Jerusalem. [8]I also gathered for myself silver and gold and the treasure of kings and of the provinces; I got singers, both men and women, and delights of the flesh, and many concubines.[a]

9 So I became great and surpassed all who were before me in Jerusalem; also my wisdom remained with me. [10]Whatever my eyes desired I did not keep from them; I kept my heart from no pleasure, for my heart found pleasure in all my toil, and this was my reward for all my toil. [11]Then I considered all that my hands had done and the toil I had spent in doing it, and again, all was vanity and a chasing after wind,[b] and there was nothing to be gained under the sun.

Wisdom and Joy Given to One Who Pleases God

12 So I turned to consider wisdom and madness and folly; for what can the one do who comes after the king? Only what has already been done. [13]Then I saw that wisdom excels folly as light excels darkness.
[14]   The wise have eyes in their head,
        but fools walk in darkness.
Yet I perceived that the same fate befalls all of them. [15]Then I said to myself, "What happens to the fool will happen to me also; why then have I been so very wise?" And I said to myself that this also is vanity. [16]For there is no enduring remembrance of the wise or of fools, seeing that in the days to come all will have been long forgotten. How can the wise die just like fools? [17]So I hated life, because what is done under the sun was grievous to me; for all is vanity and a chasing after wind.[b]

18 I hated all my toil in which I had toiled under the sun, seeing that I must leave it to those who come after me [19]—and who knows whether they will be wise or foolish? Yet they will be master of all for which I toiled and used my wisdom under the sun. This also is vanity. [20]So I turned and gave my heart up to despair concerning all the toil of my labors under the sun, [21]because sometimes one who has toiled with wisdom and knowledge and skill must leave all to be enjoyed by another who did not toil for it. This also is vanity and a great evil. [22]What do mortals get from all the toil and strain with which they toil under the sun? [23]For all their days are full of pain, and their work is a vexation; even at night their minds do not rest. This also is vanity.

24 There is nothing better for mortals than to eat and drink, and find enjoyment in their toil. This also, I saw, is

Testing What Is Good

ECCLESIASTES 2.1

How like a teacher to suggest another test, but so far the Teacher has limited the scope of his tests to pleasure and achievements! Today's culture also seems bent on testing the meaning of achievement, pleasure and materialism. But why not test the meaningfulness of relationships? Apply this test to your encounter with God. In what ways do you find meaning in God's presence? What "achievements" is God accomplishing through you? How are you "relating" to God? Which areas of your life with God need a tune-up? Which area seems like a good place for God and you to begin that work?

---

a Meaning of Heb uncertain   *b* Or *a feeding on wind*. See Hos 12.1

A Present Shaped by the Future

ECCLESIASTES 3.11

God has given us a sense of past and future—even putting eternity in our hearts. Our present is affected not only by our past but also by the future to which God is calling us. On one half of a sheet of paper make a list of some things God might be calling you to do. Then, on the other half, list the things that you may need to relinquish to make time for responding to God's call. As you review it, ask yourself if you see signs that this "making room" has already begun.

See Meeting God in Everyday Life

from the hand of God; [25]for apart from him[a] who can eat or who can have enjoyment? [26]For to the one who pleases him God gives wisdom and knowledge and joy; but to the sinner he gives the work of gathering and heaping, only to give to one who pleases God. This also is vanity and a chasing after wind.[b]

Everything Has Its Time

3 For everything there is a season, and a time for every matter under heaven:

[2] a time to be born, and a time to die;
a time to plant, and a time to pluck up what is planted;
[3] a time to kill, and a time to heal;
a time to break down, and a time to build up;
[4] a time to weep, and a time to laugh;
a time to mourn, and a time to dance;
[5] a time to throw away stones, and a time to gather stones together;
a time to embrace, and a time to refrain from embracing;
[6] a time to seek, and a time to lose;
a time to keep, and a time to throw away;
[7] a time to tear, and a time to sew;
a time to keep silence, and a time to speak;
[8] a time to love, and a time to hate;
a time for war, and a time for peace.

The God-Given Task

9 What gain have the workers from their toil? [10]I have seen the business that God has given to everyone to be busy with. [11]He has made everything suitable for its time; moreover he has put a sense of past and future into their minds, yet they cannot find out what God has done from the beginning to the end. [12]I know that there is nothing better for them than to be happy and enjoy themselves as long as they live; [13]moreover, it is God's gift that all should eat and drink and take pleasure in all their toil. [14]I know that whatever God does endures forever; nothing can be added to it, nor anything taken from it; God has done this, so that all should stand in awe before him. [15]That which is, already has been; that which is to be, already is; and God seeks out what has gone by.[c]

Judgment and the Future Belong to God

16 Moreover I saw under the sun that in the place of justice, wickedness was there, and in the place of righteousness, wickedness was there as well. [17]I said in my heart, God will judge the righteous and the wicked, for he has appointed a time for every matter, and for every work. [18]I said in my heart with regard to human beings that God is testing them to show that they are but animals. [19]For the fate of humans and the fate of animals is the same; as one dies, so dies the other. They all have the same breath, and humans have no advantage over the animals; for all is vanity. [20]All go to one place; all are from the dust, and all turn to dust again. [21]Who knows whether

a Gk Syr: Heb *apart from me*   *b* Or *a feeding on wind.* See Hos 12.1
c Heb *what is pursued*

the human spirit goes upward and the spirit of animals goes downward to the earth? [22] So I saw that there is nothing better than that all should enjoy their work, for that is their lot; who can bring them to see what will be after them?

4 Again I saw all the oppressions that are practiced under the sun. Look, the tears of the oppressed—with no one to comfort them! On the side of their oppressors there was power—with no one to comfort them. [2] And I thought the dead, who have already died, more fortunate than the living, who are still alive; [3] but better than both is the one who has not yet been, and has not seen the evil deeds that are done under the sun.

4 Then I saw that all toil and all skill in work come from one person's envy of another. This also is vanity and a chasing after wind.[a]

5   Fools fold their hands
      and consume their own flesh.
6   Better is a handful with quiet
      than two handfuls with toil,
      and a chasing after wind.[a]

7 Again, I saw vanity under the sun: [8] the case of solitary individuals, without sons or brothers; yet there is no end to all their toil, and their eyes are never satisfied with riches. "For whom am I toiling," they ask, "and depriving myself of pleasure?" This also is vanity and an unhappy business.

The Value of a Friend

9 Two are better than one, because they have a good reward for their toil. [10] For if they fall, one will lift up the other; but woe to one who is alone and falls and does not have another to help. [11] Again, if two lie together, they keep warm; but how can one keep warm alone? [12] And though one might prevail against another, two will withstand one. A threefold cord is not quickly broken.

13 Better is a poor but wise youth than an old but foolish king, who will no longer take advice. [14] One can indeed come out of prison to reign, even though born poor in the kingdom. [15] I saw all the living who, moving about under the sun, follow that[b] youth who replaced the king;[c] [16] there was no end to all those people whom he led. Yet those who come later will not rejoice in him. Surely this also is vanity and a chasing after wind.[a]

Reverence, Humility, and Contentment

5[d] Guard your steps when you go to the house of God; to draw near to listen is better than the sacrifice offered by fools; for they do not know how to keep from doing evil.[e] [2][f] Never be rash with your mouth, nor let your heart be quick to utter a word before God, for God is in heaven, and you upon earth; therefore let your words be few.

3 For dreams come with many cares, and a fool's voice with many words.

4 When you make a vow to God, do not delay fulfilling it; for he has no pleasure in fools. Fulfill what you vow. [5] It

---

Motivated by Envy

ECCLESIASTES 4.4

The Teacher offers a startling insight: Envy may be at the root of our hard work and achievement. Envy shifts our focus from what God has given us to what has been given to others. It estranges us from others and causes discontent with ourselves and our lot in life. Think of a few people you envy or have envied, and write their names in your journal or on a piece of paper. Add a few words describing what you envy about them. Finally, for each point make note of something God has given you. Carry the list with you until you read again from this book. Express your thanks to God.

See Meeting God in Community

---

a Or *a feeding on wind.* See Hos 12.1   b Heb *the second*   c Heb *him*
d Ch 4.17 in Heb   e Cn: Heb *they do not know how to do evil*   f Ch 5.1 in Heb

How Much Is Enough?

ECCLESIASTES 5.10–14

One of the Teacher's key questions in his struggle with "vanity" or meaninglessness seems to be "How much is enough?"

Quiz yourself for a few minutes on "enough-ness." Make a list down the side of a sheet of paper, including such things as love, money, rest, food, clothing, entertainment, exercise, spiritual self-examination, assurance of God's presence and so forth. Mark "yes" after those of which you believe you have enough. For the others, write a sentence describing your current needs. Pray for God's assistance in your appraisal; discern the difference between your desires and your needs. Finish by asking God, "What do I need to know about having enough?"

See Meeting God in Prayer

is better that you should not vow than that you should vow and not fulfill it. [6]Do not let your mouth lead you into sin, and do not say before the messenger that it was a mistake; why should God be angry at your words, and destroy the work of your hands?

7 With many dreams come vanities and a multitude of words;[a] but fear God.

8 If you see in a province the oppression of the poor and the violation of justice and right, do not be amazed at the matter; for the high official is watched by a higher, and there are yet higher ones over them. [9]But all things considered, this is an advantage for a land: a king for a plowed field.[a]

10 The lover of money will not be satisfied with money; nor the lover of wealth, with gain. This also is vanity.

11 When goods increase, those who eat them increase; and what gain has their owner but to see them with his eyes?

12 Sweet is the sleep of laborers, whether they eat little or much; but the surfeit of the rich will not let them sleep.

13 There is a grievous ill that I have seen under the sun: riches were kept by their owners to their hurt, [14]and those riches were lost in a bad venture; though they are parents of children, they have nothing in their hands. [15]As they came from their mother's womb, so they shall go again, naked as they came; they shall take nothing for their toil, which they may carry away with their hands. [16]This also is a grievous ill: just as they came, so shall they go; and what gain do they have from toiling for the wind? [17]Besides, all their days they eat in darkness, in much vexation and sickness and resentment.

18 This is what I have seen to be good: it is fitting to eat and drink and find enjoyment in all the toil with which one toils under the sun the few days of the life God gives us; for this is our lot. [19]Likewise all to whom God gives wealth and possessions and whom he enables to enjoy them, and to accept their lot and find enjoyment in their toil—this is the gift of God. [20]For they will scarcely brood over the days of their lives, because God keeps them occupied with the joy of their hearts.

The Frustration of Desires

6 There is an evil that I have seen under the sun, and it lies heavy upon humankind: [2]those to whom God gives wealth, possessions, and honor, so that they lack nothing of all that they desire, yet God does not enable them to enjoy these things, but a stranger enjoys them. This is vanity; it is a grievous ill. [3]A man may beget a hundred children, and live many years; but however many are the days of his years, if he does not enjoy life's good things, or has no burial, I say that a stillborn child is better off than he. [4]For it comes into vanity and goes into darkness, and in darkness its name is covered; [5]moreover it has not seen the sun or known anything; yet it finds rest rather than he. [6]Even though he should live a thousand years twice over, yet enjoy no good—do not all go to one place?

a Meaning of Heb uncertain

7 All human toil is for the mouth, yet the appetite is not satisfied. ⁸For what advantage have the wise over fools? And what do the poor have who know how to conduct themselves before the living? ⁹Better is the sight of the eyes than the wandering of desire; this also is vanity and a chasing after wind.^a

10 Whatever has come to be has already been named, and it is known what human beings are, and that they are not able to dispute with those who are stronger. ¹¹The more words, the more vanity, so how is one the better? ¹²For who knows what is good for mortals while they live the few days of their vain life, which they pass like a shadow? For who can tell them what will be after them under the sun?

A Disillusioned View of Life

7 A good name is better than precious ointment,
and the day of death, than the day of birth.
² It is better to go to the house of mourning
than to go to the house of feasting;
for this is the end of everyone,
and the living will lay it to heart.
³ Sorrow is better than laughter,
for by sadness of countenance the heart is
made glad.
⁴ The heart of the wise is in the house of mourning;
but the heart of fools is in the house of mirth.
⁵ It is better to hear the rebuke of the wise
than to hear the song of fools.
⁶ For like the crackling of thorns under a pot,
so is the laughter of fools;
this also is vanity.
⁷ Surely oppression makes the wise foolish,
and a bribe corrupts the heart.
⁸ Better is the end of a thing than its beginning;
the patient in spirit are better than the proud in
spirit.
⁹ Do not be quick to anger,
for anger lodges in the bosom of fools.
¹⁰ Do not say, "Why were the former days better
than these?"
For it is not from wisdom that you ask this.
¹¹ Wisdom is as good as an inheritance,
an advantage to those who see the sun.
¹² For the protection of wisdom is like the protection
of money,
and the advantage of knowledge is that wisdom
gives life to the one who possesses it.
¹³ Consider the work of God;
who can make straight what he has made
crooked?

14 In the day of prosperity be joyful, and in the day of adversity consider; God has made the one as well as the other, so that mortals may not find out anything that will come after them.

The Riddles of Life

15 In my vain life I have seen everything; there are righteous people who perish in their righteousness, and there

Wise Person or Cynic?

ECCLESIASTES 7.10–14

Jesus is known for how he asked questions. He was inquisitive, but not cynical. How would he have reacted to the questions the Teacher asks and discusses here? With what attitude would Jesus have asked them? Reread Ecclesiastes 7.10–12. What word or phrase or action attracts your attention? Reflect on this word or phrase or action. Why is it meaningful to you? Write down the key words such as *protection*, *money* and *wisdom*. Reflect on each of them. What questions might you ask God? Remain silent and open to receive insight from God.

See Meeting God in Scripture

Wisdom Brings Light

ECCLESIASTES 8.1

"We have hints that there is a way of life vastly richer and deeper than all this hurried existence, a life of unhurried serenity and peace and power. We have known some people who have found this deep Center of living. We've seen such lives, integrated, unworried by the tangles of close decisions, unhurried, cheery, fresh, positive. These are not people of dallying idleness nor of obviously mooning meditation; they are busy carrying their full load as well as we are, but without any chafing of the shoulders with the burden, with quiet joy and springing step. They are poised and at peace."

—THOMAS KELLY,
—*A Testament of Devotion*

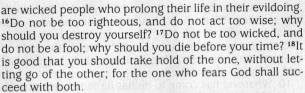

are wicked people who prolong their life in their evildoing. [16]Do not be too righteous, and do not act too wise; why should you destroy yourself? [17]Do not be too wicked, and do not be a fool; why should you die before your time? [18]It is good that you should take hold of the one, without letting go of the other; for the one who fears God shall succeed with both.

19 Wisdom gives strength to the wise more than ten rulers that are in a city.

20 Surely there is no one on earth so righteous as to do good without ever sinning.

21 Do not give heed to everything that people say, or you may hear your servant cursing you; [22]your heart knows that many times you have yourself cursed others.

23 All this I have tested by wisdom; I said, "I will be wise," but it was far from me. [24]That which is, is far off, and deep, very deep; who can find it out? [25]I turned my mind to know and to search out and to seek wisdom and the sum of things, and to know that wickedness is folly and that foolishness is madness. [26]I found more bitter than death the woman who is a trap, whose heart is snares and nets, whose hands are fetters; one who pleases God escapes her, but the sinner is taken by her. [27]See, this is what I found, says the Teacher,[a] adding one thing to another to find the sum, [28]which my mind has sought repeatedly, but I have not found. One man among a thousand I found, but a woman among all these I have not found. [29]See, this alone I found, that God made human beings straightforward, but they have devised many schemes.

Obey the King and Enjoy Yourself

8 Who is like the wise man?
 And who knows the interpretation of a thing?
Wisdom makes one's face shine,
 and the hardness of one's countenance is changed.

2 Keep[b] the king's command because of your sacred oath. [3]Do not be terrified; go from his presence, do not delay when the matter is unpleasant, for he does whatever he pleases. [4]For the word of the king is powerful, and who can say to him, "What are you doing?" [5]Whoever obeys a command will meet no harm, and the wise mind will know the time and way. [6]For every matter has its time and way, although the troubles of mortals lie heavy upon them. [7]Indeed, they do not know what is to be, for who can tell them how it will be? [8]No one has power over the wind[c] to restrain the wind,[c] or power over the day of death; there is no discharge from the battle, nor does wickedness deliver those who practice it. [9]All this I observed, applying my mind to all that is done under the sun, while one person exercises authority over another to the other's hurt.

God's Ways Are Inscrutable

10 Then I saw the wicked buried; they used to go in and out of the holy place, and were praised in the city where they had done such things.[d] This also is vanity. [11]Because sentence against an evil deed is not executed speed-

---

a Qoheleth, traditionally rendered *Preacher*   b Heb *I keep*   c Or *breath*
d Meaning of Heb uncertain

ily, the human heart is fully set to do evil. ¹²Though sinners do evil a hundred times and prolong their lives, yet I know that it will be well with those who fear God, because they stand in fear before him, ¹³but it will not be well with the wicked, neither will they prolong their days like a shadow, because they do not stand in fear before God.

14 There is a vanity that takes place on earth, that there are righteous people who are treated according to the conduct of the wicked, and there are wicked people who are treated according to the conduct of the righteous. I said that this also is vanity. ¹⁵So I commend enjoyment, for there is nothing better for people under the sun than to eat, and drink, and enjoy themselves, for this will go with them in their toil through the days of life that God gives them under the sun.

16 When I applied my mind to know wisdom, and to see the business that is done on earth, how one's eyes see sleep neither day nor night, ¹⁷then I saw all the work of God, that no one can find out what is happening under the sun. However much they may toil in seeking, they will not find it out; even though those who are wise claim to know, they cannot find it out.

Take Life as It Comes

9 All this I laid to heart, examining it all, how the righteous and the wise and their deeds are in the hand of God; whether it is love or hate one does not know. Everything that confronts them ²is vanity,ᵃ since the same fate comes to all, to the righteous and the wicked, to the good and the evil,ᵇ to the clean and the unclean, to those who sacrifice and those who do not sacrifice. As are the good, so are the sinners; those who swear are like those who shun an oath. ³This is an evil in all that happens under the sun, that the same fate comes to everyone. Moreover, the hearts of all are full of evil; madness is in their hearts while they live, and after that they go to the dead. ⁴But whoever is joined with all the living has hope, for a living dog is better than a dead lion. ⁵The living know that they will die, but the dead know nothing; they have no more reward, and even the memory of them is lost. ⁶Their love and their hate and their envy have already perished; never again will they have any share in all that happens under the sun.

7 Go, eat your bread with enjoyment, and drink your wine with a merry heart; for God has long ago approved what you do. ⁸Let your garments always be white; do not let oil be lacking on your head. ⁹Enjoy life with the wife whom you love, all the days of your vain life that are given you under the sun, because that is your portion in life and in your toil at which you toil under the sun. ¹⁰Whatever your hand finds to do, do with your might; for there is no work or thought or knowledge or wisdom in Sheol, to which you are going.

11 Again I saw that under the sun the race is not to the swift, nor the battle to the strong, nor bread to the wise, nor riches to the intelligent, nor favor to the skillful; but time and chance happen to them all. ¹²For no one can anticipate the time of disaster. Like fish taken in a cruel

Content With Mystery

ECCLESIASTES 8.16–17

The Teacher seems to be accepting the idea that God is unsearchable: "Then I saw all the work of God, that no one can find out what is happening under the sun." Make a list of the things you don't know and understand about God, humanity, science and relationships. (If you wish, walk around your house or apartment and touch things that represent them—a musical instrument, a box of bleach, a book, a wedding photo.)

Consider offering a prayer of acknowledgment to God that you don't understand these things and don't need to understand them. Let your acknowledgment of unknowing become an act of worship of the God who knows what you don't know.

See Meeting God in Prayer

A Little Folly

ECCLESIASTES 10.1

Why do we sometimes beat ourselves up over "a little folly" of the past? Perhaps you carry within yourself a pesky burden from the past—a regret, a remnant of guilt, a nagging memory? Ponder it for a moment in silence before God: What do I have invested in this foible that prompts me to hold on to it? What is God calling me to do to rid myself of this memory? An admission to a friend or mentor? A small act of restitution? A selfless act that proves I intend to travel a different road from now on?

net, and like birds caught in a snare, so mortals are snared at a time of calamity, when it suddenly falls upon them.

Wisdom Superior to Folly

13 I have also seen this example of wisdom under the sun, and it seemed great to me. ¹⁴There was a little city with few people in it. A great king came against it and besieged it, building great siegeworks against it. ¹⁵Now there was found in it a poor wise man, and he by his wisdom delivered the city. Yet no one remembered that poor man. ¹⁶So I said, "Wisdom is better than might; yet the poor man's wisdom is despised, and his words are not heeded."

¹⁷ The quiet words of the wise are more to be heeded
     than the shouting of a ruler among fools.
¹⁸ Wisdom is better than weapons of war,
     but one bungler destroys much good.

Miscellaneous Observations

10 Dead flies make the perfumer's ointment give
          off a foul odor;
        so a little folly outweighs wisdom and honor.
² The heart of the wise inclines to the right,
     but the heart of a fool to the left.
³ Even when fools walk on the road, they lack
          sense,
     and show to everyone that they are fools.
⁴ If the anger of the ruler rises against you, do not
          leave your post,
     for calmness will undo great offenses.

5 There is an evil that I have seen under the sun, as great an error as if it proceeded from the ruler: ⁶folly is set in many high places, and the rich sit in a low place. ⁷I have seen slaves on horseback, and princes walking on foot like slaves.

⁸ Whoever digs a pit will fall into it;
     and whoever breaks through a wall will be
          bitten by a snake.
⁹ Whoever quarries stones will be hurt by them;
     and whoever splits logs will be endangered by
          them.
¹⁰ If the iron is blunt, and one does not whet the
          edge,
     then more strength must be exerted;
     but wisdom helps one to succeed.
¹¹ If the snake bites before it is charmed,
     there is no advantage in a charmer.

¹² Words spoken by the wise bring them favor,
     but the lips of fools consume them.
¹³ The words of their mouths begin in foolishness,
     and their talk ends in wicked madness;
¹⁴ yet fools talk on and on.
     No one knows what is to happen,
     and who can tell anyone what the future holds?
¹⁵ The toil of fools wears them out,
     for they do not even know the way to town.
¹⁶ Alas for you, O land, when your king is a servant,ᵃ

a Or a child

and your princes feast in the morning!

17 Happy are you, O land, when your king is a nobleman,
and your princes feast at the proper time—
for strength, and not for drunkenness!

18 Through sloth the roof sinks in,
and through indolence the house leaks.

19 Feasts are made for laughter;
wine gladdens life,
and money meets every need.

20 Do not curse the king, even in your thoughts,
or curse the rich, even in your bedroom;
for a bird of the air may carry your voice,
or some winged creature tell the matter.

The Value of Diligence

11 Send out your bread upon the waters,
for after many days you will get it back.

2 Divide your means seven ways, or even eight,
for you do not know what disaster may happen
on earth.

3 When clouds are full,
they empty rain on the earth;
whether a tree falls to the south or to the north,
in the place where the tree falls, there it will lie.

4 Whoever observes the wind will not sow;
and whoever regards the clouds will not reap.

5 Just as you do not know how the breath comes to the bones in the mother's womb, so you do not know the work of God, who makes everything.

6 In the morning sow your seed, and at evening do not let your hands be idle; for you do not know which will prosper, this or that, or whether both alike will be good.

Youth and Old Age

7 Light is sweet, and it is pleasant for the eyes to see the sun.

8 Even those who live many years should rejoice in them all; yet let them remember that the days of darkness will be many. All that comes is vanity.

9 Rejoice, young man, while you are young, and let your heart cheer you in the days of your youth. Follow the inclination of your heart and the desire of your eyes, but know that for all these things God will bring you into judgment.

10 Banish anxiety from your mind, and put away pain from your body; for youth and the dawn of life are vanity.

12 Remember your creator in the days of your youth, before the days of trouble come, and the years draw near when you will say, "I have no pleasure in them"; 2before the sun and the light and the moon and the stars are darkened and the clouds return with*a* the rain; 3in the day when the guards of the house tremble, and the strong men are bent, and the women who grind cease working because they are few, and those who look through the windows see dimly; 4when the doors on the street are shut, and the sound of the grinding is low, and one rises up at the sound of a bird, and all the daughters of song are brought low; 5when one is afraid of heights, and terrors

---

Enjoy the Day

ECCLESIASTES 11.9

Ponder the seemingly paradoxical message of this passage: Be happy, but plan on facing judgment. Does this resonate with any situations you face today?

Try this exercise: Read the text slowly—reading it twice is preferable. Listen for a word or phrase that stands out—but don't rush to claim the first thing that comes to mind. Use that word or phrase to pray back to God the truth God has given you. Be quiet before God, being attentive to anything God may say to you about plans for the future.

See *Meeting God in Everyday Life*

---

a Or *after*; Heb *'ahar*

The Days of Your Youth

ECCLESIASTES 12.1–7

The Teacher writes a moving poem describing an old age of growing infirmity and perhaps bitterness. He probably uses "youth" to mean the days of good health. Honor God when things are well with you, he says, because should poor health and discouragement come, God may seem far away and uncaring. Cultivate your relationship with God now so that you may rely on it in times of trial.

Suppose the day comes when the power of your memory is fading. Yet placed in a prominent place where you live is a card or a nice sheet of paper (perhaps framed). On that card you wrote years before (today), you will read ten things you wanted most to remember throughout your life. What will you read on that card?

are in the road; the almond tree blossoms, the grasshopper drags itself along[a] and desire fails; because all must go to their eternal home, and the mourners will go about the streets; [6]before the silver cord is snapped,[b] and the golden bowl is broken, and the pitcher is broken at the fountain, and the wheel broken at the cistern, [7]and the dust returns to the earth as it was, and the breath[c] returns to God who gave it. [8]Vanity of vanities, says the Teacher;[d] all is vanity.

Epilogue

9 Besides being wise, the Teacher[d] also taught the people knowledge, weighing and studying and arranging many proverbs. [10]The Teacher[d] sought to find pleasing words, and he wrote words of truth plainly.

11 The sayings of the wise are like goads, and like nails firmly fixed are the collected sayings that are given by one shepherd.[e] [12]Of anything beyond these, my child, beware. Of making many books there is no end, and much study is a weariness of the flesh.

13 The end of the matter; all has been heard. Fear God, and keep his commandments; for that is the whole duty of everyone. [14]For God will bring every deed into judgment, including[f] every secret thing, whether good or evil.

a Or is a burden   b Syr Vg Compare Gk: Heb is removed   c Or the spirit   d Qoheleth, traditionally rendered Preacher   e Meaning of Heb uncertain   f Or into the judgment on

THE SONG OF SOLOMON

The Lover and the Beloved

KEY VERSE:

Let him kiss me with the kisses of his mouth.—Song of Solomon 1.2

Song of Solomon, thought to be written by Solomon, is an exquisite piece of Hebrew poetry that communicates two themes interwoven in a love song. On one level, it is an evocative depiction of the love between a woman and a man. On another level, it is a parable portraying the love between God and God's people. There are a number of references in the Old Testament in which human love is used to describe our relationship with God, and Song of Solomon is part of that poetic tradition.

The Song of Solomon is frankly sensual. But it is also meant to be a hymn describing the rapture and mystery of the covenant relationship between God and his people. The language points to the love that is the root of all our loves—the love that is the source of our beings. This breathtaking poem is about longing—God's longing for us and our longing for God in return—a longing signified by a kiss.

As you read Song of Solomon, sense—in the ardent desire of these lovers for each other—God's longing for you and your longing for God. Can you fully take in how passionately God loves you? Do you long for God as deeply as God longs for you? As you read and meditate on Song of Solomon, begin to understand God's ardent desire for relationship with you. Let it make all the difference in the way you worship and pray.

"Love then the Lord thy God with the entire and full affection of the heart; love him with all the vigilance and foresight of the reason, love him with the full strength and vigor of the soul, so that for his love you would not fear even to die; as it is written in a . . . verse of this Canticle: Love is strong as death . . ."

—BERNARD OF CLAIRVAUX,
Sermon XX on The Song of Songs

A Lover's Kiss

SONG OF SOLOMON 1.2

There is within each of us a restless yearning, a longing for more, a desire to be met, to be embraced, to be surrendered to Love's keeping. We may have known God as Creator, as guide, even as friend. But there is in each heart also an insistent, underlying longing to know and be known even more intimately. What aspects of yourself do you tend to withhold from God? Can you make a list of your thoughts, hopes, yearnings, ideas or activities that seem to exist apart from God's knowledge or attention? For each one, try to think of some small steps that you might take, literally or symbolically, to offer God access to them.

See Meeting God in Prayer

1 The Song of Songs, which is Solomon's.

Colloquy of Bride and Friends

2 Let him kiss me with the kisses of his mouth!
   For your love is better than wine,
3   your anointing oils are fragrant,
   your name is perfume poured out;
     therefore the maidens love you.
4 Draw me after you, let us make haste.
     The king has brought me into his chambers.
   We will exult and rejoice in you;
     we will extol your love more than wine;
     rightly do they love you.

5 I am black and beautiful,
     O daughters of Jerusalem,
   like the tents of Kedar,
     like the curtains of Solomon.
6 Do not gaze at me because I am dark,
     because the sun has gazed on me.
   My mother's sons were angry with me;
     they made me keeper of the vineyards,
     but my own vineyard I have not kept!
7 Tell me, you whom my soul loves,
     where you pasture your flock,
     where you make it lie down at noon;
   for why should I be like one who is veiled
     beside the flocks of your companions?

8 If you do not know,
     O fairest among women,
   follow the tracks of the flock,
     and pasture your kids
     beside the shepherds' tents.

Colloquy of Bridegroom, Friends, and Bride

9 I compare you, my love,
     to a mare among Pharaoh's chariots.
10 Your cheeks are comely with ornaments,
     your neck with strings of jewels.
11 We will make you ornaments of gold,
     studded with silver.

12 While the king was on his couch,
     my nard gave forth its fragrance.
13 My beloved is to me a bag of myrrh
     that lies between my breasts.
14 My beloved is to me a cluster of henna blossoms
     in the vineyards of En-gedi.

15 Ah, you are beautiful, my love;
     ah, you are beautiful;
     your eyes are doves.
16 Ah, you are beautiful, my beloved,
     truly lovely.
   Our couch is green;

17 the beams of our house are cedar,
    our rafters[a] are pine.

2 I am a rose[b] of Sharon,
    a lily of the valleys.

2 As a lily among brambles,
    so is my love among maidens.

3 As an apple tree among the trees of the wood,
    so is my beloved among young men.
  With great delight I sat in his shadow,
    and his fruit was sweet to my taste.

4 He brought me to the banqueting house,
    and his intention toward me was love.

5 Sustain me with raisins,
    refresh me with apples;
  for I am faint with love.

6 O that his left hand were under my head,
    and that his right hand embraced me!

7 I adjure you, O daughters of Jerusalem,
    by the gazelles or the wild does:
  do not stir up or awaken love
    until it is ready!

Springtime Rhapsody

8 The voice of my beloved!
    Look, he comes,
  leaping upon the mountains,
    bounding over the hills.

9 My beloved is like a gazelle
    or a young stag.
  Look, there he stands
    behind our wall,
  gazing in at the windows,
    looking through the lattice.

10 My beloved speaks and says to me:
   "Arise, my love, my fair one,
    and come away;

11 for now the winter is past,
    the rain is over and gone.

12 The flowers appear on the earth;
    the time of singing has come,
  and the voice of the turtledove
    is heard in our land.

13 The fig tree puts forth its figs,
    and the vines are in blossom;
    they give forth fragrance.
  Arise, my love, my fair one,
    and come away.

14 O my dove, in the clefts of the rock,
    in the covert of the cliff,
  let me see your face,
    let me hear your voice;
  for your voice is sweet,
    and your face is lovely.

The Soul's Springtime

SONG OF SOLOMON 2.10–13

Can you recall your delight at the first sign of spring, when the early crocuses first push their way through the last icy crust of snow? Similarly, God's love has a way of breaking through our times of trial and exile and waking us from lethargy and despair.

Do you sense something within yourself that is dormant or frozen? Is there a broken relationship, a sin that you cannot seem to put behind you, or an indifference to God's love for you? Whatever it is, in prayer ask that you will be open to God breaking through with the sweet, fresh growth of his presence in you.

See Meeting God in Prayer

---

a Meaning of Heb uncertain   *b* Heb *crocus*

Lovers Seek One Another

SONG OF SOLOMON 3.1–5

Sometimes we feel as if we are chasing God when we approach him in prayer, so desperate are we to be near him and to express ourselves to him, much like the beloved searches everywhere for her lover in order to hold him. The next time you pray, be aware of the postures you assume and what they might mean. If you kneel and rest your head on your hands or bow your head or bend over and fold your hands—these may be signs of reverence or sometimes self-protection. Try new positions as you pray. One time-honored way is the *orans* position, standing with arms outstretched and face lifted. Another possibility is to sit with an open posture, arms extended and palms upward in a more vulnerable posture. Another is to stand as if you are just about to meet someone you love deeply. Experiment with other postures that express the way you feel.

See *Meeting God in Worship*

882

15 Catch us the foxes,
    the little foxes,
that ruin the vineyards—
    for our vineyards are in blossom."

16 My beloved is mine and I am his;
    he pastures his flock among the lilies.
17 Until the day breathes
    and the shadows flee,
turn, my beloved, be like a gazelle
    or a young stag on the cleft mountains.[a]

Love's Dream

3 Upon my bed at night
    I sought him whom my soul loves;
I sought him, but found him not;
    I called him, but he gave no answer.[b]
2 "I will rise now and go about the city,
    in the streets and in the squares;
I will seek him whom my soul loves."
    I sought him, but found him not.
3 The sentinels found me,
    as they went about in the city.
"Have you seen him whom my soul loves?"
4 Scarcely had I passed them,
    when I found him whom my soul loves.
I held him, and would not let him go
    until I brought him into my mother's house,
    and into the chamber of her that conceived me.
5 I adjure you, O daughters of Jerusalem,
    by the gazelles or the wild does:
do not stir up or awaken love
    until it is ready!

The Groom and His Party Approach

6 What is that coming up from the wilderness,
    like a column of smoke,
perfumed with myrrh and frankincense,
    with all the fragrant powders of the merchant?
7 Look, it is the litter of Solomon!
    Around it are sixty mighty men
    of the mighty men of Israel,
8 all equipped with swords
    and expert in war,
each with his sword at his thigh
    because of alarms by night.
9 King Solomon made himself a palanquin
    from the wood of Lebanon.
10 He made its posts of silver,
    its back of gold, its seat of purple;
its interior was inlaid with love.[c]
    Daughters of Jerusalem,
11   come out.
Look, O daughters of Zion,
    at King Solomon,

a Or on the mountains of Bether: meaning of Heb uncertain   b Gk: Heb lacks this line   c Meaning of Heb uncertain

at the crown with which his mother crowned him
  on the day of his wedding,
  on the day of the gladness of his heart.

The Bride's Beauty Extolled

4 How beautiful you are, my love,
  how very beautiful!
Your eyes are doves
  behind your veil.
Your hair is like a flock of goats,
  moving down the slopes of Gilead.
² Your teeth are like a flock of shorn ewes
  that have come up from the washing,
all of which bear twins,
  and not one among them is bereaved.
³ Your lips are like a crimson thread,
  and your mouth is lovely.
Your cheeks are like halves of a pomegranate
  behind your veil.
⁴ Your neck is like the tower of David,
  built in courses;
on it hang a thousand bucklers,
  all of them shields of warriors.
⁵ Your two breasts are like two fawns,
  twins of a gazelle,
  that feed among the lilies.
⁶ Until the day breathes
  and the shadows flee,
I will hasten to the mountain of myrrh
  and the hill of frankincense.
⁷ You are altogether beautiful, my love;
  there is no flaw in you.
⁸ Come with me from Lebanon, my bride;
  come with me from Lebanon.
Depart*ᵃ* from the peak of Amana,
  from the peak of Senir and Hermon,
from the dens of lions,
  from the mountains of leopards.

⁹ You have ravished my heart, my sister, my bride,
  you have ravished my heart with a glance of
    your eyes,
  with one jewel of your necklace.
¹⁰ How sweet is your love, my sister, my bride!
  how much better is your love than wine,
  and the fragrance of your oils than any spice!
¹¹ Your lips distill nectar, my bride;
  honey and milk are under your tongue;
  the scent of your garments is like the scent of
    Lebanon.
¹² A garden locked is my sister, my bride,
  a garden locked, a fountain sealed.
¹³ Your channel*ᵇ* is an orchard of pomegranates
  with all choicest fruits,
  henna with nard,

Seen Through God's Eyes

SONG OF SOLOMON 4.10

Can it be? Am I really beautiful? you ask. Indeed, God greatly delights in you. You probably are well aware of the ways your spirit tends to become disfigured by the pressures of the world—made smaller, greedier, more defensive, haughty, judgmental, bitter or frightened. But can you see yourself through God's eyes, created in God's image and likeness? Ask the One who made you to open your eyes to the beauty of your life. How might God describe your best characteristics? Can you imagine the words God might use to sing your praises to someone else?

See Meeting God in the Created Order

---

a Or *Look*   *b* Meaning of Heb uncertain

Called by God

SONG OF SOLOMON 5.2–5

God's call to us is a call that woos us, just like the knock at the door and the quiet call of the beloved. In what ways do you sometimes find it hard to open yourself to God? What emotions do you feel when you make yourself vulnerable to God? Sit quietly and become aware of your body. Do you feel tension or resistance as you think about God? Breathe deeply and relax. Draw, paint, or sculpt an image that portrays trust and openness before God.

See Meeting God in Worship

14 nard and saffron, calamus and cinnamon,
　　with all trees of frankincense,
myrrh and aloes,
　　with all chief spices—
15 a garden fountain, a well of living water,
　　and flowing streams from Lebanon.

16 Awake, O north wind,
　　and come, O south wind!
Blow upon my garden
　　that its fragrance may be wafted abroad.
Let my beloved come to his garden,
　　and eat its choicest fruits.

5 I come to my garden, my sister, my bride;
　　I gather my myrrh with my spice,
　　I eat my honeycomb with my honey,
　　I drink my wine with my milk.

Eat, friends, drink,
　　and be drunk with love.

Another Dream

2 I slept, but my heart was awake.
Listen! my beloved is knocking.
"Open to me, my sister, my love,
　　my dove, my perfect one;
for my head is wet with dew,
　　my locks with the drops of the night."
3 I had put off my garment;
　　how could I put it on again?
I had bathed my feet;
　　how could I soil them?
4 My beloved thrust his hand into the opening,
　　and my inmost being yearned for him.
5 I arose to open to my beloved,
　　and my hands dripped with myrrh,
my fingers with liquid myrrh,
　　upon the handles of the bolt.
6 I opened to my beloved,
　　but my beloved had turned and was gone.
My soul failed me when he spoke.
I sought him, but did not find him;
　　I called him, but he gave no answer.
7 Making their rounds in the city
　　the sentinels found me;
they beat me, they wounded me,
　　they took away my mantle,
　　those sentinels of the walls.
8 I adjure you, O daughters of Jerusalem,
　　if you find my beloved,
tell him this:
　　I am faint with love.

Colloquy of Friends and Bride

9 What is your beloved more than another beloved,
　　O fairest among women?

What is your beloved more than another beloved,
    that you thus adjure us?

10 My beloved is all radiant and ruddy,
    distinguished among ten thousand.
11 His head is the finest gold;
    his locks are wavy,
      black as a raven.
12 His eyes are like doves
    beside springs of water,
  bathed in milk,
    fitly set.*a*
13 His cheeks are like beds of spices,
    yielding fragrance.
  His lips are lilies,
    distilling liquid myrrh.
14 His arms are rounded gold,
    set with jewels.
  His body is ivory work,*a*
    encrusted with sapphires.*b*
15 His legs are alabaster columns,
    set upon bases of gold.
  His appearance is like Lebanon,
    choice as the cedars.
16 His speech is most sweet,
    and he is altogether desirable.
  This is my beloved and this is my friend,
    O daughters of Jerusalem.

6 Where has your beloved gone,
    O fairest among women?
  Which way has your beloved turned,
    that we may seek him with you?

2 My beloved has gone down to his garden,
    to the beds of spices,
  to pasture his flock in the gardens,
    and to gather lilies.
3 I am my beloved's and my beloved is mine;
    he pastures his flock among the lilies.

The Bride's Matchless Beauty

4 You are beautiful as Tirzah, my love,
    comely as Jerusalem,
    terrible as an army with banners.
5 Turn away your eyes from me,
    for they overwhelm me!
  Your hair is like a flock of goats,
    moving down the slopes of Gilead.
6 Your teeth are like a flock of ewes,
    that have come up from the washing;
  all of them bear twins,
    and not one among them is bereaved.
7 Your cheeks are like halves of a pomegranate
    behind your veil.

Belonging

SONG OF SOLOMON 6.3

The maiden's beloved has gone to his favorite spot, a spot where he feels most accepted, safe, loved and valued. Remember a time of romance in your own life. Perhaps it was a walk on the beach or a stroll through the park, a quiet dinner with lively and intimate conversation. Do you remember how you felt at one of those moments? Relaxed and available? Open to being known deeply by the other? This is the attitude God wishes to foster in us as we pray.

Try to imagine an ideal place to meet God. Picture in your mind's eye the details of the setting. Where are you? Is it cool or warm? Outdoors or inside? What might God say to you that would lead you into a time together in which you are fully trusting and fully vulnerable? What might you and God rejoice in together, celebrate together?

See Meeting God in Prayer

---

a Meaning of Heb uncertain   *b* Heb *lapis lazuli*

A Unique Love

The lover gives the beloved a wonderful compliment: She is unique, one-of-a-kind, and therefore, her perfect self. There is no other standard.

God loves us uniquely because he created us that way—unique and incomparable. We don't have to compete for his love or push anyone aside to find intimacy with him. The psalmist seemed to sense this: "For it was you who formed my inward parts . . . I praise you , for I am fearfully and wonderfully made . . . In your book were written all the days that were formed for me, when none of them as yet existed." (Psalm 139.13,14,16). Use these three lines from Psalm 139 as an outline for your prayer today. Pray each of these lines in turn, sharing your thoughts and feelings with the One who created you—uniquely.

8   There are sixty queens and eighty concubines,
      and maidens without number.
9   My dove, my perfect one, is the only one,
      the darling of her mother,
      flawless to her that bore her.
    The maidens saw her and called her happy;
      the queens and concubines also, and they
          praised her.
10 "Who is this that looks forth like the dawn,
      fair as the moon, bright as the sun,
      terrible as an army with banners?"

11 I went down to the nut orchard,
      to look at the blossoms of the valley,
    to see whether the vines had budded,
      whether the pomegranates were in bloom.
12 Before I was aware, my fancy set me
      in a chariot beside my prince.*a*

13 *b* Return, return, O Shulammite!
      Return, return, that we may look upon you.

    Why should you look upon the Shulammite,
      as upon a dance before two armies?*c*

Expressions of Praise

7 How graceful are your feet in sandals,
      O queenly maiden!
    Your rounded thighs are like jewels,
      the work of a master hand.
2   Your navel is a rounded bowl
      that never lacks mixed wine.
    Your belly is a heap of wheat,
      encircled with lilies.
3   Your two breasts are like two fawns,
      twins of a gazelle.
4   Your neck is like an ivory tower.
    Your eyes are pools in Heshbon,
      by the gate of Bath-rabbim.
    Your nose is like a tower of Lebanon,
      overlooking Damascus.
5   Your head crowns you like Carmel,
      and your flowing locks are like purple;
      a king is held captive in the tresses.*d*

6   How fair and pleasant you are,
      O loved one, delectable maiden!*e*
7   You are stately*f* as a palm tree,
      and your breasts are like its clusters.
8   I say I will climb the palm tree
      and lay hold of its branches.
    O may your breasts be like clusters of the vine,
      and the scent of your breath like apples,
9   and your kisses*g* like the best wine

a Cn: Meaning of Heb uncertain   *b* Ch 7.1 in Heb   *c* Or *dance of Mahanaim*   *d* Meaning of Heb uncertain   *e* Syr: Heb *in delights*   *f* Heb *This your stature is*   *g* Heb *palate*

that goes down[a] smoothly,
   gliding over lips and teeth.[b]

10 I am my beloved's,
    and his desire is for me.
11 Come, my beloved,
    let us go forth into the fields,
    and lodge in the villages;
12 let us go out early to the vineyards,
    and see whether the vines have budded,
   whether the grape blossoms have opened
    and the pomegranates are in bloom.
   There I will give you my love.
13 The mandrakes give forth fragrance,
    and over our doors are all choice fruits,
   new as well as old,
    which I have laid up for you, O my beloved.

8 O that you were like a brother to me,
    who nursed at my mother's breast!
   If I met you outside, I would kiss you,
    and no one would despise me.
2 I would lead you and bring you
    into the house of my mother,
    and into the chamber of the one who bore me.[c]
   I would give you spiced wine to drink,
    the juice of my pomegranates.
3 O that his left hand were under my head,
    and that his right hand embraced me!
4 I adjure you, O daughters of Jerusalem,
    do not stir up or awaken love
    until it is ready!

Homecoming

5 Who is that coming up from the wilderness,
    leaning upon her beloved?

   Under the apple tree I awakened you.
   There your mother was in labor with you;
    there she who bore you was in labor.

6 Set me as a seal upon your heart,
    as a seal upon your arm;
   for love is strong as death,
    passion fierce as the grave.
   Its flashes are flashes of fire,
    a raging flame.
7 Many waters cannot quench love,
    neither can floods drown it.
   If one offered for love
    all the wealth of one's house,
    it would be utterly scorned.

8 We have a little sister,
    and she has no breasts.
   What shall we do for our sister,

Awakening

SONG OF SOLOMON 8.5–6

"Passage from shadow to light, from the obscure light of the faith to the illumination of the spirit and heart's eyes. Astonished awakening of the Bride, whose eyes open in wonder on the dawn of the new creation . . . this is the very word of the Resurrection; the song of the new Easter that Paul will teach to the Ephesians: 'Wake up, O sleeper, rise from the dead, and Christ will shine on you' [Ephesians 5.14]."

—BLAISE ARMINJON,
The Cantata of Love

a Heb *down for my lover*   b Gk Syr Vg: Heb *lips of sleepers*   c Gk Syr:
Heb *my mother; she* (or *you*) *will teach me*

Drawn by Love

SONG OF SOLOMON 8.14

People who truly share a deep love are often impatient during times of separation. Sometimes they can hardly wait to be together, and they, in effect, call out to one another to "Hurry!" Thus the Shulammite cries to her beloved to be as swift as a gazelle.

If God asked you, "Will you follow me anywhere?"—how would you respond? Would you answer immediately and gladly with a resounding yes? Or would you have to think about it awhile, turning the question over in your mind before you reply? How would God view your response? What does your response say about the level of intimacy and trust between you and God?

See *Meeting God in Prayer*

on the day when she is spoken for?

9 If she is a wall,
   we will build upon her a battlement of silver;
but if she is a door,
   we will enclose her with boards of cedar.

10 I was a wall,
   and my breasts were like towers;
then I was in his eyes
   as one who brings*a* peace.

11 Solomon had a vineyard at Baal-hamon;
   he entrusted the vineyard to keepers;
   each one was to bring for its fruit a thousand
      pieces of silver.

12 My vineyard, my very own, is for myself;
   you, O Solomon, may have the thousand,
   and the keepers of the fruit two hundred!

13 O you who dwell in the gardens,
   my companions are listening for your voice;
   let me hear it.

14 Make haste, my beloved,
   and be like a gazelle
or a young stag
   upon the mountains of spices!

a Or finds

ISAIAH
Faithful Response to God's Glory

KEY VERSE:

"Holy, holy, holy is the LORD of hosts; the whole earth is full of his glory."—Isaiah 6.3

The prophet Isaiah has a message for God's people who are "defying his glorious presence" (3.8). Isaiah is called (6.9–10) to confront the people with the dire consequences of their rebellion against their God who nonetheless remains faithful to them.

Chapters 1—39 are dominated by dark and vivid pictures of the devastation that human beings invite by defying the Lord's presence and purposes. When they stubbornly refuse to respect the fabric of creation, they experience the power of God in creation as a terror. When they do not live in the holiness that God calls them to, they ultimately experience God's holiness as wrath and judgment. The people are challenged to purify themselves and give up their persistent reliance on ritual magic and political maneuvering.

Such purifying change opens God's people to the Spirit's illumination of new insight into God's loving design for Israel. Chapters 40—66 overflow with promises of divine comfort and restoration. In the new era, the Israelites are called to be a servant people who will cooperate with God's purposes for the whole of humanity— purposes greater than any they could imagine.

You can glimpse, through Isaiah's poetry, some of the very specific social situations and highly personal emotions that God's people experience. The book abounds in pathos, terror, sorrow, compassion and exultation. As you read, be alert to parallels in your own life. Pay attention to how God may be working in you—judging, purifying and filling you with a wider vision of the "glorious presence." Consider how God is calling you to cooperate with his redeeming love in the world today.

> "The world is charged with
> the grandeur of God.
> It will flame out, like shin-
> ing from shook foil . . .
> Oh, morning at the brown
> brink eastward springs—
> Because the Holy Ghost over
> the bent
> World broods with warm
> breast and with ah!
> bright wings."
> —GERARD MANLEY HOPKINS,
> "God's Grandeur"

Knowing God

ISAIAH 1.2–4

The people of Israel have turned their backs on the Holy One who dwells in their midst. They've resisted the teaching and holy practices that could have enabled them to recognize and respond to God in the intimate way in which children know their parents and domestic animals know their masters. What are the primary ways in which God becomes known to human beings? Through what experiences have you seen God's glory displayed in the world and in your own life? What are the habits that estrange you from God's divine presence in the world? Write a simple prayer of thanks to God for the ways the Lord shows himself in your life, even as you acknowledge the ways in which you have been blind to them.

See Meeting God in the Created Order

1 The vision of Isaiah son of Amoz, which he saw concerning Judah and Jerusalem in the days of Uzziah, Jotham, Ahaz, and Hezekiah, kings of Judah.

The Wickedness of Judah

2 Hear, O heavens, and listen, O earth;
   for the LORD has spoken:
 I reared children and brought them up,
   but they have rebelled against me.
3 The ox knows its owner,
   and the donkey its master's crib;
 but Israel does not know,
   my people do not understand.

4 Ah, sinful nation,
   people laden with iniquity,
 offspring who do evil,
   children who deal corruptly,
 who have forsaken the LORD,
   who have despised the Holy One of Israel,
   who are utterly estranged!

5 Why do you seek further beatings?
   Why do you continue to rebel?
 The whole head is sick,
   and the whole heart faint.
6 From the sole of the foot even to the head,
   there is no soundness in it,
 but bruises and sores
   and bleeding wounds;
 they have not been drained, or bound up,
   or softened with oil.

7 Your country lies desolate,
   your cities are burned with fire;
 in your very presence
   aliens devour your land;
   it is desolate, as overthrown by foreigners.
8 And daughter Zion is left
   like a booth in a vineyard,
 like a shelter in a cucumber field,
   like a besieged city.
9 If the LORD of hosts
   had not left us a few survivors,
 we would have been like Sodom,
   and become like Gomorrah.

10 Hear the word of the LORD,
   you rulers of Sodom!
 Listen to the teaching of our God,
   you people of Gomorrah!
11 What to me is the multitude of your sacrifices?
   says the LORD;
 I have had enough of burnt offerings of rams
   and the fat of fed beasts;
 I do not delight in the blood of bulls,
   or of lambs, or of goats.

12 When you come to appear before me,[a]
   who asked this from your hand?
   Trample my courts no more;
13 bringing offerings is futile;
   incense is an abomination to me.
   New moon and sabbath and calling of
      convocation—
   I cannot endure solemn assemblies with
      iniquity.
14 Your new moons and your appointed festivals
   my soul hates;
   they have become a burden to me,
   I am weary of bearing them.
15 When you stretch out your hands,
   I will hide my eyes from you;
   even though you make many prayers,
   I will not listen;
   your hands are full of blood.
16 Wash yourselves; make yourselves clean;
   remove the evil of your doings
   from before my eyes;
   cease to do evil,
17 learn to do good;
   seek justice,
   rescue the oppressed,
defend the orphan,
   plead for the widow.

18 Come now, let us argue it out,
   says the LORD:
though your sins are like scarlet,
   they shall be like snow;
though they are red like crimson,
   they shall become like wool.
19 If you are willing and obedient,
   you shall eat the good of the land;
20 but if you refuse and rebel,
   you shall be devoured by the sword;
   for the mouth of the LORD has spoken.

The Degenerate City

21 How the faithful city
   has become a whore!
   She that was full of justice,
righteousness lodged in her—
   but now murderers!
22 Your silver has become dross,
   your wine is mixed with water.
23 Your princes are rebels
   and companions of thieves.
Everyone loves a bribe
   and runs after gifts.
They do not defend the orphan,
   and the widow's cause does not come before
      them.

God: Against Us?

ISAIAH 1.21–25

"If God is for us" (Romans 8.31), in what sense does God say, "I will turn my hand against you"? How does God respond when humans, including yourself, go against his desires for the well-being of his creatures? Have you ever experienced God being "against" you in some way? Are you being called to take the same stance—that is, *against* yourself in order to be *for* yourself—in some area of your life? Or against another's behavior for the sake of that person's well-being? What are you called to pray for in these situations?

See *Meeting God in Everyday Life*

---

a Or see my face

A Vision of God's Kingdom

ISAIAH 2.1–4

Using the classic "spiritual reading" approach, read slowly, one or more times, Isaiah's vision of the last days. Let your heart and mind be open to words, phrases and images that seem especially vital. You might practice repeating a few of them until your heart settles on just one. Turn it over in your mind, inviting it to become part of you so that you share this vision of God's kingdom fulfilled. Let a prayer arise in response to this small jewel from the Word. End your prayer with a time of silence.

See Meeting God in Scripture

24 Therefore says the Sovereign, the LORD of hosts,
　　　the Mighty One of Israel:
　　Ah, I will pour out my wrath on my enemies,
　　　and avenge myself on my foes!
25 I will turn my hand against you;
　　　I will smelt away your dross as with lye
　　　and remove all your alloy.
26 And I will restore your judges as at the first,
　　　and your counselors as at the beginning.
　　Afterward you shall be called the city of
　　　righteousness,
　　　the faithful city.

27 Zion shall be redeemed by justice,
　　　and those in her who repent, by righteousness.
28 But rebels and sinners shall be destroyed together,
　　　and those who forsake the LORD shall be
　　　consumed.
29 For you shall be ashamed of the oaks
　　　in which you delighted;
　　and you shall blush for the gardens
　　　that you have chosen.
30 For you shall be like an oak
　　　whose leaf withers,
　　　and like a garden without water.
31 The strong shall become like tinder,
　　　and their work[a] like a spark;
　　they and their work shall burn together,
　　　with no one to quench them.

The Future House of God

2 The word that Isaiah son of Amoz saw concerning Judah and Jerusalem.

2 In days to come
　　　the mountain of the LORD's house
　　shall be established as the highest of the mountains,
　　　and shall be raised above the hills;
　　all the nations shall stream to it.
3 　　Many peoples shall come and say,
　　"Come, let us go up to the mountain of the LORD,
　　　to the house of the God of Jacob;
　　that he may teach us his ways
　　　and that we may walk in his paths."
　　For out of Zion shall go forth instruction,
　　　and the word of the LORD from Jerusalem.
4 He shall judge between the nations,
　　　and shall arbitrate for many peoples;
　　they shall beat their swords into plowshares,
　　　and their spears into pruning hooks;
　　nation shall not lift up sword against nation,
　　　neither shall they learn war any more.

Judgment Pronounced on Arrogance

5 O house of Jacob,
　　come, let us walk
　　　in the light of the LORD!

a Or its makers

6 For you have forsaken the ways of^a your people,
  O house of Jacob.
Indeed they are full of diviners^b from the east
  and of soothsayers like the Philistines,
  and they clasp hands with foreigners.
7 Their land is filled with silver and gold,
  and there is no end to their treasures;
their land is filled with horses,
  and there is no end to their chariots.
8 Their land is filled with idols;
  they bow down to the work of their hands,
  to what their own fingers have made.
9 And so people are humbled,
  and everyone is brought low—
  do not forgive them!
10 Enter into the rock,
  and hide in the dust
from the terror of the LORD,
  and from the glory of his majesty.
11 The haughty eyes of people shall be brought low,
  and the pride of everyone shall be humbled;
and the LORD alone will be exalted on that day.
12 For the LORD of hosts has a day
  against all that is proud and lofty,
  against all that is lifted up and high;^c
13 against all the cedars of Lebanon,
  lofty and lifted up;
  and against all the oaks of Bashan;
14 against all the high mountains,
  and against all the lofty hills;
15 against every high tower,
  and against every fortified wall;
16 against all the ships of Tarshish,
  and against all the beautiful craft.^d
17 The haughtiness of people shall be humbled,
  and the pride of everyone shall be brought low;
  and the LORD alone will be exalted on that day.
18 The idols shall utterly pass away.
19 Enter the caves of the rocks
  and the holes of the ground,
from the terror of the LORD,
  and from the glory of his majesty,
  when he rises to terrify the earth.
20 On that day people will throw away
  to the moles and to the bats
their idols of silver and their idols of gold,
  which they made for themselves to worship,
21 to enter the caverns of the rocks
  and the clefts in the crags,
from the terror of the LORD,
  and from the glory of his majesty,
  when he rises to terrify the earth.
22 Turn away from mortals,
  who have only breath in their nostrils,
  for of what account are they?

3 For now the Sovereign, the LORD of hosts,
  is taking away from Jerusalem and from Judah

Real Humility

ISAIAH 2.11–17

A common theme throughout scripture is that God humbles the proud. The pride Isaiah admonishes God's people for is crucially different from genuine self-esteem, which is based on a realistic acceptance of God's gifts to us and our ability to use them. Lofty haughtiness is an exaggerated confidence in our ability to control our destiny, even if that pride conceals an underlying poor self-esteem. Make a list of some of your gifts and abilities and also a list of exaggerated opinions about yourself. Offer these lists in prayer, giving thanks for those gifts and asking for God's merciful help in letting go of the exaggerations. Prayerfully ponder how best to base your self-esteem on God's gracious gift—your real abilities.

See Meeting God in Prayer

---

a Heb lacks *the ways of*   b Cn: Heb lacks *of diviners*   c Cn Compare Gk: Heb *low*   d Compare Gk: Meaning of Heb uncertain

God Confronts the Leaders

ISAIAH 3.14–15

How would the God of nations make a judgment against the leaders of his people today? Imagine Isaiah speaking to one or more leadership groups: the United Nations, the leaders of your nation, town or city government, your denomination or congregation (even yourself in any position of responsibility). What kinds of behavior would warrant the prophet's call for repentance? What attitudes would the prophet call under scrutiny? What vision of God's purposes would the prophet share with them? Pray for the Spirit to challenge, illuminate and empower those people: "May your will be done through _____."

See Meeting God in Service

support and staff—
　all support of bread,
　and all support of water—
2 warrior and soldier,
　judge and prophet,
　diviner and elder,
3 captain of fifty
　and dignitary,
　counselor and skillful magician
　and expert enchanter.
4 And I will make boys their princes,
　and babes shall rule over them.
5 The people will be oppressed,
　everyone by another
　and everyone by a neighbor;
the youth will be insolent to the elder,
　and the base to the honorable.

6 Someone will even seize a relative,
　a member of the clan, saying,
"You have a cloak;
　you shall be our leader,
and this heap of ruins
　shall be under your rule."
7 But the other will cry out on that day, saying,
"I will not be a healer;
　in my house there is neither bread nor cloak;
you shall not make me
　leader of the people."
8 For Jerusalem has stumbled
　and Judah has fallen,
because their speech and their deeds are against
　the LORD,
　defying his glorious presence.

9 The look on their faces bears witness against them;
　they proclaim their sin like Sodom,
　they do not hide it.
Woe to them!
　For they have brought evil on themselves.
10 Tell the innocent how fortunate they are,
　for they shall eat the fruit of their labors.
11 Woe to the guilty! How unfortunate they are,
　for what their hands have done shall be done to
　them.
12 My people—children are their oppressors,
　and women rule over them.
O my people, your leaders mislead you,
　and confuse the course of your paths.

13 The LORD rises to argue his case;
　he stands to judge the peoples.
14 The LORD enters into judgment
　with the elders and princes of his people:
It is you who have devoured the vineyard;
　the spoil of the poor is in your houses.
15 What do you mean by crushing my people,
　by grinding the face of the poor? says the Lord
　GOD of hosts.

16 The LORD said:
Because the daughters of Zion are haughty
   and walk with outstretched necks,
   glancing wantonly with their eyes,
mincing along as they go,
   tinkling with their feet;
17 the Lord will afflict with scabs
   the heads of the daughters of Zion,
   and the LORD will lay bare their secret parts.

18 In that day the Lord will take away the finery of the anklets, the headbands, and the crescents; 19the pendants, the bracelets, and the scarfs; 20the headdresses, the armlets, the sashes, the perfume boxes, and the amulets; 21the signet rings and nose rings; 22the festal robes, the mantles, the cloaks, and the handbags; 23the garments of gauze, the linen garments, the turbans, and the veils.

24 Instead of perfume there will be a stench;
   and instead of a sash, a rope;
and instead of well-set hair, baldness;
   and instead of a rich robe, a binding of
      sackcloth;
   instead of beauty, shame.*a*
25 Your men shall fall by the sword
   and your warriors in battle.
26 And her gates shall lament and mourn;
   ravaged, she shall sit upon the ground.

4 Seven women shall take hold of one man in that day, saying,
"We will eat our own bread and wear our own
      clothes;
just let us be called by your name;
   take away our disgrace."

The Future Glory of the Survivors in Zion

2 On that day the branch of the LORD shall be beautiful and glorious, and the fruit of the land shall be the pride and glory of the survivors of Israel. 3Whoever is left in Zion and remains in Jerusalem will be called holy, everyone who has been recorded for life in Jerusalem, 4once the Lord has washed away the filth of the daughters of Zion and cleansed the bloodstains of Jerusalem from its midst by a spirit of judgment and by a spirit of burning. 5Then the LORD will create over the whole site of Mount Zion and over its places of assembly a cloud by day and smoke and the shining of a flaming fire by night. Indeed over all the glory there will be a canopy. 6It will serve as a pavilion, a shade by day from the heat, and a refuge and a shelter from the storm and rain.

The Song of the Unfruitful Vineyard

5 Let me sing for my beloved
   my love-song concerning his vineyard:
My beloved had a vineyard
   on a very fertile hill.
2 He dug it and cleared it of stones,
   and planted it with choice vines;

The Beloved's Vineyard

ISAIAH 5.1–2

The garden is a recurring image of human life under God's providence. How has God cleared away the stones, prepared the soil and planted good things in your life as if it were a vineyard? Draw or color a picture of your vineyard, identifying all the good things—the choice vines—that are flourishing in your life by the grace of God. Give thanks for each in turn and savor the goodness of each. Now sketch in the "bad fruit" of resistance to God's gifts and calls. As you identify each in turn, ask God to show you the nature of your resistance. Pray for the Spirit to help you let go of that resistance.

See Meeting God in Everyday Life

God as Adversary

ISAIAH 5.7–19

"The Word of God is thine adversary . . . It is the adversary of thy will till it becomes the author of thy salvation . . . . It is our adversary as long as we are our own adversaries. O how goodly, how useful an 'adversary.' It does not seek our will, but our advantage. As long as thou art thine own enemy, thou hast the Word of God thine enemy; be thine own friend, and thou art in agreement with it."

—AUGUSTINE,
Sermon LIX:3

he built a watchtower in the midst of it,
    and hewed out a wine vat in it;
he expected it to yield grapes,
    but it yielded wild grapes.

3 And now, inhabitants of Jerusalem
    and people of Judah,
judge between me
    and my vineyard.
4 What more was there to do for my vineyard
    that I have not done in it?
When I expected it to yield grapes,
    why did it yield wild grapes?

5 And now I will tell you
    what I will do to my vineyard.
I will remove its hedge,
    and it shall be devoured;
I will break down its wall,
    and it shall be trampled down.
6 I will make it a waste;
    it shall not be pruned or hoed,
    and it shall be overgrown with briers and
        thorns;
I will also command the clouds
    that they rain no rain upon it.

7 For the vineyard of the LORD of hosts
    is the house of Israel,
and the people of Judah
    are his pleasant planting;
he expected justice,
    but saw bloodshed;
righteousness,
    but heard a cry!

Social Injustice Denounced

8 Ah, you who join house to house,
    who add field to field,
until there is room for no one but you,
    and you are left to live alone
    in the midst of the land!
9 The LORD of hosts has sworn in my hearing:
Surely many houses shall be desolate,
    large and beautiful houses, without inhabitant.
10 For ten acres of vineyard shall yield but one bath,
    and a homer of seed shall yield a mere ephah.*a*

11 Ah, you who rise early in the morning
    in pursuit of strong drink,
who linger in the evening
    to be inflamed by wine,
12 whose feasts consist of lyre and harp,
    tambourine and flute and wine,
but who do not regard the deeds of the LORD,
    or see the work of his hands!

896

a The Heb *bath*, *homer*, and *ephah* are measures of quantity

13 Therefore my people go into exile without
        knowledge;
    their nobles are dying of hunger,
        and their multitude is parched with thirst.

14 Therefore Sheol has enlarged its appetite
        and opened its mouth beyond measure;
    the nobility of Jerusalem*a* and her multitude go
        down,
        her throng and all who exult in her.

15 People are bowed down, everyone is brought low,
        and the eyes of the haughty are humbled.

16 But the LORD of hosts is exalted by justice,
        and the Holy God shows himself holy by
            righteousness.

17 Then the lambs shall graze as in their pasture,
        fatlings and kids*b* shall feed among the ruins.

18 Ah, you who drag iniquity along with cords of
        falsehood,
    who drag sin along as with cart ropes,

19 who say, "Let him make haste,
        let him speed his work
        that we may see it;
    let the plan of the Holy One of Israel hasten to
        fulfillment,
        that we may know it!"

20 Ah, you who call evil good
        and good evil,
    who put darkness for light
        and light for darkness,
    who put bitter for sweet
        and sweet for bitter!

21 Ah, you who are wise in your own eyes,
        and shrewd in your own sight!

22 Ah, you who are heroes in drinking wine
        and valiant at mixing drink,

23 who acquit the guilty for a bribe,
        and deprive the innocent of their rights!

Foreign Invasion Predicted

24 Therefore, as the tongue of fire devours the
        stubble,
    and as dry grass sinks down in the flame,
    so their root will become rotten,
        and their blossom go up like dust;
    for they have rejected the instruction of the LORD
        of hosts,
    and have despised the word of the Holy One of
        Israel.

25 Therefore the anger of the LORD was kindled
        against his people,
    and he stretched out his hand against them and
        struck them;
        the mountains quaked,
    and their corpses were like refuse

Filled With Glory

ISAIAH 6.1–3

The glory about which the seraphim sing hovers all about us, filling heaven and earth—shining through nature and through human beings who are open to God's goodness. Prayerfully remember a person, place or event in which you have seen or felt the glory of God. Use all your inner senses to remember the sights, sounds, feelings and smells. Allow yourself to be touched and filled with God's goodness as you repeat a prayer phrase such as, "Heaven and earth are full of your glory." Repeat this prayer exercise often, varying the recollections and building a growing collection of impressions that increase your sensitivity to God's immediate presence in the world.

See Meeting God in the Created Order

---

a Heb *her nobility*   *b* Cn Compare Gk: Heb *aliens*

God Calling

ISAIAH 6.5–8

Most "calls" aren't as dramatic as Isaiah's. Often a call is simply what is "called for" in any situation. Prayerfully imagine or recall some situation in your life—work, family, congregation. Vividly envision the setting, noting the forces at work and your thoughts and feelings in response. Imagine the possible actions. Ask the Spirit to show you what's called for, letting possible actions emerge imaginatively. Let yourself be open to God's guidance by repeating, as a prayer phrase with each breath, "Here am I"—the repeated prayer of God's servants in scripture. Prayerfully review the possibilities, seeking the one that seems closest to the Spirit of Christ. If you choose to act on this, end your prayer with "Send me!"

See *Meeting God in Service*

in the streets.
For all this his anger has not turned away,
    and his hand is stretched out still.

26 He will raise a signal for a nation far away,
    and whistle for a people at the ends of the
        earth;
Here they come, swiftly, speedily!
27 None of them is weary, none stumbles,
    none slumbers or sleeps,
not a loincloth is loose,
    not a sandal-thong broken;
28 their arrows are sharp,
    all their bows bent,
their horses' hoofs seem like flint,
    and their wheels like the whirlwind.
29 Their roaring is like a lion,
    like young lions they roar;
they growl and seize their prey,
    they carry it off, and no one can rescue.
30 They will roar over it on that day,
    like the roaring of the sea.
And if one look to the land—
    only darkness and distress;
and the light grows dark with clouds.

A Vision of God in the Temple

6 In the year that King Uzziah died, I saw the Lord sitting on a throne, high and lofty; and the hem of his robe filled the temple. 2Seraphs were in attendance above him; each had six wings: with two they covered their faces, and with two they covered their feet, and with two they flew. 3And one called to another and said:
"Holy, holy, holy is the LORD of hosts;
    the whole earth is full of his glory."
4The pivots*a* on the thresholds shook at the voices of those who called, and the house filled with smoke. 5And I said: "Woe is me! I am lost, for I am a man of unclean lips, and I live among a people of unclean lips; yet my eyes have seen the King, the LORD of hosts!"

6 Then one of the seraphs flew to me, holding a live coal that had been taken from the altar with a pair of tongs. 7The seraph*b* touched my mouth with it and said: "Now that this has touched your lips, your guilt has departed and your sin is blotted out." 8Then I heard the voice of the Lord saying, "Whom shall I send, and who will go for us?" And I said, "Here am I; send me!" 9And he said, "Go and say to this people:
    'Keep listening, but do not comprehend;
    keep looking, but do not understand.'
10 Make the mind of this people dull,
    and stop their ears,
    and shut their eyes,
so that they may not look with their eyes,
    and listen with their ears,
and comprehend with their minds,
    and turn and be healed."

a Meaning of Heb uncertain   *b* Heb *He*

11 Then I said, "How long, O Lord?" And he said:
"Until cities lie waste
   without inhabitant,
and houses without people,
   and the land is utterly desolate;
12 until the LORD sends everyone far away,
   and vast is the emptiness in the midst of the
      land.
13 Even if a tenth part remain in it,
   it will be burned again,
like a terebinth or an oak
   whose stump remains standing
      when it is felled."*a*
The holy seed is its stump.

Isaiah Reassures King Ahaz

7 In the days of Ahaz son of Jotham son of Uzziah, king of Judah, King Rezin of Aram and King Pekah son of Remaliah of Israel went up to attack Jerusalem, but could not mount an attack against it. ²When the house of David heard that Aram had allied itself with Ephraim, the heart of Ahaz*b* and the heart of his people shook as the trees of the forest shake before the wind.

3 Then the LORD said to Isaiah, Go out to meet Ahaz, you and your son Shear-jashub,*c* at the end of the conduit of the upper pool on the highway to the Fuller's Field, ⁴and say to him, Take heed, be quiet, do not fear, and do not let your heart be faint because of these two smoldering stumps of firebrands, because of the fierce anger of Rezin and Aram and the son of Remaliah. ⁵Because Aram—with Ephraim and the son of Remaliah—has plotted evil against you, saying, ⁶Let us go up against Judah and cut off Jerusalem*d* and conquer it for ourselves and make the son of Tabeel king in it; ⁷therefore thus says the Lord GOD:
It shall not stand,
   and it shall not come to pass.
8 For the head of Aram is Damascus,
   and the head of Damascus is Rezin.
(Within sixty-five years Ephraim will be shattered, no longer a people.)
9 The head of Ephraim is Samaria,
   and the head of Samaria is the son of Remaliah.
If you do not stand firm in faith,
   you shall not stand at all.

Isaiah Gives Ahaz the Sign of Immanuel

10 Again the LORD spoke to Ahaz, saying, ¹¹Ask a sign of the LORD your God; let it be deep as Sheol or high as heaven. ¹²But Ahaz said, I will not ask, and I will not put the LORD to the test. ¹³Then Isaiah*e* said: "Hear then, O house of David! Is it too little for you to weary mortals, that you weary my God also? ¹⁴Therefore the Lord himself will give you a sign. Look, the young woman*f* is with child and shall bear a son, and shall name him Immanuel.*g* ¹⁵He shall eat curds and honey by the time he knows how to refuse the evil and choose the good. ¹⁶For before the child

God With Us

ISAIAH 7.14

The sign of "Immanuel" is intended to give Ahaz and the people courage in spite of their shaking hearts (7.2). What makes your heart shake? Prayerfully imagine a situation or person that has brought you fear. Now let some tangible sign of Immanuel—God with you—become part of the scene. It may be the light of the Spirit in or around you, the presence of Jesus beside you or an affirmative phrase on your lips. Let the sense of that presence strengthen you as you continue to face what you fear. Consider imaginatively how you might act differently in the face of your fear, claiming God's abiding presence.

See Meeting God in Scripture

---

a Meaning of Heb uncertain   *b* Heb *his heart*   *c* That is *A remnant shall return*   *d* Heb *cut it off*   *e* Heb *he*   *f* Gk *the virgin*   *g* That is *God is with us*

Fearing God

ISAIAH 8.13–17

"We know that if there does exist an absolute goodness, it must hate most of what we do. That is the terrible fix we are in . . . We cannot do without it and we cannot do with it. God is the only comfort, He is also the supreme terror: the thing we need most and the thing we most want to hide from. He is our only possible ally, and we have made ourselves His enemies. Goodness is either the great safety or the great danger—depending on the way you react to it. And we have reacted the wrong way . . . If you know you are sick, you will listen to the doctor."

—C. S. LEWIS,
Mere Christianity

knows how to refuse the evil and choose the good, the land before whose two kings you are in dread will be deserted. [17]The LORD will bring on you and on your people and on your ancestral house such days as have not come since the day that Ephraim departed from Judah—the king of Assyria."

18 On that day the LORD will whistle for the fly that is at the sources of the streams of Egypt, and for the bee that is in the land of Assyria. [19]And they will all come and settle in the steep ravines, and in the clefts of the rocks, and on all the thornbushes, and on all the pastures.

20 On that day the Lord will shave with a razor hired beyond the River—with the king of Assyria—the head and the hair of the feet, and it will take off the beard as well.

21 On that day one will keep alive a young cow and two sheep, [22]and will eat curds because of the abundance of milk that they give; for everyone that is left in the land shall eat curds and honey.

23 On that day every place where there used to be a thousand vines, worth a thousand shekels of silver, will become briers and thorns. [24]With bow and arrows one will go there, for all the land will be briers and thorns; [25]and as for all the hills that used to be hoed with a hoe, you will not go there for fear of briers and thorns; but they will become a place where cattle are let loose and where sheep tread.

Isaiah's Son a Sign of the Assyrian Invasion

8 Then the LORD said to me, Take a large tablet and write on it in common characters, "Belonging to Maher-shal-al-hash-baz,"[a] [2]and have it attested[b] for me by reliable witnesses, the priest Uriah and Zechariah son of Jeberechiah. [3]And I went to the prophetess, and she conceived and bore a son. Then the LORD said to me, Name him Maher-shalal-hash-baz; [4]for before the child knows how to call "My father" or "My mother," the wealth of Damascus and the spoil of Samaria will be carried away by the king of Assyria.

5 The LORD spoke to me again: [6]Because this people has refused the waters of Shiloah that flow gently, and melt in fear before[c] Rezin and the son of Remaliah; [7]therefore, the Lord is bringing up against it the mighty flood waters of the River, the king of Assyria and all his glory; it will rise above all its channels and overflow all its banks; [8]it will sweep on into Judah as a flood, and, pouring over, it will reach up to the neck; and its outspread wings will fill the breadth of your land, O Immanuel.

9 Band together, you peoples, and be dismayed;
  listen, all you far countries;
 gird yourselves and be dismayed;
  gird yourselves and be dismayed!
10 Take counsel together, but it shall be brought to
   naught;
  speak a word, but it will not stand,
   for God is with us.[d]

a That is *The spoil speeds, the prey hastens*   b Q Ms Gk Syr:
MT *and I caused to be attested*   c Cn: Meaning of Heb uncertain
d Heb *immanu el*

11 For the LORD spoke thus to me while his hand was strong upon me, and warned me not to walk in the way of this people, saying: ¹²Do not call conspiracy all that this people calls conspiracy, and do not fear what it fears, or be in dread. ¹³But the LORD of hosts, him you shall regard as holy; let him be your fear, and let him be your dread. ¹⁴He will become a sanctuary, a stone one strikes against; for both houses of Israel he will become a rock one stumbles over—a trap and a snare for the inhabitants of Jerusalem. ¹⁵And many among them shall stumble; they shall fall and be broken; they shall be snared and taken.

Disciples of Isaiah

16 Bind up the testimony, seal the teaching among my disciples. ¹⁷I will wait for the LORD, who is hiding his face from the house of Jacob, and I will hope in him. ¹⁸See, I and the children whom the LORD has given me are signs and portents in Israel from the LORD of hosts, who dwells on Mount Zion. ¹⁹Now if people say to you, "Consult the ghosts and the familiar spirits that chirp and mutter; should not a people consult their gods, the dead on behalf of the living, ²⁰for teaching and for instruction?" surely, those who speak like this will have no dawn! ²¹They will pass through the land,ᵃ greatly distressed and hungry; when they are hungry, they will be enraged and will curseᵇ their king and their gods. They will turn their faces upward, ²²or they will look to the earth, but will see only distress and darkness, the gloom of anguish; and they will be thrust into thick darkness.ᶜ

The Righteous Reign of the Coming King

9ᵈ But there will be no gloom for those who were in anguish. In the former time he brought into contempt the land of Zebulun and the land of Naphtali, but in the latter time he will make glorious the way of the sea, the land beyond the Jordan, Galilee of the nations.
2ᵉ The people who walked in darkness
 have seen a great light;
those who lived in a land of deep darkness—
 on them light has shined.
3 You have multiplied the nation,
 you have increased its joy;
they rejoice before you
 as with joy at the harvest,
 as people exult when dividing plunder.
4 For the yoke of their burden,
 and the bar across their shoulders,
 the rod of their oppressor,
 you have broken as on the day of Midian.
5 For all the boots of the tramping warriors
 and all the garments rolled in blood
 shall be burned as fuel for the fire.
6 For a child has been born for us,
 a son given to us;
authority rests upon his shoulders;
 and he is named
Wonderful Counselor, Mighty God,

The Royal Child

ISAIAH 9.1–7

Take time to enter deeply into this vision about the coming of the royal child by reading the passage aloud to yourself and then prayerfully allowing your imagination to give life to the sequence of images in the text. Envision the light dawning on people who live in great darkness; the breaking of the bar of oppression; the stilling of the fever of war; the appearance of the divinely given Child who brings the time of justice and peace. Let yourself see the child vividly; perhaps the child is shining with God's light. Imagine that light touching your life. Imagine the light bringing light to the darkness in the world. You might accompany your meditation with selections from Handel's *Messiah*.

See Meeting God in Scripture

---

a Heb *it* *b* Or *curse by* *c* Meaning of Heb uncertain *d* Ch 8.23 in Heb *e* Ch 9.1 in Heb

The Wrath of God

ISAIAH 9.12–21

"We speak, indeed, of the 'wrath' of God . . . it is something which is assumed in order to discipline by stern means those sinners who have committed many and grievous sins. The language used regarding the wrath of God is to be understood figuratively . . . for it is as if one were to call the words of a physician 'threats,' when he tells his patients, 'I will have to use the knife, and apply cauteries, if you do not obey my prescriptions, and regulate your diet and mode of life in such a way as I direct you.' "

—ORIGEN OF ALEXANDRIA,
Contra Celsus

See Meeting God in Scripture

Everlasting Father, Prince of Peace.
7 His authority shall grow continually,
    and there shall be endless peace
for the throne of David and his kingdom.
    He will establish and uphold it
with justice and with righteousness
    from this time onward and forevermore.
The zeal of the LORD of hosts will do this.

Judgment on Arrogance and Oppression

8 The Lord sent a word against Jacob,
    and it fell on Israel;
9 and all the people knew it—
    Ephraim and the inhabitants of Samaria—
but in pride and arrogance of heart they said:
10 "The bricks have fallen,
    but we will build with dressed stones;
the sycamores have been cut down,
    but we will put cedars in their place."
11 So the LORD raised adversaries[a] against them,
    and stirred up their enemies,
12 the Arameans on the east and the Philistines on
      the west,
    and they devoured Israel with open mouth.
For all this his anger has not turned away;
    his hand is stretched out still.

13 The people did not turn to him who struck them,
    or seek the LORD of hosts.
14 So the LORD cut off from Israel head and tail,
    palm branch and reed in one day—
15 elders and dignitaries are the head,
    and prophets who teach lies are the tail;
16 for those who led this people led them astray,
    and those who were led by them were left in
      confusion.
17 That is why the Lord did not have pity on[b] their
      young people,
    or compassion on their orphans and widows;
for everyone was godless and an evildoer,
    and every mouth spoke folly.
For all this his anger has not turned away;
    his hand is stretched out still.

18 For wickedness burned like a fire,
    consuming briers and thorns;
it kindled the thickets of the forest,
    and they swirled upward in a column of smoke.
19 Through the wrath of the LORD of hosts
    the land was burned,
and the people became like fuel for the fire;
    no one spared another.
20 They gorged on the right, but still were hungry,
    and they devoured on the left, but were not
      satisfied;
they devoured the flesh of their own kindred;[c]

a Cn: Heb *the adversaries of Rezin*   *b* Q Ms: MT *rejoice over*   *c* Or *arm*

21 Manasseh devoured Ephraim, and Ephraim
        Manasseh,
    and together they were against Judah.
For all this his anger has not turned away;
    his hand is stretched out still.

10 Ah, you who make iniquitous decrees,
        who write oppressive statutes,
2   to turn aside the needy from justice
        and to rob the poor of my people of their right,
    that widows may be your spoil,
        and that you may make the orphans your prey!
3   What will you do on the day of punishment,
        in the calamity that will come from far away?
    To whom will you flee for help,
        and where will you leave your wealth,
4   so as not to crouch among the prisoners
        or fall among the slain?
    For all this his anger has not turned away;
        his hand is stretched out still.

Arrogant Assyria Also Judged

5   Ah, Assyria, the rod of my anger—
        the club in their hands is my fury!
6   Against a godless nation I send him,
        and against the people of my wrath I command
            him,
    to take spoil and seize plunder,
        and to tread them down like the mire of the
            streets.
7   But this is not what he intends,
        nor does he have this in mind;
    but it is in his heart to destroy,
        and to cut off nations not a few.
8   For he says:
    "Are not my commanders all kings?
9   Is not Calno like Carchemish?
        Is not Hamath like Arpad?
        Is not Samaria like Damascus?
10 As my hand has reached to the kingdoms of the
            idols
        whose images were greater than those of
            Jerusalem and Samaria,
11 shall I not do to Jerusalem and her idols
        what I have done to Samaria and her images?"

12 When the Lord has finished all his work on Mount
Zion and on Jerusalem, he*a* will punish the arrogant boasting of the king of Assyria and his haughty pride. 13For he
says:
    "By the strength of my hand I have done it,
        and by my wisdom, for I have understanding;
    I have removed the boundaries of peoples,
        and have plundered their treasures;
        like a bull I have brought down those who sat
            on thrones.
14 My hand has found, like a nest,

The Boastful Servant

ISAIAH 10.13

The king of Assyria boasts that
he is a self-made man, succeeding "by the strength of [his
own] hand," when he is actually being an unwitting servant of
God. Is there any accomplishment for which any human can
take real credit? Take time to
review, in a spirit of openness
to God, one or more achievements you feel proud to have
accomplished. What factors, in
addition to your effort, contributed to your success? What
about inborn talents? Past mentors and teachers? Current
sources of financial, emotional
or spiritual support? Are there
any specific gifts or graces you
can attribute directly to God?
Frame a short prayer of thanks.
Consider writing a thank-you
note to someone who has supported you in some way.

See Meeting God in Community

a Heb *I*

903

Enemies and God

ISAIAH 10.15–16

God punishes Assyria for its arrogance after using this brutal nation to execute divine judgment on Israel (see 10.5). Do you think God actually raises up the enemy, or rather, does he work to bring some good out of the enemy's evil actions? How does God's judgment against our enemies work in everyday life? In your experiences, has an enemy, opponent or opposing force ever been an important catalyst for good—or the occasion for learning some important lessons? Who are your current opponents, and what might you be able to learn from these relationships? How might you act on Jesus' command to "Love your enemies, do good to those who hate you, bless those who curse you, pray for those who abuse you" (Luke 6.27–28)?

See Meeting God in Community

the wealth of the peoples;
and as one gathers eggs that have been forsaken,
so I have gathered all the earth;
and there was none that moved a wing,
or opened its mouth, or chirped."

15 Shall the ax vaunt itself over the one who
wields it,
or the saw magnify itself against the one who
handles it?
As if a rod should raise the one who lifts it up,
or as if a staff should lift the one who is not
wood!
16 Therefore the Sovereign, the Lord of hosts,
will send wasting sickness among his stout
warriors,
and under his glory a burning will be kindled,
like the burning of fire.
17 The light of Israel will become a fire,
and his Holy One a flame;
and it will burn and devour
his thorns and briers in one day.
18 The glory of his forest and his fruitful land
the Lord will destroy, both soul and body,
and it will be as when an invalid wastes away.
19 The remnant of the trees of his forest will be so
few
that a child can write them down.

The Repentant Remnant of Israel

20 On that day the remnant of Israel and the survivors of the house of Jacob will no more lean on the one who struck them, but will lean on the Lord, the Holy One of Israel, in truth. 21A remnant will return, the remnant of Jacob, to the mighty God. 22For though your people Israel were like the sand of the sea, only a remnant of them will return. Destruction is decreed, overflowing with righteousness. 23For the Lord God of hosts will make a full end, as decreed, in all the earth.[a]

24 Therefore thus says the Lord God of hosts: O my people, who live in Zion, do not be afraid of the Assyrians when they beat you with a rod and lift up their staff against you as the Egyptians did. 25For in a very little while my indignation will come to an end, and my anger will be directed to their destruction. 26The Lord of hosts will wield a whip against them, as when he struck Midian at the rock of Oreb; his staff will be over the sea, and he will lift it as he did in Egypt. 27On that day his burden will be removed from your shoulder, and his yoke will be destroyed from your neck.

He has gone up from Rimmon,[b]
28 he has come to Aiath;
he has passed through Migron,
at Michmash he stores his baggage;
29 they have crossed over the pass,
at Geba they lodge for the night;

---

a Or land   b Cn: Heb and his yoke from your neck, and a yoke will be destroyed because of fatness

Ramah trembles,
  Gibeah of Saul has fled.
30 Cry aloud, O daughter Gallim!
  Listen, O Laishah!
  Answer her, O Anathoth!
31 Madmenah is in flight,
  the inhabitants of Gebim flee for safety.
32 This very day he will halt at Nob,
  he will shake his fist
    at the mount of daughter Zion,
    the hill of Jerusalem.

33 Look, the Sovereign, the LORD of hosts,
  will lop the boughs with terrifying power;
  the tallest trees will be cut down,
  and the lofty will be brought low.
34 He will hack down the thickets of the forest with
    an ax,
  and Lebanon with its majestic trees*a* will fall.

The Peaceful Kingdom

11 A shoot shall come out from the stump of Jesse,
  and a branch shall grow out of his roots.
2 The spirit of the LORD shall rest on him,
  the spirit of wisdom and understanding,
  the spirit of counsel and might,
  the spirit of knowledge and the fear of the LORD.
3 His delight shall be in the fear of the LORD.

He shall not judge by what his eyes see,
  or decide by what his ears hear;
4 but with righteousness he shall judge the poor,
  and decide with equity for the meek of the
    earth;
he shall strike the earth with the rod of his mouth,
  and with the breath of his lips he shall kill the
    wicked.
5 Righteousness shall be the belt around his waist,
  and faithfulness the belt around his loins.

6 The wolf shall live with the lamb,
  the leopard shall lie down with the kid,
the calf and the lion and the fatling together,
  and a little child shall lead them.
7 The cow and the bear shall graze,
  their young shall lie down together;
  and the lion shall eat straw like the ox.
8 The nursing child shall play over the hole of the
    asp,
  and the weaned child shall put its hand on the
    adder's den.
9 They will not hurt or destroy
  on all my holy mountain;
for the earth will be full of the knowledge of the
    LORD
  as the waters cover the sea.

Peace With Animals

ISAIAH 11.6–9

"Out of devotion a fisherman offered [Francis] a waterfowl. He took it gladly and opened his hands to let it go, but it did not want to. He prayed for a long time with his eyes turned to heaven. After more than an hour, he came back to himself as if from another realm, and gently told the bird again to go away and praise God. Having received his permission with a blessing, the bird expressed its joy in the movements of its body and flew away."

—BONAVENTURA,
The Life of St. Francis

a Cn Compare Gk Vg: Heb *with a majestic one*

Song of Salvation

ISAIAH 12.1–6

This exultant passage is traditionally used in Jewish prayer as part of the *havdalah*, a ceremony that marks the end of the sabbath, because it looks ahead to the final redemption God promises to Israel and the nations. Recite this song of praise or chant it in a monotone or to a simple melody. Let your heart be open to one phrase that particularly draws your attention. Let that phrase become a breath prayer—a short phrase repeated for a period of time aloud, then continued silently. If you find your mind wandering, simply return to the inner repetition of the phrase, letting it turn your heart and mind toward a sense of God's goodness.

See *Meeting God in Scripture*

Return of the Remnant of Israel and Judah

10 On that day the root of Jesse shall stand as a signal to the peoples; the nations shall inquire of him, and his dwelling shall be glorious.

11 On that day the Lord will extend his hand yet a second time to recover the remnant that is left of his people, from Assyria, from Egypt, from Pathros, from Ethiopia,*a* from Elam, from Shinar, from Hamath, and from the coastlands of the sea.

12 He will raise a signal for the nations,
  and will assemble the outcasts of Israel,
and gather the dispersed of Judah
  from the four corners of the earth.
13 The jealousy of Ephraim shall depart,
  the hostility of Judah shall be cut off;
Ephraim shall not be jealous of Judah,
  and Judah shall not be hostile towards Ephraim.
14 But they shall swoop down on the backs of the
    Philistines in the west,
  together they shall plunder the people of the east.
They shall put forth their hand against Edom and
    Moab,
  and the Ammonites shall obey them.
15 And the LORD will utterly destroy
  the tongue of the sea of Egypt;
and will wave his hand over the River
  with his scorching wind;
and will split it into seven channels,
  and make a way to cross on foot;
16 so there shall be a highway from Assyria
  for the remnant that is left of his people,
as there was for Israel
  when they came up from the land of Egypt.

Thanksgiving and Praise

12 You will say in that day:
  I will give thanks to you, O LORD,
  for though you were angry with me,
your anger turned away,
  and you comforted me.

2 Surely God is my salvation;
  I will trust, and will not be afraid,
for the LORD GOD*b* is my strength and my might;
  he has become my salvation.

3 With joy you will draw water from the wells of salvation. 4And you will say in that day:
  Give thanks to the LORD,
    call on his name;
  make known his deeds among the nations;
    proclaim that his name is exalted.

5 Sing praises to the LORD, for he has done
    gloriously;
  let this be known*c* in all the earth.

a Or *Nubia;* Heb *Cush*   *b* Heb *for Yah,* the LORD   *c* Or *this is made known*

⁶ Shout aloud and sing for joy, O royal*ᵃ* Zion,
    for great in your midst is the Holy One of Israel.

Proclamation against Babylon

13 The oracle concerning Babylon that Isaiah son of Amoz saw.

² On a bare hill raise a signal,
    cry aloud to them;
wave the hand for them to enter
    the gates of the nobles.
³ I myself have commanded my consecrated ones,
    have summoned my warriors, my proudly
        exulting ones,
    to execute my anger.

⁴ Listen, a tumult on the mountains
    as of a great multitude!
Listen, an uproar of kingdoms,
    of nations gathering together!
The Lᴏʀᴅ of hosts is mustering
    an army for battle.
⁵ They come from a distant land,
    from the end of the heavens,
the Lᴏʀᴅ and the weapons of his indignation,
    to destroy the whole earth.

⁶ Wail, for the day of the Lᴏʀᴅ is near;
    it will come like destruction from the Almighty!*ᵇ*
⁷ Therefore all hands will be feeble,
    and every human heart will melt,
⁸   and they will be dismayed.
Pangs and agony will seize them;
    they will be in anguish like a woman in labor.
They will look aghast at one another;
    their faces will be aflame.
⁹ See, the day of the Lᴏʀᴅ comes,
    cruel, with wrath and fierce anger,
to make the earth a desolation,
    and to destroy its sinners from it.
¹⁰ For the stars of the heavens and their
        constellations
    will not give their light;
the sun will be dark at its rising,
    and the moon will not shed its light.
¹¹ I will punish the world for its evil,
    and the wicked for their iniquity;
I will put an end to the pride of the arrogant,
    and lay low the insolence of tyrants.
¹² I will make mortals more rare than fine gold,
    and humans than the gold of Ophir.
¹³ Therefore I will make the heavens tremble,
    and the earth will be shaken out of its place,
at the wrath of the Lᴏʀᴅ of hosts
    in the day of his fierce anger.
¹⁴ Like a hunted gazelle,
    or like sheep with no one to gather them,

Prayer Sounds

ISAIAH 13.6

Wailing, chanting, shouting and "noise"—joyful or otherwise—were common parts of ancient prayer. Experiment with sounds in your prayers: a loud repeated "hallelujah!" or a repeated sound of wonder and praise such as "ah!" Try a simple singsong chant as a prayer, such as "Here am I." You might offer your feelings about some difficulty you face—or that someone close to you faces—toward God with a low moan such as "ohhhh" or whatever sound comes naturally to you. Such sounds are the nonverbal expression of powerful feelings, even when they accompany words. Allow them to express feelings "too deep for words" (Romans 8.26) as well. By such "groanings" the Spirit may speak through you.

See Meeting God in Prayer

---

a Or *O inhabitant of*   *b* Traditional rendering of Heb *Shaddai*

Divine Compassion

ISAIAH 14.1

"The ground of compassion is love and the working of compassion keeps us in love. Compassion is a sweet gracious working in love, mingled with abundant kindness: for compassion works at taking care of us and makes all things become good. Compassion allows us to fail measurably and in as much as we fail in so much we fall . . . our failing is fearful, and our falling is shameful, but in all this the sweet eye of kindness and love never leaves us, nor does the working of compassion cease."

—JULIAN OF NORWICH,
Revelations of Divine Love

all will turn to their own people,
and all will flee to their own lands.
15 Whoever is found will be thrust through,
and whoever is caught will fall by the sword.
16 Their infants will be dashed to pieces
before their eyes;
their houses will be plundered,
and their wives ravished.
17 See, I am stirring up the Medes against them,
who have no regard for silver
and do not delight in gold.
18 Their bows will slaughter the young men;
they will have no mercy on the fruit of the
womb;
their eyes will not pity children.
19 And Babylon, the glory of kingdoms,
the splendor and pride of the Chaldeans,
will be like Sodom and Gomorrah
when God overthrew them.
20 It will never be inhabited
or lived in for all generations;
Arabs will not pitch their tents there,
shepherds will not make their flocks lie down
there.
21 But wild animals will lie down there,
and its houses will be full of howling creatures;
there ostriches will live,
and there goat-demons will dance.
22 Hyenas will cry in its towers,
and jackals in the pleasant palaces;
its time is close at hand,
and its days will not be prolonged.

Restoration of Judah

14 But the LORD will have compassion on Jacob and will again choose Israel, and will set them in their own land; and aliens will join them and attach themselves to the house of Jacob. 2And the nations will take them and bring them to their place, and the house of Israel will possess the nations[a] as male and female slaves in the LORD's land; they will take captive those who were their captors, and rule over those who oppressed them.

Downfall of the King of Babylon

3 When the LORD has given you rest from your pain and turmoil and the hard service with which you were made to serve, 4you will take up this taunt against the king of Babylon:
How the oppressor has ceased!
How his insolence[b] has ceased!
5 The LORD has broken the staff of the wicked,
the scepter of rulers,
6 that struck down the peoples in wrath
with unceasing blows,
that ruled the nations in anger
with unrelenting persecution.
7 The whole earth is at rest and quiet;

908

a Heb *them*   *b* Q Ms Compare Gk Syr Vg: Meaning of MT uncertain

they break forth into singing.
8 The cypresses exult over you,
the cedars of Lebanon, saying,
"Since you were laid low,
no one comes to cut us down."
9 Sheol beneath is stirred up
to meet you when you come;
it rouses the shades to greet you,
all who were leaders of the earth;
it raises from their thrones
all who were kings of the nations.
10 All of them will speak
and say to you:
"You too have become as weak as we!
You have become like us!"
11 Your pomp is brought down to Sheol,
and the sound of your harps;
maggots are the bed beneath you,
and worms are your covering.

12 How you are fallen from heaven,
O Day Star, son of Dawn!
How you are cut down to the ground,
you who laid the nations low!
13 You said in your heart,
"I will ascend to heaven;
I will raise my throne
above the stars of God;
I will sit on the mount of assembly
on the heights of Zaphon;*a*
14 I will ascend to the tops of the clouds,
I will make myself like the Most High."
15 But you are brought down to Sheol,
to the depths of the Pit.
16 Those who see you will stare at you,
and ponder over you:
"Is this the man who made the earth tremble,
who shook kingdoms,
17 who made the world like a desert
and overthrew its cities,
who would not let his prisoners go home?"
18 All the kings of the nations lie in glory,
each in his own tomb;
19 but you are cast out, away from your grave,
like loathsome carrion,*b*
clothed with the dead, those pierced by the
sword,
who go down to the stones of the Pit,
like a corpse trampled underfoot.
20 You will not be joined with them in burial,
because you have destroyed your land,
you have killed your people.

May the descendants of evildoers
nevermore be named!
21 Prepare slaughter for his sons
because of the guilt of their father.*c*

Dark Images

ISAIAH 14.9–21

Slowly read Israel's taunt of rejoicing over Babylon's downfall (which actually begins in 14.4). Pay attention especially to the images of destruction typical of many passages in these prophetic writings. What emotions does this vivid poetry arouse in you? Spend some time journaling about them, or use crayons to draw a picture of your emotions about this passage. Then ponder: How do you think God feels about the fall of such a violent, oppressive civilization? The same as ancient Israel does? What questions do you have about similar passages of such destruction? Take your questions into prayer and ponder them in God's presence.

See *Meeting God in Scripture*

God's Hand Over the Nations

ISAIAH 14.26

Pray for the nations of the world by opening your heart and mind to the Spirit's working and by envisioning the whole planet as if you were seeing it from a satellite. Behold the deep blue seas, the rusty, greenish continents, the dazzling swirl of clouds. Imagine the planet surrounded by the light of God's compassionate justice, seeing "the whole world in his hands." Offer your own love for the world to God. Bring specific concerns for world situations into your prayer by asking God to illuminate that section of the world with the light of his love and the touch of his hand. Listen for God calling you to specific action.

See Meeting God in the Created Order

Let them never rise to possess the earth
    or cover the face of the world with cities.

22 I will rise up against them, says the LORD of hosts, and will cut off from Babylon name and remnant, offspring and posterity, says the LORD. [23]And I will make it a possession of the hedgehog, and pools of water, and I will sweep it with the broom of destruction, says the LORD of hosts.

An Oracle concerning Assyria

24 The LORD of hosts has sworn:
    As I have designed,
        so shall it be;
    and as I have planned,
        so shall it come to pass:
25 I will break the Assyrian in my land,
        and on my mountains trample him under foot;
    his yoke shall be removed from them,
        and his burden from their shoulders.
26 This is the plan that is planned
        concerning the whole earth;
    and this is the hand that is stretched out
        over all the nations.
27 For the LORD of hosts has planned,
        and who will annul it?
    His hand is stretched out,
        and who will turn it back?

An Oracle concerning Philistia

28 In the year that King Ahaz died this oracle came:

29 Do not rejoice, all you Philistines,
        that the rod that struck you is broken,
    for from the root of the snake will come forth an
            adder,
        and its fruit will be a flying fiery serpent.
30 The firstborn of the poor will graze,
        and the needy lie down in safety;
    but I will make your root die of famine,
        and your remnant I[a] will kill.
31 Wail, O gate; cry, O city;
        melt in fear, O Philistia, all of you!
    For smoke comes out of the north,
        and there is no straggler in its ranks.

32 What will one answer the messengers of the
            nation?
    "The LORD has founded Zion,
        and the needy among his people
        will find refuge in her."

An Oracle concerning Moab

15 An oracle concerning Moab.

    Because Ar is laid waste in a night,
        Moab is undone;
    because Kir is laid waste in a night,

a Q Ms Vg: MT *he*

Moab is undone.
2 Dibon*a* has gone up to the temple,
     to the high places to weep;
  over Nebo and over Medeba
     Moab wails.
  On every head is baldness,
     every beard is shorn;
3 in the streets they bind on sackcloth;
     on the housetops and in the squares
     everyone wails and melts in tears.
4 Heshbon and Elealeh cry out,
     their voices are heard as far as Jahaz;
  therefore the loins of Moab quiver;*b*
     his soul trembles.
5 My heart cries out for Moab;
     his fugitives flee to Zoar,
     to Eglath-shelishiyah.
  For at the ascent of Luhith
     they go up weeping;
  on the road to Horonaim
     they raise a cry of destruction;
6 the waters of Nimrim
     are a desolation;
  the grass is withered, the new growth fails,
     the verdure is no more.
7 Therefore the abundance they have gained
     and what they have laid up
  they carry away
     over the Wadi of the Willows.
8 For a cry has gone
     around the land of Moab;
  the wailing reaches to Eglaim,
     the wailing reaches to Beer-elim.
9 For the waters of Dibon*c* are full of blood;
     yet I will bring upon Dibon*c* even more—
  a lion for those of Moab who escape,
     for the remnant of the land.

16 Send lambs
       to the ruler of the land,
    from Sela, by way of the desert,
       to the mount of daughter Zion.
2 Like fluttering birds,
     like scattered nestlings,
  so are the daughters of Moab
     at the fords of the Arnon.
3 "Give counsel,
     grant justice;
  make your shade like night
     at the height of noon;
  hide the outcasts,
     do not betray the fugitive;
4 let the outcasts of Moab
     settle among you;
  be a refuge to them
     from the destroyer."

When the oppressor is no more,

Interceding for Sinners

ISAIAH 15.1–9

The prophet not only thunders against sin, his "heart cries out" over the sinner as well. This vivid portrait (15.1–16.14) of the distress of Israel's enemy Moab shows how deeply the prophet shares God's compassionate grief for those who suffer, even if their suffering is a result of their own destructive behavior. Intercede today for people caught in a web of destruction— trapped, perhaps, by a harmful relationship or an addiction. Bring to mind anyone you know personally. Spend a few minutes surrounding each one in prayer for God's compassionate help—asking God to awaken and heal each of them.

See Meeting God in Prayer

---

a Cn: Heb *the house and Dibon*   *b* Cn Compare Gk Syr: Heb *the armed men of Moab cry aloud*   *c* Q Ms Vg Compare Syr: MT *Dimon*

"My Heart Throbs"

ISAIAH 16.11

"Our rabbis taught, When the Egyptian armies were drowning in the sea, the Heavenly Hosts broke out in songs of jubilation. God silenced them and said, 'My creatures are perishing, and you sing praises?' "

—*The Talmud*

and destruction has ceased,
and marauders have vanished from the land,
5 then a throne shall be established in steadfast love
in the tent of David,
and on it shall sit in faithfulness
a ruler who seeks justice
and is swift to do what is right.

6 We have heard of the pride of Moab
—how proud he is!—
of his arrogance, his pride, and his insolence;
his boasts are false.
7 Therefore let Moab wail,
let everyone wail for Moab.
Mourn, utterly stricken,
for the raisin cakes of Kir-hareseth.

8 For the fields of Heshbon languish,
and the vines of Sibmah,
whose clusters once made drunk
the lords of the nations,
reached to Jazer
and strayed to the desert;
their shoots once spread abroad
and crossed over the sea.
9 Therefore I weep with the weeping of Jazer
for the vines of Sibmah;
I drench you with my tears,
O Heshbon and Elealeh;
for the shout over your fruit harvest
and your grain harvest has ceased.
10 Joy and gladness are taken away
from the fruitful field;
and in the vineyards no songs are sung,
no shouts are raised;
no treader treads out wine in the presses;
the vintage-shout is hushed.*a*
11 Therefore my heart throbs like a harp for Moab,
and my very soul for Kir-heres.

12 When Moab presents himself, when he wearies himself upon the high place, when he comes to his sanctuary to pray, he will not prevail.

13 This was the word that the LORD spoke concerning Moab in the past. 14But now the LORD says, In three years, like the years of a hired worker, the glory of Moab will be brought into contempt, in spite of all its great multitude; and those who survive will be very few and feeble.

An Oracle concerning Damascus

17 An oracle concerning Damascus.

See, Damascus will cease to be a city,
and will become a heap of ruins.
2 Her towns will be deserted forever;*b*
they will be places for flocks,
which will lie down, and no one will make them
afraid.

a Gk: Heb *I have hushed*   *b* Cn Compare Gk: Heb *the cities of Aroer are deserted*

³ The fortress will disappear from Ephraim,
  and the kingdom from Damascus;
and the remnant of Aram will be
  like the glory of the children of Israel,
                    says the Lord of hosts.

⁴ On that day
    the glory of Jacob will be brought low,
    and the fat of his flesh will grow lean.
⁵ And it shall be as when reapers gather standing
      grain
    and their arms harvest the ears,
  and as when one gleans the ears of grain
    in the Valley of Rephaim.
⁶ Gleanings will be left in it,
    as when an olive tree is beaten—
  two or three berries
    in the top of the highest bough,
  four or five
    on the branches of a fruit tree,
                    says the Lord God of Israel.

7 On that day people will regard their Maker, and their
eyes will look to the Holy One of Israel; ⁸they will not have
regard for the altars, the work of their hands, and they will
not look to what their own fingers have made, either the
sacred poles*a* or the altars of incense.

9 On that day their strong cities will be like the deserted places of the Hivites and the Amorites,*b* which they deserted because of the children of Israel, and there will be
desolation.

¹⁰ For you have forgotten the God of your salvation,
    and have not remembered the Rock of your
      refuge;
  therefore, though you plant pleasant plants
    and set out slips of an alien god,
¹¹ though you make them grow on the day that you
      plant them,
    and make them blossom in the morning that
      you sow;
  yet the harvest will flee away
    in a day of grief and incurable pain.

¹² Ah, the thunder of many peoples,
    they thunder like the thundering of the sea!
  Ah, the roar of nations,
    they roar like the roaring of mighty waters!
¹³ The nations roar like the roaring of many waters,
    but he will rebuke them, and they will flee far
      away,
  chased like chaff on the mountains before the wind
    and whirling dust before the storm.
¹⁴ At evening time, lo, terror!
    Before morning, they are no more.
  This is the fate of those who despoil us,
    and the lot of those who plunder us.

---

a Heb *Asherim*   b Cn Compare Gk: Heb *places of the wood and the highest bough*

Looking to the Maker

ISAIAH 17.7

"I don't say anything," said an old Irish peasant about his quiet, solitary visits to the church. "I just look at God, and God looks at me." He was practicing the ancient, contemplative Prayer of Simple Regard (also known as centering prayer) by turning his heart and soul toward God.

Sit quietly. Spend some time becoming aware of the miracle of your breathing, which helps you focus your attention on the moment. Frame within your mind a word or an image that turns you toward God. As you become more focused and still, you will become aware of God's presence with you—beyond all words and images.

See *Meeting God in Prayer*

God's Sunshine

ISAIAH 18.4

"I live in the sunshine of God's presence . . . I just let God shine upon me, without words or images or thoughts. I think all that matters in prayer is that we should want God to take possession of us. And if that wanting is deep enough, then anything we feel we want to do in prayer will work . . . I feel it's God's process . . . and that what goes on is God's business. My business is just to be attentive to Him, just to be waiting for God, for God to be what He wants . . . The spiritual is not there for use. The spiritual is there for blessing. You just . . . hold out your hands to receive it."

—SISTER WENDY BECKETT,
Sister Wendy in Conversation with Bill Moyers

An Oracle concerning Ethiopia

18 Ah, land of whirring wings
   beyond the rivers of Ethiopia,[a]
² sending ambassadors by the Nile
   in vessels of papyrus on the waters!
Go, you swift messengers,
   to a nation tall and smooth,
to a people feared near and far,
   a nation mighty and conquering,
   whose land the rivers divide.

³ All you inhabitants of the world,
   you who live on the earth,
when a signal is raised on the mountains, look!
   When a trumpet is blown, listen!
⁴ For thus the LORD said to me:
I will quietly look from my dwelling
   like clear heat in sunshine,
   like a cloud of dew in the heat of harvest.
⁵ For before the harvest, when the blossom is over
   and the flower becomes a ripening grape,
he will cut off the shoots with pruning hooks,
   and the spreading branches he will hew away.
⁶ They shall all be left
   to the birds of prey of the mountains
   and to the animals of the earth.
And the birds of prey will summer on them,
   and all the animals of the earth will winter on
      them.

7 At that time gifts will be brought to the LORD of hosts from[b] a people tall and smooth, from a people feared near and far, a nation mighty and conquering, whose land the rivers divide, to Mount Zion, the place of the name of the LORD of hosts.

An Oracle concerning Egypt

19 An oracle concerning Egypt.

See, the LORD is riding on a swift cloud
   and comes to Egypt;
the idols of Egypt will tremble at his presence,
   and the heart of the Egyptians will melt within
      them.
² I will stir up Egyptians against Egyptians,
   and they will fight, one against the other,
   neighbor against neighbor,
   city against city, kingdom against kingdom;
³ the spirit of the Egyptians within them will be
      emptied out,
   and I will confound their plans;
they will consult the idols and the spirits of the dead
   and the ghosts and the familiar spirits;
⁴ I will deliver the Egyptians
   into the hand of a hard master;
a fierce king will rule over them,
   says the Sovereign, the LORD of hosts.

a Or *Nubia*; Heb *Cush*   *b* Q Ms Gk Vg: MT *of*

5 The waters of the Nile will be dried up,
  and the river will be parched and dry;
6 its canals will become foul,
  and the branches of Egypt's Nile will diminish
  and dry up,
  reeds and rushes will rot away.
7 There will be bare places by the Nile,
  on the brink of the Nile;
  and all that is sown by the Nile will dry up,
  be driven away, and be no more.
8 Those who fish will mourn;
  all who cast hooks in the Nile will lament,
  and those who spread nets on the water will
  languish.
9 The workers in flax will be in despair,
  and the carders and those at the loom will grow
  pale.
10 Its weavers will be dismayed,
  and all who work for wages will be grieved.

11 The princes of Zoan are utterly foolish;
  the wise counselors of Pharaoh give stupid
  counsel.
  How can you say to Pharaoh,
  "I am one of the sages,
  a descendant of ancient kings"?
12 Where now are your sages?
  Let them tell you and make known
  what the LORD of hosts has planned against
  Egypt.
13 The princes of Zoan have become fools,
  and the princes of Memphis are deluded;
  those who are the cornerstones of its tribes
  have led Egypt astray.
14 The LORD has poured into them[a]
  a spirit of confusion;
  and they have made Egypt stagger in all its doings
  as a drunkard staggers around in vomit.
15 Neither head nor tail, palm branch or reed,
  will be able to do anything for Egypt.

16 On that day the Egyptians will be like women, and
tremble with fear before the hand that the LORD of hosts
raises against them. [17]And the land of Judah will become
a terror to the Egyptians; everyone to whom it is mentioned will fear because of the plan that the LORD of hosts
is planning against them.

Egypt, Assyria, and Israel Blessed

18 On that day there will be five cities in the land of
Egypt that speak the language of Canaan and swear allegiance to the LORD of hosts. One of these will be called
the City of the Sun.

19 On that day there will be an altar to the LORD in the
center of the land of Egypt, and a pillar to the LORD at its
border. [20]It will be a sign and a witness to the LORD of hosts
in the land of Egypt; when they cry to the LORD because

What Is Wisdom?

ISAIAH 19.11–15

For hundreds of years, the intellect of Egyptian wise men has
been the nation's pride. But
their knowledge does not save
them from destruction.

The wisdom that we have
from God is unlike human
wisdom (see 1 Corinthians
1.20–31). It goes beyond any
worldly knowledge—beyond intellectual understanding; it
leads to salvation. What does
godly wisdom mean to you? In
what ways do you seek it? How
do you depend on human wisdom to make your decisions?
In what ways does it shape
your lifestyle? How do you discern between God's wisdom
and human wisdom? How can
they become integrated? How
can you filter intellectual
knowledge through the lens
of God's wisdom?

Interior Pain

ISAIAH 21.3–8

"How the poor heart is afflicted
when, as though abandoned by
love, she looks everywhere, and
does not find it as it seems to
her. She does not find it in the
exterior senses . . . nor in the
imagination . . . nor in the understanding; and although at
last she finds in the summit
and supreme point of the spirit
where the divine love resides,
still she does not recognize it
and does not think that it is
what it is, for the greatness of
the distress and darkness prevents her from experiencing its
sweetness . . . But what can
the soul in this case do? . . .
She . . . has only the power to
let herself die in the hands of
the will of God."

—FRANCIS DE SALES,
Treatise on the Love of God

of oppressors, he will send them a savior, and will defend and deliver them. 21The Lord will make himself known to the Egyptians; and the Egyptians will know the Lord on that day, and will worship with sacrifice and burnt offering, and they will make vows to the Lord and perform them. 22The Lord will strike Egypt, striking and healing; they will return to the Lord, and he will listen to their supplications and heal them.

23 On that day there will be a highway from Egypt to Assyria, and the Assyrian will come into Egypt, and the Egyptian into Assyria, and the Egyptians will worship with the Assyrians. 24 On that day Israel will be the third with Egypt and Assyria, a blessing in the midst of the earth, 25whom the Lord of hosts has blessed, saying, "Blessed be Egypt my people, and Assyria the work of my hands, and Israel my heritage."

Isaiah Dramatizes the Conquest of Egypt and Ethiopia

20 In the year that the commander-in-chief, who was sent by King Sargon of Assyria, came to Ashdod and fought against it and took it— 2at that time the Lord had spoken to Isaiah son of Amoz, saying, "Go, and loose the sackcloth from your loins and take your sandals off your feet," and he had done so, walking naked and barefoot. 3Then the Lord said, "Just as my servant Isaiah has walked naked and barefoot for three years as a sign and a portent against Egypt and Ethiopia,*a* 4so shall the king of Assyria lead away the Egyptians as captives and the Ethiopians*b* as exiles, both the young and the old, naked and barefoot, with buttocks uncovered, to the shame of Egypt. 5And they shall be dismayed and confounded because of Ethiopia*a* their hope and of Egypt their boast. 6In that day the inhabitants of this coastland will say, 'See, this is what has happened to those in whom we hoped and to whom we fled for help and deliverance from the king of Assyria! And we, how shall we escape?'"

Oracles concerning Babylon, Edom, and Arabia

21 The oracle concerning the wilderness of the sea.

As whirlwinds in the Negeb sweep on,
   it comes from the desert,
   from a terrible land.
2 A stern vision is told to me;
   the betrayer betrays,
   and the destroyer destroys.
Go up, O Elam,
   lay siege, O Media;
all the sighing she has caused
   I bring to an end.
3 Therefore my loins are filled with anguish;
   pangs have seized me,
   like the pangs of a woman in labor;
I am bowed down so that I cannot hear,
   I am dismayed so that I cannot see.
4 My mind reels, horror has appalled me;

a Or Nubia; Heb Cush   b Or Nubians; Heb Cushites

the twilight I longed for
has been turned for me into trembling.

5 They prepare the table,
they spread the rugs,
they eat, they drink.
Rise up, commanders,
oil the shield!

6 For thus the Lord said to me:
"Go, post a lookout,
let him announce what he sees.

7 When he sees riders, horsemen in pairs,
riders on donkeys, riders on camels,
let him listen diligently,
very diligently."

8 Then the watcher[a] called out:
"Upon a watchtower I stand, O Lord,
continually by day,
and at my post I am stationed
throughout the night.

9 Look, there they come, riders,
horsemen in pairs!"
Then he responded,
"Fallen, fallen is Babylon;
and all the images of her gods
lie shattered on the ground."

10 O my threshed and winnowed one,
what I have heard from the LORD of hosts,
the God of Israel, I announce to you.

11 The oracle concerning Dumah.

One is calling to me from Seir,
"Sentinel, what of the night?
Sentinel, what of the night?"

12 The sentinel says:
"Morning comes, and also the night.
If you will inquire, inquire;
come back again."

13 The oracle concerning the desert plain.

In the scrub of the desert plain you will lodge,
O caravans of Dedanites.

14 Bring water to the thirsty,
meet the fugitive with bread,
O inhabitants of the land of Tema.

15 For they have fled from the swords,
from the drawn sword,
from the bent bow,
and from the stress of battle.

16 For thus the Lord said to me: Within a year, according to the years of a hired worker, all the glory of Kedar will come to an end; [17]and the remaining bows of Kedar's warriors will be few; for the LORD, the God of Israel, has spoken.

a Q Ms: MT *a lion*

The Sentinel

ISAIAH 21.11

Isaiah's images of the lookout and the sentinel, or watchman, represent those who remain alert to report oncoming trouble. In our day, whom is God calling to make us aware of possible threats to our communal well-being—potential difficulties that we might otherwise overlook? How does their prophetic concern reflect God's loving mindfulness of our good? Have any of these "sentinels" influenced your attitudes, actions or prayers? Have your own eyes been opened to a problem others do not see? How does this awareness affect your living and your praying?

See Meeting God in Community

Good Grief

ISAIAH 22.11–13

Jerusalem disregards the Lord Almighty's call for weeping and mourning, exhibiting instead a revelry inappropriate to the city's dire situation.

When are tears not only appropriate, but virtually demanded? What kinds of things does God call us to mourn about—in the world and in our own lives? What price do we pay for suppressing real responses of mourning and grief? Why are the mourners called "blessed" (Matthew 5.4)? Is there anything in your life, or in the world, that you are currently being called to mourn? What good can come out of such mourning? Place any grief or sorrow you feel into God's hands, asking the Spirit to work through it for good and sustain you in the midst of it.

See Meeting God in Prayer

A Warning of Destruction of Jerusalem

22 The oracle concerning the valley of vision.

What do you mean that you have gone up,
  all of you, to the housetops,
2 you that are full of shoutings,
  tumultuous city, exultant town?
Your slain are not slain by the sword,
  nor are they dead in battle.
3 Your rulers have all fled together;
  they were captured without the use of a bow.*a*
All of you who were found were captured,
  though they had fled far away.*b*
4 Therefore I said:
Look away from me,
  let me weep bitter tears;
do not try to comfort me
  for the destruction of my beloved people.

5 For the Lord God of hosts has a day
  of tumult and trampling and confusion
  in the valley of vision,
a battering down of walls
  and a cry for help to the mountains.
6 Elam bore the quiver
  with chariots and cavalry,*c*
  and Kir uncovered the shield.
7 Your choicest valleys were full of chariots,
  and the cavalry took their stand at the gates.
8 He has taken away the covering of Judah.

On that day you looked to the weapons of the House of the Forest, 9and you saw that there were many breaches in the city of David, and you collected the waters of the lower pool. 10You counted the houses of Jerusalem, and you broke down the houses to fortify the wall. 11You made a reservoir between the two walls for the water of the old pool. But you did not look to him who did it, or have regard for him who planned it long ago.

12 In that day the Lord God of hosts
  called to weeping and mourning,
  to baldness and putting on sackcloth;
13 but instead there was joy and festivity,
  killing oxen and slaughtering sheep,
  eating meat and drinking wine.
"Let us eat and drink,
  for tomorrow we die."
14 The Lord of hosts has revealed himself in my ears:
Surely this iniquity will not be forgiven you until
    you die,
  says the Lord God of hosts.

Denunciation of Self-Seeking Officials

15 Thus says the Lord God of hosts: Come, go to this steward, to Shebna, who is master of the household, and

a Or *without their bows*   *b* Gk Syr Vg: Heb *fled from far away*
c Meaning of Heb uncertain

say to him: ¹⁶What right do you have here? Who are your relatives here, that you have cut out a tomb here for yourself, cutting a tomb on the height, and carving a habitation for yourself in the rock? ¹⁷The LORD is about to hurl you away violently, my fellow. He will seize firm hold on you, ¹⁸whirl you round and round, and throw you like a ball into a wide land; there you shall die, and there your splendid chariots shall lie, O you disgrace to your master's house! ¹⁹I will thrust you from your office, and you will be pulled down from your post.

20 On that day I will call my servant Eliakim son of Hilkiah, ²¹and will clothe him with your robe and bind your sash on him. I will commit your authority to his hand, and he shall be a father to the inhabitants of Jerusalem and to the house of Judah. ²²I will place on his shoulder the key of the house of David; he shall open, and no one shall shut; he shall shut, and no one shall open. ²³I will fasten him like a peg in a secure place, and he will become a throne of honor to his ancestral house. ²⁴And they will hang on him the whole weight of his ancestral house, the offspring and issue, every small vessel, from the cups to all the flagons. ²⁵On that day, says the LORD of hosts, the peg that was fastened in a secure place will give way; it will be cut down and fall, and the load that was on it will perish, for the LORD has spoken.

An Oracle concerning Tyre

23 The oracle concerning Tyre.

Wail, O ships of Tarshish,
   for your fortress is destroyed.ᵃ
When they came in from Cyprus
   they learned of it.
² Be still, O inhabitants of the coast,
   O merchants of Sidon,
your messengers crossed over the seaᵇ
³   and were on the mighty waters;
your revenue was the grain of Shihor,
   the harvest of the Nile;
   you were the merchant of the nations.
⁴ Be ashamed, O Sidon, for the sea has spoken,
   the fortress of the sea, saying:
"I have neither labored nor given birth,
   I have neither reared young men
   nor brought up young women."
⁵ When the report comes to Egypt,
   they will be in anguish over the report about
      Tyre.
⁶ Cross over to Tarshish—
   wail, O inhabitants of the coast!
⁷ Is this your exultant city
   whose origin is from days of old,
whose feet carried her
   to settle far away?
⁸ Who has planned this
   against Tyre, the bestower of crowns,
whose merchants were princes,

The Key of David

ISAIAH 22.22

The key is a powerful symbol of access to resources, abilities and powers. Take your set of keys and, holding each key in turn, think about the door it opens. How is each area— house, file cabinet, car, office— beneficial (or dangerous) to your soul? What opportunities to serve God does each area afford? How do the blessings you experience in each area prompt thanksgiving within you? As you hold each key, bring any desires or needs connected with its meaning into the light of God's loving concern.

See Meeting God in Everyday Life

ᵃ Cn Compare verse 14: Heb *for it is destroyed, without houses*   ᵇ Q Ms: MT *crossing over the sea, they replenished you*

A Polluted Earth

ISAIAH 24.1–5

Violation of God's intentions for creation has resulted in a planet polluted by humans who are seemingly bent on its devastation. How is God concerned for creation and its creatures? How are we called to care for creation and to carry out God's plan for it? How can you, in prayer, join in creation's "eager longing" for the full disclosure of God's kingdom (Romans 8.19)? What is one activity in your life that honors God as Creator? Give thanks for that activity. Also name one activity that ignores God's role as Creator and offer contrition for it.

See *Meeting God in the Created Order*

whose traders were the honored of the earth?
9   The LORD of hosts has planned it—
      to defile the pride of all glory,
      to shame all the honored of the earth.
10   Cross over to your own land,
      O ships of*a* Tarshish;
      this is a harbor*b* no more.
11   He has stretched out his hand over the sea,
      he has shaken the kingdoms;
      the LORD has given command concerning Canaan
      to destroy its fortresses.
12   He said:
      You will exult no longer,
      O oppressed virgin daughter Sidon;
      rise, cross over to Cyprus—
      even there you will have no rest.

13 Look at the land of the Chaldeans! This is the people; it was not Assyria. They destined Tyre for wild animals. They erected their siege towers, they tore down her palaces, they made her a ruin.*c*
14   Wail, O ships of Tarshish,
      for your fortress is destroyed.
15From that day Tyre will be forgotten for seventy years, the lifetime of one king. At the end of seventy years, it will happen to Tyre as in the song about the prostitute:
16   Take a harp,
      go about the city,
      you forgotten prostitute!
   Make sweet melody,
      sing many songs,
      that you may be remembered.
17At the end of seventy years, the LORD will visit Tyre, and she will return to her trade, and will prostitute herself with all the kingdoms of the world on the face of the earth. 18Her merchandise and her wages will be dedicated to the LORD; her profits*d* will not be stored or hoarded, but her merchandise will supply abundant food and fine clothing for those who live in the presence of the LORD.

Impending Judgment on the Earth

24 Now the Lord is about to lay waste the earth
      and make it desolate,
      and he will twist its surface and scatter its
         inhabitants.
2   And it shall be, as with the people, so with the
         priest;
      as with the slave, so with his master;
      as with the maid, so with her mistress;
   as with the buyer, so with the seller;
      as with the lender, so with the borrower;
      as with the creditor, so with the debtor.
3   The earth shall be utterly laid waste and utterly
         despoiled;
      for the LORD has spoken this word.

4   The earth dries up and withers,

a Cn Compare Gk: Heb *like the Nile, daughter*   *b* Cn: Heb *restraint*
c Meaning of Heb uncertain   *d* Heb *it*

the world languishes and withers;
the heavens languish together with the earth.
5 The earth lies polluted
under its inhabitants;
for they have transgressed laws,
violated the statutes,
broken the everlasting covenant.
6 Therefore a curse devours the earth,
and its inhabitants suffer for their guilt;
therefore the inhabitants of the earth dwindled,
and few people are left.
7 The wine dries up,
the vine languishes,
all the merry-hearted sigh.
8 The mirth of the timbrels is stilled,
the noise of the jubilant has ceased,
the mirth of the lyre is stilled.
9 No longer do they drink wine with singing;
strong drink is bitter to those who drink it.
10 The city of chaos is broken down,
every house is shut up so that no one can enter.
11 There is an outcry in the streets for lack of wine;
all joy has reached its eventide;
the gladness of the earth is banished.
12 Desolation is left in the city,
the gates are battered into ruins.
13 For thus it shall be on the earth
and among the nations,
as when an olive tree is beaten,
as at the gleaning when the grape harvest is
ended.

14 They lift up their voices, they sing for joy;
they shout from the west over the majesty of
the LORD.
15 Therefore in the east give glory to the LORD;
in the coastlands of the sea glorify the name of
the LORD, the God of Israel.
16 From the ends of the earth we hear songs of
praise,
of glory to the Righteous One.
But I say, I pine away,
I pine away. Woe is me!
For the treacherous deal treacherously,
the treacherous deal very treacherously.

17 Terror, and the pit, and the snare
are upon you, O inhabitant of the earth!
18 Whoever flees at the sound of the terror
shall fall into the pit;
and whoever climbs out of the pit
shall be caught in the snare.
For the windows of heaven are opened,
and the foundations of the earth tremble.
19 The earth is utterly broken,
the earth is torn asunder,
the earth is violently shaken.
20 The earth staggers like a drunkard,
it sways like a hut;

We Hear Singing

ISAIAH 24.16

"Holy, holy, holy,
the Lord God Almighty,
who was and is and is to
come . . .
You are worthy, our Lord
and God,
to receive glory and honor
and power,
for you created all things,
and by your will they existed
and were created."
—Revelation 4.8,11

"A Feast of Rich Food"

ISAIAH 25.6–7

In this image of gracious abundance, God prepares a "feast of rich food" for all peoples. God's will for us is that we "may have life, and have abundantly" (John 10.10). But God's will is often hidden from us by the "shroud," an effect of sin. What activities or spiritual practices help you to delight in God's abundant goodness? Does such delight come through nature? Through other people? From deep within your soul? From scripture and sacred writings? What creates a "shroud" that keeps you from such nourishing delight? Take some time to remember a delightful moment and relive it. Store it in your heart as a liberating remembrance when the "shroud" exerts power over you.

See Meeting God in Everyday Life

---

its transgression lies heavy upon it,
and it falls, and will not rise again.

21 On that day the LORD will punish
the host of heaven in heaven,
and on earth the kings of the earth.
22 They will be gathered together
like prisoners in a pit;
they will be shut up in a prison,
and after many days they will be punished.
23 Then the moon will be abashed,
and the sun ashamed;
for the LORD of hosts will reign
on Mount Zion and in Jerusalem,
and before his elders he will manifest his glory.

Praise for Deliverance from Oppression

25 O LORD, you are my God;
I will exalt you, I will praise your name;
for you have done wonderful things,
plans formed of old, faithful and sure.
2 For you have made the city a heap,
the fortified city a ruin;
the palace of aliens is a city no more,
it will never be rebuilt.
3 Therefore strong peoples will glorify you;
cities of ruthless nations will fear you.
4 For you have been a refuge to the poor,
a refuge to the needy in their distress,
a shelter from the rainstorm and a shade from
the heat.
When the blast of the ruthless was like a winter
rainstorm,
5 the noise of aliens like heat in a dry place,
you subdued the heat with the shade of clouds;
the song of the ruthless was stilled.

6 On this mountain the LORD of hosts will make for
all peoples
a feast of rich food, a feast of well-aged wines,
of rich food filled with marrow, of well-aged
wines strained clear.
7 And he will destroy on this mountain
the shroud that is cast over all peoples,
the sheet that is spread over all nations;
8 he will swallow up death forever.
Then the Lord GOD will wipe away the tears from
all faces,
and the disgrace of his people he will take away
from all the earth,
for the LORD has spoken.
9 It will be said on that day,
Lo, this is our God; we have waited for him, so
that he might save us.
This is the LORD for whom we have waited;
let us be glad and rejoice in his salvation.
10 For the hand of the LORD will rest on this
mountain.

The Moabites shall be trodden down in their place
as straw is trodden down in a dung-pit.

11 Though they spread out their hands in the midst
of it,
as swimmers spread out their hands to swim,
their pride will be laid low despite the struggle*a*
of their hands.

12 The high fortifications of his walls will be brought
down,
laid low, cast to the ground, even to the dust.

Judah's Song of Victory

26 On that day this song will be sung in the land
of Judah:
We have a strong city;
he sets up victory
like walls and bulwarks.

2 Open the gates,
so that the righteous nation that keeps faith
may enter in.

3 Those of steadfast mind you keep in peace—
in peace because they trust in you.

4 Trust in the LORD forever,
for in the LORD GOD*b*
you have an everlasting rock.

5 For he has brought low
the inhabitants of the height;
the lofty city he lays low.
He lays it low to the ground,
casts it to the dust.

6 The foot tramples it,
the feet of the poor,
the steps of the needy.

7 The way of the righteous is level;
O Just One, you make smooth the path of the
righteous.

8 In the path of your judgments,
O LORD, we wait for you;
your name and your renown
are the soul's desire.

9 My soul yearns for you in the night,
my spirit within me earnestly seeks you.
For when your judgments are in the earth,
the inhabitants of the world learn righteousness.

10 If favor is shown to the wicked,
they do not learn righteousness;
in the land of uprightness they deal perversely
and do not see the majesty of the LORD.

11 O LORD, your hand is lifted up,
but they do not see it.
Let them see your zeal for your people, and be
ashamed.
Let the fire for your adversaries consume them.

12 O LORD, you will ordain peace for us,
for indeed, all that we have done, you have
done for us.

Rooted in Peace

ISAIAH 26.3

"Thou wilt keep him in perfect peace, whose mind is stayed on thee," reads the King James Version, hugging the shape of the original Hebrew metaphor. The image is that of a tent rope "stayed," or tied, to a long peg in the ground, securing the tent in the windy desert. That image was key to the Desert Fathers' practice of repeating a prayer phrase "in the heart" with each breath. The mind is trained to be "stayed" in God-awareness, rooted in God's peace. Choose a short phrase or a single word from this passage. Practice repeating that word or phrase for a few minutes and again whenever you remember it today. Return to it often in the days and weeks ahead.

See Meeting God in Prayer

---

a Meaning of Heb uncertain   *b* Heb *in Yah, the* LORD

The Dead Shall Live

ISAIAH 26.19

"The soul comes from the dereliction and self-naughting of Calvary—from that unimaginable darkness of mind and loneliness of heart—into the world of . . . reality ablaze with God, which here and now awaits us . . . He shall roll back the heavy stone that shut us in that Cave of Illusion, the sepulchre of earthly imagination. Then we amazed and exultant shall come out to see before us a world renewed and yet the same: lit by that new colour known to those who see Creation with the eyes of God . . . Because [the soul] was not afraid to enter His darkness, lit only by the faint lantern of humble and self-giving love, now it is inundated with the Uncreated Light."

—EVELYN UNDERHILL,
The Spiral Way

13 O LORD our God,
   other lords besides you have ruled over us,
   but we acknowledge your name alone.
14 The dead do not live;
   shades do not rise—
because you have punished and destroyed them,
   and wiped out all memory of them.
15 But you have increased the nation, O LORD,
   you have increased the nation; you are glorified;
   you have enlarged all the borders of the land.

16 O LORD, in distress they sought you,
   they poured out a prayer[a]
   when your chastening was on them.
17 Like a woman with child,
   who writhes and cries out in her pangs
   when she is near her time,
so were we because of you, O LORD;
18   we were with child, we writhed,
   but we gave birth only to wind.
We have won no victories on earth,
   and no one is born to inhabit the world.
19 Your dead shall live, their corpses[b] shall rise.
   O dwellers in the dust, awake and sing for joy!
For your dew is a radiant dew,
   and the earth will give birth to those long dead.[c]

20 Come, my people, enter your chambers,
   and shut your doors behind you;
hide yourselves for a little while
   until the wrath is past.
21 For the LORD comes out from his place
   to punish the inhabitants of the earth for their
      iniquity;
the earth will disclose the blood shed on it,
   and will no longer cover its slain.

Israel's Redemption

27 On that day the LORD with his cruel and great and strong sword will punish Leviathan the fleeing serpent, Leviathan the twisting serpent, and he will kill the dragon that is in the sea.

2   On that day:
A pleasant vineyard, sing about it!
3   I, the LORD, am its keeper;
   every moment I water it.
I guard it night and day
   so that no one can harm it;
4   I have no wrath.
If it gives me thorns and briers,
   I will march to battle against it.
   I will burn it up.
5   Or else let it cling to me for protection,
   let it make peace with me,
   let it make peace with me.

a Meaning of Heb uncertain   *b* Cn Compare Syr Tg: Heb *my corpse*
c Heb *to the shades*

⁶ In days to come*a* Jacob shall take root,
   Israel shall blossom and put forth shoots,
   and fill the whole world with fruit.

⁷ Has he struck them down as he struck down those
      who struck them?
   Or have they been killed as their killers were
      killed?
⁸ By expulsion,*b* by exile you struggled against them;
   with his fierce blast he removed them in the
      day of the east wind.
⁹ Therefore by this the guilt of Jacob will be
      expiated,
   and this will be the full fruit of the removal of
      his sin:
   when he makes all the stones of the altars
      like chalkstones crushed to pieces,
   no sacred poles*c* or incense altars will remain
      standing.
¹⁰ For the fortified city is solitary,
   a habitation deserted and forsaken, like the
      wilderness;
   the calves graze there,
      there they lie down, and strip its branches.
¹¹ When its boughs are dry, they are broken;
   women come and make a fire of them.
   For this is a people without understanding;
   therefore he that made them will not have
      compassion on them,
   he that formed them will show them no favor.

12 On that day the LORD will thresh from the channel
of the Euphrates to the Wadi of Egypt, and you will be
gathered one by one, O people of Israel. ¹³And on that day
a great trumpet will be blown, and those who were lost in
the land of Assyria and those who were driven out to the
land of Egypt will come and worship the LORD on the holy
mountain at Jerusalem.

Judgment on Corrupt Rulers, Priests, and Prophets

28 Ah, the proud garland of the drunkards of Ephraim,
   and the fading flower of its glorious beauty,
   which is on the head of those bloated with rich
      food, of those overcome with wine!
² See, the Lord has one who is mighty and strong;
   like a storm of hail, a destroying tempest,
   like a storm of mighty, overflowing waters;
   with his hand he will hurl them down to the
      earth.
³ Trampled under foot will be
   the proud garland of the drunkards of Ephraim.
⁴ And the fading flower of its glorious beauty,
   which is on the head of those bloated with rich
      food,
   will be like a first-ripe fig before the summer;
   whoever sees it, eats it up
   as soon as it comes to hand.

Divine Attributes

ISAIAH 28.2–6

In this passage, Isaiah ponders the attributes of God: glory, beauty, justice, love and strength. What aspects of God are especially important to you? Make your own list. Then consider where you see any of these attributes at work in people you know or in yourself. Say a short prayer of thanks such as, "I thank you for the spirit of glory at work in Brad's poetry." Use a one-sentence expression of thanksgiving, on the spot, when you encounter this aspect of God throughout the day.

See Meeting God in Everyday Life

---

a Heb *Those to come*   *b* Meaning of Heb uncertain   *c* Heb *Asherim*

Trust: The Sure Foundation

ISAIAH 28.16

Much more than a continuous state of mind, trusting is a repeated choice of risk in a relationship. What characteristics in others invite you to trust them? To distrust? What do you know, or hope, about God that calls you to trust the Lord in daily life? Name some experiences in which you trusted God. What were the results? Are there areas of your life where your trust in God is not very sure? Write a personal prayer to express your trust—and your need for more trust—in God: "O God, I trust you because _____. O God, I'm not sure how to trust you for _____." Keep adding, from time to time, to this prayer.

See Meeting God in Everyday Life

5 In that day the LORD of hosts will be a garland of glory,
    and a diadem of beauty, to the remnant of his people;
6 and a spirit of justice to the one who sits in judgment,
    and strength to those who turn back the battle at the gate.

7 These also reel with wine
    and stagger with strong drink;
the priest and the prophet reel with strong drink,
    they are confused with wine,
    they stagger with strong drink;
they err in vision,
    they stumble in giving judgment.
8 All tables are covered with filthy vomit;
    no place is clean.

9 "Whom will he teach knowledge,
    and to whom will he explain the message?
Those who are weaned from milk,
    those taken from the breast?
10 For it is precept upon precept, precept upon precept,
    line upon line, line upon line,
    here a little, there a little."[a]

11 Truly, with stammering lip
    and with alien tongue
he will speak to this people,
12 to whom he has said,
"This is rest;
    give rest to the weary;
and this is repose";
    yet they would not hear.
13 Therefore the word of the LORD will be to them,
    "Precept upon precept, precept upon precept,
    line upon line, line upon line,
    here a little, there a little;"[a]
in order that they may go, and fall backward,
    and be broken, and snared, and taken.

14 Therefore hear the word of the LORD, you scoffers
    who rule this people in Jerusalem.
15 Because you have said, "We have made a covenant with death,
    and with Sheol we have an agreement;
when the overwhelming scourge passes through
    it will not come to us;
for we have made lies our refuge,
    and in falsehood we have taken shelter";
16 therefore thus says the Lord GOD,
    See, I am laying in Zion a foundation stone,
    a tested stone,
a precious cornerstone, a sure foundation:
    "One who trusts will not panic."

a Meaning of Heb of this verse uncertain

We are to pray

during our reading so that

God might enable us

to properly understand

himself and his will and

open to us one door after the

other into his Word.

PHILIPP JAKOB SPENER (1635-1705)

The Necessary and Useful Reading of the Holy Scriptures

Come before the Lord and begin to read. Stop reading when you feel the Lord drawing you inwardly to himself. Now, simply remain in stillness. Stay there for a while.

JEANNE GUYON (1648–1717)

Experiencing the Depths of Jesus Christ

Our own curiosity often hinders us in reading the Scriptures, because we wish to understand and argue when we should simply read on with humility, simplicity and faith.

THOMAS À KEMPIS (c. 1380-1471)

Imitation of Christ

Where the Spirit does not open the Scripture, the Scripture is not understood even though it is read.

MARTIN LUTHER (1483-1546)

17 And I will make justice the line,
   and righteousness the plummet;
hail will sweep away the refuge of lies,
   and waters will overwhelm the shelter.
18 Then your covenant with death will be annulled,
   and your agreement with Sheol will not stand;
when the overwhelming scourge passes through
   you will be beaten down by it.
19 As often as it passes through, it will take you;
   for morning by morning it will pass through,
   by day and by night;
and it will be sheer terror to understand the
   message.
20 For the bed is too short to stretch oneself on it,
   and the covering too narrow to wrap oneself in it.
21 For the LORD will rise up as on Mount Perazim,
   he will rage as in the valley of Gibeon
to do his deed—strange is his deed!—
   and to work his work—alien is his work!
22 Now therefore do not scoff,
   or your bonds will be made stronger;
for I have heard a decree of destruction
   from the Lord GOD of hosts upon the whole land.

23 Listen, and hear my voice;
   Pay attention, and hear my speech.
24 Do those who plow for sowing plow continually?
   Do they continually open and harrow their
      ground?
25 When they have leveled its surface,
   do they not scatter dill, sow cummin,
and plant wheat in rows
   and barley in its proper place,
   and spelt as the border?
26 For they are well instructed;
   their God teaches them.

27 Dill is not threshed with a threshing sledge,
   nor is a cart wheel rolled over cummin;
but dill is beaten out with a stick,
   and cummin with a rod.
28 Grain is crushed for bread,
   but one does not thresh it forever;
one drives the cart wheel and horses over it,
   but does not pulverize it.
29 This also comes from the LORD of hosts;
   he is wonderful in counsel,
   and excellent in wisdom.

The Siege of Jerusalem

29 Ah, Ariel, Ariel,
   the city where David encamped!
Add year to year;
   let the festivals run their round.
2 Yet I will distress Ariel,
   and there shall be moaning and lamentation,
   and Jerusalem[a] shall be to me like an Ariel.[b]

God's Rebuke

ISAIAH 28.19–22

"When thou for sin rebukest
   man,
Forthwith he waxeth woe
   and wan:
Bitterness fills our bowels;
   all our hearts
   Pine, and decay,
   And drop away,
And carry with them
   th' other parts.

"But thou wilt sin and grief
   destroy;
That so the broken bones
   may joy,
And tune together in a well
   set song,
   Full of his praises,
   Who dead men raises,
Fractures well cur'd make us
   more strong."
   —GEORGE HERBERT,
      "Repentance"

---

a Heb she   b Probable meaning, altar hearth; compare Ezek 43.15

The Prayer of the Heart

ISAIAH 29.13

Our hearts are the vital center of both desire and will and the wellspring of action. We often rationalize the truth in our hearts by creating false self-images with our "lips."

"Putting the mind into the heart" is a traditional Eastern Orthodox practice meant to heal this split. Sit quietly, focusing in the very center of your chest, imagining an inner space or heart-cave. You may find it helpful to imagine this area filled with the light of God. Or with each breath, repeat a name of God. Imagine that your conscious awareness settles down inside this heart-space, surrounded by God's light or the sacred divine name. Practice letting your prayers come from this heart-space.

See Meeting God in Prayer

3   And like David[a] I will encamp against you;
    I will besiege you with towers
    and raise siegeworks against you.
4   Then deep from the earth you shall speak,
    from low in the dust your words shall come;
    your voice shall come from the ground like the
        voice of a ghost,
    and your speech shall whisper out of the dust.

5   But the multitude of your foes[b] shall be like small
        dust,
    and the multitude of tyrants like flying chaff.
    And in an instant, suddenly,
6   you will be visited by the LORD of hosts
    with thunder and earthquake and great noise,
        with whirlwind and tempest, and the flame of a
            devouring fire.
7   And the multitude of all the nations that fight
        against Ariel,
    all that fight against her and her stronghold,
        and who distress her,
    shall be like a dream, a vision of the night.
8   Just as when a hungry person dreams of eating
        and wakes up still hungry,
    or a thirsty person dreams of drinking
        and wakes up faint, still thirsty,
    so shall the multitude of all the nations be
        that fight against Mount Zion.

9   Stupefy yourselves and be in a stupor,
        blind yourselves and be blind!
    Be drunk, but not from wine;
        stagger, but not from strong drink!
10 For the LORD has poured out upon you
        a spirit of deep sleep;
    he has closed your eyes, you prophets,
        and covered your heads, you seers.

11 The vision of all this has become for you like the words of a sealed document. If it is given to those who can read, with the command, "Read this," they say, "We cannot, for it is sealed." 12And if it is given to those who cannot read, saying, "Read this," they say, "We cannot read."

13   The Lord said:
    Because these people draw near with their mouths
        and honor me with their lips,
        while their hearts are far from me,
    and their worship of me is a human
            commandment learned by rote;
14 so I will again do
        amazing things with this people,
        shocking and amazing.
    The wisdom of their wise shall perish,
        and the discernment of the discerning shall be
            hidden.

a Gk: Meaning of Heb uncertain   *b* Cn: Heb *strangers*

15 Ha! You who hide a plan too deep for the Lord,
  whose deeds are in the dark,
  and who say, "Who sees us? Who knows us?"
16 You turn things upside down!
  Shall the potter be regarded as the clay?
 Shall the thing made say of its maker,
  "He did not make me";
 or the thing formed say of the one who formed it,
  "He has no understanding"?

Hope for the Future

17 Shall not Lebanon in a very little while
  become a fruitful field,
  and the fruitful field be regarded as a forest?
18 On that day the deaf shall hear
  the words of a scroll,
 and out of their gloom and darkness
  the eyes of the blind shall see.
19 The meek shall obtain fresh joy in the Lord,
  and the neediest people shall exult in the
    Holy One of Israel.
20 For the tyrant shall be no more,
  and the scoffer shall cease to be;
  all those alert to do evil shall be cut off—
21 those who cause a person to lose a lawsuit,
  who set a trap for the arbiter in the gate,
  and without grounds deny justice to the one in
    the right.

22 Therefore thus says the Lord, who redeemed Abraham, concerning the house of Jacob:
 No longer shall Jacob be ashamed,
  no longer shall his face grow pale.
23 For when he sees his children,
  the work of my hands, in his midst,
  they will sanctify my name;
 they will sanctify the Holy One of Jacob,
  and will stand in awe of the God of Israel.
24 And those who err in spirit will come to
    understanding,
  and those who grumble will accept instruction.

The Futility of Reliance on Egypt

30 Oh, rebellious children, says the Lord,
  who carry out a plan, but not mine;
 who make an alliance, but against my will,
  adding sin to sin;
2 who set out to go down to Egypt
  without asking for my counsel,
 to take refuge in the protection of Pharaoh,
  and to seek shelter in the shadow of Egypt;
3 Therefore the protection of Pharaoh shall become
    your shame,
  and the shelter in the shadow of Egypt your
    humiliation.
4 For though his officials are at Zoan
  and his envoys reach Hanes,
5 everyone comes to shame
  through a people that cannot profit them,

We Are the Clay

ISAIAH 29.16

Clay is more than merely inert matter. It often seems to have a life and integrity all its own. All potters know that they must form a relationship with the pliable, crystalline clay to shape it into durable, strong vessels. Find some real clay and practice feeling both its innate integrity and your ability to mold it into various shapes. Notice how the clay becomes more pliable and "alive" the more you work with it. Ponder how this relationship is like the one you have with the divine potter. Consider the various means or tools God uses to shape your spiritual life. How do those means change you and bring out the best aspects of your God-given nature?

See *Meeting God in Scripture*

929

Remembering to Trust

ISAIAH 30.15

Israel refuses to cultivate the habit of trusting in God's faithful presence in all circumstances. Trust can be strengthened by the practice of "remembering God" in the midst of new or difficult situations. Personalizing a sacred phrase and committing it to heart can be such a reminder. Introduce one of these phrases—"In returning and rest you shall be saved" or "in quietness and in trust shall be your strength"—into a quiet time of meditative prayer, repeating the phrase several times. As you pray, review any situation you might face that challenges your ability to trust in God, in your God-given abilities or in other people.

See Meeting God in Everyday Life

that brings neither help nor profit,
   but shame and disgrace.

6 An oracle concerning the animals of the Negeb.
   Through a land of trouble and distress,
      of lioness and roaring[a] lion,
      of viper and flying serpent,
   they carry their riches on the backs of donkeys,
      and their treasures on the humps of camels,
      to a people that cannot profit them.
7 For Egypt's help is worthless and empty,
   therefore I have called her,
   "Rahab who sits still."[b]

A Rebellious People

8 Go now, write it before them on a tablet,
      and inscribe it in a book,
   so that it may be for the time to come
      as a witness forever.
9 For they are a rebellious people,
      faithless children,
   children who will not hear
      the instruction of the LORD;
10 who say to the seers, "Do not see";
      and to the prophets, "Do not prophesy to us
         what is right;
   speak to us smooth things,
      prophesy illusions,
11 leave the way, turn aside from the path,
      let us hear no more about the Holy One of Israel."
12 Therefore thus says the Holy One of Israel:
   Because you reject this word,
      and put your trust in oppression and deceit,
      and rely on them;
13 therefore this iniquity shall become for you
      like a break in a high wall, bulging out, and
         about to collapse,
      whose crash comes suddenly, in an instant;
14 its breaking is like that of a potter's vessel
      that is smashed so ruthlessly
   that among its fragments not a sherd is found
      for taking fire from the hearth,
      or dipping water out of the cistern.

15 For thus said the Lord GOD, the Holy One of Israel:
   In returning and rest you shall be saved;
      in quietness and in trust shall be your strength.
   But you refused [16]and said,
   "No! We will flee upon horses"—
      therefore you shall flee!
   and, "We will ride upon swift steeds"—
      therefore your pursuers shall be swift!
17 A thousand shall flee at the threat of one,
      at the threat of five you shall flee,
   until you are left
      like a flagstaff on the top of a mountain,
      like a signal on a hill.

a Cn: Heb *from them*   *b* Meaning of Heb uncertain

God's Promise to Zion

18 Therefore the LORD waits to be gracious to you;
  therefore he will rise up to show mercy to you.
  For the LORD is a God of justice;
  blessed are all those who wait for him.

19 Truly, O people in Zion, inhabitants of Jerusalem, you shall weep no more. He will surely be gracious to you at the sound of your cry; when he hears it, he will answer you. 20 Though the Lord may give you the bread of adversity and the water of affliction, yet your Teacher will not hide himself any more, but your eyes shall see your Teacher. 21 And when you turn to the right or when you turn to the left, your ears shall hear a word behind you, saying, "This is the way; walk in it." 22 Then you will defile your silver-covered idols and your gold-plated images. You will scatter them like filthy rags; you will say to them, "Away with you!"

23 He will give rain for the seed with which you sow the ground, and grain, the produce of the ground, which will be rich and plenteous. On that day your cattle will graze in broad pastures; 24 and the oxen and donkeys that till the ground will eat silage, which has been winnowed with shovel and fork. 25 On every lofty mountain and every high hill there will be brooks running with water—on a day of the great slaughter, when the towers fall. 26 Moreover the light of the moon will be like the light of the sun, and the light of the sun will be sevenfold, like the light of seven days, on the day when the LORD binds up the injuries of his people, and heals the wounds inflicted by his blow.

Judgment on Assyria

27 See, the name of the LORD comes from far away,
  burning with his anger, and in thick rising
      smoke;[a]
  his lips are full of indignation,
    and his tongue is like a devouring fire;
28 his breath is like an overflowing stream
    that reaches up to the neck—
  to sift the nations with the sieve of destruction,
    and to place on the jaws of the peoples a bridle
      that leads them astray.

29 You shall have a song as in the night when a holy festival is kept; and gladness of heart, as when one sets out to the sound of the flute to go to the mountain of the LORD, to the Rock of Israel. 30 And the LORD will cause his majestic voice to be heard and the descending blow of his arm to be seen, in furious anger and a flame of devouring fire, with a cloudburst and tempest and hailstones. 31 The Assyrian will be terror-stricken at the voice of the LORD, when he strikes with his rod. 32 And every stroke of the staff of punishment that the LORD lays upon him will be to the sound of timbrels and lyres; battling with brandished arm he will fight with him. 33 For his burning place[b] has long been prepared; truly it is made ready for the king,[c] its pyre made deep and wide, with fire and wood in abundance; the breath of the LORD, like a stream of sulfur, kindles it.

a Meaning of Heb uncertain b Or Topheth c Or Molech

The Divine Teacher

ISAIAH 30.20–21

God is our ultimate teacher and guide who uses many methods to instruct us. Are there lessons God seems to be repeating so that you would learn them well? How is God instructing you right now, in this period of your life? Take time to remember, with love and with thanksgiving, some of the people who have been God's agents in teaching you. Consider also those who have taught you by the difficulty or opposition they have brought into your life, thereby helping you clarify your values and find new strength in dealing with those difficulties. Can you give thanks for these occasions of learning too? Consider writing a note of thanks as soon as possible to one of the people God has used to teach you.

See *Meeting God in Community*

God Is Like . . .

ISAIAH 31.4–5

Animal similes are often used in scripture to communicate God's character and qualities. God is compared to an eagle (Deuteronomy 32.11), a lamb (John 1.29), and even the serpent of healing and wisdom (Numbers 21.9; John 3.14). Isaiah uses the simile of a lion to describe God's fearlessness and power as the defender of Israel and that of a great bird to describe God's soaring and overarching protection. Choose one of these images to ponder. Draw or find a picture of this animal, observing the qualities that characterize it. Imagine that God is with you, embodying one of these qualities. Ask God to help you manifest this quality toward others.

See *Meeting God in the Created Order*

Alliance with Egypt Is Futile

31 Alas for those who go down to Egypt for help
  and who rely on horses,
who trust in chariots because they are many
  and in horsemen because they are very strong,
but do not look to the Holy One of Israel
  or consult the LORD!
² Yet he too is wise and brings disaster;
  he does not call back his words,
but will rise against the house of the evildoers,
  and against the helpers of those who work
    iniquity.
³ The Egyptians are human, and not God;
  their horses are flesh, and not spirit.
When the LORD stretches out his hand,
  the helper will stumble, and the one helped will
    fall,
  and they will all perish together.

⁴ For thus the LORD said to me,
As a lion or a young lion growls over its prey,
  and—when a band of shepherds is called out
    against it—
is not terrified by their shouting
  or daunted at their noise,
so the LORD of hosts will come down
  to fight upon Mount Zion and upon its hill.
⁵ Like birds hovering overhead, so the LORD of hosts
    will protect Jerusalem;
he will protect and deliver it,
  he will spare and rescue it.

6 Turn back to him whom you*a* have deeply betrayed, O people of Israel. ⁷For on that day all of you shall throw away your idols of silver and idols of gold, which your hands have sinfully made for you.
⁸ "Then the Assyrian shall fall by a sword, not of
    mortals;
  and a sword, not of humans, shall devour him;
he shall flee from the sword,
  and his young men shall be put to forced labor.
⁹ His rock shall pass away in terror,
  and his officers desert the standard in panic,"
says the LORD, whose fire is in Zion,
  and whose furnace is in Jerusalem.

Government with Justice Predicted

32 See, a king will reign in righteousness,
  and princes will rule with justice.
² Each will be like a hiding place from the wind,
  a covert from the tempest,
like streams of water in a dry place,
  like the shade of a great rock in a weary land.
³ Then the eyes of those who have sight will not be
    closed,
  and the ears of those who have hearing will
    listen.

a Heb *they*

4 The minds of the rash will have good judgment,
  and the tongues of stammerers will speak
    readily and distinctly.
5 A fool will no longer be called noble,
  nor a villain said to be honorable.
6 For fools speak folly,
  and their minds plot iniquity:
to practice ungodliness,
  to utter error concerning the LORD,
to leave the craving of the hungry unsatisfied,
  and to deprive the thirsty of drink.
7 The villainies of villains are evil;
  they devise wicked devices
to ruin the poor with lying words,
  even when the plea of the needy is right.
8 But those who are noble plan noble things,
  and by noble things they stand.

Complacent Women Warned of Disaster

9 Rise up, you women who are at ease, hear my voice;
  you complacent daughters, listen to my speech.
10 In little more than a year
  you will shudder, you complacent ones;
for the vintage will fail,
  the fruit harvest will not come.
11 Tremble, you women who are at ease,
  shudder, you complacent ones;
strip, and make yourselves bare,
  and put sackcloth on your loins.
12 Beat your breasts for the pleasant fields,
  for the fruitful vine,
13 for the soil of my people
  growing up in thorns and briers;
yes, for all the joyous houses
  in the jubilant city.
14 For the palace will be forsaken,
  the populous city deserted;
the hill and the watchtower
  will become dens forever,
the joy of wild asses,
  a pasture for flocks;
15 until a spirit from on high is poured out on us,
  and the wilderness becomes a fruitful field,
  and the fruitful field is deemed a forest.

The Peace of God's Reign

16 Then justice will dwell in the wilderness,
  and righteousness abide in the fruitful field.
17 The effect of righteousness will be peace,
  and the result of righteousness, quietness and
    trust forever.
18 My people will abide in a peaceful habitation,
  in secure dwellings, and in quiet resting places.
19 The forest will disappear completely,[a]
  and the city will be utterly laid low.
20 Happy will you be who sow beside every stream,
  who let the ox and the donkey range freely.

_a_ Cn: Heb _And it will hail when the forest comes down_

Peaceful Dwelling Places

ISAIAH 32.14–20

The prophet envisions how God's people will return to a life of a renewed connection to creation and to the Spirit—a return that leads them to "quietness and trust." What natural landscape helps you shed the stress of an overburdened life, renew the wholeness of your soul and body, and find a renewed sense of the presence of God's glory? Visit that place now in your heart, imagining its sights and sounds with all your inner senses. Rest in this remembered landscape, opening heart and mind to God in trustful prayer. Know that this place—your sanctuary—is always available.

"The King in His Beauty"

"But still I lay awake, and then our Lord opened my spiritual eyes, and showed me my soul in the midst of my heart. I saw my soul as wide as if it were a kingdom, and from the state which I saw in it, it seemed to me as if it were a fine city. In the midst of this city sits our Lord Jesus, true God and true man, a handsome person and tall, honourable, the greatest lord. And I saw him splendidly clad in honours. He sits erect there in the soul, in peace and rest . . . And my soul is blessedly occupied by the divinity, sovereign power, sovereign wisdom, sovereign goodness."

—JULIAN OF NORWICH,
Showings

A Prophecy of Deliverance from Foes

33 Ah, you destroyer,
who yourself have not been destroyed;
you treacherous one,
with whom no one has dealt treacherously!
When you have ceased to destroy,
you will be destroyed;
and when you have stopped dealing treacherously,
you will be dealt with treacherously.

2 O LORD, be gracious to us; we wait for you.
Be our arm every morning,
our salvation in the time of trouble.
3 At the sound of tumult, peoples fled;
before your majesty, nations scattered.
4 Spoil was gathered as the caterpillar gathers;
as locusts leap, they leaped*a* upon it.
5 The LORD is exalted, he dwells on high;
he filled Zion with justice and righteousness;
6 he will be the stability of your times,
abundance of salvation, wisdom, and
knowledge;
the fear of the LORD is Zion's treasure.*b*

7 Listen! the valiant*a* cry in the streets;
the envoys of peace weep bitterly.
8 The highways are deserted,
travelers have quit the road.
The treaty is broken,
its oaths*c* are despised,
its obligation*d* is disregarded.
9 The land mourns and languishes;
Lebanon is confounded and withers away;
Sharon is like a desert;
and Bashan and Carmel shake off their leaves.

10 "Now I will arise," says the LORD,
"now I will lift myself up;
now I will be exalted.
11 You conceive chaff, you bring forth stubble;
your breath is a fire that will consume you.
12 And the peoples will be as if burned to lime,
like thorns cut down, that are burned in the fire."

13 Hear, you who are far away, what I have done;
and you who are near, acknowledge my might.
14 The sinners in Zion are afraid;
trembling has seized the godless:
"Who among us can live with the devouring fire?
Who among us can live with everlasting
flames?"
15 Those who walk righteously and speak uprightly,
who despise the gain of oppression,
who wave away a bribe instead of accepting it,
who stop their ears from hearing of bloodshed
and shut their eyes from looking on evil,

a Meaning of Heb uncertain   *b* Heb *his treasure*; meaning of Heb uncertain   *c* Q Ms: MT *cities*   *d* Or *everyone*

16 they will live on the heights;
        their refuge will be the fortresses of rocks;
        their food will be supplied, their water assured.

The Land of the Majestic King

17 Your eyes will see the king in his beauty;
        they will behold a land that stretches far away.
18 Your mind will muse on the terror:
        "Where is the one who counted?
        Where is the one who weighed the tribute?
        Where is the one who counted the towers?"
19 No longer will you see the insolent people,
        the people of an obscure speech that you
            cannot comprehend,
        stammering in a language that you cannot
            understand.
20 Look on Zion, the city of our appointed festivals!
        Your eyes will see Jerusalem,
        a quiet habitation, an immovable tent,
    whose stakes will never be pulled up,
        and none of whose ropes will be broken.
21 But there the LORD in majesty will be for us
        a place of broad rivers and streams,
        where no galley with oars can go,
            nor stately ship can pass.
22 For the LORD is our judge, the LORD is our ruler,
        the LORD is our king; he will save us.

23 Your rigging hangs loose;
        it cannot hold the mast firm in its place,
        or keep the sail spread out.

    Then prey and spoil in abundance will be divided;
        even the lame will fall to plundering.
24 And no inhabitant will say, "I am sick";
        the people who live there will be forgiven their
            iniquity.

Judgment on the Nations

34 Draw near, O nations, to hear;
        O peoples, give heed!
    Let the earth hear, and all that fills it;
        the world, and all that comes from it.
2   For the LORD is enraged against all the nations,
        and furious against all their hordes;
        he has doomed them, has given them over for
            slaughter.
3   Their slain shall be cast out,
        and the stench of their corpses shall rise;
        the mountains shall flow with their blood.
4   All the host of heaven shall rot away,
        and the skies roll up like a scroll.
    All their host shall wither
        like a leaf withering on a vine,
        or fruit withering on a fig tree.

5   When my sword has drunk its fill in the heavens,
        lo, it will descend upon Edom,
        upon the people I have doomed to judgment.

The Place

ISAIAH 33.21

In Judaism, "the Place" is one of God's names, for God is seen as the Place in which everything else lives: "In him we live and move and have our being" (Acts 17.28). Try this traditional meditation: As you sit quietly, become aware of the space immediately around you. Become aware of your breathing as a gift of God. Now imaginatively expand your awareness beyond the confines of this space—imagine breathing in the air from the rest of the building. From the outside environment. From the city or town. From the surrounding countryside. Then breathe in from the whole region, country, planet—and then from God's infinite space. Breathe in the breath of God, "the Place" of all existence.

See Meeting God in Prayer

935

The Place of the Wild

ISAIAH 34.11–17

Oppressive humanity, symbolized by Edom, gives way to an entire ecosystem filled with wildlife. In this passage, which contains one of scripture's most extensive lists of animals, that ecosystem symbolizes the purification of the land from human sin—and the land subsequently brims with new life.

What are your attitudes toward the animals God has created? Do you view them as a blessed wonder or a cursed nuisance? What place is given to wild birds and animals in your neighborhood? What can you do to provide for them and offer them protection? Take a walk with keen eyes and an awakened heart, noticing with thanksgiving each of God's creatures you encounter. Look at them as God's creatures. Let your prayers include all creatures imperiled by human heedlessness and greed.

See *Meeting God in the Created Order*

6 The LORD has a sword; it is sated with blood,
    it is gorged with fat,
  with the blood of lambs and goats,
    with the fat of the kidneys of rams.
  For the LORD has a sacrifice in Bozrah,
    a great slaughter in the land of Edom.
7 Wild oxen shall fall with them,
    and young steers with the mighty bulls.
  Their land shall be soaked with blood,
    and their soil made rich with fat.

8 For the LORD has a day of vengeance,
    a year of vindication by Zion's cause.*a*
9 And the streams of Edom*b* shall be turned into
      pitch,
    and her soil into sulfur;
  her land shall become burning pitch.
10 Night and day it shall not be quenched;
    its smoke shall go up forever.
  From generation to generation it shall lie waste;
    no one shall pass through it forever and ever.
11 But the hawk*c* and the hedgehog*c* shall possess it;
    the owl*c* and the raven shall live in it.
  He shall stretch the line of confusion over it,
    and the plummet of chaos over*d* its nobles.
12 They shall name it No Kingdom There,
    and all its princes shall be nothing.
13 Thorns shall grow over its strongholds,
    nettles and thistles in its fortresses.
  It shall be the haunt of jackals,
    an abode for ostriches.
14 Wildcats shall meet with hyenas,
    goat-demons shall call to each other;
  there too Lilith shall repose,
    and find a place to rest.
15 There shall the owl nest
    and lay and hatch and brood in its shadow;
  there too the buzzards shall gather,
    each one with its mate.
16 Seek and read from the book of the LORD:
    Not one of these shall be missing;
    none shall be without its mate.
  For the mouth of the LORD has commanded,
    and his spirit has gathered them.
17 He has cast the lot for them,
    his hand has portioned it out to them with the
      line;
  they shall possess it forever,
    from generation to generation they shall live
      in it.

The Return of the Redeemed to Zion

35 The wilderness and the dry land shall be glad,
    the desert shall rejoice and blossom;
  like the crocus ²it shall blossom abundantly,
    and rejoice with joy and singing.
  The glory of Lebanon shall be given to it,

a Or *of recompense by Zion's defender*   *b* Heb *her streams*
c Identification uncertain   *d* Heb lacks *over*

the majesty of Carmel and Sharon.
They shall see the glory of the LORD,
    the majesty of our God.

3 Strengthen the weak hands,
    and make firm the feeble knees.
4 Say to those who are of a fearful heart,
    "Be strong, do not fear!
Here is your God.
    He will come with vengeance,
with terrible recompense.
    He will come and save you."

5 Then the eyes of the blind shall be opened,
    and the ears of the deaf unstopped;
6 then the lame shall leap like a deer,
    and the tongue of the speechless sing for joy.
For waters shall break forth in the wilderness,
    and streams in the desert;
7 the burning sand shall become a pool,
    and the thirsty ground springs of water;
the haunt of jackals shall become a swamp,[a]
    the grass shall become reeds and rushes.

8 A highway shall be there,
    and it shall be called the Holy Way;
the unclean shall not travel on it,[b]
    but it shall be for God's people;[c]
    no traveler, not even fools, shall go astray.
9 No lion shall be there,
    nor shall any ravenous beast come up on it;
they shall not be found there,
    but the redeemed shall walk there.
10 And the ransomed of the LORD shall return,
    and come to Zion with singing;
everlasting joy shall be upon their heads;
    they shall obtain joy and gladness,
    and sorrow and sighing shall flee away.

Sennacherib Threatens Jerusalem

36 In the fourteenth year of King Hezekiah, King Sennacherib of Assyria came up against all the fortified cities of Judah and captured them. 2 The king of Assyria sent the Rabshakeh from Lachish to King Hezekiah at Jerusalem, with a great army. He stood by the conduit of the upper pool on the highway to the Fuller's Field. 3 And there came out to him Eliakim son of Hilkiah, who was in charge of the palace, and Shebna the secretary, and Joah son of Asaph, the recorder.

4 The Rabshakeh said to them, "Say to Hezekiah: Thus says the great king, the king of Assyria: On what do you base this confidence of yours? 5 Do you think that mere words are strategy and power for war? On whom do you now rely, that you have rebelled against me? 6 See, you are relying on Egypt, that broken reed of a staff, which will pierce the hand of anyone who leans on it. Such is Pharaoh king of Egypt to all who rely on him. 7 But if you say

---

Restoration and Healing

ISAIAH 35.4–10

Practice *lectio divina* ("divine reading") with this picture of God's saving activity. What words or phrases seem to need emphasis as you slowly read the entire section aloud? What comes to mind as you choose one word or phrase and spend some time brooding on it? What thoughts, feelings, memories or associations emerge? What might God be trying to say to you through this cluster of associations? Express in prayer your heartfelt response to what you have seen.

See *Meeting God in Scripture*

---

a Cn: Heb *in the haunt of jackals is her resting place*   b Or *pass it by*
c Cn: Heb *for them*

The Field Commander

ISAIAH 36.11–16

Who are the *Rabshakehs*, or field commanders, in your life—people who by their words or behavior threaten to undermine your trust in God? Who is enticing you to compromise your values? What are the situations where trust in God seems to elude you? In what areas do doubts arise about divine grace? Health? Money? Personal confrontations? As you ponder one or more of these situations, repeat Isaiah's words: "Thus says the LORD: Do not be afraid" (37.6). Ask the Spirit to show you ways to trust God in these encounters.

See Meeting God in Everyday Life

to me, 'We rely on the LORD our God,' is it not he whose high places and altars Hezekiah has removed, saying to Judah and to Jerusalem, 'You shall worship before this altar'? ⁸Come now, make a wager with my master the king of Assyria: I will give you two thousand horses, if you are able on your part to set riders on them. ⁹How then can you repulse a single captain among the least of my master's servants, when you rely on Egypt for chariots and for horsemen? ¹⁰Moreover, is it without the LORD that I have come up against this land to destroy it? The LORD said to me, Go up against this land, and destroy it."

11 Then Eliakim, Shebna, and Joah said to the Rabshakeh, "Please speak to your servants in Aramaic, for we understand it; do not speak to us in the language of Judah within the hearing of the people who are on the wall." ¹²But the Rabshakeh said, "Has my master sent me to speak these words to your master and to you, and not to the people sitting on the wall, who are doomed with you to eat their own dung and drink their own urine?"

13 Then the Rabshakeh stood and called out in a loud voice in the language of Judah, "Hear the words of the great king, the king of Assyria! ¹⁴Thus says the king: 'Do not let Hezekiah deceive you, for he will not be able to deliver you. ¹⁵Do not let Hezekiah make you rely on the LORD by saying, The LORD will surely deliver us; this city will not be given into the hand of the king of Assyria.' ¹⁶Do not listen to Hezekiah; for thus says the king of Assyria: 'Make your peace with me and come out to me; then everyone of you will eat from your own vine and your own fig tree and drink water from your own cistern, ¹⁷until I come and take you away to a land like your own land, a land of grain and wine, a land of bread and vineyards. ¹⁸Do not let Hezekiah mislead you by saying, The LORD will save us. Has any of the gods of the nations saved their land out of the hand of the king of Assyria? ¹⁹Where are the gods of Hamath and Arpad? Where are the gods of Sepharvaim? Have they delivered Samaria out of my hand? ²⁰Who among all the gods of these countries have saved their countries out of my hand, that the LORD should save Jerusalem out of my hand?' "

21 But they were silent and answered him not a word, for the king's command was, "Do not answer him." ²²Then Eliakim son of Hilkiah, who was in charge of the palace, and Shebna the secretary, and Joah son of Asaph, the recorder, came to Hezekiah with their clothes torn, and told him the words of the Rabshakeh.

Hezekiah Consults Isaiah

37 When King Hezekiah heard it, he tore his clothes, covered himself with sackcloth, and went into the house of the LORD. ²And he sent Eliakim, who was in charge of the palace, and Shebna the secretary, and the senior priests, covered with sackcloth, to the prophet Isaiah son of Amoz. ³They said to him, "Thus says Hezekiah, This day is a day of distress, of rebuke, and of disgrace; children have come to the birth, and there is no strength to bring them forth. ⁴It may be that the LORD your God heard the words of the Rabshakeh, whom his master the king of Assyria has sent to mock the living God, and will rebuke the words that the LORD your God has heard; therefore lift up your prayer for the remnant that is left."

5 When the servants of King Hezekiah came to Isaiah, [6]Isaiah said to them, "Say to your master, 'Thus says the LORD: Do not be afraid because of the words that you have heard, with which the servants of the king of Assyria have reviled me. [7]I myself will put a spirit in him, so that he shall hear a rumor, and return to his own land; I will cause him to fall by the sword in his own land.' "

8 The Rabshakeh returned, and found the king of Assyria fighting against Libnah; for he had heard that the king had left Lachish. [9]Now the king[a] heard concerning King Tirhakah of Ethiopia,[b] "He has set out to fight against you." When he heard it, he sent messengers to Hezekiah, saying, [10]"Thus shall you speak to King Hezekiah of Judah: Do not let your God on whom you rely deceive you by promising that Jerusalem will not be given into the hand of the king of Assyria. [11]See, you have heard what the kings of Assyria have done to all lands, destroying them utterly. Shall you be delivered? [12]Have the gods of the nations delivered them, the nations that my predecessors destroyed, Gozan, Haran, Rezeph, and the people of Eden who were in Telassar? [13]Where is the king of Hamath, the king of Arpad, the king of the city of Sepharvaim, the king of Hena, or the king of Ivvah?"

Hezekiah's Prayer

14 Hezekiah received the letter from the hand of the messengers and read it; then Hezekiah went up to the house of the LORD and spread it before the LORD. [15]And Hezekiah prayed to the LORD, saying: [16]"O LORD of hosts, God of Israel, who are enthroned above the cherubim, you are God, you alone, of all the kingdoms of the earth; you have made heaven and earth. [17]Incline your ear, O LORD, and hear; open your eyes, O LORD, and see; hear all the words of Sennacherib, which he has sent to mock the living God. [18]Truly, O LORD, the kings of Assyria have laid waste all the nations and their lands, [19]and have hurled their gods into the fire, though they were no gods, but the work of human hands—wood and stone—and so they were destroyed. [20]So now, O LORD our God, save us from his hand, so that all the kingdoms of the earth may know that you alone are the LORD."

21 Then Isaiah son of Amoz sent to Hezekiah, saying: "Thus says the LORD, the God of Israel: Because you have prayed to me concerning King Sennacherib of Assyria, [22]this is the word that the LORD has spoken concerning him:

> She despises you, she scorns you—
>   virgin daughter Zion;
> she tosses her head—behind your back,
>   daughter Jerusalem.

[23] "Whom have you mocked and reviled?
>   Against whom have you raised your voice
> and haughtily lifted your eyes?
>   Against the Holy One of Israel!

The Heavenly Hosts

ISAIAH 37.16

"O glorious living light,
   which lives in Divinity!
Angels who fix your eyes
   with ardent desire . . .
On him with Whom your
   desires can never be
   sated!
O glorious joy to live in your
   form and nature!

"O angels with shining faces
   who guard the people,
O ye archangels, who take
   just souls into Heaven,
And you, O virtues and
   powers, O principalities,
. . . dominions and
   thrones . . .

"And you, cherubim and
   seraphim, seal of God's
   secrets,
Praise be to you all, who
   behold the heart of the
   Father,
And see the Ancient of Days
   spring forth in the
   fountain,
And His inner power appear
   like a face from His
   heart."

—HILDEGARD OF BINGEN,
"Symphony of the Blessed"

See Meeting God in Worship

"For the Sake of . . ."

ISAIAH 37.35

Scripture says that God performs deeds "for the sake of David" or "for the sake of Christ" or "for the sake of God's own mercy" or "name" or "praise," showing us that God is moved to do good for the well-being of another or for the glory of his own attributes.

Think of three or four good things, however small, you have done recently. Why did you perform those actions? For whose sake? What might you have done for the sake of someone's good opinion of you? Which attributes of God awaken your sense of praise? What deed can you perform today for the sake of that facet of God?

See Meeting God in Service

24 By your servants you have mocked the Lord,
  and you have said, 'With my many chariots
I have gone up the heights of the mountains,
  to the far recesses of Lebanon;
I felled its tallest cedars,
  its choicest cypresses;
I came to its remotest height,
  its densest forest.
25 I dug wells
  and drank waters,
I dried up with the sole of my foot
  all the streams of Egypt.'

26 "Have you not heard
  that I determined it long ago?
I planned from days of old
  what now I bring to pass,
that you should make fortified cities
  crash into heaps of ruins,
27 while their inhabitants, shorn of strength,
  are dismayed and confounded;
they have become like plants of the field
  and like tender grass,
like grass on the housetops,
  blighted[a] before it is grown.

28 "I know your rising up[b] and your sitting down,
  your going out and coming in,
  and your raging against me.
29 Because you have raged against me
  and your arrogance has come to my ears,
I will put my hook in your nose
  and my bit in your mouth;
I will turn you back on the way
  by which you came.

30 "And this shall be the sign for you: This year eat what grows of itself, and in the second year what springs from that; then in the third year sow, reap, plant vineyards, and eat their fruit. 31 The surviving remnant of the house of Judah shall again take root downward, and bear fruit upward; 32 for from Jerusalem a remnant shall go out, and from Mount Zion a band of survivors. The zeal of the Lord of hosts will do this.

33 "Therefore thus says the Lord concerning the king of Assyria: He shall not come into this city, shoot an arrow there, come before it with a shield, or cast up a siege ramp against it. 34 By the way that he came, by the same he shall return; he shall not come into this city, says the Lord. 35 For I will defend this city to save it, for my own sake and for the sake of my servant David."

Sennacherib's Defeat and Death

36 Then the angel of the Lord set out and struck down one hundred eighty-five thousand in the camp of the Assyrians; when morning dawned, they were all dead bodies. 37 Then King Sennacherib of Assyria left, went home,

a With 2 Kings 19.26: Heb *field*   *b* Q Ms Gk: MT lacks *your rising up*

and lived at Nineveh. **38**As he was worshiping in the house of his god Nisroch, his sons Adrammelech and Sharezer killed him with the sword, and they escaped into the land of Ararat. His son Esar-haddon succeeded him.

Hezekiah's Illness

38 In those days Hezekiah became sick and was at the point of death. The prophet Isaiah son of Amoz came to him, and said to him, "Thus says the LORD: Set your house in order, for you shall die; you shall not recover." **2**Then Hezekiah turned his face to the wall, and prayed to the LORD: **3**"Remember now, O LORD, I implore you, how I have walked before you in faithfulness with a whole heart, and have done what is good in your sight." And Hezekiah wept bitterly.

4 Then the word of the LORD came to Isaiah: **5**"Go and say to Hezekiah, Thus says the LORD, the God of your ancestor David: I have heard your prayer, I have seen your tears; I will add fifteen years to your life. **6**I will deliver you and this city out of the hand of the king of Assyria, and defend this city.

7 "This is the sign to you from the LORD, that the LORD will do this thing that he has promised: **8**See, I will make the shadow cast by the declining sun on the dial of Ahaz turn back ten steps." So the sun turned back on the dial the ten steps by which it had declined.*a*

9 A writing of King Hezekiah of Judah, after he had been sick and had recovered from his sickness:
10   I said: In the noontide of my days
     I must depart;
  I am consigned to the gates of Sheol
     for the rest of my years.
11   I said, I shall not see the LORD
     in the land of the living;
  I shall look upon mortals no more
     among the inhabitants of the world.
12   My dwelling is plucked up and removed from me
     like a shepherd's tent;
  like a weaver I have rolled up my life;
     he cuts me off from the loom;
  from day to night you bring me to an end;*a*
13   I cry for help*b* until morning;
  like a lion he breaks all my bones;
     from day to night you bring me to an end.*a*

14   Like a swallow or a crane*a* I clamor,
     I moan like a dove.
  My eyes are weary with looking upward.
     O Lord, I am oppressed; be my security!
15   But what can I say? For he has spoken to me,
     and he himself has done it.
  All my sleep has fled*c*
     because of the bitterness of my soul.

16   O Lord, by these things people live,
     and in all these is the life of my spirit.*a*

"Set Your House in Order"

ISAIAH 38.1

Memento mori, the remembrance of death, is a long-neglected Christian practice designed to increase a sense of the importance of living well here and now. If you knew that you had only one more day to live, what three things would you do? How do these three things highlight the most important things in your life? How do they relate to God's values? Prayerfully consider beginning to do one or more of these things in the next twenty-four hours.

See Meeting God in Everyday Life

---

a Meaning of Heb uncertain   *b* Cn: Meaning of Heb uncertain
c Cn Compare Syr: Heb *I will walk slowly all my years*

The Advantage of Pain

ISAIAH 38.17

Hezekiah gives thanks for the difficulties he faces. God can use challenges, tragedies, diseases and other difficulties, whatever their cause, to strengthen and purify us. Prayerfully recall some of the occasions when you have been able to say, "It was for my benefit that I suffered such anguish." Recall the gifts—perhaps of strength, endurance, patience, increased faith, deeper wisdom—that came from your experience, and give God thanks. Today, remember people who may be facing difficulty and surround them in your prayer with God's supportive care.

See Meeting God in Everyday Life

Oh, restore me to health and make me live!
¹⁷ Surely it was for my welfare
    that I had great bitterness;
but you have held back*ᵃ* my life
    from the pit of destruction,
for you have cast all my sins
    behind your back.
¹⁸ For Sheol cannot thank you,
    death cannot praise you;
those who go down to the Pit cannot hope
    for your faithfulness.
¹⁹ The living, the living, they thank you,
    as I do this day;
fathers make known to children
    your faithfulness.

²⁰ The LORD will save me,
    and we will sing to stringed instruments*ᵇ*
all the days of our lives,
    at the house of the LORD.

21 Now Isaiah had said, "Let them take a lump of figs, and apply it to the boil, so that he may recover." ²²Hezekiah also had said, "What is the sign that I shall go up to the house of the LORD?"

Envoys from Babylon Welcomed

39 At that time King Merodach-baladan son of Baladan of Babylon sent envoys with letters and a present to Hezekiah, for he heard that he had been sick and had recovered. ²Hezekiah welcomed them; he showed them his treasure house, the silver, the gold, the spices, the precious oil, his whole armory, all that was found in his storehouses. There was nothing in his house or in all his realm that Hezekiah did not show them. ³Then the prophet Isaiah came to King Hezekiah and said to him, "What did these men say? From where did they come to you?" Hezekiah answered, "They have come to me from a far country, from Babylon." ⁴He said, "What have they seen in your house?" Hezekiah answered, "They have seen all that is in my house; there is nothing in my storehouses that I did not show them."

5 Then Isaiah said to Hezekiah, "Hear the word of the LORD of hosts: ⁶Days are coming when all that is in your house, and that which your ancestors have stored up until this day, shall be carried to Babylon; nothing shall be left, says the LORD. ⁷Some of your own sons who are born to you shall be taken away; they shall be eunuchs in the palace of the king of Babylon." ⁸Then Hezekiah said to Isaiah, "The word of the LORD that you have spoken is good." For he thought, "There will be peace and security in my days."

God's People Are Comforted

40 Comfort, O comfort my people,
    says your God.
²   Speak tenderly to Jerusalem,

a Cn Compare Gk Vg: Heb *loved*   *b* Heb *my stringed instruments*

and cry to her
 that she has served her term,
  that her penalty is paid,
 that she has received from the LORD's hand
  double for all her sins.

3 A voice cries out:
 "In the wilderness prepare the way of the LORD,
  make straight in the desert a highway for our
   God.
4 Every valley shall be lifted up,
  and every mountain and hill be made low;
 the uneven ground shall become level,
  and the rough places a plain.
5 Then the glory of the LORD shall be revealed,
  and all people shall see it together,
 for the mouth of the LORD has spoken."

6 A voice says, "Cry out!"
  And I said, "What shall I cry?"
 All people are grass,
  their constancy is like the flower of the field.
7 The grass withers, the flower fades,
  when the breath of the LORD blows upon it;
  surely the people are grass.
8 The grass withers, the flower fades;
  but the word of our God will stand forever.
9 Get you up to a high mountain,
  O Zion, herald of good tidings;*a*
 lift up your voice with strength,
  O Jerusalem, herald of good tidings,*b*
  lift it up, do not fear;
 say to the cities of Judah,
  "Here is your God!"
10 See, the Lord GOD comes with might,
  and his arm rules for him;
 his reward is with him,
  and his recompense before him.
11 He will feed his flock like a shepherd;
  he will gather the lambs in his arms,
 and carry them in his bosom,
  and gently lead the mother sheep.

12 Who has measured the waters in the hollow of his
   hand
  and marked off the heavens with a span,
 enclosed the dust of the earth in a measure,
  and weighed the mountains in scales
  and the hills in a balance?
13 Who has directed the spirit of the LORD,
  or as his counselor has instructed him?
14 Whom did he consult for his enlightenment,
  and who taught him the path of justice?
 Who taught him knowledge,
  and showed him the way of understanding?
15 Even the nations are like a drop from a bucket,
  and are accounted as dust on the scales;

Good News of Comfort

ISAIAH 40.1–11

Slowly read this famous and familiar passage, which was so important to the writers of the New Testament. Open your heart and mind to the words or phrases that seem to leap off the page at you. Circle them or write them on another sheet of paper. Slowly reread the passage, paying attention to the emotions named in the text or that the text evokes in you. Spend time pondering this cluster of words and feelings, seeing if you can discern a particular pattern or theme in your response to the passage. What might the Spirit be trying to show you through the patterns in your response to the Word?

See Meeting God in Scripture

---

a Or *O herald of good tidings to Zion*   *b* Or *O herald of good tidings to Jerusalem*

"To Whom... Will You Liken God?"

ISAIAH 40.18

The Hebrews reject idols in favor of the Holy One, whom they describe in conceptual images such as lord, light, wind, fire—metaphors and symbols of a reality that no one image can capture. Drawing from scripture, spiritual reading and your own experience, think of some significant metaphors for God— those that are the most meaningful to you. See how many times you can complete the phrase "God is . . . ." Express those metaphors in prayer, such as: "O Living One, you are a refreshing breeze cooling the heat of my agitation." As you read the rest of Isaiah, find other images and metaphors for God and make them into brief sentence prayers.

See Meeting God in Prayer

see, he takes up the isles like fine dust.
16 Lebanon would not provide fuel enough,
  nor are its animals enough for a burnt offering.
17 All the nations are as nothing before him;
  they are accounted by him as less than nothing
    and emptiness.

18 To whom then will you liken God,
  or what likeness compare with him?
19 An idol? —A workman casts it,
  and a goldsmith overlays it with gold,
  and casts for it silver chains.
20 As a gift one chooses mulberry wood*a*
  —wood that will not rot—
then seeks out a skilled artisan
  to set up an image that will not topple.

21 Have you not known? Have you not heard?
  Has it not been told you from the beginning?
  Have you not understood from the foundations
    of the earth?
22 It is he who sits above the circle of the earth,
  and its inhabitants are like grasshoppers;
who stretches out the heavens like a curtain,
  and spreads them like a tent to live in;
23 who brings princes to naught,
  and makes the rulers of the earth as nothing.

24 Scarcely are they planted, scarcely sown,
  scarcely has their stem taken root in the earth,
when he blows upon them, and they wither,
  and the tempest carries them off like stubble.

25 To whom then will you compare me,
  or who is my equal? says the Holy One.
26 Lift up your eyes on high and see:
  Who created these?
He who brings out their host and numbers them,
  calling them all by name;
because he is great in strength,
  mighty in power,
  not one is missing.

27 Why do you say, O Jacob,
  and speak, O Israel,
"My way is hidden from the Lord,
  and my right is disregarded by my God"?
28 Have you not known? Have you not heard?
The Lord is the everlasting God,
  the Creator of the ends of the earth.
He does not faint or grow weary;
  his understanding is unsearchable.
29 He gives power to the faint,
  and strengthens the powerless.
30 Even youths will faint and be weary,
  and the young will fall exhausted;

a Meaning of Heb uncertain

³¹ but those who wait for the L<small>ORD</small> shall renew their
> strength,
> they shall mount up with wings like eagles,
> they shall run and not be weary,
> they shall walk and not faint.

Israel Assured of God's Help

41 Listen to me in silence, O coastlands;
> let the peoples renew their strength;
> let them approach, then let them speak;
> let us together draw near for judgment.

² Who has roused a victor from the east,
> summoned him to his service?
> He delivers up nations to him,
> and tramples kings under foot;
> he makes them like dust with his sword,
> like driven stubble with his bow.
³ He pursues them and passes on safely,
> scarcely touching the path with his feet.
⁴ Who has performed and done this,
> calling the generations from the beginning?
> I, the L<small>ORD</small>, am first,
> and will be with the last.
⁵ The coastlands have seen and are afraid,
> the ends of the earth tremble;
> they have drawn near and come.
⁶ Each one helps the other,
> saying to one another, "Take courage!"
⁷ The artisan encourages the goldsmith,
> and the one who smooths with the hammer
> encourages the one who strikes the anvil,
> saying of the soldering, "It is good";
> and they fasten it with nails so that it cannot be
> moved.
⁸ But you, Israel, my servant,
> Jacob, whom I have chosen,
> the offspring of Abraham, my friend;
⁹ you whom I took from the ends of the earth,
> and called from its farthest corners,
> saying to you, "You are my servant,
> I have chosen you and not cast you off";
¹⁰ do not fear, for I am with you,
> do not be afraid, for I am your God;
> I will strengthen you, I will help you,
> I will uphold you with my victorious right hand.

¹¹ Yes, all who are incensed against you
> shall be ashamed and disgraced;
> those who strive against you
> shall be as nothing and shall perish.
¹² You shall seek those who contend with you,
> but you shall not find them;
> those who war against you
> shall be as nothing at all.
¹³ For I, the L<small>ORD</small> your God,
> hold your right hand;
> it is I who say to you, "Do not fear,
> I will help you."

God's Friend

ISAIAH 41.8

Abraham and Moses were God's "friends." Jeremiah prayed to God as an intimate, lifelong friend as well: "My Father, you are the friend of my youth" (Jeremiah 3.4).

What are the "seeds" of relationship—the elements that create a human friendship? What elements nurture a friendship? Bring to mind the friends you enjoy and give thanks for them. How can your human friendships help you cultivate a deeper friendship with God? What does God's desire for friendship with us show us about him? Why does God want friends? Why would God want your friendship?

See Meeting God in Community

"The Poor and Needy"

ISAIAH 41.17

"The human righteousness required by God . . . has necessarily the character of a vindication of right in favour of the threatened innocent, the oppressed poor, widows, orphans and aliens . . . God always takes his stand unconditionally and passionately on this side, and on this side alone: against the lofty, and on behalf of the lowly; against those who already enjoy right and privilege, and on behalf of those who are denied and deprived of it."

—KARL BARTH,
Church Dogmatics

14 Do not fear, you worm Jacob,
  you insect[a] Israel!
I will help you, says the LORD;
  your Redeemer is the Holy One of Israel.
15 Now, I will make of you a threshing sledge,
  sharp, new, and having teeth;
you shall thresh the mountains and crush them,
  and you shall make the hills like chaff.
16 You shall winnow them and the wind shall carry
      them away,
  and the tempest shall scatter them.
Then you shall rejoice in the LORD;
  in the Holy One of Israel you shall glory.

17 When the poor and needy seek water,
  and there is none,
  and their tongue is parched with thirst,
I the LORD will answer them,
  I the God of Israel will not forsake them.
18 I will open rivers on the bare heights,[b]
  and fountains in the midst of the valleys;
I will make the wilderness a pool of water,
  and the dry land springs of water.
19 I will put in the wilderness the cedar,
  the acacia, the myrtle, and the olive;
I will set in the desert the cypress,
  the plane and the pine together,
20 so that all may see and know,
  all may consider and understand,
that the hand of the LORD has done this,
  the Holy One of Israel has created it.

The Futility of Idols

21 Set forth your case, says the LORD;
  bring your proofs, says the King of Jacob.
22 Let them bring them, and tell us
  what is to happen.
Tell us the former things, what they are,
  so that we may consider them,
and that we may know their outcome;
  or declare to us the things to come.
23 Tell us what is to come hereafter,
  that we may know that you are gods;
do good, or do harm,
  that we may be afraid and terrified.
24 You, indeed, are nothing
  and your work is nothing at all;
  whoever chooses you is an abomination.

25 I stirred up one from the north, and he has come,
  from the rising of the sun he was summoned by
      name.[c]
He shall trample[d] on rulers as on mortar,
  as the potter treads clay.
26 Who declared it from the beginning, so that we
      might know,

a Syr: Heb *men of*   b Or *trails*   c Cn Compare Q Ms Gk: MT *and he shall call on my name*   d Cn: Heb *come*

and beforehand, so that we might say, "He is
right"?
There was no one who declared it, none who
proclaimed,
none who heard your words.
27 I first have declared it to Zion,[a]
and I give to Jerusalem a herald of good tidings.
28 But when I look there is no one;
among these there is no counselor
who, when I ask, gives an answer.
29 No, they are all a delusion;
their works are nothing;
their images are empty wind.

The Servant, a Light to the Nations

42 Here is my servant, whom I uphold,
my chosen, in whom my soul delights;
I have put my spirit upon him;
he will bring forth justice to the nations.
2 He will not cry or lift up his voice,
or make it heard in the street;
3 a bruised reed he will not break,
and a dimly burning wick he will not quench;
he will faithfully bring forth justice.
4 He will not grow faint or be crushed
until he has established justice in the earth;
and the coastlands wait for his teaching.

5 Thus says God, the LORD,
who created the heavens and stretched them
out,
who spread out the earth and what comes from
it,
who gives breath to the people upon it
and spirit to those who walk in it:
6 I am the LORD, I have called you in righteousness,
I have taken you by the hand and kept you;
I have given you as a covenant to the people,[b]
a light to the nations,
7 to open the eyes that are blind,
to bring out the prisoners from the dungeon,
from the prison those who sit in darkness.
8 I am the LORD, that is my name;
my glory I give to no other,
nor my praise to idols.
9 See, the former things have come to pass,
and new things I now declare;
before they spring forth,
I tell you of them.

A Hymn of Praise

10 Sing to the LORD a new song,
his praise from the end of the earth!
Let the sea roar[c] and all that fills it,
the coastlands and their inhabitants.
11 Let the desert and its towns lift up their voice,
the villages that Kedar inhabits;

"A Dimly Burning Wick"

ISAIAH 42.3

God's strong servant of justice
is compassionate and gentle
with the "bruised reeds" and
the "dimly burning wicks"—the
broken and the weak. Opening
yourself to the Spirit, let God's
compassionate presence surround you. Ask yourself: Is
there a part of myself that is
bruised or just dimly burning?
An ability or interest that I am
hesitant to pursue or express?
Feelings I don't want to face?
Let any hesitant or injured aspect of yourself come out into
the accepting, enabling love of
the servants, which is like a
gentle breath on a dimly burning wick. Then receive back this
aspect of yourself with compassion. Let the servant's love
strengthen and heal the tenta-
tive, weak part of yourself.

a Cn: Heb First to Zion—Behold, behold them   b Meaning of Heb uncertain
c Cn Compare Ps 96.11; 98.7: Heb Those who go down to the sea

Blinded Servants

ISAIAH 42.18–20

Although Israel is God's designated messenger to the nations, it is blind and deaf to the Spirit's work in the world. How have you been blind to God's work in your life—in ways that kept you from cooperating with that work? What, or who, opened your eyes to the grace at work in that situation? In what ways do you see God at work in your religious community, even though the community may be blind to them? Pray for wisdom. How might you communicate what you see to those who do not see it? In what spirit would you best do that sharing?

See Meeting God in Community

let the inhabitants of Sela sing for joy,
  let them shout from the tops of the mountains.
12 Let them give glory to the LORD,
  and declare his praise in the coastlands.
13 The LORD goes forth like a soldier,
  like a warrior he stirs up his fury;
he cries out, he shouts aloud,
  he shows himself mighty against his foes.

14 For a long time I have held my peace,
  I have kept still and restrained myself;
now I will cry out like a woman in labor,
  I will gasp and pant.
15 I will lay waste mountains and hills,
  and dry up all their herbage;
I will turn the rivers into islands,
  and dry up the pools.
16 I will lead the blind
  by a road they do not know,
by paths they have not known
  I will guide them.
I will turn the darkness before them into light,
  the rough places into level ground.
These are the things I will do,
  and I will not forsake them.
17 They shall be turned back and utterly put to shame—
  those who trust in carved images,
who say to cast images,
  "You are our gods."

18 Listen, you that are deaf;
  and you that are blind, look up and see!
19 Who is blind but my servant,
  or deaf like my messenger whom I send?
Who is blind like my dedicated one,
  or blind like the servant of the LORD?
20 He sees many things, but does[a] not observe them;
  his ears are open, but he does not hear.

Israel's Disobedience

21 The LORD was pleased, for the sake of his righteousness,
  to magnify his teaching and make it glorious.
22 But this is a people robbed and plundered,
  all of them are trapped in holes
  and hidden in prisons;
they have become a prey with no one to rescue,
  a spoil with no one to say, "Restore!"
23 Who among you will give heed to this,
  who will attend and listen for the time to come?
24 Who gave up Jacob to the spoiler,
  and Israel to the robbers?
Was it not the LORD, against whom we have sinned,
  in whose ways they would not walk,
  and whose law they would not obey?

a Heb *You see many things but do*

25 So he poured upon him the heat of his anger
   and the fury of war;
   it set him on fire all around, but he did not
       understand;
   it burned him, but he did not take it to heart.

Restoration and Protection Promised

43 But now thus says the Lord,
   he who created you, O Jacob,
   he who formed you, O Israel:
   Do not fear, for I have redeemed you;
   I have called you by name, you are mine.
2 When you pass through the waters, I will be with
       you;
   and through the rivers, they shall not
       overwhelm you;
   when you walk through fire you shall not be
       burned,
   and the flame shall not consume you.
3 For I am the Lord your God,
   the Holy One of Israel, your Savior.
   I give Egypt as your ransom,
   Ethiopia*a* and Seba in exchange for you.
4 Because you are precious in my sight,
   and honored, and I love you,
   I give people in return for you,
   nations in exchange for your life.
5 Do not fear, for I am with you;
   I will bring your offspring from the east,
   and from the west I will gather you;
6 I will say to the north, "Give them up,"
   and to the south, "Do not withhold;
   bring my sons from far away
   and my daughters from the end of the earth—
7 everyone who is called by my name,
   whom I created for my glory,
   whom I formed and made."

8 Bring forth the people who are blind, yet have eyes,
   who are deaf, yet have ears!
9 Let all the nations gather together,
   and let the peoples assemble.
   Who among them declared this,
   and foretold to us the former things?
   Let them bring their witnesses to justify them,
   and let them hear and say, "It is true."
10 You are my witnesses, says the Lord,
   and my servant whom I have chosen,
   so that you may know and believe me
   and understand that I am he.
   Before me no god was formed,
   nor shall there be any after me.
11 I, I am the Lord,
   and besides me there is no savior.
12 I declared and saved and proclaimed,
   when there was no strange god among you;
   and you are my witnesses, says the Lord.

"You Are My Witnesses"

ISAIAH 43.10

Witnessing is, simply, reporting one's encounter with the holy. More personal than giving speeches about doctrinal principles, witnessing is simply telling what you have seen and heard. Be on the lookout for the holy today. How do you see God, God's glory, God's mercy at work? How have you witnessed God's grace in action? Rehearse in your mind how you might share this with someone you love. Then share it simply and naturally, without undue drama, before the week is out: "I want to share something I saw . . ."

See Meeting God in Community

The Redeeming God

ISAIAH 43.14–28

After a time of silent openness before God, read this passage, keeping in mind the essence of redemption—God's rescuing and rehabilitating love. Write down phrases or images that show God bringing his people out of bondage, sin and limitation into new life. Savor one or two of the phrases that seem to resonate most deeply with you. Let one phrase become a repetitive prayer, such as, "O Redeemer, break down all the bars that hold me back from loving more." Wait receptively in silence. Be receptive to any ways that God's redeeming grace, for which you have prayed might show itself in your life. Be ready to perform any actions on your part that might help you welcome it.

See Meeting God in Scripture

13 I am God, and also henceforth I am He;
　　there is no one who can deliver from my hand;
　　I work and who can hinder it?

14 Thus says the LORD,
　　your Redeemer, the Holy One of Israel:
For your sake I will send to Babylon
　　and break down all the bars,
　　and the shouting of the Chaldeans will be
　　　turned to lamentation.*a*

15 I am the LORD, your Holy One,
　　the Creator of Israel, your King.

16 Thus says the LORD,
　　who makes a way in the sea,
　　a path in the mighty waters,

17 who brings out chariot and horse,
　　army and warrior;
they lie down, they cannot rise,
　　they are extinguished, quenched like a wick:

18 Do not remember the former things,
　　or consider the things of old.

19 I am about to do a new thing;
　　now it springs forth, do you not perceive it?
I will make a way in the wilderness
　　and rivers in the desert.

20 The wild animals will honor me,
　　the jackals and the ostriches;
for I give water in the wilderness,
　　rivers in the desert,
to give drink to my chosen people,

21 　　the people whom I formed for myself
so that they might declare my praise.

22 Yet you did not call upon me, O Jacob;
　　but you have been weary of me, O Israel!

23 You have not brought me your sheep for burnt
　　　offerings,
　　or honored me with your sacrifices.
I have not burdened you with offerings,
　　or wearied you with frankincense.

24 You have not bought me sweet cane with money,
　　or satisfied me with the fat of your sacrifices.
But you have burdened me with your sins;
　　you have wearied me with your iniquities.

25 I, I am He
　　who blots out your transgressions for my own
　　　sake,
　　and I will not remember your sins.

26 Accuse me, let us go to trial;
　　set forth your case, so that you may be proved
　　　right.

27 Your first ancestor sinned,
　　and your interpreters transgressed against me.

28 Therefore I profaned the princes of the sanctuary,
　　I delivered Jacob to utter destruction,
　　and Israel to reviling.

a Meaning of Heb uncertain

God's Blessing on Israel

44 But now hear, O Jacob my servant,
Israel whom I have chosen!
2 Thus says the LORD who made you,
who formed you in the womb and will help you:
Do not fear, O Jacob my servant,
Jeshurun whom I have chosen.
3 For I will pour water on the thirsty land,
and streams on the dry ground;
I will pour my spirit upon your descendants,
and my blessing on your offspring.
4 They shall spring up like a green tamarisk,
like willows by flowing streams.
5 This one will say, "I am the LORD's,"
another will be called by the name of Jacob,
yet another will write on the hand, "The LORD's,"
and adopt the name of Israel.

6 Thus says the LORD, the King of Israel,
and his Redeemer, the LORD of hosts:
I am the first and I am the last;
besides me there is no god.
7 Who is like me? Let them proclaim it,
let them declare and set it forth before me.
Who has announced from of old the things to
come?*a*
Let them tell us*b* what is yet to be.
8 Do not fear, or be afraid;
have I not told you from of old and declared it?
You are my witnesses!
Is there any god besides me?
There is no other rock; I know not one.

The Absurdity of Idol Worship

9 All who make idols are nothing, and the things they delight in do not profit; their witnesses neither see nor know. And so they will be put to shame. 10 Who would fashion a god or cast an image that can do no good? 11 Look, all its devotees shall be put to shame; the artisans too are merely human. Let them all assemble, let them stand up; they shall be terrified, they shall all be put to shame.

12 The ironsmith fashions it*c* and works it over the coals, shaping it with hammers, and forging it with his strong arm; he becomes hungry and his strength fails, he drinks no water and is faint. 13 The carpenter stretches a line, marks it out with a stylus, fashions it with planes, and marks it with a compass; he makes it in human form, with human beauty, to be set up in a shrine. 14 He cuts down cedars or chooses a holm tree or an oak and lets it grow strong among the trees of the forest. He plants a cedar and the rain nourishes it. 15 Then it can be used as fuel. Part of it he takes and warms himself; he kindles a fire and bakes bread. Then he makes a god and worships it, makes it a carved image and bows down before it. 16 Half of it he burns in the fire; over this half he roasts meat, eats it and is satisfied. He also warms himself and

God the Rock

ISAIAH 44.8

God is not only "above" us but also "beneath" us, firm as rock. This image of God as Rock appears more than thirty times in scripture. God, the Rock, is often pictured as a huge, craggy refuge indented with caves where one can hide from a threat or find shelter from the scorching desert sun. Sit quietly, eyes closed, allowing your breathing to center your attention and calm your mind. Call on God as your Rock. Envision yourself settling into just such a "cleft" of the Rock. With each breath, entrust yourself more deeply to the abiding stability of the Almighty God. Hide yourself in the deep, warm shelter of the bedrock, the Savior. Sing, "The Cleft of the Rock."

See Meeting God in Scripture

---

a Cn: Heb *from my placing an eternal people and things to come*   *b* Tg:
Heb *them*   *c* Cn: Heb *an ax*

The Song of Creation

ISAIAH 44.23

Hebrew poetry, such as that announcing Isaiah's commissioning vision (see chapter 6), is filled with the songs that pour forth from angels, creatures and the earth in praise of God.

Go for a prayerful walk in your neighborhood or in a nearby natural area. Practice listening to the sounds of creation—the breeze in the trees, the call of birds, the rustle of animals! Hear them as music. Experiment with your humming, mimicking a bird, finding the note in a machine's drone—offering these sounds as praise. End by singing a familiar hymn or repeating the refrain, "Bless the LORD, all his works" (Psalm 103.22).

See Meeting God in the Created Order

says, "Ah, I am warm, I can feel the fire!" ¹⁷The rest of it he makes into a god, his idol, bows down to it and worships it; he prays to it and says, "Save me, for you are my god!"

18 They do not know, nor do they comprehend; for their eyes are shut, so that they cannot see, and their minds as well, so that they cannot understand. ¹⁹No one considers, nor is there knowledge or discernment to say, "Half of it I burned in the fire; I also baked bread on its coals, I roasted meat and have eaten. Now shall I make the rest of it an abomination? Shall I fall down before a block of wood?" ²⁰He feeds on ashes; a deluded mind has led him astray, and he cannot save himself or say, "Is not this thing in my right hand a fraud?"

Israel Is Not Forgotten

21 Remember these things, O Jacob,
    and Israel, for you are my servant;
 I formed you, you are my servant;
    O Israel, you will not be forgotten by me.
22 I have swept away your transgressions like a cloud,
    and your sins like mist;
 return to me, for I have redeemed you.

23 Sing, O heavens, for the LORD has done it;
    shout, O depths of the earth;
 break forth into singing, O mountains,
    O forest, and every tree in it!
 For the LORD has redeemed Jacob,
    and will be glorified in Israel.

24 Thus says the LORD, your Redeemer,
    who formed you in the womb:
 I am the LORD, who made all things,
    who alone stretched out the heavens,
    who by myself spread out the earth;
25 who frustrates the omens of liars,
    and makes fools of diviners;
 who turns back the wise,
    and makes their knowledge foolish;
26 who confirms the word of his servant,
    and fulfills the prediction of his messengers;
 who says of Jerusalem, "It shall be inhabited,"
    and of the cities of Judah, "They shall be rebuilt,
    and I will raise up their ruins";
27 who says to the deep, "Be dry—
    I will dry up your rivers";
28 who says of Cyrus, "He is my shepherd,
    and he shall carry out all my purpose";
 and who says of Jerusalem, "It shall be rebuilt,"
    and of the temple, "Your foundation shall be
       laid."

Cyrus, God's Instrument

45 Thus says the Lord to his anointed, to Cyrus,
    whose right hand I have grasped
 to subdue nations before him
    and strip kings of their robes,
 to open doors before him—

and the gates shall not be closed:

2 I will go before you
   and level the mountains,[a]
   I will break in pieces the doors of bronze
   and cut through the bars of iron,

3 I will give you the treasures of darkness
   and riches hidden in secret places,
   so that you may know that it is I, the LORD,
   the God of Israel, who call you by your name.

4 For the sake of my servant Jacob,
   and Israel my chosen,
   I call you by your name,
   I surname you, though you do not know me.

5 I am the LORD, and there is no other;
   besides me there is no god.
   I arm you, though you do not know me,

6 so that they may know, from the rising of the sun
   and from the west, that there is no one besides
   me;
   I am the LORD, and there is no other.

7 I form light and create darkness,
   I make weal and create woe;
   I the LORD do all these things.

8 Shower, O heavens, from above,
   and let the skies rain down righteousness;
   let the earth open, that salvation may spring up,[b]
   and let it cause righteousness to sprout up also;
   I the LORD have created it.

9 Woe to you who strive with your Maker,
   earthen vessels with the potter![c]
   Does the clay say to the one who fashions it,
   "What are you making"?
   or "Your work has no handles"?

10 Woe to anyone who says to a father, "What are
   you begetting?"
   or to a woman, "With what are you in labor?"

11 Thus says the LORD,
   the Holy One of Israel, and its Maker:
   Will you question me[d] about my children,
   or command me concerning the work of my
   hands?

12 I made the earth,
   and created humankind upon it;
   it was my hands that stretched out the heavens,
   and I commanded all their host.

13 I have aroused Cyrus[e] in righteousness,
   and I will make all his paths straight;
   he shall build my city
   and set my exiles free,
   not for price or reward,
   says the LORD of hosts.

14 Thus says the LORD:
   The wealth of Egypt and the merchandise of
   Ethiopia,[f]

The Giver of Light and Darkness

ISAIAH 45.7

"Blessed art thou,
O Lord our God,
King of the universe,
who formest light
and createst darkness,
who makest peace,
and createst all things:

"In mercy thou bringest
light to the earth and to
    those who dwell thereon,
and in Thy goodness
renewest continually each
    day
the miracle of creation . . .

"O Lord of our strength,
sheltering Rock,
Shield of our salvation!
Thou art a stronghold
unto us.

"All Thy hosts in heaven
continually declare
Thy high praises . . .
for the bright luminaries
which Thou hast made;
all shall glorify Thee."

—*Jewish Morning Prayer*

See *Meeting God in Worship*

---

a Q Ms Gk: MT *the swellings*   *b* Q Ms: MT *that they may bring forth salvation*   *c* Cn: Heb *with the potsherds,* or *with the potters*   *d* Cn: Heb *Ask me of things to come*   *e* Heb *him*   *f* Or *Nubia*; Heb *Cush*

When God Hides

ISAIAH 45.15

Is it in the nature of the Holy
One to hide or is God's hiddenness the result of our ignorance
and misperceptions? Is God's
grace always present in the
same way for us, or does God
change the way grace appears—
including in the situations
where it seems there is no grace
visible? How do you respond
when God seems hidden to
you? What means have you discovered to help you through
such periods? What advice
would you give to another person undergoing a period of divine hiddenness?

See Meeting God in Community

and the Sabeans, tall of stature,
shall come over to you and be yours,
they shall follow you;
they shall come over in chains and bow down
to you.
They will make supplication to you, saying,
"God is with you alone, and there is no other;
there is no god besides him."

15 Truly, you are a God who hides himself,
O God of Israel, the Savior.
16 All of them are put to shame and confounded,
the makers of idols go in confusion together.
17 But Israel is saved by the LORD
with everlasting salvation;
you shall not be put to shame or confounded
to all eternity.

18 For thus says the LORD,
who created the heavens
(he is God!),
who formed the earth and made it
(he established it;
he did not create it a chaos,
he formed it to be inhabited!):
I am the LORD, and there is no other.
19 I did not speak in secret,
in a land of darkness;
I did not say to the offspring of Jacob,
"Seek me in chaos."
I the LORD speak the truth,
I declare what is right.

Idols Cannot Save Babylon

20 Assemble yourselves and come together,
draw near, you survivors of the nations!
They have no knowledge—
those who carry about their wooden idols,
and keep on praying to a god
that cannot save.
21 Declare and present your case;
let them take counsel together!
Who told this long ago?
Who declared it of old?
Was it not I, the LORD?
There is no other god besides me,
a righteous God and a Savior;
there is no one besides me.

22 Turn to me and be saved,
all the ends of the earth!
For I am God, and there is no other.
23 By myself I have sworn,
from my mouth has gone forth in righteousness
a word that shall not return:
"To me every knee shall bow,
every tongue shall swear."

24 Only in the LORD, it shall be said of me,
are righteousness and strength;

all who were incensed against him
    shall come to him and be ashamed.
25 In the LORD all the offspring of Israel
    shall triumph and glory.

46 Bel bows down, Nebo stoops,
    their idols are on beasts and cattle;
these things you carry are loaded
    as burdens on weary animals.
2 They stoop, they bow down together;
    they cannot save the burden,
but themselves go into captivity.

3 Listen to me, O house of Jacob,
    all the remnant of the house of Israel,
who have been borne by me from your birth,
    carried from the womb;
4 even to your old age I am he,
    even when you turn gray I will carry you.
I have made, and I will bear;
    I will carry and will save.

5 To whom will you liken me and make me equal,
    and compare me, as though we were alike?
6 Those who lavish gold from the purse,
    and weigh out silver in the scales—
they hire a goldsmith, who makes it into a god;
    then they fall down and worship!
7 They lift it to their shoulders, they carry it,
    they set it in its place, and it stands there;
    it cannot move from its place.
If one cries out to it, it does not answer
    or save anyone from trouble.

8 Remember this and consider,*a*
    recall it to mind, you transgressors,
9   remember the former things of old;
for I am God, and there is no other;
    I am God, and there is no one like me,
10 declaring the end from the beginning
    and from ancient times things not yet done,
saying, "My purpose shall stand,
    and I will fulfill my intention,"
11 calling a bird of prey from the east,
    the man for my purpose from a far country.
I have spoken, and I will bring it to pass;
    I have planned, and I will do it.

12 Listen to me, you stubborn of heart,
    you who are far from deliverance:
13 I bring near my deliverance, it is not far off,
    and my salvation will not tarry;
I will put salvation in Zion,
    for Israel my glory.

Aging Into God

ISAIAH 46.4

In the depths of our souls, we are ageless. The child we once were who remains within, as well as the old sage we might become, emerge sometimes with thoughts or words that surprise us with their wisdom. Prayerfully review the various periods of your short life—infancy, childhood, adolescence, adulthood. For each period, bring to mind an image of yourself. Invite the Spirit to show you ways God showed grace to you then. Let this self-portrait continue through your aging. Envision yourself growing in grace and affirming your trust in the God who continues to "carry you."

See Meeting God in Everyday Life

Sit in Silence

ISAIAH 47.4–5

This passage constitutes God's scathing indictment of Babylon, which had placed all of its trust in human knowledge, in sorcery and magic, and in its own self-sufficiency. The nation is sent into silence and darkness to ponder its refusal to acknowledge the "LORD of hosts . . . the Holy One of Israel."

How are silence and darkness conducive to repentance? Consider spending some time sitting alone in a darkened, silent room. Ask God to show you the ways in which you rely on other people and other things. Listen to God in the silence and darkness. End your session in a prayer of repentance. Ask God for his forgiveness in Christ Jesus and for the grace to renew your trust in God alone.

See Meeting God in Prayer

The Humiliation of Babylon

47 Come down and sit in the dust,
   virgin daughter Babylon!
Sit on the ground without a throne,
   daughter Chaldea!
For you shall no more be called
   tender and delicate.
2 Take the millstones and grind meal,
   remove your veil,
strip off your robe, uncover your legs,
   pass through the rivers.
3 Your nakedness shall be uncovered,
   and your shame shall be seen.
I will take vengeance,
   and I will spare no one.
4 Our Redeemer—the LORD of hosts is his name—
   is the Holy One of Israel.

5 Sit in silence, and go into darkness,
   daughter Chaldea!
For you shall no more be called
   the mistress of kingdoms.
6 I was angry with my people,
   I profaned my heritage;
I gave them into your hand,
   you showed them no mercy;
on the aged you made your yoke
   exceedingly heavy.
7 You said, "I shall be mistress forever,"
   so that you did not lay these things to heart
   or remember their end.

8 Now therefore hear this, you lover of pleasures,
   who sit securely,
who say in your heart,
   "I am, and there is no one besides me;
I shall not sit as a widow
   or know the loss of children"—
9 both these things shall come upon you
   in a moment, in one day:
the loss of children and widowhood
   shall come upon you in full measure,
in spite of your many sorceries
   and the great power of your enchantments.

10 You felt secure in your wickedness;
   you said, "No one sees me."
Your wisdom and your knowledge
   led you astray,
and you said in your heart,
   "I am, and there is no one besides me."
11 But evil shall come upon you,
   which you cannot charm away;
disaster shall fall upon you,
   which you will not be able to ward off;
and ruin shall come on you suddenly,
   of which you know nothing.

12 Stand fast in your enchantments
    and your many sorceries,
    with which you have labored from your youth;
perhaps you may be able to succeed,
    perhaps you may inspire terror.
13 You are weary with your many consultations;
    let those who study[a] the heavens
stand up and save you,
    those who gaze at the stars,
and at each new moon predict
    what[b] shall befall you.

14 See, they are like stubble,
    the fire consumes them;
they cannot deliver themselves
    from the power of the flame.
No coal for warming oneself is this,
    no fire to sit before!
15 Such to you are those with whom you have
        labored,
    who have trafficked with you from your youth;
they all wander about in their own paths;
    there is no one to save you.

God the Creator and Redeemer

48 Hear this, O house of Jacob,
    who are called by the name of Israel,
    and who came forth from the loins[c] of Judah;
who swear by the name of the LORD,
    and invoke the God of Israel,
    but not in truth or right.
2 For they call themselves after the holy city,
    and lean on the God of Israel;
    the LORD of hosts is his name.

3 The former things I declared long ago,
    they went out from my mouth and I made them
        known;
    then suddenly I did them and they came to pass.
4 Because I know that you are obstinate,
    and your neck is an iron sinew
    and your forehead brass,
5 I declared them to you from long ago,
    before they came to pass I announced them to
        you,
so that you would not say, "My idol did them,
    my carved image and my cast image
        commanded them."

6 You have heard; now see all this;
    and will you not declare it?
From this time forward I make you hear new
        things,
    hidden things that you have not known.
7 They are created now, not long ago;
    before today you have never heard of them,
    so that you could not say, "I already knew them."

True Invocation

ISAIAH 48.1

Babylon's "sorceries" (47.12) are not the practice Israel is called to. Rather, Israel is called to invoke the "God of Israel" in truth and righteousness. Invocation involves calling on God to be present and to act according to one or more of his divine roles or attributes. Choose a name or attribute of God such as holiness, justice, truth, love, compassion, beauty or peace. Or use one of the ancient names of God in Hebrew or Greek, such as *Adonai* or *Kyrios* (Lord), *El Elyon* (God Most High), *Hokhma* (Wisdom). Add to this name a prayer phrase of need or desire: "Hear my prayer . . . I need you!" Gently, fervently, play this prayer over in your mind throughout the day.

See Meeting God in Worship

---

a Meaning of Heb uncertain   *b* Gk Syr Compare Vg: Heb *from what*
c Cn: Heb *waters*

Like a River

ISAIAH 48.17–18

Through Isaiah God declares that he is the Israelites' loving teacher who directs and teaches them what is best for them. If only they had paid attention to him, their peace would have been like a river.

Ponder that simile. The image of peace like a river is commonly used in songs and sermons, but what does it really mean to you? Picture a flowing river, perhaps one near your home or one farther away. What does it sound like? What kinds of things grow within it and on its banks? Think about how it continues to flow while you are sleeping, working, playing. Find a picture of a river, or draw or paint one yourself. Place it where you can see it from time to time. Let it remind you of the peace that flows from knowing and paying attention to God.

See Meeting God in the Created Order

8 You have never heard, you have never known,
   from of old your ear has not been opened.
 For I knew that you would deal very treacherously,
   and that from birth you were called a rebel.

9 For my name's sake I defer my anger,
   for the sake of my praise I restrain it for you,
   so that I may not cut you off.
10 See, I have refined you, but not like*a* silver;
   I have tested you in the furnace of adversity.
11 For my own sake, for my own sake, I do it,
   for why should my name*b* be profaned?
   My glory I will not give to another.

12 Listen to me, O Jacob,
   and Israel, whom I called:
 I am He; I am the first,
   and I am the last.
13 My hand laid the foundation of the earth,
   and my right hand spread out the heavens;
 when I summon them,
   they stand at attention.

14 Assemble, all of you, and hear!
   Who among them has declared these things?
 The Lord loves him;
   he shall perform his purpose on Babylon,
   and his arm shall be against the Chaldeans.
15 I, even I, have spoken and called him,
   I have brought him, and he will prosper in his
     way.
16 Draw near to me, hear this!
   From the beginning I have not spoken in secret,
   from the time it came to be I have been there.
 And now the Lord God has sent me and his spirit.

17 Thus says the Lord,
   your Redeemer, the Holy One of Israel:
 I am the Lord your God,
   who teaches you for your own good,
   who leads you in the way you should go.
18 O that you had paid attention to my
     commandments!
   Then your prosperity would have been like a
     river,
   and your success like the waves of the sea;
19 your offspring would have been like the sand,
   and your descendants like its grains;
 their name would never be cut off
   or destroyed from before me.

20 Go out from Babylon, flee from Chaldea,
   declare this with a shout of joy, proclaim it,
 send it forth to the end of the earth;
   say, "The Lord has redeemed his servant
     Jacob!"

a Cn: Heb *with*   *b* Gk Old Latin: Heb *for why should it*

21 They did not thirst when he led them through the
   deserts;
   he made water flow for them from the rock;
   he split open the rock and the water gushed out.

22 "There is no peace," says the LORD, "for the
   wicked."

The Servant's Mission

49 Listen to me, O coastlands,
   pay attention, you peoples from far away!
   The LORD called me before I was born,
   while I was in my mother's womb he named me.
2 He made my mouth like a sharp sword,
   in the shadow of his hand he hid me;
   he made me a polished arrow,
   in his quiver he hid me away.
3 And he said to me, "You are my servant,
   Israel, in whom I will be glorified."
4 But I said, "I have labored in vain,
   I have spent my strength for nothing and vanity;
   yet surely my cause is with the LORD,
   and my reward with my God."

5 And now the LORD says,
   who formed me in the womb to be his servant,
   to bring Jacob back to him,
   and that Israel might be gathered to him,
   for I am honored in the sight of the LORD,
   and my God has become my strength—
6 he says,
   "It is too light a thing that you should be my servant
   to raise up the tribes of Jacob
   and to restore the survivors of Israel;
   I will give you as a light to the nations,
   that my salvation may reach to the end of the
   earth."

7 Thus says the LORD,
   the Redeemer of Israel and his Holy One,
   to one deeply despised, abhorred by the nations,
   the slave of rulers,
   "Kings shall see and stand up,
   princes, and they shall prostrate themselves,
   because of the LORD, who is faithful,
   the Holy One of Israel, who has chosen you."

Zion's Children to Be Brought Home

8 Thus says the LORD:
   In a time of favor I have answered you,
   on a day of salvation I have helped you;
   I have kept you and given you
   as a covenant to the people,*a*
   to establish the land,
   to apportion the desolate heritages;
9 saying to the prisoners, "Come out,"
   to those who are in darkness, "Show yourselves."

Named Before Birth

ISAIAH 49.1–6

God has known, named and gifted his servant from before his birth: "You knit me together in my mother's womb" (Psalm 139.13). The servant's gifts are shaped for God's special purposes.

God has given each of us such native talents that can be developed for service. What unique, inborn qualities and talents do you possess? What have you always had a knack for? What activities do you feel naturally less equipped to do? How can you offer your innate abilities for carrying on God's work in the world? What native talents need further development? Give thanks for the qualities or talents that have shown themselves in your life. Pray for guidance, and let the Spirit show you one way to use a developed ability, however modest, to do God's will today—or one way to further develop a neglected talent.

See *Meeting God in Service*

---

a Meaning of Heb uncertain

God's Mothering Love

ISAIAH 49.15

"I know not where I came from, when I came into this life-in-death . . . I only know that the gifts Your mercy provided sustained me from the first moment . . . Thus, for my sustenance and my delight I had woman's milk; yet it was not my mother or my nurses who stored their breasts for me: it was Yourself, using them to give me the food of my infancy, according to Your ordinance and the riches set by You at every level of creation . . . For it was by the love implanted in them by You that they gave so willingly that milk which by Your gift flowed in the breasts . . . All good things are from You, O God."

—AUGUSTINE,
Confessions

They shall feed along the ways,
  on all the bare heights*a* shall be their pasture;
10 they shall not hunger or thirst,
  neither scorching wind nor sun shall strike them down,
for he who has pity on them will lead them,
  and by springs of water will guide them.
11 And I will turn all my mountains into a road,
  and my highways shall be raised up.
12 Lo, these shall come from far away,
  and lo, these from the north and from the west,
  and these from the land of Syene.*b*

13 Sing for joy, O heavens, and exult, O earth;
  break forth, O mountains, into singing!
For the LORD has comforted his people,
  and will have compassion on his suffering ones.

14 But Zion said, "The LORD has forsaken me,
  my Lord has forgotten me."
15 Can a woman forget her nursing child,
  or show no compassion for the child of her womb?
Even these may forget,
  yet I will not forget you.
16 See, I have inscribed you on the palms of my hands;
  your walls are continually before me.
17 Your builders outdo your destroyers,*c*
  and those who laid you waste go away from you.
18 Lift up your eyes all around and see;
  they all gather, they come to you.
As I live, says the LORD,
  you shall put all of them on like an ornament,
  and like a bride you shall bind them on.

19 Surely your waste and your desolate places
  and your devastated land—
surely now you will be too crowded for your inhabitants,
  and those who swallowed you up will be far away.
20 The children born in the time of your bereavement
  will yet say in your hearing:
"The place is too crowded for me;
  make room for me to settle."
21 Then you will say in your heart,
  "Who has borne me these?
I was bereaved and barren,
  exiled and put away—
so who has reared these?
I was left all alone—
  where then have these come from?"

22 Thus says the Lord GOD:
  I will soon lift up my hand to the nations,

a Or *the trails* *b* Q Ms: MT *Sinim* *c* Or *Your children come swiftly; your destroyers*

and raise my signal to the peoples;
and they shall bring your sons in their bosom,
and your daughters shall be carried on their
shoulders.
23 Kings shall be your foster fathers,
and their queens your nursing mothers.
With their faces to the ground they shall bow
down to you,
and lick the dust of your feet.
Then you will know that I am the LORD;
those who wait for me shall not be put to shame.

24 Can the prey be taken from the mighty,
or the captives of a tyrant[a] be rescued?
25 But thus says the LORD:
Even the captives of the mighty shall be taken,
and the prey of the tyrant be rescued;
for I will contend with those who contend with you,
and I will save your children.
26 I will make your oppressors eat their own flesh,
and they shall be drunk with their own blood as
with wine.
Then all flesh shall know
that I am the LORD your Savior,
and your Redeemer, the Mighty One of Jacob.

50 Thus says the LORD:
Where is your mother's bill of divorce
with which I put her away?
Or which of my creditors is it
to whom I have sold you?
No, because of your sins you were sold,
and for your transgressions your mother was
put away.
2 Why was no one there when I came?
Why did no one answer when I called?
Is my hand shortened, that it cannot redeem?
Or have I no power to deliver?
By my rebuke I dry up the sea,
I make the rivers a desert;
their fish stink for lack of water,
and die of thirst.[b]
3 I clothe the heavens with blackness,
and make sackcloth their covering.

The Servant's Humiliation and Vindication

4 The Lord GOD has given me
the tongue of a teacher,[c]
that I may know how to sustain
the weary with a word.
Morning by morning he wakens—
wakens my ear
to listen as those who are taught.
5 The Lord GOD has opened my ear,
and I was not rebellious,
I did not turn backward.
6 I gave my back to those who struck me,

Partnership With God

ISAIAH 50.1

Isaiah uses the image of the marriage commitment to describe our partnership with God, and divorce as an image for the breakdown of that covenant of fidelity. Write down, in your journal or on a sheet of paper, the nature of your covenant with God. What do you believe God has promised to do for you, with you and through you? In what specific ways have you committed yourself to be in relationship with God? Note anything that may be interfering with your faithfulness to this covenant or any areas of relationship that may need more attention. Pray for guidance about how to grow more deeply into your partnership with God.

See Meeting God in Prayer

a Q Ms Syr Vg: MT *of a righteous person*   b Or *die on the thirsty ground*
c Cn: Heb *of those who are taught*

"Morning by Morning"

ISAIAH 50.4–9

What is your wake up routine? In what ways do you intentionally turn your heart and mind to God at the beginning of your day? Experiment with ways to practice the divine presence of God at waking, such as placing a sacred symbol or picture on the wall opposite your bed; keeping a Bible or devotional manual at your bedside; using a journal to jot down significant dreams or capture ideas that may come to you in the twilight between sleeping and waking. Choose an "awakening prayer" that can rise easily to your lips, such as, "O God, you are my God, I seek you, my soul thirsts for you." (Psalm 63.1).

See Meeting God in Worship

and my cheeks to those who pulled out the
    beard;
I did not hide my face
    from insult and spitting.
7   The Lord GOD helps me;
        therefore I have not been disgraced;
    therefore I have set my face like flint,
        and I know that I shall not be put to shame;
8   he who vindicates me is near.
    Who will contend with me?
        Let us stand up together.
    Who are my adversaries?
        Let them confront me.
9   It is the Lord GOD who helps me;
        who will declare me guilty?
    All of them will wear out like a garment;
        the moth will eat them up.

10   Who among you fears the LORD
        and obeys the voice of his servant,
    who walks in darkness
        and has no light,
    yet trusts in the name of the LORD
        and relies upon his God?
11   But all of you are kindlers of fire,
        lighters of firebrands.*
    Walk in the flame of your fire,
        and among the brands that you have kindled!
    This is what you shall have from my hand:
        you shall lie down in torment.

Blessings in Store for God's People

51 Listen to me, you that pursue righteousness,
        you that seek the LORD.
    Look to the rock from which you were hewn,
        and to the quarry from which you were dug.
2   Look to Abraham your father
        and to Sarah who bore you;
    for he was but one when I called him,
        but I blessed him and made him many.
3   For the LORD will comfort Zion;
        he will comfort all her waste places,
    and will make her wilderness like Eden,
        her desert like the garden of the LORD;
    joy and gladness will be found in her,
        thanksgiving and the voice of song.

4   Listen to me, my people,
        and give heed to me, my nation;
    for a teaching will go out from me,
        and my justice for a light to the peoples.
5   I will bring near my deliverance swiftly,
        my salvation has gone out
        and my arms will rule the peoples;
    the coastlands wait for me,
        and for my arm they hope.

a Syr: Heb *you gird yourselves with firebrands*

⁶ Lift up your eyes to the heavens,
    and look at the earth beneath;
for the heavens will vanish like smoke,
    the earth will wear out like a garment,
    and those who live on it will die like gnats;^a
but my salvation will be forever,
    and my deliverance will never be ended.

⁷ Listen to me, you who know righteousness,
    you people who have my teaching in your
        hearts;
do not fear the reproach of others,
    and do not be dismayed when they revile you.
⁸ For the moth will eat them up like a garment,
    and the worm will eat them like wool;
but my deliverance will be forever,
    and my salvation to all generations.

⁹ Awake, awake, put on strength,
    O arm of the LORD!
Awake, as in days of old,
    the generations of long ago!
Was it not you who cut Rahab in pieces,
    who pierced the dragon?
¹⁰ Was it not you who dried up the sea,
    the waters of the great deep;
who made the depths of the sea a way
    for the redeemed to cross over?
¹¹ So the ransomed of the LORD shall return,
    and come to Zion with singing;
everlasting joy shall be upon their heads;
    they shall obtain joy and gladness,
    and sorrow and sighing shall flee away.

¹² I, I am he who comforts you;
    why then are you afraid of a mere mortal who
        must die,
    a human being who fades like grass?
¹³ You have forgotten the LORD, your Maker,
    who stretched out the heavens
    and laid the foundations of the earth.
You fear continually all day long
    because of the fury of the oppressor,
who is bent on destruction.
    But where is the fury of the oppressor?
¹⁴ The oppressed shall speedily be released;
    they shall not die and go down to the Pit,
    nor shall they lack bread.
¹⁵ For I am the LORD your God,
    who stirs up the sea so that its waves roar—
    the LORD of hosts is his name.
¹⁶ I have put my words in your mouth,
    and hidden you in the shadow of my hand,
stretching out^b the heavens
    and laying the foundations of the earth,
    and saying to Zion, "You are my people."

"My Teaching in Your Hearts"

ISAIAH 51.7

Memorization of key Bible passages and wise sayings has traditionally been part of "learning by heart." Our actions are influenced by what we have stored in our hearts and carry with us into each encounter and situation we face. The ancient meanings of "read" include "learn, mark and inwardly digest" (Episcopal *Book of Common Prayer*) as well. How much of God's teaching is stored in your heart? Take pencil and paper and prayerfully recall all the scripture passages you can remember without consulting a written text. Write until you cannot remember more. Place an asterisk next to the passage that is most important to you. Decide on a verse, perhaps from this chapter, that you wish to commit to your heart today, and take it as your prayer for the day.

See *Meeting God in Scripture*

---

a Or *in like manner*   *b* Syr: Heb *planting*

"Beautiful Garments"

ISAIAH 52.1

In scripture, garments are often symbolic of the state of one's soul. As you close your eyes, become aware of the vitality of all your present emotions, named and unnamed. If this emotional energy could express itself as a costume of some sort, what might it be? Let it appear spontaneously in your imagination. Savor the sensations of being dressed this way. Name your emotions to God in prayer. Now ask the Spirit to decorate, augment or transform your garments, however it will, to your good. Note any new emotions or attitudes that emerge as change proceeds.

See Meeting God in Scripture

17 Rouse yourself, rouse yourself!
    Stand up, O Jerusalem,
you who have drunk at the hand of the LORD
    the cup of his wrath,
who have drunk to the dregs
    the bowl of staggering.

18 There is no one to guide her
    among all the children she has borne;
there is no one to take her by the hand
    among all the children she has brought up.

19 These two things have befallen you
    —who will grieve with you?—
devastation and destruction, famine and sword—
    who will comfort you?[a]

20 Your children have fainted,
    they lie at the head of every street
    like an antelope in a net;
they are full of the wrath of the LORD,
    the rebuke of your God.

21 Therefore hear this, you who are wounded,[b]
    who are drunk, but not with wine:

22 Thus says your Sovereign, the LORD,
    your God who pleads the cause of his people:
See, I have taken from your hand the cup of
        staggering;
you shall drink no more
    from the bowl of my wrath.

23 And I will put it into the hand of your tormentors,
    who have said to you,
    "Bow down, that we may walk on you";
and you have made your back like the ground
    and like the street for them to walk on.

Let Zion Rejoice

52 Awake, awake,
    put on your strength, O Zion!
Put on your beautiful garments,
    O Jerusalem, the holy city;
for the uncircumcised and the unclean
    shall enter you no more.

2 Shake yourself from the dust, rise up,
    O captive[c] Jerusalem;
loose the bonds from your neck,
    O captive daughter Zion!

3 For thus says the LORD: You were sold for nothing, and you shall be redeemed without money. 4 For thus says the Lord GOD: Long ago, my people went down into Egypt to reside there as aliens; the Assyrian, too, has oppressed them without cause. 5 Now therefore what am I doing here, says the LORD, seeing that my people are taken away without cause? Their rulers howl, says the LORD, and continually, all day long, my name is despised. 6 Therefore my people shall know my name; therefore in that day they shall know that it is I who speak; here am I.

a Q Ms Gk Syr Vg: MT *how may I comfort you?*   *b* Or *humbled*
c Cn: Heb *rise up, sit*

7 How beautiful upon the mountains
  are the feet of the messenger who announces
    peace,
who brings good news,
  who announces salvation,
  who says to Zion, "Your God reigns."
8 Listen! Your sentinels lift up their voices,
  together they sing for joy;
for in plain sight they see
  the return of the LORD to Zion.
9 Break forth together into singing,
  you ruins of Jerusalem;
for the LORD has comforted his people,
  he has redeemed Jerusalem.
10 The LORD has bared his holy arm
  before the eyes of all the nations;
and all the ends of the earth shall see
  the salvation of our God.

11 Depart, depart, go out from there!
  Touch no unclean thing;
go out from the midst of it, purify yourselves,
  you who carry the vessels of the LORD.
12 For you shall not go out in haste,
  and you shall not go in flight;
for the LORD will go before you,
  and the God of Israel will be your rear guard.

The Suffering Servant

13 See, my servant shall prosper;
  he shall be exalted and lifted up,
  and shall be very high.
14 Just as there were many who were astonished at
    him[a]
  —so marred was his appearance, beyond
    human semblance,
  and his form beyond that of mortals—
15 so he shall startle[b] many nations;
  kings shall shut their mouths because of him;
for that which had not been told them they shall
    see,
  and that which they had not heard they shall
    contemplate.

53 Who has believed what we have heard?
  And to whom has the arm of the LORD been
    revealed?
2 For he grew up before him like a young plant,
  and like a root out of dry ground;
he had no form or majesty that we should look at
    him,
  nothing in his appearance that we should desire
    him.
3 He was despised and rejected by others;
  a man of suffering[c] and acquainted with
    infirmity;
and as one from whom others hide their faces[d]
  he was despised, and we held him of no account.

God Before and Behind

ISAIAH 52.12

Before setting out on your next errand, or before going to bed tonight, use this traditional invocation of God's protective presence, symbolized by the four great archangels of Jewish and Christian tradition. As you say, "May God 'give his angels charge over [me], to keep [me] in all [my] ways,'" imagine that strong Michael, the captain of the heavenly hosts, stands behind you; that beautiful Gabriel, herald of good tidings, is at your right hand; that compassionate Raphael, angel of healing, is at your left; and that Uriel, angel of light, stands before you. Pray aloud if you wish, "May strong Michael stand behind me."

See Meeting God in Scripture

a Syr Tg: Heb *you*   b Meaning of Heb uncertain   c Or *a man of sorrows*   d Or *as one who hides his face from us*

The Suffering Servant

ISAIAH 53.1–12

This passage is the very heart of Isaiah, for it turns our attention to the One who bore the price of the redemption of Israel—and of humankind—on his shoulders. Read this passage slowly and meditatively. What phrases or images capture your heart? Let that word or phrase bring you face to face with Jesus Christ, who alone can heal you and bring you peace. Rest in silence before him, and let him surround you with his gracious, redeeming love.

See Meeting God in Scripture

4 Surely he has borne our infirmities
  and carried our diseases;
yet we accounted him stricken,
  struck down by God, and afflicted.
5 But he was wounded for our transgressions,
  crushed for our iniquities;
upon him was the punishment that made us
    whole,
  and by his bruises we are healed.
6 All we like sheep have gone astray;
  we have all turned to our own way,
and the LORD has laid on him
  the iniquity of us all.

7 He was oppressed, and he was afflicted,
  yet he did not open his mouth;
like a lamb that is led to the slaughter,
  and like a sheep that before its shearers is
    silent,
  so he did not open his mouth.
8 By a perversion of justice he was taken away.
  Who could have imagined his future?
For he was cut off from the land of the living,
  stricken for the transgression of my people.
9 They made his grave with the wicked
  and his tomb[a] with the rich,[b]
although he had done no violence,
  and there was no deceit in his mouth.

10 Yet it was the will of the LORD to crush him with
    pain.[c]
When you make his life an offering for sin,[d]
  he shall see his offspring, and shall prolong his
    days;
through him the will of the LORD shall prosper.
11   Out of his anguish he shall see light;[e]
he shall find satisfaction through his knowledge.
  The righteous one,[f] my servant, shall make
    many righteous,
  and he shall bear their iniquities.
12 Therefore I will allot him a portion with the great,
  and he shall divide the spoil with the strong;
because he poured out himself to death,
  and was numbered with the transgressors;
yet he bore the sin of many,
  and made intercession for the transgressors.

The Eternal Covenant of Peace

54 Sing, O barren one who did not bear;
  burst into song and shout,
  you who have not been in labor!
For the children of the desolate woman will be
    more
  than the children of her that is married, says
    the LORD.

---

a Q Ms: MT *and in his death*   b Cn: Heb *with a rich person*   c Or *by
disease*; meaning of Heb uncertain   d Meaning of Heb uncertain
e Q Mss: MT lacks *light*   f Or *and he shall find satisfaction. Through his
knowledge, the righteous one*

2 Enlarge the site of your tent,
 and let the curtains of your habitations be
  stretched out;
do not hold back; lengthen your cords
 and strengthen your stakes.
3 For you will spread out to the right and to the left,
 and your descendants will possess the nations
 and will settle the desolate towns.

4 Do not fear, for you will not be ashamed;
 do not be discouraged, for you will not suffer
  disgrace;
for you will forget the shame of your youth,
 and the disgrace of your widowhood you will
  remember no more.
5 For your Maker is your husband,
 the LORD of hosts is his name;
the Holy One of Israel is your Redeemer,
 the God of the whole earth he is called.
6 For the LORD has called you
 like a wife forsaken and grieved in spirit,
like the wife of a man's youth when she is cast
  off,
 says your God.
7 For a brief moment I abandoned you,
 but with great compassion I will gather you.
8 In overflowing wrath for a moment
 I hid my face from you,
but with everlasting love I will have compassion
  on you,
 says the LORD, your Redeemer.

9 This is like the days of Noah to me:
 Just as I swore that the waters of Noah
 would never again go over the earth,
so I have sworn that I will not be angry with you
 and will not rebuke you.
10 For the mountains may depart
 and the hills be removed,
but my steadfast love shall not depart from you,
 and my covenant of peace shall not be
  removed,
 says the LORD, who has compassion on you.

11 O afflicted one, storm-tossed, and not comforted,
 I am about to set your stones in antimony,
 and lay your foundations with sapphires.*a*
12 I will make your pinnacles of rubies,
 your gates of jewels,
 and all your wall of precious stones.
13 All your children shall be taught by the LORD,
 and great shall be the prosperity of your
  children.
14 In righteousness you shall be established;
 you shall be far from oppression, for you shall
  not fear;
 and from terror, for it shall not come near you.

After the Anguish, Light

ISAIAH 53.11

"If you but gently persevere through [the stress of dryness and darkness], you will come out at the other end of the gloom, sooner or later, into even deeper, tenderer day . . . There is each time one crucial point—to make no decisions, to change nothing during such crises . . . The crisis goes by, thus, with much fruit. What is a sense of God worth which would be at your disposal, capable of being comfortably elicited when and where you please? It is far, far more God who must hold us, than we who must hold Him. And we get trained in these darknesses into that sense of our impotence without which the very presence of God becomes a snare."

—FRIEDRICH VON HÜGEL,
Letters to a Niece

---

a Or *lapis lazuli*

Misspent Money?

ISAIAH 55.1-3

Ask the Spirit to be with you and to open your eyes as you review your expenditures over the last month or two or more. How does the way you spend your money demonstrate your values and commitments? Ponder how each expenditure may or may not conform to God's desires for your own good and the good of the community. What money is being spent for "that which does not satisfy"? During this time period, what gifts of sustenance, nourishment and empowerment have appeared in your life? Consider prayerfully how you may need to alter your expenditures so that they will bring you satisfaction as you offer them in God's service.

See Meeting God in Service

15 If anyone stirs up strife,
   it is not from me;
   whoever stirs up strife with you
   shall fall because of you.
16 See it is I who have created the smith
   who blows the fire of coals,
   and produces a weapon fit for its purpose;
   I have also created the ravager to destroy.
17 No weapon that is fashioned against you shall
   prosper,
   and you shall confute every tongue that rises
   against you in judgment.
This is the heritage of the servants of the LORD
   and their vindication from me, says the LORD.

An Invitation to Abundant Life

55 Ho, everyone who thirsts,
   come to the waters;
and you that have no money,
   come, buy and eat!
Come, buy wine and milk
   without money and without price.
2 Why do you spend your money for that which is
   not bread,
   and your labor for that which does not satisfy?
Listen carefully to me, and eat what is good,
   and delight yourselves in rich food.
3 Incline your ear, and come to me;
   listen, so that you may live.
I will make with you an everlasting covenant,
   my steadfast, sure love for David.
4 See, I made him a witness to the peoples,
   a leader and commander for the peoples.
5 See, you shall call nations that you do not know,
   and nations that do not know you shall run to
   you,
because of the LORD your God, the Holy One of
   Israel,
   for he has glorified you.

6 Seek the LORD while he may be found,
   call upon him while he is near;
7 let the wicked forsake their way,
   and the unrighteous their thoughts;
let them return to the LORD, that he may have
   mercy on them,
   and to our God, for he will abundantly pardon.
8 For my thoughts are not your thoughts,
   nor are your ways my ways, says the LORD.
9 For as the heavens are higher than the earth,
   so are my ways higher than your ways
   and my thoughts than your thoughts.

10 For as the rain and the snow come down from
   heaven,
   and do not return there until they have watered
   the earth,
making it bring forth and sprout,
   giving seed to the sower and bread to the eater,

11 so shall my word be that goes out from my mouth;
   it shall not return to me empty,
but it shall accomplish that which I purpose,
   and succeed in the thing for which I sent it.

12 For you shall go out in joy,
   and be led back in peace;
the mountains and the hills before you
   shall burst into song,
   and all the trees of the field shall clap their
      hands.
13 Instead of the thorn shall come up the cypress;
   instead of the brier shall come up the myrtle;
and it shall be to the LORD for a memorial,
   for an everlasting sign that shall not be cut off.

The Covenant Extended to All Who Obey

56 Thus says the LORD:
Maintain justice, and do what is right,
for soon my salvation will come,
   and my deliverance be revealed.

2 Happy is the mortal who does this,
   the one who holds it fast,
who keeps the sabbath, not profaning it,
   and refrains from doing any evil.

3 Do not let the foreigner joined to the LORD say,
   "The LORD will surely separate me from his
      people";
and do not let the eunuch say,
   "I am just a dry tree."
4 For thus says the LORD:
To the eunuchs who keep my sabbaths,
   who choose the things that please me
   and hold fast my covenant,
5 I will give, in my house and within my walls,
   a monument and a name
better than sons and daughters;
I will give them an everlasting name
   that shall not be cut off.

6 And the foreigners who join themselves to the LORD,
   to minister to him, to love the name of the LORD,
   and to be his servants,
all who keep the sabbath, and do not profane it,
   and hold fast my covenant—
7 these I will bring to my holy mountain,
   and make them joyful in my house of prayer;
their burnt offerings and their sacrifices
   will be accepted on my altar;
for my house shall be called a house of prayer
   for all peoples.
8 Thus says the Lord GOD,
   who gathers the outcasts of Israel,
I will gather others to them
   besides those already gathered.[a]

a Heb *besides his gathered ones*

Mercy Like Rain

ISAIAH 55.7–13

Prayerfully read this passage about God's restorative mercy toward Israel. Let yourself be open to the richness of the metaphors and phrases, perhaps envisioning the drama: God's restorative word showers down from heaven like the rain, bringing healing and fertility to the earth. As you read it a second time, notice which images or phrases seem to call for deeper attention. Ponder one or two in turn, being open to associations you might make with your memories, your current life situation or from other parts of scripture. How does God's mercy show itself in these associations? Express these ideas and feelings in a short prayer, followed by a period of silently "soaking" in God's mercy.

See Meeting God in Scripture

Taking It to Heart

ISAIAH 57.1

"The heart is stretched through suffering and enlarged. But O the agony of this enlarging of the heart, that one may be prepared to enter into the anguish of others! Yet the way of holy obedience leads out from the heart of God and extends through the Valley of the Shadow . . . He, more powerfully, speaks with you and me, to our truest selves, in our truest moments, and disquiets us with the world's needs. By inner persuasions He draws us to a few very definite tasks, our tasks, God's burdened heart particularizing His burdens in us . . . This my task matters for me and for my fellow men and for Eternity."

—THOMAS KELLY,
A Testament of Devotion

The Corruption of Israel's Rulers

9   All you wild animals,
    all you wild animals in the forest, come to
       devour!
10 Israel's*a* sentinels are blind,
    they are all without knowledge;
  they are all silent dogs
    that cannot bark;
  dreaming, lying down,
    loving to slumber.
11 The dogs have a mighty appetite;
    they never have enough.
  The shepherds also have no understanding;
    they have all turned to their own way,
    to their own gain, one and all.
12 "Come," they say, "let us*b* get wine;
    let us fill ourselves with strong drink.
  And tomorrow will be like today,
    great beyond measure."

Israel's Futile Idolatry

57   The righteous perish,
    and no one takes it to heart;
the devout are taken away,
    while no one understands.
For the righteous are taken away from calamity,
2   and they enter into peace;
those who walk uprightly
    will rest on their couches.
3   But as for you, come here,
    you children of a sorceress,
    you offspring of an adulterer and a whore.*c*
4   Whom are you mocking?
    Against whom do you open your mouth wide
    and stick out your tongue?
  Are you not children of transgression,
    the offspring of deceit—
5   you that burn with lust among the oaks,
    under every green tree;
  you that slaughter your children in the valleys,
    under the clefts of the rocks?
6   Among the smooth stones of the valley is your
          portion;
    they, they, are your lot;
  to them you have poured out a drink offering,
    you have brought a grain offering.
    Shall I be appeased for these things?
7   Upon a high and lofty mountain
    you have set your bed,
    and there you went up to offer sacrifice.
8   Behind the door and the doorpost
    you have set up your symbol;
  for, in deserting me,*d* you have uncovered your bed,
    you have gone up to it,
    you have made it wide;

a Heb *His*   *b* Q Ms Syr Vg Tg: MT *me*   *c* Heb *an adulterer and she plays the whore*   *d* Meaning of Heb uncertain

and you have made a bargain for yourself with
    them,
  you have loved their bed,
  you have gazed on their nakedness.*a*

9 You journeyed to Molech*b* with oil,
  and multiplied your perfumes;
you sent your envoys far away,
  and sent down even to Sheol.

10 You grew weary from your many wanderings,
  but you did not say, "It is useless."
You found your desire rekindled,
  and so you did not weaken.

11 Whom did you dread and fear
  so that you lied,
and did not remember me
  or give me a thought?
Have I not kept silent and closed my eyes,*c*
  and so you do not fear me?

12 I will concede your righteousness and your works,
  but they will not help you.

13 When you cry out, let your collection of idols
    deliver you!
  The wind will carry them off,
  a breath will take them away.
But whoever takes refuge in me shall possess the
    land
  and inherit my holy mountain.

A Promise of Help and Healing

14 It shall be said,
"Build up, build up, prepare the way,
  remove every obstruction from my people's
    way."

15 For thus says the high and lofty one
  who inhabits eternity, whose name is Holy:
I dwell in the high and holy place,
  and also with those who are contrite and
    humble in spirit,
to revive the spirit of the humble,
  and to revive the heart of the contrite.

16 For I will not continually accuse,
  nor will I always be angry;
for then the spirits would grow faint before me,
  even the souls that I have made.

17 Because of their wicked covetousness I was angry;
  I struck them, I hid and was angry;
but they kept turning back to their own ways.

18 I have seen their ways, but I will heal them;
  I will lead them and repay them with comfort,
creating for their mourners the fruit of the lips.*d*

19 Peace, peace, to the far and the near, says the LORD;
  and I will heal them.

20 But the wicked are like the tossing sea
  that cannot keep still;
  its waters toss up mire and mud.

21 There is no peace, says my God, for the wicked.

*a Or their phallus; Heb the hand   b Or the king   c Gk Vg: Heb silent
even for a long time   d Meaning of Heb uncertain*

"Your Collection of Idols"

ISAIAH 57.13

Idols are the ego's security system. An idol is anything we become dependent on to allay our anxiety and to comfort us. Our idol might be an insatiable desire to seek control or power instead of a humble willingness to use our gifts, trust in God, and live in healthy interdependence with others.

In what do you seek comfort and safety, power or control? Money? Attractiveness? Intellect? Self-righteousness? Doctrinal correctness? In what ways do you substitute those things for grace-filled, authentic relationships with God and others? Let your idols become visible "graven images" by listing them, sketching or drawing them with crayon or pastel, or by finding magazine pictures to make a collage of the "idols" in your life. Offer this picture to God for transformation, perhaps by burning it as you pray that all your idol-substitutes may be purified in the fire of God's love.

"The Fast That I Choose"

ISAIAH 58.6–8

Fasting in order to cleanse heart and mind for deep prayer has been, traditionally, an integral part of Jewish and Christian practice. If one also offers the money saved in food expense, the practice can be a step toward the kind of fast described in this passage. What partial or total fast from certain foods or luxuries might you undertake today and in the coming week, so that you could make an additional donation of money to support God's work? From what amusements might you fast in order to devote the time to helping others? Prayerfully consider beginning today.

See Meeting God in Service

False and True Worship

58 Shout out, do not hold back!
Lift up your voice like a trumpet!
Announce to my people their rebellion,
   to the house of Jacob their sins.
2 Yet day after day they seek me
   and delight to know my ways,
as if they were a nation that practiced righteousness
   and did not forsake the ordinance of their God;
they ask of me righteous judgments,
   they delight to draw near to God.
3 "Why do we fast, but you do not see?
   Why humble ourselves, but you do not notice?"
Look, you serve your own interest on your fast day,
   and oppress all your workers.
4 Look, you fast only to quarrel and to fight
   and to strike with a wicked fist.
Such fasting as you do today
   will not make your voice heard on high.
5 Is such the fast that I choose,
   a day to humble oneself?
Is it to bow down the head like a bulrush,
   and to lie in sackcloth and ashes?
Will you call this a fast,
   a day acceptable to the LORD?

6 Is not this the fast that I choose:
   to loose the bonds of injustice,
   to undo the thongs of the yoke,
to let the oppressed go free,
   and to break every yoke?
7 Is it not to share your bread with the hungry,
   and bring the homeless poor into your house;
when you see the naked, to cover them,
   and not to hide yourself from your own kin?
8 Then your light shall break forth like the dawn,
   and your healing shall spring up quickly;
your vindicator*a* shall go before you,
   the glory of the LORD shall be your rear guard.
9 Then you shall call, and the LORD will answer;
   you shall cry for help, and he will say, Here I am.

If you remove the yoke from among you,
   the pointing of the finger, the speaking of evil,
10 if you offer your food to the hungry
   and satisfy the needs of the afflicted,
then your light shall rise in the darkness
   and your gloom be like the noonday.
11 The LORD will guide you continually,
   and satisfy your needs in parched places,
   and make your bones strong;
and you shall be like a watered garden,
   like a spring of water,
   whose waters never fail.
12 Your ancient ruins shall be rebuilt;
   you shall raise up the foundations of many
      generations;

a Or vindication

you shall be called the repairer of the breach,
the restorer of streets to live in.

13 If you refrain from trampling the sabbath,
from pursuing your own interests on my holy
day;
if you call the sabbath a delight
and the holy day of the LORD honorable;
if you honor it, not going your own ways,
serving your own interests, or pursuing your
own affairs;[a]
14 then you shall take delight in the LORD,
and I will make you ride upon the heights of the
earth;
I will feed you with the heritage of your ancestor
Jacob,
for the mouth of the LORD has spoken.

Injustice and Oppression to Be Punished

59 See, the LORD's hand is not too short to save,
nor his ear too dull to hear.
2 Rather, your iniquities have been barriers
between you and your God,
and your sins have hidden his face from you
so that he does not hear.
3 For your hands are defiled with blood,
and your fingers with iniquity;
your lips have spoken lies,
your tongue mutters wickedness.
4 No one brings suit justly,
no one goes to law honestly;
they rely on empty pleas, they speak lies,
conceiving mischief and begetting iniquity.
5 They hatch adders' eggs,
and weave the spider's web;
whoever eats their eggs dies,
and the crushed egg hatches out a viper.
6 Their webs cannot serve as clothing;
they cannot cover themselves with what they
make.
Their works are works of iniquity,
and deeds of violence are in their hands.
7 Their feet run to evil,
and they rush to shed innocent blood;
their thoughts are thoughts of iniquity,
desolation and destruction are in their
highways.
8 The way of peace they do not know,
and there is no justice in their paths.
Their roads they have made crooked;
no one who walks in them knows peace.

9 Therefore justice is far from us,
and righteousness does not reach us;
we wait for light, and lo! there is darkness;
and for brightness, but we walk in gloom.

The Sabbath–A Delight

ISAIAH 58.13

God commands us to set aside as holy a day of rest each week. What does this command reveal about God's design for human life? What might be the benefit of a hiatus from doing as you please for one full day, especially abstinence from working at business or home tasks? What would you do with the available time? What might be the effect on relationships with family and friends? How might this "rest" affect your relationship with the Spirit? Make a plan for some sabbath time this week. Practice by taking an hour or so today to do something in a sabbath spirit.

See Meeting God in the Created Order

Society Awry

ISAIAH 59.1–21

Ponder Isaiah's vivid images of a society far gone from the "way of peace." Read the entire chapter slowly, noting and perhaps writing down words and phrases that stand out. Consider each image in turn, staying open to whatever associations from current affairs—local, national, international—come to your mind as illustrations of such social patterns. Pray that God's justice-making Spirit will enter into each situation. Ask God to show you any specific way you can contribute to the "way of peace" today. Listen for an answer.

See Meeting God in Service

10   We grope like the blind along a wall,
        groping like those who have no eyes;
    we stumble at noon as in the twilight,
        among the vigorous*a* as though we were dead.
11   We all growl like bears;
        like doves we moan mournfully.
    We wait for justice, but there is none;
        for salvation, but it is far from us.
12   For our transgressions before you are many,
        and our sins testify against us.
    Our transgressions indeed are with us,
        and we know our iniquities:
13   transgressing, and denying the LORD,
        and turning away from following our God,
    talking oppression and revolt,
        conceiving lying words and uttering them from
            the heart.
14   Justice is turned back,
        and righteousness stands at a distance;
    for truth stumbles in the public square,
        and uprightness cannot enter.
15   Truth is lacking,
        and whoever turns from evil is despoiled.

    The LORD saw it, and it displeased him
        that there was no justice.
16   He saw that there was no one,
        and was appalled that there was no one to
            intervene;
    so his own arm brought him victory,
        and his righteousness upheld him.
17   He put on righteousness like a breastplate,
        and a helmet of salvation on his head;
    he put on garments of vengeance for clothing,
        and wrapped himself in fury as in a mantle.
18   According to their deeds, so will he repay;
        wrath to his adversaries, requital to his enemies;
        to the coastlands he will render requital.
19   So those in the west shall fear the name of the
        LORD,
        and those in the east, his glory;
    for he will come like a pent-up stream
        that the wind of the LORD drives on.

20   And he will come to Zion as Redeemer,
        to those in Jacob who turn from transgression,
            says the LORD.
21And as for me, this is my covenant with them, says the LORD: my spirit that is upon you, and my words that I have put in your mouth, shall not depart out of your mouth, or out of the mouths of your children, or out of the mouths of your children's children, says the LORD, from now on and forever.

The Ingathering of the Dispersed

60 Arise, shine; for your light has come,
      and the glory of the LORD has risen upon you.

a Meaning of Heb uncertain

² For darkness shall cover the earth,
  and thick darkness the peoples;
but the LORD will arise upon you,
  and his glory will appear over you.

³ Nations shall come to your light,
  and kings to the brightness of your dawn.

⁴ Lift up your eyes and look around;
  they all gather together, they come to you;
your sons shall come from far away,
  and your daughters shall be carried on their
    nurses' arms.

⁵ Then you shall see and be radiant;
  your heart shall thrill and rejoice,ᵃ
because the abundance of the sea shall be brought
    to you,
  the wealth of the nations shall come to you.

⁶ A multitude of camels shall cover you,
  the young camels of Midian and Ephah;
  all those from Sheba shall come.
They shall bring gold and frankincense,
  and shall proclaim the praise of the LORD.

⁷ All the flocks of Kedar shall be gathered to you,
  the rams of Nebaioth shall minister to you;
they shall be acceptable on my altar,
  and I will glorify my glorious house.

⁸ Who are these that fly like a cloud,
  and like doves to their windows?

⁹ For the coastlands shall wait for me,
  the ships of Tarshish first,
to bring your children from far away,
  their silver and gold with them,
for the name of the LORD your God,
  and for the Holy One of Israel,
  because he has glorified you.

¹⁰ Foreigners shall build up your walls,
  and their kings shall minister to you;
for in my wrath I struck you down,
  but in my favor I have had mercy on you.

¹¹ Your gates shall always be open;
  day and night they shall not be shut,
so that nations shall bring you their wealth,
  with their kings led in procession.

¹² For the nation and kingdom
  that will not serve you shall perish;
  those nations shall be utterly laid waste.

¹³ The glory of Lebanon shall come to you,
  the cypress, the plane, and the pine,
to beautify the place of my sanctuary;
  and I will glorify where my feet rest.

¹⁴ The descendants of those who oppressed you
  shall come bending low to you,
and all who despised you
  shall bow down at your feet;
they shall call you the City of the LORD,
  the Zion of the Holy One of Israel.

"The Wealth of the Nations"

ISAIAH 60.5–11

Isaiah declares that God's intention is to bless all nations. What does this reveal about God's nature? What is the "wealth of the nations" that is to be brought into the kingdom—beyond the material wealth of silver and gold? Ponder the cultural wealth of a nation you may have studied or visited, especially one different from the one that looms large in your heritage and experience. What might delight God's heart about some aspect of that culture? How does it reveal the image of God reflected in human nature? What can you learn from that culture that will help you reflect God's image in your life more fully? What in that nation's life calls for intercessory prayer today?

ᵃ Heb *be enlarged*

"The Spirit of the Lord God Is Upon Me"

ISAIAH 61.1–3

According to Isaiah, what good things does God desire for his people in this proclamation of good news? How are these values apparent in Israel's best moments and in Judaism's continued witness to the one true God? How are they visible in the life of Jesus of Nazareth, who used this passage to announce his own ministry (see Luke 4.16–19)? In what ways are they at work—or missing—in the life of your spiritual community? In what ways does your life exemplify these values? Which phrase in particular calls you to express a value in action? Ask God to show you how to participate in this aspect of the Spirit's work.

See Meeting God in Community

15 Whereas you have been forsaken and hated,
  with no one passing through,
I will make you majestic forever,
  a joy from age to age.
16 You shall suck the milk of nations,
  you shall suck the breasts of kings;
and you shall know that I, the LORD, am your Savior
  and your Redeemer, the Mighty One of Jacob.

17 Instead of bronze I will bring gold,
  instead of iron I will bring silver;
instead of wood, bronze,
  instead of stones, iron.
I will appoint Peace as your overseer
  and Righteousness as your taskmaster.
18 Violence shall no more be heard in your land,
  devastation or destruction within your borders;
you shall call your walls Salvation,
  and your gates Praise.

God the Glory of Zion

19 The sun shall no longer be
  your light by day,
nor for brightness shall the moon
  give light to you by night;[a]
but the LORD will be your everlasting light,
  and your God will be your glory.
20 Your sun shall no more go down,
  or your moon withdraw itself;
for the LORD will be your everlasting light,
  and your days of mourning shall be ended.
21 Your people shall all be righteous;
  they shall possess the land forever.
They are the shoot that I planted, the work of my hands,
  so that I might be glorified.
22 The least of them shall become a clan,
  and the smallest one a mighty nation;
I am the LORD;
  in its time I will accomplish it quickly.

The Good News of Deliverance

61 The spirit of the Lord GOD is upon me,
  because the LORD has anointed me;
he has sent me to bring good news to the oppressed,
  to bind up the brokenhearted,
to proclaim liberty to the captives,
  and release to the prisoners;
2 to proclaim the year of the LORD's favor,
  and the day of vengeance of our God;
  to comfort all who mourn;
3 to provide for those who mourn in Zion—
  to give them a garland instead of ashes,
the oil of gladness instead of mourning,
  the mantle of praise instead of a faint spirit.

a Q Ms Gk Old Latin Tg: MT lacks *by night*

They will be called oaks of righteousness,
  the planting of the Lord, to display his glory.
4 They shall build up the ancient ruins,
  they shall raise up the former devastations;
they shall repair the ruined cities,
  the devastations of many generations.

5 Strangers shall stand and feed your flocks,
  foreigners shall till your land and dress your
    vines;
6 but you shall be called priests of the Lord,
  you shall be named ministers of our God;
you shall enjoy the wealth of the nations,
  and in their riches you shall glory.
7 Because their*a* shame was double,
  and dishonor was proclaimed as their lot,
therefore they shall possess a double portion;
  everlasting joy shall be theirs.

8 For I the Lord love justice,
  I hate robbery and wrongdoing;*b*
I will faithfully give them their recompense,
  and I will make an everlasting covenant with
    them.
9 Their descendants shall be known among the
    nations,
  and their offspring among the peoples;
all who see them shall acknowledge
  that they are a people whom the Lord has
    blessed.
10 I will greatly rejoice in the Lord,
  my whole being shall exult in my God;
for he has clothed me with the garments of
    salvation,
  he has covered me with the robe of
    righteousness,
as a bridegroom decks himself with a garland,
  and as a bride adorns herself with her jewels.
11 For as the earth brings forth its shoots,
  and as a garden causes what is sown in it to
    spring up,
so the Lord God will cause righteousness and
    praise
  to spring up before all the nations.

The Vindication and Salvation of Zion

62 For Zion's sake I will not keep silent,
  and for Jerusalem's sake I will not rest,
until her vindication shines out like the dawn,
  and her salvation like a burning torch.
2 The nations shall see your vindication,
  and all the kings your glory;
and you shall be called by a new name
  that the mouth of the Lord will give.
3 You shall be a crown of beauty in the hand of the
    Lord,
  and a royal diadem in the hand of your God.

Clothed by God

ISAIAH 61.10

"Let your bodies—which are
  your clothing—shine out,
for they bound in fetters
  that man whose body
  was stained. Lord, do
you
whiten my stains
at Your banquet
with Your radiance.

"Whosoever
  puts on the robe of glory
from the water and the Spirit, will destroy with its
  burning the thorny
  growth of his sins.

"Among the saints none is
  naked for they have put
  on glory;
nor is there any clad in fig
  leaves,
or stained in shame,
for they have found,
through our Lord,
the robe that belonged
to Adam and Eve."
—EPHRAIM OF SYRIA

Intercessors

ISAIAH 62.6

The sentinels "remind the LORD,"—that is, they pray continually—for the needs of the people. Intercessory prayer is a channel through which God's comforting and guiding Spirit flows. Prayerfully imagine that you are just such a sentinel, posted high on the city wall, atop a tall building or on a high hill where you can view your family, community, congregation, nation or world. What do you see that needs to be offered to God in intercessory prayer? Let those needs enter your heart. Offer to join your thoughts and concerns with God's compassionate and powerful love so that God's love will illuminate, surround and permeate the situation for which you are praying.

See Meeting God in Prayer

4 You shall no more be termed Forsaken,[a]
and your land shall no more be termed
Desolate;[b]
but you shall be called My Delight Is in Her,[c]
and your land Married;[d]
for the LORD delights in you,
and your land shall be married.
5 For as a young man marries a young woman,
so shall your builder[e] marry you,
and as the bridegroom rejoices over the bride,
so shall your God rejoice over you.
6 Upon your walls, O Jerusalem,
I have posted sentinels;
all day and all night
they shall never be silent.
You who remind the LORD,
take no rest,
7 and give him no rest
until he establishes Jerusalem
and makes it renowned throughout the earth.
8 The LORD has sworn by his right hand
and by his mighty arm:
I will not again give your grain
to be food for your enemies,
and foreigners shall not drink the wine
for which you have labored;
9 but those who garner it shall eat it
and praise the LORD,
and those who gather it shall drink it
in my holy courts.

10 Go through, go through the gates,
prepare the way for the people;
build up, build up the highway,
clear it of stones,
lift up an ensign over the peoples.
11 The LORD has proclaimed
to the end of the earth:
Say to daughter Zion,
"See, your salvation comes;
his reward is with him,
and his recompense before him."
12 They shall be called, "The Holy People,
The Redeemed of the LORD";
and you shall be called, "Sought Out,
A City Not Forsaken."

Vengeance on Edom

63 "Who is this that comes from Edom,
from Bozrah in garments stained crimson?
Who is this so splendidly robed,
marching in his great might?"

"It is I, announcing vindication,
mighty to save."

2 "Why are your robes red,

---

a Heb *Azubah*   b Heb *Shemamah*   c Heb *Hephzibah*   d Heb *Beulah*
e Cn: Heb *your sons*

and your garments like theirs who tread the
wine press?"

3 "I have trodden the wine press alone,
and from the peoples no one was with me;
I trod them in my anger
and trampled them in my wrath;
their juice spattered on my garments,
and stained all my robes.
4 For the day of vengeance was in my heart,
and the year for my redeeming work had come.
5 I looked, but there was no helper;
I stared, but there was no one to sustain me;
so my own arm brought me victory,
and my wrath sustained me.
6 I trampled down peoples in my anger,
I crushed them in my wrath,
and I poured out their lifeblood on the earth."

God's Mercy Remembered

7 I will recount the gracious deeds of the LORD,
the praiseworthy acts of the LORD,
because of all that the LORD has done for us,
and the great favor to the house of Israel
that he has shown them according to his mercy,
according to the abundance of his steadfast
love.
8 For he said, "Surely they are my people,
children who will not deal falsely";
and he became their savior
9 in all their distress.
It was no messenger[a] or angel
but his presence that saved them;[b]
in his love and in his pity he redeemed them;
he lifted them up and carried them all the days
of old.

10 But they rebelled
and grieved his holy spirit;
therefore he became their enemy;
he himself fought against them.
11 Then they[c] remembered the days of old,
of Moses his servant.[d]
Where is the one who brought them up out of the
sea
with the shepherds of his flock?
Where is the one who put within them
his holy spirit,
12 who caused his glorious arm
to march at the right hand of Moses,
who divided the waters before them
to make for himself an everlasting name,
13 who led them through the depths?
Like a horse in the desert,
they did not stumble.
14 Like cattle that go down into the valley,
the spirit of the LORD gave them rest.

a Gk: Heb anguish   b Or savior. [9]In all their distress he was distressed; the
angel of his presence saved them;   c Heb he   d Cn: Heb his people

The Divine Warrior

ISAIAH 63.3–6

"By the hand of thy
prophets . . . thou has
imaged forth the . . .
glory of thy majesty.
They saw . . . thee . . .
as a Man of War;
he striveth with his hands.

"With dew of light
his head is filled and his
locks with drops of the
night . . .
His black locks
were flowing in curls.
He is bright
and ruddy in red apparel,
when he cometh from
treading the winepresses
of Edom.

"His glory resteth upon me,
and mine upon him; he is
nigh unto me when I call
upon him.
May his treasured people
be a crown in his hand!"
—"The Hymn of Glory,"
Hebrew Prayer Book

God, Our Father

ISAIAH 63.16; 64.8

These verses are among the few places in the Hebrew Bible that God is called "Father." The emphasis here is on the father's function of judging and correcting behavior. What other facets of fatherliness does God exhibit? Which of these qualities have you seen modeled by your father or other father figures in your life? Do you have any special "fathers in God" (of any age) who have helped you develop your relationship with God? What aspect of being "fatherly" might you need to explore or deepen in your character (whether you are male or female)? Who are the fathers that may need your prayers today?

See Meeting God in Scripture

Thus you led your people,
    to make for yourself a glorious name.

A Prayer of Penitence

15 Look down from heaven and see,
    from your holy and glorious habitation.
Where are your zeal and your might?
    The yearning of your heart and your compassion?
    They are withheld from me.
16 For you are our father,
    though Abraham does not know us
    and Israel does not acknowledge us;
you, O LORD, are our father;
    our Redeemer from of old is your name.
17 Why, O LORD, do you make us stray from your ways
    and harden our heart, so that we do not fear you?
Turn back for the sake of your servants,
    for the sake of the tribes that are your heritage.
18 Your holy people took possession for a little while;
    but now our adversaries have trampled down
        your sanctuary.
19 We have long been like those whom you do not
        rule,
    like those not called by your name.

64 O that you would tear open the heavens and
    come down,
so that the mountains would quake at your
    presence—
2a as when fire kindles brushwood
    and the fire causes water to boil—
to make your name known to your adversaries,
    so that the nations might tremble at your
        presence!
3 When you did awesome deeds that we did not
    expect,
    you came down, the mountains quaked at your
        presence.
4 From ages past no one has heard,
    no ear has perceived,
no eye has seen any God besides you,
    who works for those who wait for him.
5 You meet those who gladly do right,
    those who remember you in your ways.
But you were angry, and we sinned;
    because you hid yourself we transgressed.b
6 We have all become like one who is unclean,
    and all our righteous deeds are like a filthy cloth.
We all fade like a leaf,
    and our iniquities, like the wind, take us away.
7 There is no one who calls on your name,
    or attempts to take hold of you;
for you have hidden your face from us,
    and have deliveredc us into the hand of our
        iniquity.
8 Yet, O LORD, you are our Father;
    we are the clay, and you are our potter;

a Ch 64.1 in Heb   *b* Meaning of Heb uncertain   *c* Gk Syr Old Latin Tg: Heb *melted* we are all the work of your hand.

9 Do not be exceedingly angry, O Lord,
and do not remember iniquity forever.
Now consider, we are all your people.

10 Your holy cities have become a wilderness,
Zion has become a wilderness,
Jerusalem a desolation.

11 Our holy and beautiful house,
where our ancestors praised you,
has been burned by fire,
and all our pleasant places have become ruins.

12 After all this, will you restrain yourself, O Lord?
Will you keep silent, and punish us so severely?

The Righteousness of God's Judgment

65 I was ready to be sought out by those who did not ask,
to be found by those who did not seek me.
I said, "Here I am, here I am,"
to a nation that did not call on my name.

2 I held out my hands all day long
to a rebellious people,
who walk in a way that is not good,
following their own devices;

3 a people who provoke me
to my face continually,
sacrificing in gardens
and offering incense on bricks;

4 who sit inside tombs,
and spend the night in secret places;
who eat swine's flesh,
with broth of abominable things in their vessels;

5 who say, "Keep to yourself,
do not come near me, for I am too holy for
you."
These are a smoke in my nostrils,
a fire that burns all day long.

6 See, it is written before me:
I will not keep silent, but I will repay;
I will indeed repay into their laps

7 their[a] iniquities and their[a] ancestors' iniquities
together,
                                                    says the Lord;
because they offered incense on the mountains
and reviled me on the hills,
I will measure into their laps
full payment for their actions.

8 Thus says the Lord:
As the wine is found in the cluster,
and they say, "Do not destroy it,
for there is a blessing in it,"
so I will do for my servants' sake,
and not destroy them all.

9 I will bring forth descendants[b] from Jacob,
and from Judah inheritors[c] of my mountains;
my chosen shall inherit it,
and my servants shall settle there.

The Unnoticed Presence

ISAIAH 65.1–2

God is always pressing in on our lives, whether we heed God or not, whether we ask for God or not. God is often present incognito—without drama—in and through natural events. In what places, situations or relationships has God called out to you? In what ways might God have been saying, "Here I am" to you lately? Review the last twenty-four hours of your life for glimpses of such moments. Revisit them with a greater openness to God, "turning up the volume" of your spiritual sensitivity. Be open to what God is teaching you. This exercise can be an especially fitting way to end your day.

See Meeting God in Everyday Life

---

a Gk Syr: Heb *your*   *b* Or *a descendant*   *c* Or *an inheritor*

Invoking a Blessing

ISAIAH 65.16

Invoking a blessing means calling upon "the God of faithfulness" to pour out his grace for a particular purpose. Invoking a blessing is an act of faith; it is confidently claiming a promise inherent in an attribute of God's revealed character, as in "May the God of hope fill you with all joy" (Romans 15.13). To do so connects a particular name or attribute of God with a specific human need. What blessing do you need as you face the coming day? Who in your circle of care is in need of a particular blessing? Choose an appropriate attribute of God for each blessing, and invoke the Spirit's aid: "May the God of _____ grant _____."

See Meeting God in Prayer

10 Sharon shall become a pasture for flocks,
      and the Valley of Achor a place for herds to lie down,
      for my people who have sought me.
11 But you who forsake the LORD,
      who forget my holy mountain,
    who set a table for Fortune
      and fill cups of mixed wine for Destiny;
12 I will destine you to the sword,
      and all of you shall bow down to the slaughter;
    because, when I called, you did not answer,
      when I spoke, you did not listen,
    but you did what was evil in my sight,
      and chose what I did not delight in.
13 Therefore thus says the Lord GOD:
    My servants shall eat,
      but you shall be hungry;
    my servants shall drink,
      but you shall be thirsty;
    my servants shall rejoice,
      but you shall be put to shame;
14 my servants shall sing for gladness of heart,
      but you shall cry out for pain of heart,
      and shall wail for anguish of spirit.
15 You shall leave your name to my chosen to use as a curse,
      and the Lord GOD will put you to death;
      but to his servants he will give a different name.
16 Then whoever invokes a blessing in the land
      shall bless by the God of faithfulness,
    and whoever takes an oath in the land
      shall swear by the God of faithfulness;
    because the former troubles are forgotten
      and are hidden from my sight.

The Glorious New Creation

17 For I am about to create new heavens
      and a new earth;
    the former things shall not be remembered
      or come to mind.
18 But be glad and rejoice forever
      in what I am creating;
    for I am about to create Jerusalem as a joy,
      and its people as a delight.
19 I will rejoice in Jerusalem,
      and delight in my people;
    no more shall the sound of weeping be heard in it,
      or the cry of distress.
20 No more shall there be in it
      an infant that lives but a few days,
      or an old person who does not live out a lifetime;
    for one who dies at a hundred years will be considered a youth,
      and one who falls short of a hundred will be considered accursed.
21 They shall build houses and inhabit them;
      they shall plant vineyards and eat their fruit.
22 They shall not build and another inhabit;
      they shall not plant and another eat;

for like the days of a tree shall the days of my
people be,
and my chosen shall long enjoy the work of
their hands.
23 They shall not labor in vain,
or bear children for calamity;[a]
for they shall be offspring blessed by the Lord—
and their descendants as well.
24 Before they call I will answer,
while they are yet speaking I will hear.
25 The wolf and the lamb shall feed together,
the lion shall eat straw like the ox;
but the serpent—its food shall be dust!
They shall not hurt or destroy
on all my holy mountain,
says the Lord.

The Worship God Demands

66 Thus says the Lord:
Heaven is my throne
and the earth is my footstool;
what is the house that you would build for me,
and what is my resting place?
2 All these things my hand has made,
and so all these things are mine,[b]
says the Lord.
But this is the one to whom I will look,
to the humble and contrite in spirit,
who trembles at my word.

3 Whoever slaughters an ox is like one who kills a
human being;
whoever sacrifices a lamb, like one who breaks
a dog's neck;
whoever presents a grain offering, like one who
offers swine's blood;[c]
whoever makes a memorial offering of
frankincense, like one who blesses an idol.
These have chosen their own ways,
and in their abominations they take delight;
4 I also will choose to mock[d] them,
and bring upon them what they fear;
because, when I called, no one answered,
when I spoke, they did not listen;
but they did what was evil in my sight,
and chose what did not please me.

The Lord Vindicates Zion

5 Hear the word of the Lord,
you who tremble at his word:
Your own people who hate you
and reject you for my name's sake
have said, "Let the Lord be glorified,
so that we may see your joy";
but it is they who shall be put to shame.

"Living Sacrifices"

ISAIAH 66.1–4

Our "sacrifices" or offerings are
our daily actions and habits of
mind, rather than the ineffective and odious sacrifices that
Isaiah pictures; God desires that
his people offer righteous actions and attitudes.

Recall your day so far. What
qualities and attitudes in yourself does God have to work with
today? Offer yourself as a "living sacrifice" (Romans 12.1),
saying, "Here I am being calm
. . . loving someone . . . I offer
my actions for your purposes."
Offer whatever seems unworthy
for transformation: "Here I am
disgruntled . . . or afraid . . ."
Practice pausing periodically
throughout the day to make an
offering of what you have just
been doing, asking the Spirit to
help you craft a day worthy of
God's desires for your life.

See Meeting God in Worship

a Or *sudden terror*   b Gk Syr: Heb *these things came to be*   c Meaning
of Heb uncertain   d Or *to punish*

The Nourishing Mother

ISAIAH 66.10–14

God likens himself and the holy city Jerusalem to a generous, nourishing mother, whose overflowing grace and glory renew the bodies and hearts of her children. What do such feminine images tell us about the nature of God? How is this aspect of God manifest in men and women you know? How might you address this facet of God in prayer? Where, in your daily life, is God's nurturing care most clearly evident? What spiritual practices help you open yourself to "drink deeply with delight" in such grace? How can you embody such divine generosity in your behavior?

See Meeting God in Scripture

6 Listen, an uproar from the city!
   A voice from the temple!
The voice of the LORD,
   dealing retribution to his enemies!

7 Before she was in labor
   she gave birth;
before her pain came upon her
   she delivered a son.
8 Who has heard of such a thing?
   Who has seen such things?
Shall a land be born in one day?
   Shall a nation be delivered in one moment?
Yet as soon as Zion was in labor
   she delivered her children.
9 Shall I open the womb and not deliver?
   says the LORD;
shall I, the one who delivers, shut the womb?
   says your God.

10 Rejoice with Jerusalem, and be glad for her,
   all you who love her;
rejoice with her in joy,
   all you who mourn over her—
11 that you may nurse and be satisfied
   from her consoling breast;
that you may drink deeply with delight
   from her glorious bosom.

12 For thus says the LORD:
I will extend prosperity to her like a river,
   and the wealth of the nations like an
      overflowing stream;
and you shall nurse and be carried on her arm,
   and dandled on her knees.
13 As a mother comforts her child,
   so I will comfort you;
   you shall be comforted in Jerusalem.

The Reign and Indignation of God

14 You shall see, and your heart shall rejoice;
   your bodies[a] shall flourish like the grass;
and it shall be known that the hand of the LORD is
      with his servants,
   and his indignation is against his enemies.
15 For the LORD will come in fire,
   and his chariots like the whirlwind,
to pay back his anger in fury,
   and his rebuke in flames of fire.
16 For by fire will the LORD execute judgment,
   and by his sword, on all flesh;
   and those slain by the LORD shall be many.

17 Those who sanctify and purify themselves to go into the gardens, following the one in the center, eating the flesh of pigs, vermin, and rodents, shall come to an end together, says the LORD.

a Heb *bones*

18 For I know[a] their works and their thoughts, and I am[b] coming to gather all nations and tongues; and they shall come and shall see my glory, [19]and I will set a sign among them. From them I will send survivors to the nations, to Tarshish, Put,[c] and Lud—which draw the bow—to Tubal and Javan, to the coastlands far away that have not heard of my fame or seen my glory; and they shall declare my glory among the nations. [20]They shall bring all your kindred from all the nations as an offering to the LORD, on horses, and in chariots, and in litters, and on mules, and on dromedaries, to my holy mountain Jerusalem, says the LORD, just as the Israelites bring a grain offering in a clean vessel to the house of the LORD. [21]And I will also take some of them as priests and as Levites, says the LORD.

22 For as the new heavens and the new earth,
    which I will make,
shall remain before me, says the LORD;
    so shall your descendants and your name
        remain.
23 From new moon to new moon,
    and from sabbath to sabbath,
all flesh shall come to worship before me,
says the LORD.

24 And they shall go out and look at the dead bodies of the people who have rebelled against me; for their worm shall not die, their fire shall not be quenched, and they shall be an abhorrence to all flesh.

In the End, Praise

ISAIAH 66.23

In synagogue reading as well as in printed texts, Jews traditionally end the book of Isaiah by repeating verse 23, so that they finish the reading with God's gracious goals rather than God's temporary wrath: "From new moon to new moon, and from sabbath to sabbath, all flesh shall come to worship before me, says the LORD." God's goals for humanity are restoration, community, communion and praise. Prayerfully envision "the end" or fulfillment—for yourself, for humanity, for the creation. How is your hope of this glorious end encouraged and strengthened? What passages in scripture support your hope? Describe in writing or draw a representation of your vision of the fulfillment that God intends for us. Pray that all people will come to worship God.

See Meeting God in Worship

JEREMIAH
Hope in Times of Weeping

KEY VERSE:

Is Ephraim my dear son? Is he the child I delight in? As often as I speak against him,
I still remember him. Therefore I am deeply moved for him; I will surely have mercy on him,
says the LORD.—Jeremiah 31.20

"Batter my heart, three-
personed God, for you
As yet but knock, breathe,
shine and seek to mend;
That I may rise and stand,
o'erthrow me and bend
your force to break, blow,
burn, and make me
new."

—JOHN DONNE,
Holy Sonnets 5

Who am I called to be?" "How does God intend to use my gifts?" Jeremiah wrestles with such questions and finds that God has rich purposes for his life.

Jeremiah the *prophet* is a passionate man who grieves with God for a wayward people.

Jeremiah the *proclaimer* of God's word is a man of enormous courage—speaking at great personal cost in a climate of hostility and rejection. Jeremiah the *poet* is a man of such transparency of soul that he hears God and weeps with God. Jeremiah declares to his listeners that God is a Father who wants good things for his children, such as "a pleasant land, the most beautiful heritage of all the nations" (3.19); God so deeply loves "[his] dear son . . . the child [he] delight[s] in" (31.20), that even though his children reject and deny him, he continues to show mercy. Jeremiah the *servant of God* is a man of great integrity who calls the people of God to integrity so that they might not lose their true identity as God's children.

From his perspective in the sixth century B.C., Jeremiah shows us a God who yearns for us, a God who has wonderful things in store for us, a God who grieves when we turn away. Jeremiah calls us to repent and to grieve when we fail to respond to a love that passionately desires our good. And as we respond, we discover the compassion of God, who alone can restore us.

1 The words of Jeremiah son of Hilkiah, of the priests who were in Anathoth in the land of Benjamin, ²to whom the word of the LORD came in the days of King Josiah son of Amon of Judah, in the thirteenth year of his reign. ³It came also in the days of King Jehoiakim son of Josiah of Judah, and until the end of the eleventh year of King Zedekiah son of Josiah of Judah, until the captivity of Jerusalem in the fifth month.

Jeremiah's Call and Commission

4 Now the word of the LORD came to me saying,
5   "Before I formed you in the womb I knew you,
     and before you were born I consecrated you;
     I appointed you a prophet to the nations."
⁶Then I said, "Ah, Lord GOD! Truly I do not know how to speak, for I am only a boy." ⁷But the LORD said to me,
     "Do not say, 'I am only a boy';
     for you shall go to all to whom I send you,
     and you shall speak whatever I command you.
8   Do not be afraid of them,
     for I am with you to deliver you,
                              says the LORD."
⁹Then the LORD put out his hand and touched my mouth; and the LORD said to me,
     "Now I have put my words in your mouth.
10   See, today I appoint you over nations and over
         kingdoms,
     to pluck up and to pull down,
     to destroy and to overthrow,
     to build and to plant."

11 The word of the LORD came to me, saying, "Jeremiah, what do you see?" And I said, "I see a branch of an almond tree."ᵃ ¹²Then the LORD said to me, "You have seen well, for I am watchingᵇ over my word to perform it." ¹³The word of the LORD came to me a second time, saying, "What do you see?" And I said, "I see a boiling pot, tilted away from the north."

14 Then the LORD said to me: Out of the north disaster shall break out on all the inhabitants of the land. ¹⁵For now I am calling all the tribes of the kingdoms of the north, says the LORD; and they shall come and all of them shall set their thrones at the entrance of the gates of Jerusalem, against all its surrounding walls and against all the cities of Judah. ¹⁶And I will utter my judgments against them, for all their wickedness in forsaking me; they have made offerings to other gods, and worshiped the works of their own hands. ¹⁷But you, gird up your loins; stand up and tell them everything that I command you. Do not break down before them, or I will break you before them. ¹⁸And I for my part have made you today a fortified city, an iron pillar, and a bronze wall, against the whole land— against the kings of Judah, its princes, its priests, and the people of the land. ¹⁹They will fight against you; but they shall not prevail against you, for I am with you, says the LORD, to deliver you.

The Call

JEREMIAH 1.4–5

"Before I formed you in the womb I knew you, and before you were born I consecrated you," God tells Jeremiah. Imagine yourself being received into heaven. Your life is under review—and you are told that you have achieved that for which you were sent. You did it! You were faithful! How would you respond to the news? What is it that God has made *you* for? What awakens your passion, your creativity and your sense of being true to yourself? In other words, what is your calling? Now, ask yourself what you need to do in order to fully cooperate with that calling. Bring the matter to Jesus and ask him to guide you in your vocation.

See Meeting God in Prayer

a Heb *shaqed*   *b* Heb *shoqed*

Where Is the Lord?

JEREMIAH 2.1–13

Shut your eyes and on the wide screen of your mind gaze at the spring of living water that Jeremiah mentions. What does "living water" feel like on your hands, on your face and in your mouth? In the power of your imagination, enjoy it. Return to your "big screen" and look at some still water that oozes out of a leaky pit or a stagnant cistern in the ground! What is this water like? What would it be like to touch or drink?

Letting water be an image of your relationship with God, ask yourself, "What kind of water best represents my relationship with God at the moment?" Be still. Be honest. Ask with the prophet, "Where is the Lord?" and come to God with a prayer of response.

See Meeting God in the Created Order

God Pleads with Israel to Repent

2 The word of the Lord came to me, saying: ²Go and proclaim in the hearing of Jerusalem, Thus says the Lord:
I remember the devotion of your youth,
    your love as a bride,
how you followed me in the wilderness,
    in a land not sown.
³ Israel was holy to the Lord,
    the first fruits of his harvest.
All who ate of it were held guilty;
    disaster came upon them,
                  says the Lord.

4 Hear the word of the Lord, O house of Jacob, and all the families of the house of Israel. ⁵Thus says the Lord:
What wrong did your ancestors find in me
    that they went far from me,
and went after worthless things, and became
        worthless themselves?
⁶ They did not say, "Where is the Lord
    who brought us up from the land of Egypt,
who led us in the wilderness,
    in a land of deserts and pits,
in a land of drought and deep darkness,
    in a land that no one passes through,
    where no one lives?"
⁷ I brought you into a plentiful land
    to eat its fruits and its good things.
But when you entered you defiled my land,
    and made my heritage an abomination.
⁸ The priests did not say, "Where is the Lord?"
    Those who handle the law did not know me;
the rulers*ᵃ* transgressed against me;
    the prophets prophesied by Baal,
    and went after things that do not profit.

⁹ Therefore once more I accuse you,
                  says the Lord,
    and I accuse your children's children.
¹⁰ Cross to the coasts of Cyprus and look,
    send to Kedar and examine with care;
    see if there has ever been such a thing.
¹¹ Has a nation changed its gods,
    even though they are no gods?
But my people have changed their glory
    for something that does not profit.
¹² Be appalled, O heavens, at this,
    be shocked, be utterly desolate,
                  says the Lord,
¹³ for my people have committed two evils:
    they have forsaken me,
the fountain of living water,
    and dug out cisterns for themselves,
cracked cisterns
    that can hold no water.

¹⁴ Is Israel a slave? Is he a homeborn servant?
    Why then has he become plunder?

a Heb *shepherds*

15 The lions have roared against him,
    they have roared loudly.
They have made his land a waste;
    his cities are in ruins, without inhabitant.
16 Moreover, the people of Memphis and Tahpanhes
    have broken the crown of your head.
17 Have you not brought this upon yourself
    by forsaking the LORD your God,
    while he led you in the way?
18 What then do you gain by going to Egypt,
    to drink the waters of the Nile?
Or what do you gain by going to Assyria,
    to drink the waters of the Euphrates?
19 Your wickedness will punish you,
    and your apostasies will convict you.
Know and see that it is evil and bitter
    for you to forsake the LORD your God;
    the fear of me is not in you,
                says the Lord GOD of hosts.

20 For long ago you broke your yoke
    and burst your bonds,
    and you said, "I will not serve!"
On every high hill
    and under every green tree
    you sprawled and played the whore.
21 Yet I planted you as a choice vine,
    from the purest stock.
How then did you turn degenerate
    and become a wild vine?
22 Though you wash yourself with lye
    and use much soap,
    the stain of your guilt is still before me,
                says the Lord GOD.
23 How can you say, "I am not defiled,
    I have not gone after the Baals"?
Look at your way in the valley;
    know what you have done—
a restive young camel interlacing her tracks,
24   a wild ass at home in the wilderness,
in her heat sniffing the wind!
    Who can restrain her lust?
None who seek her need weary themselves;
    in her month they will find her.
25 Keep your feet from going unshod
    and your throat from thirst.
But you said, "It is hopeless,
    for I have loved strangers,
    and after them I will go."

26 As a thief is shamed when caught,
    so the house of Israel shall be shamed—
they, their kings, their officials,
    their priests, and their prophets,
27 who say to a tree, "You are my father,"
    and to a stone, "You gave me birth."
For they have turned their backs to me,
    and not their faces.
But in the time of their trouble they say,
    "Come and save us!"

A Prodigal Departure

JEREMIAH 2.14–18

Like a defiant youth, Israel has left home and has forsaken God for what the neighbors can offer. And like a rebellious daughter, Israel has scorned the wealth of her inheritance and the love of her home and has sold herself like a whore. The stain of guilt is indelible.

In the company of God, the faithful One, consider how you have forsaken him. What appetites lure you away? What stain do you still bear? Abandon yourself to the mercy of God, in whom you will not be ashamed (see Psalm 25.20). Fast for at least one meal. When you begin to feel hungry, let your desire for food stir your desire for God, who alone can satisfy (see Psalm 16.11).

See Meeting God in Everyday Life

I've Done Nothing Wrong!

JEREMIAH 2.29–35

Israel is in denial. God has clear evidence of unfaithfulness, yet Israel insists, "I am innocent." Israel has pursued her own fancies and put her trust in things other than God.

Make a list of things of which you are allegedly "innocent." Now ask the Holy Spirit to give you freedom from denial so that you might see things God's way. Confess those sins that need confessing. Burn your list as you pray that the acknowledgment of your sins will become the seed for the planting of new life.

See Meeting God in Prayer

28 But where are your gods
    that you made for yourself?
Let them come, if they can save you,
    in your time of trouble;
for you have as many gods
    as you have towns, O Judah.

29 Why do you complain against me?
    You have all rebelled against me,
                says the LORD.

30 In vain I have struck down your children;
    they accepted no correction.
Your own sword devoured your prophets
    like a ravening lion.

31 And you, O generation, behold the word of the
    LORD![a]
Have I been a wilderness to Israel,
    or a land of thick darkness?
Why then do my people say, "We are free,
    we will come to you no more"?

32 Can a girl forget her ornaments,
    or a bride her attire?
Yet my people have forgotten me,
    days without number.

33 How well you direct your course
    to seek lovers!
So that even to wicked women
    you have taught your ways.

34 Also on your skirts is found
    the lifeblood of the innocent poor,
though you did not catch them breaking in.
    Yet in spite of all these things[a]

35 you say, "I am innocent;
    surely his anger has turned from me."
Now I am bringing you to judgment
    for saying, "I have not sinned."

36 How lightly you gad about,
    changing your ways!
You shall be put to shame by Egypt
    as you were put to shame by Assyria.

37 From there also you will come away
    with your hands on your head;
for the LORD has rejected those in whom you trust,
    and you will not prosper through them.

Unfaithful Israel

3 If[b] a man divorces his wife
    and she goes from him
and becomes another man's wife,
    will he return to her?
Would not such a land be greatly polluted?
You have played the whore with many lovers;
    and would you return to me?
                says the LORD.

2 Look up to the bare heights,[c] and see!
    Where have you not been lain with?
By the waysides you have sat waiting for lovers,
    like a nomad in the wilderness.

    a Meaning of Heb uncertain   *b* Q Ms Gk Syr: MT *Saying, If*   *c* Or *the trails*

You have polluted the land
  with your whoring and wickedness.
3 Therefore the showers have been withheld,
  and the spring rain has not come;
yet you have the forehead of a whore,
  you refuse to be ashamed.
4 Have you not just now called to me,
  "My Father, you are the friend of my youth—
5 will he be angry forever,
  will he be indignant to the end?"
This is how you have spoken,
  but you have done all the evil that you could.

A Call to Repentance

6 The LORD said to me in the days of King Josiah: Have you seen what she did, that faithless one, Israel, how she went up on every high hill and under every green tree, and played the whore there? 7And I thought, "After she has done all this she will return to me"; but she did not return, and her false sister Judah saw it. 8She*a* saw that for all the adulteries of that faithless one, Israel, I had sent her away with a decree of divorce; yet her false sister Judah did not fear, but she too went and played the whore. 9Because she took her whoredom so lightly, she polluted the land, committing adultery with stone and tree. 10Yet for all this her false sister Judah did not return to me with her whole heart, but only in pretense, says the LORD.

11 Then the LORD said to me: Faithless Israel has shown herself less guilty than false Judah. 12Go, and proclaim these words toward the north, and say:
  Return, faithless Israel,
                    says the LORD.
  I will not look on you in anger,
    for I am merciful,
                    says the LORD;
  I will not be angry forever.
13 Only acknowledge your guilt,
    that you have rebelled against the LORD your God,
  and scattered your favors among strangers under
        every green tree,
  and have not obeyed my voice,
                    says the LORD.
14 Return, O faithless children,
                    says the LORD,
    for I am your master;
  I will take you, one from a city and two from a
        family,
  and I will bring you to Zion.

15 I will give you shepherds after my own heart, who will feed you with knowledge and understanding. 16And when you have multiplied and increased in the land, in those days, says the LORD, they shall no longer say, "The ark of the covenant of the LORD." It shall not come to mind, or be remembered, or missed; nor shall another one be made. 17At that time Jerusalem shall be called the throne of the LORD, and all nations shall gather to it, to the presence of the LORD in Jerusalem, and they shall no longer stubbornly follow their own evil will. 18In those days

---

Self-Examination

JEREMIAH 3.11–18

"Help me, O Holy Spirit, to search and question myself, and honestly to answer:
Am I single-minded in seeking my God? in serving him? even in praying to him?
Do I put God first in deed? in intention? or even in desire? in hope?
What reserves do I always maintain against him? What other loves cling to? . . .
Search me thyself, O God, seek the grounds of my heart;
Look well if there be any way of wickedness in me,
any subservience to mine own ease,
any hungering and playing for mine own honour . . .
O Saviour of the world, who by thy cross and precious Blood hast redeemed us,
save me and help me, I humbly beseech thee, O Lord."

—ERIC MILNER-WHITE,
My God My Glory

See Meeting God in Prayer

Return to God!

JEREMIAH 4.1–4

Recall an experience of returning home or being reunited with someone. What were you returning from? How were you received? What emotions from that experience remain?

Today God says, "Return!" What does it mean for you to "return to God"? Write a response in your journal or on a piece of paper. Discuss your ideas with your spiritual adviser, your pastor or a companion in faith. Take whatever action is necessary for you to "return to God."

See Meeting God in Worship

the house of Judah shall join the house of Israel, and together they shall come from the land of the north to the land that I gave your ancestors for a heritage.

19   I thought
        how I would set you among my children,
     and give you a pleasant land,
        the most beautiful heritage of all the nations.
     And I thought you would call me, My Father,
        and would not turn from following me.
20   Instead, as a faithless wife leaves her husband,
        so you have been faithless to me, O house of
           Israel,

                                    says the LORD.

21   A voice on the bare heights*a* is heard,
        the plaintive weeping of Israel's children,
     because they have perverted their way,
        they have forgotten the LORD their God:
22   Return, O faithless children,
        I will heal your faithlessness.

     "Here we come to you;
        for you are the LORD our God.
23   Truly the hills are*b* a delusion,
        the orgies on the mountains.
     Truly in the LORD our God
        is the salvation of Israel.
24   "But from our youth the shameful thing has devoured all for which our ancestors had labored, their flocks and their herds, their sons and their daughters. 25Let us lie down in our shame, and let our dishonor cover us; for we have sinned against the LORD our God, we and our ancestors, from our youth even to this day; and we have not obeyed the voice of the LORD our God."

4   If you return, O Israel,

                                    says the LORD,
        if you return to me,
     if you remove your abominations from my presence,
        and do not waver,
2   and if you swear, "As the LORD lives!"
        in truth, in justice, and in uprightness,
     then nations shall be blessed*c* by him,
        and by him they shall boast.
3   For thus says the LORD to the people of Judah and to the inhabitants of Jerusalem:
     Break up your fallow ground,
        and do not sow among thorns.
4   Circumcise yourselves to the LORD,
        remove the foreskin of your hearts,
     O people of Judah and inhabitants of Jerusalem,
        or else my wrath will go forth like fire,
        and burn with no one to quench it,
     because of the evil of your doings.

Invasion and Desolation of Judah Threatened

5   Declare in Judah, and proclaim in Jerusalem, and say:
     Blow the trumpet through the land;

a Or *the trails*   *b* Gk Syr Vg: Heb *Truly from the hills is*   *c* Or *shall bless themselves*

shout aloud[a] and say,
"Gather together, and let us go
into the fortified cities!"
6 Raise a standard toward Zion,
flee for safety, do not delay,
for I am bringing evil from the north,
and a great destruction.
7 A lion has gone up from its thicket,
a destroyer of nations has set out;
he has gone out from his place
to make your land a waste;
your cities will be ruins
without inhabitant.
8 Because of this put on sackcloth,
lament and wail:
"The fierce anger of the LORD
has not turned away from us."

9 On that day, says the LORD, courage shall fail the king and the officials; the priests shall be appalled and the prophets astounded. 10 Then I said, "Ah, Lord GOD, how utterly you have deceived this people and Jerusalem, saying, 'It shall be well with you,' even while the sword is at the throat!"

11 At that time it will be said to this people and to Jerusalem: A hot wind comes from me out of the bare heights[b] in the desert toward my poor people, not to winnow or cleanse— 12 a wind too strong for that. Now it is I who speak in judgment against them.
13 Look! He comes up like clouds,
his chariots like the whirlwind;
his horses are swifter than eagles—
woe to us, for we are ruined!
14 O Jerusalem, wash your heart clean of wickedness
so that you may be saved.
How long shall your evil schemes
lodge within you?
15 For a voice declares from Dan
and proclaims disaster from Mount Ephraim.
16 Tell the nations, "Here they are!"
Proclaim against Jerusalem,
"Besiegers come from a distant land;
they shout against the cities of Judah.
17 They have closed in around her like watchers of a
field,
because she has rebelled against me,
says the LORD.
18 Your ways and your doings
have brought this upon you.
This is your doom; how bitter it is!
It has reached your very heart."

Sorrow for a Doomed Nation

19 My anguish, my anguish! I writhe in pain!
Oh, the walls of my heart!
My heart is beating wildly;
I cannot keep silent;
for I[c] hear the sound of the trumpet,

---

a Or *shout, take your weapons*: Heb *shout, fill* (your hand)   b Or *the trails*
c Another reading is *for you, O my soul*.

Listen!

JEREMIAH 4.5–8

The trumpets are sounding! Disaster is on its way—as violent and terrifying as a lion in pursuit of prey. And all the signs are being ignored!

Are you listening? What is God saying to you that you are screening out? What issue have you registered but filed in the "must look at one day" box?

Bring your calendar and a bowl of cold water to your prayer place. Pray that the Holy Spirit will deliver you from illusion. Wash your hands and feel the cleansing, refreshing cold water. Pray that God will cleanse your heart. Take out your calendar and make an appointment with God to start dealing with this issue. Leave your time of prayer saying along with Paul the apostle, "I can do all things through [Christ] who strengthens me!" (Philippians 4.13).

See Meeting God in Prayer

Disaster

JEREMIAH 4.20–28

The prophet envisions disaster after disaster for Israel. The land is desolate. The towns are deserted. The nation groans as if in the throes of death.

As you look back over the past years of your life, what private or public disaster has most affected you? What did you learn about yourself through it? What did you learn about God?

In the center of a blank page, write what you have learned about God from the experience. In the other space write down any associated thoughts; then, with paints or crayons, fill in the page with the colors you associate with the emotions that you have. Offer your work to God and pray about whatever change in attitude or behavior it has prompted in you.

See Meeting God in Prayer

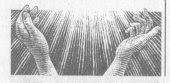

the alarm of war.
20 Disaster overtakes disaster,
  the whole land is laid waste.
Suddenly my tents are destroyed,
  my curtains in a moment.
21 How long must I see the standard,
  and hear the sound of the trumpet?
22 "For my people are foolish,
  they do not know me;
they are stupid children,
  they have no understanding.
They are skilled in doing evil,
  but do not know how to do good."

23 I looked on the earth, and lo, it was waste and void;
  and to the heavens, and they had no light.
24 I looked on the mountains, and lo, they were quaking,
  and all the hills moved to and fro.
25 I looked, and lo, there was no one at all,
  and all the birds of the air had fled.
26 I looked, and lo, the fruitful land was a desert,
  and all its cities were laid in ruins
  before the Lord, before his fierce anger.
27 For thus says the Lord: The whole land shall be a desolation; yet I will not make a full end.
28 Because of this the earth shall mourn,
  and the heavens above grow black;
for I have spoken, I have purposed;
  I have not relented nor will I turn back.

29 At the noise of horseman and archer
  every town takes to flight;
they enter thickets; they climb among rocks;
  all the towns are forsaken,
  and no one lives in them.
30 And you, O desolate one,
what do you mean that you dress in crimson,
  that you deck yourself with ornaments of gold,
  that you enlarge your eyes with paint?
In vain you beautify yourself.
  Your lovers despise you;
  they seek your life.
31 For I heard a cry as of a woman in labor,
  anguish as of one bringing forth her first child,
the cry of daughter Zion gasping for breath,
  stretching out her hands,
"Woe is me! I am fainting before killers!"

The Utter Corruption of God's People

5 Run to and fro through the streets of Jerusalem,
  look around and take note!
Search its squares and see
  if you can find one person
who acts justly
  and seeks truth—
so that I may pardon Jerusalem. *a*
2 Although they say, "As the Lord lives,"
  yet they swear falsely.

a Heb *it*

³ O LORD, do your eyes not look for truth?
You have struck them,
  but they felt no anguish;
you have consumed them,
  but they refused to take correction.
They have made their faces harder than rock;
  they have refused to turn back.

⁴ Then I said, "These are only the poor,
  they have no sense;
for they do not know the way of the LORD,
  the law of their God.
⁵ Let me go to the rich*ᵃ*
  and speak to them;
surely they know the way of the LORD,
  the law of their God."
But they all alike had broken the yoke,
  they had burst the bonds.

⁶ Therefore a lion from the forest shall kill them,
  a wolf from the desert shall destroy them.
A leopard is watching against their cities;
  everyone who goes out of them shall be torn in
    pieces—
because their transgressions are many,
  their apostasies are great.

⁷ How can I pardon you?
  Your children have forsaken me,
and have sworn by those who are no gods.
When I fed them to the full,
  they committed adultery
  and trooped to the houses of prostitutes.
⁸ They were well-fed lusty stallions,
  each neighing for his neighbor's wife.
⁹ Shall I not punish them for these things?
                              says the LORD;
  and shall I not bring retribution
    on a nation such as this?

¹⁰ Go up through her vine-rows and destroy,
  but do not make a full end;
strip away her branches,
  for they are not the LORD's.
¹¹ For the house of Israel and the house of Judah
  have been utterly faithless to me,
                              says the LORD.
¹² They have spoken falsely of the LORD,
  and have said, "He will do nothing.
No evil will come upon us,
  and we shall not see sword or famine."
¹³ The prophets are nothing but wind,
  for the word is not in them.
Thus shall it be done to them!

¹⁴ Therefore thus says the LORD, the God of hosts:
Because they*ᵇ* have spoken this word,
I am now making my words in your mouth a fire,
  and this people wood, and the fire shall devour
    them.

a Or the great   b Heb you

Denial

JEREMIAH 5.12–15

"[The Lord] will do nothing" says Israel. "No evil will come upon us." Are there attitudes or circumstances or situations in your own life, or in the life of your family or community, about which you might say dismissively, "God will do nothing!"? Are you prone to think God doesn't care about how you spend money, how you use the authority he has given you, what you eat and drink, or how you spend your time? Do you hear yourself saying, "It doesn't matter. No harm will come to me" in any of these areas?

Take all of the things about which you say "it doesn't matter" to God, and ask God if they matter. Is there something God wants you to attend to? Check it out with a prayer partner or trusted friend who will help you avoid denial or oversensitivity.

See Meeting God in Everyday Life

Boundaries

JEREMIAH 5.17–23

In defiance of the boundaries God has ordained for safety, the Israelites cross the boundaries and trust in military defense, not God (v.17). They serve "foreign gods," not Yahweh (v.19). They commit theft rather than trust God's provision (v.26). They are not just, nor do they defend the orphan and the needy (v.28). The prophets lie and the priests rule by their own authority (v.31). And worse still, the people have no problem with it!

What boundaries do you place around relationships, time, work and money? In what instances are you transgressing your own boundaries? In what ways are your boundaries in danger of being transgressed by others? Name some key areas in your life, and ask the Spirit for a gift of honesty and integrity as you look at your boundaries. Drawing on scripture and your own common sense, define new boundaries, if necessary, that are appropriate for each issue. Pray about them and refer to them at least once a month.

See Meeting God in Everyday Life

15 I am going to bring upon you
　　a nation from far away, O house of Israel,
　　　　　　　　　says the LORD.
It is an enduring nation,
　　it is an ancient nation,
a nation whose language you do not know,
　　nor can you understand what they say.
16 Their quiver is like an open tomb;
　　all of them are mighty warriors.
17 They shall eat up your harvest and your food;
　　they shall eat up your sons and your daughters;
they shall eat up your flocks and your herds;
　　they shall eat up your vines and your fig trees;
they shall destroy with the sword
　　your fortified cities in which you trust.

18 But even in those days, says the LORD, I will not make a full end of you. 19And when your people say, "Why has the LORD our God done all these things to us?" you shall say to them, "As you have forsaken me and served foreign gods in your land, so you shall serve strangers in a land that is not yours."

20 Declare this in the house of Jacob,
　　proclaim it in Judah:
21 Hear this, O foolish and senseless people,
　　who have eyes, but do not see,
　　who have ears, but do not hear.
22 Do you not fear me? says the LORD;
　　Do you not tremble before me?
I placed the sand as a boundary for the sea,
　　a perpetual barrier that it cannot pass;
though the waves toss, they cannot prevail,
　　though they roar, they cannot pass over it.
23 But this people has a stubborn and rebellious heart;
　　they have turned aside and gone away.
24 They do not say in their hearts,
　　"Let us fear the LORD our God,
who gives the rain in its season,
　　the autumn rain and the spring rain,
and keeps for us
　　the weeks appointed for the harvest."
25 Your iniquities have turned these away,
　　and your sins have deprived you of good.
26 For scoundrels are found among my people;
　　they take over the goods of others.
Like fowlers they set a trap;*a*
　　they catch human beings.
27 Like a cage full of birds,
　　their houses are full of treachery;
therefore they have become great and rich,
28 　　they have grown fat and sleek.
They know no limits in deeds of wickedness;
　　they do not judge with justice
the cause of the orphan, to make it prosper,
　　and they do not defend the rights of the needy.
29 Shall I not punish them for these things?
　　　　　　　　　says the LORD,

a Meaning of Heb uncertain

and shall I not bring retribution
on a nation such as this?
30 An appalling and horrible thing
has happened in the land:
31 the prophets prophesy falsely,
and the priests rule as the prophets direct;[a]
my people love to have it so,
but what will you do when the end comes?

The Imminence and Horror of the Invasion

6 Flee for safety, O children of Benjamin,
from the midst of Jerusalem!
Blow the trumpet in Tekoa,
and raise a signal on Beth-haccherem;
for evil looms out of the north,
and great destruction.
2 I have likened daughter Zion
to the loveliest pasture.[b]
3 Shepherds with their flocks shall come against her.
They shall pitch their tents around her;
they shall pasture, all in their places.
4 "Prepare war against her;
up, and let us attack at noon!"
"Woe to us, for the day declines,
the shadows of evening lengthen!"
5 "Up, and let us attack by night,
and destroy her palaces!"
6 For thus says the LORD of hosts:
Cut down her trees;
cast up a siege ramp against Jerusalem.
This is the city that must be punished;[c]
there is nothing but oppression within her.
7 As a well keeps its water fresh,
so she keeps fresh her wickedness;
violence and destruction are heard within her;
sickness and wounds are ever before me.
8 Take warning, O Jerusalem,
or I shall turn from you in disgust,
and make you a desolation,
an uninhabited land.

9 Thus says the LORD of hosts:
Glean[d] thoroughly as a vine
the remnant of Israel;
like a grape-gatherer, pass your hand again
over its branches.

10 To whom shall I speak and give warning,
that they may hear?
See, their ears are closed,[e]
they cannot listen.
The word of the LORD is to them an object of scorn;
they take no pleasure in it.
11 But I am full of the wrath of the LORD;
I am weary of holding it in.

a Or *rule by their own authority*   b Or *I will destroy daughter Zion, the loveliest pasture*   c Or *the city of license*   d Cn: Heb *They shall glean*   e Heb *are uncircumcised*

Anybody Listening?

JEREMIAH 6.9–10

"To whom shall I speak?" Jeremiah laments. No one is listening. The ears of Israel's people are closed to the "offense" of God's word. But the word persists, calling the people to change their minds, to see things differently—God's way—to see that there *is* sin in the land, that God *is not* honored and that judgment *is* inevitable.

Turn to a section of scripture that you usually edit out of your consciousness. Read something that "offends" you—something that just doesn't seem fair or understandable to you. In what way does it offend you? How might God use it to speak to you? Talk it over with someone in your faith community and pray about it.

See *Meeting God in Scripture*

Which Way?

JEREMIAH 6.13–16

Imagine you are at a cross-roads. You can travel either of two ways. One way is God's way. Through both its green pastures and dark valleys, you can be assured of God's companionship (see Psalm 23). The other way is not God's way, but it is attractive. What is attractive about it? What entices you to step toward it?

Paint or draw a picture of your crossroads, using color and shape to represent what your imagination has seen. Draw the Good Shepherd into the picture. Talk with him about the two ways you could go. Draw yourself on the road you really want to travel. Ask Jesus to lead you in the way that is truth and life.

See Meeting God in Everyday Life

Pour it out on the children in the street,
and on the gatherings of young men as well;
both husband and wife shall be taken,
the old folk and the very aged.

12 Their houses shall be turned over to others,
their fields and wives together;
for I will stretch out my hand
against the inhabitants of the land,
says the LORD.

13 For from the least to the greatest of them,
everyone is greedy for unjust gain;
and from prophet to priest,
everyone deals falsely.

14 They have treated the wound of my people
carelessly,
saying, "Peace, peace,"
when there is no peace.

15 They acted shamefully, they committed
abomination;
yet they were not ashamed,
they did not know how to blush.
Therefore they shall fall among those who fall;
at the time that I punish them, they shall be
overthrown,
says the LORD.

16 Thus says the LORD:
Stand at the crossroads, and look,
and ask for the ancient paths,
where the good way lies; and walk in it,
and find rest for your souls.
But they said, "We will not walk in it."

17 Also I raised up sentinels for you:
"Give heed to the sound of the trumpet!"
But they said, "We will not give heed."

18 Therefore hear, O nations,
and know, O congregation, what will happen to
them.

19 Hear, O earth; I am going to bring disaster on this
people,
the fruit of their schemes,
because they have not given heed to my words;
and as for my teaching, they have rejected it.

20 Of what use to me is frankincense that comes
from Sheba,
or sweet cane from a distant land?
Your burnt offerings are not acceptable,
nor are your sacrifices pleasing to me.

21 Therefore thus says the LORD:
See, I am laying before this people
stumbling blocks against which they shall
stumble;
parents and children together,
neighbor and friend shall perish.

22 Thus says the LORD:
See, a people is coming from the land of the north,
a great nation is stirring from the farthest parts
of the earth.

23 They grasp the bow and the javelin,

they are cruel and have no mercy,
    their sound is like the roaring sea;
they ride on horses,
    equipped like a warrior for battle,
    against you, O daughter Zion!

24 "We have heard news of them,
    our hands fall helpless;
anguish has taken hold of us,
    pain as of a woman in labor.
25 Do not go out into the field,
    or walk on the road;
for the enemy has a sword,
    terror is on every side."

26 O my poor people, put on sackcloth,
    and roll in ashes;
make mourning as for an only child,
    most bitter lamentation:
for suddenly the destroyer
    will come upon us.

27 I have made you a tester and a refiner*a* among my
    people
so that you may know and test their ways.
28 They are all stubbornly rebellious,
    going about with slanders;
they are bronze and iron,
    all of them act corruptly.
29 The bellows blow fiercely,
    the lead is consumed by the fire;
in vain the refining goes on,
    for the wicked are not removed.
30 They are called "rejected silver,"
    for the LORD has rejected them.

Jeremiah Proclaims God's Judgment on the Nation

7 The word that came to Jeremiah from the LORD: ²Stand in the gate of the LORD's house, and proclaim there this word, and say, Hear the word of the LORD, all you people of Judah, you that enter these gates to worship the LORD. ³Thus says the LORD of hosts, the God of Israel: Amend your ways and your doings, and let me dwell with you*b* in this place. ⁴Do not trust in these deceptive words: "This is*c* the temple of the LORD, the temple of the LORD, the temple of the LORD."

5 For if you truly amend your ways and your doings, if you truly act justly one with another, ⁶if you do not oppress the alien, the orphan, and the widow, or shed innocent blood in this place, and if you do not go after other gods to your own hurt, ⁷then I will dwell with you in this place, in the land that I gave of old to your ancestors forever and ever.

8 Here you are, trusting in deceptive words to no avail. ⁹Will you steal, murder, commit adultery, swear falsely, make offerings to Baal, and go after other gods that you have not known, ¹⁰and then come and stand before me in this house, which is called by my name, and say, "We are safe!"—only to go on doing all these abominations? ¹¹Has this house, which is called by my name, become a den of

---

Deceptive Words

JEREMIAH 7.1–10

"This is the temple of the LORD," says Israel, believing that somehow, by saying it, its "magic" will protect them from the reality of God's judgment.

What are the common phrases used in the liturgies and worship services of your faith community? Do you or your friends use any religious catchphrases? Ask someone to tell you what your common phrases are. Make a list of them. Give them a "reality check." Talk to your friends and to a worship leader in your church about any that you feel mask the reality of God. Pray that your speech may be authentic and free of jargon and that it may "set the believers an example in speech" (1 Timothy 4.12).

See Meeting God in Everyday Life

---

a Or *a fortress*   *b* Or *and I will let you dwell*   *c* Heb *They are*

What Is Your Guiding Light—Really?

JEREMIAH 7.21–26

Israel continues to ignore God. The people follow their own inclinations and their own counsel, and they do not turn to God. In their wayward attempts to find guidance, meaning and blessing, they sacrifice their children (32.35) and consult and worship the sun, moon and stars (8.2).

Whom or what do you unthinkingly consult before you consult God? What do you sacrifice (such as money, time or energy) without going to God first? What influences guide you—the share index, the weather, the "stars," the wills of other people? Each morning for the next week, intentionally pray for God's guidance—each moment, each day—in what you do in the situations and relationships you encounter. For each day of the week, write in your calendar, "Your word is a lamp to my feet and a light to my path" (Psalm 119.105).

See Meeting God in Everyday Life

robbers in your sight? You know, I too am watching, says the LORD. [12]Go now to my place that was in Shiloh, where I made my name dwell at first, and see what I did to it for the wickedness of my people Israel. [13]And now, because you have done all these things, says the LORD, and when I spoke to you persistently, you did not listen, and when I called you, you did not answer, [14]therefore I will do to the house that is called by my name, in which you trust, and to the place that I gave to you and to your ancestors, just what I did to Shiloh. [15]And I will cast you out of my sight, just as I cast out all your kinsfolk, all the offspring of Ephraim.

The People's Disobedience

16 As for you, do not pray for this people, do not raise a cry or prayer on their behalf, and do not intercede with me, for I will not hear you. [17]Do you not see what they are doing in the towns of Judah and in the streets of Jerusalem? [18]The children gather wood, the fathers kindle fire, and the women knead dough, to make cakes for the queen of heaven; and they pour out drink offerings to other gods, to provoke me to anger. [19]Is it I whom they provoke? says the LORD. Is it not themselves, to their own hurt? [20]Therefore thus says the Lord GOD: My anger and my wrath shall be poured out on this place, on human beings and animals, on the trees of the field and the fruit of the ground; it will burn and not be quenched.

21 Thus says the LORD of hosts, the God of Israel: Add your burnt offerings to your sacrifices, and eat the flesh. [22]For in the day that I brought your ancestors out of the land of Egypt, I did not speak to them or command them concerning burnt offerings and sacrifices. [23]But this command I gave them, "Obey my voice, and I will be your God, and you shall be my people; and walk only in the way that I command you, so that it may be well with you." [24]Yet they did not obey or incline their ear, but, in the stubbornness of their evil will, they walked in their own counsels, and looked backward rather than forward. [25]From the day that your ancestors came out of the land of Egypt until this day, I have persistently sent all my servants the prophets to them, day after day; [26]yet they did not listen to me, or pay attention, but they stiffened their necks. They did worse than their ancestors did.

27 So you shall speak all these words to them, but they will not listen to you. You shall call to them, but they will not answer you. [28]You shall say to them: This is the nation that did not obey the voice of the LORD their God, and did not accept discipline; truth has perished; it is cut off from their lips.

29   Cut off your hair and throw it away;
        raise a lamentation on the bare heights,[a]
    for the LORD has rejected and forsaken
        the generation that provoked his wrath.

30 For the people of Judah have done evil in my sight, says the LORD; they have set their abominations in the house that is called by my name, defiling it. [31]And they go on building the high place[b] of Topheth, which is in the valley of the son of Hinnom, to burn their sons and their daughters in the fire—which I did not command, nor did it come into my mind. [32]Therefore, the days are surely

a Or *the trails*   *b* Gk Tg: Heb *high places*

coming, says the LORD, when it will no more be called Topheth, or the valley of the son of Hinnom, but the valley of Slaughter: for they will bury in Topheth until there is no more room. ³³The corpses of this people will be food for the birds of the air, and for the animals of the earth; and no one will frighten them away. ³⁴And I will bring to an end the sound of mirth and gladness, the voice of the bride and bridegroom in the cities of Judah and in the streets of Jerusalem; for the land shall become a waste.

8 At that time, says the LORD, the bones of the kings of Judah, the bones of its officials, the bones of the priests, the bones of the prophets, and the bones of the inhabitants of Jerusalem shall be brought out of their tombs; ²and they shall be spread before the sun and the moon and all the host of heaven, which they have loved and served, which they have followed, and which they have inquired of and worshiped; and they shall not be gathered or buried; they shall be like dung on the surface of the ground. ³Death shall be preferred to life by all the remnant that remains of this evil family in all the places where I have driven them, says the LORD of hosts.

The Blind Perversity of the Whole Nation

4   You shall say to them, Thus says the LORD:
    When people fall, do they not get up again?
    If they go astray, do they not turn back?
5   Why then has this people*ᵃ* turned away
    in perpetual backsliding?
  They have held fast to deceit,
    they have refused to return.
6   I have given heed and listened,
    but they do not speak honestly;
  no one repents of wickedness,
    saying, "What have I done!"
  All of them turn to their own course,
    like a horse plunging headlong into battle.
7   Even the stork in the heavens
    knows its times;
  and the turtledove, swallow, and crane*ᵇ*
    observe the time of their coming;
  but my people do not know
    the ordinance of the LORD.

8   How can you say, "We are wise,
    and the law of the LORD is with us,"
  when, in fact, the false pen of the scribes
    has made it into a lie?
9   The wise shall be put to shame,
    they shall be dismayed and taken;
  since they have rejected the word of the LORD,
    what wisdom is in them?
10   Therefore I will give their wives to others
    and their fields to conquerors,
  because from the least to the greatest
    everyone is greedy for unjust gain;
  from prophet to priest
    everyone deals falsely.
11   They have treated the wound of my people
    carelessly,

At What Cost?

JEREMIAH 8.4–7

God grieves that while even the birds know how to regulate their lives, people don't do what they should naturally do—they don't get up when they fall down, nor do they turn back when they have turned away.

While in your prayer space, sketch a history of your life with God, focusing on the times you have turned away from God. Write down key words that summarize what it cost you to do so. Put yourself at God's mercy, confess your rejection of him and ask God to "renew you in his love" (Zephaniah 3.17). Put a small "stone of memorial" in a special place to remind you daily to turn back to God.

See Meeting God in Everyday Life

---

a One Ms Gk: MT *this people, Jerusalem.*   *b* Meaning of Heb uncertain

Where Is the Healing?

JEREMIAH 8.18–22

Jeremiah weeps for his people. He loves his country. At great personal cost he has declared the hard word, and no one has paid any attention. And yet the people are hurting as a result of their rejection of God! Joy is gone and grief prevails. Where is healing? Has Gilead no balm?

Do you know someone who loves people and grieves about the suffering of others? Who is a supplier of "balm" in your community? Lest their eyes be a "fountain of tears" (9.1), write them a simple letter of encouragement and offer any practical support that you can give them.

See Meeting God in Community

saying, "Peace, peace,"
    when there is no peace.
12 They acted shamefully, they committed
        abomination;
    yet they were not at all ashamed,
        they did not know how to blush.
    Therefore they shall fall among those who fall;
        at the time when I punish them, they shall be
        overthrown,
                    says the LORD.
13 When I wanted to gather them, says the LORD,
        there are[a] no grapes on the vine,
        nor figs on the fig tree;
    even the leaves are withered,
        and what I gave them has passed away from
        them.[b]

14 Why do we sit still?
    Gather together, let us go into the fortified cities
        and perish there;
    for the LORD our God has doomed us to perish,
        and has given us poisoned water to drink,
        because we have sinned against the LORD.
15 We look for peace, but find no good,
        for a time of healing, but there is terror instead.

16 The snorting of their horses is heard from Dan;
        at the sound of the neighing of their stallions
        the whole land quakes.
    They come and devour the land and all that fills it,
        the city and those who live in it.
17 See, I am letting snakes loose among you,
        adders that cannot be charmed,
        and they shall bite you,
                    says the LORD.

The Prophet Mourns for the People
18 My joy is gone, grief is upon me,
        my heart is sick.
19 Hark, the cry of my poor people
        from far and wide in the land:
    "Is the LORD not in Zion?
        Is her King not in her?"
    ("Why have they provoked me to anger with their
        images,
        with their foreign idols?")
20 "The harvest is past, the summer is ended,
        and we are not saved."
21 For the hurt of my poor people I am hurt,
        I mourn, and dismay has taken hold of me.

22 Is there no balm in Gilead?
        Is there no physician there?
    Why then has the health of my poor people
        not been restored?

9[c] O that my head were a spring of water,
        and my eyes a fountain of tears,
    so that I might weep day and night

a Or *I will make an end of them, says the* LORD. *There are*   *b* Meaning of Heb uncertain   *c* Ch 8.23 in Heb

for the slain of my poor people!
2*a* O that I had in the desert
    a traveler's lodging place,
that I might leave my people
    and go away from them!
For they are all adulterers,
    a band of traitors.

3 They bend their tongues like bows;
    they have grown strong in the land for
        falsehood, and not for truth;
for they proceed from evil to evil,
    and they do not know me, says the LORD.

4 Beware of your neighbors,
    and put no trust in any of your kin;*b*
for all your kin*c* are supplanters,
    and every neighbor goes around like a slanderer.
5 They all deceive their neighbors,
    and no one speaks the truth;
they have taught their tongues to speak lies;
    they commit iniquity and are too weary to
        repent.*d*
6 Oppression upon oppression, deceit*e* upon deceit!
    They refuse to know me, says the LORD.

7 Therefore thus says the LORD of hosts:
    I will now refine and test them,
        for what else can I do with my sinful people?*f*
8 Their tongue is a deadly arrow;
    it speaks deceit through the mouth.
They all speak friendly words to their neighbors,
    but inwardly are planning to lay an ambush.
9 Shall I not punish them for these things? says the
        LORD;
    and shall I not bring retribution
      on a nation such as this?

10 Take up*g* weeping and wailing for the mountains,
    and a lamentation for the pastures of the
        wilderness,
because they are laid waste so that no one passes
        through,
    and the lowing of cattle is not heard;
both the birds of the air and the animals
    have fled and are gone.
11 I will make Jerusalem a heap of ruins,
    a lair of jackals;
and I will make the towns of Judah a desolation,
    without inhabitant.

12 Who is wise enough to understand this? To whom has the mouth of the LORD spoken, so that they may declare it? Why is the land ruined and laid waste like a wilderness, so that no one passes through? 13And the LORD says: Because they have forsaken my law that I set before them, and have not obeyed my voice, or walked in accordance with it, 14but

---

a Ch 9.1 in Heb   *b* Heb *in a brother*   *c* Heb *for every brother*
d Cn Compare Gk: Heb *they weary themselves with iniquity.* 6*Your dwelling*
e Cn: Heb *Your dwelling in the midst of deceit*   *f* Or *my poor people*
g Gk Syr: Heb *I will take up*

What More Can Be Done?

JEREMIAH 9.5–9

In Israel no one was safe. Because the people consistently rejected God and God's ways, they have created a society in which no one trusts or honors others. The result is abuse, and abuse leads to the breakdown of society.

And what of your community? How safe is it? What about it makes you weep? Meet with a friend and walk some streets in your neighborhood—drive through your community if it is rural. Bless the houses, the people you see and the ground you are on by calling on the name of the Lord and being a bearer of God's presence into places where God may not normally be welcomed.

See Meeting God in Service

Boast Boldly

JEREMIAH 9.23–24

Gather some friends. Go around the group and talk about things each person is grateful for. In particular mention ways in which God has helped each of you. Make notes of what is said or encourage each person to keep mental notes of what is said. In prayer together give thanks for one another and what each one can, in God's grace, "boast in." Considering all the good things God has done for each of you, let your soul "boast in the LORD" (Psalm 34.2). Talk together and find some tangible way of "boasting" in God.

See Meeting God in Community

have stubbornly followed their own hearts and have gone after the Baals, as their ancestors taught them. [15]Therefore thus says the LORD of hosts, the God of Israel: I am feeding this people with wormwood, and giving them poisonous water to drink. [16]I will scatter them among nations that neither they nor their ancestors have known; and I will send the sword after them, until I have consumed them.

The People Mourn in Judgment

17   Thus says the LORD of hosts:
    Consider, and call for the mourning women to
        come;
      send for the skilled women to come;
18   let them quickly raise a dirge over us,
      so that our eyes may run down with tears,
      and our eyelids flow with water.
19   For a sound of wailing is heard from Zion:
      "How we are ruined!
      We are utterly shamed,
    because we have left the land,
      because they have cast down our dwellings."

20   Hear, O women, the word of the LORD,
      and let your ears receive the word of his mouth;
    teach to your daughters a dirge,
      and each to her neighbor a lament.
21   "Death has come up into our windows,
      it has entered our palaces,
    to cut off the children from the streets
      and the young men from the squares."
22   Speak! Thus says the LORD:
    "Human corpses shall fall
      like dung upon the open field,
    like sheaves behind the reaper,
      and no one shall gather them."

23 Thus says the LORD: Do not let the wise boast in their wisdom, do not let the mighty boast in their might, do not let the wealthy boast in their wealth; [24]but let those who boast boast in this, that they understand and know me, that I am the LORD; I act with steadfast love, justice, and righteousness in the earth, for in these things I delight, says the LORD.

25 The days are surely coming, says the LORD, when I will attend to all those who are circumcised only in the foreskin: [26]Egypt, Judah, Edom, the Ammonites, Moab, and all those with shaven temples who live in the desert. For all these nations are uncircumcised, and all the house of Israel is uncircumcised in heart.

Idolatry Has Brought Ruin on Israel

10 Hear the word that the LORD speaks to you, O house of Israel. [2]Thus says the LORD:
  Do not learn the way of the nations,
    or be dismayed at the signs of the heavens;
    for the nations are dismayed at them.
3   For the customs of the peoples are false:
    a tree from the forest is cut down,
      and worked with an ax by the hands of an artisan;
4   people deck it with silver and gold;

they fasten it with hammer and nails
    so that it cannot move.
5 Their idols[a] are like scarecrows in a cucumber field,
    and they cannot speak;
they have to be carried,
    for they cannot walk.
Do not be afraid of them,
    for they cannot do evil,
    nor is it in them to do good.

6 There is none like you, O Lord;
    you are great, and your name is great in might.
7 Who would not fear you, O King of the nations?
    For that is your due;
among all the wise ones of the nations
    and in all their kingdoms
    there is no one like you.
8 They are both stupid and foolish;
    the instruction given by idols
    is no better than wood![b]
9 Beaten silver is brought from Tarshish,
    and gold from Uphaz.
They are the work of the artisan and of the hands
        of the goldsmith;
    their clothing is blue and purple;
    they are all the product of skilled workers.
10 But the Lord is the true God;
    he is the living God and the everlasting King.
At his wrath the earth quakes,
    and the nations cannot endure his indignation.

11 Thus shall you say to them: The gods who did not make the heavens and the earth shall perish from the earth and from under the heavens.[c]

12 It is he who made the earth by his power,
    who established the world by his wisdom,
    and by his understanding stretched out the
        heavens.
13 When he utters his voice, there is a tumult of
        waters in the heavens,
    and he makes the mist rise from the ends of the
        earth.
He makes lightnings for the rain,
    and he brings out the wind from his storehouses.
14 Everyone is stupid and without knowledge;
    goldsmiths are all put to shame by their idols;
for their images are false,
    and there is no breath in them.
15 They are worthless, a work of delusion;
    at the time of their punishment they shall perish.
16 Not like these is the Lord,[d] the portion of Jacob,
    for he is the one who formed all things,
and Israel is the tribe of his inheritance;
    the Lord of hosts is his name.

The Coming Exile

17 Gather up your bundle from the ground,

The Lord Is God!

JEREMIAH 10.7–10

"No man ever saw God and lived; and yet I shall not live till I see God, and when I have seen him I shall never die. What have I ever seen in this world that hath been truly the same thing that it seemed to me? . . . As he that fears God fears nothing else, so he that sees God sees everything else. When we shall see God as he is, we shall see all things as they are, for that is their essence, as they conduce to his glory. We shall be no more deluded with outward appearances, for when this sight which we intend here comes, there will be no delusory things to be seen. All that we have made as though we saw in this world will be vanished, and I shall see nothing but God and what is in him, and I shall see him in the *flesh.*"

—JOHN DONNE,
Easter Day Sermon

See Meeting God in Worship

Covenant Keeping

JEREMIAH 11.1–8

Because promises can be easier to make than to keep, consider the covenants you have made. Make a list of them and write down the vows you made in each case. What vows were made to you? Choose some symbolic object to represent each covenant and place them before you in your prayer space. Hold each object in turn and pray for yourself in relation to each covenant. Pray for others involved. Now reflect on God's faithfulness and sing or recite:

"Great is your faithfulness,
    O God my Father,
you have fulfilled all your
        promise to me;
you never fail and your love
        is unchanging
all you have been you
        forever will be.
Great is your faithfulness."

                    —T. O. CHISHOLM

See Meeting God in Community

O you who live under siege!
¹⁸ For thus says the LORD:
I am going to sling out the inhabitants of the land
        at this time,
and I will bring distress on them,
        so that they shall feel it.

¹⁹ Woe is me because of my hurt!
        My wound is severe.
But I said, "Truly this is my punishment,
        and I must bear it."
²⁰ My tent is destroyed,
        and all my cords are broken;
my children have gone from me,
        and they are no more;
there is no one to spread my tent again,
        and to set up my curtains.
²¹ For the shepherds are stupid,
        and do not inquire of the LORD;
therefore they have not prospered,
        and all their flock is scattered.

²² Hear, a noise! Listen, it is coming—
        a great commotion from the land of the north
to make the cities of Judah a desolation,
        a lair of jackals.

²³ I know, O LORD, that the way of human beings is
        not in their control,
        that mortals as they walk cannot direct their steps.
²⁴ Correct me, O LORD, but in just measure;
        not in your anger, or you will bring me to nothing.

²⁵ Pour out your wrath on the nations that do not
        know you,
        and on the peoples that do not call on your name;
for they have devoured Jacob;
        they have devoured him and consumed him,
        and have laid waste his habitation.

Israel and Judah Have Broken the Covenant

11 The word that came to Jeremiah from the LORD: ²Hear the words of this covenant, and speak to the people of Judah and the inhabitants of Jerusalem. ³You shall say to them, Thus says the LORD, the God of Israel: Cursed be anyone who does not heed the words of this covenant, ⁴which I commanded your ancestors when I brought them out of the land of Egypt, from the iron-smelter, saying, Listen to my voice, and do all that I command you. So shall you be my people, and I will be your God, ⁵that I may perform the oath that I swore to your ancestors, to give them a land flowing with milk and honey, as at this day. Then I answered, "So be it, LORD."

6 And the LORD said to me: Proclaim all these words in the cities of Judah, and in the streets of Jerusalem: Hear the words of this covenant and do them. ⁷For I solemnly warned your ancestors when I brought them up out of the land of Egypt, warning them persistently, even to this day, saying, Obey my voice. ⁸Yet they did not obey or incline their ear, but everyone walked in the stubbornness of an

evil will. So I brought upon them all the words of this covenant, which I commanded them to do, but they did not.

9 And the LORD said to me: Conspiracy exists among the people of Judah and the inhabitants of Jerusalem. ¹⁰They have turned back to the iniquities of their ancestors of old, who refused to heed my words; they have gone after other gods to serve them; the house of Israel and the house of Judah have broken the covenant that I made with their ancestors. ¹¹Therefore, thus says the LORD, assuredly I am going to bring disaster upon them that they cannot escape; though they cry out to me, I will not listen to them. ¹²Then the cities of Judah and the inhabitants of Jerusalem will go and cry out to the gods to whom they make offerings, but they will never save them in the time of their trouble. ¹³For your gods have become as many as your towns, O Judah; and as many as the streets of Jerusalem are the altars to shame you have set up, altars to make offerings to Baal.

14 As for you, do not pray for this people, or lift up a cry or prayer on their behalf, for I will not listen when they call to me in the time of their trouble. ¹⁵What right has my beloved in my house, when she has done vile deeds? Can vows*a* and sacrificial flesh avert your doom? Can you then exult? ¹⁶The LORD once called you, "A green olive tree, fair with goodly fruit"; but with the roar of a great tempest he will set fire to it, and its branches will be consumed. ¹⁷The LORD of hosts, who planted you, has pronounced evil against you, because of the evil that the house of Israel and the house of Judah have done, provoking me to anger by making offerings to Baal.

Jeremiah's Life Threatened

18　It was the LORD who made it known to me, and I
　　　knew;
　　　then you showed me their evil deeds.
19　But I was like a gentle lamb
　　　led to the slaughter.
　　And I did not know it was against me
　　　that they devised schemes, saying,
　　"Let us destroy the tree with its fruit,
　　　let us cut him off from the land of the living,
　　　so that his name will no longer be remembered!"
20　But you, O LORD of hosts, who judge righteously,
　　　who try the heart and the mind,
　　let me see your retribution upon them,
　　　for to you I have committed my cause.

21　Therefore thus says the LORD concerning the people of Anathoth, who seek your life, and say, "You shall not prophesy in the name of the LORD, or you will die by our hand"—²²therefore thus says the LORD of hosts: I am going to punish them; the young men shall die by the sword; their sons and their daughters shall die by famine; ²³and not even a remnant shall be left of them. For I will bring disaster upon the people of Anathoth, the year of their punishment.

Jeremiah Complains to God

12　You will be in the right, O LORD,
　　　　when I lay charges against you;
　　　　but let me put my case to you.
　　　Why does the way of the guilty prosper?

a Gk: Heb *Can many*

Those Who Are Not "for" You

JEREMIAH 11.18–23

People from Jeremiah's hometown were so incensed by his words that they wanted to end his life. Ask yourself, "Who is against me?" See their faces. Name their names aloud. What are your feelings about them? Listen to the internal dialogue you might be having with them. Sense your own vulnerability— and your power to hurt them. Breathe several slow, deep breaths and welcome God into your thoughts. Slowly name each person before God, asking, "Lord, what do you think of _____?" Confess your fears and your complaints against them. Pray for God's justice and mercy to deal with them. With God's Spirit renewing yours, what unobtrusive act of kindness can you do for someone who is not "for" you?

See Meeting God in Prayer

Reaping Thorns

JEREMIAH 12.7–13

In 1944, while World War II was raging, preacher William Bower Black of St. David's Church, Auckland, New Zealand, proclaimed these words: "We must not dare lightly to assume that everything will come out all right. God does let His children wreck their boats, and our whole modern civilization may wreck itself. If it refuses to give God His rightful place, and is contemptuous of His holy law, that very law will be its destruction . . . Have we any right to believe that God will say anything less to us than he said to Israel long ago: 'You only have I known of all the families of the earth, *therefore* will I punish you for all your iniquities'?" (William Bower Black, *Thy Steadfast Hills*).

Beginning with the prayer "Lord, teach us to pray" (Luke 11.1), pray for our modern civilization. Pray for the leaders of the nation. Pray for its corporations and institutions. Pray for its citizens that we may not be abandoned "into the hands of [our] enemies."

See Meeting God in Prayer

Why do all who are treacherous thrive?
2 You plant them, and they take root;
 they grow and bring forth fruit;
 you are near in their mouths
 yet far from their hearts.
3 But you, O Lord, know me;
 You see me and test me—my heart is with you.
 Pull them out like sheep for the slaughter,
 and set them apart for the day of slaughter.
4 How long will the land mourn,
 and the grass of every field wither?
 For the wickedness of those who live in it
 the animals and the birds are swept away,
 and because people said, "He is blind to our
 ways."[a]

God Replies to Jeremiah

5 If you have raced with foot-runners and they have
 wearied you,
 how will you compete with horses?
 And if in a safe land you fall down,
 how will you fare in the thickets of the Jordan?
6 For even your kinsfolk and your own family,
 even they have dealt treacherously with you;
 they are in full cry after you;
 do not believe them,
 though they speak friendly words to you.

7 I have forsaken my house,
 I have abandoned my heritage;
 I have given the beloved of my heart
 into the hands of her enemies.
8 My heritage has become to me
 like a lion in the forest;
 she has lifted up her voice against me—
 therefore I hate her.
9 Is the hyena greedy[b] for my heritage at my
 command?
 Are the birds of prey all around her?
 Go, assemble all the wild animals;
 bring them to devour her.
10 Many shepherds have destroyed my vineyard,
 they have trampled down my portion,
 they have made my pleasant portion
 a desolate wilderness.
11 They have made it a desolation;
 desolate, it mourns to me.
 The whole land is made desolate,
 but no one lays it to heart.
12 Upon all the bare heights[c] in the desert
 spoilers have come;
 for the sword of the Lord devours
 from one end of the land to the other;
 no one shall be safe.
13 They have sown wheat and have reaped thorns,
 they have tired themselves out but profit nothing.
 They shall be ashamed of their[d] harvests
 because of the fierce anger of the Lord.

a Gk: Heb *to our future*   b Cn: Heb *Is the hyena, the bird of prey*
c Or *the trails*   d Heb *your*

14 Thus says the Lord concerning all my evil neighbors who touch the heritage that I have given my people Israel to inherit: I am about to pluck them up from their land, and I will pluck up the house of Judah from among them. ¹⁵And after I have plucked them up, I will again have compassion on them, and I will bring them again to their heritage and to their land, everyone of them. ¹⁶And then, if they will diligently learn the ways of my people, to swear by my name, "As the Lord lives," as they taught my people to swear by Baal, then they shall be built up in the midst of my people. ¹⁷But if any nation will not listen, then I will completely uproot it and destroy it, says the Lord.

The Linen Loincloth

13 Thus said the Lord to me, "Go and buy yourself a linen loincloth, and put it on your loins, but do not dip it in water." ²So I bought a loincloth according to the word of the Lord, and put it on my loins. ³And the word of the Lord came to me a second time, saying, ⁴"Take the loincloth that you bought and are wearing, and go now to the Euphrates,ᵃ and hide it there in a cleft of the rock." ⁵So I went, and hid it by the Euphrates,ᵇ as the Lord commanded me. ⁶And after many days the Lord said to me, "Go now to the Euphrates,ᵃ and take from there the loincloth that I commanded you to hide there." ⁷Then I went to the Euphrates,ᵃ and dug, and I took the loincloth from the place where I had hidden it. But now the loincloth was ruined; it was good for nothing.

8 Then the word of the Lord came to me: ⁹Thus says the Lord: Just so I will ruin the pride of Judah and the great pride of Jerusalem. ¹⁰This evil people, who refuse to hear my words, who stubbornly follow their own will and have gone after other gods to serve them and worship them, shall be like this loincloth, which is good for nothing. ¹¹For as the loincloth clings to one's loins, so I made the whole house of Israel and the whole house of Judah cling to me, says the Lord, in order that they might be for me a people, a name, a praise, and a glory. But they would not listen.

Symbol of the Wine-Jars

12 You shall speak to them this word: Thus says the Lord, the God of Israel: Every wine-jar should be filled with wine. And they will say to you, "Do you think we do not know that every wine-jar should be filled with wine?" ¹³Then you shall say to them: Thus says the Lord: I am about to fill all the inhabitants of this land—the kings who sit on David's throne, the priests, the prophets, and all the inhabitants of Jerusalem—with drunkenness. ¹⁴And I will dash them one against another, parents and children together, says the Lord. I will not pity or spare or have compassion when I destroy them.

Exile Threatened

15 Hear and give ear; do not be haughty,
   for the Lord has spoken.
16 Give glory to the Lord your God
   before he brings darkness,
 and before your feet stumble
   on the mountains at twilight;

A Linen Loincloth

JEREMIAH 13.1–11

How close are you to God today? As close as your clothing is to you? God says, "I made the whole house of Israel and the whole house of Judah cling to me . . . that they might be for me a people, a name, a praise, and a glory."

As a reminder of God's presence and God's desire to be close to you, select an article of close-fitting clothing. You might lift it before God and pray aloud, asking God to bless it. Wear it for the day as a reminder of God's desire to stay close to you. When you take it off, thank God for staying close.

See Meeting God in Everyday Life

ᵃ Or to Parah; Heb perath   ᵇ Or by Parah; Heb perath

The Mark of Forgiveness

JEREMIAH 14.1–9

Every action has consequences. Through both indifference and active choice, Israel has ignored God and now faces the consequences. Jerusalem will be devastated, its citizens exiled and the land left to perish in drought.

How do you react to this passage in light of Jesus' words to a paralyzed man, "Friend, your sins are forgiven" (Luke 5.20)? The apostle Paul says to us, "There is therefore now no condemnation for those who are in Christ Jesus" (Romans 8.1). What have been the consequences of your less-than-honorable actions? Place a bowl of water before you. Bring to Jesus any guilt or shame that you feel. Ask for forgiveness—and for the grace to forgive yourself. As a reminder of your baptism, put some water on your head and say, "I belong to Jesus Christ." Mark the inside of your palm with a small cross. For the rest of the day let it be a reminder of the mark of Jesus' forgiveness.

See Meeting God in Worship

while you look for light,
　　he turns it into gloom
　　and makes it deep darkness.
17 But if you will not listen,
　　my soul will weep in secret for your pride;
　　my eyes will weep bitterly and run down with tears,
　　because the LORD's flock has been taken captive.

18 Say to the king and the queen mother:
　　"Take a lowly seat,
　　for your beautiful crown
　　　has come down from your head."*a*
19 The towns of the Negeb are shut up
　　with no one to open them;
　　all Judah is taken into exile,
　　wholly taken into exile.

20 Lift up your eyes and see
　　those who come from the north.
　　Where is the flock that was given you,
　　　your beautiful flock?
21 What will you say when they set as head over you
　　those whom you have trained
　　　to be your allies?
　　Will not pangs take hold of you,
　　　like those of a woman in labor?
22 And if you say in your heart,
　　　"Why have these things come upon me?"
　　it is for the greatness of your iniquity
　　　that your skirts are lifted up,
　　　and you are violated.
23 Can Ethiopians*b* change their skin
　　or leopards their spots?
　　Then also you can do good
　　　who are accustomed to do evil.
24 I will scatter you*c* like chaff
　　driven by the wind from the desert.
25 This is your lot,
　　　the portion I have measured out to you, says the
　　　　LORD,
　　because you have forgotten me
　　　and trusted in lies.
26 I myself will lift up your skirts over your face,
　　　and your shame will be seen.
27 I have seen your abominations,
　　　your adulteries and neighings, your shameless
　　　　prostitutions
　　　on the hills of the countryside.
　　Woe to you, O Jerusalem!
　　　How long will it be
　　　　before you are made clean?

The Great Drought

14 The word of the LORD that came to Jeremiah concerning the drought:
2 Judah mourns
　　and her gates languish;
　　they lie in gloom on the ground,

a Gk Syr Vg: Meaning of Heb uncertain　　*b* Or *Nubians*; Heb *Cushites*
c Heb *them*

and the cry of Jerusalem goes up.
3 Her nobles send their servants for water;
    they come to the cisterns,
they find no water,
    they return with their vessels empty.
They are ashamed and dismayed
    and cover their heads,
4 because the ground is cracked.
    Because there has been no rain on the land
the farmers are dismayed;
    they cover their heads.
5 Even the doe in the field forsakes her newborn fawn
    because there is no grass.
6 The wild asses stand on the bare heights,[a]
    they pant for air like jackals;
their eyes fail
    because there is no herbage.

7 Although our iniquities testify against us,
    act, O LORD, for your name's sake;
our apostasies indeed are many,
    and we have sinned against you.
8 O hope of Israel,
    its savior in time of trouble,
why should you be like a stranger in the land,
    like a traveler turning aside for the night?
9 Why should you be like someone confused,
    like a mighty warrior who cannot give help?
Yet you, O LORD, are in the midst of us,
    and we are called by your name;
    do not forsake us!

10 Thus says the LORD concerning this people:
Truly they have loved to wander,
    they have not restrained their feet;
therefore the LORD does not accept them,
    now he will remember their iniquity
    and punish their sins.

11 The LORD said to me: Do not pray for the welfare of this people. 12 Although they fast, I do not hear their cry, and although they offer burnt offering and grain offering, I do not accept them; but by the sword, by famine, and by pestilence I consume them.

Denunciation of Lying Prophets

13 Then I said: "Ah, Lord GOD! Here are the prophets saying to them, 'You shall not see the sword, nor shall you have famine, but I will give you true peace in this place.'" 14 And the LORD said to me: The prophets are prophesying lies in my name; I did not send them, nor did I command them or speak to them. They are prophesying to you a lying vision, worthless divination, and the deceit of their own minds. 15 Therefore thus says the LORD concerning the prophets who prophesy in my name though I did not send them, and who say, "Sword and famine shall not come on this land": By sword and famine those prophets shall be consumed. 16 And the people to whom they prophesy shall be thrown out into the streets of Jerusalem, victims of

Where Are You?

JEREMIAH 14.7–9

"So when we think of the absence of God, is it not worthwhile to ask ourselves whom we blame for it? We always blame God, we always accuse Him, either straight to His face or in front of people, of being absent, of never being there when He is needed, never answering when He is addressed. At times we are more 'pious' (very much in quotes), and we say piously 'God is testing my patience, my faith, my humility.' We find all sorts of ways of turning God's judgment on us into a new way of pleasing ourselves. We are so patient that we can put up even with God!"

—ARCHBISHOP ANTHONY BLOOM,
A School for Prayer

See Meeting God in Worship

Congruence

JEREMIAH 14.19–15.1

"We acknowledge our wickedness, O Lord." *That* sounds like a genuine repentance. "Can any idols of the nations bring rain? . . . Is it not you, O LORD our God?" And *that* sounds like a genuine statement of faith. But where is the change in behavior? "Send them out of my sight, and let them go!" says God.

Are your prayers and your statements about faith congruent with your behavior? To help close the gap between your faith and your behavior, ask God to fill you with his Spirit. In each of the next nine days, focus on living one aspect of the fruit of the Spirit mentioned in Galatians 5.22–23. At the end of each day, review and journal your experience of seeking to live the fruit of the Spirit.

See Meeting God in Everyday Life

famine and sword. There shall be no one to bury them—themselves, their wives, their sons, and their daughters. For I will pour out their wickedness upon them.

17 You shall say to them this word:
  Let my eyes run down with tears night and day,
    and let them not cease,
  for the virgin daughter—my people—is struck
      down with a crushing blow,
    with a very grievous wound.
18 If I go out into the field,
    look—those killed by the sword!
  And if I enter the city,
    look—those sick with*a* famine!
  For both prophet and priest ply their trade
      throughout the land,
    and have no knowledge.

The People Plead for Mercy

19 Have you completely rejected Judah?
    Does your heart loathe Zion?
  Why have you struck us down
    so that there is no healing for us?
  We look for peace, but find no good;
    for a time of healing, but there is terror instead.
20 We acknowledge our wickedness, O LORD,
    the iniquity of our ancestors,
    for we have sinned against you.
21 Do not spurn us, for your name's sake;
    do not dishonor your glorious throne;
  remember and do not break your covenant
      with us.
22 Can any idols of the nations bring rain?
    Or can the heavens give showers?
  Is it not you, O LORD our God?
    We set our hope on you,
    for it is you who do all this.

Punishment Is Inevitable

15 Then the LORD said to me: Though Moses and Samuel stood before me, yet my heart would not turn toward this people. Send them out of my sight, and let them go! ²And when they say to you, "Where shall we go?" you shall say to them: Thus says the LORD:
  Those destined for pestilence, to pestilence,
    and those destined for the sword, to the sword;
  those destined for famine, to famine,
    and those destined for captivity, to captivity.
³And I will appoint over them four kinds of destroyers, says the LORD: the sword to kill, the dogs to drag away, and the birds of the air and the wild animals of the earth to devour and destroy. ⁴I will make them a horror to all the kingdoms of the earth because of what King Manasseh son of Hezekiah of Judah did in Jerusalem.

5 Who will have pity on you, O Jerusalem,
    or who will bemoan you?
  Who will turn aside
    to ask about your welfare?

a Heb *look—the sicknesses of*

⁶ You have rejected me, says the LORD,
  you are going backward;
so I have stretched out my hand against you and
      destroyed you—
  I am weary of relenting.
⁷ I have winnowed them with a winnowing fork
    in the gates of the land;
  I have bereaved them, I have destroyed my people;
    they did not turn from their ways.
⁸ Their widows became more numerous
    than the sand of the seas;
  I have brought against the mothers of youths
    a destroyer at noonday;
  I have made anguish and terror
    fall upon her suddenly.
⁹ She who bore seven has languished;
    she has swooned away;
  her sun went down while it was yet day;
    she has been shamed and disgraced.
  And the rest of them I will give to the sword
    before their enemies,
                              says the LORD.

Jeremiah Complains Again and Is Reassured

10 Woe is me, my mother, that you ever bore me, a man of strife and contention to the whole land! I have not lent, nor have I borrowed, yet all of them curse me. ¹¹The LORD said: Surely I have intervened in your life^a for good, surely I have imposed enemies on you in a time of trouble and in a time of distress.^b ¹²Can iron and bronze break iron from the north?

13 Your wealth and your treasures I will give as plunder, without price, for all your sins, throughout all your territory. ¹⁴I will make you serve your enemies in a land that you do not know, for in my anger a fire is kindled that shall burn forever.
¹⁵ O LORD, you know;
    remember me and visit me,
    and bring down retribution for me on my
        persecutors.
  In your forbearance do not take me away;
    know that on your account I suffer insult.
¹⁶ Your words were found, and I ate them,
    and your words became to me a joy
    and the delight of my heart;
  for I am called by your name,
    O LORD, God of hosts.
¹⁷ I did not sit in the company of merrymakers,
    nor did I rejoice;
  under the weight of your hand I sat alone,
    for you had filled me with indignation.
¹⁸ Why is my pain unceasing,
    my wound incurable,
    refusing to be healed?
  Truly, you are to me like a deceitful brook,
    like waters that fail.

¹⁹ Therefore thus says the LORD:
    If you turn back, I will take you back,

The Cost of a Call

JEREMIAH 15.15–18

Jeremiah is experiencing a "Gethsemane." Watch and pray with him. Identify with his anguish. What "cup" would you rather not drink from? What task would you rather let pass? In what ways does your vocation seem too costly at times?

Find a place to write down your responses to the book of Jeremiah, articulating that which is "precious" (v.19), honest and real. Discuss any relevant issues with someone you trust and pray together about them.

See Meeting God in Service

---

^a Heb *intervened with you*   ^b Meaning of Heb uncertain

I Don't Deserve This!

JEREMIAH 16.10–13

When things go wrong—from minor irritations to total disasters—a voice within you protests, "I don't understand! I don't deserve this!"

What has happened to you that leads you to protest like the people of Israel did (v.10)? Has someone done you an injustice? Write about the circumstances. Do you feel you are being punished? That God has looked the other way? How will you react to the situation? Find someone you trust and discuss your thoughts and feelings.

See *Meeting God in Everyday Life*

and you shall stand before me.
If you utter what is precious, and not what is worthless,
you shall serve as my mouth.
It is they who will turn to you,
not you who will turn to them.

20 And I will make you to this people
a fortified wall of bronze;
they will fight against you,
but they shall not prevail over you,
for I am with you
to save you and deliver you,

says the LORD.

21 I will deliver you out of the hand of the wicked,
and redeem you from the grasp of the ruthless.

Jeremiah's Celibacy and Message

16 The word of the LORD came to me: ²You shall not take a wife, nor shall you have sons or daughters in this place. ³For thus says the LORD concerning the sons and daughters who are born in this place, and concerning the mothers who bear them and the fathers who beget them in this land: ⁴They shall die of deadly diseases. They shall not be lamented, nor shall they be buried; they shall become like dung on the surface of the ground. They shall perish by the sword and by famine, and their dead bodies shall become food for the birds of the air and for the wild animals of the earth.

5 For thus says the LORD: Do not enter the house of mourning, or go to lament, or bemoan them; for I have taken away my peace from this people, says the LORD, my steadfast love and mercy. ⁶Both great and small shall die in this land; they shall not be buried, and no one shall lament for them; there shall be no gashing, no shaving of the head for them. ⁷No one shall break bread*ᵃ* for the mourner, to offer comfort for the dead; nor shall anyone give them the cup of consolation to drink for their fathers or their mothers. ⁸You shall not go into the house of feasting to sit with them, to eat and drink. ⁹For thus says the LORD of hosts, the God of Israel: I am going to banish from this place, in your days and before your eyes, the voice of mirth and the voice of gladness, the voice of the bridegroom and the voice of the bride.

10 And when you tell this people all these words, and they say to you, "Why has the LORD pronounced all this great evil against us? What is our iniquity? What is the sin that we have committed against the LORD our God?" ¹¹then you shall say to them: It is because your ancestors have forsaken me, says the LORD, and have gone after other gods and have served and worshiped them, and have forsaken me and have not kept my law; ¹²and because you have behaved worse than your ancestors, for here you are, every one of you, following your stubborn evil will, refusing to listen to me. ¹³Therefore I will hurl you out of this land into a land that neither you nor your ancestors have known, and there you shall serve other gods day and night, for I will show you no favor.

a Two Mss Gk: MT *break for them*

God Will Restore Israel

14 Therefore, the days are surely coming, says the LORD, when it shall no longer be said, "As the LORD lives who brought the people of Israel up out of the land of Egypt," 15but "As the LORD lives who brought the people of Israel up out of the land of the north and out of all the lands where he had driven them." For I will bring them back to their own land that I gave to their ancestors.

16 I am now sending for many fishermen, says the LORD, and they shall catch them; and afterward I will send for many hunters, and they shall hunt them from every mountain and every hill, and out of the clefts of the rocks. 17For my eyes are on all their ways; they are not hidden from my presence, nor is their iniquity concealed from my sight. 18And*a* I will doubly repay their iniquity and their sin, because they have polluted my land with the carcasses of their detestable idols, and have filled my inheritance with their abominations.

19   O LORD, my strength and my stronghold,
     my refuge in the day of trouble,
to you shall the nations come
     from the ends of the earth and say:
Our ancestors have inherited nothing but lies,
     worthless things in which there is no profit.
20   Can mortals make for themselves gods?
     Such are no gods!

21 "Therefore I am surely going to teach them, this time I am going to teach them my power and my might, and they shall know that my name is the LORD."

Judah's Sin and Punishment

17 The sin of Judah is written with an iron pen; with a diamond point it is engraved on the tablet of their hearts, and on the horns of their altars, 2while their children remember their altars and their sacred poles,*b* beside every green tree, and on the high hills, 3on the mountains in the open country. Your wealth and all your treasures I will give for spoil as the price of your sin*c* throughout all your territory. 4By your own act you shall lose the heritage that I gave you, and I will make you serve your enemies in a land that you do not know, for in my anger a fire is kindled*d* that shall burn forever.

5   Thus says the LORD:
   Cursed are those who trust in mere mortals
     and make mere flesh their strength,
     whose hearts turn away from the LORD.
6   They shall be like a shrub in the desert,
     and shall not see when relief comes.
   They shall live in the parched places of the
       wilderness,
     in an uninhabited salt land.

7   Blessed are those who trust in the LORD,
     whose trust is the LORD.

a Gk: Heb *And first*   *b* Heb *Asherim*   *c* Cn: Heb *spoil your high places for sin*   *d* Two Mss Theodotion: *you kindled*

Seek God's Blessing

JEREMIAH 17.5–8

Whose advice do you seek when the going gets tough—a friend, a counselor, a financial consultant, a self-help book? Make a list of your resources of "flesh"—people that you might call on. Rank them according to their usefulness. Now imagine what might happen if you took your tough issue to God and trusted him to help you. What might you expect of God? Pray about it. Keep praying about it. Write down your discoveries in your journal. Watch for the fruit of your prayer—changes within yourself and any evidence of God's action.

See Meeting God in Prayer

Sabbath

JEREMIAH 17.19–27

The Lord instructed Jeremiah to stand by the gate and proclaim the holiness of the sabbath. The people were not to bring loads through the gates of Jerusalem or out of their houses.

What does the sabbath mean to you? Do you ever carry loads into your sabbath time—mental or emotional burdens that might disrupt your time with God? How can you let Jesus Christ carry them for you so that you can worship without distraction (see Matthew 11.28–30)?

See Meeting God in Worship

8 They shall be like a tree planted by water,
   sending out its roots by the stream.
It shall not fear when heat comes,
   and its leaves shall stay green;
in the year of drought it is not anxious,
   and it does not cease to bear fruit.

9 The heart is devious above all else;
   it is perverse—
   who can understand it?
10 I the LORD test the mind
   and search the heart,
to give to all according to their ways,
   according to the fruit of their doings.

11 Like the partridge hatching what it did not lay,
   so are all who amass wealth unjustly;
in mid-life it will leave them,
   and at their end they will prove to be fools.

12 O glorious throne, exalted from the beginning,
   shrine of our sanctuary!
13 O hope of Israel! O LORD!
   All who forsake you shall be put to shame;
those who turn away from you*a* shall be recorded
   in the underworld,*b*
for they have forsaken the fountain of living
   water, the LORD.

Jeremiah Prays for Vindication

14 Heal me, O LORD, and I shall be healed;
   save me, and I shall be saved;
   for you are my praise.
15 See how they say to me,
   "Where is the word of the LORD?
   Let it come!"
16 But I have not run away from being a shepherd*c* in
      your service,
   nor have I desired the fatal day.
You know what came from my lips;
   it was before your face.
17 Do not become a terror to me;
   you are my refuge in the day of disaster;
18 Let my persecutors be shamed,
   but do not let me be shamed;
let them be dismayed,
   but do not let me be dismayed;
bring on them the day of disaster;
   destroy them with double destruction!

Hallow the Sabbath Day

19 Thus said the LORD to me: Go and stand in the People's Gate, by which the kings of Judah enter and by which they go out, and in all the gates of Jerusalem, ²⁰and say to them: Hear the word of the LORD, you kings of Judah, and all Judah, and all the inhabitants of Jerusalem, who enter by these gates. ²¹Thus says the LORD: For the sake of your lives, take care that you do not bear a burden on the sabbath day or bring it in by the gates of Jerusalem. ²²And do

a Heb *me*   *b* Or *in the earth*   *c* Meaning of Heb uncertain

not carry a burden out of your houses on the sabbath or do any work, but keep the sabbath day holy, as I commanded your ancestors. ²³Yet they did not listen or incline their ear; they stiffened their necks and would not hear or receive instruction.

24 But if you listen to me, says the LORD, and bring in no burden by the gates of this city on the sabbath day, but keep the sabbath day holy and do no work on it, ²⁵then there shall enter by the gates of this city kings*ᵃ* who sit on the throne of David, riding in chariots and on horses, they and their officials, the people of Judah and the inhabitants of Jerusalem; and this city shall be inhabited forever. ²⁶And people shall come from the towns of Judah and the places around Jerusalem, from the land of Benjamin, from the Shephelah, from the hill country, and from the Negeb, bringing burnt offerings and sacrifices, grain offerings and frankincense, and bringing thank offerings to the house of the LORD. ²⁷But if you do not listen to me, to keep the sabbath day holy, and to carry in no burden through the gates of Jerusalem on the sabbath day, then I will kindle a fire in its gates; it shall devour the palaces of Jerusalem and shall not be quenched.

The Potter and the Clay

18 The word that came to Jeremiah from the LORD: ²"Come, go down to the potter's house, and there I will let you hear my words." ³So I went down to the potter's house, and there he was working at his wheel. ⁴The vessel he was making of clay was spoiled in the potter's hand, and he reworked it into another vessel, as seemed good to him.

5 Then the word of the LORD came to me: ⁶Can I not do with you, O house of Israel, just as this potter has done? says the LORD. Just like the clay in the potter's hand, so are you in my hand, O house of Israel. ⁷At one moment I may declare concerning a nation or a kingdom, that I will pluck up and break down and destroy it, ⁸but if that nation, concerning which I have spoken, turns from its evil, I will change my mind about the disaster that I intended to bring on it. ⁹And at another moment I may declare concerning a nation or a kingdom that I will build and plant it, ¹⁰but if it does evil in my sight, not listening to my voice, then I will change my mind about the good that I had intended to do to it. ¹¹Now, therefore, say to the people of Judah and the inhabitants of Jerusalem: Thus says the LORD: Look, I am a potter shaping evil against you and devising a plan against you. Turn now, all of you from your evil way, and amend your ways and your doings.

Israel's Stubborn Idolatry

12 But they say, "It is no use! We will follow our own plans, and each of us will act according to the stubbornness of our evil will."

13 Therefore thus says the LORD:
    Ask among the nations:
      Who has heard the like of this?
    The virgin Israel has done
      a most horrible thing.
14 Does the snow of Lebanon leave

The Nation

JEREMIAH 18.1–11

If possible, invite a friend to share this exercise with you. Find some potter's clay or other malleable substance. Hold it and warm it in your hands. Let your fingers and your heart—not your brain—shape a symbol of your nation at its worst. Place it before God and ask God to show mercy to your nation. Crush your clay symbol. Ask the Spirit to anoint your hands and then make a symbol of how God desires your nation to be. Place it before God and ask God to bless your nation. Let your molding medium harden so that it will become your reminder to pray for your nation and the forces that shape it.

See Meeting God in Prayer

My Enemies

JEREMIAH 18.19–23

Who comes to mind under the heading "My Enemies"? What kind of "pit" have they dug for you? Draw a picture of it. Draw yourself in it. Under God's caring eye, write some key words beside your picture that describe what—in your rawest anger—you would like to happen to your "enemies." Do not ignore your honest feelings. When they are fully present, frame them within your mind as you read Luke 6.22–23,27–28. What is Jesus asking of you with regard to your "enemies"? Pray for them as you are able, trying to see them from God's perspective. What action does your prayer require of you?

See Meeting God in Prayer

the crags of Sirion?[a]
   Do the mountain[b] waters run dry,[c]
     the cold flowing streams?
15 But my people have forgotten me,
     they burn offerings to a delusion;
they have stumbled[d] in their ways,
     in the ancient roads,
and have gone into bypaths,
     not the highway,
16 making their land a horror,
     a thing to be hissed at forever.
All who pass by it are horrified
     and shake their heads.
17 Like the wind from the east,
     I will scatter them before the enemy.
I will show them my back, not my face,
     in the day of their calamity.

A Plot against Jeremiah

18 Then they said, "Come, let us make plots against Jeremiah—for instruction shall not perish from the priest, nor counsel from the wise, nor the word from the prophet. Come, let us bring charges against him,[e] and let us not heed any of his words."

19 Give heed to me, O LORD,
     and listen to what my adversaries say!
20 Is evil a recompense for good?
     Yet they have dug a pit for my life.
Remember how I stood before you
     to speak good for them,
     to turn away your wrath from them.
21 Therefore give their children over to famine;
     hurl them out to the power of the sword,
let their wives become childless and widowed.
     May their men meet death by pestilence,
     their youths be slain by the sword in battle.
22 May a cry be heard from their houses,
     when you bring the marauder suddenly upon
        them!
For they have dug a pit to catch me,
     and laid snares for my feet.
23 Yet you, O LORD, know
     all their plotting to kill me.
Do not forgive their iniquity,
     do not blot out their sin from your sight.
Let them be tripped up before you;
     deal with them while you are angry.

The Broken Earthenware Jug

19 Thus said the LORD: Go and buy a potter's earthenware jug. Take with you[f] some of the elders of the people and some of the senior priests, 2and go out to the valley of the son of Hinnom at the entry of the Potsherd Gate, and proclaim there the words that I tell you. 3You shall say: Hear the word of the LORD, O kings of Judah and inhabitants of Jerusalem. Thus says the LORD of hosts, the God

---

a Cn: Heb *of the field*   b Cn: Heb *foreign*   c Cn: Heb *Are . . . plucked up?*   d Gk Syr Vg: Heb *they made them stumble*   e Heb *strike him with the tongue*   f Syr Tg Compare Gk: Heb lacks *take with you*

of Israel: I am going to bring such disaster upon this place that the ears of everyone who hears of it will tingle. ⁴Because the people have forsaken me, and have profaned this place by making offerings in it to other gods whom neither they nor their ancestors nor the kings of Judah have known, and because they have filled this place with the blood of the innocent, ⁵and gone on building the high places of Baal to burn their children in the fire as burnt offerings to Baal, which I did not command or decree, nor did it enter my mind; ⁶therefore the days are surely coming, says the LORD, when this place shall no more be called Topheth, or the valley of the son of Hinnom, but the valley of Slaughter. ⁷And in this place I will make void the plans of Judah and Jerusalem, and will make them fall by the sword before their enemies, and by the hand of those who seek their life. I will give their dead bodies for food to the birds of the air and to the wild animals of the earth. ⁸And I will make this city a horror, a thing to be hissed at; everyone who passes by it will be horrified and will hiss because of all its disasters. ⁹And I will make them eat the flesh of their sons and the flesh of their daughters, and all shall eat the flesh of their neighbors in the siege, and in the distress with which their enemies and those who seek their life afflict them.

10 Then you shall break the jug in the sight of those who go with you, ¹¹and shall say to them: Thus says the LORD of hosts: So will I break this people and this city, as one breaks a potter's vessel, so that it can never be mended. In Topheth they shall bury until there is no more room to bury. ¹²Thus will I do to this place, says the LORD, and to its inhabitants, making this city like Topheth. ¹³And the houses of Jerusalem and the houses of the kings of Judah shall be defiled like the place of Topheth—all the houses upon whose roofs offerings have been made to the whole host of heaven, and libations have been poured out to other gods.

14 When Jeremiah came from Topheth, where the LORD had sent him to prophesy, he stood in the court of the LORD's house and said to all the people: ¹⁵Thus says the LORD of hosts, the God of Israel: I am now bringing upon this city and upon all its towns all the disaster that I have pronounced against it, because they have stiffened their necks, refusing to hear my words.

Jeremiah Persecuted by Pashhur

20 Now the priest Pashhur son of Immer, who was chief officer in the house of the LORD, heard Jeremiah prophesying these things. ²Then Pashhur struck the prophet Jeremiah, and put him in the stocks that were in the upper Benjamin Gate of the house of the LORD. ³The next morning when Pashhur released Jeremiah from the stocks, Jeremiah said to him, The LORD has named you not Pashhur but "Terror-all-around." ⁴For thus says the LORD: I am making you a terror to yourself and to all your friends; and they shall fall by the sword of their enemies while you look on. And I will give all Judah into the hand of the king of Babylon; he shall carry them captive to Babylon, and shall kill them with the sword. ⁵I will give all the wealth of this city, all its gains, all its prized belongings, and all the treasures of the kings of Judah into the hand of their enemies, who shall plunder them, and seize them, and carry them to Babylon. ⁶And you, Pashhur, and all who live in

Terror on Every Side

JEREMIAH 20.1–6

Be seated in a place that feels safe and comfortable. Using the phrase "deliver us from evil" (from the Lord's Prayer), pray for God's protection for yourself and those close to you. In the company of Jesus, your Protector, name your terrors and your greatest fears. Write them down. Focus not on them, but on Jesus, and pray for deliverance from them. Memorize: "The Lord is my helper; I will not be afraid" (Hebrews 13.6). Share with your spiritual adviser, faith companion or a counselor what has happened.

See Meeting God in Prayer

The Pits

JEREMIAH 20.7–18

Jeremiah is experiencing more than a blue mood. He feels that God has deceived him. He wrestles with inner voices that would have him question everything.

Seated in your prayer place, write an honest response to this question: "What do I say to myself when I am 'in the pits'?" Note the dominant themes of your "self-talk" at such times. Now consider what effect your melancholy has on your relationships (you might ask someone), your work, your behavior and your prayer life. What does it mean to be able to declare with Jeremiah, "The LORD is with me like a dread warrior"? How does it help to reaffirm that God can, and will, defend us?

See Meeting God in Everyday Life

your house, shall go into captivity, and to Babylon you shall go; there you shall die, and there you shall be buried, you and all your friends, to whom you have prophesied falsely.

Jeremiah Denounces His Persecutors

7 O LORD, you have enticed me,
  and I was enticed;
you have overpowered me,
  and you have prevailed.
I have become a laughingstock all day long;
  everyone mocks me.
8 For whenever I speak, I must cry out,
  I must shout, "Violence and destruction!"
For the word of the LORD has become for me
  a reproach and derision all day long.
9 If I say, "I will not mention him,
  or speak any more in his name,"
then within me there is something like a burning fire
  shut up in my bones;
I am weary with holding it in,
  and I cannot.
10 For I hear many whispering:
  "Terror is all around!
Denounce him! Let us denounce him!"
  All my close friends
  are watching for me to stumble.
"Perhaps he can be enticed,
  and we can prevail against him,
  and take our revenge on him."
11 But the LORD is with me like a dread warrior;
  therefore my persecutors will stumble,
  and they will not prevail.
They will be greatly shamed,
  for they will not succeed.
Their eternal dishonor
  will never be forgotten.
12 O LORD of hosts, you test the righteous,
  you see the heart and the mind;
let me see your retribution upon them,
  for to you I have committed my cause.

13 Sing to the LORD;
  praise the LORD!
For he has delivered the life of the needy
  from the hands of evildoers.

14 Cursed be the day
  on which I was born!
The day when my mother bore me,
  let it not be blessed!
15 Cursed be the man
  who brought the news to my father, saying,
"A child is born to you, a son,"
  making him very glad.
16 Let that man be like the cities
  that the LORD overthrew without pity;
let him hear a cry in the morning
  and an alarm at noon,
17 because he did not kill me in the womb;
  so my mother would have been my grave,

and her womb forever great.
18 Why did I come forth from the womb
    to see toil and sorrow,
    and spend my days in shame?

Jerusalem Will Fall to Nebuchadrezzar

21 This is the word that came to Jeremiah from the LORD, when King Zedekiah sent to him Pashhur son of Malchiah and the priest Zephaniah son of Maaseiah, saying, 2"Please inquire of the LORD on our behalf, for King Nebuchadrezzar of Babylon is making war against us; perhaps the LORD will perform a wonderful deed for us, as he has often done, and will make him withdraw from us."

3 Then Jeremiah said to them: 4Thus you shall say to Zedekiah: Thus says the LORD, the God of Israel: I am going to turn back the weapons of war that are in your hands and with which you are fighting against the king of Babylon and against the Chaldeans who are besieging you outside the walls; and I will bring them together into the center of this city. 5I myself will fight against you with outstretched hand and mighty arm, in anger, in fury, and in great wrath. 6And I will strike down the inhabitants of this city, both human beings and animals; they shall die of a great pestilence. 7Afterward, says the LORD, I will give King Zedekiah of Judah, and his servants, and the people in this city—those who survive the pestilence, sword, and famine—into the hands of King Nebuchadrezzar of Babylon, into the hands of their enemies, into the hands of those who seek their lives. He shall strike them down with the edge of the sword; he shall not pity them, or spare them, or have compassion.

8 And to this people you shall say: Thus says the LORD: See, I am setting before you the way of life and the way of death. 9Those who stay in this city shall die by the sword, by famine, and by pestilence; but those who go out and surrender to the Chaldeans who are besieging you shall live and shall have their lives as a prize of war. 10For I have set my face against this city for evil and not for good, says the LORD: it shall be given into the hands of the king of Babylon, and he shall burn it with fire.

Message to the House of David

11 To the house of the king of Judah say: Hear the word of the LORD, 12O house of David! Thus says the LORD:
    Execute justice in the morning,
        and deliver from the hand of the oppressor
        anyone who has been robbed,
    or else my wrath will go forth like fire,
        and burn, with no one to quench it,
        because of your evil doings.

13 See, I am against you, O inhabitant of the valley,
        O rock of the plain,

                                                                    says the LORD;
    you who say, "Who can come down against us,
        or who can enter our places of refuge?"
14 I will punish you according to the fruit of your
        doings,

                                                                    says the LORD;
    I will kindle a fire in its forest,
        and it shall devour all that is around it.

Act With Justice and Righteousness!

JEREMIAH 21.11–14

"Every plan, which aims at the welfare of a nation, in defiance of [God's] authority and laws, however apparently wise, will prove to be essentially defective, and, if persisted in, ruinous. The righteous Lord loveth righteousness, and he has engaged to plead the cause and vindicate the wrongs of the oppressed. It is righteousness that exalteth a nation; and wickedness is the present reproach, and will, sooner or later, unless repentance intervene, prove the ruin of any people . . . God forbid that any supposed profit or advantage which we derive from the groans, and agonies, and blood of the poor Africans, should draw down his heavy curse upon all that we might, otherwise, honourably and comfortably possess."

—JOHN NEWTON,
Thoughts Upon the African Slave Trade

See Meeting God in Community

Your Legacy

JEREMIAH 22.14–17

What is the legacy of a "great" national leader? A noble building named for that person—or greater justice and righteousness within the nation? What will be your legacy? Visible achievements—or quiet acts of compassion, fairness and honor?

Imagine you are a journalist. Write your own obituary. Do not write anything negative. Write the kind of obituary you would really love to have written about you—affirming all the good you want to be remembered for. Do not analyze or try to think it through logically. Under the grace of God's smile, just write. Reread it from time to time to see if there is anything you want to change or add. Pray that God will make your remaining years "fruitful."

See Meeting God in Everyday Life

Exhortation to Repent

22 Thus says the LORD: Go down to the house of the king of Judah, and speak there this word, ²and say: Hear the word of the LORD, O King of Judah sitting on the throne of David—you, and your servants, and your people who enter these gates. ³Thus says the LORD: Act with justice and righteousness, and deliver from the hand of the oppressor anyone who has been robbed. And do no wrong or violence to the alien, the orphan, and the widow, or shed innocent blood in this place. ⁴For if you will indeed obey this word, then through the gates of this house shall enter kings who sit on the throne of David, riding in chariots and on horses, they, and their servants, and their people. ⁵But if you will not heed these words, I swear by myself, says the LORD, that this house shall become a desolation. ⁶For thus says the LORD concerning the house of the king of Judah:

You are like Gilead to me,
 like the summit of Lebanon;
but I swear that I will make you a desert,
 an uninhabited city.*ᵃ*
7 I will prepare destroyers against you,
 all with their weapons;
they shall cut down your choicest cedars
 and cast them into the fire.

8 And many nations will pass by this city, and all of them will say one to another, "Why has the LORD dealt in this way with that great city?" ⁹And they will answer, "Because they abandoned the covenant of the LORD their God, and worshiped other gods and served them."

10 Do not weep for him who is dead,
 nor bemoan him;
weep rather for him who goes away,
 for he shall return no more
 to see his native land.

Message to the Sons of Josiah

11 For thus says the LORD concerning Shallum son of King Josiah of Judah, who succeeded his father Josiah, and who went away from this place: He shall return here no more, ¹²but in the place where they have carried him captive he shall die, and he shall never see this land again.

13 Woe to him who builds his house by
  unrighteousness,
 and his upper rooms by injustice;
who makes his neighbors work for nothing,
 and does not give them their wages;
14 who says, "I will build myself a spacious house
 with large upper rooms,"
and who cuts out windows for it,
 paneling it with cedar,
 and painting it with vermilion.
15 Are you a king
 because you compete in cedar?
Did not your father eat and drink
 and do justice and righteousness?
 Then it was well with him.

a Cn: Heb *uninhabited cities*

16 He judged the cause of the poor and needy;
    then it was well.
  Is not this to know me?
    says the LORD.
17 But your eyes and heart
    are only on your dishonest gain,
  for shedding innocent blood,
    and for practicing oppression and violence.
18 Therefore thus says the LORD concerning King Jehoiakim son of Josiah of Judah:
  They shall not lament for him, saying,
    "Alas, my brother!" or "Alas, sister!"
  They shall not lament for him, saying,
    "Alas, lord!" or "Alas, his majesty!"
19 With the burial of a donkey he shall be buried—
    dragged off and thrown out beyond the gates of
      Jerusalem.

20 Go up to Lebanon, and cry out,
    and lift up your voice in Bashan;
  cry out from Abarim,
    for all your lovers are crushed.
21 I spoke to you in your prosperity,
    but you said, "I will not listen."
  This has been your way from your youth,
    for you have not obeyed my voice.
22 The wind shall shepherd all your shepherds,
    and your lovers shall go into captivity;
  then you will be ashamed and dismayed
    because of all your wickedness.
23 O inhabitant of Lebanon,
    nested among the cedars,
  how you will groan*a* when pangs come upon you,
    pain as of a woman in labor!

Judgment on Coniah (Jehoiachin)

24 As I live, says the LORD, even if King Coniah son of Jehoiakim of Judah were the signet ring on my right hand, even from there I would tear you off 25and give you into the hands of those who seek your life, into the hands of those of whom you are afraid, even into the hands of King Nebuchadrezzar of Babylon and into the hands of the Chaldeans. 26I will hurl you and the mother who bore you into another country, where you were not born, and there you shall die. 27But they shall not return to the land to which they long to return.
28 Is this man Coniah a despised broken pot,
    a vessel no one wants?
  Why are he and his offspring hurled out
    and cast away in a land that they do not know?
29 O land, land, land,
    hear the word of the LORD!
30 Thus says the LORD:
  Record this man as childless,
    a man who shall not succeed in his days;
  for none of his offspring shall succeed
    in sitting on the throne of David,
    and ruling again in Judah.

---

a Gk Vg Syr: Heb *will be pitied*

Exile

JEREMIAH 22.24–30

King Coniah and his mother will be handed over to their enemies and exiled.

What is your experience of "exile"? Recall a time when you found yourself among people whose values, culture, way of life and worship were different from your own. Did you wonder if you would ever get "home" again? Write out what you learned about yourself and God through that experience.

See Meeting God in Community

Godly Leadership

JEREMIAH 23.9–19

What grieves you about the church? What has disturbed you about its leadership? What experience have you had of feeling "crushed" by those in authority?

Take these questions to your prayer place. Pray for awareness of the presence of the Good Shepherd. Pray for a particular church leader for a week, that he or she will be characterized by faithfulness to the Lord. Pray that you will be a worthy servant of God in whatever position of power you serve.

See Meeting God in Service

Restoration after Exile

23 Woe to the shepherds who destroy and scatter the sheep of my pasture! says the LORD. ²Therefore thus says the LORD, the God of Israel, concerning the shepherds who shepherd my people: It is you who have scattered my flock, and have driven them away, and you have not attended to them. So I will attend to you for your evil doings, says the LORD. ³Then I myself will gather the remnant of my flock out of all the lands where I have driven them, and I will bring them back to their fold, and they shall be fruitful and multiply. ⁴I will raise up shepherds over them who will shepherd them, and they shall not fear any longer, or be dismayed, nor shall any be missing, says the LORD.

The Righteous Branch of David

5 The days are surely coming, says the LORD, when I will raise up for David a righteous Branch, and he shall reign as king and deal wisely, and shall execute justice and righteousness in the land. ⁶In his days Judah will be saved and Israel will live in safety. And this is the name by which he will be called: "The LORD is our righteousness."

7 Therefore, the days are surely coming, says the LORD, when it shall no longer be said, "As the LORD lives who brought the people of Israel up out of the land of Egypt," ⁸but "As the LORD lives who brought out and led the offspring of the house of Israel out of the land of the north and out of all the lands where he*ᵃ* had driven them." Then they shall live in their own land.

False Prophets of Hope Denounced

9 Concerning the prophets:
My heart is crushed within me,
    all my bones shake;
I have become like a drunkard,
    like one overcome by wine,
because of the LORD
    and because of his holy words.
¹⁰ For the land is full of adulterers;
    because of the curse the land mourns,
    and the pastures of the wilderness are dried up.
Their course has been evil,
    and their might is not right.
¹¹ Both prophet and priest are ungodly;
    even in my house I have found their wickedness,
                                                    says the LORD.
¹² Therefore their way shall be to them
    like slippery paths in the darkness,
    into which they shall be driven and fall;
for I will bring disaster upon them
    in the year of their punishment,
                                                    says the LORD.
¹³ In the prophets of Samaria
    I saw a disgusting thing:
    they prophesied by Baal
    and led my people Israel astray.
¹⁴ But in the prophets of Jerusalem
    I have seen a more shocking thing:
    they commit adultery and walk in lies;

a Gk: Heb *I*

they strengthen the hands of evildoers,
so that no one turns from wickedness;
all of them have become like Sodom to me,
and its inhabitants like Gomorrah.
¹⁵ Therefore thus says the LORD of hosts concerning
the prophets:
"I am going to make them eat wormwood,
and give them poisoned water to drink;
for from the prophets of Jerusalem
ungodliness has spread throughout the land."

16 Thus says the LORD of hosts: Do not listen to the words of the prophets who prophesy to you; they are deluding you. They speak visions of their own minds, not from the mouth of the LORD. ¹⁷They keep saying to those who despise the word of the LORD, "It shall be well with you"; and to all who stubbornly follow their own stubborn hearts, they say, "No calamity shall come upon you."

¹⁸ For who has stood in the council of the LORD
so as to see and to hear his word?
Who has given heed to his word so as to
proclaim it?
¹⁹ Look, the storm of the LORD!
Wrath has gone forth,
a whirling tempest;
it will burst upon the head of the wicked.
²⁰ The anger of the LORD will not turn back
until he has executed and accomplished
the intents of his mind.
In the latter days you will understand it clearly.

²¹ I did not send the prophets,
yet they ran;
I did not speak to them,
yet they prophesied.
²² But if they had stood in my council,
then they would have proclaimed my words to
my people,
and they would have turned them from their evil
way,
and from the evil of their doings.

23 Am I a God near by, says the LORD, and not a God far off? ²⁴Who can hide in secret places so that I cannot see them? says the LORD. Do I not fill heaven and earth? says the LORD. ²⁵I have heard what the prophets have said who prophesy lies in my name, saying, "I have dreamed, I have dreamed!" ²⁶How long? Will the hearts of the prophets ever turn back—those who prophesy lies, and who prophesy the deceit of their own heart? ²⁷They plan to make my people forget my name by their dreams that they tell one another, just as their ancestors forgot my name for Baal. ²⁸Let the prophet who has a dream tell the dream, but let the one who has my word speak my word faithfully. What has straw in common with wheat? says the LORD. ²⁹Is not my word like fire, says the LORD, and like a hammer that breaks a rock in pieces? ³⁰See, therefore, I am against the prophets, says the LORD, who steal my words from one another. ³¹See, I am against the prophets, says the LORD,

What's God Got To Do With This Anyway?

JEREMIAH 23.20–37

"A Christian who was in a great deal of trouble was recounting to another the various efforts he had made to find deliverance, and concluded by saying, 'But it has all been in vain, and there is literally nothing left for me to do now but to trust the Lord.'

" 'Alas!' exclaimed his friend in a tone of the deepest commiseration, as though no greater risk were possible,— 'Alas! has it come to *that!* '"

—HANNAH WHITALL SMITH,
The Christian's Secret of a Happy Life

Abide in Me and Bear Much Fruit

JEREMIAH 24.1–10

Find two pieces of ripe fruit. Put one in the refrigerator and the other in a warm place and leave them until the one in the warm place starts to decay. Place them in front of you and spend some time looking at their particular details, feeling and smelling them and thinking of all the associations they evoke for you. Ask the Spirit to guide you. Write in your journal your response to the question: "What is God saying to me through each of these pieces of fruit?" Pray about the ideas and feelings you have. Plan how you will act if you see that an action is required. Ask God to make your life fruitful. Eat the good fruit and dispose of the bad piece of fruit.

See Meeting God in the Created Order

who use their own tongues and say, "Says the LORD." ³²See, I am against those who prophesy lying dreams, says the LORD, and who tell them, and who lead my people astray by their lies and their recklessness, when I did not send them or appoint them; so they do not profit this people at all, says the LORD.

33 When this people, or a prophet, or a priest asks you, "What is the burden of the LORD?" you shall say to them, "You are the burden,*a* and I will cast you off, says the LORD." ³⁴And as for the prophet, priest, or the people who say, "The burden of the LORD," I will punish them and their households. ³⁵Thus shall you say to one another, among yourselves, "What has the LORD answered?" or "What has the LORD spoken?" ³⁶But "the burden of the LORD" you shall mention no more, for the burden is everyone's own word, and so you pervert the words of the living God, the LORD of hosts, our God. ³⁷Thus you shall ask the prophet, "What has the LORD answered you?" or "What has the LORD spoken?" ³⁸But if you say, "the burden of the LORD," thus says the LORD: Because you have said these words, "the burden of the LORD," when I sent to you, saying, You shall not say, "the burden of the LORD," ³⁹therefore, I will surely lift you up*b* and cast you away from my presence, you and the city that I gave to you and your ancestors. ⁴⁰And I will bring upon you everlasting disgrace and perpetual shame, which shall not be forgotten.

The Good and the Bad Figs

24 The LORD showed me two baskets of figs placed before the temple of the LORD. This was after King Nebuchadrezzar of Babylon had taken into exile from Jerusalem King Jeconiah son of Jehoiakim of Judah, together with the officials of Judah, the artisans, and the smiths, and had brought them to Babylon. ²One basket had very good figs, like first-ripe figs, but the other basket had very bad figs, so bad that they could not be eaten. ³And the LORD said to me, "What do you see, Jeremiah?" I said, "Figs, the good figs very good, and the bad figs very bad, so bad that they cannot be eaten."

4 Then the word of the LORD came to me: ⁵Thus says the LORD, the God of Israel: Like these good figs, so I will regard as good the exiles from Judah, whom I have sent away from this place to the land of the Chaldeans. ⁶I will set my eyes upon them for good, and I will bring them back to this land. I will build them up, and not tear them down; I will plant them, and not pluck them up. ⁷I will give them a heart to know that I am the LORD; and they shall be my people and I will be their God, for they shall return to me with their whole heart.

8 But thus says the LORD: Like the bad figs that are so bad they cannot be eaten, so will I treat King Zedekiah of Judah, his officials, the remnant of Jerusalem who remain in this land, and those who live in the land of Egypt. ⁹I will make them a horror, an evil thing, to all the kingdoms of the earth—a disgrace, a byword, a taunt, and a curse in all the places where I shall drive them. ¹⁰And I will send sword, famine, and pestilence upon them, until they are utterly destroyed from the land that I gave to them and their ancestors.

a Gk Vg: Heb *What burden* *b* Heb Mss Gk Vg: MT *forget you*

The Babylonian Captivity Foretold

25 The word that came to Jeremiah concerning all the people of Judah, in the fourth year of King Jehoiakim son of Josiah of Judah (that was the first year of King Nebuchadrezzar of Babylon), ²which the prophet Jeremiah spoke to all the people of Judah and all the inhabitants of Jerusalem: ³For twenty-three years, from the thirteenth year of King Josiah son of Amon of Judah, to this day, the word of the LORD has come to me, and I have spoken persistently to you, but you have not listened. ⁴And though the LORD persistently sent you all his servants the prophets, you have neither listened nor inclined your ears to hear ⁵when they said, "Turn now, everyone of you, from your evil way and wicked doings, and you will remain upon the land that the LORD has given to you and your ancestors from of old and forever; ⁶do not go after other gods to serve and worship them, and do not provoke me to anger with the work of your hands. Then I will do you no harm." ⁷Yet you did not listen to me, says the LORD, and so you have provoked me to anger with the work of your hands to your own harm.

8 Therefore thus says the LORD of hosts: Because you have not obeyed my words, ⁹I am going to send for all the tribes of the north, says the LORD, even for King Nebuchadrezzar of Babylon, my servant, and I will bring them against this land and its inhabitants, and against all these nations around; I will utterly destroy them, and make them an object of horror and of hissing, and an everlasting disgrace.ᵃ ¹⁰And I will banish from them the sound of mirth and the sound of gladness, the voice of the bridegroom and the voice of the bride, the sound of the millstones and the light of the lamp. ¹¹This whole land shall become a ruin and a waste, and these nations shall serve the king of Babylon seventy years. ¹²Then after seventy years are completed, I will punish the king of Babylon and that nation, the land of the Chaldeans, for their iniquity, says the LORD, making the land an everlasting waste. ¹³I will bring upon that land all the words that I have uttered against it, everything written in this book, which Jeremiah prophesied against all the nations. ¹⁴For many nations and great kings shall make slaves of them also; and I will repay them according to their deeds and the work of their hands.

The Cup of God's Wrath

15 For thus the LORD, the God of Israel, said to me: Take from my hand this cup of the wine of wrath, and make all the nations to whom I send you drink it. ¹⁶They shall drink and stagger and go out of their minds because of the sword that I am sending among them.

17 So I took the cup from the LORD's hand, and made all the nations to whom the LORD sent me drink it: ¹⁸Jerusalem and the towns of Judah, its kings and officials, to make them a desolation and a waste, an object of hissing and of cursing, as they are today; ¹⁹Pharaoh king of Egypt, his servants, his officials, and all his people; ²⁰all the mixed people;ᵇ all the kings of the land of Uz; all the kings of the land of the Philistines—Ashkelon, Gaza, Ekron, and the remnant of Ashdod; ²¹Edom, Moab, and the Ammonites; ²²all the kings of

---

The Grapes of Wrath

JEREMIAH 25.8–14

"Outrageous!" we think. How could God call Nebuchadnezzar—a pagan emperor—"my servant"? How could God bring disaster on Jerusalem, the city that bears his name? At first glance both of these actions are difficult to comprehend, even contradictory; but sometimes God uses unpredictable means to accomplish great ends.

Identify a "godless" force in your life (or in the life of your church or nation) that God used to bring about change. When change occurred, what sacred things in your life seemed threatened? What are you saying to yourself about it now? What are you feeling? Take it to God in prayer.

See Meeting God in Everyday Life

Spreading Disaster

JEREMIAH 25.32–38

The prophet is to say to the nations, "Disaster is spreading from nation to nation." What disasters do you see spreading "from nation to nation" in today's world? Is your typical response, "Too hard! Forget it!"? Is it a response of despair? Turn to the God of nations. Bring your usual response and ask God what he thinks of it. Ask God to give you direction about a "disaster" you can pray for. Whom can you invite to pray with you?

See Meeting God in Everyday Life

Tyre, all the kings of Sidon, and the kings of the coastland across the sea; ²³Dedan, Tema, Buz, and all who have shaven temples; ²⁴all the kings of Arabia and all the kings of the mixed peoples*ᵃ* that live in the desert; ²⁵all the kings of Zimri, all the kings of Elam, and all the kings of Media; ²⁶all the kings of the north, far and near, one after another, and all the kingdoms of the world that are on the face of the earth. And after them the king of Sheshach*ᵇ* shall drink.

27 Then you shall say to them, Thus says the LORD of hosts, the God of Israel: Drink, get drunk and vomit, fall and rise no more, because of the sword that I am sending among you.

28 And if they refuse to accept the cup from your hand to drink, then you shall say to them: Thus says the LORD of hosts: You must drink! ²⁹See, I am beginning to bring disaster on the city that is called by my name, and how can you possibly avoid punishment? You shall not go unpunished, for I am summoning a sword against all the inhabitants of the earth, says the LORD of hosts.

30 You, therefore, shall prophesy against them all these words, and say to them:
The LORD will roar from on high,
  and from his holy habitation utter his voice;
he will roar mightily against his fold,
  and shout, like those who tread grapes,
  against all the inhabitants of the earth.
31   The clamor will resound to the ends of the earth,
    for the LORD has an indictment against the nations;
  he is entering into judgment with all flesh,
    and the guilty he will put to the sword,
            says the LORD.

32   Thus says the LORD of hosts:
  See, disaster is spreading
    from nation to nation,
  and a great tempest is stirring
    from the farthest parts of the earth!

33 Those slain by the LORD on that day shall extend from one end of the earth to the other. They shall not be lamented, or gathered, or buried; they shall become dung on the surface of the ground.
34   Wail, you shepherds, and cry out;
    roll in ashes, you lords of the flock,
  for the days of your slaughter have come—and
      your dispersions,*ᵃ*
  and you shall fall like a choice vessel.
35   Flight shall fail the shepherds,
    and there shall be no escape for the lords of the
      flock.
36   Hark! the cry of the shepherds,
    and the wail of the lords of the flock!
  For the LORD is despoiling their pasture,
37   and the peaceful folds are devastated,
    because of the fierce anger of the LORD.
38   Like a lion he has left his covert;
    for their land has become a waste
  because of the cruel sword,
    and because of his fierce anger.

ᵃ Meaning of Heb uncertain   *ᵇ* *Sheshach* is a cryptogram for *Babel, Babylon*

Jeremiah's Prophecies in the Temple

26 At the beginning of the reign of King Jehoiakim son of Josiah of Judah, this word came from the LORD: ²Thus says the LORD: Stand in the court of the LORD's house, and speak to all the cities of Judah that come to worship in the house of the LORD; speak to them all the words that I command you; do not hold back a word. ³It may be that they will listen, all of them, and will turn from their evil way, that I may change my mind about the disaster that I intend to bring on them because of their evil doings. ⁴You shall say to them: Thus says the LORD: If you will not listen to me, to walk in my law that I have set before you, ⁵and to heed the words of my servants the prophets whom I send to you urgently—though you have not heeded— ⁶then I will make this house like Shiloh, and I will make this city a curse for all the nations of the earth.

7 The priests and the prophets and all the people heard Jeremiah speaking these words in the house of the LORD. ⁸And when Jeremiah had finished speaking all that the LORD had commanded him to speak to all the people, then the priests and the prophets and all the people laid hold of him, saying, "You shall die! ⁹Why have you prophesied in the name of the LORD, saying, 'This house shall be like Shiloh, and this city shall be desolate, without inhabitant'?" And all the people gathered around Jeremiah in the house of the LORD.

10 When the officials of Judah heard these things, they came up from the king's house to the house of the LORD and took their seat in the entry of the New Gate of the house of the LORD. ¹¹Then the priests and the prophets said to the officials and to all the people, "This man deserves the sentence of death because he has prophesied against this city, as you have heard with your own ears."

12 Then Jeremiah spoke to all the officials and all the people, saying, "It is the LORD who sent me to prophesy against this house and this city all the words you have heard. ¹³Now therefore amend your ways and your doings, and obey the voice of the LORD your God, and the LORD will change his mind about the disaster that he has pronounced against you. ¹⁴But as for me, here I am in your hands. Do with me as seems good and right to you. ¹⁵Only know for certain that if you put me to death, you will be bringing innocent blood upon yourselves and upon this city and its inhabitants, for in truth the LORD sent me to you to speak all these words in your ears."

16 Then the officials and all the people said to the priests and the prophets, "This man does not deserve the sentence of death, for he has spoken to us in the name of the LORD our God." ¹⁷And some of the elders of the land arose and said to all the assembled people, ¹⁸"Micah of Moresheth, who prophesied during the days of King Hezekiah of Judah, said to all the people of Judah: 'Thus says the LORD of hosts,

Zion shall be plowed as a field;
Jerusalem shall become a heap of ruins,
and the mountain of the house a wooded height.'

¹⁹Did King Hezekiah of Judah and all Judah actually put him to death? Did he not fear the LORD and entreat the favor of the LORD, and did not the LORD change his mind about the disaster that he had pronounced against them? But we are about to bring great disaster on ourselves!"

Integrity at What Cost?

JEREMIAH 26.12–15

Bill died at age 81, after a life of loving and serving God with great faithfulness. As you read this prayer found in Bill's Bible, note both your resistance and your affinity to these lines:

"Lord, I am willing
to receive what you give
to lack what you withhold
to relinquish what you take
to suffer what you inflict
to be what you require."

Write out this prayer and use it as a bookmark.

See Meeting God in Worship

Can This Be God?

JEREMIAH 27.12–15

Does God really counsel submission to a foreign power? Is God really saying, "Do not listen to encouragement from your leaders"? Through the words of the prophet, God is giving unexpected direction.

Sometimes God smashes our assumptions and bypasses our neatly packaged definitions of who he is and what he will say to us. In the quiet of your prayer space, ask yourself what God is saying to you that is different from what you would expect. Ask God to confirm what you hear, and check it with the counsel of your spiritual adviser, pastor or faith companion.

See Meeting God in Scripture

20 There was another man prophesying in the name of the Lord, Uriah son of Shemaiah from Kiriath-jearim. He prophesied against this city and against this land in words exactly like those of Jeremiah. ²¹And when King Jehoiakim, with all his warriors and all the officials, heard his words, the king sought to put him to death; but when Uriah heard of it, he was afraid and fled and escaped to Egypt. ²²Then King Jehoiakim sent*ᵃ* Elnathan son of Achbor and men with him to Egypt, ²³and they took Uriah from Egypt and brought him to King Jehoiakim, who struck him down with the sword and threw his dead body into the burial place of the common people.

24 But the hand of Ahikam son of Shaphan was with Jeremiah so that he was not given over into the hands of the people to be put to death.

The Sign of the Yoke

27 In the beginning of the reign of King Zedekiah*ᵇ* son of Josiah of Judah, this word came to Jeremiah from the Lord. ²Thus the Lord said to me: Make yourself a yoke of straps and bars, and put them on your neck. ³Send word*ᶜ* to the king of Edom, the king of Moab, the king of the Ammonites, the king of Tyre, and the king of Sidon by the hand of the envoys who have come to Jerusalem to King Zedekiah of Judah. ⁴Give them this charge for their masters: Thus says the Lord of hosts, the God of Israel: This is what you shall say to your masters: ⁵It is I who by my great power and my outstretched arm have made the earth, with the people and animals that are on the earth, and I give it to whomever I please. ⁶Now I have given all these lands into the hand of King Nebuchadnezzar of Babylon, my servant, and I have given him even the wild animals of the field to serve him. ⁷All the nations shall serve him and his son and his grandson, until the time of his own land comes; then many nations and great kings shall make him their slave.

8 But if any nation or kingdom will not serve this king, Nebuchadnezzar of Babylon, and put its neck under the yoke of the king of Babylon, then I will punish that nation with the sword, with famine, and with pestilence, says the Lord, until I have completed its*ᵈ* destruction by his hand. ⁹You, therefore, must not listen to your prophets, your diviners, your dreamers,*ᵉ* your soothsayers, or your sorcerers, who are saying to you, "You shall not serve the king of Babylon." ¹⁰For they are prophesying a lie to you, with the result that you will be removed far from your land; I will drive you out, and you will perish. ¹¹But any nation that will bring its neck under the yoke of the king of Babylon and serve him, I will leave on its own land, says the Lord, to till it and live there.

12 I spoke to King Zedekiah of Judah in the same way: Bring your necks under the yoke of the king of Babylon, and serve him and his people, and live. ¹³Why should you and your people die by the sword, by famine, and by pestilence, as the Lord has spoken concerning any nation that will not serve the king of Babylon? ¹⁴Do not listen to the words of the prophets who are telling you not to serve the king of Babylon, for they are prophesying a lie to you. ¹⁵I have not sent them, says the Lord, but they are prophesying falsely in my

a Heb adds *men to Egypt*   *b* Another reading is *Jehoiakim*   *c* Cn: Heb *send them*   *d* Heb *their*   *e* Gk Syr Vg: Heb *dreams*

name, with the result that I will drive you out and you will perish, you and the prophets who are prophesying to you.

16 Then I spoke to the priests and to all this people, saying, Thus says the LORD: Do not listen to the words of your prophets who are prophesying to you, saying, "The vessels of the LORD's house will soon be brought back from Babylon," for they are prophesying a lie to you. ¹⁷Do not listen to them; serve the king of Babylon and live. Why should this city become a desolation? ¹⁸If indeed they are prophets, and if the word of the LORD is with them, then let them intercede with the LORD of hosts, that the vessels left in the house of the LORD, in the house of the king of Judah, and in Jerusalem may not go to Babylon. ¹⁹For thus says the LORD of hosts concerning the pillars, the sea, the stands, and the rest of the vessels that are left in this city, ²⁰which King Nebuchadnezzar of Babylon did not take away when he took into exile from Jerusalem to Babylon King Jeconiah son of Jehoiakim of Judah, and all the nobles of Judah and Jerusalem— ²¹thus says the LORD of hosts, the God of Israel, concerning the vessels left in the house of the LORD, in the house of the king of Judah, and in Jerusalem: ²²They shall be carried to Babylon, and there they shall stay, until the day when I give attention to them, says the LORD. Then I will bring them up and restore them to this place.

Hananiah Opposes Jeremiah and Dies

28 In that same year, at the beginning of the reign of King Zedekiah of Judah, in the fifth month of the fourth year, the prophet Hananiah son of Azzur, from Gibeon, spoke to me in the house of the LORD, in the presence of the priests and all the people, saying, ²"Thus says the LORD of hosts, the God of Israel: I have broken the yoke of the king of Babylon. ³Within two years I will bring back to this place all the vessels of the LORD's house, which King Nebuchadnezzar of Babylon took away from this place and carried to Babylon. ⁴I will also bring back to this place King Jeconiah son of Jehoiakim of Judah, and all the exiles from Judah who went to Babylon, says the LORD, for I will break the yoke of the king of Babylon."

5 Then the prophet Jeremiah spoke to the prophet Hananiah in the presence of the priests and all the people who were standing in the house of the LORD; ⁶and the prophet Jeremiah said, "Amen! May the LORD do so; may the LORD fulfill the words that you have prophesied, and bring back to this place from Babylon the vessels of the house of the LORD, and all the exiles. ⁷But listen now to this word that I speak in your hearing and in the hearing of all the people. ⁸The prophets who preceded you and me from ancient times prophesied war, famine, and pestilence against many countries and great kingdoms. ⁹As for the prophet who prophesies peace, when the word of that prophet comes true, then it will be known that the LORD has truly sent the prophet."

10 Then the prophet Hananiah took the yoke from the neck of the prophet Jeremiah, and broke it. ¹¹And Hananiah spoke in the presence of all the people, saying, "Thus says the LORD: This is how I will break the yoke of King Nebuchadnezzar of Babylon from the neck of all the nations within two years." At this, the prophet Jeremiah went his way.

12 Sometime after the prophet Hananiah had broken the yoke from the neck of the prophet Jeremiah, the word of

Peace in Our Time

JEREMIAH 28.1–9

No one wanted to face the facts. "Peace in our time," announced British Prime Minister Neville Chamberlain after signing the Munich Pact with Hitler in September 1938. And the popular press had its clairvoyants and "stars" predicting there would be no war. Events soon proved otherwise.

What is God doing that you don't want to know about? What issue would you rather not hear about from God? Ask for the double-edged sword of the Spirit to help you discern truth from wishful thinking, and write a journal entry under the heading "What I Don't Want to Hear From God." Discuss it with a trusted friend and take your answer with you the next time you go to worship. During the prayers or hymns, lift up your hesitation again before God.

See *Meeting God in Worship*

A Future With Hope

JEREMIAH 29.4–7,10–14

God is gracious! The steadfast love of the Lord never ceases (see Lamentations 3.22). Regardless of the data that might cause you to despair, God wills your well-being. So what does it mean for you to build and plant and eat? What does it mean for you to increase your family? What mental paradigm shift would allow you to be content with the provision that God has made for you? Spend the next several days giving thanks to God for all that you have. Dream of what God might yet provide. Seek God with all your heart, singing an appropriate song or hymn.

See Meeting God in Service

the LORD came to Jeremiah: ¹³Go, tell Hananiah, Thus says the LORD: You have broken wooden bars only to forge iron bars in place of them! ¹⁴For thus says the LORD of hosts, the God of Israel: I have put an iron yoke on the neck of all these nations so that they may serve King Nebuchadnezzar of Babylon, and they shall indeed serve him; I have even given him the wild animals. ¹⁵And the prophet Jeremiah said to the prophet Hananiah, "Listen, Hananiah, the LORD has not sent you, and you made this people trust in a lie. ¹⁶Therefore thus says the LORD: I am going to send you off the face of the earth. Within this year you will be dead, because you have spoken rebellion against the LORD."

17 In that same year, in the seventh month, the prophet Hananiah died.

Jeremiah's Letter to the Exiles in Babylon

29 These are the words of the letter that the prophet Jeremiah sent from Jerusalem to the remaining elders among the exiles, and to the priests, the prophets, and all the people, whom Nebuchadnezzar had taken into exile from Jerusalem to Babylon. ²This was after King Jeconiah, and the queen mother, the court officials, the leaders of Judah and Jerusalem, the artisans, and the smiths had departed from Jerusalem. ³The letter was sent by the hand of Elasah son of Shaphan and Gemariah son of Hilkiah, whom King Zedekiah of Judah sent to Babylon to King Nebuchadnezzar of Babylon. It said: ⁴Thus says the LORD of hosts, the God of Israel, to all the exiles whom I have sent into exile from Jerusalem to Babylon: ⁵Build houses and live in them; plant gardens and eat what they produce. ⁶Take wives and have sons and daughters; take wives for your sons, and give your daughters in marriage, that they may bear sons and daughters; multiply there, and do not decrease. ⁷But seek the welfare of the city where I have sent you into exile, and pray to the LORD on its behalf, for in its welfare you will find your welfare. ⁸For thus says the LORD of hosts, the God of Israel: Do not let the prophets and the diviners who are among you deceive you, and do not listen to the dreams that they dream,ᵃ ⁹for it is a lie that they are prophesying to you in my name; I did not send them, says the LORD.

10 For thus says the LORD: Only when Babylon's seventy years are completed will I visit you, and I will fulfill to you my promise and bring you back to this place. ¹¹For surely I know the plans I have for you, says the LORD, plans for your welfare and not for harm, to give you a future with hope. ¹²Then when you call upon me and come and pray to me, I will hear you. ¹³When you search for me, you will find me; if you seek me with all your heart, ¹⁴I will let you find me, says the LORD, and I will restore your fortunes and gather you from all the nations and all the places where I have driven you, says the LORD, and I will bring you back to the place from which I sent you into exile.

15 Because you have said, "The LORD has raised up prophets for us in Babylon,"— ¹⁶Thus says the LORD concerning the king who sits on the throne of David, and concerning all the people who live in this city, your kinsfolk who did not go out with you into exile: ¹⁷Thus says the LORD of hosts, I am going to let loose on them sword,

ᵃ Cn: Heb *your dreams that you cause to dream*

famine, and pestilence, and I will make them like rotten figs that are so bad they cannot be eaten. [18]I will pursue them with the sword, with famine, and with pestilence, and will make them a horror to all the kingdoms of the earth, to be an object of cursing, and horror, and hissing, and a derision among all the nations where I have driven them, [19]because they did not heed my words, says the LORD, when I persistently sent to you my servants the prophets, but they[a] would not listen, says the LORD. [20]But now, all you exiles whom I sent away from Jerusalem to Babylon, hear the word of the LORD: [21]Thus says the LORD of hosts, the God of Israel, concerning Ahab son of Kolaiah and Zedekiah son of Maaseiah, who are prophesying a lie to you in my name: I am going to deliver them into the hand of King Nebuchadrezzar of Babylon, and he shall kill them before your eyes. [22]And on account of them this curse shall be used by all the exiles from Judah in Babylon: "The LORD make you like Zedekiah and Ahab, whom the king of Babylon roasted in the fire," [23]because they have perpetrated outrage in Israel and have committed adultery with their neighbors' wives, and have spoken in my name lying words that I did not command them; I am the one who knows and bears witness, says the LORD.

The Letter of Shemaiah

24 To Shemaiah of Nehelam you shall say: [25]Thus says the LORD of hosts, the God of Israel: In your own name you sent a letter to all the people who are in Jerusalem, and to the priest Zephaniah son of Maaseiah, and to all the priests, saying, [26]The LORD himself has made you priest instead of the priest Jehoiada, so that there may be officers in the house of the LORD to control any madman who plays the prophet, to put him in the stocks and the collar. [27]So now why have you not rebuked Jeremiah of Anathoth who plays the prophet for you? [28]For he has actually sent to us in Babylon, saying, "It will be a long time; build houses and live in them, and plant gardens and eat what they produce."

29 The priest Zephaniah read this letter in the hearing of the prophet Jeremiah. [30]Then the word of the LORD came to Jeremiah: [31]Send to all the exiles, saying, Thus says the LORD concerning Shemaiah of Nehelam: Because Shemaiah has prophesied to you, though I did not send him, and has led you to trust in a lie, [32]therefore thus says the LORD: I am going to punish Shemaiah of Nehelam and his descendants; he shall not have anyone living among this people to see[b] the good that I am going to do to my people, says the LORD, for he has spoken rebellion against the LORD.

Restoration Promised for Israel and Judah

30 The word that came to Jeremiah from the LORD: [2]Thus says the LORD, the God of Israel: Write in a book all the words that I have spoken to you. [3]For the days are surely coming, says the LORD, when I will restore the fortunes of my people, Israel and Judah, says the LORD, and I will bring them back to the land that I gave to their ancestors and they shall take possession of it.

4 These are the words that the LORD spoke concerning Israel and Judah:

5 Thus says the LORD:

Listen and Obey!

JEREMIAH 29.24–32

"How beautiful obedience is. For it alone silences doubt, preserves our stability and presence of mind, our freedom of heart and firmness of will in the midst of all that might shake or disturb us. Unless we constantly bring ourselves back to Obedience, we lose our heads, and that which should be a blessing becomes a torment and a curse. We lose all sense of where we stand."

—ABBÉ DE TOURVILLE,
Letters of Direction

See *Meeting God in Scripture*

God Will Restore

JEREMIAH 30.12–17

Whom do you know who has a wound that is grievous and "incurable"? A family member? A friend? Yourself? Your nation? Journal your response to God's words: "I will restore health to you, and your wounds I will heal."

What do you feel as you listen to these words? What do you think? What images come to your mind? What action is asked of you? What will you do, and when will you do it? Make yourself accountable to a faith companion for your response.

We have heard a cry of panic,
    of terror, and no peace.
6 Ask now, and see,
    can a man bear a child?
Why then do I see every man
    with his hands on his loins like a woman in labor?
    Why has every face turned pale?
7 Alas! that day is so great
    there is none like it;
it is a time of distress for Jacob;
    yet he shall be rescued from it.

8 On that day, says the LORD of hosts, I will break the yoke from off his[a] neck, and I will burst his[a] bonds, and strangers shall no more make a servant of him. 9 But they shall serve the LORD their God and David their king, whom I will raise up for them.

10 But as for you, have no fear, my servant Jacob,
        says the LORD,
    and do not be dismayed, O Israel;
for I am going to save you from far away,
    and your offspring from the land of their captivity.
Jacob shall return and have quiet and ease,
    and no one shall make him afraid.
11 For I am with you, says the LORD, to save you;
I will make an end of all the nations
    among which I scattered you,
    but of you I will not make an end.
I will chastise you in just measure,
    and I will by no means leave you unpunished.

12 For thus says the LORD:
Your hurt is incurable,
    your wound is grievous.
13 There is no one to uphold your cause,
    no medicine for your wound,
    no healing for you.
14 All your lovers have forgotten you;
    they care nothing for you;
for I have dealt you the blow of an enemy,
    the punishment of a merciless foe,
because your guilt is great,
    because your sins are so numerous.
15 Why do you cry out over your hurt?
    Your pain is incurable.
Because your guilt is great,
    because your sins are so numerous,
    I have done these things to you.
16 Therefore all who devour you shall be devoured,
    and all your foes, everyone of them, shall go into
        captivity;
those who plunder you shall be plundered,
    and all who prey on you I will make a prey.
17 For I will restore health to you,
    and your wounds I will heal,
                                says the LORD,
because they have called you an outcast:
    "It is Zion; no one cares for her!"

a Cn: Heb *your*

18 Thus says the LORD:
I am going to restore the fortunes of the tents of
    Jacob,
  and have compassion on his dwellings;
the city shall be rebuilt upon its mound,
  and the citadel set on its rightful site.
19 Out of them shall come thanksgiving,
  and the sound of merrymakers.
I will make them many, and they shall not be few;
  I will make them honored, and they shall not be
    disdained.
20 Their children shall be as of old,
  their congregation shall be established before me;
  and I will punish all who oppress them.
21 Their prince shall be one of their own,
  their ruler shall come from their midst;
I will bring him near, and he shall approach me,
  for who would otherwise dare to approach me?
                    says the LORD.
22 And you shall be my people,
  and I will be your God.

23 Look, the storm of the LORD!
  Wrath has gone forth,
a whirling*a* tempest;
  it will burst upon the head of the wicked.
24 The fierce anger of the LORD will not turn back
  until he has executed and accomplished
  the intents of his mind.
In the latter days you will understand this.

The Joyful Return of the Exiles

31 At that time, says the LORD, I will be the God of all
the families of Israel, and they shall be my people.
2 Thus says the LORD:
The people who survived the sword
  found grace in the wilderness;
when Israel sought for rest,
3   the LORD appeared to him*b* from far away.*c*
I have loved you with an everlasting love;
  therefore I have continued my faithfulness to you.
4 Again I will build you, and you shall be built,
  O virgin Israel!
Again you shall take*d* your tambourines,
  and go forth in the dance of the merrymakers.
5 Again you shall plant vineyards
  on the mountains of Samaria;
the planters shall plant,
  and shall enjoy the fruit.
6 For there shall be a day when sentinels will call
  in the hill country of Ephraim:
"Come, let us go up to Zion,
  to the LORD our God."

7 For thus says the LORD:
Sing aloud with gladness for Jacob,
  and raise shouts for the chief of the nations;
proclaim, give praise, and say,

"With an Everlasting Love"

JEREMIAH 31.2–6

Virgin Israel? How can God call Israel "virgin" when the nation's shameful unfaithfulness has been exposed in detail by the prophet? Yet it seems that God intends the word "virgin" to mean "virgin"!

Remember that God is greater than your past. Be seated in a quiet place and listen to Jesus saying, "I am making all things new" (Revelation 21.5). Listen to the apostle Paul saying, "If anyone is in Christ, there is a new creation" (2 Corinthians 5.17). How, in the light of this, do you view yourself? Are you more aware of what is in your file of sins or are you one whom God has loved "with an everlasting love"? One spiritual adviser writes, "Say to yourself very often about everything that happens, 'God loves me! What a joy!' and reply boldly, 'And truly I love him too!' " (Abbé de Tourville).

See Meeting God in Scripture

---

a One Ms: Meaning of MT uncertain   *b* Gk: Heb *me*   *c* Or *to him long ago*   *d* Or *adorn yourself with*

Ransomed, Healed, Restored, Forgiven!

JEREMIAH 31.10–14

"The texts express two anticipations about human life restored. On the one hand, there is anticipation of the restoration of public life, safe cities, caring communities, and secure streets. On the other hand, there is anticipation of the restoration of personal and interpersonal life, happy families, domestic well-being and joy, shared food and delighted relationships. Both public and interpersonal life depend on the self-giving action of God who makes newness possible. This alternative life comes from the self-giving act of atonement wrought only by God."

—WALTER BRUEGGEMANN,
Finally Comes the Poet

See Meeting God in Everyday Life

"Save, O LORD, your people,
the remnant of Israel."

8 See, I am going to bring them from the land of the north,
and gather them from the farthest parts of the earth,
among them the blind and the lame,
those with child and those in labor, together;
a great company, they shall return here.

9 With weeping they shall come,
and with consolations[a] I will lead them back,
I will let them walk by brooks of water,
in a straight path in which they shall not stumble;
for I have become a father to Israel,
and Ephraim is my firstborn.

10 Hear the word of the LORD, O nations,
and declare it in the coastlands far away;
say, "He who scattered Israel will gather him,
and will keep him as a shepherd a flock."

11 For the LORD has ransomed Jacob,
and has redeemed him from hands too strong for him.

12 They shall come and sing aloud on the height of Zion,
and they shall be radiant over the goodness of the LORD,
over the grain, the wine, and the oil,
and over the young of the flock and the herd;
their life shall become like a watered garden,
and they shall never languish again.

13 Then shall the young women rejoice in the dance,
and the young men and the old shall be merry.
I will turn their mourning into joy,
I will comfort them, and give them gladness for sorrow.

14 I will give the priests their fill of fatness,
and my people shall be satisfied with my bounty,
says the LORD.

15 Thus says the LORD:
A voice is heard in Ramah,
lamentation and bitter weeping.
Rachel is weeping for her children;
she refuses to be comforted for her children,
because they are no more.

16 Thus says the LORD:
Keep your voice from weeping,
and your eyes from tears;
for there is a reward for your work,
says the LORD:
they shall come back from the land of the enemy;

17 there is hope for your future,
says the LORD:
your children shall come back to their own country.

18 Indeed I heard Ephraim pleading:
"You disciplined me, and I took the discipline;

a Gk Compare Vg Tg: Heb *supplications*

I was like a calf untrained.
Bring me back, let me come back,
for you are the LORD my God.
19 For after I had turned away I repented;
and after I was discovered, I struck my thigh;
I was ashamed, and I was dismayed
because I bore the disgrace of my youth."
20 Is Ephraim my dear son?
Is he the child I delight in?
As often as I speak against him,
I still remember him.
Therefore I am deeply moved for him;
I will surely have mercy on him,
says the LORD.

21 Set up road markers for yourself,
make yourself guideposts;
consider well the highway,
the road by which you went.
Return, O virgin Israel,
return to these your cities.
22 How long will you waver,
O faithless daughter?
For the LORD has created a new thing on the earth:
a woman encompasses*a* a man.

23 Thus says the LORD of hosts, the God of Israel: Once more they shall use these words in the land of Judah and in its towns when I restore their fortunes:
"The LORD bless you, O abode of righteousness,
O holy hill!"
24And Judah and all its towns shall live there together, and the farmers and those who wander*b* with their flocks.
25 I will satisfy the weary,
and all who are faint I will replenish.
26 Thereupon I awoke and looked, and my sleep was pleasant to me.

Individual Retribution

27 The days are surely coming, says the LORD, when I will sow the house of Israel and the house of Judah with the seed of humans and the seed of animals. 28And just as I have watched over them to pluck up and break down, to overthrow, destroy, and bring evil, so I will watch over them to build and to plant, says the LORD. 29In those days they shall no longer say:
"The parents have eaten sour grapes,
and the children's teeth are set on edge."
30But all shall die for their own sins; the teeth of everyone who eats sour grapes shall be set on edge.

A New Covenant

31 The days are surely coming, says the LORD, when I will make a new covenant with the house of Israel and the house of Judah. 32It will not be like the covenant that I made with their ancestors when I took them by the hand to bring them out of the land of Egypt—a covenant that they broke, though I was their husband,*c* says the LORD.

a Meaning of Heb uncertain   *b* Cn Compare Syr Vg Tg: Heb *and they shall wander*   *c* Or *master*

Road Markers and Guideposts

JEREMIAH 31.21,31–34

God has embraced you in a new covenant in Jesus Christ that is built on a relationship rather than rules. God has written "I love you" on your heart.

What is the history of your covenant relationship with God? Use your journal (or any suitable paper) to write a concise history of your relationship with God. What are the key experiences and moments of insight and decision that stand out as road markers and guideposts? As best you can, remember the dates of watershed events and put them in your calendar for the year ahead. Be sure to celebrate your anniversaries with God.

See Meeting God in Everyday Life

Free to Know the Lord

JEREMIAH 31.34

What sin, if any, stands between you and God? How big is this sin within you? So that you may know the Lord in full measure, bring your sin to God and confess it, believing that God will remember your sin no more. Give your fullest attention (rather than your intention) to God. If sin continues to block your way, confess it before a trusted friend, your spiritual adviser or your pastor (see James 5.16) and listen to the authoritative word of Jesus Christ's forgiveness that that person proclaims.

See Meeting God in Worship

³³But this is the covenant that I will make with the house of Israel after those days, says the LORD: I will put my law within them, and I will write it on their hearts; and I will be their God, and they shall be my people. ³⁴No longer shall they teach one another, or say to each other, "Know the LORD," for they shall all know me, from the least of them to the greatest, says the LORD; for I will forgive their iniquity, and remember their sin no more.

³⁵ Thus says the LORD,
who gives the sun for light by day
and the fixed order of the moon and the stars
for light by night,
who stirs up the sea so that its waves roar—
the LORD of hosts is his name:
³⁶ If this fixed order were ever to cease
from my presence, says the LORD,
then also the offspring of Israel would cease
to be a nation before me forever.

³⁷ Thus says the LORD:
If the heavens above can be measured,
and the foundations of the earth below can be
explored,
then I will reject all the offspring of Israel
because of all they have done,
says the LORD.

Jerusalem to Be Enlarged

38 The days are surely coming, says the LORD, when the city shall be rebuilt for the LORD from the tower of Hananel to the Corner Gate. ³⁹And the measuring line shall go out farther, straight to the hill Gareb, and shall then turn to Goah. ⁴⁰The whole valley of the dead bodies and the ashes, and all the fields as far as the Wadi Kidron, to the corner of the Horse Gate toward the east, shall be sacred to the LORD. It shall never again be uprooted or overthrown.

Jeremiah Buys a Field During the Siege

32 The word that came to Jeremiah from the LORD in the tenth year of King Zedekiah of Judah, which was the eighteenth year of Nebuchadrezzar. ²At that time the army of the king of Babylon was besieging Jerusalem, and the prophet Jeremiah was confined in the court of the guard that was in the palace of the king of Judah, ³where King Zedekiah of Judah had confined him. Zedekiah had said, "Why do you prophesy and say: Thus says the LORD: I am going to give this city into the hand of the king of Babylon, and he shall take it; ⁴King Zedekiah of Judah shall not escape out of the hands of the Chaldeans, but shall surely be given into the hands of the king of Babylon, and shall speak with him face to face and see him eye to eye; ⁵and he shall take Zedekiah to Babylon, and there he shall remain until I attend to him, says the LORD; though you fight against the Chaldeans, you shall not succeed?"

6 Jeremiah said, The word of the LORD came to me: ⁷Hanamel son of your uncle Shallum is going to come to you and say, "Buy my field that is at Anathoth, for the right of redemption by purchase is yours." ⁸Then my

cousin Hanamel came to me in the court of the guard, in accordance with the word of the LORD, and said to me, "Buy my field that is at Anathoth in the land of Benjamin, for the right of possession and redemption is yours; buy it for yourself." Then I knew that this was the word of the LORD.

9 And I bought the field at Anathoth from my cousin Hanamel, and weighed out the money to him, seventeen shekels of silver. ¹⁰I signed the deed, sealed it, got witnesses, and weighed the money on scales. ¹¹Then I took the sealed deed of purchase, containing the terms and conditions, and the open copy; ¹²and I gave the deed of purchase to Baruch son of Neriah son of Mahseiah, in the presence of my cousin Hanamel, in the presence of the witnesses who signed the deed of purchase, and in the presence of all the Judeans who were sitting in the court of the guard. ¹³In their presence I charged Baruch, saying, ¹⁴Thus says the LORD of hosts, the God of Israel: Take these deeds, both this sealed deed of purchase and this open deed, and put them in an earthenware jar, in order that they may last for a long time. ¹⁵For thus says the LORD of hosts, the God of Israel: Houses and fields and vineyards shall again be bought in this land.

Jeremiah Prays for Understanding

16 After I had given the deed of purchase to Baruch son of Neriah, I prayed to the LORD, saying: ¹⁷Ah Lord GOD! It is you who made the heavens and the earth by your great power and by your outstretched arm! Nothing is too hard for you. ¹⁸You show steadfast love to the thousandth generation,ᵃ but repay the guilt of parents into the laps of their children after them, O great and mighty God whose name is the LORD of hosts, ¹⁹great in counsel and mighty in deed; whose eyes are open to all the ways of mortals, rewarding all according to their ways and according to the fruit of their doings. ²⁰You showed signs and wonders in the land of Egypt, and to this day in Israel and among all humankind, and have made yourself a name that continues to this very day. ²¹You brought your people Israel out of the land of Egypt with signs and wonders, with a strong hand and outstretched arm, and with great terror; ²²and you gave them this land, which you swore to their ancestors to give them, a land flowing with milk and honey; ²³and they entered and took possession of it. But they did not obey your voice or follow your law; of all you commanded them to do, they did nothing. Therefore you have made all these disasters come upon them. ²⁴See, the siege ramps have been cast up against the city to take it, and the city, faced with sword, famine, and pestilence, has been given into the hands of the Chaldeans who are fighting against it. What you spoke has happened, as you yourself can see. ²⁵Yet you, O Lord GOD, have said to me, "Buy the field for money and get witnesses"—though the city has been given into the hands of the Chaldeans.

God's Assurance of the People's Return

26 The word of the LORD came to Jeremiah: ²⁷See, I am the LORD, the God of all flesh; is anything too hard for me? ²⁸Therefore, thus says the LORD: I am going to give this city

ᵃ Or to thousands

Witnesses

JEREMIAH 32.9–15

Witnesses to Jeremiah's land purchase included "all the Judeans who were sitting in the court of the guard" (v.12).

Do you spend money freely, or are you cautious with money? Who witnesses what you buy? Take someone with you the next time you shop. When you return, file the receipt at this page in the book of Jeremiah. Pray with your companion for all those involved in the production and sale of your purchase. What is it like for those who cannot afford what you bought? Pray for them. And from a tithe of your purchase, give to someone in need.

See Meeting God in Service

All Shall Be Well

JEREMIAH 32.42–44

"Because of our good Lord's tender love to all those who shall be saved, he quickly comforts them saying, 'The cause of this pain is sin. But all shall be well, and all shall be well, and all manner of thing shall be well.' These words were said so kindly and without a hint of blame, to me or to any who shall be saved."

—JULIAN OF NORWICH,
Enfolded in Love

See *Meeting God in Worship*

into the hands of the Chaldeans and into the hand of King Nebuchadrezzar of Babylon, and he shall take it. ²⁹The Chaldeans who are fighting against this city shall come, set it on fire, and burn it, with the houses on whose roofs offerings have been made to Baal and libations have been poured out to other gods, to provoke me to anger. ³⁰For the people of Israel and the people of Judah have done nothing but evil in my sight from their youth; the people of Israel have done nothing but provoke me to anger by the work of their hands, says the LORD. ³¹This city has aroused my anger and wrath, from the day it was built until this day, so that I will remove it from my sight ³²because of all the evil of the people of Israel and the people of Judah that they did to provoke me to anger—they, their kings and their officials, their priests and their prophets, the citizens of Judah and the inhabitants of Jerusalem. ³³They have turned their backs to me, not their faces; though I have taught them persistently, they would not listen and accept correction. ³⁴They set up their abominations in the house that bears my name, and defiled it. ³⁵They built the high places of Baal in the valley of the son of Hinnom, to offer up their sons and daughters to Molech, though I did not command them, nor did it enter my mind that they should do this abomination, causing Judah to sin.

36 Now therefore thus says the LORD, the God of Israel, concerning this city of which you say, "It is being given into the hand of the king of Babylon by the sword, by famine, and by pestilence": ³⁷See, I am going to gather them from all the lands to which I drove them in my anger and my wrath and in great indignation; I will bring them back to this place, and I will settle them in safety. ³⁸They shall be my people, and I will be their God. ³⁹I will give them one heart and one way, that they may fear me for all time, for their own good and the good of their children after them. ⁴⁰I will make an everlasting covenant with them, never to draw back from doing good to them; and I will put the fear of me in their hearts, so that they may not turn from me. ⁴¹I will rejoice in doing good to them, and I will plant them in this land in faithfulness, with all my heart and all my soul.

42 For thus says the LORD: Just as I have brought all this great disaster upon this people, so I will bring upon them all the good fortune that I now promise them. ⁴³Fields shall be bought in this land of which you are saying, It is a desolation, without human beings or animals; it has been given into the hands of the Chaldeans. ⁴⁴Fields shall be bought for money, and deeds shall be signed and sealed and witnessed, in the land of Benjamin, in the places around Jerusalem, and in the cities of Judah, of the hill country, of the Shephelah, and of the Negeb; for I will restore their fortunes, says the LORD.

Healing after Punishment

33 The word of the LORD came to Jeremiah a second time, while he was still confined in the court of the guard: ²Thus says the LORD who made the earth,ᵃ the LORD who formed it to establish it—the LORD is his name: ³Call to me and I will answer you, and will tell you great and hidden things that you have not known. ⁴For thus says the

a Gk: Heb *it*

Lord, the God of Israel, concerning the houses of this city and the houses of the kings of Judah that were torn down to make a defense against the siege ramps and before the sword:[a] 5The Chaldeans are coming in to fight[b] and to fill them with the dead bodies of those whom I shall strike down in my anger and my wrath, for I have hidden my face from this city because of all their wickedness. 6I am going to bring it recovery and healing; I will heal them and reveal to them abundance[a] of prosperity and security. 7I will restore the fortunes of Judah and the fortunes of Israel, and rebuild them as they were at first. 8I will cleanse them from all the guilt of their sin against me, and I will forgive all the guilt of their sin and rebellion against me. 9And this city[c] shall be to me a name of joy, a praise and a glory before all the nations of the earth who shall hear of all the good that I do for them; they shall fear and tremble because of all the good and all the prosperity I provide for it.

10 Thus says the Lord: In this place of which you say, "It is a waste without human beings or animals," in the towns of Judah and the streets of Jerusalem that are desolate, without inhabitants, human or animal, there shall once more be heard 11the voice of mirth and the voice of gladness, the voice of the bridegroom and the voice of the bride, the voices of those who sing, as they bring thank offerings to the house of the Lord:

"Give thanks to the Lord of hosts,
 for the Lord is good,
 for his steadfast love endures forever!"

For I will restore the fortunes of the land as at first, says the Lord.

12 Thus says the Lord of hosts: In this place that is waste, without human beings or animals, and in all its towns there shall again be pasture for shepherds resting their flocks. 13In the towns of the hill country, of the Shephelah, and of the Negeb, in the land of Benjamin, the places around Jerusalem, and in the towns of Judah, flocks shall again pass under the hands of the one who counts them, says the Lord.

The Righteous Branch and the Covenant with David

14 The days are surely coming, says the Lord, when I will fulfill the promise I made to the house of Israel and the house of Judah. 15In those days and at that time I will cause a righteous Branch to spring up for David; and he shall execute justice and righteousness in the land. 16In those days Judah will be saved and Jerusalem will live in safety. And this is the name by which it will be called: "The Lord is our righteousness."

17 For thus says the Lord: David shall never lack a man to sit on the throne of the house of Israel, 18and the levitical priests shall never lack a man in my presence to offer burnt offerings, to make grain offerings, and to make sacrifices for all time.

19 The word of the Lord came to Jeremiah: 20Thus says the Lord: If any of you could break my covenant with the day and my covenant with the night, so that day and night would not come at their appointed time, 21only then could my covenant with my servant David be broken, so that

---

This City

JEREMIAH 33.10–16

Talk with a companion (or dialogue with God) about the ways in which your community could be described as a "waste" (v.10). In what way is justice and righteousness needed? What needs to be "saved" and what issues of safety need to be addressed? Sit in a public place and observe the people and animals. What are they doing? What can you learn about them by just watching them? What spirit can you feel in your community today? As you watch and question, silently invite both the people and the animals to "Give thanks to the Lord of hosts, for the Lord is good, for his steadfast love endures forever!"

See Meeting God in Everyday Life

---

a Meaning of Heb uncertain   b Cn: Heb They are coming in to fight against the Chaldeans   c Heb And it

Free the Slaves!

JEREMIAH 34.8–16

The Hebrews who owned other Hebrews as slaves freed them, but later they changed their minds because it was expedient! What an irony—when God's action in freeing the Hebrew people from slavery was the heart of their national identity! But before you "throw stones," listen to God's voice in this passage proclaiming justice. Who is enslaved because of our own society's economic systems? Who is in bondage because of our society's lifestyle preferences? Who, beyond your conscious awareness, might be in bondage to serve your needs and wants? Contact an aid agency and find out. See what you can do to make a difference. Share what you learn with others in your faith community and take some specific group action.

See *Meeting God in Service*

he would not have a son to reign on his throne, and my covenant with my ministers the Levites. ²²Just as the host of heaven cannot be numbered and the sands of the sea cannot be measured, so I will increase the offspring of my servant David, and the Levites who minister to me.

23 The word of the LORD came to Jeremiah: ²⁴Have you not observed how these people say, "The two families that the LORD chose have been rejected by him," and how they hold my people in such contempt that they no longer regard them as a nation? ²⁵Thus says the LORD: Only if I had not established my covenant with day and night and the ordinances of heaven and earth, ²⁶would I reject the offspring of Jacob and of my servant David and not choose any of his descendants as rulers over the offspring of Abraham, Isaac, and Jacob. For I will restore their fortunes, and will have mercy upon them.

Death in Captivity Predicted for Zedekiah

34 The word that came to Jeremiah from the LORD, when King Nebuchadrezzar of Babylon and all his army and all the kingdoms of the earth and all the peoples under his dominion were fighting against Jerusalem and all its cities: ²Thus says the LORD, the God of Israel: Go and speak to King Zedekiah of Judah and say to him: Thus says the LORD: I am going to give this city into the hand of the king of Babylon, and he shall burn it with fire. ³And you yourself shall not escape from his hand, but shall surely be captured and handed over to him; you shall see the king of Babylon eye to eye and speak with him face to face; and you shall go to Babylon. ⁴Yet hear the word of the LORD, O King Zedekiah of Judah! Thus says the LORD concerning you: You shall not die by the sword; ⁵you shall die in peace. And as spices were burned*ᵃ* for your ancestors, the earlier kings who preceded you, so they shall burn spices*ᵇ* for you and lament for you, saying, "Alas, lord!" For I have spoken the word, says the LORD.

6 Then the prophet Jeremiah spoke all these words to Zedekiah king of Judah, in Jerusalem, ⁷when the army of the king of Babylon was fighting against Jerusalem and against all the cities of Judah that were left, Lachish and Azekah; for these were the only fortified cities of Judah that remained.

Treacherous Treatment of Slaves

8 The word that came to Jeremiah from the LORD, after King Zedekiah had made a covenant with all the people in Jerusalem to make a proclamation of liberty to them— ⁹that all should set free their Hebrew slaves, male and female, so that no one should hold another Judean in slavery. ¹⁰And they obeyed, all the officials and all the people who had entered into the covenant that all would set free their slaves, male or female, so that they would not be enslaved again; they obeyed and set them free. ¹¹But afterward they turned around and took back the male and female slaves they had set free, and brought them again into subjection as slaves. ¹²The word of the LORD came to Jeremiah from the LORD: ¹³Thus says the LORD, the God of Israel: I myself made a covenant with your ancestors when I brought them out of the land of Egypt, out of the house

a Heb *as there was burning*   *b* Heb *shall burn*

of slavery, saying, ¹⁴"Every seventh year each of you must set free any Hebrews who have been sold to you and have served you six years; you must set them free from your service." But your ancestors did not listen to me or incline their ears to me. ¹⁵You yourselves recently repented and did what was right in my sight by proclaiming liberty to one another, and you made a covenant before me in the house that is called by my name; ¹⁶but then you turned around and profaned my name when each of you took back your male and female slaves, whom you had set free according to their desire, and you brought them again into subjection to be your slaves. ¹⁷Therefore, thus says the Lord: You have not obeyed me by granting a release to your neighbors and friends; I am going to grant a release to you, says the Lord—a release to the sword, to pestilence, and to famine. I will make you a horror to all the kingdoms of the earth. ¹⁸And those who transgressed my covenant and did not keep the terms of the covenant that they made before me, I will make like*a* the calf when they cut it in two and passed between its parts: ¹⁹the officials of Judah, the officials of Jerusalem, the eunuchs, the priests, and all the people of the land who passed between the parts of the calf ²⁰shall be handed over to their enemies and to those who seek their lives. Their corpses shall become food for the birds of the air and the wild animals of the earth. ²¹And as for King Zedekiah of Judah and his officials, I will hand them over to their enemies and to those who seek their lives, to the army of the king of Babylon, which has withdrawn from you. ²²I am going to command, says the Lord, and will bring them back to this city; and they will fight against it, and take it, and burn it with fire. The towns of Judah I will make a desolation without inhabitant.

The Rechabites Commended

35 The word that came to Jeremiah from the Lord in the days of King Jehoiakim son of Josiah of Judah: ²Go to the house of the Rechabites, and speak with them, and bring them to the house of the Lord, into one of the chambers; then offer them wine to drink. ³So I took Jaazaniah son of Jeremiah son of Habazziniah, and his brothers, and all his sons, and the whole house of the Rechabites. ⁴I brought them to the house of the Lord into the chamber of the sons of Hanan son of Igdaliah, the man of God, which was near the chamber of the officials, above the chamber of Maaseiah son of Shallum, keeper of the threshold. ⁵Then I set before the Rechabites pitchers full of wine, and cups; and I said to them, "Have some wine." ⁶But they answered, "We will drink no wine, for our ancestor Jonadab son of Rechab commanded us, 'You shall never drink wine, neither you nor your children; ⁷nor shall you ever build a house, or sow seed; nor shall you plant a vineyard, or even own one; but you shall live in tents all your days, that you may live many days in the land where you reside.' ⁸We have obeyed the charge of our ancestor Jonadab son of Rechab in all that he commanded us, to drink no wine all our days, ourselves, our wives, our sons, or our daughters, ⁹and not to build houses to live in. We have no vineyard or field or seed; ¹⁰but we have lived in tents, and

Different

JEREMIAH 35.1–11

The Recabites were different. They chose to live in tents, work as shepherds and abstain from wine, shunning the more sophisticated, settled ways of some of God's people. God made them an example of obedience and faithfulness.

Think about committed Christians you may know who practice their faith differently than you do. Choose someone you trust and respect, and talk to that person about his or her most important convictions. Ask them honest questions and list the differences between you and that person. With this passage before you, pray over your list, asking God for new insights or reaffirmation of your own convictions.

See Meeting God in Community

Attending to the Word

When you hear the Word of God read publicly, are you attentive or does your mind tend to wander? To sharpen your hearing make a pact with some friends to fast for at least one meal, praying that your appetite for God's Word would be sharpened. Select a passage of scripture and then meet together. Choose a good reader. Listen to God's Word as it is read aloud. Follow the reading with times of silent reflection, prayer and discussion about what you have heard. Finish with a simple meal commemorating the fact that together you live by both bread and the Word (see Deuteronomy 8.3).

See Meeting God in Scripture

have obeyed and done all that our ancestor Jonadab commanded us. ¹¹But when King Nebuchadrezzar of Babylon came up against the land, we said, 'Come, and let us go to Jerusalem for fear of the army of the Chaldeans and the army of the Arameans.' That is why we are living in Jerusalem."

12 Then the word of the LORD came to Jeremiah: ¹³Thus says the LORD of hosts, the God of Israel: Go and say to the people of Judah and the inhabitants of Jerusalem, Can you not learn a lesson and obey my words? says the LORD. ¹⁴The command has been carried out that Jonadab son of Rechab gave to his descendants to drink no wine; and they drink none to this day, for they have obeyed their ancestor's command. But I myself have spoken to you persistently, and you have not obeyed me. ¹⁵I have sent to you all my servants the prophets, sending them persistently, saying, "Turn now everyone of you from your evil way, and amend your doings, and do not go after other gods to serve them, and then you shall live in the land that I gave to you and your ancestors." But you did not incline your ear or obey me. ¹⁶The descendants of Jonadab son of Rechab have carried out the command that their ancestor gave them, but this people has not obeyed me. ¹⁷Therefore, thus says the LORD, the God of hosts, the God of Israel: I am going to bring on Judah and on all the inhabitants of Jerusalem every disaster that I have pronounced against them; because I have spoken to them and they have not listened, I have called to them and they have not answered.

18 But to the house of the Rechabites Jeremiah said: Thus says the LORD of hosts, the God of Israel: Because you have obeyed the command of your ancestor Jonadab, and kept all his precepts, and done all that he commanded you, ¹⁹therefore thus says the LORD of hosts, the God of Israel: Jonadab son of Rechab shall not lack a descendant to stand before me for all time.

The Scroll Read in the Temple

36 In the fourth year of King Jehoiakim son of Josiah of Judah, this word came to Jeremiah from the LORD: ²Take a scroll and write on it all the words that I have spoken to you against Israel and Judah and all the nations, from the day I spoke to you, from the days of Josiah until today. ³It may be that when the house of Judah hears of all the disasters that I intend to do to them, all of them may turn from their evil ways, so that I may forgive their iniquity and their sin.

4 Then Jeremiah called Baruch son of Neriah, and Baruch wrote on a scroll at Jeremiah's dictation all the words of the LORD that he had spoken to him. ⁵And Jeremiah ordered Baruch, saying, "I am prevented from entering the house of the LORD; ⁶so you go yourself, and on a fast day in the hearing of the people in the LORD's house you shall read the words of the LORD from the scroll that you have written at my dictation. You shall read them also in the hearing of all the people of Judah who come up from their towns. ⁷It may be that their plea will come before the LORD, and that all of them will turn from their evil ways, for great is the anger and wrath that the LORD has pronounced against this people." ⁸And Baruch son of Neriah

did all that the prophet Jeremiah ordered him about reading from the scroll the words of the LORD in the LORD's house.

9 In the fifth year of King Jehoiakim son of Josiah of Judah, in the ninth month, all the people in Jerusalem and all the people who came from the towns of Judah to Jerusalem proclaimed a fast before the LORD. ¹⁰Then, in the hearing of all the people, Baruch read the words of Jeremiah from the scroll, in the house of the LORD, in the chamber of Gemariah son of Shaphan the secretary, which was in the upper court, at the entry of the New Gate of the LORD's house.

The Scroll Read in the Palace

11 When Micaiah son of Gemariah son of Shaphan heard all the words of the LORD from the scroll, ¹²he went down to the king's house, into the secretary's chamber; and all the officials were sitting there: Elishama the secretary, Delaiah son of Shemaiah, Elnathan son of Achbor, Gemariah son of Shaphan, Zedekiah son of Hananiah, and all the officials. ¹³And Micaiah told them all the words that he had heard, when Baruch read the scroll in the hearing of the people. ¹⁴Then all the officials sent Jehudi son of Nethaniah son of Shelemiah son of Cushi to say to Baruch, "Bring the scroll that you read in the hearing of the people, and come." So Baruch son of Neriah took the scroll in his hand and came to them. ¹⁵And they said to him, "Sit down and read it to us." So Baruch read it to them. ¹⁶When they heard all the words, they turned to one another in alarm, and said to Baruch, "We certainly must report all these words to the king." ¹⁷Then they questioned Baruch, "Tell us now, how did you write all these words? Was it at his dictation?" ¹⁸Baruch answered them, "He dictated all these words to me, and I wrote them with ink on the scroll." ¹⁹Then the officials said to Baruch, "Go and hide, you and Jeremiah, and let no one know where you are."

Jehoiakim Burns the Scroll

20 Leaving the scroll in the chamber of Elishama the secretary, they went to the court of the king; and they reported all the words to the king. ²¹Then the king sent Jehudi to get the scroll, and he took it from the chamber of Elishama the secretary; and Jehudi read it to the king and all the officials who stood beside the king. ²²Now the king was sitting in his winter apartment (it was the ninth month), and there was a fire burning in the brazier before him. ²³As Jehudi read three or four columns, the king*a* would cut them off with a penknife and throw them into the fire in the brazier, until the entire scroll was consumed in the fire that was in the brazier. ²⁴Yet neither the king, nor any of his servants who heard all these words, was alarmed, nor did they tear their garments. ²⁵Even when Elnathan and Delaiah and Gemariah urged the king not to burn the scroll, he would not listen to them. ²⁶And the king commanded Jerahmeel the king's son and Seraiah son of Azriel and Shelemiah son of Abdeel to arrest the secretary Baruch and the prophet Jeremiah. But the LORD hid them.

a Heb he

What Fire Will Not Destroy

JEREMIAH 36.20–26

You may have never burned a Bible as King Jehoiakim contemptuously burned Jeremiah's manuscript, but have you neglected God's Word? Neglect can nullify the Word as effectively as fire.

Place a Bible before you. Light a candle so that it shines on it. Ask God to give you a burning desire to hear what the Word is saying. Read a familiar passage as if for the first time. Dwell on it so that you might hear something new. Fire could not destroy what God had spoken to Jeremiah, and death could not destroy God's Word spoken in Jesus; pray that you and your faith community experience new life in your desire to listen to, and act on, God's Word.

See *Meeting God in Scripture*

Jerusalem! Jerusalem!

JEREMIAH 37.8–10

"Jerusalem, Jerusalem, the city that kills the prophets and stones those who are sent to it! How often have I desired to gather your children together as a hen gathers her brood under her wings, and you were not willing! See, your house is left to you, desolate."

—Matthew 23.37–38

See Meeting God in Service

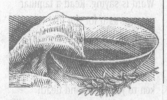

Jeremiah Dictates Another

27 Now, after the king had burned the scroll with the words that Baruch wrote at Jeremiah's dictation, the word of the LORD came to Jeremiah: **28**Take another scroll and write on it all the former words that were in the first scroll, which King Jehoiakim of Judah has burned. **29**And concerning King Jehoiakim of Judah you shall say: Thus says the LORD, You have dared to burn this scroll, saying, Why have you written in it that the king of Babylon will certainly come and destroy this land, and will cut off from it human beings and animals? **30**Therefore thus says the LORD concerning King Jehoiakim of Judah: He shall have no one to sit upon the throne of David, and his dead body shall be cast out to the heat by day and the frost by night. **31**And I will punish him and his offspring and his servants for their iniquity; I will bring on them, and on the inhabitants of Jerusalem, and on the people of Judah, all the disasters with which I have threatened them—but they would not listen.

32 Then Jeremiah took another scroll and gave it to the secretary Baruch son of Neriah, who wrote on it at Jeremiah's dictation all the words of the scroll that King Jehoiakim of Judah had burned in the fire; and many similar words were added to them.

Zedekiah's Vain Hope

37 Zedekiah son of Josiah, whom King Nebuchadrezzar of Babylon made king in the land of Judah, succeeded Coniah son of Jehoiakim. **2**But neither he nor his servants nor the people of the land listened to the words of the LORD that he spoke through the prophet Jeremiah.

3 King Zedekiah sent Jehucal son of Shelemiah and the priest Zephaniah son of Maaseiah to the prophet Jeremiah saying, "Please pray for us to the LORD our God." **4**Now Jeremiah was still going in and out among the people, for he had not yet been put in prison. **5**Meanwhile, the army of Pharaoh had come out of Egypt; and when the Chaldeans who were besieging Jerusalem heard news of them, they withdrew from Jerusalem.

6 Then the word of the LORD came to the prophet Jeremiah: **7**Thus says the LORD, God of Israel: This is what the two of you shall say to the king of Judah, who sent you to me to inquire of me: Pharaoh's army, which set out to help you, is going to return to its own land, to Egypt. **8**And the Chaldeans shall return and fight against this city; they shall take it and burn it with fire. **9**Thus says the LORD: Do not deceive yourselves, saying, "The Chaldeans will surely go away from us," for they will not go away. **10**Even if you defeated the whole army of Chaldeans who are fighting against you, and there remained of them only wounded men in their tents, they would rise up and burn this city with fire.

Jeremiah Is Imprisoned

11 Now when the Chaldean army had withdrawn from Jerusalem at the approach of Pharaoh's army, **12**Jeremiah set out from Jerusalem to go to the land of Benjamin to receive his share of property*ᵃ* among the people there.

a Meaning of Heb uncertain

¹³When he reached the Benjamin Gate, a sentinel there named Irijah son of Shelemiah son of Hananiah arrested the prophet Jeremiah saying, "You are deserting to the Chaldeans." ¹⁴And Jeremiah said, "That is a lie; I am not deserting to the Chaldeans." But Irijah would not listen to him, and arrested Jeremiah and brought him to the officials. ¹⁵The officials were enraged at Jeremiah, and they beat him and imprisoned him in the house of the secretary Jonathan, for it had been made a prison. ¹⁶Thus Jeremiah was put in the cistern house, in the cells, and remained there many days.

17 Then King Zedekiah sent for him, and received him. The king questioned him secretly in his house, and said, "Is there any word from the LORD?" Jeremiah said, "There is!" Then he said, "You shall be handed over to the king of Babylon." ¹⁸Jeremiah also said to King Zedekiah, "What wrong have I done to you or your servants or this people, that you have put me in prison? ¹⁹Where are your prophets who prophesied to you, saying, 'The king of Babylon will not come against you and against this land'? ²⁰Now please hear me, my lord king: be good enough to listen to my plea, and do not send me back to the house of the secretary Jonathan to die there." ²¹So King Zedekiah gave orders, and they committed Jeremiah to the court of the guard; and a loaf of bread was given him daily from the bakers' street, until all the bread of the city was gone. So Jeremiah remained in the court of the guard.

Jeremiah in the Cistern

38 Now Shephatiah son of Mattan, Gedaliah son of Pashhur, Jucal son of Shelemiah, and Pashhur son of Malchiah heard the words that Jeremiah was saying to all the people, ²Thus says the LORD, Those who stay in this city shall die by the sword, by famine, and by pestilence; but those who go out to the Chaldeans shall live; they shall have their lives as a prize of war, and live. ³Thus says the LORD, This city shall surely be handed over to the army of the king of Babylon and be taken. ⁴Then the officials said to the king, "This man ought to be put to death, because he is discouraging the soldiers who are left in this city, and all the people, by speaking such words to them. For this man is not seeking the welfare of this people, but their harm." ⁵King Zedekiah said, "Here he is; he is in your hands; for the king is powerless against you." ⁶So they took Jeremiah and threw him into the cistern of Malchiah, the king's son, which was in the court of the guard, letting Jeremiah down by ropes. Now there was no water in the cistern, but only mud, and Jeremiah sank in the mud.

Jeremiah Is Rescued by Ebed-melech

7 Ebed-melech the Ethiopian,ᵃ a eunuch in the king's house, heard that they had put Jeremiah into the cistern. The king happened to be sitting at the Benjamin Gate, ⁸So Ebed-melech left the king's house and spoke to the king, ⁹"My lord king, these men have acted wickedly in all they did to the prophet Jeremiah by throwing him into the cistern to die there of hunger, for there is no bread left in the city." ¹⁰Then the king commanded Ebed-melech the Ethiopian,ᵃ "Take three men with you from here, and pull the

Deliverance From Denial and Disaster

JEREMIAH 38.14–16

We ask to hear the truth, but if we do not like what we hear, can we choose to ignore it? And if we do ignore the truth, what is the cost?

Ask the Spirit to bless your imagination and guide you as you explore the truth. Imagine you are having a conversation with Jeremiah and that you are writing as you talk together. Jeremiah asks you a question about some matter that you do not want anyone else to know about at this stage. Write his question down. On the next line write your response—whatever comes to mind. Ignoring any inner voices that say, "This is silly. You're just inventing this," keep writing until your conversation is finished. Read what you have written. Take it to the Lord and ask for deliverance from denial, delusion and disaster. If it seems right, share what has happened to you with a trusted person such as your spiritual adviser, faith companion or pastor.

See Meeting God in Worship

prophet Jeremiah up from the cistern before he dies." ¹¹So Ebed-melech took the men with him and went to the house of the king, to a wardrobe of*ᵃ* the storehouse, and took from there old rags and worn-out clothes, which he let down to Jeremiah in the cistern by ropes. ¹²Then Ebed-melech the Ethiopian*ᵇ* said to Jeremiah, "Just put the rags and clothes between your armpits and the ropes." Jeremiah did so. ¹³Then they drew Jeremiah up by the ropes and pulled him out of the cistern. And Jeremiah remained in the court of the guard.

Zedekiah Consults Jeremiah Again

14 King Zedekiah sent for the prophet Jeremiah and received him at the third entrance of the temple of the LORD. The king said to Jeremiah, "I have something to ask you; do not hide anything from me." ¹⁵Jeremiah said to Zedekiah, "If I tell you, you will put me to death, will you not? And if I give you advice, you will not listen to me." ¹⁶So King Zedekiah swore an oath in secret to Jeremiah, "As the LORD lives, who gave us our lives, I will not put you to death or hand you over to these men who seek your life."

17 Then Jeremiah said to Zedekiah, "Thus says the LORD, the God of hosts, the God of Israel, If you will only surrender to the officials of the king of Babylon, then your life shall be spared, and this city shall not be burned with fire, and you and your house shall live. ¹⁸But if you do not surrender to the officials of the king of Babylon, then this city shall be handed over to the Chaldeans, and they shall burn it with fire, and you yourself shall not escape from their hand." ¹⁹King Zedekiah said to Jeremiah, "I am afraid of the Judeans who have deserted to the Chaldeans, for I might be handed over to them and they would abuse me." ²⁰Jeremiah said, "That will not happen. Just obey the voice of the LORD in what I say to you, and it shall go well with you, and your life shall be spared. ²¹But if you are determined not to surrender, this is what the LORD has shown me— ²²a vision of all the women remaining in the house of the king of Judah being led out to the officials of the king of Babylon and saying,

'Your trusted friends have seduced you
    and have overcome you;
Now that your feet are stuck in the mud,
    they desert you.'

²³All your wives and your children shall be led out to the Chaldeans, and you yourself shall not escape from their hand, but shall be seized by the king of Babylon; and this city shall be burned with fire."

24 Then Zedekiah said to Jeremiah, "Do not let anyone else know of this conversation, or you will die. ²⁵If the officials should hear that I have spoken with you, and they should come and say to you, 'Just tell us what you said to the king; do not conceal it from us, or we will put you to death. What did the king say to you?' ²⁶then you shall say to them, 'I was presenting my plea to the king not to send me back to the house of Jonathan to die there.' " ²⁷All the officials did come to Jeremiah and questioned him; and he answered them in the very words the king had commanded. So they stopped questioning him, for the conversation had not been overheard. ²⁸And Jeremiah

a Cn: Heb *to under*   *b* Or *Nubian*; Heb *Cushite*

remained in the court of the guard until the day that Jerusalem was taken.

The Fall of Jerusalem

39 In the ninth year of King Zedekiah of Judah, in the tenth month, King Nebuchadrezzar of Babylon and all his army came against Jerusalem and besieged it; ²in the eleventh year of Zedekiah, in the fourth month, on the ninth day of the month, a breach was made in the city. ³When Jerusalem was taken,ᵃ all the officials of the king of Babylon came and sat in the middle gate: Nergal-sharezer, Samgar-nebo, Sarsechim the Rabsaris, Nergal-sharezer the Rabmag, with all the rest of the officials of the king of Babylon. ⁴When King Zedekiah of Judah and all the soldiers saw them, they fled, going out of the city at night by way of the king's garden through the gate between the two walls; and they went toward the Arabah. ⁵But the army of the Chaldeans pursued them, and overtook Zedekiah in the plains of Jericho; and when they had taken him, they brought him up to King Nebuchadrezzar of Babylon, at Riblah, in the land of Hamath; and he passed sentence on him. ⁶The king of Babylon slaughtered the sons of Zedekiah at Riblah before his eyes; also the king of Babylon slaughtered all the nobles of Judah. ⁷He put out the eyes of Zedekiah, and bound him in fetters to take him to Babylon. ⁸The Chaldeans burned the king's house and the houses of the people, and broke down the walls of Jerusalem. ⁹Then Nebuzaradan the captain of the guard exiled to Babylon the rest of the people who were left in the city, those who had deserted to him, and the people who remained. ¹⁰Nebuzaradan the captain of the guard left in the land of Judah some of the poor people who owned nothing, and gave them vineyards and fields at the same time.

Jeremiah, Set Free, Remembers Ebed-melech

11 King Nebuchadrezzar of Babylon gave command concerning Jeremiah through Nebuzaradan, the captain of the guard, saying, ¹²"Take him, look after him well and do him no harm, but deal with him as he may ask you." ¹³So Nebuzaradan the captain of the guard, Nebushazban the Rabsaris, Nergal-sharezer the Rabmag, and all the chief officers of the king of Babylon sent ¹⁴and took Jeremiah from the court of the guard. They entrusted him to Gedaliah son of Ahikam son of Shaphan to be brought home. So he stayed with his own people.

15 The word of the LORD came to Jeremiah while he was confined in the court of the guard: ¹⁶Go and say to Ebed-melech the Ethiopian:ᵇ Thus says the LORD of hosts, the God of Israel: I am going to fulfill my words against this city for evil and not for good, and they shall be accomplished in your presence on that day. ¹⁷But I will save you on that day, says the LORD, and you shall not be handed over to those whom you dread. ¹⁸For I will surely save you, and you shall not fall by the sword; but you shall have your life as a prize of war, because you have trusted in me, says the LORD.

Jerusalem Falls

JEREMIAH 39.1–10

"God help us. With great skill and energy we have ignored the state of the human heart. With politics and economics we have denied the heart's needs. With eloquence, wit and reason we have belittled the heart's wisdom. With sophistication and style, with science and technology, we have drowned out the voice of the soul. The primitive voice, the innocent voice. The truth. We cannot hear our heart's truth and thus we have betrayed and belittled ourselves and pledged madness to our children. With skill and pride we have made for ourselves an unhappy society. God be with us. Amen."

—MICHAEL LEUNIG,
A Common Prayer

ᵃ This clause has been transposed from 38.28   ᵇ Or *Nubian*; Heb *Cushite*

Why Do the Wicked Prosper?

JEREMIAH 41.1–3

Gedaliah is a generous man who is prepared to believe the best. He dismisses Ishmael's threat, but Ishmael treacherously murders him as they eat together.

Look at some current news sources and political commentaries and find someone who might be an "Ishmael" in our era. Place a newspaper clipping about that person before you in your prayer place. (If you do not have a clipping, write his or her name in large print on a sheet of paper and place that before you.) Pray that the love of God will touch that person. Pray that those within his or her sphere of influence will be delivered from evil.

See Meeting God in Everyday Life

Jeremiah with Gedaliah the Governor

40 The word that came to Jeremiah from the LORD after Nebuzaradan the captain of the guard had let him go from Ramah, when he took him bound in fetters along with all the captives of Jerusalem and Judah who were being exiled to Babylon. ²The captain of the guard took Jeremiah and said to him, "The LORD your God threatened this place with this disaster; ³and now the LORD has brought it about, and has done as he said, because all of you sinned against the LORD and did not obey his voice. Therefore this thing has come upon you. ⁴Now look, I have just released you today from the fetters on your hands. If you wish to come with me to Babylon, come, and I will take good care of you; but if you do not wish to come with me to Babylon, you need not come. See, the whole land is before you; go wherever you think it good and right to go. ⁵If you remain,ᵃ then return to Gedaliah son of Ahikam son of Shaphan, whom the king of Babylon appointed governor of the towns of Judah, and stay with him among the people; or go wherever you think it right to go." So the captain of the guard gave him an allowance of food and a present, and let him go. ⁶Then Jeremiah went to Gedaliah son of Ahikam at Mizpah, and stayed with him among the people who were left in the land.

7 When all the leaders of the forces in the open country and their troops heard that the king of Babylon had appointed Gedaliah son of Ahikam governor in the land, and had committed to him men, women, and children, those of the poorest of the land who had not been taken into exile to Babylon, ⁸they went to Gedaliah at Mizpah—Ishmael son of Nethaniah, Johanan son of Kareah, Seraiah son of Tanhumeth, the sons of Ephai the Netophathite, Jezaniah son of the Maacathite, they and their troops. ⁹Gedaliah son of Ahikam son of Shaphan swore to them and their troops, saying, "Do not be afraid to serve the Chaldeans. Stay in the land and serve the king of Babylon, and it shall go well with you. ¹⁰As for me, I am staying at Mizpah to represent you before the Chaldeans who come to us; but as for you, gather wine and summer fruits and oil, and store them in your vessels, and live in the towns that you have taken over." ¹¹Likewise, when all the Judeans who were in Moab and among the Ammonites and in Edom and in other lands heard that the king of Babylon had left a remnant in Judah and had appointed Gedaliah son of Ahikam son of Shaphan as governor over them, ¹²then all the Judeans returned from all the places to which they had been scattered and came to the land of Judah, to Gedaliah at Mizpah; and they gathered wine and summer fruits in great abundance.

13 Now Johanan son of Kareah and all the leaders of the forces in the open country came to Gedaliah at Mizpah ¹⁴and said to him, "Are you at all aware that Baalis king of the Ammonites has sent Ishmael son of Nethaniah to take your life?" But Gedaliah son of Ahikam would not believe them. ¹⁵Then Johanan son of Kareah spoke secretly to Gedaliah at Mizpah, "Please let me go and kill Ishmael son of Nethaniah, and no one else will know. Why should he take your life, so that all the Judeans who are gathered

a Syr: Meaning of Heb uncertain

around you would be scattered, and the remnant of Judah would perish?" [16]But Gedaliah son of Ahikam said to Johanan son of Kareah, "Do not do such a thing, for you are telling a lie about Ishmael."

Insurrection against Gedaliah

41 In the seventh month, Ishmael son of Nethaniah son of Elishama, of the royal family, one of the chief officers of the king, came with ten men to Gedaliah son of Ahikam, at Mizpah. As they ate bread together there at Mizpah, [2]Ishmael son of Nethaniah and the ten men with him got up and struck down Gedaliah son of Ahikam son of Shaphan with the sword and killed him, because the king of Babylon had appointed him governor in the land. [3]Ishmael also killed all the Judeans who were with Gedaliah at Mizpah, and the Chaldean soldiers who happened to be there.

4 On the day after the murder of Gedaliah, before anyone knew of it, [5]eighty men arrived from Shechem and Shiloh and Samaria, with their beards shaved and their clothes torn, and their bodies gashed, bringing grain offerings and incense to present at the temple of the LORD. [6]And Ishmael son of Nethaniah came out from Mizpah to meet them, weeping as he came. As he met them, he said to them, "Come to Gedaliah son of Ahikam." [7]When they reached the middle of the city, Ishmael son of Nethaniah and the men with him slaughtered them, and threw them[a] into a cistern. [8]But there were ten men among them who said to Ishmael, "Do not kill us, for we have stores of wheat, barley, oil, and honey hidden in the fields." So he refrained, and did not kill them along with their companions.

9 Now the cistern into which Ishmael had thrown all the bodies of the men whom he had struck down was the large cistern[b] that King Asa had made for defense against King Baasha of Israel; Ishmael son of Nethaniah filled that cistern with those whom he had killed. [10]Then Ishmael took captive all the rest of the people who were in Mizpah, the king's daughters and all the people who were left at Mizpah, whom Nebuzaradan, the captain of the guard, had committed to Gedaliah son of Ahikam. Ishmael son of Nethaniah took them captive and set out to cross over to the Ammonites.

11 But when Johanan son of Kareah and all the leaders of the forces with him heard of all the crimes that Ishmael son of Nethaniah had done, [12]they took all their men and went to fight against Ishmael son of Nethaniah. They came upon him at the great pool that is in Gibeon. [13]And when all the people who were with Ishmael saw Johanan son of Kareah and all the leaders of the forces with him, they were glad. [14]So all the people whom Ishmael had carried away captive from Mizpah turned around and came back, and went to Johanan son of Kareah. [15]But Ishmael son of Nethaniah escaped from Johanan with eight men, and went to the Ammonites. [16]Then Johanan son of Kareah and all the leaders of the forces with him took all the rest of the people whom Ishmael son of Nethaniah had carried away captive[c] from Mizpah after he had slain Ged-

a Syr: Heb lacks *and threw them*; compare verse 9   b Gk: Heb *whom he had killed by the hand of Gedaliah*   c Cn: Heb *whom he recovered from Ishmael son of Nethaniah*

Go Where? Do What?

JEREMIAH 42.1–6

The quandary the officers face is where to go and what to do. To stay where they are may bring reprisals from Babylon. To escape to Egypt could bring safety, but it carries with it a *de facto* admission of guilt. The people ask Jeremiah to pray to the Lord for guidance.

Whom do you ask to pray for you when you are in a quandary? What feedback do you give that person? Pray for her or him. Send a simple note of thanks. If you have asked no one to pray for you, consider who that person might be. Approach him or her. Present your request for prayer and discuss how you will stay in contact with one another.

See Meeting God in Community

Deceitful Heart

JEREMIAH 42.7–17

You say you believe God is with you always, but how solid is that belief in practice?

The Lord says, "Do not be afraid . . . for I am with you to save you and rescue you . . . . I will grant you mercy."

Do you really believe this or do your worries get the better of you? Write about an experience you have had in which you knew God's saving, rescuing compassion. Write a few lines about what you have learned about God as you have reflected on your experience. Now apply what you have learned to a present experience of difficulty. Pray that God will save you from the duplicity of a deceitful heart. Pray that you will be blessed with the gift of a trust in God that is bigger than your worries.

See *Meeting God in Worship*

aliah son of Ahikam—soldiers, women, children, and eunuchs, whom Johanan brought back from Gibeon.[a] 17And they set out, and stopped at Geruth Chimham near Bethlehem, intending to go to Egypt 18because of the Chaldeans; for they were afraid of them, because Ishmael son of Nethaniah had killed Gedaliah son of Ahikam, whom the king of Babylon had made governor over the land.

Jeremiah Advises Survivors Not to Migrate

42 Then all the commanders of the forces, and Johanan son of Kareah and Azariah[b] son of Hoshaiah, and all the people from the least to the greatest, approached 2the prophet Jeremiah and said, "Be good enough to listen to our plea, and pray to the LORD your God for us—for all this remnant. For there are only a few of us left out of many, as your eyes can see. 3Let the LORD your God show us where we should go and what we should do." 4The prophet Jeremiah said to them, "Very well: I am going to pray to the LORD your God as you request, and whatever the LORD answers you I will tell you; I will keep nothing back from you." 5They in their turn said to Jeremiah, "May the LORD be a true and faithful witness against us if we do not act according to everything that the LORD your God sends us through you. 6Whether it is good or bad, we will obey the voice of the LORD our God to whom we are sending you, in order that it may go well with us when we obey the voice of the LORD our God."

7 At the end of ten days the word of the LORD came to Jeremiah. 8Then he summoned Johanan son of Kareah and all the commanders of the forces who were with him, and all the people from the least to the greatest, 9and said to them, "Thus says the LORD, the God of Israel, to whom you sent me to present your plea before him: 10If you will only remain in this land, then I will build you up and not pull you down; I will plant you, and not pluck you up; for I am sorry for the disaster that I have brought upon you. 11Do not be afraid of the king of Babylon, as you have been; do not be afraid of him, says the LORD, for I am with you, to save you and to rescue you from his hand. 12I will grant you mercy, and he will have mercy on you and restore you to your native soil. 13But if you continue to say, 'We will not stay in this land,' thus disobeying the voice of the LORD your God 14and saying, 'No, we will go to the land of Egypt, where we shall not see war, or hear the sound of the trumpet, or be hungry for bread, and there we will stay,' 15then hear the word of the LORD, O remnant of Judah. Thus says the LORD of hosts, the God of Israel: If you are determined to enter Egypt and go to settle there, 16then the sword that you fear shall overtake you there, in the land of Egypt; and the famine that you dread shall follow close after you into Egypt; and there you shall die. 17All the people who have determined to go to Egypt to settle there shall die by the sword, by famine, and by pestilence; they shall have no remnant or survivor from the disaster that I am bringing upon them.

18 "For thus says the LORD of hosts, the God of Israel: Just as my anger and my wrath were poured out on the inhabitants of Jerusalem, so my wrath will be poured out on

a Meaning of Heb uncertain   *b* Gk: Heb *Jezaniah*

you when you go to Egypt. You shall become an object of execration and horror, of cursing and ridicule. You shall see this place no more. ¹⁹The LORD has said to you, O remnant of Judah, Do not go to Egypt. Be well aware that I have warned you today ²⁰that you have made a fatal mistake. For you yourselves sent me to the LORD your God, saying, 'Pray for us to the LORD our God, and whatever the LORD our God says, tell us and we will do it.' ²¹So I have told you today, but you have not obeyed the voice of the LORD your God in anything that he sent me to tell you. ²²Be well aware, then, that you shall die by the sword, by famine, and by pestilence in the place where you desire to go and settle."

Taken to Egypt, Jeremiah Warns of Judgment

43 When Jeremiah finished speaking to all the people all these words of the LORD their God, with which the LORD their God had sent him to them, ²Azariah son of Hoshaiah and Johanan son of Kareah and all the other insolent men said to Jeremiah, "You are telling a lie. The LORD our God did not send you to say, 'Do not go to Egypt to settle there'; ³but Baruch son of Neriah is inciting you against us, to hand us over to the Chaldeans, in order that they may kill us or take us into exile in Babylon." ⁴So Johanan son of Kareah and all the commanders of the forces and all the people did not obey the voice of the LORD, to stay in the land of Judah. ⁵But Johanan son of Kareah and all the commanders of the forces took all the remnant of Judah who had returned to settle in the land of Judah from all the nations to which they had been driven— ⁶the men, the women, the children, the princesses, and everyone whom Nebuzaradan the captain of the guard had left with Gedaliah son of Ahikam son of Shaphan; also the prophet Jeremiah and Baruch son of Neriah. ⁷And they came into the land of Egypt, for they did not obey the voice of the LORD. And they arrived at Tahpanhes.

8 Then the word of the LORD came to Jeremiah in Tahpanhes: ⁹Take some large stones in your hands, and bury them in the clay pavement[a] that is at the entrance to Pharaoh's palace in Tahpanhes. Let the Judeans see you do it, ¹⁰and say to them, Thus says the LORD of hosts, the God of Israel: I am going to send and take my servant King Nebuchadrezzar of Babylon, and he[b] will set his throne above these stones that I have buried, and he will spread his royal canopy over them. ¹¹He shall come and ravage the land of Egypt, giving

those who are destined for pestilence, to
        pestilence,
    and those who are destined for captivity, to
        captivity,
    and those who are destined for the sword, to the
        sword.

¹²He[c] shall kindle a fire in the temples of the gods of Egypt; and he shall burn them and carry them away captive; and he shall pick clean the land of Egypt, as a shepherd picks his cloak clean of vermin; and he shall depart from there safely. ¹³He shall break the obelisks of Heliopolis, which is in the land of Egypt; and the temples of the gods of Egypt he shall burn with fire.

Where Can I Flee From Your Presence?

JEREMIAH 43.8–13

Where can you run to get away from God? You can immerse yourself in the busyness of work. You can let your life be taken over by the demands of a relationship. You can fill yourself with food and drink and entertaining diversions. You can escape to any "Egypt" of your own making.

Find a small stone. Set it apart as a reminder of God's sovereign presence in your life. Put it in your pocket or wallet so that it goes where you go. Touch it at various times throughout the day and, as you do so, ask yourself if you are headed toward God or toward your "Egypt."

See Meeting God in Everyday Life

---

a Meaning of Heb uncertain   *b* Gk Syr: Heb *I*   *c* Gk Syr Vg: Heb *I*

Whose Word Will Stand?

JEREMIAH 44.15–19

The world is full of words—advice from politicians, researchers, sociologists, economists, statisticians, preachers, teachers and consultants. Then there are the words of your own heart—its desires, preferences and inclinations. How does God get a word in?

Place a map of your community and a picture of yourself in front of you. Put a Bible on top of them and say a prayer for your community and for yourself. Pray that the word of God and the good that God seeks will prevail through and over the torrent of words that stream through you and your community today.

See Meeting God in Everyday Life

Denunciation of Persistent Idolatry

44 The word that came to Jeremiah for all the Judeans living in the land of Egypt, at Migdol, at Tahpanhes, at Memphis, and in the land of Pathros, ²Thus says the LORD of hosts, the God of Israel: You yourselves have seen all the disaster that I have brought on Jerusalem and on all the towns of Judah. Look at them; today they are a desolation, without an inhabitant in them, ³because of the wickedness that they committed, provoking me to anger, in that they went to make offerings and serve other gods that they had not known, neither they, nor you, nor your ancestors. ⁴Yet I persistently sent to you all my servants the prophets, saying, "I beg you not to do this abominable thing that I hate!" ⁵But they did not listen or incline their ear, to turn from their wickedness and make no offerings to other gods. ⁶So my wrath and my anger were poured out and kindled in the towns of Judah and in the streets of Jerusalem; and they became a waste and a desolation, as they still are today. ⁷And now thus says the LORD God of hosts, the God of Israel: Why are you doing such great harm to yourselves, to cut off man and woman, child and infant, from the midst of Judah, leaving yourselves without a remnant? ⁸Why do you provoke me to anger with the works of your hands, making offerings to other gods in the land of Egypt where you have come to settle? Will you be cut off and become an object of cursing and ridicule among all the nations of the earth? ⁹Have you forgotten the crimes of your ancestors, of the kings of Judah, of their*a* wives, your own crimes and those of your wives, which they committed in the land of Judah and in the streets of Jerusalem? ¹⁰They have shown no contrition or fear to this day, nor have they walked in my law and my statutes that I set before you and before your ancestors.

11 Therefore thus says the LORD of hosts, the God of Israel: I am determined to bring disaster on you, to bring all Judah to an end. ¹²I will take the remnant of Judah who are determined to come to the land of Egypt to settle, and they shall perish, everyone; in the land of Egypt they shall fall; by the sword and by famine they shall perish; from the least to the greatest, they shall die by the sword and by famine; and they shall become an object of execration and horror, of cursing and ridicule. ¹³I will punish those who live in the land of Egypt, as I have punished Jerusalem, with the sword, with famine, and with pestilence, ¹⁴so that none of the remnant of Judah who have come to settle in the land of Egypt shall escape or survive or return to the land of Judah. Although they long to go back to live there, they shall not go back, except some fugitives.

15 Then all the men who were aware that their wives had been making offerings to other gods, and all the women who stood by, a great assembly, all the people who lived in Pathros in the land of Egypt, answered Jeremiah: ¹⁶"As for the word that you have spoken to us in the name of the LORD, we are not going to listen to you. ¹⁷Instead, we will do everything that we have vowed, make offerings to the queen of heaven and pour out libations to her, just as we and our ancestors, our kings and our officials, used to do in the towns of Judah and in the streets of Jerusalem.

a Heb *his*

We used to have plenty of food, and prospered, and saw no misfortune. ¹⁸But from the time we stopped making offerings to the queen of heaven and pouring out libations to her, we have lacked everything and have perished by the sword and by famine." ¹⁹And the women said,ᵃ "Indeed we will go on making offerings to the queen of heaven and pouring out libations to her; do you think that we made cakes for her, marked with her image, and poured out libations to her without our husbands' being involved?"

20 Then Jeremiah said to all the people, men and women, all the people who were giving him this answer: ²¹"As for the offerings that you made in the towns of Judah and in the streets of Jerusalem, you and your ancestors, your kings and your officials, and the people of the land, did not the Lord remember them? Did it not come into his mind? ²²The Lord could no longer bear the sight of your evil doings, the abominations that you committed; therefore your land became a desolation and a waste and a curse, without inhabitant, as it is to this day. ²³It is because you burned offerings, and because you sinned against the Lord and did not obey the voice of the Lord or walk in his law and in his statutes and in his decrees, that this disaster has befallen you, as is still evident today."

24 Jeremiah said to all the people and all the women, "Hear the word of the Lord, all you Judeans who are in the land of Egypt, ²⁵Thus says the Lord of hosts, the God of Israel: You and your wives have accomplished in deeds what you declared in words, saying, 'We are determined to perform the vows that we have made, to make offerings to the queen of heaven and to pour out libations to her.' By all means, keep your vows and make your libations! ²⁶Therefore hear the word of the Lord, all you Judeans who live in the land of Egypt: Lo, I swear by my great name, says the Lord, that my name shall no longer be pronounced on the lips of any of the people of Judah in all the land of Egypt, saying, 'As the Lord God lives.' ²⁷I am going to watch over them for harm and not for good; all the people of Judah who are in the land of Egypt shall perish by the sword and by famine, until not one is left. ²⁸And those who escape the sword shall return from the land of Egypt to the land of Judah, few in number; and all the remnant of Judah, who have come to the land of Egypt to settle, shall know whose words will stand, mine or theirs! ²⁹This shall be the sign to you, says the Lord, that I am going to punish you in this place, in order that you may know that my words against you will surely be carried out: ³⁰Thus says the Lord, I am going to give Pharaoh Hophra, king of Egypt, into the hands of his enemies, those who seek his life, just as I gave King Zedekiah of Judah into the hand of King Nebuchadrezzar of Babylon, his enemy who sought his life."

A Word of Comfort to Baruch

45 The word that the prophet Jeremiah spoke to Baruch son of Neriah, when he wrote these words in a scroll at the dictation of Jeremiah, in the fourth year of King Jehoiakim son of Josiah of Judah: ²Thus says the Lord, the God of Israel, to you, O Baruch: ³You said, "Woe is me! The Lord has added sorrow to my pain; I am weary

You Too, Baruch!

JEREMIAH 45.1–5

What is happening to the secretary? He is getting the job done effectively—ready, willing and available to Jeremiah, taking his dictation, acting on his behalf in this great and noble service of making the word of God available to the community. But he says, "I am weary . . ."

What is your "but"? If you were completing the sentence, "I want to serve you, God, but . . . ," what would come next? What would you rather be doing with your life? What wearies you? What "great things" would you rather seek for yourself? God's word will be different from the word God had for Baruch, but God has a word for you. Write about your "but . . ." and your weariness and take them to God. Make an appointment to talk with your pastor or a trusted friend about any vocational issues that arise for you.

See *Meeting God in Service*

Prayer for the Perishing

"I believe in the HOLY PRIEST-HOOD OF THY SAINTS, and that I too am a priest, with power to appear before the Father, and in the prayer that avails much bring down blessing on the perishing around me.

"I believe in the POWER OF THY PRECIOUS BLOOD to cleanse from all sin, to give me perfect confidence toward God, and bring me near in the full assurance of faith that my intercession will be heard . . .

"In this faith I yield myself this day to God, as one of His anointed priests, to stand before His face to intercede in behalf of sinners, and to come out and bless in His name."

—ANDREW MURRAY,
With Christ in the School of Prayer

See Meeting God in Prayer

with my groaning, and I find no rest." [4]Thus you shall say to him, "Thus says the LORD: I am going to break down what I have built, and pluck up what I have planted—that is, the whole land. [5]And you, do you seek great things for yourself? Do not seek them; for I am going to bring disaster upon all flesh, says the LORD; but I will give you your life as a prize of war in every place to which you may go."

Judgment on Egypt

46 The word of the LORD that came to the prophet Jeremiah concerning the nations.

2 Concerning Egypt, about the army of Pharaoh Neco, king of Egypt, which was by the river Euphrates at Carchemish and which King Nebuchadrezzar of Babylon defeated in the fourth year of King Jehoiakim son of Josiah of Judah:

[3] Prepare buckler and shield,
    and advance for battle!
[4] Harness the horses;
    mount the steeds!
Take your stations with your helmets,
    whet your lances,
    put on your coats of mail!
[5] Why do I see them terrified?
    They have fallen back;
their warriors are beaten down,
    and have fled in haste.
They do not look back—
    terror is all around!
          says the LORD.
[6] The swift cannot flee away,
    nor can the warrior escape;
in the north by the river Euphrates
    they have stumbled and fallen.

[7] Who is this, rising like the Nile,
    like rivers whose waters surge?
[8] Egypt rises like the Nile,
    like rivers whose waters surge.
It said, Let me rise, let me cover the earth,
    let me destroy cities and their inhabitants.
[9] Advance, O horses,
    and dash madly, O chariots!
Let the warriors go forth:
    Ethiopia[a] and Put who carry the shield,
    the Ludim, who draw[b] the bow.
[10] That day is the day of the Lord GOD of hosts,
    a day of retribution,
    to gain vindication from his foes.
The sword shall devour and be sated,
    and drink its fill of their blood.
For the Lord GOD of hosts holds a sacrifice
    in the land of the north by the river Euphrates.
[11] Go up to Gilead, and take balm,
    O virgin daughter Egypt!
In vain you have used many medicines;
    there is no healing for you.
[12] The nations have heard of your shame,
    and the earth is full of your cry;

a Or Nubia; Heb Cush   *b* Cn: Heb *who grasp, who draw*

for warrior has stumbled against warrior;
 both have fallen together.

Babylonia Will Strike Egypt

13 The word that the LORD spoke to the prophet Jeremiah about the coming of King Nebuchadrezzar of Babylon to attack the land of Egypt:

14 Declare in Egypt, and proclaim in Migdol;
 proclaim in Memphis and Tahpanhes;
 Say, "Take your stations and be ready,
 for the sword shall devour those around you."
15 Why has Apis fled?[a]
 Why did your bull not stand?
 —because the LORD thrust him down.
16 Your multitude stumbled[b] and fell,
 and one said to another,[c]
 "Come, let us go back to our own people
 and to the land of our birth,
 because of the destroying sword."
17 Give Pharaoh, king of Egypt, the name
 "Braggart who missed his chance."

18 As I live, says the King,
 whose name is the LORD of hosts,
 one is coming
 like Tabor among the mountains,
 and like Carmel by the sea.
19 Pack your bags for exile,
 sheltered daughter Egypt!
 For Memphis shall become a waste,
 a ruin, without inhabitant.

20 A beautiful heifer is Egypt—
 a gadfly from the north lights upon her.
21 Even her mercenaries in her midst
 are like fatted calves;
 they too have turned and fled together,
 they did not stand;
 for the day of their calamity has come upon them,
 the time of their punishment.

22 She makes a sound like a snake gliding away;
 for her enemies march in force,
 and come against her with axes,
 like those who fell trees.
23 They shall cut down her forest,
   says the LORD,
 though it is impenetrable,
 because they are more numerous
 than locusts;
 they are without number.
24 Daughter Egypt shall be put to shame;
 she shall be handed over to a people from the
 north.

25 The LORD of hosts, the God of Israel, said: See, I am bringing punishment upon Amon of Thebes, and Pharaoh, and Egypt and her gods and her kings, upon Pharaoh and

---

Before the Floods

JEREMIAH 46.25—47.3

The twentieth century has been called the bloodiest century in human history. And even today terror floods into the lives of people everywhere—the terror of an invading army or a crime syndicate, the terror of a street gang or a random attacker, the terror of domestic violence or child abduction. People cry out. Parents are helpless to protect their children. Help is nowhere to be found.

What is happening within you as you consider such things? What thoughts do you have? How do you feel? How is your faith in God engaged? Drawing on your responses to these questions, write a prayer to God. Set aside some special time to plead for those who are facing terror.

See Meeting God in Prayer

---

a Gk: Heb *Why was it swept away*   b Gk: Meaning of Heb uncertain
c Gk: Heb *and fell one to another and they said*

God of Nations

JEREMIAH 47.6—48.2

When viewed from the inside of a sanctuary—when, from where you sit, all seems well—God's judgment, especially God's judgment on other nations, does not seem to be a matter of immediate concern. But all nations stand in judgment or in blessing before God, the One judging the "strongholds and treasures" in which each nation trusts. Pray for God's mercy to be showered on the nation you call your own. Pray on behalf of several other nations too.

See Meeting God in Prayer

those who trust in him. [26]I will hand them over to those who seek their life, to King Nebuchadrezzar of Babylon and his officers. Afterward Egypt shall be inhabited as in the days of old, says the LORD.

God Will Save Israel

27 But as for you, have no fear, my servant Jacob,
    and do not be dismayed, O Israel;
for I am going to save you from far away,
    and your offspring from the land of their
       captivity.
Jacob shall return and have quiet and ease,
    and no one shall make him afraid.
28 As for you, have no fear, my servant Jacob,
                says the LORD,
    for I am with you.
I will make an end of all the nations
    among which I have banished you,
    but I will not make an end of you!
I will chastise you in just measure,
    and I will by no means leave you unpunished.

Judgment on the Philistines

47 The word of the LORD that came to the prophet Jeremiah concerning the Philistines, before Pharaoh attacked Gaza:

2 Thus says the LORD:
See, waters are rising out of the north
    and shall become an overflowing torrent;
they shall overflow the land and all that fills it,
    the city and those who live in it.
People shall cry out,
    and all the inhabitants of the land shall wail.
3 At the noise of the stamping of the hoofs of his
       stallions,
    at the clatter of his chariots, at the rumbling of
       their wheels,
parents do not turn back for children,
    so feeble are their hands,
4 because of the day that is coming
    to destroy all the Philistines,
to cut off from Tyre and Sidon
    every helper that remains.
For the LORD is destroying the Philistines,
    the remnant of the coastland of Caphtor.
5 Baldness has come upon Gaza,
    Ashkelon is silenced.
O remnant of their power![a]
    How long will you gash yourselves?
6 Ah, sword of the LORD!
    How long until you are quiet?
Put yourself into your scabbard,
    rest and be still!
7 How can it[b] be quiet,
    when the LORD has given it an order?
Against Ashkelon and against the seashore—
    there he has appointed it.

a Gk: Heb *their valley*   *b* Gk Vg: Heb *you*

Judgment on Moab

48 Concerning Moab.

Thus says the LORD of hosts, the God of Israel:
　Alas for Nebo, it is laid waste!
　　Kiriathaim is put to shame, it is taken;
　the fortress is put to shame and broken down;
2　　the renown of Moab is no more.
　In Heshbon they planned evil against her:
　　"Come, let us cut her off from being a nation!"
　You also, O Madmen, shall be brought to silence;[a]
　　the sword shall pursue you.

3　Hark! a cry from Horonaim,
　　"Desolation and great destruction!"
4　"Moab is destroyed!"
　　her little ones cry out.
5　For at the ascent of Luhith
　　they go[b] up weeping bitterly;
　for at the descent of Horonaim
　　they have heard the distressing cry of anguish.
6　Flee! Save yourselves!
　　Be like a wild ass[c] in the desert!

7　Surely, because you trusted in your strongholds[d]
　　　and your treasures,
　　you also shall be taken;
　Chemosh shall go out into exile,
　　with his priests and his attendants.
8　The destroyer shall come upon every town,
　　and no town shall escape;
　the valley shall perish,
　　and the plain shall be destroyed,
　　as the LORD has spoken.

9　Set aside salt for Moab,
　　for she will surely fall;
　her towns shall become a desolation,
　　with no inhabitant in them.

10 Accursed is the one who is slack in doing the work of the LORD; and accursed is the one who keeps back the sword from bloodshed.

11　Moab has been at ease from his youth,
　　settled like wine[e] on its dregs;
　he has not been emptied from vessel to vessel,
　　nor has he gone into exile;
　therefore his flavor has remained
　　and his aroma is unspoiled.
12 Therefore, the time is surely coming, says the LORD, when I shall send to him decanters to decant him, and empty his vessels, and break his[f] jars in pieces. 13Then Moab shall be ashamed of Chemosh, as the house of Israel was ashamed of Bethel, their confidence.

Down From Glory

JEREMIAH 48.12–20

In the time of Augustine, the churches of North Africa were just as flourishing as the beautiful woodlands and fields that he described. Today, where is the church in North Africa? Where are the woodlands and fields? Forests become deserts, churches rise and fall like nations; individual fellowships and entire denominations come and go.

　Gather with others from your church. Make a list of the glories of the tradition in which your faith community stands. What are the forces that could bring it down from glory? Agree together on how you might pray for your church and discuss what practical actions you can take to work for its health and well-being.

See Meeting God in Community

---

a The place-name *Madmen* sounds like the Hebrew verb *to be silent*
b Cn: Heb *he goes*　　*c* Gk Aquila: Heb *like Aroer*　　*d* Gk: Heb *works*
e Heb lacks *like wine*　　*f* Gk Aquila: Heb *their*

Like a Flute

JEREMIAH 48.29–39

Pride and arrogance can be smashed as easily as a piece of pottery, for the Lord will have none of it. Yet God grieves that it should be so.

What is the pride and arrogance of your nation that may grieve God? Let a piece of crockery represent the pride and arrogance of your nation. Play some solemn music to represent the grief of God, and smash the crockery before God. Pray for the mercy of God to cover the land—its people, its institutions, governments, corporations and societies. Close by singing a prayer of contrition, using music as your accompaniment.

See Meeting God in Service

14 How can you say, "We are heroes
        and mighty warriors"?
15 The destroyer of Moab and his towns has come up,
        and the choicest of his young men have gone
                down to slaughter,
        says the King, whose name is the Lord of hosts.
16 The calamity of Moab is near at hand
        and his doom approaches swiftly.
17 Mourn over him, all you his neighbors,
        and all who know his name;
    say, "How the mighty scepter is broken,
        the glorious staff!"

18 Come down from glory,
        and sit on the parched ground,
        enthroned daughter Dibon!
    For the destroyer of Moab has come up against you;
        he has destroyed your strongholds.
19 Stand by the road and watch,
        you inhabitant of Aroer!
    Ask the man fleeing and the woman escaping;
        say, "What has happened?"
20 Moab is put to shame, for it is broken down;
        wail and cry!
    Tell it by the Arnon,
        that Moab is laid waste.

21 Judgment has come upon the tableland, upon Holon, and Jahzah, and Mephaath, 22and Dibon, and Nebo, and Beth-diblathaim, 23and Kiriathaim, and Beth-gamul, and Beth-meon, 24and Kerioth, and Bozrah, and all the towns of the land of Moab, far and near. 25The horn of Moab is cut off, and his arm is broken, says the Lord.

26 Make him drunk, because he magnified himself against the Lord; let Moab wallow in his vomit; he too shall become a laughingstock. 27Israel was a laughingstock for you, though he was not caught among thieves; but whenever you spoke of him you shook your head!

28 Leave the towns, and live on the rock,
        O inhabitants of Moab!
    Be like the dove that nests
        on the sides of the mouth of a gorge.
29 We have heard of the pride of Moab—
        he is very proud—
    of his loftiness, his pride, and his arrogance,
        and the haughtiness of his heart.
30 I myself know his insolence, says the Lord;
        his boasts are false,
        his deeds are false.
31 Therefore I wail for Moab;
        I cry out for all Moab;
        for the people of Kir-heres I mourn.
32 More than for Jazer I weep for you,
        O vine of Sibmah!
    Your branches crossed over the sea,
        reached as far as Jazer;*a*
    upon your summer fruits and your vintage
        the destroyer has fallen.

a Two Mss and Isa 16.8: MT *the sea of Jazer*

33 Gladness and joy have been taken away
  from the fruitful land of Moab;
I have stopped the wine from the wine presses;
  no one treads them with shouts of joy;
  the shouting is not the shout of joy.

34 Heshbon and Elealeh cry out;[a] as far as Jahaz they utter their voice, from Zoar to Horonaim and Eglath-shelishiyah. For even the waters of Nimrim have become desolate. 35And I will bring to an end in Moab, says the LORD, those who offer sacrifice at a high place and make offerings to their gods. 36Therefore my heart moans for Moab like a flute, and my heart moans like a flute for the people of Kir-heres; for the riches they gained have perished.

37 For every head is shaved and every beard cut off; on all the hands there are gashes, and on the loins sackcloth. 38On all the housetops of Moab and in the squares there is nothing but lamentation; for I have broken Moab like a vessel that no one wants, says the LORD. 39How it is broken! How they wail! How Moab has turned his back in shame! So Moab has become a derision and a horror to all his neighbors.

40 For thus says the LORD:
  Look, he shall swoop down like an eagle,
    and spread his wings against Moab;
41 the towns[b] shall be taken
    and the strongholds seized.
  The hearts of the warriors of Moab, on that day,
    shall be like the heart of a woman in labor.
42 Moab shall be destroyed as a people,
    because he magnified himself against the LORD.
43 Terror, pit, and trap
    are before you, O inhabitants of Moab!
          says the LORD.
44 Everyone who flees from the terror
    shall fall into the pit,
  and everyone who climbs out of the pit
    shall be caught in the trap.
  For I will bring these things[c] upon Moab
    in the year of their punishment,
          says the LORD.

45 In the shadow of Heshbon
    fugitives stop exhausted;
  for a fire has gone out from Heshbon,
    a flame from the house of Sihon;
  it has destroyed the forehead of Moab,
    the scalp of the people of tumult.[d]
46 Woe to you, O Moab!
    The people of Chemosh have perished,
  for your sons have been taken captive,
    and your daughters into captivity.
47 Yet I will restore the fortunes of Moab
    in the latter days, says the LORD.
  Thus far is the judgment on Moab.

Can Chemosh Save You?

JEREMIAH 48.45–47

Chemosh is the national god of Moab (see Judges 11.24). Chemosh cannot save anyone. His people are destroyed. His sons and daughters are taken captive.

What is the "Chemosh" in your life? What god have you been serving—your anxiety, your ambition, your property? In prayer, bring your vulnerable "Chemosh" before Yahweh, the Lord your God, in some symbolic form. Talk to God about your allegiance to false gods. And when you are ready, write a pledge of allegiance to Jesus Christ. Say it to Jesus in the presence of your "Chemosh" symbol. Tape it to your "Chemosh" symbol and begin each day of the next week with your pledge of allegiance to Jesus.

See Meeting God in Worship

a Cn: Heb *From the cry of Heshbon to Elealeh* b Or *Kerioth* c Gk Syr: Heb *bring upon it* d Or *of Shaon*

Exposed!

JEREMIAH 49.7–10

Esau will be stripped! The nation is to be exposed. Who can hide from the Almighty? "For there is nothing hidden, except to be disclosed; nor is anything secret, except to come to light" (Mark 4.22).

What is your emotional response to Jesus' words? What would you be ashamed of if all your thoughts and actions were revealed? Before whom would you be ashamed? Confess your shame to Jesus and pray: "In you, O LORD, I seek refuge; do not let me ever be put to shame; in your righteousness deliver me" (Psalm 31.1).

See Meeting God in Prayer

Judgment on the Ammonites

49 Concerning the Ammonites.

Thus says the LORD:

Has Israel no sons?
Has he no heir?
Why then has Milcom dispossessed Gad,
and his people settled in its towns?
2 Therefore, the time is surely coming,
says the LORD,
when I will sound the battle alarm
against Rabbah of the Ammonites;
it shall become a desolate mound,
and its villages shall be burned with fire;
then Israel shall dispossess those who
dispossessed him,
says the LORD.

3 Wail, O Heshbon, for Ai is laid waste!
Cry out, O daughters*a* of Rabbah!
Put on sackcloth,
lament, and slash yourselves with whips!*b*
For Milcom shall go into exile,
with his priests and his attendants.
4 Why do you boast in your strength?
Your strength is ebbing,
O faithless daughter.
You trusted in your treasures, saying,
"Who will attack me?"
5 I am going to bring terror upon you,
says the Lord GOD of hosts,
from all your neighbors,
and you will be scattered, each headlong,
with no one to gather the fugitives.

6 But afterward I will restore the fortunes of the Ammonites, says the LORD.

Judgment on Edom

7 Concerning Edom.

Thus says the LORD of hosts:

Is there no longer wisdom in Teman?
Has counsel perished from the prudent?
Has their wisdom vanished?
8 Flee, turn back, get down low,
inhabitants of Dedan!
For I will bring the calamity of Esau upon him,
the time when I punish him.
9 If grape-gatherers came to you,
would they not leave gleanings?
If thieves came by night,
even they would pillage only what they wanted.
10 But as for me, I have stripped Esau bare,
I have uncovered his hiding places,
and he is not able to conceal himself.
His offspring are destroyed, his kinsfolk
and his neighbors; and he is no more.
11 Leave your orphans, I will keep them alive;
and let your widows trust in me.

a Or *villages*   *b* Cn: Meaning of Heb uncertain

12 For thus says the Lord: If those who do not deserve to drink the cup still have to drink it, shall you be the one to go unpunished? You shall not go unpunished; you must drink it. ¹³For by myself I have sworn, says the Lord, that Bozrah shall become an object of horror and ridicule, a waste, and an object of cursing; and all her towns shall be perpetual wastes.

¹⁴ I have heard tidings from the Lord,
    and a messenger has been sent among the
      nations:
    "Gather yourselves together and come against her,
      and rise up for battle!"
¹⁵ For I will make you least among the nations,
    despised by humankind.
¹⁶ The terror you inspire
    and the pride of your heart have deceived you,
    you who live in the clefts of the rock,ᵃ
    who hold the height of the hill.
Although you make your nest as high as the
      eagle's,
    from there I will bring you down,
                     says the Lord.

17 Edom shall become an object of horror; everyone who passes by it will be horrified and will hiss because of all its disasters. ¹⁸As when Sodom and Gomorrah and their neighbors were overthrown, says the Lord, no one shall live there, nor shall anyone settle in it. ¹⁹Like a lion coming up from the thickets of the Jordan against a perennial pasture, I will suddenly chase Edomᵇ away from it; and I will appoint over it whomever I choose.ᶜ For who is like me? Who can summon me? Who is the shepherd who can stand before me? ²⁰Therefore hear the plan that the Lord has made against Edom and the purposes that he has formed against the inhabitants of Teman: Surely the little ones of the flock shall be dragged away; surely their fold shall be appalled at their fate. ²¹At the sound of their fall the earth shall tremble; the sound of their cry shall be heard at the Red Sea.ᵈ ²²Look, he shall mount up and swoop down like an eagle, and spread his wings against Bozrah, and the heart of the warriors of Edom in that day shall be like the heart of a woman in labor.

Judgment on Damascus

23 Concerning Damascus.

Hamath and Arpad are confounded,
    for they have heard bad news;
they melt in fear, they are troubled like the seaᵉ
    that cannot be quiet.
²⁴ Damascus has become feeble, she turned to flee,
    and panic seized her;
anguish and sorrows have taken hold of her,
    as of a woman in labor.
²⁵ How the famous city is forsaken,ᶠ
    the joyful town!ᵍ

Alas! The Young Ones!

JEREMIAH 49.17–22

Even the young will be dragged away! How can the young ever escape what happens to their elders?

What is happening to the young people in your community? What is our society exposing them to? Young people often grow up to perpetuate the abuse that they experienced themselves. Who is there to care for them, guide them and protect them in the vulnerability of their formative years? Carefully consider a supportive action you can do for a little one this week while you pray for the young in your community, those who care for them and the agencies that exist to support them.

See Meeting God in Service

ᵃ Or *of Sela*   ᵇ Heb *him*   ᶜ Or *and I will single out the choicest of his rams:* Meaning of Heb uncertain   ᵈ Or *Sea of Reeds*   ᵉ Cn: Heb *there is trouble in the sea*   ᶠ Vg: Heb *is not forsaken*   ᵍ Syr Vg Tg: Heb *the town of my joy*

Budgeting for Defense

JEREMIAH 49.35–39

The "bow of Elam" is no defense against Yahweh, the Almighty, even though it is the mainstay of Elam's might.

What is the mainstay of your defense? Your self-defense skills? Your personality or your income? Your words, your wit or your wisdom? And against what do you need to defend yourself?

Recall an incident in which God has been your defender. In the light of that experience, meditate on Psalm 59. Memorize the verses that speak the most emphatically to you, so that when you're in danger, they may bring you to God, "the mainstay" of your defense.

See Meeting God in Scripture

26 Therefore her young men shall fall in her squares,
    and all her soldiers shall be destroyed in that day,
        says the LORD of hosts.
27 And I will kindle a fire at the wall of Damascus,
    and it shall devour the strongholds of Ben-hadad.

Judgment on Kedar and Hazor

28 Concerning Kedar and the kingdoms of Hazor that King Nebuchadrezzar of Babylon defeated.

Thus says the LORD:
Rise up, advance against Kedar!
    Destroy the people of the east!
29 Take their tents and their flocks,
    their curtains and all their goods;
carry off their camels for yourselves,
    and a cry shall go up: "Terror is all around!"
30 Flee, wander far away, hide in deep places,
    O inhabitants of Hazor!
        says the LORD.
For King Nebuchadrezzar of Babylon
    has made a plan against you
    and formed a purpose against you.

31 Rise up, advance against a nation at ease,
    that lives secure,
        says the LORD,
    that has no gates or bars,
    that lives alone.
32 Their camels shall become booty,
    their herds of cattle a spoil.
I will scatter to every wind
    those who have shaven temples,
and I will bring calamity
    against them from every side,
        says the LORD.
33 Hazor shall become a lair of jackals,
    an everlasting waste;
no one shall live there,
    nor shall anyone settle in it.

Judgment on Elam

34 The word of the LORD that came to the prophet Jeremiah concerning Elam, at the beginning of the reign of King Zedekiah of Judah.

35 Thus says the LORD of hosts: I am going to break the bow of Elam, the mainstay of their might; 36and I will bring upon Elam the four winds from the four quarters of heaven; and I will scatter them to all these winds, and there shall be no nation to which the exiles from Elam shall not come. 37I will terrify Elam before their enemies, and before those who seek their life; I will bring disaster upon them, my fierce anger, says the LORD. I will send the sword after them, until I have consumed them; 38and I will set my throne in Elam, and destroy their king and officials, says the LORD.

39 But in the latter days I will restore the fortunes of Elam, says the LORD.

Judgment on Babylon

50 The word that the LORD spoke concerning Babylon, concerning the land of the Chaldeans, by the prophet Jeremiah:

2 Declare among the nations and proclaim,
    set up a banner and proclaim,
    do not conceal it, say:
Babylon is taken,
    Bel is put to shame,
    Merodach is dismayed.
Her images are put to shame,
    her idols are dismayed.

3 For out of the north a nation has come up against her; it shall make her land a desolation, and no one shall live in it; both human beings and animals shall flee away.

4 In those days and in that time, says the LORD, the people of Israel shall come, they and the people of Judah together; they shall come weeping as they seek the LORD their God. 5They shall ask the way to Zion, with faces turned toward it, and they shall come and join*a* themselves to the LORD by an everlasting covenant that will never be forgotten.

6 My people have been lost sheep; their shepherds have led them astray, turning them away on the mountains; from mountain to hill they have gone, they have forgotten their fold. 7All who found them have devoured them, and their enemies have said, "We are not guilty, because they have sinned against the LORD, the true pasture, the LORD, the hope of their ancestors."

8 Flee from Babylon, and go out of the land of the Chaldeans, and be like male goats leading the flock. 9For I am going to stir up and bring against Babylon a company of great nations from the land of the north; and they shall array themselves against her; from there she shall be taken. Their arrows are like the arrows of a skilled warrior who does not return empty-handed. 10Chaldea shall be plundered; all who plunder her shall be sated, says the LORD.

11 Though you rejoice, though you exult,
    O plunderers of my heritage,
though you frisk about like a heifer on the grass,
    and neigh like stallions,
12 your mother shall be utterly shamed,
    and she who bore you shall be disgraced.
Lo, she shall be the last of the nations,
    a wilderness, dry land, and a desert.
13 Because of the wrath of the LORD she shall not be
        inhabited,
    but shall be an utter desolation;
everyone who passes by Babylon shall be appalled
    and hiss because of all her wounds.
14 Take up your positions around Babylon,
    all you that bend the bow;
shoot at her, spare no arrows,
    for she has sinned against the LORD.

What You Give Is What You Get!

JEREMIAH 50.7–10

Babylon might well excuse herself by saying, "Not guilty! These Israelites have sinned against the Lord and have gotten what they deserve! We have acted in the service of their God anyway!" Babylon is a violent nation and the violence she inflicts will inevitably be the violence she receives.

How do you deal with violence that is directed at you? Think of a situation in which you feel you have the right to retaliate. Read Matthew 5.43–45 and think again about your desire to retaliate. What do you feel? Write your honest response and pray about it. On a card write, "A soft answer turns away wrath" (Proverbs 15.1), and carry it with you in your wallet or purse.

See Meeting God in Scripture

a Gk: Heb *toward it. Come! They shall join*

Restoration

JEREMIAH 50.17–20

"As the word is spoken one more time, we move through the wearisome death-ridden days of our life and come back once again to Easter to be stunned into disbelief, and then beyond disbelief, to be stunned to life, now filled with fear and trembling . . . The sermon for such a time shames the Prince [of Darkness] and we become yet again more nearly human. The Author of the text laughs in delight, the way that Author has laughed only at creation and at Easter, but laughs again when the sermon carries the day against the prose of the Dark Prince who wants no new poetry in the region he thinks he governs. Where the poetry is sounded, the Prince knows a little of the territory has been lost to its true Ruler. The newly claimed territory becomes a new home of freedom, justice, peace, and abiding joy."

—WALTER BRUEGGEMANN,
Finally Comes the Poet

See *Meeting God in Worship*

15 Raise a shout against her from all sides,
    "She has surrendered;
her bulwarks have fallen,
    her walls are thrown down."
For this is the vengeance of the LORD:
    take vengeance on her,
    do to her as she has done.
16 Cut off from Babylon the sower,
    and the wielder of the sickle in time of harvest;
because of the destroying sword
    all of them shall return to their own people,
    and all of them shall flee to their own land.

17 Israel is a hunted sheep driven away by lions. First the king of Assyria devoured it, and now at the end King Nebuchadrezzar of Babylon has gnawed its bones. 18 Therefore, thus says the LORD of hosts, the God of Israel: I am going to punish the king of Babylon and his land, as I punished the king of Assyria. 19 I will restore Israel to its pasture, and it shall feed on Carmel and in Bashan, and on the hills of Ephraim and in Gilead its hunger shall be satisfied. 20 In those days and at that time, says the LORD, the iniquity of Israel shall be sought, and there shall be none; and the sins of Judah, and none shall be found; for I will pardon the remnant that I have spared.

21 Go up to the land of Merathaim;[a]
    go up against her,
and attack the inhabitants of Pekod[b]
    and utterly destroy the last of them,[c]
                                says the LORD;
    do all that I have commanded you.
22 The noise of battle is in the land,
    and great destruction!
23 How the hammer of the whole earth
    is cut down and broken!
How Babylon has become
    a horror among the nations!
24 You set a snare for yourself and you were caught,
        O Babylon,
    but you did not know it;
you were discovered and seized,
    because you challenged the LORD.
25 The LORD has opened his armory,
    and brought out the weapons of his wrath,
for the Lord GOD of hosts has a task to do
    in the land of the Chaldeans.
26 Come against her from every quarter;
    open her granaries;
pile her up like heaps of grain, and destroy her
        utterly;
    let nothing be left of her.
27 Kill all her bulls,
    let them go down to the slaughter.
Alas for them, their day has come,
    the time of their punishment!

---

a Or *of Double Rebellion*   *b* Or *of Punishment*   *c* Tg: Heb *destroy after them*

28 Listen! Fugitives and refugees from the land of Babylon are coming to declare in Zion the vengeance of the LORD our God, vengeance for his temple.

29 Summon archers against Babylon, all who bend the bow. Encamp all around her; let no one escape. Repay her according to her deeds; just as she has done, do to her—for she has arrogantly defied the LORD, the Holy One of Israel. ³⁰Therefore her young men shall fall in her squares, and all her soldiers shall be destroyed on that day, says the LORD.

31 I am against you, O arrogant one,
  says the Lord GOD of hosts;
for your day has come,
  the time when I will punish you.
32 The arrogant one shall stumble and fall,
  with no one to raise him up,
and I will kindle a fire in his cities,
  and it will devour everything around him.

33 Thus says the LORD of hosts: The people of Israel are oppressed, and so too are the people of Judah; all their captors have held them fast and refuse to let them go. ³⁴Their Redeemer is strong; the LORD of hosts is his name. He will surely plead their cause, that he may give rest to the earth, but unrest to the inhabitants of Babylon.

35 A sword against the Chaldeans, says the LORD,
  and against the inhabitants of Babylon,
  and against her officials and her sages!
36 A sword against the diviners,
  so that they may become fools!
A sword against her warriors,
  so that they may be destroyed!
37 A sword against her*a* horses and against her*a*
    chariots,
  and against all the foreign troops in her midst,
  so that they may become women!
A sword against all her treasures,
  that they may be plundered!
38 A drought*b* against her waters,
  that they may be dried up!
For it is a land of images,
  and they go mad over idols.

39 Therefore wild animals shall live with hyenas in Babylon,*c* and ostriches shall inhabit her; she shall never again be peopled, or inhabited for all generations. ⁴⁰As when God overthrew Sodom and Gomorrah and their neighbors, says the LORD, so no one shall live there, nor shall anyone settle in her.

41 Look, a people is coming from the north;
  a mighty nation and many kings
  are stirring from the farthest parts of the earth.
42 They wield bow and spear,
  they are cruel and have no mercy.
The sound of them is like the roaring sea;

Set Me Free!

JEREMIAH 50.33–34

The people of Israel and Judah are oppressed. Their captors hold them fast and refuse to let them go. Yet there is a Redeemer! "The LORD of hosts is his name."

What oppresses you? What situation, what attitude, what behavior holds you fast? What would redemption look like for you?

Take two large sheets of paper, a dinner plate and a crayon. Trace a circle around the plate on each sheet of paper. Using paint or crayons, illustrate your oppression in the first circle, paying particular attention to color. In the same way illustrate your redemption. Pray about your responses, seeking God's freedom from that which oppresses you.

See Meeting God in Worship

---

a Cn: Heb *his*   *b* Another reading is *A sword*   *c* Heb lacks *in Babylon*

Like a Lion

JEREMIAH 50.44–46

From your awareness of the news from television, radio or the newspaper, note the people who seem to wield oppressive power today. Imagine how that person would react to a lion suddenly emerging from the thickets and bearing down on them. Who can challenge a lion?

Pray for that Jesus, the Lion of Judah, will challenge the powers of this world and hold them in check.

See Meeting God in Service

they ride upon horses,
    set in array as a warrior for battle,
      against you, O daughter Babylon!

43 The king of Babylon heard news of them,
    and his hands fell helpless;
anguish seized him,
    pain like that of a woman in labor.

44 Like a lion coming up from the thickets of the Jordan against a perennial pasture, I will suddenly chase them away from her; and I will appoint over her whomever I choose.[a] For who is like me? Who can summon me? Who is the shepherd who can stand before me? 45Therefore hear the plan that the LORD has made against Babylon, and the purposes that he has formed against the land of the Chaldeans: Surely the little ones of the flock shall be dragged away; surely their[b] fold shall be appalled at their fate. 46At the sound of the capture of Babylon the earth shall tremble, and her cry shall be heard among the nations.

51 Thus says the LORD:
    I am going to stir up a destructive wind[c]
      against Babylon
      and against the inhabitants of Leb-qamai;[d]
2 and I will send winnowers to Babylon,
    and they shall winnow her.
They shall empty her land
    when they come against her from every side
    on the day of trouble.
3 Let not the archer bend his bow,
    and let him not array himself in his coat of mail.
Do not spare her young men;
    utterly destroy her entire army.
4 They shall fall down slain in the land of the
    Chaldeans,
    and wounded in her streets.
5 Israel and Judah have not been forsaken
    by their God, the LORD of hosts,
though their land is full of guilt
    before the Holy One of Israel.

6 Flee from the midst of Babylon,
    save your lives, each of you!
Do not perish because of her guilt,
    for this is the time of the LORD's vengeance;
    he is repaying her what is due.
7 Babylon was a golden cup in the LORD's hand,
    making all the earth drunken;
the nations drank of her wine,
    and so the nations went mad.
8 Suddenly Babylon has fallen and is shattered;
    wail for her!
Bring balm for her wound;
    perhaps she may be healed.

a Or *and I will single out the choicest of her rams*: Meaning of Heb uncertain b Syr Gk Tg Compare 49.20: Heb lacks *their*   c Or *stir up the spirit of a destroyer*   d *Leb-qamai* is a cryptogram for *Kasdim*, Chaldea

9 We tried to heal Babylon,
  but she could not be healed.
Forsake her, and let each of us go
  to our own country;
for her judgment has reached up to heaven
  and has been lifted up even to the skies.
10 The Lord has brought forth our vindication;
  come, let us declare in Zion
  the work of the Lord our God.

11 Sharpen the arrows!
  Fill the quivers!
The Lord has stirred up the spirit of the kings of the
Medes, because his purpose concerning Babylon is to destroy it, for that is the vengeance of the Lord, vengeance
for his temple.
12 Raise a standard against the walls of Babylon;
  make the watch strong;
post sentinels;
  prepare the ambushes;
for the Lord has both planned and done
  what he spoke concerning the inhabitants of
  Babylon.
13 You who live by mighty waters,
  rich in treasures,
your end has come,
  the thread of your life is cut.
14 The Lord of hosts has sworn by himself:
Surely I will fill you with troops like a swarm of
  locusts,
  and they shall raise a shout of victory over you.

15 It is he who made the earth by his power,
  who established the world by his wisdom,
and by his understanding stretched out the
  heavens.
16 When he utters his voice there is a tumult of
  waters in the heavens,
  and he makes the mist rise from the ends of the
  earth.
He makes lightnings for the rain,
  and he brings out the wind from his
  storehouses.
17 Everyone is stupid and without knowledge;
  goldsmiths are all put to shame by their idols;
for their images are false,
  and there is no breath in them.
18 They are worthless, a work of delusion;
  at the time of their punishment they shall
  perish.
19 Not like these is the Lord,[a] the portion of Jacob,
  for he is the one who formed all things,
and Israel is the tribe of his inheritance;
  the Lord of hosts is his name.

Israel the Creator's Instrument

20 You are my war club, my weapon of battle:
with you I smash nations;
  with you I destroy kingdoms;

Freedom After the Fall!

JEREMIAH 51.7–10

How the mighty fall! Like a cup that falls and is broken—a gold cup at that—Babylon falls and is broken.

What, or who, has power over you—an organization, a person, your finances, your appetites? Compare that power with the power of God. What needs to happen in order for you to experience freedom?

Climb to the top of a hill or some small rise in your neighborhood—somewhere not too public. In a strong voice repeat the apostle Paul's words at least a dozen times: "For freedom Christ has set us free. Stand firm, therefore, and do not submit again to a yoke of slavery" (Galatians 5.1). Let your body absorb the power of the words, and assign some part of your anatomy (like your left shoulder) to hold the truth of the words for you so that, touching that part of your body later, you can remind yourself of the power of God that is setting you free.

See Meeting God in Worship

---

a Heb lacks *the Lord*

The Hammer of the Lord

JEREMIAH 51.20–23

Babylon was supreme. It could do as it pleased. But now its power is checked. It will no longer be an enemy but will fall under God's war club. Death, too, was once supreme. It could do as it pleased. But now it is checked. It can claim no victory and has no sting because it has fallen under the hammer of Jesus Christ's resurrection power (see 1 Corinthians 15.55–56).

Take something hard, like a walnut, and place it on a piece of wood. Pick up a hammer. Swing it around and feel its weight. Bang it onto the wood with all the strength you can manage. Now take the hard object you have selected. Imagine it as "Death." Swing the hammer high. Bring it down on the hard object and smash it in the name of the Lord! What thoughts did this experience raise? How did you feel? Pray about your responses.

See Meeting God in Everyday Life

21 with you I smash the horse and its rider;
with you I smash the chariot and the charioteer;
22 with you I smash man and woman;
with you I smash the old man and the boy;
with you I smash the young man and the girl;
23 with you I smash shepherds and their flocks;
with you I smash farmers and their teams;
with you I smash governors and deputies.

The Doom of Babylon

24 I will repay Babylon and all the inhabitants of Chaldea before your very eyes for all the wrong that they have done in Zion, says the LORD.

25 I am against you, O destroying mountain,
says the LORD,
that destroys the whole earth;
I will stretch out my hand against you,
and roll you down from the crags,
and make you a burned-out mountain.
26 No stone shall be taken from you for a corner
and no stone for a foundation,
but you shall be a perpetual waste,
says the LORD.

27 Raise a standard in the land,
blow the trumpet among the nations;
prepare the nations for war against her,
summon against her the kingdoms,
Ararat, Minni, and Ashkenaz;
appoint a marshal against her,
bring up horses like bristling locusts.
28 Prepare the nations for war against her,
the kings of the Medes, with their governors and
deputies,
and every land under their dominion.
29 The land trembles and writhes,
for the LORD's purposes against Babylon stand,
to make the land of Babylon a desolation,
without inhabitant.
30 The warriors of Babylon have given up fighting,
they remain in their strongholds;
their strength has failed,
they have become women;
her buildings are set on fire,
her bars are broken.
31 One runner runs to meet another,
and one messenger to meet another,
to tell the king of Babylon
that his city is taken from end to end:
32 the fords have been seized,
the marshes have been burned with fire,
and the soldiers are in panic.
33 For thus says the LORD of hosts, the God of Israel:
Daughter Babylon is like a threshing floor
at the time when it is trodden;
yet a little while
and the time of her harvest will come.

34 "King Nebuchadrezzar of Babylon has devoured me,
　　he has crushed me;
　he has made me an empty vessel,
　　he has swallowed me like a monster;
　he has filled his belly with my delicacies,
　　he has spewed me out.
35 May my torn flesh be avenged on Babylon,"
　　the inhabitants of Zion shall say.
　"May my blood be avenged on the inhabitants of
　　Chaldea,"
　　Jerusalem shall say.
36 Therefore thus says the LORD:
　I am going to defend your cause
　　and take vengeance for you.
　I will dry up her sea
　　and make her fountain dry;
37 and Babylon shall become a heap of ruins,
　　a den of jackals,
　an object of horror and of hissing,
　　without inhabitant.

38 Like lions they shall roar together;
　　they shall growl like lions' whelps.
39 When they are inflamed, I will set out their drink
　　and make them drunk, until they become merry
　and then sleep a perpetual sleep
　　and never wake, says the LORD.
40 I will bring them down like lambs to the slaughter,
　　like rams and goats.

41 How Sheshach[a] is taken,
　　the pride of the whole earth seized!
　How Babylon has become
　　an object of horror among the nations!
42 The sea has risen over Babylon;
　　she has been covered by its tumultuous waves.
43 Her cities have become an object of horror,
　　a land of drought and a desert,
　a land in which no one lives,
　　and through which no mortal passes.
44 I will punish Bel in Babylon,
　　and make him disgorge what he has swallowed.
　The nations shall no longer stream to him;
　　the wall of Babylon has fallen.

45 Come out of her, my people!
　　Save your lives, each of you,
　　from the fierce anger of the LORD!
46 Do not be fainthearted or fearful
　　at the rumors heard in the land—
　one year one rumor comes,
　　the next year another,
　rumors of violence in the land
　　and of ruler against ruler.

47 Assuredly, the days are coming
　　when I will punish the images of Babylon;
　her whole land shall be put to shame,
　　and all her slain shall fall in her midst.

a Sheshach is a cryptogram for Babel, Babylon

I Will Defend You

JEREMIAH 51.34–37

Jerusalem has been ravished, her flesh violated and her delicacy gutted. Have you been the victim of violence—brutal or subtle? What has been the effect on your emotions, your mind, your spirit or your body? What healing have you sought? Is there still more healing to do? Meditate on the images of God's justice at work against Babylon. What redress have you sought against your abuser? Pray for strength to forgive that person and for courage not to allow continuing abuse in the future. Journal your responses and share any issues that arise within you with your pastor, spiritual adviser or counselor.

See Meeting God in Scripture

A Holy Picture

JEREMIAH 51.47–53

There is death and destruction on all sides. Babylon will be leveled. But in the face of the disaster, "Remember the LORD . . . and let Jerusalem come into your mind."

What are the central images of your faith? What "icon" of God's presence can you hold in your mind when you face nothing but calamity? Under threat of death Stephen looked to Jesus (see Acts 7.55). With paint or crayon make a holy picture that illustrates the central image of your faith.

See Meeting God in Worship

48 Then the heavens and the earth,
and all that is in them,
shall shout for joy over Babylon;
for the destroyers shall come against them out
of the north,
says the LORD.
49 Babylon must fall for the slain of Israel,
as the slain of all the earth have fallen because
of Babylon.

50 You survivors of the sword,
go, do not linger!
Remember the LORD in a distant land,
and let Jerusalem come into your mind:
51 We are put to shame, for we have heard insults;
dishonor has covered our face,
for aliens have come
into the holy places of the LORD's house.

52 Therefore the time is surely coming, says the LORD,
when I will punish her idols,
and through all her land
the wounded shall groan.
53 Though Babylon should mount up to heaven,
and though she should fortify her strong height,
from me destroyers would come upon her,
says the LORD.

54 Listen!—a cry from Babylon!
A great crashing from the land of the Chaldeans!
55 For the LORD is laying Babylon waste,
and stilling her loud clamor.
Their waves roar like mighty waters,
the sound of their clamor resounds;
56 for a destroyer has come against her,
against Babylon;
her warriors are taken,
their bows are broken;
for the LORD is a God of recompense,
he will repay in full.
57 I will make her officials and her sages drunk,
also her governors, her deputies, and her
warriors;
they shall sleep a perpetual sleep and never wake,
says the King, whose name is the LORD of hosts.

58 Thus says the LORD of hosts:
The broad wall of Babylon
shall be leveled to the ground,
and her high gates
shall be burned with fire.
The peoples exhaust themselves for nothing,
and the nations weary themselves only for fire.*a*

Jeremiah's Command to Seraiah

59 The word that the prophet Jeremiah commanded Seraiah son of Neriah son of Mahseiah, when he went with King Zedekiah of Judah to Babylon, in the fourth year of

a Gk Syr Compare Hab 2.13: Heb *and the nations for fire, and they are weary*

his reign. Seraiah was the quartermaster. [60]Jeremiah wrote in a[a] scroll all the disasters that would come on Babylon, all these words that are written concerning Babylon. [61]And Jeremiah said to Seraiah: "When you come to Babylon, see that you read all these words, [62]and say, 'O LORD, you yourself threatened to destroy this place so that neither human beings nor animals shall live in it, and it shall be desolate forever.' [63]When you finish reading this scroll, tie a stone to it, and throw it into the middle of the Euphrates, [64]and say, 'Thus shall Babylon sink, to rise no more, because of the disasters that I am bringing on her.' "[b]

Thus far are the words of Jeremiah.

The Destruction of Jerusalem Reviewed

52 Zedekiah was twenty-one years old when he began to reign; he reigned eleven years in Jerusalem. His mother's name was Hamutal daughter of Jeremiah of Libnah. [2]He did what was evil in the sight of the LORD, just as Jehoiakim had done. [3]Indeed, Jerusalem and Judah so angered the LORD that he expelled them from his presence.

Zedekiah rebelled against the king of Babylon. [4]And in the ninth year of his reign, in the tenth month, on the tenth day of the month, King Nebuchadrezzar of Babylon came with all his army against Jerusalem, and they laid siege to it; they built siegeworks against it all around. [5]So the city was besieged until the eleventh year of King Zedekiah. [6]On the ninth day of the fourth month the famine became so severe in the city that there was no food for the people of the land. [7]Then a breach was made in the city wall;[c] and all the soldiers fled and went out from the city by night by the way of the gate between the two walls, by the king's garden, though the Chaldeans were all around the city. They went in the direction of the Arabah. [8]But the army of the Chaldeans pursued the king, and overtook Zedekiah in the plains of Jericho; and all his army was scattered, deserting him. [9]Then they captured the king, and brought him up to the king of Babylon at Riblah in the land of Hamath, and he passed sentence on him. [10]The king of Babylon killed the sons of Zedekiah before his eyes, and also killed all the officers of Judah at Riblah. [11]He put out the eyes of Zedekiah, and bound him in fetters, and the king of Babylon took him to Babylon, and put him in prison until the day of his death.

12 In the fifth month, on the tenth day of the month—which was the nineteenth year of King Nebuchadrezzar, king of Babylon—Nebuzaradan the captain of the bodyguard who served the king of Babylon, entered Jerusalem. [13]He burned the house of the LORD, the king's house, and all the houses of Jerusalem; every great house he burned down. [14]All the army of the Chaldeans, who were with the captain of the guard, broke down all the walls around Jerusalem. [15]Nebuzaradan the captain of the guard carried into exile some of the poorest of the people and the rest of the people who were left in the city and the deserters who had defected to the king of Babylon, together with the rest of the artisans. [16]But Nebuzaradan the captain of the guard left some of the poorest people of the land to be vinedressers and tillers of the soil.

So Will Babylon Sink

JEREMIAH 51.59–64

Write on a piece of paper the name of an evil force in the world—such as domestic violence, dishonesty, pornography or embezzlement. Write some words from the Bible about this evil and what you understand to be God's perspective. Attach the paper to a stone with string or a rubber band and throw it into a pond, river or lake. Recite, "So will this evil sink to rise no more." What practical action will affirm your prayer?

See Meeting God in Scripture

---

a Or *one*   *b* Gk: Heb *on her. And they shall weary themselves*
c Heb lacks *wall*

Celebrating Release

JEREMIAH 52.31–34

King Jehoiachin is free. The king of Babylon treats him kindly. His status is raised. He is invited to the king's table and treated with honor.

What is your experience of being freed by Jesus? How have you experienced his kindness? How has God raised you and honored you?

Prepare a meal fit for a king. Invite two or more of your companions in faith and share the meal with them. Intentionally talk together about your experience of God's kindness in Jesus Christ. Celebrate the goodness of God. "Taste and see that the LORD is good" (Psalm 34.8).

See Meeting God in Worship

17 The pillars of bronze that were in the house of the LORD, and the stands and the bronze sea that were in the house of the LORD, the Chaldeans broke in pieces, and carried all the bronze to Babylon. ¹⁸They took away the pots, the shovels, the snuffers, the basins, the ladles, and all the vessels of bronze used in the temple service. ¹⁹The captain of the guard took away the small bowls also, the firepans, the basins, the pots, the lampstands, the ladles, and the bowls for libation, both those of gold and those of silver. ²⁰As for the two pillars, the one sea, the twelve bronze bulls that were under the sea, and the stands,ᵃ which King Solomon had made for the house of the LORD, the bronze of all these vessels was beyond weighing. ²¹As for the pillars, the height of the one pillar was eighteen cubits, its circumference was twelve cubits; it was hollow and its thickness was four fingers. ²²Upon it was a capital of bronze; the height of the capital was five cubits; latticework and pomegranates, all of bronze, encircled the top of the capital. And the second pillar had the same, with pomegranates. ²³There were ninety-six pomegranates on the sides; all the pomegranates encircling the latticework numbered one hundred.

24 The captain of the guard took the chief priest Seraiah, the second priest Zephaniah, and the three guardians of the threshold; ²⁵and from the city he took an officer who had been in command of the soldiers, and seven men of the king's council who were found in the city; the secretary of the commander of the army who mustered the people of the land; and sixty men of the people of the land who were found inside the city. ²⁶Then Nebuzaradan the captain of the guard took them, and brought them to the king of Babylon at Riblah. ²⁷And the king of Babylon struck them down, and put them to death at Riblah in the land of Hamath. So Judah went into exile out of its land.

28 This is the number of the people whom Nebuchadrezzar took into exile: in the seventh year, three thousand twenty-three Judeans; ²⁹in the eighteenth year of Nebuchadrezzar he took into exile from Jerusalem eight hundred thirty-two persons; ³⁰in the twenty-third year of Nebuchadrezzar, Nebuzaradan the captain of the guard took into exile of the Judeans seven hundred forty-five persons; all the persons were four thousand six hundred.

Jehoiachin Favored in Captivity

31 In the thirty-seventh year of the exile of King Jehoiachin of Judah, in the twelfth month, on the twenty-fifth day of the month, King Evil-merodach of Babylon, in the year he began to reign, showed favor to King Jehoiachin of Judah and brought him out of prison; ³²he spoke kindly to him, and gave him a seat above the seats of the other kings who were with him in Babylon. ³³So Jehoiachin put aside his prison clothes, and every day of his life he dined regularly at the king's table. ³⁴For his allowance, a regular daily allowance was given him by the king of Babylon, as long as he lived, up to the day of his death.

a Cn: Heb *that were under the stands*

A Personal Lamentation

After reading these verses, close your eyes and remember a time you felt absolutely alone and defeated. Write your own description of that anguished point in your life. Feel free to make parallels to the scripture verses. Try to use vivid language as you detail the rejection and hopelessness you felt. Read your "lamentation" aloud and offer your words to the God who has never left you, even when you felt alone.

See Meeting God in Prayer

The Deserted City

1 How lonely sits the city
    that once was full of people!
How like a widow she has become,
    she that was great among the nations!
She that was a princess among the provinces
    has become a vassal.

2 She weeps bitterly in the night,
    with tears on her cheeks;
among all her lovers
    she has no one to comfort her;
all her friends have dealt treacherously with her,
    they have become her enemies.

3 Judah has gone into exile with suffering
    and hard servitude;
she lives now among the nations,
    and finds no resting place;
her pursuers have all overtaken her
    in the midst of her distress.

4 The roads to Zion mourn,
    for no one comes to the festivals;
all her gates are desolate,
    her priests groan;
her young girls grieve,*a*
    and her lot is bitter.

5 Her foes have become the masters,
    her enemies prosper,
because the LORD has made her suffer
    for the multitude of her transgressions;
her children have gone away,
    captives before the foe.

6 From daughter Zion has departed
    all her majesty.
Her princes have become like stags
    that find no pasture;
they fled without strength
    before the pursuer.

7 Jerusalem remembers,
    in the days of her affliction and wandering,
all the precious things
    that were hers in days of old.
When her people fell into the hand of the foe,
    and there was no one to help her,
the foe looked on mocking
    over her downfall.

8 Jerusalem sinned grievously,
    so she has become a mockery;
all who honored her despise her,
    for they have seen her nakedness;
she herself groans,
    and turns her face away.

9 Her uncleanness was in her skirts;
    she took no thought of her future;
her downfall was appalling,

a Meaning of Heb uncertain

LAMENTATIONS
Afflicted and Comforted

KEY VERSE:

The steadfast love of the LORD never ceases, his mercies never come to an end.

—Lamentations 3.22

Although many Biblical books contain poignant expressions of grief in poetry and song, Lamentations is the only Old Testament book composed solely of such expressions. The author grieves over the destruction of Jerusalem, the Hebrew people's infidelity to God and the punishment that comes at the hands of the Babylonians when his people turned from God.

Like the author of Lamentations, we can turn to God in times of anguish and pain. We can pour out our sorrow from the depths of our souls as we look for God's healing love. Turning to God also means taking responsibility for our actions, repenting of misdeeds and accepting the new life that God offers us. No matter what our personal pain or sorrow, Lamentations tells us, God is the Rock to whom we can turn. Whatever our afflictions, God's loving arms reach out to comfort us.

"O sometimes the shadows
    are deep,
And rough seems the path
    to my goal,
And sorrows, sometimes
    how they sweep
Like tempests down over the
    soul!
O then to the Rock let me
    fly,
To the Rock that is higher
    than I!
O near to the Rock let me
    keep
If blessings or sorrows
    prevail,
Or climbing the mountain
    way steep,
Or walking the shadowy
    vale.
O then to the Rock let me
    fly,
to the Rock that is higher
    than I!"

—ERASTUS JOHNSON

with none to comfort her.
"O LORD, look at my affliction,
 for the enemy has triumphed!"

10 Enemies have stretched out their hands
   over all her precious things;
she has even seen the nations
   invade her sanctuary,
those whom you forbade
   to enter your congregation.

11 All her people groan
   as they search for bread;
they trade their treasures for food
   to revive their strength.
Look, O LORD, and see
   how worthless I have become.

12 Is it nothing to you,*a* all you who pass by?
   Look and see
if there is any sorrow like my sorrow,
   which was brought upon me,
which the LORD inflicted
   on the day of his fierce anger.

13 From on high he sent fire;
   it went deep into my bones;
he spread a net for my feet;
   he turned me back;
he has left me stunned,
   faint all day long.

14 My transgressions were bound*a* into a yoke;
   by his hand they were fastened together;
they weigh on my neck,
   sapping my strength;
the Lord handed me over
   to those whom I cannot withstand.

15 The LORD has rejected
   all my warriors in the midst of me;
he proclaimed a time against me
   to crush my young men;
the Lord has trodden as in a wine press
   the virgin daughter Judah.

16 For these things I weep;
   my eyes flow with tears;
for a comforter is far from me,
   one to revive my courage;
my children are desolate,
   for the enemy has prevailed.

17 Zion stretches out her hands,
   but there is no one to comfort her;
the LORD has commanded against Jacob
   that his neighbors should become his foes;
Jerusalem has become
   a filthy thing among them.

18 The LORD is in the right,
   for I have rebelled against his word;
but hear, all you peoples,

Rest for the Soul

LAMENTATIONS 1.14

Place a heavy beach towel or blanket on your shoulders, feeling the weight that is a symbol of the sins that "weigh on [your] neck." What does the weight mean to you? In what ways would such a load, pressing down on your neck and shoulders, restrict your movement? How does the weight affect how you feel inside? With your eyes closed, reach up to slowly take the weight off as you recall Jesus' words: "Come to me, all you that are weary and are carrying burdens, and I will give you rest." Give thanks that Jesus has taken the weight of your sins and promised "rest for your [soul]" (Matthew 11.28–29).

See Meeting God in Scripture

---

a Meaning of Heb uncertain

Low As Low Can Be

LAMENTATIONS 1.20

Utterly discouraged, the author goes straight to God and pours out his distress and torment. Why is God willing to listen to his problems and complaints? Why does he feel safe in God's care?

Do you feel safe in God's care? Why or why not? How does your sense of safety influence the kinds of concerns you take to God in prayer? In those times when you feel that "inside, there is only death," how do you move on? After expressing your deepest feelings, what should you do next? In other words, how does a heart-to-heart talk with God enable you to stop complaining and start taking positive action?

See Meeting God in Prayer

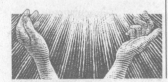

and behold my suffering;
  my young women and young men
    have gone into captivity.

19 I called to my lovers
    but they deceived me;
my priests and elders
    perished in the city
while seeking food
    to revive their strength.

20 See, O LORD, how distressed I am;
    my stomach churns,
my heart is wrung within me,
    because I have been very rebellious.
In the street the sword bereaves;
    in the house it is like death.

21 They heard how I was groaning,
    with no one to comfort me.
All my enemies heard of my trouble;
    they are glad that you have done it.
Bring on the day you have announced,
    and let them be as I am.

22 Let all their evil doing come before you;
    and deal with them
as you have dealt with me
    because of all my transgressions;
for my groans are many
    and my heart is faint.

God's Warnings Fulfilled

2 How the Lord in his anger
    has humiliated[a] daughter Zion!
He has thrown down from heaven to earth
    the splendor of Israel;
he has not remembered his footstool
    in the day of his anger.

2 The Lord has destroyed without mercy
    all the dwellings of Jacob;
in his wrath he has broken down
    the strongholds of daughter Judah;
he has brought down to the ground in dishonor
    the kingdom and its rulers.

3 He has cut down in fierce anger
    all the might of Israel;
he has withdrawn his right hand from them
    in the face of the enemy;
he has burned like a flaming fire in Jacob,
    consuming all around.

4 He has bent his bow like an enemy,
    with his right hand set like a foe;
he has killed all in whom we took pride
    in the tent of daughter Zion;
he has poured out his fury like fire.

5 The Lord has become like an enemy;
    he has destroyed Israel.
He has destroyed all its palaces,

a Meaning of Heb uncertain

laid in ruins its strongholds,
and multiplied in daughter Judah
mourning and lamentation.

6 He has broken down his booth like a garden,
he has destroyed his tabernacle;
the LORD has abolished in Zion
festival and sabbath,
and in his fierce indignation has spurned
king and priest.

7 The Lord has scorned his altar,
disowned his sanctuary;
he has delivered into the hand of the enemy
the walls of her palaces;
a clamor was raised in the house of the LORD
as on a day of festival.

8 The LORD determined to lay in ruins
the wall of daughter Zion;
he stretched the line;
he did not withhold his hand from destroying;
he caused rampart and wall to lament;
they languish together.

9 Her gates have sunk into the ground;
he has ruined and broken her bars;
her king and princes are among the nations;
guidance is no more,
and her prophets obtain
no vision from the LORD.

10 The elders of daughter Zion
sit on the ground in silence;
they have thrown dust on their heads
and put on sackcloth;
the young girls of Jerusalem
have bowed their heads to the ground.

11 My eyes are spent with weeping;
my stomach churns;
my bile is poured out on the ground
because of the destruction of my people,
because infants and babes faint
in the streets of the city.

12 They cry to their mothers,
"Where is bread and wine?"
as they faint like the wounded
in the streets of the city,
as their life is poured out
on their mothers' bosom.

13 What can I say for you, to what compare you,
O daughter Jerusalem?
To what can I liken you, that I may comfort you,
O virgin daughter Zion?
For vast as the sea is your ruin;
who can heal you?

14 Your prophets have seen for you
false and deceptive visions;
they have not exposed your iniquity
to restore your fortunes,

Jesus Can Heal

LAMENTATIONS 2.13

Divide a piece of paper into two columns. On the left side, make a list of those wounds that you carry—from times you have felt hurt, abandoned, misunderstood, physically injured or emotionally bruised. Be specific. On the right hand side, across from each listed hurt, write the words: "Who can heal you? Jesus can." When you feel your lists are complete, prayerfully read the lists as a litany, so that as you name each hurt, you hear the response: "Who can heal you? Jesus can."

See Meeting God in Prayer

Pour Out Your Heart

LAMENTATIONS 2.19

Fill a pitcher with water and place it on a table along with a large bowl. Sit in front of the bowl and pitcher and enter into a quiet time of prayer. Imagine yourself as the water in the pitcher, God as the bowl. Slowly pour the water into the bowl as you talk to God. Say whatever is on your mind. Follow the scriptural directive: "Pour out your heart like water before the presence of the Lord!" When all of the water is in the bowl, immerse your hands in the bowl. Let the bowl symbolize how God's love surrounds you just as the water is able to accept you as it surrounds your hands.

See Meeting God in Prayer

but have seen oracles for you
    that are false and misleading.

15 All who pass along the way
    clap their hands at you;
they hiss and wag their heads
    at daughter Jerusalem;
"Is this the city that was called
    the perfection of beauty,
    the joy of all the earth?"

16 All your enemies
    open their mouths against you;
they hiss, they gnash their teeth,
    they cry: "We have devoured her!
Ah, this is the day we longed for;
    at last we have seen it!"

17 The LORD has done what he purposed,
    he has carried out his threat;
as he ordained long ago,
    he has demolished without pity;
he has made the enemy rejoice over you,
    and exalted the might of your foes.

18 Cry aloud*a* to the Lord!
    O wall of daughter Zion!
Let tears stream down like a torrent
    day and night!
Give yourself no rest,
    your eyes no respite!

19 Arise, cry out in the night,
    at the beginning of the watches!
Pour out your heart like water
    before the presence of the Lord!
Lift your hands to him
    for the lives of your children,
who faint for hunger
    at the head of every street.

20 Look, O LORD, and consider!
    To whom have you done this?
Should women eat their offspring,
    the children they have borne?
Should priest and prophet be killed
    in the sanctuary of the Lord?

21 The young and the old are lying
    on the ground in the streets;
my young women and my young men
    have fallen by the sword;
in the day of your anger you have killed them,
    slaughtering without mercy.

22 You invited my enemies from all around
    as if for a day of festival;
and on the day of the anger of the LORD
    no one escaped or survived;
those whom I bore and reared
    my enemy has destroyed.

a Cn: Heb *Their heart cried*

God's Steadfast Love Endures

3 I am one who has seen affliction
under the rod of God's[a] wrath;
2 he has driven and brought me
into darkness without any light;
3 against me alone he turns his hand,
again and again, all day long.

4 He has made my flesh and my skin waste away,
and broken my bones;
5 he has besieged and enveloped me
with bitterness and tribulation;
6 he has made me sit in darkness
like the dead of long ago.

7 He has walled me about so that I cannot escape;
he has put heavy chains on me;
8 though I call and cry for help,
he shuts out my prayer;
9 he has blocked my ways with hewn stones,
he has made my paths crooked.

10 He is a bear lying in wait for me,
a lion in hiding;
11 he led me off my way and tore me to pieces;
he has made me desolate;
12 he bent his bow and set me
as a mark for his arrow.

13 He shot into my vitals
the arrows of his quiver;
14 I have become the laughingstock of all my people,
the object of their taunt-songs all day long.
15 He has filled me with bitterness,
he has sated me with wormwood.

16 He has made my teeth grind on gravel,
and made me cower in ashes;
17 my soul is bereft of peace;
I have forgotten what happiness is;
18 so I say, "Gone is my glory,
and all that I had hoped for from the LORD."

19 The thought of my affliction and my homelessness
is wormwood and gall!
20 My soul continually thinks of it
and is bowed down within me.
21 But this I call to mind,
and therefore I have hope:

22 The steadfast love of the LORD never ceases,[b]
his mercies never come to an end;
23 they are new every morning;
great is your faithfulness.
24 "The LORD is my portion," says my soul,
"therefore I will hope in him."

25 The LORD is good to those who wait for him,
to the soul that seeks him.
26 It is good that one should wait quietly
for the salvation of the LORD.
27 It is good for one to bear

But This I Call to Mind

LAMENTATIONS 3.19–26

The author speaks on behalf of the Hebrew people who are suffering in the midst of God's discipline. In intense images, we feel with the one who says, "the thought of my affliction and my homelessness is wormwood and the gall!" and then continues, "But . . . The steadfast love of the LORD never ceases." Verses 21–26 are a turning point in this chapter. Read these verses again and again, pausing between readings to meditate on what they mean for you today. Let the words seep deep within you until you feel ready, no matter what happens in your life, to proclaim, "But . . . The LORD is good to those who wait for him."

See Meeting God in Scripture

Kept in God's Love

Thou who art—also within
    us,
May all see Thee—in me
    also,
May I prepare the way for
    Thee,
May I thank Thee for all that
    shall fall to my lot,
May I also not forget the
    needs of others,
Keep me in Thy love
As Thou wouldst that all
    should be kept in mine.
May everything in this my
    being be directed to Thy
    glory
And may I never despair
For I am under Thy hand,
And in Thee is all power
    and goodness.
Give me a pure heart—that I
    may see Thee,
A humble heart—that I may
    hear Thee,
A heart of love—that I may
    serve Thee,
A heart of faith—that I may
    abide in Thee."

—DAG HAMMARSKJÖLD,
Markings

28 the yoke in youth,
to sit alone in silence
    when the Lord has imposed it,
29 to put one's mouth to the dust
    (there may yet be hope),
30 to give one's cheek to the smiter,
    and be filled with insults.

31 For the Lord will not
    reject forever.
32 Although he causes grief, he will have compassion
    according to the abundance of his steadfast love;
33 for he does not willingly afflict
    or grieve anyone.

34 When all the prisoners of the land
    are crushed under foot,
35 when human rights are perverted
    in the presence of the Most High,
36 when one's case is subverted
    —does the Lord not see it?

37 Who can command and have it done,
    if the Lord has not ordained it?
38 Is it not from the mouth of the Most High
    that good and bad come?
39 Why should any who draw breath complain
    about the punishment of their sins?

40 Let us test and examine our ways,
    and return to the LORD.
41 Let us lift up our hearts as well as our hands
    to God in heaven.
42 We have transgressed and rebelled,
    and you have not forgiven.

43 You have wrapped yourself with anger and
      pursued us,
    killing without pity;
44 you have wrapped yourself with a cloud
    so that no prayer can pass through.
45 You have made us filth and rubbish
    among the peoples.

46 All our enemies
    have opened their mouths against us;
47 panic and pitfall have come upon us,
    devastation and destruction.
48 My eyes flow with rivers of tears
    because of the destruction of my people.

49 My eyes will flow without ceasing,
    without respite,
50 until the LORD from heaven
    looks down and sees.
51 My eyes cause me grief
    at the fate of all the young women in my city.

52 Those who were my enemies without cause
    have hunted me like a bird;
53 they flung me alive into a pit
    and hurled stones on me;
54 water closed over my head;
    I said, "I am lost."

55 I called on your name, O LORD,
   from the depths of the pit;
56 you heard my plea, "Do not close your ear
   to my cry for help, but give me relief!"
57 You came near when I called on you;
   you said, "Do not fear!"

58 You have taken up my cause, O Lord,
   you have redeemed my life.
59 You have seen the wrong done to me, O LORD;
   judge my cause.
60 You have seen all their malice,
   all their plots against me.

61 You have heard their taunts, O LORD,
   all their plots against me.
62 The whispers and murmurs of my assailants
   are against me all day long.
63 Whether they sit or rise—see,
   I am the object of their taunt-songs.

64 Pay them back for their deeds, O LORD,
   according to the work of their hands!
65 Give them anguish of heart;
   your curse be on them!
66 Pursue them in anger and destroy them
   from under the LORD's heavens.

The Punishment of Zion

4 How the gold has grown dim,
   how the pure gold is changed!
The sacred stones lie scattered
   at the head of every street.

2 The precious children of Zion,
   worth their weight in fine gold—
how they are reckoned as earthen pots,
   the work of a potter's hands!

3 Even the jackals offer the breast
   and nurse their young,
but my people has become cruel,
   like the ostriches in the wilderness.

4 The tongue of the infant sticks
   to the roof of its mouth for thirst;
the children beg for food,
   but no one gives them anything.

5 Those who feasted on delicacies
   perish in the streets;
those who were brought up in purple
   cling to ash heaps.

6 For the chastisement[a] of my people has been greater
   than the punishment[b] of Sodom,
which was overthrown in a moment,
   though no hand was laid on it.[c]

7 Her princes were purer than snow,
   whiter than milk;
their bodies were more ruddy than coral,
   their hair[c] like sapphire.[d]

Help Is on the Way

LAMENTATIONS 3.55–58

Imagine yourself at the bottom of a dark, dank pit from which you can see no escape. Is anyone within earshot as you cry out in panic? Smell the mustiness; feel the dampness of the earthen walls seeping into your clothes. Goose bumps rise on your skin as you feel the cold and realize that you are all alone with no hope of escape. "Help!" you cry, and then from afar you hear a strong voice respond, "Do not fear!"

How does God come to you? What help does God offer? What else does God say to you? How will you respond, both inwardly and outwardly?

See Meeting God in Scripture

---

a Or *iniquity*   b Or *sin*   c Meaning of Heb uncertain   d Or *lapis lazuli*

Content With Nothing Less

LAMENTATIONS 4:7–19

"It is too much, Lord! It is too much for me! Please give these sorts of favors and consolations to the sinners and people who do not know you at all, in order to attract them to Your service. As for me, who have the happiness of knowing You by faith, it seems to me that *that* ought to be sufficient for me. But because I ought to refuse nothing from so rich and liberal a hand as Yours, I accept, my God, the favors You do for me. Having received them, I beg You to let me return to You what You have given me, for You well know that it is not your gifts that I look for and desire but it is Yourself, and I can be content with nothing less!"

—BROTHER LAWRENCE,
The Practice of the Presence of God

8 Now their visage is blacker than soot;
    they are not recognized in the streets.
Their skin has shriveled on their bones;
    it has become as dry as wood.

9 Happier were those pierced by the sword
    than those pierced by hunger,
whose life drains away, deprived
    of the produce of the field.

10 The hands of compassionate women
    have boiled their own children;
they became their food
    in the destruction of my people.

11 The LORD gave full vent to his wrath;
    he poured out his hot anger,
and kindled a fire in Zion
    that consumed its foundations.

12 The kings of the earth did not believe,
    nor did any of the inhabitants of the world,
that foe or enemy could enter
    the gates of Jerusalem.

13 It was for the sins of her prophets
    and the iniquities of her priests,
who shed the blood of the righteous
    in the midst of her.

14 Blindly they wandered through the streets,
    so defiled with blood
that no one was able
    to touch their garments.

15 "Away! Unclean!" people shouted at them;
    "Away! Away! Do not touch!"
So they became fugitives and wanderers;
    it was said among the nations,
    "They shall stay here no longer."

16 The LORD himself has scattered them,
    he will regard them no more;
no honor was shown to the priests,
    no favor to the elders.

17 Our eyes failed, ever watching
    vainly for help;
we were watching eagerly
    for a nation that could not save.

18 They dogged our steps
    so that we could not walk in our streets;
our end drew near; our days were numbered;
    for our end had come.

19 Our pursuers were swifter
    than the eagles in the heavens;
they chased us on the mountains,
    they lay in wait for us in the wilderness.

20 The LORD's anointed, the breath of our life,
    was taken in their pits—
the one of whom we said, "Under his shadow
    we shall live among the nations."

21 Rejoice and be glad, O daughter Edom,
　　you that live in the land of Uz;
　but to you also the cup shall pass;
　　you shall become drunk and strip yourself bare.

22 The punishment of your iniquity, O daughter Zion,
　　is accomplished,
　he will keep you in exile no longer;
　but your iniquity, O daughter Edom, he will punish,
　　he will uncover your sins.

A Plea for Mercy

5 Remember, O Lord, what has befallen us;
　　look, and see our disgrace!
2 Our inheritance has been turned over to strangers,
　　our homes to aliens.
3 We have become orphans, fatherless;
　　our mothers are like widows.
4 We must pay for the water we drink;
　　the wood we get must be bought.
5 With a yoke*a* on our necks we are hard driven;
　　we are weary, we are given no rest.
6 We have made a pact with*b* Egypt and Assyria,
　　to get enough bread.
7 Our ancestors sinned; they are no more,
　　and we bear their iniquities.
8 Slaves rule over us;
　　there is no one to deliver us from their hand.
9 We get our bread at the peril of our lives,
　　because of the sword in the wilderness.
10 Our skin is black as an oven
　　from the scorching heat of famine.
11 Women are raped in Zion,
　　virgins in the towns of Judah.
12 Princes are hung up by their hands;
　　no respect is shown to the elders.
13 Young men are compelled to grind,
　　and boys stagger under loads of wood.
14 The old men have left the city gate,
　　the young men their music.
15 The joy of our hearts has ceased;
　　our dancing has been turned to mourning.
16 The crown has fallen from our head;
　　woe to us, for we have sinned!
17 Because of this our hearts are sick,
　　because of these things our eyes have grown dim:
18 because of Mount Zion, which lies desolate;
　　jackals prowl over it.

19 But you, O Lord, reign forever;
　　your throne endures to all generations.
20 Why have you forgotten us completely?
　　Why have you forsaken us these many days?
21 Restore us to yourself, O Lord, that we may be
　　restored;
　renew our days as of old—
22 unless you have utterly rejected us,
　　and are angry with us beyond measure.

A Safe Place

LAMENTATIONS 5.21

We may not have an attachment to a place as the Hebrew people did to their holy city, Jerusalem, but we know what it is to need a home. We desire a safe place where we are loved and accepted, known and cherished despite all our flaws. If we are lucky, we have family, friends or a community that provides us with nurture, acceptance and support. But even when we move to a new location and must begin again to build a loving community, God is with us, offering that home and safe place we deeply need. Copy verse 21 onto a 3x5 card and put it where you can see it often. Pray it frequently until it becomes your own personal prayer.

See Meeting God in Prayer

WAYS of MEETING GOD

Meeting God in Scripture

In every era, in myriad places and in all kinds of circumstances, people have testified that the Bible speaks powerfully—that the Word of God can and does change lives. But perhaps you feel that your own experience with reading the Bible pales in significance when compared to such a standard. You feel like the woman who confessed, "Surely there has to be a way to get more out of my Bible reading!" Your times with the Bible yield much of value and interest—but transformation?

> Christian meditation . . . is letting a special word or phrase that you discovered in the first phase of reading sink into your heart.

That is another matter. You learn facts—places and names—but have yet to hear God's voice. As much as you value the insights gained, you long to meet God.

When you read and study scripture it is possible to grow beyond an intellectual knowledge of the Bible to the transformation of your heart. The Bible can become "a lamp to [your] feet and a light to [your] path" (Psalm 119.105). You can go to the heart of the matter and meet the Author. The eighteenth-century bishop Tikhon of Zodonsk articulated well what can happen: "Whenever you read the Gospel," he wrote, "Christ Himself is speaking to you. And while you read, you are praying and talking to Him." Reading and studying the Bible can become more fulfilling than anything you have previously experienced.

But how? Fortunately we are heirs to several helpful approaches. The great spiritual writers of the past have given us a legacy that engages mind and heart, intellect and will. They have suggested ways that help us derive life from the text and so become agents of life for others.

Divine Reading. In the history of Christian spirituality, the oldest and best-known approach to Bible reading is called "spiritual reading" or "divine reading" (the Latin is *lectio divina*). The practice dates back to at least the fourth century, but the idea behind it is even more ancient. Spiritual reading entails a fourfold approach:

First, read slowly. Choose a relatively short passage of a Biblical book (no more than several paragraphs or a short chapter), and read meditatively, prayerfully. In this phase you are a seeker, looking for the "word within the Word." Watch for a key phrase or word that jumps out at you or promises to have special meaning for you. Concern yourself not so much with the *amount* you are reading as the *depth* with which you read. It is better to dwell profoundly on one word or phrase than to skim the surface of several chapters. Read with your own life and choices in view, recalling Paul's injunction that God's word to us is "useful for teaching, for reproof, for correction, and for training in righteousness" (2 Timothy 3.16).

Second, meditate. Christian meditation is not stream-of-consciousness or free association, nor is it Eastern transcendental meditation. Rather, it is letting a special word or phrase that you discovered in the first phase of reading sink into your heart. It is what the Biblical writers had in mind when they spoke of "meditating" on the book of the law "day and night" (Joshua 1.8, Psalm 1.2). For example, when you are reading Psalm 23, perhaps you linger at the phrase, "The LORD is my shepherd." For reasons that may not be immediately apparent, the word "my" stands out. You are struck by the idea that God can be—and wants to be—*your* shepherd. In this second phase of spiritual reading, stay with that thought. Use whatever study skills and related materials that are available to you to enrich your reflection. Bring mind, will and emotions to the enterprise. This meditative stage is comparable to walking around a great statue, viewing it from multiple vantage points. You are like Mary, Jesus' mother, who heard of the angel's announcement and "treasured" and "pondered" what she had heard (Luke 2.19).

Third, pray the text. You have listened; now you respond—that is, you form a prayer that expresses your response to the idea. You "pray it back to God." You are, in effect, engaging God in dialogue. In the case of "The LORD is my shepherd," your response could easily be a prayer of gratitude. It might be a prolonged recollection of all of the ways that God has been present with you over the years, shepherding you through life. This phase of divine reading is in reality not separate from the other aspects but flows through all of them, so that you are continually converting the text into a prayer, a prayer formed by God's revealed will. What you have read is woven through what you tell God. You thereby acknowledge that God's Word "shall not return . . . empty, but it shall accomplish that which [God] purposes]" (Isaiah 55.11).

Fourth, contemplate. That is, rest. In divine reading you eventually arrive at the place at which you no longer work on the text but allow it to work itself into you. You let it soak into your deepest being. You are not straining for additional insights; you simply are savoring an encounter—with God's truth and with God himself. You enjoy the rest that Jesus promised those who come to him (see Matthew 11.28). Quietly, when ready, move toward the moment in which you ask God to show you how to live out what you have experienced.

Spiritual reading enables God to "speak and show" in ways that transform the written Word into a living Word—just for you. Then, having "[tasted] and [seen] that the LORD is good" (Psalm 34.8), you move outward in daily living to become a blessing to others.

Ignatian Reading. Attributed to Ignatius of Loyola (1491–1556) and articulated in his "Spiritual Exercises," the Ignatian method of reading the Bible likewise invites us to enter actively and fully into the text. It encourages detachment from either ego-driven success or fear-motivated anxiety, leaving the soul free to obey God's stirrings.

Generally, Ignatian reading works best with narrative material in which actual characters lived a story of faith. The idea is to place yourself into the text as a careful observer—a "fly on the wall," if you will. Ignatius commended the use of the five senses in such meditation. You taste, hear, see, smell and feel your way through the passage. Occasionally you become one of the characters, seeing the story unfold from his or her viewpoint. Most of all, the aim is to help you perceive the narrative from the viewpoint of Jesus so that you may more fully participate in his mind, heart and work.

> Whatever method you use at any given time, . . . pray for a "Scriptural mind" that is obedient, faithful to the historic Christian tradition, Christ-centered and personal.

For the sake of practice, you might like to concentrate on John 18.1–11 and spend five days reading it. Each day, imagine yourself as a different one of the characters: Judas, a soldier, Peter, the high priest's servant or Jesus. As you enter vicariously into the position of each character, ask God to teach you how to live in greater fidelity and obedience—which is the ultimate aim of the Ignatian method of reading scripture and of Ignatian spirituality in general.

Franciscan Reading. While not a direct by-product of the teachings of Francis of Assisi, Franciscan reading exhibits primary qualities of Franciscan spirituality, such as action, spontaneity, love, praise, beauty and delight in creation. Like Ignatian reflection, Franciscan reading involves the mental process of entering personally into the text. But this method is more fluid. It allows the encounter with God to incorporate ordinary activities and daily experiences.

For example, turn in your Bible to Isaiah 53 and read through this chapter. To help you enter into its message and reflect on Jesus' sacrificial death on the cross, the Franciscan method would invite you to take actions such as these: If you have a model of a cross with Jesus on it, you might hold it in your hand, gazing at the details of the Lord's crucified body. You might sing a hymn such as "O Sacred Head, Now Wounded" or "The Old Rugged Cross." You might look through today's newspaper and identify places in the world where people are suffering. You might write a poem or paint a picture to capture what you are thinking and feeling. In the Franciscan spirit, you would allow your emotions to be expressed through an activity. You would be encouraged to "feel" something of what Jesus experienced on your behalf. You would saturate the entire experience with prayer, asking God to make you an instrument of peace in the lives of those who are suffering.

To be sure, these methods do not exhaust our options for formative reading. You might use the fruit of the Spirit described in Galatians 5.22–23 as a lens through which you read, asking yourself how a particular passage might deepen love, joy, peace, patience, kindness, goodness, gentleness, faithfulness and self-control in your life. You might use what some have called the Fivefold Question (What does this passage say about God's nature? What does it say about human nature? What does it say about how God relates to people? What does it suggest about how I might pray? What does it suggest about how I might act?).

Whatever method you use at any given time, an underlying attitude of openness to seeking truth should be adopted. We pray for a "scriptural mind" that is obedient, faithful to the historic Christian tradition, Christ-centered and personal. We must desire to find truth and be willing to apply it to our own lives and our relationships with others. Apart from such foundational commitments, any method becomes mere technique. With them, any of the methods of reading scripture can become a true means of grace.

See Page 1498 for the next Ways of Meeting God *article.*

EZEKIEL

Confronting the Holy

KEY VERSE:

"Then the nations that are left all around you shall know that I, the LORD, have rebuilt the ruined places, and replanted that which was desolate; I, the LORD, have spoken, and I will do it."—Ezekiel 36.36

"Brokenness and wounding do not occur in order to break human dignity but to open the heart so God can act."
—MARTIN MARTY,
A Cry of Absence

Many people know this book primarily by the author's vision of a valley of dry bones. But in these pages we also meet a priest and prophet who agonizes over the poor choices of the leaders of Israel, who bemoans the sins of the people and who condemns the desecration performed by neighboring nations.

With words and images that seem abrasive at times—yet always penetrating—Ezekiel invites us to look to the One whom we worship. He calls us to worship God with authenticity (14.6). Through his account we meet a God who is angry and disappointed (9.9), a God who laments the disasters that will come upon unjust nations (30.1–4), and a God who cares for people as a shepherd cares for a flock of sheep (34.1–24). This God holds people accountable for their actions (23.35), desires to make a new covenant of peace (34.25), and longs to put a new heart and a new spirit in them (36.26). We meet a God who will gather in the scattered exiles (36.24), restore the nation to the tribes of Israel (47.13) and reestablish the centrality of worship (43.1–5). Renewal will flow like a river to all the land (47.1).

Woven throughout the book of Ezekiel is the refrain, "Then they will know that I am the LORD." As you read Ezekiel, you may find yourself confronted and challenged, loved and renewed, and ready to sing the refrain, "Now I know that you are the Lord my God." Pray for openness to hear the words of Ezekiel and a soft heart with which to accompany him into the presence of God.

The Vision of the Chariot

1 In the thirtieth year, in the fourth month, on the fifth day of the month, as I was among the exiles by the river Chebar, the heavens were opened, and I saw visions of God. ²On the fifth day of the month (it was the fifth year of the exile of King Jehoiachin), ³the word of the LORD came to the priest Ezekiel son of Buzi, in the land of the Chaldeans by the river Chebar; and the hand of the LORD was on him there.

4 As I looked, a stormy wind came out of the north: a great cloud with brightness around it and fire flashing forth continually, and in the middle of the fire, something like gleaming amber. ⁵In the middle of it was something like four living creatures. This was their appearance: they were of human form. ⁶Each had four faces, and each of them had four wings. ⁷Their legs were straight, and the soles of their feet were like the sole of a calf's foot; and they sparkled like burnished bronze. ⁸Under their wings on their four sides they had human hands. And the four had their faces and their wings thus: ⁹their wings touched one another; each of them moved straight ahead, without turning as they moved. ¹⁰As for the appearance of their faces: the four had the face of a human being, the face of a lion on the right side, the face of an ox on the left side, and the face of an eagle; ¹¹such were their faces. Their wings were spread out above; each creature had two wings, each of which touched the wing of another, while two covered their bodies. ¹²Each moved straight ahead; wherever the spirit would go, they went, without turning as they went. ¹³In the middle of*a* the living creatures there was something that looked like burning coals of fire, like torches moving to and fro among the living creatures; the fire was bright, and lightning issued from the fire. ¹⁴The living creatures darted to and fro, like a flash of lightning.

15 As I looked at the living creatures, I saw a wheel on the earth beside the living creatures, one for each of the four of them.*b* ¹⁶As for the appearance of the wheels and their construction: their appearance was like the gleaming of beryl; and the four had the same form, their construction being something like a wheel within a wheel. ¹⁷When they moved, they moved in any of the four directions without veering as they moved. ¹⁸Their rims were tall and awesome, for the rims of all four were full of eyes all around. ¹⁹When the living creatures moved, the wheels moved beside them; and when the living creatures rose from the earth, the wheels rose. ²⁰Wherever the spirit would go, they went, and the wheels rose along with them; for the spirit of the living creatures was in the wheels. ²¹When they moved, the others moved; when they stopped, the others stopped; and when they rose from the earth, the wheels rose along with them; for the spirit of the living creatures was in the wheels.

22 Over the heads of the living creatures there was something like a dome, shining like crystal,*c* spread out above their heads. ²³Under the dome their wings were stretched out straight, one toward another; and each of the creatures had two wings covering its body. ²⁴When they moved, I heard the sound of their wings like the sound of

---

a Gk OL: Heb *And the appearance of*   *b* Heb *of their faces*   *c* Gk: Heb *like the awesome crystal*

Awestruck

EZEKIEL 1.22—2.1

Carefully read this description of the "glory of the LORD." Read it again and then close your eyes and fix this image firmly in your mind. Keep it there for a period of time. What is your response to God's glory? What posture expresses your response? Is it to stand with your arms raised in praise? Or is it to lie prostrate on the floor and experience utter humility in the presence of God? Or is it to kneel in quiet adoration at the splendor of God? Repeat in prayer: "The glory of the Lord" or "Holy is God."

See *Meeting God in Prayer*

A Meal of Words

EZEKIEL 3.1–3

The writer of Psalm 119.103 suggests that God's words are "sweeter than honey." Ezekiel carries the imagery even further by eating a scroll. Ezekiel was to let God's words fill him completely so that he could fulfill his commission to preach to Israel. Though the scroll contained words of woe and mourning, it tasted sweet to God's servant.

Spiritual teachers throughout the centuries have encouraged us to to savor the sweetness of the Word of God as we come into God's presence in prayer. What scripture passages have you "tasted" and "digested" so that they have become part of you? What passages do you know from memory? What passages do you frequently return to for nourishment? Write out a passage that "tastes" especially sweet to you.

See *Meeting God in Scripture*.

mighty waters, like the thunder of the Almighty,[a] a sound of tumult like the sound of an army; when they stopped, they let down their wings. 25And there came a voice from above the dome over their heads; when they stopped, they let down their wings.

26 And above the dome over their heads there was something like a throne, in appearance like sapphire;[b] and seated above the likeness of a throne was something that seemed like a human form. 27Upward from what appeared like the loins I saw something like gleaming amber, something that looked like fire enclosed all around; and downward from what looked like the loins I saw something that looked like fire, and there was a splendor all around. 28Like the bow in a cloud on a rainy day, such was the appearance of the splendor all around. This was the appearance of the likeness of the glory of the LORD.

When I saw it, I fell on my face, and I heard the voice of someone speaking.

The Vision of the Scroll

2 He said to me: O mortal,[c] stand up on your feet, and I will speak with you. 2And when he spoke to me, a spirit entered into me and set me on my feet; and I heard him speaking to me. 3He said to me, Mortal, I am sending you to the people of Israel, to a nation[d] of rebels who have rebelled against me; they and their ancestors have transgressed against me to this very day. 4The descendants are impudent and stubborn. I am sending you to them, and you shall say to them, "Thus says the Lord GOD." 5Whether they hear or refuse to hear (for they are a rebellious house), they shall know that there has been a prophet among them. 6And you, O mortal, do not be afraid of them, and do not be afraid of their words, though briers and thorns surround you and you live among scorpions; do not be afraid of their words, and do not be dismayed at their looks, for they are a rebellious house. 7You shall speak my words to them, whether they hear or refuse to hear; for they are a rebellious house.

8 But you, mortal, hear what I say to you; do not be rebellious like that rebellious house; open your mouth and eat what I give you. 9I looked, and a hand was stretched out to me, and a written scroll was in it. 10He spread it before me; it had writing on the front and on the back, and written on it were words of lamentation and mourning and woe.

3 He said to me, O mortal, eat what is offered to you; eat this scroll, and go, speak to the house of Israel. 2So I opened my mouth, and he gave me the scroll to eat. 3He said to me, Mortal, eat this scroll that I give you and fill your stomach with it. Then I ate it; and in my mouth it was as sweet as honey.

4 He said to me: Mortal, go to the house of Israel and speak my very words to them. 5For you are not sent to a people of obscure speech and difficult language, but to the house of Israel— 6not to many peoples of obscure speech and difficult language, whose words you cannot understand. Surely, if I sent you to them, they would listen to you. 7But the house of Israel will not listen to you, for they

a Traditional rendering of Heb *Shaddai*   *b* Or *lapis lazuli*   *c* Or *son of man*; Heb *ben adam* (and so throughout the book when Ezekiel is addressed)   *d* Syr: Heb *to nations*

are not willing to listen to me; because all the house of Israel have a hard forehead and a stubborn heart. [8]See, I have made your face hard against their faces, and your forehead hard against their foreheads. [9]Like the hardest stone, harder than flint, I have made your forehead; do not fear them or be dismayed at their looks, for they are a rebellious house. [10]He said to me: Mortal, all my words that I shall speak to you receive in your heart and hear with your ears; [11]then go to the exiles, to your people, and speak to them. Say to them, "Thus says the Lord GOD"; whether they hear or refuse to hear.

Ezekiel at the River Chebar

12 Then the spirit lifted me up, and as the glory of the LORD rose[a] from its place, I heard behind me the sound of loud rumbling; [13]it was the sound of the wings of the living creatures brushing against one another, and the sound of the wheels beside them, that sounded like a loud rumbling. [14]The spirit lifted me up and bore me away; I went in bitterness in the heat of my spirit, the hand of the LORD being strong upon me. [15]I came to the exiles at Tel-abib, who lived by the river Chebar.[b] And I sat there among them, stunned, for seven days.

16 At the end of seven days, the word of the LORD came to me: [17]Mortal, I have made you a sentinel for the house of Israel; whenever you hear a word from my mouth, you shall give them warning from me. [18]If I say to the wicked, "You shall surely die," and you give them no warning, or speak to warn the wicked from their wicked way, in order to save their life, those wicked persons shall die for their iniquity; but their blood I will require at your hand. [19]But if you warn the wicked, and they do not turn from their wickedness, or from their wicked way, they shall die for their iniquity; but you will have saved your life. [20]Again, if the righteous turn from their righteousness and commit iniquity, and I lay a stumbling block before them, they shall die; because you have not warned them, they shall die for their sin, and their righteous deeds that they have done shall not be remembered; but their blood I will require at your hand. [21]If, however, you warn the righteous not to sin, and they do not sin, they shall surely live, because they took warning; and you will have saved your life.

Ezekiel Isolated and Silenced

22 Then the hand of the LORD was upon me there; and he said to me, Rise up, go out into the valley, and there I will speak with you. [23]So I rose up and went out into the valley; and the glory of the LORD stood there, like the glory that I had seen by the river Chebar; and I fell on my face. [24]The spirit entered into me, and set me on my feet; and he spoke with me and said to me: Go, shut yourself inside your house. [25]As for you, mortal, cords shall be placed on you, and you shall be bound with them, so that you cannot go out among the people; [26]and I will make your tongue cling to the roof of your mouth, so that you shall be speechless and unable to reprove them; for they are a rebellious house. [27]But when I speak with you, I will open your mouth, and you shall say to them, "Thus says the Lord

a Cn: Heb *and blessed be the glory of the LORD*   b Two Mss Syr: Heb *Chebar, and to where they lived.* Another reading is *Chebar, and I sat where they sat*

An Obedient Word

EZEKIEL 3.16–17

"Even the awkwardly spoken word, if only it come out of an obedient heart, is better than a word unspoken in disobedience. Even the prayer that seems ineffectual and may perhaps be ridiculed may have left behind a seed of blessing. Indeed, even if no fruit is created in the spiritual sense, so that a soul comes nearer to God, still there is one thing that has happened: a testimony has been given in the Biblical sense. And this precisely is our task, a hard task, but a glorious task."

—ERICH SCHICK,
quoted in *A Guide to Prayer*

Days of Bread and Water

EZEKIEL 4.6–9

Ezekiel was to foreshadow the suffering of the Israelites by lying on his side for many days and eating only bread and drinking only water. He symbolically bore the sins of Israel, calling the people's attention to their sin.

There are people suffering today under poverty and oppression. Who calls our attention to the plight of the needy? What does it cost them? Offer a prayer of thanks for those who have been given a prophetic calling. Is there anyone you know in such a ministry whom you could call or to whom you could send a word of encouragement? For one meal today have bread and water, and remember the poor and hungry.

See *Meeting God in Service*

GOD"; let those who will hear, hear; and let those who refuse to hear, refuse; for they are a rebellious house.

The Siege of Jerusalem Portrayed

4 And you, O mortal, take a brick and set it before you. On it portray a city, Jerusalem; ²and put siegeworks against it, and build a siege wall against it, and cast up a ramp against it; set camps also against it, and plant battering rams against it all around. ³Then take an iron plate and place it as an iron wall between you and the city; set your face toward it, and let it be in a state of siege, and press the siege against it. This is a sign for the house of Israel.

4 Then lie on your left side, and place the punishment of the house of Israel upon it; you shall bear their punishment for the number of the days that you lie there. ⁵For I assign to you a number of days, three hundred ninety days, equal to the number of the years of their punishment; and so you shall bear the punishment of the house of Israel. ⁶When you have completed these, you shall lie down a second time, but on your right side, and bear the punishment of the house of Judah; forty days I assign you, one day for each year. ⁷You shall set your face toward the siege of Jerusalem, and with your arm bared you shall prophesy against it. ⁸See, I am putting cords on you so that you cannot turn from one side to the other until you have completed the days of your siege.

9 And you, take wheat and barley, beans and lentils, millet and spelt; put them into one vessel, and make bread for yourself. During the number of days that you lie on your side, three hundred ninety days, you shall eat it. ¹⁰The food that you eat shall be twenty shekels a day by weight; at fixed times you shall eat it. ¹¹And you shall drink water by measure, one-sixth of a hin; at fixed times you shall drink. ¹²You shall eat it as a barley-cake, baking it in their sight on human dung. ¹³The LORD said, "Thus shall the people of Israel eat their bread, unclean, among the nations to which I will drive them." ¹⁴Then I said, "Ah Lord GOD! I have never defiled myself; from my youth up until now I have never eaten what died of itself or was torn by animals, nor has carrion flesh come into my mouth." ¹⁵Then he said to me, "See, I will let you have cow's dung instead of human dung, on which you may prepare your bread."

16 Then he said to me, Mortal, I am going to break the staff of bread in Jerusalem; they shall eat bread by weight and with fearfulness; and they shall drink water by measure and in dismay. ¹⁷Lacking bread and water, they will look at one another in dismay, and waste away under their punishment.

A Sword against Jerusalem

5 And you, O mortal, take a sharp sword; use it as a barber's razor and run it over your head and your beard; then take balances for weighing, and divide the hair. ²One third of the hair you shall burn in the fire inside the city, when the days of the siege are completed; one third you shall take and strike with the sword all around the city;ᵃ and one third you shall scatter to the wind, and I will unsheathe the sword after them. ³Then you shall take from these a small number, and bind them in the skirts of your

a Heb *it*

robe. [4]From these, again, you shall take some, throw them into the fire and burn them up; from there a fire will come out against all the house of Israel.

5 Thus says the Lord GOD: This is Jerusalem; I have set her in the center of the nations, with countries all around her. [6]But she has rebelled against my ordinances and my statutes, becoming more wicked than the nations and the countries all around her, rejecting my ordinances and not following my statutes. [7]Therefore thus says the Lord GOD: Because you are more turbulent than the nations that are all around you, and have not followed my statutes or kept my ordinances, but have acted according to the ordinances of the nations that are all around you; [8]therefore thus says the Lord GOD: I, I myself, am coming against you; I will execute judgments among you in the sight of the nations. [9]And because of all your abominations, I will do to you what I have never yet done, and the like of which I will never do again. [10]Surely, parents shall eat their children in your midst, and children shall eat their parents; I will execute judgments on you, and any of you who survive I will scatter to every wind. [11]Therefore, as I live, says the Lord GOD, surely, because you have defiled my sanctuary with all your detestable things and with all your abominations— therefore I will cut you down;[a] my eye will not spare, and I will have no pity. [12]One third of you shall die of pestilence or be consumed by famine among you; one third shall fall by the sword around you; and one third I will scatter to every wind and will unsheathe the sword after them.

13 My anger shall spend itself, and I will vent my fury on them and satisfy myself; and they shall know that I, the LORD, have spoken in my jealousy, when I spend my fury on them. [14]Moreover I will make you a desolation and an object of mocking among the nations around you, in the sight of all that pass by. [15]You shall be[b] a mockery and a taunt, a warning and a horror, to the nations around you, when I execute judgments on you in anger and fury, and with furious punishments—I, the LORD, have spoken— [16]when I loose against you[c] my deadly arrows of famine, arrows for destruction, which I will let loose to destroy you, and when I bring more and more famine upon you, and break your staff of bread. [17]I will send famine and wild animals against you, and they will rob you of your children; pestilence and bloodshed shall pass through you; and I will bring the sword upon you. I, the LORD, have spoken.

Judgment on Idolatrous Israel

6 The word of the LORD came to me: [2]O mortal, set your face toward the mountains of Israel, and prophesy against them, [3]and say, You mountains of Israel, hear the word of the Lord GOD! Thus says the Lord GOD to the mountains and the hills, to the ravines and the valleys: I, I myself will bring a sword upon you, and I will destroy your high places. [4]Your altars shall become desolate, and your incense stands shall be broken; and I will throw down your slain in front of your idols. [5]I will lay the corpses of the people of Israel in front of their idols; and I will scatter your bones around your altars. [6]Wherever you live, your towns shall be waste and your high places ruined, so that your al-

On Not Choosing Idols

EZEKIEL 6.1–4

"Every time you make a choice you are turning the central part of you, the part of you that chooses, into something a little different from what it was before. And taking your life as a whole, with all your innumerable choices, all your life long you are slowly turning this central thing either into a Heavenly creature or into a hellish creature: either into a creature that is in harmony with God, with other creatures, and with itself, or else into one that is in a state of war and hatred with God, and with its fellow creatures, and with itself. To be the one kind of creature is Heaven; that is, it is joy, and peace and knowledge, and power. To be the other means madness, horror, idiocy, rage, impotence and eternal loneliness. Each of us at each moment is progressing to the one state or the other."

—C. S. LEWIS,
Mere Christianity

---

a Another reading is *I will withdraw*   *b* Gk Syr Vg Tg: Heb *It shall be*
c Heb *them*

Dealing With the Doom

EZEKIEL 7.1–4

By this point in Ezekiel's account we have read several chapters forecasting punishment and desolations. And more hard words of doom and judgment follow in subsequent chapters. In the middle of reading such difficult words, it sometimes helps to realize that behind God's wrath is his broken heart (see 6.9). God loves the people of Jerusalem, but his heart is torn in two as the nation continues to worship idols and make unholy alliances. As a parent disciplines a child out of love, so God is forced to correct Israel. Spend a few moments meditating on how you may have broken God's heart and what might need correcting within you. Ask God for help in making amends.

See Meeting God in Prayer

tars will be waste and ruined,[a] your idols broken and destroyed, your incense stands cut down, and your works wiped out. [7]The slain shall fall in your midst; then you shall know that I am the LORD.

8 But I will spare some. Some of you shall escape the sword among the nations and be scattered through the countries. [9]Those of you who escape shall remember me among the nations where they are carried captive, how I was crushed by their wanton heart that turned away from me, and their wanton eyes that turned after their idols. Then they will be loathsome in their own sight for the evils that they have committed, for all their abominations. [10]And they shall know that I am the LORD; I did not threaten in vain to bring this disaster upon them.

11 Thus says the Lord GOD: Clap your hands and stamp your foot, and say, Alas for all the vile abominations of the house of Israel! For they shall fall by the sword, by famine, and by pestilence. [12]Those far off shall die of pestilence; those nearby shall fall by the sword; and any who are left and are spared shall die of famine. Thus I will spend my fury upon them. [13]And you shall know that I am the LORD, when their slain lie among their idols around their altars, on every high hill, on all the mountain tops, under every green tree, and under every leafy oak, wherever they offered pleasing odor to all their idols. [14]I will stretch out my hand against them, and make the land desolate and waste, throughout all their settlements, from the wilderness to Riblah.[b] Then they shall know that I am the LORD.

Impending Disaster

7 The word of the LORD came to me: [2]You, O mortal, thus says the Lord GOD to the land of Israel:
An end! The end has come
    upon the four corners of the land.
[3] Now the end is upon you,
    I will let loose my anger upon you;
    I will judge you according to your ways,
    I will punish you for all your abominations.
[4] My eye will not spare you, I will have no pity.
    I will punish you for your ways,
    while your abominations are among you.
Then you shall know that I am the LORD.

5 Thus says the Lord GOD:
Disaster after disaster! See, it comes.
[6]   An end has come, the end has come.
    It has awakened against you; see, it comes!
[7] Your doom[c] has come to you,
    O inhabitant of the land.
    The time has come, the day is near—
    of tumult, not of reveling on the mountains.
[8] Soon now I will pour out my wrath upon you;
    I will spend my anger against you.
    I will judge you according to your ways,
    and punish you for all your abominations.
[9] My eye will not spare; I will have no pity.
    I will punish you according to your ways,
    while your abominations are among you.
Then you shall know that it is I the LORD who strike.

a Syr Vg Tg: Heb *and be made guilty*   b Another reading is *Diblah*
c Meaning of Heb uncertain

¹⁰ See, the day! See, it comes!
  Your doom*ᵃ* has gone out.
The rod has blossomed, pride has budded.
¹¹   Violence has grown into a rod of wickedness.
None of them shall remain,
    not their abundance, not their wealth;
    no pre-eminence among them.*ᵃ*
¹² The time has come, the day draws near;
    let not the buyer rejoice, nor the seller mourn,
    for wrath is upon all their multitude.
¹³For the sellers shall not return to what has been sold as
long as they remain alive. For the vision concerns all their
multitude; it shall not be revoked. Because of their iniquity,
they cannot maintain their lives.*ᵃ*
¹⁴   They have blown the horn and made everything
        ready;
    but no one goes to battle,
    for my wrath is upon all their multitude.
¹⁵   The sword is outside, pestilence and famine are
        inside;
    those in the field die by the sword;
    those in the city—famine and pestilence devour
        them.
¹⁶   If any survivors escape,
    they shall be found on the mountains
    like doves of the valleys,
    all of them moaning over their iniquity.
¹⁷   All hands shall grow feeble,
    all knees turn to water.
¹⁸   They shall put on sackcloth,
    horror shall cover them.
    Shame shall be on all faces,
    baldness on all their heads.
¹⁹   They shall fling their silver into the streets,
    their gold shall be treated as unclean.
Their silver and gold cannot save them on the day of the
wrath of the Lᴏʀᴅ. They shall not satisfy their hunger or fill
their stomachs with it. For it was the stumbling block of
their iniquity. ²⁰From their*ᵇ* beautiful ornament, in which
they took pride, they made their abominable images, their
detestable things; therefore I will make of it an unclean
thing to them.
²¹   I will hand it over to strangers as booty,
    to the wicked of the earth as plunder;
    they shall profane it.
²²   I will avert my face from them,
    so that they may profane my treasured*ᶜ* place;
    the violent shall enter it,
    they shall profane it.
²³   Make a chain!*ᵃ*
    For the land is full of bloody crimes;
    the city is full of violence.
²⁴   I will bring the worst of the nations
    to take possession of their houses.
    I will put an end to the arrogance of the strong,
    and their holy places shall be profaned.
²⁵   When anguish comes, they will seek peace,
    but there shall be none.
²⁶   Disaster comes upon disaster,

Silver and Gold

EZEKIEL 7.19–20

Some people in Jerusalem turn
their silver and gold into images to worship, but their idols
cannot save them or satisfy
their hunger.

Write down some of your
thoughts and recollections
about money and your relationship to it. You might address
things your parents taught you
about money or write about
factors that influenced your attitudes about money. Think
about the first money you
earned, the most money you've
made, or your decisions about
giving or tithing. As you read
what you have written, consider
those attitudes and actions for
which you need to ask forgiveness. What can you celebrate?
In what ways do you need
God's guidance?

See Meeting God in Everyday Life

---

a Meaning of Heb uncertain   *b* Syr Symmachus: Heb *its*   *c* Or *secret*

Turning From Violence

EZEKIEL 8.17

God is already angry with the people of Jerusalem, but they provoke him even more by "fill[ing] the land with violence."

Because it is "news," violence tends to dominate the media coverage and is typically recorded in graphic and colorful detail. Therefore it is especially important to remember and support acts of peace and reconciliation. Find newspaper articles about those whose efforts bring about peace and reconciliation and pray for those efforts. Or make a list of actions that you could do to help bring about peace. Ask God to help you bring peace into troubled situations. Do something from the list each day this week.

See Meeting God in Service

rumor follows rumor;
they shall keep seeking a vision from the prophet;
    instruction shall perish from the priest,
    and counsel from the elders.
27 The king shall mourn,
    the prince shall be wrapped in despair,
    and the hands of the people of the land shall
        tremble.
According to their way I will deal with them;
    according to their own judgments I will judge
        them.
And they shall know that I am the LORD.

Abominations in the Temple

8 In the sixth year, in the sixth month, on the fifth day of the month, as I sat in my house, with the elders of Judah sitting before me, the hand of the Lord GOD fell upon me there. ²I looked, and there was a figure that looked like a human being;*a* below what appeared to be its loins it was fire, and above the loins it was like the appearance of brightness, like gleaming amber. ³It stretched out the form of a hand, and took me by a lock of my head; and the spirit lifted me up between earth and heaven, and brought me in visions of God to Jerusalem, to the entrance of the gateway of the inner court that faces north, to the seat of the image of jealousy, which provokes to jealousy. ⁴And the glory of the God of Israel was there, like the vision that I had seen in the valley.

5 Then God*b* said to me, "O mortal, lift up your eyes now in the direction of the north." So I lifted up my eyes toward the north, and there, north of the altar gate, in the entrance, was this image of jealousy. ⁶He said to me, "Mortal, do you see what they are doing, the great abominations that the house of Israel are committing here, to drive me far from my sanctuary? Yet you will see still greater abominations."

7 And he brought me to the entrance of the court; I looked, and there was a hole in the wall. ⁸Then he said to me, "Mortal, dig through the wall"; and when I dug through the wall, there was an entrance. ⁹He said to me, "Go in, and see the vile abominations that they are committing here." ¹⁰So I went in and looked; there, portrayed on the wall all around, were all kinds of creeping things, and loathsome animals, and all the idols of the house of Israel. ¹¹Before them stood seventy of the elders of the house of Israel, with Jaazaniah son of Shaphan standing among them. Each had his censer in his hand, and the fragrant cloud of incense was ascending. ¹²Then he said to me, "Mortal, have you seen what the elders of the house of Israel are doing in the dark, each in his room of images? For they say, 'The LORD does not see us, the LORD has forsaken the land.'" ¹³He said also to me, "You will see still greater abominations that they are committing."

14 Then he brought me to the entrance of the north gate of the house of the LORD; women were sitting there weeping for Tammuz. ¹⁵Then he said to me, "Have you seen this, O mortal? You will see still greater abominations than these."

16 And he brought me into the inner court of the house of the LORD; there, at the entrance of the temple of the LORD, between the porch and the altar, were about twenty-

a Gk: Heb *like fire*   *b* Heb *he*

five men, with their backs to the temple of the Lord, and their faces toward the east, prostrating themselves to the sun toward the east. [17]Then he said to me, "Have you seen this, O mortal? Is it not bad enough that the house of Judah commits the abominations done here? Must they fill the land with violence, and provoke my anger still further? See, they are putting the branch to their nose! [18]Therefore I will act in wrath; my eye will not spare, nor will I have pity; and though they cry in my hearing with a loud voice, I will not listen to them."

The Slaughter of the Idolaters

9 Then he cried in my hearing with a loud voice, saying, "Draw near, you executioners of the city, each with his destroying weapon in his hand." [2]And six men came from the direction of the upper gate, which faces north, each with his weapon for slaughter in his hand; among them was a man clothed in linen, with a writing case at his side. They went in and stood beside the bronze altar.

3 Now the glory of the God of Israel had gone up from the cherub on which it rested to the threshold of the house. The Lord called to the man clothed in linen, who had the writing case at his side; [4]and said to him, "Go through the city, through Jerusalem, and put a mark on the foreheads of those who sigh and groan over all the abominations that are committed in it." [5]To the others he said in my hearing, "Pass through the city after him, and kill; your eye shall not spare, and you shall show no pity. [6]Cut down old men, young men and young women, little children and women, but touch no one who has the mark. And begin at my sanctuary." So they began with the elders who were in front of the house. [7]Then he said to them, "Defile the house, and fill the courts with the slain. Go!" So they went out and killed in the city. [8]While they were killing, and I was left alone, I fell prostrate on my face and cried out, "Ah Lord God! will you destroy all who remain of Israel as you pour out your wrath upon Jerusalem?" [9]He said to me, "The guilt of the house of Israel and Judah is exceedingly great; the land is full of bloodshed and the city full of perversity; for they say, 'The Lord has forsaken the land, and the Lord does not see.' [10]As for me, my eye will not spare, nor will I have pity, but I will bring down their deeds upon their heads."

11 Then the man clothed in linen, with the writing case at his side, brought back word, saying, "I have done as you commanded me."

God's Glory Leaves Jerusalem

10 Then I looked, and above the dome that was over the heads of the cherubim there appeared above them something like a sapphire,[a] in form resembling a throne. [2]He said to the man clothed in linen, "Go within the wheelwork underneath the cherubim; fill your hands with burning coals from among the cherubim, and scatter them over the city." He went in as I looked on. [3]Now the cherubim were standing on the south side of the house when the man went in; and a cloud filled the inner court. [4]Then the glory of the Lord rose up from the cherub to the threshold of the house; the house was filled with the cloud, and the court was full of the brightness of the glory of the

The Mark of Lament

EZEKIEL 9.4–11

The man clothed in linen is instructed to go throughout Jerusalem and mark the foreheads of those who "sigh and groan" over the sins of the city. The mark saved them from death.

Even in times of great wrongdoing and impending judgment there are good people and good things that should be preserved, even cherished. Consider how you can become one who sighs and groans over corruption. Pray for wisdom and discernment to preserve and reinforce the good.

See Meeting God in Service

---

a Or lapis lazuli

Forgiveness

EZEKIEL 11.12

"Lord, I have fallen again—
     a human clod!
Selfish I was, and heedless
     to offend,
Stood on my rights. Thy
     own child would not
     send
Away his shreds of nothing
     for the whole God!
Wretched, to thee who
     savest, low I bend:
Give me the power to let my
     rag-tag rights go
In the great wind that from
     thy gulf doth blow."
—GEORGE MACDONALD,
Diary of an Old Soul

LORD. ⁵The sound of the wings of the cherubim was heard as far as the outer court, like the voice of God Almighty*a* when he speaks.

6 When he commanded the man clothed in linen, "Take fire from within the wheelwork, from among the cherubim," he went in and stood beside a wheel. ⁷And a cherub stretched out his hand from among the cherubim to the fire that was among the cherubim, took some of it and put it into the hands of the man clothed in linen, who took it and went out. ⁸The cherubim appeared to have the form of a human hand under their wings.

9 I looked, and there were four wheels beside the cherubim, one beside each cherub; and the appearance of the wheels was like gleaming beryl. ¹⁰And as for their appearance, the four looked alike, something like a wheel within a wheel. ¹¹When they moved, they moved in any of the four directions without veering as they moved; but in whatever direction the front wheel faced, the others followed without veering as they moved. ¹²Their entire body, their rims, their spokes, their wings, and the wheels—the wheels of the four of them—were full of eyes all around. ¹³As for the wheels, they were called in my hearing "the wheelwork." ¹⁴Each one had four faces: the first face was that of the cherub, the second face was that of a human being, the third that of a lion, and the fourth that of an eagle.

15 The cherubim rose up. These were the living creatures that I saw by the river Chebar. ¹⁶When the cherubim moved, the wheels moved beside them; and when the cherubim lifted up their wings to rise up from the earth, the wheels at their side did not veer. ¹⁷When they stopped, the others stopped, and when they rose up, the others rose up with them; for the spirit of the living creatures was in them.

18 Then the glory of the LORD went out from the threshold of the house and stopped above the cherubim. ¹⁹The cherubim lifted up their wings and rose up from the earth in my sight as they went out with the wheels beside them. They stopped at the entrance of the east gate of the house of the LORD; and the glory of the God of Israel was above them.

20 These were the living creatures that I saw underneath the God of Israel by the river Chebar; and I knew that they were cherubim. ²¹Each had four faces, each four wings, and underneath their wings something like human hands. ²²As for what their faces were like, they were the same faces whose appearance I had seen by the river Chebar. Each one moved straight ahead.

Judgment on Wicked Counselors

11 The spirit lifted me up and brought me to the east gate of the house of the LORD, which faces east. There, at the entrance of the gateway, were twenty-five men; among them I saw Jaazaniah son of Azzur, and Pelatiah son of Benaiah, officials of the people. ²He said to me, "Mortal, these are the men who devise iniquity and who give wicked counsel in this city; ³they say, 'The time is not near to build houses; this city is the pot, and we are the meat.' ⁴Therefore prophesy against them; prophesy, O mortal."

5 Then the spirit of the LORD fell upon me, and he said to me, "Say, Thus says the LORD: This is what you think, O house of Israel; I know the things that come into your

a Traditional rendering of Heb *El Shaddai*

mind. ⁶You have killed many in this city, and have filled its streets with the slain. ⁷Therefore thus says the Lord GOD: The slain whom you have placed within it are the meat, and this city is the pot; but you shall be taken out of it. ⁸You have feared the sword; and I will bring the sword upon you, says the Lord GOD. ⁹I will take you out of it and give you over to the hands of foreigners, and execute judgments upon you. ¹⁰You shall fall by the sword; I will judge you at the border of Israel. And you shall know that I am the LORD. ¹¹This city shall not be your pot, and you shall not be the meat inside it; I will judge you at the border of Israel. ¹²Then you shall know that I am the LORD, whose statutes you have not followed, and whose ordinances you have not kept, but you have acted according to the ordinances of the nations that are around you."

13 Now, while I was prophesying, Pelatiah son of Benaiah died. Then I fell down on my face, cried with a loud voice, and said, "Ah Lord GOD! will you make a full end of the remnant of Israel?"

God Will Restore Israel

14 Then the word of the LORD came to me: ¹⁵Mortal, your kinsfolk, your own kin, your fellow exiles,*ᵃ* the whole house of Israel, all of them, are those of whom the inhabitants of Jerusalem have said, "They have gone far from the LORD; to us this land is given for a possession." ¹⁶Therefore say: Thus says the Lord GOD: Though I removed them far away among the nations, and though I scattered them among the countries, yet I have been a sanctuary to them for a little while*ᵇ* in the countries where they have gone. ¹⁷Therefore say: Thus says the Lord GOD: I will gather you from the peoples, and assemble you out of the countries where you have been scattered, and I will give you the land of Israel. ¹⁸When they come there, they will remove from it all its detestable things and all its abominations. ¹⁹I will give them one*ᶜ* heart, and put a new spirit within them; I will remove the heart of stone from their flesh and give them a heart of flesh, ²⁰so that they may follow my statutes and keep my ordinances and obey them. Then they shall be my people, and I will be their God. ²¹But as for those whose heart goes after their detestable things and their abominations,*ᵈ* I will bring their deeds upon their own heads, says the Lord GOD.

22 Then the cherubim lifted up their wings, with the wheels beside them; and the glory of the God of Israel was above them. ²³And the glory of the LORD ascended from the middle of the city, and stopped on the mountain east of the city. ²⁴The spirit lifted me up and brought me in a vision by the spirit of God into Chaldea, to the exiles. Then the vision that I had seen left me. ²⁵And I told the exiles all the things that the LORD had shown me.

Judah's Captivity Portrayed

12 The word of the LORD came to me: ²Mortal, you are living in the midst of a rebellious house, who have eyes to see but do not see, who have ears to hear but do not hear; ³for they are a rebellious house. Therefore, mortal, prepare for yourself an exile's baggage, and go into exile by

---

A New Heart

EZEKIEL 11.17–21

In the midst of pain and destruction, God speaks a word of hope. The people shall be gathered together and be given a new heart and a new spirit so they will be responsive to God's call.

A new heart is soft and resilient and responsive to God's grace.

Cut two hearts of the same size out of paper or cloth. Staple, glue or sew the two hearts together, leaving a small opening so that you can stuff the heart with tissue or cotton. Then close the opening. The heart you have made is not flat or hard, but puffed and soft and resilient. Holding the heart you have crafted, meditate on being open to God's leading today. Pray this prayer: "God, give me an open heart, a heart of flesh, a heart that is soft to your touch."

---

a Gk Syr: Heb *people of your kindred*   *b* Or *to some extent*   *c* Another reading is *a new*   *d* Cn: Heb *And to the heart of their detestable things and their abominations their heart goes*

Trust the Vision

EZEKIEL 12.22–25

Will God follow through on the punishments Ezekiel has prophesied? Will he keep his promises sooner—or later? The people rationalize, saying, as humans are wont to do: It can't happen to us. This is way off in the future. We don't have to deal with this now. God follows through even if it seems to take a long time. "I the LORD will speak the word that I speak, and it will be fulfilled. It will no longer be delayed." God persistently calls to us even as we ignore his still, small voice.

Just as surely, God keeps his promises as he fulfills judgment and works for good even in the midst of sorrow or despair. Recall some occasions when you wondered if God had stopped listening. Were you tempted to not bother to talk to God anymore? Or were you certain God would speak in due time? Share your times of doubt with a friend in the faith. Spend some time in prayer thinking about the times when God's promises have been fulfilled in your life.

See *Meeting God in Everyday Life*

day in their sight; you shall go like an exile from your place to another place in their sight. Perhaps they will understand, though they are a rebellious house. [4]You shall bring out your baggage by day in their sight, as baggage for exile; and you shall go out yourself at evening in their sight, as those do who go into exile. [5]Dig through the wall in their sight, and carry the baggage through it. [6]In their sight you shall lift the baggage on your shoulder, and carry it out in the dark; you shall cover your face, so that you may not see the land; for I have made you a sign for the house of Israel.

[7] I did just as I was commanded. I brought out my baggage by day, as baggage for exile, and in the evening I dug through the wall with my own hands; I brought it out in the dark, carrying it on my shoulder in their sight.

[8] In the morning the word of the LORD came to me: [9]Mortal, has not the house of Israel, the rebellious house, said to you, "What are you doing?" [10]Say to them, "Thus says the Lord GOD: This oracle concerns the prince in Jerusalem and all the house of Israel in it." [11]Say, "I am a sign for you: as I have done, so shall it be done to them; they shall go into exile, into captivity." [12]And the prince who is among them shall lift his baggage on his shoulder in the dark, and shall go out; he[a] shall dig through the wall and carry it through; he shall cover his face, so that he may not see the land with his eyes. [13]I will spread my net over him, and he shall be caught in my snare; and I will bring him to Babylon, the land of the Chaldeans, yet he shall not see it; and he shall die there. [14]I will scatter to every wind all who are around him, his helpers and all his troops; and I will unsheathe the sword behind them. [15]And they shall know that I am the LORD, when I disperse them among the nations and scatter them through the countries. [16]But I will let a few of them escape from the sword, from famine and pestilence, so that they may tell of all their abominations among the nations where they go; then they shall know that I am the LORD.

Judgment Not Postponed

[17] The word of the LORD came to me: [18]Mortal, eat your bread with quaking, and drink your water with trembling and with fearfulness; [19]and say to the people of the land, Thus says the Lord GOD concerning the inhabitants of Jerusalem in the land of Israel: They shall eat their bread with fearfulness, and drink their water in dismay, because their land shall be stripped of all it contains, on account of the violence of all those who live in it. [20]The inhabited cities shall be laid waste, and the land shall become a desolation; and you shall know that I am the LORD.

[21] The word of the LORD came to me: [22]Mortal, what is this proverb of yours about the land of Israel, which says, "The days are prolonged, and every vision comes to nothing"? [23]Tell them therefore, "Thus says the Lord GOD: I will put an end to this proverb, and they shall use it no more as a proverb in Israel." But say to them, The days are near, and the fulfillment of every vision. [24]For there shall no longer be any false vision or flattering divination within the house of Israel. [25]But I the LORD will speak the word that I speak, and it will be fulfilled. It will no longer be delayed;

a Gk Syr: Heb *they*

but in your days, O rebellious house, I will speak the word and fulfill it, says the Lord GOD.

26 The word of the LORD came to me: [27]Mortal, the house of Israel is saying, "The vision that he sees is for many years ahead; he prophesies for distant times." [28]Therefore say to them, Thus says the Lord GOD: None of my words will be delayed any longer, but the word that I speak will be fulfilled, says the Lord GOD.

False Prophets Condemned

13 The word of the LORD came to me: [2]Mortal, prophesy against the prophets of Israel who are prophesying; say to those who prophesy out of their own imagination: "Hear the word of the LORD!" [3]Thus says the Lord GOD, Alas for the senseless prophets who follow their own spirit, and have seen nothing! [4]Your prophets have been like jackals among ruins, O Israel. [5]You have not gone up into the breaches, or repaired a wall for the house of Israel, so that it might stand in battle on the day of the LORD. [6]They have envisioned falsehood and lying divination; they say, "Says the LORD," when the LORD has not sent them, and yet they wait for the fulfillment of their word! [7]Have you not seen a false vision or uttered a lying divination, when you have said, "Says the LORD," even though I did not speak?

8 Therefore thus says the Lord GOD: Because you have uttered falsehood and envisioned lies, I am against you, says the Lord GOD. [9]My hand will be against the prophets who see false visions and utter lying divinations; they shall not be in the council of my people, nor be enrolled in the register of the house of Israel, nor shall they enter the land of Israel; and you shall know that I am the Lord GOD. [10]Because, in truth, because they have misled my people, saying, "Peace," when there is no peace; and because, when the people build a wall, these prophets[a] smear whitewash on it. [11]Say to those who smear whitewash on it that it shall fall. There will be a deluge of rain,[b] great hailstones will fall, and a stormy wind will break out. [12]When the wall falls, will it not be said to you, "Where is the whitewash you smeared on it?" [13]Therefore thus says the Lord GOD: In my wrath I will make a stormy wind break out, and in my anger there shall be a deluge of rain, and hailstones in wrath to destroy it. [14]I will break down the wall that you have smeared with whitewash, and bring it to the ground, so that its foundation will be laid bare; when it falls, you shall perish within it; and you shall know that I am the LORD. [15]Thus I will spend my wrath upon the wall, and upon those who have smeared it with whitewash; and I will say to you, The wall is no more, nor those who smeared it— [16]the prophets of Israel who prophesied concerning Jerusalem and saw visions of peace for it, when there was no peace, says the Lord GOD.

17 As for you, mortal, set your face against the daughters of your people, who prophesy out of their own imagination; prophesy against them [18]and say, Thus says the Lord GOD: Woe to the women who sew bands on all wrists, and make veils for the heads of persons of every height, in the hunt for human lives! Will you hunt down lives among my people, and maintain your own lives? [19]You have profaned me among my people for handfuls of barley and for

a Heb *they*   *b* Heb *rain and you*

Discernment

EZEKIEL 13.10–16

Ezekiel prophesies against false prophets who mislead the people and proclaim peace when in fact Babylon is about to destroy Jerusalem. They are like whitewashed walls that look good but do not seal against storms and cannot stand against wind and rain. Their words and their actions deceive the people.

Are there true prophets today? Who is calling the church to reach out to the lost and care for the lonely? Whose words are reflected in their deeds? Spend a few minutes in prayer that is discerning, and ask God to help you pay heed to modern-day prophets who speak God's true words.

See Meeting God in Service

Repent and Turn

EZEKIEL 14.6

"To repent is to come to your senses. It is not so much something you do as something that happens. True repentance spends less time looking at the past and saying, 'I'm sorry,' than to the future and saying 'Wow!' "

—FREDERICK BUECHNER,
Wishful Thinking

pieces of bread, putting to death persons who should not die and keeping alive persons who should not live, by your lies to my people, who listen to lies.

20 Therefore thus says the Lord GOD: I am against your bands with which you hunt lives;*ª* I will tear them from your arms, and let the lives go free, the lives that you hunt down like birds. ²¹I will tear off your veils, and save my people from your hands; they shall no longer be prey in your hands; and you shall know that I am the LORD. ²²Because you have disheartened the righteous falsely, although I have not disheartened them, and you have encouraged the wicked not to turn from their wicked way and save their lives; ²³therefore you shall no longer see false visions or practice divination; I will save my people from your hand. Then you will know that I am the LORD.

God's Judgments Justified

14 Certain elders of Israel came to me and sat down before me. ²And the word of the LORD came to me: ³Mortal, these men have taken their idols into their hearts, and placed their iniquity as a stumbling block before them; shall I let myself be consulted by them? ⁴Therefore speak to them, and say to them, Thus says the Lord GOD: Any of those of the house of Israel who take their idols into their hearts and place their iniquity as a stumbling block before them, and yet come to the prophet—I the LORD will answer those who come with the multitude of their idols, ⁵in order that I may take hold of the hearts of the house of Israel, all of whom are estranged from me through their idols.

6 Therefore say to the house of Israel, Thus says the Lord GOD: Repent and turn away from your idols; and turn away your faces from all your abominations. ⁷For any of those of the house of Israel, or of the aliens who reside in Israel, who separate themselves from me, taking their idols into their hearts and placing their iniquity as a stumbling block before them, and yet come to a prophet to inquire of me by him, I the LORD will answer them myself. ⁸I will set my face against them; I will make them a sign and a byword and cut them off from the midst of my people; and you shall know that I am the LORD.

9 If a prophet is deceived and speaks a word, I, the LORD, have deceived that prophet, and I will stretch out my hand against him, and will destroy him from the midst of my people Israel. ¹⁰And they shall bear their punishment—the punishment of the inquirer and the punishment of the prophet shall be the same— ¹¹so that the house of Israel may no longer go astray from me, nor defile themselves any more with all their transgressions. Then they shall be my people, and I will be their God, says the Lord GOD.

12 The word of the LORD came to me: ¹³Mortal, when a land sins against me by acting faithlessly, and I stretch out my hand against it, and break its staff of bread and send famine upon it, and cut off from it human beings and animals, ¹⁴even if Noah, Daniel,*ᵇ* and Job, these three, were in it, they would save only their own lives by their righteousness, says the Lord GOD. ¹⁵If I send wild animals through the land to ravage it, so that it is made desolate, and no one may pass through because of the animals; ¹⁶even if these three men were in it, as I live, says the Lord GOD, they

a Gk Syr: Heb *lives for birds* *b* Or, as otherwise read, *Danel* would save neither sons nor daughters; they alone would be saved, but the land would be desolate. ¹⁷Or if I bring a sword upon that land and say, "Let a sword pass through the land," and I cut off human beings and animals from it; ¹⁸though these three men were in it, as I live, says the Lord God, they would save neither sons nor daughters, but they alone would be saved. ¹⁹Or if I send a pestilence into that land, and pour out my wrath upon it with blood, to cut off humans and animals from it; ²⁰even if Noah, Daniel,ᵃ and Job were in it, as I live, says the Lord God, they would save neither son nor daughter; they would save only their own lives by their righteousness.

21 For thus says the Lord God: How much more when I send upon Jerusalem my four deadly acts of judgment, sword, famine, wild animals, and pestilence, to cut off humans and animals from it! ²²Yet, survivors shall be left in it, sons and daughters who will be brought out; they will come out to you. When you see their ways and their deeds, you will be consoled for the evil that I have brought upon Jerusalem, for all that I have brought upon it. ²³They shall console you, when you see their ways and their deeds; and you shall know that it was not without cause that I did all that I have done in it, says the Lord God.

The Useless Vine

15 The word of the Lord came to me: ²O mortal, how does the wood of the vine surpass all other wood—
the vine branch that is among the trees of the
forest?
³ Is wood taken from it to make anything?
Does one take a peg from it on which to hang
any object?
⁴ It is put in the fire for fuel;
when the fire has consumed both ends of it
and the middle of it is charred,
is it useful for anything?
⁵ When it was whole it was used for nothing;
how much less—when the fire has consumed it,
and it is charred—
can it ever be used for anything!

6 Therefore thus says the Lord God: Like the wood of the vine among the trees of the forest, which I have given to the fire for fuel, so I will give up the inhabitants of Jerusalem. ⁷I will set my face against them; although they escape from the fire, the fire shall still consume them; and you shall know that I am the Lord, when I set my face against them. ⁸And I will make the land desolate, because they have acted faithlessly, says the Lord God.

God's Faithless Bride

16 The word of the Lord came to me: ²Mortal, make known to Jerusalem her abominations, ³and say, Thus says the Lord God to Jerusalem: Your origin and your birth were in the land of the Canaanites; your father was an Amorite, and your mother a Hittite. ⁴As for your birth, on the day you were born your navel cord was not cut, nor were you washed with water to cleanse you, nor rubbed with salt, nor wrapped in cloths. ⁵No eye pitied you, to do

The Vine

EZEKIEL 15.1–8

Ezekiel employs a harsh and bitter image to convince the people how serious their unfaithfulness is in God's eyes. He compares them to the wood of vines—wood that is of little value in making anything useful and is useless even as firewood.

Difficult as it may be, recall a time in your adult life when you were severely, but appropriately, criticized. Can you remember the guilt and shame you felt? How did you respond? Did you try to defend yourself or did you admit your mistakes? How did you seek forgiveness? Write a prayer of confession that is specific to you alone and to your own particular failings. Offer it to God in prayer. Ask God to show you in some concrete way the forgiveness he offers you.

See Meeting God in Everyday Life

ᵃ Or, as otherwise read, *Danel*

Looking for Love

EZEKIEL 16.26–29

God compares Jerusalem to an unfaithful bride. She is the masthead of a nation that has turned away from the loving intentions of God. She is looking for love in all the wrong places, worshiping idols and forging unholy alliances.

The apostle John refers to the New Testament church as the bride of Christ (see Revelation 19.7). Sometimes churches turn away from following their one true love. Draw a picture of your church and write "Jesus Christ" in the center of the picture. All around the outside of the building write or picture some of the temptations that may distract your church from following Jesus. Refer to your drawing as you pray.

See Meeting God in Community

any of these things for you out of compassion for you; but you were thrown out in the open field, for you were abhorred on the day you were born.

6 I passed by you, and saw you flailing about in your blood. As you lay in your blood, I said to you, "Live!⁷and grow up*a* like a plant of the field." You grew up and became tall and arrived at full womanhood;*b* your breasts were formed, and your hair had grown; yet you were naked and bare.

8 I passed by you again and looked on you; you were at the age for love. I spread the edge of my cloak over you, and covered your nakedness: I pledged myself to you and entered into a covenant with you, says the Lord GOD, and you became mine. ⁹Then I bathed you with water and washed off the blood from you, and anointed you with oil. ¹⁰I clothed you with embroidered cloth and with sandals of fine leather; I bound you in fine linen and covered you with rich fabric.*c* ¹¹I adorned you with ornaments: I put bracelets on your arms, a chain on your neck, ¹²a ring on your nose, earrings in your ears, and a beautiful crown upon your head. ¹³You were adorned with gold and silver, while your clothing was of fine linen, rich fabric,*c* and embroidered cloth. You had choice flour and honey and oil for food. You grew exceedingly beautiful, fit to be a queen. ¹⁴Your fame spread among the nations on account of your beauty, for it was perfect because of my splendor that I had bestowed on you, says the Lord GOD.

15 But you trusted in your beauty, and played the whore because of your fame, and lavished your whorings on any passer-by.*d* ¹⁶You took some of your garments, and made for yourself colorful shrines, and on them played the whore; nothing like this has ever been or ever shall be.*c* ¹⁷You also took your beautiful jewels of my gold and my silver that I had given you, and made for yourself male images, and with them played the whore; ¹⁸and you took your embroidered garments to cover them, and set my oil and my incense before them. ¹⁹Also my bread that I gave you— I fed you with choice flour and oil and honey—you set it before them as a pleasing odor; and so it was, says the Lord GOD. ²⁰You took your sons and your daughters, whom you had borne to me, and these you sacrificed to them to be devoured. As if your whorings were not enough! ²¹You slaughtered my children and delivered them up as an offering to them. ²²And in all your abominations and your whorings you did not remember the days of your youth, when you were naked and bare, flailing about in your blood.

23 After all your wickedness (woe, woe to you! says the Lord GOD), ²⁴you built yourself a platform and made yourself a lofty place in every square; ²⁵at the head of every street you built your lofty place and prostituted your beauty, offering yourself to every passer-by, and multiplying your whoring. ²⁶You played the whore with the Egyptians, your lustful neighbors, multiplying your whoring, to provoke me to anger. ²⁷Therefore I stretched out my hand against you, reduced your rations, and gave you up to the will of your enemies, the daughters of the Philistines, who were ashamed of your lewd behavior. ²⁸You played the whore with the Assyrians, because you were insatiable; you

a Gk Syr: Heb *Live! I made you a myriad*   b Cn: Heb *ornament of ornaments*
c Meaning of Heb uncertain   d Heb adds *let it be his*

played the whore with them, and still you were not satisfied. [29]You multiplied your whoring with Chaldea, the land of merchants; and even with this you were not satisfied.

30 How sick is your heart, says the Lord God, that you did all these things, the deeds of a brazen whore; [31]building your platform at the head of every street, and making your lofty place in every square! Yet you were not like a whore, because you scorned payment. [32]Adulterous wife, who receives strangers instead of her husband! [33]Gifts are given to all whores; but you gave your gifts to all your lovers, bribing them to come to you from all around for your whorings. [34]So you were different from other women in your whorings: no one solicited you to play the whore; and you gave payment, while no payment was given to you; you were different.

35 Therefore, O whore, hear the word of the Lord: [36]Thus says the Lord God, Because your lust was poured out and your nakedness uncovered in your whoring with your lovers, and because of all your abominable idols, and because of the blood of your children that you gave to them, [37]therefore, I will gather all your lovers, with whom you took pleasure, all those you loved and all those you hated; I will gather them against you from all around, and will uncover your nakedness to them, so that they may see all your nakedness. [38]I will judge you as women who commit adultery and shed blood are judged, and bring blood upon you in wrath and jealousy. [39]I will deliver you into their hands, and they shall throw down your platform and break down your lofty places; they shall strip you of your clothes and take your beautiful objects and leave you naked and bare. [40]They shall bring up a mob against you, and they shall stone you and cut you to pieces with their swords. [41]They shall burn your houses and execute judgments on you in the sight of many women; I will stop you from playing the whore, and you shall also make no more payments. [42]So I will satisfy my fury on you, and my jealousy shall turn away from you; I will be calm, and will be angry no longer. [43]Because you have not remembered the days of your youth, but have enraged me with all these things; therefore, I have returned your deeds upon your head, says the Lord God.

Have you not committed lewdness beyond all your abominations? [44]See, everyone who uses proverbs will use this proverb about you, "Like mother, like daughter." [45]You are the daughter of your mother, who loathed her husband and her children; and you are the sister of your sisters, who loathed their husbands and their children. Your mother was a Hittite and your father an Amorite. [46]Your elder sister is Samaria, who lived with her daughters to the north of you; and your younger sister, who lived to the south of you, is Sodom with her daughters. [47]You not only followed their ways, and acted according to their abominations; within a very little time you were more corrupt than they in all your ways. [48]As I live, says the Lord God, your sister Sodom and her daughters have not done as you and your daughters have done. [49]This was the guilt of your sister Sodom: she and her daughters had pride, excess of food, and prosperous ease, but did not aid the poor and needy. [50]They were haughty, and did abominable things before me; therefore I removed them when I saw it. [51]Samaria has not committed half your sins; you have committed more abominations than they, and have made your sisters appear righteous by all the abomi-

Hope Is Never Far Away

EZEKIEL 16.48–55

Jerusalem has been a faithless bride. Ezekiel has vividly described her behavior and condemned her ways. Yet hope is never far away and God's love is stronger than his judgment. "I will restore . . . your own fortunes."

Assume a posture of disgrace or shame. You might bow your head and body, for example, or lie facedown on the floor. Now act out a gradual awakening to restoration. Is it a quiet movement of chastened confidence or a joyous prancing of great leaps? Imagine what it is like to return to your true love and be forgiven and embraced. Turn around and around. Enjoy being restored to oneness with the love of your life.

See Meeting God in Scripture

God's Memory, Our Memory

EZEKIEL 16.60–63

Some people may have agile memories, but God's capacity to remember is infinite. God remembers the covenant of love he made with Abraham and Sarah, even though Israel repeatedly breaks the covenant and runs after other gods. It is as if God is saying, "I remember my covenant. I remember my promise of love. I remember, and I forgive." Let that picture of God sink into your heart.

Our memories often bring to mind the shameful things we have done. Our memories of shame have taught us to be humble: "that you may remember and be confounded, and never open your mouth again because of your shame." But our memories of God's faithfulness also teach us to return again and again to a God who remembers to love us. Let your memories of God's faithfulness and forgiveness move you to pray with thanksgiving. You may wish to write your prayer in your journal.

See Meeting God in Prayer

nations that you have committed. ⁵²Bear your disgrace, you also, for you have brought about for your sisters a more favorable judgment; because of your sins in which you acted more abominably than they, they are more in the right than you. So be ashamed, you also, and bear your disgrace, for you have made your sisters appear righteous.

53 I will restore their fortunes, the fortunes of Sodom and her daughters and the fortunes of Samaria and her daughters, and I will restore your own fortunes along with theirs, ⁵⁴in order that you may bear your disgrace and be ashamed of all that you have done, becoming a consolation to them. ⁵⁵As for your sisters, Sodom and her daughters shall return to their former state, Samaria and her daughters shall return to their former state, and you and your daughters shall return to your former state. ⁵⁶Was not your sister Sodom a byword in your mouth in the day of your pride, ⁵⁷before your wickedness was uncovered? Now you are a mockery to the daughters of Aram*ᵃ* and all her neighbors, and to the daughters of the Philistines, those all around who despise you. ⁵⁸You must bear the penalty of your lewdness and your abominations, says the LORD.

An Everlasting Covenant

59 Yes, thus says the Lord GOD: I will deal with you as you have done, you who have despised the oath, breaking the covenant; ⁶⁰yet I will remember my covenant with you in the days of your youth, and I will establish with you an everlasting covenant. ⁶¹Then you will remember your ways, and be ashamed when I*ᵇ* take your sisters, both your elder and your younger, and give them to you as daughters, but not on account of my*ᶜ* covenant with you. ⁶²I will establish my covenant with you, and you shall know that I am the LORD, ⁶³in order that you may remember and be confounded, and never open your mouth again because of your shame, when I forgive you all that you have done, says the Lord GOD.

The Two Eagles and the Vine

17 The word of the LORD came to me: ²O mortal, propound a riddle, and speak an allegory to the house of Israel. ³Say: Thus says the Lord GOD:

A great eagle, with great wings and long pinions,
  rich in plumage of many colors,
  came to the Lebanon.
He took the top of the cedar,
⁴ broke off its topmost shoot;
he carried it to a land of trade,
  set it in a city of merchants.
⁵ Then he took a seed from the land,
  placed it in fertile soil;
a plant*ᵈ* by abundant waters,
  he set it like a willow twig.
⁶ It sprouted and became a vine
  spreading out, but low;
its branches turned toward him,
  its roots remained where it stood.
So it became a vine;
  it brought forth branches,
  put forth foliage.

a Another reading is *Edom* *b* Syr: Heb *you* *c* Heb lacks *my*
d Meaning of Heb uncertain

7 There was another great eagle,
   with great wings and much plumage.
And see! This vine stretched out
   its roots toward him;
it shot out its branches toward him,
   so that he might water it.
From the bed where it was planted
8   it was transplanted
to good soil by abundant waters,
   so that it might produce branches
   and bear fruit
   and become a noble vine.
9Say: Thus says the Lord God:
   Will it prosper?
Will he not pull up its roots,
   cause its fruit to rot*a* and wither,
   its fresh sprouting leaves to fade?
No strong arm or mighty army will be needed
   to pull it from its roots.
10 When it is transplanted, will it thrive?
When the east wind strikes it,
   will it not utterly wither,
   wither on the bed where it grew?

11 Then the word of the Lord came to me: 12Say now to the rebellious house: Do you not know what these things mean? Tell them: The king of Babylon came to Jerusalem, took its king and its officials, and brought them back with him to Babylon. 13He took one of the royal offspring and made a covenant with him, putting him under oath (he had taken away the chief men of the land), 14so that the kingdom might be humble and not lift itself up, and that by keeping his covenant it might stand. 15But he rebelled against him by sending ambassadors to Egypt, in order that they might give him horses and a large army. Will he succeed? Can one escape who does such things? Can he break the covenant and yet escape? 16As I live, says the Lord God, surely in the place where the king resides who made him king, whose oath he despised, and whose covenant with him he broke—in Babylon he shall die. 17Pharaoh with his mighty army and great company will not help him in war, when ramps are cast up and siege walls built to cut off many lives. 18Because he despised the oath and broke the covenant, because he gave his hand and yet did all these things, he shall not escape. 19Therefore thus says the Lord God: As I live, I will surely return upon his head my oath that he despised, and my covenant that he broke. 20I will spread my net over him, and he shall be caught in my snare; I will bring him to Babylon and enter into judgment with him there for the treason he has committed against me. 21All the pick*b* of his troops shall fall by the sword, and the survivors shall be scattered to every wind; and you shall know that I, the Lord, have spoken.

Israel Exalted at Last

22 Thus says the Lord God:
I myself will take a sprig
   from the lofty top of a cedar;
   I will set it out.
I will break off a tender one

A New Branch Bears Fruit

EZEKIEL 17.22–24

"Later the soul will bring forth fruit exactly in the measure in which the inner life is developed in it. If there is no inner life, however great may be the zeal, the high intention, the hard work, no fruit will come forth; it is like a spring that would give out sanctity to others but cannot, having none to give; one can only give that which one has. It is in solitude, in that lonely life alone with God, in profound recollection of soul, in forgetfulness of all created things, that God gives himself to the soul that thus gives itself whole and entire to him."

—CHARLES DE FOUCAULD,
Meditations of a Hermit

a Meaning of Heb uncertain   *b* Another reading is *fugitives*

Bearing Our Own Responsibility

EZEKIEL 18.19–20

"It's not my fault" is a familiar refrain. We complain that our parents didn't love us enough. Our schools gave us an inadequate education. Our bosses didn't spend enough time with us, so we didn't know what was expected of us. There is always someone we can blame if we choose to.

Here in Ezekiel neither the sins nor the blessings are transferred to the next generation. There is to be no blaming others for troubles and no resting on the righteousness of someone else. This is an ethic of personal responsibility. When have you blamed others for your problems? Taken credit for another's efforts? Take some time to write in your journal about your own ethic of responsibility.

See Meeting God in Everyday Life

from the topmost of its young twigs;
I myself will plant it
on a high and lofty mountain.
23 On the mountain height of Israel
I will plant it,
in order that it may produce boughs and bear fruit,
and become a noble cedar.
Under it every kind of bird will live;
in the shade of its branches will nest
winged creatures of every kind.
24 All the trees of the field shall know
that I am the LORD.
I bring low the high tree,
I make high the low tree;
I dry up the green tree
and make the dry tree flourish.
I the LORD have spoken;
I will accomplish it.

Individual Retribution

18 The word of the LORD came to me: ²What do you mean by repeating this proverb concerning the land of Israel, "The parents have eaten sour grapes, and the children's teeth are set on edge"? ³As I live, says the Lord GOD, this proverb shall no more be used by you in Israel. ⁴Know that all lives are mine; the life of the parent as well as the life of the child is mine: it is only the person who sins that shall die.

5 If a man is righteous and does what is lawful and right— ⁶if he does not eat upon the mountains or lift up his eyes to the idols of the house of Israel, does not defile his neighbor's wife or approach a woman during her menstrual period, ⁷does not oppress anyone, but restores to the debtor his pledge, commits no robbery, gives his bread to the hungry and covers the naked with a garment, ⁸does not take advance or accrued interest, withholds his hand from iniquity, executes true justice between contending parties, ⁹follows my statutes, and is careful to observe my ordinances, acting faithfully—such a one is righteous; he shall surely live, says the Lord GOD.

10 If he has a son who is violent, a shedder of blood, ¹¹who does any of these things (though his father*a* does none of them), who eats upon the mountains, defiles his neighbor's wife, ¹²oppresses the poor and needy, commits robbery, does not restore the pledge, lifts up his eyes to the idols, commits abomination, ¹³takes advance or accrued interest; shall he then live? He shall not. He has done all these abominable things; he shall surely die; his blood shall be upon himself.

14 But if this man has a son who sees all the sins that his father has done, considers, and does not do likewise, ¹⁵who does not eat upon the mountains or lift up his eyes to the idols of the house of Israel, does not defile his neighbor's wife, ¹⁶does not wrong anyone, exacts no pledge, commits no robbery, but gives his bread to the hungry and covers the naked with a garment, ¹⁷withholds his hand from iniquity,*b* takes no advance or accrued interest, observes my ordinances, and follows my statutes; he shall not die for his father's iniquity; he shall surely live. ¹⁸As for his father, be-

a Heb *he*   *b* Gk: Heb *the poor*

cause he practiced extortion, robbed his brother, and did what is not good among his people, he dies for his iniquity. 19 Yet you say, "Why should not the son suffer for the iniquity of the father?" When the son has done what is lawful and right, and has been careful to observe all my statutes, he shall surely live. 20 The person who sins shall die. A child shall not suffer for the iniquity of a parent, nor a parent suffer for the iniquity of a child; the righteousness of the righteous shall be his own, and the wickedness of the wicked shall be his own.

21 But if the wicked turn away from all their sins that they have committed and keep all my statutes and do what is lawful and right, they shall surely live; they shall not die. 22 None of the transgressions that they have committed shall be remembered against them; for the righteousness that they have done they shall live. 23 Have I any pleasure in the death of the wicked, says the Lord God, and not rather that they should turn from their ways and live? 24 But when the righteous turn away from their righteousness and commit iniquity and do the same abominable things that the wicked do, shall they live? None of the righteous deeds that they have done shall be remembered; for the treachery of which they are guilty and the sin they have committed, they shall die.

25 Yet you say, "The way of the Lord is unfair." Hear now, O house of Israel: Is my way unfair? Is it not your ways that are unfair? 26 When the righteous turn away from their righteousness and commit iniquity, they shall die for it; for the iniquity that they have committed they shall die. 27 Again, when the wicked turn away from the wickedness they have committed and do what is lawful and right, they shall save their life. 28 Because they considered and turned away from all the transgressions that they had committed, they shall surely live; they shall not die. 29 Yet the house of Israel says, "The way of the Lord is unfair." O house of Israel, are my ways unfair? Is it not your ways that are unfair?

30 Therefore I will judge you, O house of Israel, all of you according to your ways, says the Lord God. Repent and turn from all your transgressions; otherwise iniquity will be your ruin.*a* 31 Cast away from you all the transgressions that you have committed against me, and get yourselves a new heart and a new spirit! Why will you die, O house of Israel? 32 For I have no pleasure in the death of anyone, says the Lord God. Turn, then, and live.

Israel Degraded

19 As for you, raise up a lamentation for the princes of Israel, 2 and say:
What a lioness was your mother
  among lions!
She lay down among young lions,
  rearing her cubs.
3 She raised up one of her cubs;
    he became a young lion,
  and he learned to catch prey;
    he devoured humans.
4 The nations sounded an alarm against him;
    he was caught in their pit;
  and they brought him with hooks
    to the land of Egypt.

A New Heart

EZEKIEL 18.30–32

"We are speaking about a mystery for which words are inadequate. It is the mystery that the heart, which is the center of our being, is transformed by God into his own heart, a heart large enough to embrace the entire universe. Through prayer we can carry in our heart all human pain and sorrow, all conflicts and agonies, all torture and war, all hunger, loneliness, and misery, not because of some great psychological or emotional capacity, but because God's heart has become one with ours."

—HENRI J. M. NOUWEN,
The Way of the Heart

---

a Or so that they shall not be a stumbling block of iniquity to you

Lamentation

EZEKIEL 19.9–14

Life does not always go smoothly, even in the best of times, even for those born with seemingly everything going for them. The best-laid plans—like those for the finest youths of the Davidic dynasty—can go awry. Where does one go when disaster turns life into a dry and thirsty land? The Hebrews believed you could go to God and complain. Their prayers of lament told God in strong language what they believed to be wrong and why God should intervene. Their prayers were full of anguish but also full of faith that God would intervene.

Try writing a lament. Tell God about your concern, your anger, and why you feel God should intervene in the circumstances that trouble you. End by reaffirming your trust in God and thanking him for hearing your prayer.

See Meeting God in Scripture

5 When she saw that she was thwarted,
    that her hope was lost,
she took another of her cubs
    and made him a young lion.
6 He prowled among the lions;
    he became a young lion,
and he learned to catch prey;
    he devoured people.
7 And he ravaged their strongholds, *a*
    and laid waste their towns;
the land was appalled, and all in it,
    at the sound of his roaring.
8 The nations set upon him
    from the provinces all around;
they spread their net over him;
    he was caught in their pit.
9 With hooks they put him in a cage,
    and brought him to the king of Babylon;
they brought him into custody,
    so that his voice should be heard no more
    on the mountains of Israel.
10 Your mother was like a vine in a vineyard *b*
    transplanted by the water,
fruitful and full of branches
    from abundant water.
11 Its strongest stem became
    a ruler's scepter; *c*
it towered aloft
    among the thick boughs;
it stood out in its height
    with its mass of branches.
12 But it was plucked up in fury,
    cast down to the ground;
the east wind dried it up;
    its fruit was stripped off,
its strong stem was withered;
    the fire consumed it.
13 Now it is transplanted into the wilderness,
    into a dry and thirsty land.
14 And fire has gone out from its stem,
    has consumed its branches and fruit,
so that there remains in it no strong stem,
    no scepter for ruling.

This is a lamentation, and it is used as a lamentation.

Israel's Continuing Rebellion

20 In the seventh year, in the fifth month, on the tenth day of the month, certain elders of Israel came to consult the LORD, and sat down before me. ²And the word of the LORD came to me: ³Mortal, speak to the elders of Israel, and say to them: Thus says the Lord GOD: Why are you coming? To consult me? As I live, says the Lord GOD, I will not be consulted by you. ⁴Will you judge them, mortal, will you judge them? Then let them know the abominations of their ancestors, ⁵and say to them: Thus says the Lord GOD: On the day when I chose Israel, I swore to the offspring of the house of Jacob—making myself known to them in the land

a Heb *his widows*   *b* Cn: Heb *in your blood*   *c* Heb *Its strongest stems became rulers' scepters*

of Egypt—I swore to them, saying, I am the Lord your God. ⁶On that day I swore to them that I would bring them out of the land of Egypt into a land that I had searched out for them, a land flowing with milk and honey, the most glorious of all lands. ⁷And I said to them, Cast away the detestable things your eyes feast on, every one of you, and do not defile yourselves with the idols of Egypt; I am the Lord your God. ⁸But they rebelled against me and would not listen to me; not one of them cast away the detestable things their eyes feasted on, nor did they forsake the idols of Egypt.

Then I thought I would pour out my wrath upon them and spend my anger against them in the midst of the land of Egypt. ⁹But I acted for the sake of my name, that it should not be profaned in the sight of the nations among whom they lived, in whose sight I made myself known to them in bringing them out of the land of Egypt. ¹⁰So I led them out of the land of Egypt and brought them into the wilderness. ¹¹I gave them my statutes and showed them my ordinances, by whose observance everyone shall live. ¹²Moreover I gave them my sabbaths, as a sign between me and them, so that they might know that I the Lord sanctify them. ¹³But the house of Israel rebelled against me in the wilderness; they did not observe my statutes but rejected my ordinances, by whose observance everyone shall live; and my sabbaths they greatly profaned.

Then I thought I would pour out my wrath upon them in the wilderness, to make an end of them. ¹⁴But I acted for the sake of my name, so that it should not be profaned in the sight of the nations, in whose sight I had brought them out. ¹⁵Moreover I swore to them in the wilderness that I would not bring them into the land that I had given them, a land flowing with milk and honey, the most glorious of all lands, ¹⁶because they rejected my ordinances and did not observe my statutes, and profaned my sabbaths; for their heart went after their idols. ¹⁷Nevertheless my eye spared them, and I did not destroy them or make an end of them in the wilderness.

18 I said to their children in the wilderness, Do not follow the statutes of your parents, nor observe their ordinances, nor defile yourselves with their idols. ¹⁹I the Lord am your God; follow my statutes, and be careful to observe my ordinances, ²⁰and hallow my sabbaths that they may be a sign between me and you, so that you may know that I the Lord am your God. ²¹But the children rebelled against me; they did not follow my statutes, and were not careful to observe my ordinances, by whose observance everyone shall live; they profaned my sabbaths.

Then I thought I would pour out my wrath upon them and spend my anger against them in the wilderness. ²²But I withheld my hand, and acted for the sake of my name, so that it should not be profaned in the sight of the nations, in whose sight I had brought them out. ²³Moreover I swore to them in the wilderness that I would scatter them among the nations and disperse them through the countries, ²⁴because they had not executed my ordinances, but had rejected my statutes and profaned my sabbaths, and their eyes were set on their ancestors' idols. ²⁵Moreover I gave them statutes that were not good and ordinances by which they could not live. ²⁶I defiled them through their very gifts,

The Gift of Sabbath

EZEKIEL 20.10–13

When is your sabbath? What day is your special time to rest in God? When do you cease being busy and just stop to acknowledge your Creator, your Savior?

In a wonderfully poignant lament, God expresses his distress at the misuse of the sabbath: "I gave them my sabbaths, as a sign between me and them, so that they might know that I the Lord sanctify them." The sabbath is a gift to us so that we will remember that God made us to be holy.

Take a look at your week and set aside a sabbath time—a time and a place to focus on God. A whole day is wonderful. An hour is a start. Try to be aware during the whole period of time that God wants to be with you as much (or more!) as you want to be with God. Allow yourself to dwell in God's holy presence.

See Meeting God in the Created Order

Wilderness Journeys

EZEKIEL 20.34–37,41–44

Our lives are shaped by wilderness experiences. Like the Israelites in exile, we experience times and places in which we search for our authentic selves. Wilderness journeys often involve suffering, purifying, examining, wandering, correcting and remembering. God always accompanies us in the wilderness to help us discover our identity and lead us home.

Take a sheet of paper and draw or paint a picture of your wilderness. Where are you on the journey through it? Just beginning? Lost and searching for direction? Almost home? Are there any companions with you? Do you have a title for your wilderness picture?

See Meeting God in Scripture

in their offering up all their firstborn, in order that I might horrify them, so that they might know that I am the LORD.

27 Therefore, mortal, speak to the house of Israel and say to them, Thus says the Lord GOD: In this again your ancestors blasphemed me, by dealing treacherously with me. ²⁸For when I had brought them into the land that I swore to give them, then wherever they saw any high hill or any leafy tree, there they offered their sacrifices and presented the provocation of their offering; there they sent up their pleasing odors, and there they poured out their drink offerings. ²⁹(I said to them, What is the high place to which you go? So it is called Bamah^a to this day.) ³⁰Therefore say to the house of Israel, Thus says the Lord GOD: Will you defile yourselves after the manner of your ancestors and go astray after their detestable things? ³¹When you offer your gifts and make your children pass through the fire, you defile yourselves with all your idols to this day. And shall I be consulted by you, O house of Israel? As I live, says the Lord GOD, I will not be consulted by you.

32 What is in your mind shall never happen—the thought, "Let us be like the nations, like the tribes of the countries, and worship wood and stone."

God Will Restore Israel

33 As I live, says the Lord GOD, surely with a mighty hand and an outstretched arm, and with wrath poured out, I will be king over you. ³⁴I will bring you out from the peoples and gather you out of the countries where you are scattered, with a mighty hand and an outstretched arm, and with wrath poured out; ³⁵and I will bring you into the wilderness of the peoples, and there I will enter into judgment with you face to face. ³⁶As I entered into judgment with your ancestors in the wilderness of the land of Egypt, so I will enter into judgment with you, says the Lord GOD. ³⁷I will make you pass under the staff, and will bring you within the bond of the covenant. ³⁸I will purge out the rebels among you, and those who transgress against me; I will bring them out of the land where they reside as aliens, but they shall not enter the land of Israel. Then you shall know that I am the LORD.

39 As for you, O house of Israel, thus says the Lord GOD: Go serve your idols, everyone of you now and hereafter, if you will not listen to me; but my holy name you shall no more profane with your gifts and your idols.

40 For on my holy mountain, the mountain height of Israel, says the Lord GOD, there all the house of Israel, all of them, shall serve me in the land; there I will accept them, and there I will require your contributions and the choicest of your gifts, with all your sacred things. ⁴¹As a pleasing odor I will accept you, when I bring you out from the peoples, and gather you out of the countries where you have been scattered; and I will manifest my holiness among you in the sight of the nations. ⁴²You shall know that I am the LORD, when I bring you into the land of Israel, the country that I swore to give to your ancestors. ⁴³There you shall remember your ways and all the deeds by which you have polluted yourselves; and you shall loathe yourselves for all the evils that you have committed. ⁴⁴And you shall know that I am the LORD, when I deal with you for my name's

a That is High Place

sake, not according to your evil ways, or corrupt deeds, O house of Israel, says the Lord God.

A Prophecy against the Negeb

45[a] The word of the LORD came to me: 46Mortal, set your face toward the south, preach against the south, and prophesy against the forest land in the Negeb; 47say to the forest of the Negeb, Hear the word of the LORD: Thus says the Lord God, I will kindle a fire in you, and it shall devour every green tree in you and every dry tree; the blazing flame shall not be quenched, and all faces from south to north shall be scorched by it. 48All flesh shall see that I the LORD have kindled it; it shall not be quenched. 49Then I said, "Ah Lord God! they are saying of me, 'Is he not a maker of allegories?' "

The Drawn Sword of God

21[b] The word of the LORD came to me: 2Mortal, set your face toward Jerusalem and preach against the sanctuaries; prophesy against the land of Israel 3and say to the land of Israel, Thus says the LORD: I am coming against you, and will draw my sword out of its sheath, and will cut off from you both righteous and wicked. 4Because I will cut off from you both righteous and wicked, therefore my sword shall go out of its sheath against all flesh from south to north; 5and all flesh shall know that I the LORD have drawn my sword out of its sheath; it shall not be sheathed again. 6Moan therefore, mortal; moan with breaking heart and bitter grief before their eyes. 7And when they say to you, "Why do you moan?" you shall say, "Because of the news that has come. Every heart will melt and all hands will be feeble, every spirit will faint and all knees will turn to water. See, it comes and it will be fulfilled," says the Lord God.

8 And the word of the LORD came to me: 9Mortal, prophesy and say: Thus says the Lord; Say:

A sword, a sword is sharpened,
 it is also polished;
10 it is sharpened for slaughter,
 honed to flash like lightning!
How can we make merry?
 You have despised the rod,
 and all discipline.[c]
11 The sword[d] is given to be polished,
 to be grasped in the hand;
it is sharpened, the sword is polished,
 to be placed in the slayer's hand.
12 Cry and wail, O mortal,
 for it is against my people;
it is against all Israel's princes;
 they are thrown to the sword,
 together with my people.
Ah! Strike the thigh!
13For consider: What! If you despise the rod, will it not happen?[c] says the Lord God.
14 And you, mortal, prophesy;
 strike hand to hand.
Let the sword fall twice, thrice;
 it is a sword for killing.
A sword for great slaughter—

Song of the Sword

EZEKIEL 21.4–12

Kneeling is a posture of humility; it is the posture of a person seeking forgiveness or the prayer position of someone seeking to discern God's will.

As God calls the Israelites to repent, so might we experience a call to confess our sins. Find a comfortable place and imagine that your knees are "turning to water" so that you have to assume a posture of kneeling. Use this posture to offer a prayer of confession. Let the image of the sword help you let go of that which limits your discipleship. Rise from your knees renewed and forgiven.

See Meeting God in Scripture

Trouble Is Coming

EZEKIEL 21.25–28

"Count each affliction,
whether light or grave,
God's messenger
sent down to thee;
do thou
with courtesy receive him."

—AUBREY THOMAS DE VERE,
"Sorrow"

it surrounds them;
15 therefore hearts melt
and many stumble.
At all their gates I have set
the point[a] of the sword.
Ah! It is made for flashing,
it is polished[b] for slaughter.
16 Attack to the right!
Engage to the left!
—wherever your edge is directed.
17 I too will strike hand to hand,
I will satisfy my fury;
I the LORD have spoken.

18 The word of the LORD came to me: [19]Mortal, mark out two roads for the sword of the king of Babylon to come; both of them shall issue from the same land. And make a signpost, make it for a fork in the road leading to a city; [20]mark out the road for the sword to come to Rabbah of the Ammonites or to Judah and to[c] Jerusalem the fortified. [21]For the king of Babylon stands at the parting of the way, at the fork in the two roads, to use divination; he shakes the arrows, he consults the teraphim,[d] he inspects the liver. [22]Into his right hand comes the lot for Jerusalem, to set battering rams, to call out for slaughter, for raising the battle cry, to set battering rams against the gates, to cast up ramps, to build siege towers. [23]But to them it will seem like a false divination; they have sworn solemn oaths; but he brings their guilt to remembrance, bringing about their capture.

24 Therefore thus says the Lord GOD: Because you have brought your guilt to remembrance, in that your transgressions are uncovered, so that in all your deeds your sins appear—because you have come to remembrance, you shall be taken in hand.[e]
25 As for you, vile, wicked prince of Israel,
you whose day has come,
the time of final punishment,
26 thus says the Lord GOD:
Remove the turban, take off the crown;
things shall not remain as they are.
Exalt that which is low,
abase that which is high.
27 A ruin, a ruin, a ruin—
I will make it!
(Such has never occurred.)
Until he comes whose right it is;
to him I will give it.

28 As for you, mortal, prophesy, and say, Thus says the Lord GOD concerning the Ammonites, and concerning their reproach; say:
A sword, a sword! Drawn for slaughter,
polished to consume,[f] to flash like lightning.
29 Offering false visions for you,
divining lies for you,
they place you over the necks
of the vile, wicked ones—
those whose day has come,
the time of final punishment.
30 Return it to its sheath!

a Meaning of Heb uncertain   b Tg: Heb wrapped up   c Gk Syr: Heb Judah in   d Or the household gods   e Or be taken captive   f Cn: Heb to contain

In the place where you were created,
in the land of your origin,
I will judge you.
[31] I will pour out my indignation upon you,
with the fire of my wrath
I will blow upon you.
I will deliver you into brutish hands,
those skillful to destroy.
[32] You shall be fuel for the fire,
your blood shall enter the earth;
you shall be remembered no more,
for I the Lord have spoken.

The Bloody City

22 The word of the Lord came to me: [2]You, mortal, will you judge, will you judge the bloody city? Then declare to it all its abominable deeds. [3]You shall say, Thus says the Lord God: A city! Shedding blood within itself; its time has come; making its idols, defiling itself. [4]You have become guilty by the blood that you have shed, and defiled by the idols that you have made; you have brought your day near, the appointed time of your years has come. Therefore I have made you a disgrace before the nations, and a mockery to all the countries. [5]Those who are near and those who are far from you will mock you, you infamous one, full of tumult.

6 The princes of Israel in you, everyone according to his power, have been bent on shedding blood. [7]Father and mother are treated with contempt in you; the alien residing within you suffers extortion; the orphan and the widow are wronged in you. [8]You have despised my holy things, and profaned my sabbaths. [9]In you are those who slander to shed blood, those in you who eat upon the mountains, who commit lewdness in your midst. [10]In you they uncover their fathers' nakedness; in you they violate women in their menstrual periods. [11]One commits abomination with his neighbor's wife; another lewdly defiles his daughter-in-law; another in you defiles his sister, his father's daughter. [12]In you, they take bribes to shed blood; you take both advance interest and accrued interest, and make gain of your neighbors by extortion; and you have forgotten me, says the Lord God.

13 See, I strike my hands together at the dishonest gain you have made, and at the blood that has been shed within you. [14]Can your courage endure, or can your hands remain strong in the days when I shall deal with you? I the Lord have spoken, and I will do it. [15]I will scatter you among the nations and disperse you through the countries, and I will purge your filthiness out of you. [16]And I[a] shall be profaned through you in the sight of the nations; and you shall know that I am the Lord.

17 The word of the Lord came to me: [18]Mortal, the house of Israel has become dross to me; all of them, silver,[b] bronze, tin, iron, and lead. In the smelter they have become dross. [19]Therefore thus says the Lord God: Because you have all become dross, I will gather you into the midst of Jerusalem. [20]As one gathers silver, bronze, iron, lead, and tin into a smelter, to blow the fire upon them in order to melt them; so I will gather you in my anger and in my

If We Forget

EZEKIEL 22.12

The list of sins in this chapter is overwhelming: idolatry, injustice, violence, slander, adultery, fornication, extortion. Yet perhaps the most basic sin is that the people of Judah have forgotten God. They have forgotten their key relationship with the One who would curb their wandering and sinning.

We are in deep trouble if we forget to keep our eyes on God. Make a list of the good things that you have received from God. Begin each line with, "I remember when . . ." or "I remember the time . . ." Offer a prayer of thanksgiving when you have finished the list. Add to the list as you remember other blessings. Hang the list in a prominent place to help keep your heart, mind and soul focused on God and the blessings he has given you.

See Meeting God in Everyday Life

Stand in the Breach

EZEKIEL 22.29–31

Imagine walking along a river-bank; heavy rains have caused the river to rise to a dangerous level. Sandbagging efforts have contained the river thus far, but you see a trickle of water seeping through the sandbags and know that the break could bring damage to the town. You see a shovel and sandbags left over from the night before and you set to work. You discover a surge of energy that keeps you strong; your shouts bring others to help you repair the breach.

God is looking for us to "stand in the breach." What are the problems of the day? Secularism? Racism? Poverty? Violence? Greed? Abuse and addictions? How might you be called on to stand in the gap? Which of your friends might help you address these problems? Choose one problem you can respond today.

See *Meeting God in Service*

wrath, and I will put you in and melt you. ²¹I will gather you and blow upon you with the fire of my wrath, and you shall be melted within it. ²²As silver is melted in a smelter, so you shall be melted in it; and you shall know that I the LORD have poured out my wrath upon you.

23 The word of the LORD came to me: ²⁴Mortal, say to it: You are a land that is not cleansed, not rained upon in the day of indignation. ²⁵Its princes*a* within it are like a roaring lion tearing the prey; they have devoured human lives; they have taken treasure and precious things; they have made many widows within it. ²⁶Its priests have done violence to my teaching and have profaned my holy things; they have made no distinction between the holy and the common, nei-ther have they taught the difference between the unclean and the clean, and they have disregarded my sabbaths, so that I am profaned among them. ²⁷Its officials within it are like wolves tearing the prey, shedding blood, destroying lives to get dishonest gain. ²⁸Its prophets have smeared white-wash on their behalf, seeing false visions and divining lies for them, saying, "Thus says the Lord GOD," when the LORD has not spoken. ²⁹The people of the land have practiced extor-tion and committed robbery; they have oppressed the poor and needy, and have extorted from the alien without redress. ³⁰And I sought for anyone among them who would repair the wall and stand in the breach before me on behalf of the land, so that I would not destroy it; but I found no one. ³¹Therefore I have poured out my indignation upon them; I have consumed them with the fire of my wrath; I have re-turned their conduct upon their heads, says the Lord GOD.

Oholah and Oholibah

23 The word of the LORD came to me: ²Mortal, there were two women, the daughters of one mother; ³they played the whore in Egypt; they played the whore in their youth; their breasts were caressed there, and their vir-gin bosoms were fondled. ⁴Oholah was the name of the elder and Oholibah the name of her sister. They became mine, and they bore sons and daughters. As for their names, Oholah is Samaria, and Oholibah is Jerusalem.

5 Oholah played the whore while she was mine; she lusted after her lovers the Assyrians, warriors*b* ⁶clothed in blue, governors and commanders, all of them handsome young men, mounted horsemen. ⁷She bestowed her favors upon them, the choicest men of Assyria all of them; and she defiled herself with all the idols of everyone for whom she lusted. ⁸She did not give up her whorings that she had practiced since Egypt; for in her youth men had lain with her and fondled her virgin bosom and poured out their lust upon her. ⁹Therefore I delivered her into the hands of her lovers, into the hands of the Assyrians, for whom she lust-ed. ¹⁰These uncovered her nakedness; they seized her sons and her daughters; and they killed her with the sword. Judgment was executed upon her, and she became a by-word among women.

11 Her sister Oholibah saw this, yet she was more cor-rupt than she in her lusting and in her whorings, which were worse than those of her sister. ¹²She lusted after the Assyrians, governors and commanders, warriors*b* clothed

a Gk: Heb *indignation.* ²⁵*A conspiracy of its prophets*   *b* Meaning of Heb uncertain in full armor, mounted horsemen, all of them handsome young men. ¹³And I saw that she was defiled; they both took the same way. ¹⁴But she carried her whorings further; she saw male figures carved on the wall, images of the Chaldeans portrayed in vermilion, ¹⁵with belts around their waists, with flowing turbans on their heads, all of them looking like officers—a picture of Babylonians whose native land was Chaldea. ¹⁶When she saw them she lusted after them, and sent messengers to them in Chaldea. ¹⁷And the Babylonians came to her into the bed of love, and they defiled her with their lust; and after she defiled herself with them, she turned from them in disgust. ¹⁸When she carried on her whorings so openly and flaunted her nakedness, I turned in disgust from her, as I had turned from her sister. ¹⁹Yet she increased her whorings, remembering the days of her youth, when she played the whore in the land of Egypt ²⁰and lusted after her paramours there, whose members were like those of donkeys, and whose emission was like that of stallions. ²¹Thus you longed for the lewdness of your youth, when the Egyptians*ᵃ* fondled your bosom and caressed*ᵇ* your young breasts.

22 Therefore, O Oholibah, thus says the Lord God: I will rouse against you your lovers from whom you turned in disgust, and I will bring them against you from every side: ²³the Babylonians and all the Chaldeans, Pekod and Shoa and Koa, and all the Assyrians with them, handsome young men, governors and commanders all of them, officers and warriors,*ᶜ* all of them riding on horses. ²⁴They shall come against you from the north*ᵈ* with chariots and wagons and a host of peoples; they shall set themselves against you on every side with buckler, shield, and helmet, and I will commit the judgment to them, and they shall judge you according to their ordinances. ²⁵I will direct my indignation against you, in order that they may deal with you in fury. They shall cut off your nose and your ears, and your survivors shall fall by the sword. They shall seize your sons and your daughters, and your survivors shall be devoured by fire. ²⁶They shall also strip you of your clothes and take away your fine jewels. ²⁷So I will put an end to your lewdness and your whoring brought from the land of Egypt; you shall not long for them, or remember Egypt any more. ²⁸For thus says the Lord God: I will deliver you into the hands of those whom you hate, into the hands of those from whom you turned in disgust; ²⁹and they shall deal with you in hatred, and take away all the fruit of your labor, and leave you naked and bare, and the nakedness of your whorings shall be exposed. Your lewdness and your whorings ³⁰have brought this upon you, because you played the whore with the nations, and polluted yourself with their idols. ³¹You have gone the way of your sister; therefore I will give her cup into your hand. ³²Thus says the Lord God:

You shall drink your sister's cup,
   deep and wide;
you shall be scorned and derided,
   it holds so much.
33   You shall be filled with drunkenness and sorrow.
   A cup of horror and desolation
     is the cup of your sister Samaria;

Consequences

EZEKIEL 23.22–31

God is angry. The language is graphic and violent. "They shall cut off your noses and your ears, and your survivors shall fall by the sword." In the face of the Israelites' persistent sin, a loving God has become an angry God who brings punishment for their sin.

Have you angered God? Have the Christians and the churches of today angered God? Have the nations of the world angered God? Struggle with these questions. What might be the consequences of our faithlessness and our injustices? Be honest and blunt in your reflections. Ask for forgiveness in your prayer.

See Meeting God in Prayer

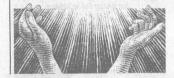

a Two Mss: MT *from Egypt*   *b* Cn: Heb *for the sake of*   *c* Compare verses 6 and 12: Heb *officers and called ones*   *d* Gk: Meaning of Heb uncertain

A Boiling, Purifying Pot

EZEKIEL 24.1–5

Ezekiel chooses another graphic image to symbolize the trouble that Jerusalem is in. The king of Babylon has laid siege to the city; the citizens will feel like they are being roasted in a pot. The Israelites' worship of other gods, their misplaced confidence in other nations and their neglect of the poor have gotten them into deep water—hot water.

Draw a picture of a large pot and put into it your personality traits and harmful actions that need to be purified. Place into the water all the "isms" (such as racism, sexism, and the like) that need to be boiled clean. In what ways does your church or country need to be purified?

See Meeting God in Scripture

34   you shall drink it and drain it out,
        and gnaw its sherds,
        and tear out your breasts;
for I have spoken, says the Lord GOD. [35]Therefore thus says the Lord GOD: Because you have forgotten me and cast me behind your back, therefore bear the consequences of your lewdness and whorings.

36 The LORD said to me: Mortal, will you judge Oholah and Oholibah? Then declare to them their abominable deeds. [37]For they have committed adultery, and blood is on their hands; with their idols they have committed adultery; and they have even offered up to them for food the children whom they had borne to me. [38]Moreover this they have done to me: they have defiled my sanctuary on the same day and profaned my sabbaths. [39]For when they had slaughtered their children for their idols, on the same day they came into my sanctuary to profane it. This is what they did in my house.

40 They even sent for men to come from far away, to whom a messenger was sent, and they came. For them you bathed yourself, painted your eyes, and decked yourself with ornaments; [41]you sat on a stately couch, with a table spread before it on which you had placed my incense and my oil. [42]The sound of a raucous multitude was around her, with many of the rabble brought in drunken from the wilderness; and they put bracelets on the arms[a] of the women, and beautiful crowns upon their heads.

43 Then I said, Ah, she is worn out with adulteries, but they carry on their sexual acts with her. [44]For they have gone in to her, as one goes in to a whore. Thus they went in to Oholah and to Oholibah, wanton women. [45]But righteous judges shall declare them guilty of adultery and of bloodshed; because they are adulteresses and blood is on their hands.

46 For thus says the Lord GOD: Bring up an assembly against them, and make them an object of terror and of plunder. [47]The assembly shall stone them and with their swords they shall cut them down; they shall kill their sons and their daughters, and burn up their houses. [48]Thus will I put an end to lewdness in the land, so that all women may take warning and not commit lewdness as you have done. [49]They shall repay you for your lewdness, and you shall bear the penalty for your sinful idolatry; and you shall know that I am the Lord GOD.

The Boiling Pot

24 In the ninth year, in the tenth month, on the tenth day of the month, the word of the LORD came to me: [2]Mortal, write down the name of this day, this very day. The king of Babylon has laid siege to Jerusalem this very day. [3]And utter an allegory to the rebellious house and say to them, Thus says the Lord GOD:

        Set on the pot, set it on,
            pour in water also;
4   put in it the pieces,
            all the good pieces, the thigh and the shoulder;
            fill it with choice bones.
5   Take the choicest one of the flock,
            pile the logs[b] under it;

a Heb *hands*   *b* Compare verse 10: Heb *the bones*

boil its pieces,[a]
seethe[b] also its bones in it.

6 Therefore thus says the Lord GOD:
Woe to the bloody city,
    the pot whose rust is in it,
    whose rust has not gone out of it!
Empty it piece by piece,
    making no choice at all.[c]
7 For the blood she shed is inside it;
    she placed it on a bare rock;
she did not pour it out on the ground,
    to cover it with earth.
8 To rouse my wrath, to take vengeance,
    I have placed the blood she shed
    on a bare rock,
so that it may not be covered.
9 Therefore thus says the Lord GOD:
Woe to the bloody city!
    I will even make the pile great.
10 Heap up the logs, kindle the fire;
    boil the meat well, mix in the spices,
    let the bones be burned.
11 Stand it empty upon the coals,
    so that it may become hot, its copper glow,
    its filth melt in it, its rust be consumed.
12 In vain I have wearied myself;[d]
    its thick rust does not depart.
    To the fire with its rust![e]
13 Yet, when I cleansed you in your filthy lewdness,
    you did not become clean from your filth;
you shall not again be cleansed
    until I have satisfied my fury upon you.
14 I the LORD have spoken; the time is coming, I will act. I will not refrain, I will not spare, I will not relent. According to your ways and your doings I will judge you, says the Lord GOD.

Ezekiel's Bereavement

15 The word of the LORD came to me: 16 Mortal, with one blow I am about to take away from you the delight of your eyes; yet you shall not mourn or weep, nor shall your tears run down. 17 Sigh, but not aloud; make no mourning for the dead. Bind on your turban, and put your sandals on your feet; do not cover your upper lip or eat the bread of mourners.[f] 18 So I spoke to the people in the morning, and at evening my wife died. And on the next morning I did as I was commanded.

19 Then the people said to me, "Will you not tell us what these things mean for us, that you are acting this way?" 20 Then I said to them: The word of the LORD came to me: 21 Say to the house of Israel, Thus says the Lord GOD: I will profane my sanctuary, the pride of your power, the delight of your eyes, and your heart's desire; and your sons and your daughters whom you left behind shall fall by the sword. 22 And you shall do as I have done; you shall not cover your upper lip or eat the bread of mourners.[f] 23 Your turbans shall

Hold On

EZEKIEL 24.18–24

Ezekiel is instructed not to grieve for his dead wife. The traditional rites of mourning are to be dispensed with, so that the people will ask Ezekiel why he isn't grieving. This unusual behavior allows Ezekiel to pronounce a dire warning in a way so vivid that the people cannot possibly miss its meaning.

We sometimes miss warnings we should have heeded. We can often see them clearly after the fact but, unfortunately, not so clearly beforehand. Have you found a way to develop your spiritual antennae? What subtle clues do you look for as warnings regarding your actions, behaviors or relationships? What major warnings have you missed in the past? Ask God to help you see more clearly so you do not miss the signs God gives you for your benefit.

See Meeting God in Everyday Life

---

a Two Mss: Heb *its boilings*   *b* Cn: Heb *its bones seethe*   *c* Heb *piece, no lot has fallen on it*   *d* Cn: Meaning of Heb uncertain   *e* Meaning of Heb uncertain   *f* Vg Tg: Heb *of men*

The Misfortune of Others

EZEKIEL 25.6–7

Some of the nations around Judah clap their hands and stamp their feet at the destruction of Jerusalem. But God will not allow his people to be mocked, so he promises that destruction will come to those jeering nations as well as to Jerusalem.

When have you taken pleasure in the misfortunes of others? Have you laughed when the butt of the joke is a vulnerable and unfortunate person? What causes this tendency in so many of us? Is it relief that the misfortune is not our own? Consider today your own vulnerability. With God's help look for an occasion to help someone who is suffering misfortune.

See Meeting God in Service

be on your heads and your sandals on your feet; you shall not mourn or weep, but you shall pine away in your iniquities and groan to one another. ²⁴Thus Ezekiel shall be a sign to you; you shall do just as he has done. When this comes, then you shall know that I am the Lord GOD.

25 And you, mortal, on the day when I take from them their stronghold, their joy and glory, the delight of their eyes and their heart's affection, and also*ᵃ* their sons and their daughters, ²⁶on that day, one who has escaped will come to you to report to you the news. ²⁷On that day your mouth shall be opened to the one who has escaped, and you shall speak and no longer be silent. So you shall be a sign to them; and they shall know that I am the LORD.

Proclamation against Ammon

25 The word of the LORD came to me: ²Mortal, set your face toward the Ammonites and prophesy against them. ³Say to the Ammonites, Hear the word of the Lord GOD: Thus says the Lord GOD, Because you said, "Aha!" over my sanctuary when it was profaned, and over the land of Israel when it was made desolate, and over the house of Judah when it went into exile; ⁴therefore I am handing you over to the people of the east for a possession. They shall set their encampments among you and pitch their tents in your midst; they shall eat your fruit, and they shall drink your milk. ⁵I will make Rabbah a pasture for camels and Ammon a fold for flocks. Then you shall know that I am the LORD. ⁶For thus says the Lord GOD: Because you have clapped your hands and stamped your feet and rejoiced with all the malice within you against the land of Israel, ⁷therefore I have stretched out my hand against you, and will hand you over as plunder to the nations. I will cut you off from the peoples and will make you perish out of the countries; I will destroy you. Then you shall know that I am the LORD.

Proclamation against Moab

8 Thus says the Lord GOD: Because Moab*ᵇ* said, The house of Judah is like all the other nations, ⁹therefore I will lay open the flank of Moab from the towns*ᶜ* on its frontier, the glory of the country, Beth-jeshimoth, Baal-meon, and Kiriathaim. ¹⁰I will give it along with Ammon to the people of the east as a possession. Thus Ammon shall be remembered no more among the nations, ¹¹and I will execute judgments upon Moab. Then they shall know that I am the LORD.

Proclamation against Edom

12 Thus says the Lord GOD: Because Edom acted revengefully against the house of Judah and has grievously offended in taking vengeance upon them, ¹³therefore thus says the Lord GOD, I will stretch out my hand against Edom, and cut off from it humans and animals, and I will make it desolate; from Teman even to Dedan they shall fall by the sword. ¹⁴I will lay my vengeance upon Edom by the hand of my people Israel; and they shall act in Edom according to my anger and according to my wrath; and they shall know my vengeance, says the Lord GOD.

a Heb lacks *and also*   *b* Gk Old Latin: Heb *Moab and Seir*   *c* Heb *towns from its towns*

Proclamation against Philistia

15 Thus says the Lord GOD: Because with unending hostilities the Philistines acted in vengeance, and with malice of heart took revenge in destruction; [16]therefore thus says the Lord GOD, I will stretch out my hand against the Philistines, cut off the Cherethites, and destroy the rest of the seacoast. [17]I will execute great vengeance on them with wrathful punishments. Then they shall know that I am the LORD, when I lay my vengeance on them.

Proclamation against Tyre

26 In the eleventh year, on the first day of the month, the word of the LORD came to me: [2]Mortal, because Tyre said concerning Jerusalem,

"Aha, broken is the gateway of the peoples;
    it has swung open to me;
I shall be replenished,
    now that it is wasted,"

[3]therefore, thus says the Lord GOD:

See, I am against you, O Tyre!
    I will hurl many nations against you,
    as the sea hurls its waves.
4 They shall destroy the walls of Tyre
    and break down its towers.
I will scrape its soil from it
    and make it a bare rock.
5 It shall become, in the midst of the sea,
    a place for spreading nets.
I have spoken, says the Lord GOD.
    It shall become plunder for the nations,
6   and its daughter-towns in the country
    shall be killed by the sword.
Then they shall know that I am the LORD.

7 For thus says the Lord GOD: I will bring against Tyre from the north King Nebuchadrezzar of Babylon, king of kings, together with horses, chariots, cavalry, and a great and powerful army.

8   Your daughter-towns in the country
    he shall put to the sword.
He shall set up a siege wall against you,
    cast up a ramp against you,
    and raise a roof of shields against you.
9   He shall direct the shock of his battering rams
        against your walls
    and break down your towers with his axes.
10   His horses shall be so many
    that their dust shall cover you.
At the noise of cavalry, wheels, and chariots
    your very walls shall shake,
when he enters your gates
    like those entering a breached city.
11   With the hoofs of his horses
    he shall trample all your streets.
He shall put your people to the sword,
    and your strong pillars shall fall to the ground.
12   They will plunder your riches
    and loot your merchandise;
they shall break down your walls
    and destroy your fine houses.
Your stones and timber and soil

Silence the Songs

EZEKIEL 26.13–14

A prophecy is directed against Tyre because Tyre failed to come to the aid of its ally Jerusalem. The king of Babylon will destroy the city of Tyre so completely that it will never be rebuilt. In poignant detail Ezekiel records, "I will silence the music of your songs; the sound of your lyres shall be heard no more. I will make you a bare rock; you shall be a place for spreading nets. You shall never again be rebuilt." Days of sadness and lament are coming to the city of Tyre.

Sometimes it's beneficial to allow ourselves a day for sadness and lament, for grieving the loss of dreams, loved ones or other precious things. Find a passage in a novel or poem or find a piece of music that expresses the sadness you sometimes feel. Let yourself feel that sadness and ask God to be with you in that experience. Thank God for sharing your sadness.

See Meeting God in Prayer

A Solid Ship

EZEKIEL 27.1–9

The island city of Tyre is compared to a beautiful ship constructed of precious wood and exquisite fabrics from many nations. An exotic and cosmopolitan showplace, the city was like a lovely jewel of the sea. But the people were puffed up with pride; they thought they were invincible. And yet Ezekiel prophesies that the ship (the nation) will sink because it is built on the shaky foundation of prosperity (28.5).

What is your foundation? What are the strong planks of your faith? What experiences bind your heart and spirit into a weather-resistant craft? What scripture passages bolt your life into a sturdy ship? Who is the wind in your sails?

See Meeting God in Scripture

they shall cast into the water.
13 I will silence the music of your songs;
   the sound of your lyres shall be heard no more.
14 I will make you a bare rock;
   you shall be a place for spreading nets.
You shall never again be rebuilt,
   for I the LORD have spoken,
   says the Lord GOD.

15 Thus says the Lord GOD to Tyre: Shall not the coastlands shake at the sound of your fall, when the wounded groan, when slaughter goes on within you? 16Then all the princes of the sea shall step down from their thrones; they shall remove their robes and strip off their embroidered garments. They shall clothe themselves with trembling, and shall sit on the ground; they shall tremble every moment, and be appalled at you. 17And they shall raise a lamentation over you, and say to you:

How you have vanished*a* from the seas,
   O city renowned,
once mighty on the sea,
   you and your inhabitants,*b*
who imposed your*c* terror
   on all the mainland!*d*
18 Now the coastlands tremble
   on the day of your fall;
the coastlands by the sea
   are dismayed at your passing.

19 For thus says the Lord GOD: When I make you a city laid waste, like cities that are not inhabited, when I bring up the deep over you, and the great waters cover you, 20then I will thrust you down with those who descend into the Pit, to the people of long ago, and I will make you live in the world below, among primeval ruins, with those who go down to the Pit, so that you will not be inhabited or have a place*e* in the land of the living. 21I will bring you to a dreadful end, and you shall be no more; though sought for, you will never be found again, says the Lord GOD.

Lamentation over Tyre

27 The word of the LORD came to me: 2Now you, mortal, raise a lamentation over Tyre, 3and say to Tyre, which sits at the entrance to the sea, merchant of the peoples on many coastlands, Thus says the Lord GOD:

O Tyre, you have said,
   "I am perfect in beauty."
4 Your borders are in the heart of the seas;
   your builders made perfect your beauty.
5 They made all your planks
   of fir trees from Senir;
they took a cedar from Lebanon
   to make a mast for you.
6 From oaks of Bashan
   they made your oars;
they made your deck of pines*f*
   from the coasts of Cyprus,
   inlaid with ivory.

a Gk OL Aquila: Heb *have vanished, O inhabited one,*   *b* Heb *it and its inhabitants*   *c* Heb *their*   *d* Cn: Heb *its inhabitants*   *e* Gk: Heb *I will give beauty*   *f* Or *boxwood*

7 Of fine embroidered linen from Egypt
was your sail,
serving as your ensign;
blue and purple from the coasts of Elishah
was your awning.
8 The inhabitants of Sidon and Arvad
were your rowers;
skilled men of Zemer*a* were within you,
they were your pilots.
9 The elders of Gebal and its artisans were within you,
caulking your seams;
all the ships of the sea with their mariners were
within you,
to barter for your wares.
10 Paras*b* and Lud and Put
were in your army,
your mighty warriors;
they hung shield and helmet in you;
they gave you splendor.
11 Men of Arvad and Helech*c*
were on your walls all around;
men of Gamad were at your towers.
They hung their quivers all around your walls;
they made perfect your beauty.

12 Tarshish did business with you out of the abundance of your great wealth; silver, iron, tin, and lead they exchanged for your wares. 13 Javan, Tubal, and Meshech traded with you; they exchanged human beings and vessels of bronze for your merchandise. 14 Beth-togarmah exchanged for your wares horses, war horses, and mules. 15 The Rhodians*d* traded with you; many coastlands were your own special markets; they brought you in payment ivory tusks and ebony. 16 Edom*e* did business with you because of your abundant goods; they exchanged for your wares turquoise, purple, embroidered work, fine linen, coral, and rubies. 17 Judah and the land of Israel traded with you; they exchanged for your merchandise wheat from Minnith, millet,*f* honey, oil, and balm. 18 Damascus traded with you for your abundant goods—because of your great wealth of every kind—wine of Helbon, and white wool. 19 Vedan and Javan from Uzal*f* entered into trade for your wares; wrought iron, cassia, and sweet cane were bartered for your merchandise. 20 Dedan traded with you in saddlecloths for riding. 21 Arabia and all the princes of Kedar were your favored dealers in lambs, rams, and goats; in these they did business with you. 22 The merchants of Sheba and Raamah traded with you; they exchanged for your wares the best of all kinds of spices, and all precious stones, and gold. 23 Haran, Canneh, Eden, the merchants of Sheba, Asshur, and Chilmad traded with you. 24 These traded with you in choice garments, in clothes of blue and embroidered work, and in carpets of colored material, bound with cords and made secure; in these they traded with you.*g* 25 The ships of Tarshish traveled for you in your trade.

So you were filled and heavily laden
in the heart of the seas.

---

a Cn Compare Gen 10.18: Heb *your skilled men, O Tyre*   *b* Or *Persia*
c Or *and your army*   *d* Gk: Heb *The Dedanites*   *e* Another reading is
Aram   *f* Meaning of Heb uncertain   *g* Cn: Heb *in your market*

The East Wind Blows

EZEKIEL 27.12–36

The east wind has sunk Tyre. The proud nation and its mighty fleet have come to an end. Tyre's wealth and pomp cannot save the city. Its fame does not last. The lament over Tyre is a warning to us: Our plans are to be Christ-centered; our goals are to be Spirit-driven. When we ask God to direct us, we have no reason to fear the force of the east wind.

Write down three or four of the most important goals in your life. Ask tough, searching questions about these goals. What part did God play in crafting these plans? Offer your goals to God in prayer and ask the Lord to examine them. Revise them (if need be) according to God's plans for you.

See Meeting God in Everyday Life

Be Not Proud

EZEKIEL 28.2

"If there is any good in you, believe that there is much more in others so that you may preserve humility. It hurts you not to submit to everyone, but it hurts you most of all to prefer yourself to even one other person."

—THOMAS À KEMPIS,
The Imitation of Christ

26 Your rowers have brought you
    into the high seas.
The east wind has wrecked you
    in the heart of the seas.
27 Your riches, your wares, your merchandise,
    your mariners and your pilots,
your caulkers, your dealers in merchandise,
    and all your warriors within you,
with all the company
    that is with you,
sink into the heart of the seas
    on the day of your ruin.
28 At the sound of the cry of your pilots
    the countryside shakes,
29 and down from their ships
    come all that handle the oar.
The mariners and all the pilots of the sea
    stand on the shore
30 and wail aloud over you,
    and cry bitterly.
They throw dust on their heads
    and wallow in ashes;
31 they make themselves bald for you,
    and put on sackcloth,
and they weep over you in bitterness of soul,
    with bitter mourning.
32 In their wailing they raise a lamentation for you,
    and lament over you:
"Who was ever destroyed[a] like Tyre
    in the midst of the sea?
33 When your wares came from the seas,
    you satisfied many peoples;
with your abundant wealth and merchandise
    you enriched the kings of the earth.
34 Now you are wrecked by the seas,
    in the depths of the waters;
your merchandise and all your crew
    have sunk with you.
35 All the inhabitants of the coastlands
    are appalled at you;
and their kings are horribly afraid,
    their faces are convulsed.
36 The merchants among the peoples hiss at you;
    you have come to a dreadful end
    and shall be no more forever."

Proclamation against the King of Tyre

28 The word of the LORD came to me: 2Mortal, say to the prince of Tyre, Thus says the Lord GOD:
Because your heart is proud
    and you have said, "I am a god;
I sit in the seat of the gods,
    in the heart of the seas,"
yet you are but a mortal, and no god,
    though you compare your mind
    with the mind of a god.
3 You are indeed wiser than Daniel;[b]
    no secret is hidden from you;
4 by your wisdom and your understanding

a Tg Vg: Heb *like silence*   *b* Or, as otherwise read, *Danel*

you have amassed wealth for yourself,
and have gathered gold and silver
into your treasuries.
5 By your great wisdom in trade
you have increased your wealth,
and your heart has become proud in your wealth.
6 Therefore thus says the Lord GOD:
Because you compare your mind
with the mind of a god,
7 therefore, I will bring strangers against you,
the most terrible of the nations;
they shall draw their swords against the beauty of
your wisdom
and defile your splendor.
8 They shall thrust you down to the Pit,
and you shall die a violent death
in the heart of the seas.
9 Will you still say, "I am a god,"
in the presence of those who kill you,
though you are but a mortal, and no god,
in the hands of those who wound you?
10 You shall die the death of the uncircumcised
by the hand of foreigners;
for I have spoken, says the Lord GOD.

Lamentation over the King of Tyre

11 Moreover the word of the LORD came to me: 12Mortal,
raise a lamentation over the king of Tyre, and say to him,
Thus says the Lord GOD:
You were the signet of perfection,*a*
full of wisdom and perfect in beauty.
13 You were in Eden, the garden of God;
every precious stone was your covering,
carnelian, chrysolite, and moonstone,
beryl, onyx, and jasper,
sapphire,*b* turquoise, and emerald;
and worked in gold were your settings
and your engravings.*a*
On the day that you were created
they were prepared.
14 With an anointed cherub as guardian I placed you;*a*
you were on the holy mountain of God;
you walked among the stones of fire.
15 You were blameless in your ways
from the day that you were created,
until iniquity was found in you.
16 In the abundance of your trade
you were filled with violence, and you sinned;
so I cast you as a profane thing from the mountain
of God,
and the guardian cherub drove you out
from among the stones of fire.
17 Your heart was proud because of your beauty;
you corrupted your wisdom for the sake of your
splendor.
I cast you to the ground;
I exposed you before kings,
to feast their eyes on you.

Blameless

EZEKIEL 28.15

The prophet is eloquent and comprehensive as he laments the problems in Tyre. The country and its leaders are guilty of arrogance, idolatry and injustice. There is very little that is good about Tyre. Yet, in the midst of Ezekiel's diatribe, he inserts a word of hope: "You were blameless in your ways from the day that you were created, until iniquity was found in you."

However far we may stray from God's chosen path for us, we carry deep within us the image of God. We are born under God's watchful eye, and we are forever in God's heart. Do you believe that you are precious in God's eyes? Can you sense that God's love has been there for you since the moment you came into being? (See Psalm 139.13–16.) Try writing a prayer of thanksgiving that expresses your joy at being loved.

See Meeting God in Scripture

a Meaning of Heb uncertain   *b* Or *lapis lazuli*

Gather the Scattered

EZEKIEL 28.25–26

"Hope is the primary prophetic idiom not because of the general dynamic of history or because of the signs of the times but because the prophet speaks to a people who, willy-nilly, are God's people. Hope is what this community must do because it is God's community invited to be in God's pilgrimage. And as Israel is invited to grieve God's grief over the ending, so Israel is now invited to hope in God's promises."

—WALTER BRUEGGEMANN,
The Prophetic Imagination

¹⁸ By the multitude of your iniquities,
　　in the unrighteousness of your trade,
　　you profaned your sanctuaries.
　So I brought out fire from within you;
　　it consumed you,
　and I turned you to ashes on the earth
　　in the sight of all who saw you.
¹⁹ All who know you among the peoples
　　are appalled at you;
　you have come to a dreadful end
　　and shall be no more forever.

Proclamation against Sidon

20 The word of the LORD came to me: ²¹Mortal, set your face toward Sidon, and prophesy against it, ²²and say, Thus says the Lord GOD:

　I am against you, O Sidon,
　　and I will gain glory in your midst.
　They shall know that I am the LORD
　　when I execute judgments in it,
　　and manifest my holiness in it;
²³　for I will send pestilence into it,
　　and bloodshed into its streets;
　and the dead shall fall in its midst,
　　by the sword that is against it on every side.
　And they shall know that I am the LORD.

24 The house of Israel shall no longer find a pricking brier or a piercing thorn among all their neighbors who have treated them with contempt. And they shall know that I am the Lord GOD.

Future Blessing for Israel

25 Thus says the Lord GOD: When I gather the house of Israel from the peoples among whom they are scattered, and manifest my holiness in them in the sight of the nations, then they shall settle on their own soil that I gave to my servant Jacob. ²⁶They shall live in safety in it, and shall build houses and plant vineyards. They shall live in safety, when I execute judgments upon all their neighbors who have treated them with contempt. And they shall know that I am the LORD their God.

Proclamation against Egypt

29 In the tenth year, in the tenth month, on the twelfth day of the month, the word of the LORD came to me: ²Mortal, set your face against Pharaoh king of Egypt, and prophesy against him and against all Egypt; ³speak, and say, Thus says the Lord GOD:

　I am against you,
　　Pharaoh king of Egypt,
　the great dragon sprawling
　　in the midst of its channels,
　saying, "My Nile is my own;
　　I made it for myself."
⁴　I will put hooks in your jaws,
　　and make the fish of your channels stick to your
　　　scales.
　I will draw you up from your channels,
　　with all the fish of your channels
　　sticking to your scales.

5 I will fling you into the wilderness,
    you and all the fish of your channels;
you shall fall in the open field,
    and not be gathered and buried.
To the animals of the earth and to the birds of the air
    I have given you as food.

6 Then all the inhabitants of Egypt shall know
    that I am the LORD
because you[a] were a staff of reed
    to the house of Israel;

7 when they grasped you with the hand, you broke,
    and tore all their shoulders;
and when they leaned on you, you broke,
    and made all their legs unsteady.[b]

8 Therefore, thus says the Lord GOD: I will bring a sword upon you, and will cut off from you human being and animal; 9and the land of Egypt shall be a desolation and a waste. Then they shall know that I am the LORD.

Because you[c] said, "The Nile is mine, and I made it," 10therefore, I am against you, and against your channels, and I will make the land of Egypt an utter waste and desolation, from Migdol to Syene, as far as the border of Ethiopia.[d] 11No human foot shall pass through it, and no animal foot shall pass through it; it shall be uninhabited forty years. 12I will make the land of Egypt a desolation among desolated countries; and her cities shall be a desolation forty years among cities that are laid waste. I will scatter the Egyptians among the nations, and disperse them among the countries.

13 Further, thus says the Lord GOD: At the end of forty years I will gather the Egyptians from the peoples among whom they were scattered; 14and I will restore the fortunes of Egypt, and bring them back to the land of Pathros, the land of their origin; and there they shall be a lowly kingdom. 15It shall be the most lowly of the kingdoms, and never again exalt itself above the nations; and I will make them so small that they will never again rule over the nations. 16The Egyptians[e] shall never again be the reliance of the house of Israel; they will recall their iniquity, when they turned to them for aid. Then they shall know that I am the Lord GOD.

Babylonia Will Plunder Egypt

17 In the twenty-seventh year, in the first month, on the first day of the month, the word of the LORD came to me: 18Mortal, King Nebuchadrezzar of Babylon made his army labor hard against Tyre; every head was made bald and every shoulder was rubbed bare; yet neither he nor his army got anything from Tyre to pay for the labor that he had expended against it. 19Therefore thus says the Lord GOD: I will give the land of Egypt to King Nebuchadrezzar of Babylon; and he shall carry off its wealth and despoil it and plunder it; and it shall be the wages for his army. 20I have given him the land of Egypt as his payment for which he labored, because they worked for me, says the Lord GOD.

21 On that day I will cause a horn to sprout up for the house of Israel, and I will open your lips among them. Then they shall know that I am the LORD.

A Day of Clouds

EZEKIEL 29.17—30.3

Most often "the day of the LORD" referred to God's judgment, though later it was associated with the day of Israel's restoration. The "day of the LORD" or the "day of clouds" urges us to look out for trouble.

Imagine "a day of clouds," dark and threatening. The clouds beckon you to consider the course of your life. What have you been putting off? What is really important that you want to do before the rain comes and washes out the possibilities? The clouds are a call to sort your priorities, to take care of business before the storms roll in. Let the guidance and promises of God be a place of shelter for your prayer and reflection. Make some plans to take action.

See Meeting God in Scripture

---

a Gk Syr Vg: Heb *they*   b Syr: Heb *stand*   c Gk Syr Vg: Heb *he*
d Or *Nubia*; Heb *Cush*   e Heb *It*

Idols and Images

EZEKIEL 30.13

Take a look around your house or apartment. Begin by looking at the walls. What images are most prevalent? What meaning do the pictures convey? Is there any religious art? A cross? An icon? Look at your books. Is the Bible clearly visible? What objects rest on your shelves? What magazines, newspapers or catalogs do you see? How prominent a place does the television or computer or stereo have? Do any of the things in your house tempt you to turn away from God, cause you to miss worship services, or neglect prayer or Bible study? What activities take up most of your time? Can you affirm the words of scripture, "As for me and my household, we will serve the LORD" (Joshua 24.15)?

See Meeting God in Everyday Life

Lamentation for Egypt

30 The word of the LORD came to me: ²Mortal, prophesy, and say, Thus says the Lord GOD:
Wail, "Alas for the day!"
³   For a day is near,
        the day of the LORD is near;
    it will be a day of clouds,
        a time of doom*ª* for the nations.
⁴   A sword shall come upon Egypt,
        and anguish shall be in Ethiopia,*ᵇ*
    when the slain fall in Egypt,
        and its wealth is carried away,
        and its foundations are torn down.

⁵Ethiopia,*ᵇ* and Put, and Lud, and all Arabia, and Libya,*ᶜ* and the people of the allied land*ᵈ* shall fall with them by the sword.

⁶   Thus says the LORD:
    Those who support Egypt shall fall,
        and its proud might shall come down;
    from Migdol to Syene
        they shall fall within it by the sword,
    says the Lord GOD.
⁷   They shall be desolated among other desolated
                countries,
        and their cities shall lie among cities laid waste.
⁸   Then they shall know that I am the LORD,
        when I have set fire to Egypt,
        and all who help it are broken.

9 On that day, messengers shall go out from me in ships to terrify the unsuspecting Ethiopians;*ᵉ* and anguish shall come upon them on the day of Egypt's doom;*ᶠ* for it is coming!

10 Thus says the Lord GOD:
    I will put an end to the hordes of Egypt,
        by the hand of King Nebuchadrezzar of Babylon.
¹¹   He and his people with him, the most terrible of the
                nations,
        shall be brought in to destroy the land;
    and they shall draw their swords against Egypt,
        and fill the land with the slain.
¹²   I will dry up the channels,
        and will sell the land into the hand of evildoers;
    I will bring desolation upon the land and everything
                in it
        by the hand of foreigners;
    I the LORD have spoken.

13 Thus says the Lord GOD:
    I will destroy the idols
        and put an end to the images in Memphis;
    there shall no longer be a prince in the land of Egypt;
        so I will put fear in the land of Egypt.
¹⁴   I will make Pathros a desolation,
        and will set fire to Zoan,
        and will execute acts of judgment on Thebes.

---

a Heb lacks *of doom*   *b* Or *Nubia*; Heb *Cush*   *c* Compare Gk Syr Vg: Heb *Cub*   *d* Meaning of Heb uncertain   *e* Or *Nubians*; Heb *Cush*   *f* Heb *the day of Egypt*

15 I will pour my wrath upon Pelusium,
 the stronghold of Egypt,
 and cut off the hordes of Thebes.
16 I will set fire to Egypt;
 Pelusium shall be in great agony;
Thebes shall be breached,
 and Memphis face adversaries by day.
17 The young men of On and of Pi-beseth shall fall by
 the sword;
 and the cities themselves*a* shall go into captivity.
18 At Tehaphnehes the day shall be dark,
 when I break there the dominion of Egypt,
and its proud might shall come to an end;
 the city*b* shall be covered by a cloud,
 and its daughter-towns shall go into captivity.
19 Thus I will execute acts of judgment on Egypt.
 Then they shall know that I am the LORD.

Proclamation against Pharaoh

20 In the eleventh year, in the first month, on the seventh day of the month, the word of the LORD came to me: 21Mortal, I have broken the arm of Pharaoh king of Egypt; it has not been bound up for healing or wrapped with a bandage, so that it may become strong to wield the sword. 22Therefore thus says the Lord GOD: I am against Pharaoh king of Egypt, and will break his arms, both the strong arm and the one that was broken; and I will make the sword fall from his hand. 23I will scatter the Egyptians among the nations, and disperse them throughout the lands. 24I will strengthen the arms of the king of Babylon, and put my sword in his hand; but I will break the arms of Pharaoh, and he will groan before him with the groans of one mortally wounded. 25I will strengthen the arms of the king of Babylon, but the arms of Pharaoh shall fall. And they shall know that I am the LORD, when I put my sword into the hand of the king of Babylon. He shall stretch it out against the land of Egypt, 26and I will scatter the Egyptians among the nations and disperse them throughout the countries. Then they shall know that I am the LORD.

The Lofty Cedar

31 In the eleventh year, in the third month, on the first day of the month, the word of the LORD came to me: 2Mortal, say to Pharaoh king of Egypt and to his hordes:
 Whom are you like in your greatness?
3 Consider Assyria, a cedar of Lebanon,
 with fair branches and forest shade,
  and of great height,
  its top among the clouds.*c*
4 The waters nourished it,
 the deep made it grow tall,
making its rivers flow*d*
 around the place it was planted,
sending forth its streams
 to all the trees of the field.
5 So it towered high
 above all the trees of the field;
 its boughs grew large

Like a Tree Planted by the Water

EZEKIEL 31.3–9

The tree image is woven throughout scripture. There is the tree of knowledge in the Garden of Eden, the tree turned into a cross on the hill of Calvary and the tree of life in Revelation. This passage in Ezekiel presents a beautiful description of a cedar. Yet this glorious tree, with deep roots, bountiful branches and grand height, is a symbol of a nation that is infested with sinful pride. And this tree—this nation—is about to be felled because of that pride.

Pay attention today to small, humble trees. The mighty oaks and cedars may be felled in a storm in which the smaller trees remain standing. Perhaps you might sit under a small tree and pray for the gift of humility.

See Meeting God in the Created Order

---

a Heb *and they* *b* Heb *she* *c* Gk: Heb *thick boughs* *d* Gk: Heb *rivers going*

Seeing Ourselves

EZEKIEL 32.1–3

How do we think of ourselves? Do we see ourselves with the eyes of God? Or do we measure ourselves by the standards of the world? The lament over Egypt and its pharaoh focuses on their pride and arrogance: "You consider yourself a lion . . . . you are like a dragon."

One way God measures nations, its leaders and its people is with the yardstick of compassion. Are the poor, the strangers and the hurting being taken care of? Are the people caring and loving in their attitudes and actions?

Choose a special friend whom you trust and discuss these questions with that person. Begin with your nation, your community or your church. Then ask for your friend's candid and honest help in examining yourself. Have you fallen into arrogant habits without realizing it? In what ways do you express compassion regularly?

See Meeting God in Community

and its branches long,
from abundant water in its shoots.
6 All the birds of the air
made their nests in its boughs;
under its branches all the animals of the field
gave birth to their young;
and in its shade
all great nations lived.
7 It was beautiful in its greatness,
in the length of its branches;
for its roots went down
to abundant water.
8 The cedars in the garden of God could not rival it,
nor the fir trees equal its boughs;
the plane trees were as nothing
compared with its branches;
no tree in the garden of God
was like it in beauty.
9 I made it beautiful
with its mass of branches,
the envy of all the trees of Eden
that were in the garden of God.

10 Therefore thus says the Lord GOD: Because it[a] towered high and set its top among the clouds,[b] and its heart was proud of its height, 11I gave it into the hand of the prince of the nations; he has dealt with it as its wickedness deserves. I have cast it out. 12Foreigners from the most terrible of the nations have cut it down and left it. On the mountains and in all the valleys its branches have fallen, and its boughs lie broken in all the watercourses of the land; and all the peoples of the earth went away from its shade and left it.
13 On its fallen trunk settle
all the birds of the air,
and among its boughs lodge
all the wild animals.
14All this is in order that no trees by the waters may grow to lofty height or set their tops among the clouds,[b] and that no trees that drink water may reach up to them in height.
For all of them are handed over to death,
to the world below;
along with all mortals,
with those who go down to the Pit.

15 Thus says the Lord GOD: On the day it went down to Sheol I closed the deep over it and covered it; I restrained its rivers, and its mighty waters were checked. I clothed Lebanon in gloom for it, and all the trees of the field fainted because of it. 16I made the nations quake at the sound of its fall, when I cast it down to Sheol with those who go down to the Pit; and all the trees of Eden, the choice and best of Lebanon, all that were well watered, were consoled in the world below. 17They also went down to Sheol with it, to those killed by the sword, along with its allies,[c] those who lived in its shade among the nations.

18 Which among the trees of Eden was like you in glory and in greatness? Now you shall be brought down with the trees of Eden to the world below; you shall lie among the uncircumcised, with those who are killed by the sword. This is Pharaoh and all his horde, says the Lord GOD.

a Syr Vg: Heb *you*   b Gk: Heb *thick boughs*   c Heb *its arms*

Lamentation over Pharaoh and Egypt

32 In the twelfth year, in the twelfth month, on the first day of the month, the word of the LORD came to me: ²Mortal, raise a lamentation over Pharaoh king of Egypt, and say to him:

> You consider yourself a lion among the nations,
> but you are like a dragon in the seas;
> you thrash about in your streams,
> trouble the water with your feet,
> and foul your*ᵃ* streams.

3 Thus says the Lord GOD:
> In an assembly of many peoples
> I will throw my net over you;
> and I*ᵇ* will haul you up in my dragnet.

4 I will throw you on the ground,
> on the open field I will fling you,
> and will cause all the birds of the air to settle on you,
> and I will let the wild animals of the whole earth
> gorge themselves with you.

5 I will strew your flesh on the mountains,
> and fill the valleys with your carcass.*ᶜ*

6 I will drench the land with your flowing blood
> up to the mountains,
> and the watercourses will be filled with you.

7 When I blot you out, I will cover the heavens,
> and make their stars dark;
> I will cover the sun with a cloud,
> and the moon shall not give its light.

8 All the shining lights of the heavens
> I will darken above you,
> and put darkness on your land,
> says the Lord GOD.

9 I will trouble the hearts of many peoples,
> as I carry you captive*ᵈ* among the nations,
> into countries you have not known.

10 I will make many peoples appalled at you;
> their kings shall shudder because of you.
> When I brandish my sword before them,
> they shall tremble every moment
> for their lives, each one of them,
> on the day of your downfall.

11 For thus says the Lord GOD:
> The sword of the king of Babylon shall come
> against you.

12 I will cause your hordes to fall
> by the swords of mighty ones,
> all of them most terrible among the nations.
> They shall bring to ruin the pride of Egypt,
> and all its hordes shall perish.

13 I will destroy all its livestock
> from beside abundant waters;
> and no human foot shall trouble them any more,
> nor shall the hoofs of cattle trouble them.

14 Then I will make their waters clear,
> and cause their streams to run like oil, says the
> Lord GOD.

15 When I make the land of Egypt desolate

---

a Heb *their*   *b* Gk Vg: Heb *they*   *c* Symmachus Syr Vg: Heb *your height*
d Gk: Heb *bring your destruction*

Chant

EZEKIEL 32.15–16

Music is a powerful force that can be used to build up or tear down, to make people happy or sad. It can articulate love or revitalize revolution or express otherwise inexpressible sadness.

In this passage, the women chant a lament for Egypt, a nation that squandered so much of its potential. What opportunities in our society are wasted through greed, addictions, violence and ignorance? Try writing a chant, a lament, over potential left unfulfilled. Sing your lament for the people and nations who waste potential and leave possibilities unexplored.

See Meeting God in Scripture

Blow the Trumpet

EZEKIEL 33.1–9

The sentinel is to blow the trumpet when the enemy approaches. Likewise, the responsibility for warning the people of impending doom was squarely on the prophet Ezekiel's shoulders. In some communities today, a central siren announces that bad weather threatens or a civil threat exists. Trumpet blasts and loud sirens serve the same purpose: to alert the people who hear them to impending danger.

Are you in danger? Have you drifted away from God? Do your deeds match your words? Is your religious community in danger because it does not take God's Word seriously? Who is sounding a trumpet blast? Is the nation in trouble? Are you called to be a sentinel? Is there an injustice or a wrong to which no one is paying attention? Is it time to raise your trumpet?

See Meeting God in Community

and when the land is stripped of all that fills it,
when I strike down all who live in it,
then they shall know that I am the LORD.
16 This is a lamentation; it shall be chanted.
The women of the nations shall chant it.
Over Egypt and all its hordes they shall chant it,
says the Lord GOD.

Dirge over Egypt

17 In the twelfth year, in the first month,*a* on the fifteenth day of the month, the word of the LORD came to me:
18 Mortal, wail over the hordes of Egypt,
and send them down,
with Egypt*b* and the daughters of majestic nations,
to the world below,
with those who go down to the Pit.
19 "Whom do you surpass in beauty?
Go down! Be laid to rest with the uncircumcised!"
20 They shall fall among those who are killed by the sword. Egypt*c* has been handed over to the sword; carry away both it and its hordes. 21 The mighty chiefs shall speak of them, with their helpers, out of the midst of Sheol: "They have come down, they lie still, the uncircumcised, killed by the sword."

22 Assyria is there, and all its company, their graves all around it, all of them killed, fallen by the sword. 23 Their graves are set in the uttermost parts of the Pit. Its company is all around its grave, all of them killed, fallen by the sword, who spread terror in the land of the living.

24 Elam is there, and all its hordes around its grave; all of them killed, fallen by the sword, who went down uncircumcised into the world below, who spread terror in the land of the living. They bear their shame with those who go down to the Pit. 25 They have made Elam*b* a bed among the slain with all its hordes, their graves all around it, all of them uncircumcised, killed by the sword; for terror of them was spread in the land of the living, and they bear their shame with those who go down to the Pit; they are placed among the slain.

26 Meshech and Tubal are there, and all their multitude, their graves all around them, all of them uncircumcised, killed by the sword; for they spread terror in the land of the living. 27 And they do not lie with the fallen warriors of long ago*d* who went down to Sheol with their weapons of war, whose swords were laid under their heads, and whose shields*e* are upon their bones; for the terror of the warriors was in the land of the living. 28 So you shall be broken and lie among the uncircumcised, with those who are killed by the sword.

29 Edom is there, its kings and all its princes, who for all their might are laid with those who are killed by the sword; they lie with the uncircumcised, with those who go down to the Pit.

30 The princes of the north are there, all of them, and all the Sidonians, who have gone down in shame with the slain, for all the terror that they caused by their might; they lie uncircumcised with those who are killed by the sword, and bear their shame with those who go down to the Pit.

31 When Pharaoh sees them, he will be consoled for all

a Gk: Heb lacks *in the first month*   *b* Heb *it*   *c* Heb *It*   *d* Gk Old Latin: Heb *of the uncircumcised*   *e* Cn: Heb *iniquities*

his hordes—Pharaoh and all his army, killed by the sword, says the Lord GOD. [32]For he[a] spread terror in the land of the living; therefore he shall be laid to rest among the uncircumcised, with those who are slain by the sword—Pharaoh and all his multitude, says the Lord GOD.

Ezekiel Israel's Sentry

33 The word of the LORD came to me: [2]O Mortal, speak to your people and say to them, If I bring the sword upon a land, and the people of the land take one of their number as their sentinel; [3]and if the sentinel sees the sword coming upon the land and blows the trumpet and warns the people; [4]then if any who hear the sound of the trumpet do not take warning, and the sword comes and takes them away, their blood shall be upon their own heads. [5]They heard the sound of the trumpet and did not take warning; their blood shall be upon themselves. But if they had taken warning, they would have saved their lives. [6]But if the sentinel sees the sword coming and does not blow the trumpet, so that the people are not warned, and the sword comes and takes any of them, they are taken away in their iniquity, but their blood I will require at the sentinel's hand.

[7] So you, mortal, I have made a sentinel for the house of Israel; whenever you hear a word from my mouth, you shall give them warning from me. [8]If I say to the wicked, "O wicked ones, you shall surely die," and you do not speak to warn the wicked to turn from their ways, the wicked shall die in their iniquity, but their blood I will require at your hand. [9]But if you warn the wicked to turn from their ways, and they do not turn from their ways, the wicked shall die in their iniquity, but you will have saved your life.

God's Justice and Mercy

[10] Now you, mortal, say to the house of Israel, Thus you have said: "Our transgressions and our sins weigh upon us, and we waste away because of them; how then can we live?" [11]Say to them, As I live, says the Lord GOD, I have no pleasure in the death of the wicked, but that the wicked turn from their ways and live; turn back, turn back from your evil ways; for why will you die, O house of Israel? [12]And you, mortal, say to your people, The righteousness of the righteous shall not save them when they transgress; and as for the wickedness of the wicked, it shall not make them stumble when they turn from their wickedness; and the righteous shall not be able to live by their righteousness[b] when they sin. [13]Though I say to the righteous that they shall surely live, yet if they trust in their righteousness and commit iniquity, none of their righteous deeds shall be remembered; but in the iniquity that they have committed they shall die. [14]Again, though I say to the wicked, "You shall surely die," yet if they turn from their sin and do what is lawful and right— [15]if the wicked restore the pledge, give back what they have taken by robbery, and walk in the statutes of life, committing no iniquity—they shall surely live, they shall not die. [16]None of the sins that they have committed shall be remembered against them; they have done what is lawful and right, they shall surely live.

[17] Yet your people say, "The way of the Lord is not just," when it is their own way that is not just. [18]When the righteous

---

Turn Back to God

EZEKIEL 33.11–16

"And then he showed me a little thing, the size of a hazelnut, lying in the palm of my hand, as it seemed to me. It was as round as a ball. I looked at it with the eye of my understanding and thought, *What can this be?* It was answered generally thus: 'It is all that is made.' I marveled that it could last, for it was so little that it could suddenly have become nothing. I was answered in my understanding, 'It lasts and ever shall, for God loves it.' And so everything has being by the love of God. In this little thing I saw three properties. The first is that God made it, the second that God loves it, and the third that God keeps it."

—JULIAN OF NORWICH,
Showings

The Whole Person Obeys

EZEKIEL 33.31–33

The people of Israel are physically present at worship, but their minds and hearts are somewhere else. Although they listen to the word of God, they have no intention of obeying it.

Draw a large picture of a person. (Artistic ability not required!) Next to the mouth you have drawn, write words of flattery that you might use—that are only partially true or hollow-sounding—to praise others. Draw a heart and inside of it write words of greed you might use to express some of your attitudes about money and possessions. Lastly, near the feet write some words that define those things that draw you away from the path of discipleship. Now draw another person and put words of kindness by the mouth, words of love and compassion inside the heart, and words of service next to the feet. Offer a prayer that your whole being might be responsive to God's guidance.

See Meeting God in Prayer

turn from their righteousness, and commit iniquity, they shall die for it.[a] [19]And when the wicked turn from their wickedness, and do what is lawful and right, they shall live by it.[a] [20]Yet you say, "The way of the Lord is not just." O house of Israel, I will judge all of you according to your ways!

The Fall of Jerusalem

21 In the twelfth year of our exile, in the tenth month, on the fifth day of the month, someone who had escaped from Jerusalem came to me and said, "The city has fallen." [22]Now the hand of the LORD had been upon me the evening before the fugitive came; but he had opened my mouth by the time the fugitive came to me in the morning; so my mouth was opened, and I was no longer unable to speak.

The Survivors in Judah

23 The word of the LORD came to me: [24]Mortal, the inhabitants of these waste places in the land of Israel keep saying, "Abraham was only one man, yet he got possession of the land; but we are many; the land is surely given us to possess." [25]Therefore say to them, Thus says the Lord GOD: You eat flesh with the blood, and lift up your eyes to your idols, and shed blood; shall you then possess the land? [26]You depend on your swords, you commit abominations, and each of you defiles his neighbor's wife; shall you then possess the land? [27]Say this to them, Thus says the Lord GOD: As I live, surely those who are in the waste places shall fall by the sword; and those who are in the open field I will give to the wild animals to be devoured; and those who are in strongholds and in caves shall die by pestilence. [28]I will make the land a desolation and a waste, and its proud might shall come to an end; and the mountains of Israel shall be so desolate that no one will pass through. [29]Then they shall know that I am the LORD, when I have made the land a desolation and a waste because of all their abominations that they have committed.

30 As for you, mortal, your people who talk together about you by the walls, and at the doors of the houses, say to one another, each to a neighbor, "Come and hear what the word is that comes from the LORD." [31]They come to you as people come, and they sit before you as my people, and they hear your words, but they will not obey them. For flattery is on their lips, but their heart is set on their gain. [32]To them you are like a singer of love songs,[b] one who has a beautiful voice and plays well on an instrument; they hear what you say, but they will not do it. [33]When this comes—and come it will!—then they shall know that a prophet has been among them.

Israel's False Shepherds

34 The word of the LORD came to me: [2]Mortal, prophesy against the shepherds of Israel: prophesy, and say to them—to the shepherds: Thus says the Lord GOD: Ah, you shepherds of Israel who have been feeding yourselves! Should not shepherds feed the sheep? [3]You eat the fat, you clothe yourselves with the wool, you slaughter the fatlings; but you do not feed the sheep. [4]You have not strengthened the weak, you have not healed the sick, you have not bound up the injured, you have not brought back

a Heb *them*   *b* Cn: Heb *like a love song*

the strayed, you have not sought the lost, but with force and harshness you have ruled them. ⁵So they were scattered, because there was no shepherd; and scattered, they became food for all the wild animals. ⁶My sheep were scattered, they wandered over all the mountains and on every high hill; my sheep were scattered over all the face of the earth, with no one to search or seek for them.

7 Therefore, you shepherds, hear the word of the LORD: ⁸As I live, says the Lord GOD, because my sheep have become a prey, and my sheep have become food for all the wild animals, since there was no shepherd; and because my shepherds have not searched for my sheep, but the shepherds have fed themselves, and have not fed my sheep; ⁹therefore, you shepherds, hear the word of the LORD: ¹⁰Thus says the Lord GOD, I am against the shepherds; and I will demand my sheep at their hand, and put a stop to their feeding the sheep; no longer shall the shepherds feed themselves. I will rescue my sheep from their mouths, so that they may not be food for them.

God, the True Shepherd

11 For thus says the Lord GOD: I myself will search for my sheep, and will seek them out. ¹²As shepherds seek out their flocks when they are among their scattered sheep, so I will seek out my sheep. I will rescue them from all the places to which they have been scattered on a day of clouds and thick darkness. ¹³I will bring them out from the peoples and gather them from the countries, and will bring them into their own land; and I will feed them on the mountains of Israel, by the watercourses, and in all the inhabited parts of the land. ¹⁴I will feed them with good pasture, and the mountain heights of Israel shall be their pasture; there they shall lie down in good grazing land, and they shall feed on rich pasture on the mountains of Israel. ¹⁵I myself will be the shepherd of my sheep, and I will make them lie down, says the Lord GOD. ¹⁶I will seek the lost, and I will bring back the strayed, and I will bind up the injured, and I will strengthen the weak, but the fat and the strong I will destroy. I will feed them with justice.

17 As for you, my flock, thus says the Lord GOD: I shall judge between sheep and sheep, between rams and goats: ¹⁸Is it not enough for you to feed on the good pasture, but you must tread down with your feet the rest of your pasture? When you drink of clear water, must you foul the rest with your feet? ¹⁹And must my sheep eat what you have trodden with your feet, and drink what you have fouled with your feet?

20 Therefore, thus says the Lord GOD to them: I myself will judge between the fat sheep and the lean sheep. ²¹Because you pushed with flank and shoulder, and butted at all the weak animals with your horns until you scattered them far and wide, ²²I will save my flock, and they shall no longer be ravaged; and I will judge between sheep and sheep.

23 I will set up over them one shepherd, my servant David, and he shall feed them: he shall feed them and be their shepherd. ²⁴And I, the LORD, will be their God, and my servant David shall be prince among them; I, the LORD, have spoken.

25 I will make with them a covenant of peace and banish wild animals from the land, so that they may live in the

The Good Shepherd

EZEKIEL 34.1–31

The people of Israel are like abandoned sheep. Their leaders have been poor shepherds who have not gathered them, nursed their wounds, fed them or protected them from danger. So God promises that he will lead them himself and place over them a shepherd like David, thereby promising to establish a new covenant of peace through the coming Messiah.

Turn to either Psalm 23 or John 10 (or both) and read these familiar texts that tell of the caring, guiding role of the shepherd. Reflect on ways in which you need to be cared for. Are you lost? Are you carrying wounds or resentments that get in the way of joyful living? Are you hungry for spiritual food? Has someone given you false guidance? Imagine a plentiful pasture and a gentle shepherd. Repeat as a prayer guide, "The LORD is my shepherd, I shall not want" (Psalm 23.1).

See Meeting God in Scripture

Hope and Restoration

EZEKIEL 36.8–12

After many chapters of doom and gloom, the prophet speaks a word of hope and restoration. The people will come home from exile, the towns will be rebuilt and the land will once again become fruitful. God promises them, "I will do more good to you than ever before."

Restoration is a word of hope. Think about times of restoration in your life—a restoration to health, a renewal of your family life after an absence or separation, a restoration of prosperity after a transition or loss. Perhaps you could plant a tree or a garden as an affirmation of trust in God's ability to bring about hope and restoration.

See Meeting God in Everyday Life

wild and sleep in the woods securely. ²⁶I will make them and the region around my hill a blessing; and I will send down the showers in their season; they shall be showers of blessing. ²⁷The trees of the field shall yield their fruit, and the earth shall yield its increase. They shall be secure on their soil; and they shall know that I am the LORD, when I break the bars of their yoke, and save them from the hands of those who enslaved them. ²⁸They shall no more be plunder for the nations, nor shall the animals of the land devour them; they shall live in safety, and no one shall make them afraid. ²⁹I will provide for them a splendid vegetation so that they shall no more be consumed with hunger in the land, and no longer suffer the insults of the nations. ³⁰They shall know that I, the LORD their God, am with them, and that they, the house of Israel, are my people, says the Lord GOD. ³¹You are my sheep, the sheep of my pasture*ᵃ* and I am your God, says the Lord GOD.

Judgment on Mount Seir

35 The word of the LORD came to me: ²Mortal, set your face against Mount Seir, and prophesy against it, ³and say to it, Thus says the Lord GOD:

I am against you, Mount Seir;
  I stretch out my hand against you
  to make you a desolation and a waste.
⁴ I lay your towns in ruins;
  you shall become a desolation,
  and you shall know that I am the LORD.

⁵Because you cherished an ancient enmity, and gave over the people of Israel to the power of the sword at the time of their calamity, at the time of their final punishment; ⁶therefore, as I live, says the Lord GOD, I will prepare you for blood, and blood shall pursue you; since you did not hate bloodshed, bloodshed shall pursue you. ⁷I will make Mount Seir a waste and a desolation; and I will cut off from it all who come and go. ⁸I will fill its mountains with the slain; on your hills and in your valleys and in all your watercourses those killed with the sword shall fall. ⁹I will make you a perpetual desolation, and your cities shall never be inhabited. Then you shall know that I am the LORD.

10 Because you said, "These two nations and these two countries shall be mine, and we will take possession of them,"—although the LORD was there— ¹¹therefore, as I live, says the Lord GOD, I will deal with you according to the anger and envy that you showed because of your hatred against them; and I will make myself known among you,*ᵇ* when I judge you. ¹²You shall know that I, the LORD, have heard all the abusive speech that you uttered against the mountains of Israel, saying, "They are laid desolate, they are given us to devour." ¹³And you magnified yourselves against me with your mouth, and multiplied your words against me; I heard it. ¹⁴Thus says the Lord GOD: As the whole earth rejoices, I will make you desolate. ¹⁵As you rejoiced over the inheritance of the house of Israel, because it was desolate, so I will deal with you; you shall be desolate, Mount Seir, and all Edom, all of it. Then they shall know that I am the LORD.

a Gk OL: Heb *pasture, you are people*   *b* Gk: Heb *them*

Blessing on Israel

36 And you, mortal, prophesy to the mountains of Israel, and say: O mountains of Israel, hear the word of the LORD. ²Thus says the Lord GOD: Because the enemy said of you, "Aha!" and, "The ancient heights have become our possession," ³therefore prophesy, and say: Thus says the Lord GOD: Because they made you desolate indeed, and crushed you from all sides, so that you became the possession of the rest of the nations, and you became an object of gossip and slander among the people; ⁴therefore, O mountains of Israel, hear the word of the Lord GOD: Thus says the Lord GOD to the mountains and the hills, the watercourses and the valleys, the desolate wastes and the deserted towns, which have become a source of plunder and an object of derision to the rest of the nations all around; ⁵therefore thus says the Lord GOD: I am speaking in my hot jealousy against the rest of the nations, and against all Edom, who, with wholehearted joy and utter contempt, took my land as their possession, because of its pasture, to plunder it. ⁶Therefore prophesy concerning the land of Israel, and say to the mountains and hills, to the watercourses and valleys, Thus says the Lord GOD: I am speaking in my jealous wrath, because you have suffered the insults of the nations; ⁷therefore thus says the Lord GOD: I swear that the nations that are all around you shall themselves suffer insults.

8 But you, O mountains of Israel, shall shoot out your branches, and yield your fruit to my people Israel; for they shall soon come home. ⁹See now, I am for you; I will turn to you, and you shall be tilled and sown; ¹⁰and I will multiply your population, the whole house of Israel, all of it; the towns shall be inhabited and the waste places rebuilt; ¹¹and I will multiply human beings and animals upon you. They shall increase and be fruitful; and I will cause you to be inhabited as in your former times, and will do more good to you than ever before. Then you shall know that I am the LORD. ¹²I will lead people upon you—my people Israel—and they shall possess you, and you shall be their inheritance. No longer shall you bereave them of children.

13 Thus says the Lord GOD: Because they say to you, "You devour people, and you bereave your nation of children," ¹⁴therefore you shall no longer devour people and no longer bereave your nation of children, says the Lord GOD; ¹⁵and no longer will I let you hear the insults of the nations, no longer shall you bear the disgrace of the peoples; and no longer shall you cause your nation to stumble, says the Lord GOD.

The Renewal of Israel

16 The word of the LORD came to me: ¹⁷Mortal, when the house of Israel lived on their own soil, they defiled it with their ways and their deeds; their conduct in my sight was like the uncleanness of a woman in her menstrual period. ¹⁸So I poured out my wrath upon them for the blood that they had shed upon the land, and for the idols with which they had defiled it. ¹⁹I scattered them among the nations, and they were dispersed through the countries; in accordance with their conduct and their deeds I judged them. ²⁰But when they came to the nations, wherever they came, they profaned my holy name, in that it was said of them, "These are the people

---

Clean and New

EZEKIEL 36.16–28

The images in this passage are like sunshine after a long, hard winter. Ezekiel declares that the nation and the people will be sprinkled with clean water and given a new spirit and a new heart. The relationship between God and Israel is to be restored.

What does this passage say about God's character? What does it say about our need for forgiveness and salvation? How might you pray to God, who is seeking you at this very moment? Sprinkle a little water on yourself and remember how God's love and forgiveness bring you the sense of being fresh and newly cleansed. Better still, "Remember your baptism and be thankful" (United Methodist "Service of Baptism Covenant I").

See Meeting God in Worship

In the Valley

EZEKIEL 37.1–14

Join Ezekiel in his visit to the valley of dry bones. Imagine you are there, looking out over the barren, dry landscape covered with bleached white bones. The smell of dust and decay is acrid in your nostrils. You wonder with Ezekiel, "How can these bones live again?"

Tell the bones to hear the word of the Lord and live. Watch and listen as the bones shake and rattle, bone meeting bone as they snap together.

Then breath comes from the four winds as you call it to come. Hear the rush of the wind and feel its breeze. See the movement of breath in the bellies and chests of the flesh. See the bones become living people and begin to dance. Now read verses 12–14. Ask God to continue to breathe life into you and your congregation.

See Meeting God in Scripture

of the LORD, and yet they had to go out of his land." [21] But I had concern for my holy name, which the house of Israel had profaned among the nations to which they came.

22 Therefore say to the house of Israel, Thus says the Lord GOD: It is not for your sake, O house of Israel, that I am about to act, but for the sake of my holy name, which you have profaned among the nations to which you came. [23] I will sanctify my great name, which has been profaned among the nations, and which you have profaned among them; and the nations shall know that I am the LORD, says the Lord GOD, when through you I display my holiness before their eyes. [24] I will take you from the nations, and gather you from all the countries, and bring you into your own land. [25] I will sprinkle clean water upon you, and you shall be clean from all your uncleannesses, and from all your idols I will cleanse you. [26] A new heart I will give you, and a new spirit I will put within you; and I will remove from your body the heart of stone and give you a heart of flesh. [27] I will put my spirit within you, and make you follow my statutes and be careful to observe my ordinances. [28] Then you shall live in the land that I gave to your ancestors; and you shall be my people, and I will be your God. [29] I will save you from all your uncleannesses, and I will summon the grain and make it abundant and lay no famine upon you. [30] I will make the fruit of the tree and the produce of the field abundant, so that you may never again suffer the disgrace of famine among the nations. [31] Then you shall remember your evil ways, and your dealings that were not good; and you shall loathe yourselves for your iniquities and your abominable deeds. [32] It is not for your sake that I will act, says the Lord GOD; let that be known to you. Be ashamed and dismayed for your ways, O house of Israel.

33 Thus says the Lord GOD: On the day that I cleanse you from all your iniquities, I will cause the towns to be inhabited, and the waste places shall be rebuilt. [34] The land that was desolate shall be tilled, instead of being the desolation that it was in the sight of all who passed by. [35] And they will say, "This land that was desolate has become like the garden of Eden; and the waste and desolate and ruined towns are now inhabited and fortified." [36] Then the nations that are left all around you shall know that I, the LORD, have rebuilt the ruined places, and replanted that which was desolate; I, the LORD, have spoken, and I will do it.

37 Thus says the Lord GOD: I will also let the house of Israel ask me to do this for them: to increase their population like a flock. [38] Like the flock for sacrifices,[a] like the flock at Jerusalem during her appointed festivals, so shall the ruined towns be filled with flocks of people. Then they shall know that I am the LORD.

The Valley of Dry Bones

37 The hand of the LORD came upon me, and he brought me out by the spirit of the LORD and set me down in the middle of a valley; it was full of bones. [2] He led me all around them; there were very many lying in the valley, and they were very dry. [3] He said to me, "Mortal, can these bones live?" I answered, "O Lord GOD, you know." [4] Then he said to me, "Prophesy to these bones, and say to them: O dry bones, hear the word of the LORD. [5] Thus says the Lord GOD to these bones: I will cause breath[b] to enter

a Heb *flock of holy things*   *b* Or *spirit*

you, and you shall live. [6]I will lay sinews on you, and will cause flesh to come upon you, and cover you with skin, and put breath[a] in you, and you shall live; and you shall know that I am the Lord."

7 So I prophesied as I had been commanded; and as I prophesied, suddenly there was a noise, a rattling, and the bones came together, bone to its bone. [8]I looked, and there were sinews on them, and flesh had come upon them, and skin had covered them; but there was no breath in them. [9]Then he said to me, "Prophesy to the breath, prophesy, mortal, and say to the breath:[b] Thus says the Lord God: Come from the four winds, O breath,[b] and breathe upon these slain, that they may live." [10]I prophesied as he commanded me, and the breath came into them, and they lived, and stood on their feet, a vast multitude.

11 Then he said to me, "Mortal, these bones are the whole house of Israel. They say, 'Our bones are dried up, and our hope is lost; we are cut off completely.' [12]Therefore prophesy, and say to them, Thus says the Lord God: I am going to open your graves, and bring you up from your graves, O my people; and I will bring you back to the land of Israel. [13]And you shall know that I am the Lord, when I open your graves, and bring you up from your graves, O my people. [14]I will put my spirit within you, and you shall live, and I will place you on your own soil; then you shall know that I, the Lord, have spoken and will act, says the Lord."

The Two Sticks

15 The word of the Lord came to me: [16]Mortal, take a stick and write on it, "For Judah, and the Israelites associated with it"; then take another stick and write on it, "For Joseph (the stick of Ephraim) and all the house of Israel associated with it"; [17]and join them together into one stick, so that they may become one in your hand. [18]And when your people say to you, "Will you not show us what you mean by these?" [19]say to them, Thus says the Lord God: I am about to take the stick of Joseph (which is in the hand of Ephraim) and the tribes of Israel associated with it; and I will put the stick of Judah upon it,[c] and make them one stick, in order that they may be one in my hand. [20]When the sticks on which you write are in your hand before their eyes, [21]then say to them, Thus says the Lord God: I will take the people of Israel from the nations among which they have gone, and will gather them from every quarter, and bring them to their own land. [22]I will make them one nation in the land, on the mountains of Israel; and one king shall be king over them all. Never again shall they be two nations, and never again shall they be divided into two kingdoms. [23]They shall never again defile themselves with their idols and their detestable things, or with any of their transgressions. I will save them from all the apostasies into which they have fallen,[d] and will cleanse them. Then they shall be my people, and I will be their God.

24 My servant David shall be king over them; and they shall all have one shepherd. They shall follow my ordinances and be careful to observe my statutes. [25]They shall live in the land that I gave to my servant Jacob, in which your ancestors lived; they and their children and their children's children shall live there forever; and my servant David shall be their

An Everlasting Covenant

EZEKIEL 37.24–28

"O Fairness, so ancient, and yet so new! I love you too late. Look, you were internal, and I external. And I looked for you in external things. Unlovely, I rushed thoughtlessly among the things of beauty you made. You were with me, but I was not with you. Those things kept me far from you, even though unless they were in you they would not be at all. You called and cried aloud and forced open my deafness. You gleamed and shone and chased away my blindness. You exhaled a fragrance, and I drew in my breath and still pant after you. I tasted and still hunger and thirst. You touched me, and I burned for your peace."

—AUGUSTINE,
Confessions

---

a Or *spirit*   b Or *wind* or *spirit*   c Heb *I will put them upon it*
d Another reading is *from all the settlements in which they have sinned*

When What Looks Like Disaster Isn't

EZEKIEL 38.16

A nation from the north is coming like a dark cloud to crush Israel, but the ultimate defeat of that marauding nation will show that God is still in charge.

Remember a time in your life when some disaster threatened the "end" of your world. Can you remember how you felt, what you did? With the gift of hindsight, note how where you have been has brought you to where you are today. How are you a different person because of that experience? How did God bring you to a new day? Did you thank God? If not, today is a good day for a prayer of thanksgiving.

See Meeting God in Everyday Life

prince forever. ²⁶I will make a covenant of peace with them; it shall be an everlasting covenant with them; and I will bless*ᵃ* them and multiply them, and will set my sanctuary among them forevermore. ²⁷My dwelling place shall be with them; and I will be their God, and they shall be my people. ²⁸Then the nations shall know that I the LORD sanctify Israel, when my sanctuary is among them forevermore.

Invasion by Gog

38 The word of the LORD came to me: ²Mortal, set your face toward Gog, of the land of Magog, the chief prince of Meshech and Tubal. Prophesy against him ³and say: Thus says the Lord GOD: I am against you, O Gog, chief prince of Meshech and Tubal; ⁴I will turn you around and put hooks into your jaws, and I will lead you out with all your army, horses and horsemen, all of them clothed in full armor, a great company, all of them with shield and buckler, wielding swords. ⁵Persia, Ethiopia,*ᵇ* and Put are with them, all of them with buckler and helmet; ⁶Gomer and all its troops; Beth-togarmah from the remotest parts of the north with all its troops—many peoples are with you.

7 Be ready and keep ready, you and all the companies that are assembled around you, and hold yourselves in reserve for them. ⁸After many days you shall be mustered; in the latter years you shall go against a land restored from war, a land where people were gathered from many nations on the mountains of Israel, which had long lain waste; its people were brought out from the nations and now are living in safety, all of them. ⁹You shall advance, coming on like a storm; you shall be like a cloud covering the land, you and all your troops, and many peoples with you.

10 Thus says the Lord GOD: On that day thoughts will come into your mind, and you will devise an evil scheme. ¹¹You will say, "I will go up against the land of unwalled villages; I will fall upon the quiet people who live in safety, all of them living without walls, and having no bars or gates"; ¹²to seize spoil and carry off plunder; to assail the waste places that are now inhabited, and the people who were gathered from the nations, who are acquiring cattle and goods, who live at the center*ᶜ* of the earth. ¹³Sheba and Dedan and the merchants of Tarshish and all its young warriors*ᵈ* will say to you, "Have you come to seize spoil? Have you assembled your horde to carry off plunder, to carry away silver and gold, to take away cattle and goods, to seize a great amount of booty?"

14 Therefore, mortal, prophesy, and say to Gog: Thus says the Lord GOD: On that day when my people Israel are living securely, you will rouse yourself*ᵉ* ¹⁵and come from your place out of the remotest parts of the north, you and many peoples with you, all of them riding on horses, a great horde, a mighty army; ¹⁶you will come up against my people Israel, like a cloud covering the earth. In the latter days I will bring you against my land, so that the nations may know me, when through you, O Gog, I display my holiness before their eyes.

Judgment on Gog

17 Thus says the Lord GOD: Are you he of whom I spoke

a Tg: Heb *give*   *b* Or *Nubia*; Heb *Cush*   *c* Heb *navel*   *d* Heb *young lions*
e Gk: Heb *will you not know?*

in former days by my servants the prophets of Israel, who in those days prophesied for years that I would bring you against them? ¹⁸On that day, when Gog comes against the land of Israel, says the Lord GOD, my wrath shall be aroused. ¹⁹For in my jealousy and in my blazing wrath I declare: On that day there shall be a great shaking in the land of Israel; ²⁰the fish of the sea, and the birds of the air, and the animals of the field, and all creeping things that creep on the ground, and all human beings that are on the face of the earth, shall quake at my presence, and the mountains shall be thrown down, and the cliffs shall fall, and every wall shall tumble to the ground. ²¹I will summon the sword against Gog*ᵃ* inᵇ all my mountains, says the Lord GOD; the swords of all will be against their comrades. ²²With pestilence and bloodshed I will enter into judgment with him; and I will pour down torrential rains and hailstones, fire and sulfur, upon him and his troops and the many peoples that are with him. ²³So I will display my greatness and my holiness and make myself known in the eyes of many nations. Then they shall know that I am the LORD.

Gog's Armies Destroyed

39 And you, mortal, prophesy against Gog, and say: Thus says the Lord GOD: I am against you, O Gog, chief prince of Meshech and Tubal! ²I will turn you around and drive you forward, and bring you up from the remotest parts of the north, and lead you against the mountains of Israel. ³I will strike your bow from your left hand, and will make your arrows drop out of your right hand. ⁴You shall fall upon the mountains of Israel, you and all your troops and the peoples that are with you; I will give you to birds of prey of every kind and to the wild animals to be devoured. ⁵You shall fall in the open field; for I have spoken, says the Lord GOD. ⁶I will send fire on Magog and on those who live securely in the coastlands; and they shall know that I am the LORD.

7 My holy name I will make known among my people Israel; and I will not let my holy name be profaned any more; and the nations shall know that I am the LORD, the Holy One in Israel. ⁸It has come! It has happened, says the Lord GOD. This is the day of which I have spoken.

9 Then those who live in the towns of Israel will go out and make fires of the weapons and burn them—bucklers and shields, bows and arrows, handpikes and spears—and they will make fires of them for seven years. ¹⁰They will not need to take wood out of the field or cut down any trees in the forests, for they will make their fires of the weapons; they will despoil those who despoiled them, and plunder those who plundered them, says the Lord GOD.

The Burial of Gog

11 On that day I will give to Gog a place for burial in Israel, the Valley of the Travelersᶜ east of the sea; it shall block the path of the travelers, for there Gog and all his horde will be buried; it shall be called the Valley of Hamon-gog.ᵈ ¹²Seven months the house of Israel shall spend burying them, in order to cleanse the land. ¹³All the people of the land shall bury them; and it will bring them honor on the day that I show my glory, says the Lord GOD. ¹⁴They will set

a Heb *him*   *b* Heb *to* or *for*   *c* Or *of the Abarim*   *d* That is, *the Horde of Gog*

Hide and Seek

EZEKIEL 39.11–29

We often think that it is we humans who hide from God and God who seeks us. But here in this passage we have the image of God hiding from humanity, or at least turning away: "[I] hid my face from them."

The mystics have written of experiencing these times when God seems distant or absent. Jesus experienced such a time as he hung on the cross on our behalf (see Matthew 27.46). Does God seem distant or absent from you right now? Why do you think such moments or seasons occur? What do you think is necessary for you to restore a keen awareness of God's presence? Read Psalm 51 for one answer.

See Meeting God in Prayer

Visions

EZEKIEL 40.1–4

There are many kinds of sight. We speak of plain sight (seeing what is right before us) and hindsight (clarity of sight when we look back at something that has already happened). Just as important is insight, the perception of deeper layers of wisdom and meaning. Insight has an element of mystery or grace, because we can't manufacture it; it is a gift from God.

Do you have insight? How can you humbly share it with others? Have you ever had a vision? What was it about? Was it a personal vision or for the wider community? Have you shared the vision with anyone? What steps have you taken to act on this gift from God?

See Meeting God in Community

apart men to pass through the land regularly and bury any invaders*a* who remain on the face of the land, so as to cleanse it; for seven months they shall make their search. [15]As the searchers*a* pass through the land, anyone who sees a human bone shall set up a sign by it, until the buriers have buried it in the Valley of Hamon-gog.*b* [16](A city Hamonah*c* is there also.) Thus they shall cleanse the land.

17 As for you, mortal, thus says the Lord GOD: Speak to the birds of every kind and to all the wild animals: Assemble and come, gather from all around to the sacrificial feast that I am preparing for you, a great sacrificial feast on the mountains of Israel, and you shall eat flesh and drink blood. [18]You shall eat the flesh of the mighty, and drink the blood of the princes of the earth—of rams, of lambs, and of goats, of bulls, all of them fatlings of Bashan. [19]You shall eat fat until you are filled, and drink blood until you are drunk, at the sacrificial feast that I am preparing for you. [20]And you shall be filled at my table with horses and charioteers,*d* with warriors and all kinds of soldiers, says the Lord GOD.

Israel Restored to the Land

21 I will display my glory among the nations; and all the nations shall see my judgment that I have executed, and my hand that I have laid on them. [22]The house of Israel shall know that I am the LORD their God, from that day forward. [23]And the nations shall know that the house of Israel went into captivity for their iniquity, because they dealt treacherously with me. So I hid my face from them and gave them into the hand of their adversaries, and they all fell by the sword. [24]I dealt with them according to their uncleanness and their transgressions, and hid my face from them.

25 Therefore thus says the Lord GOD: Now I will restore the fortunes of Jacob, and have mercy on the whole house of Israel; and I will be jealous for my holy name. [26]They shall forget*e* their shame, and all the treachery they have practiced against me, when they live securely in their land with no one to make them afraid, [27]when I have brought them back from the peoples and gathered them from their enemies' lands, and through them have displayed my holiness in the sight of many nations. [28]Then they shall know that I am the LORD their God because I sent them into exile among the nations, and then gathered them into their own land. I will leave none of them behind; [29]and I will never again hide my face from them, when I pour out my spirit upon the house of Israel, says the Lord GOD.

The Vision of the New Temple

40 In the twenty-fifth year of our exile, at the beginning of the year, on the tenth day of the month, in the fourteenth year after the city was struck down, on that very day, the hand of the LORD was upon me, and he brought me there. [2]He brought me, in visions of God, to the land of Israel, and set me down upon a very high mountain, on which was a structure like a city to the south. [3]When he brought me there, a man was there, whose appearance shone like bronze, with a linen cord and a measuring reed in his hand; and he was standing in the gateway. [4]The man said to me, "Mortal, look closely and lis-

a Heb *travelers*   *b* That is, *the Horde of Gog*   *c* That is *The Horde*
d Heb *chariots*   *e* Another reading is *They shall bear*

ten attentively, and set your mind upon all that I shall show you, for you were brought here in order that I might show it to you; declare all that you see to the house of Israel."

5 Now there was a wall all around the outside of the temple area. The length of the measuring reed in the man's hand was six long cubits, each being a cubit and a handbreadth in length; so he measured the thickness of the wall, one reed; and the height, one reed. [6]Then he went into the gateway facing east, going up its steps, and measured the threshold of the gate, one reed deep.[a] There were [7]recesses, and each recess was one reed wide and one reed deep; and the space between the recesses, five cubits; and the threshold of the gate by the vestibule of the gate at the inner end was one reed deep. [8]Then he measured the inner vestibule of the gateway, one cubit. [9]Then he measured the vestibule of the gateway, eight cubits; and its pilasters, two cubits; and the vestibule of the gate was at the inner end. [10]There were three recesses on either side of the east gate; the three were of the same size; and the pilasters on either side were of the same size. [11]Then he measured the width of the opening of the gateway, ten cubits; and the width of the gateway, thirteen cubits. [12]There was a barrier before the recesses, one cubit on either side; and the recesses were six cubits on either side. [13]Then he measured the gate from the back[b] of the one recess to the back[b] of the other, a width of twenty-five cubits, from wall to wall.[c] [14]He measured[d] also the vestibule, twenty cubits; and the gate next to the pilaster on every side of the court.[e] [15]From the front of the gate at the entrance to the end of the inner vestibule of the gate was fifty cubits. [16]The recesses and their pilasters had windows, with shutters[e] on the inside of the gateway all around, and the vestibules also had windows on the inside all around; and on the pilasters were palm trees.

17 Then he brought me into the outer court; there were chambers there, and a pavement, all around the court; thirty chambers fronted on the pavement. [18]The pavement ran along the side of the gates, corresponding to the length of the gates; this was the lower pavement. [19]Then he measured the distance from the inner front of[f] the lower gate to the outer front of the inner court, one hundred cubits.[g]

20 Then he measured the gate of the outer court that faced north—its depth and width. [21]Its recesses, three on either side, and its pilasters and its vestibule were of the same size as those of the first gate; its depth was fifty cubits, and its width twenty-five cubits. [22]Its windows, its vestibule, and its palm trees were of the same size as those of the gate that faced toward the east. Seven steps led up to it; and its vestibule was on the inside.[h] [23]Opposite the gate on the north, as on the east, was a gate to the inner court; he measured from gate to gate, one hundred cubits.

24 Then he led me toward the south, and there was a gate on the south; and he measured its pilasters and its vestibule; they had the same dimensions as the others. [25]There were windows all around in it and in its vestibule, like the windows of the others; its depth was fifty cubits, and its width twenty-five cubits. [26]There were seven steps leading up to it; its vestibule was on the inside.[h] It had palm

The Measure of Worship

EZEKIEL 40.20–27

"When we come to a service of worship, we should come to participate, to bring our praise and honor and thanks—as well as our needs—and lay them at God's feet in the midst of this great mixed community of the present and the past. In this act, we are lifted out of our private world into a public one, out of our personal situations into a social situation . . . The humbling, enlarging, encompassing fellowship into which the church's corporate exercise sweeps us is a part of the Christian experience that we dare not forgo if we are able to attend."

—DOUGLAS STEERE,
Dimensions of Prayer

See *Meeting God in Worship*

---

a Heb *deep, and one threshold, one reed deep*   b Gk: Heb *roof*
c Heb *opening facing opening*   d Heb *made*   e Meaning of Heb uncertain
f Compare Gk: Heb *from before*   g Heb adds *the east and the north*
h Gk: Heb *before them*

The Most Holy Place

EZEKIEL 41.4

For the Israelites the most holy place had profound significance. For most people, having a place to pray is very important. Where is your most holy place of prayer? Do you have a room or area in your home designated to use for prayer and meditation? What sets it apart? Are there special pictures or objects in the room? Do you light candles? Is there a special chair? Do you keep a Bible, journal and other spiritual books nearby? Perhaps your holy place is in a church or small chapel. Or perhaps it is outside.

God can be present anywhere, of course, but often a designated place helps us turn our hearts and minds toward God. If you do not have a special holy place for prayer, consider finding or making one. Visit your holy place as often as you can.

See *Meeting God in Prayer*

trees on its pilasters, one on either side. [27]There was a gate on the south of the inner court; and he measured from gate to gate toward the south, one hundred cubits.

28 Then he brought me to the inner court by the south gate, and he measured the south gate; it was of the same dimensions as the others. [29]Its recesses, its pilasters, and its vestibule were of the same size as the others; and there were windows all around in it and in its vestibule; its depth was fifty cubits, and its width twenty-five cubits. [30]There were vestibules all around, twenty-five cubits deep and five cubits wide. [31]Its vestibule faced the outer court, and palm trees were on its pilasters, and its stairway had eight steps.

32 Then he brought me to the inner court on the east side, and he measured the gate; it was of the same size as the others. [33]Its recesses, its pilasters, and its vestibule were of the same dimensions as the others; and there were windows all around in it and in its vestibule; its depth was fifty cubits, and its width twenty-five cubits. [34]Its vestibule faced the outer court, and it had palm trees on its pilasters, on either side; and its stairway had eight steps.

35 Then he brought me to the north gate, and he measured it; it had the same dimensions as the others. [36]Its recesses, its pilasters, and its vestibule were of the same size as the others;[a] and it had windows all around. Its depth was fifty cubits, and its width twenty-five cubits. [37]Its vestibule[b] faced the outer court, and it had palm trees on its pilasters, on either side; and its stairway had eight steps.

38 There was a chamber with its door in the vestibule of the gate,[c] where the burnt offering was to be washed. [39]And in the vestibule of the gate were two tables on either side, on which the burnt offering and the sin offering and the guilt offering were to be slaughtered. [40]On the outside of the vestibule[d] at the entrance of the north gate were two tables; and on the other side of the vestibule of the gate were two tables. [41]Four tables were on the inside, and four tables on the outside of the side of the gate, eight tables, on which the sacrifices were to be slaughtered. [42]There were also four tables of hewn stone for the burnt offering, a cubit and a half long, and one cubit and a half wide, and one cubit high, on which the instruments were to be laid with which the burnt offerings and the sacrifices were slaughtered. [43]There were pegs, one handbreadth long, fastened all around the inside. And on the tables the flesh of the offering was to be laid.

44 On the outside of the inner gateway there were chambers for the singers in the inner court, one[e] at the side of the north gate facing south, the other at the side of the east gate facing north. [45]He said to me, "This chamber that faces south is for the priests who have charge of the temple, [46]and the chamber that faces north is for the priests who have charge of the altar; these are the descendants of Zadok, who alone among the descendants of Levi may come near to the LORD to minister to him." [47]He measured the court, one hundred cubits deep, and one hundred cubits wide, a square; and the altar was in front of the temple.

The Temple

48 Then he brought me to the vestibule of the temple

a One Ms: Compare verses 29 and 33: MT lacks *were of the same size as the others* b Gk Vg Compare verses 26, 31, 34: Heb *pilasters* c Cn: Heb *at the pilasters of the gates* d Cn: Heb *to him who goes up* e Heb lacks *one*

and measured the pilasters of the vestibule, five cubits on either side; and the width of the gate was fourteen cubits; and the sidewalls of the gate were three cubits[a] on either side. [49]The depth of the vestibule was twenty cubits, and the width twelve[b] cubits; ten steps led up[c] to it; and there were pillars beside the pilasters on either side.

41 Then he brought me to the nave, and measured the pilasters; on each side six cubits was the width of the pilasters.[d] [2]The width of the entrance was ten cubits; and the sidewalls of the entrance were five cubits on either side. He measured the length of the nave, forty cubits, and its width, twenty cubits. [3]Then he went into the inner room and measured the pilasters of the entrance, two cubits; and the width of the entrance, six cubits; and the sidewalls[e] of the entrance, seven cubits. [4]He measured the depth of the room, twenty cubits, and its width, twenty cubits, beyond the nave. And he said to me, This is the most holy place.

5 Then he measured the wall of the temple, six cubits thick; and the width of the side chambers, four cubits, all around the temple. [6]The side chambers were in three stories, one over another, thirty in each story. There were offsets[f] all around the wall of the temple to serve as supports for the side chambers, so that they should not be supported by the wall of the temple. [7]The passageway[g] of the side chambers widened from story to story; for the structure was supplied with a stairway all around the temple. For this reason the structure became wider from story to story. One ascended from the bottom story to the uppermost story by way of the middle one. [8]I saw also that the temple had a raised platform all around; the foundations of the side chambers measured a full reed of six long cubits. [9]The thickness of the outer wall of the side chambers was five cubits; and the free space between the side chambers of the temple [10]and the chambers of the court was a width of twenty cubits all around the temple on every side. [11]The side chambers opened onto the area left free, one door toward the north, and another door toward the south; and the width of the part that was left free was five cubits all around.

12 The building that was facing the temple yard on the west side was seventy cubits wide; and the wall of the building was five cubits thick all around, and its depth ninety cubits.

13 Then he measured the temple, one hundred cubits deep; and the yard and the building with its walls, one hundred cubits deep; [14]also the width of the east front of the temple and the yard, one hundred cubits.

15 Then he measured the depth of the building facing the yard at the west, together with its galleries[h] on either side, one hundred cubits.

The nave of the temple and the inner room and the outer[i] vestibule [16]were paneled,[j] and, all around, all three had windows with recessed[k] frames. Facing the threshold the temple was paneled with wood all around, from the floor up to the windows (now the windows were covered), [17]to the space above the door, even to the inner room, and

The Table of the Lord

EZEKIEL 41.15–22

"Whenever we come together around the table, take bread, bless it, break it, and give it to one another, saying, 'The Body of Christ,' we know that Jesus is among us not as a vague memory of a person who lived long ago but as a real, life-giving presence that transforms us. By eating the Body of Christ, we become the living Christ and we are enabled to discover our own chosenness and blessedness, acknowledge our brokenness, and trust that all we live we live for others. Thus, we, like Jesus himself, become food for the world."

—HENRI J. M. NOUWEN,
Bread for the Journey

See *Meeting God in Worship*

---

a Gk: Heb *and the width of the gate was three cubits*   *b* Gk: Heb *eleven*
c Gk: Heb *and by steps that went up*   *d* Compare Gk: Heb *tent*   *e* Gk: Heb
width   *f* Gk Compare 1 Kings 6.6: Heb *they entered*   *g* Cn: Heb *it was*
surrounded   *h* Cn: Meaning of Heb uncertain   *i* Gk: Heb *of the court*
j Gk: Heb *the thresholds*   *k* Cn Compare Gk 1 Kings 6.4: Meaning of Heb
uncertain

Clothed With the Spirit

EZEKIEL 42.13–14

All of us think about what is appropriate clothing for worship and for work. It is even more important to think about clothing ourselves with appropriate attitudes.

Paul counsels us to clothe ourselves with "compassion, kindness, humility, meekness and patience . . . Above all, clothe yourself with love" (Colossians 3.12–14). Wherever we go and whomever we meet, this attire should reveal God's presence. Each morning this week, as you dress, mentally label one item of clothing with a specifically Christian virtue—one aspect of the fruit of the Spirit perhaps (see Galatians 5.22–23). Choose a new characteristic each day. All through the day let that piece of clothing remind you of how you are growing more Christlike.

See Meeting God in Scripture

on the outside. And on all the walls all around in the inner room and the nave there was a pattern.[a] [18]It was formed of cherubim and palm trees, a palm tree between cherub and cherub. Each cherub had two faces: [19]a human face turned toward the palm tree on the one side, and the face of a young lion turned toward the palm tree on the other side. They were carved on the whole temple all around; [20]from the floor to the area above the door, cherubim and palm trees were carved on the wall.[b]

21 The doorposts of the nave were square. In front of the holy place was something resembling [22]an altar of wood, three cubits high, two cubits long, and two cubits wide;[c] its corners, its base,[d] and its walls were of wood. He said to me, "This is the table that stands before the LORD." [23]The nave and the holy place had each a double door. [24]The doors had two leaves apiece, two swinging leaves for each door. [25]On the doors of the nave were carved cherubim and palm trees, such as were carved on the walls; and there was a canopy of wood in front of the vestibule outside. [26]And there were recessed windows and palm trees on either side, on the sidewalls of the vestibule.[e]

The Holy Chambers and the Outer Wall

42 Then he led me out into the outer court, toward the north, and he brought me to the chambers that were opposite the temple yard and opposite the building on the north. [2]The length of the building that was on the north side[f] was[g] one hundred cubits, and the width fifty cubits. [3]Across the twenty cubits that belonged to the inner court, and facing the pavement that belonged to the outer court, the chambers rose[h] gallery[i] by gallery[i] in three stories. [4]In front of the chambers was a passage on the inner side, ten cubits wide and one hundred cubits deep,[j] and its[k] entrances were on the north. [5]Now the upper chambers were narrower, for the galleries[i] took more away from them than from the lower and middle chambers in the building. [6]For they were in three stories, and they had no pillars like the pillars of the outer[l] court; for this reason the upper chambers were set back from the ground more than the lower and the middle ones. [7]There was a wall outside parallel to the chambers, toward the outer court, opposite the chambers, fifty cubits long. [8]For the chambers on the outer court were fifty cubits long, while those opposite the temple were one hundred cubits long. [9]At the foot of these chambers ran a passage that one entered from the east in order to enter them from the outer court. [10]The width of the passage[m] was fixed by the wall of the court.

On the south[n] also, opposite the vacant area and opposite the building, there were chambers [11]with a passage in front of them; they were similar to the chambers on the north, of the same length and width, with the same exits[o] and arrangements and doors. [12]So the entrances of the chambers to the south were entered through the entrance at the head of the corresponding passage, from the east, along the matching wall.[i]

13 Then he said to me, "The north chambers and the

---

a Heb *measures*   b Cn Compare verse 25: Heb *and the wall*   c Gk: Heb lacks *two cubits wide*   d Gk: Heb *length*   e Cn: Heb *vestibule. And the side chambers of the temple and the canopies*   f Gk: Heb *door*   g Gk: Heb *before the length*   h Heb lacks *the chambers rose*   i Meaning of Heb uncertain   j Gk Syr: Heb *a way of one cubit*   k Heb *their*   l Gk: Heb lacks *outer*   m Heb lacks *of the passage*   n Gk: Heb *east*   o Heb *and all their exits*

south chambers opposite the vacant area are the holy chambers, where the priests who approach the Lord shall eat the most holy offerings; there they shall deposit the most holy offerings—the grain offering, the sin offering, and the guilt offering—for the place is holy. ¹⁴When the priests enter the holy place, they shall not go out of it into the outer court without laying there the vestments in which they minister, for these are holy; they shall put on other garments before they go near to the area open to the people."

15 When he had finished measuring the interior of the temple area, he led me out by the gate that faces east, and measured the temple area all around. ¹⁶He measured the east side with the measuring reed, five hundred cubits by the measuring reed. ¹⁷Then he turned and measured*a* the north side, five hundred cubits by the measuring reed. ¹⁸Then he turned and measured*a* the south side, five hundred cubits by the measuring reed. ¹⁹Then he turned to the west side and measured, five hundred cubits by the measuring reed. ²⁰He measured it on the four sides. It had a wall around it, five hundred cubits long and five hundred cubits wide, to make a separation between the holy and the common.

The Divine Glory Returns to the Temple

43 Then he brought me to the gate, the gate facing east. ²And there, the glory of the God of Israel was coming from the east; the sound was like the sound of mighty waters; and the earth shone with his glory. ³The*b* vision I saw was like the vision that I had seen when he came to destroy the city, and*c* like the vision that I had seen by the river Chebar; and I fell upon my face. ⁴As the glory of the Lord entered the temple by the gate facing east, ⁵the spirit lifted me up, and brought me into the inner court; and the glory of the Lord filled the temple.

6 While the man was standing beside me, I heard someone speaking to me out of the temple. ⁷He said to me: Mortal, this is the place of my throne and the place for the soles of my feet, where I will reside among the people of Israel forever. The house of Israel shall no more defile my holy name, neither they nor their kings, by their whoring, and by the corpses of their kings at their death.*d* ⁸When they placed their threshold by my threshold and their doorposts beside my doorposts, with only a wall between me and them, they were defiling my holy name by their abominations that they committed; therefore I have consumed them in my anger. ⁹Now let them put away their idolatry and the corpses of their kings far from me, and I will reside among them forever.

10 As for you, mortal, describe the temple to the house of Israel, and let them measure the pattern; and let them be ashamed of their iniquities. ¹¹When they are ashamed of all that they have done, make known to them the plan of the temple, its arrangement, its exits and its entrances, and its whole form—all its ordinances and its entire plan and all its laws; and write it down in their sight, so that they may observe and follow the entire plan and all its ordinances. ¹²This is the law of the temple: the whole territory on the top of the mountain all around shall be most holy. This is the law of the temple.

Preparing to Worship

EZEKIEL 43.1–5

Worship ushers us into the presence of God with sights and sounds. Encountering God may sound like the "sound of mighty waters." It may be as bright as the radiance of the sun. Ezekiel uses vivid words to describe the experience of meeting God in his vision of the temple. Not all our worship will be so dramatic, but we can always enter worship expecting to meet the holy, living God.

How do you prepare for worship? Do you have times during the week for individual prayer and worship? Do you get plenty of rest the night before? Do you give yourself time to get to worship services without having to rush? Do you pray for openness—that through the words and music you might hear the word of God? This week be ready to let "the glory of the Lord" fill your house of worship.

See Meeting God in Worship

---

a Gk: Heb *measuring reed all around. He measured*   *b* Gk: Heb *Like the vision*   *c* Syr: Heb *and the visions*   *d* Or *on their high places*

Facedown Worship

The glory of the Lord is so awesome, so brilliant, that Ezekiel can only fall to the ground facedown. Follow Ezekiel's example and lie facedown in God's presence. As you assume this posture, think about God. How is he so awesome that you cannot look at him? What is so grand about God that you cannot approach or talk to him? Let that kind of reverence and awe sink in. Ponder God's goodness and mercy that reveals your shame. Do you find that tears come more easily as you lie prostrate?

Rest and remain in that posture for a few moments, and know that the God who is awesome is also forgiving, slow to anger, and full of compassion and kindness. Add this posture of prayer to your practice of communing with God.

See Meeting God in Prayer

The Altar

13 These are the dimensions of the altar by cubits (the cubit being one cubit and a handbreadth): its base shall be one cubit high,*a* and one cubit wide, with a rim of one span around its edge. This shall be the height of the altar: ¹⁴From the base on the ground to the lower ledge, two cubits, with a width of one cubit; and from the smaller ledge to the larger ledge, four cubits, with a width of one cubit; ¹⁵and the altar hearth, four cubits; and from the altar hearth projecting upward, four horns. ¹⁶The altar hearth shall be square, twelve cubits long by twelve wide. ¹⁷The ledge also shall be square, fourteen cubits long by fourteen wide, with a rim around it half a cubit wide, and its surrounding base, one cubit. Its steps shall face east.

18 Then he said to me: Mortal, thus says the Lord GOD: These are the ordinances for the altar: On the day when it is erected for offering burnt offerings upon it and for dashing blood against it, ¹⁹you shall give to the levitical priests of the family of Zadok, who draw near to me to minister to me, says the Lord GOD, a bull for a sin offering. ²⁰And you shall take some of its blood, and put it on the four horns of the altar, and on the four corners of the ledge, and upon the rim all around; thus you shall purify it and make atonement for it. ²¹You shall also take the bull of the sin offering, and it shall be burnt in the appointed place belonging to the temple, outside the sacred area.

22 On the second day you shall offer a male goat without blemish for a sin offering; and the altar shall be purified, as it was purified with the bull. ²³When you have finished purifying it, you shall offer a bull without blemish and a ram from the flock without blemish. ²⁴You shall present them before the LORD, and the priests shall throw salt on them and offer them up as a burnt offering to the LORD. ²⁵For seven days you shall provide daily a goat for a sin offering; also a bull and a ram from the flock, without blemish, shall be provided. ²⁶Seven days shall they make atonement for the altar and cleanse it, and so consecrate it. ²⁷When these days are over, then from the eighth day onward the priests shall offer upon the altar your burnt offerings and your offerings of well-being; and I will accept you, says the Lord GOD.

The Closed Gate

44 Then he brought me back to the outer gate of the sanctuary, which faces east; and it was shut. ²The LORD said to me: This gate shall remain shut; it shall not be opened, and no one shall enter by it; for the LORD, the God of Israel, has entered by it; therefore it shall remain shut. ³Only the prince, because he is a prince, may sit in it to eat food before the LORD; he shall enter by way of the vestibule of the gate, and shall go out by the same way.

Admission to the Temple

4 Then he brought me by way of the north gate to the front of the temple; and I looked, and lo! the glory of the LORD filled the temple of the LORD; and I fell upon my face. ⁵The LORD said to me: Mortal, mark well, look closely, and listen attentively to all that I shall tell you concerning all the ordinances of the temple of the LORD and all its laws; and mark

a Gk: Heb lacks *high*

well those who may be admitted to*a* the temple and all those who are to be excluded from the sanctuary. 6Say to the rebellious house,*b* to the house of Israel, Thus says the Lord GOD: O house of Israel, let there be an end to all your abominations 7in admitting foreigners, uncircumcised in heart and flesh, to be in my sanctuary, profaning my temple when you offer to me my food, the fat and the blood. You*c* have broken my covenant with all your abominations. 8And you have not kept charge of my sacred offerings; but you have appointed foreigners*d* to act for you in keeping my charge in my sanctuary.

9 Thus says the Lord GOD: No foreigner, uncircumcised in heart and flesh, of all the foreigners who are among the people of Israel, shall enter my sanctuary. 10But the Levites who went far from me, going astray from me after their idols when Israel went astray, shall bear their punishment. 11They shall be ministers in my sanctuary, having oversight at the gates of the temple, and serving in the temple; they shall slaughter the burnt offering and the sacrifice for the people, and they shall attend on them and serve them. 12Because they ministered to them before their idols and made the house of Israel stumble into iniquity, therefore I have sworn concerning them, says the Lord GOD, that they shall bear their punishment. 13They shall not come near to me, to serve me as priest, nor come near any of my sacred offerings, the things that are most sacred; but they shall bear their shame, and the consequences of the abominations that they have committed. 14Yet I will appoint them to keep charge of the temple, to do all its chores, all that is to be done in it.

The Levitical Priests

15 But the levitical priests, the descendants of Zadok, who kept the charge of my sanctuary when the people of Israel went astray from me, shall come near to me to minister to me; and they shall attend me to offer me the fat and the blood, says the Lord GOD. 16It is they who shall enter my sanctuary, it is they who shall approach my table, to minister to me, and they shall keep my charge. 17When they enter the gates of the inner court, they shall wear linen vestments; they shall have nothing of wool on them, while they minister at the gates of the inner court, and within. 18They shall have linen turbans on their heads, and linen undergarments on their loins; they shall not bind themselves with anything that causes sweat. 19When they go out into the outer court to the people, they shall remove the vestments in which they have been ministering, and lay them in the holy chambers; and they shall put on other garments, so that they may not communicate holiness to the people with their vestments. 20They shall not shave their heads or let their locks grow long; they shall only trim the hair of their heads. 21No priest shall drink wine when he enters the inner court. 22They shall not marry a widow, or a divorced woman, but only a virgin of the stock of the house of Israel, or a widow who is the widow of a priest. 23They shall teach my people the difference between the holy and the common, and show them how to distinguish between the unclean and the clean. 24In a controversy they shall act as judges, and they shall decide it according to my judgments. They shall keep my laws and my statutes regarding

a Cn: Heb *the entrance of*   *b* Gk: Heb lacks *house*   *c* Gk Syr Vg: Heb *They*
d Heb lacks *foreigners*

The Care of God's Servants

EZEKIEL 44.15,16,29–31

Ezekiel reminds the people that they are responsible for the care and support of the priests.

Call to mind those who are your shepherds (chapter 34), teachers (44.23) and priests. Who guides your spiritual life? A number of names may come to mind.

How do you care for those who minister to you? Do you remember them in your prayers each day? Do you send them a note of thanks or encouragement? Have you ever given them a gift for Easter or Christmas? Have you invited them over for a meal or taken them out to lunch? Are you honest in your praise and gentle in your criticism? Today is a good day to do something caring for your "shepherd."

See Meeting God in Service

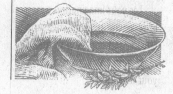

An Honest Ephah and an Honest Bath

EZEKIEL 45.10–11

An ephah was a dry measure. For a time of meditation, find a measuring cup and some measuring spoons. Hold the measuring spoons and imagine measuring some virtues as you would measure spices. Do you give your children the full tablespoon of patience? Do you pour out a full quart of joy to your spouse? Do you give your employer the full cup of an honest day's work? What else do you measure out?

Now hold the measuring cup and pour a liquid into it (a bath was a liquid measure). Pour out the oil of gladness in gratitude for your parents and the wine of compassion for those who need it. Pour out tears of sorrow and tears of joy for your friends. What would go into your cup?

Let your imagination soar a little as you hold the measuring spoons and cup. God wants to make something good out of your life.

See Meeting God in Everyday Life

all my appointed festivals, and they shall keep my sabbaths holy. 25They shall not defile themselves by going near to a dead person; for father or mother, however, and for son or daughter, and for brother or unmarried sister they may defile themselves. 26After he has become clean, they shall count seven days for him. 27On the day that he goes into the holy place, into the inner court, to minister in the holy place, he shall offer his sin offering, says the Lord GOD.

28 This shall be their inheritance: I am their inheritance; and you shall give them no holding in Israel; I am their holding. 29They shall eat the grain offering, the sin offering, and the guilt offering; and every devoted thing in Israel shall be theirs. 30The first of all the first fruits of all kinds, and every offering of all kinds from all your offerings, shall belong to the priests; you shall also give to the priests the first of your dough, in order that a blessing may rest on your house. 31The priests shall not eat of anything, whether bird or animal, that died of itself or was torn by animals.

The Holy District

45 When you allot the land as an inheritance, you shall set aside for the LORD a portion of the land as a holy district, twenty-five thousand cubits long and twenty*ᵃ* thousand cubits wide; it shall be holy throughout its entire extent. 2Of this, a square plot of five hundred by five hundred cubits shall be for the sanctuary, with fifty cubits for an open space around it. 3In the holy district you shall measure off a section twenty-five thousand cubits long and ten thousand wide, in which shall be the sanctuary, the most holy place. 4It shall be a holy portion of the land; it shall be for the priests, who minister in the sanctuary and approach the LORD to minister to him; and it shall be both a place for their houses and a holy place for the sanctuary. 5Another section, twenty-five thousand cubits long and ten thousand cubits wide, shall be for the Levites who minister at the temple, as their holding for cities to live in.*ᵇ*

6 Alongside the portion set apart as the holy district you shall assign as a holding for the city an area five thousand cubits wide, and twenty-five thousand cubits long; it shall belong to the whole house of Israel.

7 And to the prince shall belong the land on both sides of the holy district and the holding of the city, alongside the holy district and the holding of the city, on the west and on the east, corresponding in length to one of the tribal portions, and extending from the western to the eastern boundary 8of the land. It is to be his property in Israel. And my princes shall no longer oppress my people; but they shall let the house of Israel have the land according to their tribes.

9 Thus says the Lord GOD: Enough, O princes of Israel! Put away violence and oppression, and do what is just and right. Cease your evictions of my people, says the Lord GOD.

Weights and Measures

10 You shall have honest balances, an honest ephah, and an honest bath.*ᶜ* 11The ephah and the bath shall be of the same measure, the bath containing one-tenth of a homer, and the ephah one-tenth of a homer; the homer shall be the standard measure. 12The shekel shall be twen-

a Gk: Heb *ten*   *b* Gk: Heb *as their holding, twenty chambers*   *c* A Heb measure of volume

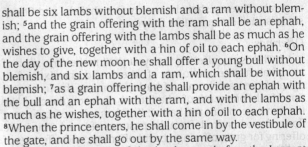

Morning by Morning

EZEKIEL 46.13–14

Worship at the temple was not just for the great festivals, sabbaths and new moons, but each day, "morning by morning," there were to be rituals of praise and sacrifice.

Though we no longer practice animal sacrifice in worship, the instruction to worship God daily is a lasting ordinance for all time. "Morning by morning" is a wonderful expression of God's faithfulness in the beloved hymn: "Great is thy faithfulness! Great is thy faithfulness! Morning by morning new mercies I see; all I have needed thy hand has provided; great is thy faithfulness, Lord, unto me" (Thomas O. Chisholm, "Great Is Thy Faithfulness").

What prayer do you say or song do you sing "morning by morning" to declare your praise?

shall be six lambs without blemish and a ram without blemish; [5]and the grain offering with the ram shall be an ephah, and the grain offering with the lambs shall be as much as he wishes to give, together with a hin of oil to each ephah. [6]On the day of the new moon he shall offer a young bull without blemish, and six lambs and a ram, which shall be without blemish; [7]as a grain offering he shall provide an ephah with the bull and an ephah with the ram, and with the lambs as much as he wishes, together with a hin of oil to each ephah. [8]When the prince enters, he shall come in by the vestibule of the gate, and he shall go out by the same way.

9 When the people of the land come before the LORD at the appointed festivals, whoever enters by the north gate to worship shall go out by the south gate; and whoever enters by the south gate shall go out by the north gate: they shall not return by way of the gate by which they entered, but shall go out straight ahead. [10]When they come in, the prince shall come in with them; and when they go out, he shall go out.

11 At the festivals and the appointed seasons the grain offering with a young bull shall be an ephah, and with a ram an ephah, and with the lambs as much as one wishes to give, together with a hin of oil to an ephah. [12]When the prince provides a freewill offering, either a burnt offering or offerings of well-being as a freewill offering to the LORD, the gate facing east shall be opened for him; and he shall offer his burnt offering or his offerings of well-being as he does on the sabbath day. Then he shall go out, and after he has gone out the gate shall be closed.

13 He shall provide a lamb, a yearling, without blemish, for a burnt offering to the LORD daily; morning by morning he shall provide it. [14]And he shall provide a grain offering with it morning by morning regularly, one-sixth of an ephah, and one-third of a hin of oil to moisten the choice flour, as a grain offering to the LORD; this is the ordinance for all time. [15]Thus the lamb and the grain offering and the oil shall be provided, morning by morning, as a regular burnt offering.

16 Thus says the Lord GOD: If the prince makes a gift to any of his sons out of his inheritance,[a] it shall belong to his sons, it is their holding by inheritance. [17]But if he makes a gift out of his inheritance to one of his servants, it shall be his to the year of liberty; then it shall revert to the prince; only his sons may keep a gift from his inheritance. [18]The prince shall not take any of the inheritance of the people, thrusting them out of their holding; he shall give his sons their inheritance out of his own holding, so that none of my people shall be dispossessed of their holding.

19 Then he brought me through the entrance, which was at the side of the gate, to the north row of the holy chambers for the priests; and there I saw a place at the extreme western end of them. [20]He said to me, "This is the place where the priests shall boil the guilt offering and the sin offering, and where they shall bake the grain offering, in order not to bring them out into the outer court and so communicate holiness to the people."

21 Then he brought me out to the outer court, and led me past the four corners of the court; and in each corner of the court there was a court— [22]in the four corners of the court were small[b] courts, forty cubits long and thirty wide; the four were of the same size. [23]On the inside, around

a Gk: Heb *it is his inheritance*   *b* Gk Syr Vg: Meaning of Heb uncertain

ty gerahs. Twenty shekels, twenty-five shekels, and fifteen shekels shall make a mina for you.

Offerings

13 This is the offering that you shall make: one-sixth of an ephah from each homer of wheat, and one-sixth of an ephah from each homer of barley, ¹⁴and as the fixed portion of oil,^a one-tenth of a bath from each cor (the cor,^b like the homer, contains ten baths); ¹⁵and one sheep from every flock of two hundred, from the pastures of Israel. This is the offering for grain offerings, burnt offerings, and offerings of well-being, to make atonement for them, says the Lord God. ¹⁶All the people of the land shall join with the prince in Israel in making this offering. ¹⁷But this shall be the obligation of the prince regarding the burnt offerings, grain offerings, and drink offerings, at the festivals, the new moons, and the sabbaths, all the appointed festivals of the house of Israel: he shall provide the sin offerings, grain offerings, the burnt offerings, and the offerings of well-being, to make atonement for the house of Israel.

Festivals

18 Thus says the Lord God: In the first month, on the first day of the month, you shall take a young bull without blemish, and purify the sanctuary. ¹⁹The priest shall take some of the blood of the sin offering and put it on the doorposts of the temple, the four corners of the ledge of the altar, and the posts of the gate of the inner court. ²⁰You shall do the same on the seventh day of the month for anyone who has sinned through error or ignorance; so you shall make atonement for the temple.

21 In the first month, on the fourteenth day of the month, you shall celebrate the festival of the passover, and for seven days unleavened bread shall be eaten. ²²On that day the prince shall provide for himself and all the people of the land a young bull for a sin offering. ²³And during the seven days of the festival he shall provide as a burnt offering to the Lord seven young bulls and seven rams without blemish, on each of the seven days; and a male goat daily for a sin offering. ²⁴He shall provide as a grain offering an ephah for each bull, an ephah for each ram, and a hin of oil to each ephah. ²⁵In the seventh month, on the fifteenth day of the month and for the seven days of the festival, he shall make the same provision for sin offerings, burnt offerings, and grain offerings, and for the oil.

Miscellaneous Regulations

46 Thus says the Lord God: The gate of the inner court that faces east shall remain closed on the six working days; but on the sabbath day it shall be opened and on the day of the new moon it shall be opened. ²The prince shall enter by the vestibule of the gate from outside, and shall take his stand by the post of the gate. The priests shall offer his burnt offering and his offerings of well-being, and he shall bow down at the threshold of the gate. Then he shall go out, but the gate shall not be closed until evening. ³The people of the land shall bow down at the entrance of that gate before the Lord on the sabbaths and on the new moons. ⁴The burnt offering that the prince offers to the Lord on the sabbath day

---

Open the Gates of Worship

EZEKIEL 46.1

"O my God, let me remember with gratitude and confess to you your mercies toward me. Let my bones be bathed in your love and let them say, 'Lord who is like unto thee? You have broken my bonds apart, I will offer to you the sacrifice of thanksgiving.' And how you broke them I will declare and all who worship you will say when they hear these things: 'Blessed be the Lord in heaven and earth, great and wonderful is his name.' "

—AUGUSTINE,
Confessions

---

a Cn: Heb *oil, the bath the oil*   b Vg: Heb *homer*

Compassion for the Foreigner

EZEKIEL 47.21–23

When the people of Israel return from captivity, the land is to be divided equally among the tribes. The foreigners and aliens who are living among them are also to receive an allotment. They are to be considered citizens of Israel. God's grace knows no boundaries.

Dorotheus of Gaza, a sixth-century monk, suggested that love can be viewed as a compass with God in the center. "To move toward God, then, human beings move from the circumference along the various radii of the circle to the center. But at the same time, the closer they are to God, the closer they become to one another; and the closer they are to one another, the closer they become to God." All the people you meet today, whatever the color of their skin or their station in life, are gifts to help you move closer to God.

18 On the east side, between Hauran and Damascus; along the Jordan between Gilead and the land of Israel; to the eastern sea and as far as Tamar.*a* This shall be the east side.

19 On the south side, it shall run from Tamar as far as the waters of Meribath-kadesh, from there along the Wadi of Egypt*b* to the Great Sea. This shall be the south side.

20 On the west side, the Great Sea shall be the boundary to a point opposite Lebo-hamath. This shall be the west side.

21 So you shall divide this land among you according to the tribes of Israel. 22 You shall allot it as an inheritance for yourselves and for the aliens who reside among you and have begotten children among you. They shall be to you as citizens of Israel; with you they shall be allotted an inheritance among the tribes of Israel. 23 In whatever tribe aliens reside, there you shall assign them their inheritance, says the Lord GOD.

The Tribal Portions

48 These are the names of the tribes: Beginning at the northern border, on the Hethlon road,*c* from Lebo-hamath, as far as Hazar-enon (which is on the border of Damascus, with Hamath to the north), and*d* extending from the east side to the west,*e* Dan, one portion. 2 Adjoining the territory of Dan, from the east side to the west, Asher, one portion. 3 Adjoining the territory of Asher, from the east side to the west, Naphtali, one portion. 4 Adjoining the territory of Naphtali, from the east side to the west, Manasseh, one portion. 5 Adjoining the territory of Manasseh, from the east side to the west, Ephraim, one portion. 6 Adjoining the territory of Ephraim, from the east side to the west, Reuben, one portion. 7 Adjoining the territory of Reuben, from the east side to the west, Judah, one portion.

8 Adjoining the territory of Judah, from the east side to the west, shall be the portion that you shall set apart, twenty-five thousand cubits in width, and in length equal to one of the tribal portions, from the east side to the west, with the sanctuary in the middle of it. 9 The portion that you shall set apart for the LORD shall be twenty-five thousand cubits in length, and twenty*f* thousand in width. 10 These shall be the allotments of the holy portion: the priests shall have an allotment measuring twenty-five thousand cubits on the northern side, ten thousand cubits in width on the western side, ten thousand in width on the eastern side, and twenty-five thousand in length on the southern side, with the sanctuary of the LORD in the middle of it. 11 This shall be for the consecrated priests, the descendants*g* of Zadok, who kept my charge, who did not go astray when the people of Israel went astray, as the Levites did. 12 It shall belong to them as a special portion from the holy portion of the land, a most holy place, adjoining the territory of the Levites. 13 Alongside the territory of the priests, the Levites shall have an allotment twenty-five thousand cubits in length and ten thousand in width. The whole length shall be twenty-five thousand cubits and the width twenty*h* thousand. 14 They shall not sell or exchange any of it; they shall not transfer this choice portion of the land, for it is holy to the LORD.

a Compare Syr: Heb *you shall measure*   b Heb lacks *of Egypt*
c Compare 47.15: Heb *by the side of the way*   d Cn: Heb *and they shall be his*   e Gk Compare verses 2-8: Heb *the east side the west*   f Compare 45.1: Heb *ten*   g One Ms Gk: Heb *of the descendants*   h Gk: Heb *ten*

each of the four courts[a] was a row of masonry, with hearths made at the bottom of the rows all around. [24]Then he said to me, "These are the kitchens where those who serve at the temple shall boil the sacrifices of the people."

Water Flowing from the Temple

47 Then he brought me back to the entrance of the temple; there, water was flowing from below the threshold of the temple toward the east (for the temple faced east); and the water was flowing down from below the south end of the threshold of the temple, south of the altar. [2]Then he brought me out by way of the north gate, and led me around on the outside to the outer gate that faces toward the east;[b] and the water was coming out on the south side.

3 Going on eastward with a cord in his hand, the man measured one thousand cubits, and then led me through the water; and it was ankle-deep. [4]Again he measured one thousand, and led me through the water; and it was knee-deep. Again he measured one thousand, and led me through the water; and it was up to the waist. [5]Again he measured one thousand, and it was a river that I could not cross, for the water had risen; it was deep enough to swim in, a river that could not be crossed. [6]He said to me, "Mortal, have you seen this?"

Then he led me back along the bank of the river. [7]As I came back, I saw on the bank of the river a great many trees on the one side and on the other. [8]He said to me, "This water flows toward the eastern region and goes down into the Arabah; and when it enters the sea, the sea of stagnant waters, the water will become fresh. [9]Wherever the river goes,[c] every living creature that swarms will live, and there will be very many fish, once these waters reach there. It will become fresh; and everything will live where the river goes. [10]People will stand fishing beside the sea[d] from En-gedi to En-eglaim; it will be a place for the spreading of nets; its fish will be of a great many kinds, like the fish of the Great Sea. [11]But its swamps and marshes will not become fresh; they are to be left for salt. [12]On the banks, on both sides of the river, there will grow all kinds of trees for food. Their leaves will not wither nor their fruit fail, but they will bear fresh fruit every month, because the water for them flows from the sanctuary. Their fruit will be for food, and their leaves for healing."

The New Boundaries of the Land

13 Thus says the Lord GOD: These are the boundaries by which you shall divide the land for inheritance among the twelve tribes of Israel. Joseph shall have two portions. [14]You shall divide it equally; I swore to give it to your ancestors, and this land shall fall to you as your inheritance.

15 This shall be the boundary of the land: On the north side, from the Great Sea by way of Hethlon to Lebo-hamath, and on to Zedad,[e] [16]Berothah, Sibraim (which lies between the border of Damascus and the border of Hamath), as far as Hazer-hatticon, which is on the border of Hauran. [17]So the boundary shall run from the sea to Hazar-enon, which is north of the border of Damascus, with the border of Hamath to the north.[b] This shall be the north side.

Water of Life

EZEKIEL 47.7–12

The water flows from the throne of God. From under the temple the water flows to change the salty water of the Dead Sea into a freshwater sea of life. It irrigates the desert into an orchard of fruit trees, where the fruit provides food and the leaves bring healing. Can you see this in your mind's eye?

Walk beside a stream or river. Or turn on a faucet for ten seconds. Touch the water. Listen to the sound of running water. Hold a few drops of water in your cupped hands. Marvel at such a precious gift. Drink a glass of water slowly and mindfully. Be aware of its life-giving properties as you swallow it. Imagine a stream of water flowing from God's throne to the place where you live and work. Offer thanksgiving to Almighty God.

See Meeting God in the Created Order

a Heb *the four of them*   b Meaning of Heb uncertain   c Gk Syr Vg Tg: Heb *the two rivers go*   d Heb *it*   e Gk: Heb *Lebo-zedad*, [16]*Hamath*

1155

15 The remainder, five thousand cubits in width and twenty-five thousand in length, shall be for ordinary use for the city, for dwellings and for open country. In the middle of it shall be the city; ¹⁶and these shall be its dimensions: the north side four thousand five hundred cubits, the south side four thousand five hundred, the east side four thousand five hundred, and the west side four thousand five hundred. ¹⁷The city shall have open land: on the north two hundred fifty cubits, on the south two hundred fifty, on the east two hundred fifty, on the west two hundred fifty. ¹⁸The remainder of the length alongside the holy portion shall be ten thousand cubits to the east, and ten thousand to the west, and it shall be alongside the holy portion. Its produce shall be food for the workers of the city. ¹⁹The workers of the city, from all the tribes of Israel, shall cultivate it. ²⁰The whole portion that you shall set apart shall be twenty-five thousand cubits square, that is, the holy portion together with the property of the city.

21 What remains on both sides of the holy portion and of the property of the city shall belong to the prince. Extending from the twenty-five thousand cubits of the holy portion to the east border, and westward from the twenty-five thousand cubits to the west border, parallel to the tribal portions, it shall belong to the prince. The holy portion with the sanctuary of the temple in the middle of it, ²²and the property of the Levites and of the city, shall be in the middle of that which belongs to the prince. The portion of the prince shall lie between the territory of Judah and the territory of Benjamin.

23 As for the rest of the tribes: from the east side to the west, Benjamin, one portion. ²⁴Adjoining the territory of Benjamin, from the east side to the west, Simeon, one portion. ²⁵Adjoining the territory of Simeon, from the east side to the west, Issachar, one portion. ²⁶Adjoining the territory of Issachar, from the east side to the west, Zebulun, one portion. ²⁷Adjoining the territory of Zebulun, from the east side to the west, Gad, one portion. ²⁸And adjoining the territory of Gad to the south, the boundary shall run from Tamar to the waters of Meribath-kadesh, from there along the Wadi of Egypt*ᵃ* to the Great Sea. ²⁹This is the land that you shall allot as an inheritance among the tribes of Israel, and these are their portions, says the Lord God.

30 These shall be the exits of the city: On the north side, which is to be four thousand five hundred cubits by measure, ³¹three gates, the gate of Reuben, the gate of Judah, and the gate of Levi, the gates of the city being named after the tribes of Israel. ³²On the east side, which is to be four thousand five hundred cubits, three gates, the gate of Joseph, the gate of Benjamin, and the gate of Dan. ³³On the south side, which is to be four thousand five hundred cubits by measure, three gates, the gate of Simeon, the gate of Issachar, and the gate of Zebulun. ³⁴On the west side, which is to be four thousand five hundred cubits, three gates,*ᵇ* the gate of Gad, the gate of Asher, and the gate of Naphtali. ³⁵The circumference of the city shall be eighteen thousand cubits. And the name of the city from that time on shall be, The Lord is There.

The Lord Is There

EZEKIEL 48.35

Ezekiel has lived through bad alliances, the destruction of Jerusalem, the captivity in Babylon. Now, at the end of his ministry, he has a vision of the new Jerusalem, which will be known as the "the Lord is There." We have been on a journey with this incredible prophet and his colorful words and actions. The book ends in hope, but our journey goes on, and we know that wherever we are, "the Lord is There."

Take a moment to thank God for the prophet Ezekiel. Make some notes in your journal or in the margin of this Bible about how your life has been affected by this major prophet. Have you claimed some sabbath time, created a holy place, tried some new prayer postures, written some prayers, become more compassionate? Remember, wherever you are, wherever you go, "the Lord is There."

See Meeting God in Prayer

DANIEL
The Power to Stand

KEY VERSE:

"We will not serve your gods and we will not worship the golden statue that you have set up."

—Daniel 3.18

"The most desirable prayer is that where we can quite pour out our soul and freely talk with God. But it is not this alone which is acceptable to him. 'Love one' said a holy man, 'that perseveres in dry duty.' Beware of thinking even this is labour lost. God does much work in the heart even at those seasons."

—JOHN WESLEY,
Letter to Miss March, June 1771

The book of Daniel is a story of intrigue and mystery, of dreams and visions and miracles. It is also the story of four young men who find the power to stand firm while living in a culture whose values oppose their faith.

Daniel, Hananiah, Mishael and Azariah are carried away as captives to Babylon when Jerusalem falls. They are of royal and noble lineage—four of the finest young men of Judah—and so they are chosen for special roles. They are given new names (Belteshazzar, Shadrach, Meshach and Abednego) and are to be educated and groomed for service in Nebuchadnezzar's court, learning the literature, language and customs of Babylon.

The four young men refuse to worship the image the king has set up. The advisers to the Babylonian king oppose the young men for expressing their faith, and they plot against them. The young men, however, pray for one another and stand together. Daniel rises to a place of power in the kingdom as an interpreter of the king's dreams, and he writes down his visions of how God will work in human events.

The book of Daniel shows how the faithful can triumph even in difficult situations by remaining true to God and living by God's standards despite opposition from the culture. Their reliance on one another and on the power of prayer are models that all of us can use as a pattern for our lives, whatever the difficult situations in which we find ourselves.

23 To you, O God of my ancestors,
  I give thanks and praise,
for you have given me wisdom and power,
  and have now revealed to me what we asked of
    you,
  for you have revealed to us what the king
    ordered."

Daniel Interprets the Dream

24 Therefore Daniel went to Arioch, whom the king had appointed to destroy the wise men of Babylon, and said to him, "Do not destroy the wise men of Babylon; bring me in before the king, and I will give the king the interpretation." 25 Then Arioch quickly brought Daniel before the king and said to him: "I have found among the exiles from Judah a man who can tell the king the interpretation." 26 The king said to Daniel, whose name was Belteshazzar, "Are you able to tell me the dream that I have seen and its interpretation?" 27 Daniel answered the king, "No wise men, enchanters, magicians, or diviners can show to the king the mystery that the king is asking, 28 but there is a God in heaven who reveals mysteries, and he has disclosed to King Nebuchadnezzar what will happen at the end of days. Your dream and the visions of your head as you lay in bed were these: 29 To you, O king, as you lay in bed, came thoughts of what would be hereafter, and the revealer of mysteries disclosed to you what is to be. 30 But as for me, this mystery has not been revealed to me because of any wisdom that I have more than any other living being, but in order that the interpretation may be known to the king and that you may understand the thoughts of your mind.

31 "You were looking, O king, and lo! there was a great statue. This statue was huge, its brilliance extraordinary; it was standing before you, and its appearance was frightening. 32 The head of that statue was of fine gold, its chest and arms of silver, its middle and thighs of bronze, 33 its legs of iron, its feet partly of iron and partly of clay. 34 As you looked on, a stone was cut out, not by human hands, and it struck the statue on its feet of iron and clay and broke them in pieces. 35 Then the iron, the clay, the bronze, the silver, and the gold, were all broken in pieces and became like the chaff of the summer threshing floors; and the wind carried them away, so that not a trace of them could be found. But the stone that struck the statue became a great mountain and filled the whole earth.

36 "This was the dream; now we will tell the king its interpretation. 37 You, O king, the king of kings—to whom the God of heaven has given the kingdom, the power, the might, and the glory, 38 into whose hand he has given human beings, wherever they live, the wild animals of the field, and the birds of the air, and whom he has established as ruler over them all—you are the head of gold. 39 After you shall arise another kingdom inferior to yours, and yet a third kingdom of bronze, which shall rule over the whole earth. 40 And there shall be a fourth kingdom, strong as iron; just as iron crushes and smashes everything,*a* it shall crush and shatter all these. 41 As you saw the feet and toes partly of potter's clay and partly of iron, it shall be a divided kingdom; but some of the strength of iron shall be in it, as you

---

Dream Talker

DANIEL 2.20–23

God does not communicate with us only in our waking hours. Paying attention to our dreams can be a way of paying attention to God. Recurring patterns in our dreams—such as feelings of deep love or a sense of searching for something lost—can help us to understand more deeply our spiritual needs. Consider writing down your dreams when you awaken. If you record even snippets of dreams, you will gradually remember more and more of your dreams. Look for connections between your dreams and the events of your waking hours. Ask God to show you the meaning of your dreams so that you would gain understanding of them.

See Meeting God in Everyday Life

---

a Gk Theodotion Syr Vg: Aram adds *and like iron that crushes*

Speak Up!

DANIEL 2.46–47

Because Daniel spoke up, the king gave God credit for Daniel's wisdom. Living in a culture that is not always receptive to expressions of personal belief, we are sometimes reluctant to mention our faith. Think about how you speak in the company of nonbelievers. What subjects do you refer to? Do those you work with and enjoy leisure activities with know from your conversations that you are a believer? What conclusions about believers' interests and behavior might they draw from your example? When we mention serving God or talk with excitement about the role of faith in our lives, we may be inviting others to think about spiritual things. Like the king of Babylon, they may be moved to ponder who God is and how God is working in the world.

See *Meeting God in Community*

saw the iron mixed with the clay. ⁴²As the toes of the feet were part iron and part clay, so the kingdom shall be partly strong and partly brittle. ⁴³As you saw the iron mixed with clay, so will they mix with one another in marriage,ᵃ but they will not hold together, just as iron does not mix with clay. ⁴⁴And in the days of those kings the God of heaven will set up a kingdom that shall never be destroyed, nor shall this kingdom be left to another people. It shall crush all these kingdoms and bring them to an end, and it shall stand forever; ⁴⁵just as you saw that a stone was cut from the mountain not by hands, and that it crushed the iron, the bronze, the clay, the silver, and the gold. The great God has informed the king what shall be hereafter. The dream is certain, and its interpretation trustworthy."

Daniel and His Friends Promoted

46 Then King Nebuchadnezzar fell on his face, worshiped Daniel, and commanded that a grain offering and incense be offered to him. ⁴⁷The king said to Daniel, "Truly, your God is God of gods and Lord of kings and a revealer of mysteries, for you have been able to reveal this mystery!" ⁴⁸Then the king promoted Daniel, gave him many great gifts, and made him ruler over the whole province of Babylon and chief prefect over all the wise men of Babylon. ⁴⁹Daniel made a request of the king, and he appointed Shadrach, Meshach, and Abednego over the affairs of the province of Babylon. But Daniel remained at the king's court.

The Golden Image

3 King Nebuchadnezzar made a golden statue whose height was sixty cubits and whose width was six cubits; he set it up on the plain of Dura in the province of Babylon. ²Then King Nebuchadnezzar sent for the satraps, the prefects, and the governors, the counselors, the treasurers, the justices, the magistrates, and all the officials of the provinces, to assemble and come to the dedication of the statue that King Nebuchadnezzar had set up. ³So the satraps, the prefects, and the governors, the counselors, the treasurers, the justices, the magistrates, and all the officials of the provinces, assembled for the dedication of the statue that King Nebuchadnezzar had set up. When they were standing before the statue that Nebuchadnezzar had set up, ⁴the herald proclaimed aloud, "You are commanded, O peoples, nations, and languages, ⁵that when you hear the sound of the horn, pipe, lyre, trigon, harp, drum, and entire musical ensemble, you are to fall down and worship the golden statue that King Nebuchadnezzar has set up. ⁶Whoever does not fall down and worship shall immediately be thrown into a furnace of blazing fire." ⁷Therefore, as soon as all the peoples heard the sound of the horn, pipe, lyre, trigon, harp, drum, and entire musical ensemble, all the peoples, nations, and languages fell down and worshiped the golden statue that King Nebuchadnezzar had set up.

8 Accordingly, at this time certain Chaldeans came forward and denounced the Jews. ⁹They said to King Nebuchadnezzar, "O king, live forever! ¹⁰You, O king, have made a decree, that everyone who hears the sound of the horn, pipe, lyre, trigon, harp, drum, and entire musical ensemble, shall fall down and worship the golden statue, ¹¹and who-

a Aram *by human seed*

ever does not fall down and worship shall be thrown into a furnace of blazing fire. ¹²There are certain Jews whom you have appointed over the affairs of the province of Babylon: Shadrach, Meshach, and Abednego. These pay no heed to you, O king. They do not serve your gods and they do not worship the golden statue that you have set up."

13 Then Nebuchadnezzar in furious rage commanded that Shadrach, Meshach, and Abednego be brought in; so they brought those men before the king. ¹⁴Nebuchadnezzar said to them, "Is it true, O Shadrach, Meshach, and Abednego, that you do not serve my gods and you do not worship the golden statue that I have set up? ¹⁵Now if you are ready when you hear the sound of the horn, pipe, lyre, trigon, harp, drum, and entire musical ensemble to fall down and worship the statue that I have made, well and good.ᵃ But if you do not worship, you shall immediately be thrown into a furnace of blazing fire, and who is the god that will deliver you out of my hands?"

16 Shadrach, Meshach, and Abednego answered the king, "O Nebuchadnezzar, we have no need to present a defense to you in this matter. ¹⁷If our God whom we serve is able to deliver us from the furnace of blazing fire and out of your hand, O king, let him deliver us.ᵇ ¹⁸But if not, be it known to you, O king, that we will not serve your gods and we will not worship the golden statue that you have set up."

The Fiery Furnace

19 Then Nebuchadnezzar was so filled with rage against Shadrach, Meshach, and Abednego that his face was distorted. He ordered the furnace heated up seven times more than was customary, ²⁰and ordered some of the strongest guards in his army to bind Shadrach, Meshach, and Abednego and to throw them into the furnace of blazing fire. ²¹So the men were bound, still wearing their tunics,ᶜ their trousers,ᶜ their hats, and their other garments, and they were thrown into the furnace of blazing fire. ²²Because the king's command was urgent and the furnace was so overheated, the raging flames killed the men who lifted Shadrach, Meshach, and Abednego. ²³But the three men, Shadrach, Meshach, and Abednego, fell down, bound, into the furnace of blazing fire.

24 Then King Nebuchadnezzar was astonished and rose up quickly. He said to his counselors, "Was it not three men that we threw bound into the fire?" They answered the king, "True, O king." ²⁵He replied, "But I see four men unbound, walking in the middle of the fire, and they are not hurt; and the fourth has the appearance of a god."ᵈ ²⁶Nebuchadnezzar then approached the door of the furnace of blazing fire and said, "Shadrach, Meshach, and Abednego, servants of the Most High God, come out! Come here!" So Shadrach, Meshach, and Abednego came out from the fire. ²⁷And the satraps, the prefects, the governors, and the king's counselors gathered together and saw that the fire had not had any power over the bodies of those men; the hair of their heads was not singed, their tunicsᶜ were not harmed, and not even the smell of fire came from them. ²⁸Nebuchadnezzar said, "Blessed be the God of Shadrach,

---

But If Not . . .

DANIEL 3.18

It is showdown time—pitting God against the officials who are trying to have the Hebrews killed. Shadrach, Meshach and Abednego make a stand for their faith, telling their accusers that God will deliver them, but even if God does not, they still will remain faithful.

"But if not" is a phrase we all may have occasion to use. "God will heal my friend of this disease, but if not . . ." "God will keep our business from failing, but if not . . . " Consider an area of your life where you expect or want God to do something specific, in a certain way. On a piece of paper, write down a phrase or draw a symbol that represents this area and your desire concerning it. Hold this before God in prayer. Then take a felt-tip marker or dark pen and write over your phrase or symbol, "God's will be done, no matter what might happen."

See Meeting God in Scripture

ᵃ Aram lacks *well and good*   ᵇ Or *If our God whom we serve is able to deliver us, he will deliver us from the furnace of blazing fire and out of your hand, O king.*   ᶜ Meaning of Aram word uncertain   ᵈ Aram *a son of the gods*

Imagine the Heat!

DANIEL 3.19–30

The Hebrews are thrown into the fiery furnace, but they are not burned. Do you believe that spectacular miracles like this happen today? On the other hand, is there such a thing as a small miracle? Anytime God intervenes in our lives, it is a miracle. Can you identify times when God intervened in your life or in the life of someone close to you? What "miracles" have you seen recently? Think of a situation in which you want God to act. Lift up this situation before God and watch for a miracle.

See Meeting God in Prayer

Meshach, and Abednego, who has sent his angel and delivered his servants who trusted in him. They disobeyed the king's command and yielded up their bodies rather than serve and worship any god except their own God. ²⁹Therefore I make a decree: Any people, nation, or language that utters blasphemy against the God of Shadrach, Meshach, and Abednego shall be torn limb from limb, and their houses laid in ruins; for there is no other god who is able to deliver in this way." ³⁰Then the king promoted Shadrach, Meshach, and Abednego in the province of Babylon.

Nebuchadnezzar's Second Dream

4ᵃ King Nebuchadnezzar to all peoples, nations, and languages that live throughout the earth: May you have abundant prosperity! ²The signs and wonders that the Most High God has worked for me I am pleased to recount.
³   How great are his signs,
       how mighty his wonders!
     His kingdom is an everlasting kingdom,
       and his sovereignty is from generation to
         generation.
⁴ᵇ I, Nebuchadnezzar, was living at ease in my home and prospering in my palace. ⁵I saw a dream that frightened me; my fantasies in bed and the visions of my head terrified me. ⁶So I made a decree that all the wise men of Babylon should be brought before me, in order that they might tell me the interpretation of the dream. ⁷Then the magicians, the enchanters, the Chaldeans, and the diviners came in, and I told them the dream, but they could not tell me its interpretation. ⁸At last Daniel came in before me—he who was named Belteshazzar after the name of my god, and who is endowed with a spirit of the holy godsᶜ—and I told him the dream: ⁹"O Belteshazzar, chief of the magicians, I know that you are endowed with a spirit of the holy godsᶜ and that no mystery is too difficult for you. Hearᵈ the dream that I saw; tell me its interpretation.
¹⁰ᵉ   Upon my bed this is what I saw;
       there was a tree at the center of the earth,
         and its height was great.
¹¹   The tree grew great and strong,
       its top reached to heaven,
       and it was visible to the ends of the whole earth.
¹²   Its foliage was beautiful,
         its fruit abundant,
       and it provided food for all.
     The animals of the field found shade under it,
         the birds of the air nested in its branches,
       and from it all living beings were fed.
13. "I continued looking, in the visions of my head as I lay in bed, and there was a holy watcher, coming down from heaven. ¹⁴He cried aloud and said:
     'Cut down the tree and chop off its branches,
       strip off its foliage and scatter its fruit.
     Let the animals flee from beneath it
       and the birds from its branches.
¹⁵   But leave its stump and roots in the ground,

ᵃ Ch 3.31 in Aram   ᵇ Ch 4.1 in Aram   ᶜ Or *a holy, divine spirit*
ᵈ Theodotion: Aram *The visions of*   ᵉ Theodotion Syr Compare Gk: Aram adds *The visions of my head*

with a band of iron and bronze,
 in the tender grass of the field.
Let him be bathed with the dew of heaven,
 and let his lot be with the animals of the field
 in the grass of the earth.
16 Let his mind be changed from that of a human,
 and let the mind of an animal be given to him.
 And let seven times pass over him.
17 The sentence is rendered by decree of the watchers,
 the decision is given by order of the holy ones,
 in order that all who live may know
 that the Most High is sovereign over the kingdom
 of mortals;
 he gives it to whom he will
 and sets over it the lowliest of human beings.'

18 "This is the dream that I, King Nebuchadnezzar, saw. Now you, Belteshazzar, declare the interpretation, since all the wise men of my kingdom are unable to tell me the interpretation. You are able, however, for you are endowed with a spirit of the holy gods."[a]

Daniel Interprets the Second Dream

19 Then Daniel, who was called Belteshazzar, was severely distressed for a while. His thoughts terrified him. The king said, "Belteshazzar, do not let the dream or the interpretation terrify you." Belteshazzar answered, "My lord, may the dream be for those who hate you, and its interpretation for your enemies! 20The tree that you saw, which grew great and strong, so that its top reached to heaven and was visible to the end of the whole earth, 21whose foliage was beautiful and its fruit abundant, and which provided food for all, under which animals of the field lived, and in whose branches the birds of the air had nests— 22it is you, O king! You have grown great and strong. Your greatness has increased and reaches to heaven, and your sovereignty to the ends of the earth. 23And whereas the king saw a holy watcher coming down from heaven and saying, 'Cut down the tree and destroy it, but leave its stump and roots in the ground, with a band of iron and bronze, in the grass of the field; and let him be bathed with the dew of heaven, and let his lot be with the animals of the field, until seven times pass over him'— 24this is the interpretation, O king, and it is a decree of the Most High that has come upon my lord the king: 25You shall be driven away from human society, and your dwelling shall be with the wild animals. You shall be made to eat grass like oxen, you shall be bathed with the dew of heaven, and seven times shall pass over you, until you have learned that the Most High has sovereignty over the kingdom of mortals, and gives it to whom he will. 26As it was commanded to leave the stump and roots of the tree, your kingdom shall be re-established for you from the time that you learn that Heaven is sovereign. 27Therefore, O king, may my counsel be acceptable to you: atone for[b] your sins with righteousness, and your iniquities with mercy to the oppressed, so that your prosperity may be prolonged."

Nebuchadnezzar's Humiliation

28 All this came upon King Nebuchadnezzar. 29At the

Hard Words

DANIEL 4.1–27

Have you ever had someone ask you for advice when what that person really needed to hear was difficult for you to say? That's the situation in which Daniel finds himself. His interpretation of the king's dream is harsh, but Daniel is obliged to tell the king the truth.

Think about a time when you had to say something difficult to a friend or family member. Paul's words to the Ephesians set the standard of "speaking the truth in love" (Ephesians 4.15). We may shy away from speaking the truth for fear that we will offend those we love. Ask God to fill you with love as you speak the truth to those who trust you.

See Meeting God in Community

---

a Or *a holy, divine spirit*   *b* Aram *break off*

Desecrating the Holy

DANIEL 5.2–4

The king desecrates the temple goblets by using them to toast idols. He takes the holy things of God and uses them to praise the unholy "gods" of Babylon.

We would never do something like this, would we? We would never use God's people or God's house for our own ends. But we all hear stories about scandals within the religious community, situations in which people misuse what belongs to God. Think about a scandal you've heard about. Does it involve money? Sexual misconduct? Abuse of power or trust? Pray for the people involved. What do you want God to do? Think about your own motives for doing what you do among God's people. Examine yourself. What do you want to say to God about this?

See *Meeting God in Prayer*

end of twelve months he was walking on the roof of the royal palace of Babylon, [30]and the king said, "Is this not magnificent Babylon, which I have built as a royal capital by my mighty power and for my glorious majesty?" [31]While the words were still in the king's mouth, a voice came from heaven: "O King Nebuchadnezzar, to you it is declared: The kingdom has departed from you! [32]You shall be driven away from human society, and your dwelling shall be with the animals of the field. You shall be made to eat grass like oxen, and seven times shall pass over you, until you have learned that the Most High has sovereignty over the kingdom of mortals and gives it to whom he will." [33]Immediately the sentence was fulfilled against Nebuchadnezzar. He was driven away from human society, ate grass like oxen, and his body was bathed with the dew of heaven, until his hair grew as long as eagles' feathers and his nails became like birds' claws.

Nebuchadnezzar Praises God

34 When that period was over, I, Nebuchadnezzar, lifted my eyes to heaven, and my reason returned to me.
> I blessed the Most High,
> > and praised and honored the one who lives forever.
> For his sovereignty is an everlasting sovereignty,
> > and his kingdom endures from generation to generation.
35   All the inhabitants of the earth are accounted as nothing,
> > and he does what he wills with the host of heaven
> > and the inhabitants of the earth.
> There is no one who can stay his hand
> > or say to him, "What are you doing?"

[36]At that time my reason returned to me; and my majesty and splendor were restored to me for the glory of my kingdom. My counselors and my lords sought me out, I was re-established over my kingdom, and still more greatness was added to me. [37]Now I, Nebuchadnezzar, praise and extol and honor the King of heaven,
> for all his works are truth,
> > and his ways are justice;
> and he is able to bring low
> > those who walk in pride.

Belshazzar's Feast

5 King Belshazzar made a great festival for a thousand of his lords, and he was drinking wine in the presence of the thousand.
2 Under the influence of the wine, Belshazzar commanded that they bring in the vessels of gold and silver that his father Nebuchadnezzar had taken out of the temple in Jerusalem, so that the king and his lords, his wives, and his concubines might drink from them. [3]So they brought in the vessels of gold and silver[a] that had been taken out of the temple, the house of God in Jerusalem, and the king and his lords, his wives, and his concubines drank from them. [4]They drank the wine and praised the gods of gold and silver, bronze, iron, wood, and stone.

a Theodotion Vg: Aram lacks *and silver*

The Writing on the Wall

5 Immediately the fingers of a human hand appeared and began writing on the plaster of the wall of the royal palace, next to the lampstand. The king was watching the hand as it wrote. [6]Then the king's face turned pale, and his thoughts terrified him. His limbs gave way, and his knees knocked together. [7]The king cried aloud to bring in the enchanters, the Chaldeans, and the diviners; and the king said to the wise men of Babylon, "Whoever can read this writing and tell me its interpretation shall be clothed in purple, have a chain of gold around his neck, and rank third in the kingdom." [8]Then all the king's wise men came in, but they could not read the writing or tell the king the interpretation. [9]Then King Belshazzar became greatly terrified and his face turned pale, and his lords were perplexed.

10 The queen, when she heard the discussion of the king and his lords, came into the banqueting hall. The queen said, "O king, live forever! Do not let your thoughts terrify you or your face grow pale. [11]There is a man in your kingdom who is endowed with a spirit of the holy gods.[a] In the days of your father he was found to have enlightenment, understanding, and wisdom like the wisdom of the gods. Your father, King Nebuchadnezzar, made him chief of the magicians, enchanters, Chaldeans, and diviners,[b] [12]because an excellent spirit, knowledge, and understanding to interpret dreams, explain riddles, and solve problems were found in this Daniel, whom the king named Belteshazzar. Now let Daniel be called, and he will give the interpretation."

The Writing on the Wall Interpreted

13 Then Daniel was brought in before the king. The king said to Daniel, "So you are Daniel, one of the exiles of Judah, whom my father the king brought from Judah? [14]I have heard of you that a spirit of the gods[c] is in you, and that enlightenment, understanding, and excellent wisdom are found in you. [15]Now the wise men, the enchanters, have been brought in before me to read this writing and tell me its interpretation, but they were not able to give the interpretation of the matter. [16]But I have heard that you can give interpretations and solve problems. Now if you are able to read the writing and tell me its interpretation, you shall be clothed in purple, have a chain of gold around your neck, and rank third in the kingdom."

17 Then Daniel answered in the presence of the king, "Let your gifts be for yourself, or give your rewards to someone else! Nevertheless I will read the writing to the king and let him know the interpretation. [18]O king, the Most High God gave your father Nebuchadnezzar kingship, greatness, glory, and majesty. [19]And because of the greatness that he gave him, all peoples, nations, and languages trembled and feared before him. He killed those he wanted to kill, kept alive those he wanted to keep alive, honored those he wanted to honor, and degraded those he wanted to degrade. [20]But when his heart was lifted up and his spirit was hardened so that he acted proudly, he was deposed from his kingly throne, and his glory was stripped from him. [21]He was driven from human society, and his mind

The Search for Meaning

DANIEL 5.5–16

Daniel helps others make sense of life's mysteries. This passage makes it clear that such a skill is a divine gift. Do you know someone who is truly wise, someone who has a gift for helping others make sense of confusion? Do you have this gift? Give thanks for those who have helped you to see the way before you in a confusing time.

See Meeting God in Community

---

a Or *a holy, divine spirit*   b Aram adds *the king your father*   c Or *a divine spirit*

In God's Hand

All people, even those who are not believers, are held in God's hand. Think about this. God holds each of us— even those who do not recognize that it is God who gives them breath—in his hand. Imagine yourself in God's hand, and there, right beside you, is someone whose beliefs are very different from yours. Perhaps it is someone who has done heinous things or someone you have hated for years. Yet you both are there. And God gives breath to both of you. What do you feel? What does this say to you about God?

See Meeting God in Worship

was made like that of an animal. His dwelling was with the wild asses, he was fed grass like oxen, and his body was bathed with the dew of heaven, until he learned that the Most High God has sovereignty over the kingdom of mortals, and sets over it whomever he will. ²²And you, Belshazzar his son, have not humbled your heart, even though you knew all this! ²³You have exalted yourself against the Lord of heaven! The vessels of his temple have been brought in before you, and you and your lords, your wives and your concubines have been drinking wine from them. You have praised the gods of silver and gold, of bronze, iron, wood, and stone, which do not see or hear or know; but the God in whose power is your very breath, and to whom belong all your ways, you have not honored.

24 "So from his presence the hand was sent and this writing was inscribed: ²⁵And this is the writing that was inscribed: MENE, MENE, TEKEL, and PARSIN. ²⁶This is the interpretation of the matter: MENE, God has numbered the days of*ᵃ* your kingdom and brought it to an end; ²⁷TEKEL, you have been weighed on the scales and found wanting; ²⁸PERES,*ᵇ* your kingdom is divided and given to the Medes and Persians."

29 Then Belshazzar gave the command, and Daniel was clothed in purple, a chain of gold was put around his neck, and a proclamation was made concerning him that he should rank third in the kingdom.

30 That very night Belshazzar, the Chaldean king, was killed. ³¹*ᶜ*And Darius the Mede received the kingdom, being about sixty-two years old.

The Plot against Daniel

6 It pleased Darius to set over the kingdom one hundred twenty satraps, stationed throughout the whole kingdom, ²and over them three presidents, including Daniel; to these the satraps gave account, so that the king might suffer no loss. ³Soon Daniel distinguished himself above all the other presidents and satraps because an excellent spirit was in him, and the king planned to appoint him over the whole kingdom. ⁴So the presidents and the satraps tried to find grounds for complaint against Daniel in connection with the kingdom. But they could find no grounds for complaint or any corruption, because he was faithful, and no negligence or corruption could be found in him. ⁵The men said, "We shall not find any ground for complaint against this Daniel unless we find it in connection with the law of his God."

6 So the presidents and satraps conspired and came to the king and said to him, "O King Darius, live forever! ⁷All the presidents of the kingdom, the prefects and the satraps, the counselors and the governors are agreed that the king should establish an ordinance and enforce an interdict, that whoever prays to anyone, divine or human, for thirty days, except to you, O king, shall be thrown into a den of lions. ⁸Now, O king, establish the interdict and sign the document, so that it cannot be changed, according to the law of the Medes and the Persians, which cannot be revoked." ⁹Therefore King Darius signed the document and interdict.

Daniel in the Lions' Den

10 Although Daniel knew that the document had been signed, he continued to go to his house, which had win-

a Aram lacks *the days of*   *b* The singular of *Parsin*   *c* Ch 6.1 in Aram

dows in its upper room open toward Jerusalem, and to get down on his knees three times a day to pray to his God and praise him, just as he had done previously. ¹¹The conspirators came and found Daniel praying and seeking mercy before his God. ¹²Then they approached the king and said concerning the interdict, "O king! Did you not sign an interdict, that anyone who prays to anyone, divine or human, within thirty days except to you, O king, shall be thrown into a den of lions?" The king answered, "The thing stands fast, according to the law of the Medes and Persians, which cannot be revoked." ¹³Then they responded to the king, "Daniel, one of the exiles from Judah, pays no attention to you, O king, or to the interdict you have signed, but he is saying his prayers three times a day."

14 When the king heard the charge, he was very much distressed. He was determined to save Daniel, and until the sun went down he made every effort to rescue him. ¹⁵Then the conspirators came to the king and said to him, "Know, O king, that it is a law of the Medes and Persians that no interdict or ordinance that the king establishes can be changed."

16 Then the king gave the command, and Daniel was brought and thrown into the den of lions. The king said to Daniel, "May your God, whom you faithfully serve, deliver you!" ¹⁷A stone was brought and laid on the mouth of the den, and the king sealed it with his own signet and with the signet of his lords, so that nothing might be changed concerning Daniel. ¹⁸Then the king went to his palace and spent the night fasting; no food was brought to him, and sleep fled from him.

Daniel Saved from the Lions

19 Then, at break of day, the king got up and hurried to the den of lions. ²⁰When he came near the den where Daniel was, he cried out anxiously to Daniel, "O Daniel, servant of the living God, has your God whom you faithfully serve been able to deliver you from the lions?" ²¹Daniel then said to the king, "O king, live forever! ²²My God sent his angel and shut the lions' mouths so that they would not hurt me, because I was found blameless before him; and also before you, O king, I have done no wrong." ²³Then the king was exceedingly glad and commanded that Daniel be taken up out of the den. So Daniel was taken up out of the den, and no kind of harm was found on him, because he had trusted in his God. ²⁴The king gave a command, and those who had accused Daniel were brought and thrown into the den of lions—they, their children, and their wives. Before they reached the bottom of the den the lions overpowered them and broke all their bones in pieces.

25 Then King Darius wrote to all peoples and nations of every language throughout the whole world: "May you have abundant prosperity! ²⁶I make a decree, that in all my royal dominion people should tremble and fear before the God of Daniel:

> For he is the living God,
> > enduring forever.
> His kingdom shall never be destroyed,
> > and his dominion has no end.

²⁷ He delivers and rescues,

Caught in the System

DANIEL 6.10–18

Jealous officials set up a law to force the king into throwing Daniel into the lions' den. The system assumes a life of its own; once the machinery starts, the king cannot stop it and rescue Daniel even though he wants to. But God intervenes to shut the mouths of the lions.

Think about the social systems in our society—welfare, health, corporate and political systems—that sometimes help but often hurt people (not to mention the snares of sweatshop labor and the drug culture). We feel powerless to make changes that will keep people from being ground up in the machinery of the system. In what situations might you call out to God to "shut the lions' mouths"? What systems seem out of control—too powerful for us to make a difference? Where do you need to stand firm? What helps you to remember that God is with you?

See Meeting God in Service

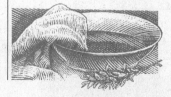

A Fearsome Vision

DANIEL 7.1–14

Like many visions of judgment, this one is full of symbols that can be interpreted many different ways. Most interpreters say the four beasts represent four kingdoms that will rise and fall. But the vision also offers hope in its picture of the "Ancient One," the One who will ultimately triumph over all kingdoms, good and bad. Read again verses 9 and 10 and draw a picture to represent the One who holds the victory. What colors will you use? What emotions does the picture evoke in you? What feelings would you want your picture to evoke in those who might see it?

See Meeting God in Scripture

he works signs and wonders in heaven and on earth;
> for he has saved Daniel
> from the power of the lions."

²⁸So this Daniel prospered during the reign of Darius and the reign of Cyrus the Persian.

Visions of the Four Beasts

7 In the first year of King Belshazzar of Babylon, Daniel had a dream and visions of his head as he lay in bed. Then he wrote down the dream:ᵃ ²I,ᵇ Daniel, saw in my vision by night the four winds of heaven stirring up the great sea, ³and four great beasts came up out of the sea, different from one another. ⁴The first was like a lion and had eagles' wings. Then, as I watched, its wings were plucked off, and it was lifted up from the ground and made to stand on two feet like a human being; and a human mind was given to it. ⁵Another beast appeared, a second one, that looked like a bear. It was raised up on one side, had three tusksᶜ in its mouth among its teeth and was told, "Arise, devour many bodies!" ⁶After this, as I watched, another appeared, like a leopard. The beast had four wings of a bird on its back and four heads; and dominion was given to it. ⁷After this I saw in the visions by night a fourth beast, terrifying and dreadful and exceedingly strong. It had great iron teeth and was devouring, breaking in pieces, and stamping what was left with its feet. It was different from all the beasts that preceded it, and it had ten horns. ⁸I was considering the horns, when another horn appeared, a little one coming up among them; to make room for it, three of the earlier horns were plucked up by the roots. There were eyes like human eyes in this horn, and a mouth speaking arrogantly.

Judgment before the Ancient One

9   As I watched,
> thrones were set in place,
>> and an Ancient Oneᵈ took his throne,
> his clothing was white as snow,
>> and the hair of his head like pure wool;
> his throne was fiery flames,
>> and its wheels were burning fire.
10   A stream of fire issued
> and flowed out from his presence.
> A thousand thousands served him,
>> and ten thousand times ten thousand stood attending him.
> The court sat in judgment,
>> and the books were opened.

¹¹I watched then because of the noise of the arrogant words that the horn was speaking. And as I watched, the beast was put to death, and its body destroyed and given over to be burned with fire. ¹²As for the rest of the beasts, their dominion was taken away, but their lives were prolonged for a season and a time. ¹³As I watched in the night visions,
> I saw one like a human beingᵉ
>> coming with the clouds of heaven.
> And he came to the Ancient Oneᶠ

a Q Ms Theodotion: MT adds *the beginning of the words; he said*
b Theodotion: Aram *Daniel answered and said, "I*   c Or *ribs*   d Aram *an Ancient of Days*   e Aram *one like a son of man*   f Aram *the Ancient of Days*

and was presented before him.
[14] To him was given dominion
and glory and kingship,
that all peoples, nations, and languages
should serve him.
His dominion is an everlasting dominion
that shall not pass away,
and his kingship is one
that shall never be destroyed.

Daniel's Visions Interpreted

15 As for me, Daniel, my spirit was troubled within me,[a] and the visions of my head terrified me. [16]I approached one of the attendants to ask him the truth concerning all this. So he said that he would disclose to me the interpretation of the matter: [17]"As for these four great beasts, four kings shall arise out of the earth. [18]But the holy ones of the Most High shall receive the kingdom and possess the kingdom forever—forever and ever."

19 Then I desired to know the truth concerning the fourth beast, which was different from all the rest, exceedingly terrifying, with its teeth of iron and claws of bronze, and which devoured and broke in pieces, and stamped what was left with its feet; [20]and concerning the ten horns that were on its head, and concerning the other horn, which came up and to make room for which three of them fell out—the horn that had eyes and a mouth that spoke arrogantly, and that seemed greater than the others. [21]As I looked, this horn made war with the holy ones and was prevailing over them, [22]until the Ancient One[b] came; then judgment was given for the holy ones of the Most High, and the time arrived when the holy ones gained possession of the kingdom.

23 This is what he said: "As for the fourth beast,
there shall be a fourth kingdom on earth
that shall be different from all the other kingdoms;
it shall devour the whole earth,
and trample it down, and break it to pieces.
[24] As for the ten horns,
out of this kingdom ten kings shall arise,
and another shall arise after them.
This one shall be different from the former ones,
and shall put down three kings.
[25] He shall speak words against the Most High,
shall wear out the holy ones of the Most High,
and shall attempt to change the sacred seasons
and the law;
and they shall be given into his power
for a time, two times,[c] and half a time.
[26] Then the court shall sit in judgment,
and his dominion shall be taken away,
to be consumed and totally destroyed.
[27] The kingship and dominion
and the greatness of the kingdoms under the
whole heaven
shall be given to the people of the holy ones of
the Most High;
their kingdom shall be an everlasting kingdom,
and all dominions shall serve and obey them."

Faith Responds to Fear

DANIEL 7.15

Daniel's vision frightens and unsettles him, and so he asks for help. Think about your own life. What is it that you fear? Do you imagine terrible possibilities? Are there troublesome situations facing you that you need help understanding? How can you follow Daniel's example? Consider talking with a trusted friend, a counselor or a pastor if you find that fears intrude on your ability to face daily life with peace.

See *Meeting God in Community*

a Aram *troubled in its sheath*   b Aram *the Ancient of Days*   c Aram *a time, times*

Who Can Break This?

DANIEL 8.23–25

When deceit seems to prosper, Gabriel's words remind us that we are not alone and that we do not work alone to overcome evil. We must do what we can, but evil is overcome finally "not by human hands" but by the power of God. This is good news for us. God will keep on working until evil is defeated.

Bring to mind a situation in which evil and deceit seem to dominate. Now envision the light of God's power flooding into that situation. Envision yourself as a torchbearer, carrying God's light on a pole. Approach the situation, praying for God's power to be with you and within you. Plant the torch in the middle of the situation and, in your mind's eye, leave it there as a reminder that God is at work.

See Meeting God in Scripture

28 Here the account ends. As for me, Daniel, my thoughts greatly terrified me, and my face turned pale; but I kept the matter in my mind.

Vision of a Ram and a Goat

8 In the third year of the reign of King Belshazzar a vision appeared to me, Daniel, after the one that had appeared to me at first. [2]In the vision I was looking and saw myself in Susa the capital, in the province of Elam,[a] and I was by the river Ulai.[b] [3]I looked up and saw a ram standing beside the river.[c] It had two horns. Both horns were long, but one was longer than the other, and the longer one came up second. [4]I saw the ram charging westward and northward and southward. All beasts were powerless to withstand it, and no one could rescue from its power; it did as it pleased and became strong.

5 As I was watching, a male goat appeared from the west, coming across the face of the whole earth without touching the ground. The goat had a horn[d] between its eyes. [6]It came toward the ram with the two horns that I had seen standing beside the river,[c] and it ran at it with savage force. [7]I saw it approaching the ram. It was enraged against it and struck the ram, breaking its two horns. The ram did not have power to withstand it; it threw the ram down to the ground and trampled upon it, and there was no one who could rescue the ram from its power. [8]Then the male goat grew exceedingly great; but at the height of its power, the great horn was broken, and in its place there came up four prominent horns toward the four winds of heaven.

9 Out of one of them came another[e] horn, a little one, which grew exceedingly great toward the south, toward the east, and toward the beautiful land. [10]It grew as high as the host of heaven. It threw down to the earth some of the host and some of the stars, and trampled on them. [11]Even against the prince of the host it acted arrogantly; it took the regular burnt offering away from him and overthrew the place of his sanctuary. [12]Because of wickedness, the host was given over to it together with the regular burnt offering;[f] it cast truth to the ground, and kept prospering in what it did. [13]Then I heard a holy one speaking, and another holy one said to the one that spoke, "For how long is this vision concerning the regular burnt offering, the transgression that makes desolate, and the giving over of the sanctuary and host to be trampled?"[f] [14]And he answered him,[g] "For two thousand three hundred evenings and mornings; then the sanctuary shall be restored to its rightful state."

Gabriel Interprets the Vision

15 When I, Daniel, had seen the vision, I tried to understand it. Then someone appeared standing before me, having the appearance of a man, [16]and I heard a human voice by the Ulai, calling, "Gabriel, help this man understand the vision." [17]So he came near where I stood; and when he came, I became frightened and fell prostrate. But he said to me, "Understand, O mortal,[h] that the vision is for the time of the end."

a Gk Theodotion: MT Q Ms repeat *in the vision I was looking*   *b* Or *the Ulai Gate*   *c* Or *gate*   *d* Theodotion: Gk *one horn*; Heb *a horn of vision*
e Cn Compare 7.8: Heb *one*   *f* Meaning of Heb uncertain
g Gk Theodotion Syr Vg: Heb *me*   *h* Heb *son of man*

18 As he was speaking to me, I fell into a trance, face to the ground; then he touched me and set me on my feet. ¹⁹He said, "Listen, and I will tell you what will take place later in the period of wrath; for it refers to the appointed time of the end. ²⁰As for the ram that you saw with the two horns, these are the kings of Media and Persia. ²¹The male goat*a* is the king of Greece, and the great horn between its eyes is the first king. ²²As for the horn that was broken, in place of which four others arose, four kingdoms shall arise from his*b* nation, but not with his power.

23   At the end of their rule,
      when the transgressions have reached their full
         measure,
    a king of bold countenance shall arise,
      skilled in intrigue.
24   He shall grow strong in power,*c*
      shall cause fearful destruction,
      and shall succeed in what he does.
    He shall destroy the powerful
      and the people of the holy ones.
25   By his cunning
      he shall make deceit prosper under his hand,
      and in his own mind he shall be great.
    Without warning he shall destroy many
      and shall even rise up against the Prince of princes.
    But he shall be broken, and not by human hands.

²⁶The vision of the evenings and the mornings that has been told is true. As for you, seal up the vision, for it refers to many days from now."

27 So I, Daniel, was overcome and lay sick for some days; then I arose and went about the king's business. But I was dismayed by the vision and did not understand it.

Daniel's Prayer for the People

9 In the first year of Darius son of Ahasuerus, by birth a Mede, who became king over the realm of the Chaldeans— ²in the first year of his reign, I, Daniel, perceived in the books the number of years that, according to the word of the LORD to the prophet Jeremiah, must be fulfilled for the devastation of Jerusalem, namely, seventy years.

3 Then I turned to the Lord God, to seek an answer by prayer and supplication with fasting and sackcloth and ashes. ⁴I prayed to the LORD my God and made confession, saying,

"Ah, Lord, great and awesome God, keeping covenant and steadfast love with those who love you and keep your commandments, ⁵we have sinned and done wrong, acted wickedly and rebelled, turning aside from your commandments and ordinances. ⁶We have not listened to your servants the prophets, who spoke in your name to our kings, our princes, and our ancestors, and to all the people of the land.

7 "Righteousness is on your side, O Lord, but open shame, as at this day, falls on us, the people of Judah, the inhabitants of Jerusalem, and all Israel, those who are near and those who are far away, in all the lands to which you have driven them, because of the treachery that they have committed against you. ⁸Open shame, O LORD, falls on us, our kings, our officials, and our ancestors, because we have sinned against you. ⁹To the Lord our God belong mercy and

God's Fidelity

DANIEL 9.4–5,9,13,18

Daniel is praying again. He begins by praising God for his steadfastness in keeping the covenant with his people. God has shown great mercy and love even though his people have not kept faith. That is the story of this people over and over again. Look back over your life for evidence of God's "great mercies" and love shown toward you. Especially look for times when your faithfulness waned but God's did not. Reflect on God's faithfulness. How has God loved you? Through whom has God loved you? Make a list of instances of God's faithfulness and carry it with you for the next several days. Each time you see the list or think of it, place your hand on your heart as an acknowledgment that God's faithfulness is as steady as the rhythm of your beating heart.

See Meeting God in Everyday Life

---

a Or *shaggy male goat*   *b* Gk Theodotion Vg: Heb *the*   *c* Theodotion and one Gk Ms: Heb repeats (from 8.22) *but not with his power*

For the Nation

DANIEL 9.20

Daniel offers a model of confessing on behalf of a nation and praying for it. What might you confess on behalf of your nation today? What might you ask God to do for your nation? And what is your prayer for nations other than your own? Write on a small card or piece of paper something to remind you to pray for your country, and place the card near your television, radio or stack of news magazines. For the next week, "pray through the news." Pray about the people, systems and situations mentioned in the news stories.

See Meeting God in Prayer

forgiveness, for we have rebelled against him, [10]and have not obeyed the voice of the LORD our God by following his laws, which he set before us by his servants the prophets.

11 "All Israel has transgressed your law and turned aside, refusing to obey your voice. So the curse and the oath written in the law of Moses, the servant of God, have been poured out upon us, because we have sinned against you. [12]He has confirmed his words, which he spoke against us and against our rulers, by bringing upon us a calamity so great that what has been done against Jerusalem has never before been done under the whole heaven. [13]Just as it is written in the law of Moses, all this calamity has come upon us. We did not entreat the favor of the LORD our God, turning from our iniquities and reflecting on his[a] fidelity. [14]So the LORD kept watch over this calamity until he brought it upon us. Indeed, the LORD our God is right in all that he has done; for we have disobeyed his voice.

15 "And now, O Lord our God, who brought your people out of the land of Egypt with a mighty hand and made your name renowned even to this day—we have sinned, we have done wickedly. [16]O Lord, in view of all your righteous acts, let your anger and wrath, we pray, turn away from your city Jerusalem, your holy mountain; because of our sins and the iniquities of our ancestors, Jerusalem and your people have become a disgrace among all our neighbors. [17]Now therefore, O our God, listen to the prayer of your servant and to his supplication, and for your own sake, Lord,[b] let your face shine upon your desolated sanctuary. [18]Incline your ear, O my God, and hear. Open your eyes and look at our desolation and the city that bears your name. We do not present our supplication before you on the ground of our righteousness, but on the ground of your great mercies. [19]O Lord, hear; O Lord, forgive; O Lord, listen and act and do not delay! For your own sake, O my God, because your city and your people bear your name!"

The Seventy Weeks

20 While I was speaking, and was praying and confessing my sin and the sin of my people Israel, and presenting my supplication before the LORD my God on behalf of the holy mountain of my God— [21]while I was speaking in prayer, the man Gabriel, whom I had seen before in a vision, came to me in swift flight at the time of the evening sacrifice. [22]He came[c] and said to me, "Daniel, I have now come out to give you wisdom and understanding. [23]At the beginning of your supplications a word went out, and I have come to declare it, for you are greatly beloved. So consider the word and understand the vision:

24 "Seventy weeks are decreed for your people and your holy city: to finish the transgression, to put an end to sin, and to atone for iniquity, to bring in everlasting righteousness, to seal both vision and prophet, and to anoint a most holy place.[d] [25]Know therefore and understand: from the time that the word went out to restore and rebuild Jerusalem until the time of an anointed prince, there shall be seven weeks; and for sixty-two weeks it shall be built again with streets and moat, but in a troubled time. [26]After the sixty-two weeks, an anointed one shall be cut off and shall have nothing, and the

---

a Heb *your*   *b* Theodotion Vg Compare Syr: Heb *for the Lord's sake*
c Gk Syr: Heb *He made to understand*   *d* Or *thing* or *one*

troops of the prince who is to come shall destroy the city and the sanctuary. Its[a] end shall come with a flood, and to the end there shall be war. Desolations are decreed. 27He shall make a strong covenant with many for one week, and for half of the week he shall make sacrifice and offering cease; and in their place[b] shall be an abomination that desolates, until the decreed end is poured out upon the desolator."

Conflict of Nations and Heavenly Powers

10 In the third year of King Cyrus of Persia a word was revealed to Daniel, who was named Belteshazzar. The word was true, and it concerned a great conflict. He understood the word, having received understanding in the vision. 2 At that time I, Daniel, had been mourning for three weeks. 3I had eaten no rich food, no meat or wine had entered my mouth, and I had not anointed myself at all, for the full three weeks. 4On the twenty-fourth day of the first month, as I was standing on the bank of the great river (that is, the Tigris), 5I looked up and saw a man clothed in linen, with a belt of gold from Uphaz around his waist. 6His body was like beryl, his face like lightning, his eyes like flaming torches, his arms and legs like the gleam of burnished bronze, and the sound of his words like the roar of a multitude. 7I, Daniel, alone saw the vision; the people who were with me did not see the vision, though a great trembling fell upon them, and they fled and hid themselves. 8So I was left alone to see this great vision. My strength left me, and my complexion grew deathly pale, and I retained no strength. 9Then I heard the sound of his words; and when I heard the sound of his words, I fell into a trance, face to the ground.

10 But then a hand touched me and roused me to my hands and knees. 11He said to me, "Daniel, greatly beloved, pay attention to the words that I am going to speak to you. Stand on your feet, for I have now been sent to you." So while he was speaking this word to me, I stood up trembling. 12He said to me, "Do not fear, Daniel, for from the first day that you set your mind to gain understanding and to humble yourself before your God, your words have been heard, and I have come because of your words. 13But the prince of the kingdom of Persia opposed me twenty-one days. So Michael, one of the chief princes, came to help me, and I left him there with the prince of the kingdom of Persia,[c] 14and have come to help you understand what is to happen to your people at the end of days. For there is a further vision for those days."

15 While he was speaking these words to me, I turned my face toward the ground and was speechless. 16Then one in human form touched my lips, and I opened my mouth to speak, and said to the one who stood before me, "My lord, because of the vision such pains have come upon me that I retain no strength. 17How can my lord's servant talk with my lord? For I am shaking,[d] no strength remains in me, and no breath is left in me."

18 Again one in human form touched me and strengthened me. 19He said, "Do not fear, greatly beloved, you are safe. Be strong and courageous!" When he spoke to me, I was strengthened and said, "Let my lord speak, for you have strengthened me." 20Then he said, "Do you know why I have come to you? Now I must return to fight against the

Answers to Prayer

DANIEL 10.10–18

Daniel has been praying and fasting for three weeks. The heavenly messenger says Daniel's words have been heard from the first day that he started to pray.

The absence of a visible answer does not mean our prayers are not heard. Some prayers are answered quickly, but sometimes we must persevere in prayer and "pray without ceasing" (1 Thessalonians 5.17). Write down on a slip of paper the names of the persons or situations that have dominated your prayers. On the same slip of paper, write, "My words have been heard, and God is sending help." Place the paper in a place where you will see it frequently as a reminder that persistent prayer matters and that God responds to your perseverance.

See Meeting God in Prayer

a Or His   b Cn: Meaning of Heb uncertain   c Gk Theodotion: Heb I was left there with the kings of Persia   d Gk: Heb from now

History Through God's Eyes

DANIEL 11.6–24

In this extended passage, God gives Daniel a gift—the ability to see his contemporary situation against the backdrop of the divine time line of the universe. No matter how bleak or dark the human story appears to be—God is ultimately in control and will bring the kingdom to fruition.

How does the knowledge that God is in control of history help give you perspective on your own situation? Find a time line of Biblical history in a Bible reference book, or look in a world historical atlas in order to envision all of human history. Or read the first three chapters of Genesis and the last three of Revelation in one sitting. What is God saying to you about your place in history?

See Meeting God in Scripture

prince of Persia, and when I am through with him, the prince of Greece will come. ²¹But I am to tell you what is inscribed in the book of truth. There is no one with me who contends against these princes except Michael, your prince.

11 ¹As for me, in the first year of Darius the Mede, I stood up to support and strengthen him.

2 "Now I will announce the truth to you. Three more kings shall arise in Persia. The fourth shall be far richer than all of them, and when he has become strong through his riches, he shall stir up all against the kingdom of Greece. ³Then a warrior king shall arise, who shall rule with great dominion and take action as he pleases. ⁴And while still rising in power, his kingdom shall be broken and divided toward the four winds of heaven, but not to his posterity, nor according to the dominion with which he ruled; for his kingdom shall be uprooted and go to others besides these.

5 "Then the king of the south shall grow strong, but one of his officers shall grow stronger than he and shall rule a realm greater than his own realm. ⁶After some years they shall make an alliance, and the daughter of the king of the south shall come to the king of the north to ratify the agreement. But she shall not retain her power, and his offspring shall not endure. She shall be given up, she and her attendants and her child and the one who supported her.

"In those times ⁷a branch from her roots shall rise up in his place. He shall come against the army and enter the fortress of the king of the north, and he shall take action against them and prevail. ⁸Even their gods, with their idols and with their precious vessels of silver and gold, he shall carry off to Egypt as spoils of war. For some years he shall refrain from attacking the king of the north; ⁹then the latter shall invade the realm of the king of the south, but will return to his own land.

10 "His sons shall wage war and assemble a multitude of great forces, which shall advance like a flood and pass through, and again shall carry the war as far as his fortress. ¹¹Moved with rage, the king of the south shall go out and do battle against the king of the north, who shall muster a great multitude, which shall, however, be defeated by his enemy. ¹²When the multitude has been carried off, his heart shall be exalted, and he shall overthrow tens of thousands, but he shall not prevail. ¹³For the king of the north shall again raise a multitude, larger than the former, and after some years*a* he shall advance with a great army and abundant supplies.

14 "In those times many shall rise against the king of the south. The lawless among your own people shall lift themselves up in order to fulfill the vision, but they shall fail. ¹⁵Then the king of the north shall come and throw up siegeworks, and take a well-fortified city. And the forces of the south shall not stand, not even his picked troops, for there shall be no strength to resist. ¹⁶But he who comes against him shall take the actions he pleases, and no one shall withstand him. He shall take a position in the beautiful land, and all of it shall be in his power. ¹⁷He shall set his mind to come with the strength of his whole kingdom, and he shall bring terms of peace*b* and perform them. In order to destroy the kingdom,*c* he shall give him a woman in marriage; but it shall not succeed or be to his advantage. ¹⁸Afterward he shall turn to the coastlands, and shall cap-

---

a Heb *and at the end of the times years*   *b* Gk: Heb *kingdom, and upright ones with him*   *c* Heb *it*

ture many. But a commander shall put an end to his insolence; indeed,[a] he shall turn his insolence back upon him.
¹⁹Then he shall turn back toward the fortresses of his own
land, but he shall stumble and fall, and shall not be found.

20 "Then shall arise in his place one who shall send an
official for the glory of the kingdom; but within a few days
he shall be broken, though not in anger or in battle. ²¹In his
place shall arise a contemptible person on whom royal
majesty had not been conferred; he shall come in without
warning and obtain the kingdom through intrigue. ²²Armies
shall be utterly swept away and broken before him, and the
prince of the covenant as well. ²³And after an alliance is
made with him, he shall act deceitfully and become strong
with a small party. ²⁴Without warning he shall come into
the richest parts[b] of the province and do what none of his
predecessors had ever done, lavishing plunder, spoil, and
wealth on them. He shall devise plans against strongholds,
but only for a time. ²⁵He shall stir up his power and determination against the king of the south with a great army,
and the king of the south shall wage war with a much
greater and stronger army. But he shall not succeed, for
plots shall be devised against him ²⁶by those who eat of
the royal rations. They shall break him, his army shall be
swept away, and many shall fall slain. ²⁷The two kings, their
minds bent on evil, shall sit at one table and exchange lies.
But it shall not succeed, for there remains an end at the
time appointed. ²⁸He shall return to his land with great
wealth, but his heart shall be set against the holy covenant.
He shall work his will, and return to his own land.

29 "At the time appointed he shall return and come into
the south, but this time it shall not be as it was before. ³⁰For
ships of Kittim shall come against him, and he shall lose
heart and withdraw. He shall be enraged and take action
against the holy covenant. He shall turn back and pay heed
to those who forsake the holy covenant. ³¹Forces sent by
him shall occupy and profane the temple and fortress. They
shall abolish the regular burnt offering and set up the abomination that makes desolate. ³²He shall seduce with intrigue
those who violate the covenant; but the people who are
loyal to their God shall stand firm and take action. ³³The
wise among the people shall give understanding to many;
for some days, however, they shall fall by sword and flame,
and suffer captivity and plunder. ³⁴When they fall victim,
they shall receive a little help, and many shall join them in-
sincerely. ³⁵Some of the wise shall fall, so that they may be
refined, purified, and cleansed,[c] until the time of the end,
for there is still an interval until the time appointed.

36 "The king shall act as he pleases. He shall exalt himself
and consider himself greater than any god, and shall speak
horrendous things against the God of gods. He shall prosper
until the period of wrath is completed, for what is determined shall be done. ³⁷He shall pay no respect to the gods of
his ancestors, or to the one beloved by women; he shall pay
no respect to any other god, for he shall consider himself
greater than all. ³⁸He shall honor the god of fortresses instead of these; a god whom his ancestors did not know he
shall honor with gold and silver, with precious stones and
costly gifts. ³⁹He shall deal with the strongest fortresses by

God in Politics

DANIEL 11.29–32

Monarchs rise and monarchs
fall. Countries overcome one
another and are conquered in
turn. God is involved. God is
not apolitical—he directs the
drama of world events "at the
time appointed."

Are you to be one of the
players? Is it the appointed
time for you to be involved in
political matters? Are you being
called to be God's servant in
shaping the history of humankind in one way or another? Do you ask God to guide
and shape your political views
and help you make wise decisions at the polls?

See Meeting God in Service

Rest in Peace

DANIEL 12.12–13

Rest? In the midst of receiving this confusing and troubling vision, Daniel is urged by God's messenger to do exactly that. The things that will be done, *will* be done—in God's time. Daniel cannot hurry the events or hasten his understanding of them. Until God's appointed time, he is told to rest.

Reflect on your recent prayers and isolate something you are troubled about or do not understand. Draw a picture to remind you of this situation, fold the paper and offer this concern to God. Remind yourself that you cannot hurry or slow down the resolution of some events. Place the folded paper in your Bible as a symbol of leaving the problem or situation in God's hand.

See *Meeting God in Everyday Life*

the help of a foreign god. Those who acknowledge him he shall make more wealthy, and shall appoint them as rulers over many, and shall distribute the land for a price.

The Time of the End

40 "At the time of the end the king of the south shall attack him. But the king of the north shall rush upon him like a whirlwind, with chariots and horsemen, and with many ships. He shall advance against countries and pass through like a flood. ⁴¹He shall come into the beautiful land, and tens of thousands shall fall victim, but Edom and Moab and the main part of the Ammonites shall escape from his power. ⁴²He shall stretch out his hand against the countries, and the land of Egypt shall not escape. ⁴³He shall become ruler of the treasures of gold and of silver, and all the riches of Egypt; and the Libyans and the Ethiopians*ᵃ* shall follow in his train. ⁴⁴But reports from the east and the north shall alarm him, and he shall go out with great fury to bring ruin and complete destruction to many. ⁴⁵He shall pitch his palatial tents between the sea and the beautiful holy mountain. Yet he shall come to his end, with no one to help him.

The Resurrection of the Dead

12 "At that time Michael, the great prince, the protector of your people, shall arise. There shall be a time of anguish, such as has never occurred since nations first came into existence. But at that time your people shall be delivered, everyone who is found written in the book. ²Many of those who sleep in the dust of the earth*ᵇ* shall awake, some to everlasting life, and some to shame and everlasting contempt. ³Those who are wise shall shine like the brightness of the sky,*ᶜ* and those who lead many to righteousness, like the stars forever and ever. ⁴But you, Daniel, keep the words secret and the book sealed until the time of the end. Many shall be running back and forth, and evil*ᵈ* shall increase."

5 Then I, Daniel, looked, and two others appeared, one standing on this bank of the stream and one on the other. ⁶One of them said to the man clothed in linen, who was upstream, "How long shall it be until the end of these wonders?" ⁷The man clothed in linen, who was upstream, raised his right hand and his left hand toward heaven. And I heard him swear by the one who lives forever that it would be for a time, two times, and half a time,*ᵉ* and that when the shattering of the power of the holy people comes to an end, all these things would be accomplished. ⁸I heard but could not understand; so I said, "My lord, what shall be the outcome of these things?" ⁹He said, "Go your way, Daniel, for the words are to remain secret and sealed until the time of the end. ¹⁰Many shall be purified, cleansed, and refined, but the wicked shall continue to act wickedly. None of the wicked shall understand, but those who are wise shall understand. ¹¹From the time that the regular burnt offering is taken away and the abomination that desolates is set up, there shall be one thousand two hundred ninety days. ¹²Happy are those who persevere and attain the thousand three hundred thirty-five days. ¹³But you, go your way,*ᶠ* and rest; you shall rise for your reward at the end of the days."

a Or *Nubians*; Heb *Cushites*   *b* Or *the land of dust*   *c* Or *dome*
d Cn Compare Gk: Heb *knowledge*   *e* Heb *a time, times, and a half*
f Gk Theodotion: Heb adds *to the end*

HOSEA

Unwavering Love

KEY VERSE:

Return, O Israel, to the LORD your God.—Hosea 14.1

I n the book of Hosea, God calls, confronts and woos the people of Israel. Herein unfolds the account of a rebellious Israel—a people looking to idols rather than to God. God directs the prophet Hosea to marry Gomer, a prostitute, to be a living metaphor of God's unwavering love to his unfaithful people. Hosea marries Gomer, knowing she will be repeatedly unfaithful. God instructs Hosea to remain faithful regardless of Gomer's behavior. Hosea obeys (3.1–2), and, while the people deserve God's wrath, through the drama of his life Hosea demonstrates God's constant love for Israel.

The Israelites vacillate between clinging to idol worship and crying out to God for help. Israel's sin is so great that the people become "detestable like the thing they [love]" (9.10). Yet in a dramatic flood of compassion, God acts—not as a human being would, but as only God can (11.8–11). God chooses to forgive his people and draw them near once again.

This book has much to say about the human propensity to look anywhere but to God for meaning and comfort. Even more vividly it reminds us of the wonder of God's faithful love to persistently unfaithful people. Why does God repeatedly forgive and love a people who deserve only judgment? As passionately as anywhere in scripture, the book of Hosea speaks of God's intention to be Israel's faithful, loving spouse. As you read Hosea let God nurture in you an intimacy with him that is the fruit of knowing and receiving him in spirit and in truth.

"O eternal Father! . . . O eternal, infinite God! O mad lover! And you have need of your creature? It seems so to me, for you act as if you could not live without her, in spite of the fact that you are Life itself, and everything has life from you and nothing can have life without you. Why then are you so mad? Because you have fallen in love with what you have made! You are pleased and delighted over her within yourself, as if you were drunk with desire for her salvation. She runs away from you and you go looking for her. She strays and you draw closer to her. You clothed yourself in our humanity, and nearer than that you could not have come."

—CATHERINE OF SIENA,
The Dialogue

A Radical Obedience

HOSEA 1.1–2.5

God calls Hosea to make a covenant with a woman identified from the beginning as a prostitute. God is asking for radical obedience from Hosea; Hosea must give up much to follow God.

How do you respond when God asks you to obey in radical ways? Think of a time when the cost of discipleship required courage and a relinquishment of your own preferences or plans. Is God asking you to follow him in a radical way right now? Write a prayer asking God to help you be willing to relinquish your will, plans and life to him.

See Meeting God in Prayer

1 The word of the LORD that came to Hosea son of Beeri, in the days of Kings Uzziah, Jotham, Ahaz, and Hezekiah of Judah, and in the days of King Jeroboam son of Joash of Israel.

The Family of Hosea

2 When the LORD first spoke through Hosea, the LORD said to Hosea, "Go, take for yourself a wife of whoredom and have children of whoredom, for the land commits great whoredom by forsaking the LORD." 3 So he went and took Gomer daughter of Diblaim, and she conceived and bore him a son.

4 And the LORD said to him, "Name him Jezreel;*a* for in a little while I will punish the house of Jehu for the blood of Jezreel, and I will put an end to the kingdom of the house of Israel. 5 On that day I will break the bow of Israel in the valley of Jezreel."

6 She conceived again and bore a daughter. Then the LORD said to him, "Name her Lo-ruhamah,*b* for I will no longer have pity on the house of Israel or forgive them. 7 But I will have pity on the house of Judah, and I will save them by the LORD their God; I will not save them by bow, or by sword, or by war, or by horses, or by horsemen."

8 When she had weaned Lo-ruhamah, she conceived and bore a son. 9 Then the LORD said, "Name him Lo-ammi,*c* for you are not my people and I am not your God."*d*

The Restoration of Israel

10*e* Yet the number of the people of Israel shall be like the sand of the sea, which can be neither measured nor numbered; and in the place where it was said to them, "You are not my people," it shall be said to them, "Children of the living God." 11 The people of Judah and the people of Israel shall be gathered together, and they shall appoint for themselves one head; and they shall take possession of*f* the land, for great shall be the day of Jezreel. **2***g* Say to your brother,*h* Ammi,*i* and to your sister,*j* Ruhamah.*k*

Israel's Infidelity, Punishment, and Redemption

2 Plead with your mother, plead—
    for she is not my wife,
    and I am not her husband—
that she put away her whoring from her face,
    and her adultery from between her breasts,
3 or I will strip her naked
    and expose her as in the day she was born,
    and make her like a wilderness,
    and turn her into a parched land,
    and kill her with thirst.
4 Upon her children also I will have no pity,
    because they are children of whoredom.
5 For their mother has played the whore;
    she who conceived them has acted shamefully.
    For she said, "I will go after my lovers;

---

a That is *God sows* *b* That is *Not pitied* *c* That is *Not my people*
d Heb *I am not yours* *e* Ch 2.1 in Heb *f* Heb *rise up from* *g* Ch 2.3
in Heb *h* Gk: Heb *brothers* *i* That is *My people* *j* Gk Vg: Heb *sisters*
k That is *Pitied*

they give me my bread and my water,
   my wool and my flax, my oil and my drink."
6 Therefore I will hedge up her*a* way with thorns;
   and I will build a wall against her,
   so that she cannot find her paths.
7 She shall pursue her lovers,
   but not overtake them;
and she shall seek them,
   but shall not find them.
Then she shall say, "I will go
   and return to my first husband,
   for it was better with me then than now."
8 She did not know
   that it was I who gave her
   the grain, the wine, and the oil,
and who lavished upon her silver
   and gold that they used for Baal.
9 Therefore I will take back
   my grain in its time,
   and my wine in its season;
and I will take away my wool and my flax,
   which were to cover her nakedness.
10 Now I will uncover her shame
   in the sight of her lovers,
   and no one shall rescue her out of my hand.
11 I will put an end to all her mirth,
   her festivals, her new moons, her sabbaths,
   and all her appointed festivals.
12 I will lay waste her vines and her fig trees,
   of which she said,
"These are my pay,
   which my lovers have given me."
I will make them a forest,
   and the wild animals shall devour them.
13 I will punish her for the festival days of the Baals,
   when she offered incense to them
and decked herself with her ring and jewelry,
   and went after her lovers,
   and forgot me, says the LORD.

14 Therefore, I will now allure her,
   and bring her into the wilderness,
   and speak tenderly to her.
15 From there I will give her her vineyards,
   and make the Valley of Achor a door of hope.
There she shall respond as in the days of her
      youth,
   as at the time when she came out of the land of
      Egypt.
16 On that day, says the LORD, you will call me, "My husband," and no longer will you call me, "My Baal."*b* 17 For I
will remove the names of the Baals from her mouth, and
they shall be mentioned by name no more. 18 I will make
for you*c* a covenant on that day with the wild animals, the
birds of the air, and the creeping things of the ground; and
I will abolish*d* the bow, the sword, and war from the land;
and I will make you lie down in safety. 19 And I will take
you for my wife forever; I will take you for my wife in righteousness and in justice, in steadfast love, and in mercy.

Reality and Restoration

HOSEA 2.14–20

Imagine standing in a valley named "Trouble" (Achor means trouble) and in the far distance you see a doorway labeled "Hope." What do you hope is on the other side of that door? From where you stand in the valley, what lies between you and the door? What steps must you take to go through the Valley of Trouble and walk through the door into renewal? How can focusing on God's intimate, committed love deliver, heal and transform you? Pray through Psalm 23, 91 or 103 for more guidance.

See Meeting God in Scripture

a Gk Syr: Heb *your*   *b* That is, *"My master"*   *c* Heb *them*   *d* Heb *break*

Compassionate Beyond Words

HOSEA 2.19—3.5

"The thing which may for long prevent the soul from thus accepting the Lord, is that it forgets to think of Him always and above all as compassionate. Yet in everything, that is the first idea we must try to have about Him. We shall be quite differently affected by [God's] great splendor if we first realize that He to whom it belongs and who offers it to us is compassionate beyond all words. How gladly shall we then rejoice in [God's] Divine splendors! For they are the splendors of the All-Compassionate, the Intimate, and the Familiar God."

—ABBÉ DE TOURVILLE,
Letters of Direction

²⁰I will take you for my wife in faithfulness; and you shall know the LORD.
21　On that day I will answer, says the LORD,
　　I will answer the heavens
　　　and they shall answer the earth;
22　and the earth shall answer the grain, the wine,
　　　and the oil,
　　and they shall answer Jezreel;ᵃ
23　and I will sow himᵇ for myself in the land.
　And I will have pity on Lo-ruhamah,ᶜ
　　and I will say to Lo-ammi,ᵈ "You are my
　　　people";
　and he shall say, "You are my God."

Further Assurances of God's Redeeming Love

3 The LORD said to me again, "Go, love a woman who has a lover and is an adulteress, just as the LORD loves the people of Israel, though they turn to other gods and love raisin cakes." ²So I bought her for fifteen shekels of silver and a homer of barley and a measure of wine.ᵉ ³And I said to her, "You must remain as mine for many days; you shall not play the whore, you shall not have intercourse with a man, nor I with you." ⁴For the Israelites shall remain many days without king or prince, without sacrifice or pillar, without ephod or teraphim. ⁵Afterward the Israelites shall return and seek the LORD their God, and David their king; they shall come in awe to the LORD and to his goodness in the latter days.

God Accuses Israel

4 Hear the word of the LORD, O people of Israel;
　　for the LORD has an indictment against the
　　　inhabitants of the land.
　There is no faithfulness or loyalty,
　　and no knowledge of God in the land.
2　Swearing, lying, and murder,
　　and stealing and adultery break out;
　　bloodshed follows bloodshed.
3　Therefore the land mourns,
　　and all who live in it languish;
　together with the wild animals
　　and the birds of the air,
　　even the fish of the sea are perishing.

4　Yet let no one contend,
　　and let none accuse,
　　for with you is my contention, O priest.ᶠ
5　You shall stumble by day;
　　the prophet also shall stumble with you by
　　　night,
　　and I will destroy your mother.
6　My people are destroyed for lack of knowledge;
　　because you have rejected knowledge,
　　I reject you from being a priest to me.
　And since you have forgotten the law of your God,
　　I also will forget your children.

---

a That is God sows   b Cn: Heb her   c That is Not pitied   d That is Not my people   e Gk: Heb a homer of barley and a lethech of barley   f Cn: Meaning of Heb uncertain

7 The more they increased,
the more they sinned against me;
they changed[a] their glory into shame.
8 They feed on the sin of my people;
they are greedy for their iniquity.
9 And it shall be like people, like priest;
I will punish them for their ways,
and repay them for their deeds.
10 They shall eat, but not be satisfied;
they shall play the whore, but not multiply;
because they have forsaken the LORD
to devote themselves to 11whoredom.

The Idolatry of Israel

Wine and new wine
take away the understanding.
12 My people consult a piece of wood,
and their divining rod gives them oracles.
For a spirit of whoredom has led them astray,
and they have played the whore, forsaking their
God.
13 They sacrifice on the tops of the mountains,
and make offerings upon the hills,
under oak, poplar, and terebinth,
because their shade is good.

Therefore your daughters play the whore,
and your daughters-in-law commit adultery.
14 I will not punish your daughters when they play
the whore,
nor your daughters-in-law when they commit
adultery;
for the men themselves go aside with whores,
and sacrifice with temple prostitutes;
thus a people without understanding comes to
ruin.

15 Though you play the whore, O Israel,
do not let Judah become guilty.
Do not enter into Gilgal,
or go up to Beth-aven,
and do not swear, "As the LORD lives."
16 Like a stubborn heifer,
Israel is stubborn;
can the LORD now feed them
like a lamb in a broad pasture?

17 Ephraim is joined to idols—
let him alone.
18 When their drinking is ended, they indulge in
sexual orgies;
they love lewdness more than their glory.[b]
19 A wind has wrapped them[c] in its wings,
and they shall be ashamed because of their
altars.[d]

a Ancient Heb tradition: MT *I will change*   b Cn Compare Gk: Meaning
of Heb uncertain   c Heb *her*   d Gk Syr: Heb *sacrifices*

Consulting a Wooden Idol

HOSEA 4.6–7

To worship idols is to allow something or someone (other than God) the power to appropriate our attention, steal our affections, and dictate our choices and actions. When we worship idols we tend to substitute the most paltry things for the comfort and security God provides.

Reflect on your own spiritual pilgrimage. How do you give power to paltry substitutes rather than commit to trust in God? What do you gain from idolatry? Is it ever worth it? How have you made the choice to give God the holy place, the first place, in your life? Is God in that place today? How do you know?

See *Meeting God in Prayer*

Vulnerability and Obedience

HOSEA 5.5–6

We read in these verses that when the people look for God, God has "withdrawn from them." What a poignant picture! To help you meditate, write these two verses from Hosea in your journal. Then, between the lines of this Hosea passage, write out this promise from Deuteronomy 4.29 with a different color pen: "From there you will seek the LORD your God, and you will find him if you search after him with all your heart and soul." Turn your reflection toward God and ask him to reveal himself to you as you pray.

See Meeting God in Everyday Life

Impending Judgment on Israel and Judah

5 Hear this, O priests!
  Give heed, O house of Israel!
Listen, O house of the king!
  For the judgment pertains to you;
for you have been a snare at Mizpah,
  and a net spread upon Tabor,
2 and a pit dug deep in Shittim;*a*
  but I will punish all of them.

3 I know Ephraim,
  and Israel is not hidden from me;
for now, O Ephraim, you have played the whore;
  Israel is defiled.
4 Their deeds do not permit them
  to return to their God.
For the spirit of whoredom is within them,
  and they do not know the LORD.

5 Israel's pride testifies against him;
  Ephraim*b* stumbles in his guilt;
  Judah also stumbles with them.
6 With their flocks and herds they shall go
  to seek the LORD,
but they will not find him;
  he has withdrawn from them.
7 They have dealt faithlessly with the LORD;
  for they have borne illegitimate children.
  Now the new moon shall devour them along
    with their fields.

8 Blow the horn in Gibeah,
  the trumpet in Ramah.
Sound the alarm at Beth-aven;
  look behind you, Benjamin!
9 Ephraim shall become a desolation
  in the day of punishment;
among the tribes of Israel
  I declare what is sure.
10 The princes of Judah have become
  like those who remove the landmark;
on them I will pour out
  my wrath like water.
11 Ephraim is oppressed, crushed in judgment,
  because he was determined to go after vanity.*c*
12 Therefore I am like maggots to Ephraim,
  and like rottenness to the house of Judah.
13 When Ephraim saw his sickness,
  and Judah his wound,
then Ephraim went to Assyria,
  and sent to the great king.*d*
But he is not able to cure you
  or heal your wound.
14 For I will be like a lion to Ephraim,
  and like a young lion to the house of Judah.
I myself will tear and go away;
  I will carry off, and no one shall rescue.

a Cn: Meaning of Heb uncertain   *b* Heb *Israel and Ephraim*
c Gk: Meaning of Heb uncertain   *d* Cn: Heb *to a king who will contend*

¹⁵ I will return again to my place
 until they acknowledge their guilt and seek my
 face.
 In their distress they will beg my favor:

A Call to Repentance

6 "Come, let us return to the LORD;
 for it is he who has torn, and he will heal us;
 he has struck down, and he will bind us up.

² After two days he will revive us;
 on the third day he will raise us up,
 that we may live before him.

³ Let us know, let us press on to know the LORD;
 his appearing is as sure as the dawn;
 he will come to us like the showers,
 like the spring rains that water the earth."

Impenitence of Israel and Judah

⁴ What shall I do with you, O Ephraim?
 What shall I do with you, O Judah?
 Your love is like a morning cloud,
 like the dew that goes away early.

⁵ Therefore I have hewn them by the prophets,
 I have killed them by the words of my mouth,
 and my^a judgment goes forth as the light.

⁶ For I desire steadfast love and not sacrifice,
 the knowledge of God rather than burnt
 offerings.

⁷ But at^b Adam they transgressed the covenant;
 there they dealt faithlessly with me.

⁸ Gilead is a city of evildoers,
 tracked with blood.

⁹ As robbers lie in wait^c for someone,
 so the priests are banded together;^d
 they murder on the road to Shechem,
 they commit a monstrous crime.

¹⁰ In the house of Israel I have seen a horrible thing;
 Ephraim's whoredom is there, Israel is defiled.

¹¹ For you also, O Judah, a harvest is appointed.

When I would restore the fortunes of my people,

7 ¹ when I would heal Israel,
 the corruption of Ephraim is revealed,
 and the wicked deeds of Samaria;
 for they deal falsely,
 the thief breaks in,
 and the bandits raid outside.

² But they do not consider
 that I remember all their wickedness.
 Now their deeds surround them,
 they are before my face.

³ By their wickedness they make the king glad,
 and the officials by their treachery.

⁴ They are all adulterers;
 they are like a heated oven,
 whose baker does not need to stir the fire,

To Desire God Forever

HOSEA 6.3

"What is that sweet thing that comes sometimes to touch me at the thought of God? . . . I struggle deliciously to prevent myself [from] leaving this thing which I desire to embrace forever."

—HUGH OF ST. VICTOR

---

^a Gk Syr: Heb *your* ^b Cn: Heb *like* ^c Cn: Meaning of Heb uncertain
^d Syr: Heb *are a company*

What Prevents Our Return?

HOSEA 7.10–11

Despite God's judgment—despite God's repeated attempts to call the people back—Israel steadfastly refuses to turn back and seek God. Instead the Israelites turn to alliances with foreign nations to find the help they need.

When you are "stressed out" or distressed, to what or to whom do you turn first? Food? Alcohol? Television? Your credit card? Sports? Your friends? Make a list of "foreign alliances" you are tempted to turn to. Study your list. What do any of these things or people offer you that God cannot? How might God become your true source of life, contentment and health?

See Meeting God in Prayer

from the kneading of the dough until it is
leavened.
⁵ On the day of our king the officials
became sick with the heat of wine;
he stretched out his hand with mockers.
⁶ For they are kindled*a* like an oven, their heart
burns within them;
all night their anger smolders;
in the morning it blazes like a flaming fire.
⁷ All of them are hot as an oven,
and they devour their rulers.
All their kings have fallen;
none of them calls upon me.
⁸ Ephraim mixes himself with the peoples;
Ephraim is a cake not turned.
⁹ Foreigners devour his strength,
but he does not know it;
gray hairs are sprinkled upon him,
but he does not know it.
¹⁰ Israel's pride testifies against*b* him;
yet they do not return to the Lᴏʀᴅ their God,
or seek him, for all this.

Futile Reliance on the Nations

¹¹ Ephraim has become like a dove,
silly and without sense;
they call upon Egypt, they go to Assyria.
¹² As they go, I will cast my net over them;
I will bring them down like birds of the air;
I will discipline them according to the report
made to their assembly.*c*
¹³ Woe to them, for they have strayed from me!
Destruction to them, for they have rebelled
against me!
I would redeem them,
but they speak lies against me.
¹⁴ They do not cry to me from the heart,
but they wail upon their beds;
they gash themselves for grain and wine;
they rebel against me.
¹⁵ It was I who trained and strengthened their arms,
yet they plot evil against me.
¹⁶ They turn to that which does not profit;*d*
they have become like a defective bow;
their officials shall fall by the sword
because of the rage of their tongue.
So much for their babbling in the land of Egypt.

Israel's Apostasy

8 Set the trumpet to your lips!
One like a vulture*c* is over the house of the
Lᴏʀᴅ,
because they have broken my covenant,
and transgressed my law.
² Israel cries to me,
"My God, we—Israel—know you!"

a Gk Syr: Heb *brought near*   *b* Or *humbles*   *c* Meaning of Heb uncertain   *d* Cn: Meaning of Heb uncertain

³ Israel has spurned the good;
  the enemy shall pursue him.

⁴ They made kings, but not through me;
  they set up princes, but without my knowledge.
With their silver and gold they made idols
  for their own destruction.

⁵ Your calf is rejected, O Samaria.
  My anger burns against them.
How long will they be incapable of innocence?

⁶ For it is from Israel,
an artisan made it;
  it is not God.
The calf of Samaria
  shall be broken to pieces.ᵃ

⁷ For they sow the wind,
  and they shall reap the whirlwind.
The standing grain has no heads,
  it shall yield no meal;
if it were to yield,
  foreigners would devour it.

⁸ Israel is swallowed up;
  now they are among the nations
  as a useless vessel.

⁹ For they have gone up to Assyria,
  a wild ass wandering alone;
Ephraim has bargained for lovers.

¹⁰ Though they bargain with the nations,
  I will now gather them up.
They shall soon writhe
  under the burden of kings and princes.

¹¹ When Ephraim multiplied altars to expiate sin,
  they became to him altars for sinning.

¹² Though I write for him the multitude of my
    instructions,
  they are regarded as a strange thing.

¹³ Though they offer choice sacrifices,ᵇ
  though they eat flesh,
  the Lord does not accept them.
Now he will remember their iniquity,
  and punish their sins;
  they shall return to Egypt.

¹⁴ Israel has forgotten his Maker,
  and built palaces;
and Judah has multiplied fortified cities;
  but I will send a fire upon his cities,
  and it shall devour his strongholds.

Punishment for Israel's Sin

9 Do not rejoice, O Israel!
  Do not exultᶜ as other nations do;
for you have played the whore, departing from
    your God.
  You have loved a prostitute's pay
  on all threshing floors.

The Way Rejected

HOSEA 8.14

Thinking themselves safe the Israelites "forget" God, preferring instead to rely on their palaces and fortified towns. Do they really think God can be so easily outmaneuvered or put off? Consider your own life. Find someone you trust with whom you can discuss your attitudes toward God. Do you gladly welcome God into the scenes of your daily life? With your mentor consider whether there are times when you tend to evade or avoid God and hide behind your accomplishments or possessions.

See *Meeting God in Community*

ᵃ Or *shall go up in flames*   ᵇ Cn: Meaning of Heb uncertain   ᶜ Gk: Heb
To exultation

Subtle Deformation

HOSEA 9.1–4

"When it is true that the image you carry in your mind can affect your physical, mental and emotional life, then it becomes a crucial question as to which images we expose ourselves or allow ourselves to be exposed to."

—HENRI J. M. NOUWEN,
Gracias

2 Threshing floor and wine vat shall not feed them,
   and the new wine shall fail them.
3 They shall not remain in the land of the LORD;
   but Ephraim shall return to Egypt,
   and in Assyria they shall eat unclean food.

4 They shall not pour drink offerings of wine to the
      LORD,
   and their sacrifices shall not please him.
Such sacrifices shall be like mourners' bread;
   all who eat of it shall be defiled;
for their bread shall be for their hunger only;
   it shall not come to the house of the LORD.

5 What will you do on the day of appointed festival,
   and on the day of the festival of the LORD?
6 For even if they escape destruction,
   Egypt shall gather them,
   Memphis shall bury them.
Nettles shall possess their precious things of
      silver;[a]
   thorns shall be in their tents.

7 The days of punishment have come,
   the days of recompense have come;
   Israel cries,[b]
"The prophet is a fool,
   the man of the spirit is mad!"
Because of your great iniquity,
   your hostility is great.
8 The prophet is a sentinel for my God over
      Ephraim,
   yet a fowler's snare is on all his ways,
   and hostility in the house of his God.
9 They have deeply corrupted themselves
   as in the days of Gibeah;
he will remember their iniquity,
   he will punish their sins.

10 Like grapes in the wilderness,
      I found Israel.
Like the first fruit on the fig tree,
      in its first season,
      I saw your ancestors.
But they came to Baal-peor,
   and consecrated themselves to a thing of
      shame,
   and became detestable like the thing they
      loved.
11 Ephraim's glory shall fly away like a bird—
   no birth, no pregnancy, no conception!
12 Even if they bring up children,
   I will bereave them until no one is left.
Woe to them indeed
   when I depart from them!
13 Once I saw Ephraim as a young palm planted in a
      lovely meadow,[a]
   but now Ephraim must lead out his children for
      slaughter.

a Meaning of Heb uncertain   *b* Cn Compare Gk: Heb *shall know*

14 Give them, O Lord—
    what will you give?
Give them a miscarrying womb
    and dry breasts.

15 Every evil of theirs began at Gilgal;
    there I came to hate them.
Because of the wickedness of their deeds
    I will drive them out of my house.
I will love them no more;
    all their officials are rebels.

16 Ephraim is stricken,
    their root is dried up,
    they shall bear no fruit.
Even though they give birth,
    I will kill the cherished offspring of their womb.

17 Because they have not listened to him,
    my God will reject them;
    they shall become wanderers among the
        nations.

Israel's Sin and Captivity

10 Israel is a luxuriant vine
    that yields its fruit.
The more his fruit increased
    the more altars he built;
as his country improved,
    he improved his pillars.
2 Their heart is false;
    now they must bear their guilt.
The Lord[a] will break down their altars,
    and destroy their pillars.

3 For now they will say:
    "We have no king,
for we do not fear the Lord,
    and a king—what could he do for us?"
4 They utter mere words;
    with empty oaths they make covenants;
so litigation springs up like poisonous weeds
    in the furrows of the field.
5 The inhabitants of Samaria tremble
    for the calf[b] of Beth-aven.
Its people shall mourn for it,
    and its idolatrous priests shall wail[c] over it,
    over its glory that has departed from it.
6 The thing itself shall be carried to Assyria
    as tribute to the great king.[d]
Ephraim shall be put to shame,
    and Israel shall be ashamed of his idol.[e]

7 Samaria's king shall perish
    like a chip on the face of the waters.
8 The high places of Aven, the sin of Israel,
    shall be destroyed.
Thorn and thistle shall grow up
    on their altars.

The Sign of Unfruitfulness

HOSEA 9.10–16

As a new bride Israel has been ripe with promise, but she turns away from God, the very source of her fruitfulness. She consecrates herself to idols and reaps the consequences of unfaithfulness—she becomes barren and unable to sustain her children.

A fruitful life is a result of following God, yet fruitful abundance can also lead to complacency. How can you keep from taking God's blessings for granted? What keeps your zeal and your desire for God fresh and new? How can being accountable to others in the community keep you fruitful?

See Meeting God in Community

---

a Heb *he*   b Gk Syr: Heb *calves*   c Cn: Heb *exult*   d Cn: Heb *to a king who will contend*   e Cn: Heb *counsel*

In Praise of the Gardener

HOSEA 10.12

Using the metaphor of a vine for your life in Christ Jesus, map out your history. Be creative and extend the metaphor with other horticultural illustrations from scripture (see Matthew 13.1–23; John 15.1–8; Galatians 5.22–23). Where did God plant you? What made you grow in one direction and not another? Where did you branch off in the wrong direction? How did God prune you and discipline you? Who were the people who came along and watered and nourished you? What experiences have stimulated you to seek the light of the Lord? What fruit are you bearing?

See Meeting God in Scripture

They shall say to the mountains, Cover us,
and to the hills, Fall on us.

9 Since the days of Gibeah you have sinned, O Israel;
there they have continued.
Shall not war overtake them in Gibeah?
10 I will come*a* against the wayward people to punish them;
and nations shall be gathered against them
when they are punished*b* for their double iniquity.

11 Ephraim was a trained heifer
that loved to thresh,
and I spared her fair neck;
but I will make Ephraim break the ground;
Judah must plow;
Jacob must harrow for himself.
12 Sow for yourselves righteousness;
reap steadfast love;
break up your fallow ground;
for it is time to seek the LORD,
that he may come and rain righteousness upon you.

13 You have plowed wickedness,
you have reaped injustice,
you have eaten the fruit of lies.
Because you have trusted in your power
and in the multitude of your warriors,
14 therefore the tumult of war shall rise against your people,
and all your fortresses shall be destroyed,
as Shalman destroyed Beth-arbel on the day of battle
when mothers were dashed in pieces with their children.
15 Thus it shall be done to you, O Bethel,
because of your great wickedness.
At dawn the king of Israel
shall be utterly cut off.

God's Compassion Despite Israel's Ingratitude

11 When Israel was a child, I loved him,
and out of Egypt I called my son.
2 The more I*c* called them,
the more they went from me;*d*
they kept sacrificing to the Baals,
and offering incense to idols.

3 Yet it was I who taught Ephraim to walk,
I took them up in my*e* arms;
but they did not know that I healed them.
4 I led them with cords of human kindness,
with bands of love.
I was to them like those
who lift infants to their cheeks.*f*
I bent down to them and fed them.

a Cn Compare Gk: Heb *In my desire*   b Gk: Heb *bound*   c Gk: Heb *they*
d Gk: Heb *them*   e Gk Syr Vg: Heb *his*   f Or *who ease the yoke on their jaws*

5 They shall return to the land of Egypt,
   and Assyria shall be their king,
   because they have refused to return to me.
6 The sword rages in their cities,
   it consumes their oracle-priests,
   and devours because of their schemes.
7 My people are bent on turning away from me.
   To the Most High they call,
   but he does not raise them up at all.ᵃ

8 How can I give you up, Ephraim?
   How can I hand you over, O Israel?
   How can I make you like Admah?
   How can I treat you like Zeboiim?
   My heart recoils within me;
   my compassion grows warm and tender.
9 I will not execute my fierce anger;
   I will not again destroy Ephraim;
   for I am God and no mortal,
   the Holy One in your midst,
   and I will not come in wrath.ᵃ

10 They shall go after the LORD,
    who roars like a lion;
   when he roars,
    his children shall come trembling from the
     west.
11 They shall come trembling like birds from Egypt,
    and like doves from the land of Assyria;
    and I will return them to their homes, says the
     LORD.

12ᵇ Ephraim has surrounded me with lies,
    and the house of Israel with deceit;
   but Judah still walksᶜ with God,
    and is faithful to the Holy One.

12 Ephraim herds the wind,
    and pursues the east wind all day long;
   they multiply falsehood and violence;
    they make a treaty with Assyria,
    and oil is carried to Egypt.

The Long History of Rebellion

2 The LORD has an indictment against Judah,
   and will punish Jacob according to his ways,
   and repay him according to his deeds.
3 In the womb he tried to supplant his brother,
   and in his manhood he strove with God.
4 He strove with the angel and prevailed,
   he wept and sought his favor;
   he met him at Bethel,
   and there he spoke with him.ᵈ
5 The LORD the God of hosts,
   the LORD is his name!
6 But as for you, return to your God,
   hold fast to love and justice,
   and wait continually for your God.

Nurture in Spite of Nature

HOSEA 11.1–3

Using a tender picture of a father teaching a child to walk, Hosea relays God's nurturing love to his people. God's nature is to guide us, while our nature is to wander, much like a headstrong two-year-old in a crowded mall.

In what ways do you allow God to guide you and lead you step by step? What traits, attitudes and desires cause you to pull away from God's guiding hand? What happens when you insist on having your own way? Do you get lost among the "giants" around you? Do you fall on your face? At what point do you turn and look for God? Does God ever really lose track of his children?

See Meeting God in Everyday Life

---

a Meaning of Heb uncertain   b Ch 12.1 in Heb   c Heb roams or rules
d Gk Syr: Heb us

The Sum of What We Hold Dear

HOSEA 13.1–3

Israel offends God by sinning more and more, until the people are crafting silver idols. Do you ascribe too much worth to things, position, security or human recognition? Have they become idols? Have you started to resemble the sum of what you hold dear?

Sketch a large figure to represent yourself. Inside the head write down some of the things you are thinking about most. In the area of the heart, name three or four things that are claiming your emotional energy. On the hands name two projects or activities that are presently occupying most of your time. Repeat this process for any part of the body that applies. Does your portrait look like an idol? Or does it resemble a child of your heavenly Father? In what ways are you content with this picture? Concerned?

See Meeting God in Everyday Life

7 A trader, in whose hands are false balances,
he loves to oppress.
8 Ephraim has said, "Ah, I am rich,
I have gained wealth for myself;
in all of my gain
no offense has been found in me
that would be sin."*a*
9 I am the Lord your God
from the land of Egypt;
I will make you live in tents again,
as in the days of the appointed festival.
10 I spoke to the prophets;
it was I who multiplied visions,
and through the prophets I will bring
destruction.
11 In Gilead*b* there is iniquity,
they shall surely come to nothing.
In Gilgal they sacrifice bulls,
so their altars shall be like stone heaps
on the furrows of the field.
12 Jacob fled to the land of Aram,
there Israel served for a wife,
and for a wife he guarded sheep.*c*
13 By a prophet the Lord brought Israel up from
Egypt,
and by a prophet he was guarded.
14 Ephraim has given bitter offense,
so his Lord will bring his crimes down on him
and pay him back for his insults.

Relentless Judgment on Israel

13 When Ephraim spoke, there was trembling;
he was exalted in Israel;
but he incurred guilt through Baal and died.
2 And now they keep on sinning
and make a cast image for themselves,
idols of silver made according to their
understanding,
all of them the work of artisans.
"Sacrifice to these," they say.*d*
People are kissing calves!
3 Therefore they shall be like the morning mist
or like the dew that goes away early,
like chaff that swirls from the threshing floor
or like smoke from a window.

4 Yet I have been the Lord your God
ever since the land of Egypt;
you know no God but me,
and besides me there is no savior.
5 It was I who fed*e* you in the wilderness,
in the land of drought.
6 When I fed*f* them, they were satisfied;
they were satisfied, and their heart was proud;
therefore they forgot me.

a Meaning of Heb uncertain   *b* Compare Syr: Heb *Gilead*   *c* Heb lacks
sheep   *d* Cn Compare Gk: Heb *To these they say sacrifices of people*
e Gk Syr: Heb *knew*   *f* Cn: Heb *according to their pasture*

7 So I will become like a lion to them,
      like a leopard I will lurk beside the way.
8 I will fall upon them like a bear robbed of her cubs,
      and will tear open the covering of their heart;
   there I will devour them like a lion,
      as a wild animal would mangle them.

9 I will destroy you, O Israel;
      who can help you?[a]
10 Where now is[b] your king, that he may save you?
      Where in all your cities are your rulers,
   of whom you said,
      "Give me a king and rulers"?
11 I gave you a king in my anger,
      and I took him away in my wrath.

12 Ephraim's iniquity is bound up;
      his sin is kept in store.
13 The pangs of childbirth come for him,
      but he is an unwise son;
   for at the proper time he does not present himself
      at the mouth of the womb.

14 Shall I ransom them from the power of Sheol?
      Shall I redeem them from Death?
   O Death, where are[c] your plagues?
      O Sheol, where is[c] your destruction?
      Compassion is hidden from my eyes.

15 Although he may flourish among rushes,[d]
      the east wind shall come, a blast from the LORD,
         rising from the wilderness;
   and his fountain shall dry up,
      his spring shall be parched.
   It shall strip his treasury
      of every precious thing.
16[e] Samaria shall bear her guilt,
      because she has rebelled against her God;
   they shall fall by the sword,
      their little ones shall be dashed in pieces,
      and their pregnant women ripped open.

A Plea for Repentance

14 Return, O Israel, to the LORD your God,
      for you have stumbled because of your iniquity.
2 Take words with you
      and return to the LORD;
   say to him,
      "Take away all guilt;
   accept that which is good,
      and we will offer
      the fruit[f] of our lips.
3 Assyria shall not save us;
      we will not ride upon horses;
   we will say no more, 'Our God,'
      to the work of our hands.
   In you the orphan finds mercy."

Take Words With You

HOSEA 14.1–4

Hosea advises the people of God to take this simple offering to God: ""Take away all guilt; accept that which is good, and we will offer the fruit of our lips." And God replies with gracious compassion: "I will heal their disloyalty; I will love them freely."

What "words" do you take with you when you go into God's presence? Are they the words of confession as in verse 2? Do you offer God an exuberant, resounding YES? Do you go before God offering "a sacrifice of praise . . . . the fruit of lips that confess his name" (Hebrews 13.15)? Be silent before God, whom no words can describe, yet who is approachable and knowable. What does God say to you in your silence?

See Meeting God in Prayer

---

a Gk Syr: Heb *for in me is your help*   b Gk Syr Vg: Heb *I will be*
c Gk Syr: Heb *I will be*   d Or *among brothers*   e Ch 14.1 in Heb
f Gk Syr: Heb *bulls*

Love Triumphant

HOSEA 14.5–9

"Once I 'know' God, that is, once I experience God's love as the love in which all my human experiences are anchored, I can only desire one thing: to be in that love. 'Being' anywhere else, then, is shown to be illusory and eventually lethal . . . The great temptation is to use our many obvious failures and disappointments in our lives to convince ourselves that we are really not worth being loved . . . But for a person of faith the opposite is true. The many failures may open that place where we have nothing to brag about but everything to be loved for."

—HENRI J. M. NOUWEN,
Gracias

Assurance of Forgiveness

4 I will heal their disloyalty;
  I will love them freely,
  for my anger has turned from them.
5 I will be like the dew to Israel;
  he shall blossom like the lily,
  he shall strike root like the forests of Lebanon.^a
6 His shoots shall spread out;
  his beauty shall be like the olive tree,
  and his fragrance like that of Lebanon.
7 They shall again live beneath my^b shadow,
  they shall flourish as a garden;^c
they shall blossom like the vine,
  their fragrance shall be like the wine of
    Lebanon.

8 O Ephraim, what have I^d to do with idols?
  It is I who answer and look after you.^e
I am like an evergreen cypress;
  your faithfulness^f comes from me.
9 Those who are wise understand these things;
  those who are discerning know them.
For the ways of the LORD are right,
  and the upright walk in them,
  but transgressors stumble in them.

a Cn: Heb *like Lebanon*   *b* Heb *his*   *c* Cn: Heb *they shall grow grain*
d Or *What more has Ephraim*   *e* Heb *him*   *f* Heb *your fruit*

JOEL

The Coming Day of the Lord

KEY VERSES:

Then afterward I will pour out my spirit on all flesh; your sons and your daughters shall prophesy, your old men shall dream dreams, and your young men shall see visions . . . in those days, I will pour out my spirit . . . Then everyone who calls on the name of the LORD shall be saved.—Joel 2.28–29,32

I s the day of the Lord a day of judgment or a day of salvation? Is it a day of wrath or a day of restoration? As we read Joel's prophecy, we discover that it is both. God's earlier judgment against the apostasy of Judah is reversed, not by the actions of the people, but by God's loving determination to restore his people to fellowship and life. This prophecy is a debate within the very mind of God—the people of Judah deserve judgment (a plague of locusts) and yet God wants to offer the people miraculous mercy (the gift of abundant life).

God waits for each of us to rend our hearts, to repent and to receive in faith the salvation that God desires to give us. Through the prophet Joel, God invites you to listen. You will be standing on holy ground as you read, for the message of the book of Joel is that God's arms are extended to you, inviting you to return to him so that you may stand in God's presence in the day of the Lord—a day when God's Spirit would be poured out on all people.

> "Courage, then, O soul most beautiful, you now know that your Beloved, whom you long for, dwells hidden within your breast; strive, therefore, to be truly hidden with your Beloved, and then you will embrace him, and be conscious of his presence with loving affection."
>
> —JOHN OF THE CROSS,
> *A Spiritual Canticle of the Soul*

The Lament

JOEL 1.5–12

The devastation of Judah is complete. An invasion of locusts has plunged the nation into famine. Joel calls all in the land—the drunkards, the young women, the priests, the farmers, the vine growers—to lament their waywardness and repent of their sins.

Reflect: Why does the prophet refer to Judah's destruction in agricultural and ecological terms? Is it a merely figurative destruction or is it a literal one? Have you ever wept or mourned over the destruction of a land and its people? What repercussions does human sin have on creation? What repercussions might your own ignorance, carelessness or greed have on the environment? How do you think God views ecological devastation? After considering these questions respond by finding a Scripture passage that reflects God's joy in his created world and pray through it.

See Meeting God in the Created Order

1 The word of the LORD that came to Joel son of Pethuel:

Lament over the Ruin of the Country

2 Hear this, O elders,
   give ear, all inhabitants of the land!
Has such a thing happened in your days,
   or in the days of your ancestors?
3 Tell your children of it,
   and let your children tell their children,
   and their children another generation.

4 What the cutting locust left,
   the swarming locust has eaten.
What the swarming locust left,
   the hopping locust has eaten,
and what the hopping locust left,
   the destroying locust has eaten.

5 Wake up, you drunkards, and weep;
   and wail, all you wine-drinkers,
over the sweet wine,
   for it is cut off from your mouth.
6 For a nation has invaded my land,
   powerful and innumerable;
its teeth are lions' teeth,
   and it has the fangs of a lioness.
7 It has laid waste my vines,
   and splintered my fig trees;
it has stripped off their bark and thrown it down;
   their branches have turned white.

8 Lament like a virgin dressed in sackcloth
   for the husband of her youth.
9 The grain offering and the drink offering are
      cut off
   from the house of the LORD.
The priests mourn,
   the ministers of the LORD.
10 The fields are devastated,
   the ground mourns;
for the grain is destroyed,
   the wine dries up,
   the oil fails.

11 Be dismayed, you farmers,
   wail, you vinedressers,
over the wheat and the barley;
   for the crops of the field are ruined.
12 The vine withers,
   the fig tree droops.
Pomegranate, palm, and apple—
   all the trees of the field are dried up;
surely, joy withers away
   among the people.

A Call to Repentance and Prayer

13 Put on sackcloth and lament, you priests;
   wail, you ministers of the altar.
Come, pass the night in sackcloth,
   you ministers of my God!

Grain offering and drink offering
    are withheld from the house of your God.

14 Sanctify a fast,
    call a solemn assembly.
Gather the elders
    and all the inhabitants of the land
to the house of the LORD your God,
    and cry out to the LORD.

15 Alas for the day!
For the day of the LORD is near,
    and as destruction from the Almighty[a] it comes.
16 Is not the food cut off
    before our eyes,
joy and gladness
    from the house of our God?

17 The seed shrivels under the clods,[b]
    the storehouses are desolate;
the granaries are ruined
    because the grain has failed.
18 How the animals groan!
    The herds of cattle wander about
because there is no pasture for them;
    even the flocks of sheep are dazed.[c]

19 To you, O LORD, I cry.
For fire has devoured
    the pastures of the wilderness,
and flames have burned
    all the trees of the field.
20 Even the wild animals cry to you
    because the watercourses are dried up,
and fire has devoured
    the pastures of the wilderness.

2 Blow the trumpet in Zion;
    sound the alarm on my holy mountain!
Let all the inhabitants of the land tremble,
    for the day of the LORD is coming, it is near—
2 a day of darkness and gloom,
    a day of clouds and thick darkness!
Like blackness spread upon the mountains
    a great and powerful army comes;
their like has never been from of old,
    nor will be again after them
    in ages to come.

3 Fire devours in front of them,
    and behind them a flame burns.
Before them the land is like the garden of Eden,
    but after them a desolate wilderness,
    and nothing escapes them.

4 They have the appearance of horses,
    and like war-horses they charge.
5 As with the rumbling of chariots,

Sackcloth and Fasting

JOEL 1.13–14

Joel is calling the priests who serve at the altar in the temple to lead the people of the nation in a "solemn assembly" or special service of repentance. They are to "pass the night in sackcloth" and "sanctify a fast" as signs of their heartfelt penitence and humility before God. Their very lives and the life of the nation depend on how they respond to the prophet's call.

How can you designate a special time of confession and repentance on behalf of your nation, your family or yourself? Might it be a late-night vigil once a week? A weekend retreat during the season of Advent or Lent? A day of fasting once a month? Consider wearing a dark scarf or stole around your shoulders during your confessional prayer time as an outward sign of inward humility.

a Traditional rendering of Heb *Shaddai*   b Meaning of Heb uncertain
c Compare Gk Syr Vg: Meaning of Heb uncertain

Rend Your Heart

JOEL 2.12–14

Tear a piece of cloth or an old garment in two. Watch what happens. What do you notice? Does it require effort to tear it? What noise does the fabric make? In this passage God commands the Judeans to rend their hearts and return to the Lord God. "The sacrifice acceptable to God is a broken spirit; a broken and contrite heart . . . [God] will not despise" (Psalm 51.17). Such a return to God is a deliberate act of will on our part. Such repentance requires effort. It may involve wrenching pain as we give up the excesses, false security and comfortable, destructive ruts we are fond of. It may leave some raw edges and cause bits of fluff to fly as the fabric of our ego rips. None of us can do this apart from the help of our gracious and compassionate God. What deliberate steps will you take to open your heart to God and walk steadfastly in God's way?

See *Meeting God in Scripture*

they leap on the tops of the mountains,
like the crackling of a flame of fire
    devouring the stubble,
like a powerful army
    drawn up for battle.

6 Before them peoples are in anguish,
    all faces grow pale. *a*
7 Like warriors they charge,
    like soldiers they scale the wall.
Each keeps to its own course,
    they do not swerve from *b* their paths.
8 They do not jostle one another,
    each keeps to its own track;
they burst through the weapons
    and are not halted.
9 They leap upon the city,
    they run upon the walls;
they climb up into the houses,
    they enter through the windows like a thief.

10 The earth quakes before them,
    the heavens tremble.
The sun and the moon are darkened,
    and the stars withdraw their shining.
11 The LORD utters his voice
    at the head of his army;
how vast is his host!
    Numberless are those who obey his command.
Truly the day of the LORD is great;
    terrible indeed—who can endure it?

12 Yet even now, says the LORD,
    return to me with all your heart,
with fasting, with weeping, and with mourning;
13   rend your hearts and not your clothing.
Return to the LORD, your God,
    for he is gracious and merciful,
slow to anger, and abounding in steadfast love,
    and relents from punishing.
14 Who knows whether he will not turn and relent,
    and leave a blessing behind him,
a grain offering and a drink offering
    for the LORD, your God?

15 Blow the trumpet in Zion;
    sanctify a fast;
call a solemn assembly;
16   gather the people.
Sanctify the congregation;
    assemble the aged;
gather the children,
    even infants at the breast.
Let the bridegroom leave his room,
    and the bride her canopy.

17 Between the vestibule and the altar
    let the priests, the ministers of the LORD, weep.

a Meaning of Heb uncertain   *b* Gk Syr Vg: Heb *they do not take a pledge along*

Let them say, "Spare your people, O LORD,
  and do not make your heritage a mockery,
  a byword among the nations.
Why should it be said among the peoples,
  'Where is their God?' "

God's Response and Promise

18 Then the LORD became jealous for his land,
  and had pity on his people.
19 In response to his people the LORD said:
I am sending you
  grain, wine, and oil,
  and you will be satisfied;
and I will no more make you
  a mockery among the nations.

20 I will remove the northern army far from you,
  and drive it into a parched and desolate land,
  its front into the eastern sea,
  and its rear into the western sea;
its stench and foul smell will rise up.
  Surely he has done great things!

21 Do not fear, O soil;
  be glad and rejoice,
  for the LORD has done great things!
22 Do not fear, you animals of the field,
  for the pastures of the wilderness are green;
the tree bears its fruit,
  the fig tree and vine give their full yield.

23 O children of Zion, be glad
  and rejoice in the LORD your God;
for he has given the early rain[a] for your vindication,
  he has poured down for you abundant rain,
  the early and the later rain, as before.
24 The threshing floors shall be full of grain,
  the vats shall overflow with wine and oil.

25 I will repay you for the years
  that the swarming locust has eaten,
the hopper, the destroyer, and the cutter,
  my great army, which I sent against you.

26 You shall eat in plenty and be satisfied,
  and praise the name of the LORD your God,
  who has dealt wondrously with you.
And my people shall never again be put to shame.
27 You shall know that I am in the midst of Israel,
  and that I, the LORD, am your God and there is no
    other.
And my people shall never again be put to shame.

God's Spirit Poured Out

28[b] Then afterward
  I will pour out my spirit on all flesh;
your sons and your daughters shall prophesy,
  your old men shall dream dreams,
  and your young men shall see visions.

God's Jealousy

JOEL 2.18–20

We generally think of jealousy as a negative trait or feeling, but have you ever thought of jealousy as redemptive? God's "jealousy" is the fountainhead of his great love for us. God is zealous to carry out his purpose of salvation for his people, even when they turn away. God's yearning for us is stronger than his anger and wrath. How is God's yearning for your attention and your companionship being expressed to you? How does God call you into communion? How does God's still, small voice whisper to you that he wants you to spend time with him? Offer thanksgiving for God's jealous, wooing, pursuing love.

See Meeting God in Prayer

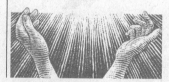

The Gift of the Spirit

JOEL 2.28–29

God promises to pour out his Spirit on all people, an event that would signify a new era in the advancement of God's kingdom. Joel's prophecy is fulfilled when the Holy Spirit is poured out on the disciples gathered in Jerusalem (see Acts 2). This wonderful gift of the Holy Spirit is given to all who "repent, and [are] baptized . . . in the name of Jesus Christ" (Acts 2.38). The Holy Spirit reveals God's will, renews our energy, redeems us, restores the covenant relationship and removes our fear. Recall a Pentecost experience in your own life. How are you experiencing the gift of the Holy Spirit today?

29 Even on the male and female slaves,
    in those days, I will pour out my spirit.

30 I will show portents in the heavens and on the earth, blood and fire and columns of smoke. ³¹The sun shall be turned to darkness, and the moon to blood, before the great and terrible day of the LORD comes. ³²Then everyone who calls on the name of the LORD shall be saved; for in Mount Zion and in Jerusalem there shall be those who escape, as the LORD has said, and among the survivors shall be those whom the LORD calls.

3 ᵃ For then, in those days and at that time, when I restore the fortunes of Judah and Jerusalem, ²I will gather all the nations and bring them down to the valley of Jehoshaphat, and I will enter into judgment with them there, on account of my people and my heritage Israel, because they have scattered them among the nations. They have divided my land, ³and cast lots for my people, and traded boys for prostitutes, and sold girls for wine, and drunk it down.

4 What are you to me, O Tyre and Sidon, and all the regions of Philistia? Are you paying me back for something? If you are paying me back, I will turn your deeds back upon your own heads swiftly and speedily. ⁵For you have taken my silver and my gold, and have carried my rich treasures into your temples.ᵇ ⁶You have sold the people of Judah and Jerusalem to the Greeks, removing them far from their own border. ⁷But now I will rouse them to leave the places to which you have sold them, and I will turn your deeds back upon your own heads. ⁸I will sell your sons and your daughters into the hand of the people of Judah, and they will sell them to the Sabeans, to a nation far away; for the LORD has spoken.

Judgment in the Valley of Jehoshaphat

9 Proclaim this among the nations:
Prepare war,ᶜ
    stir up the warriors.
Let all the soldiers draw near,
    let them come up.
10 Beat your plowshares into swords,
    and your pruning hooks into spears;
    let the weakling say, "I am a warrior."

11 Come quickly,ᵈ
    all you nations all around,
    gather yourselves there.
Bring down your warriors, O LORD.
12 Let the nations rouse themselves,
    and come up to the valley of Jehoshaphat;
for there I will sit to judge
    all the neighboring nations.

13 Put in the sickle,
    for the harvest is ripe.
Go in, tread,
    for the wine press is full.
The vats overflow,
    for their wickedness is great.

a Ch 4.1 in Heb   b Or *palaces*   c Heb *sanctify war*   d Meaning of Heb uncertain

14 Multitudes, multitudes,
 in the valley of decision!
For the day of the LORD is near
 in the valley of decision.
15 The sun and the moon are darkened,
 and the stars withdraw their shining.

16 The LORD roars from Zion,
 and utters his voice from Jerusalem,
 and the heavens and the earth shake.
But the LORD is a refuge for his people,
 a stronghold for the people of Israel.

The Glorious Future of Judah
17 So you shall know that I, the LORD your God,
 dwell in Zion, my holy mountain.
And Jerusalem shall be holy,
 and strangers shall never again pass through it.

18 In that day
the mountains shall drip sweet wine,
 the hills shall flow with milk,
and all the stream beds of Judah
 shall flow with water;
a fountain shall come forth from the house of the
 LORD
 and water the Wadi Shittim.

19 Egypt shall become a desolation
 and Edom a desolate wilderness,
because of the violence done to the people of
 Judah,
 in whose land they have shed innocent blood.
20 But Judah shall be inhabited forever,
 and Jerusalem to all generations.
21 I will avenge their blood, and I will not clear the
 guilty,*a*
 for the LORD dwells in Zion.

Hills Flow With Milk

JOEL 3.17–21

After lengthy descriptions of war and judgment, the book of Joel concludes with a moving poetic description of the restoration of Judah. Destruction is not God's final word for Judah or for the people of God. The final word is unimaginable grace—grace made visible in a verdant land with plentiful water and abundant harvests. The rhythm of God's life in us, revealed in Jesus Christ, is *death and* resurrection. Nothing that happens to us is so bad that it cannot be redeemed.

Think of the low points in your life. Write descriptions of four or five of them on the left side of a piece of paper. Label that column "death." Opposite each entry, write down how God led you through "the valley," strengthened you, redeemed the situation. Label that column "resurrection."

See Meeting God in Everyday Life

---

a Gk Syr: Heb *I will hold innocent their blood that I have not held innocent*

AMOS

Let Justice Roll

KEY VERSE:

But let justice roll down like waters, and righteousness like an ever-flowing stream.—Amos 5.24

> "The Lord is gentle; the Lord is slow to anger; the Lord is gracious. But the Lord is also just. The Lord is also faithful. God gives you space for correction, but you love the delay of judgment more than the amendment of your ways."
>
> —AUGUSTINE, *Commentary on John's Gospel*, Treatise 33

Perhaps nowhere in the Bible is God's desire for justice and righteousness more explicitly proclaimed than in the book of Amos. Again and again Amos details the sins of a society that thinks it has it all together—it is prospering economically and militarily as it proclaims faith in the one true God. But Amos peers beneath the prosperous and religious surface, and what he sees spells doom for Israel.

The name *Amos* aptly means "burden bearer," and this prophet bears the burden of announcing some painful truths to errant Israel. Amos is not a prophet by trade but a herdsman and cultivator of sycamore-fig trees. This outdoorsman-tradesman declares the word of the Lord in terms familiar to him: vineyards and trees, marketplaces and caravan customs.

Amos is not an easy or comforting book to read, but its words are as relevant today as they were almost three thousand years ago. We simply cannot get around the book's hard-hitting truth: If we misuse power or have gained wealth unjustly, if we are indifferent to the suffering of the distressed and disadvantaged, we are to stop and "seek God and live." As you read this book, try to see ways in which you are similar to the people of Israel, no matter how disturbing it may be to do so.

Like any good prophet, Amos offers hope as well as reproach. There is no mistaking the kind of life God desires for us, and that life is an existence far more meaningful and fulfilling than any we could ever imagine in the midst of our comfortable complacency.

1 The words of Amos, who was among the shepherds of Tekoa, which he saw concerning Israel in the days of King Uzziah of Judah and in the days of King Jeroboam son of Joash of Israel, two years[a] before the earthquake.

Judgment on Israel's Neighbors

2 And he said:

The LORD roars from Zion,
  and utters his voice from Jerusalem;
the pastures of the shepherds wither,
  and the top of Carmel dries up.

3 Thus says the LORD:
For three transgressions of Damascus,
  and for four, I will not revoke the punishment;[b]
because they have threshed Gilead
  with threshing sledges of iron.
4 So I will send a fire on the house of Hazael,
  and it shall devour the strongholds of
      Ben-hadad.
5 I will break the gate bars of Damascus,
  and cut off the inhabitants from the Valley of
      Aven,
and the one who holds the scepter from Beth-eden;
  and the people of Aram shall go into exile to Kir,
                      says the LORD.

6 Thus says the LORD:
For three transgressions of Gaza,
  and for four, I will not revoke the punishment;[b]
because they carried into exile entire
      communities,
  to hand them over to Edom.
7 So I will send a fire on the wall of Gaza,
  fire that shall devour its strongholds.
8 I will cut off the inhabitants from Ashdod,
  and the one who holds the scepter from
      Ashkelon;
I will turn my hand against Ekron,
  and the remnant of the Philistines shall perish,
                      says the Lord GOD.

9 Thus says the LORD:
For three transgressions of Tyre,
  and for four, I will not revoke the punishment;[b]
because they delivered entire communities over to
      Edom,
  and did not remember the covenant of kinship.
10 So I will send a fire on the wall of Tyre,
  fire that shall devour its strongholds.

11 Thus says the LORD:
For three transgressions of Edom,
  and for four, I will not revoke the punishment;[b]
because he pursued his brother with the sword
  and cast off all pity;
he maintained his anger perpetually,[c]
  and kept his wrath[d] forever.

Thus Says the Lord

AMOS 1.1–11

Amos begins by prophesying, not about Israel's sins, but about the sins of its neighbors. Perhaps Israel feels pretty smug at this point. It's always easy to recognize the sins of others. After all, God had chosen the Israelites, so their nation would always be prosperous and safe, wouldn't it? It's those *other* people who deserve God's judgment. Perhaps Israel is glad that the Lord is finally going to do something about "those people"—the people of Damascus, Gaza, Tyre and Edom.

Who are those you might label "those people"? What are their sins? How do you distinguish yourself from them? Ask God to help you identify with them in your mutual need for confession and repentance.

See Meeting God in Community

---

a Or *during two years*   *b* Heb *cause it to return*   *c* Syr Vg: Heb *and his anger tore perpetually*   *d* Gk Syr Vg: Heb *and his wrath kept*

Beneath the Surface

AMOS 2.6–8

Wait! Does Amos say *Israel?* But the Lord has chosen Israel! And Israel worships the Lord. How can a God-fearing nation sell the righteous and the needy? How can such a nation trample on people who are poor and deny justice to the oppressed? Amos sees corruption and exploitation beneath the surface of Israel's society— things Israel either hasn't seen or has turned a blind eye toward.

How are nations today corrupt in similar ways? What sins do you think Amos would point out in your town? How do you participate in these sins? Offer prayers of confession on behalf of yourself and your community.

See Meeting God in Prayer

1204

¹² So I will send a fire on Teman,
    and it shall devour the strongholds of Bozrah.
¹³ Thus says the LORD:
    For three transgressions of the Ammonites,
      and for four, I will not revoke the punishment;*ᵃ*
    because they have ripped open pregnant women
      in Gilead
    in order to enlarge their territory.
¹⁴ So I will kindle a fire against the wall of Rabbah,
    fire that shall devour its strongholds,
with shouting on the day of battle,
    with a storm on the day of the whirlwind;
¹⁵ then their king shall go into exile,
    he and his officials together,
                says the LORD.

2 Thus says the LORD:
For three transgressions of Moab,
    and for four, I will not revoke the punishment;*ᵃ*
because he burned to lime
    the bones of the king of Edom.
² So I will send a fire on Moab,
    and it shall devour the strongholds of Kerioth,
and Moab shall die amid uproar,
    amid shouting and the sound of the trumpet;
³ I will cut off the ruler from its midst,
    and will kill all its officials with him,
                says the LORD.

Judgment on Judah
⁴ Thus says the LORD:
For three transgressions of Judah,
    and for four, I will not revoke the punishment;*ᵃ*
because they have rejected the law of the LORD,
    and have not kept his statutes,
but they have been led astray by the same lies
    after which their ancestors walked.
⁵ So I will send a fire on Judah,
    and it shall devour the strongholds of Jerusalem.

Judgment on Israel
⁶ Thus says the LORD:
For three transgressions of Israel,
    and for four, I will not revoke the punishment;*ᵃ*
because they sell the righteous for silver,
    and the needy for a pair of sandals—
⁷ they who trample the head of the poor into the
      dust of the earth,
    and push the afflicted out of the way;
father and son go in to the same girl,
    so that my holy name is profaned;
⁸ they lay themselves down beside every altar
    on garments taken in pledge;
and in the house of their God they drink
    wine bought with fines they imposed.

⁹ Yet I destroyed the Amorite before them,
    whose height was like the height of cedars,

a Heb *cause it to return*

and who was as strong as oaks;
I destroyed his fruit above,
and his roots beneath.

10 Also I brought you up out of the land of Egypt,
and led you forty years in the wilderness,
to possess the land of the Amorite.

11 And I raised up some of your children to be
prophets
and some of your youths to be nazirites.*a*
Is it not indeed so, O people of Israel?

says the LORD.

12 But you made the nazirites*a* drink wine,
and commanded the prophets,
saying, "You shall not prophesy."

13 So, I will press you down in your place,
just as a cart presses down
when it is full of sheaves.*b*

14 Flight shall perish from the swift,
and the strong shall not retain their strength,
nor shall the mighty save their lives;

15 those who handle the bow shall not stand,
and those who are swift of foot shall not save
themselves,
nor shall those who ride horses save their lives;

16 and those who are stout of heart among the
mighty
shall flee away naked in that day,

says the LORD.

Israel's Guilt and Punishment

3 Hear this word that the LORD has spoken against you,
O people of Israel, against the whole family that I
brought up out of the land of Egypt:

2 You only have I known
of all the families of the earth;
therefore I will punish you
for all your iniquities.

3 Do two walk together
unless they have made an appointment?

4 Does a lion roar in the forest,
when it has no prey?
Does a young lion cry out from its den,
if it has caught nothing?

5 Does a bird fall into a snare on the earth,
when there is no trap for it?
Does a snare spring up from the ground,
when it has taken nothing?

6 Is a trumpet blown in a city,
and the people are not afraid?
Does disaster befall a city,
unless the LORD has done it?

7 Surely the Lord GOD does nothing,
without revealing his secret
to his servants the prophets.

8 The lion has roared;

A Covenant Broken

AMOS 3.2

How does the first half of this verse cause you to feel? Honored? Secure? Loved? What happens when you read the second half of the verse? Imagine Israel hearing these words for the first time and experiencing such a reversal of emotions. The Israelites may feel betrayed—until they remember that their relationship with God is a covenant relationship! God rescued them from Egypt, bringing them to a good place where they are to love God and keep God's commandments.

Try to remember some occasions from childhood when you were punished. Can you remember occasions when you were undeservedly punished? Can you also remember times when you deserved your punishment? Now try to recall being punished by someone you loved and who loved you. Write a short paragraph or two describing that event. What does your story reveal about love and punishment?

See Meeting God in Prayer

---

a That is, *those separated* or *those consecrated* *b* Meaning of Heb uncertain

Harsh Words

AMOS 4.1–3

Imagine entering a worship service, eagerly anticipating an inspiring message from the dynamic, young preacher. But instead the message the young preacher delivers is confrontational, directive, even appalling! You are called a "cow of Bashan." You're told you have much more wealth and power than you need and that you obtained it at the expense of people who are poor and needy—that you are overly ambitious, a social climber, a corporate ladder-climber.

How do you react? Are you defensive? Do you deny everything and hope everyone else got the message that, of course, wasn't directed at you? Or do you humbly begin to examine your own conscience and ask God to illumine your heart? Do you ask: "How have I treated others to get what I have? How have I claimed credit that others deserved? Whom have I ignored in order to get ahead?" Ask God to show you how to pray regarding these situations.

See Meeting God in Worship

who will not fear?
The Lord God has spoken;
    who can but prophesy?

9 Proclaim to the strongholds in Ashdod,
    and to the strongholds in the land of Egypt,
and say, "Assemble yourselves on Mount[a]
        Samaria,
    and see what great tumults are within it,
    and what oppressions are in its midst."
10 They do not know how to do right, says the Lord,
    those who store up violence and robbery in
        their strongholds.
11 Therefore thus says the Lord God:
An adversary shall surround the land,
    and strip you of your defense;
    and your strongholds shall be plundered.

12 Thus says the Lord: As the shepherd rescues from the mouth of the lion two legs, or a piece of an ear, so shall the people of Israel who live in Samaria be rescued, with the corner of a couch and part[b] of a bed.

13 Hear, and testify against the house of Jacob,
    says the Lord God, the God of hosts:
14 On the day I punish Israel for its transgressions,
    I will punish the altars of Bethel,
and the horns of the altar shall be cut off
    and fall to the ground.
15 I will tear down the winter house as well as the
        summer house;
    and the houses of ivory shall perish,
    and the great houses[c] shall come to an end,
                    says the Lord.

4 Hear this word, you cows of Bashan
    who are on Mount Samaria,
who oppress the poor, who crush the needy,
    who say to their husbands, "Bring something to
        drink!"
2 The Lord God has sworn by his holiness:
    The time is surely coming upon you,
when they shall take you away with hooks,
    even the last of you with fishhooks.
3 Through breaches in the wall you shall leave,
    each one straight ahead;
    and you shall be flung out into Harmon,[b]
                    says the Lord.

4 Come to Bethel—and transgress;
    to Gilgal—and multiply transgression;
bring your sacrifices every morning,
    your tithes every three days;
5 bring a thank offering of leavened bread,
    and proclaim freewill offerings, publish them;
for so you love to do, O people of Israel!
                    says the Lord God.

a Gk Syr: Heb *the mountains of* b Meaning of Heb uncertain
c Or *many houses*

Israel Rejects Correction

6 I gave you cleanness of teeth in all your cities,
  and lack of bread in all your places,
yet you did not return to me,

           says the LORD.

7 And I also withheld the rain from you
  when there were still three months to the
    harvest;
I would send rain on one city,
  and send no rain on another city;
one field would be rained upon,
  and the field on which it did not rain withered;
8 so two or three towns wandered to one town
  to drink water, and were not satisfied;
yet you did not return to me,

           says the LORD.

9 I struck you with blight and mildew;
  I laid waste *a* your gardens and your vineyards;
  the locust devoured your fig trees and your olive
    trees;
yet you did not return to me,

           says the LORD.

10 I sent among you a pestilence after the manner of
    Egypt;
I killed your young men with the sword;
I carried away your horses;*b*
  and I made the stench of your camp go up into
    your nostrils;
yet you did not return to me,

           says the LORD.

11 I overthrew some of you,
  as when God overthrew Sodom and Gomorrah,
  and you were like a brand snatched from the fire;
yet you did not return to me,

           says the LORD.

12 Therefore thus I will do to you, O Israel;
  because I will do this to you,
  prepare to meet your God, O Israel!

13 For lo, the one who forms the mountains, creates
    the wind,
  reveals his thoughts to mortals,
makes the morning darkness,
  and treads on the heights of the earth—
  the LORD, the God of hosts, is his name!

A Lament for Israel's Sin

5 Hear this word that I take up over you in lamentation,
  O house of Israel:
2 Fallen, no more to rise,
  is maiden Israel;
forsaken on her land,
  with no one to raise her up.

a Cn: Heb *the multitude of*   *b* Heb *with the captivity of your horses*

You Did Not Return to Me

AMOS 4.6–13

Amos outlines each step that God has taken in order to compel his people to acknowledge his sovereignty and return to him, but Amos also demonstrates how the people thwarted (at least temporarily) God's will by exercising free will and choosing to turn away. The Israelites had encountered God during many difficult times throughout their history, yet the Lord declares to them, "You did not return to me."

Have you encountered God's discipline? In what ways? Make a list of actions God has taken in your life in an effort to turn you back to himself. In what way do you need to return to God now? Consider this question for a moment and then paraphrase verse 13, using it as a prayer of acknowledgment of God's sovereignty in your life.

See Meeting God in Everyday Life

A Fulfilling Life

AMOS 5.4–6,14–15

In just four words God tells Israel what is necessary to live a life of fulfillment: "Seek me and live." But God—and therefore life—isn't to be found in showy, empty worship or in riches gained by perverting justice and exploiting the poor. We can know the true joy of God's gift of life only when justice is our rule and when righteousness, rather than evil, determines our choices.

Take the words "Seek me and live" with you into each situation and circumstance of your day. Consider what it would mean to "seek God and live" in each one of them.

See Meeting God in Scripture

3 For thus says the Lord GOD:
The city that marched out a thousand
    shall have a hundred left,
and that which marched out a hundred
    shall have ten left.ᵃ

4 For thus says the LORD to the house of Israel:
Seek me and live;
5   but do not seek Bethel,
and do not enter into Gilgal
    or cross over to Beer-sheba;
for Gilgal shall surely go into exile,
    and Bethel shall come to nothing.

6 Seek the LORD and live,
    or he will break out against the house of Joseph
        like fire,
    and it will devour Bethel, with no one to
        quench it.
7 Ah, you that turn justice to wormwood,
    and bring righteousness to the ground!

8 The one who made the Pleiades and Orion,
    and turns deep darkness into the morning,
    and darkens the day into night,
who calls for the waters of the sea,
    and pours them out on the surface of the earth,
the LORD is his name,
9 who makes destruction flash out against the
        strong,
    so that destruction comes upon the fortress.

10 They hate the one who reproves in the gate,
    and they abhor the one who speaks the truth.
11 Therefore because you trample on the poor
    and take from them levies of grain,
you have built houses of hewn stone,
    but you shall not live in them;
you have planted pleasant vineyards,
    but you shall not drink their wine.
12 For I know how many are your transgressions,
    and how great are your sins—
you who afflict the righteous, who take a bribe,
    and push aside the needy in the gate.
13 Therefore the prudent will keep silent in such a
        time;
    for it is an evil time.

14 Seek good and not evil,
    that you may live;
and so the LORD, the God of hosts, will be with
        you,
    just as you have said.
15 Hate evil and love good,
    and establish justice in the gate;
it may be that the LORD, the God of hosts,
    will be gracious to the remnant of Joseph.

a Heb adds to the house of Israel

16 Therefore thus says the LORD, the God of hosts,
        the Lord:
    In all the squares there shall be wailing;
        and in all the streets they shall say, "Alas! alas!"
    They shall call the farmers to mourning,
        and those skilled in lamentation, to wailing;
17 in all the vineyards there shall be wailing,
        for I will pass through the midst of you,
                                                    says the LORD.

The Day of the LORD a Dark Day

18 Alas for you who desire the day of the LORD!
        Why do you want the day of the LORD?
    It is darkness, not light;
19   as if someone fled from a lion,
        and was met by a bear;
    or went into the house and rested a hand against
        the wall,
        and was bitten by a snake.
20 Is not the day of the LORD darkness, not light,
        and gloom with no brightness in it?

21 I hate, I despise your festivals,
        and I take no delight in your solemn assemblies.
22 Even though you offer me your burnt offerings
        and grain offerings,
        I will not accept them;
    and the offerings of well-being of your fatted
        animals
        I will not look upon.
23 Take away from me the noise of your songs;
        I will not listen to the melody of your harps.
24 But let justice roll down like waters,
        and righteousness like an ever-flowing stream.

25 Did you bring to me sacrifices and offerings the
forty years in the wilderness, O house of Israel? 26 You shall
take up Sakkuth your king, and Kaiwan your star-god, your
images,*a* which you made for yourselves; 27 therefore I will
take you into exile beyond Damascus, says the LORD,
whose name is the God of hosts.

Complacent Self-Indulgence Will Be Punished

6 Alas for those who are at ease in Zion,
        and for those who feel secure on Mount Samaria,
    the notables of the first of the nations,
        to whom the house of Israel resorts!
2 Cross over to Calneh, and see;
        from there go to Hamath the great;
        then go down to Gath of the Philistines.
    Are you better*b* than these kingdoms?
        Or is your*c* territory greater than their*d*
        territory,
3 O you that put far away the evil day,
        and bring near a reign of violence?

4 Alas for those who lie on beds of ivory,
        and lounge on their couches,

True Worship

AMOS 5.21–24

If worshipers forget God's true nature, if they do not love justice and righteousness, then all of their worship and its accoutrements count for nothing. What place do justice and righteousness occupy in your worship? How could your worship more fully include these characteristics? What other forms of worship might you embrace in order to do so? How could you increase your love of justice and righteousness? What would that mean in your life? Would some attitudes need to change? What about your actions? Would your prayers change in any way? As you worship and pray, ask God to help you answer these questions.

See Meeting God in Worship

a Heb *your images, your star-god*   *b* Or *Are they better*   *c* Heb *their*
d Heb *your*

We've Done It!

AMOS 6.13

One of the Israelites' sins is their belief that they have accomplished great things on their own. They seem to have forgotten that God has brought them out of Egypt into a good land and has continued to protect them and provide for them.

Like the Israelites we may lapse into similar thinking, particularly when things are going well. As you go about your daily activity, make a special effort to recall how God has benefited you, and then thank God for the blessings you enjoy.

See Meeting God in Everyday Life

and eat lambs from the flock,
and calves from the stall;
5 who sing idle songs to the sound of the harp,
and like David improvise on instruments of
music;
6 who drink wine from bowls,
and anoint themselves with the finest oils,
but are not grieved over the ruin of Joseph!
7 Therefore they shall now be the first to go into
exile,
and the revelry of the loungers shall pass away.

8 The Lord God has sworn by himself
(says the Lord, the God of hosts):
I abhor the pride of Jacob
and hate his strongholds;
and I will deliver up the city and all that is in it.

9 If ten people remain in one house, they shall die. 10 And if a relative, one who burns the dead,[a] shall take up the body to bring it out of the house, and shall say to someone in the innermost parts of the house, "Is anyone else with you?" the answer will come, "No." Then the relative[b] shall say, "Hush! We must not mention the name of the Lord."

11 See, the Lord commands,
and the great house shall be shattered to bits,
and the little house to pieces.
12 Do horses run on rocks?
Does one plow the sea with oxen?[c]
But you have turned justice into poison
and the fruit of righteousness into wormwood—
13 you who rejoice in Lo-debar,[d]
who say, "Have we not by our own strength
taken Karnaim[e] for ourselves?"
14 Indeed, I am raising up against you a nation,
O house of Israel, says the Lord, the God of
hosts,
and they shall oppress you from Lebo-hamath
to the Wadi Arabah.

Locusts, Fire, and a Plumb Line

7 This is what the Lord God showed me: he was forming locusts at the time the latter growth began to sprout (it was the latter growth after the king's mowings). 2 When they had finished eating the grass of the land, I said,

"O Lord God, forgive, I beg you!
How can Jacob stand?
He is so small!"
3 The Lord relented concerning this;
"It shall not be," said the Lord.

4 This is what the Lord God showed me: the Lord God was calling for a shower of fire,[f] and it devoured the great deep and was eating up the land. 5 Then I said,

a Or *who makes a burning for him*   *b* Heb *he*   *c* Or *Does one plow them with oxen*   *d* Or *in a thing of nothingness*   *e* Or *horns*   *f* Or *for a judgment by fire*

"O Lord God, cease, I beg you!
How can Jacob stand?
He is so small!"
6 The Lord relented concerning this;
"This also shall not be," said the Lord God.

7 This is what he showed me: the Lord was standing beside a wall built with a plumb line, with a plumb line in his hand. 8And the Lord said to me, "Amos, what do you see?" And I said, "A plumb line." Then the Lord said,
"See, I am setting a plumb line
in the midst of my people Israel;
I will never again pass them by;
9 the high places of Isaac shall be made desolate,
and the sanctuaries of Israel shall be laid waste,
and I will rise against the house of Jeroboam
with the sword."

Amaziah Complains to the King

10 Then Amaziah, the priest of Bethel, sent to King Jeroboam of Israel, saying, "Amos has conspired against you in the very center of the house of Israel; the land is not able to bear all his words. 11For thus Amos has said,
'Jeroboam shall die by the sword,
and Israel must go into exile
away from his land.' "
12And Amaziah said to Amos, "O seer, go, flee away to the land of Judah, earn your bread there, and prophesy there; 13but never again prophesy at Bethel, for it is the king's sanctuary, and it is a temple of the kingdom."
14 Then Amos answered Amaziah, "I am[a] no prophet, nor a prophet's son; but I am[a] a herdsman, and a dresser of sycamore trees, 15and the Lord took me from following the flock, and the Lord said to me, 'Go, prophesy to my people Israel.'
16 "Now therefore hear the word of the Lord.
You say, 'Do not prophesy against Israel,
and do not preach against the house of Isaac.'
17 Therefore thus says the Lord:
'Your wife shall become a prostitute in the city,
and your sons and your daughters shall fall by
the sword,
and your land shall be parceled out by line;
you yourself shall die in an unclean land,
and Israel shall surely go into exile away from
its land.' "

The Basket of Fruit

8 This is what the Lord God showed me—a basket of summer fruit.[b] 2He said, "Amos, what do you see?" And I said, "A basket of summer fruit."[b] Then the Lord said to me,
"The end[c] has come upon my people Israel;
I will never again pass them by.
3 The songs of the temple[d] shall become wailings in
that day,"
says the Lord God;
"the dead bodies shall be many,
cast out in every place. Be silent!"

Prophesy Somewhere Else!

AMOS 7.12–13

Picture this scene: Amos is being told, "Go away! Stand on another street corner! Find another pulpit! Your message doesn't please us! Go spread your gloom and doom elsewhere!" This scene seems almost comical until we ask ourselves how many times we have done the same thing in one way or another. Have you ever heard an unsettling message, which may have come from God, but responded by dismissing the prophet entirely?

Write a prayer, asking that you be able to discern God's word in the many voices around you. Use a breath prayer—such as, "Immanuel—God with us, let me be open to hearing your word"—to remind you to listen for God's word today.

See *Meeting God in Worship*

a Or was   b Heb *qayits*   c Heb *qets*   d Or *palace*

Famine

AMOS 8.11–14

A famine is coming, but this famine is different. It is not food that the people will lack; they will experience a dearth of hearing the words of the Lord. Place yourself in the scenario in verse 12. You search everywhere for a word of guidance, a word of comfort, a word of redemption from the Lord, but you are unable to find it anywhere. Your need is so acute, so painful that you stagger beneath its burden. Perhaps you thought that God would always be there, patiently waiting for you to come back to him. Will you ever hear God again?

What word is God asking you to hear today? What are you waiting for? What is stopping you?

See Meeting God in Scripture

4 Hear this, you that trample on the needy,
and bring to ruin the poor of the land,
5 saying, "When will the new moon be over
so that we may sell grain;
and the sabbath,
so that we may offer wheat for sale?
We will make the ephah small and the shekel great,
and practice deceit with false balances,
6 buying the poor for silver
and the needy for a pair of sandals,
and selling the sweepings of the wheat."

7 The LORD has sworn by the pride of Jacob:
Surely I will never forget any of their deeds.
8 Shall not the land tremble on this account,
and everyone mourn who lives in it,
and all of it rise like the Nile,
and be tossed about and sink again, like the Nile of Egypt?

9 On that day, says the Lord GOD,
I will make the sun go down at noon,
and darken the earth in broad daylight.
10 I will turn your feasts into mourning,
and all your songs into lamentation;
I will bring sackcloth on all loins,
and baldness on every head;
I will make it like the mourning for an only son,
and the end of it like a bitter day.

11 The time is surely coming, says the Lord GOD,
when I will send a famine on the land;
not a famine of bread, or a thirst for water,
but of hearing the words of the LORD.
12 They shall wander from sea to sea,
and from north to east;
they shall run to and fro, seeking the word of the LORD,
but they shall not find it.

13 In that day the beautiful young women and the young men
shall faint for thirst.
14 Those who swear by Ashimah of Samaria,
and say, "As your god lives, O Dan,"
and, "As the way of Beer-sheba lives"—
they shall fall, and never rise again.

The Destruction of Israel

9 I saw the LORD standing beside*a* the altar, and he said:
Strike the capitals until the thresholds shake,
and shatter them on the heads of all the people;*b*
and those who are left I will kill with the sword;
not one of them shall flee away,
not one of them shall escape.

a Or *on*   *b* Heb *all of them*

2 Though they dig into Sheol,
    from there shall my hand take them;
  though they climb up to heaven,
    from there I will bring them down.
3 Though they hide themselves on the top of
        Carmel,
    from there I will search out and take them;
  and though they hide from my sight at the bottom
        of the sea,
    there I will command the sea-serpent, and it
        shall bite them.
4 And though they go into captivity in front of their
        enemies,
    there I will command the sword, and it shall kill
        them;
  and I will fix my eyes on them
    for harm and not for good.

5 The Lord, God of hosts,
  he who touches the earth and it melts,
    and all who live in it mourn,
  and all of it rises like the Nile,
    and sinks again, like the Nile of Egypt;
6 who builds his upper chambers in the heavens,
    and founds his vault upon the earth;
  who calls for the waters of the sea,
    and pours them out upon the surface of the
        earth—
  the Lord is his name.

7 Are you not like the Ethiopians[a] to me,
    O people of Israel? says the Lord.
  Did I not bring Israel up from the land of Egypt,
    and the Philistines from Caphtor and the
        Arameans from Kir?
8 The eyes of the Lord God are upon the sinful
        kingdom,
    and I will destroy it from the face of the earth
    —except that I will not utterly destroy the house
        of Jacob,
                                    says the Lord.

9 For lo, I will command,
    and shake the house of Israel among all the
        nations
  as one shakes with a sieve,
    but no pebble shall fall to the ground.
10 All the sinners of my people shall die by the
        sword,
    who say, "Evil shall not overtake or meet us."

The Restoration of David's Kingdom

11 On that day I will raise up
    the booth of David that is fallen,
  and repair its[b] breaches,
    and raise up its[c] ruins,
    and rebuild it as in the days of old;

Nowhere to Hide

AMOS 9.2–10

We like to take comfort in knowing that God is always with us. We delight in the comforting proximity of God, which we read about in Psalm 139. We savor the thought that God formed us in our mother's womb and will never leave us. But in the book of Amos this inescapable God is not a comforting figure. The Israelites are told that, no matter where they might try to hide, God will find them. They have abused the covenant relationship by not accepting its accompanying responsibilities.

Why might you want to hide from God? Is there a responsibility in your relationship with God that you've refused to embrace? What do you need to pray now, so that you no longer have to hide from God? Write in your journal your anticipation of that time.

See Meeting God in Prayer

---

a Or Nubians; Heb Cushites   b Gk: Heb their   c Gk: Heb his

Restoration

AMOS 9.11–15

A glimmer of hope finally appears: "I will restore the fortunes of my people Israel." Notice the rich lavishness of the restoration: "The mountains shall drip sweet wine, and all the hills shall flow with it." But until that time the people of Israel must live with the consequences of their actions. Like the Israelites we often have to live with the consequences of our wrongful actions. What consequences are you presently living with? How are you experiencing God's grace and forgiveness in spite of them? Can you imagine the lush restoration God has planned for you? How does the promise and picture of future restoration help you through your present difficulties?

See Meeting God in the Created Order

12 in order that they may possess the remnant of
    Edom
    and all the nations who are called by my name,
    says the LORD who does this.

13 The time is surely coming, says the LORD,
    when the one who plows shall overtake the one
    who reaps,
    and the treader of grapes the one who sows the
    seed;
the mountains shall drip sweet wine,
    and all the hills shall flow with it.

14 I will restore the fortunes of my people Israel,
    and they shall rebuild the ruined cities and
    inhabit them;
they shall plant vineyards and drink their wine,
    and they shall make gardens and eat their fruit.

15 I will plant them upon their land,
    and they shall never again be plucked up
    out of the land that I have given them,
                    says the LORD your God.

OBADIAH

God's Passion for Justice

KEY VERSE:

For the day of the LORD is near against all the nations. As you have done, it shall be done to you; your deeds shall return on your own head.—Obadiah 15

No one likes to be treated unfairly or see others so treated. When injustices occur, it helps to know that God is watching and will see that justice ultimately prevails.

Although the book of Obadiah gives us very little information about the prophet, it reiterates God's zeal for justice, a theme that is woven throughout the prophetic books. Therefore God pledges to bring judgment on the people of Edom, who stand by (and even cause harm) while their Israelite kinfolk are conquered (v.11). Obadiah declares that God will bring "the day of the LORD," a day of judgment for all nations (vv.15–16). God will not forget those who are treated unfairly!

In these twenty-one verses we are once again impressed with God's passion for justice. And we know that in the end all nations and people—indeed, all of life—belong to God. "And the kingdom shall be the LORD's" (v.21).

> "Truly at the day of judgment we shall not be examined on what we have read, but what we have done; not how well we have spoken, but how religiously we have lived."
>
> —THOMAS À KEMPIS,
> *The Imitation of Christ*

Standing By, Doing Nothing

OBADIAH 11

Sometimes to take no action is to act. The Edomites were guilty of ignoring the plight of God's people. They did nothing to stop the attacks on Judah; in fact they rejoiced! The Edomites even joined in the looting that followed the Babylonian capture of Judah.

Read the newspaper or listen to a news broadcast today with the goal of listening for God's call concerning some contemporary dilemma. Pray about the situation. Then perhaps write a letter, mail a check or make a phone call to express your concern. Let this be one day when you do not turn aside from the cries of the needy or oppressed. Ask God to make you aware of those who may need your help or who may need to hear your voice today.

See Meeting God in Service

Proud Edom Will Be Brought Low

1 The vision of Obadiah.

Thus says the Lord GOD concerning Edom:
We have heard a report from the LORD,
   and a messenger has been sent among the
      nations:
"Rise up! Let us rise against it for battle!"
2 I will surely make you least among the nations;
   you shall be utterly despised.
3 Your proud heart has deceived you,
   you that live in the clefts of the rock,*a*
   whose dwelling is in the heights.
You say in your heart,
   "Who will bring me down to the ground?"
4 Though you soar aloft like the eagle,
   though your nest is set among the stars,
   from there I will bring you down,
                  says the LORD.

Pillage and Slaughter Will Repay Edom's Cruelty

5 If thieves came to you,
   if plunderers by night
   —how you have been destroyed!—
   would they not steal only what they wanted?
If grape-gatherers came to you,
   would they not leave gleanings?
6 How Esau has been pillaged,
   his treasures searched out!
7 All your allies have deceived you,
   they have driven you to the border;
your confederates have prevailed against you;
   those who ate*b* your bread have set a trap for
      you—
there is no understanding of it.
8 On that day, says the LORD,
   I will destroy the wise out of Edom,
   and understanding out of Mount Esau.
9 Your warriors shall be shattered, O Teman,
   so that everyone from Mount Esau will be cut off.

Edom Mistreated His Brother

10 For the slaughter and violence done to your brother
      Jacob,
   shame shall cover you,
   and you shall be cut off forever.
11 On the day that you stood aside,
   on the day that strangers carried off his wealth,
and foreigners entered his gates
   and cast lots for Jerusalem,
   you too were like one of them.
12 But you should not have gloated*c* over*d* your brother
   on the day of his misfortune;
you should not have rejoiced over the people of
      Judah
   on the day of their ruin;
   you should not have boasted

a Or *clefts of Sela*   *b* Cn: Heb lacks *those who ate*   *c* Heb *But do not gloat* (and similarly through verse 14)   *d* Heb *on the day of*

on the day of distress.
13 You should not have entered the gate of my people
on the day of their calamity;
you should not have joined in the gloating over
Judah's[a] disaster
on the day of his calamity;
you should not have looted his goods
on the day of his calamity.
14 You should not have stood at the crossings
to cut off his fugitives;
you should not have handed over his survivors
on the day of distress.

15 For the day of the LORD is near against all the
nations.
As you have done, it shall be done to you;
your deeds shall return on your own head.
16 For as you have drunk on my holy mountain,
all the nations around you shall drink;
they shall drink and gulp down,[b]
and shall be as though they had never been.

Israel's Final Triumph

17 But on Mount Zion there shall be those that escape,
and it shall be holy;
and the house of Jacob shall take possession of
those who dispossessed them.
18 The house of Jacob shall be a fire,
the house of Joseph a flame,
and the house of Esau stubble;
they shall burn them and consume them,
and there shall be no survivor of the house of
Esau;
for the LORD has spoken.
19 Those of the Negeb shall possess Mount Esau,
and those of the Shephelah the land of the
Philistines;
they shall possess the land of Ephraim and the land
of Samaria,
and Benjamin shall possess Gilead.
20 The exiles of the Israelites who are in Halah[c]
shall possess[d] Phoenicia as far as Zarephath;
and the exiles of Jerusalem who are in Sepharad
shall possess the towns of the Negeb.
21 Those who have been saved[e] shall go up to Mount
Zion
to rule Mount Esau;
and the kingdom shall be the LORD's.

Your Deeds Shall Return

OBADIAH 15

The proverb, "You reap what you sow," is similar to these words of Obadiah. It is a word of warning: As you have treated others, so will you be treated.

Today is a good day to seek forgiveness for your actions and to make amends to anyone you may have hurt. Bring to mind anyone who may have something against you. Lift them to God in prayer and ask for forgiveness and for wisdom in seeking reconciliation. Let your prayer guide you in the steps you should take in making amends.

See Meeting God in Prayer

---

a Heb *his*   b Meaning of Heb uncertain   c Cn: Heb *in this army*
d Cn: Meaning of Heb uncertain   e Or *Saviors*

JONAH
Running From God

KEY VERSE:

"Should I not be concerned about Nineveh, that great city?"—Jonah 4.11

"I fled Him, down the
  nights and down the
  days;
I fled Him, down the arches
  of the years;
I fled Him, down the
  labyrinthine ways
Of my own mind; and in the
  mist of tears
I hid from Him."
—FRANCIS THOMPSON,
The Hound of Heaven

At first glance the book of Jonah is an account of the strangest two-way journey ever described: A reluctant prophet flees in fear as far away as ships could sail, only to return to land within the belly of a giant fish. But the story of Jonah's strange journey underlines a great truth about God: God can use even a stubborn and reluctant prophet to bring the truth to those who need to hear it. In spite of Jonah's ungracious willfulness, God's compassion prevails—the entire population of Nineveh repents and experiences God's healing love.

This fascinating story makes us wonder if Jonah ever clearly grasped that "the love of God is broader than the measure of the mind," as an old hymn says so well. God's compassion is so great and unwavering that we, like Jonah, struggle to believe it. We wince at the prospect of having to imitate it, particularly when we need to demonstrate it to certain people.

As you read this book, you might identify with Jonah's struggle as he first does the wrong thing and then finally does the right thing but with a wrong heart. Perhaps you have felt at odds with what God has asked you to do, and so you've offered a stiff handshake or a fake smile. You've kept people at a distance whom God would have you love. Let God penetrate the areas of your life in which you barely cooperate or even resist. Experience God's wonderfully embracing love for you—and for others—even when you feel tempted to run.

Jonah Tries to Run Away from God

1 Now the word of the LORD came to Jonah son of Amittai, saying, ²"Go at once to Nineveh, that great city, and cry out against it; for their wickedness has come up before me." ³But Jonah set out to flee to Tarshish from the presence of the LORD. He went down to Joppa and found a ship going to Tarshish; so he paid his fare and went on board, to go with them to Tarshish, away from the presence of the LORD.

4 But the LORD hurled a great wind upon the sea, and such a mighty storm came upon the sea that the ship threatened to break up. ⁵Then the mariners were afraid, and each cried to his god. They threw the cargo that was in the ship into the sea, to lighten it for them. Jonah, meanwhile, had gone down into the hold of the ship and had lain down, and was fast asleep. ⁶The captain came and said to him, "What are you doing sound asleep? Get up, call on your god! Perhaps the god will spare us a thought so that we do not perish."

7 The sailors*ᵃ* said to one another, "Come, let us cast lots, so that we may know on whose account this calamity has come upon us." So they cast lots, and the lot fell on Jonah. ⁸Then they said to him, "Tell us why this calamity has come upon us. What is your occupation? Where do you come from? What is your country? And of what people are you?" ⁹"I am a Hebrew," he replied. "I worship the LORD, the God of heaven, who made the sea and the dry land." ¹⁰Then the men were even more afraid, and said to him, "What is this that you have done!" For the men knew that he was fleeing from the presence of the LORD, because he had told them so.

11 Then they said to him, "What shall we do to you, that the sea may quiet down for us?" For the sea was growing more and more tempestuous. ¹²He said to them, "Pick me up and throw me into the sea; then the sea will quiet down for you; for I know it is because of me that this great storm has come upon you." ¹³Nevertheless the men rowed hard to bring the ship back to land, but they could not, for the sea grew more and more stormy against them. ¹⁴Then they cried out to the LORD, "Please, O LORD, we pray, do not let us perish on account of this man's life. Do not make us guilty of innocent blood; for you, O LORD, have done as it pleased you." ¹⁵So they picked Jonah up and threw him into the sea; and the sea ceased from its raging. ¹⁶Then the men feared the LORD even more, and they offered a sacrifice to the LORD and made vows.

17*ᵇ* But the LORD provided a large fish to swallow up Jonah; and Jonah was in the belly of the fish three days and three nights.

A Psalm of Thanksgiving

2 Then Jonah prayed to the LORD his God from the belly of the fish, ²saying,

"I called to the LORD out of my distress,
    and he answered me;
out of the belly of Sheol I cried,
    and you heard my voice.
³ You cast me into the deep,

God of *All?*

JONAH 1.2–3

Jonah and his people have a keen awareness of their relationship with God. Error creeps in when Jonah begins to consider God his exclusive possession. Jonah would rather flee from God than give up his narrow views about who deserves to know God and experience God's mercy.

Think about those whom you consider impervious to change. Are you tempted to steer clear of them? Are you trying to ignore God's clear leading to become involved? How can you let Jonah's negative example remind you that God is not willing that anyone should perish (2 Peter 3.9)? In prayer, name two or three people desperately in need of God's gracious intervention.

See Meeting God in Service

---

a Heb *They*   *b* Ch 2.1 in Heb

No Foxhole Faith

JONAH 2.4–9

The wartime expression "There are no atheists in foxholes" is illustrated well by Jonah's cry to God. It's easy to remember God when we're in trouble and forget to practice God's presence in ordinary times. Use this exercise to recall God's tender deliverance of you in the past: Recall a situation in which you were displaced or threatened in some way. How deeply into despair did you sink? What caused you to remember God and pray? What did you learn from your experience? How has that experience taught you to call on God when trouble looms? Rest in silent assurance, enjoying the steady sense of God's presence in this ordinary moment.

See Meeting God in Everyday Life

into the heart of the seas,
　and the flood surrounded me;
all your waves and your billows
　passed over me.
4　Then I said, 'I am driven away
　　from your sight;
how*ᵃ* shall I look again
　upon your holy temple?'
5　The waters closed in over me;
　　the deep surrounded me;
weeds were wrapped around my head
6　　at the roots of the mountains.
I went down to the land
　whose bars closed upon me forever;
yet you brought up my life from the Pit,
　O LORD my God.
7　As my life was ebbing away,
　　I remembered the LORD;
and my prayer came to you,
　into your holy temple.
8　Those who worship vain idols
　　forsake their true loyalty.
9　But I with the voice of thanksgiving
　　will sacrifice to you;
what I have vowed I will pay.
　Deliverance belongs to the LORD!"

¹⁰Then the LORD spoke to the fish, and it spewed Jonah out upon the dry land.

Conversion of Nineveh

3 The word of the LORD came to Jonah a second time, saying, ²"Get up, go to Nineveh, that great city, and proclaim to it the message that I tell you." ³So Jonah set out and went to Nineveh, according to the word of the LORD. Now Nineveh was an exceedingly large city, a three days' walk across. ⁴Jonah began to go into the city, going a day's walk. And he cried out, "Forty days more, and Nineveh shall be overthrown!" ⁵And the people of Nineveh believed God; they proclaimed a fast, and everyone, great and small, put on sackcloth.

6 When the news reached the king of Nineveh, he rose from his throne, removed his robe, covered himself with sackcloth, and sat in ashes. ⁷Then he had a proclamation made in Nineveh: "By the decree of the king and his nobles: No human being or animal, no herd or flock, shall taste anything. They shall not feed, nor shall they drink water. ⁸Human beings and animals shall be covered with sackcloth, and they shall cry mightily to God. All shall turn from their evil ways and from the violence that is in their hands. ⁹Who knows? God may relent and change his mind; he may turn from his fierce anger, so that we do not perish."

10 When God saw what they did, how they turned from their evil ways, God changed his mind about the calamity that he had said he would bring upon them; and he did not do it.

a Theodotion: Heb *surely*

Jonah's Anger

4 But this was very displeasing to Jonah, and he became angry. [2]He prayed to the LORD and said, "O LORD! Is not this what I said while I was still in my own country? That is why I fled to Tarshish at the beginning; for I knew that you are a gracious God and merciful, slow to anger, and abounding in steadfast love, and ready to relent from punishing. [3]And now, O LORD, please take my life from me, for it is better for me to die than to live." [4]And the LORD said, "Is it right for you to be angry?" [5]Then Jonah went out of the city and sat down east of the city, and made a booth for himself. He sat under it in the shade, waiting to see what would become of the city.

6 The LORD God appointed a bush,[a] and made it come up over Jonah, to give shade over his head, to save him from his discomfort; so Jonah was very happy about the bush. [7]But when dawn came up the next day, God appointed a worm that attacked the bush, so that it withered. [8]When the sun rose, God prepared a sultry east wind, and the sun beat down on the head of Jonah so that he was faint and asked that he might die. He said, "It is better for me to die than to live."

Jonah Is Reproved

9 But God said to Jonah, "Is it right for you to be angry about the bush?" And he said, "Yes, angry enough to die." [10]Then the LORD said, "You are concerned about the bush, for which you did not labor and which you did not grow; it came into being in a night and perished in a night. [11]And should I not be concerned about Nineveh, that great city, in which there are more than a hundred and twenty thousand persons who do not know their right hand from their left, and also many animals?"

"Should I Not Be Concerned?"

JONAH 4.11

Jonah is pouting—dangerously close to a tantrum. And why? Because God's sweeping, inclusive love extends to even "those people" whom our protagonist has been conditioned to hold in low regard. God's ways are not Jonah's ways, and Jonah makes it known loud and clear.

Alas, when the story ends, we have not discovered how Jonah responds. But we can proceed to discover what's in our own hearts. Bring to mind someone or some group of people whom you resent—perhaps for what seem to be good reasons. Paraphrase this verse, including information about those people so that in prayer you can express concern for them by using God's own words.

See Meeting God in Prayer

---

a Heb *qiqayon*, possibly *the castor bean plant*

MICAH
What God Requires

KEY VERSE:

He has told you, O mortal, what is good; and what does the LORD *require of you but to do justice,*
and to love kindness, and to walk humbly with your God?—Micah 6.8

"Where people let loose their minds after the love of outward things and are more engaged in pursuing the profits and seeking the friendships of this world than to be inwardly acquainted with the way of true peace, such walk in a vain shadow while the true comfort of life is wanting."

—JOHN WOOLMAN,
The Journal of John Woolman

Micah looks beneath the surface of Judah's society and sees fundamental flaws that will result in the nation's downfall. Greed and dishonesty permeate the nation, and the result is a compromised legal system, a callous disregard for the poor and an unethical business practice. Ironically all this takes place while Judah publicly professes to be faithful to the one true God and to the divine law handed down to the people during their wilderness wandering. They are hypocrites; their religion is a sham and God is angry.

Micah's prophetic words give us occasion to ask ourselves several questions: How can I be willing to hear all that God has to say, even when it is unpleasant? How might God be speaking to me about my thoughts and activities in light of the faith I profess? How do I need to participate in calling society to account for being less than it professes to be? How can I claim for myself Micah's hope for a time when a just and peaceful world will be God's prized possession? How open am I to acknowledging God's presence in every area of my life?

1
The word of the LORD that came to Micah of Moresheth in the days of Kings Jotham, Ahaz, and Hezekiah of Judah, which he saw concerning Samaria and Jerusalem.

Judgment Pronounced against Samaria

2 Hear, you peoples, all of you;
   listen, O earth, and all that is in it;
and let the Lord GOD be a witness against you,
   the Lord from his holy temple.
3 For lo, the LORD is coming out of his place,
   and will come down and tread upon the high
      places of the earth.
4 Then the mountains will melt under him
   and the valleys will burst open,
like wax near the fire,
   like waters poured down a steep place.
5 All this is for the transgression of Jacob
   and for the sins of the house of Israel.
What is the transgression of Jacob?
   Is it not Samaria?
And what is the high place[a] of Judah?
   Is it not Jerusalem?
6 Therefore I will make Samaria a heap in the open
      country,
   a place for planting vineyards.
I will pour down her stones into the valley,
   and uncover her foundations.
7 All her images shall be beaten to pieces,
   all her wages shall be burned with fire,
   and all her idols I will lay waste;
for as the wages of a prostitute she gathered them,
   and as the wages of a prostitute they shall again
      be used.

The Doom of the Cities of Judah

8 For this I will lament and wail;
   I will go barefoot and naked;
I will make lamentation like the jackals,
   and mourning like the ostriches.
9 For her wound[b] is incurable.
   It has come to Judah;
it has reached to the gate of my people,
   to Jerusalem.

10 Tell it not in Gath,
      weep not at all;
   in Beth-leaphrah
      roll yourselves in the dust.
11 Pass on your way,
      inhabitants of Shaphir,
      in nakedness and shame;
   the inhabitants of Zaanan
      do not come forth;
   Beth-ezel is wailing
      and shall remove its support from you.
12 For the inhabitants of Maroth
      wait anxiously for good,

The Lord Is Coming!

MICAH 1.1–7

What a picture Micah's words bring to mind! "The LORD is coming out of his place, and will come and tread upon the high places of the earth." The power of God's touch on the earth is so awesome that "the mountains will melt under him and the valleys will burst open."

To say that God's presence among us brings radical change is a gross understatement. When we ask God into our lives, we can expect transformation of earthshaking proportions. How would you respond to an announcement of God's presence upon the earth—a place nearby? What does it mean for God to come from his dwelling place and radically change you—even a part of you that you would prefer to leave undisturbed?

See Meeting God in the Created Order

---

a Heb *what are the high places*   *b* Gk Syr Vg: Heb *wounds*

Devising Evil

MICAH 2.1–6

Micah accuses the people of Judah of planning "evil deeds on their beds!" They aren't planning heinous crimes like serial murder or mass genocide, but their nighttime scheming results in the misuse of power in their day-to-day dealings with people.

How does this passage challenge you to consider what kind of thought life you might be indulging in during your leisure time? Consider what you could do or say during those restful moments instead of pondering how to acquire more or get more done to advance your agenda. How could you use those moments to connect with God and consider God's agenda?

See Meeting God in Everyday Life

yet disaster has come down from the LORD
    to the gate of Jerusalem.
13 Harness the steeds to the chariots,
        inhabitants of Lachish;
it was the beginning of sin
        to daughter Zion,
for in you were found
        the transgressions of Israel.
14 Therefore you shall give parting gifts
        to Moresheth-gath;
the houses of Achzib shall be a deception
        to the kings of Israel.
15 I will again bring a conqueror upon you,
        inhabitants of Mareshah;
the glory of Israel
        shall come to Adullam.
16 Make yourselves bald and cut off your hair
        for your pampered children;
make yourselves as bald as the eagle,
        for they have gone from you into exile.

Social Evils Denounced

2 Alas for those who devise wickedness
        and evil deeds^a on their beds!
When the morning dawns, they perform it,
        because it is in their power.
2 They covet fields, and seize them;
        houses, and take them away;
they oppress householder and house,
        people and their inheritance.
3 Therefore thus says the LORD:
Now, I am devising against this family an evil
        from which you cannot remove your necks;
and you shall not walk haughtily,
        for it will be an evil time.
4 On that day they shall take up a taunt song against
            you,
        and wail with bitter lamentation,
and say, "We are utterly ruined;
        the LORD^b alters the inheritance of my people;
how he removes it from me!
        Among our captors^c he parcels out our fields."
5 Therefore you will have no one to cast the line by
            lot
        in the assembly of the LORD.

6 "Do not preach"—thus they preach—
        "one should not preach of such things;
        disgrace will not overtake us."
7 Should this be said, O house of Jacob?
        Is the LORD's patience exhausted?
        Are these his doings?
Do not my words do good
        to one who walks uprightly?
8 But you rise up against my people^d as an enemy;
        you strip the robe from the peaceful,^e
from those who pass by trustingly
        with no thought of war.

a Cn: Heb *work evil*   *b* Heb *he*   *c* Cn: Heb *the rebellious*   *d* Cn: Heb
But yesterday my people rose   *e* Cn: Heb *from before a garment*

9   The women of my people you drive out
        from their pleasant houses;
    from their young children you take away
        my glory forever.
10 Arise and go;
        for this is no place to rest,
    because of uncleanness that destroys
        with a grievous destruction.*a*
11 If someone were to go about uttering empty
        falsehoods,
    saying, "I will preach to you of wine and strong
        drink,"
    such a one would be the preacher for this
        people!

A Promise for the Remnant of Israel

12 I will surely gather all of you, O Jacob,
        I will gather the survivors of Israel;
    I will set them together
        like sheep in a fold,
    like a flock in its pasture;
        it will resound with people.
13 The one who breaks out will go up before them;
        they will break through and pass the gate,
        going out by it.
    Their king will pass on before them,
        the LORD at their head.

Wicked Rulers and Prophets

3   And I said:
    Listen, you heads of Jacob
        and rulers of the house of Israel!
    Should you not know justice?—
2   you who hate the good and love the evil,
    who tear the skin off my people,*b*
        and the flesh off their bones;
3   who eat the flesh of my people,
        flay their skin off them,
    break their bones in pieces,
        and chop them up like meat*c* in a kettle,
        like flesh in a caldron.

4   Then they will cry to the LORD,
        but he will not answer them;
    he will hide his face from them at that time,
        because they have acted wickedly.

5   Thus says the LORD concerning the prophets
        who lead my people astray,
    who cry "Peace"
        when they have something to eat,
    but declare war against those
        who put nothing into their mouths.
6   Therefore it shall be night to you, without vision,
        and darkness to you, without revelation.
    The sun shall go down upon the prophets,
        and the day shall be black over them;
7   the seers shall be disgraced,
        and the diviners put to shame;

Empty Falsehoods

MICAH 2.11

Micah must not only proclaim an unpopular message, but he must also contend with false prophets whose message is that God requires only business as usual of his chosen people. Notice the sarcasm in verse 11. Write down the verse and carry it with you as you go about your day today. Be on the lookout for those who would deceive others. What message is being proclaimed today that seems to be just what people want to hear? What messages today are unpopular? How can you discredit the false messages and support God's true messages and messengers today?

See Meeting God in Everyday Life

---

a Meaning of Heb uncertain   *b* Heb *from them*   *c* Gk: Heb *as*

An Invitation

Place yourself in the midst of this text. You hear the invitation: "Come, let us go up to the mountain of the LORD . . . that he may teach us his ways and that we may walk in his paths."

What is your response to the invitation? What would beating "swords into plowshares" and "spears into pruning hooks" look like in your life? What weapons—words, facial expressions, invitation lists—that you sometimes wield could become tools of peace? Is this message a welcome word to you, or is it one you would rather not hear because it requires too much from you? Why?

See Meeting God in Scripture

they shall all cover their lips,
for there is no answer from God.
8 But as for me, I am filled with power,
with the spirit of the LORD,
and with justice and might,
to declare to Jacob his transgression
and to Israel his sin.

9 Hear this, you rulers of the house of Jacob
and chiefs of the house of Israel,
who abhor justice
and pervert all equity,
10 who build Zion with blood
and Jerusalem with wrong!
11 Its rulers give judgment for a bribe,
its priests teach for a price,
its prophets give oracles for money;
yet they lean upon the LORD and say,
"Surely the LORD is with us!
No harm shall come upon us."
12 Therefore because of you
Zion shall be plowed as a field;
Jerusalem shall become a heap of ruins,
and the mountain of the house a wooded
height.

Peace and Security through Obedience

4 In days to come
the mountain of the LORD's house
shall be established as the highest of the
mountains,
and shall be raised up above the hills.
Peoples shall stream to it,
2 and many nations shall come and say:
"Come, let us go up to the mountain of the LORD,
to the house of the God of Jacob;
that he may teach us his ways
and that we may walk in his paths."
For out of Zion shall go forth instruction,
and the word of the LORD from Jerusalem.
3 He shall judge between many peoples,
and shall arbitrate between strong nations far
away;
they shall beat their swords into plowshares,
and their spears into pruning hooks;
nation shall not lift up sword against nation,
neither shall they learn war any more;
4 but they shall all sit under their own vines and
under their own fig trees,
and no one shall make them afraid;
for the mouth of the LORD of hosts has spoken.

5 For all the peoples walk,
each in the name of its god,
but we will walk in the name of the LORD our God
forever and ever.

Restoration Promised after Exile

6 In that day, says the LORD,
I will assemble the lame

and gather those who have been driven away,
    and those whom I have afflicted.
7 The lame I will make the remnant,
    and those who were cast off, a strong nation;
and the LORD will reign over them in Mount Zion
    now and forevermore.

8 And you, O tower of the flock,
    hill of daughter Zion,
to you it shall come,
    the former dominion shall come,
    the sovereignty of daughter Jerusalem.

9 Now why do you cry aloud?
    Is there no king in you?
Has your counselor perished,
    that pangs have seized you like a woman in
        labor?
10 Writhe and groan,*a* O daughter Zion,
    like a woman in labor;
for now you shall go forth from the city
    and camp in the open country;
    you shall go to Babylon.
There you shall be rescued,
    there the LORD will redeem you
    from the hands of your enemies.

11 Now many nations
    are assembled against you,
saying, "Let her be profaned,
    and let our eyes gaze upon Zion."
12 But they do not know
    the thoughts of the LORD;
they do not understand his plan,
    that he has gathered them as sheaves to the
        threshing floor.
13 Arise and thresh,
    O daughter Zion,
for I will make your horn iron
    and your hoofs bronze;
you shall beat in pieces many peoples,
    and shall*b* devote their gain to the LORD,
    their wealth to the Lord of the whole earth.

5 *c* Now you are walled around with a wall;*d*
    siege is laid against us;
with a rod they strike the ruler of Israel
    upon the cheek.

The Ruler from Bethlehem

2 *e* But you, O Bethlehem of Ephrathah,
    who are one of the little clans of Judah,
from you shall come forth for me
    one who is to rule in Israel,
whose origin is from of old,
    from ancient days.
3 Therefore he shall give them up until the time
    when she who is in labor has brought forth;

The Other Side of Ruin–Restoration

MICAH 4.6–13

Micah's message of restoration tells us three things: (1) God will ultimately prevail in spite of the prevalence of evil; (2) it is no accident that individuals and nations suffer the consequences of the evil they do; and (3) no matter how complete individual or national ruin seems, restoration awaits beyond the ruin.

Do you hear this message with a sense of hope or doom? How have you experienced suffering as a consequence of evil? In what ways have you seen God restore people, churches, communities? How has God restored you? Make this your breath prayer (a short prayer repeated frequently) today: "O God who acts in history, restore me to a right relationship with you."

See *Meeting God in Scripture*

---

a Meaning of Heb uncertain   *b* Gk Syr Tg: Heb *and I will*   *c* Ch 4.14 in
Heb   *d* Cn Compare Gk: Meaning of Heb uncertain   *e* Ch 5.1 in Heb

The One of Peace

MICAH 5.2–5

In this passage Micah describes a future deliverer who will once and for all time restore Judah to its rightful place among the nations. The source of this new leader's power is proclaimed in verses 4–5. What kind of leader do these verses describe? Think about the areas in your life where you serve in a leadership role—perhaps on your block, at work, among friends, with children. Evaluate your leadership in the light of these verses. If our nation looked for these qualities in its leaders, how would the nation be affected?

See Meeting God in Community

then the rest of his kindred shall return
    to the people of Israel.
4 And he shall stand and feed his flock in the strength
    of the LORD,
    in the majesty of the name of the LORD his God.
And they shall live secure, for now he shall be great
    to the ends of the earth;
5 and he shall be the one of peace.

If the Assyrians come into our land
    and tread upon our soil,[a]
we will raise against them seven shepherds
    and eight installed as rulers.
6 They shall rule the land of Assyria with the sword,
    and the land of Nimrod with the drawn sword;[b]
they[c] shall rescue us from the Assyrians
    if they come into our land
    or tread within our border.

The Future Role of the Remnant

7 Then the remnant of Jacob,
    surrounded by many peoples,
shall be like dew from the LORD,
    like showers on the grass,
which do not depend upon people
    or wait for any mortal.
8 And among the nations the remnant of Jacob,
    surrounded by many peoples,
shall be like a lion among the animals of the forest,
    like a young lion among the flocks of sheep,
which, when it goes through, treads down
    and tears in pieces, with no one to deliver.
9 Your hand shall be lifted up over your adversaries,
    and all your enemies shall be cut off.

10 In that day, says the LORD,
    I will cut off your horses from among you
    and will destroy your chariots;
11 and I will cut off the cities of your land
    and throw down all your strongholds;
12 and I will cut off sorceries from your hand,
    and you shall have no more soothsayers;
13 and I will cut off your images
    and your pillars from among you,
and you shall bow down no more
    to the work of your hands;
14 and I will uproot your sacred poles[d] from among
      you
    and destroy your towns.
15 And in anger and wrath I will execute vengeance
    on the nations that did not obey.

God Challenges Israel

6 Hear what the LORD says:
    Rise, plead your case before the mountains,
    and let the hills hear your voice.
2 Hear, you mountains, the controversy of the LORD,
    and you enduring foundations of the earth;

a Gk: Heb *in our palaces*   b Cn: Heb *in its entrances*   c Heb *he*
d Heb *Asherim*

for the Lord has a controversy with his people,
and he will contend with Israel.

3 "O my people, what have I done to you?
In what have I wearied you? Answer me!
4 For I brought you up from the land of Egypt,
and redeemed you from the house of slavery;
and I sent before you Moses,
Aaron, and Miriam.
5 O my people, remember now what King Balak of
Moab devised,
what Balaam son of Beor answered him,
and what happened from Shittim to Gilgal,
that you may know the saving acts of the Lord."

What God Requires

6 "With what shall I come before the Lord,
and bow myself before God on high?
Shall I come before him with burnt offerings,
with calves a year old?
7 Will the Lord be pleased with thousands of rams,
with ten thousands of rivers of oil?
Shall I give my firstborn for my transgression,
the fruit of my body for the sin of my soul?"
8 He has told you, O mortal, what is good;
and what does the Lord require of you
but to do justice, and to love kindness,
and to walk humbly with your God?

Cheating and Violence to Be Punished

9 The voice of the Lord cries to the city
(it is sound wisdom to fear your name):
Hear, O tribe and assembly of the city!*a*
10 Can I forget*b* the treasures of wickedness in the
house of the wicked,
and the scant measure that is accursed?
11 Can I tolerate wicked scales
and a bag of dishonest weights?
12 Your*c* wealthy are full of violence;
your*d* inhabitants speak lies,
with tongues of deceit in their mouths.
13 Therefore I have begun*e* to strike you down,
making you desolate because of your sins.
14 You shall eat, but not be satisfied,
and there shall be a gnawing hunger within you;
you shall put away, but not save,
and what you save, I will hand over to the sword.
15 You shall sow, but not reap;
you shall tread olives, but not anoint yourselves
with oil;
you shall tread grapes, but not drink wine.
16 For you have kept the statutes of Omri*f*
and all the works of the house of Ahab,
and you have followed their counsels.
Therefore I will make you a desolation, and your*g*
inhabitants an object of hissing;
so you shall bear the scorn of my people.

What the Lord Requires

MICAH 6.6–8

Let this passage speak directly to you. Slowly read the passage aloud. (You may want to read it more than once.) Is there a word or phrase or image that particularly draws your attention? Reflect on that word or phrase or image. Why is it important? Wait silently, asking yourself what God might be trying to say to you in this passage. Pray that God will reveal the meaning of this passage to you and then hide the meaning deep in your heart.

See Meeting God in Scripture

---

a Cn Compare Gk: Heb *tribe, and who has appointed it yet?*   b Cn: Meaning of Heb uncertain   c Heb *Whose*   d Heb *whose*   e Gk Syr Vg: Heb *have made sick*   f Gk Syr Vg Tg: Heb *the statutes of Omri are kept*   g Heb *its*

Hopeful Waiting

MICAH 7.1–7

Read aloud verses 1–6 of Micah's lament. Can you identify with Micah's despair over a society lacking justice and mercy? Make a list of the problems of our society that cause you to despair.

Micah's lament does not end in despair however. He declares he will "look to the LORD" and "wait for" the God of his salvation. Micah's faith allows him to rise above his despair and continue to work for God. Pray through your list of our society's dilemmas. Ask God to act in these areas and to show you how it may be possible for you to address them. When you are finished, write verse 7 in red ink across your list and read it aloud.

See Meeting God in Scripture

The Total Corruption of the People

7 Woe is me! For I have become like one who,
  after the summer fruit has been gathered,
  after the vintage has been gleaned,
finds no cluster to eat;
  there is no first-ripe fig for which I hunger.
2 The faithful have disappeared from the land,
  and there is no one left who is upright;
they all lie in wait for blood,
  and they hunt each other with nets.
3 Their hands are skilled to do evil;
  the official and the judge ask for a bribe,
and the powerful dictate what they desire;
  thus they pervert justice.*ᵃ*
4 The best of them is like a brier,
  the most upright of them a thorn hedge.
The day of their*ᵇ* sentinels, of their*ᵇ* punishment,
  has come;
  now their confusion is at hand.
5 Put no trust in a friend,
  have no confidence in a loved one;
guard the doors of your mouth
  from her who lies in your embrace;
6 for the son treats the father with contempt,
  the daughter rises up against her mother,
the daughter-in-law against her mother-in-law;
  your enemies are members of your own
    household.
7 But as for me, I will look to the LORD,
  I will wait for the God of my salvation;
  my God will hear me.

Penitence and Trust in God

8 Do not rejoice over me, O my enemy;
  when I fall, I shall rise;
when I sit in darkness,
  the LORD will be a light to me.
9 I must bear the indignation of the LORD,
  because I have sinned against him,
until he takes my side
  and executes judgment for me.
He will bring me out to the light;
  I shall see his vindication.
10 Then my enemy will see,
  and shame will cover her who said to me,
  "Where is the LORD your God?"
My eyes will see her downfall;*ᶜ*
  now she will be trodden down
  like the mire of the streets.

A Prophecy of Restoration

11 A day for the building of your walls!
  In that day the boundary shall be far extended.
12 In that day they will come to you
  from Assyria to*ᵈ* Egypt,
and from Egypt to the River,
  from sea to sea and from mountain to mountain.

a Cn: Heb *they weave it*   *b* Heb *your*   *c* Heb lacks *downfall*   *d* One Ms:
MT *Assyria and cities of*

13 But the earth will be desolate
because of its inhabitants,
for the fruit of their doings.

14 Shepherd your people with your staff,
the flock that belongs to you,
which lives alone in a forest
in the midst of a garden land;
let them feed in Bashan and Gilead
as in the days of old.
15 As in the days when you came out of the land of
Egypt,
show us*a* marvelous things.
16 The nations shall see and be ashamed
of all their might;
they shall lay their hands on their mouths;
their ears shall be deaf;
17 they shall lick dust like a snake,
like the crawling things of the earth;
they shall come trembling out of their fortresses;
they shall turn in dread to the LORD our God,
and they shall stand in fear of you.

God's Compassion and Steadfast Love

18 Who is a God like you, pardoning iniquity
and passing over the transgression
of the remnant of your*b* possession?
He does not retain his anger forever,
because he delights in showing clemency.
19 He will again have compassion upon us;
he will tread our iniquities under foot.
You will cast all our*c* sins
into the depths of the sea.
20 You will show faithfulness to Jacob
and unswerving loyalty to Abraham,
as you have sworn to our ancestors
from the days of old.

A Compassionate and Loving God

MICAH 7.18–20

The book of Micah closes with God's assurance of compassion and steadfast love: God does not "stay angry forever." In light of this passage, reflect on the state of your heart right now. In what ways do you need assurance of God's forgiveness and love? Write on a piece of paper, "[You delight] in showing clemency. [You] will again have compassion upon us." Carry this message of hope with you today, and at the end of the day reread the words and thank God for the compassion and steadfast love he offers to you. Exult in the freedom that the knowledge of your forgiveness brings.

See Meeting God in Scripture

---

a Cn: Heb *I will show him*   *b* Heb *his*   *c* Gk Syr Vg Tg: Heb *their*

NAHUM

Woe and Reassurance

KEY VERSE:

Look! On the mountains the feet of one who brings good tidings, who proclaims peace! Celebrate your festivals, O Judah, fulfill your vows, for never again shall the wicked invade you; they are utterly cut off.—Nahum 1.15

"And though this world,
  with devils filled,
Should threaten to undo us,
We will not fear, for God
  hath willed
His truth to triumph
  through us:
The Prince of Darkness grim,
We tremble not for him;
His rage we can endure,
For lo his doom is sure,
One little word shall fell
  him."

—MARTIN LUTHER,
"A Mighty Fortress Is Our God"

The prophet Nahum is given a vision, and with poetic passion he tells the world what he sees. His call is to announce that God opposes the arrogant Assyrian empire and will bring about the downfall of Nineveh, the proud city of Assyria. Nahum's descriptions are astonishingly powerful. "Ah! City of bloodshed, utterly deceitful, full of booty—no end to the plunder! The crack of whip and rumble of wheel, galloping horse and bounding chariot!" (3.1–3). The language is terse and clear: "There is no assuaging your hurt, your wound is mortal" (3.19).

Among the Israelites, though, there will be rejoicing. The images of destruction also contain a word of hope for the people of Israel, long oppressed by the Assyrians: "Look, there on the mountains, the feet of one who brings good news, who proclaims peace!" (1.15). Nahum calls us to look at our own arrogance and faithlessness and welcome the herald who brings us news of peace and hope.

1
An oracle concerning Nineveh. The book of the vision of Nahum of Elkosh.

The Consuming Wrath of God

2 A jealous and avenging God is the LORD,
    the LORD is avenging and wrathful;
the LORD takes vengeance on his adversaries
    and rages against his enemies.
3 The LORD is slow to anger but great in power,
    and the LORD will by no means clear the guilty.

His way is in whirlwind and storm,
    and the clouds are the dust of his feet.
4 He rebukes the sea and makes it dry,
    and he dries up all the rivers;
Bashan and Carmel wither,
    and the bloom of Lebanon fades.
5 The mountains quake before him,
    and the hills melt;
the earth heaves before him,
    the world and all who live in it.

6 Who can stand before his indignation?
    Who can endure the heat of his anger?
His wrath is poured out like fire,
    and by him the rocks are broken in pieces.
7 The LORD is good,
    a stronghold in a day of trouble;
he protects those who take refuge in him,
8   even in a rushing flood.
He will make a full end of his adversaries,[a]
    and will pursue his enemies into darkness.
9 Why do you plot against the LORD?
    He will make an end;
no adversary will rise up twice.
10 Like thorns they are entangled,
    like drunkards they are drunk;
they are consumed like dry straw.
11 From you one has gone out
    who plots evil against the LORD,
    one who counsels wickedness.

Good News for Judah

12 Thus says the LORD,
"Though they are at full strength and many,[b]
    they will be cut off and pass away.
Though I have afflicted you,
    I will afflict you no more.
13 And now I will break off his yoke from you
    and snap the bonds that bind you."

14 The LORD has commanded concerning you:
    "Your name shall be perpetuated no longer;
from the house of your gods I will cut off
    the carved image and the cast image.
I will make your grave, for you are worthless."

God Is Wholly Holy

NAHUM 1.3,6–7

Although our God is caring and compassionate, his holiness cannot tolerate wrongdoing and evil. They simply cannot co-exist. God's indignation at evil is consuming and complete.

God's anger with us is assuaged in Christ Jesus, yet God asks us to be holy because he is holy (see 1 Peter 1.16). Is there anything in your life, past or present, that cannot dwell alongside God's holiness within your redeemed spirit? Is there anything for which you need to ask forgiveness? As an act of confession, list your wrongdoings. Confess them to the Lord who "protects those who take refuge in him." Roll up that piece of paper and throw it away, or burn it. Experience the joy that comes from letting God cleanse you from all your sin.

See Meeting God in Prayer

Behold, Good Tidings Are Coming

NAHUM 1.15

Imagine yourself a captive in a walled city. As you look out through holes in the city wall, you see hills and mountains—beautiful and green, yet inaccessible to you. You have almost given up hope of ever being free. Then you hear a trumpet sound and people shouting. Someone is coming toward the city; someone is coming with good news. Your captivity is over! You are free to go! Peace is coming to you!

You have heard the good news. What barriers have been overcome? How has your life been transformed? Who brings the word of peace to you? Who will attend a celebration with you? What will you do to celebrate? Throw a party? Write a prayer of thanksgiving?

See Meeting God in Scripture

15*a* Look! On the mountains the feet of one
who brings good tidings,
who proclaims peace!
Celebrate your festivals, O Judah,
fulfill your vows,
for never again shall the wicked invade you;
they are utterly cut off.

The Destruction of the Wicked City

2 A shatterer*b* has come up against you.
Guard the ramparts;
watch the road;
gird your loins;
collect all your strength.

2 (For the LORD is restoring the majesty of Jacob,
as well as the majesty of Israel,
though ravagers have ravaged them
and ruined their branches.)

3 The shields of his warriors are red;
his soldiers are clothed in crimson.
The metal on the chariots flashes
on the day when he musters them;
the chargers*c* prance.

4 The chariots race madly through the streets,
they rush to and fro through the squares;
their appearance is like torches,
they dart like lightning.

5 He calls his officers;
they stumble as they come forward;
they hasten to the wall,
and the mantelet*d* is set up.

6 The river gates are opened,
the palace trembles.

7 It is decreed*d* that the city*e* be exiled,
its slave women led away,
moaning like doves
and beating their breasts.

8 Nineveh is like a pool
whose waters*f* run away.
"Halt! Halt!"—
but no one turns back.

9 "Plunder the silver,
plunder the gold!
There is no end of treasure!
An abundance of every precious thing!"

10 Devastation, desolation, and destruction!
Hearts faint and knees tremble,
all loins quake,
all faces grow pale!

11 What became of the lions' den,
the cave*g* of the young lions,
where the lion goes,
and the lion's cubs, with no one to disturb them?

a Ch 2.1 in Heb   *b* Cn: Heb *scatterer*   *c* Cn Compare Gk Syr: Heb *cypresses*   *d* Meaning of Heb uncertain   *e* Heb *it*   *f* Cn Compare Gk: Heb *a pool, from the days that she has become, and they*   *g* Cn: Heb *pasture*

12 The lion has torn enough for his whelps
  and strangled prey for his lionesses;
he has filled his caves with prey
  and his dens with torn flesh.

13 See, I am against you, says the LORD of hosts, and I will burn your[a] chariots in smoke, and the sword shall devour your young lions; I will cut off your prey from the earth, and the voice of your messengers shall be heard no more.

Ruin Imminent and Inevitable

3 Ah! City of bloodshed,
  utterly deceitful, full of booty—
  no end to the plunder!
2 The crack of whip and rumble of wheel,
  galloping horse and bounding chariot!
3 Horsemen charging,
  flashing sword and glittering spear,
piles of dead,
  heaps of corpses,
dead bodies without end—
  they stumble over the bodies!
4 Because of the countless debaucheries of the
    prostitute,
  gracefully alluring, mistress of sorcery,
who enslaves[b] nations through her debaucheries,
  and peoples through her sorcery,
5 I am against you,
  says the LORD of hosts,
  and will lift up your skirts over your face;
and I will let nations look on your nakedness
  and kingdoms on your shame.
6 I will throw filth at you
  and treat you with contempt,
  and make you a spectacle.
7 Then all who see you will shrink from you and say,
  "Nineveh is devastated; who will bemoan her?"
  Where shall I seek comforters for you?

8 Are you better than Thebes[c]
  that sat by the Nile,
with water around her,
  her rampart a sea,
  water her wall?
9 Ethiopia[d] was her strength,
  Egypt too, and that without limit;
  Put and the Libyans were her[e] helpers.

10 Yet she became an exile,
  she went into captivity;
even her infants were dashed in pieces
  at the head of every street;
lots were cast for her nobles,
  all her dignitaries were bound in fetters.
11 You also will be drunken,
  you will go into hiding;[f]
you will seek
  a refuge from the enemy.

Not Pride but Humility

NAHUM 3.8–11

"Let God do as He likes; consider yourself as a picture which a great master is proposing to paint; but take courage, for I foresee that it will take some time to grind and powder the colors, and then to lay them on, combine them and shade them. All you have to do is to keep the canvas ready, well-cleaned and fastened on its two motionless pivots, the one being self-humiliation . . . the other a complete self-abandonment pushed to the point of losing your will altogether in the will of God."

—JEAN-PIERRE DE CAUSSADE,
in *Living Water, An Anthology
of Letters of Direction*

a Heb *her*   b Heb *sells*   c Heb *No-amon*   d Or *Nubia;* Heb *Cush*
e Gk: Heb *your*   f Meaning of Heb uncertain

No Hope, New Hope

NAHUM 3.12–19

There is no hope for Nineveh. She is doomed. Sometimes we feel hopeless ourselves: when a job we count on falls through; a troubling report from the doctor changes all our plans; a relationship unravels and we are left alone and desolate. Or despair may grip us during those times when we realize our faithlessness has caused unnecessary pain to ourselves, to others, even to God. "There is no assuaging your hurt, your wound is mortal." All seems hopeless.

But we must remember that although life may at times seem helpless and hopeless, there is hope for us in Jesus Christ. Light a candle. It is a simple act of faith that reaffirms that Jesus is the light of the world (John 8.12) who casts out darkness and hopelessness. Give thanks for the light.

See Meeting God in Everyday Life

12 All your fortresses are like fig trees
    with first-ripe figs—
if shaken they fall
    into the mouth of the eater.
13 Look at your troops:
    they are women in your midst.
The gates of your land
    are wide open to your foes;
    fire has devoured the bars of your gates.

14 Draw water for the siege,
    strengthen your forts;
trample the clay,
    tread the mortar,
    take hold of the brick mold!
15 There the fire will devour you,
    the sword will cut you off.
    It will devour you like the locust.

Multiply yourselves like the locust,
    multiply like the grasshopper!
16 You increased your merchants
    more than the stars of the heavens.
    The locust sheds its skin and flies away.
17 Your guards are like grasshoppers,
    your scribes like swarms[a] of locusts
settling on the fences
    on a cold day—
when the sun rises, they fly away;
    no one knows where they have gone.

18 Your shepherds are asleep,
    O king of Assyria;
    your nobles slumber.
Your people are scattered on the mountains
    with no one to gather them.
19 There is no assuaging your hurt,
    your wound is mortal.
All who hear the news about you
    clap their hands over you.
For who has ever escaped
    your endless cruelty?

a Meaning of Heb uncertain

HABAKKUK

Waiting and Hoping

KEY VERSE:

For there is still a vision for the appointed time; it speaks of the end, and does not lie. If it seems to tarry, wait for it; it will surely come, it will not delay.—Habakkuk 2.3

Habakkuk, a seventh-century B.C. Judean prophet, is pressed between the two horns of a dilemma of faith. On one side are his people, the people of God, living as faithlessly as though they are not God's people at all. On the other side are surrounding nations whose "own might is their god" (1.11), yet who have been given a role in punishing God's errant people. As the pressure mounts Habakkuk cries out to the Lord, "Why do you look on the treacherous, and are silent when the wicked swallow those more righteous than they?" (1.13), Habakkuk is restless, hungry for answers. The result is a prophet's narrative of waiting and hoping, hoping and waiting.

Although Habakkuk never receives complete answers to his difficult questions about justice and fairness, he does receive a word from the Lord that encourages him. A book that begins in a desperate cry ends with a song declaring that "God, the Lord is my strength; he makes my feet like the feet of a deer, and makes me tread upon the heights" (3.19). As the prophet waits through trouble, he has a sure and certain hope that God will save him.

As you read these three intense chapters, recall times when it seemed to you that life was unfair, that there were more questions than answers or that God was slow to reveal his purposes. When have you prayed, "How long . . .?" When have you sensed that God was telling you to "wait" for insight or resolution to a problem? Where have you found hope in such times?

> "Nothing that is worth doing can be achieved in a lifetime; therefore, we must be saved by hope. Nothing which is true or beautiful or good makes complete sense in any immediate context of history; therefore, we must be saved by faith."
>
> —REINHOLD NIEBUHR,
> *Justice and Mercy*

Questioning God

HABAKKUK 1.1–4

We don't readily think that questioning God is a faithful expression of prayer, but the Bible contains many instances in which prayer became an avenue for confronting or questioning God. Think of a time when you, like Habakkuk, have wanted to confront God with an experience of unfairness, an untimely death, a frustrating circumstance, an injustice, intense suffering. Have you felt that it was permissible to express those emotions in prayer? Could you find the language? Habakkuk's prayer begins, "O Lord, how long, . . . ?" Based on your circumstances or perceptions of the world and its needs, how would you conclude this question with your own words?

See Meeting God in Prayer

1 The oracle that the prophet Habakkuk saw.

The Prophet's Complaint

2 O Lord, how long shall I cry for help,
    and you will not listen?
Or cry to you "Violence!"
    and you will not save?
3 Why do you make me see wrongdoing
    and look at trouble?
Destruction and violence are before me;
    strife and contention arise.
4 So the law becomes slack
    and justice never prevails.
The wicked surround the righteous—
    therefore judgment comes forth perverted.

5 Look at the nations, and see!
    Be astonished! Be astounded!
For a work is being done in your days
    that you would not believe if you were told.
6 For I am rousing the Chaldeans,
    that fierce and impetuous nation,
who march through the breadth of the earth
    to seize dwellings not their own.
7 Dread and fearsome are they;
    their justice and dignity proceed from
      themselves.
8 Their horses are swifter than leopards,
    more menacing than wolves at dusk;
    their horses charge.
Their horsemen come from far away;
    they fly like an eagle swift to devour.
9 They all come for violence,
    with faces pressing[a] forward;
    they gather captives like sand.
10 At kings they scoff,
    and of rulers they make sport.
They laugh at every fortress,
    and heap up earth to take it.
11 Then they sweep by like the wind;
    they transgress and become guilty;
    their own might is their god!

12 Are you not from of old,
    O Lord my God, my Holy One?
    You[b] shall not die.
O Lord, you have marked them for judgment;
    and you, O Rock, have established them for
      punishment.
13 Your eyes are too pure to behold evil,
    and you cannot look on wrongdoing;
why do you look on the treacherous,
    and are silent when the wicked swallow
      those more righteous than they?
14 You have made people like the fish of the sea,
    like crawling things that have no ruler.

a Meaning of Heb uncertain   *b* Ancient Heb tradition: MT *We*

15 The enemy*a* brings all of them up with a hook;
   he drags them out with his net,
he gathers them in his seine;
   so he rejoices and exults.
16 Therefore he sacrifices to his net
   and makes offerings to his seine;
for by them his portion is lavish,
   and his food is rich.
17 Is he then to keep on emptying his net,
   and destroying nations without mercy?

God's Reply to the Prophet's Complaint

2 I will stand at my watchpost,
   and station myself on the rampart;
I will keep watch to see what he will say to me,
   and what he*b* will answer concerning my
      complaint.
2 Then the LORD answered me and said:
Write the vision;
   make it plain on tablets,
   so that a runner may read it.
3 For there is still a vision for the appointed time;
   it speaks of the end, and does not lie.
If it seems to tarry, wait for it;
   it will surely come, it will not delay.
4 Look at the proud!
   Their spirit is not right in them,
   but the righteous live by their faith.*c*
5 Moreover, wealth*d* is treacherous;
   the arrogant do not endure.
They open their throats wide as Sheol;
   like Death they never have enough.
They gather all nations for themselves,
   and collect all peoples as their own.

The Woes of the Wicked

6 Shall not everyone taunt such people and, with mocking riddles, say about them,
   "Alas for you who heap up what is not your own!"
   How long will you load yourselves with goods
      taken in pledge?
7 Will not your own creditors suddenly rise,
   and those who make you tremble wake up?
   Then you will be booty for them.
8 Because you have plundered many nations,
   all that survive of the peoples shall plunder you—
because of human bloodshed, and violence to the
      earth,
   to cities and all who live in them.

9 "Alas for you who get evil gain for your houses,
   setting your nest on high
   to be safe from the reach of harm!"
10 You have devised shame for your house
   by cutting off many peoples;
   you have forfeited your life.
11 The very stones will cry out from the wall,
   and the plaster*e* will respond from the woodwork.

Waiting for God

HABAKKUK 2.1–3

The writer Anthony Padovano once observed that "we wait for everything that is really worth having . . . We even wait for God." Waiting in the Biblical tradition is not passive or forgetful, but active, eager, yearning and engaged. Habakkuk determines to wait on God for resolution of his crisis; God, in turn, bids him, "If it seems to tarry, wait." What are you waiting for most fervently for yourself? For your loved ones? Your church? Your community? The world? Name these things before God in prayer, claiming God's promises. Wait for their fulfillment with the same attentiveness as the Bible's best "waiters."

See Meeting God in Prayer

a Heb *He*   b Syr: Heb *I*   c Or *faithfulness*   d Other Heb Mss read *wine*
e Or *beam*

The Earth Filled

HABAKKUK 2.14–17

Christians have not always associated salvation with concern for God's creation, but we are becoming more aware of how intertwined the two are. The Word of God, through the prophet Habakkuk, proclaims that the whole creation is drawn into human abuses (v.8) but that it is also subject to God's redemption (v.14). Meditate on a scene in nature you can see from where you are sitting. Or imagine yourself in a beautiful natural setting. Offer confession on behalf of all humankind for the many ways we have misused creation. Consider how God cares for the place where you are or that you are imagining, then envision in your mind's eye how the knowledge of God's glory will fill all the earth.

See Meeting God in the Created Order

12 "Alas for you who build a town by bloodshed,
  and found a city on iniquity!"
13 Is it not from the LORD of hosts
  that peoples labor only to feed the flames,
  and nations weary themselves for nothing?
14 But the earth will be filled
  with the knowledge of the glory of the LORD,
  as the waters cover the sea.

15 "Alas for you who make your neighbors drink,
  pouring out your wrath*a* until they are drunk,
  in order to gaze on their nakedness!"
16 You will be sated with contempt instead of glory.
  Drink, you yourself, and stagger!*b*
The cup in the LORD's right hand
  will come around to you,
  and shame will come upon your glory!
17 For the violence done to Lebanon will overwhelm
    you;
  the destruction of the animals will terrify you—*c*
because of human bloodshed and violence to the
    earth,
  to cities and all who live in them.

18 What use is an idol
  once its maker has shaped it—
  a cast image, a teacher of lies?
For its maker trusts in what has been made,
  though the product is only an idol that cannot
    speak!
19 Alas for you who say to the wood, "Wake up!"
  to silent stone, "Rouse yourself!"
  Can it teach?
See, it is gold and silver plated,
  and there is no breath in it at all.

20 But the LORD is in his holy temple;
  let all the earth keep silence before him!

3 A prayer of the prophet Habakkuk according to Shigionoth.

The Prophet's Prayer

2 O LORD, I have heard of your renown,
  and I stand in awe, O LORD, of your work.
In our own time revive it;
  in our own time make it known;
  in wrath may you remember mercy.
3 God came from Teman,
  the Holy One from Mount Paran.   *Selah*
His glory covered the heavens,
  and the earth was full of his praise.
4 The brightness was like the sun;
  rays came forth from his hand,
  where his power lay hidden.
5 Before him went pestilence,
  and plague followed close behind.
6 He stopped and shook the earth;

---

a Or *poison*   *b* Q Ms Gk: MT *be uncircumcised*   *c* Gk Syr: Meaning of Heb uncertain

he looked and made the nations tremble.
The eternal mountains were shattered;
    along his ancient pathways
    the everlasting hills sank low.
7 I saw the tents of Cushan under affliction;
    the tent-curtains of the land of Midian trembled.
8 Was your wrath against the rivers,[a] O LORD?
    Or your anger against the rivers,[a]
    or your rage against the sea,[b]
when you drove your horses,
    your chariots to victory?
9 You brandished your naked bow,
    sated[c] were the arrows at your command.[d]   Selah
    You split the earth with rivers.
10 The mountains saw you, and writhed;
    a torrent of water swept by;
the deep gave forth its voice.
    The sun[e] raised high its hands;
11 the moon[f] stood still in its exalted place,
    at the light of your arrows speeding by,
    at the gleam of your flashing spear.
12 In fury you trod the earth,
    in anger you trampled nations.
13 You came forth to save your people,
    to save your anointed.
You crushed the head of the wicked house,
    laying it bare from foundation to roof.[d]   Selah
14 You pierced with their[g] own arrows the head[h] of his
    warriors,[i]
    who came like a whirlwind to scatter us,[j]
    gloating as if ready to devour the poor who were
      in hiding.
15 You trampled the sea with your horses,
    churning the mighty waters.

16 I hear, and I tremble within;
    my lips quiver at the sound.
Rottenness enters into my bones,
    and my steps tremble[k] beneath me.
I wait quietly for the day of calamity
    to come upon the people who attack us.

Trust and Joy in the Midst of Trouble

17 Though the fig tree does not blossom,
    and no fruit is on the vines;
though the produce of the olive fails,
    and the fields yield no food;
though the flock is cut off from the fold,
    and there is no herd in the stalls,
18 yet I will rejoice in the LORD;
    I will exult in the God of my salvation.
19 GOD, the Lord, is my strength;
    he makes my feet like the feet of a deer,
    and makes me tread upon the heights.[l]

To the leader: with stringed[m] instruments.

The Place for *Yet*

HABAKKUK 3.17–19

The conclusion of Habakkuk could be a mourner's litany—no figs, no fruit, no food, no flocks—of all the prophet and his people have lost or fear to lose. Instead Habakkuk's list of potential or real catastrophes is turned on its head with one simple word: *yet*. That one word becomes the turning point and Habakkuk's anxiety becomes triumph; what could have been a dirge has become a dance.

    Construct your own "mourner's litany," listing things you've lost or things you fear you might lose. Now add that faith word, *yet*, and borrow language from Habakkuk to express your assurance of God's provision in all circumstances.

See Meeting God in Everyday Life

---

a Or *against River*   b Or *against Sea*   c Cn: Heb *oaths*   d Meaning of
Heb uncertain   e Heb *It*   f Heb *sun, moon*   g Heb *his*   h Or *leader*
i Vg Compare Gk Syr: Meaning of Heb uncertain   j Heb *me*
k Cn Compare Gk: Meaning of Heb uncertain   l Heb *my heights*
m Heb *my stringed*

ZEPHANIAH

Quieted by God's Love

KEY VERSE:

The LORD, your God, is in your midst, a warrior who gives victory; he will rejoice over you with gladness, he will renew you in his love; he will exult over you with loud singing.—Zephaniah 3.17

"One time, I was under very great suffering in my spirit and under the very sense of death; but when I came out of it, standing in the will of God, a heavenly breathing arose in my soul to the Lord. Then did I see the heavens opened and the glory of God shined over all."

—GEORGE FOX,
Journal

A day of judgment is coming quickly, says the prophet Zephaniah, when God is going to make a clean sweep of Judah and the nations around her. In these three chapters we learn that the priests, prophets, leaders and people are involved in idol worship (1.4–5), are complacent in doing justice while accumulating quantities of gold and silver (1.12,18), and are arrogantly rebelling against God's instructions (3.11). Yet hope and promise are woven through the predictions of darkness and gloom.

The humble and righteous will find shelter on the day of trouble and ruin (2.3), and the lowly and meek will remain as a faithful remnant (3.12–13). The greatest word of hope comes at the end of Zephaniah in a chorus of praise in which God promises to keep the nation from the impending disaster, to gather all the scattered people and bring them home, and to reestablish the Judeans as a people of honor and blessing (3.14–20).

Though we may have different idols and face different threats, the call of Zephaniah is just as important for us today—it is a call to live a life of humble obedience before God. We are to be aware of what God has done in the past and let that remembrance keep us humbly walking on the right path. There must always be room in our lives for praise, because God delights in us, quiets us with his love and rejoices over us with singing.

1 The word of the Lord that came to Zephaniah son of Cushi son of Gedaliah son of Amariah son of Hezekiah, in the days of King Josiah son of Amon of Judah.

The Coming Judgment on Judah

2 I will utterly sweep away everything
    from the face of the earth, says the Lord.
3 I will sweep away humans and animals;
    I will sweep away the birds of the air
    and the fish of the sea.
I will make the wicked stumble.*a*
    I will cut off humanity
    from the face of the earth, says the Lord.
4 I will stretch out my hand against Judah,
    and against all the inhabitants of Jerusalem;
and I will cut off from this place every remnant of
    Baal
    and the name of the idolatrous priests;*b*
5 those who bow down on the roofs
    to the host of the heavens;
those who bow down and swear to the Lord,
    but also swear by Milcom;*c*
6 those who have turned back from following the
    Lord,
    who have not sought the Lord or inquired of him.

7 Be silent before the Lord God!
    For the day of the Lord is at hand;
the Lord has prepared a sacrifice,
    he has consecrated his guests.
8 And on the day of the Lord's sacrifice
I will punish the officials and the king's sons
    and all who dress themselves in foreign attire.
9 On that day I will punish
    all who leap over the threshold,
who fill their master's house
    with violence and fraud.

10 On that day, says the Lord,
    a cry will be heard from the Fish Gate,
a wail from the Second Quarter,
    a loud crash from the hills.
11 The inhabitants of the Mortar wail,
    for all the traders have perished;
    all who weigh out silver are cut off.
12 At that time I will search Jerusalem with lamps,
    and I will punish the people
who rest complacently*d* on their dregs,
    those who say in their hearts,
"The Lord will not do good,
    nor will he do harm."
13 Their wealth shall be plundered,
    and their houses laid waste.
Though they build houses,
    they shall not inhabit them;
though they plant vineyards,
    they shall not drink wine from them.

A Clean Sweep

ZEPHANIAH 1.2–4

Zephaniah cuts straight to the heart of the matter. Israel is in trouble; destruction is coming because of her idolatry. It will touch the royal court, all people, and even animals, fish and birds. God will "sweep away everything."

Find a broom and look for a place to begin sweeping. Pay attention to the sound the broom makes, the way the dirt falls into a line, how much effort and repetition it takes to get the area really clean. Give your full attention to sweeping.

You may wish to write in a journal about the experience and start reflecting on what needs to be cleaned up in your life. If God took a broom to your spiritual life, what would be swept away? Invite God to come in and begin this work.

See Meeting God in Everyday Life

---

a Cn: Heb *sea, and those who cause the wicked to stumble*   *b* Compare Gk: Heb *the idolatrous priests with the priests*   *c* Gk Mss Syr Vg: Heb *Malcam* (or, *their king*)   *d* Heb *who thicken*

To Be Humble and Just

ZEPHANIAH 2.1–3

The great day of the Lord is coming soon, and the prophet says it will be a day of judgment and ruin. List all the abuses that Zephaniah condemns (see, for example, 1.9,11,12). Think of some injustices in our world today and add them to your list. Pray for the day when God will come to clean up all the trouble, sorrow and pain.

While these verses contain judgment, they also convey the hope that those who humble themselves and pursue righteousness will be sheltered from God's wrath. In a time of prayer, tilt your head back so your eyes focus on the heavens and then extend your arms as you would to welcome a long lost friend. In prayer give thanks that Jesus Christ has become our righteousness before God.

The Great Day of the Lord

14 The great day of the Lord is near,
 near and hastening fast;
 the sound of the day of the Lord is bitter,
 the warrior cries aloud there.
15 That day will be a day of wrath,
 a day of distress and anguish,
 a day of ruin and devastation,
 a day of darkness and gloom,
 a day of clouds and thick darkness,
16 a day of trumpet blast and battle cry
 against the fortified cities
 and against the lofty battlements.

17 I will bring such distress upon people
 that they shall walk like the blind;
 because they have sinned against the Lord,
 their blood shall be poured out like dust,
 and their flesh like dung.
18 Neither their silver nor their gold
 will be able to save them
 on the day of the Lord's wrath;
 in the fire of his passion
 the whole earth shall be consumed;
 for a full, a terrible end
 he will make of all the inhabitants of the earth.

Judgment on Israel's Enemies

2 Gather together, gather,
 O shameless nation,
2 before you are driven away
 like the drifting chaff,[a]
 before there comes upon you
 the fierce anger of the Lord,
 before there comes upon you
 the day of the Lord's wrath.
3 Seek the Lord, all you humble of the land,
 who do his commands;
 seek righteousness, seek humility;
 perhaps you may be hidden
 on the day of the Lord's wrath.

4 For Gaza shall be deserted,
 and Ashkelon shall become a desolation;
 Ashdod's people shall be driven out at noon,
 and Ekron shall be uprooted.

5 Ah, inhabitants of the seacoast,
 you nation of the Cherethites!
 The word of the Lord is against you,
 O Canaan, land of the Philistines;
 and I will destroy you until no inhabitant is left.
6 And you, O seacoast, shall be pastures,
 meadows for shepherds
 and folds for flocks.
7 The seacoast shall become the possession
 of the remnant of the house of Judah,
 on which they shall pasture,

a Cn Compare Gk Syr: Heb *before a decree is born; like chaff a day has passed away*

and in the houses of Ashkelon
    they shall lie down at evening.
For the LORD their God will be mindful of them
    and restore their fortunes.

8 I have heard the taunts of Moab
    and the revilings of the Ammonites,
how they have taunted my people
    and made boasts against their territory.
9 Therefore, as I live, says the LORD of hosts,
    the God of Israel,
Moab shall become like Sodom
    and the Ammonites like Gomorrah,
a land possessed by nettles and salt pits,
    and a waste forever.
The remnant of my people shall plunder them,
    and the survivors of my nation shall possess
        them.
10 This shall be their lot in return for their pride,
    because they scoffed and boasted
against the people of the LORD of hosts.
11 The LORD will be terrible against them;
    he will shrivel all the gods of the earth,
and to him shall bow down,
    each in its place,
    all the coasts and islands of the nations.

12 You also, O Ethiopians,*a*
    shall be killed by my sword.

13 And he will stretch out his hand against the north,
    and destroy Assyria;
and he will make Nineveh a desolation,
    a dry waste like the desert.
14 Herds shall lie down in it,
    every wild animal;*b*
the desert owl*c* and the screech owl*c*
    shall lodge on its capitals;
the owl*d* shall hoot at the window,
    the raven*e* croak on the threshold;
    for its cedar work will be laid bare.
15 Is this the exultant city
    that lived secure,
that said to itself,
    "I am, and there is no one else"?
What a desolation it has become,
    a lair for wild animals!
Everyone who passes by it
    hisses and shakes the fist.

The Wickedness of Jerusalem

3 Ah, soiled, defiled,
    oppressing city!
2 It has listened to no voice;
    it has accepted no correction.
It has not trusted in the LORD;
    it has not drawn near to its God.

Pride Goes Before a Fall

ZEPHANIAH 2.10,15

"Recollection is the only cure for your haughtiness, the sharpness of your contemptuous criticism, the sallies of your imagination, your impatience with inferiors, your love of pleasure and all your other faults. It is an excellent remedy, but it needs frequent repetition. You are like a good watch, which needs constant winding . . . Expect nothing of yourself, but all things of God. Knowledge of our own hopeless, incorrigible weakness, with unreserved confidence in God's power, are the true foundations of all spiritual life."

—FRANÇOIS FÉNELON,
in *Living Water, An Anthology
of Letters of Direction*

---

a Or *Nubians*; Heb *Cushites*   *b* Tg Compare Gk: Heb *nation*   *c* Meaning of Heb uncertain   *d* Cn: Heb *a voice*   *e* Gk Vg: Heb *desolation*

Look, See, Remember

ZEPHANIAH 3.7

The prophet's words convey God's anguish: "Surely the city will fear me, it will accept correction;" *Surely* the people of Jerusalem remember how God brought them from Egypt. *Surely* they can see what has happened to other nations. *Surely* they know that God is a God of justice. But the people continue in their corrupt ways.

To help you remember what God has done, make a list of blessings and corrections that you have received from God. Give thanks for the ways that God has touched your life and kept you on the right path. Give thanks for corrections and lessons learned that you can now count as blessings.

See *Meeting God in Everyday Life*

3 The officials within it
    are roaring lions;
its judges are evening wolves
    that leave nothing until the morning.
4 Its prophets are reckless,
    faithless persons;
its priests have profaned what is sacred,
    they have done violence to the law.
5 The LORD within it is righteous;
    he does no wrong.
Every morning he renders his judgment,
    each dawn without fail;
    but the unjust knows no shame.

6 I have cut off nations;
    their battlements are in ruins;
I have laid waste their streets
    so that no one walks in them;
their cities have been made desolate,
    without people, without inhabitants.
7 I said, "Surely the city*a* will fear me,
    it will accept correction;
it will not lose sight*b*
    of all that I have brought upon it."
But they were the more eager
    to make all their deeds corrupt.

Punishment and Conversion of the Nations

8 Therefore wait for me, says the LORD,
    for the day when I arise as a witness.
For my decision is to gather nations,
    to assemble kingdoms,
to pour out upon them my indignation,
    all the heat of my anger;
for in the fire of my passion
    all the earth shall be consumed.

9 At that time I will change the speech of the peoples
    to a pure speech,
that all of them may call on the name of the LORD
    and serve him with one accord.
10 From beyond the rivers of Ethiopia*c*
    my suppliants, my scattered ones,
    shall bring my offering.

11 On that day you shall not be put to shame
    because of all the deeds by which you have
        rebelled against me;
for then I will remove from your midst
    your proudly exultant ones,
and you shall no longer be haughty
    in my holy mountain.
12 For I will leave in the midst of you
    a people humble and lowly.
They shall seek refuge in the name of the LORD—
13   the remnant of Israel;
they shall do no wrong
    and utter no lies,

a Heb *it*   *b* Gk Syr: Heb *its dwelling will not be cut off*   *c* Or *Nubia;* Heb *Cush*

The actions of our savior are so rich in meaning that every soul that ponders them finds in them its own share of spiritual food to nourish it and bring it to salvation.

CATHERINE OF SIENA (1347-1380)

The Life of Catherine of Siena

what knowledge can result from adapting the meaning of the Scriptures to suit one's own likes? The true sage discovers, through the Spirit's wisdom, the hidden mysteries to which the Scriptures bear witness.

PETER OF DAMASKOS (TWELFTH CENTURY?)
The Philokalia (Volume Three)

We should accept with simplicity whatever understanding the Lord gives us; and what he doesn't we shouldn't tire ourselves over. For one word of God's will contain within itself a thousand mysteries.

TERESA OF AVILA (1515-1582)

Meditation on the Song of Songs

If you want
true knowledge
of the Scriptures,
try to secure steadfast
humility of heart,
to carry you by the
perfection of love
not to knowledge that
puffs up, but that
enlightens.

JOHN CASSIAN (c. 365–c. 435)
Conferences, Book XIV

nor shall a deceitful tongue
  be found in their mouths.
Then they will pasture and lie down,
  and no one shall make them afraid.

A Song of Joy

14 Sing aloud, O daughter Zion;
    shout, O Israel!
  Rejoice and exult with all your heart,
    O daughter Jerusalem!
15 The LORD has taken away the judgments against
      you,
    he has turned away your enemies.
  The king of Israel, the LORD, is in your midst;
    you shall fear disaster no more.
16 On that day it shall be said to Jerusalem:
  Do not fear, O Zion;
    do not let your hands grow weak.
17 The LORD, your God, is in your midst,
    a warrior who gives victory;
  he will rejoice over you with gladness,
    he will renew you*a* in his love;
  he will exult over you with loud singing
18   as on a day of festival.*b*
  I will remove disaster from you,*c*
    so that you will not bear reproach for it.
19 I will deal with all your oppressors
    at that time.
  And I will save the lame
    and gather the outcast,
  and I will change their shame into praise
    and renown in all the earth.
20 At that time I will bring you home,
    at the time when I gather you;
  for I will make you renowned and praised
    among all the peoples of the earth,
  when I restore your fortunes
    before your eyes, says the LORD.

From Disaster to Celebration

ZEPHANIAH 3.14–20

In the middle of troubles and pain, there is a promise of joy. The threat of destruction is over and hope springs up once again. Using the image of a mother who comforts a child she has disciplined, God reminds his people of his great love. Reread the passage slowly, noting the words or phrases of promise that particularly speak to you. Use these words or phrases to write a prayer based on this passage. Ask God to fulfill the promises you are waiting on to be fulfilled. Praise God for making such wonderful promises.

See Meeting God in Scripture

---

a Gk Syr: Heb *he will be silent*   *b* Gk Syr: Meaning of Heb uncertain
c Cn: Heb *I will remove from you; they were*

HAGGAI

Examine Your Ways

KEY VERSES:

Then the word of the LORD came by the prophet Haggai, saying: Is it a time for you yourselves to live in your paneled houses, while this house lies in ruins?—Haggai 1.3–4

"During the darkest periods of history, quite often a small number of men and women, scattered throughout the world, have been able to reverse the course of historical evolutions. This was only possible because they hoped beyond all hope. What had been bound for disintegration then entered into the current of a new dynamism."
—BROTHER ROGER OF TAIZÉ

Haggai encourages his listeners to anticipate that the rebuilding of the temple will set in motion a new chain of events that will reveal God's powerful presence. Haggai, a prophet in the court of King Darius (about 520 B.C.), wants to inspire the Israelites and capture their imaginations with the vision of a rebuilt Jerusalem, where God will once again be honored and praised.

Beaten down and focused on survival under alien rule, God's people are in despair. They have returned from exile physically but haven't yet returned "home" to God—they haven't begun to rebuild God's house. They can see failed crops and a government in chaos; they cannot see hope for their future.

As you read these two short chapters containing Haggai's oracles, reflect on these questions: Have you ever felt so oppressed by events in your life that you lost your focus on God? Do you in some way long for the "good old days" when things were better for you? Are you dissatisfied with the present? Have you given up on God and decided that you have to take care of things yourself? Haggai will help you put things in perspective, for his message is that hope in God is always the best option.

The Command to Rebuild the Temple

1 In the second year of King Darius, in the sixth month, on the first day of the month, the word of the Lord came by the prophet Haggai to Zerubbabel son of Shealtiel, governor of Judah, and to Joshua son of Jehozadak, the high priest: ²Thus says the Lord of hosts: These people say the time has not yet come to rebuild the Lord's house. ³Then the word of the Lord came by the prophet Haggai, saying: ⁴Is it a time for you yourselves to live in your paneled houses, while this house lies in ruins? ⁵Now therefore thus says the Lord of hosts: Consider how you have fared. ⁶You have sown much, and harvested little; you eat, but you never have enough; you drink, but you never have your fill; you clothe yourselves, but no one is warm; and you that earn wages earn wages to put them into a bag with holes.

7 Thus says the Lord of hosts: Consider how you have fared. ⁸Go up to the hills and bring wood and build the house, so that I may take pleasure in it and be honored, says the Lord. ⁹You have looked for much, and, lo, it came to little; and when you brought it home, I blew it away. Why? says the Lord of hosts. Because my house lies in ruins, while all of you hurry off to your own houses. ¹⁰Therefore the heavens above you have withheld the dew, and the earth has withheld its produce. ¹¹And I have called for a drought on the land and the hills, on the grain, the new wine, the oil, on what the soil produces, on human beings and animals, and on all their labors.

12 Then Zerubbabel son of Shealtiel, and Joshua son of Jehozadak, the high priest, with all the remnant of the people, obeyed the voice of the Lord their God, and the words of the prophet Haggai, as the Lord their God had sent him; and the people feared the Lord. ¹³Then Haggai, the messenger of the Lord, spoke to the people with the Lord's message, saying, I am with you, says the Lord. ¹⁴And the Lord stirred up the spirit of Zerubbabel son of Shealtiel, governor of Judah, and the spirit of Joshua son of Jehozadak, the high priest, and the spirit of all the remnant of the people; and they came and worked on the house of the Lord of hosts, their God, ¹⁵on the twenty-fourth day of the month, in the sixth month.

The Future Glory of the Temple

2 In the second year of King Darius, ¹in the seventh month, on the twenty-first day of the month, the word of the Lord came by the prophet Haggai, saying: ²Speak now to Zerubbabel son of Shealtiel, governor of Judah, and to Joshua son of Jehozadak, the high priest, and to the remnant of the people, and say, ³Who is left among you that saw this house in its former glory? How does it look to you now? Is it not in your sight as nothing? ⁴Yet now take courage, O Zerubbabel, says the Lord; take courage, O Joshua, son of Jehozadak, the high priest; take courage, all you people of the land, says the Lord; work, for I am with you, says the Lord of hosts, ⁵according to the promise that I made you when you came out of Egypt. My spirit abides among you; do not fear. ⁶For thus says the Lord of hosts: Once again, in a little while, I will shake the heavens and the earth and the sea and the dry land; ⁷and I will shake all the nations, so that the treasure of all nations shall come, and I will fill this house with splendor, says the Lord of

A Personal Letter

HAGGAI 2.4–5

Scripture is our personal love letter from God, if only we can hear the voice of the One who is calling out our name. We may not be called "Zerubbabel" or "Joshua," but these verses nevertheless speak to us as they spoke to those in King Darius's court long ago.

In what way do you need courage in your life today? How do you need the strength of God's Spirit? Substitute your own name so that you hear, "Yet now take courage, _____, . . . for I am with you . . . My spirit abides among you; do not fear." Accept this personal promise; feel courage grow within you as you realize that the God who spoke through Haggai speaks to you today.

See Meeting God in Scripture

Seed Ready to Grow

HAGGAI 2.18–19

Just as the people of God have been hurt and scarred by their long and painful exile from their native land, there are times when we too may feel that the pain of past hurts keeps us from enjoying a fruitful present. "Not so!" says God, who uses all of our experiences, positive and negative, for good. "Is there any seed left in the barn?" What remains within you that, with nurture, might flourish and grow into something beautiful? No matter what your past may have been, God offers you the chance to plant new seeds, nourish a new life, look toward the future with hope. What seeds are in you, ready to sprout? Hear gladly God's promise to you: "From this day on I will bless you."

See Meeting God in Everyday Life

hosts. **8**The silver is mine, and the gold is mine, says the LORD of hosts. **9**The latter splendor of this house shall be greater than the former, says the LORD of hosts; and in this place I will give prosperity, says the LORD of hosts.

A Rebuke and a Promise

10 On the twenty-fourth day of the ninth month, in the second year of Darius, the word of the LORD came by the prophet Haggai, saying: **11**Thus says the LORD of hosts: Ask the priests for a ruling: **12**If one carries consecrated meat in the fold of one's garment, and with the fold touches bread, or stew, or wine, or oil, or any kind of food, does it become holy? The priests answered, "No." **13**Then Haggai said, "If one who is unclean by contact with a dead body touches any of these, does it become unclean?" The priests answered, "Yes, it becomes unclean." **14**Haggai then said, So is it with this people, and with this nation before me, says the LORD; and so with every work of their hands; and what they offer there is unclean. **15**But now, consider what will come to pass from this day on. Before a stone was placed upon a stone in the LORD's temple, **16**how did you fare?*a* When one came to a heap of twenty measures, there were but ten; when one came to the wine vat to draw fifty measures, there were but twenty. **17**I struck you and all the products of your toil with blight and mildew and hail; yet you did not return to me, says the LORD. **18**Consider from this day on, from the twenty-fourth day of the ninth month. Since the day that the foundation of the LORD's temple was laid, consider: **19**Is there any seed left in the barn? Do the vine, the fig tree, the pomegranate, and the olive tree still yield nothing? From this day on I will bless you.

God's Promise to Zerubbabel

20 The word of the LORD came a second time to Haggai on the twenty-fourth day of the month: **21**Speak to Zerubbabel, governor of Judah, saying, I am about to shake the heavens and the earth, **22**and to overthrow the throne of kingdoms; I am about to destroy the strength of the kingdoms of the nations, and overthrow the chariots and their riders; and the horses and their riders shall fall, every one by the sword of a comrade. **23**On that day, says the LORD of hosts, I will take you, O Zerubbabel my servant, son of Shealtiel, says the LORD, and make you like a signet ring; for I have chosen you, says the LORD of hosts.

a Gk: Heb *since they were*

ZECHARIAH

Not by Might

KEY VERSES:

*Thus says the LORD of hosts: I will save my people from the east country and from the west country;
and I will bring them to live in Jerusalem. They shall be my people and I will be their God,
in faithfulness and in righteousness.—Zechariah 8.7–8*

Zechariah seems to say, "Let's start over, refocus ourselves on God and get busy." The task at hand is the rebuilding of the temple that has lain in ruins since its destruction by the Babylonians. The focus for the future is on rebuilding the spiritual life of a people who have endured humiliation and exile. To complicate the problem, the people are apathetic about their task and indifferent to the call to restore their worship to its former glory. But the prophet reminds the returned exiles that they have a golden opportunity to renew their relationship with God—God is waiting to wrap loving arms around this people who had previously snubbed their Creator.

So too God stands ready to quiet each of us with his love if we earnestly desire to receive that love. In God's strength we can rebuild that which has been broken down. With God's vision we can look toward a future of new possibilities. What is God saying to you about your future? Are you open to this motivating, energizing, divine love—love that offers new life in this world and in eternity?

> "In this temple of God, in this divine dwelling place, God alone rejoices with the soul in the deepest silence. There is no reason for the intellect to stir or seek anything, for the Lord who created it wishes to give it repose here."
>
> —TERESA OF AVILA,
> *The Interior Castle*

Rebuilding My House

ZECHARIAH 1.2–6,16

God, speaking through Zechariah, extends an invitation to the people of Judah to partner with him in rebuilding the temple, "I have returned to Jerusalem with compassion; my house shall be built in it."

God wants to help you rebuild as well. If you think of your life as your spiritual house, what might need some work? Is the substructure—your spiritual foundation—solid? Are all the rooms—the facets of your life—used for the right purposes? Are you conscientious about upkeep—daily spiritual practices? What about renovation—growing in the knowledge of Jesus Christ? When the measuring line of the Master Builder is laid out, how do you measure up? Let Jesus come to you with mercy and build alongside you.

See Meeting God in Everyday Life

Israel Urged to Repent

1 In the eighth month, in the second year of Darius, the word of the LORD came to the prophet Zechariah son of Berechiah son of Iddo, saying: ²The LORD was very angry with your ancestors. ³Therefore say to them, Thus says the LORD of hosts: Return to me, says the LORD of hosts, and I will return to you, says the LORD of hosts. ⁴Do not be like your ancestors, to whom the former prophets proclaimed, "Thus says the LORD of hosts, Return from your evil ways and from your evil deeds." But they did not hear or heed me, says the LORD. ⁵Your ancestors, where are they? And the prophets, do they live forever? ⁶But my words and my statutes, which I commanded my servants the prophets, did they not overtake your ancestors? So they repented and said, "The LORD of hosts has dealt with us according to our ways and deeds, just as he planned to do."

First Vision: The Horsemen

7 On the twenty-fourth day of the eleventh month, the month of Shebat, in the second year of Darius, the word of the LORD came to the prophet Zechariah son of Berechiah son of Iddo; and Zechariah[a] said, ⁸In the night I saw a man riding on a red horse! He was standing among the myrtle trees in the glen; and behind him were red, sorrel, and white horses. ⁹Then I said, "What are these, my lord?" The angel who talked with me said to me, "I will show you what they are." ¹⁰So the man who was standing among the myrtle trees answered, "They are those whom the LORD has sent to patrol the earth." ¹¹Then they spoke to the angel of the LORD who was standing among the myrtle trees, "We have patrolled the earth, and lo, the whole earth remains at peace." ¹²Then the angel of the LORD said, "O LORD of hosts, how long will you withhold mercy from Jerusalem and the cities of Judah, with which you have been angry these seventy years?" ¹³Then the LORD replied with gracious and comforting words to the angel who talked with me. ¹⁴So the angel who talked with me said to me, Proclaim this message: Thus says the LORD of hosts; I am very jealous for Jerusalem and for Zion. ¹⁵And I am extremely angry with the nations that are at ease; for while I was only a little angry, they made the disaster worse. ¹⁶Therefore, thus says the LORD, I have returned to Jerusalem with compassion; my house shall be built in it, says the LORD of hosts, and the measuring line shall be stretched out over Jerusalem. ¹⁷Proclaim further: Thus says the LORD of hosts: My cities shall again overflow with prosperity; the LORD will again comfort Zion and again choose Jerusalem.

Second Vision: The Horns and the Smiths

18[b] And I looked up and saw four horns. ¹⁹I asked the angel who talked with me, "What are these?" And he answered me, "These are the horns that have scattered Judah, Israel, and Jerusalem." ²⁰Then the LORD showed me four blacksmiths. ²¹And I asked, "What are they coming to do?" He answered, "These are the horns that scattered Judah, so that no head could be raised; but these have come to terrify them, to strike down the horns of the nations that lifted up their horns against the land of Judah to scatter its people."[c]

a Heb *and he*   *b* Ch 2.1 in Heb   *c* Heb *it*

Third Vision: The Man with a Measuring Line

2 [a] I looked up and saw a man with a measuring line in his hand. ²Then I asked, "Where are you going?" He answered me, "To measure Jerusalem, to see what is its width and what is its length." ³Then the angel who talked with me came forward, and another angel came forward to meet him, ⁴and said to him, "Run, say to that young man: Jerusalem shall be inhabited like villages without walls, because of the multitude of people and animals in it. ⁵For I will be a wall of fire all around it, says the LORD, and I will be the glory within it."

Interlude: An Appeal to the Exiles

6 Up, up! Flee from the land of the north, says the LORD; for I have spread you abroad like the four winds of heaven, says the LORD. ⁷Up! Escape to Zion, you that live with daughter Babylon. ⁸For thus said the LORD of hosts (after his glory[b] sent me) regarding the nations that plundered you: Truly, one who touches you touches the apple of my eye.[c] ⁹See now, I am going to raise[d] my hand against them, and they shall become plunder for their own slaves. Then you will know that the LORD of hosts has sent me. ¹⁰Sing and rejoice, O daughter Zion! For lo, I will come and dwell in your midst, says the LORD. ¹¹Many nations shall join themselves to the LORD on that day, and shall be my people; and I will dwell in your midst. And you shall know that the LORD of hosts has sent me to you. ¹²The LORD will inherit Judah as his portion in the holy land, and will again choose Jerusalem.

13 Be silent, all people, before the LORD; for he has roused himself from his holy dwelling.

Fourth Vision: Joshua and Satan

3 Then he showed me the high priest Joshua standing before the angel of the LORD, and Satan[e] standing at his right hand to accuse him. ²And the LORD said to Satan,[e] "The LORD rebuke you, O Satan![e] The LORD who has chosen Jerusalem rebuke you! Is not this man a brand plucked from the fire?" ³Now Joshua was dressed with filthy clothes as he stood before the angel. ⁴The angel said to those who were standing before him, "Take off his filthy clothes." And to him he said, "See, I have taken your guilt away from you, and I will clothe you with festal apparel." ⁵And I said, "Let them put a clean turban on his head." So they put a clean turban on his head and clothed him with the apparel; and the angel of the LORD was standing by.

6 Then the angel of the LORD assured Joshua, saying ⁷"Thus says the LORD of hosts: If you will walk in my ways and keep my requirements, then you shall rule my house and have charge of my courts, and I will give you the right of access among those who are standing here. ⁸Now listen, Joshua, high priest, you and your colleagues who sit before you! For they are an omen of things to come: I am going to bring my servant the Branch. ⁹For on the stone that I have set before Joshua, on a single stone with seven facets, I will engrave its inscription, says the LORD of hosts, and I will remove the guilt of this land in a single day. ¹⁰On that day,

---

a Ch 2.5 in Heb   b Cn: Heb *after glory he*   c Heb *his eye*   d Or *wave*
e Or *the Accuser*; Heb *the Adversary*

Walk in My Ways

ZECHARIAH 3.3–7

Read this passage—replacing the name of Joshua with your own name—so that the story becomes your own story. Close your eyes and reenact the encounter between yourself and the angel. Pay close attention to detail. What does the angel look like? How would you describe your dirty clothes? How do you feel when the angel clothes you with a new garment and puts a clean turban on your head? What happens within you when you hear God's charge to you (v.7)? Enjoy the sense of renewal that comes when your sins are washed away and you are "clean," ready to begin again.

See Meeting God in Scripture

1253

By My Spirit

ZECHARIAH 4.6

The definitions of "might" and "power" probably depend on one's position, culture, personality or era, yet the words of God through the angel's mouth apply to any time or place: "Not by might nor by power, but by my spirit, says the LORD of hosts."

Along one side of a sheet of paper, write down some of the images that come to mind when you think of might and power. Do you see a soldier in full battle gear or a wealthy person who has widespread economic influence? Perhaps you see a forceful leader with a persuasive personality. On the other side of the paper, write down images that come to mind when you think of "by my spirit." Look for other passages of scripture that will help you develop this concept.

says the LORD of hosts, you shall invite each other to come under your vine and fig tree."

Fifth Vision: The Lampstand and Olive Trees

4 The angel who talked with me came again, and wakened me, as one is wakened from sleep. ²He said to me, "What do you see?" And I said, "I see a lampstand all of gold, with a bowl on the top of it; there are seven lamps on it, with seven lips on each of the lamps that are on the top of it. ³And by it there are two olive trees, one on the right of the bowl and the other on its left." ⁴I said to the angel who talked with me, "What are these, my lord?" ⁵Then the angel who talked with me answered me, "Do you not know what these are?" I said, "No, my lord." ⁶He said to me, "This is the word of the LORD to Zerubbabel: Not by might, nor by power, but by my spirit, says the LORD of hosts. ⁷What are you, O great mountain? Before Zerubbabel you shall become a plain; and he shall bring out the top stone amid shouts of 'Grace, grace to it!' "

8 Moreover the word of the LORD came to me, saying, ⁹"The hands of Zerubbabel have laid the foundation of this house; his hands shall also complete it. Then you will know that the LORD of hosts has sent me to you. ¹⁰For whoever has despised the day of small things shall rejoice, and shall see the plummet in the hand of Zerubbabel.

"These seven are the eyes of the LORD, which range through the whole earth." ¹¹Then I said to him, "What are these two olive trees on the right and the left of the lampstand?" ¹²And a second time I said to him, "What are these two branches of the olive trees, which pour out the oilᵃ through the two golden pipes?" ¹³He said to me, "Do you not know what these are?" I said, "No, my lord." ¹⁴Then he said, "These are the two anointed ones who stand by the Lord of the whole earth."

Sixth Vision: The Flying Scroll

5 Again I looked up and saw a flying scroll. ²And he said to me, "What do you see?" I answered, "I see a flying scroll; its length is twenty cubits, and its width ten cubits." ³Then he said to me, "This is the curse that goes out over the face of the whole land; for everyone who steals shall be cut off according to the writing on one side, and everyone who swears falselyᵇ shall be cut off according to the writing on the other side. ⁴I have sent it out, says the LORD of hosts, and it shall enter the house of the thief, and the house of anyone who swears falsely by my name; and it shall abide in that house and consume it, both timber and stones."

Seventh Vision: The Woman in a Basket

5 Then the angel who talked with me came forward and said to me, "Look up and see what this is that is coming out." ⁶I said, "What is it?" He said, "This is a basketᶜ coming out." And he said, "This is their iniquityᵈ in all the land." ⁷Then a leaden cover was lifted, and there was a woman sitting in the basket!ᶜ ⁸And he said, "This is Wickedness." So he thrust her back into the basket,ᶜ and pressed the leaden weight down on its mouth. ⁹Then I

a Cn: Heb gold   b The word *falsely* added from verse 4   c Heb *ephah*
d Gk Compare Syr: Heb *their eye*

looked up and saw two women coming forward. The wind was in their wings; they had wings like the wings of a stork, and they lifted up the basket*ᵃ* between earth and sky. ¹⁰Then I said to the angel who talked with me, "Where are they taking the basket?"*ᵃ* ¹¹He said to me, "To the land of Shinar, to build a house for it; and when this is prepared, they will set the basket*ᵃ* down there on its base."

Eighth Vision: Four Chariots

6 And again I looked up and saw four chariots coming out from between two mountains—mountains of bronze. ²The first chariot had red horses, the second chariot black horses, ³the third chariot white horses, and the fourth chariot dappled gray*ᵇ* horses. ⁴Then I said to the angel who talked with me, "What are these, my lord?" ⁵The angel answered me, "These are the four winds*ᶜ* of heaven going out, after presenting themselves before the Lord of all the earth. ⁶The chariot with the black horses goes toward the north country, the white ones go toward the west country,*ᵈ* and the dappled ones go toward the south country." ⁷When the steeds came out, they were impatient to get off and patrol the earth. And he said, "Go, patrol the earth." So they patrolled the earth. ⁸Then he cried out to me, "Lo, those who go toward the north country have set my spirit at rest in the north country."

The Coronation of the Branch

9 The word of the LORD came to me: ¹⁰Collect silver and gold*ᵉ* from the exiles—from Heldai, Tobijah, and Jedaiah—who have arrived from Babylon; and go the same day to the house of Josiah son of Zephaniah. ¹¹Take the silver and gold and make a crown,*ᶠ* and set it on the head of the high priest Joshua son of Jehozadak; ¹²say to him: Thus says the LORD of hosts: Here is a man whose name is Branch: for he shall branch out in his place, and he shall build the temple of the LORD. ¹³It is he that shall build the temple of the LORD; he shall bear royal honor, and shall sit upon his throne and rule. There shall be a priest by his throne, with peaceful understanding between the two of them. ¹⁴And the crown*ᵍ* shall be in the care of Heldai,*ʰ* Tobijah, Jedaiah, and Josiah*ⁱ* son of Zephaniah, as a memorial in the temple of the LORD.

15 Those who are far off shall come and help to build the temple of the LORD; and you shall know that the LORD of hosts has sent me to you. This will happen if you diligently obey the voice of the LORD your God.

Hypocritical Fasting Condemned

7 In the fourth year of King Darius, the word of the LORD came to Zechariah on the fourth day of the ninth month, which is Chislev. ²Now the people of Bethel had sent Sharezer and Regem-melech and their men, to entreat the favor of the LORD, ³and to ask the priests of the house of the LORD of hosts and the prophets, "Should I mourn and practice abstinence in the fifth month, as I have done for so many years?" ⁴Then the word of the LORD of hosts came to

Visions and Prophecies

ZECHARIAH 5.3–6.12

The visions that came to Zechariah contain powerful and vivid images that encourage God's people to live in anticipation of the coming of the Messiah. The prophet describes a flying scroll, a woman in a basket, and four chariots—images we are not apt to forget.

Sketch these three images or have an artistic friend draw them for you. Spend some time looking at each one and give your imagination time to absorb them. What insights do these images illustrate for you? Try describing them in your own words, as if telling a story to a friend, and use the pictures to illustrate each point you make.

See Meeting God in Scripture

---

a Heb *ephah*   *b* Compare Gk: Meaning of Heb uncertain   *c* Or *spirits*
d Cn: Heb *go after them*   *e* Cn Compare verse 11: Heb lacks *silver and gold*
f Gk Mss Syr Tg: Heb *crowns*   *g* Gk Syr: Heb *crowns*   *h* Syr Compare
verse 10: Heb *Helem*   *i* Syr Compare verse 10: Heb *Hen*

Justice, Mercy and Compassion

ZECHARIAH 7.8–10

Read these verses in Zechariah; then compare them to the following passages: Micah 6.8; Isaiah 58.6–10; Matthew 25.34–40. What do these passages have in common? To whom are we called to reach out? Think of your own life. How much contact do you have with people who are homeless, with children who need care and guidance, with people who are new in your neighborhood or with people whose basic needs are not being met? Are you ready to go out of your way to meet their needs? Talk to God about how you might be able to make a difference; then make a commitment to do acts of justice, mercy and compassion.

See Meeting God in Service

me: ⁵Say to all the people of the land and the priests: When you fasted and lamented in the fifth month and in the seventh, for these seventy years, was it for me that you fasted? ⁶And when you eat and when you drink, do you not eat and drink only for yourselves? ⁷Were not these the words that the LORD proclaimed by the former prophets, when Jerusalem was inhabited and in prosperity, along with the towns around it, and when the Negeb and the Shephelah were inhabited?

Punishment for Rejecting God's Demands

8 The word of the LORD came to Zechariah, saying: ⁹Thus says the LORD of hosts: Render true judgments, show kindness and mercy to one another; ¹⁰do not oppress the widow, the orphan, the alien, or the poor; and do not devise evil in your hearts against one another. ¹¹But they refused to listen, and turned a stubborn shoulder, and stopped their ears in order not to hear. ¹²They made their hearts adamant in order not to hear the law and the words that the LORD of hosts had sent by his spirit through the former prophets. Therefore great wrath came from the LORD of hosts. ¹³Just as, when I*ᵃ* called, they would not hear, so, when they called, I would not hear, says the LORD of hosts, ¹⁴and I scattered them with a whirlwind among all the nations that they had not known. Thus the land they left was desolate, so that no one went to and fro, and a pleasant land was made desolate.

God's Promises to Zion

8 The word of the LORD of hosts came to me, saying: ²Thus says the LORD of hosts: I am jealous for Zion with great jealousy, and I am jealous for her with great wrath. ³Thus says the LORD: I will return to Zion, and will dwell in the midst of Jerusalem; Jerusalem shall be called the faithful city, and the mountain of the LORD of hosts shall be called the holy mountain. ⁴Thus says the LORD of hosts: Old men and old women shall again sit in the streets of Jerusalem, each with staff in hand because of their great age. ⁵And the streets of the city shall be full of boys and girls playing in its streets. ⁶Thus says the LORD of hosts: Even though it seems impossible to the remnant of this people in these days, should it also seem impossible to me, says the LORD of hosts? ⁷Thus says the LORD of hosts: I will save my people from the east country and from the west country; ⁸and I will bring them to live in Jerusalem. They shall be my people and I will be their God, in faithfulness and in righteousness.

9 Thus says the LORD of hosts: Let your hands be strong—you that have recently been hearing these words from the mouths of the prophets who were present when the foundation was laid for the rebuilding of the temple, the house of the LORD of hosts. ¹⁰For before those days there were no wages for people or for animals, nor was there any safety from the foe for those who went out or came in, and I set them all against one another. ¹¹But now I will not deal with the remnant of this people as in the former days, says the LORD of hosts. ¹²For there shall be a sowing of peace; the vine shall yield its fruit, the ground shall give its produce, and the skies shall give their dew; and I

a Heb *he*

will cause the remnant of this people to possess all these things. ¹³Just as you have been a cursing among the nations, O house of Judah and house of Israel, so I will save you and you shall be a blessing. Do not be afraid, but let your hands be strong.

14 For thus says the LORD of hosts: Just as I purposed to bring disaster upon you, when your ancestors provoked me to wrath, and I did not relent, says the LORD of hosts, ¹⁵so again I have purposed in these days to do good to Jerusalem and to the house of Judah; do not be afraid. ¹⁶These are the things that you shall do: Speak the truth to one another, render in your gates judgments that are true and make for peace, ¹⁷do not devise evil in your hearts against one another, and love no false oath; for all these are things that I hate, says the LORD.

Joyful Fasting

18 The word of the LORD of hosts came to me, saying: ¹⁹Thus says the LORD of hosts: The fast of the fourth month, and the fast of the fifth, and the fast of the seventh, and the fast of the tenth, shall be seasons of joy and gladness, and cheerful festivals for the house of Judah: therefore love truth and peace.

Many Peoples Drawn to Jerusalem

20 Thus says the LORD of hosts: Peoples shall yet come, the inhabitants of many cities; ²¹the inhabitants of one city shall go to another, saying, "Come, let us go to entreat the favor of the LORD, and to seek the LORD of hosts; I myself am going." ²²Many peoples and strong nations shall come to seek the LORD of hosts in Jerusalem, and to entreat the favor of the LORD. ²³Thus says the LORD of hosts: In those days ten men from nations of every language shall take hold of a Jew, grasping his garment and saying, "Let us go with you, for we have heard that God is with you."

Judgment on Israel's Enemies

9

An Oracle.

The word of the LORD is against the land of Hadrach
  and will rest upon Damascus.
For to the LORD belongs the capital*ᵃ* of Aram,*ᵇ*
  as do all the tribes of Israel;
² Hamath also, which borders on it,
  Tyre and Sidon, though they are very wise.
³ Tyre has built itself a rampart,
  and heaped up silver like dust,
  and gold like the dirt of the streets.
⁴ But now, the Lord will strip it of its possessions
  and hurl its wealth into the sea,
  and it shall be devoured by fire.

⁵ Ashkelon shall see it and be afraid;
  Gaza too, and shall writhe in anguish;
  Ekron also, because its hopes are withered.
The king shall perish from Gaza;
  Ashkelon shall be uninhabited;

Godliness Is Attractive

ZECHARIAH 8.23

What compels ten persons from a variety of backgrounds to follow this man on his journey? What is it about this man that makes it so obvious that God is with him?

People who exhibit God's character attract others to God. Have you ever been so impressed by someone's faith that you wanted to imitate it? Can you think of anyone whose example has brought you closer to the One who made you? Can you think of a group whose love for God and each other was so contagious that you wanted to be one of them? Give thanks for the people who, by the way they lived and shared their faith, have brought you closer to God. Write them a note expressing your appreciation.

See Meeting God in Everyday Life

---

a Heb *eye*   *b* Cn: Heb *of Adam* (or *of humankind*)

Clean, Ready and Worthy

ZECHARIAH 9.9–12

"We are made clean by contrition, ready by compassion, and worthy by our true desire for God. These are three means, as I understood, by which all souls come to heaven, that is to say, those who have been sinners on earth and will be saved . . . For our courteous Lord does not want his servants to despair over falling often or falling deeply. Our falling does not prevent him from loving us. Peace and love are always working in us, but we are not always in peace and love. God wants us to take heed that God is the foundation of all our whole life in love. Furthermore, God is our everlasting protector and mightily defends us against all our most dangerous and fierce enemies."

—JULIAN OF NORWICH,
Showings

6 a mongrel people shall settle in Ashdod,
   and I will make an end of the pride of Philistia.
7 I will take away its blood from its mouth,
   and its abominations from between its teeth;
   it too shall be a remnant for our God;
   it shall be like a clan in Judah,
   and Ekron shall be like the Jebusites.
8 Then I will encamp at my house as a guard,
   so that no one shall march to and fro;
   no oppressor shall again overrun them,
   for now I have seen with my own eyes.

The Coming Ruler of God's People

9 Rejoice greatly, O daughter Zion!
   Shout aloud, O daughter Jerusalem!
   Lo, your king comes to you;
   triumphant and victorious is he,
   humble and riding on a donkey,
   on a colt, the foal of a donkey.
10 He[a] will cut off the chariot from Ephraim
   and the war-horse from Jerusalem;
   and the battle bow shall be cut off,
   and he shall command peace to the nations;
   his dominion shall be from sea to sea,
   and from the River to the ends of the earth.

11 As for you also, because of the blood of my
      covenant with you,
   I will set your prisoners free from the waterless
      pit.
12 Return to your stronghold, O prisoners of hope;
   today I declare that I will restore to you double.
13 For I have bent Judah as my bow;
   I have made Ephraim its arrow.
   I will arouse your sons, O Zion,
   against your sons, O Greece,
   and wield you like a warrior's sword.

14 Then the LORD will appear over them,
   and his arrow go forth like lightning;
   the Lord GOD will sound the trumpet
   and march forth in the whirlwinds of the south.
15 The LORD of hosts will protect them,
   and they shall devour and tread down the
      slingers;[b]
   they shall drink their blood[c] like wine,
   and be full like a bowl,
   drenched like the corners of the altar.

16 On that day the LORD their God will save them
   for they are the flock of his people;
   for like the jewels of a crown
   they shall shine on his land.
17 For what goodness and beauty are his!
   Grain shall make the young men flourish,
   and new wine the young women.

a Gk: Heb *I*   *b* Cn: Heb *the slingstones*   *c* Gk: Heb *shall drink*

Restoration of Judah and Israel

10 Ask rain from the LORD
in the season of the spring rain,
from the LORD who makes the storm clouds,
who gives showers of rain to you,[a]
the vegetation in the field to everyone.
2 For the teraphim[b] utter nonsense,
and the diviners see lies;
the dreamers tell false dreams,
and give empty consolation.
Therefore the people wander like sheep;
they suffer for lack of a shepherd.

3 My anger is hot against the shepherds,
and I will punish the leaders;[c]
for the LORD of hosts cares for his flock, the house
of Judah,
and will make them like his proud war-horse.
4 Out of them shall come the cornerstone,
out of them the tent peg,
out of them the battle bow,
out of them every commander.
5 Together they shall be like warriors in battle,
trampling the foe in the mud of the streets;
they shall fight, for the LORD is with them,
and they shall put to shame the riders on horses.

6 I will strengthen the house of Judah,
and I will save the house of Joseph.
I will bring them back because I have compassion
on them,
and they shall be as though I had not rejected
them;
for I am the LORD their God and I will answer
them.
7 Then the people of Ephraim shall become like
warriors,
and their hearts shall be glad as with wine.
Their children shall see it and rejoice,
their hearts shall exult in the LORD.

8 I will signal for them and gather them in,
for I have redeemed them,
and they shall be as numerous as they were
before.
9 Though I scattered them among the nations,
yet in far countries they shall remember me,
and they shall rear their children and return.
10 I will bring them home from the land of Egypt,
and gather them from Assyria;
I will bring them to the land of Gilead and to
Lebanon,
until there is no room for them.
11 They[d] shall pass through the sea of distress,
and the waves of the sea shall be struck down,
and all the depths of the Nile dried up.
The pride of Assyria shall be laid low,
and the scepter of Egypt shall depart.

Give God the Credit

ZECHARIAH 9.16—10.10

The prophet Zechariah reminds his listeners that it is God, not the Canaanite god Baal, who is in charge of the weather and all things. Baal may not be our "god of choice" today, but the one true God still isn't getting credit for all he does.

In common speech today, God gets little credit: "Boy, that was lucky!" someone may say after a narrow escape from death. "Things are sure looking up for me," another may report. "Fate is smiling on me, that's for sure." How often do we hear "I've been really blessed by God" or "Thanks to God, I've made it through"? Take some quiet time to reflect on the language you use and the attitude you express when describing good things that happen to you.

See Meeting God in Everyday Life

---

a Heb *them*   *b* Or *household gods*   *c* Or *male goats*   *d* Gk: Heb *He*

Gathered and Redeemed

ZECHARIAH 10.8–12

"O most blessed grace, although I be tempted and vexed with many tribulations, yet I will fear no evil, so long as thou art with me. Grace alone and by itself is my strength; this alone giveth advice and help. This is stronger than all enemies, and wiser than all the wise. Let thy grace therefore, O Lord, always follow me through thy Son Jesus Christ. Amen."

—DOUGLAS V. STEERE,
in *The Imitation of Christ (Selections)*

12 I will make them strong in the LORD,
   and they shall walk in his name,
          says the LORD.

11 Open your doors, O Lebanon,
   so that fire may devour your cedars!
2 Wail, O cypress, for the cedar has fallen,
   for the glorious trees are ruined!
Wail, oaks of Bashan,
   for the thick forest has been felled!
3 Listen, the wail of the shepherds,
   for their glory is despoiled!
Listen, the roar of the lions,
   for the thickets of the Jordan are destroyed!

Two Kinds of Shepherds

4 Thus said the LORD my God: Be a shepherd of the flock doomed to slaughter. 5Those who buy them kill them and go unpunished; and those who sell them say, "Blessed be the LORD, for I have become rich"; and their own shepherds have no pity on them. 6For I will no longer have pity on the inhabitants of the earth, says the LORD. I will cause them, every one, to fall each into the hand of a neighbor, and each into the hand of the king; and they shall devastate the earth, and I will deliver no one from their hand.

7 So, on behalf of the sheep merchants, I became the shepherd of the flock doomed to slaughter. I took two staffs; one I named Favor, the other I named Unity, and I tended the sheep. 8In one month I disposed of the three shepherds, for I had become impatient with them, and they also detested me. 9So I said, "I will not be your shepherd. What is to die, let it die; what is to be destroyed, let it be destroyed; and let those that are left devour the flesh of one another!" 10I took my staff Favor and broke it, annulling the covenant that I had made with all the peoples. 11So it was annulled on that day, and the sheep merchants, who were watching me, knew that it was the word of the LORD. 12I then said to them, "If it seems right to you, give me my wages; but if not, keep them." So they weighed out as my wages thirty shekels of silver. 13Then the LORD said to me, "Throw it into the treasury"*a*—this lordly price at which I was valued by them. So I took the thirty shekels of silver and threw them into the treasury*a* in the house of the LORD. 14Then I broke my second staff Unity, annulling the family ties between Judah and Israel.

15 Then the LORD said to me: Take once more the implements of a worthless shepherd. 16For I am now raising up in the land a shepherd who does not care for the perishing, or seek the wandering,*b* or heal the maimed, or nourish the healthy,*c* but devours the flesh of the fat ones, tearing off even their hoofs.
17 Oh, my worthless shepherd,
   who deserts the flock!
May the sword strike his arm
   and his right eye!
Let his arm be completely withered,
   his right eye utterly blinded!

a Syr: Heb *it to the potter*   *b* Syr Compare Gk Vg: Heb *the youth*
c Meaning of Heb uncertain

Jerusalem's Victory

12
An Oracle.

The word of the LORD concerning Israel: Thus says the LORD, who stretched out the heavens and founded the earth and formed the human spirit within: ²See, I am about to make Jerusalem a cup of reeling for all the surrounding peoples; it will be against Judah also in the siege against Jerusalem. ³On that day I will make Jerusalem a heavy stone for all the peoples; all who lift it shall grievously hurt themselves. And all the nations of the earth shall come together against it. ⁴On that day, says the LORD, I will strike every horse with panic, and its rider with madness. But on the house of Judah I will keep a watchful eye, when I strike every horse of the peoples with blindness. ⁵Then the clans of Judah shall say to themselves, "The inhabitants of Jerusalem have strength through the LORD of hosts, their God."

6 On that day I will make the clans of Judah like a blazing pot on a pile of wood, like a flaming torch among sheaves; and they shall devour to the right and to the left all the surrounding peoples, while Jerusalem shall again be inhabited in its place, in Jerusalem.

7 And the LORD will give victory to the tents of Judah first, that the glory of the house of David and the glory of the inhabitants of Jerusalem may not be exalted over that of Judah. ⁸On that day the LORD will shield the inhabitants of Jerusalem so that the feeblest among them on that day shall be like David, and the house of David shall be like God, like the angel of the LORD, at their head. ⁹And on that day I will seek to destroy all the nations that come against Jerusalem.

Mourning for the Pierced One

10 And I will pour out a spirit of compassion and supplication on the house of David and the inhabitants of Jerusalem, so that, when they look on the one*ᵃ* whom they have pierced, they shall mourn for him, as one mourns for an only child, and weep bitterly over him, as one weeps over a firstborn. ¹¹On that day the mourning in Jerusalem will be as great as the mourning for Hadad-rimmon in the plain of Megiddo. ¹²The land shall mourn, each family by itself; the family of the house of David by itself, and their wives by themselves; the family of the house of Nathan by itself, and their wives by themselves; ¹³the family of the house of Levi by itself, and their wives by themselves; the family of the Shimeites by itself, and their wives by themselves; ¹⁴and all the families that are left, each by itself, and their wives by themselves.

13
On that day a fountain shall be opened for the house of David and the inhabitants of Jerusalem, to cleanse them from sin and impurity.

Idolatry Cut Off

2 On that day, says the LORD of hosts, I will cut off the names of the idols from the land, so that they shall be remembered no more; and also I will remove from the land the prophets and the unclean spirit. ³And if any prophets

---

To Be Saved

ZECHARIAH 13.1

"To be saved does not mean to be a little encouraged, a little comforted, a little relieved. It means to be pulled like a log from a burning fire."

—KARL BARTH,
Deliverance to the Captives

---

a Heb *on me*

God Rules

ZECHARIAH 14.9

The day will come when God is acknowledged as "king over all the earth." What if that day was today? Write a description of what the world would be like if every living being recognized God's power and loving presence. God's Spirit would be like perfume in the air we breathe; there would be no more violence; each person would be fully conformed to the likeness of Jesus. Try to imagine what it would be like if everyone in the world lived in the fullness of faith. After you have written as many things as you can imagine, talk to God about any ways you might be part of helping to bring more of that kingdom ideal to fruition.

See Meeting God in Scripture

appear again, their fathers and mothers who bore them will say to them, "You shall not live, for you speak lies in the name of the LORD"; and their fathers and their mothers who bore them shall pierce them through when they prophesy. ⁴On that day the prophets will be ashamed, every one, of their visions when they prophesy; they will not put on a hairy mantle in order to deceive, ⁵but each of them will say, "I am no prophet, I am a tiller of the soil; for the land has been my possession*ᵃ* since my youth." ⁶And if anyone asks them, "What are these wounds on your chest?"*ᵇ* the answer will be "The wounds I received in the house of my friends."

The Shepherd Struck, the Flock Scattered

7   "Awake, O sword, against my shepherd,
    against the man who is my associate,"
                        says the LORD of hosts.
  Strike the shepherd, that the sheep may be
    scattered;
  I will turn my hand against the little ones.
8   In the whole land, says the LORD,
    two-thirds shall be cut off and perish,
    and one-third shall be left alive.
9   And I will put this third into the fire,
    refine them as one refines silver,
    and test them as gold is tested.
  They will call on my name,
    and I will answer them.
  I will say, "They are my people";
    and they will say, "The LORD is our God."

Future Warfare and Final Victory

14 See, a day is coming for the LORD, when the plunder taken from you will be divided in your midst. ²For I will gather all the nations against Jerusalem to battle, and the city shall be taken and the houses looted and the women raped; half the city shall go into exile, but the rest of the people shall not be cut off from the city. ³Then the LORD will go forth and fight against those nations as when he fights on a day of battle. ⁴On that day his feet shall stand on the Mount of Olives, which lies before Jerusalem on the east; and the Mount of Olives shall be split in two from east to west by a very wide valley; so that one half of the Mount shall withdraw northward, and the other half southward. ⁵And you shall flee by the valley of the LORD's mountain,*ᶜ* for the valley between the mountains shall reach to Azal;*ᵈ* and you shall flee as you fled from the earthquake in the days of King Uzziah of Judah. Then the LORD my God will come, and all the holy ones with him.

6 On that day there shall not be*ᵉ* either cold or frost.*ᶠ* ⁷And there shall be continuous day (it is known to the LORD), not day and not night, for at evening time there shall be light.

8 On that day living waters shall flow out from Jerusalem, half of them to the eastern sea and half of them to the western sea; it shall continue in summer as in winter.

a Cn: Heb *for humankind has caused me to possess*   *b* Heb *wounds between your hands*   *c* Heb *my mountains*   *d* Meaning of Heb uncertain   *e* Cn: Heb *there shall not be light*   *f* Compare Gk Syr Vg Tg: Meaning of Heb uncertain

9 And the LORD will become king over all the earth; on that day the LORD will be one and his name one.

10 The whole land shall be turned into a plain from Geba to Rimmon south of Jerusalem. But Jerusalem shall remain aloft on its site from the Gate of Benjamin to the place of the former gate, to the Corner Gate, and from the Tower of Hananel to the king's wine presses. ¹¹And it shall be inhabited, for never again shall it be doomed to destruction; Jerusalem shall abide in security.

12 This shall be the plague with which the LORD will strike all the peoples that wage war against Jerusalem: their flesh shall rot while they are still on their feet; their eyes shall rot in their sockets, and their tongues shall rot in their mouths. ¹³On that day a great panic from the LORD shall fall on them, so that each will seize the hand of a neighbor, and the hand of the one will be raised against the hand of the other; ¹⁴even Judah will fight at Jerusalem. And the wealth of all the surrounding nations shall be collected— gold, silver, and garments in great abundance. ¹⁵And a plague like this plague shall fall on the horses, the mules, the camels, the donkeys, and whatever animals may be in those camps.

16 Then all who survive of the nations that have come against Jerusalem shall go up year after year to worship the King, the LORD of hosts, and to keep the festival of booths.ᵃ ¹⁷If any of the families of the earth do not go up to Jerusalem to worship the King, the LORD of hosts, there will be no rain upon them. ¹⁸And if the family of Egypt do not go up and present themselves, then on them shallᵇ come the plague that the LORD inflicts on the nations that do not go up to keep the festival of booths.ᵃ ¹⁹Such shall be the punishment of Egypt and the punishment of all the nations that do not go up to keep the festival of booths.ᵃ

20 On that day there shall be inscribed on the bells of the horses, "Holy to the LORD." And the cooking pots in the house of the LORD shall be as holy asᶜ the bowls in front of the altar; ²¹and every cooking pot in Jerusalem and Judah shall be sacred to the LORD of hosts, so that all who sacrifice may come and use them to boil the flesh of the sacrifice. And there shall no longer be tradersᵈ in the house of the LORD of hosts on that day.

Holy to the Lord!

ZECHARIAH 14.20

Zechariah envisions a time when even the horses have "Holy to the LORD" engraved on their bells. Close your eyes and in your imagination take a walk through your home: "Holy to the LORD" is written above each doorway and woven into the carpet under your feet. In each room "Holy to the LORD" is inscribed on the furniture and objects. How does it feel to see these words on a chair, a lamp, a picture on the wall? No matter where you go, you are reminded of God's power and goodness; you are reminded that everything, no matter how ordinary, becomes holy when it is consecrated to God. As you step outside your home, you realize that the same words are invisibly written on your skin. The reminder is everywhere. HOLY TO THE LORD!

See Meeting God in Scripture

MALACHI

Keeping Promises

KEY VERSE:

Ever since the days of your ancestors you have turned aside from my statutes and
have not kept them. Return to me, and I will return to you, says the LORD of hosts.
But you say, "How shall we return?"—Malachi 3.7

To worship is to quicken the conscience by the holiness of God, to feed the mind with the truth of God, to purge the imagination by the beauty of God, to open the heart to the love of God, to devote the will to the purpose of God.

—WILLIAM TEMPLE

In the book of Malachi, it is the prophet's words, not his person, that demand our attention. We know next to nothing about the prophet himself, but we find in his writing a vibrant word from God (the name of the book means "my messenger").

Malachi, using a question-and-answer device, challenges the people to mend their ways. The prophet warns the priests about offering blemished sacrifices (1.8) and giving false teachings (2.8). He confronts the people about mixed marriages and divorce (2.10–16) and about not paying a full tithe (3.8–9). The day of judgment is coming, he declares, and it will be like a fire—it will burn away evil and refine what is good.

Amid Malachi's warnings and judgment, the prophet tells of some wonderful blessings that will belong to those who are faithful and obedient to God. Those who are generous and bring a full tithe to God will see God "open the window of heaven . . . and pour down for [them] an overflowing blessing" (3.10). Those who revere and honor God will see the sun of righteousness "rise, with healing in its wings" (4.2). Malachi calls us to return to a life of honest worship, truthful speech and generous compassion. Listen with your heart, respond with your deeds, and the Lord will come to you!

1

An oracle. The word of the LORD to Israel by Malachi.*a*

Israel Preferred to Edom

2 I have loved you, says the LORD. But you say, "How have you loved us?" Is not Esau Jacob's brother? says the LORD. Yet I have loved Jacob **3**but I have hated Esau; I have made his hill country a desolation and his heritage a desert for jackals. **4**If Edom says, "We are shattered but we will rebuild the ruins," the LORD of hosts says: They may build, but I will tear down, until they are called the wicked country, the people with whom the LORD is angry forever. **5**Your own eyes shall see this, and you shall say, "Great is the LORD beyond the borders of Israel!"

Corruption of the Priesthood

6 A son honors his father, and servants their master. If then I am a father, where is the honor due me? And if I am a master, where is the respect due me? says the LORD of hosts to you, O priests, who despise my name. You say, "How have we despised your name?" **7**By offering polluted food on my altar. And you say, "How have we polluted it?"*b* By thinking that the LORD's table may be despised. **8**When you offer blind animals in sacrifice, is that not wrong? And when you offer those that are lame or sick, is that not wrong? Try presenting that to your governor; will he be pleased with you or show you favor? says the LORD of hosts. **9**And now implore the favor of God, that he may be gracious to us. The fault is yours. Will he show favor to any of you? says the LORD of hosts. **10**Oh, that someone among you would shut the temple*c* doors, so that you would not kindle fire on my altar in vain! I have no pleasure in you, says the LORD of hosts, and I will not accept an offering from your hands. **11**For from the rising of the sun to its setting my name is great among the nations, and in every place incense is offered to my name, and a pure offering; for my name is great among the nations, says the LORD of hosts. **12**But you profane it when you say that the Lord's table is polluted, and the food for it*d* may be despised. **13**"What a weariness this is," you say, and you sniff at me,*e* says the LORD of hosts. You bring what has been taken by violence or is lame or sick, and this you bring as your offering! Shall I accept that from your hand? says the LORD. **14**Cursed be the cheat who has a male in the flock and vows to give it, and yet sacrifices to the Lord what is blemished; for I am a great King, says the LORD of hosts, and my name is reverenced among the nations.

2

And now, O priests, this command is for you. **2**If you will not listen, if you will not lay it to heart to give glory to my name, says the LORD of hosts, then I will send the curse on you and I will curse your blessings; indeed I have already cursed them,*f* because you do not lay it to heart. **3**I will rebuke your offspring, and spread dung on your faces, the dung of your offerings, and I will put you out of my presence.*g*

4 Know, then, that I have sent this command to you, that my covenant with Levi may hold, says the LORD of

Offering Less Than the Best

MALACHI 1.13–14

We may not comprehend the necessity of the animal sacrifices that were common practice in the Old Testament, but we understand all too well the prophet's disgust with offerings that were less than the best. In our spiritual life we sometimes offer God less than our best: We try to squeeze prayer in at the end of a crowded day and end up falling asleep; we go wearily to worship services after staying up too late the night before; we skip Bible study because we don't have time.

God desires our best "from the rising of the sun to its setting" (v.11), and our best is not tired prayers, halfhearted study or short-lived compassion. Review your spiritual disciplines of prayer, worship and Bible study. Write a prayer of confession for your "less than best" efforts or a prayer of thanksgiving for your ability to be faithful. Ask God to help you as you grow to be the very best he intends you to be.

See *Meeting God in Prayer*

---

a Or *by my messenger*   *b* Gk: Heb *you*   *c* Heb lacks *temple*
d Compare Syr Tg: Heb *its fruit, its food*   *e* Another reading is *at it*
f Heb *it*   *g* Cn Compare Gk Syr: Heb *and he shall bear you to it*

The Lips and the Mouth

MALACHI 2.4–9

The prophet decries a priesthood that has become complacent and corrupt. Steady as iron, though, he upholds God's clear standards of righteousness.

Draw a picture of a mouth. On one side of the mouth write some of the words you have used to hurt, mislead or create trouble. On the other side write words you have used to comfort, guide and maintain peace. Try to speak a few words of encouragement, guidance or peace to everyone you meet today. Pray that the words you speak will be a blessing to others.

See Meeting God in Everyday Life

hosts. ⁵My covenant with him was a covenant of life and well-being, which I gave him; this called for reverence, and he revered me and stood in awe of my name. ⁶True instruction was in his mouth, and no wrong was found on his lips. He walked with me in integrity and uprightness, and he turned many from iniquity. ⁷For the lips of a priest should guard knowledge, and people should seek instruction from his mouth, for he is the messenger of the Lord of hosts. ⁸But you have turned aside from the way; you have caused many to stumble by your instruction; you have corrupted the covenant of Levi, says the Lord of hosts, ⁹and so I make you despised and abased before all the people, inasmuch as you have not kept my ways but have shown partiality in your instruction.

The Covenant Profaned by Judah

10 Have we not all one father? Has not one God created us? Why then are we faithless to one another, profaning the covenant of our ancestors? ¹¹Judah has been faithless, and abomination has been committed in Israel and in Jerusalem; for Judah has profaned the sanctuary of the Lord, which he loves, and has married the daughter of a foreign god. ¹²May the Lord cut off from the tents of Jacob anyone who does this—any to witness*a* or answer, or to bring an offering to the Lord of hosts.

13 And this you do as well: You cover the Lord's altar with tears, with weeping and groaning because he no longer regards the offering or accepts it with favor at your hand. ¹⁴You ask, "Why does he not?" Because the Lord was a witness between you and the wife of your youth, to whom you have been faithless, though she is your companion and your wife by covenant. ¹⁵Did not one God make her?*b* Both flesh and spirit are his.*c* And what does the one God*d* desire? Godly offspring. So look to yourselves, and do not let anyone be faithless to the wife of his youth. ¹⁶For I hate*e* divorce, says the Lord, the God of Israel, and covering one's garment with violence, says the Lord of hosts. So take heed to yourselves and do not be faithless.

17 You have wearied the Lord with your words. Yet you say, "How have we wearied him?" By saying, "All who do evil are good in the sight of the Lord, and he delights in them." Or by asking, "Where is the God of justice?"

The Coming Messenger

3 See, I am sending my messenger to prepare the way before me, and the Lord whom you seek will suddenly come to his temple. The messenger of the covenant in whom you delight—indeed, he is coming, says the Lord of hosts. ²But who can endure the day of his coming, and who can stand when he appears?

For he is like a refiner's fire and like fullers' soap; ³he will sit as a refiner and purifier of silver, and he will purify the descendants of Levi and refine them like gold and silver, until they present offerings to the Lord in righteousness.*f* ⁴Then the offering of Judah and Jerusalem will

a Cn Compare Gk: Heb *arouse*   *b* Or *Has he not made one?*   *c* Cn: Heb
and a remnant of spirit was his   *d* Heb *he*   *e* Cn: Heb *he hates*
f Or *right offerings to the Lord*

be pleasing to the LORD as in the days of old and as in former years.

5 Then I will draw near to you for judgment; I will be swift to bear witness against the sorcerers, against the adulterers, against those who swear falsely, against those who oppress the hired workers in their wages, the widow and the orphan, against those who thrust aside the alien, and do not fear me, says the LORD of hosts.

6 For I the LORD do not change; therefore you, O children of Jacob, have not perished. [7]Ever since the days of your ancestors you have turned aside from my statutes and have not kept them. Return to me, and I will return to you, says the LORD of hosts. But you say, "How shall we return?"

Do Not Rob God

8 Will anyone rob God? Yet you are robbing me! But you say, "How are we robbing you?" In your tithes and offerings! [9]You are cursed with a curse, for you are robbing me—the whole nation of you! [10]Bring the full tithe into the storehouse, so that there may be food in my house, and thus put me to the test, says the LORD of hosts; see if I will not open the windows of heaven for you and pour down for you an overflowing blessing. [11]I will rebuke the locust[a] for you, so that it will not destroy the produce of your soil; and your vine in the field shall not be barren, says the LORD of hosts. [12]Then all nations will count you happy, for you will be a land of delight, says the LORD of hosts.

13 You have spoken harsh words against me, says the LORD. Yet you say, "How have we spoken against you?" [14]You have said, "It is vain to serve God. What do we profit by keeping his command or by going about as mourners before the LORD of hosts? [15]Now we count the arrogant happy; evildoers not only prosper, but when they put God to the test they escape."

The Reward of the Faithful

16 Then those who revered the LORD spoke with one another. The LORD took note and listened, and a book of remembrance was written before him of those who revered the LORD and thought on his name. [17]They shall be mine, says the LORD of hosts, my special possession on the day when I act, and I will spare them as parents spare their children who serve them. [18]Then once more you shall see the difference between the righteous and the wicked, between one who serves God and one who does not serve him.

The Great Day of the LORD

4[b] See, the day is coming, burning like an oven, when all the arrogant and all evildoers will be stubble; the day that comes shall burn them up, says the LORD of hosts, so that it will leave them neither root nor branch. [2]But for you who revere my name the sun of righteousness shall rise, with healing in its wings. You shall go out leaping like calves from the stall. [3]And you shall tread down the wicked, for they will be ashes under the soles of your feet, on the day when I act, says the LORD of hosts.

A Messenger Comes in Many Ways

MALACHI 3.1–4

"[God's] appeals come through the conversations of good people, or from sermons, or through the reading of good books; and there are many other ways . . . in which God calls. Or they come through sicknesses and trials, or by means of truths which God teaches us at times when we are engaged in prayer; however feeble such prayers may be, God values them highly. You must not despise this first favor, nor be disconsolate, even though you have not responded immediately to the Lord's call; for his majesty is quite prepared to wait for many days, and even years, especially when he sees we are persevering and have good desires."

—TERESA OF AVILA,
The Interior Castle

---

a Heb *devourer*   b Ch 4.1-6 are Ch 3.19-24 in Heb

On That Day

MALACHI 4.1–3

Whatever judgment occurs on the day of the Lord, those who revere God will experience that day as one of rejoicing in their salvation and renewal: "You shall go out leaping like calves released from the stall."

Think of the rays of the sun as white or golden birds that bring healing to your mind, body and spirit. How would those wings of healing enfold and touch you with warmth and healing? Imagine these birds flying out over your neighborhood and community. Where would they bring healing and salvation? Next see the birds winging their way over the country and around the world. Where would you ask God to send healing and renewal? Where is the sun of righteousness needed? Draw a picture of your bird of healing or write a prayer of thanksgiving.

See Meeting God in Scripture

4 Remember the teaching of my servant Moses, the statutes and ordinances that I commanded him at Horeb for all Israel.

5 Lo, I will send you the prophet Elijah before the great and terrible day of the LORD comes. 6He will turn the hearts of parents to their children and the hearts of children to their parents, so that I will not come and strike the land with a curse.ᵃ

a Or a ban of utter destruction

THE
NEW TESTAMENT

THE GOSPEL ACCORDING TO
MATTHEW

Promises That Come True

KEY VERSE:

"Do not think that I have come to abolish the law or the prophets; I have come not to abolish but to fulfill."—Matthew 5.17

Matthew writes this Gospel in the early church period when the church is predominantly Jewish. Matthew frequently cites passages from the Old Testament that are fulfilled in the coming of Jesus the Messiah, a watershed event in the long tradition of ancient Judaism. Matthew's intent is that those who read his Gospel, whether Jews or Gentiles, will see themselves as participants in the grand sweep of God's purposes in history. The coming of Jesus, says Matthew, is the culmination of all our waiting.

Matthew almost seems astonished that God should become incarnate in Jesus Christ, that people could see and hear and touch the Almighty God. As you read Matthew's Gospel, try to imagine yourself as a Jew in Gospel times. Your people have waited a thousand years for fulfillment. You have studied and remembered all the ancient prophecies and now, for the first time, they make sense. Suddenly, Almighty God is among your people. Emmanuel, *God is with us*, is present and active in the day-to-day life of the people—healing, feeding, teaching—bringing the Word of God personally to the people of God.

As you read this Gospel, remember that Jesus is still *God with us*. He is God incarnate, with us in the Holy Spirit. What questions would you like to ask him? What would you like him to explain? What do you need him to do for you? What can you do for him? Make these questions the prayers of your heart.

"The Gospel is a public exhibition of the Son of God manifested in the flesh to deliver a ruined world, and to restore men from death to life. It is justly called a good and joyful message, for it contains perfect happiness. Its object is to commence the reign of God, and by means of our deliverance from the corruption of the flesh, and of our renewal by the Spirit, to conduct us to the heavenly glory."

—JOHN CALVIN,
Institutes of the Christian Religion

Your Past Doesn't Dictate Your Future

The genealogy of Jesus is a startling testimony to God's power to overcome the sin of humankind. This is by no means a "pure" family tree: Judah visited prostitutes; Rahab was a prostitute; David committed adultery and murder; Solomon flirted with idols. Yet through these imperfect people, God was able to preserve his promises and shape earthly events to prepare the way for the Messiah. In what ways have you departed from God's will for you? How has God called you back? How do you see God working to keep you on track with his purposes, even through your times of spiritual dryness and perceived distance from God?

The Genealogy of Jesus the Messiah

1 An account of the genealogy*a* of Jesus the Messiah,*b* the son of David, the son of Abraham.

2 Abraham was the father of Isaac, and Isaac the father of Jacob, and Jacob the father of Judah and his brothers, *3*and Judah the father of Perez and Zerah by Tamar, and Perez the father of Hezron, and Hezron the father of Aram, *4*and Aram the father of Aminadab, and Aminadab the father of Nahshon, and Nahshon the father of Salmon, *5*and Salmon the father of Boaz by Rahab, and Boaz the father of Obed by Ruth, and Obed the father of Jesse, *6*and Jesse the father of King David.

And David was the father of Solomon by the wife of Uriah, *7*and Solomon the father of Rehoboam, and Rehoboam the father of Abijah, and Abijah the father of Asaph,*c* *8*and Asaph*c* the father of Jehoshaphat, and Jehoshaphat the father of Joram, and Joram the father of Uzziah, *9*and Uzziah the father of Jotham, and Jotham the father of Ahaz, and Ahaz the father of Hezekiah, *10*and Hezekiah the father of Manasseh, and Manasseh the father of Amos,*d* and Amos*d* the father of Josiah, *11*and Josiah the father of Jechoniah and his brothers, at the time of the deportation to Babylon.

12 And after the deportation to Babylon: Jechoniah was the father of Salathiel, and Salathiel the father of Zerubbabel, *13*and Zerubbabel the father of Abiud, and Abiud the father of Eliakim, and Eliakim the father of Azor, *14*and Azor the father of Zadok, and Zadok the father of Achim, and Achim the father of Eliud, *15*and Eliud the father of Eleazar, and Eleazar the father of Matthan, and Matthan the father of Jacob, *16*and Jacob the father of Joseph the husband of Mary, of whom Jesus was born, who is called the Messiah.*e*

17 So all the generations from Abraham to David are fourteen generations; and from David to the deportation to Babylon, fourteen generations; and from the deportation to Babylon to the Messiah,*e* fourteen generations.

The Birth of Jesus the Messiah

18 Now the birth of Jesus the Messiah*b* took place in this way. When his mother Mary had been engaged to Joseph, but before they lived together, she was found to be with child from the Holy Spirit. *19*Her husband Joseph, being a righteous man and unwilling to expose her to public disgrace, planned to dismiss her quietly. *20*But just when he had resolved to do this, an angel of the Lord appeared to him in a dream and said, "Joseph, son of David, do not be afraid to take Mary as your wife, for the child conceived in her is from the Holy Spirit. *21*She will bear a son, and you are to name him Jesus, for he will save his people from their sins." *22*All this took place to fulfill what had been spoken by the Lord through the prophet:

23 "Look, the virgin shall conceive and bear a son,
    and they shall name him Emmanuel,"

which means, "God is with us." *24*When Joseph awoke

a Or *birth*   *b* Or *Jesus Christ*   *c* Other ancient authorities read *Asa*
d Other ancient authorities read *Amon*   *e* Or *the Christ*

from sleep, he did as the angel of the Lord commanded him; he took her as his wife, [25]but had no marital relations with her until she had borne a son;[a] and he named him Jesus.

The Visit of the Wise Men

2 In the time of King Herod, after Jesus was born in Bethlehem of Judea, wise men[b] from the East came to Jerusalem, [2]asking, "Where is the child who has been born king of the Jews? For we observed his star at its rising,[c] and have come to pay him homage." [3]When King Herod heard this, he was frightened, and all Jerusalem with him; [4]and calling together all the chief priests and scribes of the people, he inquired of them where the Messiah[d] was to be born. [5]They told him, "In Bethlehem of Judea; for so it has been written by the prophet:

[6] 'And you, Bethlehem, in the land of Judah,
    are by no means least among the rulers of Judah;
  for from you shall come a ruler
    who is to shepherd[e] my people Israel.' "

7 Then Herod secretly called for the wise men[b] and learned from them the exact time when the star had appeared. [8]Then he sent them to Bethlehem, saying, "Go and search diligently for the child; and when you have found him, bring me word so that I may also go and pay him homage." [9]When they had heard the king, they set out; and there, ahead of them, went the star that they had seen at its rising,[c] until it stopped over the place where the child was. [10]When they saw that the star had stopped,[f] they were overwhelmed with joy. [11]On entering the house, they saw the child with Mary his mother; and they knelt down and paid him homage. Then, opening their treasure chests, they offered him gifts of gold, frankincense, and myrrh. [12]And having been warned in a dream not to return to Herod, they left for their own country by another road.

The Escape to Egypt

13 Now after they had left, an angel of the Lord appeared to Joseph in a dream and said, "Get up, take the child and his mother, and flee to Egypt, and remain there until I tell you; for Herod is about to search for the child, to destroy him." [14]Then Joseph[g] got up, took the child and his mother by night, and went to Egypt, [15]and remained there until the death of Herod. This was to fulfill what had been spoken by the Lord through the prophet, "Out of Egypt I have called my son."

The Massacre of the Infants

16 When Herod saw that he had been tricked by the wise men,[b] he was infuriated, and he sent and killed all the children in and around Bethlehem who were two years old or under, according to the time that he had learned from the wise men.[b] [17]Then was fulfilled what had been spoken through the prophet Jeremiah:

---

a Other ancient authorities read *her firstborn son*   b Or *astrologers*; Gk *magi*   c Or *in the East*   d Or *the Christ*   e Or *rule*   f Gk *saw the star*   g Gk *he*

Reasons of the Heart

MATTHEW 2.2

The wise men come to worship Jesus. Later others come to him for healing and forgiveness, to learn from him, or in hopes of gaining material blessings or power. Imagine you are a contemporary of Jesus and you have just heard about him. Who told you about Jesus? What did that person say about Jesus? What was the first thing you said? What did you think about just before falling asleep that night? What do you seek now? Ask God to help you find it. Or ask God to teach you, as you read this Gospel, what you should be seeking.

See Meeting God in Worship

Cooperating With God

MATTHEW 2.15; 3.1

Joseph takes the young Jesus to Egypt and stays there to fulfill what God has said through the prophets. Later John the Baptist prepares the way for the Messiah by preaching repentance. Each man makes life choices that God uses to fulfill the covenant of salvation.

Take a short trip out of town; spend the night alone and reflect on how your life can be part of God's purpose. (As an alternative, take a leisurely walk some morning or afternoon.) Ask yourself: How can I cooperate with God's designs for my life? Do I have any unique qualities that might reflect a certain purpose? What promise might I help fulfill?

See Meeting God in Everyday Life

18 "A voice was heard in Ramah,
    wailing and loud lamentation,
  Rachel weeping for her children;
    she refused to be consoled, because they are no
      more."

The Return from Egypt

19 When Herod died, an angel of the Lord suddenly appeared in a dream to Joseph in Egypt and said, 20 "Get up, take the child and his mother, and go to the land of Israel, for those who were seeking the child's life are dead." 21 Then Joseph*a* got up, took the child and his mother, and went to the land of Israel. 22 But when he heard that Archelaus was ruling over Judea in place of his father Herod, he was afraid to go there. And after being warned in a dream, he went away to the district of Galilee. 23 There he made his home in a town called Nazareth, so that what had been spoken through the prophets might be fulfilled, "He will be called a Nazorean."

The Proclamation of John the Baptist

3 In those days John the Baptist appeared in the wilderness of Judea, proclaiming, 2 "Repent, for the kingdom of heaven has come near."*b* 3 This is the one of whom the prophet Isaiah spoke when he said,

  "The voice of one crying out in the wilderness:
  'Prepare the way of the Lord,
    make his paths straight.' "

4 Now John wore clothing of camel's hair with a leather belt around his waist, and his food was locusts and wild honey. 5 Then the people of Jerusalem and all Judea were going out to him, and all the region along the Jordan, 6 and they were baptized by him in the river Jordan, confessing their sins.

7 But when he saw many Pharisees and Sadducees coming for baptism, he said to them, "You brood of vipers! Who warned you to flee from the wrath to come? 8 Bear fruit worthy of repentance. 9 Do not presume to say to yourselves, 'We have Abraham as our ancestor'; for I tell you, God is able from these stones to raise up children to Abraham. 10 Even now the ax is lying at the root of the trees; every tree therefore that does not bear good fruit is cut down and thrown into the fire.

11 "I baptize you with*c* water for repentance, but one who is more powerful than I is coming after me; I am not worthy to carry his sandals. He will baptize you with*c* the Holy Spirit and fire. 12 His winnowing fork is in his hand, and he will clear his threshing floor and will gather his wheat into the granary; but the chaff he will burn with unquenchable fire."

The Baptism of Jesus

13 Then Jesus came from Galilee to John at the Jordan, to be baptized by him. 14 John would have prevented him, saying, "I need to be baptized by you, and do you come to me?" 15 But Jesus answered him, "Let it be so now; for it is proper for us in this way to fulfill all righteousness."

a Gk *he*   *b* Or *is at hand*   *c* Or *in*

Then he consented. ¹⁶And when Jesus had been baptized, just as he came up from the water, suddenly the heavens were opened to him and he saw the Spirit of God descending like a dove and alighting on him. ¹⁷And a voice from heaven said, "This is my Son, the Beloved,ᵃ with whom I am well pleased."

The Temptation of Jesus

4 Then Jesus was led up by the Spirit into the wilderness to be tempted by the devil. ²He fasted forty days and forty nights, and afterwards he was famished. ³The tempter came and said to him, "If you are the Son of God, command these stones to become loaves of bread." ⁴But he answered, "It is written,

'One does not live by bread alone,
   but by every word that comes from the mouth of
      God.' "

5 Then the devil took him to the holy city and placed him on the pinnacle of the temple, ⁶saying to him, "If you are the Son of God, throw yourself down; for it is written,

'He will command his angels concerning you,'
   and 'On their hands they will bear you up,
so that you will not dash your foot against a
   stone.' "

⁷Jesus said to him, "Again it is written, 'Do not put the Lord your God to the test.' "

8 Again, the devil took him to a very high mountain and showed him all the kingdoms of the world and their splendor; ⁹and he said to him, "All these I will give you, if you will fall down and worship me." ¹⁰Jesus said to him, "Away with you, Satan! for it is written,

'Worship the Lord your God,
   and serve only him.' "

¹¹Then the devil left him, and suddenly angels came and waited on him.

Jesus Begins His Ministry in Galilee

12 Now when Jesusᵇ heard that John had been arrested, he withdrew to Galilee. ¹³He left Nazareth and made his home in Capernaum by the sea, in the territory of Zebulun and Naphtali, ¹⁴so that what had been spoken through the prophet Isaiah might be fulfilled:

¹⁵ "Land of Zebulun, land of Naphtali,
      on the road by the sea, across the Jordan, Galilee
         of the Gentiles—
¹⁶ the people who sat in darkness
      have seen a great light,
   and for those who sat in the region and shadow of
         death
   light has dawned."

¹⁷From that time Jesus began to proclaim, "Repent, for the kingdom of heaven has come near."ᶜ

Jesus Calls the First Disciples

18 As he walked by the Sea of Galilee, he saw two brothers, Simon, who is called Peter, and Andrew his brother, casting a net into the sea—for they were fisher-

The Temptation of Legitimate Needs

MATTHEW 4.1–4

After forty days of fasting, Jesus' need for food was understandably acute. Satan uses this legitimate need to tempt Jesus to "prove" his significance and power.

Temptation often results from such legitimate needs. What needs do you have in your life that aren't being met? Are you tempted to meet those needs in illegitimate ways? Put yourself in Jesus' sandals; imagine his hunger after a forty-day fast. Consider fasting for a day to more fully experience the kinds of sensations Jesus did. How can the strength Jesus exhibits and words he speaks encourage you?

ᵃ Or *my beloved Son*   ᵇ Gk *he*   ᶜ Or *is at hand*

Life With Others

MATTHEW 5.3–10

If every member of your community made a concerted effort to become poor in spirit, meek, merciful, pure in heart, and prone to promoting peace, how would your community be transformed? How do these beatitudes bring people together? Reflect on this passage by looking at the harm done by the opposite attitudes. What usually follows in the wake of a haughty spirit? What happens when people become demanding? Divisive? Critical? How can God use you in your church, circle of friends, or neighborhood to reflect the character of the Spirit of Jesus?

See Meeting God in Community

men. ¹⁹And he said to them, "Follow me, and I will make you fish for people." ²⁰Immediately they left their nets and followed him. ²¹As he went from there, he saw two other brothers, James son of Zebedee and his brother John, in the boat with their father Zebedee, mending their nets, and he called them. ²²Immediately they left the boat and their father, and followed him.

Jesus Ministers to Crowds of People

23 Jesus*a* went throughout Galilee, teaching in their synagogues and proclaiming the good news*b* of the kingdom and curing every disease and every sickness among the people. ²⁴So his fame spread throughout all Syria, and they brought to him all the sick, those who were afflicted with various diseases and pains, demoniacs, epileptics, and paralytics, and he cured them. ²⁵And great crowds followed him from Galilee, the Decapolis, Jerusalem, Judea, and from beyond the Jordan.

The Beatitudes

5 When Jesus*c* saw the crowds, he went up the mountain; and after he sat down, his disciples came to him. ²Then he began to speak, and taught them, saying:

3 "Blessed are the poor in spirit, for theirs is the kingdom of heaven.

4 "Blessed are those who mourn, for they will be comforted.

5 "Blessed are the meek, for they will inherit the earth.

6 "Blessed are those who hunger and thirst for righteousness, for they will be filled.

7 "Blessed are the merciful, for they will receive mercy.

8 "Blessed are the pure in heart, for they will see God.

9 "Blessed are the peacemakers, for they will be called children of God.

10 "Blessed are those who are persecuted for righteousness' sake, for theirs is the kingdom of heaven.

11 "Blessed are you when people revile you and persecute you and utter all kinds of evil against you falsely*d* on my account. ¹²Rejoice and be glad, for your reward is great in heaven, for in the same way they persecuted the prophets who were before you.

Salt and Light

13 "You are the salt of the earth; but if salt has lost its taste, how can its saltiness be restored? It is no longer good for anything, but is thrown out and trampled under foot.

14 "You are the light of the world. A city built on a hill cannot be hid. ¹⁵No one after lighting a lamp puts it under the bushel basket, but on the lampstand, and it gives light to all in the house. ¹⁶In the same way, let your light shine before others, so that they may see your good works and give glory to your Father in heaven.

The Law and the Prophets

17 "Do not think that I have come to abolish the law or the prophets; I have come not to abolish but to fulfill. ¹⁸For

a Gk *He*   *b* Gk *gospel*   *c* Gk *he*   *d* Other ancient authorities lack *falsely*

truly I tell you, until heaven and earth pass away, not one letter,[a] not one stroke of a letter, will pass from the law until all is accomplished. ¹⁹Therefore, whoever breaks[b] one of the least of these commandments, and teaches others to do the same, will be called least in the kingdom of heaven; but whoever does them and teaches them will be called great in the kingdom of heaven. ²⁰For I tell you, unless your righteousness exceeds that of the scribes and Pharisees, you will never enter the kingdom of heaven.

Concerning Anger

21 "You have heard that it was said to those of ancient times, 'You shall not murder'; and 'whoever murders shall be liable to judgment.' ²²But I say to you that if you are angry with a brother or sister,[c] you will be liable to judgment; and if you insult[d] a brother or sister,[e] you will be liable to the council; and if you say, 'You fool,' you will be liable to the hell[f] of fire. ²³So when you are offering your gift at the altar, if you remember that your brother or sister[g] has something against you, ²⁴leave your gift there before the altar and go; first be reconciled to your brother or sister,[g] and then come and offer your gift. ²⁵Come to terms quickly with your accuser while you are on the way to court[h] with him, or your accuser may hand you over to the judge, and the judge to the guard, and you will be thrown into prison. ²⁶Truly I tell you, you will never get out until you have paid the last penny.

Concerning Adultery

27 "You have heard that it was said, 'You shall not commit adultery.' ²⁸But I say to you that everyone who looks at a woman with lust has already committed adultery with her in his heart. ²⁹If your right eye causes you to sin, tear it out and throw it away; it is better for you to lose one of your members than for your whole body to be thrown into hell.[f] ³⁰And if your right hand causes you to sin, cut it off and throw it away; it is better for you to lose one of your members than for your whole body to go into hell.[f]

Concerning Divorce

31 "It was also said, 'Whoever divorces his wife, let him give her a certificate of divorce.' ³²But I say to you that anyone who divorces his wife, except on the ground of unchastity, causes her to commit adultery; and whoever marries a divorced woman commits adultery.

Concerning Oaths

33 "Again, you have heard that it was said to those of ancient times, 'You shall not swear falsely, but carry out the vows you have made to the Lord.' ³⁴But I say to you, Do not swear at all, either by heaven, for it is the throne of God, ³⁵or by the earth, for it is his footstool, or by Jerusalem, for it is the city of the great King. ³⁶And do not swear by your head, for you cannot make one hair white or black. ³⁷Let your word be 'Yes, Yes' or 'No, No'; anything more than this comes from the evil one.[i]

---

a Gk *one iota*   b Or *annuls*   c Gk *a brother*; other ancient authorities add *without cause*   d Gk *say Raca to* (an obscure term of abuse)   e Gk *a brother*   f Gk *Gehenna*   g Gk *your brother*   h Gk lacks *to court*   i Or *evil*

A Positive Ethic

MATTHEW 5.48

One thing that set Jesus' teaching so radically apart from that of the religious leaders is that the religious leaders emphasized what people *shouldn't* do while Jesus stressed the positive nature of our calling—what we *should* do. It's not enough to refrain from killing our enemies; we are called to love them and pray for them. Think about your own shortcomings and how you might counteract each one with a positive virtue. For example, instead of being critical, learn to encourage; instead of hoarding wealth, learn to be generous, and so on. Ask God to help you go beyond merely desiring change to being transformed into his likeness.

See Meeting God in Service

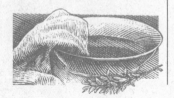

Concerning Retaliation

38 "You have heard that it was said, 'An eye for an eye and a tooth for a tooth.' 39But I say to you, Do not resist an evildoer. But if anyone strikes you on the right cheek, turn the other also; 40and if anyone wants to sue you and take your coat, give your cloak as well; 41and if anyone forces you to go one mile, go also the second mile. 42Give to everyone who begs from you, and do not refuse anyone who wants to borrow from you.

Love for Enemies

43 "You have heard that it was said, 'You shall love your neighbor and hate your enemy.' 44But I say to you, Love your enemies and pray for those who persecute you, 45so that you may be children of your Father in heaven; for he makes his sun rise on the evil and on the good, and sends rain on the righteous and on the unrighteous. 46For if you love those who love you, what reward do you have? Do not even the tax collectors do the same? 47And if you greet only your brothers and sisters,*a* what more are you doing than others? Do not even the Gentiles do the same? 48Be perfect, therefore, as your heavenly Father is perfect.

Concerning Almsgiving

6 "Beware of practicing your piety before others in order to be seen by them; for then you have no reward from your Father in heaven.

2 "So whenever you give alms, do not sound a trumpet before you, as the hypocrites do in the synagogues and in the streets, so that they may be praised by others. Truly I tell you, they have received their reward. 3But when you give alms, do not let your left hand know what your right hand is doing, 4so that your alms may be done in secret; and your Father who sees in secret will reward you.*b*

Concerning Prayer

5 "And whenever you pray, do not be like the hypocrites; for they love to stand and pray in the synagogues and at the street corners, so that they may be seen by others. Truly I tell you, they have received their reward. 6But whenever you pray, go into your room and shut the door and pray to your Father who is in secret; and your Father who sees in secret will reward you.*b*

7 "When you are praying, do not heap up empty phrases as the Gentiles do; for they think that they will be heard because of their many words. 8Do not be like them, for your Father knows what you need before you ask him.

9 "Pray then in this way:
　　Our Father in heaven,
　　　　hallowed be your name.
10　　Your kingdom come.
　　Your will be done,
　　　　on earth as it is in heaven.
11　　Give us this day our daily bread.*c*
12　　And forgive us our debts,
　　　　as we also have forgiven our debtors.

a Gk *your brothers*　*b* Other ancient authorities add *openly*　*c* Or *our bread for tomorrow*

13 And do not bring us to the time of trial,[a] but rescue us from the evil one.[b] 14For if you forgive others their trespasses, your heavenly Father will also forgive you; 15but if you do not forgive others, neither will your Father forgive your trespasses.

Concerning Fasting

16 "And whenever you fast, do not look dismal, like the hypocrites, for they disfigure their faces so as to show others that they are fasting. Truly I tell you, they have received their reward. 17But when you fast, put oil on your head and wash your face, 18so that your fasting may be seen not by others but by your Father who is in secret; and your Father who sees in secret will reward you.[c]

Concerning Treasures

19 "Do not store up for yourselves treasures on earth, where moth and rust[d] consume and where thieves break in and steal; 20but store up for yourselves treasures in heaven, where neither moth nor rust[d] consumes and where thieves do not break in and steal. 21For where your treasure is, there your heart will be also.

The Sound Eye

22 "The eye is the lamp of the body. So, if your eye is healthy, your whole body will be full of light; 23but if your eye is unhealthy, your whole body will be full of darkness. If then the light in you is darkness, how great is the darkness!

Serving Two Masters

24 "No one can serve two masters; for a slave will either hate the one and love the other, or be devoted to the one and despise the other. You cannot serve God and wealth.[e]

Do Not Worry

25 "Therefore I tell you, do not worry about your life, what you will eat or what you will drink,[f] or about your body, what you will wear. Is not life more than food, and the body more than clothing? 26Look at the birds of the air; they neither sow nor reap nor gather into barns, and yet your heavenly Father feeds them. Are you not of more value than they? 27And can any of you by worrying add a single hour to your span of life?[g] 28And why do you worry about clothing? Consider the lilies of the field, how they grow; they neither toil nor spin, 29yet I tell you, even Solomon in all his glory was not clothed like one of these. 30But if God so clothes the grass of the field, which is alive today and tomorrow is thrown into the oven, will he not much more clothe you—you of little faith? 31Therefore do not worry, saying, 'What will we eat?' or 'What will we drink?' or 'What will we wear?' 32For it is the Gentiles who strive for all these things; and indeed your heavenly Father

---

Praying Like Jesus

MATTHEW 6.9–13

Someone once approached a teacher and asked her how to cultivate a deeper prayer life. "Say the Lord's Prayer," she replied, "but take an hour to say it." Far from being a quick, rote form, this prayer Jesus taught us can become a life-giving pattern for rich communion. Take time now to slowly and meditatively pray the phrases of this prayer. Consider each clause an invitation to be specific and personal.

See Meeting God in Prayer

---

a Or *us into temptation*   b Or *from evil.* Other ancient authorities add, in some form, *For the kingdom and the power and the glory are yours forever. Amen.*   c Other ancient authorities add *openly*   d Gk *eating*
e Gk *mammon*   f Other ancient authorities lack *or what you will drink*
g Or *add one cubit to your height*

Cry of the Heart

MATTHEW 6.33

Righteousness doesn't come naturally or passively to us. We have to seek it. In fact it is something we're told to seek *first*, along with God's kingdom. What are your primary pursuits? What do you value most? What do you think about as you lie awake at night or drive down the road in the middle of the day? What aspect of your life occupies most of your energy? How does your life reflect your desire to seek God's kingdom and experience his righteousness?

See Meeting God in Everyday Life

knows that you need all these things. [33]But strive first for the kingdom of God[a] and his[b] righteousness, and all these things will be given to you as well.

34 "So do not worry about tomorrow, for tomorrow will bring worries of its own. Today's trouble is enough for today.

Judging Others

7 "Do not judge, so that you may not be judged. [2]For with the judgment you make you will be judged, and the measure you give will be the measure you get. [3]Why do you see the speck in your neighbor's[c] eye, but do not notice the log in your own eye? [4]Or how can you say to your neighbor,[d] 'Let me take the speck out of your eye,' while the log is in your own eye? [5]You hypocrite, first take the log out of your own eye, and then you will see clearly to take the speck out of your neighbor's[e] eye.

Profaning the Holy

6 "Do not give what is holy to dogs; and do not throw your pearls before swine, or they will trample them under foot and turn and maul you.

Ask, Search, Knock

7 "Ask, and it will be given you; search, and you will find; knock, and the door will be opened for you. [8]For everyone who asks receives, and everyone who searches finds, and for everyone who knocks, the door will be opened. [9]Is there anyone among you who, if your child asks for bread, will give a stone? [10]Or if the child asks for a fish, will give a snake? [11]If you then, who are evil, know how to give good gifts to your children, how much more will your Father in heaven give good things to those who ask him!

The Golden Rule

12 "In everything do to others as you would have them do to you; for this is the law and the prophets.

The Narrow Gate

13 "Enter through the narrow gate; for the gate is wide and the road is easy[e] that leads to destruction, and there are many who take it. [14]For the gate is narrow and the road is hard that leads to life, and there are few who find it.

A Tree and Its Fruit

15 "Beware of false prophets, who come to you in sheep's clothing but inwardly are ravenous wolves. [16]You will know them by their fruits. Are grapes gathered from thorns, or figs from thistles? [17]In the same way, every good tree bears good fruit, but the bad tree bears bad fruit. [18]A good tree cannot bear bad fruit, nor can a bad tree bear good fruit. [19]Every tree that does not bear good fruit is cut down and thrown into the fire. [20]Thus you will know them by their fruits.

a Other ancient authorities lack *of God*   *b* Or *its*   *c* Gk *brother's*
d Gk *brother*   *e* Other ancient authorities read *for the road is wide and easy*

Concerning Self-Deception

21 "Not everyone who says to me, 'Lord, Lord,' will enter the kingdom of heaven, but only the one who does the will of my Father in heaven. ²²On that day many will say to me, 'Lord, Lord, did we not prophesy in your name, and cast out demons in your name, and do many deeds of power in your name?' ²³Then I will declare to them, 'I never knew you; go away from me, you evildoers.'

Hearers and Doers

24 "Everyone then who hears these words of mine and acts on them will be like a wise man who built his house on rock. ²⁵The rain fell, the floods came, and the winds blew and beat on that house, but it did not fall, because it had been founded on rock. ²⁶And everyone who hears these words of mine and does not act on them will be like a foolish man who built his house on sand. ²⁷The rain fell, and the floods came, and the winds blew and beat against that house, and it fell—and great was its fall!"

28 Now when Jesus had finished saying these things, the crowds were astounded at his teaching, ²⁹for he taught them as one having authority, and not as their scribes.

Jesus Cleanses a Leper

8 When Jesus^a had come down from the mountain, great crowds followed him; ²and there was a leper^b who came to him and knelt before him, saying, "Lord, if you choose, you can make me clean." ³He stretched out his hand and touched him, saying, "I do choose. Be made clean!" Immediately his leprosy^b was cleansed. ⁴Then Jesus said to him, "See that you say nothing to anyone; but go, show yourself to the priest, and offer the gift that Moses commanded, as a testimony to them."

Jesus Heals a Centurion's Servant

5 When he entered Capernaum, a centurion came to him, appealing to him ⁶and saying, "Lord, my servant is lying at home paralyzed, in terrible distress." ⁷And he said to him, "I will come and cure him." ⁸The centurion answered, "Lord, I am not worthy to have you come under my roof; but only speak the word, and my servant will be healed. ⁹For I also am a man under authority, with soldiers under me; and I say to one, 'Go,' and he goes, and to another, 'Come,' and he comes, and to my slave, 'Do this,' and the slave does it." ¹⁰When Jesus heard him, he was amazed and said to those who followed him, "Truly I tell you, in no one^c in Israel have I found such faith. ¹¹I tell you, many will come from east and west and will eat with Abraham and Isaac and Jacob in the kingdom of heaven, ¹²while the heirs of the kingdom will be thrown into the outer darkness, where there will be weeping and gnashing of teeth." ¹³And to the centurion Jesus said, "Go; let it be done for you according to your faith." And the servant was healed in that hour.

---

a Gk *he*　　*b* The terms *leper* and *leprosy* can refer to several diseases
c Other ancient authorities read *Truly I tell you, not even*

The Solid Rock

MATTHEW 7.24–27

Picture two houses—one built on rock and one built on sand. You might recall news footage of beachfront houses tumbling into the sea as a storm surge rips the sand from their pilings. Or picture a lighthouse standing firm against pounding waves. Which of these pictures most resembles your life? Does it have characteristics of each? What storms of life are raging against you? In what way do you feel yourself tottering? How can you stand firm? What makes the difference? How can Jesus Christ become your sure foundation, your solid rock? You might crystallize this image by taking paper and colored pencils and drawing a representation of yourself as a house being battered by wind and waves.

See *Meeting God in Scripture*

Connecting Benefits

MATTHEW 8.14–17

"What is undoubtedly spoken about the impurities of the soul, Matthew applies to bodily diseases . . . [Matthew] states not merely the benefit conferred by Christ on those sick persons, but the purpose for which he healed their diseases . . . . He gave sight to the blind, in order to show that he is 'the light of the world.' He restored life to the dead, to prove that he is 'the resurrection and the life.' Similar observations might be made as to those who were lame or had palsy. Following out this analogy, let us connect those benefits, which Christ bestowed on men in the flesh, with the design which is stated to us by Matthew, that he was sent by the Father, to relieve us from all evil and miseries."

—JOHN CALVIN,
Institutes of the Christian Religion

Jesus Heals Many at Peter's House

14 When Jesus entered Peter's house, he saw his mother-in-law lying in bed with a fever; [15]he touched her hand, and the fever left her, and she got up and began to serve him. [16]That evening they brought to him many who were possessed with demons; and he cast out the spirits with a word, and cured all who were sick. [17]This was to fulfill what had been spoken through the prophet Isaiah, "He took our infirmities and bore our diseases."

Would-Be Followers of Jesus

18 Now when Jesus saw great crowds around him, he gave orders to go over to the other side. [19]A scribe then approached and said, "Teacher, I will follow you wherever you go." [20]And Jesus said to him, "Foxes have holes, and birds of the air have nests; but the Son of Man has nowhere to lay his head." [21]Another of his disciples said to him, "Lord, first let me go and bury my father." [22]But Jesus said to him, "Follow me, and let the dead bury their own dead."

Jesus Stills the Storm

23 And when he got into the boat, his disciples followed him. [24]A windstorm arose on the sea, so great that the boat was being swamped by the waves; but he was asleep. [25]And they went and woke him up, saying, "Lord, save us! We are perishing!" [26]And he said to them, "Why are you afraid, you of little faith?" Then he got up and rebuked the winds and the sea; and there was a dead calm. [27]They were amazed, saying, "What sort of man is this, that even the winds and the sea obey him?"

Jesus Heals the Gadarene Demoniacs

28 When he came to the other side, to the country of the Gadarenes,[a] two demoniacs coming out of the tombs met him. They were so fierce that no one could pass that way. [29]Suddenly they shouted, "What have you to do with us, Son of God? Have you come here to torment us before the time?" [30]Now a large herd of swine was feeding at some distance from them. [31]The demons begged him, "If you cast us out, send us into the herd of swine." [32]And he said to them, "Go!" So they came out and entered the swine; and suddenly, the whole herd rushed down the steep bank into the sea and perished in the water. [33]The swineherds ran off, and on going into the town, they told the whole story about what had happened to the demoniacs. [34]Then the whole town came out to meet Jesus; and when they saw him, they begged him to leave their neighborhood. 9 [1]And after getting into a boat he crossed the sea and came to his own town.

Jesus Heals a Paralytic

2 And just then some people were carrying a paralyzed man lying on a bed. When Jesus saw their faith, he said to the paralytic, "Take heart, son; your sins are forgiven." [3]Then some of the scribes said to themselves, "This man is blaspheming." [4]But Jesus, perceiving their thoughts,

a Other ancient authorities read *Gergesenes*; others, *Gerasenes*

said, "Why do you think evil in your hearts? [5]For which is easier, to say, 'Your sins are forgiven,' or to say, 'Stand up and walk'? [6]But so that you may know that the Son of Man has authority on earth to forgive sins"—he then said to the paralytic—"Stand up, take your bed and go to your home." [7]And he stood up and went to his home. [8]When the crowds saw it, they were filled with awe, and they glorified God, who had given such authority to human beings.

The Call of Matthew

9 As Jesus was walking along, he saw a man called Matthew sitting at the tax booth; and he said to him, "Follow me." And he got up and followed him.

10 And as he sat at dinner[a] in the house, many tax collectors and sinners came and were sitting[b] with him and his disciples. [11]When the Pharisees saw this, they said to his disciples, "Why does your teacher eat with tax collectors and sinners?" [12]But when he heard this, he said, "Those who are well have no need of a physician, but those who are sick. [13]Go and learn what this means, 'I desire mercy, not sacrifice.' For I have come to call not the righteous but sinners."

The Question about Fasting

14 Then the disciples of John came to him, saying, "Why do we and the Pharisees fast often,[c] but your disciples do not fast?" [15]And Jesus said to them, "The wedding guests cannot mourn as long as the bridegroom is with them, can they? The days will come when the bridegroom is taken away from them, and then they will fast. [16]No one sews a piece of unshrunk cloth on an old cloak, for the patch pulls away from the cloak, and a worse tear is made. [17]Neither is new wine put into old wineskins; otherwise, the skins burst, and the wine is spilled, and the skins are destroyed; but new wine is put into fresh wineskins, and so both are preserved."

A Girl Restored to Life and a Woman Healed

18 While he was saying these things to them, suddenly a leader of the synagogue[d] came in and knelt before him, saying, "My daughter has just died; but come and lay your hand on her, and she will live." [19]And Jesus got up and followed him, with his disciples. [20]Then suddenly a woman who had been suffering from hemorrhages for twelve years came up behind him and touched the fringe of his cloak, [21]for she said to herself, "If I only touch his cloak, I will be made well." [22]Jesus turned, and seeing her he said, "Take heart, daughter; your faith has made you well." And instantly the woman was made well. [23]When Jesus came to the leader's house and saw the flute players and the crowd making a commotion, [24]he said, "Go away; for the girl is not dead but sleeping." And they laughed at him. [25]But when the crowd had been put outside, he went in and took her by the hand, and the girl got up. [26]And the report of this spread throughout that district.

Follow Me

MATTHEW 9.9

The invitation Jesus gives to Matthew is remarkably blunt and open-ended: "Follow me." Jesus offers no explanation and no incentives such as, "Follow me, and I'll do this for you. Follow me, and we'll go here and there." This is a blind call, a two-word command that comes without any promise: "Follow me." If Jesus looked into your eyes today and said, "Follow me," how would you respond? What would you have to give up? What would be most difficult to give up? Place yourself in Matthew's shoes and try to imagine the turmoil he must have felt; consider whether you're willing to give such blind allegiance to your Lord.

See Meeting God in Scripture

---

a Gk *reclined*   *b* Gk *were reclining*   *c* Other ancient authorities lack *often*
d Gk lacks *of the synagogue*

Pouring Light Into Darkness

MATTHEW 9.35–38

As Jesus walks through Judea, he brings people back from the dead, heals others of long-standing diseases, frees some from demons and freely offers the wonderful news that God is at work in the world. He dismantles hell every step of the way, destroying it with the word and works of God.

Your daily passage through the streets to your office and your home may not be quite so dramatic; but how, realistically, can you help to bring God's kingdom? Start by taking notice of the people around you. Become aware of their needs for compassion and for God's love and truth. How can you bring God's light into dark situations as the Holy Spirit works through you?

See *Meeting God in Service*

Jesus Heals Two Blind Men

27 As Jesus went on from there, two blind men followed him, crying loudly, "Have mercy on us, Son of David!" ²⁸When he entered the house, the blind men came to him; and Jesus said to them, "Do you believe that I am able to do this?" They said to him, "Yes, Lord." ²⁹Then he touched their eyes and said, "According to your faith let it be done to you." ³⁰And their eyes were opened. Then Jesus sternly ordered them, "See that no one knows of this." ³¹But they went away and spread the news about him throughout that district.

Jesus Heals One Who Was Mute

32 After they had gone away, a demoniac who was mute was brought to him. ³³And when the demon had been cast out, the one who had been mute spoke; and the crowds were amazed and said, "Never has anything like this been seen in Israel." ³⁴But the Pharisees said, "By the ruler of the demons he casts out the demons."ᵃ

The Harvest Is Great, the Laborers Few

35 Then Jesus went about all the cities and villages, teaching in their synagogues, and proclaiming the good news of the kingdom, and curing every disease and every sickness. ³⁶When he saw the crowds, he had compassion for them, because they were harassed and helpless, like sheep without a shepherd. ³⁷Then he said to his disciples, "The harvest is plentiful, but the laborers are few; ³⁸therefore ask the Lord of the harvest to send out laborers into his harvest."

The Twelve Apostles

10 Then Jesusᵇ summoned his twelve disciples and gave them authority over unclean spirits, to cast them out, and to cure every disease and every sickness. ²These are the names of the twelve apostles: first, Simon, also known as Peter, and his brother Andrew; James son of Zebedee, and his brother John; ³Philip and Bartholomew; Thomas and Matthew the tax collector; James son of Alphaeus, and Thaddaeus;ᶜ ⁴Simon the Cananaean, and Judas Iscariot, the one who betrayed him.

The Mission of the Twelve

5 These twelve Jesus sent out with the following instructions: "Go nowhere among the Gentiles, and enter no town of the Samaritans, ⁶but go rather to the lost sheep of the house of Israel. ⁷As you go, proclaim the good news, 'The kingdom of heaven has come near.'ᵈ ⁸Cure the sick, raise the dead, cleanse the lepers,ᵉ cast out demons. You received without payment; give without payment. ⁹Take no gold, or silver, or copper in your belts, ¹⁰no bag for your journey, or two tunics, or sandals, or a staff; for laborers deserve their food. ¹¹Whatever town or village you enter, find out who in it is worthy, and stay there until you leave. ¹²As you enter the house, greet it. ¹³If the house is worthy, let your peace come upon it; but

---

a Other ancient authorities lack this verse   b Gk *he*   c Other ancient authorities read *Lebbaeus*, or *Lebbaeus called Thaddaeus*   d Or *is at hand*   e The terms *leper* and *leprosy* can refer to several diseases

if it is not worthy, let your peace return to you. ¹⁴If anyone will not welcome you or listen to your words, shake off the dust from your feet as you leave that house or town. ¹⁵Truly I tell you, it will be more tolerable for the land of Sodom and Gomorrah on the day of judgment than for that town.

Coming Persecutions

16 "See, I am sending you out like sheep into the midst of wolves; so be wise as serpents and innocent as doves. ¹⁷Beware of them, for they will hand you over to councils and flog you in their synagogues; ¹⁸and you will be dragged before governors and kings because of me, as a testimony to them and the Gentiles. ¹⁹When they hand you over, do not worry about how you are to speak or what you are to say; for what you are to say will be given to you at that time; ²⁰for it is not you who speak, but the Spirit of your Father speaking through you. ²¹Brother will betray brother to death, and a father his child, and children will rise against parents and have them put to death; ²²and you will be hated by all because of my name. But the one who endures to the end will be saved. ²³When they persecute you in one town, flee to the next; for truly I tell you, you will not have gone through all the towns of Israel before the Son of Man comes.

24 "A disciple is not above the teacher, nor a slave above the master; ²⁵it is enough for the discile to be like the teacher, and the slave like the master. If they have called the master of the house Beelzebul, how much more will they malign those of his household!

Whom to Fear

26 "So have no fear of them; for nothing is covered up that will not be uncovered, and nothing secret that will not become known. ²⁷What I say to you in the dark, tell in the light; and what you hear whispered, proclaim from the housetops. ²⁸Do not fear those who kill the body but cannot kill the soul; rather fear him who can destroy both soul and body in hell.ᵃ ²⁹Are not two sparrows sold for a penny? Yet not one of them will fall to the ground apart from your Father. ³⁰And even the hairs of your head are all counted. ³¹So do not be afraid; you are of more value than many sparrows.

32 "Everyone therefore who acknowledges me before others, I also will acknowledge before my Father in heaven; ³³but whoever denies me before others, I also will deny before my Father in heaven.

Not Peace, but a Sword

34 "Do not think that I have come to bring peace to the earth; I have not come to bring peace, but a sword.
³⁵ For I have come to set a man against his father,
and a daughter against her mother,
and a daughter-in-law against her mother-in-law;
³⁶ and one's foes will be members of one's own
household.
³⁷Whoever loves father or mother more than me is not

Where the Pain Comes From

MATTHEW 10.34

"It is true that there is something painful in beginning to practice piety, but this pain does not arise from the beginnings of piety within us, but from the impiety that is still there. If our senses were not opposed to penance and our corruption were not opposed to God's purity, there would be nothing painful about it. As for us, we only suffer in so far as our natural vice resists supernatural grace . . . The cruelest war that God can wage on people in this life is to leave them without the war he came to bring. 'I did not come to bring peace, but a sword.' "

—BLAISE PASCAL,
Pensees

What Do You Hear and See?

MATTHEW 11.4–6

Jesus invites John's followers to tell others what they see and hear. If you were one of them, what report would you give? What stories would you tell? What teaching would you remember? What events would lead you to fall down and worship Jesus? Is there anything about his life and teaching that would embarrass you? Is there anything that would make you want to rebel or turn away? Imagine Jesus looking into your eyes, saying, "Blessed is anyone who takes no offense at me." How will you respond?

See Meeting God in Scripture

worthy of me; and whoever loves son or daughter more than me is not worthy of me; [38]and whoever does not take up the cross and follow me is not worthy of me. [39]Those who find their life will lose it, and those who lose their life for my sake will find it.

Rewards

40 "Whoever welcomes you welcomes me, and whoever welcomes me welcomes the one who sent me. [41]Whoever welcomes a prophet in the name of a prophet will receive a prophet's reward; and whoever welcomes a righteous person in the name of a righteous person will receive the reward of the righteous; [42]and whoever gives even a cup of cold water to one of these little ones in the name of a disciple—truly I tell you, none of these will lose their reward."

11 Now when Jesus had finished instructing his twelve disciples, he went on from there to teach and proclaim his message in their cities.

Messengers from John the Baptist

2 When John heard in prison what the Messiah[a] was doing, he sent word by his[b] disciples [3]and said to him, "Are you the one who is to come, or are we to wait for another?" [4]Jesus answered them, "Go and tell John what you hear and see: [5]the blind receive their sight, the lame walk, the lepers[c] are cleansed, the deaf hear, the dead are raised, and the poor have good news brought to them. [6]And blessed is anyone who takes no offense at me."

Jesus Praises John the Baptist

7 As they went away, Jesus began to speak to the crowds about John: "What did you go out into the wilderness to look at? A reed shaken by the wind? [8]What then did you go out to see? Someone[d] dressed in soft robes? Look, those who wear soft robes are in royal palaces. [9]What then did you go out to see? A prophet?[e] Yes, I tell you, and more than a prophet. [10]This is the one about whom it is written,

'See, I am sending my messenger ahead of you,
who will prepare your way before you.'

[11]Truly I tell you, among those born of women no one has arisen greater than John the Baptist; yet the least in the kingdom of heaven is greater than he. [12]From the days of John the Baptist until now the kingdom of heaven has suffered violence,[f] and the violent take it by force. [13]For all the prophets and the law prophesied until John came; [14]and if you are willing to accept it, he is Elijah who is to come. [15]Let anyone with ears[g] listen!

16 "But to what will I compare this generation? It is like children sitting in the marketplaces and calling to one another,

---

a Or *the Christ*   b Other ancient authorities read *two of his*   c The terms *leper* and *leprosy* can refer to several diseases   d Or *Why then did you go out? To see someone*   e Other ancient authorities read *Why then did you go out? To see a prophet?*   f Or *has been coming violently*   g Other ancient authorities add *to hear*

17 'We played the flute for you, and you did not dance;
    we wailed, and you did not mourn.'
18 For John came neither eating nor drinking, and they say, 'He has a demon'; 19 the Son of Man came eating and drinking, and they say, 'Look, a glutton and a drunkard, a friend of tax collectors and sinners!' Yet wisdom is vindicated by her deeds."[a]

Woes to Unrepentant Cities

20 Then he began to reproach the cities in which most of his deeds of power had been done, because they did not repent. 21 "Woe to you, Chorazin! Woe to you, Bethsaida! For if the deeds of power done in you had been done in Tyre and Sidon, they would have repented long ago in sackcloth and ashes. 22 But I tell you, on the day of judgment it will be more tolerable for Tyre and Sidon than for you. 23 And you, Capernaum,
    will you be exalted to heaven?
        No, you will be brought down to Hades.
For if the deeds of power done in you had been done in Sodom, it would have remained until this day. 24 But I tell you that on the day of judgment it will be more tolerable for the land of Sodom than for you."

Jesus Thanks His Father

25 At that time Jesus said, "I thank[b] you, Father, Lord of heaven and earth, because you have hidden these things from the wise and the intelligent and have revealed them to infants; 26 yes, Father, for such was your gracious will.[c] 27 All things have been handed over to me by my Father; and no one knows the Son except the Father, and no one knows the Father except the Son and anyone to whom the Son chooses to reveal him.

28 "Come to me, all you that are weary and are carrying heavy burdens, and I will give you rest. 29 Take my yoke upon you, and learn from me; for I am gentle and humble in heart, and you will find rest for your souls. 30 For my yoke is easy, and my burden is light."

Plucking Grain on the Sabbath

12 At that time Jesus went through the grainfields on the sabbath; his disciples were hungry, and they began to pluck heads of grain and to eat. 2 When the Pharisees saw it, they said to him, "Look, your disciples are doing what is not lawful to do on the sabbath." 3 He said to them, "Have you not read what David did when he and his companions were hungry? 4 He entered the house of God and ate the bread of the Presence, which it was not lawful for him or his companions to eat, but only for the priests. 5 Or have you not read in the law that on the sabbath the priests in the temple break the sabbath and yet are guiltless? 6 I tell you, something greater than the temple is here. 7 But if you had known what this means, 'I desire mercy and not sacrifice,' you would not have condemned the guiltless. 8 For the Son of Man is lord of the sabbath."

The Son Revealing the Father

MATTHEW 11.28–30

Imagine yourself bent low under a heavy burden. What burden are you carrying? What is weighing you down? Jesus is saying to you, "Come to me, all you that are weary and are carrying heavy burdens, and I will give you rest." Imagine yourself joining a stream of people making their way toward Jesus. When you stand before him, he gently lifts the burden from your back. He encourages you to stand straight, and you feel the weariness leaving your body. "Take my yoke," he says. On your shoulder he places a stole or shawl, a sign of your special ministry in his name. And he hands you a certificate, your own commission from him. What does it say? Write out a copy to keep and to refer to regularly.

See Meeting God in Scripture

---

a Other ancient authorities read *children*   b Or *praise*   c Or *for so it was well-pleasing in your sight*

The World's Enmity Toward God

MATTHEW 12.14

The religious leaders join in a conspiracy to destroy Jesus. They misunderstand and condemn everything he does. He heals people and the Pharisees reproach him for violating the sabbath. He casts out a demon and his opponents accuse him of using demonic power. Those of us who have come to know Jesus as Savior, Friend and Lord may sometimes forget that the world is in enmity toward Jesus Christ. We pursue God in a world hostile to his name. We pray to a God whom other people ignore or disdain. How does the world's enmity affect your own relationship with God? How does it stifle your witness? How does the world's attitude toward God affect your behavior at home? At work? In your neighborhood? Pray for the courage to take a stand for God even in the midst of hostility.

See Meeting God in Everyday Life

The Man with a Withered Hand

9 He left that place and entered their synagogue; ¹⁰a man was there with a withered hand, and they asked him, "Is it lawful to cure on the sabbath?" so that they might accuse him. ¹¹He said to them, "Suppose one of you has only one sheep and it falls into a pit on the sabbath; will you not one lay hold of it and lift it out? ¹²How much more valuable is a human being than a sheep! So it is lawful to do good on the sabbath." ¹³Then he said to the man, "Stretch out your hand." He stretched it out, and it was restored, as sound as the other. ¹⁴But the Pharisees went out and conspired against him, how to destroy him.

God's Chosen Servant

15 When Jesus became aware of this, he departed. Many crowds*a* followed him, and he cured all of them, ¹⁶and he ordered them not to make him known. ¹⁷This was to fulfill what had been spoken through the prophet Isaiah:

18   "Here is my servant, whom I have chosen,
    my beloved, with whom my soul is well pleased.
  I will put my Spirit upon him,
    and he will proclaim justice to the Gentiles.
19   He will not wrangle or cry aloud,
    nor will anyone hear his voice in the streets.
20   He will not break a bruised reed
    or quench a smoldering wick
  until he brings justice to victory.
21   And in his name the Gentiles will hope."

Jesus and Beelzebul

22 Then they brought to him a demoniac who was blind and mute; and he cured him, so that the one who had been mute could speak and see. ²³All the crowds were amazed and said, "Can this be the Son of David?" ²⁴But when the Pharisees heard it, they said, "It is only by Beelzebul, the ruler of the demons, that this fellow casts out the demons." ²⁵He knew what they were thinking and said to them, "Every kingdom divided against itself is laid waste, and no city or house divided against itself will stand. ²⁶If Satan casts out Satan, he is divided against himself; how then will his kingdom stand? ²⁷If I cast out demons by Beelzebul, by whom do your own exorcists*b* cast them out? Therefore they will be your judges. ²⁸But if it is by the Spirit of God that I cast out demons, then the kingdom of God has come to you. ²⁹Or how can one enter a strong man's house and plunder his property, without first tying up the strong man? Then indeed the house can be plundered. ³⁰Whoever is not with me is against me, and whoever does not gather with me scatters. ³¹Therefore I tell you, people will be forgiven for every sin and blasphemy, but blasphemy against the Spirit will not be forgiven. ³²Whoever speaks a word against the Son of Man will be forgiven, but whoever speaks against the Holy Spirit will not be forgiven, either in this age or in the age to come.

a Other ancient authorities lack *crowds*   *b* Gk *sons*

A Tree and Its Fruit

33 "Either make the tree good, and its fruit good; or make the tree bad, and its fruit bad; for the tree is known by its fruit. 34You brood of vipers! How can you speak good things, when you are evil? For out of the abundance of the heart the mouth speaks. 35The good person brings good things out of a good treasure, and the evil person brings evil things out of an evil treasure. 36I tell you, on the day of judgment you will have to give an account for every careless word you utter; 37for by your words you will be justified, and by your words you will be condemned."

The Sign of Jonah

38 Then some of the scribes and Pharisees said to him, "Teacher, we wish to see a sign from you." 39But he answered them, "An evil and adulterous generation asks for a sign, but no sign will be given to it except the sign of the prophet Jonah. 40For just as Jonah was three days and three nights in the belly of the sea monster, so for three days and three nights the Son of Man will be in the heart of the earth. 41The people of Nineveh will rise up at the judgment with this generation and condemn it, because they repented at the proclamation of Jonah, and see, something greater than Jonah is here! 42The queen of the South will rise up at the judgment with this generation and condemn it, because she came from the ends of the earth to listen to the wisdom of Solomon, and see, something greater than Solomon is here!

The Return of the Unclean Spirit

43 "When the unclean spirit has gone out of a person, it wanders through waterless regions looking for a resting place, but it finds none. 44Then it says, 'I will return to my house from which I came.' When it comes, it finds it empty, swept, and put in order. 45Then it goes and brings along seven other spirits more evil than itself, and they enter and live there; and the last state of that person is worse than the first. So will it be also with this evil generation."

The True Kindred of Jesus

46 While he was still speaking to the crowds, his mother and his brothers were standing outside, wanting to speak to him. 47Someone told him, "Look, your mother and your brothers are standing outside, wanting to speak to you."[a] 48But to the one who had told him this, Jesus[b] replied, "Who is my mother, and who are my brothers?" 49And pointing to his disciples, he said, "Here are my mother and my brothers! 50For whoever does the will of my Father in heaven is my brother and sister and mother."

The Parable of the Sower

13 That same day Jesus went out of the house and sat beside the sea. 2Such great crowds gathered around him that he got into a boat and sat there, while the whole crowd stood on the beach. 3And he told them many

---

The Good Soil

MATTHEW 13.1–9

If weather allows, read this parable outside—preferably near a garden—and consider the application of this parable to your own life. Consider the seeds you have planted. What will give your seeds the best chance to grow? What are the troubles that keep the seeds from growing? What has been carried off without ever growing at all? Which plants have been choked by the thorns of materialism or busyness? What has started well, but never taken root? What has flourished? What will it take to enrich the soil of your heart so that it is fertile? Draw the picture that Jesus describes, and take time to creatively depict each element.

See Meeting God in Scripture

---

a Other ancient authorities lack verse 47   b Gk he

1289

A Balanced Spirituality

MATTHEW 13.23

Jesus says that the mark of good soil is that it produces a good crop: a hundred times what was sown, sixty times, or thirty times, but always something. Many Christians sense the tension between *being* and *doing* in the Christian life—between the contemplative life of prayer and the active life of performing good deeds. Yet it's not a matter of choosing one or the other, but of balancing the two.

Which side of the spectrum do you most readily gravitate toward? Are you "running on empty," without a foundation of prayer? Or are you so focused on the inner life that you're neglecting your social responsibility? How can you discern the unique balance of prayer and action to which God is calling you? How can you develop the element that is deficient in your life? What do you need to do to come to your own balance?

See Meeting God in Everyday Life

things in parables, saying: "Listen! A sower went out to sow. ⁴And as he sowed, some seeds fell on the path, and the birds came and ate them up. ⁵Other seeds fell on rocky ground, where they did not have much soil, and they sprang up quickly, since they had no depth of soil. ⁶But when the sun rose, they were scorched; and since they had no root, they withered away. ⁷Other seeds fell among thorns, and the thorns grew up and choked them. ⁸Other seeds fell on good soil and brought forth grain, some a hundredfold, some sixty, some thirty. ⁹Let anyone with ears^a listen!"

The Purpose of the Parables

10 Then the disciples came and asked him, "Why do you speak to them in parables?" ¹¹He answered, "To you it has been given to know the secrets^b of the kingdom of heaven, but to them it has not been given. ¹²For to those who have, more will be given, and they will have an abundance; but from those who have nothing, even what they have will be taken away. ¹³The reason I speak to them in parables is that 'seeing they do not perceive, and hearing they do not listen, nor do they understand.' ¹⁴With them indeed is fulfilled the prophecy of Isaiah that says:

'You will indeed listen, but never understand,
    and you will indeed look, but never perceive.
¹⁵ For this people's heart has grown dull,
        and their ears are hard of hearing,
            and they have shut their eyes;
        so that they might not look with their eyes,
    and listen with their ears,
    and understand with their heart and turn—
        and I would heal them.'

¹⁶But blessed are your eyes, for they see, and your ears, for they hear. ¹⁷Truly I tell you, many prophets and righteous people longed to see what you see, but did not see it, and to hear what you hear, but did not hear it.

The Parable of the Sower Explained

18 "Hear then the parable of the sower. ¹⁹When anyone hears the word of the kingdom and does not understand it, the evil one comes and snatches away what is sown in the heart; this is what was sown on the path. ²⁰As for what was sown on rocky ground, this is the one who hears the word and immediately receives it with joy; ²¹yet such a person has no root, but endures only for a while, and when trouble or persecution arises on account of the word, that person immediately falls away.^c ²²As for what was sown among thorns, this is the one who hears the word, but the cares of the world and the lure of wealth choke the word, and it yields nothing. ²³But as for what was sown on good soil, this is the one who hears the word and understands it, who indeed bears fruit and yields, in one case a hundredfold, in another sixty, and in another thirty."

The Parable of Weeds among the Wheat

24 He put before them another parable: "The kingdom

a Other ancient authorities add *to hear*   *b* Or *mysteries*   *c* Gk *stumbles* of heaven may be compared to someone who sowed good seed in his field; ²⁵but while everybody was asleep, an enemy came and sowed weeds among the wheat, and then went away. ²⁶So when the plants came up and bore grain, then the weeds appeared as well. ²⁷And the slaves of the householder came and said to him, 'Master, did you not sow good seed in your field? Where, then, did these weeds come from?' ²⁸He answered, 'An enemy has done this.' The slaves said to him, 'Then do you want us to go and gather them?' ²⁹But he replied, 'No; for in gathering the weeds you would uproot the wheat along with them. ³⁰Let both of them grow together until the harvest; and at harvest time I will tell the reapers, Collect the weeds first and bind them in bundles to be burned, but gather the wheat into my barn.' "

The Parable of the Mustard Seed

31 He put before them another parable: "The kingdom of heaven is like a mustard seed that someone took and sowed in his field; ³²it is the smallest of all the seeds, but when it has grown it is the greatest of shrubs and becomes a tree, so that the birds of the air come and make nests in its branches."

The Parable of the Yeast

33 He told them another parable: "The kingdom of heaven is like yeast that a woman took and mixed in with*ᵃ* three measures of flour until all of it was leavened."

The Use of Parables

34 Jesus told the crowds all these things in parables; without a parable he told them nothing. ³⁵This was to fulfill what had been spoken through the prophet:*ᵇ*
  "I will open my mouth to speak in parables;
    I will proclaim what has been hidden from the
      foundation of the world."*ᶜ*

Jesus Explains the Parable of the Weeds

36 Then he left the crowds and went into the house. And his disciples approached him, saying, "Explain to us the parable of the weeds of the field." ³⁷He answered, "The one who sows the good seed is the Son of Man; ³⁸the field is the world, and the good seed are the children of the kingdom; the weeds are the children of the evil one, ³⁹and the enemy who sowed them is the devil; the harvest is the end of the age, and the reapers are angels. ⁴⁰Just as the weeds are collected and burned up with fire, so will it be at the end of the age. ⁴¹The Son of Man will send his angels, and they will collect out of his kingdom all causes of sin and all evildoers, ⁴²and they will throw them into the furnace of fire, where there will be weeping and gnashing of teeth. ⁴³Then the righteous will shine like the sun in the kingdom of their Father. Let anyone with ears*ᵈ* listen!

Three Parables

44 "The kingdom of heaven is like treasure hidden in a

A Vintage Find

MATTHEW 13.44–46

An antique table, a vintage bottle of wine, or a rare first-edition book is priced according to the market demand—whatever the buyer is willing to pay for it. Jesus asserts that the kingdom of heaven is so valuable that people would gladly give all they have to possess it. Imagine God standing before you with a gift—the kingdom of heaven—just for you. What will it mean for you if you receive it? But wait, your hands are full! You cannot receive God's gift until you put down what you are holding. What is it? Are you willing to put it down to receive God's gift?

See Meeting God in Scripture

---

a Gk *hid in*   *b* Other ancient authorities read *the prophet Isaiah*   *c* Other ancient authorities lack *of the world*   *d* Other ancient authorities add *to hear*

Looking Up to Heaven

MATTHEW 14.18–21

The Christian life is not a matter of doing great things *for* God. That's religion. Christianity is doing great things *with* God. That's the life of Jesus Christ in us. How can you adopt a spirit of "[looking] up to heaven" as you go through your day? Some Christian traditions have created symbols for this purpose (a crucifix, a cross worn around the neck, a painting of a Biblical scene, and so on). If you were to create a symbol that would remind you of your dependence on God, what would it be? Where would you put it? What are some other things you could do to maintain an attitude of consistently "[looking] up to heaven"?

See Meeting God in Everyday Life

field, which someone found and hid; then in his joy he goes and sells all that he has and buys that field.

45 "Again, the kingdom of heaven is like a merchant in search of fine pearls; ⁴⁶on finding one pearl of great value, he went and sold all that he had and bought it.

47 "Again, the kingdom of heaven is like a net that was thrown into the sea and caught fish of every kind; ⁴⁸when it was full, they drew it ashore, sat down, and put the good into baskets but threw out the bad. ⁴⁹So it will be at the end of the age. The angels will come out and separate the evil from the righteous ⁵⁰and throw them into the furnace of fire, where there will be weeping and gnashing of teeth.

Treasures New and Old

51 "Have you understood all this?" They answered, "Yes." ⁵²And he said to them, "Therefore every scribe who has been trained for the kingdom of heaven is like the master of a household who brings out of his treasure what is new and what is old." ⁵³When Jesus had finished these parables, he left that place.

The Rejection of Jesus at Nazareth

54 He came to his hometown and began to teach the people*ᵃ* in their synagogue, so that they were astounded and said, "Where did this man get this wisdom and these deeds of power? ⁵⁵Is not this the carpenter's son? Is not his mother called Mary? And are not his brothers James and Joseph and Simon and Judas? ⁵⁶And are not all his sisters with us? Where then did this man get all this?" ⁵⁷And they took offense at him. But Jesus said to them, "Prophets are not without honor except in their own country and in their own house." ⁵⁸And he did not do many deeds of power there, because of their unbelief.

The Death of John the Baptist

14 At that time Herod the ruler*ᵇ* heard reports about Jesus; ²and he said to his servants, "This is John the Baptist; he has been raised from the dead, and for this reason these powers are at work in him." ³For Herod had arrested John, bound him, and put him in prison on account of Herodias, his brother Philip's wife,*ᶜ* ⁴because John had been telling him, "It is not lawful for you to have her." ⁵Though Herod*ᵈ* wanted to put him to death, he feared the crowd, because they regarded him as a prophet. ⁶But when Herod's birthday came, the daughter of Herodias danced before the company, and she pleased Herod ⁷so much that he promised on oath to grant her whatever she might ask. ⁸Prompted by her mother, she said, "Give me the head of John the Baptist here on a platter." ⁹The king was grieved, yet out of regard for his oaths and for the guests, he commanded it to be given; ¹⁰he sent and had John beheaded in the prison. ¹¹The head was brought on a platter and given to the girl, who brought it to her mother. ¹²His disciples came and took the body and buried it; then they went and told Jesus.

a Gk *them* *b* Gk *tetrarch* *c* Other ancient authorities read *his brother's wife* *d* Gk *he*

Feeding the Five Thousand

13 Now when Jesus heard this, he withdrew from there in a boat to a deserted place by himself. But when the crowds heard it, they followed him on foot from the towns. [14]When he went ashore, he saw a great crowd; and he had compassion for them and cured their sick. [15]When it was evening, the disciples came to him and said, "This is a deserted place, and the hour is now late; send the crowds away so that they may go into the villages and buy food for themselves." [16]Jesus said to them, "They need not go away; you give them something to eat." [17]They replied, "We have nothing here but five loaves and two fish." [18]And he said, "Bring them here to me." [19]Then he ordered the crowds to sit down on the grass. Taking the five loaves and the two fish, he looked up to heaven, and blessed and broke the loaves, and gave them to the disciples, and the disciples gave them to the crowds. [20]And all ate and were filled; and they took up what was left over of the broken pieces, twelve baskets full. [21]And those who ate were about five thousand men, besides women and children.

Jesus Walks on the Water

22 Immediately he made the disciples get into the boat and go on ahead to the other side, while he dismissed the crowds. [23]And after he had dismissed the crowds, he went up the mountain by himself to pray. When evening came, he was there alone, [24]but by this time the boat, battered by the waves, was far from the land,[a] for the wind was against them. [25]And early in the morning he came walking toward them on the sea. [26]But when the disciples saw him walking on the sea, they were terrified, saying, "It is a ghost!" And they cried out in fear. [27]But immediately Jesus spoke to them and said, "Take heart, it is I; do not be afraid."

28 Peter answered him, "Lord, if it is you, command me to come to you on the water." [29]He said, "Come." So Peter got out of the boat, started walking on the water, and came toward Jesus. [30]But when he noticed the strong wind,[b] he became frightened, and beginning to sink, he cried out, "Lord, save me!" [31]Jesus immediately reached out his hand and caught him, saying to him, "You of little faith, why did you doubt?" [32]When they got into the boat, the wind ceased. [33]And those in the boat worshiped him, saying, "Truly you are the Son of God."

Jesus Heals the Sick in Gennesaret

34 When they had crossed over, they came to land at Gennesaret. [35]After the people of that place recognized him, they sent word throughout the region and brought all who were sick to him, [36]and begged him that they might touch even the fringe of his cloak; and all who touched it were healed.

The Tradition of the Elders

15 Then Pharisees and scribes came to Jesus from Jerusalem and said, [2]"Why do your disciples break

a Other ancient authorities read was out on the sea   b Other ancient authorities read the wind

Full Reliance

MATTHEW 14.22–33

"The wind was actually boisterous, the waves were actually high, but Peter did not see them at first. He did not reckon with them, he simply recognized his Lord and stepped out in recognition of him, and walked on the water. Then he began to reckon with the actual things, and down he went instantly. Why could not our Lord have enabled him to walk at the bottom of the waves as well as on the top of them? . . . We step right out on God over some things, then self-consideration enters in and down we go . . . Immediately you look at [circumstances and] you are overwhelmed, you cannot recognize Jesus, and the rebuke comes: 'Wherefore didst thou doubt?' Let actual circumstances be what they may, keep recognizing Jesus, maintain complete reliance on him."

—OSWALD CHAMBERS,
My Utmost for His Highest

Loving the Whole Person

MATTHEW 15.29–37

The physical, practical nature of Jesus' ministry is remarkable. Not only does he teach deep truths, but he also heals people who are sick or disabled and takes time to feed a crowd of hungry people.

In what ways can you minister to people—caring for the "whole person"—as Jesus did? To whom might you reach out today? While you may or may not have the gift of healing, what gifts do you have that you can use to relieve hardship and suffering? Do you share in Jesus' compassion? If not, what might be standing in your way?

See Meeting God in Service

the tradition of the elders? For they do not wash their hands before they eat." ³He answered them, "And why do you break the commandment of God for the sake of your tradition? ⁴For God said,ᵃ 'Honor your father and your mother,' and, 'Whoever speaks evil of father or mother must surely die.' ⁵But you say that whoever tells father or mother, 'Whatever support you might have had from me is given to God,'ᵇ then that person need not honor the father.ᶜ ⁶So, for the sake of your tradition, you make void the wordᵈ of God. ⁷You hypocrites! Isaiah prophesied rightly about you when he said:

8 'This people honors me with their lips,
but their hearts are far from me;
9 in vain do they worship me,
teaching human precepts as doctrines.' "

Things That Defile

10 Then he called the crowd to him and said to them, "Listen and understand: ¹¹it is not what goes into the mouth that defiles a person, but it is what comes out of the mouth that defiles." ¹²Then the disciples approached and said to him, "Do you know that the Pharisees took offense when they heard what you said?" ¹³He answered, "Every plant that my heavenly Father has not planted will be uprooted. ¹⁴Let them alone; they are blind guides of the blind.ᵉ And if one blind person guides another, both will fall into a pit." ¹⁵But Peter said to him, "Explain this parable to us." ¹⁶Then he said, "Are you also still without understanding? ¹⁷Do you not see that whatever goes into the mouth enters the stomach, and goes out into the sewer? ¹⁸But what comes out of the mouth proceeds from the heart, and this is what defiles. ¹⁹For out of the heart come evil intentions, murder, adultery, fornication, theft, false witness, slander. ²⁰These are what defile a person, but to eat with unwashed hands does not defile."

The Canaanite Woman's Faith

21 Jesus left that place and went away to the district of Tyre and Sidon. ²²Just then a Canaanite woman from that region came out and started shouting, "Have mercy on me, Lord, Son of David; my daughter is tormented by a demon." ²³But he did not answer her at all. And his disciples came and urged him, saying, "Send her away, for she keeps shouting after us." ²⁴He answered, "I was sent only to the lost sheep of the house of Israel." ²⁵But she came and knelt before him, saying, "Lord, help me." ²⁶He answered, "It is not fair to take the children's food and throw it to the dogs." ²⁷She said, "Yes, Lord, yet even the dogs eat the crumbs that fall from their masters' table." ²⁸Then Jesus answered her, "Woman, great is your faith! Let it be done for you as you wish." And her daughter was healed instantly.

Jesus Cures Many People

29 After Jesus had left that place, he passed along the

---

a Other ancient authorities read *commanded, saying*   b Or *is an offering*
c Other ancient authorities add *or the mother*   d Other ancient authorities
read *law*; others, *commandment*   e Other ancient authorities lack *of the blind*

Sea of Galilee, and he went up the mountain, where he sat down. ³⁰Great crowds came to him, bringing with them the lame, the maimed, the blind, the mute, and many others. They put them at his feet, and he cured them, ³¹so that the crowd was amazed when they saw the mute speaking, the maimed whole, the lame walking, and the blind seeing. And they praised the God of Israel.

Feeding the Four Thousand

32 Then Jesus called his disciples to him and said, "I have compassion for the crowd, because they have been with me now for three days and have nothing to eat; and I do not want to send them away hungry, for they might faint on the way." ³³The disciples said to him, "Where are we to get enough bread in the desert to feed so great a crowd?" ³⁴Jesus asked them, "How many loaves have you?" They said, "Seven, and a few small fish." ³⁵Then ordering the crowd to sit down on the ground, ³⁶he took the seven loaves and the fish; and after giving thanks he broke them and gave them to the disciples, and the disciples gave them to the crowds. ³⁷And all of them ate and were filled; and they took up the broken pieces left over, seven baskets full. ³⁸Those who had eaten were four thousand men, besides women and children. ³⁹After sending away the crowds, he got into the boat and went to the region of Magadan.ᵃ

The Demand for a Sign

16 The Pharisees and Sadducees came, and to test Jesusᵇ they asked him to show them a sign from heaven. ²He answered them, "When it is evening, you say, 'It will be fair weather, for the sky is red.' ³And in the morning, 'It will be stormy today, for the sky is red and threatening.' You know how to interpret the appearance of the sky, but you cannot interpret the signs of the times.ᶜ ⁴An evil and adulterous generation asks for a sign, but no sign will be given to it except the sign of Jonah." Then he left them and went away.

The Yeast of the Pharisees and Sadducees

5 When the disciples reached the other side, they had forgotten to bring any bread. ⁶Jesus said to them, "Watch out, and beware of the yeast of the Pharisees and Sadducees." ⁷They said to one another, "It is because we have brought no bread." ⁸And becoming aware of it, Jesus said, "You of little faith, why are you talking about having no bread? ⁹Do you still not perceive? Do you not remember the five loaves for the five thousand, and how many baskets you gathered? ¹⁰Or the seven loaves for the four thousand, and how many baskets you gathered? ¹¹How could you fail to perceive that I was not speaking about bread? Beware of the yeast of the Pharisees and Sadducees!" ¹²Then they understood that he had not told them to beware of the yeast of bread, but of the teaching of the Pharisees and Sadducees.

What Really Matters

MATTHEW 16.1–6

When Jesus chastises the religious leaders of his day for failing to read "the signs of the times," he's referring to their preoccupation with rules and their lack of spiritual insight. The Pharisees and Sadducees, obsessed with arguing the finer points of the law, missed seeing the very embodiment of the law, Jesus Christ himself.

What issues preoccupy you today? Do you tend to focus on central issues or peripheral ones—the big picture or the details? How does getting caught up in rules distort your faith or disrupt community life? Make a list of the actual rules you live by, not just the rules you *think* should govern your life. Do they reflect Jesus' priorities? Seek God's guidance as you reflect on them.

See Meeting God in Everyday Life

---

a Other ancient authorities read *Magdala* or *Magdalan*   *b* Gk *him*
c Other ancient authorities lack ²*When it is . . . of the times*

A Chance to Grow

MATTHEW 16.24–26

"Individuality is the husk of the personal life. Individuality is all elbows, it separates and isolates . . . but individuality must go in order that the personal life may come out and be brought into fellowship with God . . . God wants to bring you into union with himself, but unless you are willing to give up your right to deny yourself he cannot. 'Let him deny himself'—deny his independent right to himself, then the real life has a chance to grow."

—OSWALD CHAMBERS,
My Utmost for His Highest

Peter's Declaration about Jesus

13 Now when Jesus came into the district of Caesarea Philippi, he asked his disciples, "Who do people say that the Son of Man is?" ¹⁴And they said, "Some say John the Baptist, but others Elijah, and still others Jeremiah or one of the prophets." ¹⁵He said to them, "But who do you say that I am?" ¹⁶Simon Peter answered, "You are the Messiah,ᵃ the Son of the living God." ¹⁷And Jesus answered him, "Blessed are you, Simon son of Jonah! For flesh and blood has not revealed this to you, but my Father in heaven. ¹⁸And I tell you, you are Peter,ᵇ and on this rockᶜ I will build my church, and the gates of Hades will not prevail against it. ¹⁹I will give you the keys of the kingdom of heaven, and whatever you bind on earth will be bound in heaven, and whatever you loose on earth will be loosed in heaven." ²⁰Then he sternly ordered the disciples not to tell anyone that he wasᵈ the Messiah.ᵃ

Jesus Foretells His Death and Resurrection

21 From that time on, Jesus began to show his disciples that he must go to Jerusalem and undergo great suffering at the hands of the elders and chief priests and scribes, and be killed, and on the third day be raised. ²²And Peter took him aside and began to rebuke him, saying, "God forbid it, Lord! This must never happen to you." ²³But he turned and said to Peter, "Get behind me, Satan! You are a stumbling block to me; for you are setting your mind not on divine things but on human things."

The Cross and Self-Denial

24 Then Jesus told his disciples, "If any want to become my followers, let them deny themselves and take up their cross and follow me. ²⁵For those who want to save their life will lose it, and those who lose their life for my sake will find it. ²⁶For what will it profit them if they gain the whole world but forfeit their life? Or what will they give in return for their life?

27 "For the Son of Man is to come with his angels in the glory of his Father, and then he will repay everyone for what has been done. ²⁸Truly I tell you, there are some standing here who will not taste death before they see the Son of Man coming in his kingdom."

The Transfiguration

17 Six days later, Jesus took with him Peter and James and his brother John and led them up a high mountain, by themselves. ²And he was transfigured before them, and his face shone like the sun, and his clothes became dazzling white. ³Suddenly there appeared to them Moses and Elijah, talking with him. ⁴Then Peter said to Jesus, "Lord, it is good for us to be here; if you wish, Iᵉ will make three dwellingsᶠ here, one for you, one for Moses, and one for Elijah." ⁵While he was still speaking, suddenly a bright cloud overshadowed them, and from the cloud a voice said, "This is my Son, the Beloved;ᵍ with him I am

a Or *the Christ*   b Gk *Petros*   c Gk *petra*   d Other ancient authorities add *Jesus*   e Other ancient authorities read *we*   f Or *tents*   g Or *my beloved Son*

well pleased; listen to him!" [6]When the disciples heard this, they fell to the ground and were overcome by fear. [7]But Jesus came and touched them, saying, "Get up and do not be afraid." [8]And when they looked up, they saw no one except Jesus himself alone.

9 As they were coming down the mountain, Jesus ordered them, "Tell no one about the vision until after the Son of Man has been raised from the dead." [10]And the disciples asked him, "Why, then, do the scribes say that Elijah must come first?" [11]He replied, "Elijah is indeed coming and will restore all things; [12]but I tell you that Elijah has already come, and they did not recognize him, but they did to him whatever they pleased. So also the Son of Man is about to suffer at their hands." [13]Then the disciples understood that he was speaking to them about John the Baptist.

Jesus Cures a Boy with a Demon

14 When they came to the crowd, a man came to him, knelt before him, [15]and said, "Lord, have mercy on my son, for he is an epileptic and he suffers terribly; he often falls into the fire and often into the water. [16]And I brought him to your disciples, but they could not cure him." [17]Jesus answered, "You faithless and perverse generation, how much longer must I be with you? How much longer must I put up with you? Bring him here to me." [18]And Jesus rebuked the demon,[a] and it[b] came out of him, and the boy was cured instantly. [19]Then the disciples came to Jesus privately and said, "Why could we not cast it out?" [20]He said to them, "Because of your little faith. For truly I tell you, if you have faith the size of a[c] mustard seed, you will say to this mountain, 'Move from here to there,' and it will move; and nothing will be impossible for you."[d]

Jesus Again Foretells His Death and Resurrection

22 As they were gathering[e] in Galilee, Jesus said to them, "The Son of Man is going to be betrayed into human hands, [23]and they will kill him, and on the third day he will be raised." And they were greatly distressed.

Jesus and the Temple Tax

24 When they reached Capernaum, the collectors of the temple tax[f] came to Peter and said, "Does your teacher not pay the temple tax?"[f] [25]He said, "Yes, he does." And when he came home, Jesus spoke of it first, asking, "What do you think, Simon? From whom do kings of the earth take toll or tribute? From their children or from others?" [26]When Peter[g] said, "From others," Jesus said to him, "Then the children are free. [27]However, so that we do not give offense to them, go to the sea and cast a hook; take the first fish that comes up; and when you open its mouth, you will find a coin;[h] take that and give it to them for you and me."

A Child's Heart

MATTHEW 18.1–5

Spend time with your children, visit a playground or volunteer to assist in a church school class. Prayerfully watch the children interact and play. What quality in children does Jesus prize so highly? How can you humble yourself like a child? What does it mean to "welcome" a child in Jesus' name? Why do you think that Jesus never said, "Unless you become like an adult . . ."? Why did he choose children to be our example? How can you become childlike without becoming childish? Pray slowly and thoughtfully through Psalm 131.

---

a Gk it or him   b Gk the demon   c Gk faith as a grain of   d Other ancient authorities add verse 21, But this kind does not come out except by prayer and fasting   e Other ancient authorities read living   f Gk didrachma   g Gk he   h Gk stater; the stater was worth two didrachmas

The Incredible Freedom of Forgiveness

MATTHEW 18.21–34

As Christians we are to "reflect" God's Spirit so that others will see and know God. In this passage Jesus asks us to lavish the same forgiveness on others that God has so graciously given to us. Take a few moments to put yourself in the first debtor's position: How does it feel to be forgiven such a large sum? Imagine the weight removed from your shoulders as the entire debt is canceled. Now think of those to whom you can offer the same forgiveness that you have received from God.

See Meeting God in Prayer

True Greatness

18 At that time the disciples came to Jesus and asked, "Who is the greatest in the kingdom of heaven?" ²He called a child, whom he put among them, ³and said, "Truly I tell you, unless you change and become like children, you will never enter the kingdom of heaven. ⁴Whoever becomes humble like this child is the greatest in the kingdom of heaven. ⁵Whoever welcomes one such child in my name welcomes me.

Temptations to Sin

6 "If any of you put a stumbling block before one of these little ones who believe in me, it would be better for you if a great millstone were fastened around your neck and you were drowned in the depth of the sea. ⁷Woe to the world because of stumbling blocks! Occasions for stumbling are bound to come, but woe to the one by whom the stumbling block comes!

8 "If your hand or your foot causes you to stumble, cut it off and throw it away; it is better for you to enter life maimed or lame than to have two hands or two feet and to be thrown into the eternal fire. ⁹And if your eye causes you to stumble, tear it out and throw it away; it is better for you to enter life with one eye than to have two eyes and to be thrown into the hell*ᵃ* of fire.

The Parable of the Lost Sheep

10 "Take care that you do not despise one of these little ones; for, I tell you, in heaven their angels continually see the face of my Father in heaven.*ᵇ* ¹²What do you think? If a shepherd has a hundred sheep, and one of them has gone astray, does he not leave the ninety-nine on the mountains and go in search of the one that went astray? ¹³And if he finds it, truly I tell you, he rejoices over it more than over the ninety-nine that never went astray. ¹⁴So it is not the will of your*ᶜ* Father in heaven that one of these little ones should be lost.

Reproving Another Who Sins

15 "If another member of the church*ᵈ* sins against you,*ᵉ* go and point out the fault when the two of you are alone. If the member listens to you, you have regained that one.*ᶠ* ¹⁶But if you are not listened to, take one or two others along with you, so that every word may be confirmed by the evidence of two or three witnesses. ¹⁷If the member refuses to listen to them, tell it to the church; and if the offender refuses to listen even to the church, let such a one be to you as a Gentile and a tax collector. ¹⁸Truly I tell you, whatever you bind on earth will be bound in heaven, and whatever you loose on earth will be loosed in heaven. ¹⁹Again, truly I tell you, if two of you agree on earth about anything you ask, it will be done for you by my Father in heaven. ²⁰For where two or three are gathered in my name, I am there among them."

a Gk *Gehenna*   *b* Other ancient authorities add verse 11, *For the Son of Man came to save the lost*   *c* Other ancient authorities read *my*   *d* Gk *If your brother*   *e* Other ancient authorities lack *against you*   *f* Gk *the brother*

Forgiveness

21 Then Peter came and said to him, "Lord, if another member of the church*a* sins against me, how often should I forgive? As many as seven times?" ²²Jesus said to him, "Not seven times, but, I tell you, seventy-seven*b* times.

The Parable of the Unforgiving Servant

23 "For this reason the kingdom of heaven may be compared to a king who wished to settle accounts with his slaves. ²⁴When he began the reckoning, one who owed him ten thousand talents*c* was brought to him; ²⁵and, as he could not pay, his lord ordered him to be sold, together with his wife and children and all his possessions, and payment to be made. ²⁶So the slave fell on his knees before him, saying, 'Have patience with me, and I will pay you everything.' ²⁷And out of pity for him, the lord of that slave released him and forgave him the debt. ²⁸But that same slave, as he went out, came upon one of his fellow slaves who owed him a hundred denarii;*d* and seizing him by the throat, he said, 'Pay what you owe.' ²⁹Then his fellow slave fell down and pleaded with him, 'Have patience with me, and I will pay you.' ³⁰But he refused; then he went and threw him into prison until he would pay the debt. ³¹When his fellow slaves saw what had happened, they were greatly distressed, and they went and reported to their lord all that had taken place. ³²Then his lord summoned him and said to him, 'You wicked slave! I forgave you all that debt because you pleaded with me. ³³Should you not have had mercy on your fellow slave, as I had mercy on you?' ³⁴And in anger his lord handed him over to be tortured until he would pay his entire debt. ³⁵So my heavenly Father will also do to every one of you, if you do not forgive your brother or sister*e* from your heart."

Teaching about Divorce

19 When Jesus had finished saying these things, he left Galilee and went to the region of Judea beyond the Jordan. ²Large crowds followed him, and he cured them there.

3 Some Pharisees came to him, and to test him they asked, "Is it lawful for a man to divorce his wife for any cause?" ⁴He answered, "Have you not read that the one who made them at the beginning 'made them male and female,' ⁵and said, 'For this reason a man shall leave his father and mother and be joined to his wife, and the two shall become one flesh'? ⁶So they are no longer two, but one flesh. Therefore what God has joined together, let no one separate." ⁷They said to him, "Why then did Moses command us to give a certificate of dismissal and to divorce her?" ⁸He said to them, "It was because you were so hard-hearted that Moses allowed you to divorce your wives, but from the beginning it was not so. ⁹And I say to you, whoever divorces his wife, except for unchastity, and marries another commits adultery."*f*

Strong Hearts, Soft Hearts

MATTHEW 19.1–12

Moses had allowed divorce primarily to protect the vulnerable women who were put away without due cause. But Jesus goes to the heart of the matter.

After Jesus' words on marriage and divorce, we may conclude that marriage is not for the hardhearted, or as the disciples conclude, for the fainthearted (see v.10). Marriage, often the most difficult of human relationships, requires grace-filled, soft hearts to succeed, and even more important, to honor the Creator who made men and women "male and female." Make your own marriage—or those of friends or family members—a subject of your prayers today. Pray that God will give both partners strong, soft hearts for each other and a generous measure of divine grace.

See Meeting God in Community

---

a Gk *if my brother*   *b* Or *seventy times seven*   *c* A talent was worth more than fifteen years' wages of a laborer   *d* The denarius was the usual day's wage for a laborer   *e* Gk *brother*   *f* Other ancient authorities read *except on the ground of unchastity, causes her to commit adultery*; others add at the end of the verse *and he who marries a divorced woman commits adultery*

The Same Reward

MATTHEW 20.1–16

How would you feel if you were one of the first workers to be hired? Imagine your excitement when you see the latecomers receiving a generous reward, and then your frustration when you receive the same amount. Now place yourself in the position of the latecomers: How do you feel receiving your reward and then hearing the early arrivals complain about how you've been treated? Next put yourself in the position of the landowner: What goes through your mind as some of the workers protest your policies? With which group do you most identify? What can you learn from the reaction of the other workers? What might you be missing by focusing only on your own perspective?

See Meeting God in Scripture

10 His disciples said to him, "If such is the case of a man with his wife, it is better not to marry." [11]But he said to them, "Not everyone can accept this teaching, but only those to whom it is given. [12]For there are eunuchs who have been so from birth, and there are eunuchs who have been made eunuchs by others, and there are eunuchs who have made themselves eunuchs for the sake of the kingdom of heaven. Let anyone accept this who can."

Jesus Blesses Little Children

13 Then little children were being brought to him in order that he might lay his hands on them and pray. The disciples spoke sternly to those who brought them; [14]but Jesus said, "Let the little children come to me, and do not stop them; for it is to such as these that the kingdom of heaven belongs." [15]And he laid his hands on them and went on his way.

The Rich Young Man

16 Then someone came to him and said, "Teacher, what good deed must I do to have eternal life?" [17]And he said to him, "Why do you ask me about what is good? There is only one who is good. If you wish to enter into life, keep the commandments." [18]He said to him, "Which ones?" And Jesus said, "You shall not murder; You shall not commit adultery; You shall not steal; You shall not bear false witness; [19]Honor your father and mother; also, You shall love your neighbor as yourself." [20]The young man said to him, "I have kept all these;[a] what do I still lack?" [21]Jesus said to him, "If you wish to be perfect, go, sell your possessions, and give the money[b] to the poor, and you will have treasure in heaven; then come, follow me." [22]When the young man heard this word, he went away grieving, for he had many possessions.

23 Then Jesus said to his disciples, "Truly I tell you, it will be hard for a rich person to enter the kingdom of heaven. [24]Again I tell you, it is easier for a camel to go through the eye of a needle than for someone who is rich to enter the kingdom of God." [25]When the disciples heard this, they were greatly astounded and said, "Then who can be saved?" [26]But Jesus looked at them and said, "For mortals it is impossible, but for God all things are possible."

27 Then Peter said in reply, "Look, we have left everything and followed you. What then will we have?" [28]Jesus said to them, "Truly I tell you, at the renewal of all things, when the Son of Man is seated on the throne of his glory, you who have followed me will also sit on twelve thrones, judging the twelve tribes of Israel. [29]And everyone who has left houses or brothers or sisters or father or mother or children or fields, for my name's sake, will receive a hundredfold,[c] and will inherit eternal life. [30]But many who are first will be last, and the last will be first.

The Laborers in the Vineyard

20 "For the kingdom of heaven is like a landowner who went out early in the morning to hire laborers for his vineyard. [2]After agreeing with the laborers for the

a Other ancient authorities add from my youth   b Gk lacks the money
c Other ancient authorities read manifold

usual daily wage,*a* he sent them into his vineyard. ³When he went out about nine o'clock, he saw others standing idle in the marketplace; ⁴and he said to them, 'You also go into the vineyard, and I will pay you whatever is right.' So they went. ⁵When he went out again about noon and about three o'clock, he did the same. ⁶And about five o'clock he went out and found others standing around; and he said to them, 'Why are you standing here idle all day?' ⁷They said to him, 'Because no one has hired us.' He said to them, 'You also go into the vineyard.' ⁸When evening came, the owner of the vineyard said to his manager, 'Call the laborers and give them their pay, beginning with the last and then going to the first.' ⁹When those hired about five o'clock came, each of them received the usual daily wage.*a* ¹⁰Now when the first came, they thought they would receive more; but each of them also received the usual daily wage.*a* ¹¹And when they received it, they grumbled against the landowner, ¹²saying, 'These last worked only one hour, and you have made them equal to us who have borne the burden of the day and the scorching heat.' ¹³But he replied to one of them, 'Friend, I am doing you no wrong; did you not agree with me for the usual daily wage?*a* ¹⁴Take what belongs to you and go; I choose to give to this last the same as I give to you. ¹⁵Am I not allowed to do what I choose with what belongs to me? Or are you envious because I am generous?'*b* ¹⁶So the last will be first, and the first will be last."*c*

A Third Time Jesus Foretells His Death and Resurrection

17 While Jesus was going up to Jerusalem, he took the twelve disciples aside by themselves, and said to them on the way, ¹⁸"See, we are going up to Jerusalem, and the Son of Man will be handed over to the chief priests and scribes, and they will condemn him to death; ¹⁹then they will hand him over to the Gentiles to be mocked and flogged and crucified; and on the third day he will be raised."

The Request of the Mother of James and John

20 Then the mother of the sons of Zebedee came to him with her sons, and kneeling before him, she asked a favor of him. ²¹And he said to her, "What do you want?" She said to him, "Declare that these two sons of mine will sit, one at your right hand and one at your left, in your kingdom." ²²But Jesus answered, "You do not know what you are asking. Are you able to drink the cup that I am about to drink?"*d* They said to him, "We are able." ²³He said to them, "You will indeed drink my cup, but to sit at my right hand and at my left, this is not mine to grant, but it is for those for whom it has been prepared by my Father."

24 When the ten heard it, they were angry with the two brothers. ²⁵But Jesus called them to him and said, "You know that the rulers of the Gentiles lord it over them, and their great ones are tyrants over them. ²⁶It will not be so among you; but whoever wishes to be great among you

The Quest for Greatness

MATTHEW 20.20–28

The human quest for greatness and power has caused untold meaningless bloodshed. But ironically God's call to servant-hood caused the most meaning-ful bloodshed of all—Jesus' own sacrifice on the cross.

If you want to know the true aim and direction of your life, ask yourself these questions: Where do I expend my greatest effort and energy? Is it to dominate others and gain control? Or is it to love and serve them? What is more important to me—taking charge, or meeting needs? Do I prefer to act in secret or do I have a burning desire to be recognized? What would Jesus say about your answers?

See Meeting God in Service

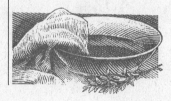

a Gk *a denarius*   b Gk *is your eye evil because I am good?*   c Other ancient authorities add *for many are called but few are chosen*   d Other ancient authorities add *or to be baptized with the baptism that I am baptized with?*

1301

Palm Sunday

MATTHEW 21.1–11

Imagine yourself in the crowd as Jesus rides into Jerusalem. You are in the street near the city gate—a street packed with people. The shouts and cries around you are deafening. The smell of unwashed humanity mingles with the aroma of the smoke blowing down from the temple sacrifices. "What is happening?" you ask some of the others in the crowd. Why are they there? Why are they waving branches and shouting? What do you feel as Jesus rides by? What do you want to do?

See Meeting God in Scripture

must be your servant, ²⁷and whoever wishes to be first among you must be your slave; ²⁸just as the Son of Man came not to be served but to serve, and to give his life a ransom for many."

Jesus Heals Two Blind Men

29 As they were leaving Jericho, a large crowd followed him. ³⁰There were two blind men sitting by the roadside. When they heard that Jesus was passing by, they shouted, "Lord,ᵃ have mercy on us, Son of David!" ³¹The crowd sternly ordered them to be quiet; but they shouted even more loudly, "Have mercy on us, Lord, Son of David!" ³²Jesus stood still and called them, saying, "What do you want me to do for you?" ³³They said to him, "Lord, let our eyes be opened." ³⁴Moved with compassion, Jesus touched their eyes. Immediately they regained their sight and followed him.

Jesus' Triumphal Entry into Jerusalem

21 When they had come near Jerusalem and had reached Bethphage, at the Mount of Olives, Jesus sent two disciples, ²saying to them, "Go into the village ahead of you, and immediately you will find a donkey tied, and a colt with her; untie them and bring them to me. ³If anyone says anything to you, just say this, 'The Lord needs them.' And he will send them immediately.ᵇ" ⁴This took place to fulfill what had been spoken through the prophet, saying,

⁵   "Tell the daughter of Zion,
     Look, your king is coming to you,
         humble, and mounted on a donkey,
             and on a colt, the foal of a donkey."

⁶The disciples went and did as Jesus had directed them; ⁷they brought the donkey and the colt, and put their cloaks on them, and he sat on them. ⁸A very large crowdᶜ spread their cloaks on the road, and others cut branches from the trees and spread them on the road. ⁹The crowds that went ahead of him and that followed were shouting,

    "Hosanna to the Son of David!
    Blessed is the one who comes in the name of the
        Lord!
    Hosanna in the highest heaven!"

¹⁰When he entered Jerusalem, the whole city was in turmoil, asking, "Who is this?" ¹¹The crowds were saying, "This is the prophet Jesus from Nazareth in Galilee."

Jesus Cleanses the Temple

12 Then Jesus entered the templeᵈ and drove out all who were selling and buying in the temple, and he overturned the tables of the money changers and the seats of those who sold doves. ¹³He said to them, "It is written,
    'My house shall be called a house of prayer';
        but you are making it a den of robbers."

14 The blind and the lame came to him in the temple, and he cured them. ¹⁵But when the chief priests and the scribes saw the amazing things that he did, and heardᵉ

ᵃ Other ancient authorities lack *Lord*   ᵇ Or *'The Lord needs them and will send them back immediately.'*   ᶜ Or *Most of the crowd*   ᵈ Other ancient authorities add *of God*   ᵉ Gk lacks *heard*

the children crying out in the temple, "Hosanna to the Son of David," they became angry [16]and said to him, "Do you hear what these are saying?" Jesus said to them, "Yes; have you never read,

'Out of the mouths of infants and nursing babies
    you have prepared praise for yourself'?"

[17]He left them, went out of the city to Bethany, and spent the night there.

Jesus Curses the Fig Tree

18 In the morning, when he returned to the city, he was hungry. [19]And seeing a fig tree by the side of the road, he went to it and found nothing at all on it but leaves. Then he said to it, "May no fruit ever come from you again!" And the fig tree withered at once. [20]When the disciples saw it, they were amazed, saying, "How did the fig tree wither at once?" [21]Jesus answered them, "Truly I tell you, if you have faith and do not doubt, not only will you do what has been done to the fig tree, but even if you say to this mountain, 'Be lifted up and thrown into the sea,' it will be done. [22]Whatever you ask for in prayer with faith, you will receive."

The Authority of Jesus Questioned

23 When he entered the temple, the chief priests and the elders of the people came to him as he was teaching, and said, "By what authority are you doing these things, and who gave you this authority?" [24]Jesus said to them, "I will also ask you one question; if you tell me the answer, then I will also tell you by what authority I do these things. [25]Did the baptism of John come from heaven, or was it of human origin?" And they argued with one another, "If we say, 'From heaven,' he will say to us, 'Why then did you not believe him?' [26]But if we say, 'Of human origin,' we are afraid of the crowd; for all regard John as a prophet." [27]So they answered Jesus, "We do not know." And he said to them, "Neither will I tell you by what authority I am doing these things.

The Parable of the Two Sons

28 "What do you think? A man had two sons; he went to the first and said, 'Son, go and work in the vineyard today.' [29]He answered, 'I will not'; but later he changed his mind and went. [30]The father[a] went to the second and said the same; and he answered, 'I go, sir'; but he did not go. [31]Which of the two did the will of his father?" They said, "The first." Jesus said to them, "Truly I tell you, the tax collectors and the prostitutes are going into the kingdom of God ahead of you. [32]For John came to you in the way of righteousness and you did not believe him, but the tax collectors and the prostitutes believed him; and even after you saw it, you did not change your minds and believe him.

The Parable of the Wicked Tenants

33 "Listen to another parable. There was a landowner who planted a vineyard, put a fence around it, dug a wine

---

People-Pleasing Paralysis

MATTHEW 21.23–27

The chief priests and elders are caught—and paralyzed—by their desire to please the crowd. If they answer Jesus' question one way, they will bring shame on themselves; if they answer it the other, they may lose the people's favor. The moral vacuum created by people-pleasing destroys integrity—and reduces leadership to the emptiness of a popularity contest. Have you been in situations where you felt caught between your principles and your desire to be popular? What did you do? Where is the next conflict most likely to come from? How can you be prepared to respond with integrity?

See Meeting God in Everyday Life

---

a Gk *He*

A Generous Invitation

MATTHEW 22.1–14

What astonishing excuses people will give for declining the invitation to God's kingdom! Imagine God sending that invitation to you. God is throwing a party—and you are invited. But the party is occurring right now, and the invitation requires an immediate response. You'd really like to go. What is holding you back? What must you get finished before you go? What dream of your own are you pursuing? Do God's repeated calls nag at your conscience? Do they make you angry or resentful? Now imagine you see others responding—people who are homeless, young children, people who are very old. Put aside whatever you have been doing and join them. As you arrive at the party, God embraces you and says, "I'm so glad you've come!"

See Meeting God in Scripture

press in it, and built a watchtower. Then he leased it to tenants and went to another country. ³⁴When the harvest time had come, he sent his slaves to the tenants to collect his produce. ³⁵But the tenants seized his slaves and beat one, killed another, and stoned another. ³⁶Again he sent other slaves, more than the first; and they treated them in the same way. ³⁷Finally he sent his son to them, saying, 'They will respect my son.' ³⁸But when the tenants saw the son, they said to themselves, 'This is the heir; come, let us kill him and get his inheritance.' ³⁹So they seized him, threw him out of the vineyard, and killed him. ⁴⁰Now when the owner of the vineyard comes, what will he do to those tenants?" ⁴¹They said to him, "He will put those wretches to a miserable death, and lease the vineyard to other tenants who will give him the produce at the harvest time."

42 Jesus said to them, "Have you never read in the scriptures:

'The stone that the builders rejected
  has become the cornerstone;ᵃ
this was the Lord's doing,
  and it is amazing in our eyes'?

⁴³Therefore I tell you, the kingdom of God will be taken away from you and given to a people that produces the fruits of the kingdom.ᵇ ⁴⁴The one who falls on this stone will be broken to pieces; and it will crush anyone on whom it falls."ᶜ

45 When the chief priests and the Pharisees heard his parables, they realized that he was speaking about them. ⁴⁶They wanted to arrest him, but they feared the crowds, because they regarded him as a prophet.

The Parable of the Wedding Banquet

22 Once more Jesus spoke to them in parables, saying: ²"The kingdom of heaven may be compared to a king who gave a wedding banquet for his son. ³He sent his slaves to call those who had been invited to the wedding banquet, but they would not come. ⁴Again he sent other slaves, saying, 'Tell those who have been invited: Look, I have prepared my dinner, my oxen and my fat calves have been slaughtered, and everything is ready; come to the wedding banquet.' ⁵But they made light of it and went away, one to his farm, another to his business, ⁶while the rest seized his slaves, mistreated them, and killed them. ⁷The king was enraged. He sent his troops, destroyed those murderers, and burned their city. ⁸Then he said to his slaves, 'The wedding is ready, but those invited were not worthy. ⁹Go therefore into the main streets, and invite everyone you find to the wedding banquet.' ¹⁰Those slaves went out into the streets and gathered all whom they found, both good and bad; so the wedding hall was filled with guests.

11 "But when the king came in to see the guests, he noticed a man there who was not wearing a wedding robe, ¹²and he said to him, 'Friend, how did you get in here without a wedding robe?' And he was speechless. ¹³Then the king said to the attendants, 'Bind him hand and foot,

a Or *keystone*   *b* Gk *the fruits of it*   *c* Other ancient authorities lack verse 44

and throw him into the outer darkness, where there will be weeping and gnashing of teeth.' [14]For many are called, but few are chosen."

The Question about Paying Taxes

15 Then the Pharisees went and plotted to entrap him in what he said. [16]So they sent their disciples to him, along with the Herodians, saying, "Teacher, we know that you are sincere, and teach the way of God in accordance with truth, and show deference to no one; for you do not regard people with partiality. [17]Tell us, then, what you think. Is it lawful to pay taxes to the emperor, or not?" [18]But Jesus, aware of their malice, said, "Why are you putting me to the test, you hypocrites? [19]Show me the coin used for the tax." And they brought him a denarius. [20]Then he said to them, "Whose head is this, and whose title?" [21]They answered, "The emperor's." Then he said to them, "Give therefore to the emperor the things that are the emperor's, and to God the things that are God's." [22]When they heard this, they were amazed; and they left him and went away.

The Question about the Resurrection

23 The same day some Sadducees came to him, saying there is no resurrection;[a] and they asked him a question, saying, [24]"Teacher, Moses said, 'If a man dies childless, his brother shall marry the widow, and raise up children for his brother.' [25]Now there were seven brothers among us; the first married, and died childless, leaving the widow to his brother. [26]The second did the same, so also the third, down to the seventh. [27]Last of all, the woman herself died. [28]In the resurrection, then, whose wife of the seven will she be? For all of them had married her."

29 Jesus answered them, "You are wrong, because you know neither the scriptures nor the power of God. [30]For in the resurrection they neither marry nor are given in marriage, but are like angels[b] in heaven. [31]And as for the resurrection of the dead, have you not read what was said to you by God, [32]'I am the God of Abraham, the God of Isaac, and the God of Jacob'? He is God not of the dead, but of the living." [33]And when the crowd heard it, they were astounded at his teaching.

The Greatest Commandment

34 When the Pharisees heard that he had silenced the Sadducees, they gathered together, [35]and one of them, a lawyer, asked him a question to test him. [36]"Teacher, which commandment in the law is the greatest?" [37]He said to him, " 'You shall love the Lord your God with all your heart, and with all your soul, and with all your mind.' [38]This is the greatest and first commandment. [39]And a second is like it: 'You shall love your neighbor as yourself.' [40]On these two commandments hang all the law and the prophets."

The Question about David's Son

41 Now while the Pharisees were gathered together, Jesus asked them this question: [42]"What do you think of

To Cling to God

MATTHEW 22.34–40

"In order that we may know how to love ourselves, an end has been established for us to which we are to refer all our action, so that we may attain to bliss. For if we love ourselves, our one wish is to achieve blessedness. Now this end is to cling to God. Thus, if we know how to love ourselves, the commandment to love our neighbor bids us to do all we can to bring our neighbor to love God. This is the worship of God; this is true religion; this is the right kind of devotion; this is the service which is owed to God alone."

—AUGUSTINE,
The City of God

---

a Other ancient authorities read *who say that there is no resurrection*
b Other ancient authorities add *of God*

Whitewashed Tombs

MATTHEW 23.27–28

By using the phrase "white-washed tombs" to describe the religious leaders, Jesus evokes one of the most powerful images in literature. On the outside the religious leaders' holiness looks impressive; inside there is nothing but death and decay. Think of other instances where appearances belie reality (a tree with a rotten core, a car with no engine, a crooked judge). Ask God to help you see how your inner life contradicts your outer life. Where do they agree? How might God work to build more "holy integrity" within you?

See Meeting God in Prayer

the Messiah?[a] Whose son is he?" They said to him, "The son of David." [43]He said to them, "How is it then that David by the Spirit[b] calls him Lord, saying,

[44] 'The Lord said to my Lord,
"Sit at my right hand,
until I put your enemies under your feet" '?

[45]If David thus calls him Lord, how can he be his son?" [46]No one was able to give him an answer, nor from that day did anyone dare to ask him any more questions.

Jesus Denounces Scribes and Pharisees

23 Then Jesus said to the crowds and to his disciples, [2]"The scribes and the Pharisees sit on Moses' seat; [3]therefore, do whatever they teach you and follow it; but do not do as they do, for they do not practice what they teach. [4]They tie up heavy burdens, hard to bear,[c] and lay them on the shoulders of others; but they themselves are unwilling to lift a finger to move them. [5]They do all their deeds to be seen by others; for they make their phylacteries broad and their fringes long. [6]They love to have the place of honor at banquets and the best seats in the synagogues, [7]and to be greeted with respect in the marketplaces, and to have people call them rabbi. [8]But you are not to be called rabbi, for you have one teacher, and you are all students.[d] [9]And call no one your father on earth, for you have one Father—the one in heaven. [10]Nor are you to be called instructors, for you have one instructor, the Messiah.[e] [11]The greatest among you will be your servant. [12]All who exalt themselves will be humbled, and all who humble themselves will be exalted.

13 "But woe to you, scribes and Pharisees, hypocrites! For you lock people out of the kingdom of heaven. For you do not go in yourselves, and when others are going in, you stop them.[f] [15]Woe to you, scribes and Pharisees, hypocrites! For you cross sea and land to make a single convert, and you make the new convert twice as much a child of hell[g] as yourselves.

16 "Woe to you, blind guides, who say, 'Whoever swears by the sanctuary is bound by nothing, but whoever swears by the gold of the sanctuary is bound by the oath.' [17]You blind fools! For which is greater, the gold or the sanctuary that has made the gold sacred? [18]And you say, 'Whoever swears by the altar is bound by nothing, but whoever swears by the gift that is on the altar is bound by the oath.' [19]How blind you are! For which is greater, the gift or the altar that makes the gift sacred? [20]So whoever swears by the altar, swears by it and by everything on it; [21]and whoever swears by the sanctuary, swears by it and by the one who dwells in it; [22]and whoever swears by heaven, swears by the throne of God and by the one who is seated upon it.

23 "Woe to you, scribes and Pharisees, hypocrites! For you tithe mint, dill, and cummin, and have neglected the weightier matters of the law: justice and mercy and faith.

a Or *Christ*   b Gk *in spirit*   c Other ancient authorities lack *hard to bear*   d Gk *brothers*   e Or *the Christ*   f Other authorities add here (or after verse 12) verse 14, *Woe to you, scribes and Pharisees, hypocrites! For you devour widows' houses and for the sake of appearance you make long prayers; therefore you will receive the greater condemnation*   g Gk *Gehenna*

It is these you ought to have practiced without neglecting the others. ²⁴You blind guides! You strain out a gnat but swallow a camel!

25 "Woe to you, scribes and Pharisees, hypocrites! For you clean the outside of the cup and of the plate, but inside they are full of greed and self-indulgence. ²⁶You blind Pharisee! First clean the inside of the cup,ᵃ so that the outside also may become clean.

27 "Woe to you, scribes and Pharisees, hypocrites! For you are like whitewashed tombs, which on the outside look beautiful, but inside they are full of the bones of the dead and of all kinds of filth. ²⁸So you also on the outside look righteous to others, but inside you are full of hypocrisy and lawlessness.

29 "Woe to you, scribes and Pharisees, hypocrites! For you build the tombs of the prophets and decorate the graves of the righteous, ³⁰and you say, 'If we had lived in the days of our ancestors, we would not have taken part with them in shedding the blood of the prophets.' ³¹Thus you testify against yourselves that you are descendants of those who murdered the prophets. ³²Fill up, then, the measure of your ancestors. ³³You snakes, you brood of vipers! How can you escape being sentenced to hell?ᵇ ³⁴Therefore I send you prophets, sages, and scribes, some of whom you will kill and crucify, and some you will flog in your synagogues and pursue from town to town, ³⁵so that upon you may come all the righteous blood shed on earth, from the blood of righteous Abel to the blood of Zechariah son of Barachiah, whom you murdered between the sanctuary and the altar. ³⁶Truly I tell you, all this will come upon this generation.

The Lament over Jerusalem

37 "Jerusalem, Jerusalem, the city that kills the prophets and stones those who are sent to it! How often have I desired to gather your children together as a hen gathers her brood under her wings, and you were not willing! ³⁸See, your house is left to you, desolate.ᶜ ³⁹For I tell you, you will not see me again until you say, 'Blessed is the one who comes in the name of the Lord.' "

The Destruction of the Temple Foretold

24 As Jesus came out of the temple and was going away, his disciples came to point out to him the buildings of the temple. ²Then he asked them, "You see all these, do you not? Truly I tell you, not one stone will be left here upon another; all will be thrown down."

Signs of the End of the Age

3 When he was sitting on the Mount of Olives, the disciples came to him privately, saying, "Tell us, when will this be, and what will be the sign of your coming and of the end of the age?" ⁴Jesus answered them, "Beware that no one leads you astray. ⁵For many will come in my name, saying, 'I am the Messiah!'ᵈ and they will lead many astray. ⁶And you will hear of wars and rumors of wars; see that you are not alarmed; for this must take place, but the

A Sobering Promise

MATTHEW 24.4–14

Not many of the popular "Bible promises" books include this promise: "They will hand you over to be tortured and will put you to death, and you will be hated by all nations because of my name." Is your faith such that you would be willing to face violence and ridicule—even death—rather than disown Jesus? Write down the things you do to please other people (tell jokes, succeed in business, devote attention to appearance); ask yourself how many of those things you would be willing to give up if you were called to do so. How would you cope if a number of people around you disliked or ignored you?

See Meeting God in Scripture

---

a Other ancient authorities add *and of the plate*   b Gk *Gehenna*   c Other ancient authorities lack *desolate*   d Or *the Christ*

Expectant Living

MATTHEW 24.36–44

Jesus stresses the importance of watching vigilantly for his return. What does it mean to "keep awake"? Imagine yourself a sentry or a ship's deckhand standing a late night watch. What things might tempt you to drop your guard? Competing concerns? Fatigue? Distractions? Spend some time thinking about how believing in Jesus Christ's return, and waiting expectantly for it, can help you live the Christian life. What do you want to be doing when the Master returns? Are you doing that now? Pray this ancient prayer from *The Book of Common Prayer*: "Guide us waking, O Lord, and guard us sleeping, that awake we may watch with Christ and asleep we may rest in peace."

See Meeting God in Prayer

end is not yet. [7]For nation will rise against nation, and kingdom against kingdom, and there will be famines[a] and earthquakes in various places: [8]all this is but the beginning of the birth pangs.

Persecutions Foretold

[9] "Then they will hand you over to be tortured and will put you to death, and you will be hated by all nations because of my name. [10]Then many will fall away,[b] and they will betray one another and hate one another. [11]And many false prophets will arise and lead many astray. [12]And because of the increase of lawlessness, the love of many will grow cold. [13]But the one who endures to the end will be saved. [14]And this good news[c] of the kingdom will be proclaimed throughout the world, as a testimony to all the nations; and then the end will come.

The Desolating Sacrilege

[15] "So when you see the desolating sacrilege standing in the holy place, as was spoken of by the prophet Daniel (let the reader understand), [16]then those in Judea must flee to the mountains; [17]the one on the housetop must not go down to take what is in the house; [18]the one in the field must not turn back to get a coat. [19]Woe to those who are pregnant and to those who are nursing infants in those days! [20]Pray that your flight may not be in winter or on a sabbath. [21]For at that time there will be great suffering, such as has not been from the beginning of the world until now, no, and never will be. [22]And if those days had not been cut short, no one would be saved; but for the sake of the elect those days will be cut short. [23]Then if anyone says to you, 'Look! Here is the Messiah!'[d] or 'There he is!'—do not believe it. [24]For false messiahs[e] and false prophets will appear and produce great signs and omens, to lead astray, if possible, even the elect. [25]Take note, I have told you beforehand. [26]So, if they say to you, 'Look! He is in the wilderness,' do not go out. If they say, 'Look! He is in the inner rooms,' do not believe it. [27]For as the lightning comes from the east and flashes as far as the west, so will be the coming of the Son of Man. [28]Wherever the corpse is, there the vultures will gather.

The Coming of the Son of Man

[29] "Immediately after the suffering of those days
the sun will be darkened,
    and the moon will not give its light;
the stars will fall from heaven,
    and the powers of heaven will be shaken.
[30]Then the sign of the Son of Man will appear in heaven, and then all the tribes of the earth will mourn, and they will see 'the Son of Man coming on the clouds of heaven' with power and great glory. [31]And he will send out his angels with a loud trumpet call, and they will gather his elect from the four winds, from one end of heaven to the other.

The Lesson of the Fig Tree

[32] "From the fig tree learn its lesson: as soon as its

a Other ancient authorities add *and pestilences*   *b* Or *stumble*   *c* Or *gospel*   *d* Or *the Christ*   *e* Or *christs*

branch becomes tender and puts forth its leaves, you know that summer is near. ³³So also, when you see all these things, you know that he*a* is near, at the very gates. ³⁴Truly I tell you, this generation will not pass away until all these things have taken place. ³⁵Heaven and earth will pass away, but my words will not pass away.

The Necessity for Watchfulness

36 "But about that day and hour no one knows, neither the angels of heaven, nor the Son,*b* but only the Father. ³⁷For as the days of Noah were, so will be the coming of the Son of Man. ³⁸For as in those days before the flood they were eating and drinking, marrying and giving in marriage, until the day Noah entered the ark, ³⁹and they knew nothing until the flood came and swept them all away, so too will be the coming of the Son of Man. ⁴⁰Then two will be in the field; one will be taken and one will be left. ⁴¹Two women will be grinding meal together; one will be taken and one will be left. ⁴²Keep awake therefore, for you do not know on what day*c* your Lord is coming. ⁴³But understand this: if the owner of the house had known in what part of the night the thief was coming, he would have stayed awake and would not have let his house be broken into. ⁴⁴Therefore you also must be ready, for the Son of Man is coming at an unexpected hour.

The Faithful or the Unfaithful Slave

45 "Who then is the faithful and wise slave, whom his master has put in charge of his household, to give the other slaves*d* their allowance of food at the proper time? ⁴⁶Blessed is that slave whom his master will find at work when he arrives. ⁴⁷Truly I tell you, he will put that one in charge of all his possessions. ⁴⁸But if that wicked slave says to himself, 'My master is delayed,' ⁴⁹and he begins to beat his fellow slaves, and eats and drinks with drunkards, ⁵⁰the master of that slave will come on a day when he does not expect him and at an hour that he does not know. ⁵¹He will cut him in pieces*e* and put him with the hypocrites, where there will be weeping and gnashing of teeth.

The Parable of the Ten Bridesmaids

25 "Then the kingdom of heaven will be like this. Ten bridesmaids*f* took their lamps and went to meet the bridegroom.*g* ²Five of them were foolish, and five were wise. ³When the foolish took their lamps, they took no oil with them; ⁴but the wise took flasks of oil with their lamps. ⁵As the bridegroom was delayed, all of them became drowsy and slept. ⁶But at midnight there was a shout, 'Look! Here is the bridegroom! Come out to meet him.' ⁷Then all those bridesmaids*f* got up and trimmed their lamps. ⁸The foolish said to the wise, 'Give us some of your oil, for our lamps are going out.' ⁹But the wise replied, 'No! there will not be enough for you and for us; you had better go to the dealers and buy some for yourselves.' ¹⁰And while they went to buy it, the bridegroom

---

No Impossible Duty

MATTHEW 25.14–30

"There are diversities of gifts in the kingdom of God, and these gifts are divided to 'every man according to his own ability.' I may have five talents or two or only one. I may be called to do twenty things or one thing. My responsibility is simply to do that which I am called to do, and nothing more . . . . Many Christians make the further mistake of looking upon every act of service as a perpetual obligation. They think because it was right for them to give a tract to one person in a railway train, for instance, that they are always to give tracts to everybody. In this way they burden themselves with an impossible duty."

—HANNAH WHITALL SMITH,
The Christian's Secret of a Happy Life

---

a Or *it*   *b* Other ancient authorities lack *nor the Son*   *c* Other ancient authorities read *at what hour*   *d* Gk *to give them*   *e* Or *cut him off*   *f* Gk *virgins*   *g* Other ancient authorities add *and the bride*

A Heavenly Greeting

MATTHEW 25.31–46

Jesus reminds his followers that discipleship is about doing his work in his name. This parable inspired Christians of earlier times to list "works of mercy." Seven of these works deal with physical needs: feeding the hungry, giving drink to the thirsty, clothing the naked, harboring the stranger, visiting the sick, ministering to prisoners and burying the dead. Seven others deal with spiritual needs: converting the sinner, instructing the ignorant, counseling the doubtful, comforting the sorrowful, bearing wrongs patiently, forgiving injuries, and praying for others. How have these works of mercy been part of your own ministry for Jesus Christ? How could they be part of it in the future? What type of things will God commend you for when you are judged? Write out the greeting with which you hope God will meet you.

See *Meeting God in Scripture*

came, and those who were ready went with him into the wedding banquet; and the door was shut. ¹¹Later the other bridesmaids*a* came also, saying, 'Lord, lord, open to us.' ¹²But he replied, 'Truly I tell you, I do not know you.' ¹³Keep awake therefore, for you know neither the day nor the hour.*b*

The Parable of the Talents

14 "For it is as if a man, going on a journey, summoned his slaves and entrusted his property to them; ¹⁵to one he gave five talents,*c* to another two, to another one, to each according to his ability. Then he went away. ¹⁶The one who had received the five talents went off at once and traded with them, and made five more talents. ¹⁷In the same way, the one who had the two talents made two more talents. ¹⁸But the one who had received the one talent went off and dug a hole in the ground and hid his master's money. ¹⁹After a long time the master of those slaves came and settled accounts with them. ²⁰Then the one who had received the five talents came forward, bringing five more talents, saying, 'Master, you handed over to me five talents; see, I have made five more talents.' ²¹His master said to him, 'Well done, good and trustworthy slave; you have been trustworthy in a few things, I will put you in charge of many things; enter into the joy of your master.' ²²And the one with the two talents also came forward, saying, 'Master, you handed over to me two talents; see, I have made two more talents.' ²³His master said to him, 'Well done, good and trustworthy slave; you have been trustworthy in a few things, I will put you in charge of many things; enter into the joy of your master.' ²⁴Then the one who had received the one talent also came forward, saying, 'Master, I knew that you were a harsh man, reaping where you did not sow, and gathering where you did not scatter seed; ²⁵so I was afraid, and I went and hid your talent in the ground. Here you have what is yours.' ²⁶But his master replied, 'You wicked and lazy slave! You knew, did you, that I reap where I did not sow, and gather where I did not scatter? ²⁷Then you ought to have invested my money with the bankers, and on my return I would have received what was my own with interest. ²⁸So take the talent from him, and give it to the one with the ten talents. ²⁹For to all those who have, more will be given, and they will have an abundance; but from those who have nothing, even what they have will be taken away. ³⁰As for this worthless slave, throw him into the outer darkness, where there will be weeping and gnashing of teeth.'

The Judgment of the Nations

31 "When the Son of Man comes in his glory, and all the angels with him, then he will sit on the throne of his glory. ³²All the nations will be gathered before him, and he will separate people one from another as a shepherd separates the sheep from the goats, ³³and he will put the sheep at his right hand and the goats at the left. ³⁴Then the king will say to those at his right hand, 'Come, you that are blessed by my Father, inherit the kingdom pre-

a Gk *virgins*   *b* Other ancient authorities add *in which the Son of Man is coming*   *c* A talent was worth more than fifteen years' wages of a laborer

pared for you from the foundation of the world; ³⁵for I was hungry and you gave me food, I was thirsty and you gave me something to drink, I was a stranger and you welcomed me, ³⁶I was naked and you gave me clothing, I was sick and you took care of me, I was in prison and you visited me.' ³⁷Then the righteous will answer him, 'Lord, when was it that we saw you hungry and gave you food, or thirsty and gave you something to drink? ³⁸And when was it that we saw you a stranger and welcomed you, or naked and gave you clothing? ³⁹And when was it that we saw you sick or in prison and visited you?' ⁴⁰And the king will answer them, 'Truly I tell you, just as you did it to one of the least of these who are members of my family,[a] you did it to me.' ⁴¹Then he will say to those at his left hand, 'You that are accursed, depart from me into the eternal fire prepared for the devil and his angels; ⁴²for I was hungry and you gave me no food, I was thirsty and you gave me nothing to drink, ⁴³I was a stranger and you did not welcome me, naked and you did not give me clothing, sick and in prison and you did not visit me.' ⁴⁴Then they also will answer, 'Lord, when was it that we saw you hungry or thirsty or a stranger or naked or sick or in prison, and did not take care of you?' ⁴⁵Then he will answer them, 'Truly I tell you, just as you did not do it to one of the least of these, you did not do it to me.' ⁴⁶And these will go away into eternal punishment, but the righteous into eternal life."

The Plot to Kill Jesus

26 When Jesus had finished saying all these things, he said to his disciples, ²"You know that after two days the Passover is coming, and the Son of Man will be handed over to be crucified."

3 Then the chief priests and the elders of the people gathered in the palace of the high priest, who was called Caiaphas, ⁴and they conspired to arrest Jesus by stealth and kill him. ⁵But they said, "Not during the festival, or there may be a riot among the people."

The Anointing at Bethany

6 Now while Jesus was at Bethany in the house of Simon the leper,[b] ⁷a woman came to him with an alabaster jar of very costly ointment, and she poured it on his head as he sat at the table. ⁸But when the disciples saw it, they were angry and said, "Why this waste? ⁹For this ointment could have been sold for a large sum, and the money given to the poor." ¹⁰But Jesus, aware of this, said to them, "Why do you trouble the woman? She has performed a good service for me. ¹¹For you always have the poor with you, but you will not always have me. ¹²By pouring this ointment on my body she has prepared me for burial. ¹³Truly I tell you, wherever this good news[c] is proclaimed in the whole world, what she has done will be told in remembrance of her."

Judas Agrees to Betray Jesus

14 Then one of the twelve, who was called Judas Iscar-

A Scandalous, "Wasteful" Love

MATTHEW 26.6–13

There are no "how to" books for love. When the disciples chastise the woman for "wasting" her fragrant and expensive oil, they disconnect their hearts from their heads; they can't understand the draw and depth of her passionate and holy affection.

Have you ever done something "extravagant" or "wasteful" out of love for another person? When have you done something like that out of love for God? How do you let Jesus know you love him? How can you show Jesus extravagant love today?

See Meeting God in Worship

a Gk *these my brothers*   b The terms *leper* and *leprosy* can refer to several diseases   c Or *gospel*

Absolute Surrender

MATTHEW 26.39–42

Jesus' prayer—"Not what I want, but what you want"—displays a remarkable surrender to the will of his Father. Jesus knew full well the hatred, violence and separation from God that he was about to face. Try to imagine the depth of Jesus' dread. Spend some time meditating on these hardships, which Jesus eventually accepted.

Sometimes our will can come into conflict with God's will. Is there a "little" surrender you can offer to God to help build up your maturity in preparation for those times when greater conflicts arise? How might the spiritual disciplines help you in this? One beginning might be simply to contemplate Jesus' prayer for a while, slowly repeating, "Not what I want, but what you want."

See *Meeting God in Prayer*

iot, went to the chief priests ¹⁵and said, "What will you give me if I betray him to you?" They paid him thirty pieces of silver. ¹⁶And from that moment he began to look for an opportunity to betray him.

The Passover with the Disciples

17 On the first day of Unleavened Bread the disciples came to Jesus, saying, "Where do you want us to make the preparations for you to eat the Passover?" ¹⁸He said, "Go into the city to a certain man, and say to him, 'The Teacher says, My time is near; I will keep the Passover at your house with my disciples.' " ¹⁹So the disciples did as Jesus had directed them, and they prepared the Passover meal.

20 When it was evening, he took his place with the twelve;*a* ²¹and while they were eating, he said, "Truly I tell you, one of you will betray me." ²²And they became greatly distressed and began to say to him one after another, "Surely not I, Lord?" ²³He answered, "The one who has dipped his hand into the bowl with me will betray me. ²⁴The Son of Man goes as it is written of him, but woe to that one by whom the Son of Man is betrayed! It would have been better for that one not to have been born." ²⁵Judas, who betrayed him, said, "Surely not I, Rabbi?" He replied, "You have said so."

The Institution of the Lord's Supper

26 While they were eating, Jesus took a loaf of bread, and after blessing it he broke it, gave it to the disciples, and said, "Take, eat; this is my body." ²⁷Then he took a cup, and after giving thanks he gave it to them, saying, "Drink from it, all of you; ²⁸for this is my blood of the*b* covenant, which is poured out for many for the forgiveness of sins. ²⁹I tell you, I will never again drink of this fruit of the vine until that day when I drink it new with you in my Father's kingdom."

30 When they had sung the hymn, they went out to the Mount of Olives.

Peter's Denial Foretold

31 Then Jesus said to them, "You will all become deserters because of me this night; for it is written,

'I will strike the shepherd,
and the sheep of the flock will be scattered.'
³²But after I am raised up, I will go ahead of you to Galilee." ³³Peter said to him, "Though all become deserters because of you, I will never desert you." ³⁴Jesus said to him, "Truly I tell you, this very night, before the cock crows, you will deny me three times." ³⁵Peter said to him, "Even though I must die with you, I will not deny you." And so said all the disciples.

Jesus Prays in Gethsemane

36 Then Jesus went with them to a place called Gethsemane; and he said to his disciples, "Sit here while I go over there and pray." ³⁷He took with him Peter and the two sons of Zebedee, and began to be grieved and agitated. ³⁸Then he said to them, "I am deeply grieved, even to

---

a Other ancient authorities add *disciples*   *b* Other ancient authorities add *new*

death; remain here, and stay awake with me." ³⁹And going a little farther, he threw himself on the ground and prayed, "My Father, if it is possible, let this cup pass from me; yet not what I want but what you want." ⁴⁰Then he came to the disciples and found them sleeping; and he said to Peter, "So, could you not stay awake with me one hour? ⁴¹Stay awake and pray that you may not come into the time of trial;ᵃ the spirit indeed is willing, but the flesh is weak." ⁴²Again he went away for the second time and prayed, "My Father, if this cannot pass unless I drink it, your will be done." ⁴³Again he came and found them sleeping, for their eyes were heavy. ⁴⁴So leaving them again, he went away and prayed for the third time, saying the same words. ⁴⁵Then he came to the disciples and said to them, "Are you still sleeping and taking your rest? See, the hour is at hand, and the Son of Man is betrayed into the hands of sinners. ⁴⁶Get up, let us be going. See, my betrayer is at hand."

The Betrayal and Arrest of Jesus

47 While he was still speaking, Judas, one of the twelve, arrived; with him was a large crowd with swords and clubs, from the chief priests and the elders of the people. ⁴⁸Now the betrayer had given them a sign, saying, "The one I will kiss is the man; arrest him." ⁴⁹At once he came up to Jesus and said, "Greetings, Rabbi!" and kissed him. ⁵⁰Jesus said to him, "Friend, do what you are here to do." Then they came and laid hands on Jesus and arrested him. ⁵¹Suddenly, one of those with Jesus put his hand on his sword, drew it, and struck the slave of the high priest, cutting off his ear. ⁵²Then Jesus said to him, "Put your sword back into its place; for all who take the sword will perish by the sword. ⁵³Do you think that I cannot appeal to my Father, and he will at once send me more than twelve legions of angels? ⁵⁴But how then would the scriptures be fulfilled, which say it must happen in this way?" ⁵⁵At that hour Jesus said to the crowds, "Have you come out with swords and clubs to arrest me as though I were a bandit? Day after day I sat in the temple teaching, and you did not arrest me. ⁵⁶But all this has taken place, so that the scriptures of the prophets may be fulfilled." Then all the disciples deserted him and fled.

Jesus before the High Priest

57 Those who had arrested Jesus took him to Caiaphas the high priest, in whose house the scribes and the elders had gathered. ⁵⁸But Peter was following him at a distance, as far as the courtyard of the high priest; and going inside, he sat with the guards in order to see how this would end. ⁵⁹Now the chief priests and the whole council were looking for false testimony against Jesus so that they might put him to death, ⁶⁰but they found none, though many false witnesses came forward. At last two came forward ⁶¹and said, "This fellow said, 'I am able to destroy the temple of God and to build it in three days.' " ⁶²The high priest stood up and said, "Have you no answer? What is it that they testify against you?" ⁶³But Jesus was silent. Then the high

Failure Times Two

MATTHEW 26.69–27.5

Each of these two disciples fails Jesus miserably. Compare and contrast their actions and reactions. Why does Peter disown Jesus? Why do you think Judas betrays Jesus? How does Peter react to his own disloyalty afterward? Judas? How might each of them have responded differently? What is the outcome of their actions? Do you think Jesus would have forgiven Judas if Judas and asked him for forgiveness? What is God saying to you through this passage? How does this passage prompt you to pray today?

See Meeting God in Scripture

priest said to him, "I put you under oath before the living God, tell us if you are the Messiah,ᵃ the Son of God." ⁶⁴Jesus said to him, "You have said so. But I tell you,

From now on you will see the Son of Man
    seated at the right hand of Power
    and coming on the clouds of heaven."

⁶⁵Then the high priest tore his clothes and said, "He has blasphemed! Why do we still need witnesses? You have now heard his blasphemy. ⁶⁶What is your verdict?" They answered, "He deserves death." ⁶⁷Then they spat in his face and struck him; and some slapped him, ⁶⁸saying, "Prophesy to us, you Messiah!ᵃ Who is it that struck you?"

Peter's Denial of Jesus

69 Now Peter was sitting outside in the courtyard. A servant-girl came to him and said, "You also were with Jesus the Galilean." ⁷⁰But he denied it before all of them, saying, "I do not know what you are talking about." ⁷¹When he went out to the porch, another servant-girl saw him, and she said to the bystanders, "This man was with Jesus of Nazareth."ᵇ ⁷²Again he denied it with an oath, "I do not know the man." ⁷³After a little while the bystanders came up and said to Peter, "Certainly you are also one of them, for your accent betrays you." ⁷⁴Then he began to curse, and he swore an oath, "I do not know the man!" At that moment the cock crowed. ⁷⁵Then Peter remembered what Jesus had said: "Before the cock crows, you will deny me three times." And he went out and wept bitterly.

Jesus Brought before Pilate

27 When morning came, all the chief priests and the elders of the people conferred together against Jesus in order to bring about his death. ²They bound him, led him away, and handed him over to Pilate the governor.

The Suicide of Judas

3 When Judas, his betrayer, saw that Jesusᶜ was condemned, he repented and brought back the thirty pieces of silver to the chief priests and the elders. ⁴He said, "I have sinned by betraying innocentᵈ blood." But they said, "What is that to us? See to it yourself." ⁵Throwing down the pieces of silver in the temple, he departed; and he went and hanged himself. ⁶But the chief priests, taking the pieces of silver, said, "It is not lawful to put them into the treasury, since they are blood money." ⁷After conferring together, they used them to buy the potter's field as a place to bury foreigners. ⁸For this reason that field has been called the Field of Blood to this day. ⁹Then was fulfilled what had been spoken through the prophet Jeremiah,ᵉ "And they tookᶠ the thirty pieces of silver, the price of the one on whom a price had been set,ᵍ on whom some of the people of Israel had set a price, ¹⁰and they gaveʰ them for the potter's field, as the Lord commanded me."

a Or *Christ*   b Gk *the Nazorean*   c Gk *he*   d Other ancient authorities read *righteous*   e Other ancient authorities read *Zechariah* or *Isaiah*   f Or *I took*   g Or *the price of the precious One*   h Other ancient authorities read *I gave*

Pilate Questions Jesus

11 Now Jesus stood before the governor; and the governor asked him, "Are you the King of the Jews?" Jesus said, "You say so." [12]But when he was accused by the chief priests and elders, he did not answer. [13]Then Pilate said to him, "Do you not hear how many accusations they make against you?" [14]But he gave him no answer, not even to a single charge, so that the governor was greatly amazed.

Barabbas or Jesus?

15 Now at the festival the governor was accustomed to release a prisoner for the crowd, anyone whom they wanted. [16]At that time they had a notorious prisoner, called Jesus[a] Barabbas. [17]So after they had gathered, Pilate said to them, "Whom do you want me to release for you, Jesus[a] Barabbas or Jesus who is called the Messiah?"[b] [18]For he realized that it was out of jealousy that they had handed him over. [19]While he was sitting on the judgment seat, his wife sent word to him, "Have nothing to do with that innocent man, for today I have suffered a great deal because of a dream about him." [20]Now the chief priests and the elders persuaded the crowds to ask for Barabbas and to have Jesus killed. [21]The governor again said to them, "Which of the two do you want me to release for you?" And they said, "Barabbas." [22]Pilate said to them, "Then what should I do with Jesus who is called the Messiah?"[b] All of them said, "Let him be crucified!" [23]Then he asked, "Why, what evil has he done?" But they shouted all the more, "Let him be crucified!"

Pilate Hands Jesus over to Be Crucified

24 So when Pilate saw that he could do nothing, but rather that a riot was beginning, he took some water and washed his hands before the crowd, saying, "I am innocent of this man's blood;[c] see to it yourselves." [25]Then the people as a whole answered, "His blood be on us and on our children!" [26]So he released Barabbas for them; and after flogging Jesus, he handed him over to be crucified.

The Soldiers Mock Jesus

27 Then the soldiers of the governor took Jesus into the governor's headquarters,[d] and they gathered the whole cohort around him. [28]They stripped him and put a scarlet robe on him, [29]and after twisting some thorns into a crown, they put it on his head. They put a reed in his right hand and knelt before him and mocked him, saying, "Hail, King of the Jews!" [30]They spat on him, and took the reed and struck him on the head. [31]After mocking him, they stripped him of the robe and put his own clothes on him. Then they led him away to crucify him.

The Crucifixion of Jesus

32 As they went out, they came upon a man from Cyrene named Simon; they compelled this man to carry his cross. [33]And when they came to a place called Golgotha (which means Place of a Skull), [34]they offered him wine to drink, mixed with gall; but when he tasted it, he would not

---

At the Cross

MATTHEW 27.32–55

Imagine that you are standing on Golgotha while Jesus is being crucified. Look around you. Listen to the sound of the hammer pounding nails into soft flesh, the thud of the cross as it is lifted into position. Look at the people there with you. Some are mocking, some weeping. What are you doing? Do you talk to others or keep to yourself? What are your thoughts and feelings as the sky grows dark and as Jesus cries out?

Sing a hymn such as "Go to Dark Gethsemane," "When I Survey the Wondrous Cross" or "Were You There?" What emotions do you experience as you sing? How have you encountered the reality of Jesus' death through these hymns?

See Meeting God in Scripture

---

a Other ancient authorities lack *Jesus*   b Or *the Christ*   c Other ancient authorities read *this righteous blood*, or *this righteous man's blood*   d Gk *the praetorium*

A Promise Fulfilled

MATTHEW 28.1–10

Matthew begins his Gospel with a promise given and he ends it with a promise fulfilled. Yet nobody on earth expected the promise to be fulfilled exactly in the way it was. Have you ever doubted one of God's promises because it seemed so long in coming to fulfillment? On a sheet of paper, draw a symbol or simple representation of that time of doubt. What helped you to persevere? What can you learn from the fear, confusion and doubt of the disciples? From the attempts of the authorities to smother the hope of Jesus' followers by sealing the tomb and placing guards in front of it? From the joy of the women who first saw Jesus risen from the dead?

See Meeting God in Everyday Life

drink it. ³⁵And when they had crucified him, they divided his clothes among themselves by casting lots;*a* ³⁶then they sat down there and kept watch over him. ³⁷Over his head they put the charge against him, which read, "This is Jesus, the King of the Jews."

38 Then two bandits were crucified with him, one on his right and one on his left. ³⁹Those who passed by derided*b* him, shaking their heads ⁴⁰and saying, "You who would destroy the temple and build it in three days, save yourself! If you are the Son of God, come down from the cross." ⁴¹In the same way the chief priests also, along with the scribes and elders, were mocking him, saying, ⁴²"He saved others; he cannot save himself.*c* He is the King of Israel; let him come down from the cross now, and we will believe in him. ⁴³He trusts in God; let God deliver him now, if he wants to; for he said, 'I am God's Son.' " ⁴⁴The bandits who were crucified with him also taunted him in the same way.

The Death of Jesus

45 From noon on, darkness came over the whole land*d* until three in the afternoon. ⁴⁶And about three o'clock Jesus cried with a loud voice, "Eli, Eli, lema sabachthani?" that is, "My God, my God, why have you forsaken me?" ⁴⁷When some of the bystanders heard it, they said, "This man is calling for Elijah." ⁴⁸At once one of them ran and got a sponge, filled it with sour wine, put it on a stick, and gave it to him to drink. ⁴⁹But the others said, "Wait, let us see whether Elijah will come to save him."*e* ⁵⁰Then Jesus cried again with a loud voice and breathed his last.*f* ⁵¹At that moment the curtain of the temple was torn in two, from top to bottom. The earth shook, and the rocks were split. ⁵²The tombs also were opened, and many bodies of the saints who had fallen asleep were raised. ⁵³After his resurrection they came out of the tombs and entered the holy city and appeared to many. ⁵⁴Now when the centurion and those with him, who were keeping watch over Jesus, saw the earthquake and what took place, they were terrified and said, "Truly this man was God's Son!"*g*

55 Many women were also there, looking on from a distance; they had followed Jesus from Galilee and had provided for him. ⁵⁶Among them were Mary Magdalene, and Mary the mother of James and Joseph, and the mother of the sons of Zebedee.

The Burial of Jesus

57 When it was evening, there came a rich man from Arimathea, named Joseph, who was also a disciple of Jesus. ⁵⁸He went to Pilate and asked for the body of Jesus; then Pilate ordered it to be given to him. ⁵⁹So Joseph took the body and wrapped it in a clean linen cloth ⁶⁰and laid it in his own new tomb, which he had hewn in the rock. He then rolled a great stone to the door of the tomb and went away. ⁶¹Mary Magdalene and the other Mary were there, sitting opposite the tomb.

a Other ancient authorities add *in order that what had been spoken through the prophet might be fulfilled, "They divided my clothes among themselves, and for my clothing they cast lots."*   *b* Or *blasphemed*   *c* Or *is he unable to save himself?*   *d* Or *earth*   *e* Other ancient authorities add *And another took a spear and pierced his side, and out came water and blood*   *f* Or *gave up his spirit*   *g* Or *a son of God*

The Guard at the Tomb

62 The next day, that is, after the day of Preparation, the chief priests and the Pharisees gathered before Pilate [63]and said, "Sir, we remember what that impostor said while he was still alive, 'After three days I will rise again.' [64]Therefore command the tomb to be made secure until the third day; otherwise his disciples may go and steal him away, and tell the people, 'He has been raised from the dead,' and the last deception would be worse than the first." [65]Pilate said to them, "You have a guard[a] of soldiers; go, make it as secure as you can."[b] [66]So they went with the guard and made the tomb secure by sealing the stone.

The Resurrection of Jesus

28 After the sabbath, as the first day of the week was dawning, Mary Magdalene and the other Mary went to see the tomb. [2]And suddenly there was a great earthquake; for an angel of the Lord, descending from heaven, came and rolled back the stone and sat on it. [3]His appearance was like lightning, and his clothing white as snow. [4]For fear of him the guards shook and became like dead men. [5]But the angel said to the women, "Do not be afraid; I know that you are looking for Jesus who was crucified. [6]He is not here; for he has been raised, as he said. Come, see the place where he[c] lay. [7]Then go quickly and tell his disciples, 'He has been raised from the dead,'[d] and indeed he is going ahead of you to Galilee; there you will see him.' This is my message for you." [8]So they left the tomb quickly with fear and great joy, and ran to tell his disciples. [9]Suddenly Jesus met them and said, "Greetings!" And they came to him, took hold of his feet, and worshiped him. [10]Then Jesus said to them, "Do not be afraid; go and tell my brothers to go to Galilee; there they will see me."

The Report of the Guard

11 While they were going, some of the guard went into the city and told the chief priests everything that had happened. [12]After the priests[e] had assembled with the elders, they devised a plan to give a large sum of money to the soldiers, [13]telling them, "You must say, 'His disciples came by night and stole him away while we were asleep.' [14]If this comes to the governor's ears, we will satisfy him and keep you out of trouble." [15]So they took the money and did as they were directed. And this story is still told among the Jews to this day.

The Commissioning of the Disciples

16 Now the eleven disciples went to Galilee, to the mountain to which Jesus had directed them. [17]When they saw him, they worshiped him; but some doubted. [18]And Jesus came and said to them, "All authority in heaven and on earth has been given to me. [19]Go therefore and make disciples of all nations, baptizing them in the name of the Father and of the Son and of the Holy Spirit, [20]and teaching them to obey everything that I have commanded you. And remember, I am with you always, to the end of the age."[f]

A Great Commission

MATTHEW 28.16–20

Read the Great Commission in verses 19 and 20 as if Jesus were speaking directly to you. To what part of the world is he sending you? What is your role in making disciples? How can you extend his invitation to everyone you meet? Where will you find support in fulfilling this commission? What help do you need from God? From other people? Remember this final promise from Jesus: "And remember I am with you always, to the end of the age."

See Meeting God in Service

---

a Or *Take a guard*   *b* Gk *you know how*   *c* Other ancient authorities read *the Lord*   *d* Other ancient authorities lack *from the dead*   *e* Gk *they*   *f* Other ancient authorities add *Amen*

The Gospel According to
MARK
What It Costs to Follow Jesus

KEY VERSE:

*"For the Son of Man came not to be served but to serve, and to give his life
a ransom for many."—Mark 10.45*

"To go one's way under the sign of the cross is not misery and desperation, but peace and refreshment for the soul, it is the highest joy. Then we do not walk under our self-made laws and burdens, but under the yoke of him who knows us and who walks under the yoke with us. Under his yoke we are certain of his nearness and communion."

—DIETRICH BONHOEFFER,
The Cost of Discipleship

What did it cost Jesus to do the work of his Father? What will it cost you to follow Jesus? You will find the answers to both questions in the Gospel of Mark. In this fast-paced narrative the apostle Mark reveals what it cost Jesus to do this work: He was persecuted by the Pharisees (Mark 3.6); he had to address the bewilderment expressed by his family (3.21); he was rejected by his hometown crowd (6.3–4); he relinquished both his privacy (6.30–34) and material goods. When accused, he did not defend himself (14.61).

Mark also outlines the cost of following Jesus. As much as we prefer to identify ourselves with Jesus in his role of conquering king, we are also called to become like him as servants, reconciling those around us to God. Just as Jesus spoke the truth to the confused and the corrupt, so must we. Just as he addressed the physical needs of the crowds who followed him, so must we. Just as he sought to heal the broken places of people's hearts, so must we.

As you read this account, let the forward momentum of Mark's narrative instill within you a sense of urgency. The time to follow Jesus is now. As you read about Jesus' words and works, ask God what he is calling you to be and do. What do you need to know about the power of Jesus and the servant heart of Jesus in order to be conformed to his image for the sake of others?

The Proclamation of John the Baptist

1 The beginning of the good news*a* of Jesus Christ, the Son of God.*b*

2 As it is written in the prophet Isaiah,*c*

"See, I am sending my messenger ahead of you,*d*
who will prepare your way;

3 the voice of one crying out in the wilderness:
'Prepare the way of the Lord,
make his paths straight,' "

4 John the baptizer appeared*e* in the wilderness, proclaiming a baptism of repentance for the forgiveness of sins. 5 And people from the whole Judean countryside and all the people of Jerusalem were going out to him, and were baptized by him in the river Jordan, confessing their sins. 6 Now John was clothed with camel's hair, with a leather belt around his waist, and he ate locusts and wild honey. 7 He proclaimed, "The one who is more powerful than I is coming after me; I am not worthy to stoop down and untie the thong of his sandals. 8 I have baptized you with*f* water; but he will baptize you with*f* the Holy Spirit."

The Baptism of Jesus

9 In those days Jesus came from Nazareth of Galilee and was baptized by John in the Jordan. 10 And just as he was coming up out of the water, he saw the heavens torn apart and the Spirit descending like a dove on him. 11 And a voice came from heaven, "You are my Son, the Beloved;*g* with you I am well pleased."

The Temptation of Jesus

12 And the Spirit immediately drove him out into the wilderness. 13 He was in the wilderness forty days, tempted by Satan; and he was with the wild beasts; and the angels waited on him.

The Beginning of the Galilean Ministry

14 Now after John was arrested, Jesus came to Galilee, proclaiming the good news*a* of God,*h* 15 and saying, "The time is fulfilled, and the kingdom of God has come near;*i* repent, and believe in the good news."*a*

Jesus Calls the First Disciples

16 As Jesus passed along the Sea of Galilee, he saw Simon and his brother Andrew casting a net into the sea— for they were fishermen. 17 And Jesus said to them, "Follow me and I will make you fish for people." 18 And immediately they left their nets and followed him. 19 As he went a little farther, he saw James son of Zebedee and his brother John, who were in their boat mending the nets. 20 Immediately he called them; and they left their father Zebedee in the boat with the hired men, and followed him.

The Man with an Unclean Spirit

21 They went to Capernaum; and when the sabbath came, he entered the synagogue and taught. 22 They were astounded at his teaching, for he taught them as one hav-

Grasping the Nets

MARK 1.16–18

The disciples' fishing nets represent their income, their sense of accomplishment and their identity as enterprising fish-catching businessmen. They've probably handled these nets most of their lives. No wonder they find it difficult to let go of them!

Imagine yourself clutching the tightly woven cords of the fishing nets—how familiar they feel, how secure. But Jesus is standing near you, gazing at you with a look of invitation that's somehow irresistible. He's asking you to let go of the nets and find your security in him. Jesus walks daily through your life, calling you to follow him. What is God asking you to let go of today? What do you need to relinquish in order to conform your heart to the heart of Jesus Christ?

See Meeting God in Scripture

a Or *gospel*   *b* Other ancient authorities lack *the Son of God*   *c* Other ancient authorities read *in the prophets*   *d* Gk *before your face*   *e* Other ancient authorities read *John was baptizing*   *f* Or *in*   *g* Or *my beloved Son*   *h* Other ancient authorities read *of the kingdom*   *i* Or *is at hand*

Time Out From Service

MARK 1.29–35

On the morning after an exhausting day of healing and driving out evil spirits, it would be understandable if Jesus slept in. Although it is likely that he was tired, he got up early to go off alone to pray. What do you suppose Jesus prayed about? How do you explain the apparent longing in his heart to talk to God?

Reflect on your life. How do times of intense service affect you? In what ways do they prompt you to converse with God about them? What is God saying to you about your acts of service?

See Meeting God in Prayer

ing authority, and not as the scribes. 23Just then there was in their synagogue a man with an unclean spirit, 24and he cried out, "What have you to do with us, Jesus of Nazareth? Have you come to destroy us? I know who you are, the Holy One of God." 25But Jesus rebuked him, saying, "Be silent, and come out of him!" 26And the unclean spirit, convulsing him and crying with a loud voice, came out of him. 27They were all amazed, and they kept on asking one another, "What is this? A new teaching—with authority! He*a* commands even the unclean spirits, and they obey him." 28At once his fame began to spread throughout the surrounding region of Galilee.

Jesus Heals Many at Simon's House

29 As soon as they*b* left the synagogue, they entered the house of Simon and Andrew, with James and John. 30Now Simon's mother-in-law was in bed with a fever, and they told him about her at once. 31He came and took her by the hand and lifted her up. Then the fever left her, and she began to serve them.

32 That evening, at sundown, they brought to him all who were sick or possessed with demons. 33And the whole city was gathered around the door. 34And he cured many who were sick with various diseases, and cast out many demons; and he would not permit the demons to speak, because they knew him.

A Preaching Tour in Galilee

35 In the morning, while it was still very dark, he got up and went out to a deserted place, and there he prayed. 36And Simon and his companions hunted for him. 37When they found him, they said to him, "Everyone is searching for you." 38He answered, "Let us go on to the neighboring towns, so that I may proclaim the message there also; for that is what I came out to do." 39And he went throughout Galilee, proclaiming the message in their synagogues and casting out demons.

Jesus Cleanses a Leper

40 A leper*c* came to him begging him, and kneeling*d* he said to him, "If you choose, you can make me clean." 41Moved with pity,*e* Jesus*f* stretched out his hand and touched him, and said to him, "I do choose. Be made clean!" 42Immediately the leprosy*c* left him, and he was made clean. 43After sternly warning him he sent him away at once, 44saying to him, "See that you say nothing to anyone; but go, show yourself to the priest, and offer for your cleansing what Moses commanded, as a testimony to them." 45But he went out and began to proclaim it freely, and to spread the word, so that Jesus*f* could no longer go into a town openly, but stayed out in the country; and people came to him from every quarter.

Jesus Heals a Paralytic

2 When he returned to Capernaum after some days, it was reported that he was at home. 2So many gathered

a Or *A new teaching! With authority he*　　*b* Other ancient authorities read *he*
c The terms *leper* and *leprosy* can refer to several diseases　　*d* Other ancient authorities lack *kneeling*　　*e* Other ancient authorities read *anger*
f Gk *he*

around that there was no longer room for them, not even in front of the door; and he was speaking the word to them. [3]Then some people[a] came, bringing to him a paralyzed man, carried by four of them. [4]And when they could not bring him to Jesus because of the crowd, they removed the roof above him; and after having dug through it, they let down the mat on which the paralytic lay. [5]When Jesus saw their faith, he said to the paralytic, "Son, your sins are forgiven." [6]Now some of the scribes were sitting there, questioning in their hearts, [7]"Why does this fellow speak in this way? It is blasphemy! Who can forgive sins but God alone?" [8]At once Jesus perceived in his spirit that they were discussing these questions among themselves; and he said to them, "Why do you raise such questions in your hearts? [9]Which is easier, to say to the paralytic, 'Your sins are forgiven,' or to say, 'Stand up and take your mat and walk'? [10]But so that you may know that the Son of Man has authority on earth to forgive sins"—he said to the paralytic— [11]"I say to you, stand up, take your mat and go to your home." [12]And he stood up, and immediately took the mat and went out before all of them; so that they were all amazed and glorified God, saying, "We have never seen anything like this!"

Jesus Calls Levi

13 Jesus[b] went out again beside the sea; the whole crowd gathered around him, and he taught them. [14]As he was walking along, he saw Levi son of Alphaeus sitting at the tax booth, and he said to him, "Follow me." And he got up and followed him.

15 And as he sat at dinner[c] in Levi's[d] house, many tax collectors and sinners were also sitting[e] with Jesus and his disciples—for there were many who followed him. [16]When the scribes of[f] the Pharisees saw that he was eating with sinners and tax collectors, they said to his disciples, "Why does he eat[g] with tax collectors and sinners?" [17]When Jesus heard this, he said to them, "Those who are well have no need of a physician, but those who are sick; I have come to call not the righteous but sinners."

The Question about Fasting

18 Now John's disciples and the Pharisees were fasting; and people[a] came and said to him, "Why do John's disciples and the disciples of the Pharisees fast, but your disciples do not fast?" [19]Jesus said to them, "The wedding guests cannot fast while the bridegroom is with them, can they? As long as they have the bridegroom with them, they cannot fast. [20]The days will come when the bridegroom is taken away from them, and then they will fast on that day.

21 "No one sews a piece of unshrunk cloth on an old cloak; otherwise, the patch pulls away from it, the new from the old, and a worse tear is made. [22]And no one puts new wine into old wineskins; otherwise, the wine will burst the skins, and the wine is lost, and so are the skins; but one puts new wine into fresh wineskins."[h]

---

a Gk they   b Gk He   c Gk reclined   d Gk his   e Gk reclining
f Other ancient authorities read and   g Other ancient authorities add and drink   h Other ancient authorities lack but one puts new wine into fresh wineskins

Self-Created Limits

MARK 2.15–17

"To die to our neighbors means to stop judging them, to stop evaluating them, and thus to become free to be compassionate. Compassion can never coexist with judgment because judgment creates the distance, the distinction, which prevent us from really being with each other. Often quite unconsciously we classify people as very good, good, neutral, bad, and very bad. These judgments influence deeply the thoughts, words, and actions. These self-created limits prevent us from being available to people and shrivel up our compassion."

—HENRI J. M. NOUWEN,
The Way of the Heart

Being With Him

MARK 3.14

What are the advantages of "hanging out" with someone? Jesus must have thought this was important because he appointed the twelve so that they might "be with him." If you were to "hang out" with God all day, what would you talk about? What phrases might God use in his conversation with you? What would it be like to have an all-day companion who is intensely interested in you? How would you feel—after such a day—about going out to reflect God's concerns? How would such a day of "hanging out" with God prepare you to be sent out to preach?

See Meeting God in Community

Pronouncement about the Sabbath

23 One sabbath he was going through the grainfields; and as they made their way his disciples began to pluck heads of grain. [24]The Pharisees said to him, "Look, why are they doing what is not lawful on the sabbath?" [25]And he said to them, "Have you never read what David did when he and his companions were hungry and in need of food? [26]He entered the house of God, when Abiathar was high priest, and ate the bread of the Presence, which it is not lawful for any but the priests to eat, and he gave some to his companions." [27]Then he said to them, "The sabbath was made for humankind, and not humankind for the sabbath; [28]so the Son of Man is lord even of the sabbath."

The Man with a Withered Hand

3 Again he entered the synagogue, and a man was there who had a withered hand. [2]They watched him to see whether he would cure him on the sabbath, so that they might accuse him. [3]And he said to the man who had the withered hand, "Come forward." [4]Then he said to them, "Is it lawful to do good or to do harm on the sabbath, to save life or to kill?" But they were silent. [5]He looked around at them with anger; he was grieved at their hardness of heart and said to the man, "Stretch out your hand." He stretched it out, and his hand was restored. [6]The Pharisees went out and immediately conspired with the Herodians against him, how to destroy him.

A Multitude at the Seaside

7 Jesus departed with his disciples to the sea, and a great multitude from Galilee followed him; [8]hearing all that he was doing, they came to him in great numbers from Judea, Jerusalem, Idumea, beyond the Jordan, and the region around Tyre and Sidon. [9]He told his disciples to have a boat ready for him because of the crowd, so that they would not crush him; [10]for he had cured many, so that all who had diseases pressed upon him to touch him. [11]Whenever the unclean spirits saw him, they fell down before him and shouted, "You are the Son of God!" [12]But he sternly ordered them not to make him known.

Jesus Appoints the Twelve

13 He went up the mountain and called to him those whom he wanted, and they came to him. [14]And he appointed twelve, whom he also named apostles,[a] to be with him, and to be sent out to proclaim the message, [15]and to have authority to cast out demons. [16]So he appointed the twelve:[b] Simon (to whom he gave the name Peter); [17]James son of Zebedee and John the brother of James (to whom he gave the name Boanerges, that is, Sons of Thunder); [18]and Andrew, and Philip, and Bartholomew, and Matthew, and Thomas, and James son of Alphaeus, and Thaddaeus, and Simon the Cananaean, [19]and Judas Iscariot, who betrayed him.

Jesus and Beelzebul

Then he went home; [20]and the crowd came together

---

a Other ancient authorities lack *whom he also named apostles*   b Other ancient authorities lack *So he appointed the twelve*

again, so that they could not even eat. [21]When his family heard it, they went out to restrain him, for people were saying, "He has gone out of his mind." [22]And the scribes who came down from Jerusalem said, "He has Beelzebul, and by the ruler of the demons he casts out demons." [23]And he called them to him, and spoke to them in parables, "How can Satan cast out Satan? [24]If a kingdom is divided against itself, that kingdom cannot stand. [25]And if a house is divided against itself, that house will not be able to stand. [26]And if Satan has risen up against himself and is divided, he cannot stand, but his end has come. [27]But no one can enter a strong man's house and plunder his property without first tying up the strong man; then indeed the house can be plundered.

28 "Truly I tell you, people will be forgiven for their sins and whatever blasphemies they utter; [29]but whoever blasphemes against the Holy Spirit can never have forgiveness, but is guilty of an eternal sin"— [30]for they had said, "He has an unclean spirit."

The True Kindred of Jesus

31 Then his mother and his brothers came; and standing outside, they sent to him and called him. [32]A crowd was sitting around him; and they said to him, "Your mother and your brothers and sisters[a] are outside, asking for you." [33]And he replied, "Who are my mother and my brothers?" [34]And looking at those who sat around him, he said, "Here are my mother and my brothers! [35]Whoever does the will of God is my brother and sister and mother."

The Parable of the Sower

4 Again he began to teach beside the sea. Such a very large crowd gathered around him that he got into a boat on the sea and sat there, while the whole crowd was beside the sea on the land. [2]He began to teach them many things in parables, and in his teaching he said to them: [3]"Listen! A sower went out to sow. [4]And as he sowed, some seed fell on the path, and the birds came and ate it up. [5]Other seed fell on rocky ground, where it did not have much soil, and it sprang up quickly, since it had no depth of soil. [6]And when the sun rose, it was scorched; and since it had no root, it withered away. [7]Other seed fell among thorns, and the thorns grew up and choked it, and it yielded no grain. [8]Other seed fell into good soil and brought forth grain, growing up and increasing and yielding thirty and sixty and a hundredfold." [9]And he said, "Let anyone with ears to hear listen!"

The Purpose of the Parables

10 When he was alone, those who were around him along with the twelve asked him about the parables. [11]And he said to them, "To you has been given the secret[b] of the kingdom of God, but for those outside, everything comes in parables; [12]in order that
   'they may indeed look, but not perceive,
     and may indeed listen, but not understand;
   so that they may not turn again and be forgiven.' "
13 And he said to them, "Do you not understand this parable? Then how will you understand all the parables?

Looking Inwardly With Courage

MARK 4.13–20

"Jesus doesn't take us aside and explain things to us all the time; He explains things to us as we are able to understand them. It is slow work—so slow that it takes God all of time and eternity to make a man or woman conform to His purpose. We can only be used by God after we allow Him to show us the deep, hidden areas of our own character. It is astounding how ignorant we are about ourselves! We don't even recognize the envy, laziness or pride within us when we see it. But Jesus will reveal to us everything we have held within ourselves before His grace began to work. How many of us have learned to look inwardly with courage?"
—OSWALD CHAMBERS,
My Utmost for His Highest

---

a Other ancient authorities lack *and sisters*   b Or *mystery*

To Trust or Not to Trust

MARK 4.35–41

Whether it's a family estrangement, a church dispute or a national disaster, we sometimes find ourselves asking, "God, don't you care . . . ?" Imagine yourself on this life-threatening voyage. You've bailed water for hours. Your legs are bruised from being banged about the boat by the heaving waves. You are cold, wet and bone-weary. With a hoarse voice you ask, "Teacher, do you not care . . . ?"

What about this passage touches you the most? That Jesus could control an uncontrollable force? That Jesus was surprised by their fear? That the disciples expected Jesus to intervene, but then, when he did, they were astounded that he could help? What does this passage say to you about the mystery of God's presence in seemingly uncontrollable circumstances?

See *Meeting God in the Created Order*

[14]The sower sows the word. [15]These are the ones on the path where the word is sown: when they hear, Satan immediately comes and takes away the word that is sown in them. [16]And these are the ones sown on rocky ground: when they hear the word, they immediately receive it with joy. [17]But they have no root, and endure only for a while; then, when trouble or persecution arises on account of the word, immediately they fall away.[a] [18]And others are those sown among the thorns: these are the ones who hear the word, [19]but the cares of the world, and the lure of wealth, and the desire for other things come in and choke the word, and it yields nothing. [20]And these are the ones sown on the good soil: they hear the word and accept it and bear fruit, thirty and sixty and a hundredfold."

A Lamp under a Bushel Basket

21 He said to them, "Is a lamp brought in to be put under the bushel basket, or under the bed, and not on the lampstand? [22]For there is nothing hidden, except to be disclosed; nor is anything secret, except to come to light. [23]Let anyone with ears to hear listen!" [24]And he said to them, "Pay attention to what you hear; the measure you give will be the measure you get, and still more will be given you. [25]For to those who have, more will be given; and from those who have nothing, even what they have will be taken away."

The Parable of the Growing Seed

26 He also said, "The kingdom of God is as if someone would scatter seed on the ground, [27]and would sleep and rise night and day, and the seed would sprout and grow, he does not know how. [28]The earth produces of itself, first the stalk, then the head, then the full grain in the head. [29]But when the grain is ripe, at once he goes in with his sickle, because the harvest has come."

The Parable of the Mustard Seed

30 He also said, "With what can we compare the kingdom of God, or what parable will we use for it? [31]It is like a mustard seed, which, when sown upon the ground, is the smallest of all the seeds on earth; [32]yet when it is sown it grows up and becomes the greatest of all shrubs, and puts forth large branches, so that the birds of the air can make nests in its shade."

The Use of Parables

33 With many such parables he spoke the word to them, as they were able to hear it; [34]he did not speak to them except in parables, but he explained everything in private to his disciples.

Jesus Stills a Storm

35 On that day, when evening had come, he said to them, "Let us go across to the other side." [36]And leaving the crowd behind, they took him with them in the boat, just as he was. Other boats were with him. [37]A great windstorm arose, and the waves beat into the boat, so that the boat was already being swamped. [38]But he was in the stern, asleep on the cushion; and they woke him up and said to

a Or *stumble*

him, "Teacher, do you not care that we are perishing?" [39]He woke up and rebuked the wind, and said to the sea, "Peace! Be still!" Then the wind ceased, and there was a dead calm. [40]He said to them, "Why are you afraid? Have you still no faith?" [41]And they were filled with great awe and said to one another, "Who then is this, that even the wind and the sea obey him?"

Jesus Heals the Gerasene Demoniac

5 They came to the other side of the sea, to the country of the Gerasenes.[a] [2]And when he had stepped out of the boat, immediately a man out of the tombs with an unclean spirit met him. [3]He lived among the tombs; and no one could restrain him any more, even with a chain; [4]for he had often been restrained with shackles and chains, but the chains he wrenched apart, and the shackles he broke in pieces; and no one had the strength to subdue him. [5]Night and day among the tombs and on the mountains he was always howling and bruising himself with stones. [6]When he saw Jesus from a distance, he ran and bowed down before him; [7]and he shouted at the top of his voice, "What have you to do with me, Jesus, Son of the Most High God? I adjure you by God, do not torment me." [8]For he had said to him, "Come out of the man, you unclean spirit!" [9]Then Jesus[b] asked him, "What is your name?" He replied, "My name is Legion; for we are many." [10]He begged him earnestly not to send them out of the country. [11]Now there on the hillside a great herd of swine was feeding; [12]and the unclean spirits[c] begged him, "Send us into the swine; let us enter them." [13]So he gave them permission. And the unclean spirits came out and entered the swine; and the herd, numbering about two thousand, rushed down the steep bank into the sea, and were drowned in the sea.

14 The swineherds ran off and told it in the city and in the country. Then people came to see what it was that had happened. [15]They came to Jesus and saw the demoniac sitting there, clothed and in his right mind, the very man who had had the legion; and they were afraid. [16]Those who had seen what had happened to the demoniac and to the swine reported it. [17]Then they began to beg Jesus[d] to leave their neighborhood. [18]As he was getting into the boat, the man who had been possessed by demons begged him that he might be with him. [19]But Jesus[b] refused, and said to him, "Go home to your friends, and tell them how much the Lord has done for you, and what mercy he has shown you." [20]And he went away and began to proclaim in the Decapolis how much Jesus had done for him; and everyone was amazed.

A Girl Restored to Life and a Woman Healed

21 When Jesus had crossed again in the boat[e] to the other side, a great crowd gathered around him; and he was by the sea. [22]Then one of the leaders of the synagogue named Jairus came and, when he saw him, fell at his feet [23]and begged him repeatedly, "My little daughter is at the point of death. Come and lay your hands on her, so that she may be made well, and live." [24]So he went with him.

And a large crowd followed him and pressed in on him.

When It Hurts to Stick Around

MARK 5.18–20

When we've been hurt or embarrassed by a group of people, it can be tough to sense God saying that we need to stay with those people for a while longer in order to become the person God wants us to be.

Read Mark 5.1–20, then reread verses 18–20. What word or phrase in these verses attracts your attention? Reflect on this word or phrase. What new insights come to you as you turn it over in your mind? Rest in silence, being open to anything God may want to impress on you. How does this passage touch your life today?

See Meeting God in Scripture

---

a Other ancient authorities read *Gergesenes*; others, *Gadarenes*   *b* Gk *he*
c Gk *they*   *d* Gk *him*   *e* Other ancient authorities lack *in the boat*

Telling God Where It Hurts

MARK 5.27–35

Something about Jesus captivates this woman and prompts her to appear in public, even though she has suffered from a lengthy and intensely personal disease. She recognizes his love and power and trusts him enough to touch him, even though she is ritually "unclean." Do you feel safe enough with God to trust him with everything, even the most embarrassing things? How might it contribute to your healing to tell God about your intensely personal problems, even though he is already aware of them? How might God respond to you? If you wish, paraphrase God's response from Mark 5.34: "Your faith has made you well; go in peace, and be healed of your disease."

See Meeting God in Prayer

²⁵Now there was a woman who had been suffering from hemorrhages for twelve years. ²⁶She had endured much under many physicians, and had spent all that she had; and she was no better, but rather grew worse. ²⁷She had heard about Jesus, and came up behind him in the crowd and touched his cloak, ²⁸for she said, "If I but touch his clothes, I will be made well." ²⁹Immediately her hemorrhage stopped; and she felt in her body that she was healed of her disease. ³⁰Immediately aware that power had gone forth from him, Jesus turned about in the crowd and said, "Who touched my clothes?" ³¹And his disciples said to him, "You see the crowd pressing in on you; how can you say, 'Who touched me?'" ³²He looked all around to see who had done it. ³³But the woman, knowing what had happened to her, came in fear and trembling, fell down before him, and told him the whole truth. ³⁴He said to her, "Daughter, your faith has made you well; go in peace, and be healed of your disease."

35 While he was still speaking, some people came from the leader's house to say, "Your daughter is dead. Why trouble the teacher any further?" ³⁶But overhearing*a* what they said, Jesus said to the leader of the synagogue, "Do not fear, only believe." ³⁷He allowed no one to follow him except Peter, James, and John, the brother of James. ³⁸When they came to the house of the leader of the synagogue, he saw a commotion, people weeping and wailing loudly. ³⁹When he had entered, he said to them, "Why do you make a commotion and weep? The child is not dead but sleeping." ⁴⁰And they laughed at him. Then he put them all outside, and took the child's father and mother and those who were with him, and went in where the child was. ⁴¹He took her by the hand and said to her, "Talitha cum," which means, "Little girl, get up!" ⁴²And immediately the girl got up and began to walk about (she was twelve years of age). At this they were overcome with amazement. ⁴³He strictly ordered them that no one should know this, and told them to give her something to eat.

The Rejection of Jesus at Nazareth

6 He left that place and came to his hometown, and his disciples followed him. ²On the sabbath he began to teach in the synagogue, and many who heard him were astounded. They said, "Where did this man get all this? What is this wisdom that has been given to him? What deeds of power are being done by his hands! ³Is not this the carpenter, the son of Mary*b* and brother of James and Joses and Judas and Simon, and are not his sisters here with us?" And they took offense*c* at him. ⁴Then Jesus said to them, "Prophets are not without honor, except in their hometown, and among their own kin, and in their own house." ⁵And he could do no deed of power there, except that he laid his hands on a few sick people and cured them. ⁶And he was amazed at their unbelief.

The Mission of the Twelve

Then he went about among the villages teaching. ⁷He called the twelve and began to send them out two by two, and gave them authority over the unclean spirits. ⁸He or-

a Or *ignoring*; other ancient authorities read *hearing*   *b* Other ancient authorities read *son of the carpenter and of Mary*   *c* Or *stumbled*

dered them to take nothing for their journey except a staff; no bread, no bag, no money in their belts; [9]but to wear sandals and not to put on two tunics. [10]He said to them, "Wherever you enter a house, stay there until you leave the place. [11]If any place will not welcome you and they refuse to hear you, as you leave, shake off the dust that is on your feet as a testimony against them." [12]So they went out and proclaimed that all should repent. [13]They cast out many demons, and anointed with oil many who were sick and cured them.

The Death of John the Baptist

14 King Herod heard of it, for Jesus'[a] name had become known. Some were[b] saying, "John the baptizer has been raised from the dead; and for this reason these powers are at work in him." [15]But others said, "It is Elijah." And others said, "It is a prophet, like one of the prophets of old." [16]But when Herod heard of it, he said, "John, whom I beheaded, has been raised."

17 For Herod himself had sent men who arrested John, bound him, and put him in prison on account of Herodias, his brother Philip's wife, because Herod[c] had married her. [18]For John had been telling Herod, "It is not lawful for you to have your brother's wife." [19]And Herodias had a grudge against him, and wanted to kill him. But she could not, [20]for Herod feared John, knowing that he was a righteous and holy man, and he protected him. When he heard him, he was greatly perplexed;[d] and yet he liked to listen to him. [21]But an opportunity came when Herod on his birthday gave a banquet for his courtiers and officers and for the leaders of Galilee. [22]When his daughter Herodias[e] came in and danced, she pleased Herod and his guests; and the king said to the girl, "Ask me for whatever you wish, and I will give it." [23]And he solemnly swore to her, "Whatever you ask me, I will give you, even half of my kingdom." [24]She went out and said to her mother, "What should I ask for?" She replied, "The head of John the baptizer." [25]Immediately she rushed back to the king and requested, "I want you to give me at once the head of John the Baptist on a platter." [26]The king was deeply grieved; yet out of regard for his oaths and for the guests, he did not want to refuse her. [27]Immediately the king sent a soldier of the guard with orders to bring John's[a] head. He went and beheaded him in the prison, [28]brought his head on a platter, and gave it to the girl. Then the girl gave it to her mother. [29]When his disciples heard about it, they came and took his body, and laid it in a tomb.

Feeding the Five Thousand

30 The apostles gathered around Jesus, and told him all that they had done and taught. [31]He said to them, "Come away to a deserted place all by yourselves and rest a while." For many were coming and going, and they had no leisure even to eat. [32]And they went away in the boat to a deserted place by themselves. [33]Now many saw them going and recognized them, and they hurried there on foot from all the towns and arrived ahead of them. [34]As he went ashore,

Empty and Filled

MARK 6.30–34

Jesus and the disciples give up a quiet time of fellowship because Jesus has compassion on the crowd and stops to teach and feed them. As much as we'd like to think that the Christian life will be happy and comfortable, "dying to self" often requires us to give up both our time and our personal preferences. When our service is costly, when we empty ourselves, God can fill our hearts with compassion.

Who is like that "great crowd" in your own situation? Who is like a "sheep without a shepherd"? How is God asking you to use your unique skills for a particular task? Perhaps you're not sure whether God is prompting you to go to "a deserted place all by [yourself] and rest awhile"—or compelling you to get back to work? What do you need to ask God with respect to this issue?

See Meeting God in Service

a Gk *his*   b Other ancient authorities read *He was*   c Gk *he*   d Other ancient authorities read *he did many things*   e Other ancient authorities read *the daughter of Herodias herself*

The Folly of the Distant Heart

MARK 7.6–7

Sometimes we mistakenly think that if we know facts about God and do good deeds, we're on the right track spiritually. But God wants our love to be authentic. A hypocrite, according to this Biblical definition, is a person whose heart doesn't match his or her words, actions and beliefs.

Paraphrase and personalize Mark 7.6 along these lines: "God, I honor you with my _____ (actions, words, priorities), but my heart is far from you." Confess this to God and then ask God to fill you with a genuine love that you can express with your heart, your head and your hands.

See Meeting God in Prayer

he saw a great crowd; and he had compassion for them, because they were like sheep without a shepherd; and he began to teach them many things. ³⁵When it grew late, his disciples came to him and said, "This is a deserted place, and the hour is now very late; ³⁶send them away so that they may go into the surrounding country and villages and buy something for themselves to eat." ³⁷But he answered them, "You give them something to eat." They said to him, "Are we to go and buy two hundred denariiᵃ worth of bread, and give it to them to eat?" ³⁸And he said to them, "How many loaves have you? Go and see." When they had found out, they said, "Five, and two fish." ³⁹Then he ordered them to get all the people to sit down in groups on the green grass. ⁴⁰So they sat down in groups of hundreds and of fifties. ⁴¹Taking the five loaves and the two fish, he looked up to heaven, and blessed and broke the loaves, and gave them to his disciples to set before the people; and he divided the two fish among them all. ⁴²And all ate and were filled; ⁴³and they took up twelve baskets full of broken pieces and of the fish. ⁴⁴Those who had eaten the loaves numbered five thousand men.

Jesus Walks on the Water

45 Immediately he made his disciples get into the boat and go on ahead to the other side, to Bethsaida, while he dismissed the crowd. ⁴⁶After saying farewell to them, he went up on the mountain to pray.

47 When evening came, the boat was out on the sea, and he was alone on the land. ⁴⁸When he saw that they were straining at the oars against an adverse wind, he came towards them early in the morning, walking on the sea. He intended to pass them by. ⁴⁹But when they saw him walking on the sea, they thought it was a ghost and cried out; ⁵⁰for they all saw him and were terrified. But immediately he spoke to them and said, "Take heart, it is I; do not be afraid." ⁵¹Then he got into the boat with them and the wind ceased. And they were utterly astounded, ⁵²for they did not understand about the loaves, but their hearts were hardened.

Healing the Sick in Gennesaret

53 When they had crossed over, they came to land at Gennesaret and moored the boat. ⁵⁴When they got out of the boat, people at once recognized him, ⁵⁵and rushed about that whole region and began to bring the sick on mats to wherever they heard he was. ⁵⁶And wherever he went, into villages or cities or farms, they laid the sick in the marketplaces, and begged him that they might touch even the fringe of his cloak; and all who touched it were healed.

The Tradition of the Elders

7 Now when the Pharisees and some of the scribes who had come from Jerusalem gathered around him, ²they noticed that some of his disciples were eating with defiled hands, that is, without washing them. ³(For the Pharisees, and all the Jews, do not eat unless they thoroughly wash their hands,ᵇ thus observing the tradition of the elders;

---

a The denarius was the usual day's wage for a laborer   *b* Meaning of Gk uncertain

[4] and they do not eat anything from the market unless they wash it;[a] and there are also many other traditions that they observe, the washing of cups, pots, and bronze kettles.[b]) [5] So the Pharisees and the scribes asked him, "Why do your disciples not live[c] according to the tradition of the elders, but eat with defiled hands?" [6] He said to them, "Isaiah prophesied rightly about you hypocrites, as it is written,

'This people honors me with their lips,
    but their hearts are far from me;
[7] in vain do they worship me,
    teaching human precepts as doctrines.'

[8] You abandon the commandment of God and hold to human tradition."

9 Then he said to them, "You have a fine way of rejecting the commandment of God in order to keep your tradition! [10] For Moses said, 'Honor your father and your mother'; and, 'Whoever speaks evil of father or mother must surely die.' [11] But you say that if anyone tells father or mother, 'Whatever support you might have had from me is Corban' (that is, an offering to God[d])— [12] then you no longer permit doing anything for a father or mother, [13] thus making void the word of God through your tradition that you have handed on. And you do many things like this."

14 Then he called the crowd again and said to them, "Listen to me, all of you, and understand: [15] there is nothing outside a person that by going in can defile, but the things that come out are what defile."[e]

17 When he had left the crowd and entered the house, his disciples asked him about the parable. [18] He said to them, "Then do you also fail to understand? Do you not see that whatever goes into a person from outside cannot defile, [19] since it enters, not the heart but the stomach, and goes out into the sewer?" (Thus he declared all foods clean.) [20] And he said, "It is what comes out of a person that defiles. [21] For it is from within, from the human heart, that evil intentions come: fornication, theft, murder, [22] adultery, avarice, wickedness, deceit, licentiousness, envy, slander, pride, folly. [23] All these evil things come from within, and they defile a person."

The Syrophoenician Woman's Faith

24 From there he set out and went away to the region of Tyre.[f] He entered a house and did not want anyone to know he was there. Yet he could not escape notice, [25] but a woman whose little daughter had an unclean spirit immediately heard about him, and she came and bowed down at his feet. [26] Now the woman was a Gentile, of Syrophoenician origin. She begged him to cast the demon out of her daughter. [27] He said to her, "Let the children be fed first, for it is not fair to take the children's food and throw it to the dogs." [28] But she answered him, "Sir,[g] even the dogs under the table eat the children's crumbs." [29] Then he said to her, "For saying that, you may go—the demon has left your daughter." [30] So she went home, found the child lying on the bed, and the demon gone.

---

a Other ancient authorities read *and when they come from the marketplace, they do not eat unless they purify themselves*   b Other ancient authorities add *and beds*   c Gk *walk*   d Gk lacks *to God*   e Other ancient authorities add verse 16, *"Let anyone with ears to hear listen"*   f Other ancient authorities add *and Sidon*   g Or *Lord*; other ancient authorities prefix *Yes*

God's Personal Touch

MARK 7.33–35

The way that Jesus heals this man requires that Jesus touch the man's head and face, perhaps even cradling the man's face in his hands. We can't help but wonder how long it has been since this person has been treated so gently.

Picture yourself face-to-face with Jesus and needing a healing touch. In what way does Jesus touch you? With a gentle pat on the back to encourage you? With his hands on your shoulders, looking you squarely in the eyes in order to get your attention? Cradling your face with compassion because you have been left out and rejected? Enjoy that image for several moments. Ask God to show you someone who needs to be touched in the same way.

See Meeting God in Service

Remembering God's Grace

MARK 8.16–21

Hungry once again, the disciples forget that providing for their needs is Jesus' specialty. On an even deeper level, they don't understand that Jesus is the Christ, who changes water to wine and feeds five thousand people with five loaves.

Our experiences of God—the times when he has rescued, comforted, confronted and challenged us—should teach us to rely on his miraculous power. They should help us remember how he has cared for us in the past. In our human weakness, however, we forget, and our forgetfulness hardens our hearts. Recall the last time God confronted, comforted or guided you. If you wish, write about that occasion for a minute or two and place it with other reflections in a journal as a way of deepening your trust in God's willingness and ability to care for you.

See *Meeting God in Everyday Life*

Jesus Cures a Deaf Man

31 Then he returned from the region of Tyre, and went by way of Sidon towards the Sea of Galilee, in the region of the Decapolis. ³²They brought to him a deaf man who had an impediment in his speech; and they begged him to lay his hand on him. ³³He took him aside in private, away from the crowd, and put his fingers into his ears, and he spat and touched his tongue. ³⁴Then looking up to heaven, he sighed and said to him, "Ephphatha," that is, "Be opened." ³⁵And immediately his ears were opened, his tongue was released, and he spoke plainly. ³⁶Then Jesus*a* ordered them to tell no one; but the more he ordered them, the more zealously they proclaimed it. ³⁷They were astounded beyond measure, saying, "He has done everything well; he even makes the deaf to hear and the mute to speak."

Feeding the Four Thousand

8 In those days when there was again a great crowd without anything to eat, he called his disciples and said to them, ²"I have compassion for the crowd, because they have been with me now for three days and have nothing to eat. ³If I send them away hungry to their homes, they will faint on the way—and some of them have come from a great distance." ⁴His disciples replied, "How can one feed these people with bread here in the desert?" ⁵He asked them, "How many loaves do you have?" They said, "Seven." ⁶Then he ordered the crowd to sit down on the ground; and he took the seven loaves, and after giving thanks he broke them and gave them to his disciples to distribute; and they distributed them to the crowd. ⁷They had also a few small fish; and after blessing them, he ordered that these too should be distributed. ⁸They ate and were filled; and they took up the broken pieces left over, seven baskets full. ⁹Now there were about four thousand people. And he sent them away. ¹⁰And immediately he got into the boat with his disciples and went to the district of Dalmanutha.*b*

The Demand for a Sign

11 The Pharisees came and began to argue with him, asking him for a sign from heaven, to test him. ¹²And he sighed deeply in his spirit and said, "Why does this generation ask for a sign? Truly I tell you, no sign will be given to this generation." ¹³And he left them, and getting into the boat again, he went across to the other side.

The Yeast of the Pharisees and of Herod

14 Now the disciples*c* had forgotten to bring any bread; and they had only one loaf with them in the boat. ¹⁵And he cautioned them, saying, "Watch out—beware of the yeast of the Pharisees and the yeast of Herod."*d* ¹⁶They said to one another, "It is because we have no bread." ¹⁷And becoming aware of it, Jesus said to them, "Why are you talking about having no bread? Do you still not perceive or understand? Are your hearts hardened? ¹⁸Do you have eyes, and fail to see? Do you have ears, and fail to hear? And do you not remember? ¹⁹When I broke the five loaves for the five thou-

---

a Gk *he*   *b* Other ancient authorities read *Mageda* or *Magdala*   *c* Gk *they*
d Other ancient authorities read *the Herodians*

sand, how many baskets full of broken pieces did you collect?" They said to him, "Twelve." [20]"And the seven for the four thousand, how many baskets full of broken pieces did you collect?" And they said to him, "Seven." [21]Then he said to them, "Do you not yet understand?"

Jesus Cures a Blind Man at Bethsaida

22 They came to Bethsaida. Some people[a] brought a blind man to him and begged him to touch him. [23]He took the blind man by the hand and led him out of the village; and when he had put saliva on his eyes and laid his hands on him, he asked him, "Can you see anything?" [24]And the man[b] looked up and said, "I can see people, but they look like trees, walking." [25]Then Jesus[b] laid his hands on his eyes again; and he looked intently and his sight was restored, and he saw everything clearly. [26]Then he sent him away to his home, saying, "Do not even go into the village."[c]

Peter's Declaration about Jesus

27 Jesus went on with his disciples to the villages of Caesarea Philippi; and on the way he asked his disciples, "Who do people say that I am?" [28]And they answered him, "John the Baptist; and others, Elijah; and still others, one of the prophets." [29]He asked them, "But who do you say that I am?" Peter answered him, "You are the Messiah."[d] [30]And he sternly ordered them not to tell anyone about him.

Jesus Foretells His Death and Resurrection

31 Then he began to teach them that the Son of Man must undergo great suffering, and be rejected by the elders, the chief priests, and the scribes, and be killed, and after three days rise again. [32]He said all this quite openly. And Peter took him aside and began to rebuke him. [33]But turning and looking at his disciples, he rebuked Peter and said, "Get behind me, Satan! For you are setting your mind not on divine things but on human things."

34 He called the crowd with his disciples, and said to them, "If any want to become my followers, let them deny themselves and take up their cross and follow me. [35]For those who want to save their life will lose it, and those who lose their life for my sake, and for the sake of the gospel,[e] will save it. [36]For what will it profit them to gain the whole world and forfeit their life? [37]Indeed, what can they give in return for their life? [38]Those who are ashamed of me and of my words[f] in this adulterous and sinful generation, of them the Son of Man will also be ashamed when he comes in the glory of his Father with the holy angels." [1]And he said to them, "Truly I tell you, there are some standing here who will not taste death until they see that the kingdom of God has come with[g] power."

The Transfiguration

2 Six days later, Jesus took with him Peter and James and John, and led them up a high mountain apart, by themselves. And he was transfigured before them, [3]and his clothes became dazzling white, such as no one[h] on earth

---

a Gk They   b Gk he   c Other ancient authorities add or tell anyone in the village   d Or the Christ   e Other ancient authorities read lose their life for the sake of the gospel   f Other ancient authorities read and of mine   g Or in   h Gk no fuller

---

Broken Bread, Poured Out Wine

MARK 8.35

"The ecclesiastical idea of a servant of God is not Jesus Christ's idea. His idea is that we serve Him by being the servants of other [people]. The real test of the saint is not preaching the gospel, but washing disciples' feet, that is, doing the things that do not count in the actual estimate of [others] but count everything in the estimate of God. Jesus Christ's idea of a New Testament saint [is] not one who proclaims the gospel merely, but one who becomes broken bread and poured out wine in the hands of Jesus Christ for other lives."

—OSWALD CHAMBERS,
My Utmost for His Highest

Honest Doubt

MARK 9.24

The father of this burned and broken boy is surprisingly honest about his lack of faith. Because he wants so much for Jesus to help his son, he might have been motivated to equivocate. Jesus honors his honesty with compassion and respect.

Fold your hands with your fingers intertwined. Imagine that one hand is your belief in God's power to redeem a person or situation and that your other hand is your doubt. Ask God to help you overcome your doubts and to work in that situation to bring about renewal and healing.

See Meeting God in Prayer

could bleach them. [4]And there appeared to them Elijah with Moses, who were talking with Jesus. [5]Then Peter said to Jesus, "Rabbi, it is good for us to be here; let us make three dwellings,[a] one for you, one for Moses, and one for Elijah." [6]He did not know what to say, for they were terrified. [7]Then a cloud overshadowed them, and from the cloud there came a voice, "This is my Son, the Beloved;[b] listen to him!" [8]Suddenly when they looked around, they saw no one with them any more, but only Jesus.

The Coming of Elijah

9 As they were coming down the mountain, he ordered them to tell no one about what they had seen, until after the Son of Man had risen from the dead. [10]So they kept the matter to themselves, questioning what this rising from the dead could mean. [11]Then they asked him, "Why do the scribes say that Elijah must come first?" [12]He said to them, "Elijah is indeed coming first to restore all things. How then is it written about the Son of Man, that he is to go through many sufferings and be treated with contempt? [13]But I tell you that Elijah has come, and they did to him whatever they pleased, as it is written about him."

The Healing of a Boy with a Spirit

14 When they came to the disciples, they saw a great crowd around them, and some scribes arguing with them. [15]When the whole crowd saw him, they were immediately overcome with awe, and they ran forward to greet him. [16]He asked them, "What are you arguing about with them?" [17]Someone from the crowd answered him, "Teacher, I brought you my son; he has a spirit that makes him unable to speak; [18]and whenever it seizes him, it dashes him down; and he foams and grinds his teeth and becomes rigid; and I asked your disciples to cast it out, but they could not do so." [19]He answered them, "You faithless generation, how much longer must I be among you? How much longer must I put up with you? Bring him to me." [20]And they brought the boy[c] to him. When the spirit saw him, immediately it convulsed the boy,[c] and he fell on the ground and rolled about, foaming at the mouth. [21]Jesus[d] asked the father, "How long has this been happening to him?" And he said, "From childhood. [22]It has often cast him into the fire and into the water, to destroy him; but if you are able to do anything, have pity on us and help us." [23]Jesus said to him, "If you are able!—All things can be done for the one who believes." [24]Immediately the father of the child cried out,[e] "I believe; help my unbelief!" [25]When Jesus saw that a crowd came running together, he rebuked the unclean spirit, saying to it, "You spirit that keeps this boy from speaking and hearing, I command you, come out of him, and never enter him again!" [26]After crying out and convulsing him terribly, it came out, and the boy was like a corpse, so that most of them said, "He is dead." [27]But Jesus took him by the hand and lifted him up, and he was able to stand. [28]When he had entered the house, his disciples asked him privately, "Why could we not cast it out?" [29]He said to them, "This kind can come out only through prayer."[f]

a Or *tents*   b Or *my beloved Son*   c Gk *him*   d Gk *He*   e Other ancient authorities add *with tears*   f Other ancient authorities add *and fasting*

Jesus Again Foretells His Death and Resurrection

30 They went on from there and passed through Galilee. He did not want anyone to know it; ³¹for he was teaching his disciples, saying to them, "The Son of Man is to be betrayed into human hands, and they will kill him, and three days after being killed, he will rise again." ³²But they did not understand what he was saying and were afraid to ask him.

Who Is the Greatest?

33 Then they came to Capernaum; and when he was in the house he asked them, "What were you arguing about on the way?" ³⁴But they were silent, for on the way they had argued with one another who was the greatest. ³⁵He sat down, called the twelve, and said to them, "Whoever wants to be first must be last of all and servant of all." ³⁶Then he took a little child and put it among them; and taking it in his arms, he said to them, ³⁷"Whoever welcomes one such child in my name welcomes me, and whoever welcomes me welcomes not me but the one who sent me."

Another Exorcist

38 John said to him, "Teacher, we saw someone*a* casting out demons in your name, and we tried to stop him, because he was not following us." ³⁹But Jesus said, "Do not stop him; for no one who does a deed of power in my name will be able soon afterward to speak evil of me. ⁴⁰Whoever is not against us is for us. ⁴¹For truly I tell you, whoever gives you a cup of water to drink because you bear the name of Christ will by no means lose the reward.

Temptations to Sin

42 "If any of you put a stumbling block before one of these little ones who believe in me,*b* it would be better for you if a great millstone were hung around your neck and you were thrown into the sea. ⁴³If your hand causes you to stumble, cut it off; it is better for you to enter life maimed than to have two hands and to go to hell,*c* to the unquenchable fire.*d* ⁴⁵And if your foot causes you to stumble, cut it off; it is better for you to enter life lame than to have two feet and to be thrown into hell.*c,d* ⁴⁷And if your eye causes you to stumble, tear it out; it is better for you to enter the kingdom of God with one eye than to have two eyes and to be thrown into hell,*c* ⁴⁸where their worm never dies, and the fire is never quenched.

49 "For everyone will be salted with fire.*e* ⁵⁰Salt is good; but if salt has lost its saltiness, how can you season it?*f* Have salt in yourselves, and be at peace with one another."

Teaching about Divorce

10 He left that place and went to the region of Judea and*g* beyond the Jordan. And crowds again gathered around him; and, as was his custom, he again taught them.

No Competition

MARK 9.38–41

Sometimes we tend to become competitive with other people, organizations or churches. When we're competitive we feel threatened. We're driven to prove we possess a special knowledge, a better method or a more honorable motive. We sometimes become territorial when someone who is not "one of us" does what we do. What if they would do it better? We want the kingdom of God to be advanced, but we want to be able to claim the credit for our corner of it.

Read this passage again and ponder these questions: What does this passage teach me about competition and God's kingdom? What can I pray for those toward whom I feel competitive?

See Meeting God in Community

---

a Other ancient authorities add *who does not follow us*   *b* Other ancient authorities lack *in me*   *c* Gk *Gehenna*   *d* Verses 44 and 46 (which are identical with verse 48) are lacking in the best ancient authorities   *e* Other ancient authorities either add or substitute *and every sacrifice will be salted with salt*   *f* Or *how can you restore its saltiness?*   *g* Other ancient authorities lack *and*

All Things Are Possible

MARK 10.21–27

The dashing young star of this passage is also a meticulously religious person. Jesus pierces his heart, however, by demanding that he surrender the wealth and position that he values more than God.

Imagine yourself face-to-face with Jesus. You are self-possessed, well-mannered, and surrounded by your accomplishments. Your motives are honorable. Imagine Jesus looking into your eyes so that you know the depth of his love for you. Now imagine him asking you to give up something that is very precious to you. You cringe. "O Lord, not that!" Now Jesus is telling you that all things are possible with God. What do you need to say to God in response?

See Meeting God in Scripture

2 Some Pharisees came, and to test him they asked, "Is it lawful for a man to divorce his wife?" ³He answered them, "What did Moses command you?" ⁴They said, "Moses allowed a man to write a certificate of dismissal and to divorce her." ⁵But Jesus said to them, "Because of your hardness of heart he wrote this commandment for you. ⁶But from the beginning of creation, 'God made them male and female.' ⁷'For this reason a man shall leave his father and mother and be joined to his wife,ᵃ ⁸and the two shall become one flesh.' So they are no longer two, but one flesh. ⁹Therefore what God has joined together, let no one separate."

10 Then in the house the disciples asked him again about this matter. ¹¹He said to them, "Whoever divorces his wife and marries another commits adultery against her; ¹²and if she divorces her husband and marries another, she commits adultery."

Jesus Blesses Little Children

13 People were bringing little children to him in order that he might touch them; and the disciples spoke sternly to them. ¹⁴But when Jesus saw this, he was indignant and said to them, "Let the little children come to me; do not stop them; for it is to such as these that the kingdom of God belongs. ¹⁵Truly I tell you, whoever does not receive the kingdom of God as a little child will never enter it." ¹⁶And he took them up in his arms, laid his hands on them, and blessed them.

The Rich Man

17 As he was setting out on a journey, a man ran up and knelt before him, and asked him, "Good Teacher, what must I do to inherit eternal life?" ¹⁸Jesus said to him, "Why do you call me good? No one is good but God alone. ¹⁹You know the commandments: 'You shall not murder; You shall not commit adultery; You shall not steal; You shall not bear false witness; You shall not defraud; Honor your father and mother.' " ²⁰He said to him, "Teacher, I have kept all these since my youth." ²¹Jesus, looking at him, loved him and said, "You lack one thing; go, sell what you own, and give the moneyᵇ to the poor, and you will have treasure in heaven; then come, follow me." ²²When he heard this, he was shocked and went away grieving, for he had many possessions.

23 Then Jesus looked around and said to his disciples, "How hard it will be for those who have wealth to enter the kingdom of God!" ²⁴And the disciples were perplexed at these words. But Jesus said to them again, "Children, how hard it isᶜ to enter the kingdom of God! ²⁵It is easier for a camel to go through the eye of a needle than for someone who is rich to enter the kingdom of God." ²⁶They were greatly astounded and said to one another,ᵈ "Then who can be saved?" ²⁷Jesus looked at them and said, "For mortals it is impossible, but not for God; for God all things are possible."

28 Peter began to say to him, "Look, we have left everything and followed you." ²⁹Jesus said, "Truly I tell you, there is no one who has left house or brothers or sisters or moth-

a Other ancient authorities lack *and be joined to his wife*   b Gk lacks *the money*   c Other ancient authorities add *for those who trust in riches*   d Other ancient authorities read *to him*

er or father or children or fields, for my sake and for the sake of the good news,*a* ³⁰who will not receive a hundredfold now in this age—houses, brothers and sisters, mothers and children, and fields, with persecutions—and in the age to come eternal life. ³¹But many who are first will be last, and the last will be first."

A Third Time Jesus Foretells His Death and Resurrection

32 They were on the road, going up to Jerusalem, and Jesus was walking ahead of them; they were amazed, and those who followed were afraid. He took the twelve aside again and began to tell them what was to happen to him, ³³saying, "See, we are going up to Jerusalem, and the Son of Man will be handed over to the chief priests and the scribes, and they will condemn him to death; then they will hand him over to the Gentiles; ³⁴they will mock him, and spit upon him, and flog him, and kill him; and after three days he will rise again."

The Request of James and John

35 James and John, the sons of Zebedee, came forward to him and said to him, "Teacher, we want you to do for us whatever we ask of you." ³⁶And he said to them, "What is it you want me to do for you?" ³⁷And they said to him, "Grant us to sit, one at your right hand and one at your left, in your glory." ³⁸But Jesus said to them, "You do not know what you are asking. Are you able to drink the cup that I drink, or be baptized with the baptism that I am baptized with?" ³⁹They replied, "We are able." Then Jesus said to them, "The cup that I drink you will drink; and with the baptism with which I am baptized, you will be baptized; ⁴⁰but to sit at my right hand or at my left is not mine to grant, but it is for those for whom it has been prepared."

41 When the ten heard this, they began to be angry with James and John. ⁴²So Jesus called them and said to them, "You know that among the Gentiles those whom they recognize as their rulers lord it over them, and their great ones are tyrants over them. ⁴³But it is not so among you; but whoever wishes to become great among you must be your servant, ⁴⁴and whoever wishes to be first among you must be slave of all. ⁴⁵For the Son of Man came not to be served but to serve, and to give his life a ransom for many."

The Healing of Blind Bartimaeus

46 They came to Jericho. As he and his disciples and a large crowd were leaving Jericho, Bartimaeus son of Timaeus, a blind beggar, was sitting by the roadside. ⁴⁷When he heard that it was Jesus of Nazareth, he began to shout out and say, "Jesus, Son of David, have mercy on me!" ⁴⁸Many sternly ordered him to be quiet, but he cried out even more loudly, "Son of David, have mercy on me!" ⁴⁹Jesus stood still and said, "Call him here." And they called the blind man, saying to him, "Take heart; get up, he is calling you." ⁵⁰So throwing off his cloak, he sprang up and came to Jesus. ⁵¹Then Jesus said to him, "What do you want me to do for you?" The blind man said to him, "My teacher,*b* let me see again." ⁵²Jesus said to him, "Go; your faith has made you well." Immediately he regained his sight and followed him on the way.

---

a Or *gospel*   *b* Aramaic *Rabbouni*

A Place of Importance

MARK 10.35–40

James and John use their friendship with Jesus in order to manipulate him into giving them a place beside him, thinking it will bring them prestige and power. It must not have seemed improper to them at the time, nor do our "order-placing" prayers look that bad to us. If we're honest, a lot of our prayers consist of politely telling God how things should be.

Think about a troublesome situation in your life. Write a prayer that tells God how you think things should be. Read it. Now write a prayer that is full of your questions rather than full of your answers.

See Meeting God in Prayer

Prayer for All Nations

MARK 11.17

Praying for people we know can be difficult—praying for people we don't know is even more challenging. Jesus said the temple was a place of prayer for all nations. The court of the Gentiles was to be a place where all people could come to God.

Try praying for other nations in one of these ways: Choose a particular nation or group of people for whom you have compassion (those who live with famine conditions in Africa, people in South America who are losing their rainforest habitat, those who live under the threat of genocide). Pray for them and their troubling situation. Or turn to the world news section of your newspaper or in a magazine and pray for the nations mentioned there. Turn to the "restaurant" category in the Yellow Pages of your telephone book and pray for the nations represented by various ethnic restaurants.

See *Meeting God in Community*

Jesus' Triumphal Entry into Jerusalem

11 When they were approaching Jerusalem, at Bethphage and Bethany, near the Mount of Olives, he sent two of his disciples ²and said to them, "Go into the village ahead of you, and immediately as you enter it, you will find tied there a colt that has never been ridden; untie it and bring it. ³If anyone says to you, 'Why are you doing this?' just say this, 'The Lord needs it and will send it back here immediately.' " ⁴They went away and found a colt tied near a door, outside in the street. As they were untying it, ⁵some of the bystanders said to them, "What are you doing, untying the colt?" ⁶They told them what Jesus had said; and they allowed them to take it. ⁷Then they brought the colt to Jesus and threw their cloaks on it; and he sat on it. ⁸Many people spread their cloaks on the road, and others spread leafy branches that they had cut in the fields. ⁹Then those who went ahead and those who followed were shouting,

"Hosanna!
   Blessed is the one who comes in the name of the
      Lord!
¹⁰   Blessed is the coming kingdom of our ancestor
      David!
   Hosanna in the highest heaven!"

11 Then he entered Jerusalem and went into the temple; and when he had looked around at everything, as it was already late, he went out to Bethany with the twelve.

Jesus Curses the Fig Tree

12 On the following day, when they came from Bethany, he was hungry. ¹³Seeing in the distance a fig tree in leaf, he went to see whether perhaps he would find anything on it. When he came to it, he found nothing but leaves, for it was not the season for figs. ¹⁴He said to it, "May no one ever eat fruit from you again." And his disciples heard it.

Jesus Cleanses the Temple

15 Then they came to Jerusalem. And he entered the temple and began to drive out those who were selling and those who were buying in the temple, and he overturned the tables of the money changers and the seats of those who sold doves; ¹⁶and he would not allow anyone to carry anything through the temple. ¹⁷He was teaching and saying, "Is it not written,

'My house shall be called a house of prayer for all
      the nations'?
   But you have made it a den of robbers."
¹⁸And when the chief priests and the scribes heard it, they kept looking for a way to kill him; for they were afraid of him, because the whole crowd was spellbound by his teaching. ¹⁹And when evening came, Jesus and his disciples*a* went out of the city.

The Lesson from the Withered Fig Tree

20 In the morning as they passed by, they saw the fig tree withered away to its roots. ²¹Then Peter remembered and said to him, "Rabbi, look! The fig tree that you cursed has withered." ²²Jesus answered them, "Have*b* faith in God.

a Gk *they*: other ancient authorities read *he*   *b* Other ancient authorities read "*If you have*

²³Truly I tell you, if you say to this mountain, 'Be taken up and thrown into the sea,' and if you do not doubt in your heart, but believe that what you say will come to pass, it will be done for you. ²⁴So I tell you, whatever you ask for in prayer, believe that you have received[a] it, and it will be yours.

25 "Whenever you stand praying, forgive, if you have anything against anyone; so that your Father in heaven may also forgive you your trespasses."[b]

Jesus' Authority Is Questioned

27 Again they came to Jerusalem. As he was walking in the temple, the chief priests, the scribes, and the elders came to him ²⁸and said, "By what authority are you doing these things? Who gave you this authority to do them?" ²⁹Jesus said to them, "I will ask you one question; answer me, and I will tell you by what authority I do these things. ³⁰Did the baptism of John come from heaven, or was it of human origin? Answer me." ³¹They argued with one another, "If we say, 'From heaven,' he will say, 'Why then did you not believe him?' ³²But shall we say, 'Of human origin'?"— they were afraid of the crowd, for all regarded John as truly a prophet. ³³So they answered Jesus, "We do not know." And Jesus said to them, "Neither will I tell you by what authority I am doing these things."

The Parable of the Wicked Tenants

12 Then he began to speak to them in parables. "A man planted a vineyard, put a fence around it, dug a pit for the wine press, and built a watchtower; then he leased it to tenants and went to another country. ²When the season came, he sent a slave to the tenants to collect from them his share of the produce of the vineyard. ³But they seized him, and beat him, and sent him away empty-handed. ⁴And again he sent another slave to them; this one they beat over the head and insulted. ⁵Then he sent another, and that one they killed. And so it was with many others; some they beat, and others they killed. ⁶He had still one other, a beloved son. Finally he sent him to them, saying, 'They will respect my son.' ⁷But those tenants said to one another, 'This is the heir; come, let us kill him, and the inheritance will be ours.' ⁸So they seized him, killed him, and threw him out of the vineyard. ⁹What then will the owner of the vineyard do? He will come and destroy the tenants and give the vineyard to others. ¹⁰Have you not read this scripture:

'The stone that the builders rejected
    has become the cornerstone;[c]
¹¹ this was the Lord's doing,
    and it is amazing in our eyes'?"

12 When they realized that he had told this parable against them, they wanted to arrest him, but they feared the crowd. So they left him and went away.

The Question about Paying Taxes

13 Then they sent to him some Pharisees and some Herodians to trap him in what he said. ¹⁴And they came

---

The New Way of Faith

MARK 11.12–14,20–24

The fig tree is no longer bearing fruit and Jesus curses it to illustrate a point to the disciples. The old ways of the temple culture and the Pharisees are past the point of being able to bear fruit. Then Jesus tells the disciples how the new covenant is characterized by faith (v.22), direct access to God through grace (v.24) and forgiveness (v.25).

Examine yourself in God's presence today. Are you bearing the fruit of faith, grace and forgiveness? How might an unforgiving spirit be causing your faith to shrivel? How can you open up the channels of God's grace so that Jesus' life-giving power can flow freely and so that you can bear fruit?

---

a Other ancient authorities read *are receiving*   *b* Other ancient authorities add verse 26, *"But if you do not forgive, neither will your Father in heaven forgive your trespasses."*   *c* Or *keystone*

A Spark of God's Love

MARK 12.28–31

"The two great commandments . . . . are contained in the first two words of the Lord's Prayer, and a Christian should never say "Our Father" without feeling an awakening of the love of God and his neighbor . . . It is love which is the voice of the heart. Love God and you will be always speaking to him. Ask God to open your heart and kindle in it a spark of his love."

—JEAN NICHOLAS GROU,
How to Pray

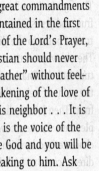

and said to him, "Teacher, we know that you are sincere, and show deference to no one; for you do not regard people with partiality, but teach the way of God in accordance with truth. Is it lawful to pay taxes to the emperor, or not? [15]Should we pay them, or should we not?" But knowing their hypocrisy, he said to them, "Why are you putting me to the test? Bring me a denarius and let me see it." [16]And they brought one. Then he said to them, "Whose head is this, and whose title?" They answered, "The emperor's." [17]Jesus said to them, "Give to the emperor the things that are the emperor's, and to God the things that are God's." And they were utterly amazed at him.

The Question about the Resurrection

18 Some Sadducees, who say there is no resurrection, came to him and asked him a question, saying, [19]"Teacher, Moses wrote for us that if a man's brother dies, leaving a wife but no child, the man[a] shall marry the widow and raise up children for his brother. [20]There were seven brothers; the first married and, when he died, left no children; [21]and the second married the widow[b] and died, leaving no children; and the third likewise; [22]none of the seven left children. Last of all the woman herself died. [23]In the resurrection[c] whose wife will she be? For the seven had married her."

24 Jesus said to them, "Is not this the reason you are wrong, that you know neither the scriptures nor the power of God? [25]For when they rise from the dead, they neither marry nor are given in marriage, but are like angels in heaven. [26]And as for the dead being raised, have you not read in the book of Moses, in the story about the bush, how God said to him, 'I am the God of Abraham, the God of Isaac, and the God of Jacob'? [27]He is God not of the dead, but of the living; you are quite wrong."

The First Commandment

28 One of the scribes came near and heard them disputing with one another, and seeing that he answered them well, he asked him, "Which commandment is the first of all?" [29]Jesus answered, "The first is, 'Hear, O Israel: the Lord our God, the Lord is one; [30]you shall love the Lord your God with all your heart, and with all your soul, and with all your mind, and with all your strength.' [31]The second is this, 'You shall love your neighbor as yourself.' There is no other commandment greater than these." [32]Then the scribe said to him, "You are right, Teacher; you have truly said that 'he is one, and besides him there is no other'; [33]and 'to love him with all the heart, and with all the understanding, and with all the strength,' and 'to love one's neighbor as oneself,'—this is much more important than all whole burnt offerings and sacrifices." [34]When Jesus saw that he answered wisely, he said to him, "You are not far from the kingdom of God." After that no one dared to ask him any question.

The Question about David's Son

35 While Jesus was teaching in the temple, he said, "How can the scribes say that the Messiah[d] is the son of David? [36]David himself, by the Holy Spirit, declared,

a Gk *his brother*   *b* Gk *her*   *c* Other ancient authorities add *when they rise*   *d* Or *the Christ*

'The Lord said to my Lord,
  "Sit at my right hand,
    until I put your enemies under your feet." '
[37]David himself calls him Lord; so how can he be his son?" And the large crowd was listening to him with delight.

Jesus Denounces the Scribes

38 As he taught, he said, "Beware of the scribes, who like to walk around in long robes, and to be greeted with respect in the marketplaces, [39]and to have the best seats in the synagogues and places of honor at banquets! [40]They devour widows' houses and for the sake of appearance say long prayers. They will receive the greater condemnation."

The Widow's Offering

41 He sat down opposite the treasury, and watched the crowd putting money into the treasury. Many rich people put in large sums. [42]A poor widow came and put in two small copper coins, which are worth a penny. [43]Then he called his disciples and said to them, "Truly I tell you, this poor widow has put in more than all those who are contributing to the treasury. [44]For all of them have contributed out of their abundance; but she out of her poverty has put in everything she had, all she had to live on."

The Destruction of the Temple Foretold

13 As he came out of the temple, one of his disciples said to him, "Look, Teacher, what large stones and what large buildings!" [2]Then Jesus asked him, "Do you see these great buildings? Not one stone will be left here upon another; all will be thrown down."

3 When he was sitting on the Mount of Olives opposite the temple, Peter, James, John, and Andrew asked him privately, [4]"Tell us, when will this be, and what will be the sign that all these things are about to be accomplished?" [5]Then Jesus began to say to them, "Beware that no one leads you astray. [6]Many will come in my name and say, 'I am he!'[a] and they will lead many astray. [7]When you hear of wars and rumors of wars, do not be alarmed; this must take place, but the end is still to come. [8]For nation will rise against nation, and kingdom against kingdom; there will be earthquakes in various places; there will be famines. This is but the beginning of the birth pangs.

Persecution Foretold

9 "As for yourselves, beware; for they will hand you over to councils; and you will be beaten in synagogues; and you will stand before governors and kings because of me, as a testimony to them. [10]And the good news[b] must first be proclaimed to all nations. [11]When they bring you to trial and hand you over, do not worry beforehand about what you are to say; but say whatever is given you at that time, for it is not you who speak, but the Holy Spirit. [12]Brother will betray brother to death, and a father his child, and children will rise against parents and have them put to death; [13]and you will be hated by all because of my name. But the one who endures to the end will be saved.

a Gk *I am*   b Gk *gospel*

In Jesus' Eyes

MARK 12.41–44

As Jesus watches the people give their money, he interprets the scene differently than the other onlookers. He reckons the widow's two copper coins a treasure and the rich people's large offerings inconsequential. What does this tell us about the way God views what we offer? About the way God measures generosity?

Imagine that you are one of the disciples in this scene. What is God teaching you today about giving? About the state of your heart? What will you ask yourself the next time you put money into the temple treasury?

See Meeting God in Scripture

Beware

MARK 13.9–11, 32–37

Jesus tells his followers that they are to "watch themselves" so that they are not distracted by the cataclysmic events going on around them. They are to be spiritually aware and ready to proclaim the truth in tough times.

Do you ever face tough questions about your faith? Are you ready to give a passionate and compelling answer when asked why you have the hope that you have (see 1 Peter 3.15)? What can you do to prepare for such a time, even though you may not know what will be specifically asked of you? How can you be ready to let the Holy Spirit speak through you?

The Desolating Sacrilege

14 "But when you see the desolating sacrilege set up where it ought not to be (let the reader understand), then those in Judea must flee to the mountains; ¹⁵the one on the housetop must not go down or enter the house to take anything away; ¹⁶the one in the field must not turn back to get a coat. ¹⁷Woe to those who are pregnant and to those who are nursing infants in those days! ¹⁸Pray that it may not be in winter. ¹⁹For in those days there will be suffering, such as has not been from the beginning of the creation that God created until now, no, and never will be. ²⁰And if the Lord had not cut short those days, no one would be saved; but for the sake of the elect, whom he chose, he has cut short those days. ²¹And if anyone says to you at that time, 'Look! Here is the Messiah!'ᵃ or 'Look! There he is!'—do not believe it. ²²False messiahsᵇ and false prophets will appear and produce signs and omens, to lead astray, if possible, the elect. ²³But be alert; I have already told you everything.

The Coming of the Son of Man

24 "But in those days, after that suffering,
  the sun will be darkened,
    and the moon will not give its light,
²⁵ and the stars will be falling from heaven,
    and the powers in the heavens will be shaken.
²⁶Then they will see 'the Son of Man coming in clouds' with great power and glory. ²⁷Then he will send out the angels, and gather his elect from the four winds, from the ends of the earth to the ends of heaven.

The Lesson of the Fig Tree

28 "From the fig tree learn its lesson: as soon as its branch becomes tender and puts forth its leaves, you know that summer is near. ²⁹So also, when you see these things taking place, you know that heᶜ is near, at the very gates. ³⁰Truly I tell you, this generation will not pass away until all these things have taken place. ³¹Heaven and earth will pass away, but my words will not pass away.

The Necessity for Watchfulness

32 "But about that day or hour no one knows, neither the angels in heaven, nor the Son, but only the Father. ³³Beware, keep alert;ᵈ for you do not know when the time will come. ³⁴It is like a man going on a journey, when he leaves home and puts his slaves in charge, each with his work, and commands the doorkeeper to be on the watch. ³⁵Therefore, keep awake—for you do not know when the master of the house will come, in the evening, or at midnight, or at cockcrow, or at dawn, ³⁶or else he may find you asleep when he comes suddenly. ³⁷And what I say to you I say to all: Keep awake."

The Plot to Kill Jesus

14 It was two days before the Passover and the festival of Unleavened Bread. The chief priests and the scribes were looking for a way to arrest Jesusᵉ by stealth and kill him; ²for they said, "Not during the festival, or there may be a riot among the people."

a Or the Christ b Or christs c Or it d Other ancient authorities add and pray e Gk him

The Anointing at Bethany

3 While he was at Bethany in the house of Simon the leper,[a] as he sat at the table, a woman came with an alabaster jar of very costly ointment of nard, and she broke open the jar and poured the ointment on his head. [4]But some were there who said to one another in anger, "Why was the ointment wasted in this way? [5]For this ointment could have been sold for more than three hundred denarii,[b] and the money given to the poor." And they scolded her. [6]But Jesus said, "Let her alone; why do you trouble her? She has performed a good service for me. [7]For you always have the poor with you, and you can show kindness to them whenever you wish; but you will not always have me. [8]She has done what she could; she has anointed my body beforehand for its burial. [9]Truly I tell you, wherever the good news[c] is proclaimed in the whole world, what she has done will be told in remembrance of her."

Judas Agrees to Betray Jesus

10 Then Judas Iscariot, who was one of the twelve, went to the chief priests in order to betray him to them. [11]When they heard it, they were greatly pleased, and promised to give him money. So he began to look for an opportunity to betray him.

The Passover with the Disciples

12 On the first day of Unleavened Bread, when the Passover lamb is sacrificed, his disciples said to him, "Where do you want us to go and make the preparations for you to eat the Passover?" [13]So he sent two of his disciples, saying to them, "Go into the city, and a man carrying a jar of water will meet you; follow him, [14]and wherever he enters, say to the owner of the house, 'The Teacher asks, Where is my guest room where I may eat the Passover with my disciples?' [15]He will show you a large room upstairs, furnished and ready. Make preparations for us there." [16]So the disciples set out and went to the city, and found everything as he had told them; and they prepared the Passover meal.

17 When it was evening, he came with the twelve. [18]And when they had taken their places and were eating, Jesus said, "Truly I tell you, one of you will betray me, one who is eating with me." [19]They began to be distressed and to say to him one after another, "Surely, not I?" [20]He said to them, "It is one of the twelve, one who is dipping bread[d] into the bowl[e] with me. [21]For the Son of Man goes as it is written of him, but woe to that one by whom the Son of Man is betrayed! It would have been better for that one not to have been born."

The Institution of the Lord's Supper

22 While they were eating, he took a loaf of bread, and after blessing it he broke it, gave it to them, and said, "Take; this is my body." [23]Then he took a cup, and after giving thanks he gave it to them, and all of them drank from it. [24]He said to them, "This is my blood of the[f] covenant, which is poured out for many. [25]Truly I tell you, I will never

---

a The terms *leper* and *leprosy* can refer to several diseases
b The denarius was the usual day's wage for a laborer   c Or *gospel*
d Gk lacks *bread*   e Other ancient authorities read *same bowl*   f Other ancient authorities add *new*

The Melted Will

MARK 14.35–36

Sometimes we underestimate what it cost Jesus to submit his will to the Father's. What was the price of saying yes to the Father as Jesus faced the cross?

Light a candle. Scoop up some of the melted wax as it drips down the side. Press it between your fingers and think of a situation or event that requires you to surrender your will. Sing an appropriate song such as "Have Thine Own Way, Lord," and pray that God will open your heart and make it as pliable as warm wax.

again drink of the fruit of the vine until that day when I drink it new in the kingdom of God."

Peter's Denial Foretold

26 When they had sung the hymn, they went out to the Mount of Olives. ²⁷And Jesus said to them, "You will all become deserters; for it is written,

'I will strike the shepherd,
and the sheep will be scattered.'

²⁸But after I am raised up, I will go before you to Galilee." ²⁹Peter said to him, "Even though all become deserters, I will not." ³⁰Jesus said to him, "Truly I tell you, this day, this very night, before the cock crows twice, you will deny me three times." ³¹But he said vehemently, "Even though I must die with you, I will not deny you." And all of them said the same.

Jesus Prays in Gethsemane

32 They went to a place called Gethsemane; and he said to his disciples, "Sit here while I pray." ³³He took with him Peter and James and John, and began to be distressed and agitated. ³⁴And he said to them, "I am deeply grieved, even to death; remain here, and keep awake." ³⁵And going a little farther, he threw himself on the ground and prayed that, if it were possible, the hour might pass from him. ³⁶He said, "Abba,ᵃ Father, for you all things are possible; remove this cup from me; yet, not what I want, but what you want." ³⁷He came and found them sleeping; and he said to Peter, "Simon, are you asleep? Could you not keep awake one hour? ³⁸Keep awake and pray that you may not come into the time of trial;ᵇ the spirit indeed is willing, but the flesh is weak." ³⁹And again he went away and prayed, saying the same words. ⁴⁰And once more he came and found them sleeping, for their eyes were very heavy; and they did not know what to say to him. ⁴¹He came a third time and said to them, "Are you still sleeping and taking your rest? Enough! The hour has come; the Son of Man is betrayed into the hands of sinners. ⁴²Get up, let us be going. See, my betrayer is at hand."

The Betrayal and Arrest of Jesus

43 Immediately, while he was still speaking, Judas, one of the twelve, arrived; and with him there was a crowd with swords and clubs, from the chief priests, the scribes, and the elders. ⁴⁴Now the betrayer had given them a sign, saying, "The one I will kiss is the man; arrest him and lead him away under guard." ⁴⁵So when he came, he went up to him at once and said, "Rabbi!" and kissed him. ⁴⁶Then they laid hands on him and arrested him. ⁴⁷But one of those who stood near drew his sword and struck the slave of the high priest, cutting off his ear. ⁴⁸Then Jesus said to them, "Have you come out with swords and clubs to arrest me as though I were a bandit? ⁴⁹Day after day I was with you in the temple teaching, and you did not arrest me. But let the scriptures be fulfilled." ⁵⁰All of them deserted him and fled.

51 A certain young man was following him, wearing nothing but a linen cloth. They caught hold of him, ⁵²but he left the linen cloth and ran off naked.

a Aramaic for *Father*   *b* Or *into temptation*

Jesus before the Council

53 They took Jesus to the high priest; and all the chief priests, the elders, and the scribes were assembled. 54Peter had followed him at a distance, right into the courtyard of the high priest; and he was sitting with the guards, warming himself at the fire. 55Now the chief priests and the whole council were looking for testimony against Jesus to put him to death; but they found none. 56For many gave false testimony against him, and their testimony did not agree. 57Some stood up and gave false testimony against him, saying, 58"We heard him say, 'I will destroy this temple that is made with hands, and in three days I will build another, not made with hands.' " 59But even on this point their testimony did not agree. 60Then the high priest stood up before them and asked Jesus, "Have you no answer? What is it that they testify against you?" 61But he was silent and did not answer. Again the high priest asked him, "Are you the Messiah,[a] the Son of the Blessed One?" 62Jesus said, "I am; and

'you will see the Son of Man
seated at the right hand of the Power,'
and 'coming with the clouds of heaven.' "

63Then the high priest tore his clothes and said, "Why do we still need witnesses? 64You have heard his blasphemy! What is your decision?" All of them condemned him as deserving death. 65Some began to spit on him, to blindfold him, and to strike him, saying to him, "Prophesy!" The guards also took him over and beat him.

Peter Denies Jesus

66 While Peter was below in the courtyard, one of the servant-girls of the high priest came by. 67When she saw Peter warming himself, she stared at him and said, "You also were with Jesus, the man from Nazareth." 68But he denied it, saying, "I do not know or understand what you are talking about." And he went out into the forecourt.[b] Then the cock crowed.[c] 69And the servant-girl, on seeing him, began again to say to the bystanders, "This man is one of them." 70But again he denied it. Then after a little while the bystanders again said to Peter, "Certainly you are one of them; for you are a Galilean." 71But he began to curse, and he swore an oath, "I do not know this man you are talking about." 72At that moment the cock crowed for the second time. Then Peter remembered that Jesus had said to him, "Before the cock crows twice, you will deny me three times." And he broke down and wept.

Jesus before Pilate

15 As soon as it was morning, the chief priests held a consultation with the elders and scribes and the whole council. They bound Jesus, led him away, and handed him over to Pilate. 2Pilate asked him, "Are you the King of the Jews?" He answered him, "You say so." 3Then the chief priests accused him of many things. 4Pilate asked him again, "Have you no answer? See how many charges they bring against you." 5But Jesus made no further reply, so that Pilate was amazed.

To Proclaim the Christ

MARK 14.61–62

At his trial Jesus, beaten and bedraggled, proclaims himself the Christ. Such a declaration must seem ridiculous to those gathered—that the man whom they are about to execute is the Messiah.

Are you called to proclaim Jesus the Christ to people to whom that reality might seem foreign or even ridiculous? To people who are sick or dying? To doubt-ridden people? To people who are destitute? To proud and self-sufficient people? In what ways might God want you to communicate divine truth? Do you have a friend with whom you could discuss this and who would pray for you?

See Meeting God in Community

---

a Or the Christ   b Or gateway   c Other ancient authorities lack Then the cock crowed

Tender, Wise and Strong

MARK 15.16–20

"It is the cup that Thou didst drink, Lord Jesus, more than ought else that renders Thee love-worthy; it is the work of our redemption that supremely claims our love. He put up with people who tried to catch Him in His talk, carped at His actions, mocked His suffering and even upbraided Him in death. This love of His is tender, wise and strong. Tender in that He took on Him our flesh; careful and wise in that He guarded against sin; and strong in that He suffered death. I trust myself entirely to Him who willed to save me, knew the way to do it, and had the power to carry out the work. He has sought me out and called me by His grace."

—BERNARD OF CLAIRVAUX,
*Selections from the Writings
of Bernard of Clairvaux*

Pilate Hands Jesus over to Be Crucified

6 Now at the festival he used to release a prisoner for them, anyone for whom they asked. [7]Now a man called Barabbas was in prison with the rebels who had committed murder during the insurrection. [8]So the crowd came and began to ask Pilate to do for them according to his custom. [9]Then he answered them, "Do you want me to release for you the King of the Jews?" [10]For he realized that it was out of jealousy that the chief priests had handed him over. [11]But the chief priests stirred up the crowd to have him release Barabbas for them instead. [12]Pilate spoke to them again, "Then what do you wish me to do[a] with the man you call[b] the King of the Jews?" [13]They shouted back, "Crucify him!" [14]Pilate asked them, "Why, what evil has he done?" But they shouted all the more, "Crucify him!" [15]So Pilate, wishing to satisfy the crowd, released Barabbas for them; and after flogging Jesus, he handed him over to be crucified.

The Soldiers Mock Jesus

16 Then the soldiers led him into the courtyard of the palace (that is, the governor's headquarters[c]); and they called together the whole cohort. [17]And they clothed him in a purple cloak; and after twisting some thorns into a crown, they put it on him. [18]And they began saluting him, "Hail, King of the Jews!" [19]They struck his head with a reed, spat upon him, and knelt down in homage to him. [20]After mocking him, they stripped him of the purple cloak and put his own clothes on him. Then they led him out to crucify him.

The Crucifixion of Jesus

21 They compelled a passer-by, who was coming in from the country, to carry his cross; it was Simon of Cyrene, the father of Alexander and Rufus. [22]Then they brought Jesus[d] to the place called Golgotha (which means the place of a skull). [23]And they offered him wine mixed with myrrh; but he did not take it. [24]And they crucified him, and divided his clothes among them, casting lots to decide what each should take.

25 It was nine o'clock in the morning when they crucified him. [26]The inscription of the charge against him read, "The King of the Jews." [27]And with him they crucified two bandits, one on his right and one on his left.[e] [29]Those who passed by derided[f] him, shaking their heads and saying, "Aha! You who would destroy the temple and build it in three days, [30]save yourself, and come down from the cross!" [31]In the same way the chief priests, along with the scribes, were also mocking him among themselves and saying, "He saved others; he cannot save himself. [32]Let the Messiah,[g] the King of Israel, come down from the cross now, so that we may see and believe." Those who were crucified with him also taunted him.

The Death of Jesus

33 When it was noon, darkness came over the whole land[h] until three in the afternoon. [34]At three o'clock Jesus

a Other ancient authorities read *what should I do*   b Other ancient authorities lack *the man you call*   c Gk *the praetorium*   d Gk *him*
e Other ancient authorities add verse 28, *And the scripture was fulfilled that says, "And he was counted among the lawless."*   f Or *blasphemed*   g Or *the Christ*   h Or *earth*

cried out with a loud voice, "Eloi, Eloi, lema sabachthani?" which means, "My God, my God, why have you forsaken me?"[a] **35**When some of the bystanders heard it, they said, "Listen, he is calling for Elijah." **36**And someone ran, filled a sponge with sour wine, put it on a stick, and gave it to him to drink, saying, "Wait, let us see whether Elijah will come to take him down." **37**Then Jesus gave a loud cry and breathed his last. **38**And the curtain of the temple was torn in two, from top to bottom. **39**Now when the centurion, who stood facing him, saw that in this way he[b] breathed his last, he said, "Truly this man was God's Son!"[c]

40 There were also women looking on from a distance; among them were Mary Magdalene, and Mary the mother of James the younger and of Joses, and Salome. **41**These used to follow him and provided for him when he was in Galilee; and there were many other women who had come up with him to Jerusalem.

The Burial of Jesus

42 When evening had come, and since it was the day of Preparation, that is, the day before the sabbath, **43**Joseph of Arimathea, a respected member of the council, who was also himself waiting expectantly for the kingdom of God, went boldly to Pilate and asked for the body of Jesus. **44**Then Pilate wondered if he were already dead; and summoning the centurion, he asked him whether he had been dead for some time. **45**When he learned from the centurion that he was dead, he granted the body to Joseph. **46**Then Joseph[d] bought a linen cloth, and taking down the body,[e] wrapped it in the linen cloth, and laid it in a tomb that had been hewn out of the rock. He then rolled a stone against the door of the tomb. **47**Mary Magdalene and Mary the mother of Joses saw where the body[e] was laid.

The Resurrection of Jesus

16 When the sabbath was over, Mary Magdalene, and Mary the mother of James, and Salome bought spices, so that they might go and anoint him. **2**And very early on the first day of the week, when the sun had risen, they went to the tomb. **3**They had been saying to one another, "Who will roll away the stone for us from the entrance to the tomb?" **4**When they looked up, they saw that the stone, which was very large, had already been rolled back. **5**As they entered the tomb, they saw a young man, dressed in a white robe, sitting on the right side; and they were alarmed. **6**But he said to them, "Do not be alarmed; you are looking for Jesus of Nazareth, who was crucified. He has been raised; he is not here. Look, there is the place they laid him. **7**But go, tell his disciples and Peter that he is going ahead of you to Galilee; there you will see him, just as he told you." **8**So they went out and fled from the tomb, for terror and amazement had seized them; and they said nothing to anyone, for they were afraid.[f]

---

a Other ancient authorities read *made me a reproach*   *b* Other ancient authorities add *cried out and*   *c* Or *a son of God*   *d* Gk *he*   *e* Gk *it*
f Some of the most ancient authorities bring the book to a close at the end of verse 8. One authority concludes the book with the shorter ending; others include the shorter ending and then continue with verses 9-20. In most authorities verses 9-20 follow immediately after verse 8, though in some of these authorities the passage is marked as being doubtful.

Were You There?

MARK 15.37–39

Read this passage, taking on the role of the Roman centurion. Feel the weight of the armor on your shoulders. Listen to the pathos of Jesus' loud cry. Do you see the blood and sweat drip from his body? Now he is quiet. You notice that his breathing and heartbeat have ceased. You declare: "Truly this man was God's Son!"

Position your body in a way that expresses this phrase—facedown on the floor, standing with your hands raised or stooping over in grief. Thank Jesus the Savior for his redeeming love.

See Meeting God in Worship

Encountering the Unexpected

MARK 16.4–8

Meeting an angel is so shocking to this group of women that they leave the garden trembling and bewildered. Even though Jesus had told them to expect his resurrection, they are still astounded at what the angel has told them.

Read the passage slowly and sit quietly. Wait in silence, being content to enjoy God's Word. What word, phrase or image impresses you and stays with you? Reflect on this word or phrase. Why do you think it is important? What is God's message to you? How will you respond when you meet him unexpectedly? Ask God what you need to learn from this passage.

See Meeting God in Scripture

THE SHORTER ENDING OF MARK

⟦And all that had been commanded them they told briefly to those around Peter. And afterward Jesus himself sent out through them, from east to west, the sacred and imperishable proclamation of eternal salvation.[a]⟧

THE LONGER ENDING OF MARK

Jesus Appears to Mary Magdalene

9 ⟦Now after he rose early on the first day of the week, he appeared first to Mary Magdalene, from whom he had cast out seven demons. [10]She went out and told those who had been with him, while they were mourning and weeping. [11]But when they heard that he was alive and had been seen by her, they would not believe it.

Jesus Appears to Two Disciples

12 After this he appeared in another form to two of them, as they were walking into the country. [13]And they went back and told the rest, but they did not believe them.

Jesus Commissions the Disciples

14 Later he appeared to the eleven themselves as they were sitting at the table; and he upbraided them for their lack of faith and stubbornness, because they had not believed those who saw him after he had risen.[b] [15]And he said to them, "Go into all the world and proclaim the good news[c] to the whole creation. [16]The one who believes and is baptized will be saved; but the one who does not believe will be condemned. [17]And these signs will accompany those who believe: by using my name they will cast out demons; they will speak in new tongues; [18]they will pick up snakes in their hands,[d] and if they drink any deadly thing, it will not hurt them; they will lay their hands on the sick, and they will recover."

The Ascension of Jesus

19 So then the Lord Jesus, after he had spoken to them, was taken up into heaven and sat down at the right hand of God. [20]And they went out and proclaimed the good news everywhere, while the Lord worked with them and confirmed the message by the signs that accompanied it.[a]⟧

---

a Other ancient authorities add *Amen*   b Other ancient authorities add, in whole or in part, *And they excused themselves, saying, "This age of lawlessness and unbelief is under Satan, who does not allow the truth and power of God to prevail over the unclean things of the spirits. Therefore reveal your righteousness now"—thus they spoke to Christ. And Christ replied to them, "The term of years of Satan's power has been fulfilled, but other terrible things draw near. And for those who have sinned I was handed over to death, that they may return to the truth and sin no more, that they may inherit the spiritual and imperishable glory of righteousness that is in heaven."*   c Or *gospel*
d Other ancient authorities lack *in their hands*

THE GOSPEL ACCORDING TO
LUKE
Life of Prayer, Life of Compassion

KEY VERSES:

"Lord, teach us to pray."—Luke 11.1

"Which of these . . . was a neighbor? . . . Go and do likewise."—Luke 10.36–37

In the Gospel of Luke, Luke the physician draws a portrait of Jesus the Savior, who brings the love of God to earth and draws the people of God to heaven. Luke conveys his fascination with this Jesus, a man of both prayer and action, who could be continually mindful of God and yet be fully present with people as an attentive, empathetic healer. Jesus modeled perfect communication with his heavenly Father (the Lord's Prayer) and perfect compassion for those his culture considered outcasts (the parable of the Good Samaritan).

Jesus' life and teachings reconcile some of the contrasts that exist within the spiritual life, blending spiritual with physical (6.24–27), feasting with fasting (5.33–35), compassion with confrontation (6.9), and solitude with community (6.12–16).

Jesus moved beyond the restrictions of Jewish society, welcoming anyone with a seeking heart and granting the forgiveness of God to those the "righteous" Jewish leaders had rejected (6.20–26; 21.1–4). He engaged women, as well as men, in ministry (8.1–3; 23.55—24.11). For Luke, the only Gentile Gospel writer, this was good news indeed, for Jesus brought reconciliation to the Gentile world.

Let the book of Luke help you discover what it means to live an inward life of prayer and an outward life of compassion. When you struggle to balance "doing" with "being," imitate Jesus Christ, who practiced an ongoing rhythm of ministry and sabbath rest. How can you serve God in the same radical way? How can you maintain this rhythm in your personal life?

> "Let one who cannot be alone beware of community . . . Let one who is not in community beware of being alone."
> —DIETRICH BONHOEFFER,
> *Life Together*

Silences

LUKE 1.20–23

Like Abraham and Sarah, Zechariah expresses doubt when God promises that a child will be born to him and his wife in their old age. As a result God silences Zechariah until the child is born. What if you were to receive the most precious desire of your heart today? How would you respond? Reflect on this in a journal or notebook, using words or art. Also reflect on the times when you may have experienced periods of doubt, silence, waiting or listening. Such spiritual stillness can be a prelude to some new birth in your life, as it was for Zechariah and Elizabeth.

See Meeting God in Everyday Life

Dedication to Theophilus

1 Since many have undertaken to set down an orderly account of the events that have been fulfilled among us, ²just as they were handed on to us by those who from the beginning were eyewitnesses and servants of the word, ³I too decided, after investigating everything carefully from the very first,ᵃ to write an orderly account for you, most excellent Theophilus, ⁴so that you may know the truth concerning the things about which you have been instructed.

The Birth of John the Baptist Foretold

5 In the days of King Herod of Judea, there was a priest named Zechariah, who belonged to the priestly order of Abijah. His wife was a descendant of Aaron, and her name was Elizabeth. ⁶Both of them were righteous before God, living blamelessly according to all the commandments and regulations of the Lord. ⁷But they had no children, because Elizabeth was barren, and both were getting on in years.

8 Once when he was serving as priest before God and his section was on duty, ⁹he was chosen by lot, according to the custom of the priesthood, to enter the sanctuary of the Lord and offer incense. ¹⁰Now at the time of the incense offering, the whole assembly of the people was praying outside. ¹¹Then there appeared to him an angel of the Lord, standing at the right side of the altar of incense. ¹²When Zechariah saw him, he was terrified; and fear overwhelmed him. ¹³But the angel said to him, "Do not be afraid, Zechariah, for your prayer has been heard. Your wife Elizabeth will bear you a son, and you will name him John. ¹⁴You will have joy and gladness, and many will rejoice at his birth, ¹⁵for he will be great in the sight of the Lord. He must never drink wine or strong drink; even before his birth he will be filled with the Holy Spirit. ¹⁶He will turn many of the people of Israel to the Lord their God. ¹⁷With the spirit and power of Elijah he will go before him, to turn the hearts of parents to their children, and the disobedient to the wisdom of the righteous, to make ready a people prepared for the Lord." ¹⁸Zechariah said to the angel, "How will I know that this is so? For I am an old man, and my wife is getting on in years." ¹⁹The angel replied, "I am Gabriel. I stand in the presence of God, and I have been sent to speak to you and to bring you this good news. ²⁰But now, because you did not believe my words, which will be fulfilled in their time, you will become mute, unable to speak, until the day these things occur."

21 Meanwhile the people were waiting for Zechariah, and wondered at his delay in the sanctuary. ²²When he did come out, he could not speak to them, and they realized that he had seen a vision in the sanctuary. He kept motioning to them and remained unable to speak. ²³When his time of service was ended, he went to his home.

24 After those days his wife Elizabeth conceived, and for five months she remained in seclusion. She said, ²⁵"This is what the Lord has done for me when he looked

a Or for a long time

favorably on me and took away the disgrace I have endured among my people."

The Birth of Jesus Foretold

26 In the sixth month the angel Gabriel was sent by God to a town in Galilee called Nazareth, [27]to a virgin engaged to a man whose name was Joseph, of the house of David. The virgin's name was Mary. [28]And he came to her and said, "Greetings, favored one! The Lord is with you."[a] [29]But she was much perplexed by his words and pondered what sort of greeting this might be. [30]The angel said to her, "Do not be afraid, Mary, for you have found favor with God. [31]And now, you will conceive in your womb and bear a son, and you will name him Jesus. [32]He will be great, and will be called the Son of the Most High, and the Lord God will give to him the throne of his ancestor David. [33]He will reign over the house of Jacob forever, and of his kingdom there will be no end." [34]Mary said to the angel, "How can this be, since I am a virgin?"[b] [35]The angel said to her, "The Holy Spirit will come upon you, and the power of the Most High will overshadow you; therefore the child to be born[c] will be holy; he will be called Son of God. [36]And now, your relative Elizabeth in her old age has also conceived a son; and this is the sixth month for her who was said to be barren. [37]For nothing will be impossible with God." [38]Then Mary said, "Here am I, the servant of the Lord; let it be with me according to your word." Then the angel departed from her.

Mary Visits Elizabeth

39 In those days Mary set out and went with haste to a Judean town in the hill country, [40]where she entered the house of Zechariah and greeted Elizabeth. [41]When Elizabeth heard Mary's greeting, the child leaped in her womb. And Elizabeth was filled with the Holy Spirit [42]and exclaimed with a loud cry, "Blessed are you among women, and blessed is the fruit of your womb. [43]And why has this happened to me, that the mother of my Lord comes to me? [44]For as soon as I heard the sound of your greeting, the child in my womb leaped for joy. [45]And blessed is she who believed that there would be[d] a fulfillment of what was spoken to her by the Lord."

Mary's Song of Praise

46 And Mary[e] said,
"My soul magnifies the Lord,
[47]   and my spirit rejoices in God my Savior,
[48] for he has looked with favor on the lowliness of
   his servant.
      Surely, from now on all generations will call me
      blessed;
[49] for the Mighty One has done great things for me,
   and holy is his name.
[50] His mercy is for those who fear him
   from generation to generation.
[51] He has shown strength with his arm;
   he has scattered the proud in the thoughts of
      their hearts.

Spiritual Friendship

LUKE 1.39–45

"What happiness, what security, what joy to have someone to whom you dare to speak on terms of equality as to another self," wrote the twelfth-century monk Aelred of Rievaulx in *Spiritual Friendship*. What an apt description of Mary and Elizabeth's spiritual kinship as both women face unusual, yet joyous, circumstances! Recall some of the special friendships you've experienced during your lifetime. Call a friend or share a meal together, and reminisce about your friendship. Tell your friend some of the ways in which you consider him or her a blessing.

See Meeting God in Community

---

a Other ancient authorities add *Blessed are you among women*   *b* Gk *I do not know a man*   *c* Other ancient authorities add *of you*   *d* Or *believed, for there will be*   *e* Other ancient authorities read *Elizabeth*

Zechariah's Song

LUKE 1.67–79

Although many of our prayers tend to become "wish lists," Zechariah's prayer is full of acknowledgment of what God has done in the past and will do in the future. He worships God using the special name "Most High" and proclaims God's "tender mercy" (1.78). Try finishing these sentences: "God, I praise you because you have . . ." "I look forward to the day when you will . . ." "O God, I am filled with awe and wonder that you . . ."

See *Meeting God in Worship*

52 He has brought down the powerful from their
    thrones,
    and lifted up the lowly;
53 he has filled the hungry with good things,
    and sent the rich away empty.
54 He has helped his servant Israel,
    in remembrance of his mercy,
55 according to the promise he made to our ancestors,
    to Abraham and to his descendants forever."

56 And Mary remained with her about three months and then returned to her home.

The Birth of John the Baptist

57 Now the time came for Elizabeth to give birth, and she bore a son. 58 Her neighbors and relatives heard that the Lord had shown his great mercy to her, and they rejoiced with her.

59 On the eighth day they came to circumcise the child, and they were going to name him Zechariah after his father. 60 But his mother said, "No; he is to be called John." 61 They said to her, "None of your relatives has this name." 62 Then they began motioning to his father to find out what name he wanted to give him. 63 He asked for a writing tablet and wrote, "His name is John." And all of them were amazed. 64 Immediately his mouth was opened and his tongue freed, and he began to speak, praising God. 65 Fear came over all their neighbors, and all these things were talked about throughout the entire hill country of Judea. 66 All who heard them pondered them and said, "What then will this child become?" For, indeed, the hand of the Lord was with him.

Zechariah's Prophecy

67 Then his father Zechariah was filled with the Holy Spirit and spoke this prophecy:
68 "Blessed be the Lord God of Israel,
    for he has looked favorably on his people and
      redeemed them.
69 He has raised up a mighty savior[a] for us
    in the house of his servant David,
70 as he spoke through the mouth of his holy
      prophets from of old,
71 that we would be saved from our enemies and
    from the hand of all who hate us.
72 Thus he has shown the mercy promised to our
      ancestors,
    and has remembered his holy covenant,
73 the oath that he swore to our ancestor Abraham,
    to grant us 74 that we, being rescued from the
      hands of our enemies,
    might serve him without fear, 75 in holiness and
      righteousness
    before him all our days.
76 And you, child, will be called the prophet of the
    Most High;
    for you will go before the Lord to prepare his
      ways,
77 to give knowledge of salvation to his people
    by the forgiveness of their sins.

a Gk *a horn of salvation*

[78] By the tender mercy of our God,
  the dawn from on high will break upon[a] us,
[79] to give light to those who sit in darkness and in
    the shadow of death,
  to guide our feet into the way of peace."

80 The child grew and became strong in spirit, and he was in the wilderness until the day he appeared publicly to Israel.

The Birth of Jesus

2 In those days a decree went out from Emperor Augustus that all the world should be registered. [2]This was the first registration and was taken while Quirinius was governor of Syria. [3]All went to their own towns to be registered. [4]Joseph also went from the town of Nazareth in Galilee to Judea, to the city of David called Bethlehem, because he was descended from the house and family of David. [5]He went to be registered with Mary, to whom he was engaged and who was expecting a child. [6]While they were there, the time came for her to deliver her child. [7]And she gave birth to her firstborn son and wrapped him in bands of cloth, and laid him in a manger, because there was no place for them in the inn.

The Shepherds and the Angels

8 In that region there were shepherds living in the fields, keeping watch over their flock by night. [9]Then an angel of the Lord stood before them, and the glory of the Lord shone around them, and they were terrified. [10]But the angel said to them, "Do not be afraid; for see—I am bringing you good news of great joy for all the people: [11]to you is born this day in the city of David a Savior, who is the Messiah,[b] the Lord. [12]This will be a sign for you: you will find a child wrapped in bands of cloth and lying in a manger." [13]And suddenly there was with the angel a multitude of the heavenly host,[c] praising God and saying,

[14] "Glory to God in the highest heaven,
  and on earth peace among those whom he
    favors!"[d]

15 When the angels had left them and gone into heaven, the shepherds said to one another, "Let us go now to Bethlehem and see this thing that has taken place, which the Lord has made known to us." [16]So they went with haste and found Mary and Joseph, and the child lying in the manger. [17]When they saw this, they made known what had been told them about this child; [18]and all who heard it were amazed at what the shepherds told them. [19]But Mary treasured all these words and pondered them in her heart. [20]The shepherds returned, glorifying and praising God for all they had heard and seen, as it had been told them.

Jesus Is Named

21 After eight days had passed, it was time to circumcise the child; and he was called Jesus, the name given by the angel before he was conceived in the womb.

---

a Other ancient authorities read *has broken upon*   b Or *the Christ*
c Gk *army*   d Other ancient authorities read *peace, goodwill among people*

Singing With Angels

LUKE 1.68; 2.14

Everyone is singing—Mary (1.46–55), Zechariah, Simeon (2.28–32), the angels! Sing a song of praise—such as "Angels We Have Heard on High" (especially the chorus)—in the shower, in the woods or in the car. Sing where no one can hear you so that you can sing exuberantly and can embellish your song of praise with worshipful gestures or movements. Experiment with the joy of worshiping God—let inward singing permeate your activities. Another option: Sing the African-American spiritual "Guide My Feet" (based on Luke 1.79).

See Meeting God in Worship

Praying With Anna and Simeon

LUKE 2.22–38

An offering of doves or pigeons is a sign of poverty. Imagine the elderly Simeon and Anna holding the infant Jesus and welcoming this young, poor family. Simeon's prayer identifying Jesus as "a light for revelation . . . and for glory" indicates how much he wants to see God's penetrating light and glory displayed on earth (2.32). We can guess Anna's heart aches to see the redemption of Israel (2.38). What situations today need to be penetrated by God's light? Youth separated from older adults? Rich from poor? Try holding a symbol of these situations in your hand (a related newspaper article, a committee agenda, a child's hat, a family member's pain medication) and praying Simeon's prayer. Or write the prayer that you imagine Anna might have prayed.

See Meeting God in Community

Jesus Is Presented in the Temple

22 When the time came for their purification according to the law of Moses, they brought him up to Jerusalem to present him to the Lord 23(as it is written in the law of the Lord, "Every firstborn male shall be designated as holy to the Lord"), 24and they offered a sacrifice according to what is stated in the law of the Lord, "a pair of turtledoves or two young pigeons."

25 Now there was a man in Jerusalem whose name was Simeon;*a* this man was righteous and devout, looking forward to the consolation of Israel, and the Holy Spirit rested on him. 26It had been revealed to him by the Holy Spirit that he would not see death before he had seen the Lord's Messiah.*b* 27Guided by the Spirit, Simeon*c* came into the temple; and when the parents brought in the child Jesus, to do for him what was customary under the law, 28Simeon*d* took him in his arms and praised God, saying,

29 "Master, now you are dismissing your servant*e* in peace,
    according to your word;
30 for my eyes have seen your salvation,
31 which you have prepared in the presence of all peoples,
32 a light for revelation to the Gentiles
    and for glory to your people Israel."

33 And the child's father and mother were amazed at what was being said about him. 34Then Simeon*a* blessed them and said to his mother Mary, "This child is destined for the falling and the rising of many in Israel, and to be a sign that will be opposed 35so that the inner thoughts of many will be revealed—and a sword will pierce your own soul too."

36 There was also a prophet, Anna*f* the daughter of Phanuel, of the tribe of Asher. She was of a great age, having lived with her husband seven years after her marriage, 37then as a widow to the age of eighty-four. She never left the temple but worshiped there with fasting and prayer night and day. 38At that moment she came, and began to praise God and to speak about the child*g* to all who were looking for the redemption of Jerusalem.

The Return to Nazareth

39 When they had finished everything required by the law of the Lord, they returned to Galilee, to their own town of Nazareth. 40The child grew and became strong, filled with wisdom; and the favor of God was upon him.

The Boy Jesus in the Temple

41 Now every year his parents went to Jerusalem for the festival of the Passover. 42And when he was twelve years old, they went up as usual for the festival. 43When the festival was ended and they started to return, the boy Jesus stayed behind in Jerusalem, but his parents did not know it. 44Assuming that he was in the group of travelers, they went a day's journey. Then they started to look for him among their relatives and friends. 45When they did not find him, they returned to Jerusalem to search for him.

a Gk *Symeon*   *b* Or *the Lord's Christ*   *c* Gk *In the Spirit, he*   *d* Gk *he*   *e* Gk *slave*   *f* Gk *Hanna*   *g* Gk *him*

⁴⁶After three days they found him in the temple, sitting among the teachers, listening to them and asking them questions. ⁴⁷And all who heard him were amazed at his understanding and his answers. ⁴⁸When his parents*a* saw him they were astonished; and his mother said to him, "Child, why have you treated us like this? Look, your father and I have been searching for you in great anxiety." ⁴⁹He said to them, "Why were you searching for me? Did you not know that I must be in my Father's house?"*b* ⁵⁰But they did not understand what he said to them. ⁵¹Then he went down with them and came to Nazareth, and was obedient to them. His mother treasured all these things in her heart.

52 And Jesus increased in wisdom and in years,*c* and in divine and human favor.

The Proclamation of John the Baptist

3 In the fifteenth year of the reign of Emperor Tiberius, when Pontius Pilate was governor of Judea, and Herod was ruler*d* of Galilee, and his brother Philip ruler*d* of the region of Ituraea and Trachonitis, and Lysanias ruler*d* of Abilene, ²during the high priesthood of Annas and Caiaphas, the word of God came to John son of Zechariah in the wilderness. ³He went into all the region around the Jordan, proclaiming a baptism of repentance for the forgiveness of sins, ⁴as it is written in the book of the words of the prophet Isaiah,

"The voice of one crying out in the wilderness:
'Prepare the way of the Lord,
    make his paths straight.
⁵ Every valley shall be filled,
    and every mountain and hill shall be made low,
  and the crooked shall be made straight,
    and the rough ways made smooth;
⁶ and all flesh shall see the salvation of God.' "

7 John said to the crowds that came out to be baptized by him, "You brood of vipers! Who warned you to flee from the wrath to come? ⁸Bear fruits worthy of repentance. Do not begin to say to yourselves, 'We have Abraham as our ancestor'; for I tell you, God is able from these stones to raise up children to Abraham. ⁹Even now the ax is lying at the root of the trees; every tree therefore that does not bear good fruit is cut down and thrown into the fire."

10 And the crowds asked him, "What then should we do?" ¹¹In reply he said to them, "Whoever has two coats must share with anyone who has none; and whoever has food must do likewise." ¹²Even tax collectors came to be baptized, and they asked him, "Teacher, what should we do?" ¹³He said to them, "Collect no more than the amount prescribed for you." ¹⁴Soldiers also asked him, "And we, what should we do?" He said to them, "Do not extort money from anyone by threats or false accusation, and be satisfied with your wages."

15 As the people were filled with expectation, and all were questioning in their hearts concerning John, whether he might be the Messiah,*e* ¹⁶John answered all of them by saying, "I baptize you with water; but one who is more

Treasuring . . .

LUKE 2.41–52

Mary reacts to crises by pondering or treasuring in her heart what God says or does. She does this when she faces the shame of becoming an unwed mother; when she responds to the shepherds' visit in a stable; and, in this passage, when she copes with the increasing independence of her twelve-year-old son (1.29; 2.19,51). How might Mary's response be an example to you? How could you respond more contemplatively and prayerfully to the events in your life? What event in your life needs more pondering instead of worrying, fixing or withdrawing?

See Meeting God in Everyday Life

---

a Gk *they*   *b* Or *be about my Father's interests?*   *c* Or *in stature*
d Gk *tetrarch*   *e* Or *the Christ*

Revolutionary Simplicity

LUKE 3.7–20

John the Baptist thunders a revolutionary message that costs him his life. He is imprisoned and killed by Herod for nothing less than the radical condemnation of those in power: "The ax is lying at the root of the trees" (3.9; see also 3.19). Yet when the crowd asks, "What then should we do?" John suggests sharing their extra coats and food with others and living honestly. Find some extra cans of food and an extra jacket to take to a homeless shelter. Hold them in your hands. What might happen within you when you take them to the shelter? What revolution might take place within your heart if you chose to make generosity your lifestyle? What might happen to your need for security and control? Commit to one simple act at a time. Mark a date on your calendar that is a month from now; when that date arrives, assess any change you might have experienced within yourself.

See Meeting God in Community

powerful than I is coming; I am not worthy to untie the thong of his sandals. He will baptize you with[a] the Holy Spirit and fire. [17]His winnowing fork is in his hand, to clear his threshing floor and to gather the wheat into his granary; but the chaff he will burn with unquenchable fire."

18 So, with many other exhortations, he proclaimed the good news to the people. [19]But Herod the ruler,[b] who had been rebuked by him because of Herodias, his brother's wife, and because of all the evil things that Herod had done, [20]added to them all by shutting up John in prison.

The Baptism of Jesus

21 Now when all the people were baptized, and when Jesus also had been baptized and was praying, the heaven was opened, [22]and the Holy Spirit descended upon him in bodily form like a dove. And a voice came from heaven, "You are my Son, the Beloved;[c] with you I am well pleased."[d]

The Ancestors of Jesus

23 Jesus was about thirty years old when he began his work. He was the son (as was thought) of Joseph son of Heli, [24]son of Matthat, son of Levi, son of Melchi, son of Jannai, son of Joseph, [25]son of Mattathias, son of Amos, son of Nahum, son of Esli, son of Naggai, [26]son of Maath, son of Mattathias, son of Semein, son of Josech, son of Joda, [27]son of Joanan, son of Rhesa, son of Zerubbabel, son of Shealtiel,[e] son of Neri, [28]son of Melchi, son of Addi, son of Cosam, son of Elmadam, son of Er, [29]son of Joshua, son of Eliezer, son of Jorim, son of Matthat, son of Levi, [30]son of Simeon, son of Judah, son of Joseph, son of Jonam, son of Eliakim, [31]son of Melea, son of Menna, son of Mattatha, son of Nathan, son of David, [32]son of Jesse, son of Obed, son of Boaz, son of Sala,[f] son of Nahshon, [33]son of Amminadab, son of Admin, son of Arni,[g] son of Hezron, son of Perez, son of Judah, [34]son of Jacob, son of Isaac, son of Abraham, son of Terah, son of Nahor, [35]son of Serug, son of Reu, son of Peleg, son of Eber, son of Shelah, [36]son of Cainan, son of Arphaxad, son of Shem, son of Noah, son of Lamech, [37]son of Methuselah, son of Enoch, son of Jared, son of Mahalaleel, son of Cainan, [38]son of Enos, son of Seth, son of Adam, son of God.

The Temptation of Jesus

4 Jesus, full of the Holy Spirit, returned from the Jordan and was led by the Spirit in the wilderness, [2]where for forty days he was tempted by the devil. He ate nothing at all during those days, and when they were over, he was famished. [3]The devil said to him, "If you are the Son of God, command this stone to become a loaf of bread." [4]Jesus answered him, "It is written, 'One does not live by bread alone.' "

5 Then the devil[h] led him up and showed him in an instant all the kingdoms of the world. [6]And the devil[h] said to him, "To you I will give their glory and all this authority; for it has been given over to me, and I give it to any-

a Or in   *b* Gk *tetrarch*   *c* Or *my beloved Son*   *d* Other ancient authorities read *You are my Son, today I have begotten you*   *e* Gk *Salathiel*   *f* Other ancient authorities read *Salmon*   *g* Other ancient authorities read *Amminadab, son of Aram*; others vary widely   *h* Gk *he*

one I please. [7]If you, then, will worship me, it will all be yours." [8]Jesus answered him, "It is written,

'Worship the Lord your God,
and serve only him.' "

9 Then the devil[a] took him to Jerusalem, and placed him on the pinnacle of the temple, saying to him, "If you are the Son of God, throw yourself down from here, [10]for it is written,

'He will command his angels concerning you,
to protect you,'

[11]and

'On their hands they will bear you up,
so that you will not dash your foot against a
stone.' "

[12]Jesus answered him, "It is said, 'Do not put the Lord your God to the test.' " [13]When the devil had finished every test, he departed from him until an opportune time.

The Beginning of the Galilean Ministry

14 Then Jesus, filled with the power of the Spirit, returned to Galilee, and a report about him spread through all the surrounding country. [15]He began to teach in their synagogues and was praised by everyone.

The Rejection of Jesus at Nazareth

16 When he came to Nazareth, where he had been brought up, he went to the synagogue on the sabbath day, as was his custom. He stood up to read, [17]and the scroll of the prophet Isaiah was given to him. He unrolled the scroll and found the place where it was written:
[18] "The Spirit of the Lord is upon me,
because he has anointed me
to bring good news to the poor.
He has sent me to proclaim release to the captives
and recovery of sight to the blind,
to let the oppressed go free,
[19] to proclaim the year of the Lord's favor."
[20]And he rolled up the scroll, gave it back to the attendant, and sat down. The eyes of all in the synagogue were fixed on him. [21]Then he began to say to them, "Today this scripture has been fulfilled in your hearing." [22]All spoke well of him and were amazed at the gracious words that came from his mouth. They said, "Is not this Joseph's son?" [23]He said to them, "Doubtless you will quote to me this proverb, 'Doctor, cure yourself!' And you will say, 'Do here also in your hometown the things that we have heard you did at Capernaum.' " [24]And he said, "Truly I tell you, no prophet is accepted in the prophet's hometown. [25]But the truth is, there were many widows in Israel in the time of Elijah, when the heaven was shut up three years and six months, and there was a severe famine over all the land; [26]yet Elijah was sent to none of them except to a widow at Zarephath in Sidon. [27]There were also many lepers[b] in Israel in the time of the prophet Elisha, and none of them was cleansed except Naaman the Syrian." [28]When they heard this, all in the synagogue were filled with rage. [29]They got up, drove him out of the town, and led him to the brow of the hill on which their town was built, so that

Jesus Walks

LUKE 4.16–30

Picture yourself with Jesus in the hometown synagogue he attended "as was his custom." Listen as Jesus stands up to read the words of Isaiah 61.1–2 (Luke 4.18–19). Notice how the people become angry when Jesus highlights God's love for the Gentiles (Luke 4.25–27). Go along as the outraged people drive him out of town and try to hurl him from a cliff. Now picture yourself in a conflict in which you take an unpopular stand on someone's behalf. Enjoy the sense of security you feel as Jesus walks with you in the midst of a crowd of irate people. What is Jesus saying to you?

See Meeting God in Community

they might hurl him off the cliff. [30]But he passed through the midst of them and went on his way.

The Man with an Unclean Spirit

31 He went down to Capernaum, a city in Galilee, and was teaching them on the sabbath. [32]They were astounded at his teaching, because he spoke with authority. [33]In the synagogue there was a man who had the spirit of an unclean demon, and he cried out with a loud voice, [34]"Let us alone! What have you to do with us, Jesus of Nazareth? Have you come to destroy us? I know who you are, the Holy One of God." [35]But Jesus rebuked him, saying, "Be silent, and come out of him!" When the demon had thrown him down before them, he came out of him without having done him any harm. [36]They were all amazed and kept saying to one another, "What kind of utterance is this? For with authority and power he commands the unclean spirits, and out they come!" [37]And a report about him began to reach every place in the region.

Healings at Simon's House

38 After leaving the synagogue he entered Simon's house. Now Simon's mother-in-law was suffering from a high fever, and they asked him about her. [39]Then he stood over her and rebuked the fever, and it left her. Immediately she got up and began to serve them.

40 As the sun was setting, all those who had any who were sick with various kinds of diseases brought them to him; and he laid his hands on each of them and cured them. [41]Demons also came out of many, shouting, "You are the Son of God!" But he rebuked them and would not allow them to speak, because they knew that he was the Messiah.[a]

Jesus Preaches in the Synagogues

42 At daybreak he departed and went into a deserted place. And the crowds were looking for him; and when they reached him, they wanted to prevent him from leaving them. [43]But he said to them, "I must proclaim the good news of the kingdom of God to the other cities also; for I was sent for this purpose." [44]So he continued proclaiming the message in the synagogues of Judea.[b]

Jesus Calls the First Disciples

5 Once while Jesus[c] was standing beside the lake of Gennesaret, and the crowd was pressing in on him to hear the word of God, [2]he saw two boats there at the shore of the lake; the fishermen had gone out of them and were washing their nets. [3]He got into one of the boats, the one belonging to Simon, and asked him to put out a little way from the shore. Then he sat down and taught the crowds from the boat. [4]When he had finished speaking, he said to Simon, "Put out into the deep water and let down your nets for a catch." [5]Simon answered, "Master, we have worked all night long but have caught nothing. Yet if you say so, I will let down the nets." [6]When they had done this, they caught so many fish that their nets were beginning to break. [7]So they signaled their partners in the other boat to come and help them. And they came and filled

a Or *the Christ*   *b* Other ancient authorities read *Galilee*   *c* Gk *he* both boats, so that they began to sink. **8**But when Simon Peter saw it, he fell down at Jesus' knees, saying, "Go away from me, Lord, for I am a sinful man!" **9**For he and all who were with him were amazed at the catch of fish that they had taken; **10**and so also were James and John, sons of Zebedee, who were partners with Simon. Then Jesus said to Simon, "Do not be afraid; from now on you will be catching people." **11**When they had brought their boats to shore, they left everything and followed him.

Jesus Cleanses a Leper

12 Once, when he was in one of the cities, there was a man covered with leprosy.*a* When he saw Jesus, he bowed with his face to the ground and begged him, "Lord, if you choose, you can make me clean." **13**Then Jesus*b* stretched out his hand, touched him, and said, "I do choose. Be made clean." Immediately the leprosy*a* left him. **14**And he ordered him to tell no one. "Go," he said, "and show yourself to the priest, and, as Moses commanded, make an offering for your cleansing, for a testimony to them." **15**But now more than ever the word about Jesus*c* spread abroad; many crowds would gather to hear him and to be cured of their diseases. **16**But he would withdraw to deserted places and pray.

Jesus Heals a Paralytic

17 One day, while he was teaching, Pharisees and teachers of the law were sitting near by (they had come from every village of Galilee and Judea and from Jerusalem); and the power of the Lord was with him to heal.*d* **18**Just then some men came, carrying a paralyzed man on a bed. They were trying to bring him in and lay him before Jesus;*c* **19**but finding no way to bring him in because of the crowd, they went up on the roof and let him down with his bed through the tiles into the middle of the crowd*e* in front of Jesus. **20**When he saw their faith, he said, "Friend,*f* your sins are forgiven you." **21**Then the scribes and the Pharisees began to question, "Who is this who is speaking blasphemies? Who can forgive sins but God alone?" **22**When Jesus perceived their questionings, he answered them, "Why do you raise such questions in your hearts? **23**Which is easier, to say, 'Your sins are forgiven you,' or to say, 'Stand up and walk'? **24**But so that you may know that the Son of Man has authority on earth to forgive sins"—he said to the one who was paralyzed—"I say to you, stand up and take your bed and go to your home." **25**Immediately he stood up before them, took what he had been lying on, and went to his home, glorifying God. **26**Amazement seized all of them, and they glorified God and were filled with awe, saying, "We have seen strange things today."

Jesus Calls Levi

27 After this he went out and saw a tax collector named Levi, sitting at the tax booth; and he said to him, "Follow me." **28**And he got up, left everything, and followed him.
29 Then Levi gave a great banquet for him in his house;

Transforming the Beloved

LUKE 5.4–6

"We have worked all night long but have caught nothing." Simon's words might also describe the dark night of the soul: "The soul has to go on loving in the emptiness, or at least go on wanting to love, though it may only be with an infinitesimal part of itself. Then, one day, God will come to show himself to this soul and reveal the beauty of the world to it" (Simone Weil, *Waiting for God*). It is often in periods of seeming fruitlessness that Jesus Christ reveals his power, and in times of darkness that God sheds the greatest light. Are you enduring a period of fruitlessness or darkness? Ask Jesus to tell you where to "let down your nets" in order to see his power revealed.

See Meeting God in Everyday Life

---

a The terms *leper* and *leprosy* can refer to several diseases   *b* Gk *he*
c Gk *him*   *d* Other ancient authorities read *was present to heal them*
e Gk *into the midst*   *f* Gk *Man*

Open to the Wonder of God

LUKE 5.26-32

The word *paradox* occurs only once in scripture: They "were filled with awe, saying, 'We have seen strange [*paradoxa*] things today' " (5.26). As onlookers watch the healing of the paralytic, they wonder that the power to heal comes not from the righteous, authoritative Pharisees, but from the peasant preacher, Jesus (5.17–26). Wonder at the unexpected, the paradoxical, often opens one's soul to God. Ponder the unexpected ways in which Jesus reveals divine power and glory. Is there anything about Jesus Christ that seems paradoxical to you? In what unconventional ways might God be speaking to you now? Close your eyes and bask in wonder at the mystery of Jesus Christ.

See Meeting God in Worship

and there was a large crowd of tax collectors and others sitting at the table*a* with them. ³⁰The Pharisees and their scribes were complaining to his disciples, saying, "Why do you eat and drink with tax collectors and sinners?" ³¹Jesus answered, "Those who are well have no need of a physician, but those who are sick; ³²I have come to call not the righteous but sinners to repentance."

The Question about Fasting

33 Then they said to him, "John's disciples, like the disciples of the Pharisees, frequently fast and pray, but your disciples eat and drink." ³⁴Jesus said to them, "You cannot make wedding guests fast while the bridegroom is with them, can you? ³⁵The days will come when the bridegroom will be taken away from them, and then they will fast in those days." ³⁶He also told them a parable: "No one tears a piece from a new garment and sews it on an old garment; otherwise the new will be torn, and the piece from the new will not match the old. ³⁷And no one puts new wine into old wineskins; otherwise the new wine will burst the skins and will be spilled, and the skins will be destroyed. ³⁸But new wine must be put into fresh wineskins. ³⁹And no one after drinking old wine desires new wine, but says, 'The old is good.' "*b*

The Question about the Sabbath

6 One sabbath*c* while Jesus*d* was going through the grainfields, his disciples plucked some heads of grain, rubbed them in their hands, and ate them. ²But some of the Pharisees said, "Why are you doing what is not lawful*e* on the sabbath?" ³Jesus answered, "Have you not read what David did when he and his companions were hungry? ⁴He entered the house of God and took and ate the bread of the Presence, which it is not lawful for any but the priests to eat, and gave some to his companions?" ⁵Then he said to them, "The Son of Man is lord of the sabbath."

The Man with a Withered Hand

6 On another sabbath he entered the synagogue and taught, and there was a man there whose right hand was withered. ⁷The scribes and the Pharisees watched him to see whether he would cure on the sabbath, so that they might find an accusation against him. ⁸Even though he knew what they were thinking, he said to the man who had the withered hand, "Come and stand here." He got up and stood there. ⁹Then Jesus said to them, "I ask you, is it lawful to do good or to do harm on the sabbath, to save life or to destroy it?" ¹⁰After looking around at all of them, he said to him, "Stretch out your hand." He did so, and his hand was restored. ¹¹But they were filled with fury and discussed with one another what they might do to Jesus.

Jesus Chooses the Twelve Apostles

12 Now during those days he went out to the mountain to pray; and he spent the night in prayer to God. ¹³And when day came, he called his disciples and chose twelve of them, whom he also named apostles: ¹⁴Simon, whom

a Gk *reclining*   *b* Other ancient authorities read *better*; others lack verse 39   *c* Other ancient authorities read *On the second first sabbath*
d Gk *he*   *e* Other ancient authorities add *to do*

he named Peter, and his brother Andrew, and James, and John, and Philip, and Bartholomew, ¹⁵and Matthew, and Thomas, and James son of Alphaeus, and Simon, who was called the Zealot, ¹⁶and Judas son of James, and Judas Iscariot, who became a traitor.

Jesus Teaches and Heals

17 He came down with them and stood on a level place, with a great crowd of his disciples and a great multitude of people from all Judea, Jerusalem, and the coast of Tyre and Sidon. ¹⁸They had come to hear him and to be healed of their diseases; and those who were troubled with unclean spirits were cured. ¹⁹And all in the crowd were trying to touch him, for power came out from him and healed all of them.

Blessings and Woes

20 Then he looked up at his disciples and said:
"Blessed are you who are poor,
   for yours is the kingdom of God.
²¹ "Blessed are you who are hungry now,
   for you will be filled.
"Blessed are you who weep now,
   for you will laugh.
22 "Blessed are you when people hate you, and when they exclude you, revile you, and defame you[a] on account of the Son of Man. ²³Rejoice in that day and leap for joy, for surely your reward is great in heaven; for that is what their ancestors did to the prophets.
²⁴ "But woe to you who are rich,
   for you have received your consolation.
²⁵ "Woe to you who are full now,
   for you will be hungry.
"Woe to you who are laughing now,
   for you will mourn and weep.
26 "Woe to you when all speak well of you, for that is what their ancestors did to the false prophets.

Love for Enemies

27 "But I say to you that listen, Love your enemies, do good to those who hate you, ²⁸bless those who curse you, pray for those who abuse you. ²⁹If anyone strikes you on the cheek, offer the other also; and from anyone who takes away your coat do not withhold even your shirt. ³⁰Give to everyone who begs from you; and if anyone takes away your goods, do not ask for them again. ³¹Do to others as you would have them do to you.
32 "If you love those who love you, what credit is that to you? For even sinners love those who love them. ³³If you do good to those who do good to you, what credit is that to you? For even sinners do the same. ³⁴If you lend to those from whom you hope to receive, what credit is that to you? Even sinners lend to sinners, to receive as much again. ³⁵But love your enemies, do good, and lend, expecting nothing in return.[b] Your reward will be great, and you will be children of the Most High; for he is kind to the ungrateful and the wicked. ³⁶Be merciful, just as your Father is merciful.

---

a Gk *cast out your name as evil*   *b* Other ancient authorities read *despairing of no one*

Divine Rhythm: Solitude and Community

LUKE 6.12–16

Jesus prays alone all night; in the morning he calls the twelve to work alongside him. How do you balance solitude and community in your life? In what ways are your practices of solitude and community out of balance? Consider designing a pattern—called by some a "rule of life"—to maintain a rhythm of time apart for prayer and reflection and time spent with others. Consider how you can ensure neither is shortchanged. Do you spend your entire workweek with others? Your weekends entirely alone? What could you do differently? Write down some of your ideas and discuss them with a friend.

See Meeting God in Prayer

1359

Blessing the Difficult

LUKE 6.32–36

Read this passage and then reread it slowly as you do this exercise (*lectio divina* or "divine reading"): Listen for a word or phrase that stands out—don't rush to the most obvious one first. Continue to be quiet before God. What do you think happens within you as you love your enemy? What does it teach you about yourself? Respond to whatever God is telling you through this passage.

See Meeting God in Prayer

Judging Others

37 "Do not judge, and you will not be judged; do not condemn, and you will not be condemned. Forgive, and you will be forgiven; **38**give, and it will be given to you. A good measure, pressed down, shaken together, running over, will be put into your lap; for the measure you give will be the measure you get back."

39 He also told them a parable: "Can a blind person guide a blind person? Will not both fall into a pit? **40**A disciple is not above the teacher, but everyone who is fully qualified will be like the teacher. **41**Why do you see the speck in your neighbor's*a* eye, but do not notice the log in your own eye? **42**Or how can you say to your neighbor,*b* 'Friend,*b* let me take out the speck in your eye,' when you yourself do not see the log in your own eye? You hypocrite, first take the log out of your own eye, and then you will see clearly to take the speck out of your neighbor's*a* eye.

A Tree and Its Fruit

43 "No good tree bears bad fruit, nor again does a bad tree bear good fruit; **44**for each tree is known by its own fruit. Figs are not gathered from thorns, nor are grapes picked from a bramble bush. **45**The good person out of the good treasure of the heart produces good, and the evil person out of evil treasure produces evil; for it is out of the abundance of the heart that the mouth speaks.

The Two Foundations

46 "Why do you call me 'Lord, Lord,' and do not do what I tell you? **47**I will show you what someone is like who comes to me, hears my words, and acts on them. **48**That one is like a man building a house, who dug deeply and laid the foundation on rock; when a flood arose, the river burst against that house but could not shake it, because it had been well built.*c* **49**But the one who hears and does not act is like a man who built a house on the ground without a foundation. When the river burst against it, immediately it fell, and great was the ruin of that house."

Jesus Heals a Centurion's Servant

7 After Jesus*d* had finished all his sayings in the hearing of the people, he entered Capernaum. **2**A centurion there had a slave whom he valued highly, and who was ill and close to death. **3**When he heard about Jesus, he sent some Jewish elders to him, asking him to come and heal his slave. **4**When they came to Jesus, they appealed to him earnestly, saying, "He is worthy of having you do this for him, **5**for he loves our people, and it is he who built our synagogue for us." **6**And Jesus went with them, but when he was not far from the house, the centurion sent friends to say to him, "Lord, do not trouble yourself, for I am not worthy to have you come under my roof; **7**therefore I did not presume to come to you. But only speak the word, and let my servant be healed. **8**For I also am a man set under authority, with soldiers under me; and I say to one, 'Go,' and he goes, and to another, 'Come,' and he comes, and to my slave, 'Do this,' and the slave does it." **9**When

a Gk *brother's*   *b* Gk *brother*   *c* Other ancient authorities read *founded upon the rock*   *d* Gk *he*

Jesus heard this he was amazed at him, and turning to the crowd that followed him, he said, "I tell you, not even in Israel have I found such faith." [10]When those who had been sent returned to the house, they found the slave in good health.

Jesus Raises the Widow's Son at Nain

11 Soon afterwards[a] he went to a town called Nain, and his disciples and a large crowd went with him. [12]As he approached the gate of the town, a man who had died was being carried out. He was his mother's only son, and she was a widow; and with her was a large crowd from the town. [13]When the Lord saw her, he had compassion for her and said to her, "Do not weep." [14]Then he came forward and touched the bier, and the bearers stood still. And he said, "Young man, I say to you, rise!" [15]The dead man sat up and began to speak, and Jesus[b] gave him to his mother. [16]Fear seized all of them; and they glorified God, saying, "A great prophet has risen among us!" and "God has looked favorably on his people!" [17]This word about him spread throughout Judea and all the surrounding country.

Messengers from John the Baptist

18 The disciples of John reported all these things to him. So John summoned two of his disciples [19]and sent them to the Lord to ask, "Are you the one who is to come, or are we to wait for another?" [20]When the men had come to him, they said, "John the Baptist has sent us to you to ask, 'Are you the one who is to come, or are we to wait for another?' " [21]Jesus[c] had just then cured many people of diseases, plagues, and evil spirits, and had given sight to many who were blind. [22]And he answered them, "Go and tell John what you have seen and heard: the blind receive their sight, the lame walk, the lepers[d] are cleansed, the deaf hear, the dead are raised, the poor have good news brought to them. [23]And blessed is anyone who takes no offense at me."

24 When John's messengers had gone, Jesus[b] began to speak to the crowds about John:[e] "What did you go out into the wilderness to look at? A reed shaken by the wind? [25]What then did you go out to see? Someone[f] dressed in soft robes? Look, those who put on fine clothing and live in luxury are in royal palaces. [26]What then did you go out to see? A prophet? Yes, I tell you, and more than a prophet. [27]This is the one about whom it is written,

'See, I am sending my messenger ahead of you,
who will prepare your way before you.'

[28]I tell you, among those born of women no one is greater than John; yet the least in the kingdom of God is greater than he." [29](And all the people who heard this, including the tax collectors, acknowledged the justice of God,[g] because they had been baptized with John's baptism. [30]But by refusing to be baptized by him, the Pharisees and the lawyers rejected God's purpose for themselves.)

31 "To what then will I compare the people of this gen-

The Journey to Belief

LUKE 7.18–23

"Perhaps it is all a mistake, this business about Christianity . . . Perhaps all this talk about God and Jesus Christ and the salvation of [human beings] is a collection of fairy tales . . . Perhaps it is a mistake to preach love in a hate-torn world, to rescue those who are in need, to teach the children, to comfort the lonely and the dying. But if it is, after all, a mistake, then it is a beautiful mistake. If Christianity should turn out, after all, to be true, then unbelief will have been a very ugly mistake."

—KAJ MUNK,
By the Rivers of Babylon

See Meeting God in Community

---

a Other ancient authorities read *Next day*   b Gk *he*   c Gk *He*
d The terms *leper* and *leprosy* can refer to several diseases   e Gk *him*
f Or *Why then did you go out? To see someone*   g Or *praised God*

Twin Spiritual Paths

LUKE 7.33–34

Two men, two spiritual paths, two traditions exist in creative tension: the ascetic path of John the Baptist, who lived mainly in the desert, and the path of the Son of Man, who spent much of his time in cities crowded with people. These paths intersect when God calls us to retreat in order to prepare for service.

Are you being called to streamline your lifestyle so that you have more time for solitude, prayer and reflection? Or are you being called to mix more with people in the world as a friend of "sinners"? How might the cultivation of a simple, modest lifestyle better prepare you to live as Jesus did, in the world but not of the world?

See *Meeting God in Community*

eration, and what are they like? 32They are like children sitting in the marketplace and calling to one another,

'We played the flute for you, and you did not dance;
we wailed, and you did not weep.'

33For John the Baptist has come eating no bread and drinking no wine, and you say, 'He has a demon'; 34the Son of Man has come eating and drinking, and you say, 'Look, a glutton and a drunkard, a friend of tax collectors and sinners!' 35Nevertheless, wisdom is vindicated by all her children."

A Sinful Woman Forgiven

36 One of the Pharisees asked Jesus[a] to eat with him, and he went into the Pharisee's house and took his place at the table. 37And a woman in the city, who was a sinner, having learned that he was eating in the Pharisee's house, brought an alabaster jar of ointment. 38She stood behind him at his feet, weeping, and began to bathe his feet with her tears and to dry them with her hair. Then she continued kissing his feet and anointing them with the ointment. 39Now when the Pharisee who had invited him saw it, he said to himself, "If this man were a prophet, he would have known who and what kind of woman this is who is touching him—that she is a sinner." 40Jesus spoke up and said to him, "Simon, I have something to say to you." "Teacher," he replied, "speak." 41"A certain creditor had two debtors; one owed five hundred denarii,[b] and the other fifty. 42When they could not pay, he canceled the debts for both of them. Now which of them will love him more?" 43Simon answered, "I suppose the one for whom he canceled the greater debt." And Jesus[c] said to him, "You have judged rightly." 44Then turning toward the woman, he said to Simon, "Do you see this woman? I entered your house; you gave me no water for my feet, but she has bathed my feet with her tears and dried them with her hair. 45You gave me no kiss, but from the time I came in she has not stopped kissing my feet. 46You did not anoint my head with oil, but she has anointed my feet with ointment. 47Therefore, I tell you, her sins, which were many, have been forgiven; hence she has shown great love. But the one to whom little is forgiven, loves little." 48Then he said to her, "Your sins are forgiven." 49But those who were at the table with him began to say among themselves, "Who is this who even forgives sins?" 50And he said to the woman, "Your faith has saved you; go in peace."

Some Women Accompany Jesus

8 Soon afterwards he went on through cities and villages, proclaiming and bringing the good news of the kingdom of God. The twelve were with him, 2as well as some women who had been cured of evil spirits and infirmities: Mary, called Magdalene, from whom seven demons had gone out, 3and Joanna, the wife of Herod's steward Chuza, and Susanna, and many others, who provided for them[d] out of their resources.

---

a Gk *him*   b The denarius was the usual day's wage for a laborer
c Gk *he*   d Other ancient authorities read *him*

The Parable of the Sower

4 When a great crowd gathered and people from town after town came to him, he said in a parable: [5]"A sower went out to sow his seed; and as he sowed, some fell on the path and was trampled on, and the birds of the air ate it up. [6]Some fell on the rock; and as it grew up, it withered for lack of moisture. [7]Some fell among thorns, and the thorns grew with it and choked it. [8]Some fell into good soil, and when it grew, it produced a hundredfold." As he said this, he called out, "Let anyone with ears to hear listen!"

The Purpose of the Parables

9 Then his disciples asked him what this parable meant. [10]He said, "To you it has been given to know the secrets[a] of the kingdom of God; but to others I speak[b] in parables, so that

'looking they may not perceive,
and listening they may not understand.'

The Parable of the Sower Explained

11 "Now the parable is this: The seed is the word of God. [12]The ones on the path are those who have heard; then the devil comes and takes away the word from their hearts, so that they may not believe and be saved. [13]The ones on the rock are those who, when they hear the word, receive it with joy. But these have no root; they believe only for a while and in a time of testing fall away. [14]As for what fell among the thorns, these are the ones who hear; but as they go on their way, they are choked by the cares and riches and pleasures of life, and their fruit does not mature. [15]But as for that in the good soil, these are the ones who, when they hear the word, hold it fast in an honest and good heart, and bear fruit with patient endurance.

A Lamp under a Jar

16 "No one after lighting a lamp hides it under a jar, or puts it under a bed, but puts it on a lampstand, so that those who enter may see the light. [17]For nothing is hidden that will not be disclosed, nor is anything secret that will not become known and come to light. [18]Then pay attention to how you listen; for to those who have, more will be given; and from those who do not have, even what they seem to have will be taken away."

The True Kindred of Jesus

19 Then his mother and his brothers came to him, but they could not reach him because of the crowd. [20]And he was told, "Your mother and your brothers are standing outside, wanting to see you." [21]But he said to them, "My mother and my brothers are those who hear the word of God and do it."

Jesus Calms a Storm

22 One day he got into a boat with his disciples, and he said to them, "Let us go across to the other side of the lake." So they put out, [23]and while they were sailing he fell asleep. A windstorm swept down on the lake, and the

Letting the Word Grow

LUKE 8.11–15

Attending to God's voice requires effort. We're so unaccustomed to listening that we often let God's messages go unnoticed. Or we hear God speaking to us, but we don't let the words take root in our inner being. Pleasures and problems quickly overshadow them. What does it say about God that he continues to plant seeds even though people don't nurture them? What does it say about our human nature that we're so easily distracted? What do you want to say to God, or to ask God, about these issues? What does this passage tell you that you need to do in order to hear God better?

Spiritual Family

LUKE 8.19–21

Jesus provides a startling definition of his family: "those who hear the word of God and do it." Consider the various ages and stages of your life. Who has been that kind of "family" for you? What have these "family members" taught you? Diligence? Sensitivity? Courage? Try making a gratitude list, noting the names of people to whom you are grateful and what these people have contributed to your life. As you make your list, thank God for these people and ponder how God wants you to participate in the lives of these spiritual "family members."

See *Meeting God in Community*

boat was filling with water, and they were in danger. [24]They went to him and woke him up, shouting, "Master, Master, we are perishing!" And he woke up and rebuked the wind and the raging waves; they ceased, and there was a calm. [25]He said to them, "Where is your faith?" They were afraid and amazed, and said to one another, "Who then is this, that he commands even the winds and the water, and they obey him?"

Jesus Heals the Gerasene Demoniac

26 Then they arrived at the country of the Gerasenes,[a] which is opposite Galilee. [27]As he stepped out on land, a man of the city who had demons met him. For a long time he had worn[b] no clothes, and he did not live in a house but in the tombs. [28]When he saw Jesus, he fell down before him and shouted at the top of his voice, "What have you to do with me, Jesus, Son of the Most High God? I beg you, do not torment me"— [29]for Jesus[c] had commanded the unclean spirit to come out of the man. (For many times it had seized him; he was kept under guard and bound with chains and shackles, but he would break the bonds and be driven by the demon into the wilds.) [30]Jesus then asked him, "What is your name?" He said, "Legion"; for many demons had entered him. [31]They begged him not to order them to go back into the abyss.

32 Now there on the hillside a large herd of swine was feeding; and the demons[d] begged Jesus[e] to let them enter these. So he gave them permission. [33]Then the demons came out of the man and entered the swine, and the herd rushed down the steep bank into the lake and was drowned.

34 When the swineherds saw what had happened, they ran off and told it in the city and in the country. [35]Then people came out to see what had happened, and when they came to Jesus, they found the man from whom the demons had gone sitting at the feet of Jesus, clothed and in his right mind. And they were afraid. [36]Those who had seen it told them how the one who had been possessed by demons had been healed. [37]Then all the people of the surrounding country of the Gerasenes[a] asked Jesus[e] to leave them; for they were seized with great fear. So he got into the boat and returned. [38]The man from whom the demons had gone begged that he might be with him; but Jesus[c] sent him away, saying, [39]"Return to your home, and declare how much God has done for you." So he went away, proclaiming throughout the city how much Jesus had done for him.

A Girl Restored to Life and a Woman Healed

40 Now when Jesus returned, the crowd welcomed him, for they were all waiting for him. [41]Just then there came a man named Jairus, a leader of the synagogue. He fell at Jesus' feet and begged him to come to his house, [42]for he had an only daughter, about twelve years old, who was dying.

As he went, the crowds pressed in on him. [43]Now there was a woman who had been suffering from hemorrhages

---

a Other ancient authorities read *Gadarenes*; others, *Gergesenes*   b Other ancient authorities read *a man of the city who had had demons for a long time met him. He wore*   c Gk *he*   d Gk *they*   e Gk *him*

for twelve years; and though she had spent all she had on physicians,*a* no one could cure her. **44**She came up behind him and touched the fringe of his clothes, and immediately her hemorrhage stopped. **45**Then Jesus asked, "Who touched me?" When all denied it, Peter*b* said, "Master, the crowds surround you and press in on you." **46**But Jesus said, "Someone touched me; for I noticed that power had gone out from me." **47**When the woman saw that she could not remain hidden, she came trembling; and falling down before him, she declared in the presence of all the people why she had touched him, and how she had been immediately healed. **48**He said to her, "Daughter, your faith has made you well; go in peace."

49 While he was still speaking, someone came from the leader's house to say, "Your daughter is dead; do not trouble the teacher any longer." **50**When Jesus heard this, he replied, "Do not fear. Only believe, and she will be saved." **51**When he came to the house, he did not allow anyone to enter with him, except Peter, John, and James, and the child's father and mother. **52**They were all weeping and wailing for her; but he said, "Do not weep; for she is not dead but sleeping." **53**And they laughed at him, knowing that she was dead. **54**But he took her by the hand and called out, "Child, get up!" **55**Her spirit returned, and she got up at once. Then he directed them to give her something to eat. **56**Her parents were astounded; but he ordered them to tell no one what had happened.

The Mission of the Twelve

9 Then Jesus*c* called the twelve together and gave them power and authority over all demons and to cure diseases, **2**and he sent them out to proclaim the kingdom of God and to heal. **3**He said to them, "Take nothing for your journey, no staff, nor bag, nor bread, nor money—not even an extra tunic. **4**Whatever house you enter, stay there, and leave from there. **5**Wherever they do not welcome you, as you are leaving that town shake the dust off your feet as a testimony against them." **6**They departed and went through the villages, bringing the good news and curing diseases everywhere.

Herod's Perplexity

7 Now Herod the ruler*d* heard about all that had taken place, and he was perplexed, because it was said by some that John had been raised from the dead, **8**by some that Elijah had appeared, and by others that one of the ancient prophets had arisen. **9**Herod said, "John I beheaded; but who is this about whom I hear such things?" And he tried to see him.

Feeding the Five Thousand

10 On their return the apostles told Jesus*e* all they had done. He took them with him and withdrew privately to a city called Bethsaida. **11**When the crowds found out about it, they followed him; and he welcomed them, and spoke to them about the kingdom of God, and healed those who needed to be cured.

---

a Other ancient authorities lack *and though she had spent all she had on physicians*   *b* Other ancient authorities add *and those who were with him*   *c* Gk *he*   *d* Gk *tetrarch*   *e* Gk *him*

When Life Is Interrupted

LUKE 8.40–56

Read this Scripture passage aloud; then reread it silently. Allow an "inner video" to play, visualizing each character and hearing each one converse with Jesus: Jairus comes to Jesus on behalf of his dying twelve-year-old daughter . . . Jesus works his way through the crowds . . . A woman who has been bleeding for twelve years touches Jesus' clothing . . . The disciples become angry . . . The woman is afraid as she is singled out . . . Jesus says, "Daughter, your faith has made you well; go in peace." Then, to Jairus, Jesus says, "Do not fear. Only believe." Listen to Jesus' words as if they were spoken to you: "Do not fear. Only believe." Rest in God's presence.

See Meeting God in Scripture

Taking Inventory

LUKE 9.10–17

Imagine that you are one of the disciples, returning tired from teaching, healing and driving out demons. You have so many questions to ask Jesus. Then you hear about the execution of John the Baptist. Jesus invites you to retreat; you long to go to a quiet spot to rest and grieve. Suddenly a crowd of people arrives, asking for help. When you ask Jesus to send them away, he says, "You give them something to eat." But you protest, "I have no more than _____." In order to fill in the blank, take an inventory of the resources of your life: your personal, family, intellectual, material, physical and spiritual resources. Picture yourself placing these resources in Jesus' hands, one by one, until the last resource is yourself—resting in Jesus' arms.

See Meeting God in Community

12 The day was drawing to a close, and the twelve came to him and said, "Send the crowd away, so that they may go into the surrounding villages and countryside, to lodge and get provisions; for we are here in a deserted place." 13But he said to them, "You give them something to eat." They said, "We have no more than five loaves and two fish—unless we are to go and buy food for all these people." 14For there were about five thousand men. And he said to his disciples, "Make them sit down in groups of about fifty each." 15They did so and made them all sit down. 16And taking the five loaves and the two fish, he looked up to heaven, and blessed and broke them, and gave them to the disciples to set before the crowd. 17And all ate and were filled. What was left over was gathered up, twelve baskets of broken pieces.

Peter's Declaration about Jesus

18 Once when Jesus*a* was praying alone, with only the disciples near him, he asked them, "Who do the crowds say that I am?" 19They answered, "John the Baptist; but others, Elijah; and still others, that one of the ancient prophets has arisen." 20He said to them, "But who do you say that I am?" Peter answered, "The Messiah*b* of God."

Jesus Foretells His Death and Resurrection

21 He sternly ordered and commanded them not to tell anyone, 22saying, "The Son of Man must undergo great suffering, and be rejected by the elders, chief priests, and scribes, and be killed, and on the third day be raised."

23 Then he said to them all, "If any want to become my followers, let them deny themselves and take up their cross daily and follow me. 24For those who want to save their life will lose it, and those who lose their life for my sake will save it. 25What does it profit them if they gain the whole world, but lose or forfeit themselves? 26Those who are ashamed of me and of my words, of them the Son of Man will be ashamed when he comes in his glory and the glory of the Father and of the holy angels. 27But truly I tell you, there are some standing here who will not taste death before they see the kingdom of God."

The Transfiguration

28 Now about eight days after these sayings Jesus*a* took with him Peter and John and James, and went up on the mountain to pray. 29And while he was praying, the appearance of his face changed, and his clothes became dazzling white. 30Suddenly they saw two men, Moses and Elijah, talking to him. 31They appeared in glory and were speaking of his departure, which he was about to accomplish at Jerusalem. 32Now Peter and his companions were weighed down with sleep; but since they had stayed awake,*c* they saw his glory and the two men who stood with him. 33Just as they were leaving him, Peter said to Jesus, "Master, it is good for us to be here; let us make three dwellings,*d* one for you, one for Moses, and one for Elijah"—not knowing what he said. 34While he was saying this, a cloud came and overshadowed them; and they were terrified as they entered the cloud. 35Then from the

a Gk *he* *b* Or *The Christ* *c* Or *but when they were fully awake*
d Or *tents*

cloud came a voice that said, "This is my Son, my Chosen;[a] listen to him!" [36]When the voice had spoken, Jesus was found alone. And they kept silent and in those days told no one any of the things they had seen.

Jesus Heals a Boy with a Demon

37 On the next day, when they had come down from the mountain, a great crowd met him. [38]Just then a man from the crowd shouted, "Teacher, I beg you to look at my son; he is my only child. [39]Suddenly a spirit seizes him, and all at once he[b] shrieks. It convulses him until he foams at the mouth; it mauls him and will scarcely leave him. [40]I begged your disciples to cast it out, but they could not." [41]Jesus answered, "You faithless and perverse generation, how much longer must I be with you and bear with you? Bring your son here." [42]While he was coming, the demon dashed him to the ground in convulsions. But Jesus rebuked the unclean spirit, healed the boy, and gave him back to his father. [43]And all were astounded at the greatness of God.

Jesus Again Foretells His Death

While everyone was amazed at all that he was doing, he said to his disciples, [44]"Let these words sink into your ears: The Son of Man is going to be betrayed into human hands." [45]But they did not understand this saying; its meaning was concealed from them, so that they could not perceive it. And they were afraid to ask him about this saying.

True Greatness

46 An argument arose among them as to which one of them was the greatest. [47]But Jesus, aware of their inner thoughts, took a little child and put it by his side, [48]and said to them, "Whoever welcomes this child in my name welcomes me, and whoever welcomes me welcomes the one who sent me; for the least among all of you is the greatest."

Another Exorcist

49 John answered, "Master, we saw someone casting out demons in your name, and we tried to stop him, because he does not follow with us." [50]But Jesus said to him, "Do not stop him; for whoever is not against you is for you."

A Samaritan Village Refuses to Receive Jesus

51 When the days drew near for him to be taken up, he set his face to go to Jerusalem. [52]And he sent messengers ahead of him. On their way they entered a village of the Samaritans to make ready for him; [53]but they did not receive him, because his face was set toward Jerusalem. [54]When his disciples James and John saw it, they said, "Lord, do you want us to command fire to come down from heaven and consume them?"[c] [55]But he turned and rebuked them. [56]Then[d] they went on to another village.

---

a Other ancient authorities read *my Beloved*   b Or *it*   c Other ancient authorities add *as Elijah did*   d Other ancient authorities read *rebuked them, and said, "You do not know what spirit you are of, [56]for the Son of Man has not come to destroy the lives of human beings but to save them." Then*

Going to the Mountain to Pray

LUKE 9.28–36

Notice the concrete elements in this mystical event: Jesus and the three disciples climb a mountain to pray. As Jesus prays, his face is transformed and his clothes appear as dazzling light. Moses and Elijah appear and speak to Jesus. A cloud envelopes them and a voice tells them to listen to Jesus, God's beloved, chosen One.

God uses real, concrete things to reveal Jesus Christ glorified,—a mountain, a face, clothes, bodies from the past, a cloud. What observable, physical response to Jesus' glory (kneeling, laying prostrate, twirling in delight) would communicate worship to our majestic God?

See Meeting God in Worship

Go Forth and Travel Lightly!

LUKE 10.1–12

When Jesus sends the seventy out to prepare the people for his coming, he instructs them to travel lightly. They are not to attempt to control how their needs will be met or how people will respond to them. Why does God want us to serve as disciples without having control over resources or circumstances? Why do we seem to need to control these things? What do your answers suggest about how you can pray about these issues?

See Meeting God in Community

Would-Be Followers of Jesus

57 As they were going along the road, someone said to him, "I will follow you wherever you go." 58And Jesus said to him, "Foxes have holes, and birds of the air have nests; but the Son of Man has nowhere to lay his head." 59To another he said, "Follow me." But he said, "Lord, first let me go and bury my father." 60But Jesus*a* said to him, "Let the dead bury their own dead; but as for you, go and proclaim the kingdom of God." 61Another said, "I will follow you, Lord; but let me first say farewell to those at my home." 62Jesus said to him, "No one who puts a hand to the plow and looks back is fit for the kingdom of God."

The Mission of the Seventy

10 After this the Lord appointed seventy*b* others and sent them on ahead of him in pairs to every town and place where he himself intended to go. 2He said to them, "The harvest is plentiful, but the laborers are few; therefore ask the Lord of the harvest to send out laborers into his harvest. 3Go on your way. See, I am sending you out like lambs into the midst of wolves. 4Carry no purse, no bag, no sandals; and greet no one on the road. 5Whatever house you enter, first say, 'Peace to this house!' 6And if anyone is there who shares in peace, your peace will rest on that person; but if not, it will return to you. 7Remain in the same house, eating and drinking whatever they provide, for the laborer deserves to be paid. Do not move about from house to house. 8Whenever you enter a town and its people welcome you, eat what is set before you; 9cure the sick who are there, and say to them, 'The kingdom of God has come near to you.'*c* 10But whenever you enter a town and they do not welcome you, go out into its streets and say, 11'Even the dust of your town that clings to our feet, we wipe off in protest against you. Yet know this: the kingdom of God has come near.'*d* 12I tell you, on that day it will be more tolerable for Sodom than for that town.

Woes to Unrepentant Cities

13 "Woe to you, Chorazin! Woe to you, Bethsaida! For if the deeds of power done in you had been done in Tyre and Sidon, they would have repented long ago, sitting in sackcloth and ashes. 14But at the judgment it will be more tolerable for Tyre and Sidon than for you. 15And you, Capernaum,

will you be exalted to heaven?
No, you will be brought down to Hades.

16 "Whoever listens to you listens to me, and whoever rejects you rejects me, and whoever rejects me rejects the one who sent me."

The Return of the Seventy

17 The seventy*b* returned with joy, saying, "Lord, in your name even the demons submit to us!" 18He said to them, "I watched Satan fall from heaven like a flash of lightning. 19See, I have given you authority to tread on snakes and scorpions, and over all the power of the

a Gk *he*   *b* Other ancient authorities read *seventy-two for you*   *c* Or *is at hand*   *d* Or *is at hand*

enemy; and nothing will hurt you. ²⁰Nevertheless, do not rejoice at this, that the spirits submit to you, but rejoice that your names are written in heaven."

Jesus Rejoices

21 At that same hour Jesus*ᵃ* rejoiced in the Holy Spirit*ᵇ* and said, "I thank*ᶜ* you, Father, Lord of heaven and earth, because you have hidden these things from the wise and the intelligent and have revealed them to infants; yes, Father, for such was your gracious will.*ᵈ* ²²All things have been handed over to me by my Father; and no one knows who the Son is except the Father, or who the Father is except the Son and anyone to whom the Son chooses to reveal him."

23 Then turning to the disciples, Jesus*ᵃ* said to them privately, "Blessed are the eyes that see what you see! ²⁴For I tell you that many prophets and kings desired to see what you see, but did not see it, and to hear what you hear, but did not hear it."

The Parable of the Good Samaritan

25 Just then a lawyer stood up to test Jesus.*ᵉ* "Teacher," he said, "what must I do to inherit eternal life?" ²⁶He said to him, "What is written in the law? What do you read there?" ²⁷He answered, "You shall love the Lord your God with all your heart, and with all your soul, and with all your strength, and with all your mind; and your neighbor as yourself." ²⁸And he said to him, "You have given the right answer; do this, and you will live."

29 But wanting to justify himself, he asked Jesus, "And who is my neighbor?" ³⁰Jesus replied, "A man was going down from Jerusalem to Jericho, and fell into the hands of robbers, who stripped him, beat him, and went away, leaving him half dead. ³¹Now by chance a priest was going down that road; and when he saw him, he passed by on the other side. ³²So likewise a Levite, when he came to the place and saw him, passed by on the other side. ³³But a Samaritan while traveling came near him; and when he saw him, he was moved with pity. ³⁴He went to him and bandaged his wounds, having poured oil and wine on them. Then he put him on his own animal, brought him to an inn, and took care of him. ³⁵The next day he took out two denarii,*ᶠ* gave them to the innkeeper, and said, 'Take care of him; and when I come back, I will repay you whatever more you spend.' ³⁶Which of these three, do you think, was a neighbor to the man who fell into the hands of the robbers?" ³⁷He said, "The one who showed him mercy." Jesus said to him, "Go and do likewise."

Jesus Visits Martha and Mary

38 Now as they went on their way, he entered a certain village, where a woman named Martha welcomed him into her home. ³⁹She had a sister named Mary, who sat at the Lord's feet and listened to what he was saying. ⁴⁰But Martha was distracted by her many tasks; so she came to him and asked, "Lord, do you not care that my sister has left me to do all the work by myself? Tell her then to help

---

a Gk *he*   *b* Other authorities read *in the spirit*   *c* Or *praise*   *d* Or *for so it was well-pleasing in your sight*   *e* Gk *him*   *f* The denarius was the usual day's wage for a laborer

Lord, Don't You Care?

LUKE 10.38–42

Put yourself in Martha's place. You have worked hard to offer the Lord hospitality, using all the skills you have and providing the sumptuous feast that is fitting for your honored guest. Hot and tired, your face contorts with annoyance when you see Mary just sitting at Jesus' feet. You ask, "Lord, do you not care that my sister has left me to do all the work by myself?"

Let Jesus address you lovingly, personally: "_____, you are worried and distracted by many things." Tell Jesus "the many things" bothering you. Hear Jesus say to you: "_____, there is need of only one thing." What is the one thing that's needed now in life? Allow a word or phrase to rise within you. Repeat it slowly, letting that word or phrase carry your concerns, one by one, into the heart of God.

See Meeting God in Prayer

The Personal Sermon

LUKE 11.1-4

"Frequently when I come to a certain part of 'Our Father' or to a petition, I land in such rich thoughts that I leave behind all set prayers. When such rich, good thoughts arrive, then one should leave the other commandments aside and offer room to those thoughts and listen in stillness and for all the world not put up obstructions. For then the Holy Spirit . . . is preaching and one word from [that] sermon is better than a thousand of our prayers. I have often learned more from one such prayer than I could have received from much reading and writing."

—MARTIN LUTHER

See *Meeting God in Worship*

me." ⁴¹But the Lord answered her, "Martha, Martha, you are worried and distracted by many things; ⁴²there is need of only one thing.ᵃ Mary has chosen the better part, which will not be taken away from her."

The Lord's Prayer

11 He was praying in a certain place, and after he had finished, one of his disciples said to him, "Lord, teach us to pray, as John taught his disciples." ²He said to them, "When you pray, say:
> Father,ᵇ hallowed be your name.
> Your kingdom come.ᶜ
³ Give us each day our daily bread.ᵈ
⁴ And forgive us our sins,
> for we ourselves forgive everyone indebted
> to us.
> And do not bring us to the time of trial."ᵉ

Perseverance in Prayer

5 And he said to them, "Suppose one of you has a friend, and you go to him at midnight and say to him, 'Friend, lend me three loaves of bread; ⁶for a friend of mine has arrived, and I have nothing to set before him.' ⁷And he answers from within, 'Do not bother me; the door has already been locked, and my children are with me in bed; I cannot get up and give you anything.' ⁸I tell you, even though he will not get up and give him anything because he is his friend, at least because of his persistence he will get up and give him whatever he needs.

9 "So I say to you, Ask, and it will be given you; search, and you will find; knock, and the door will be opened for you. ¹⁰For everyone who asks receives, and everyone who searches finds, and for everyone who knocks, the door will be opened. ¹¹Is there anyone among you who, if your child asks forᶠ a fish, will give a snake instead of a fish? ¹²Or if the child asks for an egg, will give a scorpion? ¹³If you then, who are evil, know how to give good gifts to your children, how much more will the heavenly Father give the Holy Spiritᵍ to those who ask him!"

Jesus and Beelzebul

14 Now he was casting out a demon that was mute; when the demon had gone out, the one who had been mute spoke, and the crowds were amazed. ¹⁵But some of them said, "He casts out demons by Beelzebul, the ruler of the demons." ¹⁶Others, to test him, kept demanding from him a sign from heaven. ¹⁷But he knew what they were thinking and said to them, "Every kingdom divided against itself becomes a desert, and house falls on house. ¹⁸If Satan also is divided against himself, how will his kingdom stand? —for you say that I cast out the demons by Beelzebul. ¹⁹Now if I cast out the demons by Beelzebul, by whom do your exorcistsʰ cast them out? Therefore they

---

a Other ancient authorities read *few things are necessary, or only one* *b* Other ancient authorities read *Our Father in heaven* *c* A few ancient authorities read *Your Holy Spirit come upon us and cleanse us.* Other ancient authorities add *Your will be done, on earth as in heaven* *d* Or *our bread for tomorrow* *e* Or *us into temptation.* Other ancient authorities add *but rescue us from the evil one* (or *from evil*) *f* Other ancient authorities add *bread, will give a stone; or if your child asks for* *g* Other ancient authorities read *the Father give the Holy Spirit from heaven* *h* Gk *sons*

will be your judges. **20**But if it is by the finger of God that I cast out the demons, then the kingdom of God has come to you. **21**When a strong man, fully armed, guards his castle, his property is safe. **22**But when one stronger than he attacks him and overpowers him, he takes away his armor in which he trusted and divides his plunder. **23**Whoever is not with me is against me, and whoever does not gather with me scatters.

The Return of the Unclean Spirit

24 "When the unclean spirit has gone out of a person, it wanders through waterless regions looking for a resting place, but not finding any, it says, 'I will return to my house from which I came.' **25**When it comes, it finds it swept and put in order. **26**Then it goes and brings seven other spirits more evil than itself, and they enter and live there; and the last state of that person is worse than the first."

True Blessedness

27 While he was saying this, a woman in the crowd raised her voice and said to him, "Blessed is the womb that bore you and the breasts that nursed you!" **28**But he said, "Blessed rather are those who hear the word of God and obey it!"

The Sign of Jonah

29 When the crowds were increasing, he began to say, "This generation is an evil generation; it asks for a sign, but no sign will be given to it except the sign of Jonah. **30**For just as Jonah became a sign to the people of Nineveh, so the Son of Man will be to this generation. **31**The queen of the South will rise at the judgment with the people of this generation and condemn them, because she came from the ends of the earth to listen to the wisdom of Solomon, and see, something greater than Solomon is here! **32**The people of Nineveh will rise up at the judgment with this generation and condemn it, because they repented at the proclamation of Jonah, and see, something greater than Jonah is here!

The Light of the Body

33 "No one after lighting a lamp puts it in a cellar,*a* but on the lampstand so that those who enter may see the light. **34**Your eye is the lamp of your body. If your eye is healthy, your whole body is full of light; but if it is not healthy, your body is full of darkness. **35**Therefore consider whether the light in you is not darkness. **36**If then your whole body is full of light, with no part of it in darkness, it will be as full of light as when a lamp gives you light with its rays."

Jesus Denounces Pharisees and Lawyers

37 While he was speaking, a Pharisee invited him to dine with him; so he went in and took his place at the table. **38**The Pharisee was amazed to see that he did not first wash before dinner. **39**Then the Lord said to him, "Now you Pharisees clean the outside of the cup and of the dish, but inside you are full of greed and wickedness.

Your Life Mission

LUKE 11.33–36

A "healthy eye" is an eye that floods the body with light. In *Man's Search for Meaning*, Victor Frankl wrote that a person with a *why* to live can survive almost any *how*. What is your focused *why* for living? Try finishing this sentence: "My purpose for being on this earth is . . ." Close your eyes and identify what gives you inner joy and fulfillment. What is your passion—your mission? Summarize this single vision in a sentence and write it on a small card, or express it artistically. Look at it from time to time and pray. How do you sense God's affirmation about being called in this direction?

See Meeting God in Community

---

a Other ancient authorities add *or under the bushel basket*

Making Christ Known

LUKE 11.42–44; 12.1–3

Jesus Christ is reflected in us through the seamless integrity of our worship—expressed both in the words we whisper privately and in the love with which we carry out our deeds. The "yeast of the Pharisees"—hypocrisy of the heart—must be rooted out. Read this passage twice, slowly the second time. Sit quietly, allowing a word or phrase to stand out. Reflect on this word or phrase or action. Why is it meaningful to you? Use that word or phrase to pray back to God the truth God has given you. Be quiet before God and attentive to anything God may be showing you.

See Meeting God in Scripture

40 You fools! Did not the one who made the outside make the inside also? 41 So give for alms those things that are within; and see, everything will be clean for you.

42 "But woe to you Pharisees! For you tithe mint and rue and herbs of all kinds, and neglect justice and the love of God; it is these you ought to have practiced, without neglecting the others. 43 Woe to you Pharisees! For you love to have the seat of honor in the synagogues and to be greeted with respect in the marketplaces. 44 Woe to you! For you are like unmarked graves, and people walk over them without realizing it."

45 One of the lawyers answered him, "Teacher, when you say these things, you insult us too." 46 And he said, "Woe also to you lawyers! For you load people with burdens hard to bear, and you yourselves do not lift a finger to ease them. 47 Woe to you! For you build the tombs of the prophets whom your ancestors killed. 48 So you are witnesses and approve of the deeds of your ancestors; for they killed them, and you build their tombs. 49 Therefore also the Wisdom of God said, 'I will send them prophets and apostles, some of whom they will kill and persecute,' 50 so that this generation may be charged with the blood of all the prophets shed since the foundation of the world, 51 from the blood of Abel to the blood of Zechariah, who perished between the altar and the sanctuary. Yes, I tell you, it will be charged against this generation. 52 Woe to you lawyers! For you have taken away the key of knowledge; you did not enter yourselves, and you hindered those who were entering."

53 When he went outside, the scribes and the Pharisees began to be very hostile toward him and to cross-examine him about many things, 54 lying in wait for him, to catch him in something he might say.

A Warning against Hypocrisy

12 Meanwhile, when the crowd gathered by the thousands, so that they trampled on one another, he began to speak first to his disciples, "Beware of the yeast of the Pharisees, that is, their hypocrisy. 2 Nothing is covered up that will not be uncovered, and nothing secret that will not become known. 3 Therefore whatever you have said in the dark will be heard in the light, and what you have whispered behind closed doors will be proclaimed from the housetops.

Exhortation to Fearless Confession

4 "I tell you, my friends, do not fear those who kill the body, and after that can do nothing more. 5 But I will warn you whom to fear: fear him who, after he has killed, has authority[a] to cast into hell.[b] Yes, I tell you, fear him! 6 Are not five sparrows sold for two pennies? Yet not one of them is forgotten in God's sight. 7 But even the hairs of your head are all counted. Do not be afraid; you are of more value than many sparrows.

8 "And I tell you, everyone who acknowledges me before others, the Son of Man also will acknowledge before the angels of God; 9 but whoever denies me before others will be denied before the angels of God. 10 And everyone who speaks a word against the Son of Man will be forgiv-

a Or *power*   *b* Gk *Gehenna*

en; but whoever blasphemes against the Holy Spirit will not be forgiven. [11]When they bring you before the synagogues, the rulers, and the authorities, do not worry about how[a] you are to defend yourselves or what you are to say; [12]for the Holy Spirit will teach you at that very hour what you ought to say."

The Parable of the Rich Fool

13 Someone in the crowd said to him, "Teacher, tell my brother to divide the family inheritance with me." [14]But he said to him, "Friend, who set me to be a judge or arbitrator over you?" [15]And he said to them, "Take care! Be on your guard against all kinds of greed; for one's life does not consist in the abundance of possessions." [16]Then he told them a parable: "The land of a rich man produced abundantly. [17]And he thought to himself, 'What should I do, for I have no place to store my crops?' [18]Then he said, 'I will do this: I will pull down my barns and build larger ones, and there I will store all my grain and my goods. [19]And I will say to my soul, Soul, you have ample goods laid up for many years; relax, eat, drink, be merry.' [20]But God said to him, 'You fool! This very night your life is being demanded of you. And the things you have prepared, whose will they be?' [21]So it is with those who store up treasures for themselves but are not rich toward God."

Do Not Worry

22 He said to his disciples, "Therefore I tell you, do not worry about your life, what you will eat, or about your body, what you will wear. [23]For life is more than food, and the body more than clothing. [24]Consider the ravens: they neither sow nor reap, they have neither storehouse nor barn, and yet God feeds them. Of how much more value are you than the birds! [25]And can any of you by worrying add a single hour to your span of life?[b] [26]If then you are not able to do so small a thing as that, why do you worry about the rest? [27]Consider the lilies, how they grow: they neither toil nor spin;[c] yet I tell you, even Solomon in all his glory was not clothed like one of these. [28]But if God so clothes the grass of the field, which is alive today and tomorrow is thrown into the oven, how much more will he clothe you—you of little faith! [29]And do not keep striving for what you are to eat and what you are to drink, and do not keep worrying. [30]For it is the nations of the world that strive after all these things, and your Father knows that you need them. [31]Instead, strive for his[d] kingdom, and these things will be given to you as well.

32 "Do not be afraid, little flock, for it is your Father's good pleasure to give you the kingdom. [33]Sell your possessions, and give alms. Make purses for yourselves that do not wear out, an unfailing treasure in heaven, where no thief comes near and no moth destroys. [34]For where your treasure is, there your heart will be also.

Watchful Slaves

35 "Be dressed for action and have your lamps lit; [36]be like those who are waiting for their master to return from

Focused Solely on God

LUKE 12.22–34

"Indeed the very heart of this work is nothing else but a naked intent toward God for God's own sake. I call it a naked intent because it is utterly disinterested. In this work the perfect artisan does not seek personal gain or exemption from suffering. One desires only God and God alone. One is so fascinated by the God one loves and so concerned that God's will be done on earth that one neither notices nor cares about one's own ease or anxiety. In reality it amounts to a yearning for God, a longing to see and taste God as much as is possible in this life."

—ANONYMOUS,
The Cloud of Unknowing

---

a Other ancient authorities add *or what*   b Or *add a cubit to your stature*
c Other ancient authorities read *Consider the lilies; they neither spin nor weave*   d Other ancient authorities read *God's*

Let Jesus Carry Your Stress

LUKE 12.49–53

Although we'd like to believe that the walk of faith is all light and warmth, we can't avoid the reality that it can also be fiery: "I came to bring fire to the earth." Being a disciple of Jesus is costly. Loyalty to Jesus Christ may cause division rather than peace. Referring to the cross and his resurrection as a "baptism," Jesus says, "What stress I am under until it is completed!"

A life of faith isn't about being happy and popular, but about aligning ourselves with Jesus. Picture Jesus carrying each stress in your life to the cross, one by one, as each thought of a personal or family conflict comes to your mind. Finally, picture yourself being baptized—dying with Jesus, then rising to walk in newness of life.

the wedding banquet, so that they may open the door for him as soon as he comes and knocks. ³⁷Blessed are those slaves whom the master finds alert when he comes; truly I tell you, he will fasten his belt and have them sit down to eat, and he will come and serve them. ³⁸If he comes during the middle of the night, or near dawn, and finds them so, blessed are those slaves.

39 "But know this: if the owner of the house had known at what hour the thief was coming, he*a* would not have let his house be broken into. ⁴⁰You also must be ready, for the Son of Man is coming at an unexpected hour."

The Faithful or the Unfaithful Slave

41 Peter said, "Lord, are you telling this parable for us or for everyone?" ⁴²And the Lord said, "Who then is the faithful and prudent manager whom his master will put in charge of his slaves, to give them their allowance of food at the proper time? ⁴³Blessed is that slave whom his master will find at work when he arrives. ⁴⁴Truly I tell you, he will put that one in charge of all his possessions. ⁴⁵But if that slave says to himself, 'My master is delayed in coming,' and if he begins to beat the other slaves, men and women, and to eat and drink and get drunk, ⁴⁶the master of that slave will come on a day when he does not expect him and at an hour that he does not know, and will cut him in pieces,*b* and put him with the unfaithful. ⁴⁷That slave who knew what his master wanted, but did not prepare himself or do what was wanted, will receive a severe beating. ⁴⁸But the one who did not know and did what deserved a beating will receive a light beating. From everyone to whom much has been given, much will be required; and from the one to whom much has been entrusted, even more will be demanded.

Jesus the Cause of Division

49 "I came to bring fire to the earth, and how I wish it were already kindled! ⁵⁰I have a baptism with which to be baptized, and what stress I am under until it is completed! ⁵¹Do you think that I have come to bring peace to the earth? No, I tell you, but rather division! ⁵²From now on five in one household will be divided, three against two and two against three; ⁵³they will be divided:
> father against son
> and son against father,
> mother against daughter
> and daughter against mother,
> mother-in-law against her daughter-in-law
> and daughter-in-law against mother-in-law."

Interpreting the Time

54 He also said to the crowds, "When you see a cloud rising in the west, you immediately say, 'It is going to rain'; and so it happens. ⁵⁵And when you see the south wind blowing, you say, 'There will be scorching heat'; and it happens. ⁵⁶You hypocrites! You know how to interpret the appearance of earth and sky, but why do you not know how to interpret the present time?

a Other ancient authorities add *would have watched and* *b* Or *cut him off*

Settling with Your Opponent

57 "And why do you not judge for yourselves what is right? 58Thus, when you go with your accuser before a magistrate, on the way make an effort to settle the case,*a* or you may be dragged before the judge, and the judge hand you over to the officer, and the officer throw you in prison. 59I tell you, you will never get out until you have paid the very last penny."

Repent or Perish

13 At that very time there were some present who told him about the Galileans whose blood Pilate had mingled with their sacrifices. 2He asked them, "Do you think that because these Galileans suffered in this way they were worse sinners than all other Galileans? 3No, I tell you; but unless you repent, you will all perish as they did. 4Or those eighteen who were killed when the tower of Siloam fell on them—do you think that they were worse offenders than all the others living in Jerusalem? 5No, I tell you; but unless you repent, you will all perish just as they did."

The Parable of the Barren Fig Tree

6 Then he told this parable: "A man had a fig tree planted in his vineyard; and he came looking for fruit on it and found none. 7So he said to the gardener, 'See here! For three years I have come looking for fruit on this fig tree, and still I find none. Cut it down! Why should it be wasting the soil?' 8He replied, 'Sir, let it alone for one more year, until I dig around it and put manure on it. 9If it bears fruit next year, well and good; but if not, you can cut it down.' "

Jesus Heals a Crippled Woman

10 Now he was teaching in one of the synagogues on the sabbath. 11And just then there appeared a woman with a spirit that had crippled her for eighteen years. She was bent over and was quite unable to stand up straight. 12When Jesus saw her, he called her over and said, "Woman, you are set free from your ailment." 13When he laid his hands on her, immediately she stood up straight and began praising God. 14But the leader of the synagogue, indignant because Jesus had cured on the sabbath, kept saying to the crowd, "There are six days on which work ought to be done; come on those days and be cured, and not on the sabbath day." 15But the Lord answered him and said, "You hypocrites! Does not each of you on the sabbath untie his ox or his donkey from the manger, and lead it away to give it water? 16And ought not this woman, a daughter of Abraham whom Satan bound for eighteen long years, be set free from this bondage on the sabbath day?" 17When he said this, all his opponents were put to shame; and the entire crowd was rejoicing at all the wonderful things that he was doing.

The Parable of the Mustard Seed

18 He said therefore, "What is the kingdom of God like? And to what should I compare it? 19It is like a mustard

Set Free

LUKE 13.10–13

The wounds of people's infirmities rarely escape Jesus' notice and he is always ready to offer a healing touch. Walk around the room bent over, as the woman in this passage does, to see how the world looks from her vantage point. How does it feel to walk that way? What are the burdens that weigh you down and bend you over? Take a deep breath and stand up straight, offering your burdens to God. Raise your hands in praise to God, who declares you have been "set free!" Take note of any part of your body in which you feel tightness or pain—your neck, shoulders, lower back. Inhale and exhale deeply. From what does God want to set you free?

See Meeting God in the Created Order

a Gk *settle with him*

As a Hen Gathers Her Brood

LUKE 13.31–35

As he contemplates Jerusalem, the Holy City of David, Jesus is filled with sorrow at the reluctance of God's chosen people to allow him to gather them in as a mother hen gathers, warms and protects her chicks.

Let this image of Jesus as nurturer guide you as you pray today. Read Psalm 91 to help you sharpen your awareness of God as your protector and nurturer. How can you nestle under the wings of God? In what ways do you need to be warmed in mind and spirit? What, if any, resistance are you experiencing as you contemplate this image?

See Meeting God in Scripture

seed that someone took and sowed in the garden; it grew and became a tree, and the birds of the air made nests in its branches."

The Parable of the Yeast

20 And again he said, "To what should I compare the kingdom of God? [21]It is like yeast that a woman took and mixed in with[a] three measures of flour until all of it was leavened."

The Narrow Door

22 Jesus[b] went through one town and village after another, teaching as he made his way to Jerusalem. [23]Someone asked him, "Lord, will only a few be saved?" He said to them, [24]"Strive to enter through the narrow door; for many, I tell you, will try to enter and will not be able. [25]When once the owner of the house has got up and shut the door, and you begin to stand outside and to knock at the door, saying, 'Lord, open to us,' then in reply he will say to you, 'I do not know where you come from.' [26]Then you will begin to say, 'We ate and drank with you, and you taught in our streets.' [27]But he will say, 'I do not know where you come from; go away from me, all you evildoers!' [28]There will be weeping and gnashing of teeth when you see Abraham and Isaac and Jacob and all the prophets in the kingdom of God, and you yourselves thrown out. [29]Then people will come from east and west, from north and south, and will eat in the kingdom of God. [30]Indeed, some are last who will be first, and some are first who will be last."

The Lament over Jerusalem

31 At that very hour some Pharisees came and said to him, "Get away from here, for Herod wants to kill you." [32]He said to them, "Go and tell that fox for me,[c] 'Listen, I am casting out demons and performing cures today and tomorrow, and on the third day I finish my work. [33]Yet today, tomorrow, and the next day I must be on my way, because it is impossible for a prophet to be killed outside of Jerusalem.' [34]Jerusalem, Jerusalem, the city that kills the prophets and stones those who are sent to it! How often have I desired to gather your children together as a hen gathers her brood under her wings, and you were not willing! [35]See, your house is left to you. And I tell you, you will not see me until the time comes when[d] you say, 'Blessed is the one who comes in the name of the Lord.' "

Jesus Heals the Man with Dropsy

14 On one occasion when Jesus[e] was going to the house of a leader of the Pharisees to eat a meal on the sabbath, they were watching him closely. [2]Just then, in front of him, there was a man who had dropsy. [3]And Jesus asked the lawyers and Pharisees, "Is it lawful to cure people on the sabbath, or not?" [4]But they were silent. So Jesus[e] took him and healed him, and sent him away. [5]Then he said to them, "If one of you has a child[f] or an ox that has fallen into a well, will you not immediately pull it out on a sabbath day?" [6]And they could not reply to this.

a Gk *hid in*   b Gk *He*   c Gk lacks *for me*   d Other ancient authorities lack *the time comes when*   e Gk *he*   f Other ancient authorities read *a donkey*

Humility and Hospitality

7 When he noticed how the guests chose the places of honor, he told them a parable. 8"When you are invited by someone to a wedding banquet, do not sit down at the place of honor, in case someone more distinguished than you has been invited by your host; 9and the host who invited both of you may come and say to you, 'Give this person your place,' and then in disgrace you would start to take the lowest place. 10But when you are invited, go and sit down at the lowest place, so that when your host comes, he may say to you, 'Friend, move up higher'; then you will be honored in the presence of all who sit at the table with you. 11For all who exalt themselves will be humbled, and those who humble themselves will be exalted."

12 He said also to the one who had invited him, "When you give a luncheon or a dinner, do not invite your friends or your brothers or your relatives or rich neighbors, in case they may invite you in return, and you would be repaid. 13But when you give a banquet, invite the poor, the crippled, the lame, and the blind. 14And you will be blessed, because they cannot repay you, for you will be repaid at the resurrection of the righteous."

The Parable of the Great Dinner

15 One of the dinner guests, on hearing this, said to him, "Blessed is anyone who will eat bread in the kingdom of God!" 16Then Jesus*a* said to him, "Someone gave a great dinner and invited many. 17At the time for the dinner he sent his slave to say to those who had been invited, 'Come; for everything is ready now.' 18But they all alike began to make excuses. The first said to him, 'I have bought a piece of land, and I must go out and see it; please accept my regrets.' 19Another said, 'I have bought five yoke of oxen, and I am going to try them out; please accept my regrets.' 20Another said, 'I have just been married, and therefore I cannot come.' 21So the slave returned and reported this to his master. Then the owner of the house became angry and said to his slave, 'Go out at once into the streets and lanes of the town and bring in the poor, the crippled, the blind, and the lame.' 22And the slave said, 'Sir, what you ordered has been done, and there is still room.' 23Then the master said to the slave, 'Go out into the roads and lanes, and compel people to come in, so that my house may be filled. 24For I tell you,*b* none of those who were invited will taste my dinner.' "

The Cost of Discipleship

25 Now large crowds were traveling with him; and he turned and said to them, 26"Whoever comes to me and does not hate father and mother, wife and children, brothers and sisters, yes, and even life itself, cannot be my disciple. 27Whoever does not carry the cross and follow me cannot be my disciple. 28For which of you, intending to build a tower, does not first sit down and estimate the cost, to see whether he has enough to complete it? 29Otherwise, when he has laid a foundation and is not able to finish, all who see it will begin to ridicule him, 30saying, 'This fellow began to build and was not able to finish.' 31Or what king,

---

Hospitality Within the Heart of Christ

LUKE 14.12–14

"Let all guests who arrive be received like Christ, for he is going to say, 'I came as a guest, and you received me.' And to all let due honor be shown . . . In reception of the poor and of pilgrims the greatest care and solicitude should be shown, because it is especially in them that Christ is received."

—*The Rule of Saint Benedict*

Reassuring Words, Empowering Words

LUKE 15.11–32

Read this passage silently and create an "inner video" of it. Converse with each character: the younger prodigal son; the angry, perfectionist older son; the heartbroken father; and the unseen mother. With whom do you identify most? Why? Return to the older sibling, identifying your own dutiful, resentful feelings. Hear God's reassuring words: "You are always with me." God invites you to claim your inheritance: "All that is mine is yours." Repeat these empowering words. Let them become your prayer of thanksgiving as you offer yourself to God: "You are always with me, and all that is mine is yours."

See Meeting God in Scripture

going out to wage war against another king, will not sit down first and consider whether he is able with ten thousand to oppose the one who comes against him with twenty thousand? ³²If he cannot, then, while the other is still far away, he sends a delegation and asks for the terms of peace. ³³So therefore, none of you can become my disciple if you do not give up all your possessions.

About Salt

34 "Salt is good; but if salt has lost its taste, how can its saltiness be restored?*a* ³⁵It is fit neither for the soil nor for the manure pile; they throw it away. Let anyone with ears to hear listen!"

The Parable of the Lost Sheep

15 Now all the tax collectors and sinners were coming near to listen to him. ²And the Pharisees and the scribes were grumbling and saying, "This fellow welcomes sinners and eats with them."

3 So he told them this parable: ⁴"Which one of you, having a hundred sheep and losing one of them, does not leave the ninety-nine in the wilderness and go after the one that is lost until he finds it? ⁵When he has found it, he lays it on his shoulders and rejoices. ⁶And when he comes home, he calls together his friends and neighbors, saying to them, 'Rejoice with me, for I have found my sheep that was lost.' ⁷Just so, I tell you, there will be more joy in heaven over one sinner who repents than over ninety-nine righteous persons who need no repentance.

The Parable of the Lost Coin

8 "Or what woman having ten silver coins,*b* if she loses one of them, does not light a lamp, sweep the house, and search carefully until she finds it? ⁹When she has found it, she calls together her friends and neighbors, saying, 'Rejoice with me, for I have found the coin that I had lost.' ¹⁰Just so, I tell you, there is joy in the presence of the angels of God over one sinner who repents."

The Parable of the Prodigal and His Brother

11 Then Jesus*c* said, "There was a man who had two sons. ¹²The younger of them said to his father, 'Father, give me the share of the property that will belong to me.' So he divided his property between them. ¹³A few days later the younger son gathered all he had and traveled to a distant country, and there he squandered his property in dissolute living. ¹⁴When he had spent everything, a severe famine took place throughout that country, and he began to be in need. ¹⁵So he went and hired himself out to one of the citizens of that country, who sent him to his fields to feed the pigs. ¹⁶He would gladly have filled himself with*d* the pods that the pigs were eating; and no one gave him anything. ¹⁷But when he came to himself he said, 'How many of my father's hired hands have bread enough and to spare, but here I am dying of hunger! ¹⁸I will get up and go to my father, and I will say to him, "Father, I have sinned against heaven and before you; ¹⁹I am no longer worthy to be

a Or how can it be used for seasoning? *b Gk drachmas, each worth about a day's wage for a laborer* *c Gk he* *d Other ancient authorities read filled his stomach with*

called your son; treat me like one of your hired hands.' '
²⁰So he set off and went to his father. But while he was still
far off, his father saw him and was filled with compassion; he ran and put his arms around him and kissed him.
²¹Then the son said to him, 'Father, I have sinned against
heaven and before you; I am no longer worthy to be called
your son.'ᵃ ²²But the father said to his slaves, 'Quickly,
bring out a robe—the best one—and put it on him; put a
ring on his finger and sandals on his feet. ²³And get the
fatted calf and kill it, and let us eat and celebrate; ²⁴for this
son of mine was dead and is alive again; he was lost and
is found!' And they began to celebrate.

25 "Now his elder son was in the field; and when he
came and approached the house, he heard music and
dancing. ²⁶He called one of the slaves and asked what was
going on. ²⁷He replied, 'Your brother has come, and your
father has killed the fatted calf, because he has got him
back safe and sound.' ²⁸Then he became angry and refused to go in. His father came out and began to plead
with him. ²⁹But he answered his father, 'Listen! For all
these years I have been working like a slave for you, and
I have never disobeyed your command; yet you have
never given me even a young goat so that I might celebrate with my friends. ³⁰But when this son of yours came
back, who has devoured your property with prostitutes,
you killed the fatted calf for him!' ³¹Then the fatherᵇ said
to him, 'Son, you are always with me, and all that is mine
is yours. ³²But we had to celebrate and rejoice, because
this brother of yours was dead and has come to life; he
was lost and has been found.' "

The Parable of the Dishonest Manager

16 Then Jesusᵇ said to the disciples, "There was a rich
man who had a manager, and charges were
brought to him that this man was squandering his property. ²So he summoned him and said to him, 'What is this
that I hear about you? Give me an accounting of your management, because you cannot be my manager any longer.'
³Then the manager said to himself, 'What will I do, now
that my master is taking the position away from me? I am
not strong enough to dig, and I am ashamed to beg. ⁴I
have decided what to do so that, when I am dismissed as
manager, people may welcome me into their homes.' ⁵So,
summoning his master's debtors one by one, he asked the
first, 'How much do you owe my master?' ⁶He answered,
'A hundred jugs of olive oil.' He said to him, 'Take your
bill, sit down quickly, and make it fifty.' ⁷Then he asked another, 'And how much do you owe?' He replied, 'A hundred
containers of wheat.' He said to him, 'Take your bill and
make it eighty.' ⁸And his master commended the dishonest manager because he had acted shrewdly; for the children of this age are more shrewd in dealing with their own
generation than are the children of light. ⁹And I tell you,
make friends for yourselves by means of dishonest
wealthᶜ so that when it is gone, they may welcome you
into the eternal homes.ᵈ

10 "Whoever is faithful in a very little is faithful also in
much; and whoever is dishonest in a very little is dishon-

Choosing God's Riches

LUKE 16.10–13

We are being trained to be
trustworthy with God's "true
riches" when we are given little
and prove trustworthy with it.
Sometimes we struggle, however, to keep choosing "true
riches" over worldly wealth.
Read this passage twice. What
word or phrase draws your attention? Reflect on this word or
phrase. What comes to you as
you reflect on it? Remain silent
and open to insight from God.
In what way does this passage
touch your life today?

See Meeting God in Scripture

---

a Other ancient authorities add *Treat me like one of your hired servants*
b Gk *he*   c Gk *mammon*   d Gk *tents*

Letting Go of Possessions

LUKE 16.19–31

Jesus, in this story of the rich man and Lazarus, illustrates how difficult it is to love God and your neighbor when one's treasure is great wealth and possessions.

Imagine yourself in the scene of Lazarus and the rich man. With which character do you identify more? What would you like to ask each character? Try asking Jesus how you can let go of your attachment to money, intelligence and privilege. What would it mean to relinquish everything to God? (See also 18.18–30.)

est also in much. ¹¹If then you have not been faithful with the dishonest wealth,ᵃ who will entrust to you the true riches? ¹²And if you have not been faithful with what belongs to another, who will give you what is your own? ¹³No slave can serve two masters; for a slave will either hate the one and love the other, or be devoted to the one and despise the other. You cannot serve God and wealth."ᵃ

The Law and the Kingdom of God

14 The Pharisees, who were lovers of money, heard all this, and they ridiculed him. ¹⁵So he said to them, "You are those who justify yourselves in the sight of others; but God knows your hearts; for what is prized by human beings is an abomination in the sight of God.

16 "The law and the prophets were in effect until John came; since then the good news of the kingdom of God is proclaimed, and everyone tries to enter it by force.ᵇ ¹⁷But it is easier for heaven and earth to pass away, than for one stroke of a letter in the law to be dropped.

18 "Anyone who divorces his wife and marries another commits adultery, and whoever marries a woman divorced from her husband commits adultery.

The Rich Man and Lazarus

19 "There was a rich man who was dressed in purple and fine linen and who feasted sumptuously every day. ²⁰And at his gate lay a poor man named Lazarus, covered with sores, ²¹who longed to satisfy his hunger with what fell from the rich man's table; even the dogs would come and lick his sores. ²²The poor man died and was carried away by the angels to be with Abraham.ᶜ The rich man also died and was buried. ²³In Hades, where he was being tormented, he looked up and saw Abraham far away with Lazarus by his side.ᵈ ²⁴He called out, 'Father Abraham, have mercy on me, and send Lazarus to dip the tip of his finger in water and cool my tongue; for I am in agony in these flames.' ²⁵But Abraham said, 'Child, remember that during your lifetime you received your good things, and Lazarus in like manner evil things; but now he is comforted here, and you are in agony. ²⁶Besides all this, between you and us a great chasm has been fixed, so that those who might want to pass from here to you cannot do so, and no one can cross from there to us.' ²⁷He said, 'Then, father, I beg you to send him to my father's house— ²⁸for I have five brothers—that he may warn them, so that they will not also come into this place of torment.' ²⁹Abraham replied, 'They have Moses and the prophets; they should listen to them.' ³⁰He said, 'No, father Abraham; but if someone goes to them from the dead, they will repent.' ³¹He said to him, 'If they do not listen to Moses and the prophets, neither will they be convinced even if someone rises from the dead.' "

Some Sayings of Jesus

17 Jesusᵉ said to his disciples, "Occasions for stumbling are bound to come, but woe to anyone by whom they come! ²It would be better for you if a millstone were hung around your neck and you were thrown

ᵃ Gk mammon   ᵇ Or everyone is strongly urged to enter it   ᶜ Gk to Abraham's bosom   ᵈ Gk in his bosom   ᵉ Gk He

into the sea than for you to cause one of these little ones to stumble. ³Be on your guard! If another disciple*a* sins, you must rebuke the offender, and if there is repentance, you must forgive. ⁴And if the same person sins against you seven times a day, and turns back to you seven times and says, 'I repent,' you must forgive."

5 The apostles said to the Lord, "Increase our faith!" ⁶The Lord replied, "If you had faith the size of a*b* mustard seed, you could say to this mulberry tree, 'Be uprooted and planted in the sea,' and it would obey you.

7 "Who among you would say to your slave who has just come in from plowing or tending sheep in the field, 'Come here at once and take your place at the table'? ⁸Would you not rather say to him, 'Prepare supper for me, put on your apron and serve me while I eat and drink; later you may eat and drink'? ⁹Do you thank the slave for doing what was commanded? ¹⁰So you also, when you have done all that you were ordered to do, say, 'We are worthless slaves; we have done only what we ought to have done!' "

Jesus Cleanses Ten Lepers

11 On the way to Jerusalem Jesus*c* was going through the region between Samaria and Galilee. ¹²As he entered a village, ten lepers*d* approached him. Keeping their distance, ¹³they called out, saying, "Jesus, Master, have mercy on us!" ¹⁴When he saw them, he said to them, "Go and show yourselves to the priests." And as they went, they were made clean. ¹⁵Then one of them, when he saw that he was healed, turned back, praising God with a loud voice. ¹⁶He prostrated himself at Jesus'*e* feet and thanked him. And he was a Samaritan. ¹⁷Then Jesus asked, "Were not ten made clean? But the other nine, where are they? ¹⁸Was none of them found to return and give praise to God except this foreigner?" ¹⁹Then he said to him, "Get up and go on your way; your faith has made you well."

The Coming of the Kingdom

20 Once Jesus*c* was asked by the Pharisees when the kingdom of God was coming, and he answered, "The kingdom of God is not coming with things that can be observed; ²¹nor will they say, 'Look, here it is!' or 'There it is!' For, in fact, the kingdom of God is among*f* you."

22 Then he said to the disciples, "The days are coming when you will long to see one of the days of the Son of Man, and you will not see it. ²³They will say to you, 'Look there!' or 'Look here!' Do not go, do not set off in pursuit. ²⁴For as the lightning flashes and lights up the sky from one side to the other, so will the Son of Man be in his day.*g* ²⁵But first he must endure much suffering and be rejected by this generation. ²⁶Just as it was in the days of Noah, so too it will be in the days of the Son of Man. ²⁷They were eating and drinking, and marrying and being given in marriage, until the day Noah entered the ark, and the flood came and destroyed all of them. ²⁸Likewise, just as it was in the days of Lot: they were eating and drinking, buying and selling, planting and building, ²⁹but on the day

Praying With the Tenth Leper

LUKE 17.11–19

"If in your lifetime the only prayer you offer is Thanks, that would suffice," wrote Meister Eckhart. Sit comfortably, close your eyes and begin to repeat the word *gracias!* (Spanish for "thanks") or *grazia!* (Italian). Recall the events that have occurred in the last week (conversations with friends, small tasks accomplished, rest and relaxation, appointments kept) and, after each event comes to mind, offer thanks. Because *gracias!* (or *grazia!*) means "grace" as well as "thanks," you can continue praying this way when you think of difficulties. To the God who provides grace under pressure, you can say, "Thank you for being with me."

See Meeting God in Everyday Life

---

a Gk *your brother*   *b* Gk *faith as a grain of*   *c* Gk *he*   *d* The terms *leper* and *leprosy* can refer to several diseases   *e* Gk *his*   *f* Or *within*   *g* Other ancient authorities lack *in his day*

Receiving the Kingdom

LUKE 18.15–17

"Whoever does not receive the kingdom of God as a little child will never enter it." What spiritual truth could you learn from children that would help you receive (take in or take possession of) the kingdom of God? Call to mind the faces of a child or two, or go to a place where you might spend time with children (a playground or church nursery). Recall the children you know—their questions, stories, attitudes about life. Ponder this question: What would it mean to "receive the kingdom of God" like a child? What would it mean for you to embrace the childlike faith within you?

See Meeting God in the Created Order

that Lot left Sodom, it rained fire and sulfur from heaven and destroyed all of them ³⁰—it will be like that on the day that the Son of Man is revealed. ³¹On that day, anyone on the housetop who has belongings in the house must not come down to take them away; and likewise anyone in the field must not turn back. ³²Remember Lot's wife. ³³Those who try to make their life secure will lose it, but those who lose their life will keep it. ³⁴I tell you, on that night there will be two in one bed; one will be taken and the other left. ³⁵There will be two women grinding meal together; one will be taken and the other left."*ᵃ* ³⁷Then they asked him, "Where, Lord?" He said to them, "Where the corpse is, there the vultures will gather."

The Parable of the Widow and the Unjust Judge

18 Then Jesus*ᵇ* told them a parable about their need to pray always and not to lose heart. ²He said, "In a certain city there was a judge who neither feared God nor had respect for people. ³In that city there was a widow who kept coming to him and saying, 'Grant me justice against my opponent.' ⁴For a while he refused; but later he said to himself, 'Though I have no fear of God and no respect for anyone, ⁵yet because this widow keeps bothering me, I will grant her justice, so that she may not wear me out by continually coming.' "*ᶜ* ⁶And the Lord said, "Listen to what the unjust judge says. ⁷And will not God grant justice to his chosen ones who cry to him day and night? Will he delay long in helping them? ⁸I tell you, he will quickly grant justice to them. And yet, when the Son of Man comes, will he find faith on earth?"

The Parable of the Pharisee and the Tax Collector

9 He also told this parable to some who trusted in themselves that they were righteous and regarded others with contempt: ¹⁰"Two men went up to the temple to pray, one a Pharisee and the other a tax collector. ¹¹The Pharisee, standing by himself, was praying thus, 'God, I thank you that I am not like other people: thieves, rogues, adulterers, or even like this tax collector. ¹²I fast twice a week; I give a tenth of all my income.' ¹³But the tax collector, standing far off, would not even look up to heaven, but was beating his breast and saying, 'God, be merciful to me, a sinner!' ¹⁴I tell you, this man went down to his home justified rather than the other; for all who exalt themselves will be humbled, but all who humble themselves will be exalted."

Jesus Blesses Little Children

15 People were bringing even infants to him that he might touch them; and when the disciples saw it, they sternly ordered them not to do it. ¹⁶But Jesus called for them and said, "Let the little children come to me, and do not stop them; for it is to such as these that the kingdom of God belongs. ¹⁷Truly I tell you, whoever does not receive the kingdom of God as a little child will never enter it."

---

a Other ancient authorities add verse 36, *"Two will be in the field; one will be taken and the other left."* b Gk *he* c Or *so that she may not finally come and slap me in the face*

The Rich Ruler

18 A certain ruler asked him, "Good Teacher, what must I do to inherit eternal life?" ¹⁹Jesus said to him, "Why do you call me good? No one is good but God alone. ²⁰You know the commandments: 'You shall not commit adultery; You shall not murder; You shall not steal; You shall not bear false witness; Honor your father and mother.' " ²¹He replied, "I have kept all these since my youth." ²²When Jesus heard this, he said to him, "There is still one thing lacking. Sell all that you own and distribute the money*a* to the poor, and you will have treasure in heaven; then come, follow me." ²³But when he heard this, he became sad; for he was very rich. ²⁴Jesus looked at him and said, "How hard it is for those who have wealth to enter the kingdom of God! ²⁵Indeed, it is easier for a camel to go through the eye of a needle than for someone who is rich to enter the kingdom of God."

26 Those who heard it said, "Then who can be saved?" ²⁷He replied, "What is impossible for mortals is possible for God."

28 Then Peter said, "Look, we have left our homes and followed you." ²⁹And he said to them, "Truly I tell you, there is no one who has left house or wife or brothers or parents or children, for the sake of the kingdom of God, ³⁰who will not get back very much more in this age, and in the age to come eternal life."

A Third Time Jesus Foretells His Death and Resurrection

31 Then he took the twelve aside and said to them, "See, we are going up to Jerusalem, and everything that is written about the Son of Man by the prophets will be accomplished. ³²For he will be handed over to the Gentiles; and he will be mocked and insulted and spat upon. ³³After they have flogged him, they will kill him, and on the third day he will rise again." ³⁴But they understood nothing about all these things; in fact, what he said was hidden from them, and they did not grasp what was said.

Jesus Heals a Blind Beggar Near Jericho

35 As he approached Jericho, a blind man was sitting by the roadside begging. ³⁶When he heard a crowd going by, he asked what was happening. ³⁷They told him, "Jesus of Nazareth*b* is passing by." ³⁸Then he shouted, "Jesus, Son of David, have mercy on me!" ³⁹Those who were in front sternly ordered him to be quiet; but he shouted even more loudly, "Son of David, have mercy on me!" ⁴⁰Jesus stood still and ordered the man to be brought to him; and when he came near, he asked him, ⁴¹"What do you want me to do for you?" He said, "Lord, let me see again." ⁴²Jesus said to him, "Receive your sight; your faith has saved you." ⁴³Immediately he regained his sight and followed him, glorifying God; and all the people, when they saw it, praised God.

Jesus and Zacchaeus

19 He entered Jericho and was passing through it. ²A man was there named Zacchaeus; he was a chief tax collector and was rich. ³He was trying to see who Jesus

---

The Prayer of the Heart

LUKE 18.13,38

The ancient "Jesus prayer" is based on the words of the tax collector in the temple and of the blind beggar. Using this prayer can help you pray continually (see 1 Thessalonians 5.17). It can be done as naturally as breathing: "O Lord Jesus Christ, [Son of God] (*inhaling, receiving*), have mercy [on me, a sinner] (*exhaling, surrendering*)." Get up and do an everyday task (cook a meal, clean a bathroom, get dressed), reciting the "Jesus prayer" as you do so. Come back and rest in God's presence. Keep this prayer in your heart throughout the day; let the awareness of God's presence permeate all your activities.

See Meeting God in Worship

---

a Gk lacks *the money*   *b* Gk *the Nazorean*

Jesus Notices "the Little People"

LUKE 19.1–10

Imagine that you are Zacchaeus, a hated tax collector. Consider how Zacchaeus may have felt when singled out in the crowd by Jesus, someone everyone wanted to meet. Jesus wants to talk to you—you are the focus of his attention. Picture the face of someone who is a reflection of Jesus' loving attention to you. Bask in the joy of being chosen and loved by God.

Now reflect on Zacchaeus's response to Jesus. Because Zacchaeus was a short man, he was probably used to being overlooked. (The Hebrew word for "the poor" [v.8] also means "the little people" of the earth, those who may be discounted or overlooked.) Do you ever feel overlooked or passed over by people? What is your response to Jesus as he singles you out?

See Meeting God in Scripture

was, but on account of the crowd he could not, because he was short in stature. ⁴So he ran ahead and climbed a sycamore tree to see him, because he was going to pass that way. ⁵When Jesus came to the place, he looked up and said to him, "Zacchaeus, hurry and come down; for I must stay at your house today." ⁶So he hurried down and was happy to welcome him. ⁷All who saw it began to grumble and said, "He has gone to be the guest of one who is a sinner." ⁸Zacchaeus stood there and said to the Lord, "Look, half of my possessions, Lord, I will give to the poor; and if I have defrauded anyone of anything, I will pay back four times as much." ⁹Then Jesus said to him, "Today salvation has come to this house, because he too is a son of Abraham. ¹⁰For the Son of Man came to seek out and to save the lost."

The Parable of the Ten Pounds

11 As they were listening to this, he went on to tell a parable, because he was near Jerusalem, and because they supposed that the kingdom of God was to appear immediately. ¹²So he said, "A nobleman went to a distant country to get royal power for himself and then return. ¹³He summoned ten of his slaves, and gave them ten pounds,ᵃ and said to them, 'Do business with these until I come back.' ¹⁴But the citizens of his country hated him and sent a delegation after him, saying, 'We do not want this man to rule over us.' ¹⁵When he returned, having received royal power, he ordered these slaves, to whom he had given the money, to be summoned so that he might find out what they had gained by trading. ¹⁶The first came forward and said, 'Lord, your pound has made ten more pounds.' ¹⁷He said to him, 'Well done, good slave! Because you have been trustworthy in a very small thing, take charge of ten cities.' ¹⁸Then the second came, saying, 'Lord, your pound has made five pounds.' ¹⁹He said to him, 'And you, rule over five cities.' ²⁰Then the other came, saying, 'Lord, here is your pound. I wrapped it up in a piece of cloth, ²¹for I was afraid of you, because you are a harsh man; you take what you did not deposit, and reap what you did not sow.' ²²He said to him, 'I will judge you by your own words, you wicked slave! You knew, did you, that I was a harsh man, taking what I did not deposit and reaping what I did not sow? ²³Why then did you not put my money into the bank? Then when I returned, I could have collected it with interest.' ²⁴He said to the bystanders, 'Take the pound from him and give it to the one who has ten pounds.' ²⁵(And they said to him, 'Lord, he has ten pounds!') ²⁶'I tell you, to all those who have, more will be given; but from those who have nothing, even what they have will be taken away. ²⁷But as for these enemies of mine who did not want me to be king over them—bring them here and slaughter them in my presence.' "

Jesus' Triumphal Entry into Jerusalem

28 After he had said this, he went on ahead, going up to Jerusalem.

29 When he had come near Bethphage and Bethany, at the place called the Mount of Olives, he sent two of the

---

a The mina, rendered here by *pound,* was about three months' wages for a laborer disciples, [30]saying, "Go into the village ahead of you, and as you enter it you will find tied there a colt that has never been ridden. Untie it and bring it here. [31]If anyone asks you, 'Why are you untying it?' just say this, 'The Lord needs it.' " [32]So those who were sent departed and found it as he had told them. [33]As they were untying the colt, its owners asked them, "Why are you untying the colt?" [34]They said, "The Lord needs it." [35]Then they brought it to Jesus; and after throwing their cloaks on the colt, they set Jesus on it. [36]As he rode along, people kept spreading their cloaks on the road. [37]As he was now approaching the path down from the Mount of Olives, the whole multitude of the disciples began to praise God joyfully with a loud voice for all the deeds of power that they had seen, [38]saying,

"Blessed is the king
  who comes in the name of the Lord!
Peace in heaven,
  and glory in the highest heaven!"

[39]Some of the Pharisees in the crowd said to him, "Teacher, order your disciples to stop." [40]He answered, "I tell you, if these were silent, the stones would shout out."

Jesus Weeps over Jerusalem

41 As he came near and saw the city, he wept over it, [42]saying, "If you, even you, had only recognized on this day the things that make for peace! But now they are hidden from your eyes. [43]Indeed, the days will come upon you, when your enemies will set up ramparts around you and surround you, and hem you in on every side. [44]They will crush you to the ground, you and your children within you, and they will not leave within you one stone upon another; because you did not recognize the time of your visitation from God."[a]

Jesus Cleanses the Temple

45 Then he entered the temple and began to drive out those who were selling things there; [46]and he said, "It is written,

'My house shall be a house of prayer';
  but you have made it a den of robbers.'"

47 Every day he was teaching in the temple. The chief priests, the scribes, and the leaders of the people kept looking for a way to kill him; [48]but they did not find anything they could do, for all the people were spellbound by what they heard.

The Authority of Jesus Questioned

20 One day, as he was teaching the people in the temple and telling the good news, the chief priests and the scribes came with the elders [2]and said to him, "Tell us, by what authority are you doing these things? Who is it who gave you this authority?" [3]He answered them, "I will also ask you a question, and you tell me: [4]Did the baptism of John come from heaven, or was it of human origin?" [5]They discussed it with one another, saying, "If we say, 'From heaven,' he will say, 'Why did you not believe him?' [6]But if we say, 'Of human origin,' all the people will stone us; for they are convinced that John was a prophet." [7]So they answered that they did not know where it came

---

What Would the Stones Say?

LUKE 19.28–40

Picture yourself in the multitude during Jesus' triumphal entry and allow the scene to unfold. Imagine the sun beating down on your head, the shouts of the crowd, the odors of animals and people. Look how the people are spreading their cloaks in the road like a carpet. Join the chorus, "Blessed is the king who comes . . .! Peace in heaven, and glory in the highest heaven!" Notice the disapproval of the religious leaders: "Teacher, order your disciples to stop." Jesus responds: "If [they] were silent, the stones would shout out." What would the stones say? Try expressing your unspoken cries of joy in your journal.

See *Meeting God in Worship*

Love the Questions!

LUKE 20.1–47

In Luke 20 the religious authorities ask Jesus three questions in order to trick him. Jesus responds by asking them twice as many questions and by telling them a parable. You might want to list the questions in this chapter of Luke and ponder why Jesus asks so many of them. Then ask yourself, "Do I respond to people's problems with *my* answers or do I listen to them and ask them helpful questions?" The poet Rainer Maria Rilke wrote, "Be patient toward all that is unsolved in your heart and try to love the questions themselves." Do you offer your own questions to God in your prayer life? Try writing a prayer consisting only of questions.

See Meeting God in Prayer

from. ⁸Then Jesus said to them, "Neither will I tell you by what authority I am doing these things."

The Parable of the Wicked Tenants

9 He began to tell the people this parable: "A man planted a vineyard, and leased it to tenants, and went to another country for a long time. ¹⁰When the season came, he sent a slave to the tenants in order that they might give him his share of the produce of the vineyard; but the tenants beat him and sent him away empty-handed. ¹¹Next he sent another slave; that one also they beat and insulted and sent away empty-handed. ¹²And he sent still a third; this one also they wounded and threw out. ¹³Then the owner of the vineyard said, 'What shall I do? I will send my beloved son; perhaps they will respect him.' ¹⁴But when the tenants saw him, they discussed it among themselves and said, 'This is the heir; let us kill him so that the inheritance may be ours.' ¹⁵So they threw him out of the vineyard and killed him. What then will the owner of the vineyard do to them? ¹⁶He will come and destroy those tenants and give the vineyard to others." When they heard this, they said, "Heaven forbid!" ¹⁷But he looked at them and said, "What then does this text mean:
  'The stone that the builders rejected
    has become the cornerstone'?ᵃ
¹⁸Everyone who falls on that stone will be broken to pieces; and it will crush anyone on whom it falls." ¹⁹When the scribes and chief priests realized that he had told this parable against them, they wanted to lay hands on him at that very hour, but they feared the people.

The Question about Paying Taxes

20 So they watched him and sent spies who pretended to be honest, in order to trap him by what he said, so as to hand him over to the jurisdiction and authority of the governor. ²¹So they asked him, "Teacher, we know that you are right in what you say and teach, and you show deference to no one, but teach the way of God in accordance with truth. ²²Is it lawful for us to pay taxes to the emperor, or not?" ²³But he perceived their craftiness and said to them, ²⁴"Show me a denarius. Whose head and whose title does it bear?" They said, "The emperor's." ²⁵He said to them, "Then give to the emperor the things that are the emperor's, and to God the things that are God's." ²⁶And they were not able in the presence of the people to trap him by what he said; and being amazed by his answer, they became silent.

The Question about the Resurrection

27 Some Sadducees, those who say there is no resurrection, came to him ²⁸and asked him a question, "Teacher, Moses wrote for us that if a man's brother dies, leaving a wife but no children, the manᵇ shall marry the widow and raise up children for his brother. ²⁹Now there were seven brothers; the first married, and died childless; ³⁰then the second ³¹and the third married her, and so in the same way all seven died childless. ³²Finally the woman also died. ³³In the resurrection, therefore, whose wife will the woman be? For the seven had married her."

a Or *keystone*   *b* Gk *his brother*

34 Jesus said to them, "Those who belong to this age marry and are given in marriage; 35but those who are considered worthy of a place in that age and in the resurrection from the dead neither marry nor are given in marriage. 36Indeed they cannot die anymore, because they are like angels and are children of God, being children of the resurrection. 37And the fact that the dead are raised Moses himself showed, in the story about the bush, where he speaks of the Lord as the God of Abraham, the God of Isaac, and the God of Jacob. 38Now he is God not of the dead, but of the living; for to him all of them are alive." 39Then some of the scribes answered, "Teacher, you have spoken well." 40For they no longer dared to ask him another question.

The Question about David's Son

41 Then he said to them, "How can they say that the Messiah*a* is David's son? 42For David himself says in the book of Psalms,

'The Lord said to my Lord,
"Sit at my right hand,
43   until I make your enemies your footstool." '
44David thus calls him Lord; so how can he be his son?"

Jesus Denounces the Scribes

45 In the hearing of all the people he said to the*b* disciples, 46"Beware of the scribes, who like to walk around in long robes, and love to be greeted with respect in the marketplaces, and to have the best seats in the synagogues and places of honor at banquets. 47They devour widows' houses and for the sake of appearance say long prayers. They will receive the greater condemnation."

The Widow's Offering

21 He looked up and saw rich people putting their gifts into the treasury; 2he also saw a poor widow put in two small copper coins. 3He said, "Truly I tell you, this poor widow has put in more than all of them; 4for all of them have contributed out of their abundance, but she out of her poverty has put in all she had to live on."

The Destruction of the Temple Foretold

5 When some were speaking about the temple, how it was adorned with beautiful stones and gifts dedicated to God, he said, 6"As for these things that you see, the days will come when not one stone will be left upon another; all will be thrown down."

Signs and Persecutions

7 They asked him, "Teacher, when will this be, and what will be the sign that this is about to take place?" 8And he said, "Beware that you are not led astray; for many will come in my name and say, 'I am he!'*c* and, 'The time is near!'*d* Do not go after them. 9"When you hear of wars and insurrections, do not be terrified; for these things must take place first, but the end will not follow immediately." 10Then he said to them, "Nation will rise against nation, and kingdom against kingdom; 11there will be great earthquakes, and in various

The Poor Widow, Our Teacher

LUKE 21.1–4

Luke shows Jesus pointing to forgotten people as agents of God's love to privileged people. Here a poor widow (typically a recipient of charity) becomes our teacher, prefiguring Jesus Christ's self-giving love. Can you recall an occasion when a person whom the world might ignore became a special symbol of God's love in your life or a window through which you could see God? Reflect on it with God. Whom might God be using to teach you now? Try exploring these questions in your journal and see if any connections come to you or reflect on this idea with a friend.

See Meeting God in Community

Pay Attention to Today!

LUKE 21.7–38

Jesus warns about preoccupation with end-times predictions (21.8) and instead commands simple attentiveness to God's presence every moment of every day: "Be alert at all times" (21.36). How can you nurture what Jean-Pierre de Caussade called "the sacrament of the present moment"? He described it this way: "This discovery of divine action in everything that happens, each moment, is the most subtle wisdom possible regarding the ways of God in this life." What practices help you cultivate this simple attentiveness?

See Meeting God in Everyday Life

places famines and plagues; and there will be dreadful portents and great signs from heaven.

12 "But before all this occurs, they will arrest you and persecute you; they will hand you over to synagogues and prisons, and you will be brought before kings and governors because of my name. ¹³This will give you an opportunity to testify. ¹⁴So make up your minds not to prepare your defense in advance; ¹⁵for I will give you words*a* and a wisdom that none of your opponents will be able to withstand or contradict. ¹⁶You will be betrayed even by parents and brothers, by relatives and friends; and they will put some of you to death. ¹⁷You will be hated by all because of my name. ¹⁸But not a hair of your head will perish. ¹⁹By your endurance you will gain your souls.

The Destruction of Jerusalem Foretold

20 "When you see Jerusalem surrounded by armies, then know that its desolation has come near.*b* ²¹Then those in Judea must flee to the mountains, and those inside the city must leave it, and those out in the country must not enter it; ²²for these are days of vengeance, as a fulfillment of all that is written. ²³Woe to those who are pregnant and to those who are nursing infants in those days! For there will be great distress on the earth and wrath against this people; ²⁴they will fall by the edge of the sword and be taken away as captives among all nations; and Jerusalem will be trampled on by the Gentiles, until the times of the Gentiles are fulfilled.

The Coming of the Son of Man

25 "There will be signs in the sun, the moon, and the stars, and on the earth distress among nations confused by the roaring of the sea and the waves. ²⁶People will faint from fear and foreboding of what is coming upon the world, for the powers of the heavens will be shaken. ²⁷Then they will see 'the Son of Man coming in a cloud' with power and great glory. ²⁸Now when these things begin to take place, stand up and raise your heads, because your redemption is drawing near."

The Lesson of the Fig Tree

29 Then he told them a parable: "Look at the fig tree and all the trees; ³⁰as soon as they sprout leaves you can see for yourselves and know that summer is already near. ³¹So also, when you see these things taking place, you know that the kingdom of God is near. ³²Truly I tell you, this generation will not pass away until all things have taken place. ³³Heaven and earth will pass away, but my words will not pass away.

Exhortation to Watch

34 "Be on guard so that your hearts are not weighed down with dissipation and drunkenness and the worries of this life, and that day does not catch you unexpectedly, ³⁵like a trap. For it will come upon all who live on the face of the whole earth. ³⁶Be alert at all times, praying that you may have the strength to escape all these things that will take place, and to stand before the Son of Man."

37 Every day he was teaching in the temple, and at

a Gk *a mouth*   *b* Or *is at hand*

night he would go out and spend the night on the Mount of Olives, as it was called. [38]And all the people would get up early in the morning to listen to him in the temple.

The Plot to Kill Jesus

22 Now the festival of Unleavened Bread, which is called the Passover, was near. [2]The chief priests and the scribes were looking for a way to put Jesus[a] to death, for they were afraid of the people.

3 Then Satan entered into Judas called Iscariot, who was one of the twelve; [4]he went away and conferred with the chief priests and officers of the temple police about how he might betray him to them. [5]They were greatly pleased and agreed to give him money. [6]So he consented and began to look for an opportunity to betray him to them when no crowd was present.

The Preparation of the Passover

7 Then came the day of Unleavened Bread, on which the Passover lamb had to be sacrificed. [8]So Jesus[b] sent Peter and John, saying, "Go and prepare the Passover meal for us that we may eat it." [9]They asked him, "Where do you want us to make preparations for it?" [10]"Listen," he said to them, "when you have entered the city, a man carrying a jar of water will meet you; follow him into the house he enters [11]and say to the owner of the house, 'The teacher asks you, "Where is the guest room, where I may eat the Passover with my disciples?" ' [12]He will show you a large room upstairs, already furnished. Make preparations for us there." [13]So they went and found everything as he had told them; and they prepared the Passover meal.

The Institution of the Lord's Supper

14 When the hour came, he took his place at the table, and the apostles with him. [15]He said to them, "I have eagerly desired to eat this Passover with you before I suffer; [16]for I tell you, I will not eat it[c] until it is fulfilled in the kingdom of God." [17]Then he took a cup, and after giving thanks he said, "Take this and divide it among yourselves; [18]for I tell you that from now on I will not drink of the fruit of the vine until the kingdom of God comes." [19]Then he took a loaf of bread, and when he had given thanks, he broke it and gave it to them, saying, "This is my body, which is given for you. Do this in remembrance of me." [20]And he did the same with the cup after supper, saying, "This cup that is poured out for you is the new covenant in my blood.[d] [21]But see, the one who betrays me is with me, and his hand is on the table. [22]For the Son of Man is going as it has been determined, but woe to that one by whom he is betrayed!" [23]Then they began to ask one another which one of them it could be who would do this.

The Dispute about Greatness

24 A dispute also arose among them as to which one of them was to be regarded as the greatest. [25]But he said to them, "The kings of the Gentiles lord it over them; and those in authority over them are called benefactors. [26]But

---

What It Means to Live in Christ

LUKE 22.24–27

"The church is the church only when it exists for others. To make a start, it should give away all its property to those in need. The church must share in the secular problems of ordinary human life, not dominating, but helping and serving. It must tell people of every calling what it means to live in Christ, to exist for others. It must not under-estimate the importance of human example (which has its origins in the humanity of Jesus and is so important in Paul's teaching); it is not abstract argument, but example, that gives its word emphasis and power."

—DIETRICH BONHOEFFER,
Letters and Papers from Prison

---

a Gk *him*   *b* Gk *he*   *c* Other ancient authorities read *never eat it again*
d Other ancient authorities lack, in whole or in part, verses 19b-20 (*which is given . . . in my blood*)

This Bitter Cup

LUKE 22.39–46

"Jesus, my gentle Jesus,
Walking in the dark of the
    garden—
The Garden of Gethsemane,
Saying to the three
    disciples:
Sorrow is in my soul—
Even unto death;
Tarry ye here a little while,
And watch with me.

"Jesus, my burdened Jesus,
Praying in the dark of the
    garden—
The Garden of Gethsemane.
Saying: Father,
Oh, Father,
This bitter cup,
This bitter cup,
Let it pass from me.

"Jesus, my sorrowing Jesus,
The sweat like drops of
    blood upon his brow,
Talking with his Father,
While the three disciples
    slept,
Saying: Father,
Oh, Father,
Not as I will,
Not as I will,
But let thy will be done."
—JAMES WELDON JOHNSON,
    "God's Trombones"

not so with you; rather the greatest among you must become like the youngest, and the leader like one who serves. [27]For who is greater, the one who is at the table or the one who serves? Is it not the one at the table? But I am among you as one who serves.

28 "You are those who have stood by me in my trials; [29]and I confer on you, just as my Father has conferred on me, a kingdom, [30]so that you may eat and drink at my table in my kingdom, and you will sit on thrones judging the twelve tribes of Israel.

Jesus Predicts Peter's Denial

31 "Simon, Simon, listen! Satan has demanded[a] to sift all of you like wheat, [32]but I have prayed for you that your own faith may not fail; and you, when once you have turned back, strengthen your brothers." [33]And he said to him, "Lord, I am ready to go with you to prison and to death!" [34]Jesus[b] said, "I tell you, Peter, the cock will not crow this day, until you have denied three times that you know me."

Purse, Bag, and Sword

35 He said to them, "When I sent you out without a purse, bag, or sandals, did you lack anything?" They said, "No, not a thing." [36]He said to them, "But now, the one who has a purse must take it, and likewise a bag. And the one who has no sword must sell his cloak and buy one. [37]For I tell you, this scripture must be fulfilled in me, 'And he was counted among the lawless'; and indeed what is written about me is being fulfilled." [38]They said, "Lord, look, here are two swords." He replied, "It is enough."

Jesus Prays on the Mount of Olives

39 He came out and went, as was his custom, to the Mount of Olives; and the disciples followed him. [40]When he reached the place, he said to them, "Pray that you may not come into the time of trial."[c] [41]Then he withdrew from them about a stone's throw, knelt down, and prayed, [42]"Father, if you are willing, remove this cup from me; yet, not my will but yours be done." [[[43]Then an angel from heaven appeared to him and gave him strength. [44]In his anguish he prayed more earnestly, and his sweat became like great drops of blood falling down on the ground.]][d] [45]When he got up from prayer, he came to the disciples and found them sleeping because of grief, [46]and he said to them, "Why are you sleeping? Get up and pray that you may not come into the time of trial."[c]

The Betrayal and Arrest of Jesus

47 While he was still speaking, suddenly a crowd came, and the one called Judas, one of the twelve, was leading them. He approached Jesus to kiss him; [48]but Jesus said to him, "Judas, is it with a kiss that you are betraying the Son of Man?" [49]When those who were around him saw what was coming, they asked, "Lord, should we strike with the sword?" [50]Then one of them struck the slave of the high priest and cut off his right ear. [51]But Jesus said, "No more of this!" And he touched his ear and healed him.

a Or has obtained permission   b Gk He   c Or into temptation
d Other ancient authorities lack verses 43 and 44

⁵²Then Jesus said to the chief priests, the officers of the temple police, and the elders who had come for him, "Have you come out with swords and clubs as if I were a bandit? ⁵³When I was with you day after day in the temple, you did not lay hands on me. But this is your hour, and the power of darkness!"

Peter Denies Jesus

54 Then they seized him and led him away, bringing him into the high priest's house. But Peter was following at a distance. ⁵⁵When they had kindled a fire in the middle of the courtyard and sat down together, Peter sat among them. ⁵⁶Then a servant-girl, seeing him in the firelight, stared at him and said, "This man also was with him." ⁵⁷But he denied it, saying, "Woman, I do not know him." ⁵⁸A little later someone else, on seeing him, said, "You also are one of them." But Peter said, "Man, I am not!" ⁵⁹Then about an hour later still another kept insisting, "Surely this man also was with him; for he is a Galilean." ⁶⁰But Peter said, "Man, I do not know what you are talking about!" At that moment, while he was still speaking, the cock crowed. ⁶¹The Lord turned and looked at Peter. Then Peter remembered the word of the Lord, how he had said to him, "Before the cock crows today, you will deny me three times." ⁶²And he went out and wept bitterly.

The Mocking and Beating of Jesus

63 Now the men who were holding Jesus began to mock him and beat him; ⁶⁴they also blindfolded him and kept asking him, "Prophesy! Who is it that struck you?" ⁶⁵They kept heaping many other insults on him.

Jesus before the Council

66 When day came, the assembly of the elders of the people, both chief priests and scribes, gathered together, and they brought him to their council. ⁶⁷They said, "If you are the Messiah,[a] tell us." He replied, "If I tell you, you will not believe; ⁶⁸and if I question you, you will not answer. ⁶⁹But from now on the Son of Man will be seated at the right hand of the power of God." ⁷⁰All of them asked, "Are you, then, the Son of God?" He said to them, "You say that I am." ⁷¹Then they said, "What further testimony do we need? We have heard it ourselves from his own lips!"

Jesus before Pilate

23 Then the assembly rose as a body and brought Jesus[b] before Pilate. ²They began to accuse him, saying, "We found this man perverting our nation, forbidding us to pay taxes to the emperor, and saying that he himself is the Messiah, a king."[c] ³Then Pilate asked him, "Are you the king of the Jews?" He answered, "You say so." ⁴Then Pilate said to the chief priests and the crowds, "I find no basis for an accusation against this man." ⁵But they were insistent and said, "He stirs up the people by teaching throughout all Judea, from Galilee where he began even to this place."

The Lord Turns and Looks

LUKE 22.56–62

Jesus confronts his delinquent disciple, Peter, simply by looking at him. What sort of look might it have been? Hold in your hand an object that, for you, represents some kind of denial of Jesus' lordship in your life (money, a book, a certain piece of clothing). As you hold it, close your eyes. Imagine Jesus turning and gazing at you with eyes of rebuke—and love. Ask yourself, "Why have I held on to this? What makes me think I need it?" Let go of the object and look to Jesus again.

---

a Or *the Christ*   b Gk *him*   c Or *is an anointed king*

Meditating on Forgiveness at the Cross

LUKE 23.34

If you're experiencing pain in a relationship with a child, spouse, friend or coworker, picture Jesus on the cross, sharing the pain that you feel over the relationship. If there are persons you cannot forgive, open your arms wide, breathe deeply and let Jesus Christ pray within you: "Father, forgive them; for they do not know what they are doing." Feel free to admit that humanly you cannot forgive, but that with Jesus it is possible. Consider practicing this exercise several days a week, for a month. Don't be discouraged if a *feeling* of forgiveness doesn't come; for the time being, be content that God has forgiven those involved in the situation.

See Meeting God in Prayer

Jesus before Herod

6 When Pilate heard this, he asked whether the man was a Galilean. 7And when he learned that he was under Herod's jurisdiction, he sent him off to Herod, who was himself in Jerusalem at that time. 8When Herod saw Jesus, he was very glad, for he had been wanting to see him for a long time, because he had heard about him and was hoping to see him perform some sign. 9He questioned him at some length, but Jesus[a] gave him no answer. 10The chief priests and the scribes stood by, vehemently accusing him. 11Even Herod with his soldiers treated him with contempt and mocked him; then he put an elegant robe on him, and sent him back to Pilate. 12That same day Herod and Pilate became friends with each other; before this they had been enemies.

Jesus Sentenced to Death

13 Pilate then called together the chief priests, the leaders, and the people, 14and said to them, "You brought me this man as one who was perverting the people; and here I have examined him in your presence and have not found this man guilty of any of your charges against him. 15Neither has Herod, for he sent him back to us. Indeed, he has done nothing to deserve death. 16I will therefore have him flogged and release him."[b]

18 Then they all shouted out together, "Away with this fellow! Release Barabbas for us!" 19(This was a man who had been put in prison for an insurrection that had taken place in the city, and for murder.) 20Pilate, wanting to release Jesus, addressed them again; 21but they kept shouting, "Crucify, crucify him!" 22A third time he said to them, "Why, what evil has he done? I have found in him no ground for the sentence of death; I will therefore have him flogged and then release him." 23But they kept urgently demanding with loud shouts that he should be crucified; and their voices prevailed. 24So Pilate gave his verdict that their demand should be granted. 25He released the man they asked for, the one who had been put in prison for insurrection and murder, and he handed Jesus over as they wished.

The Crucifixion of Jesus

26 As they led him away, they seized a man, Simon of Cyrene, who was coming from the country, and they laid the cross on him, and made him carry it behind Jesus. 27A great number of the people followed him, and among them were women who were beating their breasts and wailing for him. 28But Jesus turned to them and said, "Daughters of Jerusalem, do not weep for me, but weep for yourselves and for your children. 29For the days are surely coming when they will say, 'Blessed are the barren, and the wombs that never bore, and the breasts that never nursed.' 30Then they will begin to say to the mountains, 'Fall on us'; and to the hills, 'Cover us.' 31For if they do this when the wood is green, what will happen when it is dry?"

32 Two others also, who were criminals, were led away to be put to death with him. 33When they came to the

a Gk *he*   *b* Here, or after verse 19, other ancient authorities add verse 17, *Now he was obliged to release someone for them at the festival*

place that is called The Skull, they crucified Jesus[a] there with the criminals, one on his right and one on his left. ⟦ [34]Then Jesus said, "Father, forgive them; for they do not know what they are doing."⟧[b] And they cast lots to divide his clothing. [35]And the people stood by, watching; but the leaders scoffed at him, saying, "He saved others; let him save himself if he is the Messiah[c] of God, his chosen one!" [36]The soldiers also mocked him, coming up and offering him sour wine, [37]and saying, "If you are the King of the Jews, save yourself!" [38]There was also an inscription over him,[d] "This is the King of the Jews."

39 One of the criminals who were hanged there kept deriding[e] him and saying, "Are you not the Messiah?[c] Save yourself and us!" [40]But the other rebuked him, saying, "Do you not fear God, since you are under the same sentence of condemnation? [41]And we indeed have been condemned justly, for we are getting what we deserve for our deeds, but this man has done nothing wrong." [42]Then he said, "Jesus, remember me when you come into[f] your kingdom." [43]He replied, "Truly I tell you, today you will be with me in Paradise."

The Death of Jesus

44 It was now about noon, and darkness came over the whole land[g] until three in the afternoon, [45]while the sun's light failed;[h] and the curtain of the temple was torn in two. [46]Then Jesus, crying with a loud voice, said, "Father, into your hands I commend my spirit." Having said this, he breathed his last. [47]When the centurion saw what had taken place, he praised God and said, "Certainly this man was innocent."[i] [48]And when all the crowds who had gathered there for this spectacle saw what had taken place, they returned home, beating their breasts. [49]But all his acquaintances, including the women who had followed him from Galilee, stood at a distance, watching these things.

The Burial of Jesus

50 Now there was a good and righteous man named Joseph, who, though a member of the council, [51]had not agreed to their plan and action. He came from the Jewish town of Arimathea, and he was waiting expectantly for the kingdom of God. [52]This man went to Pilate and asked for the body of Jesus. [53]Then he took it down, wrapped it in a linen cloth, and laid it in a rock-hewn tomb where no one had ever been laid. [54]It was the day of Preparation, and the sabbath was beginning.[j] [55]The women who had come with him from Galilee followed, and they saw the tomb and how his body was laid. [56]Then they returned, and prepared spices and ointments.

On the sabbath they rested according to the commandment.

The Resurrection of Jesus

24 But on the first day of the week, at early dawn, they came to the tomb, taking the spices that they

---

Standing by Christ

LUKE 23.39–43

"What I call the haven is the Cross. If it cannot be given me to deserve one day to share the Cross of Christ, at least may I share that of the good thief. Of all the beings other than Christ of whom the Gospel tells us, the good thief is by far the one I most envy. To have been at the side of Christ and in the same state during the crucifixion seems to me a far more enviable privilege than to be at the right hand of his glory."

—SIMONE WEIL,
Waiting for God

---

a Gk *him*   b Other ancient authorities lack the sentence *Then Jesus . . . what they are doing*   c Or *the Christ*   d Other ancient authorities add *written in Greek and Latin and Hebrew* (that is, *Aramaic*)
e Or *blaspheming*   f Other ancient authorities read *in*   g Or *earth*
h Or *the sun was eclipsed.* Other ancient authorities read *the sun was darkened*   i Or *righteous*   j Gk *was dawning*

Journeying to Emmaus

LUKE 24.13–36

Following the sequence of events in this passage, note the ways the hidden Christ is revealed. In your journal reflect how God speaks to you through the following elements:

- Body movement (walking, exercising)
- Conversation (discussing, talking)
- Listening (attentive to stories, feelings)
- Printed and spoken word (interpreting Scripture)
- Nature (sunset, beauty)
- Friendship (empathizing with sadness, joy)
- Hospitality (inviting, visiting)
- Prayer (blessing the bread)
- Communion (breaking the bread)
- Knowing without evidence (as he vanished they knew who he was)
- Surprise (the guest was really the host; the stranger was really a friend)
- Celebrating the memory (sharing how their hearts burned)

See Meeting God in the Created Order

had prepared. ²They found the stone rolled away from the tomb, ³but when they went in, they did not find the body.ᵃ ⁴While they were perplexed about this, suddenly two men in dazzling clothes stood beside them. ⁵The womenᵇ were terrified and bowed their faces to the ground, but the menᶜ said to them, "Why do you look for the living among the dead? He is not here, but has risen.ᵈ ⁶Remember how he told you, while he was still in Galilee, ⁷that the Son of Man must be handed over to sinners, and be crucified, and on the third day rise again." ⁸Then they remembered his words, ⁹and returning from the tomb, they told all this to the eleven and to all the rest. ¹⁰Now it was Mary Magdalene, Joanna, Mary the mother of James, and the other women with them who told this to the apostles. ¹¹But these words seemed to them an idle tale, and they did not believe them. ¹²But Peter got up and ran to the tomb; stooping and looking in, he saw the linen cloths by themselves; then he went home, amazed at what had happened.ᵉ

The Walk to Emmaus

13 Now on that same day two of them were going to a village called Emmaus, about seven milesᶠ from Jerusalem, ¹⁴and talking with each other about all these things that had happened. ¹⁵While they were talking and discussing, Jesus himself came near and went with them, ¹⁶but their eyes were kept from recognizing him. ¹⁷And he said to them, "What are you discussing with each other while you walk along?" They stood still, looking sad.ᵍ ¹⁸Then one of them, whose name was Cleopas, answered him, "Are you the only stranger in Jerusalem who does not know the things that have taken place there in these days?" ¹⁹He asked them, "What things?" They replied, "The things about Jesus of Nazareth,ʰ who was a prophet mighty in deed and word before God and all the people, ²⁰and how our chief priests and leaders handed him over to be condemned to death and crucified him. ²¹But we had hoped that he was the one to redeem Israel.ⁱ Yes, and besides all this, it is now the third day since these things took place. ²²Moreover, some women of our group astounded us. They were at the tomb early this morning, ²³and when they did not find his body there, they came back and told us that they had indeed seen a vision of angels who said that he was alive. ²⁴Some of those who were with us went to the tomb and found it just as the women had said; but they did not see him." ²⁵Then he said to them, "Oh, how foolish you are, and how slow of heart to believe all that the prophets have declared! ²⁶Was it not necessary that the Messiahʲ should suffer these things and then enter into his glory?" ²⁷Then beginning with Moses and all the prophets, he interpreted to them the things about himself in all the scriptures.

28 As they came near the village to which they were going, he walked ahead as if he were going on. ²⁹But they urged him strongly, saying, "Stay with us, because it is al-

a Other ancient authorities add *of the Lord Jesus*   *b* Gk *They*   *c* Gk *but they*   *d* Other ancient authorities lack *He is not here, but has risen*   *e* Other ancient authorities lack verse 12   *f* Gk *sixty stadia;* other ancient authorities read *a hundred sixty stadia*   *g* Other ancient authorities read *walk along, looking sad?"*   *h* Other ancient authorities read *Jesus the Nazorean*   *i* Or *to set Israel free*   *j* Or *the Christ*

most evening and the day is now nearly over." So he went in to stay with them. ³⁰When he was at the table with them, he took bread, blessed and broke it, and gave it to them. ³¹Then their eyes were opened, and they recognized him; and he vanished from their sight. ³²They said to each other, "Were not our hearts burning within us*a* while he was talking to us on the road, while he was opening the scriptures to us?" ³³That same hour they got up and returned to Jerusalem; and they found the eleven and their companions gathered together. ³⁴They were saying, "The Lord has risen indeed, and he has appeared to Simon!" ³⁵Then they told what had happened on the road, and how he had been made known to them in the breaking of the bread.

Jesus Appears to His Disciples

36 While they were talking about this, Jesus himself stood among them and said to them, "Peace be with you."*b* ³⁷They were startled and terrified, and thought that they were seeing a ghost. ³⁸He said to them, "Why are you frightened, and why do doubts arise in your hearts? ³⁹Look at my hands and my feet; see that it is I myself. Touch me and see; for a ghost does not have flesh and bones as you see that I have." ⁴⁰And when he had said this, he showed them his hands and his feet.*c* ⁴¹While in their joy they were disbelieving and still wondering, he said to them, "Have you anything here to eat?" ⁴²They gave him a piece of broiled fish, ⁴³and he took it and ate in their presence.

44 Then he said to them, "These are my words that I spoke to you while I was still with you—that everything written about me in the law of Moses, the prophets, and the psalms must be fulfilled." ⁴⁵Then he opened their minds to understand the scriptures, ⁴⁶and he said to them, "Thus it is written, that the Messiah*d* is to suffer and to rise from the dead on the third day, ⁴⁷and that repentance and forgiveness of sins is to be proclaimed in his name to all nations, beginning from Jerusalem. ⁴⁸You are witnesses*e* of these things. ⁴⁹And see, I am sending upon you what my Father promised; so stay here in the city until you have been clothed with power from on high."

The Ascension of Jesus

50 Then he led them out as far as Bethany, and, lifting up his hands, he blessed them. ⁵¹While he was blessing them, he withdrew from them and was carried up into heaven.*f* ⁵²And they worshiped him, and*g* returned to Jerusalem with great joy; ⁵³and they were continually in the temple blessing God.*h*

Pointing Toward Eternity

LUKE 24.39–53

"The day of resurrection!
Earth tell it out abroad;
the Passover of gladness,
the Passover of God.
From death to life eternal,
from earth unto the sky,
our Christ has brought us
over with hymns of victory."
—JOHN OF DAMASCUS

---

a Other ancient authorities lack *within us*   *b* Other ancient authorities lack *and said to them, "Peace be with you."*   *c* Other ancient authorities lack verse 40   *d* Or *the Christ*   *e* Or *nations. Beginning from Jerusalem* ⁴⁸*you are witnesses*   *f* Other ancient authorities lack *and was carried up into heaven*   *g* Other ancient authorities lack *worshiped him, and*   *h* Other ancient authorities add *Amen*

THE GOSPEL ACCORDING TO
JOHN
Living in the Light

KEY VERSES:

The Word became flesh and lived among us, and we have seen his glory . . . . In him was life,
and the life was the light of all people.—John 1.14,4

> "You called, you cried, you shattered my deafness. You sparkled, you blazed, you drove away my blindness. You shed your fragrance, and I drew in my breath, and I pant for you. I tasted and now I hunger and thirst. You touched me, and now I burn with longing for your peace."
>
> —AUGUSTINE,
> *Confessions*

The light is shining. It is a light that defies our ability to capture and define. The light has a voice that speaks life to us. The light has hands that hold and heal us. The light has a name—Jesus, the son of Mary, the Son of God.

The light became flesh. The light conquers darkness and turns death into life. Into situations as ordinary as a catering problem at a wedding or as deeply troubling as a death in the family, this light beams a transforming power. When the light is present, everything is changed. When the light is present in us, we are changed. We have eternal life. We are restored to the glory that our Creator God intended.

Many situations in the book of John may resemble your personal situations. As you read you might ask yourself, "What is God doing here, and how can I be open to allow God to work within me?" As you participate in a community of believers, you might ask, "What is God doing among us?"

John calls his community of Jews and non-Jews to follow the revolutionary—and sometimes unpopular—way of Jesus. He shows that the way of Jesus is full of challenge and adventure—full of the risk involved when we let go and trust. The way might be hard. But in Jesus we find grace and truth. In Jesus we will "have life, and have abundantly!" (John 10.10). John urges us to dwell in the light of Jesus, so that we might carry the death-defying love of God into the world.

The Word Became Flesh

1 In the beginning was the Word, and the Word was with God, and the Word was God. ²He was in the beginning with God. ³All things came into being through him, and without him not one thing came into being. What has come into being ⁴in him was life,ᵃ and the life was the light of all people. ⁵The light shines in the darkness, and the darkness did not overcome it.

6 There was a man sent from God, whose name was John. ⁷He came as a witness to testify to the light, so that all might believe through him. ⁸He himself was not the light, but he came to testify to the light. ⁹The true light, which enlightens everyone, was coming into the world.ᵇ

10 He was in the world, and the world came into being through him; yet the world did not know him. ¹¹He came to what was his own,ᶜ and his own people did not accept him. ¹²But to all who received him, who believed in his name, he gave power to become children of God, ¹³who were born, not of blood or of the will of the flesh or of the will of man, but of God.

14 And the Word became flesh and lived among us, and we have seen his glory, the glory as of a father's only son,ᵈ full of grace and truth. ¹⁵(John testified to him and cried out, "This was he of whom I said, 'He who comes after me ranks ahead of me because he was before me.' ") ¹⁶From his fullness we have all received, grace upon grace. ¹⁷The law indeed was given through Moses; grace and truth came through Jesus Christ. ¹⁸No one has ever seen God. It is God the only Son,ᵉ who is close to the Father's heart,ᶠ who has made him known.

The Testimony of John the Baptist

19 This is the testimony given by John when the Jews sent priests and Levites from Jerusalem to ask him, "Who are you?" ²⁰He confessed and did not deny it, but confessed, "I am not the Messiah."ᵍ ²¹And they asked him, "What then? Are you Elijah?" He said, "I am not." "Are you the prophet?" He answered, "No." ²²Then they said to him, "Who are you? Let us have an answer for those who sent us. What do you say about yourself?" ²³He said,

"I am the voice of one crying out in the
    wilderness,
'Make straight the way of the Lord,' "

as the prophet Isaiah said.

24 Now they had been sent from the Pharisees. ²⁵They asked him, "Why then are you baptizing if you are neither the Messiah,ᵍ nor Elijah, nor the prophet?" ²⁶John answered them, "I baptize with water. Among you stands one whom you do not know, ²⁷the one who is coming after me; I am not worthy to untie the thong of his sandal." ²⁸This took place in Bethany across the Jordan where John was baptizing.

The Lamb of God

29 The next day he saw Jesus coming toward him and

A Light Shines

JOHN 1.1–18

John's rich, resonating words sound out like a majestic overture. Imagine trumpets and drums as the great themes of this Gospel are declared: "In the beginning was the Word"; "in him was life"; "the light shines"; "darkness did not overcome it." As you walk around the room, read this passage again aloud, as loudly as the text suggests to you. As you read, listen for a word or phrase that catches your attention. Repeat it and let it expand within your spirit. Sense its power. Give it the center stage of your consciousness and let it speak. When you are ready, let this experience serve as the foundation for a prayer of reflection.

See Meeting God in Scripture

ᵃ Or ³through him. And without him not one thing came into being that has come into being. ⁴In him was life   ᵇ Or He was the true light that enlightens everyone coming into the world   ᶜ Or to his own home   ᵈ Or the Father's only Son   ᵉ Other ancient authorities read It is an only Son, God, or It is the only Son   ᶠ Gk bosom   ᵍ Or the Christ

Where Are You Staying?

JOHN 1.35–39

Two seekers ask Jesus where he is staying. Jesus says, "Come and see." It is an invitation to his lodgings—and into discipleship with him.

Invite Jesus to come and see where you are staying. Invite him into your living space. Talk to him as you show him around. Show him those aspects of your home and your possessions that delight you. Then ask Jesus to sit with you. When Jesus asks where your spirit is residing, how might you respond? Write a dialogue with Jesus about where you are "staying." Be truthful. Trust him. Pray through the thoughts and emotions you experience during that dialogue. If appropriate, share your experience with someone you trust.

See Meeting God in Everyday Life

declared, "Here is the Lamb of God who takes away the sin of the world! [30]This is he of whom I said, 'After me comes a man who ranks ahead of me because he was before me.' [31]I myself did not know him; but I came baptizing with water for this reason, that he might be revealed to Israel." [32]And John testified, "I saw the Spirit descending from heaven like a dove, and it remained on him. [33]I myself did not know him, but the one who sent me to baptize with water said to me, 'He on whom you see the Spirit descend and remain is the one who baptizes with the Holy Spirit.' [34]And I myself have seen and have testified that this is the Son of God."[a]

The First Disciples of Jesus

35 The next day John again was standing with two of his disciples, [36]and as he watched Jesus walk by, he exclaimed, "Look, here is the Lamb of God!" [37]The two disciples heard him say this, and they followed Jesus. [38]When Jesus turned and saw them following, he said to them, "What are you looking for?" They said to him, "Rabbi" (which translated means Teacher), "where are you staying?" [39]He said to them, "Come and see." They came and saw where he was staying, and they remained with him that day. It was about four o'clock in the afternoon. [40]One of the two who heard John speak and followed him was Andrew, Simon Peter's brother. [41]He first found his brother Simon and said to him, "We have found the Messiah" (which is translated Anointed[b]). [42]He brought Simon[c] to Jesus, who looked at him and said, "You are Simon son of John. You are to be called Cephas" (which is translated Peter[d]).

Jesus Calls Philip and Nathanael

43 The next day Jesus decided to go to Galilee. He found Philip and said to him, "Follow me." [44]Now Philip was from Bethsaida, the city of Andrew and Peter. [45]Philip found Nathanael and said to him, "We have found him about whom Moses in the law and also the prophets wrote, Jesus son of Joseph from Nazareth." [46]Nathanael said to him, "Can anything good come out of Nazareth?" Philip said to him, "Come and see." [47]When Jesus saw Nathanael coming toward him, he said of him, "Here is truly an Israelite in whom there is no deceit!" [48]Nathanael asked him, "Where did you get to know me?" Jesus answered, "I saw you under the fig tree before Philip called you." [49]Nathanael replied, "Rabbi, you are the Son of God! You are the King of Israel!" [50]Jesus answered, "Do you believe because I told you that I saw you under the fig tree? You will see greater things than these." [51]And he said to him, "Very truly, I tell you,[e] you will see heaven opened and the angels of God ascending and descending upon the Son of Man."

The Wedding at Cana

2 On the third day there was a wedding in Cana of Galilee, and the mother of Jesus was there. [2]Jesus and his

a Other ancient authorities read *is God's chosen one*   b Or *Christ*
c Gk *him*   d From the word for *rock* in Aramaic (*kepha*) and Greek (*petra*), respectively   e Both instances of the Greek word for *you* in this verse are plural

disciples had also been invited to the wedding. ³When the wine gave out, the mother of Jesus said to him, "They have no wine." ⁴And Jesus said to her, "Woman, what concern is that to you and to me? My hour has not yet come." ⁵His mother said to the servants, "Do whatever he tells you." ⁶Now standing there were six stone water jars for the Jewish rites of purification, each holding twenty or thirty gallons. ⁷Jesus said to them, "Fill the jars with water." And they filled them up to the brim. ⁸He said to them, "Now draw some out, and take it to the chief steward." So they took it. ⁹When the steward tasted the water that had become wine, and did not know where it came from (though the servants who had drawn the water knew), the steward called the bridegroom ¹⁰and said to him, "Everyone serves the good wine first, and then the inferior wine after the guests have become drunk. But you have kept the good wine until now." ¹¹Jesus did this, the first of his signs, in Cana of Galilee, and revealed his glory; and his disciples believed in him.

12 After this he went down to Capernaum with his mother, his brothers, and his disciples; and they remained there a few days.

Jesus Cleanses the Temple

13 The Passover of the Jews was near, and Jesus went up to Jerusalem. ¹⁴In the temple he found people selling cattle, sheep, and doves, and the money changers seated at their tables. ¹⁵Making a whip of cords, he drove all of them out of the temple, both the sheep and the cattle. He also poured out the coins of the money changers and overturned their tables. ¹⁶He told those who were selling the doves, "Take these things out of here! Stop making my Father's house a marketplace!" ¹⁷His disciples remembered that it was written, "Zeal for your house will consume me." ¹⁸The Jews then said to him, "What sign can you show us for doing this?" ¹⁹Jesus answered them, "Destroy this temple, and in three days I will raise it up." ²⁰The Jews then said, "This temple has been under construction for forty-six years, and will you raise it up in three days?" ²¹But he was speaking of the temple of his body. ²²After he was raised from the dead, his disciples remembered that he had said this; and they believed the scripture and the word that Jesus had spoken.

23 When he was in Jerusalem during the Passover festival, many believed in his name because they saw the signs that he was doing. ²⁴But Jesus on his part would not entrust himself to them, because he knew all people ²⁵and needed no one to testify about anyone; for he himself knew what was in everyone.

Nicodemus Visits Jesus

3 Now there was a Pharisee named Nicodemus, a leader of the Jews. ²He came to Jesus*a* by night and said to him, "Rabbi, we know that you are a teacher who has come from God; for no one can do these signs that you do apart from the presence of God." ³Jesus answered him, "Very truly, I tell you, no one can see the kingdom of God without being born from above."*b* ⁴Nicodemus said to him,

a Gk *him* *b* Or *born anew*

Doing What Jesus Says

JOHN 2.1–11

Sometimes the things God asks us to do just don't seem to make sense! Jesus says, "Fill the jars with water." But why fill up the jars with water when it is wine that has run out? Even though it seems to make no sense, the servants do as they are told. The water becomes premium wine. The hosts experience honor rather than shame.

You may ask, "What am I running out of? What shortages are my family, my faith community or my neighborhood likely to encounter?" Tell Jesus about them. What does Jesus ask you to do in response? What act of obedience does Jesus ask of you so that the situation might be transformed? What do you envision Jesus doing as you cooperate with him?

See Meeting God in Community

You Choose

Nicodemus admires Jesus and has many questions to ask, but he has much to lose—security, position and power—if he is public about his admiration, so he seeks Jesus under the cover of darkness. Yet Jesus asks the Pharisee to do something much more profound and much more difficult than putting his lifestyle in jeopardy—he asks him to be "born from above."

Ask the Spirit to bless your imagination and your senses as you take your place in the story as Nicodemus. What is happening? What do you see? What do you hear—around you and from Jesus? Smell the evening air. Feel the breeze. Ask Jesus to speak to you about your fears and questions. Ask what being "born from above" could mean for you right now. Let Jesus enlighten your lack of understanding, your stubborn resistance or your glad acceptance. Carry the experience in your heart during the coming week.

See Meeting God in Everyday Life

"How can anyone be born after having grown old? Can one enter a second time into the mother's womb and be born?" ⁵Jesus answered, "Very truly, I tell you, no one can enter the kingdom of God without being born of water and Spirit. ⁶What is born of the flesh is flesh, and what is born of the Spirit is spirit.ᵃ ⁷Do not be astonished that I said to you, 'Youᵇ must be born from above.'ᶜ ⁸The windᵃ blows where it chooses, and you hear the sound of it, but you do not know where it comes from or where it goes. So it is with everyone who is born of the Spirit." ⁹Nicodemus said to him, "How can these things be?" ¹⁰Jesus answered him, "Are you a teacher of Israel, and yet you do not understand these things?

11 "Very truly, I tell you, we speak of what we know and testify to what we have seen; yet youᵈ do not receive our testimony. ¹²If I have told you about earthly things and you do not believe, how can you believe if I tell you about heavenly things? ¹³No one has ascended into heaven except the one who descended from heaven, the Son of Man.ᵉ ¹⁴And just as Moses lifted up the serpent in the wilderness, so must the Son of Man be lifted up, ¹⁵that whoever believes in him may have eternal life.ᶠ

16 "For God so loved the world that he gave his only Son, so that everyone who believes in him may not perish but may have eternal life.

17 "Indeed, God did not send the Son into the world to condemn the world, but in order that the world might be saved through him. ¹⁸Those who believe in him are not condemned; but those who do not believe are condemned already, because they have not believed in the name of the only Son of God. ¹⁹And this is the judgment, that the light has come into the world, and people loved darkness rather than light because their deeds were evil. ²⁰For all who do evil hate the light and do not come to the light, so that their deeds may not be exposed. ²¹But those who do what is true come to the light, so that it may be clearly seen that their deeds have been done in God."ᶠ

Jesus and John the Baptist

22 After this Jesus and his disciples went into the Judean countryside, and he spent some time there with them and baptized. ²³John also was baptizing at Aenon near Salim because water was abundant there; and people kept coming and were being baptized ²⁴—John, of course, had not yet been thrown into prison.

25 Now a discussion about purification arose between John's disciples and a Jew.ᵍ ²⁶They came to John and said to him, "Rabbi, the one who was with you across the Jordan, to whom you testified, here he is baptizing, and all are going to him." ²⁷John answered, "No one can receive anything except what has been given from heaven. ²⁸You yourselves are my witnesses that I said, 'I am not the Messiah,ʰ but I have been sent ahead of him.' ²⁹He who has the bride is the bridegroom. The friend of the bridegroom, who stands and hears him, rejoices greatly at the bride-

---

a The same Greek word means both *wind* and *spirit*   *b* The Greek word for *you* here is plural   *c* Or *anew*   *d* The Greek word for *you* here and in verse 12 is plural   *e* Other ancient authorities add *who is in heaven*
f Some interpreters hold that the quotation concludes with verse 15
g Other ancient authorities read *the Jews*   *h* Or *the Christ*

groom's voice. For this reason my joy has been fulfilled. [30]He must increase, but I must decrease."[a]

The One Who Comes from Heaven

31 The one who comes from above is above all; the one who is of the earth belongs to the earth and speaks about earthly things. The one who comes from heaven is above all. [32]He testifies to what he has seen and heard, yet no one accepts his testimony. [33]Whoever has accepted his testimony has certified[b] this, that God is true. [34]He whom God has sent speaks the words of God, for he gives the Spirit without measure. [35]The Father loves the Son and has placed all things in his hands. [36]Whoever believes in the Son has eternal life; whoever disobeys the Son will not see life, but must endure God's wrath.

Jesus and the Woman of Samaria

4 Now when Jesus[c] learned that the Pharisees had heard, "Jesus is making and baptizing more disciples than John" [2]—although it was not Jesus himself but his disciples who baptized— [3]he left Judea and started back to Galilee. [4]But he had to go through Samaria. [5]So he came to a Samaritan city called Sychar, near the plot of ground that Jacob had given to his son Joseph. [6]Jacob's well was there, and Jesus, tired out by his journey, was sitting by the well. It was about noon.

7 A Samaritan woman came to draw water, and Jesus said to her, "Give me a drink." [8](His disciples had gone to the city to buy food.) [9]The Samaritan woman said to him, "How is it that you, a Jew, ask a drink of me, a woman of Samaria?" (Jews do not share things in common with Samaritans.)[d] [10]Jesus answered her, "If you knew the gift of God, and who it is that is saying to you, 'Give me a drink,' you would have asked him, and he would have given you living water." [11]The woman said to him, "Sir, you have no bucket, and the well is deep. Where do you get that living water? [12]Are you greater than our ancestor Jacob, who gave us the well, and with his sons and his flocks drank from it?" [13]Jesus said to her, "Everyone who drinks of this water will be thirsty again, [14]but those who drink of the water that I will give them will never be thirsty. The water that I will give will become in them a spring of water gushing up to eternal life." [15]The woman said to him, "Sir, give me this water, so that I may never be thirsty or have to keep coming here to draw water."

16 Jesus said to her, "Go, call your husband, and come back." [17]The woman answered him, "I have no husband." Jesus said to her, "You are right in saying, 'I have no husband'; [18]for you have had five husbands, and the one you have now is not your husband. What you have said is true!" [19]The woman said to him, "Sir, I see that you are a prophet. [20]Our ancestors worshiped on this mountain, but you[e] say that the place where people must worship is in Jerusalem." [21]Jesus said to her, "Woman, believe me, the hour is coming when you will worship the Father neither on this mountain nor in Jerusalem. [22]You worship what

---

a Some interpreters hold that the quotation continues through verse 36
b Gk *set a seal to*   c Other ancient authorities read *the Lord*   d Other ancient authorities lack this sentence   e The Greek word for *you* here and in verses 21 and 22 is plural

Over the Line

JOHN 4.7–9

The Samaritans are considered "unclean." Jews don't associate with Samaritans, John reminds us. To do so is to cross over the line of propriety. And Jesus dares to talk to a Samaritan woman alone! The two discuss thirst (physical and spiritual), relationships and religion. As he speaks Jesus crosses the boundary of his culture's notion of what is acceptable and what is not. His disciples are surprised—even shocked (v.27).

Who is "over the line" in your way of thinking? How can you expand your ideas of what is acceptable so that you can meet the needs of "the unacceptable" as Jesus did? What is Jesus waiting to teach you and show you about yourself?

See Meeting God in Service

Living Water

JOHN 4.13–15

Walk around the room as you read verses 13 through 15 aloud three times. Put the Bible down and walk around the room again, reciting the text three more times. Now, seated comfortably, with this text and a glass of water in front of you, name your thirsts. Pray the same request that the Samaritan woman made of Jesus: "Sir, give me this water." Drink the water as you receive Jesus' gift, a spring of water that gushes up to eternal life. Rest in God's presence. As you go out into the world, let the water of eternal life flow through your heart and out to others through your words and actions.

See Meeting God in Scripture

you do not know; we worship what we know, for salvation is from the Jews. ²³But the hour is coming, and is now here, when the true worshipers will worship the Father in spirit and truth, for the Father seeks such as these to worship him. ²⁴God is spirit, and those who worship him must worship in spirit and truth." ²⁵The woman said to him, "I know that Messiah is coming" (who is called Christ). "When he comes, he will proclaim all things to us." ²⁶Jesus said to her, "I am he,ᵃ the one who is speaking to you."

27 Just then his disciples came. They were astonished that he was speaking with a woman, but no one said, "What do you want?" or, "Why are you speaking with her?" ²⁸Then the woman left her water jar and went back to the city. She said to the people, ²⁹"Come and see a man who told me everything I have ever done! He cannot be the Messiah,ᵇ can he?" ³⁰They left the city and were on their way to him.

31 Meanwhile the disciples were urging him, "Rabbi, eat something." ³²But he said to them, "I have food to eat that you do not know about." ³³So the disciples said to one another, "Surely no one has brought him something to eat?" ³⁴Jesus said to them, "My food is to do the will of him who sent me and to complete his work. ³⁵Do you not say, 'Four months more, then comes the harvest'? But I tell you, look around you, and see how the fields are ripe for harvesting. ³⁶The reaper is already receivingᶜ wages and is gathering fruit for eternal life, so that sower and reaper may rejoice together. ³⁷For here the saying holds true, 'One sows and another reaps.' ³⁸I sent you to reap that for which you did not labor. Others have labored, and you have entered into their labor."

39 Many Samaritans from that city believed in him because of the woman's testimony, "He told me everything I have ever done." ⁴⁰So when the Samaritans came to him, they asked him to stay with them; and he stayed there two days. ⁴¹And many more believed because of his word. ⁴²They said to the woman, "It is no longer because of what you said that we believe, for we have heard for ourselves, and we know that this is truly the Savior of the world."

Jesus Returns to Galilee

43 When the two days were over, he went from that place to Galilee ⁴⁴(for Jesus himself had testified that a prophet has no honor in the prophet's own country). ⁴⁵When he came to Galilee, the Galileans welcomed him, since they had seen all that he had done in Jerusalem at the festival; for they too had gone to the festival.

Jesus Heals an Official's Son

46 Then he came again to Cana in Galilee where he had changed the water into wine. Now there was a royal official whose son lay ill in Capernaum. ⁴⁷When he heard that Jesus had come from Judea to Galilee, he went and begged him to come down and heal his son, for he was at the point of death. ⁴⁸Then Jesus said to him, "Unless youᵈ see signs and wonders you will not believe." ⁴⁹The official said

---

a Gk *I am*   *b* Or *the Christ*   *c* Or ³⁵ . . . *the fields are already ripe for harvesting.* ³⁶*The reaper is receiving*   *d* Both instances of the Greek word for *you* in this verse are plural

to him, "Sir, come down before my little boy dies." [50]Jesus said to him, "Go; your son will live." The man believed the word that Jesus spoke to him and started on his way. [51]As he was going down, his slaves met him and told him that his child was alive. [52]So he asked them the hour when he began to recover, and they said to him, "Yesterday at one in the afternoon the fever left him." [53]The father realized that this was the hour when Jesus had said to him, "Your son will live." So he himself believed, along with his whole household. [54]Now this was the second sign that Jesus did after coming from Judea to Galilee.

Jesus Heals on the Sabbath

5 After this there was a festival of the Jews, and Jesus went up to Jerusalem.

2 Now in Jerusalem by the Sheep Gate there is a pool, called in Hebrew[a] Beth-zatha,[b] which has five porticoes. [3]In these lay many invalids—blind, lame, and paralyzed.[c] [5]One man was there who had been ill for thirty-eight years. [6]When Jesus saw him lying there and knew that he had been there a long time, he said to him, "Do you want to be made well?" [7]The sick man answered him, "Sir, I have no one to put me into the pool when the water is stirred up; and while I am making my way, someone else steps down ahead of me." [8]Jesus said to him, "Stand up, take your mat and walk." [9]At once the man was made well, and he took up his mat and began to walk.

Now that day was a sabbath. [10]So the Jews said to the man who had been cured, "It is the sabbath; it is not lawful for you to carry your mat." [11]But he answered them, "The man who made me well said to me, 'Take up your mat and walk.'" [12]They asked him, "Who is the man who said to you, 'Take it up and walk'?" [13]Now the man who had been healed did not know who it was, for Jesus had disappeared in[d] the crowd that was there. [14]Later Jesus found him in the temple and said to him, "See, you have been made well! Do not sin any more, so that nothing worse happens to you." [15]The man went away and told the Jews that it was Jesus who had made him well. [16]Therefore the Jews started persecuting Jesus, because he was doing such things on the sabbath. [17]But Jesus answered them, "My Father is still working, and I also am working." [18]For this reason the Jews were seeking all the more to kill him, because he was not only breaking the sabbath, but was also calling God his own Father, thereby making himself equal to God.

The Authority of the Son

19 Jesus said to them, "Very truly, I tell you, the Son can do nothing on his own, but only what he sees the Father doing; for whatever the Father[e] does, the Son does likewise. [20]The Father loves the Son and shows him all that he himself is doing; and he will show him greater works than these, so that you will be astonished. [21]Indeed, just as the

---

At a Distance

JOHN 4.46–54

"Anticipation. God is fixing it right now, even though I can't see how. Anticipation. While I am trying to figure it out, God has already worked it out. Learn how to wait with the expectancy that God is doing something about it. Anticipation. Faith is relational, not conceptual: 'What we will yet be, has not been revealed.'"

—JEREMIAH A. WRIGHT, JR.,
What Makes You So Strong?

---

a That is, *Aramaic*   b Other ancient authorities read *Bethesda*, others *Bethsaida*   c Other ancient authorities add, wholly or in part, *waiting for the stirring of the water;* [4]*for an angel of the Lord went down at certain seasons into the pool, and stirred up the water; whoever stepped in first after the stirring of the water was made well from whatever disease that person had.*   d Or *had left because of*   e Gk *that one*

The Son Gives Life

JOHN 5.1–15

Jesus has challenged this man to change—a man who has good reasons for being the way he is. But still Jesus asks him, "Do you want to be made well?" Jesus' question is purposely ambiguous.

Picture the scene with yourself in the role of the person with a disability. Jesus asks you, "Do you want to be made well?" What do you think of the question? How does it make you feel? How do you answer Jesus? Ask the Spirit to enlighten your heart and mind. Write a letter to Jesus, asking him to help you discern any resistance to wellness that you hold within you.

See Meeting God in Scripture

Father raises the dead and gives them life, so also the Son gives life to whomever he wishes. ²²The Father judges no one but has given all judgment to the Son, ²³so that all may honor the Son just as they honor the Father. Anyone who does not honor the Son does not honor the Father who sent him. ²⁴Very truly, I tell you, anyone who hears my word and believes him who sent me has eternal life, and does not come under judgment, but has passed from death to life.

25 "Very truly, I tell you, the hour is coming, and is now here, when the dead will hear the voice of the Son of God, and those who hear will live. ²⁶For just as the Father has life in himself, so he has granted the Son also to have life in himself; ²⁷and he has given him authority to execute judgment, because he is the Son of Man. ²⁸Do not be astonished at this; for the hour is coming when all who are in their graves will hear his voice ²⁹and will come out— those who have done good, to the resurrection of life, and those who have done evil, to the resurrection of condemnation.

Witnesses to Jesus

30 "I can do nothing on my own. As I hear, I judge; and my judgment is just, because I seek to do not my own will but the will of him who sent me.

31 "If I testify about myself, my testimony is not true. ³²There is another who testifies on my behalf, and I know that his testimony to me is true. ³³You sent messengers to John, and he testified to the truth. ³⁴Not that I accept such human testimony, but I say these things so that you may be saved. ³⁵He was a burning and shining lamp, and you were willing to rejoice for a while in his light. ³⁶But I have a testimony greater than John's. The works that the Father has given me to complete, the very works that I am doing, testify on my behalf that the Father has sent me. ³⁷And the Father who sent me has himself testified on my behalf. You have never heard his voice or seen his form, ³⁸and you do not have his word abiding in you, because you do not believe him whom he has sent.

39 "You search the scriptures because you think that in them you have eternal life; and it is they that testify on my behalf. ⁴⁰Yet you refuse to come to me to have life. ⁴¹I do not accept glory from human beings. ⁴²But I know that you do not have the love of God in*a* you. ⁴³I have come in my Father's name, and you do not accept me; if another comes in his own name, you will accept him. ⁴⁴How can you believe when you accept glory from one another and do not seek the glory that comes from the one who alone is God? ⁴⁵Do not think that I will accuse you before the Father; your accuser is Moses, on whom you have set your hope. ⁴⁶If you believed Moses, you would believe me, for he wrote about me. ⁴⁷But if you do not believe what he wrote, how will you believe what I say?"

Feeding the Five Thousand

6 After this Jesus went to the other side of the Sea of Galilee, also called the Sea of Tiberias.*b* ²A large crowd kept following him, because they saw the signs that he

a Or *among*   *b* Gk *of Galilee of Tiberias*

was doing for the sick. ³Jesus went up the mountain and sat down there with his disciples. ⁴Now the Passover, the festival of the Jews, was near. ⁵When he looked up and saw a large crowd coming toward him, Jesus said to Philip, "Where are we to buy bread for these people to eat?" ⁶He said this to test him, for he himself knew what he was going to do. ⁷Philip answered him, "Six months' wages*a* would not buy enough bread for each of them to get a little." ⁸One of his disciples, Andrew, Simon Peter's brother, said to him, ⁹"There is a boy here who has five barley loaves and two fish. But what are they among so many people?" ¹⁰Jesus said, "Make the people sit down." Now there was a great deal of grass in the place; so they*b* sat down, about five thousand in all. ¹¹Then Jesus took the loaves, and when he had given thanks, he distributed them to those who were seated; so also the fish, as much as they wanted. ¹²When they were satisfied, he told his disciples, "Gather up the fragments left over, so that nothing may be lost." ¹³So they gathered them up, and from the fragments of the five barley loaves, left by those who had eaten, they filled twelve baskets. ¹⁴When the people saw the sign that he had done, they began to say, "This is indeed the prophet who is to come into the world."

15 When Jesus realized that they were about to come and take him by force to make him king, he withdrew again to the mountain by himself.

Jesus Walks on the Water

16 When evening came, his disciples went down to the sea, ¹⁷got into a boat, and started across the sea to Capernaum. It was now dark, and Jesus had not yet come to them. ¹⁸The sea became rough because a strong wind was blowing. ¹⁹When they had rowed about three or four miles,*c* they saw Jesus walking on the sea and coming near the boat, and they were terrified. ²⁰But he said to them, "It is I;*d* do not be afraid." ²¹Then they wanted to take him into the boat, and immediately the boat reached the land toward which they were going.

The Bread from Heaven

22 The next day the crowd that had stayed on the other side of the sea saw that there had been only one boat there. They also saw that Jesus had not got into the boat with his disciples, but that his disciples had gone away alone. ²³Then some boats from Tiberias came near the place where they had eaten the bread after the Lord had given thanks.*e* ²⁴So when the crowd saw that neither Jesus nor his disciples were there, they themselves got into the boats and went to Capernaum looking for Jesus.

25 When they found him on the other side of the sea, they said to him, "Rabbi, when did you come here?" ²⁶Jesus answered them, "Very truly, I tell you, you are looking for me, not because you saw signs, but because you ate your fill of the loaves. ²⁷Do not work for the food that perishes, but for the food that endures for eternal life, which the Son of Man will give you. For it is on him that God the

The Sovereign One

JOHN 6.13–15

The crowd that gathers around Jesus is impressed with him. They have seen him miraculously provide lunch for thousands. They want to make him king. But Jesus refuses to be co-opted.

Jesus will not be enlisted into our causes—no matter how laudable they may seem to us—if they do not conform to the will of God. Using the words of Psalm 139, invite God to examine your heart. Confess (perhaps in the presence of someone you trust) ways in which you have desired Jesus for what he could do for your cause, rather than desiring Jesus for himself. Spend some time with Jesus, enjoying him for his own sake. Repeat a simple phrase such as, "Jesus, you are all I want."

See Meeting God in Prayer

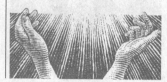

---

a Gk *Two hundred denarii*; the denarius was the usual day's wage for a laborer   *b* Gk *the men*   *c* Gk *about twenty-five or thirty stadia*   *d* Gk *I am*   *e* Other ancient authorities lack *after the Lord had given thanks*

Living Bread

JOHN 6.35

Think about how it feels to be hungry—hungry in your stomach and hungry in your soul. Then think of the best bread you have ever tasted. Smell its yeasty aroma. What does it look like? Feel its crust and its soft interior with your fingers. Taste it. Savor the experience. What kinds of things are like bread for you—savory, filling, satisfying? Write down some descriptive words that come to you. What does it mean for you to "eat" the bread Jesus offers? At your earliest opportunity (according to your custom), take your place at the communion table of the Lord and receive the bread of remembrance, the bread of life.

See Meeting God in Worship

Father has set his seal." [28]Then they said to him, "What must we do to perform the works of God?" [29]Jesus answered them, "This is the work of God, that you believe in him whom he has sent." [30]So they said to him, "What sign are you going to give us then, so that we may see it and believe you? What work are you performing? [31]Our ancestors ate the manna in the wilderness; as it is written, 'He gave them bread from heaven to eat.' " [32]Then Jesus said to them, "Very truly, I tell you, it was not Moses who gave you the bread from heaven, but it is my Father who gives you the true bread from heaven. [33]For the bread of God is that which[a] comes down from heaven and gives life to the world." [34]They said to him, "Sir, give us this bread always."

[35] Jesus said to them, "I am the bread of life. Whoever comes to me will never be hungry, and whoever believes in me will never be thirsty. [36]But I said to you that you have seen me and yet do not believe. [37]Everything that the Father gives me will come to me, and anyone who comes to me I will never drive away; [38]for I have come down from heaven, not to do my own will, but the will of him who sent me. [39]And this is the will of him who sent me, that I should lose nothing of all that he has given me, but raise it up on the last day. [40]This is indeed the will of my Father, that all who see the Son and believe in him may have eternal life; and I will raise them up on the last day."

[41] Then the Jews began to complain about him because he said, "I am the bread that came down from heaven." [42]They were saying, "Is not this Jesus, the son of Joseph, whose father and mother we know? How can he now say, 'I have come down from heaven'?" [43]Jesus answered them, "Do not complain among yourselves. [44]No one can come to me unless drawn by the Father who sent me; and I will raise that person up on the last day. [45]It is written in the prophets, 'And they shall all be taught by God.' Everyone who has heard and learned from the Father comes to me. [46]Not that anyone has seen the Father except the one who is from God; he has seen the Father. [47]Very truly, I tell you, whoever believes has eternal life. [48]I am the bread of life. [49]Your ancestors ate the manna in the wilderness, and they died. [50]This is the bread that comes down from heaven, so that one may eat of it and not die. [51]I am the living bread that came down from heaven. Whoever eats of this bread will live forever; and the bread that I will give for the life of the world is my flesh."

[52] The Jews then disputed among themselves, saying, "How can this man give us his flesh to eat?" [53]So Jesus said to them, "Very truly, I tell you, unless you eat the flesh of the Son of Man and drink his blood, you have no life in you. [54]Those who eat my flesh and drink my blood have eternal life, and I will raise them up on the last day; [55]for my flesh is true food and my blood is true drink. [56]Those who eat my flesh and drink my blood abide in me, and I in them. [57]Just as the living Father sent me, and I live because of the Father, so whoever eats me will live because of me. [58]This is the bread that came down from heaven, not like that which your ancestors ate, and they died. But the one who eats this bread will live forever." [59]He said these things while he was teaching in the synagogue at Capernaum.

a Or *he who*

The Words of Eternal Life

60 When many of his disciples heard it, they said, "This teaching is difficult; who can accept it?" [61]But Jesus, being aware that his disciples were complaining about it, said to them, "Does this offend you? [62]Then what if you were to see the Son of Man ascending to where he was before? [63]It is the spirit that gives life; the flesh is useless. The words that I have spoken to you are spirit and life. [64]But among you there are some who do not believe." For Jesus knew from the first who were the ones that did not believe, and who was the one that would betray him. [65]And he said, "For this reason I have told you that no one can come to me unless it is granted by the Father."

66 Because of this many of his disciples turned back and no longer went about with him. [67]So Jesus asked the twelve, "Do you also wish to go away?" [68]Simon Peter answered him, "Lord, to whom can we go? You have the words of eternal life. [69]We have come to believe and know that you are the Holy One of God."[a] [70]Jesus answered them, "Did I not choose you, the twelve? Yet one of you is a devil." [71]He was speaking of Judas son of Simon Iscariot,[b] for he, though one of the twelve, was going to betray him.

The Unbelief of Jesus' Brothers

7 After this Jesus went about in Galilee. He did not wish[c] to go about in Judea because the Jews were looking for an opportunity to kill him. [2]Now the Jewish festival of Booths[d] was near. [3]So his brothers said to him, "Leave here and go to Judea so that your disciples also may see the works you are doing; [4]for no one who wants[e] to be widely known acts in secret. If you do these things, show yourself to the world." [5](For not even his brothers believed in him.) [6]Jesus said to them, "My time has not yet come, but your time is always here. [7]The world cannot hate you, but it hates me because I testify against it that its works are evil. [8]Go to the festival yourselves. I am not[f] going to this festival, for my time has not yet fully come." [9]After saying this, he remained in Galilee.

Jesus at the Festival of Booths

10 But after his brothers had gone to the festival, then he also went, not publicly but as it were[g] in secret. [11]The Jews were looking for him at the festival and saying, "Where is he?" [12]And there was considerable complaining about him among the crowds. While some were saying, "He is a good man," others were saying, "No, he is deceiving the crowd." [13]Yet no one would speak openly about him for fear of the Jews.

14 About the middle of the festival Jesus went up into the temple and began to teach. [15]The Jews were astonished at it, saying, "How does this man have such learning,[h] when he has never been taught?" [16]Then Jesus answered them, "My teaching is not mine but his who

"To Whom Can We Go?"

JOHN 6.66–69

Sometimes the things Jesus says are just too hard. Many of Jesus' disciples just can't accept his teaching—that he is "the bread of life" (see 6.35–58). They decide to leave. What is Jesus asking you to face that seems too hard for you right now? To whom will you go? Your friend? Your counselor? Your therapist? Your spiritual adviser? They will surely help. But who has the words of eternal life? When life is too hard, do you *really* believe in the Holy One of God? It may help to write your response. Go to Jesus and tell him about those things that seem too hard for you.

---

a Other ancient authorities read *the Christ, the Son of the living God*
b Other ancient authorities read *Judas Iscariot son of Simon;* others, *Judas son of Simon from Karyot* (Kerioth)   c Other ancient authorities read *was not at liberty*   d Or *Tabernacles*   e Other ancient authorities read *wants it*   f Other ancient authorities add *yet*   g Other ancient authorities lack *as it were*   h Or *this man know his letters*

Let the Waters Flow

JOHN 7.37–39

Jesus is the source of living water. And this water is to have many conduits—the hearts of believers. From the believer's heart will flow rivers of living water! Because it is sometimes hard to own the good that has happened through us, ask the Spirit to bring to mind people who have been refreshed by the living water of Jesus that has flowed from you. Give thanks for them. Pray that God will refresh them again today. Give thanks for the living water of Jesus.

See Meeting God in Prayer

sent me. [17]Anyone who resolves to do the will of God will know whether the teaching is from God or whether I am speaking on my own. [18]Those who speak on their own seek their own glory; but the one who seeks the glory of him who sent him is true, and there is nothing false in him.

19 "Did not Moses give you the law? Yet none of you keeps the law. Why are you looking for an opportunity to kill me?" [20]The crowd answered, "You have a demon! Who is trying to kill you?" [21]Jesus answered them, "I performed one work, and all of you are astonished. [22]Moses gave you circumcision (it is, of course, not from Moses, but from the patriarchs), and you circumcise a man on the sabbath. [23]If a man receives circumcision on the sabbath in order that the law of Moses may not be broken, are you angry with me because I healed a man's whole body on the sabbath? [24]Do not judge by appearances, but judge with right judgment."

Is This the Christ?

25 Now some of the people of Jerusalem were saying, "Is not this the man whom they are trying to kill? [26]And here he is, speaking openly, but they say nothing to him! Can it be that the authorities really know that this is the Messiah?[a] [27]Yet we know where this man is from; but when the Messiah[a] comes, no one will know where he is from." [28]Then Jesus cried out as he was teaching in the temple, "You know me, and you know where I am from. I have not come on my own. But the one who sent me is true, and you do not know him. [29]I know him, because I am from him, and he sent me." [30]Then they tried to arrest him, but no one laid hands on him, because his hour had not yet come. [31]Yet many in the crowd believed in him and were saying, "When the Messiah[a] comes, will he do more signs than this man has done?"[b]

Officers Are Sent to Arrest Jesus

32 The Pharisees heard the crowd muttering such things about him, and the chief priests and Pharisees sent temple police to arrest him. [33]Jesus then said, "I will be with you a little while longer, and then I am going to him who sent me. [34]You will search for me, but you will not find me; and where I am, you cannot come." [35]The Jews said to one another, "Where does this man intend to go that we will not find him? Does he intend to go to the Dispersion among the Greeks and teach the Greeks? [36]What does he mean by saying, 'You will search for me and you will not find me' and 'Where I am, you cannot come'?"

Rivers of Living Water

37 On the last day of the festival, the great day, while Jesus was standing there, he cried out, "Let anyone who is thirsty come to me, [38]and let the one who believes in me drink. As[c] the scripture has said, 'Out of the believer's heart[d] shall flow rivers of living water.' " [39]Now he said this

a Or *the Christ*   b Other ancient authorities read *is doing*   c Or *come to me and drink.* [38]*The one who believes in me, as*   d Gk *out of his belly* about the Spirit, which believers in him were to receive; for as yet there was no Spirit,*a* because Jesus was not yet glorified.

Division among the People

40 When they heard these words, some in the crowd said, "This is really the prophet." *41*Others said, "This is the Messiah."*b* But some asked, "Surely the Messiah*b* does not come from Galilee, does he? *42*Has not the scripture said that the Messiah*b* is descended from David and comes from Bethlehem, the village where David lived?" *43*So there was a division in the crowd because of him. *44*Some of them wanted to arrest him, but no one laid hands on him.

The Unbelief of Those in Authority

45 Then the temple police went back to the chief priests and Pharisees, who asked them, "Why did you not arrest him?" *46*The police answered, "Never has anyone spoken like this!" *47*Then the Pharisees replied, "Surely you have not been deceived too, have you? *48*Has any one of the authorities or of the Pharisees believed in him? *49*But this crowd, which does not know the law—they are accursed." *50*Nicodemus, who had gone to Jesus*c* before, and who was one of them, asked, *51*"Our law does not judge people without first giving them a hearing to find out what they are doing, does it?" *52*They replied, "Surely you are not also from Galilee, are you? Search and you will see that no prophet is to arise from Galilee."

The Woman Caught in Adultery

8 ⟦*53*Then each of them went home, *1*while Jesus went to the Mount of Olives. *2*Early in the morning he came again to the temple. All the people came to him and he sat down and began to teach them. *3*The scribes and the Pharisees brought a woman who had been caught in adultery; and making her stand before all of them, *4*they said to him, "Teacher, this woman was caught in the very act of committing adultery. *5*Now in the law Moses commanded us to stone such women. Now what do you say?" *6*They said this to test him, so that they might have some charge to bring against him. Jesus bent down and wrote with his finger on the ground. *7*When they kept on questioning him, he straightened up and said to them, "Let anyone among you who is without sin be the first to throw a stone at her." *8*And once again he bent down and wrote on the ground.*d* *9*When they heard it, they went away, one by one, beginning with the elders; and Jesus was left alone with the woman standing before him. *10*Jesus straightened up and said to her, "Woman, where are they? Has no one condemned you?" *11*She said, "No one, sir."*e* And Jesus said, "Neither do I condemn you. Go your way, and from now on do not sin again."⟧*f*

---

a Other ancient authorities read *for as yet the Spirit* (others, *Holy Spirit*) *had not been given*   *b* Or *the Christ*   *c* Gk *him*   *d* Other ancient authorities add *the sins of each of them*   *e* Or *Lord*   *f* The most ancient authorities lack 7.53—8.11; other authorities add the passage here or after 7.36 or after 21.25 or after Luke 21.38, with variations of text; some mark the passage as doubtful.

Standing in the Light of Life

JOHN 8.1–11

In this passage Jesus declares to a shamed woman that she is not condemned, and then he invites her to leave her life of sin and walk in the light.

Sometimes we too readily believe another's words of condemnation rather than seek the word of Jesus. Jesus invites us to come out of the darkness and death of condemnation and into the light of life. Stand in sunlight or lamplight. Open yourself to Jesus as the light of the world. Welcome his light into your soul and ask Jesus to stand in that place with you. Let him transform the darkness in you into light.

See Meeting God in the Created Order

What Makes You, You?

JOHN 8.31–33

Jesus is challenging a group of people whose identity is firmly entrenched in their religious culture. The Pharisees are proudly saying, "We are descendants of Abraham," as if that is all that is needed to be right with God.

Jesus calls us into the identity of being his disciples—into a truth that will set us free. What gives you your identity? A birth certificate or a passport? Your income or your education? A neighborhood or a relationship? Make a list of several aspects of your life that form the basis of your identity. Write the name of Jesus beside each one. Pray over each item on your list and ask that your allegiance to Jesus be the foundation of each aspect of your life.

Jesus the Light of the World

12 Again Jesus spoke to them, saying, "I am the light of the world. Whoever follows me will never walk in darkness but will have the light of life." [13]Then the Pharisees said to him, "You are testifying on your own behalf; your testimony is not valid." [14]Jesus answered, "Even if I testify on my own behalf, my testimony is valid because I know where I have come from and where I am going, but you do not know where I come from or where I am going. [15]You judge by human standards;[a] I judge no one. [16]Yet even if I do judge, my judgment is valid; for it is not I alone who judge, but I and the Father[b] who sent me. [17]In your law it is written that the testimony of two witnesses is valid. [18]I testify on my own behalf, and the Father who sent me testifies on my behalf." [19]Then they said to him, "Where is your Father?" Jesus answered, "You know neither me nor my Father. If you knew me, you would know my Father also." [20]He spoke these words while he was teaching in the treasury of the temple, but no one arrested him, because his hour had not yet come.

Jesus Foretells His Death

21 Again he said to them, "I am going away, and you will search for me, but you will die in your sin. Where I am going, you cannot come." [22]Then the Jews said, "Is he going to kill himself? Is that what he means by saying, 'Where I am going, you cannot come'?" [23]He said to them, "You are from below, I am from above; you are of this world, I am not of this world. [24]I told you that you would die in your sins, for you will die in your sins unless you believe that I am he."[c] [25]They said to him, "Who are you?" Jesus said to them, "Why do I speak to you at all?[d] [26]I have much to say about you and much to condemn; but the one who sent me is true, and I declare to the world what I have heard from him." [27]They did not understand that he was speaking to them about the Father. [28]So Jesus said, "When you have lifted up the Son of Man, then you will realize that I am he,[c] and that I do nothing on my own, but I speak these things as the Father instructed me. [29]And the one who sent me is with me; he has not left me alone, for I always do what is pleasing to him." [30]As he was saying these things, many believed in him.

True Disciples

31 Then Jesus said to the Jews who had believed in him, "If you continue in my word, you are truly my disciples; [32]and you will know the truth, and the truth will make you free." [33]They answered him, "We are descendants of Abraham and have never been slaves to anyone. What do you mean by saying, 'You will be made free'?"

34 Jesus answered them, "Very truly, I tell you, everyone who commits sin is a slave to sin. [35]The slave does not have a permanent place in the household; the son has a place there forever. [36]So if the Son makes you free, you will be free indeed. [37]I know that you are descendants of Abraham; yet you look for an opportunity to kill me, because there is no place in you for my word. [38]I declare what I

a Gk according to the flesh   b Other ancient authorities read he   c Gk I am   d Or What I have told you from the beginning have seen in the Father's presence; as for you, you should do what you have heard from the Father."[a]

Jesus and Abraham

39 They answered him, "Abraham is our father." Jesus said to them, "If you were Abraham's children, you would be doing[b] what Abraham did, [40]but now you are trying to kill me, a man who has told you the truth that I heard from God. This is not what Abraham did. [41]You are indeed doing what your father does." They said to him, "We are not illegitimate children; we have one father, God himself." [42]Jesus said to them, "If God were your Father, you would love me, for I came from God and now I am here. I did not come on my own, but he sent me. [43]Why do you not understand what I say? It is because you cannot accept my word. [44]You are from your father the devil, and you choose to do your father's desires. He was a murderer from the beginning and does not stand in the truth, because there is no truth in him. When he lies, he speaks according to his own nature, for he is a liar and the father of lies. [45]But because I tell the truth, you do not believe me. [46]Which of you convicts me of sin? If I tell the truth, why do you not believe me? [47]Whoever is from God hears the words of God. The reason you do not hear them is that you are not from God."

48 The Jews answered him, "Are we not right in saying that you are a Samaritan and have a demon?" [49]Jesus answered, "I do not have a demon; but I honor my Father, and you dishonor me. [50]Yet I do not seek my own glory; there is one who seeks it and he is the judge. [51]Very truly, I tell you, whoever keeps my word will never see death." [52]The Jews said to him, "Now we know that you have a demon. Abraham died, and so did the prophets; yet you say, 'Whoever keeps my word will never taste death.' [53]Are you greater than our father Abraham, who died? The prophets also died. Who do you claim to be?" [54]Jesus answered, "If I glorify myself, my glory is nothing. It is my Father who glorifies me, he of whom you say, 'He is our God,' [55]though you do not know him. But I know him; if I would say that I do not know him, I would be a liar like you. But I do know him and I keep his word. [56]Your ancestor Abraham rejoiced that he would see my day; he saw it and was glad." [57]Then the Jews said to him, "You are not yet fifty years old, and have you seen Abraham?"[c] [58]Jesus said to them, "Very truly, I tell you, before Abraham was, I am." [59]So they picked up stones to throw at him, but Jesus hid himself and went out of the temple.

A Man Born Blind Receives Sight

9 As he walked along, he saw a man blind from birth. [2]His disciples asked him, "Rabbi, who sinned, this man or his parents, that he was born blind?" [3]Jesus answered, "Neither this man nor his parents sinned; he was born blind so that God's works might be revealed in him. [4]We[d] must work the works of him who sent me[e] while it is day; night is coming when no one can work. [5]As long as I

---

a Other ancient authorities read *you do what you have heard from your father*   b Other ancient authorities read *If you are Abraham's children, then do*   c Other ancient authorities read *has Abraham seen you?*
d Other ancient authorities read *I*   e Other ancient authorities read *us*

Owning the Action of Jesus

JOHN 9.1–11,20–22

The Pharisees are hostile to Jesus and what he is doing. As a result, the parents of the blind man are fearful. We would expect them to be thankfully proclaiming that their son can see for the first time! They are afraid to speak up and testify to the power and goodness of the man who performed the miracle.

How free are you to speak of what Jesus has done for you? Whatever your situation, how can you let your gratitude to Jesus be as full as it needs to be? Name any hostile people or forces that you are encountering when you share your faith and bring them into the light of Jesus' redeeming power.

"Though I Was Blind, Now I See!"

JOHN 9.25

Fill a bowl with water. As you sit in a comfortable position, focus your attention on Jesus. Ask him to cover you and fill you with healing light. Ask him to show you some part of your life to which you are blind—perhaps a responsibility you don't see or an attitude that blinds you to the truth of a situation. Ask Jesus to enable you to see what he wants you to see. Wash your eyes with the water, praying that you may see with the eyes of Jesus. Ask Jesus to empower you to take whatever action your renewed spiritual sight requires.

See Meeting God in Prayer

am in the world, I am the light of the world." ⁶When he had said this, he spat on the ground and made mud with the saliva and spread the mud on the man's eyes, ⁷saying to him, "Go, wash in the pool of Siloam" (which means Sent). Then he went and washed and came back able to see. ⁸The neighbors and those who had seen him before as a beggar began to ask, "Is this not the man who used to sit and beg?" ⁹Some were saying, "It is he." Others were saying, "No, but it is someone like him." He kept saying, "I am the man." ¹⁰But they kept asking him, "Then how were your eyes opened?" ¹¹He answered, "The man called Jesus made mud, spread it on my eyes, and said to me, 'Go to Siloam and wash.' Then I went and washed and received my sight." ¹²They said to him, "Where is he?" He said, "I do not know."

The Pharisees Investigate the Healing

13 They brought to the Pharisees the man who had formerly been blind. ¹⁴Now it was a sabbath day when Jesus made the mud and opened his eyes. ¹⁵Then the Pharisees also began to ask him how he had received his sight. He said to them, "He put mud on my eyes. Then I washed, and now I see." ¹⁶Some of the Pharisees said, "This man is not from God, for he does not observe the sabbath." But others said, "How can a man who is a sinner perform such signs?" And they were divided. ¹⁷So they said again to the blind man, "What do you say about him? It was your eyes he opened." He said, "He is a prophet."

18 The Jews did not believe that he had been blind and had received his sight until they called the parents of the man who had received his sight ¹⁹and asked them, "Is this your son, who you say was born blind? How then does he now see?" ²⁰His parents answered, "We know that this is our son, and that he was born blind; ²¹but we do not know how it is that now he sees, nor do we know who opened his eyes. Ask him; he is of age. He will speak for himself." ²²His parents said this because they were afraid of the Jews; for the Jews had already agreed that anyone who confessed Jesus[a] to be the Messiah[b] would be put out of the synagogue. ²³Therefore his parents said, "He is of age; ask him."

24 So for the second time they called the man who had been blind, and they said to him, "Give glory to God! We know that this man is a sinner." ²⁵He answered, "I do not know whether he is a sinner. One thing I do know, that though I was blind, now I see." ²⁶They said to him, "What did he do to you? How did he open your eyes?" ²⁷He answered them, "I have told you already, and you would not listen. Why do you want to hear it again? Do you also want to become his disciples?" ²⁸Then they reviled him, saying, "You are his disciple, but we are disciples of Moses. ²⁹We know that God has spoken to Moses, but as for this man, we do not know where he comes from." ³⁰The man answered, "Here is an astonishing thing! You do not know where he comes from, and yet he opened my eyes. ³¹We know that God does not listen to sinners, but he does listen to one who worships him and obeys his will. ³²Never since the world began has it been heard that anyone

a Gk *him*   *b* Or *the Christ*

opened the eyes of a person born blind. ³³If this man were not from God, he could do nothing." ³⁴They answered him, "You were born entirely in sins, and are you trying to teach us?" And they drove him out.

Spiritual Blindness

35 Jesus heard that they had driven him out, and when he found him, he said, "Do you believe in the Son of Man?"ᵃ ³⁶He answered, "And who is he, sir?ᵇ Tell me, so that I may believe in him." ³⁷Jesus said to him, "You have seen him, and the one speaking with you is he." ³⁸He said, "Lord,ᵇ I believe." And he worshiped him. ³⁹Jesus said, "I came into this world for judgment so that those who do not see may see, and those who do see may become blind." ⁴⁰Some of the Pharisees near him heard this and said to him, "Surely we are not blind, are we?" ⁴¹Jesus said to them, "If you were blind, you would not have sin. But now that you say, 'We see,' your sin remains.

Jesus the Good Shepherd

10 "Very truly, I tell you, anyone who does not enter the sheepfold by the gate but climbs in by another way is a thief and a bandit. ²The one who enters by the gate is the shepherd of the sheep. ³The gatekeeper opens the gate for him, and the sheep hear his voice. He calls his own sheep by name and leads them out. ⁴When he has brought out all his own, he goes ahead of them, and the sheep follow him because they know his voice. ⁵They will not follow a stranger, but they will run from him because they do not know the voice of strangers." ⁶Jesus used this figure of speech with them, but they did not understand what he was saying to them.

7 So again Jesus said to them, "Very truly, I tell you, I am the gate for the sheep. ⁸All who came before me are thieves and bandits; but the sheep did not listen to them. ⁹I am the gate. Whoever enters by me will be saved, and will come in and go out and find pasture. ¹⁰The thief comes only to steal and kill and destroy. I came that they may have life, and have it abundantly.

11 "I am the good shepherd. The good shepherd lays down his life for the sheep. ¹²The hired hand, who is not the shepherd and does not own the sheep, sees the wolf coming and leaves the sheep and runs away—and the wolf snatches them and scatters them. ¹³The hired hand runs away because a hired hand does not care for the sheep. ¹⁴I am the good shepherd. I know my own and my own know me, ¹⁵just as the Father knows me and I know the Father. And I lay down my life for the sheep. ¹⁶I have other sheep that do not belong to this fold. I must bring them also, and they will listen to my voice. So there will be one flock, one shepherd. ¹⁷For this reason the Father loves me, because I lay down my life in order to take it up again. ¹⁸No one takesᶜ it from me, but I lay it down of my own accord. I have power to lay it down, and I have power to take it up again. I have received this command from my Father."

a Other ancient authorities read *the Son of God*   b *Sir* and *Lord* translate the same Greek word   c Other ancient authorities read *has taken*

The Good Shepherd

JOHN 10.11–18

Jesus is the Good Shepherd. The shepherd cares for you. He knows your name. He will protect you and guard you from those who want to destroy you. And he knows the path that lies ahead of you.

What is ahead of you right now? With crayon or paint, draw or paint a picture of it. Are you walking into green pastures or dark valleys? Draw Jesus in your picture. Think about the implications of Jesus' presence. Envisioning Jesus ahead of you as you walk, pray about what is happening to you.

See *Meeting God in Everyday Life*

Those Who Hear

JOHN 10.22–30

"Whatever we now strive for, or are justly eager for, or blamelessly desire, when we come to the vision of God, we shall require no more . . . . An impure heart cannot see that which is seen only by the pure in heart. You will be repelled, driven back from it, and will not see it."

—AUGUSTINE,
"Purity of Heart"

---

19 Again the Jews were divided because of these words. ²⁰Many of them were saying, "He has a demon and is out of his mind. Why listen to him?" ²¹Others were saying, "These are not the words of one who has a demon. Can a demon open the eyes of the blind?"

Jesus Is Rejected by the Jews

22 At that time the festival of the Dedication took place in Jerusalem. It was winter, ²³and Jesus was walking in the temple, in the portico of Solomon. ²⁴So the Jews gathered around him and said to him, "How long will you keep us in suspense? If you are the Messiah,ᵃ tell us plainly." ²⁵Jesus answered, "I have told you, and you do not believe. The works that I do in my Father's name testify to me; ²⁶but you do not believe, because you do not belong to my sheep. ²⁷My sheep hear my voice. I know them, and they follow me. ²⁸I give them eternal life, and they will never perish. No one will snatch them out of my hand. ²⁹What my Father has given me is greater than all else, and no one can snatch it out of the Father's hand.ᵇ ³⁰The Father and I are one."

31 The Jews took up stones again to stone him. ³²Jesus replied, "I have shown you many good works from the Father. For which of these are you going to stone me?" ³³The Jews answered, "It is not for a good work that we are going to stone you, but for blasphemy, because you, though only a human being, are making yourself God." ³⁴Jesus answered, "Is it not written in your law,ᶜ 'I said, you are gods'? ³⁵If those to whom the word of God came were called 'gods'—and the scripture cannot be annulled—³⁶can you say that the one whom the Father has sanctified and sent into the world is blaspheming because I said, 'I am God's Son'? ³⁷If I am not doing the works of my Father, then do not believe me. ³⁸But if I do them, even though you do not believe me, believe the works, so that you may know and understandᵈ that the Father is in me and I am in the Father." ³⁹Then they tried to arrest him again, but he escaped from their hands.

40 He went away again across the Jordan to the place where John had been baptizing earlier, and he remained there. ⁴¹Many came to him, and they were saying, "John performed no sign, but everything that John said about this man was true." ⁴²And many believed in him there.

The Death of Lazarus

11 Now a certain man was ill, Lazarus of Bethany, the village of Mary and her sister Martha. ²Mary was the one who anointed the Lord with perfume and wiped his feet with her hair; her brother Lazarus was ill. ³So the sisters sent a message to Jesus,ᵉ "Lord, he whom you love is ill." ⁴But when Jesus heard it, he said, "This illness does not lead to death; rather it is for God's glory, so that the Son of God may be glorified through it." ⁵Accordingly, though Jesus loved Martha and her sister and Lazarus,

---

a Or the Christ   b Other ancient authorities read My Father who has given them to me is greater than all, and no one can snatch them out of the Father's hand   c Other ancient authorities read in the law   d Other ancient authorities lack and understand; others read and believe   e Gk him

⁶after having heard that Lazarus*a* was ill, he stayed two days longer in the place where he was.

7 Then after this he said to the disciples, "Let us go to Judea again." ⁸The disciples said to him, "Rabbi, the Jews were just now trying to stone you, and are you going there again?" ⁹Jesus answered, "Are there not twelve hours of daylight? Those who walk during the day do not stumble, because they see the light of this world. ¹⁰But those who walk at night stumble, because the light is not in them." ¹¹After saying this, he told them, "Our friend Lazarus has fallen asleep, but I am going there to awaken him." ¹²The disciples said to him, "Lord, if he has fallen asleep, he will be all right." ¹³Jesus, however, had been speaking about his death, but they thought that he was referring merely to sleep. ¹⁴Then Jesus told them plainly, "Lazarus is dead. ¹⁵For your sake I am glad I was not there, so that you may believe. But let us go to him." ¹⁶Thomas, who was called the Twin,*b* said to his fellow disciples, "Let us also go, that we may die with him."

Jesus the Resurrection and the Life

17 When Jesus arrived, he found that Lazarus*a* had already been in the tomb four days. ¹⁸Now Bethany was near Jerusalem, some two miles*c* away, ¹⁹and many of the Jews had come to Martha and Mary to console them about their brother. ²⁰When Martha heard that Jesus was coming, she went and met him, while Mary stayed at home. ²¹Martha said to Jesus, "Lord, if you had been here, my brother would not have died. ²²But even now I know that God will give you whatever you ask of him." ²³Jesus said to her, "Your brother will rise again." ²⁴Martha said to him, "I know that he will rise again in the resurrection on the last day." ²⁵Jesus said to her, "I am the resurrection and the life.*d* Those who believe in me, even though they die, will live, ²⁶and everyone who lives and believes in me will never die. Do you believe this?" ²⁷She said to him, "Yes, Lord, I believe that you are the Messiah,*e* the Son of God, the one coming into the world."

Jesus Weeps

28 When she had said this, she went back and called her sister Mary, and told her privately, "The Teacher is here and is calling for you." ²⁹And when she heard it, she got up quickly and went to him. ³⁰Now Jesus had not yet come to the village, but was still at the place where Martha had met him. ³¹The Jews who were with her in the house, consoling her, saw Mary get up quickly and go out. They followed her because they thought that she was going to the tomb to weep there. ³²When Mary came where Jesus was and saw him, she knelt at his feet and said to him, "Lord, if you had been here, my brother would not have died." ³³When Jesus saw her weeping, and the Jews who came with her also weeping, he was greatly disturbed in spirit and deeply moved. ³⁴He said, "Where have you laid him?" They said to him, "Lord, come and see." ³⁵Jesus began to weep. ³⁶So the Jews said, "See how he loved him!" ³⁷But

Resurrection and Life

JOHN 11.21–26

Jesus is "the resurrection and the life." Is your perception of the future determined by the certainty of your death or by your faith in Jesus? Is your life determined by the ability to make life "happen" or by the power of Jesus' presence within you to give you life? Find a quiet place and a quiet moment. Quiet your body and slowly breathe the life of Jesus' presence in. Hold your breath and let your mind and heart say, "Jesus, my life!" Slowly breathe "death" out. Hold your breath and let your mind and heart say, "Jesus, my resurrection!" Repeat these phrases a few times. Let Jesus speak of resurrection and life to you.

See *Meeting God in Scripture*

a Gk *he* *b* Gk *Didymus* *c* Gk *fifteen stadia* *d* Other ancient authorities lack *and the life* *e* Or *the Christ*

Jesus Wept Too

JOHN 11.32-37

Jesus wept too. The Word made flesh knows the pain and the loss that death causes us. He does not minimize our feelings. He knows about our grief and is with us in the midst of it. Through today's newspaper, radio or television broadcast, or personal contact, learn about a situation that is likely to be causing grief to someone. Imagine yourself in that person's place. Grieve alongside him or her. Share that grief with Jesus. With the wings of imagination, go into that situation with Jesus, inviting him to "come and see" (v.34). Ask him to bring his resurrection life and light to the ones who are grieving. Just as Mary and Martha trusted him to know what to do, you trust him too.

See *Meeting God in Everyday Life*

some of them said, "Could not he who opened the eyes of the blind man have kept this man from dying?"

Jesus Raises Lazarus to Life

38 Then Jesus, again greatly disturbed, came to the tomb. It was a cave, and a stone was lying against it. [39]Jesus said, "Take away the stone." Martha, the sister of the dead man, said to him, "Lord, already there is a stench because he has been dead four days." [40]Jesus said to her, "Did I not tell you that if you believed, you would see the glory of God?" [41]So they took away the stone. And Jesus looked upward and said, "Father, I thank you for having heard me. [42]I knew that you always hear me, but I have said this for the sake of the crowd standing here, so that they may believe that you sent me." [43]When he had said this, he cried with a loud voice, "Lazarus, come out!" [44]The dead man came out, his hands and feet bound with strips of cloth, and his face wrapped in a cloth. Jesus said to them, "Unbind him, and let him go."

The Plot to Kill Jesus

45 Many of the Jews therefore, who had come with Mary and had seen what Jesus did, believed in him. [46]But some of them went to the Pharisees and told them what he had done. [47]So the chief priests and the Pharisees called a meeting of the council, and said, "What are we to do? This man is performing many signs. [48]If we let him go on like this, everyone will believe in him, and the Romans will come and destroy both our holy place[a] and our nation." [49]But one of them, Caiaphas, who was high priest that year, said to them, "You know nothing at all! [50]You do not understand that it is better for you to have one man die for the people than to have the whole nation destroyed." [51]He did not say this on his own, but being high priest that year he prophesied that Jesus was about to die for the nation, [52]and not for the nation only, but to gather into one the dispersed children of God. [53]So from that day on they planned to put him to death.

54 Jesus therefore no longer walked about openly among the Jews, but went from there to a town called Ephraim in the region near the wilderness; and he remained there with the disciples.

55 Now the Passover of the Jews was near, and many went up from the country to Jerusalem before the Passover to purify themselves. [56]They were looking for Jesus and were asking one another as they stood in the temple, "What do you think? Surely he will not come to the festival, will he?" [57]Now the chief priests and the Pharisees had given orders that anyone who knew where Jesus[b] was should let them know, so that they might arrest him.

Mary Anoints Jesus

12 Six days before the Passover Jesus came to Bethany, the home of Lazarus, whom he had raised from the dead. [2]There they gave a dinner for him. Martha served, and Lazarus was one of those at the table with him. [3]Mary took a pound of costly perfume made of pure

a Or *our temple*; Greek *our place*   *b* Gk *he*

nard, anointed Jesus' feet, and wiped them[a] with her hair. The house was filled with the fragrance of the perfume. [4]But Judas Iscariot, one of his disciples (the one who was about to betray him), said, [5]"Why was this perfume not sold for three hundred denarii[b] and the money given to the poor?" [6](He said this not because he cared about the poor, but because he was a thief; he kept the common purse and used to steal what was put into it.) [7]Jesus said, "Leave her alone. She bought it[c] so that she might keep it for the day of my burial. [8]You always have the poor with you, but you do not always have me."

The Plot to Kill Lazarus

9 When the great crowd of the Jews learned that he was there, they came not only because of Jesus but also to see Lazarus, whom he had raised from the dead. [10]So the chief priests planned to put Lazarus to death as well, [11]since it was on account of him that many of the Jews were deserting and were believing in Jesus.

Jesus' Triumphal Entry into Jerusalem

12 The next day the great crowd that had come to the festival heard that Jesus was coming to Jerusalem. [13]So they took branches of palm trees and went out to meet him, shouting,

"Hosanna!
  Blessed is the one who comes in the name of the
    Lord—
      the King of Israel!"

[14]Jesus found a young donkey and sat on it; as it is written:
[15] "Do not be afraid, daughter of Zion.
  Look, your king is coming,
    sitting on a donkey's colt!"

[16]His disciples did not understand these things at first; but when Jesus was glorified, then they remembered that these things had been written of him and had been done to him. [17]So the crowd that had been with him when he called Lazarus out of the tomb and raised him from the dead continued to testify.[d] [18]It was also because they heard that he had performed this sign that the crowd went to meet him. [19]The Pharisees then said to one another, "You see, you can do nothing. Look, the world has gone after him!"

Some Greeks Wish to See Jesus

20 Now among those who went up to worship at the festival were some Greeks. [21]They came to Philip, who was from Bethsaida in Galilee, and said to him, "Sir, we wish to see Jesus." [22]Philip went and told Andrew; then Andrew and Philip went and told Jesus. [23]Jesus answered them, "The hour has come for the Son of Man to be glorified. [24]Very truly, I tell you, unless a grain of wheat falls into the earth and dies, it remains just a single grain; but if it dies, it bears much fruit. [25]Those who love their life lose it, and those who hate their life in this world will keep it for eternal life. [26]Whoever serves me must follow me, and where

Pouring Out Love

JOHN 12.1–8

Mary anoints Jesus in a grand and extravagant gesture of uninhibited love. Though others criticize her, Jesus accepts her gift and affirms her faith and love. She anoints him with nard, a fragrant ointment, in symbolic preparation for his death—his own gesture of love, a gesture so vast that it will have cosmic repercussions: The Son of God will pour out his life for the forgiveness of sins. What unexpected and extravagant act of love can you perform today? How can you be a gift to others? What can you do that will be a reflection of the love of Jesus?

See Meeting God in Service

---

a Gk *his feet*   b Three hundred denarii would be nearly a year's wages for a laborer   c Gk lacks *She bought it*   d Other ancient authorities read *with him began to testify that he had called . . . from the dead*

That Jesus May Be Seen

JOHN 12.20–32

The Greeks come from a culture with a vast tradition of learning, philosophy and culture. Yet they come to see Jesus because they have needs.

In our own day we have an explosion of information available, but we are also more aware than ever that human need abounds. What human needs seem most urgent in our own day? Take a relaxed position. Breathe in and let your body and mind grow quiet. Imagine you are a sponge, soaking up the life of Jesus into every part of your being. Then pray that Jesus will be "lifted up" and so visible in you that others will desire to know him for themselves and will go to him to have their needs met.

See *Meeting God in Service*

I am, there will my servant be also. Whoever serves me, the Father will honor.

Jesus Speaks about His Death

27 "Now my soul is troubled. And what should I say—'Father, save me from this hour'? No, it is for this reason that I have come to this hour. ²⁸Father, glorify your name." Then a voice came from heaven, "I have glorified it, and I will glorify it again." ²⁹The crowd standing there heard it and said that it was thunder. Others said, "An angel has spoken to him." ³⁰Jesus answered, "This voice has come for your sake, not for mine. ³¹Now is the judgment of this world; now the ruler of this world will be driven out. ³²And I, when I am lifted up from the earth, will draw all people[a] to myself." ³³He said this to indicate the kind of death he was to die. ³⁴The crowd answered him, "We have heard from the law that the Messiah[b] remains forever. How can you say that the Son of Man must be lifted up? Who is this Son of Man?" ³⁵Jesus said to them, "The light is with you for a little longer. Walk while you have the light, so that the darkness may not overtake you. If you walk in the darkness, you do not know where you are going. ³⁶While you have the light, believe in the light, so that you may become children of light."

The Unbelief of the People

After Jesus had said this, he departed and hid from them. ³⁷Although he had performed so many signs in their presence, they did not believe in him. ³⁸This was to fulfill the word spoken by the prophet Isaiah:

"Lord, who has believed our message,
   and to whom has the arm of the Lord been
      revealed?"

³⁹And so they could not believe, because Isaiah also said,
40   "He has blinded their eyes
      and hardened their heart,
   so that they might not look with their eyes,
      and understand with their heart and turn—
      and I would heal them."

⁴¹Isaiah said this because[c] he saw his glory and spoke about him. ⁴²Nevertheless many, even of the authorities, believed in him. But because of the Pharisees they did not confess it, for fear that they would be put out of the synagogue; ⁴³for they loved human glory more than the glory that comes from God.

Summary of Jesus' Teaching

44 Then Jesus cried aloud: "Whoever believes in me believes not in me but in him who sent me. ⁴⁵And whoever sees me sees him who sent me. ⁴⁶I have come as light into the world, so that everyone who believes in me should not remain in the darkness. ⁴⁷I do not judge anyone who hears my words and does not keep them, for I came not to judge the world, but to save the world. ⁴⁸The one who rejects me and does not receive my word has a judge; on the last day the word that I have spoken will serve as judge, ⁴⁹for I have not spoken on my own, but the Father who sent me has

a Other ancient authorities read *all things*   *b* Or *the Christ*   *c* Other ancient witnesses read *when*

himself given me a commandment about what to say and what to speak. ⁵⁰And I know that his commandment is eternal life. What I speak, therefore, I speak just as the Father has told me."

Jesus Washes the Disciples' Feet

13 Now before the festival of the Passover, Jesus knew that his hour had come to depart from this world and go to the Father. Having loved his own who were in the world, he loved them to the end. ²The devil had already put it into the heart of Judas son of Simon Iscariot to betray him. And during supper ³Jesus, knowing that the Father had given all things into his hands, and that he had come from God and was going to God, ⁴got up from the table,ᵃ took off his outer robe, and tied a towel around himself. ⁵Then he poured water into a basin and began to wash the disciples' feet and to wipe them with the towel that was tied around him. ⁶He came to Simon Peter, who said to him, "Lord, are you going to wash my feet?" ⁷Jesus answered, "You do not know now what I am doing, but later you will understand." ⁸Peter said to him, "You will never wash my feet." Jesus answered, "Unless I wash you, you have no share with me." ⁹Simon Peter said to him, "Lord, not my feet only but also my hands and my head!" ¹⁰Jesus said to him, "One who has bathed does not need to wash, except for the feet,ᵇ but is entirely clean. And youᶜ are clean, though not all of you." ¹¹For he knew who was to betray him; for this reason he said, "Not all of you are clean."

12 After he had washed their feet, had put on his robe, and had returned to the table, he said to them, "Do you know what I have done to you? ¹³You call me Teacher and Lord—and you are right, for that is what I am. ¹⁴So if I, your Lord and Teacher, have washed your feet, you also ought to wash one another's feet. ¹⁵For I have set you an example, that you also should do as I have done to you. ¹⁶Very truly, I tell you, servantsᵈ are not greater than their master, nor are messengers greater than the one who sent them. ¹⁷If you know these things, you are blessed if you do them. ¹⁸I am not speaking of all of you; I know whom I have chosen. But it is to fulfill the scripture, 'The one who ate my breadᵉ has lifted his heel against me.' ¹⁹I tell you this now, before it occurs, so that when it does occur, you may believe that I am he.ᶠ ²⁰Very truly, I tell you, whoever receives one whom I send receives me; and whoever receives me receives him who sent me."

Jesus Foretells His Betrayal

21 After saying this Jesus was troubled in spirit, and declared, "Very truly, I tell you, one of you will betray me." ²²The disciples looked at one another, uncertain of whom he was speaking. ²³One of his disciples—the one whom Jesus loved—was reclining next to him; ²⁴Simon Peter therefore motioned to him to ask Jesus of whom he was speaking. ²⁵So while reclining next to Jesus, he asked him, "Lord, who is it?" ²⁶Jesus answered, "It is the one to whom

---

Receiving and Giving

JOHN 13.1–20

Like Peter we may resist being served. When someone serves us we feel vulnerable and out of control. Despite our self-sufficiency and our need for control, Jesus wants to serve us—not just in order to benefit us, but also to show us how to serve others. Can you name something Jesus has done for you? Write about it or paint a representation of it. Discover the safety, love and grace within Jesus' service. Go and perform an act of loving service for another person. Celebrate the fact that when someone receives your service, Jesus is received also.

See Meeting God in the Created Order

---

a Gk *from supper*   b Other ancient authorities lack *except for the feet*
c The Greek word for *you* here is plural   d Gk *slaves*   e Other ancient
authorities read *ate bread with me*   f Gk *I am*

Love in Action

JOHN 13.34

"God also showed me that any 'love' for him meant *nothing* unless I was truly able to love from my heart my brother or sister in Christ. As the Lord put various names into my mind I began to write letters to about twelve people asking for forgiveness for hurting them, for still being inwardly angry against them—or whatever. It was the most painful pruning and purging I can remember in my entire Christian life. But fruitful! Already some replies to my letters have reduced me to tears!"

—DAVID WATSON,
Fear No Evil

I give this piece of bread when I have dipped it in the dish."*a* So when he had dipped the piece of bread, he gave it to Judas son of Simon Iscariot.*b* ²⁷After he received the piece of bread,*c* Satan entered into him. Jesus said to him, "Do quickly what you are going to do." ²⁸Now no one at the table knew why he said this to him. ²⁹Some thought that, because Judas had the common purse, Jesus was telling him, "Buy what we need for the festival"; or, that he should give something to the poor. ³⁰So, after receiving the piece of bread, he immediately went out. And it was night.

The New Commandment

31 When he had gone out, Jesus said, "Now the Son of Man has been glorified, and God has been glorified in him. ³²If God has been glorified in him,*d* God will also glorify him in himself and will glorify him at once. ³³Little children, I am with you only a little longer. You will look for me; and as I said to the Jews so now I say to you, 'Where I am going, you cannot come.' ³⁴I give you a new commandment, that you love one another. Just as I have loved you, you also should love one another. ³⁵By this everyone will know that you are my disciples, if you have love for one another."

Jesus Foretells Peter's Denial

36 Simon Peter said to him, "Lord, where are you going?" Jesus answered, "Where I am going, you cannot follow me now; but you will follow afterward." ³⁷Peter said to him, "Lord, why can I not follow you now? I will lay down my life for you." ³⁸Jesus answered, "Will you lay down your life for me? Very truly, I tell you, before the cock crows, you will have denied me three times.

Jesus the Way to the Father

14 "Do not let your hearts be troubled. Believe*e* in God, believe also in me. ²In my Father's house there are many dwelling places. If it were not so, would I have told you that I go to prepare a place for you?*f* ³And if I go and prepare a place for you, I will come again and will take you to myself, so that where I am, there you may be also. ⁴And you know the way to the place where I am going."*g* ⁵Thomas said to him, "Lord, we do not know where you are going. How can we know the way?" ⁶Jesus said to him, "I am the way, and the truth, and the life. No one comes to the Father except through me. ⁷If you know me, you will know*h* my Father also. From now on you do know him and have seen him."

8 Philip said to him, "Lord, show us the Father, and we will be satisfied." ⁹Jesus said to him, "Have I been with you all this time, Philip, and you still do not know me? Whoever has seen me has seen the Father. How can you say, 'Show us the Father'? ¹⁰Do you not believe that I am in the Father and the Father is in me? The words that I say to

a Gk *dipped it* *b* Other ancient authorities read *Judas Iscariot son of Simon*; others, *Judas son of Simon from Karyot* (Kerioth) *c* Gk *After the piece of bread* *d* Other ancient authorities lack *If God has been glorified in him* *e* Or *You believe* *f* Or *If it were not so, I would have told you; for I go to prepare a place for you* *g* Other ancient authorities read *Where I am going you know, and the way you know* *h* Other ancient authorities read *If you had known me, you would have known*

you I do not speak on my own; but the Father who dwells in me does his works. ¹¹Believe me that I am in the Father and the Father is in me; but if you do not, then believe me because of the works themselves. ¹²Very truly, I tell you, the one who believes in me will also do the works that I do and, in fact, will do greater works than these, because I am going to the Father. ¹³I will do whatever you ask in my name, so that the Father may be glorified in the Son. ¹⁴If in my name you ask me*ᵃ* for anything, I will do it.

The Promise of the Holy Spirit

15 "If you love me, you will keep*ᵇ* my commandments. ¹⁶And I will ask the Father, and he will give you another Advocate,*ᶜ* to be with you forever. ¹⁷This is the Spirit of truth, whom the world cannot receive, because it neither sees him nor knows him. You know him, because he abides with you, and he will be in*ᵈ* you.

18 "I will not leave you orphaned; I am coming to you. ¹⁹In a little while the world will no longer see me, but you will see me; because I live, you also will live. ²⁰On that day you will know that I am in my Father, and you in me, and I in you. ²¹They who have my commandments and keep them are those who love me; and those who love me will be loved by my Father, and I will love them and reveal myself to them." ²²Judas (not Iscariot) said to him, "Lord, how is it that you will reveal yourself to us, and not to the world?" ²³Jesus answered him, "Those who love me will keep my word, and my Father will love them, and we will come to them and make our home with them. ²⁴Whoever does not love me does not keep my words; and the word that you hear is not mine, but is from the Father who sent me.

25 "I have said these things to you while I am still with you. ²⁶But the Advocate,*ᶜ* the Holy Spirit, whom the Father will send in my name, will teach you everything, and remind you of all that I have said to you. ²⁷Peace I leave with you; my peace I give to you. I do not give to you as the world gives. Do not let your hearts be troubled, and do not let them be afraid. ²⁸You heard me say to you, 'I am going away, and I am coming to you.' If you loved me, you would rejoice that I am going to the Father, because the Father is greater than I. ²⁹And now I have told you this before it occurs, so that when it does occur, you may believe. ³⁰I will no longer talk much with you, for the ruler of this world is coming. He has no power over me; ³¹but I do as the Father has commanded me, so that the world may know that I love the Father. Rise, let us be on our way.

Jesus the True Vine

15 "I am the true vine, and my Father is the vine-grower. ²He removes every branch in me that bears no fruit. Every branch that bears fruit he prunes*ᵉ* to make it bear more fruit. ³You have already been cleansed*ᵉ* by the word that I have spoken to you. ⁴Abide in me as I abide in you. Just as the branch cannot bear fruit by itself unless it abides in the vine, neither can you unless you abide in me.

---

a Other ancient authorities lack *me*   *b* Other ancient authorities read *me, keep*   *c* Or *Helper*   *d* Or *among*   *e* The same Greek root refers to pruning and cleansing

---

Troubles and Trust

JOHN 14.1

"Do not let your hearts be troubled." Jesus is saying we can trust him. He is telling us to "believe" in God—not a generic "god" but "the Father" to whom he leads us. We make a choice to trust him and the Father to bear our troubles for us.

So what is troubling you? Feel the intensity of that problem. Listen to its demands. Face its immensity and offer it in complete abandonment to God. Pray, "Lord, I choose you." Take the prayer with you and repeat it many times. Let God shoulder your trouble. Jesus is promising that you will not be orphaned and left to face your troubles alone.

See Meeting God in Prayer

Bearing Fruit

JOHN 15.1–5

Draw a vine. Watch each branch grow under your pencil. Note that no branch is more important than another. Each branch is dependent on the main stem. Let your vine do what vines are supposed to do, and draw some fruit growing from the branch that passes on all the necessary nutrients from the vine. Grounded in the self-giving love of Jesus, the true vine, talk with other people in your faith community about an action you can take together that will show love as visibly as fruit.

See Meeting God in Service

⁵I am the vine, you are the branches. Those who abide in me and I in them bear much fruit, because apart from me you can do nothing. ⁶Whoever does not abide in me is thrown away like a branch and withers; such branches are gathered, thrown into the fire, and burned. ⁷If you abide in me, and my words abide in you, ask for whatever you wish, and it will be done for you. ⁸My Father is glorified by this, that you bear much fruit and become*ᵃ* my disciples. ⁹As the Father has loved me, so I have loved you; abide in my love. ¹⁰If you keep my commandments, you will abide in my love, just as I have kept my Father's commandments and abide in his love. ¹¹I have said these things to you so that my joy may be in you, and that your joy may be complete.

12 "This is my commandment, that you love one another as I have loved you. ¹³No one has greater love than this, to lay down one's life for one's friends. ¹⁴You are my friends if you do what I command you. ¹⁵I do not call you servants*ᵇ* any longer, because the servant*ᶜ* does not know what the master is doing; but I have called you friends, because I have made known to you everything that I have heard from my Father. ¹⁶You did not choose me but I chose you. And I appointed you to go and bear fruit, fruit that will last, so that the Father will give you whatever you ask him in my name. ¹⁷I am giving you these commands so that you may love one another.

The World's Hatred

18 "If the world hates you, be aware that it hated me before it hated you. ¹⁹If you belonged to the world,*ᵈ* the world would love you as its own. Because you do not belong to the world, but I have chosen you out of the world— therefore the world hates you. ²⁰Remember the word that I said to you, 'Servants*ᵉ* are not greater than their master.' If they persecuted me, they will persecute you; if they kept my word, they will keep yours also. ²¹But they will do all these things to you on account of my name, because they do not know him who sent me. ²²If I had not come and spoken to them, they would not have sin; but now they have no excuse for their sin. ²³Whoever hates me hates my Father also. ²⁴If I had not done among them the works that no one else did, they would not have sin. But now they have seen and hated both me and my Father. ²⁵It was to fulfill the word that is written in their law, 'They hated me without a cause.'

26 "When the Advocate*ᶠ* comes, whom I will send to you from the Father, the Spirit of truth who comes from the Father, he will testify on my behalf. ²⁷You also are to testify because you have been with me from the beginning.

16 "I have said these things to you to keep you from stumbling. ²They will put you out of the synagogues. Indeed, an hour is coming when those who kill you will think that by doing so they are offering worship to God. ³And they will do this because they have not known the Father or me. ⁴But I have said these things to you so

a Or *be* *b* Gk *slaves* *c* Gk *slave* *d* Gk *were of the world*
e Gk *Slaves* *f* Or *Helper*

that when their hour comes you may remember that I told you about them.

The Work of the Spirit

"I did not say these things to you from the beginning, because I was with you. ⁵But now I am going to him who sent me; yet none of you asks me, 'Where are you going?' ⁶But because I have said these things to you, sorrow has filled your hearts. ⁷Nevertheless I tell you the truth: it is to your advantage that I go away, for if I do not go away, the Advocate*a* will not come to you; but if I go, I will send him to you. ⁸And when he comes, he will prove the world wrong about*b* sin and righteousness and judgment: ⁹about sin, because they do not believe in me; ¹⁰about righteousness, because I am going to the Father and you will see me no longer; ¹¹about judgment, because the ruler of this world has been condemned.

12 "I still have many things to say to you, but you cannot bear them now. ¹³When the Spirit of truth comes, he will guide you into all the truth; for he will not speak on his own, but will speak whatever he hears, and he will declare to you the things that are to come. ¹⁴He will glorify me, because he will take what is mine and declare it to you. ¹⁵All that the Father has is mine. For this reason I said that he will take what is mine and declare it to you.

Sorrow Will Turn into Joy

16 "A little while, and you will no longer see me, and again a little while, and you will see me." ¹⁷Then some of his disciples said to one another, "What does he mean by saying to us, 'A little while, and you will no longer see me, and again a little while, and you will see me'; and 'Because I am going to the Father'?" ¹⁸They said, "What does he mean by this 'a little while'? We do not know what he is talking about." ¹⁹Jesus knew that they wanted to ask him, so he said to them, "Are you discussing among yourselves what I meant when I said, 'A little while, and you will no longer see me, and again a little while, and you will see me'? ²⁰Very truly, I tell you, you will weep and mourn, but the world will rejoice; you will have pain, but your pain will turn into joy. ²¹When a woman is in labor, she has pain, because her hour has come. But when her child is born, she no longer remembers the anguish because of the joy of having brought a human being into the world. ²²So you have pain now; but I will see you again, and your hearts will rejoice, and no one will take your joy from you. ²³On that day you will ask nothing of me.*c* Very truly, I tell you, if you ask anything of the Father in my name, he will give it to you.*d* ²⁴Until now you have not asked for anything in my name. Ask and you will receive, so that your joy may be complete.

Peace for the Disciples

25 "I have said these things to you in figures of speech. The hour is coming when I will no longer speak to you in figures, but will tell you plainly of the Father. ²⁶On that day you will ask in my name. I do not say to you that I will ask

Dare to Be Different

JOHN 15.18—16.4

Jesus is referring to "the world" as a force opposed to him—a force that hates him and will hate his followers by association. Jesus and his followers are in many ways "countercultural." In what ways are you different from "the world"? How much do you participate in the world's games of "achieve, succeed and win"? Talk with others about how your church can be an "alternative community" controlled by God's love. Ask the Spirit to help you and your faith community pray for your church and for the world. Agree on a way in which you can focus your prayer for the next week.

See Meeting God in Community

---

a Or *Helper*   *b* Or *convict the world of*   *c* Or *will ask me no question*
d Other ancient authorities read *Father, he will give it to you in my name*

Pray Boldly

JOHN 16.23–33

We are called to pray boldly. With the kind of fervent prayer that brought down the Iron Curtain or the Berlin Wall, ask of the Father, in Jesus' name, that his power will overcome political corruption, economic bondage, pedophilia, terrorism or whatever problem God's love requires you to address. Pray against despair and discouragement in spite of the evidence of the power of evil, "for the Father himself loves you." With holy imagination, see more "iron curtains" falling.

See Meeting God in Prayer

the Father on your behalf; ²⁷for the Father himself loves you, because you have loved me and have believed that I came from God.ᵃ ²⁸I came from the Father and have come into the world; again, I am leaving the world and am going to the Father."

29 His disciples said, "Yes, now you are speaking plainly, not in any figure of speech! ³⁰Now we know that you know all things, and do not need to have anyone question you; by this we believe that you came from God." ³¹Jesus answered them, "Do you now believe? ³²The hour is coming, indeed it has come, when you will be scattered, each one to his home, and you will leave me alone. Yet I am not alone because the Father is with me. ³³I have said this to you, so that in me you may have peace. In the world you face persecution. But take courage; I have conquered the world!"

Jesus Prays for His Disciples

17 After Jesus had spoken these words, he looked up to heaven and said, "Father, the hour has come; glorify your Son so that the Son may glorify you, ²since you have given him authority over all people,ᵇ to give eternal life to all whom you have given him. ³And this is eternal life, that they may know you, the only true God, and Jesus Christ whom you have sent. ⁴I glorified you on earth by finishing the work that you gave me to do. ⁵So now, Father, glorify me in your own presence with the glory that I had in your presence before the world existed.

6 "I have made your name known to those whom you gave me from the world. They were yours, and you gave them to me, and they have kept your word. ⁷Now they know that everything you have given me is from you; ⁸for the words that you gave to me I have given to them, and they have received them and know in truth that I came from you; and they have believed that you sent me. ⁹I am asking on their behalf; I am not asking on behalf of the world, but on behalf of those whom you gave me, because they are yours. ¹⁰All mine are yours, and yours are mine; and I have been glorified in them. ¹¹And now I am no longer in the world, but they are in the world, and I am coming to you. Holy Father, protect them in your name that you have given me, so that they may be one, as we are one. ¹²While I was with them, I protected them in your name thatᶜ you have given me. I guarded them, and not one of them was lost except the one destined to be lost,ᵈ so that the scripture might be fulfilled. ¹³But now I am coming to you, and I speak these things in the world so that they may have my joy made complete in themselves.ᵉ ¹⁴I have given them your word, and the world has hated them because they do not belong to the world, just as I do not belong to the world. ¹⁵I am not asking you to take them out of the world, but I ask you to protect them from the evil one.ᶠ ¹⁶They do not belong to the world, just as I do not belong to the world. ¹⁷Sanctify them in the truth; your word is truth. ¹⁸As you have sent me into the world, so I

ᵃ Other ancient authorities read *the Father*   ᵇ Gk *flesh*   ᶜ Other ancient authorities read *protected in your name those whom*   ᵈ Gk *except the son of destruction*   ᵉ Or *among themselves*   ᶠ Or *from evil*

have sent them into the world. ¹⁹And for their sakes I sanctify myself, so that they also may be sanctified in truth.

20 "I ask not only on behalf of these, but also on behalf of those who will believe in me through their word, ²¹that they may all be one. As you, Father, are in me and I am in you, may they also be in us,ᵃ so that the world may believe that you have sent me. ²²The glory that you have given me I have given them, so that they may be one, as we are one, ²³I in them and you in me, that they may become completely one, so that the world may know that you have sent me and have loved them even as you have loved me. ²⁴Father, I desire that those also, whom you have given me, may be with me where I am, to see my glory, which you have given me because you loved me before the foundation of the world.

25 "Righteous Father, the world does not know you, but I know you; and these know that you have sent me. ²⁶I made your name known to them, and I will make it known, so that the love with which you have loved me may be in them, and I in them."

The Betrayal and Arrest of Jesus

18 After Jesus had spoken these words, he went out with his disciples across the Kidron valley to a place where there was a garden, which he and his disciples entered. ²Now Judas, who betrayed him, also knew the place, because Jesus often met there with his disciples. ³So Judas brought a detachment of soldiers together with police from the chief priests and the Pharisees, and they came there with lanterns and torches and weapons. ⁴Then Jesus, knowing all that was to happen to him, came forward and asked them, "Whom are you looking for?" ⁵They answered, "Jesus of Nazareth."ᵇ Jesus replied, "I am he."ᶜ Judas, who betrayed him, was standing with them. ⁶When Jesusᵈ said to them, "I am he,"ᶜ they stepped back and fell to the ground. ⁷Again he asked them, "Whom are you looking for?" And they said, "Jesus of Nazareth."ᵇ ⁸Jesus answered, "I told you that I am he.ᶜ So if you are looking for me, let these men go." ⁹This was to fulfill the word that he had spoken, "I did not lose a single one of those whom you gave me." ¹⁰Then Simon Peter, who had a sword, drew it, struck the high priest's slave, and cut off his right ear. The slave's name was Malchus. ¹¹Jesus said to Peter, "Put your sword back into its sheath. Am I not to drink the cup that the Father has given me?"

Jesus before the High Priest

12 So the soldiers, their officer, and the Jewish police arrested Jesus and bound him. ¹³First they took him to Annas, who was the father-in-law of Caiaphas, the high priest that year. ¹⁴Caiaphas was the one who had advised the Jews that it was better to have one person die for the people.

Peter Denies Jesus

15 Simon Peter and another disciple followed Jesus. Since that disciple was known to the high priest, he went

---

In Unity

JOHN 17.20–23

This is no typical deathbed prayer Jesus is praying. Jesus is praying for unity with God, asking the Father to make believers one as he and the Father are one. And Jesus is praying for his followers' oneness with him and with the Father.

Unity may be hard for us to achieve, but the glory of God is visible when we live in unity. When we do, the death-defying life of God is expressed. In what ways might you be experiencing disunity? Ask God to show you what actions you will need to take. Carry within your mind a picture of Jesus praying for unity.

See Meeting God in Community

Are You With Him?

JOHN 18.15–17

We are quick to point out and condemn the evil we see in Judas. But Peter? His betrayal is even more disturbing, perhaps because it is generated by Peter's need for self-preservation, a trait we recognize in ourselves. His loyalty to Jesus is requiring much more of him than he is prepared to give up—his safety and security.

Is there someone in your school, your workplace or your family who is asking something like, "You are not also one of this man's disciples, are you?" What is your reply? Find an object that might symbolize your reply. What color is it? What properties does it have? When you are ready, speak to Jesus about your reflections.

See *Meeting God in Scripture*

with Jesus into the courtyard of the high priest, [16]but Peter was standing outside at the gate. So the other disciple, who was known to the high priest, went out, spoke to the woman who guarded the gate, and brought Peter in. [17]The woman said to Peter, "You are not also one of this man's disciples, are you?" He said, "I am not." [18]Now the slaves and the police had made a charcoal fire because it was cold, and they were standing around it and warming themselves. Peter also was standing with them and warming himself.

The High Priest Questions Jesus

19 Then the high priest questioned Jesus about his disciples and about his teaching. [20]Jesus answered, "I have spoken openly to the world; I have always taught in synagogues and in the temple, where all the Jews come together. I have said nothing in secret. [21]Why do you ask me? Ask those who heard what I said to them; they know what I said." [22]When he had said this, one of the police standing nearby struck Jesus on the face, saying, "Is that how you answer the high priest?" [23]Jesus answered, "If I have spoken wrongly, testify to the wrong. But if I have spoken rightly, why do you strike me?" [24]Then Annas sent him bound to Caiaphas the high priest.

Peter Denies Jesus Again

25 Now Simon Peter was standing and warming himself. They asked him, "You are not also one of his disciples, are you?" He denied it and said, "I am not." [26]One of the slaves of the high priest, a relative of the man whose ear Peter had cut off, asked, "Did I not see you in the garden with him?" [27]Again Peter denied it, and at that moment the cock crowed.

Jesus before Pilate

28 Then they took Jesus from Caiaphas to Pilate's headquarters.[a] It was early in the morning. They themselves did not enter the headquarters,[a] so as to avoid ritual defilement and to be able to eat the Passover. [29]So Pilate went out to them and said, "What accusation do you bring against this man?" [30]They answered, "If this man were not a criminal, we would not have handed him over to you." [31]Pilate said to them, "Take him yourselves and judge him according to your law." The Jews replied, "We are not permitted to put anyone to death." [32](This was to fulfill what Jesus had said when he indicated the kind of death he was to die.)

33 Then Pilate entered the headquarters[a] again, summoned Jesus, and asked him, "Are you the King of the Jews?" [34]Jesus answered, "Do you ask this on your own, or did others tell you about me?" [35]Pilate replied, "I am not a Jew, am I? Your own nation and the chief priests have handed you over to me. What have you done?" [36]Jesus answered, "My kingdom is not from this world. If my kingdom were from this world, my followers would be fighting to keep me from being handed over to the Jews. But as it is, my kingdom is not from here." [37]Pilate asked him, "So you are a king?" Jesus answered, "You say that I am a

a Gk *the praetorium*

king. For this I was born, and for this I came into the world, to testify to the truth. Everyone who belongs to the truth listens to my voice." [38]Pilate asked him, "What is truth?"

Jesus Sentenced to Death

After he had said this, he went out to the Jews again and told them, "I find no case against him. [39]But you have a custom that I release someone for you at the Passover. Do you want me to release for you the King of the Jews?" [40]They shouted in reply, "Not this man, but Barabbas!" Now Barabbas was a bandit.

19 Then Pilate took Jesus and had him flogged. [2]And the soldiers wove a crown of thorns and put it on his head, and they dressed him in a purple robe. [3]They kept coming up to him, saying, "Hail, King of the Jews!" and striking him on the face. [4]Pilate went out again and said to them, "Look, I am bringing him out to you to let you know that I find no case against him." [5]So Jesus came out, wearing the crown of thorns and the purple robe. Pilate said to them, "Here is the man!" [6]When the chief priests and the police saw him, they shouted, "Crucify him! Crucify him!" Pilate said to them, "Take him yourselves and crucify him; I find no case against him." [7]The Jews answered him, "We have a law, and according to that law he ought to die because he has claimed to be the Son of God."

8 Now when Pilate heard this, he was more afraid than ever. [9]He entered his headquarters[a] again and asked Jesus, "Where are you from?" But Jesus gave him no answer. [10]Pilate therefore said to him, "Do you refuse to speak to me? Do you not know that I have power to release you, and power to crucify you?" [11]Jesus answered him, "You would have no power over me unless it had been given you from above; therefore the one who handed me over to you is guilty of a greater sin." [12]From then on Pilate tried to release him, but the Jews cried out, "If you release this man, you are no friend of the emperor. Everyone who claims to be a king sets himself against the emperor."

13 When Pilate heard these words, he brought Jesus outside and sat[b] on the judge's bench at a place called The Stone Pavement, or in Hebrew[c] Gabbatha. [14]Now it was the day of Preparation for the Passover; and it was about noon. He said to the Jews, "Here is your King!" [15]They cried out, "Away with him! Away with him! Crucify him!" Pilate asked them, "Shall I crucify your King?" The chief priests answered, "We have no king but the emperor." [16]Then he handed him over to them to be crucified.

The Crucifixion of Jesus

So they took Jesus; [17]and carrying the cross by himself, he went out to what is called The Place of the Skull, which in Hebrew[c] is called Golgotha. [18]There they crucified him, and with him two others, one on either side, with Jesus between them. [19]Pilate also had an inscription written and put on the cross. It read, "Jesus of Nazareth,[d] the King of the Jews." [20]Many of the Jews read this inscription, be-

---

Here Is Your King

JOHN 19.1–15

Jesus is dressed in purple and wearing a crown that mocks him rather than honors him. Though Jesus looks nothing like royalty, Pilate says cynically, "Here is your king!" The tragedy of this moment is not only Jesus' impending death but that the people fail to recognize God in Jesus Christ.

Will you recognize your King today? Jesus may be in the child who needs you to listen to her troubles. Jesus may be in the neighbor who needs a ride to the doctor's office. Jesus may be in the person being shouted at and abused, for whom you might intervene. Ask Jesus to give you the vision to see him today. Ask for the grace to see Jesus in the people you meet so that you may serve your God and King (see Matthew 25.31–46).

See *Meeting God in Worship*

Jesus in the Hour of Death

In great dignity, and in the serenity of complete trust, Jesus dies. The blood spilled, like the blood of the Passover lamb, is for our deliverance—the ultimate act of a heart generous with the fullness of God's love.

Pray for those who are dying. Pray for those who are dying for lack of love. Pray for yourself in the hour of your death. And in the presence of a love "so amazing, so divine," with confidence in your voice, sing:

"When I tread the verge of
    Jordan,
bid my anxious fears
    subside;
death of death and hell's
    destruction,
land me safe on Canaan's
    side.
Songs of praises, songs of
    praises,
I will ever sing to you; I will
    ever sing to you."
    —HARRY EMERSON FOSDICK,
"Guide Me, O Thou Great Jehovah"

See *Meeting God in Worship*

cause the place where Jesus was crucified was near the city; and it was written in Hebrew,[a] in Latin, and in Greek. [21]Then the chief priests of the Jews said to Pilate, "Do not write, 'The King of the Jews,' but, 'This man said, I am King of the Jews.'" [22]Pilate answered, "What I have written I have written." [23]When the soldiers had crucified Jesus, they took his clothes and divided them into four parts, one for each soldier. They also took his tunic; now the tunic was seamless, woven in one piece from the top. [24]So they said to one another, "Let us not tear it, but cast lots for it to see who will get it." This was to fulfill what the scripture says,

"They divided my clothes among themselves,
    and for my clothing they cast lots."

[25]And that is what the soldiers did.

Meanwhile, standing near the cross of Jesus were his mother, and his mother's sister, Mary the wife of Clopas, and Mary Magdalene. [26]When Jesus saw his mother and the disciple whom he loved standing beside her, he said to his mother, "Woman, here is your son." [27]Then he said to the disciple, "Here is your mother." And from that hour the disciple took her into his own home.

[28] After this, when Jesus knew that all was now finished, he said (in order to fulfill the scripture), "I am thirsty." [29]A jar full of sour wine was standing there. So they put a sponge full of the wine on a branch of hyssop and held it to his mouth. [30]When Jesus had received the wine, he said, "It is finished." Then he bowed his head and gave up his spirit.

Jesus' Side Is Pierced

[31] Since it was the day of Preparation, the Jews did not want the bodies left on the cross during the sabbath, especially because that sabbath was a day of great solemnity. So they asked Pilate to have the legs of the crucified men broken and the bodies removed. [32]Then the soldiers came and broke the legs of the first and of the other who had been crucified with him. [33]But when they came to Jesus and saw that he was already dead, they did not break his legs. [34]Instead, one of the soldiers pierced his side with a spear, and at once blood and water came out. [35](He who saw this has testified so that you also may believe. His testimony is true, and he knows[b] that he tells the truth.) [36]These things occurred so that the scripture might be fulfilled, "None of his bones shall be broken." [37]And again another passage of scripture says, "They will look on the one whom they have pierced."

The Burial of Jesus

[38] After these things, Joseph of Arimathea, who was a disciple of Jesus, though a secret one because of his fear of the Jews, asked Pilate to let him take away the body of Jesus. Pilate gave him permission; so he came and removed his body. [39]Nicodemus, who had at first come to Jesus by night, also came, bringing a mixture of myrrh and aloes, weighing about a hundred pounds. [40]They took the body of Jesus and wrapped it with the spices in linen cloths, according to the burial custom of the Jews. [41]Now

a That is, Aramaic   b Or there is one who knows

there was a garden in the place where he was crucified, and in the garden there was a new tomb in which no one had ever been laid. ⁴²And so, because it was the Jewish day of Preparation, and the tomb was nearby, they laid Jesus there.

The Resurrection of Jesus

20 Early on the first day of the week, while it was still dark, Mary Magdalene came to the tomb and saw that the stone had been removed from the tomb. ²So she ran and went to Simon Peter and the other disciple, the one whom Jesus loved, and said to them, "They have taken the Lord out of the tomb, and we do not know where they have laid him." ³Then Peter and the other disciple set out and went toward the tomb. ⁴The two were running together, but the other disciple outran Peter and reached the tomb first. ⁵He bent down to look in and saw the linen wrappings lying there, but he did not go in. ⁶Then Simon Peter came, following him, and went into the tomb. He saw the linen wrappings lying there, ⁷and the cloth that had been on Jesus' head, not lying with the linen wrappings but rolled up in a place by itself. ⁸Then the other disciple, who reached the tomb first, also went in, and he saw and believed; ⁹for as yet they did not understand the scripture, that he must rise from the dead. ¹⁰Then the disciples returned to their homes.

Jesus Appears to Mary Magdalene

11 But Mary stood weeping outside the tomb. As she wept, she bent over to look[a] into the tomb; ¹²and she saw two angels in white, sitting where the body of Jesus had been lying, one at the head and the other at the feet. ¹³They said to her, "Woman, why are you weeping?" She said to them, "They have taken away my Lord, and I do not know where they have laid him." ¹⁴When she had said this, she turned around and saw Jesus standing there, but she did not know that it was Jesus. ¹⁵Jesus said to her, "Woman, why are you weeping? Whom are you looking for?" Supposing him to be the gardener, she said to him, "Sir, if you have carried him away, tell me where you have laid him, and I will take him away." ¹⁶Jesus said to her, "Mary!" She turned and said to him in Hebrew,[b] "Rabbouni!" (which means Teacher). ¹⁷Jesus said to her, "Do not hold on to me, because I have not yet ascended to the Father. But go to my brothers and say to them, 'I am ascending to my Father and your Father, to my God and your God.' " ¹⁸Mary Magdalene went and announced to the disciples, "I have seen the Lord"; and she told them that he had said these things to her.

Jesus Appears to the Disciples

19 When it was evening on that day, the first day of the week, and the doors of the house where the disciples had met were locked for fear of the Jews, Jesus came and stood among them and said, "Peace be with you." ²⁰After he said this, he showed them his hands and his side. Then the disciples rejoiced when they saw the Lord. ²¹Jesus said to them again, "Peace be with you. As the Father has sent

He Speaks Your Name

JOHN 20.1–18

Joseph of Arimathea offers a tomb for Jesus' body. Nicodemus says his good-bye to Jesus with a generous gift of burial spices (see 19.38–40). Peter and John (the "other disciple") see an empty tomb with the linen burial cloths "rolled up." Mary weeps before the gardener—until he says her name!

Jesus, the risen One, knows your name too. Be very still and use every one of your senses. Listen as Jesus says your name. Listen. Sense, think and feel what it means for you to hear Jesus say your name.

See Meeting God in Scripture

---

a Gk lacks *to look*   *b* That is, *Aramaic*

He Knows What We Need

JOHN 20.24–29

We are sometimes scornful of Thomas, giving him the nickname "doubting Thomas." But he is not unlike many of us. He needs the data. He needs the visuals. He needs to touch Jesus' wounds in order for his faith to take root and grow. Jesus accepts that. He knows what we need.

What do you need from Jesus in order for your faith to bloom? Write it down. Say it aloud. Tell another person perhaps. Tell Jesus. And wait, watch and wonder.

See *Meeting God in Worship*

me, so I send you." ²²When he had said this, he breathed on them and said to them, "Receive the Holy Spirit. ²³If you forgive the sins of any, they are forgiven them; if you retain the sins of any, they are retained."

Jesus and Thomas

24 But Thomas (who was called the Twin[a]), one of the twelve, was not with them when Jesus came. ²⁵So the other disciples told him, "We have seen the Lord." But he said to them, "Unless I see the mark of the nails in his hands, and put my finger in the mark of the nails and my hand in his side, I will not believe."

26 A week later his disciples were again in the house, and Thomas was with them. Although the doors were shut, Jesus came and stood among them and said, "Peace be with you." ²⁷Then he said to Thomas, "Put your finger here and see my hands. Reach out your hand and put it in my side. Do not doubt but believe." ²⁸Thomas answered him, "My Lord and my God!" ²⁹Jesus said to him, "Have you believed because you have seen me? Blessed are those who have not seen and yet have come to believe."

The Purpose of This Book

30 Now Jesus did many other signs in the presence of his disciples, which are not written in this book. ³¹But these are written so that you may come to believe[b] that Jesus is the Messiah,[c] the Son of God, and that through believing you may have life in his name.

Jesus Appears to Seven Disciples

21 After these things Jesus showed himself again to the disciples by the Sea of Tiberias; and he showed himself in this way. ²Gathered there together were Simon Peter, Thomas called the Twin,[a] Nathanael of Cana in Galilee, the sons of Zebedee, and two others of his disciples. ³Simon Peter said to them, "I am going fishing." They said to him, "We will go with you." They went out and got into the boat, but that night they caught nothing.

4 Just after daybreak, Jesus stood on the beach; but the disciples did not know that it was Jesus. ⁵Jesus said to them, "Children, you have no fish, have you?" They answered him, "No." ⁶He said to them, "Cast the net to the right side of the boat, and you will find some." So they cast it, and now they were not able to haul it in because there were so many fish. ⁷That disciple whom Jesus loved said to Peter, "It is the Lord!" When Simon Peter heard that it was the Lord, he put on some clothes, for he was naked, and jumped into the sea. ⁸But the other disciples came in the boat, dragging the net full of fish, for they were not far from the land, only about a hundred yards[d] off.

9 When they had gone ashore, they saw a charcoal fire there, with fish on it, and bread. ¹⁰Jesus said to them, "Bring some of the fish that you have just caught." ¹¹So Simon Peter went aboard and hauled the net ashore, full of large fish, a hundred fifty-three of them; and though there were so many, the net was not torn. ¹²Jesus said to them, "Come and have breakfast." Now none of the disciples

a Gk *Didymus*   b Other ancient authorities read *may continue to believe*
c Or *the Christ*   d Gk *two hundred cubits*

dared to ask him, "Who are you?" because they knew it was the Lord. [13]Jesus came and took the bread and gave it to them, and did the same with the fish. [14]This was now the third time that Jesus appeared to the disciples after he was raised from the dead.

Jesus and Peter

15 When they had finished breakfast, Jesus said to Simon Peter, "Simon son of John, do you love me more than these?" He said to him, "Yes, Lord; you know that I love you." Jesus said to him, "Feed my lambs." [16]A second time he said to him, "Simon son of John, do you love me?" He said to him, "Yes, Lord; you know that I love you." Jesus said to him, "Tend my sheep." [17]He said to him the third time, "Simon son of John, do you love me?" Peter felt hurt because he said to him the third time, "Do you love me?" And he said to him, "Lord, you know everything; you know that I love you." Jesus said to him, "Feed my sheep. [18]Very truly, I tell you, when you were younger, you used to fasten your own belt and to go wherever you wished. But when you grow old, you will stretch out your hands, and someone else will fasten a belt around you and take you where you do not wish to go." [19](He said this to indicate the kind of death by which he would glorify God.) After this he said to him, "Follow me."

Jesus and the Beloved Disciple

20 Peter turned and saw the disciple whom Jesus loved following them; he was the one who had reclined next to Jesus at the supper and had said, "Lord, who is it that is going to betray you?" [21]When Peter saw him, he said to Jesus, "Lord, what about him?" [22]Jesus said to him, "If it is my will that he remain until I come, what is that to you? Follow me!" [23]So the rumor spread in the community[a] that this disciple would not die. Yet Jesus did not say to him that he would not die, but, "If it is my will that he remain until I come, what is that to you?"[b]

24 This is the disciple who is testifying to these things and has written them, and we know that his testimony is true. [25]But there are also many other things that Jesus did; if every one of them were written down, I suppose that the world itself could not contain the books that would be written.

The Food of Love

JOHN 21.1–19

Jesus turned water into wine at a wedding reception. He provided lunch for thousands. And in this passage, even after his glorious resurrection we see him caring for his own by providing fish and bread for breakfast.

In the same warm, companionable way, Jesus is with you now, asking, "Do you love me?" How will you respond? Whether it is an honest "no," a "give me a bit more time," or an unequivocal "yes," Jesus wants to share his gifts of nourishment and life with you. He wants you to care for others with nothing less than his own love. As you conclude your reading of this Gospel, go out in the name of Jesus with a specific act or word of love.

See Meeting God in Service

THE ACTS OF THE APOSTLES

The Good News Spreads Under the Spirit's Guidance

KEY VERSE:

"But you will receive power when the Holy Spirit has come upon you; and you will be my witnesses in Jerusalem, in all Judea and Samaria, and to the ends of the earth."—Acts 1.8

"In this manner the church proceeds on its pilgrim way . . . with the persecutions of the world on one side, and on the other the consolations of God."
—AUGUSTINE,
The City of God

This book might well be called "The Acts of the Holy Spirit." From beginning to end the Spirit guides the spread of the gospel from Jerusalem to Rome itself. Poured out on the day of Pentecost with "a sound like the rush of a violent wind" and "divided tongues as of fire" (Acts 2.2–3), the Spirit changes lives, alters plans and transforms situations. The Spirit empowers the early Christians to stand up to authorities, to face down mobs, to speak to hostile audiences, and to hold fast through suffering even to death—all for the sake of the Good News of Jesus Christ. At the same time, the Spirit impels them far beyond their comfort zones into missions to the Samaritans and Gentiles and to people from all levels of society.

God's Spirit is active in our own lives—comforting, encouraging, strengthening, nudging. When have you felt led, like the early disciples, in a particular direction? When have you been the channel of God's love to someone else? When have you experienced a shower of grace when you needed it most? And when have you found resources of strength to do what seemed impossible? You have experienced the work of the Spirit, sent by Jesus Christ who is "exalted at the right hand of God . . . and [who has] received from the Father the promise of the Holy Spirit [and] has poured out this that you both see and hear" (2.33).

The Promise of the Holy Spirit

1 In the first book, Theophilus, I wrote about all that Jesus did and taught from the beginning ²until the day when he was taken up to heaven, after giving instructions through the Holy Spirit to the apostles whom he had chosen. ³After his suffering he presented himself alive to them by many convincing proofs, appearing to them during forty days and speaking about the kingdom of God. ⁴While staying*ᵃ* with them, he ordered them not to leave Jerusalem, but to wait there for the promise of the Father. "This," he said, "is what you have heard from me; ⁵for John baptized with water, but you will be baptized with*ᵇ* the Holy Spirit not many days from now."

The Ascension of Jesus

6 So when they had come together, they asked him, "Lord, is this the time when you will restore the kingdom to Israel?" ⁷He replied, "It is not for you to know the times or periods that the Father has set by his own authority. ⁸But you will receive power when the Holy Spirit has come upon you; and you will be my witnesses in Jerusalem, in all Judea and Samaria, and to the ends of the earth." ⁹When he had said this, as they were watching, he was lifted up, and a cloud took him out of their sight. ¹⁰While he was going and they were gazing up toward heaven, suddenly two men in white robes stood by them. ¹¹They said, "Men of Galilee, why do you stand looking up toward heaven? This Jesus, who has been taken up from you into heaven, will come in the same way as you saw him go into heaven."

Matthias Chosen to Replace Judas

12 Then they returned to Jerusalem from the mount called Olivet, which is near Jerusalem, a sabbath day's journey away. ¹³When they had entered the city, they went to the room upstairs where they were staying, Peter, and John, and James, and Andrew, Philip and Thomas, Bartholomew and Matthew, James son of Alphaeus, and Simon the Zealot, and Judas son of*ᶜ* James. ¹⁴All these were constantly devoting themselves to prayer, together with certain women, including Mary the mother of Jesus, as well as his brothers.

15 In those days Peter stood up among the believers*ᵈ* (together the crowd numbered about one hundred twenty persons) and said, ¹⁶"Friends,*ᵉ* the scripture had to be fulfilled, which the Holy Spirit through David foretold concerning Judas, who became a guide for those who arrested Jesus— ¹⁷for he was numbered among us and was allotted his share in this ministry." ¹⁸(Now this man acquired a field with the reward of his wickedness; and falling headlong,*ᶠ* he burst open in the middle and all his bowels gushed out. ¹⁹This became known to all the residents of Jerusalem, so that the field was called in their language Hakeldama, that is, Field of Blood.) ²⁰"For it is written in the book of Psalms,

'Let his homestead become desolate,
     and let there be no one to live in it';

and

'Let another take his position of overseer.'

²¹So one of the men who have accompanied us during all

a Or eating   b Or by   c Or the brother of   d Gk brothers   e Gk Men, brothers   f Or swelling up

A Question to Ponder

ACTS 1.11

Do you sometimes allow prayer, Bible study or other spiritual exercises to become substitutes for your mission as a Christian rather than allow them to become the power sources for that mission? Write a dialogue between yourself and God. Begin with God asking you what the angel asked the first Christians: "Why do you stand looking up toward heaven?" How would you respond? What do you think God would say to your response? Writing it out will keep the dialogue focused.

Your Picture of the Spirit

ACTS 2.1–4

How do you picture the Holy
Spirit? Here the Spirit is likened
to a violent wind and tongues
of fire. In Matthew 3.16 the
Spirit is compared to a descending dove. Elsewhere the
Spirit is experienced through
various gifts (see 1 Corinthians
12.4–11) and fruit (see Galatians 5.22–23). Try praising
God with your hands as you
draw or paint your own image
or images of the Spirit.

See Meeting God in Worship

the time that the Lord Jesus went in and out among us,
²²beginning from the baptism of John until the day when
he was taken up from us—one of these must become a witness with us to his resurrection." ²³So they proposed two,
Joseph called Barsabbas, who was also known as Justus,
and Matthias. ²⁴Then they prayed and said, "Lord, you
know everyone's heart. Show us which one of these two
you have chosen ²⁵to take the place*a* in this ministry and
apostleship from which Judas turned aside to go to his own
place." ²⁶And they cast lots for them, and the lot fell on
Matthias; and he was added to the eleven apostles.

The Coming of the Holy Spirit

2 When the day of Pentecost had come, they were all together in one place. ²And suddenly from heaven there
came a sound like the rush of a violent wind, and it filled
the entire house where they were sitting. ³Divided tongues,
as of fire, appeared among them, and a tongue rested on
each of them. ⁴All of them were filled with the Holy Spirit
and began to speak in other languages, as the Spirit gave
them ability.

5 Now there were devout Jews from every nation under
heaven living in Jerusalem. ⁶And at this sound the crowd
gathered and was bewildered, because each one heard
them speaking in the native language of each. ⁷Amazed
and astonished, they asked, "Are not all these who are
speaking Galileans? ⁸And how is it that we hear, each of us,
in our own native language? ⁹Parthians, Medes, Elamites,
and residents of Mesopotamia, Judea and Cappadocia, Pontus and Asia, ¹⁰Phrygia and Pamphylia, Egypt and the parts
of Libya belonging to Cyrene, and visitors from Rome, both
Jews and proselytes, ¹¹Cretans and Arabs—in our own languages we hear them speaking about God's deeds of
power." ¹²All were amazed and perplexed, saying to one
another, "What does this mean?" ¹³But others sneered and
said, "They are filled with new wine."

Peter Addresses the Crowd

14 But Peter, standing with the eleven, raised his voice
and addressed them, "Men of Judea and all who live in
Jerusalem, let this be known to you, and listen to what I
say. ¹⁵Indeed, these are not drunk, as you suppose, for it is
only nine o'clock in the morning. ¹⁶No, this is what was
spoken through the prophet Joel:

¹⁷ 'In the last days it will be, God declares,
that I will pour out my Spirit upon all flesh,
and your sons and your daughters shall prophesy,
and your young men shall see visions,
and your old men shall dream dreams.
¹⁸ Even upon my slaves, both men and women,
in those days I will pour out my Spirit;
and they shall prophesy.
¹⁹ And I will show portents in the heaven above
and signs on the earth below,
blood, and fire, and smoky mist.
²⁰ The sun shall be turned to darkness
and the moon to blood,
before the coming of the Lord's great and
glorious day.

a Other ancient authorities read *the share*

21   Then everyone who calls on the name of the Lord
          shall be saved.'
22 "You that are Israelites,[a] listen to what I have to say:
Jesus of Nazareth,[b] a man attested to you by God with
deeds of power, wonders, and signs that God did through
him among you, as you yourselves know— [23]this man,
handed over to you according to the definite plan and fore-
knowledge of God, you crucified and killed by the hands of
those outside the law. [24]But God raised him up, having
freed him from death,[c] because it was impossible for him
to be held in its power. [25]For David says concerning him,
     'I saw the Lord always before me,
          for he is at my right hand so that I will not be
               shaken;
26   therefore my heart was glad, and my tongue
               rejoiced;
          moreover my flesh will live in hope.
27   For you will not abandon my soul to Hades,
          or let your Holy One experience corruption.
28   You have made known to me the ways of life;
          you will make me full of gladness with your
               presence.'
29 "Fellow Israelites,[d] I may say to you confidently of our
ancestor David that he both died and was buried, and his
tomb is with us to this day. [30]Since he was a prophet, he
knew that God had sworn with an oath to him that he would
put one of his descendants on his throne. [31]Foreseeing this,
David[e] spoke of the resurrection of the Messiah,[f] saying,
     'He was not abandoned to Hades,
          nor did his flesh experience corruption.'
[32]This Jesus God raised up, and of that all of us are witnesses. [33]Being therefore exalted at[g] the right hand of God,
and having received from the Father the promise of the
Holy Spirit, he has poured out this that you both see and
hear. [34]For David did not ascend into the heavens, but he
himself says,
     'The Lord said to my Lord,
          "Sit at my right hand,
35   until I make your enemies your footstool." '
[36]Therefore let the entire house of Israel know with certainty that God has made him both Lord and Messiah,[h] this
Jesus whom you crucified."

The First Converts

37 Now when they heard this, they were cut to the heart
and said to Peter and to the other apostles, "Brothers,[d] what
should we do?" [38]Peter said to them, "Repent, and be baptized every one of you in the name of Jesus Christ so that
your sins may be forgiven; and you will receive the gift of
the Holy Spirit. [39]For the promise is for you, for your children, and for all who are far away, everyone whom the Lord
our God calls to him." [40]And he testified with many other
arguments and exhorted them, saying, "Save yourselves
from this corrupt generation." [41]So those who welcomed
his message were baptized, and that day about three thousand persons were added. [42]They devoted themselves to
the apostles' teaching and fellowship, to the breaking of
bread and the prayers.

Rising to New Life

ACTS 2.24

"Christ has risen and death has
been cast down. Christ has
risen and the devils have fallen.
Christ has risen and the angels
rejoice. Christ has risen and
there are no corpses left in the
sepulcher. For Christ in rising
from the dead is the firstfruits
of those that sleep. To him be
glory and power for ever and
ever. Amen."

—JOHN CHRYSOSTOM,
"Those Invited"

a Gk *Men, Israelites*   *b* Gk *the Nazorean*   *c* Gk *the pains of death*
d Gk *Men, brothers*   *e* Gk *he*   *f* Or *the Christ*   *g* Or *by*   *h* Or *Christ*

The Gift You Really Need

ACTS 3.1–10

The beggar thinks he knows the extent of what he can ask for, but Peter gives him something much better. Do you limit God's giving by specifying what you want rather than receiving what God wants to give you? Imagine yourself as the beggar, crying out to Peter and John. What do you ask for? What do you really want? Healing of body or soul? Forgiveness? Hear Peter, as an instrument of Christ's Spirit, speak to you: "In the name of Jesus Christ of Nazareth . . ." What is the gift he offers?

See Meeting God in Scripture

Life among the Believers

43 Awe came upon everyone, because many wonders and signs were being done by the apostles. ⁴⁴All who believed were together and had all things in common; ⁴⁵they would sell their possessions and goods and distribute the proceeds*ᵃ* to all, as any had need. ⁴⁶Day by day, as they spent much time together in the temple, they broke bread at home*ᵇ* and ate their food with glad and generous*ᶜ* hearts, ⁴⁷praising God and having the goodwill of all the people. And day by day the Lord added to their number those who were being saved.

Peter Heals a Crippled Beggar

3 One day Peter and John were going up to the temple at the hour of prayer, at three o'clock in the afternoon. ²And a man lame from birth was being carried in. People would lay him daily at the gate of the temple called the Beautiful Gate so that he could ask for alms from those entering the temple. ³When he saw Peter and John about to go into the temple, he asked them for alms. ⁴Peter looked intently at him, as did John, and said, "Look at us." ⁵And he fixed his attention on them, expecting to receive something from them. ⁶But Peter said, "I have no silver or gold, but what I have I give you; in the name of Jesus Christ of Nazareth,*ᵈ* stand up and walk." ⁷And he took him by the right hand and raised him up; and immediately his feet and ankles were made strong. ⁸Jumping up, he stood and began to walk, and he entered the temple with them, walking and leaping and praising God. ⁹All the people saw him walking and praising God, ¹⁰and they recognized him as the one who used to sit and ask for alms at the Beautiful Gate of the temple; and they were filled with wonder and amazement at what had happened to him.

Peter Speaks in Solomon's Portico

11 While he clung to Peter and John, all the people ran together to them in the portico called Solomon's Portico, utterly astonished. ¹²When Peter saw it, he addressed the people, "You Israelites,*ᵉ* why do you wonder at this, or why do you stare at us, as though by our own power or piety we had made him walk? ¹³The God of Abraham, the God of Isaac, and the God of Jacob, the God of our ancestors has glorified his servant*ᶠ* Jesus, whom you handed over and rejected in the presence of Pilate, though he had decided to release him. ¹⁴But you rejected the Holy and Righteous One and asked to have a murderer given to you, ¹⁵and you killed the Author of life, whom God raised from the dead. To this we are witnesses. ¹⁶And by faith in his name, his name itself has made this man strong, whom you see and know; and the faith that is through Jesus*ᵍ* has given him this perfect health in the presence of all of you.

17 "And now, friends,*ʰ* I know that you acted in ignorance, as did also your rulers. ¹⁸In this way God fulfilled what he had foretold through all the prophets, that his Messiah*ⁱ* would suffer. ¹⁹Repent therefore, and turn to God so that your sins may be wiped out, ²⁰so that times of refreshing may come from the presence of the Lord, and that

---

a Gk *them* *b* Or *from house to house* *c* Or *sincere* *d* Gk *the Nazorean*
e Gk *Men, Israelites* *f* Or *child* *g* Gk *him* *h* Gk *brothers* *i* Or *his Christ*

he may send the Messiah[a] appointed for you, that is, Jesus, [21]who must remain in heaven until the time of universal restoration that God announced long ago through his holy prophets. [22]Moses said, 'The Lord your God will raise up for you from your own people[b] a prophet like me. You must listen to whatever he tells you. [23]And it will be that everyone who does not listen to that prophet will be utterly rooted out of the people.' [24]And all the prophets, as many as have spoken, from Samuel and those after him, also predicted these days. [25]You are the descendants of the prophets and of the covenant that God gave to your ancestors, saying to Abraham, 'And in your descendants all the families of the earth shall be blessed.' [26]When God raised up his servant,[c] he sent him first to you, to bless you by turning each of you from your wicked ways."

Peter and John before the Council

4 While Peter and John[d] were speaking to the people, the priests, the captain of the temple, and the Sadducees came to them, [2]much annoyed because they were teaching the people and proclaiming that in Jesus there is the resurrection of the dead. [3]So they arrested them and put them in custody until the next day, for it was already evening. [4]But many of those who heard the word believed; and they numbered about five thousand.

5 The next day their rulers, elders, and scribes assembled in Jerusalem, [6]with Annas the high priest, Caiaphas, John,[e] and Alexander, and all who were of the high-priestly family. [7]When they had made the prisoners[f] stand in their midst, they inquired, "By what power or by what name did you do this?" [8]Then Peter, filled with the Holy Spirit, said to them, "Rulers of the people and elders, [9]if we are questioned today because of a good deed done to someone who was sick and are asked how this man has been healed, [10]let it be known to all of you, and to all the people of Israel, that this man is standing before you in good health by the name of Jesus Christ of Nazareth,[g] whom you crucified, whom God raised from the dead. [11]This Jesus[h] is

'the stone that was rejected by you, the builders;
    it has become the cornerstone.'[i]

[12]There is salvation in no one else, for there is no other name under heaven given among mortals by which we must be saved."

13 Now when they saw the boldness of Peter and John and realized that they were uneducated and ordinary men, they were amazed and recognized them as companions of Jesus. [14]When they saw the man who had been cured standing beside them, they had nothing to say in opposition. [15]So they ordered them to leave the council while they discussed the matter with one another. [16]They said, "What will we do with them? For it is obvious to all who live in Jerusalem that a notable sign has been done through them; we cannot deny it. [17]But to keep it from spreading further among the people, let us warn them to speak no more to anyone in this name." [18]So they called them and ordered them not to speak or teach at all in the name of Jesus. [19]But Peter and John answered them, "Whether it is right in

Holy Boldness

ACTS 4.13–20

People are amazed at Peter and John's boldness as they preach the Good News in spite of warnings from the religious authorities. Are there areas of your own life in which you pay more attention to human rules than to God's call? Pray for opportunities to share the gospel and for the boldness to use those opportunities. You might also pray for pastors and missionaries, evangelists and others engaged in spreading the Word. Be specific as you pray.

See Meeting God in Prayer

---

a Or *the Christ*   b Gk *brothers*   c Or *child*   d Gk *While they*   e Other ancient authorities read *Jonathan*   f Gk *them*   g Gk *the Nazorean* h Gk *This*   i Or *keystone*

The Blessed Community

ACTS 4.32–33

" 'See how these Christians love one another' might well have been a spontaneous exclamation in the days of the apostles. The Holy Fellowship, the Blessed Community has always astonished those who stood without it. The sharing of physical goods in the primitive church is only an outcropping of a profoundly deeper sharing of a Life, the base and center of which is obscured to those who are still oriented about self, rather than about God."

—THOMAS KELLY,
A Testament of Devotion

See *Meeting God in Community*

God's sight to listen to you rather than to God, you must judge; [20]for we cannot keep from speaking about what we have seen and heard." [21]After threatening them again, they let them go, finding no way to punish them because of the people, for all of them praised God for what had happened. [22]For the man on whom this sign of healing had been performed was more than forty years old.

The Believers Pray for Boldness

23 After they were released, they went to their friends[a] and reported what the chief priests and the elders had said to them. [24]When they heard it, they raised their voices together to God and said, "Sovereign Lord, who made the heaven and the earth, the sea, and everything in them, [25]it is you who said by the Holy Spirit through our ancestor David, your servant:[b]

'Why did the Gentiles rage,
 and the peoples imagine vain things?
26   The kings of the earth took their stand,
  and the rulers have gathered together
   against the Lord and against his Messiah.'[c]

[27]For in this city, in fact, both Herod and Pontius Pilate, with the Gentiles and the peoples of Israel, gathered together against your holy servant[b] Jesus, whom you anointed, [28]to do whatever your hand and your plan had predestined to take place. [29]And now, Lord, look at their threats, and grant to your servants[d] to speak your word with all boldness, [30]while you stretch out your hand to heal, and signs and wonders are performed through the name of your holy servant[b] Jesus." [31]When they had prayed, the place in which they were gathered together was shaken; and they were all filled with the Holy Spirit and spoke the word of God with boldness.

The Believers Share Their Possessions

32 Now the whole group of those who believed were of one heart and soul, and no one claimed private ownership of any possessions, but everything they owned was held in common. [33]With great power the apostles gave their testimony to the resurrection of the Lord Jesus, and great grace was upon them all. [34]There was not a needy person among them, for as many as owned lands or houses sold them and brought the proceeds of what was sold. [35]They laid it at the apostles' feet, and it was distributed to each as any had need. [36]There was a Levite, a native of Cyprus, Joseph, to whom the apostles gave the name Barnabas (which means "son of encouragement"). [37]He sold a field that belonged to him, then brought the money, and laid it at the apostles' feet.

Ananias and Sapphira

5 But a man named Ananias, with the consent of his wife Sapphira, sold a piece of property; [2]with his wife's knowledge, he kept back some of the proceeds, and brought only a part and laid it at the apostles' feet. [3]"Ananias," Peter asked, "why has Satan filled your heart to lie to the Holy Spirit and to keep back part of the proceeds of the land? [4]While it remained unsold, did it not remain your own? And after it was sold, were not the proceeds at your

a Gk *their own*   *b* Or *child*   *c* Or *his Christ*   *d* Gk *slaves*

disposal? How is it that you have contrived this deed in your heart? You did not lie to us[a] but to God!" [5]Now when Ananias heard these words, he fell down and died. And great fear seized all who heard of it. [6]The young men came and wrapped up his body,[b] then carried him out and buried him.

7 After an interval of about three hours his wife came in, not knowing what had happened. [8]Peter said to her, "Tell me whether you and your husband sold the land for such and such a price." And she said, "Yes, that was the price." [9]Then Peter said to her, "How is it that you have agreed together to put the Spirit of the Lord to the test? Look, the feet of those who have buried your husband are at the door, and they will carry you out." [10]Immediately she fell down at his feet and died. When the young men came in they found her dead, so they carried her out and buried her beside her husband. [11]And great fear seized the whole church and all who heard of these things.

The Apostles Heal Many

12 Now many signs and wonders were done among the people through the apostles. And they were all together in Solomon's Portico. [13]None of the rest dared to join them, but the people held them in high esteem. [14]Yet more than ever believers were added to the Lord, great numbers of both men and women, [15]so that they even carried out the sick into the streets, and laid them on cots and mats, in order that Peter's shadow might fall on some of them as he came by. [16]A great number of people would also gather from the towns around Jerusalem, bringing the sick and those tormented by unclean spirits, and they were all cured.

The Apostles Are Persecuted

17 Then the high priest took action; he and all who were with him (that is, the sect of the Sadducees), being filled with jealousy, [18]arrested the apostles and put them in the public prison. [19]But during the night an angel of the Lord opened the prison doors, brought them out, and said, [20]"Go, stand in the temple and tell the people the whole message about this life." [21]When they heard this, they entered the temple at daybreak and went on with their teaching.

When the high priest and those with him arrived, they called together the council and the whole body of the elders of Israel, and sent to the prison to have them brought. [22]But when the temple police went there, they did not find them in the prison; so they returned and reported, [23]"We found the prison securely locked and the guards standing at the doors, but when we opened them, we found no one inside." [24]Now when the captain of the temple and the chief priests heard these words, they were perplexed about them, wondering what might be going on. [25]Then someone arrived and announced, "Look, the men whom you put in prison are standing in the temple and teaching the people!" [26]Then the captain went with the temple police and brought them, but without violence, for they were afraid of being stoned by the people.

27 When they had brought them, they had them stand

Putting God to the Test

ACTS 5.9

Ananias and Sapphira keep a little for themselves while claiming to give all they have. It is their little secret, a hedge in case following Jesus doesn't work out. When their secret is revealed, they die. Are you holding back from full commitment, waiting to see how things work out before getting fully involved? What secret do you cling to for fear that others will think less of you if they learn it? You might take time now to confess—not only to God, but to a Christian friend whose guidance you trust.

See Meeting God in Community

Rejoicing in Suffering

ACTS 5.41

Have you suffered "dishonor for the sake of the name"? Has being faithful created uncomfortable situations for you? How did you respond? If you have never experienced firsthand the cost of discipleship, why do you think that is so? For the apostles, suffering was a badge of honor, a declaration of worthiness. Is your Christianity so low-key that it offends no one or even is unnoticed outside of the church setting? If no one knows for sure you are a Christian, what badge are you wearing?

See Meeting God in Everyday Life

before the council. The high priest questioned them, ²⁸saying, "We gave you strict orders not to teach in this name,ᵃ yet here you have filled Jerusalem with your teaching and you are determined to bring this man's blood on us." ²⁹But Peter and the apostles answered, "We must obey God rather than any human authority.ᵇ ³⁰The God of our ancestors raised up Jesus, whom you had killed by hanging him on a tree. ³¹God exalted him at his right hand as Leader and Savior that he might give repentance to Israel and forgiveness of sins. ³²And we are witnesses to these things, and so is the Holy Spirit whom God has given to those who obey him."

33 When they heard this, they were enraged and wanted to kill them. ³⁴But a Pharisee in the council named Gamaliel, a teacher of the law, respected by all the people, stood up and ordered the men to be put outside for a short time. ³⁵Then he said to them, "Fellow Israelites,ᶜ consider carefully what you propose to do to these men. ³⁶For some time ago Theudas rose up, claiming to be somebody, and a number of men, about four hundred, joined him; but he was killed, and all who followed him were dispersed and disappeared. ³⁷After him Judas the Galilean rose up at the time of the census and got people to follow him; he also perished, and all who followed him were scattered. ³⁸So in the present case, I tell you, keep away from these men and let them alone; because if this plan or this undertaking is of human origin, it will fail; ³⁹but if it is of God, you will not be able to overthrow them—in that case you may even be found fighting against God!"

They were convinced by him, ⁴⁰and when they had called in the apostles, they had them flogged. Then they ordered them not to speak in the name of Jesus, and let them go. ⁴¹As they left the council, they rejoiced that they were considered worthy to suffer dishonor for the sake of the name. ⁴²And every day in the temple and at homeᵈ they did not cease to teach and proclaim Jesus as the Messiah.ᵉ

Seven Chosen to Serve

6 Now during those days, when the disciples were increasing in number, the Hellenists complained against the Hebrews because their widows were being neglected in the daily distribution of food. ²And the twelve called together the whole community of the disciples and said, "It is not right that we should neglect the word of God in order to wait on tables.ᶠ ³Therefore, friends,ᵍ select from among yourselves seven men of good standing, full of the Spirit and of wisdom, whom we may appoint to this task, ⁴while we, for our part, will devote ourselves to prayer and to serving the word." ⁵What they said pleased the whole community, and they chose Stephen, a man full of faith and the Holy Spirit, together with Philip, Prochorus, Nicanor, Timon, Parmenas, and Nicolaus, a proselyte of Antioch. ⁶They had these men stand before the apostles, who prayed and laid their hands on them.

7 The word of God continued to spread; the number of the disciples increased greatly in Jerusalem, and a great many of the priests became obedient to the faith.

---

a Other ancient authorities read *Did we not give you strict orders not to teach in this name?*   *b* Gk *than men*   *c* Gk *Men, Israelites*   *d* Or *from house to house*   *e* Or *the Christ*   *f* Or *keep accounts*   *g* Gk *brothers*

The Arrest of Stephen

8 Stephen, full of grace and power, did great wonders and signs among the people. 9Then some of those who belonged to the synagogue of the Freedmen (as it was called), Cyrenians, Alexandrians, and others of those from Cilicia and Asia, stood up and argued with Stephen. 10But they could not withstand the wisdom and the Spirit*a* with which he spoke. 11Then they secretly instigated some men to say, "We have heard him speak blasphemous words against Moses and God." 12They stirred up the people as well as the elders and the scribes; then they suddenly confronted him, seized him, and brought him before the council. 13They set up false witnesses who said, "This man never stops saying things against this holy place and the law; 14for we have heard him say that this Jesus of Nazareth*b* will destroy this place and will change the customs that Moses handed on to us." 15And all who sat in the council looked intently at him, and they saw that his face was like the face of an angel.

Stephen's Speech to the Council

7 Then the high priest asked him, "Are these things so?" 2And Stephen replied:

"Brothers*c* and fathers, listen to me. The God of glory appeared to our ancestor Abraham when he was in Mesopotamia, before he lived in Haran, 3and said to him, 'Leave your country and your relatives and go to the land that I will show you.' 4Then he left the country of the Chaldeans and settled in Haran. After his father died, God had him move from there to this country in which you are now living. 5He did not give him any of it as a heritage, not even a foot's length, but promised to give it to him as his possession and to his descendants after him, even though he had no child. 6And God spoke in these terms, that his descendants would be resident aliens in a country belonging to others, who would enslave them and mistreat them during four hundred years. 7'But I will judge the nation that they serve,' said God, 'and after that they shall come out and worship me in this place.' 8Then he gave him the covenant of circumcision. And so Abraham*d* became the father of Isaac and circumcised him on the eighth day; and Isaac became the father of Jacob, and Jacob of the twelve patriarchs.

9 "The patriarchs, jealous of Joseph, sold him into Egypt; but God was with him, 10and rescued him from all his afflictions, and enabled him to win favor and to show wisdom when he stood before Pharaoh, king of Egypt, who appointed him ruler over Egypt and over all his household. 11Now there came a famine throughout Egypt and Canaan, and great suffering, and our ancestors could find no food. 12But when Jacob heard that there was grain in Egypt, he sent our ancestors there on their first visit. 13On the second visit Joseph made himself known to his brothers, and Joseph's family became known to Pharaoh. 14Then Joseph sent and invited his father Jacob and all his relatives to come to him, seventy-five in all; 15so Jacob went down to Egypt. He himself died there as well as our ancestors, 16and their bodies*e* were brought back to Shechem and laid in the

Telling the Story of Salvation

ACTS 7.1–38

When Stephen talks about God's activity in human history, he starts with Abraham, Isaac, Jacob, Joseph and Moses.

Think of the ways you might recall the most important events and people in your life. For example, you might revisit your family home, reflect on a family tree, write in a journal or browse through a photo album. Can you, like Stephen, see God's hand in the big and small events of your life? Use paper and pen to briefly describe, or draw a picture of, an important event in your life. With the benefit of hindsight, where do you see God at work in what happened? How might this event fit into God's larger scheme for your life?

See Meeting God in Everyday Life

a Or *spirit* b Gk *the Nazorean* c Gk *Men, brothers* d Gk *he*
e Gk *they*

To Kill Virtue's Adversary

ACTS 7.24

"Moses teaches us to take our
stand with virtue as with a
kinsman and to kill virtue's adversary. The victory of true religion is the death of idolatry. So
also injustice is killed by righteousness and arrogance is
slain by humility."

—GREGORY OF NYSSA,
The Life of Moses Book II

tomb that Abraham had bought for a sum of silver from the
sons of Hamor in Shechem.

17 "But as the time drew near for the fulfillment of the
promise that God had made to Abraham, our people in
Egypt increased and multiplied [18]until another king who
had not known Joseph ruled over Egypt. [19]He dealt craftily
with our race and forced our ancestors to abandon their infants so that they would die. [20]At this time Moses was born,
and he was beautiful before God. For three months he was
brought up in his father's house; [21]and when he was abandoned, Pharaoh's daughter adopted him and brought him
up as her own son. [22]So Moses was instructed in all the wisdom of the Egyptians and was powerful in his words and
deeds.

23 "When he was forty years old, it came into his heart
to visit his relatives, the Israelites.[a] [24]When he saw one of
them being wronged, he defended the oppressed man and
avenged him by striking down the Egyptian. [25]He supposed
that his kinsfolk would understand that God through him
was rescuing them, but they did not understand. [26]The next
day he came to some of them as they were quarreling and
tried to reconcile them, saying, 'Men, you are brothers;
why do you wrong each other?' [27]But the man who was
wronging his neighbor pushed Moses[b] aside, saying, 'Who
made you a ruler and a judge over us? [28]Do you want to kill
me as you killed the Egyptian yesterday?' [29]When he heard
this, Moses fled and became a resident alien in the land of
Midian. There he became the father of two sons.

30 "Now when forty years had passed, an angel appeared to him in the wilderness of Mount Sinai, in the
flame of a burning bush. [31]When Moses saw it, he was
amazed at the sight; and as he approached to look, there
came the voice of the Lord: [32]'I am the God of your ancestors, the God of Abraham, Isaac, and Jacob.' Moses began to
tremble and did not dare to look. [33]Then the Lord said to
him, 'Take off the sandals from your feet, for the place
where you are standing is holy ground. [34]I have surely seen
the mistreatment of my people who are in Egypt and have
heard their groaning, and I have come down to rescue
them. Come now, I will send you to Egypt.'

35 "It was this Moses whom they rejected when they
said, 'Who made you a ruler and a judge?' and whom God
now sent as both ruler and liberator through the angel who
appeared to him in the bush. [36]He led them out, having
performed wonders and signs in Egypt, at the Red Sea, and
in the wilderness for forty years. [37]This is the Moses who
said to the Israelites, 'God will raise up a prophet for you
from your own people[c] as he raised me up.' [38]He is the one
who was in the congregation in the wilderness with the
angel who spoke to him at Mount Sinai, and with our ancestors; and he received living oracles to give to us. [39]Our
ancestors were unwilling to obey him; instead, they pushed
him aside, and in their hearts they turned back to Egypt,
[40]saying to Aaron, 'Make gods for us who will lead the way
for us; as for this Moses who led us out from the land of
Egypt, we do not know what has happened to him.' [41]At
that time they made a calf, offered a sacrifice to the idol,
and reveled in the works of their hands. [42]But God turned

a Gk *his brothers, the sons of Israel*   *b* Gk *him*   *c* Gk *your brothers*

away from them and handed them over to worship the host of heaven, as it is written in the book of the prophets:

'Did you offer to me slain victims and sacrifices
    forty years in the wilderness, O house of Israel?
⁴³   No; you took along the tent of Moloch,
    and the star of your god Rephan,
      the images that you made to worship;
  so I will remove you beyond Babylon.'

44 "Our ancestors had the tent of testimony in the wilderness, as God[a] directed when he spoke to Moses, ordering him to make it according to the pattern he had seen. ⁴⁵Our ancestors in turn brought it in with Joshua when they dispossessed the nations that God drove out before our ancestors. And it was there until the time of David, ⁴⁶who found favor with God and asked that he might find a dwelling place for the house of Jacob.[b] ⁴⁷But it was Solomon who built a house for him. ⁴⁸Yet the Most High does not dwell in houses made with human hands;[c] as the prophet says,

⁴⁹ 'Heaven is my throne,
    and the earth is my footstool.
  What kind of house will you build for me, says the
      Lord,
    or what is the place of my rest?
⁵⁰   Did not my hand make all these things?'

51 "You stiff-necked people, uncircumcised in heart and ears, you are forever opposing the Holy Spirit, just as your ancestors used to do. ⁵²Which of the prophets did your ancestors not persecute? They killed those who foretold the coming of the Righteous One, and now you have become his betrayers and murderers. ⁵³You are the ones that received the law as ordained by angels, and yet you have not kept it."

The Stoning of Stephen

54 When they heard these things, they became enraged and ground their teeth at Stephen.[d] ⁵⁵But filled with the Holy Spirit, he gazed into heaven and saw the glory of God and Jesus standing at the right hand of God. ⁵⁶"Look," he said, "I see the heavens opened and the Son of Man standing at the right hand of God!" ⁵⁷But they covered their ears, and with a loud shout all rushed together against him. ⁵⁸Then they dragged him out of the city and began to stone him; and the witnesses laid their coats at the feet of a young man named Saul. ⁵⁹While they were stoning Stephen, he prayed, "Lord Jesus, receive my spirit." ⁶⁰Then he knelt down and cried out in a loud voice, "Lord, do not hold this sin against them." When he had said this, he died.[e]

8 ¹And Saul approved of their killing him.

Saul Persecutes the Church

That day a severe persecution began against the church in Jerusalem, and all except the apostles were scattered throughout the countryside of Judea and Samaria. ²Devout men buried Stephen and made loud lamentation over him. ³But Saul was ravaging the church by entering house after

---

The Crowd at Stephen's Stoning

ACTS 7.44–60

This might be a good passage with which to try the Ignatian approach described in the article *Meeting God in Scripture*. Imagine yourself as part of the crowd at Stephen's stoning. Begin by rereading the story of Stephen's arrest and speech beginning at 6.8. Picture the crowded council room. Listen to the accusations against Stephen and to his defense against those allegations. How do those around you react to Stephen calling them "stiff-necked people . . . forever opposing the Holy Spirit"? Try talking with them. How do you react? Follow the mob as they take Stephen out to stone him. How does his witness affect you? Do you get caught up in the mob's anger? You might "debrief" by writing a description of what you have seen, heard and felt.

Purchasing God

ACTS 8.18–21

Simon the sorcerer tried to buy the Spirit's power, and ever since that time the practice of purchasing church offices has been called "simony." There are less obvious ways we try to purchase God's favor. Sometimes we pray, "O God, if you'll do this [or give me that], then I'll be good [or go to church every Sunday or become a minister]." When have you tried to bargain with God? What is it that God really wants? (See Psalm 51.16–17 and Micah 6.8.) You might want to pray a brief prayer of surrender, freely offering God your heart, your will, your life—to use as he wills.

house; dragging off both men and women, he committed them to prison.

Philip Preaches in Samaria

4 Now those who were scattered went from place to place, proclaiming the word. 5Philip went down to the city*a* of Samaria and proclaimed the Messiah*b* to them. 6The crowds with one accord listened eagerly to what was said by Philip, hearing and seeing the signs that he did, 7for unclean spirits, crying with loud shrieks, came out of many who were possessed; and many others who were paralyzed or lame were cured. 8So there was great joy in that city.

9 Now a certain man named Simon had previously practiced magic in the city and amazed the people of Samaria, saying that he was someone great. 10All of them, from the least to the greatest, listened to him eagerly, saying, "This man is the power of God that is called Great." 11And they listened eagerly to him because for a long time he had amazed them with his magic. 12But when they believed Philip, who was proclaiming the good news about the kingdom of God and the name of Jesus Christ, they were baptized, both men and women. 13Even Simon himself believed. After being baptized, he stayed constantly with Philip and was amazed when he saw the signs and great miracles that took place.

14 Now when the apostles at Jerusalem heard that Samaria had accepted the word of God, they sent Peter and John to them. 15The two went down and prayed for them that they might receive the Holy Spirit 16(for as yet the Spirit had not come*c* upon any of them; they had only been baptized in the name of the Lord Jesus). 17Then Peter and John*d* laid their hands on them, and they received the Holy Spirit. 18Now when Simon saw that the Spirit was given through the laying on of the apostles' hands, he offered them money, 19saying, "Give me also this power so that anyone on whom I lay my hands may receive the Holy Spirit." 20But Peter said to him, "May your silver perish with you, because you thought you could obtain God's gift with money! 21You have no part or share in this, for your heart is not right before God. 22Repent therefore of this wickedness of yours, and pray to the Lord that, if possible, the intent of your heart may be forgiven you. 23For I see that you are in the gall of bitterness and the chains of wickedness." 24Simon answered, "Pray for me to the Lord, that nothing of what you*e* have said may happen to me."

25 Now after Peter and John*f* had testified and spoken the word of the Lord, they returned to Jerusalem, proclaiming the good news to many villages of the Samaritans.

Philip and the Ethiopian Eunuch

26 Then an angel of the Lord said to Philip, "Get up and go toward the south*g* to the road that goes down from Jerusalem to Gaza." (This is a wilderness road.) 27So he got up and went. Now there was an Ethiopian eunuch, a court official of the Candace, queen of the Ethiopians, in charge of her entire treasury. He had come to Jerusalem to worship 28and was returning home; seated in his chariot, he was

a Other ancient authorities read *a city*   b Or *the Christ*   c Gk *fallen*
d Gk *they*   e The Greek word for *you* and the verb *pray* are plural
f Gk *after they*   g Or *go at noon*

reading the prophet Isaiah. ²⁹Then the Spirit said to Philip, "Go over to this chariot and join it." ³⁰So Philip ran up to it and heard him reading the prophet Isaiah. He asked, "Do you understand what you are reading?" ³¹He replied, "How can I, unless someone guides me?" And he invited Philip to get in and sit beside him. ³²Now the passage of the scripture that he was reading was this:

"Like a sheep he was led to the slaughter,
    and like a lamb silent before its shearer,
        so he does not open his mouth.
³³   In his humiliation justice was denied him.
    Who can describe his generation?
        For his life is taken away from the earth."

³⁴The eunuch asked Philip, "About whom, may I ask you, does the prophet say this, about himself or about someone else?" ³⁵Then Philip began to speak, and starting with this scripture, he proclaimed to him the good news about Jesus. ³⁶As they were going along the road, they came to some water; and the eunuch said, "Look, here is water! What is to prevent me from being baptized?"*ᵃ* ³⁸He commanded the chariot to stop, and both of them, Philip and the eunuch, went down into the water, and Philip*ᵇ* baptized him. ³⁹When they came up out of the water, the Spirit of the Lord snatched Philip away; the eunuch saw him no more, and went on his way rejoicing. ⁴⁰But Philip found himself at Azotus, and as he was passing through the region, he proclaimed the good news to all the towns until he came to Caesarea.

The Conversion of Saul

9 Meanwhile Saul, still breathing threats and murder against the disciples of the Lord, went to the high priest ²and asked him for letters to the synagogues at Damascus, so that if he found any who belonged to the Way, men or women, he might bring them bound to Jerusalem. ³Now as he was going along and approaching Damascus, suddenly a light from heaven flashed around him. ⁴He fell to the ground and heard a voice saying to him, "Saul, Saul, why do you persecute me?" ⁵He asked, "Who are you, Lord?" The reply came, "I am Jesus, whom you are persecuting. ⁶But get up and enter the city, and you will be told what you are to do." ⁷The men who were traveling with him stood speechless because they heard the voice but saw no one. ⁸Saul got up from the ground, and though his eyes were open, he could see nothing; so they led him by the hand and brought him into Damascus. ⁹For three days he was without sight, and neither ate nor drank.

10 Now there was a disciple in Damascus named Ananias. The Lord said to him in a vision, "Ananias." He answered, "Here I am, Lord." ¹¹The Lord said to him, "Get up and go to the street called Straight, and at the house of Judas look for a man of Tarsus named Saul. At this moment he is praying, ¹²and he has seen in a vision*ᶜ* a man named Ananias come in and lay his hands on him so that he might regain his sight." ¹³But Ananias answered, "Lord, I have heard from many about this man, how much evil he has

Seeing Opportunities to Witness

ACTS 8.29–39

An angel of the Lord gives instructions to Philip and he is led to a chariot on a desert road. There he finds an unexpected occasion to tell the good news of Jesus. Such opportunities are all around us, though we often let them pass unnoticed. You might look back over the last day or so. Did you ignore someone's pain or offer polite sympathy instead of a word of hope or love? When might you have invited someone to come to a worship service or a Bible study? Were there occasions when you could have witnessed about your own faith? Ask God to give you the vision to see such opportunities in the coming days as well as the courage to act on them.

See Meeting God in Service

Before and After

ACTS 9.13–16

Ananias is afraid to go to Saul (Paul) because he knows only who Saul *has been*, not who he *is becoming* since his encounter with Jesus Christ. You might try drawing simple cartoons to illustrate the "before" and "after" versions of Paul. What are the outward changes? How might you illustrate the inward ones? What if you were to try the same exercise with yourself? What changes has Jesus made in your life? What is still "in process"? You might go even further and illustrate the "ideal you" that you are becoming in Jesus.

done to your saints in Jerusalem; [14]and here he has authority from the chief priests to bind all who invoke your name." [15]But the Lord said to him, "Go, for he is an instrument whom I have chosen to bring my name before Gentiles and kings and before the people of Israel; [16]I myself will show him how much he must suffer for the sake of my name." [17]So Ananias went and entered the house. He laid his hands on Saul[a] and said, "Brother Saul, the Lord Jesus, who appeared to you on your way here, has sent me so that you may regain your sight and be filled with the Holy Spirit." [18]And immediately something like scales fell from his eyes, and his sight was restored. Then he got up and was baptized, [19]and after taking some food, he regained his strength.

Saul Preaches in Damascus

For several days he was with the disciples in Damascus, [20]and immediately he began to proclaim Jesus in the synagogues, saying, "He is the Son of God." [21]All who heard him were amazed and said, "Is not this the man who made havoc in Jerusalem among those who invoked this name? And has he not come here for the purpose of bringing them bound before the chief priests?" [22]Saul became increasingly more powerful and confounded the Jews who lived in Damascus by proving that Jesus[b] was the Messiah.[c]

Saul Escapes from the Jews

23 After some time had passed, the Jews plotted to kill him, [24]but their plot became known to Saul. They were watching the gates day and night so that they might kill him; [25]but his disciples took him by night and let him down through an opening in the wall,[d] lowering him in a basket.

Saul in Jerusalem

26 When he had come to Jerusalem, he attempted to join the disciples; and they were all afraid of him, for they did not believe that he was a disciple. [27]But Barnabas took him, brought him to the apostles, and described for them how on the road he had seen the Lord, who had spoken to him, and how in Damascus he had spoken boldly in the name of Jesus. [28]So he went in and out among them in Jerusalem, speaking boldly in the name of the Lord. [29]He spoke and argued with the Hellenists; but they were attempting to kill him. [30]When the believers[e] learned of it, they brought him down to Caesarea and sent him off to Tarsus.

31 Meanwhile the church throughout Judea, Galilee, and Samaria had peace and was built up. Living in the fear of the Lord and in the comfort of the Holy Spirit, it increased in numbers.

The Healing of Aeneas

32 Now as Peter went here and there among all the believers,[f] he came down also to the saints living in Lydda. [33]There he found a man named Aeneas, who had been bedridden for eight years, for he was paralyzed. [34]Peter said to him, "Aeneas, Jesus Christ heals you; get up and make

a Gk *him*   b Gk *that this*   c Or *the Christ*   d Gk *through the wall*
e Gk *brothers*   f Gk *all of them*

your bed!" And immediately he got up. ³⁵And all the residents of Lydda and Sharon saw him and turned to the Lord.

Peter in Lydda and Joppa

36 Now in Joppa there was a disciple whose name was Tabitha, which in Greek is Dorcas.ᵃ She was devoted to good works and acts of charity. ³⁷At that time she became ill and died. When they had washed her, they laid her in a room upstairs. ³⁸Since Lydda was near Joppa, the disciples, who heard that Peter was there, sent two men to him with the request, "Please come to us without delay." ³⁹So Peter got up and went with them; and when he arrived, they took him to the room upstairs. All the widows stood beside him, weeping and showing tunics and other clothing that Dorcas had made while she was with them. ⁴⁰Peter put all of them outside, and then he knelt down and prayed. He turned to the body and said, "Tabitha, get up." Then she opened her eyes, and seeing Peter, she sat up. ⁴¹He gave her his hand and helped her up. Then calling the saints and widows, he showed her to be alive. ⁴²This became known throughout Joppa, and many believed in the Lord. ⁴³Meanwhile he stayed in Joppa for some time with a certain Simon, a tanner.

Peter and Cornelius

10 In Caesarea there was a man named Cornelius, a centurion of the Italian Cohort, as it was called. ²He was a devout man who feared God with all his household; he gave alms generously to the people and prayed constantly to God. ³One afternoon at about three o'clock he had a vision in which he clearly saw an angel of God coming in and saying to him, "Cornelius." ⁴He stared at him in terror and said, "What is it, Lord?" He answered, "Your prayers and your alms have ascended as a memorial before God. ⁵Now send men to Joppa for a certain Simon who is called Peter; ⁶he is lodging with Simon, a tanner, whose house is by the seaside." ⁷When the angel who spoke to him had left, he called two of his slaves and a devout soldier from the ranks of those who served him, ⁸and after telling them everything, he sent them to Joppa.

9 About noon the next day, as they were on their journey and approaching the city, Peter went up on the roof to pray. ¹⁰He became hungry and wanted something to eat; and while it was being prepared, he fell into a trance. ¹¹He saw the heaven opened and something like a large sheet coming down, being lowered to the ground by its four corners. ¹²In it were all kinds of four-footed creatures and reptiles and birds of the air. ¹³Then he heard a voice saying, "Get up, Peter; kill and eat." ¹⁴But Peter said, "By no means, Lord; for I have never eaten anything that is profane or unclean." ¹⁵The voice said to him again, a second time, "What God has made clean, you must not call profane." ¹⁶This happened three times, and the thing was suddenly taken up to heaven.

17 Now while Peter was greatly puzzled about what to make of the vision that he had seen, suddenly the men sent by Cornelius appeared. They were asking for Simon's house and were standing by the gate. ¹⁸They called out to ask whether Simon, who was called Peter, was staying

---

What's Stopping You?

ACTS 10.9–16

Peter was unwilling to visit Gentiles because they ate unclean animals. Then God showed him a vision. You might put yourself in Peter's place. See a great sheet coming down and opening. What are the things inside that make you cry, "By no means, Lord"? What makes you hold back? A different race or ethnic group? A dirty house? A lifestyle you find strange or repugnant? As you look around you, hear God's word to you: "What God has made clean, you must not call profane." What can you do to move from prayer to action?

See Meeting God in Service

ᵃ The name Tabitha in Aramaic and the name Dorcas in Greek mean
a gazelle

Who Is Acceptable?

ACTS 10.34–35

"I truly understand that God shows no partiality, but in every nation anyone who fears him and does what is right is acceptable to him." What an amazing statement! Turn this sentence over and over in your mind. Mull it over until you have extracted all its truth. Take it in little bites: no partiality . . . every nation . . . is acceptable. What do you learn about God's love? What call do you hear to change your attitude toward others? What good news do you hear for yourself?

See *Meeting God in Service*

there. [19]While Peter was still thinking about the vision, the Spirit said to him, "Look, three[a] men are searching for you. [20]Now get up, go down, and go with them without hesitation; for I have sent them." [21]So Peter went down to the men and said, "I am the one you are looking for; what is the reason for your coming?" [22]They answered, "Cornelius, a centurion, an upright and God-fearing man, who is well spoken of by the whole Jewish nation, was directed by a holy angel to send for you to come to his house and to hear what you have to say." [23]So Peter[b] invited them in and gave them lodging.

The next day he got up and went with them, and some of the believers[c] from Joppa accompanied him. [24]The following day they came to Caesarea. Cornelius was expecting them and had called together his relatives and close friends. [25]On Peter's arrival Cornelius met him, and falling at his feet, worshiped him. [26]But Peter made him get up, saying, "Stand up; I am only a mortal." [27]And as he talked with him, he went in and found that many had assembled; [28]and he said to them, "You yourselves know that it is unlawful for a Jew to associate with or to visit a Gentile; but God has shown me that I should not call anyone profane or unclean. [29]So when I was sent for, I came without objection. Now may I ask why you sent for me?"

30 Cornelius replied, "Four days ago at this very hour, at three o'clock, I was praying in my house when suddenly a man in dazzling clothes stood before me. [31]He said, 'Cornelius, your prayer has been heard and your alms have been remembered before God. [32]Send therefore to Joppa and ask for Simon, who is called Peter; he is staying in the home of Simon, a tanner, by the sea.' [33]Therefore I sent for you immediately, and you have been kind enough to come. So now all of us are here in the presence of God to listen to all that the Lord has commanded you to say."

Gentiles Hear the Good News

34 Then Peter began to speak to them: "I truly understand that God shows no partiality, [35]but in every nation anyone who fears him and does what is right is acceptable to him. [36]You know the message he sent to the people of Israel, preaching peace by Jesus Christ—he is Lord of all. [37]That message spread throughout Judea, beginning in Galilee after the baptism that John announced: [38]how God anointed Jesus of Nazareth with the Holy Spirit and with power; how he went about doing good and healing all who were oppressed by the devil, for God was with him. [39]We are witnesses to all that he did both in Judea and in Jerusalem. They put him to death by hanging him on a tree; [40]but God raised him on the third day and allowed him to appear, [41]not to all the people but to us who were chosen by God as witnesses, and who ate and drank with him after he rose from the dead. [42]He commanded us to preach to the people and to testify that he is the one ordained by God as judge of the living and the dead. [43]All the prophets testify about him that everyone who believes in him receives forgiveness of sins through his name."

a One ancient authority reads *two*; others lack the word   *b* Gk *he*
c Gk *brothers*

Gentiles Receive the Holy Spirit

44 While Peter was still speaking, the Holy Spirit fell upon all who heard the word. ⁴⁵The circumcised believers who had come with Peter were astounded that the gift of the Holy Spirit had been poured out even on the Gentiles, ⁴⁶for they heard them speaking in tongues and extolling God. Then Peter said, ⁴⁷"Can anyone withhold the water for baptizing these people who have received the Holy Spirit just as we have?" ⁴⁸So he ordered them to be baptized in the name of Jesus Christ. Then they invited him to stay for several days.

Peter's Report to the Church at Jerusalem

11 Now the apostles and the believers[a] who were in Judea heard that the Gentiles had also accepted the word of God. ²So when Peter went up to Jerusalem, the circumcised believers[b] criticized him, ³saying, "Why did you go to uncircumcised men and eat with them?" ⁴Then Peter began to explain it to them, step by step, saying, ⁵"I was in the city of Joppa praying, and in a trance I saw a vision. There was something like a large sheet coming down from heaven, being lowered by its four corners; and it came close to me. ⁶As I looked at it closely I saw four-footed animals, beasts of prey, reptiles, and birds of the air. ⁷I also heard a voice saying to me, 'Get up, Peter; kill and eat.' ⁸But I replied, 'By no means, Lord; for nothing profane or unclean has ever entered my mouth.' ⁹But a second time the voice answered from heaven, 'What God has made clean, you must not call profane.' ¹⁰This happened three times; then everything was pulled up again to heaven. ¹¹At that very moment three men, sent to me from Caesarea, arrived at the house where we were. ¹²The Spirit told me to go with them and not to make a distinction between them and us.[c] These six brothers also accompanied me, and we entered the man's house. ¹³He told us how he had seen the angel standing in his house and saying, 'Send to Joppa and bring Simon, who is called Peter; ¹⁴he will give you a message by which you and your entire household will be saved.' ¹⁵And as I began to speak, the Holy Spirit fell upon them just as it had upon us at the beginning. ¹⁶And I remembered the word of the Lord, how he had said, 'John baptized with water, but you will be baptized with the Holy Spirit.' ¹⁷If then God gave them the same gift that he gave us when we believed in the Lord Jesus Christ, who was I that I could hinder God?" ¹⁸When they heard this, they were silenced. And they praised God, saying, "Then God has given even to the Gentiles the repentance that leads to life."

The Church in Antioch

19 Now those who were scattered because of the persecution that took place over Stephen traveled as far as Phoenicia, Cyprus, and Antioch, and they spoke the word to no one except Jews. ²⁰But among them were some men of Cyprus and Cyrene who, on coming to Antioch, spoke to the Hellenists[d] also, proclaiming the Lord Jesus. ²¹The hand of the Lord was with them, and a great number became be-

Praising God for the Spirit's Work

ACTS 11.17–18

Peter was amazed when the Spirit was poured out on Cornelius and his household. The other disciples were also astonished to hear of it. But they praised God for giving grace "even to the Gentiles." As you think about the world around you, where does the Spirit's activity astound you? Name people whom you have written off as unreachable who are finding Jesus Christ. How are people experiencing the Spirit's power in ways that you find strange or that make you uncomfortable? What attitudes or traditions do you cherish that might be hindering God? What do you see that makes you praise God for this gift of "repentance that leads to life"?

a Gk *brothers*   *b* Gk lacks *believers*   *c* Or *not to hesitate*   *d* Other ancient authorities read *Greeks*

The Chains Fall Off

ACTS 12.5–8

Use your imagination to put yourself in Peter's place. Reread the passage. See the cell, the guards, the chains. What are the chains that bind you? What keeps you captive, unable to move freely? Even as you remain in bondage, know that others are praying for your release. You might join them, asking God for help. See an angel appear before you. Feel the angel's touch. Hear the words, "Get up quickly." Picture yourself getting up as the chains fall off. You stand free, able to walk out of captivity. Hear the angel call you to follow him. Where can you go to tell what God has done for you? Whom do you need to tell?

See Meeting God in Scripture

lievers and turned to the Lord. [22]News of this came to the ears of the church in Jerusalem, and they sent Barnabas to Antioch. [23]When he came and saw the grace of God, he rejoiced, and he exhorted them all to remain faithful to the Lord with steadfast devotion; [24]for he was a good man, full of the Holy Spirit and of faith. And a great many people were brought to the Lord. [25]Then Barnabas went to Tarsus to look for Saul, [26]and when he had found him, he brought him to Antioch. So it was that for an entire year they met with[a] the church and taught a great many people, and it was in Antioch that the disciples were first called "Christians."

27 At that time prophets came down from Jerusalem to Antioch. [28]One of them named Agabus stood up and predicted by the Spirit that there would be a severe famine over all the world; and this took place during the reign of Claudius. [29]The disciples determined that according to their ability, each would send relief to the believers[b] living in Judea; [30]this they did, sending it to the elders by Barnabas and Saul.

James Killed and Peter Imprisoned

12 About that time King Herod laid violent hands upon some who belonged to the church. [2]He had James, the brother of John, killed with the sword. [3]After he saw that it pleased the Jews, he proceeded to arrest Peter also. (This was during the festival of Unleavened Bread.) [4]When he had seized him, he put him in prison and handed him over to four squads of soldiers to guard him, intending to bring him out to the people after the Passover. [5]While Peter was kept in prison, the church prayed fervently to God for him.

Peter Delivered from Prison

6 The very night before Herod was going to bring him out, Peter, bound with two chains, was sleeping between two soldiers, while guards in front of the door were keeping watch over the prison. [7]Suddenly an angel of the Lord appeared and a light shone in the cell. He tapped Peter on the side and woke him, saying, "Get up quickly." And the chains fell off his wrists. [8]The angel said to him, "Fasten your belt and put on your sandals." He did so. Then he said to him, "Wrap your cloak around you and follow me." [9]Peter[c] went out and followed him; he did not realize that what was happening with the angel's help was real; he thought he was seeing a vision. [10]After they had passed the first and the second guard, they came before the iron gate leading into the city. It opened for them of its own accord, and they went outside and walked along a lane, when suddenly the angel left him. [11]Then Peter came to himself and said, "Now I am sure that the Lord has sent his angel and rescued me from the hands of Herod and from all that the Jewish people were expecting."

12 As soon as he realized this, he went to the house of Mary, the mother of John whose other name was Mark, where many had gathered and were praying. [13]When he knocked at the outer gate, a maid named Rhoda came to answer. [14]On recognizing Peter's voice, she was so overjoyed that, instead of opening the gate, she ran in and an-

a Or were guests of   b Gk brothers   c Gk He

nounced that Peter was standing at the gate. ¹⁵They said to her, "You are out of your mind!" But she insisted that it was so. They said, "It is his angel." ¹⁶Meanwhile Peter continued knocking; and when they opened the gate, they saw him and were amazed. ¹⁷He motioned to them with his hand to be silent, and described for them how the Lord had brought him out of the prison. And he added, "Tell this to James and to the believers."ᵃ Then he left and went to another place.

18 When morning came, there was no small commotion among the soldiers over what had become of Peter. ¹⁹When Herod had searched for him and could not find him, he examined the guards and ordered them to be put to death. Then he went down from Judea to Caesarea and stayed there.

The Death of Herod

20 Now Herodᵇ was angry with the people of Tyre and Sidon. So they came to him in a body; and after winning over Blastus, the king's chamberlain, they asked for a reconciliation, because their country depended on the king's country for food. ²¹On an appointed day Herod put on his royal robes, took his seat on the platform, and delivered a public address to them. ²²The people kept shouting, "The voice of a god, and not of a mortal!" ²³And immediately, because he had not given the glory to God, an angel of the Lord struck him down, and he was eaten by worms and died.

24 But the word of God continued to advance and gain adherents. ²⁵Then after completing their mission Barnabas and Saul returned toᶜ Jerusalem and brought with them John, whose other name was Mark.

Barnabas and Saul Commissioned

13 Now in the church at Antioch there were prophets and teachers: Barnabas, Simeon who was called Niger, Lucius of Cyrene, Manaen a member of the court of Herod the ruler,ᵈ and Saul. ²While they were worshiping the Lord and fasting, the Holy Spirit said, "Set apart for me Barnabas and Saul for the work to which I have called them." ³Then after fasting and praying they laid their hands on them and sent them off.

The Apostles Preach in Cyprus

4 So, being sent out by the Holy Spirit, they went down to Seleucia; and from there they sailed to Cyprus. ⁵When they arrived at Salamis, they proclaimed the word of God in the synagogues of the Jews. And they had John also to assist them. ⁶When they had gone through the whole island as far as Paphos, they met a certain magician, a Jewish false prophet, named Bar-Jesus. ⁷He was with the proconsul, Sergius Paulus, an intelligent man, who summoned Barnabas and Saul and wanted to hear the word of God. ⁸But the magician Elymas (for that is the translation of his name) opposed them and tried to turn the proconsul away from the faith. ⁹But Saul, also known as Paul, filled with the Holy Spirit, looked intently at him ¹⁰and said, "You son of the devil, you enemy of all righteousness, full of all deceit

Called Through Community

ACTS 13.1–3

How often do you pray for God to set apart and empower leaders for your church? How often is this need mentioned in prayer during worship or other group gatherings? You might want to suggest this concern during worship or at a meeting. You might even offer to lead such a time of prayer. Perhaps you could read this passage and then suggest a time of silent prayer, focusing on the need to hear God's call. Or you might pray for the spiritual empowerment of those who already have positions of leadership, mentioning them by name or even laying hands on them as you pray.

See Meeting God in Community

---

a Gk *brothers*   *b* Gk *he*   *c* Other ancient authorities read *from*
d Gk *tetrarch*

Perverting the Right Ways of the Lord

ACTS 13.8–12

When Paul speaks of "making crooked the straight paths of the Lord," he is reacting to an opponent's attempt to distort the Christian message in order to attack it. Where in your own life have you found yourself falsely under attack? In what ways were you able to stand firm? How were you able to display the love of Jesus Christ? Recall ways in which God was gracious in supporting you. Ask God for forgiveness for those times in which you did not stand firm. Commit the incident into God's hands, knowing he can bring good out of it, as he did for Paul.

See Meeting God in Prayer

and villainy, will you not stop making crooked the straight paths of the Lord? ¹¹And now listen—the hand of the Lord is against you, and you will be blind for a while, unable to see the sun." Immediately mist and darkness came over him, and he went about groping for someone to lead him by the hand. ¹²When the proconsul saw what had happened, he believed, for he was astonished at the teaching about the Lord.

Paul and Barnabas in Antioch of Pisidia

13 Then Paul and his companions set sail from Paphos and came to Perga in Pamphylia. John, however, left them and returned to Jerusalem; ¹⁴but they went on from Perga and came to Antioch in Pisidia. And on the sabbath day they went into the synagogue and sat down. ¹⁵After the reading of the law and the prophets, the officials of the synagogue sent them a message, saying, "Brothers, if you have any word of exhortation for the people, give it." ¹⁶So Paul stood up and with a gesture began to speak:

"You Israelites,ᵃ and others who fear God, listen. ¹⁷The God of this people Israel chose our ancestors and made the people great during their stay in the land of Egypt, and with uplifted arm he led them out of it. ¹⁸For about forty years he put up withᵇ them in the wilderness. ¹⁹After he had destroyed seven nations in the land of Canaan, he gave them their land as an inheritance ²⁰for about four hundred fifty years. After that he gave them judges until the time of the prophet Samuel. ²¹Then they asked for a king; and God gave them Saul son of Kish, a man of the tribe of Benjamin, who reigned for forty years. ²²When he had removed him, he made David their king. In his testimony about him he said, 'I have found David, son of Jesse, to be a man after my heart, who will carry out all my wishes.' ²³Of this man's posterity God has brought to Israel a Savior, Jesus, as he promised; ²⁴before his coming John had already proclaimed a baptism of repentance to all the people of Israel. ²⁵And as John was finishing his work, he said, 'What do you suppose that I am? I am not he. No, but one is coming after me; I am not worthy to untie the thong of the sandalsᶜ on his feet.'

26 "My brothers, you descendants of Abraham's family, and others who fear God, to usᵈ the message of this salvation has been sent. ²⁷Because the residents of Jerusalem and their leaders did not recognize him or understand the words of the prophets that are read every sabbath, they fulfilled those words by condemning him. ²⁸Even though they found no cause for a sentence of death, they asked Pilate to have him killed. ²⁹When they had carried out everything that was written about him, they took him down from the tree and laid him in a tomb. ³⁰But God raised him from the dead; ³¹and for many days he appeared to those who came up with him from Galilee to Jerusalem, and they are now his witnesses to the people. ³²And we bring you the good news that what God promised to our ancestors ³³he has fulfilled for us, their children, by raising Jesus; as also it is written in the second psalm,

'You are my Son;
    today I have begotten you.'

a Gk *Men, Israelites*   *b* Other ancient authorities read *cared for*
c Gk *untie the sandals*   *d* Other ancient authorities read *you*

³⁴As to his raising him from the dead, no more to return to corruption, he has spoken in this way,

'I will give you the holy promises made to David.'

³⁵Therefore he has also said in another psalm,

'You will not let your Holy One experience
corruption.'

³⁶For David, after he had served the purpose of God in his own generation, died,ᵃ was laid beside his ancestors, and experienced corruption; ³⁷but he whom God raised up experienced no corruption. ³⁸Let it be known to you therefore, my brothers, that through this man forgiveness of sins is proclaimed to you; ³⁹by this Jesusᵇ everyone who believes is set free from all those sinsᶜ from which you could not be freed by the law of Moses. ⁴⁰Beware, therefore, that what the prophets said does not happen to you:

⁴¹   'Look, you scoffers!
        Be amazed and perish,
    for in your days I am doing a work,
        a work that you will never believe, even if
            someone tells you.' "

42 As Paul and Barnabasᵈ were going out, the people urged them to speak about these things again the next sabbath. ⁴³When the meeting of the synagogue broke up, many Jews and devout converts to Judaism followed Paul and Barnabas, who spoke to them and urged them to continue in the grace of God.

44 The next sabbath almost the whole city gathered to hear the word of the Lord.ᵉ ⁴⁵But when the Jews saw the crowds, they were filled with jealousy; and blaspheming, they contradicted what was spoken by Paul. ⁴⁶Then both Paul and Barnabas spoke out boldly, saying, "It was necessary that the word of God should be spoken first to you. Since you reject it and judge yourselves to be unworthy of eternal life, we are now turning to the Gentiles. ⁴⁷For so the Lord has commanded us, saying,

'I have set you to be a light for the Gentiles,
    so that you may bring salvation to the ends of the
        earth.' "

48 When the Gentiles heard this, they were glad and praised the word of the Lord; and as many as had been destined for eternal life became believers. ⁴⁹Thus the word of the Lord spread throughout the region. ⁵⁰But the Jews incited the devout women of high standing and the leading men of the city, and stirred up persecution against Paul and Barnabas, and drove them out of their region. ⁵¹So they shook the dust off their feet in protest against them, and went to Iconium. ⁵²And the disciples were filled with joy and with the Holy Spirit.

Paul and Barnabas in Iconium

14 The same thing occurred in Iconium, where Paul and Barnabasᵈ went into the Jewish synagogue and spoke in such a way that a great number of both Jews and Greeks became believers. ²But the unbelieving Jews stirred up the Gentiles and poisoned their minds against the brothers. ³So they remained for a long time, speaking boldly for the Lord, who testified to the word of his grace by granting signs and wonders to be done through them. ⁴But the resi-

---

His Poverty, Our Riches

ACTS 13.38–39

"Become like Christ, since Christ has become like us . . . He has become inferior to make us superior; he has become poor to enrich us by his poverty; he has taken the condition of a slave to procure freedom for us; he has come on earth to bring us to heaven; he has been tempted to see us triumph; he has been dishonored to cover us with glory; he has died to save us; he has ascended to heaven to draw us to himself, we who lie prostrate because of falling into sin."

—GREGORY OF NAZIANZUS,
"Sermon I: On Easter" in *The Paschal Mystery*

ᵃ Gk *fell asleep*   ᵇ Gk *this*   ᶜ Gk *all*   ᵈ Gk *they*   ᵉ Other ancient authorities read *God*

All Good Gifts

ACTS 14.17

A hymn reminds us, "All good gifts around us are sent from heaven above." Another urges us to count our blessings and to name them one by one. Now might be a good time to do that. Write them down to make the exercise more concrete. How long a list can you make of the blessings in your life—the people, things and events for which you are thankful? When you have run out of ideas, go back over the list again, thanking God for each of these good gifts. Keep the list handy so you can come back to it when you need to remind yourself of what you truly appreciate in your life.

See Meeting God in Worship

dents of the city were divided; some sided with the Jews, and some with the apostles. ⁵And when an attempt was made by both Gentiles and Jews, with their rulers, to mistreat them and to stone them, ⁶the apostles*ᵃ* learned of it and fled to Lystra and Derbe, cities of Lycaonia, and to the surrounding country; ⁷and there they continued proclaiming the good news.

Paul and Barnabas in Lystra and Derbe

8 In Lystra there was a man sitting who could not use his feet and had never walked, for he had been crippled from birth. ⁹He listened to Paul as he was speaking. And Paul, looking at him intently and seeing that he had faith to be healed, ¹⁰said in a loud voice, "Stand upright on your feet." And the man*ᵇ* sprang up and began to walk. ¹¹When the crowds saw what Paul had done, they shouted in the Lycaonian language, "The gods have come down to us in human form!" ¹²Barnabas they called Zeus, and Paul they called Hermes, because he was the chief speaker. ¹³The priest of Zeus, whose temple was just outside the city,*ᶜ* brought oxen and garlands to the gates; he and the crowds wanted to offer sacrifice. ¹⁴When the apostles Barnabas and Paul heard of it, they tore their clothes and rushed out into the crowd, shouting, ¹⁵"Friends,*ᵈ* why are you doing this? We are mortals just like you, and we bring you good news, that you should turn from these worthless things to the living God, who made the heaven and the earth and the sea and all that is in them. ¹⁶In past generations he allowed all the nations to follow their own ways; ¹⁷yet he has not left himself without a witness in doing good—giving you rains from heaven and fruitful seasons, and filling you with food and your hearts with joy." ¹⁸Even with these words, they scarcely restrained the crowds from offering sacrifice to them.

19 But Jews came there from Antioch and Iconium and won over the crowds. Then they stoned Paul and dragged him out of the city, supposing that he was dead. ²⁰But when the disciples surrounded him, he got up and went into the city. The next day he went on with Barnabas to Derbe.

The Return to Antioch in Syria

21 After they had proclaimed the good news to that city and had made many disciples, they returned to Lystra, then on to Iconium and Antioch. ²²There they strengthened the souls of the disciples and encouraged them to continue in the faith, saying, "It is through many persecutions that we must enter the kingdom of God." ²³And after they had appointed elders for them in each church, with prayer and fasting they entrusted them to the Lord in whom they had come to believe.

24 Then they passed through Pisidia and came to Pamphylia. ²⁵When they had spoken the word in Perga, they went down to Attalia. ²⁶From there they sailed back to Antioch, where they had been commended to the grace of God for the work*ᵉ* that they had completed. ²⁷When they arrived, they called the church together and related all that God had done with them, and how he had opened a door

a Gk *they*   *b* Gk *he*   *c* Or *The priest of Zeus-Outside-the-City*   *d* Gk *Men*
e Or *committed in the grace of God to the work*

of faith for the Gentiles. [28]And they stayed there with the disciples for some time.

The Council at Jerusalem

15 Then certain individuals came down from Judea and were teaching the brothers, "Unless you are circumcised according to the custom of Moses, you cannot be saved." [2]And after Paul and Barnabas had no small dissension and debate with them, Paul and Barnabas and some of the others were appointed to go up to Jerusalem to discuss this question with the apostles and the elders. [3]So they were sent on their way by the church, and as they passed through both Phoenicia and Samaria, they reported the conversion of the Gentiles, and brought great joy to all the believers.[a] [4]When they came to Jerusalem, they were welcomed by the church and the apostles and the elders, and they reported all that God had done with them. [5]But some believers who belonged to the sect of the Pharisees stood up and said, "It is necessary for them to be circumcised and ordered to keep the law of Moses."

6 The apostles and the elders met together to consider this matter. [7]After there had been much debate, Peter stood up and said to them, "My brothers,[b] you know that in the early days God made a choice among you, that I should be the one through whom the Gentiles would hear the message of the good news and become believers. [8]And God, who knows the human heart, testified to them by giving them the Holy Spirit, just as he did to us; [9]and in cleansing their hearts by faith he has made no distinction between them and us. [10]Now therefore why are you putting God to the test by placing on the neck of the disciples a yoke that neither our ancestors nor we have been able to bear? [11]On the contrary, we believe that we will be saved through the grace of the Lord Jesus, just as they will."

12 The whole assembly kept silence, and listened to Barnabas and Paul as they told of all the signs and wonders that God had done through them among the Gentiles. [13]After they finished speaking, James replied, "My brothers,[b] listen to me. [14]Simeon has related how God first looked favorably on the Gentiles, to take from among them a people for his name. [15]This agrees with the words of the prophets, as it is written,

[16] 'After this I will return,
  and I will rebuild the dwelling of David, which has
      fallen;
    from its ruins I will rebuild it,
      and I will set it up,
[17] so that all other peoples may seek the Lord—
    even all the Gentiles over whom my name has
        been called.
      Thus says the Lord, who has been making
        these things [18]known from long ago.'[c]

[19]Therefore I have reached the decision that we should not trouble those Gentiles who are turning to God, [20]but we should write to them to abstain only from things polluted by idols and from fornication and from whatever has been strangled[d] and from blood. [21]For in every city, for genera-

---

a Gk brothers   b Gk Men, brothers   c Other ancient authorities read
things. [18]Known to God from of old are all his works.'   d Other ancient
authorities lack and from whatever has been strangled

Extra Burdens

ACTS 15.10

The earliest Christian leaders decided not to put on the necks of the disciples a yoke too heavy to bear. Though we could point to many instances where leaders do heap on extra burdens, perhaps the heaviest burdens are those we heap on ourselves. What expectations do you have for yourself that continue to be a source of guilt? What private vows do you find impossible to keep? You might imagine yourself yoked to all these burdens, bent down under their weight. Ask God to break the yoke, release you from the weight of guilt and help you to stand tall, supported with grace. Thank God for setting you free.

See Meeting God in Scripture

Receiving Exhortations

ACTS 15.22–31

When the Jerusalem council met to deliberate and to discern God's will, they knew they needed the collective wisdom of the group. When the decision was delivered, the people read it and "rejoiced at the exortation." Imagine that a present-day equivalent of the council is addressing a pressing issue in your life. How difficult would it be for you to consider the prayerful insights of others? On the other hand, in what situations might God want you to rely on your own prayerful insight?

See Meeting God in Community

tions past, Moses has had those who proclaim him, for he has been read aloud every sabbath in the synagogues."

The Council's Letter to Gentile Believers

22 Then the apostles and the elders, with the consent of the whole church, decided to choose men from among their members[a] and to send them to Antioch with Paul and Barnabas. They sent Judas called Barsabbas, and Silas, leaders among the brothers, 23with the following letter: "The brothers, both the apostles and the elders, to the believers[b] of Gentile origin in Antioch and Syria and Cilicia, greetings. 24Since we have heard that certain persons who have gone out from us, though with no instructions from us, have said things to disturb you and have unsettled your minds,[c] 25we have decided unanimously to choose representatives[d] and send them to you, along with our beloved Barnabas and Paul, 26who have risked their lives for the sake of our Lord Jesus Christ. 27We have therefore sent Judas and Silas, who themselves will tell you the same things by word of mouth. 28For it has seemed good to the Holy Spirit and to us to impose on you no further burden than these essentials: 29that you abstain from what has been sacrificed to idols and from blood and from what is strangled[e] and from fornication. If you keep yourselves from these, you will do well. Farewell."

30 So they were sent off and went down to Antioch. When they gathered the congregation together, they delivered the letter. 31When its members[f] read it, they rejoiced at the exhortation. 32Judas and Silas, who were themselves prophets, said much to encourage and strengthen the believers.[b] 33After they had been there for some time, they were sent off in peace by the believers[b] to those who had sent them.[g] 35But Paul and Barnabas remained in Antioch, and there, with many others, they taught and proclaimed the word of the Lord.

Paul and Barnabas Separate

36 After some days Paul said to Barnabas, "Come, let us return and visit the believers[b] in every city where we proclaimed the word of the Lord and see how they are doing." 37Barnabas wanted to take with them John called Mark. 38But Paul decided not to take with them one who had deserted them in Pamphylia and had not accompanied them in the work. 39The disagreement became so sharp that they parted company; Barnabas took Mark with him and sailed away to Cyprus. 40But Paul chose Silas and set out, the believers[b] commending him to the grace of the Lord. 41He went through Syria and Cilicia, strengthening the churches.

Timothy Joins Paul and Silas

16 Paul[h] went on also to Derbe and to Lystra, where there was a disciple named Timothy, the son of a Jewish woman who was a believer; but his father was a Greek. 2He was well spoken of by the believers[b] in Lystra and Iconium. 3Paul wanted Timothy to accompany him;

a Gk *from among them*   b Gk *brothers*   c Other ancient authorities add saying, 'You must be circumcised and keep the law.'   d Gk *men*   e Other ancient authorities lack *and from what is strangled*   f Gk *When they*   g Other ancient authorities add verse 34, *But it seemed good to Silas to remain there*   h Gk *He*

and he took him and had him circumcised because of the Jews who were in those places, for they all knew that his father was a Greek. **4**As they went from town to town, they delivered to them for observance the decisions that had been reached by the apostles and elders who were in Jerusalem. **5**So the churches were strengthened in the faith and increased in numbers daily.

Paul's Vision of the Man of Macedonia

6 They went through the region of Phrygia and Galatia, having been forbidden by the Holy Spirit to speak the word in Asia. **7**When they had come opposite Mysia, they attempted to go into Bithynia, but the Spirit of Jesus did not allow them; **8**so, passing by Mysia, they went down to Troas. **9**During the night Paul had a vision: there stood a man of Macedonia pleading with him and saying, "Come over to Macedonia and help us." **10**When he had seen the vision, we immediately tried to cross over to Macedonia, being convinced that God had called us to proclaim the good news to them.

The Conversion of Lydia

11 We set sail from Troas and took a straight course to Samothrace, the following day to Neapolis, **12**and from there to Philippi, which is a leading city of the district*a* of Macedonia and a Roman colony. We remained in this city for some days. **13**On the sabbath day we went outside the gate by the river, where we supposed there was a place of prayer; and we sat down and spoke to the women who had gathered there. **14**A certain woman named Lydia, a worshiper of God, was listening to us; she was from the city of Thyatira and a dealer in purple cloth. The Lord opened her heart to listen eagerly to what was said by Paul. **15**When she and her household were baptized, she urged us, saying, "If you have judged me to be faithful to the Lord, come and stay at my home." And she prevailed upon us.

Paul and Silas in Prison

16 One day, as we were going to the place of prayer, we met a slave-girl who had a spirit of divination and brought her owners a great deal of money by fortune-telling. **17**While she followed Paul and us, she would cry out, "These men are slaves of the Most High God, who proclaim to you*b* a way of salvation." **18**She kept doing this for many days. But Paul, very much annoyed, turned and said to the spirit, "I order you in the name of Jesus Christ to come out of her." And it came out that very hour.

19 But when her owners saw that their hope of making money was gone, they seized Paul and Silas and dragged them into the marketplace before the authorities. **20**When they had brought them before the magistrates, they said, "These men are disturbing our city; they are Jews **21**and are advocating customs that are not lawful for us as Romans to adopt or observe." **22**The crowd joined in attacking them, and the magistrates had them stripped of their clothing and ordered them to be beaten with rods. **23**After they had given them a severe flogging, they threw them into prison and ordered the jailer to keep them securely. **24**Following

---

Receiving God's Guidance

ACTS 16.6–10

How have you experienced God's call or God's guidance during your life? Through dreams like the one Paul had? Through "closed doors" you could come to accept as God's will? Have you heard God speak through the voices of friends, through unexpected opportunities, through gut feelings? As you listen prayerfully to the people, things and events in your life right now, where can you hear God? What responses could you make? What response will you make?

See *Meeting God in Everyday Life*

---

a Other authorities read *a city of the first district*   *b* Other ancient authorities read *to us*

An Earthshaking Experience

ACTS 16.25–34

This is a powerful story to play out in the imagination. You might want to imagine yourself in the role of the jailer. As you drift off to sleep, you are puzzled to hear your prisoners singing God's praises while chained in their cells. Then you awake with a start as an earthquake shakes open the prison doors. Terrified, you hear Paul call out, "Do not harm yourself." Imagine your unrestrained joy when you and all your family are baptized. What other emotions do you experience? What parallels do you see in your own Christian experience? You might conclude with rejoicing that you too have "become a believer in God."

See Meeting God in Scripture

these instructions, he put them in the innermost cell and fastened their feet in the stocks.

25 About midnight Paul and Silas were praying and singing hymns to God, and the prisoners were listening to them. ²⁶Suddenly there was an earthquake, so violent that the foundations of the prison were shaken; and immediately all the doors were opened and everyone's chains were unfastened. ²⁷When the jailer woke up and saw the prison doors wide open, he drew his sword and was about to kill himself, since he supposed that the prisoners had escaped. ²⁸But Paul shouted in a loud voice, "Do not harm yourself, for we are all here." ²⁹The jailer*ᵃ* called for lights, and rushing in, he fell down trembling before Paul and Silas. ³⁰Then he brought them outside and said, "Sirs, what must I do to be saved?" ³¹They answered, "Believe on the Lord Jesus, and you will be saved, you and your household." ³²They spoke the word of the Lord*ᵇ* to him and to all who were in his house. ³³At the same hour of the night he took them and washed their wounds; then he and his entire family were baptized without delay. ³⁴He brought them up into the house and set food before them; and he and his entire household rejoiced that he had become a believer in God.

35 When morning came, the magistrates sent the police, saying, "Let those men go." ³⁶And the jailer reported the message to Paul, saying, "The magistrates sent word to let you go; therefore come out now and go in peace." ³⁷But Paul replied, "They have beaten us in public, uncondemned, men who are Roman citizens, and have thrown us into prison; and now are they going to discharge us in secret? Certainly not! Let them come and take us out themselves." ³⁸The police reported these words to the magistrates, and they were afraid when they heard that they were Roman citizens; ³⁹so they came and apologized to them. And they took them out and asked them to leave the city. ⁴⁰After leaving the prison they went to Lydia's home; and when they had seen and encouraged the brothers and sisters*ᶜ* there, they departed.

The Uproar in Thessalonica

17 After Paul and Silas*ᵈ* had passed through Amphipolis and Apollonia, they came to Thessalonica, where there was a synagogue of the Jews. ²And Paul went in, as was his custom, and on three sabbath days argued with them from the scriptures, ³explaining and proving that it was necessary for the Messiah*ᵉ* to suffer and to rise from the dead, and saying, "This is the Messiah,*ᵉ* Jesus whom I am proclaiming to you." ⁴Some of them were persuaded and joined Paul and Silas, as did a great many of the devout Greeks and not a few of the leading women. ⁵But the Jews became jealous, and with the help of some ruffians in the marketplaces they formed a mob and set the city in an uproar. While they were searching for Paul and Silas to bring them out to the assembly, they attacked Jason's house. ⁶When they could not find them, they dragged Jason and some believers*ᶜ* before the city authorities,*ᶠ* shouting, "These people who have been turning the world upside down have come here also, ⁷and Jason has entertained them as guests. They are all acting contrary to the decrees

a Gk *He*   *b* Other ancient authorities read *word of God*   *c* Gk *brothers*
d Gk *they*   *e* Or *the Christ*   *f* Gk *politarchs*

of the emperor, saying that there is another king named Jesus." [8]The people and the city officials were disturbed when they heard this, [9]and after they had taken bail from Jason and the others, they let them go.

Paul and Silas in Beroea

10 That very night the believers[a] sent Paul and Silas off to Beroea; and when they arrived, they went to the Jewish synagogue. [11]These Jews were more receptive than those in Thessalonica, for they welcomed the message very eagerly and examined the scriptures every day to see whether these things were so. [12]Many of them therefore believed, including not a few Greek women and men of high standing. [13]But when the Jews of Thessalonica learned that the word of God had been proclaimed by Paul in Beroea as well, they came there too, to stir up and incite the crowds. [14]Then the believers[a] immediately sent Paul away to the coast, but Silas and Timothy remained behind. [15]Those who conducted Paul brought him as far as Athens; and after receiving instructions to have Silas and Timothy join him as soon as possible, they left him.

Paul in Athens

16 While Paul was waiting for them in Athens, he was deeply distressed to see that the city was full of idols. [17]So he argued in the synagogue with the Jews and the devout persons, and also in the marketplace[b] every day with those who happened to be there. [18]Also some Epicurean and Stoic philosophers debated with him. Some said, "What does this babbler want to say?" Others said, "He seems to be a proclaimer of foreign divinities." (This was because he was telling the good news about Jesus and the resurrection.) [19]So they took him and brought him to the Areopagus and asked him, "May we know what this new teaching is that you are presenting? [20]It sounds rather strange to us, so we would like to know what it means." [21]Now all the Athenians and the foreigners living there would spend their time in nothing but telling or hearing something new.

22 Then Paul stood in front of the Areopagus and said, "Athenians, I see how extremely religious you are in every way. [23]For as I went through the city and looked carefully at the objects of your worship, I found among them an altar with the inscription, 'To an unknown god.' What therefore you worship as unknown, this I proclaim to you. [24]The God who made the world and everything in it, he who is Lord of heaven and earth, does not live in shrines made by human hands, [25]nor is he served by human hands, as though he needed anything, since he himself gives to all mortals life and breath and all things. [26]From one ancestor[c] he made all nations to inhabit the whole earth, and he allotted the times of their existence and the boundaries of the places where they would live, [27]so that they would search for God[d] and perhaps grope for him and find him—though indeed he is not far from each one of us. [28]For 'In him we live and move and have our being'; as even some of your own poets have said,

'For we too are his offspring.'

[29]Since we are God's offspring, we ought not to think that

When in Athens

ACTS 17.16–32

When the apostle Paul speaks to the people of Athens, he addresses them in the context of their culture. He begins with a common area of interest and speaks to them with respect. He speaks of the "unknown god," with whom they are familiar. He uses vocabulary they understand. And yet he delivers the gospel in its entirety and without watering it down.

Do you know anyone who needs to hear the gospel? How can you present the gospel to that individual within the context of the culture he or she knows and understands? Think about the kind of vocabulary you might use. Pray for the wisdom and creativity to think of a way to approach that person.

See *Meeting God in Community*

---

a Gk *brothers*   *b* Or *civic center*; Gk *agora*   *c* Gk *From one*; other ancient authorities read *From one blood*   *d* Other ancient authorities read *the Lord*

Shaking off the Dust

ACTS 18.6

Sometimes we have to admit defeat in our efforts to spread the gospel. The hardest part of this process is learning to shake off the dust and get on with our lives. How do defeats, hurts or broken relationships still weigh you down? You might want to name the defeat, then shake out your clothes while saying, "I am leaving you behind. Through Jesus Christ you have no more power over me. I will go on as God leads me." What new beginning is God calling you to? (See also Acts 22.19–21 and Matthew 10.14.)

See Meeting God in Service

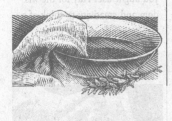

the deity is like gold, or silver, or stone, an image formed by the art and imagination of mortals. ³⁰While God has overlooked the times of human ignorance, now he commands all people everywhere to repent, ³¹because he has fixed a day on which he will have the world judged in righteousness by a man whom he has appointed, and of this he has given assurance to all by raising him from the dead."

32 When they heard of the resurrection of the dead, some scoffed; but others said, "We will hear you again about this." ³³At that point Paul left them. ³⁴But some of them joined him and became believers, including Dionysius the Areopagite and a woman named Damaris, and others with them.

Paul in Corinth

18 After this Paul*a* left Athens and went to Corinth. ²There he found a Jew named Aquila, a native of Pontus, who had recently come from Italy with his wife Priscilla, because Claudius had ordered all Jews to leave Rome. Paul*b* went to see them, ³and, because he was of the same trade, he stayed with them, and they worked together—by trade they were tentmakers. ⁴Every sabbath he would argue in the synagogue and would try to convince Jews and Greeks.

5 When Silas and Timothy arrived from Macedonia, Paul was occupied with proclaiming the word,*c* testifying to the Jews that the Messiah*d* was Jesus. ⁶When they opposed and reviled him, in protest he shook the dust from his clothes*e* and said to them, "Your blood be on your own heads! I am innocent. From now on I will go to the Gentiles." ⁷Then he left the synagogue*f* and went to the house of a man named Titius*g* Justus, a worshiper of God; his house was next door to the synagogue. ⁸Crispus, the official of the synagogue, became a believer in the Lord, together with all his household; and many of the Corinthians who heard Paul became believers and were baptized. ⁹One night the Lord said to Paul in a vision, "Do not be afraid, but speak and do not be silent; ¹⁰for I am with you, and no one will lay a hand on you to harm you, for there are many in this city who are my people." ¹¹He stayed there a year and six months, teaching the word of God among them.

12 But when Gallio was proconsul of Achaia, the Jews made a united attack on Paul and brought him before the tribunal. ¹³They said, "This man is persuading people to worship God in ways that are contrary to the law." ¹⁴Just as Paul was about to speak, Gallio said to the Jews, "If it were a matter of crime or serious villainy, I would be justified in accepting the complaint of you Jews; ¹⁵but since it is a matter of questions about words and names and your own law, see to it yourselves; I do not wish to be a judge of these matters." ¹⁶And he dismissed them from the tribunal. ¹⁷Then all of them*h* seized Sosthenes, the official of the synagogue, and beat him in front of the tribunal. But Gallio paid no attention to any of these things.

Paul's Return to Antioch

18 After staying there for a considerable time, Paul said

a Gk *he*   b Gk *He*   c Gk *with the word*   d Or *the Christ*   e Gk *reviled him, he shook out his clothes*   f Gk *left there*   g Other ancient authorities read *Titus*   h Other ancient authorities read *all the Greeks*

farewell to the believers*a* and sailed for Syria, accompanied by Priscilla and Aquila. At Cenchreae he had his hair cut, for he was under a vow. **19**When they reached Ephesus, he left them there, but first he himself went into the synagogue and had a discussion with the Jews. **20**When they asked him to stay longer, he declined; **21**but on taking leave of them, he said, "I*b* will return to you, if God wills." Then he set sail from Ephesus.

22 When he had landed at Caesarea, he went up to Jerusalem*c* and greeted the church, and then went down to Antioch. **23**After spending some time there he departed and went from place to place through the region of Galatia*d* and Phrygia, strengthening all the disciples.

Ministry of Apollos

24 Now there came to Ephesus a Jew named Apollos, a native of Alexandria. He was an eloquent man, well-versed in the scriptures. **25**He had been instructed in the Way of the Lord; and he spoke with burning enthusiasm and taught accurately the things concerning Jesus, though he knew only the baptism of John. **26**He began to speak boldly in the synagogue; but when Priscilla and Aquila heard him, they took him aside and explained the Way of God to him more accurately. **27**And when he wished to cross over to Achaia, the believers*a* encouraged him and wrote to the disciples to welcome him. On his arrival he greatly helped those who through grace had become believers, **28**for he powerfully refuted the Jews in public, showing by the scriptures that the Messiah*e* is Jesus.

Paul in Ephesus

19 While Apollos was in Corinth, Paul passed through the interior regions and came to Ephesus, where he found some disciples. **2**He said to them, "Did you receive the Holy Spirit when you became believers?" They replied, "No, we have not even heard that there is a Holy Spirit." **3**Then he said, "Into what then were you baptized?" They answered, "Into John's baptism." **4**Paul said, "John baptized with the baptism of repentance, telling the people to believe in the one who was to come after him, that is, in Jesus." **5**On hearing this, they were baptized in the name of the Lord Jesus. **6**When Paul had laid his hands on them, the Holy Spirit came upon them, and they spoke in tongues and prophesied— **7**altogether there were about twelve of them.

8 He entered the synagogue and for three months spoke out boldly, and argued persuasively about the kingdom of God. **9**When some stubbornly refused to believe and spoke evil of the Way before the congregation, he left them, taking the disciples with him, and argued daily in the lecture hall of Tyrannus.*f* **10**This continued for two years, so that all the residents of Asia, both Jews and Greeks, heard the word of the Lord.

The Sons of Sceva

11 God did extraordinary miracles through Paul, **12**so that

---

a Gk *brothers*   *b* Other ancient authorities read *I must at all costs keep the approaching festival in Jerusalem, but I*   *c* Gk *went up*   *d* Gk *the Galatian region*   *e* Or *the Christ*   *f* Other ancient authorities read *of a certain Tyrannus, from eleven o'clock in the morning to four in the afternoon*

Receive the Holy Spirit

ACTS 19.1–2

Paul asks, "Did you receive the Holy Spirit when you became believers?" How have you experienced the Spirit in your life? In the extraordinary ways of speaking in tongues or performing miracles so often described in Acts? In the steady working of spiritual gifts? (See 1 Corinthians 12.4–11 and Ephesians 4.11–13.) In the quiet grace of the fruit of the Spirit? (See Galatians 5.22–23.) You might welcome the Spirit's presence with a hymn-prayer such as "Come, Holy Ghost, Our Souls Inspire," "Spirit of God, Descend Upon My Heart" or "Spirit of the Living God, Fall Afresh on Me."

See *Meeting God in Worship*

Who Must Lose?

The silversmiths of Ephesus see the gospel as a threat to their livelihood. Certainly when lives are changed, those who profited from the old way must lose. What companies or businesses in your area would be threatened if more people took Christian discipleship seriously? Could they change? Or would they have to start over from scratch? What about your own livelihood? Are there changes you could implement in order to support a more Christian lifestyle?

See Meeting God in Community

when the handkerchiefs or aprons that had touched his skin were brought to the sick, their diseases left them, and the evil spirits came out of them. ¹³Then some itinerant Jewish exorcists tried to use the name of the Lord Jesus over those who had evil spirits, saying, "I adjure you by the Jesus whom Paul proclaims." ¹⁴Seven sons of a Jewish high priest named Sceva were doing this. ¹⁵But the evil spirit said to them in reply, "Jesus I know, and Paul I know; but who are you?" ¹⁶Then the man with the evil spirit leaped on them, mastered them all, and so overpowered them that they fled out of the house naked and wounded. ¹⁷When this became known to all residents of Ephesus, both Jews and Greeks, everyone was awestruck; and the name of the Lord Jesus was praised. ¹⁸Also many of those who became believers confessed and disclosed their practices. ¹⁹A number of those who practiced magic collected their books and burned them publicly; when the value of these books*ᵃ* was calculated, it was found to come to fifty thousand silver coins. ²⁰So the word of the Lord grew mightily and prevailed.

The Riot in Ephesus

21 Now after these things had been accomplished, Paul resolved in the Spirit to go through Macedonia and Achaia, and then to go on to Jerusalem. He said, "After I have gone there, I must also see Rome." ²²So he sent two of his helpers, Timothy and Erastus, to Macedonia, while he himself stayed for some time longer in Asia.

23 About that time no little disturbance broke out concerning the Way. ²⁴A man named Demetrius, a silversmith who made silver shrines of Artemis, brought no little business to the artisans. ²⁵These he gathered together, with the workers of the same trade, and said, "Men, you know that we get our wealth from this business. ²⁶You also see and hear that not only in Ephesus but in almost the whole of Asia this Paul has persuaded and drawn away a considerable number of people by saying that gods made with hands are not gods. ²⁷And there is danger not only that this trade of ours may come into disrepute but also that the temple of the great goddess Artemis will be scorned, and she will be deprived of her majesty that brought all Asia and the world to worship her."

28 When they heard this, they were enraged and shouted, "Great is Artemis of the Ephesians!" ²⁹The city was filled with the confusion; and people*ᵇ* rushed together to the theater, dragging with them Gaius and Aristarchus, Macedonians who were Paul's travel companions. ³⁰Paul wished to go into the crowd, but the disciples would not let him; ³¹even some officials of the province of Asia,*ᶜ* who were friendly to him, sent him a message urging him not to venture into the theater. ³²Meanwhile, some were shouting one thing, some another; for the assembly was in confusion, and most of them did not know why they had come together. ³³Some of the crowd gave instructions to Alexander, whom the Jews had pushed forward. And Alexander motioned for silence and tried to make a defense before the people. ³⁴But when they recognized that he was a Jew, for about two hours all of them shouted in unison, "Great is Artemis of the Ephesians!" ³⁵But when the town clerk had

a Gk *them*   *b* Gk *they*   *c* Gk *some of the Asiarchs* quieted the crowd, he said, "Citizens of Ephesus, who is there that does not know that the city of the Ephesians is the temple keeper of the great Artemis and of the statue that fell from heaven?*a* ³⁶Since these things cannot be denied, you ought to be quiet and do nothing rash. ³⁷You have brought these men here who are neither temple robbers nor blasphemers of our*b* goddess. ³⁸If therefore Demetrius and the artisans with him have a complaint against anyone, the courts are open, and there are proconsuls; let them bring charges there against one another. ³⁹If there is anything further*c* you want to know, it must be settled in the regular assembly. ⁴⁰For we are in danger of being charged with rioting today, since there is no cause that we can give to justify this commotion." ⁴¹When he had said this, he dismissed the assembly.

Paul Goes to Macedonia and Greece

20 After the uproar had ceased, Paul sent for the disciples; and after encouraging them and saying farewell, he left for Macedonia. ²When he had gone through those regions and had given the believers*d* much encouragement, he came to Greece, ³where he stayed for three months. He was about to set sail for Syria when a plot was made against him by the Jews, and so he decided to return through Macedonia. ⁴He was accompanied by Sopater son of Pyrrhus from Beroea, by Aristarchus and Secundus from Thessalonica, by Gaius from Derbe, and by Timothy, as well as by Tychicus and Trophimus from Asia. ⁵They went ahead and were waiting for us in Troas; ⁶but we sailed from Philippi after the days of Unleavened Bread, and in five days we joined them in Troas, where we stayed for seven days.

Paul's Farewell Visit to Troas

7 On the first day of the week, when we met to break bread, Paul was holding a discussion with them; since he intended to leave the next day, he continued speaking until midnight. ⁸There were many lamps in the room upstairs where we were meeting. ⁹A young man named Eutychus, who was sitting in the window, began to sink off into a deep sleep while Paul talked still longer. Overcome by sleep, he fell to the ground three floors below and was picked up dead. ¹⁰But Paul went down, and bending over him took him in his arms, and said, "Do not be alarmed, for his life is in him." ¹¹Then Paul went upstairs, and after he had broken bread and eaten, he continued to converse with them until dawn; then he left. ¹²Meanwhile they had taken the boy away alive and were not a little comforted.

The Voyage from Troas to Miletus

13 We went ahead to the ship and set sail for Assos, intending to take Paul on board there; for he had made this arrangement, intending to go by land himself. ¹⁴When he met us in Assos, we took him on board and went to Mitylene. ¹⁵We sailed from there, and on the following day we arrived opposite Chios. The next day we touched at Samos, and*e* the day after that we came to Miletus. ¹⁶For Paul had

Resurrection Power

ACTS 20.7–12

Even a wearying three-hour sermon can lead to an experience of God's resurrection power. When have you most vividly felt God's presence or power in worship? What made that experience come alive? As you reflect on the experience, what do you recognize about your own need for God? What can you learn about God's ways of reaching out to you? What difference did the presence of the worshiping community make?

See Meeting God in Worship

---

a Meaning of Gk uncertain   *b* Other ancient authorities read *your*
c Other ancient authorities read *about other matters*   *d* Gk *given them*
e Other ancient authorities add *after remaining at Trogyllium*

Genuine Community

"I have community with others and I shall continue to have it only through Jesus Christ. The more genuine and the deeper our community becomes, the more surely will everything between us recede, the more clearly and purely will Jesus Christ and his work become the one and only thing that is vital between us."

—DIETRICH BONHOEFFER,
Life Together

decided to sail past Ephesus, so that he might not have to spend time in Asia; he was eager to be in Jerusalem, if possible, on the day of Pentecost.

Paul Speaks to the Ephesian Elders

17 From Miletus he sent a message to Ephesus, asking the elders of the church to meet him. ¹⁸When they came to him, he said to them:

"You yourselves know how I lived among you the entire time from the first day that I set foot in Asia, ¹⁹serving the Lord with all humility and with tears, enduring the trials that came to me through the plots of the Jews. ²⁰I did not shrink from doing anything helpful, proclaiming the message to you and teaching you publicly and from house to house, ²¹as I testified to both Jews and Greeks about repentance toward God and faith toward our Lord Jesus. ²²And now, as a captive to the Spirit,ᵃ I am on my way to Jerusalem, not knowing what will happen to me there, ²³except that the Holy Spirit testifies to me in every city that imprisonment and persecutions are waiting for me. ²⁴But I do not count my life of any value to myself, if only I may finish my course and the ministry that I received from the Lord Jesus, to testify to the good news of God's grace.

25 "And now I know that none of you, among whom I have gone about proclaiming the kingdom, will ever see my face again. ²⁶Therefore I declare to you this day that I am not responsible for the blood of any of you, ²⁷for I did not shrink from declaring to you the whole purpose of God. ²⁸Keep watch over yourselves and over all the flock, of which the Holy Spirit has made you overseers, to shepherd the church of Godᵇ that he obtained with the blood of his own Son.ᶜ ²⁹I know that after I have gone, savage wolves will come in among you, not sparing the flock. ³⁰Some even from your own group will come distorting the truth in order to entice the disciples to follow them. ³¹Therefore be alert, remembering that for three years I did not cease night or day to warn everyone with tears. ³²And now I commend you to God and to the message of his grace, a message that is able to build you up and to give you the inheritance among all who are sanctified. ³³I coveted no one's silver or gold or clothing. ³⁴You know for yourselves that I worked with my own hands to support myself and my companions. ³⁵In all this I have given you an example that by such work we must support the weak, remembering the words of the Lord Jesus, for he himself said, 'It is more blessed to give than to receive.' "

36 When he had finished speaking, he knelt down with them all and prayed. ³⁷There was much weeping among them all; they embraced Paul and kissed him, ³⁸grieving especially because of what he had said, that they would not see him again. Then they brought him to the ship.

Paul's Journey to Jerusalem

21 When we had parted from them and set sail, we came by a straight course to Cos, and the next day to Rhodes, and from there to Patara.ᵈ ²When we found a ship bound for Phoenicia, we went on board and set sail.

ᵃ Or *And now, bound in the spirit*   ᵇ Other ancient authorities read *of the Lord*   ᶜ Or *with his own blood;* Gk *with the blood of his Own*   ᵈ Other ancient authorities add *and Myra*

3We came in sight of Cyprus; and leaving it on our left, we sailed to Syria and landed at Tyre, because the ship was to unload its cargo there. 4We looked up the disciples and stayed there for seven days. Through the Spirit they told Paul not to go on to Jerusalem. 5When our days there were ended, we left and proceeded on our journey; and all of them, with wives and children, escorted us outside the city. There we knelt down on the beach and prayed 6and said farewell to one another. Then we went on board the ship, and they returned home.

7 When we had finished*a* the voyage from Tyre, we arrived at Ptolemais; and we greeted the believers*b* and stayed with them for one day. 8The next day we left and came to Caesarea; and we went into the house of Philip the evangelist, one of the seven, and stayed with him. 9He had four unmarried daughters*c* who had the gift of prophecy. 10While we were staying there for several days, a prophet named Agabus came down from Judea. 11He came to us and took Paul's belt, bound his own feet and hands with it, and said, "Thus says the Holy Spirit, 'This is the way the Jews in Jerusalem will bind the man who owns this belt and will hand him over to the Gentiles.' " 12When we heard this, we and the people there urged him not to go up to Jerusalem. 13Then Paul answered, "What are you doing, weeping and breaking my heart? For I am ready not only to be bound but even to die in Jerusalem for the name of the Lord Jesus." 14Since he would not be persuaded, we remained silent except to say, "The Lord's will be done."

15 After these days we got ready and started to go up to Jerusalem. 16Some of the disciples from Caesarea also came along and brought us to the house of Mnason of Cyprus, an early disciple, with whom we were to stay.

Paul Visits James at Jerusalem

17 When we arrived in Jerusalem, the brothers welcomed us warmly. 18The next day Paul went with us to visit James; and all the elders were present. 19After greeting them, he related one by one the things that God had done among the Gentiles through his ministry. 20When they heard it, they praised God. Then they said to him, "You see, brother, how many thousands of believers there are among the Jews, and they are all zealous for the law. 21They have been told about you that you teach all the Jews living among the Gentiles to forsake Moses, and that you tell them not to circumcise their children or observe the customs. 22What then is to be done? They will certainly hear that you have come. 23So do what we tell you. We have four men who are under a vow. 24Join these men, go through the rite of purification with them, and pay for the shaving of their heads. Thus all will know that there is nothing in what they have been told about you, but that you yourself observe and guard the law. 25But as for the Gentiles who have become believers, we have sent a letter with our judgment that they should abstain from what has been sacrificed to idols and from blood and from what is strangled*d* and from fornication." 26Then Paul took the men, and the next day, having purified himself, he entered the temple with them,

Why Are You Weeping?

ACTS 21.13–14

How can we best support loved ones who face trouble? Paul seems to find his companions' weeping less than helpful. Do you pray that your loved ones may find relief from their problems or that they may find the courage and strength to face them? Sometimes the best we can do is what Paul's friends did: Be silent except to say, "The Lord's will be done." For what friends or family members do you need to offer that prayer today? You might also want to pray for yourself, for the willingness to release them into God's care.

See *Meeting God in Prayer*

a Or *continued*   *b* Gk *brothers*   *c* Gk *four daughters, virgins,*   *d* Other ancient authorities lack *and from what is strangled*

1465

Paul's Conversion

ACTS 22.6–11

As Paul tells his story, you might try picturing the event as if you had been there with Paul as a traveling companion. See the road as you walk toward Damascus. Feel the heat of the sun, smell the animals, taste the blowing dust. Do you see the bright light or only Paul's reaction as he falls, blinded? Imagine yourself helping him up, asking what has happened. What does he say? What is your response? After imagining the story as a bystander, you might try putting yourself in the role of Paul. Is your experience of the event different?

See Meeting God in Scripture

making public the completion of the days of purification when the sacrifice would be made for each of them.

Paul Arrested in the Temple

27 When the seven days were almost completed, the Jews from Asia, who had seen him in the temple, stirred up the whole crowd. They seized him, ²⁸shouting, "Fellow Israelites, help! This is the man who is teaching everyone everywhere against our people, our law, and this place; more than that, he has actually brought Greeks into the temple and has defiled this holy place." ²⁹For they had previously seen Trophimus the Ephesian with him in the city, and they supposed that Paul had brought him into the temple. ³⁰Then all the city was aroused, and the people rushed together. They seized Paul and dragged him out of the temple, and immediately the doors were shut. ³¹While they were trying to kill him, word came to the tribune of the cohort that all Jerusalem was in an uproar. ³²Immediately he took soldiers and centurions and ran down to them. When they saw the tribune and the soldiers, they stopped beating Paul. ³³Then the tribune came, arrested him, and ordered him to be bound with two chains; he inquired who he was and what he had done. ³⁴Some in the crowd shouted one thing, some another; and as he could not learn the facts because of the uproar, he ordered him to be brought into the barracks. ³⁵When Paul*ᵃ* came to the steps, the violence of the mob was so great that he had to be carried by the soldiers. ³⁶The crowd that followed kept shouting, "Away with him!"

Paul Defends Himself

37 Just as Paul was about to be brought into the barracks, he said to the tribune, "May I say something to you?" The tribune*ᵇ* replied, "Do you know Greek? ³⁸Then you are not the Egyptian who recently stirred up a revolt and led the four thousand assassins out into the wilderness?" ³⁹Paul replied, "I am a Jew, from Tarsus in Cilicia, a citizen of an important city; I beg you, let me speak to the people." ⁴⁰When he had given him permission, Paul stood on the steps and motioned to the people for silence; and when there was a great hush, he addressed them in the Hebrew*ᶜ* language, saying:

22 "Brothers and fathers, listen to the defense that I now make before you."

2 When they heard him addressing them in Hebrew,*ᶜ* they became even more quiet. Then he said:

3 "I am a Jew, born in Tarsus in Cilicia, but brought up in this city at the feet of Gamaliel, educated strictly according to our ancestral law, being zealous for God, just as all of you are today. ⁴I persecuted this Way up to the point of death by binding both men and women and putting them in prison, ⁵as the high priest and the whole council of elders can testify about me. From them I also received letters to the brothers in Damascus, and I went there in order to bind those who were there and to bring them back to Jerusalem for punishment.

Paul Tells of His Conversion

6 "While I was on my way and approaching Damascus,

a Gk *he*　　*b* Gk *He*　　*c* That is, *Aramaic*

about noon a great light from heaven suddenly shone about me. [7]I fell to the ground and heard a voice saying to me, 'Saul, Saul, why are you persecuting me?' [8]I answered, 'Who are you, Lord?' Then he said to me, 'I am Jesus of Nazareth[a] whom you are persecuting.' [9]Now those who were with me saw the light but did not hear the voice of the one who was speaking to me. [10]I asked, 'What am I to do, Lord?' The Lord said to me, 'Get up and go to Damascus; there you will be told everything that has been assigned to you to do.' [11]Since I could not see because of the brightness of that light, those who were with me took my hand and led me to Damascus.

12 "A certain Ananias, who was a devout man according to the law and well spoken of by all the Jews living there, [13]came to me; and standing beside me, he said, 'Brother Saul, regain your sight!' In that very hour I regained my sight and saw him. [14]Then he said, 'The God of our ancestors has chosen you to know his will, to see the Righteous One and to hear his own voice; [15]for you will be his witness to all the world of what you have seen and heard. [16]And now why do you delay? Get up, be baptized, and have your sins washed away, calling on his name.'

Paul Sent to the Gentiles

17 "After I had returned to Jerusalem and while I was praying in the temple, I fell into a trance [18]and saw Jesus[b] saying to me, 'Hurry and get out of Jerusalem quickly, because they will not accept your testimony about me.' [19]And I said, 'Lord, they themselves know that in every synagogue I imprisoned and beat those who believed in you. [20]And while the blood of your witness Stephen was shed, I myself was standing by, approving and keeping the coats of those who killed him.' [21]Then he said to me, 'Go, for I will send you far away to the Gentiles.' "

Paul and the Roman Tribune

22 Up to this point they listened to him, but then they shouted, "Away with such a fellow from the earth! For he should not be allowed to live." [23]And while they were shouting, throwing off their cloaks, and tossing dust into the air, [24]the tribune directed that he was to be brought into the barracks, and ordered him to be examined by flogging, to find out the reason for this outcry against him. [25]But when they had tied him up with thongs,[c] Paul said to the centurion who was standing by, "Is it legal for you to flog a Roman citizen who is uncondemned?" [26]When the centurion heard that, he went to the tribune and said to him, "What are you about to do? This man is a Roman citizen." [27]The tribune came and asked Paul,[b] "Tell me, are you a Roman citizen?" And he said, "Yes." [28]The tribune answered, "It cost me a large sum of money to get my citizenship." Paul said, "But I was born a citizen." [29]Immediately those who were about to examine him drew back from him; and the tribune also was afraid, for he realized that Paul was a Roman citizen and that he had bound him.

Paul before the Council

30 Since he wanted to find out what Paul[d] was being accused of by the Jews, the next day he released him and or-

Those We Cannot Reach

ACTS 22.19–21

Jesus told Paul to leave Jerusalem because Paul could not effectively preach the gospel to the people there. They knew too much of his past to accept his changed life. It can be both frustrating and humbling to admit that there are some people who will never listen to what we have to say. Whom have you tried to reach out to, only to be rebuffed? Relatives? Old friends? Inactive church members? Can you accept Jesus' permission to leave them and go on to others who may be more responsive? Express your love for them as you commit them to Jesus' care. Then listen for his call to pursue new opportunities.

---

a Gk *the Nazorean*   *b* Gk *him*   *c* Or *up for the lashes*   *d* Gk *he*

Take Courage

ACTS 23.11

Who are your enemies? Are there people or groups who criticize you or belittle you personally? People who stand against what is important to you? What particular temptations must you struggle with? What spiritual powers seem to be opposing you? (See Ephesians 6.10–12.) You might try to picture your enemies surrounding you, trying to reach you. But Jesus stands next to you, and they cannot come into his light. Hear his word to you: "Keep up your courage!" He tells you that your battle is not yet over, for he has more for you to do. As you stand with him in his light, hear again his words, "Keep up your courage!"

dered the chief priests and the entire council to meet. He brought Paul down and had him stand before them.

23 While Paul was looking intently at the council he said, "Brothers,[a] up to this day I have lived my life with a clear conscience before God." 2Then the high priest Ananias ordered those standing near him to strike him on the mouth. 3At this Paul said to him, "God will strike you, you whitewashed wall! Are you sitting there to judge me according to the law, and yet in violation of the law you order me to be struck?" 4Those standing nearby said, "Do you dare to insult God's high priest?" 5And Paul said, "I did not realize, brothers, that he was high priest; for it is written, 'You shall not speak evil of a leader of your people.' "

6 When Paul noticed that some were Sadducees and others were Pharisees, he called out in the council, "Brothers, I am a Pharisee, a son of Pharisees. I am on trial concerning the hope of the resurrection[b] of the dead." 7When he said this, a dissension began between the Pharisees and the Sadducees, and the assembly was divided. 8(The Sadducees say that there is no resurrection, or angel, or spirit; but the Pharisees acknowledge all three.) 9Then a great clamor arose, and certain scribes of the Pharisees' group stood up and contended, "We find nothing wrong with this man. What if a spirit or an angel has spoken to him?" 10When the dissension became violent, the tribune, fearing that they would tear Paul to pieces, ordered the soldiers to go down, take him by force, and bring him into the barracks.

11 That night the Lord stood near him and said, "Keep up your courage! For just as you have testified for me in Jerusalem, so you must bear witness also in Rome."

The Plot to Kill Paul

12 In the morning the Jews joined in a conspiracy and bound themselves by an oath neither to eat nor drink until they had killed Paul. 13There were more than forty who joined in this conspiracy. 14They went to the chief priests and elders and said, "We have strictly bound ourselves by an oath to taste no food until we have killed Paul. 15Now then, you and the council must notify the tribune to bring him down to you, on the pretext that you want to make a more thorough examination of his case. And we are ready to do away with him before he arrives."

16 Now the son of Paul's sister heard about the ambush; so he went and gained entrance to the barracks and told Paul. 17Paul called one of the centurions and said, "Take this young man to the tribune, for he has something to report to him." 18So he took him, brought him to the tribune, and said, "The prisoner Paul called me and asked me to bring this young man to you; he has something to tell you." 19The tribune took him by the hand, drew him aside privately, and asked, "What is it that you have to report to me?" 20He answered, "The Jews have agreed to ask you to bring Paul down to the council tomorrow, as though they were going to inquire more thoroughly into his case. 21But do not be persuaded by them, for more than forty of their men are lying in ambush for him. They have bound themselves by an oath neither to eat nor drink until they kill him. They are ready now and are waiting for your consent." 22So the tri-

a Gk Men, brothers   b Gk concerning hope and resurrection

bune dismissed the young man, ordering him, "Tell no one that you have informed me of this."

Paul Sent to Felix the Governor

23 Then he summoned two of the centurions and said, "Get ready to leave by nine o'clock tonight for Caesarea with two hundred soldiers, seventy horsemen, and two hundred spearmen. 24Also provide mounts for Paul to ride, and take him safely to Felix the governor." 25He wrote a letter to this effect:

26 "Claudius Lysias to his Excellency the governor Felix, greetings. 27This man was seized by the Jews and was about to be killed by them, but when I had learned that he was a Roman citizen, I came with the guard and rescued him. 28Since I wanted to know the charge for which they accused him, I had him brought to their council. 29I found that he was accused concerning questions of their law, but was charged with nothing deserving death or imprisonment. 30When I was informed that there would be a plot against the man, I sent him to you at once, ordering his accusers also to state before you what they have against him.ᵃ"

31 So the soldiers, according to their instructions, took Paul and brought him during the night to Antipatris. 32The next day they let the horsemen go on with him, while they returned to the barracks. 33When they came to Caesarea and delivered the letter to the governor, they presented Paul also before him. 34On reading the letter, he asked what province he belonged to, and when he learned that he was from Cilicia, 35he said, "I will give you a hearing when your accusers arrive." Then he ordered that he be kept under guard in Herod's headquarters.ᵇ

Paul before Felix at Caesarea

24 Five days later the high priest Ananias came down with some elders and an attorney, a certain Tertullus, and they reported their case against Paul to the governor. 2When Paulᶜ had been summoned, Tertullus began to accuse him, saying:

"Your Excellency,ᵈ because of you we have long enjoyed peace, and reforms have been made for this people because of your foresight. 3We welcome this in every way and everywhere with utmost gratitude. 4But, to detain you no further, I beg you to hear us briefly with your customary graciousness. 5We have, in fact, found this man a pestilent fellow, an agitator among all the Jews throughout the world, and a ringleader of the sect of the Nazarenes.ᵉ 6He even tried to profane the temple, and so we seized him.ᶠ 8By examining him yourself you will be able to learn from him concerning everything of which we accuse him."

9 The Jews also joined in the charge by asserting that all this was true.

A Shield From Vanity

ACTS 24.5

"It is good for us to have trials and troubles at times, for they often remind us that we are on probation and ought not to hope in any worldly thing. It is good for us sometimes to suffer contradiction, to be misjudged by others even though we do well and mean well. These things help us to be humble and shield us from vanity. When to all outward appearances others give us no credit, when they do not think well of us, then we are more inclined to seek God, who sees our hearts. Therefore, we ought to root ourselves so firmly in God that we will not need human consolations."

—THOMAS À KEMPIS,
The Imitation of Christ

---

a Other ancient authorities add *Farewell*   *b* Gk *praetorium*   *c* Gk *he*
d Gk lacks *Your Excellency*   *e* Gk *Nazoreans*   *f* Other ancient authorities add *and we would have judged him according to our law.* 7*But the chief captain Lysias came and with great violence took him out of our hands,* 8*commanding his accusers to come before you.*

Doing Your Best

"Therefore I do my best always to have a clear conscience toward God and all people." What a statement Paul makes! Can you make such a claim? When are you inspired to do your best? When do you feel it is okay to slack off, to offer less than your best? What are some specific occasions recently when you have done less than you could have? Did you let others down? Did you let God down? What can you do now to clear your conscience? Is it enough to ask forgiveness, or are there other actions you need to take as well?

See Meeting God in Prayer

Paul's Defense before Felix

10 When the governor motioned to him to speak, Paul replied:

"I cheerfully make my defense, knowing that for many years you have been a judge over this nation. ¹¹As you can find out, it is not more than twelve days since I went up to worship in Jerusalem. ¹²They did not find me disputing with anyone in the temple or stirring up a crowd either in the synagogues or throughout the city. ¹³Neither can they prove to you the charge that they now bring against me. ¹⁴But this I admit to you, that according to the Way, which they call a sect, I worship the God of our ancestors, believing everything laid down according to the law or written in the prophets. ¹⁵I have a hope in God—a hope that they themselves also accept—that there will be a resurrection of both[a] the righteous and the unrighteous. ¹⁶Therefore I do my best always to have a clear conscience toward God and all people. ¹⁷Now after some years I came to bring alms to my nation and to offer sacrifices. ¹⁸While I was doing this, they found me in the temple, completing the rite of purification, without any crowd or disturbance. ¹⁹But there were some Jews from Asia—they ought to be here before you to make an accusation, if they have anything against me. ²⁰Or let these men here tell what crime they had found when I stood before the council, ²¹unless it was this one sentence that I called out while standing before them, 'It is about the resurrection of the dead that I am on trial before you today.' "

22 But Felix, who was rather well informed about the Way, adjourned the hearing with the comment, "When Lysias the tribune comes down, I will decide your case." ²³Then he ordered the centurion to keep him in custody, but to let him have some liberty and not to prevent any of his friends from taking care of his needs.

Paul Held in Custody

24 Some days later when Felix came with his wife Drusilla, who was Jewish, he sent for Paul and heard him speak concerning faith in Christ Jesus. ²⁵And as he discussed justice, self-control, and the coming judgment, Felix became frightened and said, "Go away for the present; when I have an opportunity, I will send for you." ²⁶At the same time he hoped that money would be given him by Paul, and for that reason he used to send for him very often and converse with him.

27 After two years had passed, Felix was succeeded by Porcius Festus; and since he wanted to grant the Jews a favor, Felix left Paul in prison.

Paul Appeals to the Emperor

25 Three days after Festus had arrived in the province, he went up from Caesarea to Jerusalem ²where the chief priests and the leaders of the Jews gave him a report against Paul. They appealed to him ³and requested, as a favor to them against Paul,[b] to have him transferred to Jerusalem. They were, in fact, planning an ambush to kill him along the way. ⁴Festus replied that Paul was being kept at Caesarea, and that he himself intended to go there short-

a Other ancient authorities read *of the dead, both of*   *b* Gk *him*

ly. ⁵"So," he said, "let those of you who have the authority come down with me, and if there is anything wrong about the man, let them accuse him."

6 After he had stayed among them not more than eight or ten days, he went down to Caesarea; the next day he took his seat on the tribunal and ordered Paul to be brought. ⁷When he arrived, the Jews who had gone down from Jerusalem surrounded him, bringing many serious charges against him, which they could not prove. ⁸Paul said in his defense, "I have in no way committed an offense against the law of the Jews, or against the temple, or against the emperor." ⁹But Festus, wishing to do the Jews a favor, asked Paul, "Do you wish to go up to Jerusalem and be tried there before me on these charges?" ¹⁰Paul said, "I am appealing to the emperor's tribunal; this is where I should be tried. I have done no wrong to the Jews, as you very well know. ¹¹Now if I am in the wrong and have committed something for which I deserve to die, I am not trying to escape death; but if there is nothing to their charges against me, no one can turn me over to them. I appeal to the emperor." ¹²Then Festus, after he had conferred with his council, replied, "You have appealed to the emperor; to the emperor you will go."

Festus Consults King Agrippa

13 After several days had passed, King Agrippa and Bernice arrived at Caesarea to welcome Festus. ¹⁴Since they were staying there several days, Festus laid Paul's case before the king, saying, "There is a man here who was left in prison by Felix. ¹⁵When I was in Jerusalem, the chief priests and the elders of the Jews informed me about him and asked for a sentence against him. ¹⁶I told them that it was not the custom of the Romans to hand over anyone before the accused had met the accusers face to face and had been given an opportunity to make a defense against the charge. ¹⁷So when they met here, I lost no time, but on the next day took my seat on the tribunal and ordered the man to be brought. ¹⁸When the accusers stood up, they did not charge him with any of the crimes*ᵃ* that I was expecting. ¹⁹Instead they had certain points of disagreement with him about their own religion and about a certain Jesus, who had died, but whom Paul asserted to be alive. ²⁰Since I was at a loss how to investigate these questions, I asked whether he wished to go to Jerusalem and be tried there on these charges.*ᵇ* ²¹But when Paul had appealed to be kept in custody for the decision of his Imperial Majesty, I ordered him to be held until I could send him to the emperor." ²²Agrippa said to Festus, "I would like to hear the man myself." "Tomorrow," he said, "you will hear him."

Paul Brought before Agrippa

23 So on the next day Agrippa and Bernice came with great pomp, and they entered the audience hall with the military tribunes and the prominent men of the city. Then Festus gave the order and Paul was brought in. ²⁴And Festus said, "King Agrippa and all here present with us, you see this man about whom the whole Jewish community petitioned me, both in Jerusalem and here, shouting that he ought not to live any longer. ²⁵But I found that he had done

Praying for Justice

ACTS 25.18–19

The quest for truth and justice is often a difficult one. How might you undergird it with prayer? One possibility might be to attend a trial in your area or follow a trial through newspaper accounts, not to come to some judgment but simply to pray for all of those involved: defendant and accuser, defense attorney and prosecutor, judge and jury. Pray for wisdom and courage and patience. Pray for the Spirit's guidance.

See Meeting God in Everyday Life

---

a Other ancient authorities read *with anything*   *b* Gk *on them*

Kicking Against the Goads

ACTS 26.14–16

This third report of Paul's conversion is the first one to include these words of Jesus: "It hurts you to kick against the goads." Where in your own life have you "kicked against" God's guidance? What have you lost by insisting on your own way rather than God's? How have you been hurt? What is God prodding you toward now? You might write out answers to three questions: What is God calling me to be? What is God calling me to do? What specific actions can I take to respond to these calls?

See Meeting God in Service

nothing deserving death; and when he appealed to his Imperial Majesty, I decided to send him. 26But I have nothing definite to write to our sovereign about him. Therefore I have brought him before all of you, and especially before you, King Agrippa, so that, after we have examined him, I may have something to write— 27for it seems to me unreasonable to send a prisoner without indicating the charges against him."

Paul Defends Himself before Agrippa

26 Agrippa said to Paul, "You have permission to speak for yourself." Then Paul stretched out his hand and began to defend himself:

2 "I consider myself fortunate that it is before you, King Agrippa, I am to make my defense today against all the accusations of the Jews, 3because you are especially familiar with all the customs and controversies of the Jews; therefore I beg of you to listen to me patiently.

4 "All the Jews know my way of life from my youth, a life spent from the beginning among my own people and in Jerusalem. 5They have known for a long time, if they are willing to testify, that I have belonged to the strictest sect of our religion and lived as a Pharisee. 6And now I stand here on trial on account of my hope in the promise made by God to our ancestors, 7a promise that our twelve tribes hope to attain, as they earnestly worship day and night. It is for this hope, your Excellency,*a* that I am accused by Jews! 8Why is it thought incredible by any of you that God raises the dead?

9 "Indeed, I myself was convinced that I ought to do many things against the name of Jesus of Nazareth.*b* 10And that is what I did in Jerusalem; with authority received from the chief priests, I not only locked up many of the saints in prison, but I also cast my vote against them when they were being condemned to death. 11By punishing them often in all the synagogues I tried to force them to blaspheme; and since I was so furiously enraged at them, I pursued them even to foreign cities.

Paul Tells of His Conversion

12 "With this in mind, I was traveling to Damascus with the authority and commission of the chief priests, 13when at midday along the road, your Excellency,*a* I saw a light from heaven, brighter than the sun, shining around me and my companions. 14When we had all fallen to the ground, I heard a voice saying to me in the Hebrew*c* language, 'Saul, Saul, why are you persecuting me? It hurts you to kick against the goads.' 15I asked, 'Who are you, Lord?' The Lord answered, 'I am Jesus whom you are persecuting. 16But get up and stand on your feet; for I have appeared to you for this purpose, to appoint you to serve and testify to the things in which you have seen me*d* and to those in which I will appear to you. 17I will rescue you from your people and from the Gentiles—to whom I am sending you 18to open their eyes so that they may turn from darkness to light and from the power of Satan to God, so that they may receive forgiveness of sins and a place among those who are sanctified by faith in me.'

a Gk *O king*   *b* Gk *the Nazorean*   *c* That is, *Aramaic*   *d* Other ancient authorities read *the things that you have seen*

Paul Tells of His Preaching

19 "After that, King Agrippa, I was not disobedient to the heavenly vision, [20]but declared first to those in Damascus, then in Jerusalem and throughout the countryside of Judea, and also to the Gentiles, that they should repent and turn to God and do deeds consistent with repentance. [21]For this reason the Jews seized me in the temple and tried to kill me. [22]To this day I have had help from God, and so I stand here, testifying to both small and great, saying nothing but what the prophets and Moses said would take place: [23]that the Messiah[a] must suffer, and that, by being the first to rise from the dead, he would proclaim light both to our people and to the Gentiles."

Paul Appeals to Agrippa to Believe

24 While he was making this defense, Festus exclaimed, "You are out of your mind, Paul! Too much learning is driving you insane!" [25]But Paul said, "I am not out of my mind, most excellent Festus, but I am speaking the sober truth. [26]Indeed the king knows about these things, and to him I speak freely; for I am certain that none of these things has escaped his notice, for this was not done in a corner. [27]King Agrippa, do you believe the prophets? I know that you believe." [28]Agrippa said to Paul, "Are you so quickly persuading me to become a Christian?"[b] [29]Paul replied, "Whether quickly or not, I pray to God that not only you but also all who are listening to me today might become such as I am—except for these chains."

30 Then the king got up, and with him the governor and Bernice and those who had been seated with them; [31]and as they were leaving, they said to one another, "This man is doing nothing to deserve death or imprisonment." [32]Agrippa said to Festus, "This man could have been set free if he had not appealed to the emperor."

Paul Sails for Rome

27 When it was decided that we were to sail for Italy, they transferred Paul and some other prisoners to a centurion of the Augustan Cohort, named Julius. [2]Embarking on a ship of Adramyttium that was about to set sail to the ports along the coast of Asia, we put to sea, accompanied by Aristarchus, a Macedonian from Thessalonica. [3]The next day we put in at Sidon; and Julius treated Paul kindly, and allowed him to go to his friends to be cared for. [4]Putting out to sea from there, we sailed under the lee of Cyprus, because the winds were against us. [5]After we had sailed across the sea that is off Cilicia and Pamphylia, we came to Myra in Lycia. [6]There the centurion found an Alexandrian ship bound for Italy and put us on board. [7]We sailed slowly for a number of days and arrived with difficulty off Cnidus, and as the wind was against us, we sailed under the lee of Crete off Salmone. [8]Sailing past it with difficulty, we came to a place called Fair Havens, near the city of Lasea.

9 Since much time had been lost and sailing was now dangerous, because even the Fast had already gone by, Paul advised them, [10]saying, "Sirs, I can see that the voyage will be with danger and much heavy loss, not only of the cargo

Praying for Conversions

ACTS 26.28–29

Join your prayer to Paul's, praying that those who hear the gospel proclaimed may become Christians, "whether quickly or not." It may help to make a list of friends, neighbors or family members who are not followers of Jesus. Through your praying bring each one into the presence of Jesus. Note that this kind of prayer is not the same as praying for these people to become members of your church or simply praying for your church to grow. All your concern should be focused on the goal that these individuals meet and follow Jesus, in Jesus' own way and time.

See Meeting God in Prayer

Encouraged by Rest, Food and Prayer

ACTS 27.33–36

After fourteen days of being pitched and tossed about on the Adriatic Sea, the crew is near exhaustion and ready to jump ship. Paul intervenes with much-needed food and encouragement.

In our days of fast food and hurried meals, we are tempted to overlook the ministry of a shared meal and the fellowship of breaking bread, as was common in the early church (see 2.46). A pot of bean soup or a loaf of freshly baked bread can communicate volumes of care and concern to one who is sad, lonely, discouraged or sick. Ask God to show you someone who needs encouragement. Make plans to take a meal to a shut-in. Include with the meal a written prayer or scripture verse, or a book or CD that will nourish that person spiritually. Take a young person out to a good restaurant or invite a family to your home for a hearty meal soon.

See Meeting God in Community

and the ship, but also of our lives." ¹¹But the centurion paid more attention to the pilot and to the owner of the ship than to what Paul said. ¹²Since the harbor was not suitable for spending the winter, the majority was in favor of putting to sea from there, on the chance that somehow they could reach Phoenix, where they could spend the winter. It was a harbor of Crete, facing southwest and northwest.

The Storm at Sea

13 When a moderate south wind began to blow, they thought they could achieve their purpose; so they weighed anchor and began to sail past Crete, close to the shore. ¹⁴But soon a violent wind, called the northeaster, rushed down from Crete.*ᵃ* ¹⁵Since the ship was caught and could not be turned head-on into the wind, we gave way to it and were driven. ¹⁶By running under the lee of a small island called Cauda*ᵇ* we were scarcely able to get the ship's boat under control. ¹⁷After hoisting it up they took measures*ᶜ* to undergird the ship; then, fearing that they would run on the Syrtis, they lowered the sea anchor and so were driven. ¹⁸We were being pounded by the storm so violently that on the next day they began to throw the cargo overboard, ¹⁹and on the third day with their own hands they threw the ship's tackle overboard. ²⁰When neither sun nor stars appeared for many days, and no small tempest raged, all hope of our being saved was at last abandoned.

21 Since they had been without food for a long time, Paul then stood up among them and said, "Men, you should have listened to me and not have set sail from Crete and thereby avoided this damage and loss. ²²I urge you now to keep up your courage, for there will be no loss of life among you, but only of the ship. ²³For last night there stood by me an angel of the God to whom I belong and whom I worship, ²⁴and he said, 'Do not be afraid, Paul; you must stand before the emperor; and indeed, God has granted safety to all those who are sailing with you.' ²⁵So keep up your courage, men, for I have faith in God that it will be exactly as I have been told. ²⁶But we will have to run aground on some island."

27 When the fourteenth night had come, as we were drifting across the sea of Adria, about midnight the sailors suspected that they were nearing land. ²⁸So they took soundings and found twenty fathoms; a little farther on they took soundings again and found fifteen fathoms. ²⁹Fearing that we might run on the rocks, they let down four anchors from the stern and prayed for day to come. ³⁰But when the sailors tried to escape from the ship and had lowered the boat into the sea, on the pretext of putting out anchors from the bow, ³¹Paul said to the centurion and the soldiers, "Unless these men stay in the ship, you cannot be saved." ³²Then the soldiers cut away the ropes of the boat and set it adrift.

33 Just before daybreak, Paul urged all of them to take some food, saying, "Today is the fourteenth day that you have been in suspense and remaining without food, having eaten nothing. ³⁴Therefore I urge you to take some food, for it will help you survive; for none of you will lose a hair from your heads." ³⁵After he had said this, he took bread; and giving thanks to God in the presence of all, he broke it and

a Gk *it*   *b* Other ancient authorities read *Clauda*   *c* Gk *helps*

began to eat. ³⁶Then all of them were encouraged and took food for themselves. ³⁷(We were in all two hundred seventy-six*a* persons in the ship.) ³⁸After they had satisfied their hunger, they lightened the ship by throwing the wheat into the sea.

The Shipwreck

39 In the morning they did not recognize the land, but they noticed a bay with a beach, on which they planned to run the ship ashore, if they could. ⁴⁰So they cast off the anchors and left them in the sea. At the same time they loosened the ropes that tied the steering-oars; then hoisting the foresail to the wind, they made for the beach. ⁴¹But striking a reef,*b* they ran the ship aground; the bow stuck and remained immovable, but the stern was being broken up by the force of the waves. ⁴²The soldiers' plan was to kill the prisoners, so that none might swim away and escape; ⁴³but the centurion, wishing to save Paul, kept them from carrying out their plan. He ordered those who could swim to jump overboard first and make for the land, ⁴⁴and the rest to follow, some on planks and others on pieces of the ship. And so it was that all were brought safely to land.

Paul on the Island of Malta

28 After we had reached safety, we then learned that the island was called Malta. ²The natives showed us unusual kindness. Since it had begun to rain and was cold, they kindled a fire and welcomed all of us around it. ³Paul had gathered a bundle of brushwood and was putting it on the fire, when a viper, driven out by the heat, fastened itself on his hand. ⁴When the natives saw the creature hanging from his hand, they said to one another, "This man must be a murderer; though he has escaped from the sea, justice has not allowed him to live." ⁵He, however, shook off the creature into the fire and suffered no harm. ⁶They were expecting him to swell up or drop dead, but after they had waited a long time and saw that nothing unusual had happened to him, they changed their minds and began to say that he was a god.

7 Now in the neighborhood of that place were lands belonging to the leading man of the island, named Publius, who received us and entertained us hospitably for three days. ⁸It so happened that the father of Publius lay sick in bed with fever and dysentery. Paul visited him and cured him by praying and putting his hands on him. ⁹After this happened, the rest of the people on the island who had diseases also came and were cured. ¹⁰They bestowed many honors on us, and when we were about to sail, they put on board all the provisions we needed.

Paul Arrives at Rome

11 Three months later we set sail on a ship that had wintered at the island, an Alexandrian ship with the Twin Brothers as its figurehead. ¹²We put in at Syracuse and stayed there for three days; ¹³then we weighed anchor and came to Rhegium. After one day there a south wind sprang up, and on the second day we came to Puteoli. ¹⁴There we found believers*c* and were invited to stay with them for

---

Facing Fear

ACTS 28.1–10

After surviving a shipwreck, Paul gathers firewood and is bitten by a snake! Danger can strike in the midst of everyday activities. What "everyday" danger do you fear? How does that fear affect your life? What would happen if your worst fear came true? Can you offer your fear to God? You might want to draw your fear or sculpt it from wire or clay, so that you can face it as you pray for God's deliverance.

See Meeting God in Everyday Life

---

a Other ancient authorities read *seventy-six*; others, *about seventy-six*
b Gk *place of two seas*   c Gk *brothers*

A Visit With Paul

ACTS 28.28–31

The book of Acts ends with Paul living serenely in Rome, where he "welcomed all who came to him." You might imagine yourself as one of those visitors. What would you want to talk about with Paul? What would you ask him? How do you think he would answer? Your imagination will be more focused if you write out a "transcript" of your visit.

See *Meeting God in Scripture*

seven days. And so we came to Rome. [15] The believers[a] from there, when they heard of us, came as far as the Forum of Appius and Three Taverns to meet us. On seeing them, Paul thanked God and took courage.

16 When we came into Rome, Paul was allowed to live by himself, with the soldier who was guarding him.

Paul and Jewish Leaders in Rome

17 Three days later he called together the local leaders of the Jews. When they had assembled, he said to them, "Brothers, though I had done nothing against our people or the customs of our ancestors, yet I was arrested in Jerusalem and handed over to the Romans. [18] When they had examined me, the Romans[b] wanted to release me, because there was no reason for the death penalty in my case. [19] But when the Jews objected, I was compelled to appeal to the emperor—even though I had no charge to bring against my nation. [20] For this reason therefore I have asked to see you and speak with you,[c] since it is for the sake of the hope of Israel that I am bound with this chain." [21] They replied, "We have received no letters from Judea about you, and none of the brothers coming here has reported or spoken anything evil about you. [22] But we would like to hear from you what you think, for with regard to this sect we know that everywhere it is spoken against."

Paul Preaches in Rome

23 After they had set a day to meet with him, they came to him at his lodgings in great numbers. From morning until evening he explained the matter to them, testifying to the kingdom of God and trying to convince them about Jesus both from the law of Moses and from the prophets. [24] Some were convinced by what he had said, while others refused to believe. [25] So they disagreed with each other; and as they were leaving, Paul made one further statement: "The Holy Spirit was right in saying to your ancestors through the prophet Isaiah,

26 'Go to this people and say,
You will indeed listen, but never understand,
and you will indeed look, but never perceive.
27 For this people's heart has grown dull,
and their ears are hard of hearing,
and they have shut their eyes;
so that they might not look with their eyes,
and listen with their ears,
and understand with their heart and turn—
and I would heal them.'

[28] Let it be known to you then that this salvation of God has been sent to the Gentiles; they will listen."[d]

30 He lived there two whole years at his own expense[e] and welcomed all who came to him, [31] proclaiming the kingdom of God and teaching about the Lord Jesus Christ with all boldness and without hindrance.

a Gk *brothers*   *b* Gk *they*   *c* Or *I have asked you to see me and speak with me*   *d* Other ancient authorities add verse 29, *And when he had said these words, the Jews departed, arguing vigorously among themselves*   *e* Or *in his own hired dwelling*

The Letter of Paul to the

ROMANS

The Old Self and the New Self

KEY VERSE:

But God proves his love for us in that while we still were sinners
Christ died for us.—Romans 5.8

Like a parent giving a gift to a child out of pure love, God gives us the gift of salvation. We do not have to do anything to deserve it, and we never could be good enough to earn it. In the book of Romans, the apostle Paul writes a treatise on the love of God. God's love is redeeming love, for every one of us is "under the power of sin" (3.9) and controlled by our human nature; we all "fall short of the glory of God" (3.23). God initiates our redemption even before we are aware of our need of it. In response to God's love, we are to turn our entire lives toward God so that, day by day, we are transformed—a process (5.1–4) that involves heart (2.29), mind (8.5–6), will (7.14–15) and actions (12.9–21)—as we become new persons who want what God wants (12.2).

Romans is a theological book, but it is also a realistic, practical discussion of how growing into fullness of life in Christ is a matter of mind, heart and spirit. Throughout our inner struggles and our struggles with others, we are drawn by God's incredible love in Christ Jesus, which seeks us out and bears us along in the spiritual life. Nothing that we have done, or ever could do, can separate us from the love that God offers us in Christ Jesus our Lord.

"Carefully note this point: When you find the phrase 'the righteousness of God' in Scripture, do not think that it means the essential, inner righteousness of God . . . Otherwise you will be frightened by it. Know rather that . . . it means the grace and the mercy of God poured out into us through Christ, whereby we are considered pious and righteous before Him. And it is called the righteousness or the piety of God because not we but God works it in us by His grace."

—MARTIN LUTHER,
in *What Luther Says*, 3909

All Creation Is God's

ROMANS 1.19–21

God has made himself knowable and readily visible in the creation he has made. God's Spirit has been present in the world from its beginning. When we are observant, creation reveals the eternal power and wondrous beauty of the Creator.

Set aside a half hour to go for a stroll. As you walk, pray for awareness of anything that might speak to you of God. Breathe deeply. If something attracts you, stop and give it your full attention. Let God speak to you in whatever form that experience may take. Look for some small object to bring back with you as a reminder of your meeting with God, and place it where you can see it for the next few days.

See Meeting God in the Created Order

Salutation

1 Paul, a servant*a* of Jesus Christ, called to be an apostle, set apart for the gospel of God, ²which he promised beforehand through his prophets in the holy scriptures, ³the gospel concerning his Son, who was descended from David according to the flesh ⁴and was declared to be Son of God with power according to the spirit*b* of holiness by resurrection from the dead, Jesus Christ our Lord, ⁵through whom we have received grace and apostleship to bring about the obedience of faith among all the Gentiles for the sake of his name, ⁶including yourselves who are called to belong to Jesus Christ,

7 To all God's beloved in Rome, who are called to be saints:

Grace to you and peace from God our Father and the Lord Jesus Christ.

Prayer of Thanksgiving

8 First, I thank my God through Jesus Christ for all of you, because your faith is proclaimed throughout the world. ⁹For God, whom I serve with my spirit by announcing the gospel*c* of his Son, is my witness that without ceasing I remember you always in my prayers, ¹⁰asking that by God's will I may somehow at last succeed in coming to you. ¹¹For I am longing to see you so that I may share with you some spiritual gift to strengthen you— ¹²or rather so that we may be mutually encouraged by each other's faith, both yours and mine. ¹³I want you to know, brothers and sisters,*d* that I have often intended to come to you (but thus far have been prevented), in order that I may reap some harvest among you as I have among the rest of the Gentiles. ¹⁴I am a debtor both to Greeks and to barbarians, both to the wise and to the foolish ¹⁵—hence my eagerness to proclaim the gospel to you also who are in Rome.

The Power of the Gospel

16 For I am not ashamed of the gospel; it is the power of God for salvation to everyone who has faith, to the Jew first and also to the Greek. ¹⁷For in it the righteousness of God is revealed through faith for faith; as it is written, "The one who is righteous will live by faith."*e*

The Guilt of Humankind

18 For the wrath of God is revealed from heaven against all ungodliness and wickedness of those who by their wickedness suppress the truth. ¹⁹For what can be known about God is plain to them, because God has shown it to them. ²⁰Ever since the creation of the world his eternal power and divine nature, invisible though they are, have been understood and seen through the things he has made. So they are without excuse; ²¹for though they knew God, they did not honor him as God or give thanks to him, but they became futile in their thinking, and their senseless minds were darkened. ²²Claiming to be wise, they became fools; ²³and they exchanged the glory of the

a Gk *slave*   *b* Or *Spirit*   *c* Gk *my spirit in the gospel*   *d* Gk *brothers*
e Or *The one who is righteous through faith will live*

immortal God for images resembling a mortal human being or birds or four-footed animals or reptiles.

24 Therefore God gave them up in the lusts of their hearts to impurity, to the degrading of their bodies among themselves, 25because they exchanged the truth about God for a lie and worshiped and served the creature rather than the Creator, who is blessed forever! Amen.

26 For this reason God gave them up to degrading passions. Their women exchanged natural intercourse for unnatural, 27and in the same way also the men, giving up natural intercourse with women, were consumed with passion for one another. Men committed shameless acts with men and received in their own persons the due penalty for their error.

28 And since they did not see fit to acknowledge God, God gave them up to a debased mind and to things that should not be done. 29They were filled with every kind of wickedness, evil, covetousness, malice. Full of envy, murder, strife, deceit, craftiness, they are gossips, 30slanderers, God-haters,*a* insolent, haughty, boastful, inventors of evil, rebellious toward parents, 31foolish, faithless, heartless, ruthless. 32They know God's decree, that those who practice such things deserve to die—yet they not only do them but even applaud others who practice them.

The Righteous Judgment of God

2 Therefore you have no excuse, whoever you are, when you judge others; for in passing judgment on another you condemn yourself, because you, the judge, are doing the very same things. 2You say,*b* "We know that God's judgment on those who do such things is in accordance with truth." 3Do you imagine, whoever you are, that when you judge those who do such things and yet do them yourself, you will escape the judgment of God? 4Or do you despise the riches of his kindness and forbearance and patience? Do you not realize that God's kindness is meant to lead you to repentance? 5But by your hard and impenitent heart you are storing up wrath for yourself on the day of wrath, when God's righteous judgment will be revealed. 6For he will repay according to each one's deeds: 7to those who by patiently doing good seek for glory and honor and immortality, he will give eternal life; 8while for those who are self-seeking and who obey not the truth but wickedness, there will be wrath and fury. 9There will be anguish and distress for everyone who does evil, the Jew first and also the Greek, 10but glory and honor and peace for everyone who does good, the Jew first and also the Greek. 11For God shows no partiality.

12 All who have sinned apart from the law will also perish apart from the law, and all who have sinned under the law will be judged by the law. 13For it is not the hearers of the law who are righteous in God's sight, but the doers of the law who will be justified. 14When Gentiles, who do not possess the law, do instinctively what the law requires, these, though not having the law, are a law to themselves. 15They show that what the law requires is written on their

God's Kindness

ROMANS 2.4

"God's kindness is meant to lead [us] to repentance"; all the means that God uses to bring us to faith are expressions of that kindness. Even before we are aware that we need or want to know God, he reaches out to draw us toward himself.

What is your first memory of awareness of God? What circumstances led you to repentance? Who was instrumental in bringing you to an awareness of God's love? Try to recall your first memory of praying or wanting to pray, the person who first mentioned God to you, the person who taught you your first "memory verse." In more recent times, who has helped you learn about God or inspired you to want to know God more deeply? Give thanks for the kindnesses that have nurtured your faith. Take the time to write a thank-you note to someone who has been an expression of God's kindness in your life.

See Meeting God in Everyday Life

A Matter of the Heart

ROMANS 2.28–29

Many common expressions acknowledge the importance of the heart in our daily language. When we speak openly and honestly, we "speak from the heart." To truly understand, we "get to the heart" of a matter. The heart is the place of deepest knowing. When the heart is cluttered, resistant or hardened, it can keep us closed to God and alienated from other people. An uncluttered heart is the work of a lifetime, a work we cannot achieve alone.

Set aside time to be quiet and ask Jesus to inspect your heart. Is it open and ready to welcome God? Or is it cluttered? What does the clutter look like? Write about, or draw a description of, the areas of your heart that are not prepared to welcome God. Tell Jesus why you have closed off those areas.

hearts, to which their own conscience also bears witness; and their conflicting thoughts will accuse or perhaps excuse them [16]on the day when, according to my gospel, God, through Jesus Christ, will judge the secret thoughts of all.

The Jews and the Law

17 But if you call yourself a Jew and rely on the law and boast of your relation to God [18]and know his will and determine what is best because you are instructed in the law, [19]and if you are sure that you are a guide to the blind, a light to those who are in darkness, [20]a corrector of the foolish, a teacher of children, having in the law the embodiment of knowledge and truth, [21]you, then, that teach others, will you not teach yourself? While you preach against stealing, do you steal? [22]You that forbid adultery, do you commit adultery? You that abhor idols, do you rob temples? [23]You that boast in the law, do you dishonor God by breaking the law? [24]For, as it is written, "The name of God is blasphemed among the Gentiles because of you."

25 Circumcision indeed is of value if you obey the law; but if you break the law, your circumcision has become uncircumcision. [26]So, if those who are uncircumcised keep the requirements of the law, will not their uncircumcision be regarded as circumcision? [27]Then those who are physically uncircumcised but keep the law will condemn you that have the written code and circumcision but break the law. [28]For a person is not a Jew who is one outwardly, nor is true circumcision something external and physical. [29]Rather, a person is a Jew who is one inwardly, and real circumcision is a matter of the heart—it is spiritual and not literal. Such a person receives praise not from others but from God.

3 Then what advantage has the Jew? Or what is the value of circumcision? [2]Much, in every way. For in the first place the Jews[a] were entrusted with the oracles of God. [3]What if some were unfaithful? Will their faithlessness nullify the faithfulness of God? [4]By no means! Although everyone is a liar, let God be proved true, as it is written,

"So that you may be justified in your words,
    and prevail in your judging."[b]

[5]But if our injustice serves to confirm the justice of God, what should we say? That God is unjust to inflict wrath on us? (I speak in a human way.) [6]By no means! For then how could God judge the world? [7]But if through my falsehood God's truthfulness abounds to his glory, why am I still being condemned as a sinner? [8]And why not say (as some people slander us by saying that we say), "Let us do evil so that good may come"? Their condemnation is deserved!

None Is Righteous

9 What then? Are we any better off?[c] No, not at all; for we have already charged that all, both Jews and Greeks, are under the power of sin, [10]as it is written:

a Gk *they*   *b* Gk *when you are being judged*   *c* Or *at any disadvantage?*

"There is no one who is righteous, not even one;

¹¹   there is no one who has understanding,
        there is no one who seeks God.

¹² All have turned aside, together they have become
        worthless;
    there is no one who shows kindness,
        there is not even one."

¹³ "Their throats are opened graves;
        they use their tongues to deceive."
    "The venom of vipers is under their lips."

¹⁴   "Their mouths are full of cursing and
        bitterness."

¹⁵ "Their feet are swift to shed blood;

¹⁶   ruin and misery are in their paths,

¹⁷ and the way of peace they have not known."

¹⁸   "There is no fear of God before their eyes."

19 Now we know that whatever the law says, it speaks to those who are under the law, so that every mouth may be silenced, and the whole world may be held accountable to God. ²⁰For "no human being will be justified in his sight" by deeds prescribed by the law, for through the law comes the knowledge of sin.

Righteousness through Faith

21 But now, apart from law, the righteousness of God has been disclosed, and is attested by the law and the prophets, ²²the righteousness of God through faith in Jesus Christ^a for all who believe. For there is no distinction, ²³since all have sinned and fall short of the glory of God; ²⁴they are now justified by his grace as a gift, through the redemption that is in Christ Jesus, ²⁵whom God put forward as a sacrifice of atonement^b by his blood, effective through faith. He did this to show his righteousness, because in his divine forbearance he had passed over the sins previously committed; ²⁶it was to prove at the present time that he himself is righteous and that he justifies the one who has faith in Jesus.^c

27 Then what becomes of boasting? It is excluded. By what law? By that of works? No, but by the law of faith. ²⁸For we hold that a person is justified by faith apart from works prescribed by the law. ²⁹Or is God the God of Jews only? Is he not the God of Gentiles also? Yes, of Gentiles also, ³⁰since God is one; and he will justify the circumcised on the ground of faith and the uncircumcised through that same faith. ³¹Do we then overthrow the law by this faith? By no means! On the contrary, we uphold the law.

The Example of Abraham

4 What then are we to say was gained by^d Abraham, our ancestor according to the flesh? ²For if Abraham was justified by works, he has something to boast about, but not before God. ³For what does the scripture say? "Abraham believed God, and it was reckoned to him as righteousness." ⁴Now to one who works, wages are not reckoned as a gift but as something due. ⁵But to one who

---

The Gift of Righteousness

ROMANS 3.21–24

Paul points out that, regardless of how "nice" or "good" we feel we are, to be human is to be deeply and terminally flawed. God in Christ Jesus covers us perfectly and fully with righteousness—flaws and all. Jesus loves us so much that he redeemed us at the price of his own life.

Imagine Jesus kneeling before you. He wants to pour out his love and grace to you; as a symbol of love and grace, he is pouring out water to wash your feet. As he gazes up at you with eyes of love and acceptance, what emotions do you experience? What will you say to him? What do you envision Jesus saying to you?

See Meeting God in Scripture

---

*a Or through the faith of Jesus Christ   b Or a place of atonement
c Or who has the faith of Jesus   d Other ancient authorities read say
about*

Living in Faith

ROMANS 4.16–19

Abraham believed God even when things looked impossible; because of Abraham's faith, God considered him righteous. To have faith is to walk along a path without a map and to believe that Almighty God knows the way and walks with us. It is an act of will, not of emotion, when we hand over the control of our lives to the only One who will neither become lost nor lose us.

Think of some troubling situations that you would like to surrender to God's control. Is it difficult for you to think about letting go of them? Write a description of one of them on a piece of paper and place it in the palm of your hand. Then, raising your hands, transfer your concern to the nail-scarred palms of Jesus. What emotions do you experience? Talk to God about them, and listen carefully for God's response.

See *Meeting God in Everyday Life*

without works trusts him who justifies the ungodly, such faith is reckoned as righteousness. ⁶So also David speaks of the blessedness of those to whom God reckons righteousness apart from works:

7 "Blessed are those whose iniquities are forgiven,
and whose sins are covered;
8 blessed is the one against whom the Lord will not
reckon sin."

9 Is this blessedness, then, pronounced only on the circumcised, or also on the uncircumcised? We say, "Faith was reckoned to Abraham as righteousness." ¹⁰How then was it reckoned to him? Was it before or after he had been circumcised? It was not after, but before he was circumcised. ¹¹He received the sign of circumcision as a seal of the righteousness that he had by faith while he was still uncircumcised. The purpose was to make him the ancestor of all who believe without being circumcised and who thus have righteousness reckoned to them, ¹²and likewise the ancestor of the circumcised who are not only circumcised but who also follow the example of the faith that our ancestor Abraham had before he was circumcised.

God's Promise Realized through Faith

13 For the promise that he would inherit the world did not come to Abraham or to his descendants through the law but through the righteousness of faith. ¹⁴If it is the adherents of the law who are to be the heirs, faith is null and the promise is void. ¹⁵For the law brings wrath; but where there is no law, neither is there violation.

16 For this reason it depends on faith, in order that the promise may rest on grace and be guaranteed to all his descendants, not only to the adherents of the law but also to those who share the faith of Abraham (for he is the father of all of us, ¹⁷as it is written, "I have made you the father of many nations")—in the presence of the God in whom he believed, who gives life to the dead and calls into existence the things that do not exist. ¹⁸Hoping against hope, he believed that he would become "the father of many nations," according to what was said, "So numerous shall your descendants be." ¹⁹He did not weaken in faith when he considered his own body, which was already*a* as good as dead (for he was about a hundred years old), or when he considered the barrenness of Sarah's womb. ²⁰No distrust made him waver concerning the promise of God, but he grew strong in his faith as he gave glory to God, ²¹being fully convinced that God was able to do what he had promised. ²²Therefore his faith*b* "was reckoned to him as righteousness." ²³Now the words, "it was reckoned to him," were written not for his sake alone, ²⁴but for ours also. It will be reckoned to us who believe in him who raised Jesus our Lord from the dead, ²⁵who was handed over to death for our trespasses and was raised for our justification.

a Other ancient authorities lack *already*   *b* Gk *Therefore it*

Results of Justification

5 Therefore, since we are justified by faith, we[a] have peace with God through our Lord Jesus Christ, [2]through whom we have obtained access[b] to this grace in which we stand; and we[c] boast in our hope of sharing the glory of God. [3]And not only that, but we[c] also boast in our sufferings, knowing that suffering produces endurance, [4]and endurance produces character, and character produces hope, [5]and hope does not disappoint us, because God's love has been poured into our hearts through the Holy Spirit that has been given to us.

6 For while we were still weak, at the right time Christ died for the ungodly. [7]Indeed, rarely will anyone die for a righteous person—though perhaps for a good person someone might actually dare to die. [8]But God proves his love for us in that while we still were sinners Christ died for us. [9]Much more surely then, now that we have been justified by his blood, will we be saved through him from the wrath of God.[d] [10]For if while we were enemies, we were reconciled to God through the death of his Son, much more surely, having been reconciled, will we be saved by his life. [11]But more than that, we even boast in God through our Lord Jesus Christ, through whom we have now received reconciliation.

Adam and Christ

12 Therefore, just as sin came into the world through one man, and death came through sin, and so death spread to all because all have sinned— [13]sin was indeed in the world before the law, but sin is not reckoned when there is no law. [14]Yet death exercised dominion from Adam to Moses, even over those whose sins were not like the transgression of Adam, who is a type of the one who was to come.

15 But the free gift is not like the trespass. For if the many died through the one man's trespass, much more surely have the grace of God and the free gift in the grace of the one man, Jesus Christ, abounded for the many. [16]And the free gift is not like the effect of the one man's sin. For the judgment following one trespass brought condemnation, but the free gift following many trespasses brings justification. [17]If, because of the one man's trespass, death exercised dominion through that one, much more surely will those who receive the abundance of grace and the free gift of righteousness exercise dominion in life through the one man, Jesus Christ.

18 Therefore just as one man's trespass led to condemnation for all, so one man's act of righteousness leads to justification and life for all. [19]For just as by the one man's disobedience the many were made sinners, so by the one man's obedience the many will be made righteous. [20]But law came in, with the result that the trespass multiplied; but where sin increased, grace abounded all the more, [21]so that, just as sin exercised dominion in death, so grace

---

The Gift of Life

ROMANS 5.6–8

Our consumer-driven culture tempts us to speak glibly about sacrifice and self-denial: "I'd give my right arm for tickets to that game." "That ice cream is to die for." Do we take in the amazing reality of such wondrous love—that Jesus not only *offered* to die for us, but he actually did? If we fully absorbed this truth, would we not walk day by day in awe?

Repeat verse 8 slowly, personalizing it: "While I was still a sinner, Christ died for me." Can you understand why? Would you die for someone else? Would you willingly take the punishment someone else deserved? What kind of connection would you have to have with someone to put yourself in that person's place? Write a letter to the One who died for you, expressing what you think and feel about his wondrous sacrifice for you.

---

a Other ancient authorities read *let us*   b Other ancient authorities add *by faith*   c Or *let us*   d Gk *the wrath*

Service That Frees

ROMANS 6.20–23

Every person serves something—giving his or her energies to some goal, desire, person or organization. And after we serve long enough, we identify with that master and take on its characteristics. What do you serve? Ask God to make you aware of your motives and loyalties. Set aside some time to think about how you are spending your time and energy. In what ways have you made choices to serve God? Are you growing more Christlike? Who, or what, claims your loyalty? Who are your other "gods"? What is the payoff for serving them?

See Meeting God in Service

might also exercise dominion through justification[a] leading to eternal life through Jesus Christ our Lord.

Dying and Rising with Christ

6 What then are we to say? Should we continue in sin in order that grace may abound? ²By no means! How can we who died to sin go on living in it? ³Do you not know that all of us who have been baptized into Christ Jesus were baptized into his death? ⁴Therefore we have been buried with him by baptism into death, so that, just as Christ was raised from the dead by the glory of the Father, so we too might walk in newness of life.

5 For if we have been united with him in a death like his, we will certainly be united with him in a resurrection like his. ⁶We know that our old self was crucified with him so that the body of sin might be destroyed, and we might no longer be enslaved to sin. ⁷For whoever has died is freed from sin. ⁸But if we have died with Christ, we believe that we will also live with him. ⁹We know that Christ, being raised from the dead, will never die again; death no longer has dominion over him. ¹⁰The death he died, he died to sin, once for all; but the life he lives, he lives to God. ¹¹So you also must consider yourselves dead to sin and alive to God in Christ Jesus.

12 Therefore, do not let sin exercise dominion in your mortal bodies, to make you obey their passions. ¹³No longer present your members to sin as instruments[b] of wickedness, but present yourselves to God as those who have been brought from death to life, and present your members to God as instruments[b] of righteousness. ¹⁴For sin will have no dominion over you, since you are not under law but under grace.

Slaves of Righteousness

15 What then? Should we sin because we are not under law but under grace? By no means! ¹⁶Do you not know that if you present yourselves to anyone as obedient slaves, you are slaves of the one whom you obey, either of sin, which leads to death, or of obedience, which leads to righteousness? ¹⁷But thanks be to God that you, having once been slaves of sin, have become obedient from the heart to the form of teaching to which you were entrusted, ¹⁸and that you, having been set free from sin, have become slaves of righteousness. ¹⁹I am speaking in human terms because of your natural limitations.[c] For just as you once presented your members as slaves to impurity and to greater and greater iniquity, so now present your members as slaves to righteousness for sanctification.

20 When you were slaves of sin, you were free in regard to righteousness. ²¹So what advantage did you then get from the things of which you now are ashamed? The end of those things is death. ²²But now that you have been freed from sin and enslaved to God, the advantage you get is sanctification. The end is eternal life. ²³For the wages of sin is death, but the free gift of God is eternal life in Christ Jesus our Lord.

a Or *righteousness*   *b* Or *weapons*   *c* Gk *the weakness of your flesh*

An Analogy from Marriage

7 Do you not know, brothers and sisters[a]—for I am speaking to those who know the law—that the law is binding on a person only during that person's lifetime? [2]Thus a married woman is bound by the law to her husband as long as he lives; but if her husband dies, she is discharged from the law concerning the husband. [3]Accordingly, she will be called an adulteress if she lives with another man while her husband is alive. But if her husband dies, she is free from that law, and if she marries another man, she is not an adulteress.

4 In the same way, my friends,[a] you have died to the law through the body of Christ, so that you may belong to another, to him who has been raised from the dead in order that we may bear fruit for God. [5]While we were living in the flesh, our sinful passions, aroused by the law, were at work in our members to bear fruit for death. [6]But now we are discharged from the law, dead to that which held us captive, so that we are slaves not under the old written code but in the new life of the Spirit.

The Law and Sin

7 What then should we say? That the law is sin? By no means! Yet, if it had not been for the law, I would not have known sin. I would not have known what it is to covet if the law had not said, "You shall not covet." [8]But sin, seizing an opportunity in the commandment, produced in me all kinds of covetousness. Apart from the law sin lies dead. [9]I was once alive apart from the law, but when the commandment came, sin revived [10]and I died, and the very commandment that promised life proved to be death to me. [11]For sin, seizing an opportunity in the commandment, deceived me and through it killed me. [12]So the law is holy, and the commandment is holy and just and good.

13 Did what is good, then, bring death to me? By no means! It was sin, working death in me through what is good, in order that sin might be shown to be sin, and through the commandment might become sinful beyond measure.

The Inner Conflict

14 For we know that the law is spiritual; but I am of the flesh, sold into slavery under sin.[b] [15]I do not understand my own actions. For I do not do what I want, but I do the very thing I hate. [16]Now if I do what I do not want, I agree that the law is good. [17]But in fact it is no longer I that do it, but sin that dwells within me. [18]For I know that nothing good dwells within me, that is, in my flesh. I can will what is right, but I cannot do it. [19]For I do not do the good I want, but the evil I do not want is what I do. [20]Now if I do what I do not want, it is no longer I that do it, but sin that dwells within me.

21 So I find it to be a law that when I want to do what is good, evil lies close at hand. [22]For I delight in the law of God in my inmost self, [23]but I see in my members another law at war with the law of my mind, making me captive

---

The Reality of Struggle

ROMANS 7.15,21–25

Paul was no stranger to the struggle against the sinful nature. He knew what it was like to want to do one thing and yet do another. On a daily basis we fall short of being who God wants us to be and of doing what God wants us to do.

Is there one area of your life where you have experienced continual struggle, perhaps for years? Tell God about your struggles. End your prayer by reading Romans 8.1–2 as God's promise to you. Ask God's Spirit to live in you, and find some object to carry with you as a reminder of the Spirit within you—a cross, a small rock, a written verse from scripture. Keep this symbol where you can touch it when you need to remember that you live by grace.

See Meeting God in Everyday Life

Enlightening Our Spirits

ROMANS 8.26–27

Watching 3-D movies requires special glasses. While wearing these glasses viewers see a dramatically different picture. The glasses make it possible to see to a depth or perspective that is otherwise impossible. Without the presence of the Holy Spirit in us, we cannot see with God's perspective. The Spirit enlightens "the eyes of [our] heart" (Ephesians 1.18) so we can understand the hope to which God calls us.

Pray for an awareness of God's Spirit within you. Then, allowing God's Spirit to give you perspective, take time to write about some issue—perhaps a difficult moment at work or at home, or something you've read about in the daily newspaper. Allow the Spirit to give you ongoing insight about what you have written.

See Meeting God in Everyday Life

to the law of sin that dwells in my members. ²⁴Wretched man that I am! Who will rescue me from this body of death? ²⁵Thanks be to God through Jesus Christ our Lord!

So then, with my mind I am a slave to the law of God, but with my flesh I am a slave to the law of sin.

Life in the Spirit

8 There is therefore now no condemnation for those who are in Christ Jesus. ²For the law of the Spirit[a] of life in Christ Jesus has set you[b] free from the law of sin and of death. ³For God has done what the law, weakened by the flesh, could not do: by sending his own Son in the likeness of sinful flesh, and to deal with sin,[c] he condemned sin in the flesh, ⁴so that the just requirement of the law might be fulfilled in us, who walk not according to the flesh but according to the Spirit.[a] ⁵For those who live according to the flesh set their minds on the things of the flesh, but those who live according to the Spirit[a] set their minds on the things of the Spirit.[a] ⁶To set the mind on the flesh is death, but to set the mind on the Spirit[a] is life and peace. ⁷For this reason the mind that is set on the flesh is hostile to God; it does not submit to God's law—indeed it cannot, ⁸and those who are in the flesh cannot please God.

9 But you are not in the flesh; you are in the Spirit,[a] since the Spirit of God dwells in you. Anyone who does not have the Spirit of Christ does not belong to him. ¹⁰But if Christ is in you, though the body is dead because of sin, the Spirit[a] is life because of righteousness. ¹¹If the Spirit of him who raised Jesus from the dead dwells in you, he who raised Christ[d] from the dead will give life to your mortal bodies also through[e] his Spirit that dwells in you.

12 So then, brothers and sisters,[f] we are debtors, not to the flesh, to live according to the flesh— ¹³for if you live according to the flesh, you will die; but if by the Spirit you put to death the deeds of the body, you will live. ¹⁴For all who are led by the Spirit of God are children of God. ¹⁵For you did not receive a spirit of slavery to fall back into fear, but you have received a spirit of adoption. When we cry, "Abba![g] Father!" ¹⁶it is that very Spirit bearing witness[h] with our spirit that we are children of God, ¹⁷and if children, then heirs, heirs of God and joint heirs with Christ— if, in fact, we suffer with him so that we may also be glorified with him.

Future Glory

18 I consider that the sufferings of this present time are not worth comparing with the glory about to be revealed to us. ¹⁹For the creation waits with eager longing for the revealing of the children of God; ²⁰for the creation was subjected to futility, not of its own will but by the will of the one who subjected it, in hope ²¹that the creation itself will be set free from its bondage to decay and will obtain the

a Or *spirit*   *b* Here the Greek word *you* is singular number; other ancient authorities read *me* or *us*   *c* Or *and as a sin offering*   *d* Other ancient authorities read *the Christ* or *Christ Jesus* or *Jesus Christ*   *e* Other ancient authorities read *on account of*   *f* Gk *brothers*   *g* Aramaic for *Father*   *h* Or *¹⁵a spirit of adoption, by which we cry, "Abba! Father!" ¹⁶The Spirit itself bears witness*

freedom of the glory of the children of God. [22]We know that the whole creation has been groaning in labor pains until now; [23]and not only the creation, but we ourselves, who have the first fruits of the Spirit, groan inwardly while we wait for adoption, the redemption of our bodies. [24]For in[a] hope we were saved. Now hope that is seen is not hope. For who hopes[b] for what is seen? [25]But if we hope for what we do not see, we wait for it with patience.

26 Likewise the Spirit helps us in our weakness; for we do not know how to pray as we ought, but that very Spirit intercedes[c] with sighs too deep for words. [27]And God,[d] who searches the heart, knows what is the mind of the Spirit, because the Spirit[e] intercedes for the saints according to the will of God.[f]

28 We know that all things work together for good[g] for those who love God, who are called according to his purpose. [29]For those whom he foreknew he also predestined to be conformed to the image of his Son, in order that he might be the firstborn within a large family.[h] [30]And those whom he predestined he also called; and those whom he called he also justified; and those whom he justified he also glorified.

God's Love in Christ Jesus

31 What then are we to say about these things? If God is for us, who is against us? [32]He who did not withhold his own Son, but gave him up for all of us, will he not with him also give us everything else? [33]Who will bring any charge against God's elect? It is God who justifies. [34]Who is to condemn? It is Christ Jesus, who died, yes, who was raised, who is at the right hand of God, who indeed intercedes for us.[i] [35]Who will separate us from the love of Christ? Will hardship, or distress, or persecution, or famine, or nakedness, or peril, or sword? [36]As it is written,
> "For your sake we are being killed all day long;
>   we are accounted as sheep to be slaughtered."

[37]No, in all these things we are more than conquerors through him who loved us. [38]For I am convinced that neither death, nor life, nor angels, nor rulers, nor things present, nor things to come, nor powers, [39]nor height, nor depth, nor anything else in all creation, will be able to separate us from the love of God in Christ Jesus our Lord.

God's Election of Israel

9 I am speaking the truth in Christ—I am not lying; my conscience confirms it by the Holy Spirit— [2]I have great sorrow and unceasing anguish in my heart. [3]For I could wish that I myself were accursed and cut off from Christ for the sake of my own people,[j] my kindred according to the flesh. [4]They are Israelites, and to them belong the adoption, the glory, the covenants, the giving of the law, the worship, and the promises; [5]to them belong the

---

Utterly Inseparable

ROMANS 8.35–39

"Can a woman forget her nursing child, or show no compassion for the child of her womb? Even these may forget, yet I will never forget you. See, I have inscribed you on the palms of my hands" (Isaiah 49.15–16).

Find an old tree whose roots are deeply entwined with the earth and with other roots, or find moss that has grown on a tree trunk. Or at the beach find a shell that has attached itself to a rock. Look for other examples of such deep inseparability. As you hold or look at these objects, speak the words of this passage, using them as a description for the One who holds you close.

See Meeting God in Scripture

---

a Or *by*   *b* Other ancient authorities read *awaits*   *c* Other ancient authorities add *for us*   *d* Gk *the one*   *e* Gk *he* or *it*   *f* Gk *according to God*   *g* Other ancient authorities read *God makes all things work together for good,* or *in all things God works for good*   *h* Gk *among many brothers*   *i* Or *Is it Christ Jesus . . . for us?*   *j* Gk *my brothers*

A Greater Purpose

ROMANS 9.14–18,24

Paul reminds us that we are not aware of God's greater design. The reasons that he has mercy on some and not on others remain a mystery to our finite minds.

We do know, however, that God's infinite wisdom is motivated by his infinite love. He sometimes uses negative circumstances to achieve his divine purposes. What qualifies as a closed door or a momentous defeat today may look quite different a few months or years down the road. With God's involvement, what seems like defeat can become a door to life.

Look back on your life and identify events that seemed completely negative at the time. Can you see any good that God has brought from them? Can you see how they are like pieces of a puzzle that, when fit together, have made you the person you are today? Offer to God the memories and experiences that still make no sense to you and that continue to be a source of pain.

See Meeting God in Everyday Life

patriarchs, and from them, according to the flesh, comes the Messiah,*a* who is over all, God blessed forever.*b* Amen.

6 It is not as though the word of God had failed. For not all Israelites truly belong to Israel, 7and not all of Abraham's children are his true descendants; but "It is through Isaac that descendants shall be named for you." 8This means that it is not the children of the flesh who are the children of God, but the children of the promise are counted as descendants. 9For this is what the promise said, "About this time I will return and Sarah shall have a son." 10Nor is that all; something similar happened to Rebecca when she had conceived children by one husband, our ancestor Isaac. 11Even before they had been born or had done anything good or bad (so that God's purpose of election might continue, 12not by works but by his call) she was told, "The elder shall serve the younger." 13As it is written,

> "I have loved Jacob,
> but I have hated Esau."

14 What then are we to say? Is there injustice on God's part? By no means! 15For he says to Moses,

> "I will have mercy on whom I have mercy,
> and I will have compassion on whom I have compassion."

16So it depends not on human will or exertion, but on God who shows mercy. 17For the scripture says to Pharaoh, "I have raised you up for the very purpose of showing my power in you, so that my name may be proclaimed in all the earth." 18So then he has mercy on whomever he chooses, and he hardens the heart of whomever he chooses.

God's Wrath and Mercy

19 You will say to me then, "Why then does he still find fault? For who can resist his will?" 20But who indeed are you, a human being, to argue with God? Will what is molded say to the one who molds it, "Why have you made me like this?" 21Has the potter no right over the clay, to make out of the same lump one object for special use and another for ordinary use? 22What if God, desiring to show his wrath and to make known his power, has endured with much patience the objects of wrath that are made for destruction; 23and what if he has done so in order to make known the riches of his glory for the objects of mercy, which he has prepared beforehand for glory— 24including us whom he has called, not from the Jews only but also from the Gentiles? 25As indeed he says in Hosea,

> "Those who were not my people I will call 'my people,'
> and her who was not beloved I will call 'beloved.' "

26 "And in the very place where it was said to them,
> 'You are not my people,'
> there they shall be called children of the living God."

a Or *the Christ*   *b* Or *Messiah, who is God over all, blessed forever*; or *Messiah. May he who is God over all be blessed forever*

27 And Isaiah cries out concerning Israel, "Though the number of the children of Israel were like the sand of the sea, only a remnant of them will be saved; ²⁸for the Lord will execute his sentence on the earth quickly and decisively."ᵃ ²⁹And as Isaiah predicted,

"If the Lord of hosts had not left survivorsᵇ to us,
we would have fared like Sodom
and been made like Gomorrah."

Israel's Unbelief

30 What then are we to say? Gentiles, who did not strive for righteousness, have attained it, that is, righteousness through faith; ³¹but Israel, who did strive for the righteousness that is based on the law, did not succeed in fulfilling that law. ³²Why not? Because they did not strive for it on the basis of faith, but as if it were based on works. They have stumbled over the stumbling stone, ³³as it is written,

"See, I am laying in Zion a stone that will make
people stumble, a rock that will make them
fall,
and whoever believes in himᶜ will not be put to
shame."

10 Brothers and sisters,ᵈ my heart's desire and prayer to God for them is that they may be saved. ²I can testify that they have a zeal for God, but it is not enlightened. ³For, being ignorant of the righteousness that comes from God, and seeking to establish their own, they have not submitted to God's righteousness. ⁴For Christ is the end of the law so that there may be righteousness for everyone who believes.

Salvation Is for All

5 Moses writes concerning the righteousness that comes from the law, that "the person who does these things will live by them." ⁶But the righteousness that comes from faith says, "Do not say in your heart, 'Who will ascend into heaven?' " (that is, to bring Christ down) ⁷"or 'Who will descend into the abyss?' " (that is, to bring Christ up from the dead). ⁸But what does it say?

"The word is near you,
on your lips and in your heart"

(that is, the word of faith that we proclaim); ⁹becauseᵉ if you confess with your lips that Jesus is Lord and believe in your heart that God raised him from the dead, you will be saved. ¹⁰For one believes with the heart and so is justified, and one confesses with the mouth and so is saved. ¹¹The scripture says, "No one who believes in him will be put to shame." ¹²For there is no distinction between Jew and Greek; the same Lord is Lord of all and is generous to all who call on him. ¹³For, "Everyone who calls on the name of the Lord shall be saved."

14 But how are they to call on one in whom they have not believed? And how are they to believe in one of whom

---

Faith in Jesus

ROMANS 10.9–13

Paul's unequivocal affirmation—that faith in Jesus is the only possible way to become righteous before God—allows no theological room for legalism to creep into our thinking. Legalism kept the Pharisees from accepting God's grace, and it remains a snare today. Rule keeping allows one to be religious without relinquishing pride or power to Almighty God. It is a way of avoiding the necessity of saying "Jesus is Lord."

In what ways are you tempted to think legalistically? Are there any attitudes of self-righteousness, selfishness or pride that you hang on to? Do you rely on an illusion of your own goodness for spiritual security? Search the corners of your heart with the Spirit's help. Write a paragraph about that search, and then respond by relinquishing pride and control to Jesus. Conclude by writing "Jesus is Lord" across that paragraph.

---

a Other ancient authorities read *for he will finish his work and cut it short in righteousness, because the Lord will make the sentence shortened on the earth*   b Or *descendants*; Gk *seed*   c Or *trusts in it*   d Gk *Brothers*   e Or *namely, that*

God's Initiative, Our Response

ROMANS 10.21–11.1,5–6

Scripture tells many stories of men and women whose choice to believe that God is God has placed them among God's "remnant" people. It was not their deeds or their titles that qualified them, but their decision to remain in relationship to God and therefore open to his guidance, correction and saving faithfulness.

Read these verses from Romans aloud, slowly. Where do you find yourself in them? Holding out your hands to another? Turning away from a gift? Accepting it? Trying to work your way to God? Wherever you are led, use that as a topic for prayer. Tell God where you are being led, and give him your response. Remember that any experience of God is a gift of grace and not your own work.

See Meeting God in Scripture

they have never heard? And how are they to hear without someone to proclaim him? ¹⁵And how are they to proclaim him unless they are sent? As it is written, "How beautiful are the feet of those who bring good news!" ¹⁶But not all have obeyed the good news;*ᵃ* for Isaiah says, "Lord, who has believed our message?" ¹⁷So faith comes from what is heard, and what is heard comes through the word of Christ.*ᵇ*

18 But I ask, have they not heard? Indeed they have; for
"Their voice has gone out to all the earth,
    and their words to the ends of the world."
¹⁹Again I ask, did Israel not understand? First Moses says,
"I will make you jealous of those who are not a
        nation;
    with a foolish nation I will make you angry."
²⁰Then Isaiah is so bold as to say,
"I have been found by those who did not seek me;
    I have shown myself to those who did not ask
        for me."
²¹But of Israel he says, "All day long I have held out my hands to a disobedient and contrary people."

Israel's Rejection Is Not Final

11 I ask, then, has God rejected his people? By no means! I myself am an Israelite, a descendant of Abraham, a member of the tribe of Benjamin. ²God has not rejected his people whom he foreknew. Do you not know what the scripture says of Elijah, how he pleads with God against Israel? ³"Lord, they have killed your prophets, they have demolished your altars; I alone am left, and they are seeking my life." ⁴But what is the divine reply to him? "I have kept for myself seven thousand who have not bowed the knee to Baal." ⁵So too at the present time there is a remnant, chosen by grace. ⁶But if it is by grace, it is no longer on the basis of works, otherwise grace would no longer be grace.*ᶜ*

7 What then? Israel failed to obtain what it was seeking. The elect obtained it, but the rest were hardened, ⁸as it is written,
"God gave them a sluggish spirit,
    eyes that would not see
    and ears that would not hear,
down to this very day."
⁹And David says,
"Let their table become a snare and a trap,
    a stumbling block and a retribution for them;
¹⁰ let their eyes be darkened so that they cannot see,
    and keep their backs forever bent."

The Salvation of the Gentiles

11 So I ask, have they stumbled so as to fall? By no means! But through their stumbling*ᵈ* salvation has come to the Gentiles, so as to make Israel*ᵉ* jealous. ¹²Now if their stumbling*ᵈ* means riches for the world, and if their defeat

a Or *gospel*   *b* Or *about Christ*; other ancient authorities read *of God*
c Other ancient authorities add *But if it is by works, it is no longer
on the basis of grace, otherwise work would no longer be work*
d Gk *transgression*   *e* Gk *them*

means riches for Gentiles, how much more will their full inclusion mean!

13 Now I am speaking to you Gentiles. Inasmuch then as I am an apostle to the Gentiles, I glorify my ministry [14]in order to make my own people[a] jealous, and thus save some of them. [15]For if their rejection is the reconciliation of the world, what will their acceptance be but life from the dead! [16]If the part of the dough offered as first fruits is holy, then the whole batch is holy; and if the root is holy, then the branches also are holy.

17 But if some of the branches were broken off, and you, a wild olive shoot, were grafted in their place to share the rich root[b] of the olive tree, [18]do not boast over the branches. If you do boast, remember that it is not you that support the root, but the root that supports you. [19]You will say, "Branches were broken off so that I might be grafted in." [20]That is true. They were broken off because of their unbelief, but you stand only through faith. So do not become proud, but stand in awe. [21]For if God did not spare the natural branches, perhaps he will not spare you.[c] [22]Note then the kindness and the severity of God: severity toward those who have fallen, but God's kindness toward you, provided you continue in his kindness; otherwise you also will be cut off. [23]And even those of Israel,[d] if they do not persist in unbelief, will be grafted in, for God has the power to graft them in again. [24]For if you have been cut from what is by nature a wild olive tree and grafted, contrary to nature, into a cultivated olive tree, how much more will these natural branches be grafted back into their own olive tree.

All Israel Will Be Saved

25 So that you may not claim to be wiser than you are, brothers and sisters,[e] I want you to understand this mystery: a hardening has come upon part of Israel, until the full number of the Gentiles has come in. [26]And so all Israel will be saved; as it is written,

"Out of Zion will come the Deliverer;
    he will banish ungodliness from Jacob."
[27] "And this is my covenant with them,
    when I take away their sins."

[28]As regards the gospel they are enemies of God[f] for your sake; but as regards election they are beloved, for the sake of their ancestors; [29]for the gifts and the calling of God are irrevocable. [30]Just as you were once disobedient to God but have now received mercy because of their disobedience, [31]so they have now been disobedient in order that, by the mercy shown to you, they too may now[g] receive mercy. [32]For God has imprisoned all in disobedience so that he may be merciful to all.

33 O the depth of the riches and wisdom and knowledge of God! How unsearchable are his judgments and how inscrutable his ways!
[34] "For who has known the mind of the Lord?
    Or who has been his counselor?"

Connected

ROMANS 11.16

As branches grafted into a tree become part of the tree and dependent on the tree, taking on the character and nature of the tree, so we as believers are grafted into Jesus Christ.

With your eyes closed, picture a tree. Begin to imagine yourself as a part of the tree. You are connected to the sturdy central trunk and to all the other branches through that trunk. How did you become a part of this tree? What do you share? What is yours alone? Do you give anything to the tree? Stay with this picture, being open to whatever images and emotions come to you. Conclude by drawing or writing your experience, and use that as your prayer to God.

See Meeting God in Scripture

---

a Gk *my flesh*   b Other ancient authorities read *the richness*   c Other ancient authorities read *neither will he spare you*   d Gk lacks *of Israel*
e Gk *brothers*   f Gk lacks *of God*   g Other ancient authorities lack *now*

Creator, Creation and Call

ROMANS 12.3–6

Plants give off oxygen in photosynthesis and thus provide oxygen for respiration for human beings and animals. Human beings and animals give off carbon dioxide for plants to use. This interdependence that God has built into all creation is the pattern for our life in Jesus Christ. We all worship the same God and face many of the same problems, yet each of us experiences life—and God—in unique ways. Our unique perspective may provide just the right pathway for others to gain insight to apply to their lives. Each of us belongs to others and each of us is to offer our unique gifts and talents to help the body grow.

What are your spiritual gifts? How do you use them as part of the body of Christ? Ask God to help you review your gifts and service. Are you mutually dependent on others in the body, or are you a "lone ranger"? In what ways can you offer yourself as a "living sacrifice" (v.1)?

See Meeting God in Community

^{35} "Or who has given a gift to him,
      to receive a gift in return?"
^{36}For from him and through him and to him are all things. To him be the glory forever. Amen.

The New Life in Christ

12 I appeal to you therefore, brothers and sisters,^{a} by the mercies of God, to present your bodies as a living sacrifice, holy and acceptable to God, which is your spiritual^b worship. ^{2}Do not be conformed to this world,^{c} but be transformed by the renewing of your minds, so that you may discern what is the will of God—what is good and acceptable and perfect.^{d}

3 For by the grace given to me I say to everyone among you not to think of yourself more highly than you ought to think, but to think with sober judgment, each according to the measure of faith that God has assigned. ^{4}For as in one body we have many members, and not all the members have the same function, ^{5}so we, who are many, are one body in Christ, and individually we are members one of another. ^{6}We have gifts that differ according to the grace given to us: prophecy, in proportion to faith; ^{7}ministry, in ministering; the teacher, in teaching; ^{8}the exhorter, in exhortation; the giver, in generosity; the leader, in diligence; the compassionate, in cheerfulness.

Marks of the True Christian

9 Let love be genuine; hate what is evil, hold fast to what is good; ^{10}love one another with mutual affection; outdo one another in showing honor. ^{11}Do not lag in zeal, be ardent in spirit, serve the Lord.^{e} ^{12}Rejoice in hope, be patient in suffering, persevere in prayer. ^{13}Contribute to the needs of the saints; extend hospitality to strangers.

14 Bless those who persecute you; bless and do not curse them. ^{15}Rejoice with those who rejoice, weep with those who weep. ^{16}Live in harmony with one another; do not be haughty, but associate with the lowly;^{f} do not claim to be wiser than you are. ^{17}Do not repay anyone evil for evil, but take thought for what is noble in the sight of all. ^{18}If it is possible, so far as it depends on you, live peaceably with all. ^{19}Beloved, never avenge yourselves, but leave room for the wrath of God;^{g} for it is written, "Vengeance is mine, I will repay, says the Lord." ^{20}No, "if your enemies are hungry, feed them; if they are thirsty, give them something to drink; for by doing this you will heap burning coals on their heads." ^{21}Do not be overcome by evil, but overcome evil with good.

Being Subject to Authorities

13 Let every person be subject to the governing authorities; for there is no authority except from God, and those authorities that exist have been instituted by God. ^{2}Therefore whoever resists authority resists what God has appointed, and those who resist will incur judgment. ^{3}For rulers are not a terror to good conduct, but to bad. Do

a Gk *brothers*   *b* Or *reasonable*   *c* Gk *age*   *d* Or *what is the good and acceptable and perfect will of God*   *e* Other ancient authorities read *serve the opportune time*   *f* Or *give yourselves to humble tasks*   *g* Gk *the wrath*

you wish to have no fear of the authority? Then do what is good, and you will receive its approval; ⁴for it is God's servant for your good. But if you do what is wrong, you should be afraid, for the authority*ᵃ* does not bear the sword in vain! It is the servant of God to execute wrath on the wrongdoer. ⁵Therefore one must be subject, not only because of wrath but also because of conscience. ⁶For the same reason you also pay taxes, for the authorities are God's servants, busy with this very thing. ⁷Pay to all what is due them—taxes to whom taxes are due, revenue to whom revenue is due, respect to whom respect is due, honor to whom honor is due.

Love for One Another

8 Owe no one anything, except to love one another; for the one who loves another has fulfilled the law. ⁹The commandments, "You shall not commit adultery; You shall not murder; You shall not steal; You shall not covet"; and any other commandment, are summed up in this word, "Love your neighbor as yourself." ¹⁰Love does no wrong to a neighbor; therefore, love is the fulfilling of the law.

An Urgent Appeal

11 Besides this, you know what time it is, how it is now the moment for you to wake from sleep. For salvation is nearer to us now than when we became believers; ¹²the night is far gone, the day is near. Let us then lay aside the works of darkness and put on the armor of light; ¹³let us live honorably as in the day, not in reveling and drunkenness, not in debauchery and licentiousness, not in quarreling and jealousy. ¹⁴Instead, put on the Lord Jesus Christ, and make no provision for the flesh, to gratify its desires.

Do Not Judge Another

14 Welcome those who are weak in faith,*ᵇ* but not for the purpose of quarreling over opinions. ²Some believe in eating anything, while the weak eat only vegetables. ³Those who eat must not despise those who abstain, and those who abstain must not pass judgment on those who eat; for God has welcomed them. ⁴Who are you to pass judgment on servants of another? It is before their own lord that they stand or fall. And they will be upheld, for the Lord*ᶜ* is able to make them stand.

5 Some judge one day to be better than another, while others judge all days to be alike. Let all be fully convinced in their own minds. ⁶Those who observe the day, observe it in honor of the Lord. Also those who eat, eat in honor of the Lord, since they give thanks to God; while those who abstain, abstain in honor of the Lord and give thanks to God.

7 We do not live to ourselves, and we do not die to ourselves. ⁸If we live, we live to the Lord, and if we die, we die to the Lord; so then, whether we live or whether we die, we are the Lord's. ⁹For to this end Christ died and lived again, so that he might be Lord of both the dead and the living.

God Knows Our Needs

ROMANS 14.5–6

"Abbot Mark once said to Abbot Arsenius: It is good, is it not, to have nothing in your cell that just gives you pleasure? For example, once I knew a brother who had a little wildflower that came up in his cell, and he pulled it out by the roots. Well, said Abbot Arsenius, that is all right. But each man should act according to his own spiritual way. And if one were not able to get along without the flower, he should plant it again" (Thomas Merton, trans., *The Wisdom of the Desert*).

Take some time to think about the ways in which you worship best. Is it through prayer, solitude, serving others, working with your hands? Set aside a time to worship in that way. Or set aside time to worship in a setting that communicates joy and peace to you: in a garden, by a body of water, with another person, in silence, or using a piece of music or words of scripture. Rest in that peace. All good things are gifts from God.

See Meeting God in Worship

The Gift of Harmony

ROMANS 15.5–6

The early Christians stood out in their culture because of the love and care they showed one another. The love they showed to each other is the same love they experienced from knowing Jesus Christ. "We love because [God] first loved us" (1 John 4.19). The heart of the gospel and the hope of our lives are connected: God's loving steadfastness toward us gives us the resources to live with and to love each other.

Read these verses slowly aloud to yourself. As you read, what touches your heart? Stop reading and focus your attention on that point. What is the call, the hope, the concern or the need that these verses reveal to you, however faint it may be? Open your mind and heart to God's leading. Slowly read these verses again, taking the time to personalize them so that they become your own prayer of petition or prayer of response.

See Meeting God in Scripture

10 Why do you pass judgment on your brother or sister?[a] Or you, why do you despise your brother or sister?[a] For we will all stand before the judgment seat of God.[b] [11]For it is written,

"As I live, says the Lord, every knee shall bow
to me,
and every tongue shall give praise to[c] God."

[12]So then, each of us will be accountable to God.[d]

Do Not Make Another Stumble

13 Let us therefore no longer pass judgment on one another, but resolve instead never to put a stumbling block or hindrance in the way of another.[e] [14]I know and am persuaded in the Lord Jesus that nothing is unclean in itself; but it is unclean for anyone who thinks it unclean. [15]If your brother or sister[a] is being injured by what you eat, you are no longer walking in love. Do not let what you eat cause the ruin of one for whom Christ died. [16]So do not let your good be spoken of as evil. [17]For the kingdom of God is not food and drink but righteousness and peace and joy in the Holy Spirit. [18]The one who thus serves Christ is acceptable to God and has human approval. [19]Let us then pursue what makes for peace and for mutual upbuilding. [20]Do not, for the sake of food, destroy the work of God. Everything is indeed clean, but it is wrong for you to make others fall by what you eat; [21]it is good not to eat meat or drink wine or do anything that makes your brother or sister[a] stumble.[f] [22]The faith that you have, have as your own conviction before God. Blessed are those who have no reason to condemn themselves because of what they approve. [23]But those who have doubts are condemned if they eat, because they do not act from faith;[g] for whatever does not proceed from faith[g] is sin.[h]

Please Others, Not Yourselves

15 We who are strong ought to put up with the failings of the weak, and not to please ourselves. [2]Each of us must please our neighbor for the good purpose of building up the neighbor. [3]For Christ did not please himself; but, as it is written, "The insults of those who insult you have fallen on me." [4]For whatever was written in former days was written for our instruction, so that by steadfastness and by the encouragement of the scriptures we might have hope. [5]May the God of steadfastness and encouragement grant you to live in harmony with one another, in accordance with Christ Jesus, [6]so that together you may with one voice glorify the God and Father of our Lord Jesus Christ.

The Gospel for Jews and Gentiles Alike

7 Welcome one another, therefore, just as Christ has welcomed you, for the glory of God. [8]For I tell you that Christ has become a servant of the circumcised on behalf of the truth of God in order that he might confirm the

a Gk *brother*   b Other ancient authorities read *of Christ*   c Or *confess*
d Other ancient authorities lack *to God*   e Gk *of a brother*   f Other ancient authorities add *or be upset or be weakened*   g Or *conviction*
h Other authorities, some ancient, add here 16.25-27

promises given to the patriarchs, [9]and in order that the Gentiles might glorify God for his mercy. As it is written,

"Therefore I will confess[a] you among the Gentiles,
and sing praises to your name";

[10]and again he says,

"Rejoice, O Gentiles, with his people";

[11]and again,

"Praise the Lord, all you Gentiles,
and let all the peoples praise him";

[12]and again Isaiah says,

"The root of Jesse shall come,
the one who rises to rule the Gentiles;
in him the Gentiles shall hope."

[13]May the God of hope fill you with all joy and peace in believing, so that you may abound in hope by the power of the Holy Spirit.

Paul's Reason for Writing So Boldly

14 I myself feel confident about you, my brothers and sisters,[b] that you yourselves are full of goodness, filled with all knowledge, and able to instruct one another. [15]Nevertheless on some points I have written to you rather boldly by way of reminder, because of the grace given me by God [16]to be a minister of Christ Jesus to the Gentiles in the priestly service of the gospel of God, so that the offering of the Gentiles may be acceptable, sanctified by the Holy Spirit. [17]In Christ Jesus, then, I have reason to boast of my work for God. [18]For I will not venture to speak of anything except what Christ has accomplished[c] through me to win obedience from the Gentiles, by word and deed, [19]by the power of signs and wonders, by the power of the Spirit of God,[d] so that from Jerusalem and as far around as Illyricum I have fully proclaimed the good news[e] of Christ. [20]Thus I make it my ambition to proclaim the good news,[e] not where Christ has already been named, so that I do not build on someone else's foundation, [21]but as it is written,

"Those who have never been told of him shall see,
and those who have never heard of him shall
understand."

Paul's Plan to Visit Rome

22 This is the reason that I have so often been hindered from coming to you. [23]But now, with no further place for me in these regions, I desire, as I have for many years, to come to you [24]when I go to Spain. For I do hope to see you on my journey and to be sent on by you, once I have enjoyed your company for a little while. [25]At present, however, I am going to Jerusalem in a ministry to the saints; [26]for Macedonia and Achaia have been pleased to share their resources with the poor among the saints at Jerusalem. [27]They were pleased to do this, and indeed they owe it to them; for if the Gentiles have come to share in their spiritual blessings, they ought also to be of service to them in material things. [28]So, when I have completed this, and have delivered to them what has been collected,[f] I will set

---

The Community of Prayer

ROMANS 15.22–32

We need each other. The faithfulness of the Christian community supports us when we stumble, and we support others in turn. Whether they like it or not, believers are woven together into a large, interdependent family. When we pray for another or are prayed for, we live out the reality of this connection.

Take a piece of woven fabric. Pull a thread or two out of the fabric and notice what happens to the remaining piece. Look at the threads you pulled out and notice their sudden isolation, smallness and weakness when compared to the larger fabric. Imagine God weaving the fabric, and imagine yourself as a thread in that fabric. How does that experience form and inform your prayer?

See Meeting God in Community

---

a Or *thank*   *b* Gk *brothers*   *c* Gk *speak of those things that Christ has not accomplished*   *d* Other ancient authorities read *of the Spirit* or *of the Holy Spirit*   *e* Or *gospel*   *f* Gk *have sealed to them this fruit*

Individual Greetings; Community Life

ROMANS 16.1–16

Even as much as Paul was teacher and theologian and apostle to the people of Rome, he was a good friend and "family" as well.

Who are the people who make up your spiritual network? Draw a "family tree" and name some of the members who share your branch. Include those you pray and worship with, your "soul friends" or authors who have taught and mentored you. Write notes of greeting and appreciation to some of them.

See Meeting God in Community

out by way of you to Spain; [29]and I know that when I come to you, I will come in the fullness of the blessing[a] of Christ.

30 I appeal to you, brothers and sisters,[b] by our Lord Jesus Christ and by the love of the Spirit, to join me in earnest prayer to God on my behalf, [31]that I may be rescued from the unbelievers in Judea, and that my ministry[c] to Jerusalem may be acceptable to the saints, [32]so that by God's will I may come to you with joy and be refreshed in your company. [33]The God of peace be with all of you.[d] Amen.

Personal Greetings

16 I commend to you our sister Phoebe, a deacon[e] of the church at Cenchreae, [2]so that you may welcome her in the Lord as is fitting for the saints, and help her in whatever she may require from you, for she has been a benefactor of many and of myself as well.

3 Greet Prisca and Aquila, who work with me in Christ Jesus, [4]and who risked their necks for my life, to whom not only I give thanks, but also all the churches of the Gentiles. [5]Greet also the church in their house. Greet my beloved Epaenetus, who was the first convert[f] in Asia for Christ. [6]Greet Mary, who has worked very hard among you. [7]Greet Andronicus and Junia,[g] my relatives[h] who were in prison with me; they are prominent among the apostles, and they were in Christ before I was. [8]Greet Ampliatus, my beloved in the Lord. [9]Greet Urbanus, our co-worker in Christ, and my beloved Stachys. [10]Greet Apelles, who is approved in Christ. Greet those who belong to the family of Aristobulus. [11]Greet my relative[i] Herodion. Greet those in the Lord who belong to the family of Narcissus. [12]Greet those workers in the Lord, Tryphaena and Tryphosa. Greet the beloved Persis, who has worked hard in the Lord. [13]Greet Rufus, chosen in the Lord; and greet his mother—a mother to me also. [14]Greet Asyncritus, Phlegon, Hermes, Patrobas, Hermas, and the brothers and sisters[a] who are with them. [15]Greet Philologus, Julia, Nereus and his sister, and Olympas, and all the saints who are with them. [16]Greet one another with a holy kiss. All the churches of Christ greet you.

Final Instructions

17 I urge you, brothers and sisters,[b] to keep an eye on those who cause dissensions and offenses, in opposition to the teaching that you have learned; avoid them. [18]For such people do not serve our Lord Christ, but their own appetites,[j] and by smooth talk and flattery they deceive the hearts of the simple-minded. [19]For while your obedience is known to all, so that I rejoice over you, I want you to be wise in what is good and guileless in what is evil. [20]The God of peace will shortly crush Satan under your feet. The grace of our Lord Jesus Christ be with you.[k]

a Other ancient authorities add *of the gospel*   b Gk *brothers*   c Other ancient authorities read *my bringing of a gift*   d One ancient authority adds 16.25-27 here   e Or *minister*   f Gk *first fruits*   g Or *Junias*; other ancient authorities read *Julia*   h Or *compatriots*   i Or *compatriot*   j Gk *their own belly*   k Other ancient authorities lack this sentence

21 Timothy, my co-worker, greets you; so do Lucius and Jason and Sosipater, my relatives.*a*

22 I Tertius, the writer of this letter, greet you in the Lord.*b*

23 Gaius, who is host to me and to the whole church, greets you. Erastus, the city treasurer, and our brother Quartus, greet you.*c*

Final Doxology

25 Now to God*d* who is able to strengthen you according to my gospel and the proclamation of Jesus Christ, according to the revelation of the mystery that was kept secret for long ages ²⁶but is now disclosed, and through the prophetic writings is made known to all the Gentiles, according to the command of the eternal God, to bring about the obedience of faith— ²⁷to the only wise God, through Jesus Christ, to whom*e* be the glory forever! Amen.*f*

To God Be the Glory

ROMANS 16.25–27

God has made known to us the mystery of faith: We can know God in an intimate way through the incarnation of Jesus Christ. God is accessible and available. God is "for us," and that is reason to shout and to sing: "To the only wise God through Jesus Christ, to whom be the glory forever! Amen."

Let these last verses become a dialogue with God as you pray them. What particular word or phrase draws your attention? As you keep that word or phrase in your mind, let God lead you further: What do you need to disclose? How do you need to be strengthened? Comforted? What prompts you to cry, "Glory to God"? Return to these verses again, changing the wording so that it becomes your personal response to who God is and what God has done.

---

a Or *compatriots*   *b* Or *I Tertius, writing this letter in the Lord, greet you*
c Other ancient authorities add verse 24, *The grace of our Lord Jesus Christ be with all of you. Amen.*   *d* Gk *the one*   *e* Other ancient authorities lack *to whom.* The verse then reads, *to the only wise God be the glory through Jesus Christ forever. Amen.*   *f* Other ancient authorities lack 16.25-27 or include it after 14.23 or 15.33; others put verse 24 after verse 27

WAYS *of* MEETING GOD

Meeting God in Community

We were not created to live in isolation. No person "is an island, entire of itself," wrote the poet John Donne. While no one questions the need for periods of solitude and refreshment in our lives, faith tends to thrive most readily when shared and experienced with others. Without the connections community affords us, we experience what someone once called "spiritual loneliness." For we meet God not just as we sit alone in quiet corners but in and through the people with whom we live, work and interact as we go through our daily routine.

> We meet God not just as we sit alone in quiet corners but in and through the people with whom we live, work and interact as we go through our daily routine.

Relationships present us with both a remarkable privilege and an awesome responsibility. Proverbs 27.17 tells us that "iron sharpens iron, and one person sharpens [and shapes] . . . another." As other people's lives touch ours, they help to form our faith and make us who we are. As we touch others, we reflect God's love to them.

Relationships with other believers have extraordinary power in our lives because Jesus is present in them. Jesus knew how important people are in conveying God's grace and presence. "Where two or three are gathered in my name," he said, "I am there among them" (Matthew 18.20). Within our churches, small groups, families and friendships, we learn from one another. We find encouragement. We challenge one another to follow God more faithfully. Other Christians enable us to walk as we should when we might otherwise have strayed or wandered. God uses relationships to form us, and relationships form us so that God can use us.

Power for Growth and Change. The Bible offers many examples of the formational power of relationships. The story of Ruth and Naomi demonstrates how the presence of other believers can enable us to do what we can't do alone. Ruth is a foreigner, a "Moabitess" who has married Naomi's son. When Naomi's husband and her sons (including Ruth's husband) die, she grieves, saying, "The hand of the LORD has turned against me" (Ruth 1.13). Ruth, also widowed, chooses to stay with Naomi rather than return to her own kin. Ruth speaks the words that are well-known and much-loved: "Where you go, I will go; where you lodge I will lodge; your people shall be my people, and your God my God" (Ruth 1.16). Just think of the magnitude of the change those words brought about! Something in this relationship makes Ruth willing to leave her family and country to adopt Naomi's faith. The younger woman seeks guidance from Naomi and in turn cares for her. Through their loving relationship Naomi is released from the bitterness of her losses, and Ruth is drawn into relationship with the God of Israel. Eventually Ruth even becomes the ancestor of Jesus the Messiah (see Matthew 1.5).

Elijah and Elisha offer an example of the way God uses the power of relationships to build strong leaders. God, employing Elijah as Elisha's mentor, makes a dramatic difference in the life of the younger man who is eager to serve God faithfully. Elijah, a famous prophet, is near the end of his ministry when God tells him to seek out and anoint Elisha as his successor. Elijah throws his cloak over Elisha's shoulders as the younger man walks behind his plow and his oxen, publicly calling Elisha to a new way of life. What a dramatic act! Elisha leaves his farm work to become Elijah's attendant (see 1 Kings 19.16–21), following the prophet and seeking to learn from him. He refuses to leave his mentor and asks for "a double share" of the spirit that has made Elijah great (see 2 Kings 2.9). One man is clearly the teacher and the other the student, and, like Elijah, Elisha acknowledges that God is at the center of his life and ministry. Through his relationship with Elijah, he develops the courage, faith and skills to carry on the work of the prophet as God's spokesman.

In the New Testament Mary and Elizabeth offer us yet another example of how relationships help us mature in faith. Their relationship illustrates the value of sharing mutual insight and encouragement. According to the Gospel of Luke, young Mary is visited by the angel Gabriel, who tells her that she will bear a son who will be the Messiah. Mary, "much perplexed by his words" (Luke 1.29), hurries to visit her older cousin Elizabeth, who is also pregnant. Though Mary has told the angel that she wants to be obedient to God's will, she is surely also confused and frightened. But after Elizabeth speaks to her, Mary breaks into a song of praise to God; her faith has been strengthened. Mary spends three months with Elizabeth, who supports her and in turn is supported in the joyful yet sacrificial work to which God has called both of them. Mary discovered, as many have, that when we are hesitant to face what lies ahead, spending time with someone who knows us and shares our faith can help us see more clearly and understand more deeply the issues we need to deal with. It fortifies us to move forward in faith.

Soul Friends. Throughout the history of the church, writers and leaders have echoed this message. In the twelfth century, Aelred of Rievaulx said that Christian friendship can be "a step to raise us to the love and knowledge of God." He also spoke of the joy of having a friend with "whom you need have no fear to confess your failings; one to whom you can unblushingly make known what progress you have made in the spiritual life; one to whom you can entrust all the secrets of your heart and before whom you can place all your plans." Teresa of Avila wrote in the sixteenth century of how "it is a great advantage for us to be able to consult someone who knows us, so that we may learn to know ourselves." John Wesley went so far as to declare that there is no such thing as a solitary Christian.

What these Christians from various times and places learned is that God uses close and continuing relationships to form us into the image of Jesus. As we share both our high moments and our low, pray for one another, help each other and work together toward common goals, we reflect Jesus and acknowledge Jesus' presence with us.

Nurturing Your Own Soul Friends. To begin to meet God in community you may want to reach out to other believers with whom you can discuss your spiritual journey. Such conversation helps you to sort out what you know about yourself and about God. It may be especially valuable if you make this a deliberate action. Ask one or two mature individuals—with whom you can exchange thoughts and prayers with confidence and assurance of confidentiality—to meet with you. This practice has traditionally been called "spiritual guidance," "spiritual direction" or "spiritual friendship." This kind of conversation may also occur in the context of worship services, church school classes and small groups. One-on-one relationships and small groups allow for a depth of interaction not possible in larger, more formal settings. They allow us to pray aloud for one another with potentially life-changing results. As Alan Jones, an essayist on Christian friendship, stated, "We cannot help but tremble on the brink of surrender, but it is our companions who give us the courage to jump."

> At their best, relationships with other believers not only shield us in difficult times but also help us to confront our imperfections.

Spend Time Observing the Lives of Faithful Christians. The New Testament tells us repeatedly that we become like Jesus by spending time with those who are his friends. We look at those who have led us, consider the outcome of their faith and then choose to imitate them (see Hebrews 13.7). Some find it a good discipline to think periodically about someone whose faith they admire. Consider approaching one or more such people to ask them how God has been at work in their lives. (For Biblical examples of this process, see 1 Corinthians 4.6; Philippians 3.17; 1 Thessalonians 1.6; and 2 Thessalonians 3.9.)

Stay Active in a Church Community. As happens within our immediate family circle, when we rub shoulders with others we are continually confronted with reminders of our weaknesses and brokenness. We wound others and are wounded by them. Romans 12.18 acknowledges that living with others can be difficult, urging, "If it is possible, so far as it depends on you, live peaceably with all." While imperfections abound within what Paul calls "the body of Christ," God still uses the company of believers to grace our lives and transform the world (see Romans 12.4–5; 1 Corinthians 12.12; and Ephesians 5.30). We cannot do without our fellow believers. The writer of the letter to the Hebrews urges Christians not to neglect to meet together (Hebrews 10.25). At their best, relationships with other believers not only shield us in difficult times but also help us to confront our imperfections. We find a place to mutually speak "the truth in love" (Ephesians 4.15).

View Your Involvement With Other Believers as an Opportunity to Help. It is a privilege to nurture another person, to be trusted to hear another's dreams and concerns, to pray for someone. In so doing we may discover myriad ways to use the gifts that God has given us to benefit our family in Christ as well as for our own growth and enjoyment. As we help others, we too will be helped. As we comfort and teach and encourage, we will be comforted, taught and encouraged in turn. As we experience community, we find our own lives enriched, in turn providing us with more to give to others.

See Page 1578 for the next Ways of Meeting God *article.*

THE FIRST LETTER OF PAUL TO THE
CORINTHIANS

The Way of Love

KEY VERSES:

Love is patient; love is kind; love is not envious or boastful or arrogant or rude. It does not insist on its own way; it is not irritable or resentful; it does not rejoice in wrongdoing, but rejoices in the truth. It bears all things, believes all things, hopes all things, endures all things.—1 Corinthians 13.4–7

"Love in its nature makes a human being like God, as far as is possible for a human being. The soul is intoxicated by the effects of it. Its characteristics are a fountain of faith, an abyss of patience, an ocean of humility."

—JOHN CLIMACUS,
in *Drinking from the Fountain: A Patristic Breviary*

In the apostle Paul's first letter to the Corinthians we encounter a missionary whose spirit is being transformed by the Holy Spirit. Paul urges the people of the Corinthian church to be likewise transformed by the Spirit of God. Paul admits that he is not a clever, eloquent orator but a childlike man who is "foolish" enough to preach the cross (1.17—2.16). His servant posture cuts through the barriers of human factions to pull together a community of believers who will proclaim in one voice that Jesus is Lord.

As you read Paul's letter and meditate on it, imagine yourself in the presence of the apostle, a seasoned spiritual teacher who crowns his letter with the often–quoted essay on love. Envision yourself telling Paul how hard it is for you to uphold this standard of love when you've had a spat with your spouse or felt misunderstood by your friend. Then turn your thoughts toward God in prayer. Ask God to help you cross the bridge between love in the abstract ("Of course I love people, but I can't stand my next-door neighbor!") and love in the concrete ("I know if I can learn to love my neighbor, then it won't be so hard to love other people"). How might such prayerful interaction with what Paul writes help you to become more loving—and part of a more loving community in Jesus Christ?

Salutation

1 Paul, called to be an apostle of Christ Jesus by the will of God, and our brother Sosthenes,

2 To the church of God that is in Corinth, to those who are sanctified in Christ Jesus, called to be saints, together with all those who in every place call on the name of our Lord Jesus Christ, both their Lord*a* and ours:

3 Grace to you and peace from God our Father and the Lord Jesus Christ.

4 I give thanks to my*b* God always for you because of the grace of God that has been given you in Christ Jesus, *5*for in every way you have been enriched in him, in speech and knowledge of every kind— *6*just as the testimony of*c* Christ has been strengthened among you— *7*so that you are not lacking in any spiritual gift as you wait for the revealing of our Lord Jesus Christ. *8*He will also strengthen you to the end, so that you may be blameless on the day of our Lord Jesus Christ. *9*God is faithful; by him you were called into the fellowship of his Son, Jesus Christ our Lord.

Divisions in the Church

10 Now I appeal to you, brothers and sisters,*d* by the name of our Lord Jesus Christ, that all of you be in agreement and that there be no divisions among you, but that you be united in the same mind and the same purpose. *11*For it has been reported to me by Chloe's people that there are quarrels among you, my brothers and sisters.*e* *12*What I mean is that each of you says, "I belong to Paul," or "I belong to Apollos," or "I belong to Cephas," or "I belong to Christ." *13*Has Christ been divided? Was Paul crucified for you? Or were you baptized in the name of Paul? *14*I thank God*f* that I baptized none of you except Crispus and Gaius, *15*so that no one can say that you were baptized in my name. *16*(I did baptize also the household of Stephanas; beyond that, I do not know whether I baptized anyone else.) *17*For Christ did not send me to baptize but to proclaim the gospel, and not with eloquent wisdom, so that the cross of Christ might not be emptied of its power.

Christ the Power and Wisdom of God

18 For the message about the cross is foolishness to those who are perishing, but to us who are being saved it is the power of God. *19*For it is written,

"I will destroy the wisdom of the wise,
 and the discernment of the discerning I will
  thwart."

*20*Where is the one who is wise? Where is the scribe? Where is the debater of this age? Has not God made foolish the wisdom of the world? *21*For since, in the wisdom of God, the world did not know God through wisdom, God decided, through the foolishness of our proclamation, to save those who believe. *22*For Jews demand signs and Greeks desire wisdom, *23*but we proclaim Christ crucified, a stumbling block to Jews and foolishness to Gentiles, *24*but to those who are the called, both Jews and Greeks, Christ the power of God and the wisdom of God. *25*For God's foolish-

The Cross Is Good News

1 CORINTHIANS 1.17–18

Think of the cross on which the Savior of the world hung. The grisly story it tells seems to suggest anything but God's glory, yet by the sacrifice of Jesus Christ on the cross we are saved. Jesus, hanging in agony upon it, was powerless, yet in him resides the power to redeem humankind from sin and death. There is nothing eloquent about the cross, yet it preaches the world's best sermon.

Let the weight of this paradox sink into your heart. In what ways do you feel emotionally or spiritually weak? In what ways are you drained and exhausted? Are you living with self-condemnation or guilt? Write down your responses. Then rethink them in the light of the good news Paul conveys to the Corinthians in this powerful opening passage. Appropriate the power of God to renew your spirit with life and forgiveness.

See Meeting God in Worship

a Gk *theirs*   *b* Other ancient authorities lack *my*   *c* Or *to*
d Gk *brothers*   *e* Gk *my brothers*   *f* Other ancient authorities read *I am thankful*

God's Secret Wisdom

1 CORINTHIANS 2.3–7

We live in a culture that values power and self-reliance. It seems that the Corinthians held the same assumptions about human righteousness that we do today: Moral standards are set by human wisdom, not by God's wisdom; privileges are acquired through noble birth, not by being born in a stable; truth is found in the testimony of clever minds, not in the fear and trembling uttered by humble prophets.

What, then, is the secret wisdom of which Paul speaks in this passage? What cherished illusions about the way to grow spiritually does it shatter? How does Paul's message prompt you to pray? For more perfect understanding? For a greater capacity for spiritual discernment? Or simply for putting on the mind of Christ Jesus?

See Meeting God in Prayer

ness is wiser than human wisdom, and God's weakness is stronger than human strength.

26 Consider your own call, brothers and sisters:[a] not many of you were wise by human standards,[b] not many were powerful, not many were of noble birth. [27]But God chose what is foolish in the world to shame the wise; God chose what is weak in the world to shame the strong; [28]God chose what is low and despised in the world, things that are not, to reduce to nothing things that are, [29]so that no one[c] might boast in the presence of God. [30]He is the source of your life in Christ Jesus, who became for us wisdom from God, and righteousness and sanctification and redemption, [31]in order that, as it is written, "Let the one who boasts, boast in[d] the Lord."

Proclaiming Christ Crucified

2 When I came to you, brothers and sisters,[a] I did not come proclaiming the mystery[e] of God to you in lofty words or wisdom. [2]For I decided to know nothing among you except Jesus Christ, and him crucified. [3]And I came to you in weakness and in fear and in much trembling. [4]My speech and my proclamation were not with plausible words of wisdom,[f] but with a demonstration of the Spirit and of power, [5]so that your faith might rest not on human wisdom but on the power of God.

The True Wisdom of God

6 Yet among the mature we do speak wisdom, though it is not a wisdom of this age or of the rulers of this age, who are doomed to perish. [7]But we speak God's wisdom, secret and hidden, which God decreed before the ages for our glory. [8]None of the rulers of this age understood this; for if they had, they would not have crucified the Lord of glory. [9]But, as it is written,

"What no eye has seen, nor ear heard,
nor the human heart conceived,
what God has prepared for those who love him"—

[10]these things God has revealed to us through the Spirit; for the Spirit searches everything, even the depths of God. [11]For what human being knows what is truly human except the human spirit that is within? So also no one comprehends what is truly God's except the Spirit of God. [12]Now we have received not the spirit of the world, but the Spirit that is from God, so that we may understand the gifts bestowed on us by God. [13]And we speak of these things in words not taught by human wisdom but taught by the Spirit, interpreting spiritual things to those who are spiritual.[g]

14 Those who are unspiritual[h] do not receive the gifts of God's Spirit, for they are foolishness to them, and they are unable to understand them because they are spiritually discerned. [15]Those who are spiritual discern all things, and they are themselves subject to no one else's scrutiny.

[16] "For who has known the mind of the Lord
so as to instruct him?"

But we have the mind of Christ.

---

a Gk *brothers*   *b* Gk *according to the flesh*   *c* Gk *no flesh*   *d* Or *of*
e Other ancient authorities read *testimony*   *f* Other ancient authorities
read *the persuasiveness of wisdom*   *g* Or *interpreting spiritual things in
spiritual language,* or *comparing spiritual things with spiritual*   *h* Or *natural*

On Divisions in the Corinthian Church

3 And so, brothers and sisters,[a] I could not speak to you as spiritual people, but rather as people of the flesh, as infants in Christ. [2]I fed you with milk, not solid food, for you were not ready for solid food. Even now you are still not ready, [3]for you are still of the flesh. For as long as there is jealousy and quarreling among you, are you not of the flesh, and behaving according to human inclinations? [4]For when one says, "I belong to Paul," and another, "I belong to Apollos," are you not merely human?

5 What then is Apollos? What is Paul? Servants through whom you came to believe, as the Lord assigned to each. [6]I planted, Apollos watered, but God gave the growth. [7]So neither the one who plants nor the one who waters is anything, but only God who gives the growth. [8]The one who plants and the one who waters have a common purpose, and each will receive wages according to the labor of each. [9]For we are God's servants, working together; you are God's field, God's building.

10 According to the grace of God given to me, like a skilled master builder I laid a foundation, and someone else is building on it. Each builder must choose with care how to build on it. [11]For no one can lay any foundation other than the one that has been laid; that foundation is Jesus Christ. [12]Now if anyone builds on the foundation with gold, silver, precious stones, wood, hay, straw— [13]the work of each builder will become visible, for the Day will disclose it, because it will be revealed with fire, and the fire will test what sort of work each has done. [14]If what has been built on the foundation survives, the builder will receive a reward. [15]If the work is burned up, the builder will suffer loss; the builder will be saved, but only as through fire.

16 Do you not know that you are God's temple and that God's Spirit dwells in you?[b] [17]If anyone destroys God's temple, God will destroy that person. For God's temple is holy, and you are that temple.

18 Do not deceive yourselves. If you think that you are wise in this age, you should become fools so that you may become wise. [19]For the wisdom of this world is foolishness with God. For it is written,

"He catches the wise in their craftiness,"

[20]and again,

"The Lord knows the thoughts of the wise,
   that they are futile."

[21]So let no one boast about human leaders. For all things are yours, [22]whether Paul or Apollos or Cephas or the world or life or death or the present or the future—all belong to you, [23]and you belong to Christ, and Christ belongs to God.

The Ministry of the Apostles

4 Think of us in this way, as servants of Christ and stewards of God's mysteries. [2]Moreover, it is required of stewards that they be found trustworthy. [3]But with me it is a very small thing that I should be judged by you or by any human court. I do not even judge myself. [4]I am not aware of anything against myself, but I am not thereby acquitted. It is the Lord who judges me. [5]Therefore do not pronounce judgment before the time, before the Lord comes, who will

---

Building the House of God

1 CORINTHIANS 3.9–17

Have you ever had the experience of building your own home? If you have, you know about the importance of starting with a straight, solid foundation. Paul says any foundation other than Jesus Christ will never support the church. Anything built on any other foundation will one day topple over. What is the foundation of your spiritual life? What is the foundation of your worshiping community? Are there some things that must change in order for Jesus Christ to become the only foundation? Picture yourself building on this foundation, laying the first stone. Of what does it consist— "gold, silver, precious stones, wood, hay, straw" (3.12)? Is your house built in such a way that it is impervious to most natural disasters, or is it likely to fall down in a windstorm or collapse in a flood? How could you build it better?

See Meeting God in Scripture

---

a Gk *brothers*   *b* In verses 16 and 17 the Greek word for *you* is plural

Foolish for Christ

1 CORINTHIANS 4.9–13

Who would ever want to look like a fool? Yet that is what Paul asks followers of Christ to be. Who would ever want to come across as a spectacle? Yet Paul would show us off, in all our weakness, "to the world, to angels and to mortals."

In what ways are you a fool for Christ? What behaviors and attitudes do others see as foolish in you: blessing those who curse you, enduring persecution and misunderstanding without comment, answering slander with kindness, letting others take precedence? Write such events in your spiritual journal or on a note card and review them with this passage in mind.

See Meeting God in Everyday Life

bring to light the things now hidden in darkness and will disclose the purposes of the heart. Then each one will receive commendation from God.

6 I have applied all this to Apollos and myself for your benefit, brothers and sisters,*a* so that you may learn through us the meaning of the saying, "Nothing beyond what is written," so that none of you will be puffed up in favor of one against another. 7For who sees anything different in you?*b* What do you have that you did not receive? And if you received it, why do you boast as if it were not a gift?

8 Already you have all you want! Already you have become rich! Quite apart from us you have become kings! Indeed, I wish that you had become kings, so that we might be kings with you! 9For I think that God has exhibited us apostles as last of all, as though sentenced to death, because we have become a spectacle to the world, to angels and to mortals. 10We are fools for the sake of Christ, but you are wise in Christ. We are weak, but you are strong. You are held in honor, but we in disrepute. 11To the present hour we are hungry and thirsty, we are poorly clothed and beaten and homeless, 12and we grow weary from the work of our own hands. When reviled, we bless; when persecuted, we endure; 13when slandered, we speak kindly. We have become like the rubbish of the world, the dregs of all things, to this very day.

Fatherly Admonition

14 I am not writing this to make you ashamed, but to admonish you as my beloved children. 15For though you might have ten thousand guardians in Christ, you do not have many fathers. Indeed, in Christ Jesus I became your father through the gospel. 16I appeal to you, then, be imitators of me. 17For this reason I sent*c* you Timothy, who is my beloved and faithful child in the Lord, to remind you of my ways in Christ Jesus, as I teach them everywhere in every church. 18But some of you, thinking that I am not coming to you, have become arrogant. 19But I will come to you soon, if the Lord wills, and I will find out not the talk of these arrogant people but their power. 20For the kingdom of God depends not on talk but on power. 21What would you prefer? Am I to come to you with a stick, or with love in a spirit of gentleness?

Sexual Immorality Defiles the Church

5 It is actually reported that there is sexual immorality among you, and of a kind that is not found even among pagans; for a man is living with his father's wife. 2And you are arrogant! Should you not rather have mourned, so that he who has done this would have been removed from among you?

3 For though absent in body, I am present in spirit; and as if present I have already pronounced judgment 4in the name of the Lord Jesus on the man who has done such a thing.*d* When you are assembled, and my spirit is present with the power of our Lord Jesus, 5you are to hand this man

a Gk *brothers*   *b* Or *Who makes you different from another?*   *c* Or *am sending*   *d* Or *on the man who has done such a thing in the name of the Lord Jesus*

over to Satan for the destruction of the flesh, so that his spirit may be saved in the day of the Lord.[a]

6 Your boasting is not a good thing. Do you not know that a little yeast leavens the whole batch of dough? [7]Clean out the old yeast so that you may be a new batch, as you really are unleavened. For our paschal lamb, Christ, has been sacrificed. [8]Therefore, let us celebrate the festival, not with the old yeast, the yeast of malice and evil, but with the unleavened bread of sincerity and truth.

Sexual Immorality Must Be Judged

9 I wrote to you in my letter not to associate with sexually immoral persons— [10]not at all meaning the immoral of this world, or the greedy and robbers, or idolaters, since you would then need to go out of the world. [11]But now I am writing to you not to associate with anyone who bears the name of brother or sister[b] who is sexually immoral or greedy, or is an idolater, reviler, drunkard, or robber. Do not even eat with such a one. [12]For what have I to do with judging those outside? Is it not those who are inside that you are to judge? [13]God will judge those outside. "Drive out the wicked person from among you."

Lawsuits among Believers

6 When any of you has a grievance against another, do you dare to take it to court before the unrighteous, instead of taking it before the saints? [2]Do you not know that the saints will judge the world? And if the world is to be judged by you, are you incompetent to try trivial cases? [3]Do you not know that we are to judge angels—to say nothing of ordinary matters? [4]If you have ordinary cases, then, do you appoint as judges those who have no standing in the church? [5]I say this to your shame. Can it be that there is no one among you wise enough to decide between one believer[b] and another, [6]but a believer[b] goes to court against a believer[b]—and before unbelievers at that?

7 In fact, to have lawsuits at all with one another is already a defeat for you. Why not rather be wronged? Why not rather be defrauded? [8]But you yourselves wrong and defraud—and believers[c] at that?

9 Do you not know that wrongdoers will not inherit the kingdom of God? Do not be deceived! Fornicators, idolaters, adulterers, male prostitutes, sodomites, [10]thieves, the greedy, drunkards, revilers, robbers—none of these will inherit the kingdom of God. [11]And this is what some of you used to be. But you were washed, you were sanctified, you were justified in the name of the Lord Jesus Christ and in the Spirit of our God.

Glorify God in Body and Spirit

12 "All things are lawful for me," but not all things are beneficial. "All things are lawful for me," but I will not be dominated by anything. [13]"Food is meant for the stomach and the stomach for food,"[d] and God will destroy both one and the other. The body is meant not for fornication but for the Lord, and the Lord for the body. [14]And God raised the Lord and will also raise us by his power. [15]Do you not know that your bodies are members of Christ? Should I therefore

---

Honoring God With Your Body

1 CORINTHIANS 6.12–20

The bread of sincerity and truth that Paul advises us to eat nourishes the spirit much like a loaf of bread satisifies hunger. What happens, then, when sexual immorality replaces integrity? When overindulgence replaces self-control? The body is not separate from the soul; what nourishes one nourishes the other. What destroys or degrades one destroys or degrades the other.

If you were asked to speak to young people in your church about sexual morality and the sanctity of marriage, how might you paraphrase or expand the argument Paul gives here? How much of your own lecture do you need to hear?

See Meeting God in Everyday Life

---

a Other ancient authorities add *Jesus*   b Gk *brother*   c Gk *brothers*
d The quotation may extend to the word *other*

The Balm of Fidelity

1 CORINTHIANS 7.1–7,17–24

"Without a little wisp of fidelity simmering within, life can become distasteful enough to make a marriage come crashing down, to send men and women through foolish pursuits of power, gambling, promiscuity, and exotic interludes, to a feverish chase after fantasized heights through dangerous drugs. Nothing of this can heal the tediousness of a life lived outside simple loyalty to a daily task. No human banality can substitute for the balm of fidelity."

—ADRIAN VAN KAAM,
The Music of Eternity

take the members of Christ and make them members of a prostitute? Never! ¹⁶Do you not know that whoever is united to a prostitute becomes one body with her? For it is said, "The two shall be one flesh." ¹⁷But anyone united to the Lord becomes one spirit with him. ¹⁸Shun fornication! Every sin that a person commits is outside the body; but the fornicator sins against the body itself. ¹⁹Or do you not know that your body is a temple*a* of the Holy Spirit within you, which you have from God, and that you are not your own? ²⁰For you were bought with a price; therefore glorify God in your body.

Directions concerning Marriage

7 Now concerning the matters about which you wrote: "It is well for a man not to touch a woman." ²But because of cases of sexual immorality, each man should have his own wife and each woman her own husband. ³The husband should give to his wife her conjugal rights, and likewise the wife to her husband. ⁴For the wife does not have authority over her own body, but the husband does; likewise the husband does not have authority over his own body, but the wife does. ⁵Do not deprive one another except perhaps by agreement for a set time, to devote yourselves to prayer, and then come together again, so that Satan may not tempt you because of your lack of self-control. ⁶This I say by way of concession, not of command. ⁷I wish that all were as I myself am. But each has a particular gift from God, one having one kind and another a different kind.

8 To the unmarried and the widows I say that it is well for them to remain unmarried as I am. ⁹But if they are not practicing self-control, they should marry. For it is better to marry than to be aflame with passion.

10 To the married I give this command—not I but the Lord—that the wife should not separate from her husband ¹¹(but if she does separate, let her remain unmarried or else be reconciled to her husband), and that the husband should not divorce his wife.

12 To the rest I say—I and not the Lord—that if any believer*b* has a wife who is an unbeliever, and she consents to live with him, he should not divorce her. ¹³And if any woman has a husband who is an unbeliever, and he consents to live with her, she should not divorce him. ¹⁴For the unbelieving husband is made holy through his wife, and the unbelieving wife is made holy through her husband. Otherwise, your children would be unclean, but as it is, they are holy. ¹⁵But if the unbelieving partner separates, let it be so; in such a case the brother or sister is not bound. It is to peace that God has called you.*c* ¹⁶Wife, for all you know, you might save your husband. Husband, for all you know, you might save your wife.

The Life That the Lord Has Assigned

17 However that may be, let each of you lead the life that the Lord has assigned, to which God called you. This is my rule in all the churches. ¹⁸Was anyone at the time of his call already circumcised? Let him not seek to remove the marks of circumcision. Was anyone at the time of his call uncircumcised? Let him not seek circumcision. ¹⁹Circumci-

a Or *sanctuary*   *b* Gk *brother*   *c* Other ancient authorities read *us*

sion is nothing, and uncircumcision is nothing; but obeying the commandments of God is everything. [20]Let each of you remain in the condition in which you were called.

21 Were you a slave when called? Do not be concerned about it. Even if you can gain your freedom, make use of your present condition now more than ever.[a] [22]For whoever was called in the Lord as a slave is a freed person belonging to the Lord, just as whoever was free when called is a slave of Christ. [23]You were bought with a price; do not become slaves of human masters. [24]In whatever condition you were called, brothers and sisters,[b] there remain with God.

The Unmarried and the Widows

25 Now concerning virgins, I have no command of the Lord, but I give my opinion as one who by the Lord's mercy is trustworthy. [26]I think that, in view of the impending[c] crisis, it is well for you to remain as you are. [27]Are you bound to a wife? Do not seek to be free. Are you free from a wife? Do not seek a wife. [28]But if you marry, you do not sin, and if a virgin marries, she does not sin. Yet those who marry will experience distress in this life,[d] and I would spare you that. [29]I mean, brothers and sisters,[b] the appointed time has grown short; from now on, let even those who have wives be as though they had none, [30]and those who mourn as though they were not mourning, and those who rejoice as though they were not rejoicing, and those who buy as though they had no possessions, [31]and those who deal with the world as though they had no dealings with it. For the present form of this world is passing away.

32 I want you to be free from anxieties. The unmarried man is anxious about the affairs of the Lord, how to please the Lord; [33]but the married man is anxious about the affairs of the world, how to please his wife, [34]and his interests are divided. And the unmarried woman and the virgin are anxious about the affairs of the Lord, so that they may be holy in body and spirit; but the married woman is anxious about the affairs of the world, how to please her husband. [35]I say this for your own benefit, not to put any restraint upon you, but to promote good order and unhindered devotion to the Lord.

36 If anyone thinks that he is not behaving properly toward his fiancée,[e] if his passions are strong, and so it has to be, let him marry as he wishes; it is no sin. Let them marry. [37]But if someone stands firm in his resolve, being under no necessity but having his own desire under control, and has determined in his own mind to keep her as his fiancée,[e] he will do well. [38]So then, he who marries his fiancée[e] does well; and he who refrains from marriage will do better.

39 A wife is bound as long as her husband lives. But if the husband dies,[f] she is free to marry anyone she wishes, only in the Lord. [40]But in my judgment she is more blessed if she remains as she is. And I think that I too have the Spirit of God.

Food Offered to Idols

8 Now concerning food sacrificed to idols: we know that "all of us possess knowledge." Knowledge puffs up, but

---

Undivided Devotion

1 CORINTHIANS 7.35

"The greatest difficulty in conversion, is to win the heart to God; and the greatest difficulty after conversion, is to keep the heart with God."

—JOHN FLAVEL,
Keeping the Heart

---

a Or *avail yourself of the opportunity*   b Gk *brothers*   c Or *present*
d Gk *in the flesh*   e Gk *virgin*   f Gk *falls asleep*

Undivided Devotion

1 CORINTHIANS 8.9–12

Many of the same issues that threatened to divide the Christian community in Corinth still plague us today. For example, the problem of an inflated ego (knowledge that puffs us up) is not easily overcome in a culture in which people make choices based on their own preferences and perceptions. The main challenge Paul proposes is that Christians are to be motivated first and foremost by love.

Search your conscience. How are your actions—no matter how justifiable or innocent they may seem in your eyes— likely to affect the faith of those who are not confident or strong in their faith? Is your exercise of Christian freedom likely to undermine someone's faith? Try to be specific. Ask God for forgiveness and guidance—and trust that you will reap the spiritual fruit of which Paul speaks.

See *Meeting God in Community*

love builds up. ²Anyone who claims to know something does not yet have the necessary knowledge; ³but anyone who loves God is known by him.

4 Hence, as to the eating of food offered to idols, we know that "no idol in the world really exists," and that "there is no God but one." ⁵Indeed, even though there may be so-called gods in heaven or on earth—as in fact there are many gods and many lords— ⁶yet for us there is one God, the Father, from whom are all things and for whom we exist, and one Lord, Jesus Christ, through whom are all things and through whom we exist.

7 It is not everyone, however, who has this knowledge. Since some have become so accustomed to idols until now, they still think of the food they eat as food offered to an idol; and their conscience, being weak, is defiled. ⁸"Food will not bring us close to God."ᵃ We are no worse off if we do not eat, and no better off if we do. ⁹But take care that this liberty of yours does not somehow become a stumbling block to the weak. ¹⁰For if others see you, who possess knowledge, eating in the temple of an idol, might they not, since their conscience is weak, be encouraged to the point of eating food sacrificed to idols? ¹¹So by your knowledge those weak believers for whom Christ died are destroyed.ᵇ ¹²But when you thus sin against members of your family,ᶜ and wound their conscience when it is weak, you sin against Christ. ¹³Therefore, if food is a cause of their falling,ᵈ I will never eat meat, so that I may not cause one of themᵉ to fall.

The Rights of an Apostle

9 Am I not free? Am I not an apostle? Have I not seen Jesus our Lord? Are you not my work in the Lord? ²If I am not an apostle to others, at least I am to you; for you are the seal of my apostleship in the Lord.

3 This is my defense to those who would examine me. ⁴Do we not have the right to our food and drink? ⁵Do we not have the right to be accompanied by a believing wife,ᶠ as do the other apostles and the brothers of the Lord and Cephas? ⁶Or is it only Barnabas and I who have no right to refrain from working for a living? ⁷Who at any time pays the expenses for doing military service? Who plants a vineyard and does not eat any of its fruit? Or who tends a flock and does not get any of its milk?

8 Do I say this on human authority? Does not the law also say the same? ⁹For it is written in the law of Moses, "You shall not muzzle an ox while it is treading out the grain." Is it for oxen that God is concerned? ¹⁰Or does he not speak entirely for our sake? It was indeed written for our sake, for whoever plows should plow in hope and whoever threshes should thresh in hope of a share in the crop. ¹¹If we have sown spiritual good among you, is it too much if we reap your material benefits? ¹²If others share this rightful claim on you, do not we still more?

Nevertheless, we have not made use of this right, but we endure anything rather than put an obstacle in the way of the gospel of Christ. ¹³Do you not know that those who are employed in the temple service get their food from the

---

a The quotation may extend to the end of the verse   *b* Gk *the weak brother . . . is destroyed*   *c* Gk *against the brothers*   *d* Gk *my brother's falling*   *e* Gk *cause my brother*   *f* Gk *a sister as wife*

temple, and those who serve at the altar share in what is sacrificed on the altar? ¹⁴In the same way, the Lord commanded that those who proclaim the gospel should get their living by the gospel.

15 But I have made no use of any of these rights, nor am I writing this so that they may be applied in my case. Indeed, I would rather die than that—no one will deprive me of my ground for boasting! ¹⁶If I proclaim the gospel, this gives me no ground for boasting, for an obligation is laid on me, and woe to me if I do not proclaim the gospel! ¹⁷For if I do this of my own will, I have a reward; but if not of my own will, I am entrusted with a commission. ¹⁸What then is my reward? Just this: that in my proclamation I may make the gospel free of charge, so as not to make full use of my rights in the gospel.

19 For though I am free with respect to all, I have made myself a slave to all, so that I might win more of them. ²⁰To the Jews I became as a Jew, in order to win Jews. To those under the law I became as one under the law (though I myself am not under the law) so that I might win those under the law. ²¹To those outside the law I became as one outside the law (though I am not free from God's law but am under Christ's law) so that I might win those outside the law. ²²To the weak I became weak, so that I might win the weak. I have become all things to all people, that I might by all means save some. ²³I do it all for the sake of the gospel, so that I may share in its blessings.

24 Do you not know that in a race the runners all compete, but only one receives the prize? Run in such a way that you may win it. ²⁵Athletes exercise self-control in all things; they do it to receive a perishable wreath, but we an imperishable one. ²⁶So I do not run aimlessly, nor do I box as though beating the air; ²⁷but I punish my body and enslave it, so that after proclaiming to others I myself should not be disqualified.

Warnings from Israel's History

10 I do not want you to be unaware, brothers and sisters,ᵃ that our ancestors were all under the cloud, and all passed through the sea, ²and all were baptized into Moses in the cloud and in the sea, ³and all ate the same spiritual food, ⁴and all drank the same spiritual drink. For they drank from the spiritual rock that followed them, and the rock was Christ. ⁵Nevertheless, God was not pleased with most of them, and they were struck down in the wilderness.

6 Now these things occurred as examples for us, so that we might not desire evil as they did. ⁷Do not become idolaters as some of them did; as it is written, "The people sat down to eat and drink, and they rose up to play." ⁸We must not indulge in sexual immorality as some of them did, and twenty-three thousand fell in a single day. ⁹We must not put Christᵇ to the test, as some of them did, and were destroyed by serpents. ¹⁰And do not complain as some of them did, and were destroyed by the destroyer. ¹¹These things happened to them to serve as an example, and they were written down to instruct us, on whom the ends of the ages have come. ¹²So if you think you are standing, watch out that you do not fall. ¹³No testing has overtaken you that

---

Building Up the Body of Christ

1 CORINTHIANS 10.23–24

" 'All things are lawful,' but not all things are beneficial. 'All things are lawful,' but not all things build up." Contrast Paul's sense of what it means to follow Jesus Christ in true liberation from the law with the "anything goes" freedom that allows the individual to do whatever feels right. How are Christians to balance freedom with concern for the good of others?

In what ways do gratification of desires, a need to acquire possessions, or a slavery to addictions replace Jesus Christ as your source of fulfillment? In what ways do you allow a judgmental attitude or a posture of superiority over weaker members to prevent you from accepting others in the body of Christ? How could you go about correcting these arrogant and judgmental traits in yourself as well as helping others to do so?

See Meeting God in Community

Overcoming Conflicts

1 CORINTHIANS 10.31–33

Disagreements, arguments, differences of opinion—such conflicts divide Christians from God and from one another. Handling the conflicts that threaten Christian unity is unthinkable without a spirit of charity. That spirit begins to grow when we put aside self-promotion and allow the love Jesus Christ plants in our hearts to permeate all of our attitudes and activities. Try to live the gospel today. As you eat your supper, drink a glass of water, drive your car, stop at the grocery store, speak to someone on the phone, dust the living room furniture, dress your child, write a letter or engage in any other ordinary activity, be conscious of doing it all thankfully, with a grateful disposition "for the glory of God."

See Meeting God in Everyday Life

is not common to everyone. God is faithful, and he will not let you be tested beyond your strength, but with the testing he will also provide the way out so that you may be able to endure it.

14 Therefore, my dear friends,*a* flee from the worship of idols. 15I speak as to sensible people; judge for yourselves what I say. 16The cup of blessing that we bless, is it not a sharing in the blood of Christ? The bread that we break, is it not a sharing in the body of Christ? 17Because there is one bread, we who are many are one body, for we all partake of the one bread. 18Consider the people of Israel;*b* are not those who eat the sacrifices partners in the altar? 19What do I imply then? That food sacrificed to idols is anything, or that an idol is anything? 20No, I imply that what pagans sacrifice, they sacrifice to demons and not to God. I do not want you to be partners with demons. 21You cannot drink the cup of the Lord and the cup of demons. You cannot partake of the table of the Lord and the table of demons. 22Or are we provoking the Lord to jealousy? Are we stronger than he?

Do All to the Glory of God

23 "All things are lawful," but not all things are beneficial. "All things are lawful," but not all things build up. 24Do not seek your own advantage, but that of the other. 25Eat whatever is sold in the meat market without raising any question on the ground of conscience, 26for "the earth and its fullness are the Lord's." 27If an unbeliever invites you to a meal and you are disposed to go, eat whatever is set before you without raising any question on the ground of conscience. 28But if someone says to you, "This has been offered in sacrifice," then do not eat it, out of consideration for the one who informed you, and for the sake of conscience— 29I mean the other's conscience, not your own. For why should my liberty be subject to the judgment of someone else's conscience? 30If I partake with thankfulness, why should I be denounced because of that for which I give thanks?

31 So, whether you eat or drink, or whatever you do, do everything for the glory of God. 32Give no offense to Jews or to Greeks or to the church of God, 33just as I try to please everyone in everything I do, not seeking my own advantage, but that of many, so that they may be saved.
11 1Be imitators of me, as I am of Christ.

Head Coverings

2 I commend you because you remember me in everything and maintain the traditions just as I handed them on to you. 3But I want you to understand that Christ is the head of every man, and the husband*c* is the head of his wife,*d* and God is the head of Christ. 4Any man who prays or prophesies with something on his head disgraces his head, 5but any woman who prays or prophesies with her head unveiled disgraces her head—it is one and the same thing as having her head shaved. 6For if a woman will not veil herself, then she should cut off her hair; but if it is disgraceful for a woman to have her hair cut off or to be

a Gk *my beloved*   *b* Gk *Israel according to the flesh*   *c* The same Greek word means *man* or *husband*   *d* Or *head of the woman* shaved, she should wear a veil. ⁷For a man ought not to have his head veiled, since he is the image and reflection[a] of God; but woman is the reflection[a] of man. ⁸Indeed, man was not made from woman, but woman from man. ⁹Neither was man created for the sake of woman, but woman for the sake of man. ¹⁰For this reason a woman ought to have a symbol of[b] authority on her head,[c] because of the angels. ¹¹Nevertheless, in the Lord woman is not independent of man or man independent of woman. ¹²For just as woman came from man, so man comes through woman; but all things come from God. ¹³Judge for yourselves: is it proper for a woman to pray to God with her head unveiled? ¹⁴Does not nature itself teach you that if a man wears long hair, it is degrading to him, ¹⁵but if a woman has long hair, it is her glory? For her hair is given to her for a covering. ¹⁶But if anyone is disposed to be contentious—we have no such custom, nor do the churches of God.

Abuses at the Lord's Supper

17 Now in the following instructions I do not commend you, because when you come together it is not for the better but for the worse. ¹⁸For, to begin with, when you come together as a church, I hear that there are divisions among you; and to some extent I believe it. ¹⁹Indeed, there have to be factions among you, for only so will it become clear who among you are genuine. ²⁰When you come together, it is not really to eat the Lord's supper. ²¹For when the time comes to eat, each of you goes ahead with your own supper, and one goes hungry and another becomes drunk. ²²What! Do you not have homes to eat and drink in? Or do you show contempt for the church of God and humiliate those who have nothing? What should I say to you? Should I commend you? In this matter I do not commend you!

The Institution of the Lord's Supper

23 For I received from the Lord what I also handed on to you, that the Lord Jesus on the night when he was betrayed took a loaf of bread, ²⁴and when he had given thanks, he broke it and said, "This is my body that is for[d] you. Do this in remembrance of me." ²⁵In the same way he took the cup also, after supper, saying, "This cup is the new covenant in my blood. Do this, as often as you drink it, in remembrance of me." ²⁶For as often as you eat this bread and drink the cup, you proclaim the Lord's death until he comes.

Partaking of the Supper Unworthily

27 Whoever, therefore, eats the bread or drinks the cup of the Lord in an unworthy manner will be answerable for the body and blood of the Lord. ²⁸Examine yourselves, and only then eat of the bread and drink of the cup. ²⁹For all who eat and drink[e] without discerning the body,[f] eat and drink judgment against themselves. ³⁰For this reason many of you are weak and ill, and some have died.[g] ³¹But if we judged ourselves, we would not be judged. ³²But when we

---

The Bread of Life, the Cup of Salvation

1 CORINTHIANS 11.23–25

Because this passage brings us to the heart of our faith, it is important not to rush past it, but to consciously enter the presence of Almighty God. The Corinthians are taking the Eucharistic feast too lightly. Go with the apostle Paul to visit, in your imagination, into the upper room where Jesus ate the Last Supper with his disciples. Imagine yourself and Paul in that awesome setting with Jesus and the others. Picture all of the details of the setting. Hear Jesus' words concerning the bread and wine. Join in receiving the elements when they are passed. How do you feel about being present? Try to recall that feeling the next time you partake at the Lord's Table. How is Paul's perspective on that Last Supper evident in this passage?

See Meeting God in Worship

---

a Or glory   b Gk lacks a symbol of   c Or have freedom of choice regarding her head   d Other ancient authorities read is broken for   e Other ancient authorities add in an unworthy manner,   f Other ancient authorities read the Lord's body   g Gk fallen asleep

Unity in Diversity

1 CORINTHIANS 12.4–6,13,26

Paul proposes that unity in diversity is central to life in the Christian community. He sees in the community different gifts but the same Spirit; different services and deeds but the same God working through them; an array of people called to be baptized—Jews and Greeks, slaves and free—who are part of the same body. How might the words of this passage influence the way you relate to people in the church? The way in which you pray? To bring the message of Paul closer to home, name someone you know who is suffering. Think of another person who has recently been honored or acknowledged in some way. Think of someone who exhibits each of the spiritual gifts listed in verses 28 through 30.

See Meeting God in Community

are judged by the Lord, we are disciplined[a] so that we may not be condemned along with the world.

33 So then, my brothers and sisters,[b] when you come together to eat, wait for one another. 34If you are hungry, eat at home, so that when you come together, it will not be for your condemnation. About the other things I will give instructions when I come.

Spiritual Gifts

12 Now concerning spiritual gifts,[c] brothers and sisters,[b] I do not want you to be uninformed. 2You know that when you were pagans, you were enticed and led astray to idols that could not speak. 3Therefore I want you to understand that no one speaking by the Spirit of God ever says "Let Jesus be cursed!" and no one can say "Jesus is Lord" except by the Holy Spirit.

4 Now there are varieties of gifts, but the same Spirit; 5and there are varieties of services, but the same Lord; 6and there are varieties of activities, but it is the same God who activates all of them in everyone. 7To each is given the manifestation of the Spirit for the common good. 8To one is given through the Spirit the utterance of wisdom, and to another the utterance of knowledge according to the same Spirit, 9to another faith by the same Spirit, to another gifts of healing by the one Spirit, 10to another the working of miracles, to another prophecy, to another the discernment of spirits, to another various kinds of tongues, to another the interpretation of tongues. 11All these are activated by one and the same Spirit, who allots to each one individually just as the Spirit chooses.

One Body with Many Members

12 For just as the body is one and has many members, and all the members of the body, though many, are one body, so it is with Christ. 13For in the one Spirit we were all baptized into one body—Jews or Greeks, slaves or free—and we were all made to drink of one Spirit.

14 Indeed, the body does not consist of one member but of many. 15If the foot would say, "Because I am not a hand, I do not belong to the body," that would not make it any less a part of the body. 16And if the ear would say, "Because I am not an eye, I do not belong to the body," that would not make it any less a part of the body. 17If the whole body were an eye, where would the hearing be? If the whole body were hearing, where would the sense of smell be? 18But as it is, God arranged the members in the body, each one of them, as he chose. 19If all were a single member, where would the body be? 20As it is, there are many members, yet one body. 21The eye cannot say to the hand, "I have no need of you," nor again the head to the feet, "I have no need of you." 22On the contrary, the members of the body that seem to be weaker are indispensable, 23and those members of the body that we think less honorable we clothe with greater honor, and our less respectable members are treated with greater respect; 24whereas our more respectable members do not need this. But God has so arranged the body, giving the greater honor to the inferior member, 25that there may be no dissension within the

a Or When we are judged, we are being disciplined by the Lord
b Gk brothers   c Or spiritual persons

body, but the members may have the same care for one another. ²⁶If one member suffers, all suffer together with it; if one member is honored, all rejoice together with it.

27 Now you are the body of Christ and individually members of it. ²⁸And God has appointed in the church first apostles, second prophets, third teachers; then deeds of power, then gifts of healing, forms of assistance, forms of leadership, various kinds of tongues. ²⁹Are all apostles? Are all prophets? Are all teachers? Do all work miracles? ³⁰Do all possess gifts of healing? Do all speak in tongues? Do all interpret? ³¹But strive for the greater gifts. And I will show you a still more excellent way.

The Gift of Love

13 If I speak in the tongues of mortals and of angels, but do not have love, I am a noisy gong or a clanging cymbal. ²And if I have prophetic powers, and understand all mysteries and all knowledge, and if I have all faith, so as to remove mountains, but do not have love, I am nothing. ³If I give away all my possessions, and if I hand over my body so that I may boast,ᵃ but do not have love, I gain nothing.

4 Love is patient; love is kind; love is not envious or boastful or arrogant ⁵or rude. It does not insist on its own way; it is not irritable or resentful; ⁶it does not rejoice in wrongdoing, but rejoices in the truth. ⁷It bears all things, believes all things, hopes all things, endures all things.

8 Love never ends. But as for prophecies, they will come to an end; as for tongues, they will cease; as for knowledge, it will come to an end. ⁹For we know only in part, and we prophesy only in part; ¹⁰but when the complete comes, the partial will come to an end. ¹¹When I was a child, I spoke like a child, I thought like a child, I reasoned like a child; when I became an adult, I put an end to childish ways. ¹²For now we see in a mirror, dimly,ᵇ but then we will see face to face. Now I know only in part; then I will know fully, even as I have been fully known. ¹³And now faith, hope, and love abide, these three; and the greatest of these is love.

Gifts of Prophecy and Tongues

14 Pursue love and strive for the spiritual gifts, and especially that you may prophesy. ²For those who speak in a tongue do not speak to other people but to God; for nobody understands them, since they are speaking mysteries in the Spirit. ³On the other hand, those who prophesy speak to other people for their upbuilding and encouragement and consolation. ⁴Those who speak in a tongue build up themselves, but those who prophesy build up the church. ⁵Now I would like all of you to speak in tongues, but even more to prophesy. One who prophesies is greater than one who speaks in tongues, unless someone interprets, so that the church may be built up.

6 Now, brothers and sisters,ᶜ if I come to you speaking in tongues, how will I benefit you unless I speak to you in some revelation or knowledge or prophecy or teaching? ⁷It is the same way with lifeless instruments that produce sound, such as the flute or the harp. If they do not give dis-

---

Follow the Way of Love

1 CORINTHIANS 14.1

"The Holy Spirit has enabled people to speak with tongues, and to prophesy. But the light that most necessarily attends it is a light to discern the fallacies of flesh and blood, to reject the irreligious maxims of the world, and to practice those degrees of trust in God and love to people, whose foundation is not so much in the present appearances of things, as in some that are yet to come. The object which this light brings us most immediately to know is ourselves. And by virtue of this, one that is born of God and has a lively hope, may indeed see far into the ways of Providence and farther yet into the Holy Scriptures."

—JOHN WESLEY,
from his sermon "On the Holy Spirit"

ᵃ Other ancient authorities read *body to be burned*   ᵇ Gk *in a riddle*
ᶜ Gk *brothers*

Growing Spiritually Mature

1 CORINTHIANS 14.20–40

The Corinthian Christians continue to try Paul's patience. Instead of focusing on God in grateful unity, they persist in competing for the most impressive manifestation of spiritual gifts. Paul declares that they should "do not be children in your thinking" and conduct their worship in an orderly and fitting manner.

What are some childish behaviors you would like to correct in yourself as you grow spiritually mature? What about whining when things go wrong? Or calling attention to your accomplishments? Perhaps you choose the safer and more familiar course rather than take risks for the sake of spiritual maturity. Write a letter to yourself similar to one Paul might write to you.

See Meeting God in Everyday Life

tinct notes, how will anyone know what is being played? [8]And if the bugle gives an indistinct sound, who will get ready for battle? [9]So with yourselves; if in a tongue you utter speech that is not intelligible, how will anyone know what is being said? For you will be speaking into the air. [10]There are doubtless many different kinds of sounds in the world, and nothing is without sound. [11]If then I do not know the meaning of a sound, I will be a foreigner to the speaker and the speaker a foreigner to me. [12]So with yourselves; since you are eager for spiritual gifts, strive to excel in them for building up the church.

13 Therefore, one who speaks in a tongue should pray for the power to interpret. [14]For if I pray in a tongue, my spirit prays but my mind is unproductive. [15]What should I do then? I will pray with the spirit, but I will pray with the mind also; I will sing praise with the spirit, but I will sing praise with the mind also. [16]Otherwise, if you say a blessing with the spirit, how can anyone in the position of an outsider say the "Amen" to your thanksgiving, since the outsider does not know what you are saying? [17]For you may give thanks well enough, but the other person is not built up. [18]I thank God that I speak in tongues more than all of you; [19]nevertheless, in church I would rather speak five words with my mind, in order to instruct others also, than ten thousand words in a tongue.

20 Brothers and sisters,[a] do not be children in your thinking; rather, be infants in evil, but in thinking be adults. [21]In the law it is written,

"By people of strange tongues
  and by the lips of foreigners
 I will speak to this people;
  yet even then they will not listen to me,"

says the Lord. [22]Tongues, then, are a sign not for believers but for unbelievers, while prophecy is not for unbelievers but for believers. [23]If, therefore, the whole church comes together and all speak in tongues, and outsiders or unbelievers enter, will they not say that you are out of your mind? [24]But if all prophesy, an unbeliever or outsider who enters is reproved by all and called to account by all. [25]After the secrets of the unbeliever's heart are disclosed, that person will bow down before God and worship him, declaring, "God is really among you."

Orderly Worship

26 What should be done then, my friends?[a] When you come together, each one has a hymn, a lesson, a revelation, a tongue, or an interpretation. Let all things be done for building up. [27]If anyone speaks in a tongue, let there be only two or at most three, and each in turn; and let one interpret. [28]But if there is no one to interpret, let them be silent in church and speak to themselves and to God. [29]Let two or three prophets speak, and let the others weigh what is said. [30]If a revelation is made to someone else sitting nearby, let the first person be silent. [31]For you can all prophesy one by one, so that all may learn and all be encouraged. [32]And the spirits of prophets are subject to the prophets, [33]for God is a God not of disorder but of peace.

(As in all the churches of the saints, [34]women should be silent in the churches. For they are not permitted to speak,

a Gk *brothers*

but should be subordinate, as the law also says. ³⁵If there is anything they desire to know, let them ask their husbands at home. For it is shameful for a woman to speak in church.*ᵃ* ³⁶Or did the word of God originate with you? Or are you the only ones it has reached?)

37 Anyone who claims to be a prophet, or to have spiritual powers, must acknowledge that what I am writing to you is a command of the Lord. ³⁸Anyone who does not recognize this is not to be recognized. ³⁹So, my friends,*ᵇ* be eager to prophesy, and do not forbid speaking in tongues; ⁴⁰but all things should be done decently and in order.

The Resurrection of Christ

15 Now I would remind you, brothers and sisters,*ᶜ* of the good news*ᵈ* that I proclaimed to you, which you in turn received, in which also you stand, ²through which also you are being saved, if you hold firmly to the message that I proclaimed to you—unless you have come to believe in vain.

3 For I handed on to you as of first importance what I in turn had received: that Christ died for our sins in accordance with the scriptures, ⁴and that he was buried, and that he was raised on the third day in accordance with the scriptures, ⁵and that he appeared to Cephas, then to the twelve. ⁶Then he appeared to more than five hundred brothers and sisters*ᶜ* at one time, most of whom are still alive, though some have died.*ᵉ* ⁷Then he appeared to James, then to all the apostles. ⁸Last of all, as to one untimely born, he appeared also to me. ⁹For I am the least of the apostles, unfit to be called an apostle, because I persecuted the church of God. ¹⁰But by the grace of God I am what I am, and his grace toward me has not been in vain. On the contrary, I worked harder than any of them—though it was not I, but the grace of God that is with me. ¹¹Whether then it was I or they, so we proclaim and so you have come to believe.

The Resurrection of the Dead

12 Now if Christ is proclaimed as raised from the dead, how can some of you say there is no resurrection of the dead? ¹³If there is no resurrection of the dead, then Christ has not been raised; ¹⁴and if Christ has not been raised, then our proclamation has been in vain and your faith has been in vain. ¹⁵We are even found to be misrepresenting God, because we testified of God that he raised Christ—whom he did not raise if it is true that the dead are not raised. ¹⁶For if the dead are not raised, then Christ has not been raised. ¹⁷If Christ has not been raised, your faith is futile and you are still in your sins. ¹⁸Then those also who have died*ᵉ* in Christ have perished. ¹⁹If for this life only we have hoped in Christ, we are of all people most to be pitied.

20 But in fact Christ has been raised from the dead, the first fruits of those who have died.*ᵉ* ²¹For since death came through a human being, the resurrection of the dead has also come through a human being; ²²for as all die in Adam, so all will be made alive in Christ. ²³But each in his own order: Christ the first fruits, then at his coming those who

Saved by the Gospel

1 CORINTHIANS 15.1–2

Consider your journey of faith. Do you remember the moment when you accepted Jesus Christ as your Savior and Lord? When you decided that for the rest of your life you would "hold firmly to the message"? Let this passage ignite your commitment to let the Bible be your companion every day. Think of ways to pass on the saving word of the gospel to your spouse, children, friends, coworkers and even to the people you encounter in your daily routine. Conclude by meditating on Paul's bottom line: "By the grace of God I am what I am" (v.10).

See Meeting God in Scripture

---

a Other ancient authorities put verses 34-35 after verse 40   *b* Gk *my brothers*   *c* Gk *brothers*   *d* Or *gospel*   *e* Gk *fallen asleep*

Death Swallowed in Victory

1 CORINTHIANS 15.20–26

In radiant faith Paul proclaims the victory of the resurrection of the dead in the power of Christ Jesus. Read this passage slowly. Find some garden seeds. Hold one in the palm of your hand. Notice how small it is, perhaps no bigger than the head of a pin, how dry and dead it looks. Yet you know that if you bury it, it will produce a plant. Allow this simple illustration from nature to reawaken your awe in the resurrection. Let what happened on Easter morning fill your mind and imagination with wonder. Open your heart to contemplative prayer. Let the Orthodox greeting, "My Joy! Christ is risen!" be ever on your lips.

See Meeting God in Everyday Life

belong to Christ. **24**Then comes the end,*ᵃ* when he hands over the kingdom to God the Father, after he has destroyed every ruler and every authority and power. **25**For he must reign until he has put all his enemies under his feet. **26**The last enemy to be destroyed is death. **27**For "God*ᵇ* has put all things in subjection under his feet." But when it says, "All things are put in subjection," it is plain that this does not include the one who put all things in subjection under him. **28**When all things are subjected to him, then the Son himself will also be subjected to the one who put all things in subjection under him, so that God may be all in all.

29 Otherwise, what will those people do who receive baptism on behalf of the dead? If the dead are not raised at all, why are people baptized on their behalf?

30 And why are we putting ourselves in danger every hour? **31**I die every day! That is as certain, brothers and sisters,*ᶜ* as my boasting of you—a boast that I make in Christ Jesus our Lord. **32**If with merely human hopes I fought with wild animals at Ephesus, what would I have gained by it? If the dead are not raised,

"Let us eat and drink,
  for tomorrow we die."

33Do not be deceived:

"Bad company ruins good morals."

34Come to a sober and right mind, and sin no more; for some people have no knowledge of God. I say this to your shame.

The Resurrection Body

35 But someone will ask, "How are the dead raised? With what kind of body do they come?" **36**Fool! What you sow does not come to life unless it dies. **37**And as for what you sow, you do not sow the body that is to be, but a bare seed, perhaps of wheat or of some other grain. **38**But God gives it a body as he has chosen, and to each kind of seed its own body. **39**Not all flesh is alike, but there is one flesh for human beings, another for animals, another for birds, and another for fish. **40**There are both heavenly bodies and earthly bodies, but the glory of the heavenly is one thing, and that of the earthly is another. **41**There is one glory of the sun, and another glory of the moon, and another glory of the stars; indeed, star differs from star in glory.

42 So it is with the resurrection of the dead. What is sown is perishable, what is raised is imperishable. **43**It is sown in dishonor, it is raised in glory. It is sown in weakness, it is raised in power. **44**It is sown a physical body, it is raised a spiritual body. If there is a physical body, there is also a spiritual body. **45**Thus it is written, "The first man, Adam, became a living being"; the last Adam became a life-giving spirit. **46**But it is not the spiritual that is first, but the physical, and then the spiritual. **47**The first man was from the earth, a man of dust; the second man is*ᵈ* from heaven. **48**As was the man of dust, so are those who are of the dust; and as is the man of heaven, so are those who are of heaven. **49**Just as we have borne the image of the man of dust, we will*ᵉ* also bear the image of the man of heaven.

50 What I am saying, brothers and sisters,*ᶜ* is this: flesh and blood cannot inherit the kingdom of God, nor does the

a Or *Then come the rest*   *b* Gk *he*   *c* Gk *brothers*   *d* Other ancient authorities add *the Lord*   *e* Other ancient authorities read *let us*

perishable inherit the imperishable. [51]Listen, I will tell you a mystery! We will not all die,[a] but we will all be changed, [52]in a moment, in the twinkling of an eye, at the last trumpet. For the trumpet will sound, and the dead will be raised imperishable, and we will be changed. [53]For this perishable body must put on imperishability, and this mortal body must put on immortality. [54]When this perishable body puts on imperishability, and this mortal body puts on immortality, then the saying that is written will be fulfilled:

"Death has been swallowed up in victory."

[55]   "Where, O death, is your victory?
      Where, O death, is your sting?"

[56]The sting of death is sin, and the power of sin is the law. [57]But thanks be to God, who gives us the victory through our Lord Jesus Christ.

58 Therefore, my beloved,[b] be steadfast, immovable, always excelling in the work of the Lord, because you know that in the Lord your labor is not in vain.

The Collection for the Saints

16 Now concerning the collection for the saints: you should follow the directions I gave to the churches of Galatia. [2]On the first day of every week, each of you is to put aside and save whatever extra you earn, so that collections need not be taken when I come. [3]And when I arrive, I will send any whom you approve with letters to take your gift to Jerusalem. [4]If it seems advisable that I should go also, they will accompany me.

Plans for Travel

5 I will visit you after passing through Macedonia—for I intend to pass through Macedonia— [6]and perhaps I will stay with you or even spend the winter, so that you may send me on my way, wherever I go. [7]I do not want to see you now just in passing, for I hope to spend some time with you, if the Lord permits. [8]But I will stay in Ephesus until Pentecost, [9]for a wide door for effective work has opened to me, and there are many adversaries.

10 If Timothy comes, see that he has nothing to fear among you, for he is doing the work of the Lord just as I am; [11]therefore let no one despise him. Send him on his way in peace, so that he may come to me; for I am expecting him with the brothers.

12 Now concerning our brother Apollos, I strongly urged him to visit you with the other brothers, but he was not at all willing[c] to come now. He will come when he has the opportunity.

Final Messages and Greetings

13 Keep alert, stand firm in your faith, be courageous, be strong. [14]Let all that you do be done in love.

15 Now, brothers and sisters,[d] you know that members of the household of Stephanas were the first converts in Achaia, and they have devoted themselves to the service of the saints; [16]I urge you to put yourselves at the service of such people, and of everyone who works and toils with them. [17]I rejoice at the coming of Stephanas and Fortunatus and Achaicus, because they have made up for your ab-

Death, Be Not Proud

1 CORINTHIANS 15.35–58

Death, be not proud,
   though some have
   called thee
Mighty and dreadful, for
   thou art not so;
For those whom thou
   think'st thou dost
   overthrow
Die not, poor Death, nor yet
   canst thou kill me.
From rest and sleep, which
   but thy pictures be,
Much pleasure; then from
   thee much more must
   flow
And soonest our best men
   with thee do go,
Rest of their bones, and
   soul's delivery.
Thou are slave to fate,
   chance, kings, and
   desperate men,
And dost with poison, war,
   and sickness dwell,
And poppy or charms can
   make us sleep as well
And better than thy stroke;
   why swell'st thou then?
One short sleep past, we
   wake eternally
And death shall be no more;
   Death, thou shalt die.

—JOHN DONNE,
"Holy Sonnets" 10

a Gk *fall asleep*   b Gk *beloved brothers*   c Or *it was not at all God's will for him*   d Gk *brothers*

Sowing the Seeds

1 CORINTHIANS 16.1–2

Giving, says Paul, should be a way of life, not a spur-of-the-moment gesture. Set aside money regularly, planning prayerfully how much to give to your church and how much to contribute to other causes. Give joyfully and without condescension as you are blessed. Consider how by your giving you carry on the mission begun in Jesus Christ and continued by the apostle Paul—a mission of peace, courage and above all—love. End your reading of 1 Corinthians with a prayer for a heart of love. Starting today let your actions speak as loudly as your words.

See Meeting God in Service

sence; [18]for they refreshed my spirit as well as yours. So give recognition to such persons.

19 The churches of Asia send greetings. Aquila and Prisca, together with the church in their house, greet you warmly in the Lord. [20]All the brothers and sisters[a] send greetings. Greet one another with a holy kiss.

21 I, Paul, write this greeting with my own hand. [22]Let anyone be accursed who has no love for the Lord. Our Lord, come![b] [23]The grace of the Lord Jesus be with you. [24]My love be with all of you in Christ Jesus.[c]

---

a Gk *brothers*   b Gk *Marana tha.* These Aramaic words can also be read *Maran atha,* meaning *Our Lord has come*   c Other ancient authorities add *Amen*

THE SECOND LETTER OF PAUL TO THE
CORINTHIANS

Our Hope for New Life

KEY VERSES:

So if anyone is in Christ, there is a new creation: everything old has passed away; see, everything has become new! All this is from God, who reconciled us to himself through Christ, and has given us the ministry of reconciliation; that is, in Christ God was reconciling the world to himself, not counting their trespasses against them.—2 Corinthians 5.17–19

One of the greatest obstacles facing us on the road to spiritual formation is our lack of appreciation for our infinite worth in the eyes of God. No matter what faults and failings may hamper us on our way home to our Father's house, God loves and forgives and welcomes us. One of the gifts the apostle Paul gives his readers in this ardent and honest letter is a renewed sense of worthiness to minister in the name of Jesus Christ. Paul applies correction but he also encourages his readers with an appraisal of their worth: They are "the aroma of Christ" (2.15); Christ's "ambassadors" (5.20); "the temple of God" (6.16). Paul's encouragement is not meant to produce pride in his readers but to remind them that "Christ Jesus is in [them]" (13.5). His Spirit forms, reforms and transforms us "into the same image from one degree of glory to another" (3.18).

The spirit of servanthood dies, as Paul sees it, when we try to become "super-apostles" (12.11), incapable of admitting that we are vulnerable, suffering, wounded creatures. We can unlock the door to Christian service only with the key of our weaknesses. Paul boasts of his "weaknesses, so that the power of Christ may dwell in [him]" (12.9).

As you read this letter, reflect on your ministry, whatever it may be. What do you think makes you competent to serve? What are your strengths in Christ Jesus? How are his strengths apparent through your weaknesses?

"The holy Church includes many people, men, women, and children without number. They are all quite different from one another in birth, in size, in nationality and language, in style of living and age, in trades and opinions, in clothes and customs, in knowledge and rank, in welfare and in appearance. They are nonetheless all of them in the self-same Church. Thanks to her, they are all reborn, newly created in the Spirit."

—MAXIMUS THE CONFESSOR,
in *Drinking from the Fountain: A Patristic Breviary*

Yes!

2 CORINTHIANS 1.3–11,18–22

Paul declares that "in [Jesus Christ] every one of God's promises is a 'Yes.' " As you read these two passages, make a list of the verb phrases that describe God's promised actions toward us. Let them lead you to awareness of God's love and saving grace. Begin with the phrase "consoles us in all our affliction." After each phrase, think of an example of how God has kept that promise to you. Then write "Yes!" after each one, and keep the list in your Bible or journal.

See Meeting God in Prayer

Salutation

1 Paul, an apostle of Christ Jesus by the will of God, and Timothy our brother,

To the church of God that is in Corinth, including all the saints throughout Achaia:

2 Grace to you and peace from God our Father and the Lord Jesus Christ.

Paul's Thanksgiving after Affliction

3 Blessed be the God and Father of our Lord Jesus Christ, the Father of mercies and the God of all consolation, ⁴who consoles us in all our affliction, so that we may be able to console those who are in any affliction with the consolation with which we ourselves are consoled by God. ⁵For just as the sufferings of Christ are abundant for us, so also our consolation is abundant through Christ. ⁶If we are being afflicted, it is for your consolation and salvation; if we are being consoled, it is for your consolation, which you experience when you patiently endure the same sufferings that we are also suffering. ⁷Our hope for you is unshaken; for we know that as you share in our sufferings, so also you share in our consolation.

8 We do not want you to be unaware, brothers and sisters,ᵃ of the affliction we experienced in Asia; for we were so utterly, unbearably crushed that we despaired of life itself. ⁹Indeed, we felt that we had received the sentence of death so that we would rely not on ourselves but on God who raises the dead. ¹⁰He who rescued us from so deadly a peril will continue to rescue us; on him we have set our hope that he will rescue us again, ¹¹as you also join in helping us by your prayers, so that many will give thanks on ourᵇ behalf for the blessing granted us through the prayers of many.

The Postponement of Paul's Visit

12 Indeed, this is our boast, the testimony of our conscience: we have behaved in the world with franknessᶜ and godly sincerity, not by earthly wisdom but by the grace of God—and all the more toward you. ¹³For we write you nothing other than what you can read and also understand; I hope you will understand until the end— ¹⁴as you have already understood us in part—that on the day of the Lord Jesus we are your boast even as you are our boast.

15 Since I was sure of this, I wanted to come to you first, so that you might have a double favor;ᵈ ¹⁶I wanted to visit you on my way to Macedonia, and to come back to you from Macedonia and have you send me on to Judea. ¹⁷Was I vacillating when I wanted to do this? Do I make my plans according to ordinary human standards,ᵉ ready to say "Yes, yes" and "No, no" at the same time? ¹⁸As surely as God is faithful, our word to you has not been "Yes and No." ¹⁹For the Son of God, Jesus Christ, whom we proclaimed among you, Silvanus and Timothy and I, was not "Yes and No"; but in him it is always "Yes." ²⁰For in him every one of God's promises is a "Yes." For this reason it is through him that we say the "Amen," to the glory of God. ²¹But it is God who establishes us with you in Christ and has anointed us, ²²by

---

a Gk *brothers*   b Other ancient authorities read *your*   c Other ancient authorities read *holiness*   d Other ancient authorities read *pleasure*   e Gk *according to the flesh*

putting his seal on us and giving us his Spirit in our hearts as a first installment.

23 But I call on God as witness against me: it was to spare you that I did not come again to Corinth. ²⁴I do not mean to imply that we lord it over your faith; rather, we are workers with you for your joy, because you stand firm in the faith. ¹So I made up my mind not to make you another painful visit. ²For if I cause you pain, who is there to make me glad but the one whom I have pained? ³And I wrote as I did, so that when I came, I might not suffer pain from those who should have made me rejoice; for I am confident about all of you, that my joy would be the joy of all of you. ⁴For I wrote you out of much distress and anguish of heart and with many tears, not to cause you pain, but to let you know the abundant love that I have for you.

Forgiveness for the Offender

5 But if anyone has caused pain, he has caused it not to me, but to some extent—not to exaggerate it—to all of you. ⁶This punishment by the majority is enough for such a person; ⁷so now instead you should forgive and console him, so that he may not be overwhelmed by excessive sorrow. ⁸So I urge you to reaffirm your love for him. ⁹I wrote for this reason: to test you and to know whether you are obedient in everything. ¹⁰Anyone whom you forgive, I also forgive. What I have forgiven, if I have forgiven anything, has been for your sake in the presence of Christ. ¹¹And we do this so that we may not be outwitted by Satan; for we are not ignorant of his designs.

Paul's Anxiety in Troas

12 When I came to Troas to proclaim the good news of Christ, a door was opened for me in the Lord; ¹³but my mind could not rest because I did not find my brother Titus there. So I said farewell to them and went on to Macedonia.

14 But thanks be to God, who in Christ always leads us in triumphal procession, and through us spreads in every place the fragrance that comes from knowing him. ¹⁵For we are the aroma of Christ to God among those who are being saved and among those who are perishing; ¹⁶to the one a fragrance from death to death, to the other a fragrance from life to life. Who is sufficient for these things? ¹⁷For we are not peddlers of God's word like so many;ᵃ but in Christ we speak as persons of sincerity, as persons sent from God and standing in his presence.

Ministers of the New Covenant

3 Are we beginning to commend ourselves again? Surely we do not need, as some do, letters of recommendation to you or from you, do we? ²You yourselves are our letter, written on ourᵇ hearts, to be known and read by all; ³and you show that you are a letter of Christ, prepared by us, written not with ink but with the Spirit of the living God, not on tablets of stone but on tablets of human hearts.

4 Such is the confidence that we have through Christ toward God. ⁵Not that we are competent of ourselves to claim anything as coming from us; our competence is from God,

The Fragrance of Christ

2 CORINTHIANS 2.14–3.6

Often what we remember about people is not so much what they said or did but who they were—their identity, their spirit. How do you want people to remember you? Pray that by your very presence you may spread the knowledge of Jesus Christ, the living God, as sweet fragrance fills a room. What kind of "letter of recommendation" for Christ does your life offer? What would you like to edit out or add? What do you want the Spirit of God to write on the hearts of people who serve you day by day as "ministers of a new covenant"?

See Meeting God in Everyday Life

ᵃ Other ancient authorities read *like the others*   ᵇ Other ancient authorities read *your*

A Treasure in Clay Jars

2 CORINTHIANS 4.5–7

Paul reflects on the mystery of God's transforming love. We are like humble, everyday clay pots and yet God has filled us with "the light of the knowledge of the glory of God in the face of Christ." God hides this treasure in ordinary vessels to show that the power is his, not ours. What do you see when you look at yourself—the simple clay pot or the divine glory it contains? What do others see in you—the glory of God in a clay pot, or a clay pot trying to look like a treasure chest? A clay pot with the lid tightly closed? A clay pot with a hole in the bottom? A pot with cracks through which God's glory shines? Pray for more awareness of God's presence in you and in everyone you meet.

See Meeting God in the Created Order

⁶who has made us competent to be ministers of a new covenant, not of letter but of spirit; for the letter kills, but the Spirit gives life.

7 Now if the ministry of death, chiseled in letters on stone tablets,ᵃ came in glory so that the people of Israel could not gaze at Moses' face because of the glory of his face, a glory now set aside, ⁸how much more will the ministry of the Spirit come in glory? ⁹For if there was glory in the ministry of condemnation, much more does the ministry of justification abound in glory! ¹⁰Indeed, what once had glory has lost its glory because of the greater glory; ¹¹for if what was set aside came through glory, much more has the permanent come in glory!

12 Since, then, we have such a hope, we act with great boldness, ¹³not like Moses, who put a veil over his face to keep the people of Israel from gazing at the end of the glory thatᵇ was being set aside. ¹⁴But their minds were hardened. Indeed, to this very day, when they hear the reading of the old covenant, that same veil is still there, since only in Christ is it set aside. ¹⁵Indeed, to this very day whenever Moses is read, a veil lies over their minds; ¹⁶but when one turns to the Lord, the veil is removed. ¹⁷Now the Lord is the Spirit, and where the Spirit of the Lord is, there is freedom. ¹⁸And all of us, with unveiled faces, seeing the glory of the Lord as though reflected in a mirror, are being transformed into the same image from one degree of glory to another; for this comes from the Lord, the Spirit.

Treasure in Clay Jars

4 Therefore, since it is by God's mercy that we are engaged in this ministry, we do not lose heart. ²We have renounced the shameful things that one hides; we refuse to practice cunning or to falsify God's word; but by the open statement of the truth we commend ourselves to the conscience of everyone in the sight of God. ³And even if our gospel is veiled, it is veiled to those who are perishing. ⁴In their case the god of this world has blinded the minds of the unbelievers, to keep them from seeing the light of the gospel of the glory of Christ, who is the image of God. ⁵For we do not proclaim ourselves; we proclaim Jesus Christ as Lord and ourselves as your slaves for Jesus' sake. ⁶For it is the God who said, "Let light shine out of darkness," who has shone in our hearts to give the light of the knowledge of the glory of God in the face of Jesus Christ.

7 But we have this treasure in clay jars, so that it may be made clear that this extraordinary power belongs to God and does not come from us. ⁸We are afflicted in every way, but not crushed; perplexed, but not driven to despair; ⁹persecuted, but not forsaken; struck down, but not destroyed; ¹⁰always carrying in the body the death of Jesus, so that the life of Jesus may also be made visible in our bodies. ¹¹For while we live, we are always being given up to death for Jesus' sake, so that the life of Jesus may be made visible in our mortal flesh. ¹²So death is at work in us, but life in you.

13 But just as we have the same spirit of faith that is in accordance with scripture—"I believed, and so I spoke"— we also believe, and so we speak, ¹⁴because we know that the one who raised the Lord Jesus will raise us also with Jesus, and will bring us with you into his presence. ¹⁵Yes,

a Gk on stones   b Gk of what

everything is for your sake, so that grace, as it extends to more and more people, may increase thanksgiving, to the glory of God.

Living by Faith

16 So we do not lose heart. Even though our outer nature is wasting away, our inner nature is being renewed day by day. ¹⁷For this slight momentary affliction is preparing us for an eternal weight of glory beyond all measure, ¹⁸because we look not at what can be seen but at what cannot be seen; for what can be seen is temporary, but what cannot be seen is eternal.

5 For we know that if the earthly tent we live in is destroyed, we have a building from God, a house not made with hands, eternal in the heavens. ²For in this tent we groan, longing to be clothed with our heavenly dwelling— ³if indeed, when we have taken it off*ᵃ* we will not be found naked. ⁴For while we are still in this tent, we groan under our burden, because we wish not to be unclothed but to be further clothed, so that what is mortal may be swallowed up by life. ⁵He who has prepared us for this very thing is God, who has given us the Spirit as a guarantee.

6 So we are always confident; even though we know that while we are at home in the body we are away from the Lord— ⁷for we walk by faith, not by sight. ⁸Yes, we do have confidence, and we would rather be away from the body and at home with the Lord. ⁹So whether we are at home or away, we make it our aim to please him. ¹⁰For all of us must appear before the judgment seat of Christ, so that each may receive recompense for what has been done in the body, whether good or evil.

The Ministry of Reconciliation

11 Therefore, knowing the fear of the Lord, we try to persuade others; but we ourselves are well known to God, and I hope that we are also well known to your consciences. ¹²We are not commending ourselves to you again, but giving you an opportunity to boast about us, so that you may be able to answer those who boast in outward appearance and not in the heart. ¹³For if we are beside ourselves, it is for God; if we are in our right mind, it is for you. ¹⁴For the love of Christ urges us on, because we are convinced that one has died for all; therefore all have died. ¹⁵And he died for all, so that those who live might live no longer for themselves, but for him who died and was raised for them.

16 From now on, therefore, we regard no one from a human point of view;*ᵇ* even though we once knew Christ from a human point of view,*ᵇ* we know him no longer in that way. ¹⁷So if anyone is in Christ, there is a new creation: everything old has passed away; see, everything has become new! ¹⁸All this is from God, who reconciled us to himself through Christ, and has given us the ministry of reconciliation; ¹⁹that is, in Christ God was reconciling the world to himself,*ᶜ* not counting their trespasses against them, and entrusting the message of reconciliation to us. ²⁰So we are ambassadors for Christ, since God is making his appeal through us; we entreat you on behalf of Christ,

---

An Appeal to Be Reconciled

2 CORINTHIANS 5.17–20

"What unparalleled condescension and divinely tender mercies are displayed in [these verses]! Did the judge ever beseech a condemned criminal to accept pardon? Does the creditor ever beseech a ruined debtor to receive an acquittal in full? Yet our almighty Lord, and our eternal Judge, not only vouchsafes to offer these blessings, but invites us, entreats us, and, with the most tender importunity, solicits us not to reject them."

—JOHN WESLEY,
Explanatory Notes Upon the New Testament

---

a Other ancient authorities read *put it on*   *b* Gk *according to the flesh*
c Or *God was in Christ reconciling the world to himself*

Temples of the Living God

2 CORINTHIANS 6.16–18

We are God's temple, for God dwells in us. It is through us that others see God's face. Through us others experience God's love, comfort, healing and forgiveness. Like all dwellings, sacred and secular, we are in need of maintenance.

What has to be swept out of your life today to make your whole being a more fitting dwelling for God? Whether you have to dust a little corner still permeated by the darkness of doubt or whether you have to run the vacuum throughout the house to sweep from your system the last traces of lingering sin is for you to decide. The important thing is to open wide the doors of your temple so that the Spirit of God can enter. Ask God to help you prepare a place for the One who wants to live in you and walk with you.

See Meeting God in Prayer

be reconciled to God. ²¹For our sake he made him to be sin who knew no sin, so that in him we might become the righteousness of God.

6 As we work together with him,ᵃ we urge you also not to accept the grace of God in vain. ²For he says,
"At an acceptable time I have listened to you,
and on a day of salvation I have helped you."
See, now is the acceptable time; see, now is the day of salvation! ³We are putting no obstacle in anyone's way, so that no fault may be found with our ministry, ⁴but as servants of God we have commended ourselves in every way: through great endurance, in afflictions, hardships, calamities, ⁵beatings, imprisonments, riots, labors, sleepless nights, hunger; ⁶by purity, knowledge, patience, kindness, holiness of spirit, genuine love, ⁷truthful speech, and the power of God; with the weapons of righteousness for the right hand and for the left; ⁸in honor and dishonor, in ill repute and good repute. We are treated as impostors, and yet are true; ⁹as unknown, and yet are well known; as dying, and see—we are alive; as punished, and yet not killed; ¹⁰as sorrowful, yet always rejoicing; as poor, yet making many rich; as having nothing, and yet possessing everything.

11 We have spoken frankly to you Corinthians; our heart is wide open to you. ¹²There is no restriction in our affections, but only in yours. ¹³In return—I speak as to children—open wide your hearts also.

The Temple of the Living God

14 Do not be mismatched with unbelievers. For what partnership is there between righteousness and lawlessness? Or what fellowship is there between light and darkness? ¹⁵What agreement does Christ have with Beliar? Or what does a believer share with an unbeliever? ¹⁶What agreement has the temple of God with idols? For weᵇ are the temple of the living God; as God said,
"I will live in them and walk among them,
and I will be their God,
and they shall be my people.
¹⁷ Therefore come out from them,
and be separate from them, says the Lord,
and touch nothing unclean;
then I will welcome you,
¹⁸ and I will be your father,
and you shall be my sons and daughters,
says the Lord Almighty."

7 Since we have these promises, beloved, let us cleanse ourselves from every defilement of body and of spirit, making holiness perfect in the fear of God.

Paul's Joy at the Church's Repentance

2 Make room in your heartsᶜ for us; we have wronged no one, we have corrupted no one, we have taken advantage of no one. ³I do not say this to condemn you, for I said before that you are in our hearts, to die together and to live together. ⁴I often boast about you; I have great pride in you; I am filled with consolation; I am overjoyed in all our affliction.

5 For even when we came into Macedonia, our bodies

ᵃ Gk *As we work together*   ᵇ Other ancient authorities read *you*
ᶜ Gk lacks *in your hearts*

had no rest, but we were afflicted in every way—disputes without and fears within. [6]But God, who consoles the downcast, consoled us by the arrival of Titus, [7]and not only by his coming, but also by the consolation with which he was consoled about you, as he told us of your longing, your mourning, your zeal for me, so that I rejoiced still more. [8]For even if I made you sorry with my letter, I do not regret it (though I did regret it, for I see that I grieved you with that letter, though only briefly). [9]Now I rejoice, not because you were grieved, but because your grief led to repentance; for you felt a godly grief, so that you were not harmed in any way by us. [10]For godly grief produces a repentance that leads to salvation and brings no regret, but worldly grief produces death. [11]For see what earnestness this godly grief has produced in you, what eagerness to clear yourselves, what indignation, what alarm, what longing, what zeal, what punishment! At every point you have proved yourselves guiltless in the matter. [12]So although I wrote to you, it was not on account of the one who did the wrong, nor on account of the one who was wronged, but in order that your zeal for us might be made known to you before God. [13]In this we find comfort.

In addition to our own consolation, we rejoiced still more at the joy of Titus, because his mind has been set at rest by all of you. [14]For if I have been somewhat boastful about you to him, I was not disgraced; but just as everything we said to you was true, so our boasting to Titus has proved true as well. [15]And his heart goes out all the more to you, as he remembers the obedience of all of you, and how you welcomed him with fear and trembling. [16]I rejoice, because I have complete confidence in you.

Encouragement to Be Generous

8 We want you to know, brothers and sisters,[a] about the grace of God that has been granted to the churches of Macedonia; [2]for during a severe ordeal of affliction, their abundant joy and their extreme poverty have overflowed in a wealth of generosity on their part. [3]For, as I can testify, they voluntarily gave according to their means, and even beyond their means, [4]begging us earnestly for the privilege[b] of sharing in this ministry to the saints— [5]and this, not merely as we expected; they gave themselves first to the Lord and, by the will of God, to us, [6]so that we might urge Titus that, as he had already made a beginning, so he should also complete this generous undertaking[c] among you. [7]Now as you excel in everything—in faith, in speech, in knowledge, in utmost eagerness, and in our love for you[d]—so we want you to excel also in this generous undertaking.[c]

8 I do not say this as a command, but I am testing the genuineness of your love against the earnestness of others. [9]For you know the generous act[e] of our Lord Jesus Christ, that though he was rich, yet for your sakes he became poor, so that by his poverty you might become rich. [10]And in this matter I am giving my advice: it is appropriate for you who began last year not only to do something but even to desire to do something— [11]now finish doing it, so that your eagerness may be matched by completing it according to

---

Cultivating the Life of Holiness

2 CORINTHIANS 7.1

"The beginner must realize that in order to give delight to the Lord he is starting to cultivate a garden on very barren soil, full of abominable weeds. His Majesty pulls up the weeds and plants good seed . . . . And with the help of God we must strive like good gardeners to get these plants to grow and take pains to water them so that they don't wither but come to bud and flower and give forth a most pleasant fragrance to provide refreshment for this Lord of ours. Then He will often come to take delight in this garden and find His joy among these virtues."

—TERESA OF AVILA,
The Book of Her Life

---

a Gk *brothers*   b Gk *grace*   c Gk *this grace*   d Other ancient authorities read *your love for us*   e Gk *the grace*

From Contemplation to Action

2 CORINTHIANS 8.2–15

Teresa of Avila and John of the Cross remind us that the only true test of contemplation or oneness with God is the charity that flows from it. The apostle Paul declares, as he makes an appeal for financial support, that giving is an essential test of the sincerity of love. Even today it is not easy to ask people to reach into their pockets and contribute generously to a ministry. What do Paul's words of appeal and conviction communicate afresh to you? What examples of others' generosity inspire you to give more freely? What does it mean to give not only out of your abundance but also out of your poverty?

See Meeting God in Community

your means. ¹²For if the eagerness is there, the gift is acceptable according to what one has—not according to what one does not have. ¹³I do not mean that there should be relief for others and pressure on you, but it is a question of a fair balance between ¹⁴your present abundance and their need, so that their abundance may be for your need, in order that there may be a fair balance. ¹⁵As it is written,

"The one who had much did not have too much,
 and the one who had little did not have too little."

Commendation of Titus

16 But thanks be to God who put in the heart of Titus the same eagerness for you that I myself have. ¹⁷For he not only accepted our appeal, but since he is more eager than ever, he is going to you of his own accord. ¹⁸With him we are sending the brother who is famous among all the churches for his proclaiming the good news;*a* ¹⁹and not only that, but he has also been appointed by the churches to travel with us while we are administering this generous undertaking*b* for the glory of the Lord himself*c* and to show our goodwill. ²⁰We intend that no one should blame us about this generous gift that we are administering, ²¹for we intend to do what is right not only in the Lord's sight but also in the sight of others. ²²And with them we are sending our brother whom we have often tested and found eager in many matters, but who is now more eager than ever because of his great confidence in you. ²³As for Titus, he is my partner and co-worker in your service; as for our brothers, they are messengers*d* of the churches, the glory of Christ. ²⁴Therefore openly before the churches, show them the proof of your love and of our reason for boasting about you.

The Collection for Christians at Jerusalem

9 Now it is not necessary for me to write you about the ministry to the saints, ²for I know your eagerness, which is the subject of my boasting about you to the people of Macedonia, saying that Achaia has been ready since last year; and your zeal has stirred up most of them. ³But I am sending the brothers in order that our boasting about you may not prove to have been empty in this case, so that you may be ready, as I said you would be; ⁴otherwise, if some Macedonians come with me and find that you are not ready, we would be humiliated—to say nothing of you—in this undertaking.*e* ⁵So I thought it necessary to urge the brothers to go on ahead to you, and arrange in advance for this bountiful gift that you have promised, so that it may be ready as a voluntary gift and not as an extortion.

6 The point is this: the one who sows sparingly will also reap sparingly, and the one who sows bountifully will also reap bountifully. ⁷Each of you must give as you have made up your mind, not reluctantly or under compulsion, for God loves a cheerful giver. ⁸And God is able to provide you with every blessing in abundance, so that by always having enough of everything, you may share abundantly in every good work. ⁹As it is written,

"He scatters abroad, he gives to the poor;
 his righteousness*f* endures forever."

a Or *the gospel* *b* Gk *this grace* *c* Other ancient authorities lack *himself* *d* Gk *apostles* *e* Other ancient authorities add *of boasting* *f* Or *benevolence*

¹⁰He who supplies seed to the sower and bread for food will supply and multiply your seed for sowing and increase the harvest of your righteousness.ᵃ ¹¹You will be enriched in every way for your great generosity, which will produce thanksgiving to God through us; ¹²for the rendering of this ministry not only supplies the needs of the saints but also overflows with many thanksgivings to God. ¹³Through the testing of this ministry you glorify God by your obedience to the confession of the gospel of Christ and by the generosity of your sharing with them and with all others, ¹⁴while they long for you and pray for you because of the surpassing grace of God that he has given you. ¹⁵Thanks be to God for his indescribable gift!

Paul Defends His Ministry

10 I myself, Paul, appeal to you by the meekness and gentleness of Christ—I who am humble when face to face with you, but bold toward you when I am away!— ²I ask that when I am present I need not show boldness by daring to oppose those who think we are acting according to human standards.ᵇ ³Indeed, we live as human beings,ᶜ but we do not wage war according to human standards;ᵇ ⁴for the weapons of our warfare are not merely human,ᵈ but they have divine power to destroy strongholds. We destroy arguments ⁵and every proud obstacle raised up against the knowledge of God, and we take every thought captive to obey Christ. ⁶We are ready to punish every disobedience when your obedience is complete.

7 Look at what is before your eyes. If you are confident that you belong to Christ, remind yourself of this, that just as you belong to Christ, so also do we. ⁸Now, even if I boast a little too much of our authority, which the Lord gave for building you up and not for tearing you down, I will not be ashamed of it. ⁹I do not want to seem as though I am trying to frighten you with my letters. ¹⁰For they say, "His letters are weighty and strong, but his bodily presence is weak, and his speech contemptible." ¹¹Let such people understand that what we say by letter when absent, we will also do when present.

12 We do not dare to classify or compare ourselves with some of those who commend themselves. But when they measure themselves by one another, and compare themselves with one another, they do not show good sense. ¹³We, however, will not boast beyond limits, but will keep within the field that God has assigned to us, to reach out even as far as you. ¹⁴For we were not overstepping our limits when we reached you; we were the first to come all the way to you with the good newsᵉ of Christ. ¹⁵We do not boast beyond limits, that is, in the labors of others; but our hope is that, as your faith increases, our sphere of action among you may be greatly enlarged, ¹⁶so that we may proclaim the good newsᵉ in lands beyond you, without boasting of work already done in someone else's sphere of action. ¹⁷"Let the one who boasts, boast in the Lord." ¹⁸For it is not those who commend themselves that are approved, but those whom the Lord commends.

Sowing Generously

2 CORINTHIANS 9.5–12

"It is not enough to help the poor. We must help them with generosity and without grumbling. And it is not enough to help them without grumbling. We must help them gladly and happily. When the poor are helped there ought to be these two conditions: generosity and joy . . . By showing great joyfulness you will succeed in enabling your brother or sister to overcome their sensitivity. They will understand that in your opinion receiving is just as beautiful as giving. By showing bad temper, on the other hand, far from cheering them up you will be depressing them even further. If you give gladly, even if you give only a little, it is a big gift. If you give unwillingly, even if you give a big gift, you turn it into a small one."

—JOHN CHRYSOSTOM,
On the Letter to the Romans

See *Meeting God in Community*

---

a Or *benevolence*   *b* Gk *according to the flesh*   *c* Gk *in the flesh*
d Gk *fleshly*   *e* Or *the gospel*

Boasting in the Cross

2 CORINTHIANS 11.21–30

The cross of Jesus Christ is the horizon against which Paul sees everything else. He sees in the cross the whole meaning of every imprisonment, every flogging, every exposure to death he endures. Picture yourself standing with Paul at the foot of the cross. Rub your fingers against the rough wood. Look up at the crossbars on which the Savior hung. Imagine the pain of this horrendous way of death. No wonder Paul boasts about his sufferings. What are they? All these sufferings have gained for him a wealth of meaning. What are you suffering for the cross of Christ? Are you growing in compassion through the pain? Growing in courage?

Paul and the False Apostles

11 I wish you would bear with me in a little foolishness. Do bear with me! ²I feel a divine jealousy for you, for I promised you in marriage to one husband, to present you as a chaste virgin to Christ. ³But I am afraid that as the serpent deceived Eve by its cunning, your thoughts will be led astray from a sincere and pure*ᵃ* devotion to Christ. ⁴For if someone comes and proclaims another Jesus than the one we proclaimed, or if you receive a different spirit from the one you received, or a different gospel from the one you accepted, you submit to it readily enough. ⁵I think that I am not in the least inferior to these super-apostles. ⁶I may be untrained in speech, but not in knowledge; certainly in every way and in all things we have made this evident to you.

7 Did I commit a sin by humbling myself so that you might be exalted, because I proclaimed God's good news*ᵇ* to you free of charge? ⁸I robbed other churches by accepting support from them in order to serve you. ⁹And when I was with you and was in need, I did not burden anyone, for my needs were supplied by the friends*ᶜ* who came from Macedonia. So I refrained and will continue to refrain from burdening you in any way. ¹⁰As the truth of Christ is in me, this boast of mine will not be silenced in the regions of Achaia. ¹¹And why? Because I do not love you? God knows I do!

12 And what I do I will also continue to do, in order to deny an opportunity to those who want an opportunity to be recognized as our equals in what they boast about. ¹³For such boasters are false apostles, deceitful workers, disguising themselves as apostles of Christ. ¹⁴And no wonder! Even Satan disguises himself as an angel of light. ¹⁵So it is not strange if his ministers also disguise themselves as ministers of righteousness. Their end will match their deeds.

Paul's Sufferings as an Apostle

16 I repeat, let no one think that I am a fool; but if you do, then accept me as a fool, so that I too may boast a little. ¹⁷What I am saying in regard to this boastful confidence, I am saying not with the Lord's authority, but as a fool; ¹⁸since many boast according to human standards,*ᵈ* I will also boast. ¹⁹For you gladly put up with fools, being wise yourselves! ²⁰For you put up with it when someone makes slaves of you, or preys upon you, or takes advantage of you, or puts on airs, or gives you a slap in the face. ²¹To my shame, I must say, we were too weak for that!

But whatever anyone dares to boast of—I am speaking as a fool—I also dare to boast of that. ²²Are they Hebrews? So am I. Are they Israelites? So am I. Are they descendants of Abraham? So am I. ²³Are they ministers of Christ? I am talking like a madman—I am a better one: with far greater labors, far more imprisonments, with countless floggings, and often near death. ²⁴Five times I have received from the Jews the forty lashes minus one. ²⁵Three times I was beaten with rods. Once I received a stoning. Three times I was shipwrecked; for a night and a day I was adrift at sea; ²⁶on

a Other ancient authorities lack *and pure*   *b* Gk *the gospel of God*
c Gk *brothers*   *d* Gk *according to the flesh*

frequent journeys, in danger from rivers, danger from bandits, danger from my own people, danger from Gentiles, danger in the city, danger in the wilderness, danger at sea, danger from false brothers and sisters;[a] 27in toil and hardship, through many a sleepless night, hungry and thirsty, often without food, cold and naked. 28And, besides other things, I am under daily pressure because of my anxiety for all the churches. 29Who is weak, and I am not weak? Who is made to stumble, and I am not indignant?

30 If I must boast, I will boast of the things that show my weakness. 31The God and Father of the Lord Jesus (blessed be he forever!) knows that I do not lie. 32In Damascus, the governor[b] under King Aretas guarded the city of Damascus in order to[c] seize me, 33but I was let down in a basket through a window in the wall,[d] and escaped from his hands.

Paul's Visions and Revelations

12 It is necessary to boast; nothing is to be gained by it, but I will go on to visions and revelations of the Lord. 2I know a person in Christ who fourteen years ago was caught up to the third heaven—whether in the body or out of the body I do not know; God knows. 3And I know that such a person—whether in the body or out of the body I do not know; God knows— 4was caught up into Paradise and heard things that are not to be told, that no mortal is permitted to repeat. 5On behalf of such a one I will boast, but on my own behalf I will not boast, except of my weaknesses. 6But if I wish to boast, I will not be a fool, for I will be speaking the truth. But I refrain from it, so that no one may think better of me than what is seen in me or heard from me, 7even considering the exceptional character of the revelations. Therefore, to keep[e] me from being too elated, a thorn was given me in the flesh, a messenger of Satan to torment me, to keep me from being too elated.[f] 8Three times I appealed to the Lord about this, that it would leave me, 9but he said to me, "My grace is sufficient for you, for power[g] is made perfect in weakness." So, I will boast all the more gladly of my weaknesses, so that the power of Christ may dwell in me. 10Therefore I am content with weaknesses, insults, hardships, persecutions, and calamities for the sake of Christ; for whenever I am weak, then I am strong.

Paul's Concern for the Corinthian Church

11 I have been a fool! You forced me to it. Indeed you should have been the ones commending me, for I am not at all inferior to these super-apostles, even though I am nothing. 12The signs of a true apostle were performed among you with utmost patience, signs and wonders and mighty works. 13How have you been worse off than the other churches, except that I myself did not burden you? Forgive me this wrong!

14 Here I am, ready to come to you this third time. And I will not be a burden, because I do not want what is yours but you; for children ought not to lay up for their parents,

Walking in the Truth

2 CORINTHIANS 12.7–10

The classical definition of humility offered by Teresa of Avila is to walk in the truth of who we are. This means accepting our weaknesses and our limitations as gifts of God as well as our strengths and talents.

Given that definition, what does walking in the truth mean for you? How can you regard yourself as God regards you? How can you become more grateful for the way God has created you—in light of both your strengths and weaknesses? Meditate on these words and let them give you the courage to fulfill your calling as a minister of the new covenant. "My grace is sufficient for you, for power is made perfect in weakness."

See Meeting God in Service

---

a Gk brothers   b Gk ethnarch   c Other ancient authorities read and
wanted to   d Gk through the wall   e Other ancient authorities read To
keep   f Other ancient authorities lack to keep me from being too elated
g Other ancient authorities read my power

Spending All for God

2 CORINTHIANS 12.14–18

"As children of the darkness that rules through fear, self-interest, greed, and power, our great motivators are survival and self-preservation. But as children of the light who know that perfect love casts out all fear, it becomes possible to give away all that we have for others. As children of the light, we prepare ourselves to become true martyrs, people who witness with their whole lives to the unlimited love of God. Giving all thus becomes gaining all . . . Every time I take a step in the direction of generosity, I know I am moving from fear to love."

—HENRI J. M. NOUWEN,
The Return of the Prodigal Son:
A Story of Homecoming

but parents for their children. ¹⁵I will most gladly spend and be spent for you. If I love you more, am I to be loved less? ¹⁶Let it be assumed that I did not burden you. Nevertheless (you say) since I was crafty, I took you in by deceit. ¹⁷Did I take advantage of you through any of those whom I sent to you? ¹⁸I urged Titus to go, and sent the brother with him. Titus did not take advantage of you, did he? Did we not conduct ourselves with the same spirit? Did we not take the same steps?

19 Have you been thinking all along that we have been defending ourselves before you? We are speaking in Christ before God. Everything we do, beloved, is for the sake of building you up. ²⁰For I fear that when I come, I may find you not as I wish, and that you may find me not as you wish; I fear that there may perhaps be quarreling, jealousy, anger, selfishness, slander, gossip, conceit, and disorder. ²¹I fear that when I come again, my God may humble me before you, and that I may have to mourn over many who previously sinned and have not repented of the impurity, sexual immorality, and licentiousness that they have practiced.

Further Warning

13 This is the third time I am coming to you. "Any charge must be sustained by the evidence of two or three witnesses." ²I warned those who sinned previously and all the others, and I warn them now while absent, as I did when present on my second visit, that if I come again, I will not be lenient— ³since you desire proof that Christ is speaking in me. He is not weak in dealing with you, but is powerful in you. ⁴For he was crucified in weakness, but lives by the power of God. For we are weak in him,ᵃ but in dealing with you we will live with him by the power of God.

5 Examine yourselves to see whether you are living in the faith. Test yourselves. Do you not realize that Jesus Christ is in you?—unless, indeed, you fail to meet the test! ⁶I hope you will find out that we have not failed. ⁷But we pray to God that you may not do anything wrong—not that we may appear to have met the test, but that you may do what is right, though we may seem to have failed. ⁸For we cannot do anything against the truth, but only for the truth. ⁹For we rejoice when we are weak and you are strong. This is what we pray for, that you may become perfect. ¹⁰So I write these things while I am away from you, so that when I come, I may not have to be severe in using the authority that the Lord has given me for building up and not for tearing down.

Final Greetings and Benediction

11 Finally, brothers and sisters,ᵇ farewell.ᶜ Put things in order, listen to my appeal,ᵈ agree with one another, live in peace; and the God of love and peace will be with you. ¹²Greet one another with a holy kiss. All the saints greet you.

13 The grace of the Lord Jesus Christ, the love of God, and the communion ofᵉ the Holy Spirit be with all of you.

ᵃ Other ancient authorities read *with him*   ᵇ Gk *brothers*   ᶜ Or *rejoice*
ᵈ Or *encourage one another*   ᵉ Or *and the sharing in*

THE LETTER OF PAUL TO THE
GALATIANS
In Step With the Spirit

KEY VERSE:

If we live by the Spirit, let us also be guided by the Spirit.—Galatians 5.25

Parades are fun to watch, but it takes great concentration to march in one, especially if one is playing an instrument or carrying a flag. Bands designate a leader to set the proper cadence; the challenge for each band member is to stay in step—and not only when the band is in front of the viewing stand!

Paul's letter to the Galatians explores some of the difficulties that can cause Christians to get out of step as they follow Jesus Christ. Paul warns his readers against misunderstanding the role of the law, pursuing the dead end of human effort, and concentrating on external religious practice while neglecting their inner life.

Paul's letter is a refreshing message for the Galatians—and for us today: We don't have to struggle to be in control of our spiritual life. God wants to guide us as we walk in step with the Holy Spirit so that we experience God's gracious freedom, guidance and renewing joy. As you read this letter, consider how your own lifestyle reflects the pace and power of the Holy Spirit. Be careful to notice those areas in which God is calling you to get in step with the Spirit.

"Is there not a soul among you who sometimes hears the Spirit of the Son crying in his inmost heart, 'Abba, Father'? (Galatians 4.6). Let him who feels himself loved by the Father realize that he is moved by the same Spirit as the Son. Trust without reserve. Be of good courage."

—BERNARD OF CLAIRVAUX,
Selected Works

Called by Grace

GALATIANS 1.13–17

As a zealous Pharisee, Paul had been out of step with God's Spirit. Steeped in a tradition of law, he had relied on his own strength and ability. But all that changed when he met Jesus on the road to Damascus. Getting in step with the Spirit meant discovering and following God's way, not his own.

Retrace your spiritual history. You may, like Paul, be able to pinpoint a specific occasion when you fell into step with Jesus Christ (Acts 9.1–19). Or your life might resemble the more gradual pattern of Timothy's experience (2 Timothy 3.14–15). How have you experienced God's grace? How has God revealed Jesus Christ to you? Where is God still calling you to change, to get in step with the Spirit? What is blocking you? You might ask for God's help in overcoming the obstacles or in listening for direction. Consider the possibility of recording your reflections in a journal as a way of deepening your experiences of God's grace.

See Meeting God in Everyday Life

Salutation

1 Paul an apostle—sent neither by human commission nor from human authorities, but through Jesus Christ and God the Father, who raised him from the dead— ²and all the members of God's family*ᵃ* who are with me,

To the churches of Galatia:

3 Grace to you and peace from God our Father and the Lord Jesus Christ, ⁴who gave himself for our sins to set us free from the present evil age, according to the will of our God and Father, ⁵to whom be the glory forever and ever. Amen.

There Is No Other Gospel

6 I am astonished that you are so quickly deserting the one who called you in the grace of Christ and are turning to a different gospel— ⁷not that there is another gospel, but there are some who are confusing you and want to pervert the gospel of Christ. ⁸But even if we or an angel*ᵇ* from heaven should proclaim to you a gospel contrary to what we proclaimed to you, let that one be accursed! ⁹As we have said before, so now I repeat, if anyone proclaims to you a gospel contrary to what you received, let that one be accursed!

10 Am I now seeking human approval, or God's approval? Or am I trying to please people? If I were still pleasing people, I would not be a servant*ᶜ* of Christ.

Paul's Vindication of His Apostleship

11 For I want you to know, brothers and sisters,*ᵈ* that the gospel that was proclaimed by me is not of human origin; ¹²for I did not receive it from a human source, nor was I taught it, but I received it through a revelation of Jesus Christ. 13 You have heard, no doubt, of my earlier life in Judaism. I was violently persecuting the church of God and was trying to destroy it. ¹⁴I advanced in Judaism beyond many among my people of the same age, for I was far more zealous for the traditions of my ancestors. ¹⁵But when God, who had set me apart before I was born and called me through his grace, was pleased ¹⁶to reveal his Son to me,*ᵉ* so that I might proclaim him among the Gentiles, I did not confer with any human being, ¹⁷nor did I go up to Jerusalem to those who were already apostles before me, but I went away at once into Arabia, and afterwards I returned to Damascus.

18 Then after three years I did go up to Jerusalem to visit Cephas and stayed with him fifteen days; ¹⁹but I did not see any other apostle except James the Lord's brother. ²⁰In what I am writing to you, before God, I do not lie! ²¹Then I went into the regions of Syria and Cilicia, ²²and I was still unknown by sight to the churches of Judea that are in Christ; ²³they only heard it said, "The one who formerly was persecuting us is now proclaiming the faith he once tried to destroy." ²⁴And they glorified God because of me.

Paul and the Other Apostles

2 Then after fourteen years I went up again to Jerusalem with Barnabas, taking Titus along with me. ²I went up in response to a revelation. Then I laid before them (though only in a private meeting with the acknowledged leaders) the gospel that I proclaim among the Gentiles, in order to make

a Gk *all the brothers*   *b* Or *a messenger*   *c* Gk *slave*   *d* Gk *brothers*
e Gk *in me*

sure that I was not running, or had not run, in vain. ³But even Titus, who was with me, was not compelled to be circumcised, though he was a Greek. ⁴But because of false believers*a* secretly brought in, who slipped in to spy on the freedom we have in Christ Jesus, so that they might enslave us— ⁵we did not submit to them even for a moment, so that the truth of the gospel might always remain with you. ⁶And from those who were supposed to be acknowledged leaders (what they actually were makes no difference to me; God shows no partiality)—those leaders contributed nothing to me. ⁷On the contrary, when they saw that I had been entrusted with the gospel for the uncircumcised, just as Peter had been entrusted with the gospel for the circumcised ⁸(for he who worked through Peter making him an apostle to the circumcised also worked through me in sending me to the Gentiles), ⁹and when James and Cephas and John, who were acknowledged pillars, recognized the grace that had been given to me, they gave to Barnabas and me the right hand of fellowship, agreeing that we should go to the Gentiles and they to the circumcised. ¹⁰They asked only one thing, that we remember the poor, which was actually what I was*b* eager to do.

Paul Rebukes Peter at Antioch

11 But when Cephas came to Antioch, I opposed him to his face, because he stood self-condemned; ¹²for until certain people came from James, he used to eat with the Gentiles. But after they came, he drew back and kept himself separate for fear of the circumcision faction. ¹³And the other Jews joined him in this hypocrisy, so that even Barnabas was led astray by their hypocrisy. ¹⁴But when I saw that they were not acting consistently with the truth of the gospel, I said to Cephas before them all, "If you, though a Jew, live like a Gentile and not like a Jew, how can you compel the Gentiles to live like Jews?"*c*

Jews and Gentiles Are Saved by Faith

15 We ourselves are Jews by birth and not Gentile sinners; ¹⁶yet we know that a person is justified*d* not by the works of the law but through faith in Jesus Christ.*e* And we have come to believe in Christ Jesus, so that we might be justified by faith in Christ,*f* and not by doing the works of the law, because no one will be justified by the works of the law. ¹⁷But if, in our effort to be justified in Christ, we ourselves have been found to be sinners, is Christ then a servant of sin? Certainly not! ¹⁸But if I build up again the very things that I once tore down, then I demonstrate that I am a transgressor. ¹⁹For through the law I died to the law, so that I might live to God. I have been crucified with Christ; ²⁰and it is no longer I who live, but it is Christ who lives in me. And the life I now live in the flesh I live by faith in the Son of God,*g* who loved me and gave himself for me. ²¹I do not nullify the grace of God; for if justification*h* comes through the law, then Christ died for nothing.

New Life at the Center

GALATIANS 2.20

Imagine that someone has asked you to create a film of your life using this verse as the theme. What scenes would you include to represent your life before Jesus Christ came to live in you? After? What is different? Why? Whom would you cast for the major parts? What message do you hope your viewers will receive by watching your life? Pay attention to the details. Be open to ways in which you can thank God for the whole picture, even if some parts are painful to watch.

See Meeting God in Everyday Life

---

a Gk *false brothers*   *b* Or *had been*   *c* Some interpreters hold that the quotation extends into the following paragraph   *d* Or *reckoned as righteous;* and so elsewhere   *e* Or *the faith of Jesus Christ*   *f* Or *the faith of Christ*   *g* Or *by the faith of the Son of God*   *h* Or *righteousness*

Consider Abraham

GALATIANS 3.6–9

Our society is hungry for heroes. So many of our "all-stars" in politics, entertainment, sports and even in the church have fallen and disappointed us. While Abraham was not perfect, he was different. He was a person of faith. The Bible speaks of faith as both belief (assenting to the content of Christianity) and trust (depending on God for all our needs). Living out that faith—living in step with the Spirit—is risky, especially in the uncertainties of life. God repeatedly asked Abraham to step out into the unknown.

Reflect on your own life. How have you been blessed in living by faith? In what way is God calling you to live by faith? Identify some contemporary heroes of faith who can encourage you to walk in step with God's Spirit.

See Meeting God in Everyday Life

Law or Faith

3 You foolish Galatians! Who has bewitched you? It was before your eyes that Jesus Christ was publicly exhibited as crucified! ²The only thing I want to learn from you is this: Did you receive the Spirit by doing the works of the law or by believing what you heard? ³Are you so foolish? Having started with the Spirit, are you now ending with the flesh? ⁴Did you experience so much for nothing?—if it really was for nothing. ⁵Well then, does God[a] supply you with the Spirit and work miracles among you by your doing the works of the law, or by your believing what you heard?

6 Just as Abraham "believed God, and it was reckoned to him as righteousness," ⁷so, you see, those who believe are the descendants of Abraham. ⁸And the scripture, foreseeing that God would justify the Gentiles by faith, declared the gospel beforehand to Abraham, saying, "All the Gentiles shall be blessed in you." ⁹For this reason, those who believe are blessed with Abraham who believed.

10 For all who rely on the works of the law are under a curse; for it is written, "Cursed is everyone who does not observe and obey all the things written in the book of the law." ¹¹Now it is evident that no one is justified before God by the law; for "The one who is righteous will live by faith."[b] ¹²But the law does not rest on faith; on the contrary, "Whoever does the works of the law[c] will live by them." ¹³Christ redeemed us from the curse of the law by becoming a curse for us—for it is written, "Cursed is everyone who hangs on a tree"— ¹⁴in order that in Christ Jesus the blessing of Abraham might come to the Gentiles, so that we might receive the promise of the Spirit through faith.

The Promise to Abraham

15 Brothers and sisters,[d] I give an example from daily life: once a person's will[e] has been ratified, no one adds to it or annuls it. ¹⁶Now the promises were made to Abraham and to his offspring;[f] it does not say, "And to offsprings,"[g] as of many; but it says, "And to your offspring,"[f] that is, to one person, who is Christ. ¹⁷My point is this: the law, which came four hundred thirty years later, does not annul a covenant previously ratified by God, so as to nullify the promise. ¹⁸For if the inheritance comes from the law, it no longer comes from the promise; but God granted it to Abraham through the promise.

The Purpose of the Law

19 Why then the law? It was added because of transgressions, until the offspring[f] would come to whom the promise had been made; and it was ordained through angels by a mediator. ²⁰Now a mediator involves more than one party; but God is one.

21 Is the law then opposed to the promises of God? Certainly not! For if a law had been given that could make alive, then righteousness would indeed come through the law. ²²But the scripture has imprisoned all things under the power of sin, so that what was promised through faith in Jesus Christ[h] might be given to those who believe.

23 Now before faith came, we were imprisoned and

---

a Gk *he*   *b* Or *The one who is righteous through faith will live*   *c* Gk *does them*   *d* Gk *Brothers*   *e* Or *covenant* (as in verse 17)   *f* Gk *seed*   *g* Gk *seeds*   *h* Or *through the faith of Jesus Christ*

guarded under the law until faith would be revealed.
²⁴Therefore the law was our disciplinarian until Christ
came, so that we might be justified by faith. ²⁵But now that
faith has come, we are no longer subject to a disciplinarian,
²⁶for in Christ Jesus you are all children of God through
faith. ²⁷As many of you as were baptized into Christ have
clothed yourselves with Christ. ²⁸There is no longer Jew or
Greek, there is no longer slave or free, there is no longer
male and female; for all of you are one in Christ Jesus.
²⁹And if you belong to Christ, then you are Abraham's offspring,ᵃ heirs according to the promise.

4 My point is this: heirs, as long as they are minors, are
no better than slaves, though they are the owners of all
the property; ²but they remain under guardians and trustees until the date set by the father. ³So with us; while we
were minors, we were enslaved to the elemental spiritsᵇ of
the world. ⁴But when the fullness of time had come, God
sent his Son, born of a woman, born under the law, ⁵in
order to redeem those who were under the law, so that we
might receive adoption as children. ⁶And because you are
children, God has sent the Spirit of his Son into ourᶜ hearts,
crying, "Abba!ᵈ Father!" ⁷So you are no longer a slave but a
child, and if a child then also an heir, through God.ᵉ

Paul Reproves the Galatians

8 Formerly, when you did not know God, you were enslaved to beings that by nature are not gods. ⁹Now, however, that you have come to know God, or rather to be known
by God, how can you turn back again to the weak and beggarly elemental spirits?ᶠ How can you want to be enslaved
to them again? ¹⁰You are observing special days, and
months, and seasons, and years. ¹¹I am afraid that my work
for you may have been wasted.

12 Friends,ᵍ I beg you, become as I am, for I also have become as you are. You have done me no wrong. ¹³You know
that it was because of a physical infirmity that I first announced the gospel to you; ¹⁴though my condition put you to
the test, you did not scorn or despise me, but welcomed me
as an angel of God, as Christ Jesus. ¹⁵What has become of the
goodwill you felt? For I testify that, had it been possible, you
would have torn out your eyes and given them to me. ¹⁶Have
I now become your enemy by telling you the truth? ¹⁷They
make much of you, but for no good purpose; they want to exclude you, so that you may make much of them. ¹⁸It is good
to be made much of for a good purpose at all times, and not
only when I am present with you. ¹⁹My little children, for
whom I am again in the pain of childbirth until Christ is
formed in you, ²⁰I wish I were present with you now and
could change my tone, for I am perplexed about you.

The Allegory of Hagar and Sarah

21 Tell me, you who desire to be subject to the law, will
you not listen to the law? ²²For it is written that Abraham
had two sons, one by a slave woman and the other by a
free woman. ²³One, the child of the slave, was born according to the flesh; the other, the child of the free woman,
was born through the promise. ²⁴Now this is an allegory:

God's Life in Us

GALATIANS 4.19

"True religion is a union of the
soul with God, a real participation of the Divine nature, the
very image of God drawn upon
the soul, or, in the apostle's
phrase, 'Christ is formed in
you.'"

—HENRY SCOUGAL,
The Life of God in the Soul of Man

---

a Gk *seed*   b Or *the rudiments*   c Other ancient authorities read *your*
d Aramaic for *Father*   e Other ancient authorities read *an heir of God
through Christ*   f Or *beggarly rudiments*   g Gk *Brothers*

Free to Love Responsibly

GALATIANS 5.13–15

While Christian freedom is a wonderful gift, it carries responsibility along with it. God expects those who follow the Spirit to walk in love rather than to serve the sinful nature. Furthermore, walking in step with the Spirit is communal as well as individual. Personal, spiritual formation is only half of the process. As representatives of Jesus Christ, we are called to live out our faith by loving our neighbor and treating others as if they were Jesus (see Matthew 25.35–36).

Use the newspaper or evening news broadcast to pray this scripture. Consider which stories reflect love and which ones abuse freedom and reflect a lack of love. How do the news stories and this scripture challenge you to some form of responsible action? If Jesus were watching the news with you, how might he respond and encourage you to respond?

See Meeting God in Community

these women are two covenants. One woman, in fact, is Hagar, from Mount Sinai, bearing children for slavery. [25]Now Hagar is Mount Sinai in Arabia[a] and corresponds to the present Jerusalem, for she is in slavery with her children. [26]But the other woman corresponds to the Jerusalem above; she is free, and she is our mother. [27]For it is written,

"Rejoice, you childless one, you who bear no
        children,
    burst into song and shout, you who endure no
        birth pangs;
for the children of the desolate woman are more
        numerous
    than the children of the one who is married."

[28]Now you,[b] my friends,[c] are children of the promise, like Isaac. [29]But just as at that time the child who was born according to the flesh persecuted the child who was born according to the Spirit, so it is now also. [30]But what does the scripture say? "Drive out the slave and her child; for the child of the slave will not share the inheritance with the child of the free woman." [31]So then, friends,[c] we are children, not of the slave but of the free woman. [1]For freedom Christ has set us free. Stand firm, therefore, and do not submit again to a yoke of slavery.

The Nature of Christian Freedom

2 Listen! I, Paul, am telling you that if you let yourselves be circumcised, Christ will be of no benefit to you. [3]Once again I testify to every man who lets himself be circumcised that he is obliged to obey the entire law. [4]You who want to be justified by the law have cut yourselves off from Christ; you have fallen away from grace. [5]For through the Spirit, by faith, we eagerly wait for the hope of righteousness. [6]For in Christ Jesus neither circumcision nor uncircumcision counts for anything; the only thing that counts is faith working[d] through love.

7 You were running well; who prevented you from obeying the truth? [8]Such persuasion does not come from the one who calls you. [9]A little yeast leavens the whole batch of dough. [10]I am confident about you in the Lord that you will not think otherwise. But whoever it is that is confusing you will pay the penalty. [11]But my friends,[c] why am I still being persecuted if I am still preaching circumcision? In that case the offense of the cross has been removed. [12]I wish those who unsettle you would castrate themselves!

13 For you were called to freedom, brothers and sisters;[c] only do not use your freedom as an opportunity for self-indulgence,[e] but through love become slaves to one another. [14]For the whole law is summed up in a single commandment, "You shall love your neighbor as yourself." [15]If, however, you bite and devour one another, take care that you are not consumed by one another.

The Works of the Flesh

16 Live by the Spirit, I say, and do not gratify the desires of the flesh. [17]For what the flesh desires is opposed to the Spirit, and what the Spirit desires is opposed to the flesh; for these are opposed to each other, to prevent you from

---

a Other ancient authorities read *For Sinai is a mountain in Arabia* *b* Other ancient authorities read *we* *c* Gk *brothers* *d* Or *made effective* *e* Gk *the flesh*

doing what you want. ¹⁸But if you are led by the Spirit, you are not subject to the law. ¹⁹Now the works of the flesh are obvious: fornication, impurity, licentiousness, ²⁰idolatry, sorcery, enmities, strife, jealousy, anger, quarrels, dissensions, factions, ²¹envy,*ᵃ* drunkenness, carousing, and things like these. I am warning you, as I warned you before: those who do such things will not inherit the kingdom of God.

The Fruit of the Spirit

22 By contrast, the fruit of the Spirit is love, joy, peace, patience, kindness, generosity, faithfulness, ²³gentleness, and self-control. There is no law against such things. ²⁴And those who belong to Christ Jesus have crucified the flesh with its passions and desires. ²⁵If we live by the Spirit, let us also be guided by the Spirit. ²⁶Let us not become conceited, competing against one another, envying one another.

Bear One Another's Burdens

6 My friends,*ᵇ* if anyone is detected in a transgression, you who have received the Spirit should restore such a one in a spirit of gentleness. Take care that you yourselves are not tempted. ²Bear one another's burdens, and in this way you will fulfill*ᶜ* the law of Christ. ³For if those who are nothing think they are something, they deceive themselves. ⁴All must test their own work; then that work, rather than their neighbor's work, will become a cause for pride. ⁵For all must carry their own loads.

6 Those who are taught the word must share in all good things with their teacher.

7 Do not be deceived; God is not mocked, for you reap whatever you sow. ⁸If you sow to your own flesh, you will reap corruption from the flesh; but if you sow to the Spirit, you will reap eternal life from the Spirit. ⁹So let us not grow weary in doing what is right, for we will reap at harvest time, if we do not give up. ¹⁰So then, whenever we have an opportunity, let us work for the good of all, and especially for those of the family of faith.

Final Admonitions and Benediction

11 See what large letters I make when I am writing in my own hand! ¹²It is those who want to make a good showing in the flesh that try to compel you to be circumcised—only that they may not be persecuted for the cross of Christ. ¹³Even the circumcised do not themselves obey the law, but they want you to be circumcised so that they may boast about your flesh. ¹⁴May I never boast of anything except the cross of our Lord Jesus Christ, by which*ᵈ* the world has been crucified to me, and I to the world. ¹⁵For*ᵉ* neither circumcision nor uncircumcision is anything; but a new creation is everything! ¹⁶As for those who will follow this rule—peace be upon them, and mercy, and upon the Israel of God.

17 From now on, let no one make trouble for me; for I carry the marks of Jesus branded on my body.

18 May the grace of our Lord Jesus Christ be with your spirit, brothers and sisters.*ᶠ* Amen.

Keeping in Step With the Spirit

GALATIANS 5.22–26

To be in step with the Spirit is to live in such a way that we reflect the fruit of the Spirit and the characteristics of Jesus Christ.

Slowly read this passage. What word or phrase attracts your attention? Reflect on this word or phrase. What new insights surface as you continue to meditate on it? How does it touch your emotions? How does it stir your heart to pray? Gently rest in silence, being open to any impressions from God. In a journal (or on any piece of paper) write down your impressions and experiences so you can return to them later in the day.

See *Meeting God in Scripture*

---

a Other ancient authorities add *murder*   *b* Gk *Brothers*   *c* Other ancient authorities read *in this way fulfill*   *d* Or *through whom*   *e* Other ancient authorities add *in Christ Jesus*   *f* Gk *brothers*

THE LETTER OF PAUL TO THE
EPHESIANS
Rooted in Love

KEY VERSES:

I pray . . . that Christ may dwell in your hearts through faith, as you are being rooted and grounded in love. I pray that you may have the power to comprehend, with all the saints, what is the breadth and length and height and depth, and to know the love of Christ that surpasses knowledge.—Ephesians 3.16–19

"Our real problem, in failing to center down, is not a lack of time; it is, I fear, in too many of us, lack of joyful, enthusiastic delight in [God], lack of deep, deep-drawing love directed toward him at every hour of the day and night."

—THOMAS KELLY,
A Testament of Devotion

Paul's letter to the Ephesians reminds us of the importance of roots. The health of a tree is dependent on the health of its root system. Roots reach deep into the soil to draw up the necessary nourishment to sustain the tree. Deep roots create stability and help the tree withstand the storms of life. Likewise, when we are rooted in the powerful and boundless love of Jesus, we are prepared to face the challenges of living in a stormy world.

This letter calls us to imitate God (5.1) as the means of developing healthy roots. That task is made possible by being in a community of love with other Christians (4.12–16). Furthermore, our life is energized by the unconditional grace of Jesus rather than by our own human efforts (2.4–10). Throughout this letter Paul offers prayers for his readers.

Pay attention to your own root system as you read and pray through Ephesians. Pray that Jesus Christ will dwell within your heart more and more so that you are equipped to face the realities of life. Consider the spiritual habits that have sustained you in the past. What new resources does this book offer to you? How can you encourage others in the healthy planting of their roots deep into Jesus?

Salutation

1 Paul, an apostle of Christ Jesus by the will of God,

To the saints who are in Ephesus and are faithful*ᵃ* in Christ Jesus:

2 Grace to you and peace from God our Father and the Lord Jesus Christ.

Spiritual Blessings in Christ

3 Blessed be the God and Father of our Lord Jesus Christ, who has blessed us in Christ with every spiritual blessing in the heavenly places, ⁴just as he chose us in Christ*ᵇ* before the foundation of the world to be holy and blameless before him in love. ⁵He destined us for adoption as his children through Jesus Christ, according to the good pleasure of his will, ⁶to the praise of his glorious grace that he freely bestowed on us in the Beloved. ⁷In him we have redemption through his blood, the forgiveness of our trespasses, according to the riches of his grace ⁸that he lavished on us. With all wisdom and insight ⁹he has made known to us the mystery of his will, according to his good pleasure that he set forth in Christ, ¹⁰as a plan for the fullness of time, to gather up all things in him, things in heaven and things on earth. ¹¹In Christ we have also obtained an inheritance,*ᶜ* having been destined according to the purpose of him who accomplishes all things according to his counsel and will, ¹²so that we, who were the first to set our hope on Christ, might live for the praise of his glory. ¹³In him you also, when you had heard the word of truth, the gospel of your salvation, and had believed in him, were marked with the seal of the promised Holy Spirit; ¹⁴this*ᵈ* is the pledge of our inheritance toward redemption as God's own people, to the praise of his glory.

Paul's Prayer

15 I have heard of your faith in the Lord Jesus and your love*ᵉ* toward all the saints, and for this reason ¹⁶I do not cease to give thanks for you as I remember you in my prayers. ¹⁷I pray that the God of our Lord Jesus Christ, the Father of glory, may give you a spirit of wisdom and revelation as you come to know him, ¹⁸so that, with the eyes of your heart enlightened, you may know what is the hope to which he has called you, what are the riches of his glorious inheritance among the saints, ¹⁹and what is the immeasurable greatness of his power for us who believe, according to the working of his great power. ²⁰God*ᶠ* put this power to work in Christ when he raised him from the dead and seated him at his right hand in the heavenly places, ²¹far above all rule and authority and power and dominion, and above every name that is named, not only in this age but also in the age to come. ²²And he has put all things under his feet and has made him the head over all things for the church, ²³which is his body, the fullness of him who fills all in all.

a Other ancient authorities lack *in Ephesus,* reading *saints who are also faithful*   *b* Gk *in him*   *c* Or *been made a heritage*   *d* Other ancient authorities read *who*   *e* Other ancient authorities lack *and your love*   *f* Gk *He*

Chosen by Love

EPHESIANS 1.3–8

When the Bible speaks of love it is more than a sentimental or romantic concept. Love reveals the compassionate heart of God for us and God's active presence with us. We recognize God's love by paying attention to what God does on our behalf. Notice the verbs Paul uses to describe God's actions:

- blessed
- chose
- predestined
- adopted
- bestowed
- loves
- lavished

What does each verb express about God's nature? How does each verb invite you to experience your spiritual blessings in Christ? Write a brief paragraph or compose a poem about what you notice.

See Meeting God in Everyday Life

Built Into the Cornerstone

EPHESIANS 2.19–22

Imagine that you are watching God build a "household," a "holy temple" within the setting of your church community. What needs to be cleared away before the foundation can be laid? What is the foundation made of? Now God comes to add you to the building. Where does God place you? What is your function within the whole? How can you use your spiritual gifts to work alongside others in order to build up the church of Jesus Christ? What can you do to promote the building of this spiritual dwelling place for God?

See Meeting God in Community

From Death to Life

2 You were dead through the trespasses and sins [2]in which you once lived, following the course of this world, following the ruler of the power of the air, the spirit that is now at work among those who are disobedient. [3]All of us once lived among them in the passions of our flesh, following the desires of flesh and senses, and we were by nature children of wrath, like everyone else. [4]But God, who is rich in mercy, out of the great love with which he loved us [5]even when we were dead through our trespasses, made us alive together with Christ[a]—by grace you have been saved— [6]and raised us up with him and seated us with him in the heavenly places in Christ Jesus, [7]so that in the ages to come he might show the immeasurable riches of his grace in kindness toward us in Christ Jesus. [8]For by grace you have been saved through faith, and this is not your own doing; it is the gift of God— [9]not the result of works, so that no one may boast. [10]For we are what he has made us, created in Christ Jesus for good works, which God prepared beforehand to be our way of life.

One in Christ

11 So then, remember that at one time you Gentiles by birth,[b] called "the uncircumcision" by those who are called "the circumcision"—a physical circumcision made in the flesh by human hands— [12]remember that you were at that time without Christ, being aliens from the commonwealth of Israel, and strangers to the covenants of promise, having no hope and without God in the world. [13]But now in Christ Jesus you who once were far off have been brought near by the blood of Christ. [14]For he is our peace; in his flesh he has made both groups into one and has broken down the dividing wall, that is, the hostility between us. [15]He has abolished the law with its commandments and ordinances, that he might create in himself one new humanity in place of the two, thus making peace, [16]and might reconcile both groups to God in one body[c] through the cross, thus putting to death that hostility through it.[d] [17]So he came and proclaimed peace to you who were far off and peace to those who were near; [18]for through him both of us have access in one Spirit to the Father. [19]So then you are no longer strangers and aliens, but you are citizens with the saints and also members of the household of God, [20]built upon the foundation of the apostles and prophets, with Christ Jesus himself as the cornerstone.[e] [21]In him the whole structure is joined together and grows into a holy temple in the Lord; [22]in whom you also are built together spiritually[f] into a dwelling place for God.

Paul's Ministry to the Gentiles

3 This is the reason that I Paul am a prisoner for[g] Christ Jesus for the sake of you Gentiles— [2]for surely you have already heard of the commission of God's grace that was given me for you, [3]and how the mystery was made known to me by revelation, as I wrote above in a few words, [4]a reading of which will enable you to perceive my understanding of the mystery of Christ. [5]In former generations

a Other ancient authorities read *in Christ*   b Gk *in the flesh*
c Or *reconcile both of us in one body for God*   d Or *in him,* or *in himself*
e Or *keystone*   f Gk *in the Spirit*   g Or *of*

this mystery*a* was not made known to humankind, as it has now been revealed to his holy apostles and prophets by the Spirit: ⁶that is, the Gentiles have become fellow heirs, members of the same body, and sharers in the promise in Christ Jesus through the gospel.

7 Of this gospel I have become a servant according to the gift of God's grace that was given me by the working of his power. ⁸Although I am the very least of all the saints, this grace was given to me to bring to the Gentiles the news of the boundless riches of Christ, ⁹and to make everyone see*b* what is the plan of the mystery hidden for ages in*c* God who created all things; ¹⁰so that through the church the wisdom of God in its rich variety might now be made known to the rulers and authorities in the heavenly places. ¹¹This was in accordance with the eternal purpose that he has carried out in Christ Jesus our Lord, ¹²in whom we have access to God in boldness and confidence through faith in him.*d* ¹³I pray therefore that you*e* may not lose heart over my sufferings for you; they are your glory.

Prayer for the Readers

14 For this reason I bow my knees before the Father,*f* ¹⁵from whom every family*g* in heaven and on earth takes its name. ¹⁶I pray that, according to the riches of his glory, he may grant that you may be strengthened in your inner being with power through his Spirit, ¹⁷and that Christ may dwell in your hearts through faith, as you are being rooted and grounded in love. ¹⁸I pray that you may have the power to comprehend, with all the saints, what is the breadth and length and height and depth, ¹⁹and to know the love of Christ that surpasses knowledge, so that you may be filled with all the fullness of God.

20 Now to him who by the power at work within us is able to accomplish abundantly far more than all we can ask or imagine, ²¹to him be glory in the church and in Christ Jesus to all generations, forever and ever. Amen.

Unity in the Body of Christ

4 I therefore, the prisoner in the Lord, beg you to lead a life worthy of the calling to which you have been called, ²with all humility and gentleness, with patience, bearing with one another in love, ³making every effort to maintain the unity of the Spirit in the bond of peace. ⁴There is one body and one Spirit, just as you were called to the one hope of your calling, ⁵one Lord, one faith, one baptism, ⁶one God and Father of all, who is above all and through all and in all.

7 But each of us was given grace according to the measure of Christ's gift. ⁸Therefore it is said,

"When he ascended on high he made captivity
    itself a captive;
  he gave gifts to his people."

⁹(When it says, "He ascended," what does it mean but that he had also descended*h* into the lower parts of the earth? ¹⁰He who descended is the same one who ascended far above all the heavens, so that he might fill all things.) ¹¹The gifts he gave were that some would be apostles, some prophets, some evangelists, some pastors and teachers,

---

A "Walking Prayer"

EPHESIANS 3.14–19

Perhaps because we use the word "love" so carelessly, people do not take it seriously. Listen to the conversations that fill your day. You will likely hear people say, "I love that car!" (or restaurant, dress, tie, CD).

Paul had a deeper and more formative principle in mind when he prayed that the Ephesians be "rooted and grounded in love." To be rooted in love is to experience the boundless love of Jesus Christ. Use this passage as a "walking prayer." As you go about your day, frequently and gently repeat the phrase "rooted in love." Pray this phrase as you meet people, participate in activities, make decisions, drive your vehicle, and so forth. What might happen to each person or activity if they were rooted in the love of Jesus Christ? What might happen to you?

See *Meeting God in Everyday Life*

---

a Gk *it*   *b* Other ancient authorities read *to bring to light*   *c* Or *by*
d Or *the faith of him*   *e* Or *I*   *f* Other ancient authorities add *of our Lord Jesus Christ*   *g* Gk *fatherhood*   *h* Other ancient authorities add *first*

The Language of Love

EPHESIANS 4.14–16

Love is never lived out in isolation; rather it is integrated into every relationship. As we become rooted in the love of Jesus, we grow in integrity and truth. Lying denies God's love (see v.25), while honesty inspires maturity and unity in any group of which we are members.

Prayerfully reflect on this scripture, inviting Jesus to guide you as you review the ways in which you speak with others. How do you speak to God, to those closest to you and to others you meet throughout the day? How do you deal with difficult people? Try monitoring your speech for a few days, listening to how frequently you speak the language of love.

See Meeting God in Community

[12]to equip the saints for the work of ministry, for building up the body of Christ, [13]until all of us come to the unity of the faith and of the knowledge of the Son of God, to maturity, to the measure of the full stature of Christ. [14]We must no longer be children, tossed to and fro and blown about by every wind of doctrine, by people's trickery, by their craftiness in deceitful scheming. [15]But speaking the truth in love, we must grow up in every way into him who is the head, into Christ, [16]from whom the whole body, joined and knit together by every ligament with which it is equipped, as each part is working properly, promotes the body's growth in building itself up in love.

The Old Life and the New

17 Now this I affirm and insist on in the Lord: you must no longer live as the Gentiles live, in the futility of their minds. [18]They are darkened in their understanding, alienated from the life of God because of their ignorance and hardness of heart. [19]They have lost all sensitivity and have abandoned themselves to licentiousness, greedy to practice every kind of impurity. [20]That is not the way you learned Christ! [21]For surely you have heard about him and were taught in him, as truth is in Jesus. [22]You were taught to put away your former way of life, your old self, corrupt and deluded by its lusts, [23]and to be renewed in the spirit of your minds, [24]and to clothe yourselves with the new self, created according to the likeness of God in true righteousness and holiness.

Rules for the New Life

25 So then, putting away falsehood, let all of us speak the truth to our neighbors, for we are members of one another. [26]Be angry but do not sin; do not let the sun go down on your anger, [27]and do not make room for the devil. [28]Thieves must give up stealing; rather let them labor and work honestly with their own hands, so as to have something to share with the needy. [29]Let no evil talk come out of your mouths, but only what is useful for building up,[a] as there is need, so that your words may give grace to those who hear. [30]And do not grieve the Holy Spirit of God, with which you were marked with a seal for the day of redemption. [31]Put away from you all bitterness and wrath and anger and wrangling and slander, together with all malice, [32]and be kind to one another, tenderhearted, forgiving one another, as God in Christ has forgiven you.[b] [1]Therefore be imitators of God, as beloved children, [2]and live in love, as Christ loved us[c] and gave himself up for us, a fragrant offering and sacrifice to God.

Renounce Pagan Ways

3 But fornication and impurity of any kind, or greed, must not even be mentioned among you, as is proper among saints. [4]Entirely out of place is obscene, silly, and vulgar talk; but instead, let there be thanksgiving. [5]Be sure of this, that no fornicator or impure person, or one who is greedy (that is, an idolater), has any inheritance in the kingdom of Christ and of God.

6 Let no one deceive you with empty words, for because

a Other ancient authorities read *building up faith*   *b* Other ancient authorities read *us*   *c* Other ancient authorities read *you*

of these things the wrath of God comes on those who are disobedient. [7]Therefore do not be associated with them. [8]For once you were darkness, but now in the Lord you are light. Live as children of light— [9]for the fruit of the light is found in all that is good and right and true. [10]Try to find out what is pleasing to the Lord. [11]Take no part in the unfruitful works of darkness, but instead expose them. [12]For it is shameful even to mention what such people do secretly; [13]but everything exposed by the light becomes visible, [14]for everything that becomes visible is light. Therefore it says,
"Sleeper, awake!
    Rise from the dead,
    and Christ will shine on you."

15 Be careful then how you live, not as unwise people but as wise, [16]making the most of the time, because the days are evil. [17]So do not be foolish, but understand what the will of the Lord is. [18]Do not get drunk with wine, for that is debauchery; but be filled with the Spirit, [19]as you sing psalms and hymns and spiritual songs among yourselves, singing and making melody to the Lord in your hearts, [20]giving thanks to God the Father at all times and for everything in the name of our Lord Jesus Christ.

The Christian Household

21 Be subject to one another out of reverence for Christ.
22 Wives, be subject to your husbands as you are to the Lord. [23]For the husband is the head of the wife just as Christ is the head of the church, the body of which he is the Savior. [24]Just as the church is subject to Christ, so also wives ought to be, in everything, to their husbands.
25 Husbands, love your wives, just as Christ loved the church and gave himself up for her, [26]in order to make her holy by cleansing her with the washing of water by the word, [27]so as to present the church to himself in splendor, without a spot or wrinkle or anything of the kind—yes, so that she may be holy and without blemish. [28]In the same way, husbands should love their wives as they do their own bodies. He who loves his wife loves himself. [29]For no one ever hates his own body, but he nourishes and tenderly cares for it, just as Christ does for the church, [30]because we are members of his body.[a] [31]"For this reason a man will leave his father and mother and be joined to his wife, and the two will become one flesh." [32]This is a great mystery, and I am applying it to Christ and the church. [33]Each of you, however, should love his wife as himself, and a wife should respect her husband.

Children and Parents

6 Children, obey your parents in the Lord,[b] for this is right. [2]"Honor your father and mother"—this is the first commandment with a promise: [3]"so that it may be well with you and you may live long on the earth."
4 And, fathers, do not provoke your children to anger, but bring them up in the discipline and instruction of the Lord.

Slaves and Masters

5 Slaves, obey your earthly masters with fear and trem-

Good Roots Produce Healthy Fruit

EPHESIANS 5.8–11

God's love transforms us. As we begin to experience this incredible love we move from darkness to light. As a child of the light we bear the fruit of light and love. Imagine yourself as a fruit tree. Light a candle and, within its circle of illumination, draw your tree on paper with crayons or markers. What kind of fruit do you bear? Is your fruit the kind that "is pleasing to the Lord"? Who is nourished by your fruit? How can you offer yourself and your fruit for God's glory?

See Meeting God in Worship

---

a Other ancient authorities add *of his flesh and of his bones*   b Other ancient authorities lack *in the Lord*

The Ministry of Intercession

EPHESIANS 6.18–20

Paul offers three helpful guidelines for rooting our lives in prayer: depending on the Spirit, praying wherever we are, and using different forms or methods. He reminds us that prayer confronts and weakens the powers of darkness (see v.12) that seek to destroy God's love. Being rooted in love calls us to pray for others.

As you pray, remember to intercede in love for those who are:

- struggling with depression or doubt
- facing persecution and turmoil
- seeking to communicate the gospel of Jesus Christ
- trying to find hope and direction
- wrestling with failing health

Establish the habit of intercessory prayer by writing the name of at least one person on each day of your planning calendar for the next month to remind you to pray daily for others.

See Meeting God in Service

bling, in singleness of heart, as you obey Christ; 6not only while being watched, and in order to please them, but as slaves of Christ, doing the will of God from the heart. 7Render service with enthusiasm, as to the Lord and not to men and women, 8knowing that whatever good we do, we will receive the same again from the Lord, whether we are slaves or free.

9 And, masters, do the same to them. Stop threatening them, for you know that both of you have the same Master in heaven, and with him there is no partiality.

The Whole Armor of God

10 Finally, be strong in the Lord and in the strength of his power. 11Put on the whole armor of God, so that you may be able to stand against the wiles of the devil. 12For our[a] struggle is not against enemies of blood and flesh, but against the rulers, against the authorities, against the cosmic powers of this present darkness, against the spiritual forces of evil in the heavenly places. 13Therefore take up the whole armor of God, so that you may be able to withstand on that evil day, and having done everything, to stand firm. 14Stand therefore, and fasten the belt of truth around your waist, and put on the breastplate of righteousness. 15As shoes for your feet put on whatever will make you ready to proclaim the gospel of peace. 16With all of these,[b] take the shield of faith, with which you will be able to quench all the flaming arrows of the evil one. 17Take the helmet of salvation, and the sword of the Spirit, which is the word of God.

18 Pray in the Spirit at all times in every prayer and supplication. To that end keep alert and always persevere in supplication for all the saints. 19Pray also for me, so that when I speak, a message may be given to me to make known with boldness the mystery of the gospel,[c] 20for which I am an ambassador in chains. Pray that I may declare it boldly, as I must speak.

Personal Matters and Benediction

21 So that you also may know how I am and what I am doing, Tychicus will tell you everything. He is a dear brother and a faithful minister in the Lord. 22I am sending him to you for this very purpose, to let you know how we are, and to encourage your hearts.

23 Peace be to the whole community,[d] and love with faith, from God the Father and the Lord Jesus Christ. 24Grace be with all who have an undying love for our Lord Jesus Christ.[e]

a Other ancient authorities read *your*   b Or *In all circumstances*   c Other ancient authorities lack *of the gospel*   d Gk *to the brothers*   e Other ancient authorities add *Amen*

THE LETTER OF PAUL TO THE
PHILIPPIANS
A Work in Progress

KEY VERSE:

I am confident of this, that the one who began a good work among you will bring it to completion by the day of Jesus Christ.—Philippians 1.6

One of the characteristics of our contemporary culture is impatience. Advances in technology encourage us to demand ever more in less time. Unfortunately the continued pressure to rush everything has reduced our ability to wait for anything.

Some aspects of life, however, cannot be rushed. Spiritual growth is no different than physical growth—both require time and great patience. And when we experience growth, it is not always easy to detect. Progress sometimes seems meager. Perhaps that is why Christians have often been called a pilgrim people. Our lives reflect the process of God's work more than any polished final product.

In an age of instant gratification, the apostle Paul proclaims a countercultural message. He reminds us to be patient because God's work in us is not finished. Regardless of how long we have been concentrating on growing spiritually, we are still beginners—and always will be—until we reach heaven. Paul encourages us to press on and not give up. He emphasizes that Christian maturity is a process of cooperating with God's presence and power in our lives.

The message of Philippians is one of patience and hope. Perhaps this book will renew your stagnant life or give you permission to seek excellence rather than perfection in all you do. Regardless of where you find yourself, let these words inspire and invite you into deeper participation with the God who seeks to join you in spiritual partnership.

"Those who think that they have arrived, have lost their way. Those who think they have reached their goal, have missed it. Those who think they are saints, are demons. An important part of the spiritual life is to keep longing, waiting, hoping, expecting."

—HENRI J. M. NOUWEN,
The Genesee Diary

God's Work Will Be Completed

PHILIPPIANS 1.3–6

In this letter Paul warmly and joyfully expresses the confidence that God will complete the work of faith and growth in those who are in Christ Jesus. Paul's prayer for his readers is that they may grow in love, in knowledge and insight, and that they may produce the harvest of righteousness.

It's important to look at where we've been and where God is taking us in our spiritual lives (see Psalm 77.11; 105.5; 143.5). If you have been following Jesus for a number of years, recall what your life was like at the beginning of your journey. How have you grown? If you are a more recent Christian, reflect on the promises and faithfulness of God, who calls you to spiritual maturity. What specific aspect of hope or encouragement does this passage offer? Draw a picture that illustrates God's work in your life today. What colors will you select? Do the colors have any particular significance?

See Meeting God in Everyday Life

Salutation

1 Paul and Timothy, servants*ᵃ* of Christ Jesus,
To all the saints in Christ Jesus who are in Philippi, with the bishops*ᵇ* and deacons:*ᶜ*
2 Grace to you and peace from God our Father and the Lord Jesus Christ.

Paul's Prayer for the Philippians

3 I thank my God every time I remember you, ⁴constantly praying with joy in every one of my prayers for all of you, ⁵because of your sharing in the gospel from the first day until now. ⁶I am confident of this, that the one who began a good work among you will bring it to completion by the day of Jesus Christ. ⁷It is right for me to think this way about all of you, because you hold me in your heart,*ᵈ* for all of you share in God's grace*ᵉ* with me, both in my imprisonment and in the defense and confirmation of the gospel. ⁸For God is my witness, how I long for all of you with the compassion of Christ Jesus. ⁹And this is my prayer, that your love may overflow more and more with knowledge and full insight ¹⁰to help you to determine what is best, so that in the day of Christ you may be pure and blameless, ¹¹having produced the harvest of righteousness that comes through Jesus Christ for the glory and praise of God.

Paul's Present Circumstances

12 I want you to know, beloved,*ᶠ* that what has happened to me has actually helped to spread the gospel, ¹³so that it has become known throughout the whole imperial guard*ᵍ* and to everyone else that my imprisonment is for Christ; ¹⁴and most of the brothers and sisters,*ᶠ* having been made confident in the Lord by my imprisonment, dare to speak the word*ʰ* with greater boldness and without fear.

15 Some proclaim Christ from envy and rivalry, but others from goodwill. ¹⁶These proclaim Christ out of love, knowing that I have been put here for the defense of the gospel; ¹⁷the others proclaim Christ out of selfish ambition, not sincerely but intending to increase my suffering in my imprisonment. ¹⁸What does it matter? Just this, that Christ is proclaimed in every way, whether out of false motives or true; and in that I rejoice.

Yes, and I will continue to rejoice, ¹⁹for I know that through your prayers and the help of the Spirit of Jesus Christ this will turn out for my deliverance. ²⁰It is my eager expectation and hope that I will not be put to shame in any way, but that by my speaking with all boldness, Christ will be exalted now as always in my body, whether by life or by death. ²¹For to me, living is Christ and dying is gain. ²²If I am to live in the flesh, that means fruitful labor for me; and I do not know which I prefer. ²³I am hard pressed between the two: my desire is to depart and be with Christ, for that is far better; ²⁴but to remain in the flesh is more necessary for you. ²⁵Since I am convinced of this, I know that I will remain and continue with all of you for your progress and joy in faith, ²⁶so that I may share abundantly in your boasting in Christ Jesus when I come to you again.

a Gk *slaves*   *b* Or *overseers*   *c* Or *overseers and helpers*   *d* Or *because I hold you in my heart*   *e* Gk *in grace*   *f* Gk *brothers*   *g* Gk *whole praetorium*   *h* Other ancient authorities read *word of God*

27 Only, live your life in a manner worthy of the gospel of Christ, so that, whether I come and see you or am absent and hear about you, I will know that you are standing firm in one spirit, striving side by side with one mind for the faith of the gospel, 28and are in no way intimidated by your opponents. For them this is evidence of their destruction, but of your salvation. And this is God's doing. 29For he has graciously granted you the privilege not only of believing in Christ, but of suffering for him as well— 30since you are having the same struggle that you saw I had and now hear that I still have.

Imitating Christ's Humility

2 If then there is any encouragement in Christ, any consolation from love, any sharing in the Spirit, any compassion and sympathy, 2make my joy complete: be of the same mind, having the same love, being in full accord and of one mind. 3Do nothing from selfish ambition or conceit, but in humility regard others as better than yourselves. 4Let each of you look not to your own interests, but to the interests of others. 5Let the same mind be in you that was*a* in Christ Jesus,

6   who, though he was in the form of God,
      did not regard equality with God
      as something to be exploited,
7   but emptied himself,
      taking the form of a slave,
      being born in human likeness.
   And being found in human form,
8   he humbled himself
      and became obedient to the point of death—
      even death on a cross.

9   Therefore God also highly exalted him
      and gave him the name
      that is above every name,
10   so that at the name of Jesus
      every knee should bend,
      in heaven and on earth and under the earth,
11   and every tongue should confess
      that Jesus Christ is Lord,
      to the glory of God the Father.

Shining as Lights in the World

12 Therefore, my beloved, just as you have always obeyed me, not only in my presence, but much more now in my absence, work out your own salvation with fear and trembling; 13for it is God who is at work in you, enabling you both to will and to work for his good pleasure.

14 Do all things without murmuring and arguing, 15so that you may be blameless and innocent, children of God without blemish in the midst of a crooked and perverse generation, in which you shine like stars in the world. 16It is by your holding fast to the word of life that I can boast on the day of Christ that I did not run in vain or labor in vain. 17But even if I am being poured out as a libation over the sacrifice and the offering of your faith, I am glad and rejoice with all of you— 18and in the same way you also must be glad and rejoice with me.

a Or *that you have*

Working In, Working Out

PHILIPPIANS 2.12–14

"You have to work out with concentration and care what God works in; not work your own salvation, but work it out, while you base resolutely in unshaken faith on the complete and perfect Redemption of the Lord . . . God is the source of your will, therefore you are able to work out [God's] will."

—OSWALD CHAMBERS,
My Utmost for His Highest

Claiming the Prize

PHILIPPIANS 3.12–14

In this passage the apostle Paul shares his vision of the eternal prize—a prize that Christ Jesus has already won, yet a prize that prompts the apostle to look heavenward.

What prize do you reach for? (See also 3.7–11.)

What vision do Paul's words prompt in you concerning your life in Christ? Be open to any insight or impressions from God. Based on this passage, write three goals for your own life in Christ.

See Meeting God in Scripture

Timothy and Epaphroditus

19 I hope in the Lord Jesus to send Timothy to you soon, so that I may be cheered by news of you. 20I have no one like him who will be genuinely concerned for your welfare. 21All of them are seeking their own interests, not those of Jesus Christ. 22But Timothy's*a* worth you know, how like a son with a father he has served with me in the work of the gospel. 23I hope therefore to send him as soon as I see how things go with me; 24and I trust in the Lord that I will also come soon.

25 Still, I think it necessary to send to you Epaphroditus—my brother and co-worker and fellow soldier, your messenger*b* and minister to my need; 26for he has been longing for*c* all of you, and has been distressed because you heard that he was ill. 27He was indeed so ill that he nearly died. But God had mercy on him, and not only on him but on me also, so that I would not have one sorrow after another. 28I am the more eager to send him, therefore, in order that you may rejoice at seeing him again, and that I may be less anxious. 29Welcome him then in the Lord with all joy, and honor such people, 30because he came close to death for the work of Christ,*d* risking his life to make up for those services that you could not give me.

3 Finally, my brothers and sisters,*e* rejoice*f* in the Lord.

Breaking with the Past

To write the same things to you is not troublesome to me, and for you it is a safeguard.

2 Beware of the dogs, beware of the evil workers, beware of those who mutilate the flesh!*g* 3For it is we who are the circumcision, who worship in the Spirit of God*h* and boast in Christ Jesus and have no confidence in the flesh—4even though I, too, have reason for confidence in the flesh.

If anyone else has reason to be confident in the flesh, I have more: 5circumcised on the eighth day, a member of the people of Israel, of the tribe of Benjamin, a Hebrew born of Hebrews; as to the law, a Pharisee; 6as to zeal, a persecutor of the church; as to righteousness under the law, blameless.

7 Yet whatever gains I had, these I have come to regard as loss because of Christ. 8More than that, I regard everything as loss because of the surpassing value of knowing Christ Jesus my Lord. For his sake I have suffered the loss of all things, and I regard them as rubbish, in order that I may gain Christ 9and be found in him, not having a righteousness of my own that comes from the law, but one that comes through faith in Christ,*i* the righteousness from God based on faith. 10I want to know Christ*j* and the power of his resurrection and the sharing of his sufferings by becoming like him in his death, 11if somehow I may attain the resurrection from the dead.

Pressing toward the Goal

12 Not that I have already obtained this or have already

---

a Gk *his*   *b* Gk *apostle*   *c* Other ancient authorities read *longing to see*
d Other ancient authorities read *of the Lord*   *e* Gk *my brothers*
f Or *farewell*   *g* Gk *the mutilation*   *h* Other ancient authorities read
worship God in spirit   *i* Or *through the faith of Christ*   *j* Gk *him*

reached the goal;[a] but I press on to make it my own, because Christ Jesus has made me his own. [13]Beloved,[b] I do
not consider that I have made it my own;[c] but this one
thing I do: forgetting what lies behind and straining forward
to what lies ahead, [14]I press on toward the goal for the prize
of the heavenly[d] call of God in Christ Jesus. [15]Let those of us
then who are mature be of the same mind; and if you think
differently about anything, this too God will reveal to you.
[16]Only let us hold fast to what we have attained.

17 Brothers and sisters,[b] join in imitating me, and observe those who live according to the example you have in
us. [18]For many live as enemies of the cross of Christ; I have
often told you of them, and now I tell you even with tears.
[19]Their end is destruction; their god is the belly; and their
glory is in their shame; their minds are set on earthly
things. [20]But our citizenship[e] is in heaven, and it is from
there that we are expecting a Savior, the Lord Jesus Christ.
[21]He will transform the body of our humiliation[f] that it may
be conformed to the body of his glory,[g] by the power that
also enables him to make all things subject to himself.
4 [1]Therefore, my brothers and sisters,[h] whom I love and
long for, my joy and crown, stand firm in the Lord in
this way, my beloved.

Exhortations

2 I urge Euodia and I urge Syntyche to be of the same
mind in the Lord. [3]Yes, and I ask you also, my loyal companion,[i] help these women, for they have struggled beside
me in the work of the gospel, together with Clement and
the rest of my co-workers, whose names are in the book of
life.

4 Rejoice[j] in the Lord always; again I will say, Rejoice.[j]
[5]Let your gentleness be known to everyone. The Lord is
near. [6]Do not worry about anything, but in everything by
prayer and supplication with thanksgiving let your requests
be made known to God. [7]And the peace of God, which surpasses all understanding, will guard your hearts and your
minds in Christ Jesus.

8 Finally, beloved,[k] whatever is true, whatever is honorable, whatever is just, whatever is pure, whatever is pleasing, whatever is commendable, if there is any excellence
and if there is anything worthy of praise, think about[l] these
things. [9]Keep on doing the things that you have learned
and received and heard and seen in me, and the God of
peace will be with you.

Acknowledgment of the Philippians' Gift

10 I rejoice[m] in the Lord greatly that now at last you have
revived your concern for me; indeed, you were concerned
for me, but had no opportunity to show it.[n] [11]Not that I am
referring to being in need; for I have learned to be content
with whatever I have. [12]I know what it is to have little, and
I know what it is to have plenty. In any and all circumstances I have learned the secret of being well-fed and of

---

Inventory of Peace

PHILIPPIANS 4.4–9

What images and impressions
does the word "peace" create
for you? The word peace has
rich Biblical connotations of
reconciliation, wholeness,
health and unity. The apostle
Paul often greets fellow Christians with the words *grace and
peace* (see Romans 1.7; 1 Corinthians 1.3; Galatians 1.3).

Read and ponder these
words of scripture. Make two
columns on a page of your journal. In one column list some of
the things that rob you of
peace. In the other column note
some things that give you a
sense of peace. Which column
reflects the condition you find
yourself in most often? How
can this scripture passage guide
you into greater peace?

See *Meeting God in Scripture*

---

a Or *have already been made perfect*   b Gk *Brothers*   c Other ancient
authorities read *my own yet*   d Gk *upward*   e Or *commonwealth*
f Or *our humble bodies*   g Or *his glorious body*   h Gk *my brothers*
i Or *loyal Syzygus*   j Or *Farewell*   k Gk *brothers*   l Gk *take account of*
m Gk *I rejoiced*   n Gk lacks *to show it*

Renewing Abundance

PHILIPPIANS 4.19

"Providence is the almighty and ever present power of God by which [God] upholds, as with [God's] hand, heaven and earth and all creatures, and so rules them that leaf and blade, rain and drought, fruitful and lean years, food and drink, health and sickness, prosperity and poverty—all things, in fact, come to us not by chance but from [God's] fatherly hand."

—*Heidelberg Catechism*, Lord's Day 10, Question and Answer 27

See *Meeting God in the Created Order*

going hungry, of having plenty and of being in need. [13]I can do all things through him who strengthens me. [14]In any case, it was kind of you to share my distress.

15 You Philippians indeed know that in the early days of the gospel, when I left Macedonia, no church shared with me in the matter of giving and receiving, except you alone. [16]For even when I was in Thessalonica, you sent me help for my needs more than once. [17]Not that I seek the gift, but I seek the profit that accumulates to your account. [18]I have been paid in full and have more than enough; I am fully satisfied, now that I have received from Epaphroditus the gifts you sent, a fragrant offering, a sacrifice acceptable and pleasing to God. [19]And my God will fully satisfy every need of yours according to his riches in glory in Christ Jesus. [20]To our God and Father be glory forever and ever. Amen.

Final Greetings and Benediction

21 Greet every saint in Christ Jesus. The friends*a* who are with me greet you. [22]All the saints greet you, especially those of the emperor's household.

23 The grace of the Lord Jesus Christ be with your spirit.*b*

a Gk *brothers*   *b* Other ancient authorities add *Amen*

THE LETTER OF PAUL TO THE
COLOSSIANS
A Heart Set on God

KEY VERSE:

So if you have been raised with Christ, seek the things that are above, where Christ is,
seated at the right hand of God.—Colossians 3.1

Sometimes we fool ourselves, believing it is more difficult to live today than two thousand years ago. However the Christians of the first century faced equal or greater challenges to their faith. The apostle Paul seeks to etch deeply into human hearts the truth that meaning and purpose do not come through any exclusive knowledge or superior spirituality. Rather they are firmly established in the life of Jesus Christ, in whom God was pleased to dwell with all the divine fullness. Paul understands the serious crisis before his readers and seeks to weave these words into a fabric of practical guidance that clothes them with hearts that seek to focus on God. In pondering these words of Scripture, remember that the Bible uses the word "heart" to speak of mind, soul and will. How can the book of Colossians help you devote your life to God in all of these areas?

"O to grace how great a
debtor daily I'm
constrained to be!
Let thy goodness, like a
fetter, bind my
wandering heart to thee.
Prone to wander, Lord, I
feel it, prone to leave
the God I love;
Here's my heart, O take and
seal it; seal it for thy
courts above."
—ROBERT ROBINSON,
"Come, Thou Fount of Every Blessing"

Motivated Living

COLOSSIANS 1.15–20

This beautiful hymn to Jesus Christ contains several wonderful images of his supremacy. List them using your own words. Then choose one of these images and meditate on it. Draw, paint or fashion some sort of creative expression that reflects your experience of pondering this scripture. Keep it in your place of prayer to encourage you daily.

See Meeting God in the Created Order

Salutation

1 Paul, an apostle of Christ Jesus by the will of God, and Timothy our brother,

2 To the saints and faithful brothers and sisters*a* in Christ in Colossae:

Grace to you and peace from God our Father.

Paul Thanks God for the Colossians

3 In our prayers for you we always thank God, the Father of our Lord Jesus Christ, *4*for we have heard of your faith in Christ Jesus and of the love that you have for all the saints, *5*because of the hope laid up for you in heaven. You have heard of this hope before in the word of the truth, the gospel *6*that has come to you. Just as it is bearing fruit and growing in the whole world, so it has been bearing fruit among yourselves from the day you heard it and truly comprehended the grace of God. *7*This you learned from Epaphras, our beloved fellow servant.*b* He is a faithful minister of Christ on your*c* behalf, *8*and he has made known to us your love in the Spirit.

9 For this reason, since the day we heard it, we have not ceased praying for you and asking that you may be filled with the knowledge of God's*d* will in all spiritual wisdom and understanding, *10*so that you may lead lives worthy of the Lord, fully pleasing to him, as you bear fruit in every good work and as you grow in the knowledge of God. *11*May you be made strong with all the strength that comes from his glorious power, and may you be prepared to endure everything with patience, while joyfully *12*giving thanks to the Father, who has enabled*e* you*f* to share in the inheritance of the saints in the light. *13*He has rescued us from the power of darkness and transferred us into the kingdom of his beloved Son, *14*in whom we have redemption, the forgiveness of sins.*g*

The Supremacy of Christ

15 He is the image of the invisible God, the firstborn of all creation; *16*for in*h* him all things in heaven and on earth were created, things visible and invisible, whether thrones or dominions or rulers or powers—all things have been created through him and for him. *17*He himself is before all things, and in*h* him all things hold together. *18*He is the head of the body, the church; he is the beginning, the firstborn from the dead, so that he might come to have first place in everything. *19*For in him all the fullness of God was pleased to dwell, *20*and through him God was pleased to reconcile to himself all things, whether on earth or in heaven, by making peace through the blood of his cross.

21 And you who were once estranged and hostile in mind, doing evil deeds, *22*he has now reconciled*i* in his fleshly body*j* through death, so as to present you holy and blameless and irreproachable before him— *23*provided that you continue securely established and steadfast in the faith, without shifting from the hope promised by the gospel that you heard, which has been proclaimed to every creature under heaven. I, Paul, became a servant of this gospel.

a Gk *brothers*   *b* Gk *slave*   *c* Other ancient authorities read *our*
d Gk *his*   *e* Other ancient authorities read *called*   *f* Other ancient
authorities read *us*   *g* Other ancient authorities add *through his blood*
h Or *by*   *i* Other ancient authorities read *you have now been reconciled*
j Gk *in the body of his flesh*

Paul's Interest in the Colossians

24 I am now rejoicing in my sufferings for your sake, and in my flesh I am completing what is lacking in Christ's afflictions for the sake of his body, that is, the church. 25I became its servant according to God's commission that was given to me for you, to make the word of God fully known, 26the mystery that has been hidden throughout the ages and generations but has now been revealed to his saints. 27To them God chose to make known how great among the Gentiles are the riches of the glory of this mystery, which is Christ in you, the hope of glory. 28It is he whom we proclaim, warning everyone and teaching everyone in all wisdom, so that we may present everyone mature in Christ. 29For this I toil and struggle with all the energy that he powerfully inspires within me.

2 For I want you to know how much I am struggling for you, and for those in Laodicea, and for all who have not seen me face to face. 2I want their hearts to be encouraged and united in love, so that they may have all the riches of assured understanding and have the knowledge of God's mystery, that is, Christ himself,*a* 3in whom are hidden all the treasures of wisdom and knowledge. 4I am saying this so that no one may deceive you with plausible arguments. 5For though I am absent in body, yet I am with you in spirit, and I rejoice to see your morale and the firmness of your faith in Christ.

Fullness of Life in Christ

6 As you therefore have received Christ Jesus the Lord, continue to live your lives*b* in him, 7rooted and built up in him and established in the faith, just as you were taught, abounding in thanksgiving.

8 See to it that no one takes you captive through philosophy and empty deceit, according to human tradition, according to the elemental spirits of the universe,*c* and not according to Christ. 9For in him the whole fullness of deity dwells bodily, 10and you have come to fullness in him, who is the head of every ruler and authority. 11In him also you were circumcised with a spiritual circumcision,*d* by putting off the body of the flesh in the circumcision of Christ; 12when you were buried with him in baptism, you were also raised with him through faith in the power of God, who raised him from the dead. 13And when you were dead in trespasses and the uncircumcision of your flesh, God*e* made you*f* alive together with him, when he forgave us all our trespasses, 14erasing the record that stood against us with its legal demands. He set this aside, nailing it to the cross. 15He disarmed*g* the rulers and authorities and made a public example of them, triumphing over them in it.

16 Therefore do not let anyone condemn you in matters of food and drink or of observing festivals, new moons, or sabbaths. 17These are only a shadow of what is to come, but the substance belongs to Christ. 18Do not let anyone disqualify you, insisting on self-abasement and worship of angels, dwelling*h* on visions,*i* puffed up without cause by a

---

Experiencing the Mystery

COLOSSIANS 1.27

Our western world has a strong desire to analyze and explain everything. While knowledge and understanding are essential for the Christian, there are some aspects of the faith that defy explanation. John Calvin, the sixteenth-century Swiss reformer, understood this. As he was struggling to understand Jesus' presence in the Lord's Supper, he reached a point where he confessed, "I would rather experience than understand it" (John Calvin, *Institutes of the Christian Religion*). What would it mean for you to experience this verse? Seek the Spirit's guidance as you pray and ponder the good news that Jesus Christ is in you. Use your imagination as you engage this scripture and quietly rest in this mystery. Conclude your time with a prayer of gratitude and commitment. Create some symbol or picture to remind you of Christ's indwelling presence in your life.

See *Meeting God in Scripture*

---

a Other ancient authorities read *of the mystery of God, both of the Father and of Christ*   *b* Gk *to walk*   *c* Or *the rudiments of the world*   *d* Gk *a circumcision made without hands*   *e* Gk *he*   *f* Other ancient authorities read *made us*; others, *made*   *g* Or *divested himself of*   *h* Other ancient authorities read *not dwelling*   *i* Meaning of Gk uncertain

Guidelines for a Healthy Heart

COLOSSIANS 3.1–4

Your physical heart requires a balanced diet to remain healthy. Your spiritual heart is no different. It too requires a healthy diet to function and equip you to know the love, grace, forgiveness, wonder and joy of God.

Where do you normally set your heart? How does that help you experience God? How does that hinder you from experiencing God? What spiritual habits encourage you in cultivating a heart for God? What is the greatest competition for your heart? How does that affect your relationship with God? What one request would you like to ask of Jesus to help you set your heart on things above? Record it and pay attention to how God answers your prayer.

See *Meeting God in Prayer*

human way of thinking,[a] [19]and not holding fast to the head, from whom the whole body, nourished and held together by its ligaments and sinews, grows with a growth that is from God.

Warnings against False Teachers

20 If with Christ you died to the elemental spirits of the universe,[b] why do you live as if you still belonged to the world? Why do you submit to regulations, [21]"Do not handle, Do not taste, Do not touch"? [22]All these regulations refer to things that perish with use; they are simply human commands and teachings. [23]These have indeed an appearance of wisdom in promoting self-imposed piety, humility, and severe treatment of the body, but they are of no value in checking self-indulgence.[c]

The New Life in Christ

3 So if you have been raised with Christ, seek the things that are above, where Christ is, seated at the right hand of God. [2]Set your minds on things that are above, not on things that are on earth, [3]for you have died, and your life is hidden with Christ in God. [4]When Christ who is your[d] life is revealed, then you also will be revealed with him in glory.

5 Put to death, therefore, whatever in you is earthly: fornication, impurity, passion, evil desire, and greed (which is idolatry). [6]On account of these the wrath of God is coming on those who are disobedient.[e] [7]These are the ways you also once followed, when you were living that life.[f] [8]But now you must get rid of all such things—anger, wrath, malice, slander, and abusive[g] language from your mouth. [9]Do not lie to one another, seeing that you have stripped off the old self with its practices [10]and have clothed yourselves with the new self, which is being renewed in knowledge according to the image of its creator. [11]In that renewal[h] there is no longer Greek and Jew, circumcised and uncircumcised, barbarian, Scythian, slave and free; but Christ is all and in all!

12 As God's chosen ones, holy and beloved, clothe yourselves with compassion, kindness, humility, meekness, and patience. [13]Bear with one another and, if anyone has a complaint against another, forgive each other; just as the Lord[i] has forgiven you, so you also must forgive. [14]Above all, clothe yourselves with love, which binds everything together in perfect harmony. [15]And let the peace of Christ rule in your hearts, to which indeed you were called in the one body. And be thankful. [16]Let the word of Christ[j] dwell in you richly; teach and admonish one another in all wisdom; and with gratitude in your hearts sing psalms, hymns, and spiritual songs to God.[k] [17]And whatever you do, in word or deed, do everything in the name of the Lord Jesus, giving thanks to God the Father through him.

Rules for Christian Households

18 Wives, be subject to your husbands, as is fitting in

a Gk *by the mind of his flesh*   b Or *the rudiments of the world*   c Or *are of no value, serving only to indulge the flesh*   d Other authorities read *our*   e Other ancient authorities lack *on those who are disobedient* (Gk *the children of disobedience*)   f Or *living among such people*   g Or *filthy*   h Gk *its creator*, [ii]*where*   i Other ancient authorities read *just as Christ*   j Other ancient authorities read *of God*, or *of the Lord*   k Other ancient authorities read *to the Lord*

the Lord. [19]Husbands, love your wives and never treat them harshly.

20 Children, obey your parents in everything, for this is your acceptable duty in the Lord. [21]Fathers, do not provoke your children, or they may lose heart. [22]Slaves, obey your earthly masters[a] in everything, not only while being watched and in order to please them, but wholeheartedly, fearing the Lord.[a] [23]Whatever your task, put yourselves into it, as done for the Lord and not for your masters,[b] [24]since you know that from the Lord you will receive the inheritance as your reward; you serve[c] the Lord Christ. [25]For the wrongdoer will be paid back for whatever wrong has been done, and there is no partiality. [1]Masters, treat your slaves justly and fairly, for you know that you also have a Master in heaven.

Further Instructions

2 Devote yourselves to prayer, keeping alert in it with thanksgiving. [3]At the same time pray for us as well that God will open to us a door for the word, that we may declare the mystery of Christ, for which I am in prison, [4]so that I may reveal it clearly, as I should.

5 Conduct yourselves wisely toward outsiders, making the most of the time.[d] [6]Let your speech always be gracious, seasoned with salt, so that you may know how you ought to answer everyone.

Final Greetings and Benediction

7 Tychicus will tell you all the news about me; he is a beloved brother, a faithful minister, and a fellow servant[e] in the Lord. [8]I have sent him to you for this very purpose, so that you may know how we are[f] and that he may encourage your hearts; [9]he is coming with Onesimus, the faithful and beloved brother, who is one of you. They will tell you about everything here.

10 Aristarchus my fellow prisoner greets you, as does Mark the cousin of Barnabas, concerning whom you have received instructions—if he comes to you, welcome him. [11]And Jesus who is called Justus greets you. These are the only ones of the circumcision among my co-workers for the kingdom of God, and they have been a comfort to me. [12]Epaphras, who is one of you, a servant[e] of Christ Jesus, greets you. He is always wrestling in his prayers on your behalf, so that you may stand mature and fully assured in everything that God wills. [13]For I testify for him that he has worked hard for you and for those in Laodicea and in Hierapolis. [14]Luke, the beloved physician, and Demas greet you. [15]Give my greetings to the brothers and sisters[g] in Laodicea, and to Nympha and the church in her house. [16]And when this letter has been read among you, have it read also in the church of the Laodiceans; and see that you read also the letter from Laodicea. [17]And say to Archippus, "See that you complete the task that you have received in the Lord."

18 I, Paul, write this greeting with my own hand. Remember my chains. Grace be with you.[h]

---

a In Greek the same word is used for *master* and *Lord*   b Gk *not for men*
c Or *you are slaves of*, or *be slaves of*   d Or *opportunity*   e Gk *slave*
f Other authorities read *that I may know how you are*   g Gk *brothers*
h Other ancient authorities add *Amen*

Supportive Care for Seeking Hearts

COLOSSIANS 4.7–9

Soul friends are a special gift from God. Tychicus served in that capacity for Paul by being a beloved brother, a faithful minister and a fellow servant.

Do you have a Tychicus in your life? How has he or she supported you in your faith? When have you last told this person how glad you are to have him or her in your life? For whom are you a Tychicus? How do you seek to encourage his or her heart in Jesus Christ? Remember, in particular, the wonderful opportunity of supporting children and young people as they seek to know Jesus. This week select one person whose heart you can encourage for God.

See *Meeting God in Service*

THE FIRST LETTER OF PAUL TO THE
THESSALONIANS

Waiting in Holiness

KEY VERSE:

And may he so strengthen your hearts in holiness that you may be blameless before our God and Father at the coming of our Lord Jesus with all his saints.—1 Thessalonians 3.13

"Finish, then, thy new creation; pure and spotless let us be;
Let us see thy great salvation perfectly restored in thee:
Changed from glory into glory, till in heaven we take our place,
Till we cast our crowns before thee, lost in wonder, love and praise."
—CHARLES WESLEY, "Love Divine, All Loves Excelling"

How often don't we wish for a friend who could give us spiritual help—not just casual advice, but powerful counsel that would lead us to a closer relationship with God (2.12). The Christians of Thessalonica had such a friend in the apostle Paul. As he writes, Paul is open about his affection for them, his longing to be their guide and religious instructor, and his pride in their success in living lives worthy of God's calling. He is thrilled when Timothy reports that the faith and love Paul remembered as characteristic of them was still alive and flourishing among these faithful converts.

Paul's affection for the Thessalonians is so endearing that we might be reminded of a similar friend of our own. Imagine returning home one day and finding a letter waiting in the mail from just such an old friend. More than once you have wished you could sit and talk with this friend because he or she is a good listener and always knows just what to say to point you in the right direction.

Now imagine that this friend is someone like Paul, a person of considerable stature, who is keenly interested in the things you do, say and think. In your last letter to this friend, what did you write about? What was weighing heavily on your heart? What joys did you share? Now how does this person's letter of response to you begin? What concern seems most important? What does your friend wish for you most of all? Read the book of 1 Thessalonians as if it were such a letter, written just for you and your faith community.

Salutation

1 Paul, Silvanus, and Timothy,

To the church of the Thessalonians in God the Father and the Lord Jesus Christ:

Grace to you and peace.

The Thessalonians' Faith and Example

2 We always give thanks to God for all of you and mention you in our prayers, constantly ³remembering before our God and Father your work of faith and labor of love and steadfastness of hope in our Lord Jesus Christ. ⁴For we know, brothers and sisters*ᵃ* beloved by God, that he has chosen you, ⁵because our message of the gospel came to you not in word only, but also in power and in the Holy Spirit and with full conviction; just as you know what kind of persons we proved to be among you for your sake. ⁶And you became imitators of us and of the Lord, for in spite of persecution you received the word with joy inspired by the Holy Spirit, ⁷so that you became an example to all the believers in Macedonia and in Achaia. ⁸For the word of the Lord has sounded forth from you not only in Macedonia and Achaia, but in every place your faith in God has become known, so that we have no need to speak about it. ⁹For the people of those regions*ᵇ* report about us what kind of welcome we had among you, and how you turned to God from idols, to serve a living and true God, ¹⁰and to wait for his Son from heaven, whom he raised from the dead— Jesus, who rescues us from the wrath that is coming.

Paul's Ministry in Thessalonica

2 You yourselves know, brothers and sisters,*ᵃ* that our coming to you was not in vain, ²but though we had already suffered and been shamefully mistreated at Philippi, as you know, we had courage in our God to declare to you the gospel of God in spite of great opposition. ³For our appeal does not spring from deceit or impure motives or trickery, ⁴but just as we have been approved by God to be entrusted with the message of the gospel, even so we speak, not to please mortals, but to please God who tests our hearts. ⁵As you know and as God is our witness, we never came with words of flattery or with a pretext for greed; ⁶nor did we seek praise from mortals, whether from you or from others, ⁷though we might have made demands as apostles of Christ. But we were gentle*ᶜ* among you, like a nurse tenderly caring for her own children. ⁸So deeply do we care for you that we are determined to share with you not only the gospel of God but also our own selves, because you have become very dear to us.

9 You remember our labor and toil, brothers and sisters;*ᵃ* we worked night and day, so that we might not burden any of you while we proclaimed to you the gospel of God. ¹⁰You are witnesses, and God also, how pure, upright, and blameless our conduct was toward you believers. ¹¹As you know, we dealt with each one of you like a father with his children, ¹²urging and encouraging you and pleading that you lead a life worthy of God, who calls you into his own kingdom and glory.

13 We also constantly give thanks to God for this, that

Thank You, My Friend in Christ

1 THESSALONIANS 1.1

The apostle Paul is very appreciative of his partners in ministry. In the opening verse of this letter, he mentions two of them, Silvanus and Timothy. Paul knows he needs others to share the mission of spreading the Good News as well as to bolster him when he is discouraged. Paul's gratitude prompts us to reflect on our own friendships rooted in a shared faith and a common mission.

Who are the people who have shared your journey and made a difference in your life with Jesus Christ? Sometimes a letter is the best way to tell them how grateful you are for their presence in your life. To which friend will you write today? How was that friend transparent enough to let the presence of Jesus shine through them on your behalf? How did that friend influence your prayer life? What plan do you have for writing your other friends?

See Meeting God in Community

A Pastor's Prayer

1 THESSALONIANS 3.9–13

What a wonderful prayer Paul offers for his friends in Thessalonica! Picture in your mind someone who has been important in helping you to grow in Jesus Christ: a former pastor, evangelist, teacher or other mentor. Picture this person praying for you with the same insight and concern Paul shows in these words. Read these words slowly and carefully so that they sink in. Rejoice in the knowledge that this person prays for you, if not with these exact words, then with other words of love flowing from their spirit.

Close your prayer time by thanking God for this person and the ways in which this person touches your life. Lift your thanks to God also for his continuing presence as he strengthens your heart in holiness.

See Meeting God in Community

when you received the word of God that you heard from us, you accepted it not as a human word but as what it really is, God's word, which is also at work in you believers. [14]For you, brothers and sisters,[a] became imitators of the churches of God in Christ Jesus that are in Judea, for you suffered the same things from your own compatriots as they did from the Jews, [15]who killed both the Lord Jesus and the prophets,[b] and drove us out; they displease God and oppose everyone [16]by hindering us from speaking to the Gentiles so that they may be saved. Thus they have constantly been filling up the measure of their sins; but God's wrath has overtaken them at last.[c]

Paul's Desire to Visit the Thessalonians Again

17 As for us, brothers and sisters,[a] when, for a short time, we were made orphans by being separated from you—in person, not in heart—we longed with great eagerness to see you face to face. [18]For we wanted to come to you—certainly I, Paul, wanted to again and again—but Satan blocked our way. [19]For what is our hope or joy or crown of boasting before our Lord Jesus at his coming? Is it not you? [20]Yes, you are our glory and joy!

3 Therefore when we could bear it no longer, we decided to be left alone in Athens; [2]and we sent Timothy, our brother and co-worker for God in proclaiming[d] the gospel of Christ, to strengthen and encourage you for the sake of your faith, [3]so that no one would be shaken by these persecutions. Indeed, you yourselves know that this is what we are destined for. [4]In fact, when we were with you, we told you beforehand that we were to suffer persecution; so it turned out, as you know. [5]For this reason, when I could bear it no longer, I sent to find out about your faith; I was afraid that somehow the tempter had tempted you and that our labor had been in vain.

Timothy's Encouraging Report

6 But Timothy has just now come to us from you, and has brought us the good news of your faith and love. He has told us also that you always remember us kindly and long to see us—just as we long to see you. [7]For this reason, brothers and sisters,[a] during all our distress and persecution we have been encouraged about you through your faith. [8]For we now live, if you continue to stand firm in the Lord. [9]How can we thank God enough for you in return for all the joy that we feel before our God because of you? [10]Night and day we pray most earnestly that we may see you face to face and restore whatever is lacking in your faith.

11 Now may our God and Father himself and our Lord Jesus direct our way to you. [12]And may the Lord make you increase and abound in love for one another and for all, just as we abound in love for you. [13]And may he so strengthen your hearts in holiness that you may be blameless before our God and Father at the coming of our Lord Jesus with all his saints.

a Gk *brothers*   *b* Other ancient authorities read *their own prophets*
c Or *completely* or *forever*   *d* Gk lacks *proclaiming*

A Life Pleasing to God

4 Finally, brothers and sisters,[a] we ask and urge you in the Lord Jesus that, as you learned from us how you ought to live and to please God (as, in fact, you are doing), you should do so more and more. [2]For you know what instructions we gave you through the Lord Jesus. [3]For this is the will of God, your sanctification: that you abstain from fornication; [4]that each one of you know how to control your own body[b] in holiness and honor, [5]not with lustful passion, like the Gentiles who do not know God; [6]that no one wrong or exploit a brother or sister[c] in this matter, because the Lord is an avenger in all these things, just as we have already told you beforehand and solemnly warned you. [7]For God did not call us to impurity but in holiness. [8]Therefore whoever rejects this rejects not human authority but God, who also gives his Holy Spirit to you.

9 Now concerning love of the brothers and sisters,[a] you do not need to have anyone write to you, for you yourselves have been taught by God to love one another; [10]and indeed you do love all the brothers and sisters[a] throughout Macedonia. But we urge you, beloved,[a] to do so more and more, [11]to aspire to live quietly, to mind your own affairs, and to work with your hands, as we directed you, [12]so that you may behave properly toward outsiders and be dependent on no one.

The Coming of the Lord

13 But we do not want you to be uninformed, brothers and sisters,[a] about those who have died,[d] so that you may not grieve as others do who have no hope. [14]For since we believe that Jesus died and rose again, even so, through Jesus, God will bring with him those who have died.[d] [15]For this we declare to you by the word of the Lord, that we who are alive, who are left until the coming of the Lord, will by no means precede those who have died.[d] [16]For the Lord himself, with a cry of command, with the archangel's call and with the sound of God's trumpet, will descend from heaven, and the dead in Christ will rise first. [17]Then we who are alive, who are left, will be caught up in the clouds together with them to meet the Lord in the air; and so we will be with the Lord forever. [18]Therefore encourage one another with these words.

5 Now concerning the times and the seasons, brothers and sisters,[a] you do not need to have anything written to you. [2]For you yourselves know very well that the day of the Lord will come like a thief in the night. [3]When they say, "There is peace and security," then sudden destruction will come upon them, as labor pains come upon a pregnant woman, and there will be no escape! [4]But you, beloved,[a] are not in darkness, for that day to surprise you like a thief; [5]for you are all children of light and children of the day; we are not of the night or of darkness. [6]So then let us not fall asleep as others do, but let us keep awake and be sober; [7]for those who sleep sleep at night, and those who are drunk get drunk at night. [8]But since we belong to the day, let us be sober, and put on the breastplate of faith and love, and for a helmet the hope of salvation. [9]For God has des-

Meeting the Lord

1 THESSALONIANS 4.16–18

When Paul talks about meeting the Lord in the air, the image is of a welcoming committee going out from a town to greet and escort a visiting dignitary.

Imagine that you are appointed to head such a welcoming committee to prepare for Jesus' coming to your church or your town. How would you greet him? What would you say? What parts of your community would you eagerly show him? What parts would you rather hide? How would your own life stand up to his gaze? What in your community or your life would you wish to change before he arrived? What might be preventing you from making the change? Why not begin right now?

See Meeting God in Scripture

---

a Gk *brothers*   b Or *how to take a wife for himself*   c Gk *brothers*
d Gk *fallen asleep*

Demands and Priorities

1 THESSALONIANS 5.12–22

Living a life of unity and peace with others can be difficult and demanding. Before you read (or reread) this section of Paul's letter, make your own list of the tough demands made on you by living with your family, spouse, children, parents, roommates and friends. Add the demands of your church life, your job or other role or responsibility. Then compare it with Paul's list. How are Paul's demands different from yours?

We set priorities by appraising the demands made by others in light of our own sense of our identity and our calling from God. As you look over your list, ask God to help you decide which demands need to be priorities and which demands need to be dismissed. Pray also for the strength and encouragement of the Holy Spirit as you seek to live out these decisions.

See Meeting God in Everyday Life

tined us not for wrath but for obtaining salvation through our Lord Jesus Christ, [10]who died for us, so that whether we are awake or asleep we may live with him. [11]Therefore encourage one another and build up each other, as indeed you are doing.

Final Exhortations, Greetings, and Benediction

12 But we appeal to you, brothers and sisters,[a] to respect those who labor among you, and have charge of you in the Lord and admonish you; [13]esteem them very highly in love because of their work. Be at peace among yourselves. [14]And we urge you, beloved,[a] to admonish the idlers, encourage the fainthearted, help the weak, be patient with all of them. [15]See that none of you repays evil for evil, but always seek to do good to one another and to all. [16]Rejoice always, [17]pray without ceasing, [18]give thanks in all circumstances; for this is the will of God in Christ Jesus for you. [19]Do not quench the Spirit. [20]Do not despise the words of prophets,[b] [21]but test everything; hold fast to what is good; [22]abstain from every form of evil.

23 May the God of peace himself sanctify you entirely; and may your spirit and soul and body be kept sound[c] and blameless at the coming of our Lord Jesus Christ. [24]The one who calls you is faithful, and he will do this.

25 Beloved,[d] pray for us.

26 Greet all the brothers and sisters[a] with a holy kiss. [27]I solemnly command you by the Lord that this letter be read to all of them.[e]

28 The grace of our Lord Jesus Christ be with you.[f]

---

a Gk *brothers* *b* Gk *despise prophecies* *c* Or *complete* *d* Gk *Brothers*
e Gk *to all the brothers* *f* Other ancient authorities add *Amen*

THE SECOND LETTER OF PAUL TO THE
THESSALONIANS
A Life Worthy of God's Calling

KEY VERSE:

To this end we always pray for you, asking that our God will make you worthy of his call and will fulfill by his power every good resolve and work of faith.—2 Thessalonians 1.11

The early church in Thessalonica is buzzing with predictions of Jesus' second coming. For some the fearful "end times" are troubling to contemplate. Others want only to wait passively for Jesus' return. The timing of this final event is uncertain, and many, in a state of paralysis, have given up their work and sit idly, awaiting the end of the world.

The author of this letter pointedly reminds his readers of who is in charge of all these things. The apostle Paul admonishes the Thessalonians not to be shaken but to have faith (2.2), remembering that God has chosen them.

Paul also confronts the destructiveness of fear and anxiety. They are to remain steadfast in their faith in the same way God is steadfast in his love for them (2.16). Idleness only adds to the problem of worry, he says; and he tells them to earn their own way (3.11–12) and live their lives as models of love and perseverance (3.5).

Take time to reflect on your fears as you read 2 Thessalonians. Which fears can you surrender to God? How could a fuller measure of faith in God dispel your feelings of being overwhelmed and hopeless in your daily life? What do you need to allow God to handle so that you can experience a turnabout in your ability to handle your fears? As you read this letter, let yourself experience the presence of the One who can calm all your fears.

"Some Christians seem to think that all the requirements of a holy life are met when there is very active and successful Christian work; and because they do so much for the Lord in public they feel a liberty to be cross and ugly and un-Christlike in private . . . If we are to walk as Christ walked, it must be in private as well as in public, at home as well as abroad; and it must be every hour all day long, and not at stated periods or on certain fixed occasions . . . It is in daily homely living, indeed, that practical piety can best show itself."

—HANNAH WHITALL SMITH,
The Christian's Secret of a Happy Life

A Portrait of a Church

2 THESSALONIANS 1.1–4

With just a few words, the author paints a picture of a thriving church that, despite problems, is filled with love, faith and steadfastness.

Try painting a portrait of your church. You might use words similar to those used in these verses. Or you might try representing your church pictorially, using crayons, markers or paints. What attributes would you honor? What problems would you need to illustrate?

As you work on this portrait, say a prayer for your church. Give thanks for what is good and confess problems that need God's correction. Ask God to bless all the individuals who are a part of your church, especially those in leadership positions.

Salutation

1 Paul, Silvanus, and Timothy,
To the church of the Thessalonians in God our Father and the Lord Jesus Christ:
2 Grace to you and peace from God our[a] Father and the Lord Jesus Christ.

Thanksgiving

3 We must always give thanks to God for you, brothers and sisters,[b] as is right, because your faith is growing abundantly, and the love of everyone of you for one another is increasing. 4Therefore we ourselves boast of you among the churches of God for your steadfastness and faith during all your persecutions and the afflictions that you are enduring.

The Judgment at Christ's Coming

5 This is evidence of the righteous judgment of God, and is intended to make you worthy of the kingdom of God, for which you are also suffering. 6For it is indeed just of God to repay with affliction those who afflict you, 7and to give relief to the afflicted as well as to us, when the Lord Jesus is revealed from heaven with his mighty angels 8in flaming fire, inflicting vengeance on those who do not know God and on those who do not obey the gospel of our Lord Jesus. 9These will suffer the punishment of eternal destruction, separated from the presence of the Lord and from the glory of his might, 10when he comes to be glorified by his saints and to be marveled at on that day among all who have believed, because our testimony to you was believed. 11To this end we always pray for you, asking that our God will make you worthy of his call and will fulfill by his power every good resolve and work of faith, 12so that the name of our Lord Jesus may be glorified in you, and you in him, according to the grace of our God and the Lord Jesus Christ.

The Man of Lawlessness

2 As to the coming of our Lord Jesus Christ and our being gathered together to him, we beg you, brothers and sisters,[b] 2not to be quickly shaken in mind or alarmed, either by spirit or by word or by letter, as though from us, to the effect that the day of the Lord is already here. 3Let no one deceive you in any way; for that day will not come unless the rebellion comes first and the lawless one[c] is revealed, the one destined for destruction.[d] 4He opposes and exalts himself above every so-called god or object of worship, so that he takes his seat in the temple of God, declaring himself to be God. 5Do you not remember that I told you these things when I was still with you? 6And you know what is now restraining him, so that he may be revealed when his time comes. 7For the mystery of lawlessness is already at work, but only until the one who now restrains it is removed. 8And then the lawless one will be revealed, whom the Lord Jesus[e] will destroy[f] with the breath of his mouth, annihilating him by the mani-

---

a Other ancient authorities read *the*   b Gk *brothers*   c Gk *the man of lawlessness*; other ancient authorities read *the man of sin*   d Gk *the son of destruction*   e Other ancient authorities lack *Jesus*   f Other ancient authorities read *consume*

festation of his coming. ⁹The coming of the lawless one is apparent in the working of Satan, who uses all power, signs, lying wonders, ¹⁰and every kind of wicked deception for those who are perishing, because they refused to love the truth and so be saved. ¹¹For this reason God sends them a powerful delusion, leading them to believe what is false, ¹²so that all who have not believed the truth but took pleasure in unrighteousness will be condemned.

Chosen for Salvation

13 But we must always give thanks to God for you, brothers and sisters[a] beloved by the Lord, because God chose you as the first fruits[b] for salvation through sanctification by the Spirit and through belief in the truth. ¹⁴For this purpose he called you through our proclamation of the good news,[c] so that you may obtain the glory of our Lord Jesus Christ. ¹⁵So then, brothers and sisters,[a] stand firm and hold fast to the traditions that you were taught by us, either by word of mouth or by our letter.

16 Now may our Lord Jesus Christ himself and God our Father, who loved us and through grace gave us eternal comfort and good hope, ¹⁷comfort your hearts and strengthen them in every good work and word.

Request for Prayer

3 Finally, brothers and sisters,[a] pray for us, so that the word of the Lord may spread rapidly and be glorified everywhere, just as it is among you, ²and that we may be rescued from wicked and evil people; for not all have faith. ³But the Lord is faithful; he will strengthen you and guard you from the evil one.[d] ⁴And we have confidence in the Lord concerning you, that you are doing and will go on doing the things that we command. ⁵May the Lord direct your hearts to the love of God and to the steadfastness of Christ.

Warning against Idleness

6 Now we command you, beloved,[a] in the name of our Lord Jesus Christ, to keep away from believers who are[e] living in idleness and not according to the tradition that they[f] received from us. ⁷For you yourselves know how you ought to imitate us; we were not idle when we were with you, ⁸and we did not eat anyone's bread without paying for it; but with toil and labor we worked night and day, so that we might not burden any of you. ⁹This was not because we do not have that right, but in order to give you an example to imitate. ¹⁰For even when we were with you, we gave you this command: Anyone unwilling to work should not eat. ¹¹For we hear that some of you are living in idleness, mere busybodies, not doing any work. ¹²Now such persons we command and exhort in the Lord Jesus Christ to do their work quietly and to earn their own living. ¹³Brothers and sisters,[g] do not be weary in doing what is right.

14 Take note of those who do not obey what we say in this letter; have nothing to do with them, so that they may

---

Prevenient Grace

2 THESSALONIANS 2.13–15

Sometimes we talk about making a decision for Jesus Christ as if our decision initiated God's presence in our lives. Here the author reminds the Thessalonians that God chose them for salvation and called them to the Lord Jesus Christ through Paul's preaching. Theologians speak of "prevenient" grace—God's gifts to us "coming before" we even thought or even knew to ask. God may have touched your life and drawn you through family devotions, a church school teacher or a Vacation Bible School program, a campfire sing-a-long, religious programming on television or Christian themes powerfully depicted in a movie, a Gideon Bible in a motel room, a friend whose example inspired you, or countless other ways.

Try making a list of different examples of prevenient grace in your life. Where can you see God going before you, drawing you nearer in ways that at the time you didn't recognize as God's grace at work in your life? Close by reading the list aloud and thanking God for each item.

---

a Gk *brothers*   b Other ancient authorities read *from the beginning*
c Or *through our gospel*   d Or *from evil*   e Gk *from every brother who is*
f Other ancient authorities read *you*   g Gk *Brothers*

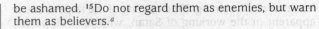
Receiving God's Grace

"We cannot escape the dangers, which abound in life, without the actual and continual help of God. Let us then pray to God for it continually. How can we pray to God without being with God? How can we be with God but in thinking of God often? And how can we often think of God, but by a holy habit, which we should form of it? . . . This is the best and easiest method I know; and as I use no other, I advise all the world to it."

—BROTHER LAWRENCE,
The Practice of the Presence of God

be ashamed. ¹⁵Do not regard them as enemies, but warn them as believers.ᵃ

Final Greetings and Benediction

16 Now may the Lord of peace himself give you peace at all times in all ways. The Lord be with all of you.

17 I, Paul, write this greeting with my own hand. This is the mark in every letter of mine; it is the way I write. ¹⁸The grace of our Lord Jesus Christ be with all of you.ᵇ

a Gk *a brother*   *b* Other ancient authorities add *Amen*

We should search

the Scriptures carefully,

in humility and

with the counsel

of experienced people,

learning not merely theoretically

but by putting into practice

what we read.

PETER OF DAMASKOS (TWELFTH CENTURY?)

The Philokalia (Volume Three)

At any price, give me the book of God! Here is knowledge enough for me. In God's presence I open, I read this book, for this end: to find the **way** to heaven.

JOHN WESLEY (1703-1791)

Sermons on Several Occasions

In our meditation we ponder the chosen text on the strength of the promise that it has something utterly personal to say to us for this day and for our Christian life.

DIETRICH BONHOEFFER (1906-1945)
Life Together

Just as you

do not analyze the words of someone *you love*, but accept them as they are said to you, accept the Word of Scripture and ponder it in your **heart**.

DIETRICH BONHOEFFER (1906-1945)

The Way to Freedom

THE FIRST LETTER OF PAUL TO
TIMOTHY
Guidelines for Godliness

KEY VERSE:

*Pay close attention to yourself and to your teaching; continue in these things, for in doing this
you will save both yourself and your hearers.—1 Timothy 4.16*

As the young pastor Timothy's mentor and friend, the apostle Paul writes to his "loyal child in the faith" with words of instruction and encouragement. Timothy is pastor of the Ephesian church, which is facing all the problems of a growing institution, not the least of which is keeping the church's love for Jesus Christ fresh and fervent (see Revelation 2.4). Timothy has to manage the church's internal affairs such as personnel, structure, worship and doctrinal struggles as well as to combat the continuing persecution and false teachings coming from outside and inside the church.

The book of 1 Timothy is primarily a call to godliness in the broadest sense. Paul summons the Ephesians to godliness characterized by right doctrine, orderly worship and holy relationships. He addresses the mission of the church, the qualifications of leaders and social concerns such as the care of widows.

To be godly is to imitate God in holiness; such a calling affects every part of our being, from our beliefs to our behavior, from our attitudes to our actions, and from our relationships to our worship. There isn't an element of human existence that isn't radically and profoundly altered by this call to Christian living that Paul refers to as godliness. Consider studying this book with a sheet of paper with the word "godliness" written at the top. Ask God to broaden your view of godliness and to remove the limits of how you might have previously defined godliness. Ask God to show you areas of your life that need to be anointed with new holiness.

> "As a good Christian should consider every place as holy because God is there, so he should look upon every part of his life as a matter of holiness because it is to be offered unto God."
>
> —WILLIAM LAW,
> *A Serious Call to a Devout and Holy Life*

Dynamic Hope

1 TIMOTHY 1.1

Paul calls Christ Jesus our "hope." The word "hope" (*elpis*) means something very different from "wishful thinking." This hope connotes absolute certainty. At the top of a sheet of paper write the words "Because of Jesus." Below it list all the "absolute certainties" you can count on because of Jesus Christ. What can you expect in this life? What certainties do you face in eternity? What is the difference between having this certain hope in a *person*—Jesus Christ—and having hope in a cause or a political agenda?

Salutation

1 Paul, an apostle of Christ Jesus by the command of God our Savior and of Christ Jesus our hope,

2 To Timothy, my loyal child in the faith:

Grace, mercy, and peace from God the Father and Christ Jesus our Lord.

Warning against False Teachers

3 I urge you, as I did when I was on my way to Macedonia, to remain in Ephesus so that you may instruct certain people not to teach any different doctrine, ⁴and not to occupy themselves with myths and endless genealogies that promote speculations rather than the divine training*a* that is known by faith. ⁵But the aim of such instruction is love that comes from a pure heart, a good conscience, and sincere faith. ⁶Some people have deviated from these and turned to meaningless talk, ⁷desiring to be teachers of the law, without understanding either what they are saying or the things about which they make assertions.

8 Now we know that the law is good, if one uses it legitimately. ⁹This means understanding that the law is laid down not for the innocent but for the lawless and disobedient, for the godless and sinful, for the unholy and profane, for those who kill their father or mother, for murderers, ¹⁰fornicators, sodomites, slave traders, liars, perjurers, and whatever else is contrary to the sound teaching ¹¹that conforms to the glorious gospel of the blessed God, which he entrusted to me.

Gratitude for Mercy

12 I am grateful to Christ Jesus our Lord, who has strengthened me, because he judged me faithful and appointed me to his service, ¹³even though I was formerly a blasphemer, a persecutor, and a man of violence. But I received mercy because I had acted ignorantly in unbelief, ¹⁴and the grace of our Lord overflowed for me with the faith and love that are in Christ Jesus. ¹⁵The saying is sure and worthy of full acceptance, that Christ Jesus came into the world to save sinners—of whom I am the foremost. ¹⁶But for that very reason I received mercy, so that in me, as the foremost, Jesus Christ might display the utmost patience, making me an example to those who would come to believe in him for eternal life. ¹⁷To the King of the ages, immortal, invisible, the only God, be honor and glory forever and ever.*b* Amen.

18 I am giving you these instructions, Timothy, my child, in accordance with the prophecies made earlier about you, so that by following them you may fight the good fight, ¹⁹having faith and a good conscience. By rejecting conscience, certain persons have suffered shipwreck in the faith; ²⁰among them are Hymenaeus and Alexander, whom I have turned over to Satan, so that they may learn not to blaspheme.

Instructions concerning Prayer

2 First of all, then, I urge that supplications, prayers, intercessions, and thanksgivings be made for everyone, ²for kings and all who are in high positions, so that we may

a Or *plan*   *b* Gk *to the ages of the ages*

lead a quiet and peaceable life in all godliness and dignity. ³This is right and is acceptable in the sight of God our Savior, ⁴who desires everyone to be saved and to come to the knowledge of the truth. ⁵For

there is one God;
there is also one mediator between God and humankind,
Christ Jesus, himself human,

⁶ who gave himself a ransom for all

—this was attested at the right time. ⁷For this I was appointed a herald and an apostle (I am telling the truth,ᵃ I am not lying), a teacher of the Gentiles in faith and truth.

8 I desire, then, that in every place the men should pray, lifting up holy hands without anger or argument; ⁹also that the women should dress themselves modestly and decently in suitable clothing, not with their hair braided, or with gold, pearls, or expensive clothes, ¹⁰but with good works, as is proper for women who profess reverence for God. ¹¹Let a womanᵇ learn in silence with full submission. ¹²I permit no womanᵇ to teach or to have authority over a man;ᶜ she is to keep silent. ¹³For Adam was formed first, then Eve; ¹⁴and Adam was not deceived, but the woman was deceived and became a transgressor. ¹⁵Yet she will be saved through childbearing, provided they continue in faith and love and holiness, with modesty.

Qualifications of Bishops

3 The saying is sure:ᵈ whoever aspires to the office of bishopᵉ desires a noble task. ²Now a bishopᶠ must be above reproach, married only once,ᵍ temperate, sensible, respectable, hospitable, an apt teacher, ³not a drunkard, not violent but gentle, not quarrelsome, and not a lover of money. ⁴He must manage his own household well, keeping his children submissive and respectful in every way— ⁵for if someone does not know how to manage his own household, how can he take care of God's church? ⁶He must not be a recent convert, or he may be puffed up with conceit and fall into the condemnation of the devil. ⁷Moreover, he must be well thought of by outsiders, so that he may not fall into disgrace and the snare of the devil.

Qualifications of Deacons

8 Deacons likewise must be serious, not double-tongued, not indulging in much wine, not greedy for money; ⁹they must hold fast to the mystery of the faith with a clear conscience. ¹⁰And let them first be tested; then, if they prove themselves blameless, let them serve as deacons. ¹¹Womenʰ likewise must be serious, not slanderers, but temperate, faithful in all things. ¹²Let deacons be married only once,ⁱ and let them manage their children and their households well; ¹³for those who serve well as deacons gain a good standing for themselves and great boldness in the faith that is in Christ Jesus.

---

a Other ancient authorities add *in Christ*   b Or *wife*   c Or *her husband*
d Some interpreters place these words at the end of the previous paragraph. Other ancient authorities read *The saying is commonly accepted*
e Or *overseer*   f Or *an overseer*   g Gk *the husband of one wife*
h Or *Their wives*, or *Women deacons*   i Gk *be husbands of one wife*

Holy Hands

1 TIMOTHY 2.8

When Paul mentions "holy hands" lifted up in prayer, many images might come to mind, but the two ideas Paul specifically mentions here are "without anger or argument." Have you ever experienced extra difficulty in prayer while in the midst of a contentious relationship?

As you pray, look at your hands. Are they "holy hands"? Clench them into fists. What situations or people are making you angry? Ask God to take away your anger as you slowly relax and open your hands. What relationships need reconciliation or healing? Imagine the other person held in your hands as you lift him or her up to God. Ask for God's blessing on the relationship. Finally, spread your raised hands apart in praise and thanksgiving.

See Meeting God in Community

Taking Care of the Soul

1 TIMOTHY 4.11–16

Imagine that God gave you two plants to take care of, leaving you in charge of watering them, fertilizing them and making sure they get enough (but not too much) sun. In a way, Paul gives us this kind of challenge in verse 16. The two "plants" we are to watch over are our life and our doctrine. How can you create a favorable environment for both of these plants to grow? What essential elements do you provide for them? Write out a "gardening" plan for both your life and your doctrine.

The Mystery of Our Religion

14 I hope to come to you soon, but I am writing these instructions to you so that, ¹⁵if I am delayed, you may know how one ought to behave in the household of God, which is the church of the living God, the pillar and bulwark of the truth. ¹⁶Without any doubt, the mystery of our religion is great:

> He*ᵃ* was revealed in flesh,
> vindicated*ᵇ* in spirit,*ᶜ*
> seen by angels,
> proclaimed among Gentiles,
> believed in throughout the world,
> taken up in glory.

False Asceticism

4 Now the Spirit expressly says that in later*ᵈ* times some will renounce the faith by paying attention to deceitful spirits and teachings of demons, ²through the hypocrisy of liars whose consciences are seared with a hot iron. ³They forbid marriage and demand abstinence from foods, which God created to be received with thanksgiving by those who believe and know the truth. ⁴For everything created by God is good, and nothing is to be rejected, provided it is received with thanksgiving; ⁵for it is sanctified by God's word and by prayer.

A Good Minister of Jesus Christ

6 If you put these instructions before the brothers and sisters,*ᵉ* you will be a good servant*ᶠ* of Christ Jesus, nourished on the words of the faith and of the sound teaching that you have followed. ⁷Have nothing to do with profane myths and old wives' tales. Train yourself in godliness, ⁸for, while physical training is of some value, godliness is valuable in every way, holding promise for both the present life and the life to come. ⁹The saying is sure and worthy of full acceptance. ¹⁰For to this end we toil and struggle,*ᵍ* because we have our hope set on the living God, who is the Savior of all people, especially of those who believe.

11 These are the things you must insist on and teach. ¹²Let no one despise your youth, but set the believers an example in speech and conduct, in love, in faith, in purity. ¹³Until I arrive, give attention to the public reading of scripture,*ʰ* to exhorting, to teaching. ¹⁴Do not neglect the gift that is in you, which was given to you through prophecy with the laying on of hands by the council of elders.*ⁱ* ¹⁵Put these things into practice, devote yourself to them, so that all may see your progress. ¹⁶Pay close attention to yourself and to your teaching; continue in these things, for in doing this you will save both yourself and your hearers.

Duties toward Believers

5 Do not speak harshly to an older man,*ʲ* but speak to him as to a father, to younger men as brothers, ²to older women as mothers, to younger women as sisters—with absolute purity.

3 Honor widows who are really widows. ⁴If a widow has

a Gk *Who*; other ancient authorities read *God*; others, *Which*   *b* Or *justified* *c* Or *by the Spirit*   *d* Or *the last*   *e* Gk *brothers*   *f* Or *deacon*   *g* Other ancient authorities read *suffer reproach*   *h* Gk *to the reading*   *i* Gk *by the presbytery*   *j* Or *an elder*, or *a presbyter*

children or grandchildren, they should first learn their religious duty to their own family and make some repayment to their parents; for this is pleasing in God's sight. [5]The real widow, left alone, has set her hope on God and continues in supplications and prayers night and day; [6]but the widow[a] who lives for pleasure is dead even while she lives. [7]Give these commands as well, so that they may be above reproach. [8]And whoever does not provide for relatives, and especially for family members, has denied the faith and is worse than an unbeliever.

9 Let a widow be put on the list if she is not less than sixty years old and has been married only once;[b] [10]she must be well attested for her good works, as one who has brought up children, shown hospitality, washed the saints' feet, helped the afflicted, and devoted herself to doing good in every way. [11]But refuse to put younger widows on the list; for when their sensual desires alienate them from Christ, they want to marry, [12]and so they incur condemnation for having violated their first pledge. [13]Besides that, they learn to be idle, gadding about from house to house; and they are not merely idle, but also gossips and busybodies, saying what they should not say. [14]So I would have younger widows marry, bear children, and manage their households, so as to give the adversary no occasion to revile us. [15]For some have already turned away to follow Satan. [16]If any believing woman[c] has relatives who are really widows, let her assist them; let the church not be burdened, so that it can assist those who are real widows.

17 Let the elders who rule well be considered worthy of double honor,[d] especially those who labor in preaching and teaching; [18]for the scripture says, "You shall not muzzle an ox while it is treading out the grain," and, "The laborer deserves to be paid." [19]Never accept any accusation against an elder except on the evidence of two or three witnesses. [20]As for those who persist in sin, rebuke them in the presence of all, so that the rest also may stand in fear. [21]In the presence of God and of Christ Jesus and of the elect angels, I warn you to keep these instructions without prejudice, doing nothing on the basis of partiality. [22]Do not ordain[e] anyone hastily, and do not participate in the sins of others; keep yourself pure.

23 No longer drink only water, but take a little wine for the sake of your stomach and your frequent ailments.

24 The sins of some people are conspicuous and precede them to judgment, while the sins of others follow them there. [25]So also good works are conspicuous; and even when they are not, they cannot remain hidden.

6 Let all who are under the yoke of slavery regard their masters as worthy of all honor, so that the name of God and the teaching may not be blasphemed. [2]Those who have believing masters must not be disrespectful to them on the ground that they are members of the church;[f] rather they must serve them all the more, since those who benefit by their service are believers and beloved.[g]

---

a Gk *she*   *b* Gk *the wife of one husband*   *c* Other ancient authorities read *believing man or woman*; others, *believing man*   *d* Or *compensation*   *e* Gk *Do not lay hands on*   *f* Gk *are brothers*   *g* Or *since they are believers and beloved, who devote themselves to good deeds*

The Weight of Words

1 TIMOTHY 6.3–5

Throughout this letter, Paul addresses people who are fascinated with fanciful and false doctrines. Read through this list and try to discern any contemporary applications. What kinds of current discussions tend to do nothing but create controversy? What forms of debate lead to envy? Quarreling? Malicious talk? Evil suspicions? Constant friction? Now turn this around and imagine the kinds of conversation that build unity. Pray and think about ways in which your words can lead to encouragement instead of envy, reconciliation instead of quarreling, sincere appreciation instead of malicious talk, and expressions of confidence and support instead of evil suspicions. Ask God to allow you to turn at least one "controversial" conversation into a "unifying" one in the next twenty-four hours.

See *Meeting God in Everyday Life*

The Pursuit of Growth

1 TIMOTHY 6:11

Copy this verse down on a piece of paper (or commit it to memory), then go outside and start walking. Pick a point on the horizon and as you walk toward it, prayerfully consider what activities mentioned throughout this letter will help you to "pursue" righteousness and godliness. Start running (or at least pick up the pace) for just a short while. What is the significance of the sense of urgency Paul conveys (see also 1 Corinthians 9:24–25)? Once you reach your destination, turn around and walk back, prayerfully considering Paul's words about growing in endurance. Are your legs tired? What makes you spiritually tired? How can you get in better shape spiritually?

False Teaching and True Riches

Teach and urge these duties. ³Whoever teaches otherwise and does not agree with the sound words of our Lord Jesus Christ and the teaching that is in accordance with godliness, ⁴is conceited, understanding nothing, and has a morbid craving for controversy and for disputes about words. From these come envy, dissension, slander, base suspicions, ⁵and wrangling among those who are depraved in mind and bereft of the truth, imagining that godliness is a means of gain.ᵃ ⁶Of course, there is great gain in godliness combined with contentment; ⁷for we brought nothing into the world, so thatᵇ we can take nothing out of it; ⁸but if we have food and clothing, we will be content with these. ⁹But those who want to be rich fall into temptation and are trapped by many senseless and harmful desires that plunge people into ruin and destruction. ¹⁰For the love of money is a root of all kinds of evil, and in their eagerness to be rich some have wandered away from the faith and pierced themselves with many pains.

The Good Fight of Faith

11 But as for you, man of God, shun all this; pursue righteousness, godliness, faith, love, endurance, gentleness. ¹²Fight the good fight of the faith; take hold of the eternal life, to which you were called and for which you madeᶜ the good confession in the presence of many witnesses. ¹³In the presence of God, who gives life to all things, and of Christ Jesus, who in his testimony before Pontius Pilate made the good confession, I charge you ¹⁴to keep the commandment without spot or blame until the manifestation of our Lord Jesus Christ, ¹⁵which he will bring about at the right time—he who is the blessed and only Sovereign, the King of kings and Lord of lords. ¹⁶It is he alone who has immortality and dwells in unapproachable light, whom no one has ever seen or can see; to him be honor and eternal dominion. Amen.

17 As for those who in the present age are rich, command them not to be haughty, or to set their hopes on the uncertainty of riches, but rather on God who richly provides us with everything for our enjoyment. ¹⁸They are to do good, to be rich in good works, generous, and ready to share, ¹⁹thus storing up for themselves the treasure of a good foundation for the future, so that they may take hold of the life that really is life.

Personal Instructions and Benediction

20 Timothy, guard what has been entrusted to you. Avoid the profane chatter and contradictions of what is falsely called knowledge; ²¹by professing it some have missed the mark as regards the faith.

Grace be with you.ᵈ

---

a Other ancient authorities add *Withdraw yourself from such people*
b Other ancient authorities read *world—it is certain that*   c Gk *confessed*
d The Greek word for *you* here is plural; in other ancient authorities it is singular. Other ancient authorities add *Amen*

THE SECOND LETTER OF PAUL TO
TIMOTHY
Faithfulness Under Pressure

KEY VERSE:

*As for you, always be sober, endure suffering, do the work of an evangelist,
carry out your ministry fully.*—2 Timothy 4.5

Do you ever live through seasons in which the entire world seems bent on distracting you from God's calling? As you seek to serve God, are you hampered by pressures and opposition? If so, this letter will offer you profound encouragement. Whether your frustrations stem from the pressure of meeting many obligations, a feeling of weariness, or the experience of open opposition or ridicule, you will find empathy in Paul's and Timothy's experiences. Even as they face many of these same pressures, Paul urges Timothy to persevere and remain faithful in his ministry.

While most of the New Testament books are written to churches, this one is written to an individual. The situation in which Paul and Timothy find themselves is a veritable pressure cooker. Paul is in prison, the church is being persecuted, opposition is hot and fierce—even from those who call themselves Christians, and Timothy is trying to stay true to his work in the midst of doctrinal confusion and hardship. Paul's letter is a stirring call to Timothy to remain faithful under pressure, and its relevance has been proven in every generation.

Before you reflect on the specific teachings of this book, take a personal inventory of the challenges you have faced in serving God. What has made it most difficult for you to fulfill a calling that you believe God has given you? What is the biggest obstacle you currently face? Even as you confront your own struggles, prepare to be challenged and encouraged by Paul's words to his friend Timothy. Within these chapters you may find the keys to remaining faithful under pressure in your own life.

"Trials are a further benefit to true religion because they not only manifest its truth but they also enhance its genuine beauty and attractiveness. True virtue is loveliest when it is oppressed. The divine excellency of real Christianity is best exhibited when it is under the greatest trials."

—JONATHAN EDWARDS,
Treatise Concerning Religious Affections

Guard the Truth

2 TIMOTHY 1.14

Picture yourself as a guard, like Timothy, given charge of protecting God's truth. Who, or what, are the enemies you need to watch out for? What might cause a guard to fail—weariness, lack of attention, carelessness, distractions? What arena would be the most probable scene of battle? Guards need proper equipment and good backup. What has God provided for you as you stand guard? What is the difference between guarding something against being corrupted or damaged and guarding something from being stolen? What is the particular challenge of guarding "truth" as opposed to guarding a person or physical object?

Salutation

1 Paul, an apostle of Christ Jesus by the will of God, for the sake of the promise of life that is in Christ Jesus, 2 To Timothy, my beloved child:

Grace, mercy, and peace from God the Father and Christ Jesus our Lord.

Thanksgiving and Encouragement

3 I am grateful to God—whom I worship with a clear conscience, as my ancestors did—when I remember you constantly in my prayers night and day. ⁴Recalling your tears, I long to see you so that I may be filled with joy. ⁵I am reminded of your sincere faith, a faith that lived first in your grandmother Lois and your mother Eunice and now, I am sure, lives in you. ⁶For this reason I remind you to rekindle the gift of God that is within you through the laying on of my hands; ⁷for God did not give us a spirit of cowardice, but rather a spirit of power and of love and of self-discipline.

8 Do not be ashamed, then, of the testimony about our Lord or of me his prisoner, but join with me in suffering for the gospel, relying on the power of God, ⁹who saved us and called us with a holy calling, not according to our works but according to his own purpose and grace. This grace was given to us in Christ Jesus before the ages began, ¹⁰but it has now been revealed through the appearing of our Savior Christ Jesus, who abolished death and brought life and immortality to light through the gospel. ¹¹For this gospel I was appointed a herald and an apostle and a teacher,ᵃ ¹²and for this reason I suffer as I do. But I am not ashamed, for I know the one in whom I have put my trust, and I am sure that he is able to guard until that day what I have entrusted to him.ᵇ ¹³Hold to the standard of sound teaching that you have heard from me, in the faith and love that are in Christ Jesus. ¹⁴Guard the good treasure entrusted to you, with the help of the Holy Spirit living in us.

15 You are aware that all who are in Asia have turned away from me, including Phygelus and Hermogenes. ¹⁶May the Lord grant mercy to the household of Onesiphorus, because he often refreshed me and was not ashamed of my chain; ¹⁷when he arrived in Rome, he eagerlyᶜ searched for me and found me ¹⁸—may the Lord grant that he will find mercy from the Lord on that day! And you know very well how much service he rendered in Ephesus.

A Good Soldier of Christ Jesus

2 You then, my child, be strong in the grace that is in Christ Jesus; ²and what you have heard from me through many witnesses entrust to faithful people who will be able to teach others as well. ³Share in suffering like a good soldier of Christ Jesus. ⁴No one serving in the army gets entangled in everyday affairs; the soldier's aim is to please the enlisting officer. ⁵And in the case of an athlete, no one is crowned without competing according to the rules. ⁶It is the farmer who does the work who ought to have the first share of the crops. ⁷Think over what I say, for the Lord will give you understanding in all things.

8 Remember Jesus Christ, raised from the dead, a de-

a Other ancient authorities add *of the Gentiles*   *b* Or *what has been entrusted to me*   *c* Or *promptly*

scendant of David—that is my gospel, ⁹for which I suffer hardship, even to the point of being chained like a criminal. But the word of God is not chained. ¹⁰Therefore I endure everything for the sake of the elect, so that they may also obtain the salvation that is in Christ Jesus, with eternal glory. ¹¹The saying is sure:

If we have died with him, we will also live with him;
¹² if we endure, we will also reign with him;
   if we deny him, he will also deny us;
¹³ if we are faithless, he remains faithful—
   for he cannot deny himself.

A Worker Approved by God

14 Remind them of this, and warn them before God[a] that they are to avoid wrangling over words, which does no good but only ruins those who are listening. ¹⁵Do your best to present yourself to God as one approved by him, a worker who has no need to be ashamed, rightly explaining the word of truth. ¹⁶Avoid profane chatter, for it will lead people into more and more impiety, ¹⁷and their talk will spread like gangrene. Among them are Hymenaeus and Philetus, ¹⁸who have swerved from the truth by claiming that the resurrection has already taken place. They are upsetting the faith of some. ¹⁹But God's firm foundation stands, bearing this inscription: "The Lord knows those who are his," and, "Let everyone who calls on the name of the Lord turn away from wickedness."

20 In a large house there are utensils not only of gold and silver but also of wood and clay, some for special use, some for ordinary. ²¹All who cleanse themselves of the things I have mentioned[b] will become special utensils, dedicated and useful to the owner of the house, ready for every good work. ²²Shun youthful passions and pursue righteousness, faith, love, and peace, along with those who call on the Lord from a pure heart. ²³Have nothing to do with stupid and senseless controversies; you know that they breed quarrels. ²⁴And the Lord's servant[c] must not be quarrelsome but kindly to everyone, an apt teacher, patient, ²⁵correcting opponents with gentleness. God may perhaps grant that they will repent and come to know the truth, ²⁶and that they may escape from the snare of the devil, having been held captive by him to do his will.[d]

Godlessness in the Last Days

3 You must understand this, that in the last days distressing times will come. ²For people will be lovers of themselves, lovers of money, boasters, arrogant, abusive, disobedient to their parents, ungrateful, unholy, ³inhuman, implacable, slanderers, profligates, brutes, haters of good, ⁴treacherous, reckless, swollen with conceit, lovers of pleasure rather than lovers of God, ⁵holding to the outward form of godliness but denying its power. Avoid them! ⁶For among them are those who make their way into households and captivate silly women, overwhelmed by their sins and swayed by all kinds of desires, ⁷who are always being instructed and can never arrive at a knowledge of the truth. ⁸As Jannes and Jambres opposed Moses, so these people, of corrupt mind and counterfeit faith, also oppose

Flee and Pursue

2 TIMOTHY 2.22

"We are both to run away from spiritual danger and to run after spiritual good, both to flee from the one in order to escape it and to pursue the other in order to attain it. This double duty of Christians—negative and positive—is the consistent, reiterated teaching of Scripture. Thus, we are to deny ourselves and to follow Christ. We are to put off what belongs to the old life and put on what belongs to the new life . . . It is the ruthless rejection of the one in combination with the relentless pursuit of the other which Scripture enjoins upon us as the secret of holiness."

—JOHN STOTT,
Guard the Gospel

See *Meeting God in Scripture*

---

a Other ancient authorities read *the Lord*   b Gk *of these things*
c Gk *slave*   d Or *by him, to do his* (that is, God's) *will*

Ripe or Rotting?

2 TIMOTHY 3.13–15

Paul contrasts two images in these verses. The first image is of wicked people and impostors, who go from "bad to worse"; the second image is of Timothy, who continues to grow in keeping with the good start he received, becoming mature.

Imagine two pieces of fruit—one that has a rotten spot that is getting ever worse, and the other that is wholesome, firm and just beginning to ripen. What is there in your spiritual life that resembles the rotten fruit? What can be done to keep the rot from spreading? What is like the ripening fruit? What will keep it growing toward full maturity? Ask God for whatever help you need to prevent rot and encourage growth.

the truth. [9]But they will not make much progress, because, as in the case of those two men,[a] their folly will become plain to everyone.

Paul's Charge to Timothy

10 Now you have observed my teaching, my conduct, my aim in life, my faith, my patience, my love, my steadfastness, [11]my persecutions, and my suffering the things that happened to me in Antioch, Iconium, and Lystra. What persecutions I endured! Yet the Lord rescued me from all of them. [12]Indeed, all who want to live a godly life in Christ Jesus will be persecuted. [13]But wicked people and impostors will go from bad to worse, deceiving others and being deceived. [14]But as for you, continue in what you have learned and firmly believed, knowing from whom you learned it, [15]and how from childhood you have known the sacred writings that are able to instruct you for salvation through faith in Christ Jesus. [16]All scripture is inspired by God and is[b] useful for teaching, for reproof, for correction, and for training in righteousness, [17]so that everyone who belongs to God may be proficient, equipped for every good work.

4 In the presence of God and of Christ Jesus, who is to judge the living and the dead, and in view of his appearing and his kingdom, I solemnly urge you: [2]proclaim the message; be persistent whether the time is favorable or unfavorable; convince, rebuke, and encourage, with the utmost patience in teaching. [3]For the time is coming when people will not put up with sound doctrine, but having itching ears, they will accumulate for themselves teachers to suit their own desires, [4]and will turn away from listening to the truth and wander away to myths. [5]As for you, always be sober, endure suffering, do the work of an evangelist, carry out your ministry fully.

6 As for me, I am already being poured out as a libation, and the time of my departure has come. [7]I have fought the good fight, I have finished the race, I have kept the faith. [8]From now on there is reserved for me the crown of righteousness, which the Lord, the righteous judge, will give me on that day, and not only to me but also to all who have longed for his appearing.

Personal Instructions

9 Do your best to come to me soon, [10]for Demas, in love with this present world, has deserted me and gone to Thessalonica; Crescens has gone to Galatia,[c] Titus to Dalmatia. [11]Only Luke is with me. Get Mark and bring him with you, for he is useful in my ministry. [12]I have sent Tychicus to Ephesus. [13]When you come, bring the cloak that I left with Carpus at Troas, also the books, and above all the parchments. [14]Alexander the coppersmith did me great harm; the Lord will pay him back for his deeds. [15]You also must beware of him, for he strongly opposed our message.

16 At my first defense no one came to my support, but all deserted me. May it not be counted against them! [17]But the Lord stood by me and gave me strength, so that through me the message might be fully proclaimed and all the Gentiles might hear it. So I was rescued from the lion's

a Gk lacks *two men* b Or *Every scripture inspired by God is also* c Other ancient authorities read *Gaul*

mouth. ¹⁸The Lord will rescue me from every evil attack and save me for his heavenly kingdom. To him be the glory forever and ever. Amen.

Final Greetings and Benediction

19 Greet Prisca and Aquila, and the household of Onesiphorus. ²⁰Erastus remained in Corinth; Trophimus I left ill in Miletus. ²¹Do your best to come before winter. Eubulus sends greetings to you, as do Pudens and Linus and Claudia and all the brothers and sisters.ᵃ

22 The Lord be with your spirit. Grace be with you.ᵇ

Friends

2 TIMOTHY 4.19–21

In his pressure-packed pursuit to plant churches, live a holy life and serve God, Paul clearly remains a very relational person. At the end of this letter, Paul affectionately greets several friends, companions and fellow believers—a refreshing end to a somewhat somber letter. If you were writing a letter back to a member of your church, what friends might you inquire about? To whom would you want your greetings passed along? How do relationships encourage us in our pursuit of God? What role do relationships play in dealing with pressure? How might you begin to build additional "spiritual friendships"? (See Hebrews 10.24–25.)

See *Meeting God in Community*

---

a Gk *all the brothers*   *b* The Greek word for *you* here is plural. Other ancient authorities add *Amen*

WAYS of MEETING GOD

Meeting God in Everyday Life

"We live lives of little things," someone once said. We are occupied most often with the details of ordinary life. Driving to the office or factory, putting supper on the table, taking feverish kids to the doctor—these are the things that fill our hours. When we meet God, that encounter often takes place in and through everyday circumstances. Growing spiritually will mean "living to God on common occasions," as Horace Bushnell expressed it. Inevitably we cultivate our spiritual lives not just in quiet solitude but in the activity of everyday life. We realize that God speaks to us not just in sky-rending revelations but also in the intimacy of quiet conversation with our spouse, the freshness of a child's spontaneous observation, the warmth of a bubbling pot of chili, the comfort of a family-night ritual.

> The Bible leaves no doubt that God works through the inner and outer details of our everyday lives. And if God is present in such moments, we cannot let them slide into oblivion.

How do we meet God in the midst of our stressful, busy lives? How do we recognize the signs that, in Avery Brooke's wonderful phrase, lie "hidden in plain sight"?

Two intentions will help us:

Remember God's Deeds. The Bible leaves no doubt that God works through the inner and outer details of our everyday lives. And if God is present in such moments, we cannot let them slide into oblivion: "Watch yourselves closely, so as neither to forget the things that your eyes have seen nor to let them slip from your mind all the days of your life" (Deuteronomy 4.9). The psalmist, recalling God's careful involvement in Israel's history, vowed, "I will call to mind the deeds of the LORD; I will remember your wonders of old" (Psalm 77.11).

The act of remembering helped the people of Israel to keep events from the past vital in the present. Just as we pull out a photo album on a rainy day in order to recall the significant moments of our lives—to review the snapshots of graduations and confirmations, visits and vacations—so God wanted the people of Israel to keep their holy history vividly present in their minds. And they were to remember God's good deeds corporately, as a people. Recollection was a community event. As they gathered in various ways, the people recalled aloud the moments that had given them identity as people of God—when God led them to freedom from Egyptian bondage, gave them commandments and instruction, gave them life. "Remember the former things of old," Isaiah enjoined the people, speaking on God's behalf (Isaiah 46.9). The Israelites' very identity depended on the God who had acted in their history. To forget God's acts would have meant to forget that God had called and chosen them.

God's call to remember carried over into New Testament times. Jesus urged his followers to recall God's work of redemption in his own life, death and resurrection. "Do this in remembrance of me," Jesus said at the Last Supper (Luke 22.19). Communion, in which we partake of the bread and the cup, is a supreme act of remembering. We also meet God through recalling what he has done for us personally. With David the psalmist we make certain that we "do not forget all [God's] benefits" in our daily lives (Psalm 103.2). To jog his readers' memories, David then recited specific benefits. He was not indulging in nostalgia but was gleaning from the past all that the Lord did and said. When we remember the Lord's deeds, we likewise keep in the forefront of our minds what God has already shown us; we live in continuity with the events that have shaped us. We recall the blessings of last year and the hardships of last week, remembering how God walked beside us and sometimes carried us in our moments of weakness and woundedness.

Conscious recollection requires discipline. In our live-for-the-moment culture, we may find the act of remembering more difficult than ancient people did. We are prone to become distracted by the details of the moment. We forget to "read life backwards." But memory can be a powerful resource for keeping our spiritual perspective alive.

One practical aid to this holy remembering is keeping a journal. Many find it helpful to jot down prayers, record insights from Bible readings or put on paper the events that seem to be leading somewhere—events that have left an impression on them. Keeping a journal can be done in a way that meets your own needs and preferences. Journaling need not be an elaborate affair or something you slavishly perform every day. It can be as simple as you wish and as occasional as meets your need. If you have never used a journal, try taking a blank bound book, a spiral notebook or a binder full of paper—and then simply write. Make your writing an act of sanctified listening. When you write down your thoughts and ideas and emotions, they take definition and shape. You may find that as you write, you begin to untangle your confusion about what you are hearing from God. You may hear God speaking in ways in which you may not have been attentive otherwise.

Do not allow yourself to relegate to a fuzzy memory the significant things going on within and around you. "The simplest ink," says an old Chinese proverb, "is more reliable than the finest mind." Writing becomes a way to extract a deeper meaning from what has happened to you. It becomes an act of remembering.

Leaf back through your journal pages every few weeks. Notice how God's purposes seem to be emerging in what has happened—and in what hasn't happened. Thank God for prayers that have been answered. Continue to lift up to God themes that emerge from what you've written, themes that reveal your heart's desires. And watch for a greater sense of personal direction. Keeping a journal, wrote Ronald Klug, is "like walking into a messy room—toys and clothes and books piled around—and slowly picking things up and putting them in their right places again. The room 'feels good' and I can go on living there. In a similar way, my journal helps me sort out things in my life and restore some internal order."

We can practice the art of remembering when we meet with family and friends. Conversations at family reunions might move beyond talk of sports or vacations to reflections about how God has proven himself faithful in our family's past and present stories. And when we go to church, worship can be an exercise in remembering. Spiritual growth groups, church school classes—any gathering of believers—can be an occasion to track God's actions in our midst. We recall all the ways God has been faithful. We "testify." And as we do, we find ourselves reminded of who God is through what he has done.

> Open-eyed reflection allows us to see God's hand at work or grasp insights we might otherwise have been too busy to notice.

Reflect on God's Deeds. Reflection—alert awareness of what is happening now—returns us to the present moment. Open-eyed reflection allows us to see God's hand at work or grasp insights we might otherwise have been too busy to notice. The Bible sometimes uses the word "meditation" for this kind of thoughtful reflection. We are not talking about the meditation of Eastern religions, nor a privatized, overly individualistic quest for religious experience. Biblical meditation is always God-centered. It often focuses on God's Word revealed in scripture. And it often has to do with God's activity. "On your wondrous works, I will meditate," David exults in Psalm 145.5. Just three verses earlier he had vowed, "Every day I will bless you." An awareness of what God is doing and the impulse to praise God go hand-in-hand.

Events of daily life therefore belong in our daily prayers. In the Lord's Prayer

Jesus directed us to pray for God's will to be done on earth, not just in heaven—which means in our everyday lives as well. Knowing how much daily matters affect us, Jesus even encouraged his followers to pray for "daily bread"—the everyday sustenance that keeps our physical bodies going. The likelihood that Jesus worked as a carpenter during his early adult years implies that God, through Jesus Christ's incarnation, has for all time graced daily work. And God notices when "bad" things happen and operates through events so that, as the apostle Paul wrote, "We know that all things work together for good for those who love God" (Romans 8.28). All the realities of life, then, constitute the grist for our conversations with God.

As we pray about the things that happen to us from moment to moment, we will begin to cultivate a spiritual alertness. Jean-Pierre de Caussade wrote of "the sacrament of the present moment." He meant that the very place where we are, the very things that we do, can mediate God's presence. Writing of Mary and Joseph, Jesus' parents, de Caussade asks, "What do they discern beneath the seemingly everyday events which occupy them? What is seen is similar to what happens to the rest of [hu]mankind. But what is unseen, that which faith discovers and unravels, is nothing less than God fulfilling his mighty purpose . . . God reveals himself to the humble in small things."

This reflection can take place in the workplace, where many of us spend much of our time. Martin Luther, one of the prime figures of the Protestant Reformation, argued that not just priest or nun, but also milkmaid or blacksmith, could become deeply conscious of God's presence. This can happen in our family times and during our leisure times. Thomas Kelly writes, "a life of little whispered words of adoration, of praise, of prayer, of worship can be breathed all through the day."

Staying alert to God's presence may be as simple as pausing to acknowledge that God is near. It may mean taking a few moments to pray during a lunch hour or coffee break. It may mean occasionally looking out the window to drink in the beauty of God's creation or really paying attention to the people with whom we live. And it certainly means allowing everyday blessings—a sunset, a smile from a friend—to remind us of God and point us back to him in gratitude.

See Page 164 for the first Ways of Meeting God *article.*

The Letter of Paul to
TITUS

Keeping Your Focus

KEY VERSE:

I left you behind in Crete for this reason, so that you should put in order what remained to be done, and should appoint elders in every town, as I directed you.—Titus 1.5

"I earnestly beseech you all in the name of God, and for the sake of your people's souls, that you do not do your ministry carelessly and superficially. Do it vigorously and with all your might. Make it your great and serious business . . ."

—RICHARD BAXTER,
The Reformed Pastor

Have you ever heard of the phrase "medical triage"? It refers to the practice of responding to natural or human disasters. When the injured are so many and the physicians are so few, doctors and nurses must set priorities and work systematically; otherwise they'd be overwhelmed and the situation would take much longer to bring under control.

On a spiritual level, this was the challenge Titus faced. He is left on the Mediterranean island of Crete to supervise a church planted among a particularly unruly people. The people of Crete were renowned for their malicious savagery and unrestrained passions. The idiom "to play the Cretan" meant to be a liar. Even Epimenides, one of Crete's own philosophers, chastised his homeland's moral character. These are the issues Paul takes up with Titus. By giving concrete advice in a clear framework, Paul seems to be saying, "Don't be overwhelmed, stay focused, appoint qualified elders, challenge false teaching, pass on pure doctrine and don't forget the importance of good deeds."

In this letter Paul encapsulates the heart of true Christianity. Titus is overwhelmed, so Paul focuses only on what was most important. The challenge Titus faced long ago can result in something good for us today, for in this letter we are presented with the bedrock essence of our faith. If you were left alone on an island to nurture a Christian church that had been planted in this culture, what would you emphasize? How would you bring order? What would be your primary message?

Salutation

1 Paul, a servant[a] of God and an apostle of Jesus Christ, for the sake of the faith of God's elect and the knowledge of the truth that is in accordance with godliness, [2]in the hope of eternal life that God, who never lies, promised before the ages began— [3]in due time he revealed his word through the proclamation with which I have been entrusted by the command of God our Savior,

4 To Titus, my loyal child in the faith we share:

Grace[b] and peace from God the Father and Christ Jesus our Savior.

Titus in Crete

5 I left you behind in Crete for this reason, so that you should put in order what remained to be done, and should appoint elders in every town, as I directed you: [6]someone who is blameless, married only once,[c] whose children are believers, not accused of debauchery and not rebellious. [7]For a bishop,[d] as God's steward, must be blameless; he must not be arrogant or quick-tempered or addicted to wine or violent or greedy for gain; [8]but he must be hospitable, a lover of goodness, prudent, upright, devout, and self-controlled. [9]He must have a firm grasp of the word that is trustworthy in accordance with the teaching, so that he may be able both to preach with sound doctrine and to refute those who contradict it.

10 There are also many rebellious people, idle talkers and deceivers, especially those of the circumcision; [11]they must be silenced, since they are upsetting whole families by teaching for sordid gain what it is not right to teach. [12]It was one of them, their very own prophet, who said,

"Cretans are always liars, vicious brutes, lazy
    gluttons."

[13]That testimony is true. For this reason rebuke them sharply, so that they may become sound in the faith, [14]not paying attention to Jewish myths or to commandments of those who reject the truth. [15]To the pure all things are pure, but to the corrupt and unbelieving nothing is pure. Their very minds and consciences are corrupted. [16]They profess to know God, but they deny him by their actions. They are detestable, disobedient, unfit for any good work.

Teach Sound Doctrine

2 But as for you, teach what is consistent with sound doctrine. [2]Tell the older men to be temperate, serious, prudent, and sound in faith, in love, and in endurance.

3 Likewise, tell the older women to be reverent in behavior, not to be slanderers or slaves to drink; they are to teach what is good, [4]so that they may encourage the young women to love their husbands, to love their children, [5]to be self-controlled, chaste, good managers of the household, kind, being submissive to their husbands, so that the word of God may not be discredited.

6 Likewise, urge the younger men to be self-controlled. [7]Show yourself in all respects a model of good works, and in your teaching show integrity, gravity, [8]and sound speech

---

a Gk slave   b Other ancient authorities read Grace, mercy,   c Gk husband of one wife   d Or an overseer

The Power of a Pure Source

TITUS 1.15

Take out some food coloring and a clear drinking glass. Fill the glass with water; then add a few drops of food coloring. Notice how the small stain begins to spread. With a little stirring, it colors all the water. Imagine trying to separate the dye from the water. Sounds impossible, doesn't it?

Now hold the glass under a running faucet. Watch as eventually the clear, pure water completely replaces the dyed water in the glass. What might you infer about your spiritual life from this experiment? What are the stains that have colored your life? Anger, fear, despair, self-righteousness, addictions? Ask Jesus to give you the living water of the Spirit to blot out the stains and cleanse you completely.

Changed Saints

TITUS 3.3–5

"Even true Christians still have remnants of a contrary spirit and may even be guilty of behavior offensive to such a spirit. But this I affirm, there are no true Christians who live in the prevailing power of such a spirit so that it becomes truly their character. The Scripture speaks of no real Christians who have an ugly, selfish, angry, and contentious spirit. Nothing can be more contradictory than a morose, hard, closed, and spiteful Christian. [While] allowances must be made for our natural human temperament . . . we see that in the early church converts were remarkably changed."

—JONATHAN EDWARDS,
Treatise Concerning Religious Affections

that cannot be censured; then any opponent will be put to shame, having nothing evil to say of us.

9 Tell slaves to be submissive to their masters and to give satisfaction in every respect; they are not to talk back, [10]not to pilfer, but to show complete and perfect fidelity, so that in everything they may be an ornament to the doctrine of God our Savior.

11 For the grace of God has appeared, bringing salvation to all,[a] [12]training us to renounce impiety and worldly passions, and in the present age to live lives that are self-controlled, upright, and godly, [13]while we wait for the blessed hope and the manifestation of the glory of our great God and Savior,[b] Jesus Christ. [14]He it is who gave himself for us that he might redeem us from all iniquity and purify for himself a people of his own who are zealous for good deeds.

15 Declare these things; exhort and reprove with all authority.[c] Let no one look down on you.

Maintain Good Deeds

3 Remind them to be subject to rulers and authorities, to be obedient, to be ready for every good work, [2]to speak evil of no one, to avoid quarreling, to be gentle, and to show every courtesy to everyone. [3]For we ourselves were once foolish, disobedient, led astray, slaves to various passions and pleasures, passing our days in malice and envy, despicable, hating one another. [4]But when the goodness and loving kindness of God our Savior appeared, [5]he saved us, not because of any works of righteousness that we had done, but according to his mercy, through the water[d] of rebirth and renewal by the Holy Spirit. [6]This Spirit he poured out on us richly through Jesus Christ our Savior, [7]so that, having been justified by his grace, we might become heirs according to the hope of eternal life. [8]The saying is sure.

I desire that you insist on these things, so that those who have come to believe in God may be careful to devote themselves to good works; these things are excellent and profitable to everyone. [9]But avoid stupid controversies, genealogies, dissensions, and quarrels about the law, for they are unprofitable and worthless. [10]After a first and second admonition, have nothing more to do with anyone who causes divisions, [11]since you know that such a person is perverted and sinful, being self-condemned.

Final Messages and Benediction

12 When I send Artemas to you, or Tychicus, do your best to come to me at Nicopolis, for I have decided to spend the winter there. [13]Make every effort to send Zenas the lawyer and Apollos on their way, and see that they lack nothing. [14]And let people learn to devote themselves to good works in order to meet urgent needs, so that they may not be unproductive.

15 All who are with me send greetings to you. Greet those who love us in the faith.

Grace be with all of you.[e]

a Or *has appeared to all, bringing salvation*   b Or *of the great God and our Savior*   c Gk *commandment*   d Gk *washing*   e Other ancient authorities add *Amen*

THE LETTER OF PAUL TO
PHILEMON
A Plea for Reconciliation

KEY VERSE:

So if you consider me your partner, welcome him as you would welcome me.—Philemon 17

This brief letter leads us into the middle of a difficult situation in the early church, one with parallels to our time. Philemon was a first-century Christian living in Asia Minor. His slave Onesimus escaped and met the imprisoned apostle Paul, who shared the gospel with him. Then Paul wrote this gracious and respectful letter encouraging Philemon to take back Onesimus—"no longer as a slave, but . . . [as] a beloved brother" (v.16).

Consider Philemon's options. Should he free Onesimus and risk total chaos among the other slaves, who might fake conversions to win their freedom? Should he punish Onesimus for running away? Should he return Onesimus to Paul? Or should he do what Paul suggests—welcome him home as a brother in Christ Jesus?

Welcoming people into our church communities after they have a change of heart can be a problem for us. If they have hurt us in the past, we may want to offer only the cold heart and closed fist of judgment. We may feel little eagerness to remove the stigma associated with their former reputations. After all, what will everyone else think if it looks like we are too easy on them?

But Paul takes a different approach by regarding other Christians as family members. Philemon is twice addressed as "brother." Apphia is a "sister." Because Onesimus is now a Christian, he, too, must be called "brother." The apostle Paul encourages Philemon to do the hard thing—the right thing. His letter asks us to do the same in the difficult relationships we may face in our own churches.

"We are to be gospel people. We are not to be our own law; we are not to be the centers of our own universe; we are not to be unaware, unconcerned, unlistening to all the others. We are to be the formers of the human community, and we are to be formed by it as well. That is the function of authority . . . Authority is more than the preservation of law or the maintenance of order. Authority is the call to growth."

—JOAN CHITTISTER, O.S.B.,
Wisdom Distilled from the Daily: Living the Rule of St. Benedict Today

Asking a Favor

PHILEMON 13-14

Paul writes to request a favor of a friend. He could use his authority to force Philemon to comply, but he wants Philemon to make the choice freely.

Paul's actions give us something to wonder about. How do we seek to get our way? Do we simply ask, or do we use authority, guilt or other forms of manipulation? You might ask those around you to help assess your approach.

It takes real faith—in others and in God—to state your case and then trust that whatever happens will be okay. Are you involved in urging an individual or group to make a particular decision? Ask God to give you the wisdom to present your opinion well and the courage to allow others the freedom to decide for themselves.

See Meeting God in Community

Salutation

1 Paul, a prisoner of Christ Jesus, and Timothy our brother,[a]

To Philemon our dear friend and co-worker, [2]to Apphia our sister,[b] to Archippus our fellow soldier, and to the church in your house:
3 Grace to you and peace from God our Father and the Lord Jesus Christ.

Philemon's Love and Faith

4 When I remember you[c] in my prayers, I always thank my God [5]because I hear of your love for all the saints and your faith toward the Lord Jesus. [6]I pray that the sharing of your faith may become effective when you perceive all the good that we[d] may do for Christ. [7]I have indeed received much joy and encouragement from your love, because the hearts of the saints have been refreshed through you, my brother.

Paul's Plea for Onesimus

8 For this reason, though I am bold enough in Christ to command you to do your duty, [9]yet I would rather appeal to you on the basis of love—and I, Paul, do this as an old man, and now also as a prisoner of Christ Jesus.[e] [10]I am appealing to you for my child, Onesimus, whose father I have become during my imprisonment. [11]Formerly he was useless to you, but now he is indeed useful[f] both to you and to me. [12]I am sending him, that is, my own heart, back to you. [13]I wanted to keep him with me, so that he might be of service to me in your place during my imprisonment for the gospel; [14]but I preferred to do nothing without your consent, in order that your good deed might be voluntary and not something forced. [15]Perhaps this is the reason he was separated from you for a while, so that you might have him back forever, [16]no longer as a slave but more than a slave, a beloved brother—especially to me but how much more to you, both in the flesh and in the Lord.

17 So if you consider me your partner, welcome him as you would welcome me. [18]If he has wronged you in any way, or owes you anything, charge that to my account. [19]I, Paul, am writing this with my own hand: I will repay it. I say nothing about your owing me even your own self. [20]Yes, brother, let me have this benefit from you in the Lord! Refresh my heart in Christ. [21]Confident of your obedience, I am writing to you, knowing that you will do even more than I say.

22 One thing more—prepare a guest room for me, for I am hoping through your prayers to be restored to you.

Final Greetings and Benediction

23 Epaphras, my fellow prisoner in Christ Jesus, sends greetings to you,[g] [24]and so do Mark, Aristarchus, Demas, and Luke, my fellow workers.

25 The grace of the Lord Jesus Christ be with your spirit.[h]

---

a Gk *the brother*   b Gk *the sister*   c From verse 4 through verse 21, *you* is singular   d Other ancient authorities read *you* (plural)   e Or *as an ambassador of Christ Jesus, and now also his prisoner*   f The name Onesimus means *useful* or (compare verse 20) *beneficial*   g Here *you* is singular   h Other ancient authorities add *Amen*

THE LETTER TO THE
HEBREWS
A New and Better Way

KEY VERSE:

For this reason he is the mediator of a new covenant, so that those who are called may receive the promised eternal inheritance, because a death has occurred that redeems them from the transgressions under the first covenant.—Hebrews 9.15

Some people think that, in religious matters, tradition is all-important. Some, on the other hand, will have nothing to do with tradition; they forever want to be on the "cutting edge." Ideally, though, the best of the new is that which grows from and builds on the depth and wisdom of the older traditions.

For the writer of Hebrews, the new covenant of Jesus Christ represented the fullness and completion of the revelation of God's love for humanity—the revelation God began with the old covenant. In fact the Old Testament itself pointed to the unfolding of the new covenant of love in Jesus Christ—a new and superior way that would supersede the old.

As you read and meditate on these pages of Scripture, notice how often they refer to Jesus' ministry as "superior to" or "better" than the ministry of the old covenant. This book is about faith—God's faithfulness to us in giving us his Son, "the reflection of God's glory and the exact imprint of [God's] very being" (1.3), and our faithful response of "looking to Jesus" (12.2). Open up any areas in your life in which you need to renew your trust and dependence on the promises of God and the provisions of Jesus Christ through the Holy Spirit.

"Our faith in Jesus is most real. We believe in those dear wounds of His as we believe in nothing else; there is no fact so sure to us as that He was slain, and He has redeemed us to God by His blood. We believe in the brightness of His glory; for nothing seems to us so necessarily true as that He who was obedient unto death should, as His due reward, be crowned with glory and honour."

—CHARLES H. SPURGEON,
An All Around Ministry

The Reflection of God's Glory

HEBREWS 1.1–4

Jesus Christ is the Son of God! Consider what that means to God. Then consider what that means to you. Notice what God has done through Jesus (spoken, created, sustained and saved). List some of the ways you have experienced this "superior" ministry of Jesus Christ in your life.

After reading and pondering this passage, close your eyes and imagine how you would depict Jesus through painting, sculpture, music or poetry based on this Scripture. What characteristics of Jesus would you try to emphasize? You might want to create the work of art you have imagined.

See *Meeting God in Scripture*

God Has Spoken by His Son

1 Long ago God spoke to our ancestors in many and various ways by the prophets, [2]but in these last days he has spoken to us by a Son,[a] whom he appointed heir of all things, through whom he also created the worlds. [3]He is the reflection of God's glory and the exact imprint of God's very being, and he sustains[b] all things by his powerful word. When he had made purification for sins, he sat down at the right hand of the Majesty on high, [4]having become as much superior to angels as the name he has inherited is more excellent than theirs.

The Son Is Superior to Angels

[5] For to which of the angels did God ever say,
"You are my Son;
    today I have begotten you"?
Or again,
"I will be his Father,
    and he will be my Son"?
[6]And again, when he brings the firstborn into the world, he says,
"Let all God's angels worship him."
[7]Of the angels he says,
"He makes his angels winds,
    and his servants flames of fire."
[8]But of the Son he says,
"Your throne, O God, is[c] forever and ever,
    and the righteous scepter is the scepter of your[d]
        kingdom.
[9] You have loved righteousness and hated
        wickedness;
therefore God, your God, has anointed you
    with the oil of gladness beyond your
        companions."
[10]And,
"In the beginning, Lord, you founded the earth,
    and the heavens are the work of your hands;
[11] they will perish, but you remain;
    they will all wear out like clothing;
[12] like a cloak you will roll them up,
    and like clothing[e] they will be changed.
But you are the same,
    and your years will never end."
[13]But to which of the angels has he ever said,
"Sit at my right hand
    until I make your enemies a footstool for your
        feet"?
[14]Are not all angels[f] spirits in the divine service, sent to serve for the sake of those who are to inherit salvation?

Warning to Pay Attention

2 Therefore we must pay greater attention to what we have heard, so that we do not drift away from it. [2]For if the message declared through angels was valid, and every transgression or disobedience received a just penalty, [3]how can we escape if we neglect so great a salvation? It was declared at first through the Lord, and it was attest-

a Or *the Son*   b Or *bears along*   c Or *God is your throne*   d Other ancient authorities read *his*   e Other ancient authorities lack *like clothing*   f Gk *all of them*

ed to us by those who heard him, ⁴while God added his testimony by signs and wonders and various miracles, and by gifts of the Holy Spirit, distributed according to his will.

Exaltation through Abasement

5 Now God*ᵃ* did not subject the coming world, about which we are speaking, to angels. ⁶But someone has testified somewhere,

"What are human beings that you are mindful of
them,*ᵇ*
or mortals, that you care for them?*ᶜ*
⁷ You have made them for a little while lower*ᵈ* than
the angels;
you have crowned them with glory and honor,*ᵉ*
⁸ subjecting all things under their feet."

Now in subjecting all things to them, God*ᵃ* left nothing outside their control. As it is, we do not yet see everything in subjection to them, ⁹but we do see Jesus, who for a little while was made lower*ᶠ* than the angels, now crowned with glory and honor because of the suffering of death, so that by the grace of God*ᵍ* he might taste death for everyone.

10 It was fitting that God,*ᵃ* for whom and through whom all things exist, in bringing many children to glory, should make the pioneer of their salvation perfect through sufferings. ¹¹For the one who sanctifies and those who are sanctified all have one Father.*ʰ* For this reason Jesus*ᵃ* is not ashamed to call them brothers and sisters,*ⁱ* ¹²saying,

"I will proclaim your name to my brothers and
sisters,*ⁱ*
in the midst of the congregation I will praise
you."

¹³And again,

"I will put my trust in him."

And again,

"Here am I and the children whom God has given
me."

14 Since, therefore, the children share flesh and blood, he himself likewise shared the same things, so that through death he might destroy the one who has the power of death, that is, the devil, ¹⁵and free those who all their lives were held in slavery by the fear of death. ¹⁶For it is clear that he did not come to help angels, but the descendants of Abraham. ¹⁷Therefore he had to become like his brothers and sisters*ⁱ* in every respect, so that he might be a merciful and faithful high priest in the service of God, to make a sacrifice of atonement for the sins of the people. ¹⁸Because he himself was tested by what he suffered, he is able to help those who are being tested.

Moses a Servant, Christ a Son

3 Therefore, brothers and sisters,*ⁱ* holy partners in a heavenly calling, consider that Jesus, the apostle and high priest of our confession, ²was faithful to the one who appointed him, just as Moses also "was faithful in all*ʲ*

---

a Gk he   b Gk What is man that you are mindful of him?   c Gk or the
son of man that you care for him? In the Hebrew of Psalm 8.4-6 both man
and son of man refer to all humankind   d Or them only a little lower
e Other ancient authorities add and set them over the works of your hands
f Or who was made a little lower   g Other ancient authorities read apart
from God   h Gk are all of one   i Gk brothers   j Other ancient
authorities lack all

Freedom From Fear

HEBREWS 2.14–18

Life can be pretty scary! And the powers of darkness delight in shifting our focus from Jesus to our fears and problems. But listen to the good news: "Because he himself suffered when he was tempted, he is able to help those who are being tempted."

What are your greatest fears? In what ways do you feel enslaved by your fears? How do you feel about the process of aging and the reality that you (and all your loved ones) will someday die? Picture a situation in which you feel afraid. Invite Jesus to sit beside you. Slowly repeat verse 18. Memorize it and recall it whenever you feel that fear is taking control of your mind or emotions.

See Meeting God in Scripture

Don't Be Disqualified!

HEBREWS 3.12–14

How sad to read the letters DNF ("did not finish") behind the name of an athlete for whatever the reason—a sprain, exhaustion, violation of a rule, or an equipment problem. It's sad, too, when we Christians don't finish "the race that is set before us" (see 12.1). One of our greatest spiritual challenges is to protect our hearts from becoming hardened and to stay receptive to God's action in our lives.

Take some time to gently examine your life. Are there any habits that draw you away from God? What helps you to draw nearer to Jesus Christ and deepen your relationship with him? Who has been your cheerleader—one who has encouraged you to be faithful? Conclude by renewing your commitment to God through a tangible act of dedication.

See Meeting God in Everyday Life

God's[a] house." [3]Yet Jesus[b] is worthy of more glory than Moses, just as the builder of a house has more honor than the house itself. [4](For every house is built by someone, but the builder of all things is God.) [5]Now Moses was faithful in all God's[a] house as a servant, to testify to the things that would be spoken later. [6]Christ, however, was faithful over God's[a] house as a son, and we are his house if we hold firm[c] the confidence and the pride that belong to hope.

Warning against Unbelief

[7] Therefore, as the Holy Spirit says,
"Today, if you hear his voice,
[8]   do not harden your hearts as in the rebellion,
        as on the day of testing in the wilderness,
[9]   where your ancestors put me to the test,
        though they had seen my works [10]for forty years.
Therefore I was angry with that generation,
and I said, 'They always go astray in their hearts,
and they have not known my ways.'
[11]   As in my anger I swore,
'They will not enter my rest.' "
[12]Take care, brothers and sisters,[d] that none of you may have an evil, unbelieving heart that turns away from the living God. [13]But exhort one another every day, as long as it is called "today," so that none of you may be hardened by the deceitfulness of sin. [14]For we have become partners of Christ, if only we hold our first confidence firm to the end. [15]As it is said,
"Today, if you hear his voice,
do not harden your hearts as in the rebellion."
[16]Now who were they who heard and yet were rebellious? Was it not all those who left Egypt under the leadership of Moses? [17]But with whom was he angry forty years? Was it not those who sinned, whose bodies fell in the wilderness? [18]And to whom did he swear that they would not enter his rest, if not to those who were disobedient? [19]So we see that they were unable to enter because of unbelief.

The Rest That God Promised

4 Therefore, while the promise of entering his rest is still open, let us take care that none of you should seem to have failed to reach it. [2]For indeed the good news came to us just as to them; but the message they heard did not benefit them, because they were not united by faith with those who listened.[e] [3]For we who have believed enter that rest, just as God[f] has said,
"As in my anger I swore,
'They shall not enter my rest,' "
though his works were finished at the foundation of the world. [4]For in one place it speaks about the seventh day as follows, "And God rested on the seventh day from all his works." [5]And again in this place it says, "They shall not enter my rest." [6]Since therefore it remains open for some to enter it, and those who formerly received the good news failed to enter because of disobedience, [7]again he

---

a Gk *his*   b Gk *this one*   c Other ancient authorities add *to the end*
d Gk *brothers*   e Other ancient authorities read *it did not meet with faith in those who listened*   f Gk *he*

sets a certain day—"today"—saying through David much later, in the words already quoted,

"Today, if you hear his voice,
do not harden your hearts."

[8]For if Joshua had given them rest, God[a] would not speak later about another day. [9]So then, a sabbath rest still remains for the people of God; [10]for those who enter God's rest also cease from their labors as God did from his. [11]Let us therefore make every effort to enter that rest, so that no one may fall through such disobedience as theirs.

12 Indeed, the word of God is living and active, sharper than any two-edged sword, piercing until it divides soul from spirit, joints from marrow; it is able to judge the thoughts and intentions of the heart. [13]And before him no creature is hidden, but all are naked and laid bare to the eyes of the one to whom we must render an account.

Jesus the Great High Priest

14 Since, then, we have a great high priest who has passed through the heavens, Jesus, the Son of God, let us hold fast to our confession. [15]For we do not have a high priest who is unable to sympathize with our weaknesses, but we have one who in every respect has been tested[b] as we are, yet without sin. [16]Let us therefore approach the throne of grace with boldness, so that we may receive mercy and find grace to help in time of need.

5 Every high priest chosen from among mortals is put in charge of things pertaining to God on their behalf, to offer gifts and sacrifices for sins. [2]He is able to deal gently with the ignorant and wayward, since he himself is subject to weakness; [3]and because of this he must offer sacrifice for his own sins as well as for those of the people. [4]And one does not presume to take this honor, but takes it only when called by God, just as Aaron was.

5 So also Christ did not glorify himself in becoming a high priest, but was appointed by the one who said to him,

"You are my Son,
today I have begotten you";

[6]as he says also in another place,

"You are a priest forever,
according to the order of Melchizedek."

7 In the days of his flesh, Jesus[a] offered up prayers and supplications, with loud cries and tears, to the one who was able to save him from death, and he was heard because of his reverent submission. [8]Although he was a Son, he learned obedience through what he suffered; [9]and having been made perfect, he became the source of eternal salvation for all who obey him, [10]having been designated by God a high priest according to the order of Melchizedek.

Warning against Falling Away

11 About this[c] we have much to say that is hard to explain, since you have become dull in understanding. [12]For though by this time you ought to be teachers, you need someone to teach you again the basic elements of the oracles of God. You need milk, not solid food; [13]for everyone who lives on milk, being still an infant, is unskilled in the word of righteousness. [14]But solid food is for the mature,

Help for the Asking

HEBREWS 4.14–16

What would it be like to "approach [God's] throne"? Does that phrase invoke a mental image of the angels and awesome glory of Isaiah 6? Read this passage again, lingering over the phrases "sympathize with our weaknesses . . . tested as we are . . . throne of grace." Imagine yourself approaching God's throne and finding Jesus there; he smiles and calls you "friend." What do you ask of him? What gift does he give you? You might conclude by singing a hymn such as "What a Friend We Have in Jesus" or "Jesus Is All the World to Me."

See Meeting God in Prayer

---

a Gk *he*   *b* Or *tempted*   *c* Or *him*

Confidence in God's Promises

"One of the chief needs in our waiting upon God, one of the deepest secrets of its blessedness and blessing, is a quiet, confident persuasion that it is not in vain. Have courage and believe that God will hear and help. We are waiting on a God who could never disappoint His people."

—ANDREW MURRAY,
Waiting on God

for those whose faculties have been trained by practice to distinguish good from evil.

The Peril of Falling Away

6 Therefore let us go on toward perfection,[a] leaving behind the basic teaching about Christ, and not laying again the foundation: repentance from dead works and faith toward God, [2]instruction about baptisms, laying on of hands, resurrection of the dead, and eternal judgment. [3]And we will do[b] this, if God permits. [4]For it is impossible to restore again to repentance those who have once been enlightened, and have tasted the heavenly gift, and have shared in the Holy Spirit, [5]and have tasted the goodness of the word of God and the powers of the age to come, [6]and then have fallen away, since on their own they are crucifying again the Son of God and are holding him up to contempt. [7]Ground that drinks up the rain falling on it repeatedly, and that produces a crop useful to those for whom it is cultivated, receives a blessing from God. [8]But if it produces thorns and thistles, it is worthless and on the verge of being cursed; its end is to be burned over.

9 Even though we speak in this way, beloved, we are confident of better things in your case, things that belong to salvation. [10]For God is not unjust; he will not overlook your work and the love that you showed for his sake[c] in serving the saints, as you still do. [11]And we want each one of you to show the same diligence so as to realize the full assurance of hope to the very end, [12]so that you may not become sluggish, but imitators of those who through faith and patience inherit the promises.

The Certainty of God's Promise

13 When God made a promise to Abraham, because he had no one greater by whom to swear, he swore by himself, [14]saying, "I will surely bless you and multiply you." [15]And thus Abraham,[d] having patiently endured, obtained the promise. [16]Human beings, of course, swear by someone greater than themselves, and an oath given as confirmation puts an end to all dispute. [17]In the same way, when God desired to show even more clearly to the heirs of the promise the unchangeable character of his purpose, he guaranteed it by an oath, [18]so that through two unchangeable things, in which it is impossible that God would prove false, we who have taken refuge might be strongly encouraged to seize the hope set before us. [19]We have this hope, a sure and steadfast anchor of the soul, a hope that enters the inner shrine behind the curtain, [20]where Jesus, a forerunner on our behalf, has entered, having become a high priest forever according to the order of Melchizedek.

The Priestly Order of Melchizedek

7 This "King Melchizedek of Salem, priest of the Most High God, met Abraham as he was returning from defeating the kings and blessed him"; [2]and to him Abraham apportioned "one-tenth of everything." His name, in the first place, means "king of righteousness"; next he is also king of Salem, that is, "king of peace." [3]Without father,

---

a Or *toward maturity*   b Other ancient authorities read *let us do*
c Gk *for his name*   d Gk *he*

without mother, without genealogy, having neither beginning of days nor end of life, but resembling the Son of God, he remains a priest forever.

4 See how great he is! Even[a] Abraham the patriarch gave him a tenth of the spoils. [5]And those descendants of Levi who receive the priestly office have a commandment in the law to collect tithes[b] from the people, that is, from their kindred,[c] though these also are descended from Abraham. [6]But this man, who does not belong to their ancestry, collected tithes[b] from Abraham and blessed him who had received the promises. [7]It is beyond dispute that the inferior is blessed by the superior. [8]In the one case, tithes are received by those who are mortal; in the other, by one of whom it is testified that he lives. [9]One might even say that Levi himself, who receives tithes, paid tithes through Abraham, [10]for he was still in the loins of his ancestor when Melchizedek met him.

Another Priest, Like Melchizedek

11 Now if perfection had been attainable through the levitical priesthood—for the people received the law under this priesthood—what further need would there have been to speak of another priest arising according to the order of Melchizedek, rather than one according to the order of Aaron? [12]For when there is a change in the priesthood, there is necessarily a change in the law as well. [13]Now the one of whom these things are spoken belonged to another tribe, from which no one has ever served at the altar. [14]For it is evident that our Lord was descended from Judah, and in connection with that tribe Moses said nothing about priests.

15 It is even more obvious when another priest arises, resembling Melchizedek, [16]one who has become a priest, not through a legal requirement concerning physical descent, but through the power of an indestructible life. [17]For it is attested of him,

"You are a priest forever,
according to the order of Melchizedek."

[18]There is, on the one hand, the abrogation of an earlier commandment because it was weak and ineffectual [19](for the law made nothing perfect); there is, on the other hand, the introduction of a better hope, through which we approach God.

20 This was confirmed with an oath; for others who became priests took their office without an oath, [21]but this one became a priest with an oath, because of the one who said to him,

"The Lord has sworn
and will not change his mind,
'You are a priest forever' "—

[22]accordingly Jesus has also become the guarantee of a better covenant.

23 Furthermore, the former priests were many in number, because they were prevented by death from continuing in office; [24]but he holds his priesthood permanently, because he continues forever. [25]Consequently he is able for all time to save[d] those who approach God through him, since he always lives to make intercession for them.

---

a Other ancient authorities lack *Even*   b Or *a tenth*   c Gk *brothers*
d Or *able to save completely*

An Anchor for the Soul

HEBREWS 6.17–20

Many people seem overwhelmed by a chronic, low-grade hopelessness. Adrift in a sea of busyness and pressure, they are looking for something to grab hold of—anything to keep them afloat.

What is your greatest source of hope? In what areas of your life are you most in need of hope? Hebrews speaks of hope as an "anchor of the soul." Reflect on that image. What other symbol or image would remind you of hope? Draw or find a picture of that item, and hang it in a prominent place where you can see it and let it strengthen you.

Jesus, Our Intercessor

HEBREWS 7.23–28

The good news is that Jesus never gives up! He continues until he completes each task that has been set before him. Jesus lives always to offer prayers for you. Sit quietly and imagine Jesus praying for you. What do you sense about his method of prayer? How does it feel to know that Jesus, the great high priest, is praying to the Father on your behalf? How might his prayers differ from your prayers for yourself? From the prayers of others on your behalf? How can Jesus help you as you intercede for other people?

See Meeting God in Prayer

26 For it was fitting that we should have such a high priest, holy, blameless, undefiled, separated from sinners, and exalted above the heavens. [27]Unlike the other[a] high priests, he has no need to offer sacrifices day after day, first for his own sins, and then for those of the people; this he did once for all when he offered himself. [28]For the law appoints as high priests those who are subject to weakness, but the word of the oath, which came later than the law, appoints a Son who has been made perfect forever.

Mediator of a Better Covenant

8 Now the main point in what we are saying is this: we have such a high priest, one who is seated at the right hand of the throne of the Majesty in the heavens, [2]a minister in the sanctuary and the true tent[b] that the Lord, and not any mortal, has set up. [3]For every high priest is appointed to offer gifts and sacrifices; hence it is necessary for this priest also to have something to offer. [4]Now if he were on earth, he would not be a priest at all, since there are priests who offer gifts according to the law. [5]They offer worship in a sanctuary that is a sketch and shadow of the heavenly one; for Moses, when he was about to erect the tent,[b] was warned, "See that you make everything according to the pattern that was shown you on the mountain." [6]But Jesus[c] has now obtained a more excellent ministry, and to that degree he is the mediator of a better covenant, which has been enacted through better promises. [7]For if that first covenant had been faultless, there would have been no need to look for a second one.

8 God[d] finds fault with them when he says:
"The days are surely coming, says the Lord,
    when I will establish a new covenant with the
        house of Israel
    and with the house of Judah;
[9]   not like the covenant that I made with their
        ancestors,
    on the day when I took them by the hand to
        lead them out of the land of Egypt;
    for they did not continue in my covenant,
    and so I had no concern for them, says the
        Lord.
[10]   This is the covenant that I will make with the
        house of Israel
    after those days, says the Lord:
    I will put my laws in their minds,
        and write them on their hearts,
    and I will be their God,
        and they shall be my people.
[11]   And they shall not teach one another
        or say to each other, 'Know the Lord,'
    for they shall all know me,
        from the least of them to the greatest.
[12]   For I will be merciful toward their iniquities,
        and I will remember their sins no more."
[13]In speaking of "a new covenant," he has made the first one obsolete. And what is obsolete and growing old will soon disappear.

a Gk lacks *other*   *b* Or *tabernacle*   *c* Gk *he*   *d* Gk *He*

The Earthly and the Heavenly Sanctuaries

9 Now even the first covenant had regulations for worship and an earthly sanctuary. ²For a tent[a] was constructed, the first one, in which were the lampstand, the table, and the bread of the Presence;[b] this is called the Holy Place. ³Behind the second curtain was a tent[a] called the Holy of Holies. ⁴In it stood the golden altar of incense and the ark of the covenant overlaid on all sides with gold, in which there were a golden urn holding the manna, and Aaron's rod that budded, and the tablets of the covenant; ⁵above it were the cherubim of glory overshadowing the mercy seat.[c] Of these things we cannot speak now in detail.

6 Such preparations having been made, the priests go continually into the first tent[a] to carry out their ritual duties; ⁷but only the high priest goes into the second, and he but once a year, and not without taking the blood that he offers for himself and for the sins committed unintentionally by the people. ⁸By this the Holy Spirit indicates that the way into the sanctuary has not yet been disclosed as long as the first tent[a] is still standing. ⁹This is a symbol[d] of the present time, during which gifts and sacrifices are offered that cannot perfect the conscience of the worshiper, ¹⁰but deal only with food and drink and various baptisms, regulations for the body imposed until the time comes to set things right.

11 But when Christ came as a high priest of the good things that have come,[e] then through the greater and perfect[f] tent[a] (not made with hands, that is, not of this creation), ¹²he entered once for all into the Holy Place, not with the blood of goats and calves, but with his own blood, thus obtaining eternal redemption. ¹³For if the blood of goats and bulls, with the sprinkling of the ashes of a heifer, sanctifies those who have been defiled so that their flesh is purified, ¹⁴how much more will the blood of Christ, who through the eternal Spirit[g] offered himself without blemish to God, purify our[h] conscience from dead works to worship the living God!

15 For this reason he is the mediator of a new covenant, so that those who are called may receive the promised eternal inheritance, because a death has occurred that redeems them from the transgressions under the first covenant.[i] ¹⁶Where a will[i] is involved, the death of the one who made it must be established. ¹⁷For a will[i] takes effect only at death, since it is not in force as long as the one who made it is alive. ¹⁸Hence not even the first covenant was inaugurated without blood. ¹⁹For when every commandment had been told to all the people by Moses in accordance with the law, he took the blood of calves and goats,[j] with water and scarlet wool and hyssop, and sprinkled both the scroll itself and all the people, ²⁰saying, "This is the blood of the covenant that God has ordained for you." ²¹And in the same way he sprinkled with the blood both the tent[a] and all the vessels used in worship. ²²Indeed, under the law almost everything is purified with

---

a Or tabernacle   b Gk the presentation of the loaves   c Or the place of atonement   d Gk parable   e Other ancient authorities read good things to come   f Gk more perfect   g Other ancient authorities read Holy Spirit   h Other ancient authorities read your   i The Greek word used here means both covenant and will   j Other ancient authorities lack and goats

Inner Cleansing

HEBREWS 9.13–14

Making a good impression is important. Yet we may become so preoccupied with our outward appearance that we neglect our inner heart and conscience. Jesus comes to cleanse all aspects of our lives. His Spirit begins by renewing our hearts and his work radiates through our attitudes and actions. You may already be conscious of your faults. Are you as familiar with Jesus' cleansing? You might picture your faults as trash cluttering the floor of a room that represents your conscience. Let the Spirit pour through your inner room like a flood—cleansing, purifying and renewing. Envision the room transformed into a chapel where God is worshiped and glorified. You may want to conclude by slowly and reflectively repeating the Lord's Prayer.

A New and Different High Priest

HEBREWS 9.25–28

The human priests of the Old Testament had to continually offer up sacrifices for themselves and the people they represented in order to be cleansed from their sin. Jesus is a different high priest. He offered his life as a sacrifice only once and for all time.

Allow yourself to reflect on the significance of Jesus' sacrifice. What does it mean to you? How does it affect the way in which you live? What words could you use to describe Jesus' extravagant gift to you? Record these words in your journal. How do you express your gratitude to God for Jesus, your high priest?

See Meeting God in Worship

blood, and without the shedding of blood there is no forgiveness of sins.

Christ's Sacrifice Takes Away Sin

23 Thus it was necessary for the sketches of the heavenly things to be purified with these rites, but the heavenly things themselves need better sacrifices than these. 24For Christ did not enter a sanctuary made by human hands, a mere copy of the true one, but he entered into heaven itself, now to appear in the presence of God on our behalf. 25Nor was it to offer himself again and again, as the high priest enters the Holy Place year after year with blood that is not his own; 26for then he would have had to suffer again and again since the foundation of the world. But as it is, he has appeared once for all at the end of the age to remove sin by the sacrifice of himself. 27And just as it is appointed for mortals to die once, and after that the judgment, 28so Christ, having been offered once to bear the sins of many, will appear a second time, not to deal with sin, but to save those who are eagerly waiting for him.

Christ's Sacrifice Once for All

10 Since the law has only a shadow of the good things to come and not the true form of these realities, it*a* can never, by the same sacrifices that are continually offered year after year, make perfect those who approach. 2Otherwise, would they not have ceased being offered, since the worshipers, cleansed once for all, would no longer have any consciousness of sin? 3But in these sacrifices there is a reminder of sin year after year. 4For it is impossible for the blood of bulls and goats to take away sins. 5Consequently, when Christ*b* came into the world, he said,

"Sacrifices and offerings you have not desired,
　but a body you have prepared for me;
6　in burnt offerings and sin offerings
　　you have taken no pleasure.
7　Then I said, 'See, God, I have come to do your
　　will, O God'
　　(in the scroll of the book*c* it is written of me)."

8When he said above, "You have neither desired nor taken pleasure in sacrifices and offerings and burnt offerings and sin offerings" (these are offered according to the law), 9then he added, "See, I have come to do your will." He abolishes the first in order to establish the second. 10And it is by God's will*d* that we have been sanctified through the offering of the body of Jesus Christ once for all.

11 And every priest stands day after day at his service, offering again and again the same sacrifices that can never take away sins. 12But when Christ*e* had offered for all time a single sacrifice for sins, "he sat down at the right hand of God," 13and since then has been waiting "until his enemies would be made a footstool for his feet." 14For by a single offering he has perfected for all time those who are sanctified. 15And the Holy Spirit also testifies to us, for after saying,
16　"This is the covenant that I will make with them

a Other ancient authorities read *they*　*b* Gk *he*　*c* Meaning of Gk uncertain　*d* Gk *by that will*　*e* Gk *this one*

after those days, says the Lord:
I will put my laws in their hearts,
    and I will write them on their minds,"
[17]he also adds,
    "I will remember[a] their sins and their lawless
        deeds no more."
[18]Where there is forgiveness of these, there is no longer any offering for sin.

A Call to Persevere

19 Therefore, my friends,[b] since we have confidence to enter the sanctuary by the blood of Jesus, [20]by the new and living way that he opened for us through the curtain (that is, through his flesh), [21]and since we have a great priest over the house of God, [22]let us approach with a true heart in full assurance of faith, with our hearts sprinkled clean from an evil conscience and our bodies washed with pure water. [23]Let us hold fast to the confession of our hope without wavering, for he who has promised is faithful. [24]And let us consider how to provoke one another to love and good deeds, [25]not neglecting to meet together, as is the habit of some, but encouraging one another, and all the more as you see the Day approaching.

26 For if we willfully persist in sin after having received the knowledge of the truth, there no longer remains a sacrifice for sins, [27]but a fearful prospect of judgment, and a fury of fire that will consume the adversaries. [28]Anyone who has violated the law of Moses dies without mercy "on the testimony of two or three witnesses." [29]How much worse punishment do you think will be deserved by those who have spurned the Son of God, profaned the blood of the covenant by which they were sanctified, and outraged the Spirit of grace? [30]For we know the one who said, "Vengeance is mine, I will repay." And again, "The Lord will judge his people." [31]It is a fearful thing to fall into the hands of the living God.

32 But recall those earlier days when, after you had been enlightened, you endured a hard struggle with sufferings, [33]sometimes being publicly exposed to abuse and persecution, and sometimes being partners with those so treated. [34]For you had compassion for those who were in prison, and you cheerfully accepted the plundering of your possessions, knowing that you yourselves possessed something better and more lasting. [35]Do not, therefore, abandon that confidence of yours; it brings a great reward. [36]For you need endurance, so that when you have done the will of God, you may receive what was promised. [37]For yet

"in a very little while,
    the one who is coming will come and will not
        delay;
[38]   but my righteous one will live by faith.
    My soul takes no pleasure in anyone who
        shrinks back."
[39]But we are not among those who shrink back and so are lost, but among those who have faith and so are saved.

The Overcoming Power of Faith

HEBREWS 10.19–25

Life is filled with pain and challenges that tax the human spirit. Some respond to life's pain by taking refuge in materialism and hedonism or by dulling the pain with addictions. Some people choose to become hard and bitter. But Jesus offers us a "new and living way," a way of hope and reconciliation.

Find a comfortable place where you can relax and read these verses with both your head and your heart. Read the passage twice, slowly. What phrase or word speaks to you? Examine that phrase or word more closely. What attracts you to it? What does it mean to you? Allow this phrase or word to touch your heart. What emotions does it stir within you? Turn it into a prayer for yourself or others. Continue to savor these verses. Open your heart and mind to any impressions God's Spirit may wish to communicate to you.

See Meeting God in Scripture

The Beauty of Faith

"Faith is a living, daring confidence in God's grace. It is so sure and certain that a [person] could stake his [or her] life on it a thousand times."

—MARTIN LUTHER

The Meaning of Faith

11 Now faith is the assurance of things hoped for, the conviction of things not seen. ²Indeed, by faith*a* our ancestors received approval. ³By faith we understand that the worlds were prepared by the word of God, so that what is seen was made from things that are not visible.*b*

The Examples of Abel, Enoch, and Noah

4 By faith Abel offered to God a more acceptable*c* sacrifice than Cain's. Through this he received approval as righteous, God himself giving approval to his gifts; he died, but through his faith*d* he still speaks. ⁵By faith Enoch was taken so that he did not experience death; and "he was not found, because God had taken him." For it was attested before he was taken away that "he had pleased God." ⁶And without faith it is impossible to please God, for whoever would approach him must believe that he exists and that he rewards those who seek him. ⁷By faith Noah, warned by God about events as yet unseen, respected the warning and built an ark to save his household; by this he condemned the world and became an heir to the righteousness that is in accordance with faith.

The Faith of Abraham

8 By faith Abraham obeyed when he was called to set out for a place that he was to receive as an inheritance; and he set out, not knowing where he was going. ⁹By faith he stayed for a time in the land he had been promised, as in a foreign land, living in tents, as did Isaac and Jacob, who were heirs with him of the same promise. ¹⁰For he looked forward to the city that has foundations, whose architect and builder is God. ¹¹By faith he received power of procreation, even though he was too old—and Sarah herself was barren—because he considered him faithful who had promised.*e* ¹²Therefore from one person, and this one as good as dead, descendants were born, "as many as the stars of heaven and as the innumerable grains of sand by the seashore."

13 All of these died in faith without having received the promises, but from a distance they saw and greeted them. They confessed that they were strangers and foreigners on the earth, ¹⁴for people who speak in this way make it clear that they are seeking a homeland. ¹⁵If they had been thinking of the land that they had left behind, they would have had opportunity to return. ¹⁶But as it is, they desire a better country, that is, a heavenly one. Therefore God is not ashamed to be called their God; indeed, he has prepared a city for them.

17 By faith Abraham, when put to the test, offered up Isaac. He who had received the promises was ready to offer up his only son, ¹⁸of whom he had been told, "It is through Isaac that descendants shall be named for you." ¹⁹He considered the fact that God is able even to raise someone from the dead—and figuratively speaking, he did receive him back. ²⁰By faith Isaac invoked blessings for the future on Jacob and Esau. ²¹By faith Jacob, when

a Gk *by this*   *b* Or *was not made out of visible things*   *c* Gk *greater*
d Gk *through it*   *e* Or *By faith Sarah herself, though barren, received power to conceive, even when she was too old, because she considered him faithful who had promised.*

dying, blessed each of the sons of Joseph, "bowing in worship over the top of his staff." [22]By faith Joseph, at the end of his life, made mention of the exodus of the Israelites and gave instructions about his burial.[a]

The Faith of Moses

23 By faith Moses was hidden by his parents for three months after his birth, because they saw that the child was beautiful; and they were not afraid of the king's edict.[b] [24]By faith Moses, when he was grown up, refused to be called a son of Pharaoh's daughter, [25]choosing rather to share ill-treatment with the people of God than to enjoy the fleeting pleasures of sin. [26]He considered abuse suffered for the Christ[c] to be greater wealth than the treasures of Egypt, for he was looking ahead to the reward. [27]By faith he left Egypt, unafraid of the king's anger; for he persevered as though[d] he saw him who is invisible. [28]By faith he kept the Passover and the sprinkling of blood, so that the destroyer of the firstborn would not touch the firstborn of Israel.[e]

The Faith of Other Israelite Heroes

29 By faith the people passed through the Red Sea as if it were dry land, but when the Egyptians attempted to do so they were drowned. [30]By faith the walls of Jericho fell after they had been encircled for seven days. [31]By faith Rahab the prostitute did not perish with those who were disobedient,[f] because she had received the spies in peace.

32 And what more should I say? For time would fail me to tell of Gideon, Barak, Samson, Jephthah, of David and Samuel and the prophets— [33]who through faith conquered kingdoms, administered justice, obtained promises, shut the mouths of lions, [34]quenched raging fire, escaped the edge of the sword, won strength out of weakness, became mighty in war, put foreign armies to flight. [35]Women received their dead by resurrection. Others were tortured, refusing to accept release, in order to obtain a better resurrection. [36]Others suffered mocking and flogging, and even chains and imprisonment. [37]They were stoned to death, they were sawn in two,[g] they were killed by the sword; they went about in skins of sheep and goats, destitute, persecuted, tormented— [38]of whom the world was not worthy. They wandered in deserts and mountains, and in caves and holes in the ground.

39 Yet all these, though they were commended for their faith, did not receive what was promised, [40]since God had provided something better so that they would not, apart from us, be made perfect.

The Example of Jesus

12 Therefore, since we are surrounded by so great a cloud of witnesses, let us also lay aside every weight and the sin that clings so closely,[h] and let us run with perseverance the race that is set before us, [2]looking to Jesus the pioneer and perfecter of our faith, who for

Heroes of Faith

HEBREWS 11.32–34

This eleventh chapter of Hebrews introduces us to some of the heroes of the faith who demonstrated both belief and action. Who are some of the men and women who have become your own heroes of the faith? How did the trials they faced strengthen them? In the past and the present, how have they assisted you in living your faith? Make a list of your heroes and place it at this passage as a bookmark.

See Meeting God in Everyday Life

---

a Gk his bones   b Other ancient authorities add By faith Moses, when he was grown up, killed the Egyptian, because he observed the humiliation of his people (Gk brothers)   c Or the Messiah   d Or because   e Gk would not touch them   f Or unbelieving   g Other ancient authorities add they were tempted   h Other ancient authorities read sin that easily distracts

Therefore, Consider Jesus!

HEBREWS 12.1–3

These verses are filled with action verbs. Notice the verb phrases used to describe Jesus' actions on our behalf. Reflect on what Jesus has done for the sake of "the joy that was set before him":

"endured the cross"

"disregarding its shame"

"has taken his seat"

Ponder the verb phrases that describe our response:

"lay aside"

"run with perseverance"

"look to"

"consider him"

"not grow weary or lose heart"

How many of these action verbs capture the essence of your response to Jesus Christ? In what areas of your life would you like to deepen your faith? Spend some time in prayer with Jesus about that desire, repeating your need to him over the course of the next days and weeks.

See Meeting God in Everyday Life

the sake of[a] the joy that was set before him endured the cross, disregarding its shame, and has taken his seat at the right hand of the throne of God.

3 Consider him who endured such hostility against himself from sinners,[b] so that you may not grow weary or lose heart. [4]In your struggle against sin you have not yet resisted to the point of shedding your blood. [5]And you have forgotten the exhortation that addresses you as children—

"My child, do not regard lightly the discipline of
  the Lord,
  or lose heart when you are punished by him;
[6] for the Lord disciplines those whom he loves,
  and chastises every child whom he accepts."

[7]Endure trials for the sake of discipline. God is treating you as children; for what child is there whom a parent does not discipline? [8]If you do not have that discipline in which all children share, then you are illegitimate and not his children. [9]Moreover, we had human parents to discipline us, and we respected them. Should we not be even more willing to be subject to the Father of spirits and live? [10]For they disciplined us for a short time as seemed best to them, but he disciplines us for our good, in order that we may share his holiness. [11]Now, discipline always seems painful rather than pleasant at the time, but later it yields the peaceful fruit of righteousness to those who have been trained by it.

12 Therefore lift your drooping hands and strengthen your weak knees, [13]and make straight paths for your feet, so that what is lame may not be put out of joint, but rather be healed.

Warnings against Rejecting God's Grace

14 Pursue peace with everyone, and the holiness without which no one will see the Lord. [15]See to it that no one fails to obtain the grace of God; that no root of bitterness springs up and causes trouble, and through it many become defiled. [16]See to it that no one becomes like Esau, an immoral and godless person, who sold his birthright for a single meal. [17]You know that later, when he wanted to inherit the blessing, he was rejected, for he found no chance to repent,[c] even though he sought the blessing[d] with tears.

18 You have not come to something[e] that can be touched, a blazing fire, and darkness, and gloom, and a tempest, [19]and the sound of a trumpet, and a voice whose words made the hearers beg that not another word be spoken to them. [20](For they could not endure the order that was given, "If even an animal touches the mountain, it shall be stoned to death." [21]Indeed, so terrifying was the sight that Moses said, "I tremble with fear.") [22]But you have come to Mount Zion and to the city of the living God, the heavenly Jerusalem, and to innumerable angels in festal gathering, [23]and to the assembly[f] of the firstborn who are enrolled in heaven, and to God the judge of all, and to the spirits of the righteous made perfect, [24]and to Jesus,

a Or *who instead of*   *b* Other ancient authorities read *such hostility from sinners against themselves*   *c* Or *no chance to change his father's mind*   *d* Gk *it*   *e* Other ancient authorities read *a mountain*   *f* Or *angels, and to the festal gathering* [23]*and assembly*

the mediator of a new covenant, and to the sprinkled blood that speaks a better word than the blood of Abel.

25 See that you do not refuse the one who is speaking; for if they did not escape when they refused the one who warned them on earth, how much less will we escape if we reject the one who warns from heaven! ²⁶At that time his voice shook the earth; but now he has promised, "Yet once more I will shake not only the earth but also the heaven." ²⁷This phrase, "Yet once more," indicates the removal of what is shaken—that is, created things—so that what cannot be shaken may remain. ²⁸Therefore, since we are receiving a kingdom that cannot be shaken, let us give thanks, by which we offer to God an acceptable worship with reverence and awe; ²⁹for indeed our God is a consuming fire.

Service Well-Pleasing to God

13 Let mutual love continue. ²Do not neglect to show hospitality to strangers, for by doing that some have entertained angels without knowing it. ³Remember those who are in prison, as though you were in prison with them; those who are being tortured, as though you yourselves were being tortured.ᵃ ⁴Let marriage be held in honor by all, and let the marriage bed be kept undefiled; for God will judge fornicators and adulterers. ⁵Keep your lives free from the love of money, and be content with what you have; for he has said, "I will never leave you or forsake you." ⁶So we can say with confidence,

"The Lord is my helper;
    I will not be afraid.
What can anyone do to me?"

7 Remember your leaders, those who spoke the word of God to you; consider the outcome of their way of life, and imitate their faith. ⁸Jesus Christ is the same yesterday and today and forever. ⁹Do not be carried away by all kinds of strange teachings; for it is well for the heart to be strengthened by grace, not by regulations about food,ᵇ which have not benefited those who observe them. ¹⁰We have an altar from which those who officiate in the tentᶜ have no right to eat. ¹¹For the bodies of those animals whose blood is brought into the sanctuary by the high priest as a sacrifice for sin are burned outside the camp. ¹²Therefore Jesus also suffered outside the city gate in order to sanctify the people by his own blood. ¹³Let us then go to him outside the camp and bear the abuse he endured. ¹⁴For here we have no lasting city, but we are looking for the city that is to come. ¹⁵Through him, then, let us continually offer a sacrifice of praise to God, that is, the fruit of lips that confess his name. ¹⁶Do not neglect to do good and to share what you have, for such sacrifices are pleasing to God.

17 Obey your leaders and submit to them, for they are keeping watch over your souls and will give an account. Let them do this with joy and not with sighing—for that would be harmful to you.

18 Pray for us; we are sure that we have a clear conscience, desiring to act honorably in all things. ¹⁹I urge you all the more to do this, so that I may be restored to you very soon.

Worship That Makes a Difference

HEBREWS 12.28–29

Worship is our grateful response to all that Jesus has accomplished and all he continues to do on our behalf. Unfortunately many people think of worship in terms of what they can receive from God rather than what they can offer to God.

What is your definition of worship? What happens when you gather with other Christians to worship? What principles does this passage provide to guide your worship? Read these verses before you worship next Sunday. As you worship seek to participate as fully and freely as possible. How conscious are you of God's awesome majesty? Of God's nearness and intimate love? Follow up by rereading this scripture and reflecting on your experience in light of it.

See Meeting God in Worship

---

a Gk were in the body   b Gk not by foods   c Or tabernacle

Receive the Benediction

HEBREWS 13.20–21

The author of Hebrews offers you this blessing. What posture indicates openness or receptivity for you? You might adopt that posture as you receive this blessing. Reread it slowly. All of this is for you: Jesus Christ's death and resurrection; the new covenant; the perfect equipment for serving God; power to know and do God's will; participation in Christ's glory. Spend some time pondering each of these gifts, accepting each one and thanking God for it. Finish by singing the doxology "Praise God, From Whom All Blessings Flow."

See Meeting God in Everyday Life

Benediction

20 Now may the God of peace, who brought back from the dead our Lord Jesus, the great shepherd of the sheep, by the blood of the eternal covenant, 21make you complete in everything good so that you may do his will, working among us*a* that which is pleasing in his sight, through Jesus Christ, to whom be the glory forever and ever. Amen.

Final Exhortation and Greetings

22 I appeal to you, brothers and sisters,*b* bear with my word of exhortation, for I have written to you briefly. 23I want you to know that our brother Timothy has been set free; and if he comes in time, he will be with me when I see you. 24Greet all your leaders and all the saints. Those from Italy send you greetings. 25Grace be with all of you.*c*

a Other ancient authorities read *you*   *b* Gk *brothers*   *c* Other ancient authorities add *Amen*

THE LETTER OF
JAMES
Faith at Work

KEY VERSE:

But be doers of the word, and not merely hearers who deceive themselves.—James 1.22

J ames could be said to have one objective in writing this letter: to assist the churches to whom he writes to live well, that is, to work out their faith in good deeds and holy habits. The straightforward, commonsense approach of this letter is refreshing, although it might challenge and confront those who are comfortable in certain patterns of neglect or indifference toward others. "Be doers . . . not hearers who deceive themselves" (1.22). "Understand this" (1.19). "You do well if you really fulfill the royal law" (2.8). These are the directives of a writer who is intent on reiterating or fleshing out the ancient words of the prophet Micah: "He has told you, O mortal, what is good; and what does the LORD require of you but to do justice, and to love kindness, and to walk humbly with your God" (Micah 6.8).

As you contemplate these chapters, let them be like candles lighting your soul, life and habits. How do they describe you or your church? How do they challenge you toward greater faithfulness in loving others? In the down-to-brass-tacks spirit of this letter, consider this question throughout: What are specific and concrete ways in which I can respond to what I am reading? Ask God to lead you into authentic behaviors and attitudes that—in challenging ways and ways that may very well stretch you perhaps—will put your faith to work.

"For when we ask how good a person is, we do not ask what they believe or what they hope for but what they live."
—AUGUSTINE,
Enchiridion

Endurance

JAMES 1.2–9

The word "endurance" appears often in James. The meaning of this word in Greek has to do with "rising above" a circumstance while at the same time "holding on" within that circumstance. The exercise of endurance is central to James's lessons on faithfulness.

What are some circumstances in your life or in your church in which the practice of "rising above while holding on" is called for? What would it mean to regard these circumstances as "nothing but joy"? When in the past have you endured a difficult situation and found that it bore the fruit of joy?

Salutation

1 James, a servant[a] of God and of the Lord Jesus Christ, To the twelve tribes in the Dispersion: Greetings.

Faith and Wisdom

2 My brothers and sisters,[b] whenever you face trials of any kind, consider it nothing but joy, [3]because you know that the testing of your faith produces endurance; [4]and let endurance have its full effect, so that you may be mature and complete, lacking in nothing.

5 If any of you is lacking in wisdom, ask God, who gives to all generously and ungrudgingly, and it will be given you. [6]But ask in faith, never doubting, for the one who doubts is like a wave of the sea, driven and tossed by the wind; [7, 8]for the doubter, being double-minded and unstable in every way, must not expect to receive anything from the Lord.

Poverty and Riches

9 Let the believer[c] who is lowly boast in being raised up, [10]and the rich in being brought low, because the rich will disappear like a flower in the field. [11]For the sun rises with its scorching heat and withers the field; its flower falls, and its beauty perishes. It is the same way with the rich; in the midst of a busy life, they will wither away.

Trial and Temptation

12 Blessed is anyone who endures temptation. Such a one has stood the test and will receive the crown of life that the Lord[d] has promised to those who love him. [13]No one, when tempted, should say, "I am being tempted by God"; for God cannot be tempted by evil and he himself tempts no one. [14]But one is tempted by one's own desire, being lured and enticed by it; [15]then, when that desire has conceived, it gives birth to sin, and that sin, when it is fully grown, gives birth to death. [16]Do not be deceived, my beloved.[e]

17 Every generous act of giving, with every perfect gift, is from above, coming down from the Father of lights, with whom there is no variation or shadow due to change.[f] [18]In fulfillment of his own purpose he gave us birth by the word of truth, so that we would become a kind of first fruits of his creatures.

Hearing and Doing the Word

19 You must understand this, my beloved:[e] let everyone be quick to listen, slow to speak, slow to anger; [20]for your anger does not produce God's righteousness. [21]Therefore rid yourselves of all sordidness and rank growth of wickedness, and welcome with meekness the implanted word that has the power to save your souls.

22 But be doers of the word, and not merely hearers who deceive themselves. [23]For if any are hearers of the word and not doers, they are like those who look at themselves[g] in a mirror; [24]for they look at themselves and, on going away, immediately forget what they were like. [25]But

---

a Gk *slave*   b Gk *brothers*   c Gk *brother*   d Gk *he*; other ancient authorities read *God*   e Gk *my beloved brothers*   f Other ancient authorities read *variation due to a shadow of turning*   g Gk *at the face of his birth*

those who look into the perfect law, the law of liberty, and persevere, being not hearers who forget but doers who act—they will be blessed in their doing.

26 If any think they are religious, and do not bridle their tongues but deceive their hearts, their religion is worthless. [27] Religion that is pure and undefiled before God, the Father, is this: to care for orphans and widows in their distress, and to keep oneself unstained by the world.

Warning against Partiality

2 My brothers and sisters,[a] do you with your acts of favoritism really believe in our glorious Lord Jesus Christ?[b] [2] For if a person with gold rings and in fine clothes comes into your assembly, and if a poor person in dirty clothes also comes in, [3] and if you take notice of the one wearing the fine clothes and say, "Have a seat here, please," while to the one who is poor you say, "Stand there," or, "Sit at my feet,"[c] [4] have you not made distinctions among yourselves, and become judges with evil thoughts? [5] Listen, my beloved brothers and sisters.[d] Has not God chosen the poor in the world to be rich in faith and to be heirs of the kingdom that he has promised to those who love him? [6] But you have dishonored the poor. Is it not the rich who oppress you? Is it not they who drag you into court? [7] Is it not they who blaspheme the excellent name that was invoked over you?

8 You do well if you really fulfill the royal law according to the scripture, "You shall love your neighbor as yourself." [9] But if you show partiality, you commit sin and are convicted by the law as transgressors. [10] For whoever keeps the whole law but fails in one point has become accountable for all of it. [11] For the one who said, "You shall not commit adultery," also said, "You shall not murder." Now if you do not commit adultery but if you murder, you have become a transgressor of the law. [12] So speak and so act as those who are to be judged by the law of liberty. [13] For judgment will be without mercy to anyone who has shown no mercy; mercy triumphs over judgment.

Faith without Works Is Dead

14 What good is it, my brothers and sisters,[d] if you say you have faith but do not have works? Can faith save you? [15] If a brother or sister is naked and lacks daily food, [16] and one of you says to them, "Go in peace; keep warm and eat your fill," and yet you do not supply their bodily needs, what is the good of that? [17] So faith by itself, if it has no works, is dead.

18 But someone will say, "You have faith and I have works." Show me your faith apart from your works, and I by my works will show you my faith. [19] You believe that God is one; you do well. Even the demons believe—and shudder. [20] Do you want to be shown, you senseless person, that faith apart from works is barren? [21] Was not our ancestor Abraham justified by works when he offered his son Isaac on the altar? [22] You see that faith was active along with his works, and faith was brought to completion by the works. [23] Thus the scripture was fulfilled that says, "Abraham believed God, and it was reckoned to him as righteousness,"

Loving All the Same

JAMES 2.3–13

A rabbi asked the question of his disciples, "When do we know that light has appeared out of darkness?" One student answered, "When we can tell the difference between a dog and a lamb?" "No," said the rabbi. Another student answered, "When we can tell the difference between a palm tree and a fig tree?" "No," said the rabbi. "When, then, do we know?" the disciples asked their teacher. "We know that light has appeared out of darkness when someone can look in the face of any human being and see the face of a sister or brother."

See *Meeting God in Service*

a Gk *My brothers*   b Or *hold the faith of our glorious Lord Jesus Christ without acts of favoritism*   c Gk *Sit under my footstool*   d Gk *brothers*

1605

Guarding the Heart

JAMES 3.6–12

"A brother asked Abba Sisois, 'I long to guard my heart.' The old man said to him, 'And how can we guard the heart if our tongue leaves the door of the fortress open?' "

—from *Western Asceticism*

and he was called the friend of God. ²⁴You see that a person is justified by works and not by faith alone. ²⁵Likewise, was not Rahab the prostitute also justified by works when she welcomed the messengers and sent them out by another road? ²⁶For just as the body without the spirit is dead, so faith without works is also dead.

Taming the Tongue

3 Not many of you should become teachers, my brothers and sisters,^a for you know that we who teach will be judged with greater strictness. ²For all of us make many mistakes. Anyone who makes no mistakes in speaking is perfect, able to keep the whole body in check with a bridle. ³If we put bits into the mouths of horses to make them obey us, we guide their whole bodies. ⁴Or look at ships: though they are so large that it takes strong winds to drive them, yet they are guided by a very small rudder wherever the will of the pilot directs. ⁵So also the tongue is a small member, yet it boasts of great exploits.

How great a forest is set ablaze by a small fire! ⁶And the tongue is a fire. The tongue is placed among our members as a world of iniquity; it stains the whole body, sets on fire the cycle of nature,^b and is itself set on fire by hell.^c ⁷For every species of beast and bird, of reptile and sea creature, can be tamed and has been tamed by the human species, ⁸but no one can tame the tongue—a restless evil, full of deadly poison. ⁹With it we bless the Lord and Father, and with it we curse those who are made in the likeness of God. ¹⁰From the same mouth come blessing and cursing. My brothers and sisters,^d this ought not to be so. ¹¹Does a spring pour forth from the same opening both fresh and brackish water? ¹²Can a fig tree, my brothers and sisters,^e yield olives, or a grapevine figs? No more can salt water yield fresh.

Two Kinds of Wisdom

13 Who is wise and understanding among you? Show by your good life that your works are done with gentleness born of wisdom. ¹⁴But if you have bitter envy and selfish ambition in your hearts, do not be boastful and false to the truth. ¹⁵Such wisdom does not come down from above, but is earthly, unspiritual, devilish. ¹⁶For where there is envy and selfish ambition, there will also be disorder and wickedness of every kind. ¹⁷But the wisdom from above is first pure, then peaceable, gentle, willing to yield, full of mercy and good fruits, without a trace of partiality or hypocrisy. ¹⁸And a harvest of righteousness is sown in peace for^f those who make peace.

Friendship with the World

4 Those conflicts and disputes among you, where do they come from? Do they not come from your cravings that are at war within you? ²You want something and do not have it; so you commit murder. And you covet^g something and cannot obtain it; so you engage in disputes and conflicts. You do not have, because you do not ask. ³You ask and do not receive, because you ask wrongly, in order to spend what you get on your pleasures. ⁴Adulterers! Do

a Gk brothers   b Or wheel of birth   c Gk Gehenna   d Gk My brothers
e Gk my brothers   f Or by   g Or you murder and you covet

you not know that friendship with the world is enmity with God? Therefore whoever wishes to be a friend of the world becomes an enemy of God. ⁵Or do you suppose that it is for nothing that the scripture says, "God*a* yearns jealously for the spirit that he has made to dwell in us"? ⁶But he gives all the more grace; therefore it says,

"God opposes the proud,
but gives grace to the humble."

⁷Submit yourselves therefore to God. Resist the devil, and he will flee from you. ⁸Draw near to God, and he will draw near to you. Cleanse your hands, you sinners, and purify your hearts, you double-minded. ⁹Lament and mourn and weep. Let your laughter be turned into mourning and your joy into dejection. ¹⁰Humble yourselves before the Lord, and he will exalt you.

Warning against Judging Another

11 Do not speak evil against one another, brothers and sisters.*b* Whoever speaks evil against another or judges another, speaks evil against the law and judges the law; but if you judge the law, you are not a doer of the law but a judge. ¹²There is one lawgiver and judge who is able to save and to destroy. So who, then, are you to judge your neighbor?

Boasting about Tomorrow

13 Come now, you who say, "Today or tomorrow we will go to such and such a town and spend a year there, doing business and making money." ¹⁴Yet you do not even know what tomorrow will bring. What is your life? For you are a mist that appears for a little while and then vanishes. ¹⁵Instead you ought to say, "If the Lord wishes, we will live and do this or that." ¹⁶As it is, you boast in your arrogance; all such boasting is evil. ¹⁷Anyone, then, who knows the right thing to do and fails to do it, commits sin.

Warning to Rich Oppressors

5 Come now, you rich people, weep and wail for the miseries that are coming to you. ²Your riches have rotted, and your clothes are moth-eaten. ³Your gold and silver have rusted, and their rust will be evidence against you, and it will eat your flesh like fire. You have laid up treasure*c* for the last days. ⁴Listen! The wages of the laborers who mowed your fields, which you kept back by fraud, cry out, and the cries of the harvesters have reached the ears of the Lord of hosts. ⁵You have lived on the earth in luxury and in pleasure; you have fattened your hearts in a day of slaughter. ⁶You have condemned and murdered the righteous one, who does not resist you.

Patience in Suffering

7 Be patient, therefore, beloved,*b* until the coming of the Lord. The farmer waits for the precious crop from the earth, being patient with it until it receives the early and the late rains. ⁸You also must be patient. Strengthen your hearts, for the coming of the Lord is near.*d* ⁹Beloved,*e* do not grumble against one another, so that you may not be judged. See, the Judge is standing at the doors! ¹⁰As an example of suffering and patience, beloved,*b* take the prophets who spoke

Faith and Tomorrow's Work

JAMES 4.13–17

In the Mexican culture, *si Dios quiere* ("if God wishes") is a common expression that refers to the tenuous nature of daily living and future planning. James conveys the same idea. He prompts his readers to live by an awareness of the radical contingency of their lives: "Instead, you ought to say, 'If it is the Lord's will, we will live and do . . .'" Examine your life; in what ways do you act as though tomorrow and the future are within your own control? Consider ways in which you could be more intentional in surrendering your plans to God and more open to divine guidance.

See Meeting God in Everyday Life

---

a Gk *He*   *b* Gk *brothers*   *c* Or *will eat your flesh, since you have stored up fire*   *d* Or *is at hand*   *e* Gk *Brothers*

The Community of Care

JAMES 5.13–20

Augustine once referred to the "walls of the church" as those braces and boundaries within which individuals who belong to the church are held. James closes his letter by describing those "walls" or means of grace—prayer, confession, healing, restoration—that benefit both the individual and the whole community. Recall an instance in which the church has provided for you in a time of specific need. Now think of less visible or dramatic ways in which your faith community has been a channel of God's grace in your life. In what ways can you become such a caring presence to a brother or sister, or to your congregation as a whole? Ask God to guide you in discerning and fulfilling that calling.

See Meeting God in Community

in the name of the Lord. ¹¹Indeed we call blessed those who showed endurance. You have heard of the endurance of Job, and you have seen the purpose of the Lord, how the Lord is compassionate and merciful.

12 Above all, my beloved,ᵃ do not swear, either by heaven or by earth or by any other oath, but let your "Yes" be yes and your "No" be no, so that you may not fall under condemnation.

The Prayer of Faith

13 Are any among you suffering? They should pray. Are any cheerful? They should sing songs of praise. ¹⁴Are any among you sick? They should call for the elders of the church and have them pray over them, anointing them with oil in the name of the Lord. ¹⁵The prayer of faith will save the sick, and the Lord will raise them up; and anyone who has committed sins will be forgiven. ¹⁶Therefore confess your sins to one another, and pray for one another, so that you may be healed. The prayer of the righteous is powerful and effective. ¹⁷Elijah was a human being like us, and he prayed fervently that it might not rain, and for three years and six months it did not rain on the earth. ¹⁸Then he prayed again, and the heaven gave rain and the earth yielded its harvest.

19 My brothers and sisters,ᵇ if anyone among you wanders from the truth and is brought back by another, ²⁰you should know that whoever brings back a sinner from wandering will save the sinner'sᶜ soul from death and will cover a multitude of sins.

a Gk *brothers*   *b* Gk *My brothers*   *c* Gk *his*

THE FIRST LETTER OF
PETER

Christians Under Construction

KEY VERSE:

I have written this short letter to encourage you and to testify that this is the true grace of God.
Stand fast in it.—1 Peter 5.12

Standing fast in the true grace of God transforms all of life. How simple it sounds. How seldom it is achieved! Peter knows this from personal experience. He knows how easy it is to wobble and fall. With a pastor's heart of compassion, he writes to Christians scattered in many places and facing a variety of tests and trials. His warm, encouraging letter reminds them first of the blessings and hope they already have in Jesus Christ. With that confident assurance they have every reason to be diligent in putting aside anything that could hold them back from full enjoyment of salvation.

The Christian life is no glowing dream world though. Peter is realistic. Believers are to hold on in the midst of political challenges, slavery, abuse, questions from unbelievers, and suffering and pain. Standing fast in these situations requires a clear sense of God's gracious presence. It also demands a disciplined commitment to living daily according to Jesus' example. Peter gives down-to-earth, specific guidance. This is Christianity in everyday clothes.

Even outright persecution is not to shake Jesus' followers from standing fast. As painful and puzzling as it is to suffer because of their faith, Peter's readers can be encouraged because of his gentle reminder that they share in Christ's sufferings.

Peter shows the care of a wise shepherd in the way he writes to his readers. His letter encourages us to care for others in the same way. Humbled, disciplined and strengthened by the power of Jesus Christ, we can stand firm in the amazing, true grace of God.

"The many uses of the word in English convince me that grace is indeed amazing—truly our last best word. It contains the essence of the gospel as a drop of water can contain the image of the sun. The world thirsts for grace in ways it does not even recognize; little wonder the hymn 'Amazing Grace' edged its way into the Top Ten charts two hundred years after composition. For a society that seems adrift, without moorings, I know of no better place to drop the anchor of faith."

—PHILIP YANCEY,
What's So Amazing About Grace?

Inheritance Guaranteed!

1 PETER 1.1–12

If you found out today that you had inherited a million dollars from a rich relative, what difference would it make to the way you live? Be specific: "I would . . ." Now come back from dreaming to reality! You actually do have an inheritance—and it is worth infinitely more than a million dollars. Read this entire passage and write down every word or phrase that speaks of the riches you have in Jesus Christ. Then repeat several times: "This is my inheritance. It can never perish, spoil or fade." What difference will this knowledge make in the way you live? Be specific. Write a thank-you letter to God, expressing what this inheritance means to you.

See Meeting God in Everyday Life

Salutation

1 Peter, an apostle of Jesus Christ,
To the exiles of the Dispersion in Pontus, Galatia, Cappadocia, Asia, and Bithynia, [2]who have been chosen and destined by God the Father and sanctified by the Spirit to be obedient to Jesus Christ and to be sprinkled with his blood:
May grace and peace be yours in abundance.

A Living Hope

3 Blessed be the God and Father of our Lord Jesus Christ! By his great mercy he has given us a new birth into a living hope through the resurrection of Jesus Christ from the dead, [4]and into an inheritance that is imperishable, undefiled, and unfading, kept in heaven for you, [5]who are being protected by the power of God through faith for a salvation ready to be revealed in the last time. [6]In this you rejoice,[a] even now for a little while you have had to suffer various trials, [7]so that the genuineness of your faith—being more precious than gold that, though perishable, is tested by fire—may be found to result in praise and glory and honor when Jesus Christ is revealed. [8]Although you have not seen[b] him, you love him; and even though you do not see him now, you believe in him and rejoice with an indescribable and glorious joy, [9]for you are receiving the outcome of your faith, the salvation of your souls.

10 Concerning this salvation, the prophets who prophesied of the grace that was to be yours made careful search and inquiry, [11]inquiring about the person or time that the Spirit of Christ within them indicated when it testified in advance to the sufferings destined for Christ and the subsequent glory. [12]It was revealed to them that they were serving not themselves but you, in regard to the things that have now been announced to you through those who brought you good news by the Holy Spirit sent from heaven—things into which angels long to look!

A Call to Holy Living

13 Therefore prepare your minds for action;[c] discipline yourselves; set all your hope on the grace that Jesus Christ will bring you when he is revealed. [14]Like obedient children, do not be conformed to the desires that you formerly had in ignorance. [15]Instead, as he who called you is holy, be holy yourselves in all your conduct; [16]for it is written, "You shall be holy, for I am holy."

17 If you invoke as Father the one who judges all people impartially according to their deeds, live in reverent fear during the time of your exile. [18]You know that you were ransomed from the futile ways inherited from your ancestors, not with perishable things like silver or gold, [19]but with the precious blood of Christ, like that of a lamb without defect or blemish. [20]He was destined before the foundation of the world, but was revealed at the end of the ages for your sake. [21]Through him you have come to trust in God, who raised him from the dead and gave him glory, so that your faith and hope are set on God.

22 Now that you have purified your souls by your obe-

a Or Rejoice in this   b Other ancient authorities read known   c Gk gird up the loins of your mind dience to the truth[a] so that you have genuine mutual love, love one another deeply[b] from the heart.[c] ²³You have been born anew, not of perishable but of imperishable seed, through the living and enduring word of God.[d] ²⁴For

> "All flesh is like grass
> and all its glory like the flower of grass.
> The grass withers,
> and the flower falls,
> ²⁵ but the word of the Lord endures forever."

That word is the good news that was announced to you.

The Living Stone and a Chosen People

2 Rid yourselves, therefore, of all malice, and all guile, insincerity, envy, and all slander. ²Like newborn infants, long for the pure, spiritual milk, so that by it you may grow into salvation— ³if indeed you have tasted that the Lord is good.

4 Come to him, a living stone, though rejected by mortals yet chosen and precious in God's sight, and ⁵like living stones, let yourselves be built[e] into a spiritual house, to be a holy priesthood, to offer spiritual sacrifices acceptable to God through Jesus Christ. ⁶For it stands in scripture:

> "See, I am laying in Zion a stone,
> a cornerstone chosen and precious;
> and whoever believes in him[f] will not be put to
>   shame."

⁷To you then who believe, he is precious; but for those who do not believe,

> "The stone that the builders rejected
> has become the very head of the corner,"

⁸and

> "A stone that makes them stumble,
> and a rock that makes them fall."

They stumble because they disobey the word, as they were destined to do.

9 But you are a chosen race, a royal priesthood, a holy nation, God's own people,[g] in order that you may proclaim the mighty acts of him who called you out of darkness into his marvelous light.

> ¹⁰ Once you were not a people,
> but now you are God's people;
> once you had not received mercy,
> but now you have received mercy.

Live as Servants of God

11 Beloved, I urge you as aliens and exiles to abstain from the desires of the flesh that wage war against the soul. ¹²Conduct yourselves honorably among the Gentiles, so that, though they malign you as evildoers, they may see your honorable deeds and glorify God when he comes to judge.[h]

13 For the Lord's sake accept the authority of every human institution,[i] whether of the emperor as supreme, ¹⁴or of governors, as sent by him to punish those who do wrong and to praise those who do right. ¹⁵For it is God's will that by doing right you should silence the ignorance of the

---

a Other ancient authorities add *through the Spirit*   *b* Or *constantly*
c Other ancient authorities read *a pure heart*   *d* Or *through the word of the living and enduring God*   *e* Or *you yourselves are being built*   *f* Or *it*
g Gk *a people for his possession*   *h* Gk *God on the day of visitation*
i Or *every institution ordained for human beings*

A Chosen People

1 PETER 2.9–10

How confident are you that you are personally chosen by God and that you really *belong*? The need for a strong sense of belonging touches deep and vulnerable places in the spirit. Gently envision God coming toward you right now. How close will you let God come? What posture does God take? What is your response? Do you move? Do you say anything? What emotions rise within you? Is there anything God wants to say to you? Describe the experience you envision by writing down or drawing what happens.

Free, Yet Costly Love

1 PETER 3.8–12

"Do not hesitate to love and to love deeply. You might be afraid of the pain that deep love can cause. When those you love deeply reject you, leave you, or die, your heart will be broken. But that should not hold you back from loving deeply. The pain that comes from deep love makes your love ever more fruitful. It is like a plow that breaks the ground to allow the seed to take root and grow into a strong plant."

—HENRI J. M. NOUWEN,
The Inner Voice of Love

foolish. ¹⁶As servants[a] of God, live as free people, yet do not use your freedom as a pretext for evil. ¹⁷Honor everyone. Love the family of believers.[b] Fear God. Honor the emperor.

The Example of Christ's Suffering

18 Slaves, accept the authority of your masters with all deference, not only those who are kind and gentle but also those who are harsh. ¹⁹For it is a credit to you if, being aware of God, you endure pain while suffering unjustly. ²⁰If you endure when you are beaten for doing wrong, what credit is that? But if you endure when you do right and suffer for it, you have God's approval. ²¹For to this you have been called, because Christ also suffered for you, leaving you an example, so that you should follow in his steps.
²² "He committed no sin,
      and no deceit was found in his mouth."
²³When he was abused, he did not return abuse; when he suffered, he did not threaten; but he entrusted himself to the one who judges justly. ²⁴He himself bore our sins in his body on the cross,[c] so that, free from sins, we might live for righteousness; by his wounds[d] you have been healed. ²⁵For you were going astray like sheep, but now you have returned to the shepherd and guardian of your souls.

Wives and Husbands

3 Wives, in the same way, accept the authority of your husbands, so that, even if some of them do not obey the word, they may be won over without a word by their wives' conduct, ²when they see the purity and reverence of your lives. ³Do not adorn yourselves outwardly by braiding your hair, and by wearing gold ornaments or fine clothing; ⁴rather, let your adornment be the inner self with the lasting beauty of a gentle and quiet spirit, which is very precious in God's sight. ⁵It was in this way long ago that the holy women who hoped in God used to adorn themselves by accepting the authority of their husbands. ⁶Thus Sarah obeyed Abraham and called him lord. You have become her daughters as long as you do what is good and never let fears alarm you.

7 Husbands, in the same way, show consideration for your wives in your life together, paying honor to the woman as the weaker sex,[e] since they too are also heirs of the gracious gift of life—so that nothing may hinder your prayers.

Suffering for Doing Right

8 Finally, all of you, have unity of spirit, sympathy, love for one another, a tender heart, and a humble mind. ⁹Do not repay evil for evil or abuse for abuse; but, on the contrary, repay with a blessing. It is for this that you were called—that you might inherit a blessing. ¹⁰For
"Those who desire life
      and desire to see good days,
   let them keep their tongues from evil
      and their lips from speaking deceit;
¹¹   let them turn away from evil and do good;
      let them seek peace and pursue it.
¹²   For the eyes of the Lord are on the righteous,
      and his ears are open to their prayer.
   But the face of the Lord is against those who do evil."

a Gk *slaves*   b Gk *Love the brotherhood*   c Or *carried up our sins in his body to the tree*   d Gk *bruise*   e Gk *vessel*

13 Now who will harm you if you are eager to do what is good? ¹⁴But even if you do suffer for doing what is right, you are blessed. Do not fear what they fear,ᵃ and do not be intimidated, ¹⁵but in your hearts sanctify Christ as Lord. Always be ready to make your defense to anyone who demands from you an accounting for the hope that is in you; ¹⁶yet do it with gentleness and reverence.ᵇ Keep your conscience clear, so that, when you are maligned, those who abuse you for your good conduct in Christ may be put to shame. ¹⁷For it is better to suffer for doing good, if suffering should be God's will, than to suffer for doing evil. ¹⁸For Christ also sufferedᶜ for sins once for all, the righteous for the unrighteous, in order to bring youᵈ to God. He was put to death in the flesh, but made alive in the spirit, ¹⁹in which also he went and made a proclamation to the spirits in prison, ²⁰who in former times did not obey, when God waited patiently in the days of Noah, during the building of the ark, in which a few, that is, eight persons, were saved through water. ²¹And baptism, which this prefigured, now saves you—not as a removal of dirt from the body, but as an appeal to God forᵉ a good conscience, through the resurrection of Jesus Christ, ²²who has gone into heaven and is at the right hand of God, with angels, authorities, and powers made subject to him.

Good Stewards of God's Grace

4 Since therefore Christ suffered in the flesh,ᶠ arm yourselves also with the same intention (for whoever has suffered in the flesh has finished with sin), ²so as to live for the rest of your earthly lifeᵍ no longer by human desires but by the will of God. ³You have already spent enough time in doing what the Gentiles like to do, living in licentiousness, passions, drunkenness, revels, carousing, and lawless idolatry. ⁴They are surprised that you no longer join them in the same excesses of dissipation, and so they blaspheme.ʰ ⁵But they will have to give an accounting to him who stands ready to judge the living and the dead. ⁶For this is the reason the gospel was proclaimed even to the dead, so that, though they had been judged in the flesh as everyone is judged, they might live in the spirit as God does.

7 The end of all things is near;ⁱ therefore be serious and discipline yourselves for the sake of your prayers. ⁸Above all, maintain constant love for one another, for love covers a multitude of sins. ⁹Be hospitable to one another without complaining. ¹⁰Like good stewards of the manifold grace of God, serve one another with whatever gift each of you has received. ¹¹Whoever speaks must do so as one speaking the very words of God; whoever serves must do so with the strength that God supplies, so that God may be glorified in all things through Jesus Christ. To him belong the glory and the power forever and ever. Amen.

Suffering as a Christian

12 Beloved, do not be surprised at the fiery ordeal that is taking place among you to test you, as though something strange were happening to you. ¹³But rejoice insofar as you

---

Gentle Answers

1 PETER 3.13–17

How attractive do Christians make Christianity? Gentle, respectful answers accounting for the hope that is in us are made authentic when matched by the nonverbal messages of our attitudes and behavior. Think of three people with whom you have regular contact. Ask Jesus to help you as you formulate what you would say to each one if he or she asked about your faith in Jesus Christ. Speak your answers aloud as if the person were sitting opposite you. Now reflect on what each person sees and experiences in interaction with you in everyday life. Do your words and lifestyle match? Bring your answer to Jesus in prayer.

See Meeting God in Service

---

a Gk *their fear*   b Or *respect*   c Other ancient authorities read *died*
d Other ancient authorities read *us*   e Or *a pledge to God from*   f Other ancient authorities add *for us*; others, *for you*   g Gk *rest of the time in the flesh*   h Or *they malign you*   i Or *is at hand*

True Grace

1 PETER 4.12–5.14

Peter writes this letter to encourage his readers to stand fast in the true grace of God. Pause and expectantly open your heart for a gift of true grace personally underlined for you somewhere in this page of God's Word. Now read slowly right through the passage, noting any special phrases, words or verses that attract your attention. Choose the one that draws you most strongly and return to it. Read that phrase or verse aloud, emphasizing different key words on each reading. Then quiet your spirit and let the words nestle in a safe place within your heart. Let this gift of grace grow and bear fruit.

See *Meeting God in Scripture*

are sharing Christ's sufferings, so that you may also be glad and shout for joy when his glory is revealed. [14]If you are reviled for the name of Christ, you are blessed, because the spirit of glory,[a] which is the Spirit of God, is resting on you.[b] [15]But let none of you suffer as a murderer, a thief, a criminal, or even as a mischief maker. [16]Yet if any of you suffers as a Christian, do not consider it a disgrace, but glorify God because you bear this name. [17]For the time has come for judgment to begin with the household of God; if it begins with us, what will be the end for those who do not obey the gospel of God? [18]And

"If it is hard for the righteous to be saved,
    what will become of the ungodly and the sinners?"

[19]Therefore, let those suffering in accordance with God's will entrust themselves to a faithful Creator, while continuing to do good.

Tending the Flock of God

5 Now as an elder myself and a witness of the sufferings of Christ, as well as one who shares in the glory to be revealed, I exhort the elders among you [2]to tend the flock of God that is in your charge, exercising the oversight,[c] not under compulsion but willingly, as God would have you do it[d]—not for sordid gain but eagerly. [3]Do not lord it over those in your charge, but be examples to the flock. [4]And when the chief shepherd appears, you will win the crown of glory that never fades away. [5]In the same way, you who are younger must accept the authority of the elders.[e] And all of you must clothe yourselves with humility in your dealings with one another, for

"God opposes the proud,
    but gives grace to the humble."

6 Humble yourselves therefore under the mighty hand of God, so that he may exalt you in due time. [7]Cast all your anxiety on him, because he cares for you. [8]Discipline yourselves, keep alert.[f] Like a roaring lion your adversary the devil prowls around, looking for someone to devour. [9]Resist him, steadfast in your faith, for you know that your brothers and sisters[g] in all the world are undergoing the same kinds of suffering. [10]And after you have suffered for a little while, the God of all grace, who has called you to his eternal glory in Christ, will himself restore, support, strengthen, and establish you. [11]To him be the power forever and ever. Amen.

Final Greetings and Benediction

12 Through Silvanus, whom I consider a faithful brother, I have written this short letter to encourage you and to testify that this is the true grace of God. Stand fast in it. [13]Your sister church[h] in Babylon, chosen together with you, sends you greetings; and so does my son Mark. [14]Greet one another with a kiss of love.

Peace to all of you who are in Christ.[i]

---

a Other ancient authorities add *and of power*   b Other ancient authorities add *On their part he is blasphemed, but on your part he is glorified*   c Other ancient authorities lack *exercising the oversight*   d Other ancient authorities lack *as God would have you do it*   e Or *of those who are older*   f Or *be vigilant*   g Gk *your brotherhood*   h Gk *She who is*   i Other ancient authorities add *Amen*

THE SECOND LETTER OF
PETER
Listening for Truth

KEY VERSE:
Grow in the grace and knowledge of our Lord and Savior Jesus Christ.—2 Peter 3.18

Would you prefer a godly life or a wallow in the mud (2.22)? Given the choice, most Christians would choose a godly life! Peter dramatically contrasts those two choices. He asserts that everything needed for living a godly life has already been given us in Christ Jesus; it is simply waiting to be appropriated. If this is the case, who would ever be diverted? "Well," says Peter, "plenty of people!" He pulls no punches. The examples he uses do not make for pleasant reading. Yet, shock tactics have their place in demanding our attention.

These particular shock tactics provide the basis for Peter's heartfelt exhortation that his readers be on the lookout for similar issues that might undermine their faith. God is patient and leaves time for each generation of believers to identify the options and choose salvation and life. But the day will come when time has run out. How much better to be actively involved in growing in grace than to be caught unprepared.

The message of this letter is very contemporary. Nothing has changed—God provides everything we need for a life of godliness. We face the same challenge the early Christians did—to grow in our knowledge and experience of holiness in Jesus Christ. Nothing has changed, either, in the human capacity to distort, scoff at or simply disbelieve the grace of God. We, like the recipients of Peter's letter, have been forewarned: Stay away from the mud and discover the green pastures of godliness!

"Let all our employment be to *know* God: the more one *knows* him, the more one *desires* to know him. And as knowledge is commonly the measure of *love*, the deeper and more extensive our *knowledge* shall be, the greater will be our *love*: and if our *love* of God were great we would love him equally in pains and pleasures."

—BROTHER LAWRENCE,
The Practice of the Presence of God

You Have Everything You Need

2 PETER 1.1–4

"In technology you have this horizontal progress where you must start at one point and move to another and then another. But that is not the way to build a life of prayer. In prayer we discover what we already have. You start where you are and you deepen what you already have, and you realize that you are already there. We already have everything, but we don't know it and we don't experience it. Everything has been given to us in Christ. All we need is to experience what we already possess."

—THOMAS MERTON,
as quoted in *Thomas Merton/Monk:
A Monastic Tribute*

Salutation

1 Simeon[a] Peter, a servant[b] and apostle of Jesus Christ,
To those who have received a faith as precious as ours through the righteousness of our God and Savior Jesus Christ:[c]

2 May grace and peace be yours in abundance in the knowledge of God and of Jesus our Lord.

The Christian's Call and Election

3 His divine power has given us everything needed for life and godliness, through the knowledge of him who called us by[d] his own glory and goodness. [4]Thus he has given us, through these things, his precious and very great promises, so that through them you may escape from the corruption that is in the world because of lust, and may become participants of the divine nature. [5]For this very reason, you must make every effort to support your faith with goodness, and goodness with knowledge, [6]and knowledge with self-control, and self-control with endurance, and endurance with godliness, [7]and godliness with mutual[e] affection, and mutual[e] affection with love. [8]For if these things are yours and are increasing among you, they keep you from being ineffective and unfruitful in the knowledge of our Lord Jesus Christ. [9]For anyone who lacks these things is nearsighted and blind, and is forgetful of the cleansing of past sins. [10]Therefore, brothers and sisters,[f] be all the more eager to confirm your call and election, for if you do this, you will never stumble. [11]For in this way, entry into the eternal kingdom of our Lord and Savior Jesus Christ will be richly provided for you.

12 Therefore I intend to keep on reminding you of these things, though you know them already and are established in the truth that has come to you. [13]I think it right, as long as I am in this body,[g] to refresh your memory, [14]since I know that my death[h] will come soon, as indeed our Lord Jesus Christ has made clear to me. [15]And I will make every effort so that after my departure you may be able at any time to recall these things.

Eyewitnesses of Christ's Glory

16 For we did not follow cleverly devised myths when we made known to you the power and coming of our Lord Jesus Christ, but we had been eyewitnesses of his majesty. [17]For he received honor and glory from God the Father when that voice was conveyed to him by the Majestic Glory, saying, "This is my Son, my Beloved,[i] with whom I am well pleased." [18]We ourselves heard this voice come from heaven, while we were with him on the holy mountain.

19 So we have the prophetic message more fully confirmed. You will do well to be attentive to this as to a lamp shining in a dark place, until the day dawns and the morning star rises in your hearts. [20]First of all you must understand this, that no prophecy of scripture is a matter of one's own interpretation, [21]because no prophecy ever came by human will, but men and women moved by the Holy Spirit spoke from God.[j]

a Other ancient authorities read *Simon*   *b* Gk *slave*   *c* Or *of our God and the Savior Jesus Christ*   *d* Other ancient authorities read *through*
e Gk *brotherly*   *f* Gk *brothers*   *g* Gk *tent*   *h* Gk *the putting off of my tent*
i Other ancient authorities read *my beloved Son*   *j* Other ancient authorities read *but moved by the Holy Spirit saints of God spoke*

False Prophets and Their Punishment

2 But false prophets also arose among the people, just as there will be false teachers among you, who will secretly bring in destructive opinions. They will even deny the Master who bought them—bringing swift destruction on themselves. ²Even so, many will follow their licentious ways, and because of these teachers[a] the way of truth will be maligned. ³And in their greed they will exploit you with deceptive words. Their condemnation, pronounced against them long ago, has not been idle, and their destruction is not asleep.

4 For if God did not spare the angels when they sinned, but cast them into hell[b] and committed them to chains[c] of deepest darkness to be kept until the judgment; ⁵and if he did not spare the ancient world, even though he saved Noah, a herald of righteousness, with seven others, when he brought a flood on a world of the ungodly; ⁶and if by turning the cities of Sodom and Gomorrah to ashes he condemned them to extinction[d] and made them an example of what is coming to the ungodly;[e] ⁷and if he rescued Lot, a righteous man greatly distressed by the licentiousness of the lawless ⁸(for that righteous man, living among them day after day, was tormented in his righteous soul by their lawless deeds that he saw and heard), ⁹then the Lord knows how to rescue the godly from trial, and to keep the unrighteous under punishment until the day of judgment ¹⁰—especially those who indulge their flesh in depraved lust, and who despise authority.

Bold and willful, they are not afraid to slander the glorious ones,[f] ¹¹whereas angels, though greater in might and power, do not bring against them a slanderous judgment from the Lord.[g] ¹²These people, however, are like irrational animals, mere creatures of instinct, born to be caught and killed. They slander what they do not understand, and when those creatures are destroyed,[h] they also will be destroyed, ¹³suffering[i] the penalty for doing wrong. They count it a pleasure to revel in the daytime. They are blots and blemishes, reveling in their dissipation[j] while they feast with you. ¹⁴They have eyes full of adultery, insatiable for sin. They entice unsteady souls. They have hearts trained in greed. Accursed children! ¹⁵They have left the straight road and have gone astray, following the road of Balaam son of Bosor,[k] who loved the wages of doing wrong, ¹⁶but was rebuked for his own transgression; a speechless donkey spoke with a human voice and restrained the prophet's madness.

17 These are waterless springs and mists driven by a storm; for them the deepest darkness has been reserved. ¹⁸For they speak bombastic nonsense, and with licentious desires of the flesh they entice people who have just[l] escaped from those who live in error. ¹⁹They promise them freedom, but they themselves are slaves of corruption; for people are slaves to whatever masters them. ²⁰For if, after they have escaped the defilements of the world through the knowledge of our Lord and Savior Jesus Christ, they are again entangled in them and overpowered, the last state

---

Slave or Free?

2 PETER 2.17–20

Peter does not mince words: "People are slaves to whatever masters them." Given all the examples he has just identified, we had better take his cautionary words seriously.

What controls you? What hinders your freedom and growth in Jesus Christ? Is it fear? The opinions of others? Laziness? An addiction? An unforgiving spirit? Greed? Or something else? Take time to let the Spirit reveal what enslaves you. Stand up and let your body feel as it would if bound with restricting ropes. Ask God to reveal the freedom Christ Jesus has won for you. As you see each rope being untied, move your body more and more freely and joyfully. End by assuming a posture that expresses your grateful commitment to true freedom.

---

a Gk *because of them*   b Gk *Tartaros*   c Other ancient authorities read *pits*   d Other ancient authorities lack *to extinction*   e Other ancient authorities read *an example to those who were to be ungodly*   f Or *angels*; Gk *glories*   g Other ancient authorities read *before the Lord*; others lack the phrase   h Gk *in their destruction*   i Other ancient authorities read *receiving*   j Other ancient authorities read *love-feasts*   k Other ancient authorities read *Beor*   l Other ancient authorities read *actually*

A Day to Look Forward To

2 PETER 3.1–18

As children, most of us felt as though Christmas day would never come. We looked forward to it eagerly for weeks—weeks that seemed like years! The anticipation filled us with excitement and imagination and prompted all kinds of preparation for the big day. Another big day is coming. But this time we don't know the date!

Suppose you knew that Jesus would return this year or next month or next week. What difference would that make in your plans and priorities? How would you feel? What preparation would you make? "Well, get on with it!" says Peter in effect. This could be the day. Let eager anticipation motivate your choices.

has become worse for them than the first. [21]For it would have been better for them never to have known the way of righteousness than, after knowing it, to turn back from the holy commandment that was passed on to them. [22]It has happened to them according to the true proverb,

"The dog turns back to its own vomit,"

and,

"The sow is washed only to wallow in the mud."

The Promise of the Lord's Coming

3 This is now, beloved, the second letter I am writing to you; in them I am trying to arouse your sincere intention by reminding you [2]that you should remember the words spoken in the past by the holy prophets, and the commandment of the Lord and Savior spoken through your apostles. [3]First of all you must understand this, that in the last days scoffers will come, scoffing and indulging their own lusts [4]and saying, "Where is the promise of his coming? For ever since our ancestors died,[a] all things continue as they were from the beginning of creation!" [5]They deliberately ignore this fact, that by the word of God heavens existed long ago and an earth was formed out of water and by means of water, [6]through which the world of that time was deluged with water and perished. [7]But by the same word the present heavens and earth have been reserved for fire, being kept until the day of judgment and destruction of the godless.

8 But do not ignore this one fact, beloved, that with the Lord one day is like a thousand years, and a thousand years are like one day. [9]The Lord is not slow about his promise, as some think of slowness, but is patient with you,[b] not wanting any to perish, but all to come to repentance. [10]But the day of the Lord will come like a thief, and then the heavens will pass away with a loud noise, and the elements will be dissolved with fire, and the earth and everything that is done on it will be disclosed.[c]

11 Since all these things are to be dissolved in this way, what sort of persons ought you to be in leading lives of holiness and godliness, [12]waiting for and hastening[d] the coming of the day of God, because of which the heavens will be set ablaze and dissolved, and the elements will melt with fire? [13]But, in accordance with his promise, we wait for new heavens and a new earth, where righteousness is at home.

Final Exhortation and Doxology

14 Therefore, beloved, while you are waiting for these things, strive to be found by him at peace, without spot or blemish; [15]and regard the patience of our Lord as salvation. So also our beloved brother Paul wrote to you according to the wisdom given him, [16]speaking of this as he does in all his letters. There are some things in them hard to understand, which the ignorant and unstable twist to their own destruction, as they do the other scriptures. [17]You therefore, beloved, since you are forewarned, beware that you are not carried away with the error of the lawless and lose your own stability. [18]But grow in the grace and knowledge of our Lord and Savior Jesus Christ. To him be the glory both now and to the day of eternity. Amen.[e]

a Gk our fathers fell asleep   b Other ancient authorities read on your account   c Other ancient authorities read will be burned up
d Or earnestly desiring   e Other ancient authorities lack Amen

THE FIRST LETTER OF
JOHN
Living in Love

KEY VERSE:

God is love, and those who abide in love abide in God, and God abides in them.—1 John 4.16

John's letter paints a panoramic portrait of love the way God sees it. As we read and pray through these brief but powerful pages, two facets of Biblical love seem to stand out. First, before we are able to practice or walk in love, we must have some awareness of its nature. Love is grounded in God (4.8,16) and is most clearly depicted in Jesus Christ, who sacrificially offered his life for us (3.16; 4.10). John calls us to the same kind of sacrificial love in which our actions align with our words in truth. (3.18).

Second, the apostle John connects love with obedience. Obedience is our joyful response to the love of Jesus Christ, which allows us to live in him and he in us (2.3–5; 2 John 5–6). We are commanded to walk in love not only when it is convenient for us but each day because we are children of God (5.2).

As you reflect on these words, review your experience of God's incredible love for you. Think about how you express that love to others. And as you join John in pondering this message, prayerfully ask God to help you to see him more clearly, love him more dearly and follow him more nearly as you mirror his love day by day.

"O most merciful Redeemer, friend and brother, may we know thee more clearly, love thee more dearly, and follow thee more nearly, for thine own sake."

—RICHARD OF CHICHESTER

Imitating Christ

1 JOHN 2.3–6

Jesus' message is clear and bracing: He commands us to follow him and walk in the same way in which he himself walked (see Matthew 8.22; John 21.19). It's not possible for us to do this through our own effort, but we can walk in him when he lives within us. Otherwise Jesus would not have given us this command!

As you reflect on these verses, describe in your own words how Jesus walked. How might you follow his example? How have you already experienced this? In what situations is it most difficult to practice? How will you ask for his help in fulfilling this command? Before turning away from this scripture passage, think about a hymn or song that best captures this theme for you. Sing or hum it throughout the day as a way of internalizing this passage.

See Meeting God in Everyday Life

The Word of Life

1 We declare to you what was from the beginning, what we have heard, what we have seen with our eyes, what we have looked at and touched with our hands, concerning the word of life— ²this life was revealed, and we have seen it and testify to it, and declare to you the eternal life that was with the Father and was revealed to us— ³we declare to you what we have seen and heard so that you also may have fellowship with us; and truly our fellowship is with the Father and with his Son Jesus Christ. ⁴We are writing these things so that our[a] joy may be complete.

God Is Light

5 This is the message we have heard from him and proclaim to you, that God is light and in him there is no darkness at all. ⁶If we say that we have fellowship with him while we are walking in darkness, we lie and do not do what is true; ⁷but if we walk in the light as he himself is in the light, we have fellowship with one another, and the blood of Jesus his Son cleanses us from all sin. ⁸If we say that we have no sin, we deceive ourselves, and the truth is not in us. ⁹If we confess our sins, he who is faithful and just will forgive us our sins and cleanse us from all unrighteousness. ¹⁰If we say that we have not sinned, we make him a liar, and his word is not in us.

Christ Our Advocate

2 My little children, I am writing these things to you so that you may not sin. But if anyone does sin, we have an advocate with the Father, Jesus Christ the righteous; ²and he is the atoning sacrifice for our sins, and not for ours only but also for the sins of the whole world.

3 Now by this we may be sure that we know him, if we obey his commandments. ⁴Whoever says, "I have come to know him," but does not obey his commandments, is a liar, and in such a person the truth does not exist; ⁵but whoever obeys his word, truly in this person the love of God has reached perfection. By this we may be sure that we are in him: ⁶whoever says, "I abide in him," ought to walk just as he walked.

A New Commandment

7 Beloved, I am writing you no new commandment, but an old commandment that you have had from the beginning; the old commandment is the word that you have heard. ⁸Yet I am writing you a new commandment that is true in him and in you, because[b] the darkness is passing away and the true light is already shining. ⁹Whoever says, "I am in the light," while hating a brother or sister,[c] is still in the darkness. ¹⁰Whoever loves a brother or sister[d] lives in the light, and in such a person[e] there is no cause for stumbling. ¹¹But whoever hates another believer[f] is in the darkness, walks in the darkness, and does not know the way to go, because the darkness has brought on blindness.

¹² I am writing to you, little children,
   because your sins are forgiven on account of his
   name.

a Other ancient authorities read *your*   b Or *that*   c Gk *hating a brother*
d Gk *loves a brother*   e Or *in it*   f Gk *hates a brother*

13 I am writing to you, fathers,
　　because you know him who is from the
　　　beginning.
　I am writing to you, young people,
　　because you have conquered the evil one.
14 I write to you, children,
　　because you know the Father.
　I write to you, fathers,
　　because you know him who is from the
　　　beginning.
　I write to you, young people,
　　because you are strong
　　and the word of God abides in you,
　　　and you have overcome the evil one.

15 Do not love the world or the things in the world. The love of the Father is not in those who love the world; ¹⁶for all that is in the world—the desire of the flesh, the desire of the eyes, the pride in riches—comes not from the Father but from the world. ¹⁷And the world and its desire*a* are passing away, but those who do the will of God live forever.

Warning against Antichrists

18 Children, it is the last hour! As you have heard that antichrist is coming, so now many antichrists have come. From this we know that it is the last hour. ¹⁹They went out from us, but they did not belong to us; for if they had belonged to us, they would have remained with us. But by going out they made it plain that none of them belongs to us. ²⁰But you have been anointed by the Holy One, and all of you have knowledge.*b* ²¹I write to you, not because you do not know the truth, but because you know it, and you know that no lie comes from the truth. ²²Who is the liar but the one who denies that Jesus is the Christ?*c* This is the antichrist, the one who denies the Father and the Son. ²³No one who denies the Son has the Father; everyone who confesses the Son has the Father also. ²⁴Let what you heard from the beginning abide in you. If what you heard from the beginning abides in you, then you will abide in the Son and in the Father. ²⁵And this is what he has promised us,*d* eternal life.

26 I write these things to you concerning those who would deceive you. ²⁷As for you, the anointing that you received from him abides in you, and so you do not need anyone to teach you. But as his anointing teaches you about all things, and is true and is not a lie, and just as it has taught you, abide in him.*e*

28 And now, little children, abide in him, so that when he is revealed we may have confidence and not be put to shame before him at his coming.

Children of God

29 If you know that he is righteous, you may be sure that
3 everyone who does right has been born of him. ¹See what love the Father has given us, that we should be called children of God; and that is what we are. The reason the world does not know us is that it did not know him. ²Beloved, we are God's children now; what we will be has not yet been revealed. What we do know is this: when he*e*

---

a Or *the desire for it*　　*b* Other ancient authorities read *you know all things*
c Or *the Messiah*　　*d* Other ancient authorities read *you*　　*e* Or *it*

Love in Actions

1 JOHN 3.16–18

Many people think they *know* something when in reality they only know *about* it. They are limited by secondhand knowledge—a poor substitute for the real thing! We know the love of Jesus Christ because he laid down his life for us. And John reminds us that the best way to experience that love is to express it. How might you demonstrate that love to God? How might you demonstrate love to those who are closest to you, to your friends or associates at work, school, church, to those who are in need, or maybe even to a person you don't particularly like? Create a symbol or reminder to encourage you to make love visible to others. Carry it with you or place it on your mirror or in another prominent spot.

See Meeting God in Everyday Life

is revealed, we will be like him, for we will see him as he is. ³And all who have this hope in him purify themselves, just as he is pure.

4 Everyone who commits sin is guilty of lawlessness; sin is lawlessness. ⁵You know that he was revealed to take away sins, and in him there is no sin. ⁶No one who abides in him sins; no one who sins has either seen him or known him. ⁷Little children, let no one deceive you. Everyone who does what is right is righteous, just as he is righteous. ⁸Everyone who commits sin is a child of the devil; for the devil has been sinning from the beginning. The Son of God was revealed for this purpose, to destroy the works of the devil. ⁹Those who have been born of God do not sin, because God's seed abides in them;*a* they cannot sin, because they have been born of God. ¹⁰The children of God and the children of the devil are revealed in this way: all who do not do what is right are not from God, nor are those who do not love their brothers and sisters.*b*

Love One Another

11 For this is the message you have heard from the beginning, that we should love one another. ¹²We must not be like Cain who was from the evil one and murdered his brother. And why did he murder him? Because his own deeds were evil and his brother's righteous. ¹³Do not be astonished, brothers and sisters,*c* that the world hates you. ¹⁴We know that we have passed from death to life because we love one another. Whoever does not love abides in death. ¹⁵All who hate a brother or sister*b* are murderers, and you know that murderers do not have eternal life abiding in them. ¹⁶We know love by this, that he laid down his life for us—and we ought to lay down our lives for one another. ¹⁷How does God's love abide in anyone who has the world's goods and sees a brother or sister*d* in need and yet refuses help?

18 Little children, let us love, not in word or speech, but in truth and action. ¹⁹And by this we will know that we are from the truth and will reassure our hearts before him ²⁰whenever our hearts condemn us; for God is greater than our hearts, and he knows everything. ²¹Beloved, if our hearts do not condemn us, we have boldness before God; ²²and we receive from him whatever we ask, because we obey his commandments and do what pleases him.

23 And this is his commandment, that we should believe in the name of his Son Jesus Christ and love one another, just as he has commanded us. ²⁴All who obey his commandments abide in him, and he abides in them. And by this we know that he abides in us, by the Spirit that he has given us.

Testing the Spirits

4 Beloved, do not believe every spirit, but test the spirits to see whether they are from God; for many false prophets have gone out into the world. ²By this you know the Spirit of God: every spirit that confesses that Jesus Christ has come in the flesh is from God, ³and every spirit that does not confess Jesus*e* is not from God. And this is the

a Or *because the children of God abide in him*   *b* Gk *his brother*
c Gk *brothers*   *d* Gk *brother*   *e* Other ancient authorities read *does away with Jesus* (Gk *dissolves Jesus*)

spirit of the antichrist, of which you have heard that it is coming; and now it is already in the world. ⁴Little children, you are from God, and have conquered them; for the one who is in you is greater than the one who is in the world. ⁵They are from the world; therefore what they say is from the world, and the world listens to them. ⁶We are from God. Whoever knows God listens to us, and whoever is not from God does not listen to us. From this we know the spirit of truth and the spirit of error.

God Is Love

7 Beloved, let us love one another, because love is from God; everyone who loves is born of God and knows God. ⁸Whoever does not love does not know God, for God is love. ⁹God's love was revealed among us in this way: God sent his only Son into the world so that we might live through him. ¹⁰In this is love, not that we loved God but that he loved us and sent his Son to be the atoning sacrifice for our sins. ¹¹Beloved, since God loved us so much, we also ought to love one another. ¹²No one has ever seen God; if we love one another, God lives in us, and his love is perfected in us.

13 By this we know that we abide in him and he in us, because he has given us of his Spirit. ¹⁴And we have seen and do testify that the Father has sent his Son as the Savior of the world. ¹⁵God abides in those who confess that Jesus is the Son of God, and they abide in God. ¹⁶So we have known and believe the love that God has for us.

God is love, and those who abide in love abide in God, and God abides in them. ¹⁷Love has been perfected among us in this: that we may have boldness on the day of judgment, because as he is, so are we in this world. ¹⁸There is no fear in love, but perfect love casts out fear; for fear has to do with punishment, and whoever fears has not reached perfection in love. ¹⁹We love*a* because he first loved us. ²⁰Those who say, "I love God," and hate their brothers or sisters,*b* are liars; for those who do not love a brother or sister*c* whom they have seen, cannot love God whom they have not seen. ²¹The commandment we have from him is this: those who love God must love their brothers and sisters*b* also.

Faith Conquers the World

5 Everyone who believes that Jesus is the Christ*d* has been born of God, and everyone who loves the parent loves the child. ²By this we know that we love the children of God, when we love God and obey his commandments. ³For the love of God is this, that we obey his commandments. And his commandments are not burdensome, ⁴for whatever is born of God conquers the world. And this is the victory that conquers the world, our faith. ⁵Who is it that conquers the world but the one who believes that Jesus is the Son of God?

Testimony concerning the Son of God

6 This is the one who came by water and blood, Jesus Christ, not with the water only but with the water and the blood. And the Spirit is the one that testifies, for the Spirit

God Is Love

1 JOHN 4.16–18

God is love. What a simple, yet powerful description of God's nature! Slowly and carefully read these verses again. What phrase captures your attention? Gently savor this scripture. What attracts you to it? What does it mean to you? How have you experienced it in your life? As you continue to slowly ponder and pray this phrase, what emotions do you feel stirring within your heart? Allow God's Spirit the freedom to impress you with any insights, reminders or invitations. Conclude by thanking God for your time together.

See Meeting God in Scripture

---

a Other ancient authorities add *him*; others add *God*   *b* Gk *brothers*
c Gk *brother*   *d* Or *the Messiah*

Accept No Substitutes!

1 JOHN 5.21

God alone is worthy to receive our devotion and love. Sometimes, however, we allow people and things to take God's place at the center of our lives; they become idols.

Use your imagination and enter into a conversation with Jesus. Where are the two of you? What are you talking about? As your time unfolds, imagine Jesus gently but firmly asking, "My friend, who are the idols in your life? What competes with me for your love? I desire to fill you with my grace—with myself—and to be your first love." How is God's Holy Spirit calling you to respond? What do you notice about the look on Jesus' face? What emotions are you experiencing. Record your insights in your journal.

See *Meeting God in Everyday Life*

is the truth. [7]There are three that testify:[a] [8]the Spirit and the water and the blood, and these three agree. [9]If we receive human testimony, the testimony of God is greater; for this is the testimony of God that he has testified to his Son. [10]Those who believe in the Son of God have the testimony in their hearts. Those who do not believe in God[b] have made him a liar by not believing in the testimony that God has given concerning his Son. [11]And this is the testimony: God gave us eternal life, and this life is in his Son. [12]Whoever has the Son has life; whoever does not have the Son of God does not have life.

Epilogue

13 I write these things to you who believe in the name of the Son of God, so that you may know that you have eternal life.

14 And this is the boldness we have in him, that if we ask anything according to his will, he hears us. [15]And if we know that he hears us in whatever we ask, we know that we have obtained the requests made of him. [16]If you see your brother or sister[c] committing what is not a mortal sin, you will ask, and God[d] will give life to such a one—to those whose sin is not mortal. There is sin that is mortal; I do not say that you should pray about that. [17]All wrongdoing is sin, but there is sin that is not mortal.

18 We know that those who are born of God do not sin, but the one who was born of God protects them, and the evil one does not touch them. [19]We know that we are God's children, and that the whole world lies under the power of the evil one. [20]And we know that the Son of God has come and has given us understanding so that we may know him who is true;[e] and we are in him who is true, in his Son Jesus Christ. He is the true God and eternal life.

21 Little children, keep yourselves from idols.[f]

THE SECOND LETTER OF
JOHN
Walking in Love

KEY VERSE:

This is the commandment just as you have heard it from the beginning—you must walk in it.—2 John 6

The challenging words of Amy Carmichael mirror John's message: Biblical love is contagious! Love is a dynamic, blazing flame that awakens us by its power, passion and reality. However, our life experiences remind us that not everyone is inspired by the integrity of love. As strange as it may seem, some are equally motivated by error. This brief letter summarizes the battle being waged within the believer between walking in love and walking in error. True love—expressed in obedience—produces the richness of delight in God (v.6). But walking in error and heresy yields the emptiness of deception and danger (vv.7–11). John alerts us to the same potential pitfalls today. As you read this short book, don't underestimate the importance of its message. Whom or what do you welcome into your life? Do those people, activities and experiences encourage you to walk in love or in error?

"You will, I believe and trust, become more and more in love with a crucified Saviour. He wants lovers. Oh how tepid is the love of so many who call themselves by His name. How tepid our own—my own—in comparison with the lava fires of His eternal love. I pray that you may be an ardent lover, the kind of lover who sets others on fire."

—AMY CARMICHAEL,
Candles in the Dark,

Remember the Command: Walk in Love!

2 JOHN 4–6

Parents and teachers can readily grasp the message of these verses. John's heart is overflowing with joy that others within the church are living out the truth of walking in love. In our own day, when many relationships both within and outside the church are fractured by greed and the desire for ease and self-advancement, it is both wise and necessary to follow this Biblical counsel.

What does it mean for you to walk in love with those significant people in your life? What is the greatest hurdle you have to overcome to walk in love? How much joy does your church bring to Jesus Christ by the way its people interact inside the church? By the way those people interact with those outside the church? As you reflect on these questions write a "love letter" to Jesus about your intentions to walk in love.

See Meeting God in Community

Salutation

1 The elder to the elect lady and her children, whom I love in the truth, and not only I but also all who know the truth, ²because of the truth that abides in us and will be with us forever:

3 Grace, mercy, and peace will be with us from God the Father and from*ᵃ* Jesus Christ, the Father's Son, in truth and love.

Truth and Love

4 I was overjoyed to find some of your children walking in the truth, just as we have been commanded by the Father. ⁵But now, dear lady, I ask you, not as though I were writing you a new commandment, but one we have had from the beginning, let us love one another. ⁶And this is love, that we walk according to his commandments; this is the commandment just as you have heard it from the beginning—you must walk in it.

7 Many deceivers have gone out into the world, those who do not confess that Jesus Christ has come in the flesh; any such person is the deceiver and the antichrist! ⁸Be on your guard, so that you do not lose what we*ᵇ* have worked for, but may receive a full reward. ⁹Everyone who does not abide in the teaching of Christ, but goes beyond it, does not have God; whoever abides in the teaching has both the Father and the Son. ¹⁰Do not receive into the house or welcome anyone who comes to you and does not bring this teaching; ¹¹for to welcome is to participate in the evil deeds of such a person.

Final Greetings

12 Although I have much to write to you, I would rather not use paper and ink; instead I hope to come to you and talk with you face to face, so that our joy may be complete.

13 The children of your elect sister send you their greetings.*ᶜ*

a Other ancient authorities add *the Lord*   *b* Other ancient authorities read *you*   *c* Other ancient authorities add *Amen*

THE THIRD LETTER OF
JOHN
Walking in Truth

KEY VERSE:

I have no greater joy than this, to hear that my children are walking in the truth.—3 John 4

What a startling comparison John paints on the canvas of this book of holy Scripture. Two specific individuals are mentioned by name to illustrate the importance of personal character. Diotrephes, who is characterized by self-love, exhibits an inhospitable attitude that ravages the Christian community (vv.9–10). In stark contrast is Demetrius, whose reputation for truthful living is affirmed by everyone (v.12). His life is marked by integrity, and John holds him up as a fitting model for his readers. It is evident from John's words that walking in truth is more than speaking the correct words. It requires the formation of character that is honest and is worthy of God. Indeed John's third letter could serve as a New Testament counterpoint to Micah's great ethical summary of the law: "He has told you, O mortal, what is good; and what does the LORD require of you but to do justice, and to love kindness, and to walk humbly with your God?" (Micah 6.8). What will you do today to rise to John Huss's challenges to pursue truth?

"Therefore, O faithful Christian, search for truth, hear truth, learn truth, love truth, speak the truth, hold the truth, defend the truth till death!"

—JOHN HUSS,
Exposition of Faith

The Source of True Health

3 JOHN 2–4

Our society is health conscious, a phenomenon that is clearly confirmed by the number of health publications, vitamins and supplements, kinds of exercise equipment and assorted experimental healing techniques that are available on the market. And modern medicine is finally discovering the reality, which scripture has consistently communicated, that there is a connection between the health of our spirit and the health of our bodies. We rarely hear, however, that one of the basic principles of a healthful life is truth!

When our lives are characterized by honesty and integrity, we reduce the need to conceal or deceive. Our level of peace goes up and our stress level goes down. Jesus was telling the gospel truth when he reminded us that the truth sets us free (see John 8.32). Where do you most need this freedom in your life? How are you being challenged to walk in greater truth? Spend some moments quietly seeking and listening to God's Spirit. If possible, share your insights with a trusted friend who can pray with you and encourage you to walk in the truth.

Salutation

1 The elder to the beloved Gaius, whom I love in truth.

Gaius Commended for His Hospitality

2 Beloved, I pray that all may go well with you and that you may be in good health, just as it is well with your soul. ³I was overjoyed when some of the friends*a* arrived and testified to your faithfulness to the truth, namely how you walk in the truth. ⁴I have no greater joy than this, to hear that my children are walking in the truth.

5 Beloved, you do faithfully whatever you do for the friends,*a* even though they are strangers to you; ⁶they have testified to your love before the church. You will do well to send them on in a manner worthy of God; ⁷for they began their journey for the sake of Christ,*b* accepting no support from non-believers.*c* ⁸Therefore we ought to support such people, so that we may become co-workers with the truth.

Diotrephes and Demetrius

9 I have written something to the church; but Diotrephes, who likes to put himself first, does not acknowledge our authority. ¹⁰So if I come, I will call attention to what he is doing in spreading false charges against us. And not content with those charges, he refuses to welcome the friends,*a* and even prevents those who want to do so and expels them from the church.

11 Beloved, do not imitate what is evil but imitate what is good. Whoever does good is from God; whoever does evil has not seen God. ¹²Everyone has testified favorably about Demetrius, and so has the truth itself. We also testify for him,*d* and you know that our testimony is true.

Final Greetings

13 I have much to write to you, but I would rather not write with pen and ink; ¹⁴instead I hope to see you soon, and we will talk together face to face.

15 Peace to you. The friends send you their greetings. Greet the friends there, each by name.

a Gk *brothers*   *b* Gk *for the sake of the name*   *c* Gk *the Gentiles*
d Gk lacks *for him*

THE LETTER OF
JUDE
Standing Firm

KEY VERSE:

Keep yourselves in the love of God; look forward to the mercy of our Lord Jesus Christ
that leads to eternal life.—Jude 21

This little book is short, sharp and salutary. Jude sets out to write an enthusiastic letter about the wonders of salvation but finds himself writing strong, stern words instead. He is motivated by love of God and love for his readers.

Jude (said by tradition to be the brother of Jesus as well as his servant) burns with passion for the purity of the faith; he can't bear to see it undermined. But that is exactly what is happening, and a warning must be issued. With anguish and energy Jude startles his readers into taking notice. At the beginning and end of the letter, Jude speaks of the mercy, peace, love, power and security that are available in Jesus Christ. In the middle of the letter, Jude gives graphic examples of the awful possibility of perverting what Jesus offers. Though the examples Jude gives certainly would have evoked powerful memories for his original readers, some of them may seem irrelevant to us in our culture and our time. We can't escape the significance of this letter however. God's Spirit, who inspired Jude's letter, asks us to consider what might pervert God's grace in our day. What behavior, lifestyle, attitudes or destructive talk do we need to address? Do we need to wake up? After all, we are nearer to the "last time" than Jude's readers were! May his passionate words kindle the fire of love in our hearts. Be warned. Take action. Keep yourself in the love of God.

> "It is not easy under everyday conditions to learn and maintain the art of steadfast attention to God; yet no art could more certainly serve his purposes than this. 'One loving spirit sets another on fire.' "
>
> —EVELYN UNDERHILL,
> *The Golden Sequence*

Beware of Intruders!

JUDE 1–19

Jude issues a wake-up call to those of his readers whose spiritual lives are being subtly undermined. There are intruders in the community of faith—distorters of the truth, who are turning abundant mercy, peace and love into waterless clouds and fruitless trees. Do you ever have the uncomfortable feeling that there is subtle conflict going on within you? Within your community of faith? Prayerfully reflect on your faith community. What symbols or descriptions might represent various influences, both negative and positive? Name what you can celebrate and that for which you can give thanks! Then ask for the Spirit's help to name and deal with the intruders that undermine your peace.

See *Meeting God in Community*

Salutation

1 Jude,[a] a servant[b] of Jesus Christ and brother of James,

To those who are called, who are beloved[c] in[d] God the Father and kept safe for[d] Jesus Christ:

2 May mercy, peace, and love be yours in abundance.

Occasion of the Letter

3 Beloved, while eagerly preparing to write to you about the salvation we share, I find it necessary to write and appeal to you to contend for the faith that was once for all entrusted to the saints. [4]For certain intruders have stolen in among you, people who long ago were designated for this condemnation as ungodly, who pervert the grace of our God into licentiousness and deny our only Master and Lord, Jesus Christ.[e]

Judgment on False Teachers

5 Now I desire to remind you, though you are fully informed, that the Lord, who once for all saved[f] a people out of the land of Egypt, afterward destroyed those who did not believe. [6]And the angels who did not keep their own position, but left their proper dwelling, he has kept in eternal chains in deepest darkness for the judgment of the great day. [7]Likewise, Sodom and Gomorrah and the surrounding cities, which, in the same manner as they, indulged in sexual immorality and pursued unnatural lust,[g] serve as an example by undergoing a punishment of eternal fire.

8 Yet in the same way these dreamers also defile the flesh, reject authority, and slander the glorious ones.[h] [9]But when the archangel Michael contended with the devil and disputed about the body of Moses, he did not dare to bring a condemnation of slander[i] against him, but said, "The Lord rebuke you!" [10]But these people slander whatever they do not understand, and they are destroyed by those things that, like irrational animals, they know by instinct. [11]Woe to them! For they go the way of Cain, and abandon themselves to Balaam's error for the sake of gain, and perish in Korah's rebellion. [12]These are blemishes[j] on your love-feasts, while they feast with you without fear, feeding themselves.[k] They are waterless clouds carried along by the winds; autumn trees without fruit, twice dead, uprooted; [13]wild waves of the sea, casting up the foam of their own shame; wandering stars, for whom the deepest darkness has been reserved forever.

14 It was also about these that Enoch, in the seventh generation from Adam, prophesied, saying, "See, the Lord is coming[l] with ten thousands of his holy ones, [15]to execute judgment on all, and to convict everyone of all the deeds of ungodliness that they have committed in such an ungodly way, and of all the harsh things that ungodly sinners have spoken against him." [16]These are grumblers and malcontents; they indulge their own lusts; they are bombastic in speech, flattering people to their own advantage.

a Gk *Judas*   b Gk *slave*   c Other ancient authorities read *sanctified*   d Or *by*   e Or *the only Master and our Lord Jesus Christ*   f Other ancient authorities read *though you were once for all fully informed, that Jesus* (or *Joshua*) *who saved*   g Gk *went after other flesh*   h Or *angels*; Gk *glories*   i Or *condemnation for blasphemy*   j Or *reefs*   k Or *without fear. They are shepherds who care only for themselves*   l Gk *came*

Warnings and Exhortations

17 But you, beloved, must remember the predictions of the apostles of our Lord Jesus Christ; ¹⁸for they said to you, "In the last time there will be scoffers, indulging their own ungodly lusts." ¹⁹It is these worldly people, devoid of the Spirit, who are causing divisions. ²⁰But you, beloved, build yourselves up on your most holy faith; pray in the Holy Spirit; ²¹keep yourselves in the love of God; look forward to the mercy of our Lord Jesus Christ that leads to*a* eternal life. ²²And have mercy on some who are wavering; ²³save others by snatching them out of the fire; and have mercy on still others with fear, hating even the tunic defiled by their bodies.*b*

Benediction

24 Now to him who is able to keep you from falling, and to make you stand without blemish in the presence of his glory with rejoicing, ²⁵to the only God our Savior, through Jesus Christ our Lord, be glory, majesty, power, and authority, before all time and now and forever. Amen.

Securely Loved

JUDE 20–25

Being made aware of the weak spots and the distortions in our life of faith can be a devastating as well as a defining experience. Where is the secure ground, we ask? How can we be sure we aren't following a wild wave or a wandering star to nowhere? Stay in the center of God's love, answers Jude. This is the axis around which faith, prayer, hope and mercy revolve. Close your eyes and picture the center "pole" of God's love. Where are you in relation to it? Let the prayer picture develop. Notice what the Spirit shows you. Afterward you may want to draw or write down your key insights. Read verses 24–25 as a final assurance of blessing and a powerful shout of praise to God.

a Gk *Christ to*   b Gk *by the flesh*. The Greek text of verses 22–23 is uncertain at several points

THE REVELATION TO JOHN

A Kingdom of Priests

KEY VERSES:

To him who loves us and freed us from our sins by his blood, and made us to be a kingdom,
priests serving his God and Father, to him be glory and dominion forever and ever.
Amen.—Revelation 1.5–6

> "Christ's Cross has become the key to a history whose purpose is to separate the City of God from the city of this world, which has Babylon for its symbolic name."
>
> —THOMAS MERTON,
> *Bread in the Wilderness*

The book of Revelation paints sweeping landscapes of two worlds: the sinful world that will pass away ("Fallen, fallen is Babylon the Great!" [18.2]) and, in contrast, a new world established in Jesus Christ that is the true home of all believers ("I saw the holy city, the new Jerusalem, coming down out of heaven from God" [21.2]).

There are many interpretations of this apocalyptic book. Some interpret it as exclusively futuristic and place the events of the book in the end times. This view, however, avoids the call to radical discipleship at the heart of John's vision. Revelation can be seen as a map of the Christian's spiritual journey from citizenship in Babylon to citizenship in the new Jerusalem. Babylon represents all the destructive, self-centered, dehumanizing effects of sin in this world, while Jerusalem represents the healing and liberation of new life in Christ. Redeemed in the blood of the Lamb of God, believers find a new identity in Jesus Christ and become "priests" of God who represent the presence of God in the fallen world.

As you meditate on John's vision, try to put aside all your preconceptions about Revelation and listen to the voice of the Spirit speaking to your heart about your true life as a "priest" in God's kingdom. Listen for God's call for you to become what you were created to be—a beloved child created in the image of God, a member of God's kingdom. Let the love of God become evident in you as you live in profound integrity and wholeness.

Introduction and Salutation

1 The revelation of Jesus Christ, which God gave him to show his servants[a] what must soon take place; he made[b] it known by sending his angel to his servant[c] John, [2]who testified to the word of God and to the testimony of Jesus Christ, even to all that he saw.

3 Blessed is the one who reads aloud the words of the prophecy, and blessed are those who hear and who keep what is written in it; for the time is near.

4 John to the seven churches that are in Asia:

Grace to you and peace from him who is and who was and who is to come, and from the seven spirits who are before his throne, [5]and from Jesus Christ, the faithful witness, the firstborn of the dead, and the ruler of the kings of the earth.

To him who loves us and freed[d] us from our sins by his blood, [6]and made[b] us to be a kingdom, priests serving[e] his God and Father, to him be glory and dominion forever and ever. Amen.

7 Look! He is coming with the clouds;
   every eye will see him,
      even those who pierced him;
         and on his account all the tribes of the earth
            will wail.
So it is to be. Amen.

8 "I am the Alpha and the Omega," says the Lord God, who is and who was and who is to come, the Almighty.

A Vision of Christ

9 I, John, your brother who share with you in Jesus the persecution and the kingdom and the patient endurance, was on the island called Patmos because of the word of God and the testimony of Jesus.[f] [10]I was in the spirit[g] on the Lord's day, and I heard behind me a loud voice like a trumpet [11]saying, "Write in a book what you see and send it to the seven churches, to Ephesus, to Smyrna, to Pergamum, to Thyatira, to Sardis, to Philadelphia, and to Laodicea."

12 Then I turned to see whose voice it was that spoke to me, and on turning I saw seven golden lampstands, [13]and in the midst of the lampstands I saw one like the Son of Man, clothed with a long robe and with a golden sash across his chest. [14]His head and his hair were white as white wool, white as snow; his eyes were like a flame of fire, [15]his feet were like burnished bronze, refined as in a furnace, and his voice was like the sound of many waters. [16]In his right hand he held seven stars, and from his mouth came a sharp, two-edged sword, and his face was like the sun shining with full force.

17 When I saw him, I fell at his feet as though dead. But he placed his right hand on me, saying, "Do not be afraid; I am the first and the last, [18]and the living one. I was dead, and see, I am alive forever and ever; and I have the keys of Death and of Hades. [19]Now write what you have seen, what is, and what is to take place after this. [20]As for the mystery of the seven stars that you saw in my right hand,

---

Radical Reorientation

REVELATION 1.10–20

John is so disturbed when he encounters God that he falls "at his feet as though dead." God's presence has a way of disrupting our carefully structured world. We tend to expect God to fit neatly into our agendas, our perspectives and our lifestyle. Make a list of your attitudes that limit who God can be in your life. Alongside this list write down some characteristics of your lifestyle that could restrict God's presence in your activities. Also examine your expectations for the future. How could they hinder God's purposes for you? What would you need to do to let this awesome and merciful God disrupt the structures of your life?

See Meeting God in Everyday Life

---

a Gk *slaves*   b Gk *and he made*   c Gk *slave*   d Other ancient authorities read *washed*   e Gk *priests to*   f Or *testimony to Jesus*   g Or *in the Spirit*

Cold Orthodoxy

The Ephesian church appears to be strong; in reality it has a serious problem that threatens its very existence in the body of Christ. What is the nature of the love [it] had at first"? (See Acts 19.10,19–20.) What are the signs of its faithfulness? What are the signs of your faithfulness? Are there ways in which your discipleship has become a set of habits and not a living relationship with God? Write a letter to yourself or your church—one you could envision Jesus himself writing. In light of such a letter, what changes in your discipleship do you need to make?

and the seven golden lampstands: the seven stars are the angels of the seven churches, and the seven lampstands are the seven churches.

The Message to Ephesus

2 "To the angel of the church in Ephesus write: These are the words of him who holds the seven stars in his right hand, who walks among the seven golden lampstands:

2 "I know your works, your toil and your patient endurance. I know that you cannot tolerate evildoers; you have tested those who claim to be apostles but are not, and have found them to be false. ³I also know that you are enduring patiently and bearing up for the sake of my name, and that you have not grown weary. ⁴But I have this against you, that you have abandoned the love you had at first. ⁵Remember then from what you have fallen; repent, and do the works you did at first. If not, I will come to you and remove your lampstand from its place, unless you repent. ⁶Yet this is to your credit: you hate the works of the Nicolaitans, which I also hate. ⁷Let anyone who has an ear listen to what the Spirit is saying to the churches. To everyone who conquers, I will give permission to eat from the tree of life that is in the paradise of God.

The Message to Smyrna

8 "And to the angel of the church in Smyrna write: These are the words of the first and the last, who was dead and came to life:

9 "I know your affliction and your poverty, even though you are rich. I know the slander on the part of those who say that they are Jews and are not, but are a synagogue of Satan. ¹⁰Do not fear what you are about to suffer. Beware, the devil is about to throw some of you into prison so that you may be tested, and for ten days you will have affliction. Be faithful until death, and I will give you the crown of life. ¹¹Let anyone who has an ear listen to what the Spirit is saying to the churches. Whoever conquers will not be harmed by the second death.

The Message to Pergamum

12 "And to the angel of the church in Pergamum write: These are the words of him who has the sharp two-edged sword:

13 "I know where you are living, where Satan's throne is. Yet you are holding fast to my name, and you did not deny your faith in me*a* even in the days of Antipas my witness, my faithful one, who was killed among you, where Satan lives. ¹⁴But I have a few things against you: you have some there who hold to the teaching of Balaam, who taught Balak to put a stumbling block before the people of Israel, so that they would eat food sacrificed to idols and practice fornication. ¹⁵So you also have some who hold to the teaching of the Nicolaitans. ¹⁶Repent then. If not, I will come to you soon and make war against them with the sword of my mouth. ¹⁷Let anyone who has an ear listen to what the Spirit is saying to the churches. To everyone who conquers I will give some of the hidden manna, and I will give a white stone, and on the white stone is written

a Or *deny my faith*

a new name that no one knows except the one who receives it.

The Message to Thyatira

18 "And to the angel of the church in Thyatira write: These are the words of the Son of God, who has eyes like a flame of fire, and whose feet are like burnished bronze: 19 "I know your works—your love, faith, service, and patient endurance. I know that your last works are greater than the first. 20But I have this against you: you tolerate that woman Jezebel, who calls herself a prophet and is teaching and beguiling my servants*a* to practice fornication and to eat food sacrificed to idols. 21I gave her time to repent, but she refuses to repent of her fornication. 22Beware, I am throwing her on a bed, and those who commit adultery with her I am throwing into great distress, unless they repent of her doings; 23and I will strike her children dead. And all the churches will know that I am the one who searches minds and hearts, and I will give to each of you as your works deserve. 24But to the rest of you in Thyatira, who do not hold this teaching, who have not learned what some call 'the deep things of Satan,' to you I say, I do not lay on you any other burden; 25only hold fast to what you have until I come. 26To everyone who conquers and continues to do my works to the end,

I will give authority over the nations;
27 to rule*b* them with an iron rod,
    as when clay pots are shattered—
28even as I also received authority from my Father. To the one who conquers I will also give the morning star. 29Let anyone who has an ear listen to what the Spirit is saying to the churches.

The Message to Sardis

3 "And to the angel of the church in Sardis write: These are the words of him who has the seven spirits of God and the seven stars:

"I know your works; you have a name of being alive, but you are dead. 2Wake up, and strengthen what remains and is on the point of death, for I have not found your works perfect in the sight of my God. 3Remember then what you received and heard; obey it, and repent. If you do not wake up, I will come like a thief, and you will not know at what hour I will come to you. 4Yet you have still a few persons in Sardis who have not soiled their clothes; they will walk with me, dressed in white, for they are worthy. 5If you conquer, you will be clothed like them in white robes, and I will not blot your name out of the book of life; I will confess your name before my Father and before his angels. 6Let anyone who has an ear listen to what the Spirit is saying to the churches.

The Message to Philadelphia

7 "And to the angel of the church in Philadelphia write: These are the words of the holy one, the true one,
    who has the key of David,
        who opens and no one will shut,
            who shuts and no one opens:
8 "I know your works. Look, I have set before you an

Dead or Alive?

REVELATION 3.1–6

Imagine that you are a citizen of the impregnable city of Sardis, set atop a promontory. Only twice in many centuries has your city ever been captured by an enemy. On both occasions your ancestors were so confident in their security that they failed to set a watch during a siege. The enemy scaled the cliffs at night and captured the city. What is Jesus saying to you as a citizen of this city? How can you set a watch against the enemies of your soul? If Jesus were to come right now, would it be well with your soul? What changes do you need to make?

---

a Gk *slaves*   *b* Or *to shepherd*

Opening the Door

Are there any closed doors in your heart? Are there doors that you have not dared open to allow Jesus in? What are the spiritual and emotional prisons that keep you from him? Try to still the inner "noise" of distracting thoughts and listen for Jesus' knock of love on the door. Picture yourself in a room with a closed door. What is the name on the door (indulgence, impatience, anger, lust, _____)? Go to that door. Open it to Jesus' presence. Give him permission to enter and nurture you to wholeness.

open door, which no one is able to shut. I know that you have but little power, and yet you have kept my word and have not denied my name. [9]I will make those of the synagogue of Satan who say that they are Jews and are not, but are lying—I will make them come and bow down before your feet, and they will learn that I have loved you. [10]Because you have kept my word of patient endurance, I will keep you from the hour of trial that is coming on the whole world to test the inhabitants of the earth. [11]I am coming soon; hold fast to what you have, so that no one may seize your crown. [12]If you conquer, I will make you a pillar in the temple of my God; you will never go out of it. I will write on you the name of my God, and the name of the city of my God, the new Jerusalem that comes down from my God out of heaven, and my own new name. [13]Let anyone who has an ear listen to what the Spirit is saying to the churches.

The Message to Laodicea

14 "And to the angel of the church in Laodicea write: The words of the Amen, the faithful and true witness, the origin[a] of God's creation:

15 "I know your works; you are neither cold nor hot. I wish that you were either cold or hot. [16]So, because you are lukewarm, and neither cold nor hot, I am about to spit you out of my mouth. [17]For you say, 'I am rich, I have prospered, and I need nothing.' You do not realize that you are wretched, pitiable, poor, blind, and naked. [18]Therefore I counsel you to buy from me gold refined by fire so that you may be rich; and white robes to clothe you and to keep the shame of your nakedness from being seen; and salve to anoint your eyes so that you may see. [19]I reprove and discipline those whom I love. Be earnest, therefore, and repent. [20]Listen! I am standing at the door, knocking; if you hear my voice and open the door, I will come in to you and eat with you, and you with me. [21]To the one who conquers I will give a place with me on my throne, just as I myself conquered and sat down with my Father on his throne. [22]Let anyone who has an ear listen to what the Spirit is saying to the churches."

The Heavenly Worship

4 After this I looked, and there in heaven a door stood open! And the first voice, which I had heard speaking to me like a trumpet, said, "Come up here, and I will show you what must take place after this." [2]At once I was in the spirit,[b] and there in heaven stood a throne, with one seated on the throne! [3]And the one seated there looks like jasper and carnelian, and around the throne is a rainbow that looks like an emerald. [4]Around the throne are twenty-four thrones, and seated on the thrones are twenty-four elders, dressed in white robes, with golden crowns on their heads. [5]Coming from the throne are flashes of lightning, and rumblings and peals of thunder, and in front of the throne burn seven flaming torches, which are the seven spirits of God; [6]and in front of the throne there is something like a sea of glass, like crystal.

Around the throne, and on each side of the throne, are four living creatures, full of eyes in front and behind: [7]the

a Or *beginning*   *b* Or *in the Spirit*

first living creature like a lion, the second living creature like an ox, the third living creature with a face like a human face, and the fourth living creature like a flying eagle. [8]And the four living creatures, each of them with six wings, are full of eyes all around and inside. Day and night without ceasing they sing,

"Holy, holy, holy,
the Lord God the Almighty,
who was and is and is to come."

[9]And whenever the living creatures give glory and honor and thanks to the one who is seated on the throne, who lives forever and ever, [10]the twenty-four elders fall before the one who is seated on the throne and worship the one who lives forever and ever; they cast their crowns before the throne, singing,

[11] "You are worthy, our Lord and God,
to receive glory and honor and power,
for you created all things,
and by your will they existed and were
created."

The Scroll and the Lamb

5 Then I saw in the right hand of the one seated on the throne a scroll written on the inside and on the back, sealed[a] with seven seals; [2]and I saw a mighty angel proclaiming with a loud voice, "Who is worthy to open the scroll and break its seals?" [3]And no one in heaven or on earth or under the earth was able to open the scroll or to look into it. [4]And I began to weep bitterly because no one was found worthy to open the scroll or to look into it. [5]Then one of the elders said to me, "Do not weep. See, the Lion of the tribe of Judah, the Root of David, has conquered, so that he can open the scroll and its seven seals."

6 Then I saw between the throne and the four living creatures and among the elders a Lamb standing as if it had been slaughtered, having seven horns and seven eyes, which are the seven spirits of God sent out into all the earth. [7]He went and took the scroll from the right hand of the one who was seated on the throne. [8]When he had taken the scroll, the four living creatures and the twenty-four elders fell before the Lamb, each holding a harp and golden bowls full of incense, which are the prayers of the saints. [9]They sing a new song:

"You are worthy to take the scroll
and to open its seals,
for you were slaughtered and by your blood you
ransomed for God
saints from[b] every tribe and language and
people and nation;
[10] you have made them to be a kingdom and priests
serving[c] our God,
and they will reign on earth."

11 Then I looked, and I heard the voice of many angels surrounding the throne and the living creatures and the elders; they numbered myriads of myriads and thousands of thousands, [12]singing with full voice,

"Worthy is the Lamb that was slaughtered

Priestly Character

REVELATION 4.4–11

Read this vision of the throne of God several times and then reenact it as a prayerful recommitment to priestly discipleship. Make a paper crown for yourself and write on it "The Control of My Life." Falling down before God, acknowledge him with the prayer in verse 8. In a spirit of worship give him freedom to be God in your life. Finally, lay down your crown before him! Let him be in control of your life. Meditate on how you can carry into your daily life and relationships an inner attitude of falling down before God, worshiping him and placing your "crown" before him.

See Meeting God in Everyday Life

---

a Or written on the inside, and sealed on the back   b Gk ransomed for God from   c Gk priests to

"Worthy Is the Lamb"

REVELATION 5.11–14

We may be among the many Christians who have a very well-developed intellectual understanding of Jesus, his life, his death, his resurrection and what it all means for us. But sometimes our spirit and emotions do not catch up with our intellect. Find a CD, cassette tape or record of Handel's *Messiah*. Play the selection "Worthy Is the Lamb" and let the music lead you into worship. Or for a more contemporary musical offering, play Michael Card's "You Are Worthy," from his CD *Unveiled Hope*. Let the music sink into your soul until it expresses your adoration of the Lamb. You might try something similar with the other songs on Card's CD, which sets many of the songs of praise and adoration in Revelation to music. Then try singing the scripture in your heart and mind throughout the day.

See Meeting God in Worship

to receive power and wealth and wisdom and
   might
and honor and glory and blessing!"
¹³Then I heard every creature in heaven and on earth and under the earth and in the sea, and all that is in them, singing,
   "To the one seated on the throne and to the Lamb
   be blessing and honor and glory and might
   forever and ever!"
¹⁴And the four living creatures said, "Amen!" And the elders fell down and worshiped.

The Seven Seals

6 Then I saw the Lamb open one of the seven seals, and I heard one of the four living creatures call out, as with a voice of thunder, "Come!"ᵃ ²I looked, and there was a white horse! Its rider had a bow; a crown was given to him, and he came out conquering and to conquer.

3 When he opened the second seal, I heard the second living creature call out, "Come!"ᵃ ⁴And out cameᵇ another horse, bright red; its rider was permitted to take peace from the earth, so that people would slaughter one another; and he was given a great sword.

5 When he opened the third seal, I heard the third living creature call out, "Come!"ᵃ I looked, and there was a black horse! Its rider held a pair of scales in his hand, ⁶and I heard what seemed to be a voice in the midst of the four living creatures saying, "A quart of wheat for a day's pay,ᶜ and three quarts of barley for a day's pay,ᶜ but do not damage the olive oil and the wine!"

7 When he opened the fourth seal, I heard the voice of the fourth living creature call out, "Come!"ᵃ ⁸I looked and there was a pale green horse! Its rider's name was Death, and Hades followed with him; they were given authority over a fourth of the earth, to kill with sword, famine, and pestilence, and by the wild animals of the earth.

9 When he opened the fifth seal, I saw under the altar the souls of those who had been slaughtered for the word of God and for the testimony they had given; ¹⁰they cried out with a loud voice, "Sovereign Lord, holy and true, how long will it be before you judge and avenge our blood on the inhabitants of the earth?" ¹¹They were each given a white robe and told to rest a little longer, until the number would be complete both of their fellow servantsᵈ and of their brothers and sisters,ᵉ who were soon to be killed as they themselves had been killed.

12 When he opened the sixth seal, I looked, and there came a great earthquake; the sun became black as sackcloth, the full moon became like blood, ¹³and the stars of the sky fell to the earth as the fig tree drops its winter fruit when shaken by a gale. ¹⁴The sky vanished like a scroll rolling itself up, and every mountain and island was removed from its place. ¹⁵Then the kings of the earth and the magnates and the generals and the rich and the powerful, and everyone, slave and free, hid in the caves and among the rocks of the mountains, ¹⁶calling to the mountains and rocks, "Fall on us and hide us from the face of the one seated on the throne and from the wrath of the

a Or "Go!"   *b* Or *went*   *c* Gk *a denarius*   *d* Gk *slaves*   *e* Gk *brothers*

Lamb; [17]for the great day of their wrath has come, and who is able to stand?"

The 144,000 of Israel Sealed

7 After this I saw four angels standing at the four corners of the earth, holding back the four winds of the earth so that no wind could blow on earth or sea or against any tree. [2]I saw another angel ascending from the rising of the sun, having the seal of the living God, and he called with a loud voice to the four angels who had been given power to damage earth and sea, [3]saying, "Do not damage the earth or the sea or the trees, until we have marked the servants[a] of our God with a seal on their foreheads."

4 And I heard the number of those who were sealed, one hundred forty-four thousand, sealed out of every tribe of the people of Israel:

5 From the tribe of Judah twelve thousand sealed,
   from the tribe of Reuben twelve thousand,
   from the tribe of Gad twelve thousand,
6 from the tribe of Asher twelve thousand,
   from the tribe of Naphtali twelve thousand,
   from the tribe of Manasseh twelve thousand,
7 from the tribe of Simeon twelve thousand,
   from the tribe of Levi twelve thousand,
   from the tribe of Issachar twelve thousand,
8 from the tribe of Zebulun twelve thousand,
   from the tribe of Joseph twelve thousand,
   from the tribe of Benjamin twelve thousand sealed.

The Multitude from Every Nation

9 After this I looked, and there was a great multitude that no one could count, from every nation, from all tribes and peoples and languages, standing before the throne and before the Lamb, robed in white, with palm branches in their hands. [10]They cried out in a loud voice, saying,
   "Salvation belongs to our God who is seated on
      the throne, and to the Lamb!"
[11]And all the angels stood around the throne and around the elders and the four living creatures, and they fell on their faces before the throne and worshiped God, [12]singing,
   "Amen! Blessing and glory and wisdom
   and thanksgiving and honor
   and power and might
   be to our God forever and ever! Amen."
13 Then one of the elders addressed me, saying, "Who are these, robed in white, and where have they come from?" [14]I said to him, "Sir, you are the one that knows." Then he said to me, "These are they who have come out of the great ordeal; they have washed their robes and made them white in the blood of the Lamb.
15   For this reason they are before the throne of God,
      and worship him day and night within his
         temple,
      and the one who is seated on the throne will
         shelter them.
16   They will hunger no more, and thirst no more;
      the sun will not strike them,
      nor any scorching heat;

When the World Falls Apart

REVELATION 6.12–17

In this vision everything familiar to the people of the earth—the mighty and powerful people as well as the ordinary people—is shaken. The things that seem most permanent and dependable—the sun, moon, stars and sky—are passing away.

God has a way of disrupting our familiar landmarks—the settled ruts of our lives—leaving us disoriented among the broken pieces of our world, so that we learn to acknowledge his sovereign control in our lives. What are the familiar landmarks of your life? Values you've absorbed but never examined? Familiar but unbiblical ways of dealing with problems? Unhealthy patterns of relating to others? Into which of these do you sense God's presence as a disruption? How are you responding to that disruption?

See Meeting God in the Created Order

Prayer That Shakes the World

REVELATION 8.3–5

In John's vision the prayers of the saints are offered with fire as a sacrifice to God and God's power is released into the world, which is shaken to its foundations.

Choose the letter that best completes the sentence: Prayer (a) puts everything in God's hands; (b) changes me; (c) invites God's disruptive but transforming presence into my life; (d) is costly; or (e) all of the above. What do you need to sacrifice as an offering of prayer? Try this experiment: When praying about an urgent concern in your life, see if you can abandon (sacrifice) your desired "solution" and be genuinely receptive to God's resolution—no matter what it may be. Write down your prayer and preserve it at this point in your Bible. Keep track of how God answers.

See Meeting God in Prayer

---

17 for the Lamb at the center of the throne will be
their shepherd,
and he will guide them to springs of the water
of life,
and God will wipe away every tear from their
eyes."

The Seventh Seal and the Golden Censer

8 When the Lamb opened the seventh seal, there was silence in heaven for about half an hour. 2And I saw the seven angels who stand before God, and seven trumpets were given to them.

3 Another angel with a golden censer came and stood at the altar; he was given a great quantity of incense to offer with the prayers of all the saints on the golden altar that is before the throne. 4And the smoke of the incense, with the prayers of the saints, rose before God from the hand of the angel. 5Then the angel took the censer and filled it with fire from the altar and threw it on the earth; and there were peals of thunder, rumblings, flashes of lightning, and an earthquake.

The Seven Trumpets

6 Now the seven angels who had the seven trumpets made ready to blow them.

7 The first angel blew his trumpet, and there came hail and fire, mixed with blood, and they were hurled to the earth; and a third of the earth was burned up, and a third of the trees were burned up, and all green grass was burned up.

8 The second angel blew his trumpet, and something like a great mountain, burning with fire, was thrown into the sea. 9A third of the sea became blood, a third of the living creatures in the sea died, and a third of the ships were destroyed.

10 The third angel blew his trumpet, and a great star fell from heaven, blazing like a torch, and it fell on a third of the rivers and on the springs of water. 11The name of the star is Wormwood. A third of the waters became wormwood, and many died from the water, because it was made bitter.

12 The fourth angel blew his trumpet, and a third of the sun was struck, and a third of the moon, and a third of the stars, so that a third of their light was darkened; a third of the day was kept from shining, and likewise the night.

13 Then I looked, and I heard an eagle crying with a loud voice as it flew in midheaven, "Woe, woe, woe to the inhabitants of the earth, at the blasts of the other trumpets that the three angels are about to blow!"

9 And the fifth angel blew his trumpet, and I saw a star that had fallen from heaven to earth, and he was given the key to the shaft of the bottomless pit; 2he opened the shaft of the bottomless pit, and from the shaft rose smoke like the smoke of a great furnace, and the sun and the air were darkened with the smoke from the shaft. 3Then from the smoke came locusts on the earth, and they were given authority like the authority of scorpions of the earth. 4They were told not to damage the grass of the earth or any green growth or any tree, but only those people who do

not have the seal of God on their foreheads. ⁵They were allowed to torture them for five months, but not to kill them, and their torture was like the torture of a scorpion when it stings someone. ⁶And in those days people will seek death but will not find it; they will long to die, but death will flee from them.

7 In appearance the locusts were like horses equipped for battle. On their heads were what looked like crowns of gold; their faces were like human faces, ⁸their hair like women's hair, and their teeth like lions' teeth; ⁹they had scales like iron breastplates, and the noise of their wings was like the noise of many chariots with horses rushing into battle. ¹⁰They have tails like scorpions, with stingers, and in their tails is their power to harm people for five months. ¹¹They have as king over them the angel of the bottomless pit; his name in Hebrew is Abaddon,ᵃ and in Greek he is called Apollyon.ᵇ

12 The first woe has passed. There are still two woes to come.

13 Then the sixth angel blew his trumpet, and I heard a voice from the fourᶜ horns of the golden altar before God, ¹⁴saying to the sixth angel who had the trumpet, "Release the four angels who are bound at the great river Euphrates." ¹⁵So the four angels were released, who had been held ready for the hour, the day, the month, and the year, to kill a third of humankind. ¹⁶The number of the troops of cavalry was two hundred million; I heard their number. ¹⁷And this was how I saw the horses in my vision: the riders wore breastplates the color of fire and of sapphireᵈ and of sulfur; the heads of the horses were like lions' heads, and fire and smoke and sulfur came out of their mouths. ¹⁸By these three plagues a third of humankind was killed, by the fire and smoke and sulfur coming out of their mouths. ¹⁹For the power of the horses is in their mouths and in their tails; their tails are like serpents, having heads; and with them they inflict harm.

20 The rest of humankind, who were not killed by these plagues, did not repent of the works of their hands or give up worshiping demons and idols of gold and silver and bronze and stone and wood, which cannot see or hear or walk. ²¹And they did not repent of their murders or their sorceries or their fornication or their thefts.

The Angel with the Little Scroll

10 And I saw another mighty angel coming down from heaven, wrapped in a cloud, with a rainbow over his head; his face was like the sun, and his legs like pillars of fire. ²He held a little scroll open in his hand. Setting his right foot on the sea and his left foot on the land, ³he gave a great shout, like a lion roaring. And when he shouted, the seven thunders sounded. ⁴And when the seven thunders had sounded, I was about to write, but I heard a voice from heaven saying, "Seal up what the seven thunders have said, and do not write it down." ⁵Then the angel whom I saw standing on the sea and the land

raised his right hand to heaven
⁶ and swore by him who lives forever and ever,
who created heaven and what is in it, the earth and what

The Blindness of Sin

REVELATION 9.13–21

This portion of John's vision is a terrifying picture of the destructiveness of sin (vv.13–19). Even more frightening is the blindness of sin (vv.20–21). Name some people who are in a destructive bondage to sin and who persist in it, even though they know what the consequences will be. Are there Biblical restrictions or requirements that you'd rather not notice? What is the price you are paying to resist God's commands? What would obedience cost you? What behaviors would you have to change? What attitudes would you have to alter? What relationships would have to be different?

See Meeting God in Everyday Life

ᵃ That is, *Destruction* ᵇ That is, *Destroyer* ᶜ Other ancient authorities lack *four* ᵈ Gk *hyacinth*

Feeding on the Word

REVELATION 10.8–10

The promises of God's Word often seem as "sweet as honey" when we first receive them: "I came that they may have life, and have it abundantly" (John 10.10). When we begin to internalize the Word, however, we begin to realize that the promises may require a radical response from us: "If any want to become my followers, let them deny themselves and take up their cross and follow me" (Matthew 16.24). There is a temptation to claim the promises without committing to the relationship with God in which the promises are grounded. Jot down a few of God's promises you claim for yourself. What are the commitments God is asking from you in response to each promise?

See Meeting God in Service

is in it, and the sea and what is in it: "There will be no more delay, ⁷but in the days when the seventh angel is to blow his trumpet, the mystery of God will be fulfilled, as he announced to his servants[a] the prophets."

8 Then the voice that I had heard from heaven spoke to me again, saying, "Go, take the scroll that is open in the hand of the angel who is standing on the sea and on the land." ⁹So I went to the angel and told him to give me the little scroll; and he said to me, "Take it, and eat; it will be bitter to your stomach, but sweet as honey in your mouth." ¹⁰So I took the little scroll from the hand of the angel and ate it; it was sweet as honey in my mouth, but when I had eaten it, my stomach was made bitter.

11 Then they said to me, "You must prophesy again about many peoples and nations and languages and kings."

The Two Witnesses

11 Then I was given a measuring rod like a staff, and I was told, "Come and measure the temple of God and the altar and those who worship there, ²but do not measure the court outside the temple; leave that out, for it is given over to the nations, and they will trample over the holy city for forty-two months. ³And I will grant my two witnesses authority to prophesy for one thousand two hundred sixty days, wearing sackcloth."

4 These are the two olive trees and the two lampstands that stand before the Lord of the earth. ⁵And if anyone wants to harm them, fire pours from their mouth and consumes their foes; anyone who wants to harm them must be killed in this manner. ⁶They have authority to shut the sky, so that no rain may fall during the days of their prophesying, and they have authority over the waters to turn them into blood, and to strike the earth with every kind of plague, as often as they desire.

7 When they have finished their testimony, the beast that comes up from the bottomless pit will make war on them and conquer them and kill them, ⁸and their dead bodies will lie in the street of the great city that is prophetically[b] called Sodom and Egypt, where also their Lord was crucified. ⁹For three and a half days members of the peoples and tribes and languages and nations will gaze at their dead bodies and refuse to let them be placed in a tomb; ¹⁰and the inhabitants of the earth will gloat over them and celebrate and exchange presents, because these two prophets had been a torment to the inhabitants of the earth.

11 But after the three and a half days, the breath[c] of life from God entered them, and they stood on their feet, and those who saw them were terrified. ¹²Then they[d] heard a loud voice from heaven saying to them, "Come up here!" And they went up to heaven in a cloud while their enemies watched them. ¹³At that moment there was a great earthquake, and a tenth of the city fell; seven thousand people were killed in the earthquake, and the rest were terrified and gave glory to the God of heaven.

14 The second woe has passed. The third woe is coming very soon.

a Gk *slaves*   b Or *allegorically*; Gk *spiritually*   c Or *the spirit*
d Other ancient authorities read *I*

The Seventh Trumpet

15 Then the seventh angel blew his trumpet, and there were loud voices in heaven, saying,

"The kingdom of the world has become the
kingdom of our Lord
and of his Messiah,[a]
and he will reign forever and ever."

16 Then the twenty-four elders who sit on their thrones before God fell on their faces and worshiped God, [17]singing,

"We give you thanks, Lord God Almighty,
who are and who were,
for you have taken your great power
and begun to reign.
18 The nations raged,
but your wrath has come,
and the time for judging the dead,
for rewarding your servants,[b] the prophets
and saints and all who fear your name,
both small and great,
and for destroying those who destroy the earth."

19 Then God's temple in heaven was opened, and the ark of his covenant was seen within his temple; and there were flashes of lightning, rumblings, peals of thunder, an earthquake, and heavy hail.

The Woman and the Dragon

12 A great portent appeared in heaven: a woman clothed with the sun, with the moon under her feet, and on her head a crown of twelve stars. [2]She was pregnant and was crying out in birth pangs, in the agony of giving birth. [3]Then another portent appeared in heaven: a great red dragon, with seven heads and ten horns, and seven diadems on his heads. [4]His tail swept down a third of the stars of heaven and threw them to the earth. Then the dragon stood before the woman who was about to bear a child, so that he might devour her child as soon as it was born. [5]And she gave birth to a son, a male child, who is to rule[c] all the nations with a rod of iron. But her child was snatched away and taken to God and to his throne; [6]and the woman fled into the wilderness, where she has a place prepared by God, so that there she can be nourished for one thousand two hundred sixty days.

Michael Defeats the Dragon

7 And war broke out in heaven; Michael and his angels fought against the dragon. The dragon and his angels fought back, [8]but they were defeated, and there was no longer any place for them in heaven. [9]The great dragon was thrown down, that ancient serpent, who is called the Devil and Satan, the deceiver of the whole world—he was thrown down to the earth, and his angels were thrown down with him.
10 Then I heard a loud voice in heaven, proclaiming,

"Now have come the salvation and the power
and the kingdom of our God
and the authority of his Messiah,[a]
for the accuser of our comrades[d] has been thrown
down,

The Depths of God's Love

REVELATION 12.1–6

How does this vision help you understand the phrase "the foundation of the world in the book of life of the Lamb that was slaughtered," mentioned in Revelation 13.8? John here reveals to us the profound meaning of Jesus' redeeming death on the cross—not as a simple event, but as a revelation of the very nature of God. The cross is not simply something God *did*, but it is a revelation of who God *is*! God offers his very being to you for your healing. In what way are you wounded and in pain? Do you carry within you unhealed memories? Damaged emotions? Addiction? Picture God touching each place that hurts. See yourself receiving God's love, healing, protection and freedom as God transforms your broken spirit into a whole one.

See Meeting God in the Created Order

---

a Gk *Christ*   *b* Gk *slaves*   *c* Or *to shepherd*   *d* Gk *brothers*

Seeing the Unseen

REVELATION 12.10–11

Paul says to the Corinthians, "So we do not lose heart. Even though our outer nature is wasting away, our inner nature is being renewed day by day. For this slight momentary affliction is preparing for us an eternal weight of glory beyond all measure, because *we look not at what can be seen but at what cannot be seen; for what can be seen is temporary, but what cannot be seen is eternal*" (2 Corinthians 4.16–18, emphasis added). In light of this, and of this vision of God's victory in Jesus Christ, reflect on some event in your life from the past week. Did you perceive that event in terms of the impossible circumstances of the situation, or did you see it in the light of God's sure victory in Christ? How could you have lived it out differently? What lies ahead of you today? How do you think it looks through God's eyes?

See Meeting God in Everyday Life

who accuses them day and night before our
God.
11 But they have conquered him by the blood of the
Lamb
and by the word of their testimony,
for they did not cling to life even in the face of
death.
12 Rejoice then, you heavens
and those who dwell in them!
But woe to the earth and the sea,
for the devil has come down to you
with great wrath,
because he knows that his time is short!"

The Dragon Fights Again on Earth

13 So when the dragon saw that he had been thrown down to the earth, he pursued[a] the woman who had given birth to the male child. 14But the woman was given the two wings of the great eagle, so that she could fly from the serpent into the wilderness, to her place where she is nourished for a time, and times, and half a time. 15Then from his mouth the serpent poured water like a river after the woman, to sweep her away with the flood. 16But the earth came to the help of the woman; it opened its mouth and swallowed the river that the dragon had poured from his mouth. 17Then the dragon was angry with the woman, and went off to make war on the rest of her children, those who keep the commandments of God and hold the testimony of Jesus.

The First Beast

18 Then the dragon[b] took his stand on the sand of the seashore. 13 1And I saw a beast rising out of the sea, having ten horns and seven heads; and on its horns were ten diadems, and on its heads were blasphemous names. 2And the beast that I saw was like a leopard, its feet were like a bear's, and its mouth was like a lion's mouth. And the dragon gave it his power and his throne and great authority. 3One of its heads seemed to have received a death-blow, but its mortal wound[c] had been healed. In amazement the whole earth followed the beast. 4They worshiped the dragon, for he had given his authority to the beast, and they worshiped the beast, saying, "Who is like the beast, and who can fight against it?"

5 The beast was given a mouth uttering haughty and blasphemous words, and it was allowed to exercise authority for forty-two months. 6It opened its mouth to utter blasphemies against God, blaspheming his name and his dwelling, that is, those who dwell in heaven. 7Also it was allowed to make war on the saints and to conquer them.[d] It was given authority over every tribe and people and language and nation, 8and all the inhabitants of the earth will worship it, everyone whose name has not been written from the foundation of the world in the book of life of the Lamb that was slaughtered.[e]

9 Let anyone who has an ear listen:

a Or persecuted   b Gk Then he; other ancient authorities read Then I stood   c Gk the plague of its death   d Other ancient authorities lack this sentence   e Or written in the book of life of the Lamb that was slaughtered from the foundation of the world

10 If you are to be taken captive,
    into captivity you go;
  if you kill with the sword,
    with the sword you must be killed.

Here is a call for the endurance and faith of the saints.

The Second Beast

11 Then I saw another beast that rose out of the earth; it had two horns like a lamb and it spoke like a dragon. ¹²It exercises all the authority of the first beast on its behalf, and it makes the earth and its inhabitants worship the first beast, whose mortal wound*ᵃ* had been healed. ¹³It performs great signs, even making fire come down from heaven to earth in the sight of all; ¹⁴and by the signs that it is allowed to perform on behalf of the beast, it deceives the inhabitants of earth, telling them to make an image for the beast that had been wounded by the sword*ᵇ* and yet lived; ¹⁵and it was allowed to give breath*ᶜ* to the image of the beast so that the image of the beast could even speak and cause those who would not worship the image of the beast to be killed. ¹⁶Also it causes all, both small and great, both rich and poor, both free and slave, to be marked on the right hand or the forehead, ¹⁷so that no one can buy or sell who does not have the mark, that is, the name of the beast or the number of its name. ¹⁸This calls for wisdom: let anyone with understanding calculate the number of the beast, for it is the number of a person. Its number is six hundred sixty-six.*ᵈ*

The Lamb and the 144,000

14 Then I looked, and there was the Lamb, standing on Mount Zion! And with him were one hundred forty-four thousand who had his name and his Father's name written on their foreheads. ²And I heard a voice from heaven like the sound of many waters and like the sound of loud thunder; the voice I heard was like the sound of harpists playing on their harps, ³and they sing a new song before the throne and before the four living creatures and before the elders. No one could learn that song except the one hundred forty-four thousand who have been redeemed from the earth. ⁴It is these who have not defiled themselves with women, for they are virgins; these follow the Lamb wherever he goes. They have been redeemed from humankind as first fruits for God and the Lamb, ⁵and in their mouth no lie was found; they are blameless.

The Messages of the Three Angels

6 Then I saw another angel flying in midheaven, with an eternal gospel to proclaim to those who live*ᵉ* on the earth—to every nation and tribe and language and people. ⁷He said in a loud voice, "Fear God and give him glory, for the hour of his judgment has come; and worship him who made heaven and earth, the sea and the springs of water."

8 Then another angel, a second, followed, saying, "Fallen, fallen is Babylon the great! She has made all nations drink of the wine of the wrath of her fornication."

a Gk whose plague of its death   b Or that had received the plague of the sword   c Or spirit   d Other ancient authorities read six hundred sixteen e Gk sit

The Mark of the Beast

REVELATION 13.1–18

Read this chapter describing the beast out of the sea and beast out of earth. Write down a few words that describe each one. What emotions do these descriptions evoke in you? What happens within you as you reread verse 8? How do you picture the book of life that belongs to the Lamb? How does that verse encourage you? Reread also verses 10 and 18. How do these verses lead you to pray? In what ways might patient endurance and wisdom help you in the trials and tribulations you face today?

Walking on Water

REVELATION 15.2–4

Those who have been victorious over the beast and his image stand beside the sea and sing the song of Moses and of the Lamb, a song of deliverance. Those who have conquered the world of fallen Babylon (the beast, its image and its number) "by the blood of the Lamb and by the word of their testimony" (12.11) can sing the song of God's deliverance today.

Throughout the morning today, reflect on God's great, amazing love that created you as God's beloved child (your identity and value) and calls you to wholeness (your purpose). During the afternoon, bow your heart in awe before the Holy One who is your true life. In the evening, look back on how the world's false values are crumbling beneath your feet.

See Meeting God in Worship

9 Then another angel, a third, followed them, crying with a loud voice, "Those who worship the beast and its image, and receive a mark on their foreheads or on their hands, ¹⁰they will also drink the wine of God's wrath, poured unmixed into the cup of his anger, and they will be tormented with fire and sulfur in the presence of the holy angels and in the presence of the Lamb. ¹¹And the smoke of their torment goes up forever and ever. There is no rest day or night for those who worship the beast and its image and for anyone who receives the mark of its name."

12 Here is a call for the endurance of the saints, those who keep the commandments of God and hold fast to the faith of*ᵃ* Jesus.

13 And I heard a voice from heaven saying, "Write this: Blessed are the dead who from now on die in the Lord." "Yes," says the Spirit, "they will rest from their labors, for their deeds follow them."

Reaping the Earth's Harvest

14 Then I looked, and there was a white cloud, and seated on the cloud was one like the Son of Man, with a golden crown on his head, and a sharp sickle in his hand! ¹⁵Another angel came out of the temple, calling with a loud voice to the one who sat on the cloud, "Use your sickle and reap, for the hour to reap has come, because the harvest of the earth is fully ripe." ¹⁶So the one who sat on the cloud swung his sickle over the earth, and the earth was reaped.

17 Then another angel came out of the temple in heaven, and he too had a sharp sickle. ¹⁸Then another angel came out from the altar, the angel who has authority over fire, and he called with a loud voice to him who had the sharp sickle, "Use your sharp sickle and gather the clusters of the vine of the earth, for its grapes are ripe." ¹⁹So the angel swung his sickle over the earth and gathered the vintage of the earth, and he threw it into the great wine press of the wrath of God. ²⁰And the wine press was trodden outside the city, and blood flowed from the wine press, as high as a horse's bridle, for a distance of about two hundred miles.*ᵇ*

The Angels with the Seven Last Plagues

15 Then I saw another portent in heaven, great and amazing: seven angels with seven plagues, which are the last, for with them the wrath of God is ended.

2 And I saw what appeared to be a sea of glass mixed with fire, and those who had conquered the beast and its image and the number of its name, standing beside the sea of glass with harps of God in their hands. ³And they sing the song of Moses, the servant*ᶜ* of God, and the song of the Lamb:

> "Great and amazing are your deeds,
>   Lord God the Almighty!
> Just and true are your ways,
>   King of the nations!*ᵈ*
> 4   Lord, who will not fear
>   and glorify your name?

a Or *to their faith in*   *b* Gk *one thousand six hundred stadia*   *c* Gk *slave*
d Other ancient authorities read *the ages*

For you alone are holy.
All nations will come
and worship before you,
for your judgments have been revealed."

5 After this I looked, and the temple of the tent*a* of witness in heaven was opened, [6]and out of the temple came the seven angels with the seven plagues, robed in pure bright linen,*b* with golden sashes across their chests. [7]Then one of the four living creatures gave the seven angels seven golden bowls full of the wrath of God, who lives forever and ever; [8]and the temple was filled with smoke from the glory of God and from his power, and no one could enter the temple until the seven plagues of the seven angels were ended.

The Bowls of God's Wrath

16 Then I heard a loud voice from the temple telling the seven angels, "Go and pour out on the earth the seven bowls of the wrath of God."

2 So the first angel went and poured his bowl on the earth, and a foul and painful sore came on those who had the mark of the beast and who worshiped its image.

3 The second angel poured his bowl into the sea, and it became like the blood of a corpse, and every living thing in the sea died.

4 The third angel poured his bowl into the rivers and the springs of water, and they became blood. [5]And I heard the angel of the waters say,

"You are just, O Holy One, who are and were,
for you have judged these things;
[6]   because they shed the blood of saints and
prophets,
you have given them blood to drink.
It is what they deserve!"
[7]And I heard the altar respond,
"Yes, O Lord God, the Almighty,
your judgments are true and just!"

8 The fourth angel poured his bowl on the sun, and it was allowed to scorch people with fire; [9]they were scorched by the fierce heat, but they cursed the name of God, who had authority over these plagues, and they did not repent and give him glory.

10 The fifth angel poured his bowl on the throne of the beast, and its kingdom was plunged into darkness; people gnawed their tongues in agony, [11]and cursed the God of heaven because of their pains and sores, and they did not repent of their deeds.

12 The sixth angel poured his bowl on the great river Euphrates, and its water was dried up in order to prepare the way for the kings from the east. [13]And I saw three foul spirits like frogs coming from the mouth of the dragon, from the mouth of the beast, and from the mouth of the false prophet. [14]These are demonic spirits, performing signs, who go abroad to the kings of the whole world, to assemble them for battle on the great day of God the Almighty. [15]("See, I am coming like a thief! Blessed is the one who stays awake and is clothed,*c* not going about

The Wrath of God

REVELATION 15.7–16.11

Imagine yourself sitting comfortably in an easy chair on the top of a hill. See yourself rejoicing that the trustworthiness of the law of gravity provides you with security and stability. Now picture yourself getting up and tripping, tumbling painfully down the hill. How has gravity changed? Has gravity suddenly become mean, punitive, judgmental, retributive, angry? Of course not! It's still gravity. Now apply that illustration to the sense of wholeness and well-being that accompanies your response to God's love and the sense of disruption and anxiety that comes when you reject God's love. Rejoice that, even in the midst of our self-imposed pain and anguish, God persistently seeks our redemption (note the reminder of the possibility of repentance in 16.9,11).

---

a Or *tabernacle*   *b* Other ancient authorities read *stone*   *c* Gk *and keeps his robes*

Fatal Attraction

REVELATION 17.4–6

John seems to be describing a horrendous monster who is, nonetheless, adorned with great beauty and power. Babylon the great, the mother of whores, is a vision of rich royal fabrics, jewels and gold. John is "greatly amazed."

What aspects of the world's allure attract you? Power? The promise of control? The security of abundance? The possibility of fame and popularity? Don't be too quick to deny any attraction to these. The time may be right for a spiritual inventory. Where does the needle of the compass of your soul point? Toward power or powerlessness? Toward control or consecration? Toward abundance or simplicity? Toward fame or humility? Toward popularity or servanthood?

See Meeting God in Prayer

naked and exposed to shame.") ¹⁶And they assembled them at the place that in Hebrew is called Harmagedon.

17 The seventh angel poured his bowl into the air, and a loud voice came out of the temple, from the throne, saying, "It is done!" ¹⁸And there came flashes of lightning, rumblings, peals of thunder, and a violent earthquake, such as had not occurred since people were upon the earth, so violent was that earthquake. ¹⁹The great city was split into three parts, and the cities of the nations fell. God remembered great Babylon and gave her the wine-cup of the fury of his wrath. ²⁰And every island fled away, and no mountains were to be found; ²¹and huge hailstones, each weighing about a hundred pounds,ᵃ dropped from heaven on people, until they cursed God for the plague of the hail, so fearful was that plague.

The Great Whore and the Beast

17 Then one of the seven angels who had the seven bowls came and said to me, "Come, I will show you the judgment of the great whore who is seated on many waters, ²with whom the kings of the earth have committed fornication, and with the wine of whose fornication the inhabitants of the earth have become drunk." ³So he carried me away in the spiritᵇ into a wilderness, and I saw a woman sitting on a scarlet beast that was full of blasphemous names, and it had seven heads and ten horns. ⁴The woman was clothed in purple and scarlet, and adorned with gold and jewels and pearls, holding in her hand a golden cup full of abominations and the impurities of her fornication; ⁵and on her forehead was written a name, a mystery: "Babylon the great, mother of whores and of earth's abominations." ⁶And I saw that the woman was drunk with the blood of the saints and the blood of the witnesses to Jesus.

When I saw her, I was greatly amazed. ⁷But the angel said to me, "Why are you so amazed? I will tell you the mystery of the woman, and of the beast with seven heads and ten horns that carries her. ⁸The beast that you saw was, and is not, and is about to ascend from the bottomless pit and go to destruction. And the inhabitants of the earth, whose names have not been written in the book of life from the foundation of the world, will be amazed when they see the beast, because it was and is not and is to come.

9 "This calls for a mind that has wisdom: the seven heads are seven mountains on which the woman is seated; also, they are seven kings, ¹⁰of whom five have fallen, one is living, and the other has not yet come; and when he comes, he must remain only a little while. ¹¹As for the beast that was and is not, it is an eighth but it belongs to the seven, and it goes to destruction. ¹²And the ten horns that you saw are ten kings who have not yet received a kingdom, but they are to receive authority as kings for one hour, together with the beast. ¹³These are united in yielding their power and authority to the beast; ¹⁴they will make war on the Lamb, and the Lamb will conquer them, for he is Lord of lords and King of kings, and those with him are called and chosen and faithful."

15 And he said to me, "The waters that you saw, where

a Gk weighing about a talent   b Or in the Spirit

the whore is seated, are peoples and multitudes and nations and languages. ¹⁶And the ten horns that you saw, they and the beast will hate the whore; they will make her desolate and naked; they will devour her flesh and burn her up with fire. ¹⁷For God has put it into their hearts to carry out his purpose by agreeing to give their kingdom to the beast, until the words of God will be fulfilled. ¹⁸The woman you saw is the great city that rules over the kings of the earth."

The Fall of Babylon

18 After this I saw another angel coming down from heaven, having great authority; and the earth was made bright with his splendor. ²He called out with a mighty voice,

"Fallen, fallen is Babylon the great!
It has become a dwelling place of demons,
a haunt of every foul spirit,
a haunt of every foul bird,
a haunt of every foul and hateful beast.ᵃ

³ For all the nations have drunkᵇ
of the wine of the wrath of her fornication,
and the kings of the earth have committed
fornication with her,
and the merchants of the earth have grown rich
from the powerᶜ of her luxury."

4 Then I heard another voice from heaven saying,
"Come out of her, my people,
so that you do not take part in her sins,
and so that you do not share in her plagues;

⁵ for her sins are heaped high as heaven,
and God has remembered her iniquities.

⁶ Render to her as she herself has rendered,
and repay her double for her deeds;
mix a double draught for her in the cup she
mixed.

⁷ As she glorified herself and lived luxuriously,
so give her a like measure of torment and grief.
Since in her heart she says,
'I rule as a queen;
I am no widow,
and I will never see grief,'

⁸ therefore her plagues will come in a single day—
pestilence and mourning and famine—
and she will be burned with fire;
for mighty is the Lord God who judges her."

9 And the kings of the earth, who committed fornication and lived in luxury with her, will weep and wail over her when they see the smoke of her burning; ¹⁰they will stand far off, in fear of her torment, and say,

"Alas, alas, the great city,
Babylon, the mighty city!
For in one hour your judgment has come."

11 And the merchants of the earth weep and mourn for her, since no one buys their cargo anymore, ¹²cargo of gold, silver, jewels and pearls, fine linen, purple, silk and

---

ᵃ Other ancient authorities lack the words *a haunt of every foul beast* and attach the words *and hateful* to the previous line so as to read *a haunt of every foul and hateful bird*   ᵇ Other ancient authorities read *She has made all nations drink*   ᶜ Or *resources*

A Peculiar People

REVELATION 18.1–5

What does it mean to be a citizen of God's kingdom in a world shaped by the destructive and dehumanizing values of Babylon? List characteristics of your community that reflect the values and structures of fallen Babylon, especially those that impinge on your life. Reflect on what citizenship in the new Jerusalem looks like. What specific steps can you take to incarnate the liberating and healing presence of the new Jerusalem?

See Meeting God in Community

1649

A Tenuous Livelihood

REVELATION 18.11–19

Isn't it interesting that economic issues are in the forefront of this passage about those who mourn the fall of Babylon? Economic issues were also central in the early days of the church (Acts 2.44–45)! The link between our attitudes toward money and our spiritual lives is reflected in Jesus' words: "For where your treasure is, there your heart will be also" (Matthew 6.21). What are the values that shape your economic philosophy? In a few paragraphs write a description of your economic worldview. Ask God to examine your values and priorities with you.

See Meeting God in Service

scarlet, all kinds of scented wood, all articles of ivory, all articles of costly wood, bronze, iron, and marble, ¹³cinnamon, spice, incense, myrrh, frankincense, wine, olive oil, choice flour and wheat, cattle and sheep, horses and chariots, slaves—and human lives.ᵃ

14 "The fruit for which your soul longed
      has gone from you,
  and all your dainties and your splendor
      are lost to you,
      never to be found again!"

¹⁵The merchants of these wares, who gained wealth from her, will stand far off, in fear of her torment, weeping and mourning aloud,

16 "Alas, alas, the great city,
      clothed in fine linen,
          in purple and scarlet,
      adorned with gold,
          with jewels, and with pearls!

17 For in one hour all this wealth has been laid
          waste!"

And all shipmasters and seafarers, sailors and all whose trade is on the sea, stood far off ¹⁸and cried out as they saw the smoke of her burning,

  "What city was like the great city?"

¹⁹And they threw dust on their heads, as they wept and mourned, crying out,

  "Alas, alas, the great city,
      where all who had ships at sea
      grew rich by her wealth!
  For in one hour she has been laid waste."

20 Rejoice over her, O heaven, you saints and apostles and prophets! For God has given judgment for you against her.

21 Then a mighty angel took up a stone like a great millstone and threw it into the sea, saying,

  "With such violence Babylon the great city
      will be thrown down,
      and will be found no more;

22 and the sound of harpists and minstrels and of
          flutists and trumpeters
      will be heard in you no more;
  and an artisan of any trade
      will be found in you no more;
  and the sound of the millstone
      will be heard in you no more;

23 and the light of a lamp
      will shine in you no more;
  and the voice of bridegroom and bride
      will be heard in you no more;
  for your merchants were the magnates of the
          earth,
      and all nations were deceived by your sorcery.

24 And in youᵇ was found the blood of prophets and
          of saints,
      and of all who have been slaughtered on earth."

The Rejoicing in Heaven

19 After this I heard what seemed to be the loud voice of a great multitude in heaven, saying,

a Or chariots, and human bodies and souls   b Gk her

"Hallelujah!
Salvation and glory and power to our God,
2   for his judgments are true and just;
he has judged the great whore
who corrupted the earth with her fornication,
and he has avenged on her the blood of his
servants."[a]
[3]Once more they said,
"Hallelujah!
The smoke goes up from her forever and ever."
[4]And the twenty-four elders and the four living creatures fell down and worshiped God who is seated on the throne, saying,
"Amen. Hallelujah!"
5 And from the throne came a voice saying,
"Praise our God,
all you his servants,[a]
and all who fear him,
small and great."
[6]Then I heard what seemed to be the voice of a great multitude, like the sound of many waters and like the sound of mighty thunderpeals, crying out,
"Hallelujah!
For the Lord our God
the Almighty reigns.
7   Let us rejoice and exult
and give him the glory,
for the marriage of the Lamb has come,
and his bride has made herself ready;
8   to her it has been granted to be clothed
with fine linen, bright and pure"—
for the fine linen is the righteous deeds of the saints.

9 And the angel said[b] to me, "Write this: Blessed are those who are invited to the marriage supper of the Lamb." And he said to me, "These are true words of God." [10]Then I fell down at his feet to worship him, but he said to me, "You must not do that! I am a fellow servant[c] with you and your comrades[d] who hold the testimony of Jesus.[e] Worship God! For the testimony of Jesus[e] is the spirit of prophecy."

The Rider on the White Horse

11 Then I saw heaven opened, and there was a white horse! Its rider is called Faithful and True, and in righteousness he judges and makes war. [12]His eyes are like a flame of fire, and on his head are many diadems; and he has a name inscribed that no one knows but himself. [13]He is clothed in a robe dipped in[f] blood, and his name is called The Word of God. [14]And the armies of heaven, wearing fine linen, white and pure, were following him on white horses. [15]From his mouth comes a sharp sword with which to strike down the nations, and he will rule[g] them with a rod of iron; he will tread the wine press of the fury of the wrath of God the Almighty. [16]On his robe and on his thigh he has a name inscribed, "King of kings and Lord of lords."

The Bride and the Groom

REVELATION 19.5–8

"The bride sets all this perfection and preparedness before her beloved, the Son of God, with the desire that He transform her from the spiritual marriage, to which He desired to bring her in this Church Militant, to the glorious marriage of the Triumphant. May the most sweet Jesus, bridegroom of faithful souls, be pleased to bring all who invoke His name to this glorious marriage. To Him be honor and glory, together with the Father and the Holy Spirit, *in saecula saeculorum.* Amen."

—JOHN OF THE CROSS,
The Spiritual Canticle

---

a Gk *slaves*   b Gk *he said*   c Gk *slave*   d Gk *brothers*   e Or *to Jesus*
f Other ancient authorities read *sprinkled with*   g Or *will shepherd*

Reigning With Christ

REVELATION 20.4–6

Compare Ephesians 2.1–6 with Revelation 20.4–6. Paul is describing in Ephesians what John is seeing in Revelation. Often we can grasp things with our minds (as Paul was so good at doing) more readily than with our hearts (as John was prone to do). These passages are excellent spiritual checklists: Are there vestiges of darkness in me? Have I claimed all my rights as a citizen of Christ's kingdom? Have I washed my soul in the blood of the Lamb of God? Is my life seated with him? Am I reigning with Christ? Am I living out my priestly life in Christ? If the images don't seem to have meaning for you, ask yourself why not. Choose the image that seems most difficult for you and ask God to make it a spiritual reality for you.

The Beast and Its Armies Defeated

17 Then I saw an angel standing in the sun, and with a loud voice he called to all the birds that fly in midheaven, "Come, gather for the great supper of God, [18]to eat the flesh of kings, the flesh of captains, the flesh of the mighty, the flesh of horses and their riders—flesh of all, both free and slave, both small and great." [19]Then I saw the beast and the kings of the earth with their armies gathered to make war against the rider on the horse and against his army. [20]And the beast was captured, and with it the false prophet who had performed in its presence the signs by which he deceived those who had received the mark of the beast and those who worshiped its image. These two were thrown alive into the lake of fire that burns with sulfur. [21]And the rest were killed by the sword of the rider on the horse, the sword that came from his mouth; and all the birds were gorged with their flesh.

The Thousand Years

20 Then I saw an angel coming down from heaven, holding in his hand the key to the bottomless pit and a great chain. [2]He seized the dragon, that ancient serpent, who is the Devil and Satan, and bound him for a thousand years, [3]and threw him into the pit, and locked and sealed it over him, so that he would deceive the nations no more, until the thousand years were ended. After that he must be let out for a little while.

4 Then I saw thrones, and those seated on them were given authority to judge. I also saw the souls of those who had been beheaded for their testimony to Jesus[a] and for the word of God. They had not worshiped the beast or its image and had not received its mark on their foreheads or their hands. They came to life and reigned with Christ a thousand years. [5](The rest of the dead did not come to life until the thousand years were ended.) This is the first resurrection. [6]Blessed and holy are those who share in the first resurrection. Over these the second death has no power, but they will be priests of God and of Christ, and they will reign with him a thousand years.

Satan's Doom

7 When the thousand years are ended, Satan will be released from his prison [8]and will come out to deceive the nations at the four corners of the earth, Gog and Magog, in order to gather them for battle; they are as numerous as the sands of the sea. [9]They marched up over the breadth of the earth and surrounded the camp of the saints and the beloved city. And fire came down from heaven[b] and consumed them. [10]And the devil who had deceived them was thrown into the lake of fire and sulfur, where the beast and the false prophet were, and they will be tormented day and night forever and ever.

The Dead Are Judged

11 Then I saw a great white throne and the one who sat on it; the earth and the heaven fled from his presence, and no place was found for them. [12]And I saw the dead,

a Or for the testimony of Jesus   b Other ancient authorities read from God, out of heaven, or out of heaven from God

great and small, standing before the throne, and books were opened. Also another book was opened, the book of life. And the dead were judged according to their works, as recorded in the books. ¹³And the sea gave up the dead that were in it, Death and Hades gave up the dead that were in them, and all were judged according to what they had done. ¹⁴Then Death and Hades were thrown into the lake of fire. This is the second death, the lake of fire; ¹⁵and anyone whose name was not found written in the book of life was thrown into the lake of fire.

The New Heaven and the New Earth

21 Then I saw a new heaven and a new earth; for the first heaven and the first earth had passed away, and the sea was no more. ²And I saw the holy city, the new Jerusalem, coming down out of heaven from God, prepared as a bride adorned for her husband. ³And I heard a loud voice from the throne saying,

"See, the home*a* of God is among mortals.
He will dwell*b* with them;
they will be his peoples,*c*
and God himself will be with them;*d*
⁴ he will wipe every tear from their eyes.
Death will be no more;
mourning and crying and pain will be no more,
for the first things have passed away."

5 And the one who was seated on the throne said, "See, I am making all things new." Also he said, "Write this, for these words are trustworthy and true." ⁶Then he said to me, "It is done! I am the Alpha and the Omega, the beginning and the end. To the thirsty I will give water as a gift from the spring of the water of life. ⁷Those who conquer will inherit these things, and I will be their God and they will be my children. ⁸But as for the cowardly, the faithless,*e* the polluted, the murderers, the fornicators, the sorcerers, the idolaters, and all liars, their place will be in the lake that burns with fire and sulfur, which is the second death."

Vision of the New Jerusalem

9 Then one of the seven angels who had the seven bowls full of the seven last plagues came and said to me, "Come, I will show you the bride, the wife of the Lamb." ¹⁰And in the spirit*f* he carried me away to a great, high mountain and showed me the holy city Jerusalem coming down out of heaven from God. ¹¹It has the glory of God and a radiance like a very rare jewel, like jasper, clear as crystal. ¹²It has a great, high wall with twelve gates, and at the gates twelve angels, and on the gates are inscribed the names of the twelve tribes of the Israelites; ¹³on the east three gates, on the north three gates, on the south three gates, and on the west three gates. ¹⁴And the wall of the city has twelve foundations, and on them are the twelve names of the twelve apostles of the Lamb.

15 The angel*g* who talked to me had a measuring rod of gold to measure the city and its gates and walls. ¹⁶The city lies foursquare, its length the same as its width; and he measured the city with his rod, fifteen hundred miles;*h*

All Things New

REVELATION 21.3–7

List the "old things" that hold you in bondage to your past—the hidden addiction that fills your heart with fear, the destructive habit that brings death to your hopes and dreams, the unhealed memories that cause you sorrow, the damaged emotions that inflict pain on your spirit. Then, at each point, read and affirm Revelation 21.3. When you sense in your spirit the reality of God's loving presence with you, hear God say, "I am making all things new!" This exercise may be helpful to you as a daily discipline until the awareness of God's deliverance and healing permeates your heart and calms your spirit.

See Meeting God in the Created Order

---

a Gk *the tabernacle*   *b* Gk *will tabernacle*   *c* Other ancient authorities read *people*   *d* Other ancient authorities add *and be their God*   *e* Or *the unbelieving*   *f* Or *in the Spirit*   *g* Gk *He*   *h* Gk *twelve thousand stadia*

The Gates Are Open

REVELATION 21.25—22.5

Access to God's realm, the new Jerusalem, is available to all who wash their robes in the blood of the Lamb. Its gates are never shut. Read this passage slowly and meditatively until a phrase or sentence stands out. Stay with that word or phrase until you hear God speaking to you. What response will you make? Rest in God's presence.

See *Meeting God in Prayer*

its length and width and height are equal. [17]He also measured its wall, one hundred forty-four cubits[a] by human measurement, which the angel was using. [18]The wall is built of jasper, while the city is pure gold, clear as glass. [19]The foundations of the wall of the city are adorned with every jewel; the first was jasper, the second sapphire, the third agate, the fourth emerald, [20]the fifth onyx, the sixth carnelian, the seventh chrysolite, the eighth beryl, the ninth topaz, the tenth chrysoprase, the eleventh jacinth, the twelfth amethyst. [21]And the twelve gates are twelve pearls, each of the gates is a single pearl, and the street of the city is pure gold, transparent as glass.

22 I saw no temple in the city, for its temple is the Lord God the Almighty and the Lamb. [23]And the city has no need of sun or moon to shine on it, for the glory of God is its light, and its lamp is the Lamb. [24]The nations will walk by its light, and the kings of the earth will bring their glory into it. [25]Its gates will never be shut by day—and there will be no night there. [26]People will bring into it the glory and the honor of the nations. [27]But nothing unclean will enter it, nor anyone who practices abomination or falsehood, but only those who are written in the Lamb's book of life.

The River of Life

22 Then the angel[b] showed me the river of the water of life, bright as crystal, flowing from the throne of God and of the Lamb [2]through the middle of the street of the city. On either side of the river is the tree of life[c] with its twelve kinds of fruit, producing its fruit each month; and the leaves of the tree are for the healing of the nations. [3]Nothing accursed will be found there any more. But the throne of God and of the Lamb will be in it, and his servants[d] will worship him; [4]they will see his face, and his name will be on their foreheads. [5]And there will be no more night; they need no light of lamp or sun, for the Lord God will be their light, and they will reign forever and ever.

6 And he said to me, "These words are trustworthy and true, for the Lord, the God of the spirits of the prophets, has sent his angel to show his servants[d] what must soon take place."

7 "See, I am coming soon! Blessed is the one who keeps the words of the prophecy of this book."

Epilogue and Benediction

8 I, John, am the one who heard and saw these things. And when I heard and saw them, I fell down to worship at the feet of the angel who showed them to me; [9]but he said to me, "You must not do that! I am a fellow servant[e] with you and your comrades[f] the prophets, and with those who keep the words of this book. Worship God!"

10 And he said to me, "Do not seal up the words of the prophecy of this book, for the time is near. [11]Let the evildoer still do evil, and the filthy still be filthy, and the righteous still do right, and the holy still be holy."

12 "See, I am coming soon; my reward is with me, to

a That is, almost seventy-five yards   b Gk *he*   c Or *the Lamb.* [2]*In the middle of the street of the city, and on either side of the river, is the tree of life*   d Gk *slaves*   e Gk *slave*   f Gk *brothers*

repay according to everyone's work. ¹³I am the Alpha and the Omega, the first and the last, the beginning and the end."

14 Blessed are those who wash their robes,ᵃ so that they will have the right to the tree of life and may enter the city by the gates. ¹⁵Outside are the dogs and sorcerers and fornicators and murderers and idolaters, and everyone who loves and practices falsehood.

16 "It is I, Jesus, who sent my angel to you with this testimony for the churches. I am the root and the descendant of David, the bright morning star."

¹⁷ The Spirit and the bride say, "Come."
   And let everyone who hears say, "Come."
   And let everyone who is thirsty come.
   Let anyone who wishes take the water of life as a
      gift.

18 I warn everyone who hears the words of the prophecy of this book: if anyone adds to them, God will add to that person the plagues described in this book; ¹⁹if anyone takes away from the words of the book of this prophecy, God will take away that person's share in the tree of life and in the holy city, which are described in this book.

20 The one who testifies to these things says, "Surely I am coming soon."
   Amen. Come, Lord Jesus!

21 The grace of the Lord Jesus be with all the saints. Amen.ᵇ

The Spirit and the Bride

REVELATION 22.17

As the final notes of Revelation sound out, a clear bell of invitation chimes: "Come!"

Whoever is thirsty, whoever is in need, whoever will accept the free gift of the water of life is invited by the Spirit and the bride to simply "come." God awaits you with open hands—gentle, healing and life-giving hands. Read these final chapters of Revelation over until you hear the invitation of God resound in you. Then go out and, with joy, share the invitation with someone else who needs the gift of life.

a Other ancient authorities read *do his commandments*   b Other ancient authorities lack *all*; others lack *the saints*; others lack *Amen*

1655

TOPICAL INDEX
TO ENTRY POINTS
AND WAYS OF MEETING GOD

INDEX OF QUOTATIONS

TOPICAL INDEX
TO ENTRY POINTS AND WAYS OF MEETING GOD

Abundance 922
Abundance and Poverty 210
Abuse 405
Acceptance 141, 325, 590, 1043, 1156,
1401, 1448
Access to God 1654
Acclaim 1301, 1303
Accountability 387
Addiction 764
Adoration 164
Advice 411, 652, 1015, 1456
Aging 773, 955
Ambition 428
Angels 119, 939, 965
Anger 836, 849
Anointing 110, 481
Answered Prayer 435
Anxiety 739, 802
Art 117
Assertiveness 52
Atonement 1, 108, 128, 147, 1596, 1643
Attentiveness 1388
Attitudes 145
Authority 248, 412, 533, 1585
Beatitudes 1276
Belief 656, 1361
Benediction 1602
Bitterness 35
Blessing (Human) 179, 982, 1360
Blessings (God's) 66, 69, 237, 259, 1378
Boasting 903
Body of Christ 1511
Boldness 75, 275, 1411, 1437
Boundaries 221, 296, 507, 996
Breath of God 1140
Breath Prayer 906
Burdens 1287
Burnout 459
Business 254, 837
Busyness 444, 846
Celebration 353, 505, 608, 626
Centering Prayer 912
Change 358
Character 575
Childlike 1297

Children 512, 1297, 1382
Choices 279, 300, 446, 614, 1095, 1274,
1484, 1510
Choosing Life 23
Christian Character 367
Christian Meditation 1087
Christian Walk 1531, 1626
Christlikeness 1453, 1524, 1563, 1620
Cleansing 138, 143, 144, 199, 286, 587,
612, 1120, 1139, 1243, 1253, 1595
Clothing 964, 1009, 1148
Comfort 271, 649, 662
Commemoration 646
Commitment 146, 215, 262, 409, 1553
Communion With God 113, 744, 1199,
1251, 1322
Community 1347, 1464, 1495
Community Worship 102, 551
Companionship 4
Compassion 336, 473, 640, 1321, 1329
Compassion (God's) 908
Competition 1333
Complacency 584, 1189
Complaining 168, 654, 768, 1078
Compromise 516, 583, 1423, 1426
Confession 5, 129, 135, 280, 324, 524, 616,
717, 861, 1038, 1115, 1174
Conflict 31, 322, 858, 1356, 1512, 1569
Conformity 203
Confrontation 78, 310, 1165
Conscience 339, 408, 678, 1470
Consecration 46, 110, 806, 1263
Consequences 190, 218, 279, 449, 599, 1119
Contentment 228, 253, 261, 295, 872, 1032
Control 82, 366, 1368
Conversion 1446, 1466
Conviction 214
Correction 1096, 1205, 1207, 1246, 1247
Corruption 1202
Counsel 651
Courage 273, 285, 363, 364, 408, 619,
1249, 1468
Covenant 18, 77, 628, 1006
Creation 251, 781, 820, 821, 823, 834,
889, 920, 1478

Creative Worship 749
Crisis 487, 492
Culture 975
Curses 410
Dance 396, 531, 834
Dark Night of the Soul 559, 647
Dealing with Enemies 1007, 1028, 1635
Death 49, 271, 448, 549, 1070, 1416,
1428, 1519
Deceit 1172
Deception 1225, 1630, 1631
Decisions 614
Dedication 441, 586
Defeat 1460
Defense 1064
Delight in God 1540
Deliverance 312, 425
Denial 990, 995, 1048
Depression 724, 1020
Desiring God 124, 299, 722, 728, 745, 1141,
1185, 1195, 1373, 1396
Despair 779
Dignity 7
Disappointment 268
Discernment 30, 50, 55, 315, 329, 528, 574,
800, 869, 948, 1103, 1631
Discipleship 1013, 1318, 1393, 1398,
1407, 1637
Discouragement 498, 605, 756
Doubt 63, 1316, 1332
Dreams 1161
Economic Fears 83
Emotions 657, 697
Emptiness 341
Encountering God 41
Encouragement 1002
Enemies 904
Environment 161, 1196
Envy 372, 871
Eternal Life 1402
Eternity 985, 1519
Ethics 247
Evil 456
Excellence 618, 1265
Exile 1023
Expressing Emotions 714, 720, 1080
Failure 331, 489, 635, 1314
Fairness 224, 1300
Faith 63, 667, 1072, 1220, 1337, 1382,
1403, 1482, 1598
Faith Traditions 209, 602, 603, 1059
Faithfulness 518, 961, 1590, 1634
Faithfulness (God's) 701, 1173
False Security 1061
Family 490, 515, 624
Family (God's) 48, 1364, 1491, 1496
Family Expectations 173
Family Relationships 38, 64

Fasting 239, 337, 611, 972, 989, 1197
Fathers 980
Fear 529, 605, 655, 740, 772, 1171,
1324, 1365, 1475, 1589
Fellowship 333, 359, 1438
Fidelity 1508
Finances 159, 217
Fitting In 356
Following God 303, 888, 1292
Following Jesus 1283, 1506, 1619
Forgiveness 130, 137, 158, 374, 593, 594,
715, 1010, 1298, 1392
Foundation 1124
Franciscan Reading 1082
Freedom 88, 641, 797, 1069, 1074, 1234,
1295, 1375, 1450, 1455, 1617
Friendship . . . 371, 390, 945, 1349, 1557, 1559,
1577
Fruit of the Spirit 1012, 1539
Fruitfulness 895, 1026, 1189, 1289, 1422
Fruitlessness 1357
Frustration 260
Fulfillment 68, 985
Gatekeepers 544
Generational Sin 45, 427, 762
Generations 208, 815
Generosity 838, 1528, 1529
Gifts and Talents 122, 176, 540, 751, 959,
1159, 1294, 1309
Giving 59, 156, 242, 309, 630, 1339
Gloating 1122
Goals 1125
God the Father 227, 716, 748
God's Anger 902
God's Call 15, 226, 288, 533, 1226,
1319, 1472, 1536
God's Care 11, 88, 343, 1413
God's Compassion 305, 426
God's Creation 711
God's Design 16, 719
God's Glory 532, 690, 897, 1091, 1588
God's Goodness 718, 900
God's Guidance . . . 100, 313, 369, 377, 710, 931,
1000, 1191, 1457
God's Hands 616
God's Help 457, 478, 497, 527, 695,
742, 1083
God's Image 615
God's Kingdom 733, 788
God's Leading 89
God's Mercy 536, 767
God's Nature 944, 984, 1541
God's Omniscience 42, 817
God's Perspective 1644
God's Plan 50, 229, 569, 771, 811
God's Presence . . . 17, 43, 101, 114, 234, 289,
328, 349, 395, 436, 508, 523,
696, 709, 914, 1146, 1157

God's Promises 197, 560, 1102, 1522
God's Protection 238, 270, 274, 281,
                          318, 477, 537, 847, 951,
                                1019, 1376, 1487
God's Provision 96, 235, 291, 361, 627, 1137
God's Service 609
God's Silence 1011
God's Sovereignty 54, 174, 323, 1142, 1639
God's Standard 502
God's Ways 345
God's Will 81, 827, 1163, 1488, 1549
God's Word 2, 264, 596, 625, 693, 707,
                    796, 848, 864, 896, 1044, 1045,
                            1054, 1092, 1642
God's Wrath 1647
Godliness 1257
Good and Evil 404
Goodness 381
Government 452
Grace 6, 148, 277, 370, 600, 1201, 1285,
                                1485, 1565
Gratitude 91, 302, 1004, 1210, 1454
Greatness 565
Greed 112, 402, 464
Grief 393, 480, 613, 918, 1133
Grief (God's) 8, 613, 1416
Guidance 186, 206, 378, 800, 844, 1051
Guilt 717, 1105, 1455
Habits 190, 220, 290, 495
Halfheartedness 582
Happiness 255
Haughtiness 1245
Healing 45, 474, 500, 572, 762, 947, 1034,
              1071, 1079, 1155, 1268, 1282, 1326,
                    1329, 1365, 1375, 1404, 1643
Hearing God 316, 319, 761, 775, 993, 997,
              1030, 1048, 1211, 1267, 1363, 1429
Heartspace 928
Helping Others 401, 578, 672, 754, 789,
                                    860, 1294
Helplessness 73
Heritage 461
Heroes of Faith 1599
Hiding from God 1187, 1213, 1218
History 1176
Holiness . . . 27, 125, 134, 236, 506, 1526, 1527
Holiness (Christian) 1331, 1567
Holiness (God's) 149, 170, 194, 673, 1233
Holy Spirit 373, 1200, 1434, 1449, 1461,
                                1486, 1515
Holy Spirit's Power 330, 1254
Home 1085
Homecoming 415, 804
Honesty 768, 1332
Hope 10, 25, 434, 460, 499, 580, 674,
                    700, 746, 1181, 1236, 1568, 1593
Hospitality 29, 340, 375, 561, 1377, 1474
Hostility 1288

Human Body 823
Human Value 12, 823, 852
Humility 139, 400, 447, 712, 798, 1126
Hunger 418
Hypocrisy 406, 1306, 1328
Identity 19, 1409, 1523, 1646
Idolatry 465, 583, 595, 1624
Idols 971, 1130, 1183
Ignatian Reading 1082
Illness 244, 500, 1282
Indifference 1216
Infertility 512
Inheritance 1610
Injustice 841, 1244
Insight 835, 1144
Integrity 1628
Integrity of Worship 1372
Interceding for Society 1008
Interceding for the Nation 1017, 1060
Intercession 107, 385, 391, 403, 469, 910,
              911, 978, 1028, 1050, 1056, 1058,
                    1118, 1160, 1336, 1473, 1546
Intimacy with God 1182
Invitation 1655
Irritation 80
Jesus Prayer 1383
Jesus' Presence 1405
Jesus' Return 1618
Job Worries 83
Journaling 1579
Joy 307, 1458
Judging Others 1322
Judgment 151, 379, 909
Justice 293, 321, 323, 334, 389, 392, 668,
                    765, 862, 946, 1204, 1471
Kindness 344, 399, 479, 1479
Kingdom of God 892, 1262
Kinship 37
Knowing God 890, 1615
Lamentation 1076
Leaders 539, 564, 601, 610, 1151
Leadership . . . 94, 152, 153, 169, 187, 188, 196,
              248, 311, 394, 413, 496, 585, 894,
                    1024, 1228, 1303, 1451, 1499
Lectio Divina 1086
Legacy 1022
Legalism 1295, 1489
Life Mission 1371
Lifestyle 467, 1362, 1633
Light 105, 705, 1397
Listening 305, 653, 660
Listening to God 167, 350, 1370, 1394
Livelihood 1462
Living for God 494
Living in Community 99, 1501
Living Water 988
Loneliness 663, 708, 724, 1498
Lord's Prayer 859

Lord's Supper 175, 1406, 1513
Loss 25, 72, 352, 520, 598
Love 150, 1302, 1311, 1338, 1387, 1420,
                            1431, 1612, 1623
Love (God's) 22, 704, 722, 763, 770, 809,
                            1035, 1194
Love (Jesus') 1344
Loving God 240, 879
Loyalty 639
Making Amends 1217
Martyrdom 1442
Materialism 734
Meditation . . . 70, 270, 422, 689, 758, 799, 1279
Meeting God 74, 213, 885
Memorial 258, 276
Memorization 963
Memory 1108
Mentors 624, 638, 753, 759, 1560
Mercy 195, 222, 249, 538, 969, 1231, 1310
Ministry 76, 306, 1087
Miracles 79, 1164
Money 968, 1039, 1097, 1380, 1650
Morning Prayer 814, 962, 1154, 1320
Mothers 866
Motives 1166
Mourning 1241
Music 368, 472, 542, 632, 691
Mutual Support 207
Mystery 823, 875, 1555
Names 47
Names of God 267, 699, 957
Nature 421, 686, 687, 698, 729, 777, 905,
                            932, 936, 952, 1240
Needs 1430
Neighbors 98, 828
Oath 571
Obedience 160, 327, 346, 791, 1032,
                            1136, 1180, 1390, 1399
Offerings 126, 154, 163, 212
Open to God 884, 1490
Openhearted 1480
Opposition 188
Pain 664, 669, 680, 942
Parenting 172, 414, 429, 825
Passover 85, 246
Peace 81, 317, 455, 567, 772, 923, 1551
Peer Pressure 417
Persecution 1307
Perseverance 967, 1452, 1603
Personal Worship 551
Petition 21, 165, 326, 337, 347, 355, 443,
                            1424, 1436
Pilgrimage 803
Planning 1607
Politics 1177
Possessions 637
Power 320
Power of Words 666

Praise . . 314, 548, 577, 780, 818, 819, 1385, 1497
Prayer 283, 514, 650, 738, 801, 1290, 1335,
                            1367, 1640
Prayer (Answered) 24, 284, 1175
Prayer Posture 328, 1345
Praying the Bible 166
Preparedness 1129
Preparing to Worship 121, 1149
Pressure 283
Pride 13, 475, 1131
Priorities . . 171, 265, 437, 685, 941, 1280, 1562
Problems 189
Prophecy 78, 205, 466, 480, 1031, 1255
Purity 131, 216, 736, 1507
Purpose 868
Questions 692, 1238, 1386
Rebellion 1186
Rebirth 924, 1400, 1535
Rebuilding 1252
Rebuke 132, 927, 1206
Reconciliation 44, 536, 589, 1525
Redemption 787, 950, 966, 1067, 1352
Reflecting God's Glory 116
Reflection 87
Refreshment 93, 766, 1408
Refuge 732
Regret 876
Rejoicing 644
Relationships 177, 522, 623
Relying on God 1330
Remembering 193, 225, 232, 241, 301, 491,
                            676, 774, 1441, 1578
Renewal 86, 252, 604, 634, 881, 933,
                            1101, 1272, 1653
Repentance 442, 463, 567, 593, 683,
                            1104, 1197, 1198, 1647
Resentment 1221
Respect 416
Rest 287, 1077, 1366
Resting in God 53, 397, 793, 1178
Restoration 142, 338, 1066, 1138, 1227
Resurrection 887, 1395, 1415, 1435, 1518
Revenge . . . 35, 62, 97, 157, 383, 785, 856, 1065
Reverence 529, 1150
Rhythm 1359
Righteousness 140, 1477, 1572
Ritual 109
Rivalry 642
Role Models 424
Roots 386
Rule of Life 1359
Sabbath 111, 155
Sabbath Rest 973, 1016, 1113
Sacred Meals 357
Sadness 1123
Salvation 137, 1483, 1558
Searching 682
Security 342

Seeking God 67, 570, 752, 783, 882, 1117,
1143, 1184, 1208
Self-esteem 883, 893, 1384
Self-examination 678, 811, 991, 1323, 1652
Self-image 14, 420, 636, 722, 778, 809, 886,
987, 1127, 1132, 1611
Selfishness 476
Self-reliance 431, 568
Self-sacrifice 32, 326, 525, 588, 983,
1327, 1575
Self-will 34
Serenity 842
Servanthood 606, 621, 1532, 1538
Service 127, 230, 243, 288, 365, 439, 471,
479, 523, 541, 556, 620, 622,
940, 989, 1367, 1419, 1427
Shame 612, 1062
Silence 956, 1348
Simony 1444
Simplicity 843, 1354
Sin 784
Singing 517
Singing Praise 90, 201, 1350, 1351
Slavery 1042
Sleeplessness 677
Social Unrest 974, 1003
Solitude 103, 658, 1355
Soul Friends 1500
Sounds of Prayer 907
Speaking Out 211, 865
Speech 812, 833, 857, 863, 999, 1259,
1266, 1544, 1571
Spiritual Disciplines 290, 741, 1433, 1556
Spiritual Dryness 184, 185, 954, 1114
Spiritual Evaluation . . . 233, 360, 430, 549, 679,
831, 1281
Spiritual Formation . . . 3, 65, 503, 855, 878, 929
Spiritual Gifts 1492, 1514
Spiritual Growth . . . 737, 757, 1190, 1250, 1278,
1296, 1570, 1600
Spiritual History 57, 1534
Spiritual Journey 219, 250, 257, 292, 398,
491, 703, 706, 730, 755,
1001, 1037, 1548
Spiritual Maturity 351, 1498, 1516, 1576
Spiritual Warfare . . 202, 281, 388, 451, 526, 592,
1232, 1284
Status 506, 637
Stewardship 251, 327, 546, 1520
Stress 1374
Struggle 200, 1485
Submitting to God 1342
Success 829
Suffering . . . 640, 648, 661, 681, 725, 994, 1075,
1081, 1112, 1440
Support 297, 1465
Surrender 191, 282, 294, 554, 880, 1029,
1109, 1291, 1334, 1391, 1636

Teachers 486
Temptation 566, 1275
Testing 26, 942
Thanksgiving 180, 501, 591, 633, 735, 925,
1381, 1561
The Body of Christ 519
The Church 511, 521, 1389, 1432, 1521,
1542, 1564, 1608, 1651
The Cross 1503
The Gospel 1271, 1517
The Trinity 1533
Thoughts 1225
Tongue 1606
Tradition 590
Tranparency 1439
Transformation 308, 1223, 1584
Treasuring 1353
Trials 1014, 1469, 1573
Trouble 60, 1181, 1421
Trust 1421
Trust in God 926, 930, 938, 1025, 1324
Truth 573, 1574, 1627, 1628
Unity 376, 380, 510, 807, 1425, 1494
Values 39, 256, 1192
Vanity 805
Violence 223, 483, 1071, 1098
Vision 1144, 1412
Vocation 543, 987, 1055
Vows 162, 178, 215, 399
Waiting on God 20, 709, 713, 850, 1230,
1239, 1592
Walking Prayer 1543
War 493
Warning 1121
Watchfulness 231, 917, 1134, 1308
Water 9, 33, 354, 1583
Weakness 27, 370, 795
Wealth 1299
Wealth 1379
Welcome 192
Wholeheartedness 810
Wisdom 432, 433, 445, 675, 688, 790, 826,
830, 832, 874, 915, 1504
Witnessing 726, 949, 1162, 1219, 1284,
1320, 1340, 1343, 1417, 1445,
1459, 1467, 1613
Wonder 1358
Work 629
Worldliness 1621, 1648
Worry 1052
Worship 120, 154, 245, 438, 450, 562,
702, 1145, 1209, 1264,
1273, 1493, 1601
Woundedness 1325
Wrath (God's) 22, 263
Wrestling With God 58
Youth 462, 1063
Zeal 482, 484

INDEX OF QUOTATIONS
TO ENTRY POINTS AND WAYS OF MEETING GOD

Page 1   Julian of Norwich (c.1342–c.1413). Taken from *Showings*.

Page 7   From *Addiction and Grace* by Gerald May. Copyright ©1988 by Gerald May. Published by Harper-San Francisco, San Francisco, CA.

Page 12   Peter Brown. Quoted from *The Body and Society*, from *American Council of Learned Societies Lectures on the History of Religion, No. 13*. Copyright ©1988. Published by Columbia University Press, New York, NY.

Page 16   Quoted from *The Path of Life* by Cyprian Smith. Copyright ©1995 by Cyprian Smith. Published by Morehouse Publications, Harrisburg, PA.

Page 19   From *Nama Japa: Prayer of the Name* by Sister Vandana. Copyright ©1984. Published by South Asia Books, Bombay (Columbia, MO).

Page 22   from *True Prayer: An Invitation to Christian Spirituality* by Kenneth Leech. Copyright ©1995 by Kenneth Leech. Published by Morehouse Publications, Harrisburg, PA.

Page 27   From *To Believe in Jesus* by Ruth Burrows. Copyright ©1978. Published by Dimension Books, Denville, NJ.

Page 32   Rufus Jones (1863–1948) is quoted in *Daily Readings from Quaker Spirituality, (Western Classics of Spirituality Series)*. Copyright ©1987. Published by Paulist Press, Mahwah, NJ.

Page 36   From *Holiness* by Donald Nicholl. Copyright ©1981. Published by Seabury Press.

Page 40   From *Praying the Psalms* by Walter Brueggemann. Copyright ©1982,1986. Published by St. Mary's Press, Winona, MN.

Page 43   F.W. Robertson. From "Jacob's Wrestling" in *Ten Sermons* (quoted in Otto *The Idea of the Holy*, Galaxy Books, trans. by John W. Harvey). Copyright ©1958. Oxford University Press, New York, NY.

Page 46   From *Addiction and Grace* by Gerald May. Copyright ©1988 by Gerald May. Published by Harper-San Francisco, San Francisco, CA.

Page 49   Bede (673–735) from *A History of the English Church and People*. Copyright ©1955. Published by Penguin Classics, New York.

Page 53   From *Daily Readings from Quaker Spirituality, (Western Classics of Spirituality Series)* by Caroline Stephen. Copyright ©1987. Published by Paulist Press, Mahwah, NJ.

Page 56   From *The Cloud of Unknowing* an anonymous, 14th century work. Copyright ©1981. Published by Paulist Press, Mahwah, NJ.

Page 58   From *A Tree Full of Angels* by Macrina Wiederkehr. Copyright ©1990 by Macrina Wiederkehr. Published by HarperSanFrancisco, San Francisco, CA.

Page 60   Thomas Brown. From *Daily Readings from Quaker Spirituality (Western Classics of Spirituality Series)*. Copyright ©1987. Published by Paulist Press, Mahwah, NJ.

Page 67   Henry Suso (1295–1366) from *Works*. Copyright ©1958. Published by Oxford University Press, New York, NY.

Page 70   Francis de Sales (1567–1622) from *Introduction to the Devout Life*. Copyright ©1972. Published by Doubleday Image Books, New York.

Page 71   "Prayer at Easter Vigil" is quoted from the Roman Missal.

Page 76   From *Creative Ministry* by Henri J.M. Nouwen. Copyright ©1971 by Henri J. M. Nouwen. Published by Doubleday Image Books, New York.

Page 89   Dietrich Bonhoeffer (1906–1945) from *The Mystery of Easter*. Copyright ©1997. Published by Crossroad Publishing, New York.

Page 92   Thomas Merton (1915–1968) from *No Man Is an Island*. Copyright ©1955 by the Trustees of the Merton Legacy Fund. Published by Harcourt Brace, and Co., New York, NY.

Page 96   "Little Girls in Church" by Kathleen Norris. Copyright ©1995 by Kathleen Norris. Published by the University of Pittsburgh Press, Pittsburgh, PA.

Page 99   Catherine of Siena (1347–1380) from *The Dialogue*, edited by Suzanne Noffke. Copyright ©1980. Published by Paulist Press, Mahwah, NJ.

Page 105   Origen (c.185–c.254) from *Homilies on Exodus*. Copyright ©1982. Published by Catholic University of America, Washington, DC.

Page 114   Gregory of Nyssa (330–395) from *The Life of Moses,* translated by Abraham Malherbe and Everett Ferguson. Copyright ©1978. Published by Paulist Press, Mahwah, NJ.

Page 120   Thomas à Kempis (1380–1471) from *The Imitation of Christ*.

Page 124   John of the Cross (1542–1591) from *The Dark Night of the Soul, Selected Writings (Classics of Western Spirituality Series)*. Copyright ©1987. Published by Paulist Press, Mahwah, NJ.

Page 125   John Calvin (1509–1564) from the *Institutes of the Christian Religion*. Edited by John T. McNeill. Copyright ©1960. Published by Westminster John Knox Press, Louisville KY.

Page 138   Martin Luther (1483–1546) from Sermon II in Volume 52 of *Luther's Works*, edited by Hans Hillerbrand. Copyright ©1974. Published Augsburg Fortress Press, Minneapolis, MN.

Page 140   Catherine of Siena (1347–1380) from *The Dialogue,* edited by Suzanne Noffke. Copyright ©1980. Published by Published by Paulist Press, Mahwah, NJ.

Page 148   Augustine (354–430) from "Admonition and Grace."

Page 168   Augustine (354–430) from *Confessions*.

Page 202   Teresa of Avila (1515–1582) from *The Interior Castle*.

Page 214   John Woolman (1720–1772) from *The Journal of John Woolman*.

Page 216   Francis de Sales (1567–1622) from *Introduction to the Devout Life*. Copyright ©1972. Published by Doubleday Image Books, New York.

Page 225   Francis de Sales (1567–1622) from *Introduction to the Devout Life*. Copyright ©1972. Published by Doubleday Image Books, New York.

Page 231   Thomas à Kempis (1380–1471) from *The Imitation of Christ*.

Page 236   Francis de Sales (1567–1622) from *Introduction to the Devout Life*. Copyright ©1972. Published by Doubleday Image Books, New York.

Page 240   Augustine (354–430) from *Sermons and Expositions*.

Page 244   From *The Cloud of Unknowing,* an anonymous, 14th century work. Copyright ©1981. Published by Paulist Press, Mahwah, NJ.

Page 253   Francis de Sales (1567–1622) from *Introduction to the Devout Life*. Copyright ©1972. Published by Doubleday Image Books, New York.

Page 261   Blaise Pascal (1623–1662) from *Pensees*.

Page 269   Thomas à Kempis (1380–1471) from *The Imitation of Christ*.

Page 272   Evelyn Underhill (1875–1941) from *The Ways of the Spirit*, edited by Grace Adolphsen Brame. Copyright ©1990. Published by Crossroad Publishing, New York.

Page 395   Francis de Sales (1567–1622) from *Introduction to the Devout Life*. Copyright ©1972. Published by Doubleday Image Books, New York.

Page 396   Mechtild of Magdeburg (c. 1212–c. 1280) from *Flowing Light of the Godhead*, Book I (*Classics of Western Spirituality Series*). Copyright ©1998. Published by Paulist Press, Mahwah, NJ.

Page 404   Francois Fenelon (1651–1715) from *Spiritual Letters* to Women (Letter 7). Copyright ©1984 by Zondervan Publishing House. Published by the Zondervan Corporation, Grand Rapids, MI.

Page 408   A quotation attributed to Pastor Martin Niemoeller (1892–1984).

Page 426   From *Time for God* by Leslie D. Weatherhead. Copyright ©1967. Published by Abingdon Press, Nashville, TN.

Page 430   From *Taste and See: A Personal Guide to the Spiritual Life* by William O. Paulsell. Copyright ©1976. Published by Chalice Press, St. Louis, MO.

Page 433   Augustine (354–430) from *Enchiridion*.

Page 440   Augustine (354–430) from *On The Presence of God*, Letter 187, from *Augustine of Hippo: Selected Writings*, translation and introduction by Mary T. Clark. Copyright ©1984. Published by Paulist Press, Mahwah, NJ.

Page 447   From *The Talmud*, Numbers Rabba, Bemidhar, IV, 20, edited by Rabbi Steinsaltz. Copyright ©1998. Published by Random House, New York.

Page 452   From *The Talmud*, Deuteronomy Rabba, V, 1 and 3. Copyright ©1998. Published by Random House, New York.

Page 454   From *Taste and See: A Personal Guide to the Spiritual Life* by William O. Paulsell. Copyright ©1976. Published by Chalice Press, St. Louis, MO.

Page 456   From *People of the Lie* by M. Scott Peck. Copyright ©1983 by M. Scott Peck. Published by Simon & Schuster, New York, NY.

Page 468   Evelyn Underhill (1875–1941) from *The Spiritual Life: Great Spiritual Truths for Everyday Life* (*Mystical Series of the World*). Copyright ©1955. Morehouse Publications, Harrisburg, PA.

Page 476   From *Workbook on the Seven Deadly Sins* by Maxie Dunham, Kimberly Dunham Reisman. Copyright ©1997 by Maxie Dunham, Kimberly Dunham Reisman. Published by Upper Room Books, Nashville, TN. Reprinted by permission of Upper Room Books. All rights reserved.

Page 488   From *Your God is Too Small* by J.B. Phillips. Copyright ©1976. Published by Simon & Schuster, New York, NY.

Page 505   William Law (1686–1761) from *A Serious Call to a Devout and Holy Life*.

Page 509   From the *Lumen Gentium* Chapter 2, Vatican Council II, (1962–1965), *The Concilar and Post Concilar Documents*, edited by Austin Flannery, O.P. Copyright ©1975. Liturgical Press, Collegeville, MN.

Page 511   From *The Book of Discipline of the United Methodist Church*. Copyright ©1992. United Methodist Publishing House, Nashville.

Page 517   From *A Testament of Devotion* by Thomas R. Kelly. Copyright ©1941 by Harper & Row Publishers, Inc. Renewed ©1969 by Lois Lael Kelly Statler.

Page 518   Frederick Lucian Hosmer. "Forward through the Ages," # 555, United Methodist Hymnal. (1908).

Page 520   From *Eighth Day of Creation* by Elizabeth O'Connor. Copyright ©1971. Word Books, Nashville, TN.

Page 521   Eberhard Arnold (1883–1935) from *God's Revolution*. Copyright ©1984. Plough Publishing of the Bruderhof Foundation, Farmington, PA.

Page 526   Cyprian of Carthage (d. 258). From *Letter 1*.

Page 530   Augustine (354–430) from *The City of God*, Book 17 Chapter 14.

Page 534   Charles Wesley (1707–1788) from a hymn.

Page 536 Macarius the Great (300–390). Quoted in *Sayings of the Desert Fathers*, edited by Sister Benedicta Ward. Copyright ©1975. Published by Cistercian Publications, Inc., Kalamazoo, MI.

Page 540 John Bunyan (1628–1688) from *Grace Abounding to the Chief of Sinners*.

Page 543 Thomas Merton (1915–1968) from *No Man Is an Island*. Copyright ©1955 by the Trustees of the Merton Legacy Fund. Published by Harcourt Brace, New York, NY.

Page 546 Cyprian of Carthage (d. 258). Treatise "On the Lord's Prayer."

Page 550 From Augustine (354–430) from *Confessions*, Book I.

Page 554 John Wesley (1703–1791) from *Journal*.

Page 559 From *The Cloud of Unknowing,* an anonymous, 14th century work. Copyright ©1981. Published by Paulist Press, Mahwah, NJ.

Page 566 Thomas à Kempis (1380–1471) from *The Imitation of Christ*.

Page 567 Anonymous Franciscan (late 19th century), often attributed to St. Francis. Hymn # 481, United Methodist Hymnal.

Page 570 Annie S. Hawks. "I Need Thee Every Hour," Hymn # 397, United Methodist Hymnal.

Page 577 Augustine (354–430) from *Confessions*.

Page 581 Ignatius of Loyola (1491–1556) from *The Spiritual Exercises*.

Page 586 George B. Robson. Hymn # 607, United Methodist Hymnal.

Page 588 Teresa of Avila (1515–1582) from *The Interior Castle*.

Page 591 From *Prayer and the Common Life* by Georgia Harkness. Copyright ©1948. Published by Abingdon/Cokesbury, Nashville, TN.

Page 593 Mius of Belos is quoted in *Sayings of the Desert Fathers*, edited by Sister Benedicta Ward. Copyright ©1975. Published by Cistercian Publications, Inc., Kalamazoo, MI.

Page 597 From *The Passover Haggadah* (traditional), edited by Nahum Glatzer. Copyright ©1953, 1969. Published by Schocken Books (Knopf), New York.

Page 600 John Bunyan (1628–1688) from *Grace Abounding to the Chief of Sinners*.

Page 606 Francis de Sales (1567–1622) from *Introduction to the Devout Life*. Copyright ©1972. Published by Doubleday Image Books, .

Page 615 Dorothy Day (1897–1980) from *The Long Loneliness*. Copyright ©1952. Harper & Row, New York.

Page 618 From *Community and Growth* by Jean Vanier. Copyright ©1979. Published by Paulist Press Mahwah, NJ.

Page 621 Ephraim of Syria, (c. 300), from *Repentance*. Copyright ©1984. Published by Paulist Press, Mahwah, NJ.

Page 629 Brother Lawrence (c.1605–1691) from *The Practice of the Presence of God*.

Page 631 Evelyn Underhill (1875–1941) from *The School of Charity*. Copyright ©1991. Published by Morehouse Publications, Harrisburg, PA.

Page 636 From *Reversed Thunder* by Eugene Peterson. Copyright ©1988 by Eugene Peterson. Published by HarperSan Francisco, San Francisco, CA.

Page 641 Dietrich Bonhoeffer (1906 1945) from *Ethics*, edited by Eberhard Bethge, translated by Neville Horton Smith. Copyright ©1995. Simon & Schuster, New York, NY.

Page 647 John of the Cross (1542–1591) from *The Dark Night of the Soul, from Selected Writings (Classics of Western Spirituality Series)*. Copyright ©1987. Published by Paulist Press, Mahwah, NJ.

Page 665 John of the Cross (1542–1591). *The Dark Night of the Soul* from *Selected Writings (Classics of Western Spirituality Series)*. Copyright ©1987. Published by Paulist Press, Mahwah, NJ.

Page 671 From *The Cloud of Unknowing,* an anonymous, 14th century work. Copyright ©1981. Published by Paulist Press, Mahwah, NJ.

Page 680   C. S. Lewis (1898–1963) from *The Problem of Pain*. Copyright ©1996. Touchstone Books, Simon & Schuster, New York, NY.

Page 684   Augustine (354–430) from *Enchiridion*.

Page 690   John Calvin (1509–1564) from *Institutes of the Christian Religion,* edited by John T. McNeill. Copyright ©1960. Published by Westminster John Knox Press, Louisville, KY.

Page 693   Thomas Merton (1915–1968) from *Bread in the Wilderness*. Copyright ©1953, 1997 by the Trustees of the Merton Legacy Fund. Published by New Directions, Norfolk, CN.

Page 716   Evelyn Underhill (1875–1941) from *Abba*. Copyright ©1992. Published by Morehouse Publications, Harrisburg, PA.

Page 721   John Cassian (c. 360–430) from *The Conferences of Cassian*

Page 726   From *Praying the Psalms* by Walter Brueggemann. Copyright ©1982,1986. Published by St. Mary's Press, Winona, MN.

Page 727   Thomas à Kempis (1380–1471) from *The Imitation of Christ*.

Page 742   Hadewijch of Antwerp (c. 1200) from *The Complete Works*, translated by Columba Hart. Copyright ©1980. Published by Paulist Press, Mahwah, NJ.

Page 750   From *Reaching Out: The Three Movements of the Spiritual Life* by Henri J.M. Nouwen. Copyright ©1975. Published by Doubleday, New York, NY.

Page 770   From *Here and Now* by Henri J.M. Nouwen. Copyright ©1994. Published by Crossroad Publishing Co, Inc., New York, NY.

Page 776   John Ruusbroec (1293–1381) from *The Spiritual Espousals*, introduction and translation by James A. Wiseman. Copyright ©1985. Published by Paulist Press, Mahwah, NJ.

Page 792   Thomas Merton (1915–1968) from *New Seeds of Contemplation*. Copyright ©1961 by the Trustees of the Merton Legacy Fund. Published by New Directions Books, Norfolk, CN.

Page 801   Dietrich Bonhoeffer (1906–1945) from *Life Together*. Copyright ©1954. Published by Augsburg Fortress Press, Minneapolis, MN.

Page 816   Evelyn Underhill (1875–1941) from *The Spiritual Life: Great Spiritual Truths for Everyday Life (Mystical Series of the World)*. Copyright ©1955. Published by Morehouse Publications, Harrisburg, PA.

Page 820   Elizabeth Barrett Browning (1806–1861) from "Aurora Leigh," book VII, line 820.

Page 821   Gerard Manley Hopkins (1844–1889). "God's Grandeur" from *The Poems and Prose of Gerard Manley Hopkins*.

Page 821   John Calvin (1509–1564) from *Institutes of the Christian Religion,* edited by John T. McNeill. Copyright ©1960. Published by Westminster John Knox Press, Louisville, KY.

Page 822   From *The Story of My Heart: My Autobiography* by Richard Jefferies with an introduction by Elizabeth Jennings. Copyright ©1968. Published in London by Macmillan.

Page 824   Augustine (354–430) from *Confessions*.

Page 827   Jean-Pierre de Caussade (1675–1751) from *Abandonment to Divine Providence*. Copyright ©1975. Published by Doubleday, New York, NY.

Page 832   *The Wisdom of Solomon from the Old Testament Apocrypha* (NRSV). Copyright ©1989 by the Division of Christian Education of the National Council of Churches of Christ in the U.S.A., New York, NY.

Page 839   From *The Sarum Primer*.

Page 842   Reinhold Niebuhr (1893–1971) from *Justice and Mercy*. Copyright ©1974 by Reinhold Niebuhr. Published by Westminster John Knox Press, Louisville, KY.

Page 845   William Law (1686–1761) from *A Serious Call to a Devout and Holy Life*.

Page 849   Hildegard of Bingen (1098–1179). *Scivias* from *Creation and Christ: The Wisdom of Hildegard of Bingen*, translated by Columba Hart and Jane Bishop; edited by Kathleen A. Walsh. Copyright ©1996. Published by Paulist Press, Mahwah, NJ.

Page 854 Phoebe Palmer (1807–1874) from *Entire Devotion to God.* Copyright ©1979. Published by Schmul Publishing, Salem, Ohio.

Page 864 Peter of Damaskos, (c 1100) from *Philokalia*, Vol. III compiled by St. Nikodimos of the Holy Mountain and St. Makarios of Corinth; translated from the Greek and edited by G.E.H. Palmer, Philip Sherrard, Kallistos Ware. Copyright ©1979, 1983. Published by Faber & Faber, London.

Page 867 Jean-Pierre de Caussade (1675–1751) from *The Sacrament of the Present Moment*, translated by Kitty Muggeridge. Copyright ©1989. Published by HarperSanFrancisco, San Francisco, CA.

Page 874 From *A Testament of Devotion* by Thomas R. Kelly. Copyright ©1941 by Harper & Row Publishers, Inc. Renewed ©1969 by Lois Lael Kelly Statler.

Page 879 Bernard of Clairvaux (1090–1153) from *Sermon XX on the Song of Songs.* Copyright ©1987. Published by Paulist Press, Mahwah, NJ.

Page 887 Blaise Arminjon from *The Cantata of Love: A Verse-by-Verse Reading of the Song of Songs,* translated by Nelly Marans. Copyright ©1988. Published by Ignatius Press, San Francisco, CA.

Page 889 Gerard Manley Hopkins (1844–1889). "God's Grandeur." From *Poems and Prose of Gerard Manley Hopkins.*

Page 896 Augustine (354–430) from *Sermon LIX:3.*

Page 900 C. S. Lewis (1898–1963) from *Mere Christianity.* Copyright ©1952. Published by Simon & Schuster, New York, NY.

Page 902 Origen of Alexandria (c.185–c.254) from *Contra Celsus.*

Page 905 Bonaventura (1221–1274) from *The Life of St. Francis* translated by Ewart Cousins. Copyright ©1978. Published by Paulist Press, Mahwah, NJ.

Page 908 Julian of Norwich (c.1342–c.1413) from *Revelations of Divine Love.*

Page 912 From *The Talmud*, edited by Rabbi Steinsaltz. Copyright ©1998. Published by Random House, New York.

Page 914 Sister Wendy Beckett from *"Sister Wendy in Conversation with Bill Moyers.* Copyright ©1997. Broadcast by WGBH-TV Boston.

Page 916 Francis de Sales (1567–1622) from *Treatise of the Love of God.* Copyright ©1973. Published by Morehouse Publications, Harrisburg, PA.

Page 924 Evelyn Underhill (1875–1941) from *The Spiral Way.*

Page 927 George Herbert (1593–1633) from "Repentance" in *George Herbert: The Country Parson,* edited John Wal Jr. (*Classics of Western Spirituality Series*). Copyright ©1981. Published by Paulist Press, Mahwah, NJ.

Page 934 Julian of Norwich (c.1342–c.1413) from *Showings.*

Page 939 Hildegard of Bingen (1098–1179) from *"Symphony of the Blessed,* Vision 13, translated by Columba Hart and Jane Bishop. Copyright ©1990. Published by Paulist Press, Mahwah, NJ.

Page 946 Karl Barth (1886–1968) from *Church Dogmatics, Vol. 2,* edited by G.W. Bromiley, T.F. Torrance. Copyright ©1957. Published by Books International Inc., Herndon, VA.

Page 953 *Jewish Morning Prayer.* Copyright ©1956. Published by Prayer Book Press (subs. of Media Judaica, Inc.) Bridgeport, CT.

Page 960 Augustine (354–430) from *Confessions.*

Page 967 Friedrich von Hugel (1852–1925) from *Letters to a Niece (Letters from Baron Friedrich von Hugel to a Niece),* edited by Gwendolyn Green. Copyright ©1928. Published by J.M. Dent & Sons, (subs of Orion House) London.

Page 970 From *A Testament of Devotion* by Thomas R. Kelly. Copyright ©1941 by Harper & Row Publishers, Inc. Renewed ©1969 by Lois Lael Kelly Statler.

Page 977 Ephraim of Syria, (c.300) from *Ephraim the Syrian,* edited by K. McVey (*Classics of Western Spirituality Series*). Copyright ©1989. Published by Paulist Press, Mahwah, NJ.

Page 979 "The Hymn of Glory" from the *Hebrew Prayer Book.* (a traditional Jewish chant translated by T.H. Phillips in "Daily Prayers"). Published by Hebrew Publishing Co., Spencetown, New York.

Page 986 John Donne (1573–1631) from *Holy Sonnets 5.*

Page 991 Eric Milner-White (1884–1963) from *My God, My Glory.* Copyright ©1967. Published by S.P.C.K., London.

Page 1005 John Donne (1573–1631) from *Easter Day Sermon.*

Page 1006 T.O. Chisholm."Great is Your Faithfulness," #260 from *Hymns for Today's Church.* Copyright ©1925, 1951. Published by Hope Publishing, Carol Stream, IL.

Page 1011 From *A School for Prayer* by Archbishop Anthony Bloom. Copyright ©1970. Published by Libra Books, San Diego, CA.

Page 1021 John Newton (1725–1807) from *Thoughts Upon the African Slave Trade.*

Page 1025 Hannah Whithall Smith (1832–1911) from *The Christian's Secret of a Happy Life.*

Page 1035 Abbé de Tourville from *Letters of Direction: Thoughts on the Spiritual Life from the Letters of the Abbé de Tourville.* Copyright ©1987. Published by Morehouse Publications, Harrisburg, PA.

Page 1038 From *Finally Comes the Poet* by Walter Brueggemann. Copyright ©1989. Published by Augsburg Fortress Publishers, Minneapolis, MN.

Page 1040 Julian of Norwich (c.1342–c.1413) from *Enfolded in Love: Daily Readings from Julian of Norwich.* Copyright ©1980. Published by Darton, Longman and Todd, London.

Page 1051 From *A Common Prayer* by Michael Leunig. Copyright ©1991. Published by HarperSan Francisco, San Francisco, CA.

Page 1056 Andrew Murray (1828–1917) from *With Christ in the School of Prayer.* Copyright ©1965. Published by Whitaker House, New Kensington, PA.

Page 1066 From *Finally Comes The Poet* by Walter Brueggemann. Copyright ©1989. Published by Augsburg Fortress Press, Minneapolis, MN.

Page 1035 Erastus Johnson. "The Gospel," from *The United Methodist Hymnal.*

Page 1082 Dag Hammarskjold (1905–1961) from *Markings.* Copyright ©1966. Published by Knopf (division of Random House), New York.

Page 1084 Brother Lawrence (c.1605–1691) from *The Practice of the Presence of God.*

Page 1090 From *A Cry of Absence: Reflections for the Winter of the Heart* by Martin Marty, illustrated by Susan Teumer Marty. Copyright ©1983. Published by Harper & Row, New York.

Page 1093 Erich Schick. Quoted in *A Guide to Prayer for Ministers* by Job and Shawchuck. Copyright ©1983. Published by Upper Room Books, Nashville, TN. Used by permission.

Page 1095 C. S. Lewis (1898–1963) from *Mere Christianity.* Copyright ©1952. Published by Simon & Schuster, New York, NY.

Page 1100 George MacDonald (1824–1905) from *Diary of an Old Soul.* Copyright ©1994. Published by Augsburg Fortress Press, Minneapolis, MN.

Page 1104 From *Wishful Thinking* by Fredrick Buechner. Copyright ©1973. Published by Harper & Row, New York, NY.

Page 1109 Charles de Foucauld (1858–1916) from *Meditations of a Hermit, translation by Charlotte Balfour.* Copyright ©1981, 1983. Published by Orbis Books, Maryknoll, New York.

Page 1111 From *The Way of the Heart: Desert Spirituality and Contemporary Ministry* by Henri J. M. Nouwen. Copyright ©1981 by Henri J. M. Nouwen. Published by Seabury Press, New York.

Page 1116 Aubrey Thomas de Vere (1814–1902). "Sorrow."

Page 1126 Thomas à Kempis (1380–1471) from *The Imitation of Christ.*

Page 1128 From *The Prophetic Imagination* by Walter Brueggemann. Copyright ©1978 by Walter Brueggemann. Published by Augsburg Fortress Press Philadelphia, PA.

Page 1135 Julian of Norwich (c.1342–c.1413) from *Showings.*

Page 1141 Augustine (354–430) from *Confessions*.

Page 1145 From *Dimensions of Prayer* by Douglas V. Steere. Copyright ©1961, 1997. Published by Upper Room Books, Nashville, TN.

Page 1147 From *Bread for the Journey* by Henri J. M. Nouwen. Copyright ©1997 by Henri J. M. Nouwen. Published by HarperSan Francisco, San Francisco CA.

Page 1153 Augustine (354–430) from *Confessions*.

Page 1156 Dorotheus of Gaza, (c. 500). From *Discourses and Sayings, translated by Eric P. Wheeler*. Copyright ©1977. Published by Cistercian Publications, Inc., Kalamazoo, MI.

Page 1158 John Wesley (1703–1791) from *Letter to Miss March*.

Page 1179 Catherine of Siena (1347–1380) from *The Dialogue,* edited by Suzanne Noffke. Copyright ©1980. Published by Paulist Press, Mahwah, NJ.

Page 1182 From *Letters of Direction: Thoughts on the Spiritual Life from the Letters of the Abbé de Tourville.* Copyright ©1959, 1987. Published by Morehouse Publications, Harrisburg, PA.

Page 1185 Hugh of St. Victor (c.1096–1141) from *The Graces of Interior Prayer*. Published by Kegan Paul, International, Ltd., London

Page 1188 From *Gracias, A Latin American Journal* by Henri J.M. Nouwen. Copyright ©1983. Published by Harper & Row, San Francisco, CA.

Page 1194 From *Gracias, A Latin American Journal* by Henri J. M. Nouwen. Copyright ©1983. Published by Harper & Row, San Francisco, CA.

Page 1195 John of the Cross (1542–1591) from *The Spiritual Canticle*. Copyright ©1987. Published by Paulist Press, Mahwah, NJ.

Page 1202 Augustine (354–430) from *Commentary on John's Gospel,* Treatise 33.

Page 1215 Thomas à Kempis (1380–1471) from *The Imitation of Christ*.

Page 1218 Francis Thompson (1859–1907). "The Hound of Heaven."

Page 1222 John Woolman (1720–1772) from *The Journal of John Woolman*.

Page 1232 Martin Luther (1483–1546) from "A Mighty Fortress is Our God" translated by Fredrick H. Hedge.

Page 1235 Jean-Pierre de Caussade (1675–1751) from *Living Water: an Anthology of Letters of Direction*, selected and introduced by Robin Baird-Smith. Copyright ©1987. Published in Grand Rapids, MI, by W.B. Eerdmans Co.

Page 1237 Reinhold Niebuhr (1892–1971) from *Justice and Mercy*. Copyright ©1974, 1991. Published by Westminster John Knox Press, Louisville, KY.

Page 1242 George Fox (1624–1691) from *Journal*.

Page 1253 Francois Fenelon (1651–1715) from *Living Water: An Anthology of Letters of Direction,* selected and introduced by Robin Baird-Smith. Copyright ©1987. Published in Grand Rapids, MI by W.B. Eerdmans Co.

Page 1245 Brother Roger of Taize from *The Dorothy Day Book: Selections from Her Writings*, edited and introduced by Michael Garvey. Copyright ©1996. Published in Springfield, IL, by Templegate Publishers.

Page 1251 Teresa of Avila (1515–1582) from *The Interior Castle*.

Page 1258 Julian of Norwich (c.1342–c.1413) from *Showings*.

Page 1260 Thomas à Kempis (1380–1471) from *The Imitation of Christ: Living Selections from the Great Devotional Classics,* edited by Douglas V. Steere. Copyright ©1950. Reprinted with permission from Upper Room Books, Nashville, TN.

Page 1261 Karl Barth (1886–1968) from *Deliverance to the Captives, translated by Marguerite Wieser*. Copyright ©1961. Published by Harper & Row, New York.

Page 1264 William Temple (1881–1944).

Page 1267 Teresa of Avila (1515–1582) from *The Interior Castle.*

Page 1271 John Calvin (1509–1564) from *Institutes of the Christian Religion*, edited by John T. McNeill. Copyright ©1960. Published by Westminster John Knox Press, Louisville, KY.

Page 1277 From *The Reality of the Spiritual World* by Thomas R. Kelly. Copyright ©1942. Published by PendleHill Publications, Wallingford, PA.

Page 1282 John Calvin (1509–1564) from *Institutes of the Christian Religion,* edited by John T. McNeill. Copyright ©1960. Published by Westminster John Knox Press, Louisville, KY.

Page 1285 Blaise Pascal (1623–1662) from *Pensees.*

Page 1293 Oswald Chambers (1874–1917) from *My Utmost for His Highest.* Copyright ©1935 by Dodd Mead & Co. Renewed ©1963 by The Oswald Chambers Publications Assn. Ltd., and is used by permission of Discovery House Publishers, Box 3566, Grand Rapids, MI. All rights reserved.

Page 1296 Oswald Chambers (1874–1917) from *My Utmost for His Highest.* Copyright ©1935 by Dodd Mead & Co. Renewed ©1963 by The Oswald Chambers Publications Assn. Ltd., and is used by permission of Discovery House Publishers, Box 3566, Grand Rapids, MI. All rights reserved.

Page 1305 Augustine (354–430) from *The City of God.*

Page 1309 Hannah Whithall Smith (1832–1911) from *The Christian's Secret of a Happy Life.*

Page 1313 John Calvin (1509–1564) from *Institutes of the Christian Religion,* edited by John T. McNeill. Copyright ©1960. Published by Westminster John Knox Press, Louisville, KY.

Page 1318 Dietrich Bonhoeffer (1906–1945) from *The Cost of Discipleship.* Copyright ©1995. Published by Simon & Schuster, New York, NY.

Page 1321 Henri J.M. Nouwen from *The Way of the Heart: Desert Spirituality and Contemporary Ministry.* Copyright ©1981 by Henri J. M. Nouwen. Published by Seabury Press, New York, NY.

Page 1323 Oswald Chambers (1874–1917) from *My Utmost for His Highest.* Copyright ©1935 by Dodd Mead & Co. Renewed ©1963 by The Oswald Chambers Publications Assn. Ltd., and is used by permission of Discovery House Publishers, Box 3566, Grand Rapids, MI. All rights reserved.

Page 1331 Oswald Chambers (1874–1917) from *My Utmost for His Highest.* Copyright ©1935 by Dodd Mead & Co. Renewed ©1963 by The Oswald Chambers Publications Assn. Ltd., and is used by permission of Discovery House Publishers, Box 3566, Grand Rapids, MI. All rights reserved.

Page 1338 From *How to Pray* by Jean Nicholas Grou. Copyright ©1982. Published by James Clark and Co., Cambridge, England.

Page 1344 Bernard of Clairvaux (1090–1153) from *Selections from the Writings of Bernard Clairvaux*, edited by Douglas V. Steere. Copyright ©1952. Published by A.R. Mowbray & Co., London.

Page 1347 Dietrich Bonhoeffer (1906–1945) from *Life Together*, translated by John W. Doberstein. Copyright ©1954. Published by Harper & Row, New York.

Page 1349 Aelred of Rievaulx (1109–1167) from "On Spiritual Friendship," translated by Mary Eugenia Laker, SSND. Copyright ©1974. Published by Cistercian Publications Inc., Kalamazoo, MI.

Page 1357 Simone Weil (1909–1943) from *Waiting for God.* Copyright ©1973. Published by Putnam & Sons, New York, NY.

Page 1361 From *By the Rivers of Babylon* by Kaj Munk. Copyright ©1945. Published in Blair, Nebraska: Lutheran Publishing House, Copyright ©1945. Reprinted with permission from Augsburg Fortress Press, Minneapolis, MN.

Page 1370 Martin Luther (1483–1546). Quoted from "A Pamphlet on Prayer" in *Luther and the Mystics* edited by Bengt Hoffman. Copyright ©1976. Published by Augsburg Fortress Press, Minneapolis, MN.

Page 1373 From *The Cloud of Unknowing,* an anonymous, 14th century work. Copyright ©1981. Published by Paulist Press, Mahwah, NJ.

Page 1377 From *The Rule of St. Benedict.* Copyright ©1975. Published by Liturgical Press, Collegeville, MN.

Page 1389 Dietrich Bonhoeffer (1906–1945) from *Letters and Papers from Prison,* edited by Eberhard Bethge. Copyright ©1971, 1972. Published by Simon & Schuster, New York, NY.

Page 1529 John Chrysostom (d.407) from *On the Letter to the Romans.*

Page 1532 From *The Return of the Prodigal Son: A Story of Homecoming* by Henri J. M. Nouwen. Copyright ©1992 by Henri J.M. Nouwen. Published by Doubleday, Image Books, New York.

Page 1534 Bernard of Clairvaux (1090–1153) from *Selected Works: translation and foreword by G.R. Evans.* Copyright ©1987. Published by Paulist Press, Mahwah, NJ.

Page 1537 Henry Scougal (1650–1678) from *The Life of God in the Soul of Man.* Copyright ©1992. Published by GAM Publications, Sterling, VA.

Page 1540 From *A Testament of Devotion* by Thomas R. Kelly. Copyright ©1941 by Harper & Row Publishers, Inc. Renewed ©1969 by Lois Lael Kelly Statler.

Page 1547 From *The Genesee Diary* by Henri J. M. Nouwen. Copyright ©1981 by Henri J. M. Nouwen. Published by Image Books, Doubleday Publishing, New York.

Page 1549 Oswald Chambers (1874–1917) from *My Utmost for His Highest.* Copyright ©1935 by Dodd Mead & Co. Renewed ©1963 by The Oswald Chambers Publications Assn. Ltd., and is used by permission of Discovery House Publishers, Box 3566, Grand Rapids, MI. All rights reserved.

Page 1552 *Heidelberg Catechism.* Copyright ©1963. Published by Pilgrim Press, Cleveland, OH.

Page 1553 Robert Robinson. "Come Thou Fount of Every Blessing," #400, United Methodist Hymnal.

Page 1558 Charles Wesley (1707–1788). *"Love Divine, All Loves Excelling."*

Page 1563 Hannah Whithall Smith (1832–1911) from *The Christian's Secret of a Happy Life.*

Page 1566 Brother Lawrence (c.1605–1691) from *The Practice of the Presence of God.*

Page 1557 William Law (1686–1761) from *A Serious Call to a Devout and Holy Life.*

Page 1573 Jonathan Edwards (1703–1758) from *Treatise Concerning Religious Affections.*

Page 1575 From *Guard the Gospel: the Message of 2 Timothy* by John R.W. Stott. Copyright ©1973. Published in Downer's Grove, IL by Inter Varsity Press.

Page 1579 From *Sermons For New Life,* by Horace Bushnell; revised edition quoted in Weavings, May/June25, 1987. Copyright ©1901. Published in New York by Charles Scribner's Sons

Page 1580 Jean-Pierre de Caussade (1675–1751) from *The Sacrament of the Present Moment,* translated by Kitty Muggeridge. Copyright ©1989. Published in San Francisco by Harper & Row.

Page 1580 From *Keeping a Spiritual Journal* by Ronald Klug. Copyright ©1983. Published by Augsburg Press, Minneapolis, MN.

Page 1581 From *A Testament of Devotion* by Thomas R. Kelly. Copyright ©1941 by Harper & Row Publishers, Inc. Renewed ©1969 by Lois Lael Kelly Statler.

Page 1582 From *The Reformed Pastor* by Richard Baxter. Copyright ©1979. Published by Banner of Truth Publications, Carlisle, PA.

Page 1584 Jonathan Edwards (1703–1758) from a *Treatise Concerning Religious Affections.*

Page 1585 *Wisdom Distilled from the Daily: Living the Rule of St. Benedict Today* by Joan Chittister, OSB. Copyright ©1991. Published by HarperSanFrancisco.

Page 1588 Charles H. Spurgeon (1834–1892) from *An All Around Ministry.* Copyright ©1983. Published by Pilgrim Publications, Pasadena, TX.

Page 1592 Andrew Murray (1828–1917) from *Waiting on God.* Copyright ©1992. Published by the Christian Literature Crusade, Fort Washington, PA.

Page 1598 Martin Luther (1483–1546) from *Topical Encyclopedia of Living Quotations,* #1010, edited by Sherwood Wirt. Copyright ©1982. Published by Bethany House Publishers, Minneapolis, MN.

Page 1603 Augustine (354–430) from *Enchiridion.*

Page 1606 From *Western Asceticism,* edited by Owen Chadwick. Copyright ©1979. Published by Westminster John Knox Press, Louisville, KY.

Page 1609 From *What's So Amazing About Grace?* by Phillip Yancey. Copyright ©1997 by Phillip Yancey. Published by the Zondervan Corporation, Grand Rapids, MI. Used with permission.

Page 1612 From *The Inner Voice of Love* by Henri J.M. Nouwen. Copyright ©1996 by Henri J. M. Nouwen. Published by Doubleday, New York.

Page 1615 Brother Lawrence (c.1605–1691) from *The Practice of the Presence of God.*

Page 1616 Thomas Merton (1915–1968). Quoted in *Thomas Merton/ Monk: A Monastic Tribute,* edited by Patrick Hart. Copyright ©1983. Published by Cistercian Publications Inc., Kalamazoo, MI.

Page 1619 Richard of Chichester, (c. 1200), "Three Things I Pray," Hymn # 493, United Methodist Hymnal.

Page 1621 Bernard of Clairvaux (1090–1153) from *The Love of God, and Spiritual Friendship,* abridged, edited, and introduced by James M. Houston. Copyright ©1983. Published by Multnomah Press, Sisters, OR.

Page 1625 Amy Carmichael (1867–1951) from *Candles in the Dark.* Copyright ©1982. Published by the Christian Literature Crusade, Fort Washington, PA.

Page 1627 John Huss (1373–1415) from *Exposition of Faith.*

Page 1629 Evelyn Underhill (1875–1941) from *An Anthology of the Love of God from the Writings of Evelyn Underhill.* Copyright ©1976. Published by A.R. Mowbray & Co., London.

Page 1632 From *Bread in the Wilderness* by Thomas Merton. Copyright ©1997 by the Trustees of the Merton Legacy Fund. Published by New Directions, New York.

Page 1651 John of the Cross (1542–1591) from *The Spiritual Canticle.* Copyright ©1987. Published by Paulist Press, Mahwah, NJ.

Spiritual Formation Bible:
GROWING IN INTIMACY WITH GOD THROUGH SCRIPTURE

General Editor, Timothy Jones

Project Management and Editorial, Ruth DeJager

Editorial Assistance, Natalie Block

Art Direction, Cindy Davis

Interior Design, Sharon Wright,
Belmont, MI

Interior Art, Clint Hanson

Calligraphic Design, Bruce Gore

Proofreading, Peachtree Editorial and Proofreading Service,
Peachtree City, GA

Interior Typesetting, Multnomah Graphics,
Troutdale, OR

Printing, R. R. Donnelley & Sons,
Crawfordsville, IN